Peterson's® How to Get Money for College 2019

PETERSON'S®

About Peterson's

Peterson's® has been your trusted educational publisher for over 50 years. It's a milestone we're quite proud of, as we continue to offer the most accurate, dependable, high-quality educational content in the field, providing you with everything you need to succeed. No matter where you are on your academic or professional path, you can rely on Peterson's for its books, online information, expert test-prep tools, the most up-to-date education exploration data, and the highest quality career success resources—everything you need to achieve your education goals. For our complete line of products, visit www.petersons.com.

For more information about Peterson's range of educational products, contact Peterson's, 8740 Lucent Blvd., Suite 400, Highlands Ranch, CO 80129, or find us online at www.petersons.com.

Previous editions published as *How to Get Money for College* © 2009, 2010, 2011, 2012, 2013, 2014, 2015, 2016, 2017; *Peterson's College Money Handbook* © 1983, 1984, 1985, 1986, 1987, 1988, 1989, 1990, 1991, 1997, 1998, 1999, 2000, 2001, 2002, 2003, 2004, 2005, 2006, 2007, 2008; and as *Paying Less for College* © 1992, 1993, 1994, 1995, 1996

FAFSA® is a registered trademark of the U.S. Department of Education.

ISSN 1544-2330
ISBN: 978-0-7689-4231-6

Printed in the United States of America

10 9 8 7 6 5 4 3 2 1   20 19 18

Thirty-sixth Edition

Contents

A Note from the Peterson's® Editors

The news media seem to constantly remind us that a college education is expensive. It certainly appears to be beyond the means of many Americans. The sticker price for four years at state-supported colleges can be more than $45,000, and private colleges and universities can cost more than $150,000. And these numbers continue to rise.

But there is good news. The system operates to provide the needed money so that most families and students are able to afford a college education while making only a reasonable financial sacrifice. However, because the college financial aid system is complex, finding the money is often easier said than done. That is why the process demands study, planning, calculation, flexibility, filling out forms, and meeting deadlines. Fortunately, for most people, it can produce positive results. There are many ways to manage college costs and many channels through which you can receive help. Be sure to take full advantage of the opportunities that have been opened up to students and their families by the many organizations, foundations, and businesses that have organized to help you with the burden of college expenses.

For nearly forty years, Peterson's has given students and parents the most comprehensive, up-to-date information on how to get their fair share of the financial aid pie. *Peterson's How to Get Money for College* is both a quick reference and a comprehensive resource that puts valuable information about college costs and financial aid opportunities at your fingertips.

- **The ABC's of Paying for College** provides insight into federal financial aid programs that are available, offers an overview of the financial aid landscape, walks you through the process of filing for aid, and provides proven tips on how to successfully navigate the financial aid process to obtain the federal, state, and institutional aid you deserve.

- The **Quick-Reference Chart** offers a snapshot comparison of the financial aid programs available at more than 2,400 four-year institutions across the country.

- The **Profiles of College Financial Aid Programs** provide unbiased financial aid data for each of the more than 2,400 four-year institutions listed.

- The **Appendix** lists the state scholarship and grant programs offered by all fifty states and the District of Columbia.

- The six **Indexes** included in the back of the book allow you to search for specific award programs based on a variety of criteria, including merit-based awards, athletic grants, ROTC programs, and much more.

Peterson's publishes a full line of books—financial aid, education exploration, test prep, and career preparation. Peterson's publications can be found at high school guidance offices, college libraries and career centers, and your local bookstore and library. Peterson's books are also available at www.petersonsbooks.com.

We welcome any comments or suggestions you may have about this publication. Your feedback will help us make educational dreams possible for you—and others like you.

The ABC's of Paying for College

What You Need to Know About the FAFSA®

The Free Application for Federal Student Aid or FAFSA® (https://fafsa.ed.gov/FAFSA/app/fafsa) is a critical form that anyone seeking college financial aid must complete.

WHY YOU MUST FILE THE FAFSA®

The FAFSA® is required in order for a student to be considered for any type of federal financial aid, including grants and loans. Even if you think your family makes too much for you to qualify for need-based aid, you should still complete the FAFSA®. For one thing, many people are surprised to find that they may actually qualify for need-based aid—the eligibility for which is determined by a number of factors, in addition to household income.

Also, the FAFSA® is required to apply for students loans (for which there is no need-based element such as income limits). If you don't initially think you want to apply for student loans but later change your mind, having a completed FAFSA® already on file will help speed up the process.

In addition, most schools will require a student to have a completed FAFSA® on file before the student can be considered for any school-based aid programs such as scholarships. A completed FAFSA® is also required for federal work study jobs.

IT'S EASIER TO FILE ONLINE

While you can opt to print and complete a paper version of the FAFSA®, it is much quicker and easier to complete the online version. The system walks you through the process and can alert you to sections you can skip if they don't apply to you.

If you have completed a FAFSA® in the past, some of your information will be automatically entered when you start to work on your newest one, giving you a head start. You will further save a lot of time by using the IRS data retrieval tool, which will be discussed later in this article.

Filing online means your form will be processed faster, and it also eliminates the worry that your paperwork will be lost or delayed in the mail.

For those who want or need to print and submit a paper version of the FAFSA®, you can print a PDF version of the FAFSA® online. Students and parents can request up to three copies of the paper FAFSA® (in English or Spanish) by calling the Federal Student Aid Information Center toll-free at 800-4-FED-AID.

THE NEW FEDERAL STUDENT AID ID

In order for a student to complete the online FAFSA®, he or she must obtain a Federal Student Aid (FSA) ID. You can get this online at https://fsaid.ed.gov/npas/index.htm. The FSA ID replaced the PIN system that was previously used prior to May 2015. Parents of dependent students also need to obtain their own FSA ID in order to sign their child's FAFSA® electronically online.

The FSA ID can be used to access several federal aid-related websites, including FAFSA.gov and StudentLoans.gov. It consists of a username and password and can be used to electronically sign Federal Student Aid documents, access your personal records, and make binding legal obligations. The FSA ID is beneficial in several ways:

- It removes your personally identifiable information (PII), such as your Social Security number, from your log-in credentials.

- It creates a more secure and efficient way to verify your information when you log in to access to your federal student aid information online.

- It gives you the ability to easily update your personal information.

- It allows you to easily retrieve your username and password by requesting a secure code be sent to your e-mail address or by answering challenge questions.

It's relatively simple to create an FSA ID and should only take a few minutes. In addition, you will have an opportunity to link your current Federal Student Aid PIN (if you already have one) to your FSA ID. The final step is to confirm your e-mail address. You will receive a secure code to the e-mail address you provided when you set up your FSA ID. Once you retrieve the code from your e-mail account and enter it—to confirm your e-mail address is valid—you will be able to use this e-mail address instead of your username to log in to any of the federal aid-related websites, making the log-in process even simpler for you and your parents.

When you initially create your FSA ID, your information will need to be verified with the Social Security Administration. This process can take anywhere from one to three days. For that reason, it's a good idea to take care of setting up your FSA ID as early as possible, so it will be all set when you are ready to begin completing your FAFSA®.

IMPORTANT NOTE: Since your FSA ID provides access to your personal information and is used to sign online documents, it's imperative that you protect this ID. Don't share it with *anyone* or write it down in an insecure location—you could place yourself at great risk for identify theft.

If your FSA ID is lost or stolen, you must do one of the following:

- Contact Federal Student Aid's Customer Service center at 800-433-3243 (toll-free).

- Update your username and password by selecting "Edit My FSA ID."

- Disable your FSA ID so that no one can use it by selecting "Edit My FSA ID" and then selecting "Disable my FSA ID."

INFORMATION YOU WILL NEED

Completing your FAFSA® (or updating one you have already started) will be much easier if you have some basic information and documentation handy when you prepare to complete the form. The first section of the FAFSA® involves your basic personal information that you should know offhand, such as your name, address, and Social Security number. After that, you will need to provide details about your income, assets, and other financial issues. If you file taxes, much of this information will be taken from your tax return. If you haven't yet completed your taxes for that year, you can enter estimated figures and update the form with the final numbers later.

If you're a student who is married, you will also need to provide information about your spouse and their finances. If you're a dependent student, information about one or both or your parents and their finances will be required.

You will also need to provide information about the school(s) you attend or plan to attend. If you haven't made your final school choices yet, you can list the ones you know at this point and add others later.

BE MINDFUL OF DEADLINES

The new FAFSA® for the upcoming school year is available online starting on October 1. It is smart to complete your FAFSA® as early as possible. If you file taxes, you will need information from your tax return (and from your parents, too, if you are a dependent student). However, you can complete your FAFSA® before you file your tax return by entering estimated information and then returning to the online system and making any necessary updates once you have filed your taxes.

For federal aid, the final deadline to submit your FAFSA® is June 30 at the end of the school year for which you are applying. So for the 2018–19 school year, the final deadline to submit your FAFSA® would be June 30, 2019. However, you would normally want to apply for aid before the start of a semester—and ideally, as far in advance as possible. That's because schools frequently require all of your financial aid to be processed (or at least be in process) before your registration is considered official.

It can sometimes be tricky to keep track of other financial aid deadlines because the deadlines for different types of aid can vary by state and school. Be sure to check with your school—or the schools you are considering attending—to find out their financial aid deadlines so you can get all of your forms submitted in time.

Check the website for your state's department of education to find out the deadlines to submit the FAFSA® and other forms in order to be considered for any state-funded financial aid that may be available to you.

DEPENDENCY

One of the biggest misconceptions—or most misunderstood aspects of the FAFSA® and financial aid—is that a student can simply declare himself or herself independent, and then their parents' information will not be considered. In the past, dependency wasn't viewed in such strict terms, and it was easier for a student who lived on their own to be considered independent.

It's important to keep in mind that dependency for financial aid purposes has nothing to do with tax status or whether a student's parents claimed the student as a dependent on their tax return. Dependency for taxes and financial aid are two completely different and separate things.

There are now strict criteria that determine a student's dependency status. To be considered independent, a student must meet one of the following conditions:

- Age 24 or older by December 31 of the school year for which the student is applying for aid

- Married

- Have children or other dependents for whom the student provides more than half of their support

- Currently serving in the military

- Having been homeless, in foster care, or a ward of the court

Even if one of these conditions applies, that doesn't necessarily grant the student automatic independent status. There may still be additional required documentation or other conditions that must be met.

IRS DATA RETRIEVAL TOOL

A common complaint about the FAFSA® is that it takes too long to complete. But a fairly recent change has made the form considerably less time-consuming for many people. The IRS Data Retrieval tool now allows the tax information of students or parents to be automatically imported into the FAFSA®.

Once you reach the section of the online FAFSA® that deals with financial information of the student (and parent, if applicable), you will see a button that says "Link to IRS" if that option is available to you. You will then follow the steps to log into the IRS system and have your information transferred to your FAFSA®. In order to access the Data Retrieval Tool, the information you enter on the IRS login screen—including your name, address, and filing status—must exactly match the information on your most recent tax return.

Those who decide to skip this step for whatever reason should know that there's a good chance they will then be required to submit copies of their tax return and possibly even an IRS transcript in order to verify their tax information. (An IRS transcript is an official document that must be obtained from the IRS. That can be a time-consuming and inconvenient process, so you are usually better off just using the IRA data retrieval tool in the first place.)

There are certain situations in which the FAFSA® will not allow you to use the Data Retrieval Tool. This tool is not an option for students or parents who are married and filed as Married Filing Separately, are married and filed as Head of Household, filed a Form 1040X amended tax return, or filed a Puerto Rican or foreign tax return. If you fall into one of these categories, you will need to enter your tax information manually.

Also, if you have just filed your tax return within a few weeks prior to completing the FAFSA®, your current information may not be in the IRS system yet and may not be accessible by the Data Retrieval Tool.

PARENTS' MARITAL STATUS

For dependent students, their parents' marital status can have a big impact on financial aid eligibility. If the parents are married, financial information for both parents must be reported. If the parents are separated but still living together, they are still listed as "married or remarried" on the FAFSA®. Parents who are legally separated or living in separate households are classified as "divorced or separated."

If parents are divorced, the FAFSA® must be completed by the parent with whom the student lived with most during the previous twelve-month period. If the student lived equally with both parents, the form would be completed by the parent who provided the most support.

LISTING SCHOOL CHOICES

When completing the FAFSA®, you must specify which colleges should receive the report generated by your FAFSA® application. On the paper FAFSA®, you can only list four colleges. On the online version, you can list ten. If you complete the paper version and want to have your information provided to more than four schools, you can go online to the FAFSA® website after your form has been processed and add more schools to your list (up to a total of ten).

From a federal aid standpoint, it doesn't matter in what order you list the colleges. However, the FAFSA® instructions note that for state aid purposes, you may want to list the colleges in order of preference. Keep in mind that each school on your list will see everything on your FAFSA®—including the names of the other colleges you have listed. There have been reports that schools are using students' college listings to determine how likely a specific student is to attend their particular school (based on the theory that students tend to list colleges in the order of how much they want to attend each). The speculation is that a college may reserve its best financial aid offers for students who seem most interested in attending. While most schools won't confirm that practice, it is probably in your best interest to list your colleges in order of the ones you most want to attend.

Falsifying Information on Your FAFSA® Could Bring Big Problems

With the cost of college rising each year and college graduates saddled with more than $1 trillion in debt to pay for their postsecondary studies, more and more families are desperate to secure payment-free options for higher education. Nothing illuminates this fact better than the meteoric rise in applications for financial aid through the annually Free Application for Federal Student Aid (FAFSA). In the 2004–05 academic year, more than 11 million students sent in FAFSA applications. Less than seven years later, that number doubled to more than 22 million. With more and more students applying for federal financial aid, there is, unfortunately, an increased temptation to commit fraud. Parents try to do whatever they can to lower their Expected Family Contribution (EFC), and sometimes this can lead to falsifying information. This is a big no-no, but that doesn't stop people from trying.

A quick search on Google, and you can find parents and students asking boldly, "Do people lying on their FAFSA really get caught?" or "How do I hide the fact that I have money from FAFSA?" Cheating on the FAFSA seems as intuitive as forgetting to report that second job you have to the Internal Revenue Service.

A report released by the Government Accountability Office, the Congress-created financial watchdog, found that fifteen for-profit universities encouraged fraud and/or engaged in deceptive marketing practices. The report stated that one college admission worker encouraged an undercover applicant to not report $250,000 in savings on the student's FAFSA. Another college representative told an undercover applicant to falsify the number of dependents he had from 0 to 3.

It all seems so deceptively easy—giving thousands of dollars in savings to a student's uncle temporarily to hide that asset; writing down grandma's address to gain in-state tuition rates; forgetting to mention your true immigration status; or the extreme example of one Alaskan woman who used a false identity. In that situation, after claiming she suffered from years of child abuse, the woman used an obscure federal law to secure a new identity to hide from her accused abuser. (The abuser she named was never charged with a crime.) She received a new social security number and card. But instead of living a new life in anonymity, she used her *old* identity to apply for federal student loans—a lot of them. Arrested and convicted, the woman was sentenced to five years in prison and ordered to pay back nearly $1 million.

The prospect of going to jail for filling out false information on your FAFSA application may not have crossed your mind, but it is certainly a possibility. Falsifying information—knowingly or unknowingly—is a federal crime. It is punishable by up to $20,000 in fines and up to five years in prison. And though there are books offering tantalizing options to "game," the federal student aid system—do not be tempted.

You do not want to start your college career by committing a crime against the government. It's just not worth it. Your FAFSA is checked against your IRS documents by professionals who do not want to take the chance that they will use their precious scarce financial aid resources to support students who really do not need it. Students who falsify information to get financial aid leave deserving cash-strapped students out in the cold. Fortunately, though, fraud in the federal aid system is low—a recent government study found that about 5 percent of applications contain false information.

Even if you do not intend to defraud the government, inaccurate information on your FAFSA can get you into trouble. It is critical that you fill the application out as accurately as possible. It may look like an innocuous document, but it amounts to a partnership between you and the federal government, and it is essential that partnership is based upon trust.

Here are some tips to avoid making mistakes on your FAFSA that could cost you financial aid or even your freedom:

- Accurately report your assets, address, dependents, income, and so on. It just doesn't make sense to lie. All that information is easily verifiable. Income includes wages, tips, social security payments, child support payments, and other untaxed income. But retirement income such as those in a 401K or IRA does not have to be reported. Check with your tax advisor when filling out your FAFSA application.

- Fill out your FAFSA completely. Mistakes can cost you time as you might have to reapply, and that will literally cost you money.

- Avoid books, consultants, and websites that promise to lower your EFC by questionable means. Trying to "game," the federal aid system is just going to cause you headaches.

College is expensive, and families are smart to try to lower that expense as much as possible. But planning, saving, and focusing on academic pursuits to garner scholarships and grants is a much better way of acquiring money for college than trying to put one over on the federal government. Being honest is always the best policy—especially when applying for federal financial aid.

Tips for Financing Your Child's College Education

by Don Betterton

Given the lifelong benefit of a college degree (college graduates are projected to earn in a lifetime $1 million more than those with only a high school diploma), higher education is a worthwhile investment. However, it is also an expensive one made even more difficult to manage by cost increases that have outpaced both inflation and gains in family income. The reality of higher education economics is that paying for a child's college education is an issue that shows no sign of getting easier.

Because of the high cost involved (even the most inexpensive four-year education at a public institution costs about $10,000 a year), good information about college budgets and strategies for reducing the "sticker price" is essential. You have made a good start by taking the time to read *Peterson's How to Get Money for College*. In the pages that follow, you will find valuable information about the four main sources of aid—federal, state, institutional, and private. Before you learn about the various programs, however, it will be helpful if you have an overview of how the college financial aid system operates and what long-range financing strategies are available.

FINANCIAL AID

Financial aid refers to money that is awarded to a student, usually in a "package" that consists of gift aid (commonly called a scholarship or grant), a student loan, and/or a campus job.

COLLEGE COSTS

The starting point for organizing a plan to pay for your child's college education is to make a good estimate of the yearly cost of attendance. You can use the **College Cost Worksheet** on the next page to do this.

To estimate your college costs for 2018–19, refer to the tuition and fees and room and board figures shown in the **College Cost Worksheet**. If your child will commute from your home, use $2,500 instead of the college's room and board charges and $900 for transportation. We have used $800 for books and $1,500 for personal expenses. Finally, estimate the cost of two round trips if your home is more than a few hundred miles from the college. Add the items to calculate the total budget. You should now have a reasonably good estimate of college costs for 2018–19. (To determine the costs for later years, adding 4 percent per year will probably give you a fairly accurate estimate.)

DO YOU QUALIFY FOR NEED-BASED AID?

The next step is to evaluate whether or not you are likely to qualify for financial aid based on need. This step is critical, since more than 90 percent of the yearly total of $128 billion in student aid is awarded only after a determination is made that the family lacks sufficient financial resources to pay the full cost of college on its own. To judge your chance of receiving need-based aid, it is necessary to estimate an Expected Family Contribution (EFC) according to a government formula known as the Federal Methodology (FM). The official Federal Student Aid Website provides a FAFSA4caster tool (similar to an EFC calculator) that helps you get a head start on the financial aid process, including getting an early estimate of your eligibility for federal aid. The tool will also allow you to transfer the information provided into the actual Free Application for Federal Student Aid (FAFSA) form when you are ready to complete it. You can find the tool on the Fafsa.ed.gov website.

APPLYING FOR NEED-BASED AID

Because the federal government provides about 67 percent of all aid awarded, the application, FAFSA®, and need evaluation process is controlled by the U.S. Department of Education. In addition, nearly every state that offers student assistance uses the federal government's system to award its own aid. Furthermore, in addition to arranging for the payment of federal and state aid, many colleges use the FAFSA to award their own funds to eligible students. (Note: In addition to the FAFSA, many private colleges and universities also ask the family to complete the CSS/Financial Aid PROFILE® application.)

The FAFSA is your "passport" to receiving your share of the billions of dollars awarded annually in need-based aid. If you didn't read the first article in this section about the FAFSA, go back and take a look at it now. You will find the latest information on the FAFSA, including important details on the change from the PIN to the new FSA ID.

AWARDING AID

The colleges you list on the FAFSA will receive your information in order to calculate a financial aid award in a package that

College Cost Worksheet

	College 1	College 2	College 3	Commuter College
Tuition and Fees	_____	_____	_____	_____
Room and Board	_____	_____	_____	$2,500
Books	$ 800	$ 800	$ 800	$ 750
Personal Expenses	$1,500	$1,500	$1,500	$1,500
Travel	_____	_____	_____	$ 900
Total Budget	_____	_____	_____	_____

typically includes aid from at least one of the major sources—federal, state, college, or private. In addition, the award will probably consist of a combination of a scholarship, grant, loan, or campus job. These last two pieces—loan and job—are called self-help aid because they require effort on your child's part (that is, the aid must be either earned through work or paid back later). Scholarships or grants are outright gifts that have no such obligation.

It is important that you understand each part of the package. You'll want to know, for example, how much aid is a gift, the interest rate and repayment terms of the student loan, or how many hours per week the campus job requires. There should be an enclosure with the award letter that answers these questions. If not, make a list of your questions and call or visit the financial aid office.

Once you understand the terms of each item in the award letter, you should turn your attention to the "bottom line"—how much you will have to pay at each college where your child is accepted. In addition to understanding the aid award, this means having a good estimate of the college budget so you can

accurately calculate how much you and your child will have to contribute. (Often, an aid package does not cover the entire need.) Colleges differ in how much detail they include in their award notifications. Many colleges provide full information—types and amounts of aid, yearly costs, and the EFC for the parent and student shares. If these important items are missing or incomplete, you can do the work on your own. (See the **Comparing Financial Aid Awards and Family Contribution Worksheet** on the next page.) For example, if the award letter only shows the college's direct charges—tuition, room, and board— you need to estimate indirect costs such as books, personal expenses, and travel. Then subtract the total aid awarded from the yearly cost to get the EFC. A portion of that amount may be your child's contribution (35 percent of student assets and 50 percent of student earnings over $2,200) and the remainder is the parental share. If you can afford this amount at your child's first-choice college, the financial aid system has worked well for you, and your child's college enrollment plans can go forward.

How Need Is Calculated and Aid Is Awarded

	College 1	College 2
Total Cost of Attendance	$10,000	$ 24,000
− Expected Family Contribution	− 5,500	− 5,500
= Financial Need	$ 4,500	$ 18,500
− Grant Aid Awarded	− 675	−14,575
− Campus Job (Work-Study) Awarded	− 1,400	− 1,300
− Student Loan Awarded	− 2,425	− 2,625
= Unmet Need	0	0

Note: Sometimes an institution is unable to meet all need. The amount of unmet need is called "the gap."

Comparing Financial Aid Awards and Family Contribution Worksheet

	College 1	College 2	College 3
Cost of Attendance	_____	_____	_____
Aid Awarded	_____	_____	_____
Grant/Scholarship	_____	_____	_____
Loan	_____	_____	_____
Job	_____	_____	_____
Total Aid	_____	_____	_____
Expected Family Contribution	_____	_____	_____
Student Contribution	_____	_____	_____
Parent Contribution	_____	_____	_____

But if you think your EFC is too high, you should contact the college's financial aid office and ask whether additional aid is available. Many private high-cost colleges are willing to work with families to help make attendance at their institutions possible. Most colleges also allow applicants to appeal their financial aid awards, the budget used for you, or any of the elements used to determine the family contribution, especially if there are extenuating circumstances or if the information has changed since the application was submitted. Some colleges may also reconsider an award based on a "competitive appeal," the submission of a more favorable award letter from another college.

If your appeal is unsuccessful and there is still a gap between the expected family contribution and what you feel you can pay from income and savings, you are left with two choices. One option is for your child to attend a college where paying your share of the bill will not be a problem. (This assumes that an affordable option was included on your child's original list of colleges, a wise admission application strategy.) The second is to look into alternate methods of financing. At this stage, parental loans and tuition payment plans are the best financing options. A parental loan can bring the yearly cost down to a manageable level by spreading payments over a number of years. This is the type of financing that families use when purchasing a home or automobile. A tuition payment plan is essentially a short-term loan and allows you to pay the costs over ten to twelve months. It is an option for families who have the resources available but need help with managing their cash flow.

NON-NEED-BASED AID

Regardless of whether you might qualify for a need-based award, it is always worthwhile to look into merit, or non-need, scholarships from sources such as foundations, agencies, religious groups, and service organizations. For a family that isn't eligible for need-based aid, merit scholarships are the only form of gift aid available. If your child later qualifies for a need-based award, a merit scholarship can be quite helpful in providing additional resources if the aid does not fully cover the costs. Even if the college meets 100 percent of need, a merit scholarship reduces the self-help (loan and job) portion of an award.

In searching for merit-based scholarships, keep in mind that there are relatively few awards (compared to those that are need-based), and most of them are highly competitive. Use the following checklist in your search.

- Take advantage of any scholarships for which your child is automatically eligible based on parents' employer benefits, military service, association or church membership, other affiliations, or student or parent attributes (ethnic background, nationality, and so on). Company or union tuition remissions are the most common examples of these awards.

- Look for other awards for which your child might be eligible based on the previous characteristics and affiliations but where there is a selection process and an application is required. Free computerized searches are available on the Internet. (You should not pay a fee for a scholarship search.) Peterson's free scholarship search can be accessed by logging on to www.petersons.com/finaid. Scholarship directories, such as *Peterson's Scholarships, Grants & Prizes*, which details more than 3,800 scholarship programs, and *Peterson's Best Scholarships for Best Students* are useful resources and can be found in bookstores, high school guidance offices, or your local library. You can also find these books at www.petersonsbooks.com.

- See if your state has a merit scholarship program.

- Look into national scholarship competitions. High school guidance counselors usually know about these scholarships. Examples of these awards are the National Meritt Scholarship Program, the Coca-Cola Scholarship, Gates Millennium Scholars, Intel Science Talent Search, and the U.S. Senate Youth Program.

- ROTC (Reserve Officers' Training Corps) scholarships are offered by the Army, Navy, Air Force, and Marine Corps. A full ROTC scholarship covers tuition, fees, textbook costs, and, in some cases, a stipend. Acceptance of an ROTC scholarship entails a commitment to take military science courses and to serve for a specific number of years as an officer in the sponsoring branch of the service. Competition is heavy, and preference may be given to students in certain fields of study, such as engineering, languages, science, and health professions. Application procedures vary by service. Contact an armed services recruiter or high school guidance counselor for further information.

- Investigate community scholarships. High school guidance counselors usually have a list of these awards, and announcements are published in local newspapers. Most common are awards given by service organizations like the American Legion, Rotary International, and the local women's club.

- If your child is strong academically or is very talented in fields such as athletics or performing/creative arts, you may want to consider colleges that offer their own merit awards to gifted students they wish to enroll. Refer to the Non-Need Scholarships for Undergraduates index in the back part of this guide.

In addition to merit scholarships, there are loan and job opportunities for students who do not qualify for need-based aid. Some of the organizations that sponsor scholarships—for example, the Air Force Aid Society—also provide loans.

Work opportunities during the academic year are another type of assistance that is not restricted to aid recipients. Many colleges will, after assigning jobs to students on aid, open campus positions to all students looking for work. In addition, there are usually off-campus employment opportunities available to everyone.

FINANCING YOUR CHILD'S COLLEGE EDUCATION

"Financing" means putting together resources to pay the balance due the college over and above payments from the primary sources of aid—grants, scholarships, student loans, and jobs. Financing strategies are important because the high cost of a college education today often requires a family, whether or not it receives aid, to think about stretching its college payment beyond the four-year period of enrollment. For high-cost colleges, it is not unreasonable to think about a 10-4-10 plan: ten years of saving; four years of paying college bills out of current income, savings, and borrowing; and ten years to repay a parental loan.

Note

A point of clarification about whether to put college savings in your name or your child's: If you are certain that your child will not be a candidate for need-based aid, there may be a tax advantage to accumulating money in his or her name. However, when it comes to maximizing aid eligibility, it is important to understand that student assets are assessed at a 20 percent rate and parental assets at about 5 percent. Therefore, if your college savings are in your child's name, it may be wise to reestablish title to these funds before applying for financial aid. You should contact your financial planner or accountant before making any modifications to your asset structure.

Savings

Although saving for college is always a good idea, many families are unclear about its advantages. Some families do not save because after normal living expenses have been covered, they do not have much money to set aside. An affordable but regular savings plan through a payroll deduction is usually the answer to the problem of spending your entire paycheck every month.

The second reason why saving for college is not a high priority is the belief that the financial aid system penalizes a family by lowering aid eligibility. The Federal Methodology of need determination is very kind to families that save. In fact, savings are ignored completely for most families that earn less than $50,000. Savings in the form of home equity, retirement plans, and most annuities are excluded from the calculation. And even when savings are counted, a maximum of 5 percent of the total is expected each year. In other words, if a family has $40,000 in savings after an asset protection allowance is considered, the contribution is no greater than $2,000. Given the impact of compound interest it is easy to see that a long-term savings plan can make paying for college much easier.

A sensible savings plan is important because of the financial advantage of saving compared to borrowing. The amount of money students borrow for college is now greater than the amount they receive in grants and scholarships. With loans becoming so widespread, savings should be carefully con-

What Is CSS/Financial Aid PROFILE

There are many complexities in the financial aid process: knowing which aid is merit-based and which aid is need-based; understanding the difference between grants, loans, and work-study; and determining whether funds are from federal, state, institutional, or private sources.

In addition, the aid application process itself can be confusing. It can involve more than the Free Application for Federal Student Aid (FAFSA) and the Federal Methodology (FM). Many colleges feel that the federal aid system (FAFSA and FM) does not collect or evaluate information thoroughly enough for them to award their own institutional funds. These colleges have made an arrangement with the College Scholarship Service, a branch of the College Board, to establish a separate application system.

The application is called the CSS/Financial Aid PROFILE®, and the need-analysis formula is referred to as the Institutional Methodology (IM). If you apply for financial aid at one of the colleges that uses the PROFILE, the admission material will state that the PROFILE is required in addition to the FAFSA. You should read the information carefully and file the PROFILE to meet the earliest college deadline. Before you can receive the PROFILE, however, you must register, either by phone or online at https://student.collegeboard.org/css-financial-aid-profile, providing enough basic information so the PROFILE package can be designed specifically for you. The FAFSA is free, but there is a charge for the PROFILE. As with the FAFSA, the PROFILE can be submitted via the Internet.

In addition to the requirement by certain colleges that you submit both the FAFSA and PROFILE (when used, the PROFILE is always in addition to the FAFSA; it does not replace it), you should understand that each system has its own method for analyzing a family's ability to pay for college. The main differences between PROFILE's Institutional Methodology and the FAFSA's Federal Methodology are:

- PROFILE includes equity in the family home as an asset; the FAFSA doesn't.

- PROFILE takes a broader look at assets not included on the FAFSA.

- PROFILE expects a minimum student contribution, usually in the form of summer earnings; the FAFSA has no such minimum.

- PROFILE may collect information on the noncustodial parent; the FAFSA does not.

- PROFILE allows for more professional judgment than the FAFSA. Medical expenses, private secondary school costs, and a variety of special circumstances are considered under PROFILE, subject to the discretion of the aid counselor on campus.

- PROFILE includes information on assets not reported on the FAFSA, including life insurance, annuities, retirement plans, etc.

To summarize: PROFILE's Institutional Methodology tends to be both more complete in its data collection and more rigorous in its analysis than the FAFSA's Federal Methodology. When IM results are compared to FM results for thousands of applicants, IM will usually come up with a somewhat higher expected parental contribution than FM.

Creditworthiness

If you will be borrowing to pay for your child's college education, making sure you qualify for a loan is critical. For the most part, that means your credit record must be free of default or delinquency. You can check your credit history with one or more of the following three major credit bureaus and clean up any adverse information that appears. The numbers below will offer specific information on what you need to provide to obtain a report. All of the credit bureaus accept credit report requests over their Web sites. You will usually be asked to provide your full name, phone number, social security number, birth date, and addresses for the last five years. You are entitled to a free report from each bureau.

Equifax Credit Information	Trans Union	Experian
P.O. Box 740241	800-888-4213	888-397-3742
Atlanta, GA 30374	http://www.transunion.com	http://www.experian.com
800-685-1111		
http://www.equifax.com		

sidered as an alternative to borrowing. Your incentive for saving is that a dollar saved is a dollar not borrowed.

Borrowing

Once you've calculated your "bottom-line" parental contribution and determined that the amount is not affordable out of your current income and assets, the most likely alternative is borrowing. Beginning July 1, 2010, as a result of the Health Care and Education Reconciliation Act, federal student loans are no longer made by private lenders under the Federal Family Education Loan (FFEL) Program. Instead, all new federal student loans come directly from the U.S. Department of Education under the Direct Loan Program, which offers subsidized and unsubsidized (Stafford) loans for students, PLUS loans for parents and graduate/professional students, and consolidation loans for both students and parents. For additional information, go online to https://studentloans.gov/myDirectLoan/index.action or call 800-4-FED-AID (toll-free).

For the Direct PLUS Loan, parents must complete a Direct PLUS Loan application and promissory note, contained in a single form that can be obtained from a school's financial aid office. The yearly limit on a PLUS Loan is equal to the student's cost of attendance minus any other financial aid the student receives. For example, if your cost of attendance is $6,000, and you receive $4,500 in other financial aid, your parents can borrow up to $1,500. Loans are disbursed between July 1 and June 30 of each year and have a fixed interest rate throughout the life of the loan. The rate for undergraduate students will never exceed 8.25%. Interest is charged on a PLUS Loan from the date of the first disbursement until the loan is paid in full. A PLUS Loan made to the parent cannot be transferred to the student. The parent is responsible for repaying the PLUS Loan. For more details about PLUS Loans, visit www.direct.ed.gov/about.html.

MAKE FINANCIAL AID WORK FOR YOU

If you are like millions of families that benefit from financial aid, it is likely that your child's college plans can go forward without undue worry about the costs involved. The key is to understand the financial aid system and to follow the best path for your family. The result of good information and good planning should be that you will receive your fair share of the billions of dollars available each year and that the cost of college will not prevent your child from attending.

Don Betterton is a former Director of Undergraduate Financial Aid at Princeton University and a Certified College Planner (CCP).

Residency: Its Impact on Tuition

When it comes to college tuition at a state school, a student's *in-state* or *out-of-state* status can often make a big difference. For those students who are unable to cover a school's price tag, it can often be quite frustrating. However, there is a legitimate reason why colleges charge more to out-of-state students, even if this happens to be thousands more. And here's why.

Public universities receive public funding by way of tax dollars paid by state residents. A large chunk of money that these public universities get each year are paid by taxpayers who live in that state. It only make sense then that in-state students should catch a break in tuition costs since their families, as residents, have helped pay for the public universities' operating costs.

Another reason for in-state tuition to be less expensive is because states want to offer an incentive to keep their residents in state. Their investment for keeping their students in-state pays off when a student graduates and starts working in-state as well, essentially helping boost the economy from within, and contributing to the social and cultural climate of the state.

RECIPROCITY

In some cases, a public college or university will offer in-state tuition to out-of-state students. Typically this happens when a program of study is not available to the student in his or her home state, or the states make an agreement with one another to offer in-state or close to in-state tuition to students from each other's states. For example, the Western Undergraduate Exchange (WUE) program offers out-of-state students tuition at 1.5 times as much as in-state tuition; states included are Alaska, Arizona, California, Colorado, Hawaii, Idaho, Montana, Nevada, New Mexico, North Dakota, South Dakota, Utah, Washington, and Wyoming.

Check with your high school guidance counselor and/or the financial aid office at your school(s) of interest to see if there are any options like this in your state

IN-STATE REQUIREMENTS

In-state requirements and establishing residency varies state to state, but you can always ask your prospective school what is required to establish residency. Typically it takes at least one year of living in the state, and you will be required to perform certain tasks, such as obtaining a driver's license in the state, filing taxes in the state, and so on. You may need to demonstrate that you are in the state for years to come—not only for the duration of your undergraduate education. It is important that you research this thoroughly and contact the school to be sure you are taking the right steps to obtain residency.

Although not easy, some students may find a way to move to the state they want to go to school in a year (or two) before they even apply. If you want to attend an out-of-state institution and cannot afford the out-of-state tuition, establishing residency is crucial to lowering your tuition cost and ensuring you will be able to afford to attend until graduation. Establishing residency might also open up other financial aid opportunities as well, so be sure to ask if there are any scholarships, grants, or other sources of funding available only to in-state students. Whether or not you want to obtain residency will have to do with your specific financial situation, so you should be sure to weigh your all of your options carefully before making your decision.

Federal Financial Aid Programs

There are a number of sources of financial aid available to students: federal and state governments, private agencies, and the colleges themselves. In addition, there are three different forms of aid: grants, earnings, and loans.

The federal government is the single largest source of financial aid for students. In recent years, the U.S. Department of Education's student financial aid programs made more than $80 billion available in loans, grants, and other aid to 14 million students. At present, there are four federal grant programs—Federal Pell Grant, Federal Supplemental Educational Opportunity Grant (FSEOG), Teacher Education Assistance for College and Higher Education (TEACH) Grant, and Iraq and Afghanistan Service Grant. There are two federal loan programs: Federal Perkins Loan Program and the William D. Ford Federal Direct Loan Program. The federal government also has a job program, Federal Work-Study Program (FWS), which helps colleges provide employment for students. In addition to the student aid programs, there are also tuition tax credits and deductions. They are the American Opportunity Credit, the Lifetime Learning Credit, the Tuition and Fees Tax Deduction, and the Student Loan Interest Tax Deduction. Also, there is AmeriCorps. AmeriCorps will pay the interest that is accrued on qualified student loans for members who complete the service program.

The majority of federal higher education loans are made in the Direct Loan Program, which makes available two kinds of loans: loans to students and PLUS loans to parents or to graduate or professional students. These loans are either subsidized or unsubsidized. Subsidized loans are made on the basis of demonstrated student need, and the interest is paid by the government during the time the student is in school or deferment. For the unsubsidized (non-need-based) loans and PLUS loans, interest begins to accrue as funds are disbursed.

All new federal student loans come directly from the U.S. Department of Education under the Direct Loan Program. Students interested in receiving federal student aid should continue to complete a Free Application for Federal Student Aid (FAFSA) for each school year that they wish to be considered for aid. For more information about applying for federal student aid, call 800-4-FED-AID (800-433-3243)(toll-free) or visit www.fafsa.ed.gov.

FEDERAL PELL GRANT

The Federal Pell Grant is the largest grant program; more than 9 million students receive Pell Grants annually. This grant is intended to be the starting point of assistance for lower-income families. Eligibility for a Pell Grant is based on the Expected Family Contribution. The amount you receive will depend on your EFC and the cost of education at the college you will attend. The highest award depends on how much funding the program receives from the government. For the 2018–19 award year (July 1, 2018 to June 30, 2019), the maximum award is $5,920. As of July 1, 2012, a student can not receive a Federal Pell Grant for more than 12 semesters or the equivalent. A student will receive notice when he/she is close to their limit.

FEDERAL SUPPLEMENTAL EDUCATIONAL OPPORTUNITY GRANT (FSEOG)

As its name implies, Federal Supplemental Educational Opportunity Grants provide additional need-based federal grant money to supplement the Federal Pell Grant Program. Each participating college is given funds to award to especially needy students. The maximum award is $4,000 per year, but the amount you receive depends on the college's awarding policy, the availability of FSEOG funds, the total cost of education, and the amount of other aid awarded.

FEDERAL WORK-STUDY PROGRAM (FWS)

This program provides jobs for students who demonstrate need. Salaries are paid by funds from the federal government as well as the college. Students work on an hourly basis on or off campus and must be paid at least the federal minimum wage. Students may earn only up to the amount awarded in the financial aid package.

FEDERAL PERKINS LOAN PROGRAM

This is a low-interest (5%) loan for students with exceptional financial need. Perkins Loans are made through the college's financial aid office with the college as the lender. Undergraduate students can borrow a maximum of $5,500 per year, and there is a cumulative limit of $27,500. The annual limit for graduate and professional-degree-seeking students is $8,500 with a total cumulative limit (including the $27,500) of $60,000. Borrowers may take up to ten years to repay the loan, beginning nine months after they graduate, leave school, or drop below half-time status. No interest accrues while they are in school, and, under certain conditions (e.g., they teach in low-income areas, work in law enforcement, are full-time nurses or medical technicians, serve as Peace Corps or VISTA volunteers, etc.), some or all of the loan can be cancelled. In addition, payments can be deferred under certain conditions such as unemployment.

FEDERAL DIRECT LOANS

A Direct Loan is borrowed directly from the U.S. Department of Education through the college's financial aid office.

Federal Financial Aid Programs

Name of Program	Type of Program	Maximum Award Per Year
Federal Pell Grant	need-based grant	$6,095
Federal Supplemental Educational Opportunity Grant (FSEOG)	need-based grant	$4,000
Teacher Education Assistance for College and Higher Education (TEACH) Grants	need/merit	up to $4,000 a year for undergraduates
Iraq and Afghanistan Service Grant	need/merit	$6,095 (based on strict criteria being met)
Federal Work-Study Program (FWS)	need-based part-time job	no maximum
Federal Perkins Loan Program	need-based loan	$5,500
Subsidized Federal Direct Loan	need-based grant student loan	$3,500 (first year)
Unsubsidized Federal Direct Loan	non-need based	$5,500 (first year, dependent student)

The interest rate on Direct Subsidized and Unsubsidized Loans for undergraduates with a first disbursement date between July 1, 2018, and June 30, 2019, is 4.29 percent. For those loans with a first disbursement date between July 1, 2017, and June 30, 2018, the interest rate was 4.29 percent.

The maximum amount dependent students may borrow in any one year is $5,500 for freshmen, $6,500 for sophomores, and $7,500 for juniors and seniors, with a maximum of $31,000 for the total undergraduate program (of which not more than $23,000 can be subsidized). The maximum amount independent students can borrow is $9,500 for freshmen (of which no more than $3,500 can be subsidized), $10,500 for sophomores (of which no more than $4,500 can be subsidized), and $12,500 for juniors and seniors (of which no more than $5,500 can be subsidized). Independent students can borrow up to $57,500 (of which no more than $23,000 can be subsidized) for the total undergraduate program. Borrowers may be charged a small origination fee, which is deducted from the loan proceeds. See the helpful, easy-to-read chart on the next page for maximum annual and total subsidized and unsubsidized loan limits.

To apply for a Federal Student Loan, you must first complete the FAFSA to determine eligibility for a subsidized loan and then complete a separate loan application that is submitted to the Department of Education. The Department of Education will send a master promissory for completion. The proceeds of the loan, less the origination fee, will be sent to the college to be either credited to your account or released to you directly. Direct loans are processed by the financial aid office as part of the overall financial aid package.

Once the repayment period starts, borrowers of both subsidized and unsubsidized Federal Direct Loans have to pay a combination of interest and principal monthly for up to a 25-year period. There are a number of repayment options as well as opportunities to consolidate federal loans. There are also provisions for extended repayments, deferments, and repayment forbearance, if needed. Note: If you received a Direct Subsidized Loan that was first disbursed between July 1, 2012, and July 1, 2014, you are responsible for paying any interest that accrued during your grace period (first six months after graduation). If you choose not to pay the interest that accrued during your grace period, the interest will be added to your principal balance.

DIRECT PLUS LOANS

PLUS loans are for parents of dependent students to help families with the cost of education. There is no needs test to qualify. For Direct PLUS Loans first disbursed on or after July 1, 2017, and before July 1, 2018, the interest rate is 7%. For Direct PLUS Loans first disbursed on or after July 1, 2018, and before July 1, 2019, the interest rate is 5%. There is no yearly limit; you

Maximum Annual and Total Subsidized and Unsubsidized Loan Limits as of July 1, 2015

Year	Dependent Students (except students whose parents are unable to obtain PLUS Loans)	Independent Students (and dependent undergraduate students whose parents are unable to obtain PLUS Loans)
First-Year Undergraduate	$5,500—No more than $3,500 of this amount may be in subsidized loans.	$9,500—No more than $3,500 of this amount may be in subsidized loans.
Second-Year Undergraduate	$6,500—No more than $4,500 of this amount may be in subsidized loans.	$10,500—No more than $4,500 of this amount may be in subsidized loans.
Third-Year and Beyond Undergraduate	$7,500 per year—No more than $5,500 of this amount may be in subsidized loans.	$12,500 per year—No more than $5,500 of this amount may be in subsidized loans.
Graduate or Professional Degree Students	Not Applicable	$20,500
Maximum Total Debt from Subsidized and Unsubsidized Loans	$31,000—No more than $23,000 of this amount may be in subsidized loans.	$57,500 for undergraduates—No more than $23,000 of this amount may be in subsidized loans. $138,500 for graduate or professional students—No more than $65,500 of this amount may be in subsidized loans. The graduate debt limit includes all federal loans received for undergraduate study.

Source: https://studentaid.ed.gov/sa/types/loans/subsidized-unsubsidized

can borrow up to the cost of your child's education, less other financial aid received. Repayment begins sixty days after the funds are disbursed. The origination fee is approximately 4 percent and may be subtracted from the proceeds. Parent borrowers must generally have a good credit record to qualify.

AMERICAN OPPORTUNITY CREDIT AND LIFETIME LEARNING CREDIT

Tuition tax credits allow families to reduce their tax bill by the out-of-pocket college tuition expense. Unlike a tax deduction, which is modified according to your tax bracket, a tax credit is a dollar-for-dollar reduction in taxes paid.

There are two programs: the American Opportunity Credit and the Lifetime Learning Credit. As is true of many federal programs, there are numerous rules and restrictions that apply. You should check with your tax preparer, financial adviser, or IRS Publication 970 for information about your own particular situation.

American Opportunity Credit

The American Opportunity Credit (formerly the Hope Credit) can be claimed for expenses for the first four years of postsecondary education. This is a change from the previous Hope Credit. The American Opportunity Credit can be claimed now through tax-year 2018 for expenses for course-related books, supplies, and equipment. It is a tax credit of up to $2,500 of the cost of qualifying tuition and expenses, and up to 40 percent of the credit is refundable (up to $1,000).

Eligibility also differs from the former Hope Credit. A taxpayer who pays qualified tuition and related expenses and whose federal income tax return has a modified adjusted gross income of $80,000 or less ($160,000 or less for joint filers) is eligible for the credit. The credit is reduced ratably if a taxpayer's modified adjusted gross income exceeds those amounts. A taxpayer whose modified adjusted gross income is greater than $90,000 ($180,000 for joint filers) cannot benefit from this credit.

For more information about the American Opportunity Tax Credit, go online to http://www.irs.gov/uac/American-Opportunity-Tax-Credit:-Questions-and-Answers.

Lifetime Learning Credit

The Lifetime Learning Credit is the counterpart of the American Opportunity Credit. The qualifying taxpayer can claim an annual tax credit of up to $2,000—20 percent of the first $10,000 of tuition. The credit is available for net tuition and fees, less grant aid. The total credit available is limited to $2,000 per year per taxpayer (or joint-filing couple). There is no limit on the number of years the lifetime learning credit can be claimed for each student. However, a taxpayer cannot claim both the American Opportunity Credit and Lifetime Learning Credit for the same student in one year. For more information, visit http://www.irs.gov/Individuals/LLC.

TUITION AND FEES TAX DEDUCTION

The Tuition and Fees Tax Deduction could reduce taxable income by as much as $4,000. This deduction is taken as an adjustment to income, which means you can claim this deduction even if you do not itemize deductions on Schedule A of Form 1040. This deduction may benefit taxpayers who do not qualify for either the American Opportunity Credit or Lifetime Learning Credit.

Up to $4,000 may be deducted for tuition and fees required for enrollment or attendance at an eligible postsecondary institution. Personal living and family expenses, including room and board, insurance, medical, and transportation, are not deductible expenses.

The exact amount of the Tuition and Fees Tax Deduction depends on the amount of qualified tuition and related expenses paid for one's self, spouse, or dependents, and your Adjusted Gross Income. Consult the IRS or your tax preparer for more information.

STUDENT LOAN INTEREST TAX DEDUCTION

If you made student loan interest payments, you may be able to reduce your taxable income by up to $2,500. You should check with your lender with regards to the amount of interest you paid if you did not receive an IRS Form 1098-E and your tax preparer or IRS Publication 970 for additional information, which can be found online at http://www.irs.gov/publications/p970/ch04.html.

AMERICORPS

AmeriCorps is a national umbrella group of service programs for students. Participants work in a public or private nonprofit agency and provide service to the community in one of four priority areas: education, human services, the environment, and public safety. For all AmeriCorps programs, members receive a modest living allowance, and some programs provide housing. Individuals may not save much money during their year of service, but most find the living allowance to be adequate to cover their needs. AmeriCorps members who complete a term of service also receive an AmeriCorps Education Award. Many student-loan lenders will postpone the repayment of student loans during service in AmeriCorps, and AmeriCorps will pay the interest that is accrued on qualified student loans for members who complete the service program. Participants can work before, during, or after college and can use the funds to either pay current educational expenses or repay federal student loans. For more information, visit http://www.nationalservice.gov/programs/americorps.

College Financial Aid: Impressing the Financial Aid Counselor

The best way to impress a financial aid counselor is to be prepared and do as much research as you can before your meeting. You want to build a positive relationship with the individuals in the financial aid office as they often are the ones who will ultimately help you receive the most financial aid possible, including scholarships and grants.

Here are some things to know and do:

- Be aware of the school's financial aid application deadline.
- Meet with the financial aid counselor as soon as possible.
- Keep copies of everything that will help complete your application.
- Check with the financial aid office to make sure your file is complete and that everything was filled out correctly.
- Speak with the financial aid officer about any scholarships you receive, whether they are from the school itself or from outside of the school.
- Never be late to an appointment, and call to cancel if you need to do so.

ACTION ITEMS

Be sure to gather and submit any documentation that will provide a truthful claim of your financial situation, and always ask for a confirmation of submission. Don't lie about anything in your financial aid application, and always be open to discussing your situation. Financial aid counselors are here to help.

Be patient. Financial aid decisions can take time. Appeals can typically take more time than usual, as well as the fact that committees usually only meet a couple of times a month to review appeal submissions. Ask your financial aid counselor about an expected date, and if you haven't heard from him/her in a couple of weeks at minimum, call them to follow up.

While you want to be assertive and make sure that your questions are answered to your satisfaction, you also want to be sure you are polite and respectful. Politeness goes a long way. Often financial aid counselors will work with you every year when applying for scholarships, grants, and loans, so you want to be sure you establish a good long-term relationship.

Keep these "DO" tips in mind:

- Do call ahead to make an appointment—otherwise you might be waiting all day to speak with the counselor.
- Do make a list of any questions or concerns you have.
- Do ask what requirements are needed in order to keep getting aid in the future, for example a minimum GPA.
- Do compare your family's expected contribution (EFC) with other schools, and ask the counselor to explain the differences.
- Do ask about employment opportunities on campus.
- Do fill out and submit all applications by the deadline.
- Do ask what changes in your financial situation can affect your award.
- Do ask if outside scholarships will affect your financial aid award.
- Do thank the counselor for helping you.

Remember, financial aid counselors are there to help you. While some may seem rude or be rushed, it doesn't mean that you have to be as well. Patience goes a long way in getting the help you need.

Keep these "DON'T" tips in mind:

- Don't try to compare your award with others as each situation is different. Ask your counselor if you have any questions.
- Don't discuss consumer debt with your counselor. Consumer debt will not be taken into account.
- Don't give up; you can always apply again the following year.
- Don't take out students loans just because you can. Loans HAVE to be repaid, usually with interest. Only take out loans that you absolutely need.
- Don't be ashamed to discuss your personal finances, including bankruptcy, child-support, medical expenses, and anything else that may affect your ability to pay for tuition.

Keep these tips in mind as you are meeting with your financial aid counselor, and always remember that they are there to help you find the best financial aid package as possible.

Inside the Federal Work-Study Program

I f you're like millions of other families with college-age youth you may have had that moment. It's the stomach-churching wrinkle in time when you realize that the gap between the amount of money you've saved for your child's college education and the cost of that dream university seems as insurmountable as crossing the ocean on a surfboard. Even as you fill out the Free Application for Federal Student Aid (FAFSA) and your child gets the award letter from the college, the sticker shock can be depressing. But there is glimmer of hope, and it's called the Federal Work-Study Program (FWS).

The federally funded FWS, formerly known as the College Campus Work-Study Program, was a part of the anti-poverty legislation that swept the country in the 1960s. FWS partners with 3,400 institutions in the country to pay students to work on a college or university campus. Looking at the words "work study," may instill fear in some parent's hearts. They may think of nightmarish scenarios where their son or daughter spends so much time guarding the science building that they won't have time for their studies. This isn't necessarily true. There are several aspects to the federally supported work-study program that makes it an attractive option for students looking to lower their college bill.

WORK-STUDY CAN BE A VALUABLE EXPERIENCE

The Federal Work-Study (FWS) Program is a federal student aid program that provides part-time employment while you are enrolled in school to help pay your education expenses. The Federal Work-Study Program emphasizes, whenever possible, employment in civic education and work that is related to your course of study.

If you work on campus, you'll most likely work for your school. If you work off campus, your employer might be a private nonprofit organization or a public agency, and the work performed must be in the public interest.

Colleges and universities like that the FWS is federally subsidized, so they will offer this option as part of a financial aid package first because it saves them money. So send your FASFA as early as possible, especially if you want to beat out the millions of students who seek work-study jobs! Also, don't forget to indicate on your FASFA that you are interested in a work-study job.

In addition, it may be best to choose work-study over outside employment. You may believe that work is work, but when it comes to work-study jobs that sentiment is not true. Work-study jobs are usually better for students because the payment you receive is NOT counted against you when applying for financial aid. This could make a huge difference in how much aid you receive from your chosen institution.

WORK-STUDY JOBS—NOT ALWAYS "BORING"

Not all work-study jobs have to be through educational institutions. The program also funds jobs at a federal, state, or local public agency; a private nonprofit organization; or even a private for-profit organization. Check and see if your school has a partnership with an off-campus workplace. You might be able to find a work-study position in your field of study. This allows you to gain valuable experience and not just collect "man hours" while you pay down your college price tag.

Still, the type of job a student is privy to largely depends upon the intuition's work-study program. Some programs focus on interesting options such as janitorial services, cafeteria work, or even telemarketer. But with a little ingenuity, students can find a work-study assignment that fits their academic and financial need. For example, at Colorado College, a private school in Colorado Springs, work-study students can apply for jobs as diverse as stage manager for theater productions or work off campus at a nonprofit such as the Children's Literacy Center. To ensure you get a work-study position that fits your career goals, it's best to talk to officials at your institution early and often about available work-study options. For example, according to the U.S. Department of Education, a college must use 7 percent of its work-study funds to support students "working in community service jobs, including reading tutors for preschool age or elementary school children, mathematics tutors for students enrolled in elementary school through ninth grade, literacy tutors in a family literacy project performing family literacy activities, or emergency preparedness and response." When you talk to your institution's financial aid office you might mention your experience in any of these areas. This won't guarantee you a "better" work-study job, but it certainly can't hurt.

TAKE ANOTHER LOOK AT WORK-STUDY

With flexible hours, guaranteed pay and the ability to help your institution and community, the work-study option is an attractive way for students to pay for their college education. Do not over look its benefits. Indicate work-study on your FAFSA application, and apply early. Who knows? You could end up as a tennis racquet stringer at Colorado College. For more information about FWS, go to http://www2.ed.gov/programs/fws/index.html.

Analyzing Financial Aid Award Letters

by Richard Woodland

You have just received the financial aid award letters. Now what? This is the time to do a detailed analysis of each college's offer to help you pay for your child's education. Remember, accepting financial aid is a family matter. More often than not, parents need to borrow money to send their dependent children to college. You need to clearly understand the types of aid you and your child are being offered. How much is "free" money in the form of grants and/or scholarships that does not have to be repaid? If your financial aid award package includes loans, what are the terms and conditions for these loans? A good tool to have with you is the federal government's most recent issue of *Funding Your Education* or *Do You Need Money for College? Federal Student Aid at a Glance,* available from the school's financial aid office or at http://www.fsapubs.gov. This publication is very helpful in explaining the federal grant and loan programs that are usually a part of the aid package.

Let's take a minute to explain what is meant by "financial aid award package." A college will offer an aid applicant a combination of aid types, "packaged" in the form of grants and scholarships, loans, and a work-study job, based on the information provided on the FAFSA and/or another application. Many schools use a priority filing date, which guarantees that all applications received by this date will be considered for the full range of institutional aid programs available. Late applicants (by even one day!) often are only awarded the basic aid programs from state and federal sources. *It is important to apply on time.*

EVALUATE EACH LETTER

As each award letter comes in, read it through carefully. The following are some critical points to consider:

- **Does the Cost of Attendance (COA) include all projected costs?** Each award letter should state the school's academic year COA. Tuition, fees, room, board, books, transportation, and personal expenses are what normally make up the COA. Does the award letter itemize all these components? Or does it omit some? This is crucial because this is what you will need to budget for. If you need additional information, be sure to contact the financial aid office. They will be glad to provide you with information or answer any questions you may have about their costs.

- **What is your Expected Family Contribution (EFC)?** Is the school's—not just the federal government's—EFC listed on the award letter? Some schools may require a higher EFC than you expected. Be aware that the EFC may increase or decrease each year depending on the information you provide on the renewal FAFSA or other financial aid application.

- **Is there unmet need?** Does the aid package cover the difference between the COA and the EFC? Not every school can cover your full need. If the aid package does not cover your full need, does the information with the award letter provide you with alternative loan options? If not, contact the financial aid office for more information.

- **Is the scholarship renewable for four years?** If your child is awarded a scholarship based on scholastic achievement or talent, you need to ask these questions: Is there a minimum grade point average he has to maintain? Can he switch majors but keep the scholarship? Does he need to participate in an "honors college" program to maintain the scholarship? If he needs to change to part-time status, will the award amount be prorated, or does he need to maintain full-time status? If it is an athletic or "special talent" scholarship, will he continue to receive the award if for some reason he cannot continue with the specific program? Renewal of scholarship funds is often the biggest misunderstanding between families and colleges. Be sure you clearly understand the terms and conditions of all grants and scholarships.

- **What will the college do to your child's award if she receives outside, noninstitutional scholarships?** Will the award be used to cover unmet need or reduce her student loans? Will the college reduce her institutional grants or scholarships? Or will they reduce her work-study award? (This is a good time to compare each school's policy on this matter.) Remember, your overall aid cannot total more than the COA, and many programs cannot exceed your financial need.

- **What are the interest rates of the loans that are offered?** Did another school offer you more than one loan and why? *Do not* sign the award letter until you understand your loan obligations. Again, *Funding Education Beyond High School: The Guide to Federal Student Aid* can be very helpful with this part of the analysis.

- **Is the school likely to cover the same expenses every year?** In particular, ask if grant or scholarship funds are normally reduced or increased after the freshman year, even if family income and EFC remain the same. Some colleges will increase the self-help (loan, job) percentage every year but not necessarily the free money.

- **If work-study was awarded, how many hours a week will your child be expected to work?** If you feel working that many hours will have a negative impact on your child's academic performance, you may want to request that the awarded job funds be changed to a loan. You must ask immediately because funds are limited. Many schools are flexible with these funds early in the process.

- **What happens if (or more likely, when) tuition increases?** Check with the financial aid office to find out what its policy is for renewing an aid package. If, for example, tuition increases by 5 percent each of the next three years and your EFC remains the same, what will happen to your scholarships, grants, and loans?

You can always appeal your award letter if you feel that your needs are not being met, if your family situation has changed, or if you have received a better award from a competitive school. You have the right to ask for a reconsideration of your award. (Do not use the word *negotiate*.) When asking for reconsideration, be sure to provide the aid officer with all relevant information.

COMPARE LETTERS

After you have received and reviewed all the award letters from the schools your child is considering, the next step is to compare them and determine which schools are offering the best aid packages. Following are three sample award letters and a sample spreadsheet that shows you how to analyze and compare each school's awards.

(Note: These award letters are simply for discussion purposes. They should not be considered to be representative award letters with an EFC of $9,550.)

Once you have entered all the information into a spreadsheet of your own and come up with the balances, here are some things to consider for each school:

- **How much is the balance?** Ideally, your balance should be $0, but look to see which school has the lowest balance amount.

- **What part of the aid package comes in the form of grants and scholarships?** It is important to note this because these awards (gift aid) do not have to be paid back.

- **Look at the loans.** Usually, the best financial deal contains more money in scholarships and less in loan dollars. Based on expected freshman-year borrowing, determine the debt burden at each school once your child graduates. You have to multiply the amount of your loan by four or five years, depending on how long it will take for your child to graduate.

UNIVERSITY A
FINANCIAL AID AWARD LETTER
2018-2019

Date: 4/21/18
ID#: 0000000009

Dear Jane Smith,
We are pleased to inform you that you are eligible to receive the financial assistance indictate in the area labled "Your Financial Aid."
We estimated your budget based on the following assumptions:

In-state resident and living on campus.

	FALL	SPRING	TOTAL
Tuition and Fees	$3,849	$3,849	$7,698
Room & Board	3,769	3,770	7,539
Books	420	420	840
Transportation	973	974	1,947
Personal expenses	369	369	738
Estimated Coast of Attendance	**$9,380**	**$9,382**	**$18,762**

Your Financial Aid

	FALL	SPRING	TOTAL
Federal Pell Grant	$1,950	$1,950	$3,900
Federal Direct Subsidized Loan	$1,750	$1,750	$3,500
State Grant	432	432	864
Total Financial Aid	**$4,132**	**$4,132**	**$8,264**
Unmet Need	**$5,248**	**$5,250**	**$10,498**

What to Do Next:
- Verify that accurate assumptions have been used to determine your awards.
- Carefully review and follow the instructions on the Data Changes Form.
- To reduce or decline all or part of your loans, you must complete and return the Data Changes Form.
- We will assume you fully accept the awards above unless you submit changes to us immediately.
- Return corrections and required documents promptly.
- Retain this letter for your records.

UNIVERSITY B
FINANCIAL AID AWARD LETTER
2018-2019

Date: 4/21/18
ID#: 0000000009

Dear Jane Smith,
We are pleased to inform you that you are eligible to receive the financial assistance indictate in the area labled "Your Financial Aid."
We estimated your budget based on the following assumptions:

Nonresident and living on campus.

	FALL	SPRING	TOTAL
Tuition and Fees	$9,805	$9,085	$18,170
Room & Board	2,835	2,835	5,670
Books	410	410	820
Transportation	875	875	1,750
Personal Expenses	378	377	755
Estimated Coast of Attendance	**$13,583**	**$13,582**	**$27,165**

Your Financial Aid

	FALL	SPRING	TOTAL
Federal Pell Grant	$1,950	$1,950	$3,900
Federal SEOG Grant	225	225	450
Academic Excellence Scholarship	500	500	1,000
Federal Work-Study	1,050	1,050	2,100
Federal Perkins Loan Program	1,250	1,250	2,500
Subsidized Federal Stafford Student Loan	1,750	1,750	3,500
University Student Loan	2,000	2,000	4,000
Total Financial Aid	**$8,725**	**$8,725**	**$17,450**
Unmet Need	**$4,858**	**$4,857**	**$9,715**

What to Do Next:
- Verify that accurate assumptions have been used to determine your awards.
- Carefully review and follow the instructions on the Data Changes Form.
- To reduce or decline all or part of your loans, you must complete and return the Data Changes Form.
- We will assume you fully accept the awards above unless you submit changes to us immediately.
- Return corrections and required documents promptly.
- Retain this letter for your records.

UNIVERSITY C
FINANCIAL AID AWARD LETTER
2018-2019

Date: 4/21/18
ID#: 0000000009

Dear Jane Smith,
We are pleased to inform you that you are eligible to receive the financial assistance indictate in the area lablcd "Your Financial Aid."
We estimated your budget based on the following assumptions:

Living on campus.

	FALL	SPRING	TOTAL
Tuition and Fees	$14,955	$14,955	$29,910
Room & Board	4,194	4,193	8,387
Books	450	450	900
Transportation	350	350	700
Personal Expenses	1,295	1,293	2,588
Estimated Coast of Attendance	**$21,244**	**$21,241**	**$42,485**

Your Financial Aid

	FALL	SPRING	TOTAL
Institutional Grant	$10,805	$10,805	$21,610
Federal Pell Grant	$1,950	$1,950	$3,900
Federal SEOG Grant	2,000	2,000	4,000
Federal Work-Study Program	1,713	1,712	3,425
Total Financial Aid	**$16,468**	**$16,467**	**$32,935**
Unmet Need	**$4,776**	**$4,774**	**$9,550**

What to Do Next:
■ Verify that accurate assumptions have been used to determine your awards.
■ Carefully review and follow the instructions on the Data Changes Form.
■ To reduce or decline all or part of your loans, you must complete and return the Data Changes Form.
■ We will assume you fully accept the awards above unless you submit changes to us immediately.
■ Return corrections and required documents promptly.
■ Retain this letter for your records.

Comparison Grid

	University A (State University)	University B (Nonresident State University)	University C (Private College)
Cost of Attendance	$18,762	$27,165	$42,485
Tuition and Fees	7,698	18,170	29,910
Room & Board	7,539	5,670	8,367
Books	840	820	900
Transportation	1,947	1,750	700
Personal Expenses	738	755	2,558
Grants and Scholarships	4,764	5,350	29,510
Loans	3,500	10,000	0
Work-Study	0	2,00	3,425
Expected Family Contribution	9,550	9,550	9,550
Balance	$948	$165	$0

Some things to notice:
- At all schools, the federal Pell Grant remains the same.
- The loan amounts varied greatly among these schools.
- Even though University C (a private college) has the highest "sticker price," the net cost is less than the state schools.
- University B is a state university, but you are classified as an out-of-state resident (or nonresident). Many Students in this situation find that the higher out-of-state costs combined with lower grant aid make this a costly decision.
- All schools assume that you will be residing in on-campus housing. But if you choose to commute to University A, you would save a substatial amount because you would not have the $7,539 room and board cost.

And remember that the loan amounts will probably increase each year. You also should take into consideration that you will have to borrow even more as the COA increases each year. To determine the best loan deal, consider:
- —What are the terms of the loans?
- —What are interest rates?
- —Do you pay the yearly interest rate during enrollment or is the interest subsidized or paid by the government?
- —Is any money due during enrollment or is it deferred until after graduation? Figuring out how much you will owe at each school at graduation will give you a clear picture of what your financial situation will be after graduation.

However, unless cost is your only concern, you shouldn't simply choose the school offering the lowest loan amounts. Many other factors need to be considered, such as academic and social environment. And you should never reject a school based solely on insufficient financial aid. Consult with an aid administrator to discuss possible alternatives.

Finally, if the college that costs the most is still the one your child wants to attend, there are a number of ways to find money to cover the gap between the aid package and your actual cost, including paying more than the EFC figure, increasing student borrowing, working more hours, and taking out a PLUS loan.

Richard Woodland is Vice President of Development for ProEd Solutions. He previously served as Director of Financial Aid at Rutgers University–Camden and as Director of Student Services and Financial Assistance at the Curtis Institute of Music.

The "Non-Offer"—Dealing With a Low Financial Aid Letter

by Ken O'Connor
Chief Impact Officer, Invite Education

When the last of college financial aid award letters are sent out, plenty of congratulations are in order to families that have their choice school lined up with their funding eligibility ready to go.

But there's a less publicized occurrence that's common as well: the disappointment of realizing that the financial aid awards cannot cover enough of the costs of a preferred college. In certain cases, I call it the "Non-Offer," when a family of modest means applies to a school with the hopes of gaining enough funding to make it affordable, and the school responds with limited awards.

GOING TO A STATE SCHOOL THAT IS OUT OF YOUR STATE

It's often discussed how affordable state schools are in comparison to private schools. But this is not the case when a person wants to attend a state school that is out of their state of residence. In an interesting twist of budgetary fate, state schools looking to boost their revenues may admit many students from out of state, charging them the full out-of-state tuition, plus requiring them to live on campus freshman year. For many state schools, pulling students from out of state is a financial win, practically doubling or even tripling the tuition costs but also leaving one less seat for an in-state student who was hoping to attend locally on discounted (in-state) tuition. Receiving an award letter with a $30,000+ shortfall in the first year adds up to a fair warning. Yes, you are invited to join this school—all you need is enough extra money over four years that could buy a 1-BR, mid-market condo.

UNDERSTANDING THE REAL COST OF STUDENT LOANS

Many 18 year olds are excited just to get away from their parents, and going away to college seems to provide the perfect venue until you take a step back and look at the real costs. I used the 1-BR condo example earlier to help illustrate in real terms *cost versus value*.[1]

Cost is an issue only in the absence of Value: What is most valuable to your child at 18?

Without real-world context, it's simply impossible for teenagers to understand the long-term implications of debt.

But they do value independence—or at least the perception of it. To get around this, I use examples of property values, mortgage, and rent payments as the closest comparison to large student loan debt (!).

So, go ahead and run the numbers with a loan calculator. No fancy math required. $120k @ 6% would require payments of around $1,332 per month over ten years and cost about $40,000 in interest. Now look at the student's major. Question: Does this seem at all reasonable for an undergraduate degree from this particular institution? It's tough to justify, but once it's realized that the amount of debt used for their education would be enough to purchase real estate, then the young student at least has some context of their college costs. It's up to them to respond by evaluating this school option accordingly, while parents can more clearly see what they would be cosigning for.

RE-CHART THE COURSE

There's no time for optimism or pessimism when making the final school choice. It's time for *realism* in the decision-making process, given the short time ahead.

Here are three things to consider:

1. **Appeal for additional funding—if there is a legitimate reason to do so.** Real financial aid appeals are necessary due to specific circumstances including, but not limited to, a parent being laid-off, divorce, or a major medical issue and its ensuing expenses. In these types of appeals, documentation is required to prove that the financial need of the family has increased greatly due to such major life circumstances. If you are asking the school for more funding without one of these documentable circumstances, it will not go very far. If your student is looking at a $20,000–$30,000 gap per year without the cash to pay for it, you cannot expect a financial aid office to fund the difference.

2. **Eliminate the options that are not financially feasible.** It's time to say no and entertain the process of elimination. This is tough as some students grow quite attached to a preferred school choice, but they are going to have to get over it when it's simply unaffordable. Financial discipline is in short supply, but it's needed now more than ever during these uneasy economic times.

3. **Focus on your next simple step forward.** Take the pragmatic approach to affordability and value in higher education. Attend a school close by, and commute from home. Community college is still the go-to option to complete a substantial amount of required college credits while preparing to transfer to a four-year degree institution elsewhere.

What Long-Term Planners Learn From This

The last thing you want is to be stuck between a rock and a hard place, but that's exactly where most middle-income families are when financial aid award letters finally arrive. Avoid this by having these key areas well understood.

- Aptitude: Planning well for college also means honestly accounting for the student's aptitude. Early testing, excellent grades, and incredible mental acuity far above the average can be spotted rather quickly, even before starting high school. There will always be winners on the high end of the intelligence spectrum who have everything to gain from the college admissions process. This is a minority of students, so if your child is not on this level, it's not anyone's fault. It's better to be honest about your child's capabilities than to dream that somehow they will magically receive a perfect on the SAT® or ACT®. In such cases, expect college to remain an expense covered mainly by income, savings, student loans, and perhaps some need-based aid. If it turns out your child is able to earn a scholarship, it's an additional blessing, but good planners know well in advance the odds of qualifying and make up the difference by locating and applying for as many opportunities as they can find.

- Savings: It's cheaper to save than to borrow.[2] Planners remember this every month they contribute to their child's 529 plan by Kindergarten—or perhaps much earlier. They already know college is expensive, and if they, as a parent are already experienced with student loan debt, they may be even more motivated to save so their child can avoid it. College savings are up this past year,[3] with increases in assets and new accounts being opened. This is a good sign, as truly the entire higher education system is dealing with a flux of funding, where state support has dwindled, and the Parent Plus loan[4] may be subject to change in credit-approval criteria in the future. Without any savings, college options are just further limited to scholarship and financial aid eligibility that may or may not be robust when the child finally graduates high school.

REFERENCES

1. *http://www.theatlantic.com/education/archive/2015/10/the-allure-of-the-out-of-state-student/410656/*

2. *https://b2b.inviteeducation.com/2016/04/05/top-5-reasons-for-529/*

3. *http://time.com/money/4259055/saving-more-for-college-529-plan/*

4. *http://www.studentloanborrowerassistance.org/new-rules-plus-loan-credit-checks/*

Ken O'Connor has served parents and students for over fifteen years with high-quality knowledge and information about the college financing process. Ken developed his expertise as a financial aid officer, working face-to-face with families creating college payment strategies. At Invite Education, he continues to help thousands of families make smart college choices through the use of educational planning technology, blending his practical wisdom with in-depth knowledge of the financial aid process. He holds a B.S. an MBA in Finance from Fairleigh Dickinson University in New Jersey.

Parents' and Students' Common Questions Answered

Q *Are a student's chances of being admitted to a college reduced if the student applies for financial aid?*

A Generally no. Nearly all colleges have a policy of "need-blind" admissions, which means that a student's financial need is not taken into account in the admission decision. There are a few selective colleges, however, that do consider ability to pay before deciding whether or not to admit a student. Some colleges will mention this in their literature; others may not. The best advice is to apply for financial aid if the student needs assistance to attend college.

Q *Are parents penalized for saving money for college?*

A No. As a matter of fact, families that have made a concerted effort to save money for college are in a much better position than those that have not. For example, a student from a family that has saved money may not have to borrow as much. Furthermore, the "taxing rate" on savings is quite low—only about 5 percent of the parents' assets are assessed and neither the home equity nor retirement savings are included. For example, a single 40-year-old parent who saved $40,000 for college expenses will have about $1,900 counted as part of the parental contribution. Two parents, if the older one is 40 years old (a parent's age factors into the formulation), would have about $300 counted. (Note: The "taxing rate" for student assets is much higher—20 percent—compared to 5 percent for parents.)

Q *How does the financial aid system work in cases of divorce or separation? How are stepparents treated?*

A In cases of divorce or separation, the financial aid application(s) should be completed by the parent with whom the student lived for the longest period of time in the past twelve months (custodial parent). If the custodial parent has remarried, the stepparent is considered a family member and must complete the application along with the biological parent. If your family has any special circumstances, you should discuss these directly with the financial aid office. (Note: Colleges that award their own aid may ask the noncustodial biological parent to complete a separate aid application and a contribution will be calculated.)

Q *When are students considered independent of parental support in applying for financial aid?*

A The student must be at least 24 years of age in order to be considered independent. If younger than 24, the student must be married, be a graduate or professional student, have legal dependents other than a spouse, be an orphan or ward of the court, or be a veteran of the armed forces or on active military duty. However, in very unusual situations, students who can clearly document estrangement from their parents can appeal to the financial aid office for additional consideration.

Q *What can a family do if a job loss occurs?*

A Financial aid eligibility is based on the previous year's income. Currently, the family's 2017 income would be reported to determine eligibility for the 2018–19 academic year. It is possible that that income tax return may not reflect the family's current financial situation, due to a job loss or other hardship. So, families should discuss the situation directly with the financial aid office and be prepared to provide appropriate documentation.

Q *When my daughter first went to college, we applied for financial aid and were denied because our Expected Family Contribution was too high. Now, my son is a high school senior, and we will soon have two in college. Will we get the same results?*

A The results will definitely be different. Both your son and your daughter should apply. As described earlier, need-based financial aid is based on your Expected Family Contribution, or EFC. When you have two children in college, this amount is divided in half for each child.

Q *I've heard about the "middle-income squeeze" in regard to financial aid. What is it?*

A The so-called "middle-income squeeze" is the idea that low-income families qualify for aid, high-income families have adequate resources to pay for education, and those in the middle are not eligible for aid but do not have the ability to pay full college costs. There is no provision in the Federal Methodology that treats middle-income students differently than others (such as an income cutoff for eligibility). The Expected Family Contribution rises proportionately as income and assets increase. If a middle-income family does not qualify for aid, it is because the need analysis formula yields a contribution that exceeds college costs. But keep in mind that if a $65,000-income family does not qualify for grant aid at a public university with a $16,000 cost, the same family will likely be eligible for aid at a private college with a cost of $25,000 or more. Also, there are loan programs available to parents and students that are not based on need. Middle-income families should realize, however, that many of the grant programs funded by federal and state governments are directed at lower-income families. It is therefore likely that a larger share of an aid package for a middle-income student will consist of loans rather than grants.

Q *Given our financial condition, my daughter will be receiving financial aid. We will help out as much as we can, and, in fact, we ourselves will be borrowing. But I am concerned that she will have to take on a lot of loans in order to go to the college of her choice. Does she have any options?*

A She does. If offered a loan, she can decline all or part of it. One option is for her to ask in the financial aid office to have some of the loan changed to a work-study job. If this is not possible, she can find her own part-time work. Often there is an employment office on campus that can help her locate a job. In most cases, the more she works, the less she has to borrow. It is important to remember that the education loans offered to students have very attractive terms and conditions, with flexible repayment options. Students should look upon these loans as a long-term investment that will reap significant rewards.

Q *What are some easy ways to improve my chances of receiving aid?*

A When filling out your scholarship or financial aid application, it's important to remember that the smallest mistake could hurt your chances for landing free money, or even worse, it could disqualify you completely from an awards contest. Grants and scholarships are highly competitive, so it's a good idea to make a list of what's needed and make sure you have everything before submitting your application. If you are submitting an essay, have another pair of eyes look at it for any spelling and grammar errors. Keep a file on everything you're applying for so that you don't miss any elements of an application. Make sure you're using reputable sites to conduct your free scholarship searches. If you have to pay to apply for an award or look for scholarships, chances are you're being scammed. In a nutshell, the best advice is to follow all directions, and make sure that you meet all deadlines.

In addition, when filling out the FAFSA®, it's important to pay close attention to the details, since any errors may delay the application process. These days, it's preferable to fill out the FAFSA® online, since mailed forms can take weeks to process. If you're confused or concerned about something on the application, contact the Federal Student Aid Information Center at 1-800-4FED-AID; questions can also be asked through the FAFSA® Website. Your college's financial aid office should also be able to assist you. The FAFSA® is available this year starting October 1, and it's essential that you don't miss the deadline to apply. The sooner you apply, the sooner you'll know the kind of funding package you are likely to receive, and this will help you determine if you need to apply for any additional aid.

Q *Is it possible to change your financial aid package?*

A Yes. Most colleges have an appeal process. A request to change a need-based loan to a work-study job is usually approved if funds are available. A request to consider special financial circumstances may also be granted. At most colleges, a request for more grant money is rarely approved unless it is based on a change in the information reported. Applicants should speak with the financial aid office if they have concerns about their financial package. Some colleges may even respond to a competitive appeal, that is, a request to match another college's offer.

Q *The cost of attending college seems to be going up so much faster than the Consumer Price Index. Why is that, and how can I plan for my child's four years?*

A The cost of higher education cannot be compared to the Consumer Price Index (CPI). The CPI does not take into account most of the costs faced by colleges. For example, the dollars that universities spend on grants and scholarships have risen rapidly. Many universities have increased enrollment of students from less affluent families, further increasing the need for institutional financial aid. Colleges are expected to be on the cutting edge of technology, not only in research but also in the classroom and in the library. Many colleges have deferred needed maintenance and repairs that can now no longer be put off. In addition, there is market pressure to provide many expensive lifestyle amenities that were not expected ten years ago. In general, you can expect that college costs will rise at least 2 to 3 percent faster than inflation.

Q *I'm struggling with the idea that all students should apply to the college of their choice, regardless of cost, because financial aid will level the playing field. I feel I will be penalized because I have saved for college. My son has been required to save half of his allowance since age six for his college education. Will that count against him when he applies for financial aid? It's difficult to explain to him that his college choices may be limited because of the responsible choices and sacrifices we have made as a family. What can we do to make the most of our situation?*

A In general, it is always better to have planned ahead for college by saving. Families that have put away sufficient funds to pay for college will quickly realize that they have made the burden easier for themselves and their children. In today's college financing world, schools assume that paying for the cost of attendance is a ten-year commitment. So by saving when your child is young, you reap significant advantages from compound interest on the assets and reduce the need to borrow as much while in school. This should reduce the number of years after college that you will be burdened with loans. Families should spend the student's assets first, since the financial aid formulas count these more heavily than parental assets. Then, after the first year, you can explain to the college how you spent these assets, and why you might now need assistance. When looking at parental information, the income of the family is by far the most important component. Contrary to popular belief, parental assets play a minor role in the calculation of need. With this strategy, you have done the right thing, and in the long run, it should prove to be a wise financial plan.

Picking the right college also involves other factors. Students should select the colleges to which they are going to apply in two ways. First, and most important, is to look at colleges that meet your son's academic and lifestyle interests. Most experts will tell him to pick a few "reach" schools (i.e., schools where he is not sure he has the grades and scores required) and at least one or two academically "safe" schools. He should also select one or two financially "safe" schools that you are sure you can afford with either moderate or little financial aid. Most students do not get into all of their first-choice schools, and not everyone can afford the schools to which they are admitted. By working closely with the guidance office in high school and the admissions and financial aid offices at the college, you can maximize your options.

Q *My son was awarded a $2,500 scholarship. This can be split and used for two years. When filling out the FAFSA®, do we have to claim the full amount, or just the $1,250 he plans to use the first year?*

A Congratulations to your son on the scholarship. Nowhere on the FAFSA® should you report this scholarship. It is not considered income or an asset. However, once you choose a school to attend, you must notify the financial aid office for its advice on how to take the funds. But remember, do NOT report it on the FAFSA®.

Q *I will be receiving a scholarship from my local high school. How will this scholarship be treated in my financial aid award?*

A Federal student aid regulations specify that all forms of aid must be included within the defined level of need. This means that additional aid, such as outside scholarships, must be combined with any need-based aid you receive; it may not be kept separate and used to reduce your family's contribution. If the college has not filled 100 percent of your need, it will usually allow outside scholarships to close the gap. Once your total need has been met, the college must reduce other aid and replace it with the outside award. Most colleges will allow you to use some, if not all, of an outside scholarship to replace self-help aid (loans and Federal Work-Study Program awards) rather than grant aid.

Q *Is there enough aid available to make it worthwhile for me to consider colleges that are more expensive than I can afford?*

A Definitely. More than $100 billion in aid is awarded to undergraduates every year. With more than half of all enrolled students qualifying for some type of assistance, this totals more than $5,500 per student. You should view financial aid as a large, national system of tuition discounts, some given according to a student's ability and talent, others based on what a student's family can afford to pay. If you qualify for need-based financial aid, you will essentially pay only your calculated family contribution, regardless of the cost of the college. You will not pay the "sticker price" (the cost of attendance listed in the college catalog) but a lower rate that is reduced by the amount of aid you receive. No college should be ruled out until after financial aid is considered. In addition, when deciding which college to attend, consider that the short-term cost of a college education is only one criterion. If the college meets your educational needs and you are convinced it can launch you on an exciting career, a significant up-front investment may turn out to be a bargain over the long run.

Q *If I don't qualify for need-based aid, what options are available?*

A You should try to put together your own aid package to help reduce your parents' share. There are three sources to look into. First, search for merit scholarships. Second, seek employment, during both the summer and the academic year. The student employment office should be able to help you find a campus job. Third, look into borrowing. Even if you don't qualify for the need-based loan programs, the unsubsidized Federal Direct Loan is available to all students. The terms and conditions are the same as the subsidized loan programs except that interest accrues while you are in college.

After you have contributed what you can through scholarships, employment, and loans, your parents will be faced with their share of the college bill. Many colleges have monthly payment plans that allow families to spread their payments over the academic year. If these monthly payments turn out to be more than your parents can afford, they can take out a parent loan. By borrowing from the college itself, from a commercial agency or lender, or through PLUS, your parents can extend the payments over a ten-year period or longer. Borrowing reduces the monthly obligation to its lowest level, but the total amount paid will be the highest due to principal and interest payments. Before making a decision on where to borrow parental loan funds, be sure to first check with the financial aid office to determine what is the best source of alternative funds.

Q *After applying to college and receiving a financial award letter, am I able to back out of attending if I can't afford it?*

A Of course! This actually happens quite often. If you end up not being able to afford the college you applied to, don't worry. The first step would be to contact the financial aid office just to make sure the award is accurate and there aren't any other ways to cover the costs of attendance, for example a scholarship and/or grant. You never know what may have been missed in the initial application.

Second, if there aren't any other funds that can be awarded, send the admissions office an e-mail letting them know you won't be able to attend, thanking them for their time. They will greatly appreciate your e-mail, and it will help to stay on good terms with the school if you decide to apply again. Never burn bridges!

How to Use This Guide

QUICK-REFERENCE CHART

The amount of aid available at colleges can vary greatly. "College Costs At-a-Glance" lists the percent of freshmen who applied for and received need-based gift aid and the percent of those whose need was fully met. Also listed are the average freshman financial aid package, the average cost after aid, and the average indebtedness upon graduation.

PROFILES OF COLLEGE FINANCIAL AID PROGRAMS

After the federal government, colleges provide the largest amount of financial aid to students. In addition, they control most of the money channeled to students from the federal government. The amount and makeup of your financial aid package will depend on the institution's particular circumstances and its decisions concerning your application. The main section of this book shows you the pattern and extent of each college's current awards. The profiles present detailed factual and statistical data for each school in a uniform format to enable easy, quick references and comparisons. Items that could not be collected in time for publication for specific institutions do not appear in those institutions' profiles. Colleges that supplied no data are listed by name and address only so that you do not overlook them in your search for colleges.

There is much anecdotal evidence that students and their families fail to apply for financial aid under the misconception that student aid goes only to poor families. Financial need in the context of college expenses is not the same as being needy in the broad social context. Middle-class families typically qualify for need-based financial aid; at expensive schools, even upper-middle income families can qualify for need-based financial aid. Peterson's encourages you to apply for financial aid whether or not you think that you will qualify.

To help you understand the definition and significance of each item, the following outline of the profile format explains what is covered in each section. The term college or colleges is frequently used throughout to refer to any institution of higher education, regardless of its official definition.

The College

The name of the college is the official name as it appears on the institution's charter. The city and state listed are the official location of the school. The subhead line shows tuition and required fees, as they were charged to the majority of full-time undergraduate students in the 2017–18 academic year. Any exceptions to the 2017–18 academic year are so noted. For a public institution, the tuition and fees shown are for state residents, and this is noted. If a college's annual expenses are expressed as a comprehensive fee (including full-time tuition, mandatory fees, and college room and board), this is noted, as are any unusual definitions, such as tuition only. The average undergraduate aid package is the average total package of grant, loan, and work-study aid that was awarded to meet the officially defined financial need of full-time undergraduates enrolled in fall 2017 (or fall 2016) who applied for financial aid, were determined to have need, and then actually received financial aid. This information appears in more detail in each profile.

About the Institution

This paragraph gives the reader a brief introduction to a college. It contains the following elements:

Institutional Control

Private institutions are designated as *independent* (nonprofit), *independent/religious* (sponsored by or affiliated with a religious group or having a nondenominational or interdenominational religious orientation), or *proprietary* (profit-making). Public institutions are designated by their primary source of support, such as *federal*, *state*, *commonwealth* (Puerto Rico), *territory* (U.S. territories), *county*, *district* (an administrative unit of public education, often having boundaries different from those of units of local government), *state-and locally-supported* ("locally" refers to county, district, or city), *state-supported* (funded by the state), or *state-related* (funded primarily by the state but administered autonomously).

Type of Student Body

The categories are *men* (100 percent of student body), *coed-primarily men*, *women* (100 percent of student body), *coed-primarily women*, and *coed*. A few schools are designated as *undergraduate: women only, graduate: coed* or *undergraduate: men only, graduate: coed*.

Degrees Awarded

Associate, bachelor's (baccalaureate), *master's, doctoral* (doctorate), and *first professional* (in such fields as law and medicine). There are no institutions in this book that award the associate degree only. Many award the bachelor's as the highest degree.

Number of Undergraduate Majors

This shows the number of academic fields in which the institution offers associate and/or bachelor's degrees. The purpose of this is to give you an indication of the range of subjects available.

Enrollment

These figures are based on the actual number of full-time and part-time students enrolled in degree programs as of fall 2017 (or 2016 if the 2017 figure was not available). In most instances, they are designated as *total enrollment* (for the specific college or university) and *freshmen*. If the institution is a university and its total enrollment figure includes graduate students, a separate figure for *undergraduates* may be provided. If the profiled institution is a subunit of a university, the figures may be designated *total university enrollment* for the entire university and *total unit enrollment* for the specific subunit.

Methodology Used for Determining Need

Private colleges usually have larger financial aid programs, but public colleges usually have lower sticker prices, especially for in-state or local students. At a public college, your financial need will be less, and you will receive a smaller financial aid package. This note on whether a college uses federal (FAFSA®) or institutional methodology (usually CSS/ Financial Aid PRO-FILE®) will let you know whether you will have to complete one or two kinds of financial aid application forms. Federal Methodology is the needs-analysis formula used by the U.S. Department of Education to determine the Expected Family Contribution (EFC), which, when subtracted from the cost of attendance at an institution, determines the financial need of a student. There is no relative advantage or disadvantage to using one methodology over the other.

Undergraduate Expenses

If provided by the institution, the one-time application fee is listed. Costs are given for the 2018–19 academic year or for the 2017–18 academic year if 2018–19 figures were not yet available. (Peterson's collects information for freshmen specifically.) Annual expenses may be expressed as a comprehensive fee (including full-time tuition, mandatory fees, and college room and board) or may be given as separate figures for full-time tuition, fees, room and board, or room only. For public institutions where tuition differs according to state residence, separate figures are given for area or state residents and for nonresidents. Part-time tuition is expressed in terms of a per-unit rate (per credit, per semester hour, etc.), as specified by the institution.

The tuition structure at some institutions is complex. Freshmen and sophomores may be charged a different rate from that charged juniors and seniors, a professional or vocational division may have a different fee structure from the liberal arts division of the same institution, or part-time tuition may be prorated on a sliding scale according to the number of credit hours taken. Tuition and fees may vary according to academic program, campus/location, class time (day, evening, weekend), course/credit load, course level, degree level, reciprocity agreements, and student level. If tuition and fees differ for international students, the rate charged is listed.

Room and board charges are reported as a double occupancy and nineteen meals per week plan or the equivalent and may vary according to board plan selected, campus/location, gender, type of housing facility, or student level. If no college-owned or -operated housing facilities are offered, the phrase *college housing not available* will appear.

If a college offers a *guaranteed tuition* plan, it promises that the tuition rate of an entering student will not increase for the entire term of enrollment, from entrance to graduation. Other payment plans might include *tuition prepayment*, which allows an entering student to lock in the current tuition rate for the entire term of enrollment by paying the full amount in advance rather than year by year, and *installment* and *deferred* *payment* plans, which allow students to delay the payment of the full tuition.

Guaranteed tuition and tuition prepayment help you to plan the total cost of education and can save you from the financial distress sometimes caused by tuition hikes. Colleges that offer such plans may also help you to arrange financing, which in the long run can cost less than the total of four years of increasing tuition rates. Deferred payment or installment payments may better fit your personal financial situation, especially if you do not qualify for financial aid and, due to other financial commitments, find that obtaining the entire amount due is burdensome. Carefully investigate these plans, however, to see what premium you may pay at the end to allow you to defer immediate payment.

Freshman Financial Aid

Usually, these are actual figures for the 2016–17 term, beginning in fall 2016; figures may also be estimated for the 2017–18 term. The particular term for which these data apply is indicated. The figures are for degree-seeking full-time freshman students. The first figure is the number of freshmen who applied for any kind of financial aid. The next figure is the percentage of those freshmen financial aid applicants who were determined to have financial need—that is, through the formal needs-assessment process, had a cálculated expected family contribution that was less than the total college cost. The next figure is the percentage of this group of eligible freshmen who received any financial aid. The next figure is the percentage of this preceding group of eligible aid recipients whose need was fully met by financial aid. The *Average percent of need met* is the average percentage of financial need met for freshmen who received any need-based aid. The *Average financial aid package* is the average dollar amount awarded (need-based or non-need-based) to freshmen who applied for aid, were deemed eligible, and received any aid; awards used to reduce the expected family contribution are excluded from this average. The final line in most profiles is the percentage of freshmen who had no financial need but who received non-need-based aid other than athletic scholarships or special-group tuition benefits.

What do these data mean to you? If financial aid is important in your comparison of colleges, the relative percentage of students who received any aid, whose need was fully met, and the average percentage of need met have the most weight. These figures reflect the relative abundance of student aid available to the average eligible applicant. The average dollar amount of the aid package has real meaning, but only in relation to the college's expense; you will be especially interested in the difference between this figure and the costs figure, which is what the average student (in any given statistical group, there actually may be no average individual) will have to pay. Of course, if the financial aid package is largely loans rather than grants, you will have to pay this amount eventually. Relative differences in the figures of the number of students who apply for aid and who are deemed eligible can hinge on any number of factors: the relative sticker price of the college, the relative level of wealth of the students' families, the proportion of only children in college and students with siblings in college (families with two or more children in college are more likely to apply for aid and be considered eligible), or the relative sophistication in financial aid matters (or quality of college counseling they may have received) of the students and their families. While these may be interesting, they will not mean too much to most students and families. If you are among the unlucky (or, perhaps, lucky) families who do not qualify for need-based financial aid, the final sentence of this paragraph in the profile will be of interest because it reveals the relative policies that the college has in distributing merit-based aid to students who cannot demonstrate need.

Undergraduate Financial Aid

This is the parallel paragraph to the Freshman Financial Aid paragraph. The same definitions apply, except that the group being considered is degree-seeking full-time under-graduate students (including freshmen).

There are cases of students who chose a particular college because they received a really generous financial aid package in their freshman year and then had to scramble to pay the tuition bill in their later years. If a financial aid package is a key factor in the decision to attend a particular college, you want to be certain that the package offered to all undergraduates is not too far from that offered to freshmen. The key figures are those for the percentage of students who received any aid, the percentage of financial aid recipients whose need was fully met, the average percentage of need met, and the dollar figure of the average financial aid package. Generally, colleges assume that after the freshman year, students develop study habits and time-man-agement skills that will allow them to take on part-time and summer employment without hurting their academic perfor-mance. So, the proportion of self-help aid (work-study and student loans) in the financial aid package tends to increase after the freshman year. This pattern, which is true of most col-leges, can be verified in the freshman-undergraduate figures in the paragraph on Gift Aid (Need-Based).

Gift Aid (Need-Based)

Total amount is the total dollar figure in 2017–18 (esti-mated) or 2016–17 (actual) of need-based scholarships and grant (gift) aid awarded to degree-seeking full-time and part-time students that was used to meet financial need. The per-centages of this aid from federal, state, institutional (college or university), and external (e.g., foundations, civic organizations, etc.) sources are shown. *Receiving aid* shows the percentages (and number, in parentheses) of freshmen and of all under-graduates who applied for aid, were considered eligible, and received any need-based gift aid. *Average award* is the average dollar amount of awards to freshmen and all undergraduates who applied for aid, were considered eligible, and received any need-based gift aid. *Scholarships, grants, and awards* cites major categories of need-based gift aid provided by the college; these include Federal Pell Grants, Federal Supplemental Educational Opportunity Grants (FSEOG), state scholarships, private scholarships, college/university gift aid from institutional funds, United Negro College Fund aid, Federal Nursing Schol-arships, and others.

Scholarships and grants are gifts awarded to students that do not need to be repaid. These are preferable to loans, which have to be repaid, or work-study wages, which may take time away from studies and personal pursuits. The total amount of need-based gift aid has to be placed into the context of the total number of undergraduate students (shown in the About the Institution paragraph) and the relative expense of the insti-tution. Filing the FAFSA® automatically puts you in line to receive any available federal grants for which you may qualify. However, if the college being considered has a higher than usual proportion of gift aid coming from state, institutional, or external sources, be sure to check with the financial aid office to find out what these sources may be and how to apply for them. For almost all colleges, the percentage of freshmen receiving need-based gift aid will be higher than the percentage of all undergraduates receiving need-based gift aid. However, if you are dependent on need-based gift aid and the particular college under consideration shows a sharper drop from the freshman to undergraduate years than other colleges of a similar type, you might want to think about how this change will affect your ability to pay for later years at this college.

Gift Aid (Non-Need-Based)

Total amount is the total dollar figure in 2017–18 (esti-mated) or 2016–17 (actual) of non-need-based scholarships and grant (gift) aid awarded to degree-seeking full-time and part-time students. Non-need-based aid that was used to meet financial need is not included in this total. The percentages of this aid from federal, state, institutional (college or university), and external (e.g., National Merit Scholarships, civic, religious, fraternal organizations, etc.) sources are shown. *Receiving aid* shows the percentages (and number, in parentheses) of freshmen and of all undergraduates who were determined to have need and received non-need-based gift aid. *Average award* is the average dollar amount of awards to freshmen and all undergraduates determined to have no need but received non-need-based awards. *Scholarships, grants, and awards by category* cites the major categories in which non-need-based awards are available and the number of awards made in that category (in parentheses, the total dollar value of these awards). The cate-gories listed are *Academic interests/achievement, Creative arts/performance, Special achievements/activities*, and *Special charac-teristics. Tuition waivers* indicate special categories of students (minority students, children of alumni, college employees or children of employees, adult students, and senior citizens) who may qualify for a full or partial waiver of tuition. *ROTC* indi-cates Army, Naval, and Air Force ROTC programs that are offered on campus; a program offered by arrangement on another campus is indicated by the word *cooperative.*

This section covers college-administered scholarships awarded to undergraduates on the basis of merit or personal attributes without regard to need. If you do not qualify for financial aid but nevertheless lack the resources to pay for college, non-need-based awards will be of special interest to you. Some personal characteristics are completely beyond an individual's control, and talents and achievements take a number of years to develop or attain. However, certain criteria for these awards, such as religious involvement, community service, and special academic interests can be attained in a relatively brief period of time. ROTC programs offer such benefits as tuition, the cost of textbooks, and living allowances. In return, you must fulfill a service obligation after graduating from college. Because they can be a significant help in paying for college, these programs have become quite competitive. Certain subject areas, such as nursing, health care, or the technical fields, are in stronger demand than others. Among the obligations to consider about ROTC are that you must spend a regular portion of your available time in military training programs and that ROTC entails a multiyear commitment after your graduation to serve as an officer in the armed services branch sponsoring the program.

Loans

The figures here represent loans that are part of the financial aid award package. *Student loans* represents the total dollar amount of loans from all sources to full-time and part-time degree-seeking undergraduates or their parents. *Average need-based loan* represents the percentage of these loans that goes to meet financial need, and the percentage that goes to pay the non-need portion (the expected family contribution) are indicated. The percentage of a past graduating class who borrowed through any loan program (except parent loans) while enrolled at the college is shown, as is the average dollar figure per-borrower of cumulative undergraduate indebtedness (this does not include loans from other institutions). *Parent loans* shows the total amount borrowed through parent loan programs as well as the percentages that were applied to the need-based and non-needbased portions of financial need. *Programs* indicates the major loan programs available to undergraduates. These include Direct Student Loans (subsidized and unsubsidized and PLUS), Perkins Loans, Federal Nursing Loans, state loans, college/university loans, and other types.

Note: As a result of the Health Care and Education Reconciliation Act, as of July 1, 2010, federal student loans are no longer made by private lenders under the Federal Family Education Loan (FFEL) Program. Instead, all new federal student loans come directly from the U.S. Department of Education under the Direct Loan Program. Any FFEL loans noted in this section of an institution's profile are no longer available.

Loans are forms of aid that must be repaid with interest. Most people will borrow money to pay college costs. The loans available through financial aid programs are offered at very favorable interest rates. In comparing colleges, the dollar amount of total indebtedness is a factor to be considered. Typically, this amount would increase proportionate to the tuition. However, if it does not, this could mean that the college provides relatively generous grant or work-study aid rather than loans in its financial aid package.

Work-Study

The total dollar amounts, number, and average dollar amount of *Federal work-study* (FWS) jobs appear first. The total dollar figure of *State or other work-study/employment*, if available, is shown, as is the percentage of those dollars that go to meet financial need. The number of part-time jobs available on campus to undergraduates, other than work-study, is shown last.

FWS is a federally funded program that enables students with demonstrated need to earn money by working on or off campus, usually in a nonprofit organization. FWS jobs are a special category of jobs that are open to students only through the financial aid office. Other kinds of part-time jobs are routinely available at most colleges and may vary widely. In comparing colleges, you may find characteristic differences in how the "self-help" amounts (loans and work-study) are apportioned.

Athletic Awards

The total dollar amount of athletic scholarships given by the college to undergraduate students, including percentages that are need-based and non-need-based, is indicated.

Applying for Financial Aid

Required financial aid forms include the FAFSA® (Free Application for Federal Student Aid), the institution's own form, CSS/Financial Aid PROFILE, a state aid form, a noncustodial (divorced/separated) parent's statement, a business/farm supplement, and others. The college's financial aid application deadline is noted as the *Financial aid deadline* and is shown in one of three ways: as a specific date if it is an absolute deadline; noted as *continuous*, which means processing goes on without a deadline or until all available aid has been awarded; or as a date with the note *(priority)*, meaning that you are encouraged to apply before that date in order to have the best chance of obtaining aid. *Notification date* is listed as either a specific date or *continuous*. The date by which a reply to the college with the decision to accept or decline its financial aid package is listed as either a specific date or as a number of weeks from the date of notification.

Be prepared to check early with the colleges as to exactly which forms will be required. All colleges require the FAFSA® for students applying for federal aid. In most cases, colleges have a limited amount of funds set aside to use as financial aid. It is possible that the first eligible students will get a larger share of what is available.

Contact

The name, title, address, telephone and fax numbers, and e-mail address of the person to contact for further information (student financial aid contact) are given at the end of the profile. You should feel free to write or call for any materials you need or if you have questions.

APPENDIX

This section lists nearly 300 state-specific grants and loans. Award amounts, number of awards, eligibility requirements, application requirements, and deadlines are given for all programs.

INDEXES

Six indexes in the back of the book allow you to search for particular award programs based on the following criteria:

Non-Need Scholarships for Undergraduates

This index lists the colleges that report that they offer scholarships based on academic interests, abilities, achievements, or personal characteristics other than financial need. Specific categories appear in alphabetical order under the following broad groups:

- Academic Interests/Achievements
- Creative Arts/Performance
- Special Achievements/Activities
- Special Characteristics

See the index for specific categories in each group.

Athletic Grants for Undergraduates

This index lists the colleges that report offering scholarships on the basis of athletic abilities.

Co-op Programs

This index lists colleges that report offering cooperative education programs. These are formal arrangements with off-campus employers that are designed to allow students to combine study and work, often in a position related to the student's field of study. Salaries typically are set at regular marketplace levels, and academic credit is often given.

ROTC Programs

This index lists colleges that offer Reserve Officers' Training Corps programs. The index is arranged by the branch of service that sponsors the program.

Tuition Waivers

This index lists colleges that report offering full or partial tuition waivers for certain categories of students. A majority of colleges offer tuition waivers to employees or children of employees.

Because this benefit is so common and the affected employees usually are aware of it, no separate index of schools offering this option is provided. However, this information is included in the individual college profiles.

Tuition Payment Alternatives

This index lists colleges that report offering tuition payment alternatives. These payment alternatives include deferred payment plans, guaranteed tuition plans, installment payment plans, and prepayment plans.

DATA COLLECTION PROCEDURES

The data contained in the college chart, profiles, and indexes were collected in winter and spring 2018 through *Peterson's Annual Survey of Undergraduate Financial Aid* and *Peterson's Annual Survey of Undergraduate Institutions*. Questionnaires were sent to the more than 4,100 institutions of higher education that are accredited in the United States and U.S. territories and offer full four- or five-year baccalaureate degrees via full-time on-campus programs of study. Officials at the colleges—usually financial aid or admission officers but sometimes registrars or institutional research staff members—completed and returned the forms. Peterson's has every reason to believe that the data presented in this book are accurate. However, students should always confirm costs and other facts with a specific school at the time of application, since colleges can and do change policies and fees whenever necessary.

The state aid data presented in *Peterson's How to Get Money for College* was submitted by state officials (usually the director of the state scholarship commission) to Peterson's in the spring of 2018. Because regulations for any government-sponsored program may be changed at any time, you should request written descriptive materials from the office administering a program in which you are interested.

CRITERIA FOR INCLUSION IN THIS BOOK

To be included in this guide, an institution must have full accreditation or be a candidate for accreditation (preaccreditation) status by an institutional or specialized accrediting body recognized by the U.S. Department of Education or the Council for Higher Education Accreditation (CHEA). Institutional accrediting bodies, which review each institution as a whole, include the six regional associations of schools and colleges (Middle States, New England, North Central, Northwest, Southern, and Western), each of which is responsible for a specified portion of the United States and its territories. Other institutional accrediting bodies are national in scope and accredit specific kinds of institutions (e.g., Bible colleges, independent colleges, and rabbinical and Talmudic schools). Program registration by the New York State Board of Regents is considered to be the equivalent of institutional accreditation, since the board requires that all programs offered by an institution meet its standards before recognition is granted. There are recognized specialized or professional accrediting bodies in more than forty different fields, each of which is authorized to accredit institutions or specific programs in its particular field. For specialized institutions that offer programs in one field only, we designate this to be the equivalent of institutional accreditation. A full explanation of the accrediting process and complete information on recognized, institutional (regional and national) and specialized accrediting bodies can be found online at www.chea.org or at www.ed.gov/admins/finaid/accred/index.html.

Quick-Reference Chart

College Costs At-a-Glance

by Michael Steidel
Dean of Admission, Carnegie Mellon University

To help shed some light on the typical patterns of financial aid offered by colleges, we have prepared the following chart. This chart can help you to better understand financial aid practices in general, form realistic expectations about the amounts of aid that might be provided by specific colleges or universities, and prepare for meaningful discussions with the financial aid officers at colleges being considered. The data appearing in the chart have been supplied by the schools themselves and are also shown in the individual college profiles.

Tuition and fees are based on the total of full-time tuition and mandatory fees for the 2016–2017 academic year or for the 2015–2016 academic year if 2016–2017 figures are not available. More information about these costs, as well as the costs of room and board and the year for which they are current, can be found in the individual college profiles. For institutions that have two or more tuition rates for different categories of students or types of programs, the lowest rate is used in figuring the cost.

The colleges are listed alphabetically by state. An "NR" in any individual column indicates that the applicable data element was "Not Reported."

The chart is divided into eight columns of information for each college:

1. Institutional Control
Whether the school is independent (ind.), including independent, independent–religious, and proprietary, or public (pub.), including federal, state, commonwealth, territory, county, district, city, state, local, and state-related.

2. Tuition and Fees
Based on the total of full-time tuition and mandatory fees. An asterisk indicates that the school includes room and board in their mandatory fees.

3. Room and Board
If a school has room and board costs that vary according to the type of accommodation and meal plan, either the lowest figures are represented or the figures are for the most common room arrangement and a full meal plan. If a school has only housing arrangements, a dagger appears to the right of the number. An "NA" will appear in this column if no college-owned or -operated housing facilities are offered.

4. Percent of Eligible Freshmen Receiving Need-Based Gift Awards
Calculated by dividing the number of freshman students determined to have need who received need-based gift aid by the number of full-time freshmen.

5. Percent of Freshmen Whose Need Was Fully Met
Calculated by dividing the number of freshman students whose financial need was fully met by the number of freshmen with need.

6. Average Financial Aid Package for Freshmen
The average dollar amount from all sources, including *gift aid* (scholarships and grants) and *self-help* (jobs and loans), awarded to freshmen receiving aid. Note that this aid package may exceed tuition and fees if the average aid package included coverage of room and board expenses.

7. Average Net Cost After Aid
Average aid package subtracted from published costs (tuition, fees, room, and board) to produce what the average student will have to pay.

8. Average Indebtedness Upon Graduation
Average per-student indebtedness of graduating seniors.

Because personal situations vary widely, it is very important to note that an individual's aid package can be quite different from the averages. Moreover, the data shown for each school can fluctuate widely from year to year, depending on the number of applicants, the amount of need to be met, and the financial resources and policies of the college. Peterson's intent in presenting this chart is to provide you with useful facts and figures that can serve as general guidelines in the pursuit of financial aid. We caution you to use the data only as a jumping-off point for further investigation and analysis, not as a means to rank or select colleges.

After you have narrowed down the choice of colleges based on academic and personal criteria, we recommend that you carefully study this chart. From it, you can develop a list of questions for financial aid officers at the colleges under serious consideration. Here are just a few questions you might want to ask: About the Institution

- What are the specific types and sources of aid provided to freshmen at this school?

- What factors does this college consider in determining whether a financial aid applicant is qualified for its need-based aid programs?

- How does the college determine the combination of types of aid that make up an individual's package?

- How are non-need-based awards treated: as a part of the aid package or as a part of the parental/family contribution?

- Does this school "guarantee" financial aid and, if so, how is its policy implemented? Guaranteed aid means that, by policy, 100 percent of need is met for all students judged to have need. Implementation determines *how* need is met and varies widely from school to school. For example, grade point average may determine the apportioning of scholarship, loan, and work-study aid. Rules for freshmen may be different from those for upperclass students.

- To what degree is the admission process "need-blind"? Need-blind means that admission decisions are made without regard to the student's need for financial aid.

- What are the norms and practices for upperclass students? Peterson's chart presents information on *freshmen* financial aid only; however, the financial aid office should be able and willing to provide you with comparable figures for upper-

class students. A college might offer a wonderful package for the freshman year, then leave students mostly on their own to fund the remaining three years. Or the school may provide a higher proportion of scholarship money for freshmen, then rebalance its aid packages to contain more self-help aid (loans and work-study) in upperclass years. There is an assumption that, all other factors being equal, students who have settled into the pattern of college time management can handle more work-study hours than freshmen. Grade point average, tuition increases, changes in parental financial circumstances, and other factors may also affect the redistribution.

College Costs At-a-Glance

	Institutional Control ind.=independent; pub.=public	Tuition and Fees	Room and Board	Percent of Eligible Freshmen Receiving Need-Based Gift Awards	Percent of Freshmen Whose Need Was Fully Met	Average Financial Aid Package for Freshmen	Average Net Cost After Aid	Average Indebtedness Upon Graduation
Alabama								
Alabama State University	pub.	$11,068	$6050	86%	31%	$16,694	$424	$34,691
Amridge University	ind.	$9900	NA	100%	100%	$5518	$4382	$11,179
Athens State University	pub.	$6690	NA	NR	NR	NR	NR	NR
Auburn University	pub.	$10,968	$13,332	85%	18%	$11,644	$12,656	$29,295
Auburn University at Montgomery	pub.	$8236	$6980	75%	9%	$8229	$6987	$27,007
Birmingham-Southern College	ind.	$17,650	$12,300	61%	30%	$31,335	—	$30,084
Faulkner University	ind.	$21,690	$7550	71%	8%	$15,296	$13,944	$33,622
Huntingdon College	ind.	$26,400	$9500	100%	15%	$19,451	$16,449	$32,201
Jacksonville State University	pub.	$10,020	$7898	44%	NR	$10,352	$7566	NR
Samford University	ind.	$31,650	$10,550	99%	24%	$19,155	$23,045	$27,539
Spring Hill College	ind.	$37,584	$13,070	84%	25%	$36,147	$14,507	NR
Troy University	pub.	$12,155	$7946	56%	NR	$3648	$16,453	NR
Tuskegee University	ind.	N/R	NR	72%	50%	$20,500	—	$26,500
United States Sports Academy	ind.	$15,972	NR	NR	NR	NR	NR	NR
The University of Alabama	pub.	$10,780	$9974	80%	29%	$16,254	$4500	$34,305
The University of Alabama at Birmingham	pub.	$10,635	$11,682	59%	17%	$10,049	$12,268	$34,872
The University of Alabama in Huntsville	pub.	$10,280	$9748	94%	30%	$14,044	$5984	$29,396
University of Montevallo	pub.	$12,400	$7512	96%	21%	$13,266	$6646	$33,755
University of North Alabama	pub.	$10,370	$7684	53%	3%	$8735	$9319	$28,283
The University of West Alabama	pub.	$9204	$7080	70%	2%	$11,087	$5197	$25,114
Alaska								
Alaska Bible College	ind.	$9600	$5700	NR	NR	NR	NR	NR
Alaska Pacific University	ind.	$20,830	$8230	NR	NR	NR	NR	NR
University of Alaska Anchorage	pub.	$6186	$11,962	89%	20%	$9685	$8463	$27,188
University of Alaska Fairbanks	pub.	$8800	$8930	92%	22%	$8457	$9273	$22,155
Arizona								
Arizona Christian University	ind.	$2546	$10,674	100%	21%	$16,008	—	NR
Arizona State University at the Downtown Phoenix campus	pub.	N/R	NR	99%	21%	$17,692	—	$24,368
Arizona State University at the Polytechnic campus	pub.	N/R	NR	96%	26%	$14,727	—	$26,797
Arizona State University at the Tempe campus	pub.	$10,522	NR	99%	22%	$16,638	—	$23,237
Arizona State University at the West campus	pub.	N/R	NR	98%	22%	$15,123	—	$24,498
Embry-Riddle Aeronautical University–Prescott	ind.	$34,662	$10,468	89%	NR	$17,718	$27,412	NR
Northern Arizona University	pub.	$11,060	$9944	69%	13%	$13,241	$7763	$24,413
The University of Arizona	pub.	$12,200	$12,550	99%	18%	$16,047	$8703	$23,956
Arkansas								
Arkansas Tech University	pub.	$8880	$7338	80%	6%	$9235	$6983	$24,816
Harding University	ind.	$19,190	$6894	97%	22%	$12,898	$13,186	$31,007
Henderson State University	pub.	$8311	$7320	68%	13%	$9279	$6352	$20,638
Hendrix College	ind.	$45,790	$12,284	100%	32%	$41,885	$16,189	$27,786
John Brown University	ind.	$26,928	$9224	86%	20%	$21,504	$14,648	$24,467
Lyon College	ind.	$27,340	$8780	99%	25%	$23,396	$12,724	$26,353

NA = not applicable; NR = not reported; * = includes room and board; † = room only; — = not available.

College Costs At-a-Glance

	Institutional Control ind.=independent; pub.=public	Tuition and Fees	Room and Board	Percent of Eligible Freshmen Receiving Need-Based Gift Awards	Percent of Freshmen Whose Need Was Fully Met	Average Financial Aid Package for Freshmen	Average Net Cost After Aid	Average Indebtedness Upon Graduation
Ouachita Baptist University	ind.	$26,790	$7880	98%	37%	$23,214	$11,456	$28,406
Philander Smith College	ind.	$12,714	$5192	99%	4%	$12,704	$5202	$46,965
Southern Arkansas University–Magnolia	pub.	$8346	$6028	70%	42%	$12,154	$2220	$22,616
University of Arkansas	pub.	$9062	$10,704	83%	13%	$9398	$10,368	$26,242
University of Arkansas at Little Rock	pub.	$9430	$5900	99%	NR	$13,731	$1599	NR
University of Central Arkansas	pub.	$8524	$6518	NR	NR	NR	NR	NR
Williams Baptist College	ind.	$17,320	$7600	82%	NR	$16,169	$8751	$22,747
California								
Academy of Art University	ind.	$27,810	$16,648	79%	3%	$10,984	$33,474	NR
Alliant International University–San Diego	ind.	$17,510	NA	57%	NR	$12,950	$4560	NR
American Jewish University	ind.	N/R	NR	40%	NR	$29,592	—	$30,000
Azusa Pacific University	ind.	$37,506	$5770†	82%	15%	$25,615	$17,661	$31,277
Biola University	ind.	$38,448	$10,972	100%	14%	$22,083	$27,337	$35,489
California Baptist University	ind.	$33,478	$12,160	98%	24%	$24,142	$21,496	$38,324
California Christian College	ind.	$9330	$4950†	100%	NR	$3365	$10,915	NR
California College of the Arts	ind.	$49,138	$10,136†	100%	11%	$33,562	$25,712	$32,017
California Institute of Technology	ind.	$49,908	$14,796	100%	100%	$46,321	$18,383	$16,777
California Lutheran University	ind.	$41,363	$13,320	100%	25%	$37,400	$17,283	$34,220
California Polytechnic State University, San Luis Obispo	pub.	$9432	$13,115	95%	11%	$9996	$12,551	$21,852
California State Polytechnic University, Pomona	pub.	$7297	$14,514	80%	1%	$10,386	$11,425	$22,228
California State University, Chico	pub.	$12,516	$12,536	76%	15%	$17,631	$7421	NR
California State University, Dominguez Hills	pub.	$8132	$12,540	88%	1%	$5730	$14,942	$15,880
California State University, Fresno	pub.	N/R	NR	92%	16%	$12,505	—	$18,308
California State University, Fullerton	pub.	$6850	$15,642	80%	8%	$9132	$13,360	$14,965
California State University, Long Beach	pub.	$6798	$12,750	82%	63%	$12,577	$6971	$19,062
California State University Maritime Academy	pub.	$8360	$12,807	96%	8%	NR	NR	$24,052
California State University, Monterey Bay	pub.	$7043	$12,396	83%	14%	$11,840	$7599	$19,962
California State University, Northridge	pub.	$6870	$10,402	83%	NR	$11,212	$6060	$16,876
California State University, Sacramento	pub.	$6934	$14,396	96%	8%	$10,662	$10,668	$20,052
California State University, San Bernardino	pub.	$6656	$12,711	98%	64%	$9590	$9777	$21,555
California State University, San Marcos	pub.	$13,390	$13,227	93%	4%	$10,484	$16,133	$23,734
California State University, Stanislaus	pub.	$7038	$8670	90%	99%	$16,904	—	$18,960
Chapman University	ind.	$52,724	$15,828	91%	18%	$35,342	$33,210	$26,926
Claremont McKenna College	ind.	$52,825	$16,220	97%	97%	$51,688	$17,357	$21,421
Concordia University Irvine	ind.	$35,400	$11,300	100%	14%	$25,612	$21,088	$32,754
Dominican University of California	ind.	$44,690	$14,650	100%	17%	$30,693	$28,647	$37,827
FIDM/Fashion Institute of Design & Merchandising, Los Angeles Campus	ind.	$32,945	NA	NR	NR	NR	NR	NR
Harvey Mudd College	ind.	$54,636	$17,592	95%	100%	$42,654	$29,574	$25,041
Hope International University	ind.	$31,800	$9930	69%	2%	$13,008	$28,722	$26,733
Humboldt State University	pub.	$7492	$13,056	95%	8%	$13,988	$6560	$24,638
John Paul the Great Catholic University	ind.	$26,100	$7650†	100%	2%	$14,238	$19,512	NR

NA = not applicable; NR = not reported; * = includes room and board; † = room only; — = not available.

College Costs At-a-Glance

	Institutional Control ind.=independent; pub.=public	Tuition and Fees	Room and Board	Percent of Eligible Freshmen Receiving Need-Based Gift Awards	Percent of Freshmen Whose Need Was Fully Met	Average Financial Aid Package for Freshmen	Average Net Cost After Aid	Average Indebtedness Upon Graduation
Laguna College of Art & Design	ind.	$30,700	$10,000†	NR	NR	NR	NR	$38,000
La Sierra University	ind.	$32,130	$8250	100%	10%	$25,608	$14,772	NR
Loyola Marymount University	ind.	$46,136	$14,690	95%	27%	$28,854	$31,972	$32,560
Marymount California University	ind.	$35,884	$14,412	100%	30%	$35,846	$14,450	$31,562
Mills College	ind.	$30,257	$13,448	92%	18%	$49,500	—	$29,954
Mount Saint Mary's University	ind.	$41,170	$12,235	98%	6%	$34,579	$18,826	$35,161
Occidental College	ind.	$52,838	$14,968	99%	100%	$48,188	$19,618	$32,008
Pepperdine University	ind.	$53,932	$15,320	100%	16%	$39,938	$29,314	$31,410
Pitzer College	ind.	$52,236	$16,264	100%	100%	$46,934	$21,566	$20,947
Point Loma Nazarene University	ind.	$35,700	$10,450	99%	19%	$23,148	$23,002	$35,414
Pomona College	ind.	$52,780	$16,716	100%	100%	$52,748	$16,748	$17,408
Saint Mary's College of California	ind.	$47,280	$15,370	98%	1%	$34,854	$27,796	$31,356
San Diego State University	pub.	$7460	$15,966	62%	8%	$9700	$13,726	$19,633
San Francisco Art Institute	ind.	$46,534	$15,709	86%	10%	$16,709	$45,534	$27,137
San Francisco Conservatory of Music	ind.	$44,810	$16,160	100%	26%	$27,500	$33,470	$42,000
San Francisco State University	pub.	$7254	$13,248	96%	27%	$17,230	$3272	$19,347
San Jose State University	pub.	$7417	$14,107	95%	72%	$19,745	$1779	$19,303
Santa Clara University	ind.	$49,858	$14,487	88%	43%	$38,585	$25,760	$28,808
Scripps College	ind.	$52,966	$16,294	99%	100%	$46,467	$22,793	$19,639
Soka University of America	ind.	$32,980	$12,530	100%	63%	$35,003	$10,507	$23,441
Sonoma State University	pub.	$7724	$13,554	74%	4%	$10,986	$10,292	$20,797
Southern California Institute of Architecture	ind.	N/R	NA	89%	22%	$17,318	—	$39,287
Stanford University	ind.	$49,617	$15,112	98%	95%	$53,337	$11,392	$20,205
Thomas Aquinas College	ind.	$24,500	$7950	84%	100%	$19,352	$13,098	$19,269
University of California, Berkeley	pub.	$14,170	$15,716	96%	23%	$24,668	$5218	$18,197
University of California, Davis	pub.	$14,463	$15,765	98%	25%	$25,819	$4409	$19,124
University of California, Irvine	pub.	$15,516	$14,829	98%	25%	$23,886	$6459	$19,745
University of California, Los Angeles	pub.	$13,584	$15,143	96%	28%	$24,405	$4322	$22,013
University of California, Merced	pub.	$13,598	$16,790	99%	26%	$29,416	$972	$19,551
University of California, Riverside	pub.	$15,642	$17,000	98%	22%	$26,448	$6194	$21,104
University of California, San Diego	pub.	$14,050	$13,307	97%	36%	$24,736	$2621	$21,430
University of California, Santa Barbara	pub.	$14,472	$15,673	97%	25%	$25,612	$4533	$20,665
University of California, Santa Cruz	pub.	$14,028	$16,055	96%	23%	$25,549	$4534	$22,804
University of La Verne	ind.	$41,450	$13,140	100%	5%	$34,198	$20,392	$33,384
University of San Diego	ind.	$49,358	$12,980	99%	17%	$33,801	$28,537	$30,854
University of San Francisco	ind.	$48,066	$14,830	98%	7%	$40,446	$22,450	$48,201
University of Southern California	ind.	$54,323	$14,885	87%	88%	$52,795	$16,413	$29,080
University of the Pacific	ind.	$46,346	$13,356	99%	15%	$37,952	$21,750	$28,759
Vanguard University of Southern California	ind.	$33,700	NR	66%	100%	$16,513	$17,187	$31,614
Westmont College	ind.	$44,044	$13,886	100%	27%	$35,292	$22,638	$33,407
Whittier College	ind.	$46,120	$13,328	86%	18%	$39,034	$20,414	$32,258
William Jessup University	ind.	$30,550	$11,075	99%	17%	$25,313	$16,312	$25,670

NA = not applicable; NR = not reported; * = includes room and board; † = room only; — = not available.

College Costs At-a-Glance

	Institutional Control ind.=independent; pub.=public	Tuition and Fees	Room and Board	Percent of Eligible Freshmen Receiving Need-Based Gift Awards	Percent of Freshmen Whose Need Was Fully Met	Average Financial Aid Package for Freshmen	Average Net Cost After Aid	Average Indebtedness Upon Graduation
Colorado								
Adams State University	pub.	$9444	$7215	96%	10%	$13,775	$2884	$24,958
The Colorado College	ind.	$52,818	$12,076	97%	100%	$49,928	$14,966	$20,742
Colorado Mesa University	pub.	$8972	$10,735	86%	18%	$8920	$10,787	$28,101
Colorado School of Mines	pub.	$18,386	$11,897	56%	24%	$15,356	$14,927	$32,221
Colorado State University	pub.	$11,488	$11,514	85%	35%	$11,572	$11,430	$26,348
Fort Lewis College	pub.	$5609	$9416	92%	15%	$15,593	—	$20,988
Metropolitan State University of Denver	pub.	$7352	NA	87%	5%	$7475	—	$25,805
Platt College	ind.	N/R	NA	50%	NR	$6095	—	$43,477
Regis University	ind.	$36,810	$11,560	99%	20%	$32,981	$15,389	$28,153
University of Colorado Boulder	pub.	$12,086	$13,998	76%	46%	$15,834	$10,250	$27,680
University of Colorado Colorado Springs	pub.	$10,201	$10,100	55%	4%	$7880	$12,421	$25,042
University of Colorado Denver	pub.	$11,258	$12,190	81%	2%	$8889	$14,559	$20,941
University of Denver	ind.	$50,556	$13,005	99%	31%	$41,860	$21,701	$31,526
University of Northern Colorado	pub.	$9545	$10,982	84%	24%	$14,042	$6485	$24,844
Western State Colorado University	pub.	$9802	$9546	93%	3%	$11,049	$8299	$26,950
Connecticut								
Albertus Magnus College	ind.	$31,490	$14,016	94%	8%	$27,993	$17,513	$36,908
Central Connecticut State University	pub.	$10,225	$11,816	82%	11%	$8747	$13,294	$5831
Charter Oak State College	pub.	$9771	NA	NR	NR	NR	NR	NR
Connecticut College	ind.	$52,850	$14,590	96%	100%	$40,993	$26,447	$31,884
Fairfield University	ind.	$47,165	$14,280	82%	33%	$34,178	$27,267	$32,186
Mitchell College	ind.	N/R	NR	100%	6%	$22,393	—	$36,430
Post University	ind.	$29,550	$10,600	NR	NR	NR	NR	$20,246
Quinnipiac University	ind.	$47,960	$14,990	99%	17%	$28,944	$34,006	$48,894
Sacred Heart University	ind.	$39,820	$14,770	100%	15%	$20,600	$33,990	$42,033
Trinity College	ind.	N/R	NR	97%	100%	$50,836	—	$25,958
University of Bridgeport	ind.	$32,250	$13,590	88%	6%	$30,815	$15,025	$21,200
University of Hartford	ind.	$40,694	$12,476	99%	14%	$27,225	$25,945	NR
University of New Haven	ind.	$38,170	$15,610	100%	14%	$23,746	$30,034	$49,941
University of Saint Joseph	ind.	$39,172	$11,428	100%	19%	$29,484	$21,116	$38,916
Wesleyan University	ind.	$52,474	$14,466	94%	100%	$51,412	$15,528	$22,930
Western Connecticut State University	pub.	$10,458	$12,416	88%	14%	$8838	$14,036	$35,177
Yale University	ind.	$51,400	$15,500	100%	100%	$56,320	$10,580	$13,050
Delaware								
Delaware State University	pub.	$7868	$11,054	70%	8%	$11,863	$7059	$36,812
University of Delaware	pub.	$13,160	$12,332	94%	11%	$13,284	$12,208	$34,144
District of Columbia								
American University	ind.	$48,459	$14,880	95%	46%	$38,374	$24,965	NR
The Catholic University of America	ind.	$44,060	$14,316	98%	42%	$31,104	$27,272	$36,542
Georgetown University	ind.	$52,300	$16,670	94%	100%	$46,703	$22,267	$23,387

NA = not applicable; NR = not reported; * = includes room and board; † = room only; — = not available.

College Costs At-a-Glance

	Institutional Control ind.=independent; pub.=public	Tuition and Fees	Room and Board	Percent of Eligible Freshmen Receiving Need-Based Gift Awards	Percent of Freshmen Whose Need Was Fully Met	Average Financial Aid Package for Freshmen	Average Net Cost After Aid	Average Indebtedness Upon Graduation
The George Washington University	ind.	$53,518	$13,000	97%	51%	$46,348	$20,170	$33,305
Florida								
Ave Maria University	ind.	N/R	NR	99%	24%	$18,407	—	$24,294
The Baptist College of Florida	ind.	$11,100	$4138	100%	3%	$10,151	$5087	$24,444
Barry University	ind.	$29,700	$11,100	88%	6%	$27,266	$13,534	$38,176
Bethune-Cookman University	ind.	$14,410	$8912	100%	4%	$15,903	$7419	$40,601
Carlos Albizu University, Miami Campus	ind.	$12,444	NA	100%	NR	$8901	$3543	NR
Eckerd College	ind.	$43,044	$12,162	100%	47%	$35,564	$19,642	$33,484
Embry-Riddle Aeronautical University–Daytona	ind.	$35,714	$11,438	85%	NR	$19,457	$27,695	NR
Embry-Riddle Aeronautical University–Worldwide	ind.	$9076	NR	81%	NR	$8513	$563	NR
Flagler College	ind.	$18,950	$11,340	100%	16%	$13,239	$17,051	$30,039
Florida Agricultural and Mechanical University	pub.	$5785	$10,594	83%	16%	$14,953	$1426	$7454
Florida Atlantic University	pub.	$6039	$10,388	84%	18%	$13,295	$3132	$22,818
Florida Gulf Coast University	pub.	$6118	$8620	64%	8%	$9419	$5319	$24,879
Florida Institute of Technology	ind.	$41,850	$12,880	100%	37%	$38,128	$16,602	$33,135
Florida International University	pub.	$6558	$10,882	79%	8%	$7826	$9614	$20,022
Florida National University	ind.	$13,850	NA	98%	NR	NR	NR	$10,982
Florida Southern College	ind.	$34,774	$11,204	100%	33%	$29,865	$16,113	$25,493
Florida State University	pub.	$6507	$10,458	94%	21%	$14,486	$2479	$23,679
Jacksonville University	ind.	$35,260	$13,950	100%	24%	$31,030	$18,180	NR
Johnson University Florida	ind.	$16,060	$6700	100%	13%	$11,487	$11,273	$28,906
Keiser University	ind.	N/R	NA	96%	100%	$6831	—	NR
Lynn University	ind.	$38,210	$12,170	88%	100%	$22,362	$28,018	$32,533
New College of Florida	pub.	$6916	$9264	90%	26%	$16,063	$117	$16,297
Nova Southeastern University	ind.	$29,940	$12,550	99%	17%	$32,899	$9591	$32,127
Palm Beach Atlantic University	ind.	$31,450	$10,130	100%	18%	$23,523	$18,057	$26,907
Ringling College of Art and Design	ind.	$46,420	$14,670	100%	9%	$24,796	$36,294	$46,575
Rollins College	ind.	$49,760	$14,740	100%	32%	$40,224	$24,276	$32,700
Saint Leo University	ind.	$21,970	$10,570	100%	16%	$22,815	$9725	$40,359
St. Thomas University	ind.	$31,080	$11,700	NR	NR	NR	NR	NR
Southeastern University	ind.	$25,360	$9550	71%	14%	$15,729	$19,181	$29,810
Stetson University	ind.	$46,030	$13,052	99%	25%	$36,918	$22,164	$31,457
Trinity College of Florida	ind.	$16,340	$6975	100%	9%	$11,294	$12,021	$31,757
University of Central Florida	pub.	$6368	$10,011	63%	9%	$8544	$7835	$21,818
University of Florida	pub.	$6381	$9910	59%	28%	$13,685	$2606	$22,192
University of Miami	ind.	$48,484	$13,666	79%	74%	$46,432	$15,718	$25,000
University of North Florida	pub.	$6394	$9772	66%	10%	$9495	$6671	$18,787
University of South Florida	pub.	$6410	$10,325	89%	13%	$11,668	$5067	$21,799
The University of Tampa	ind.	$28,426	$10,502	98%	10%	$17,346	$21,582	$32,048
University of West Florida	pub.	$6359	$9942	99%	16%	$10,648	$5653	NR
Valencia College	pub.	$2473	NA	NR	NR	NR	NR	NR
Webber International University	ind.	$26,116	$9294	100%	9%	$20,282	$15,128	$26,682

NA = not applicable; NR = not reported; * = includes room and board; † = room only; — = not available.

College Costs At-a-Glance

	Institutional Control ind.=independent; pub.=public	Tuition and Fees	Room and Board	Percent of Eligible Freshmen Receiving Need-Based Gift Awards	Percent of Freshmen Whose Need Was Fully Met	Average Financial Aid Package for Freshmen	Average Net Cost After Aid	Average Indebtedness Upon Graduation
Georgia								
Agnes Scott College	ind.	$41,160	$12,330	100%	20%	$36,505	$16,985	$32,276
Albany State University	pub.	$5675	$8874	88%	8%	$4838	$9711	NR
Berry College	ind.	$35,176	$12,260	100%	26%	$30,171	$17,265	$27,378
Brenau University	ind.	$29,050	$12,418	100%	15%	$24,066	$17,402	$34,058
Clayton State University	pub.	$6410	$10,490	92%	4%	$11,230	$5670	$30,423
College of Coastal Georgia	pub.	$3971	$9520	100%	27%	$6897	$6594	$25,455
Columbus State University	pub.	$7200	$10,550	71%	18%	$10,502	$7248	$30,503
Covenant College	ind.	$34,330	$10,260	98%	39%	$29,124	$15,466	$26,184
Emmanuel College	ind.	$19,710	$7888	100%	20%	$15,412	$12,186	$24,840
Emory University	ind.	$51,306	$14,456	95%	100%	$44,118	$21,644	$28,262
Georgia College & State University	pub.	$9346	$12,538	34%	20%	$11,051	$10,833	$30,407
Georgia Institute of Technology	pub.	$12,418	$14,126	44%	52%	$14,735	$11,809	$32,398
Georgia Southern University	pub.	$6890	$9650	92%	15%	$10,636	$5904	$29,724
Georgia Southwestern State University	pub.	$6332	$7910	66%	14%	$10,015	$4227	$25,775
Georgia State University	pub.	$10,858	$14,392	66%	6%	$12,541	$12,709	$30,167
Kennesaw State University	pub.	$7432	$11,467	49%	9%	$9659	$9240	NR
LaGrange College	ind.	$29,480	$11,630	92%	17%	$24,446	$16,664	$35,580
Life University	ind.	$11,715	$14,400	71%	NR	$11,000	$15,115	$29,500
Mercer University	ind.	$36,000	$12,153	100%	44%	$37,448	$10,705	$26,429
Middle Georgia State University	pub.	$4608	$7614	NR	NR	NR	NR	NR
Morehouse College	ind.	$27,574	$13,438	98%	NR	$23,454	$17,558	$31,833
Oglethorpe University	ind.	$36,825	$12,960	100%	19%	$33,750	$16,035	$28,495
Piedmont College	ind.	$24,464	$9870	100%	20%	$22,356	$11,978	$29,160
Savannah College of Art and Design	ind.	$36,630	$14,550	99%	10%	$17,140	$34,040	$39,022
Spelman College	ind.	$28,181	$13,461	99%	46%	$15,660	$25,982	$32,427
Thomas University	ind.	$16,940	$7040	88%	NR	NR	NR	NR
Toccoa Falls College	ind.	$22,744	$8330	100%	14%	$17,190	$13,884	$26,653
Truett McConnell University	ind.	$19,480	$7400	100%	16%	$16,788	$10,092	$29,757
University of Georgia	pub.	$11,818	$10,060	99%	28%	$13,999	$7879	$23,403
University of North Georgia	pub.	$7395	$10,800	91%	63%	$10,077	$8118	$12,345
University of West Georgia	pub.	$7292	$10,218	69%	70%	$8411	$9099	$29,000
Valdosta State University	pub.	$6410	$7900	88%	16%	$16,833	—	$28,318
Wesleyan College	ind.	$22,370	$9570	97%	26%	$22,740	$9200	$31,565
Young Harris College	ind.	N/R	NR	100%	23%	$23,810	—	$27,173
Hawaii								
Chaminade University of Honolulu	ind.	$25,374	$13,630	93%	9%	$18,292	$20,712	$26,191
Hawai`i Pacific University	ind.	$25,980	$14,800	99%	10%	$19,107	$21,673	$27,481
University of Hawaii at Manoa	pub.	$11,970	$13,689	99%	36%	$15,477	$10,182	$24,233
Idaho								
Boise State University	pub.	$7326	$7750	64%	19%	$11,233	$3843	$27,974

NA = not applicable; NR = not reported; * = includes room and board; † = room only; — = not available.

College Costs At-a-Glance

	Institutional Control ind.=independent; pub.=public	Tuition and Fees	Room and Board	Percent of Eligible Freshmen Receiving Need-Based Gift Awards	Percent of Freshmen Whose Need Was Fully Met	Average Financial Aid Package for Freshmen	Average Net Cost After Aid	Average Indebtedness Upon Graduation
The College of Idaho	ind.	$30,155	$9697	48%	28%	$25,141	$14,711	$7202
Idaho State University	pub.	$7166	$7024	78%	7%	$8422	$5768	$29,340
Lewis-Clark State College	pub.	N/R	NR	68%	14%	$7809	—	$27,370
Northwest Nazarene University	ind.	$29,300	$7400	72%	26%	$25,716	$10,984	$34,288
University of Idaho	pub.	$7488	$8670	62%	34%	$13,930	$2228	$25,145
Illinois								
Augustana College	ind.	$42,135	$10,572	100%	25%	$32,193	$20,514	$34,964
Aurora University	ind.	$24,260	$11,700	97%	9%	$22,277	$13,683	$27,117
Benedictine University	ind.	$34,290	$9480	75%	NR	$23,114	$20,656	$23,959
Blessing-Rieman College of Nursing & Health Sciences	ind.	$25,050	NR	NR	NR	NR	NR	NR
Bradley University	ind.	$32,930	$10,310	100%	15%	$25,763	$17,477	$28,432
Columbia College Chicago	ind.	$27,309	$14,012	94%	17%	$10,539	$30,782	$33,208
Concordia University Chicago	ind.	$32,078	$9748	100%	22%	$24,093	$17,733	$22,804
DePaul University	ind.	$38,410	NR	89%	16%	$25,812	$12,598	$30,115
Dominican University	ind.	$33,434	$10,241	100%	12%	$25,099	$18,576	$28,659
Eastern Illinois University	pub.	$11,678	$9736	80%	8%	$13,760	$7654	$30,695
Elmhurst College	ind.	$37,055	$10,366	100%	26%	$26,913	$20,508	$29,925
Eureka College	ind.	$25,390	$9370	100%	12%	$17,273	$17,487	$34,180
Governors State University	pub.	$11,746	$10,104	82%	6%	$11,833	$10,017	NR
Greenville University	ind.	$27,108	$9448	100%	9%	$20,921	$15,635	$28,724
Illinois College	ind.	$33,090	$9280	100%	27%	$29,646	$12,724	$32,740
Illinois Institute of Technology	ind.	N/R	NR	99%	22%	$41,478	—	$32,671
Illinois Wesleyan University	ind.	$47,636	$10,984	100%	20%	$36,363	$22,257	$36,036
Judson University	ind.	$29,860	$9988	14%	14%	$25,767	$14,081	$39,021
Knox College	ind.	$46,554	$9870	99%	33%	$38,565	$17,859	$31,235
Lakeview College of Nursing	ind.	$15,610	NA	NR	NR	NR	NR	NR
Lewis University	ind.	$32,450	$10,578	100%	25%	$28,160	$14,868	$34,006
Loyola University Chicago	ind.	$43,808	NR	98%	18%	$36,370	$7438	$34,973
McKendree University	ind.	$30,520	$9920	100%	26%	$21,989	$18,451	$28,375
Millikin University	ind.	$33,066	$11,082	83%	35%	$27,477	$16,671	$33,146
Monmouth College	ind.	$37,674	$8966	100%	29%	$35,129	$11,511	$33,333
Moody Bible Institute	ind.	N/R	NR	98%	13%	$5045	—	$15,715
North Central College	ind.	$37,749	$10,650	100%	21%	$28,633	$19,766	$38,267
Northeastern Illinois University	pub.	$13,420	$11,424	100%	5%	$10,174	$14,670	$15,819
Northern Illinois University	pub.	$12,262	$10,880	96%	9%	$14,067	$9075	$34,708
Northwestern University	ind.	$52,678	$16,047	97%	100%	$50,668	$18,057	$19,718
Olivet Nazarene University	ind.	$34,940	$7900	100%	22%	$30,970	$11,870	$33,847
Principia College	ind.	$29,470	$11,610	100%	48%	$33,381	$7699	$18,335
Resurrection University	ind.	$38,448	NA	NR	NR	NR	NR	NR
Robert Morris University Illinois	ind.	$28,530	NR	98%	6%	$17,401	$11,129	$34,382
Rockford University	ind.	$30,930	$8660	99%	8%	$23,142	$16,448	$38,951
Saint Francis Medical Center College of Nursing	ind.	$21,057	$1850†	NR	NR	NR	NR	NR

NA = not applicable; NR = not reported; * = includes room and board; † = room only; — = not available.

College Costs At-a-Glance

	Institutional Control ind.=independent; pub.=public	Tuition and Fees	Room and Board	Percent of Eligible Freshmen Receiving Need-Based Gift Awards	Percent of Freshmen Whose Need Was Fully Met	Average Financial Aid Package for Freshmen	Average Net Cost After Aid	Average Indebtedness Upon Graduation
School of the Art Institute of Chicago	ind.	$47,420	$15,490	NR	NR	NR	NR	NR
Southern Illinois University Carbondale	pub.	$13,936	$10,622	69%	13%	$17,101	$7457	$29,637
Trinity Christian College	ind.	$29,950	$9790	100%	23%	$23,576	$16,164	$29,978
University of Chicago	ind.	$54,825	$15,726	99%	100%	$54,438	$16,113	$23,401
University of Illinois at Chicago	pub.	$13,614	$10,960	88%	9%	$14,792	$9782	$23,076
University of Illinois at Springfield	pub.	$12,445	$11,660	98%	25%	$16,424	$7681	$25,313
University of Illinois at Urbana–Champaign	pub.	$15,868	$11,308	88%	12%	$17,394	$9782	$25,550
University of St. Francis	ind.	$32,320	NR	100%	22%	$27,256	$5064	$32,838
VanderCook College of Music	ind.	$28,434	$12,074	78%	NR	$14,295	$26,213	$42,886
Western Illinois University	pub.	$11,267	$9630	84%	21%	$13,592	$7305	$29,422
Wheaton College	ind.	$36,420	$10,180	100%	18%	$27,369	$19,231	$27,543
Indiana								
Ball State University	pub.	$9774	$10,034	72%	38%	$14,375	$5433	$28,295
Bethel College	ind.	$28,590	$9000	NR	NR	NR	NR	$33,565
Butler University	ind.	$41,120	$14,690	99%	12%	$25,981	$29,829	$40,393
Calumet College of Saint Joseph	ind.	$19,870	NA	70%	12%	$13,753	$6117	$24,431
Crossroads Bible College	ind.	N/R	NR	NR	NR	NR	NR	$37,497
DePauw University	ind.	$47,838	$12,529	100%	32%	$42,524	$17,843	$23,635
Earlham College	ind.	$46,450	$10,400	100%	55%	$43,032	$13,818	$27,830
Franklin College	ind.	$30,920	$9215	100%	15%	$22,156	$17,979	$36,145
Goshen College	ind.	$33,700	$10,650	100%	21%	$30,536	$13,814	$27,062
Hanover College	ind.	$36,520	$11,230	100%	36%	$29,008	$18,742	$30,835
Huntington University	ind.	$25,540	$8456	100%	3%	$20,385	$13,611	$32,515
Indiana State University	pub.	$8916	$9883	67%	15%	$11,415	$7384	$28,092
Indiana University Bloomington	pub.	$10,681	NR	86%	33%	$14,159	—	$28,792
Indiana University East	pub.	$7344	NA	94%	20%	$8755	—	$22,392
Indiana University Kokomo	pub.	$7344	NA	88%	18%	$7844	—	$23,664
Indiana University Northwest	pub.	$7344	NA	85%	16%	$8104	—	$28,241
Indiana University–Purdue University Indianapolis	pub.	$9465	NR	87%	25%	$11,684	—	$29,065
Indiana University South Bend	pub.	$7344	NR	90%	17%	$8201	—	$25,780
Indiana University Southeast	pub.	$7344	NR	89%	12%	$8008	—	$23,845
Indiana Wesleyan University	ind.	$25,980	$8312	78%	62%	$30,090	$4202	$30,355
Manchester University	ind.	$32,758	$9580	100%	22%	$31,221	$11,117	$32,920
Oakland City University	ind.	$24,000	$9900	81%	NR	$23,488	$10,412	NR
Purdue University	pub.	$9992	$10,030	72%	40%	$13,452	$6570	$27,617
Rose-Hulman Institute of Technology	ind.	$45,762	$14,061	100%	76%	$31,203	$28,620	$45,345
Saint Mary-of-the-Woods College	ind.	$29,510	$10,914	100%	NR	$28,166	$12,258	NR
Saint Mary's College	ind.	$40,800	$12,100	99%	17%	$34,444	$18,456	$33,698
Taylor University	ind.	$32,885	$9245	100%	33%	$25,071	$17,059	$28,094
Trine University	ind.	$31,540	$10,570	100%	17%	$28,583	$13,527	$38,161
University of Evansville	ind.	$36,416	$12,460	96%	46%	$31,459	$17,417	$30,533
University of Indianapolis	ind.	$28,390	$9988	67%	12%	$21,998	$16,380	$36,320

NA = not applicable; NR = not reported; * = includes room and board; † = room only; — = not available.

College Costs At-a-Glance

	Institutional Control ind.=independent; pub.=public	Tuition and Fees	Room and Board	Percent of Eligible Freshmen Receiving Need-Based Gift Awards	Percent of Freshmen Whose Need Was Fully Met	Average Financial Aid Package for Freshmen	Average Net Cost After Aid	Average Indebtedness Upon Graduation
University of Notre Dame	ind.	$53,391	$15,410	96%	99%	$47,455	$21,346	$29,254
University of Southern Indiana	pub.	$7970	$8838	62%	26%	$9426	$7382	$24,568
Valparaiso University	ind.	$40,260	$11,860	100%	45%	$31,812	$20,308	$37,978
Wabash College	ind.	$43,650	$9850	99%	94%	$40,879	$12,621	$35,726
Iowa								
Allen College	ind.	$18,226	$7281	NR	NR	NR	NR	NR
Buena Vista University	ind.	$32,854	$9490	100%	19%	$29,904	$12,440	$36,299
Central College	ind.	N/R	NR	100%	15%	$31,856	—	$34,273
Clarke University	ind.	$33,350	$9600	100%	28%	$27,084	$15,866	$39,907
Coe College	ind.	$45,000	$9480	100%	21%	$37,433	$17,047	$36,022
Cornell College	ind.	$42,299	$9384	100%	28%	$30,926	$20,757	$34,130
Dordt College	ind.	N/R	NR	99%	49%	$25,520	—	$29,481
Drake University	ind.	$41,396	$10,158	99%	32%	$29,236	$22,318	$34,600
Graceland University	ind.	$29,240	$8760	100%	15%	$26,960	$11,040	$32,120
Grinnell College	ind.	$52,392	$12,810	100%	100%	$47,058	$18,144	$19,392
Iowa State University of Science and Technology	pub.	$8636	$8546	99%	20%	$13,195	$3987	$27,643
Iowa Wesleyan University	ind.	$30,500	$10,500	73%	13%	$25,803	$15,197	$33,152
Loras College	ind.	$34,184	$8275	100%	32%	$28,297	$14,162	$34,156
Luther College	ind.	$42,290	$9460	100%	39%	$38,605	$13,145	$36,685
Morningside College	ind.	$30,390	$9390	68%	23%	$25,670	$14,110	$36,449
Mount Mercy University	ind.	$31,998	$9534	100%	23%	$25,722	$15,810	$25,739
Northwestern College	ind.	$31,100	$9200	89%	65%	$25,084	$15,216	$32,164
St. Ambrose University	ind.	$30,894	$10,470	100%	25%	$23,589	$17,775	NR
Simpson College	ind.	$39,144	$8380	99%	29%	$31,851	$15,673	$38,155
University of Dubuque	ind.	$29,710	$9450	99%	14%	$27,325	$11,835	$30,353
The University of Iowa	pub.	$7486	$10,450	71%	34%	$15,835	$2101	$28,405
University of Northern Iowa	pub.	$8699	$8781	58%	16%	$8210	$9270	$23,887
Upper Iowa University	ind.	$30,450	$8460	98%	NR	$28,429	$10,481	$26,488
Wartburg College	ind.	$41,280	$9995	100%	20%	$30,254	$21,021	$37,551
Kansas								
Baker University	ind.	$28,880	$8310	91%	NR	$25,695	$11,495	$31,937
Barclay College	ind.	$19,640	$9350	100%	NR	$19,548	$9442	$19,926
Benedictine College	ind.	$28,480	$9900	100%	42%	$24,665	$13,715	$29,196
Bethel College	ind.	$28,540	$8850	83%	28%	$25,737	$11,653	$5633
Emporia State University	pub.	$6345	$8684	100%	15%	$9538	$5491	$22,816
Fort Hays State University	pub.	$4007	$7615	91%	8%	$7296	$4326	$26,568
Kansas State University	pub.	$10,135	$9430	55%	24%	$13,500	$6065	$28,318
Kansas Wesleyan University	ind.	$29,500	$9500	88%	13%	$20,665	$18,335	$34,526
MidAmerica Nazarene University	ind.	$30,736	$8708	100%	75%	$25,049	$14,395	$33,018
Newman University	ind.	$30,564	$8406	96%	29%	$14,494	$24,476	$25,963
Pittsburg State University	pub.	$7100	$7700	42%	NR	$6013	$8787	$24,389
Southwestern College	ind.	$30,150	$7760	100%	15%	$23,788	$14,122	$39,231

NA = not applicable; NR = not reported; * = includes room and board; † = room only; — = not available.

College Costs At-a-Glance

	Institutional Control ind.=independent; pub.=public	Tuition and Fees	Room and Board	Percent of Eligible Freshmen Receiving Need-Based Gift Awards	Percent of Freshmen Whose Need Was Fully Met	Average Financial Aid Package for Freshmen	Average Net Cost After Aid	Average Indebtedness Upon Graduation
Sterling College	ind.	$24,485	$8580	94%	14%	$20,964	$12,101	$28,221
The University of Kansas	pub.	$10,824	$10,060	87%	45%	$16,455	$4429	$28,462
Wichita State University	pub.	$8325	$6782	62%	25%	$7704	$7403	$25,380
Kentucky								
Alice Lloyd College	ind.	$2150	$6880	99%	7%	$13,132	—	$10,141
Bellarmine University	ind.	$41,800	$12,250	100%	24%	$36,193	$17,857	$31,377
Berea College	ind.	$560	$6534	100%	NR	$34,670	—	$7468
Campbellsville University	ind.	$25,400	$8000	100%	21%	$22,539	$10,861	$21,756
Centre College	ind.	$41,700	$10,480	100%	37%	$34,441	$17,739	$24,917
Clear Creek Baptist Bible College	ind.	N/R	NR	100%	NR	$8488	—	NR
Eastern Kentucky University	pub.	$8996	$9728	63%	31%	$12,365	$6359	$33,102
Georgetown College	ind.	$38,650	$9780	100%	100%	$37,938	$10,492	$31,267
Kentucky State University	pub.	$7796	$6690	100%	13%	$12,640	$1846	$29,553
Lindsey Wilson College	ind.	$24,850	$9385	99%	25%	NR	NR	$28,870
Morehead State University	pub.	$8950	$9436	66%	19%	$12,594	$5792	$26,623
Murray State University	pub.	$8340	$8906	92%	22%	$11,656	$5590	$27,564
Northern Kentucky University	pub.	$9744	$9732	59%	24%	$11,887	$7589	$27,612
Thomas More College	ind.	$30,270	$7592	100%	26%	$23,123	$14,739	$32,908
Transylvania University	ind.	$38,750	$10,460	100%	26%	$29,177	$20,033	$30,595
Union College	ind.	$26,080	$7400	97%	12%	$20,956	$12,524	$32,691
University of Kentucky	pub.	$13,134	$12,184	42%	19%	$12,112	$13,206	$31,374
University of Louisville	pub.	$11,264	$8700	98%	22%	$13,208	$6756	$23,556
University of Pikeville	ind.	$20,950	$7800	100%	50%	$20,100	$8650	$23,876
Western Kentucky University	pub.	$10,202	$8350	62%	24%	$13,958	$4594	$27,654
Louisiana								
Centenary College of Louisiana	ind.	$36,580	$13,400	100%	25%	$28,259	$21,721	$32,900
Grambling State University	pub.	$7435	$10,054	100%	NR	$3744	$13,745	$47,162
Louisiana College	ind.	$16,000	$5274	100%	24%	$14,112	$7162	$26,285
Louisiana State University and Agricultural & Mechanical College	pub.	$11,374	$11,750	96%	22%	$15,330	$7794	$24,933
Louisiana Tech University	pub.	$9645	$6360	98%	23%	$11,667	$4338	$22,262
Loyola University New Orleans	ind.	$39,692	$13,380	100%	15%	$35,842	$17,230	$29,946
Nicholls State University	pub.	$7886	$9790	96%	13%	$10,845	$6831	NR
Southeastern Louisiana University	pub.	$8153	$8340	66%	11%	$9407	$7086	$20,164
Tulane University	ind.	$52,960	$14,536	98%	67%	$45,405	$22,091	$33,717
University of Louisiana at Lafayette	pub.	N/R	NR	83%	13%	$10,178	—	NR
University of Louisiana at Monroe	pub.	$8470	$7454	69%	20%	$8402	$7522	NR
University of New Orleans	pub.	$8694	$10,575	83%	17%	$9946	$9323	$20,723
Maine								
Bates College	ind.	$52,042	$14,678	100%	100%	$47,276	$19,444	$20,715
Bowdoin College	ind.	$51,848	$14,132	100%	100%	$47,275	$18,705	$23,174
Colby College	ind.	$53,120	$13,660	100%	100%	$51,118	$15,662	$34,745

NA = not applicable; NR = not reported; * = includes room and board; † = room only; — = not available.

College Costs At-a-Glance

	Institutional Control ind.=independent; pub.=public	Tuition and Fees	Room and Board	Percent of Eligible Freshmen Receiving Need-Based Gift Awards	Percent of Freshmen Whose Need Was Fully Met	Average Financial Aid Package for Freshmen	Average Net Cost After Aid	Average Indebtedness Upon Graduation
College of the Atlantic	ind.	$43,542	$9747	100%	9%	$47,010	$6279	$24,228
Husson University	ind.	$17,600	$9830	86%	12%	$15,351	$12,079	$33,412
Thomas College	ind.	N/R	NR	99%	12%	$21,043	—	$31,142
Unity College	ind.	$28,350	$10,400	100%	13%	$21,099	$17,651	NR
University of Maine	pub.	$10,902	$10,136	100%	20%	$14,897	$6141	$34,741
University of Maine at Fort Kent	pub.	$8115	$7910	94%	46%	$10,644	$5381	$24,096
University of Maine at Machias	pub.	$7726	$8490	100%	65%	$14,303	$1913	$25,702
University of Maine at Presque Isle	pub.	$8034	$8406	99%	50%	$12,155	$4285	$23,574
University of New England	ind.	$36,530	$13,580	NR	NR	NR	NR	NR
University of Southern Maine	pub.	$9220	$9200	100%	40%	$14,808	$3612	NR
Maryland								
Bowie State University	pub.	$8063	$11,340	78%	17%	$9389	$10,014	$29,433
Frostburg State University	pub.	$8914	$9210	80%	17%	$10,469	$7655	$29,802
Goucher College	ind.	$43,440	$12,670	100%	25%	$37,562	$18,548	$33,702
Hood College	ind.	$39,492	$12,700	100%	12%	$34,658	$17,534	$35,823
Loyola University Maryland	ind.	$47,725	$14,150	69%	90%	$32,616	$29,259	$33,969
McDaniel College	ind.	$41,800	$11,110	100%	24%	$39,191	$13,719	$34,099
Morgan State University	pub.	$7767	$10,650	80%	7%	$11,310	$7107	$34,578
Mount St. Mary's University	ind.	$40,550	$12,830	100%	23%	$32,667	$20,713	$36,112
Peabody Conservatory of The Johns Hopkins University	ind.	N/R	NR	55%	33%	$7095	—	$30,737
St. John's College	ind.	$51,670	$12,234	98%	23%	$42,027	$21,877	NR
St. Mary's College of Maryland	pub.	$14,496	$12,816	92%	5%	$15,606	$11,706	$21,911
Salisbury University	pub.	$9582	$11,550	87%	14%	$8990	$12,142	$26,940
Stevenson University	ind.	$36,182	$13,130	100%	21%	$25,847	$23,465	$37,000
Towson University	pub.	$9694	$12,544	58%	12%	$10,462	$11,776	$26,460
University of Maryland, Baltimore County	pub.	$11,518	$11,486	91%	19%	$11,914	$11,090	$27,221
University of Maryland, College Park	pub.	$10,399	$12,082	76%	19%	$11,813	$10,668	$28,122
University of Maryland University College	pub.	$7296	NA	78%	NR	$5144	$2152	NR
Washington College	ind.	$47,006	$12,190	99%	18%	$35,772	$23,424	$30,462
Massachusetts								
Amherst College	ind.	$54,310	$14,190	100%	100%	$53,209	$15,291	$19,075
Assumption College	ind.	$40,958	$12,684	100%	25%	$28,121	$25,521	NR
Babson College	ind.	$51,104	$16,312	95%	100%	$42,799	$24,617	$35,013
Bay Path University	ind.	$33,557	$12,799	100%	8%	$30,290	$16,066	$41,614
Becker College	ind.	$39,200	$13,800	100%	NR	$22,731	$30,269	NR
Bentley University	ind.	$49,880	$16,320	99%	41%	$35,924	$30,276	$31,889
Berklee College of Music	ind.	N/R	NR	35%	9%	$17,962	—	$50,177
Boston Architectural College	ind.	$21,174	NA	80%	NR	$14,481	$6693	NR
Boston Baptist College	ind.	$6300	$3500	86%	29%	NR	NR	NR
Boston College	ind.	$53,346	$14,142	91%	100%	$41,768	$25,720	$20,481
Boston University	ind.	$52,082	$15,270	99%	32%	$47,702	$19,650	$40,089
Brandeis University	ind.	$53,537	$14,906	98%	94%	$44,761	$23,682	$33,522

NA = not applicable; NR = not reported; * = includes room and board; † = room only; — = not available.

College Costs At-a-Glance

	Institutional Control ind.=independent; pub.=public	Tuition and Fees	Room and Board	Percent of Eligible Freshmen Receiving Need-Based Gift Awards	Percent of Freshmen Whose Need Was Fully Met	Average Financial Aid Package for Freshmen	Average Net Cost After Aid	Average Indebtedness Upon Graduation
Bridgewater State University	pub.	$10,312	$13,000	83%	11%	$8523	$14,789	$28,680
Clark University	ind.	$45,730	$9170	99%	29%	$32,004	$22,896	$34,305
College of the Holy Cross	ind.	$50,630	$13,690	85%	100%	$40,451	$23,869	$26,258
Curry College	ind.	$39,720	$15,885	100%	12%	$30,765	$24,840	$45,947
Dean College	ind.	$39,434	$16,836	84%	8%	$27,040	$29,230	$48,717
Elms College	ind.	$35,788	$13,106	100%	9%	$28,556	$20,338	$38,539
Emmanuel College	ind.	$39,804	$14,994	100%	30%	$29,383	$25,415	NR
Endicott College	ind.	$33,050	$15,276	98%	9%	$21,066	$27,260	$44,159
Fisher College	ind.	$31,384	$15,926	100%	NR	$27,235	$20,075	$12,724
Fitchburg State University	pub.	$10,155	$10,676	77%	NR	$10,177	$10,654	$26,316
Framingham State University	pub.	$9920	$11,820	85%	27%	$9900	$11,840	$30,781
Franklin W. Olin College of Engineering	ind.	$51,080	$16,300	100%	100%	$50,941	$16,439	$23,098
Gordon College	ind.	$37,400	$11,070	100%	18%	$27,047	$21,423	$37,780
Harvard University	ind.	$48,949	$16,660	100%	100%	$55,354	$10,255	$15,114
Hult International Business School	ind.	N/R	NR	100%	NR	$11,442	—	$12,343
Lasell College	ind.	$36,000	$15,400	100%	13%	$29,059	$22,341	$41,455
Lesley University	ind.	$27,600	$16,230	100%	9%	$19,144	$24,686	$23,000
Massachusetts College of Art and Design	pub.	$13,200	$13,500	88%	NR	$11,504	$15,196	$26,792
Massachusetts College of Liberal Arts	pub.	$10,135	$10,724	78%	81%	$15,219	$5640	$27,883
Massachusetts Institute of Technology	ind.	$51,832	$15,510	98%	100%	$47,524	$19,818	$20,048
Massachusetts Maritime Academy	pub.	$8398	$12,306	67%	31%	$17,027	$3677	$37,414
MCPHS University	ind.	$32,705	$16,400	100%	40%	$9948	$39,157	$58,012
Merrimack College	ind.	$40,190	$15,225	100%	12%	$24,754	$30,661	NR
Mount Holyoke College	ind.	$49,998	$14,660	100%	100%	$41,558	$23,100	$23,872
New England Conservatory of Music	ind.	$46,930	$15,700	100%	31%	$28,909	$33,721	$33,003
Nichols College	ind.	$34,000	$13,800	100%	24%	$32,635	$15,165	$34,873
Northeastern University	ind.	$49,497	$16,240	97%	100%	$39,377	$26,360	NR
Pine Manor College	ind.	$30,860	$13,430	100%	6%	$26,900	$17,390	$34,970
Simmons College	ind.	$40,800	$15,200	100%	12%	$32,115	$23,885	$39,942
Smith College	ind.	$50,044	$16,730	99%	100%	$50,844	$15,930	$24,501
Springfield College	ind.	N/R	NR	100%	12%	$28,265	—	$42,329
Stonehill College	ind.	$41,300	$15,760	99%	46%	$28,838	$28,222	$36,502
Suffolk University	ind.	$38,566	NR	90%	33%	$31,817	$6749	$28,859
Tufts University	ind.	$54,318	$14,054	96%	100%	$46,384	$21,988	$27,367
University of Massachusetts Amherst	pub.	$15,411	$12,258	93%	14%	$17,495	$10,174	$31,860
University of Massachusetts Boston	pub.	$13,828	NA	94%	38%	$15,304	—	$27,109
University of Massachusetts Dartmouth	pub.	$13,571	$12,936	93%	33%	$17,203	$9304	$31,992
University of Massachusetts Lowell	pub.	$14,800	$12,496	92%	43%	$16,799	$10,497	$32,744
Wellesley College	ind.	$51,148	$15,836	97%	100%	$49,612	$17,372	$18,370
Wentworth Institute of Technology	ind.	$34,977	$13,844	89%	10%	$19,571	$29,250	$59,419
Western New England University	ind.	$35,740	$13,442	100%	14%	$26,141	$23,041	$36,517
Westfield State University	pub.	$9715	$10,689	74%	9%	$8186	$12,218	$29,050

NA = not applicable; NR = not reported; * = includes room and board; † = room only; — = not available.

College Costs At-a-Glance

	Institutional Control ind.=independent; pub.=public	Tuition and Fees	Room and Board	Percent of Eligible Freshmen Receiving Need-Based Gift Awards	Percent of Freshmen Whose Need Was Fully Met	Average Financial Aid Package for Freshmen	Average Net Cost After Aid	Average Indebtedness Upon Graduation
Wheaton College	ind.	$52,626	$13,424	100%	84%	$44,651	$21,399	$35,058
Williams College	ind.	$53,550	$14,150	100%	100%	$56,486	$11,214	$16,230
Worcester Polytechnic Institute	ind.	$48,628	$14,218	100%	58%	$34,841	$28,005	NR
Worcester State University	pub.	$9532	$12,006	89%	36%	$16,144	$5394	$29,137
Michigan								
Albion College	ind.	$45,590	$12,380	100%	16%	$44,414	$13,556	$44,140
Alma College	ind.	$38,768	$10,642	100%	17%	$31,054	$18,356	$39,264
Andrews University	ind.	$28,436	$9078	61%	27%	$29,011	$8503	$31,845
Aquinas College	ind.	$32,574	$9332	100%	21%	$25,933	$15,973	$29,755
Calvin College	ind.	$33,100	$9990	100%	20%	$25,195	$17,895	$31,478
Central Michigan University	pub.	$12,510	$9736	93%	56%	$14,438	$7808	$33,635
Cornerstone University	ind.	$24,500	$9300	100%	16%	$22,748	$11,052	$33,729
Eastern Michigan University	pub.	$13,649	$9672	71%	6%	$10,667	$12,654	$30,205
Ferris State University	pub.	$12,180	$9894	83%	17%	$13,160	$8914	$35,600
Grand Valley State University	pub.	$11,994	$9000	87%	16%	$10,902	$10,092	$29,675
Hillsdale College	ind.	$26,742	$10,610	54%	36%	$19,899	$17,453	$28,171
Hope College	ind.	$34,010	$10,310	88%	25%	$27,577	$16,743	$33,033
Kalamazoo College	ind.	$48,516	$9756	98%	54%	$42,907	$15,365	$31,789
Kuyper College	ind.	$21,090	$7254	100%	8%	$16,518	$11,826	$36,147
Lake Superior State University	pub.	N/R	NR	95%	24%	$12,640	—	$27,405
Lawrence Technological University	ind.	$32,130	$9500	99%	24%	$24,490	$17,140	$32,572
Michigan State University	pub.	$14,460	$9976	68%	17%	$14,029	$10,407	$32,310
Michigan Technological University	pub.	$15,074	$10,477	86%	18%	$16,495	$9056	$35,834
Northern Michigan University	pub.	$10,490	$10,328	71%	19%	$9613	$11,205	$31,075
Northwood University, Michigan Campus	ind.	$26,080	$10,170	75%	29%	$20,656	$15,594	$31,992
Olivet College	ind.	N/R	NR	91%	14%	$19,120	—	$26,872
Saginaw Valley State University	pub.	$9819	$9465	94%	NR	NR	NR	$31,695
University of Detroit Mercy	ind.	$41,158	$9452	99%	8%	$37,388	$13,222	$36,968
University of Michigan	pub.	$14,826	$11,198	82%	75%	$27,050	—	$25,712
University of Michigan–Dearborn	pub.	$12,472	NA	79%	10%	$10,866	$1606	$25,759
University of Michigan–Flint	pub.	$11,334	$8437	71%	2%	$11,613	$8158	$33,258
Walsh College of Accountancy and Business Administration	ind.	$16,935	NA	NR	NR	NR	NR	NR
Wayne State University	pub.	$13,776	$10,106	72%	9%	$12,247	$11,635	$27,960
Western Michigan University	pub.	$11,943	$9848	87%	30%	$14,180	$7611	$35,602
Minnesota								
Augsburg University	ind.	$38,800	$10,280	100%	13%	$32,783	$16,297	$38,176
Bemidji State University	pub.	N/R	NR	65%	7%	$8434	—	$27,171
Bethany Lutheran College	ind.	$27,780	$8040	100%	21%	$21,015	$14,805	$31,654
Bethel University	ind.	$37,300	$10,520	100%	23%	$30,215	$17,605	$36,990
Carleton College	ind.	$52,782	$13,632	100%	100%	$47,776	$18,638	$21,035
College of Saint Benedict	ind.	$43,738	$10,742	99%	38%	$35,942	$18,538	$42,833
The College of St. Scholastica	ind.	$37,212	$9710	78%	27%	$31,038	$15,884	$41,133

NA = not applicable; NR = not reported; * = includes room and board; † = room only; — = not available.

College Costs At-a-Glance

	Institutional Control ind.=independent; pub.=public	Tuition and Fees	Room and Board	Percent of Eligible Freshmen Receiving Need-Based Gift Awards	Percent of Freshmen Whose Need Was Fully Met	Average Financial Aid Package for Freshmen	Average Net Cost After Aid	Average Indebtedness Upon Graduation
Concordia College	ind.	$38,378	$8040	98%	29%	$30,121	$16,297	NR
Concordia University, St. Paul	ind.	$22,775	$9000	100%	16%	$17,906	$13,869	$34,686
Gustavus Adolphus College	ind.	$45,100	$9910	100%	60%	$38,506	$16,504	NR
Hamline University	ind.	$41,298	$10,358	100%	22%	$32,000	$19,656	$34,935
Macalester College	ind.	$54,344	$12,156	99%	100%	$47,580	$18,920	$24,381
Martin Luther College	ind.	$14,680	$5790	99%	17%	$12,508	$7962	$23,239
Minnesota State University Mankato	pub.	$8663	$8475	83%	15%	$9733	$7405	$31,483
Minnesota State University Moorhead	pub.	$8496	$9280	66%	NR	$2706	$15,070	$32,713
St. Catherine University	ind.	$38,349	$9196	85%	37%	$38,300	$9245	$38,199
Saint John's University	ind.	$43,356	$10,116	99%	36%	$35,367	$18,105	$41,698
Saint Mary's University of Minnesota	ind.	$35,140	$9080	99%	24%	$27,733	$16,487	$39,917
St. Olaf College	ind.	$47,840	$5200	100%	93%	$41,392	$11,648	$27,002
University of Minnesota, Crookston	pub.	$12,202	$7658	99%	31%	$14,771	$5089	$26,696
University of Minnesota, Duluth	pub.	$13,344	$7608	93%	29%	$13,155	$7797	$30,445
University of Minnesota, Twin Cities Campus	pub.	$14,417	$9852	87%	26%	$13,686	$10,583	$26,568
University of St. Thomas	ind.	$41,133	$10,054	98%	26%	$29,564	$21,623	$40,983
Winona State University	pub.	$9379	$8730	74%	11%	$6613	$11,496	$33,873
Mississippi								
Alcorn State University	pub.	$6888	$9731	100%	14%	$14,918	$1701	$35,680
Belhaven University	ind.	$25,300	$8500	77%	8%	$19,199	$14,601	NR
Blue Mountain College	ind.	$11,760	$6125	99%	20%	$11,593	$6292	$19,084
Jackson State University	pub.	$7946	$9552	85%	10%	$12,592	$4906	$29,864
Millsaps College	ind.	$39,910	$13,730	99%	23%	$35,521	$18,119	$33,569
Mississippi State University	pub.	$8318	$9614	97%	30%	$16,612	$1320	$30,721
University of Mississippi	pub.	$8290	$10,502	93%	19%	$13,656	$5136	$30,731
University of Southern Mississippi	pub.	$8108	$10,638	63%	31%	$13,096	$5650	$27,859
Missouri								
Central Methodist University	ind.	$24,420	$7940	65%	23%	$20,642	$11,718	NR
College of the Ozarks	ind.	$460	$7400	100%	NR	$18,500	—	NR
Columbia College	ind.	$22,704	NR	76%	19%	$16,983	$5721	$26,312
Conception Seminary College	ind.	$21,576	$12,809	100%	25%	$23,285	$11,100	$31,817
Cox College	ind.	$10,270	NA	83%	NR	$3375	$6895	NR
Culver-Stockton College	ind.	$26,680	$8520	100%	19%	$21,156	$14,044	$29,105
Drury University	ind.	$28,365	$9040	100%	25%	$21,933	$15,472	$31,137
Evangel University	ind.	$23,421	$4304†	100%	14%	$18,494	$9231	$30,443
Goldfarb School of Nursing at Barnes-Jewish College	ind.	$20,188	NA	NR	NR	NR	NR	NR
Harris-Stowe State University	pub.	$5340	$6500†	56%	61%	$11,146	$694	NR
Kansas City Art Institute	ind.	$37,550	$10,400	100%	18%	NR	NR	$25,000
Lincoln University	pub.	$7632	$6770	91%	3%	$17,962	—	$32,928
Lindenwood University	ind.	$16,960	$8800	89%	17%	$15,902	$9858	$32,774
Logan University	ind.	$8400	NA	67%	NR	$12,539	—	NR
Maryville University of Saint Louis	ind.	$28,470	$10,088	100%	13%	$20,091	$18,467	$29,849

NA = not applicable; NR = not reported; * = includes room and board; † = room only; — = not available.

College Costs At-a-Glance

	Institutional Control ind.=independent; pub.=public	Tuition and Fees	Room and Board	Percent of Eligible Freshmen Receiving Need-Based Gift Awards	Percent of Freshmen Whose Need Was Fully Met	Average Financial Aid Package for Freshmen	Average Net Cost After Aid	Average Indebtedness Upon Graduation
Missouri Baptist University	ind.	$26,020	$10,380	80%	40%	$23,313	$13,087	$27,951
Missouri Southern State University	pub.	$6067	NR	81%	17%	$8972	—	$25,314
Missouri State University	pub.	$7306	$8537	85%	18%	$9294	$6549	$25,714
Missouri University of Science and Technology	pub.	$8460	$10,094	94%	14%	$16,722	$1832	$27,500
Missouri Valley College	ind.	$20,600	$9150	100%	3%	$17,674	$12,076	$31,508
Missouri Western State University	pub.	$6842	$8102	NR	NR	NR	NR	NR
Northwest Missouri State University	pub.	$9571	$9770	91%	48%	$11,144	$8197	$28,332
Rockhurst University	ind.	$36,590	$9970	100%	29%	$30,058	$16,502	$26,198
St. Louis College of Pharmacy	ind.	$30,010	$12,285	96%	19%	$17,193	$25,102	NR
Saint Louis University	ind.	$42,166	$10,996	97%	51%	$32,013	$21,149	$21,292
Southeast Missouri State University	pub.	$7185	$8715	95%	17%	$9718	$6182	$27,991
Southwest Baptist University	ind.	$24,010	$7720	86%	25%	$23,107	$8623	$29,429
Truman State University	pub.	$7656	$8630	99%	41%	$13,306	$2980	$24,938
University of Central Missouri	pub.	$7520	$8536	60%	14%	$8853	$7203	$27,481
University of Missouri	pub.	$9787	$10,676	89%	17%	$12,455	$8008	$27,364
University of Missouri–St. Louis	pub.	$10,275	$9363	86%	29%	$14,284	$5354	$25,873
Washington University in St. Louis	ind.	$53,399	$16,440	96%	100%	$48,169	$21,670	$22,592
Webster University	ind.	$27,100	$11,050	86%	21%	$27,407	$10,743	$29,867
Westminster College	ind.	N/R	NR	100%	68%	$24,896	—	$29,691
William Jewell College	ind.	$34,400	$9930	100%	60%	$31,927	$12,403	$33,326
William Woods University	ind.	$24,185	$9700	100%	NR	$18,004	$15,881	$32,728
Montana								
Carroll College	ind.	$34,480	$9608	98%	27%	$26,459	$17,629	$30,640
Montana State University	pub.	$7223	$9250	77%	41%	$1154	$15,319	$27,254
Montana State University Billings	pub.	$5826	$7510	89%	34%	$9959	$3377	$26,780
Montana Tech of The University of Montana	pub.	$7411	$9828	87%	22%	$10,327	$6912	$27,926
Rocky Mountain College	ind.	$28,512	$8330	100%	17%	$24,276	$12,566	$29,452
University of Montana	pub.	$7244	$9544	65%	12%	$12,033	$4755	$30,000
The University of Montana Western	pub.	$5502	$7744	76%	NR	$3603	$9643	NR
University of Providence	ind.	$25,318	$9200	71%	8%	$21,363	$13,155	$31,642
Nebraska								
College of Saint Mary	ind.	$20,350	$7700	100%	38%	$16,535	$11,515	$35,259
Concordia University, Nebraska	ind.	$32,220	$8470	100%	29%	$26,541	$14,149	$27,722
Creighton University	ind.	$39,916	$11,036	100%	30%	$29,125	$21,827	$35,766
Doane University	ind.	$32,250	$9090	100%	39%	$26,137	$15,203	$28,240
Nebraska Christian College of Hope International University	ind.	$16,830	$9130	60%	7%	$10,227	$15,733	$18,479
Nebraska Methodist College	ind.	$15,980	$6300†	100%	14%	$11,629	$10,651	$37,215
Union College	ind.	$23,780	$7070	100%	25%	$19,425	$11,425	$35,893
University of Nebraska at Kearney	pub.	$7326	$9688	92%	30%	$12,008	$5006	$19,538
University of Nebraska–Lincoln	pub.	$8887	$11,044	84%	20%	$14,958	$4973	$22,918
Wayne State College	pub.	$6824	$7430	73%	50%	$9940	$4314	NR

NA = not applicable; NR = not reported; * = includes room and board; † = room only; — = not available.

College Costs At-a-Glance

	Institutional Control ind.=independent; pub.=public	Tuition and Fees	Room and Board	Percent of Eligible Freshmen Receiving Need-Based Gift Awards	Percent of Freshmen Whose Need Was Fully Met	Average Financial Aid Package for Freshmen	Average Net Cost After Aid	Average Indebtedness Upon Graduation
Nevada								
University of Nevada, Las Vegas	pub.	$7800	$10,780	71%	21%	$8288	$10,292	$21,333
University of Nevada, Reno	pub.	$7764	$10,868	90%	10%	$8300	$10,332	$22,650
New Hampshire								
Dartmouth College	ind.	$52,950	$15,159	94%	100%	$52,069	$16,040	$19,571
Franklin Pierce University	ind.	$34,995	$13,082	100%	23%	$26,482	$21,595	$41,661
Keene State College	pub.	$13,868	$10,736	78%	14%	$12,507	$12,097	$40,195
New England College	ind.	$36,954	$13,874	98%	4%	$27,668	$23,160	$37,450
Northeast Catholic College	ind.	N/R	NR	100%	90%	$17,581	—	$18,186
Plymouth State University	pub.	N/R	NR	100%	17%	$9992	—	$39,319
Saint Anselm College	ind.	$41,200	$14,500	100%	27%	$28,104	$27,596	$36,567
Southern New Hampshire University	ind.	$31,136	$12,278	60%	15%	$22,182	$21,232	$40,327
Thomas More College of Liberal Arts	ind.	$21,600	$9700	100%	9%	$18,012	$13,288	$26,828
University of New Hampshire	pub.	$18,499	$11,588	79%	17%	$24,020	$6067	$33,013
University of New Hampshire at Manchester	pub.	$14,860	NA	60%	20%	$13,266	$1594	$30,423
New Jersey								
Caldwell University	ind.	$34,715	$13,300	100%	8%	$31,389	$16,626	$25,114
The College of New Jersey	pub.	$16,149	$13,200	50%	12%	$11,899	$17,450	$37,787
Drew University	ind.	$39,500	$14,108	100%	15%	$44,763	$8845	$24,058
Fairleigh Dickinson University, Florham Campus	ind.	$41,780	$13,130	100%	16%	$41,927	$12,983	$42,122
Fairleigh Dickinson University, Metropolitan Campus	ind.	$39,446	$13,086	100%	10%	$40,106	$12,426	$40,151
Felician University	ind.	$34,315	$12,885	81%	10%	$30,379	$16,821	NR
Georgian Court University	ind.	$32,260	$10,808	98%	24%	$33,169	$9899	$39,006
Kean University	pub.	$12,107	$13,513	74%	1%	$10,551	$15,069	$32,277
Monmouth University	ind.	$36,732	$13,552	82%	94%	$28,429	$21,855	$30,985
Montclair State University	pub.	$12,455	$13,466	69%	12%	$9632	$16,289	$28,070
New Jersey City University	pub.	$11,431	$12,446	87%	2%	$12,419	$11,458	$27,173
New Jersey Institute of Technology	pub.	$16,898	$13,300	100%	17%	$13,628	$16,570	$40,979
Princeton University	ind.	$49,330	$16,290	100%	100%	$54,310	$11,310	$9005
Ramapo College of New Jersey	pub.	$14,080	$12,180	51%	3%	$11,418	$14,842	$10,082
Rider University	ind.	$41,310	$14,700	100%	14%	$34,344	$21,666	$35,332
Rowan University	pub.	$13,108	$11,688	48%	16%	$9618	$15,178	$31,900
Rutgers University–Camden	pub.	$14,501	$12,094	78%	5%	$15,736	$10,859	$32,781
Rutgers University–Newark	pub.	$14,085	$13,266	86%	3%	$15,122	$12,229	$29,077
Rutgers University–New Brunswick	pub.	$14,638	$12,452	65%	6%	$15,044	$12,046	$32,601
Saint Peter's University	ind.	N/R	NR	99%	7%	$33,384	—	$22,317
Stevens Institute of Technology	ind.	$52,202	$15,244	68%	17%	$31,639	$35,807	$38,402
Stockton University	pub.	$13,404	$12,120	77%	26%	$17,797	$7727	$33,629
Thomas Edison State University	pub.	$7300	NA	NR	NR	NR	NR	NR
William Paterson University of New Jersey	pub.	$12,804	$11,218	76%	29%	$11,881	$12,141	$33,355

NA = not applicable; NR = not reported; * = includes room and board; † = room only; — = not available.

College Costs At-a-Glance

	Institutional Control ind.=independent; pub.=public	Tuition and Fees	Room and Board	Percent of Eligible Freshmen Receiving Need-Based Gift Awards	Percent of Freshmen Whose Need Was Fully Met	Average Financial Aid Package for Freshmen	Average Net Cost After Aid	Average Indebtedness Upon Graduation
New Mexico								
New Mexico Highlands University	pub.	$6454	$7654	98%	6%	$8591	$5517	$19,391
New Mexico Institute of Mining and Technology	pub.	$7183	$8202	54%	20%	$11,791	$3594	$26,817
New Mexico State University	pub.	$6461	$8686	98%	14%	$12,054	$3093	$21,019
St. John's College	ind.	$53,218	$12,148	100%	32%	$45,500	$19,866	$26,990
New York								
Adelphi University	ind.	$37,170	$15,500	73%	16%	$21,500	$31,170	$35,285
Alfred University	ind.	$33,484	$12,516	100%	15%	$31,102	$14,898	$35,987
Bard College	ind.	$52,915	$15,066	97%	30%	$50,218	$17,763	$26,904
Barnard College	ind.	$52,662	$16,100	97%	97%	$50,619	$18,143	$23,276
Baruch College of the City University of New York	pub.	$7115	NR	96%	10%	$6115	$1000	$5642
Binghamton University, State University of New York	pub.	$9523	$14,577	80%	15%	$13,199	$10,901	$27,022
Buffalo State College, State University of New York	pub.	$7976	$12,982	92%	28%	$13,807	$7151	$26,495
Canisius College	ind.	$28,488	$11,300	100%	24%	$34,108	$5680	$33,694
Cazenovia College	ind.	$33,656	$14,210	100%	25%	$36,189	$11,677	$35,863
City College of the City University of New York	pub.	N/R	NR	94%	77%	$9212	—	NR
Clarkson University	ind.	$49,444	$14,908	99%	21%	$45,835	$18,517	$24,500
Colgate University	ind.	$53,980	$13,520	100%	100%	$53,246	$14,254	$24,761
The College at Brockport, State University of New York	pub.	$8154	$12,904	77%	12%	$11,532	$9526	$30,416
The College of New Rochelle	ind.	$37,760	$14,562	NR	NR	NR	NR	$35,430
The College of Saint Rose	ind.	$32,574	$12,714	74%	16%	$24,052	$21,236	$37,506
College of Staten Island of the City University of New York	pub.	$7089	$13,900†	94%	5%	$8489	$12,500	NR
Columbia University	ind.	$57,208	$13,618	99%	100%	$59,830	$10,996	NR
Cornell University	ind.	$52,853	$14,380	98%	100%	$47,860	$19,373	$25,542
The Culinary Institute of America	ind.	$31,616	$10,870	95%	9%	$18,382	$24,104	$51,200
Daemen College	ind.	$27,990	$12,696	100%	16%	$30,169	$10,517	$35,530
Davis College	ind.	$16,300	$7700	97%	NR	$9924	$14,076	$9381
Dominican College	ind.	$29,000	$13,150	100%	12%	$26,111	$16,039	$32,859
Elmira College	ind.	$41,900	$12,000	100%	17%	$32,600	$21,300	$29,601
Eugene Lang College of Liberal Arts	ind.	$46,340	$16,250	84%	10%	$26,201	$36,389	$62,290
Farmingdale State College	pub.	$8076	$12,892	90%	9%	$8390	$12,578	$22,105
Fashion Institute of Technology	pub.	$7463	$13,945	73%	47%	$10,679	$10,729	$25,074
Fordham University	ind.	$50,986	$17,445	97%	32%	$36,410	$32,021	$35,735
Hamilton College	ind.	$52,770	$13,400	100%	100%	$46,050	$20,120	$19,281
Hartwick College	ind.	$45,510	$12,460	100%	15%	$39,511	$18,459	$27,653
Hilbert College	ind.	$22,350	$9350	100%	19%	$16,942	$14,758	$19,613
Hobart and William Smith Colleges	ind.	$55,255	$14,035	99%	64%	$36,231	$33,059	$33,600
Hofstra University	ind.	$43,960	$14,930	99%	26%	$33,000	$25,890	NR
Hunter College of the City University of New York	pub.	$6980	$4857†	91%	32%	$9039	$2798	$12,122
Iona College	ind.	$37,682	$14,832	44%	14%	$26,200	$26,314	$32,487
Ithaca College	ind.	$43,978	$15,562	97%	57%	$38,729	$20,811	$42,016

NA = not applicable; NR = not reported; * = includes room and board; † = room only; — = not available.

College Costs At-a-Glance

	Institutional Control ind.=independent; pub.=public	Tuition and Fees	Room and Board	Percent of Eligible Freshmen Receiving Need-Based Gift Awards	Percent of Freshmen Whose Need Was Fully Met	Average Financial Aid Package for Freshmen	Average Net Cost After Aid	Average Indebtedness Upon Graduation
John Jay College of Criminal Justice of the City University of New York	pub.	$7070	$20,007	92%	NR	$8610	$18,467	NR
The Juilliard School	ind.	$43,520	$15,990	100%	33%	$38,790	$20,720	$33,025
Keuka College	ind.	$30,946	$11,452	83%	9%	$26,000	$16,398	NR
The King's College	ind.	$36,450	$16,840†	100%	16%	$26,538	$26,752	$34,271
Lehman College of the City University of New York	pub.	$7010	NR	95%	1%	$11,322	—	$4410
Le Moyne College	ind.	$34,625	$13,780	100%	28%	$27,000	$21,405	$35,209
Long Island University–LIU Brooklyn	ind.	$36,978	$13,720	82%	2%	$25,945	$24,753	$46,578
Long Island University–LIU Post	ind.	$36,978	$13,720	56%	6%	$28,850	$21,848	$36,533
Manhattan College	ind.	$42,087	$15,600	88%	NR	$25,262	$32,425	$39,443
Manhattanville College	ind.	$38,820	$14,520	83%	11%	$28,326	$25,014	$33,850
Marist College	ind.	$36,680	$15,900	98%	26%	$27,579	$25,001	$37,681
Marymount Manhattan College	ind.	$33,778	$16,832	100%	7%	$19,019	$31,591	$26,742
Medgar Evers College of the City University of New York	pub.	$6650	NA	98%	3%	$8900	—	NR
Mercy College	ind.	$18,713	$13,900	90%	2%	$15,270	$17,343	$30,258
Metropolitan College of New York	ind.	$19,180	NA	100%	2%	$13,461	$5719	NR
Molloy College	ind.	$30,310	$14,712	98%	11%	$19,410	$25,612	$33,197
Morrisville State College	pub.	$8309	$13,238	86%	NR	$10,586	$10,961	$28,402
Mount Saint Mary College	ind.	$31,118	$15,108	99%	19%	$23,758	$22,468	$28,313
Nazareth College of Rochester	ind.	$33,324	$13,410	100%	37%	$28,120	$18,614	$40,958
The New School College of Performing Arts	ind.	$46,340	$16,250	32%	4%	$16,338	$46,252	$77,353
The New School for Public Engagement	ind.	$30,860	$16,250	100%	NR	$19,538	$27,572	NR
New York Institute of Technology	ind.	$36,890	$14,290	79%	NR	$29,280	$21,900	NR
New York School of Interior Design	ind.	N/R	NR	100%	NR	$11,321	—	$65,401
Niagara University	ind.	$33,500	$13,200	98%	56%	$28,761	$17,939	$34,214
Parsons School of Design	ind.	$47,920	$15,000	94%	11%	$25,388	$37,532	$70,361
Pratt Institute	ind.	$51,870	$12,622	43%	13%	$29,698	$34,794	$37,926
Queens College of the City University of New York	pub.	$7138	$15,352	92%	3%	$5503	$16,987	$14,738
Rensselaer Polytechnic Institute	ind.	$53,880	$15,260	100%	22%	$40,705	$28,435	NR
Roberts Wesleyan College	ind.	$30,936	$10,430	100%	20%	$25,757	$15,609	$34,679
Rochester Institute of Technology	ind.	$40,068	$12,666	95%	77%	$28,468	$24,266	$38,927
The Sage Colleges	ind.	$30,857	$12,618	78%	NR	NR	NR	$30,905
St. Bonaventure University	ind.	$33,331	$11,815	73%	23%	$29,259	$15,887	$15,101
St. John Fisher College	ind.	$33,120	$12,150	100%	38%	$24,214	$21,056	$38,639
St. John's University	ind.	$40,520	$17,020	74%	16%	$30,684	$26,856	$32,831
St. Joseph's College, Long Island Campus	ind.	$26,560	NA	99%	38%	$17,996	$8564	$30,358
St. Joseph's College, New York	ind.	$26,550	NR	100%	24%	$18,764	$7786	$21,123
St. Lawrence University	ind.	$54,846	$14,134	100%	22%	$45,856	$23,124	$32,627
St. Thomas Aquinas College	ind.	$30,750	$12,750	100%	18%	$16,500	$27,000	$28,750
Sarah Lawrence College	ind.	$54,010	$14,856	98%	18%	$36,059	$32,807	$19,610
School of Visual Arts	ind.	$39,900	$20,400	89%	5%	$19,728	$40,572	$47,989
Siena College	ind.	$36,975	$15,000	100%	27%	$30,196	$21,779	$35,827
Skidmore College	ind.	$52,446	$14,004	100%	100%	$47,700	$18,750	$23,916

NA = not applicable; NR = not reported; * = includes room and board; † = room only; — = not available.

College Costs At-a-Glance

	Institutional Control ind.=independent; pub.=public	Tuition and Fees	Room and Board	Percent of Eligible Freshmen Receiving Need-Based Gift Awards	Percent of Freshmen Whose Need Was Fully Met	Average Financial Aid Package for Freshmen	Average Net Cost After Aid	Average Indebtedness Upon Graduation
State University of New York at Fredonia	pub.	$8288	$12,490	81%	23%	$13,113	$7665	$27,586
State University of New York at New Paltz	pub.	$7975	$12,642	60%	7%	$12,457	$8160	$26,385
State University of New York at Oswego	pub.	$8191	$13,740	96%	7%	$12,201	$9730	$28,429
State University of New York at Plattsburgh	pub.	$8164	$12,988	91%	22%	$14,667	$6485	$29,865
State University of New York College at Cortland	pub.	$8300	$12,410	66%	12%	$14,939	$5771	$29,111
State University of New York College at Geneseo	pub.	$8408	$13,214	76%	11%	$9567	$12,055	$25,148
State University of New York College at Potsdam	pub.	$8221	$12,830	85%	6%	$18,264	$2787	$28,797
State University of New York College of Agriculture and Technology at Cobleskill	pub.	$8139	$13,182	88%	1%	$8392	$12,929	$29,645
State University of New York College of Environmental Science and Forestry	pub.	$8568	$16,140	98%	35%	$11,625	$13,083	$26,679
State University of New York College of Technology at Canton	pub.	$8129	$12,450	87%	19%	$11,077	$9502	$31,499
State University of New York Maritime College	pub.	$8074	$12,134	71%	NR	$4278	$15,930	$36,503
State University of New York Polytechnic Institute	pub.	$7998	$12,440	97%	100%	$12,153	$8285	NR
Stony Brook University, State University of New York	pub.	$9257	$13,446	94%	16%	$14,202	$8501	$26,219
Syracuse University	ind.	$46,755	$15,558	93%	55%	$38,450	$23,863	$38,918
Union College	ind.	$53,490	$13,119	97%	100%	$43,345	$23,264	$34,221
University at Albany, State University of New York	pub.	$9490	$13,864	89%	7%	$11,672	$11,682	$27,329
University at Buffalo, the State University of New York	pub.	$9828	$13,782	75%	6%	$10,937	$12,673	$25,598
University of Rochester	ind.	$53,825	$15,860	100%	93%	$50,139	$19,546	$29,013
Utica College	ind.	$20,676	$10,834	95%	6%	$14,484	$17,026	$31,694
Vassar College	ind.	$55,210	$12,900	100%	100%	$52,284	$15,826	$19,439
Vaughn College of Aeronautics and Technology	ind.	$24,877	$14,185	88%	15%	$8084	$30,978	$32,014
Villa Maria College	ind.	$22,080	NA	NR	NR	NR	NR	$22,658
Webb Institute	ind.	$50,175	$15,050	100%	NR	$50,500	$14,725	$17,870
Wells College	ind.	$39,600	$13,730	100%	19%	$32,620	$20,710	$35,287
North Carolina								
Appalachian State University	pub.	$7303	$8174	77%	17%	$9021	$6456	$22,855
Barton College	ind.	$30,880	$10,120	98%	14%	$21,454	$19,546	$26,477
Belmont Abbey College	ind.	N/R	NR	100%	11%	$13,110	—	$25,610
Campbell University	ind.	$31,190	$10,840	74%	34%	$29,970	$12,060	$29,975
Carolina Christian College	ind.	$13,950	NA	67%	67%	$9500	$4450	NR
Catawba College	ind.	$30,520	$10,488	68%	31%	$26,659	$14,349	$31,471
Charlotte Christian College and Theological Seminary	ind.	$10,468	NA	NR	NR	NR	NR	$33,034
Chowan University	ind.	$24,980	$9400	100%	5%	$21,497	$12,883	$38,443
Davidson College	ind.	$49,949	$13,954	100%	100%	$47,564	$16,339	$20,431
Duke University	ind.	$53,500	$14,798	96%	100%	$53,831	$14,467	$23,819
East Carolina University	pub.	$7143	$9835	68%	8%	$9640	$7338	$28,918
Elon University	ind.	$35,318	$12,230	89%	18%	$19,885	$27,663	$30,458
Gardner-Webb University	ind.	$30,730	$5100	80%	24%	$27,388	$8442	$31,926
Guilford College	ind.	$34,215	$10,222	99%	67%	$29,257	$15,180	$35,392
High Point University	ind.	$35,118	$14,130	99%	10%	$15,623	$33,625	$37,025

NA = not applicable; NR = not reported; * = includes room and board; † = room only; — = not available.

College Costs At-a-Glance

	Institutional Control ind.=independent; pub.=public	Tuition and Fees	Room and Board	Percent of Eligible Freshmen Receiving Need-Based Gift Awards	Percent of Freshmen Whose Need Was Fully Met	Average Financial Aid Package for Freshmen	Average Net Cost After Aid	Average Indebtedness Upon Graduation
Johnson C. Smith University	ind.	$18,236	$7100	95%	4%	$16,143	$9193	$35,769
Lees-McRae College	ind.	$26,198	$10,758	86%	NR	$24,172	$12,784	NR
Lenoir-Rhyne University	ind.	$35,350	$12,150	100%	18%	$30,392	$17,108	$28,485
Meredith College	ind.	$35,916	$10,718	100%	16%	$28,267	$18,367	$34,959
Methodist University	ind.	$32,860	$12,295	100%	10%	$24,664	$20,491	$33,978
Montreat College	ind.	N/R	NR	100%	8%	$21,786	—	$21,802
North Carolina Agricultural and Technical State University	pub.	$6526	$7260	88%	9%	$11,444	$2342	$34,379
North Carolina State University	pub.	$9100	$11,078	95%	23%	$13,222	$6956	$24,053
Pfeiffer University	ind.	$29,574	$10,958	86%	12%	$21,854	$18,678	$15,939
Piedmont International University	ind.	$10,100	$7185	100%	5%	$8055	$9230	NR
St. Andrews University	ind.	$25,618	NR	99%	10%	$21,097	$4521	$26,209
Saint Augustine's University	ind.	$17,890	$7692	100%	NR	$10,315	$15,267	$19,500
Salem College	ind.	$28,566	$11,640	NR	NR	NR	NR	NR
University of North Carolina at Asheville	pub.	$7145	$9106	93%	26%	$12,857	$3394	$23,824
The University of North Carolina at Chapel Hill	pub.	$8986	$11,190	92%	83%	$17,732	$2444	$22,214
The University of North Carolina at Charlotte	pub.	$7023	$10,780	73%	11%	$9103	$8700	$27,453
The University of North Carolina at Greensboro	pub.	$7164	$8834	73%	22%	$12,287	$3711	$26,841
The University of North Carolina at Pembroke	pub.	$5955	$8782	86%	7%	$9498	$5239	$25,831
The University of North Carolina Wilmington	pub.	$7048	$9736	86%	16%	$8348	$8436	$24,605
Wake Forest University	ind.	$53,322	$16,032	96%	100%	$49,145	$20,209	$35,434
Western Carolina University	pub.	$7191	$9164	96%	12%	$11,338	$5017	$15,669
North Dakota								
Minot State University	pub.	$6810	$6140	98%	34%	$9946	$3004	$23,400
University of Jamestown	ind.	$21,976	$7570	100%	32%	$14,942	$14,604	$27,238
University of North Dakota	pub.	$8447	$8226	85%	49%	$14,780	$1893	NR
Valley City State University	pub.	$7406	$6328	99%	56%	$13,848	—	$27,050
Ohio								
Allegheny Wesleyan College	ind.	N/R	NR	100%	100%	$10,000	—	NR
Baldwin Wallace University	ind.	$32,586	$9554	100%	32%	$28,852	$13,288	$36,426
Bluffton University	ind.	$32,766	$10,800	99%	15%	$26,786	$16,780	$36,796
Bowling Green State University	pub.	$11,057	$8918	90%	17%	$13,781	$6194	$30,814
Capital University	ind.	$35,466	$10,842	97%	33%	$30,669	$15,639	$32,515
Case Western Reserve University	ind.	$47,500	$14,784	98%	96%	$46,967	$15,317	$32,377
Cedarville University	ind.	$30,270	$7360	71%	35%	$22,070	$15,560	$29,582
Central State University	pub.	$6246	$9934	100%	5%	$8934	$7246	NR
Cleveland Institute of Art	ind.	$40,655	$10,800	100%	7%	$26,456	$24,999	$37,195
Cleveland Institute of Music	ind.	N/R	NR	100%	34%	$35,778	—	$25,994
Cleveland State University	pub.	$9696	$12,000	89%	8%	$9234	$12,462	$29,380
The College of Wooster	ind.	$48,600	$11,400	97%	55%	$42,174	$17,826	$30,053
Columbus College of Art & Design	ind.	$35,375	$9370	100%	11%	$26,973	$17,772	$32,258
Defiance College	ind.	$32,730	$10,220	100%	11%	$23,953	$18,997	NR
Denison University	ind.	$50,440	$12,330	100%	79%	$47,566	$15,204	$27,823

NA = not applicable; NR = not reported; * = includes room and board; † = room only; — = not available.

College Costs At-a-Glance

	Institutional Control ind.=independent; pub.=public	Tuition and Fees	Room and Board	Percent of Eligible Freshmen Receiving Need-Based Gift Awards	Percent of Freshmen Whose Need Was Fully Met	Average Financial Aid Package for Freshmen	Average Net Cost After Aid	Average Indebtedness Upon Graduation
Franciscan University of Steubenville	ind.	$26,430	$8400	100%	18%	$17,368	$17,462	$34,222
Heidelberg University	ind.	$31,000	$10,400	100%	22%	$24,888	$16,512	$35,872
Hiram College	ind.	$34,300	$10,290	NR	NR	NR	NR	NR
John Carroll University	ind.	$39,790	$11,580	98%	23%	$31,209	$20,161	$30,860
Kent State University	pub.	$10,012	$10,916	51%	16%	$11,138	$9790	$32,790
Kent State University at Geauga	pub.	$5664	NA	71%	7%	$6284	—	NR
Kent State University at Stark	pub.	$5664	NA	66%	15%	$6470	—	NR
Kenyon College	ind.	$55,930	$12,510	96%	100%	$45,275	$23,165	$21,404
Malone University	ind.	$30,860	$9500	100%	15%	$27,995	$12,365	$33,330
Marietta College	ind.	$36,040	$11,320	84%	42%	$34,019	$13,341	$40,196
Miami University	pub.	$14,578	$12,725	86%	29%	$16,002	$11,301	$29,434
Mount Carmel College of Nursing	ind.	$13,442	$5000†	82%	8%	$5984	$12,458	$36,309
Mount St. Joseph University	ind.	$30,100	$9442	100%	18%	$24,612	$14,930	NR
Mount Vernon Nazarene University	ind.	$29,194	$8170	100%	53%	$25,284	$12,080	$25,745
Muskingum University	ind.	$28,516	$11,480	100%	26%	$25,880	$14,116	$33,490
Oberlin College	ind.	$53,460	$14,402	95%	100%	$42,825	$25,037	$29,781
Ohio Northern University	ind.	$32,260	$11,650	100%	24%	$27,782	$16,128	NR
The Ohio State University	pub.	$10,591	$12,252	94%	24%	$14,976	$7867	$28,158
Ohio University	pub.	$11,896	$11,498	90%	41%	$9672	$13,722	$27,993
Ohio University–Chillicothe	pub.	N/R	NA	87%	13%	$6471	—	$27,993
Ohio University–Eastern	pub.	$5050	NA	90%	10%	$5787	—	$27,993
Ohio University–Lancaster	pub.	N/R	NA	85%	18%	$5511	—	$27,993
Ohio University–Southern Campus	pub.	N/R	NA	95%	15%	$5725	—	$27,993
Ohio University–Zanesville	pub.	$5076	NA	86%	11%	$5835	—	$27,993
Ohio Wesleyan University	ind.	$45,740	$12,430	100%	16%	$36,981	$21,189	$35,221
Shawnee State University	pub.	$8556	$10,864	72%	5%	$8662	$10,758	$30,554
Tiffin University	ind.	$25,000	$11,200	100%	16%	$19,092	$17,108	$36,819
The University of Akron	pub.	$10,270	$12,296	56%	14%	$9343	$13,223	$32,033
University of Cincinnati	pub.	$11,000	$11,118	74%	7%	$8688	$13,430	$25,877
The University of Findlay	ind.	$33,320	$9720	100%	27%	$28,326	$14,714	$37,424
The University of Toledo	pub.	$9240	$11,151	98%	9%	$10,896	$9495	$28,260
Ursuline College	ind.	$32,390	$10,776	100%	12%	$29,874	$13,292	$34,189
Wittenberg University	ind.	$39,500	$10,356	100%	27%	$34,185	$15,671	$35,242
Wright State University	pub.	$8730	$11,376	86%	21%	$9870	$10,236	$30,677
Wright State University–Lake Campus	pub.	$5842	$10,584	84%	30%	$7143	$9283	$22,549
Xavier University	ind.	$37,230	$12,150	68%	11%	$24,999	$24,381	$10,217
Youngstown State University	pub.	$8899	NR	78%	13%	$9269	—	$31,759
Oklahoma								
Cameron University	pub.	$6180	$5452	88%	6%	$7985	$3647	$23,961
East Central University	pub.	$6600	$6730	77%	31%	$5792	$7538	$24,171
Northeastern State University	pub.	$6334	$7020	93%	83%	$11,859	$1495	$21,268
Oklahoma Baptist University	ind.	$28,258	$7350	75%	26%	$24,504	$11,104	$24,451

NA = not applicable; **NR** = not reported; ***** = includes room and board; **†** = room only; **—** = not available.

College Costs At-a-Glance

	Institutional Control ind.=independent; pub.=public	Tuition and Fees	Room and Board	Percent of Eligible Freshmen Receiving Need-Based Gift Awards	Percent of Freshmen Whose Need Was Fully Met	Average Financial Aid Package for Freshmen	Average Net Cost After Aid	Average Indebtedness Upon Graduation
Oklahoma Christian University	ind.	$22,760	$8190	53%	48%	$23,205	$7745	$28,438
Oklahoma City University	ind.	$31,026	$8896	98%	86%	$23,951	$15,971	$27,209
Oklahoma State University	pub.	$8738	$8558	79%	17%	$14,954	$2342	$23,790
Oral Roberts University	ind.	$27,728	$9450	100%	49%	$27,859	$9319	$32,745
Rogers State University	pub.	$6870	$8050	91%	5%	$9422	$5498	$16,164
Southeastern Oklahoma State University	pub.	$6750	$6568	68%	12%	$13,097	$221	$16,542
Southwestern Oklahoma State University	pub.	$7005	$5500	99%	16%	$5769	$6736	$18,520
University of Central Oklahoma	pub.	$7099	$8050	70%	16%	$10,459	$4690	$26,939
University of Oklahoma	pub.	$9063	$10,588	46%	77%	$13,004	$6647	$29,283
University of Science and Arts of Oklahoma	pub.	$7200	NR	100%	21%	$11,011	—	$22,351
The University of Tulsa	ind.	$41,024	$11,116	92%	38%	$34,596	$17,544	$34,869
Oregon								
Corban University	ind.	$33,040	$10,231	100%	18%	$22,607	$20,664	$31,408
Eastern Oregon University	pub.	$8362	$9250	94%	29%	$10,515	$7097	$31,314
George Fox University	ind.	$34,866	$10,886	97%	42%	$24,100	$21,652	$29,207
Lewis & Clark College	ind.	$48,988	$12,096	97%	45%	$39,084	$22,000	$27,591
Linfield College	ind.	$41,576	$11,770	81%	25%	$36,595	$16,751	$34,244
Northwest Christian University	ind.	$28,680	$8800	100%	26%	$24,111	$13,369	$28,740
Oregon Health & Science University	pub.	$19,602	NA	NR	NR	NR	NR	NR
Oregon State University	pub.	$10,797	$12,540	85%	13%	$12,911	$10,426	$26,749
Pacific University	ind.	N/R	NR	69%	17%	$34,829	—	$36,001
Portland State University	pub.	$8783	$12,831	77%	7%	$10,928	$10,686	$26,867
Reed College	ind.	$54,200	$13,670	100%	94%	$42,917	$24,953	$17,467
Southern Oregon University	pub.	$9286	$12,831	67%	12%	$8651	$13,466	$23,603
University of Oregon	pub.	$11,571	$12,450	78%	7%	$11,038	$12,983	$26,164
University of Portland	ind.	N/R	NR	80%	7%	$30,658	—	$31,815
Warner Pacific College	ind.	$24,500	$9300	75%	20%	$22,286	$11,514	$28,471
Western Oregon University	pub.	$9198	$10,203	86%	10%	$9878	$9523	$29,565
Willamette University	ind.	$50,074	$12,440	97%	30%	$35,088	$27,426	$32,117
Pennsylvania								
Albright College	ind.	$45,302	$12,070	100%	11%	$41,714	$15,658	$38,599
Allegheny College	ind.	$47,540	$12,140	100%	27%	$42,666	$17,014	NR
Bloomsburg University of Pennsylvania	pub.	$10,500	$9430	65%	9%	$8411	$11,519	$35,407
Bryn Mawr College	ind.	$50,500	$15,910	100%	100%	$47,447	$18,963	$25,448
Bucknell University	ind.	$53,986	$13,150	69%	NR	$37,500	$29,636	$33,000
Cairn University	ind.	$27,279	$10,294	98%	11%	$24,301	$13,272	$35,717
Carlow University	ind.	$28,596	$11,108	100%	22%	$24,457	$15,247	NR
Carnegie Mellon University	ind.	$55,465	$14,418	97%	94%	$44,812	$25,071	$31,077
Cedar Crest College	ind.	$39,216	$11,544	100%	16%	$30,533	$20,227	$44,032
Chatham University	ind.	$37,611	$12,090	88%	23%	$29,499	$20,202	$35,303
Chestnut Hill College	ind.	$36,180	$11,000	82%	28%	$30,165	$17,015	$42,527
Clarion University of Pennsylvania	pub.	$10,890	$11,058	83%	4%	$9315	$12,633	$35,277

NA = not applicable; NR = not reported; * = includes room and board; † = room only; — = not available.

College Costs At-a-Glance

	Institutional Control ind.=independent; pub.=public	Tuition and Fees	Room and Board	Percent of Eligible Freshmen Receiving Need-Based Gift Awards	Percent of Freshmen Whose Need Was Fully Met	Average Financial Aid Package for Freshmen	Average Net Cost After Aid	Average Indebtedness Upon Graduation
Delaware Valley University	ind.	$38,000	$13,950	99%	14%	$29,940	$22,010	$45,953
DeSales University	ind.	$36,100	$12,800	100%	25%	$27,969	$20,931	$42,536
Dickinson College	ind.	$52,930	$13,236	97%	92%	$44,642	$21,524	$25,881
Drexel University	ind.	$52,002	$13,890	100%	34%	$42,948	$22,944	NR
Duquesne University	ind.	$36,394	$12,114	100%	24%	$25,928	$22,580	$43,637
Eastern University	ind.	$32,882	$11,254	87%	21%	$25,020	$19,116	$37,225
East Stroudsburg University of Pennsylvania	pub.	$10,298	$8672	95%	47%	$8679	$10,291	$24,182
Elizabethtown College	ind.	$46,940	$11,370	100%	29%	$34,258	$24,052	$42,316
Franklin & Marshall College	ind.	$54,380	$13,580	100%	100%	$52,315	$15,645	$27,011
Gannon University	ind.	N/R	NR	99%	20%	$26,530	—	NR
Geneva College	ind.	$26,980	$10,170	100%	20%	$20,435	$16,715	$35,440
Gettysburg College	ind.	$52,640	$12,570	98%	90%	$40,147	$25,063	$31,323
Grove City College	ind.	$17,254	$9400	100%	13%	$7989	$18,665	$40,747
Gwynedd Mercy University	ind.	$33,520	$11,980	100%	14%	$26,574	$18,926	$46,139
Harrisburg University of Science and Technology	ind.	$23,900	$6800†	99%	17%	$21,553	$9147	$34,547
Haverford College	ind.	$52,754	$15,958	100%	100%	$49,905	$18,807	$15,000
Holy Family University	ind.	$30,346	$13,576	99%	16%	$25,350	$18,572	$36,609
Indiana University of Pennsylvania	pub.	$12,146	$12,488	71%	9%	$11,469	$13,165	$39,833
Juniata College	ind.	$45,597	$12,521	100%	16%	$37,720	$20,398	$38,478
King's College	ind.	$35,830	$12,410	100%	21%	$26,789	$21,451	$38,625
Kutztown University of Pennsylvania	pub.	$9987	$10,282	63%	7%	$8384	$11,885	$40,084
Lafayette College	ind.	$50,850	$15,040	98%	100%	$49,946	$15,944	$32,974
Lancaster Bible College	ind.	N/R	NR	99%	30%	$19,703	—	$33,818
La Roche College	ind.	$28,564	$11,556	78%	37%	$32,879	$7241	$27,298
La Salle University	ind.	$29,500	$14,690	99%	14%	$32,533	$11,657	$37,002
Lebanon Valley College	ind.	$43,650	$11,860	100%	17%	$35,396	$20,114	$43,588
Lehigh University	ind.	$50,740	$13,120	91%	75%	$46,421	$17,439	$35,440
Lincoln University	pub.	$10,636	$9738	95%	4%	$11,744	$8630	$41,630
Lock Haven University of Pennsylvania	pub.	$10,576	$9968	71%	96%	$11,774	$8770	$34,863
Lycoming College	ind.	$40,090	$12,568	100%	13%	$39,141	$13,517	NR
Mansfield University of Pennsylvania	pub.	$12,316	$11,928	74%	40%	$10,164	$14,080	$36,624
Marywood University	ind.	$34,910	$13,900	100%	21%	$28,187	$20,623	$41,880
Messiah College	ind.	$35,160	$10,520	100%	17%	$25,467	$20,213	$37,399
Millersville University of Pennsylvania	pub.	$11,858	$13,440	72%	6%	$7836	$17,462	$31,476
Misericordia University	ind.	$33,240	$13,960	100%	26%	$25,752	$21,448	$47,764
Moravian College	ind.	$43,636	$13,378	100%	16%	$32,824	$24,190	$33,096
Mount Aloysius College	ind.	$22,430	$10,338	100%	NR	$15,500	$17,268	$36,899
Muhlenberg College	ind.	$50,830	$11,420	100%	27%	$37,050	$25,200	$32,241
Neumann University	ind.	$30,050	$12,520	62%	59%	$23,372	$19,198	$39,694
Peirce College	ind.	$15,060	NA	NR	NR	NR	NR	NR
Penn State Abington	pub.	$14,516	NR	67%	11%	$10,966	$3550	$31,007
Penn State Altoona	pub.	$15,190	$11,280	51%	26%	$9941	$16,529	$41,629

NA = not applicable; NR = not reported; * = includes room and board; † = room only; — = not available.

College Costs At-a-Glance

	Institutional Control ind.=independent; pub.=public	Tuition and Fees	Room and Board	Percent of Eligible Freshmen Receiving Need-Based Gift Awards	Percent of Freshmen Whose Need Was Fully Met	Average Financial Aid Package for Freshmen	Average Net Cost After Aid	Average Indebtedness Upon Graduation
Penn State Beaver	pub.	$13,694	$11,280	53%	30%	$11,325	$13,649	$35,924
Penn State Berks	pub.	$15,190	$12,400	53%	25%	$9582	$18,008	$39,022
Penn State Brandywine	pub.	$14,460	$11,860	55%	18%	$10,512	$15,808	$34,353
Penn State Erie, The Behrend College	pub.	$15,190	$11,280	48%	32%	$10,282	$16,188	$39,977
Penn State Greater Allegheny	pub.	$13,694	$11,280	63%	25%	$13,195	$11,779	$37,163
Penn State Harrisburg	pub.	$15,190	$12,940	51%	23%	$10,055	$18,075	$42,315
Penn State Hazleton	pub.	$14,460	$11,280	59%	24%	$12,610	$13,130	$45,703
Penn State Lehigh Valley	pub.	$14,460	NA	61%	14%	$10,837	$3623	$38,922
Penn State New Kensington	pub.	$13,694	NR	57%	20%	$10,178	$3516	$38,989
Penn State Schuylkill	pub.	$14,398	$8426	68%	19%	$11,653	$11,171	$38,360
Penn State Shenango	pub.	$13,324	NA	58%	23%	$11,549	$1775	$45,746
Penn State University Park	pub.	$18,436	$11,280	36%	34%	$9620	$20,096	$37,307
Penn State Wilkes-Barre	pub.	$13,568	NA	66%	22%	$10,504	$3064	$34,805
Penn State Worthington Scranton	pub.	$14,460	NA	68%	18%	$10,717	$3743	$41,945
Penn State York	pub.	$14,460	NA	57%	16%	$9757	$4703	$39,091
Pennsylvania College of Technology	pub.	$18,840	$11,340	76%	NR	$12,300	$17,880	$7218
Point Park University	ind.	$30,130	$11,960	100%	14%	$28,190	$13,900	$27,924
Robert Morris University	ind.	$29,420	$11,180	100%	12%	$25,418	$15,182	$39,856
Rosemont College	ind.	$19,486	$11,960	99%	3%	$17,578	$13,868	$30,437
Saint Joseph's University	ind.	$43,880	$14,840	98%	23%	$30,645	$28,075	NR
Saint Vincent College	ind.	$34,830	$11,399	88%	24%	$32,283	$13,946	$46,794
Seton Hill University	ind.	$34,660	$11,280	100%	22%	$25,565	$20,375	$35,356
Shippensburg University of Pennsylvania	pub.	$12,086	$12,010	81%	7%	$9796	$14,300	$33,839
Slippery Rock University of Pennsylvania	pub.	$10,205	$10,312	65%	8%	$8777	$11,740	$34,300
Susquehanna University	ind.	$45,470	$12,090	100%	23%	$37,399	$20,161	$33,757
Swarthmore College	ind.	$50,822	$14,952	100%	100%	$52,104	$13,670	$20,209
Temple University	pub.	$16,658	$11,566	80%	30%	$19,406	$8818	$38,108
Thomas Jefferson University	ind.	N/R	NR	100%	18%	$36,481	—	$40,100
University of Pennsylvania	ind.	$55,584	$15,616	98%	100%	$49,401	$21,799	$23,224
University of Pittsburgh	pub.	$19,080	$10,950	82%	18%	$12,960	$17,070	$38,322
University of Pittsburgh at Bradford	pub.	$13,900	$9058	96%	9%	$13,499	$9459	$36,250
University of Pittsburgh at Greensburg	pub.	$13,870	$10,270	95%	15%	$12,438	$11,702	$36,358
University of Pittsburgh at Johnstown	pub.	$13,388	$9684	90%	15%	$9892	$13,180	$37,239
The University of Scranton	ind.	$43,310	$14,618	98%	14%	$27,728	$30,200	$43,530
The University of the Arts	ind.	$44,780	$16,322	100%	23%	$28,871	$32,231	$37,575
Ursinus College	ind.	$52,050	$12,750	99%	30%	$41,196	$23,604	$39,026
Villanova University	ind.	$51,284	$13,548	94%	12%	$38,853	$25,979	$34,752
Washington & Jefferson College	ind.	$46,628	$12,318	98%	13%	$38,035	$20,911	$54,184
Waynesburg University	ind.	$24,010	$9820	100%	27%	$20,026	$13,804	$31,000
West Chester University of Pennsylvania	pub.	$10,111	$9060	52%	7%	$7231	$11,940	$34,160
Westminster College	ind.	$36,230	$11,020	100%	16%	$29,849	$17,401	$43,241
Widener University	ind.	$44,166	$14,024	99%	20%	$35,505	$22,685	NR

NA = not applicable; NR = not reported; * = includes room and board; † = room only; — = not available.

College Costs At-a-Glance

	Institutional Control ind.=independent; pub.=public	Tuition and Fees	Room and Board	Percent of Eligible Freshmen Receiving Need-Based Gift Awards	Percent of Freshmen Whose Need Was Fully Met	Average Financial Aid Package for Freshmen	Average Net Cost After Aid	Average Indebtedness Upon Graduation
Wilkes University	ind.	$34,896	$14,270	100%	15%	$25,631	$23,535	$47,907
Wilson College	ind.	$24,452	$11,364	100%	7%	$20,606	$15,210	$40,623
York College of Pennsylvania	ind.	$20,100	$11,200	72%	15%	$13,712	$17,588	$41,969
Puerto Rico								
Carlos Albizu University	ind.	N/R	NA	100%	NR	$3365	—	NR
Inter American University of Puerto Rico, Bayamón Campus	ind.	$5178	$6114	99%	NR	$1379	$9913	NR
Inter American University of Puerto Rico, Ponce Campus	ind.	N/R	NA	100%	NR	NR	NR	NR
Theological University of the Caribbean	ind.	$5442	$2400	100%	NR	$2356	$5486	$8906
University of Puerto Rico–Bayamón	pub.	$2082	NA	NR	NR	NR	NR	NR
University of Puerto Rico–Mayagüez	pub.	N/R	NR	100%	NR	$5552	—	$7550
Rhode Island								
Brown University	ind.	$53,419	$14,020	93%	100%	$47,438	$20,001	$25,471
Bryant University	ind.	$43,973	$15,702	56%	30%	$25,278	$34,397	$52,949
Providence College	ind.	$48,764	$14,240	94%	27%	$32,640	$30,364	$41,383
Rhode Island College	pub.	$8776	$11,335	90%	13%	$11,033	$9078	$25,791
Roger Williams University	ind.	$32,510	$15,564	46%	11%	$19,985	$28,089	$44,225
Salve Regina University	ind.	$38,986	$14,060	100%	12%	$29,388	$23,658	$37,464
University of Rhode Island	pub.	$13,792	$7774	96%	62%	$17,526	$4040	$33,335
South Carolina								
Anderson University	ind.	$26,970	$9680	99%	21%	$21,033	$15,617	$31,042
Bob Jones University	ind.	$18,150	$6976	100%	20%	$13,519	$11,607	$21,153
The Citadel, The Military College of South Carolina	pub.	$14,368	$6600	87%	17%	$15,346	$5622	$32,039
Claflin University	ind.	$16,391	$9112	100%	7%	$17,003	$8500	$31,747
Clemson University	pub.	$14,712	$9592	94%	21%	$13,131	$11,173	$30,201
Coastal Carolina University	pub.	$11,200	$9140	51%	9%	$10,509	$9831	$37,373
Coker College	ind.	$28,684	$8824	92%	25%	$25,948	$11,560	$20,494
College of Charleston	pub.	$12,458	$12,048	80%	18%	$13,986	$10,520	$27,256
Columbia International University	ind.	$22,390	$7990	100%	15%	$18,501	$11,879	$24,132
Converse College	ind.	$18,030	$10,610	77%	17%	$15,526	$13,114	$29,814
Francis Marion University	pub.	$10,742	$7948	99%	10%	$13,021	$5669	$36,082
Furman University	ind.	$48,348	$12,158	98%	40%	$38,887	$21,619	$32,919
Newberry College	ind.	$26,424	$10,666	100%	11%	$22,497	$14,593	$22,380
Presbyterian College	ind.	$37,842	$10,298	100%	34%	$36,977	$11,163	NR
University of South Carolina	pub.	$12,262	$11,200	33%	35%	$8327	$15,135	$28,972
University of South Carolina Aiken	pub.	$10,502	$7592	96%	19%	$11,184	$6910	$27,739
University of South Carolina Upstate	pub.	N/R	NR	71%	6%	$10,456	—	$27,163
Winthrop University	pub.	$15,350	$8740	99%	14%	$14,033	$10,057	$36,147
Wofford College	ind.	$43,865	$12,685	100%	47%	$37,760	$18,790	$32,043
South Dakota								
Augustana University	ind.	$33,018	$8248	100%	20%	$27,792	$13,474	$36,950
Black Hills State University	pub.	$8602	$6820	NR	NR	NR	NR	NR

NA = not applicable; NR = not reported; * = includes room and board; † = room only; — = not available.

College Costs At-a-Glance

	Institutional Control ind.=independent; pub.=public	Tuition and Fees	Room and Board	Percent of Eligible Freshmen Receiving Need-Based Gift Awards	Percent of Freshmen Whose Need Was Fully Met	Average Financial Aid Package for Freshmen	Average Net Cost After Aid	Average Indebtedness Upon Graduation
Dakota State University	pub.	$9147	$6720	61%	9%	$7789	$8078	$29,962
Mount Marty College	ind.	$26,310	$7846	98%	56%	$29,970	$4186	$32,744
Northern State University	pub.	$8280	$7844	93%	34%	$10,057	$6067	$29,968
South Dakota State University	pub.	$8460	$7110	NR	NR	NR	NR	$31,131
University of Sioux Falls	ind.	$18,280	$7350	97%	31%	$22,378	$3252	$33,297
University of South Dakota	pub.	$8772	$7672	46%	20%	$8620	$7824	$29,686
Tennessee								
Austin Peay State University	pub.	$8225	$9170	100%	NR	$11,204	$6191	$18,044
Belmont University	ind.	$32,820	$11,680	96%	13%	$20,078	$24,422	$29,207
Bryan College	ind.	$25,600	$7300	100%	40%	$23,296	$9604	$25,666
Carson-Newman University	ind.	$27,400	$8630	99%	15%	$24,975	$11,055	$27,188
Christian Brothers University	ind.	$32,820	$7400	100%	33%	$27,968	$12,252	$30,694
Johnson University	ind.	$16,060	$6700	99%	11%	$11,285	$11,475	$24,353
King University	ind.	$29,714	$4400	99%	15%	$24,806	$9308	$24,370
Lee University	ind.	$17,690	$8300	94%	25%	$13,944	$12,046	$32,792
Lipscomb University	ind.	$32,144	$12,652	100%	21%	$24,038	$20,758	$29,673
Maryville College	ind.	$34,880	$11,424	100%	10%	$33,305	$12,999	$27,889
Middle Tennessee State University	pub.	$8948	$6408	65%	12%	$11,039	$4317	$25,717
Mid-South Christian College	ind.	$6658	$3400	100%	67%	$6000	$4058	NR
Milligan College	ind.	$33,700	$7100	100%	29%	$25,604	$15,196	$29,277
Rhodes College	ind.	$46,504	$11,290	99%	51%	$39,190	$18,604	$27,576
Sewanee: The University of the South	ind.	$45,120	$12,880	98%	35%	$37,018	$20,982	$26,772
Southern Adventist University	ind.	$21,950	$6940	96%	2%	$16,593	$12,297	$33,445
Tennessee Technological University	pub.	$8513	$9274	53%	13%	$11,596	$6191	$22,018
Tennessee Wesleyan University	ind.	$23,800	$7750	100%	24%	$16,549	$15,001	$18,540
Trevecca Nazarene University	ind.	$25,598	$8400	NR	NR	NR	NR	$29,487
Union University	ind.	$32,890	$10,200	89%	26%	$30,695	$12,395	$39,022
University of Memphis	pub.	$9701	$9366	99%	6%	$13,037	$6030	$27,002
The University of Tennessee	pub.	$12,970	$10,696	93%	22%	$14,137	$9529	$21,872
The University of Tennessee at Chattanooga	pub.	$8664	$8676	96%	19%	$10,822	$6518	$22,293
The University of Tennessee at Martin	pub.	$9236	$5976	69%	23%	$12,512	$2700	$27,335
Vanderbilt University	ind.	$47,664	$15,584	98%	100%	$50,356	$12,892	$23,973
Texas								
Abilene Christian University	ind.	$33,330	$10,378	100%	27%	$24,361	$19,347	NR
Angelo State University	pub.	$8215	$7666	86%	16%	$10,757	$5124	$24,926
Austin College	ind.	$39,010	$12,334	100%	22%	$35,402	$15,942	NR
Austin Graduate School of Theology	ind.	$8750	NA	NR	NR	NR	NR	NR
Baptist University of the Americas	ind.	$6240	$7670	NR	NR	NR	NR	NR
Baylor University	ind.	$45,542	$12,595	100%	15%	$33,682	$24,455	$44,859
Concordia University Texas	ind.	N/R	NR	100%	15%	$26,924	—	$32,509
Criswell College	ind.	$10,710	NA	80%	20%	$7824	$2886	NR
Dallas Baptist University	ind.	$28,870	$7992	64%	35%	$16,680	$20,182	$24,805

NA = not applicable; NR = not reported; * = includes room and board; † = room only; — = not available.

College Costs At-a-Glance

	Institutional Control ind.=independent; pub.=public	Tuition and Fees	Room and Board	Percent of Eligible Freshmen Receiving Need-Based Gift Awards	Percent of Freshmen Whose Need Was Fully Met	Average Financial Aid Package for Freshmen	Average Net Cost After Aid	Average Indebtedness Upon Graduation
East Texas Baptist University	ind.	$25,470	$8915	74%	14%	$19,612	$14,773	$33,823
Hardin-Simmons University	ind.	$28,990	$8080	79%	23%	$24,488	$12,582	$51,346
Houston Baptist University	ind.	$32,530	$8814	100%	10%	$27,336	$14,008	$31,767
Howard Payne University	ind.	$28,090	$8386	99%	18%	$19,362	$17,114	$34,875
Lamar University	pub.	$10,111	$8740	85%	16%	$5395	$13,456	$35,651
LeTourneau University	ind.	$30,210	$9970	100%	17%	$25,705	$14,475	$36,704
Lubbock Christian University	ind.	$21,794	$7478	100%	11%	$15,012	$14,260	$35,879
McMurry University	ind.	$26,712	$8324	100%	10%	$21,967	$13,069	$31,350
Midwestern State University	pub.	N/R	NR	92%	44%	$11,228	—	$28,468
Our Lady of the Lake University	ind.	$28,740	$9602	100%	38%	$23,250	$15,092	$34,224
Prairie View A&M University	pub.	$10,533	$8743	87%	7%	$16,636	$2640	$37,209
Rice University	ind.	$45,608	$13,850	99%	100%	$46,077	$13,381	$26,556
St. Edward's University	ind.	$43,050	$12,940	89%	13%	$37,627	$18,363	$34,812
St. Mary's University	ind.	$30,600	$10,790	100%	12%	$26,401	$14,989	$37,866
Sam Houston State University	pub.	$9890	$9180	87%	11%	$11,276	$7794	$27,920
Schreiner University	ind.	$26,900	$10,152	100%	14%	$19,144	$17,908	$29,746
Southern Methodist University	ind.	$54,493	$16,845	62%	49%	$43,715	$27,623	$32,468
Southwestern Christian College	ind.	N/R	NR	100%	62%	$12,194	—	NR
Southwestern University	ind.	$42,000	$12,000	98%	23%	$35,991	$18,009	$34,788
Stephen F. Austin State University	pub.	$9537	$8868	71%	17%	$12,423	$5982	$30,101
Tarleton State University	pub.	$9078	$9872	89%	3%	$10,478	$8472	$24,695
Texas A&M International University	pub.	$8320	$8160	98%	1%	$10,388	$6092	$17,394
Texas A&M University	pub.	$10,403	$12,250	94%	25%	$18,142	$4511	$23,505
Texas A&M University–Commerce	pub.	$8748	$8326	99%	7%	$11,948	$5126	$27,961
Texas A&M University–Corpus Christi	pub.	$8969	$10,410	81%	2%	$10,193	$9186	$16,998
Texas A&M University–Kingsville	pub.	$8462	$8760	93%	29%	$14,537	$2685	$28,347
Texas A&M University–Texarkana	pub.	$7634	$7462	91%	9%	$11,339	$3757	$19,410
Texas Christian University	ind.	$44,760	$12,360	94%	36%	$30,307	$26,813	$42,212
Texas Lutheran University	ind.	$29,960	$10,150	100%	28%	$26,587	$13,523	$32,437
Texas Southern University	pub.	N/R	NR	100%	100%	$21,430	—	$36,580
Texas State University	pub.	$10,621	$8100	85%	23%	$12,458	$6263	$26,568
Texas Tech University	pub.	$10,772	$5956	89%	15%	$14,477	$2251	$30,759
Texas Wesleyan University	ind.	$27,800	$9538	100%	13%	$24,949	$12,389	$12,360
Texas Woman's University	pub.	$9360	$8181	96%	34%	$14,927	$2614	$23,983
Trinity University	ind.	$42,976	$13,464	99%	68%	$40,226	$16,214	$40,800
University of Dallas	ind.	$38,716	$11,960	100%	28%	$34,091	$16,585	$35,161
University of Houston	pub.	$11,887	$9984	93%	17%	$12,712	$9159	$23,746
University of Houston–Clear Lake	pub.	$6873	$4852†	73%	12%	$11,771	—	NR
University of Houston–Downtown	pub.	$7832	NA	85%	2%	$8871	—	$25,747
University of Houston–Victoria	pub.	$7627	$7698	95%	16%	$11,931	$3394	NR
University of Mary Hardin-Baylor	ind.	$26,890	$8446	100%	10%	$18,700	$16,636	$43,344
University of North Texas	pub.	$11,514	$9610	66%	10%	$13,131	$7993	$25,203

NA = not applicable; NR = not reported; * = includes room and board; † = room only; — = not available.

College Costs At-a-Glance

	Institutional Control ind.=independent; pub.=public	Tuition and Fees	Room and Board	Percent of Eligible Freshmen Receiving Need-Based Gift Awards	Percent of Freshmen Whose Need Was Fully Met	Average Financial Aid Package for Freshmen	Average Net Cost After Aid	Average Indebtedness Upon Graduation
University of North Texas at Dallas	pub.	$7848	$8948	95%	11%	$10,964	$5832	$6927
University of St. Thomas	ind.	$33,580	NR	100%	10%	$27,619	$5961	$29,857
The University of Texas at Austin	pub.	$10,398	$10,070	79%	21%	$11,704	$8764	$24,883
The University of Texas at Dallas	pub.	$12,528	$11,112	89%	25%	$14,538	$9102	$23,565
The University of Texas at El Paso	pub.	$7651	$9495	NR	NR	$11,631	$5515	$22,938
The University of Texas at San Antonio	pub.	$9380	$7190	79%	12%	$10,722	$5848	$26,089
The University of Texas at Tyler	pub.	N/R	NR	86%	4%	$7321	—	$17,916
The University of Texas of the Permian Basin	pub.	$7124	$10,944	94%	24%	$9562	$8506	$19,578
The University of Texas Rio Grande Valley	pub.	$9055	$7986	98%	4%	$10,357	$6684	$14,291
University of the Incarnate Word	ind.	$29,990	$12,436	99%	12%	$28,638	$13,788	$6271
Wayland Baptist University	ind.	$19,430	$7534	100%	6%	$13,003	$13,961	$29,555
West Texas A&M University	pub.	$7885	$7196	81%	11%	$9767	$5314	$22,569
Utah								
Brigham Young University	ind.	$5620	$7628	55%	2%	$6921	$6327	$14,998
Dixie State University	pub.	$5080	$6328	90%	8%	$8655	$2753	$12,201
Neumont College of Computer Science	ind.	$24,750	$5970†	NR	NR	NR	NR	$39,623
Southern Utah University	pub.	$6676	$7067	53%	20%	$8984	$4759	$16,824
University of Utah	pub.	$8824	$9867	90%	20%	$22,575	—	$21,188
Utah State University	pub.	$7174	$6060	66%	18%	$9312	$3922	$21,328
Utah Valley University	pub.	$5652	NA	64%	20%	$7947	—	$20,832
Weber State University	pub.	$5712	$8400	74%	89%	$5144	$8968	$22,657
Westminster College	ind.	$34,040	$10,245	100%	27%	$27,193	$17,092	$28,774
Vermont								
Bennington College	ind.	$53,860	$15,610	100%	14%	$43,749	$25,721	$27,470
Champlain College	ind.	$39,818	$14,906	99%	20%	$28,236	$26,488	$38,818
Marlboro College	ind.	$40,840	$12,385	100%	33%	$44,049	$9176	$31,747
Middlebury College	ind.	$52,496	$14,968	100%	100%	$50,113	$17,351	$19,382
Saint Michael's College	ind.	$45,375	$12,220	99%	25%	$35,838	$21,757	$40,009
Southern Vermont College	ind.	$25,511	$11,000	100%	NR	$17,500	$19,011	$35,728
University of Vermont	pub.	$17,740	$12,022	99%	18%	$26,574	$3188	$28,894
Vermont Technical College	pub.	$15,510	$10,598	92%	8%	$12,492	$13,616	$29,988
Virginia								
Averett University	ind.	$33,350	$9684	100%	10%	$26,770	$16,264	$35,373
Bluefield College	ind.	$25,290	$9024	100%	12%	$18,689	$15,625	$33,772
Bridgewater College	ind.	$35,160	$12,720	100%	22%	$32,931	$14,949	$33,567
Christendom College	ind.	$26,360	$10,280	100%	NR	$18,729	$17,911	$31,877
Christopher Newport University	pub.	$13,654	$11,224	74%	21%	$9535	$15,343	$32,994
The College of William and Mary	pub.	$22,044	$11,799	90%	23%	$22,147	$11,696	$24,072
Eastern Mennonite University	ind.	$37,100	$11,160	99%	23%	$33,055	$15,205	$39,845
Emory & Henry College	ind.	$35,050	$11,820	99%	23%	$33,682	$13,188	$27,825
George Mason University	pub.	$11,724	NR	88%	3%	$14,717	—	$30,755

NA = not applicable; NR = not reported; * = includes room and board; † = room only; — = not available.

College Costs At-a-Glance

	Institutional Control ind.=independent; pub.=public	Tuition and Fees	Room and Board	Percent of Eligible Freshmen Receiving Need-Based Gift Awards	Percent of Freshmen Whose Need Was Fully Met	Average Financial Aid Package for Freshmen	Average Net Cost After Aid	Average Indebtedness Upon Graduation
Hampden-Sydney College	ind.	$45,852	$13,558	100%	26%	$33,456	$25,954	$35,921
Hampton University	ind.	$25,442	$11,218	100%	42%	$5975	$30,685	$34,131
Hollins University	ind.	$39,035	$13,520	100%	25%	$36,595	$15,960	$31,211
James Madison University	pub.	$10,830	$9822	61%	86%	$8547	$12,105	$27,656
Jefferson College of Health Sciences	ind.	$26,866	$9514	100%	NR	NR	NR	NR
Liberty University	ind.	$23,940	$9850	99%	11%	$14,553	$19,237	$21,875
Longwood University	pub.	$13,080	$10,732	NR	NR	$14,609	$9203	$28,376
Lynchburg College	ind.	$37,690	$10,680	100%	27%	$29,360	$19,010	$35,290
Mary Baldwin University	ind.	$31,085	$9410	100%	17%	$31,700	$8795	$32,679
Marymount University	ind.	$30,425	$12,805	60%	18%	$24,030	$19,200	$34,051
Old Dominion University	pub.	$10,350	$11,268	86%	19%	$12,247	$9371	$32,092
Radford University	pub.	$10,627	$9131	67%	25%	$9960	$9798	$31,463
Randolph College	ind.	$39,695	$13,580	51%	20%	$34,868	$18,407	$33,830
Randolph-Macon College	ind.	$41,300	$11,860	100%	29%	$29,326	$23,834	$34,660
Regent University	ind.	$17,478	$8250	97%	21%	$13,920	$11,808	$28,035
Roanoke College	ind.	$44,030	$13,690	100%	19%	$36,817	$20,903	$41,187
Shenandoah University	ind.	$32,530	$10,370	74%	10%	$19,644	$23,256	$34,121
Sweet Briar College	ind.	$21,000	$13,000	100%	31%	$34,928	—	$31,269
University of Mary Washington	pub.	$11,630	$11,118	69%	11%	$9573	$13,175	$29,964
University of Richmond	ind.	$52,610	$12,250	98%	84%	$48,645	$16,215	$27,125
University of Virginia	pub.	$16,146	$11,220	88%	100%	$29,009	—	$24,501
The University of Virginia's College at Wise	pub.	$9825	$10,314	91%	17%	$13,128	$7011	$21,389
Virginia Commonwealth University	pub.	$13,570	$10,187	94%	8%	$12,175	$11,582	$31,919
Virginia Military Institute	pub.	$18,214	$9236	90%	32%	$23,915	$3535	$30,367
Virginia Polytechnic Institute and State University	pub.	$13,230	$8690	71%	20%	$17,549	$4371	$30,221
Virginia State University	pub.	$8726	$10,880	80%	31%	$11,000	$8606	$28,250
Virginia Wesleyan University	ind.	$36,660	$9256	100%	12%	$26,090	$19,826	$34,212
Washington and Lee University	ind.	$50,170	$11,730	100%	100%	$51,751	$10,149	$22,651
Washington								
Central Washington University	pub.	$7849	$10,684	61%	20%	$11,110	$7423	$20,411
DigiPen Institute of Technology	ind.	$31,340	NR	53%	6%	$10,929	$20,411	$28,539
Eastern Washington University	pub.	$7109	$11,493	87%	7%	$12,429	$6173	$27,961
The Evergreen State College	pub.	$7416	$9681	94%	10%	$10,879	$6218	$21,147
Gonzaga University	ind.	$41,330	$11,550	100%	29%	$27,736	$25,144	$29,692
Northwest College of Art & Design	ind.	$20,600	NR	NR	NR	NR	NR	NR
Northwest University	ind.	$31,540	$8630	85%	16%	$16,561	$23,609	$24,930
Pacific Lutheran University	ind.	$40,722	$10,520	72%	26%	$34,019	$17,223	$26,379
Saint Martin's University	ind.	$37,356	$11,445	100%	23%	$28,575	$20,226	$30,744
Seattle Pacific University	ind.	$40,902	$11,178	100%	10%	$34,500	$17,580	$28,646
Seattle University	ind.	$42,885	$12,072	89%	14%	$35,825	$19,132	$28,848
University of Puget Sound	ind.	$49,776	$12,540	100%	16%	$35,650	$26,666	$34,791
University of Washington	pub.	$10,753	$11,691	94%	34%	$17,500	$4944	$19,880

NA = not applicable; NR = not reported; * = includes room and board; † = room only; — = not available.

College Costs At-a-Glance

	Institutional Control ind.=independent; pub.=public	Tuition and Fees	Room and Board	Percent of Eligible Freshmen Receiving Need-Based Gift Awards	Percent of Freshmen Whose Need Was Fully Met	Average Financial Aid Package for Freshmen	Average Net Cost After Aid	Average Indebtedness Upon Graduation
University of Washington, Bothell	pub.	$10,690	$10,833	93%	15%	$15,350	$6173	$18,850
University of Washington, Tacoma	pub.	$10,831	$10,230	93%	24%	$15,150	$5911	$17,480
Walla Walla University	ind.	$27,495	$7350	71%	30%	$23,317	$11,528	$33,577
Washington State University	pub.	$11,391	$11,356	95%	17%	$12,969	$9778	$26,807
Western Washington University	pub.	$7933	$11,400	90%	16%	$16,369	$2964	$15,663
Whitman College	ind.	$51,746	$13,174	99%	27%	$40,519	$24,401	$23,254
Whitworth University	ind.	$43,640	$11,496	99%	20%	$38,628	$16,508	$26,940
West Virginia								
Appalachian Bible College	ind.	$13,920	$7960	94%	NR	$13,401	$8479	$15,421
Bluefield State College	pub.	$6728	NA	82%	13%	$3300	$3428	$29,000
Concord University	pub.	$7732	$8642	88%	52%	$8000	$8374	$21,176
Fairmont State University	pub.	$9066	$9184	90%	13%	$9509	$8741	$25,291
Glenville State College	pub.	N/R	NR	83%	12%	$14,108	—	$29,608
Marshall University	pub.	$7798	$10,126	83%	25%	$12,330	$5594	$28,095
Ohio Valley University	ind.	$21,100	$7700	95%	15%	$13,511	$15,289	NR
Shepherd University	pub.	$7548	$10,500	70%	37%	$12,978	$5070	$27,686
West Virginia University	pub.	$8376	$10,576	79%	4%	$6752	$12,200	$29,358
West Virginia University Institute of Technology	pub.	$6960	$11,304	90%	6%	$7400	$10,864	$25,155
West Virginia Wesleyan College	ind.	$31,640	$8856	100%	26%	$29,339	$11,157	$31,996
Wheeling Jesuit University	ind.	$28,110	$8996	68%	26%	$29,063	$8043	$32,428
Wisconsin								
Alverno College	ind.	$28,277	$8296	98%	NR	$26,594	$9979	$36,659
Beloit College	ind.	$50,040	$8830	99%	27%	$45,818	$13,052	$27,507
Cardinal Stritch University	ind.	$28,844	$8118	100%	5%	$28,810	$8152	$31,526
Carroll University	ind.	$31,918	$9896	100%	37%	$25,791	$16,023	$35,802
Concordia University Wisconsin	ind.	$28,600	$10,530	96%	33%	$24,318	$14,812	$33,298
Edgewood College	ind.	$29,500	$11,020	100%	12%	$22,039	$18,481	$35,300
Lawrence University	ind.	$46,101	$10,032	99%	59%	$41,820	$14,313	$32,488
Marquette University	ind.	$39,900	$11,890	99%	22%	$29,812	$21,978	$37,713
Milwaukee School of Engineering	ind.	$40,749	$9408	100%	21%	$30,726	$19,431	$38,421
Mount Mary University	ind.	$30,100	$8600	100%	6%	$27,799	$10,901	$27,308
Northland College	ind.	$36,183	$9176	100%	12%	$32,280	$13,079	$28,731
St. Norbert College	ind.	$38,129	$9954	99%	22%	$25,972	$22,111	$33,794
University of Wisconsin–Eau Claire	pub.	$8816	$7538	82%	21%	$9343	$7011	$26,244
University of Wisconsin–Green Bay	pub.	$7878	$7306	80%	37%	$9325	$5859	$22,664
University of Wisconsin–La Crosse	pub.	$8922	$6206	85%	26%	$7857	$7271	$26,768
University of Wisconsin–Madison	pub.	$10,533	$10,842	83%	45%	$16,644	$4731	$27,979
University of Wisconsin–Milwaukee	pub.	$11,010	$10,728	58%	28%	$7153	$14,585	$37,131
University of Wisconsin–Parkside	pub.	$7649	$7924	73%	15%	$9687	$5886	$28,504
University of Wisconsin–River Falls	pub.	$8013	$6576	54%	2%	$6216	$8373	$27,428
University of Wisconsin–Stevens Point	pub.	$9734	$7290	72%	7%	$8688	$8336	$25,918
University of Wisconsin–Stout	pub.	$9456	$6744	54%	14%	$10,396	$5804	$30,409

NA = not applicable; NR = not reported; * = includes room and board; † = room only; — = not available.

College Costs At-a-Glance

	Institutional Control ind.=independent; pub.=public	Tuition and Fees	Room and Board	Percent of Eligible Freshmen Receiving Need-Based Gift Awards	Percent of Freshmen Whose Need Was Fully Met	Average Financial Aid Package for Freshmen	Average Net Cost After Aid	Average Indebtedness Upon Graduation
University of Wisconsin–Superior	pub.	$8109	$6730	64%	21%	$10,795	$4044	$30,285
University of Wisconsin–Whitewater	pub.	$7662	$6492	57%	38%	$7834	$6320	$24,704
Wisconsin Lutheran College	ind.	$29,725	$10,190	100%	17%	$24,748	$15,167	$32,549
Wyoming								
University of Wyoming	pub.	$5217	$10,320	68%	26%	$10,701	$4836	$22,524

NA = not applicable; NR = not reported; * = includes room and board; † = room only; — = not available.

Profiles of College Financial Aid Programs

ABILENE CHRISTIAN UNIVERSITY
Abilene, TX

Tuition & fees: $33,330	Average undergraduate aid package: $23,433

ABOUT THE INSTITUTION Independent Church of Christ, coed. *Awards:* certificates, associate, bachelor's, master's, and doctoral degrees. 65 undergraduate majors. *Total enrollment:* 5,149. Undergraduates: 3,670. Freshmen: 972. Federal methodology is used as a basis for awarding need-based institutional aid.

UNDERGRADUATE EXPENSES for 2017–2018 *Application fee:* $50. *Comprehensive fee:* $43,708 includes full-time tuition ($33,280), mandatory fees ($50), and room and board ($10,378). *College room only:* $5186. Full-time tuition and fees vary according to course load. Room and board charges vary according to board plan and housing facility. *Part-time tuition:* $1338 per credit hour. Part-time tuition and fees vary according to course load. *Payment plan:* Tuition prepayment.

FRESHMAN FINANCIAL AID (Fall 2017, est.) 828 applied for aid; of those 87% were deemed to have need. 100% of freshmen with need received aid; of those 27% had need fully met. *Average percent of need met:* 69% (excluding resources awarded to replace EFC). *Average financial aid package:* $24,361 (excluding resources awarded to replace EFC). 26% of all full-time freshmen had no need and received non-need-based gift aid.

UNDERGRADUATE FINANCIAL AID (Fall 2017, est.) 2,877 applied for aid; of those 83% were deemed to have need. 100% of undergraduates with need received aid; of those 27% had need fully met. *Average percent of need met:* 67% (excluding resources awarded to replace EFC). *Average financial aid package:* $23,433 (excluding resources awarded to replace EFC). 33% of all full-time undergraduates had no need and received non-need-based gift aid.

GIFT AID (NEED-BASED) *Total amount:* $45,629,614 (10% federal, 7% state, 80% institutional, 3% external sources). *Receiving aid:* Freshmen: 76% (717); all full-time undergraduates: 67% (2,368). *Average award:* Freshmen: $22,109; Undergraduates: $20,532. *Scholarships, grants, and awards:* Federal Pell, FSEOG, state, private, college/university gift aid from institutional funds.

GIFT AID (NON-NEED-BASED) *Total amount:* $16,849,399 (99% institutional, 1% external sources). *Receiving aid:* Freshmen: 76% (717). Undergraduates: 67% (2,356). *Average award:* Freshmen: $14,953. Undergraduates: $13,365. *Scholarships, grants, and awards by category: Academic interests/achievement:* agriculture, biological sciences, business, communication, education, engineering/technologies, English, foreign languages, general academic interests/achievements, mathematics, physical sciences, religion/biblical studies, social sciences. *Creative arts/performance:* art/fine arts, debating, journalism/publications, music, theater/drama. *Special achievements/activities:* cheerleading/drum major, leadership. *Special characteristics:* children of faculty/staff, ethnic background, first-generation college students, local/state students, members of minority groups, out-of-state students, previous college experience, relatives of clergy, religious affiliation. *Tuition waivers:* Full or partial for employees or children of employees.

LOANS *Student loans:* $24,550,013 (29% need-based, 71% non-need-based). *Average need-based loan:* Freshmen: $3466. Undergraduates: $4489. *Parent loans:* $5,611,601 (100% non-need-based). *Programs:* Federal Direct (Subsidized and Unsubsidized Stafford, PLUS), Perkins, state, private loans.

WORK-STUDY *Federal work-study:* Total amount: $64,407; jobs available. *State or other work-study/employment:* Total amount: $1,908,903 (1% need-based, 99% non-need-based). Part-time jobs available.

ATHLETIC AWARDS Total amount: $6,746,207 (53% need-based, 47% non-need-based).

APPLYING FOR FINANCIAL AID *Required financial aid form:* FAFSA. *Financial aid deadline (priority):* 3/1. *Notification date:* Continuous beginning 4/1. Students must reply within 3 weeks of notification.

CONTACT Undergraduate Admissions, Abilene Christian University, ACU Box 29000, Abilene, TX 79699-9000, 325-674-2650 or toll-free 800-460-6228. *Fax:* 325-674-2130. *E-mail:* info@admissions.acu.edu. *Website:* http://www.acu.edu/.

ABRAHAM BALDWIN AGRICULTURAL COLLEGE
Tifton, GA

CONTACT Michael Wright, Director of Student Financial Services, Abraham Baldwin Agricultural College, 2802 Moore Highway, ABAC 23, Tifton, GA 31793-2601, 229-391-4910 or toll-free 800-733-3653. *Fax:* 229-391-4871. *E-mail:* sfs@abac.edu. *Website:* http://www.abac.edu/.

ACADEMY COLLEGE
Bloomington, MN

ABOUT THE INSTITUTION Proprietary, coed. *Awards:* diplomas, associate, and bachelor's degrees. 7 undergraduate majors. *Total enrollment:* 65. Undergraduates: 65.

GIFT AID (NEED-BASED) *Scholarships, grants, and awards:* Federal Pell, FSEOG, state, private, college/university gift aid from institutional funds.

LOANS *Programs:* Federal Direct (Subsidized and Unsubsidized Stafford, PLUS), state, alternative loans.

APPLYING FOR FINANCIAL AID *Required financial aid forms:* FAFSA, institution's own form, state aid form.

CONTACT Kellye MacLeod, Director of Financial Aid, Academy College, 1101 East 78th Street, Bloomington, MN 55420, 952-851-0066 or toll-free 800-292-9149. *Fax:* 952-851-0093. *E-mail:* finaid@academycollege.edu. *Website:* http://www.academycollege.edu/.

ACADEMY OF ART UNIVERSITY
San Francisco, CA

Tuition & fees: $27,810	Average undergraduate aid package: $11,828

ABOUT THE INSTITUTION Proprietary, coed. *Awards:* certificates, associate, bachelor's, and master's degrees. 42 undergraduate majors. *Total enrollment:* 11,672. Undergraduates: 7,652. Freshmen: 813. Federal methodology is used as a basis for awarding need-based institutional aid.

UNDERGRADUATE EXPENSES for 2018–2019 *Application fee:* $50. *Comprehensive fee:* $44,458 includes full-time tuition ($27,510), mandatory fees ($300), and room and board ($16,648). Full-time tuition and fees vary according to course load. Room and board charges vary according to board plan and housing facility. *Part-time tuition:* $917 per unit. Part-time tuition and fees vary according to course load.

FRESHMAN FINANCIAL AID (Fall 2016) 331 applied for aid; of those 92% were deemed to have need. 95% of freshmen with need received aid; of those 3% had need fully met. *Average percent of need met:* 31% (excluding resources awarded to replace EFC). *Average financial aid package:* $10,984 (excluding resources awarded to replace EFC). 5% of all full-time freshmen had no need and received non-need-based gift aid.

UNDERGRADUATE FINANCIAL AID (Fall 2016) 2,115 applied for aid; of those 94% were deemed to have need. 98% of undergraduates with need received aid; of those 3% had need fully met. *Average percent of need met:* 34% (excluding resources awarded to replace EFC). *Average financial aid package:* $11,828 (excluding resources awarded to replace EFC). 1% of all full-time undergraduates had no need and received non-need-based gift aid.

GIFT AID (NEED-BASED) *Total amount:* $21,156,404 (51% federal, 12% state, 4% institutional, 33% external sources). *Receiving aid:* Freshmen: 37% (231); all full-time undergraduates: 31% (1,474). *Average award:* Freshmen: $10,479; Undergraduates: $10,925. *Scholarships, grants, and awards:* Federal Pell, FSEOG, state, private, college/university gift aid from institutional funds.

GIFT AID (NON-NEED-BASED) *Receiving aid:* Freshmen: 5% (32). Undergraduates: 3% (138). *Average award:* Freshmen: $3889. Undergraduates: $7290. *ROTC:* Army cooperative.

LOANS *Student loans:* $30,803,288 (100% need-based). 59% of past graduating class borrowed through all loan programs. *Average need-based loan:* Freshmen: $3190. Undergraduates: $3948. *Parent loans:* $21,917,043 (72% need-based, 28% non-need-based). *Programs:* Federal Direct (Subsidized and Unsubsidized Stafford, PLUS), alternative loans.

WORK-STUDY *Federal work-study:* 100 jobs averaging $4940.

ATHLETIC AWARDS Total amount: $3,741,052 (45% need-based, 55% non-need-based).

APPLYING FOR FINANCIAL AID *Required financial aid forms:* FAFSA, institution's own form. *Financial aid deadline:* Continuous. *Notification date:* Continuous beginning 3/15. Students must reply within 2 weeks of notification.

CONTACT Mr. Joe Vollaro, Executive Vice President of Financial Aid and Compliance, Academy of Art University, 79 New Montgomery Street, San Francisco, CA 94105-3410, 415-618-6528 or toll-free 800-544-ARTS. *Fax:* 415-618-6273. *E-mail:* jvollaro@academyart.edu.
Website: http://www.academyart.edu/.

ADAMS STATE UNIVERSITY
Alamosa, CO

Tuition & fees (CO res): $9444	Average undergraduate aid package: $13,827

ABOUT THE INSTITUTION State-supported, coed. *Awards:* associate, bachelor's, master's, and doctoral degrees. 78 undergraduate majors. *Total enrollment:* 3,308. Undergraduates: 1,949. Freshmen: 397. Federal methodology is used as a basis for awarding need-based institutional aid.
UNDERGRADUATE EXPENSES for 2017–2018 *Application fee:* $30. *Tuition, state resident:* full-time $5736; part-time $316 per credit hour. *Tuition, nonresident:* full-time $16,752; part-time $698 per credit hour. *Required fees:* full-time $3708; $151.19 per credit hour. Full-time tuition and fees vary according to course load. Part-time tuition and fees vary according to course load. *College room and board:* $7215; *Room only:* $4900. Room and board charges vary according to board plan and housing facility. *Payment plan:* Guaranteed tuition.
FRESHMAN FINANCIAL AID (Fall 2017, est.) 365 applied for aid; of those 81% were deemed to have need. 99% of freshmen with need received aid; of those 10% had need fully met. *Average percent of need met:* 65% (excluding resources awarded to replace EFC). *Average financial aid package:* $13,775 (excluding resources awarded to replace EFC).
UNDERGRADUATE FINANCIAL AID (Fall 2017, est.) 1,506 applied for aid; of those 80% were deemed to have need. 99% of undergraduates with need received aid; of those 6% had need fully met. *Average percent of need met:* 64% (excluding resources awarded to replace EFC). *Average financial aid package:* $13,827 (excluding resources awarded to replace EFC).
GIFT AID (NEED-BASED) *Total amount:* $10,984,314 (43% federal, 18% state, 29% institutional, 10% external sources). *Receiving aid:* Freshmen: 77% (282); all full-time undergraduates: 76% (1,140). *Average award:* Freshmen: $10,223; Undergraduates: $9080. *Scholarships, grants, and awards:* Federal Pell, FSEOG, state, private, college/university gift aid from institutional funds.
GIFT AID (NON-NEED-BASED) *Total amount:* $1,047,884 (1% federal, 2% state, 76% institutional, 21% external sources). *Receiving aid:* Freshmen: 23% (83). Undergraduates: 20% (299). *Tuition waivers:* Full or partial for employees or children of employees, senior citizens.
LOANS *Student loans:* $6,918,876 (92% need-based, 8% non-need-based). 72% of past graduating class borrowed through all loan programs. *Average indebtedness per student:* $24,958. *Average need-based loan:* Freshmen: $3222. Undergraduates: $4131. *Parent loans:* $2,104,173 (80% need-based, 20% non-need-based). *Programs:* Federal Direct (Subsidized and Unsubsidized Stafford, PLUS), Perkins, alternative loans.
WORK-STUDY *Federal work-study:* Total amount: $739,269; jobs available. *State or other work-study/employment:* Total amount: $1,584,440 (88% need-based, 12% non-need-based). Part-time jobs available.
ATHLETIC AWARDS Total amount: $1,991,413 (76% need-based, 24% non-need-based).
APPLYING FOR FINANCIAL AID *Required financial aid form:* FAFSA. *Financial aid deadline:* Continuous. *Notification date:* Continuous beginning 3/1.
CONTACT Philip Schroeder, Director of Financial Aid, Adams State University, 208 Edgemont Boulevard, Alamosa, CO 81101, 719-587-7306 or toll-free 800-824-6494. *Fax:* 719-587-7366. *E-mail:* financialaid@adams.edu.
Website: http://www.adams.edu/.

ADELPHI UNIVERSITY
Garden City, NY

Tuition & fees: $37,170	Average undergraduate aid package: $21,500

ABOUT THE INSTITUTION Independent, coed. *Awards:* certificates, associate, bachelor's, master's, and doctoral degrees. 48 undergraduate majors. *Total enrollment:* 7,978. Undergraduates: 5,266. Freshmen: 1,131. Both federal and institutional methodology are used as a basis for awarding need-based institutional aid.
UNDERGRADUATE EXPENSES for 2017–2018 *Application fee:* $40. *Comprehensive fee:* $52,670 includes full-time tuition ($35,430), mandatory fees ($1740), and room and board ($15,500). Full-time tuition and fees vary according to course level, course load, location, program, and student level. Room and board charges vary according to board plan and housing facility. *Part-time tuition:* $1080 per credit hour. *Part-time fees:* $463 per term. Part-time tuition and fees vary according to course level, course load, location, program, and student level. *Payment plan:* Tuition prepayment.
FRESHMAN FINANCIAL AID (Fall 2017, est.) 972 applied for aid; of those 86% were deemed to have need. 100% of freshmen with need received aid; of those 16% had need fully met. *Average percent of need met:* 52% (excluding resources awarded to replace EFC). *Average financial aid package:* $21,500 (excluding resources awarded to replace EFC). 14% of all full-time freshmen had no need and received non-need-based gift aid.
UNDERGRADUATE FINANCIAL AID (Fall 2017, est.) 3,910 applied for aid; of those 87% were deemed to have need. 100% of undergraduates with need received aid; of those 14% had need fully met. *Average percent of need met:* 45% (excluding resources awarded to replace EFC). *Average financial aid package:* $21,500 (excluding resources awarded to replace EFC). 20% of all full-time undergraduates had no need and received non-need-based gift aid.
GIFT AID (NEED-BASED) *Total amount:* $54,111,159 (15% federal, 9% state, 76% institutional). *Receiving aid:* Freshmen: 56% (607); all full-time undergraduates: 50% (2,405). *Average award:* Freshmen: $19,902; Undergraduates: $17,300. *Scholarships, grants, and awards:* Federal Pell, FSEOG, state, private, college/university gift aid from institutional funds, United Negro College Fund, endowed and restricted scholarships and grants.
GIFT AID (NON-NEED-BASED) *Total amount:* $19,927,035 (86% institutional, 14% external sources). *Receiving aid:* Freshmen: 53% (573). Undergraduates: 58% (2,809). *Average award:* Freshmen: $17,799. Undergraduates: $15,523. *Scholarships, grants, and awards by category:* Academic interests/achievement: 3,611 awards ($53,684,326 total): business, communication, computer science, foreign languages, general academic interests/achievements, mathematics, physical sciences. *Creative arts/performance:* 69 awards ($580,930 total): art/fine arts, cinema/film/broadcasting, dance, music, performing arts, theater/drama. *Special achievements/activities:* 496 awards ($499,750 total): community service, general special achievements/activities, leadership, memberships. *Special characteristics:* 428 awards ($4,225,637 total): adult students, children and siblings of alumni, children of faculty/staff, veterans. *Tuition waivers:* Full or partial for employees or children of employees, senior citizens. *ROTC:* Army cooperative, Air Force cooperative.
LOANS *Student loans:* $31,181,795 (41% need-based, 59% non-need-based). 61% of past graduating class borrowed through all loan programs. *Average indebtedness per student:* $35,285. *Average need-based loan:* Freshmen: $3464. Undergraduates: $4181. *Parent loans:* $16,399,284 (92% need-based, 8% non-need-based). *Programs:* Federal Direct (Subsidized and Unsubsidized Stafford, PLUS), Perkins, Federal Nursing.
WORK-STUDY *Federal work-study:* Total amount: $1,595,868; 364 jobs averaging $1835. *State or other work-study/employment:* Total amount: $4,086,804 (100% non-need-based). 1,241 part-time jobs averaging $2641.
ATHLETIC AWARDS Total amount: $3,389,575 (56% need-based, 44% non-need-based).
APPLYING FOR FINANCIAL AID *Required financial aid forms:* FAFSA, state aid form. *Financial aid deadline (priority):* 3/1. *Notification date:* Continuous beginning 12/15.
CONTACT Ms. Debra Evans, Senior Associate Director of Student Financial Services, Adelphi University, 1 South Avenue, PO Box 701, Garden City, NY 11530, 516-877-3394 or toll-free 800-ADELPHI. *Fax:* 516-877-3380. *E-mail:* evans@adelphi.edu.
Website: http://www.adelphi.edu/.

ADRIAN COLLEGE
Adrian, MI

CONTACT Mr. Matthew Rheinecker, Director of Financial Aid, Adrian College, 110 South Madison Street, Adrian, MI 49221-2575, 517-264-3109 or toll-free 800-877-2246. *Fax:* 517-264-3394. *E-mail:* mrheinecker@adrian.edu. *Website:* http://www.adrian.edu/.

ADVENTIST UNIVERSITY OF HEALTH SCIENCES
Orlando, FL

CONTACT Rebecca Valencia, Director of Financial Aid, Adventist University of Health Sciences, 671 Winyah Drive, Orlando, FL 32803, 407-303-9203 or toll-free 800-500-7747. *Fax:* 407-303-7680. *E-mail:* rebecca.valencia@adu.edu. *Website:* http://www.adu.edu/.

AGNES SCOTT COLLEGE
Decatur, GA

Tuition & fees: $41,160	Average undergraduate aid package: $36,231

ABOUT THE INSTITUTION Independent Presbyterian Church (U.S.A.), women only. *Awards:* bachelor's degrees. 36 undergraduate majors. *Total enrollment:* 921. Undergraduates: 921. Freshmen: 251. Both federal and institutional methodology are used as a basis for awarding need-based institutional aid.
UNDERGRADUATE EXPENSES for 2018–2019 *One-time required fee:* $200. *Comprehensive fee:* $53,490 includes full-time tuition ($40,920), mandatory fees ($240), and room and board ($12,330). Room and board charges vary according to board plan and housing facility. *Part-time tuition:* $1705 per credit hour. Part-time tuition and fees vary according to course load.
FRESHMAN FINANCIAL AID (Fall 2017, est.) 228 applied for aid; of those 92% were deemed to have need. 100% of freshmen with need received aid; of those 20% had need fully met. *Average percent of need met:* 85% (excluding resources awarded to replace EFC). *Average financial aid package:* $36,505 (excluding resources awarded to replace EFC). 17% of all full-time freshmen had no need and received non-need-based gift aid.
UNDERGRADUATE FINANCIAL AID (Fall 2017, est.) 743 applied for aid; of those 91% were deemed to have need. 100% of undergraduates with need received aid; of those 22% had need fully met. *Average percent of need met:* 85% (excluding resources awarded to replace EFC). *Average financial aid package:* $36,231 (excluding resources awarded to replace EFC). 23% of all full-time undergraduates had no need and received non-need-based gift aid.
GIFT AID (NEED-BASED) Total amount: $20,633,503 (9% federal, 6% state, 83% institutional, 2% external sources). *Receiving aid:* Freshmen: 83% (209); all full-time undergraduates: 76% (676). *Average award:* Freshmen: $31,186; Undergraduates: $30,022. *Scholarships, grants, and awards:* Federal Pell, FSEOG, state, private, college/university gift aid from institutional funds.
GIFT AID (NON-NEED-BASED) Total amount: $7,040,862 (7% state, 88% institutional, 5% external sources). *Receiving aid:* Freshmen: 15% (37). Undergraduates: 16% (143). *Average award:* Freshmen: $29,363. Undergraduates: $27,576. *Scholarships, grants, and awards by category:* Academic interests/achievement: general academic interests/achievements. *Creative arts/performance:* music. *Special achievements/activities:* community service, leadership. *Special characteristics:* adult students, children of educators, children of faculty/staff, international students, local/state students, religious affiliation, veterans, veterans' children. *Tuition waivers:* Full or partial for employees or children of employees. *ROTC:* Army cooperative, Air Force cooperative.
LOANS Student loans: $5,211,651 (49% need-based, 51% non-need-based). 64% of past graduating class borrowed through all loan programs. *Average indebtedness per student:* $32,276. *Average need-based loan:* Freshmen: $3388. Undergraduates: $4344. *Parent loans:* $2,178,813 (52% need-based, 48% non-need-based). *Programs:* Federal Direct (Subsidized and Unsubsidized Stafford, PLUS).

WORK-STUDY *Federal work-study:* Total amount: $667,289; jobs available. *State or other work-study/employment:* Total amount: $46,000 (100% non-need-based). Part-time jobs available.
APPLYING FOR FINANCIAL AID *Required financial aid forms:* FAFSA, federal income tax form(s). *Financial aid deadline:* 5/1 (priority: 2/15). *Notification date:* Continuous beginning 3/1. Students must reply by 5/1.
CONTACT Patrick Bonones, Director of Financial Aid, Agnes Scott College, 141 East College Avenue, Decatur, GA 30030-3797, 404-471-6395 or toll-free 800-868-8602. *Fax:* 404-471-6159. *E-mail:* finaid@agnesscott.edu. *Website:* http://www.agnesscott.edu/.

ALABAMA AGRICULTURAL AND MECHANICAL UNIVERSITY
Huntsville, AL

CONTACT Ms. Deborah Gordon, Financial Aid Officer, Alabama Agricultural and Mechanical University, PO Box 907, Huntsville, AL 35762, 256-372-4853 or toll-free 800-553-0816. *Fax:* 256-372-5407. *E-mail:* deborah.gordon@aamu.edu. *Website:* http://www.aamu.edu/.

ALABAMA STATE UNIVERSITY
Montgomery, AL

Tuition & fees (AL res): $11,068	Average undergraduate aid package: $16,124

ABOUT THE INSTITUTION State-supported, coed. *Awards:* certificates, bachelor's, master's, and doctoral degrees. 36 undergraduate majors. *Total enrollment:* 4,760. Undergraduates: 4,208. Freshmen: 967. Federal methodology is used as a basis for awarding need-based institutional aid.
UNDERGRADUATE EXPENSES for 2018–2019 *Application fee:* $25. *One-time required fee:* $150. *Tuition, state resident:* full-time $8328; part-time $347 per credit hour. *Tuition, nonresident:* full-time $16,656; part-time $694 per credit hour. *Required fees:* full-time $2740; $446 per credit hour. Full-time tuition and fees vary according to class time, course level, course load, degree level, program, and student level. Part-time tuition and fees vary according to class time, course level, course load, degree level, program, and student level. *College room and board:* $6050. Room and board charges vary according to board plan and housing facility.
FRESHMAN FINANCIAL AID (Fall 2017, est.) 780 applied for aid; of those 100% were deemed to have need. 97% of freshmen with need received aid; of those 31% had need fully met. *Average percent of need met:* 77% (excluding resources awarded to replace EFC). *Average financial aid package:* $16,694 (excluding resources awarded to replace EFC). 1% of all full-time freshmen had no need and received non-need-based gift aid.
UNDERGRADUATE FINANCIAL AID (Fall 2017, est.) 3,722 applied for aid; of those 98% were deemed to have need. 99% of undergraduates with need received aid; of those 47% had need fully met. *Average percent of need met:* 79% (excluding resources awarded to replace EFC). *Average financial aid package:* $16,124 (excluding resources awarded to replace EFC). 2% of all full-time undergraduates had no need and received non-need-based gift aid.
GIFT AID (NEED-BASED) Total amount: $16,646,453 (94% federal, 1% state, 5% institutional). *Receiving aid:* Freshmen: 67% (651); all full-time undergraduates: 81% (3,136). *Average award:* Freshmen: $5764; Undergraduates: $5368. *Scholarships, grants, and awards:* Federal Pell, FSEOG, state, private, college/university gift aid from institutional funds, United Negro College Fund.
GIFT AID (NON-NEED-BASED) Total amount: $12,522,444 (2% federal, 43% state, 48% institutional, 7% external sources). *Receiving aid:* Freshmen: 29% (280). Undergraduates: 47% (1,816). *Average award:* Freshmen: $11,803. Undergraduates: $9364. *Scholarships, grants, and awards by category:* Academic interests/achievement: general academic interests/achievements. *Creative arts/performance:* general creative arts/performance, music, theater/drama. *Special achievements/activities:* leadership. *Special characteristics:* general special characteristics, members of minority groups. *Tuition waivers:* Full or partial for employees or children of employees. *ROTC:* Army cooperative, Air Force.

LOANS *Student loans:* $23,630,475 (46% need-based, 54% non-need-based). 81% of past graduating class borrowed through all loan programs. *Average indebtedness per student:* $34,691. *Average need-based loan:* Freshmen: $3392. Undergraduates: $3809. *Parent loans:* $14,236,252 (87% need-based, 13% non-need-based). *Programs:* Federal Direct (Subsidized and Unsubsidized Stafford, PLUS), Perkins.
WORK-STUDY *Federal work-study:* Total amount: $1,424,141; 530 jobs averaging $1687. *State or other work-study/employment:* Total amount: $283,779 (100% non-need-based). 480 part-time jobs averaging $620.
ATHLETIC AWARDS Total amount: $4,181,970 (84% need-based, 16% non-need-based).
APPLYING FOR FINANCIAL AID *Required financial aid form:* FAFSA. *Financial aid deadline (priority):* 4/1. *Notification date:* Continuous beginning 5/1.
CONTACT Dr. Davida Haywood, Acting Director of Financial Aid, Alabama State University, PO Box 271, Montgomery, AL 36101-0271, 334-229-4323 or toll-free 800-253-5037. *Fax:* 334-299-4924. *E-mail:* dhaywood@alasu.edu. *Website:* http://www.alasu.edu/.

ALASKA BIBLE COLLEGE
Palmer, AK

Tuition & fees: $9600	Average undergraduate aid package: N/A

ABOUT THE INSTITUTION Independent nondenominational, coed. *Awards:* certificates, associate, and bachelor's degrees. 1 undergraduate major. *Total enrollment:* 50. Undergraduates: 50. Freshmen: 6. Institutional methodology is used as a basis for awarding need-based institutional aid.
UNDERGRADUATE EXPENSES for 2018–2019 *Application fee:* $35. *Comprehensive fee:* $15,300 includes full-time tuition ($9000), mandatory fees ($600), and room and board ($5700). *Part-time tuition:* $375 per credit hour. *Part-time fees:* $50 per term.
GIFT AID (NEED-BASED) *Total amount:* $167,876 (61% federal, 12% state, 18% institutional, 9% external sources). *Scholarships, grants, and awards:* Federal Pell, FSEOG, private, college/university gift aid from institutional funds.
GIFT AID (NON-NEED-BASED) *Scholarships, grants, and awards by category:* Academic interests/achievement: general academic interests/achievements, religion/biblical studies. Creative arts/performance: music. Special achievements/activities: religious involvement. Special characteristics: children of faculty/staff, married students, spouses of current students. *Tuition waivers:* Full or partial for employees or children of employees.
LOANS *Student loans:* $27,933 (100% need-based). *Parent loans:* $5000 (100% need-based). *Programs:* Federal Direct (Subsidized and Unsubsidized Stafford), state.
WORK-STUDY *Federal work-study:* Total amount: $5000; jobs available.
APPLYING FOR FINANCIAL AID *Required financial aid form:* FAFSA. *Financial aid deadline:* Continuous. *Notification date:* 9/1. Students must reply within 2 weeks of notification.
CONTACT Christy Coté, Financial Aid Administrator, Alaska Bible College, 248 East Elmwood Avenue, Palmer, AK 99645, 907-745-3201 or toll-free 800-478-7884. *Fax:* 907-745-3210. *E-mail:* financialaid@akbible.edu. *Website:* http://www.akbible.edu/.

ALASKA PACIFIC UNIVERSITY
Anchorage, AK

Tuition & fees: $20,830	Average undergraduate aid package: N/A

ABOUT THE INSTITUTION Independent, coed. *Awards:* certificates, associate, bachelor's, master's, and doctoral degrees. 10 undergraduate majors. *Total enrollment:* 547. Undergraduates: 294. Freshmen: 41. Federal methodology is used as a basis for awarding need-based institutional aid.
UNDERGRADUATE EXPENSES for 2018–2019 *Application fee:* $25. *Comprehensive fee:* $29,060 includes full-time tuition ($20,350), mandatory fees ($480), and room and board ($8230). Full-time tuition and fees vary according to course load, degree level, program, and reciprocity agreements. Room and board charges vary

according to board plan and housing facility. Part-time tuition and fees vary according to course load, degree level, and program.
GIFT AID (NEED-BASED) *Total amount:* $2,247,000 (22% federal, 7% state, 62% institutional, 9% external sources). *Scholarships, grants, and awards:* Federal Pell, FSEOG, state, private, college/university gift aid from institutional funds, Bureau of Indian Affairs Grants, Yellow Ribbon Grant Program, Native Alaskan Scholarships.
GIFT AID (NON-NEED-BASED) *Total amount:* $185,000 (4% state, 84% institutional, 12% external sources). *Scholarships, grants, and awards by category:* Academic interests/achievement: area/ethnic studies, biological sciences, business, communication, education, English, general academic interests/achievements, health fields, home economics, humanities, mathematics, physical sciences, religion/biblical studies, social sciences. *Creative arts/performance:* art/fine arts, journalism/publications, music, theater/drama. *Special achievements/activities:* community service, general special achievements/activities, leadership, religious involvement. *Special characteristics:* adult students, children and siblings of alumni, children of faculty/staff, ethnic background, general special characteristics, international students, local/state students, members of minority groups, out-of-state students, previous college experience, religious affiliation, veterans. *Tuition waivers:* Full or partial for employees or children of employees. *ROTC:* Air Force cooperative.
LOANS *Student loans:* $1,286,000 (94% need-based, 6% non-need-based). *Parent loans:* $175,000 (88% need-based, 12% non-need-based). *Programs:* Federal Direct (Subsidized and Unsubsidized Stafford, PLUS), state, alternative loans.
WORK-STUDY *Federal work-study:* Total amount: $38,000; jobs available. *State or other work-study/employment:* Total amount: $135,000 (90% need-based, 10% non-need-based). Part-time jobs available.
ATHLETIC AWARDS Total amount: $47,000 (6% need-based, 94% non-need-based).
APPLYING FOR FINANCIAL AID *Required financial aid form:* FAFSA. *Financial aid deadline (priority):* 2/1. *Notification date:* Continuous beginning 2/1. Students must reply by 8/1.
CONTACT Financial Aid Office, Alaska Pacific University, 4101 University Drive, Carr-Gottstein Room 106, Anchorage, AK 99508-4672, 907-564-8341 or toll-free 800-252-7528. *Fax:* 907-564-8317. *E-mail:* finaid@alaskapacific.edu. *Website:* http://www.alaskapacific.edu/.

ALBANY COLLEGE OF PHARMACY AND HEALTH SCIENCES
Albany, NY

CONTACT Kathleen Montague, Director of Financial Aid, Albany College of Pharmacy and Health Sciences, 106 New Scotland Avenue, Albany, NY 12208-3425, 518-694-7256 or toll-free 888-203-8010. *Fax:* 518-694-7322. *E-mail:* financial_aid@acphs.edu. *Website:* http://www.acphs.edu/.

ALBANY STATE UNIVERSITY
Albany, GA

Tuition & fees (GA res): $5675	Average undergraduate aid package: $4720

ABOUT THE INSTITUTION State-supported, coed. *Awards:* certificates, bachelor's, and master's degrees. 34 undergraduate majors. *Total enrollment:* 3,041. Undergraduates: 2,594. Freshmen: 437. Federal methodology is used as a basis for awarding need-based institutional aid.
UNDERGRADUATE EXPENSES for 2017–2018 *Application fee:* $25. *Tuition, state resident:* full-time $3965; part-time $165 per credit hour. *Tuition, nonresident:* full-time $14,426; part-time $601 per credit hour. *Required fees:* full-time $1710. Full-time tuition and fees vary according to course load and degree level. Part-time tuition and fees vary according to course load and degree level. *College room and board:* $8874; *Room only:* $5266. Room and board charges vary according to board plan and housing facility.
FRESHMAN FINANCIAL AID (Fall 2017, est.) 1,300 applied for aid; of those 94% were deemed to have need. 100% of freshmen with need received aid; of those 8% had need fully met. *Average percent of need met:* 71% (excluding resources

awarded to replace EFC). *Average financial aid package:* $4838 (excluding resources awarded to replace EFC). 4% of all full-time freshmen had no need and received non-need-based gift aid.

UNDERGRADUATE FINANCIAL AID (Fall 2017, est.) 3,660 applied for aid; of those 90% were deemed to have need. 100% of undergraduates with need received aid; of those 12% had need fully met. *Average percent of need met:* 72% (excluding resources awarded to replace EFC). *Average financial aid package:* $4720 (excluding resources awarded to replace EFC). 1% of all full-time undergraduates had no need and received non-need-based gift aid.

GIFT AID (NEED-BASED) *Total amount:* $9,006,939 (99% federal, 1% institutional). *Receiving aid:* Freshmen: 82% (1,077); all full-time undergraduates: 74% (2,788). *Average award:* Freshmen: $2791; Undergraduates: $2716. *Scholarships, grants, and awards:* Federal Pell, FSEOG, state, private, United Negro College Fund.

GIFT AID (NON-NEED-BASED) *Total amount:* $2,058,319 (74% state, 6% institutional, 20% external sources). *Receiving aid:* Freshmen: 34% (445). Undergraduates: 29% (1,111). *Average award:* Freshmen: $565. Undergraduates: $970. *Scholarships, grants, and awards by category: Academic interests/achievement:* biological sciences, computer science, education, general academic interests/achievements, health fields, mathematics, social sciences. *Creative arts/performance:* music. *Special characteristics:* children and siblings of alumni, local/state students. *ROTC:* Army.

LOANS *Student loans:* $15,327,042 (48% need-based, 52% non-need-based). *Average need-based loan:* Freshmen: $1769. Undergraduates: $2020. *Parent loans:* $2,668,079 (100% non-need-based). *Programs:* Federal Direct (Subsidized and Unsubsidized Stafford, PLUS), state.

WORK-STUDY *Federal work-study:* Total amount: $205,333; jobs available. *State or other work-study/employment:* Part-time jobs available.

ATHLETIC AWARDS Total amount: $790,501 (100% non-need-based).

APPLYING FOR FINANCIAL AID *Required financial aid form:* FAFSA. *Financial aid deadline:* 7/1 (priority: 2/15). *Notification date:* Continuous beginning 2/1. Students must reply by 7/1.

CONTACT Mr. Thomas A. Harris, Director of Financial Aid, Albany State University, 504 College Drive, Albany, GA 31705-2717, 229-430-4650 or toll-free 800-822-7267. *Fax:* 229-430-3936.

Website: http://www.asurams.edu/.

ALBERTUS MAGNUS COLLEGE
New Haven, CT

Tuition & fees: $31,490	Average undergraduate aid package: $17,021

ABOUT THE INSTITUTION Independent Roman Catholic, coed. *Awards:* certificates, diplomas, associate, bachelor's, and master's degrees. 45 undergraduate majors. *Total enrollment:* 1,555. Undergraduates: 1,220. Freshmen: 135. Federal methodology is used as a basis for awarding need-based institutional aid.

UNDERGRADUATE EXPENSES for 2017–2018 *Application fee:* $35. *Comprehensive fee:* $45,506 includes full-time tuition ($31,000), mandatory fees ($490), and room and board ($14,016). Full-time tuition and fees vary according to program. Room and board charges vary according to board plan. Part-time tuition and fees vary according to program.

FRESHMAN FINANCIAL AID (Fall 2017, est.) 112 applied for aid; of those 97% were deemed to have need. 100% of freshmen with need received aid; of those 8% had need fully met. *Average percent of need met:* 68% (excluding resources awarded to replace EFC). *Average financial aid package:* $27,993 (excluding resources awarded to replace EFC). 3% of all full-time freshmen had no need and received non-need-based gift aid.

UNDERGRADUATE FINANCIAL AID (Fall 2017, est.) 940 applied for aid; of those 95% were deemed to have need. 100% of undergraduates with need received aid; of those 5% had need fully met. *Average percent of need met:* 51% (excluding resources awarded to replace EFC). *Average financial aid package:* $17,021 (excluding resources awarded to replace EFC). 1% of all full-time undergraduates had no need and received non-need-based gift aid.

GIFT AID (NEED-BASED) *Total amount:* $6,201,874 (30% federal, 1% state, 69% institutional). *Receiving aid:* Freshmen: 91% (103); all full-time undergraduates: 72% (726). *Average award:* Freshmen: $19,803; Undergraduates: $12,555. *Schol-*

---

arships, grants, and awards: Federal Pell, FSEOG, state, college/university gift aid from institutional funds.

GIFT AID (NON-NEED-BASED) *Total amount:* $1,411,748 (2% state, 90% institutional, 8% external sources). *Receiving aid:* Freshmen: 42% (48). Undergraduates: 18% (186). *Average award:* Freshmen: $13,883. Undergraduates: $12,497. *Scholarships, grants, and awards by category: Academic interests/achievement:* biological sciences, business, communication, computer science, education, English, foreign languages, general academic interests/achievements, humanities, international studies, mathematics, physical sciences, premedicine, religion/biblical studies, social sciences. *Creative arts/performance:* art/fine arts, performing arts, theater/drama. *Special achievements/activities:* community service, leadership. *Special characteristics:* local/state students, religious affiliation, siblings of current students. *Tuition waivers:* Full or partial for employees or children of employees, senior citizens.

LOANS *Student loans:* $5,111,134 (44% need-based, 56% non-need-based). 83% of past graduating class borrowed through all loan programs. *Average indebtedness per student:* $36,908. *Average need-based loan:* Freshmen: $3715. Undergraduates: $4370. *Parent loans:* $594,398 (100% non-need-based). *Programs:* Federal Direct (Subsidized and Unsubsidized Stafford, PLUS), Perkins.

WORK-STUDY *Federal work-study:* Total amount: $106,090; jobs available.

APPLYING FOR FINANCIAL AID *Required financial aid form:* FAFSA. *Financial aid deadline (priority):* 3/15. *Notification date:* Continuous beginning 3/15. Students must reply within 2 weeks of notification.

CONTACT Michelle Cochran, Director of Financial Aid, Albertus Magnus College, 700 Prospect Street, New Haven, CT 06511-1189, 203-773-8508 or toll-free 800-578-9160. *Fax:* 203-773-8972. *E-mail:* financial_aid@albertus.edu.

Website: http://www.albertus.edu/.

ALBION COLLEGE
Albion, MI

Tuition & fees: $45,590	Average undergraduate aid package: $40,402

ABOUT THE INSTITUTION Independent Methodist, coed. *Awards:* bachelor's degrees. 61 undergraduate majors. *Total enrollment:* 1,568. Undergraduates: 1,568. Freshmen: 515. Federal methodology is used as a basis for awarding need-based institutional aid.

UNDERGRADUATE EXPENSES for 2018–2019 *One-time required fee:* $185. *Comprehensive fee:* $57,970 includes full-time tuition ($45,070), mandatory fees ($520), and room and board ($12,380). *College room only:* $6080. Full-time tuition and fees vary according to course load. Room and board charges vary according to board plan and housing facility. *Part-time tuition:* $1890 per semester hour. Part-time tuition and fees vary according to course load.

FRESHMAN FINANCIAL AID (Fall 2017, est.) 475 applied for aid; of those 94% were deemed to have need. 100% of freshmen with need received aid; of those 16% had need fully met. *Average percent of need met:* 93% (excluding resources awarded to replace EFC). *Average financial aid package:* $44,414 (excluding resources awarded to replace EFC). 13% of all full-time freshmen had no need and received non-need-based gift aid.

UNDERGRADUATE FINANCIAL AID (Fall 2017, est.) 1,295 applied for aid; of those 95% were deemed to have need. 100% of undergraduates with need received aid; of those 17% had need fully met. *Average percent of need met:* 87% (excluding resources awarded to replace EFC). *Average financial aid package:* $40,402 (excluding resources awarded to replace EFC). 21% of all full-time undergraduates had no need and received non-need-based gift aid.

GIFT AID (NEED-BASED) *Total amount:* $44,691,547 (7% federal, 4% state, 88% institutional, 1% external sources). *Receiving aid:* Freshmen: 86% (445); all full-time undergraduates: 79% (1,228). *Average award:* Freshmen: $40,241; Undergraduates: $35,978. *Scholarships, grants, and awards:* Federal Pell, FSEOG, state, private, college/university gift aid from institutional funds.

GIFT AID (NON-NEED-BASED) *Total amount:* $7,982,280 (97% institutional, 3% external sources). *Receiving aid:* Freshmen: 86% (442). Undergraduates: 77% (1,204). *Average award:* Freshmen: $28,917. Undergraduates: $23,988. *Scholarships, grants, and awards by category: Academic interests/achievement:* 1,163 awards ($24,072,128 total): communication, general academic interests/achievements. *Creative arts/performance:* 52 awards ($116,260 total): art/fine arts, music, performing arts, theater/drama. *Special characteristics:* 438 awards ($2,002,783 total):

children and siblings of alumni, international students, out-of-state students, relatives of clergy. *Tuition waivers:* Full or partial for employees or children of employees.
LOANS *Student loans:* $10,308,768 (45% need-based, 55% non-need-based). 64% of past graduating class borrowed through all loan programs. *Average indebtedness per student:* $44,140. *Average need-based loan:* Freshmen: $3412. Undergraduates: $4295. *Parent loans:* $3,551,672 (100% non-need-based). *Programs:* Federal Direct (Subsidized and Unsubsidized Stafford, PLUS).
WORK-STUDY *Federal work-study:* Total amount: $468,750; 355 jobs averaging $1320. *State or other work-study/employment:* Total amount: $321,074 (100% need-based). 168 part-time jobs averaging $1770.
APPLYING FOR FINANCIAL AID *Required financial aid form:* FAFSA. *Financial aid deadline (priority):* 12/1. *Notification date:* Continuous beginning 12/1.
CONTACT Dr. Robert Kniss, Director of Student Financial Services, Albion College, Kellogg Center Box 4670, Albion, MI 49224-1831, 517-629-0440 or toll-free 800-858-6770. *Fax:* 517-629-0581. *E-mail:* financialaid@albion.edu.
Website: http://www.albion.edu/.

ALBRIGHT COLLEGE
Reading, PA

Tuition & fees: $45,302	Average undergraduate aid package: $38,880

ABOUT THE INSTITUTION Independent United Methodist Church, coed. *Awards:* certificates, bachelor's, and master's degrees. 61 undergraduate majors. *Total enrollment:* 2,036. Undergraduates: 2,015. Freshmen: 465. Federal methodology is used as a basis for awarding need-based institutional aid.
UNDERGRADUATE EXPENSES for 2018–2019 *Application fee:* $35. *Comprehensive fee:* $57,372 includes full-time tuition ($44,202), mandatory fees ($1100), and room and board ($12,070). *College room only:* $6664. Full-time tuition and fees vary according to degree level. Room and board charges vary according to board plan and housing facility. *Part-time tuition:* $5526 per course. Part-time tuition and fees vary according to degree level.
FRESHMAN FINANCIAL AID (Fall 2017, est.) 452 applied for aid; of those 94% were deemed to have need. 100% of freshmen with need received aid; of those 11% had need fully met. *Average percent of need met:* 84% (excluding resources awarded to replace EFC). *Average financial aid package:* $41,714 (excluding resources awarded to replace EFC). 9% of all full-time freshmen had no need and received non-need-based gift aid.
UNDERGRADUATE FINANCIAL AID (Fall 2017, est.) 1,575 applied for aid; of those 96% were deemed to have need. 100% of undergraduates with need received aid; of those 10% had need fully met. *Average percent of need met:* 80% (excluding resources awarded to replace EFC). *Average financial aid package:* $38,880 (excluding resources awarded to replace EFC). 8% of all full-time undergraduates had no need and received non-need-based gift aid.
GIFT AID (NEED-BASED) *Total amount:* $49,650,586 (8% federal, 5% state, 84% institutional, 3% external sources). *Receiving aid:* Freshmen: 91% (423); all full-time undergraduates: 92% (1,513). *Average award:* Freshmen: $36,013; Undergraduates: $32,813. *Scholarships, grants, and awards:* Federal Pell, FSEOG, state, private, college/university gift aid from institutional funds, United Negro College Fund.
GIFT AID (NON-NEED-BASED) *Total amount:* $4,058,086 (86% institutional, 14% external sources). *Receiving aid:* Freshmen: 6% (29). Undergraduates: 6% (100). *Average award:* Freshmen: $24,885. Undergraduates: $22,066. *Scholarships, grants, and awards by category:* Academic interests/achievement: general academic interests/achievements. Creative arts/performance: art/fine arts, journalism/publications, music, theater/drama. Special achievements/activities: memberships, religious involvement. Special characteristics: children and siblings of alumni, ethnic background, local/state students, siblings of current students. *Tuition waivers:* Full or partial for employees or children of employees, adult students, senior citizens.
LOANS *Student loans:* $15,111,679 (81% need-based, 19% non-need-based). 88% of past graduating class borrowed through all loan programs. *Average indebtedness per student:* $38,599. *Average need-based loan:* Freshmen: $4907. Undergraduates: $5532. *Parent loans:* $5,263,650 (100% non-need-based). *Programs:* Federal Direct (Subsidized and Unsubsidized Stafford, PLUS).
WORK-STUDY *Federal work-study:* Total amount: $1,562,063; jobs available. *State or other work-study/employment:* Part-time jobs available.

APPLYING FOR FINANCIAL AID *Required financial aid form:* FAFSA. *Financial aid deadline:* Continuous. *Notification date:* Continuous beginning 11/15.
CONTACT Chris Hanlon, Director of Financial Aid, Albright College, PO Box 15234, Reading, PA 19612-5234, 610-921-7515 or toll-free 800-252-1856. *Fax:* 610-921-7729. *E-mail:* chanlon@albright.edu.
Website: http://www.albright.edu/.

ALCORN STATE UNIVERSITY
Lorman, MS

Tuition & fees (MS res): $6888	Average undergraduate aid package: $15,032

ABOUT THE INSTITUTION State-supported, coed. *Awards:* certificates, associate, bachelor's, and master's degrees. 29 undergraduate majors. *Total enrollment:* 3,716. Undergraduates: 3,172. Freshmen: 742. Both federal and institutional methodology are used as a basis for awarding need-based institutional aid.
UNDERGRADUATE EXPENSES for 2017–2018 *Tuition, state resident:* full-time $6888; part-time $574 per credit hour. *Tuition, nonresident:* full-time $6888; part-time $574 per credit hour. Full-time tuition and fees vary according to course load. Part-time tuition and fees vary according to course load. *College room and board:* $9731; *Room only:* $6639. Room and board charges vary according to board plan and housing facility.
FRESHMAN FINANCIAL AID (Fall 2017, est.) 525 applied for aid; of those 100% were deemed to have need. 100% of freshmen with need received aid; of those 14% had need fully met. *Average percent of need met:* 97% (excluding resources awarded to replace EFC). *Average financial aid package:* $14,918 (excluding resources awarded to replace EFC). 49% of all full-time freshmen had no need and received non-need-based gift aid.
UNDERGRADUATE FINANCIAL AID (Fall 2017, est.) 1,337 applied for aid; of those 96% were deemed to have need. 95% of undergraduates with need received aid; of those 11% had need fully met. *Average percent of need met:* 94% (excluding resources awarded to replace EFC). *Average financial aid package:* $15,032 (excluding resources awarded to replace EFC). 28% of all full-time undergraduates had no need and received non-need-based gift aid.
GIFT AID (NEED-BASED) *Total amount:* $13,702,291 (92% federal, 5% state, 3% institutional). *Receiving aid:* Freshmen: 100% (525); all full-time undergraduates: 45% (1,160). *Average award:* Freshmen: $6140; Undergraduates: $5902. *Scholarships, grants, and awards:* Federal Pell, FSEOG, state, private, college/university gift aid from institutional funds.
GIFT AID (NON-NEED-BASED) *Receiving aid:* Freshmen: 47% (246). Undergraduates: 16% (402). *Average award:* Freshmen: $8184. Undergraduates: $8158. *Scholarships, grants, and awards by category:* Academic interests/achievement: 757 awards ($8,207,003 total): general academic interests/achievements. Creative arts/performance: 263 awards ($2,513,174 total): music. Special achievements/activities: 2 awards ($9366 total): leadership. Special characteristics: 44 awards ($229,427 total): children of faculty/staff. *Tuition waivers:* Full or partial for employees or children of employees. *ROTC:* Army.
LOANS *Student loans:* $23,144,622 (38% need-based, 62% non-need-based). 97% of past graduating class borrowed through all loan programs. *Average indebtedness per student:* $35,680. *Average need-based loan:* Freshmen: $3428. Undergraduates: $3892. *Parent loans:* $3,672,798 (100% non-need-based). *Programs:* Federal Direct (Subsidized and Unsubsidized Stafford, PLUS).
WORK-STUDY *Federal work-study:* Total amount: $398,171; 381 jobs averaging $870. *State or other work-study/employment:* Part-time jobs available.
ATHLETIC AWARDS Total amount: $2,731,134 (100% non-need-based).
APPLYING FOR FINANCIAL AID *Required financial aid forms:* FAFSA, institution's own form. *Financial aid deadline (priority):* 3/15. *Notification date:* Continuous beginning 4/1. Students must reply within 4 weeks of notification.
CONTACT Mrs. Juanita M. Edwards, Director of Financial Aid, Alcorn State University, 1000 ASU Drive #28, Alcorn State, MS 39096-7500, 601-877-6190 or toll-free 800-222-6790. *Fax:* 601-877-6110. *E-mail:* juanita@alcorn.edu.
Website: http://www.alcorn.edu/.

ALDERSON BROADDUS UNIVERSITY
Philippi, WV

ABOUT THE INSTITUTION Independent American Baptist Churches in the U.S.A., coed. **Awards:** associate, bachelor's, and master's degrees. 28 undergraduate majors. **Total enrollment:** 1,052. Undergraduates: 981. Freshmen: 261.

GIFT AID (NEED-BASED) Scholarships, grants, and awards: Federal Pell, FSEOG, state, private, college/university gift aid from institutional funds, Federal Nursing, Scholarships for Disadvantaged Students (SDS), National Health Service Corps Scholarships.

GIFT AID (NON-NEED-BASED) Scholarships, grants, and awards by category: Academic interests/achievement: biological sciences, business, communication, computer science, education, general academic interests/achievements, health fields, mathematics, physical sciences, premedicine, religion/biblical studies, social sciences. Creative arts/performance: applied art and design, debating, journalism/publications, music. Special achievements/activities: general special achievements/activities, leadership. Special characteristics: children and siblings of alumni, children of faculty/staff, ethnic background, general special characteristics, international students, religious affiliation.

LOANS Programs: Federal Direct (Subsidized and Unsubsidized Stafford, PLUS), Perkins, Federal Nursing.

WORK-STUDY Federal work-study: 430 jobs averaging $1435. **State or other work-study/employment:** Total amount: $217,690 (36% need-based, 64% non-need-based). 95 part-time jobs averaging $2410.

APPLYING FOR FINANCIAL AID Required financial aid form: FAFSA.

CONTACT Amy L. King, Director of Financial Aid, Alderson Broaddus University, College Hill Road, Philippi, WV 26416, 304-457-6354 or toll-free 800-263-1549. Fax: 304-457-6391.
Website: http://www.ab.edu/.

ALFRED UNIVERSITY
Alfred, NY

Tuition & fees: $33,484	Average undergraduate aid package: $27,889

ABOUT THE INSTITUTION Independent, coed. **Awards:** certificates, bachelor's, master's, and doctoral degrees. 39 undergraduate majors. **Total enrollment:** 2,362. Undergraduates: 1,707. Freshmen: 418. Both federal and institutional methodology are used as a basis for awarding need-based institutional aid.

UNDERGRADUATE EXPENSES for 2018–2019 Application fee: $50. **Comprehensive fee:** $46,000 includes full-time tuition ($32,494), mandatory fees ($990), and room and board ($12,516). **College room only:** $6340. Full-time tuition and fees vary according to program. Room and board charges vary according to board plan and housing facility. **Part-time tuition:** $998 per credit hour. **Part-time fees:** $84 per term.

FRESHMAN FINANCIAL AID (Fall 2017, est.) 407 applied for aid; of those 91% were deemed to have need. 100% of freshmen with need received aid; of those 15% had need fully met. **Average percent of need met:** 86% (excluding resources awarded to replace EFC). **Average financial aid package:** $31,102 (excluding resources awarded to replace EFC). 2% of all full-time freshmen had no need and received non-need-based gift aid.

UNDERGRADUATE FINANCIAL AID (Fall 2017, est.) 1,456 applied for aid; of those 91% were deemed to have need. 100% of undergraduates with need received aid; of those 20% had need fully met. **Average percent of need met:** 83% (excluding resources awarded to replace EFC). **Average financial aid package:** $27,889 (excluding resources awarded to replace EFC). 6% of all full-time undergraduates had no need and received non-need-based gift aid.

GIFT AID (NEED-BASED) Total amount: $28,654,930 (14% federal, 7% state, 79% institutional). **Receiving aid:** Freshmen: 88% (368); all full-time undergraduates: 83% (1,314). **Average award:** Freshmen: $24,114; Undergraduates: $21,500. **Scholarships, grants, and awards:** Federal Pell, FSEOG, state, private, college/university gift aid from institutional funds.

GIFT AID (NON-NEED-BASED) Total amount: $2,747,807 (1% federal, 84% institutional, 15% external sources). **Receiving aid:** Freshmen: 49% (206). Undergraduates: 45% (709). **Average award:** Freshmen: $13,739. Undergraduates: $12,114. **Scholarships, grants, and awards by category:** Academic interests/

achievement: 1,308 awards ($11,758,097 total): biological sciences, business, communication, education, engineering/technologies, English, foreign languages, general academic interests/achievements, humanities, international studies, mathematics, physical sciences, premedicine, social sciences. Creative arts/performance: 48 awards ($528,400 total): art/fine arts. Special characteristics: 57 awards ($908,215 total): children of educators, children of faculty/staff. **Tuition waivers:** Full or partial for employees or children of employees. **ROTC:** Army cooperative.

LOANS Student loans: $12,403,906 (57% need-based, 43% non-need-based). 82% of past graduating class borrowed through all loan programs. Average indebtedness per student: $35,987. **Average need-based loan:** Freshmen: $5774. Undergraduates: $5940. **Parent loans:** $3,080,004 (100% non-need-based). **Programs:** Federal Direct (Subsidized and Unsubsidized Stafford, PLUS), Perkins, college/university, alternative loans.

WORK-STUDY Federal work-study: Total amount: $1,769,786; 936 jobs averaging $1861.

APPLYING FOR FINANCIAL AID Required financial aid forms: FAFSA, state aid form. **Financial aid deadline:** 3/15. **Notification date:** Continuous beginning 1/15. Students must reply by 5/1 or within 2 weeks of notification.

CONTACT Mrs. Jane Gilliland, Executive Director of Student Financial Services, Alfred University, Alumni Hall, One Saxon Drive, Alfred, NY 14802-1205, 607-871-2159 or toll-free 800-541-9229. Fax: 607-871-2252. E-mail: gilliland@alfred.edu. Website: http://www.alfred.edu/.

ALICE LLOYD COLLEGE
Pippa Passes, KY

Tuition & fees: $2150	Average undergraduate aid package: $13,681

ABOUT THE INSTITUTION Independent, coed. **Awards:** bachelor's degrees. 15 undergraduate majors. **Total enrollment:** 598. Undergraduates: 598. Freshmen: 220. Federal methodology is used as a basis for awarding need-based institutional aid.

UNDERGRADUATE EXPENSES for 2018–2019 College room only: $3300. **Part-time tuition:** $225 per credit hour. **Part-time fees:** $225 per credit hour.

FRESHMAN FINANCIAL AID (Fall 2016) 167 applied for aid; of those 94% were deemed to have need. 100% of freshmen with need received aid; of those 7% had need fully met. **Average percent of need met:** 66% (excluding resources awarded to replace EFC). **Average financial aid package:** $13,132 (excluding resources awarded to replace EFC). 13% of all full-time freshmen had no need and received non-need-based gift aid.

UNDERGRADUATE FINANCIAL AID (Fall 2016) 584 applied for aid; of those 91% were deemed to have need. 100% of undergraduates with need received aid; of those 13% had need fully met. **Average percent of need met:** 71% (excluding resources awarded to replace EFC). **Average financial aid package:** $13,681 (excluding resources awarded to replace EFC). 10% of all full-time undergraduates had no need and received non-need-based gift aid.

GIFT AID (NEED-BASED) Total amount: $5,238,281 (29% federal, 45% state, 26% institutional). **Receiving aid:** Freshmen: 93% (156); all full-time undergraduates: 90% (528). **Average award:** Freshmen: $9475; Undergraduates: $9872. **Scholarships, grants, and awards:** Federal Pell, FSEOG, state, private, college/university gift aid from institutional funds.

GIFT AID (NON-NEED-BASED) Total amount: $676,255 (37% state, 63% institutional). **Receiving aid:** Freshmen: 5% (8). Undergraduates: 9% (53). **Average award:** Freshmen: $5091. Undergraduates: $5919. **Scholarships, grants, and awards by category:** Special achievements/activities: general special achievements/activities. Special characteristics: members of minority groups.

LOANS Student loans: $1,815,037 (81% need-based, 19% non-need-based). 67% of past graduating class borrowed through all loan programs. Average indebtedness per student: $10,141. **Average need-based loan:** Freshmen: $2017. Undergraduates: $2197. **Parent loans:** $23,598 (100% non-need-based). **Programs:** Federal Direct (Subsidized and Unsubsidized Stafford, PLUS), college/university, Bagby Loans.

WORK-STUDY Federal work-study: 418 jobs averaging $2320. **State or other work-study/employment:** Total amount: $434,300 (16% need-based, 84% non-need-based). 168 part-time jobs averaging $2320.

ATHLETIC AWARDS Total amount: $171,881 (100% need-based).

APPLYING FOR FINANCIAL AID Required financial aid form: FAFSA. **Financial aid deadline (priority):** 11/1. **Notification date:** Continuous beginning 4/1. Students must reply by 7/1 or within 4 weeks of notification.

CONTACT Ms Jacqueline Stewart, Director of Financial Aid, Alice Lloyd College, 100 Purpose Road, Pippa Passes, KY 41844, 606-368-6058 or toll-free 888-280-4252. *E-mail:* jacquelinestewart@alc.edu. *Website:* http://www.alc.edu/.

ALLEGHENY COLLEGE
Meadville, PA

Tuition & fees: $47,540	Average undergraduate aid package: $41,669

ABOUT THE INSTITUTION Independent, coed. *Awards:* bachelor's degrees. 47 undergraduate majors. *Total enrollment:* 1,802. Undergraduates: 1,802. Freshmen: 484. Federal methodology is used as a basis for awarding need-based institutional aid.

UNDERGRADUATE EXPENSES for 2018–2019 *Comprehensive fee:* $59,680 includes full-time tuition ($47,040), mandatory fees ($500), and room and board ($12,140). *College room only:* $6410. Room and board charges vary according to board plan and housing facility. *Part-time tuition:* $1960 per credit hour. *Part-time fees:* $250 per term. Part-time tuition and fees vary according to course load.

FRESHMAN FINANCIAL AID (Fall 2017, est.) 449 applied for aid; of those 86% were deemed to have need. 100% of freshmen with need received aid; of those 27% had need fully met. *Average percent of need met:* 91% (excluding resources awarded to replace EFC). *Average financial aid package:* $42,666 (excluding resources awarded to replace EFC). 19% of all full-time freshmen had no need and received non-need-based gift aid.

UNDERGRADUATE FINANCIAL AID (Fall 2017, est.) 1,493 applied for aid; of those 91% were deemed to have need. 100% of undergraduates with need received aid; of those 27% had need fully met. *Average percent of need met:* 90% (excluding resources awarded to replace EFC). *Average financial aid package:* $41,669 (excluding resources awarded to replace EFC). 20% of all full-time undergraduates had no need and received non-need-based gift aid.

GIFT AID (NEED-BASED) *Total amount:* $45,729,338 (8% federal, 3% state, 86% institutional, 3% external sources). *Receiving aid:* Freshmen: 81% (388); all full-time undergraduates: 78% (1,365). *Average award:* Freshmen: $36,480; Undergraduates: $34,310. *Scholarships, grants, and awards:* Federal Pell, FSEOG, state, private, college/university gift aid from institutional funds, Veterans Education Benefits (GI Bill), Yellow Ribbon Program.

GIFT AID (NON-NEED-BASED) *Total amount:* $9,494,988 (95% institutional, 5% external sources). *Receiving aid:* Freshmen: 14% (68). Undergraduates: 12% (212). *Average award:* Freshmen: $25,905. Undergraduates: $21,604. *Scholarships, grants, and awards by category:* Academic interests/achievement: 1,632 awards ($33,319,705 total): general academic interests/achievements. *Creative arts/performance:* 8 awards ($16,000 total): art/fine arts, dance, music, performing arts, theater/drama. *Special characteristics:* 301 awards ($3,476,691 total): adult students, children of educators, children of faculty/staff, international students. *Tuition waivers:* Full or partial for employees or children of employees. *ROTC:* Army cooperative.

LOANS *Student loans:* $11,997,536 (46% need-based, 54% non-need-based). *Average need-based loan:* Freshmen: $3730. Undergraduates: $5145. *Parent loans:* $3,466,157 (100% non-need-based). *Programs:* Federal Direct (Subsidized and Unsubsidized Stafford, PLUS), Perkins, private loans.

WORK-STUDY *Federal work-study:* Total amount: $2,262,404; 917 jobs averaging $2475. *State or other work-study/employment:* Total amount: $566,650 (100% non-need-based). 116 part-time jobs averaging $4885.

APPLYING FOR FINANCIAL AID *Required financial aid form:* FAFSA. *Financial aid deadline (priority):* 2/15. *Notification date:* Continuous beginning 12/1. Students must reply by 5/1 or within 4 weeks of notification.

CONTACT Mr. Jonathan Boleratz, Director of Financial Aid, Allegheny College, 520 North Main Street, Meadville, PA 16335, 800-835-7780 or toll-free 800-521-5293. *Fax:* 814-332-2349. *E-mail:* fao@allegheny.edu. *Website:* http://www.allegheny.edu/.

ALLEGHENY WESLEYAN COLLEGE
Salem, OH

Tuition & fees: N/R	Average undergraduate aid package: $12,000

ABOUT THE INSTITUTION Independent Wesleyan, coed. 2 undergraduate majors. Institutional methodology is used as a basis for awarding need-based institutional aid.

FRESHMAN FINANCIAL AID (Fall 2016) 17 applied for aid; of those 88% were deemed to have need. 100% of freshmen with need received aid; of those 100% had need fully met. *Average percent of need met:* 90% (excluding resources awarded to replace EFC). *Average financial aid package:* $10,000 (excluding resources awarded to replace EFC). 17% of all full-time freshmen had no need and received non-need-based gift aid.

UNDERGRADUATE FINANCIAL AID (Fall 2016) 62 applied for aid; of those 94% were deemed to have need. 100% of undergraduates with need received aid; of those 41% had need fully met. *Average percent of need met:* 85% (excluding resources awarded to replace EFC). *Average financial aid package:* $12,000 (excluding resources awarded to replace EFC). 16% of all full-time undergraduates had no need and received non-need-based gift aid.

GIFT AID (NEED-BASED) *Total amount:* $260,072 (84% federal, 1% state, 13% institutional, 2% external sources). *Receiving aid:* Freshmen: 83% (15); all full-time undergraduates: 64% (43). *Average award:* Freshmen: $2400; Undergraduates: $2000. *Scholarships, grants, and awards:* Federal Pell, FSEOG, private, college/university gift aid from institutional funds.

GIFT AID (NON-NEED-BASED) *Receiving aid:* Freshmen: 67% (12). Undergraduates: 33% (22). *Average award:* Freshmen: $3500. Undergraduates: $4500. *Scholarships, grants, and awards by category:* Creative arts/performance: music.

LOANS *Student loans:* $12,000 (100% need-based). *Average need-based loan:* Freshmen: $3500. Undergraduates: $4400. *Programs:* Federal Direct (Subsidized and Unsubsidized Stafford, PLUS).

WORK-STUDY *State or other work-study/employment:* Total amount: $60,223 (100% need-based). 36 part-time jobs averaging $1700.

APPLYING FOR FINANCIAL AID *Required financial aid forms:* FAFSA, institution's own form. *Financial aid deadline (priority):* 7/31. *Notification date:* 8/15. Students must reply within 3 weeks of notification.

CONTACT Mrs. Esther Phelps, Financial Aid Director, Allegheny Wesleyan College, 2161 Woodsdale Road, Salem, OH 44460, 330-337-6403 Ext. 111 or toll-free 800-292-3153. *Fax:* 424-228-3006. *E-mail:* ephelps@awc.edu. *Website:* http://www.awc.edu/.

ALLEN COLLEGE
Waterloo, IA

Tuition & fees: $18,226	Average undergraduate aid package: $11,693

ABOUT THE INSTITUTION Independent, coed, primarily women. *Awards:* certificates, associate, bachelor's, master's, and doctoral degrees (liberal arts and general education courses offered at either University of North Iowa or Wartburg College). 5 undergraduate majors. *Total enrollment:* 622. Undergraduates: 329. Federal methodology is used as a basis for awarding need-based institutional aid.

UNDERGRADUATE EXPENSES for 2017–2018 *Application fee:* $50. *Comprehensive fee:* $25,507 includes full-time tuition ($16,884), mandatory fees ($1342), and room and board ($7281). *College room only:* $3641. Full-time tuition and fees vary according to course load, degree level, and program. *Part-time tuition:* $603 per credit hour. *Part-time fees:* $81 per credit hour. Part-time tuition and fees vary according to course load, degree level, and program.

UNDERGRADUATE FINANCIAL AID (Fall 2017, est.) 311 applied for aid; of those 87% were deemed to have need. 97% of undergraduates with need received aid; of those 5% had need fully met. *Average percent of need met:* 51% (excluding resources awarded to replace EFC). *Average financial aid package:* $11,693 (excluding resources awarded to replace EFC). 8% of all full-time undergraduates had no need and received non-need-based gift aid.

GIFT AID (NEED-BASED) *Total amount:* $2,075,381 (22% federal, 44% state, 26% institutional, 8% external sources). *Receiving aid:* All full-time undergraduates:

54% (193). *Average award:* Undergraduates: $5846. *Scholarships, grants, and awards:* Federal Pell, FSEOG, state, private, college/university gift aid from institutional funds, Federal Nursing, Scholarships for Disadvantaged Students (SDS).

GIFT AID (NON-NEED-BASED) *Total amount:* $102,981 (48% federal, 52% institutional). *Receiving aid:* Undergraduates: 12% (43). *Average award:* Undergraduates: $1250. *Scholarships, grants, and awards by category:* Academic interests/achievement: home economics. *Special achievements/activities:* community service, general special achievements/activities, leadership. *Special characteristics:* children of faculty/staff, general special characteristics, local/state students, members of minority groups, out-of-state students. *ROTC:* Army cooperative.

LOANS *Student loans:* $2,960,027 (38% need-based, 62% non-need-based). *Average need-based loan:* Undergraduates: $4797. *Parent loans:* $691,309 (100% non-need-based). *Programs:* Federal Direct (Subsidized and Unsubsidized Stafford, PLUS), Federal Nursing, college/university.

WORK-STUDY *Federal work-study:* Total amount: $43,095; 15 jobs averaging $3000.

APPLYING FOR FINANCIAL AID *Required financial aid form:* FAFSA. *Financial aid deadline:* Continuous. *Notification date:* Continuous beginning 4/1. Students must reply within 2 weeks of notification.

CONTACT Jobyna A. Johnston, Director of Financial Aid, Allen College, Barrett Forum, 1825 Logan Avenue, Waterloo, IA 50703-1990, 319-226-2515. *Fax:* 319-226-2051. *E-mail:* jobyna.johnston@allencollege.edu.
Website: http://www.allencollege.edu/.

ALLEN UNIVERSITY
Columbia, SC

CONTACT Ms. Donna Foster, Director of Financial Aid, Allen University, 1530 Harden Street, Columbia, SC 29204-1085, 803-376-5736 or toll-free 877-625-5368. *E-mail:* donnaf@allenuniversity.edu.
Website: http://www.allenuniversity.edu/.

ALLIANT INTERNATIONAL UNIVERSITY–SAN DIEGO
San Diego, CA

Tuition & fees: $17,510	Average undergraduate aid package: $14,450

ABOUT THE INSTITUTION Independent, coed. *Awards:* certificates, bachelor's, master's, and doctoral degrees. 2 undergraduate majors. *Total enrollment:* 3,046. Undergraduates: 168. Federal methodology is used as a basis for awarding need-based institutional aid.

UNDERGRADUATE EXPENSES for 2017–2018 *Application fee:* $65. *Tuition:* full-time $17,250; part-time $575 per credit hour.

FRESHMAN FINANCIAL AID (Fall 2016) 7 applied for aid; of those 100% were deemed to have need. 100% of freshmen with need received aid. *Average percent of need met:* 64% (excluding resources awarded to replace EFC). *Average financial aid package:* $12,950 (excluding resources awarded to replace EFC). 30% of all full-time freshmen had no need and received non-need-based gift aid.

UNDERGRADUATE FINANCIAL AID (Fall 2016) 103 applied for aid; of those 100% were deemed to have need. 100% of undergraduates with need received aid; of those 3% had need fully met. *Average percent of need met:* 64% (excluding resources awarded to replace EFC). *Average financial aid package:* $14,450 (excluding resources awarded to replace EFC). 7% of all full-time undergraduates had no need and received non-need-based gift aid.

GIFT AID (NEED-BASED) *Total amount:* $956,272 (58% federal, 12% state, 29% institutional, 1% external sources). *Receiving aid:* Freshmen: 40% (4); all full-time undergraduates: 6% (84). *Average award:* Freshmen: $9590; Undergraduates: $9590. *Scholarships, grants, and awards:* Federal Pell, FSEOG, state, private, college/university gift aid from institutional funds.

GIFT AID (NON-NEED-BASED) *Receiving aid:* Freshmen: 60% (6). Undergraduates: 6% (84). *Average award:* Freshmen: $4000. Undergraduates: $4000. *Scholarships, grants, and awards by category:* Academic interests/

achievement: business, education, English, general academic interests/achievements, home economics, humanities, international studies, social sciences. *Special achievements/activities:* community service, general special achievements/activities, leadership. *Special characteristics:* children and siblings of alumni, children of faculty/staff, general special characteristics, international students, local/state students, public servants, siblings of current students, spouses of current students, veterans, veterans' children. *Tuition waivers:* Full or partial for children of alumni, employees or children of employees.

LOANS *Student loans:* $571,436 (53% need-based, 47% non-need-based). *Average need-based loan:* Freshmen: $3500. Undergraduates: $5000. *Parent loans:* $35,978 (100% non-need-based). *Programs:* Federal Direct (Subsidized and Unsubsidized Stafford, PLUS), Perkins, alternative loans.

WORK-STUDY *Federal work-study:* 27 jobs averaging $4000. *State or other work-study/employment:* Part-time jobs available.

APPLYING FOR FINANCIAL AID *Required financial aid form:* FAFSA. *Financial aid deadline (priority):* 3/2. *Notification date:* Continuous beginning 3/15. Students must reply within 3 weeks of notification.

CONTACT Ms. Deborah Spindler, Director of Financial Aid, Alliant International University–San Diego, 10455 Pomerado Road, San Diego, CA 92131-1799, 858-635-4559 Ext. 4700 or toll-free 866-825-5426. *Fax:* 858-635-4848. *E-mail:* dspindler@alliant.edu.
Website: http://www.alliant.edu/.

ALMA COLLEGE
Alma, MI

Tuition & fees: $38,768	Average undergraduate aid package: $28,542

ABOUT THE INSTITUTION Independent Presbyterian, coed. *Awards:* bachelor's degrees. 39 undergraduate majors. *Total enrollment:* 1,426. Undergraduates: 1,426. Freshmen: 408. Federal methodology is used as a basis for awarding need-based institutional aid.

UNDERGRADUATE EXPENSES for 2017–2018 *Application fee:* $25. *Comprehensive fee:* $49,410 includes full-time tuition ($38,348), mandatory fees ($420), and room and board ($10,642). Room and board charges vary according to board plan and housing facility. *Part-time tuition:* $1150 per credit hour. Part-time tuition and fees vary according to course load.

FRESHMAN FINANCIAL AID (Fall 2017, est.) 398 applied for aid; of those 91% were deemed to have need. 100% of freshmen with need received aid; of those 17% had need fully met. *Average percent of need met:* 76% (excluding resources awarded to replace EFC). *Average financial aid package:* $31,054 (excluding resources awarded to replace EFC). 11% of all full-time freshmen had no need and received non-need-based gift aid.

UNDERGRADUATE FINANCIAL AID (Fall 2017, est.) 1,264 applied for aid; of those 92% were deemed to have need. 100% of undergraduates with need received aid; of those 11% had need fully met. *Average percent of need met:* 70% (excluding resources awarded to replace EFC). *Average financial aid package:* $28,542 (excluding resources awarded to replace EFC). 15% of all full-time undergraduates had no need and received non-need-based gift aid.

GIFT AID (NEED-BASED) *Total amount:* $31,108,327 (6% federal, 6% state, 86% institutional, 2% external sources). *Receiving aid:* Freshmen: 89% (363); all full-time undergraduates: 84% (1,160). *Average award:* Freshmen: $29,684; Undergraduates: $27,547. *Scholarships, grants, and awards:* Federal Pell, FSEOG, state, private, college/university gift aid from institutional funds.

GIFT AID (NON-NEED-BASED) *Total amount:* $5,367,129 (96% institutional, 4% external sources). *Receiving aid:* Freshmen: 15% (61). Undergraduates: 9% (127). *Average award:* Freshmen: $25,040. Undergraduates: $21,776. *Scholarships, grants, and awards by category:* Academic interests/achievement: 1,313 awards ($22,856,047 total): general academic interests/achievements. *Creative arts/performance:* 278 awards ($722,795 total): art/fine arts, dance, music, performing arts, theater/drama. *Special achievements/activities:* religious involvement. *Special characteristics:* 486 awards ($786,270 total): children and siblings of alumni, members of minority groups, out-of-state students, siblings of current students. *Tuition waivers:* Full or partial for employees or children of employees. *ROTC:* Army cooperative.

LOANS *Student loans:* $10,405,375 (72% need-based, 28% non-need-based). 80% of past graduating class borrowed through all loan programs. *Average indebtedness per student:* $39,264. *Average need-based loan:* Freshmen: $3191. Undergrad-

uates: $4396. *Parent loans:* $3,790,059 (54% need-based, 46% non-need-based). *Programs:* Federal Direct (Subsidized and Unsubsidized Stafford, PLUS), Perkins, college/university, alternative loans.

WORK-STUDY *Federal work-study:* Total amount: $866,550; 690 jobs averaging $1824.

APPLYING FOR FINANCIAL AID *Required financial aid form:* FAFSA. *Financial aid deadline (priority):* 3/1. *Notification date:* Continuous beginning 11/18. Students must reply within 3 weeks of notification.

CONTACT Mrs. Michelle L. McNier, Director of Financial Aid, Alma College, 614 West Superior Street, Alma, MI 48801-1599, 989-463-7347 or toll-free 800-321-ALMA. *Fax:* 989-463-7993. *E-mail:* mcnierml@alma.edu.
Website: http://www.alma.edu/.

ALVERNIA UNIVERSITY
Reading, PA

ABOUT THE INSTITUTION Independent Roman Catholic, coed. *Awards:* associate, bachelor's, master's, and doctoral degrees. 39 undergraduate majors. *Total enrollment:* 2,872. Undergraduates: 2,323. Freshmen: 345.

GIFT AID (NEED-BASED) *Scholarships, grants, and awards:* Federal Pell, FSEOG, state, private, college/university gift aid from institutional funds.

GIFT AID (NON-NEED-BASED) *Scholarships, grants, and awards by category:* Academic interests/achievement: general academic interests/achievements. *Special achievements/activities:* community service, leadership, memberships, religious involvement. *Special characteristics:* children and siblings of alumni, children of faculty/staff, general special characteristics, local/state students, siblings of current students.

LOANS *Programs:* Federal Direct (Subsidized and Unsubsidized Stafford, PLUS), Perkins.

WORK-STUDY *Federal work-study:* 981 jobs averaging $1592. *State or other work-study/employment:* Part-time jobs available.

APPLYING FOR FINANCIAL AID *Required financial aid forms:* FAFSA, state aid form.

CONTACT Ms. Christine Saadi, Director of Student Financial Planning, Alvernia University, 400 Saint Bernardine Street, Reading, PA 19607-1799, 610-796-8213 or toll-free 888-ALVERNIA (in-state). *Fax:* 610-796-8336. *E-mail:* christine.saadi@alvernia.edu.
Website: http://www.alvernia.edu/.

ALVERNO COLLEGE
Milwaukee, WI

Tuition & fees: $28,277	Average undergraduate aid package: $21,312

ABOUT THE INSTITUTION Independent Roman Catholic, undergraduate: women only; graduate: coed. *Awards:* certificates, associate, bachelor's, master's, and doctoral degrees (also offers weekend program with significant enrollment not reflected in profile). 48 undergraduate majors. *Total enrollment:* 1,942. Undergraduates: 1,312. Freshmen: 198. Federal methodology is used as a basis for awarding need-based institutional aid.

UNDERGRADUATE EXPENSES for 2017–2018 *Comprehensive fee:* $36,573 includes full-time tuition ($27,552), mandatory fees ($725), and room and board ($8296). Full-time tuition and fees vary according to program. Room and board charges vary according to board plan and housing facility. *Part-time tuition:* $1148 per credit hour. Part-time tuition and fees vary according to program.

FRESHMAN FINANCIAL AID (Fall 2017, est.) 188 applied for aid; of those 95% were deemed to have need. 100% of freshmen with need received aid. *Average financial aid package:* $26,594 (excluding resources awarded to replace EFC). 9% of all full-time freshmen had no need and received non-need-based gift aid.

UNDERGRADUATE FINANCIAL AID (Fall 2017, est.) 973 applied for aid; of those 96% were deemed to have need. 100% of undergraduates with need received aid. *Average financial aid package:* $21,312 (excluding resources awarded to replace EFC). 8% of all full-time undergraduates had no need and received non-need-based gift aid.

GIFT AID (NEED-BASED) *Total amount:* $16,686,635 (21% federal, 14% state, 63% institutional, 2% external sources). *Receiving aid:* Freshmen: 89% (175); all full-time undergraduates: 87% (893). *Average award:* Freshmen: $15,623; Undergrad-

uates: $12,685. *Scholarships, grants, and awards:* Federal Pell, FSEOG, state, private, college/university gift aid from institutional funds.

GIFT AID (NON-NEED-BASED) *Total amount:* $1,212,443 (98% institutional, 2% external sources). *Receiving aid:* Freshmen: 85% (167). Undergraduates: 79% (806). *Average award:* Freshmen: $15,043. Undergraduates: $11,782. *Scholarships, grants, and awards by category:* Academic interests/achievement: 983 awards ($8,647,343 total): education, general academic interests/achievements, library science. *Creative arts/performance:* 33 awards ($30,944 total): art/fine arts, music. *Special achievements/activities:* 8 awards ($93,986 total): community service, memberships. *Special characteristics:* 265 awards ($326,831 total): children and siblings of alumni, children of faculty/staff, ethnic background, international students, out-of-state students, religious affiliation. *Tuition waivers:* Full or partial for employees or children of employees. *ROTC:* Army cooperative, Air Force cooperative.

LOANS *Student loans:* $9,949,486 (96% need-based, 4% non-need-based). 89% of past graduating class borrowed through all loan programs. *Average indebtedness per student:* $36,659. *Average need-based loan:* Freshmen: $3193. Undergraduates: $3847. *Parent loans:* $1,847,991 (92% need-based, 8% non-need-based). *Programs:* Federal Direct (Subsidized and Unsubsidized Stafford, PLUS), Perkins, state.

WORK-STUDY *Federal work-study:* Total amount: $529,064; 263 jobs averaging $2012. *State or other work-study/employment:* Part-time jobs available.

APPLYING FOR FINANCIAL AID *Required financial aid form:* FAFSA. *Financial aid deadline (priority):* 2/1. *Notification date:* Continuous beginning 11/1. Students must reply within 2 weeks of notification.

CONTACT Ms. Amy Christen, Director of Financial Aid, Alverno College, 3400 South 43rd Street, PO Box 343922, Milwaukee, WI 53234-3922, 414-382-6040 or toll-free 800-933-3401. *Fax:* 414-382-6354. *E-mail:* amy.christen@alverno.edu.
Website: http://www.alverno.edu/.

AMERICAN ACADEMY OF ART
Chicago, IL

CONTACT Ms. Ione Fitzgerald, Director of Financial Aid, American Academy of Art, 332 South Michigan Avenue, Suite 300, Chicago, IL 60604, 312-461-0600 or toll-free 888-461-0600. *Fax:* 312-294-9570.
Website: http://www.aaart.edu/.

AMERICAN BAPTIST COLLEGE
Nashville, TN

CONTACT Miss Sharonda Campbell, Financial Aid Administrator, American Baptist College, 1800 Baptist World Center Drive, Nashville, TN 37207, 615-687-6903. *Fax:* 615-226-7855. *E-mail:* scampbell@abcnash.edu.
Website: http://www.abcnash.edu/.

AMERICAN BUSINESS & TECHNOLOGY UNIVERSITY
Saint Joseph, MO

CONTACT Financial Aid Office, American Business & Technology University, 1018 West St.Maartens Drive, Saint Joseph, MO 64506, 816-279-7000 or toll-free 800-804-1388.
Website: http://www.abtu.edu/.

AMERICAN COLLEGE FOR MEDICAL CAREERS
Orlando, FL

CONTACT Financial Aid Office, American College for Medical Careers, 5959 Lake Ellenor Drive, Orlando, FL 32809, 407-738-4488 or toll-free 888-599-7887.
Website: http://www.acmc.edu/.

AMERICAN COLLEGE OF HEALTHCARE SCIENCES
Portland, OR

CONTACT Financial Aid Office, American College of Healthcare Sciences, 5005 SW Macadam Avenue, Portland, OR 97239-3719, 503-244-0726 or toll-free 800-487-8839. *Website:* http://www.achs.edu/.

AMERICAN INTERCONTINENTAL UNIVERSITY ATLANTA
Atlanta, GA

CONTACT Financial Aid Office, American InterContinental University Atlanta, 6600 Peachtree-Dunwoody Road, 500 Embassy Row, Atlanta, GA 30328, 404-965-6500 or toll-free 800-353-1744. *Website:* http://www.aiuniv.edu/.

AMERICAN INTERCONTINENTAL UNIVERSITY HOUSTON
Houston, TX

CONTACT Financial Aid Office, American InterContinental University Houston, 9999 Richmond Avenue, Houston, TX 77042, 832-201-3600 or toll-free 888-607-9888. *Website:* http://www.aiuniv.edu/.

AMERICAN INTERCONTINENTAL UNIVERSITY ONLINE
Schaumburg, IL

CONTACT Financial Aid Office, American InterContinental University Online, 231 N. Martingale Road, 6th Floor, Schaumburg, IL 60173, 847-851-5000 or toll-free 877-701-3800. *Website:* http://www.aiuniv.edu/.

AMERICAN INTERNATIONAL COLLEGE
Springfield, MA

CONTACT Ms. Sage Stachowiak, Director of Financial Aid, American International College, 1000 State Street, Springfield, MA 01109-3189, 413-205-3521 or toll-free 800-242-3142. *Fax:* 413-205-3912. *E-mail:* sage.stachowiak@aic.edu. *Website:* http://www.aic.edu/.

AMERICAN JEWISH UNIVERSITY
Bel Air, CA

Tuition & fees: N/R	Average undergraduate aid package: $29,592

ABOUT THE INSTITUTION Independent Jewish, coed. 10 undergraduate majors. Both federal and institutional methodology are used as a basis for awarding need-based institutional aid.

FRESHMAN FINANCIAL AID (Fall 2017, est.) 15 applied for aid; of those 100% were deemed to have need. 100% of freshmen with need received aid. *Average percent of need met:* 89% (excluding resources awarded to replace EFC).

Average financial aid package: $29,592 (excluding resources awarded to replace EFC). 20% of all full-time freshmen had no need and received non-need-based gift aid.

UNDERGRADUATE FINANCIAL AID (Fall 2017, est.) 69 applied for aid; of those 100% were deemed to have need. 100% of undergraduates with need received aid. *Average percent of need met:* 93% (excluding resources awarded to replace EFC). *Average financial aid package:* $29,592 (excluding resources awarded to replace EFC). 10% of all full-time undergraduates had no need and received non-need-based gift aid.

GIFT AID (NEED-BASED) *Total amount:* $434,852 (41% federal, 26% state, 33% institutional). *Receiving aid:* Freshmen: 40% (6); all full-time undergraduates: 55% (42). *Average award:* Freshmen: $14,875; Undergraduates: $11,223. *Scholarships, grants, and awards:* Federal Pell, FSEOG, state, private, college/university gift aid from institutional funds.

GIFT AID (NON-NEED-BASED) *Receiving aid:* Freshmen: 100% (15). Undergraduates: 90% (69). *Average award:* Freshmen: $4500. Undergraduates: $7600. *Scholarships, grants, and awards by category:* Academic interests/achievement: business, general academic interests/achievements, premedicine. *Special achievements/activities:* leadership.

LOANS *Student loans:* $245,750 (51% need-based, 49% non-need-based). 90% of past graduating class borrowed through all loan programs. *Average indebtedness per student:* $30,000. *Average need-based loan:* Freshmen: $3500. Undergraduates: $3500. *Parent loans:* $88,582 (100% need-based). *Programs:* Federal Direct (Subsidized and Unsubsidized Stafford, PLUS), alternative loans.

WORK-STUDY *Federal work-study:* Total amount: $33,909; jobs available.

APPLYING FOR FINANCIAL AID *Required financial aid forms:* FAFSA, institution's own form, federal income tax form(s). *Financial aid deadline (priority):* 3/2. *Notification date:* Continuous beginning 3/15. Students must reply within 3 weeks of notification.

CONTACT Larisa Zadoyen, Director of Financial Aid, American Jewish University, 15600 Mulholland Drive, Bel Air, CA 90077-1599, 310-476-9777 Ext. 252 or toll-free 888-853-6763. *Fax:* 310-476-4613. *E-mail:* lzadoyen@aju.edu. *Website:* http://www.aju.edu/.

AMERICAN MUSICAL AND DRAMATIC ACADEMY, LOS ANGELES
Los Angeles, CA

CONTACT Financial Aid Office, American Musical and Dramatic Academy, Los Angeles, 6305 Yucca Street, Los Angeles, CA 90028, 323-469-3300 or toll-free 888-474-9444. *Website:* http://www.amda.edu/.

AMERICAN NATIONAL UNIVERSITY
Salem, VA

CONTACT Financial Aid Office, American National University, 1813 East Main Street, Salem, VA 24153, 540-986-1800 or toll-free 888-9-JOBREADY. *Website:* http://www.an.edu/.

AMERICAN SENTINEL UNIVERSITY
Aurora, CO

CONTACT Financial Aid Office, American Sentinel University, 2260 South Xanadu Way, Suite 310, Aurora, CO 80014 or toll-free 800-729-2427. *Website:* http://www.americansentinel.edu/.

AMERICAN UNIVERSITY
Washington, DC

Tuition & fees: $48,459	Average undergraduate aid package: $33,279

ABOUT THE INSTITUTION Independent Methodist, coed. *Awards:* certificates, associate, bachelor's, master's, and doctoral degrees. 70 undergraduate majors. *Total enrollment:* 13,858. Undergraduates: 8,123. Freshmen: 1,785. Institutional methodology is used as a basis for awarding need-based institutional aid.

UNDERGRADUATE EXPENSES for 2018–2019 *Application fee:* $70. *Comprehensive fee:* $63,339 includes full-time tuition ($47,640), mandatory fees ($819), and room and board ($14,880). *College room only:* $9996. Full-time tuition and fees vary according to course load. Room and board charges vary according to board plan, housing facility, and location. *Part-time tuition:* $1587 per credit hour. *Part-time fees:* $170 per term. Part-time tuition and fees vary according to course load. *Payment plan:* Tuition prepayment.

FRESHMAN FINANCIAL AID (Fall 2017, est.) 1,395 applied for aid; of those 72% were deemed to have need. 98% of freshmen with need received aid; of those 46% had need fully met. *Average percent of need met:* 91% (excluding resources awarded to replace EFC). *Average financial aid package:* $38,374 (excluding resources awarded to replace EFC). 9% of all full-time freshmen had no need and received non-need-based gift aid.

UNDERGRADUATE FINANCIAL AID (Fall 2017, est.) 4,583 applied for aid; of those 84% were deemed to have need. 98% of undergraduates with need received aid; of those 19% had need fully met. *Average percent of need met:* 72% (excluding resources awarded to replace EFC). *Average financial aid package:* $33,279 (excluding resources awarded to replace EFC). 8% of all full-time undergraduates had no need and received non-need-based gift aid.

GIFT AID (NEED-BASED) Total amount: $98,088,733 (6% federal, 84% institutional, 10% external sources). *Receiving aid:* Freshmen: 52% (926); all full-time undergraduates: 48% (3,470). *Average award:* Freshmen: $32,002; Undergraduates: $26,625. *Scholarships, grants, and awards:* Federal Pell, FSEOG, private, college/university gift aid from institutional funds.

GIFT AID (NON-NEED-BASED) Total amount: $19,385,199 (100% institutional). *Receiving aid:* Freshmen: 14% (252). Undergraduates: 15% (1,043). *Average award:* Freshmen: $14,637. Undergraduates: $14,165. *Scholarships, grants, and awards by category:* Academic interests/achievement: general academic interests/achievements. Creative arts/performance: general creative arts/performance. Special achievements/activities: general special achievements/activities, leadership, memberships. Special characteristics: ethnic background, members of minority groups, relatives of clergy. *Tuition waivers:* Full or partial for employees or children of employees. *ROTC:* Army cooperative, Air Force cooperative.

LOANS Student loans: $22,910,927 (63% need-based, 37% non-need-based). *Average need-based loan:* Freshmen: $3376. Undergraduates: $4506. *Parent loans:* $23,721,480 (100% non-need-based). *Programs:* Federal Direct (Subsidized and Unsubsidized Stafford, PLUS), Perkins, college/university.

WORK-STUDY Federal work-study: Total amount: $2,601,255; 1,700 jobs averaging $1530.

ATHLETIC AWARDS Total amount: $5,207,477 (100% non-need-based).

APPLYING FOR FINANCIAL AID Required financial aid forms: FAFSA, CSS Financial Aid PROFILE. *Financial aid deadline:* 1/15. *Notification date:* 4/1. Students must reply within 4 weeks of notification.

CONTACT Brian Lee Sang, Assistant Vice Provost of Financial Aid, American University, 4400 Massachusetts Avenue, NW, Washington, DC 20016-8001, 202-885-6500. *Fax:* 202-885-1025. *E-mail:* facounselor@american.edu. *Website:* http://www.american.edu/.

AMERICAN UNIVERSITY OF HEALTH SCIENCES
Signal Hill, CA

CONTACT Financial Aid Office, American University of Health Sciences, 1600 East Hill Street, Building #1, Signal Hill, CA 90755, 562-988-2278. *Website:* http://www.auhs.edu/.

AMERICAN UNIVERSITY OF PUERTO RICO
Bayamon, PR

CONTACT Mr. Yahaira Melendez, Financial Aid Director, American University of Puerto Rico, PO Box 2037, Bayamón, PR 00960-2037, 787-620-2040 Ext. 2031. *Fax:* 787-785-7377. *E-mail:* melendezy@aupr.edu. *Website:* http://www.aupr.edu/.

AMERICAN UNIVERSITY OF PUERTO RICO
Manati, PR

CONTACT Financial Aid Office, American University of Puerto Rico, Carretera Estatal #2 Km. 48.7, PO Box 1082, Manati, PR 00674-1082, 787-621-2835. *Website:* http://www.aupr.edu/.

AMHERST COLLEGE
Amherst, MA

Tuition & fees: $54,310	Average undergraduate aid package: $53,052

ABOUT THE INSTITUTION Independent, coed. *Awards:* bachelor's degrees. 38 undergraduate majors. *Total enrollment:* 1,836. Undergraduates: 1,836. Freshmen: 471. Both federal and institutional methodology are used as a basis for awarding need-based institutional aid.

UNDERGRADUATE EXPENSES for 2017–2018 *Application fee:* $65. *Comprehensive fee:* $68,500 includes full-time tuition ($53,430), mandatory fees ($880), and room and board ($14,190). *College room only:* $7690.

FRESHMAN FINANCIAL AID (Fall 2017, est.) 340 applied for aid; of those 80% were deemed to have need. 100% of freshmen with need received aid; of those 100% had need fully met. *Average percent of need met:* 100% (excluding resources awarded to replace EFC). *Average financial aid package:* $53,209 (excluding resources awarded to replace EFC).

UNDERGRADUATE FINANCIAL AID (Fall 2017, est.) 1,229 applied for aid; of those 90% were deemed to have need. 100% of undergraduates with need received aid; of those 100% had need fully met. *Average percent of need met:* 100% (excluding resources awarded to replace EFC). *Average financial aid package:* $53,052 (excluding resources awarded to replace EFC).

GIFT AID (NEED-BASED) Total amount: $56,862,283 (5% federal, 94% institutional, 1% external sources). *Receiving aid:* Freshmen: 58% (273); all full-time undergraduates: 57% (1,102). *Average award:* Freshmen: $52,482; Undergraduates: $51,841. *Scholarships, grants, and awards:* Federal Pell, FSEOG, state, private, college/university gift aid from institutional funds.

GIFT AID (NON-NEED-BASED) Total amount: $620,420 (100% external sources). *ROTC:* Army cooperative, Air Force cooperative.

LOANS Student loans: $2,354,059 (45% need-based, 55% non-need-based). 29% of past graduating class borrowed through all loan programs. *Average indebtedness per student:* $19,075. *Average need-based loan:* Freshmen: $454. Undergraduates: $505. *Parent loans:* $3,180,425 (100% non-need-based). *Programs:* Federal Direct (Subsidized and Unsubsidized Stafford, PLUS), Perkins, college/university.

WORK-STUDY Federal work-study: Total amount: $1,358,994; 715 jobs averaging $1901. *State or other work-study/employment:* Total amount: $333,785 (100% need-based). 171 part-time jobs averaging $1965.

APPLYING FOR FINANCIAL AID Required financial aid forms: FAFSA, CSS Financial Aid PROFILE, noncustodial (divorced/separated) parent's statement, business/farm supplement, federal income tax form(s), W-2 forms. *Financial aid deadline (priority):* 2/15. *Notification date:* 4/1. Students must reply by 5/1.

CONTACT Gail W. Holt, Dean of Financial Aid, Amherst College, B-5 Converse Hall, PO Box 5000, Amherst, MA 01002-5000, 413-542-2296. *Fax:* 413-542-2628. *E-mail:* finaid@amherst.edu. *Website:* http://www.amherst.edu/.

AMRIDGE UNIVERSITY
Montgomery, AL

Tuition & fees: $9900	Average undergraduate aid package: $9138

ABOUT THE INSTITUTION Independent Church of Christ, coed. *Awards:* associate, bachelor's, master's, and doctoral degrees. 4 undergraduate majors. *Total enrollment:* 674. Undergraduates: 318. Freshmen: 4. Both federal and institutional methodology are used as a basis for awarding need-based institutional aid.

UNDERGRADUATE EXPENSES for 2017–2018 *Application fee:* $50. *Tuition:* full-time $9000; part-time $6880 per term. *Required fees:* full-time $900; $450 per term. Full-time tuition and fees vary according to course load, program, and student level. Part-time tuition and fees vary according to course load, program, and student level. *Payment plans:* Guaranteed tuition, tuition prepayment.

FRESHMAN FINANCIAL AID (Fall 2017, est.) 5 applied for aid; of those 100% were deemed to have need. 100% of freshmen with need received aid; of those 100% had need fully met. *Average financial aid package:* $5518 (excluding resources awarded to replace EFC).

UNDERGRADUATE FINANCIAL AID (Fall 2017, est.) 146 applied for aid; of those 78% were deemed to have need. 100% of undergraduates with need received aid; of those 92% had need fully met. *Average financial aid package:* $9138 (excluding resources awarded to replace EFC).

GIFT AID (NEED-BASED) *Total amount:* $436,966 (90% federal, 9% state, 1% external sources). *Receiving aid:* Freshmen: 100% (5); all full-time undergraduates: 78% (114). *Average award:* Freshmen: $2330; Undergraduates: $2990. *Scholarships, grants, and awards:* Federal Pell, FSEOG, state, private, college/university gift aid from institutional funds.

GIFT AID (NON-NEED-BASED) *Total amount:* $1,743,487 (93% federal, 7% institutional). *Scholarships, grants, and awards by category:* Special achievements/activities: religious involvement. Special characteristics: children of educators, children of faculty/staff, veterans. *Tuition waivers:* Full or partial for employees or children of employees.

LOANS *Student loans:* $1,713,926 (100% non-need-based). *Average indebtedness per student:* $11,179. *Average need-based loan:* Freshmen: $4105. Undergraduates: $5318. *Programs:* Federal Direct (Subsidized and Unsubsidized Stafford, PLUS).

APPLYING FOR FINANCIAL AID *Required financial aid forms:* FAFSA, institution's own form, state aid form. *Financial aid deadline:* Continuous. *Notification date:* 7/30. Students must reply within 2 weeks of notification.

CONTACT Starr Fain, Director of Financial Aid, Amridge University, 1200 Taylor Road, Montgomery, AL 36117, 334-387-3877 Ext. 7523 or toll-free 888-790-8080. *Fax:* 334-387-3878. *E-mail:* starrfain@amridgeuniversity.edu.
Website: http://www.amridgeuniversity.edu/.

ANDERSON UNIVERSITY
Anderson, IN

CONTACT Mr. Kenneth Nieman, Director of Financial Aid, Anderson University, 1100 East Fifth Street, Anderson, IN 46012-3495, 765-641-4180 or toll-free 800-428-6414. *Fax:* 765-641-3831. *E-mail:* kfnieman@anderson.edu.
Website: http://www.anderson.edu/.

ANDERSON UNIVERSITY
Anderson, SC

Tuition & fees: $26,970	Average undergraduate aid package: $19,354

ABOUT THE INSTITUTION Independent Baptist, coed. *Awards:* bachelor's, master's, and doctoral degrees. 65 undergraduate majors. *Total enrollment:* 3,497. Undergraduates: 2,983. Freshmen: 681. Federal methodology is used as a basis for awarding need-based institutional aid.

UNDERGRADUATE EXPENSES for 2017–2018 *Application fee:* $25. *Comprehensive fee:* $36,650 includes full-time tuition ($24,290), mandatory fees

($2680), and room and board ($9680). *College room only:* $5030. Full-time tuition and fees vary according to course load and program. Room and board charges vary according to board plan and housing facility. *Part-time tuition:* $605 per credit hour. Part-time tuition and fees vary according to course load and program.

FRESHMAN FINANCIAL AID (Fall 2017, est.) 1,412 applied for aid; of those 83% were deemed to have need. 77% of freshmen with need received aid; of those 21% had need fully met. *Average percent of need met:* 74% (excluding resources awarded to replace EFC). *Average financial aid package:* $21,033 (excluding resources awarded to replace EFC). 8% of all full-time freshmen had no need and received non-need-based gift aid.

UNDERGRADUATE FINANCIAL AID (Fall 2017, est.) 3,350 applied for aid; of those 84% were deemed to have need. 86% of undergraduates with need received aid; of those 25% had need fully met. *Average percent of need met:* 72% (excluding resources awarded to replace EFC). *Average financial aid package:* $19,354 (excluding resources awarded to replace EFC). 11% of all full-time undergraduates had no need and received non-need-based gift aid.

GIFT AID (NEED-BASED) *Total amount:* $33,556,147 (15% federal, 26% state, 58% institutional, 1% external sources). *Receiving aid:* Freshmen: 62% (894); all full-time undergraduates: 57% (2,389). *Average award:* Freshmen: $18,777; Undergraduates: $16,574. *Scholarships, grants, and awards:* Federal Pell, FSEOG, state, private, college/university gift aid from institutional funds.

GIFT AID (NON-NEED-BASED) *Total amount:* $11,710,010 (1% federal, 29% state, 68% institutional, 2% external sources). *Receiving aid:* Freshmen: 12% (169). Undergraduates: 12% (495). *Average award:* Freshmen: $12,490. Undergraduates: $11,456. *Scholarships, grants, and awards by category:* Academic interests/achievement: 2,631 awards ($16,386,274 total): business, education, general academic interests/achievements, religion/biblical studies. Creative arts/performance: 387 awards ($930,718 total): applied art and design, art/fine arts, music, performing arts, theater/drama. Special achievements/activities: 275 awards ($327,685 total): cheerleading/drum major, leadership, memberships. Special characteristics: 1,853 awards ($5,040,508 total): children of faculty/staff, general special characteristics, international students, members of minority groups, out-of-state students, previous college experience, religious affiliation, veterans, veterans' children. *Tuition waivers:* Full or partial for employees or children of employees. *ROTC:* Army cooperative, Air Force cooperative.

LOANS *Student loans:* $16,654,664 (70% need-based, 30% non-need-based). 73% of past graduating class borrowed through all loan programs. *Average indebtedness per student:* $31,042. *Average need-based loan:* Freshmen: $3395. Undergraduates: $4284. *Parent loans:* $5618 (26% need-based, 74% non-need-based). *Programs:* Federal Direct (Subsidized and Unsubsidized Stafford, PLUS), Perkins, state, private loans.

WORK-STUDY *Federal work-study:* Total amount: $89,449; 161 jobs averaging $2000. *State or other work-study/employment:* Total amount: $96,086 (100% non-need-based). 243 part-time jobs averaging $1088.

ATHLETIC AWARDS Total amount: $3995 (29% need-based, 71% non-need-based).

APPLYING FOR FINANCIAL AID *Required financial aid form:* FAFSA. *Financial aid deadline:* 7/30 (priority: 3/1). *Notification date:* Continuous beginning 11/15. Students must reply by 5/1 or within 2 weeks of notification.

CONTACT Nancy Tate, Director of Financial Aid Services, Anderson University, 316 Boulevard, Anderson, SC 29621-4035, 864-231-2181 or toll-free 800-542-3594. *Fax:* 864-231-2008. *E-mail:* ntate@andersonuniversity.edu.
Website: http://www.andersonuniversity.edu/.

ANDREWS UNIVERSITY
Berrien Springs, MI

Tuition & fees: $28,436	Average undergraduate aid package: $31,058

ABOUT THE INSTITUTION Independent Seventh-day Adventist, coed. *Awards:* certificates, associate, bachelor's, master's, and doctoral degrees. 66 undergraduate majors. *Total enrollment:* 3,348. Undergraduates: 1,704. Freshmen: 281. Federal methodology is used as a basis for awarding need-based institutional aid.

UNDERGRADUATE EXPENSES for 2017–2018 *Application fee:* $30. *Comprehensive fee:* $37,514 includes full-time tuition ($27,456), mandatory fees ($980), and room and board ($9078). *College room only:* $4778. Full-time tuition and fees vary according to course load. Room and board charges vary according to board plan.

Part time tuition: $1111 per credit hour. Part-time fees: $124 per term. Part-time tuition and fees vary according to course load.

FRESHMAN FINANCIAL AID (Fall 2017, est.) 274 applied for aid; of those 61% were deemed to have need. 99% of freshmen with need received aid; of those 27% had need fully met. *Average percent of need met:* 86% (excluding resources awarded to replace EFC). *Average financial aid package:* $29,011 (excluding resources awarded to replace EFC). 39% of all full-time freshmen had no need and received non-need-based gift aid.

UNDERGRADUATE FINANCIAL AID (Fall 2017, est.) 869 applied for aid; of those 92% were deemed to have need. 100% of undergraduates with need received aid; of those 16% had need fully met. *Average percent of need met:* 87% (excluding resources awarded to replace EFC). *Average financial aid package:* $31,058 (excluding resources awarded to replace EFC). 39% of all full-time undergraduates had no need and received non-need-based gift aid.

GIFT AID (NEED-BASED) *Total amount:* $22,530,709 (11% federal, 1% state, 75% institutional, 13% external sources). *Receiving aid:* Freshmen: 37% (101); all full-time undergraduates: 42% (572). *Average award:* Freshmen: $5638; Undergraduates: $7052. *Scholarships, grants, and awards:* Federal Pell, FSEOG, state, private, college/university gift aid from institutional funds.

GIFT AID (NON-NEED-BASED) *Total amount:* $1,028,790 (100% external sources). *Receiving aid:* Freshmen: 61% (166). Undergraduates: 58% (787). *Average award:* Freshmen: $14,750. Undergraduates: $12,937. *Scholarships, grants, and awards by category: Academic interests/achievement:* 1,193 awards ($8,731,785 total): general academic interests/achievements. *Creative arts/performance:* 45 awards ($44,736 total): music. *Special achievements/activities:* 196 awards ($276,587 total): leadership, religious involvement. *Special characteristics:* 102 awards ($1,307,460 total): children of faculty/staff, general special characteristics, international students, spouses of current students. *Tuition waivers:* Full or partial for employees or children of employees, senior citizens.

LOANS *Student loans:* $13,621,059 (100% non-need-based). 63% of past graduating class borrowed through all loan programs. *Average indebtedness per student:* $31,845. *Average need-based loan:* Freshmen: $3298. Undergraduates: $4336. *Parent loans:* $5,173,417 (100% non-need-based). *Programs:* Federal Direct (Subsidized and Unsubsidized Stafford, PLUS), Perkins.

WORK-STUDY *Federal work-study:* Total amount: $541,075; 564 jobs averaging $959. *State or other work-study/employment:* Part-time jobs available.

APPLYING FOR FINANCIAL AID *Required financial aid forms:* FAFSA, institution's own form, CSS Financial Aid PROFILE. *Financial aid deadline:* Continuous. *Notification date:* Continuous.

CONTACT Cynthia Gammon, Assistant Director of Student Financial Services, Andrews University, Student Financial Services Administration Building, Berrien Springs, MI 49104, 800-253-2874. *Fax:* 269-471-3228. *E-mail:* sfs@andrews.edu. *Website:* http://www.andrews.edu/.

ANGELES COLLEGE
Los Angeles, CA

CONTACT Financial Aid Office, Angeles College, 3440 Wilshire Boulevard, Suite 310, Los Angeles, CA 90010, 213-487-2211. *Website:* http://www.angelescollege.edu/.

ANGELO STATE UNIVERSITY
San Angelo, TX

Tuition & fees (TX res): $8215	Average undergraduate aid package: $10,567

ABOUT THE INSTITUTION State-supported, coed. *Awards:* certificates, bachelor's, master's, and doctoral degrees. 38 undergraduate majors. *Total enrollment:* 10,417. Undergraduates: 8,798. Freshmen: 1,431. Federal methodology is used as a basis for awarding need-based institutional aid.

UNDERGRADUATE EXPENSES for 2017–2018 *Application fee:* $35. *Tuition, state resident:* full-time $5076; part-time $169.20 per credit hour. *Tuition, nonresident:* full-time $17,526; part-time $584.20 per credit hour. *Required fees:* full-time $3139. Full-time tuition and fees vary according to course load. Part-time tuition and fees vary according to course load. *College room and*

board: $7886. Room and board charges vary according to board plan and housing facility. *Payment plan:* Guaranteed tuition.

FRESHMAN FINANCIAL AID (Fall 2016) 1,371 applied for aid; of those 80% were deemed to have need. 99% of freshmen with need received aid; of those 16% had need fully met. *Average percent of need met:* 87% (excluding resources awarded to replace EFC). *Average financial aid package:* $10,757 (excluding resources awarded to replace EFC). 18% of all full-time freshmen had no need and received non-need-based gift aid.

UNDERGRADUATE FINANCIAL AID (Fall 2016) 4,039 applied for aid; of those 83% were deemed to have need. 99% of undergraduates with need received aid; of those 16% had need fully met. *Average percent of need met:* 84% (excluding resources awarded to replace EFC). *Average financial aid package:* $10,567 (excluding resources awarded to replace EFC). 19% of all full-time undergraduates had no need and received non-need-based gift aid.

GIFT AID (NEED-BASED) *Total amount:* $30,666,500 (50% federal, 50% state). *Receiving aid:* Freshmen: 61% (936); all full-time undergraduates: 58% (2,933). *Average award:* Freshmen: $3038; Undergraduates: $2905. *Scholarships, grants, and awards:* Federal Pell, FSEOG, state, private, college/university gift aid from institutional funds, Federal Nursing, Carr Academic Scholarships.

GIFT AID (NON-NEED-BASED) *Total amount:* $16,738,922 (93% institutional, 7% external sources). *Receiving aid:* Freshmen: 45% (692). Undergraduates: 37% (1,900). *Average award:* Freshmen: $3581. Undergraduates: $3788. *Scholarships, grants, and awards by category: Academic interests/achievement:* agriculture, biological sciences, business, communication, computer science, education, English, foreign languages, general academic interests/achievements, humanities, international studies, mathematics, military science, physical sciences, premedicine, social sciences. *ROTC:* Air Force.

LOANS *Student loans:* $66,391,877 (29% need-based, 71% non-need-based). 59% of past graduating class borrowed through all loan programs. *Average indebtedness per student:* $24,926. *Average need-based loan:* Freshmen: $3258. Undergraduates: $3822. *Parent loans:* $23,786,776 (100% non-need-based). *Programs:* Federal Direct (Subsidized and Unsubsidized Stafford, PLUS), Perkins, Federal Nursing, state, college/university, alternative loans.

WORK-STUDY *Federal work-study:* jobs available. *State or other work-study/employment:* Total amount: $56,197 (100% need-based). Part-time jobs available.

ATHLETIC AWARDS Total amount: $2,140,685 (100% non-need-based).

APPLYING FOR FINANCIAL AID *Required financial aid form:* FAFSA. *Financial aid deadline:* Continuous. *Notification date:* Continuous beginning 4/1. Students must reply within 4 weeks of notification.

CONTACT Mr. Ed Kerestly, Director of Financial Aid, Angelo State University, ASU Station #11015, San Angelo, TX 76909-1015, 325-942-2246 or toll-free 800-946-8627. *Fax:* 325-942-2082. *E-mail:* financial.aid@angelo.edu. *Website:* http://www.angelo.edu/.

ANNA MARIA COLLEGE
Paxton, MA

ABOUT THE INSTITUTION Independent Roman Catholic, coed. 58 undergraduate majors.

GIFT AID (NEED-BASED) *Scholarships, grants, and awards:* Federal Pell, FSEOG, state, private, college/university gift aid from institutional funds.

GIFT AID (NON-NEED-BASED) *Scholarships, grants, and awards by category: Academic interests/achievement:* general academic interests/achievements. *Creative arts/performance:* music. *Special achievements/activities:* religious involvement. *Special characteristics:* children of faculty/staff, general special characteristics, local/state students, previous college experience.

LOANS *Programs:* Federal Direct (Subsidized and Unsubsidized Stafford, PLUS), Perkins, state.

WORK-STUDY *Federal work-study:* jobs available. *State or other work-study/employment:* Part-time jobs available.

APPLYING FOR FINANCIAL AID *Required financial aid form:* FAFSA.

CONTACT Sandra J. Pereira, Director of Financial Aid, Anna Maria College, 50 Sunset Lane, Paxton, MA 01612-1198, 508-849-3363. *Fax:* 508-849-3735. *E-mail:* spereira@annamaria.edu. *Website:* http://www.annamaria.edu/.

ANTIOCH COLLEGE
Yellow Springs, OH

CONTACT Financial Aid Office, Antioch College, 1 Morgan Place, Yellow Springs, OH 45387, 937-767-1286.
Website: http://www.antiochcollege.edu/.

ANTIOCH UNIVERSITY LOS ANGELES
Culver City, CA

CONTACT Financial Aid Office, Antioch University Los Angeles, 400 Corporate Pointe, Culver City, CA 90230, 310-578-1080 or toll-free 800-726-8462.
Website: http://www.antioch.edu/los-angeles/.

ANTIOCH UNIVERSITY MIDWEST
Yellow Springs, OH

CONTACT Tricia Webb, Assistant Director of Financial Aid, Antioch University Midwest, 900 Dayton Street, Yellow Springs, OH 45387, 937-769-1883. *Fax:* 937-769-1804. *E-mail:* twebb@antioch.edu.
Website: http://www.antioch.edu/midwest/.

ANTIOCH UNIVERSITY SANTA BARBARA
Santa Barbara, CA

CONTACT Heather Nguyen, Assistant Director of Financial Aid, Antioch University Santa Barbara, 602 Anacapa Street, Santa Barbara, CA 93101, 805-962-8179 Ext. 5219 or toll-free 866-526-8462. *Fax:* 805-879-7062. *E-mail:* financialaid.ausb@antioch.edu.
Website: http://www.antioch.edu/santa-barbara/.

ANTIOCH UNIVERSITY SEATTLE
Seattle, WA

CONTACT Katy Stahl, Director of Financial Aid, Antioch University Seattle, 2326 Sixth Avenue, Seattle, WA 98121-1814, 206-268-4004 or toll-free 888-268-4477. *Fax:* 206-268-4242. *E-mail:* kstahl@antiochseattle.edu.
Website: http://www.antioch.edu/seattle/.

APEX SCHOOL OF THEOLOGY
Durham, NC

CONTACT Financial Aid Office, Apex School of Theology, 1701 T.W. Alexander Drive, Durham, NC 27703, 919-572-1625.
Website: http://www.apexsot.edu/.

APPALACHIAN BIBLE COLLEGE
Mount Hope, WV

Tuition & fees: $13,920	Average undergraduate aid package: $13,511

ABOUT THE INSTITUTION Independent nondenominational, coed. *Awards:* certificates, diplomas, associate, bachelor's, and master's degrees. 2 undergraduate majors. *Total enrollment:* 262. Undergraduates: 259. Freshmen: 41. Federal methodology is used as a basis for awarding need-based institutional aid.

UNDERGRADUATE EXPENSES for 2018–2019 *Application fee:* $35. *Comprehensive fee:* $21,880 includes full-time tuition ($13,010), mandatory fees ($910), and room and board ($7960). Full-time tuition and fees vary according to course load. Room and board charges vary according to housing facility. *Part-time tuition:* $395 per credit hour. *Part-time fees:* $42 per credit hour; $160 per term. Part-time tuition and fees vary according to course load.

FRESHMAN FINANCIAL AID (Fall 2017, est.) 54 applied for aid; of those 67% were deemed to have need. 100% of freshmen with need received aid. *Average percent of need met:* 67% (excluding resources awarded to replace EFC). *Average financial aid package:* $13,401 (excluding resources awarded to replace EFC). 5% of all full-time freshmen had no need and received non-need-based gift aid.

UNDERGRADUATE FINANCIAL AID (Fall 2017, est.) 143 applied for aid; of those 73% were deemed to have need. 100% of undergraduates with need received aid; of those 1% had need fully met. *Average percent of need met:* 64% (excluding resources awarded to replace EFC). *Average financial aid package:* $13,511 (excluding resources awarded to replace EFC). 4% of all full-time undergraduates had no need and received non-need-based gift aid.

GIFT AID (NEED-BASED) Total amount: $574,530 (84% federal, 12% state, 4% external sources). *Receiving aid:* Freshmen: 59% (34); all full-time undergraduates: 66% (103). *Average award:* Freshmen: $5338; Undergraduates: $5243. *Scholarships, grants, and awards:* Federal Pell, FSEOG, state, private, college/university gift aid from institutional funds.

GIFT AID (NON-NEED-BASED) Total amount: $1,089,157 (3% state, 81% institutional, 16% external sources). *Receiving aid:* Freshmen: 62% (36). Undergraduates: 67% (105). *Average award:* Freshmen: $6500. Undergraduates: $5885. *Scholarships, grants, and awards by category:* Academic interests/achievement: 97 awards ($200,265 total): education, general academic interests/achievements, religion/biblical studies. *Creative arts/performance:* 3 awards ($1771 total): music. *Special achievements/activities:* 9 awards ($17,600 total): community service, general special achievements/activities, leadership, religious involvement. *Special characteristics:* 141 awards ($439,486 total): children and siblings of alumni, children of educators, children of faculty/staff, children with a deceased or disabled parent, general special characteristics, international students, local/state students, married students, previous college experience, relatives of clergy, religious affiliation, siblings of current students, spouses of current students. *Tuition waivers:* Full or partial for minority students, children of alumni, employees or children of employees, senior citizens.

LOANS Student loans: $268,514 (86% need-based, 14% non-need-based). 63% of past graduating class borrowed through all loan programs. *Average indebtedness per student:* $15,421. *Average need-based loan:* Freshmen: $3146. Undergraduates: $3807. *Parent loans:* $4640 (100% need-based). *Programs:* Federal Direct (Subsidized and Unsubsidized Stafford, PLUS).

WORK-STUDY Federal work-study: Total amount: $16,588; 23 jobs averaging $721.

APPLYING FOR FINANCIAL AID Required financial aid forms: FAFSA, institution's own form. *Financial aid deadline (priority):* 6/15. *Notification date:* Continuous.

CONTACT Laura Martin, Director of Financial Aid, Appalachian Bible College, 161 College Drive, Mount Hope, WV 25880, 304-877-6428 Ext. 3247 or toll-free 800-678-9ABC. *Fax:* 304-877-5082. *E-mail:* financialaid@abc.edu.
Website: http://www.abc.edu/.

APPALACHIAN STATE UNIVERSITY
Boone, NC

Tuition & fees (NC res): $7303	Average undergraduate aid package: $9569

ABOUT THE INSTITUTION State-supported, coed. *Awards:* certificates, bachelor's, master's, and doctoral degrees. 73 undergraduate majors. *Total enrollment:* 18,811. Undergraduates: 17,017. Freshmen: 3,306. Federal methodology is used as a basis for awarding need-based institutional aid.

UNDERGRADUATE EXPENSES for 2017–2018 *Application fee:* $65. *Tuition, state resident:* full-time $4242; part-time $143 per credit hour. *Tuition, nonresident:* full-time $19,049; part-time $643.50 per credit hour. *Required fees:* full-time $3061; $19.17 per credit hour. Part-time tuition and fees vary according to course load. *College room and board:* $8174; *Room only:* $4340. Room and board charges vary according to board plan and housing facility. *Payment plan:* Guaranteed tuition.

FRESHMAN FINANCIAL AID (Fall 2017, est.) 2,830 applied for aid; of those 64% were deemed to have need. 92% of freshmen with need received aid; of those 17% had need fully met. *Average percent of need met:* 64% (excluding resources awarded to replace EFC). *Average financial aid package:* $9021 (excluding resources awarded to replace EFC). 3% of all full-time freshmen had no need and received non-need-based gift aid.

UNDERGRADUATE FINANCIAL AID (Fall 2017, est.) 11,560 applied for aid; of those 74% were deemed to have need. 94% of undergraduates with need received aid; of those 15% had need fully met. *Average percent of need met:* 66% (excluding resources awarded to replace EFC). *Average financial aid package:* $9569 (excluding resources awarded to replace EFC). 4% of all full-time undergraduates had no need and received non-need-based gift aid.

GIFT AID (NEED-BASED) *Total amount:* $49,548,252 (44% federal, 25% state, 26% institutional, 5% external sources). *Receiving aid:* Freshmen: 39% (1,279); all full-time undergraduates: 39% (6,236). *Average award:* Freshmen: $8072; Undergraduates: $7930. *Scholarships, grants, and awards:* Federal Pell, FSEOG, state, private, college/university gift aid from institutional funds.

GIFT AID (NON-NEED-BASED) *Total amount:* $4,105,902 (2% state, 64% institutional, 34% external sources). *Receiving aid:* Freshmen: 3% (87). Undergraduates: 2% (255). *Average award:* Freshmen: $6033. Undergraduates: $4198. *Scholarships, grants, and awards by category: Academic interests/achievement:* general academic interests/achievements. *Creative arts/performance:* general creative arts/performance. *Special achievements/activities:* general special achievements/activities. *Special characteristics:* general special characteristics. *Tuition waivers:* Full or partial for employees or children of employees. *ROTC:* Army.

LOANS *Student loans:* $55,399,592 (75% need-based, 25% non-need-based). 56% of past graduating class borrowed through all loan programs. *Average indebtedness per student:* $22,855. *Average need-based loan:* Freshmen: $3470. Undergraduates: $4255. *Parent loans:* $31,078,469 (67% need-based, 33% non-need-based). *Programs:* Federal Direct (Subsidized and Unsubsidized Stafford, PLUS), Perkins.

WORK-STUDY *Federal work-study:* Total amount: $857,736; jobs available.

ATHLETIC AWARDS Total amount: $4,633,939 (38% need-based, 62% non-need-based).

APPLYING FOR FINANCIAL AID *Required financial aid form:* FAFSA. *Financial aid deadline:* Continuous. *Notification date:* Continuous beginning 3/15. Students must reply within 3 weeks of notification.

CONTACT Office of Student Financial Aid, Appalachian State University, John E. Thomas Hall, ASU Box 32059, Boone, NC 28608-2059, 828-262-2190. *Fax:* 828-262-2585. *E-mail:* financialaid@appstate.edu.
Website: http://www.appstate.edu/.

AQUINAS COLLEGE
Grand Rapids, MI

Tuition & fees: $32,574	Average undergraduate aid package: $24,384

ABOUT THE INSTITUTION Independent Roman Catholic, coed. *Awards:* associate, bachelor's, and master's degrees. 72 undergraduate majors. *Total enrollment:* 1,716. Undergraduates: 1,551. Freshmen: 314. Federal methodology is used as a basis for awarding need-based institutional aid.

UNDERGRADUATE EXPENSES for 2018–2019 *Comprehensive fee:* $41,906 includes full-time tuition ($31,976), mandatory fees ($598), and room and board ($9332). *College room only:* $4376. Full-time tuition and fees vary according to course load. Room and board charges vary according to board plan and housing facility. *Part-time tuition:* $498 per credit hour. *Part-time fees:* $60 per term. Part-time tuition and fees vary according to course load.

FRESHMAN FINANCIAL AID (Fall 2017, est.) 286 applied for aid; of those 87% were deemed to have need. 100% of freshmen with need received aid; of those 21% had need fully met. *Average percent of need met:* 84% (excluding resources awarded to replace EFC). *Average financial aid package:* $25,933 (excluding resources awarded to replace EFC). 21% of all full-time freshmen had no need and received non-need-based gift aid.

UNDERGRADUATE FINANCIAL AID (Fall 2017, est.) 1,111 applied for aid; of those 91% were deemed to have need. 100% of undergraduates with need received aid; of those 20% had need fully met. *Average percent of need met:* 83% (excluding resources awarded to replace EFC). *Average financial aid package:*

$24,384 (excluding resources awarded to replace EFC). 23% of all full-time undergraduates had no need and received non-need-based gift aid.

GIFT AID (NEED-BASED) *Total amount:* $22,272,617 (11% federal, 7% state, 82% institutional). *Receiving aid:* Freshmen: 79% (248); all full-time undergraduates: 77% (1,009). *Average award:* Freshmen: $23,872; Undergraduates: $21,644. *Scholarships, grants, and awards:* Federal Pell, FSEOG, state, private, college/university gift aid from institutional funds.

GIFT AID (NON-NEED-BASED) *Total amount:* $5,098,624 (100% institutional). *Receiving aid:* Freshmen: 30% (93). Undergraduates: 26% (340). *Average award:* Freshmen: $19,774. Undergraduates: $16,822. *Scholarships, grants, and awards by category: Academic interests/achievement:* general academic interests/achievements. *Creative arts/performance:* general creative arts/performance. *Special achievements/activities:* general special achievements/activities, leadership. *Special characteristics:* children and siblings of alumni, children of faculty/staff. *Tuition waivers:* Full or partial for employees or children of employees.

LOANS *Student loans:* $6,302,141 (94% need-based, 6% non-need-based). 77% of past graduating class borrowed through all loan programs. *Average indebtedness per student:* $29,755. *Average need-based loan:* Freshmen: $2061. Undergraduates: $2740. *Parent loans:* $1,390,082 (92% need-based, 8% non-need-based). *Programs:* Federal Direct (Subsidized and Unsubsidized Stafford, PLUS).

WORK-STUDY *Federal work-study:* Total amount: $143,001; 131 jobs averaging $1026. *State or other work-study/employment:* Part-time jobs available.

ATHLETIC AWARDS Total amount: $2,249,954 (77% need-based, 23% non-need-based).

APPLYING FOR FINANCIAL AID *Required financial aid form:* FAFSA. *Financial aid deadline (priority):* 3/1. *Notification date:* Continuous beginning 11/27. Students must reply within 2 weeks of notification.

CONTACT Darcy Kampfschulte, Director of Financial Aid, Aquinas College, 1700 Fulton Street E, Grand Rapids, MI 49506-1801, 616-632-2894 or toll-free 800-678-9593. *Fax:* 616-732-4547. *E-mail:* kampfdar@aquinas.edu.
Website: http://www.aquinas.edu/.

AQUINAS COLLEGE
Nashville, TN

CONTACT Mrs. Kylie Pruitt, Director of Financial Aid, Aquinas College, 4210 Harding Road, Nashville, TN 37205-2005, 615-297-7545 Ext. 431 or toll-free 800-649-9956. *Fax:* 615-279-3891. *E-mail:* pruittk@aquinascollege.edu.
Website: http://www.aquinascollege.edu/.

ARCADIA UNIVERSITY
Glenside, PA

ABOUT THE INSTITUTION Independent Presbyterian Church (U.S.A.), coed. *Awards:* certificates, bachelor's, master's, and doctoral degrees. 61 undergraduate majors. *Total enrollment:* 3,811. Undergraduates: 2,390. Freshmen: 565.

GIFT AID (NEED-BASED) *Scholarships, grants, and awards:* Federal Pell, FSEOG, state, private, college/university gift aid from institutional funds, Academic Competitiveness Grants, National SMART Grants, TEACH Grants.

GIFT AID (NON-NEED-BASED) *Scholarships, grants, and awards by category: Academic interests/achievement:* general academic interests/achievements. *Creative arts/performance:* applied art and design, art/fine arts, theater/drama. *Special achievements/activities:* community service, general special achievements/activities, leadership, memberships. *Special characteristics:* children and siblings of alumni, relatives of clergy, religious affiliation.

LOANS *Programs:* Federal Direct (Subsidized and Unsubsidized Stafford, PLUS), Perkins.

WORK-STUDY *Federal work-study:* jobs available. *State or other work-study/employment:* Total amount: $225,675 (100% non-need-based). 140 part-time jobs averaging $1671.

APPLYING FOR FINANCIAL AID *Required financial aid forms:* FAFSA, institution's own form.

CONTACT Alison Venditti, Assistant Director of Financial Aid, Arcadia University, 450 South Easton Road, Glenside, PA 19038, 215-572-2837 or toll-free 877-ARCADIA. *Fax:* 215-572-4049. *E-mail:* vendittia@arcadia.edu.
Website: http://www.arcadia.edu/.

ARGOSY UNIVERSITY, ATLANTA
Atlanta, GA

CONTACT Financial Aid Office, Argosy University, Atlanta, 980 Hammond Drive, Suite 100, Atlanta, GA 30328, 770-671-1200 or toll-free 888-671-4777. *Website:* http://www.argosy.edu/locations/atlanta/.

ARGOSY UNIVERSITY, CHICAGO
Chicago, IL

CONTACT Financial Aid Office, Argosy University, Chicago, 225 North Michigan Avenue, Suite 1300, Chicago, IL 60601, 312-777-7600 or toll-free 800-626-4123. *Website:* http://www.argosy.edu/chicago-illinois/default.aspx.

ARGOSY UNIVERSITY, DALLAS
Farmers Branch, TX

CONTACT Financial Aid Office, Argosy University, Dallas, 5001 Lyndon B. Johnson Freeway, Heritage Square, Farmers Branch, TX 75244, 214-890-9900 or toll-free 866-954-9900. *Website:* http://www.argosy.edu/dallas-texas/default.aspx.

ARGOSY UNIVERSITY, DENVER
Denver, CO

CONTACT Financial Aid Office, Argosy University, Denver, 7600 East Eastman Avenue, Denver, CO 80231, 303-923-4110 or toll-free 866-431-5981. *Website:* http://www.argosy.edu/locations/denver/.

ARGOSY UNIVERSITY, HAWAII
Honolulu, HI

CONTACT Financial Aid Office, Argosy University, Hawaii, 1001 Bishop Street, Suite 400, Honolulu, HI 96813, 808-536-5555 or toll-free 888-323-2777. *Website:* http://www.argosy.edu/locations/hawaii/.

ARGOSY UNIVERSITY, INLAND EMPIRE
Ontario, CA

CONTACT Financial Aid Office, Argosy University, Inland Empire, 3401 Centre Lake Drive, Suite 200, Ontario, CA 91761, 909-472-0800 or toll-free 866-217-9075. *Website:* http://www.argosy.edu/locations/inland-empire/.

ARGOSY UNIVERSITY, LOS ANGELES
Los Angeles, CA

CONTACT Financial Aid Office, Argosy University, Los Angeles, 5230 Pacific Concourse, Suite 200, Los Angeles, CA 90045, 310-531-9700 or toll-free 866-505-0332. *Website:* http://www.argosy.edu/locations/los-angeles/.

ARGOSY UNIVERSITY, NASHVILLE
Nashville, TN

CONTACT Financial Aid Office, Argosy University, Nashville, 100 Centerview Drive, Suite 225, Nashville, TN 37214, 615-525-2800 or toll-free 866-833-6598. *Website:* http://www.argosy.edu/locations/nashville/.

ARGOSY UNIVERSITY, NORTHERN VIRGINIA
Arlington, VA

CONTACT Financial Aid Office, Argosy University, Northern Virginia, 1550 Wilson Boulevard, Suite 600, Arlington, VA 22209, 703-526-5800 or toll-free 866-703-2777. *Website:* http://www.argosy.edu/locations/northern-virginia/.

ARGOSY UNIVERSITY, ORANGE COUNTY
Orange, CA

CONTACT Financial Aid Office, Argosy University, Orange County, 601 South Lewis Street, Orange, CA 92868, 714-620-3700 or toll-free 800-716-9598. *Website:* http://www.argosy.edu/locations/los-angeles-orange-county/.

ARGOSY UNIVERSITY, PHOENIX
Phoenix, AZ

CONTACT Financial Aid Office, Argosy University, Phoenix, 2233 West Dunlap Avenue, Phoenix, AZ 85021, 602-216-2600 or toll-free 866-216-2777. *Website:* http://www.argosy.edu/phoenix-arizona/default.aspx.

ARGOSY UNIVERSITY, SALT LAKE CITY
Draper, UT

CONTACT Financial Aid Office, Argosy University, Salt Lake City, 121 Election Road, Suite 300, Draper, UT 84020, 801-601-5000 or toll-free 888-639-4756. *Website:* http://www.argosy.edu/locations/salt-lake-city/.

ARGOSY UNIVERSITY, SAN DIEGO
San Diego, CA

CONTACT Financial Aid Office, Argosy University, San Diego, 1615 Murray Canyon Road, Suite 100, San Diego, CA 92108, 619-321-3000 or toll-free 866-505-0333. *Website:* http://www.argosy.edu/locations/san-diego/.

ARGOSY UNIVERSITY, SAN FRANCISCO BAY AREA
Alameda, CA

CONTACT Financial Aid Office, Argosy University, San Francisco Bay Area, 1005 Atlantic Avenue, Alameda, CA 94501, 510-217-4700 or toll-free 866-215-2777. *Website:* http://www.argosy.edu/locations/san-francisco/.

ARGOSY UNIVERSITY, SARASOTA
Sarasota, FL

CONTACT Financial Aid Office, Argosy University, Sarasota, 5250 17th Street, Sarasota, FL 34235, 941-379-0404 or toll-free 800-331-5995. *Website:* http://www.argosy.edu/locations/sarasota/.

ARGOSY UNIVERSITY, SCHAUMBURG
Schaumburg, IL

CONTACT Financial Aid Office, Argosy University, Schaumburg, 999 North Plaza Drive, Suite 111, Schaumburg, IL 60173-5403, 847-969-4900 or toll-free 866-290-2777. *Website:* http://www.argosy.edu/locations/chicago-schaumburg/.

ARGOSY UNIVERSITY, SEATTLE
Seattle, WA

CONTACT Financial Aid Office, Argosy University, Seattle, 2601-A Elliott Avenue, Seattle, WA 98121, 206-283-4500 or toll-free 866-283-2777. *Website:* http://www.argosy.edu/locations/seattle/.

ARGOSY UNIVERSITY, TAMPA
Tampa, FL

CONTACT Financial Aid Office, Argosy University, Tampa, 1403 North Howard Avenue, Tampa, FL 33607, 813-393-5290 or toll-free 800-850-6488. *Website:* http://www.argosy.edu/locations/tampa/.

ARGOSY UNIVERSITY, TWIN CITIES
Eagan, MN

CONTACT Financial Aid Office, Argosy University, Twin Cities, 1515 Central Parkway, Eagan, MN 55121, 651-846-2882 or toll-free 888-844-2004. *Website:* http://www.argosy.edu/locations/twin-cities/.

ARIZONA CHRISTIAN UNIVERSITY
Phoenix, AZ

Tuition & fees: $2546	Average undergraduate aid package: $17,230

ABOUT THE INSTITUTION Independent Conservative Baptist, coed. *Awards:* associate and bachelor's degrees. 22 undergraduate majors. *Total enrollment:* 700. Undergraduates: 691. Freshmen: 153. Federal methodology is used as a basis for awarding need-based institutional aid.

**UNDERGRADUATE EXPENSES for 2018–2019 *Application fee:* $30. *Comprehensive fee:* $13,220 includes full-time tuition ($2546) and room and board ($10,674). *College room only:* $5400. Full-time tuition and fees vary according to class time, course load, and program. Room and board charges vary according to board plan. *Part-time tuition:* $1062 per credit hour. Part-time tuition and fees vary according to class time, course load, and program.

FRESHMAN FINANCIAL AID (Fall 2016) 127 applied for aid; of those 84% were deemed to have need. 97% of freshmen with need received aid; of those 21% had need fully met. *Average percent of need met:* 57% (excluding resources awarded to replace EFC). *Average financial aid package:* $16,008 (excluding resources awarded to replace EFC). 32% of all full-time freshmen had no need and received non-need-based gift aid.

UNDERGRADUATE FINANCIAL AID (Fall 2016) 492 applied for aid; of those 89% were deemed to have need. 97% of undergraduates with need received aid; of those 16% had need fully met. *Average percent of need met:* 58% (excluding resources awarded to replace EFC). *Average financial aid package:* $17,230 (excluding resources awarded to replace EFC). 18% of all full-time undergraduates had no need and received non-need-based gift aid.

**GIFT AID (NEED-BASED) *Total amount:* $1,543,322 (67% federal, 33% institutional). *Receiving aid:* Freshmen: 81% (104); all full-time undergraduates: 77% (422). *Average award:* Freshmen: $13,788; Undergraduates: $14,013. *Scholarships, grants, and awards:* Federal Pell, FSEOG, state, private, college/university gift aid from institutional funds.

**GIFT AID (NON-NEED-BASED) *Total amount:* $3,908,069 (1% federal, 94% institutional, 5% external sources). *Receiving aid:* Freshmen: 14% (18). Undergraduates: 9% (51). *Average award:* Freshmen: $13,776. Undergraduates: $13,602. *Scholarships, grants, and awards by category: Academic interests/ achievement:* general academic interests/achievements. *Creative arts/performance:* music. *Special achievements/activities:* community service, general special achievements/activities, leadership. *Tuition waivers:* Full or partial for employees or children of employees. *ROTC:* Air Force cooperative.

**LOANS *Student loans:* $2,899,711 (50% need-based, 50% non-need-based). *Average need-based loan:* Freshmen: $3164. Undergraduates: $4120. *Parent loans:* $909,612 (100% need-based). *Programs:* Federal Direct (Subsidized and Unsubsidized Stafford, PLUS).

**WORK-STUDY *Federal work-study:* jobs available.

ATHLETIC AWARDS Total amount: $2,373,828 (100% non-need-based).

**APPLYING FOR FINANCIAL AID *Required financial aid forms:* FAFSA, institution's own form. *Financial aid deadline:* Continuous. *Notification date:* Continuous beginning 4/15. Students must reply by 6/1 or within 2 weeks of notification.

CONTACT Mr. Steven Young, Director of Financial Aid, Arizona Christian University, 2625 East Cactus Road, Phoenix, AZ 85032-7042, 602-386-4115 or toll-free 800-247-2697. *Fax:* 602-404-2159. *E-mail:* steven.young@arizonachristian.edu. *Website:* http://arizonachristian.edu/.

ARIZONA COLLEGE–LAS VEGAS
Las Vegas, NV

CONTACT Financial Aid Office, Arizona College–Las Vegas, 2320 South Rancho Drive, Las Vegas, NV 89102. *Website:* http://www.arizonacollege.edu/.

ARIZONA COLLEGE–MESA
Mesa, AZ

CONTACT Financial Aid Office, Arizona College–Mesa, 163 N Dobson Road, Mesa, AZ 85201. *Website:* http://www.arizonacollege.edu/.

ARIZONA STATE UNIVERSITY AT THE DOWNTOWN PHOENIX CAMPUS
Phoenix, AZ

Tuition & fees: N/R	Average undergraduate aid package: $14,667

ABOUT THE INSTITUTION State-supported, coed. *Awards:* certificates, bachelor's, master's, and doctoral degrees. 27 undergraduate majors. *Total enrollment:* 11,465. Undergraduates: 8,902. Freshmen: 1,301. Federal methodology is used as a basis for awarding need-based institutional aid.

FRESHMAN FINANCIAL AID (Fall 2016) 1,192 applied for aid; of those 81% were deemed to have need. 100% of freshmen with need received aid; of those 21% had need fully met. *Average percent of need met:* 69% (excluding resources awarded to replace EFC). *Average financial aid package:* $17,692 (excluding resources awarded to replace EFC). 21% of all full-time freshmen had no need and received non-need-based gift aid.

UNDERGRADUATE FINANCIAL AID (Fall 2016) 6,691 applied for aid; of those 86% were deemed to have need. 100% of undergraduates with need received aid; of those 18% had need fully met. *Average percent of need met:* 58% (excluding resources awarded to replace EFC). *Average financial aid package:* $14,667 (excluding resources awarded to replace EFC). 14% of all full-time undergraduates had no need and received non-need-based gift aid.
GIFT AID (NEED-BASED) *Total amount:* $55,677,302 (35% federal, 56% institutional, 9% external sources). *Receiving aid:* Freshmen: 74% (955); all full-time undergraduates: 64% (5,251). *Average award:* Freshmen: $13,758; Undergraduates: $10,233. *Scholarships, grants, and awards:* Federal Pell, FSEOG, state, private, college/university gift aid from institutional funds, United Negro College Fund, Federal Nursing.
GIFT AID (NON-NEED-BASED) *Total amount:* $16,130,599 (6% federal, 68% institutional, 26% external sources). *Receiving aid:* Freshmen: 8% (106). Undergraduates: 5% (383). *Average award:* Freshmen: $8947. Undergraduates: $8125. *Scholarships, grants, and awards by category:* Academic interests/achievement: general academic interests/achievements. *Special achievements/activities:* leadership. *Special characteristics:* children of faculty/staff, international students, local/state students, out-of-state students. *ROTC:* Army cooperative, Naval cooperative, Air Force cooperative.
LOANS *Student loans:* $41,628,807 (75% need-based, 25% non-need-based). 63% of past graduating class borrowed through all loan programs. *Average indebtedness per student:* $24,368. *Average need-based loan:* Freshmen: $3136. Undergraduates: $4030. *Parent loans:* $22,455,895 (45% need-based, 55% non-need-based). *Programs:* Federal Direct (Subsidized and Unsubsidized Stafford, PLUS), Perkins, Federal Nursing, state, college/university, private loans from endowment funds.
WORK-STUDY *Federal work-study:* 431 jobs averaging $2689. *State or other work-study/employment:* Total amount: $4,478,308 (37% need-based, 63% non-need-based). 1,321 part-time jobs averaging $3390.
ATHLETIC AWARDS Total amount: $1,744,634 (35% need-based, 65% non-need-based).
APPLYING FOR FINANCIAL AID *Required financial aid form:* FAFSA. *Financial aid deadline (priority):* 3/1. *Notification date:* Continuous beginning 3/1.
CONTACT Financial Aid and Scholarship Services, Arizona State University at the Downtown Phoenix campus, PO Box 870412, Tempe, AZ 85287-0412, 855-278-5080. *Fax:* 480-965-9484.
Website: http://campus.asu.edu/downtown/.

ARIZONA STATE UNIVERSITY AT THE POLYTECHNIC CAMPUS
Mesa, AZ

Tuition & fees: N/R	Average undergraduate aid package: $13,973

ABOUT THE INSTITUTION State-supported, coed. *Awards:* certificates, bachelor's, master's, and doctoral degrees. 36 undergraduate majors. *Total enrollment:* 4,809. Undergraduates: 4,239. Freshmen: 581. Federal methodology is used as a basis for awarding need-based institutional aid.
FRESHMAN FINANCIAL AID (Fall 2016) 414 applied for aid; of those 73% were deemed to have need. 100% of freshmen with need received aid; of those 26% had need fully met. *Average percent of need met:* 69% (excluding resources awarded to replace EFC). *Average financial aid package:* $14,727 (excluding resources awarded to replace EFC). 25% of all full-time freshmen had no need and received non-need-based gift aid.
UNDERGRADUATE FINANCIAL AID (Fall 2016) 2,491 applied for aid; of those 84% were deemed to have need. 100% of undergraduates with need received aid; of those 20% had need fully met. *Average percent of need met:* 58% (excluding resources awarded to replace EFC). *Average financial aid package:* $13,973 (excluding resources awarded to replace EFC). 13% of all full-time undergraduates had no need and received non-need-based gift aid.
GIFT AID (NEED-BASED) *Total amount:* $18,801,920 (45% federal, 48% institutional, 7% external sources). *Receiving aid:* Freshmen: 60% (292); all full-time undergraduates: 56% (1,890). *Average award:* Freshmen: $11,683; Undergraduates: $9309. *Scholarships, grants, and awards:* Federal Pell, FSEOG, state, private, college/university gift aid from institutional funds, United Negro College Fund.

GIFT AID (NON-NEED-BASED) *Total amount:* $8,460,543 (8% federal, 41% institutional, 51% external sources). *Receiving aid:* Freshmen: 10% (48). Undergraduates: 5% (156). *Average award:* Freshmen: $8087. Undergraduates: $6948. *Scholarships, grants, and awards by category:* Academic interests/achievement: general academic interests/achievements. *Special achievements/activities:* leadership. *Special characteristics:* children of faculty/staff, international students, local/state students, out-of-state students. *ROTC:* Army cooperative, Naval cooperative, Air Force cooperative.
LOANS *Student loans:* $16,385,366 (75% need-based, 25% non-need-based). 59% of past graduating class borrowed through all loan programs. *Average indebtedness per student:* $26,797. *Average need-based loan:* Freshmen: $2915. Undergraduates: $4155. *Parent loans:* $7,649,670 (43% need-based, 57% non-need-based). *Programs:* Federal Direct (Subsidized and Unsubsidized Stafford, PLUS), Perkins, state, college/university, private loans from endowment funds.
WORK-STUDY *Federal work-study:* 197 jobs averaging $2581. *State or other work-study/employment:* Total amount: $3,031,467 (33% need-based, 67% non-need-based). 777 part-time jobs averaging $3900.
ATHLETIC AWARDS Total amount: $570,252 (29% need-based, 71% non-need-based).
APPLYING FOR FINANCIAL AID *Required financial aid form:* FAFSA. *Financial aid deadline (priority):* 3/1. *Notification date:* Continuous beginning 3/1.
CONTACT Financial Aid and Scholarship Services, Arizona State University at the Polytechnic campus, PO Box 870412, Tempe, AZ 85287-0412, 855-278-5080. *Fax:* 480-965-9484.
Website: http://campus.asu.edu/polytechnic.

ARIZONA STATE UNIVERSITY AT THE TEMPE CAMPUS
Tempe, AZ

Tuition & fees (AZ res): $10,522	Average undergraduate aid package: $14,940

ABOUT THE INSTITUTION State-supported, coed. *Awards:* certificates, bachelor's, master's, and doctoral degrees (profile includes data for the West, Polytechnic and Downtown Phoenix campuses). 96 undergraduate majors. *Total enrollment:* 51,164. Undergraduates: 42,427. Freshmen: 7,874. Federal methodology is used as a basis for awarding need-based institutional aid.
UNDERGRADUATE EXPENSES for 2017–2018 *Application fee:* $50. *Tuition, state resident:* full-time $9834; part-time $702 per credit hour. *Tuition, nonresident:* full-time $26,684; part-time $1112 per credit hour. *Required fees:* full-time $688; $196 per term. Room and board charges vary according to board plan and housing facility.
FRESHMAN FINANCIAL AID (Fall 2016) 6,648 applied for aid; of those 73% were deemed to have need. 100% of freshmen with need received aid; of those 22% had need fully met. *Average percent of need met:* 70% (excluding resources awarded to replace EFC). *Average financial aid package:* $16,638 (excluding resources awarded to replace EFC). 29% of all full-time freshmen had no need and received non-need-based gift aid.
UNDERGRADUATE FINANCIAL AID (Fall 2016) 25,918 applied for aid; of those 81% were deemed to have need. 100% of undergraduates with need received aid; of those 19% had need fully met. *Average percent of need met:* 62% (excluding resources awarded to replace EFC). *Average financial aid package:* $14,940 (excluding resources awarded to replace EFC). 22% of all full-time undergraduates had no need and received non-need-based gift aid.
GIFT AID (NEED-BASED) *Total amount:* $212,448,423 (30% federal, 63% institutional, 7% external sources). *Receiving aid:* Freshmen: 59% (4,795); all full-time undergraduates: 51% (19,605). *Average award:* Freshmen: $12,926; Undergraduates: $10,528. *Scholarships, grants, and awards:* Federal Pell, FSEOG, state, private, college/university gift aid from institutional funds, United Negro College Fund.
GIFT AID (NON-NEED-BASED) *Total amount:* $147,611,580 (1% federal, 54% institutional, 45% external sources). *Receiving aid:* Freshmen: 9% (699). Undergraduates: 5% (1,928). *Average award:* Freshmen: $9329. Undergraduates: $8329. *Scholarships, grants, and awards by category:* Academic interests/achievement: general academic interests/achievements. *Creative arts/performance:* art/fine arts, dance, music, theater/drama. *Special achievements/activities:* leadership.

Special characteristics: children of faculty/staff, international students, local/state students, out-of-state students. *Tuition waivers:* Full or partial for employees or children of employees. *ROTC:* Army, Naval, Air Force.

LOANS *Student loans:* $135,110,077 (71% need-based, 29% non-need-based). 48% of past graduating class borrowed through all loan programs. *Average indebtedness per student:* $23,237. *Average need-based loan:* Freshmen: $3123. Undergraduates: $4004. *Parent loans:* $74,913,179 (41% need-based, 59% non-need-based). *Programs:* Federal Direct (Subsidized and Unsubsidized Stafford, PLUS), Perkins, state, college/university, private loans from endowment funds.

WORK-STUDY *Federal work-study:* 1,136 jobs averaging $2470. *State or other work-study/employment:* Total amount: $21,206,062 (34% need-based, 66% non-need-based). 6,382 part-time jobs averaging $3322.

ATHLETIC AWARDS Total amount: $8,896,791 (39% need-based, 61% non-need-based).

APPLYING FOR FINANCIAL AID *Required financial aid form:* FAFSA. *Financial aid deadline (priority):* 3/1. *Notification date:* Continuous beginning 3/1.

CONTACT Financial Aid and Scholarship Services, Arizona State University at the Tempe campus, PO Box 870412, Tempe, AZ 85287-0412, 855-278-5080. *Fax:* 480-965-9484.

Website: http://www.asu.edu/.

ARIZONA STATE UNIVERSITY AT THE WEST CAMPUS
Glendale, AZ

Tuition & fees: N/R	Average undergraduate aid package: $12,895

ABOUT THE INSTITUTION State-supported, coed. *Awards:* certificates, bachelor's, master's, and doctoral degrees. 40 undergraduate majors. *Total enrollment:* 4,063. Undergraduates: 3,630. Freshmen: 522. Federal methodology is used as a basis for awarding need-based institutional aid.

FRESHMAN FINANCIAL AID (Fall 2016) 344 applied for aid; of those 83% were deemed to have need. 100% of freshmen with need received aid; of those 22% had need fully met. *Average percent of need met:* 73% (excluding resources awarded to replace EFC). *Average financial aid package:* $15,123 (excluding resources awarded to replace EFC). 17% of all full-time freshmen had no need and received non-need-based gift aid.

UNDERGRADUATE FINANCIAL AID (Fall 2016) 2,238 applied for aid; of those 89% were deemed to have need. 100% of undergraduates with need received aid; of those 15% had need fully met. *Average percent of need met:* 59% (excluding resources awarded to replace EFC). *Average financial aid package:* $12,895 (excluding resources awarded to replace EFC). 9% of all full-time undergraduates had no need and received non-need-based gift aid.

GIFT AID (NEED-BASED) *Total amount:* $17,864,312 (45% federal, 47% institutional, 8% external sources). *Receiving aid:* Freshmen: 73% (280); all full-time undergraduates: 69% (1,850). *Average award:* Freshmen: $12,364; Undergraduates: $9034. *Scholarships, grants, and awards:* Federal Pell, FSEOG, state, private, college/university gift aid from institutional funds, United Negro College Fund.

GIFT AID (NON-NEED-BASED) *Total amount:* $3,493,145 (16% federal, 54% institutional, 30% external sources). *Receiving aid:* Freshmen: 9% (36). Undergraduates: 4% (113). *Average award:* Freshmen: $7314. Undergraduates: $6743. *Scholarships, grants, and awards by category:* Academic interests/achievement: general academic interests/achievements. Special achievements/activities: leadership. *Special characteristics:* children of faculty/staff, international students, local/state students, out-of-state students. *ROTC:* Army cooperative, Naval cooperative, Air Force cooperative.

LOANS *Student loans:* $13,428,650 (79% need-based, 21% non-need-based). 64% of past graduating class borrowed through all loan programs. *Average indebtedness per student:* $24,498. *Average need-based loan:* Freshmen: $3019. Undergraduates: $4137. *Parent loans:* $3,726,335 (40% need-based, 60% non-need-based). *Programs:* Federal Direct (Subsidized and Unsubsidized Stafford, PLUS), Perkins, state, college/university, private loans from endowment funds.

WORK-STUDY *Federal work-study:* 169 jobs averaging $2277. *State or other work-study/employment:* Total amount: $1,710,408 (42% need-based, 58% non-need-based). 506 part-time jobs averaging $3380.

ATHLETIC AWARDS Total amount: $17,164 (100% need-based).

APPLYING FOR FINANCIAL AID *Required financial aid form:* FAFSA. *Financial aid deadline (priority):* 3/1. *Notification date:* Continuous beginning 3/1.

CONTACT Financial Aid and Scholarship Services, Arizona State University at the West campus, PO Box 870412, Tempe, AZ 85287-0412, 855-278-5080. *Fax:* 480-965-9484.

Website: http://campus.asu.edu/west.

ARKANSAS BAPTIST COLLEGE
Little Rock, AR

CONTACT Office of Financial Aid, Arkansas Baptist College, 1600 Bishop Street, Little Rock, AR 72202-6067, 501-374-7856.

Website: http://www.arkansasbaptist.edu/.

ARKANSAS STATE UNIVERSITY
Jonesboro, AR

CONTACT Mr. Terry Finney, Director of Financial Aid, Arkansas State University, PO Box 1620, State University, AR 72467, 870-972-2310 or toll-free 800-382-3030. *Fax:* 870-972-2794. *E-mail:* finaid@astate.edu.

Website: http://www.astate.edu/.

ARKANSAS TECH UNIVERSITY
Russellville, AR

Tuition & fees (AR res): $8880	Average undergraduate aid package: $9538

ABOUT THE INSTITUTION State-supported, coed. *Awards:* certificates, associate, bachelor's, master's, and doctoral degrees. 84 undergraduate majors. *Total enrollment:* 11,830. Undergraduates: 10,781. Freshmen: 1,846. Federal methodology is used as a basis for awarding need-based institutional aid.

UNDERGRADUATE EXPENSES for 2017–2018 *Tuition, state resident:* full-time $6780; part-time $226 per credit hour. *Tuition, nonresident:* full-time $13,560; part-time $452 per credit hour. *Required fees:* full-time $2100; $70 per credit hour. Full-time tuition and fees vary according to course load and location. Part-time tuition and fees vary according to course load and location. *College room and board:* $7338; *Room only:* $4412. Room and board charges vary according to board plan, housing facility, and location.

FRESHMAN FINANCIAL AID (Fall 2016) 1,752 applied for aid; of those 72% were deemed to have need. 98% of freshmen with need received aid; of those 6% had need fully met. *Average percent of need met:* 57% (excluding resources awarded to replace EFC). *Average financial aid package:* $9235 (excluding resources awarded to replace EFC). 19% of all full-time freshmen had no need and received non-need-based gift aid.

UNDERGRADUATE FINANCIAL AID (Fall 2016) 6,107 applied for aid; of those 76% were deemed to have need. 99% of undergraduates with need received aid; of those 9% had need fully met. *Average percent of need met:* 59% (excluding resources awarded to replace EFC). *Average financial aid package:* $9538 (excluding resources awarded to replace EFC). 13% of all full-time undergraduates had no need and received non-need-based gift aid.

GIFT AID (NEED-BASED) *Total amount:* $20,293,976 (96% federal, 4% state). *Receiving aid:* Freshmen: 55% (1,001); all full-time undergraduates: 54% (3,646). *Average award:* Freshmen: $4629; Undergraduates: $4554. *Scholarships, grants, and awards:* Federal Pell, FSEOG, state, private.

GIFT AID (NON-NEED-BASED) *Total amount:* $27,224,485 (36% state, 48% institutional, 16% external sources). *Receiving aid:* Freshmen: 47% (847). Undergraduates: 37% (2,475). *Average award:* Freshmen: $6572. Undergraduates: $6650. *Scholarships, grants, and awards by category:* Academic interests/achievement: agriculture, biological sciences, business, communication, computer science, education, engineering/technologies, English, foreign languages, general academic interests/achievements, health fields, home economics, humanities, international studies, mathematics, military science, physical sciences, premedicine, social sciences.

Creative arts/performance: art/fine arts, cinema/film/broadcasting, creative writing, journalism/publications, music, theater/drama. *Special achievements/activities:* cheerleading/drum major, general special achievements/activities, junior miss. *Special characteristics:* children of faculty/staff, general special characteristics, international students, out-of-state students, parents of current students, previous college experience, public servants, veterans, veterans' children. *Tuition waivers:* Full or partial for employees or children of employees, senior citizens. *ROTC:* Army cooperative.

LOANS *Student loans:* $39,580,407 (39% need-based, 61% non-need-based). 61% of past graduating class borrowed through all loan programs. *Average indebtedness per student:* $24,816. *Average need-based loan:* Freshmen: $2973. Undergraduates: $3601. *Parent loans:* $2,857,254 (100% non-need-based). *Programs:* Federal Direct (Subsidized and Unsubsidized Stafford, PLUS).

WORK-STUDY *Federal work-study:* jobs available. *State or other work-study/employment:* Total amount: $577,611 (20% need-based, 80% non-need-based). Part-time jobs available.

ATHLETIC AWARDS Total amount: $1,561,675 (100% non-need-based).

APPLYING FOR FINANCIAL AID *Required financial aid forms:* FAFSA, institution's own form. *Financial aid deadline (priority):* 11/15. *Notification date:* Continuous beginning 12/1. Students must reply within 2 weeks of notification.

CONTACT Niki Schwartz, Director of Student Aid, Arkansas Tech University, Brown Hall Suite 206, 105 West O Street, Russellville, AR 72801, 479-968-0399 or toll-free 800-582-6953. *Fax:* 479-964-0857. *E-mail:* fa.help@atu.edu.
Website: http://www.atu.edu/.

ARLINGTON BAPTIST UNIVERSITY
Arlington, TX

CONTACT Mr. David B. Clogston Jr., Business Manager, Arlington Baptist University, 3001 West Division Street, Arlington, TX 76012-3425, 817-461-8741 Ext. 110. *Fax:* 817-274-1138.
Website: http://www.abu.edu/.

ART ACADEMY OF CINCINNATI
Cincinnati, OH

ABOUT THE INSTITUTION Independent, coed. 11 undergraduate majors.

GIFT AID (NEED-BASED) *Scholarships, grants, and awards:* Federal Pell, FSEOG, state, private, college/university gift aid from institutional funds.

GIFT AID (NON-NEED-BASED) *Scholarships, grants, and awards by category: Creative arts/performance:* applied art and design, art/fine arts.

LOANS *Programs:* college/university, alternative loans.

WORK-STUDY *Federal work-study:* jobs available. *State or other work-study/employment:* Part-time jobs available.

APPLYING FOR FINANCIAL AID *Required financial aid form:* FAFSA.

CONTACT Ms. Dawn Reck, Director of Financial Aid, Art Academy of Cincinnati, 1212 Jackson Street, Cincinnati, OH 45202, 513-562-8773 or toll-free 800-323-5692. *Fax:* 513-562-8778. *E-mail:* financialaid@artacademy.edu.
Website: http://www.artacademy.edu/.

ARTCENTER COLLEGE OF DESIGN
Pasadena, CA

CONTACT Clema McKenzie, Director of Financial Aid, ArtCenter College of Design, 1700 Lida Street, Pasadena, CA 91103-1999, 626-396-2215. *Fax:* 626-683-8684.
Website: http://www.artcenter.edu/.

THE ART INSTITUTE OF ATLANTA
Atlanta, GA

CONTACT Financial Aid Office, The Art Institute of Atlanta, 6600 Peachtree Dunwoody Road, NE, 100 Embassy Row, Atlanta, GA 30328, 770-394-8300 or toll-free 800-275-4242.
Website: http://www.artinstitutes.edu/atlanta/.

THE ART INSTITUTE OF AUSTIN, A BRANCH OF THE ART INSTITUTE OF HOUSTON
Austin, TX

CONTACT Financial Aid Office, The Art Institute of Austin, a branch of The Art Institute of Houston, 101 W. Louis Henna Boulevard, Suite 100, Austin, TX 78728, 512-691-1707 or toll-free 866-583-7952.
Website: http://www.artinstitutes.edu/austin.

THE ART INSTITUTE OF CALIFORNIA–HOLLYWOOD, A CAMPUS OF ARGOSY UNIVERSITY
North Hollywood, CA

Financial Aid Office, The Art Institute of California–Hollywood, a campus of Argosy University, 5250 Lankershim Boulevard, North Hollywood, CA 91601, 818-299-5100 or toll-free 877-468-6232.

THE ART INSTITUTE OF CALIFORNIA–INLAND EMPIRE, A CAMPUS OF ARGOSY UNIVERSITY
San Bernardino, CA

CONTACT Financial Aid Office, The Art Institute of California–Inland Empire, a campus of Argosy University, 674 East Brier Drive, San Bernardino, CA 92408, 909-915-2100 or toll-free 800-353-0812.
Website: http://www.artinstitutes.edu/inlandempire/.

THE ART INSTITUTE OF CALIFORNIA–ORANGE COUNTY, A CAMPUS OF ARGOSY UNIVERSITY
Santa Ana, CA

CONTACT Financial Aid Office, The Art Institute of California–Orange County, a campus of Argosy University, 3601 West Sunflower Avenue, Santa Ana, CA 92704, 714-830-0200 or toll-free 888-549-3055.
Website: http://www.artinstitutes.edu/orangecounty/.

THE ART INSTITUTE OF CALIFORNIA–SACRAMENTO, A CAMPUS OF ARGOSY UNIVERSITY
Sacramento, CA

CONTACT Financial Aid Office, The Art Institute of California–Sacramento, a campus of Argosy University, 2850 Gateway Oaks Drive, Suite 100, Sacramento, CA 95833, 916-830-6320 or toll-free 800-477-1957.
Website: http://www.artinstitutes.edu/sacramento/.

THE ART INSTITUTE OF CALIFORNIA–SAN DIEGO, A CAMPUS OF ARGOSY UNIVERSITY
San Diego, CA

Financial Aid Office, The Art Institute of California–San Diego, a campus of Argosy University, 10025 Mesa Rim Road, San Diego, CA 92121, 619-546-0602 or toll-free 866-275-2422.

THE ART INSTITUTE OF CALIFORNIA–SAN FRANCISCO, A CAMPUS OF ARGOSY UNIVERSITY
San Francisco, CA

Financial Aid Office, The Art Institute of California–San Francisco, a campus of Argosy University, 1170 Market Street, San Francisco, CA 94102-4908, 415-865-0198 or toll-free 888-493-3261. Fax: 415-863-5831.

THE ART INSTITUTE OF CHARLESTON, A BRANCH OF THE ART INSTITUTE OF ATLANTA
Charleston, SC

CONTACT Financial Aid Office, The Art Institute of Charleston, a branch of The Art Institute of Atlanta, 24 North Market Street, Charleston, SC 29401, 843-727-3500 or toll-free 866-211-0107.
Website: http://www.artinstitutes.edu/charleston/.

THE ART INSTITUTE OF CHARLOTTE, A BRANCH OF MIAMI INTERNATIONAL UNIVERSITY OF ART & DESIGN
Charlotte, NC

CONTACT Financial Aid Office, The Art Institute of Charlotte, a branch of Miami International University of Art & Design, Three LakePointe Plaza, 2110 Water Ridge Parkway, Charlotte, NC 28217, 704-357-8020 or toll-free 800-872-4417.
Website: http://www.artinstitutes.edu/charlotte/.

THE ART INSTITUTE OF COLORADO
Denver, CO

CONTACT Financial Aid Office, The Art Institute of Colorado, 1200 Lincoln Street, Denver, CO 80203, 303-837-0825 or toll-free 800-275-2420.
Website: http://www.artinstitutes.edu/denver/.

THE ART INSTITUTE OF DALLAS, A BRANCH OF MIAMI INTERNATIONAL UNIVERSITY OF ART & DESIGN
Dallas, TX

CONTACT Financial Aid Office, The Art Institute of Dallas, a branch of Miami International University of Art & Design, 8080 Park Lane, Suite 100, Dallas, TX 75231-5993, 214-692-8080 or toll-free 800-275-4243.
Website: http://www.artinstitutes.edu/dallas/.

THE ART INSTITUTE OF FORT LAUDERDALE
Fort Lauderdale, FL

Financial Aid Office, The Art Institute of Fort Lauderdale, 1799 Southeast 17th Street Causeway, Fort Lauderdale, FL 33316-3000, 954-527-1799 or toll-free 800-275-7603.

THE ART INSTITUTE OF HOUSTON
Houston, TX

Financial Aid Office, The Art Institute of Houston, 4140 Southwest Freeway, Houston, TX 77027, 713-623-2040 or toll-free 800-275-4244.

THE ART INSTITUTE OF INDIANAPOLIS
Indianapolis, IN

CONTACT Financial Aid Office, The Art Institute of Indianapolis, 3500 Depauw Boulevard, Suite 1010, Indianapolis, IN 46268, 317-613-4800 or toll-free 866-441-9031.
Website: http://www.artinstitutes.edu/indianapolis/.

THE ART INSTITUTE OF LAS VEGAS
Henderson, NV

CONTACT Financial Aid Office, The Art Institute of Las Vegas, 2350 Corporate Circle Drive, Henderson, NV 89074, 702-369-9944 or toll-free 800-833-2678.
Website: http://www.artinstitutes.edu/lasvegas/.

THE ART INSTITUTE OF MICHIGAN
Novi, MI

CONTACT Financial Aid Office, The Art Institute of Michigan, 28125 Cabot Drive, Suite 120, Novi, MI 48377, 248-675-3800 or toll-free 800-479-0087.
Website: http://www.artinstitutes.edu/detroit/.

THE ART INSTITUTE OF PHILADELPHIA
Philadelphia, PA

Financial Aid Office, The Art Institute of Philadelphia, 1622 Chestnut Street, Philadelphia, PA 19103, 215-567-7080 or toll-free 800-275-2474.

THE ART INSTITUTE OF PHOENIX
Phoenix, AZ

CONTACT Financial Aid Office, The Art Institute of Phoenix, 2233 West Dunlap Avenue, Phoenix, AZ 85021-2859, 602-331-7500 or toll-free 800-474-2479. *Website:* http://www.artinstitutes.edu/phoenix/.

THE ART INSTITUTE OF PITTSBURGH
Pittsburgh, PA

Financial Aid Office, The Art Institute of Pittsburgh, 420 Boulevard of the Allies, Pittsburgh, PA 15219, 412-263-6600 or toll-free 800-275-2470.

THE ART INSTITUTE OF PORTLAND
Portland, OR

CONTACT Financial Aid Office, The Art Institute of Portland, 1122 NW Davis Street, Portland, OR 97209, 503-228-6528 or toll-free 888-228-6528. *Website:* http://www.artinstitutes.edu/portland/.

THE ART INSTITUTE OF RALEIGH-DURHAM, A BRANCH OF MIAMI INTERNATIONAL UNIVERSITY OF ART & DESIGN
Durham, NC

CONTACT Financial Aid Office, The Art Institute of Raleigh-Durham, a branch of Miami International University of Art & Design, 410 Blackwell Street, Suite 200, Durham, NC 27701, 919-317-3050 or toll-free 888-245-9593. *Website:* http://www.artinstitutes.edu/raleigh-durham.

THE ART INSTITUTE OF SAN ANTONIO, A BRANCH OF THE ART INSTITUTE OF HOUSTON
San Antonio, TX

CONTACT Financial Aid Office, The Art Institute of San Antonio, a branch of The Art Institute of Houston, 1000 IH-10 West, Suite 200, San Antonio, TX 78230, 210-338-7320 or toll-free 888-222-0040. *Website:* http://www.artinstitutes.edu/san-antonio/.

THE ART INSTITUTE OF SEATTLE
Seattle, WA

Financial Aid Office, The Art Institute of Seattle, 2323 Elliott Avenue, Seattle, WA 98121-1642, 206-448-6600 or toll-free 800-275-2471.

THE ART INSTITUTE OF TAMPA, A BRANCH OF MIAMI INTERNATIONAL UNIVERSITY OF ART & DESIGN
Tampa, FL

CONTACT Financial Aid Office, The Art Institute of Tampa, a branch of Miami International University of Art & Design, Parkside at Tampa Bay Park, 4401 North Himes Avenue, Suite 150, Tampa, FL 33614, 813-873-2112 or toll-free 866-703-3277. *Website:* http://www.artinstitutes.edu/tampa/.

THE ART INSTITUTE OF TENNESSEE–NASHVILLE, A BRANCH OF THE ART INSTITUTE OF ATLANTA
Nashville, TN

CONTACT Financial Aid Office, The Art Institute of Tennessee–Nashville, a branch of The Art Institute of Atlanta, 100 Centerview Drive, Suite 250, Nashville, TN 37214, 615-874-1067 or toll-free 866-747-5770. *Website:* http://www.artinstitutes.edu/nashville/.

THE ART INSTITUTE OF VIRGINIA BEACH, A BRANCH OF THE ART INSTITUTE OF ATLANTA
Virginia Beach, VA

CONTACT Financial Aid Office, The Art Institute of Virginia Beach, a branch of The Art Institute of Atlanta, Two Columbus Center, 4500 Main Street, Suite 100, Virginia Beach, VA 23462, 757-493-6700 or toll-free 877-437-4428. *Website:* http://www.artinstitutes.edu/virginia-beach/.

THE ART INSTITUTE OF WASHINGTON, A BRANCH OF THE ART INSTITUTE OF ATLANTA
Arlington, VA

Financial Aid Office, The Art Institute of Washington, a branch of The Art Institute of Atlanta, 1820 North Fort Myer Drive, Arlington, VA 22209, 703-247-6849 or toll-free 877-303-3771. *Fax:* 703-247-6829.

ASBURY UNIVERSITY
Wilmore, KY

ABOUT THE INSTITUTION Independent nondenominational, coed. *Awards:* associate, bachelor's, and master's degrees. 47 undergraduate majors. *Total enrollment:* 1,973. Undergraduates: 1,717. Freshmen: 318.

GIFT AID (NEED-BASED) *Scholarships, grants, and awards:* Federal Pell, FSEOG, state, private, college/university gift aid from institutional funds.

GIFT AID (NON-NEED-BASED) *Scholarships, grants, and awards by category: Academic interests/achievement:* business, general academic interests/achievements. *Creative arts/performance:* art/fine arts, music, theater/drama. *Special achievements/activities:* leadership. *Special characteristics:* children and siblings of alumni, children of faculty/staff, ethnic background, international students, out-of-state students, relatives of clergy, siblings of current students.

LOANS *Programs:* Federal Direct (Subsidized and Unsubsidized Stafford, PLUS), Perkins, college/university, private loans.

CONTACT Mr. Ronald Anderson, Director of Financial Aid, Asbury University, One Macklem Drive, Wilmore, KY 40390, 859-858-3511 Ext. 2195 or toll-free 800-888-1818. *Fax:* 859-858-9149. *E-mail:* ron.anderson@asbury.edu. *Website:* http://www.asbury.edu/.

ASHFORD UNIVERSITY
San Diego, CA

CONTACT Lisa Kramer, Director of Financial Aid, Ashford University, 400 North Bluff Boulevard, PO Box 2967, Clinton, IA 52733-2967, 563-242-4023 Ext. 1243 or toll-free 866-711-1700. *Fax:* 563-242-8684.
Website: http://www.ashford.edu/.

ASHLAND UNIVERSITY
Ashland, OH

CONTACT Mr. Stephen C. Howell, Director of Financial Aid, Ashland University, 401 College Avenue, Ashland, OH 44805-3702, 419-289-5944 or toll-free 800-882-1548. *Fax:* 419-289-5976. *E-mail:* showell@ashland.edu.
Website: http://www.ashland.edu/.

ASHWORTH COLLEGE
Norcross, GA

CONTACT Financial Aid Office, Ashworth College, 6625 The Corners Parkway, Suite 500, Norcross, GA 30092, 770-729-8400 or toll-free 800-957-5412.
Website: http://www.ashworthcollege.edu/.

ASPEN UNIVERSITY
Denver, CO

CONTACT Jennifer Quinn, Director of Financial Aid, Aspen University, 720 South Colorado Boulevard #1150N, Denver, CO 80246, 800-441-4746. *Fax:* 303-336-1144. *E-mail:* jquinn@aspen.edu.
Website: http://www.aspen.edu/.

ASSUMPTION COLLEGE
Worcester, MA

Tuition & fees: $40,958	Average undergraduate aid package: $27,681

ABOUT THE INSTITUTION Independent Roman Catholic, coed. *Awards:* certificates, bachelor's, and master's degrees. 29 undergraduate majors. *Total enrollment:* 2,334. Undergraduates: 1,940. Freshmen: 492. Federal methodology is used as a basis for awarding need-based institutional aid.
UNDERGRADUATE EXPENSES for 2018–2019 *Application fee:* $50. *Comprehensive fee:* $53,642 includes full-time tuition ($40,208), mandatory fees ($750), and room and board ($12,684). Full-time tuition and fees vary according to course load, reciprocity agreements, and student level. Room and board charges vary according to housing facility. *Part-time tuition:* $1183.67 per credit hour. Part-time tuition and fees vary according to course load.
FRESHMAN FINANCIAL AID (Fall 2017, est.) 460 applied for aid; of those 88% were deemed to have need. 100% of freshmen with need received aid; of those 25% had need fully met. *Average percent of need met:* 73% (excluding resources awarded to replace EFC). *Average financial aid package:* $28,121 (excluding resources awarded to replace EFC). 15% of all full-time freshmen had no need and received non-need-based gift aid.
UNDERGRADUATE FINANCIAL AID (Fall 2017, est.) 1,606 applied for aid; of those 90% were deemed to have need. 100% of undergraduates with need received

aid; of those 28% had need fully met. *Average percent of need met:* 76% (excluding resources awarded to replace EFC). *Average financial aid package:* $27,681 (excluding resources awarded to replace EFC). 22% of all full-time undergraduates had no need and received non-need-based gift aid.
GIFT AID (NEED-BASED) *Total amount:* $29,959,687 (7% federal, 2% state, 90% institutional, 1% external sources). *Receiving aid:* Freshmen: 82% (405); all full-time undergraduates: 75% (1,438). *Average award:* Freshmen: $23,496; Undergraduates: $22,325. *Scholarships, grants, and awards:* Federal Pell, FSEOG, state, private, college/university gift aid from institutional funds.
GIFT AID (NON-NEED-BASED) *Total amount:* $7,994,436 (99% institutional, 1% external sources). *Receiving aid:* Freshmen: 13% (65). Undergraduates: 12% (229). *Average award:* Freshmen: $16,891. Undergraduates: $15,806. *Scholarships, grants, and awards by category: Academic interests/achievement:* 1,542 awards ($23,648,057 total): general academic interests/achievements. *Creative arts/performance:* 23 awards ($176,010 total): music. *Special characteristics:* members of minority groups. *Tuition waivers:* Full or partial for employees or children of employees. *ROTC:* Army cooperative, Air Force cooperative.
LOANS *Student loans:* $14,635,684 (59% need-based, 41% non-need-based). *Average need-based loan:* Freshmen: $3448. Undergraduates: $4561. *Parent loans:* $6,433,586 (43% need-based, 57% non-need-based). *Programs:* Federal Direct (Subsidized and Unsubsidized Stafford, PLUS), Perkins, state, college/university.
WORK-STUDY *Federal work-study:* Total amount: $753,483; 456 jobs averaging $1652.
ATHLETIC AWARDS Total amount: $2,529,233 (48% need-based, 52% non-need-based).
APPLYING FOR FINANCIAL AID *Required financial aid form:* FAFSA. *Financial aid deadline:* 2/15. *Notification date:* Continuous beginning 2/16. Students must reply by 5/1.
CONTACT Lori A. Moore, Director of Financial Aid, Assumption College, 500 Salisbury Street, Worcester, MA 01609-1296, 508-767-7157 or toll-free 866-477-7776. *Fax:* 508-767-7376. *E-mail:* fa@assumption.edu.
Website: http://www.assumption.edu/.

ATENAS COLLEGE
Manati, PR

CONTACT Financial Aid Office, Atenas College, Paseo de La Atenas #101 Altos, Manati, PR 00674, 787-884-3838.
Website: http://www.atenascollege.edu/.

ATHENS STATE UNIVERSITY
Athens, AL

Tuition & fees (AL res): $6690	Average undergraduate aid package: $10,201

ABOUT THE INSTITUTION State-supported, coed. *Awards:* certificates, bachelor's, and master's degrees. 35 undergraduate majors. *Total enrollment:* 3,001. Undergraduates: 2,969. Federal methodology is used as a basis for awarding need-based institutional aid.
UNDERGRADUATE EXPENSES for 2017–2018 *Application fee:* $30. *Tuition, state resident:* full-time $5940. *Tuition, nonresident:* full-time $11,880. *Required fees:* full-time $750.
UNDERGRADUATE FINANCIAL AID (Fall 2016) 1,003 applied for aid; of those 91% were deemed to have need. 99% of undergraduates with need received aid; of those 3% had need fully met. *Average percent of need met:* 47% (excluding resources awarded to replace EFC). *Average financial aid package:* $10,201 (excluding resources awarded to replace EFC). 1% of all full-time undergraduates had no need and received non-need-based gift aid.
GIFT AID (NEED-BASED) *Total amount:* $5,269,094 (97% federal, 2% institutional, 1% external sources). *Receiving aid:* All full-time undergraduates: 48% (583). *Average award:* Undergraduates: $4110. *Scholarships, grants, and awards:* Federal Pell, FSEOG, state, private, college/university gift aid from institutional funds.
GIFT AID (NON-NEED-BASED) *Total amount:* $527,520 (16% federal, 84% institutional). *Receiving aid:* Undergraduates: 8% (97). *Average award:* Under-

graduates: $2603. *Tuition waivers:* Full or partial for employees or children of employees, senior citizens.

LOANS *Student loans:* $14,734,614 (44% need-based, 56% non-need-based). *Average need-based loan:* Undergraduates: $3326. *Programs:* Federal Direct (Subsidized and Unsubsidized Stafford, PLUS), college/university.

WORK-STUDY *Federal work-study:* jobs available.

APPLYING FOR FINANCIAL AID *Required financial aid form:* FAFSA. *Financial aid deadline:* Continuous. *Notification date:* Continuous beginning 5/1. Students must reply within 2 weeks of notification.

CONTACT Wayne Bodiford, Interim Financial Aid Director, Athens State University, 300 North Beaty Street, Athens, AL 35611, 256-233-8161 or toll-free 800-522-0272. *Fax:* 256-233-8161. *E-mail:* finaid@athens.edu. *Website:* http://www.athens.edu/.

ATLANTIC UNIVERSITY COLLEGE
Guaynabo, PR

CONTACT Mrs. Velma Aponte, Financial Aid Coordinator, Atlantic University College, Calle Colton #9, Guaynabo, PR 00970, 787-720-1092. *E-mail:* atlaneco@coqui.net. *Website:* http://www.atlanticu.edu/.

ATLANTIS UNIVERSITY
Miami, FL

CONTACT Financial Aid Office, Atlantis University, 1442 Biscayne Boulevard, Miami, FL 33132. *Website:* http://www.atlantisuniversity.edu/.

AUBURN UNIVERSITY
Auburn University, AL

Tuition & fees (AL res): $10,968	Average undergraduate aid package: $10,829

ABOUT THE INSTITUTION State-supported, coed. *Awards:* certificates, bachelor's, master's, and doctoral degrees. 149 undergraduate majors. *Total enrollment:* 29,776. Undergraduates: 23,964. Freshmen: 4,836. Federal methodology is used as a basis for awarding need-based institutional aid.

UNDERGRADUATE EXPENSES for 2017–2018 *Application fee:* $50. *Tuition, state resident:* full-time $9336; part-time $389 per semester hour. *Tuition, nonresident:* full-time $28,008; part-time $1167 per semester hour. *Required fees:* full-time $1632; $816 per term. Full-time tuition and fees vary according to program and reciprocity agreements. Part-time tuition and fees vary according to course load, program, and reciprocity agreements. *College room and board:* $13,332; *Room only:* $7860. Room and board charges vary according to board plan and housing facility.

FRESHMAN FINANCIAL AID (Fall 2016) 2,916 applied for aid; of those 59% were deemed to have need. 100% of freshmen with need received aid; of those 18% had need fully met. *Average percent of need met:* 52% (excluding resources awarded to replace EFC). *Average financial aid package:* $11,644 (excluding resources awarded to replace EFC). 30% of all full-time freshmen had no need and received non-need-based gift aid.

UNDERGRADUATE FINANCIAL AID (Fall 2016) 13,335 applied for aid; of those 54% were deemed to have need. 100% of undergraduates with need received aid; of those 13% had need fully met. *Average percent of need met:* 45% (excluding resources awarded to replace EFC). *Average financial aid package:* $10,829 (excluding resources awarded to replace EFC). 22% of all full-time undergraduates had no need and received non-need-based gift aid.

GIFT AID (NEED-BASED) *Total amount:* $43,244,237 (35% federal, 5% state, 50% institutional, 10% external sources). *Receiving aid:* Freshmen: 32% (1,469); all full-time undergraduates: 26% (5,326). *Average award:* Freshmen: $8751; Undergraduates: $7847. *Scholarships, grants, and awards:* Federal Pell, FSEOG, state, private, college/university gift aid from institutional funds.

GIFT AID (NON-NEED-BASED) *Total amount:* $59,328,032 (12% state, 65% institutional, 23% external sources). *Receiving aid:* Freshmen: 5% (242). Undergraduates: 3% (649). *Average award:* Freshmen: $7453. Undergraduates: $7249. *Scholarships, grants, and awards by category:* Academic interests/achievement: agriculture, architecture, biological sciences, business, communication, computer science, education, engineering/technologies, English, foreign languages, general academic interests/achievements, health fields, home economics, humanities, mathematics, physical sciences, premedicine, social sciences. *Creative arts/performance:* applied art and design, art/fine arts, cinema/film/broadcasting, creative writing, journalism/publications, music, performing arts, theater/drama. *Special achievements/activities:* cheerleading/drum major, leadership, memberships. *Special characteristics:* children and siblings of alumni, children of faculty/staff, children of union members/company employees, ethnic background, local/state students, married students, out-of-state students. *Tuition waivers:* Full or partial for employees or children of employees. *ROTC:* Army, Naval, Air Force.

LOANS *Student loans:* $73,515,712 (68% need-based, 32% non-need-based). 40% of past graduating class borrowed through all loan programs. *Average indebtedness per student:* $29,295. *Average need-based loan:* Freshmen: $3778. Undergraduates: $4529. *Parent loans:* $38,691,864 (55% need-based, 45% non-need-based). *Programs:* Federal Direct (Subsidized and Unsubsidized Stafford, PLUS), Perkins, Federal Nursing, college/university.

WORK-STUDY *Federal work-study:* 175 jobs averaging $4202.

ATHLETIC AWARDS Total amount: $13,619,988 (3% need-based, 97% non-need-based).

APPLYING FOR FINANCIAL AID *Required financial aid form:* FAFSA. *Financial aid deadline (priority):* 2/1. *Notification date:* Continuous beginning 10/2. Students must reply by 5/1.

CONTACT Mr. Mike Reynolds, Director of Student Financial Services, Auburn University, 203 Mary Martin Hall, Auburn University, AL 36849, 334-844-4634 or toll-free 800-AUBURN9. *Fax:* 334-844-6085. *E-mail:* finaid7@auburn.edu. *Website:* http://www.auburn.edu/.

AUBURN UNIVERSITY AT MONTGOMERY
Montgomery, AL

Tuition & fees (AL res): $8236	Average undergraduate aid package: $8263

ABOUT THE INSTITUTION State-supported, coed. *Awards:* certificates, bachelor's, master's, and doctoral degrees. 36 undergraduate majors. *Total enrollment:* 4,894. Undergraduates: 4,313. Freshmen: 673. Federal methodology is used as a basis for awarding need-based institutional aid.

UNDERGRADUATE EXPENSES for 2018–2019 *One-time required fee:* $125. *Tuition, state resident:* full-time $7536; part-time $314 per credit hour. *Tuition, nonresident:* full-time $16,994; part-time $706 per credit hour. *Required fees:* full-time $700. Full-time tuition and fees vary according to course load and degree level. Part-time tuition and fees vary according to course load and degree level. *College room and board:* $6980; *Room only:* $4580. Room and board charges vary according to housing facility.

FRESHMAN FINANCIAL AID (Fall 2016) 463 applied for aid; of those 87% were deemed to have need. 99% of freshmen with need received aid; of those 9% had need fully met. *Average percent of need met:* 56% (excluding resources awarded to replace EFC). *Average financial aid package:* $8229 (excluding resources awarded to replace EFC). 12% of all full-time freshmen had no need and received non-need-based gift aid.

UNDERGRADUATE FINANCIAL AID (Fall 2016) 2,369 applied for aid; of those 88% were deemed to have need. 99% of undergraduates with need received aid; of those 9% had need fully met. *Average percent of need met:* 58% (excluding resources awarded to replace EFC). *Average financial aid package:* $8263 (excluding resources awarded to replace EFC). 10% of all full-time undergraduates had no need and received non-need-based gift aid.

GIFT AID (NEED-BASED) *Total amount:* $10,168,769 (83% federal, 1% state, 12% institutional, 4% external sources). *Receiving aid:* Freshmen: 54% (300); all full-time undergraduates: 50% (1,548). *Average award:* Freshmen: $4639; Undergraduates: $4672. *Scholarships, grants, and awards:* Federal Pell, FSEOG, state, private, college/university gift aid from institutional funds.

GIFT AID (NON-NEED-BASED) *Total amount:* $1,850,872 (84% institutional, 16% external sources). *Receiving aid:* Freshmen: 33% (183). Undergraduates: 20% (606). *Average award:* Freshmen: $3911. Undergraduates: $3798. *Scholarships, grants, and awards by category: Academic interests/achievement:* business, education, general academic interests/achievements, military science. *Special achievements/activities:* leadership. *Special characteristics:* international students. *Tuition waivers:* Full or partial for employees or children of employees, senior citizens. *ROTC:* Army, Air Force cooperative.

LOANS *Student loans:* $17,097,516 (90% need-based, 10% non-need-based). 69% of past graduating class borrowed through all loan programs. *Average indebtedness per student:* $27,007. *Average need-based loan:* Freshmen: $2778. Undergraduates: $3463. *Parent loans:* $2,373,117 (73% need-based, 27% non-need-based). *Programs:* Federal Direct (Subsidized and Unsubsidized Stafford, PLUS), Perkins.

WORK-STUDY *Federal work-study:* 52 jobs averaging $3798.

ATHLETIC AWARDS Total amount: $2,028,628 (28% need-based, 72% non-need-based).

APPLYING FOR FINANCIAL AID *Required financial aid form:* FAFSA. *Financial aid deadline (priority):* 3/1. *Notification date:* Continuous beginning 4/15.

CONTACT Mr. Anthony Richey, Senior Director of Financial Aid, Auburn University at Montgomery, PO Box 244023, Montgomery, AL 36124-4023, 334-244-3571 or toll-free 800-227-2649. *Fax:* 334-244-3913. *E-mail:* aumfinancialaidoffice@aum.edu. *Website:* http://www.aum.edu/.

AUGSBURG UNIVERSITY
Minneapolis, MN

Tuition & fees: $38,800	Average undergraduate aid package: $29,946

ABOUT THE INSTITUTION Independent Lutheran, coed. *Awards:* certificates, bachelor's, master's, and doctoral degrees. 70 undergraduate majors. *Total enrollment:* 3,562. Undergraduates: 2,427. Freshmen: 436. Federal methodology is used as a basis for awarding need-based institutional aid.

UNDERGRADUATE EXPENSES for 2018–2019 *Comprehensive fee:* $49,080 includes full-time tuition ($38,150), mandatory fees ($650), and room and board ($10,280). *College room only:* $5350. Full-time tuition and fees vary according to class time and location. Room and board charges vary according to board plan and housing facility. *Part-time tuition:* $1192 per credit hour. Part-time tuition and fees vary according to class time and location.

FRESHMAN FINANCIAL AID (Fall 2016) 427 applied for aid; of those 92% were deemed to have need. 99% of freshmen with need received aid; of those 13% had need fully met. *Average percent of need met:* 80% (excluding resources awarded to replace EFC). *Average financial aid package:* $32,783 (excluding resources awarded to replace EFC). 17% of all full-time freshmen had no need and received non-need-based gift aid.

UNDERGRADUATE FINANCIAL AID (Fall 2016) 1,780 applied for aid; of those 92% were deemed to have need. 100% of undergraduates with need received aid; of those 12% had need fully met. *Average percent of need met:* 73% (excluding resources awarded to replace EFC). *Average financial aid package:* $29,946 (excluding resources awarded to replace EFC). 18% of all full-time undergraduates had no need and received non-need-based gift aid.

GIFT AID (NEED-BASED) *Total amount:* $39,744,544 (13% federal, 13% state, 67% institutional, 7% external sources). *Receiving aid:* Freshmen: 83% (392); all full-time undergraduates: 79% (1,621). *Average award:* Freshmen: $27,299; Undergraduates: $24,083. *Scholarships, grants, and awards:* Federal Pell, FSEOG, state, private, college/university gift aid from institutional funds, Federal Nursing.

GIFT AID (NON-NEED-BASED) *Total amount:* $8,017,234 (1% federal, 4% state, 84% institutional, 11% external sources). *Receiving aid:* Freshmen: 8% (37). Undergraduates: 7% (139). *Average award:* Freshmen: $17,787. Undergraduates: $15,419. *Scholarships, grants, and awards by category: Academic interests/achievement:* biological sciences, business, communication, computer science, education, English, foreign languages, general academic interests/achievements, health fields, international studies, mathematics, physical sciences, religion/biblical studies, social sciences. *Creative arts/performance:* art/fine arts, music, performing arts, theater/drama. *Special achievements/activities:* community service, general special achievements/activities, junior miss, leadership, religious involvement. *Special characteristics:* children and siblings of alumni, international students, members of minority

groups, relatives of clergy, siblings of current students. *Tuition waivers:* Full or partial for employees or children of employees. *ROTC:* Army cooperative, Naval cooperative, Air Force cooperative.

LOANS *Student loans:* $19,075,998 (77% need-based, 23% non-need-based). 92% of past graduating class borrowed through all loan programs. *Average indebtedness per student:* $38,176. *Average need-based loan:* Freshmen: $4321. Undergraduates: $4905. *Parent loans:* $3,654,818 (53% need-based, 47% non-need-based). *Programs:* Federal Direct (Subsidized and Unsubsidized Stafford, PLUS), Perkins, Federal Nursing, state.

WORK-STUDY *Federal work-study:* jobs available. *State or other work-study/employment:* Total amount: $2,641,309 (94% need-based, 6% non-need-based). Part-time jobs available.

APPLYING FOR FINANCIAL AID *Required financial aid form:* FAFSA. *Financial aid deadline:* 8/1 (priority: 3/15). *Notification date:* Continuous beginning 3/1. Students must reply within 3 weeks of notification.

CONTACT Mr. Paul L. Terrio, Director of Student Financial Services, Augsburg University, 2211 Riverside Avenue, Minneapolis, MN 55454-1351, 612-330-1049 or toll-free 800-788-5678. *Fax:* 612-330-1308. *E-mail:* terriop@augsburg.edu. *Website:* http://www.augsburg.edu/.

AUGUSTANA COLLEGE
Rock Island, IL

Tuition & fees: $42,135	Average undergraduate aid package: $30,840

ABOUT THE INSTITUTION Independent Evangelical Lutheran Church in America, coed. *Awards:* bachelor's degrees. 61 undergraduate majors. *Total enrollment:* 2,647. Undergraduates: 2,647. Freshmen: 735. Federal methodology is used as a basis for awarding need-based institutional aid.

UNDERGRADUATE EXPENSES for 2018–2019 *Comprehensive fee:* $52,707 includes full-time tuition ($42,135) and room and board ($10,572). *College room only:* $5079. Room and board charges vary according to board plan and housing facility. *Part-time tuition:* $1808 per credit. Part-time tuition and fees vary according to course load. *Payment plan:* Tuition prepayment.

FRESHMAN FINANCIAL AID (Fall 2016) 634 applied for aid; of those 85% were deemed to have need. 100% of freshmen with need received aid; of those 25% had need fully met. *Average percent of need met:* 87% (excluding resources awarded to replace EFC). *Average financial aid package:* $32,193 (excluding resources awarded to replace EFC). 23% of all full-time freshmen had no need and received non-need-based gift aid.

UNDERGRADUATE FINANCIAL AID (Fall 2016) 2,265 applied for aid; of those 85% were deemed to have need. 100% of undergraduates with need received aid; of those 22% had need fully met. *Average percent of need met:* 86% (excluding resources awarded to replace EFC). *Average financial aid package:* $30,840 (excluding resources awarded to replace EFC). 23% of all full-time undergraduates had no need and received non-need-based gift aid.

GIFT AID (NEED-BASED) *Total amount:* $47,092,201 (6% federal, 7% state, 86% institutional, 1% external sources). *Receiving aid:* Freshmen: 77% (534); all full-time undergraduates: 76% (1,898). *Average award:* Freshmen: $26,317; Undergraduates: $24,787. *Scholarships, grants, and awards:* Federal Pell, FSEOG, state, private, college/university gift aid from institutional funds.

GIFT AID (NON-NEED-BASED) *Total amount:* $15,280,628 (99% institutional, 1% external sources). *Receiving aid:* Freshmen: 15% (102). Undergraduates: 13% (320). *Average award:* Freshmen: $23,237. Undergraduates: $21,096. *Scholarships, grants, and awards by category: Academic interests/achievement:* 2,316 awards ($36,458,889 total): area/ethnic studies, biological sciences, business, communication, computer science, education, English, foreign languages, general academic interests/achievements, humanities, mathematics, physical sciences, religion/biblical studies, social sciences. *Creative arts/performance:* 378 awards ($1,043,178 total): art/fine arts, creative writing, music, theater/drama. *Special achievements/activities:* 49 awards ($67,824 total): leadership, religious involvement. *Special characteristics:* 751 awards ($7,542,231 total): children and siblings of alumni, children of faculty/staff, ethnic background, first-generation college students, international students, members of minority groups, out-of-state students, religious affiliation, siblings of current students. *Tuition waivers:* Full or partial for employees or children of employees.

LOANS *Student loans:* $16,111,476 (68% need-based, 32% non-need-based). 73% of past graduating class borrowed through all loan programs. *Average indebtedness*

per student: $34,964. **Average need-based loan:** Freshmen: $3888. Undergraduates: $4825. **Parent loans:** $6,251,290 (33% need-based, 67% non-need-based). **Programs:** Federal Direct (Subsidized and Unsubsidized Stafford, PLUS), Perkins.
WORK-STUDY *Federal work-study:* 1,313 jobs averaging $2339.
APPLYING FOR FINANCIAL AID *Required financial aid forms:* FAFSA, Institution's own form. *Financial aid deadline (priority):* 11/1. *Notification date:* Continuous beginning 12/15. Students must reply by 5/1.
CONTACT Ms. Sue Standley, Director of Financial Aid, Augustana College, 639 38th Street, Rock Island, IL 61201-2296, 309-794-7207 Ext. 7447 or toll-free 800-798-8100. *Fax:* 309-794-7174. *E-mail:* suestandley@augustana.edu.
Website: http://www.augustana.edu/.

AUGUSTANA UNIVERSITY
Sioux Falls, SD

Tuition & fees: $33,018	Average undergraduate aid package: $26,851

ABOUT THE INSTITUTION Independent Evangelical Lutheran Church in America, coed. *Awards:* bachelor's and master's degrees. 64 undergraduate majors. *Total enrollment:* 2,080. Undergraduates: 1,749. Freshmen: 481. Federal methodology is used as a basis for awarding need-based institutional aid.
UNDERGRADUATE EXPENSES for 2018–2019 *Comprehensive fee:* $41,266 includes full-time tuition ($32,488), mandatory fees ($530), and room and board ($8248). *College room only:* $3778. Full-time tuition and fees vary according to course load and degree level. Room and board charges vary according to board plan and housing facility. Part-time tuition and fees vary according to course load and degree level.
FRESHMAN FINANCIAL AID (Fall 2017, est.) 398 applied for aid; of those 87% were deemed to have need. 100% of freshmen with need received aid; of those 20% had need fully met. *Average percent of need met:* 89% (excluding resources awarded to replace EFC). *Average financial aid package:* $27,792 (excluding resources awarded to replace EFC). 27% of all full-time freshmen had no need and received non-need-based gift aid.
UNDERGRADUATE FINANCIAL AID (Fall 2017, est.) 1,237 applied for aid; of those 87% were deemed to have need. 100% of undergraduates with need received aid; of those 15% had need fully met. *Average percent of need met:* 86% (excluding resources awarded to replace EFC). *Average financial aid package:* $26,851 (excluding resources awarded to replace EFC). 35% of all full-time undergraduates had no need and received non-need-based gift aid.
GIFT AID (NEED-BASED) *Total amount:* $19,458,739 (10% federal, 85% institutional, 5% external sources). *Receiving aid:* Freshmen: 72% (348); all full-time undergraduates: 62% (1,048). *Average award:* Freshmen: $24,784; Undergraduates: $22,965. *Scholarships, grants, and awards:* Federal Pell, FSEOG, state, private, college/university gift aid from institutional funds, need-linked special talent scholarships, minority scholarships.
GIFT AID (NON-NEED-BASED) *Total amount:* $10,595,699 (1% federal, 97% institutional, 2% external sources). *Receiving aid:* Freshmen: 72% (344). Undergraduates: 61% (1,028). *Average award:* Freshmen: $18,116. Undergraduates: $16,217. *Scholarships, grants, and awards by category: Academic interests/achievement:* biological sciences, business, communication, computer science, education, English, foreign languages, general academic interests/achievements, health fields, home economics, humanities, international studies, mathematics, physical sciences, premedicine, religion/biblical studies, social sciences. *Creative arts/performance:* art/fine arts, creative writing, dance, journalism/publications, music, performing arts, theater/drama. *Special achievements/activities:* cheerleading/drum major, community service, general special achievements/activities, leadership, religious involvement. *Special characteristics:* adult students, children and siblings of alumni, children of current students, children of faculty/staff, ethnic background, international students, local/state students, members of minority groups, religious affiliation, siblings of current students, spouses of current students, veterans. *Tuition waivers:* Full or partial for employees or children of employees. *ROTC:* Army cooperative, Air Force cooperative.
LOANS *Student loans:* $9,801,343 (63% need-based, 37% non-need-based). 64% of past graduating class borrowed through all loan programs. *Average indebtedness per student:* $36,950. *Average need-based loan:* Freshmen: $3479. Undergraduates: $5158. *Parent loans:* $837,725 (29% need-based, 71% non-need-based). *Pro-*

grams: Federal Direct (Subsidized and Unsubsidized Stafford, PLUS), Perkins, Federal Nursing, college/university, private loans.
WORK-STUDY *Federal work-study:* Total amount: $710,580; 372 jobs averaging $1850. *State or other work-study/employment:* Total amount: $96,530 (5% need-based, 95% non-need-based). 107 part-time jobs averaging $940.
ATHLETIC AWARDS Total amount: $4,060,235 (37% need-based, 63% non-need-based).
APPLYING FOR FINANCIAL AID *Required financial aid form:* FAFSA. *Financial aid deadline (priority):* 3/1. *Notification date:* Continuous beginning 4/1. Students must reply by 5/1 or within 4 weeks of notification.
CONTACT Ms. Tresse J. Evenson, Director of Financial Aid, Augustana University, 2001 South Summit Avenue, Sioux Falls, SD 57197, 605-274-5216 or toll-free 800-727-2844. *Fax:* 605-274-5295. *E-mail:* tresse.evenson@augie.edu.
Website: http://www.augie.edu/.

AUGUSTA UNIVERSITY
Augusta, GA

ABOUT THE INSTITUTION State-supported, coed. *Awards:* certificates, associate, bachelor's, master's, and doctoral degrees. 40 undergraduate majors. *Total enrollment:* 7,938. Undergraduates: 5,133. Freshmen: 788.
GIFT AID (NEED-BASED) *Scholarships, grants, and awards:* Federal Pell, FSEOG, state, private, college/university gift aid from institutional funds, Federal Nursing.
GIFT AID (NON-NEED-BASED) *Scholarships, grants, and awards by category: Academic interests/achievement:* business, computer science, education, general academic interests/achievements, mathematics. *Creative arts/performance:* art/fine arts, music. *Special achievements/activities:* leadership. *Special characteristics:* local/state students, members of minority groups, religious affiliation, veterans.
LOANS *Programs:* Federal Direct (Subsidized and Unsubsidized Stafford, PLUS), Perkins, Federal Nursing, state, college/university.
WORK-STUDY *Federal work-study:* 169 jobs averaging $2931.
APPLYING FOR FINANCIAL AID *Required financial aid form:* FAFSA.
CONTACT Victoria Saraceno, Interim Director of Financial Aid, Augusta University, 1120 Fifteenth Street, Fanning Hall, Augusta, GA 30912-7320, 706-667-4199 or toll-free 800-519-3388. *Fax:* 706-737-1777. *E-mail:* vsaraceno@augusta.edu.
Website: http://www.augusta.edu/.

AULTMAN COLLEGE OF NURSING AND HEALTH SCIENCES
Canton, OH

CONTACT Financial Aid Office, Aultman College of Nursing and Health Sciences, 2600 6th Street, SW, Canton, OH 44710, 330-363-6347.
Website: http://www.aultmancollege.edu/.

AURORA UNIVERSITY
Aurora, IL

Tuition & fees: $24,260	Average undergraduate aid package: $20,674

ABOUT THE INSTITUTION Independent, coed. *Awards:* certificates, bachelor's, master's, and doctoral degrees. 42 undergraduate majors. *Total enrollment:* 5,833. Undergraduates: 3,933. Freshmen: 801. Federal methodology is used as a basis for awarding need-based institutional aid.
UNDERGRADUATE EXPENSES for 2018–2019 *Comprehensive fee:* $35,960 includes full-time tuition ($24,000), mandatory fees ($260), and room and board ($11,700). Full-time tuition and fees vary according to course load, location, and program. Room and board charges vary according to board plan, housing facility, and location. *Part-time tuition:* $690 per semester hour. Part-time tuition and fees vary according to course load, location, and program.

FRESHMAN FINANCIAL AID (Fall 2017, est.) 732 applied for aid; of those 91% were deemed to have need. 100% of freshmen with need received aid; of those 9% had need fully met. *Average percent of need met:* 80% (excluding resources awarded to replace EFC). *Average financial aid package:* $22,277 (excluding resources awarded to replace EFC). 16% of all full-time freshmen had no need and received non-need-based gift aid.

UNDERGRADUATE FINANCIAL AID (Fall 2017, est.) 2,989 applied for aid; of those 93% were deemed to have need. 100% of undergraduates with need received aid; of those 9% had need fully met. *Average percent of need met:* 78% (excluding resources awarded to replace EFC). *Average financial aid package:* $20,674 (excluding resources awarded to replace EFC). 17% of all full-time undergraduates had no need and received non-need-based gift aid.

GIFT AID (NEED-BASED) *Total amount:* $39,148,068 (21% federal, 18% state, 60% institutional, 1% external sources). *Receiving aid:* Freshmen: 80% (643); all full-time undergraduates: 74% (2,568). *Average award:* Freshmen: $17,908; Undergraduates: $14,929. *Scholarships, grants, and awards:* Federal Pell, FSEOG, state, private, college/university gift aid from institutional funds.

GIFT AID (NON-NEED-BASED) *Total amount:* $9,250,110 (1% federal, 1% state, 96% institutional, 2% external sources). *Receiving aid:* Freshmen: 12% (95). Undergraduates: 12% (430). *Average award:* Freshmen: $12,464. Undergraduates: $10,241. *Scholarships, grants, and awards by category: Academic interests/achievement:* 3,057 awards ($29,105,265 total): business, education, general academic interests/achievements. *Creative arts/performance:* 41 awards ($86,500 total): art/fine arts, music, theater/drama. *Special achievements/activities:* 1 award ($2000 total): leadership. *Special characteristics:* 784 awards ($1,277,889 total): children and siblings of alumni, children of current students, children of faculty/staff, general special characteristics, local/state students, out-of-state students, parents of current students, religious affiliation, siblings of current students, spouses of current students, veterans, veterans' children. *Tuition waivers:* Full or partial for children of alumni, employees or children of employees. *ROTC:* Army cooperative.

LOANS *Student loans:* $21,087,366 (75% need-based, 25% non-need-based). 79% of past graduating class borrowed through all loan programs. *Average indebtedness per student:* $27,117. *Average need-based loan:* Freshmen: $2503. Undergraduates: $3521. *Parent loans:* $3,930,166 (27% need-based, 73% non-need-based). *Programs:* Federal Direct (Subsidized and Unsubsidized Stafford, PLUS), private loans.

WORK-STUDY *Federal work-study:* Total amount: $3,869,873; 2,030 jobs averaging $1906. *State or other work-study/employment:* Total amount: $318,260 (47% need-based, 53% non-need-based). 33 part-time jobs averaging $9644.

APPLYING FOR FINANCIAL AID *Required financial aid form:* FAFSA. *Financial aid deadline:* Continuous. *Notification date:* Continuous beginning 11/15. Students must reply by 5/1.

CONTACT Ms. Heather Granart, Dean of Student Financial Services, Aurora University, 347 South Gladstone Avenue, Aurora, IL 60506-4892, 630-844-6190 or toll-free 800-742-5281. *Fax:* 630-844-6191. *E-mail:* finaid@aurora.edu. *Website:* http://www.aurora.edu/.

AUSTIN COLLEGE
Sherman, TX

Tuition & fees: $39,010	Average undergraduate aid package: $34,957

ABOUT THE INSTITUTION Independent Presbyterian, coed. *Awards:* bachelor's and master's degrees. 55 undergraduate majors. *Total enrollment:* 1,237. Undergraduates: 1,223. Freshmen: 332. Federal methodology is used as a basis for awarding need-based institutional aid.

UNDERGRADUATE EXPENSES for 2017–2018 *One-time required fee:* $25. *Comprehensive fee:* $51,344 includes full-time tuition ($38,825), mandatory fees ($185), and room and board ($12,334). *College room only:* $5750. Full-time tuition and fees vary according to student level. Room and board charges vary according to board plan and housing facility. *Part-time tuition:* $5495 per course. *Part-time fees:* $92.50 per term.

FRESHMAN FINANCIAL AID (Fall 2017, est.) 292 applied for aid; of those 85% were deemed to have need. 100% of freshmen with need received aid; of those 22% had need fully met. *Average percent of need met:* 87% (excluding resources awarded to replace EFC). *Average financial aid package:* $35,402 (excluding resources awarded to replace EFC). 25% of all full-time freshmen had no need and received non-need-based gift aid.

UNDERGRADUATE FINANCIAL AID (Fall 2017, est.) 944 applied for aid; of those 87% were deemed to have need. 100% of undergraduates with need received aid; of those 23% had need fully met. *Average percent of need met:* 86% (excluding resources awarded to replace EFC). *Average financial aid package:* $34,957 (excluding resources awarded to replace EFC). 31% of all full-time undergraduates had no need and received non-need-based gift aid.

GIFT AID (NEED-BASED) *Total amount:* $25,703,184 (9% federal, 5% state, 85% institutional, 1% external sources). *Receiving aid:* Freshmen: 75% (248); all full-time undergraduates: 67% (823). *Average award:* Freshmen: $32,493; Undergraduates: $31,269. *Scholarships, grants, and awards:* Federal Pell, FSEOG, state, private, college/university gift aid from institutional funds.

GIFT AID (NON-NEED-BASED) *Total amount:* $10,406,834 (99% institutional, 1% external sources). *Receiving aid:* Freshmen: 12% (41). Undergraduates: 10% (126). *Average award:* Freshmen: $24,114. Undergraduates: $22,504. *Scholarships, grants, and awards by category: Academic interests/achievement:* biological sciences, business, communication, computer science, education, engineering/technologies, English, foreign languages, general academic interests/achievements, home economics, humanities, international studies, mathematics, physical sciences, premedicine, religion/biblical studies, social sciences. *Creative arts/performance:* art/fine arts, music, theater/drama. *Special achievements/activities:* community service, general special achievements/activities, leadership, religious involvement. *Special characteristics:* children of faculty/staff, first-generation college students, general special characteristics, international students, local/state students, out-of-state students, previous college experience, relatives of clergy, religious affiliation, veterans. *Tuition waivers:* Full or partial for employees or children of employees.

LOANS *Student loans:* $6,345,478 (71% need-based, 29% non-need-based). *Average need-based loan:* Freshmen: $3344. Undergraduates: $4596. *Parent loans:* $2,917,153 (43% need-based, 57% non-need-based). *Programs:* Federal Direct (Subsidized and Unsubsidized Stafford, PLUS), Perkins, state, private loans.

WORK-STUDY *Federal work-study:* Total amount: $621,219; 326 jobs averaging $1875. *State or other work-study/employment:* Total amount: $143,084 (15% need-based, 85% non-need-based). 115 part-time jobs averaging $1371.

APPLYING FOR FINANCIAL AID *Required financial aid form:* FAFSA. *Financial aid deadline (priority):* 3/1. *Notification date:* Continuous beginning 12/1. Students must reply by 5/1.

CONTACT Mrs. Laurie Coulter, Executive Director of Financial Aid, Austin College, 900 North Grand Avenue, Sherman, TX 75090, 903-813-2900 or toll-free 800-596-4276 (in-state), 800-526-4276 (out-of-state). *Fax:* 903-813-3198. *E-mail:* finaid@austincollege.edu. *Website:* http://www.austincollege.edu/.

AUSTIN GRADUATE SCHOOL OF THEOLOGY
Austin, TX

Tuition & fees: $8750	Average undergraduate aid package: N/A

ABOUT THE INSTITUTION Independent Church of Christ, coed. *Awards:* bachelor's and master's degrees. 1 undergraduate major. *Total enrollment:* 36. Undergraduates: 22. Both federal and institutional methodology are used as a basis for awarding need-based institutional aid.

UNDERGRADUATE EXPENSES for 2017–2018 *Tuition:* full-time $8400; part-time $350 per credit hour. *Required fees:* full-time $350; $175 per term.

GIFT AID (NEED-BASED) *Scholarships, grants, and awards:* Federal Pell, FSEOG, college/university gift aid from institutional funds.

GIFT AID (NON-NEED-BASED) *Scholarships, grants, and awards by category: Academic interests/achievement:* religion/biblical studies. *Special achievements/activities:* religious involvement.

LOANS *Programs:* Federal Direct (Subsidized and Unsubsidized Stafford, PLUS).

WORK-STUDY Federal work-study jobs available.

APPLYING FOR FINANCIAL AID *Required financial aid forms:* FAFSA, institution's own form. *Financial aid deadline:* Continuous. *Notification date:* Continuous.

CONTACT David Arthur, Director of Financial Aid, Austin Graduate School of Theology, 7640 Guadalupe Street, Austin, TX 78752, 512-476-2772 Ext. 105 or toll-free 866-AUS-GRAD. *Fax:* 512-476-3919. *E-mail:* darthur@austingrad.edu. *Website:* http://www.austingrad.edu/.

AUSTIN PEAY STATE UNIVERSITY
Clarksville, TN

Tuition & fees (TN res): $8225	Average undergraduate aid package: $11,135

ABOUT THE INSTITUTION State-supported, coed. **Awards:** certificates, associate, bachelor's, and master's degrees. 34 undergraduate majors. **Total enrollment:** 10,463. Undergraduates: 9,591. Freshmen: 1,988. Federal methodology is used as a basis for awarding need-based institutional aid.

UNDERGRADUATE EXPENSES for 2018–2019 **Application fee:** $25. **One-time required fee:** $75. **Tuition, state resident:** full-time $6696; part-time $266 per credit hour. **Tuition, nonresident:** full-time $22,692; part-time $901 per credit hour. **Required fees:** full-time $1529. Full-time tuition and fees vary according to location and program. Part-time tuition and fees vary according to location and program. **College room and board:** $9170; **Room only:** $5520. Room and board charges vary according to board plan and housing facility.

FRESHMAN FINANCIAL AID (Fall 2016) 1,627 applied for aid; of those 86% were deemed to have need. 99% of freshmen with need received aid. **Average financial aid package:** $11,204 (excluding resources awarded to replace EFC). 13% of all full-time freshmen had no need and received non-need-based gift aid.

UNDERGRADUATE FINANCIAL AID (Fall 2016) 6,425 applied for aid; of those 88% were deemed to have need. 86% of undergraduates with need received aid. **Average financial aid package:** $11,135 (excluding resources awarded to replace EFC). 8% of all full-time undergraduates had no need and received non-need-based gift aid.

GIFT AID (NEED-BASED) Total amount: $28,205,700 (79% federal, 21% state). **Receiving aid:** Freshmen: 84% (1,378); all full-time undergraduates: 70% (4,858). **Average award:** Freshmen: $7532; Undergraduates: $7788. **Scholarships, grants, and awards:** Federal Pell, FSEOG, state, private, college/university gift aid from institutional funds.

GIFT AID (NON-NEED-BASED) Total amount: $29,616,170 (38% state, 15% institutional, 47% external sources). **Receiving aid:** Freshmen: 71% (1,175). Undergraduates: 51% (3,549). **Average award:** Freshmen: $5201. Undergraduates: $5026. **Scholarships, grants, and awards by category:** Academic interests/achievement: 980 awards ($1,730,899 total): agriculture, biological sciences, business, communication, computer science, education, English, foreign languages, general academic interests/achievements, health fields, humanities, international studies, mathematics, military science, physical sciences, social sciences. Creative arts/performance: 528 awards ($279,243 total): art/fine arts, creative writing, debating, journalism/publications, music, performing arts, theater/drama. Special achievements/activities: 245 awards ($151,860 total): general special achievements/activities, leadership, memberships. Special characteristics: 98 awards ($111,687 total): children of educators, children of faculty/staff, ethnic background, general special characteristics, members of minority groups, veterans. **Tuition waivers:** Full or partial for employees or children of employees, senior citizens. **ROTC:** Army, Air Force cooperative.

LOANS Student loans: $36,420,853 (48% need-based, 52% non-need-based). 67% of past graduating class borrowed through all loan programs. **Average indebtedness per student:** $18,044. **Average need-based loan:** Freshmen: $3198. Undergraduates: $3953. **Parent loans:** $5,132,276 (100% non-need-based). **Programs:** Federal Direct (Subsidized and Unsubsidized Stafford, PLUS), Perkins.

WORK-STUDY Federal work-study: 103 jobs averaging $2402. **State or other work-study/employment:** Total amount: $823,661 (100% non-need-based). 473 part-time jobs averaging $1741.

ATHLETIC AWARDS Total amount: $3,960,770 (100% non-need-based).

APPLYING FOR FINANCIAL AID Required financial aid form: FAFSA. **Financial aid deadline:** Continuous. **Notification date:** Continuous beginning 4/7.

CONTACT Ms. Donna Price, Director of Student Financial Aid, Austin Peay State University, PO Box 4546, Clarksville, TN 37044, 931-221-7907 or toll-free 800-844-2778. Fax: 931-221-6329. E-mail: priced@apsu.edu. Website: http://www.apsu.edu/.

AVE MARIA UNIVERSITY
Ave Maria, FL

Tuition & fees: N/R	Average undergraduate aid package: $18,502

ABOUT THE INSTITUTION Independent Roman Catholic, coed. 30 undergraduate majors. Federal methodology is used as a basis for awarding need-based institutional aid.

FRESHMAN FINANCIAL AID (Fall 2017, est.) 229 applied for aid; of those 81% were deemed to have need. 100% of freshmen with need received aid; of those 24% had need fully met. **Average percent of need met:** 75% (excluding resources awarded to replace EFC). **Average financial aid package:** $18,407 (excluding resources awarded to replace EFC). 32% of all full-time freshmen had no need and received non-need-based gift aid.

UNDERGRADUATE FINANCIAL AID (Fall 2017, est.) 725 applied for aid; of those 85% were deemed to have need. 100% of undergraduates with need received aid; of those 22% had need fully met. **Average percent of need met:** 74% (excluding resources awarded to replace EFC). **Average financial aid package:** $18,502 (excluding resources awarded to replace EFC). 38% of all full-time undergraduates had no need and received non-need-based gift aid.

GIFT AID (NEED-BASED) Total amount: $7,508,182 (15% federal, 12% state, 71% institutional, 2% external sources). **Receiving aid:** Freshmen: 65% (184); all full-time undergraduates: 60% (612). **Average award:** Freshmen: $14,914; Undergraduates: $14,290. **Scholarships, grants, and awards:** Federal Pell, FSEOG, state, private, college/university gift aid from institutional funds.

GIFT AID (NON-NEED-BASED) Total amount: $5,148,962 (14% state, 83% institutional, 3% external sources). **Receiving aid:** Freshmen: 13% (38). Undergraduates: 10% (106). **Average award:** Freshmen: $9327. Undergraduates: $9688. **Scholarships, grants, and awards by category:** Academic interests/achievement: 720 awards ($3,891,903 total): business, general academic interests/achievements. Creative arts/performance: 35 awards ($69,844 total): music. Special achievements/activities: 457 awards ($1,279,083 total): leadership, memberships, religious involvement. Special characteristics: 458 awards ($899,765 total): children of faculty/staff, religious affiliation, siblings of current students.

LOANS Student loans: $4,311,387 (63% need-based, 37% non-need-based). 60% of past graduating class borrowed through all loan programs. **Average indebtedness per student:** $24,294. **Average need-based loan:** Freshmen: $3135. Undergraduates: $3955. **Parent loans:** $1,299,825 (39% need-based, 61% non-need-based). **Programs:** Federal Direct (Subsidized and Unsubsidized Stafford, PLUS), college/university.

WORK-STUDY Federal work-study: Total amount: $105,322; 72 jobs averaging $1463. **State or other work-study/employment:** Total amount: $6171 (100% need-based). 5 part-time jobs averaging $1234.

ATHLETIC AWARDS Total amount: $2,253,849 (58% need-based, 42% non-need-based).

APPLYING FOR FINANCIAL AID Required financial aid forms: FAFSA, state aid form. **Financial aid deadline (priority):** 3/1. **Notification date:** Continuous beginning 11/1.

CONTACT Anne Hart, Director of Financial Aid, Ave Maria University, 5050 Ave Maria Boulevard, Ave Maria, FL 34142, 239-280-1669 or toll-free 877-283-8648. Fax: 239-280-2566. E-mail: amufinancialaid@avemaria.edu. Website: http://www.avemaria.edu/.

AVERETT UNIVERSITY
Danville, VA

Tuition & fees: $33,350	Average undergraduate aid package: $26,742

ABOUT THE INSTITUTION Independent Baptist General Association of Virginia, coed. **Awards:** bachelor's degrees. 54 undergraduate majors. **Total enrollment:** 929. Undergraduates: 929. Freshmen: 281. Both federal and institutional methodology are used as a basis for awarding need-based institutional aid.

UNDERGRADUATE EXPENSES for 2017–2018 **Comprehensive fee:** $43,034 includes full-time tuition ($33,350) and room and board ($9684). **College room only:** $6184. Full-time tuition and fees vary according to class time, course load, degree level, location, and program. Room and board charges vary according to board plan and housing facility. *Part-time tuition:* $1045 per credit. Part-time tuition and fees vary according to class time, course load, degree level, location, and program.

FRESHMAN FINANCIAL AID (Fall 2017, est.) 245 applied for aid; of those 96% were deemed to have need. 100% of freshmen with need received aid; of those 10% had need fully met. *Average percent of need met:* 69% (excluding resources awarded to replace EFC). *Average financial aid package:* $26,770 (excluding resources awarded to replace EFC). 14% of all full-time freshmen had no need and received non-need-based gift aid.

UNDERGRADUATE FINANCIAL AID (Fall 2017, est.) 805 applied for aid; of those 95% were deemed to have need. 100% of undergraduates with need received aid; of those 11% had need fully met. *Average percent of need met:* 72% (excluding resources awarded to replace EFC). *Average financial aid package:* $26,742 (excluding resources awarded to replace EFC). 13% of all full-time undergraduates had no need and received non-need-based gift aid.

GIFT AID (NEED-BASED) *Total amount:* $17,626,644 (13% federal, 8% state, 72% institutional, 7% external sources). *Receiving aid:* Freshmen: 86% (234); all full-time undergraduates: 86% (765). *Average award:* Freshmen: $23,023; Undergraduates: $22,850. *Scholarships, grants, and awards:* Federal Pell, FSEOG, state, private, college/university gift aid from institutional funds.

GIFT AID (NON-NEED-BASED) *Total amount:* $2,585,225 (8% state, 82% institutional, 10% external sources). *Receiving aid:* Freshmen: 7% (19). Undergraduates: 8% (75). *Average award:* Freshmen: $18,594. Undergraduates: $15,702. *Scholarships, grants, and awards by category:* Academic interests/achievement: 290 awards ($585,943 total): biological sciences, business, education, engineering/technologies, English, foreign languages, general academic interests/achievements, health fields, home economics, humanities, mathematics, physical sciences, premedicine, religion/biblical studies. *Creative arts/performance:* 10 awards ($15,000 total): art/fine arts, journalism/publications, music, theater/drama. *Special achievements/activities:* 80 awards ($99,576 total): general special achievements/activities, leadership, memberships, religious involvement. *Special characteristics:* 250 awards ($249,758 total): adult students, children and siblings of alumni, children of union members/company employees, first-generation college students, general special characteristics, international students, local/state students, out-of-state students, relatives of clergy, religious affiliation. *Tuition waivers:* Full or partial for employees or children of employees, senior citizens.

LOANS *Student loans:* $6,136,082 (84% need-based, 16% non-need-based). 79% of past graduating class borrowed through all loan programs. *Average indebtedness per student:* $35,373. *Average need-based loan:* Freshmen: $4133. Undergraduates: $4503. *Parent loans:* $4,286,725 (52% need-based, 48% non-need-based). *Programs:* Federal Direct (Subsidized and Unsubsidized Stafford, PLUS), Perkins, state, alternative loans.

WORK-STUDY *Federal work-study:* Total amount: $167,350; 244 jobs averaging $615. *State or other work-study/employment:* Part-time jobs available.

APPLYING FOR FINANCIAL AID *Required financial aid forms:* FAFSA, state aid form. *Financial aid deadline (priority):* 4/1. *Notification date:* Continuous beginning 11/1. Students must reply by 4/1 or within 2 weeks of notification.

CONTACT Carl Bradsher, Dean of Financial Assistance, Averett University, 420 West Main Street, Danville, VA 24541-3692, 434-791-5646 or toll-free 800-AVERETT. *Fax:* 434-791-5647. *E-mail:* carl.bradsher@averett.edu. *Website:* http://www.averett.edu/.

AVILA UNIVERSITY
Kansas City, MO

CONTACT Nancy Merz, Director of Financial Aid, Avila University, 11901 Wornall Road, Kansas City, MO 64145, 816-501-3782 or toll-free 800-GO-AVILA. *Fax:* 816-501-2462. *E-mail:* nancy.merz@avila.edu. *Website:* http://www.avila.edu/.

AZUSA PACIFIC UNIVERSITY
Azusa, CA

Tuition & fees: $37,506	Average undergraduate aid package: $24,503

ABOUT THE INSTITUTION Independent nondenominational, coed. *Awards:* certificates, bachelor's, master's, and doctoral degrees. 47 undergraduate majors. *Total enrollment:* 9,926. Undergraduates: 5,671. Freshmen: 1,005. Federal methodology is used as a basis for awarding need-based institutional aid.

UNDERGRADUATE EXPENSES for 2018–2019 *Tuition:* full-time $36,926; part-time $1596 per unit. Full-time tuition and fees vary according to course load and degree level. Part-time tuition and fees vary according to course load and degree level. Room and board charges vary according to board plan and housing facility.

FRESHMAN FINANCIAL AID (Fall 2016) 1,106 applied for aid; of those 78% were deemed to have need. 100% of freshmen with need received aid; of those 15% had need fully met. *Average percent of need met:* 30% (excluding resources awarded to replace EFC). *Average financial aid package:* $25,615 (excluding resources awarded to replace EFC). 21% of all full-time freshmen had no need and received non-need-based gift aid.

UNDERGRADUATE FINANCIAL AID (Fall 2016) 5,101 applied for aid; of those 77% were deemed to have need. 100% of undergraduates with need received aid; of those 14% had need fully met. *Average percent of need met:* 36% (excluding resources awarded to replace EFC). *Average financial aid package:* $24,503 (excluding resources awarded to replace EFC). 20% of all full-time undergraduates had no need and received non-need-based gift aid.

GIFT AID (NEED-BASED) *Total amount:* $66,415,333 (13% federal, 17% state, 67% institutional, 3% external sources). *Receiving aid:* Freshmen: 63% (708); all full-time undergraduates: 66% (3,443). *Average award:* Freshmen: $10,193; Undergraduates: $11,242. *Scholarships, grants, and awards:* Federal Pell, FSEOG, state, private, college/university gift aid from institutional funds.

GIFT AID (NON-NEED-BASED) *Total amount:* $26,074,644 (88% institutional, 12% external sources). *Receiving aid:* Freshmen: 67% (756). Undergraduates: 58% (3,070). *Average award:* Freshmen: $14,960. Undergraduates: $11,349. *Tuition waivers:* Full or partial for employees or children of employees. *ROTC:* Army, Air Force cooperative.

LOANS *Student loans:* $25,296,826 (80% need-based, 20% non-need-based). 70% of past graduating class borrowed through all loan programs. *Average indebtedness per student:* $31,277. *Average need-based loan:* Freshmen: $3591. Undergraduates: $4759. *Parent loans:* $14,985,352 (9% need-based, 91% non-need-based).

WORK-STUDY *Federal work-study:* jobs available. *State or other work-study/employment:* Total amount: $10,030,965 (39% need-based, 61% non-need-based). Part-time jobs available.

ATHLETIC AWARDS Total amount: $5,322,964 (43% need-based, 57% non-need-based).

APPLYING FOR FINANCIAL AID *Notification date:* Continuous.

CONTACT Todd Ross, Associate Vice-President for Undergraduate Academic and Financial Services, Azusa Pacific University, 901 East Alosta Avenue, PO Box 7000, Azusa, CA 91702-7000, 626-812-3009 or toll-free 800-TALK-APU. *E-mail:* tross@apu.edu. *Website:* http://www.apu.edu/.

BABSON COLLEGE
Wellesley, MA

Tuition & fees: $51,104	Average undergraduate aid package: $42,671

ABOUT THE INSTITUTION Independent, coed. *Awards:* certificates, bachelor's, and master's degrees. 24 undergraduate majors. *Total enrollment:* 3,329. Undergraduates: 2,342. Freshmen: 550. Both federal and institutional methodology are used as a basis for awarding need-based institutional aid.

UNDERGRADUATE EXPENSES for 2018–2019 *Application fee:* $75. *Comprehensive fee:* $67,416 includes full-time tuition ($51,104) and room and board ($16,312). Room and board charges vary according to board plan and housing facility.

FRESHMAN FINANCIAL AID (Fall 2017, est.) 291 applied for aid; of those 76% were deemed to have need. 100% of freshmen with need received aid; of those 100% had need fully met. *Average percent of need met:* 100% (excluding resources

awarded to replace EFC). *Average financial aid package:* $42,799 (excluding resources awarded to replace EFC). 5% of all full-time freshmen had no need and received non-need-based gift aid.

UNDERGRADUATE FINANCIAL AID (Fall 2017, est.) 1,077 applied for aid; of those 88% were deemed to have need. 100% of undergraduates with need received aid; of those 65% had need fully met. *Average percent of need met:* 98% (excluding resources awarded to replace EFC). *Average financial aid package:* $42,671 (excluding resources awarded to replace EFC). 6% of all full-time undergraduates had no need and received non-need-based gift aid.

GIFT AID (NEED-BASED) *Total amount:* $35,646,400 (5% federal, 1% state, 94% institutional). *Receiving aid:* Freshmen: 38% (209); all full-time undergraduates: 39% (904). *Average award:* Freshmen: $40,546; Undergraduates: $39,436. *Scholarships, grants, and awards:* Federal Pell, FSEOG, state, college/university gift aid from institutional funds.

GIFT AID (NON-NEED-BASED) *Total amount:* $3,265,600 (81% institutional, 19% external sources). *Receiving aid:* Freshmen: 4% (20). Undergraduates: 6% (145). *Average award:* Freshmen: $25,085. Undergraduates: $18,631. *Scholarships, grants, and awards by category:* Academic interests/achievement: business, general academic interests/achievements. *Special achievements/activities:* leadership. *Special characteristics:* veterans. *Tuition waivers:* Full or partial for employees or children of employees. *ROTC:* Army cooperative.

LOANS *Student loans:* $7,893,100 (42% need-based, 58% non-need-based). 40% of past graduating class borrowed through all loan programs. *Average indebtedness per student:* $35,013. *Average need-based loan:* Freshmen: $3326. Undergraduates: $4915. *Parent loans:* $3,199,600 (100% non-need-based). *Programs:* Federal Direct (Subsidized and Unsubsidized Stafford, PLUS), state.

WORK-STUDY *Federal work-study:* Total amount: $1,413,600; jobs available. *State or other work-study/employment:* Total amount: $121,600 (100% non-need-based). Part-time jobs available.

APPLYING FOR FINANCIAL AID *Required financial aid forms:* FAFSA, CSS Financial Aid PROFILE, noncustodial (divorced/separated) parent's statement, federal income tax form(s), W-2 forms, verification worksheet. *Financial aid deadline:* 2/1. *Notification date:* 4/1. Students must reply by 5/1.

CONTACT Ms. Meredith Stover, Director of Financial Aid, Babson College, Hollister Hall, Third Floor, Babson Park, MA 02457-0310, 781-239-4219 or toll-free 800-488-3696. *Fax:* 781-239-5510. *E-mail:* stoverm@babson.edu.
Website: http://www.babson.edu/.

BACONE COLLEGE
Muskogee, OK

CONTACT Mrs. Misty Oleson, Assistant Director of Financial Aid, Bacone College, 2299 Old Bacone Road, Muskogee, OK 74403-1597, 918-781-7225 or toll-free 888-682-5514 Ext. 7340. *Fax:* 866-498-1487. *E-mail:* finaid@bacone.edu.
Website: http://www.bacone.edu/.

BAIS BINYOMIN ACADEMY
Stamford, CT

CONTACT Financial Aid Office, Bais Binyomin Academy, 132 Prospect Street, Stamford, CT 06901-1202, 203-325-4351.

BAIS HAMEDRASH AND MESIVTA OF BALTIMORE
Baltimore, MD

CONTACT Financial Aid Office, Bais HaMedrash and Mesivta of Baltimore, 6823 Old Pimlico Road, Baltimore, MD 21209, 410-486-0006.

BAIS MEDRASH TORAS CHESED
Lakewood, NJ

CONTACT Financial Aid Office, Bais Medrash Toras Chesed, 910 Monmouth Avenue, Lakewood, NJ 08701.
Website: http://www.bmtc.edu/.

BAKER COLLEGE
Flint, MI

CONTACT Financial Aid Office, Baker College, Baker College System Headquarters, 1050 West Bristol Road, Flint, MI 48507, 810-766-4000 or toll-free 800-964-4299.
Website: http://www.baker.edu/.

BAKER UNIVERSITY
Baldwin City, KS

Tuition & fees: $28,880	Average undergraduate aid package: $25,766

ABOUT THE INSTITUTION Independent United Methodist, coed. *Awards:* bachelor's, master's, and doctoral degrees (profile includes information primarily for undergraduate residential campus in Baldwin City, KS). 35 undergraduate majors. *Total enrollment:* 1,159. Undergraduates: 1,159. Freshmen: 256. Federal methodology is used as a basis for awarding need-based institutional aid.

UNDERGRADUATE EXPENSES for 2017–2018 *One-time required fee:* $80. *Comprehensive fee:* $37,190 includes full-time tuition ($28,430), mandatory fees ($450), and room and board ($8310). *College room only:* $3910. Full-time tuition and fees vary according to course load, degree level, location, and program. Room and board charges vary according to board plan and housing facility. *Part-time tuition:* $890 per credit hour. *Part-time fees:* $200 per year. Part-time tuition and fees vary according to course load, degree level, location, and program.

FRESHMAN FINANCIAL AID (Fall 2016) 230 applied for aid; of those 87% were deemed to have need. 100% of freshmen with need received aid. *Average financial aid package:* $25,695 (excluding resources awarded to replace EFC). 10% of all full-time freshmen had no need and received non-need-based gift aid.

UNDERGRADUATE FINANCIAL AID (Fall 2016) 749 applied for aid; of those 87% were deemed to have need. 100% of undergraduates with need received aid. *Average financial aid package:* $25,766 (excluding resources awarded to replace EFC). 11% of all full-time undergraduates had no need and received non-need-based gift aid.

GIFT AID (NEED-BASED) *Total amount:* $3,417,382 (37% federal, 22% state, 41% institutional). *Receiving aid:* Freshmen: 76% (181); all full-time undergraduates: 65% (549). *Average award:* Freshmen: $7000; Undergraduates: $6142. *Scholarships, grants, and awards:* Federal Pell, FSEOG, state, private, college/university gift aid from institutional funds.

GIFT AID (NON-NEED-BASED) *Total amount:* $8,426,744 (88% institutional, 12% external sources). *Receiving aid:* Freshmen: 59% (141). Undergraduates: 55% (467). *Average award:* Freshmen: $8552. Undergraduates: $10,496. *Scholarships, grants, and awards by category:* Academic interests/achievement: general academic interests/achievements. *Creative arts/performance:* art/fine arts, cinema/film/broadcasting, dance, debating, journalism/publications, music, theater/drama. *Special achievements/activities:* cheerleading/drum major, leadership, religious involvement. *Special characteristics:* children and siblings of alumni, children of faculty/staff, ethnic background, international students, members of minority groups, out-of-state students, relatives of clergy, religious affiliation. *Tuition waivers:* Full or partial for employees or children of employees, senior citizens. *ROTC:* Army cooperative, Air Force cooperative.

LOANS *Student loans:* $4,065,474 (54% need-based, 46% non-need-based). 70% of past graduating class borrowed through all loan programs. *Average indebtedness per student:* $31,937. *Average need-based loan:* Freshmen: $3659. Undergraduates: $3972. *Parent loans:* $1,413,673 (100% non-need-based). *Programs:* Federal Direct (Subsidized and Unsubsidized Stafford, PLUS), Perkins, alternative loans.

WORK-STUDY *Federal work-study:* jobs available. *State or other work-study/employment:* Total amount: $94,687 (100% non-need-based). Part-time jobs available.

ATHLETIC AWARDS Total amount: $5,567,474 (100% non-need-based).

APPLYING FOR FINANCIAL AID *Required financial aid forms:* FAFSA, institution's own form. *Financial aid deadline (priority):* 3/1. *Notification date:* Continuous beginning 1/1. Students must reply by 5/1 or within 6 weeks of notification.

CONTACT Jana Parks, Financial Aid Director, Baker University, Box 65, Baldwin City, KS 66006-0065, 785-594-4595 or toll-free 800-873-4282. *Fax:* 785-594-8358. *Website:* http://www.bakeru.edu/.

BALDWIN WALLACE UNIVERSITY
Berea, OH

Tuition & fees: $32,586	Average undergraduate aid package: $26,990

ABOUT THE INSTITUTION Independent Methodist, coed. *Awards:* certificates, bachelor's, and master's degrees. 80 undergraduate majors. *Total enrollment:* 3,812. Undergraduates: 3,204. Freshmen: 685. Federal methodology is used as a basis for awarding need-based institutional aid.

UNDERGRADUATE EXPENSES for 2018–2019 *Application fee:* $25. *Comprehensive fee:* $42,140 includes full-time tuition ($32,586) and room and board ($9554). *College room only:* $5518. Full-time tuition and fees vary according to class time, course level, course load, degree level, program, and reciprocity agreements. Room and board charges vary according to housing facility. *Part-time tuition:* $1013 per credit hour. Part-time tuition and fees vary according to class time, course level, course load, degree level, program, and reciprocity agreements.

FRESHMAN FINANCIAL AID (Fall 2017, est.) 652 applied for aid; of those 88% were deemed to have need. 100% of freshmen with need received aid; of those 32% had need fully met. *Average percent of need met:* 89% (excluding resources awarded to replace EFC). *Average financial aid package:* $28,852 (excluding resources awarded to replace EFC). 15% of all full-time freshmen had no need and received non-need-based gift aid.

UNDERGRADUATE FINANCIAL AID (Fall 2017, est.) 2,586 applied for aid; of those 91% were deemed to have need. 100% of undergraduates with need received aid; of those 37% had need fully met. *Average percent of need met:* 87% (excluding resources awarded to replace EFC). *Average financial aid package:* $26,990 (excluding resources awarded to replace EFC). 18% of all full-time undergraduates had no need and received non-need-based gift aid.

GIFT AID (NEED-BASED) *Total amount:* $40,748,619 (12% federal, 6% state, 80% institutional, 2% external sources). *Receiving aid:* Freshmen: 84% (577); all full-time undergraduates: 79% (2,345). *Average award:* Freshmen: $22,838; Undergraduates: $20,876. *Scholarships, grants, and awards:* Federal Pell, FSEOG, state, private, college/university gift aid from institutional funds.

GIFT AID (NON-NEED-BASED) *Total amount:* $12,154,656 (97% institutional, 3% external sources). *Receiving aid:* Freshmen: 27% (187). Undergraduates: 29% (867). *Average award:* Freshmen: $14,894. Undergraduates: $13,504. *Scholarships, grants, and awards by category:* Academic interests/achievement: 2,663 awards ($25,612,000 total): general academic interests/achievements. Creative arts/performance: 211 awards ($947,000 total): music. Special characteristics: 1,474 awards ($4,530,000 total): children and siblings of alumni, members of minority groups, religious affiliation, siblings of current students. *Tuition waivers:* Full or partial for children of alumni, employees or children of employees. *ROTC:* Army cooperative, Air Force cooperative.

LOANS *Student loans:* $19,664,881 (52% need-based, 48% non-need-based). 76% of past graduating class borrowed through all loan programs. *Average indebtedness per student:* $36,426. *Average need-based loan:* Freshmen: $3560. Undergraduates: $4699. *Parent loans:* $9,182,437 (40% need-based, 60% non-need-based). *Programs:* Federal Direct (Subsidized and Unsubsidized Stafford, PLUS), Perkins.

WORK-STUDY *Federal work-study:* Total amount: $466,000; 960 jobs averaging $1330. *State or other work-study/employment:* Total amount: $1,848,284 (72% need-based, 28% non-need-based). 550 part-time jobs averaging $1511.

APPLYING FOR FINANCIAL AID *Required financial aid form:* FAFSA. *Financial aid deadline (priority):* 8/15. *Notification date:* Continuous beginning 12/4.

CONTACT Dr. George L. Rolleston, Director of Financial Aid, Baldwin Wallace University, 275 Eastland Road, Berea, OH 44017-2088, 440-826-2108 or toll-free 877-BW-APPLY. *Fax:* 440-826-8048. *E-mail:* grollest@bw.edu. *Website:* http://www.bw.edu/.

BALL STATE UNIVERSITY
Muncie, IN

Tuition & fees (IN res): $9774	Average undergraduate aid package: $13,416

ABOUT THE INSTITUTION State-supported, coed. *Awards:* certificates, bachelor's, master's, and doctoral degrees. 124 undergraduate majors. *Total enrollment:* 22,513. Undergraduates: 17,004. Freshmen: 3,985. Federal methodology is used as a basis for awarding need-based institutional aid.

UNDERGRADUATE EXPENSES for 2017–2018 *Application fee:* $55. *Tuition, state resident:* full-time $9112; part-time $300 per credit hour. *Tuition, nonresident:* full-time $25,280; part-time $1001 per credit hour. *Required fees:* full-time $662. Full-time tuition and fees vary according to program and reciprocity agreements. Part-time tuition and fees vary according to course load, program, and reciprocity agreements. *College room and board:* $10,034. Room and board charges vary according to board plan and housing facility.

FRESHMAN FINANCIAL AID (Fall 2017, est.) 3,835 applied for aid; of those 78% were deemed to have need. 100% of freshmen with need received aid; of those 38% had need fully met. *Average percent of need met:* 73% (excluding resources awarded to replace EFC). *Average financial aid package:* $14,375 (excluding resources awarded to replace EFC). 13% of all full-time freshmen had no need and received non-need-based gift aid.

UNDERGRADUATE FINANCIAL AID (Fall 2017, est.) 13,152 applied for aid; of those 80% were deemed to have need. 100% of undergraduates with need received aid; of those 40% had need fully met. *Average percent of need met:* 71% (excluding resources awarded to replace EFC). *Average financial aid package:* $13,416 (excluding resources awarded to replace EFC). 13% of all full-time undergraduates had no need and received non-need-based gift aid.

GIFT AID (NEED-BASED) *Total amount:* $41,492,995 (63% federal, 19% state, 18% institutional). *Receiving aid:* Freshmen: 54% (2,156); all full-time undergraduates: 43% (6,533). *Average award:* Freshmen: $6085; Undergraduates: $6216. *Scholarships, grants, and awards:* Federal Pell, FSEOG, state, private, college/university gift aid from institutional funds.

GIFT AID (NON-NEED-BASED) *Total amount:* $72,015,696 (2% federal, 35% state, 53% institutional, 10% external sources). *Receiving aid:* Freshmen: 50% (1,987). Undergraduates: 39% (5,894). *Average award:* Freshmen: $7952. Undergraduates: $8198. *Scholarships, grants, and awards by category:* Academic interests/achievement: architecture, biological sciences, business, communication, education, engineering/technologies, English, foreign languages, general academic interests/achievements, health fields, humanities, international studies, mathematics, military science, physical sciences, social sciences. *Creative arts/performance:* cinema/film/broadcasting, dance, debating, general creative arts/performance, journalism/publications, music, performing arts, theater/drama. *Special achievements/activities:* community service, general special achievements/activities, leadership. *Special characteristics:* adult students, children of faculty/staff, ethnic background, general special characteristics, international students, local/state students, members of minority groups, out-of-state students, veterans, veterans' children. *Tuition waivers:* Full or partial for employees or children of employees, senior citizens. *ROTC:* Army.

LOANS *Student loans:* $104,844,074 (39% need-based, 61% non-need-based). 72% of past graduating class borrowed through all loan programs. *Average indebtedness per student:* $28,295. *Average need-based loan:* Freshmen: $3752. Undergraduates: $4394. *Parent loans:* $25,429,219 (100% non-need-based). *Programs:* Federal Direct (Subsidized and Unsubsidized Stafford, PLUS), Perkins, college/university.

WORK-STUDY *Federal work-study:* Total amount: $3,181,665; jobs available. *State or other work-study/employment:* Total amount: $9,111,208 (100% non-need-based). Part-time jobs available.

ATHLETIC AWARDS Total amount: $7,682,438 (100% non-need-based).

APPLYING FOR FINANCIAL AID *Required financial aid form:* FAFSA. *Financial aid deadline (priority):* 4/15. *Notification date:* Continuous beginning 1/15.

CONTACT Dr. John McPherson, Assistant Vice President of Enrollment Services and Executive Director of Financial Aid and Scholarships, Ball State University, Lucina Hall, Room 245, Muncie, IN 47306, 765-285-8894 or toll-free 800-482-4BSU. *Fax:* 765-285-4247. *E-mail:* finaid@bsu.edu.
Website: http://www.bsu.edu/.

BAPTIST BIBLE COLLEGE
Springfield, MO

CONTACT Bob Kotulski, Director of Financial Aid, Baptist Bible College, 628 East Kearney, Springfield, MO 65803-3498, 417-268-6036 or toll-free 800-228-5754. *Fax:* 417-268-6694.
Website: http://www.gobbc.edu/.

THE BAPTIST COLLEGE OF FLORIDA
Graceville, FL

Tuition & fees: $11,100	Average undergraduate aid package: $9233

ABOUT THE INSTITUTION Independent Southern Baptist, coed. *Awards:* associate, bachelor's, and master's degrees. 17 undergraduate majors. *Total enrollment:* 448. Undergraduates: 427. Freshmen: 39. Federal methodology is used as a basis for awarding need-based institutional aid.

UNDERGRADUATE EXPENSES for 2017–2018 *Application fee:* $25. *Comprehensive fee:* $15,238 includes full-time tuition ($10,200), mandatory fees ($900), and room and board ($4138). Full-time tuition and fees vary according to location and program. Room and board charges vary according to board plan and housing facility. *Part-time tuition:* $340 per credit hour. *Part-time fees:* $30 per credit. Part-time tuition and fees vary according to location and program.

FRESHMAN FINANCIAL AID (Fall 2017, est.) 67 applied for aid; of those 72% were deemed to have need. 69% of freshmen with need received aid; of those 3% had need fully met. *Average percent of need met:* 42% (excluding resources awarded to replace EFC). *Average financial aid package:* $10,151 (excluding resources awarded to replace EFC). 1% of all full-time freshmen had no need and received non-need-based gift aid.

UNDERGRADUATE FINANCIAL AID (Fall 2017, est.) 367 applied for aid; of those 89% were deemed to have need. 76% of undergraduates with need received aid; of those 3% had need fully met. *Average percent of need met:* 36% (excluding resources awarded to replace EFC). *Average financial aid package:* $9233 (excluding resources awarded to replace EFC). 3% of all full-time undergraduates had no need and received non-need-based gift aid.

GIFT AID (NEED-BASED) *Total amount:* $1,781,852 (60% federal, 24% state, 13% institutional, 3% external sources). *Receiving aid:* Freshmen: 49% (33); all full-time undergraduates: 61% (241). *Average award:* Freshmen: $8666; Undergraduates: $6898. *Scholarships, grants, and awards:* Federal Pell, FSEOG, state, private, college/university gift aid from institutional funds.

GIFT AID (NON-NEED-BASED) *Total amount:* $81,546 (41% state, 30% institutional, 29% external sources). *Receiving aid:* Freshmen: 1% (1). Undergraduates: 1% (4). *Average award:* Freshmen: $1000. Undergraduates: $1471. *Scholarships, grants, and awards by category:* Academic interests/achievement: 185 awards ($273,000 total): education, religion/biblical studies. Creative arts/performance: 2 awards ($1500 total): music. Special characteristics: 158 awards ($234,531 total): children with a deceased or disabled parent, religious affiliation, spouses of current students. *Tuition waivers:* Full or partial for employees or children of employees.

LOANS *Student loans:* $1,103,298 (91% need-based, 9% non-need-based). 61% of past graduating class borrowed through all loan programs. *Average indebtedness per student:* $24,444. *Average need-based loan:* Freshmen: $2512. Undergraduates: $3697. *Parent loans:* $38,073 (53% need-based, 47% non-need-based). *Programs:* Federal Direct (Subsidized and Unsubsidized Stafford, PLUS).

WORK-STUDY *Federal work-study:* Total amount: $46,924; 24 jobs averaging $2127.

APPLYING FOR FINANCIAL AID *Required financial aid forms:* FAFSA, institution's own form, Student Fee Authorization Form. *Financial aid deadline (priority):* 7/13. *Notification date:* Continuous beginning 6/15. Students must reply within 2 weeks of notification.

BAPTIST COLLEGE OF HEALTH SCIENCES
Memphis, TN

ABOUT THE INSTITUTION Independent Southern Baptist, coed, primarily women. *Awards:* bachelor's and doctoral degrees. 10 undergraduate majors. *Total enrollment:* 1,076. Undergraduates: 1,076.

GIFT AID (NEED-BASED) *Scholarships, grants, and awards:* Federal Pell, FSEOG, state, private, college/university gift aid from institutional funds.

APPLYING FOR FINANCIAL AID *Required financial aid form:* FAFSA.

CONTACT Joanna Darden, Director of Financial Aid, Baptist College of Health Sciences, 1003 Monroe Avenue, Memphis, TN 38104, 901-227-4330 or toll-free 866-575-2247. *E-mail:* joanna.darden@bchs.edu.
Website: http://www.bchs.edu/.

BAPTIST HEALTH SYSTEM SCHOOL OF HEALTH PROFESSIONS
San Antonio, TX

CONTACT Financial Aid Office, Baptist Health System School of Health Professions, 8400 Datapoint Drive, San Antonio, TX 78229, 210-297-9636.
Website: http://www.bshp.edu/.

BAPTIST MISSIONARY ASSOCIATION THEOLOGICAL SEMINARY
Jacksonville, TX

CONTACT Dr. Philip Attebery, Dean/Registrar, Baptist Missionary Association Theological Seminary, 1530 East Pine Street, PO Box 670, Jacksonville, TX 75766-5407, 903-586-2501 or toll-free 800-259-5673. *Fax:* 903-586-0378. *E-mail:* bmatsem@bmats.edu.
Website: http://www.bmats.edu/.

BAPTIST UNIVERSITY OF THE AMERICAS
San Antonio, TX

Tuition & fees: $6240	Average undergraduate aid package: N/A

ABOUT THE INSTITUTION Independent Baptist, coed. *Awards:* certificates, diplomas, associate, and bachelor's degrees (associate degree in Cross-Cultural Studies). 7 undergraduate majors. *Total enrollment:* 195. Undergraduates: 195. Freshmen: 30. Both federal and institutional methodology are used as a basis for awarding need-based institutional aid.

UNDERGRADUATE EXPENSES for 2017–2018 *Comprehensive fee:* $13,910 includes full-time tuition ($5520), mandatory fees ($720), and room and board ($7670). *College room only:* $2500. Room and board charges vary according to housing facility. *Part-time tuition:* $230 per credit hour. *Part-time fees:* $30 per credit hour.

GIFT AID (NEED-BASED) *Scholarships, grants, and awards:* Federal Pell, FSEOG, private, college/university gift aid from institutional funds.

GIFT AID (NON-NEED-BASED) *Tuition waivers:* Full or partial for employees or children of employees.

LOANS *Programs:* Federal Direct (Subsidized and Unsubsidized Stafford).

WORK-STUDY *Federal work-study:* 4 jobs averaging $1312. *State or other work-study/employment:* 131 part-time jobs averaging $2257.

APPLYING FOR FINANCIAL AID *Required financial aid forms:* FAFSA, institution's own form. *Financial aid deadline:* Continuous. *Notification date:* Continuous.

CONTACT Mrs. Araceli G. Acosta, Financial Aid Director, Baptist University of the Americas, 7838 Barlite Boulevard, San Antonio, TX 78224, 210-924-4338 Ext. 214 or toll-free 800-721-1396. *Fax:* 210-924-2701. *E-mail:* araceli.acosta@bua.edu. *Website:* http://www.bua.edu/.

BARCLAY COLLEGE
Haviland, KS

Tuition & fees: $19,640	Average undergraduate aid package: $19,529

ABOUT THE INSTITUTION Independent Society of Friends, coed. *Awards:* certificates, associate, bachelor's, and master's degrees. 10 undergraduate majors. *Total enrollment:* 259. Undergraduates: 229. Freshmen: 39. Federal methodology is used as a basis for awarding need-based institutional aid.

UNDERGRADUATE EXPENSES for 2017–2018 *Application fee:* $15. *Comprehensive fee:* $28,990 includes full-time tuition ($15,000), mandatory fees ($4640), and room and board ($9350). Room and board charges vary according to board plan and housing facility. *Part-time tuition:* $295 per credit hour. Part-time tuition and fees vary according to course load.

FRESHMAN FINANCIAL AID (Fall 2017, est.) 20 applied for aid; of those 100% were deemed to have need. 100% of freshmen with need received aid. *Average percent of need met:* 20% (excluding resources awarded to replace EFC). *Average financial aid package:* $19,548 (excluding resources awarded to replace EFC). 9% of all full-time freshmen had no need and received non-need-based gift aid.

UNDERGRADUATE FINANCIAL AID (Fall 2017, est.) 146 applied for aid; of those 100% were deemed to have need. 100% of undergraduates with need received aid. *Average percent of need met:* 45% (excluding resources awarded to replace EFC). *Average financial aid package:* $19,529 (excluding resources awarded to replace EFC). 7% of all full-time undergraduates had no need and received non-need-based gift aid.

GIFT AID (NEED-BASED) *Total amount:* $2,387,840 (24% federal, 1% state, 72% institutional, 3% external sources). *Receiving aid:* Freshmen: 91% (20); all full-time undergraduates: 93% (146). *Average award:* Freshmen: $17,421; Undergraduates: $11,843. *Scholarships, grants, and awards:* Federal Pell, FSEOG, state, private, college/university gift aid from institutional funds.

GIFT AID (NON-NEED-BASED) *Total amount:* $285,978 (80% institutional, 20% external sources). *Receiving aid:* Freshmen: 9% (2). Undergraduates: 7% (11). *Average award:* Freshmen: $16,570. Undergraduates: $13,869. *Scholarships, grants, and awards by category: Academic interests/achievement:* 146 awards ($1,035,352 total): general academic interests/achievements. *Tuition waivers:* Full or partial for employees or children of employees.

LOANS *Student loans:* $1,204,496 (93% need-based, 7% non-need-based). 100% of past graduating class borrowed through all loan programs. *Average indebtedness per student:* $19,926. *Average need-based loan:* Freshmen: $2128. Undergraduates: $7685. *Parent loans:* $36,482 (91% need-based, 9% non-need-based). *Programs:* Federal Direct (Subsidized and Unsubsidized Stafford, PLUS).

WORK-STUDY *Federal work-study:* Total amount: $54,256; 53 jobs averaging $1545. *State or other work-study/employment:* 53 part-time jobs averaging $1545.

APPLYING FOR FINANCIAL AID *Required financial aid form:* FAFSA. *Financial aid deadline (priority):* 3/18. *Notification date:* Continuous. Students must reply by 8/1 or within 4 weeks of notification.

CONTACT Ryan Haase, Financial Aid Coordinator, Barclay College, 607 North Kingman, Haviland, KS 67059, 800-862-0226. *Fax:* 620-862-5403. *E-mail:* financialaid@barclaycollege.edu. *Website:* http://www.barclaycollege.edu/.

BARD COLLEGE
Annandale-on-Hudson, NY

Tuition & fees: $52,915	Average undergraduate aid package: $46,810

ABOUT THE INSTITUTION Independent, coed. *Awards:* bachelor's, master's, and doctoral degrees. 57 undergraduate majors. *Total enrollment:* 2,284. Undergraduates: 1,930. Freshmen: 470. Both federal and institutional methodology are used as a basis for awarding need-based institutional aid.

UNDERGRADUATE EXPENSES for 2017–2018 *Application fee:* $50. *One-time required fee:* $1635. *Comprehensive fee:* $67,981 includes full-time tuition ($52,226), mandatory fees ($689), and room and board ($15,066). Full-time tuition and fees vary according to degree level and location. Room and board charges vary according to location. *Part-time tuition:* $1635 per credit hour. Part-time tuition and fees vary according to degree level and location. *Payment plan:* Tuition prepayment.

FRESHMAN FINANCIAL AID (Fall 2017, est.) 347 applied for aid; of those 94% were deemed to have need. 100% of freshmen with need received aid; of those 30% had need fully met. *Average percent of need met:* 87% (excluding resources awarded to replace EFC). *Average financial aid package:* $50,218 (excluding resources awarded to replace EFC). 1% of all full-time freshmen had no need and received non-need-based gift aid.

UNDERGRADUATE FINANCIAL AID (Fall 2017, est.) 1,340 applied for aid; of those 95% were deemed to have need. 100% of undergraduates with need received aid; of those 25% had need fully met. *Average percent of need met:* 83% (excluding resources awarded to replace EFC). *Average financial aid package:* $46,810 (excluding resources awarded to replace EFC). 2% of all full-time undergraduates had no need and received non-need-based gift aid.

GIFT AID (NEED-BASED) *Total amount:* $51,527,328 (5% federal, 2% state, 92% institutional, 1% external sources). *Receiving aid:* Freshmen: 67% (315); all full-time undergraduates: 64% (1,242). *Average award:* Freshmen: $45,673; Undergraduates: $41,498. *Scholarships, grants, and awards:* Federal Pell, FSEOG, state, private, college/university gift aid from institutional funds.

GIFT AID (NON-NEED-BASED) *Total amount:* $774,113 (92% institutional, 8% external sources). *Average award:* Freshmen: $31,033. Undergraduates: $21,100. *Scholarships, grants, and awards by category: Special characteristics:* 16 awards ($690,398 total): children of educators, children of faculty/staff. *Tuition waivers:* Full or partial for employees or children of employees.

LOANS *Student loans:* $7,880,804 (94% need-based, 6% non-need-based). 55% of past graduating class borrowed through all loan programs. *Average indebtedness per student:* $26,904. *Average need-based loan:* Freshmen: $5134. Undergraduates: $5815. *Parent loans:* $2,926,215 (89% need-based, 11% non-need-based). *Programs:* Federal Direct (Subsidized and Unsubsidized Stafford, PLUS), Perkins.

WORK-STUDY *Federal work-study:* Total amount: $1,561,795; 873 jobs averaging $1687.

APPLYING FOR FINANCIAL AID *Required financial aid forms:* FAFSA, CSS Financial Aid PROFILE, state aid form, noncustodial (divorced/separated) parent's statement. *Financial aid deadline:* 2/15. *Notification date:* 4/1. Students must reply by 5/1 or within 2 weeks of notification.

CONTACT Denise Ann Ackerman, Director of Financial Aid, Bard College, Annandale Road, Annandale-on-Hudson, NY 12504, 845-758-7525. *Fax:* 845-758-7336. *E-mail:* finaid@bard.edu. *Website:* http://www.bard.edu/.

BARD COLLEGE AT SIMON'S ROCK
Great Barrington, MA

CONTACT Ms. Ann Murtagh Gitto, Director of Financial Aid, Bard College at Simon's Rock, 84 Alford Road, Great Barrington, MA 01230-9702, 413-528-7297 or toll-free 800-235-7186. *Fax:* 413-528-7339. *E-mail:* agitto@simons-rock.edu. *Website:* http://www.simons-rock.edu/.

BARNARD COLLEGE
New York, NY

Tuition & fees: $52,662	Average undergraduate aid package: $50,194

ABOUT THE INSTITUTION Independent, women only. **Awards:** bachelor's degrees. 51 undergraduate majors. **Total enrollment:** 2,604. Undergraduates: 2,604. Freshmen: 603. Both federal and institutional methodology are used as a basis for awarding need-based institutional aid.

UNDERGRADUATE EXPENSES for 2017–2018 **Application fee:** $75. **Comprehensive fee:** $68,762 includes full-time tuition ($50,882), mandatory fees ($1780), and room and board ($16,100). **College room only:** $9510. Room and board charges vary according to board plan and housing facility. **Part-time tuition:** $1697 per credit hour. **Payment plan:** Tuition prepayment.

FRESHMAN FINANCIAL AID (Fall 2017, est.) 309 applied for aid; of those 75% were deemed to have need. 100% of freshmen with need received aid; of those 97% had need fully met. **Average percent of need met:** 100% (excluding resources awarded to replace EFC). **Average financial aid package:** $50,619 (excluding resources awarded to replace EFC).

UNDERGRADUATE FINANCIAL AID (Fall 2017, est.) 1,124 applied for aid; of those 88% were deemed to have need. 100% of undergraduates with need received aid; of those 98% had need fully met. **Average percent of need met:** 100% (excluding resources awarded to replace EFC). **Average financial aid package:** $50,194 (excluding resources awarded to replace EFC).

GIFT AID (NEED-BASED) **Total amount:** $43,700,254 (5% federal, 2% state, 90% institutional, 3% external sources). **Receiving aid:** Freshmen: 37% (224); all full-time undergraduates: 38% (978). **Average award:** Freshmen: $46,022; Undergraduates: $43,984. **Scholarships, grants, and awards:** Federal Pell, FSEOG, state, private, college/university gift aid from institutional funds.

GIFT AID (NON-NEED-BASED) **Total amount:** $1,382,056 (2% state, 98% external sources). **Tuition waivers:** Full or partial for employees or children of employees. **ROTC:** Army cooperative, Naval cooperative, Air Force cooperative.

LOANS **Student loans:** $5,509,555 (60% need-based, 40% non-need-based). 45% of past graduating class borrowed through all loan programs. **Average indebtedness per student:** $23,276. **Average need-based loan:** Freshmen: $3237. Undergraduates: $4431. **Parent loans:** $5,468,942 (100% non-need-based). **Programs:** Federal Direct (Subsidized and Unsubsidized Stafford, PLUS), Perkins, state, college/university.

WORK-STUDY **Federal work-study:** Total amount: $536,889; 238 jobs averaging $2332. **State or other work-study/employment:** Total amount: $1,729,493 (82% need-based, 18% non-need-based). 642 part-time jobs averaging $2252.

APPLYING FOR FINANCIAL AID **Required financial aid forms:** FAFSA, CSS Financial Aid PROFILE, state aid form, noncustodial (divorced/separated) parent's statement, federal income tax form(s). **Financial aid deadline:** 2/1. **Notification date:** 3/31. Students must reply by 5/1.

CONTACT Nanette DiLauro, Director of Financial Aid, Barnard College, 3009 Broadway, New York, NY 10027-6598, 212-854-2154. *Fax:* 212-280-8794. *E-mail:* finaid@barnard.edu.
Website: http://www.barnard.edu/.

BARRY UNIVERSITY
Miami Shores, FL

Tuition & fees: $29,700	Average undergraduate aid package: $22,133

ABOUT THE INSTITUTION Independent Roman Catholic, coed. **Awards:** certificates, bachelor's, master's, and doctoral degrees. 58 undergraduate majors. **Total enrollment:** 7,358. Undergraduates: 3,505. Freshmen: 604. Federal methodology is used as a basis for awarding need-based institutional aid.

UNDERGRADUATE EXPENSES for 2018–2019 **Application fee:** $30. **Comprehensive fee:** $40,800 includes full-time tuition ($29,700) and room and board ($11,100). Room and board charges vary according to housing facility. **Part-time tuition:** $925 per credit hour. Part-time tuition and fees vary according to course load.

FRESHMAN FINANCIAL AID (Fall 2017, est.) 557 applied for aid; of those 97% were deemed to have need. 100% of freshmen with need received aid; of those 6% had

need fully met. **Average percent of need met:** 68% (excluding resources awarded to replace EFC). **Average financial aid package:** $27,266 (excluding resources awarded to replace EFC). 9% of all full-time freshmen had no need and received non-need-based gift aid.

UNDERGRADUATE FINANCIAL AID (Fall 2017, est.) 2,325 applied for aid; of those 97% were deemed to have need. 98% of undergraduates with need received aid; of those 4% had need fully met. **Average percent of need met:** 55% (excluding resources awarded to replace EFC). **Average financial aid package:** $22,133 (excluding resources awarded to replace EFC). 9% of all full-time undergraduates had no need and received non-need-based gift aid.

GIFT AID (NEED-BASED) **Total amount:** $17,390,886 (48% federal, 9% state, 43% institutional). **Receiving aid:** Freshmen: 78% (474); all full-time undergraduates: 61% (1,813). **Average award:** Freshmen: $10,631; Undergraduates: $9369. **Scholarships, grants, and awards:** Federal Pell, FSEOG, state, private, college/university gift aid from institutional funds, Federal Nursing.

GIFT AID (NON-NEED-BASED) **Total amount:** $27,214,813 (18% state, 79% institutional, 3% external sources). **Receiving aid:** Freshmen: 89% (537). Undergraduates: 70% (2,088). **Average award:** Freshmen: $10,501. Undergraduates: $10,068. **Tuition waivers:** Full or partial for employees or children of employees. **ROTC:** Army cooperative, Air Force cooperative.

LOANS **Student loans:** $17,340,029 (46% need-based, 54% non-need-based). 70% of past graduating class borrowed through all loan programs. **Average indebtedness per student:** $38,176. **Average need-based loan:** Freshmen: $3205. Undergraduates: $4290. **Parent loans:** $2,678,544 (100% non-need-based). **Programs:** Perkins, Federal Nursing, college/university, alternative loans.

WORK-STUDY **Federal work-study:** Total amount: $2,534,468; jobs available. **State or other work-study/employment:** Total amount: $349,776 (100% non-need-based). Part-time jobs available.

ATHLETIC AWARDS Total amount: $3,171,199 (100% non-need-based).

APPLYING FOR FINANCIAL AID **Required financial aid form:** FAFSA. **Financial aid deadline:** Continuous. **Notification date:** Continuous beginning 1/25.

CONTACT Mr. Dart Humeston, Director of Financial Aid, Barry University, 11300 Northeast Second Avenue, Miami Shores, FL 33161-6695, 305-899-3673 or toll-free 800-695-2279. *E-mail:* finaid@mail.barry.edu.
Website: http://www.barry.edu/.

BARTON COLLEGE
Wilson, NC

Tuition & fees: $30,880	Average undergraduate aid package: $22,703

ABOUT THE INSTITUTION Independent Christian Church (Disciples of Christ), coed. **Awards:** bachelor's and master's degrees. 35 undergraduate majors. **Total enrollment:** 960. Undergraduates: 887. Freshmen: 198. Both federal and institutional methodology are used as a basis for awarding need-based institutional aid.

UNDERGRADUATE EXPENSES for 2018–2019 **Comprehensive fee:** $41,000 includes full-time tuition ($30,880) and room and board ($10,120). **College room only:** $4360. Full-time tuition and fees vary according to class time, course load, and program. Room and board charges vary according to board plan and housing facility. **Part-time tuition:** $600 per credit hour. Part-time tuition and fees vary according to class time, course load, and program.

FRESHMAN FINANCIAL AID (Fall 2017, est.) 191 applied for aid; of those 94% were deemed to have need. 99% of freshmen with need received aid; of those 14% had need fully met. **Average percent of need met:** 64% (excluding resources awarded to replace EFC). **Average financial aid package:** $21,454 (excluding resources awarded to replace EFC). 13% of all full-time freshmen had no need and received non-need-based gift aid.

UNDERGRADUATE FINANCIAL AID (Fall 2017, est.) 759 applied for aid; of those 95% were deemed to have need. 100% of undergraduates with need received aid; of those 13% had need fully met. **Average percent of need met:** 63% (excluding resources awarded to replace EFC). **Average financial aid package:** $22,703 (excluding resources awarded to replace EFC). 12% of all full-time undergraduates had no need and received non-need-based gift aid.

GIFT AID (NEED-BASED) **Total amount:** $12,511,652 (18% federal, 17% state, 62% institutional, 3% external sources). **Receiving aid:** Freshmen: 88% (174); all full-time undergraduates: 86% (712). **Average award:** Freshmen: $18,545; Undergrad-

uates: $18,982. *Scholarships, grants, and awards:* Federal Pell, FSEOG, state, private, college/university gift aid from institutional funds.

GIFT AID (NON-NEED-BASED) *Total amount:* $1,547,335 (1% state, 95% institutional, 4% external sources). *Receiving aid:* Freshmen: 9% (17). Undergraduates: 8% (66). *Average award:* Freshmen: $12,207. Undergraduates: $11,553. *Scholarships, grants, and awards by category:* Academic interests/ *achievement:* biological sciences, business, communication, education, English, general academic interests/achievements, humanities, mathematics, physical sciences, religion/ biblical studies, social sciences. *Creative arts/performance:* art/fine arts, music, theater/drama. *Special achievements/activities:* general special achievements/activities, leadership, religious involvement. *Special characteristics:* adult students, children and siblings of alumni, children of faculty/staff, international students, local/state students, relatives of clergy, religious affiliation, siblings of current students, veterans. *Tuition waivers:* Full or partial for employees or children of employees, adult students.
LOANS *Student loans:* $5,919,422 (85% need-based, 15% non-need-based). 82% of past graduating class borrowed through all loan programs. *Average indebtedness per student:* $26,477. *Average need-based loan:* Freshmen: $3483. Undergraduates: $4168. *Parent loans:* $2,755,741 (61% need-based, 39% non-need-based). *Programs:* Federal Direct (Subsidized and Unsubsidized Stafford, PLUS), Perkins, college/university.
WORK-STUDY *Federal work-study:* Total amount: $324,082; jobs available. *State or other work-study/employment:* Part-time jobs available.
ATHLETIC AWARDS Total amount: $2,155,252 (49% need-based, 51% non-need-based).
APPLYING FOR FINANCIAL AID *Required financial aid form:* FAFSA. *Notification date:* Continuous beginning 11/1.
CONTACT Mr. Thomas Welch, Director of Financial Aid, Barton College, Box 5000, Wilson, NC 27893, 252-399-6371 or toll-free 800-345-4973. *Fax:* 252-399-6572. *E-mail:* twelch@barton.edu.
Website: http://www.barton.edu/.

BARUCH COLLEGE OF THE CITY UNIVERSITY OF NEW YORK
New York, NY

Tuition & fees (NY res): $7115	Average undergraduate aid package: $5836

ABOUT THE INSTITUTION State and locally supported, coed. *Awards:* certificates, bachelor's, and master's degrees. 25 undergraduate majors. *Total enrollment:* 18,289. Undergraduates: 15,253. Freshmen: 1,605. Federal methodology is used as a basis for awarding need-based institutional aid.
UNDERGRADUATE EXPENSES for 2018–2019 *Application fee:* $65. *Tuition, state resident:* full-time $6530; part-time $285 per credit hour. *Tuition, nonresident:* full-time $17,400; part-time $580 per credit hour. *Required fees:* full-time $585; $162.95 per term. Full-time tuition and fees vary according to course load. Part-time tuition and fees vary according to course load. Room and board charges vary according to housing facility.
FRESHMAN FINANCIAL AID (Fall 2016) 1,638 applied for aid; of those 83% were deemed to have need. 97% of freshmen with need received aid; of those 10% had need fully met. *Average percent of need met:* 45% (excluding resources awarded to replace EFC). *Average financial aid package:* $6115 (excluding resources awarded to replace EFC). 17% of all full-time freshmen had no need and received non-need-based gift aid.
UNDERGRADUATE FINANCIAL AID (Fall 2016) 9,529 applied for aid; of those 90% were deemed to have need. 95% of undergraduates with need received aid; of those 10% had need fully met. *Average percent of need met:* 24% (excluding resources awarded to replace EFC). *Average financial aid package:* $5836 (excluding resources awarded to replace EFC). 14% of all full-time undergraduates had no need and received non-need-based gift aid.
GIFT AID (NEED-BASED) *Total amount:* $67,963,486 (52% federal, 41% state, 6% institutional, 1% external sources). *Receiving aid:* Freshmen: 65% (1,272); all full-time undergraduates: 61% (7,837). *Average award:* Freshmen: $5666; Undergraduates: $5330. *Scholarships, grants, and awards:* Federal Pell, FSEOG, state, college/university gift aid from institutional funds.
GIFT AID (NON-NEED-BASED) *Receiving aid:* Freshmen: 44% (865). Undergraduates: 18% (2,272). *Average award:* Freshmen: $4434. Undergraduates: $5003. *Scholarships, grants, and awards by category:* Academic interests/

achievement: general academic interests/achievements. *Tuition waivers:* Full or partial for employees or children of employees, senior citizens. *ROTC:* Army cooperative.
LOANS *Student loans:* $22,015,173 (27% need-based, 73% non-need-based). 22% of past graduating class borrowed through all loan programs. *Average indebtedness per student:* $5642. *Average need-based loan:* Freshmen: $3186. Undergraduates: $3842. *Parent loans:* $1,468,199 (100% non-need-based). *Programs:* Federal Direct (Subsidized and Unsubsidized Stafford, PLUS), Perkins.
WORK-STUDY *Federal work-study:* 481 jobs averaging $2988. *State or other work-study/employment:* Total amount: $132,703 (100% need-based). Part-time jobs available.
APPLYING FOR FINANCIAL AID *Required financial aid forms:* FAFSA, state aid form. *Financial aid deadline (priority):* 4/15. *Notification date:* Continuous beginning 4/21. Students must reply by 6/1 or within 2 weeks of notification.
CONTACT Ms. Elizabeth Riquez, Financial Aid Services, Baruch College of the City University of New York, One Bernard Baruch Way, Box H-880, New York, NY 10010-5585, 646-312-1399. *Fax:* 646-312-1361. *E-mail:* elizabeth.riquez@baruch.cuny.edu. *Website:* http://www.baruch.cuny.edu/.

BASTYR UNIVERSITY
Kenmore, WA

Tuition & fees: N/R	Average undergraduate aid package: $15,800

ABOUT THE INSTITUTION Independent, coed. 7 undergraduate majors. Federal methodology is used as a basis for awarding need-based institutional aid.
UNDERGRADUATE FINANCIAL AID (Fall 2017, est.) 174 applied for aid; of those 99% were deemed to have need. 100% of undergraduates with need received aid. *Average percent of need met:* 57% (excluding resources awarded to replace EFC). *Average financial aid package:* $15,800 (excluding resources awarded to replace EFC).
GIFT AID (NEED-BASED) *Total amount:* $1,297,379 (32% federal, 38% state, 28% institutional, 2% external sources). *Receiving aid:* All full-time undergraduates: 70% (129). *Average award:* Undergraduates: $8850. *Scholarships, grants, and awards:* Federal Pell, FSEOG, state, private, college/university gift aid from institutional funds.
LOANS *Student loans:* $1,190,345 (44% need-based, 56% non-need-based). *Average need-based loan:* Undergraduates: $11,000. *Parent loans:* $187,853 (100% need-based). *Programs:* Federal Direct (Subsidized and Unsubsidized Stafford, PLUS), Perkins.
WORK-STUDY *Federal work-study:* Total amount: $22,548; 41 jobs averaging $1800. *State or other work-study/employment:* Total amount: $21,255 (100% need-based). 42 part-time jobs averaging $1800.
APPLYING FOR FINANCIAL AID *Financial aid deadline (priority):* 4/15. *Notification date:* Continuous. Students must reply within 4 weeks of notification.
CONTACT Katy Chapin, Financial Aid Advisor, Bastyr University, 14500 Juanita Drive NE, Kenmore, WA 98028-4966, 425-602-3085. *Fax:* 425-602-3094. *E-mail:* finaid@bastyr.edu.
Website: http://www.bastyr.edu/.

BATES COLLEGE
Lewiston, ME

Tuition & fees: $52,042	Average undergraduate aid package: $46,794

ABOUT THE INSTITUTION Independent, coed. *Awards:* bachelor's degrees. 36 undergraduate majors. *Total enrollment:* 1,787. Undergraduates: 1,787. Freshmen: 510. Institutional methodology is used as a basis for awarding need-based institutional aid.
UNDERGRADUATE EXPENSES for 2017–2018 *Application fee:* $60. *Comprehensive fee:* $66,720 includes full-time tuition ($52,042) and room and board ($14,678). *Payment plan:* Tuition prepayment.

FRESHMAN FINANCIAL AID (Fall 2017, est.) 251 applied for aid; of those 86% were deemed to have need. 100% of freshmen with need received aid; of those 100% had need fully met. *Average percent of need met:* 100% (excluding resources awarded to replace EFC). *Average financial aid package:* $47,276 (excluding resources awarded to replace EFC).

UNDERGRADUATE FINANCIAL AID (Fall 2017, est.) 836 applied for aid; of those 93% were deemed to have need. 100% of undergraduates with need received aid; of those 100% had need fully met. *Average percent of need met:* 100% (excluding resources awarded to replace EFC). *Average financial aid package:* $46,794 (excluding resources awarded to replace EFC).

GIFT AID (NEED-BASED) Total amount: $33,215,908 (3% federal, 97% institutional). *Receiving aid:* Freshmen: 42% (216); all full-time undergraduates: 43% (776). *Average award:* Freshmen: $44,063; Undergraduates: $42,804. *Scholarships, grants, and awards:* Federal Pell, FSEOG, state, private, college/university gift aid from institutional funds.

GIFT AID (NON-NEED-BASED) Total amount: $379,615 (100% external sources). *Tuition waivers:* Full or partial for employees or children of employees.

LOANS Student loans: $3,752,696 (47% need-based, 53% non-need-based). 42% of past graduating class borrowed through all loan programs. *Average indebtedness per student:* $20,715. *Average need-based loan:* Freshmen: $2190. Undergraduates: $2990. *Parent loans:* $2,758,744 (100% non-need-based). *Programs:* Federal Direct (Subsidized and Unsubsidized Stafford, PLUS), Perkins.

WORK-STUDY Federal work-study: Total amount: $729,788; jobs available. *State or other work-study/employment:* Total amount: $596,561 (100% need-based). Part-time jobs available.

APPLYING FOR FINANCIAL AID Required financial aid forms: FAFSA, CSS Financial Aid PROFILE, noncustodial (divorced/separated) parent's statement. *Financial aid deadline:* 1/1. *Notification date:* 4/1. Students must reply by 5/1.

CONTACT Ms. Wendy G. Glass, Director of Student Financial Services, Bates College, 44 Mountain Avenue, Lewiston, ME 04240, 207-786-6096 or toll-free 855-228-3755. *Fax:* 207-786-8350. *E-mail:* wglass@bates.edu. *Website:* http://www.bates.edu/.

BAYAMÓN CENTRAL UNIVERSITY
Bayamón, PR

CONTACT Financial Aid Director, Bayamón Central University, PO Box 1725, Bayamón, PR 00960-1725, 787-786-3030 Ext. 2115. *Fax:* 787-785-4365. *Website:* http://www.ucb.edu.pr/.

BAYLOR UNIVERSITY
Waco, TX

Tuition & fees: $45,542	Average undergraduate aid package: $30,498

ABOUT THE INSTITUTION Independent Baptist, coed. *Awards:* certificates, bachelor's, master's, and doctoral degrees. 126 undergraduate majors. *Total enrollment:* 17,059. Undergraduates: 14,316. Freshmen: 3,320. Federal methodology is used as a basis for awarding need-based institutional aid.

UNDERGRADUATE EXPENSES for 2018–2019 Comprehensive fee: $58,137 includes full-time tuition ($41,194), mandatory fees ($4348), and room and board ($12,595). *College room only:* $6920. Room and board charges vary according to board plan and housing facility. *Part-time tuition:* $1716 per semester hour. *Part-time fees:* $181 per semester hour.

FRESHMAN FINANCIAL AID (Fall 2017, est.) 2,682 applied for aid; of those 78% were deemed to have need. 100% of freshmen with need received aid; of those 15% had need fully met. *Average percent of need met:* 72% (excluding resources awarded to replace EFC). *Average financial aid package:* $33,682 (excluding resources awarded to replace EFC). 32% of all full-time freshmen had no need and received non-need-based gift aid.

UNDERGRADUATE FINANCIAL AID (Fall 2017, est.) 9,305 applied for aid; of those 84% were deemed to have need. 100% of undergraduates with need received aid; of those 15% had need fully met. *Average percent of need met:* 67% (excluding resources awarded to replace EFC). *Average financial aid package:*

$30,498 (excluding resources awarded to replace EFC). 36% of all full-time undergraduates had no need and received non-need-based gift aid.

GIFT AID (NEED-BASED) Total amount: $181,630,468 (8% federal, 5% state, 85% institutional, 2% external sources). *Receiving aid:* Freshmen: 63% (2,093); all full-time undergraduates: 54% (7,606). *Average award:* Freshmen: $27,714; Undergraduates: $24,420. *Scholarships, grants, and awards:* Federal Pell, FSEOG, state, college/university gift aid from institutional funds.

GIFT AID (NON-NEED-BASED) Total amount: $82,987,947 (98% institutional, 2% external sources). *Receiving aid:* Freshmen: 62% (2,066). Undergraduates: 52% (7,352). *Average award:* Freshmen: $17,488. Undergraduates: $15,059. *Scholarships, grants, and awards by category:* Academic interests/achievement: 13,330 awards ($155,014,907 total): business, communication, computer science, education, engineering/technologies, English, foreign languages, general academic interests/achievements, health fields, home economics, humanities, international studies, mathematics, military science, physical sciences, premedicine, religion/biblical studies, social sciences. Creative arts/performance: 370 awards ($2,366,188 total): art/fine arts, cinema/film/broadcasting, debating, journalism/publications, music, theater/drama. Special achievements/activities: 578 awards ($2,975,463 total): community service, leadership, religious involvement. Special characteristics: 213 awards ($6,213,037 total): children of faculty/staff, veterans, veterans' children. *Tuition waivers:* Full or partial for employees or children of employees. *ROTC:* Army, Air Force.

LOANS Student loans: $97,259,234 (66% need-based, 34% non-need-based). 52% of past graduating class borrowed through all loan programs. *Average indebtedness per student:* $44,859. *Average need-based loan:* Freshmen: $2801. Undergraduates: $3580. *Parent loans:* $37,778,467 (49% need-based, 51% non-need-based). *Programs:* Federal Direct (Subsidized and Unsubsidized Stafford, PLUS), Perkins, Federal Nursing, state, private loans.

WORK-STUDY Federal work-study: Total amount: $14,112,949; jobs available. *State or other work-study/employment:* Part-time jobs available.

ATHLETIC AWARDS Total amount: $13,839,099 (34% need-based, 66% non-need-based).

APPLYING FOR FINANCIAL AID Required financial aid forms: FAFSA, State Residency Affirmation (TX residents only). *Financial aid deadline (priority):* 2/1. *Notification date:* Continuous beginning 12/15. Students must reply by 5/1 or within 2 weeks of notification.

CONTACT Mrs. Lisa Martin, Student Financial Aid, Baylor University, PO Box 97028, Waco, TX 76798-7028, 254-710-2611 or toll-free 800-BAYLORU. *Fax:* 254-710-2695. *E-mail:* finaidtech@baylor.edu. *Website:* http://www.baylor.edu/.

BAY PATH UNIVERSITY
Longmeadow, MA

Tuition & fees: $33,557	Average undergraduate aid package: $27,333

ABOUT THE INSTITUTION Independent, undergraduate: women only; graduate: coed. *Awards:* certificates, associate, bachelor's, master's, and doctoral degrees. 30 undergraduate majors. *Total enrollment:* 3,298. Undergraduates: 1,947. Freshmen: 144. Both federal and institutional methodology are used as a basis for awarding need-based institutional aid.

UNDERGRADUATE EXPENSES for 2017–2018 Comprehensive fee: $46,356 includes full-time tuition ($33,557) and room and board ($12,799). Room and board charges vary according to board plan. *Part-time tuition:* $510 per credit hour. Part-time tuition and fees vary according to course load.

FRESHMAN FINANCIAL AID (Fall 2017, est.) 138 applied for aid; of those 97% were deemed to have need. 99% of freshmen with need received aid; of those 8% had need fully met. *Average percent of need met:* 75% (excluding resources awarded to replace EFC). *Average financial aid package:* $30,290 (excluding resources awarded to replace EFC). 5% of all full-time freshmen had no need and received non-need-based gift aid.

UNDERGRADUATE FINANCIAL AID (Fall 2017, est.) 615 applied for aid; of those 95% were deemed to have need. 100% of undergraduates with need received aid; of those 6% had need fully met. *Average percent of need met:* 72% (excluding resources awarded to replace EFC). *Average financial aid package:* $27,333 (excluding resources awarded to replace EFC). 8% of all full-time undergraduates had no need and received non-need-based gift aid.

GIFT AID (NEED-BASED) *Total amount:* $12,934,054 (14% federal, 3% state, 81% institutional, 2% external sources). *Receiving aid:* Freshmen: 92% (133); all full-time undergraduates: 92% (586). *Average award:* Freshmen: $25,346; Undergraduates: $22,108. *Scholarships, grants, and awards:* Federal Pell, FSEOG, state, private, college/university gift aid from institutional funds.
GIFT AID (NON-NEED-BASED) *Total amount:* $849,894 (99% institutional, 1% external sources). *Receiving aid:* Freshmen: 7% (10). Undergraduates: 4% (25). *Average award:* Freshmen: $18,857. Undergraduates: $13,799. *Scholarships, grants, and awards by category:* Academic interests/achievement: general academic interests/achievements. *Special characteristics:* adult students, children of faculty/staff, children with a deceased or disabled parent, general special characteristics, international students, siblings of current students. *Tuition waivers:* Full or partial for employees or children of employees. *ROTC:* Army cooperative, Air Force cooperative.
LOANS *Student loans:* $6,311,356 (80% need-based, 20% non-need-based). 90% of past graduating class borrowed through all loan programs. *Average indebtedness per student:* $41,614. *Average need-based loan:* Freshmen: $4209. Undergraduates: $4843. *Parent loans:* $1,905,765 (59% need-based, 41% non-need-based). *Programs:* Federal Direct (Subsidized and Unsubsidized Stafford, PLUS), Perkins.
WORK-STUDY *Federal work-study:* Total amount: $455,929; jobs available. *State or other work-study/employment:* Part-time jobs available.
APPLYING FOR FINANCIAL AID *Required financial aid form:* FAFSA. *Financial aid deadline (priority):* 10/1. *Notification date:* Continuous beginning 12/1. Students must reply within 2 weeks of notification.
CONTACT Stephanie King, Director of Student Financial Services, Bay Path University, 588 Longmeadow Street, Longmeadow, MA 01106-2292, 413-565-1345 or toll-free 800-782-7284 Ext. 1331. *Fax:* 413-565-1101. *E-mail:* sking@baypath.edu. *Website:* http://www.baypath.edu/.

BEACON COLLEGE
Leesburg, FL

CONTACT Mrs. Shawna L. Wells-Booth, Director of Financial Aid, Beacon College, 105 East Main Street, Leesburg, FL 34788, 352-638-9733. *Fax:* 800-360-1974. *E-mail:* financialaid@beaconcollege.edu.
Website: http://www.beaconcollege.edu/.

BECKER COLLEGE
Worcester, MA

Tuition & fees: $39,200	Average undergraduate aid package: $21,224

ABOUT THE INSTITUTION Independent, coed. *Awards:* certificates, associate, bachelor's, and master's degrees (also includes Leicester, MA small town campus). 27 undergraduate majors. *Total enrollment:* 1,892. Undergraduates: 1,882. Freshmen: 381. Federal methodology is used as a basis for awarding need-based institutional aid.
UNDERGRADUATE EXPENSES for 2018–2019 *One-time required fee:* $200. *Comprehensive fee:* $53,000 includes full-time tuition ($35,600), mandatory fees ($3600), and room and board ($13,800). Full-time tuition and fees vary according to class time, course load, and program. Room and board charges vary according to housing facility. *Part-time tuition:* $1483 per credit. Part-time tuition and fees vary according to class time, course load, and program.
FRESHMAN FINANCIAL AID (Fall 2016) 391 applied for aid; of those 93% were deemed to have need. 100% of freshmen with need received aid; of those .3% had need fully met. *Average percent of need met:* 59% (excluding resources awarded to replace EFC). *Average financial aid package:* $22,731 (excluding resources awarded to replace EFC). 11% of all full-time freshmen had no need and received non-need-based gift aid.
UNDERGRADUATE FINANCIAL AID (Fall 2016) 1,427 applied for aid; of those 95% were deemed to have need. 100% of undergraduates with need received aid; of those .2% had need fully met. *Average percent of need met:* 56% (excluding resources awarded to replace EFC). *Average financial aid package:* $21,224 (excluding resources awarded to replace EFC). 11% of all full-time undergraduates had no need and received non-need-based gift aid.

GIFT AID (NEED-BASED) *Total amount:* $28,662,804 (10% federal, 3% state, 86% institutional, 1% external sources). *Receiving aid:* Freshmen: 88% (365); all full-time undergraduates: 87% (1,362). *Average award:* Freshmen: $20,103; Undergraduates: $17,978. *Scholarships, grants, and awards:* Federal Pell, FSEOG, state, private, college/university gift aid from institutional funds.
GIFT AID (NON-NEED-BASED) *Total amount:* $2,519,083 (100% institutional). *Receiving aid:* Freshmen: 14% (57). Undergraduates: 11% (179). *Average award:* Freshmen: $14,467. Undergraduates: $12,586. *Scholarships, grants, and awards by category:* Academic interests/achievement: general academic interests/achievements. *Special achievements/activities:* leadership. *Special characteristics:* children of faculty/staff, siblings of current students. *Tuition waivers:* Full or partial for employees or children of employees. *ROTC:* Army cooperative, Naval cooperative, Air Force cooperative.
LOANS *Student loans:* $18,103,728 (91% need-based, 9% non-need-based). *Average need-based loan:* Freshmen: $2174. Undergraduates: $4124. *Parent loans:* $8,729,074 (92% need-based, 8% non-need-based). *Programs:* Federal Direct (Subsidized and Unsubsidized Stafford, PLUS), state, alternative loans.
WORK-STUDY *Federal work-study:* jobs available.
APPLYING FOR FINANCIAL AID *Required financial aid form:* FAFSA. *Financial aid deadline (priority):* 3/15. *Notification date:* Continuous beginning 12/15. Students must reply within 2 weeks of notification.
CONTACT Mr. Allen Cowett, Director of Financial Aid, Becker College, 61 Sever Street, Worcester, MA 01615-0071, 508-373-9430 or toll-free 877-5BECKER. *Fax:* 508-890-1511. *E-mail:* financialaid@becker.edu.
Website: http://www.becker.edu/.

BE'ER YAAKOV TALMUDIC SEMINARY
Spring Valley, NY

CONTACT Financial Aid Office, Be'er Yaakov Talmudic Seminary, 12 Jefferson Avenue, Spring Valley, NY 10977, 845-406-9699.

BEIS MEDRASH HEICHAL DOVID
Far Rockaway, NY

CONTACT Financial Aid Office, Beis Medrash Heichal Dovid, 257 Beach 17th Street, Far Rockaway, NY 11691, 718-868-2300.

BELHAVEN UNIVERSITY
Jackson, MS

Tuition & fees: $25,300	Average undergraduate aid package: $16,538

ABOUT THE INSTITUTION Independent Presbyterian, coed. *Awards:* certificates, associate, bachelor's, master's, and doctoral degrees. 38 undergraduate majors. *Total enrollment:* 4,458. Undergraduates: 2,482. Freshmen: 240. Federal methodology is used as a basis for awarding need-based institutional aid.
UNDERGRADUATE EXPENSES for 2018–2019 *Application fee:* $25. *Comprehensive fee:* $33,800 includes full-time tuition ($24,950), mandatory fees ($350), and room and board ($8500). Full-time tuition and fees vary according to location and program. Room and board charges vary according to housing facility. *Part-time tuition:* $425 per credit hour. Part-time tuition and fees vary according to course load, location, and program.
FRESHMAN FINANCIAL AID (Fall 2016) 213 applied for aid; of those 88% were deemed to have need. 100% of freshmen with need received aid; of those 8% had need fully met. *Average percent of need met:* 72% (excluding resources awarded to replace EFC). *Average financial aid package:* $19,199 (excluding resources awarded to replace EFC). 15% of all full-time freshmen had no need and received non-need-based gift aid.
UNDERGRADUATE FINANCIAL AID (Fall 2016) 1,134 applied for aid; of those 92% were deemed to have need. 99% of undergraduates with need received aid; of those 9% had need fully met. *Average percent of need met:* 63% (excluding resources awarded to replace EFC). *Average financial aid package:* $16,538

(excluding resources awarded to replace EFC). 18% of all full-time undergraduates had no need and received non-need-based gift aid.

GIFT AID (NEED-BASED) *Total amount:* $7,325,090 (75% federal, 3% state, 22% institutional). *Receiving aid:* Freshmen: 64% (145); all full-time undergraduates: 55% (731). *Average award:* Freshmen: $7226. *Scholarships, grants, and awards:* Federal Pell, FSEOG, state, private, college/university gift aid from institutional funds.

GIFT AID (NON-NEED-BASED) *Total amount:* $10,366,276 (1% state, 93% institutional, 6% external sources). *Receiving aid:* Freshmen: 80% (180). Undergraduates: 62% (823). *Average award:* Freshmen: $11,015. *Scholarships, grants, and awards by category: Academic interests/achievement:* biological sciences, business, communication, education, English, foreign languages, general academic interests/achievements, humanities, international studies, mathematics, premedicine, religion/biblical studies, social sciences. *Creative arts/performance:* applied art and design, art/fine arts, cinema/film/broadcasting, creative writing, dance, general creative arts/performance, journalism/publications, music, performing arts, theater/drama. *Special achievements/activities:* cheerleading/drum major, general special achievements/activities, junior miss, leadership. *Special characteristics:* children and siblings of alumni, children of faculty/staff, general special characteristics, international students, local/state students, religious affiliation, siblings of current students, veterans, veterans' children. *Tuition waivers:* Full or partial for employees or children of employees. *ROTC:* Army cooperative, Air Force cooperative.

LOANS *Student loans:* $17,104,332 (41% need-based, 59% non-need-based). *Average need-based loan:* Freshmen: $3191. Undergraduates: $4078. *Parent loans:* $2,671,608 (100% need-based). *Programs:* Federal Direct (Subsidized and Unsubsidized Stafford, PLUS), Perkins, state.

WORK-STUDY *Federal work-study:* jobs available. *State or other work-study/employment:* Total amount: $29,130 (100% non-need-based). Part-time jobs available.

APPLYING FOR FINANCIAL AID *Required financial aid form:* FAFSA. *Financial aid deadline (priority):* 3/1. *Notification date:* Continuous.

CONTACT Mrs. Debbi Braswell, Director of Financial Aid, Belhaven University, 1500 Peachtree Street, Box 159, Jackson, MS 39202-1789, 601-968-5933 or toll-free 800-960-5940. *E-mail:* dbraswell@belhaven.edu. *Website:* http://www.belhaven.edu/.

BELLARMINE UNIVERSITY
Louisville, KY

Tuition & fees: $41,800	Average undergraduate aid package: $33,094

ABOUT THE INSTITUTION Independent Roman Catholic, coed. *Awards:* certificates, bachelor's, master's, and doctoral degrees. 42 undergraduate majors. *Total enrollment:* 3,757. Undergraduates: 2,544. Freshmen: 681. Both federal and institutional methodology are used as a basis for awarding need-based institutional aid.

UNDERGRADUATE EXPENSES for 2018–2019 *Application fee:* $25. *One-time required fee:* $400. *Comprehensive fee:* $54,050 includes full-time tuition ($40,250), mandatory fees ($1550), and room and board ($12,250). *College room only:* $7630. Full-time tuition and fees vary according to course load, degree level, location, and program. Room and board charges vary according to board plan and housing facility. *Part-time tuition:* $935 per credit hour. Part-time tuition and fees vary according to course load, degree level, location, and program.

FRESHMAN FINANCIAL AID (Fall 2017, est.) 665 applied for aid; of those 88% were deemed to have need. 100% of freshmen with need received aid; of those 24% had need fully met. *Average percent of need met:* 80% (excluding resources awarded to replace EFC). *Average financial aid package:* $36,193 (excluding resources awarded to replace EFC). 13% of all full-time freshmen had no need and received non-need-based gift aid.

UNDERGRADUATE FINANCIAL AID (Fall 2017, est.) 2,174 applied for aid; of those 89% were deemed to have need. 98% of undergraduates with need received aid; of those 22% had need fully met. *Average percent of need met:* 76% (excluding resources awarded to replace EFC). *Average financial aid package:* $33,094 (excluding resources awarded to replace EFC). 19% of all full-time undergraduates had no need and received non-need-based gift aid.

GIFT AID (NEED-BASED) *Total amount:* $50,980,488 (6% federal, 11% state, 81% institutional, 2% external sources). *Receiving aid:* Freshmen: 86% (586); all full-time undergraduates: 78% (1,878). *Average award:* Freshmen: $28,051; Undergrad-

uates: $25,193. *Scholarships, grants, and awards:* Federal Pell, FSEOG, state, private, college/university gift aid from institutional funds.

GIFT AID (NON-NEED-BASED) *Total amount:* $13,386,931 (6% state, 91% institutional, 3% external sources). *Receiving aid:* Freshmen: 28% (187). Undergraduates: 24% (588). *Average award:* Freshmen: $28,206. Undergraduates: $23,565. *Scholarships, grants, and awards by category: Academic interests/achievement:* biological sciences, business, education, general academic interests/achievements, physical sciences. *Creative arts/performance:* art/fine arts, music. *Special achievements/activities:* cheerleading/drum major, community service, general special achievements/activities, leadership, religious involvement. *Special characteristics:* adult students, children and siblings of alumni, children of faculty/staff, ethnic background, international students, local/state students, members of minority groups, out-of-state students, previous college experience, religious affiliation. *Tuition waivers:* Full or partial for employees or children of employees. *ROTC:* Army cooperative, Air Force cooperative.

LOANS *Student loans:* $13,967,062 (77% need-based, 23% non-need-based). 72% of past graduating class borrowed through all loan programs. *Average indebtedness per student:* $31,377. *Average need-based loan:* Freshmen: $4068. Undergraduates: $4731. *Parent loans:* $3,402,324 (55% need-based, 45% non-need-based). *Programs:* Federal Direct (Subsidized and Unsubsidized Stafford, PLUS), Perkins, college/university.

WORK-STUDY *Federal work-study:* Total amount: $558,100; jobs available. *State or other work-study/employment:* Total amount: $220,400 (74% need-based, 26% non-need-based). Part-time jobs available.

ATHLETIC AWARDS Total amount: $3,046,858 (49% need-based, 51% non-need-based).

APPLYING FOR FINANCIAL AID *Required financial aid form:* FAFSA. *Financial aid deadline (priority):* 11/1. *Notification date:* Continuous beginning 1/31. Students must reply by 5/1.

CONTACT Ms. Heather Boutell, Director of Financial Aid, Bellarmine University, 2001 Newburg Road, Louisville, KY 40205-0671, 502-272-7300 or toll-free 800-274-4723 Ext. 8131. *Fax:* 502-272-8486. *E-mail:* hboutell@bellarmine.edu. *Website:* http://www.bellarmine.edu/.

BELLEVUE UNIVERSITY
Bellevue, NE

CONTACT Ms. Janet Yale, Director of Financial Aid, Bellevue University, 1000 Galvin Road South, Bellevue, NE 68005, 402-293-2000 or toll-free 800-756-7920. *Fax:* 402-557-5425. *Website:* http://www.bellevue.edu/.

BELLIN COLLEGE
Green Bay, WI

CONTACT Mrs. Lena C. Goodman, Director of Financial Aid, Bellin College, 3201 Eaton Road, Green Bay, WI 54311, 920-433-6638 or toll-free 800-236-8707. *Fax:* 920-433-1922. *E-mail:* lena.goodman@bellincollege.edu. *Website:* http://www.bellincollege.edu/.

BELMONT ABBEY COLLEGE
Belmont, NC

Tuition & fees: N/R	Average undergraduate aid package: $12,389

ABOUT THE INSTITUTION Independent Roman Catholic, coed. *Awards:* bachelor's degrees. 16 undergraduate majors. *Total enrollment:* 1,524. Undergraduates: 1,524. Federal methodology is used as a basis for awarding need-based institutional aid.

FRESHMAN FINANCIAL AID (Fall 2016) 325 applied for aid; of those 81% were deemed to have need. 99% of freshmen with need received aid; of those 11% had need fully met. *Average percent of need met:* 55% (excluding resources awarded to

replace EFC). *Average financial aid package:* $13,110 (excluding resources awarded to replace EFC). 30% of all full-time freshmen had no need and received non-need-based gift aid.

UNDERGRADUATE FINANCIAL AID (Fall 2016) 1,181 applied for aid; of those 86% were deemed to have need. 100% of undergraduates with need received aid; of those 10% had need fully met. *Average percent of need met:* 52% (excluding resources awarded to replace EFC). *Average financial aid package:* $12,389 (excluding resources awarded to replace EFC). 20% of all full-time undergraduates had no need and received non-need-based gift aid.

GIFT AID (NEED-BASED) *Total amount:* $4,788,428 (54% federal, 40% state, 6% institutional). *Receiving aid:* Freshmen: 73% (262); all full-time undergraduates: 67% (1,013). *Average award:* Freshmen: $9585; Undergraduates: $8458. *Scholarships, grants, and awards:* Federal Pell, FSEOG, state, private, college/university gift aid from institutional funds.

GIFT AID (NON-NEED-BASED) *Total amount:* $4,851,241 (98% institutional, 2% external sources). *Receiving aid:* Freshmen: 6% (21). Undergraduates: 4% (61). *Average award:* Freshmen: $4866. Undergraduates: $4619. *Scholarships, grants, and awards by category: Academic interests/achievement:* 867 awards ($3,291,102 total): business, education, general academic interests/achievements, humanities. *Creative arts/performance:* 18 awards ($96,176 total): theater/drama. *Special achievements/activities:* 53 awards ($298,219 total): cheerleading/drum major, religious involvement. *Special characteristics:* 32 awards ($267,014 total): children of faculty/staff.

LOANS *Student loans:* $8,467,347 (43% need-based, 57% non-need-based). 77% of past graduating class borrowed through all loan programs. *Average indebtedness per student:* $25,610. *Average need-based loan:* Freshmen: $3793. Undergraduates: $4398. *Parent loans:* $4,632,244 (37% need-based, 63% non-need-based). *Programs:* Federal Direct (Subsidized and Unsubsidized Stafford, PLUS).

WORK-STUDY *Federal work-study:* 83 jobs averaging $2000.

ATHLETIC AWARDS Total amount: $1,526,200 (11% need-based, 89% non-need-based).

APPLYING FOR FINANCIAL AID *Required financial aid form:* FAFSA. *Financial aid deadline (priority):* 2/1. *Notification date:* Continuous beginning 12/5. Students must reply within 2 weeks of notification.

CONTACT Ms. Julie Hodge, Associate Director of Financial Aid, Belmont Abbey College, 100 Belmont Mt. Holly Road, Belmont, NC 28012-1802, 704-461-7000 or toll-free 888-BAC-0110. *Fax:* 704-461-6727. *E-mail:* juliehodge@bac.edu. *Website:* http://www.belmontabbeycollege.edu/.

BELMONT UNIVERSITY
Nashville, TN

Tuition & fees: $32,820	Average undergraduate aid package: $19,176

ABOUT THE INSTITUTION Independent Christian, coed. *Awards:* certificates, bachelor's, master's, and doctoral degrees. 87 undergraduate majors. *Total enrollment:* 8,012. Undergraduates: 6,497. Freshmen: 1,568. Federal methodology is used as a basis for awarding need-based institutional aid.

UNDERGRADUATE EXPENSES for 2017–2018 *Application fee:* $50. *Comprehensive fee:* $44,500 includes full-time tuition ($31,300), mandatory fees ($1520), and room and board ($11,680). *College room only:* $6440. Full-time tuition and fees vary according to course load. Room and board charges vary according to board plan and housing facility. *Part-time tuition:* $1190 per credit hour. Part-time tuition and fees vary according to course load.

FRESHMAN FINANCIAL AID (Fall 2017, est.) 1,263 applied for aid; of those 67% were deemed to have need. 100% of freshmen with need received aid; of those 13% had need fully met. *Average percent of need met:* 61% (excluding resources awarded to replace EFC). *Average financial aid package:* $20,078 (excluding resources awarded to replace EFC). 33% of all full-time freshmen had no need and received non-need-based gift aid.

UNDERGRADUATE FINANCIAL AID (Fall 2017, est.) 4,160 applied for aid; of those 77% were deemed to have need. 100% of undergraduates with need received aid; of those 10% had need fully met. *Average percent of need met:* 56% (excluding resources awarded to replace EFC). *Average financial aid package:* $19,176 (excluding resources awarded to replace EFC). 26% of all full-time undergraduates had no need and received non-need-based gift aid.

GIFT AID (NEED-BASED) *Total amount:* $45,145,290 (11% federal, 9% state, 80% institutional). *Receiving aid:* Freshmen: 52% (814); all full-time undergraduates:

47% (2,882). *Average award:* Freshmen: $16,960; Undergraduates: $15,526. *Scholarships, grants, and awards:* Federal Pell, FSEOG, state, private, college/university gift aid from institutional funds.

GIFT AID (NON-NEED-BASED) *Total amount:* $12,528,298 (9% state, 91% institutional). *Receiving aid:* Freshmen: 7% (111). Undergraduates: 5% (318). *Average award:* Freshmen: $8348. Undergraduates: $7714. *Scholarships, grants, and awards by category: Academic interests/achievement:* biological sciences, business, general academic interests/achievements, health fields, religion/biblical studies, social sciences. *Creative arts/performance:* applied art and design, art/fine arts, cinema/film/broadcasting, creative writing, dance, general creative arts/performance, journalism/publications, music, performing arts, theater/drama. *Special achievements/activities:* cheerleading/drum major, community service, general special achievements/activities, leadership, religious involvement. *Special characteristics:* children and siblings of alumni, children of faculty/staff, local/state students, members of minority groups, siblings of current students, veterans, veterans' children. *Tuition waivers:* Full or partial for employees or children of employees, senior citizens. *ROTC:* Army cooperative, Naval cooperative, Air Force cooperative.

LOANS *Student loans:* $14,467,987 (100% need-based). 53% of past graduating class borrowed through all loan programs. *Average indebtedness per student:* $29,207. *Average need-based loan:* Freshmen: $3479. Undergraduates: $4445. *Parent loans:* $31,377,506 (81% need-based, 19% non-need-based). *Programs:* Federal Direct (Subsidized and Unsubsidized Stafford, PLUS), Perkins.

WORK-STUDY *Federal work-study:* Total amount: $2,717,633; 1,159 jobs averaging $1952.

ATHLETIC AWARDS Total amount: $5,279,808 (37% need-based, 63% non-need-based).

APPLYING FOR FINANCIAL AID *Required financial aid form:* FAFSA. *Financial aid deadline (priority):* 3/1. *Notification date:* Continuous beginning 3/15. Students must reply by 5/1 or within 2 weeks of notification.

CONTACT Mrs. Pat Smedley, Director of Student Financial Services, Belmont University, 1900 Belmont Boulevard, Nashville, TN 37212-3757, 615-460-6403. *E-mail:* pat.smedley@belmont.edu. *Website:* http://www.belmont.edu/.

BELOIT COLLEGE
Beloit, WI

Tuition & fees: $50,040	Average undergraduate aid package: $43,088

ABOUT THE INSTITUTION Independent, coed. *Awards:* bachelor's degrees. 50 undergraduate majors. *Total enrollment:* 1,402. Undergraduates: 1,402. Freshmen: 323. Both federal and institutional methodology are used as a basis for awarding need-based institutional aid.

UNDERGRADUATE EXPENSES for 2018–2019 *Comprehensive fee:* $58,870 includes full-time tuition ($49,564), mandatory fees ($476), and room and board ($8830). *College room only:* $5030. Room and board charges vary according to board plan. *Part-time tuition:* $1549 per credit hour.

FRESHMAN FINANCIAL AID (Fall 2017, est.) 250 applied for aid; of those 87% were deemed to have need. 100% of freshmen with need received aid; of those 27% had need fully met. *Average percent of need met:* 95% (excluding resources awarded to replace EFC). *Average financial aid package:* $45,818 (excluding resources awarded to replace EFC). 32% of all full-time freshmen had no need and received non-need-based gift aid.

UNDERGRADUATE FINANCIAL AID (Fall 2017, est.) 894 applied for aid; of those 89% were deemed to have need. 100% of undergraduates with need received aid; of those 29% had need fully met. *Average percent of need met:* 94% (excluding resources awarded to replace EFC). *Average financial aid package:* $43,088 (excluding resources awarded to replace EFC). 38% of all full-time undergraduates had no need and received non-need-based gift aid.

GIFT AID (NEED-BASED) *Total amount:* $25,492,007 (7% federal, 1% state, 91% institutional, 1% external sources). *Receiving aid:* Freshmen: 67% (215); all full-time undergraduates: 60% (788). *Average award:* Freshmen: $34,860; Undergraduates: $32,340. *Scholarships, grants, and awards:* Federal Pell, FSEOG, state, private, college/university gift aid from institutional funds.

GIFT AID (NON-NEED-BASED) *Total amount:* $14,468,003 (99% institutional, 1% external sources). *Receiving aid:* Freshmen: 39% (125). Undergraduates: 31% (414). *Average award:* Freshmen: $30,800. Undergraduates: $25,473. *Schol-

arships, grants, and awards by category: Academic interests/achievement: general academic interests/achievements. *Creative arts/performance:* music. *Special achievements/activities:* community service, general special achievements/activities, leadership. *Special characteristics:* siblings of current students, veterans. *Tuition waivers:* Full or partial for employees or children of employees.

LOANS *Student loans:* $7,694,876 (76% need-based, 24% non-need-based). 65% of past graduating class borrowed through all loan programs. *Average indebtedness per student:* $27,507. *Average need-based loan:* Freshmen: $6234. Undergraduates: $6822. *Parent loans:* $1,470,198 (40% need-based, 60% non-need-based). *Programs:* Federal Direct (Subsidized and Unsubsidized Stafford, PLUS), Perkins, college/university.

WORK-STUDY *Federal work-study:* Total amount: $1,074,844; jobs available. *State or other work-study/employment:* Total amount: $474,484 (10% need-based, 90% non-need-based). Part-time jobs available.

APPLYING FOR FINANCIAL AID *Required financial aid form:* FAFSA. *Financial aid deadline:* 3/1. *Notification date:* Continuous beginning 3/1. Students must reply by 5/1.

CONTACT Ms. Victoria Gack, Director of Financial Aid, Beloit College, 700 College Street, Beloit, WI 53511-5596, 608-363-2696 or toll-free 800-9-BELOIT. *Fax:* 608-363-7139. *E-mail:* gackv@beloit.edu.
Website: http://www.beloit.edu/.

BEMIDJI STATE UNIVERSITY
Bemidji, MN

Tuition & fees: N/R	Average undergraduate aid package: $9299

ABOUT THE INSTITUTION State-supported, coed. *Awards:* certificates, associate, bachelor's, and master's degrees. 70 undergraduate majors. *Total enrollment:* 5,189. Undergraduates: 4,833. Freshmen: 764. Federal methodology is used as a basis for awarding need-based institutional aid.

FRESHMAN FINANCIAL AID (Fall 2016) 666 applied for aid; of those 71% were deemed to have need. 99% of freshmen with need received aid; of those 7% had need fully met. *Average percent of need met:* 58% (excluding resources awarded to replace EFC). *Average financial aid package:* $8434 (excluding resources awarded to replace EFC). 14% of all full-time freshmen had no need and received non-need-based gift aid.

UNDERGRADUATE FINANCIAL AID (Fall 2016) 2,792 applied for aid; of those 74% were deemed to have need. 99% of undergraduates with need received aid; of those 15% had need fully met. *Average percent of need met:* 61% (excluding resources awarded to replace EFC). *Average financial aid package:* $9299 (excluding resources awarded to replace EFC). 20% of all full-time undergraduates had no need and received non-need-based gift aid.

GIFT AID (NEED-BASED) *Total amount:* $10,989,389 (63% federal, 34% state, 2% institutional, 1% external sources). *Receiving aid:* Freshmen: 40% (304); all full-time undergraduates: 42% (1,441). *Average award:* Freshmen: $5865; Undergraduates: $5878. *Scholarships, grants, and awards:* Federal Pell, FSEOG, state, private, college/university gift aid from institutional funds.

GIFT AID (NON-NEED-BASED) *Total amount:* $6,420,875 (9% federal, 10% state, 63% institutional, 18% external sources). *Receiving aid:* Freshmen: 45% (346). Undergraduates: 43% (1,450). *Average award:* Freshmen: $10,911. Undergraduates: $11,023. *Scholarships, grants, and awards by category: Academic interests/achievement:* 1,232 awards ($1,568,942 total): biological sciences, business, communication, computer science, education, engineering/technologies, English, foreign languages, general academic interests/achievements, health fields, humanities, international studies, mathematics, physical sciences, premedicine, social sciences. *Creative arts/performance:* 48 awards ($112,379 total): applied art and design, art/fine arts, cinema/film/broadcasting, creative writing, general creative arts/performance, journalism/publications, music, performing arts. *Special achievements/activities:* 18 awards ($25,100 total): general special achievements/activities, leadership. *Special characteristics:* 237 awards ($554,285 total): children and siblings of alumni, children of faculty/staff, handicapped students, international students, members of minority groups, out-of-state students, previous college experience.

LOANS *Student loans:* $24,247,541 (36% need-based, 64% non-need-based). 97% of past graduating class borrowed through all loan programs. *Average indebtedness per student:* $27,171. *Average need-based loan:* Freshmen: $3400. Undergrad-

uates: $4225. *Parent loans:* $1,046,728 (100% non-need-based). *Programs:* Federal Direct (Subsidized and Unsubsidized Stafford, PLUS), Perkins, state, alternative loans.

WORK-STUDY *Federal work-study:* 299 jobs averaging $1284. *State or other work-study/employment:* Total amount: $412,037 (100% need-based). 194 part-time jobs averaging $2124.

ATHLETIC AWARDS Total amount: $1,517,578 (100% non-need-based).

APPLYING FOR FINANCIAL AID *Required financial aid form:* FAFSA. *Financial aid deadline:* Continuous. *Notification date:* Continuous beginning 6/15.

CONTACT Financial Aid Office, Bemidji State University, 1500 Birchmont Drive NE #14, Bemidji, MN 56601-2699, 218-755-2034 or toll-free 800-475-2001. *Fax:* 218-755-4361. *E-mail:* financialaid@bemidjistate.edu.
Website: http://www.bemidjistate.edu/.

BENEDICT COLLEGE
Columbia, SC

CONTACT Mrs. Bichevia Green, Associate Director of Financial Aid, Benedict College, 1600 Harden Street, Columbia, SC 29204, 803-705-4418 or toll-free 800-868-6598. *Fax:* 803-705-6629. *E-mail:* greenb@benedict.edu.
Website: http://www.benedict.edu/.

BENEDICTINE COLLEGE
Atchison, KS

Tuition & fees: $28,480	Average undergraduate aid package: $23,698

ABOUT THE INSTITUTION Independent Roman Catholic, coed. *Awards:* certificates, diplomas, associate, bachelor's, and master's degrees. 48 undergraduate majors. *Total enrollment:* 2,167. Undergraduates: 2,071. Freshmen: 438. Federal methodology is used as a basis for awarding need-based institutional aid.

UNDERGRADUATE EXPENSES for 2017–2018 *Application fee:* $50. *Comprehensive fee:* $38,380 includes full-time tuition ($27,730), mandatory fees ($750), and room and board ($9900). *College room only:* $5400. Full-time tuition and fees vary according to course load and degree level. Room and board charges vary according to board plan and housing facility. *Part-time tuition:* $800 per credit hour. *Part-time fees:* $50 per credit hour. Part-time tuition and fees vary according to course load and degree level.

FRESHMAN FINANCIAL AID (Fall 2017, est.) 380 applied for aid; of those 82% were deemed to have need. 100% of freshmen with need received aid; of those 42% had need fully met. *Average percent of need met:* 78% (excluding resources awarded to replace EFC). *Average financial aid package:* $24,665 (excluding resources awarded to replace EFC). 29% of all full-time freshmen had no need and received non-need-based gift aid.

UNDERGRADUATE FINANCIAL AID (Fall 2017, est.) 1,441 applied for aid; of those 85% were deemed to have need. 100% of undergraduates with need received aid; of those 24% had need fully met. *Average percent of need met:* 80% (excluding resources awarded to replace EFC). *Average financial aid package:* $23,698 (excluding resources awarded to replace EFC). 32% of all full-time undergraduates had no need and received non-need-based gift aid.

GIFT AID (NEED-BASED) *Total amount:* $18,292,831 (11% federal, 3% state, 82% institutional, 4% external sources). *Receiving aid:* Freshmen: 71% (313); all full-time undergraduates: 68% (1,228). *Average award:* Freshmen: $17,596; Undergraduates: $15,796. *Scholarships, grants, and awards:* Federal Pell, FSEOG, state, private, college/university gift aid from institutional funds.

GIFT AID (NON-NEED-BASED) *Total amount:* $8,614,321 (96% institutional, 4% external sources). *Receiving aid:* Freshmen: 15% (64). Undergraduates: 12% (216). *Average award:* Freshmen: $14,098. Undergraduates: $12,748. *Scholarships, grants, and awards by category: Academic interests/achievement:* 729 awards ($8,297,287 total): general academic interests/achievements. *Creative arts/performance:* 157 awards ($134,122 total): dance, journalism/publications, music, theater/drama. *Special achievements/activities:* 77 awards ($146,925 total): cheerleading/drum major, leadership. *Special characteristics:* 83 awards ($1,694,155 total): children of

---

faculty/staff, general special characteristics. *Tuition waivers:* Full or partial for employees or children of employees, senior citizens. *ROTC:* Army cooperative.

LOANS *Student loans:* $9,455,032 (70% need-based, 30% non-need-based). 69% of past graduating class borrowed through all loan programs. *Average indebtedness per student:* $29,196. *Average need-based loan:* Freshmen: $3307. Undergraduates: $4984. *Parent loans:* $4,988,424 (33% need-based, 67% non-need-based). *Programs:* Federal Direct (Subsidized and Unsubsidized Stafford, PLUS), Perkins, alternative loans.

WORK-STUDY *Federal work-study:* Total amount: $1,249,645; 291 jobs averaging $620. *State or other work-study/employment:* Part-time jobs available.

ATHLETIC AWARDS Total amount: $4,325,937 (64% need-based, 36% non-need-based).

APPLYING FOR FINANCIAL AID *Required financial aid form:* FAFSA. *Financial aid deadline (priority):* 4/1. *Notification date:* Continuous beginning 12/15. Students must reply within 2 weeks of notification.

CONTACT Mr. Tony Tanking, Director of Financial Aid, Benedictine College, 1020 North Second Street, Atchison, KS 66002-1499, 913-360-7484 or toll-free 800-467-5340. *Fax:* 913-367-5462. *E-mail:* ttanking@benedictine.edu. *Website:* http://www.benedictine.edu/.

BENEDICTINE UNIVERSITY
Lisle, IL

Tuition & fees: $34,290	Average undergraduate aid package: $23,183

ABOUT THE INSTITUTION Independent Roman Catholic, coed. *Awards:* certificates, diplomas, bachelor's, master's, and doctoral degrees. 51 undergraduate majors. *Total enrollment:* 5,101. Undergraduates: 2,885. Freshmen: 423. Federal methodology is used as a basis for awarding need-based institutional aid.

UNDERGRADUATE EXPENSES for 2018–2019 *Application fee:* $40. *Comprehensive fee:* $43,770 includes full-time tuition ($32,700), mandatory fees ($1590), and room and board ($9480). *College room only:* $7800. Full-time tuition and fees vary according to course load, degree level, and location. Room and board charges vary according to board plan, housing facility, and location. *Part-time tuition:* $1090 per credit hour. *Part-time fees:* $60 per credit hour. Part-time tuition and fees vary according to course load, degree level, and location.

FRESHMAN FINANCIAL AID (Fall 2017, est.) 391 applied for aid; of those 94% were deemed to have need. 100% of freshmen with need received aid. *Average financial aid package:* $23,114 (excluding resources awarded to replace EFC). 6% of all full-time freshmen had no need and received non-need-based gift aid.

UNDERGRADUATE FINANCIAL AID (Fall 2017, est.) 2,074 applied for aid; of those 95% were deemed to have need. 100% of undergraduates with need received aid. *Average financial aid package:* $23,183 (excluding resources awarded to replace EFC). 15% of all full-time undergraduates had no need and received non-need-based gift aid.

GIFT AID (NEED-BASED) *Total amount:* $11,372,182 (46% federal, 31% state, 23% institutional). *Receiving aid:* Freshmen: 65% (275); all full-time undergraduates: 54% (1,329). *Average award:* Freshmen: $9585; Undergraduates: $8392. *Scholarships, grants, and awards:* Federal Pell, FSEOG, state, college/university gift aid from institutional funds.

GIFT AID (NON-NEED-BASED) *Total amount:* $26,098,470 (99% institutional, 1% external sources). *Receiving aid:* Freshmen: 78% (326). Undergraduates: 70% (1,717). *Average award:* Freshmen: $11,200. Undergraduates: $12,349. *Scholarships, grants, and awards by category: Academic interests/achievement:* general academic interests/achievements. *Creative arts/performance:* music. *Special achievements/activities:* community service, general special achievements/activities, leadership, memberships. *Special characteristics:* children and siblings of alumni, children of faculty/staff, general special characteristics, international students, local/state students, out-of-state students, relatives of clergy, siblings of current students, veterans, veterans' children. *Tuition waivers:* Full or partial for employees or children of employees. *ROTC:* Army cooperative.

LOANS *Student loans:* $14,604,481 (46% need-based, 54% non-need-based). 79% of past graduating class borrowed through all loan programs. *Average indebtedness per student:* $23,959. *Average need-based loan:* Freshmen: $3395. Undergraduates: $4594. *Parent loans:* $5,324,127 (100% non-need-based). *Programs:* Federal Direct (Subsidized and Unsubsidized Stafford, PLUS), Perkins.

WORK-STUDY *Federal work-study:* Total amount: $348,592; jobs available. *State or other work-study/employment:* Part-time jobs available.

APPLYING FOR FINANCIAL AID *Required financial aid form:* FAFSA. *Financial aid deadline:* Continuous. *Notification date:* Continuous beginning 10/28. Students must reply within 2 weeks of notification.

CONTACT Diane Battistella, Senior Associate Dean of Financial Aid, Benedictine University, 5700 College Road, Lisle, IL 60532, 630-829-6415 or toll-free 888-829-6363 (out-of-state). *Fax:* 630-829-6101. *E-mail:* dbattistella@ben.edu. *Website:* http://www.ben.edu/.

BENNETT COLLEGE
Greensboro, NC

CONTACT Ms. Keisha Ragsdale, Director of Financial Aid, Bennett College, 900 East Washington Street, Greensboro, NC 27401, 336-370-8678 or toll-free 800-413-5323. *Fax:* 336-517-2204. *E-mail:* kragsdale@bennett.edu. *Website:* http://www.bennett.edu/.

BENNINGTON COLLEGE
Bennington, VT

Tuition & fees: $53,860	Average undergraduate aid package: $41,595

ABOUT THE INSTITUTION Independent, coed. *Awards:* bachelor's and master's degrees. 88 undergraduate majors. *Total enrollment:* 851. Undergraduates: 775. Freshmen: 225. Both federal and institutional methodology are used as a basis for awarding need-based institutional aid.

UNDERGRADUATE EXPENSES for 2018–2019 *One-time required fee:* $650. *Comprehensive fee:* $69,470 includes full-time tuition ($53,160), mandatory fees ($700), and room and board ($15,610). *College room only:* $8460. Full-time tuition and fees vary according to degree level. Room and board charges vary according to board plan. *Part-time tuition:* $2215 per credit hour.

FRESHMAN FINANCIAL AID (Fall 2016) 144 applied for aid; of those 92% were deemed to have need. 100% of freshmen with need received aid; of those 14% had need fully met. *Average percent of need met:* 88% (excluding resources awarded to replace EFC). *Average financial aid package:* $43,749 (excluding resources awarded to replace EFC). 16% of all full-time freshmen had no need and received non-need-based gift aid.

UNDERGRADUATE FINANCIAL AID (Fall 2016) 446 applied for aid; of those 94% were deemed to have need. 100% of undergraduates with need received aid; of those 11% had need fully met. *Average percent of need met:* 82% (excluding resources awarded to replace EFC). *Average financial aid package:* $41,595 (excluding resources awarded to replace EFC). 28% of all full-time undergraduates had no need and received non-need-based gift aid.

GIFT AID (NEED-BASED) *Total amount:* $15,420,571 (6% federal, 92% institutional, 2% external sources). *Receiving aid:* Freshmen: 60% (132); all full-time undergraduates: 58% (418). *Average award:* Freshmen: $40,246; Undergraduates: $36,862. *Scholarships, grants, and awards:* Federal Pell, FSEOG, state, private, college/university gift aid from institutional funds.

GIFT AID (NON-NEED-BASED) *Total amount:* $6,516,710 (91% institutional, 9% external sources). *Receiving aid:* Freshmen: 5% (11). Undergraduates: 4% (26). *Average award:* Freshmen: $21,973. Undergraduates: $25,589. *Scholarships, grants, and awards by category: Academic interests/achievement:* 134 awards ($1,363,686 total): general academic interests/achievements. *Tuition waivers:* Full or partial for employees or children of employees.

LOANS *Student loans:* $2,917,257 (77% need-based, 23% non-need-based). 65% of past graduating class borrowed through all loan programs. *Average indebtedness per student:* $27,470. *Average need-based loan:* Freshmen: $2370. Undergraduates: $3558. *Parent loans:* $1,284,429 (46% need-based, 54% non-need-based). *Programs:* Federal Direct (Subsidized and Unsubsidized Stafford, PLUS).

WORK-STUDY *Federal work-study:* 349 jobs averaging $2128. *State or other work-study/employment:* Total amount: $192,200 (19% need-based, 81% non-need-based). 96 part-time jobs averaging $2134.

APPLYING FOR FINANCIAL AID *Required financial aid forms:* FAFSA, institution's own form, CSS Financial Aid PROFILE, noncustodial (divorced/separated) parent's statement, parent and student federal income tax form(s), W-2 forms. *Financial aid deadline:* 1/3. *Notification date:* 3/27. Students must reply by 5/1.

CONTACT Heather Clifford, Director of Financial Aid, Bennington College, One College Drive, Bennington, VT 05201, 802-440-4325 or toll-free 800-833-6845. *Fax:* 802-440-4880. *E-mail:* finaid@bennington.edu.
Website: http://www.bennington.edu/.

BENTLEY UNIVERSITY
Waltham, MA

Tuition & fees: $49,880	Average undergraduate aid package: $36,161

ABOUT THE INSTITUTION Independent, coed. *Awards:* certificates, bachelor's, master's, and doctoral degrees. 25 undergraduate majors. *Total enrollment:* 5,543. Undergraduates: 4,272. Freshmen: 1,018. Both federal and institutional methodology are used as a basis for awarding need-based institutional aid.

UNDERGRADUATE EXPENSES for 2018–2019 *Application fee:* $75. *Comprehensive fee:* $66,200 includes full-time tuition ($48,180), mandatory fees ($1700), and room and board ($16,320). *College room only:* $9900. Room and board charges vary according to board plan and housing facility. Part-time tuition and fees vary according to course load.

FRESHMAN FINANCIAL AID (Fall 2016) 739 applied for aid; of those 70% were deemed to have need. 100% of freshmen with need received aid; of those 41% had need fully met. *Average percent of need met:* 93% (excluding resources awarded to replace EFC). *Average financial aid package:* $35,924 (excluding resources awarded to replace EFC). 21% of all full-time freshmen had no need and received non-need-based gift aid.

UNDERGRADUATE FINANCIAL AID (Fall 2016) 2,396 applied for aid; of those 74% were deemed to have need. 100% of undergraduates with need received aid; of those 39% had need fully met. *Average percent of need met:* 93% (excluding resources awarded to replace EFC). *Average financial aid package:* $36,161 (excluding resources awarded to replace EFC). 22% of all full-time undergraduates had no need and received non-need-based gift aid.

GIFT AID (NEED-BASED) *Total amount:* $48,749,597 (7% federal, 2% state, 91% institutional). *Receiving aid:* Freshmen: 49% (514); all full-time undergraduates: 43% (1,740). *Average award:* Freshmen: $31,621; Undergraduates: $31,187. *Scholarships, grants, and awards:* Federal Pell, FSEOG, state, private, college/university gift aid from institutional funds.

GIFT AID (NON-NEED-BASED) *Total amount:* $23,007,785 (93% institutional, 7% external sources). *Receiving aid:* Freshmen: 10% (105). Undergraduates: 6% (254). *Average award:* Freshmen: $18,050. Undergraduates: $19,746. *Scholarships, grants, and awards by category:* Academic interests/achievement: 1,689 awards ($32,554,036 total): general academic interests/achievements. *Special achievements/activities:* 61 awards ($590,000 total): community service, leadership. *Special characteristics:* 93 awards ($1,794,300 total): international students, members of minority groups. *Tuition waivers:* Full or partial for employees or children of employees. *ROTC:* Army cooperative, Air Force cooperative.

LOANS *Student loans:* $18,782,302 (45% need-based, 55% non-need-based). 54% of past graduating class borrowed through all loan programs. *Average indebtedness per student:* $31,889. *Average need-based loan:* Freshmen: $4000. Undergraduates: $5062. *Parent loans:* $9,673,931 (100% non-need-based). *Programs:* Federal Direct (Subsidized and Unsubsidized Stafford, PLUS), state.

WORK-STUDY *Federal work-study:* 876 jobs averaging $1817. *State or other work-study/employment:* Total amount: $2,412,409 (100% non-need-based). 816 part-time jobs averaging $1161.

ATHLETIC AWARDS Total amount: $2,934,146 (21% need-based, 79% non-need-based).

APPLYING FOR FINANCIAL AID *Required financial aid forms:* FAFSA, CSS Financial Aid PROFILE, noncustodial (divorced/separated) parent's statement, business/farm supplement, student tax returns (including W-2 and all schedules filed). *Financial aid deadline:* 1/7. *Notification date:* 3/31.

CONTACT Katherine Anderson, Director of Financial Assistance, Bentley University, 175 Forest Street, Waltham, MA 02452-4705, 781-891-3441 or toll-free 800-523-2354. *Fax:* 781-891-2448. *E-mail:* finaid@bentley.edu.
Website: http://www.bentley.edu/.

BEREA COLLEGE
Berea, KY

Tuition & fees: $560	Average undergraduate aid package: $34,714

ABOUT THE INSTITUTION Independent, coed. *Awards:* bachelor's degrees. 34 undergraduate majors. *Total enrollment:* 1,670. Undergraduates: 1,670. Freshmen: 432. Federal methodology is used as a basis for awarding need-based institutional aid.

UNDERGRADUATE EXPENSES for 2017–2018 Financial aid is provided to all students for tuition costs.

FRESHMAN FINANCIAL AID (Fall 2016) 418 applied for aid; of those 100% were deemed to have need. 100% of freshmen with need received aid. *Average percent of need met:* 98% (excluding resources awarded to replace EFC). *Average financial aid package:* $34,670 (excluding resources awarded to replace EFC).

UNDERGRADUATE FINANCIAL AID (Fall 2016) 1,612 applied for aid; of those 100% were deemed to have need. 100% of undergraduates with need received aid. *Average percent of need met:* 95% (excluding resources awarded to replace EFC). *Average financial aid package:* $34,714 (excluding resources awarded to replace EFC).

GIFT AID (NEED-BASED) *Total amount:* $52,523,985 (13% federal, 8% state, 79% institutional). *Receiving aid:* Freshmen: 100% (418); all full-time undergraduates: 100% (1,612). *Average award:* Freshmen: $33,290; Undergraduates: $32,288. *Scholarships, grants, and awards:* Federal Pell, FSEOG, state, private, college/university gift aid from institutional funds.

LOANS *Student loans:* $1,229,873 (51% need-based, 49% non-need-based). 25% of past graduating class borrowed through all loan programs. *Average indebtedness per student:* $7468. *Average need-based loan:* Freshmen: $1197. Undergraduates: $1781. *Parent loans:* $8000 (100% need-based). *Programs:* Federal Direct (Subsidized and Unsubsidized Stafford, PLUS), Perkins, college/university.

WORK-STUDY *Federal work-study:* jobs available. *State or other work-study/employment:* Total amount: $2,242,271 (100% need-based). Part-time jobs available.

APPLYING FOR FINANCIAL AID *Required financial aid form:* FAFSA. *Financial aid deadline:* 5/1 (priority: 10/1). *Notification date:* Continuous beginning 11/1. Students must reply by 5/1.

CONTACT Theresa Lowder, Director of Student Financial Aid Services, Berea College, CPO 2172, Berea, KY 40404, 859-985-3313 or toll-free 800-326-5948. *Fax:* 859-985-3914. *E-mail:* lowdert@berea.edu.
Website: http://www.berea.edu/.

BERGIN UNIVERSITY OF CANINE STUDIES
Rohnert Park, CA

CONTACT Financial Aid Office, Bergin University of Canine Studies, 5860 Labath Avenue, Rohnert Park, CA 94928, 707-545-3647.
Website: http://www.berginu.edu/.

BERKELEY COLLEGE–NEW YORK CITY CAMPUS
New York, NY

CONTACT Office of Financial Aid, Berkeley College–New York City Campus, 3 East 43rd Street, New York, NY 10017, 800-446-5400. *E-mail:* financialaid@berkeleycollege.edu.
Website: http://www.berkeleycollege.edu/.

BERKELEY COLLEGE–WHITE PLAINS CAMPUS
White Plains, NY

CONTACT Office of Financial Aid, Berkeley College–White Plains Campus, 99 Church Street, White Plains, NY 10601, 800-446-5400. *E-mail:* financialaid@berkeleycollege.edu.
Website: http://www.berkeleycollege.edu/.

BERKELEY COLLEGE–WOODLAND PARK CAMPUS
Woodland Park, NJ

CONTACT Office of Financial Aid, Berkeley College–Woodland Park Campus, 44 Rifle Camp Road, Woodland Park, NJ 07424, 800-446-5400. *E-mail:* financialaid@berkeleycollege.edu.
Website: http://www.berkeleycollege.edu/.

BERKLEE COLLEGE OF MUSIC
Boston, MA

Tuition & fees: N/R	Average undergraduate aid package: $20,315

ABOUT THE INSTITUTION Independent, coed. 13 undergraduate majors. Both federal and institutional methodology are used as a basis for awarding need-based institutional aid.

FRESHMAN FINANCIAL AID (Fall 2017, est.) 709 applied for aid; of those 82% were deemed to have need. 93% of freshmen with need received aid; of those 9% had need fully met. *Average percent of need met:* 40% (excluding resources awarded to replace EFC). *Average financial aid package:* $17,962 (excluding resources awarded to replace EFC). 22% of all full-time freshmen had no need and received non-need-based gift aid.

UNDERGRADUATE FINANCIAL AID (Fall 2017, est.) 2,256 applied for aid; of those 87% were deemed to have need. 95% of undergraduates with need received aid; of those 7% had need fully met. *Average percent of need met:* 42% (excluding resources awarded to replace EFC). *Average financial aid package:* $20,315 (excluding resources awarded to replace EFC). 29% of all full-time undergraduates had no need and received non-need-based gift aid.

GIFT AID (NEED-BASED) *Total amount:* $31,590,585 (16% federal, 81% institutional, 3% external sources). *Receiving aid:* Freshmen: 16% (187); all full-time undergraduates: 16% (784). *Average award:* Freshmen: $5035; Undergraduates: $5064. *Scholarships, grants, and awards:* Federal Pell, FSEOG, state, private, college/university gift aid from institutional funds.

GIFT AID (NON-NEED-BASED) *Total amount:* $28,522,591 (96% institutional, 4% external sources). *Receiving aid:* Freshmen: 30% (349). Undergraduates: 25% (1,235). *Average award:* Freshmen: $17,740. Undergraduates: $18,052. *Scholarships, grants, and awards by category:* Academic interests/achievement: education, engineering/technologies, general academic interests/achievements. *Creative arts/performance:* dance, music, performing arts, theater/drama.

LOANS *Student loans:* $30,266,983 (76% need-based, 24% non-need-based). 39% of past graduating class borrowed through all loan programs. *Average indebtedness per student:* $50,177. *Average need-based loan:* Freshmen: $3464. Undergraduates: $4233. *Parent loans:* $22,788,681 (68% need-based, 32% non-need-based). *Programs:* Federal Direct (Subsidized and Unsubsidized Stafford, PLUS), Perkins, college/university.

WORK-STUDY *Federal work-study:* Total amount: $746,245; jobs available.

APPLYING FOR FINANCIAL AID *Required financial aid forms:* FAFSA, CSS Financial Aid PROFILE. *Financial aid deadline (priority):* 12/1. *Notification date:* Continuous.

CONTACT Office of Financial Aid, Berklee College of Music, 921 Boylston Street, Boston, MA 02215-3693, 617-747-2274 or toll-free 800-BERKLEE. *Fax:* 617-747-2073. *E-mail:* financialaid@berklee.edu.
Website: http://www.berklee.edu/.

BERRY COLLEGE
Mount Berry, GA

Tuition & fees: $35,176	Average undergraduate aid package: $29,832

ABOUT THE INSTITUTION Independent interdenominational, coed. *Awards:* bachelor's and master's degrees. 46 undergraduate majors. *Total enrollment:* 2,110. Undergraduates: 1,978. Freshmen: 553. Federal methodology is used as a basis for awarding need-based institutional aid.

UNDERGRADUATE EXPENSES for 2017–2018 *Comprehensive fee:* $47,436 includes full-time tuition ($34,950), mandatory fees ($226), and room and board ($12,260). *College room only:* $6930. Room and board charges vary according to board plan and housing facility. *Part-time tuition:* $1165 per credit hour.

FRESHMAN FINANCIAL AID (Fall 2017, est.) 525 applied for aid; of those 80% were deemed to have need. 100% of freshmen with need received aid; of those 26% had need fully met. *Average percent of need met:* 85% (excluding resources awarded to replace EFC). *Average financial aid package:* $30,171 (excluding resources awarded to replace EFC). 24% of all full-time freshmen had no need and received non-need-based gift aid.

UNDERGRADUATE FINANCIAL AID (Fall 2017, est.) 1,681 applied for aid; of those 82% were deemed to have need. 100% of undergraduates with need received aid; of those 25% had need fully met. *Average percent of need met:* 85% (excluding resources awarded to replace EFC). *Average financial aid package:* $29,832 (excluding resources awarded to replace EFC). 29% of all full-time undergraduates had no need and received non-need-based gift aid.

GIFT AID (NEED-BASED) *Total amount:* $34,291,596 (6% federal, 9% state, 83% institutional, 2% external sources). *Receiving aid:* Freshmen: 76% (420); all full-time undergraduates: 71% (1,378). *Average award:* Freshmen: $26,165; Undergraduates: $24,949. *Scholarships, grants, and awards:* Federal Pell, FSEOG, state, private, college/university gift aid from institutional funds.

GIFT AID (NON-NEED-BASED) *Total amount:* $11,931,962 (15% state, 81% institutional, 4% external sources). *Receiving aid:* Freshmen: 15% (85). Undergraduates: 13% (257). *Average award:* Freshmen: $16,759. Undergraduates: $15,182. *Scholarships, grants, and awards by category:* Academic interests/achievement: agriculture, business, communication, education, English, general academic interests/achievements, humanities, religion/biblical studies. *Creative arts/performance:* art/fine arts, debating, journalism/publications, music, theater/drama. *Special achievements/activities:* community service, leadership, religious involvement. *Special characteristics:* adult students, children of faculty/staff, ethnic background, first-generation college students, international students, local/state students, members of minority groups, out-of-state students, veterans, veterans' children. *Tuition waivers:* Full or partial for employees or children of employees, senior citizens.

LOANS *Student loans:* $12,899,976 (59% need-based, 41% non-need-based). 65% of past graduating class borrowed through all loan programs. *Average indebtedness per student:* $27,378. *Average need-based loan:* Freshmen: $4210. Undergraduates: $5110. *Parent loans:* $3,602,579 (32% need-based, 68% non-need-based). *Programs:* Federal Direct (Subsidized and Unsubsidized Stafford, PLUS), Perkins, state, college/university.

WORK-STUDY *Federal work-study:* Total amount: $727,206; 201 jobs averaging $3626. *State or other work-study/employment:* Total amount: $654,674 (57% need-based, 43% non-need-based). 179 part-time jobs averaging $4679.

APPLYING FOR FINANCIAL AID *Required financial aid forms:* FAFSA, CSS Financial Aid PROFILE, state aid form. *Financial aid deadline (priority):* 1/15. *Notification date:* Continuous beginning 11/1. Students must reply by 5/1.

CONTACT Mrs. Donna Childres, Director of Financial Aid, Berry College, 2277 Martha Berry Highway, NW, Mount Berry, GA 30149-5007, 706-236-1714 or toll-free 800-237-7942. *Fax:* 706-290-2160. *E-mail:* financialaid@berry.edu.
Website: http://www.berry.edu/.

BETHANY COLLEGE
Lindsborg, KS

CONTACT Ms. Amber Maneth, Office of Financial Aid, Bethany College, 335 East Swensson, Lindsborg, KS 67456-1897, 785-227-3311 Ext. 8248 or toll-free 800-826-2281. *Fax:* 785-227-2004. *E-mail:* manetha@bethanylb.edu.
Website: http://www.bethanylb.edu/.

BETHANY COLLEGE
Bethany, WV

ABOUT THE INSTITUTION Independent Christian Church (Disciples of Christ), coed. 59 undergraduate majors.

GIFT AID (NEED-BASED) *Scholarships, grants, and awards:* Federal Pell, FSEOG, state, private, college/university gift aid from institutional funds.

GIFT AID (NON-NEED-BASED) *Scholarships, grants, and awards by category:* *Academic interests/achievement:* general academic interests/achievements. *Creative arts/performance:* music. *Special achievements/activities:* community service, hobbies/interests, leadership, religious involvement. *Special characteristics:* children and siblings of alumni, children of faculty/staff, international students, local/state students, out-of-state students, relatives of clergy, religious affiliation.

LOANS *Programs:* Federal Direct (Subsidized and Unsubsidized Stafford, PLUS), Perkins, alternative loans.

WORK-STUDY *Federal work-study:* 141 jobs averaging $2000. *State or other work-study/employment:* 166 part-time jobs averaging $1500.

APPLYING FOR FINANCIAL AID *Required financial aid form:* FAFSA.

CONTACT Jason McClain, Assistant Vice President of Financial Aid, Bethany College, Center for Enrollment and Financial Aid #4, 31 East Campus Drive, Bethany, WV 26032, 304-829-7611 or toll-free 800-922-7611. *Fax:* 304-829-7142. *E-mail:* financialaid@bethanywv.edu.
Website: http://www.bethanywv.edu/.

BETHANY GLOBAL UNIVERSITY
Bloomington, MN

CONTACT Financial Aid Office, Bethany Global University, 6820 Auto Club Road, Suite C, Bloomington, MN 55438, 952-944-2121 or toll-free 800-323-3417.
Website: http://www.bethanygu.edu/.

BETHANY LUTHERAN COLLEGE
Mankato, MN

Tuition & fees: $27,780	Average undergraduate aid package: $21,147

ABOUT THE INSTITUTION Independent Lutheran, coed. *Awards:* certificates and bachelor's degrees. 34 undergraduate majors. *Total enrollment:* 651. Undergraduates: 651. Freshmen: 129. Federal methodology is used as a basis for awarding need-based institutional aid.

UNDERGRADUATE EXPENSES for 2018–2019 *One-time required fee:* $130. *Comprehensive fee:* $35,820 includes full-time tuition ($27,100), mandatory fees ($680), and room and board ($8040). Room and board charges vary according to board plan, housing facility, and student level. *Part-time tuition:* $1140 per credit hour. *Part-time fees:* $340 per term. Part-time tuition and fees vary according to course load.

FRESHMAN FINANCIAL AID (Fall 2016) 122 applied for aid; of those 92% were deemed to have need. 100% of freshmen with need received aid; of those 21% had need fully met. *Average percent of need met:* 85% (excluding resources awarded to replace EFC). *Average financial aid package:* $21,015 (excluding resources awarded to replace EFC). 13% of all full-time freshmen had no need and received non-need-based gift aid.

UNDERGRADUATE FINANCIAL AID (Fall 2016) 443 applied for aid; of those 91% were deemed to have need. 100% of undergraduates with need received aid; of those 18% had need fully met. *Average percent of need met:* 85% (excluding resources awarded to replace EFC). *Average financial aid package:* $21,147 (excluding resources awarded to replace EFC). 13% of all full-time undergraduates had no need and received non-need-based gift aid.

GIFT AID (NEED-BASED) *Total amount:* $6,154,465 (12% federal, 18% state, 69% institutional, 1% external sources). *Receiving aid:* Freshmen: 81% (112); all full-time undergraduates: 80% (405). *Average award:* Freshmen: $17,566; Undergraduates: $16,844. *Scholarships, grants, and awards:* Federal Pell, FSEOG, state, private, college/university gift aid from institutional funds.

GIFT AID (NON-NEED-BASED) *Total amount:* $1,008,047 (93% institutional, 7% external sources). *Receiving aid:* Freshmen: 13% (18). Undergraduates: 11% (56). *Average award:* Freshmen: $11,012. Undergraduates: $9435. *Scholarships, grants, and awards by category:* *Creative arts/performance:* 44 awards ($84,000 total): art/fine arts, debating, journalism/publications, music, theater/drama. *Special characteristics:* 31 awards ($582,118 total): children of faculty/staff. *Tuition waivers:* Full or partial for employees or children of employees, senior citizens. *ROTC:* Army cooperative.

LOANS *Student loans:* $3,406,552 (59% need-based, 41% non-need-based). 77% of past graduating class borrowed through all loan programs. *Average indebtedness per student:* $31,654. *Average need-based loan:* Freshmen: $4120. Undergraduates: $4829. *Parent loans:* $243,432 (29% need-based, 71% non-need-based). *Programs:* Federal Direct (Subsidized and Unsubsidized Stafford, PLUS), Perkins, state, alternative loans.

WORK-STUDY *Federal work-study:* 21 jobs averaging $1753. *State or other work-study/employment:* Total amount: $321,261 (44% need-based, 56% non-need-based). 298 part-time jobs averaging $1091.

APPLYING FOR FINANCIAL AID *Required financial aid forms:* FAFSA, institution's own form. *Financial aid deadline (priority):* 4/15. *Notification date:* Continuous beginning 12/1. Students must reply within 4 weeks of notification.

CONTACT Financial Aid Office, Bethany Lutheran College, 700 Luther Drive, Mankato, MN 56001-6163, 507-344-7328 or toll-free 800-944-3066. *Fax:* 507-344-7376. *E-mail:* finald@blc.edu.
Website: http://www.blc.edu/.

BETHEL COLLEGE
Mishawaka, IN

Tuition & fees: $28,590	Average undergraduate aid package: N/A

ABOUT THE INSTITUTION Independent Missionary Church, coed. *Awards:* associate, bachelor's, and master's degrees. 65 undergraduate majors. *Total enrollment:* 1,513. Undergraduates: 1,294. Freshmen: 233. Federal methodology is used as a basis for awarding need-based institutional aid.

UNDERGRADUATE EXPENSES for 2018–2019 *Comprehensive fee:* $37,590 includes full-time tuition ($28,140), mandatory fees ($450), and room and board ($9000). *College room only:* $4280. Full-time tuition and fees vary according to program. Room and board charges vary according to board plan and housing facility. *Part-time tuition:* $895 per credit hour. *Part-time fees:* $250 per year. Part-time tuition and fees vary according to course load and program.

GIFT AID (NEED-BASED) *Scholarships, grants, and awards:* Federal Pell, FSEOG, state, private, college/university gift aid from institutional funds, Federal Nursing.

GIFT AID (NON-NEED-BASED) *Average award:* Freshmen: $15,243. Undergraduates: $12,724. *Scholarships, grants, and awards by category:* *Academic interests/achievement:* 829 awards ($8,400,000 total): general academic interests/achievements. *Creative arts/performance:* 44 awards ($104,800 total): art/fine arts, music, theater/drama. *Special characteristics:* children of faculty/staff, general special characteristics, international students, members of minority groups. *Tuition waivers:* Full or partial for employees or children of employees. *ROTC:* Army cooperative, Air Force cooperative.

LOANS *Student loans:* 68% of past graduating class borrowed through all loan programs. *Average indebtedness per student:* $33,565. *Programs:* Federal Direct (Subsidized and Unsubsidized Stafford, PLUS), Perkins, Federal Nursing.

WORK-STUDY *Federal work-study:* 69 jobs averaging $1512.

APPLYING FOR FINANCIAL AID *Required financial aid form:* FAFSA. *Financial aid deadline:* 4/15. *Notification date:* Continuous beginning 11/1.

CONTACT Mrs. Cindi Pedersen, Director of Financial Aid, Bethel College, 1001 Bethel Circle, Mishawaka, IN 46545-5591, 574-807-7239 or toll-free 800-422-4101. *Fax:* 574-807-7122. *E-mail:* pedersc@bethelcollege.edu.
Website: http://www.bethelcollege.edu/.

BETHEL COLLEGE
North Newton, KS

Tuition & fees: $28,540	Average undergraduate aid package: $24,986

ABOUT THE INSTITUTION Independent Mennonite Church USA, coed. *Awards:* bachelor's degrees. 17 undergraduate majors. *Total enrollment:* 503. Undergraduates: 503. Freshmen: 124. Federal methodology is used as a basis for awarding need-based institutional aid.

UNDERGRADUATE EXPENSES for 2018–2019 *Comprehensive fee:* $37,390 includes full-time tuition ($28,300), mandatory fees ($240), and room and board ($8850). *College room only:* $4340. Room and board charges vary according to board plan, housing facility, and student level. *Part-time tuition:* $772.50 per credit hour. Part-time tuition and fees vary according to course load.

FRESHMAN FINANCIAL AID (Fall 2016) 92 applied for aid; of those 98% were deemed to have need. 100% of freshmen with need received aid; of those 28% had need fully met. *Average percent of need met:* 83% (excluding resources awarded to replace EFC). *Average financial aid package:* $25,737 (excluding resources awarded to replace EFC). 6% of all full-time freshmen had no need and received non-need-based gift aid.

UNDERGRADUATE FINANCIAL AID (Fall 2016) 414 applied for aid; of those 97% were deemed to have need. 100% of undergraduates with need received aid; of those 22% had need fully met. *Average percent of need met:* 82% (excluding resources awarded to replace EFC). *Average financial aid package:* $24,986 (excluding resources awarded to replace EFC). 12% of all full-time undergraduates had no need and received non-need-based gift aid.

GIFT AID (NEED-BASED) *Total amount:* $1,509,128 (69% federal, 31% state). *Receiving aid:* Freshmen: 77% (75); all full-time undergraduates: 71% (326). *Average award:* Freshmen: $5124; Undergraduates: $5398. *Scholarships, grants, and awards:* Federal Pell, FSEOG, state, college/university gift aid from institutional funds.

GIFT AID (NON-NEED-BASED) *Total amount:* $5,122,140 (93% institutional, 7% external sources). *Receiving aid:* Freshmen: 91% (88). Undergraduates: 87% (398). *Average award:* Freshmen: $16,000. Undergraduates: $12,020. *Scholarships, grants, and awards by category: Academic interests/achievement:* biological sciences, business, communication, general academic interests/achievements, home economics, mathematics, premedicine, social sciences. *Creative arts/performance:* applied art and design, art/fine arts, debating, music, theater/drama. *Special achievements/activities:* cheerleading/drum major, community service. *Special characteristics:* children and siblings of alumni, children of current students, children of faculty/staff, ethnic background, general special characteristics, international students, local/state students, previous college experience, relatives of clergy, religious affiliation, siblings of current students, spouses of current students. *Tuition waivers:* Full or partial for minority students, children of alumni, employees or children of employees, senior citizens.

LOANS *Student loans:* $2,971,540 (100% need-based). 72% of past graduating class borrowed through all loan programs. *Average indebtedness per student:* $5633. *Average need-based loan:* Freshmen: $7760. Undergraduates: $8204. *Parent loans:* $942,293 (100% non-need-based). *Programs:* Federal Direct (Subsidized and Unsubsidized Stafford, PLUS).

WORK-STUDY *Federal work-study:* jobs available. *State or other work-study/employment:* Part-time jobs available.

ATHLETIC AWARDS Total amount: $1,279,489 (100% non-need-based).

APPLYING FOR FINANCIAL AID *Required financial aid form:* FAFSA. *Financial aid deadline (priority):* 4/1. *Notification date:* Continuous beginning 2/1. Students must reply by 5/1 or within 2 weeks of notification.

CONTACT Mr. Clark Oswald, Director of Financial Aid, Bethel College, 300 East 27th Street, North Newton, KS 67117, 316-284-5232 or toll-free 800-522-1887 Ext. 230. *Fax:* 316-284-5845. *E-mail:* coswald@bethelks.edu. *Website:* http://www.bethelks.edu/.

BETHEL UNIVERSITY
St. Paul, MN

Tuition & fees: $37,300	Average undergraduate aid package: $28,736

ABOUT THE INSTITUTION Independent Baptist General Conference, coed. *Awards:* certificates, associate, bachelor's, master's, and doctoral degrees. 50 undergraduate majors. *Total enrollment:* 4,591. Undergraduates: 2,904. Freshmen: 598. Federal methodology is used as a basis for awarding need-based institutional aid.

UNDERGRADUATE EXPENSES for 2018–2019 *Comprehensive fee:* $47,820 includes full-time tuition ($37,140), mandatory fees ($160), and room and board ($10,520). *College room only:* $5830. Room and board charges vary according to board plan. *Part-time tuition:* $1550 per credit. Part-time tuition and fees vary according to course load. *Payment plan:* Tuition prepayment.

FRESHMAN FINANCIAL AID (Fall 2017, est.) 543 applied for aid; of those 85% were deemed to have need. 100% of freshmen with need received aid; of those 23% had need fully met. *Average percent of need met:* 84% (excluding resources awarded to replace EFC). *Average financial aid package:* $30,215 (excluding resources awarded to replace EFC). 20% of all full-time freshmen had no need and received non-need-based gift aid.

UNDERGRADUATE FINANCIAL AID (Fall 2017, est.) 1,994 applied for aid; of those 87% were deemed to have need. 100% of undergraduates with need received aid; of those 20% had need fully met. *Average percent of need met:* 81% (excluding resources awarded to replace EFC). *Average financial aid package:* $28,736 (excluding resources awarded to replace EFC). 23% of all full-time undergraduates had no need and received non-need-based gift aid.

GIFT AID (NEED-BASED) *Total amount:* $39,857,574 (9% federal, 11% state, 78% institutional, 2% external sources). *Receiving aid:* Freshmen: 80% (464); all full-time undergraduates: 75% (1,725). *Average award:* Freshmen: $24,855; Undergraduates: $22,874. *Scholarships, grants, and awards:* Federal Pell, FSEOG, state, private, college/university gift aid from institutional funds.

GIFT AID (NON-NEED-BASED) *Total amount:* $8,922,681 (2% federal, 94% institutional, 4% external sources). *Receiving aid:* Freshmen: 14% (80). Undergraduates: 10% (241). *Average award:* Freshmen: $15,500. Undergraduates: $13,577. *Scholarships, grants, and awards by category: Academic interests/achievement:* 2,227 awards ($29,215,088 total): general academic interests/achievements. *Creative arts/performance:* 125 awards ($466,500 total): art/fine arts, debating, music, theater/drama. *Special achievements/activities:* 282 awards ($761,743 total): community service, leadership, religious involvement. *Special characteristics:* 506 awards ($2,188,710 total): children and siblings of alumni, children of faculty/staff, out-of-state students, relatives of clergy, veterans, veterans' children. *Tuition waivers:* Full or partial for employees or children of employees. *ROTC:* Army cooperative, Air Force cooperative.

LOANS *Student loans:* $15,957,141 (64% need-based, 36% non-need-based). 73% of past graduating class borrowed through all loan programs. *Average indebtedness per student:* $36,990. *Average need-based loan:* Freshmen: $3106. Undergraduates: $3867. *Parent loans:* $2,029,572 (88% need-based, 12% non-need-based). *Programs:* Federal Direct (Subsidized and Unsubsidized Stafford, PLUS), state, alternative loans.

WORK-STUDY *Federal work-study:* Total amount: $600,000; jobs available. *State or other work-study/employment:* Total amount: $2,401,048 (69% need-based, 31% non-need-based). Part-time jobs available.

APPLYING FOR FINANCIAL AID *Required financial aid form:* FAFSA. *Financial aid deadline (priority):* 4/15. *Notification date:* Continuous beginning 3/1.

CONTACT Mr. Jeffrey D. Olson, Director of Financial Aid, Bethel University, 3900 Bethel Drive, St. Paul, MN 55112-6999, 651-638-6241 or toll-free 800-255-8706 Ext. 6242. *Fax:* 651-635-1491. *E-mail:* finaid@bethel.edu. *Website:* http://www.bethel.edu/.

BETHEL COLLEGE
Hampton, VA

CONTACT Financial Aid Office, Bethel College, 1705 Todds Lane, Hampton, VA 23666, 757-826-1426. *Website:* http://www.bcva.edu/.

BETHEL UNIVERSITY
McKenzie, TN

CONTACT Laura Bateman, Office of Financial Aid, Bethel University, 325 Cherry Avenue, McKenzie, TN 38201, 901-352-4007. *Fax:* 901-352-4069. *Website:* http://www.bethelu.edu/.

BETHESDA UNIVERSITY
Anaheim, CA

CONTACT Ms. Grace Choi, Financial Aid Administrator, Bethesda University, 730 North Euclid Street, Anaheim, CA 92801, 714-683-1413. *Fax:* 714-517-1948. *E-mail:* financialaid@bcu.edu.
Website: http://www.buc.edu/.

BETH HAMEDRASH SHAAREI YOSHER INSTITUTE
Brooklyn, NY

CONTACT Financial Aid Office, Beth HaMedrash Shaarei Yosher Institute, 4102-10 16th Avenue, Brooklyn, NY 11204, 718-854-2290.

BETH HATALMUD RABBINICAL COLLEGE
Brooklyn, NY

CONTACT Financial Aid Office, Beth Hatalmud Rabbinical College, 2127 82nd Street, Brooklyn, NY 11204, 718-259-2525.

BETHLEHEM COLLEGE & SEMINARY
Minneapolis, MN

CONTACT Financial Aid Office, Bethlehem College & Seminary, 720 13th Avenue South, Minneapolis, MN 55415.
Website: http://www.bcsmn.edu/.

BETH MEDRASH GOVOHA
Lakewood, NJ

CONTACT Financial Aid Office, Beth Medrash Govoha, 617 Sixth Street, Lakewood, NJ 08701-2797, 732-367-1060.

BETH MEDRASH MEOR YITZCHOK
Monsey, NY

CONTACT Financial Aid Office, Beth Medrash Meor Yitzchok, 85 Dykstras Way East, Monsey, NY 10952.

BETHUNE-COOKMAN UNIVERSITY
Daytona Beach, FL

Tuition & fees: $14,410	Average undergraduate aid package: $14,838

ABOUT THE INSTITUTION Independent Methodist, coed. *Awards:* bachelor's and master's degrees. 36 undergraduate majors. *Total enrollment:* 4,143. Undergraduates: 3,992. Freshmen: 1,180. Federal methodology is used as a basis for awarding need-based institutional aid.

UNDERGRADUATE EXPENSES for 2018–2019 *Application fee:* $25. *Comprehensive fee:* $23,322 includes full-time tuition ($13,440), mandatory fees ($970), and room and board ($8912). Room and board charges vary according to housing facility. *Part-time tuition:* $560 per credit hour. *Part-time fees:* $50 per credit hour. Part-time tuition and fees vary according to course load.

FRESHMAN FINANCIAL AID (Fall 2017, est.) 1,216 applied for aid; of those 97% were deemed to have need. 100% of freshmen with need received aid; of those 4% had need fully met. *Average percent of need met:* 58% (excluding resources awarded to replace EFC). *Average financial aid package:* $15,903 (excluding resources awarded to replace EFC). 3% of all full-time freshmen had no need and received non-need-based gift aid.

UNDERGRADUATE FINANCIAL AID (Fall 2017, est.) 3,565 applied for aid; of those 97% were deemed to have need. 100% of undergraduates with need received aid; of those 5% had need fully met. *Average percent of need met:* 53% (excluding resources awarded to replace EFC). *Average financial aid package:* $14,838 (excluding resources awarded to replace EFC). 3% of all full-time undergraduates had no need and received non-need-based gift aid.

GIFT AID (NEED-BASED) *Total amount:* $35,589,767 (46% federal, 26% state, 24% institutional, 4% external sources). *Receiving aid:* Freshmen: 96% (1,174); all full-time undergraduates: 92% (3,357). *Average award:* Freshmen: $12,622; Undergraduates: $11,272. *Scholarships, grants, and awards:* Federal Pell, FSEOG, state, private, college/university gift aid from institutional funds, United Negro College Fund.

GIFT AID (NON-NEED-BASED) *Total amount:* $1,517,626 (24% state, 69% institutional, 7% external sources). *Receiving aid:* Freshmen: 2% (21). Undergraduates: 3% (96). *Average award:* Freshmen: $5634. Undergraduates: $8557. *Scholarships, grants, and awards by category:* Academic interests/achievement: 128 awards ($884,925 total): general academic interests/achievements. *Tuition waivers:* Full or partial for employees or children of employees. *ROTC:* Army cooperative, Air Force cooperative.

LOANS *Student loans:* $25,945,118 (94% need-based, 6% non-need-based). 92% of past graduating class borrowed through all loan programs. *Average indebtedness per student:* $40,601. *Average need-based loan:* Freshmen: $3510. Undergraduates: $4031. *Parent loans:* $13,224,762 (83% need-based, 17% non-need-based). *Programs:* Federal Direct (Subsidized and Unsubsidized Stafford, PLUS), alternative loans.

WORK-STUDY *Federal work-study:* Total amount: $555,442; 200 jobs averaging $2500. *State or other work-study/employment:* Total amount: $12,860 (100% need-based). 100 part-time jobs averaging $2000.

ATHLETIC AWARDS Total amount: $3,962,427 (73% need-based, 27% non-need-based).

APPLYING FOR FINANCIAL AID *Required financial aid form:* FAFSA. *Financial aid deadline (priority):* 4/1. *Notification date:* Continuous beginning 3/1. Students must reply within 3 weeks of notification.

CONTACT Ms. Salina Hamilton, Director of Financial Aid, Bethune-Cookman University, 640 Dr. Mary McLeod Bethune Boulevard, Daytona Beach, FL 32114-3099, 386-481-2628 or toll-free 800-448-0228. *Fax:* 386-481-2621. *E-mail:* hamiltonsd@cookman.edu.
Website: http://www.cookman.edu/.

BET MEDRASH GADOL ATERET TORAH
Brooklyn, NY

CONTACT Financial Aid Office, Bet Medrash Gadol Ateret Torah, 1750 East Fourth Street, Brooklyn, NY 11223.

BEULAH HEIGHTS UNIVERSITY
Atlanta, GA

CONTACT Ms. Patricia Banks, Director of Financial Aid, Beulah Heights University, 892 Berne Street, SE, Atlanta, GA 30316, 404-627-2681 or toll-free 888-777-BHBC. *Fax:* 404-627-0702. *E-mail:* pat.banks@beulah.org.
Website: http://www.beulah.edu/.

BINGHAMTON UNIVERSITY, STATE UNIVERSITY OF NEW YORK
Binghamton, NY

Tuition & fees (NY res): $9523	Average undergraduate aid package: $13,677

ABOUT THE INSTITUTION State-supported, coed. *Awards:* certificates, bachelor's, master's, and doctoral degrees. 75 undergraduate majors. *Total enrollment:* 17,322. Undergraduates: 13,708. Freshmen: 2,736. Institutional methodology is used as a basis for awarding need-based institutional aid.

UNDERGRADUATE EXPENSES for 2017–2018 Application fee: $50. *Tuition, state resident:* full-time $6670; part-time $278 per credit hour. *Tuition, nonresident:* full-time $21,550; part-time $898 per credit hour. *Required fees:* full-time $2853; $115.75 per credit hour or $22.25 per term. Full-time tuition and fees vary according to program. Part-time tuition and fees vary according to course load and program. *College room and board:* $14,577; *Room only:* $9567. Room and board charges vary according to board plan and housing facility.

FRESHMAN FINANCIAL AID (Fall 2017, est.) 2,329 applied for aid; of those 62% were deemed to have need. 100% of freshmen with need received aid; of those 15% had need fully met. *Average percent of need met:* 70% (excluding resources awarded to replace EFC). *Average financial aid package:* $13,199 (excluding resources awarded to replace EFC). 2% of all full-time freshmen had no need and received non-need-based gift aid.

UNDERGRADUATE FINANCIAL AID (Fall 2017, est.) 9,510 applied for aid; of those 73% were deemed to have need. 100% of undergraduates with need received aid; of those 14% had need fully met. *Average percent of need met:* 69% (excluding resources awarded to replace EFC). *Average financial aid package:* $13,677 (excluding resources awarded to replace EFC). 3% of all full-time undergraduates had no need and received non-need-based gift aid.

GIFT AID (NEED-BASED) Total amount: $52,438,603 (37% federal, 54% state, 7% institutional, 2% external sources). *Receiving aid:* Freshmen: 43% (1,144); all full-time undergraduates: 42% (5,613). *Average award:* Freshmen: $10,101; Undergraduates: $9356. *Scholarships, grants, and awards:* Federal Pell, FSEOG, private, college/university gift aid from institutional funds.

GIFT AID (NON-NEED-BASED) Total amount: $6,066,972 (57% state, 30% institutional, 13% external sources). *Receiving aid:* Freshmen: 8% (208). Undergraduates: 4% (475). *Average award:* Freshmen: $6985. Undergraduates: $7980. *Scholarships, grants, and awards by category: Academic interests/achievement:* 402 awards ($1,998,525 total): area/ethnic studies, biological sciences, business, computer science, education, engineering/technologies, English, foreign languages, general academic interests/achievements, home economics, humanities, international studies, mathematics, physical sciences, premedicine, social sciences. *Creative arts/performance:* 29 awards ($33,700 total): art/fine arts, cinema/film/broadcasting, creative writing, dance, general creative arts/performance, journalism/publications, music, performing arts, theater/drama. *Special achievements/activities:* 43 awards ($135,830 total): community service, general special achievements/activities, leadership. *Special characteristics:* 228 awards ($1,200,800 total): adult students, children and siblings of alumni, children of faculty/staff, ethnic background, first-generation college students, general special characteristics, handicapped students, international students, local/state students, married students, members of minority groups, out-of-state students, religious affiliation, veterans, veterans' children. *ROTC:* Army cooperative, Air Force cooperative.

LOANS Student loans: $81,707,213 (75% need-based, 25% non-need-based). 51% of past graduating class borrowed through all loan programs. *Average indebtedness per student:* $27,022. *Average need-based loan:* Freshmen: $3708. Undergraduates: $5001. *Parent loans:* $14,992,655 (71% need-based, 29% non-need-based). *Programs:* Federal Direct (Subsidized and Unsubsidized Stafford, PLUS), Perkins, college/university.

WORK-STUDY Federal work-study: Total amount: $530,400; 312 jobs averaging $1483.

ATHLETIC AWARDS Total amount: $4,843,132 (100% non-need-based).

APPLYING FOR FINANCIAL AID Required financial aid forms: FAFSA, state aid form. *Financial aid deadline (priority):* 1/1. *Notification date:* Continuous beginning 1/31. Students must reply within 2 weeks of notification.

CONTACT Ms. Patricia Donahue, Director of Student Financial Aid and Student Records, Binghamton University, State University of New York, PO Box 6000, Binghamton, NY 13902-6000, 607-777-2428. *Fax:* 607-777-6897. *E-mail:* finaid@binghamton.edu.
Website: http://www.binghamton.edu/.

BIOLA UNIVERSITY
La Mirada, CA

Tuition & fees: $38,448	Average undergraduate aid package: $21,694

ABOUT THE INSTITUTION Independent interdenominational, coed. *Awards:* certificates, diplomas, bachelor's, master's, and doctoral degrees. 98 undergraduate majors. *Total enrollment:* 6,095. Undergraduates: 4,091. Freshmen: 872. Institutional methodology is used as a basis for awarding need-based institutional aid.

UNDERGRADUATE EXPENSES for 2017–2018 Application fee: $45. *One-time required fee:* $60. *Comprehensive fee:* $49,420 includes full-time tuition ($38,448) and room and board ($10,972). *College room only:* $6500. Full-time tuition and fees vary according to course load and degree level. Room and board charges vary according to board plan and housing facility. *Part-time tuition:* $1602 per credit hour. Part-time tuition and fees vary according to course load and degree level.

FRESHMAN FINANCIAL AID (Fall 2016) 726 applied for aid; of those 84% were deemed to have need. 100% of freshmen with need received aid; of those 14% had need fully met. *Average percent of need met:* 54% (excluding resources awarded to replace EFC). *Average financial aid package:* $22,083 (excluding resources awarded to replace EFC). 28% of all full-time freshmen had no need and received non-need-based gift aid.

UNDERGRADUATE FINANCIAL AID (Fall 2016) 2,984 applied for aid; of those 89% were deemed to have need. 100% of undergraduates with need received aid; of those 9% had need fully met. *Average percent of need met:* 52% (excluding resources awarded to replace EFC). *Average financial aid package:* $21,694 (excluding resources awarded to replace EFC). 31% of all full-time undergraduates had no need and received non-need-based gift aid.

GIFT AID (NEED-BASED) Total amount: $42,314,858 (14% federal, 17% state, 69% institutional). *Receiving aid:* Freshmen: 72% (607); all full-time undergraduates: 68% (2,641). *Average award:* Freshmen: $17,081; Undergraduates: $15,750. *Scholarships, grants, and awards:* Federal Pell, FSEOG, state, private, college/university gift aid from institutional funds.

GIFT AID (NON-NEED-BASED) Total amount: $11,218,941 (100% institutional). *Receiving aid:* Freshmen: 8% (65). Undergraduates: 4% (168). *Average award:* Freshmen: $12,264. Undergraduates: $8465. *Scholarships, grants, and awards by category: Academic interests/achievement:* biological sciences, communication, general academic interests/achievements. *Creative arts/performance:* cinema/film/broadcasting, journalism/publications, music, theater/drama. *Special achievements/activities:* community service, leadership. *Special characteristics:* children of faculty/staff, ethnic background, international students, members of minority groups, relatives of clergy. *Tuition waivers:* Full or partial for employees or children of employees. *ROTC:* Army cooperative, Air Force cooperative.

LOANS Student loans: $24,087,520 (77% need-based, 23% non-need-based). 67% of past graduating class borrowed through all loan programs. *Average indebtedness per student:* $35,489. *Average need-based loan:* Freshmen: $2491. Undergraduates: $3564. *Parent loans:* $13,347,920 (60% need-based, 40% non-need-based). *Programs:* Federal Direct (Subsidized and Unsubsidized Stafford, PLUS), Perkins, Federal Nursing, college/university, alternative loans.

WORK-STUDY Federal work-study: jobs available.

ATHLETIC AWARDS Total amount: $2,594,124 (48% need-based, 52% non-need-based).

APPLYING FOR FINANCIAL AID Required financial aid form: FAFSA. *Financial aid deadline (priority):* 3/2. *Notification date:* Continuous beginning 11/15.

CONTACT Office of Financial Aid, Biola University, 13800 Biola Avenue, La Mirada, CA 90639-0001, 562-903-4742 or toll-free 800-652-4652. *Fax:* 562-906-4541. *E-mail:* finaid@biola.edu.
Website: http://www.biola.edu/.

BIRMINGHAM-SOUTHERN COLLEGE
Birmingham, AL

Tuition & fees: $17,650	Average undergraduate aid package: $32,882

ABOUT THE INSTITUTION Independent Methodist, coed. *Awards:* bachelor's degrees. 42 undergraduate majors. *Total enrollment:* 1,231. Undergraduates: 1,231. Freshmen: 327. Federal methodology is used as a basis for awarding need-based institutional aid.

UNDERGRADUATE EXPENSES for 2018–2019 *Application fee:* $50. *One-time required fee:* $300. *Comprehensive fee:* $29,950 includes full-time tuition ($16,353), mandatory fees ($1297), and room and board ($12,300). *College room only:* $6950. Room and board charges vary according to board plan, housing facility, and location.

FRESHMAN FINANCIAL AID (Fall 2017, est.) 346 applied for aid; of those 81% were deemed to have need. 100% of freshmen with need received aid; of those 30% had need fully met. *Average percent of need met:* 74% (excluding resources awarded to replace EFC). *Average financial aid package:* $31,335 (excluding resources awarded to replace EFC). 19% of all full-time freshmen had no need and received non-need-based gift aid.

UNDERGRADUATE FINANCIAL AID (Fall 2017, est.) 876 applied for aid; of those 85% were deemed to have need. 100% of undergraduates with need received aid; of those 31% had need fully met. *Average percent of need met:* 74% (excluding resources awarded to replace EFC). *Average financial aid package:* $32,882 (excluding resources awarded to replace EFC). 41% of all full-time undergraduates had no need and received non-need-based gift aid.

GIFT AID (NEED-BASED) *Total amount:* $3,011,220 (44% federal, 54% institutional, 2% external sources). *Receiving aid:* Freshmen: 49% (172); all full-time undergraduates: 38% (485). *Average award:* Freshmen: $6897; Undergraduates: $6431. *Scholarships, grants, and awards:* Federal Pell, FSEOG, state, private, college/university gift aid from institutional funds.

GIFT AID (NON-NEED-BASED) *Total amount:* $30,564,670 (2% state, 94% institutional, 4% external sources). *Receiving aid:* Freshmen: 80% (280). Undergraduates: 58% (739). *Average award:* Freshmen: $22,455. Undergraduates: $21,770. *Scholarships, grants, and awards by category:* Academic interests/achievement: area/ethnic studies, biological sciences, business, communication, computer science, education, engineering/technologies, English, foreign languages, general academic interests/achievements, health fields, home economics, humanities, international studies, mathematics, physical sciences, premedicine, religion/biblical studies, social sciences. Creative arts/performance: art/fine arts, dance, music, performing arts, theater/drama. Special achievements/activities: junior miss, leadership, memberships, religious involvement. Special characteristics: adult students, children and siblings of alumni, children of faculty/staff, ethnic background, first-generation college students, general special characteristics, international students, local/state students, previous college experience, relatives of clergy, religious affiliation, veterans, veterans' children. *Tuition waivers:* Full or partial for employees or children of employees. *ROTC:* Army cooperative, Air Force cooperative.

LOANS *Student loans:* $6,178,862 (36% need-based, 64% non-need-based). 52% of past graduating class borrowed through all loan programs. *Average indebtedness per student:* $30,084. *Average need-based loan:* Freshmen: $3350. Undergraduates: $4218. *Parent loans:* $3,152,412 (100% non-need-based). *Programs:* Federal Direct (Subsidized and Unsubsidized Stafford, PLUS), Perkins, college/university.

WORK-STUDY *Federal work-study:* Total amount: $345,063; jobs available. *State or other work-study/employment:* Total amount: $166,236 (100% non-need-based). Part-time jobs available.

APPLYING FOR FINANCIAL AID *Required financial aid forms:* FAFSA, state aid form. *Financial aid deadline (priority):* 3/1. *Notification date:* 3/1. Students must reply by 5/1.

CONTACT Melissa Suzanne Burgett, Director of Financial Aid, Birmingham-Southern College, 900 Arkadelphia Road, Birmingham, AL 35254, 205-226-4688 or toll-free 800-523-5793. *Fax:* 205-226-3082. *E-mail:* finaid@bsc.edu. *Website:* http://www.bsc.edu/.

BIRTHINGWAY COLLEGE OF MIDWIFERY
Portland, OR

CONTACT Financial Aid Office, Birthingway College of Midwifery, 12113 SE Foster Road, Portland, OR 97299, 503-760-3131. *Website:* http://www.birthingway.edu/.

BLACKBURN COLLEGE
Carlinville, IL

CONTACT Mrs. Jane Kelsey, Financial Aid Administrator, Blackburn College, 700 College Avenue, Carlinville, IL 62626-1498, 217-854-3231 Ext. 4227 or toll-free 800-233-3550. *Fax:* 217-854-3731. *Website:* http://www.blackburn.edu/.

BLACK HILLS STATE UNIVERSITY
Spearfish, SD

Tuition & fees (SD res): $8602	Average undergraduate aid package: N/A

ABOUT THE INSTITUTION State-supported, coed. *Awards:* certificates, associate, bachelor's, and master's degrees. 47 undergraduate majors. *Total enrollment:* 4,178. Undergraduates: 3,947. Freshmen: 541. Federal methodology is used as a basis for awarding need-based institutional aid.

UNDERGRADUATE EXPENSES for 2018–2019 *Application fee:* $20. *Tuition, state resident:* full-time $7514; part-time $286.70 per credit hour. *Tuition, nonresident:* full-time $10,514; part-time $386.90 per credit hour. *Required fees:* full-time $1088. Full-time tuition and fees vary according to course load, location, and reciprocity agreements. Part-time tuition and fees vary according to course load, location, and reciprocity agreements. *College room and board:* $6820; *Room only:* $3467. Room and board charges vary according to board plan and housing facility.

GIFT AID (NEED-BASED) *Scholarships, grants, and awards:* Federal Pell, FSEOG, state, private, college/university gift aid from institutional funds, Academic Competitiveness Grants, National SMART Grants, TEACH Grants.

GIFT AID (NON-NEED-BASED) *Scholarships, grants, and awards by category:* Academic interests/achievement: biological sciences, business, communication, computer science, education, English, foreign languages, general academic interests/achievements, health fields, humanities, mathematics, military science, physical sciences, social sciences. Creative arts/performance: art/fine arts, music, theater/drama. *Tuition waivers:* Full or partial for children of alumni, employees or children of employees, senior citizens. *ROTC:* Army.

LOANS *Programs:* Perkins.

WORK-STUDY Federal work-study jobs available. *State or other work-study/employment:* Part-time jobs available.

APPLYING FOR FINANCIAL AID *Required financial aid form:* FAFSA. *Financial aid deadline (priority):* 3/1. *Notification date:* Continuous beginning 5/1. Students must reply within 3 weeks of notification.

CONTACT Ms. Deb Henriksen, Director of Financial Aid, Black Hills State University, 1200 University Street, Spearfish, SD 57799-9670, 605-642-6581 or toll-free 800-255-2478. *Fax:* 605-642-6913. *E-mail:* deb.henriksen@bhsu.edu. *Website:* http://www.bhsu.edu/.

BLESSING-RIEMAN COLLEGE OF NURSING & HEALTH SCIENCES
Quincy, IL

Tuition & fees: $25,050 — **Average undergraduate aid package: N/A**

ABOUT THE INSTITUTION Independent, coed, primarily women. 1 undergraduate major. Federal methodology is used as a basis for awarding need-based institutional aid.

UNDERGRADUATE EXPENSES for 2017–2018 Tuition: full-time $24,050; part-time $802 per credit hour. Full-time tuition and fees vary according to course load, degree level, program, and student level. Part-time tuition and fees vary according to course load, degree level, program, and student level.

UNDERGRADUATE FINANCIAL AID (Fall 2016) 158 applied for aid; of those 100% were deemed to have need. 100% of undergraduates with need received aid; of those 100% had need fully met. **Average percent of need met:** 100% (excluding resources awarded to replace EFC).

GIFT AID (NEED-BASED) Total amount: $1,631,972 (17% federal, 11% state, 66% institutional, 6% external sources). **Scholarships, grants, and awards:** Federal Pell, FSEOG, state, private, college/university gift aid from institutional funds.

GIFT AID (NON-NEED-BASED) Receiving aid: Undergraduates: 100% (158). **Scholarships, grants, and awards by category:** Academic interests/achievement: general academic interests/achievements. **Tuition waivers:** Full or partial for employees or children of employees.

LOANS Student loans: $858,943 (100% need-based). **Parent loans:** $72,964 (100% need-based). **Programs:** Federal Direct (Subsidized and Unsubsidized Stafford, PLUS), Federal Nursing, college/university.

APPLYING FOR FINANCIAL AID Required financial aid form: FAFSA. **Financial aid deadline:** Continuous. **Notification date:** Continuous beginning 4/1.

CONTACT Mrs. Erin McHargue, Financial Aid Coordinator, Blessing-Rieman College of Nursing & Health Sciences, Broadway at 11th Street, PO Box 7005, Quincy, IL 62301, 217-223-8400 Ext. 6993 or toll-free 800-877-9140. Fax: 217-223-1781. E-mail: mcharguee@brcn.edu.
Website: http://www.brcn.edu/.

BLOOMFIELD COLLEGE
Bloomfield, NJ

ABOUT THE INSTITUTION Independent Presbyterian Church (U.S.A.), coed. **Awards:** certificates, bachelor's, and master's degrees. 22 undergraduate majors. **Total enrollment:** 2,000. Undergraduates: 1,947. Freshmen: 507.

GIFT AID (NEED-BASED) Scholarships, grants, and awards: Federal Pell, FSEOG, state, private, college/university gift aid from institutional funds.

GIFT AID (NON-NEED-BASED) Scholarships, grants, and awards by category: Academic interests/achievement: biological sciences, business, communication, computer science, education, English, general academic interests/achievements, health fields, home economics, humanities, mathematics, physical sciences, premedicine, religion/biblical studies, social sciences. Creative arts/performance: art/fine arts, cinema/film/broadcasting, creative writing, general creative arts/performance, journalism/publications, performing arts. Special achievements/activities: community service, general special achievements/activities, leadership. Special characteristics: children and siblings of alumni, children of current students, general special characteristics, international students, local/state students, previous college experience, relatives of clergy, siblings of current students, spouses of current students, veterans.

LOANS Programs: Federal Direct (Subsidized and Unsubsidized Stafford, PLUS), private loans.

WORK-STUDY Federal work-study: 179 jobs averaging $2169. **State or other work-study/employment:** Part-time jobs available.

APPLYING FOR FINANCIAL AID Required financial aid form: FAFSA.

CONTACT Office of Financial Aid, Bloomfield College, 467 Franklin Street, Bloomfield, NJ 07003-9981, 973-748-9000 Ext. 1213 or toll-free 800-848-4555 Ext. 230. Fax: 973-748-9735.
Website: http://www.bloomfield.edu/.

BLOOMSBURG UNIVERSITY OF PENNSYLVANIA
Bloomsburg, PA

Tuition & fees (PA res): $10,500 — **Average undergraduate aid package: $9310**

ABOUT THE INSTITUTION State-supported, coed. **Awards:** certificates, bachelor's, master's, and doctoral degrees. 43 undergraduate majors. **Total enrollment:** 9,287. Undergraduates: 8,606. Freshmen: 1,861. Federal methodology is used as a basis for awarding need-based institutional aid.

UNDERGRADUATE EXPENSES for 2017–2018 Application fee: $35. **Tuition, state resident:** full-time $7492; part-time $312 per credit. **Tuition, non-resident:** full-time $18,730; part-time $780 per credit. **Required fees:** full-time $3008; $110 per credit or $75 per term. Full-time tuition and fees vary according to course load and location. Part-time tuition and fees vary according to course load and location. **College room and board:** $9430; **Room only:** $6080. Room and board charges vary according to board plan and housing facility.

FRESHMAN FINANCIAL AID (Fall 2017, est.) 1,757 applied for aid; of those 74% were deemed to have need. 99% of freshmen with need received aid; of those 9% had need fully met. **Average percent of need met:** 51% (excluding resources awarded to replace EFC). **Average financial aid package:** $8411 (excluding resources awarded to replace EFC). 5% of all full-time freshmen had no need and received non-need-based gift aid.

UNDERGRADUATE FINANCIAL AID (Fall 2017, est.) 7,058 applied for aid; of those 74% were deemed to have need. 99% of undergraduates with need received aid; of those 12% had need fully met. **Average percent of need met:** 56% (excluding resources awarded to replace EFC). **Average financial aid package:** $9310 (excluding resources awarded to replace EFC). 3% of all full-time undergraduates had no need and received non-need-based gift aid.

GIFT AID (NEED-BASED) Total amount: $21,486,343 (59% federal, 38% state, 2% institutional, 1% external sources). **Receiving aid:** Freshmen: 45% (835); all full-time undergraduates: 43% (3,351). **Average award:** Freshmen: $6160; Undergraduates: $5867. **Scholarships, grants, and awards:** Federal Pell, FSEOG, state, private, college/university gift aid from institutional funds.

GIFT AID (NON-NEED-BASED) Total amount: $4,614,186 (16% state, 49% institutional, 35% external sources). **Receiving aid:** Freshmen: 23% (418). Undergraduates: 15% (1,164). **Average award:** Freshmen: $2788. Undergraduates: $2450. **Scholarships, grants, and awards by category:** Academic interests/achievement: 1,019 awards ($1,993,867 total): biological sciences, business, communication, computer science, education, English, foreign languages, general academic interests/achievements, health fields, humanities, international studies, mathematics, physical sciences, religion/biblical studies, social sciences. Special characteristics: 264 awards ($1,059,177 total): children of faculty/staff, international students. **Tuition waivers:** Full or partial for employees or children of employees, senior citizens. **ROTC:** Army, Air Force cooperative.

LOANS Student loans: $63,109,014 (34% need-based, 66% non-need-based). 81% of past graduating class borrowed through all loan programs. **Average indebtedness per student:** $35,407. **Average need-based loan:** Freshmen: $3247. Undergraduates: $4157. **Parent loans:** $16,609,603 (100% non-need-based). **Programs:** Federal Direct (Subsidized and Unsubsidized Stafford, PLUS), state, alternative loans.

WORK-STUDY Federal work-study: Total amount: $2,552,106; 873 jobs averaging $2923. **State or other work-study/employment:** Total amount: $4,644,813 (100% non-need-based). 1,222 part-time jobs averaging $3801.

ATHLETIC AWARDS Total amount: $351,570 (100% non-need-based).

APPLYING FOR FINANCIAL AID Required financial aid form: FAFSA. **Financial aid deadline (priority):** 3/15. **Notification date:** Continuous beginning 12/1.

CONTACT Mrs. Amanda L. Kishbaugh, Interim Director of Financial Aid, Bloomsburg University of Pennsylvania, 119 Warren Student Services Center, 400 East 2nd Street, Bloomsburg, PA 17815-1301, 570-389-4279. Fax: 570-389-4795. E-mail: akishba2@bloomu.edu.
Website: http://www.bloomu.edu/.

BLUEFIELD COLLEGE
Bluefield, VA

Tuition & fees: $25,290	Average undergraduate aid package: $16,862

ABOUT THE INSTITUTION Independent Southern Baptist, coed. *Awards:* bachelor's and master's degrees. 43 undergraduate majors. *Total enrollment:* 1,000. Undergraduates: 1,754. Freshmen: 211. Federal methodology is used as a basis for awarding need-based institutional aid.

UNDERGRADUATE EXPENSES for 2018–2019 *Comprehensive fee:* $34,314 includes full-time tuition ($24,520), mandatory fees ($770), and room and board ($9024). *College room only:* $3770. Full-time tuition and fees vary according to course load and program. Room and board charges vary according to housing facility. *Part-time tuition:* $970 per credit. *Part-time fees:* $28 per credit hour. Part-time tuition and fees vary according to course load and program.

FRESHMAN FINANCIAL AID (Fall 2017, est.) 201 applied for aid; of those 96% were deemed to have need. 100% of freshmen with need received aid; of those 12% had need fully met. *Average percent of need met:* 69% (excluding resources awarded to replace EFC). *Average financial aid package:* $18,689 (excluding resources awarded to replace EFC). 8% of all full-time freshmen had no need and received non-need-based gift aid.

UNDERGRADUATE FINANCIAL AID (Fall 2017, est.) 748 applied for aid; of those 95% were deemed to have need. 100% of undergraduates with need received aid; of those 11% had need fully met. *Average percent of need met:* 66% (excluding resources awarded to replace EFC). *Average financial aid package:* $16,862 (excluding resources awarded to replace EFC). 10% of all full-time undergraduates had no need and received non-need-based gift aid.

GIFT AID (NEED-BASED) *Total amount:* $7,581,397 (33% federal, 18% state, 40% institutional, 9% external sources). *Receiving aid:* Freshmen: 91% (193); all full-time undergraduates: 87% (702). *Average award:* Freshmen: $15,576; Undergraduates: $13,152. *Scholarships, grants, and awards:* Federal Pell, FSEOG, state, private, college/university gift aid from institutional funds.

GIFT AID (NON-NEED-BASED) *Total amount:* $898,420 (24% state, 68% institutional, 8% external sources). *Receiving aid:* Freshmen: 10% (22). Undergraduates: 8% (67). *Average award:* Freshmen: $7315. Undergraduates: $6244. *Scholarships, grants, and awards by category:* Academic interests/achievement: 507 awards ($2,852,514 total): general academic interests/achievements, library science. Creative arts/performance: 41 awards ($134,200 total): art/fine arts, music, performing arts, theater/drama. Special achievements/activities: 13 awards ($55,500 total): cheerleading/drum major. Special characteristics: adult students, children of faculty/staff, first-generation college students, general special characteristics, local/state students, out-of-state students, religious affiliation, veterans, veterans' children. *Tuition waivers:* Full or partial for employees or children of employees, senior citizens.

LOANS *Student loans:* $6,218,725 (83% need-based, 17% non-need-based). 60% of past graduating class borrowed through all loan programs. *Average indebtedness per student:* $33,772. *Average need-based loan:* Freshmen: $3477. Undergraduates: $4176. *Parent loans:* $989,114 (57% need-based, 43% non-need-based). *Programs:* Federal Direct (Subsidized and Unsubsidized Stafford, PLUS), private loans.

WORK-STUDY *Federal work-study:* Total amount: $76,834; 74 jobs averaging $1038. *State or other work-study/employment:* Total amount: $4500 (39% need-based, 61% non-need-based). 12 part-time jobs averaging $375.

ATHLETIC AWARDS Total amount: $2,554,207 (66% need-based, 34% non-need-based).

APPLYING FOR FINANCIAL AID *Required financial aid forms:* FAFSA, state aid form. *Financial aid deadline (priority):* 6/1. *Notification date:* Continuous.

CONTACT Ms. Cary Grace Wright, Director of Financial Aid, Bluefield College, 3000 College Avenue, Bluefield, VA 24605, 276-326-4215 or toll-free 800-872-0175. *Fax:* 276-326-4356. *E-mail:* cwright@bluefield.edu. *Website:* http://www.bluefield.edu/.

BLUEFIELD STATE COLLEGE
Bluefield, WV

Tuition & fees (WV res): $6728	Average undergraduate aid package: $3500

ABOUT THE INSTITUTION State-supported, coed. *Awards:* associate and bachelor's degrees. 18 undergraduate majors. *Total enrollment:* 1,362. Undergraduates: 1,362. Freshmen: 226. Federal methodology is used as a basis for awarding need-based institutional aid.

UNDERGRADUATE EXPENSES for 2017–2018 *Tuition, state resident:* full-time $6728; part-time $279 per credit hour. *Tuition, nonresident:* full-time $13,032; part-time $541 per credit hour.

FRESHMAN FINANCIAL AID (Fall 2017, est.) 275 applied for aid; of those 82% were deemed to have need. 100% of freshmen with need received aid; of those 13% had need fully met. *Average percent of need met:* 65% (excluding resources awarded to replace EFC). *Average financial aid package:* $3300 (excluding resources awarded to replace EFC). 1% of all full-time freshmen had no need and received non-need-based gift aid.

UNDERGRADUATE FINANCIAL AID (Fall 2017, est.) 1,380 applied for aid; of those 83% were deemed to have need. 91% of undergraduates with need received aid; of those 13% had need fully met. *Average percent of need met:* 67% (excluding resources awarded to replace EFC). *Average financial aid package:* $3500 (excluding resources awarded to replace EFC). 1% of all full-time undergraduates had no need and received non-need-based gift aid.

GIFT AID (NEED-BASED) *Total amount:* $5,750,000 (78% federal, 22% state). *Receiving aid:* Freshmen: 66% (185); all full-time undergraduates: 70% (970). *Average award:* Freshmen: $3700; Undergraduates: $3700. *Scholarships, grants, and awards:* Federal Pell, FSEOG, state.

GIFT AID (NON-NEED-BASED) *Total amount:* $1,020,000 (39% state, 26% institutional, 35% external sources). *Receiving aid:* Freshmen: 23% (65). Undergraduates: 12% (170). *Average award:* Freshmen: $850. Undergraduates: $850. *Scholarships, grants, and awards by category:* Academic interests/achievement: engineering/technologies, general academic interests/achievements. *Special achievements/activities:* cheerleading/drum major, general special achievements/activities, junior miss, leadership. *Tuition waivers:* Full or partial for adult students, senior citizens.

LOANS *Student loans:* $7,100,000 (45% need-based, 55% non-need-based). 68% of past graduating class borrowed through all loan programs. *Average indebtedness per student:* $29,000. *Average need-based loan:* Freshmen: $3350. Undergraduates: $4250. *Parent loans:* $85,000 (100% non-need-based). *Programs:* Federal Direct (Subsidized and Unsubsidized Stafford, PLUS).

WORK-STUDY *Federal work-study:* Total amount: $130,000; 55 jobs averaging $3000. *State or other work-study/employment:* Total amount: $300 (100% non-need-based). Part-time jobs available.

ATHLETIC AWARDS Total amount: $280,000 (100% non-need-based).

APPLYING FOR FINANCIAL AID *Required financial aid forms:* FAFSA, institution's own form. *Financial aid deadline (priority):* 3/1. *Notification date:* 6/1.

CONTACT Mr. Tom Ilse, Director of Financial Aid, Bluefield State College, 219 Rock Street, Bluefield, WV 24701-2198, 304-327-4020 or toll-free 800-344-8892 Ext. 4065 (in-state), 800-654-7798 Ext. 4065 (out-of-state). *Fax:* 304-325-7747. *E-mail:* tilse@bluefieldstate.edu. *Website:* http://www.bluefieldstate.edu/.

BLUE MOUNTAIN COLLEGE
Blue Mountain, MS

Tuition & fees: $11,760	Average undergraduate aid package: $11,919

ABOUT THE INSTITUTION Independent Southern Baptist, coed. *Awards:* bachelor's and master's degrees. 24 undergraduate majors. *Total enrollment:* 601. Undergraduates: 588. Freshmen: 127. Federal methodology is used as a basis for awarding need-based institutional aid.

UNDERGRADUATE EXPENSES for 2017–2018 *Comprehensive fee:* $17,885 includes full-time tuition ($9990), mandatory fees ($1770), and room and board ($6125). Full-time tuition and fees vary according to course load, degree level, and program. Room and board charges vary according to gender, housing facility, and location. **Part-time tuition:** $333 per semester hour. **Part-time fees:** $50 per semester hour. Part-time tuition and fees vary according to course load, degree level, and program.

FRESHMAN FINANCIAL AID (Fall 2017, est.) 125 applied for aid; of those 82% were deemed to have need. 100% of freshmen with need received aid; of those 20% had need fully met. **Average percent of need met:** 67% (excluding resources awarded to replace EFC). **Average financial aid package:** $11,593 (excluding resources awarded to replace EFC). 6% of all full-time freshmen had no need and received non-need-based gift aid.

UNDERGRADUATE FINANCIAL AID (Fall 2017, est.) 526 applied for aid; of those 85% were deemed to have need. 100% of undergraduates with need received aid; of those 19% had need fully met. **Average percent of need met:** 67% (excluding resources awarded to replace EFC). **Average financial aid package:** $11,919 (excluding resources awarded to replace EFC). 7% of all full-time undergraduates had no need and received non-need-based gift aid.

GIFT AID (NEED-BASED) Total amount: $3,335,179 (41% federal, 9% state, 46% institutional, 4% external sources). **Receiving aid:** Freshmen: 81% (102); all full-time undergraduates: 83% (439). **Average award:** Freshmen: $10,157; Undergraduates: $9950. **Scholarships, grants, and awards:** Federal Pell, FSEOG, state, private, college/university gift aid from institutional funds.

GIFT AID (NON-NEED-BASED) Average award: Freshmen: $6445. Undergraduates: $5966. **Scholarships, grants, and awards by category:** Academic interests/achievement: biological sciences, business, education, English, humanities, mathematics, physical sciences, premedicine, religion/biblical studies, social sciences. Creative arts/performance: art/fine arts, music, theater/drama. Special achievements/activities: cheerleading/drum major, general special achievements/activities, leadership, memberships, religious involvement. Special characteristics: adult students, children and siblings of alumni, children of current students, children of faculty/staff, married students, parents of current students, relatives of clergy, religious affiliation, siblings of current students, spouses of current students, twins. **Tuition waivers:** Full or partial for employees or children of employees.

LOANS Student loans: $2,392,918 (53% need-based, 47% non-need-based). 49% of past graduating class borrowed through all loan programs. **Average indebtedness per student:** $19,084. **Average need-based loan:** Freshmen: $3039. Undergraduates: $3581. **Parent loans:** $242,800 (100% non-need-based). **Programs:** Federal Direct (Subsidized and Unsubsidized Stafford, PLUS).

WORK-STUDY Federal work-study: Total amount: $66,000; jobs available. **State or other work-study/employment:** Total amount: $66,000 (100% non-need-based). Part-time jobs available.

ATHLETIC AWARDS Total amount: $1,567,636 (100% need-based).

APPLYING FOR FINANCIAL AID Required financial aid form: FAFSA. **Financial aid deadline (priority):** 3/1. **Notification date:** Continuous beginning 4/1. Students must reply within 2 weeks of notification.

CONTACT Mrs. Beverly K. Hickey, Director of Financial Aid, Blue Mountain College, PO Box 160, Blue Mountain, MS 38610-0160, 662-685-4771 Ext. 141 or toll-free 800-235-0136. *Fax:* 662-685-4776. *E-mail:* bhickey@bmc.edu. *Website:* http://www.bmc.edu/.

BLUFFTON UNIVERSITY
Bluffton, OH

Tuition & fees: $32,766	Average undergraduate aid package: $27,173

ABOUT THE INSTITUTION Independent Mennonite, coed. **Awards:** certificates, bachelor's, and master's degrees. 46 undergraduate majors. **Total enrollment:** 824. Undergraduates: 748. Freshmen: 211. Both federal and institutional methodology are used as a basis for awarding need-based institutional aid.

UNDERGRADUATE EXPENSES for 2018–2019 Comprehensive fee: $43,566 includes full-time tuition ($32,316), mandatory fees ($450), and room and board ($10,800). **College room only:** $5316. Full-time tuition and fees vary according to course load, degree level, and program. Room and board charges vary according to board plan and housing facility. **Part-time tuition:** $1347 per credit hour. **Part-time fees:** $113 per term. Part-time tuition and fees vary according to course load, degree level, and program.

FRESHMAN FINANCIAL AID (Fall 2017, est.) 202 applied for aid; of those 93% were deemed to have need. 100% of freshmen with need received aid; of those 15%

had need fully met. **Average percent of need met:** 74% (excluding resources awarded to replace EFC). **Average financial aid package:** $26,786 (excluding resources awarded to replace EFC). 9% of all full-time freshmen had no need and received non-need-based gift aid.

UNDERGRADUATE FINANCIAL AID (Fall 2017, est.) 614 applied for aid; of those 94% were deemed to have need. 100% of undergraduates with need received aid; of those 14% had need fully met. **Average percent of need met:** 75% (excluding resources awarded to replace EFC). **Average financial aid package:** $27,173 (excluding resources awarded to replace EFC). 13% of all full-time undergraduates had no need and received non-need-based gift aid.

GIFT AID (NEED-BASED) Total amount: $12,504,620 (12% federal, 5% state, 80% institutional, 3% external sources). **Receiving aid:** Freshmen: 89% (187); all full-time undergraduates: 85% (572). **Average award:** Freshmen: $22,692; Undergraduates: $21,925. **Scholarships, grants, and awards:** Federal Pell, FSEOG, state, private, college/university gift aid from institutional funds.

GIFT AID (NON-NEED-BASED) Total amount: $1,891,516 (91% institutional, 9% external sources). **Receiving aid:** Freshmen: 9% (19). Undergraduates: 8% (51). **Average award:** Freshmen: $16,096. Undergraduates: $16,395. **Scholarships, grants, and awards by category:** Academic interests/achievement: 655 awards ($6,882,584 total): biological sciences, general academic interests/achievements, mathematics, physical sciences, premedicine. Creative arts/performance: 48 awards ($150,250 total): art/fine arts, music, performing arts. Special achievements/activities: 7 awards ($17,000 total): leadership. Special characteristics: 383 awards ($922,427 total): children and siblings of alumni, children of faculty/staff, international students, members of minority groups, out-of-state students, religious affiliation. **Tuition waivers:** Full or partial for employees or children of employees.

LOANS Student loans: $5,893,620 (75% need-based, 25% non-need-based). 83% of past graduating class borrowed through all loan programs. **Average indebtedness per student:** $36,796. **Average need-based loan:** Freshmen: $3384. Undergraduates: $4551. **Parent loans:** $2,204,575 (58% need-based, 42% non-need-based). **Programs:** Federal Direct (Subsidized and Unsubsidized Stafford, PLUS), Perkins, alternative loans.

WORK-STUDY Federal work-study: Total amount: $722,434; 442 jobs averaging $2306. **State or other work-study/employment:** Total amount: $390,529 (4% need-based, 96% non-need-based). 188 part-time jobs averaging $2907.

APPLYING FOR FINANCIAL AID Required financial aid form: FAFSA. **Financial aid deadline:** 10/1 (priority: 5/1). **Notification date:** Continuous beginning 11/1.

CONTACT Chris Fowler, Director of Financial Aid, Bluffton University, 1 University Drive, Bluffton, OH 45817-2104, 419-358-3266 or toll-free 800-488-3257. *Fax:* 419-358-3073. *E-mail:* fowlerc@bluffton.edu. *Website:* http://www.bluffton.edu/.

BOB JONES UNIVERSITY
Greenville, SC

Tuition & fees: $18,150	Average undergraduate aid package: $12,290

ABOUT THE INSTITUTION Independent Christian, coed. **Awards:** certificates, associate, bachelor's, master's, and doctoral degrees. 53 undergraduate majors. **Total enrollment:** 2,936. Undergraduates: 2,606. Freshmen: 596. Federal methodology is used as a basis for awarding need-based institutional aid.

UNDERGRADUATE EXPENSES for 2018–2019 Comprehensive fee: $25,126 includes full-time tuition ($17,250), mandatory fees ($900), and room and board ($6976). Full-time tuition and fees vary according to course load and program. **Part-time tuition:** $860 per credit hour. **Part-time fees:** $488 per degree program. Part-time tuition and fees vary according to course load and program.

FRESHMAN FINANCIAL AID (Fall 2017, est.) 533 applied for aid; of those 87% were deemed to have need. 100% of freshmen with need received aid; of those 20% had need fully met. **Average percent of need met:** 66% (excluding resources awarded to replace EFC). **Average financial aid package:** $13,519 (excluding resources awarded to replace EFC). 19% of all full-time freshmen had no need and received non-need-based gift aid.

UNDERGRADUATE FINANCIAL AID (Fall 2017, est.) 1,862 applied for aid; of those 89% were deemed to have need. 100% of undergraduates with need received aid; of those 16% had need fully met. **Average percent of need met:** 61% (excluding resources awarded to replace EFC). **Average financial aid package:**

$12,290 (excluding resources awarded to replace EFC). 20% of all full-time undergraduates had no need and received non-need-based gift aid.

GIFT AID (NEED-BASED) *Total amount:* $17,301,611 (25% federal, 15% state, 53% institutional, 7% external sources). *Receiving aid:* Freshmen: 78% (461); all full-time undergraduates: 71% (1,643). *Average award:* Freshmen: $12,333; Undergraduates: $10,486. *Scholarships, grants, and awards:* Federal Pell, FSEOG, state, private, college/university gift aid from institutional funds.

GIFT AID (NON-NEED-BASED) *Total amount:* $4,377,772 (27% state, 64% institutional, 9% external sources). *Receiving aid:* Freshmen: 13% (79). Undergraduates: 9% (210). *Average award:* Freshmen: $6189. Undergraduates: $5069. *Tuition waivers:* Full or partial for employees or children of employees.

LOANS *Student loans:* $5,687,807 (78% need-based, 22% non-need-based). 49% of past graduating class borrowed through all loan programs. *Average indebtedness per student:* $21,153. *Average need-based loan:* Freshmen: $2974. Undergraduates: $3814. *Parent loans:* $870,199 (47% need-based, 53% non-need-based). *Programs:* Federal Direct (Subsidized and Unsubsidized Stafford, PLUS), state, college/university.

WORK-STUDY *Federal work-study:* Total amount: $112,845; jobs available. *State or other work-study/employment:* Part-time jobs available.

APPLYING FOR FINANCIAL AID *Required financial aid form:* FAFSA. *Financial aid deadline:* Continuous. *Notification date:* Continuous beginning 4/1.

CONTACT Office of Financial Aid, Bob Jones University, 1700 Wade Hampton Boulevard, Greenville, SC 29614, 864-242-5100 Ext. 3040 or toll-free 800-252-6363. *E-mail:* finaid@bju.edu. *Website:* http://www.bju.edu/.

BOISE BIBLE COLLEGE
Boise, ID

CONTACT Beth Turner, Financial Aid Counselor, Boise Bible College, 8695 West Marigold Street, Boise, ID 83714-1220, 208-376-7731 Ext. 12 or toll-free 800-893-7755. *Fax:* 208-376-7743. *E-mail:* betht@boisebible.edu. *Website:* http://www.boisebible.edu/.

BOISE STATE UNIVERSITY
Boise, ID

Tuition & fees (ID res): $7326	Average undergraduate aid package: $10,136

ABOUT THE INSTITUTION State-supported, coed. *Awards:* certificates, associate, bachelor's, master's, and doctoral degrees. 78 undergraduate majors. *Total enrollment:* 24,154. Undergraduates: 20,767. Freshmen: 2,788. Federal methodology is used as a basis for awarding need-based institutional aid.

UNDERGRADUATE EXPENSES for 2017–2018 *Application fee:* $50. *Tuition, state resident:* full-time $5043; part-time $205 per credit hour. *Tuition, nonresident:* full-time $20,359; part-time $500 per credit hour. *Required fees:* full-time $2283; $99.71 per term. Full-time tuition and fees vary according to course load, program, and reciprocity agreements. Part-time tuition and fees vary according to course load and program. *College room and board:* $7750; *Room only:* $3850. Room and board charges vary according to board plan and housing facility.

FRESHMAN FINANCIAL AID (Fall 2016) 1,634 applied for aid; of those 99% were deemed to have need. 96% of freshmen with need received aid; of those 19% had need fully met. *Average percent of need met:* 62% (excluding resources awarded to replace EFC). *Average financial aid package:* $11,233 (excluding resources awarded to replace EFC). 6% of all full-time freshmen had no need and received non-need-based gift aid.

UNDERGRADUATE FINANCIAL AID (Fall 2016) 7,424 applied for aid; of those 99% were deemed to have need. 96% of undergraduates with need received aid; of those 14% had need fully met. *Average percent of need met:* 58% (excluding resources awarded to replace EFC). *Average financial aid package:* $10,136 (excluding resources awarded to replace EFC). 3% of all full-time undergraduates had no need and received non-need-based gift aid.

GIFT AID (NEED-BASED) *Total amount:* $34,269,259 (69% federal, 11% state, 15% institutional, 5% external sources). *Receiving aid:* Freshmen: 39% (996); all full-

time undergraduates: 40% (4,991). *Average award:* Freshmen: $5975; Undergraduates: $5750. *Scholarships, grants, and awards:* Federal Pell, FSEOG, state, private, college/university gift aid from institutional funds, Federal Nursing, Leveraging Educational Assistance Program (LEAP).

GIFT AID (NON-NEED-BASED) *Total amount:* $2,070,501 (6% state, 63% institutional, 31% external sources). *Receiving aid:* Freshmen: 4% (101). Undergraduates: 2% (208). *Average award:* Freshmen: $2895. Undergraduates: $2111. *Scholarships, grants, and awards by category:* Academic interests/achievement: architecture, area/ethnic studies, biological sciences, business, communication, computer science, education, engineering/technologies, English, foreign languages, general academic interests/achievements, health fields, home economics, humanities, international studies, mathematics, military science, physical sciences, premedicine, religion/biblical studies, social sciences. *Creative arts/performance:* art/fine arts, dance, debating, general creative arts/performance, journalism/publications, music, performing arts, theater/drama. *Special achievements/activities:* cheerleading/drum major, community service, leadership, rodeo. *Special characteristics:* ethnic background, first-generation college students, general special characteristics, handicapped students, international students, local/state students, members of minority groups, out-of-state students, previous college experience, spouses of current students, veterans, veterans' children. *Tuition waivers:* Full or partial for employees or children of employees, senior citizens. *ROTC:* Army.

LOANS *Student loans:* $56,253,800 (77% need-based, 23% non-need-based). 59% of past graduating class borrowed through all loan programs. *Average indebtedness per student:* $27,974. *Average need-based loan:* Freshmen: $3405. Undergraduates: $4386. *Parent loans:* $9,359,150 (37% need-based, 63% non-need-based). *Programs:* Federal Direct (Subsidized and Unsubsidized Stafford, PLUS), Perkins, Federal Nursing, college/university.

WORK-STUDY *Federal work-study:* 192 jobs averaging $2260. *State or other work-study/employment:* Total amount: $452,708 (100% need-based). 216 part-time jobs averaging $2090.

ATHLETIC AWARDS Total amount: $7,776,544 (90% need-based, 10% non-need-based).

APPLYING FOR FINANCIAL AID *Required financial aid form:* FAFSA. *Financial aid deadline:* 6/30 (priority: 2/15). *Notification date:* Continuous beginning 3/15. Students must reply by 4/12 or within 4 weeks of notification.

CONTACT Diana Fairchild, Office of Financial Aid and Scholarships, Boise State University, Administration Building, Room 113, Boise, ID 83725-1315, 800-824-7017 Ext. 1664 or toll-free 800-824-7017. *Fax:* 208-426-1305. *E-mail:* financialaid@boisestate.edu. *Website:* http://www.boisestate.edu/.

BON SECOURS MEMORIAL COLLEGE OF NURSING
Richmond, VA

CONTACT Financial Aid Office, Bon Secours Memorial College of Nursing, 8550 Magellan Parkway, Suite 1100, Richmond, VA 23227-1149, 804-627-5300 or toll-free 866-238-7414. *Website:* http://www.bsmcon.edu/.

BORICUA COLLEGE
New York, NY

CONTACT Ms. Rosalia Cruz, Financial Aid Administrator, Boricua College, 3755 Broadway, New York, NY 10032-1560, 212-694-1000 Ext. 611. *Fax:* 212-694-1015. *E-mail:* rcruz@boricuacollege.edu. *Website:* http://www.boricuacollege.edu/.

BOSTON ARCHITECTURAL COLLEGE
Boston, MA

Tuition & fees: $21,174	Average undergraduate aid package: $11,472

ABOUT THE INSTITUTION Independent, coed. *Awards:* certificates, bachelor's, and master's degrees. 4 undergraduate majors. *Total enrollment:* 878. Undergraduates: 472. Freshmen: 24. Federal methodology is used as a basis for awarding need-based institutional aid.

UNDERGRADUATE EXPENSES for 2017–2018 *Tuition:* full-time $20,424; part-time $1702 per credit hour. *Required fees:* full-time $750; $225 per term. Full-time tuition and fees vary according to course load and program. Part-time tuition and fees vary according to course load and program.

FRESHMAN FINANCIAL AID (Fall 2016) 5 applied for aid; of those 100% were deemed to have need. 100% of freshmen with need received aid. *Average percent of need met:* 51% (excluding resources awarded to replace EFC). *Average financial aid package:* $14,481 (excluding resources awarded to replace EFC).

UNDERGRADUATE FINANCIAL AID (Fall 2016) 98 applied for aid; of those 95% were deemed to have need. 95% of undergraduates with need received aid; of those 1% had need fully met. *Average percent of need met:* 33% (excluding resources awarded to replace EFC). *Average financial aid package:* $11,472 (excluding resources awarded to replace EFC). 7% of all full-time undergraduates had no need and received non-need-based gift aid.

GIFT AID (NEED-BASED) *Total amount:* $842,479 (49% federal, 4% state, 19% institutional, 28% external sources). *Receiving aid:* Freshmen: 36% (4); all full-time undergraduates: 57% (71). *Average award:* Freshmen: $8665; Undergraduates: $6941. *Scholarships, grants, and awards:* Federal Pell, FSEOG, state, private, college/university gift aid from institutional funds.

GIFT AID (NON-NEED-BASED) *Total amount:* $160,380 (53% institutional, 47% external sources). *Receiving aid:* Undergraduates: 1% (1). *Average award:* Undergraduates: $2740. *Scholarships, grants, and awards by category:* Academic interests/achievement: architecture, general academic interests/achievements. *Tuition waivers:* Full or partial for employees or children of employees.

LOANS *Student loans:* $1,968,958 (85% need-based, 15% non-need-based). *Average need-based loan:* Freshmen: $6999. Undergraduates: $5643. *Parent loans:* $621,506 (86% need-based, 14% non-need-based). *Programs:* Federal Direct (Subsidized and Unsubsidized Stafford, PLUS), private loans.

WORK-STUDY *Federal work-study:* 18 jobs averaging $2915.

APPLYING FOR FINANCIAL AID *Required financial aid form:* FAFSA. *Financial aid deadline (priority):* 4/15. *Notification date:* Continuous beginning 5/1. Students must reply within 2 weeks of notification.

CONTACT Ms. Janice Wilkos-Greenberg, Director of Financial Aid, Boston Architectural College, 320 Newbury Street, Boston, MA 02115, 617-585-0183. *Fax:* 617-585-0131. *E-mail:* janice.greenberg@the-bac.edu. *Website:* http://www.the-bac.edu/.

BOSTON BAPTIST COLLEGE
Boston, MA

Tuition & fees: $6300	Average undergraduate aid package: N/A

ABOUT THE INSTITUTION Independent Baptist, coed. 1 undergraduate major. Both federal and institutional methodology are used as a basis for awarding need-based institutional aid.

UNDERGRADUATE EXPENSES for 2017–2018 *Comprehensive fee:* $9800 includes full-time tuition ($5700), mandatory fees ($600), and room and board ($3500). *College room only:* $2150. Full-time tuition and fees vary according to course load and program. Room and board charges vary according to board plan. *Part-time tuition:* $475 per credit hour. *Part-time fees:* $50 per credit hour; $100 per term. Part-time tuition and fees vary according to course load and program.

FRESHMAN FINANCIAL AID (Fall 2016) 7 applied for aid; of those 100% were deemed to have need. 100% of freshmen with need received aid; of those 29% had need fully met.

UNDERGRADUATE FINANCIAL AID (Fall 2016) 69 applied for aid. 3% of all full-time undergraduates had no need and received non-need-based gift aid.

GIFT AID (NEED-BASED) *Total amount:* $755,059 (60% federal, 1% state, 38% institutional, 1% external sources). *Receiving aid:* Freshmen: 86% (6). *Scholar-ships, grants, and awards:* Federal Pell, FSEOG, state, private, college/university gift aid from institutional funds.

GIFT AID (NON-NEED-BASED) *Average award:* Undergraduates: $4000. *Scholarships, grants, and awards by category:* Academic interests/achievement: 76 awards ($288,972 total): religion/biblical studies. *Special characteristics:* 9 awards ($61,100 total): children and siblings of alumni, children of faculty/staff.

LOANS *Student loans:* $290,400 (100% need-based). *Parent loans:* $19,148 (100% need-based). *Programs:* Federal Direct (Subsidized and Unsubsidized Stafford, PLUS), state, private loans.

WORK-STUDY *Federal work-study:* 4 jobs averaging $1782.

APPLYING FOR FINANCIAL AID *Required financial aid form:* FAFSA. *Financial aid deadline:* Continuous. *Notification date:* Continuous.

CONTACT Financial Aid Office, Boston Baptist College, 950 Metropolitan Avenue, Boston, MA 02136, 617-364-3510 or toll-free 888-235-2014. *Website:* http://www.boston.edu/.

BOSTON COLLEGE
Chestnut Hill, MA

Tuition & fees: $53,346	Average undergraduate aid package: $41,056

ABOUT THE INSTITUTION Independent Roman Catholic (Jesuit), coed. *Awards:* certificates, bachelor's, master's, and doctoral degrees (also offers continuing education program with significant enrollment not reflected in profile). 48 undergraduate majors. *Total enrollment:* 13,996. Undergraduates: 9,358. Freshmen: 2,412. Institutional methodology is used as a basis for awarding need-based institutional aid.

UNDERGRADUATE EXPENSES for 2017–2018 *Application fee:* $80. *One-time required fee:* $555. *Comprehensive fee:* $67,488 includes full-time tuition ($52,500), mandatory fees ($846), and room and board ($14,142). *College room only:* $8830. Room and board charges vary according to housing facility.

FRESHMAN FINANCIAL AID (Fall 2016) 1,138 applied for aid; of those 84% were deemed to have need. 100% of freshmen with need received aid; of those 100% had need fully met. *Average percent of need met:* 100% (excluding resources awarded to replace EFC). *Average financial aid package:* $41,768 (excluding resources awarded to replace EFC). 1% of all full-time freshmen had no need and received non-need-based gift aid.

UNDERGRADUATE FINANCIAL AID (Fall 2016) 4,189 applied for aid; of those 88% were deemed to have need. 100% of undergraduates with need received aid; of those 100% had need fully met. *Average percent of need met:* 100% (excluding resources awarded to replace EFC). *Average financial aid package:* $41,056 (excluding resources awarded to replace EFC). 2% of all full-time undergraduates had no need and received non-need-based gift aid.

GIFT AID (NEED-BASED) *Total amount:* $123,934,252 (6% federal, 1% state, 91% institutional, 2% external sources). *Receiving aid:* Freshmen: 37% (867); all full-time undergraduates: 35% (3,287). *Average award:* Freshmen: $38,238; Undergraduates: $37,716. *Scholarships, grants, and awards:* Federal Pell, FSEOG, state, private, college/university gift aid from institutional funds.

GIFT AID (NON-NEED-BASED) *Total amount:* $9,558,855 (29% federal, 56% institutional, 15% external sources). *Receiving aid:* Freshmen: 1% (26). Undergraduates: 1% (85). *Average award:* Freshmen: $20,287. Undergraduates: $21,634. *Scholarships, grants, and awards by category:* Academic interests/achievement: general academic interests/achievements, military science. *Tuition waivers:* Full or partial for employees or children of employees. *ROTC:* Army cooperative, Naval cooperative, Air Force cooperative.

LOANS *Student loans:* $16,335,581 (78% need-based, 22% non-need-based). 50% of past graduating class borrowed through all loan programs. *Average indebtedness per student:* $20,481. *Average need-based loan:* Freshmen: $3347. Undergraduates: $4329. *Parent loans:* $33,802,537 (100% non-need-based). *Programs:* Perkins, Federal Nursing, state.

WORK-STUDY *Federal work-study:* jobs available.

ATHLETIC AWARDS Total amount: $19,150,031 (11% need-based, 89% non-need-based).

APPLYING FOR FINANCIAL AID *Required financial aid forms:* FAFSA, CSS Financial Aid PROFILE, business/farm supplement, federal income tax form(s), W-2 forms. *Financial aid deadline (priority):* 2/1. *Notification date:* 4/1. Students must reply by 5/1.

CONTACT Office of Student Services, Boston College, Lyons Hall, 140 Commonwealth Avenue, Chestnut Hill, MA 02467, 617-552-3300 or toll-free 800-360-2522. *Fax:* 617-552-4889. *E-mail:* studentservices@bc.edu. *Website:* http://www.bc.edu/.

CONTACT Julie Wickstrom, Executive Director of Financial Assistance, Boston University, 881 Commonwealth Avenue, Boston, MA 02215, 617-353-4176. *Fax:* 617-353-8200. *E-mail:* finaid@bu.edu. *Website:* http://www.bu.edu/.

BOSTON UNIVERSITY
Boston, MA

Tuition & fees: $52,082	Average undergraduate aid package: $42,180

ABOUT THE INSTITUTION Independent, coed. *Awards:* certificates, bachelor's, master's, and doctoral degrees. 118 undergraduate majors. *Total enrollment:* 33,355. Undergraduates: 18,080. Freshmen: 3,498. Both federal and institutional methodology are used as a basis for awarding need-based institutional aid.

UNDERGRADUATE EXPENSES for 2017–2018 *Application fee:* $80. *Comprehensive fee:* $67,352 includes full-time tuition ($50,980), mandatory fees ($1102), and room and board ($15,270). *College room only:* $10,080. Full-time tuition and fees vary according to class time and course load. Room and board charges vary according to board plan, housing facility, and location. *Part-time tuition:* $1593 per credit hour. *Part-time fees:* $60 per term. Part-time tuition and fees vary according to class time, course level, and course load. *Payment plan:* Tuition prepayment.

FRESHMAN FINANCIAL AID (Fall 2017, est.) 1,708 applied for aid; of those 88% were deemed to have need. 100% of freshmen with need received aid; of those 32% had need fully met. *Average percent of need met:* 92% (excluding resources awarded to replace EFC). *Average financial aid package:* $47,702 (excluding resources awarded to replace EFC). 5% of all full-time freshmen had no need and received non-need-based gift aid.

UNDERGRADUATE FINANCIAL AID (Fall 2017, est.) 7,333 applied for aid; of those 88% were deemed to have need. 100% of undergraduates with need received aid; of those 23% had need fully met. *Average percent of need met:* 84% (excluding resources awarded to replace EFC). *Average financial aid package:* $42,180 (excluding resources awarded to replace EFC). 7% of all full-time undergraduates had no need and received non-need-based gift aid.

GIFT AID (NEED-BASED) *Total amount:* $228,061,398 (7% federal, 1% state, 90% institutional, 2% external sources). *Receiving aid:* Freshmen: 42% (1,485); all full-time undergraduates: 39% (6,319). *Average award:* Freshmen: $43,252; Undergraduates: $36,055. *Scholarships, grants, and awards:* Federal Pell, FSEOG, state, private, college/university gift aid from institutional funds.

GIFT AID (NON-NEED-BASED) *Total amount:* $29,493,799 (71% institutional, 29% external sources). *Receiving aid:* Freshmen: 9% (323). Undergraduates: 5% (839). *Average award:* Freshmen: $24,138. Undergraduates: $20,755. *Scholarships, grants, and awards by category:* Academic interests/achievement: 1,177 awards ($20,827,879 total): engineering/technologies, general academic interests/achievements, military science. Creative arts/performance: 338 awards ($6,685,920 total): art/fine arts, music, theater/drama. Special achievements/activities: 51 awards ($2,558,008 total): general special achievements/activities, memberships. Special characteristics: 466 awards ($9,615,741 total): children and siblings of alumni, children of faculty/staff, general special characteristics, local/state students, members of minority groups, relatives of clergy, religious affiliation, veterans, veterans' children. *Tuition waivers:* Full or partial for employees or children of employees. *ROTC:* Army, Naval, Air Force.

LOANS *Student loans:* $80,717,848 (40% need-based, 60% non-need-based). 48% of past graduating class borrowed through all loan programs. *Average indebtedness per student:* $40,089. *Average need-based loan:* Freshmen: $1886. Undergraduates: $4185. *Parent loans:* $26,464,441 (37% need-based, 63% non-need-based). *Programs:* Federal Direct (Subsidized and Unsubsidized Stafford, PLUS), state.

WORK-STUDY *Federal work-study:* Total amount: $6,852,053; 3,001 jobs averaging $2283. *State or other work-study/employment:* Part-time jobs available.

ATHLETIC AWARDS Total amount: $15,212,494 (20% need-based, 80% non-need-based).

APPLYING FOR FINANCIAL AID *Required financial aid forms:* FAFSA, CSS Financial Aid PROFILE, noncustodial (divorced/separated) parent's statement. *Financial aid deadline:* 2/1. *Notification date:* 3/25. Students must reply by 5/1 or within 2 weeks of notification.

BOWDOIN COLLEGE
Brunswick, ME

Tuition & fees: $51,848	Average undergraduate aid package: $46,562

ABOUT THE INSTITUTION Independent, coed. *Awards:* bachelor's degrees. 46 undergraduate majors. *Total enrollment:* 1,816. Undergraduates: 1,816. Freshmen: 501. Institutional methodology is used as a basis for awarding need-based institutional aid.

UNDERGRADUATE EXPENSES for 2017–2018 *Application fee:* $65. *Comprehensive fee:* $65,980 includes full-time tuition ($51,344), mandatory fees ($504), and room and board ($14,132). *College room only:* $6604. Room and board charges vary according to board plan. *Part-time tuition:* $1003 per credit hour.

FRESHMAN FINANCIAL AID (Fall 2017, est.) 313 applied for aid; of those 84% were deemed to have need. 100% of freshmen with need received aid; of those 100% had need fully met. *Average percent of need met:* 100% (excluding resources awarded to replace EFC). *Average financial aid package:* $47,275 (excluding resources awarded to replace EFC). 2% of all full-time freshmen had no need and received non-need-based gift aid.

UNDERGRADUATE FINANCIAL AID (Fall 2017, est.) 925 applied for aid; of those 90% were deemed to have need. 100% of undergraduates with need received aid; of those 100% had need fully met. *Average percent of need met:* 100% (excluding resources awarded to replace EFC). *Average financial aid package:* $46,562 (excluding resources awarded to replace EFC). 2% of all full-time undergraduates had no need and received non-need-based gift aid.

GIFT AID (NEED-BASED) *Total amount:* $38,921,130 (4% federal, 91% institutional, 5% external sources). *Receiving aid:* Freshmen: 52% (262); all full-time undergraduates: 46% (832). *Average award:* Freshmen: $45,625; Undergraduates: $44,824. *Scholarships, grants, and awards:* Federal Pell, FSEOG, state, private, college/university gift aid from institutional funds.

GIFT AID (NON-NEED-BASED) *Total amount:* $1,180,093 (7% institutional, 93% external sources). *Average award:* Freshmen: $1000. Undergraduates: $1000. *Scholarships, grants, and awards by category:* Academic interests/achievement: 32 awards ($32,000 total): general academic interests/achievements. Special achievements/activities: leadership. Special characteristics: children of faculty/staff. *Tuition waivers:* Full or partial for employees or children of employees.

LOANS *Student loans:* 25% of past graduating class borrowed through all loan programs. *Average indebtedness per student:* $23,174. *Programs:* Federal Direct (Subsidized and Unsubsidized Stafford), Perkins, state.

WORK-STUDY *Federal work-study:* Total amount: $980,513; 530 jobs averaging $1850. *State or other work-study/employment:* Total amount: $465,722 (100% need-based). 252 part-time jobs averaging $1848.

APPLYING FOR FINANCIAL AID *Required financial aid forms:* FAFSA, CSS Financial Aid PROFILE, noncustodial (divorced/separated) parent's statement, business/farm supplement. *Financial aid deadline:* 2/15. *Notification date:* 3/20. Students must reply by 5/1 or within 1 week of notification.

CONTACT Mr. Michael D. Bartini, Director of Student Aid, Bowdoin College, 5300 College Station, Brunswick, ME 04011-8444, 207-725-3146. *Fax:* 207-725-3864. *E-mail:* mbartini@bowdoin.edu. *Website:* http://www.bowdoin.edu/.

BOWIE STATE UNIVERSITY
Bowie, MD

Tuition & fees (MD res): $8063	Average undergraduate aid package: $8736

ABOUT THE INSTITUTION State-supported, coed. *Awards:* certificates, bachelor's, master's, and doctoral degrees. 29 undergraduate majors. *Total*

enrollment: 5,669. Undergraduates: 4,711. Freshmen: 967. Federal methodology is used as a basis for awarding need-based institutional aid.

UNDERGRADUATE EXPENSES for 2017–2018 *Application fee:* $40. *Tuition, state resident:* full-time $5426; part-time $239 per credit hour. *Tuition, nonresident:* full-time $16,016; part-time $673 per credit hour. *Required fees:* full-time $2637; $118.52 per credit hour. Part-time tuition and fees vary according to course load. *College room and board:* $11,340; *Room only:* $7180. Room and board charges vary according to board plan and housing facility.

FRESHMAN FINANCIAL AID (Fall 2017, est.) 821 applied for aid; of those 100% were deemed to have need. 100% of freshmen with need received aid; of those 17% had need fully met. *Average percent of need met:* 45% (excluding resources awarded to replace EFC). *Average financial aid package:* $9389 (excluding resources awarded to replace EFC). 2% of all full-time freshmen had no need and received non-need-based gift aid.

UNDERGRADUATE FINANCIAL AID (Fall 2017, est.) 3,177 applied for aid; of those 100% were deemed to have need. 100% of undergraduates with need received aid; of those 15% had need fully met. *Average percent of need met:* 43% (excluding resources awarded to replace EFC). *Average financial aid package:* $8736 (excluding resources awarded to replace EFC). 1% of all full-time undergraduates had no need and received non-need-based gift aid.

GIFT AID (NEED-BASED) *Total amount:* $20,477,043 (63% federal, 20% state, 17% institutional). *Receiving aid:* Freshmen: 68% (638); all full-time undergraduates: 68% (2,472). *Average award:* Freshmen: $8405; Undergraduates: $7113. *Scholarships, grants, and awards:* Federal Pell, FSEOG, state, private, college/university gift aid from institutional funds, United Negro College Fund, Federal Nursing.

GIFT AID (NON-NEED-BASED) *Total amount:* $612,158 (10% state, 90% institutional). *Receiving aid:* Freshmen: 67% (624). Undergraduates: 64% (2,325). *Average award:* Freshmen: $5884. Undergraduates: $6408. *Scholarships, grants, and awards by category: Academic interests/achievement:* biological sciences, business, communication, computer science, engineering/technologies, mathematics, military science. *Creative arts/performance:* applied art and design, art/fine arts, general creative arts/performance, music. *Special achievements/activities:* general special achievements/activities. *Special characteristics:* first-generation college students, general special characteristics. *Tuition waivers:* Full or partial for employees or children of employees, senior citizens. *ROTC:* Army.

LOANS *Student loans:* $22,724,934 (86% need-based, 14% non-need-based). 86% of past graduating class borrowed through all loan programs. *Average indebtedness per student:* $29,433. *Average need-based loan:* Freshmen: $3425. Undergraduates: $4017. *Parent loans:* $9,052,369 (51% need-based, 49% non-need-based). *Programs:* Federal Direct (Subsidized and Unsubsidized Stafford, PLUS), Perkins, Federal Nursing, state, college/university.

WORK-STUDY *Federal work-study:* Total amount: $11,000; 85 jobs averaging $2875.

ATHLETIC AWARDS Total amount: $793,716 (72% need-based, 28% non-need-based).

APPLYING FOR FINANCIAL AID *Required financial aid forms:* FAFSA, institution's own form. *Financial aid deadline (priority):* 3/1. *Notification date:* Continuous beginning 4/1. Students must reply within 2 weeks of notification.

CONTACT Deborah Stanley, Director of Financial Aid, Bowie State University, 14000 Jericho Park Road, Bowie, MD 20715, 301-860-3543 or toll-free 877-772-6943. *Fax:* 301-860-3549. *E-mail:* dstanley@bowiestate.edu. *Website:* http://www.bowiestate.edu/.

BOWLING GREEN STATE UNIVERSITY
Bowling Green, OH

Tuition & fees (OH res): $11,057	Average undergraduate aid package: $14,097

ABOUT THE INSTITUTION State-supported, coed. *Awards:* certificates, bachelor's, master's, and doctoral degrees. 222 undergraduate majors. *Total enrollment:* 17,357. Undergraduates: 14,680. Freshmen: 3,344. Federal methodology is used as a basis for awarding need-based institutional aid.

UNDERGRADUATE EXPENSES for 2017–2018 *Application fee:* $45. *Tuition, state resident:* full-time $9096; part-time $379 per credit hour. *Tuition, nonresident:* full-time $16,632; part-time $693 per credit hour. *Required fees:* full-time $1961; $81 per credit hour. Full-time tuition and fees vary according to course load and location. Part-time tuition and fees vary according to course load and

location. *College room and board:* $8918. Room and board charges vary according to board plan and housing facility.

FRESHMAN FINANCIAL AID (Fall 2017, est.) 3,079 applied for aid; of those 76% were deemed to have need. 99% of freshmen with need received aid; of those 17% had need fully met. *Average percent of need met:* 80% (excluding resources awarded to replace EFC). *Average financial aid package:* $13,781 (excluding resources awarded to replace EFC). 20% of all full-time freshmen had no need and received non-need-based gift aid.

UNDERGRADUATE FINANCIAL AID (Fall 2017, est.) 10,783 applied for aid; of those 80% were deemed to have need. 98% of undergraduates with need received aid; of those 15% had need fully met. *Average percent of need met:* 80% (excluding resources awarded to replace EFC). *Average financial aid package:* $14,097 (excluding resources awarded to replace EFC). 20% of all full-time undergraduates had no need and received non-need-based gift aid.

GIFT AID (NEED-BASED) *Total amount:* $48,983,023 (40% federal, 9% state, 45% institutional, 6% external sources). *Receiving aid:* Freshmen: 63% (2,091); all full-time undergraduates: 55% (7,107). *Average award:* Freshmen: $7137; Undergraduates: $7209. *Scholarships, grants, and awards:* Federal Pell, FSEOG, state, private, college/university gift aid from institutional funds.

GIFT AID (NON-NEED-BASED) *Total amount:* $19,513,963 (1% federal, 3% state, 80% institutional, 16% external sources). *Receiving aid:* Freshmen: 9% (299). Undergraduates: 6% (834). *Average award:* Freshmen: $4816. Undergraduates: $5075. *Scholarships, grants, and awards by category: Academic interests/achievement:* biological sciences, business, communication, computer science, education, engineering/technologies, English, foreign languages, general academic interests/achievements, health fields, home economics, humanities, international studies, mathematics, military science, physical sciences, social sciences. *Creative arts/performance:* art/fine arts, cinema/film/broadcasting, creative writing, dance, debating, journalism/publications, music, performing arts, theater/drama. *Special achievements/activities:* general special achievements/activities, leadership. *Special characteristics:* children and siblings of alumni, children of faculty/staff, general special characteristics, international students, members of minority groups. *Tuition waivers:* Full or partial for employees or children of employees, senior citizens. *ROTC:* Army, Air Force.

LOANS *Student loans:* $73,270,178 (68% need-based, 32% non-need-based). 74% of past graduating class borrowed through all loan programs. *Average indebtedness per student:* $30,814. *Average need-based loan:* Freshmen: $3201. Undergraduates: $4107. *Parent loans:* $35,061,814 (45% need-based, 55% non-need-based). *Programs:* Federal Direct (Subsidized and Unsubsidized Stafford, PLUS), Perkins, Federal Nursing, state, college/university, alternative loans.

WORK-STUDY *Federal work-study:* Total amount: $423,654; 351 jobs averaging $1207.

ATHLETIC AWARDS Total amount: $6,828,289 (33% need-based, 67% non-need-based).

APPLYING FOR FINANCIAL AID *Required financial aid form:* FAFSA. *Financial aid deadline:* Continuous. *Notification date:* Continuous beginning 4/15. Students must reply within 3 weeks of notification.

CONTACT Betsy Johnson, Director of Student Financial Aid and Scholarships, Bowling Green State University, 319 Administration Building, Bowling Green, OH 43403, 419-372-2651. *E-mail:* betsyj@bgsu.edu. *Website:* http://www.bgsu.edu/.

BRADLEY UNIVERSITY
Peoria, IL

Tuition & fees: $32,930	Average undergraduate aid package: $23,839

ABOUT THE INSTITUTION Independent, coed. *Awards:* certificates, bachelor's, master's, and doctoral degrees. 117 undergraduate majors. *Total enrollment:* 5,844. Undergraduates: 4,649. Freshmen: 1,265. Federal methodology is used as a basis for awarding need-based institutional aid.

UNDERGRADUATE EXPENSES for 2017–2018 *Application fee:* $35. *One-time required fee:* $200. *Comprehensive fee:* $43,240 includes full-time tuition ($32,540), mandatory fees ($390), and room and board ($10,310). *College room only:* $5960. Full-time tuition and fees vary according to course load and program. Room and board charges vary according to board plan and housing facility. *Part-time tuition:* $870 per credit hour. *Part-time fees:* $390 per year. Part-time tuition and fees vary according to course load and program.

FRESHMAN FINANCIAL AID (Fall 2017, est.) 1,182 applied for aid; of those 84% were deemed to have need. 100% of freshmen with need received aid; of those 15% had need fully met. *Average percent of need met:* 76% (excluding resources awarded to replace EFC). *Average financial aid package:* $25,763 (excluding resources awarded to replace EFC). 21% of all full-time freshmen had no need and received non-need-based gift aid.

UNDERGRADUATE FINANCIAL AID (Fall 2017, est.) 3,784 applied for aid; of those 86% were deemed to have need. 99% of undergraduates with need received aid; of those 16% had need fully met. *Average percent of need met:* 72% (excluding resources awarded to replace EFC). *Average financial aid package:* $23,839 (excluding resources awarded to replace EFC). 26% of all full-time undergraduates had no need and received non-need-based gift aid.

GIFT AID (NEED-BASED) *Total amount:* $60,752,426 (11% federal, 9% state, 78% institutional, 2% external sources). *Receiving aid:* Freshmen: 78% (987); all full-time undergraduates: 66% (3,122). *Average award:* Freshmen: $21,619; Undergraduates: $18,905. *Scholarships, grants, and awards:* Federal Pell, FSEOG, state, private, college/university gift aid from institutional funds, United Negro College Fund.

GIFT AID (NON-NEED-BASED) *Total amount:* $11,143,677 (94% institutional, 6% external sources). *Receiving aid:* Freshmen: 9% (111). Undergraduates: 7% (347). *Average award:* Freshmen: $12,612. Undergraduates: $11,754. *Scholarships, grants, and awards by category:* Academic interests/achievement: general academic interests/achievements. Creative arts/performance: art/fine arts, music, theater/drama. Special achievements/activities: community service, leadership. *Special characteristics:* children and siblings of alumni, children of faculty/staff, out-of-state students. *Tuition waivers:* Full or partial for employees or children of employees, senior citizens. *ROTC:* Army.

LOANS *Student loans:* $31,058,823 (70% need-based, 30% non-need-based). 71% of past graduating class borrowed through all loan programs. *Average indebtedness per student:* $28,432. *Average need-based loan:* Freshmen: $4764. Undergraduates: $6388. *Parent loans:* $14,712,026 (45% need-based, 55% non-need-based). *Programs:* Federal Direct (Subsidized and Unsubsidized Stafford, PLUS), Perkins, Federal Nursing.

WORK-STUDY *Federal work-study:* Total amount: $706,447; 388 jobs averaging $1961.

ATHLETIC AWARDS Total amount: $4,021,105 (28% need-based, 72% non-need-based).

APPLYING FOR FINANCIAL AID *Required financial aid form:* FAFSA. *Financial aid deadline (priority):* 12/1. *Notification date:* Continuous beginning 11/15. Students must reply by 5/1 or within 2 weeks of notification.

CONTACT Debra Jackson, Director of Financial Assistance, Bradley University, 1501 West Bradley Avenue, Peoria, IL 61625, 309-677-3089 or toll-free 800-447-6460. *Fax:* 309-677-2798. *E-mail:* bufinaid@bradley.edu. *Website:* http://www.bradley.edu/.

BRANDEIS UNIVERSITY
Waltham, MA

Tuition & fees: $53,537	Average undergraduate aid package: $43,353

ABOUT THE INSTITUTION Independent, coed. *Awards:* certificates, bachelor's, master's, and doctoral degrees. 42 undergraduate majors. *Total enrollment:* 5,722. Undergraduates: 3,635. Freshmen: 858. Institutional methodology is used as a basis for awarding need-based institutional aid.

UNDERGRADUATE EXPENSES for 2017–2018 *Application fee:* $80. *Comprehensive fee:* $68,443 includes full-time tuition ($51,460), mandatory fees ($2077), and room and board ($14,906). *College room only:* $8364. Room and board charges vary according to board plan and housing facility. *Part-time tuition:* $1608 per credit. *Part-time fees:* $2077 per year. Part-time tuition and fees vary according to course load.

FRESHMAN FINANCIAL AID (Fall 2016) 550 applied for aid; of those 76% were deemed to have need. 99% of freshmen with need received aid; of those 94% had need fully met. *Average percent of need met:* 97% (excluding resources awarded to replace EFC). *Average financial aid package:* $44,761 (excluding resources awarded to replace EFC). 14% of all full-time freshmen had no need and received non-need-based gift aid.

UNDERGRADUATE FINANCIAL AID (Fall 2016) 1,991 applied for aid; of those 86% were deemed to have need. 100% of undergraduates with need received

aid; of those 72% had need fully met. *Average percent of need met:* 96% (excluding resources awarded to replace EFC). *Average financial aid package:* $43,353 (excluding resources awarded to replace EFC). 11% of all full-time undergraduates had no need and received non-need-based gift aid.

GIFT AID (NEED-BASED) *Total amount:* $65,842,092 (6% federal, 1% state, 91% institutional, 2% external sources). *Receiving aid:* Freshmen: 49% (410); all full-time undergraduates: 46% (1,657). *Average award:* Freshmen: $41,854; Undergraduates: $39,606. *Scholarships, grants, and awards:* Federal Pell, FSEOG, state, private, college/university gift aid from institutional funds.

GIFT AID (NON-NEED-BASED) *Total amount:* $8,661,508 (1% federal, 73% institutional, 26% external sources). *Receiving aid:* Freshmen: 6% (48). Undergraduates: 4% (154). *Average award:* Freshmen: $13,958. Undergraduates: $14,333. *Tuition waivers:* Full or partial for employees or children of employees. *ROTC:* Army cooperative, Air Force cooperative.

LOANS *Student loans:* $14,023,766 (62% need-based, 38% non-need-based). 54% of past graduating class borrowed through all loan programs. *Average indebtedness per student:* $33,522. *Average need-based loan:* Freshmen: $2880. Undergraduates: $4314. *Parent loans:* $5,339,910 (14% need-based, 86% non-need-based). *Programs:* Federal Direct (Subsidized and Unsubsidized Stafford, PLUS), state, college/university.

WORK-STUDY *Federal work-study:* 361 jobs averaging $2599. *State or other work-study/employment:* Total amount: $880,792 (44% need-based, 56% non-need-based). 30 part-time jobs averaging $2636.

APPLYING FOR FINANCIAL AID *Required financial aid forms:* FAFSA, CSS Financial Aid PROFILE, noncustodial (divorced/separated) parent's statement, business/farm supplement. *Financial aid deadline (priority):* 1/1. *Notification date:* 4/1. Students must reply by 5/1.

CONTACT Tim Brown, Assistant Director for Student Services, Brandeis University, Usdan Student Center, 415 South Street, Waltham, MA 02454-9110, 781-736-3700 or toll-free 800-622-0622 (out-of-state). *Fax:* 781-736-3719. *E-mail:* sfs@brandeis.edu. *Website:* http://www.brandeis.edu/.

BRANDMAN UNIVERSITY
Irvine, CA

CONTACT Financial Aid Office, Brandman University, 16355 Laguna Canyon Road, Irvine, CA 92618, 949-753-4774 or toll-free 800-746-0082. *Website:* http://www.brandman.edu/.

BRENAU UNIVERSITY
Gainesville, GA

Tuition & fees: $29,050	Average undergraduate aid package: $19,551

ABOUT THE INSTITUTION Independent, coed, primarily women. *Awards:* certificates, associate, bachelor's, master's, and doctoral degrees (also offers coed evening and weekend programs with significant enrollment not reflected in profile). 34 undergraduate majors. *Total enrollment:* 2,932. Undergraduates: 1,736. Freshmen: 310. Federal methodology is used as a basis for awarding need-based institutional aid.

UNDERGRADUATE EXPENSES for 2018–2019 *Comprehensive fee:* $41,468 includes full-time tuition ($28,650), mandatory fees ($400), and room and board ($12,418). Full-time tuition and fees vary according to class time, degree level, location, and program. *Part-time tuition:* $955 per semester hour. *Part-time fees:* $200 per term. Part-time tuition and fees vary according to program.

FRESHMAN FINANCIAL AID (Fall 2017, est.) 254 applied for aid; of those 95% were deemed to have need. 99% of freshmen with need received aid; of those 15% had need fully met. *Average percent of need met:* 63% (excluding resources awarded to replace EFC). *Average financial aid package:* $24,066 (excluding resources awarded to replace EFC). 3% of all full-time freshmen had no need and received non-need-based gift aid.

UNDERGRADUATE FINANCIAL AID (Fall 2017, est.) 958 applied for aid; of those 94% were deemed to have need. 99% of undergraduates with need received aid; of those 11% had need fully met. *Average percent of need met:* 57% (excluding resources awarded to replace EFC). *Average financial aid package:* $19,551

(excluding resources awarded to replace EFC). 3% of all full-time undergraduates had no need and received non-need-based gift aid.

GIFT AID (NEED-BASED) *Total amount:* $12,705,821 (29% federal, 14% state, 56% institutional, 1% external sources). *Receiving aid:* Freshmen: 90% (239); all full-time undergraduates: 82% (888). *Average award:* Freshmen: $19,545; Undergraduates: $14,503. *Scholarships, grants, and awards:* Federal Pell, FSEOG, state, private, college/university gift aid from institutional funds.

GIFT AID (NON-NEED-BASED) *Total amount:* $4,298,515 (11% state, 89% institutional). *Receiving aid:* Freshmen: 14% (36). Undergraduates: 9% (93). *Average award:* Freshmen: $13,706. Undergraduates: $11,907. *Scholarships, grants, and awards by category: Academic interests/achievement:* biological sciences, business, communication, education, English, general academic interests/achievements, home economics, humanities. *Creative arts/performance:* applied art and design, art/fine arts, creative writing, dance, journalism/publications, music, performing arts, theater/drama. *Special achievements/activities:* cheerleading/drum major, community service, general special achievements/activities, leadership. *Special characteristics:* children and siblings of alumni, children of faculty/staff, first-generation college students, general special characteristics, international students, members of minority groups, out-of-state students. *Tuition waivers:* Full or partial for employees or children of employees.

LOANS *Student loans:* $11,896,636 (91% need-based, 9% non-need-based). 80% of past graduating class borrowed through all loan programs. *Average indebtedness per student:* $34,058. *Average need-based loan:* Freshmen: $3748. Undergraduates: $5136. *Parent loans:* $1,694,659 (65% need-based, 35% non-need-based). *Programs:* Federal Direct (Subsidized and Unsubsidized Stafford, PLUS), Perkins, state, private loans.

WORK-STUDY *Federal work-study:* Total amount: $217,805; 134 jobs averaging $1852.

ATHLETIC AWARDS Total amount: $2,052,639 (64% need-based, 36% non-need-based).

APPLYING FOR FINANCIAL AID *Required financial aid forms:* FAFSA, state aid form. *Financial aid deadline (priority):* 3/1. *Notification date:* Continuous beginning 3/1.

CONTACT Mrs. Pam Barrett, Associate Vice President and Director of Financial Aid, Brenau University, 500 Washington Street, SE, Gainesville, GA 30501-3697, 770-534-6176 or toll-free 800-252-5119. *Fax:* 770-538-4306. *E-mail:* pbarrett@brenau.edu. *Website:* http://www.brenau.edu/.

BRESCIA UNIVERSITY
Owensboro, KY

ABOUT THE INSTITUTION Independent Roman Catholic, coed. *Awards:* certificates, associate, bachelor's, and master's degrees. 31 undergraduate majors. *Total enrollment:* 1,338. Undergraduates: 1,167. Freshmen: 121.

GIFT AID (NEED-BASED) *Scholarships, grants, and awards:* Federal Pell, FSEOG, state, private, college/university gift aid from institutional funds.

GIFT AID (NON-NEED-BASED) *Scholarships, grants, and awards by category: Academic interests/achievement:* general academic interests/achievements. *Creative arts/performance:* art/fine arts, creative writing, journalism/publications, music. *Special achievements/activities:* leadership.

LOANS *Programs:* Federal Direct (Subsidized and Unsubsidized Stafford, PLUS), Perkins, college/university, private loans.

APPLYING FOR FINANCIAL AID *Required financial aid form:* FAFSA.

CONTACT Ms. Kristi Eidson, Director of Financial Aid, Brescia University, 717 Frederica Street, Owensboro, KY 42301-3023, 270-686-4356 or toll-free 877-273-7242. *Fax:* 270-689-9563. *E-mail:* financial.aid@brescia.edu. *Website:* http://www.brescia.edu/.

BREVARD COLLEGE
Brevard, NC

ABOUT THE INSTITUTION Independent United Methodist, coed. 21 undergraduate majors.

GIFT AID (NEED-BASED) *Scholarships, grants, and awards:* Federal Pell, FSEOG, state, private, college/university gift aid from institutional funds.

GIFT AID (NON-NEED-BASED) *Scholarships, grants, and awards by category: Academic interests/achievement:* general academic interests/achievements. *Creative arts/performance:* art/fine arts, music, theater/drama. *Special achievements/activities:* cheerleading/drum major, community service, general special achievements/activities, leadership. *Special characteristics:* children of faculty/staff, international students, local/state students, previous college experience, veterans' children.

LOANS *Programs:* Federal Direct (Subsidized and Unsubsidized Stafford, PLUS), Perkins.

APPLYING FOR FINANCIAL AID *Required financial aid form:* FAFSA.

CONTACT Ms. Caron Surrett, Director of Financial Aid, Brevard College, 1 Brevard College Drive, Brevard, NC 28712, 828-884-8261 or toll-free 800-527-9090. *Fax:* 828-884-3790. *E-mail:* finaid@brevard.edu. *Website:* http://www.brevard.edu/.

BREWTON-PARKER COLLEGE
Mt. Vernon, GA

CONTACT Mrs. Shannon Mullins, Executive Director of Financial Aid, Brewton-Parker College, PO Box 197, Mt. Vernon, GA 30445-0197, 800-342-1087 Ext. 213 or toll-free 800-342-1087. *Fax:* 912-583-3598. *E-mail:* smullins@bpc.edu. *Website:* http://www.bpc.edu/.

BRIAR CLIFF UNIVERSITY
Sioux City, IA

ABOUT THE INSTITUTION Independent Roman Catholic, coed. *Awards:* certificates, associate, bachelor's, master's, and doctoral degrees. 29 undergraduate majors. *Total enrollment:* 1,316. Undergraduates: 1,117. Freshmen: 210.

GIFT AID (NEED-BASED) *Scholarships, grants, and awards:* Federal Pell, FSEOG, state, private, college/university gift aid from institutional funds.

GIFT AID (NON-NEED-BASED) *Scholarships, grants, and awards by category: Academic interests/achievement:* biological sciences, business, communication, computer science, education, English, foreign languages, general academic interests/achievements, health fields, humanities, mathematics, physical sciences, religion/biblical studies, social sciences. *Creative arts/performance:* art/fine arts, music, theater/drama. *Special achievements/activities:* leadership, religious involvement. *Special characteristics:* children and siblings of alumni, first-generation college students, international students, members of minority groups.

LOANS *Programs:* Federal Direct (Subsidized and Unsubsidized Stafford, PLUS), Perkins, alternative loans, partnership loans, Minnesota SELF Loans.

APPLYING FOR FINANCIAL AID *Required financial aid form:* FAFSA.

CONTACT Brian K. Eben, Office of Student Financial Aid, Briar Cliff University, 3303 Rebecca Street, PO Box 2100, Sioux City, IA 51104-2100, 712-279-5239 or toll-free 800-662-3303. *Fax:* 712-279-1632. *Website:* http://www.briarcliff.edu/.

BRIDGEWATER COLLEGE
Bridgewater, VA

Tuition & fees: $35,160	Average undergraduate aid package: $31,101

ABOUT THE INSTITUTION Independent Church of the Brethren, coed. *Awards:* bachelor's and master's degrees. 29 undergraduate majors. *Total enrollment:* 1,889. Undergraduates: 1,882. Freshmen: 534. Federal methodology is used as a basis for awarding need-based institutional aid.

UNDERGRADUATE EXPENSES for 2018–2019 *Comprehensive fee:* $47,880 includes full-time tuition ($34,300), mandatory fees ($860), and room and board ($12,720). Room and board charges vary according to housing facility. *Part-time tuition:* $1190 per credit hour. *Part-time fees:* $40 per term.

FRESHMAN FINANCIAL AID (Fall 2017, est.) 506 applied for aid; of those 90% were deemed to have need. 100% of freshmen with need received aid; of those 22% had need fully met. *Average percent of need met:* 85% (excluding resources awarded to replace EFC). *Average financial aid package:* $32,931 (excluding

resources awarded to replace EFC). 14% of all full-time freshmen had no need and received non-need-based gift aid.

UNDERGRADUATE FINANCIAL AID (Fall 2017, est.) 1,665 applied for aid; of those 92% were deemed to have need. 100% of undergraduates with need received aid; of those 27% had need fully met. *Average percent of need met:* 85% (excluding resources awarded to replace EFC). *Average financial aid package:* $31,101 (excluding resources awarded to replace EFC). 18% of all full-time undergraduates had no need and received non-need-based gift aid.

GIFT AID (NEED-BASED) *Total amount:* $41,535,928 (6% federal, 9% state, 84% institutional, 1% external sources). *Receiving aid:* Freshmen: 86% (457); all full-time undergraduates: 82% (1,533). *Average award:* Freshmen: $29,262; Undergraduates: $27,289. *Scholarships, grants, and awards:* Federal Pell, FSEOG, state, private, college/university gift aid from institutional funds.

GIFT AID (NON-NEED-BASED) *Total amount:* $8,094,155 (9% state, 90% institutional, 1% external sources). *Receiving aid:* Freshmen: 86% (457). Undergraduates: 82% (1,533). *Average award:* Freshmen: $22,511. Undergraduates: $20,900. *Scholarships, grants, and awards by category: Academic interests/achievement:* 1,685 awards ($31,595,180 total): general academic interests/achievements. *Creative arts/performance:* 50 awards ($100,006 total): music. *Special characteristics:* 998 awards ($4,847,355 total): children of educators, children of faculty/staff, international students, members of minority groups, out-of-state students, previous college experience, religious affiliation. *Tuition waivers:* Full or partial for employees or children of employees.

LOANS *Student loans:* $11,982,900 (74% need-based, 26% non-need-based). 81% of past graduating class borrowed through all loan programs. *Average indebtedness per student:* $33,567. *Average need-based loan:* Freshmen: $4217. Undergraduates: $4694. *Parent loans:* $5,381,702 (62% need-based, 38% non-need-based). *Programs:* Federal Direct (Subsidized and Unsubsidized Stafford, PLUS).

WORK-STUDY *Federal work-study:* Total amount: $583,179; 405 jobs averaging $1440. *State or other work-study/employment:* 100 part-time jobs averaging $1245.

APPLYING FOR FINANCIAL AID *Required financial aid forms:* FAFSA, state aid form. *Financial aid deadline (priority):* 3/1. *Notification date:* Continuous beginning 2/1. Students must reply by 5/1 or within 2 weeks of notification.

CONTACT Mr. Scott Morrison, Director of Financial Aid, Bridgewater College, 402 East College Street, Bridgewater, VA 22812-1599, 540-828-5377 or toll-free 800-759-8328. *Fax:* 540-828-5671. *E-mail:* finaid@bridgewater.edu. *Website:* http://www.bridgewater.edu/.

BRIDGEWATER STATE UNIVERSITY
Bridgewater, MA

Tuition & fees (MA res): $10,312	Average undergraduate aid package: $8148

ABOUT THE INSTITUTION State-supported, coed. *Awards:* certificates, bachelor's, and master's degrees. 81 undergraduate majors. *Total enrollment:* 11,019. Undergraduates: 9,558. Freshmen: 1,506. Federal methodology is used as a basis for awarding need-based institutional aid.

UNDERGRADUATE EXPENSES for 2018–2019 *Application fee:* $50. *Tuition, state resident:* full-time $910; part-time $38 per credit hour. *Tuition, nonresident:* full-time $7050; part-time $294 per credit hour. *Required fees:* full-time $9402; $364.50 per credit hour. Full-time tuition and fees vary according to course load. *College room and board:* $13,000; *Room only:* $8600. Room and board charges vary according to board plan and housing facility.

FRESHMAN FINANCIAL AID (Fall 2016) 1,319 applied for aid; of those 80% were deemed to have need. 99% of freshmen with need received aid; of those 11% had need fully met. *Average financial aid package:* $8523 (excluding resources awarded to replace EFC). 1% of all full-time freshmen had no need and received non-need-based gift aid.

UNDERGRADUATE FINANCIAL AID (Fall 2016) 7,044 applied for aid; of those 78% were deemed to have need. 99% of undergraduates with need received aid; of those 14% had need fully met. *Average financial aid package:* $8148 (excluding resources awarded to replace EFC). 1% of all full-time undergraduates had no need and received non-need-based gift aid.

GIFT AID (NEED-BASED) *Total amount:* $23,157,674 (59% federal, 20% state, 21% institutional). *Receiving aid:* Freshmen: 63% (871); all full-time undergraduates: 52% (4,058). *Average award:* Freshmen: $6095; Undergraduates: $5669. *Scholar-

ships, grants, and awards:* Federal Pell, FSEOG, state, college/university gift aid from institutional funds.

GIFT AID (NON-NEED-BASED) *Total amount:* $3,230,517 (1% federal, 41% state, 14% institutional, 44% external sources). *Receiving aid:* Freshmen: 13% (180). Undergraduates: 11% (889). *Average award:* Freshmen: $5322. Undergraduates: $8266. *Scholarships, grants, and awards by category: Academic interests/achievement:* general academic interests/achievements. *Special characteristics:* local/state students, members of minority groups. *Tuition waivers:* Full or partial for employees or children of employees, senior citizens. *ROTC:* Army cooperative, Air Force cooperative.

LOANS *Student loans:* $48,706,695 (44% need-based, 56% non-need-based). 77% of past graduating class borrowed through all loan programs. *Average indebtedness per student:* $28,680. *Average need-based loan:* Freshmen: $3188. Undergraduates: $3709. *Parent loans:* $10,508,032 (100% non-need-based). *Programs:* Federal Direct (Subsidized and Unsubsidized Stafford, PLUS), state.

WORK-STUDY *Federal work-study:* 395 jobs averaging $1580.

APPLYING FOR FINANCIAL AID *Required financial aid form:* FAFSA. *Financial aid deadline (priority):* 3/1. *Notification date:* Continuous beginning 4/1.

CONTACT Janet Gumbris, Office of Financial Aid, Bridgewater State University, Tillinghast Hall, Room 100, 45 School Street, Bridgewater, MA 02325-0001, 508-531-1341. *Fax:* 508-531-1728. *E-mail:* finaid@bridgew.edu. *Website:* http://www.bridgew.edu/.

BRIGHAM YOUNG UNIVERSITY
Provo, UT

Tuition & fees: $5620	Average undergraduate aid package: $7637

ABOUT THE INSTITUTION Independent The Church of Jesus Christ of Latter-day Saints, coed. *Awards:* certificates, bachelor's, master's, and doctoral degrees. 102 undergraduate majors. *Total enrollment:* 34,334. Undergraduates: 31,233. Freshmen: 5,340. Both federal and institutional methodology are used as a basis for awarding need-based institutional aid.

UNDERGRADUATE EXPENSES for 2018–2019 *Application fee:* $35. *Comprehensive fee:* $13,248 includes full-time tuition ($5620) and room and board ($7628). Room and board charges vary according to board plan, housing facility, and location. *Part-time tuition:* $294 per credit hour. Part-time tuition and fees vary according to course load.

FRESHMAN FINANCIAL AID (Fall 2016) 2,529 applied for aid; of those 64% were deemed to have need. 89% of freshmen with need received aid; of those 2% had need fully met. *Average percent of need met:* 28% (excluding resources awarded to replace EFC). *Average financial aid package:* $6921 (excluding resources awarded to replace EFC). 40% of all full-time freshmen had no need and received non-need-based gift aid.

UNDERGRADUATE FINANCIAL AID (Fall 2016) 16,073 applied for aid; of those 85% were deemed to have need. 94% of undergraduates with need received aid; of those 2% had need fully met. *Average percent of need met:* 33% (excluding resources awarded to replace EFC). *Average financial aid package:* $7637 (excluding resources awarded to replace EFC). 27% of all full-time undergraduates had no need and received non-need-based gift aid.

GIFT AID (NEED-BASED) *Total amount:* $57,857,794 (86% federal, 14% institutional). *Receiving aid:* Freshmen: 16% (801); all full-time undergraduates: 38% (10,752). *Average award:* Freshmen: $4721; Undergraduates: $5017. *Scholarships, grants, and awards:* Federal Pell, private, college/university gift aid from institutional funds.

GIFT AID (NON-NEED-BASED) *Total amount:* $73,221,496 (84% institutional, 16% external sources). *Receiving aid:* Freshmen: 21% (1,066). Undergraduates: 25% (6,866). *Average award:* Freshmen: $4216. Undergraduates: $4398. *Scholarships, grants, and awards by category: Academic interests/achievement:* general academic interests/achievements. *Creative arts/performance:* art/fine arts, music, theater/drama. *Special achievements/activities:* leadership, religious involvement. *Special characteristics:* local/state students, members of minority groups, religious affiliation. *Tuition waivers:* Full or partial for employees or children of employees. *ROTC:* Army, Air Force.

LOANS *Student loans:* $27,969,707 (55% need-based, 45% non-need-based). 26% of past graduating class borrowed through all loan programs. *Average indebtedness *per student:* $14,998. *Average need-based loan:* Freshmen: $3136. Undergraduates: $4060. *Parent loans:* $943,200 (100% non-need-based). *Programs:* Federal Direct (Subsidized and Unsubsidized Stafford, PLUS).

WORK-STUDY *State or other work-study/employment:* Part-time jobs available.

ATHLETIC AWARDS Total amount: $6,543,151 (100% non-need-based).

APPLYING FOR FINANCIAL AID *Required financial aid form:* FAFSA. *Financial aid deadline (priority):* 4/15. *Notification date:* Continuous beginning 4/1.

CONTACT Stephen E. Hill, Director of Financial Aid, Brigham Young University, C-144 ASB, Provo, UT 84602, 801-422-4104. *Fax:* 801-422-0234. *Website:* http://www.byu.edu/.

BRIGHAM YOUNG UNIVERSITY–HAWAII
Laie, HI

CONTACT Mr. Wes Duke, Director of Financial Aid, Brigham Young University–Hawaii, BYUH #1980, 55-220 Kulanui Street, Laie, HI 96762, 808-293-3530. *Fax:* 808-293-3349. *E-mail:* duekw@byuh.edu. *Website:* http://www.byuh.edu/.

BRIGHAM YOUNG UNIVERSITY–IDAHO
Rexburg, ID

CONTACT Financial Aid Office, Brigham Young University–Idaho, 525 South Center Street, Rexburg, ID 83460, 208-496-2011. *Website:* http://www.byui.edu/.

BROADVIEW ENTERTAINMENT ARTS UNIVERSITY
Salt Lake City, UT

CONTACT Office of Financial Aid, Broadview Entertainment Arts University, 240 East Morris Avenue, Salt Lake City, UT 84115, 801-300-4300 or toll-free 877-801-8889. *Fax:* 801-300-4301. *Website:* http://www.broadviewuniversity.edu/.

BROADVIEW UNIVERSITY–WEST JORDAN
West Jordan, UT

CONTACT Office of Financial Aid, Broadview University–West Jordan, 1902 West 7800 South, West Jordan, UT 84088, 801-304-4224 or toll-free 866-304-4224. *Fax:* 801-304-4229. *Website:* http://www.broadviewuniversity.edu/.

BROOKLINE COLLEGE
Phoenix, AZ

CONTACT Financial Aid Office, Brookline College, 2445 West Dunlap Avenue, Suite 100, Phoenix, AZ 85021, 602-242-6265 or toll-free 800-793-2428. *Website:* http://brooklinecollege.edu/.

BROOKLINE COLLEGE
Tempe, AZ

CONTACT Financial Aid Office, Brookline College, 1140 South Priest Drive, Tempe, AZ 85281, 480-545-8755 or toll-free 888-886-2428. *Website:* http://brooklinecollege.edu/.

BROOKLINE COLLEGE
Tucson, AZ

CONTACT Financial Aid Office, Brookline College, 5441 East 22nd Street, Suite 125, Tucson, AZ 85711, 520-748-9799 or toll-free 888-292-2428. *Website:* http://brooklinecollege.edu/.

BROOKLINE COLLEGE
Albuquerque, NM

CONTACT Financial Aid Office, Brookline College, 4201 Central Avenue NW, Suite J, Albuquerque, NM 87105-1649, 505-880-2877 or toll-free 888-660-2428. *Website:* http://brooklinecollege.edu/.

BROOKLYN COLLEGE OF THE CITY UNIVERSITY OF NEW YORK
Brooklyn, NY

CONTACT Mr. Ahad Farhang, Director of Financial Aid, Brooklyn College of the City University of New York, 2900 Bedford Avenue, Brooklyn, NY 11210-2889, 718-951-5669. *Fax:* 718-951-4778. *E-mail:* afarhang@brooklyn.cuny.edu. *Website:* http://www.brooklyn.cuny.edu/.

BROWN UNIVERSITY
Providence, RI

Tuition & fees: $53,419	Average undergraduate aid package: $49,269

ABOUT THE INSTITUTION Independent, coed. *Awards:* bachelor's, master's, and doctoral degrees. 69 undergraduate majors. *Total enrollment:* 9,781. Undergraduates: 6,926. Freshmen: 1,679. Both federal and institutional methodology are used as a basis for awarding need-based institutional aid.

UNDERGRADUATE EXPENSES for 2017–2018 *Application fee:* $75. *Comprehensive fee:* $67,439 includes full-time tuition ($52,231), mandatory fees ($1188), and room and board ($14,020). *College room only:* $8784. Room and board charges vary according to board plan. *Part-time tuition:* $6528.88 per course. Part-time tuition and fees vary according to course load.

FRESHMAN FINANCIAL AID (Fall 2017, est.) 982 applied for aid; of those 79% were deemed to have need. 100% of freshmen with need received aid; of those 100% had need fully met. *Average percent of need met:* 100% (excluding resources awarded to replace EFC). *Average financial aid package:* $47,438 (excluding resources awarded to replace EFC). 1% of all full-time freshmen had no need and received non-need-based gift aid.

UNDERGRADUATE FINANCIAL AID (Fall 2017, est.) 3,302 applied for aid; of those 89% were deemed to have need. 100% of undergraduates with need received aid; of those 100% had need fully met. *Average percent of need met:* 100% (excluding resources awarded to replace EFC). *Average financial aid package:* $49,269 (excluding resources awarded to replace EFC). 1% of all full-time undergraduates had no need and received non-need-based gift aid.

GIFT AID (NEED-BASED) *Total amount:* $133,697,718 (4% federal, 92% institutional, 4% external sources). *Receiving aid:* Freshmen: 44% (720); all full-time undergraduates: 41% (2,736). *Average award:* Freshmen: $44,435; Undergraduates:

$45,644. **Scholarships, grants, and awards:** Federal Pell, FSEOG, state, private, college/university gift aid from institutional funds.

GIFT AID (NON-NEED-BASED) Total amount: $5,818,341 (1% institutional, 99% external sources). **Average award:** Freshmen: $6889. Undergraduates: $8458. **Scholarships, grants, and awards by category:** Special characteristics: 12 awards ($95,221 total): veterans, veterans' children. **Tuition waivers:** Full or partial for employees or children of employees. **ROTC:** Army cooperative, Naval cooperative, Air Force cooperative.

LOANS Student loans: $16,295,002 (61% need-based, 39% non-need-based). 34% of past graduating class borrowed through all loan programs. **Average indebtedness per student:** $25,471. **Average need-based loan:** Freshmen: $4932. Undergraduates: $6328. **Parent loans:** $9,728,425 (2% need-based, 98% non-need-based). **Programs:** Federal Direct (Subsidized and Unsubsidized Stafford, PLUS), Perkins, college/university.

WORK-STUDY Federal work-study: Total amount: $4,290,639; 1,670 jobs averaging $2628. **State or other work-study/employment:** Total amount: $810,309 (100% need-based). 316 part-time jobs averaging $2740.

APPLYING FOR FINANCIAL AID Required financial aid forms: FAFSA, CSS Financial Aid PROFILE, noncustodial (divorced/separated) parent's statement. **Financial aid deadline:** 2/1. **Notification date:** 4/1. Students must reply by 5/1.

CONTACT Office of Financial Aid, Brown University, PO Box 1827, Providence, RI 02912, 401-863-2721. **Fax:** 401-863-7575. **E-mail:** financial_aid@brown.edu. **Website:** http://www.brown.edu/.

BRYAN COLLEGE
Dayton, TN

Tuition & fees: $25,600	Average undergraduate aid package: $21,946

ABOUT THE INSTITUTION Independent interdenominational, coed. **Awards:** certificates, diplomas, associate, bachelor's, and master's degrees. 27 undergraduate majors. **Total enrollment:** 1,592. Undergraduates: 1,401. Freshmen: 173. Federal methodology is used as a basis for awarding need-based institutional aid.

UNDERGRADUATE EXPENSES for 2017–2018 Application fee: $35. **Comprehensive fee:** $32,900 includes full-time tuition ($25,600) and room and board ($7300). **College room only:** $4550. Room and board charges vary according to housing facility. **Part-time tuition:** $1100 per credit hour.

FRESHMAN FINANCIAL AID (Fall 2017, est.) 163 applied for aid; of those 93% were deemed to have need. 100% of freshmen with need received aid; of those 40% had need fully met. **Average financial aid package:** $23,296 (excluding resources awarded to replace EFC). 1% of all full-time freshmen had no need and received non-need-based gift aid.

UNDERGRADUATE FINANCIAL AID (Fall 2017, est.) 571 applied for aid; of those 91% were deemed to have need. 100% of undergraduates with need received aid; of those 40% had need fully met. **Average financial aid package:** $21,946 (excluding resources awarded to replace EFC). 1% of all full-time undergraduates had no need and received non-need-based gift aid.

GIFT AID (NEED-BASED) Total amount: $9,527,945 (21% federal, 21% state, 57% institutional, 1% external sources). **Receiving aid:** Freshmen: 85% (151); all full-time undergraduates: 73% (489). **Average award:** Freshmen: $13,070; Undergraduates: $12,502. **Scholarships, grants, and awards:** Federal Pell, FSEOG, state, private, college/university gift aid from institutional funds.

GIFT AID (NON-NEED-BASED) Total amount: $571,499 (19% state, 80% institutional, 1% external sources). **Receiving aid:** Freshmen: 82% (145). Undergraduates: 65% (437). **Average award:** Freshmen: $18,330. Undergraduates: $26,351. **Scholarships, grants, and awards by category:** Academic interests/achievement: biological sciences, business, communication, computer science, education, English, foreign languages, general academic interests/achievements, humanities, mathematics, physical sciences, premedicine, religion/biblical studies, social sciences. Creative arts/performance: journalism/publications, music, performing arts, theater/drama. Special achievements/activities: community service, general special achievements/activities, leadership, religious involvement. Special characteristics: children and siblings of alumni, children of current students, children of educators, children of faculty/staff, general special characteristics, handicapped students, international students, local/state students, members of minority groups, relatives of clergy, spouses of current students. **Tuition waivers:** Full or partial for employees or children of employees.

LOANS Student loans: $5,033,677 (95% need-based, 5% non-need-based). 69% of past graduating class borrowed through all loan programs. **Average indebtedness per student:** $25,666. **Average need-based loan:** Freshmen: $3113. Undergraduates: $1925. **Parent loans:** $842,097 (94% need-based, 6% non-need-based). **Programs:** Federal Direct (Subsidized and Unsubsidized Stafford, PLUS), Perkins, college/university.

WORK-STUDY Federal work-study: Total amount: $528,298; jobs available.

ATHLETIC AWARDS Total amount: $1,828,327 (93% need-based, 7% non-need-based).

APPLYING FOR FINANCIAL AID Required financial aid form: FAFSA. **Financial aid deadline (priority):** 1/31. **Notification date:** Continuous beginning 11/1.

CONTACT David Haggard, Director of Financial Aid, Bryan College, 721 Bryan Drive, Dayton, TN 37321, 423-775-7339 or toll-free 800-277-9522. **Fax:** 423-775-7300. **E-mail:** finaid@bryan.edu. **Website:** http://www.bryan.edu/.

BRYAN COLLEGE OF HEALTH SCIENCES
Lincoln, NE

CONTACT Financial Aid Office, Bryan College of Health Sciences, 5035 Everett Street, Lincoln, NE 68506-1398, 402-481 3801. **Website:** http://www.bryanhealthcollege.edu/.

BRYANT & STRATTON COLLEGE–AKRON CAMPUS
Akron, OH

CONTACT Financial Aid Office, Bryant & Stratton College–Akron Campus, 190 Montrose West Avenue, Akron, OH 44321, 330-598-2500. **Website:** http://www.bryantstratton.edu/.

BRYANT & STRATTON COLLEGE–CLEVELAND CAMPUS
Cleveland, OH

CONTACT Bill Davenport, Financial Aid Supervisor, Bryant & Stratton College–Cleveland Campus, 1700 East 13th Street, Cleveland, OH 44114-3203, 216-771-1700. **Fax:** 216-771-7787. **Website:** http://www.bryantstratton.edu/.

BRYANT & STRATTON COLLEGE–HAMPTON CAMPUS
Hampton, VA

CONTACT Financial Aid Office, Bryant & Stratton College–Hampton Campus, 4410 East Claiborne Square, Suite 233, Hampton, VA 23666, 757-896-6001. **Website:** http://www.bryantstratton.edu/.

BRYANT & STRATTON COLLEGE–WAUWATOSA CAMPUS
Wauwatosa, WI

CONTACT Financial Aid Office, Bryant & Stratton College–Wauwatosa Campus, 10950 West Potter Road, Wauwatosa, WI 53226, 414-302-7000. *Website:* http://www.bryantstratton.edu/.

BRYANT UNIVERSITY
Smithfield, RI

Tuition & fees: $43,973	Average undergraduate aid package: $25,319

ABOUT THE INSTITUTION Independent, coed. *Awards:* certificates, bachelor's, and master's degrees. 78 undergraduate majors. *Total enrollment:* 3,751. Undergraduates: 3,477. Freshmen: 892. Federal methodology is used as a basis for awarding need-based institutional aid.

UNDERGRADUATE EXPENSES for 2018–2019 *Application fee:* $50. *Comprehensive fee:* $59,675 includes full-time tuition ($43,076), mandatory fees ($897), and room and board ($15,702). *College room only:* $9217. Room and board charges vary according to board plan and housing facility. *Part-time tuition:* $1067 per credit hour. Part-time tuition and fees vary according to course load.

FRESHMAN FINANCIAL AID (Fall 2017, est.) 730 applied for aid; of those 84% were deemed to have need. 100% of freshmen with need received aid; of those 30% had need fully met. *Average percent of need met:* 49% (excluding resources awarded to replace EFC). *Average financial aid package:* $25,278 (excluding resources awarded to replace EFC). 11% of all full-time freshmen had no need and received non-need-based gift aid.

UNDERGRADUATE FINANCIAL AID (Fall 2017, est.) 3,106 applied for aid; of those 67% were deemed to have need. 100% of undergraduates with need received aid; of those 30% had need fully met. *Average percent of need met:* 50% (excluding resources awarded to replace EFC). *Average financial aid package:* $25,319 (excluding resources awarded to replace EFC). 7% of all full-time undergraduates had no need and received non-need-based gift aid.

GIFT AID (NEED-BASED) *Total amount:* $33,396,503 (7% federal, 1% state, 89% institutional, 3% external sources). *Receiving aid:* Freshmen: 39% (348); all full-time undergraduates: 40% (1,351). *Average award:* Freshmen: $10,528; Undergraduates: $10,287. *Scholarships, grants, and awards:* Federal Pell, FSEOG, state, private, college/university gift aid from institutional funds.

GIFT AID (NON-NEED-BASED) *Total amount:* $22,383,154 (96% institutional, 4% external sources). *Receiving aid:* Freshmen: 51% (459). Undergraduates: 44% (1,490). *Average award:* Freshmen: $16,537. Undergraduates: $15,736. *Scholarships, grants, and awards by category:* Academic interests/achievement: 2,371 awards ($38,101,845 total): general academic interests/achievements. *Special characteristics:* 123 awards ($1,522,154 total): international students, members of minority groups, siblings of current students, veterans. *Tuition waivers:* Full or partial for employees or children of employees. *ROTC:* Army cooperative.

LOANS *Student loans:* $31,186,498 (38% need-based, 62% non-need-based). 71% of past graduating class borrowed through all loan programs. *Average indebtedness per student:* $52,949. *Average need-based loan:* Freshmen: $3799. Undergraduates: $4973. *Parent loans:* $7,703,043 (32% need-based, 68% non-need-based). *Programs:* Federal Direct (Subsidized and Unsubsidized Stafford, PLUS), Perkins, private loans.

WORK-STUDY *Federal work-study:* Total amount: $349,376; jobs available. *State or other work-study/employment:* Total amount: $1,249,738 (31% need-based, 69% non-need-based). Part-time jobs available.

ATHLETIC AWARDS Total amount: $7,925,595 (42% need-based, 58% non-need-based).

APPLYING FOR FINANCIAL AID *Required financial aid form:* FAFSA. *Financial aid deadline (priority):* 2/15. *Notification date:* 3/24. Students must reply by 5/1.

CONTACT Mr. John B. Canning, Director of Financial Aid, Bryant University, 1150 Douglas Pike, Smithfield, RI 02917-1284, 401-232-6020 or toll-free 800-622-7001. *Fax:* 401-232-6293. *E-mail:* jcanning@bryant.edu. *Website:* http://www.bryant.edu/.

BRYAN UNIVERSITY
Springfield, MO

CONTACT Financial Aid Office, Bryan University, 4255 South Nature Center Way, Springfield, MO 65804, 417-862-5700 or toll-free 855-566-0650. *Website:* http://www.bryanu.edu/.

BRYN ATHYN COLLEGE OF THE NEW CHURCH
Bryn Athyn, PA

CONTACT Wendy Cooper, Associate Director of Financial Aid, Bryn Athyn College of the New Church, Box 717, Bryn Athyn, PA 19009, 267-502-2630 or toll-free 800-767-9552. *Fax:* 267-502-4866. *E-mail:* financialaid@brynathyn.edu. *Website:* http://www.brynathyn.edu/.

BRYN MAWR COLLEGE
Bryn Mawr, PA

Tuition & fees: $50,500	Average undergraduate aid package: $47,906

ABOUT THE INSTITUTION Independent, undergraduate: women only; graduate: coed. *Awards:* certificates, bachelor's, master's, and doctoral degrees. 37 undergraduate majors. *Total enrollment:* 1,640. Undergraduates: 1,334. Freshmen: 354. Institutional methodology is used as a basis for awarding need-based institutional aid.

UNDERGRADUATE EXPENSES for 2017–2018 *Application fee:* $50. *Comprehensive fee:* $66,410 includes full-time tuition ($49,310), mandatory fees ($1190), and room and board ($15,910). *College room only:* $9080. *Part-time tuition:* $6165 per course.

FRESHMAN FINANCIAL AID (Fall 2017, est.) 228 applied for aid; of those 79% were deemed to have need. 99% of freshmen with need received aid; of those 100% had need fully met. *Average percent of need met:* 100% (excluding resources awarded to replace EFC). *Average financial aid package:* $47,447 (excluding resources awarded to replace EFC). 14% of all full-time freshmen had no need and received non-need-based gift aid.

UNDERGRADUATE FINANCIAL AID (Fall 2017, est.) 774 applied for aid; of those 90% were deemed to have need. 99% of undergraduates with need received aid; of those 100% had need fully met. *Average percent of need met:* 100% (excluding resources awarded to replace EFC). *Average financial aid package:* $47,906 (excluding resources awarded to replace EFC). 17% of all full-time undergraduates had no need and received non-need-based gift aid.

GIFT AID (NEED-BASED) *Total amount:* $29,112,669 (4% federal, 1% state, 94% institutional, 1% external sources). *Receiving aid:* Freshmen: 50% (177); all full-time undergraduates: 52% (689). *Average award:* Freshmen: $41,891; Undergraduates: $42,244. *Scholarships, grants, and awards:* Federal Pell, FSEOG, state, private, college/university gift aid from institutional funds.

GIFT AID (NON-NEED-BASED) *Total amount:* $5,292,090 (6% federal, 82% institutional, 12% external sources). *Receiving aid:* Freshmen: 8% (27). Undergraduates: 6% (84). *Average award:* Freshmen: $16,041. Undergraduates: $17,307. *Scholarships, grants, and awards by category:* Academic interests/achievement: general academic interests/achievements. *Special achievements/activities:* leadership. *ROTC:* Air Force cooperative.

LOANS *Student loans:* $4,387,954 (52% need-based, 48% non-need-based). 55% of past graduating class borrowed through all loan programs. *Average indebtedness per student:* $25,448. *Average need-based loan:* Freshmen: $2832. Undergraduates: $3545. *Parent loans:* $1,937,065 (100% non-need-based). *Programs:* Federal Direct (Subsidized and Unsubsidized Stafford, PLUS), Perkins, college/university.

WORK-STUDY *Federal work-study:* Total amount: $845,929; jobs available. *State or other work-study/employment:* Total amount: $385,886 (98% need-based, 2% non-need-based). Part-time jobs available.

APPLYING FOR FINANCIAL AID *Required financial aid forms:* FAFSA, CSS Financial Aid PROFILE, noncustodial (divorced/separated) parent's statement, parent and student tax returns or non-filer statements. *Financial aid deadline:* 1/15. *Notification date:* Continuous. Students must reply by 5/1.

CONTACT Ethel M. Desmarais, Director of Student Financial Services, Bryn Mawr College, 101 North Merion Avenue, Bryn Mawr, PA 19010-2899, 610-526-7922 or toll-free 800-BMC-1885. *Fax:* 610-526-5249. *E-mail:* edesmara@brynmawr.edu. *Website:* http://www.brynmawr.edu/.

BUCKNELL UNIVERSITY
Lewisburg, PA

Tuition & fees: $53,986	Average undergraduate aid package: $33,500

ABOUT THE INSTITUTION Independent, coed. *Awards:* bachelor's and master's degrees. 68 undergraduate majors. *Total enrollment:* 3,678. Undergraduates: 3,611. Freshmen: 973. Both federal and institutional methodology are used as a basis for awarding need-based institutional aid.

UNDERGRADUATE EXPENSES for 2017–2018 *Application fee:* $40. *Comprehensive fee:* $67,136 includes full-time tuition ($53,692), mandatory fees ($294), and room and board ($13,150). *College room only:* $8020. Room and board charges vary according to board plan and housing facility. *Part-time tuition:* $5892 per course. *Payment plan:* Tuition prepayment.

FRESHMAN FINANCIAL AID (Fall 2017, est.) 555 applied for aid; of those 73% were deemed to have need. 100% of freshmen with need received aid. *Average percent of need met:* 91% (excluding resources awarded to replace EFC). *Average financial aid package:* $37,500 (excluding resources awarded to replace EFC). 7% of all full-time freshmen had no need and received non-need-based gift aid.

UNDERGRADUATE FINANCIAL AID (Fall 2017, est.) 1,406 applied for aid; of those 92% were deemed to have need. 100% of undergraduates with need received aid. *Average percent of need met:* 91% (excluding resources awarded to replace EFC). *Average financial aid package:* $33,500 (excluding resources awarded to replace EFC). 12% of all full-time undergraduates had no need and received non-need-based gift aid.

GIFT AID (NEED-BASED) *Total amount:* $57,245,018 (3% federal, 1% state, 91% institutional, 5% external sources). *Receiving aid:* Freshmen: 29% (280); all full-time undergraduates: 34% (1,210). *Average award:* Freshmen: $32,700; Undergraduates: $29,000. *Scholarships, grants, and awards:* Federal Pell, FSEOG, state, private, college/university gift aid from institutional funds.

GIFT AID (NON-NEED-BASED) *Total amount:* $4,900,000 (100% institutional). *Receiving aid:* Freshmen: 9% (88). Undergraduates: 9% (314). *Average award:* Freshmen: $11,958. Undergraduates: $11,898. *Scholarships, grants, and awards by category:* Academic interests/achievement: 328 awards ($4,115,000 total): business, engineering/technologies, general academic interests/achievements, mathematics, physical sciences. *Creative arts/performance:* 131 awards ($819,250 total): art/fine arts, creative writing, dance, music, performing arts, theater/drama. *Special achievements/activities:* 117 awards ($6,275,344 total): general special achievements/activities, leadership. *Tuition waivers:* Full or partial for employees or children of employees. *ROTC:* Army.

LOANS *Student loans:* $11,413,341 (100% need-based). 47% of past graduating class borrowed through all loan programs. *Average indebtedness per student:* $33,000. *Average need-based loan:* Freshmen: $3500. Undergraduates: $5500. *Parent loans:* $6,361,715 (100% non-need-based). *Programs:* Federal Direct (Subsidized and Unsubsidized Stafford, PLUS), Perkins.

WORK-STUDY *Federal work-study:* Total amount: $371,112; 600 jobs averaging $1500. *State or other work-study/employment:* Total amount: $30,000 (100% need-based). 50 part-time jobs averaging $1500.

ATHLETIC AWARDS Total amount: $12,024,198 (31% need-based, 69% non-need-based).

APPLYING FOR FINANCIAL AID *Required financial aid forms:* FAFSA, CSS Financial Aid PROFILE, institution's own non-custodial form. *Financial aid deadline:* 1/15. *Notification date:* 4/1. Students must reply by 5/1.

CONTACT Andrea Leithner Stauffer, Director of Financial Aid, Bucknell University, 1 Dent Drive, Lewisburg, PA 17837, 570-577-1331. *Fax:* 570-577-1481. *E-mail:* finaid@bucknell.edu. *Website:* http://www.bucknell.edu/.

BUENA VISTA UNIVERSITY
Storm Lake, IA

Tuition & fees: $32,854	Average undergraduate aid package: $29,026

ABOUT THE INSTITUTION Independent Presbyterian Church (U.S.A.), coed. *Awards:* bachelor's and master's degrees. 64 undergraduate majors. *Total enrollment:* 964. Undergraduates: 786. Freshmen: 203. Federal methodology is used as a basis for awarding need-based institutional aid.

UNDERGRADUATE EXPENSES for 2017–2018 *Comprehensive fee:* $42,344 includes full-time tuition ($32,854) and room and board ($9490). *College room only:* $4774. Full-time tuition and fees vary according to location. Room and board charges vary according to board plan and housing facility. *Part-time tuition:* $1105 per credit hour. Part-time tuition and fees vary according to location.

FRESHMAN FINANCIAL AID (Fall 2017, est.) 199 applied for aid; of those 93% were deemed to have need. 100% of freshmen with need received aid; of those 19% had need fully met. *Average percent of need met:* 84% (excluding resources awarded to replace EFC). *Average financial aid package:* $29,904 (excluding resources awarded to replace EFC). 8% of all full-time freshmen had no need and received non-need-based gift aid.

UNDERGRADUATE FINANCIAL AID (Fall 2017, est.) 688 applied for aid; of those 92% were deemed to have need. 100% of undergraduates with need received aid; of those 21% had need fully met. *Average percent of need met:* 83% (excluding resources awarded to replace EFC). *Average financial aid package:* $29,026 (excluding resources awarded to replace EFC). 16% of all full-time undergraduates had no need and received non-need-based gift aid.

GIFT AID (NEED-BASED) *Total amount:* $14,939,216 (14% federal, 13% state, 72% institutional, 1% external sources). *Receiving aid:* Freshmen: 91% (185); all full-time undergraduates: 83% (630). *Average award:* Freshmen: $24,984; Undergraduates: $23,634. *Scholarships, grants, and awards:* Federal Pell, FSEOG, state, private, college/university gift aid from institutional funds.

GIFT AID (NON-NEED-BASED) *Total amount:* $3,209,115 (9% federal, 89% institutional, 2% external sources). *Receiving aid:* Freshmen: 13% (27). Undergraduates: 13% (98). *Average award:* Freshmen: $18,982. Undergraduates: $18,429. *Scholarships, grants, and awards by category:* Academic interests/achievement: biological sciences, business, computer science, education, general academic interests/achievements, humanities, international studies, mathematics. *Creative arts/performance:* art/fine arts, music, theater/drama. *Special achievements/activities:* general special achievements/activities, leadership. *Special characteristics:* children of faculty/staff, ethnic background, international students, out-of-state students, religious affiliation, siblings of current students. *Tuition waivers:* Full or partial for employees or children of employees. *ROTC:* Army.

LOANS *Student loans:* $5,864,146 (47% need-based, 53% non-need-based). 84% of past graduating class borrowed through all loan programs. *Average indebtedness per student:* $36,299. *Average need-based loan:* Freshmen: $4603. Undergraduates: $5359. *Parent loans:* $1,457,165 (100% non-need-based). *Programs:* Federal Direct (Subsidized and Unsubsidized Stafford, PLUS), Perkins, college/university.

WORK-STUDY *Federal work-study:* Total amount: $444,775; jobs available. *State or other work-study/employment:* Total amount: $418,980 (73% need-based, 27% non-need-based). Part-time jobs available.

APPLYING FOR FINANCIAL AID *Required financial aid form:* FAFSA. *Financial aid deadline (priority):* 6/1. *Notification date:* Continuous beginning 2/1.

CONTACT Leanne Valentine, Director of Financial Assistance, Buena Vista University, 610 West Fourth Street, Storm Lake, IA 50588, 712-749-2164 or toll-free 800-383-9600. *E-mail:* valentinel@bvu.edu. *Website:* http://www.bvu.edu/.

BUFFALO STATE COLLEGE, STATE UNIVERSITY OF NEW YORK
Buffalo, NY

Tuition & fees (NY res): $7976	Average undergraduate aid package: $12,945

ABOUT THE INSTITUTION State-supported, coed. *Awards:* certificates, bachelor's, and master's degrees. 79 undergraduate majors. *Total enrollment:* 9,516. Undergraduates: 8,527. Freshmen: 1,425. Federal methodology is used as a basis for awarding need-based institutional aid.

UNDERGRADUATE EXPENSES for 2017–2018 *Application fee:* $50. *Tuition, state resident:* full-time $6670; part-time $278 per semester hour. *Tuition, nonresident:* full-time $16,320; part-time $680 per semester hour. *Required fees:* full-time $1306; $54.50 per semester hour. Part-time tuition and fees vary according to course load. *College room and board:* $12,982; *Room only:* $7782. Room and board charges vary according to board plan, housing facility, and student level.

FRESHMAN FINANCIAL AID (Fall 2017, est.) 1,705 applied for aid; of those 100% were deemed to have need. 95% of freshmen with need received aid; of those 28% had need fully met. *Average percent of need met:* 28% (excluding resources awarded to replace EFC). *Average financial aid package:* $13,807 (excluding resources awarded to replace EFC). 16% of all full-time freshmen had no need and received non-need-based gift aid.

UNDERGRADUATE FINANCIAL AID (Fall 2017, est.) 7,111 applied for aid; of those 100% were deemed to have need. 96% of undergraduates with need received aid; of those 31% had need fully met. *Average percent of need met:* 31% (excluding resources awarded to replace EFC). *Average financial aid package:* $12,945 (excluding resources awarded to replace EFC). 13% of all full-time undergraduates had no need and received non-need-based gift aid.

GIFT AID (NEED-BASED) *Total amount:* $43,172,441 (51% federal, 49% state). *Receiving aid:* Freshmen: 83% (1,496); all full-time undergraduates: 82% (6,262). *Average award:* Freshmen: $9656; Undergraduates: $9292. *Scholarships, grants, and awards:* Federal Pell, FSEOG, state, private, college/university gift aid from institutional funds.

GIFT AID (NON-NEED-BASED) *Total amount:* $2,932,771 (1% federal, 1% state, 45% institutional, 53% external sources). *Receiving aid:* Freshmen: 16% (291). Undergraduates: 13% (1,002). *Average award:* Freshmen: $3163. Undergraduates: $2801. *Scholarships, grants, and awards by category:* Academic interests/achievement: 644 awards ($1,421,952 total): biological sciences, business, communication, computer science, education, engineering/technologies, foreign languages, general academic interests/achievements, health fields, home economics, mathematics, physical sciences, social sciences. Creative arts/performance: applied art and design, general creative arts/performance, music, performing arts, theater/drama. Special achievements/activities: general special achievements/activities. Special characteristics: general special characteristics, international students, members of minority groups, veterans, veterans' children. *Tuition waivers:* Full or partial for employees or children of employees. *ROTC:* Army cooperative.

LOANS *Student loans:* $41,131,882 (53% need-based, 47% non-need-based). 79% of past graduating class borrowed through all loan programs. *Average indebtedness per student:* $26,495. *Average need-based loan:* Freshmen: $3768. Undergraduates: $4289. *Parent loans:* $7,914,463 (100% non-need-based). *Programs:* Federal Direct (Subsidized and Unsubsidized Stafford, PLUS), Perkins.

WORK-STUDY *Federal work-study:* Total amount: $823,174; 240 jobs averaging $3744. *State or other work-study/employment:* Part-time jobs available.

APPLYING FOR FINANCIAL AID *Required financial aid form:* FAFSA. *Financial aid deadline:* 5/1 (priority: 3/1). *Notification date:* Continuous beginning 5/1.

CONTACT Connie F. Cooke, Director of Financial Aid, Buffalo State College, State University of New York, 1300 Elmwood Avenue, Buffalo, NY 14222-1095, 716-878-4902. *Fax:* 716-878-4903. *E-mail:* finaid@buffalostate.edu. *Website:* http://www.buffalostate.edu/.

BUTLER UNIVERSITY
Indianapolis, IN

Tuition & fees: $41,120	Average undergraduate aid package: $25,357

ABOUT THE INSTITUTION Independent, coed. *Awards:* certificates, bachelor's, master's, and doctoral degrees. 67 undergraduate majors. *Total enrollment:* 5,081. Undergraduates: 4,229. Freshmen: 1,054. Federal methodology is used as a basis for awarding need-based institutional aid.

UNDERGRADUATE EXPENSES for 2018–2019 *Comprehensive fee:* $55,810 includes full-time tuition ($40,160), mandatory fees ($960), and room and board ($14,690). *College room only:* $7660. Full-time tuition and fees vary according to course level, course load, degree level, and program. Room and board charges vary according to board plan and housing facility. *Part-time tuition:* $1670 per credit hour. Part-time tuition and fees vary according to course level, course load, degree level, and program.

FRESHMAN FINANCIAL AID (Fall 2017, est.) 1,029 applied for aid; of those 63% were deemed to have need. 100% of freshmen with need received aid; of those 12% had need fully met. *Average percent of need met:* 65% (excluding resources awarded to replace EFC). *Average financial aid package:* $25,981 (excluding resources awarded to replace EFC). 36% of all full-time freshmen had no need and received non-need-based gift aid.

UNDERGRADUATE FINANCIAL AID (Fall 2017, est.) 4,205 applied for aid; of those 62% were deemed to have need. 100% of undergraduates with need received aid; of those 11% had need fully met. *Average percent of need met:* 65% (excluding resources awarded to replace EFC). *Average financial aid package:* $25,357 (excluding resources awarded to replace EFC). 36% of all full-time undergraduates had no need and received non-need-based gift aid.

GIFT AID (NEED-BASED) *Total amount:* $51,833,918 (6% federal, 7% state, 79% institutional, 8% external sources). *Receiving aid:* Freshmen: 61% (639); all full-time undergraduates: 58% (2,559). *Average award:* Freshmen: $21,726; Undergraduates: $20,935. *Scholarships, grants, and awards:* Federal Pell, FSEOG, state, private, college/university gift aid from institutional funds.

GIFT AID (NON-NEED-BASED) *Total amount:* $24,991,068 (92% institutional, 8% external sources). *Receiving aid:* Freshmen: 12% (122). Undergraduates: 8% (343). *Average award:* Freshmen: $15,614. Undergraduates: $14,312. *Scholarships, grants, and awards by category:* Academic interests/achievement: biological sciences, business, communication, computer science, education, engineering/technologies, English, foreign languages, general academic interests/achievements, home economics, humanities, international studies, mathematics, physical sciences, premedicine, religion/biblical studies, social sciences. Creative arts/performance: applied art and design, art/fine arts, cinema/film/broadcasting, dance, journalism/publications, music, performing arts, theater/drama. Special characteristics: veterans, veterans' children. *Tuition waivers:* Full or partial for employees or children of employees. *ROTC:* Army cooperative, Air Force cooperative.

LOANS *Student loans:* $28,509,843 (72% need-based, 28% non-need-based). 61% of past graduating class borrowed through all loan programs. *Average indebtedness per student:* $40,393. *Average need-based loan:* Freshmen: $3426. Undergraduates: $5043. *Parent loans:* $10,808,191 (46% need-based, 54% non-need-based). *Programs:* Federal Direct (Subsidized and Unsubsidized Stafford, PLUS), Perkins.

WORK-STUDY *Federal work-study:* Total amount: $393,310; 326 jobs averaging $974.

ATHLETIC AWARDS Total amount: $5,165,954 (36% need-based, 64% non-need-based).

APPLYING FOR FINANCIAL AID *Required financial aid form:* FAFSA. *Financial aid deadline (priority):* 12/1. *Notification date:* 1/20. Students must reply within 3 weeks of notification.

CONTACT Mrs. Leslie Middleton, Associate Director of Financial Aid, Butler University, 4600 Sunset Avenue, Indianapolis, IN 46208-3485, 317-940-8200 or toll-free 888-940-8100. *Fax:* 317-940-8250. *E-mail:* lmmiddle@butler.edu. *Website:* http://www.butler.edu/.

CABARRUS COLLEGE OF HEALTH SCIENCES
Concord, NC

ABOUT THE INSTITUTION Independent, coed, primarily women. **Awards:** certificates, diplomas, associate, bachelor's, and master's degrees. 8 undergraduate majors. **Total enrollment:** 470. Undergraduates: 443. Freshmen: 23.

GIFT AID (NEED-BASED) Scholarships, grants, and awards: Federal Pell, FSEOG, state, college/university gift aid from institutional funds.

GIFT AID (NON-NEED-BASED) Scholarships, grants, and awards by category: Special characteristics: first-generation college students.

LOANS Programs: Federal Direct (Subsidized and Unsubsidized Stafford, PLUS), state.

APPLYING FOR FINANCIAL AID Required financial aid forms: FAFSA, state aid form.

CONTACT Valerie Richard, Director of Financial Aid, Cabarrus College of Health Sciences, 401 Medical Park Drive, Concord, NC 28025, 704-403-3507. Fax: 704-403-2077. E-mail: valerie.richard@carolinashealthcare.org. Website: http://www.cabarruscollege.edu/.

CABRINI UNIVERSITY
Radnor, PA

ABOUT THE INSTITUTION Independent Roman Catholic, coed. **Awards:** bachelor's, master's, and doctoral degrees. 39 undergraduate majors. **Total enrollment:** 2,436. Undergraduates: 1,650. Freshmen: 486.

GIFT AID (NEED-BASED) Scholarships, grants, and awards: Federal Pell, FSEOG, state, private, college/university gift aid from institutional funds.

GIFT AID (NON-NEED-BASED) Scholarships, grants, and awards by category: Academic interests/achievement: general academic interests/achievements. Special characteristics: children and siblings of alumni, out-of-state students, religious affiliation, siblings of current students.

LOANS Programs: Federal Direct (Subsidized and Unsubsidized Stafford, PLUS), Perkins.

APPLYING FOR FINANCIAL AID Required financial aid form: FAFSA.

CONTACT Ms. Elizabeth Gingerich, Director of Financial Aid, Cabrini University, 610 King of Prussia Road, Grace Hall, First Floor, Radnor, PA 19087-3698, 610-902-8424 or toll-free 800-848-1003. Fax: 610-902-8426. E-mail: egs34@cabrini.edu. Website: http://www.cabrini.edu/.

CAIRN UNIVERSITY
Langhorne, PA

Tuition & fees: $27,279	Average undergraduate aid package: $21,885

ABOUT THE INSTITUTION Independent nondenominational, coed. **Awards:** certificates, bachelor's, and master's degrees. 32 undergraduate majors. **Total enrollment:** 1,052. Undergraduates: 762. Freshmen: 154. Federal methodology is used as a basis for awarding need-based institutional aid.

UNDERGRADUATE EXPENSES for 2018–2019 Application fee: $25. **Comprehensive fee:** $37,573 includes full-time tuition ($26,979), mandatory fees ($300), and room and board ($10,294). **College room only:** $5389. Full-time tuition and fees vary according to course load. Room and board charges vary according to board plan and location. **Part-time tuition:** $800 per credit. Part-time tuition and fees vary according to course load.

FRESHMAN FINANCIAL AID (Fall 2017, est.) 140 applied for aid; of those 93% were deemed to have need. 100% of freshmen with need received aid; of those 11% had need fully met. **Average percent of need met:** 79% (excluding resources awarded to replace EFC). **Average financial aid package:** $24,301 (excluding resources awarded to replace EFC). 13% of all full-time freshmen had no need and received non-need-based gift aid.

UNDERGRADUATE FINANCIAL AID (Fall 2017, est.) 640 applied for aid; of those 91% were deemed to have need. 99% of undergraduates with need received aid; of those 12% had need fully met. **Average percent of need met:** 75% (excluding resources awarded to replace EFC). **Average financial aid package:** $21,885 (excluding resources awarded to replace EFC). 16% of all full-time undergraduates had no need and received non-need-based gift aid.

GIFT AID (NEED-BASED) Total amount: $9,458,029 (16% federal, 8% state, 75% institutional, 1% external sources). **Receiving aid:** Freshmen: 82% (127); all full-time undergraduates: 79% (572). **Average award:** Freshmen: $19,849; Undergraduates: $16,755. **Scholarships, grants, and awards:** Federal Pell, FSEOG, state, private, college/university gift aid from institutional funds.

GIFT AID (NON-NEED-BASED) Total amount: $1,669,467 (1% state, 97% institutional, 2% external sources). **Receiving aid:** Freshmen: 8% (12). Undergraduates: 7% (51). **Average award:** Freshmen: $17,037. Undergraduates: $12,008. **Scholarships, grants, and awards by category:** Academic interests/achievement: general academic interests/achievements. Creative arts/performance: music. Special achievements/activities: general special achievements/activities. Special characteristics: children of faculty/staff, relatives of clergy. Tuition waivers: Full or partial for employees or children of employees. ROTC: Air Force cooperative.

LOANS Student loans: $5,626,714 (78% need-based, 22% non-need-based). 82% of past graduating class borrowed through all loan programs. **Average indebtedness per student:** $35,717. **Average need-based loan:** Freshmen: $4134. Undergraduates: $5057. **Parent loans:** $848,462 (56% need-based, 44% non-need-based). **Programs:** Federal Direct (Subsidized and Unsubsidized Stafford, PLUS).

WORK-STUDY Federal work-study: Total amount: $376,870; jobs available.

APPLYING FOR FINANCIAL AID Required financial aid form: FAFSA. **Financial aid deadline (priority):** 3/1. **Notification date:** Continuous beginning 2/1. Students must reply within 2 weeks of notification.

CONTACT Mr. Stephen Cassel, Director of Financial Aid, Cairn University, 200 Manor Avenue, Langhorne, PA 19047-2990, 215-702-4243 or toll-free 800-366-0049. Fax: 215-702-4248. E-mail: scassel@cairn.edu. Website: http://cairn.edu/.

CALDWELL UNIVERSITY
Caldwell, NJ

Tuition & fees: $34,715	Average undergraduate aid package: $27,760

ABOUT THE INSTITUTION Independent Roman Catholic, coed. **Awards:** certificates, bachelor's, master's, and doctoral degrees. 33 undergraduate majors. **Total enrollment:** 2,200. Undergraduates: 1,603. Freshmen: 361. Federal methodology is used as a basis for awarding need-based institutional aid.

UNDERGRADUATE EXPENSES for 2018–2019 Application fee: $50. **Comprehensive fee:** $48,015 includes full-time tuition ($32,990), mandatory fees ($1725), and room and board ($13,300). Full-time tuition and fees vary according to course load, location, and program. Room and board charges vary according to board plan and housing facility. **Part-time tuition:** $920 per credit hour. **Part-time fees:** $230 per term. Part-time tuition and fees vary according to course load, location, and program.

FRESHMAN FINANCIAL AID (Fall 2017, est.) 287 applied for aid; of those 97% were deemed to have need. 100% of freshmen with need received aid; of those 8% had need fully met. **Average percent of need met:** 79% (excluding resources awarded to replace EFC). **Average financial aid package:** $31,389 (excluding resources awarded to replace EFC). 22% of all full-time freshmen had no need and received non-need-based gift aid.

UNDERGRADUATE FINANCIAL AID (Fall 2017, est.) 1,148 applied for aid; of those 95% were deemed to have need. 99% of undergraduates with need received aid; of those 10% had need fully met. **Average percent of need met:** 75% (excluding resources awarded to replace EFC). **Average financial aid package:** $27,760 (excluding resources awarded to replace EFC). 21% of all full-time undergraduates had no need and received non-need-based gift aid.

GIFT AID (NEED-BASED) Total amount: $24,664,384 (13% federal, 24% state, 60% institutional, 3% external sources). **Receiving aid:** Freshmen: 75% (278); all full-time undergraduates: 71% (1,047). **Average award:** Freshmen: $27,821; Undergraduates: $24,508. **Scholarships, grants, and awards:** Federal Pell, FSEOG, state, private, college/university gift aid from institutional funds.

GIFT AID (NON-NEED-BASED) Total amount: $6,783,479 (96% institutional, 4% external sources). **Receiving aid:** Freshmen: 4% (16). Undergraduates: 6% (83). **Average award:** Freshmen: $22,873. Undergraduates: $19,777. **Scholarships,**

grants, and awards by category: Academic interests/achievement: 796 awards ($13,232,442 total): general academic interests/achievements, home economics. Creative arts/performance: 47 awards ($63,425 total): art/fine arts, music. Special achievements/activities: 365 awards ($688,833 total): community service, general special achievements/activities, leadership, memberships, religious involvement. Special characteristics: 215 awards ($1,322,664 total): adult students, children and siblings of alumni, children of current students, children of educators, children of faculty/staff, general special characteristics, local/state students, parents of current students, previous college experience, public servants, relatives of clergy, religious affiliation, siblings of current students, spouses of current students, twins, veterans, veterans' children. **Tuition waivers:** Full or partial for children of alumni, employees or children of employees, adult students, senior citizens. **ROTC:** Army cooperative.

LOANS Student loans: $10,724,842 (78% need-based, 22% non-need-based). 81% of past graduating class borrowed through all loan programs. *Average indebtedness per student:* $25,114. *Average need-based loan:* Freshmen: $3243. Undergraduates: $4011. *Parent loans:* $9,326,755 (47% need-based, 53% non-need-based). *Programs:* Federal Direct (Subsidized and Unsubsidized Stafford, PLUS), state, private loans.

WORK-STUDY Federal work-study: Total amount: $165,000; 135 jobs averaging $1500. *State or other work-study/employment:* 100 part-time jobs averaging $2300.

ATHLETIC AWARDS Total amount: $1,830,189 (57% need-based, 43% non-need-based).

APPLYING FOR FINANCIAL AID *Required financial aid forms:* FAFSA, state aid form. *Financial aid deadline (priority):* 10/1. *Notification date:* Continuous beginning 11/15.

CONTACT Ms. Eileen T. Felske, Director of Financial Aid, Caldwell University, 120 Bloomfield Avenue, Caldwell, NJ 07006, 973-618-3419. *Fax:* 973-618-3650. *E-mail:* efelske@caldwell.edu.

Website: http://www.caldwell.edu/.

CALIFORNIA BAPTIST UNIVERSITY
Riverside, CA

Tuition & fees: $33,478	Average undergraduate aid package: $20,693

ABOUT THE INSTITUTION Independent Southern Baptist, coed. *Awards:* associate, bachelor's, master's, and doctoral degrees. 74 undergraduate majors. *Total enrollment:* 9,941. Undergraduates: 7,414. Freshmen: 1,413. Federal methodology is used as a basis for awarding need-based institutional aid.

UNDERGRADUATE EXPENSES for 2018–2019 *Application fee:* $45. *One-time required fee:* $310. *Comprehensive fee:* $45,638 includes full-time tuition ($31,668), mandatory fees ($1810), and room and board ($12,160). *College room only:* $5860. Full-time tuition and fees vary according to course load, location, and program. Room and board charges vary according to board plan and housing facility. *Part-time tuition:* $1218 per unit. *Part-time fees:* $175 per term. Part-time tuition and fees vary according to course load, location, and program.

FRESHMAN FINANCIAL AID (Fall 2017, est.) 1,300 applied for aid; of those 90% were deemed to have need. 97% of freshmen with need received aid; of those 24% had need fully met. *Average percent of need met:* 66% (excluding resources awarded to replace EFC). *Average financial aid package:* $24,142 (excluding resources awarded to replace EFC). 9% of all full-time freshmen had no need and received non-need-based gift aid.

UNDERGRADUATE FINANCIAL AID (Fall 2017, est.) 5,713 applied for aid; of those 90% were deemed to have need. 100% of undergraduates with need received aid; of those 16% had need fully met. *Average percent of need met:* 57% (excluding resources awarded to replace EFC). *Average financial aid package:* $20,693 (excluding resources awarded to replace EFC). 6% of all full-time undergraduates had no need and received non-need-based gift aid.

GIFT AID (NEED-BASED) Total amount: $82,030,021 (20% federal, 21% state, 58% institutional, 1% external sources). *Receiving aid:* Freshmen: 80% (1,114); all full-time undergraduates: 79% (4,987). *Average award:* Freshmen: $21,272; Undergraduates: $16,706. *Scholarships, grants, and awards:* Federal Pell, FSEOG, state, private, college/university gift aid from institutional funds, Federal Nursing.

GIFT AID (NON-NEED-BASED) Total amount: $3,643,780 (97% institutional, 3% external sources). *Receiving aid:* Freshmen: 70% (976). Undergraduates: 52% (3,255). *Average award:* Freshmen: $12,951. Undergraduates: $10,684. *Scholar-*

ships, grants, and awards by category: Academic interests/achievement: architecture, engineering/technologies, general academic interests/achievements, home economics, religion/biblical studies. Creative arts/performance: applied art and design, art/fine arts, cinema/film/broadcasting, debating, journalism/publications, music, theater/drama. Special achievements/activities: cheerleading/drum major. Special characteristics: adult students, children of faculty/staff, international students, relatives of clergy, religious affiliation, siblings of current students, veterans, veterans' children. **Tuition waivers:** Full or partial for employees or children of employees. **ROTC:** Army, Air Force cooperative.

LOANS Student loans: $52,427,527 (94% need-based, 6% non-need-based). 78% of past graduating class borrowed through all loan programs. *Average indebtedness per student:* $38,324. *Average need-based loan:* Freshmen: $3490. Undergraduates: $4622. *Parent loans:* $19,201,820 (90% need-based, 10% non-need-based). *Programs:* Federal Direct (Subsidized and Unsubsidized Stafford, PLUS), Perkins, alternative loans.

WORK-STUDY Federal work-study: Total amount: $576,276; 359 jobs averaging $893.

ATHLETIC AWARDS Total amount: $6,139,479 (90% need-based, 10% non-need-based).

APPLYING FOR FINANCIAL AID *Required financial aid forms:* FAFSA, state aid form. *Financial aid deadline (priority):* 3/2. *Notification date:* Continuous beginning 3/2. Students must reply by 6/1.

CONTACT Mr. Joshua Morey, Director of Financial Aid, California Baptist University, 8432 Magnolia Avenue, Riverside, CA 92504-3297, 951-343-4235 or toll-free 877-228-8866. *E-mail:* finaid@calbaptist.edu.

Website: http://www.calbaptist.edu/.

CALIFORNIA CHRISTIAN COLLEGE
Fresno, CA

Tuition & fees: $9330	Average undergraduate aid package: $9054

ABOUT THE INSTITUTION Independent Free Will Baptist, coed. *Awards:* associate and bachelor's degrees. 2 undergraduate majors. *Total enrollment:* 16. Undergraduates: 16. Freshmen: 3. Federal methodology is used as a basis for awarding need-based institutional aid.

UNDERGRADUATE EXPENSES for 2017–2018 *Application fee:* $40. *Tuition:* full-time $8640; part-time $360 per credit hour.

FRESHMAN FINANCIAL AID (Fall 2016) 1 applied for aid; of those 100% were deemed to have need. 100% of freshmen with need received aid. *Average percent of need met:* 30% (excluding resources awarded to replace EFC). *Average financial aid package:* $3365 (excluding resources awarded to replace EFC).

UNDERGRADUATE FINANCIAL AID (Fall 2016) 13 applied for aid; of those 100% were deemed to have need. 100% of undergraduates with need received aid. *Average percent of need met:* 46% (excluding resources awarded to replace EFC). *Average financial aid package:* $9054 (excluding resources awarded to replace EFC).

GIFT AID (NEED-BASED) Total amount: $50,272 (100% federal). *Receiving aid:* Freshmen: 100% (1); all full-time undergraduates: 56% (10). *Average award:* Freshmen: $3365; Undergraduates: $5027. *Scholarships, grants, and awards:* Federal Pell, FSEOG, state, private, college/university gift aid from institutional funds.

LOANS Student loans: $57,650 (100% need-based). *Average need-based loan:* Undergraduates: $3519. *Programs:* Federal Direct (Subsidized and Unsubsidized Stafford, PLUS).

WORK-STUDY Federal work-study: 3 jobs averaging $1470.

APPLYING FOR FINANCIAL AID *Required financial aid forms:* FAFSA, institution's own form. *Financial aid deadline (priority):* 3/2. *Notification date:* Continuous beginning 5/15.

CONTACT Mindy Scroggins, Student Finance Manager, California Christian College, 5364 East Belmont Avenue, Fresno, CA 93727, 559-251-4215 Ext. 1006. *Fax:* 559-385-2329. *E-mail:* financialaid@calchristiancollege.edu.

Website: http://www.calchristiancollege.edu/.

CALIFORNIA COAST UNIVERSITY
Santa Ana, CA

CONTACT Financial Aid Office, California Coast University, 925 North Spurgeon Street, Santa Ana, CA 92701, 714-547-9625 or toll-free 888-CCU-UNIV. *Website:* http://www.calcoast.edu/.

CALIFORNIA COLLEGE OF THE ARTS
San Francisco, CA

Tuition & fees: $49,138	Average undergraduate aid package: $32,759

ABOUT THE INSTITUTION Independent, coed. *Awards:* bachelor's and master's degrees. 22 undergraduate majors. *Total enrollment:* 1,983. Undergraduates: 1,528. Freshmen: 256. Federal methodology is used as a basis for awarding need-based institutional aid.

UNDERGRADUATE EXPENSES for 2018–2019 *Application fee:* $70. *Tuition:* full-time $48,648; part-time $2027 per unit. *Required fees:* full-time $490; $170 per term. Room and board charges vary according to housing facility.

FRESHMAN FINANCIAL AID (Fall 2017, est.) 138 applied for aid; of those 89% were deemed to have need. 100% of freshmen with need received aid; of those 11% had need fully met. *Average percent of need met:* 68% (excluding resources awarded to replace EFC). *Average financial aid package:* $33,562 (excluding resources awarded to replace EFC). 39% of all full-time freshmen had no need and received non-need-based gift aid.

UNDERGRADUATE FINANCIAL AID (Fall 2017, est.) 708 applied for aid; of those 94% were deemed to have need. 100% of undergraduates with need received aid; of those 5% had need fully met. *Average percent of need met:* 61% (excluding resources awarded to replace EFC). *Average financial aid package:* $32,759 (excluding resources awarded to replace EFC). 28% of all full-time undergraduates had no need and received non-need-based gift aid.

GIFT AID (NEED-BASED) *Total amount:* $19,461,578 (11% federal, 7% state, 77% institutional, 5% external sources). *Receiving aid:* Freshmen: 52% (123); all full-time undergraduates: 47% (662). *Average award:* Freshmen: $29,959; Undergraduates: $27,933. *Scholarships, grants, and awards:* Federal Pell, FSEOG, state, private, college/university gift aid from institutional funds.

GIFT AID (NON-NEED-BASED) *Total amount:* $5,536,590 (96% institutional, 4% external sources). *Receiving aid:* Freshmen: 45% (105). Undergraduates: 35% (494). *Average award:* Freshmen: $13,727. Undergraduates: $11,884. *Scholarships, grants, and awards by category:* Academic interests/achievement: 396 awards ($4,706,057 total): general academic interests/achievements. *Creative arts/performance:* general creative arts/performance. *Tuition waivers:* Full or partial for employees or children of employees.

LOANS *Student loans:* $2,716,022 (81% need-based, 19% non-need-based). 49% of past graduating class borrowed through all loan programs. *Average indebtedness per student:* $32,017. *Average need-based loan:* Freshmen: $3463. Undergraduates: $4665. *Parent loans:* $5,433,825 (74% need-based, 26% non-need-based). *Programs:* Federal Direct (Subsidized and Unsubsidized Stafford, PLUS), Perkins, private loans.

WORK-STUDY *Federal work-study:* Total amount: $355,385; jobs available. *State or other work-study/employment:* Total amount: $1,112,972 (100% non-need-based). Part-time jobs available.

APPLYING FOR FINANCIAL AID *Required financial aid form:* FAFSA. *Financial aid deadline (priority):* 2/1. *Notification date:* Continuous beginning 12/15. Students must reply by 5/1 or within 3 weeks of notification.

CONTACT Mr. Dewayne J. Barnes, Director of Financial Aid, California College of the Arts, 1111 Eighth Street, San Francisco, CA 94107, 415-703-9528 or toll-free 800-447-1ART. *Fax:* 415-551-9261. *E-mail:* finaid@cca.edu.
Website: http://www.cca.edu/.

CALIFORNIA COLLEGE SAN DIEGO
National City, CA

CONTACT Financial Aid Office, California College San Diego, 700 Bay Marina Drive, Suite 100, National City, CA 91950, 619-680-4421 or toll-free 800-622-3188. *Website:* http://www.cc-sd.edu/.

CALIFORNIA COLLEGE SAN DIEGO
San Diego, CA

CONTACT Raul Rivera, Senior Financial Aid Officer, California College San Diego, 6602 Convoy Court, #100, San Diego, CA 92111, 619-680-4430 Ext. 1507 or toll-free 800-622-3188. *Fax:* 619-695-5793. *E-mail:* raul.rivera@cc-sd.edu. *Website:* http://www.cc-sd.edu/.

CALIFORNIA COLLEGE SAN DIEGO
San Marcos, CA

CONTACT Financial Aid Office, California College San Diego, 277 Rancheros Drive, Suite 200, San Marcos, CA 92069, 760- 621-4333 or toll-free 800-622-3188. *Website:* http://www.cc-sd.edu/.

CALIFORNIA INSTITUTE OF INTEGRAL STUDIES
San Francisco, CA

CONTACT Financial Aid Office, California Institute of Integral Studies, 1453 Mission Street, San Francisco, CA 94103, 415-575-6122. *Fax:* 415-575-1268. *E-mail:* finaid@ciis.edu.
Website: http://www.ciis.edu/.

CALIFORNIA INSTITUTE OF TECHNOLOGY
Pasadena, CA

Tuition & fees: $49,908	Average undergraduate aid package: $49,951

ABOUT THE INSTITUTION Independent, coed. *Awards:* certificates, bachelor's, master's, and doctoral degrees. 28 undergraduate majors. *Total enrollment:* 2,238. Undergraduates: 961. Freshmen: 235. Both federal and institutional methodology are used as a basis for awarding need-based institutional aid.

UNDERGRADUATE EXPENSES for 2017–2018 *Application fee:* $75. *One-time required fee:* $500. *Comprehensive fee:* $64,704 includes full-time tuition ($48,111), mandatory fees ($1797), and room and board ($14,796). *College room only:* $8391. Room and board charges vary according to housing facility.

FRESHMAN FINANCIAL AID (Fall 2017, est.) 166 applied for aid; of those 68% were deemed to have need. 100% of freshmen with need received aid; of those 100% had need fully met. *Average percent of need met:* 100% (excluding resources awarded to replace EFC). *Average financial aid package:* $46,321 (excluding resources awarded to replace EFC).

UNDERGRADUATE FINANCIAL AID (Fall 2017, est.) 575 applied for aid; of those 86% were deemed to have need. 100% of undergraduates with need received aid; of those 100% had need fully met. *Average percent of need met:* 100% (excluding resources awarded to replace EFC). *Average financial aid package:* $49,951 (excluding resources awarded to replace EFC).

GIFT AID (NEED-BASED) *Total amount:* $21,479,398 (4% federal, 1% state, 94% institutional, 1% external sources). *Receiving aid:* Freshmen: 48% (113); all full-time undergraduates: 52% (495). *Average award:* Freshmen: $43,675; Undergrad-

uates: $45,797. **Scholarships, grants, and awards:** Federal Pell, FSEOG, state, private, college/university gift aid from institutional funds.

GIFT AID (NON-NEED-BASED) Total amount: $374,889 (100% external sources). **Receiving aid:** Undergraduates: 3. **Tuition waivers:** Full or partial for employees or children of employees. **ROTC:** Army cooperative, Air Force cooperative.

LOANS Student loans: $1,549,057 (80% need-based, 20% non-need-based). 34% of past graduating class borrowed through all loan programs. *Average indebtedness per student:* $16,777. **Average need-based loan:** Freshmen: $3125. Undergraduates: $3622. **Parent loans:** $530,932 (4% need-based, 96% non-need-based). **Programs:** Federal Direct (Subsidized and Unsubsidized Stafford, PLUS), college/university.

WORK-STUDY Federal work-study: Total amount: $829,450; 251 jobs averaging $3305. **State or other work-study/employment:** Total amount: $120,450 (93% need-based, 7% non-need-based). 47 part-time jobs averaging $2563.

APPLYING FOR FINANCIAL AID Required financial aid forms: FAFSA, institution's own form, CSS Financial Aid PROFILE, state aid form, noncustodial (divorced/separated) parent's statement, business/farm supplement. **Financial aid deadline (priority):** 2/1. **Notification date:** Continuous beginning 3/30. Students must reply by 5/1 or within 2 weeks of notification.

CONTACT Don Crewell, Director of Financial Aid, California Institute of Technology, 1200 East California Boulevard, MC 20-90, Pasadena, CA 91125-3405, 626-395-6280. *Fax:* 626-564-8136. *E-mail:* dcrewell@caltech.edu. *Website:* http://www.caltech.edu/.

CALIFORNIA INSTITUTE OF THE ARTS
Valencia, CA

ABOUT THE INSTITUTION Independent, coed. 10 undergraduate majors.

GIFT AID (NEED-BASED) Scholarships, grants, and awards: Federal Pell, FSEOG, state, private, college/university gift aid from institutional funds.

GIFT AID (NON-NEED-BASED) Scholarships, grants, and awards by category: *Creative arts/performance:* applied art and design, art/fine arts, cinema/film/broadcasting, creative writing, dance, music, performing arts, theater/drama.

LOANS Programs: Federal Direct (Subsidized and Unsubsidized Stafford, PLUS), Perkins, college/university, private loans.

WORK-STUDY Federal work-study: 280 jobs averaging $2188.

APPLYING FOR FINANCIAL AID Required financial aid form: FAFSA.

CONTACT Dr. Robin Bailey-Chen, Director of Financial Aid, California Institute of the Arts, 24700 McBean Parkway, Valencia, CA 91355-2340, 661-253-7869 or toll-free 800-545-2787. *Fax:* 661-287-3816. *E-mail:* rbaileychen@calarts.edu. *Website:* http://www.calarts.edu/.

CALIFORNIA INTERCONTINENTAL UNIVERSITY
Irvine, CA

CONTACT Financial Aid Office, California Intercontinental University, 17310 Red Hill Avenue, #200, Irvine, CA 92614, 909-396-6090 or toll-free 866-687-2258. *Website:* http://caluniversity.edu/.

CALIFORNIA LUTHERAN UNIVERSITY
Thousand Oaks, CA

Tuition & fees: $41,363	Average undergraduate aid package: $36,600

ABOUT THE INSTITUTION Independent Lutheran, coed. *Awards:* certificates, bachelor's, master's, and doctoral degrees. 55 undergraduate majors. **Total enrollment:** 4,236. Undergraduates: 2,963. Freshmen: 585. Both federal and institutional methodology are used as a basis for awarding need-based institutional aid.

UNDERGRADUATE EXPENSES for 2017–2018 **Application fee:** $25. **Comprehensive fee:** $54,683 includes full-time tuition ($40,880), mandatory fees ($483), and room and board ($13,320). **College room only:** $7150. Room and board charges vary according to board plan and housing facility. **Part-time tuition:** $1315 per unit.

FRESHMAN FINANCIAL AID (Fall 2017, est.) 575 applied for aid; of those 77% were deemed to have need. 100% of freshmen with need received aid; of those 25% had need fully met. **Average percent of need met:** 83% (excluding resources awarded to replace EFC). **Average financial aid package:** $37,400 (excluding resources awarded to replace EFC). 22% of all full-time freshmen had no need and received non-need-based gift aid.

UNDERGRADUATE FINANCIAL AID (Fall 2017, est.) 2,771 applied for aid; of those 75% were deemed to have need. 99% of undergraduates with need received aid; of those 22% had need fully met. **Average percent of need met:** 79% (excluding resources awarded to replace EFC). **Average financial aid package:** $36,600 (excluding resources awarded to replace EFC). 24% of all full-time undergraduates had no need and received non-need-based gift aid.

GIFT AID (NEED-BASED) Total amount: $65,552,593 (7% federal, 11% state, 81% institutional, 1% external sources). **Receiving aid:** Freshmen: 75% (438); all full-time undergraduates: 70% (2,002). **Average award:** Freshmen: $30,120; Undergraduates: $27,600. **Scholarships, grants, and awards:** Federal Pell, FSEOG, state, private, college/university gift aid from institutional funds.

GIFT AID (NON-NEED-BASED) Total amount: $12,783,288 (99% institutional, 1% external sources). **Receiving aid:** Freshmen: 20% (119). Undergraduates: 17% (480). **Average award:** Freshmen: $19,700. Undergraduates: $18,860. **Scholarships, grants, and awards by category:** *Academic interests/achievement:* biological sciences, business, communication, computer science, education, English, foreign languages, general academic interests/achievements, humanities, international studies, mathematics, physical sciences, religion/biblical studies, social sciences. *Creative arts/performance:* art/fine arts, creative writing, journalism/publications, music, performing arts, theater/drama. *Special achievements/activities:* community service, general special achievements/activities, leadership, religious involvement. *Special characteristics:* adult students, children and siblings of alumni, children of faculty/staff, international students, relatives of clergy, religious affiliation, veterans, veterans' children. **Tuition waivers:** Full or partial for employees or children of employees. **ROTC:** Army cooperative, Air Force cooperative.

LOANS Student loans: $16,233,108 (93% need-based, 7% non-need-based). 61% of past graduating class borrowed through all loan programs. *Average indebtedness per student:* $34,220. **Average need-based loan:** Freshmen: $3550. Undergraduates: $4840. **Parent loans:** $11,295,207 (89% need-based, 11% non-need-based). **Programs:** Federal Direct (Subsidized and Unsubsidized Stafford, PLUS), Perkins.

WORK-STUDY Federal work-study: Total amount: $669,500; 260 jobs averaging $2500. **State or other work-study/employment:** Part-time jobs available.

APPLYING FOR FINANCIAL AID Required financial aid forms: FAFSA, Cal Grant forms, GPA verification form (CA residents only). **Financial aid deadline (priority):** 3/1. **Notification date:** Continuous beginning 3/15. Students must reply by 5/1 or within 2 weeks of notification.

CONTACT Jerry McKeen, Director of Financial Aid, California Lutheran University, 60 West Olsen Road, Thousand Oaks, CA 91360-2787, 805-493-3115 or toll-free 877-258-3678. *Fax:* 805-493-3114. *E-mail:* jmckeen@callutheran.edu. *Website:* http://www.callutheran.edu/.

CALIFORNIA MIRAMAR UNIVERSITY
San Diego, CA

CONTACT Financial Aid Office, California Miramar University, 3550 Camino Del Rio North, Suite 208, San Diego, CA 92108, 858-653-3000 or toll-free 877-570-5678. *Website:* http://www.calmu.edu/.

CALIFORNIA POLYTECHNIC STATE UNIVERSITY, SAN LUIS OBISPO
San Luis Obispo, CA

Tuition & fees (CA res): $9432	Average undergraduate aid package: $10,456

ABOUT THE INSTITUTION State-supported, coed. *Awards:* certificates, bachelor's, and master's degrees. 64 undergraduate majors. *Total enrollment:* 22,188. Undergraduates: 21,297. Freshmen: 5,253. Federal methodology is used as a basis for awarding need-based institutional aid.

UNDERGRADUATE EXPENSES for 2017–2018 *Application fee:* $55. *Tuition, state resident:* full-time $5742; part-time $3330 per year. *Tuition, non-resident:* full-time $17,622; part-time $8082 per year. *Required fees:* full-time $3690; $3219 per year. Full-time tuition and fees vary according to course load, degree level, and program. Part-time tuition and fees vary according to course load, degree level, and program. *College room and board:* $13,115; *Room only:* $7792. Room and board charges vary according to housing facility.

FRESHMAN FINANCIAL AID (Fall 2016) 3,321 applied for aid; of those 50% were deemed to have need. 94% of freshmen with need received aid; of those 11% had need fully met. *Average percent of need met:* 58% (excluding resources awarded to replace EFC). *Average financial aid package:* $9996 (excluding resources awarded to replace EFC). 13% of all full-time freshmen had no need and received non-need-based gift aid.

UNDERGRADUATE FINANCIAL AID (Fall 2016) 11,669 applied for aid; of those 67% were deemed to have need. 95% of undergraduates with need received aid; of those 9% had need fully met. *Average percent of need met:* 58% (excluding resources awarded to replace EFC). *Average financial aid package:* $10,456 (excluding resources awarded to replace EFC). 13% of all full-time undergraduates had no need and received non-need-based gift aid.

GIFT AID (NEED-BASED) *Total amount:* $55,346,025 (29% federal, 34% state, 29% institutional, 8% external sources). *Receiving aid:* Freshmen: 34% (1,482); all full-time undergraduates: 35% (6,902). *Average award:* Freshmen: $3340; Undergraduates: $3563. *Scholarships, grants, and awards:* Federal Pell, FSEOG, state, private, college/university gift aid from institutional funds, TEACH Grants, California Dream Grants.

GIFT AID (NON-NEED-BASED) *Total amount:* $10,890,778 (4% state, 61% institutional, 35% external sources). *Receiving aid:* Freshmen: 2% (81). Undergraduates: 1% (246). *Average award:* Freshmen: $2916. Undergraduates: $2301. *Scholarships, grants, and awards by category:* Academic interests/achievement: agriculture, architecture, biological sciences, business, communication, computer science, education, engineering/technologies, English, foreign languages, general academic interests/achievements, health fields, home economics, humanities, international studies, library science, mathematics, military science, physical sciences, social sciences. *Creative arts/performance:* applied art and design, art/fine arts, cinema/film/broadcasting, creative writing, dance, debating, general creative arts/performance, journalism/publications, music, performing arts, theater/drama. *Special achievements/activities:* community service, leadership, rodeo. *Special characteristics:* children and siblings of alumni, general special characteristics, local/state students. *Tuition waivers:* Full or partial for employees or children of employees. *ROTC:* Army.

LOANS *Student loans:* $46,604,975 (62% need-based, 38% non-need-based). 42% of past graduating class borrowed through all loan programs. *Average indebtedness per student:* $21,852. *Average need-based loan:* Freshmen: $3347. Undergraduates: $4094. *Parent loans:* $33,239,883 (27% need-based, 73% non-need-based). *Programs:* Federal Direct (Subsidized and Unsubsidized Stafford, PLUS), Perkins, college/university, alternative loans.

WORK-STUDY *Federal work-study:* jobs available.

ATHLETIC AWARDS Total amount: $4,734,323 (32% need-based, 68% non-need-based).

APPLYING FOR FINANCIAL AID *Required financial aid form:* FAFSA. *Financial aid deadline (priority):* 3/2. *Notification date:* Continuous beginning 3/15.

CONTACT Gerrie Hatten, Interim Director of Financial Aid, California Polytechnic State University, San Luis Obispo, Administration Building, Room 212, San Luis Obispo, CA 93407, 805-756-5878. *Fax:* 805-756-7243. *E-mail:* financialaid@calpoly.edu. *Website:* http://www.calpoly.edu/.

CALIFORNIA STATE POLYTECHNIC UNIVERSITY, POMONA
Pomona, CA

Tuition & fees (CA res): $7297	Average undergraduate aid package: $11,067

ABOUT THE INSTITUTION State-supported, coed. *Awards:* bachelor's, master's, and doctoral degrees. 55 undergraduate majors. *Total enrollment:* 25,894. Undergraduates: 24,319. Freshmen: 3,786. Federal methodology is used as a basis for awarding need-based institutional aid.

UNDERGRADUATE EXPENSES for 2018–2019 *Application fee:* $55. *Tuition, state resident:* full-time $5742. *Tuition, nonresident:* full-time $17,622; part-time $264 per credit hour. *Required fees:* full-time $1555. Full-time tuition and fees vary according to course load, degree level, and program. Part-time tuition and fees vary according to course load, degree level, and program. *College room and board:* $14,514; *Room only:* $9027. Room and board charges vary according to board plan and housing facility.

FRESHMAN FINANCIAL AID (Fall 2017, est.) 3,140 applied for aid; of those 80% were deemed to have need. 96% of freshmen with need received aid; of those 1% had need fully met. *Average percent of need met:* 56% (excluding resources awarded to replace EFC). *Average financial aid package:* $10,386 (excluding resources awarded to replace EFC). 1% of all full-time freshmen had no need and received non-need-based gift aid.

UNDERGRADUATE FINANCIAL AID (Fall 2017, est.) 16,917 applied for aid; of those 88% were deemed to have need. 96% of undergraduates with need received aid; of those 3% had need fully met. *Average percent of need met:* 54% (excluding resources awarded to replace EFC). *Average financial aid package:* $11,067 (excluding resources awarded to replace EFC). 1% of all full-time undergraduates had no need and received non-need-based gift aid.

GIFT AID (NEED-BASED) *Total amount:* $164,732,919 (47% federal, 27% state, 26% institutional). *Receiving aid:* Freshmen: 53% (1,945); all full-time undergraduates: 55% (11,902). *Average award:* Freshmen: $10,039; Undergraduates: $10,122. *Scholarships, grants, and awards:* Federal Pell, FSEOG, state, private, college/university gift aid from institutional funds.

GIFT AID (NON-NEED-BASED) *Total amount:* $7,336,878 (68% state, 32% external sources). *Receiving aid:* Freshmen: 16% (600). Undergraduates: 13% (2,719). *Average award:* Freshmen: $4500. Undergraduates: $1535. *Scholarships, grants, and awards by category:* Academic interests/achievement: agriculture, architecture, area/ethnic studies, biological sciences, business, communication, computer science, education, engineering/technologies, English, foreign languages, general academic interests/achievements, humanities, international studies, mathematics, physical sciences, social sciences. *Special achievements/activities:* hobbies/interests, leadership. *Special characteristics:* children and siblings of alumni, children of current students, first-generation college students, members of minority groups. *Tuition waivers:* Full or partial for employees or children of employees. *ROTC:* Army.

LOANS *Student loans:* $65,926,212 (52% need-based, 48% non-need-based). 53% of past graduating class borrowed through all loan programs. *Average indebtedness per student:* $22,228. *Average need-based loan:* Freshmen: $3380. Undergraduates: $4454. *Parent loans:* $4,732,267 (100% non-need-based). *Programs:* Federal Direct (Subsidized and Unsubsidized Stafford, PLUS), Perkins, college/university, alternative loans.

WORK-STUDY *Federal work-study:* Total amount: $849,100; 303 jobs averaging $2802.

ATHLETIC AWARDS Total amount: $882,012 (100% non-need-based).

APPLYING FOR FINANCIAL AID *Required financial aid form:* FAFSA. *Financial aid deadline:* Continuous. *Notification date:* Continuous beginning 4/1. Students must reply within 6 weeks of notification.

CONTACT Dr. Diana Minor, Director of Financial Aid and Scholarships, California State Polytechnic University, Pomona, 3801 West Temple Avenue, Pomona, CA 91768-2557, 909-869-3704. *Fax:* 909-869-4757. *E-mail:* dyminor@cpp.edu. *Website:* http://www.cpp.edu/.

CALIFORNIA STATE UNIVERSITY, BAKERSFIELD
Bakersfield, CA

Tuition & fees: N/R	Average undergraduate aid package: $11,346

ABOUT THE INSTITUTION State-supported, coed. *Awards:* bachelor's, master's, and doctoral degrees. 30 undergraduate majors. *Total enrollment:* 9,341. Undergraduates: 8,093. Freshmen: 1,356. Federal methodology is used as a basis for awarding need-based institutional aid.

UNDERGRADUATE EXPENSES for 2017–2018 *Application fee:* $55. *Tuition, state resident:* part-time $3330 per year. *Tuition, nonresident:* part-time $8082 per year. *Required fees:* $1404 per year. Full-time tuition and fees vary according to course load. Part-time tuition and fees vary according to course load. Room and board charges vary according to board plan and housing facility.

FRESHMAN FINANCIAL AID (Fall 2016) 1,242 applied for aid; of those 85% were deemed to have need. 98% of freshmen with need received aid; of those 20% had need fully met. *Average percent of need met:* 60% (excluding resources awarded to replace EFC). *Average financial aid package:* $11,721 (excluding resources awarded to replace EFC).

UNDERGRADUATE FINANCIAL AID (Fall 2016) 6,327 applied for aid; of those 89% were deemed to have need. 98% of undergraduates with need received aid; of those 14% had need fully met. *Average percent of need met:* 55% (excluding resources awarded to replace EFC). *Average financial aid package:* $11,346 (excluding resources awarded to replace EFC).

GIFT AID (NEED-BASED) *Total amount:* $59,085,730 (42% federal, 55% state, 1% institutional, 2% external sources). *Receiving aid:* Freshmen: 75% (966); all full-time undergraduates: 72% (5,079). *Average award:* Freshmen: $10,550; Undergraduates: $9762. *Scholarships, grants, and awards:* Federal Pell, FSEOG, state, private, college/university gift aid from institutional funds, Federal Nursing.

GIFT AID (NON-NEED-BASED) *Total amount:* $575,417 (2% federal, 98% state). *Receiving aid:* Freshmen: 15% (192). Undergraduates: 12% (836). *Scholarships, grants, and awards by category:* Academic interests/achievement: biological sciences, business, communication, education, foreign languages, general academic interests/achievements, health fields, humanities, mathematics, physical sciences, premedicine, religion/biblical studies, social sciences. *Creative arts/performance:* art/fine arts, music, theater/drama. *Special achievements/activities:* community service, general special achievements/activities, leadership. *Special characteristics:* children of faculty/staff, children of union members/company employees, ethnic background, first-generation college students, local/state students, veterans. *Tuition waivers:* Full or partial for employees or children of employees, senior citizens.

LOANS *Student loans:* $20,850,538 (100% need-based). 51% of past graduating class borrowed through all loan programs. *Average indebtedness per student:* $17,454. *Average need-based loan:* Freshmen: $3541. Undergraduates: $4022. *Parent loans:* $828,590 (100% need-based). *Programs:* Federal Direct (Subsidized and Unsubsidized Stafford, PLUS), Perkins, Federal Nursing, college/university.

WORK-STUDY *Federal work-study:* jobs available.

ATHLETIC AWARDS Total amount: $2,048,610 (100% need-based).

APPLYING FOR FINANCIAL AID *Required financial aid forms:* FAFSA, state aid form. *Financial aid deadline (priority):* 3/2. *Notification date:* Continuous beginning 4/15. Students must reply within 3 weeks of notification.

CONTACT Chad Morris, Associate Director of Financial Aid and Scholarships, California State University, Bakersfield, 9001 Stockdale Highway, Bakersfield, CA 93311-1022, 661-654-3267 or toll-free 800-788-2782. *Fax:* 661-654-6800. *E-mail:* cmorris@csub.edu. *Website:* http://www.csub.edu/.

CALIFORNIA STATE UNIVERSITY CHANNEL ISLANDS
Camarillo, CA

CONTACT Financial Aid Office, California State University Channel Islands, One University Drive, Camarillo, CA 93012, 805-437-8400. *Website:* http://www.csuci.edu/.

CALIFORNIA STATE UNIVERSITY, CHICO
Chico, CA

Tuition & fees (CA res): $12,516	Average undergraduate aid package: $16,022

ABOUT THE INSTITUTION State-supported, coed. *Awards:* certificates, bachelor's, and master's degrees. 48 undergraduate majors. *Total enrollment:* 17,557. Undergraduates: 16,471. Freshmen: 2,762. Federal methodology is used as a basis for awarding need-based institutional aid.

UNDERGRADUATE EXPENSES for 2017–2018 *Application fee:* $55. *Tuition, state resident:* full-time $7044. *Tuition, nonresident:* full-time $18,204. *Required fees:* full-time $5472. Full-time tuition and fees vary according to degree level. Part-time tuition and fees vary according to course load and degree level. *College room and board:* $12,536. Room and board charges vary according to board plan and housing facility.

FRESHMAN FINANCIAL AID (Fall 2016) 2,356 applied for aid; of those 80% were deemed to have need. 97% of freshmen with need received aid; of those 15% had need fully met. *Average percent of need met:* 77% (excluding resources awarded to replace EFC). *Average financial aid package:* $17,631 (excluding resources awarded to replace EFC). 6% of all full-time freshmen had no need and received non-need-based gift aid.

UNDERGRADUATE FINANCIAL AID (Fall 2016) 12,269 applied for aid; of those 86% were deemed to have need. 98% of undergraduates with need received aid; of those 16% had need fully met. *Average percent of need met:* 74% (excluding resources awarded to replace EFC). *Average financial aid package:* $16,022 (excluding resources awarded to replace EFC). 3% of all full-time undergraduates had no need and received non-need-based gift aid.

GIFT AID (NEED-BASED) *Total amount:* $139,140,049 (26% federal, 31% state, 43% institutional). *Receiving aid:* Freshmen: 59% (1,384); all full-time undergraduates: 53% (8,312). *Average award:* Freshmen: $10,803; Undergraduates: $10,134. *Scholarships, grants, and awards:* Federal Pell, FSEOG, state, private, college/university gift aid from institutional funds, United Negro College Fund.

GIFT AID (NON-NEED-BASED) *Total amount:* $5,653,720 (39% state, 27% institutional, 34% external sources). *Receiving aid:* Freshmen: 16% (387). Undergraduates: 9% (1,331). *Average award:* Freshmen: $1611. Undergraduates: $1429. *Scholarships, grants, and awards by category:* Academic interests/achievement: agriculture, area/ethnic studies, biological sciences, business, communication, computer science, education, engineering/technologies, English, foreign languages, general academic interests/achievements, health fields, humanities, international studies, mathematics, physical sciences, social sciences. *Creative arts/performance:* applied art and design, art/fine arts, cinema/film/broadcasting, creative writing, dance, debating, general creative arts/performance, journalism/publications, music, performing arts, theater/drama. *Special achievements/activities:* community service, general special achievements/activities, hobbies/interests, leadership, memberships. *Special characteristics:* adult students, children of faculty/staff, ethnic background, first-generation college students, handicapped students, international students, local/state students, married students, members of minority groups, out-of-state students. *Tuition waivers:* Full or partial for employees or children of employees, senior citizens.

LOANS *Student loans:* $50,699,591 (59% need-based, 41% non-need-based). 62% of past graduating class borrowed through all loan programs. *Average need-based loan:* Freshmen: $3452. Undergraduates: $4653. *Parent loans:* $4,260,272 (100% need-based). *Programs:* Federal Direct (Subsidized and Unsubsidized Stafford, PLUS), Perkins, college/university.

WORK-STUDY *Federal work-study:* jobs available.

ATHLETIC AWARDS Total amount: $709,077 (100% need-based).

APPLYING FOR FINANCIAL AID *Required financial aid form:* FAFSA. *Financial aid deadline (priority):* 3/3. *Notification date:* Continuous beginning 4/3.

CONTACT Dan Reed, Director of Financial Aid and Scholarships, California State University, Chico, 400 West First Street, Student Services Center, Room 250, Chico, CA 95929-0705, 530-898-6451 or toll-free 800-542-4426 (out-of-state). *Fax:* 530-898-6883. *E-mail:* finaid@csuchico.edu. *Website:* http://www.csuchico.edu/.

CALIFORNIA STATE UNIVERSITY, DOMINGUEZ HILLS
Carson, CA

Tuition & fees (CA res): $8132	Average undergraduate aid package: $6211

ABOUT THE INSTITUTION State-supported, coed. **Awards:** certificates, bachelor's, and master's degrees. 67 undergraduate majors. **Total enrollment:** 15,179. Undergraduates: 13,116. Freshmen: 1,678. Federal methodology is used as a basis for awarding need-based institutional aid.

UNDERGRADUATE EXPENSES for 2018–2019 Application fee: $55. **Tuition, state resident:** full-time $6937; part-time $3330 per year. **Tuition, nonresident:** full-time $16,441; part-time $396 per unit. **Required fees:** full-time $1195; $1195 per year. Full-time tuition and fees vary according to course load, program, and reciprocity agreements. Part-time tuition and fees vary according to course load, program, and reciprocity agreements. **College room and board:** $12,540. Room and board charges vary according to housing facility.

FRESHMAN FINANCIAL AID (Fall 2016) 1,118 applied for aid; of those 93% were deemed to have need. 97% of freshmen with need received aid; of those 1% had need fully met. **Average percent of need met:** 34% (excluding resources awarded to replace EFC). **Average financial aid package:** $5730 (excluding resources awarded to replace EFC). 3% of all full-time freshmen had no need and received non-need-based gift aid.

UNDERGRADUATE FINANCIAL AID (Fall 2016) 6,789 applied for aid; of those 96% were deemed to have need. 98% of undergraduates with need received aid; of those 2% had need fully met. **Average percent of need met:** 34% (excluding resources awarded to replace EFC). **Average financial aid package:** $6211 (excluding resources awarded to replace EFC). 2% of all full-time undergraduates had no need and received non-need-based gift aid.

GIFT AID (NEED-BASED) Total amount: $42,913,903 (42% federal, 56% state, 1% institutional, 1% external sources). **Receiving aid:** Freshmen: 72% (885); all full-time undergraduates: 59% (5,514). **Average award:** Freshmen: $5497; Undergraduates: $5229. **Scholarships, grants, and awards:** Federal Pell, FSEOG, state, private, college/university gift aid from institutional funds.

GIFT AID (NON-NEED-BASED) Total amount: $30,260 (100% institutional). **Receiving aid:** Freshmen: 16% (198). Undergraduates: 17% (1,619). **Average award:** Freshmen: $4233. Undergraduates: $4604. **Tuition waivers:** Full or partial for employees or children of employees, senior citizens. **ROTC:** Army, Air Force cooperative.

LOANS Student loans: $16,026,742 (93% need-based, 7% non-need-based). 55% of past graduating class borrowed through all loan programs. **Average indebtedness per student:** $15,880. **Average need-based loan:** Freshmen: $1607. Undergraduates: $2337. **Parent loans:** $356,362 (61% need-based, 39% non-need-based). **Programs:** Federal Direct (Subsidized and Unsubsidized Stafford, PLUS), Perkins, college/university.

WORK-STUDY Federal work-study: 146 jobs averaging $1571.

ATHLETIC AWARDS Total amount: $251,064 (90% need-based, 10% non-need-based).

APPLYING FOR FINANCIAL AID Required financial aid form: FAFSA. **Financial aid deadline:** 5/15 (priority: 3/2). **Notification date:** Continuous beginning 3/15. Students must reply within 2 weeks of notification.

CONTACT Mrs. Delores S. Lee, Director of Financial Aid, California State University, Dominguez Hills, 1000 East Victoria Street, Carson, CA 90747-0001, 310-243-3189. Fax: 310-516-4498. E-mail: dslee@csudh.edu. Website: http://www.csudh.edu/.

CALIFORNIA STATE UNIVERSITY, EAST BAY
Hayward, CA

ABOUT THE INSTITUTION State-supported, coed. **Awards:** certificates, bachelor's, master's, and doctoral degrees. 48 undergraduate majors. **Total enrollment:** 15,435. Undergraduates: 12,998. Freshmen: 1,420.

GIFT AID (NEED-BASED) Scholarships, grants, and awards: Federal Pell, FSEOG, state, private, college/university gift aid from institutional funds.

GIFT AID (NON-NEED-BASED) Scholarships, grants, and awards by category: Academic interests/achievement: general academic interests/achievements. Creative arts/performance: music.

LOANS Programs: Federal Direct (Subsidized and Unsubsidized Stafford, PLUS), Perkins, college/university.

WORK-STUDY Federal work-study: jobs available.

APPLYING FOR FINANCIAL AID Required financial aid form: FAFSA.

CONTACT Office of Financial Aid, California State University, East Bay, 25800 Carlos Bee Boulevard, Hayward, CA 94542-3028, 510-885-2784. Fax: 510-885-2161. E-mail: finaid@csueastbay.edu. Website: http://www.csueastbay.edu/.

CALIFORNIA STATE UNIVERSITY, FRESNO
Fresno, CA

Tuition & fees: N/R	Average undergraduate aid package: $13,051

ABOUT THE INSTITUTION State-supported, coed. **Awards:** certificates, bachelor's, master's, and doctoral degrees. 87 undergraduate majors. **Total enrollment:** 24,403. Undergraduates: 21,528. Freshmen: 3,194. Federal methodology is used as a basis for awarding need-based institutional aid.

FRESHMAN FINANCIAL AID (Fall 2017, est.) 2,948 applied for aid; of those 89% were deemed to have need. 98% of freshmen with need received aid; of those 16% had need fully met. **Average percent of need met:** 72% (excluding resources awarded to replace EFC). **Average financial aid package:** $12,505 (excluding resources awarded to replace EFC). 6% of all full-time freshmen had no need and received non-need-based gift aid.

UNDERGRADUATE FINANCIAL AID (Fall 2017, est.) 15,772 applied for aid; of those 94% were deemed to have need. 98% of undergraduates with need received aid; of those 17% had need fully met. **Average percent of need met:** 79% (excluding resources awarded to replace EFC). **Average financial aid package:** $13,051 (excluding resources awarded to replace EFC). 2% of all full-time undergraduates had no need and received non-need-based gift aid.

GIFT AID (NEED-BASED) Total amount: $149,580,889 (45% federal, 55% state). **Receiving aid:** Freshmen: 72% (2,381); all full-time undergraduates: 68% (13,162). **Average award:** Freshmen: $10,879; Undergraduates: $10,486. **Scholarships, grants, and awards:** Federal Pell, FSEOG, state, private, college/university gift aid from institutional funds.

GIFT AID (NON-NEED-BASED) Total amount: $10,530,138 (33% state, 62% institutional, 5% external sources). **Receiving aid:** Freshmen: 22% (729). Undergraduates: 18% (3,451). **Average award:** Freshmen: $3085. Undergraduates: $2901. **Scholarships, grants, and awards by category:** Academic interests/achievement: 1,119 awards ($2,858,099 total): agriculture, area/ethnic studies, biological sciences, business, communication, education, engineering/technologies, English, foreign languages, general academic interests/achievements, health fields, home economics, humanities, mathematics, physical sciences, social sciences. Creative arts/performance: 182 awards ($176,397 total): art/fine arts, journalism/publications, music, theater/drama. Special achievements/activities: 22 awards ($33,198 total): community service, leadership. Special characteristics: 3 awards ($2100 total): handicapped students, local/state students. **ROTC:** Army, Air Force.

LOANS Student loans: $89,382,212 (60% need-based, 40% non-need-based). 47% of past graduating class borrowed through all loan programs. **Average indebtedness per student:** $18,308. **Average need-based loan:** Freshmen: $3183. Undergraduates: $4224. **Parent loans:** $1,195,611 (100% non-need-based). **Programs:** Federal Direct (Subsidized and Unsubsidized Stafford, PLUS), Federal Nursing, college/university, alternative loans.

WORK-STUDY Federal work-study: Total amount: $1,030,820; 183 jobs averaging $5423.

ATHLETIC AWARDS Total amount: $6,550,939 (100% non-need-based).

APPLYING FOR FINANCIAL AID Required financial aid form: FAFSA. **Financial aid deadline (priority):** 3/2. **Notification date:** Continuous beginning 4/1.

CONTACT Kelly Russell, Director of Financial Aid, California State University, Fresno, 5150 North Maple Avenue, JA64, Fresno, CA 93740, 559-278-2182. *Fax:* 559-278-4833. *E-mail:* kellyr@csufresno.edu.
Website: http://www.csufresno.edu/.

CALIFORNIA STATE UNIVERSITY, FULLERTON
Fullerton, CA

Tuition & fees (CA res): $6850	Average undergraduate aid package: $9341

ABOUT THE INSTITUTION State-supported, coed. *Awards:* certificates, bachelor's, master's, and doctoral degrees. 66 undergraduate majors. *Total enrollment:* 70,681. Undergraduates: 64,304. Federal methodology is used as a basis for awarding need-based institutional aid.

UNDERGRADUATE EXPENSES for 2017–2018 *Application fee:* $55. *Tuition, state resident:* full-time $5742; part-time $3330 per year. *Tuition, nonresident:* full-time $18,734; part-time $8082 per year. *Required fees:* full-time $1108; $1107.58 per year. Full-time tuition and fees vary according to course load, degree level, and program. Part-time tuition and fees vary according to course load, degree level, and program. *College room and board:* $15,642. Room and board charges vary according to board plan and housing facility.

FRESHMAN FINANCIAL AID (Fall 2016) 3,096 applied for aid; of those 96% were deemed to have need. 85% of freshmen with need received aid; of those 8% had need fully met. *Average percent of need met:* 75% (excluding resources awarded to replace EFC). *Average financial aid package:* $9132 (excluding resources awarded to replace EFC). 29% of all full-time freshmen had no need and received non-need-based gift aid.

UNDERGRADUATE FINANCIAL AID (Fall 2016) 18,943 applied for aid; of those 96% were deemed to have need. 89% of undergraduates with need received aid; of those 95% had need fully met. *Average percent of need met:* 76% (excluding resources awarded to replace EFC). *Average financial aid package:* $9341 (excluding resources awarded to replace EFC). 4% of all full-time undergraduates had no need and received non-need-based gift aid.

GIFT AID (NEED-BASED) *Total amount:* $182,547,571 (41% federal, 29% state, 29% institutional, 1% external sources). *Receiving aid:* Freshmen: 56% (2,008); all full-time undergraduates: 41% (14,655). *Average award:* Freshmen: $4740; Undergraduates: $5369. *Scholarships, grants, and awards:* Federal Pell, FSEOG, state, private, college/university gift aid from institutional funds, Federal Nursing.

GIFT AID (NON-NEED-BASED) *Total amount:* $1,529,476 (100% external sources). *Receiving aid:* Freshmen: 20% (710). Undergraduates: 3% (1,233). *Average award:* Freshmen: $2037. Undergraduates: $1683. *Scholarships, grants, and awards by category:* Academic interests/achievement: 1,384 awards ($1,467,192 total): area/ethnic studies, biological sciences, business, communication, computer science, education, engineering/technologies, English, foreign languages, general academic interests/achievements, health fields, home economics, humanities, international studies, mathematics, military science, physical sciences, religion/biblical studies, social sciences. *Creative arts/performance:* 136 awards ($169,830 total): art/fine arts, cinema/film/broadcasting, dance, journalism/publications, music, performing arts, theater/drama. *Special achievements/activities:* 259 awards ($309,061 total): general special achievements/activities, leadership. *Special characteristics:* 179 awards ($871,504 total): general special characteristics. *Tuition waivers:* Full or partial for employees or children of employees, senior citizens. *ROTC:* Army.

LOANS *Student loans:* $95,861,242 (42% need-based, 58% non-need-based). 42% of past graduating class borrowed through all loan programs. *Average indebtedness per student:* $14,965. *Average need-based loan:* Freshmen: $4823. Undergraduates: $1638. *Parent loans:* $5,692,342 (100% non-need-based). *Programs:* Federal Direct (Subsidized and Unsubsidized Stafford, PLUS), Perkins, college/university, private loans.

WORK-STUDY *Federal work-study:* jobs available.

ATHLETIC AWARDS Total amount: $1,176,770 (100% need-based).

APPLYING FOR FINANCIAL AID *Required financial aid form:* FAFSA. *Financial aid deadline (priority):* 3/2. *Notification date:* Continuous beginning 4/22. Students must reply within 4 weeks of notification.

CONTACT Ms. Kelly England, Interim Director of Financial Aid, California State University, Fullerton, 800 North State College Boulevard, Fullerton, CA 92831-3599, 657-278-3128. *Fax:* 657-278-7090. *E-mail:* kengland@fullerton.edu.
Website: http://www.fullerton.edu/.

CALIFORNIA STATE UNIVERSITY, LONG BEACH
Long Beach, CA

Tuition & fees (CA res): $6798	Average undergraduate aid package: $13,720

ABOUT THE INSTITUTION State-supported, coed. *Awards:* certificates, bachelor's, master's, and doctoral degrees. 148 undergraduate majors. *Total enrollment:* 37,065. Undergraduates: 31,351. Freshmen: 4,138. Federal methodology is used as a basis for awarding need-based institutional aid.

UNDERGRADUATE EXPENSES for 2018–2019 *Application fee:* $55. *Tuition, state resident:* full-time $5742. *Tuition, nonresident:* full-time $16,038. *Required fees:* full-time $1056. Full-time tuition and fees vary according to degree level and program. Part-time tuition and fees vary according to course load, degree level, and program. *College room and board:* $12,750; *Room only:* $8200. Room and board charges vary according to board plan.

FRESHMAN FINANCIAL AID (Fall 2017, est.) 3,589 applied for aid; of those 81% were deemed to have need. 97% of freshmen with need received aid; of those 63% had need fully met. *Average percent of need met:* 80% (excluding resources awarded to replace EFC). *Average financial aid package:* $12,577 (excluding resources awarded to replace EFC).

UNDERGRADUATE FINANCIAL AID (Fall 2017, est.) 23,709 applied for aid; of those 89% were deemed to have need. 96% of undergraduates with need received aid; of those 47% had need fully met. *Average percent of need met:* 78% (excluding resources awarded to replace EFC). *Average financial aid package:* $13,720 (excluding resources awarded to replace EFC).

GIFT AID (NEED-BASED) *Total amount:* $193,607,156 (41% federal, 54% state, 4% institutional, 1% external sources). *Receiving aid:* Freshmen: 56% (2,313); all full-time undergraduates: 61% (17,037). *Average award:* Freshmen: $7885; Undergraduates: $6709. *Scholarships, grants, and awards:* Federal Pell, FSEOG, state, private, college/university gift aid from institutional funds.

GIFT AID (NON-NEED-BASED) *Total amount:* $25,252 (100% federal). *Receiving aid:* Freshmen: 14% (593). Undergraduates: 21% (5,801). *Tuition waivers:* Full or partial for employees or children of employees, senior citizens. *ROTC:* Army, Air Force cooperative.

LOANS *Student loans:* $119,103,297 (58% need-based, 42% non-need-based). 50% of past graduating class borrowed through all loan programs. *Average indebtedness per student:* $19,062. *Average need-based loan:* Freshmen: $3401. Undergraduates: $3949. *Parent loans:* $3,091,662 (100% non-need-based). *Programs:* Federal Direct (Subsidized and Unsubsidized Stafford, PLUS), Perkins.

WORK-STUDY *Federal work-study:* Total amount: $4,768,920; jobs available.

ATHLETIC AWARDS Total amount: $2,628,522 (100% non-need-based).

APPLYING FOR FINANCIAL AID *Required financial aid form:* FAFSA. *Financial aid deadline (priority):* 3/2. *Notification date:* 4/1. Students must reply within 4 weeks of notification.

CONTACT Nicolas Valdivia, Office of Financial Aid, California State University, Long Beach, 1250 Bellflower Boulevard, Long Beach, CA 90840, 562-985-8403.
Website: http://www.csulb.edu/.

CALIFORNIA STATE UNIVERSITY, LOS ANGELES
Los Angeles, CA

ABOUT THE INSTITUTION State-supported, coed. *Awards:* certificates, bachelor's, master's, and doctoral degrees. 62 undergraduate majors. *Total enrollment:* 28,253. Undergraduates: 12,356. Freshmen: 3,556.

GIFT AID (NEED-BASED) *Scholarships, grants, and awards:* Federal Pell, FSEOG, state, private, college/university gift aid from institutional funds.

GIFT AID (NON-NEED-BASED) *Scholarships, grants, and awards by category:* *Academic interests/achievement:* biological sciences, business, communication, computer science, education, engineering/technologies, English, foreign languages, general academic interests/achievements, health fields, mathematics, physical sciences, social sciences. *Creative arts/performance:* art/fine arts, general creative arts/performance, journalism/publications, music, theater/drama. *Special achievements/activities:* community service, general special achievements/activities. *Special characteristics:* general special characteristics.

LOANS *Programs:* Federal Direct (Subsidized and Unsubsidized Stafford, PLUS), Perkins, Federal Nursing.

WORK-STUDY *Federal work-study:* jobs available.

APPLYING FOR FINANCIAL AID *Required financial aid form:* FAFSA.

CONTACT Tamie L. Nguyen, Director of Financial Aid, California State University, Los Angeles, 5151 State University Drive, Los Angeles, CA 90032, 323-343-6260. *Fax:* 323-343-3166. *E-mail:* tnguyen10@cslanet.calstatela.edu. *Website:* http://www.calstatela.edu/.

CALIFORNIA STATE UNIVERSITY MARITIME ACADEMY
Vallejo, CA

Tuition & fees (CA res): $8360	Average undergraduate aid package: N/A

ABOUT THE INSTITUTION State-supported, coed. *Awards:* bachelor's and master's degrees. 4 undergraduate majors. *Total enrollment:* 1,090. Undergraduates: 1,048. Freshmen: 223. Federal methodology is used as a basis for awarding need-based institutional aid.

UNDERGRADUATE EXPENSES for 2017–2018 *Application fee:* $55. *Tuition, state resident:* full-time $5472; part-time $1665 per term. *Tuition, nonresident:* full-time $11,160; part-time $396 per credit hour. *Required fees:* full-time $2888; $3198 per term. Full-time tuition and fees vary according to course load and reciprocity agreements. Part-time tuition and fees vary according to course load and reciprocity agreements. *College room and board:* $12,807. Room and board charges vary according to board plan.

FRESHMAN FINANCIAL AID (Fall 2016) 137 applied for aid; of those 88% were deemed to have need. 100% of freshmen with need received aid; of those 8% had need fully met.

UNDERGRADUATE FINANCIAL AID (Fall 2016) 575 applied for aid; of those 91% were deemed to have need. 100% of undergraduates with need received aid; of those 8% had need fully met.

GIFT AID (NEED-BASED) *Total amount:* $4,569,494 (36% federal, 48% state, 7% institutional, 9% external sources). *Receiving aid:* Freshmen: 49% (116); all full-time undergraduates: 49% (526). *Average award:* Freshmen: $8030; Undergraduates: $8575. *Scholarships, grants, and awards:* Federal Pell, FSEOG, state, private, college/university gift aid from institutional funds.

GIFT AID (NON-NEED-BASED) *Scholarships, grants, and awards by category:* *Academic interests/achievement:* business, engineering/technologies, general academic interests/achievements. *Tuition waivers:* Full or partial for employees or children of employees. *ROTC:* Naval cooperative, Air Force cooperative.

LOANS *Student loans:* $5,431,349 (37% need-based, 63% non-need-based). 74% of past graduating class borrowed through all loan programs. *Average indebtedness per student:* $24,052. *Average need-based loan:* Freshmen: $3613. Undergraduates: $4588. *Parent loans:* $2,568,767 (100% need-based). *Programs:* Federal Direct (Subsidized and Unsubsidized Stafford, PLUS).

WORK-STUDY *Federal work-study:* jobs available.

ATHLETIC AWARDS Total amount: $60,925 (100% need-based).

APPLYING FOR FINANCIAL AID *Required financial aid forms:* FAFSA, state aid form. *Financial aid deadline (priority):* 3/2. *Notification date:* Continuous beginning 3/15. Students must reply by 5/1 or within 6 weeks of notification.

CONTACT Priscilla Muha, Director of Financial Aid, California State University Maritime Academy, 200 Maritime Academy Drive, Vallejo, CA 94590-0644, 707-654-1275 or toll-free 800-561-1945. *Fax:* 707-654-1007. *E-mail:* pmuha@csum.edu. *Website:* http://www.csum.edu/.

CALIFORNIA STATE UNIVERSITY, MONTEREY BAY
Seaside, CA

Tuition & fees (CA res): $7043	Average undergraduate aid package: $11,621

ABOUT THE INSTITUTION State-supported, coed. *Awards:* bachelor's and master's degrees. 23 undergraduate majors. *Total enrollment:* 7,574. Undergraduates: 6,771. Freshmen: 926. Federal methodology is used as a basis for awarding need-based institutional aid.

UNDERGRADUATE EXPENSES for 2017–2018 *Application fee:* $55. *Tuition, state resident:* full-time $5742. *Tuition, nonresident:* full-time $17,622. *Required fees:* full-time $1301. *College room and board:* $12,396. Room and board charges vary according to board plan and housing facility.

FRESHMAN FINANCIAL AID (Fall 2017, est.) 828 applied for aid; of those 81% were deemed to have need. 95% of freshmen with need received aid; of those 14% had need fully met. *Average percent of need met:* 57% (excluding resources awarded to replace EFC). *Average financial aid package:* $11,840 (excluding resources awarded to replace EFC). 1% of all full-time freshmen had no need and received non-need-based gift aid.

UNDERGRADUATE FINANCIAL AID (Fall 2017, est.) 4,808 applied for aid; of those 90% were deemed to have need. 95% of undergraduates with need received aid; of those 12% had need fully met. *Average percent of need met:* 70% (excluding resources awarded to replace EFC). *Average financial aid package:* $11,621 (excluding resources awarded to replace EFC). 2% of all full-time undergraduates had no need and received non-need-based gift aid.

GIFT AID (NEED-BASED) *Total amount:* $37,660,223 (42% federal, 28% state, 30% institutional). *Receiving aid:* Freshmen: 57% (530); all full-time undergraduates: 58% (3,553). *Average award:* Freshmen: $10,955; Undergraduates: $9987. *Scholarships, grants, and awards:* Federal Pell, FSEOG, state, private, college/university gift aid from institutional funds.

GIFT AID (NON-NEED-BASED) *Total amount:* $1,513,000 (2% federal, 45% state, 15% institutional, 38% external sources). *Receiving aid:* Freshmen: 17% (154). Undergraduates: 10% (593). *Average award:* Freshmen: $874. Undergraduates: $1679. *Scholarships, grants, and awards by category:* *Academic interests/achievement:* business, general academic interests/achievements. *Special achievements/activities:* leadership. *Special characteristics:* children and siblings of alumni, general special characteristics, local/state students. *ROTC:* Air Force cooperative.

LOANS *Student loans:* $16,009,094 (70% need-based, 30% non-need-based). 64% of past graduating class borrowed through all loan programs. *Average indebtedness per student:* $19,962. *Average need-based loan:* Freshmen: $3363. Undergraduates: $4479. *Parent loans:* $2,701,745 (100% non-need-based). *Programs:* Federal Direct (Subsidized and Unsubsidized Stafford, PLUS), Perkins, private loans.

WORK-STUDY *Federal work-study:* Total amount: $136,632; jobs available. *State or other work-study/employment:* Part-time jobs available.

ATHLETIC AWARDS Total amount: $560,442 (100% non-need-based).

APPLYING FOR FINANCIAL AID *Required financial aid forms:* FAFSA, state aid form. *Financial aid deadline:* 8/30 (priority: 4/19). *Notification date:* Continuous beginning 2/1. Students must reply by 7/30.

CONTACT Office of Financial Aid, California State University, Monterey Bay, 100 Campus Center, Building 47, Seaside, CA 93955-8001, 831-582-5100. *Fax:* 831-582-3782. *Website:* http://www.csumb.edu/.

CALIFORNIA STATE UNIVERSITY, NORTHRIDGE
Northridge, CA

Tuition & fees (CA res): $6870	Average undergraduate aid package: $18,771

ABOUT THE INSTITUTION State-supported, coed. *Awards:* bachelor's, master's, and doctoral degrees. 59 undergraduate majors. *Total enrollment:* 39,916. Undergraduates: 35,552. Freshmen: 4,499. Federal methodology is used as a basis for awarding need-based institutional aid.

UNDERGRADUATE EXPENSES for 2017–2018 *Application fee:* $55. *Tuition, state resident:* full-time $6870. *Tuition, nonresident:* part-time $396 per unit. *College room and board:* $10,402. Room and board charges vary according to board plan and housing facility.
FRESHMAN FINANCIAL AID (Fall 2016) 4,006 applied for aid; of those 94% were deemed to have need. 100% of freshmen with need received aid. *Average financial aid package:* $11,212 (excluding resources awarded to replace EFC). 14% of all full-time freshmen had no need and received non-need-based gift aid.
UNDERGRADUATE FINANCIAL AID (Fall 2016) 23,508 applied for aid; of those 97% were deemed to have need. 100% of undergraduates with need received aid. *Average financial aid package:* $18,771 (excluding resources awarded to replace EFC). 17% of all full-time undergraduates had no need and received non-need-based gift aid.
GIFT AID (NEED-BASED) *Total amount:* $206,898,595 (43% federal, 56% state, 1% institutional). *Receiving aid:* Freshmen: 71% (3,118); all full-time undergraduates: 67% (19,387). *Average award:* Freshmen: $10,932; Undergraduates: $16,656. *Scholarships, grants, and awards:* Federal Pell, FSEOG, state, private, college/university gift aid from institutional funds.
GIFT AID (NON-NEED-BASED) *Total amount:* $9,199,226 (91% institutional, 9% external sources). *Receiving aid:* Freshmen: 15% (672). Undergraduates: 18% (5,219). *Average award:* Freshmen: $1511. Undergraduates: $1988. *Scholarships, grants, and awards by category: Academic interests/achievement:* business, communication, computer science, education, engineering/technologies, English, general academic interests/achievements, mathematics, social sciences. *Creative arts/performance:* journalism/publications, music. *Special achievements/activities:* leadership. *Tuition waivers:* Full or partial for employees or children of employees, senior citizens. *ROTC:* Army cooperative, Air Force cooperative.
LOANS *Student loans:* $70,458,204 (56% need-based, 44% non-need-based). 49% of past graduating class borrowed through all loan programs. *Average indebtedness per student:* $16,876. *Average need-based loan:* Freshmen: $4607. Undergraduates: $5999. *Parent loans:* $2,180,008 (100% non-need-based). *Programs:* Perkins.
WORK-STUDY *Federal work-study:* jobs available.
ATHLETIC AWARDS Total amount: $3,079,714 (100% non-need-based).
APPLYING FOR FINANCIAL AID *Required financial aid form:* FAFSA. *Financial aid deadline (priority):* 3/2. *Notification date:* Continuous beginning 4/1.
CONTACT Lili Vidal, Director of Financial Aid and Scholarships, California State University, Northridge, 18111 Nordhoff Street, Northridge, CA 91330-8307, 818-677-4085. *Fax:* 818-677-6787. *E-mail:* financial.aid@csun.edu.
Website: http://www.csun.edu/.

CALIFORNIA STATE UNIVERSITY, SACRAMENTO
Sacramento, CA

Tuition & fees (CA res): $6934	Average undergraduate aid package: $10,572

ABOUT THE INSTITUTION State-supported, coed. *Awards:* bachelor's, master's, and doctoral degrees. 55 undergraduate majors. *Total enrollment:* 30,670. Undergraduates: 28,064. Freshmen: 3,590. Federal methodology is used as a basis for awarding need-based institutional aid.
UNDERGRADUATE EXPENSES for 2018–2019 *Application fee:* $55. *Tuition, state resident:* full-time $5742; part-time $1665 per term. *Tuition, nonresident:* part-time $396 per credit hour. *Required fees:* full-time $1192; $731 per term. *College room and board:* $14,396; *Room only:* $9774. Room and board charges vary according to board plan and housing facility.
FRESHMAN FINANCIAL AID (Fall 2016) 3,405 applied for aid; of those 85% were deemed to have need. 96% of freshmen with need received aid; of those 8% had need fully met. *Average percent of need met:* 61% (excluding resources awarded to replace EFC). *Average financial aid package:* $10,662 (excluding resources awarded to replace EFC). 1% of all full-time freshmen had no need and received non-need-based gift aid.
UNDERGRADUATE FINANCIAL AID (Fall 2016) 19,743 applied for aid; of those 90% were deemed to have need. 96% of undergraduates with need received aid; of those 7% had need fully met. *Average percent of need met:* 60% (excluding resources awarded to replace EFC). *Average financial aid package:* $10,572

(excluding resources awarded to replace EFC). 1% of all full-time undergraduates had no need and received non-need-based gift aid.
GIFT AID (NEED-BASED) *Total amount:* $154,711,212 (42% federal, 33% state, 25% institutional). *Receiving aid:* Freshmen: 73% (2,675); all full-time undergraduates: 69% (16,037). *Average award:* Freshmen: $9142; Undergraduates: $8712. *Scholarships, grants, and awards:* Federal Pell, FSEOG, state, private, college/university gift aid from institutional funds, Federal Nursing.
GIFT AID (NON-NEED-BASED) *Total amount:* $4,337,226 (1% state, 40% institutional, 59% external sources). *Receiving aid:* Freshmen: 11% (412). Undergraduates: 6% (1,325). *Average award:* Freshmen: $992. Undergraduates: $1675. *Tuition waivers:* Full or partial for employees or children of employees. *ROTC:* Army cooperative, Air Force.
LOANS *Student loans:* $69,674,357 (55% need-based, 45% non-need-based). 54% of past graduating class borrowed through all loan programs. *Average indebtedness per student:* $20,052. *Average need-based loan:* Freshmen: $3179. Undergraduates: $4136. *Programs:* Federal Direct (Subsidized and Unsubsidized Stafford, PLUS), Perkins, Federal Nursing, college/university.
WORK-STUDY *Federal work-study:* jobs available. *State or other work-study/employment:* Part-time jobs available.
ATHLETIC AWARDS Total amount: $4,723,030 (100% need-based).
APPLYING FOR FINANCIAL AID *Required financial aid form:* FAFSA. *Financial aid deadline (priority):* 3/2. *Notification date:* Continuous beginning 4/11.
CONTACT Anita Kermes, Director of Financial Aid and Scholarships Office, California State University, Sacramento, 6000 J Street, Sacramento, CA 95819-6044, 916-278-6980. *Fax:* 916-278-6082. *E-mail:* anita.kermes@csus.edu.
Website: http://www.csus.edu/.

CALIFORNIA STATE UNIVERSITY, SAN BERNARDINO
San Bernardino, CA

Tuition & fees (CA res): $6656	Average undergraduate aid package: $9586

ABOUT THE INSTITUTION State-supported, coed. *Awards:* certificates, bachelor's, master's, and doctoral degrees. 42 undergraduate majors. *Total enrollment:* 20,461. Undergraduates: 18,243. Freshmen: 2,517. Federal methodology is used as a basis for awarding need-based institutional aid.
UNDERGRADUATE EXPENSES for 2018–2019 *Application fee:* $55. *Tuition, state resident:* full-time $5472. *Tuition, nonresident:* full-time $11,180; part-time $264 per credit hour. *Required fees:* full-time $1184. *College room and board:* $12,711. Room and board charges vary according to board plan and housing facility.
FRESHMAN FINANCIAL AID (Fall 2017, est.) 2,353 applied for aid; of those 92% were deemed to have need. 99% of freshmen with need received aid; of those 64% had need fully met. *Average percent of need met:* 85% (excluding resources awarded to replace EFC). *Average financial aid package:* $9590 (excluding resources awarded to replace EFC). 1% of all full-time freshmen had no need and received non-need-based gift aid.
UNDERGRADUATE FINANCIAL AID (Fall 2017, est.) 14,666 applied for aid; of those 95% were deemed to have need. 98% of undergraduates with need received aid; of those 60% had need fully met. *Average percent of need met:* 88% (excluding resources awarded to replace EFC). *Average financial aid package:* $9586 (excluding resources awarded to replace EFC). 1% of all full-time undergraduates had no need and received non-need-based gift aid.
GIFT AID (NEED-BASED) *Total amount:* $128,617,893 (44% federal, 34% state, 21% institutional, 1% external sources). *Receiving aid:* Freshmen: 85% (2,084); all full-time undergraduates: 81% (13,208). *Average award:* Freshmen: $9519; Undergraduates: $9648. *Scholarships, grants, and awards:* Federal Pell, FSEOG, state, private, college/university gift aid from institutional funds.
GIFT AID (NON-NEED-BASED) *Total amount:* $8,990,959 (95% institutional, 5% external sources). *Receiving aid:* Freshmen: 62% (1,509). Undergraduates: 39% (6,415). *Average award:* Freshmen: $5739. Undergraduates: $3827. *Scholarships, grants, and awards by category: Academic interests/achievement:* biological sciences, business, computer science, education, foreign languages, general academic interests/achievements, health fields, international studies, mathematics, physical sciences, social sciences. *Creative arts/performance:* art/fine arts, general creative arts/

performance, journalism/publications, music, theater/drama. *Special achievements/activities:* community service, general special achievements/activities, hobbies/interests, memberships. *Special characteristics:* children of public servants, children with a deceased or disabled parent, first-generation college students, handicapped students, veterans, veterans' children. *Tuition waivers:* Full or partial for employees or children of employees, senior citizens. *ROTC:* Army, Air Force.

LOANS *Student loans:* $38,656,034 (63% need-based, 37% non-need-based). 64% of past graduating class borrowed through all loan programs. *Average indebtedness per student:* $21,555. *Average need-based loan:* Freshmen: $3314. Undergraduates: $4187. *Parent loans:* $3,488,899 (13% need-based, 87% non-need-based). *Programs:* Federal Direct (Subsidized and Unsubsidized Stafford, PLUS), Perkins.

WORK-STUDY *Federal work-study:* Total amount: $1,731,359; 368 jobs averaging $4021.

ATHLETIC AWARDS Total amount: $691,941 (62% need-based, 38% non-need-based).

APPLYING FOR FINANCIAL AID *Required financial aid forms:* FAFSA, state aid form. *Financial aid deadline (priority):* 3/2. *Notification date:* Continuous beginning 4/1.

CONTACT Ms. Roseanna Ruiz, Director of Financial Aid, California State University, San Bernardino, 5500 University Parkway, San Bernardino, CA 92407-2397, 909-537-5227. *Fax:* 909-537-4024.
Website: http://www.csusb.edu/.

CALIFORNIA STATE UNIVERSITY, SAN MARCOS
San Marcos, CA

Tuition & fees (CA res): $13,390	Average undergraduate aid package: $10,594

ABOUT THE INSTITUTION State-supported, coed. *Awards:* bachelor's and master's degrees. 41 undergraduate majors. *Total enrollment:* 13,887. Undergraduates: 13,316. Freshmen: 2,499. Federal methodology is used as a basis for awarding need-based institutional aid.

UNDERGRADUATE EXPENSES for 2018–2019 *Application fee:* $65. *Tuition, state resident:* full-time $5742. *Tuition, nonresident:* full-time $14,670; part-time $396 per unit. *Required fees:* full-time $7648; $2433 per term. Part-time tuition and fees vary according to course load. *College room and board:* $13,227. Room and board charges vary according to housing facility.

FRESHMAN FINANCIAL AID (Fall 2016) 1,830 applied for aid; of those 80% were deemed to have need. 92% of freshmen with need received aid; of those 4% had need fully met. *Average percent of need met:* 62% (excluding resources awarded to replace EFC). *Average financial aid package:* $10,484 (excluding resources awarded to replace EFC). 1% of all full-time freshmen had no need and received non-need-based gift aid.

UNDERGRADUATE FINANCIAL AID (Fall 2016) 8,394 applied for aid; of those 87% were deemed to have need. 97% of undergraduates with need received aid; of those 3% had need fully met. *Average percent of need met:* 43% (excluding resources awarded to replace EFC). *Average financial aid package:* $10,594 (excluding resources awarded to replace EFC). 1% of all full-time undergraduates had no need and received non-need-based gift aid.

GIFT AID (NEED-BASED) *Total amount:* $65,289,917 (41% federal, 33% state, 24% institutional, 2% external sources). *Receiving aid:* Freshmen: 61% (1,250); all full-time undergraduates: 63% (6,528). *Average award:* Freshmen: $9260; Undergraduates: $8875. *Scholarships, grants, and awards:* Federal Pell, FSEOG, state, private, college/university gift aid from institutional funds.

GIFT AID (NON-NEED-BASED) *Total amount:* $178,405 (13% institutional, 87% external sources). *Receiving aid:* Freshmen: 1% (22). Undergraduates: 1% (63). *Average award:* Freshmen: $1813. Undergraduates: $1515. *Scholarships, grants, and awards by category:* Academic interests/achievement: general academic interests/achievements, mathematics. Creative arts/performance: art/fine arts. Special achievements/activities: leadership. Special characteristics: local/state students. *Tuition waivers:* Full or partial for employees or children of employees, senior citizens. *ROTC:* Army, Naval cooperative, Air Force cooperative.

LOANS *Student loans:* $35,980,067 (85% need-based, 15% non-need-based). 55% of past graduating class borrowed through all loan programs. *Average indebtedness per student:* $23,734. *Average need-based loan:* Freshmen: $3299. Undergrad-

uates: $4144. *Parent loans:* $3,022,153 (72% need-based, 28% non-need-based). *Programs:* Federal Direct (Subsidized and Unsubsidized Stafford, PLUS), Perkins, college/university.

WORK-STUDY *Federal work-study:* jobs available. *State or other work-study/employment:* Part-time jobs available.

ATHLETIC AWARDS Total amount: $718,550 (88% need-based, 12% non-need-based).

APPLYING FOR FINANCIAL AID *Required financial aid form:* FAFSA. *Financial aid deadline (priority):* 3/2. *Notification date:* Continuous beginning 3/2. Students must reply by 3/2 or within 4 weeks of notification.

CONTACT Financial Aid and Scholarships Office, California State University, San Marcos, 333 South Twin Oaks Valley Road, San Marcos, CA 92096-0001, 760-750-4850. *Fax:* 760-750-3047. *E-mail:* finaid@csusm.edu.
Website: http://www.csusm.edu/.

CALIFORNIA STATE UNIVERSITY, STANISLAUS
Turlock, CA

Tuition & fees (CA res): $7038	Average undergraduate aid package: $17,143

ABOUT THE INSTITUTION State-supported, coed. *Awards:* bachelor's, master's, and doctoral degrees. 50 undergraduate majors. *Total enrollment:* 10,003. Undergraduates: 8,891. Freshmen: 1,422. Federal methodology is used as a basis for awarding need-based institutional aid.

UNDERGRADUATE EXPENSES for 2017–2018 *Application fee:* $55. *Tuition, state resident:* full-time $5742. *Tuition, nonresident:* full-time $17,622. *Required fees:* full-time $1296. Full-time tuition and fees vary according to reciprocity agreements. Part-time tuition and fees vary according to reciprocity agreements. *College room and board:* $8670; *Room only:* $6507. Room and board charges vary according to board plan and housing facility.

FRESHMAN FINANCIAL AID (Fall 2017, est.) 1,199 applied for aid; of those 90% were deemed to have need. 100% of freshmen with need received aid; of those 99% had need fully met. *Average percent of need met:* 92% (excluding resources awarded to replace EFC). *Average financial aid package:* $16,904 (excluding resources awarded to replace EFC). 6% of all full-time freshmen had no need and received non-need-based gift aid.

UNDERGRADUATE FINANCIAL AID (Fall 2017, est.) 6,300 applied for aid; of those 93% were deemed to have need. 100% of undergraduates with need received aid; of those 99% had need fully met. *Average percent of need met:* 92% (excluding resources awarded to replace EFC). *Average financial aid package:* $17,143 (excluding resources awarded to replace EFC). 3% of all full-time undergraduates had no need and received non-need-based gift aid.

GIFT AID (NEED-BASED) *Total amount:* $112,617,439 (25% federal, 17% state, 1% institutional, 57% external sources). *Receiving aid:* Freshmen: 71% (970); all full-time undergraduates: 68% (5,136). *Average award:* Freshmen: $10,561; Undergraduates: $10,334. *Scholarships, grants, and awards:* Federal Pell, FSEOG, state, private, college/university gift aid from institutional funds.

GIFT AID (NON-NEED-BASED) *Total amount:* $7,353,353 (15% state, 57% institutional, 28% external sources). *Receiving aid:* Freshmen: 7% (93). Undergraduates: 5% (389). *Average award:* Freshmen: $2184. Undergraduates: $1901. *Scholarships, grants, and awards by category:* Academic interests/achievement: agriculture, area/ethnic studies, biological sciences, business, communication, computer science, education, English, foreign languages, general academic interests/achievements, health fields, humanities, international studies, mathematics, physical sciences, premedicine, social sciences. Creative arts/performance: art/fine arts, music. Special achievements/activities: community service, general special achievements/activities, leadership, memberships. Special characteristics: children of faculty/staff, first-generation college students, general special characteristics, local/state students. *Tuition waivers:* Full or partial for employees or children of employees.

LOANS *Student loans:* $58,253,430 (93% need-based, 7% non-need-based). 50% of past graduating class borrowed through all loan programs. *Average indebtedness per student:* $18,960. *Average need-based loan:* Freshmen: $3208. Undergraduates: $4053. *Parent loans:* $18,324,761 (76% need-based, 24% non-need-based). *Programs:* Federal Direct (Subsidized and Unsubsidized Stafford, PLUS), Perkins, private loans.

WORK-STUDY *Federal work-study:* Total amount: $2,293,782; 52 jobs averaging $3689. *State or other work-study/employment:* Part-time jobs available.

ATHLETIC AWARDS Total amount: $770,600 (66% need-based, 34% non-need-based).

APPLYING FOR FINANCIAL AID *Required financial aid forms:* FAFSA, institution's own form, state aid form. *Financial aid deadline (priority):* 3/2. *Notification date:* Continuous beginning 4/1. Students must reply within 3 weeks of notification.

CONTACT Office of Financial Aid and Scholarships, California State University, Stanislaus, One University Circle, Turlock, CA 95382, 209-667-3336 or toll-free 800-300-7420. *Fax:* 209-664-7064. *E-mail:* financial_aid@csustan.edu. *Website:* http://www.csustan.edu/.

CALIFORNIA UNIVERSITY OF MANAGEMENT AND SCIENCES
Anaheim, CA

CONTACT Financial Aid Office, California University of Management and Sciences, 721 North Euclid Street, Anaheim, CA 92801, 714-533-3946. *Website:* http://www.calums.edu/.

CALIFORNIA UNIVERSITY OF PENNSYLVANIA
California, PA

Tuition & fees: N/R	Average undergraduate aid package: $9213

ABOUT THE INSTITUTION State-supported, coed. *Awards:* certificates, associate, bachelor's, master's, and doctoral degrees. 50 undergraduate majors. *Total enrollment:* 7,788. Undergraduates: 5,557. Freshmen: 993. Federal methodology is used as a basis for awarding need-based institutional aid.

UNDERGRADUATE EXPENSES for 2018–2019 *Application fee:* $25. *Tuition, state resident:* part-time $312 per credit hour. *Tuition, nonresident:* part-time $468 per credit hour. Full-time tuition and fees vary according to course load, location, and student level. Part-time tuition and fees vary according to course load, location, and student level. *College room and board:* $10,344; *Room only:* $6592. Room and board charges vary according to board plan and housing facility.

FRESHMAN FINANCIAL AID (Fall 2016) 856 applied for aid; of those 84% were deemed to have need. 100% of freshmen with need received aid; of those 17% had need fully met. *Average percent of need met:* 53% (excluding resources awarded to replace EFC). *Average financial aid package:* $10,026 (excluding resources awarded to replace EFC). 2% of all full-time freshmen had no need and received non-need-based gift aid.

UNDERGRADUATE FINANCIAL AID (Fall 2016) 4,243 applied for aid; of those 84% were deemed to have need. 100% of undergraduates with need received aid; of those 7% had need fully met. *Average percent of need met:* 51% (excluding resources awarded to replace EFC). *Average financial aid package:* $9213 (excluding resources awarded to replace EFC). 2% of all full-time undergraduates had no need and received non-need-based gift aid.

GIFT AID (NEED-BASED) *Total amount:* $19,604,340 (52% federal, 33% state, 10% institutional, 5% external sources). *Receiving aid:* Freshmen: 65% (575); all full-time undergraduates: 62% (2,856). *Average award:* Freshmen: $6759; Undergraduates: $5997. *Scholarships, grants, and awards:* Federal Pell, FSEOG, state, private, college/university gift aid from institutional funds.

GIFT AID (NON-NEED-BASED) *Total amount:* $2,392,904 (2% federal, 4% state, 56% institutional, 38% external sources). *Receiving aid:* Freshmen: 28% (243). Undergraduates: 15% (678). *Average award:* Freshmen: $2669. Undergraduates: $4361. *Scholarships, grants, and awards by category:* Academic interests/achievement: general academic interests/achievements. Creative arts/performance: general creative arts/performance. Special achievements/activities: general special achievements/activities. Special characteristics: ethnic background, international students, members of minority groups, veterans. *Tuition waivers:* Full or partial for employees or children of employees. *ROTC:* Army.

LOANS *Student loans:* $34,139,303 (44% need-based, 56% non-need-based). 91% of past graduating class borrowed through all loan programs. *Average indebtedness per student:* $26,242. *Average need-based loan:* Freshmen: $3102. Undergraduates: $4142. *Parent loans:* $7,667,183 (100% non-need-based). *Programs:* Federal Direct (Subsidized and Unsubsidized Stafford, PLUS), Perkins.

WORK-STUDY *Federal work-study:* 666 jobs averaging $580. *State or other work-study/employment:* Total amount: $1,944,479 (27% need-based, 73% non-need-based). 1,116 part-time jobs averaging $1154.

ATHLETIC AWARDS Total amount: $1,227,166 (100% non-need-based).

APPLYING FOR FINANCIAL AID *Required financial aid form:* FAFSA. *Financial aid deadline:* Continuous. *Notification date:* Continuous beginning 12/1.

CONTACT Jeffrey Derubbo, Director of Financial Aid, California University of Pennsylvania, 250 University Avenue, California, PA 15419-1394, 724-938-4415 or toll-free 888-412-0479. *E-mail:* derubbo@calu.edu. *Website:* http://www.calu.edu/.

CALUMET COLLEGE OF SAINT JOSEPH
Whiting, IN

Tuition & fees: $19,870	Average undergraduate aid package: $13,997

ABOUT THE INSTITUTION Independent Roman Catholic, coed. *Awards:* certificates, associate, bachelor's, and master's degrees. 12 undergraduate majors. *Total enrollment:* 834. Undergraduates: 624. Freshmen: 98. Both federal and institutional methodology are used as a basis for awarding need-based institutional aid.

UNDERGRADUATE EXPENSES for 2018–2019 *Tuition:* full-time $18,900. Full-time tuition and fees vary according to course load and program. Part-time tuition and fees vary according to course load and program. *Payment plan:* Guaranteed tuition.

FRESHMAN FINANCIAL AID (Fall 2017, est.) 86 applied for aid; of those 91% were deemed to have need. 95% of freshmen with need received aid; of those 12% had need fully met. *Average percent of need met:* 51% (excluding resources awarded to replace EFC). *Average financial aid package:* $13,753 (excluding resources awarded to replace EFC). 3% of all full-time freshmen had no need and received non-need-based gift aid.

UNDERGRADUATE FINANCIAL AID (Fall 2017, est.) 384 applied for aid; of those 91% were deemed to have need. 97% of undergraduates with need received aid; of those 13% had need fully met. *Average percent of need met:* 48% (excluding resources awarded to replace EFC). *Average financial aid package:* $13,997 (excluding resources awarded to replace EFC). 3% of all full-time undergraduates had no need and received non-need-based gift aid.

GIFT AID (NEED-BASED) *Total amount:* $3,275,777 (40% federal, 34% state, 23% institutional, 3% external sources). *Receiving aid:* Freshmen: 54% (52); all full-time undergraduates: 59% (250). *Average award:* Freshmen: $11,388; Undergraduates: $9634. *Scholarships, grants, and awards:* Federal Pell, FSEOG, state, private, college/university gift aid from institutional funds, United Negro College Fund.

GIFT AID (NON-NEED-BASED) *Receiving aid:* Freshmen: 56% (54). Undergraduates: 62% (266). *Average award:* Freshmen: $1500. Undergraduates: $2427. *Scholarships, grants, and awards by category:* Academic interests/achievement: 35 awards ($127,340 total): general academic interests/achievements. Creative arts/performance: art/fine arts, creative writing, general creative arts/performance, theater/drama. Special achievements/activities: 51 awards ($67,024 total): general special achievements/activities, leadership. Special characteristics: 62 awards ($187,125 total): children and siblings of alumni, children of faculty/staff, general special characteristics, previous college experience, religious affiliation. *Tuition waivers:* Full or partial for children of alumni, employees or children of employees, senior citizens.

LOANS *Student loans:* $915,504 (84% need-based, 16% non-need-based). 80% of past graduating class borrowed through all loan programs. *Average indebtedness per student:* $24,431. *Average need-based loan:* Freshmen: $3078. Undergraduates: $3820. *Parent loans:* $335,824 (97% need-based, 3% non-need-based). *Programs:* Federal Direct (Subsidized and Unsubsidized Stafford, PLUS).

WORK-STUDY *Federal work-study:* Total amount: $17,793; 22 jobs averaging $809. *State or other work-study/employment:* Part-time jobs available.

ATHLETIC AWARDS Total amount: $1,755,858 (100% need-based).

APPLYING FOR FINANCIAL AID *Required financial aid form:* FAFSA. *Financial aid deadline (priority):* 4/15. *Notification date:* Continuous beginning 4/1.

CONTACT Lynn Miskus, Vice President for Business and Finance, Calumet College of Saint Joseph, 2400 New York Avenue, Whiting, IN 46394, 219-473-4310 or toll-free 877-700-9100. *E-mail:* lmiskus@ccsj.edu.

Website: http://www.ccsj.edu/.

CALVARY UNIVERSITY
Kansas City, MO

ABOUT THE INSTITUTION Independent nondenominational, coed. *Awards:* certificates, associate, bachelor's, and master's degrees. 34 undergraduate majors. *Total enrollment:* 271. Undergraduates: 231. Freshmen: 32.

GIFT AID (NEED-BASED) *Scholarships, grants, and awards:* Federal Pell, FSEOG, private, college/university gift aid from institutional funds.

GIFT AID (NON-NEED-BASED) *Scholarships, grants, and awards by category: Academic interests/achievement:* general academic interests/achievements, religion/biblical studies. *Creative arts/performance:* general creative arts/performance. *Special achievements/activities:* general special achievements/activities, religious involvement. *Special characteristics:* children and siblings of alumni, children of educators, children of faculty/staff, relatives of clergy, religious affiliation, siblings of current students, spouses of current students.

LOANS *Programs:* Federal Direct (Subsidized and Unsubsidized Stafford, PLUS).

WORK-STUDY *Federal work-study:* 8 jobs averaging $1687. *State or other work-study/employment:* Part-time jobs available.

APPLYING FOR FINANCIAL AID *Required financial aid forms:* FAFSA, scholarship application.

CONTACT Mr. Charles Kurtz, Assistant Director of Financial Aid, Calvary University, 15800 Calvary Road, Kansas City, MO 64147-1341, 816-425-6136 or toll-free 800-326-3960. *Fax:* 816-425-6134. *E-mail:* finaid@calvary.edu.

Website: http://www.calvary.edu/.

CALVIN COLLEGE
Grand Rapids, MI

Tuition & fees: $33,100	Average undergraduate aid package: $23,940

ABOUT THE INSTITUTION Independent Christian Reformed, coed. *Awards:* bachelor's and master's degrees. 102 undergraduate majors. *Total enrollment:* 3,840. Undergraduates: 4,282. Freshmen: 909. Both federal and institutional methodology are used as a basis for awarding need-based institutional aid.

UNDERGRADUATE EXPENSES for 2017–2018 *Application fee:* $35. *Comprehensive fee:* $43,090 includes full-time tuition ($33,100) and room and board ($9990). Full-time tuition and fees vary according to degree level, program, and student level. Room and board charges vary according to board plan and housing facility. *Part-time tuition:* $790 per credit hour. Part-time tuition and fees vary according to course load, degree level, and student level.

FRESHMAN FINANCIAL AID (Fall 2017, est.) 794 applied for aid; of those 73% were deemed to have need. 100% of freshmen with need received aid; of those 20% had need fully met. *Average percent of need met:* 77% (excluding resources awarded to replace EFC). *Average financial aid package:* $25,195 (excluding resources awarded to replace EFC). 34% of all full-time freshmen had no need and received non-need-based gift aid.

UNDERGRADUATE FINANCIAL AID (Fall 2017, est.) 2,809 applied for aid; of those 75% were deemed to have need. 100% of undergraduates with need received aid; of those 18% had need fully met. *Average percent of need met:* 73% (excluding resources awarded to replace EFC). *Average financial aid package:* $23,940 (excluding resources awarded to replace EFC). 35% of all full-time undergraduates had no need and received non-need-based gift aid.

GIFT AID (NEED-BASED) *Total amount:* $39,353,603 (10% federal, 6% state, 82% institutional, 2% external sources). *Receiving aid:* Freshmen: 66% (581); all full-time undergraduates: 59% (2,090). *Average award:* Freshmen: $20,150; Undergraduates: $18,198. *Scholarships, grants, and awards:* Federal Pell, FSEOG, state, private, college/university gift aid from institutional funds.

GIFT AID (NON-NEED-BASED) *Total amount:* $20,968,175 (97% institutional, 3% external sources). *Receiving aid:* Freshmen: 10% (85). Undergraduates: 7% (242). *Average award:* Freshmen: $15,382. Undergraduates: $11,693. *Scholarships, grants, and awards by category: Academic interests/achievement:* architecture, area/ethnic studies, biological sciences, business, communication, computer science, education, engineering/technologies, English, foreign languages, general academic interests/achievements, health fields, home economics, humanities, international studies, mathematics, physical sciences, premedicine, religion/biblical studies, social sciences. *Creative arts/performance:* applied art and design, art/fine arts, cinema/film/broadcasting, creative writing, journalism/publications, music, performing arts, theater/drama. *Special achievements/activities:* community service, leadership, religious involvement. *Special characteristics:* adult students, children and siblings of alumni, children of faculty/staff, children of union members/company employees, children of workers in trades, children with a deceased or disabled parent, ethnic background, first-generation college students, handicapped students, international students, local/state students, members of minority groups, out-of-state students, religious affiliation, twins, veterans, veterans' children. *Tuition waivers:* Full or partial for employees or children of employees. *ROTC:* Army cooperative.

LOANS *Student loans:* $20,186,776 (69% need-based, 31% non-need-based). 64% of past graduating class borrowed through all loan programs. *Average indebtedness per student:* $31,478. *Average need-based loan:* Freshmen: $3403. Undergraduates: $6077. *Parent loans:* $2,946,853 (52% need-based, 48% non-need-based). *Programs:* Federal Direct (Subsidized and Unsubsidized Stafford, PLUS), state, college/university, alternative loans.

WORK-STUDY *Federal work-study:* Total amount: $752,459; 1,217 jobs averaging $1079. *State or other work-study/employment:* Part-time jobs available.

APPLYING FOR FINANCIAL AID *Required financial aid form:* FAFSA. *Financial aid deadline (priority):* 2/1. *Notification date:* Continuous beginning 12/15.

CONTACT Ms. Emily Aungst, Financial Aid Department Assistant, Calvin College, Spoelhof Center, Grand Rapids, MI 49546, 800-688-0122. *Fax:* 616-526-6883. *E-mail:* finaid@calvin.edu.

Website: http://www.calvin.edu/.

CAMBRIDGE COLLEGE
Boston, MA

CONTACT Dr. Frank Lauder, Director of Financial Aid, Cambridge College, 1000 Massachusetts Avenue, Cambridge, MA 02138, 617-868-1000 Ext. 1440 or toll-free 800-877-4723. *Fax:* 617-349-3561. *E-mail:* francis.lauder@cambridgecollege.edu.

Website: http://www.cambridgecollege.edu/.

CAMERON UNIVERSITY
Lawton, OK

Tuition & fees (OK res): $6180	Average undergraduate aid package: $8706

ABOUT THE INSTITUTION State-supported, coed. *Awards:* associate, bachelor's, and master's degrees. 35 undergraduate majors. *Total enrollment:* 4,524. Undergraduates: 4,150. Freshmen: 638. Federal methodology is used as a basis for awarding need-based institutional aid.

UNDERGRADUATE EXPENSES for 2017–2018 *Application fee:* $25. *Tuition, state resident:* full-time $4470; part-time $149 per credit hour. *Tuition, nonresident:* full-time $13,800; part-time $460 per credit hour. *Required fees:* full-time $1710; $57 per credit hour. Full-time tuition and fees vary according to course level, course load, location, program, and student level. Part-time tuition and fees vary according to course level, course load, location, program, and student level. *College room and board:* $5452; *Room only:* $2222. Room and board charges vary according to board plan and housing facility.

FRESHMAN FINANCIAL AID (Fall 2016) 589 applied for aid; of those 88% were deemed to have need. 97% of freshmen with need received aid; of those 6% had need fully met. *Average percent of need met:* 53% (excluding resources awarded to replace EFC). *Average financial aid package:* $7985 (excluding resources awarded to replace EFC). 8% of all full-time freshmen had no need and received non-need-based gift aid.

UNDERGRADUATE FINANCIAL AID (Fall 2016) 2,344 applied for aid; of those 90% were deemed to have need. 96% of undergraduates with need received aid; of those 6% had need fully met. *Average percent of need met:* 55% (excluding resources awarded to replace EFC). *Average financial aid package:* $8706 (excluding resources awarded to replace EFC). 8% of all full-time undergraduates had no need and received non-need-based gift aid.

GIFT AID (NEED-BASED) *Total amount:* $12,734,743 (77% federal, 16% state, 3% institutional, 4% external sources). *Receiving aid:* Freshmen: 61% (441); all full-time undergraduates: 58% (1,777). *Average award:* Freshmen: $6224; Undergraduates: $6240. *Scholarships, grants, and awards:* Federal Pell, FSEOG, state, private, college/university gift aid from institutional funds.

GIFT AID (NON-NEED-BASED) *Total amount:* $1,051,892 (27% federal, 16% state, 30% institutional, 27% external sources). *Receiving aid:* Freshmen: 3% (20). Undergraduates: 2% (57). *Average award:* Freshmen: $2545. Undergraduates: $3184. *Scholarships, grants, and awards by category: Academic interests/ achievement:* agriculture, biological sciences, business, communication, computer science, education, engineering/technologies, English, foreign languages, general academic interests/achievements, home economics, mathematics, military science, physical sciences, social sciences. *Creative arts/performance:* art/fine arts, cinema/film/ broadcasting, creative writing, debating, journalism/publications, music, performing arts, theater/drama. *Special achievements/activities:* cheerleading/drum major, general special achievements/activities, leadership. *Special characteristics:* children of faculty/ staff, international students, members of minority groups, out-of-state students, veterans, veterans' children. *Tuition waivers:* Full or partial for employees or children of employees, senior citizens. *ROTC:* Army.

LOANS *Student loans:* $12,412,379 (84% need-based, 16% non-need-based). 56% of past graduating class borrowed through all loan programs. *Average indebtedness per student:* $23,961. *Average need-based loan:* Freshmen: $2926. Undergraduates: $3708. *Parent loans:* $138,604 (15% need-based, 85% non-need-based). *Programs:* Federal Direct (Subsidized and Unsubsidized Stafford, PLUS).

WORK-STUDY *Federal work-study:* 57 jobs averaging $2069. *State or other work-study/employment:* Total amount: $49,209 (72% need-based, 28% non-need-based). 261 part-time jobs averaging $2986.

ATHLETIC AWARDS Total amount: $791,743 (35% need-based, 65% non-need-based).

APPLYING FOR FINANCIAL AID *Required financial aid form:* FAFSA. *Financial aid deadline:* Continuous. *Notification date:* Continuous beginning 4/1. Students must reply by 8/1 or within 2 weeks of notification.

CONTACT Mr. Gary Garoffolo, Director of Financial Aid, Cameron University, 2800 West Gore Boulevard, Lawton, OK 73505-6377, 580-581-2293 or toll-free 888-454-7600. *Fax:* 580-581-2556. *E-mail:* ggaroffo@cameron.edu. *Website:* http://www.cameron.edu/.

CAMPBELLSVILLE UNIVERSITY
Campbellsville, KY

Tuition & fees: $25,400	Average undergraduate aid package: $19,583

ABOUT THE INSTITUTION Independent Kentucky Baptist Convention, coed. *Awards:* certificates, associate, bachelor's, master's, and doctoral degrees. 55 undergraduate majors. *Total enrollment:* 8,056. Undergraduates: 4,099. Freshmen: 540. Federal methodology is used as a basis for awarding need-based institutional aid.

UNDERGRADUATE EXPENSES for 2017–2018 *Application fee:* $20. *Comprehensive fee:* $33,400 includes full-time tuition ($24,900), mandatory fees ($500), and room and board ($8000). Full-time tuition and fees vary according to course load, location, and program. Room and board charges vary according to housing facility. *Part-time tuition:* $1038 per credit hour. *Part-time fees:* $250 per year. Part-time tuition and fees vary according to class time, course load, location, and program.

FRESHMAN FINANCIAL AID (Fall 2016) 513 applied for aid; of those 92% were deemed to have need. 100% of freshmen with need received aid; of those 21% had need fully met. *Average percent of need met:* 79% (excluding resources awarded to replace EFC). *Average financial aid package:* $22,539 (excluding resources awarded to replace EFC). 8% of all full-time freshmen had no need and received non-need-based gift aid.

UNDERGRADUATE FINANCIAL AID (Fall 2016) 1,646 applied for aid; of those 93% were deemed to have need. 100% of undergraduates with need received aid; of those 17% had need fully met. *Average percent of need met:* 76% (excluding resources awarded to replace EFC). *Average financial aid package:*

$19,583 (excluding resources awarded to replace EFC). 8% of all full-time undergraduates had no need and received non-need-based gift aid.

GIFT AID (NEED-BASED) *Total amount:* $24,288,781 (18% federal, 21% state, 57% institutional, 4% external sources). *Receiving aid:* Freshmen: 90% (470); all full-time undergraduates: 85% (1,500). *Average award:* Freshmen: $20,276; Undergraduates: $17,119. *Scholarships, grants, and awards:* Federal Pell, FSEOG, state, private, college/university gift aid from institutional funds.

GIFT AID (NON-NEED-BASED) *Total amount:* $3,173,182 (1% federal, 14% state, 71% institutional, 14% external sources). *Receiving aid:* Freshmen: 14% (72). Undergraduates: 11% (190). *Average award:* Freshmen: $14,276. Undergraduates: $11,711. *Scholarships, grants, and awards by category: Academic interests/ achievement:* biological sciences, business, communication, computer science, education, English, general academic interests/achievements, health fields, humanities, mathematics, physical sciences, premedicine, religion/biblical studies, social sciences. *Creative arts/performance:* art/fine arts, journalism/publications, music, theater/ drama. *Special achievements/activities:* cheerleading/drum major, junior miss, leadership, religious involvement. *Special characteristics:* adult students, children of educators, children of faculty/staff, international students, relatives of clergy, religious affiliation, veterans. *Tuition waivers:* Full or partial for employees or children of employees, adult students, senior citizens. *ROTC:* Army cooperative.

LOANS *Student loans:* $9,096,973 (74% need-based, 26% non-need-based). 71% of past graduating class borrowed through all loan programs. *Average indebtedness per student:* $21,756. *Average need-based loan:* Freshmen: $2834. Undergraduates: $3503. *Parent loans:* $1,524,961 (44% need-based, 56% non-need-based). *Programs:* Federal Direct (Subsidized and Unsubsidized Stafford, PLUS), Perkins.

WORK-STUDY *Federal work-study:* jobs available. *State or other work-study/employment:* Total amount: $30,880 (49% need-based, 51% non-need-based). Part-time jobs available.

ATHLETIC AWARDS Total amount: $3,318,859 (53% need-based, 47% non-need-based).

APPLYING FOR FINANCIAL AID *Required financial aid form:* FAFSA. *Financial aid deadline (priority):* 11/1. *Notification date:* Continuous beginning 12/15. Students must reply within 2 weeks of notification.

CONTACT Chris Mapes, Director of Financial Aid, Campbellsville University, 1 University Drive, Campbellsville, KY 42718, 270-789-5013 or toll-free 800-264-6014. *Fax:* 270-789-5079. *E-mail:* finaid@campbellsville.edu. *Website:* http://www.campbellsville.edu/.

CAMPBELL UNIVERSITY
Buies Creek, NC

Tuition & fees: $31,190	Average undergraduate aid package: $25,720

ABOUT THE INSTITUTION Independent North Carolina Baptist State Convention, coed. 85 undergraduate majors. Both federal and institutional methodology are used as a basis for awarding need-based institutional aid.

UNDERGRADUATE EXPENSES for 2017–2018 *Comprehensive fee:* $42,030 includes full-time tuition ($29,900), mandatory fees ($1290), and room and board ($10,840). *College room only:* $5190. Full-time tuition and fees vary according to class time, course load, location, and program. Room and board charges vary according to board plan and housing facility. *Part-time tuition:* $595 per credit hour. Part-time tuition and fees vary according to class time, course load, location, and program.

FRESHMAN FINANCIAL AID (Fall 2017, est.) 707 applied for aid; of those 75% were deemed to have need. 100% of freshmen with need received aid; of those 34% had need fully met. *Average percent of need met:* 79% (excluding resources awarded to replace EFC). *Average financial aid package:* $29,970 (excluding resources awarded to replace EFC). 23% of all full-time freshmen had no need and received non-need-based gift aid.

UNDERGRADUATE FINANCIAL AID (Fall 2017, est.) 3,005 applied for aid; of those 79% were deemed to have need. 100% of undergraduates with need received aid; of those 26% had need fully met. *Average percent of need met:* 65% (excluding resources awarded to replace EFC). *Average financial aid package:* $25,720 (excluding resources awarded to replace EFC). 17% of all full-time undergraduates had no need and received non-need-based gift aid.

GIFT AID (NEED-BASED) *Total amount:* $53,341,001 (14% federal, 14% state, 70% institutional, 2% external sources). *Receiving aid:* Freshmen: 50% (392); all full-time undergraduates: 52% (1,882). *Average award:* Freshmen: $7959; Undergrad-

uates: $7339. *Scholarships, grants, and awards:* Federal Pell, FSEOG, state, private, college/university gift aid from institutional funds.

GIFT AID (NON-NEED-BASED) *Total amount:* $11,219,962 (98% institutional, 2% external sources). *Receiving aid:* Freshmen: 67% (520). Undergraduates: 56% (2,018). *Average award:* Freshmen: $19,067. Undergraduates: $16,756. *Scholarships, grants, and awards by category:* Academic interests/achievement: 2,905 awards ($40,314,377 total): general academic interests/achievements. *Creative arts/performance:* 42 awards ($83,800 total): art/fine arts, creative writing, journalism/publications, music, theater/drama. *Special achievements/activities:* 38 awards ($138,588 total): cheerleading/drum major, religious involvement. *Special characteristics:* 900 awards ($3,042,035 total): children of faculty/staff, local/state students, out-of-state students, siblings of current students, veterans. *Tuition waivers:* Full or partial for employees or children of employees.

LOANS *Student loans:* $29,264,883 (92% need-based, 8% non-need-based). 70% of past graduating class borrowed through all loan programs. *Average indebtedness per student:* $29,975. *Average need-based loan:* Freshmen: $3213. Undergraduates: $4210. *Parent loans:* $38,651,522 (91% need-based, 9% non-need-based). *Programs:* Federal Direct (Subsidized and Unsubsidized Stafford, PLUS), Perkins, state.

WORK-STUDY *Federal work-study:* Total amount: $510,672; 288 jobs averaging $1806. *State or other work-study/employment:* Part-time jobs available.

ATHLETIC AWARDS Total amount: $3,652,888 (89% need-based, 11% non-need-based).

APPLYING FOR FINANCIAL AID *Required financial aid form:* FAFSA. *Financial aid deadline (priority):* 2/15. *Notification date:* Continuous. Students must reply within 2 weeks of notification.

CONTACT Merry M. Taylor, Financial Aid Office, Campbell University, PO Box 36, Buies Creek, NC 27506, 910-893-1310 or toll-free 800-334-4111. *Fax:* 910-814-5788. *E-mail:* taylorm@campbell.edu. *Website:* http://www.campbell.edu/.

CANISIUS COLLEGE
Buffalo, NY

Tuition & fees: $28,488	Average undergraduate aid package: $30,770

ABOUT THE INSTITUTION Independent Roman Catholic (Jesuit), coed. *Awards:* certificates, associate, bachelor's, and master's degrees. 99 undergraduate majors. *Total enrollment:* 3,464. Undergraduates: 2,396. Freshmen: 553. Federal methodology is used as a basis for awarding need-based institutional aid.

UNDERGRADUATE EXPENSES for 2018–2019 *Comprehensive fee:* $39,788 includes full-time tuition ($27,000), mandatory fees ($1488), and room and board ($11,300). *College room only:* $5764. Room and board charges vary according to board plan and housing facility. *Part-time tuition:* $999 per credit hour. *Part-time fees:* $20.50 per credit hour; $83 per term.

FRESHMAN FINANCIAL AID (Fall 2017, est.) 514 applied for aid; of those 90% were deemed to have need. 100% of freshmen with need received aid; of those 24% had need fully met. *Average percent of need met:* 85% (excluding resources awarded to replace EFC). *Average financial aid package:* $34,108 (excluding resources awarded to replace EFC). 15% of all full-time freshmen had no need and received non-need-based gift aid.

UNDERGRADUATE FINANCIAL AID (Fall 2017, est.) 1,909 applied for aid; of those 92% were deemed to have need. 100% of undergraduates with need received aid; of those 22% had need fully met. *Average percent of need met:* 79% (excluding resources awarded to replace EFC). *Average financial aid package:* $30,770 (excluding resources awarded to replace EFC). 21% of all full-time undergraduates had no need and received non-need-based gift aid.

GIFT AID (NEED-BASED) *Total amount:* $40,460,790 (10% federal, 8% state, 81% institutional, 1% external sources). *Receiving aid:* Freshmen: 84% (463); all full-time undergraduates: 75% (1,737). *Average award:* Freshmen: $27,663; Undergraduates: $24,341. *Scholarships, grants, and awards:* Federal Pell, FSEOG, state, private, college/university gift aid from institutional funds, United Negro College Fund.

GIFT AID (NON-NEED-BASED) *Total amount:* $4,215,774 (99% institutional, 1% external sources). *Receiving aid:* Freshmen: 22% (119). Undergraduates: 17% (398). *Average award:* Freshmen: $19,306. Undergraduates: $18,008. *Scholarships, grants, and awards by category:* Academic interests/achievement: 1,742

---

awards ($25,716,935 total): general academic interests/achievements. *Creative arts/performance:* 52 awards ($100,000 total): art/fine arts, music. *Special achievements/activities:* religious involvement. *Special characteristics:* 490 awards ($3,034,241 total): children and siblings of alumni, children of educators, children of faculty/staff, international students, out-of-state students, religious affiliation, veterans. *Tuition waivers:* Full or partial for employees or children of employees. *ROTC:* Army.

LOANS *Student loans:* $14,888,691 (72% need-based, 28% non-need-based). 77% of past graduating class borrowed through all loan programs. *Average indebtedness per student:* $33,694. *Average need-based loan:* Freshmen: $4188. Undergraduates: $4698. *Parent loans:* $3,057,999 (44% need-based, 56% non-need-based). *Programs:* Federal Direct (Subsidized and Unsubsidized Stafford, PLUS).

WORK-STUDY *Federal work-study:* Total amount: $944,800; 357 jobs averaging $1802. *State or other work-study/employment:* Total amount: $39,463 (98% need-based, 2% non-need-based). Part-time jobs available.

ATHLETIC AWARDS Total amount: $2,169,999 (54% need-based, 46% non-need-based).

APPLYING FOR FINANCIAL AID *Required financial aid forms:* FAFSA, state aid form. *Financial aid deadline:* Continuous. *Notification date:* Continuous beginning 12/20. Students must reply by 5/1.

CONTACT Ms. Mary Koehneke, Associate Director of Student Records and Financial Services, Canisius College, 2001 Main Street, Buffalo, NY 14208-1098, 716-888-2600 or toll-free 800-843-1517. *Fax:* 716-888-2377. *E-mail:* mkoehnek@canisius.edu. *Website:* http://www.canisius.edu/.

CAPELLA UNIVERSITY
Minneapolis, MN

CONTACT University Services, Capella University, 222 South Ninth Street, Minneapolis, MN 55402, 888-227-3552 or toll-free 866-283-7921. *Website:* http://www.capella.edu/.

CAPITAL UNIVERSITY
Columbus, OH

Tuition & fees: $35,466	Average undergraduate aid package: $28,438

ABOUT THE INSTITUTION Independent Evangelical Lutheran Church in America, coed. *Awards:* certificates, bachelor's, master's, and doctoral degrees. 60 undergraduate majors. *Total enrollment:* 3,384. Undergraduates: 2,699. Freshmen: 595. Federal methodology is used as a basis for awarding need-based institutional aid.

UNDERGRADUATE EXPENSES for 2018–2019 *Application fee:* $25. *Comprehensive fee:* $46,308 includes full-time tuition ($35,146), mandatory fees ($320), and room and board ($10,842). Full-time tuition and fees vary according to course load. Room and board charges vary according to board plan and housing facility. *Part-time tuition:* $1172 per credit hour. Part-time tuition and fees vary according to course load.

FRESHMAN FINANCIAL AID (Fall 2016) 582 applied for aid; of those 89% were deemed to have need. 100% of freshmen with need received aid; of those 33% had need fully met. *Average percent of need met:* 87% (excluding resources awarded to replace EFC). *Average financial aid package:* $30,669 (excluding resources awarded to replace EFC). 16% of all full-time freshmen had no need and received non-need-based gift aid.

UNDERGRADUATE FINANCIAL AID (Fall 2016) 2,150 applied for aid; of those 91% were deemed to have need. 100% of undergraduates with need received aid; of those 30% had need fully met. *Average percent of need met:* 80% (excluding resources awarded to replace EFC). *Average financial aid package:* $28,438 (excluding resources awarded to replace EFC). 20% of all full-time undergraduates had no need and received non-need-based gift aid.

GIFT AID (NEED-BASED) *Total amount:* $53,543,114 (7% federal, 93% institutional). *Receiving aid:* Freshmen: 82% (504); all full-time undergraduates: 76% (1,851). *Average award:* Freshmen: $25,304; Undergraduates: $23,427. *Scholarships, grants, and awards:* Federal Pell, FSEOG, state, private, college/university gift aid from institutional funds.

GIFT AID (NON-NEED-BASED) *Total amount:* $2,194,472 (2% institutional, 98% external sources). *Receiving aid:* Freshmen: 84% (517). Undergraduates: 76% (1,861). *Average award:* Freshmen: $22,863. Undergraduates: $20,185. *Scholarships, grants, and awards by category: Academic interests/achievement:* general academic interests/achievements. *Creative arts/performance:* music, performing arts. *Special achievements/activities:* hobbies/interests, leadership, religious involvement. *Special characteristics:* children and siblings of alumni, children of faculty/staff, ethnic background, international students, members of minority groups, out-of-state students, relatives of clergy, religious affiliation, siblings of current students. *Tuition waivers:* Full or partial for employees or children of employees, senior citizens. *ROTC:* Army, Air Force cooperative.

LOANS *Student loans:* $19,420,599 (39% need-based, 61% non-need-based). 80% of past graduating class borrowed through all loan programs. *Average indebtedness per student:* $32,515. *Average need-based loan:* Freshmen: $3919. Undergraduates: $4665. *Parent loans:* $7,558,133 (100% non-need-based). *Programs:* Federal Direct (Subsidized and Unsubsidized Stafford, PLUS), Perkins, Federal Nursing, college/university.

WORK-STUDY Federal work-study jobs available. *State or other work-study/employment:* Part-time jobs available.

APPLYING FOR FINANCIAL AID *Required financial aid form:* FAFSA. *Financial aid deadline (priority):* 3/1. *Notification date:* Continuous beginning 1/15. Students must reply by 5/1.

CONTACT Mr. John Brown, Director of Financial Aid, Capital University, 1 College and Main Street, Columbus, OH 43209-2394, 614-236-6511 or toll-free 866-544-6175. *Fax:* 614-236-6926. *E-mail:* finaid@capital.edu. *Website:* http://www.capital.edu/.

CAPITOL TECHNOLOGY UNIVERSITY
Laurel, MD

CONTACT Suzanne Thompson, Director of Financial Aid, Capitol Technology University, 11301 Springfield Road, Laurel, MD 20708-9759, 301-369-2800 Ext. 3037 or toll-free 800-950-1992. *Fax:* 301-369-2328. *E-mail:* sthompson@capitol-college.edu. *Website:* http://www.captechu.edu/.

CARDINAL STRITCH UNIVERSITY
Milwaukee, WI

Tuition & fees: $28,844	Average undergraduate aid package: $23,056

ABOUT THE INSTITUTION Independent Roman Catholic, coed. *Awards:* certificates, associate, bachelor's, master's, and doctoral degrees. 40 undergraduate majors. *Total enrollment:* 2,355. Undergraduates: 1,543. Freshmen: 141. Both federal and institutional methodology are used as a basis for awarding need-based institutional aid.

UNDERGRADUATE EXPENSES for 2017–2018 *Comprehensive fee:* $36,962 includes full-time tuition ($28,844) and room and board ($8118). Full-time tuition and fees vary according to degree level, program, and reciprocity agreements. Room and board charges vary according to board plan and housing facility. *Part-time tuition:* $900 per credit hour. Part-time tuition and fees vary according to course load, degree level, program, and reciprocity agreements.

FRESHMAN FINANCIAL AID (Fall 2017, est.) 92 applied for aid; of those 92% were deemed to have need. 99% of freshmen with need received aid; of those 5% had need fully met. *Average percent of need met:* 80% (excluding resources awarded to replace EFC). *Average financial aid package:* $28,810 (excluding resources awarded to replace EFC). 39% of all full-time freshmen had no need and received non-need-based gift aid.

UNDERGRADUATE FINANCIAL AID (Fall 2017, est.) 693 applied for aid; of those 90% were deemed to have need. 99% of undergraduates with need received aid; of those 10% had need fully met. *Average percent of need met:* 70% (excluding resources awarded to replace EFC). *Average financial aid package:* $23,056 (excluding resources awarded to replace EFC). 26% of all full-time undergraduates had no need and received non-need-based gift aid.

GIFT AID (NEED-BASED) *Total amount:* $11,672,725 (20% federal, 10% state, 68% institutional, 2% external sources). *Receiving aid:* Freshmen: 60% (84); all full-time undergraduates: 65% (609). *Average award:* Freshmen: $23,884; Undergraduates: $18,528. *Scholarships, grants, and awards:* Federal Pell, FSEOG, state, private, college/university gift aid from institutional funds, United Negro College Fund.

GIFT AID (NON-NEED-BASED) *Total amount:* $4,712,571 (98% institutional, 2% external sources). *Receiving aid:* Freshmen: 1% (1). Undergraduates: 4% (41). *Average award:* Freshmen: $19,678. Undergraduates: $18,306. *Scholarships, grants, and awards by category: Academic interests/achievement:* 819 awards ($8,473,220 total): general academic interests/achievements. *Creative arts/performance:* 36 awards ($68,750 total): art/fine arts, music, theater/drama. *Special characteristics:* 378 awards ($947,869 total): children and siblings of alumni, children of current students, children of faculty/staff, international students, religious affiliation, siblings of current students, spouses of current students, veterans. *Tuition waivers:* Full or partial for employees or children of employees.

LOANS *Student loans:* $7,438,718 (84% need-based, 16% non-need-based). 66% of past graduating class borrowed through all loan programs. *Average indebtedness per student:* $31,526. *Average need-based loan:* Freshmen: $3403. Undergraduates: $4046. *Parent loans:* $663,020 (51% need-based, 49% non-need-based). *Programs:* Federal Direct (Subsidized and Unsubsidized Stafford, PLUS), Perkins, state.

WORK-STUDY *Federal work-study:* Total amount: $793,037; 397 jobs averaging $2093. *State or other work-study/employment:* Total amount: $211,750 (69% need-based, 31% non-need-based). Part-time jobs available.

ATHLETIC AWARDS Total amount: $880,256 (37% need-based, 63% non-need-based).

APPLYING FOR FINANCIAL AID *Required financial aid forms:* FAFSA, institution's own form. *Financial aid deadline:* Continuous. *Notification date:* Continuous beginning 12/1. Students must reply within 2 weeks of notification.

CONTACT Financial Aid Office, Cardinal Stritch University, 6801 North Yates Road, Milwaukee, WI 53217-3985, 414-410-4048 or toll-free 800-347-8822 Ext. 4040. *E-mail:* finaid@stritch.edu. *Website:* http://www.stritch.edu/.

CAREERS UNLIMITED
Orem, UT

CONTACT Financial Aid Office, Careers Unlimited, 1176 South 1480 West, Orem, UT 84058, 801-426-8234. *Website:* http://www.ucdh.edu/.

CARIBBEAN UNIVERSITY
Bayamón, PR

CONTACT Financial Aid Office, Caribbean University, Box 493, Bayamón, PR 00960-0493, 787-780-0070. *Website:* http://www.caribbean.edu/.

CARIBBEAN UNIVERSITY–CAROLINA
Carolina, PR

CONTACT Financial Aid Office, Caribbean University–Carolina, Calle Ignacio Arzuaga #208, Carolina, PR 00985, 787-769-0007. *Website:* http://www.caribbean.edu/.

CARIBBEAN UNIVERSITY–PONCE
Ponce, PR

CONTACT Financial Aid Office, Caribbean University–Ponce, Ave. Ednita Nazario #1015, Ponce, PR 00716-7733, 787-840-2955. *Website:* http://www.caribbean.edu/.

CARIBBEAN UNIVERSITY–VEGA BAJA
Vega Baja, PR

CONTACT Financial Aid Office, Caribbean University–Vega Baja, Carr 671 K.M. 5, Sector El Criollo, Bo. Algarrobo, Vega Baja, PR 00964, 787-858-3668. *Website:* http://www.caribbean.edu/.

CARLETON COLLEGE
Northfield, MN

Tuition & fees: $52,782	Average undergraduate aid package: $48,110

ABOUT THE INSTITUTION Independent, coed. *Awards:* bachelor's degrees. 39 undergraduate majors. *Total enrollment:* 2,078. Undergraduates: 2,078. Freshmen: 522. Both federal and institutional methodology are used as a basis for awarding need-based institutional aid.

UNDERGRADUATE EXPENSES for 2017–2018 *Application fee:* $30. *Comprehensive fee:* $66,414 includes full-time tuition ($52,476), mandatory fees ($306), and room and board ($13,632). *College room only:* $7140. Room and board charges vary according to board plan.

FRESHMAN FINANCIAL AID (Fall 2016) 401 applied for aid; of those 68% were deemed to have need. 100% of freshmen with need received aid; of those 100% had need fully met. *Average percent of need met:* 100% (excluding resources awarded to replace EFC). *Average financial aid package:* $47,776 (excluding resources awarded to replace EFC). 5% of all full-time freshmen had no need and received non-need-based gift aid.

UNDERGRADUATE FINANCIAL AID (Fall 2016) 1,758 applied for aid; of those 64% were deemed to have need. 100% of undergraduates with need received aid; of those 100% had need fully met. *Average percent of need met:* 100% (excluding resources awarded to replace EFC). *Average financial aid package:* $48,110 (excluding resources awarded to replace EFC). 5% of all full-time undergraduates had no need and received non-need-based gift aid.

GIFT AID (NEED-BASED) *Total amount:* $43,515,688 (3% federal, 1% state, 92% institutional, 4% external sources). *Receiving aid:* Freshmen: 52% (271); all full-time undergraduates: 55% (1,121). *Average award:* Freshmen: $41,917; Undergraduates: $40,675. *Scholarships, grants, and awards:* Federal Pell, FSEOG, state, private, college/university gift aid from institutional funds.

GIFT AID (NON-NEED-BASED) *Total amount:* $1,339,180 (28% institutional, 72% external sources). *Receiving aid:* Freshmen: 5% (28). Undergraduates: 6% (127). *Average award:* Freshmen: $3873. Undergraduates: $4562. *Scholarships, grants, and awards by category:* Academic interests/achievement: 104 awards ($373,909 total): general academic interests/achievements. Creative arts/performance: 10 awards ($10,568 total): music. *Tuition waivers:* Full or partial for employees or children of employees.

LOANS *Student loans:* $5,948,468 (94% need-based, 6% non-need-based). 44% of past graduating class borrowed through all loan programs. *Average indebtedness per student:* $21,035. *Average need-based loan:* Freshmen: $4138. Undergraduates: $5192. *Parent loans:* $932,663 (89% need-based, 11% non-need-based). *Programs:* Federal Direct (Subsidized and Unsubsidized Stafford, PLUS), Perkins, state, college/university.

WORK-STUDY *Federal work-study:* 359 jobs averaging $2596. *State or other work-study/employment:* Total amount: $3,626,365 (59% need-based, 41% non-need-based). 1,341 part-time jobs averaging $2665.

APPLYING FOR FINANCIAL AID *Required financial aid forms:* FAFSA, CSS Financial Aid PROFILE, noncustodial (divorced/separated) parent's statement. *Financial aid deadline:* 1/15. *Notification date:* 3/31. Students must reply by 5/1 or within 2 weeks of notification.

CONTACT Mr. Rodney M. Oto, Director of Student Financial Services, Carleton College, One North College Street, Northfield, MN 55057-4001, 507-222-4138 or toll-free 800-995-2275. *Fax:* 507-222-4269. *Website:* http://www.carleton.edu/.

CARLOS ALBIZU UNIVERSITY
San Juan, PR

Tuition & fees: N/R	Average undergraduate aid package: $4925

ABOUT THE INSTITUTION Independent, coed. *Awards:* bachelor's, master's, and doctoral degrees. 3 undergraduate majors. *Total enrollment:* 919. Undergraduates: 142. Federal methodology is used as a basis for awarding need-based institutional aid.

FRESHMAN FINANCIAL AID (Fall 2017, est.) 8 applied for aid; of those 100% were deemed to have need. 100% of freshmen with need received aid. *Average percent of need met:* 100% (excluding resources awarded to replace EFC). *Average financial aid package:* $3365 (excluding resources awarded to replace EFC).

UNDERGRADUATE FINANCIAL AID (Fall 2017, est.) 147 applied for aid; of those 100% were deemed to have need. 100% of undergraduates with need received aid. *Average percent of need met:* 100% (excluding resources awarded to replace EFC). *Average financial aid package:* $4925 (excluding resources awarded to replace EFC).

GIFT AID (NEED-BASED) *Receiving aid:* Freshmen: 100% (8); all full-time undergraduates: 100% (147). *Average award:* Freshmen: $3365; Undergraduates: $4925. *Scholarships, grants, and awards:* Federal Pell, FSEOG, state, college/university gift aid from institutional funds.

GIFT AID (NON-NEED-BASED) *Scholarships, grants, and awards by category:* Academic interests/achievement: social sciences.

LOANS *Average need-based loan:* Freshmen: $1167. Undergraduates: $3000. *Programs:* Federal Direct (Subsidized and Unsubsidized Stafford, PLUS).

WORK-STUDY Federal work-study jobs available (averaging $1560).

APPLYING FOR FINANCIAL AID *Notification date:* Continuous.

CONTACT Mrs. Doris J. Quero, Director of Financial Aid, Carlos Albizu University, PO Box 9023711, San Juan, PR 00901, 787-725-6500 Ext. 1529. *Fax:* 787-721-4008. *E-mail:* dquero@albizu.edu. *Website:* http://www.albizu.edu/.

CARLOS ALBIZU UNIVERSITY, MIAMI CAMPUS
Miami, FL

Tuition & fees: $12,444	Average undergraduate aid package: $8901

ABOUT THE INSTITUTION Independent, coed. 6 undergraduate majors. Federal methodology is used as a basis for awarding need-based institutional aid.

UNDERGRADUATE EXPENSES for 2017–2018 *Tuition:* full-time $11,628; part-time $323 per credit. *Required fees:* full-time $816; $272 per term. Full-time tuition and fees vary according to course load, degree level, and program. Part-time tuition and fees vary according to course load, degree level, and program.

FRESHMAN FINANCIAL AID (Fall 2016) 7 applied for aid; of those 100% were deemed to have need. 100% of freshmen with need received aid. *Average percent of need met:* 65% (excluding resources awarded to replace EFC). *Average financial aid package:* $8901 (excluding resources awarded to replace EFC).

UNDERGRADUATE FINANCIAL AID (Fall 2016) 126 applied for aid; of those 100% were deemed to have need. 100% of undergraduates with need received aid. *Average percent of need met:* 52% (excluding resources awarded to replace EFC). *Average financial aid package:* $8901 (excluding resources awarded to replace EFC).

GIFT AID (NEED-BASED) *Total amount:* $794,600 (65% federal, 35% state). *Receiving aid:* Freshmen: 100% (7); all full-time undergraduates: 69% (126). *Average award:* Freshmen: $5540; Undergraduates: $5540. *Scholarships, grants, and awards:* Federal Pell, FSEOG, state, college/university gift aid from institutional funds.

GIFT AID (NON-NEED-BASED) *Scholarships, grants, and awards by category:* Special characteristics: children of faculty/staff. *Tuition waivers:* Full or partial for employees or children of employees.

LOANS *Student loans:* $1,104,207 (45% need-based, 55% non-need-based). *Average need-based loan:* Freshmen: $3500. Undergraduates: $4000. *Parent loans:* $13,405 (100% need-based). *Programs:* Federal Direct (Subsidized and Unsubsidized Stafford, PLUS), college/university.
WORK-STUDY *Federal work-study:* jobs available.
APPLYING FOR FINANCIAL AID *Required financial aid forms:* FAFSA, institution's own form. *Financial aid deadline (priority):* 6/1. *Notification date:* Continuous.
CONTACT Violeta Velasquez, Financial Aid Officer, Carlos Albizu University, Miami Campus, 2173 Northwest 99th Avenue, Miami, FL 33172, 305-593-1223 Ext. 3179 or toll-free 888-GO-TO-CAU (in-state), 800-GO-TO-CAU (out-of-state). *Fax:* 305-593-8902. *E-mail:* vvelasquez@albizu.edu.
Website: http://www.albizu.edu/.

CARLOW UNIVERSITY
Pittsburgh, PA

Tuition & fees: $28,596	Average undergraduate aid package: $18,975

ABOUT THE INSTITUTION Independent Roman Catholic, coed, primarily women. *Awards:* certificates, bachelor's, master's, and doctoral degrees. 28 undergraduate majors. *Total enrollment:* 2,140. Undergraduates: 1,365. Freshmen: 241. Both federal and institutional methodology are used as a basis for awarding need-based institutional aid.
UNDERGRADUATE EXPENSES for 2017–2018 *Comprehensive fee:* $39,704 includes full-time tuition ($27,950), mandatory fees ($646), and room and board ($11,108). *College room only:* $5680. Full-time tuition and fees vary according to course load, program, and reciprocity agreements. Room and board charges vary according to board plan. *Part-time tuition:* $889 per credit hour. *Part-time fees:* $13 per credit hour. Part-time tuition and fees vary according to course load, program, and reciprocity agreements.
FRESHMAN FINANCIAL AID (Fall 2016) 212 applied for aid; of those 92% were deemed to have need. 100% of freshmen with need received aid; of those 22% had need fully met. *Average percent of need met:* 75% (excluding resources awarded to replace EFC). *Average financial aid package:* $24,457 (excluding resources awarded to replace EFC).
UNDERGRADUATE FINANCIAL AID (Fall 2016) 1,085 applied for aid; of those 94% were deemed to have need. 100% of undergraduates with need received aid; of those 22% had need fully met. *Average percent of need met:* 62% (excluding resources awarded to replace EFC). *Average financial aid package:* $18,975 (excluding resources awarded to replace EFC).
GIFT AID (NEED-BASED) *Total amount:* $15,261,602 (19% federal, 16% state, 57% institutional, 8% external sources). *Receiving aid:* Freshmen: 89% (194); all full-time undergraduates: 93% (1,018). *Average award:* Freshmen: $4809; Undergraduates: $4160. *Scholarships, grants, and awards:* Federal Pell, FSEOG, state, private, college/university gift aid from institutional funds, Federal Nursing.
GIFT AID (NON-NEED-BASED) *Total amount:* $1,702,118 (1% federal, 4% state, 61% institutional, 34% external sources). *Receiving aid:* Freshmen: 42% (91). Undergraduates: 34% (370). *Scholarships, grants, and awards by category:* Academic interests/achievement: biological sciences, business, communication, computer science, education, English, general academic interests/achievements, humanities, mathematics, social sciences. *Special achievements/activities:* leadership, religious involvement. *Special characteristics:* children and siblings of alumni, children of educators, children of faculty/staff, international students, religious affiliation, siblings of current students. *Tuition waivers:* Full or partial for children of alumni, employees or children of employees, adult students. *ROTC:* Army cooperative, Naval cooperative, Air Force cooperative.
LOANS *Student loans:* $12,868,703 (80% need-based, 20% non-need-based). *Average need-based loan:* Freshmen: $3139. Undergraduates: $3342. *Parent loans:* $2,308,067 (51% need-based, 49% non-need-based). *Programs:* Federal Direct (Subsidized and Unsubsidized Stafford, PLUS), Perkins, Federal Nursing.
WORK-STUDY *Federal work-study:* jobs available.
ATHLETIC AWARDS Total amount: $785,375 (81% need-based, 19% non-need-based).
APPLYING FOR FINANCIAL AID *Required financial aid forms:* FAFSA, state aid form. *Financial aid deadline:* 5/1 (priority: 3/15). *Notification date:* Continuous beginning 12/1.

CONTACT Office of Financial Aid, Carlow University, 3333 Fifth Avenue, Pittsburgh, PA 15213-3165, 412-578-6171 or toll-free 800-333-CARLOW. *E-mail:* finaid@carlow.edu.
Website: http://www.carlow.edu/.

CARNEGIE MELLON UNIVERSITY
Pittsburgh, PA

Tuition & fees: $55,465	Average undergraduate aid package: $43,182

ABOUT THE INSTITUTION Independent, coed. *Awards:* certificates, bachelor's, master's, and doctoral degrees. 69 undergraduate majors. *Total enrollment:* 14,528. Undergraduates: 6,896. Freshmen: 1,784. Both federal and institutional methodology are used as a basis for awarding need-based institutional aid.
UNDERGRADUATE EXPENSES for 2018–2019 *Application fee:* $75. *Comprehensive fee:* $69,883 includes full-time tuition ($54,244), mandatory fees ($1221), and room and board ($14,418). *College room only:* $8450. Room and board charges vary according to board plan and housing facility. *Part-time tuition:* $753 per unit.
FRESHMAN FINANCIAL AID (Fall 2017, est.) 1,086 applied for aid; of those 68% were deemed to have need. 100% of freshmen with need received aid; of those 94% had need fully met. *Average percent of need met:* 99% (excluding resources awarded to replace EFC). *Average financial aid package:* $44,812 (excluding resources awarded to replace EFC). 3% of all full-time freshmen had no need and received non-need-based gift aid.
UNDERGRADUATE FINANCIAL AID (Fall 2017, est.) 3,206 applied for aid; of those 81% were deemed to have need. 99% of undergraduates with need received aid; of those 67% had need fully met. *Average percent of need met:* 94% (excluding resources awarded to replace EFC). *Average financial aid package:* $43,182 (excluding resources awarded to replace EFC). 5% of all full-time undergraduates had no need and received non-need-based gift aid.
GIFT AID (NEED-BASED) *Total amount:* $93,729,338 (8% federal, 91% institutional, 1% external sources). *Receiving aid:* Freshmen: 43% (721); all full-time undergraduates: 38% (2,509). *Average award:* Freshmen: $41,167; Undergraduates: $37,531. *Scholarships, grants, and awards:* Federal Pell, FSEOG, state, private, college/university gift aid from institutional funds.
GIFT AID (NON-NEED-BASED) *Total amount:* $13,672,923 (75% institutional, 25% external sources). *Receiving aid:* Freshmen: 20% (329). Undergraduates: 17% (1,147). *Average award:* Freshmen: $13,030. Undergraduates: $15,142. *Scholarships, grants, and awards by category:* Academic interests/achievement: general academic interests/achievements. Creative arts/performance: general creative arts/performance. Special achievements/activities: general special achievements/activities. Special characteristics: children of faculty/staff, general special characteristics. *Tuition waivers:* Full or partial for employees or children of employees. *ROTC:* Army cooperative, Naval, Air Force cooperative.
LOANS *Student loans:* $22,675,511 (65% need-based, 35% non-need-based). 54% of past graduating class borrowed through all loan programs. *Average indebtedness per student:* $31,077. *Average need-based loan:* Freshmen: $3423. Undergraduates: $6071. *Parent loans:* $7,521,598 (7% need-based, 93% non-need-based). *Programs:* Federal Direct (Subsidized and Unsubsidized Stafford, PLUS), Perkins.
WORK-STUDY *Federal work-study:* Total amount: $5,920,243; jobs available. *State or other work-study/employment:* Part-time jobs available.
APPLYING FOR FINANCIAL AID *Required financial aid forms:* FAFSA, CSS Financial Aid PROFILE, noncustodial (divorced/separated) parent's statement, federal income tax form(s). *Financial aid deadline (priority):* 2/15. *Notification date:* 4/15.
CONTACT Brian Hill, Director of Student Financial Services, Carnegie Mellon University, 5000 Forbes Avenue, Pittsburgh, PA 15213-3890, 412-268-8186. *Fax:* 412-268-8084. *E-mail:* thehub@andrew.cmu.edu.
Website: http://www.cmu.edu/.

CAROLINA CHRISTIAN COLLEGE
Winston-Salem, NC

Tuition & fees: $13,950	Average undergraduate aid package: $9500

ABOUT THE INSTITUTION Independent nondenominational, coed. *Awards:* associate, bachelor's, and master's degrees. 1 undergraduate major. *Total enrollment:* 53. Undergraduates: 47. Freshmen: 9. Federal methodology is used as a basis for awarding need-based institutional aid.

UNDERGRADUATE EXPENSES for 2018–2019 Application fee: $50. *One-time required fee:* $75. *Tuition:* full-time $12,500; part-time $2750 per term. *Required fees:* full-time $1450; $600 per term.

FRESHMAN FINANCIAL AID (Fall 2017, est.) 9 applied for aid; of those 100% were deemed to have need. 100% of freshmen with need received aid; of those 67% had need fully met. *Average percent of need met:* 95% (excluding resources awarded to replace EFC). *Average financial aid package:* $9500 (excluding resources awarded to replace EFC).

UNDERGRADUATE FINANCIAL AID (Fall 2017, est.) 35 applied for aid; of those 100% were deemed to have need. 100% of undergraduates with need received aid; of those 91% had need fully met. *Average percent of need met:* 95% (excluding resources awarded to replace EFC). *Average financial aid package:* $9500 (excluding resources awarded to replace EFC).

GIFT AID (NEED-BASED) Total amount: $124,500 (96% federal, 4% institutional). *Receiving aid:* Freshmen: 67% (6); all full-time undergraduates: 84% (32). *Average award:* Freshmen: $5290; Undergraduates: $5290. *Scholarships, grants, and awards:* Federal Pell, FSEOG.

GIFT AID (NON-NEED-BASED) *Scholarships, grants, and awards by category:* Academic interests/achievement: religion/biblical studies. *Tuition waivers:* Full or partial for employees or children of employees.

LOANS *Student loans:* $114,000 (100% need-based). *Average need-based loan:* Freshmen: $2000. Undergraduates: $2000. *Programs:* Federal Direct (Subsidized and Unsubsidized Stafford).

ATHLETIC AWARDS Total amount: $14,400 (100% need-based).

APPLYING FOR FINANCIAL AID *Required financial aid forms:* FAFSA, institution's own form. *Financial aid deadline:* Continuous. *Notification date:* Continuous.

CONTACT LaJada Crews, Financial Aid Officer, Carolina Christian College, 4209 Indiana Avenue, Winston-Salem, NC 27105, 336-744-0900 Ext. 201. *Fax:* 336-744-0901. *E-mail:* frontoffice@carolina.edu. *Website:* http://www.carolina.edu/.

CAROLINA COLLEGE OF BIBLICAL STUDIES
Fayetteville, NC

CONTACT Financial Aid Office, Carolina College of Biblical Studies, 817 South McPherson Church Road, Fayetteville, NC 28303, 910-323-5614. *Website:* http://carolinabiblecollege.org/.

CARROLL COLLEGE
Helena, MT

Tuition & fees: $34,480	Average undergraduate aid package: $24,914

ABOUT THE INSTITUTION Independent Roman Catholic, coed. *Awards:* certificates, associate, and bachelor's degrees. 50 undergraduate majors. *Total enrollment:* 1,352. Undergraduates: 1,352. Freshmen: 294. Federal methodology is used as a basis for awarding need-based institutional aid.

UNDERGRADUATE EXPENSES for 2017–2018 Application fee: $35. *Comprehensive fee:* $44,088 includes full-time tuition ($33,500), mandatory fees ($980), and room and board ($9608). Full-time tuition and fees vary according to program. Room and board charges vary according to board plan. *Part-time tuition:* $1395 per credit hour. *Part-time fees:* $490 per year. Part-time tuition and fees vary according to program.

FRESHMAN FINANCIAL AID (Fall 2016) 283 applied for aid; of those 84% were deemed to have need. 100% of freshmen with need received aid; of those 27% had need fully met. *Average percent of need met:* 83% (excluding resources awarded to replace EFC). *Average financial aid package:* $26,459 (excluding resources awarded to replace EFC). 27% of all full-time freshmen had no need and received non-need-based gift aid.

UNDERGRADUATE FINANCIAL AID (Fall 2016) 997 applied for aid; of those 88% were deemed to have need. 100% of undergraduates with need received aid; of those 25% had need fully met. *Average percent of need met:* 78% (excluding resources awarded to replace EFC). *Average financial aid package:* $24,914 (excluding resources awarded to replace EFC). 31% of all full-time undergraduates had no need and received non-need-based gift aid.

GIFT AID (NEED-BASED) Total amount: $15,684,218 (12% federal, 82% institutional, 6% external sources). *Receiving aid:* Freshmen: 69% (234); all full-time undergraduates: 65% (862). *Average award:* Freshmen: $21,936; Undergraduates: $19,725. *Scholarships, grants, and awards:* Federal Pell, FSEOG, state, private, college/university gift aid from institutional funds.

GIFT AID (NON-NEED-BASED) Total amount: $7,540,207 (9% federal, 83% institutional, 8% external sources). *Receiving aid:* Freshmen: 15% (51). Undergraduates: 13% (171). *Average award:* Freshmen: $15,750. Undergraduates: $14,162. *Scholarships, grants, and awards by category:* Academic interests/achievement: general academic interests/achievements. Creative arts/performance: art/fine arts, creative writing, debating, music, performing arts, theater/drama. Special achievements/activities: cheerleading/drum major, general special achievements/activities, leadership, religious involvement. Special characteristics: children of faculty/staff, children of union members/company employees, international students, religious affiliation, siblings of current students, spouses of current students, veterans. *Tuition waivers:* Full or partial for employees or children of employees, senior citizens. *ROTC:* Army.

LOANS *Student loans:* $6,373,067 (52% need-based, 48% non-need-based). 68% of past graduating class borrowed through all loan programs. *Average indebtedness per student:* $30,640. *Average need-based loan:* Freshmen: $3105. Undergraduates: $4156. *Parent loans:* $3,522,900 (41% need-based, 59% non-need-based). *Programs:* Federal Direct (Subsidized and Unsubsidized Stafford, PLUS), Perkins, private loans.

WORK-STUDY *Federal work-study:* jobs available. *State or other work-study/employment:* Part-time jobs available.

ATHLETIC AWARDS Total amount: $2,854,851 (41% need-based, 59% non-need-based).

APPLYING FOR FINANCIAL AID *Required financial aid form:* FAFSA. *Financial aid deadline (priority):* 3/1. *Notification date:* Continuous. Students must reply within 2 weeks of notification.

CONTACT Ms. Janet Riis, Director of Financial Aid, Carroll College, 1601 North Benton Avenue, Helena, MT 59625-0002, 406-447-5423 or toll-free 800-992-3648. *Fax:* 406-447-4533. *E-mail:* jriis@carroll.edu. *Website:* http://www.carroll.edu/.

CARROLL UNIVERSITY
Waukesha, WI

Tuition & fees: $31,918	Average undergraduate aid package: $24,794

ABOUT THE INSTITUTION Independent Presbyterian, coed. *Awards:* certificates, bachelor's, master's, and doctoral degrees. 77 undergraduate majors. *Total enrollment:* 3,451. Undergraduates: 2,981. Freshmen: 724. Federal methodology is used as a basis for awarding need-based institutional aid.

UNDERGRADUATE EXPENSES for 2018–2019 Comprehensive fee: $41,814 includes full-time tuition ($31,162), mandatory fees ($756), and room and board ($9896). *College room only:* $5180. Full-time tuition and fees vary according to program. Room and board charges vary according to board plan and housing facility. *Part-time tuition:* $400 per credit hour. Part-time tuition and fees vary according to course load and program.

FRESHMAN FINANCIAL AID (Fall 2017, est.) 672 applied for aid; of those 86% were deemed to have need. 100% of freshmen with need received aid; of those 37% had need fully met. *Average percent of need met:* 88% (excluding resources

awarded to replace EFC). *Average financial aid package:* $25,791 (excluding resources awarded to replace EFC). 19% of all full-time freshmen had no need and received non-need-based gift aid.

UNDERGRADUATE FINANCIAL AID (Fall 2017, est.) 2,485 applied for aid; of those 87% were deemed to have need. 100% of undergraduates with need received aid; of those 33% had need fully met. *Average percent of need met:* 87% (excluding resources awarded to replace EFC). *Average financial aid package:* $24,794 (excluding resources awarded to replace EFC). 21% of all full-time undergraduates had no need and received non-need-based gift aid.

GIFT AID (NEED-BASED) *Total amount:* $40,339,078 (8% federal, 6% state, 84% institutional, 2% external sources). *Receiving aid:* Freshmen: 81% (581); all full-time undergraduates: 78% (2,154). *Average award:* Freshmen: $21,059; Undergraduates: $19,049. *Scholarships, grants, and awards:* Federal Pell, FSEOG, state, private, college/university gift aid from institutional funds.

GIFT AID (NON-NEED-BASED) *Total amount:* $9,262,701 (2% state, 96% institutional, 2% external sources). *Receiving aid:* Freshmen: 13% (91). Undergraduates: 12% (331). *Average award:* Freshmen: $17,568. Undergraduates: $15,362. *Scholarships, grants, and awards by category:* Academic interests/achievement: 2,449 awards ($35,009,232 total): biological sciences, business, communication, computer science, education, engineering/technologies, general academic interests/achievements, health fields, humanities, international studies, mathematics, physical sciences, premedicine, social sciences. *Creative arts/performance:* 69 awards ($70,350 total): art/fine arts, journalism/publications, music, performing arts, theater/drama. *Special achievements/activities:* 67 awards ($82,689 total): general special achievements/activities, junior miss, leadership, memberships, religious involvement. *Special characteristics:* 450 awards ($1,644,509 total): adult students, children and siblings of alumni, children of current students, children of faculty/staff, general special characteristics, international students, siblings of current students, spouses of current students. *Tuition waivers:* Full or partial for employees or children of employees. *ROTC:* Army cooperative, Air Force cooperative.

LOANS *Student loans:* $19,219,287 (39% need-based, 61% non-need-based). 82% of past graduating class borrowed through all loan programs. *Average indebtedness per student:* $35,802. *Average need-based loan:* Freshmen: $3581. Undergraduates: $4542. *Parent loans:* $3,865,761 (90% need-based, 10% non-need-based). *Programs:* Federal Direct (Subsidized and Unsubsidized Stafford, PLUS), Perkins, state, college/university.

WORK-STUDY *Federal work-study:* Total amount: $1,065,895; 475 jobs averaging $2247. *State or other work-study/employment:* Total amount: $3,250,459 (100% non-need-based). 1,618 part-time jobs averaging $2298.

APPLYING FOR FINANCIAL AID *Required financial aid form:* FAFSA. *Financial aid deadline:* Continuous. *Notification date:* Continuous beginning 2/15. Students must reply by 5/1 or within 2 weeks of notification.

CONTACT Dawn Scott, Director of Financial Aid, Carroll University, 100 North East Avenue, Waukesha, WI 53186-5593, 262-524-7297 or toll-free 800-CARROLL. *Fax:* 262-951-3037. *E-mail:* dscott@carrollu.edu.
Website: http://www.carrollu.edu/.

CARSON-NEWMAN UNIVERSITY
Jefferson City, TN

Tuition & fees: $27,400	Average undergraduate aid package: $23,944

ABOUT THE INSTITUTION Independent Southern Baptist, coed. *Awards:* certificates, associate, bachelor's, master's, and doctoral degrees. 77 undergraduate majors. *Total enrollment:* 2,514. Undergraduates: 1,690. Freshmen: 395. Federal methodology is used as a basis for awarding need-based institutional aid.

UNDERGRADUATE EXPENSES for 2017–2018 *Comprehensive fee:* $36,030 includes full-time tuition ($26,200), mandatory fees ($1200), and room and board ($8630). *College room only:* $3930. Full-time tuition and fees vary according to class time and course load. Room and board charges vary according to board plan, gender, and housing facility. *Part-time tuition:* $1090 per credit hour. *Part-time fees:* $375 per term. Part-time tuition and fees vary according to class time and course load.

FRESHMAN FINANCIAL AID (Fall 2016) 455 applied for aid; of those 100% were deemed to have need. 100% of freshmen with need received aid; of those 15% had need fully met. *Average percent of need met:* 78% (excluding resources awarded to replace EFC). *Average financial aid package:* $24,975 (excluding

resources awarded to replace EFC). 6% of all full-time freshmen had no need and received non-need-based gift aid.

UNDERGRADUATE FINANCIAL AID (Fall 2016) 1,432 applied for aid; of those 100% were deemed to have need. 100% of undergraduates with need received aid; of those 21% had need fully met. *Average percent of need met:* 78% (excluding resources awarded to replace EFC). *Average financial aid package:* $23,944 (excluding resources awarded to replace EFC). 10% of all full-time undergraduates had no need and received non-need-based gift aid.

GIFT AID (NEED-BASED) *Total amount:* $25,697,015 (14% federal, 20% state, 64% institutional, 2% external sources). *Receiving aid:* Freshmen: 89% (449); all full-time undergraduates: 82% (1,397). *Average award:* Freshmen: $19,542; Undergraduates: $18,355. *Scholarships, grants, and awards:* Federal Pell, FSEOG, state, private, college/university gift aid from institutional funds, Federal Nursing.

GIFT AID (NON-NEED-BASED) *Total amount:* $3,045,790 (15% state, 81% institutional, 4% external sources). *Receiving aid:* Freshmen: 9% (46). Undergraduates: 14% (245). *Average award:* Freshmen: $10,504. Undergraduates: $10,685. *Scholarships, grants, and awards by category:* Academic interests/achievement: biological sciences, business, education, general academic interests/achievements, home economics, mathematics, military science, religion/biblical studies. *Creative arts/performance:* art/fine arts, debating, journalism/publications, music. *Special achievements/activities:* leadership, memberships. *Special characteristics:* children and siblings of alumni, members of minority groups, relatives of clergy, siblings of current students. *Tuition waivers:* Full or partial for employees or children of employees, senior citizens. *ROTC:* Army.

LOANS *Student loans:* $8,635,825 (95% need-based, 5% non-need-based). 71% of past graduating class borrowed through all loan programs. *Average indebtedness per student:* $27,188. *Average need-based loan:* Freshmen: $3014. Undergraduates: $3644. *Parent loans:* $2,707,284 (96% need-based, 4% non-need-based). *Programs:* Federal Direct (Subsidized and Unsubsidized Stafford, PLUS), Perkins, state, alternative loans.

WORK-STUDY *Federal work-study:* jobs available. *State or other work-study/employment:* Part-time jobs available.

ATHLETIC AWARDS Total amount: $4,826,292 (65% need-based, 35% non-need-based).

APPLYING FOR FINANCIAL AID *Required financial aid forms:* FAFSA, institution's own form. *Financial aid deadline (priority):* 1/16. *Notification date:* Continuous beginning 3/1. Students must reply by 5/1 or within 2 weeks of notification.

CONTACT Mrs. Danette Seale, Director of Financial Aid, Carson-Newman University, 1646 Russell Avenue, Jefferson City, TN 37760, 865-471-3247 or toll-free 800-678-9061. *Fax:* 865-471-3502. *E-mail:* dseale@cn.edu.
Website: http://www.cn.edu/.

CARTHAGE COLLEGE
Kenosha, WI

CONTACT Vatistas Vatistas, Director of Financial Aid, Carthage College, 2001 Alford Park Drive, Kenosha, WI 53140, 262-551-6001 or toll-free 800-351-4058. *Fax:* 262-551-5762. *E-mail:* vvatistas@carthage.edu.
Website: http://www.carthage.edu/.

CARVER COLLEGE
Atlanta, GA

CONTACT Financial Aid Office, Carver College, 3870 Cascade Road SW, Atlanta, GA 30331, 404-527-4520.
Website: http://www.carver.edu/.

CASE WESTERN RESERVE UNIVERSITY
Cleveland, OH

Tuition & fees: $47,500	Average undergraduate aid package: $44,122

ABOUT THE INSTITUTION Independent, coed. **Awards:** certificates, bachelor's, master's, and doctoral degrees. 72 undergraduate majors. **Total enrollment:** 11,824. Undergraduates: 5,150. Freshmen: 1,309. Both federal and institutional methodology are used as a basis for awarding need-based institutional aid.

UNDERGRADUATE EXPENSES for 2017–2018 Application fee: $70. **One-time required fee:** $540. **Comprehensive fee:** $62,284 includes full-time tuition ($47,074), mandatory fees ($426), and room and board ($14,784). **College room only:** $8570. Room and board charges vary according to board plan, housing facility, and student level. **Part-time tuition:** $1962 per credit hour. Part-time tuition and fees vary according to course load.

FRESHMAN FINANCIAL AID (Fall 2017, est.) 984 applied for aid; of those 73% were deemed to have need. 100% of freshmen with need received aid; of those 96% had need fully met. **Average percent of need met:** 99% (excluding resources awarded to replace EFC). **Average financial aid package:** $46,967 (excluding resources awarded to replace EFC). 29% of all full-time freshmen had no need and received non-need-based gift aid.

UNDERGRADUATE FINANCIAL AID (Fall 2017, est.) 2,945 applied for aid; of those 84% were deemed to have need. 100% of undergraduates with need received aid; of those 65% had need fully met. **Average percent of need met:** 89% (excluding resources awarded to replace EFC). **Average financial aid package:** $44,122 (excluding resources awarded to replace EFC). 33% of all full-time undergraduates had no need and received non-need-based gift aid.

GIFT AID (NEED-BASED) Total amount: $78,103,678 (5% federal, 2% state, 89% institutional, 4% external sources). **Receiving aid:** Freshmen: 54% (703); all full-time undergraduates: 49% (2,409). **Average award:** Freshmen: $36,474; Undergraduates: $30,713. **Scholarships, grants, and awards:** Federal Pell, FSEOG, state, private, college/university gift aid from institutional funds.

GIFT AID (NON-NEED-BASED) Total amount: $42,404,760 (94% institutional, 6% external sources). **Receiving aid:** Freshmen: 19% (248). Undergraduates: 8% (418). **Average award:** Freshmen: $23,573. Undergraduates: $23,582. **Scholarships, grants, and awards by category:** Academic interests/achievement: 3,570 awards ($75,511,515 total): biological sciences, business, communication, computer science, engineering/technologies, English, foreign languages, general academic interests/achievements, health fields, home economics, humanities, international studies, mathematics, physical sciences, premedicine, religion/biblical studies, social sciences. Creative arts/performance: 48 awards ($1,707,182 total): art/fine arts, creative writing, dance, general creative arts/performance, music, performing arts, theater/drama. Special achievements/activities: 70 awards ($261,833 total): leadership. Special characteristics: 113 awards ($5,106,489 total): children of faculty/staff. **Tuition waivers:** Full or partial for employees or children of employees. **ROTC:** Army, Air Force cooperative.

LOANS Student loans: $22,760,643 (67% need-based, 33% non-need-based). 49% of past graduating class borrowed through all loan programs. Average indebtedness per student: $32,377. **Average need-based loan:** Freshmen: $5162. Undergraduates: $6996. **Parent loans:** $10,823,803 (44% need-based, 56% non-need-based). **Programs:** Federal Direct (Subsidized and Unsubsidized Stafford, PLUS), Federal Nursing, college/university, alternative loans.

WORK-STUDY Federal work-study: Total amount: $3,942,643; 1,509 jobs averaging $2613. **State or other work-study/employment:** Total amount: $201,537 (100% need-based). 86 part-time jobs averaging $2344.

APPLYING FOR FINANCIAL AID Required financial aid forms: FAFSA, institution's own form, CSS Financial Aid PROFILE, noncustodial (divorced/separated) parent's statement. **Financial aid deadline:** 2/1. **Notification date:** Continuous beginning 3/20. Students must reply by 5/1 or within 2 weeks of notification.

CONTACT Mrs. Venus M. Puliafico, Director of University Financial Aid, Case Western Reserve University, 10900 Euclid Avenue, Cleveland, OH 44106-7049, 216-368-4530. Fax: 216-368-5054. E-mail: vxp4@case.edu. Website: http://www.case.edu/.

CASTLETON UNIVERSITY
Castleton, VT

CONTACT Kathleen O'Meara, Director of Financial Aid, Castleton University, Castleton, VT 05735, 802-468-1292 or toll-free 800-639-8521. Fax: 802-468-5237. E-mail: kathy.omeara@castleton.edu. Website: http://www.castleton.edu/.

CATAWBA COLLEGE
Salisbury, NC

Tuition & fees: $30,520	Average undergraduate aid package: $24,637

ABOUT THE INSTITUTION Independent United Church of Christ, coed. **Awards:** bachelor's and master's degrees. 42 undergraduate majors. **Total enrollment:** 1,331. Undergraduates: 1,325. Freshmen: 332. Federal methodology is used as a basis for awarding need-based institutional aid.

UNDERGRADUATE EXPENSES for 2018–2019 Comprehensive fee: $41,008 includes full-time tuition ($30,520) and room and board ($10,488). **College room only:** $6188. Full-time tuition and fees vary according to class time, course load, and degree level. Part-time tuition and fees vary according to class time, course load, and degree level.

FRESHMAN FINANCIAL AID (Fall 2016) 325 applied for aid; of those 90% were deemed to have need. 100% of freshmen with need received aid; of those 31% had need fully met. **Average percent of need met:** 81% (excluding resources awarded to replace EFC). **Average financial aid package:** $26,659 (excluding resources awarded to replace EFC). 15% of all full-time freshmen had no need and received non-need-based gift aid.

UNDERGRADUATE FINANCIAL AID (Fall 2016) 1,107 applied for aid; of those 92% were deemed to have need. 100% of undergraduates with need received aid; of those 26% had need fully met. **Average percent of need met:** 78% (excluding resources awarded to replace EFC). **Average financial aid package:** $24,637 (excluding resources awarded to replace EFC). 15% of all full-time undergraduates had no need and received non-need-based gift aid.

GIFT AID (NEED-BASED) Total amount: $5,658,240 (44% federal, 49% state, 3% institutional, 4% external sources). **Receiving aid:** Freshmen: 57% (199); all full-time undergraduates: 62% (764). **Average award:** Freshmen: $7347; Undergraduates: $6930. **Scholarships, grants, and awards:** Federal Pell, FSEOG, state, private, college/university gift aid from institutional funds.

GIFT AID (NON-NEED-BASED) Total amount: $16,358,556 (100% institutional). **Receiving aid:** Freshmen: 83% (289). Undergraduates: 73% (896). **Average award:** Freshmen: $17,652. Undergraduates: $15,130. **Scholarships, grants, and awards by category:** Academic interests/achievement: 165 awards ($1,412,440 total): business, education, general academic interests/achievements, home economics, physical sciences, premedicine. Creative arts/performance: 153 awards ($499,107 total): music, theater/drama. Special achievements/activities: 161 awards ($946,389 total): cheerleading/drum major, general special achievements/activities, leadership. Special characteristics: 56 awards ($449,320 total): children of faculty/staff, siblings of current students. **Tuition waivers:** Full or partial for employees or children of employees. **ROTC:** Army cooperative, Air Force cooperative.

LOANS Student loans: $7,593,965 (48% need-based, 52% non-need-based). 78% of past graduating class borrowed through all loan programs. Average indebtedness per student: $31,471. **Average need-based loan:** Freshmen: $3067. Undergraduates: $4290. **Parent loans:** $2,867,307 (100% non-need-based). **Programs:** Federal Direct (Subsidized and Unsubsidized Stafford, PLUS), state, college/university, alternative loans.

WORK-STUDY Federal work-study: 115 jobs averaging $1589. **State or other work-study/employment:** Total amount: $168,114 (100% need-based). 124 part-time jobs averaging $1420.

ATHLETIC AWARDS Total amount: $3,425,245 (100% non-need-based).

APPLYING FOR FINANCIAL AID Required financial aid forms: FAFSA, state aid form. **Financial aid deadline (priority):** 3/15. **Notification date:** Continuous beginning 1/15. Students must reply by 5/1 or within 2 weeks of notification.

CONTACT Kelli Hand, Director of Financial Aid, Catawba College, 2300 West Innes Street, Salisbury, NC 28144-2488, 704-637-4416 or toll-free 800-CATAWBA. *Fax:* 704-637-4252. *E-mail:* kmhand@catawba.edu. *Website:* http://www.catawba.edu/.

THE CATHOLIC UNIVERSITY OF AMERICA
Washington, DC

Tuition & fees: $44,060	Average undergraduate aid package: $30,182

ABOUT THE INSTITUTION Independent Roman Catholic Church, coed. *Awards:* certificates, bachelor's, master's, and doctoral degrees. 64 undergraduate majors. *Total enrollment:* 6,023. Undergraduates: 3,313. Freshmen: 831. Federal methodology is used as a basis for awarding need-based institutional aid.

UNDERGRADUATE EXPENSES for 2017–2018 *Application fee:* $55. *One-time required fee:* $440. *Comprehensive fee:* $58,376 includes full-time tuition ($43,300), mandatory fees ($760), and room and board ($14,316). Full-time tuition and fees vary according to program. Room and board charges vary according to board plan and housing facility. *Part-time tuition:* $1715 per credit hour. *Part-time fees:* $430 per year. Part-time tuition and fees vary according to course load and program.

FRESHMAN FINANCIAL AID (Fall 2017, est.) 692 applied for aid; of those 81% were deemed to have need. 100% of freshmen with need received aid; of those 42% had need fully met. *Average percent of need met:* 82% (excluding resources awarded to replace EFC). *Average financial aid package:* $31,104 (excluding resources awarded to replace EFC). 30% of all full-time freshmen had no need and received non-need-based gift aid.

UNDERGRADUATE FINANCIAL AID (Fall 2017, est.) 2,141 applied for aid; of those 86% were deemed to have need. 100% of undergraduates with need received aid; of those 43% had need fully met. *Average percent of need met:* 81% (excluding resources awarded to replace EFC). *Average financial aid package:* $30,182 (excluding resources awarded to replace EFC). 32% of all full-time undergraduates had no need and received non-need-based gift aid.

GIFT AID (NEED-BASED) *Total amount:* $47,306,993 (5% federal, 93% institutional, 2% external sources). *Receiving aid:* Freshmen: 66% (546); all full-time undergraduates: 56% (1,785). *Average award:* Freshmen: $27,861; Undergraduates: $26,356. *Scholarships, grants, and awards:* Federal Pell, FSEOG, state, private, college/university gift aid from institutional funds.

GIFT AID (NON-NEED-BASED) *Total amount:* $20,067,116 (99% institutional, 1% external sources). *Average award:* Freshmen: $21,690. Undergraduates: $19,597. *Scholarships, grants, and awards by category: Academic interests/achievement:* general academic interests/achievements. *Creative arts/performance:* music, theater/drama. *Special characteristics:* children and siblings of alumni, children of faculty/staff, religious affiliation, siblings of current students, twins, veterans, veterans' children. *Tuition waivers:* Full or partial for children of alumni, employees or children of employees. *ROTC:* Army cooperative, Naval cooperative, Air Force cooperative.

LOANS *Student loans:* $19,071,472 (87% need-based, 13% non-need-based). 68% of past graduating class borrowed through all loan programs. *Average indebtedness per student:* $36,542. *Average need-based loan:* Freshmen: $4080. Undergraduates: $4923. *Parent loans:* $9,800,676 (88% need-based, 12% non-need-based). *Programs:* Federal Direct (Subsidized and Unsubsidized Stafford, PLUS), district, alternative loans.

WORK-STUDY *Federal work-study:* Total amount: $401,999; 221 jobs averaging $1824.

APPLYING FOR FINANCIAL AID *Required financial aid forms:* FAFSA, CSS Financial Aid PROFILE, noncustodial (divorced/separated) parent's statement. *Financial aid deadline:* 4/10 (priority: 2/1). *Notification date:* Continuous beginning 3/20. Students must reply by 5/1 or within 2 weeks of notification.

CONTACT Ms. Mindy Schaffer, Director of Financial Aid, The Catholic University of America, 620 Michigan Avenue, NE, Washington, DC 20064, 202-319-6552 or toll-free 800-673-2772. *Fax:* 202-319-5573. *E-mail:* cua-finaid@cua.edu. *Website:* http://www.catholic.edu/.

CAZENOVIA COLLEGE
Cazenovia, NY

Tuition & fees: $33,656	Average undergraduate aid package: $33,543

ABOUT THE INSTITUTION Independent, coed. *Awards:* certificates, associate, and bachelor's degrees. 22 undergraduate majors. *Total enrollment:* 893. Undergraduates: 893. Freshmen: 165. Federal methodology is used as a basis for awarding need-based institutional aid.

UNDERGRADUATE EXPENSES for 2017–2018 *Comprehensive fee:* $47,866 includes full-time tuition ($33,068), mandatory fees ($588), and room and board ($14,210). *College room only:* $7620. Full-time tuition and fees vary according to class time, course load, and program. Room and board charges vary according to board plan and housing facility. *Part-time tuition:* $700 per credit hour. Part-time tuition and fees vary according to class time and course load.

FRESHMAN FINANCIAL AID (Fall 2017, est.) 163 applied for aid; of those 98% were deemed to have need. 100% of freshmen with need received aid; of those 25% had need fully met. *Average percent of need met:* 85% (excluding resources awarded to replace EFC). *Average financial aid package:* $36,189 (excluding resources awarded to replace EFC). 4% of all full-time freshmen had no need and received non-need-based gift aid.

UNDERGRADUATE FINANCIAL AID (Fall 2017, est.) 679 applied for aid; of those 97% were deemed to have need. 100% of undergraduates with need received aid; of those 22% had need fully met. *Average percent of need met:* 85% (excluding resources awarded to replace EFC). *Average financial aid package:* $33,543 (excluding resources awarded to replace EFC). 8% of all full-time undergraduates had no need and received non-need-based gift aid.

GIFT AID (NEED-BASED) *Total amount:* $19,789,131 (12% federal, 9% state, 78% institutional, 1% external sources). *Receiving aid:* Freshmen: 96% (159); all full-time undergraduates: 92% (659). *Average award:* Freshmen: $32,666; Undergraduates: $29,628. *Scholarships, grants, and awards:* Federal Pell, FSEOG, state, private, college/university gift aid from institutional funds.

GIFT AID (NON-NEED-BASED) *Total amount:* $1,536,309 (1% federal, 1% state, 95% institutional, 3% external sources). *Receiving aid:* Freshmen: 7% (12). Undergraduates: 8% (57). *Average award:* Freshmen: $21,011. Undergraduates: $19,125. *Scholarships, grants, and awards by category: Academic interests/achievement:* general academic interests/achievements. *Tuition waivers:* Full or partial for employees or children of employees. *ROTC:* Army cooperative, Air Force cooperative.

LOANS *Student loans:* $6,271,305 (74% need-based, 26% non-need-based). 88% of past graduating class borrowed through all loan programs. *Average indebtedness per student:* $35,863. *Average need-based loan:* Freshmen: $2406. Undergraduates: $4559. *Parent loans:* $2,410,348 (59% need-based, 41% non-need-based). *Programs:* Federal Direct (Subsidized and Unsubsidized Stafford, PLUS).

WORK-STUDY *Federal work-study:* Total amount: $224,375; jobs available.

APPLYING FOR FINANCIAL AID *Required financial aid forms:* FAFSA, noncustodial (divorced/separated) parent's statement. *Financial aid deadline (priority):* 3/1. *Notification date:* Continuous beginning 11/1. Students must reply by 5/1 or within 2 weeks of notification.

CONTACT Office of Financial Aid, Cazenovia College, 3 Sullivan Street, Cazenovia, NY 13035, 315-655-7887 or toll-free 800-654-3210. *Fax:* 315-655-7219. *E-mail:* finaid@cazenovia.edu. *Website:* http://www.cazenovia.edu/.

CEDAR CREST COLLEGE
Allentown, PA

Tuition & fees: $39,216	Average undergraduate aid package: $29,602

ABOUT THE INSTITUTION Independent United Church of Christ, coed, primarily women. *Awards:* certificates, bachelor's, and master's degrees. 41 undergraduate majors. *Total enrollment:* 1,664. Undergraduates: 1,433. Freshmen: 213. Federal methodology is used as a basis for awarding need-based institutional aid.

UNDERGRADUATE EXPENSES for 2018–2019 *Comprehensive fee:* $50,760 includes full-time tuition ($38,616), mandatory fees ($600), and room and board ($11,544). *College room only:* $5420. Full-time tuition and fees vary according to class time, course load, and program. Room and board charges vary according to board plan and housing facility. Part-time tuition and fees vary according to class time, course load, and program. **FRESHMAN FINANCIAL AID (Fall 2017, est.)** 209 applied for aid; of those 96% were deemed to have need. 100% of freshmen with need received aid; of those 16% had need fully met. *Average percent of need met:* 79% (excluding resources awarded to replace EFC). *Average financial aid package:* $30,533 (excluding resources awarded to replace EFC). 5% of all full-time freshmen had no need and received non-need-based gift aid. **UNDERGRADUATE FINANCIAL AID (Fall 2017, est.)** 693 applied for aid; of those 96% were deemed to have need. 100% of undergraduates with need received aid; of those 13% had need fully met. *Average percent of need met:* 76% (excluding resources awarded to replace EFC). *Average financial aid package:* $29,602 (excluding resources awarded to replace EFC). 1% of all full-time undergraduates had no need and received non-need-based gift aid. **GIFT AID (NEED-BASED)** *Total amount:* $16,767,769 (11% federal, 7% state, 80% institutional, 2% external sources). *Receiving aid:* Freshmen: 94% (200); all full-time undergraduates: 93% (661). *Average award:* Freshmen: $27,547; Undergraduates: $25,512. *Scholarships, grants, and awards:* Federal Pell, FSEOG, state, private, college/university gift aid from institutional funds. **GIFT AID (NON-NEED-BASED)** *Total amount:* $1,414,167 (92% institutional, 8% external sources). *Receiving aid:* Freshmen: 12% (26). Undergraduates: 10% (68). *Average award:* Freshmen: $21,997. Undergraduates: $19,374. *Scholarships, grants, and awards by category:* Academic interests/achievement: biological sciences, business, communication, education, English, general academic interests/achievements, home economics, mathematics, physical sciences. *Creative arts/performance:* art/fine arts, creative writing, dance, performing arts, theater/drama. *Special achievements/activities:* junior miss, religious involvement. *Special characteristics:* children and siblings of alumni, general special characteristics, siblings of current students. *Tuition waivers:* Full or partial for employees or children of employees. **LOANS** *Student loans:* $7,210,343 (74% need-based, 26% non-need-based). 92% of past graduating class borrowed through all loan programs. *Average indebtedness per student:* $44,032. *Average need-based loan:* Freshmen: $3355. Undergraduates: $4519. *Parent loans:* $2,600,323 (64% need-based, 36% non-need-based). *Programs:* Federal Direct (Subsidized and Unsubsidized Stafford, PLUS), Perkins, Federal Nursing. **WORK-STUDY** *Federal work-study:* Total amount: $144,000; jobs available. *State or other work-study/employment:* Total amount: $22,040 (55% need-based, 45% non-need-based). Part-time jobs available. **APPLYING FOR FINANCIAL AID** *Required financial aid form:* FAFSA. *Financial aid deadline (priority):* 5/1. *Notification date:* Continuous beginning 9/15. **CONTACT** Ms. Valerie D. Kreiser, Director of Student Financial Services, Cedar Crest College, Room 212 Blaney Hall, 100 College Drive, Allentown, PA 18104-6196, 610-606-4666 Ext. 3314 or toll-free 800-360-1222. *Fax:* 610-606-4653. *E-mail:* financialservices@cedarcrest.edu. *Website:* http://www.cedarcrest.edu/.

CEDARVILLE UNIVERSITY
Cedarville, OH

Tuition & fees: $30,270	Average undergraduate aid package: $21,864

ABOUT THE INSTITUTION Independent Baptist, coed. *Awards:* certificates, bachelor's, master's, and doctoral degrees. 71 undergraduate majors. *Total enrollment:* 3,886. Undergraduates: 3,535. Freshmen: 872. Federal methodology is used as a basis for awarding need-based institutional aid. **UNDERGRADUATE EXPENSES for 2018–2019** *Application fee:* $30. *Comprehensive fee:* $37,630 includes full-time tuition ($30,070), mandatory fees ($200), and room and board ($7360). *College room only:* $4172. Room and board charges vary according to board plan and housing facility. *Part-time tuition:* $1138 per credit. *Part-time fees:* $50 per term. Part-time tuition and fees vary according to course load. **FRESHMAN FINANCIAL AID (Fall 2017, est.)** 807 applied for aid; of those 83% were deemed to have need. 100% of freshmen with need received aid; of those 35% had need fully met. *Average percent of need met:* 22% (excluding resources awarded to replace EFC). *Average financial aid package:* $22,070 (excluding

resources awarded to replace EFC). 21% of all full-time freshmen had no need and received non-need-based gift aid. **UNDERGRADUATE FINANCIAL AID (Fall 2017, est.)** 2,521 applied for aid; of those 86% were deemed to have need. 100% of undergraduates with need received aid; of those 33% had need fully met. *Average percent of need met:* 31% (excluding resources awarded to replace EFC). *Average financial aid package:* $21,864 (excluding resources awarded to replace EFC). 18% of all full-time undergraduates had no need and received non-need-based gift aid. **GIFT AID (NEED-BASED)** *Total amount:* $10,906,725 (29% federal, 6% state, 64% institutional, 1% external sources). *Receiving aid:* Freshmen: 55% (479); all full-time undergraduates: 53% (1,651). *Average award:* Freshmen: $4141; Undergraduates: $4707. *Scholarships, grants, and awards:* Federal Pell, FSEOG, state, private, college/university gift aid from institutional funds, Federal Nursing. **GIFT AID (NON-NEED-BASED)** *Total amount:* $36,444,223 (86% institutional, 14% external sources). *Receiving aid:* Freshmen: 76% (659). Undergraduates: 66% (2,050). *Average award:* Freshmen: $12,752. Undergraduates: $12,806. *Scholarships, grants, and awards by category:* Academic interests/achievement: 1,766 awards ($11,823,467 total): general academic interests/achievements. *Creative arts/performance:* 124 awards ($451,400 total): debating, music. *Special achievements/activities:* 560 awards ($684,037 total): leadership. *Special characteristics:* 426 awards ($3,600,579 total): children of faculty/staff, ethnic background, general special characteristics, religious affiliation, veterans. *Tuition waivers:* Full or partial for employees or children of employees, adult students, senior citizens. *ROTC:* Army cooperative, Air Force cooperative. **LOANS** *Student loans:* $17,787,781 (41% need-based, 59% non-need-based). 61% of past graduating class borrowed through all loan programs. *Average indebtedness per student:* $29,582. *Average need-based loan:* Freshmen: $4161. Undergraduates: $5346. *Parent loans:* $15,230,585 (100% non-need-based). *Programs:* Federal Direct (Subsidized and Unsubsidized Stafford, PLUS), Perkins, Federal Nursing, college/university. **WORK-STUDY** *Federal work-study:* Total amount: $549,868; 240 jobs averaging $2291. *State or other work-study/employment:* Total amount: $1,977,282 (100% non-need-based). 1,439 part-time jobs averaging $1374. **ATHLETIC AWARDS** Total amount: $1,587,803 (100% non-need-based). **APPLYING FOR FINANCIAL AID** *Required financial aid form:* FAFSA. *Financial aid deadline (priority):* 3/1. *Notification date:* Continuous beginning 3/1. Students must reply within 3 weeks of notification. **CONTACT** Mr. Russell Kim Jenerette, Executive Director of Financial Aid, Cedarville University, 251 North Main Street, Cedarville, OH 45314-0601, 937-766-7866 or toll-free 800-233-2784. *Fax:* 937-766-7639. *E-mail:* kimjenerette@cedarville.edu. *Website:* http://www.cedarville.edu/.

CENTENARY COLLEGE OF LOUISIANA
Shreveport, LA

Tuition & fees: $36,580	Average undergraduate aid package: $30,528

ABOUT THE INSTITUTION Independent United Methodist, coed. *Awards:* bachelor's and master's degrees. 24 undergraduate majors. *Total enrollment:* 588. Undergraduates: 533. Freshmen: 173. Federal methodology is used as a basis for awarding need-based institutional aid. **UNDERGRADUATE EXPENSES for 2018–2019** *One-time required fee:* $250. *Comprehensive fee:* $49,980 includes full-time tuition ($36,580) and room and board ($13,400). Full-time tuition and fees vary according to course load and degree level. Room and board charges vary according to board plan, housing facility, and student level. *Part-time tuition:* $1524 per credit hour. Part-time tuition and fees vary according to course load and degree level. **FRESHMAN FINANCIAL AID (Fall 2017, est.)** 169 applied for aid; of those 82% were deemed to have need. 100% of freshmen with need received aid; of those 25% had need fully met. *Average percent of need met:* 73% (excluding resources awarded to replace EFC). *Average financial aid package:* $28,259 (excluding resources awarded to replace EFC). 20% of all full-time freshmen had no need and received non-need-based gift aid. **UNDERGRADUATE FINANCIAL AID (Fall 2017, est.)** 463 applied for aid; of those 88% were deemed to have need. 100% of undergraduates with need received aid; of those 23% had need fully met. *Average percent of need met:* 75%

(excluding resources awarded to replace EFC). **Average financial aid package:** $30,528 (excluding resources awarded to replace EFC). 21% of all full-time undergraduates had no need and received non-need-based gift aid.

GIFT AID (NEED-BASED) *Total amount:* $10,897,207 (10% federal, 11% state, 78% institutional, 1% external sources). *Receiving aid:* Freshmen: 80% (138); all full-time undergraduates: 78% (406). *Average award:* Freshmen: $25,351; Undergraduates: $26,816. *Scholarships, grants, and awards:* Federal Pell, FSEOG, state, private, college/university gift aid from institutional funds.

GIFT AID (NON-NEED-BASED) *Total amount:* $3,686,425 (7% state, 92% institutional, 1% external sources). *Receiving aid:* Freshmen: 18% (31). Undergraduates: 15% (76). *Average award:* Freshmen: $21,943. Undergraduates: $22,400. *Scholarships, grants, and awards by category:* Academic interests/achievement: 585 awards ($7,390,755 total): biological sciences, business, communication, education, engineering/technologies, English, foreign languages, general academic interests/achievements, humanities, mathematics, physical sciences, premedicine, religion/biblical studies, social sciences. *Creative arts/performance:* 81 awards ($372,750 total): art/fine arts, dance, general creative arts/performance, music, performing arts, theater/drama. *Special achievements/activities:* 52 awards ($144,201 total): community service, general special achievements/activities, hobbies/interests, religious involvement. *Special characteristics:* 108 awards ($3,008,104 total): children and siblings of alumni, children of educators, children of faculty/staff, ethnic background, first-generation college students, general special characteristics, international students, local/state students, members of minority groups, out-of-state students, relatives of clergy, religious affiliation, siblings of current students, veterans, veterans' children. *Tuition waivers:* Full or partial for employees or children of employees.

LOANS *Student loans:* $2,334,430 (49% need-based, 51% non-need-based). 75% of past graduating class borrowed through all loan programs. *Average indebtedness per student:* $32,900. *Average need-based loan:* Freshmen: $3578. Undergraduates: $4501. *Parent loans:* $1,161,411 (92% need-based, 8% non-need-based). *Programs:* Federal Direct (Subsidized and Unsubsidized Stafford, PLUS), Perkins.

WORK-STUDY *Federal work-study:* Total amount: $381,580; 167 jobs averaging $2285. *State or other work-study/employment:* Total amount: $83,865 (100% non-need-based). 53 part-time jobs averaging $1582.

APPLYING FOR FINANCIAL AID *Required financial aid form:* FAFSA. *Financial aid deadline (priority):* 11/1. *Notification date:* Continuous beginning 12/1. Students must reply by 5/1.

CONTACT Mrs. Lynette Viskozki, Director of Financial Aid, Centenary College of Louisiana, PO Box 41188, Shreveport, LA 71134-1188, 318-869-5137 or toll-free 800-234-4448. *Fax:* 318-841-7266. *E-mail:* lviskozk@centenary.edu. *Website:* http://www.centenary.edu/.

CENTENARY UNIVERSITY
Hackettstown, NJ

CONTACT Michelle Burwell, Associate Director of Financial Aid, Centenary University, 400 Jefferson Street, Hackettstown, NJ 07840-2100, 908-852-1400 Ext. 2240 or toll-free 800-236-8679. *Fax:* 908-813-2632. *E-mail:* burwellm@centenarycollege.edu. *Website:* http://www.centenaryuniversity.edu/.

CENTRAL BAPTIST COLLEGE
Conway, AR

CONTACT Christi Bell, Financial Aid Director, Central Baptist College, 1501 College Avenue, Conway, AR 72032-6470, 800-205-6872 Ext. 185 or toll-free 800-205-6872. *Fax:* 501-329-2941. *E-mail:* financialaid@cbc.edu. *Website:* http://www.cbc.edu/.

CENTRAL CHRISTIAN COLLEGE OF KANSAS
McPherson, KS

CONTACT Mike Reimer, Financial Aid Director, Central Christian College of Kansas, 1200 South Main, PO Box 1403, McPherson, KS 67460, 620-241-0723 Ext. 333 or toll-free 800-835-0078. *Fax:* 620-241-6032. *E-mail:* miker@centralchristian.edu. *Website:* http://www.centralchristian.edu/.

CENTRAL CHRISTIAN COLLEGE OF THE BIBLE
Moberly, MO

CONTACT Ms. Rhonda Dunham, Financial Aid Director, Central Christian College of the Bible, 911 East Urbandale Drive, Moberly, MO 65270-1997, 660-263-3900 Ext. 121 or toll-free 888-263-3900. *Fax:* 660-263-3936. *E-mail:* rdunham@cccb.edu. *Website:* http://www.cccb.edu/.

CENTRAL COLLEGE
Pella, IA

Tuition & fees: N/R	Average undergraduate aid package: $31,342

ABOUT THE INSTITUTION Independent Reformed Church in America, coed. 38 undergraduate majors. Federal methodology is used as a basis for awarding need-based institutional aid.

FRESHMAN FINANCIAL AID (Fall 2017, est.) 317 applied for aid; of those 91% were deemed to have need. 100% of freshmen with need received aid; of those 15% had need fully met. *Average percent of need met:* 83% (excluding resources awarded to replace EFC). *Average financial aid package:* $31,856 (excluding resources awarded to replace EFC). 10% of all full-time freshmen had no need and received non-need-based gift aid.

UNDERGRADUATE FINANCIAL AID (Fall 2017, est.) 1,070 applied for aid; of those 92% were deemed to have need. 100% of undergraduates with need received aid; of those 17% had need fully met. *Average percent of need met:* 82% (excluding resources awarded to replace EFC). *Average financial aid package:* $31,342 (excluding resources awarded to replace EFC). 17% of all full-time undergraduates had no need and received non-need-based gift aid.

GIFT AID (NEED-BASED) *Total amount:* $25,179,988 (7% federal, 9% state, 83% institutional, 1% external sources). *Receiving aid:* Freshmen: 90% (290); all full-time undergraduates: 83% (983). *Average award:* Freshmen: $28,166; Undergraduates: $26,584. *Scholarships, grants, and awards:* Federal Pell, FSEOG, state, private, college/university gift aid from institutional funds.

GIFT AID (NON-NEED-BASED) *Total amount:* $5,651,605 (5% federal, 92% institutional, 3% external sources). *Receiving aid:* Freshmen: 11% (37). Undergraduates: 10% (123). *Average award:* Freshmen: $21,284. Undergraduates: $21,100. *Scholarships, grants, and awards by category:* Academic interests/achievement: biological sciences, business, computer science, education, engineering/technologies, foreign languages, general academic interests/achievements, health fields, humanities, international studies, mathematics, physical sciences, premedicine, religion/biblical studies, social sciences. *Creative arts/performance:* art/fine arts, creative writing, music, theater/drama. *Special achievements/activities:* community service, religious involvement. *Special characteristics:* children and siblings of alumni, children of current students, children of faculty/staff, general special characteristics, handicapped students, international students, local/state students, members of minority groups, out-of-state students, previous college experience, religious affiliation, siblings of current students, twins, veterans, veterans' children.

LOANS *Student loans:* $8,380,960 (69% need-based, 31% non-need-based). 81% of past graduating class borrowed through all loan programs. *Average indebtedness per student:* $34,273. *Average need-based loan:* Freshmen: $3055. Undergraduates: $3934. *Parent loans:* $2,572,940 (32% need-based, 68% non-need-based). *Programs:* Federal Direct (Subsidized and Unsubsidized Stafford, PLUS), Perkins, college/university, alternative loans.

WORK-STUDY *Federal work-study:* Total amount: $797,594; jobs available. *State or other work-study/employment:* Total amount: $613,708 (100% non-need-based). Part-time jobs available.

APPLYING FOR FINANCIAL AID *Required financial aid form:* FAFSA. *Financial aid deadline (priority):* 12/15. *Notification date:* Continuous beginning 11/4. Students must reply by 5/1 or within 2 weeks of notification.

CONTACT Wayne Dille, Director of Financial Aid, Central College, 812 University Street, Campus Box 5800, Pella, IA 50219-1999, 641-628-5336 or toll-free 877-462-3687. *Fax:* 641-628-7199. *E-mail:* dillew@central.edu. *Website:* http://www.central.edu/.

CENTRAL CONNECTICUT STATE UNIVERSITY
New Britain, CT

Tuition & fees (CT res): $10,225	Average undergraduate aid package: $8551

ABOUT THE INSTITUTION State-supported, coed. *Awards:* certificates, bachelor's, master's, and doctoral degrees. 64 undergraduate majors. *Total enrollment:* 11,880. Undergraduates: 9,554. Freshmen: 1,433. Federal methodology is used as a basis for awarding need-based institutional aid.

UNDERGRADUATE EXPENSES for **2017–2018** *Application fee:* $50. *Tuition, state resident:* full-time $5424; part-time $226 per credit. *Tuition, non-resident:* full-time $16,882; part-time $226 per credit. *Required fees:* full-time $4801; $275 per credit or $78 per term. Full-time tuition and fees vary according to course level, course load, and program. Part-time tuition and fees vary according to course level, course load, and program. *College room and board:* $11,816; *Room only:* $6820. Room and board charges vary according to board plan and housing facility.

FRESHMAN FINANCIAL AID (Fall 2017, est.) 1,269 applied for aid; of those 83% were deemed to have need. 96% of freshmen with need received aid; of those 11% had need fully met. *Average percent of need met:* 65% (excluding resources awarded to replace EFC). *Average financial aid package:* $8747 (excluding resources awarded to replace EFC). 3% of all full-time freshmen had no need and received non-need-based gift aid.

UNDERGRADUATE FINANCIAL AID (Fall 2017, est.) 6,944 applied for aid; of those 87% were deemed to have need. 89% of undergraduates with need received aid; of those 96% had need fully met. *Average percent of need met:* 63% (excluding resources awarded to replace EFC). *Average financial aid package:* $8551 (excluding resources awarded to replace EFC). 1% of all full-time undergraduates had no need and received non-need-based gift aid.

GIFT AID (NEED-BASED) *Total amount:* $26,917,649 (55% federal, 14% state, 26% institutional, 5% external sources). *Receiving aid:* Freshmen: 58% (825); all full-time undergraduates: 49% (3,745). *Average award:* Freshmen: $6050; Undergraduates: $6573. *Scholarships, grants, and awards:* Federal Pell, FSEOG, state, college/university gift aid from institutional funds.

GIFT AID (NON-NEED-BASED) *Total amount:* $3,030,105 (100% institutional). *Receiving aid:* Freshmen: 15% (213). Undergraduates: 13% (956). *Average award:* Freshmen: $3053. Undergraduates: $3149. *Scholarships, grants, and awards by category:* Academic interests/achievement: general academic interests/achievements. *Special characteristics:* 695 awards ($1,127,935 total): members of minority groups. *Tuition waivers:* Full or partial for employees or children of employees, senior citizens. *ROTC:* Army cooperative, Air Force cooperative.

LOANS *Student loans:* $50,322,173 (41% need-based, 59% non-need-based). 61% of past graduating class borrowed through all loan programs. *Average indebtedness per student:* $5831. *Average need-based loan:* Freshmen: $3615. Undergraduates: $3356. *Parent loans:* $7,117,357 (100% non-need-based). *Programs:* Federal Direct (Subsidized and Unsubsidized Stafford, PLUS), Perkins.

WORK-STUDY *Federal work-study:* Total amount: $308,100; 275 jobs averaging $1500. *State or other work-study/employment:* Part-time jobs available.

ATHLETIC AWARDS Total amount: $3,928,456 (100% non-need-based).

APPLYING FOR FINANCIAL AID *Required financial aid form:* FAFSA. *Financial aid deadline (priority):* 3/1. *Notification date:* Continuous beginning 1/15. Students must reply by 5/1 or within 2 weeks of notification.

CONTACT Mr. Richard Bishop, Director of Financial Aid, Central Connecticut State University, Davidson Hall, Room 221, New Britain, CT 06050-4010, 860-832-2200 or toll-free 888-733-2278 (in-state). *Fax:* 860-832-3330. *E-mail:* finaid@ccsu.edu. *Website:* http://www.ccsu.edu/.

CENTRAL METHODIST UNIVERSITY
Fayette, MO

Tuition & fees: $24,420	Average undergraduate aid package: $20,911

ABOUT THE INSTITUTION Independent Methodist, coed. *Awards:* associate, bachelor's, and master's degrees. 41 undergraduate majors. *Total enrollment:* 1,060. Undergraduates: 1,060. Freshmen: 279. Federal methodology is used as a basis for awarding need-based institutional aid.

UNDERGRADUATE EXPENSES for **2018–2019** *One-time required fee:* $100. *Comprehensive fee:* $32,360 includes full-time tuition ($23,650), mandatory fees ($770), and room and board ($7940). *College room only:* $3890. Full-time tuition and fees vary according to program and reciprocity agreements. Room and board charges vary according to board plan and housing facility. *Part-time tuition:* $210 per credit hour. *Part-time fees:* $31 per credit hour. Part-time tuition and fees vary according to course load and program.

FRESHMAN FINANCIAL AID (Fall 2017, est.) 254 applied for aid; of those 90% were deemed to have need. 100% of freshmen with need received aid; of those 23% had need fully met. *Average percent of need met:* 74% (excluding resources awarded to replace EFC). *Average financial aid package:* $20,642 (excluding resources awarded to replace EFC). 13% of all full-time freshmen had no need and received non-need-based gift aid.

UNDERGRADUATE FINANCIAL AID (Fall 2017, est.) 904 applied for aid; of those 92% were deemed to have need. 100% of undergraduates with need received aid; of those 21% had need fully met. *Average percent of need met:* 75% (excluding resources awarded to replace EFC). *Average financial aid package:* $20,911 (excluding resources awarded to replace EFC). 13% of all full-time undergraduates had no need and received non-need-based gift aid.

GIFT AID (NEED-BASED) *Total amount:* $3,205,544 (68% federal, 24% state, 8% institutional). *Receiving aid:* Freshmen: 54% (148); all full-time undergraduates: 53% (554). *Average award:* Freshmen: $5417; Undergraduates: $5303. *Scholarships, grants, and awards:* Federal Pell, FSEOG, state, private, college/university gift aid from institutional funds.

GIFT AID (NON-NEED-BASED) *Total amount:* $10,024,380 (1% state, 92% institutional, 7% external sources). *Receiving aid:* Freshmen: 84% (229). Undergraduates: 81% (834). *Average award:* Freshmen: $12,957. Undergraduates: $11,700. *Scholarships, grants, and awards by category:* Academic interests/achievement: biological sciences, business, communication, computer science, education, English, foreign languages, general academic interests/achievements, health fields, humanities, mathematics, physical sciences, premedicine, religion/biblical studies, social sciences. *Creative arts/performance:* music, theater/drama. *Special achievements/activities:* cheerleading/drum major, leadership, religious involvement. *Special characteristics:* children and siblings of alumni, children of faculty/staff, general special characteristics, international students, relatives of clergy, religious affiliation, siblings of current students, spouses of current students. *Tuition waivers:* Full or partial for children of alumni, employees or children of employees. *ROTC:* Army cooperative, Air Force cooperative.

LOANS *Student loans:* $6,544,156 (43% need-based, 57% non-need-based). *Average need-based loan:* Freshmen: $3211. Undergraduates: $4246. *Parent loans:* $1,613,088 (100% non-need-based). *Programs:* Federal Direct (Subsidized and Unsubsidized Stafford, PLUS), Perkins.

WORK-STUDY *Federal work-study:* Total amount: $179,448; jobs available. *State or other work-study/employment:* Total amount: $59,521 (100% non-need-based). Part-time jobs available.

ATHLETIC AWARDS Total amount: $4,235,494 (100% non-need-based).

APPLYING FOR FINANCIAL AID *Required financial aid form:* FAFSA. *Financial aid deadline:* Continuous. *Notification date:* Continuous beginning 10/1. Students must reply by 8/1.

CONTACT Mrs. Kristen M. Gibbs, Director of Financial Assistance, Central Methodist University, 411 Central Methodist Square, Fayette, MO 65248-1198, 660-248-6244 or toll-free 888-CMU-1854 (in-state), 877-CMU-1854 (out-of-state). *Fax:* 660-248-6288. *E-mail:* kgibbs@centralmethodist.edu. *Website:* http://www.centralmethodist.edu/.

CENTRAL MICHIGAN UNIVERSITY
Mount Pleasant, MI

Tuition & fees (MI res): $12,510	Average undergraduate aid package: $13,337

ABOUT THE INSTITUTION State-supported, coed. *Awards:* certificates, bachelor's, master's, and doctoral degrees. 121 undergraduate majors. *Total enrollment:* 23,335. Undergraduates: 17,845. Freshmen: 3,076. Federal methodology is used as a basis for awarding need-based institutional aid.

UNDERGRADUATE EXPENSES for 2017–2018 *Application fee:* $35. *Tuition, state resident:* full-time $12,510; part-time $417 per credit hour. *Tuition, nonresident:* full-time $23,670; part-time $789 per credit hour. Full-time tuition and fees vary according to location. Part-time tuition and fees vary according to location. *College room and board:* $9736; *Room only:* $4868. Room and board charges vary according to board plan and housing facility.

FRESHMAN FINANCIAL AID (Fall 2016) 3,154 applied for aid; of those 76% were deemed to have need. 97% of freshmen with need received aid; of those 56% had need fully met. *Average percent of need met:* 84% (excluding resources awarded to replace EFC). *Average financial aid package:* $14,438 (excluding resources awarded to replace EFC). 23% of all full-time freshmen had no need and received non-need-based gift aid.

UNDERGRADUATE FINANCIAL AID (Fall 2016) 13,224 applied for aid; of those 79% were deemed to have need. 98% of undergraduates with need received aid; of those 37% had need fully met. *Average percent of need met:* 80% (excluding resources awarded to replace EFC). *Average financial aid package:* $13,337 (excluding resources awarded to replace EFC). 13% of all full-time undergraduates had no need and received non-need-based gift aid.

GIFT AID (NEED-BASED) *Total amount:* $54,105,197 (43% federal, 4% state, 50% institutional, 3% external sources). *Receiving aid:* Freshmen: 62% (2,156); all full-time undergraduates: 48% (8,233). *Average award:* Freshmen: $8584; Undergraduates: $6765. *Scholarships, grants, and awards:* Federal Pell, FSEOG, state, private, college/university gift aid from institutional funds.

GIFT AID (NON-NEED-BASED) *Total amount:* $15,739,733 (1% state, 91% institutional, 8% external sources). *Receiving aid:* Freshmen: 8% (287). Undergraduates: 4% (689). *Average award:* Freshmen: $5522. Undergraduates: $5471. *Scholarships, grants, and awards by category: Academic interests/achievement:* 1,504 awards ($5,074,814 total): biological sciences, business, communication, computer science, education, engineering/technologies, English, foreign languages, general academic interests/achievements, health fields, home economics, humanities, international studies, mathematics, military science, physical sciences, premedicine, religion/biblical studies, social sciences. *Creative arts/performance:* 164 awards ($300,557 total): applied art and design, art/fine arts, cinema/film/broadcasting, creative writing, dance, general creative arts/performance, journalism/publications, music, performing arts, theater/drama. *Special achievements/activities:* 1,008 awards ($6,838,410 total): general special achievements/activities, leadership. *Special characteristics:* 222 awards ($1,636,083 total): children and siblings of alumni, children of faculty/staff, ethnic background, international students, local/state students, out-of-state students. *Tuition waivers:* Full or partial for children of alumni, employees or children of employees, senior citizens. *ROTC:* Army, Air Force cooperative.

LOANS *Student loans:* $69,844,930 (77% need-based, 23% non-need-based). 73% of past graduating class borrowed through all loan programs. *Average indebtedness per student:* $33,635. *Average need-based loan:* Freshmen: $5859. Undergraduates: $7077. *Parent loans:* $37,787,710 (34% need-based, 66% non-need-based). *Programs:* Federal Direct (Subsidized and Unsubsidized Stafford, PLUS), state, college/university.

WORK-STUDY *Federal work-study:* jobs available. *State or other work-study/employment:* Total amount: $668,693 (76% need-based, 24% non-need-based). Part-time jobs available.

ATHLETIC AWARDS Total amount: $5,613,076 (29% need-based, 71% non-need-based).

Required financial aid form: FAFSA. *Financial aid deadline (priority):* 2/15. *Notification date:* Continuous beginning 3/31.

CONTACT Mr. Kirk M. Yats, Director of Scholarships and Financial Aid, Central Michigan University, 1200 South Franklin Street, Mount Pleasant, MI 48859, 989-774-3674 or toll-free 888-292-5366. *Fax:* 989-774-3634. *E-mail:* cmuosfa@cmich.edu. *Website:* http://www.cmich.edu/.

CENTRAL PENN COLLEGE
Summerdale, PA

ABOUT THE INSTITUTION Proprietary, coed. *Awards:* associate, bachelor's, and master's degrees. 25 undergraduate majors. *Total enrollment:* 1,224. Undergraduates: 1,196. Freshmen: 164.

GIFT AID (NEED-BASED) *Scholarships, grants, and awards:* Federal Pell, FSEOG, state, private, college/university gift aid from institutional funds.

GIFT AID (NON-NEED-BASED) *Scholarships, grants, and awards by category: Academic interests/achievement:* general academic interests/achievements. *Special achievements/activities:* leadership, memberships. *Special characteristics:* general special characteristics, out-of-state students.

LOANS *Programs:* Federal Direct (Subsidized and Unsubsidized Stafford, PLUS).

WORK-STUDY *Federal work-study:* jobs available. *State or other work-study/employment:* Total amount: $1,693,028 (100% non-need-based). Part-time jobs available.

APPLYING FOR FINANCIAL AID *Required financial aid forms:* FAFSA, institution's own form, state aid form.

CONTACT Kathy Shepard, Financial Aid Director, Central Penn College, College Hill and Valley Roads, Summerdale, PA 17093, 717-728-2261 or toll-free 800-759-2727. *Fax:* 717-728-2350. *E-mail:* financial-aid@centralpenn.edu. *Website:* http://www.centralpenn.edu/.

CENTRAL STATE UNIVERSITY
Wilberforce, OH

Tuition & fees (OH res): $6246	Average undergraduate aid package: $9695

ABOUT THE INSTITUTION State-supported, coed. *Awards:* bachelor's degrees. 35 undergraduate majors. *Total enrollment:* 1,784. Undergraduates: 1,784. Freshmen: 664. Federal methodology is used as a basis for awarding need-based institutional aid.

UNDERGRADUATE EXPENSES for 2017–2018 *Application fee:* $20. *Tuition, state resident:* full-time $3926; part-time $275 per credit hour. *Tuition, nonresident:* full-time $5776; part-time $625 per credit hour. *Required fees:* full-time $2320. Full-time tuition and fees vary according to course load and reciprocity agreements. Part-time tuition and fees vary according to course load and reciprocity agreements. *College room and board:* $9934; *Room only:* $5340. Room and board charges vary according to board plan and housing facility.

FRESHMAN FINANCIAL AID (Fall 2017, est.) 758 applied for aid; of those 100% were deemed to have need. 100% of freshmen with need received aid; of those 5% had need fully met. *Average percent of need met:* 5% (excluding resources awarded to replace EFC). *Average financial aid package:* $8934 (excluding resources awarded to replace EFC).

UNDERGRADUATE FINANCIAL AID (Fall 2017, est.) 1,671 applied for aid; of those 100% were deemed to have need. 100% of undergraduates with need received aid; of those 9% had need fully met. *Average percent of need met:* 9% (excluding resources awarded to replace EFC). *Average financial aid package:* $9695 (excluding resources awarded to replace EFC).

GIFT AID (NEED-BASED) *Total amount:* $11,341,207 (72% federal, 3% state, 21% institutional, 4% external sources). *Receiving aid:* Freshmen: 99% (755); all full-time undergraduates: 99% (1,668). *Average award:* Freshmen: $7384; Undergraduates: $7455. *Scholarships, grants, and awards:* Federal Pell, FSEOG, state, private, college/university gift aid from institutional funds.

GIFT AID (NON-NEED-BASED) *Scholarships, grants, and awards by category: Academic interests/achievement:* business, computer science, education, engineering/technologies, general academic interests/achievements, physical sciences.

Creative arts/performance: music. *Special characteristics:* children of faculty/staff, veterans, veterans' children. *Tuition waivers:* Full or partial for employees or children of employees, senior citizens. *ROTC:* Army.
LOANS *Student loans:* $12,107,378 (100% need-based). *Average need-based loan:* Freshmen: $3309. Undergraduates: $3803. *Parent loans:* $3,489,111 (100% need-based).
WORK-STUDY *Federal work-study:* Total amount: $1,030,797; jobs available.
ATHLETIC AWARDS Total amount: $555,891 (100% need-based).
APPLYING FOR FINANCIAL AID *Required financial aid form:* FAFSA. *Financial aid deadline (priority):* 2/15. *Notification date:* Continuous beginning 4/1. Students must reply within 2 weeks of notification.
CONTACT Sonia Slomba, Director of Student Financial Aid, Central State University, PO Box 1004, Wilberforce, OH 45384, 937-376-6579 or toll-free 800-388-CSU1 (in-state), 800-388-2781 (out-of-state). *Fax:* 937-376-6519. *E-mail:* sslomba@centralstate.edu.
Website: http://www.centralstate.edu/.

CENTRAL WASHINGTON UNIVERSITY
Ellensburg, WA

Tuition & fees (WA res): $7849	Average undergraduate aid package: $10,340

ABOUT THE INSTITUTION State-supported, coed. *Awards:* certificates, bachelor's, and master's degrees. 138 undergraduate majors. *Total enrollment:* 11,971. Undergraduates: 11,047. Freshmen: 1,665. Federal methodology is used as a basis for awarding need-based institutional aid.
UNDERGRADUATE EXPENSES for 2017–2018 *Application fee:* $50. *Tuition, state resident:* full-time $6037; part-time $224.93 per credit. *Tuition, nonresident:* full-time $20,144; part-time $695.16 per credit. *Required fees:* full-time $1812. Full-time tuition and fees vary according to course load, degree level, location, and reciprocity agreements. Part-time tuition and fees vary according to course load, degree level, location, and reciprocity agreements. *College room and board:* $10,684. Room and board charges vary according to board plan, housing facility, and location.
FRESHMAN FINANCIAL AID (Fall 2016) 1,724 applied for aid; of those 84% were deemed to have need. 89% of freshmen with need received aid; of those 20% had need fully met. *Average percent of need met:* 81% (excluding resources awarded to replace EFC). *Average financial aid package:* $11,110 (excluding resources awarded to replace EFC). 1% of all full-time freshmen had no need and received non-need-based gift aid.
UNDERGRADUATE FINANCIAL AID (Fall 2016) 8,638 applied for aid; of those 80% were deemed to have need. 95% of undergraduates with need received aid; of those 14% had need fully met. *Average percent of need met:* 68% (excluding resources awarded to replace EFC). *Average financial aid package:* $10,340 (excluding resources awarded to replace EFC). 1% of all full-time undergraduates had no need and received non-need-based gift aid.
GIFT AID (NEED-BASED) *Total amount:* $39,236,433 (46% federal, 43% state, 5% institutional, 6% external sources). *Receiving aid:* Freshmen: 41% (785); all full-time undergraduates: 46% (4,861). *Average award:* Freshmen: $8355; Undergraduates: $7706. *Scholarships, grants, and awards:* Federal Pell, FSEOG, state, private, college/university gift aid from institutional funds.
GIFT AID (NON-NEED-BASED) *Total amount:* $934,199 (2% federal, 5% state, 2% institutional, 91% external sources). *Receiving aid:* Freshmen: 22% (411). Undergraduates: 1% (143). *Average award:* Freshmen: $567. Undergraduates: $1029. *Scholarships, grants, and awards by category:* Academic interests/achievement: general academic interests/achievements. Creative arts/performance: art/fine arts, general creative arts/performance, music, theater/drama. Special achievements/activities: leadership. Special characteristics: children and siblings of alumni, children of faculty/staff, children of public servants, local/state students, members of minority groups, out-of-state students, public servants, veterans, veterans' children. *Tuition waivers:* Full or partial for employees or children of employees, senior citizens. *ROTC:* Army, Air Force.
LOANS *Student loans:* $44,470,869 (74% need-based, 26% non-need-based). 84% of past graduating class borrowed through all loan programs. *Average indebtedness per student:* $20,411. *Average need-based loan:* Freshmen: $3264. Undergraduates: $4180. *Parent loans:* $19,417,982 (29% need-based, 71% non-need-based).

Programs: Federal Direct (Subsidized and Unsubsidized Stafford, PLUS), Perkins, college/university.
WORK-STUDY *Federal work-study:* jobs available. *State or other work-study/employment:* Total amount: $343,343 (100% need-based). Part-time jobs available.
ATHLETIC AWARDS Total amount: $1,429,154 (66% need-based, 34% non-need-based).
APPLYING FOR FINANCIAL AID *Required financial aid form:* FAFSA. *Financial aid deadline (priority):* 2/1. *Notification date:* Continuous beginning 3/15. Students must reply by 6/8 or within 4 weeks of notification.
CONTACT Mr. Adrian Naranjo, Director of Student Financial Services, Central Washington University, 400 East University Way, Ellensburg, WA 98926-7495, 509-963-2091. *Fax:* 509-963-1788. *E-mail:* finaid@cwu.edu.
Website: http://www.cwu.edu/.

CENTRAL YESHIVA BETH JOSEPH
Brooklyn, NY

CONTACT Financial Aid Office, Central Yeshiva Beth Joseph, 1502 Avenue N, Brooklyn, NY 11230.
Website: http://www.centralyeshivabethjoseph.com.

CENTRAL YESHIVA TOMCHEI TMIMIM-LUBAVITCH
Brooklyn, NY

CONTACT Rabbi Moshe M. Gluckowsky, Director of Financial Aid, Central Yeshiva Tomchei Tmimim-Lubavitch, 841-853 Ocean Parkway, Brooklyn, NY 11230, 718-859-2277.

CENTRE COLLEGE
Danville, KY

Tuition & fees: $41,700	Average undergraduate aid package: $33,516

ABOUT THE INSTITUTION Independent Presbyterian Church (U.S.A.), coed. *Awards:* bachelor's degrees. 28 undergraduate majors. *Total enrollment:* 1,450. Undergraduates: 1,450. Freshmen: 401. Federal methodology is used as a basis for awarding need-based institutional aid.
UNDERGRADUATE EXPENSES for 2018–2019 *Comprehensive fee:* $52,180 includes full-time tuition ($41,700) and room and board ($10,480). *College room only:* $5240. Room and board charges vary according to housing facility. *Part-time tuition:* $1446 per credit hour.
FRESHMAN FINANCIAL AID (Fall 2017, est.) 348 applied for aid; of those 75% were deemed to have need. 100% of freshmen with need received aid; of those 37% had need fully met. *Average percent of need met:* 87% (excluding resources awarded to replace EFC). *Average financial aid package:* $34,441 (excluding resources awarded to replace EFC). 34% of all full-time freshmen had no need and received non-need-based gift aid.
UNDERGRADUATE FINANCIAL AID (Fall 2017, est.) 1,051 applied for aid; of those 80% were deemed to have need. 100% of undergraduates with need received aid; of those 32% had need fully met. *Average percent of need met:* 86% (excluding resources awarded to replace EFC). *Average financial aid package:* $33,516 (excluding resources awarded to replace EFC). 37% of all full-time undergraduates had no need and received non-need-based gift aid.
GIFT AID (NEED-BASED) *Total amount:* $25,619,221 (5% federal, 9% state, 84% institutional, 2% external sources). *Receiving aid:* Freshmen: 65% (260); all full-time undergraduates: 59% (844). *Average award:* Freshmen: $31,901; Undergraduates: $30,467. *Scholarships, grants, and awards:* Federal Pell, FSEOG, state, private, college/university gift aid from institutional funds.
GIFT AID (NON-NEED-BASED) *Total amount:* $12,621,246 (5% state, 92% institutional, 3% external sources). *Average award:* Freshmen: $23,084. Undergrad-

uates: $22,157. *Scholarships, grants, and awards by category:* Academic interests/achievement: 1,256 awards ($21,093,326 total): foreign languages. *Creative arts/performance:* 79 awards ($244,500 total): music, theater/drama. *Special achievements/activities:* 30 awards ($204,000 total): community service. *Special characteristics:* 253 awards ($4,318,308 total): children and siblings of alumni, children of faculty/staff, ethnic background, first-generation college students. *Tuition waivers:* Full or partial for employees or children of employees. *ROTC:* Army cooperative, Air Force cooperative.

LOANS *Student loans:* $5,369,118 (58% need-based, 42% non-need-based). 45% of past graduating class borrowed through all loan programs. *Average indebtedness per student:* $24,917. *Average need-based loan:* Freshmen: $3412. Undergraduates: $4615. *Parent loans:* $2,062,888 (100% non-need-based). *Programs:* Federal Direct (Subsidized and Unsubsidized Stafford, PLUS), college/university.

WORK-STUDY *Federal work-study:* Total amount: $569,500; 362 jobs averaging $1499. *State or other work-study/employment:* Total amount: $14,500 (100% need-based). Part-time jobs available.

APPLYING FOR FINANCIAL AID *Required financial aid forms:* FAFSA, institution's own form. *Financial aid deadline (priority):* 1/31. *Notification date:* Continuous beginning 2/19. Students must reply by 5/1.

CONTACT Mr. Kevin Lamb, Associate Dean of Admission and Financial Aid, Centre College, 600 West Walnut Street, Danville, KY 40422-1394, 859-238-5365 or toll-free 800-423-6236. *Fax:* 859-238-8719. *E-mail:* finaid@centre.edu. *Website:* http://www.centre.edu/.

CENTRO DE ESTUDIOS MULTIDISCIPLINARIOS
Bayamon, PR

CONTACT Financial Aid Office, Centro de Estudios Multidisciplinarios, Calle Degetau #25, Bayamon, PR 00961, 787-780-8900. *Website:* http://www.cempr.edu/.

CENTRO DE ESTUDIOS MULTIDISCIPLINARIOS
Humacao, PR

CONTACT Financial Aid Office, Centro de Estudios Multidisciplinarios, Calle Dr. Vidal #8 y #53, Humacao, PR 00791, 809-852-5505. *Website:* http://www.cempr.edu/.

CHADRON STATE COLLEGE
Chadron, NE

CONTACT Ms. Sherry Douglas, Director of Financial Aid, Chadron State College, 1000 Main Street, Chadron, NE 69337, 308-432-6230 or toll-free 800-242-3766. *Fax:* 308-432-6229. *E-mail:* finaid@csc.edu. *Website:* http://www.csc.edu/.

CHAMBERLAIN COLLEGE OF NURSING
Phoenix, AZ

CONTACT Financial Aid Office, Chamberlain College of Nursing, 2149 West Dunlap Avenue, Phoenix, AZ 85021, 602-331-2720 or toll-free 877-751-5783. *Website:* http://www.chamberlain.edu/.

CHAMBERLAIN COLLEGE OF NURSING
Rancho Cordova, CA

CONTACT Financial Aid Office, Chamberlain College of Nursing, 10971 Sun Center Drive, Rancho Cordova, CA 95670. *Website:* http://www.chamberlain.edu/.

CHAMBERLAIN COLLEGE OF NURSING
Jacksonville, FL

CONTACT Financial Aid Office, Chamberlain College of Nursing, 5200 Belfort Road, Jacksonville, FL 32256, 904-251-8110 or toll-free 877-751-5783. *Website:* http://www.chamberlain.edu/.

CHAMBERLAIN COLLEGE OF NURSING
Miramar, FL

CONTACT Financial Aid Office, Chamberlain College of Nursing, 2300 SW 145th Avenue, Miramar, FL 33027, 954-885-3510 or toll-free 877-751-5783. *Website:* http://www.chamberlain.edu/.

CHAMBERLAIN COLLEGE OF NURSING
Atlanta, GA

CONTACT Financial Aid Office, Chamberlain College of Nursing, 5775 Peachtree Dunwoody Road NE, Suite A-100, Atlanta, GA 30342, 404-250-8500 or toll-free 877-751-5783. *Website:* http://www.chamberlain.edu/.

CHAMBERLAIN COLLEGE OF NURSING
Addison, IL

CONTACT Financial Aid Office, Chamberlain College of Nursing, 1221 North Swift Road, Addison, IL 60101, 630-953-3660 or toll-free 877-751-5783. *Website:* http://www.chamberlain.edu/.

CHAMBERLAIN COLLEGE OF NURSING
Chicago, IL

CONTACT Financial Aid Office, Chamberlain College of Nursing, 3300 North Campbell Avenue, Chicago, IL 60618, 773-961-3000 or toll-free 877-751-5783. *Website:* http://www.chamberlain.edu/.

CHAMBERLAIN COLLEGE OF NURSING
Tinley Park, IL

CONTACT Financial Aid Office, Chamberlain College of Nursing, 18624 West Creek Drive, Tinley Park, IL 60477, 708-560-2000 or toll-free 877-751-5783.
Website: http://www.chamberlain.edu/.

CHAMBERLAIN COLLEGE OF NURSING
Indianapolis, IN

CONTACT Financial Aid Office, Chamberlain College of Nursing, 9100 Keystone Crossing, Indianapolis, IN 46240, 317-816-7335 or toll-free 877-751-5783.
Website: http://www.chamberlain.edu/.

CHAMBERLAIN COLLEGE OF NURSING
Troy, MI

CONTACT Financial Aid Office, Chamberlain College of Nursing, 200 Kirts Boulevard, Troy, MI 48084, 248-817-4140 or toll-free 877-751-5783.
Website: http://www.chamberlain.edu/.

CHAMBERLAIN COLLEGE OF NURSING
St. Louis, MO

CONTACT Financial Aid Counselor, Chamberlain College of Nursing, 11830 Westline Industrial Drive, Suite 106, St. Louis, MO 63146, 314-991-6200 or toll-free 877-751-5783.
Website: http://www.chamberlain.edu/.

CHAMBERLAIN COLLEGE OF NURSING
Las Vegas, NV

CONTACT Financial Aid Office, Chamberlain College of Nursing, 9901 Covington Cross Drive, Las Vegas, NV 89144, 702-786-1660 or toll-free 877-751-5783.
Website: http://www.chamberlain.edu/.

CHAMBERLAIN COLLEGE OF NURSING
North Brunswick, NJ

CONTACT Financial Aid Office, Chamberlain College of Nursing, 630 U.S. Highway 1, North Brunswick, NJ 08902, 732-875-1300 or toll-free 877-751-5783.
Website: http://www.chamberlain.edu/.

CHAMBERLAIN COLLEGE OF NURSING
Charlotte, NC

CONTACT Financial Aid Office, Chamberlain College of Nursing, 2015 Ayrsley Town Boulevard, Charlotte, NC 28273.
Website: http://www.chamberlain.edu/.

CHAMBERLAIN COLLEGE OF NURSING
Cleveland, OH

CONTACT Financial Aid Office, Chamberlain College of Nursing, 6700 Euclid Avenue, Cleveland, OH 44103, 216-361-6005 or toll-free 877-751-5783.
Website: http://www.chamberlain.edu/.

CHAMBERLAIN COLLEGE OF NURSING
Columbus, OH

CONTACT Financial Aid Office, Chamberlain College of Nursing, 1350 Alum Creek Drive, Columbus, OH 43209, 614-252-8890 or toll-free 877-751-5783.
Website: http://www.chamberlain.edu/.

CHAMBERLAIN COLLEGE OF NURSING
Houston, TX

CONTACT Financial Aid Office, Chamberlain College of Nursing, 11025 Equity Drive, Houston, TX 77041, 713-277-9800 or toll-free 877-751-5783.
Website: http://www.chamberlain.edu/.

CHAMBERLAIN COLLEGE OF NURSING
Irving, TX

CONTACT Financial Aid Office, Chamberlain College of Nursing, 4800 Regent Boulevard, Irving, TX 75063, 469-706-6705 or toll-free 866-593-8669.
Website: http://www.chamberlain.edu/.

CHAMBERLAIN COLLEGE OF NURSING
Pearland, TX

CONTACT Financial Aid Office, Chamberlain College of Nursing, 12000 Shadow Creek Parkway, Pearland, TX 77584, 832-664-7000 or toll-free 877-751-5783.
Website: http://www.chamberlain.edu/.

CHAMBERLAIN COLLEGE OF NURSING
Arlington, VA

CONTACT Financial Aid Office, Chamberlain College of Nursing, 2450 Crystal Drive, Suite 319, Arlington, VA 22202, 703-416-7300 or toll-free 877-751-5783. *Website:* http://www.chamberlain.edu/.

CHAMINADE UNIVERSITY OF HONOLULU
Honolulu, HI

Tuition & fees: $25,374	Average undergraduate aid package: $17,701

ABOUT THE INSTITUTION Independent Roman Catholic, coed. *Awards:* certificates, associate, bachelor's, and master's degrees. 23 undergraduate majors. *Total enrollment:* 1,719. Undergraduates: 1,157. Freshmen: 212. Federal methodology is used as a basis for awarding need-based institutional aid.

UNDERGRADUATE EXPENSES for 2018–2019 *Application fee:* $50. *One-time required fee:* $180. *Comprehensive fee:* $39,004 includes full-time tuition ($25,260), mandatory fees ($114), and room and board ($13,630). Full-time tuition and fees vary according to course load, location, and program. Room and board charges vary according to board plan and housing facility. *Part-time tuition:* $842 per credit. Part-time tuition and fees vary according to course load, location, and program.

FRESHMAN FINANCIAL AID (Fall 2016) 235 applied for aid; of those 79% were deemed to have need. 98% of freshmen with need received aid; of those 9% had need fully met. *Average percent of need met:* 64% (excluding resources awarded to replace EFC). *Average financial aid package:* $18,292 (excluding resources awarded to replace EFC). 28% of all full-time freshmen had no need and received non-need-based gift aid.

UNDERGRADUATE FINANCIAL AID (Fall 2016) 937 applied for aid; of those 88% were deemed to have need. 99% of undergraduates with need received aid; of those 11% had need fully met. *Average percent of need met:* 61% (excluding resources awarded to replace EFC). *Average financial aid package:* $17,701 (excluding resources awarded to replace EFC). 26% of all full-time undergraduates had no need and received non-need-based gift aid.

GIFT AID (NEED-BASED) *Receiving aid:* Freshmen: 66% (168); all full-time undergraduates: 66% (756). *Average award:* Freshmen: $4705; Undergraduates: $4608. *Scholarships, grants, and awards:* Federal Pell, FSEOG, private, college/university gift aid from institutional funds, TEACH Grants.

GIFT AID (NON-NEED-BASED) *Receiving aid:* Freshmen: 70% (178). Undergraduates: 70% (798). *Average award:* Freshmen: $10,972. Undergraduates: $8967. *Scholarships, grants, and awards by category:* Academic interests/achievement: 996 awards ($8,037,668 total): biological sciences, general academic interests/achievements, home economics, premedicine. *Special achievements/activities:* 79 awards ($1,047,654 total): community service, memberships, religious involvement. *Special characteristics:* 35 awards ($526,555 total): children of faculty/staff, ethnic background, religious affiliation, siblings of current students. *Tuition waivers:* Full or partial for employees or children of employees. *ROTC:* Army cooperative, Air Force cooperative.

LOANS *Student loans:* 64% of past graduating class borrowed through all loan programs. *Average indebtedness per student:* $26,191. *Average need-based loan:* Freshmen: $3179. Undergraduates: $4187. *Programs:* Federal Direct (Subsidized and Unsubsidized Stafford, PLUS), alternative loans.

WORK-STUDY Federal work-study jobs available.

APPLYING FOR FINANCIAL AID *Required financial aid form:* FAFSA. *Financial aid deadline:* Continuous. *Notification date:* Continuous.

CONTACT Amy Takiguchi, Director of Financial Aid, Chaminade University of Honolulu, 3140 Waialae Avenue, Honolulu, HI 96816-1578, 808-735-4780 or toll-free 800-735-3733. *Fax:* 808-739-8362. *E-mail:* finaid@chaminade.edu. *Website:* http://www.chaminade.edu/.

CHAMPLAIN COLLEGE
Burlington, VT

Tuition & fees: $39,818	Average undergraduate aid package: $25,094

ABOUT THE INSTITUTION Independent, coed. *Awards:* certificates, associate, bachelor's, and master's degrees. 36 undergraduate majors. *Total enrollment:* 3,037. Undergraduates: 2,222. Freshmen: 587. Federal methodology is used as a basis for awarding need-based institutional aid.

UNDERGRADUATE EXPENSES for 2017–2018 *Comprehensive fee:* $54,724 includes full-time tuition ($39,718), mandatory fees ($100), and room and board ($14,906). Room and board charges vary according to housing facility. *Part-time tuition:* $1658 per credit hour. *Payment plan:* Tuition prepayment.

FRESHMAN FINANCIAL AID (Fall 2017, est.) 521 applied for aid; of those 84% were deemed to have need. 100% of freshmen with need received aid; of those 20% had need fully met. *Average percent of need met:* 71% (excluding resources awarded to replace EFC). *Average financial aid package:* $28,236 (excluding resources awarded to replace EFC). 14% of all full-time freshmen had no need and received non-need-based gift aid.

UNDERGRADUATE FINANCIAL AID (Fall 2017, est.) 1,970 applied for aid; of those 88% were deemed to have need. 100% of undergraduates with need received aid; of those 15% had need fully met. *Average percent of need met:* 65% (excluding resources awarded to replace EFC). *Average financial aid package:* $25,094 (excluding resources awarded to replace EFC). 8% of all full-time undergraduates had no need and received non-need-based gift aid.

GIFT AID (NEED-BASED) *Total amount:* $33,833,896 (15% federal, 4% state, 80% institutional, 1% external sources). *Receiving aid:* Freshmen: 74% (433); all full-time undergraduates: 65% (1,641). *Average award:* Freshmen: $21,655; Undergraduates: $19,527. *Scholarships, grants, and awards:* Federal Pell, FSEOG, state, private, college/university gift aid from institutional funds.

GIFT AID (NON-NEED-BASED) *Total amount:* $8,589,188 (9% federal, 1% state, 88% institutional, 2% external sources). *Receiving aid:* Freshmen: 11% (62). Undergraduates: 6% (161). *Average award:* Freshmen: $10,778. Undergraduates: $10,660. *Scholarships, grants, and awards by category:* Academic interests/achievement: business, communication, computer science, education, general academic interests/achievements, social sciences. *Special achievements/activities:* leadership. *Special characteristics:* first-generation college students, general special characteristics, international students, members of minority groups. *Tuition waivers:* Full or partial for employees or children of employees. *ROTC:* Army cooperative.

LOANS *Student loans:* $21,916,893 (73% need-based, 27% non-need-based). 71% of past graduating class borrowed through all loan programs. *Average indebtedness per student:* $38,818. *Average need-based loan:* Freshmen: $3445. Undergraduates: $4028. *Parent loans:* $11,891,519 (52% need-based, 48% non-need-based). *Programs:* Federal Direct (Subsidized and Unsubsidized Stafford, PLUS), Perkins, state.

WORK-STUDY *Federal work-study:* Total amount: $2,739,782; jobs available.

APPLYING FOR FINANCIAL AID *Required financial aid form:* FAFSA. *Financial aid deadline:* 1/15. *Notification date:* 3/30. Students must reply by 5/1 or within 2 weeks of notification.

CONTACT Kristi Jovell, Assistant Vice President, Financial Aid and Support Services, Champlain College, 163 South Willard Street, Burlington, VT 05401, 802-860-2777 or toll-free 800-570-5858. *Fax:* 802-860-2775. *E-mail:* kjovell@champlain.edu. *Website:* http://www.champlain.edu/.

CHAPMAN UNIVERSITY
Orange, CA

Tuition & fees: $52,724	Average undergraduate aid package: $32,620

ABOUT THE INSTITUTION Independent Christian Church (Disciples of Christ), coed. *Awards:* bachelor's, master's, and doctoral degrees. 50 undergraduate majors. *Total enrollment:* 9,392. Undergraduates: 7,020. Freshmen: 1,696. Federal methodology is used as a basis for awarding need-based institutional aid.

UNDERGRADUATE EXPENSES for 2018–2019 *Application fee:* $70. *Comprehensive fee:* $68,552 includes full-time tuition ($52,340), mandatory fees ($384), and room and board ($15,828). *College room only:* $10,900. Room and board charges vary according to board plan and housing facility. *Part-time tuition:* $1625 per credit hour. Part-time tuition and fees vary according to course load. *Payment plan:* Tuition prepayment.

FRESHMAN FINANCIAL AID (Fall 2016) 1,142 applied for aid; of those 80% were deemed to have need. 100% of freshmen with need received aid; of those 18% had need fully met. *Average percent of need met:* 75% (excluding resources awarded to replace EFC). *Average financial aid package:* $35,342 (excluding resources awarded to replace EFC). 12% of all full-time freshmen had no need and received non-need-based gift aid.

UNDERGRADUATE FINANCIAL AID (Fall 2016) 3,944 applied for aid; of those 88% were deemed to have need. 100% of undergraduates with need received aid; of those 12% had need fully met. *Average percent of need met:* 69% (excluding resources awarded to replace EFC). *Average financial aid package:* $32,620 (excluding resources awarded to replace EFC). 6% of all full-time undergraduates had no need and received non-need-based gift aid.

GIFT AID (NEED-BASED) *Total amount:* $108,756,421 (5% federal, 5% state, 89% institutional, 1% external sources). *Receiving aid:* Freshmen: 55% (832); all full-time undergraduates: 51% (3,107). *Average award:* Freshmen: $17,928; Undergraduates: $16,989. *Scholarships, grants, and awards:* Federal Pell, FSEOG, state, private, college/university gift aid from institutional funds.

GIFT AID (NON-NEED-BASED) *Total amount:* $6,632,999 (98% institutional, 2% external sources). *Receiving aid:* Freshmen: 44% (660). Undergraduates: 39% (2,385). *Average award:* Freshmen: $19,066. Undergraduates: $16,916. *Scholarships, grants, and awards by category:* Academic interests/achievement: 3,627 awards ($59,085,399 total): biological sciences, general academic interests/achievements, physical sciences. *Creative arts/performance:* 274 awards ($1,072,220 total): art/fine arts, cinema/film/broadcasting, creative writing, dance, music, performing arts, theater/drama. *Special characteristics:* 155 awards ($396,697 total): children and siblings of alumni, international students, relatives of clergy. *Tuition waivers:* Full or partial for employees or children of employees. *ROTC:* Army cooperative, Air Force cooperative.

LOANS *Student loans:* $30,795,927 (90% need-based, 10% non-need-based). 59% of past graduating class borrowed through all loan programs. *Average indebtedness per student:* $26,926. *Average need-based loan:* Freshmen: $3433. Undergraduates: $4493. *Parent loans:* $38,241,426 (88% need-based, 12% non-need-based). *Programs:* Federal Direct (Subsidized and Unsubsidized Stafford), Perkins.

WORK-STUDY *Federal work-study:* 2,046 jobs averaging $2847.

APPLYING FOR FINANCIAL AID *Required financial aid forms:* FAFSA, state aid form. *Financial aid deadline (priority):* 3/2. *Notification date:* Continuous beginning 3/15. Students must reply within 3 weeks of notification.

CONTACT Mr. David Carnevale, Director of Financial Aid, Chapman University, One University Drive, Orange, CA 92866, 714-532-6049 or toll-free 888-CUAPPLY. *Fax:* 714-997-6743. *E-mail:* carneva@chapman.edu. *Website:* http://www.chapman.edu/.

CHARLES R. DREW UNIVERSITY OF MEDICINE AND SCIENCE
Los Angeles, CA

CONTACT Financial Aid Office, Charles R. Drew University of Medicine and Science, 1731 East 120th Street, Los Angeles, CA 90059, 323-563-4824. *Fax:* 323-569-0597. *Website:* http://www.cdrewu.edu/.

CHARLESTON SOUTHERN UNIVERSITY
Charleston, SC

CONTACT Mr. Jim Rhoden, Director of Admissions, Charleston Southern University, PO Box 118087, 9200 University Boulevard, Charleston, SC 29423-8087, 843-863-7050 or toll-free 800-947-7474. *Fax:* 843-863-7070. *Website:* http://www.charlestonsouthern.edu/.

CHARLOTTE CHRISTIAN COLLEGE AND THEOLOGICAL SEMINARY
Charlotte, NC

Tuition & fees: $10,468	Average undergraduate aid package: $5092

ABOUT THE INSTITUTION Independent Christian, coed. *Awards:* associate, bachelor's, master's, and doctoral degrees. 4 undergraduate majors. *Total enrollment:* 97. Undergraduates: 65. Freshmen: 2. Federal methodology is used as a basis for awarding need-based institutional aid.

UNDERGRADUATE EXPENSES for 2018–2019 *Application fee:* $50. *Tuition:* full-time $10,048; part-time $454 per credit hour. *Required fees:* full-time $420; $420 per year. Full-time tuition and fees vary according to course load and program. Part-time tuition and fees vary according to course load and program. *Payment plan:* Guaranteed tuition.

UNDERGRADUATE FINANCIAL AID (Fall 2016) 3 applied for aid; of those 100% were deemed to have need. 100% of undergraduates with need received aid; of those 100% had need fully met. *Average percent of need met:* 100% (excluding resources awarded to replace EFC). *Average financial aid package:* $5092 (excluding resources awarded to replace EFC).

GIFT AID (NEED-BASED) *Total amount:* $142,377 (82% federal, 18% institutional). *Receiving aid:* All full-time undergraduates: 100% (3). *Average award:* Undergraduates: $2960. *Scholarships, grants, and awards:* Federal Pell, FSEOG, private, college/university gift aid from institutional funds, Veterans Education Benefits (GI Bill).

GIFT AID (NON-NEED-BASED) *Total amount:* $10,959 (100% institutional). *Scholarships, grants, and awards by category:* Academic interests/achievement: 4 awards ($6550 total): education, foreign languages, general academic interests/achievements, religion/biblical studies. *Special achievements/activities:* memberships, religious involvement. *Special characteristics:* religious affiliation. *Tuition waivers:* Full or partial for employees or children of employees.

LOANS *Student loans:* $226,608 (100% need-based). 100% of past graduating class borrowed through all loan programs. *Average indebtedness per student:* $33,034. *Average need-based loan:* Undergraduates: $3500. *Programs:* Federal Direct (Subsidized and Unsubsidized Stafford, PLUS).

WORK-STUDY *Federal work-study:* 2 jobs averaging $4714.

APPLYING FOR FINANCIAL AID *Required financial aid form:* FAFSA. *Financial aid deadline:* Continuous. *Notification date:* Continuous beginning 1/15. Students must reply within 2 weeks of notification.

CONTACT Mr. Kenneth Neal Roach, Financial Aid Officer, Charlotte Christian College and Theological Seminary, 3117 Whiting Avenue, PO Box 790106, Charlotte, NC 28206-7901, 704-334-6882 Ext. 114. *Fax:* 704-334-6885. *E-mail:* kroach@charlottechristian.edu. *Website:* http://www.charlottechristian.edu/.

CHARTER COLLEGE
Vancouver, WA

CONTACT Financial Aid Office, Charter College, 17720 SE Mill Plain Boulevard, Suite 170, Vancouver, WA 98683. *Website:* http://www.chartercollege.edu/.

CHARTER OAK STATE COLLEGE
New Britain, CT

Tuition & fees (CT res): $9771	Average undergraduate aid package: $7129

ABOUT THE INSTITUTION State-supported, coed. *Awards:* certificates, associate, bachelor's, and master's degrees (offers only external degree programs). 9 undergraduate majors. *Total enrollment:* 1,500. Undergraduates: 1,416. Federal methodology is used as a basis for awarding need-based institutional aid.

UNDERGRADUATE EXPENSES for 2017–2018 *Application fee:* $75. *Tuition, state resident:* full-time $8940; part-time $298 per credit. *Tuition, non-resident:* full-time $11,760; part-time $392 per credit. *Required fees:* full-time $831; $277 per term. Full-time tuition and fees vary according to course load. Part-time tuition and fees vary according to course load.

UNDERGRADUATE FINANCIAL AID (Fall 2016) 265 applied for aid; of those 92% were deemed to have need. 98% of undergraduates with need received aid; of those 3% had need fully met. *Average percent of need met:* 44% (excluding resources awarded to replace EFC). *Average financial aid package:* $7129 (excluding resources awarded to replace EFC). 1% of all full-time undergraduates had no need and received non-need-based gift aid.

GIFT AID (NEED-BASED) *Total amount:* $2,129,210 (73% federal, 21% state, 5% institutional, 1% external sources). *Receiving aid:* All full-time undergraduates: 65% (203). *Average award:* Undergraduates: $4303. *Scholarships, grants, and awards:* Federal Pell, FSEOG, state, college/university gift aid from institutional funds, foundation grants.

GIFT AID (NON-NEED-BASED) *Total amount:* $74,600 (1% federal, 86% state, 11% institutional, 2% external sources). *Receiving aid:* Undergraduates: 1. *Average award:* Undergraduates: $1884. *Scholarships, grants, and awards by category:* Academic interests/achievement: general academic interests/achievements.

LOANS *Student loans:* $5,663,435 (76% need-based, 24% non-need-based). *Average need-based loan:* Undergraduates: $4178. *Parent loans:* $5124 (100% need-based). *Programs:* Federal Direct (Subsidized and Unsubsidized Stafford, PLUS), state, alternative loans.

APPLYING FOR FINANCIAL AID *Required financial aid form:* FAFSA. *Financial aid deadline (priority):* 7/1. *Notification date:* Continuous beginning 8/1.

CONTACT Ralph Brasure, Director of Financial Aid, Charter Oak State College, 55 Paul Manafort Drive, New Britain, CT 06053-2142, 860-515-3703. *Fax:* 860-760-6540. *E-mail:* sfa@charteroak.edu. *Website:* http://www.charteroak.edu/.

CHATHAM UNIVERSITY
Pittsburgh, PA

Tuition & fees: $37,611	Average undergraduate aid package: $26,138

ABOUT THE INSTITUTION Independent, coed, primarily women. *Awards:* certificates, bachelor's, master's, and doctoral degrees. 44 undergraduate majors. *Total enrollment:* 2,269. Undergraduates: 1,208. Freshmen: 284. Both federal and institutional methodology are used as a basis for awarding need-based institutional aid.

UNDERGRADUATE EXPENSES for 2018–2019 *Application fee:* $35. *Comprehensive fee:* $49,701 includes full-time tuition ($36,276), mandatory fees ($1335), and room and board ($12,090). *College room only:* $6240. Room and board charges vary according to board plan and housing facility. *Part-time tuition:* $880 per credit hour. Part-time tuition and fees vary according to course load.

FRESHMAN FINANCIAL AID (Fall 2017, est.) 271 applied for aid; of those 84% were deemed to have need. 100% of freshmen with need received aid; of those 23% had need fully met. *Average percent of need met:* 67% (excluding resources awarded to replace EFC). *Average financial aid package:* $29,499 (excluding resources awarded to replace EFC). 11% of all full-time freshmen had no need and received non-need-based gift aid.

UNDERGRADUATE FINANCIAL AID (Fall 2017, est.) 865 applied for aid; of those 94% were deemed to have need. 100% of undergraduates with need received aid; of those 13% had need fully met. *Average percent of need met:* 63% (excluding resources awarded to replace EFC). *Average financial aid package:* $26,138 (excluding resources awarded to replace EFC). 10% of all full-time undergraduates had no need and received non-need-based gift aid.

GIFT AID (NEED-BASED) *Total amount:* $19,137,181 (8% federal, 7% state, 84% institutional, 1% external sources). *Receiving aid:* Freshmen: 70% (200); all full-time undergraduates: 61% (558). *Average award:* Freshmen: $10,012; Undergraduates: $9112. *Scholarships, grants, and awards:* Federal Pell, FSEOG, state, private.

GIFT AID (NON-NEED-BASED) *Total amount:* $1,933,424 (90% institutional, 10% external sources). *Receiving aid:* Freshmen: 80% (228). Undergraduates: 76% (698). *Average award:* Freshmen: $17,096. Undergraduates: $16,089. *Scholar-*

ships, grants, and awards by category: Academic interests/achievement: 920 awards ($13,627,021 total): general academic interests/achievements. *Creative arts/performance:* 23 awards ($48,350 total): applied art and design, art/fine arts, music. *Special achievements/activities:* 601 awards ($1,683,500 total): leadership. *Special characteristics:* 55 awards ($342,647 total): children and siblings of alumni, children of faculty/staff, siblings of current students. *Tuition waivers:* Full or partial for employees or children of employees. *ROTC:* Army cooperative, Naval cooperative, Air Force cooperative.

LOANS *Student loans:* $5,239,288 (63% need-based, 37% non-need-based). 64% of past graduating class borrowed through all loan programs. *Average indebtedness per student:* $35,303. *Average need-based loan:* Freshmen: $3182. Undergraduates: $3963. *Parent loans:* $2,910,172 (96% need-based, 4% non-need-based). *Programs:* Federal Direct (Subsidized and Unsubsidized Stafford), Perkins.

WORK-STUDY *Federal work-study:* Total amount: $729,717; 338 jobs averaging $2200. *State or other work-study/employment:* Total amount: $200,000 (100% non-need-based). Part-time jobs available.

APPLYING FOR FINANCIAL AID *Required financial aid form:* FAFSA. *Financial aid deadline (priority):* 3/1. *Notification date:* 3/1. Students must reply within 3 weeks of notification.

CONTACT Dr. Jennifer Burns, Director of Financial Aid, Chatham University, Woodland Road, Pittsburgh, PA 15232-2826, 412-365-1849 or toll-free 800-837-1290. *Fax:* 412-365-1643. *E-mail:* jburns@chatham.edu. *Website:* http://www.chatham.edu/.

CHESTNUT HILL COLLEGE
Philadelphia, PA

Tuition & fees: $36,180	Average undergraduate aid package: $24,523

ABOUT THE INSTITUTION Independent Roman Catholic, coed. *Awards:* certificates, associate, bachelor's, master's, and doctoral degrees (profile includes figures from both traditional and accelerated (part-time) programs). 45 undergraduate majors. *Total enrollment:* 1,846. Undergraduates: 1,364. Freshmen: 207. Federal methodology is used as a basis for awarding need-based institutional aid.

UNDERGRADUATE EXPENSES for 2018–2019 *Application fee:* $35. *One-time required fee:* $475. *Comprehensive fee:* $47,180 includes full-time tuition ($35,950), mandatory fees ($230), and room and board ($11,000). Room and board charges vary according to housing facility. *Part-time tuition:* $745 per credit hour. *Part-time fees:* $230 per year. Part-time tuition and fees vary according to class time.

FRESHMAN FINANCIAL AID (Fall 2017, est.) 180 applied for aid; of those 100% were deemed to have need. 100% of freshmen with need received aid; of those 28% had need fully met. *Average percent of need met:* 63% (excluding resources awarded to replace EFC). *Average financial aid package:* $30,165 (excluding resources awarded to replace EFC). 13% of all full-time freshmen had no need and received non-need-based gift aid.

UNDERGRADUATE FINANCIAL AID (Fall 2017, est.) 885 applied for aid; of those 100% were deemed to have need. 100% of undergraduates with need received aid; of those 30% had need fully met. *Average percent of need met:* 55% (excluding resources awarded to replace EFC). *Average financial aid package:* $24,523 (excluding resources awarded to replace EFC). 12% of all full-time undergraduates had no need and received non-need-based gift aid.

GIFT AID (NEED-BASED) *Total amount:* $5,090,302 (55% federal, 31% state, 2% institutional, 12% external sources). *Receiving aid:* Freshmen: 71% (147); all full-time undergraduates: 68% (738). *Average award:* Freshmen: $9743; Undergraduates: $16,903. *Scholarships, grants, and awards:* Federal Pell, FSEOG, state, private, college/university gift aid from institutional funds.

GIFT AID (NON-NEED-BASED) *Total amount:* $120,458 (3% federal, 36% state, 22% institutional, 39% external sources). *Receiving aid:* Freshmen: 84% (174). Undergraduates: 61% (661). *Average award:* Freshmen: $14,546. Undergraduates: $14,146. *Tuition waivers:* Full or partial for employees or children of employees, senior citizens.

LOANS *Student loans:* $11,349,745 (90% need-based, 10% non-need-based). 86% of past graduating class borrowed through all loan programs. *Average indebtedness per student:* $42,527. *Average need-based loan:* Freshmen: $3318. Undergraduates: $4468. *Parent loans:* $2,821,986 (93% need-based, 7% non-need-based). *Programs:* Federal Direct (Subsidized and Unsubsidized Stafford, PLUS), alternative loans.

WORK-STUDY *Federal work-study:* Total amount: $216,750; jobs available. *State or other work-study/employment:* Part-time jobs available.

ATHLETIC AWARDS Total amount: $1,448,267 (61% need-based, 39% non-need-based).

APPLYING FOR FINANCIAL AID *Required financial aid forms:* FAFSA, state aid form, noncustodial (divorced/separated) parent's statement. *Financial aid deadline:* 6/30 (priority: 10/1). *Notification date:* Continuous beginning 10/1. Students must reply within 8 weeks of notification.

CONTACT Ms. Toshia Williams, Director of Financial Aid, Chestnut Hill College, 9601 Germantown Avenue, Philadelphia, PA 19118-2693, 215-248-7188 or toll-free 800-248-0052. *Fax:* 215-248-7217. *E-mail:* williamst@chc.edu. *Website:* http://www.chc.edu/.

CHEYNEY UNIVERSITY OF PENNSYLVANIA
Cheyney, PA

CONTACT Mr. James Brown, Director of Financial Aid, Cheyney University of Pennsylvania, 1837 University Circle, Cheyney, PA 19319, 610-399-2302 or toll-free 800-CHEYNEY. *Fax:* 610-399-2411. *E-mail:* jbrown@cheyney.edu. *Website:* http://www.cheyney.edu/.

CHICAGO STATE UNIVERSITY
Chicago, IL

CONTACT Ms. Cathy Davis, Director of Student Financial Aid, Chicago State University, 9501 South Martin Luther King Drive, Chicago, IL 60628, 773-995-2304. *E-mail:* cdavis58@csu.edu. *Website:* http://www.csu.edu/.

CHOWAN UNIVERSITY
Murfreesboro, NC

Tuition & fees: $24,980	Average undergraduate aid package: $21,151

ABOUT THE INSTITUTION Independent Baptist, coed. *Awards:* associate, bachelor's, and master's degrees. 39 undergraduate majors. *Total enrollment:* 1,503. Undergraduates: 1,498. Freshmen: 526. Federal methodology is used as a basis for awarding need-based institutional aid.

UNDERGRADUATE EXPENSES for 2018–2019 *Application fee:* $20. *Comprehensive fee:* $34,380 includes full-time tuition ($24,980) and room and board ($9400). Room and board charges vary according to board plan. *Part-time tuition:* $400 per credit hour.

FRESHMAN FINANCIAL AID (Fall 2017, est.) 495 applied for aid; of those 98% were deemed to have need. 100% of freshmen with need received aid; of those 5% had need fully met. *Average percent of need met:* 63% (excluding resources awarded to replace EFC). *Average financial aid package:* $21,497 (excluding resources awarded to replace EFC). 2% of all full-time freshmen had no need and received non-need-based gift aid.

UNDERGRADUATE FINANCIAL AID (Fall 2017, est.) 1,427 applied for aid; of those 97% were deemed to have need. 100% of undergraduates with need received aid; of those 8% had need fully met. *Average percent of need met:* 66% (excluding resources awarded to replace EFC). *Average financial aid package:* $21,151 (excluding resources awarded to replace EFC). 3% of all full-time undergraduates had no need and received non-need-based gift aid.

GIFT AID (NEED-BASED) *Total amount:* $23,274,181 (24% federal, 14% state, 60% institutional, 2% external sources). *Receiving aid:* Freshmen: 96% (484); all full-time undergraduates: 92% (1,379). *Average award:* Freshmen: $17,449; Undergraduates: $16,993. *Scholarships, grants, and awards:* Federal Pell, FSEOG, state, private, college/university gift aid from institutional funds.

GIFT AID (NON-NEED-BASED) *Total amount:* $61,289 (30% federal, 70% state). *Receiving aid:* Freshmen: 1. Undergraduates: 1% (10). *Average award:*

Freshmen: $8411. Undergraduates: $6088. *Scholarships, grants, and awards by category:* Academic interests/achievement: 1,435 awards ($6,223,716 total): general academic interests/achievements. *Creative arts/performance:* 40 awards ($71,631 total): music. *Special achievements/activities:* 582 awards ($1,640,865 total): leadership. *Special characteristics:* 39 awards ($266,482 total): children of educators, children of faculty/staff, children of public servants, children of union members/company employees, first-generation college students, general special characteristics, handicapped students, international students, local/state students, out-of-state students, public servants, relatives of clergy, religious affiliation, veterans, veterans' children. *Tuition waivers:* Full or partial for employees or children of employees.

LOANS *Student loans:* $10,173,957 (48% need-based, 52% non-need-based). 89% of past graduating class borrowed through all loan programs. *Average indebtedness per student:* $38,443. *Average need-based loan:* Freshmen: $3140. Undergraduates: $3295. *Parent loans:* $5,552,561 (100% non-need-based). *Programs:* Federal Direct (Subsidized and Unsubsidized Stafford, PLUS), Perkins, state, alternative loans.

WORK-STUDY *Federal work-study:* Total amount: $392,620; 271 jobs averaging $1449. *State or other work-study/employment:* 194 part-time jobs averaging $2669.

ATHLETIC AWARDS Total amount: $2,930,005 (100% need-based).

APPLYING FOR FINANCIAL AID *Required financial aid form:* FAFSA. *Financial aid deadline (priority):* 5/1. *Notification date:* Continuous beginning 4/1. Students must reply within 2 weeks of notification.

CONTACT Mrs. Sharon W. Rose, Director of Financial Aid, Chowan University, One University Place, Murfreesboro, NC 27855, 252-398-6535 or toll-free 888-4-CHOWAN. *Fax:* 252-398-6513. *E-mail:* roses1@chowan.edu. *Website:* http://www.chowan.edu/.

CHRISTENDOM COLLEGE
Front Royal, VA

Tuition & fees: $26,360	Average undergraduate aid package: $18,586

ABOUT THE INSTITUTION Independent Roman Catholic, coed. *Awards:* associate, bachelor's, and master's degrees. 8 undergraduate majors. *Total enrollment:* 573. Undergraduates: 493. Freshmen: 133. Institutional methodology is used as a basis for awarding need-based institutional aid.

UNDERGRADUATE EXPENSES for 2018–2019 *Comprehensive fee:* $36,640 includes full-time tuition ($25,460), mandatory fees ($900), and room and board ($10,280).

FRESHMEN FINANCIAL AID (Fall 2017, est.) 68 applied for aid; of those 100% were deemed to have need. 99% of freshmen with need received aid. *Average percent of need met:* 70% (excluding resources awarded to replace EFC). *Average financial aid package:* $18,729 (excluding resources awarded to replace EFC). 43% of all full-time freshmen had no need and received non-need-based gift aid.

UNDERGRADUATE FINANCIAL AID (Fall 2017, est.) 298 applied for aid; of those 100% were deemed to have need. 99% of undergraduates with need received aid. *Average percent of need met:* 72% (excluding resources awarded to replace EFC). *Average financial aid package:* $18,586 (excluding resources awarded to replace EFC). 27% of all full-time undergraduates had no need and received non-need-based gift aid.

GIFT AID (NEED-BASED) *Total amount:* $3,753,379 (100% institutional). *Receiving aid:* Freshmen: 46% (67); all full-time undergraduates: 62% (295). *Average award:* Freshmen: $10,418; Undergraduates: $11,914. *Scholarships, grants, and awards:* state, private, college/university gift aid from institutional funds.

GIFT AID (NON-NEED-BASED) *Total amount:* $2,491,367 (20% state, 77% institutional, 3% external sources). *Receiving aid:* Freshmen: 6% (8). Undergraduates: 7% (33). *Average award:* Freshmen: $11,639. Undergraduates: $10,678. *Scholarships, grants, and awards by category:* Academic interests/achievement: 303 awards ($2,839,724 total): general academic interests/achievements. *Special characteristics:* 72 awards ($472,770 total): siblings of current students. *Tuition waivers:* Full or partial for children of alumni, employees or children of employees.

LOANS *Student loans:* $2,804,980 (66% need-based, 34% non-need-based). 71% of past graduating class borrowed through all loan programs. *Average indebtedness per student:* $31,877. *Average need-based loan:* Freshmen: $5665. Undergraduates: $7168. *Programs:* college/university.

WORK-STUDY *State or other work-study/employment:* Total amount: $397,063 (100% non-need-based). 177 part-time jobs averaging $2243.
APPLYING FOR FINANCIAL AID *Required financial aid form:* institution's own form. *Financial aid deadline (priority):* 4/15. *Notification date:* Continuous beginning 11/1. Students must reply within 4 weeks of notification.
CONTACT Ms. Alisa Polk, Financial Aid Officer, Christendom College, 134 Christendom Drive, Front Royal, VA 22630-5103, 800-877-5456 Ext. 1214 or toll-free 800-877-5456. *Fax:* 540-631-0297. *E-mail:* apolk@christendom.edu.
Website: http://www.christendom.edu/.

CHRISTIAN BROTHERS UNIVERSITY
Memphis, TN

Tuition & fees: $32,820	Average undergraduate aid package: $24,970

ABOUT THE INSTITUTION Independent Roman Catholic, coed. *Awards:* associate, bachelor's, and master's degrees. 43 undergraduate majors. *Total enrollment:* 1,892. Undergraduates: 1,526. Freshmen: 385. Federal methodology is used as a basis for awarding need-based institutional aid.
UNDERGRADUATE EXPENSES for 2018–2019 *Application fee:* $25. *Comprehensive fee:* $40,220 includes full-time tuition ($31,900), mandatory fees ($920), and room and board ($7400). Full-time tuition and fees vary according to class time, course load, and program. Room and board charges vary according to housing facility. *Part-time tuition:* $1135 per credit hour. *Part-time fees:* $215 per term. Part-time tuition and fees vary according to class time, course load, and program.
FRESHMAN FINANCIAL AID (Fall 2017, est.) 379 applied for aid; of those 73% were deemed to have need. 100% of freshmen with need received aid; of those 33% had need fully met. *Average percent of need met:* 81% (excluding resources awarded to replace EFC). *Average financial aid package:* $27,968 (excluding resources awarded to replace EFC). 27% of all full-time freshmen had no need and received non-need-based gift aid.
UNDERGRADUATE FINANCIAL AID (Fall 2017, est.) 1,388 applied for aid; of those 69% were deemed to have need. 100% of undergraduates with need received aid; of those 29% had need fully met. *Average percent of need met:* 74% (excluding resources awarded to replace EFC). *Average financial aid package:* $24,970 (excluding resources awarded to replace EFC). 29% of all full-time undergraduates had no need and received non-need-based gift aid.
GIFT AID (NEED-BASED) *Total amount:* $18,743,223 (15% federal, 14% state, 69% institutional, 2% external sources). *Receiving aid:* Freshmen: 72% (274); all full-time undergraduates: 66% (925). *Average award:* Freshmen: $23,686; Undergraduates: $21,001. *Scholarships, grants, and awards:* Federal Pell, FSEOG, state, private, college/university gift aid from institutional funds.
GIFT AID (NON-NEED-BASED) *Total amount:* $9,841,252 (7% state, 78% institutional, 15% external sources). *Receiving aid:* Freshmen: 13% (51). Undergraduates: 10% (137). *Average award:* Freshmen: $17,916. Undergraduates: $17,121. *Scholarships, grants, and awards by category:* Academic interests/achievement: 32 awards ($215,950 total): computer science, engineering/technologies, general academic interests/achievements, mathematics. *Creative arts/performance:* 6 awards ($10,250 total): performing arts. *Special achievements/activities:* 581 awards ($1,448,803 total): general special achievements/activities, leadership, memberships. *Special characteristics:* 498 awards ($3,307,656 total): children and siblings of alumni, children of public servants, ethnic background, general special characteristics, international students, members of minority groups, out-of-state students, veterans, veterans' children. *Tuition waivers:* Full or partial for employees or children of employees.
ROTC: Army cooperative, Naval cooperative, Air Force cooperative.
LOANS *Student loans:* $6,985,220 (79% need-based, 21% non-need-based). 71% of past graduating class borrowed through all loan programs. *Average indebtedness per student:* $30,694. *Average need-based loan:* Freshmen: $3269. Undergraduates: $4006. *Parent loans:* $1,234,995 (55% need-based, 45% non-need-based). *Programs:* Federal Direct (Subsidized and Unsubsidized Stafford, PLUS), Perkins, college/university, alternative loans.
WORK-STUDY *Federal work-study:* Total amount: $87,646; 126 jobs averaging $696. *State or other work-study/employment:* Total amount: $57,501 (4% need-based, 96% non-need-based). 99 part-time jobs averaging $581.
ATHLETIC AWARDS Total amount: $2,210,503 (37% need-based, 63% non-need-based).

APPLYING FOR FINANCIAL AID *Required financial aid form:* FAFSA. *Financial aid deadline:* Continuous. *Notification date:* Continuous. Students must reply within 2 weeks of notification.
CONTACT Dr. John H. Lewis, IV, Director of Financial Aid, Christian Brothers University, 650 East Parkway South, Memphis, TN 38104, 901-321-3305 or toll-free 877-321-4CBU. *Fax:* 901-321-3327. *E-mail:* john.lewis@cbu.edu.
Website: http://www.cbu.edu/.

CHRISTOPHER NEWPORT UNIVERSITY
Newport News, VA

Tuition & fees (VA res): $13,654	Average undergraduate aid package: $9690

ABOUT THE INSTITUTION State-supported, coed. *Awards:* bachelor's and master's degrees. 39 undergraduate majors. *Total enrollment:* 5,081. Undergraduates: 4,954. Freshmen: 1,293. Federal methodology is used as a basis for awarding need-based institutional aid.
UNDERGRADUATE EXPENSES for 2017–2018 *Application fee:* $65. *Tuition, state resident:* full-time $8236; part-time $343 per credit hour. *Tuition, nonresident:* full-time $20,032; part-time $834 per credit hour. *Required fees:* full-time $5418; $225 per credit hour. Full-time tuition and fees vary according to course load. Part-time tuition and fees vary according to course load. *College room and board:* $11,224; *Room only:* $6904. Room and board charges vary according to board plan and housing facility.
FRESHMAN FINANCIAL AID (Fall 2017, est.) 1,057 applied for aid; of those 58% were deemed to have need. 93% of freshmen with need received aid; of those 21% had need fully met. *Average percent of need met:* 65% (excluding resources awarded to replace EFC). *Average financial aid package:* $9535 (excluding resources awarded to replace EFC). 19% of all full-time freshmen had no need and received non-need-based gift aid.
UNDERGRADUATE FINANCIAL AID (Fall 2017, est.) 3,208 applied for aid; of those 67% were deemed to have need. 95% of undergraduates with need received aid; of those 21% had need fully met. *Average percent of need met:* 65% (excluding resources awarded to replace EFC). *Average financial aid package:* $9690 (excluding resources awarded to replace EFC). 15% of all full-time undergraduates had no need and received non-need-based gift aid.
GIFT AID (NEED-BASED) *Total amount:* $10,138,230 (32% federal, 48% state, 20% institutional). *Receiving aid:* Freshmen: 33% (424); all full-time undergraduates: 30% (1,445). *Average award:* Freshmen: $6906; Undergraduates: $6982. *Scholarships, grants, and awards:* Federal Pell, FSEOG, state, private, college/university gift aid from institutional funds.
GIFT AID (NON-NEED-BASED) *Total amount:* $4,785,921 (2% state, 74% institutional, 24% external sources). *Receiving aid:* Freshmen: 19% (242). Undergraduates: 13% (623). *Average award:* Freshmen: $3348. Undergraduates: $2979. *Scholarships, grants, and awards by category:* Academic interests/achievement: 48 awards ($135,000 total): biological sciences, business, communication, computer science, education, engineering/technologies, English, foreign languages, general academic interests/achievements, humanities, mathematics, military science, physical sciences, premedicine, social sciences. *Creative arts/performance:* 97 awards ($206,025 total): art/fine arts, music, performing arts, theater/drama. *Special achievements/activities:* 1,071 awards ($3,122,300 total): community service, general special achievements/activities, leadership. *Special characteristics:* 47 awards ($114,600 total): adult students, first-generation college students, general special characteristics, local/state students, members of minority groups, religious affiliation. *Tuition waivers:* Full or partial for employees or children of employees, senior citizens. **ROTC:** Army.
LOANS *Student loans:* $23,634,661 (31% need-based, 69% non-need-based). 57% of past graduating class borrowed through all loan programs. *Average indebtedness per student:* $32,994. *Average need-based loan:* Freshmen: $3401. Undergraduates: $4335. *Parent loans:* $8,914,057 (100% non-need-based). *Programs:* Federal Direct (Subsidized and Unsubsidized Stafford, PLUS).
WORK-STUDY *Federal work-study:* Total amount: $102,587; 82 jobs averaging $1372. *State or other work-study/employment:* Total amount: $2,193,606 (100% non-need-based). 1,576 part-time jobs averaging $1867.

APPLYING FOR FINANCIAL AID *Required financial aid form:* FAFSA. *Financial aid deadline (priority):* 3/1. *Notification date:* Continuous beginning 3/1. Students must reply by 5/1.

CONTACT Christina Russell, Director of Financial Aid, Christopher Newport University, 1 Avenue of the Arts, Newport News, VA 23606, 757-594-7170 or toll-free 800-333-4268. *Fax:* 757-594-7113. *E-mail:* christina.russell@cnu.edu. *Website:* http://www.cnu.edu/.

CINCINNATI CHRISTIAN UNIVERSITY
Cincinnati, OH

ABOUT THE INSTITUTION Independent Church of Christ, coed. 11 undergraduate majors.

GIFT AID (NEED-BASED) *Scholarships, grants, and awards:* Federal Pell, FSEOG, state, private, college/university gift aid from institutional funds.

GIFT AID (NON-NEED-BASED) *Scholarships, grants, and awards by category:* Academic interests/achievement: education, general academic interests/achievements, religion/biblical studies. Creative arts/performance: music. Special achievements/activities: general special achievements/activities, leadership, religious involvement. Special characteristics: children of faculty/staff, international students, members of minority groups, parents of current students, siblings of current students, spouses of current students.

LOANS *Programs:* Federal Direct (Subsidized and Unsubsidized Stafford, PLUS), college/university, private loans.

APPLYING FOR FINANCIAL AID *Required financial aid form:* FAFSA.

CONTACT Marcella Farmer, Associate Director of Financial Aid, Cincinnati Christian University, 2700 Glenway Avenue, Cincinnati, OH 45204-1799, 513-244-8130 or toll-free 800-949-4228 (in-state), 800-949-4CCU (out-of-state). *Fax:* 513-244-8453. *E-mail:* financialaid@ccuniversity.edu. *Website:* http://www.ccuniversity.edu/.

CINCINNATI COLLEGE OF MORTUARY SCIENCE
Cincinnati, OH

CONTACT Ms. Pat Leon, Financial Aid Officer, Cincinnati College of Mortuary Science, 645 West North Bend Road, Cincinnati, OH 45224-1428, 513-761-2020 or toll-free 888-377-8433. *Website:* http://www.ccms.edu/.

THE CITADEL, THE MILITARY COLLEGE OF SOUTH CAROLINA
Charleston, SC

Tuition & fees (SC res): $14,368	Average undergraduate aid package: $17,136

ABOUT THE INSTITUTION State-supported, coed, primarily men. *Awards:* certificates, bachelor's, and master's degrees. 20 undergraduate majors. *Total enrollment:* 3,717. Undergraduates: 2,837. Freshmen: 687. Institutional methodology is used as a basis for awarding need-based institutional aid.

UNDERGRADUATE EXPENSES for 2017–2018 *Application fee:* $40. *Tuition, state resident:* full-time $12,056; part-time $470 per credit hour. *Tuition, nonresident:* full-time $33,819; part-time $874 per credit hour. *Required fees:* full-time $2312. Full-time tuition and fees vary according to class time, degree level, program, and student level. Part-time tuition and fees vary according to class time and program. *College room and board:* $6600.

FRESHMAN FINANCIAL AID (Fall 2017, est.) 598 applied for aid; of those 79% were deemed to have need. 97% of freshmen with need received aid; of those 17% had need fully met. *Average percent of need met:* 55% (excluding resources awarded to replace EFC). *Average financial aid package:* $15,346 (excluding resources

awarded to replace EFC). 20% of all full-time freshmen had no need and received non-need-based gift aid.

UNDERGRADUATE FINANCIAL AID (Fall 2017, est.) 1,921 applied for aid; of those 79% were deemed to have need. 97% of undergraduates with need received aid; of those 26% had need fully met. *Average percent of need met:* 62% (excluding resources awarded to replace EFC). *Average financial aid package:* $17,136 (excluding resources awarded to replace EFC). 23% of all full-time undergraduates had no need and received non-need-based gift aid.

GIFT AID (NEED-BASED) *Total amount:* $17,847,052 (17% federal, 16% state, 28% institutional, 39% external sources). *Receiving aid:* Freshmen: 58% (397); all full-time undergraduates: 47% (1,215). *Average award:* Freshmen: $14,764; Undergraduates: $16,862. *Scholarships, grants, and awards:* Federal Pell, FSEOG, state, private, college/university gift aid from institutional funds.

GIFT AID (NON-NEED-BASED) *Total amount:* $9,145,678 (1% federal, 20% state, 22% institutional, 57% external sources). *Receiving aid:* Freshmen: 9% (59). Undergraduates: 11% (288). *Average award:* Freshmen: $8233. Undergraduates: $15,228. *Scholarships, grants, and awards by category:* Academic interests/achievement: biological sciences, business, engineering/technologies, general academic interests/achievements, humanities, military science, religion/biblical studies. Creative arts/performance: journalism/publications, music. Special achievements/activities: community service, leadership, religious involvement. Special characteristics: children and siblings of alumni, children with a deceased or disabled parent, local/state students, out-of-state students, veterans, veterans' children. *Tuition waivers:* Full or partial for employees or children of employees, senior citizens. *ROTC:* Army, Naval, Air Force.

LOANS *Student loans:* $15,415,095 (81% need-based, 19% non-need-based). 64% of past graduating class borrowed through all loan programs. *Average indebtedness per student:* $32,039. *Average need-based loan:* Freshmen: $3367. Undergraduates: $4191. *Parent loans:* $10,287,212 (85% need-based, 15% non-need-based). *Programs:* Federal Direct (Subsidized and Unsubsidized Stafford, PLUS), Perkins, SC Teacher's Loan.

WORK-STUDY *Federal work-study:* Total amount: $143,389; jobs available. *State or other work-study/employment:* Part-time jobs available.

ATHLETIC AWARDS Total amount: $5,583,180 (56% need-based, 44% non-need-based).

APPLYING FOR FINANCIAL AID *Required financial aid form:* FAFSA. *Financial aid deadline (priority):* 3/1. *Notification date:* Continuous beginning 4/1. Students must reply within 2 weeks of notification.

CONTACT Lt. Col. Hank M. Fuller, Director of Financial Aid and Scholarships, The Citadel, The Military College of South Carolina, 171 Moultrie Street, Charleston, SC 29409, 843-953-5187 or toll-free 800-868-1842. *Fax:* 843-953-6759. *E-mail:* hank.fuller@citadel.edu. *Website:* http://www.citadel.edu/.

CITY COLLEGE OF THE CITY UNIVERSITY OF NEW YORK
New York, NY

Tuition & fees: N/R	Average undergraduate aid package: $9340

ABOUT THE INSTITUTION State and locally supported, coed. *Awards:* certificates, bachelor's, master's, and doctoral degrees. 66 undergraduate majors. *Total enrollment:* 16,112. Undergraduates: 13,411. Federal methodology is used as a basis for awarding need-based institutional aid.

FRESHMAN FINANCIAL AID (Fall 2016) 1,492 applied for aid; of those 90% were deemed to have need. 93% of freshmen with need received aid; of those 77% had need fully met. *Average percent of need met:* 87% (excluding resources awarded to replace EFC). *Average financial aid package:* $9212 (excluding resources awarded to replace EFC). 15% of all full-time freshmen had no need and received non-need-based gift aid.

UNDERGRADUATE FINANCIAL AID (Fall 2016) 9,399 applied for aid; of those 95% were deemed to have need. 100% of undergraduates with need received aid; of those 84% had need fully met. *Average percent of need met:* 84% (excluding resources awarded to replace EFC). *Average financial aid package:* $9340 (excluding resources awarded to replace EFC). 8% of all full-time undergraduates had no need and received non-need-based gift aid.

GIFT AID (NEED-BASED) *Total amount:* $541,871,649 (95% federal, 5% state). *Receiving aid:* Freshmen: 70% (1,175); all full-time undergraduates: 89% (8,908). *Average award:* Freshmen: $8324; Undergraduates: $8246. *Scholarships, grants, and awards:* Federal Pell, FSEOG, state, private, college/university gift aid from institutional funds.

GIFT AID (NON-NEED-BASED) *Total amount:* $16,130,311 (83% federal, 17% institutional). *Receiving aid:* Freshmen: 40% (677). Undergraduates: 55% (5,494). *Average award:* Freshmen: $3279. Undergraduates: $4410. *Scholarships, grants, and awards by category: Academic interests/achievement:* architecture, area/ethnic studies, biological sciences, communication, computer science, education, engineering/technologies, English, foreign languages, general academic interests/achievements, humanities, international studies, mathematics, premedicine, social sciences. *Creative arts/performance:* applied art and design, art/fine arts, cinema/film/broadcasting, creative writing, general creative arts/performance, music, performing arts. *Special achievements/activities:* community service, general special achievements/activities, leadership. *Special characteristics:* children and siblings of alumni, local/state students. *ROTC:* Army.

LOANS *Student loans:* $12,800,747 (47% need-based, 53% non-need-based). *Average need-based loan:* Freshmen: $2287. Undergraduates: $4249. *Parent loans:* $50,288,457 (100% need-based). *Programs:* Federal Direct (Subsidized and Unsubsidized Stafford, PLUS), Perkins.

WORK-STUDY *Federal work-study:* jobs available. *State or other work-study/employment:* Part-time jobs available.

APPLYING FOR FINANCIAL AID *Required financial aid forms:* FAFSA, state aid form. *Financial aid deadline (priority):* 3/15. *Notification date:* Continuous beginning 4/1.

CONTACT Thelma Mason, Director of Financial Aid, City College of the City University of New York, 160 Convent Avenue, Wille Administration Building, Room 104, New York, NY 10031, 212-650-5816. *Fax:* 212-650-5829. *E-mail:* tmason@ccny.cuny.edu.
Website: http://www.ccny.cuny.edu/.

CITY VISION UNIVERSITY
Kansas City, MO

CONTACT Mrs. Ann Marie Cameron-Thompson, Director of Financial Aid, City Vision University, City Vision Financial Aid, 48 Pleasant Street, Dorchester, MA 02125, 617-282-9798 Ext. 108. *Fax:* 816-256-8471. *E-mail:* financialaid@cityvision.edu. *Website:* http://www.cityvision.edu/.

CLAFLIN UNIVERSITY
Orangeburg, SC

Tuition & fees: $16,391	Average undergraduate aid package: $15,962

ABOUT THE INSTITUTION Independent United Methodist, coed. 36 undergraduate majors. Federal methodology is used as a basis for awarding need-based institutional aid.

UNDERGRADUATE EXPENSES for 2017–2018 *Comprehensive fee:* $25,503 includes full-time tuition ($15,840), mandatory fees ($551), and room and board ($9112). *College room only:* $3874. Full-time tuition and fees vary according to class time and course load. Room and board charges vary according to housing facility. *Part-time tuition:* $660 per credit hour. *Part-time fees:* $231 per term. Part-time tuition and fees vary according to class time.

FRESHMAN FINANCIAL AID (Fall 2017, est.) 480 applied for aid; of those 100% were deemed to have need. 100% of freshmen with need received aid; of those 7% had need fully met. *Average percent of need met:* 48% (excluding resources awarded to replace EFC). *Average financial aid package:* $17,003 (excluding resources awarded to replace EFC). 8% of all full-time freshmen had no need and received non-need-based gift aid.

UNDERGRADUATE FINANCIAL AID (Fall 2017, est.) 2,002 applied for aid; of those 97% were deemed to have need. 94% of undergraduates with need received aid; of those 6% had need fully met. *Average percent of need met:* 47% (excluding resources awarded to replace EFC). *Average financial aid package:* $15,962 (excluding resources awarded to replace EFC). 3% of all full-time undergraduates had no need and received non-need-based gift aid.

GIFT AID (NEED-BASED) *Total amount:* $20,130,424 (39% federal, 37% state, 15% institutional, 9% external sources). *Receiving aid:* Freshmen: 91% (475); all full-time undergraduates: 86% (1,786). *Average award:* Freshmen: $13,912; Undergraduates: $12,530. *Scholarships, grants, and awards:* Federal Pell, FSEOG, state, private, college/university gift aid from institutional funds, United Negro College Fund.

GIFT AID (NON-NEED-BASED) *Total amount:* $1,137,358 (25% state, 52% institutional, 23% external sources). *Receiving aid:* Freshmen: 5% (26). Undergraduates: 4% (79). *Average award:* Freshmen: $8254. Undergraduates: $7704. *Scholarships, grants, and awards by category: Academic interests/achievement:* general academic interests/achievements. *Creative arts/performance:* applied art and design, art/fine arts, music. *Special achievements/activities:* cheerleading/drum major. *Special characteristics:* adult students, children of faculty/staff, ethnic background, first-generation college students, international students, local/state students, relatives of clergy, religious affiliation, veterans, veterans' children. *Tuition waivers:* Full or partial for employees or children of employees.

LOANS *Student loans:* $13,598,707 (94% need-based, 6% non-need-based). 88% of past graduating class borrowed through all loan programs. *Average indebtedness per student:* $31,747. *Average need-based loan:* Freshmen: $3272. Undergraduates: $4024. *Parent loans:* $6,810,492 (85% need-based, 15% non-need-based). *Programs:* Federal Direct (Subsidized and Unsubsidized Stafford, PLUS).

WORK-STUDY *Federal work-study:* Total amount: $169,594; 233 jobs averaging $1152. *State or other work-study/employment:* Total amount: $27,110 (100% need-based). Part-time jobs available.

ATHLETIC AWARDS Total amount: $620,123 (81% need-based, 19% non-need-based).

APPLYING FOR FINANCIAL AID *Required financial aid forms:* FAFSA, institution's own form. *Financial aid deadline:* 7/15 (priority: 4/15). *Notification date:* Continuous beginning 2/1. Students must reply by 7/15 or within 2 weeks of notification.

CONTACT Ms. Terria C. Williams, Director of Financial Aid, Claflin University, Corson Hall, 400 Magnolia Street, Orangeburg, SC 29115, 803-535-5720 or toll-free 800-922-1276. *Fax:* 803-535-5383. *E-mail:* twilliams@claflin.edu. *Website:* http://www.claflin.edu/.

CLAREMONT MCKENNA COLLEGE
Claremont, CA

Tuition & fees: $52,825	Average undergraduate aid package: $49,848

ABOUT THE INSTITUTION Independent, coed. *Awards:* bachelor's and master's degrees. 32 undergraduate majors. *Total enrollment:* 1,347. Undergraduates: 1,347. Both federal and institutional methodology are used as a basis for awarding need-based institutional aid.

UNDERGRADUATE EXPENSES for 2017–2018 *Application fee:* $70. *One-time required fee:* $500. *Comprehensive fee:* $69,045 includes full-time tuition ($52,580), mandatory fees ($245), and room and board ($16,220). *College room only:* $8730. Room and board charges vary according to board plan and housing facility. *Part-time tuition:* $8763 per course. Part-time tuition and fees vary according to course load.

FRESHMAN FINANCIAL AID (Fall 2017, est.) 184 applied for aid; of those 90% were deemed to have need. 100% of freshmen with need received aid; of those 97% had need fully met. *Average percent of need met:* 100% (excluding resources awarded to replace EFC). *Average financial aid package:* $51,688 (excluding resources awarded to replace EFC). 5% of all full-time freshmen had no need and received non-need-based gift aid.

UNDERGRADUATE FINANCIAL AID (Fall 2017, est.) 624 applied for aid; of those 87% were deemed to have need. 100% of undergraduates with need received aid; of those 98% had need fully met. *Average percent of need met:* 100% (excluding resources awarded to replace EFC). *Average financial aid package:* $49,848 (excluding resources awarded to replace EFC). 5% of all full-time undergraduates had no need and received non-need-based gift aid.

GIFT AID (NEED-BASED) *Total amount:* $24,418,809 (4% federal, 4% state, 89% institutional, 3% external sources). *Receiving aid:* Freshmen: 46% (161); all full-time undergraduates: 40% (527). *Average award:* Freshmen: $49,208; Undergraduates: $46,324. *Scholarships, grants, and awards:* Federal Pell, FSEOG, state, private, college/university gift aid from institutional funds.

GIFT AID (NON-NEED-BASED) *Total amount:* $1,265,184 (91% institutional, 9% external sources). *Receiving aid:* Freshmen: 22% (76). Undergraduates: 21% (281). *Average award:* Freshmen: $20,314. Undergraduates: $16,953. *Scholarships, grants, and awards by category:* Academic interests/achievement: general academic interests/achievements, military science. *Special achievements/activities:* leadership. *Special characteristics:* veterans, veterans' children. *Tuition waivers:* Full or partial for employees or children of employees. *ROTC:* Army, Air Force cooperative.

LOANS *Student loans:* $2,250,648 (62% need-based, 38% non-need-based). 31% of past graduating class borrowed through all loan programs. *Average indebtedness per student:* $21,421. *Average need-based loan:* Freshmen: $3521. Undergraduates: $4077. *Parent loans:* $1,287,502 (100% non-need-based). *Programs:* Federal Direct (Subsidized and Unsubsidized Stafford, PLUS), Perkins, college/university, alternative loans.

WORK-STUDY *Federal work-study:* Total amount: $761,876; jobs available. *State or other work-study/employment:* Total amount: $314,680 (100% need-based). Part-time jobs available.

APPLYING FOR FINANCIAL AID *Required financial aid forms:* FAFSA, CSS Financial Aid PROFILE, state aid form, noncustodial (divorced/separated) parent's statement, business/farm supplement. *Financial aid deadline:* 2/1 (priority: 1/5). *Notification date:* Continuous beginning 4/1. Students must reply by 5/1.

CONTACT Ms. Georgette R. DeVeres, Associate Vice President and Dean of Admission and Financial Aid, Claremont McKenna College, Kravis Center, Lower Court, 888 Columbia Avenue, Claremont, CA 91711, 909-621-8356. *Fax:* 909-607-0661. *E-mail:* georgette.deveres@claremontmckenna.edu. *Website:* http://www.cmc.edu/.

CLARION UNIVERSITY OF PENNSYLVANIA
Clarion, PA

Tuition & fees (PA res): $10,890	Average undergraduate aid package: $9478

ABOUT THE INSTITUTION State-supported, coed. *Awards:* certificates, associate, bachelor's, master's, and doctoral degrees. 54 undergraduate majors. *Total enrollment:* 5,225. Undergraduates: 4,321. Freshmen: 875. Federal methodology is used as a basis for awarding need-based institutional aid.

UNDERGRADUATE EXPENSES for 2017–2018 *Application fee:* $40. *One-time required fee:* $50. *Tuition, state resident:* full-time $7492; part-time $312 per credit hour. *Tuition, nonresident:* full-time $11,238; part-time $468 per credit hour. *Required fees:* full-time $3398. Full-time tuition and fees vary according to course load, location, and program. Part-time tuition and fees vary according to location and program. *College room and board:* $11,058; *Room only:* $7350. Room and board charges vary according to board plan and housing facility.

FRESHMAN FINANCIAL AID (Fall 2017, est.) 815 applied for aid; of those 87% were deemed to have need. 98% of freshmen with need received aid; of those 4% had need fully met. *Average percent of need met:* 40% (excluding resources awarded to replace EFC). *Average financial aid package:* $9315 (excluding resources awarded to replace EFC). 7% of all full-time freshmen had no need and received non-need-based gift aid.

UNDERGRADUATE FINANCIAL AID (Fall 2017, est.) 3,198 applied for aid; of those 89% were deemed to have need. 99% of undergraduates with need received aid; of those 5% had need fully met. *Average percent of need met:* 43% (excluding resources awarded to replace EFC). *Average financial aid package:* $9478 (excluding resources awarded to replace EFC). 6% of all full-time undergraduates had no need and received non-need-based gift aid.

GIFT AID (NEED-BASED) *Total amount:* $16,097,009 (46% federal, 30% state, 17% institutional, 7% external sources). *Receiving aid:* Freshmen: 68% (579); all full-time undergraduates: 61% (2,134). *Average award:* Freshmen: $5625; Undergraduates: $5628. *Scholarships, grants, and awards:* Federal Pell, FSEOG, state, private, college/university gift aid from institutional funds, United Negro College Fund.

GIFT AID (NON-NEED-BASED) *Total amount:* $772,440 (5% state, 82% institutional, 13% external sources). *Receiving aid:* Freshmen: 29% (244). Undergraduates: 23% (803). *Average award:* Freshmen: $2388. Undergraduates: $2177. *Scholarships, grants, and awards by category:* Academic interests/achievement: biological sciences, business, communication, computer science, edu-

cation, English, foreign languages, general academic interests/achievements, health fields, humanities, international studies, library science, mathematics, military science, physical sciences, premedicine, social sciences. *Creative arts/performance:* art/fine arts, debating, general creative arts/performance, music, theater/drama. *Special achievements/activities:* community service, leadership. *Special characteristics:* children of faculty/staff, children of union members/company employees, children with a deceased or disabled parent, first-generation college students, local/state students, members of minority groups, previous college experience, spouses of current students, veterans, veterans' children. *Tuition waivers:* Full or partial for employees or children of employees, senior citizens. *ROTC:* Army.

LOANS *Student loans:* $28,663,959 (90% need-based, 10% non-need-based). 83% of past graduating class borrowed through all loan programs. *Average indebtedness per student:* $35,277. *Average need-based loan:* Freshmen: $3387. Undergraduates: $4173. *Parent loans:* $8,259,306 (90% need-based, 10% non-need-based). *Programs:* Federal Direct (Subsidized and Unsubsidized Stafford, PLUS), Perkins, alternative loans.

WORK-STUDY *Federal work-study:* Total amount: $324,329; 299 jobs averaging $1085. *State or other work-study/employment:* Total amount: $848,891 (100% need-based). 734 part-time jobs averaging $1329.

ATHLETIC AWARDS Total amount: $787,359 (80% need-based, 20% non-need-based).

APPLYING FOR FINANCIAL AID *Required financial aid forms:* FAFSA, state aid form. *Financial aid deadline (priority):* 5/1. *Notification date:* Continuous beginning 12/23.

CONTACT Ms. Sue A. Bloom, Student Financial Services, Clarion University of Pennsylvania, 122 Becht Hall, Clarion, PA 16214, 814-393-2315 or toll-free 800-672-7171. *Fax:* 814-393-2520. *E-mail:* stfinservice@clarion.edu. *Website:* http://www.clarion.edu/.

CLARK ATLANTA UNIVERSITY
Atlanta, GA

ABOUT THE INSTITUTION Independent United Methodist, coed. *Awards:* certificates, bachelor's, master's, and doctoral degrees. 28 undergraduate majors. *Total enrollment:* 3,992. Undergraduates: 3,302. Freshmen: 914.

GIFT AID (NEED-BASED) *Scholarships, grants, and awards:* Federal Pell, FSEOG, state, private, college/university gift aid from institutional funds, United Negro College Fund.

GIFT AID (NON-NEED-BASED) *Scholarships, grants, and awards by category:* Academic interests/achievement: general academic interests/achievements. Creative arts/performance: music. Special achievements/activities: general special achievements/activities, leadership. Special characteristics: general special characteristics.

LOANS *Programs:* Federal Direct (Subsidized and Unsubsidized Stafford, PLUS), Perkins.

WORK-STUDY *Federal work-study:* 201 jobs averaging $1740.

APPLYING FOR FINANCIAL AID *Required financial aid forms:* FAFSA, state aid form.

CONTACT Office of Financial Aid, Clark Atlanta University, 223 James P. Brawley Drive, Atlanta, GA 30314, 404-880-8992 or toll-free 800-688-3228. *Fax:* 404-880-8070. *E-mail:* studentfinancialaid@cau.edu. *Website:* http://www.cau.edu/.

CLARKE UNIVERSITY
Dubuque, IA

Tuition & fees: $33,350	Average undergraduate aid package: $27,131

ABOUT THE INSTITUTION Independent Roman Catholic, coed. *Awards:* associate, bachelor's, master's, and doctoral degrees. 31 undergraduate majors. *Total enrollment:* 1,032. Undergraduates: 774. Freshmen: 162. Federal methodology is used as a basis for awarding need-based institutional aid.

UNDERGRADUATE EXPENSES for 2018–2019 *Application fee:* $25. *Comprehensive fee:* $42,950 includes full-time tuition ($32,300), mandatory fees

($1050) and room and board ($9600). *College room only:* $4600. Room and board charges vary according to board plan. *Part-time tuition:* $720 per credit hour.

FRESHMAN FINANCIAL AID (Fall 2017, est.) 154 applied for aid; of those 94% were deemed to have need. 100% of freshmen with need received aid; of those 28% had need fully met. *Average percent of need met:* 79% (excluding resources awarded to replace EFC). *Average financial aid package:* $27,084 (excluding resources awarded to replace EFC). 7% of all full-time freshmen had no need and received non-need-based gift aid.

UNDERGRADUATE FINANCIAL AID (Fall 2017, est.) 636 applied for aid; of those 93% were deemed to have need. 100% of undergraduates with need received aid; of those 25% had need fully met. *Average percent of need met:* 74% (excluding resources awarded to replace EFC). *Average financial aid package:* $27,131 (excluding resources awarded to replace EFC). 13% of all full-time undergraduates had no need and received non-need-based gift aid.

GIFT AID (NEED-BASED) *Total amount:* $9,844,464 (13% federal, 9% state, 76% institutional, 2% external sources). *Receiving aid:* Freshmen: 93% (144); all full-time undergraduates: 87% (590). *Average award:* Freshmen: $23,379; Undergraduates: $21,991. *Scholarships, grants, and awards:* Federal Pell, FSEOG, state, private, college/university gift aid from institutional funds.

GIFT AID (NON-NEED-BASED) *Total amount:* $1,110,952 (99% institutional, 1% external sources). *Receiving aid:* Freshmen: 93% (144). Undergraduates: 86% (586). *Average award:* Freshmen: $25,727. Undergraduates: $22,042. *Scholarships, grants, and awards by category: Academic interests/achievement:* 689 awards ($4,927,995 total): general academic interests/achievements. *Creative arts/performance:* 55 awards ($153,138 total): art/fine arts, music, theater/drama. *Special achievements/activities:* 221 awards ($406,935 total): community service, general special achievements/activities, leadership, religious involvement. *Special characteristics:* 82 awards ($365,679 total): children and siblings of alumni, children of faculty/staff, relatives of clergy, siblings of current students. *Tuition waivers:* Full or partial for employees or children of employees. *ROTC:* Army cooperative.

LOANS *Student loans:* $7,530,387 (34% need-based, 66% non-need-based). 84% of past graduating class borrowed through all loan programs. *Average indebtedness per student:* $39,907. *Average need-based loan:* Freshmen: $2996. Undergraduates: $4489. *Parent loans:* $1,813,244 (97% need-based, 3% non-need-based). *Programs:* Federal Direct (Subsidized and Unsubsidized Stafford, PLUS), Perkins, Federal Nursing, college/university, private loans.

WORK-STUDY *Federal work-study:* Total amount: $778,000; 417 jobs averaging $2000.

ATHLETIC AWARDS Total amount: $1,856,331 (100% non-need-based).

APPLYING FOR FINANCIAL AID *Financial aid deadline:* Continuous. *Notification date:* Continuous beginning 3/15. Students must reply by 5/1 or within 2 weeks of notification.

CONTACT Kristin Look, Assistant Director of Financial Aid, Clarke University, 1550 Clarke Drive, Dubuque, IA 52001-3198, 563-588-6327 or toll-free 800-383-2345. *Fax:* 563-584-8605. *E-mail:* financialaid@clarke.edu.
Website: http://www.clarke.edu/.

CLARKSON COLLEGE
Omaha, NE

CONTACT Pam Shelton, Director of Financial Aid, Clarkson College, 101 South 42nd Street, Omaha, NE 68131-2739, 402-552-2749 or toll-free 800-647-5500. *Fax:* 402-552-6165. *E-mail:* shelton@clarksoncollege.edu.
Website: http://www.clarksoncollege.edu/.

CLARKSON UNIVERSITY
Potsdam, NY

Tuition & fees: $49,444	Average undergraduate aid package: $43,666

ABOUT THE INSTITUTION Independent, coed. *Awards:* certificates, bachelor's, master's, and doctoral degrees. 34 undergraduate majors. *Total enrollment:* 4,233. Undergraduates: 3,090. Freshmen: 677. Federal methodology is used as a basis for awarding need-based institutional aid.

UNDERGRADUATE EXPENSES for 2018–2019 *Application fee:* $50. *Comprehensive fee:* $64,352 includes full-time tuition ($48,194), mandatory fees ($1250), and room and board ($14,908). *College room only:* $8008. Full-time tuition and fees vary according to course load. Room and board charges vary according to board plan and housing facility. *Part-time tuition:* $1606 per credit hour. Part-time tuition and fees vary according to course load.

FRESHMAN FINANCIAL AID (Fall 2017, est.) 610 applied for aid; of those 93% were deemed to have need. 100% of freshmen with need received aid; of those 21% had need fully met. *Average percent of need met:* 90% (excluding resources awarded to replace EFC). *Average financial aid package:* $45,835 (excluding resources awarded to replace EFC). 14% of all full-time freshmen had no need and received non-need-based gift aid.

UNDERGRADUATE FINANCIAL AID (Fall 2017, est.) 2,588 applied for aid; of those 93% were deemed to have need. 100% of undergraduates with need received aid; of those 21% had need fully met. *Average percent of need met:* 89% (excluding resources awarded to replace EFC). *Average financial aid package:* $43,666 (excluding resources awarded to replace EFC). 16% of all full-time undergraduates had no need and received non-need-based gift aid.

GIFT AID (NEED-BASED) *Total amount:* $76,811,857 (7% federal, 3% state, 89% institutional, 1% external sources). *Receiving aid:* Freshmen: 83% (564); all full-time undergraduates: 80% (2,397). *Average award:* Freshmen: $35,300; Undergraduates: $32,061. *Scholarships, grants, and awards:* Federal Pell, FSEOG, state, private, college/university gift aid from institutional funds, Higher Education Opportunity Program (HEOP).

GIFT AID (NON-NEED-BASED) *Total amount:* $17,293,665 (11% federal, 1% state, 85% institutional, 3% external sources). *Receiving aid:* Freshmen: 13% (86). Undergraduates: 11% (339). *Average award:* Freshmen: $25,126. Undergraduates: $22,996. *Scholarships, grants, and awards by category: Academic interests/achievement:* $51,164,304 total: biological sciences, business, communication, computer science, engineering/technologies, general academic interests/achievements, humanities, mathematics, military science, physical sciences, social sciences. *Special achievements/activities:* $9,044,705 total: general special achievements/activities, leadership. *Special characteristics:* $6,367,169 total: children and siblings of alumni, children of faculty/staff, general special characteristics, international students, local/state students, members of minority groups, veterans. *Tuition waivers:* Full or partial for employees or children of employees. *ROTC:* Army, Air Force.

LOANS *Student loans:* $24,451,837 (74% need-based, 26% non-need-based). 82% of past graduating class borrowed through all loan programs. *Average indebtedness per student:* $24,500. *Average need-based loan:* Freshmen: $3577. Undergraduates: $5365. *Parent loans:* $8,001,029 (52% need-based, 48% non-need-based). *Programs:* Federal Direct (Subsidized and Unsubsidized Stafford, PLUS), Perkins, college/university, private loans.

WORK-STUDY *Federal work-study:* Total amount: $696,191; jobs available. *State or other work-study/employment:* Total amount: $541,082 (57% need-based, 43% non-need-based). 58 part-time jobs averaging $11,135.

ATHLETIC AWARDS Total amount: $76,650 (50% need-based, 50% non-need-based).

APPLYING FOR FINANCIAL AID *Required financial aid forms:* FAFSA, state aid form. *Financial aid deadline:* 3/1 (priority: 2/1). *Notification date:* Continuous beginning 2/17. Students must reply by 5/1 or within 2 weeks of notification.

CONTACT Mrs. Pamela A. Nichols, Director of Financial Aid, Clarkson University, 8 Clarkson Avenue, Box 5615, Potsdam, NY 13699, 315-268-6413 or toll-free 800-527-6577. *Fax:* 315-268-3899. *E-mail:* pnichols@clarkson.edu.
Website: http://www.clarkson.edu/.

CLARKS SUMMIT UNIVERSITY
South Abington Township, PA

ABOUT THE INSTITUTION Independent Baptist, coed. 28 undergraduate majors.

GIFT AID (NEED-BASED) *Scholarships, grants, and awards:* Federal Pell, FSEOG, state, private, college/university gift aid from institutional funds.

GIFT AID (NON-NEED-BASED) *Scholarships, grants, and awards by category: Academic interests/achievement:* education, general academic interests/achievements, religion/biblical studies. *Creative arts/performance:* general creative arts/performance, music. *Special achievements/activities:* general special achievements/activities, leadership, religious involvement. *Special characteristics:* children of faculty/staff, general special characteristics, married students.

LOANS *Programs:* Federal Direct (Subsidized and Unsubsidized Stafford, PLUS), alternative loans.

APPLYING FOR FINANCIAL AID *Required financial aid form:* FAFSA.

CONTACT Mrs. Deborah Cragle, Director of Financial Aid, Clarks Summit University, 538 Venard Road, South Abington Township, PA 18411, 570-586-2400 Ext. 9272 or toll-free 800-451-7664. *Fax:* 570-585-9470. *E-mail:* dcragle@clarkssummitu.edu.

Website: http://www.clarkssummitu.edu/.

CLARK UNIVERSITY
Worcester, MA

Tuition & fees: $45,730	Average undergraduate aid package: $32,134

ABOUT THE INSTITUTION Independent, coed. *Awards:* certificates, bachelor's, master's, and doctoral degrees. 48 undergraduate majors. *Total enrollment:* 3,153. Undergraduates: 2,240. Freshmen: 615. Institutional methodology is used as a basis for awarding need-based institutional aid.

UNDERGRADUATE EXPENSES for 2018–2019 *Application fee:* $60. *Comprehensive fee:* $54,900 includes full-time tuition ($45,380), mandatory fees ($350), and room and board ($9170). Room and board charges vary according to board plan and housing facility. *Part-time tuition:* $1376 per credit. *Payment plan:* Tuition prepayment.

FRESHMAN FINANCIAL AID (Fall 2017, est.) 477 applied for aid; of those 75% were deemed to have need. 98% of freshmen with need received aid; of those 29% had need fully met. *Average percent of need met:* 89% (excluding resources awarded to replace EFC). *Average financial aid package:* $32,004 (excluding resources awarded to replace EFC). 34% of all full-time freshmen had no need and received non-need-based gift aid.

UNDERGRADUATE FINANCIAL AID (Fall 2017, est.) 1,549 applied for aid; of those 77% were deemed to have need. 98% of undergraduates with need received aid; of those 19% had need fully met. *Average percent of need met:* 90% (excluding resources awarded to replace EFC). *Average financial aid package:* $32,134 (excluding resources awarded to replace EFC). 34% of all full-time undergraduates had no need and received non-need-based gift aid.

GIFT AID (NEED-BASED) *Total amount:* $33,116,736 (10% federal, 1% state, 89% institutional). *Receiving aid:* Freshmen: 56% (347); all full-time undergraduates: 53% (1,167). *Average award:* Freshmen: $28,199; Undergraduates: $26,780. *Scholarships, grants, and awards:* Federal Pell, FSEOG, state, college/university gift aid from institutional funds.

GIFT AID (NON-NEED-BASED) *Total amount:* $14,931,387 (100% institutional). *Receiving aid:* Freshmen: 26% (162). Undergraduates: 26% (570). *Average award:* Freshmen: $19,964. Undergraduates: $19,010. *Scholarships, grants, and awards by category:* Academic interests/achievement: general academic interests/achievements. Special achievements/activities: general special achievements/activities. *Tuition waivers:* Full or partial for employees or children of employees. *ROTC:* Army cooperative, Air Force cooperative.

LOANS *Student loans:* $10,383,909 (63% need-based, 37% non-need-based). 64% of past graduating class borrowed through all loan programs. *Average indebtedness per student:* $34,305. *Average need-based loan:* Freshmen: $3088. Undergraduates: $4754. *Parent loans:* $2,942,297 (18% need-based, 82% non-need-based). *Programs:* Federal Direct (Subsidized and Unsubsidized Stafford, PLUS), Perkins, state.

WORK-STUDY *Federal work-study:* Total amount: $1,446,576; jobs available.

APPLYING FOR FINANCIAL AID *Required financial aid forms:* FAFSA, CSS Financial Aid PROFILE, noncustodial (divorced/separated) parent's statement. *Financial aid deadline:* 1/15. *Notification date:* 2/20. Students must reply by 5/1.

CONTACT Ms. Mary Ellen Severance, Director of Financial Assistance, Clark University, 950 Main Street, Worcester, MA 01610-1477, 508-793-7478 or toll-free 800-GO-CLARK. *Fax:* 508-793-8802. *E-mail:* finaid@clarku.edu.

Website: http://www.clarku.edu/.

CLAYTON STATE UNIVERSITY
Morrow, GA

Tuition & fees (GA res): $6410	Average undergraduate aid package: $10,024

ABOUT THE INSTITUTION State-supported, coed. *Awards:* certificates, associate, bachelor's, and master's degrees. 34 undergraduate majors. *Total enrollment:* 7,003. Undergraduates: 6,555. Freshmen: 643. Federal methodology is used as a basis for awarding need-based institutional aid.

UNDERGRADUATE EXPENSES for 2017–2018 *Application fee:* $40. *Tuition, state resident:* full-time $4956; part-time $165.20 per credit hour. *Tuition, nonresident:* full-time $18,032; part-time $601.07 per credit hour. *Required fees:* full-time $1454; $727 per term. Full-time tuition and fees vary according to course load. Part-time tuition and fees vary according to course load. *College room and board:* $10,490. Room and board charges vary according to board plan and housing facility.

FRESHMAN FINANCIAL AID (Fall 2017, est.) 446 applied for aid; of those 93% were deemed to have need. 100% of freshmen with need received aid; of those 4% had need fully met. *Average percent of need met:* 52% (excluding resources awarded to replace EFC). *Average financial aid package:* $11,230 (excluding resources awarded to replace EFC). 1% of all full-time freshmen had no need and received non-need-based gift aid.

UNDERGRADUATE FINANCIAL AID (Fall 2017, est.) 3,251 applied for aid; of those 93% were deemed to have need. 100% of undergraduates with need received aid; of those 3% had need fully met. *Average percent of need met:* 47% (excluding resources awarded to replace EFC). *Average financial aid package:* $10,024 (excluding resources awarded to replace EFC). 1% of all full-time undergraduates had no need and received non-need-based gift aid.

GIFT AID (NEED-BASED) *Receiving aid:* Freshmen: 81% (381); all full-time undergraduates: 75% (2,649). *Average award:* Freshmen: $8922; Undergraduates: $7108. *Scholarships, grants, and awards:* Federal Pell, FSEOG, state, private, college/university gift aid from institutional funds, Federal Nursing.

GIFT AID (NON-NEED-BASED) *Receiving aid:* Freshmen: 6% (26). Undergraduates: 3% (118). *Average award:* Freshmen: $10,479. Undergraduates: $2045. *Tuition waivers:* Full or partial for employees or children of employees, senior citizens. *ROTC:* Army cooperative, Naval cooperative, Air Force cooperative.

LOANS *Student loans:* 84% of past graduating class borrowed through all loan programs. *Average indebtedness per student:* $30,423. *Average need-based loan:* Freshmen: $3406. Undergraduates: $4067. *Programs:* Federal Direct (Subsidized and Unsubsidized Stafford, PLUS), state.

WORK-STUDY *Federal work-study:* 67 jobs averaging $4556.

APPLYING FOR FINANCIAL AID *Required financial aid form:* FAFSA. *Financial aid deadline (priority):* 7/15. *Notification date:* Continuous beginning 4/15.

CONTACT Lakisha Sanders, Director of Financial Aid, Clayton State University, 2000 Clayton State Boulevard, Morrow, GA 30260, 678-466-4185. *Fax:* 678-466-4189. *E-mail:* financialaid@mail.clayton.edu.

Website: http://www.clayton.edu/.

CLEAR CREEK BAPTIST BIBLE COLLEGE
Pineville, KY

Tuition & fees: N/R	Average undergraduate aid package: $6566

ABOUT THE INSTITUTION Independent Southern Baptist, coed, primarily men. 2 undergraduate majors. Both federal and institutional methodology are used as a basis for awarding need-based institutional aid.

FRESHMAN FINANCIAL AID (Fall 2017, est.) 6 applied for aid; of those 67% were deemed to have need. 100% of freshmen with need received aid. *Average percent of need met:* 58% (excluding resources awarded to replace EFC). *Average financial aid package:* $8488 (excluding resources awarded to replace EFC). 33% of all full-time freshmen had no need and received non-need-based gift aid.

UNDERGRADUATE FINANCIAL AID (Fall 2017, est.) 94 applied for aid; of those 84% were deemed to have need. 100% of undergraduates with need received aid. *Average percent of need met:* 45% (excluding resources awarded to replace EFC). *Average financial aid package:* $6566 (excluding resources awarded to replace EFC). 12% of all full-time undergraduates had no need and received non-need-based gift aid.

GIFT AID (NEED-BASED) *Total amount:* $589,046 (50% federal, 37% institutional, 13% external sources). *Receiving aid:* Freshmen: 67% (4); all full-time undergraduates: 65% (79). *Average award:* Freshmen: $8488; Undergraduates: $6566. *Scholarships, grants, and awards:* Federal Pell, FSEOG, state, private, college/university gift aid from institutional funds.

GIFT AID (NON-NEED-BASED) *Total amount:* $99,217 (23% federal, 77% institutional). *Receiving aid:* Freshmen: 17% (1). Undergraduates: 29% (35). *Average award:* Freshmen: $1800. Undergraduates: $3701. *Scholarships, grants, and awards by category: Academic interests/achievement:* 3 awards ($1975 total): general academic interests/achievements. *Creative arts/performance:* 5 awards ($1250 total): music. *Special characteristics:* 2 awards ($2092 total): handicapped students, international students.

WORK-STUDY *Federal work-study:* Total amount: $38,081; 32 jobs averaging $1190.

APPLYING FOR FINANCIAL AID *Required financial aid forms:* FAFSA, institution's own form. *Financial aid deadline:* Continuous. *Notification date:* Continuous beginning 6/1.

CONTACT Mr. Sam Risner, Director of Financial Aid, Clear Creek Baptist Bible College, 300 Clear Creek Road, Pineville, KY 40977-9754, 606-337-3196 Ext. 142. *Fax:* 606-337-1631. *E-mail:* srisner@ccbbc.edu. *Website:* http://www.ccbbc.edu/.

CLEARY UNIVERSITY
Howell, MI

CONTACT Vesta Smith-Campbell, Director of Financial Aid, Cleary University, 3750 Cleary Drive, Howell, MI 48843, 517-338-3042 or toll-free 800-686-1883. *Fax:* 517-552-8022. *E-mail:* vscampbell@cleary.edu. *Website:* http://www.cleary.edu/.

CLEMSON UNIVERSITY
Clemson, SC

Tuition & fees (SC res): $14,712	Average undergraduate aid package: $11,582

ABOUT THE INSTITUTION State-supported, coed. *Awards:* certificates, bachelor's, master's, and doctoral degrees. 71 undergraduate majors. *Total enrollment:* 24,387. Undergraduates: 19,402. Freshmen: 3,649. Federal methodology is used as a basis for awarding need-based institutional aid.

UNDERGRADUATE EXPENSES for 2017–2018 *Application fee:* $70. *Tuition, state resident:* full-time $13,520; part-time $630 per credit hour. *Tuition, nonresident:* full-time $34,132; part-time $1540 per credit hour. *Required fees:* full-time $1192. Full-time tuition and fees vary according to course level, course load, location, program, and student level. Part-time tuition and fees vary according to course level, course load, location, program, and student level. *College room and board:* $9592. Room and board charges vary according to board plan, housing facility, and location.

FRESHMAN FINANCIAL AID (Fall 2017, est.) 2,985 applied for aid; of those 61% were deemed to have need. 98% of freshmen with need received aid; of those 21% had need fully met. *Average percent of need met:* 59% (excluding resources awarded to replace EFC). *Average financial aid package:* $13,131 (excluding resources awarded to replace EFC). 32% of all full-time freshmen had no need and received non-need-based gift aid.

UNDERGRADUATE FINANCIAL AID (Fall 2017, est.) 12,307 applied for aid; of those 73% were deemed to have need. 97% of undergraduates with need received aid; of those 16% had need fully met. *Average percent of need met:* 54% (excluding resources awarded to replace EFC). *Average financial aid package:* $11,582 (excluding resources awarded to replace EFC). 28% of all full-time undergraduates had no need and received non-need-based gift aid.

GIFT AID (NEED-BASED) *Total amount:* $73,390,579 (20% federal, 42% state, 32% institutional, 6% external sources). *Receiving aid:* Freshmen: 46% (1,680); all

full-time undergraduates: 39% (7,459). *Average award:* Freshmen: $10,918; Undergraduates: $9183. *Scholarships, grants, and awards:* Federal Pell, FSEOG, state, private, college/university gift aid from institutional funds, Federal Nursing.

GIFT AID (NON-NEED-BASED) *Total amount:* $59,660,022 (50% state, 45% institutional, 5% external sources). *Receiving aid:* Freshmen: 46% (1,680). Undergraduates: 39% (7,459). *Average award:* Freshmen: $6585. Undergraduates: $5071. *Scholarships, grants, and awards by category: Academic interests/achievement:* agriculture, architecture, biological sciences, business, communication, computer science, education, engineering/technologies, English, foreign languages, general academic interests/achievements, health fields, humanities, international studies, mathematics, military science, physical sciences, premedicine, social sciences. *Creative arts/performance:* applied art and design, art/fine arts, performing arts, theater/drama. *Special achievements/activities:* community service, general special achievements/activities, leadership. *Special characteristics:* children of faculty/staff, ethnic background, local/state students, members of minority groups, veterans. *Tuition waivers:* Full or partial for senior citizens. *ROTC:* Army, Air Force.

LOANS *Student loans:* $84,557,953 (77% need-based, 23% non-need-based). 46% of past graduating class borrowed through all loan programs. *Average indebtedness per student:* $30,201. *Average need-based loan:* Freshmen: $3653. Undergraduates: $4531. *Parent loans:* $33,713,633 (82% need-based, 18% non-need-based). *Programs:* Federal Direct (Subsidized and Unsubsidized Stafford, PLUS), Perkins, state, college/university.

WORK-STUDY *Federal work-study:* Total amount: $2,794,256; jobs available. *State or other work-study/employment:* 584 part-time jobs averaging $1541.

ATHLETIC AWARDS Total amount: $7,772,417 (37% need-based, 63% non-need-based).

APPLYING FOR FINANCIAL AID *Required financial aid form:* FAFSA. *Financial aid deadline (priority):* 3/1. *Notification date:* Continuous beginning 4/1. Students must reply within 3 weeks of notification.

CONTACT Mrs. Elizabeth Milam, Director of Financial Aid, Clemson University, G-01 Sikes Hall, Box 345123, Clemson, SC 29634-5123, 864-656-2280. *Fax:* 864-656-1831. *E-mail:* finaid@clemson.edu. *Website:* http://www.clemson.edu/.

CLEVELAND INSTITUTE OF ART
Cleveland, OH

Tuition & fees: $40,655	Average undergraduate aid package: $27,536

ABOUT THE INSTITUTION Independent, coed. *Awards:* bachelor's degrees. 15 undergraduate majors. *Total enrollment:* 625. Undergraduates: 625. Freshmen: 161. Federal methodology is used as a basis for awarding need-based institutional aid.

UNDERGRADUATE EXPENSES for 2017–2018 *Application fee:* $40. *Comprehensive fee:* $51,455 includes full-time tuition ($37,980), mandatory fees ($2675), and room and board ($10,800). *College room only:* $8150. Full-time tuition and fees vary according to reciprocity agreements. Room and board charges vary according to board plan and housing facility. *Part-time tuition:* $1585 per credit. *Part-time fees:* $73 per semester hour; $115 per semester hour. Part-time tuition and fees vary according to course load and reciprocity agreements.

FRESHMAN FINANCIAL AID (Fall 2016) 153 applied for aid; of those 92% were deemed to have need. 100% of freshmen with need received aid; of those 7% had need fully met. *Average percent of need met:* 59% (excluding resources awarded to replace EFC). *Average financial aid package:* $26,456 (excluding resources awarded to replace EFC). 14% of all full-time freshmen had no need and received non-need-based gift aid.

UNDERGRADUATE FINANCIAL AID (Fall 2016) 518 applied for aid; of those 95% were deemed to have need. 100% of undergraduates with need received aid; of those 9% had need fully met. *Average percent of need met:* 61% (excluding resources awarded to replace EFC). *Average financial aid package:* $27,536 (excluding resources awarded to replace EFC). 14% of all full-time undergraduates had no need and received non-need-based gift aid.

GIFT AID (NEED-BASED) *Total amount:* $10,852,039 (11% federal, 4% state, 83% institutional, 2% external sources). *Receiving aid:* Freshmen: 88% (141); all full-time undergraduates: 81% (492). *Average award:* Freshmen: $21,832; Undergraduates: $22,276. *Scholarships, grants, and awards:* Federal Pell, FSEOG, state, private, college/university gift aid from institutional funds.

GIFT AID (NON-NEED-BASED) *Total amount:* $1,438,715 (99% institutional, 1% external sources). *Receiving aid:* Freshmen: 4% (7). Undergraduates: 6% (36). *Average award:* Freshmen: $15,804. Undergraduates: $13,392. *Scholarships, grants, and awards by category: Creative arts/performance:* applied art and design, art/fine arts. *Special achievements/activities:* 6 awards ($63,795 total): leadership. *Tuition waivers:* Full or partial for employees or children of employees.

LOANS *Student loans:* $5,511,477 (83% need-based, 17% non-need-based). 79% of past graduating class borrowed through all loan programs. *Average indebtedness per student:* $37,195. *Average need-based loan:* Freshmen: $3907. Undergraduates: $4533. *Parent loans:* $2,619,282 (77% need-based, 23% non-need-based). *Programs:* Federal Direct (Subsidized and Unsubsidized Stafford, PLUS).

WORK-STUDY *Federal work-study:* Total amount: $123,326; 151 jobs averaging $1101.

APPLYING FOR FINANCIAL AID *Required financial aid form:* FAFSA. *Financial aid deadline (priority):* 3/15. *Notification date:* Continuous beginning 12/20. Students must reply by 5/1 or within 3 weeks of notification.

CONTACT Mr. Martin Joseph Carney Jr., Director of Financial Aid, Cleveland Institute of Art, 11610 Euclid Avenue, Cleveland, OH 44106-4387, 216-421-7425 or toll-free 800-223-4700. *Fax:* 216-754-3634. *E-mail:* financialaid@cia.edu. *Website:* http://www.cia.edu/.

CLEVELAND INSTITUTE OF MUSIC
Cleveland, OH

Tuition & fees: N/R	Average undergraduate aid package: $34,169

ABOUT THE INSTITUTION Independent, coed. 3 undergraduate majors. Both federal and institutional methodology are used as a basis for awarding need-based institutional aid.

FRESHMAN FINANCIAL AID (Fall 2017, est.) 46 applied for aid; of those 76% were deemed to have need. 100% of freshmen with need received aid; of those 34% had need fully met. *Average percent of need met:* 81% (excluding resources awarded to replace EFC). *Average financial aid package:* $35,778 (excluding resources awarded to replace EFC). 41% of all full-time freshmen had no need and received non-need-based gift aid.

UNDERGRADUATE FINANCIAL AID (Fall 2017, est.) 135 applied for aid; of those 83% were deemed to have need. 100% of undergraduates with need received aid; of those 26% had need fully met. *Average percent of need met:* 78% (excluding resources awarded to replace EFC). *Average financial aid package:* $34,169 (excluding resources awarded to replace EFC). 50% of all full-time undergraduates had no need and received non-need-based gift aid.

GIFT AID (NEED-BASED) *Total amount:* $3,303,659 (5% federal, 94% institutional, 1% external sources). *Receiving aid:* Freshmen: 59% (35); all full-time undergraduates: 50% (112). *Average award:* Freshmen: $31,568; Undergraduates: $29,340. *Scholarships, grants, and awards:* Federal Pell, FSEOG, state, private, college/university gift aid from institutional funds.

GIFT AID (NON-NEED-BASED) *Total amount:* $2,996,080 (98% institutional, 2% external sources). *Receiving aid:* Freshmen: 15% (9). Undergraduates: 10% (22). *Average award:* Freshmen: $24,995. Undergraduates: $23,807. *Scholarships, grants, and awards by category: Creative arts/performance:* music. *Special characteristics:* children of faculty/staff.

LOANS *Student loans:* $883,214 (69% need-based, 31% non-need-based). 50% of past graduating class borrowed through all loan programs. *Average indebtedness per student:* $25,994. *Average need-based loan:* Freshmen: $4803. Undergraduates: $5310. *Parent loans:* $573,154 (35% need-based, 65% non-need-based). *Programs:* Federal Direct (Subsidized and Unsubsidized Stafford, PLUS), private loans.

WORK-STUDY *Federal work-study:* Total amount: $96,039; jobs available. *State or other work-study/employment:* Total amount: $65,850 (6% need-based, 94% non-need-based). Part-time jobs available.

APPLYING FOR FINANCIAL AID *Required financial aid forms:* FAFSA, CSS Financial Aid PROFILE. *Financial aid deadline (priority):* 2/1. *Notification date:* 4/1. Students must reply by 5/1.

CONTACT Ms. Kristie Gripp, Director of Financial Aid, Cleveland Institute of Music, 11021 East Boulevard, Cleveland, OH 44106-1776, 216-795-3192. *Fax:* 216-707-4519. *E-mail:* kristine.gripp@cim.edu. *Website:* http://www.cim.edu/.

CLEVELAND STATE UNIVERSITY
Cleveland, OH

Tuition & fees (OH res): $9696	Average undergraduate aid package: $8932

ABOUT THE INSTITUTION State-supported, coed. *Awards:* certificates, bachelor's, master's, and doctoral degrees. 77 undergraduate majors. *Total enrollment:* 16,607. Undergraduates: 12,306. Freshmen: 1,955. Federal methodology is used as a basis for awarding need-based institutional aid.

UNDERGRADUATE EXPENSES for 2017–2018 *Application fee:* $30. *Tuition, state resident:* full-time $9636; part-time $401.50 per credit hour. *Tuition, nonresident:* full-time $13,687; part-time $570.30 per credit hour. *Required fees:* full-time $60; $49 per credit hour or $35 per term. Full-time tuition and fees vary according to course load, degree level, location, and program. Part-time tuition and fees vary according to course load, degree level, location, and program. *College room and board:* $12,000. Room and board charges vary according to board plan and housing facility.

FRESHMAN FINANCIAL AID (Fall 2017, est.) 1,630 applied for aid; of those 85% were deemed to have need. 98% of freshmen with need received aid; of those 8% had need fully met. *Average percent of need met:* 48% (excluding resources awarded to replace EFC). *Average financial aid package:* $9234 (excluding resources awarded to replace EFC). 10% of all full-time freshmen had no need and received non-need-based gift aid.

UNDERGRADUATE FINANCIAL AID (Fall 2017, est.) 7,508 applied for aid; of those 88% were deemed to have need. 98% of undergraduates with need received aid; of those 6% had need fully met. *Average percent of need met:* 47% (excluding resources awarded to replace EFC). *Average financial aid package:* $8932 (excluding resources awarded to replace EFC). 8% of all full-time undergraduates had no need and received non-need-based gift aid.

GIFT AID (NEED-BASED) *Total amount:* $38,242,633 (56% federal, 17% state, 22% institutional, 5% external sources). *Receiving aid:* Freshmen: 63% (1,205); all full-time undergraduates: 57% (5,188). *Average award:* Freshmen: $7458; Undergraduates: $6903. *Scholarships, grants, and awards:* Federal Pell, FSEOG, state, private, college/university gift aid from institutional funds.

GIFT AID (NON-NEED-BASED) *Total amount:* $4,935,042 (1% federal, 6% state, 85% institutional, 8% external sources). *Receiving aid:* Freshmen: 4% (82). Undergraduates: 3% (247). *Average award:* Freshmen: $4428. Undergraduates: $4951. *Scholarships, grants, and awards by category: Academic interests/achievement:* biological sciences, business, communication, computer science, education, engineering/technologies, English, general academic interests/achievements, home economics, humanities, mathematics, physical sciences, premedicine, social sciences. *Creative arts/performance:* art/fine arts, creative writing, dance, journalism/publications, music, performing arts, theater/drama. *Special achievements/activities:* cheerleading/drum major. *Special characteristics:* children of faculty/staff, general special characteristics, out-of-state students. *Tuition waivers:* Full or partial for employees or children of employees, senior citizens. *ROTC:* Army cooperative, Air Force cooperative.

LOANS *Student loans:* $56,012,601 (83% need-based, 17% non-need-based). 65% of past graduating class borrowed through all loan programs. *Average indebtedness per student:* $29,380. *Average need-based loan:* Freshmen: $3187. Undergraduates: $4046. *Parent loans:* $7,418,425 (49% need-based, 51% non-need-based). *Programs:* Federal Direct (Subsidized and Unsubsidized Stafford, PLUS), Perkins, state, alternative loans.

WORK-STUDY *Federal work-study:* Total amount: $849,977; 259 jobs averaging $3378. *State or other work-study/employment:* Part-time jobs available.

ATHLETIC AWARDS Total amount: $3,164,048 (36% need-based, 64% non-need-based).

APPLYING FOR FINANCIAL AID *Required financial aid forms:* FAFSA, federal income tax form(s). *Financial aid deadline (priority):* 2/15. *Notification date:* Continuous beginning 3/15. Students must reply within 4 weeks of notification.

CONTACT Financial Aid Office, Cleveland State University, 1621 Euclid Avenue, Cleveland, OH 44115, 216-687-5594 or toll-free 888-CSU-OHIO. *E-mail:* campus411@csuohio.edu. *Website:* http://www.csuohio.edu/.

CLEVELAND UNIVERSITY–KANSAS CITY
Overland Park, KS

CONTACT Financial Aid Office, Cleveland University–Kansas City, 10850 Lowell Avenue, Overland Park, KS 66210, 913-234-0600 or toll-free 800-467-2252. *Website:* http://www.cleveland.edu/.

COASTAL CAROLINA UNIVERSITY
Conway, SC

Tuition & fees (SC res): $11,200	Average undergraduate aid package: $10,256

ABOUT THE INSTITUTION State-supported, coed. *Awards:* certificates, bachelor's, master's, and doctoral degrees. 43 undergraduate majors. *Total enrollment:* 10,663. Undergraduates: 9,898. Freshmen: 2,390. Federal methodology is used as a basis for awarding need-based institutional aid.

UNDERGRADUATE EXPENSES for 2017–2018 Application fee: $45. *Tuition, state resident:* full-time $11,020; part-time $469 per credit hour. *Tuition, nonresident:* full-time $25,692; part-time $1075 per credit hour. *Required fees:* full-time $180; $5 per credit hour. Full-time tuition and fees vary according to course load, degree level, and reciprocity agreements. Part-time tuition and fees vary according to course load, degree level, and reciprocity agreements. *College room and board:* $9140; *Room only:* $5440. Room and board charges vary according to board plan and housing facility.

FRESHMAN FINANCIAL AID (Fall 2016) 2,055 applied for aid; of those 82% were deemed to have need. 99% of freshmen with need received aid; of those 9% had need fully met. *Average percent of need met:* 46% (excluding resources awarded to replace EFC). *Average financial aid package:* $10,509 (excluding resources awarded to replace EFC). 18% of all full-time freshmen had no need and received non-need-based gift aid.

UNDERGRADUATE FINANCIAL AID (Fall 2016) 7,333 applied for aid; of those 84% were deemed to have need. 99% of undergraduates with need received aid; of those 3% had need fully met. *Average percent of need met:* 46% (excluding resources awarded to replace EFC). *Average financial aid package:* $10,256 (excluding resources awarded to replace EFC). 18% of all full-time undergraduates had no need and received non-need-based gift aid.

GIFT AID (NEED-BASED) Total amount: $16,751,884 (90% federal, 10% state). *Receiving aid:* Freshmen: 38% (848); all full-time undergraduates: 38% (3,343). *Average award:* Freshmen: $5001; Undergraduates: $4826. *Scholarships, grants, and awards:* Federal Pell, FSEOG, state, private, college/university gift aid from institutional funds.

GIFT AID (NON-NEED-BASED) Total amount: $17,078,836 (64% state, 22% institutional, 14% external sources). *Receiving aid:* Freshmen: 34% (770). Undergraduates: 22% (1,970). *Average award:* Freshmen: $14,182. Undergraduates: $14,432. *Scholarships, grants, and awards by category: Academic interests/achievement:* 3,315 awards ($10,087,415 total): biological sciences, business, communication, computer science, education, English, foreign languages, general academic interests/achievements, humanities, international studies, mathematics, physical sciences, social sciences. *Creative arts/performance:* 81 awards ($113,500 total): art/fine arts, music, performing arts, theater/drama. *Special achievements/activities:* 28 awards ($24,136 total): cheerleading/drum major. *Special characteristics:* 2,570 awards ($8,096,535 total): children of faculty/staff, general special characteristics, international students, local/state students, out-of-state students, veterans' children. *Tuition waivers:* Full or partial for employees or children of employees, senior citizens. *ROTC:* Army.

LOANS Student loans: $67,845,230 (31% need-based, 69% non-need-based). 79% of past graduating class borrowed through all loan programs. *Average indebtedness per student:* $37,373. *Average need-based loan:* Freshmen: $8851. Undergraduates: $9057. *Parent loans:* $30,567,621 (100% non-need-based). *Programs:* Federal Direct (Subsidized and Unsubsidized Stafford), Perkins, state.

WORK-STUDY Federal work-study: 176 jobs averaging $1890. *State or other work-study/employment:* Total amount: $2,634,719 (100% non-need-based). 1,448 part-time jobs averaging $1820.

ATHLETIC AWARDS Total amount: $4,966,126 (100% non-need-based).

APPLYING FOR FINANCIAL AID Required financial aid form: FAFSA. *Financial aid deadline (priority):* 3/1. *Notification date:* Continuous beginning 3/1. Students must reply by 5/15.
CONTACT Ms. Wendy H. Watts, Director of Financial Aid and Scholarships, Coastal Carolina University, PO Box 261954, Conway, SC 29528-6054, 843-349-2544 or toll-free 800-277-7000. *Fax:* 843-349-2347. *E-mail:* wwatts@coastal.edu. *Website:* http://www.coastal.edu/.

COE COLLEGE
Cedar Rapids, IA

Tuition & fees: $45,000	Average undergraduate aid package: $35,630

ABOUT THE INSTITUTION Independent Presbyterian Church, coed. *Awards:* bachelor's degrees. 65 undergraduate majors. *Total enrollment:* 1,394. Undergraduates: 1,394. Freshmen: 400. Federal methodology is used as a basis for awarding need-based institutional aid.

UNDERGRADUATE EXPENSES for 2018–2019 Application fee: $30. *Comprehensive fee:* $54,480 includes full-time tuition ($44,700), mandatory fees ($300), and room and board ($9480). Room and board charges vary according to board plan and housing facility. *Part-time tuition:* $5587 per course. Part-time tuition and fees vary according to course load.

FRESHMAN FINANCIAL AID (Fall 2017, est.) 377 applied for aid; of those 92% were deemed to have need. 100% of freshmen with need received aid; of those 21% had need fully met. *Average percent of need met:* 85% (excluding resources awarded to replace EFC). *Average financial aid package:* $37,433 (excluding resources awarded to replace EFC). 14% of all full-time freshmen had no need and received non-need-based gift aid.

UNDERGRADUATE FINANCIAL AID (Fall 2017, est.) 1,197 applied for aid; of those 93% were deemed to have need. 100% of undergraduates with need received aid; of those 21% had need fully met. *Average percent of need met:* 84% (excluding resources awarded to replace EFC). *Average financial aid package:* $35,630 (excluding resources awarded to replace EFC). 17% of all full-time undergraduates had no need and received non-need-based gift aid.

GIFT AID (NEED-BASED) Total amount: $34,461,154 (6% federal, 5% state, 87% institutional, 2% external sources). *Receiving aid:* Freshmen: 86% (345); all full-time undergraduates: 83% (1,116). *Average award:* Freshmen: $33,284; Undergraduates: $30,679. *Scholarships, grants, and awards:* Federal Pell, FSEOG, state, private, college/university gift aid from institutional funds, Federal Nursing, ROTC Scholarships.

GIFT AID (NON-NEED-BASED) Total amount: $7,359,073 (2% federal, 95% institutional, 3% external sources). *Receiving aid:* Freshmen: 14% (55). Undergraduates: 13% (172). *Average award:* Freshmen: $26,569. Undergraduates: $25,052. *Scholarships, grants, and awards by category: Academic interests/achievement:* $24,358,853 total: general academic interests/achievements. *Creative arts/performance:* $598,390 total: art/fine arts, creative writing, music, performing arts, theater/drama. *Special characteristics:* $4,193,913 total: adult students, children and siblings of alumni, children of educators, children of faculty/staff, ethnic background, general special characteristics, international students, members of minority groups, religious affiliation, siblings of current students, veterans, veterans' children. *Tuition waivers:* Full or partial for employees or children of employees, adult students, senior citizens. *ROTC:* Army, Air Force cooperative.

LOANS Student loans: $9,179,255 (75% need-based, 25% non-need-based). 81% of past graduating class borrowed through all loan programs. *Average indebtedness per student:* $36,022. *Average need-based loan:* Freshmen: $3818. Undergraduates: $5144. *Parent loans:* $2,651,903 (42% need-based, 58% non-need-based). *Programs:* Federal Direct (Subsidized and Unsubsidized Stafford, PLUS), Perkins, college/university.

WORK-STUDY Federal work-study: Total amount: $1,052,394; 617 jobs averaging $1706. *State or other work-study/employment:* Total amount: $349,780 (12% need-based, 88% non-need-based). 226 part-time jobs averaging $1550.

APPLYING FOR FINANCIAL AID Required financial aid form: FAFSA. *Financial aid deadline (priority):* 3/1. *Notification date:* Continuous beginning 12/1. Students must reply by 5/1 or within 2 weeks of notification.

CONTACT Ms. Barbara Hoffman, Director of Financial Aid, Coe College, 1220 First Avenue, NE, Cedar Rapids, IA 52402-5070, 319-399-8540 or toll-free 877-225-5263. *Fax:* 319-399-8886.
Website: http://www.coe.edu/.

COGSWELL POLYTECHNICAL COLLEGE
San Jose, CA

ABOUT THE INSTITUTION Proprietary, coed. *Awards:* bachelor's and master's degrees. 6 undergraduate majors. *Total enrollment:* 608. Undergraduates: 608. Freshmen: 72.
GIFT AID (NEED-BASED) *Scholarships, grants, and awards:* Federal Pell, FSEOG, state, private, college/university gift aid from institutional funds.
LOANS *Programs:* Federal Direct (Subsidized and Unsubsidized Stafford, PLUS), private loans.
APPLYING FOR FINANCIAL AID *Required financial aid forms:* FAFSA, state aid form.
CONTACT Yariela Perez, Director of Financial Aid, Cogswell Polytechnical College, 191 Baypointe Parkway, San Jose, CA 95134, 408-498-5100 or toll-free 800-264-7955. *E-mail:* yperez@cogswell.edu.
Website: http://www.cogswell.edu/.

COKER COLLEGE
Hartsville, SC

Tuition & fees: $28,684	Average undergraduate aid package: $21,502

ABOUT THE INSTITUTION Independent, coed. *Awards:* bachelor's and master's degrees (also offers evening program with significant enrollment not reflected in profile). 39 undergraduate majors. *Total enrollment:* 1,093. Undergraduates: 1,022. Freshmen: 210. Both federal and institutional methodology are used as a basis for awarding need-based institutional aid.
UNDERGRADUATE EXPENSES for 2017–2018 *Comprehensive fee:* $37,508 includes full-time tuition ($28,464), mandatory fees ($220), and room and board ($8874). *College room only:* $4068. Full-time tuition and fees vary according to course load, degree level, location, and program. Room and board charges vary according to board plan and housing facility. *Part-time tuition:* $1186 per credit hour. Part-time tuition and fees vary according to course load, degree level, location, and program.
FRESHMAN FINANCIAL AID (Fall 2016) 243 applied for aid; of those 92% were deemed to have need. 99% of freshmen with need received aid; of those 25% had need fully met. *Average percent of need met:* 77% (excluding resources awarded to replace EFC). *Average financial aid package:* $25,948 (excluding resources awarded to replace EFC). 1% of all full-time freshmen had no need and received non-need-based gift aid.
UNDERGRADUATE FINANCIAL AID (Fall 2016) 886 applied for aid; of those 93% were deemed to have need. 99% of undergraduates with need received aid; of those 20% had need fully met. *Average percent of need met:* 70% (excluding resources awarded to replace EFC). *Average financial aid package:* $21,502 (excluding resources awarded to replace EFC). 12% of all full-time undergraduates had no need and received non-need-based gift aid.
GIFT AID (NEED-BASED) *Total amount:* $6,224,740 (44% federal, 26% state, 28% institutional, 2% external sources). *Receiving aid:* Freshmen: 80% (203); all full-time undergraduates: 78% (746). *Average award:* Freshmen: $8205; Undergraduates: $7452. *Scholarships, grants, and awards:* Federal Pell, FSEOG, state, private, college/university gift aid from institutional funds.
GIFT AID (NON-NEED-BASED) *Total amount:* $8,745,162 (6% federal, 16% state, 75% institutional, 3% external sources). *Receiving aid:* Freshmen: 86% (218). Undergraduates: 69% (659). *Average award:* Freshmen: $33,718. Undergraduates: $10,836. *Scholarships, grants, and awards by category:* Academic interests/achievement: biological sciences, general academic interests/achievements. Creative arts/performance: art/fine arts, creative writing, dance, general creative arts/performance, music, theater/drama. *Special achievements/activities:* cheerleading/drum

major, leadership. *Special characteristics:* adult students, children and siblings of alumni, children of faculty/staff, international students, local/state students, out-of-state students, previous college experience, veterans. *Tuition waivers:* Full or partial for employees or children of employees.
LOANS *Student loans:* $37,370,332 (84% need-based, 16% non-need-based). 79% of past graduating class borrowed through all loan programs. *Average indebtedness per student:* $20,494. *Average need-based loan:* Freshmen: $3,561. Undergraduates: $4277. *Parent loans:* $1,585,762 (100% non-need-based). *Programs:* Federal Direct (Subsidized and Unsubsidized Stafford, PLUS), Perkins, state, private loans.
WORK-STUDY *Federal work-study:* jobs available. *State or other work-study/employment:* Total amount: $500 (100% need-based). Part-time jobs available.
ATHLETIC AWARDS Total amount: $2,419,611 (100% non-need-based).
APPLYING FOR FINANCIAL AID *Required financial aid forms:* FAFSA, institution's own form. *Financial aid deadline:* Continuous. *Notification date:* Continuous beginning 12/15.
CONTACT Mrs. Betty Williams, Director of Student Financial Planning, Coker College, 300 East College Avenue, Hartsville, SC 29550, 843-383-8055 or toll-free 800-950-1908. *Fax:* 843-383-8056. *E-mail:* bwilliams@coker.edu.
Website: http://www.coker.edu/.

THE COLBURN SCHOOL CONSERVATORY OF MUSIC
Los Angeles, CA

ABOUT THE INSTITUTION Independent, coed. 5 undergraduate majors.
GIFT AID (NEED-BASED) *Scholarships, grants, and awards:* college/university gift aid from institutional funds.
GIFT AID (NON-NEED-BASED) *Scholarships, grants, and awards by category:* Creative arts/performance: music.
APPLYING FOR FINANCIAL AID *Required financial aid form:* institution's own form.
CONTACT Ms. Misha Starks, Registrar, The Colburn School Conservatory of Music, 200 South Grand Avenue, Los Angeles, CA 90012, 213-621-4788. *Fax:* 213-625-0371. *E-mail:* mstarks@colburnschool.edu.
Website: http://www.colburnschool.edu/.

COLBY COLLEGE
Waterville, ME

Tuition & fees: $53,120	Average undergraduate aid package: $48,467

ABOUT THE INSTITUTION Independent, coed. *Awards:* bachelor's degrees. 47 undergraduate majors. *Total enrollment:* 1,917. Undergraduates: 1,917. Freshmen: 552. Both federal and institutional methodology are used as a basis for awarding need-based institutional aid.
UNDERGRADUATE EXPENSES for 2017–2018 *Comprehensive fee:* $66,780 includes full-time tuition ($50,890), mandatory fees ($2230), and room and board ($13,660). *Part-time tuition:* $1960 per credit hour. Part-time tuition and fees vary according to course load.
FRESHMAN FINANCIAL AID (Fall 2017, est.) 297 applied for aid; of those 88% were deemed to have need. 100% of freshmen with need received aid; of those 100% had need fully met. *Average percent of need met:* 100% (excluding resources awarded to replace EFC). *Average financial aid package:* $51,118 (excluding resources awarded to replace EFC). 1% of all full-time freshmen had no need and received non-need-based gift aid.
UNDERGRADUATE FINANCIAL AID (Fall 2017, est.) 935 applied for aid; of those 87% were deemed to have need. 99% of undergraduates with need received aid; of those 99% had need fully met. *Average percent of need met:* 100% (excluding resources awarded to replace EFC). *Average financial aid package:* $48,467 (excluding resources awarded to replace EFC). 1% of all full-time undergraduates had no need and received non-need-based gift aid.
GIFT AID (NEED-BASED) *Total amount:* $37,907,180 (5% federal, 94% institutional, 1% external sources). *Receiving aid:* Freshmen: 47% (260); all full-time under-

graduates: 42% (797). *Average award:* Freshmen: $49,873; Undergraduates: $46,775. *Scholarships, grants, and awards:* Federal Pell, FSEOG, state, private, college/university gift aid from institutional funds, Colby National Merit Scholarships.

GIFT AID (NON-NEED-BASED) *Total amount:* $881,218 (31% institutional, 69% external sources). *Receiving aid:* Freshmen: 1. Undergraduates: 6. *Average award:* Freshmen: $500. Undergraduates: $433. *Scholarships, grants, and awards by category:* Academic interests/achievement: general academic interests/achievements. *Special characteristics:* general special characteristics. *Tuition waivers:* Full or partial for employees or children of employees. *ROTC:* Army cooperative.

LOANS *Student loans:* $3,114,951 (22% need-based, 78% non-need-based). 28% of past graduating class borrowed through all loan programs. *Average indebtedness per student:* $34,745. *Parent loans:* $2,069,585 (100% non-need-based). *Programs:* Federal Direct (Subsidized and Unsubsidized Stafford, PLUS), Perkins, state, alternative loans.

WORK-STUDY *Federal work-study:* Total amount: $630,211; jobs available. *State or other work-study/employment:* Total amount: $431,999 (100% need-based). Part-time jobs available.

APPLYING FOR FINANCIAL AID *Required financial aid forms:* FAFSA, CSS Financial Aid PROFILE, business/farm supplement, federal income tax form(s). *Financial aid deadline:* 2/1. *Notification date:* 4/1. Students must reply by 5/1.

CONTACT Cindy Wells, Director of Financial Aid, Colby College, 4850 Mayflower Hill, Waterville, ME 04901-8848, 207-859-4132 or toll-free 800-723-3032. *Fax:* 207-859-4828. *E-mail:* finaid@colby.edu.
Website: http://www.colby.edu/.

COLBY-SAWYER COLLEGE
New London, NH

CONTACT Ms. Beth Renzulli, Director of Financial Aid, Colby-Sawyer College, 541 Main Street, New London, NH 03257-7835, 603-526-3717 or toll-free 800-272-1015. *Fax:* 603-526-3737. *E-mail:* cscfinaid@colby-sawyer.edu.
Website: http://www.colby-sawyer.edu/.

COLEGIO UNIVERSITARIO DE SAN JUAN
San Juan, PR

CONTACT Ken Lira, Director of Financial Aid, Colegio Universitario de San Juan, 43-500 Monterey Avenue, Palm Desert, AB 92260, 760-776-7428. *Fax:* 760-776-7338. *E-mail:* klira@collegeofthedesert.edu.
Website: http://www.cunisanjuan.edu/.

COLEMAN UNIVERSITY
San Diego, CA

Tuition & fees: N/R	Average undergraduate aid package: N/A

ABOUT THE INSTITUTION Independent, coed. *Awards:* associate, bachelor's, and master's degrees. 6 undergraduate majors. *Total enrollment:* 488. Undergraduates: 477. Federal methodology is used as a basis for awarding need-based institutional aid.

GIFT AID (NEED-BASED) *Scholarships, grants, and awards:* Federal Pell, FSEOG, state.

GIFT AID (NON-NEED-BASED) *Scholarships, grants, and awards by category:* Academic interests/achievement: general academic interests/achievements. *Special characteristics:* children and siblings of alumni.

LOANS *Programs:* Federal Direct (Subsidized and Unsubsidized Stafford, PLUS).

WORK-STUDY Federal work-study jobs available.

APPLYING FOR FINANCIAL AID *Required financial aid forms:* FAFSA, institution's own form, state aid form. *Financial aid deadline:* Continuous. *Notification date:* Continuous.

CONTACT Financial Aid Office, Coleman University, 8888 Balboa Avenue, San Diego, CA 92123, 858-499-0202 or toll-free 800-430-2030. *Fax:* 858-499-0233. *E-mail:* faoffice@coleman.edu.
Website: http://www.coleman.edu/.

COLGATE UNIVERSITY
Hamilton, NY

Tuition & fees: $53,980	Average undergraduate aid package: $52,488

ABOUT THE INSTITUTION Independent, coed. *Awards:* bachelor's and master's degrees. 53 undergraduate majors. *Total enrollment:* 2,881. Undergraduates: 2,873. Freshmen: 771. Institutional methodology is used as a basis for awarding need-based institutional aid.

UNDERGRADUATE EXPENSES for 2017–2018 *Application fee:* $60. *One-time required fee:* $50. *Comprehensive fee:* $67,500 includes full-time tuition ($53,650), mandatory fees ($330), and room and board ($13,520). *College room only:* $6525. Room and board charges vary according to board plan and housing facility. *Payment plan:* Tuition prepayment.

FRESHMAN FINANCIAL AID (Fall 2017, est.) 294 applied for aid; of those 82% were deemed to have need. 100% of freshmen with need received aid; of those 100% had need fully met. *Average percent of need met:* 100% (excluding resources awarded to replace EFC). *Average financial aid package:* $53,246 (excluding resources awarded to replace EFC).

UNDERGRADUATE FINANCIAL AID (Fall 2017, est.) 1,142 applied for aid; of those 91% were deemed to have need. 100% of undergraduates with need received aid; of those 100% had need fully met. *Average percent of need met:* 100% (excluding resources awarded to replace EFC). *Average financial aid package:* $52,488 (excluding resources awarded to replace EFC).

GIFT AID (NEED-BASED) *Total amount:* $49,812,049 (3% federal, 1% state, 94% institutional, 2% external sources). *Receiving aid:* Freshmen: 31% (241); all full-time undergraduates: 36% (1,029). *Average award:* Freshmen: $49,397; Undergraduates: $48,369. *Scholarships, grants, and awards:* Federal Pell, FSEOG, state, college/university gift aid from institutional funds.

GIFT AID (NON-NEED-BASED) *Total amount:* $1,106,282 (10% state, 15% institutional, 75% external sources). *Scholarships, grants, and awards by category:* Special characteristics: 11 awards ($162,603 total): veterans, veterans' children. *Tuition waivers:* Full or partial for employees or children of employees. *ROTC:* Army cooperative.

LOANS *Student loans:* $4,448,469 (47% need-based, 53% non-need-based). 35% of past graduating class borrowed through all loan programs. *Average indebtedness per student:* $24,761. *Average need-based loan:* Freshmen: $1318. Undergraduates: $3475. *Parent loans:* $3,370,301 (100% non-need-based). *Programs:* Federal Direct (Subsidized and Unsubsidized Stafford, PLUS).

WORK-STUDY *Federal work-study:* Total amount: $1,449,747; 624 jobs averaging $2271. *State or other work-study/employment:* Total amount: $475,053 (97% need-based, 3% non-need-based). 228 part-time jobs averaging $2121.

ATHLETIC AWARDS Total amount: $12,836,041 (100% non-need-based).

APPLYING FOR FINANCIAL AID *Required financial aid forms:* FAFSA, CSS Financial Aid PROFILE, noncustodial (divorced/separated) parent's statement. *Financial aid deadline:* 1/15. *Notification date:* 3/20. Students must reply by 5/1.

CONTACT Office of Financial Aid, Colgate University, 13 Oak Drive, Hamilton, NY 13346, 315-228-7431. *Fax:* 315-228-7050. *E-mail:* finaid@colgate.edu.
Website: http://www.colgate.edu/.

THE COLLEGE AT BROCKPORT, STATE UNIVERSITY OF NEW YORK
Brockport, NY

Tuition & fees (NY res): $8154	Average undergraduate aid package: $10,755

ABOUT THE INSTITUTION State-supported, coed. *Awards:* certificates, bachelor's, and master's degrees. 46 undergraduate majors. *Total enrollment:* 8,313. Undergraduates: 7,180. Freshmen: 1,262. Federal methodology is used as a basis for awarding need-based institutional aid.

UNDERGRADUATE EXPENSES for 2018–2019 *Application fee:* $50. *Tuition, state resident:* full-time $6670; part-time $278 per credit hour. *Tuition, nonresident:* full-time $16,320; part-time $680 per credit hour. *Required fees:* full-time $1484; $61.16 per credit hour or $1484 per year. Part-time tuition and fees vary according to course load. *College room and board:* $12,904; *Room only:* $7974. Room and board charges vary according to board plan and housing facility.

FRESHMAN FINANCIAL AID (Fall 2016) 1,009 applied for aid; of those 80% were deemed to have need. 98% of freshmen with need received aid; of those 12% had need fully met. *Average percent of need met:* 66% (excluding resources awarded to replace EFC). *Average financial aid package:* $11,532 (excluding resources awarded to replace EFC). 7% of all full-time freshmen had no need and received non-need-based gift aid.

UNDERGRADUATE FINANCIAL AID (Fall 2016) 4,706 applied for aid; of those 83% were deemed to have need. 99% of undergraduates with need received aid; of those 14% had need fully met. *Average percent of need met:* 68% (excluding resources awarded to replace EFC). *Average financial aid package:* $10,755 (excluding resources awarded to replace EFC). 2% of all full-time undergraduates had no need and received non-need-based gift aid.

GIFT AID (NEED-BASED) *Total amount:* $23,760,293 (54% federal, 45% state, 1% external sources). *Receiving aid:* Freshmen: 57% (612); all full-time undergraduates: 57% (3,038). *Average award:* Freshmen: $7621; Undergraduates: $6852. *Scholarships, grants, and awards:* Federal Pell, FSEOG, state, private, college/university gift aid from institutional funds.

GIFT AID (NON-NEED-BASED) *Total amount:* $5,736,454 (9% federal, 8% state, 60% institutional, 23% external sources). *Receiving aid:* Freshmen: 25% (267). Undergraduates: 16% (835). *Average award:* Freshmen: $4610. Undergraduates: $4898. *Scholarships, grants, and awards by category: Academic interests/achievement:* 828 awards ($2,823,046 total): biological sciences, business, communication, computer science, education, English, foreign languages, general academic interests/achievements, home economics, humanities, international studies, mathematics, military science, physical sciences, premedicine, social sciences. *Creative arts/performance:* 19 awards ($16,100 total): art/fine arts, cinema/film/broadcasting, creative writing, dance, general creative arts/performance, journalism/publications, music, theater/drama. *Special achievements/activities:* 72 awards ($64,325 total): community service, general special achievements/activities, hobbies/interests, leadership, religious involvement. *Special characteristics:* 31 awards ($130,581 total): adult students, children and siblings of alumni, children of faculty/staff, ethnic background, first-generation college students, general special characteristics, international students, married students, members of minority groups, previous college experience, religious affiliation, veterans. *Tuition waivers:* Full or partial for employees or children of employees. *ROTC:* Army, Naval cooperative, Air Force cooperative.

LOANS *Student loans:* $42,735,369 (45% need-based, 55% non-need-based). 80% of past graduating class borrowed through all loan programs. *Average indebtedness per student:* $30,416. *Average need-based loan:* Freshmen: $4432. Undergraduates: $4852. *Parent loans:* $6,324,049 (100% non-need-based). *Programs:* Federal Direct (Subsidized and Unsubsidized Stafford, PLUS), Perkins, Federal Nursing, alternative loans.

WORK-STUDY *Federal work-study:* 338 jobs averaging $2475. *State or other work-study/employment:* Total amount: $1,792,101 (100% non-need-based). 986 part-time jobs averaging $1818.

APPLYING FOR FINANCIAL AID *Required financial aid forms:* FAFSA, state aid form. *Financial aid deadline (priority):* 1/1. *Notification date:* Continuous beginning 1/1. Students must reply by 2/1.

CONTACT Financial Aid Office, The College at Brockport, State University of New York, 350 New Campus Drive, Brockport, NY 14420-2937, 585-395-2501. *Fax:* 585-395-5445.
Website: http://www.brockport.edu/.

COLLEGE FOR CREATIVE STUDIES
Detroit, MI

CONTACT Office of Financial Aid, College for Creative Studies, 201 East Kirby, Detroit, MI 48202-4034, 313-664-7495 or toll-free 800-952-ARTS. *Fax:* 313-872-1521. *E-mail:* finaid@collegeforcreativestudies.edu. *Website:* http://www.collegeforcreativestudies.edu/.

COLLEGE OF BIBLICAL STUDIES–HOUSTON
Houston, TX

CONTACT Roshanna Hardison, Director of Student Financial Services, College of Biblical Studies–Houston, 7000 Regency Square Boulevard, Houston, TX 77036, 832-252-0728 or toll-free 844-227-9673. *E-mail:* roshanna.hardison@cbshouston.edu. *Website:* http://www.cbshouston.edu/.

COLLEGE OF CHARLESTON
Charleston, SC

Tuition & fees (SC res): $12,458	Average undergraduate aid package: $13,716

ABOUT THE INSTITUTION State-supported, coed. *Awards:* certificates, bachelor's, and master's degrees (also offers graduate degree programs through University of Charleston, South Carolina). 60 undergraduate majors. *Total enrollment:* 10,863. Undergraduates: 9,895. Freshmen: 1,840. Federal methodology is used as a basis for awarding need-based institutional aid.

UNDERGRADUATE EXPENSES for 2017–2018 *Application fee:* $50. *Tuition, state resident:* full-time $11,998; part-time $500 per credit hour. *Tuition, nonresident:* full-time $30,386; part-time $1266 per credit hour. *Required fees:* full-time $460; $16.25 per term or $16.25 per term. Full-time tuition and fees vary according to student level. Part-time tuition and fees vary according to course load and student level. *College room and board:* $12,048; *Room only:* $7828. Room and board charges vary according to board plan and housing facility.

FRESHMAN FINANCIAL AID (Fall 2017, est.) 1,465 applied for aid; of those 70% were deemed to have need. 95% of freshmen with need received aid; of those 18% had need fully met. *Average percent of need met:* 53% (excluding resources awarded to replace EFC). *Average financial aid package:* $13,986 (excluding resources awarded to replace EFC). 26% of all full-time freshmen had no need and received non-need-based gift aid.

UNDERGRADUATE FINANCIAL AID (Fall 2017, est.) 5,879 applied for aid; of those 78% were deemed to have need. 96% of undergraduates with need received aid; of those 16% had need fully met. *Average percent of need met:* 53% (excluding resources awarded to replace EFC). *Average financial aid package:* $13,716 (excluding resources awarded to replace EFC). 20% of all full-time undergraduates had no need and received non-need-based gift aid.

GIFT AID (NEED-BASED) *Total amount:* $29,331,714 (39% federal, 33% state, 24% institutional, 4% external sources). *Receiving aid:* Freshmen: 43% (782); all full-time undergraduates: 36% (3,252). *Average award:* Freshmen: $3404; Undergraduates: $3184. *Scholarships, grants, and awards:* Federal Pell, FSEOG, state, private, college/university gift aid from institutional funds.

GIFT AID (NON-NEED-BASED) *Total amount:* $19,358,913 (53% state, 40% institutional, 7% external sources). *Receiving aid:* Freshmen: 40% (744). Undergraduates: 24% (2,123). *Average award:* Freshmen: $11,237. Undergraduates: $11,798. *Scholarships, grants, and awards by category: Academic interests/achievement:* biological sciences, business, communication, computer science, education, engineering/technologies, English, foreign languages, general academic interests/achievements, health fields, humanities, mathematics, physical sciences, premedicine, social sciences. *Creative arts/performance:* art/fine arts, music, performing arts, theater/drama. *Special characteristics:* general special characteristics. *Tuition waivers:* Full or partial for employees or children of employees, senior citizens. *ROTC:* Air Force cooperative.

LOANS Student loans: $39,321,601 (65% need-based, 35% non-need-based). 51% of past graduating class borrowed through all loan programs. *Average indebtedness per student:* $27,256. *Average need-based loan:* Freshmen: $2911. Undergraduates: $3561. *Parent loans:* $26,946,793 (61% need-based, 39% non-need-based). *Programs:* Federal Direct (Subsidized and Unsubsidized Stafford, PLUS), Perkins.

WORK-STUDY *Federal work-study:* Total amount: $426,902; jobs available. *State or other work-study/employment:* Part-time jobs available.

ATHLETIC AWARDS Total amount: $4,620,313 (25% need-based, 75% non-need-based).

APPLYING FOR FINANCIAL AID *Required financial aid form:* FAFSA. *Financial aid deadline (priority):* 3/1. *Notification date:* Continuous beginning 4/1. Students must reply within 8 weeks of notification.

CONTACT Derwin Simpson, Student Services Manager, College of Charleston, 66 George Street, Charleston, SC 29424, 843-953-5540. *Fax:* 843-953-7192. *E-mail:* financialaid@cofc.edu. *Website:* http://www.cofc.edu/.

COLLEGE OF COASTAL GEORGIA
Brunswick, GA

Tuition & fees (GA res): $3971	Average undergraduate aid package: $6705

ABOUT THE INSTITUTION State-supported, coed. *Awards:* associate and bachelor's degrees. 23 undergraduate majors. *Total enrollment:* 3,663. Undergraduates: 3,363. Freshmen: 809. Federal methodology is used as a basis for awarding need-based institutional aid.

UNDERGRADUATE EXPENSES for 2018–2019 *Application fee:* $25. *One-time required fee:* $25. *Tuition, state resident:* full-time $2451; part-time $104.20 per credit hour. *Tuition, nonresident:* full-time $9058; part-time $384.94 per credit hour. *Required fees:* full-time $1520; $455 per term. Full-time tuition and fees vary according to course load. Part-time tuition and fees vary according to course load. *College room and board:* $9520; *Room only:* $6300. Room and board charges vary according to board plan, housing facility, and location.

FRESHMAN FINANCIAL AID (Fall 2016) 682 applied for aid; of those 70% were deemed to have need. 100% of freshmen with need received aid; of those 27% had need fully met. *Average percent of need met:* 28% (excluding resources awarded to replace EFC). *Average financial aid package:* $6897 (excluding resources awarded to replace EFC).

UNDERGRADUATE FINANCIAL AID (Fall 2016) 2,359 applied for aid; of those 82% were deemed to have need. 100% of undergraduates with need received aid; of those 45% had need fully met. *Average percent of need met:* 37% (excluding resources awarded to replace EFC). *Average financial aid package:* $6705 (excluding resources awarded to replace EFC).

GIFT AID (NEED-BASED) *Total amount:* $8,614,885 (93% federal, 7% institutional). *Receiving aid:* Freshmen: 65% (477); all full-time undergraduates: 73% (1,941). *Average award:* Freshmen: $3068; Undergraduates: $3457. *Scholarships, grants, and awards:* Federal Pell, FSEOG, state, private, college/university gift aid from institutional funds.

GIFT AID (NON-NEED-BASED) *Total amount:* $2,973,715 (92% state, 8% external sources). *Receiving aid:* Freshmen: 47% (347). Undergraduates: 33% (871). *Scholarships, grants, and awards by category:* Academic interests/achievement: 46 awards ($74,110 total): biological sciences, business, education, home economics, mathematics, premedicine, social sciences. *Creative arts/performance:* 2 awards ($2600 total): art/fine arts. *Special achievements/activities:* 4 awards ($3800 total): community service, leadership. *Special characteristics:* 28 awards ($69,686 total): first-generation college students, international students, local/state students. *Tuition waivers:* Full or partial for employees or children of employees, senior citizens.

LOANS *Student loans:* $8,334,050 (50% need-based, 50% non-need-based). 64% of past graduating class borrowed through all loan programs. *Average indebtedness per student:* $25,455. *Average need-based loan:* Freshmen: $3500. Undergraduates: $3500. *Parent loans:* $944,085 (100% non-need-based). *Programs:* Federal Direct (Subsidized and Unsubsidized Stafford, PLUS), state.

WORK-STUDY *Federal work-study:* 27 jobs averaging $3203. *State or other work-study/employment:* Total amount: $110,016 (100% need-based). Part-time jobs available.

ATHLETIC AWARDS Total amount: $332,296 (100% non-need-based).

APPLYING FOR FINANCIAL AID *Required financial aid forms:* FAFSA, state aid form. *Financial aid deadline:* 6/1 (priority: 5/1). *Notification date:* Continuous beginning 9/15.

CONTACT Ms. Terral L. Harris, Financial Aid Office, College of Coastal Georgia, One College Drive, Brunswick, GA 31520, 912-279-5722 or toll-free 800-675-7235. *Fax:* 912-264-7320. *E-mail:* finaid@ccga.edu. *Website:* http://www.ccga.edu/.

THE COLLEGE OF IDAHO
Caldwell, ID

Tuition & fees: $30,155	Average undergraduate aid package: $27,221

ABOUT THE INSTITUTION Independent, coed. *Awards:* bachelor's and master's degrees. 36 undergraduate majors. *Total enrollment:* 961. Undergraduates: 943. Freshmen: 268. Federal methodology is used as a basis for awarding need-based institutional aid.

UNDERGRADUATE EXPENSES for 2018–2019 *Comprehensive fee:* $39,852 includes full-time tuition ($29,400), mandatory fees ($755), and room and board ($9697). Room and board charges vary according to board plan and housing facility. *Part-time tuition:* $1225 per credit.

FRESHMAN FINANCIAL AID (Fall 2017, est.) 259 applied for aid; of those 86% were deemed to have need. 100% of freshmen with need received aid; of those 28% had need fully met. *Average percent of need met:* 58% (excluding resources awarded to replace EFC). *Average financial aid package:* $25,141 (excluding resources awarded to replace EFC). 28% of all full-time freshmen had no need and received non-need-based gift aid.

UNDERGRADUATE FINANCIAL AID (Fall 2017, est.) 755 applied for aid; of those 78% were deemed to have need. 100% of undergraduates with need received aid; of those 25% had need fully met. *Average percent of need met:* 50% (excluding resources awarded to replace EFC). *Average financial aid package:* $27,221 (excluding resources awarded to replace EFC). 33% of all full-time undergraduates had no need and received non-need-based gift aid.

GIFT AID (NEED-BASED) *Total amount:* $3,924,352 (34% federal, 4% state, 29% institutional, 33% external sources). *Receiving aid:* Freshmen: 34% (106); all full-time undergraduates: 33% (295). *Average award:* Freshmen: $4157; Undergraduates: $4208. *Scholarships, grants, and awards:* Federal Pell, FSEOG, state, private, college/university gift aid from institutional funds.

GIFT AID (NON-NEED-BASED) *Total amount:* $11,535,866 (95% institutional, 5% external sources). *Receiving aid:* Freshmen: 71% (223). Undergraduates: 65% (586). *Average award:* Freshmen: $22,473. Undergraduates: $19,426. *Scholarships, grants, and awards by category:* Academic interests/achievement: biological sciences, business, education, English, foreign languages, general academic interests/achievements, humanities, mathematics, physical sciences, premedicine, religion/biblical studies, social sciences. *Creative arts/performance:* art/fine arts, debating, music, performing arts, theater/drama. *Special achievements/activities:* leadership. *Special characteristics:* children and siblings of alumni, children of educators, children of faculty/staff, first-generation college students, international students, local/state students, married students, members of minority groups, out-of-state students, siblings of current students, veterans' children. *Tuition waivers:* Full or partial for employees or children of employees. *ROTC:* Army cooperative.

LOANS *Student loans:* $4,339,294 (42% need-based, 58% non-need-based). 60% of past graduating class borrowed through all loan programs. *Average indebtedness per student:* $7202. *Average need-based loan:* Freshmen: $3588. Undergraduates: $4397. *Parent loans:* $1,266,148 (100% need-based). *Programs:* Federal Direct (Subsidized and Unsubsidized Stafford, PLUS), Perkins, private loans.

WORK-STUDY *Federal work-study:* Total amount: $100,850; jobs available. *State or other work-study/employment:* Total amount: $39,700 (100% need-based). Part-time jobs available.

ATHLETIC AWARDS Total amount: $2,559,079 (100% non-need-based).

APPLYING FOR FINANCIAL AID *Required financial aid form:* FAFSA. *Financial aid deadline (priority):* 2/1. *Notification date:* Continuous beginning 1/25.

CONTACT Jennifer Worden, Director of Financial Aid Services, The College of Idaho, 2112 Cleveland Boulevard, Caldwell, ID 83605, 208-459-5307 or toll-free 800-244-3246. *Fax:* 208-459-5844. *E-mail:* jworden@collegeofidaho.edu. *Website:* http://www.collegeofidaho.edu/.

COLLEGE OF MOUNT SAINT VINCENT
Riverdale, NY

CONTACT Mr. Emmett Cooper, Director of Financial Aid, College of Mount Saint Vincent, 6301 Riverdale Avenue, Riverdale, NY 10471, 718-405-3309 or toll-free 800-665-CMSV. *Fax:* 718-405-3490. *E-mail:* emmett.cooper@mountsaintvincent.edu. *Website:* http://www.mountsaintvincent.edu/.

THE COLLEGE OF NEW JERSEY
Ewing, NJ

Tuition & fees (NJ res): $16,149	Average undergraduate aid package: $11,455

ABOUT THE INSTITUTION State-supported, coed. *Awards:* certificates, bachelor's, and master's degrees. 53 undergraduate majors. *Total enrollment:* 7,552. Undergraduates: 6,955. Freshmen: 1,542. Federal methodology is used as a basis for awarding need-based institutional aid.

UNDERGRADUATE EXPENSES for 2017–2018 *Application fee:* $75. *Tuition, state resident:* full-time $12,632; part-time $448.02 per credit hour. *Tuition, nonresident:* full-time $24,061; part-time $771.50 per credit hour. *Required fees:* full-time $3517; $134.02 per credit hour. Full-time tuition and fees vary according to course load. Part-time tuition and fees vary according to course load. *College room and board:* $13,200; *Room only:* $8696. Room and board charges vary according to board plan.

FRESHMAN FINANCIAL AID (Fall 2017, est.) 1,372 applied for aid; of those 65% were deemed to have need. 92% of freshmen with need received aid; of those 12% had need fully met. *Average percent of need met:* 40% (excluding resources awarded to replace EFC). *Average financial aid package:* $11,899 (excluding resources awarded to replace EFC). 14% of all full-time freshmen had no need and received non-need-based gift aid.

UNDERGRADUATE FINANCIAL AID (Fall 2017, est.) 4,810 applied for aid; of those 73% were deemed to have need. 95% of undergraduates with need received aid; of those 10% had need fully met. *Average percent of need met:* 43% (excluding resources awarded to replace EFC). *Average financial aid package:* $11,455 (excluding resources awarded to replace EFC). 8% of all full-time undergraduates had no need and received non-need-based gift aid.

GIFT AID (NEED-BASED) *Total amount:* $24,240,828 (25% federal, 31% state, 35% institutional, 9% external sources). *Receiving aid:* Freshmen: 27% (412); all full-time undergraduates: 23% (1,502). *Average award:* Freshmen: $11,889; Undergraduates: $11,601. *Scholarships, grants, and awards:* Federal Pell, FSEOG, state, private, college/university gift aid from institutional funds, Federal Nursing.

GIFT AID (NON-NEED-BASED) *Total amount:* $5,140,174 (83% institutional, 17% external sources). *Receiving aid:* Freshmen: 24% (370). Undergraduates: 14% (946). *Average award:* Freshmen: $5648. Undergraduates: $5116. *Scholarships, grants, and awards by category:* Academic interests/achievement: general academic interests/achievements. Creative arts/performance: art/fine arts, music. Special characteristics: children with a deceased or disabled parent, members of minority groups. *Tuition waivers:* Full or partial for employees or children of employees, senior citizens. *ROTC:* Army cooperative, Air Force cooperative.

LOANS *Student loans:* $37,866,367 (78% need-based, 22% non-need-based). 62% of past graduating class borrowed through all loan programs. *Average indebtedness per student:* $37,787. *Average need-based loan:* Freshmen: $3531. Undergraduates: $4556. *Parent loans:* $14,504,782 (43% need-based, 57% non-need-based). *Programs:* Federal Direct (Subsidized and Unsubsidized Stafford, PLUS), Perkins, Federal Nursing, private loans.

WORK-STUDY *Federal work-study:* Total amount: $182,309; jobs available.

APPLYING FOR FINANCIAL AID *Required financial aid form:* FAFSA. *Financial aid deadline:* 10/1 (priority: 3/1). *Notification date:* Continuous beginning 6/1. Students must reply within 2 weeks of notification.

CONTACT Mr. Wilbert Casaine, Executive Director of Financial Aid and Student Success, The College of New Jersey, PO Box 7718, Ewing, NJ 08628, 609-771-2602. *Fax:* 609-637-5154. *E-mail:* casainew@tcnj.edu. *Website:* http://www.tcnj.edu/.

THE COLLEGE OF NEW ROCHELLE
New Rochelle, NY

Tuition & fees: $37,760	Average undergraduate aid package: N/A

ABOUT THE INSTITUTION Independent, coed. *Awards:* certificates, bachelor's, and master's degrees (also offers a non-traditional adult program with significant enrollment not reflected in profile). 30 undergraduate majors. *Total enrollment:* 2,023. Undergraduates: 1,328. Freshmen: 186. Federal methodology is used as a basis for awarding need-based institutional aid.

UNDERGRADUATE EXPENSES for 2018–2019 *Application fee:* $35. *Comprehensive fee:* $52,322 includes full-time tuition ($36,180), mandatory fees ($1580), and room and board ($14,562). Full-time tuition and fees vary according to course load, degree level, and program. Room and board charges vary according to housing facility. *Part-time tuition:* $1206 per credit. Part-time tuition and fees vary according to course load, degree level, and program.

GIFT AID (NEED-BASED) *Scholarships, grants, and awards:* Federal Pell, FSEOG, state, private, college/university gift aid from institutional funds.

GIFT AID (NON-NEED-BASED) *Scholarships, grants, and awards by category:* Academic interests/achievement: area/ethnic studies, biological sciences, business, communication, education, English, general academic interests/achievements, health fields, humanities, mathematics, physical sciences, premedicine, religion/biblical studies, social sciences. *Creative arts/performance:* art/fine arts, creative writing, journalism/publications, music. *Special achievements/activities:* community service, general special achievements/activities, hobbies/interests, leadership, memberships, religious involvement. *Special characteristics:* children and siblings of alumni, children of faculty/staff, children of union members/company employees, children of workers in trades, general special characteristics, out-of-state students, parents of current students, previous college experience, siblings of current students, spouses of current students, spouses of deceased or disabled public servants, twins, veterans, veterans' children. *Tuition waivers:* Full or partial for employees or children of employees.

LOANS *Programs:* Federal Direct (Subsidized and Unsubsidized Stafford, PLUS), Perkins, Federal Nursing.

WORK-STUDY *Federal work-study:* jobs available. *State or other work-study/employment:* Part-time jobs available.

APPLYING FOR FINANCIAL AID *Required financial aid forms:* FAFSA, institution's own form. *Financial aid deadline:* Continuous. *Notification date:* Continuous beginning 1/1. Students must reply within 2 weeks of notification.

CONTACT Vincent Tunstall, Director of Financial Aid, The College of New Rochelle, 29 Castle Place, New Rochelle, NY 10805-2339, 914-654-5466 or toll-free 800-933-5923. *Fax:* 914-654-5420. *E-mail:* vtunstall@cnr.edu. *Website:* http://www.cnr.edu/.

COLLEGE OF SAINT BENEDICT
Saint Joseph, MN

Tuition & fees: $43,738	Average undergraduate aid package: $36,390

ABOUT THE INSTITUTION Independent Roman Catholic, women only. *Awards:* bachelor's degrees (coordinate with Saint John's University for men). 46 undergraduate majors. *Total enrollment:* 1,937. Undergraduates: 1,937. Freshmen: 519. Federal methodology is used as a basis for awarding need-based institutional aid.

UNDERGRADUATE EXPENSES for 2017–2018 *Comprehensive fee:* $54,480 includes full-time tuition ($42,690), mandatory fees ($1048), and room and board ($10,742). *College room only:* $5250. Room and board charges vary according to board plan and housing facility. *Part-time tuition:* $1779 per credit hour. Part-time tuition and fees vary according to course load.

FRESHMAN FINANCIAL AID (Fall 2017, est.) 462 applied for aid; of those 87% were deemed to have need. 100% of freshmen with need received aid; of those 38% had need fully met. *Average percent of need met:* 92% (excluding resources awarded to replace EFC). *Average financial aid package:* $35,942 (excluding resources awarded to replace EFC). 19% of all full-time freshmen had no need and received non-need-based gift aid.

UNDERGRADUATE FINANCIAL AID (Fall 2017, est.) 1,608 applied for aid; of those 89% were deemed to have need. 100% of undergraduates with need received aid; of those 31% had need fully met. *Average percent of need met:* 89% (excluding resources awarded to replace EFC). *Average financial aid package:*

$36,390 (excluding resources awarded to replace EFC). 25% of all full-time undergraduates had no need and received non-need-based gift aid.

GIFT AID (NEED-BASED) *Total amount:* $42,347,911 (6% federal, 8% state, 83% institutional, 3% external sources). *Receiving aid:* Freshmen: 76% (395); all full-time undergraduates: 73% (1,383). *Average award:* Freshmen: $31,442; Undergraduates: $30,353. *Scholarships, grants, and awards:* Federal Pell, FSEOG, state, private, college/university gift aid from institutional funds.

GIFT AID (NON-NEED-BASED) *Total amount:* $10,206,698 (1% federal, 93% institutional, 6% external sources). *Receiving aid:* Freshmen: 77% (398). Undergraduates: 70% (1,334). *Average award:* Freshmen: $20,900. Undergraduates: $19,980. *Scholarships, grants, and awards by category: Academic interests/achievement:* 1,759 awards ($29,497,827 total): computer science, engineering/technologies, general academic interests/achievements, mathematics, military science, physical sciences. *Creative arts/performance:* 227 awards ($615,500 total): art/fine arts, music, theater/drama. *Special characteristics:* 697 awards ($2,735,070 total): children and siblings of alumni, international students, out-of-state students. *Tuition waivers:* Full or partial for employees or children of employees. *ROTC:* Army cooperative.

LOANS *Student loans:* $16,218,677 (91% need-based, 9% non-need-based). 74% of past graduating class borrowed through all loan programs. *Average indebtedness per student:* $42,833. *Average need-based loan:* Freshmen: $4384. Undergraduates: $5083. *Parent loans:* $1,104,700 (89% need-based, 11% non-need-based). *Programs:* Federal Direct (Subsidized and Unsubsidized Stafford, PLUS), Perkins, state, private loans.

WORK-STUDY *Federal work-study:* Total amount: $1,053,683; 423 jobs averaging $2581. *State or other work-study/employment:* Total amount: $3,088,224 (77% need-based, 23% non-need-based). 1,005 part-time jobs averaging $2964.

APPLYING FOR FINANCIAL AID *Required financial aid form:* FAFSA. *Financial aid deadline (priority):* 3/15. *Notification date:* Continuous beginning 12/15. Students must reply by 5/1.

CONTACT Mr. Stuart Perry, Executive Director of Financial Aid, College of Saint Benedict, 37 South College Avenue, Saint Joseph, MN 56374-2099, 320-363-5388 or toll-free 800-544-1489. *Fax:* 320-363-6090. *E-mail:* sperry@csbsju.edu. *Website:* http://www.csbsju.edu/.

COLLEGE OF SAINT ELIZABETH
Morristown, NJ

ABOUT THE INSTITUTION Independent Roman Catholic, coed. *Awards:* certificates, bachelor's, master's, and doctoral degrees (also offers coed adult undergraduate degree program and coed graduate programs). 26 undergraduate majors. *Total enrollment:* 1,149. Undergraduates: 765. Freshmen: 164.

GIFT AID (NEED-BASED) *Scholarships, grants, and awards:* Federal Pell, FSEOG, state, private, college/university gift aid from institutional funds.

GIFT AID (NON-NEED-BASED) *Scholarships, grants, and awards by category: Academic interests/achievement:* general academic interests/achievements. *Special characteristics:* adult students, children and siblings of alumni.

LOANS *Programs:* Federal Direct (Subsidized and Unsubsidized Stafford), Perkins.

APPLYING FOR FINANCIAL AID *Required financial aid form:* FAFSA.

CONTACT James Kulhawy, Assistant Director of Financial Aid, College of Saint Elizabeth, 2 Convent Road, Morristown, NJ 07960-6989, 973-290-4432 or toll-free 800-210-7900. *E-mail:* jkulhaway@cse.edu. *Website:* http://www.cse.edu/.

COLLEGE OF ST. JOSEPH
Rutland, VT

CONTACT Julie Rosmus, Director of Financial Aid, College of St. Joseph, 71 Clement Road, Rutland, VT 05701-3899, 802-773-5900 Ext. 3274 or toll-free 877-270-9998. *Fax:* 802-776-5275. *E-mail:* jrosmus@csj.edu. *Website:* http://www.csj.edu/.

COLLEGE OF SAINT MARY
Omaha, NE

Tuition & fees: $20,350	Average undergraduate aid package: $14,824

ABOUT THE INSTITUTION Independent Roman Catholic, women only. *Awards:* certificates, associate, bachelor's, master's, and doctoral degrees. 30 undergraduate majors. *Total enrollment:* 1,140. Undergraduates: 832. Freshmen: 102. Federal methodology is used as a basis for awarding need-based institutional aid.

UNDERGRADUATE EXPENSES for 2018–2019 *Application fee:* $30. *Comprehensive fee:* $28,050 includes full-time tuition ($20,350) and room and board ($7700). Full-time tuition and fees vary according to program. *Part-time tuition:* $750 per credit. Part-time tuition and fees vary according to course load and program.

FRESHMAN FINANCIAL AID (Fall 2017, est.) 84 applied for aid; of those 79% were deemed to have need. 100% of freshmen with need received aid; of those 38% had need fully met. *Average percent of need met:* 81% (excluding resources awarded to replace EFC). *Average financial aid package:* $16,535 (excluding resources awarded to replace EFC). 33% of all full-time freshmen had no need and received non-need-based gift aid.

UNDERGRADUATE FINANCIAL AID (Fall 2017, est.) 670 applied for aid; of those 88% were deemed to have need. 100% of undergraduates with need received aid; of those 14% had need fully met. *Average percent of need met:* 59% (excluding resources awarded to replace EFC). *Average financial aid package:* $14,824 (excluding resources awarded to replace EFC). 17% of all full-time undergraduates had no need and received non-need-based gift aid.

GIFT AID (NEED-BASED) *Total amount:* $5,038,119 (32% federal, 5% state, 59% institutional, 4% external sources). *Receiving aid:* Freshmen: 67% (66); all full-time undergraduates: 76% (560). *Average award:* Freshmen: $13,519; Undergraduates: $9748. *Scholarships, grants, and awards:* Federal Pell, FSEOG, state, private, college/university gift aid from institutional funds, Federal Nursing.

GIFT AID (NON-NEED-BASED) *Total amount:* $1,450,522 (96% institutional, 4% external sources). *Receiving aid:* Freshmen: 18% (18). Undergraduates: 6% (44). *Average award:* Freshmen: $12,206. Undergraduates: $10,316. *Scholarships, grants, and awards by category: Academic interests/achievement:* 657 awards ($2,483,829 total): biological sciences, education, general academic interests/achievements, mathematics. *Creative arts/performance:* debating. *Special achievements/activities:* 2 awards ($2500 total): general special achievements/activities, leadership. *Special characteristics:* 16 awards ($51,895 total): children of faculty/staff, general special characteristics, international students. *Tuition waivers:* Full or partial for employees or children of employees, senior citizens. *ROTC:* Army cooperative, Air Force cooperative.

LOANS *Student loans:* $5,347,288 (82% need-based, 18% non-need-based). 74% of past graduating class borrowed through all loan programs. *Average indebtedness per student:* $35,259. *Average need-based loan:* Freshmen: $2990. Undergraduates: $5123. *Parent loans:* $1,327,391 (39% need-based, 61% non-need-based). *Programs:* Federal Direct (Subsidized and Unsubsidized Stafford, PLUS), Federal Nursing.

WORK-STUDY *Federal work-study:* Total amount: $417,417; 159 jobs averaging $2851. *State or other work-study/employment:* Total amount: $92,050 (42% need-based, 58% non-need-based). 14 part-time jobs averaging $6575.

ATHLETIC AWARDS Total amount: $732,475 (58% need-based, 42% non-need-based).

APPLYING FOR FINANCIAL AID *Required financial aid form:* FAFSA. *Financial aid deadline (priority):* 3/15. *Notification date:* Continuous beginning 12/15. Students must reply within 2 weeks of notification.

CONTACT Beth Sisk, Director of Financial Aid and the Express Center, College of Saint Mary, 7000 Mercy Road, Omaha, NE 68106, 402-399-2362 or toll-free 800-926-5534. *Fax:* 402-399-2480. *E-mail:* finaid@csm.edu. *Website:* http://www.csm.edu/.

THE COLLEGE OF SAINT ROSE
Albany, NY

Tuition & fees: $32,574	Average undergraduate aid package: $21,805

ABOUT THE INSTITUTION Independent, coed. **Awards:** certificates, bachelor's, and master's degrees. 41 undergraduate majors. **Total enrollment:** 3,950. Undergraduates: 2,523. Freshmen: 577. Federal methodology is used as a basis for awarding need-based institutional aid.

UNDERGRADUATE EXPENSES for 2018–2019 **One-time required fee:** $455. **Comprehensive fee:** $45,288 includes full-time tuition ($31,432), mandatory fees ($1142), and room and board ($12,714). **College room only:** $6394. Full-time tuition and fees vary according to course load. Room and board charges vary according to board plan and housing facility. **Part-time tuition:** $1045 per credit hour. **Part-time fees:** $33 per credit hour; $139 per term. Part-time tuition and fees vary according to course load.

FRESHMAN FINANCIAL AID (Fall 2016) 612 applied for aid; of those 93% were deemed to have need. 100% of freshmen with need received aid; of those 16% had need fully met. **Average percent of need met:** 81% (excluding resources awarded to replace EFC). **Average financial aid package:** $24,052 (excluding resources awarded to replace EFC). 9% of all full-time freshmen had no need and received non-need-based gift aid.

UNDERGRADUATE FINANCIAL AID (Fall 2016) 2,286 applied for aid; of those 93% were deemed to have need. 100% of undergraduates with need received aid; of those 15% had need fully met. **Average percent of need met:** 77% (excluding resources awarded to replace EFC). **Average financial aid package:** $21,805 (excluding resources awarded to replace EFC). 10% of all full-time undergraduates had no need and received non-need-based gift aid.

GIFT AID (NEED-BASED) Total amount: $14,450,255 (35% federal, 22% state, 40% institutional, 3% external sources). **Receiving aid:** Freshmen: 66% (422); all full-time undergraduates: 66% (1,662). **Average award:** Freshmen: $6735; Undergraduates: $7828. **Scholarships, grants, and awards:** Federal Pell, FSEOG, state, private, college/university gift aid from institutional funds.

GIFT AID (NON-NEED-BASED) Total amount: $29,937,022 (99% institutional, 1% external sources). **Receiving aid:** Freshmen: 88% (565). Undergraduates: 71% (1,774). **Average award:** Freshmen: $17,724. Undergraduates: $13,269. **Scholarships, grants, and awards by category:** Academic interests/achievement: general academic interests/achievements. Creative arts/performance: art/fine arts, music. Special achievements/activities: community service. Special characteristics: children and siblings of alumni, children of faculty/staff, children of union members/company employees, ethnic background, general special characteristics, members of minority groups, out-of-state students, siblings of current students, twins. **Tuition waivers:** Full or partial for employees or children of employees. **ROTC:** Army cooperative, Air Force cooperative.

LOANS Student loans: $13,107,157 (56% need-based, 44% non-need-based). 83% of past graduating class borrowed through all loan programs. Average indebtedness per student: $37,506. **Average need-based loan:** Freshmen: $3616. Undergraduates: $4423. **Parent loans:** $7,448,023 (79% need-based, 21% non-need-based). **Programs:** Federal Direct (Subsidized and Unsubsidized Stafford, PLUS), Perkins.

WORK-STUDY Federal work-study: jobs available. **State or other work-study/employment:** Total amount: $18,141 (100% non-need-based). Part-time jobs available.

ATHLETIC AWARDS Total amount: $2,275,863 (27% need-based, 73% non-need-based).

APPLYING FOR FINANCIAL AID Required financial aid forms: FAFSA, state aid form. **Financial aid deadline:** 5/1 (priority: 2/1). **Notification date:** 2/1. Students must reply by 5/1 or within 2 weeks of notification.

CONTACT Steven Dwire, Assistant Vice President of Financial Aid and Enrollment Management, The College of Saint Rose, 432 Western Avenue, Albertus Hall, Room 206, Albany, NY 12203-1419, 518-458-4915 or toll-free 800-637-8556. Fax: 518-454-2802. E-mail: finaid@strose.edu.
Website: http://www.strose.edu/.

THE COLLEGE OF ST. SCHOLASTICA
Duluth, MN

Tuition & fees: $37,212	Average undergraduate aid package: $26,120

ABOUT THE INSTITUTION Independent Roman Catholic Church, coed. **Awards:** certificates, bachelor's, master's, and doctoral degrees. 37 undergraduate majors. **Total enrollment:** 4,325. Undergraduates: 2,719. Freshmen: 482. Federal methodology is used as a basis for awarding need-based institutional aid.

UNDERGRADUATE EXPENSES for 2018–2019 **Comprehensive fee:** $46,922 includes full-time tuition ($36,614), mandatory fees ($598), and room and board ($9710). **College room only:** $5334. Full-time tuition and fees vary according to class time, degree level, and program. Room and board charges vary according to board plan and housing facility. **Part-time tuition:** $1148 per credit hour. Part-time tuition and fees vary according to class time, course load, degree level, and program.

FRESHMAN FINANCIAL AID (Fall 2017, est.) 457 applied for aid; of those 91% were deemed to have need. 100% of freshmen with need received aid; of those 27% had need fully met. **Average percent of need met:** 83% (excluding resources awarded to replace EFC). **Average financial aid package:** $31,038 (excluding resources awarded to replace EFC). 9% of all full-time freshmen had no need and received non-need-based gift aid.

UNDERGRADUATE FINANCIAL AID (Fall 2017, est.) 1,900 applied for aid; of those 92% were deemed to have need. 99% of undergraduates with need received aid; of those 21% had need fully met. **Average percent of need met:** 73% (excluding resources awarded to replace EFC). **Average financial aid package:** $26,120 (excluding resources awarded to replace EFC). 6% of all full-time undergraduates had no need and received non-need-based gift aid.

GIFT AID (NEED-BASED) Total amount: $10,520,980 (34% federal, 42% state, 24% institutional). **Receiving aid:** Freshmen: 68% (326); all full-time undergraduates: 60% (1,309). **Average award:** Freshmen: $7503; Undergraduates: $7595. **Scholarships, grants, and awards:** Federal Pell, FSEOG, state, private, college/university gift aid from institutional funds.

GIFT AID (NON-NEED-BASED) Total amount: $33,467,122 (1% federal, 96% institutional, 3% external sources). **Receiving aid:** Freshmen: 86% (416). Undergraduates: 68% (1,467). **Average award:** Freshmen: $19,621. Undergraduates: $18,068. **Scholarships, grants, and awards by category:** Academic interests/achievement: general academic interests/achievements. Creative arts/performance: music. Special characteristics: children and siblings of alumni, children of faculty/staff, handicapped students, international students, local/state students, previous college experience, religious affiliation, siblings of current students, spouses of current students. **Tuition waivers:** Full or partial for employees or children of employees, senior citizens. **ROTC:** Air Force cooperative.

LOANS Student loans: $20,503,154 (33% need-based, 67% non-need-based). 77% of past graduating class borrowed through all loan programs. Average indebtedness per student: $41,133. **Average need-based loan:** Freshmen: $3931. Undergraduates: $4783. **Parent loans:** $1,646,277 (100% non-need-based). **Programs:** Federal Direct (Subsidized and Unsubsidized Stafford, PLUS), Perkins, Federal Nursing, state.

WORK-STUDY Federal work-study: Total amount: $512,433; jobs available. **State or other work-study/employment:** Total amount: $1,505,666 (100% non-need-based). Part-time jobs available.

APPLYING FOR FINANCIAL AID Required financial aid form: FAFSA. **Financial aid deadline (priority):** 3/1. **Notification date:** Continuous beginning 3/1. Students must reply within 2 weeks of notification.

CONTACT Tricia Johnson, Director of Financial Aid, The College of St. Scholastica, 1200 Kenwood Avenue, Duluth, MN 55811-4199, 218-723-7027 or toll-free 800-249-6412. Fax: 218-733-2229. E-mail: tjohnson@css.edu.
Website: http://www.css.edu/.

COLLEGE OF STATEN ISLAND OF THE CITY UNIVERSITY OF NEW YORK
Staten Island, NY

Tuition & fees (NY res): $7089	Average undergraduate aid package: $8225

ABOUT THE INSTITUTION State and locally supported, coed. *Awards:* certificates, associate, bachelor's, master's, and doctoral degrees. 45 undergraduate majors. *Total enrollment:* 13,594. Undergraduates: 12,509. Freshmen: 2,729. Federal methodology is used as a basis for awarding need-based institutional aid.

UNDERGRADUATE EXPENSES for 2017–2018 *Tuition, state resident:* full-time $6530; part-time $285 per credit hour. *Tuition, nonresident:* full-time $17,400; part-time $580 per credit hour. *Required fees:* full-time $559; $181.10 per term. *Room only:* $13,900. Room and board charges vary according to housing facility.

FRESHMAN FINANCIAL AID (Fall 2016) 2,223 applied for aid; of those 89% were deemed to have need. 92% of freshmen with need received aid; of those 5% had need fully met. *Average percent of need met:* 40% (excluding resources awarded to replace EFC). *Average financial aid package:* $8489 (excluding resources awarded to replace EFC). 4% of all full-time freshmen had no need and received non-need-based gift aid.

UNDERGRADUATE FINANCIAL AID (Fall 2016) 7,704 applied for aid; of those 90% were deemed to have need. 93% of undergraduates with need received aid; of those 6% had need fully met. *Average percent of need met:* 39% (excluding resources awarded to replace EFC). *Average financial aid package:* $8225 (excluding resources awarded to replace EFC). 2% of all full-time undergraduates had no need and received non-need-based gift aid.

GIFT AID (NEED-BASED) *Total amount:* $48,629,036 (55% federal, 45% state). *Receiving aid:* Freshmen: 69% (1,706); all full-time undergraduates: 62% (5,983). *Average award:* Freshmen: $8140; Undergraduates: $7674. *Scholarships, grants, and awards:* Federal Pell, FSEOG, state, private, college/university gift aid from institutional funds.

GIFT AID (NON-NEED-BASED) *Total amount:* $4,197,266 (46% state, 23% institutional, 31% external sources). *Receiving aid:* Freshmen: 29% (718). Undergraduates: 13% (1,227). *Average award:* Freshmen: $1999. Undergraduates: $3124. *Scholarships, grants, and awards by category:* Academic interests/achievement: 13 awards ($18,860 total): area/ethnic studies, biological sciences, business, communication, computer science, education, engineering/technologies, English, foreign languages, general academic interests/achievements, home economics, humanities, international studies, mathematics, physical sciences, premedicine, social sciences. *Creative arts/performance:* 2 awards ($3290 total): applied art and design, art/fine arts, cinema/film/broadcasting, creative writing, general creative arts/performance, journalism/publications, music, performing arts, theater/drama. *Special achievements/activities:* 4 awards ($3300 total): community service, general special achievements/activities, hobbies/interests, leadership, memberships. *Special characteristics:* 6 awards ($14,420 total): adult students, children and siblings of alumni, ethnic background, general special characteristics, handicapped students, international students, local/state students, members of minority groups, out-of-state students, previous college experience, public servants, veterans, veterans' children. *Tuition waivers:* Full or partial for employees or children of employees, senior citizens.

LOANS *Student loans:* $13,929,536 (43% need-based, 57% non-need-based). 76% of past graduating class borrowed through all loan programs. *Average need-based loan:* Freshmen: $9535. Undergraduates: $8970. *Parent loans:* $1,048,489 (100% non-need-based). *Programs:* Federal Direct (Subsidized and Unsubsidized Stafford, PLUS).

WORK-STUDY *Federal work-study:* jobs available.

APPLYING FOR FINANCIAL AID *Required financial aid forms:* FAFSA, state aid form. *Financial aid deadline (priority):* 1/31. *Notification date:* Continuous beginning 2/15.

CONTACT Dr. Philippe Marius, Director of Student Financial Aid, College of Staten Island of the City University of New York, 2800 Victory Boulevard, 2A-401A, Staten Island, NY 10314-6600, 718-982-2030. *Fax:* 718-982-2037. *E-mail:* financialaid@csi.cuny.edu.
Website: http://www.csi.cuny.edu/.

COLLEGE OF THE ATLANTIC
Bar Harbor, ME

Tuition & fees: $43,542	Average undergraduate aid package: $42,122

ABOUT THE INSTITUTION Independent, coed. *Awards:* bachelor's and master's degrees. 42 undergraduate majors. *Total enrollment:* 354. Undergraduates: 349. Freshmen: 91. Both federal and institutional methodology are used as a basis for awarding need-based institutional aid.

UNDERGRADUATE EXPENSES for 2018–2019 *Application fee:* $50. *Comprehensive fee:* $53,289 includes full-time tuition ($42,993), mandatory fees ($549), and room and board ($9747). *College room only:* $6210. Full-time tuition and fees vary according to course load and degree level. Room and board charges vary according to board plan. *Part-time tuition:* $4777 per credit. *Part-time fees:* $183 per term. Part-time tuition and fees vary according to course load and degree level.

FRESHMAN FINANCIAL AID (Fall 2017, est.) 87 applied for aid; of those 91% were deemed to have need. 100% of freshmen with need received aid; of those 9% had need fully met. *Average percent of need met:* 97% (excluding resources awarded to replace EFC). *Average financial aid package:* $47,010 (excluding resources awarded to replace EFC). 13% of all full-time freshmen had no need and received non-need-based gift aid.

UNDERGRADUATE FINANCIAL AID (Fall 2017, est.) 298 applied for aid; of those 92% were deemed to have need. 100% of undergraduates with need received aid; of those 8% had need fully met. *Average percent of need met:* 96% (excluding resources awarded to replace EFC). *Average financial aid package:* $42,122 (excluding resources awarded to replace EFC). 13% of all full-time undergraduates had no need and received non-need-based gift aid.

GIFT AID (NEED-BASED) *Total amount:* $10,025,685 (5% federal, 1% state, 93% institutional, 1% external sources). *Receiving aid:* Freshmen: 87% (79); all full-time undergraduates: 83% (273). *Average award:* Freshmen: $40,936; Undergraduates: $36,071. *Scholarships, grants, and awards:* Federal Pell, FSEOG, state, private, college/university gift aid from institutional funds.

GIFT AID (NON-NEED-BASED) *Total amount:* $592,000 (95% institutional, 5% external sources). *Receiving aid:* Freshmen: 2% (2). Undergraduates: 1% (4). *Average award:* Freshmen: $17,604. Undergraduates: $14,515. *Scholarships, grants, and awards by category:* Academic interests/achievement: 42 awards ($580,639 total): general academic interests/achievements. *Tuition waivers:* Full or partial for employees or children of employees.

LOANS *Student loans:* $1,803,513 (51% need-based, 49% non-need-based). 65% of past graduating class borrowed through all loan programs. *Average indebtedness per student:* $24,228. *Average need-based loan:* Freshmen: $4047. Undergraduates: $4831. *Parent loans:* $262,497 (100% non-need-based). *Programs:* Federal Direct (Subsidized and Unsubsidized Stafford, PLUS), Perkins.

WORK-STUDY *Federal work-study:* Total amount: $509,393; 178 jobs averaging $2862. *State or other work-study/employment:* Total amount: $247,034 (88% need-based, 12% non-need-based). 85 part-time jobs averaging $2906.

APPLYING FOR FINANCIAL AID *Required financial aid forms:* FAFSA, institution's own form, noncustodial (divorced/separated) parent's statement. *Financial aid deadline:* 2/1. *Notification date:* 4/1. Students must reply by 5/1 or within 2 weeks of notification.

CONTACT Bruce Hazam, Director of Financial Aid, College of the Atlantic, 105 Eden Street, Bar Harbor, ME 04609-1198, 207-801-5645 or toll-free 800-528-0025. *Fax:* 207-288-4126. *E-mail:* bhazam@coa.edu.
Website: http://www.coa.edu/.

COLLEGE OF THE HOLY CROSS
Worcester, MA

Tuition & fees: $50,630	Average undergraduate aid package: $40,304

ABOUT THE INSTITUTION Independent Roman Catholic (Jesuit), coed. *Awards:* bachelor's degrees. 34 undergraduate majors. *Total enrollment:* 3,051. Undergraduates: 3,051. Freshmen: 818. Both federal and institutional methodology are used as a basis for awarding need-based institutional aid.

UNDERGRADUATE EXPENSES for 2017–2018 *Application fee:* $60. *Comprehensive fee:* $64,320 includes full-time tuition ($49,980), mandatory fees ($650), and room and board ($13,690). *College room only:* $7390. Room and board charges vary according to board plan and housing facility.

FRESHMAN FINANCIAL AID (Fall 2017, est.) 612 applied for aid; of those 77% were deemed to have need. 100% of freshmen with need received aid; of those 100% had need fully met. *Average percent of need met:* 100% (excluding resources awarded to replace EFC). *Average financial aid package:* $40,451 (excluding resources awarded to replace EFC). 1% of all full-time freshmen had no need and received non-need-based gift aid.

UNDERGRADUATE FINANCIAL AID (Fall 2017, est.) 1,945 applied for aid; of those 82% were deemed to have need. 100% of undergraduates with need received aid; of those 100% had need fully met. *Average percent of need met:* 100% (excluding resources awarded to replace EFC). *Average financial aid package:* $40,304 (excluding resources awarded to replace EFC). 1% of all full-time undergraduates had no need and received non-need-based gift aid.

GIFT AID (NEED-BASED) *Total amount:* $49,017,370 (6% federal, 1% state, 93% institutional). *Receiving aid:* Freshmen: 49% (401); all full-time undergraduates: 44% (1,324). *Average award:* Freshmen: $36,511; Undergraduates: $36,836. *Scholarships, grants, and awards:* Federal Pell, FSEOG, state, private, college/university gift aid from institutional funds.

GIFT AID (NON-NEED-BASED) *Total amount:* $4,409,882 (58% institutional, 42% external sources). *Receiving aid:* Freshmen: 1% (10). Undergraduates: 1% (39). *Average award:* Freshmen: $23,008. Undergraduates: $33,023. *Scholarships, grants, and awards by category:* Academic interests/achievement: general academic interests/achievements. Creative arts/performance: music. Special characteristics: children of faculty/staff. *Tuition waivers:* Full or partial for employees or children of employees. *ROTC:* Army cooperative, Naval, Air Force cooperative.

LOANS *Student loans:* $13,235,042 (83% need-based, 17% non-need-based). 52% of past graduating class borrowed through all loan programs. *Average indebtedness per student:* $26,258. *Average need-based loan:* Freshmen: $5136. Undergraduates: $5413. *Parent loans:* $10,567,672 (100% non-need-based). *Programs:* Federal Direct (Subsidized and Unsubsidized Stafford, PLUS).

WORK-STUDY *Federal work-study:* Total amount: $1,903,184; jobs available.

ATHLETIC AWARDS Total amount: $11,880,218 (30% need-based, 70% non-need-based).

APPLYING FOR FINANCIAL AID *Required financial aid forms:* FAFSA, CSS Financial Aid PROFILE, noncustodial (divorced/separated) parent's statement, business/farm supplement, federal income tax form(s). *Financial aid deadline:* 1/15. *Notification date:* 4/1. Students must reply by 5/1.

CONTACT Ms. Lynne Myers, Director of Financial Aid, College of the Holy Cross, One College Street, Worcester, MA 01610-2395, 508-793-2265 or toll-free 800-442-2421. *Fax:* 508-793-2527.
Website: http://www.holycross.edu/.

COLLEGE OF THE OZARKS
Point Lookout, MO

Tuition & fees: $460	Average undergraduate aid package: $18,500

ABOUT THE INSTITUTION Independent Presbyterian, coed. *Awards:* bachelor's degrees. 66 undergraduate majors. *Total enrollment:* 1,508. Undergraduates: 1,508. Freshmen: 368. Federal methodology is used as a basis for awarding need-based institutional aid.

UNDERGRADUATE EXPENSES for 2018–2019 *College room only:* $3700. *Part-time tuition:* $310 per credit hour. Part-time tuition and fees vary according to course load. Each student participates in the on-campus work program for 15 hours per week and two forty-hour work weeks. Earnings from participation in the work program, plus any federal and/or state aid for which students qualify, plus a College of the Ozarks Cost of Education Scholarship combine to meet each student's full tuition charge.

FRESHMAN FINANCIAL AID (Fall 2016) 361 applied for aid; of those 73% were deemed to have need. 100% of freshmen with need received aid. *Average percent of need met:* 78% (excluding resources awarded to replace EFC). *Average financial aid package:* $18,500 (excluding resources awarded to replace EFC).

UNDERGRADUATE FINANCIAL AID (Fall 2016) 1,531 applied for aid; of those 89% were deemed to have need. 100% of undergraduates with need received

aid. *Average percent of need met:* 83% (excluding resources awarded to replace EFC). *Average financial aid package:* $18,500 (excluding resources awarded to replace EFC).

GIFT AID (NEED-BASED) *Total amount:* $20,988,553 (16% federal, 6% state, 76% institutional, 2% external sources). *Receiving aid:* Freshmen: 73% (263); all full-time undergraduates: 89% (1,366). *Average award:* Freshmen: $14,188; Undergraduates: $14,188. *Scholarships, grants, and awards:* Federal Pell, FSEOG, state, private, college/university gift aid from institutional funds.

GIFT AID (NON-NEED-BASED) *Average award:* Undergraduates: $14,346. *ROTC:* Army.

WORK-STUDY *Federal work-study:* jobs available. *State or other work-study/employment:* Total amount: $2,939,227 (100% non-need-based). Part-time jobs available.

ATHLETIC AWARDS Total amount: $319,600 (100% need-based).

APPLYING FOR FINANCIAL AID *Required financial aid form:* FAFSA. *Financial aid deadline (priority):* 11/15. *Notification date:* 7/1.

CONTACT Office of Financial Aid, College of the Ozarks, PO Box 17, Point Lookout, MO 65726, 417-690-3290 or toll-free 800-222-0525. *Fax:* 417-690-3286. *Website:* http://www.cofo.edu/.

THE COLLEGE OF WILLIAM AND MARY
Williamsburg, VA

Tuition & fees (VA res): $22,044	Average undergraduate aid package: $22,087

ABOUT THE INSTITUTION State-supported, coed. *Awards:* certificates, bachelor's, master's, and doctoral degrees. 41 undergraduate majors. *Total enrollment:* 8,740. Undergraduates: 6,285. Freshmen: 1,531. Federal methodology is used as a basis for awarding need-based institutional aid.

UNDERGRADUATE EXPENSES for 2017–2018 *Application fee:* $75. *Tuition, state resident:* full-time $16,370; part-time $420 per credit hour. *Tuition, nonresident:* full-time $37,425; part-time $1195 per credit hour. *Required fees:* full-time $5674. *College room and board:* $11,799; *Room only:* $7183. Room and board charges vary according to board plan and housing facility.

FRESHMAN FINANCIAL AID (Fall 2016) 1,026 applied for aid; of those 56% were deemed to have need. 96% of freshmen with need received aid; of those 23% had need fully met. *Average percent of need met:* 78% (excluding resources awarded to replace EFC). *Average financial aid package:* $22,147 (excluding resources awarded to replace EFC). 2% of all full-time freshmen had no need and received non-need-based gift aid.

UNDERGRADUATE FINANCIAL AID (Fall 2016) 3,098 applied for aid; of those 70% were deemed to have need. 98% of undergraduates with need received aid; of those 24% had need fully met. *Average percent of need met:* 80% (excluding resources awarded to replace EFC). *Average financial aid package:* $22,087 (excluding resources awarded to replace EFC). 6% of all full-time undergraduates had no need and received non-need-based gift aid.

GIFT AID (NEED-BASED) *Total amount:* $33,982,339 (9% federal, 10% state, 77% institutional, 4% external sources). *Receiving aid:* Freshmen: 33% (490); all full-time undergraduates: 30% (1,882). *Average award:* Freshmen: $16,025; Undergraduates: $16,295. *Scholarships, grants, and awards:* Federal Pell, FSEOG, state, private, college/university gift aid from institutional funds.

GIFT AID (NON-NEED-BASED) *Total amount:* $3,873,965 (5% federal, 76% institutional, 19% external sources). *Receiving aid:* Freshmen: 16% (244). Undergraduates: 13% (805). *Average award:* Freshmen: $9120. Undergraduates: $6127. *Scholarships, grants, and awards by category:* Creative arts/performance: 47 awards ($48,638 total): music, theater/drama. Special characteristics: 183 awards ($3,249,333 total): general special characteristics. *Tuition waivers:* Full or partial for employees or children of employees, senior citizens. *ROTC:* Army.

LOANS *Student loans:* $15,492,494 (71% need-based, 29% non-need-based). 36% of past graduating class borrowed through all loan programs. *Average indebtedness per student:* $24,072. *Average need-based loan:* Freshmen: $3358. Undergraduates: $3838. *Parent loans:* $6,771,826 (64% need-based, 36% non-need-based). *Programs:* Federal Direct (Subsidized and Unsubsidized Stafford, PLUS), Perkins.

WORK-STUDY *Federal work-study:* 385 jobs averaging $1027.

ATHLETIC AWARDS Total amount: $8,224,919 (21% need-based, 79% non-need-based).
APPLYING FOR FINANCIAL AID *Required financial aid forms:* FAFSA, CSS Financial Aid PROFILE. *Financial aid deadline (priority):* 3/1. *Notification date:* Continuous beginning 3/15. Students must reply by 5/1 or within 2 weeks of notification.
CONTACT Mr. Joe Dobrota, Director of Financial Aid, The College of William and Mary, PO Box 8795, Williamsburg, VA 23187, 757-221-2425. *Fax:* 757-221-2515. *E-mail:* jdobrota@wm.edu.
Website: http://www.wm.edu/.

THE COLLEGE OF WOOSTER
Wooster, OH

Tuition & fees: $48,600	Average undergraduate aid package: $43,407

ABOUT THE INSTITUTION Independent Presbyterian Church (U.S.A.), coed. *Awards:* bachelor's degrees. 45 undergraduate majors. *Total enrollment:* 1,980. Undergraduates: 1,980. Freshmen: 568. Both federal and institutional methodology are used as a basis for awarding need-based institutional aid.
UNDERGRADUATE EXPENSES for 2017–2018 *Comprehensive fee:* $60,000 includes full-time tuition ($48,160), mandatory fees ($440), and room and board ($11,400). *College room only:* $5500. Full-time tuition and fees vary according to course load. Room and board charges vary according to board plan and housing facility. *Part-time tuition:* $1494 per credit hour. Part-time tuition and fees vary according to course load.
FRESHMAN FINANCIAL AID (Fall 2017, est.) 416 applied for aid; of those 83% were deemed to have need. 100% of freshmen with need received aid; of those 55% had need fully met. *Average percent of need met:* 95% (excluding resources awarded to replace EFC). *Average financial aid package:* $42,174 (excluding resources awarded to replace EFC). 39% of all full-time freshmen had no need and received non-need-based gift aid.
UNDERGRADUATE FINANCIAL AID (Fall 2017, est.) 1,246 applied for aid; of those 88% were deemed to have need. 100% of undergraduates with need received aid; of those 49% had need fully met. *Average percent of need met:* 93% (excluding resources awarded to replace EFC). *Average financial aid package:* $43,407 (excluding resources awarded to replace EFC). 42% of all full-time undergraduates had no need and received non-need-based gift aid.
GIFT AID (NEED-BASED) *Total amount:* $39,061,816 (5% federal, 1% state, 92% institutional, 2% external sources). *Receiving aid:* Freshmen: 59% (334); all full-time undergraduates: 54% (1,066). *Average award:* Freshmen: $34,309; Undergraduates: $32,621. *Scholarships, grants, and awards:* Federal Pell, FSEOG, state, private, college/university gift aid from institutional funds.
GIFT AID (NON-NEED-BASED) *Total amount:* $19,109,603 (96% institutional, 4% external sources). *Receiving aid:* Freshmen: 11% (63). Undergraduates: 8% (154). *Average award:* Freshmen: $27,540. Undergraduates: $24,652. *Scholarships, grants, and awards by category: Academic interests/achievement:* 1,455 awards ($33,399,545 total): general academic interests/achievements. *Creative arts/performance:* 148 awards ($629,500 total): dance, music, theater/drama. *Special achievements/activities:* 197 awards ($1,350,500 total): community service, religious involvement. *Special characteristics:* 350 awards ($10,181,094 total): children of educators, children of faculty/staff, international students, members of minority groups. *Tuition waivers:* Full or partial for employees or children of employees.
LOANS *Student loans:* $8,644,783 (67% need-based, 33% non-need-based). 54% of past graduating class borrowed through all loan programs. *Average indebtedness per student:* $30,053. *Average need-based loan:* Freshmen: $5559. Undergraduates: $5017. *Parent loans:* $3,827,393 (25% need-based, 75% non-need-based). *Programs:* Federal Direct (Subsidized and Unsubsidized Stafford, PLUS), Perkins.
WORK-STUDY *Federal work-study:* Total amount: $1,745,149; 835 jobs averaging $2045. *State or other work-study/employment:* Total amount: $575,250 (100% non-need-based). 159 part-time jobs averaging $3468.
APPLYING FOR FINANCIAL AID *Required financial aid forms:* FAFSA, institution's own form. *Financial aid deadline (priority):* 2/15. *Notification date:* Continuous beginning 3/15. Students must reply by 5/1 or within 2 weeks of notification.

CONTACT Dana Kennedy, Director of Financial Aid, The College of Wooster, Pearl House, 804 Beall Avenue, Wooster, OH 44691, 800-877-3688 or toll-free 800-877-9905. *Fax:* 330-263-2634. *E-mail:* financialaid@wooster.edu. *Website:* http://www.wooster.edu/.

COLORADO CHRISTIAN UNIVERSITY
Lakewood, CO

CONTACT Mr. Steve Woodburn, Director of Financial Aid, Colorado Christian University, 180 South Garrison Street, Lakewood, CO 80226-7499, 303-963-3230 or toll-free 800-44-FAITH. *Fax:* 303-963-3231. *E-mail:* sfs@ccu.edu. *Website:* http://www.ccu.edu/.

THE COLORADO COLLEGE
Colorado Springs, CO

Tuition & fees: $52,818	Average undergraduate aid package: $48,900

ABOUT THE INSTITUTION Independent, coed. *Awards:* certificates, bachelor's, and master's degrees (master's degree in education only). 48 undergraduate majors. *Total enrollment:* 2,114. Undergraduates: 2,101. Freshmen: 533. Both federal and institutional methodology are used as a basis for awarding need-based institutional aid.
UNDERGRADUATE EXPENSES for 2017–2018 *Application fee:* $60. *One-time required fee:* $150. *Comprehensive fee:* $64,894 includes full-time tuition ($52,380), mandatory fees ($438), and room and board ($12,076). *College room only:* $7240. Room and board charges vary according to board plan and housing facility. *Part-time tuition:* $8803 per course. *Part-time fees:* $2200.75 per credit hour. Part-time tuition and fees vary according to course load.
FRESHMAN FINANCIAL AID (Fall 2017, est.) 257 applied for aid; of those 75% were deemed to have need. 100% of freshmen with need received aid; of those 100% had need fully met. *Average percent of need met:* 100% (excluding resources awarded to replace EFC). *Average financial aid package:* $49,928 (excluding resources awarded to replace EFC). 3% of all full-time freshmen had no need and received non-need-based gift aid.
UNDERGRADUATE FINANCIAL AID (Fall 2017, est.) 801 applied for aid; of those 83% were deemed to have need. 100% of undergraduates with need received aid; of those 100% had need fully met. *Average percent of need met:* 100% (excluding resources awarded to replace EFC). *Average financial aid package:* $48,900 (excluding resources awarded to replace EFC). 6% of all full-time undergraduates had no need and received non-need-based gift aid.
GIFT AID (NEED-BASED) *Total amount:* $33,583,214 (4% federal, 96% institutional). *Receiving aid:* Freshmen: 35% (189); all full-time undergraduates: 31% (639). *Average award:* Freshmen: $47,140; Undergraduates: $45,251. *Scholarships, grants, and awards:* Federal Pell, FSEOG, state, private, college/university gift aid from institutional funds.
GIFT AID (NON-NEED-BASED) *Total amount:* $3,850,232 (40% institutional, 60% external sources). *Receiving aid:* Freshmen: 3% (14). Undergraduates: 2% (42). *Average award:* Freshmen: $17,241. Undergraduates: $14,736. *Scholarships, grants, and awards by category: Academic interests/achievement:* 177 awards ($2,524,310 total): biological sciences, general academic interests/achievements, mathematics, physical sciences. *Special characteristics:* 14 awards ($653,999 total): children of faculty/staff. *Tuition waivers:* Full or partial for employees or children of employees. *ROTC:* Army cooperative.
LOANS *Student loans:* $3,972,897 (40% need-based, 60% non-need-based). 41% of past graduating class borrowed through all loan programs. *Average indebtedness per student:* $20,742. *Average need-based loan:* Freshmen: $2885. Undergraduates: $4316. *Parent loans:* $1,412,544 (100% non-need-based). *Programs:* Federal Direct (Subsidized and Unsubsidized Stafford, PLUS), Perkins.
WORK-STUDY *Federal work-study:* Total amount: $612,082; 330 jobs averaging $1855. *State or other work-study/employment:* Total amount: $359,855 (99% need-based, 1% non-need-based). 188 part-time jobs averaging $1914.
ATHLETIC AWARDS Total amount: $2,221,832 (10% need-based, 90% non-need-based).
APPLYING FOR FINANCIAL AID *Required financial aid forms:* FAFSA, CSS Financial Aid PROFILE, noncustodial (divorced/separated) parent's statement,

federal income tax form(s), W-2 forms. *Financial aid deadline:* 2/15. *Notification date:* 3/20. Students must reply by 5/1.

CONTACT Ms. Shannon L. Amundson, Director of Financial Aid, The Colorado College, 14 East Cache La Poudre Street, Colorado Springs, CO 80903-3294, 719-389-6651 or toll-free 800-542-7214. *Fax:* 719-389-6173. *E-mail:* financialaid@coloradocollege.edu.
Website: http://www.coloradocollege.edu/.

COLORADO MESA UNIVERSITY
Grand Junction, CO

Tuition & fees (CO res): $8972	Average undergraduate aid package: $9301

ABOUT THE INSTITUTION State-supported, coed. *Awards:* certificates, associate, bachelor's, master's, and doctoral degrees. 63 undergraduate majors. *Total enrollment:* 9,735. Undergraduates: 9,595. Freshmen: 2,023. Federal methodology is used as a basis for awarding need-based institutional aid.

UNDERGRADUATE EXPENSES for 2017–2018 *Application fee:* $30. *Tuition, state resident:* full-time $8100; part-time $270 per credit hour. *Tuition, nonresident:* full-time $20,910; part-time $697 per credit hour. *Required fees:* full-time $872; $29.08 per credit hour. Full-time tuition and fees vary according to course load. Part-time tuition and fees vary according to course load. *College room and board:* $10,735; *Room only:* $5930. Room and board charges vary according to board plan and housing facility.

FRESHMAN FINANCIAL AID (Fall 2016) 1,701 applied for aid; of those 76% were deemed to have need. 99% of freshmen with need received aid; of those 18% had need fully met. *Average percent of need met:* 60% (excluding resources awarded to replace EFC). *Average financial aid package:* $8920 (excluding resources awarded to replace EFC). 11% of all full-time freshmen had no need and received non-need-based gift aid.

UNDERGRADUATE FINANCIAL AID (Fall 2016) 5,849 applied for aid; of those 80% were deemed to have need. 99% of undergraduates with need received aid; of those 17% had need fully met. *Average percent of need met:* 61% (excluding resources awarded to replace EFC). *Average financial aid package:* $9301 (excluding resources awarded to replace EFC). 7% of all full-time undergraduates had no need and received non-need-based gift aid.

GIFT AID (NEED-BASED) *Total amount:* $29,172,770 (54% federal, 21% state, 15% institutional, 10% external sources). *Receiving aid:* Freshmen: 58% (1,113); all full-time undergraduates: 54% (3,929). *Average award:* Freshmen: $7091; Undergraduates: $6936. *Scholarships, grants, and awards:* Federal Pell, FSEOG, state, private, college/university gift aid from institutional funds.

GIFT AID (NON-NEED-BASED) *Total amount:* $5,765,201 (11% federal, 1% state, 75% institutional, 13% external sources). *Receiving aid:* Freshmen: 7% (136). Undergraduates: 6% (406). *Average award:* Freshmen: $3961. Undergraduates: $3685. *Scholarships, grants, and awards by category: Academic interests/achievement:* biological sciences, business, communication, computer science, education, engineering/technologies, English, foreign languages, general academic interests/achievements, health fields, humanities, mathematics, physical sciences, social sciences. *Creative arts/performance:* art/fine arts, creative writing, dance, journalism/publications, music, performing arts, theater/drama. *Special achievements/activities:* general special achievements/activities, hobbies/interests, leadership. *Special characteristics:* adult students, first-generation college students, local/state students, out-of-state students. *Tuition waivers:* Full or partial for employees or children of employees.

LOANS *Student loans:* $40,023,870 (82% need-based, 18% non-need-based). 65% of past graduating class borrowed through all loan programs. *Average indebtedness per student:* $28,101. *Average need-based loan:* Freshmen: $3081. Undergraduates: $3729. *Parent loans:* $18,083,995 (67% need-based, 33% non-need-based). *Programs:* Federal Direct (Subsidized and Unsubsidized Stafford, PLUS), Perkins.

WORK-STUDY *Federal work-study:* jobs available. *State or other work-study/employment:* Total amount: $4,679,037 (31% need-based, 69% non-need-based). Part-time jobs available.

ATHLETIC AWARDS Total amount: $2,318,286 (44% need-based, 56% non-need-based).

APPLYING FOR FINANCIAL AID *Required financial aid form:* FAFSA. *Financial aid deadline:* Continuous. *Notification date:* Continuous.

CONTACT Mr. Curt Martin, Director of Financial Aid, Colorado Mesa University, 1100 North Avenue, Grand Junction, CO 81501-3122, 970-248-1065 or toll-free 800-982-MESA. *Fax:* 970-248-1191. *E-mail:* cumartin@coloradomesa.edu. *Website:* http://www.coloradomesa.edu/.

COLORADO MOUNTAIN COLLEGE
Glenwood Springs, CO

Tuition & fees: N/R	Average undergraduate aid package: N/A

ABOUT THE INSTITUTION District-supported, coed. 26 undergraduate majors. Both federal and institutional methodology are used as a basis for awarding need-based institutional aid.

FRESHMAN FINANCIAL AID (Fall 2016) 18% of all full-time freshmen had no need and received non-need-based gift aid.

UNDERGRADUATE FINANCIAL AID (Fall 2016) 19% of all full-time undergraduates had no need and received non-need-based gift aid.

GIFT AID (NEED-BASED) *Total amount:* $4,962,407 (70% federal, 30% state). *Average award:* Freshmen: $1764; Undergraduates: $1748. *Scholarships, grants, and awards:* Federal Pell, FSEOG, state, private, college/university gift aid from institutional funds.

GIFT AID (NON-NEED-BASED) *Total amount:* $1,426,337 (75% institutional, 25% external sources). *Average award:* Freshmen: $1127. Undergraduates: $1271. *Scholarships, grants, and awards by category: Special characteristics:* local/state students.

LOANS *Student loans:* $4,143,405 (47% need-based, 53% non-need-based). *Parent loans:* $691,048 (100% non-need-based). *Programs:* Federal Direct (Subsidized and Unsubsidized Stafford, PLUS), Perkins, Federal Nursing, state.

WORK-STUDY *Federal work-study:* jobs available. *State or other work-study/employment:* Total amount: $448,084 (38% need-based, 62% non-need-based). Part-time jobs available.

APPLYING FOR FINANCIAL AID *Required financial aid form:* FAFSA. *Financial aid deadline (priority):* 3/31. *Notification date:* Continuous.

CONTACT Mr. Thomas S. Valles, Director of Financial Aid, Colorado Mountain College, 802 Grand Avenue, Glenwood Springs, CO 81601, 970-947-8338 or toll-free 800-621-8559. *E-mail:* tvalles@coloradomtn.edu. *Website:* http://www.coloradomtn.edu/.

COLORADO MOUNTAIN COLLEGE
Leadville, CO

CONTACT Financial Aid Office, Colorado Mountain College, 901 South Highway 24, Leadville, CO 80461, 719-486-2015 or toll-free 800-621-8559.
Website: http://www.coloradomtn.edu/.

COLORADO MOUNTAIN COLLEGE
Steamboat Springs, CO

CONTACT Mr. Thomas S. Valles, Director of Financial Aid, Colorado Mountain College, 802 Grand Avenue, Glenwood Springs, CO 81601, 800-621-8559 Ext. 8338 or toll-free 800-621-8559. *Fax:* 970-947-8318. *E-mail:* finaid@coloradomtn.edu. *Website:* http://www.coloradomtn.edu/.

COLORADO SCHOOL OF MINES
Golden, CO

Tuition & fees (CO res): $18,386	Average undergraduate aid package: $13,912

ABOUT THE INSTITUTION State-supported, coed. *Awards:* certificates, bachelor's, master's, and doctoral degrees. 17 undergraduate majors. *Total*

enrollment: 5,876. Undergraduates: 4,612. Freshmen: 977. Federal methodology is used as a basis for awarding need-based institutional aid.

UNDERGRADUATE EXPENSES for 2017–2018 *Application fee:* $45. *Tuition, state resident:* full-time $16,170; part-time $539 per credit hour. *Tuition, nonresident:* full-time $35,220; part-time $1174 per credit hour. *Required fees:* full-time $2216. Full-time tuition and fees vary according to course load. *College room and board:* $11,897. Room and board charges vary according to board plan and housing facility.

FRESHMAN FINANCIAL AID (Fall 2016) 818 applied for aid; of those 58% were deemed to have need. 100% of freshmen with need received aid; of those 24% had need fully met. *Average percent of need met:* 64% (excluding resources awarded to replace EFC). *Average financial aid package:* $15,356 (excluding resources awarded to replace EFC). 37% of all full-time freshmen had no need and received non-need-based gift aid.

UNDERGRADUATE FINANCIAL AID (Fall 2016) 2,807 applied for aid; of those 70% were deemed to have need. 99% of undergraduates with need received aid; of those 22% had need fully met. *Average percent of need met:* 58% (excluding resources awarded to replace EFC). *Average financial aid package:* $13,912 (excluding resources awarded to replace EFC). 32% of all full-time undergraduates had no need and received non-need-based gift aid.

GIFT AID (NEED-BASED) *Total amount:* $16,972,422 (19% federal, 7% state, 65% institutional, 9% external sources). *Receiving aid:* Freshmen: 27% (265); all full-time undergraduates: 25% (1,083). *Average award:* Freshmen: $5626; Undergraduates: $5869. *Scholarships, grants, and awards:* Federal Pell, FSEOG, state, private, college/university gift aid from institutional funds.

GIFT AID (NON-NEED-BASED) *Total amount:* $13,686,960 (90% institutional, 10% external sources). *Receiving aid:* Freshmen: 41% (403). Undergraduates: 31% (1,342). *Average award:* Freshmen: $7948. Undergraduates: $8272. *Scholarships, grants, and awards by category:* Academic interests/achievement: 1,562 awards ($14,882,595 total): business, computer science, engineering/technologies, general academic interests/achievements, mathematics, military science, physical sciences. *Tuition waivers:* Full or partial for employees or children of employees. *ROTC:* Army, Air Force.

LOANS *Student loans:* $27,229,401 (52% need-based, 48% non-need-based). 51% of past graduating class borrowed through all loan programs. *Average indebtedness per student:* $32,221. *Average need-based loan:* Freshmen: $3155. Undergraduates: $4652. *Parent loans:* $13,450,458 (55% need-based, 45% non-need-based). *Programs:* Federal Direct (Subsidized and Unsubsidized Stafford, PLUS), Perkins, college/university.

WORK-STUDY *Federal work-study:* 384 jobs averaging $1749. *State or other work-study/employment:* Total amount: $5,062,311 (27% need-based, 73% non-need-based). 2,038 part-time jobs averaging $2428.

ATHLETIC AWARDS Total amount: $3,520,714 (36% need-based, 64% non-need-based).

APPLYING FOR FINANCIAL AID *Required financial aid form:* FAFSA. *Financial aid deadline (priority):* 3/1. *Notification date:* Continuous beginning 1/1. Students must reply by 4/1.

CONTACT Jill Robertson, Director of Financial Aid, Colorado School of Mines, 1600 Maple Street, Golden, CO 80401-1887, 303-273-3301 or toll-free 800-446-9488 Ext. 3220. *Fax:* 303-384-2252. *E-mail:* finaid@mines.edu. *Website:* http://www.mines.edu/.

level, course load, program, reciprocity agreements, and student level. *College room and board:* $11,514; *Room only:* $5578. Room and board charges vary according to board plan, housing facility, and location.

FRESHMAN FINANCIAL AID (Fall 2016) 3,968 applied for aid; of those 63% were deemed to have need. 92% of freshmen with need received aid; of those 35% had need fully met. *Average percent of need met:* 75% (excluding resources awarded to replace EFC). *Average financial aid package:* $11,572 (excluding resources awarded to replace EFC). 18% of all full-time freshmen had no need and received non-need-based gift aid.

UNDERGRADUATE FINANCIAL AID (Fall 2016) 15,747 applied for aid; of those 71% were deemed to have need. 92% of undergraduates with need received aid; of those 26% had need fully met. *Average percent of need met:* 82% (excluding resources awarded to replace EFC). *Average financial aid package:* $11,635 (excluding resources awarded to replace EFC). 14% of all full-time undergraduates had no need and received non-need-based gift aid.

GIFT AID (NEED-BASED) *Total amount:* $83,193,625 (27% federal, 12% state, 53% institutional, 8% external sources). *Receiving aid:* Freshmen: 43% (1,968); all full-time undergraduates: 33% (7,738). *Average award:* Freshmen: $8904; Undergraduates: $8223. *Scholarships, grants, and awards:* Federal Pell, FSEOG, state, private, college/university gift aid from institutional funds.

GIFT AID (NON-NEED-BASED) *Total amount:* $20,437,436 (2% federal, 2% state, 76% institutional, 20% external sources). *Receiving aid:* Freshmen: 21% (972). Undergraduates: 11% (2,488). *Average award:* Freshmen: $5215. Undergraduates: $4971. *Scholarships, grants, and awards by category:* Academic interests/achievement: 11,840 awards ($33,372,221 total): general academic interests/achievements. Creative arts/performance: 436 awards ($544,820 total): art/fine arts, creative writing, dance, music, performing arts, theater/drama. Special achievements/activities: 950 awards ($2,611,256 total): general special achievements/activities. Special characteristics: 976 awards ($5,876,498 total): children of faculty/staff, first-generation college students, international students, members of minority groups, veterans. *Tuition waivers:* Full or partial for employees or children of employees. *ROTC:* Army, Air Force.

LOANS *Student loans:* $93,094,154 (66% need-based, 34% non-need-based). 51% of past graduating class borrowed through all loan programs. *Average indebtedness per student:* $26,348. *Average need-based loan:* Freshmen: $5156. Undergraduates: $6583. *Parent loans:* $58,254,234 (36% need-based, 64% non-need-based). *Programs:* Federal Direct (Subsidized and Unsubsidized Stafford, PLUS), Perkins, private loans.

WORK-STUDY *Federal work-study:* 613 jobs averaging $2124. *State or other work-study/employment:* Total amount: $2,906,950 (58% need-based, 42% non-need-based). 1,150 part-time jobs averaging $2065.

ATHLETIC AWARDS Total amount: $9,045,353 (31% need-based, 69% non-need-based).

APPLYING FOR FINANCIAL AID *Required financial aid forms:* FAFSA, institution's own form. *Financial aid deadline (priority):* 3/1. *Notification date:* Continuous beginning 3/1.

CONTACT Office of Financial Aid, Colorado State University, Centennial Hall, 1065 Campus Delivery, Fort Collins, CO 80523-1065, 970-491-6321. *Fax:* 970-491-5010. *E-mail:* financialaid@colostate.edu. *Website:* http://www.colostate.edu/.

COLORADO STATE UNIVERSITY
Fort Collins, CO

Tuition & fees (CO res): $11,488	Average undergraduate aid package: $11,635

ABOUT THE INSTITUTION State-supported, coed. *Awards:* certificates, bachelor's, master's, and doctoral degrees. 72 undergraduate majors. *Total enrollment:* 33,237. Undergraduates: 25,903. Freshmen: 5,038. Both federal and institutional methodology are used as a basis for awarding need-based institutional aid.

UNDERGRADUATE EXPENSES for 2017–2018 *Application fee:* $50. *Tuition, state resident:* full-time $9152; part-time $415.70 per credit hour. *Tuition, nonresident:* full-time $26,660; part-time $1333 per credit hour. *Required fees:* full-time $2336; $58 per credit hour or $290.06 per term. Full-time tuition and fees vary according to course level, course load, program, reciprocity agreements, and student level. Part-time tuition and fees vary according to course

COLORADO STATE UNIVERSITY–GLOBAL CAMPUS
Greenwood Village, CO

CONTACT Financial Aid Office, Colorado State University–Global Campus, 8000 E. Maplewood Avenue, Greenwood Village, CO 80111, 720-279-0159 or toll-free 800-920-6723. *Website:* http://csuglobal.edu/.

COLORADO STATE UNIVERSITY–PUEBLO

Pueblo, CO

CONTACT Justin Streater, Associate Director of Financial Aid, Colorado State University–Pueblo, 2200 Bonforte Boulevard, Pueblo, CO 81001-4901, 719-549-2967. *Fax:* 719-549-2088. *E-mail:* justin.streater@csupueblo.edu. *Website:* http://www.csupueblo.edu/.

COLORADO TECHNICAL UNIVERSITY AURORA

Aurora, CO

CONTACT Ms. Natalie Dietsch, Financial Aid Manager, Colorado Technical University Aurora, 5775 Denver Tech Center Boulevard, Suite 100, Greenwood Village, CO 80111, 303-694-6600 or toll-free 888-309-6555. *Fax:* 303-694-6673. *Website:* http://www.coloradotech.edu/.

COLORADO TECHNICAL UNIVERSITY COLORADO SPRINGS

Colorado Springs, CO

CONTACT Jacqueline Harris, Senior Director of Student Finance Services, Colorado Technical University Colorado Springs, 4435 North Chestnut Street, Colorado Springs, CO 80907-3896, 719-598-0200 or toll-free 866-942-6555. *Fax:* 719-598-3740. *Website:* http://www.coloradotech.edu/.

COLUMBIA CENTRAL UNIVERSITY

Caguas, PR

CONTACT Financial Aid Officer, Columbia Central University, Carr 183, Km 1.7, PO Box 8517, Caguas, PR 00726, 787-743-4041 Ext. 244. *Fax:* 787-744-7031. *Website:* http://www.columbiacentral.edu/.

COLUMBIA CENTRAL UNIVERSITY

Yauco, PR

CONTACT Financial Aid Office, Columbia Central University, Calle Betances #3, Box 3062, Yauco, PR 00698, 787-856-0945. *Website:* http://www.columbiacentral.edu/.

COLUMBIA COLLEGE

Columbia, MO

Tuition & fees: $22,704	Average undergraduate aid package: $16,156

ABOUT THE INSTITUTION Independent Christian Church (Disciples of Christ), coed. *Awards:* certificates, associate, bachelor's, and master's degrees (offers continuing education program with significant enrollment not reflected in profile). 41 undergraduate majors. *Total enrollment:* 1,196. Undergraduates: 1,041. Freshmen: 174. Federal methodology is used as a basis for awarding need-based institutional aid.

UNDERGRADUATE EXPENSES for 2018–2019 *Application fee:* $35. *Tuition:* full-time $22,704; part-time $487 per credit hour. Full-time tuition and fees vary according to class time, course load, program, reciprocity agreements, and student level. Part-time tuition and fees vary according to class time, course load,

location, and reciprocity agreements. Room and board charges vary according to housing facility. *Payment plan:* Guaranteed tuition.

FRESHMAN FINANCIAL AID (Fall 2016) 177 applied for aid; of those 86% were deemed to have need. 100% of freshmen with need received aid; of those 19% had need fully met. *Average percent of need met:* 70% (excluding resources awarded to replace EFC). *Average financial aid package:* $16,983 (excluding resources awarded to replace EFC). 12% of all full-time freshmen had no need and received non-need-based gift aid.

UNDERGRADUATE FINANCIAL AID (Fall 2016) 633 applied for aid; of those 87% were deemed to have need. 99% of undergraduates with need received aid; of those 17% had need fully met. *Average percent of need met:* 62% (excluding resources awarded to replace EFC). *Average financial aid package:* $16,156 (excluding resources awarded to replace EFC). 12% of all full-time undergraduates had no need and received non-need-based gift aid.

GIFT AID (NEED-BASED) *Total amount:* $2,187,094 (59% federal, 21% state, 20% institutional). *Receiving aid:* Freshmen: 57% (116); all full-time undergraduates: 50% (406). *Average award:* Freshmen: $5249; Undergraduates: $4977. *Scholarships, grants, and awards:* Federal Pell, FSEOG, state, private, college/university gift aid from institutional funds.

GIFT AID (NON-NEED-BASED) *Total amount:* $4,664,103 (1% state, 94% institutional, 5% external sources). *Receiving aid:* Freshmen: 75% (152). Undergraduates: 59% (479). *Average award:* Freshmen: $11,232. Undergraduates: $8988. *Scholarships, grants, and awards by category:* Academic interests/achievement: 169 awards ($895,184 total): biological sciences, business, communication, computer science, education, English, general academic interests/achievements, humanities, mathematics, physical sciences, religion/biblical studies, social sciences. *Creative arts/performance:* 30 awards ($30,600 total): art/fine arts, creative writing, music. *Special achievements/activities:* 136 awards ($959,275 total): community service, general special achievements/activities, leadership, religious involvement. *Special characteristics:* 238 awards ($541,940 total): adult students, children and siblings of alumni, children of current students, children of educators, children of faculty/staff, children of union members/company employees, ethnic background, first-generation college students, general special characteristics, international students, local/state students, members of minority groups, parents of current students, previous college experience, religious affiliation, siblings of current students, spouses of current students, veterans, veterans' children. *Tuition waivers:* Full or partial for children of alumni, employees or children of employees, senior citizens. *ROTC:* Army cooperative, Naval cooperative, Air Force cooperative.

LOANS *Student loans:* $4,127,021 (37% need-based, 63% non-need-based). 61% of past graduating class borrowed through all loan programs. *Average indebtedness per student:* $26,312. *Average need-based loan:* Freshmen: $2775. Undergraduates: $3438. *Parent loans:* $922,598 (100% non-need-based). *Programs:* Federal Direct (Subsidized and Unsubsidized Stafford, PLUS).

WORK-STUDY *Federal work-study:* 156 jobs averaging $2805. *State or other work-study/employment:* Total amount: $209,858 (100% need-based). 34 part-time jobs averaging $1709.

ATHLETIC AWARDS Total amount: $2,473,950 (100% non-need-based).

APPLYING FOR FINANCIAL AID *Required financial aid form:* FAFSA. *Financial aid deadline (priority):* 3/1. *Notification date:* Continuous beginning 12/15.

CONTACT Colleen Brown, Director of Financial Aid, Columbia College, 1001 Rogers Street, Columbia, MO 65216-0002, 573-875-7362 or toll-free 800-231-2391. *Fax:* 573-875-7452. *E-mail:* ctbrown@ccis.edu. *Website:* http://www.ccis.edu/.

COLUMBIA COLLEGE

Columbia, SC

CONTACT Anita Kaminer Elliott, Director of Financial Aid, Columbia College, 1301 Columbia College Drive, Columbia, SC 29203-5998, 803-786-3612 or toll-free 800-277-1301. *Fax:* 803-786-3560. *Website:* http://www.columbiasc.edu/.

COLUMBIA COLLEGE CHICAGO
Chicago, IL

Tuition & fees: $27,309	Average undergraduate aid package: $9862

ABOUT THE INSTITUTION Independent, coed. *Awards:* certificates, bachelor's, and master's degrees. 48 undergraduate majors. *Total enrollment:* 7,312. Undergraduates: 7,027. Freshmen: 1,443. Federal methodology is used as a basis for awarding need-based institutional aid.

UNDERGRADUATE EXPENSES for 2018–2019 *Application fee:* $35. *Comprehensive fee:* $41,321 includes full-time tuition ($26,090), mandatory fees ($1219), and room and board ($14,012). Full-time tuition and fees vary according to course load and degree level. Room and board charges vary according to housing facility. *Part-time tuition:* $901 per credit hour. Part-time tuition and fees vary according to course load and degree level.

FRESHMAN FINANCIAL AID (Fall 2016) 1,397 applied for aid; of those 77% were deemed to have need. 96% of freshmen with need received aid; of those 17% had need fully met. *Average percent of need met:* 57% (excluding resources awarded to replace EFC). *Average financial aid package:* $10,539 (excluding resources awarded to replace EFC). 1% of all full-time freshmen had no need and received non-need-based gift aid.

UNDERGRADUATE FINANCIAL AID (Fall 2016) 5,923 applied for aid; of those 81% were deemed to have need. 98% of undergraduates with need received aid; of those 20% had need fully met. *Average percent of need met:* 55% (excluding resources awarded to replace EFC). *Average financial aid package:* $9862 (excluding resources awarded to replace EFC). 1% of all full-time undergraduates had no need and received non-need-based gift aid.

GIFT AID (NEED-BASED) *Total amount:* $54,738,625 (25% federal, 12% state, 61% institutional, 2% external sources). *Receiving aid:* Freshmen: 64% (980); all full-time undergraduates: 59% (4,213). *Average award:* Freshmen: $10,945; Undergraduates: $10,531. *Scholarships, grants, and awards:* Federal Pell, FSEOG, state, private, college/university gift aid from institutional funds.

GIFT AID (NON-NEED-BASED) *Total amount:* $2,069,938 (100% institutional). *Receiving aid:* Freshmen: 1% (20). Undergraduates: 3% (245). *Average award:* Freshmen: $26,900. Undergraduates: $19,659. *Scholarships, grants, and awards by category: Academic interests/achievement:* business, communication, education, English, humanities, mathematics. *Creative arts/performance:* applied art and design, art/fine arts, cinema/film/broadcasting, creative writing, dance, general creative arts/performance, journalism/publications, music, performing arts, theater/drama. *Special characteristics:* children of faculty/staff. *Tuition waivers:* Full or partial for employees or children of employees.

LOANS *Student loans:* $50,670,392 (100% need-based). 76% of past graduating class borrowed through all loan programs. *Average indebtedness per student:* $33,208. *Parent loans:* $39,630,041 (100% need-based). *Programs:* Federal Direct (Subsidized and Unsubsidized Stafford, PLUS).

WORK-STUDY *Federal work-study:* jobs available.

APPLYING FOR FINANCIAL AID *Required financial aid form:* FAFSA. *Financial aid deadline:* Continuous. *Notification date:* Continuous beginning 11/1.

CONTACT Student Financial Services, Columbia College Chicago, 600 South Michigan Avenue, Suite 303, Chicago, IL 60605, 312-369-7140. *Website:* http://www.colum.edu/.

COLUMBIA COLLEGE HOLLYWOOD
Tarzana, CA

ABOUT THE INSTITUTION Independent, coed. 5 undergraduate majors.

GIFT AID (NEED-BASED) *Scholarships, grants, and awards:* Federal Pell, FSEOG, state, private.

LOANS *Programs:* Federal Direct (Subsidized and Unsubsidized Stafford, PLUS), private loans.

WORK-STUDY *Federal work-study:* 10 jobs averaging $2000.

APPLYING FOR FINANCIAL AID *Required financial aid forms:* FAFSA, institution's own form.

CONTACT Ms. Maricela Guzman, Financial Aid Administrator, Columbia College Hollywood, 18618 Oxnard Street, Tarzana, CA 91356, 818-401-1030 or toll-free 800-785-0585. *Fax:* 818-345-8660. *E-mail:* mguzman@columbiacollege.edu. *Website:* http://www.columbiacollege.edu/.

COLUMBIA COLLEGE OF NURSING
Glendale, WI

CONTACT Wendy Hilvo, Financial Aid Director, Columbia College of Nursing, 4425 North Port Washington Road, Suite 302, Glendale, WI 53212, 414-326-2337. *Fax:* 414-326-2362. *E-mail:* financialaid@ccon.edu. *Website:* http://www.ccon.edu/.

COLUMBIA INTERNATIONAL UNIVERSITY
Columbia, SC

Tuition & fees: $22,390	Average undergraduate aid package: $18,497

ABOUT THE INSTITUTION Independent nondenominational, coed. *Awards:* certificates, associate, bachelor's, master's, and doctoral degrees. 18 undergraduate majors. *Total enrollment:* 965. Undergraduates: 497. Freshmen: 80. Federal methodology is used as a basis for awarding need-based institutional aid.

UNDERGRADUATE EXPENSES for 2017–2018 *Comprehensive fee:* $30,380 includes full-time tuition ($21,720), mandatory fees ($670), and room and board ($7990). Full-time tuition and fees vary according to course load, program, and reciprocity agreements. Room and board charges vary according to board plan and housing facility. *Part-time tuition:* $905 per semester hour. *Part-time fees:* $10 per semester hour; $185 per term. Part-time tuition and fees vary according to course load, program, and reciprocity agreements.

FRESHMAN FINANCIAL AID (Fall 2016) 84 applied for aid; of those 89% were deemed to have need. 100% of freshmen with need received aid; of those 15% had need fully met. *Average percent of need met:* 71% (excluding resources awarded to replace EFC). *Average financial aid package:* $18,501 (excluding resources awarded to replace EFC). 15% of all full-time freshmen had no need and received non-need-based gift aid.

UNDERGRADUATE FINANCIAL AID (Fall 2016) 391 applied for aid; of those 86% were deemed to have need. 100% of undergraduates with need received aid; of those 14% had need fully met. *Average percent of need met:* 69% (excluding resources awarded to replace EFC). *Average financial aid package:* $18,497 (excluding resources awarded to replace EFC). 21% of all full-time undergraduates had no need and received non-need-based gift aid.

GIFT AID (NEED-BASED) *Total amount:* $4,608,519 (20% federal, 20% state, 56% institutional, 4% external sources). *Receiving aid:* Freshmen: 85% (75); all full-time undergraduates: 78% (336). *Average award:* Freshmen: $15,381; Undergraduates: $14,494. *Scholarships, grants, and awards:* Federal Pell, FSEOG, state, private, college/university gift aid from institutional funds.

GIFT AID (NON-NEED-BASED) *Total amount:* $967,072 (17% state, 77% institutional, 6% external sources). *Receiving aid:* Freshmen: 6% (5). Undergraduates: 6% (24). *Average award:* Freshmen: $8783. Undergraduates: $6922. *Scholarships, grants, and awards by category: Academic interests/achievement:* general academic interests/achievements. *Special achievements/activities:* general special achievements/activities, leadership, religious involvement. *Special characteristics:* children and siblings of alumni, children of faculty/staff, ethnic background, international students, local/state students, members of minority groups, spouses of current students, veterans, veterans' children. *Tuition waivers:* Full or partial for employees or children of employees.

LOANS *Student loans:* $3,108,581 (75% need-based, 25% non-need-based). 61% of past graduating class borrowed through all loan programs. *Average indebtedness per student:* $24,132. *Average need-based loan:* Freshmen: $3262. Undergraduates: $4176. *Parent loans:* $487,386 (52% need-based, 48% non-need-based). *Programs:* Federal Direct (Subsidized and Unsubsidized Stafford, PLUS).

WORK-STUDY *Federal work-study:* jobs available. *State or other work-study/employment:* Part-time jobs available.

ATHLETIC AWARDS Total amount: $254,110 (76% need-based, 24% non-need-based).

APPLYING FOR FINANCIAL AID *Required financial aid forms:* FAFSA, institution's own form, state aid form. *Financial aid deadline (priority):* 4/15. *Notification date:* Continuous beginning 3/1. Students must reply within 2 weeks of notification.

CONTACT Mrs. Patty Jean Hix, Director of Financial Aid, Columbia International University, 7435 Monticello Road, Columbia, SC 29203, 800-777-2227 Ext. 5037 or toll-free 800-777-2227 Ext. 5024. *Fax:* 803-223-2505. *E-mail:* phix@ciu.edu. *Website:* http://www.ciu.edu/.

COLUMBIA UNIVERSITY
New York, NY

Tuition & fees: $57,208	Average undergraduate aid package: $58,630

ABOUT THE INSTITUTION Independent, coed. *Awards:* bachelor's, master's, and doctoral degrees. 87 undergraduate majors. *Total enrollment:* 6,231. Undergraduates: 6,231. Freshmen: 1,405. Institutional methodology is used as a basis for awarding need-based institutional aid.

UNDERGRADUATE EXPENSES for 2017–2018 *Application fee:* $85. *Comprehensive fee:* $70,826 includes full-time tuition ($54,504), mandatory fees ($2704), and room and board ($13,618). Room and board charges vary according to board plan. *Payment plan:* Tuition prepayment.

FRESHMAN FINANCIAL AID (Fall 2017, est.) 791 applied for aid; of those 91% were deemed to have need. 100% of freshmen with need received aid; of those 100% had need fully met. *Average percent of need met:* 100% (excluding resources awarded to replace EFC). *Average financial aid package:* $59,830 (excluding resources awarded to replace EFC).

UNDERGRADUATE FINANCIAL AID (Fall 2017, est.) 3,341 applied for aid; of those 94% were deemed to have need. 100% of undergraduates with need received aid; of those 94% had need fully met. *Average percent of need met:* 100% (excluding resources awarded to replace EFC). *Average financial aid package:* $58,630 (excluding resources awarded to replace EFC).

GIFT AID (NEED-BASED) *Total amount:* $168,322,528 (4% federal, 1% state, 93% institutional, 2% external sources). *Receiving aid:* Freshmen: 50% (709); all full-time undergraduates: 50% (3,118). *Average award:* Freshmen: $56,504; Undergraduates: $53,879. *Scholarships, grants, and awards:* Federal Pell, FSEOG, state, private, college/university gift aid from institutional funds.

GIFT AID (NON-NEED-BASED) *Total amount:* $807,249 (13% federal, 13% state, 74% external sources). *Receiving aid:* Freshmen: 4% (52). Undergraduates: 2% (102). *Tuition waivers:* Full or partial for employees or children of employees. *ROTC:* Army cooperative, Naval, Air Force cooperative.

LOANS *Student loans:* $9,020,854 (30% need-based, 70% non-need-based). *Average need-based loan:* Freshmen: $2620. Undergraduates: $3623. *Parent loans:* $6,549,609 (4% need-based, 96% non-need-based). *Programs:* Federal Direct (Subsidized and Unsubsidized Stafford, PLUS), college/university, alternative loans.

WORK-STUDY *Federal work-study:* Total amount: $3,566,265; jobs available. *State or other work-study/employment:* Total amount: $2,659,002 (79% need-based, 21% non-need-based). Part-time jobs available.

APPLYING FOR FINANCIAL AID *Required financial aid forms:* FAFSA, CSS Financial Aid PROFILE, noncustodial (divorced/separated) parent's statement, parent and student income tax forms. *Financial aid deadline (priority):* 2/15. *Notification date:* 4/1. Students must reply by 5/1 or within 1 week of notification.

CONTACT Office of Student Financial Services, Columbia University, Office of Financial Aid and Educational Financing, 100 Hamilton Hall, MC 2807, New York, NY 10027, 212-854-3711. *E-mail:* ugrad-finaid@columbia.edu. *Website:* http://www.columbia.edu/.

COLUMBIA UNIVERSITY SCHOOL OF GENERAL STUDIES
New York, NY

ABOUT THE INSTITUTION Independent, coed. *Awards:* certificates and bachelor's degrees. 79 undergraduate majors. *Total enrollment:* 2,068. Undergraduates: 2,068. Freshmen: 147.

GIFT AID (NEED-BASED) *Scholarships, grants, and awards:* Federal Pell, FSEOG, state, private, college/university gift aid from institutional funds.

GIFT AID (NON-NEED-BASED) *Scholarships, grants, and awards by category:* Academic interests/achievement: general academic interests/achievements.

LOANS *Programs:* Federal Direct (Subsidized and Unsubsidized Stafford, PLUS), Perkins, college/university.

APPLYING FOR FINANCIAL AID *Required financial aid forms:* FAFSA, institution's own form.

CONTACT Mr. William Skip Bailey, Director of Educational Financing, Columbia University School of General Studies, 408 Lewisohn Hall, 2970 Broadway, New York, NY 10027, 212-854-5410 or toll-free 800-895-1169. *Fax:* 212-854-6316. *E-mail:* gs_financial_aid@columbia.edu. *Website:* http://www.gs.columbia.edu/.

COLUMBUS COLLEGE OF ART & DESIGN
Columbus, OH

Tuition & fees: $35,375	Average undergraduate aid package: $24,992

ABOUT THE INSTITUTION Independent, coed. *Awards:* bachelor's and master's degrees. 12 undergraduate majors. *Total enrollment:* 1,095. Undergraduates: 1,060. Freshmen: 240. Federal methodology is used as a basis for awarding need-based institutional aid.

UNDERGRADUATE EXPENSES for 2017–2018 *Application fee:* $50. *Comprehensive fee:* $44,745 includes full-time tuition ($33,960), mandatory fees ($1415), and room and board ($9370). Full-time tuition and fees vary according to course load. Room and board charges vary according to board plan, housing facility, location, and student level. *Part-time tuition:* $1415 per credit hour. Part-time tuition and fees vary according to course load.

FRESHMAN FINANCIAL AID (Fall 2017, est.) 306 applied for aid; of those 93% were deemed to have need. 100% of freshmen with need received aid; of those 11% had need fully met. *Average percent of need met:* 64% (excluding resources awarded to replace EFC). *Average financial aid package:* $26,973 (excluding resources awarded to replace EFC). 12% of all full-time freshmen had no need and received non-need-based gift aid.

UNDERGRADUATE FINANCIAL AID (Fall 2017, est.) 873 applied for aid; of those 94% were deemed to have need. 99% of undergraduates with need received aid; of those 10% had need fully met. *Average percent of need met:* 62% (excluding resources awarded to replace EFC). *Average financial aid package:* $24,992 (excluding resources awarded to replace EFC). 18% of all full-time undergraduates had no need and received non-need-based gift aid.

GIFT AID (NEED-BASED) *Total amount:* $15,173,100 (13% federal, 5% state, 81% institutional, 1% external sources). *Receiving aid:* Freshmen: 86% (284); all full-time undergraduates: 80% (809). *Average award:* Freshmen: $21,612; Undergraduates: $18,632. *Scholarships, grants, and awards:* Federal Pell, FSEOG, state, private, college/university gift aid from institutional funds.

GIFT AID (NON-NEED-BASED) *Total amount:* $2,841,726 (99% institutional, 1% external sources). *Receiving aid:* Freshmen: 5% (17). Undergraduates: 5% (50). *Average award:* Freshmen: $13,721. Undergraduates: $13,415. *Scholarships, grants, and awards by category:* Creative arts/performance: 1,099 awards ($13,598,210 total): art/fine arts. *Special characteristics:* 15 awards ($282,464 total): children of educators, children of faculty/staff, local/state students. *Tuition waivers:* Full or partial for employees or children of employees.

LOANS *Student loans:* $8,036,405 (85% need-based, 15% non-need-based). 81% of past graduating class borrowed through all loan programs. *Average indebtedness per student:* $32,258. *Average need-based loan:* Freshmen: $6227. Undergraduates: $6805. *Parent loans:* $6,534,633 (62% need-based, 38% non-need-based).

Programs: Federal Direct (Subsidized and Unsubsidized Stafford, PLUS), Perkins, state.

WORK-STUDY *Federal work-study:* Total amount: $170,700; 142 jobs averaging $3550. *State or other work-study/employment:* 292 part-time jobs averaging $3550.

APPLYING FOR FINANCIAL AID *Required financial aid forms:* FAFSA, institution's own form, federal income tax transcript(s), verification worksheet. *Financial aid deadline (priority):* 10/15. *Notification date:* 11/1. Students must reply within 2 weeks of notification.

CONTACT Mrs. Anna Marie Schofield, Director of Financial Aid, Columbus College of Art & Design, 60 Cleveland Avenue, Columbus, OH 43215-1758, 614-224-9101 Ext. 3274 or toll-free 877-997-2223. *Fax:* 614-222-4034. *E-mail:* aschofield@ccad.edu. *Website:* http://www.ccad.edu/.

COLUMBUS STATE UNIVERSITY
Columbus, GA

Tuition & fees (GA res): $7200	Average undergraduate aid package: $9917

ABOUT THE INSTITUTION State-supported, coed. *Awards:* certificates, associate, bachelor's, master's, and doctoral degrees. 41 undergraduate majors. *Total enrollment:* 8,452. Undergraduates: 6,798. Freshmen: 958. Federal methodology is used as a basis for awarding need-based institutional aid.

UNDERGRADUATE EXPENSES for 2017–2018 *Application fee:* $40. *Tuition, state resident:* full-time $5330; part-time $177.67 per credit hour. *Tuition, nonresident:* full-time $18,812; part-time $627.07 per credit hour. *Required fees:* full-time $1870; $935 per term. Full-time tuition and fees vary according to course load, degree level, and program. Part-time tuition and fees vary according to course load, degree level, and program. *College room and board:* $10,550; *Room only:* $6580. Room and board charges vary according to board plan and housing facility.

FRESHMAN FINANCIAL AID (Fall 2017, est.) 833 applied for aid; of those 80% were deemed to have need. 100% of freshmen with need received aid; of those 18% had need fully met. *Average percent of need met:* 73% (excluding resources awarded to replace EFC). *Average financial aid package:* $10,502 (excluding resources awarded to replace EFC). 4% of all full-time freshmen had no need and received non-need-based gift aid.

UNDERGRADUATE FINANCIAL AID (Fall 2017, est.) 4,049 applied for aid; of those 82% were deemed to have need. 100% of undergraduates with need received aid; of those 18% had need fully met. *Average percent of need met:* 72% (excluding resources awarded to replace EFC). *Average financial aid package:* $9917 (excluding resources awarded to replace EFC). 4% of all full-time undergraduates had no need and received non-need-based gift aid.

GIFT AID (NEED-BASED) *Total amount:* $15,022,319 (100% federal). *Receiving aid:* Freshmen: 53% (472); all full-time undergraduates: 53% (2,417). *Average award:* Freshmen: $5018; Undergraduates: $5030. *Scholarships, grants, and awards:* Federal Pell, FSEOG, state, private, college/university gift aid from institutional funds.

GIFT AID (NON-NEED-BASED) *Total amount:* $9,763,310 (87% state, 6% institutional, 7% external sources). *Receiving aid:* Freshmen: 48% (423). Undergraduates: 31% (1,413). *Average award:* Freshmen: $1136. Undergraduates: $1543. *Scholarships, grants, and awards by category:* Academic interests/achievement: biological sciences, business, communication, computer science, education, English, general academic interests/achievements, health fields, humanities, international studies, mathematics, military science, physical sciences. *Creative arts/performance:* art/fine arts, dance, music, performing arts, theater/drama. *Special achievements/activities:* cheerleading/drum major, community service, general special achievements/activities, leadership. *Tuition waivers:* Full or partial for senior citizens. *ROTC:* Army.

LOANS *Student loans:* $34,086,718 (45% need-based, 55% non-need-based). 74% of past graduating class borrowed through all loan programs. *Average indebtedness per student:* $30,503. *Average need-based loan:* Freshmen: $3492. Undergraduates: $4277. *Parent loans:* $3,478,909 (100% non-need-based). *Programs:* Federal Direct (Subsidized and Unsubsidized Stafford, PLUS), Perkins, Federal Nursing, state, college/university.

WORK-STUDY *Federal work-study:* Total amount: $950,661; jobs available.

ATHLETIC AWARDS Total amount: $1,126,724 (100% non-need-based).

APPLYING FOR FINANCIAL AID *Required financial aid form:* FAFSA. *Financial aid deadline (priority):* 5/1. *Notification date:* Continuous beginning 5/15.

CONTACT Ms. Patricia Garrett, Associate Director of Financial Aid, Columbus State University, 4225 University Avenue, Columbus, GA 31907-5645, 706-507-8800 or toll-free 866-264-2035. *Fax:* 706-568-2230. *E-mail:* garrett_patricia2@columbusstate.edu. *Website:* http://www.columbusstate.edu/.

COMPASS COLLEGE OF CINEMATIC ARTS
Grand Rapids, MI

CONTACT Financial Aid Office, Compass College of Cinematic Arts, 41 Sheldon Boulevard SE, Grand Rapids, MI 49503, 616-988-1000. *Website:* http://www.compass.edu/.

CONCEPTION SEMINARY COLLEGE
Conception, MO

Tuition & fees: $21,576	Average undergraduate aid package: $30,220

ABOUT THE INSTITUTION Independent Roman Catholic, men only. *Awards:* certificates and bachelor's degrees. 3 undergraduate majors. *Total enrollment:* 67. Undergraduates: 67. Freshmen: 14. Federal methodology is used as a basis for awarding need-based institutional aid.

UNDERGRADUATE EXPENSES for 2018–2019 *Comprehensive fee:* $34,385 includes full-time tuition ($21,326), mandatory fees ($250), and room and board ($12,809). *College room only:* $5358. *Part-time tuition:* $200 per credit hour.

FRESHMAN FINANCIAL AID (Fall 2016) 4 applied for aid; of those 100% were deemed to have need. 100% of freshmen with need received aid; of those 25% had need fully met. *Average percent of need met:* 69% (excluding resources awarded to replace EFC). *Average financial aid package:* $23,285 (excluding resources awarded to replace EFC). 20% of all full-time freshmen had no need and received non-need-based gift aid.

UNDERGRADUATE FINANCIAL AID (Fall 2016) 35 applied for aid; of those 69% were deemed to have need. 100% of undergraduates with need received aid; of those 4% had need fully met. *Average percent of need met:* 90% (excluding resources awarded to replace EFC). *Average financial aid package:* $30,220 (excluding resources awarded to replace EFC). 24% of all full-time undergraduates had no need and received non-need-based gift aid.

GIFT AID (NEED-BASED) *Total amount:* $625,905 (23% federal, 6% institutional, 71% external sources). *Receiving aid:* Freshmen: 80% (4); all full-time undergraduates: 26% (24). *Average award:* Freshmen: $7535; Undergraduates: $6347. *Scholarships, grants, and awards:* Federal Pell, FSEOG, private, college/university gift aid from institutional funds.

GIFT AID (NON-NEED-BASED) *Total amount:* $2,459,431 (2% institutional, 98% external sources). *Receiving aid:* Freshmen: 80% (4). Undergraduates: 13% (12). *Average award:* Freshmen: $1500. Undergraduates: $2016. *Scholarships, grants, and awards by category:* Academic interests/achievement: 15 awards ($6750 total): general academic interests/achievements. *Special characteristics:* 26 awards ($101,424 total): religious affiliation. *Tuition waivers:* Full or partial for employees or children of employees.

LOANS *Student loans:* $230,044 (44% need-based, 56% non-need-based). 67% of past graduating class borrowed through all loan programs. *Average indebtedness per student:* $31,817. *Average need-based loan:* Freshmen: $3500. Undergraduates: $4941. *Parent loans:* $15,567 (100% non-need-based). *Programs:* Federal Direct (Subsidized and Unsubsidized Stafford, PLUS).

WORK-STUDY *Federal work-study:* 20 jobs averaging $876. *State or other work-study/employment:* Total amount: $33,213 (100% non-need-based). 34 part-time jobs averaging $977.

APPLYING FOR FINANCIAL AID *Required financial aid form:* FAFSA. *Financial aid deadline:* Continuous. *Notification date:* Continuous beginning 6/1. Students must reply within 4 weeks of notification.

CONTACT Br. Justin Hernandez, PhD, Financial Aid Director, Conception Seminary College, 37174 State Highway VV, Conception, MO 64433-0502, 660-944-2851. *Fax:* 660-944-2829. *E-mail:* financialaid@conception.edu. *Website:* http://www.conception.edu/.

CONCORDIA COLLEGE
Moorhead, MN

Tuition & fees: $38,378	Average undergraduate aid package: $29,701

ABOUT THE INSTITUTION Independent Evangelical Lutheran Church in America, coed. *Awards:* bachelor's and master's degrees. 55 undergraduate majors. *Total enrollment:* 2,132. Undergraduates: 2,114. Freshmen: 545. Federal methodology is used as a basis for awarding need-based institutional aid.

UNDERGRADUATE EXPENSES for 2017–2018 *Application fee:* $20. *Comprehensive fee:* $46,418 includes full-time tuition ($38,150), mandatory fees ($228), and room and board ($8040). *College room only:* $3460. Full-time tuition and fees vary according to course load and degree level. Room and board charges vary according to board plan and housing facility. *Part-time tuition:* $1435 per credit. *Part-time fees:* $114 per term. Part-time tuition and fees vary according to course load and degree level.

FRESHMAN FINANCIAL AID (Fall 2016) 490 applied for aid; of those 84% were deemed to have need. 100% of freshmen with need received aid; of those 29% had need fully met. *Average percent of need met:* 92% (excluding resources awarded to replace EFC). *Average financial aid package:* $30,121 (excluding resources awarded to replace EFC). 24% of all full-time freshmen had no need and received non-need-based gift aid.

UNDERGRADUATE FINANCIAL AID (Fall 2016) 1,726 applied for aid; of those 86% were deemed to have need. 100% of undergraduates with need received aid; of those 22% had need fully met. *Average percent of need met:* 91% (excluding resources awarded to replace EFC). *Average financial aid package:* $29,701 (excluding resources awarded to replace EFC). 26% of all full-time undergraduates had no need and received non-need-based gift aid.

GIFT AID (NEED-BASED) *Total amount:* $32,244,421 (9% federal, 8% state, 81% institutional, 2% external sources). *Receiving aid:* Freshmen: 74% (405); all full-time undergraduates: 70% (1,449). *Average award:* Freshmen: $24,460; Undergraduates: $22,228. *Scholarships, grants, and awards:* Federal Pell, FSEOG, state, private, college/university gift aid from institutional funds.

GIFT AID (NON-NEED-BASED) *Total amount:* $10,722,634 (4% federal, 91% institutional, 5% external sources). *Receiving aid:* Freshmen: 16% (86). Undergraduates: 11% (235). *Average award:* Freshmen: $18,461. Undergraduates: $15,926. *Scholarships, grants, and awards by category: Academic interests/ achievement:* general academic interests/achievements. *Creative arts/performance:* art/fine arts, debating, music, theater/drama. *Special characteristics:* international students. *Tuition waivers:* Full or partial for employees or children of employees. *ROTC:* Army cooperative, Air Force cooperative.

LOANS *Student loans:* $16,606,225 (57% need-based, 43% non-need-based). 77% of past graduating class borrowed through all loan programs. *Average need-based loan:* Freshmen: $4260. Undergraduates: $5505. *Parent loans:* $1,587,792 (24% need-based, 76% non-need-based). *Programs:* Federal Direct (Subsidized and Unsubsidized Stafford, PLUS), state, college/university, private loans.

WORK-STUDY *Federal work-study:* jobs available. *State or other work-study/employment:* Total amount: $2,319,205 (12% need-based, 88% non-need-based). Part-time jobs available.

APPLYING FOR FINANCIAL AID *Required financial aid form:* FAFSA. *Financial aid deadline:* Continuous. *Notification date:* Continuous beginning 12/15. Students must reply within 6 weeks of notification.

CONTACT Mr. Eric Addington, Associate Vice President for Enrollment and Financial Aid, Concordia College, 901 South 8th Street, Moorhead, MN 56562, 218-299-3010 or toll-free 800-699-9897. *Fax:* 218-299-3025. *E-mail:* eaddingt@cord.edu. *Website:* http://www.concordiacollege.edu/.

CONCORDIA COLLEGE–NEW YORK
Bronxville, NY

CONTACT Janice Spikereit, Director of Financial Aid, Concordia College–New York, 171 White Plains Road, Bronxville, NY 10708, 914-337-9300 Ext. 2146 or toll-free 800-YES-COLLEGE. *Fax:* 914-395-4500. *E-mail:* financialaid@concordia-ny.edu. *Website:* http://www.concordia-ny.edu/.

CONCORDIA UNIVERSITY
Portland, OR

CONTACT Mr. Robert Clarke, Director of Financial Aid, Concordia University, 2811 Northeast Holman Street, Portland, OR 97211-6099, 503-493-6555 or toll-free 800-321-9371. *Fax:* 503-280-8661. *E-mail:* jcullen@cu-portland.edu. *Website:* http://www.cu-portland.edu/.

CONCORDIA UNIVERSITY ANN ARBOR
Ann Arbor, MI

ABOUT THE INSTITUTION Independent Lutheran Church–Missouri Synod, coed. 35 undergraduate majors.

GIFT AID (NEED-BASED) *Scholarships, grants, and awards:* Federal Pell, FSEOG, state, private, college/university gift aid from institutional funds.

GIFT AID (NON-NEED-BASED) *Scholarships, grants, and awards by category: Academic interests/achievement:* business, education, general academic interests/achievements, religion/biblical studies. *Creative arts/performance:* art/fine arts, music, performing arts, theater/drama. *Special characteristics:* children and siblings of alumni, children of faculty/staff, ethnic background, general special characteristics, out-of-state students, religious affiliation, siblings of current students.

LOANS *Programs:* Federal Direct (Subsidized and Unsubsidized Stafford, PLUS), Perkins.

WORK-STUDY *Federal work-study:* jobs available. *State or other work-study/employment:* Part-time jobs available.

APPLYING FOR FINANCIAL AID *Required financial aid form:* FAFSA.

CONTACT Vicki Waschow, Financial Aid Office, Concordia University Ann Arbor, 4090 Geddes Road, Ann Arbor, MI 48105-2797, 734-995-7408 or toll-free 877-995-7520 (in-state), 877-955-7520 (out-of-state). *Fax:* 734-995-4610. *E-mail:* vicki.waschow@cuaa.edu. *Website:* http://www.cuaa.edu/.

CONCORDIA UNIVERSITY CHICAGO
River Forest, IL

Tuition & fees: $32,078	Average undergraduate aid package: $21,475

ABOUT THE INSTITUTION Independent Lutheran Church–Missouri Synod, coed. *Awards:* certificates, associate, bachelor's, master's, and doctoral degrees. 72 undergraduate majors. *Total enrollment:* 5,700. Undergraduates: 1,413. Freshmen: 327. Federal methodology is used as a basis for awarding need-based institutional aid.

UNDERGRADUATE EXPENSES for 2018–2019 *Comprehensive fee:* $41,826 includes full-time tuition ($31,146), mandatory fees ($932), and room and board ($9748). *College room only:* $6126. Full-time tuition and fees vary according to course load, degree level, and reciprocity agreements. Room and board charges vary according to board plan and housing facility. *Part-time tuition:* $937 per credit hour. Part-time tuition and fees vary according to course load, degree level, and reciprocity agreements.

FRESHMAN FINANCIAL AID (Fall 2016) 349 applied for aid; of those 91% were deemed to have need. 99% of freshmen with need received aid; of those 22% had need fully met. *Average percent of need met:* 84% (excluding resources awarded to replace EFC). *Average financial aid package:* $24,093 (excluding resources

awarded to replace EFC) 10% of all full time freshman had no need and received non-need-based gift aid.

UNDERGRADUATE FINANCIAL AID (Fall 2016) 1,273 applied for aid; of those 92% were deemed to have need. 100% of undergraduates with need received aid; of those 17% had need fully met. *Average percent of need met:* 78% (excluding resources awarded to replace EFC). *Average financial aid package:* $21,475 (excluding resources awarded to replace EFC). 11% of all full-time undergraduates had no need and received non-need-based gift aid.

GIFT AID (NEED-BASED) *Total amount:* $20,026,649 (14% federal, 11% state, 75% institutional). *Receiving aid:* Freshmen: 89% (317); all full-time undergraduates: 83% (1,135). *Average award:* Freshmen: $20,557; Undergraduates: $17,530. *Scholarships, grants, and awards:* Federal Pell, FSEOG, state, private, college/university gift aid from institutional funds.

GIFT AID (NON-NEED-BASED) *Total amount:* $3,671,196 (87% institutional, 13% external sources). *Receiving aid:* Freshmen: 14% (50). Undergraduates: 10% (137). *Average award:* Freshmen: $16,732. Undergraduates: $14,270. *Scholarships, grants, and awards by category: Academic interests/achievement:* biological sciences, business, communication, computer science, education, English, foreign languages, general academic interests/achievements, mathematics, religion/biblical studies. *Creative arts/performance:* music. *Special characteristics:* children and siblings of alumni, children of faculty/staff, international students, religious affiliation. *Tuition waivers:* Full or partial for children of alumni, employees or children of employees, senior citizens.

LOANS *Student loans:* $8,715,303 (44% need-based, 56% non-need-based). 81% of past graduating class borrowed through all loan programs. *Average indebtedness per student:* $22,804. *Average need-based loan:* Freshmen: $3088. Undergraduates: $4240. *Parent loans:* $1,792,798 (100% non-need-based). *Programs:* Federal Direct (Subsidized and Unsubsidized Stafford, PLUS), Perkins.

WORK-STUDY *Federal work-study:* jobs available. *State or other work-study/employment:* Total amount: $763,383 (100% non-need-based). Part-time jobs available.

APPLYING FOR FINANCIAL AID *Required financial aid form:* FAFSA. *Financial aid deadline:* 6/1 (priority: 12/1). *Notification date:* Continuous beginning 12/15.

CONTACT Aida Asencio-Pinto, Director of Financial Aid, Concordia University Chicago, 7400 Augusta Street, River Forest, IL 60305-1499, 708-209-3113 or toll-free 800-285-2668. *Fax:* 708-488-4102. *E-mail:* aida.asenciopinto@cuchicago.edu. *Website:* http://www.cuchicago.edu/.

CONCORDIA UNIVERSITY IRVINE
Irvine, CA

Tuition & fees: $35,400	Average undergraduate aid package: $22,186

ABOUT THE INSTITUTION Independent Lutheran Church–Missouri Synod, coed. *Awards:* associate, bachelor's, master's, and doctoral degrees (associate's degree for international students only). 29 undergraduate majors. *Total enrollment:* 4,249. Undergraduates: 1,853. Freshmen: 328. Federal methodology is used as a basis for awarding need-based institutional aid.

UNDERGRADUATE EXPENSES for 2018–2019 *Application fee:* $50. *Comprehensive fee:* $46,700 includes full-time tuition ($34,700), mandatory fees ($700), and room and board ($11,300). *College room only:* $6510. Full-time tuition and fees vary according to course load. Room and board charges vary according to board plan and housing facility. Part-time tuition and fees vary according to course load.

FRESHMAN FINANCIAL AID (Fall 2017, est.) 285 applied for aid; of those 85% were deemed to have need. 100% of freshmen with need received aid; of those 14% had need fully met. *Average percent of need met:* 71% (excluding resources awarded to replace EFC). *Average financial aid package:* $25,612 (excluding resources awarded to replace EFC). 18% of all full-time freshmen had no need and received non-need-based gift aid.

UNDERGRADUATE FINANCIAL AID (Fall 2017, est.) 1,310 applied for aid; of those 88% were deemed to have need. 99% of undergraduates with need received aid; of those 13% had need fully met. *Average percent of need met:* 61% (excluding resources awarded to replace EFC). *Average financial aid package:* $22,186 (excluding resources awarded to replace EFC). 17% of all full-time undergraduates had no need and received non-need-based gift aid.

GIFT AID (NEED-BASED) *Total amount:* $17,875,102 (14% federal, 16% state, 70% institutional). *Receiving aid:* Freshmen: 74% (242); all full-time undergraduates:

61% (1,006). *Average award:* Freshmen: $21,459; Undergraduates: $19,406. *Scholarships, grants, and awards:* Federal Pell, FSEOG, state, private, college/university gift aid from institutional funds.

GIFT AID (NON-NEED-BASED) *Total amount:* $4,679,101 (100% institutional). *Receiving aid:* Freshmen: 9% (29). Undergraduates: 6% (97). *Average award:* Freshmen: $10,228. Undergraduates: $10,787. *Scholarships, grants, and awards by category: Academic interests/achievement:* 952 awards ($8,725,538 total): general academic interests/achievements. *Creative arts/performance:* 245 awards ($1,595,026 total): debating, music, theater/drama. *Special characteristics:* 303 awards ($1,817,178 total): children of faculty/staff, first-generation college students, religious affiliation. *Tuition waivers:* Full or partial for employees or children of employees.

LOANS *Student loans:* $12,029,682 (35% need-based, 65% non-need-based). 72% of past graduating class borrowed through all loan programs. *Average indebtedness per student:* $32,754. *Average need-based loan:* Freshmen: $3409. Undergraduates: $4515. *Parent loans:* $4,688,412 (100% non-need-based). *Programs:* Federal Direct (Subsidized and Unsubsidized Stafford, PLUS), private loans.

WORK-STUDY *Federal work-study:* Total amount: $190,000; 86 jobs averaging $2238. *State or other work-study/employment:* Part-time jobs available.

ATHLETIC AWARDS Total amount: $3,722,231 (52% need-based, 48% non-need-based).

APPLYING FOR FINANCIAL AID *Required financial aid forms:* FAFSA, state aid form, department scholarship application form. *Financial aid deadline:* 3/2. *Notification date:* Continuous beginning 11/1. Students must reply within 4 weeks of notification.

CONTACT Lori McDonald, Director of Financial Aid, Concordia University Irvine, 1530 Concordia West, Irvine, CA 92612-3299, 949-214-3074 or toll-free 800-229-1200. *Fax:* 949-214-3500. *E-mail:* lori.mcdonald@cui.edu. *Website:* http://www.cui.edu/.

CONCORDIA UNIVERSITY, NEBRASKA
Seward, NE

Tuition & fees: $32,220	Average undergraduate aid package: $25,229

ABOUT THE INSTITUTION Independent Lutheran Church–Missouri Synod, coed. *Awards:* bachelor's and master's degrees. 47 undergraduate majors. *Total enrollment:* 2,520. Undergraduates: 1,684. Freshmen: 348. Federal methodology is used as a basis for awarding need-based institutional aid.

UNDERGRADUATE EXPENSES for 2018–2019 *Comprehensive fee:* $40,690 includes full-time tuition ($31,620), mandatory fees ($600), and room and board ($8470). *College room only:* $3570. Room and board charges vary according to board plan and housing facility. *Part-time tuition:* $925 per credit hour. *Part-time fees:* $150 per term.

FRESHMAN FINANCIAL AID (Fall 2017, est.) 323 applied for aid; of those 89% were deemed to have need. 100% of freshmen with need received aid; of those 29% had need fully met. *Average percent of need met:* 83% (excluding resources awarded to replace EFC). *Average financial aid package:* $26,541 (excluding resources awarded to replace EFC). 5% of all full-time freshmen had no need and received non-need-based gift aid.

UNDERGRADUATE FINANCIAL AID (Fall 2017, est.) 1,057 applied for aid; of those 89% were deemed to have need. 100% of undergraduates with need received aid; of those 26% had need fully met. *Average percent of need met:* 82% (excluding resources awarded to replace EFC). *Average financial aid package:* $25,229 (excluding resources awarded to replace EFC). 8% of all full-time undergraduates had no need and received non-need-based gift aid.

GIFT AID (NEED-BASED) *Total amount:* $17,026,611 (10% federal, 1% state, 78% institutional, 11% external sources). *Receiving aid:* Freshmen: 82% (286); all full-time undergraduates: 76% (940). *Average award:* Freshmen: $22,147; Undergraduates: $20,584. *Scholarships, grants, and awards:* Federal Pell, FSEOG, state, private, college/university gift aid from institutional funds.

GIFT AID (NON-NEED-BASED) *Total amount:* $5,004,855 (100% institutional). *Receiving aid:* Freshmen: 19% (67). Undergraduates: 14% (175). *Average award:* Freshmen: $18,275. Undergraduates: $16,989. *Scholarships, grants, and awards by category: Academic interests/achievement:* biological sciences, business, communication, computer science, education, English, general academic interests/achievements, health fields, humanities, mathematics, physical sciences, premedicine,

---

religion/biblical studies, social sciences. *Creative arts/performance:* applied art and design, art/fine arts, dance, debating, music, theater/drama. *Special achievements/activities:* cheerleading/drum major. *Special characteristics:* children and siblings of alumni, children of educators, children of faculty/staff, international students, local/state students, members of minority groups, religious affiliation, veterans, veterans' children. *Tuition waivers:* Full or partial for employees or children of employees. *ROTC:* Army cooperative, Air Force cooperative.

LOANS *Student loans:* $6,380,821 (44% need-based, 56% non-need-based). 65% of past graduating class borrowed through all loan programs. *Average indebtedness per student:* $27,722. *Average need-based loan:* Freshmen: $3612. Undergraduates: $4392. *Parent loans:* $1,896,649 (100% non-need-based). *Programs:* Federal Direct (Subsidized and Unsubsidized Stafford, PLUS), Perkins.

WORK-STUDY *Federal work-study:* Total amount: $175,000; jobs available.

ATHLETIC AWARDS Total amount: $3,775,300 (74% need-based, 26% non-need-based).

APPLYING FOR FINANCIAL AID *Required financial aid form:* FAFSA. *Financial aid deadline (priority):* 3/1. *Notification date:* Continuous beginning 3/1. Students must reply within 4 weeks of notification.

CONTACT Mr. Aaron W. Roberts, Director of Undergraduate Admissions, Concordia University, Nebraska, 800 North Columbia Avenue, Seward, NE 68434-1556, 800-535-5494. *Fax:* 402-643-4073. *E-mail:* admiss@cune.edu. *Website:* http://www.cune.edu/.

CONCORDIA UNIVERSITY, ST. PAUL
St. Paul, MN

Tuition & fees: $22,775	Average undergraduate aid package: $14,920

ABOUT THE INSTITUTION Independent Lutheran Church–Missouri Synod, coed. *Awards:* certificates, associate, bachelor's, master's, and doctoral degrees. 60 undergraduate majors. *Total enrollment:* 4,792. Undergraduates: 2,851. Freshmen: 246. Federal methodology is used as a basis for awarding need-based institutional aid.

UNDERGRADUATE EXPENSES for 2018–2019 *Comprehensive fee:* $31,775 includes full-time tuition ($22,775) and room and board ($9000). Full-time tuition and fees vary according to degree level and program. Room and board charges vary according to board plan and housing facility. *Part-time tuition:* $600 per credit. Part-time tuition and fees vary according to course load, degree level, and program.

FRESHMAN FINANCIAL AID (Fall 2017, est.) 239 applied for aid; of those 84% were deemed to have need. 100% of freshmen with need received aid; of those 16% had need fully met. *Average percent of need met:* 70% (excluding resources awarded to replace EFC). *Average financial aid package:* $17,906 (excluding resources awarded to replace EFC). 7% of all full-time freshmen had no need and received non-need-based gift aid.

UNDERGRADUATE FINANCIAL AID (Fall 2017, est.) 1,201 applied for aid; of those 87% were deemed to have need. 98% of undergraduates with need received aid; of those 11% had need fully met. *Average percent of need met:* 58% (excluding resources awarded to replace EFC). *Average financial aid package:* $14,920 (excluding resources awarded to replace EFC). 9% of all full-time undergraduates had no need and received non-need-based gift aid.

GIFT AID (NEED-BASED) *Total amount:* $12,637,929 (39% federal, 26% state, 34% institutional, 1% external sources). *Receiving aid:* Freshmen: 82% (200); all full-time undergraduates: 72% (983). *Average award:* Freshmen: $12,919; Undergraduates: $10,647. *Scholarships, grants, and awards:* Federal Pell, FSEOG, state, private, college/university gift aid from institutional funds.

GIFT AID (NON-NEED-BASED) *Total amount:* $1,479,210 (1% federal, 1% state, 98% institutional). *Receiving aid:* Freshmen: 10% (25). Undergraduates: 5% (72). *Average award:* Freshmen: $6911. Undergraduates: $5614. *Scholarships, grants, and awards by category:* Academic interests/achievement: 1,060 awards ($3,985,529 total): general academic interests/achievements, religion/biblical studies. *Creative arts/performance:* 129 awards ($117,500 total): music, theater/drama. *Special characteristics:* 265 awards ($508,546 total): children of faculty/staff, religious affiliation, veterans, veterans' children. *Tuition waivers:* Full or partial for employees or children of employees. *ROTC:* Army cooperative, Air Force cooperative.

LOANS *Student loans:* $16,403,051 (40% need-based, 60% non-need-based). 73% of past graduating class borrowed through all loan programs. *Average indebtedness per student:* $34,686. *Average need-based loan:* Freshmen: $3450. Undergrad-

uates: $4486. *Parent loans:* $1,260,780 (100% non-need-based). *Programs:* Federal Direct (Subsidized and Unsubsidized Stafford, PLUS), Perkins, state, private loans.

WORK-STUDY *Federal work-study:* Total amount: $131,937; 98 jobs averaging $2253. *State or other work-study/employment:* Total amount: $538,271 (100% need-based). 290 part-time jobs averaging $2547.

ATHLETIC AWARDS Total amount: $2,292,228 (60% need-based, 40% non-need-based).

APPLYING FOR FINANCIAL AID *Required financial aid forms:* FAFSA, state aid form. *Financial aid deadline (priority):* 5/1. *Notification date:* Continuous beginning 5/10.

CONTACT Ms. Jeanie Peck, Financial Aid Director, Concordia University, St. Paul, 1282 Concordia Avenue, St. Paul, MN 55104-5494, 651-603-6300 or toll-free 800-333-4705. *Fax:* 651-603-6298. *E-mail:* finaid@csp.edu. *Website:* http://www.csp.edu/.

CONCORDIA UNIVERSITY TEXAS
Austin, TX

Tuition & fees: N/R	Average undergraduate aid package: $23,566

ABOUT THE INSTITUTION Independent Lutheran Church–Missouri Synod, coed. 24 undergraduate majors. Federal methodology is used as a basis for awarding need-based institutional aid.

FRESHMAN FINANCIAL AID (Fall 2017, est.) 260 applied for aid; of those 85% were deemed to have need. 100% of freshmen with need received aid; of those 15% had need fully met. *Average percent of need met:* 77% (excluding resources awarded to replace EFC). *Average financial aid package:* $26,924 (excluding resources awarded to replace EFC). 18% of all full-time freshmen had no need and received non-need-based gift aid.

UNDERGRADUATE FINANCIAL AID (Fall 2017, est.) 1,127 applied for aid; of those 91% were deemed to have need. 99% of undergraduates with need received aid; of those 16% had need fully met. *Average percent of need met:* 72% (excluding resources awarded to replace EFC). *Average financial aid package:* $23,566 (excluding resources awarded to replace EFC). 17% of all full-time undergraduates had no need and received non-need-based gift aid.

GIFT AID (NEED-BASED) *Total amount:* $18,956,897 (18% federal, 13% state, 69% institutional). *Receiving aid:* Freshmen: 81% (221); all full-time undergraduates: 75% (988). *Average award:* Freshmen: $20,721; Undergraduates: $18,127. *Scholarships, grants, and awards:* Federal Pell, FSEOG, state, private, college/university gift aid from institutional funds.

GIFT AID (NON-NEED-BASED) *Total amount:* $3,951,587 (100% institutional). *Receiving aid:* Freshmen: 11% (30). Undergraduates: 10% (130). *Average award:* Freshmen: $15,450. Undergraduates: $13,856. *Scholarships, grants, and awards by category:* Academic interests/achievement: biological sciences, business, communication, computer science, education, English, foreign languages, general academic interests/achievements, home economics, international studies, mathematics, physical sciences, religion/biblical studies, social sciences. *Creative arts/performance:* music. *Special achievements/activities:* junior miss, religious involvement. *Special characteristics:* adult students, children and siblings of alumni, children of faculty/staff, international students, religious affiliation, siblings of current students, veterans, veterans' children.

LOANS *Student loans:* $10,291,969 (55% need-based, 45% non-need-based). 77% of past graduating class borrowed through all loan programs. *Average indebtedness per student:* $32,509. *Average need-based loan:* Freshmen: $5051. Undergraduates: $6276. *Parent loans:* $3,187,452 (100% non-need-based). *Programs:* Federal Direct (Subsidized and Unsubsidized Stafford, PLUS), state.

WORK-STUDY *Federal work-study:* Total amount: $598,759; 92 jobs averaging $2716.

APPLYING FOR FINANCIAL AID *Required financial aid forms:* FAFSA, state aid form. *Financial aid deadline:* Continuous. *Notification date:* Continuous beginning 2/1. Students must reply within 2 weeks of notification.

CONTACT Mr. Russell Jeffrey, Director of Student Financial Services, Concordia University Texas, 11400 Concordia University Drive, Austin, TX 78726, 512-313-4672 or toll-free 800-865-4282. *Fax:* 512-313-1670. *E-mail:* russell.jeffrey@concordia.edu. *Website:* http://www.concordia.edu/.

CONCORDIA UNIVERSITY WISCONSIN
Mequon, WI

Tuition & fees: $28,600	Average undergraduate aid package: $21,208

ABOUT THE INSTITUTION Independent Lutheran Church–Missouri Synod, coed. *Awards:* certificates, associate, bachelor's, master's, and doctoral degrees. 73 undergraduate majors. *Total enrollment:* 7,288. Undergraduates: 3,709. Freshmen: 558. Federal methodology is used as a basis for awarding need-based institutional aid.

UNDERGRADUATE EXPENSES for 2017–2018 *Comprehensive fee:* $39,130 includes full-time tuition ($28,330), mandatory fees ($270), and room and board ($10,530). *College room only:* $7970. Full-time tuition and fees vary according to program. Room and board charges vary according to board plan. Part-time tuition and fees vary according to program.

FRESHMAN FINANCIAL AID (Fall 2016) 454 applied for aid; of those 86% were deemed to have need. 100% of freshmen with need received aid; of those 33% had need fully met. *Average percent of need met:* 80% (excluding resources awarded to replace EFC). *Average financial aid package:* $24,318 (excluding resources awarded to replace EFC). 17% of all full-time freshmen had no need and received non-need-based gift aid.

UNDERGRADUATE FINANCIAL AID (Fall 2016) 2,287 applied for aid; of those 88% were deemed to have need. 100% of undergraduates with need received aid; of those 25% had need fully met. *Average percent of need met:* 71% (excluding resources awarded to replace EFC). *Average financial aid package:* $21,208 (excluding resources awarded to replace EFC). 16% of all full-time undergraduates had no need and received non-need-based gift aid.

GIFT AID (NEED-BASED) *Total amount:* $57,057,087 (17% federal, 8% state, 70% institutional, 5% external sources). *Receiving aid:* Freshmen: 78% (373); all full-time undergraduates: 74% (1,857). *Average award:* Freshmen: $16,404; Undergraduates: $13,500. *Scholarships, grants, and awards:* Federal Pell, FSEOG, state, private, college/university gift aid from institutional funds.

GIFT AID (NON-NEED-BASED) *Total amount:* $15,884,771 (100% institutional). *Receiving aid:* Freshmen: 24% (116). Undergraduates: 18% (442). *Average award:* Freshmen: $12,481. Undergraduates: $11,364. *Scholarships, grants, and awards by category: Academic interests/achievement:* religion/biblical studies. *Creative arts/performance:* music. *Special characteristics:* out-of-state students.

LOANS *Student loans:* $51,335,881 (60% need-based, 40% non-need-based). 83% of past graduating class borrowed through all loan programs. *Average indebtedness per student:* $33,298. *Average need-based loan:* Freshmen: $7197. Undergraduates: $7753. *Parent loans:* $9,167,308 (100% non-need-based). *Programs:* Federal Direct (Subsidized and Unsubsidized Stafford, PLUS), state.

WORK-STUDY *Federal work-study:* jobs available.

APPLYING FOR FINANCIAL AID *Required financial aid form:* FAFSA. *Financial aid deadline:* 4/15 (priority: 3/15). *Notification date:* Continuous beginning 2/15. Students must reply within 3 weeks of notification.

CONTACT Mr. Steven P. Taylor, Director of Financial Aid, Concordia University Wisconsin, 12800 North Lake Shore Drive, Mequon, WI 53097-2402, 262-243-4392 or toll-free 888-628-9472. *Fax:* 262-243-2992. *E-mail:* steve.taylor@cuw.edu. *Website:* http://www.cuw.edu/.

CONCORD UNIVERSITY
Athens, WV

Tuition & fees (WV res): $7732	Average undergraduate aid package: $8471

ABOUT THE INSTITUTION State-supported, coed. *Awards:* certificates, bachelor's, and master's degrees. 31 undergraduate majors. *Total enrollment:* 2,194. Undergraduates: 1,853. Freshmen: 434. Federal methodology is used as a basis for awarding need-based institutional aid.

UNDERGRADUATE EXPENSES for 2017–2018 *Tuition, state resident:* full-time $7574; part-time $316 per credit hour. *Tuition, nonresident:* full-time $16,654; part-time $694 per credit hour. *Required fees:* full-time $158. Full-time tuition and fees vary according to course load and program. Part-time tuition and fees vary according to course load and program. *College room and board:* $8642. Room and board charges vary according to board plan.

FRESHMAN FINANCIAL AID (Fall 2017, est.) 398 applied for aid; of those 87% were deemed to have need. 86% of freshmen with need received aid; of those 52% had need fully met. *Average percent of need met:* 87% (excluding resources awarded to replace EFC). *Average financial aid package:* $8000 (excluding resources awarded to replace EFC). 16% of all full-time freshmen had no need and received non-need-based gift aid.

UNDERGRADUATE FINANCIAL AID (Fall 2017, est.) 1,520 applied for aid; of those 85% were deemed to have need. 89% of undergraduates with need received aid; of those 52% had need fully met. *Average percent of need met:* 86% (excluding resources awarded to replace EFC). *Average financial aid package:* $8471 (excluding resources awarded to replace EFC). 13% of all full-time undergraduates had no need and received non-need-based gift aid.

GIFT AID (NEED-BASED) *Total amount:* $6,146,469 (70% federal, 26% state, 1% institutional, 3% external sources). *Receiving aid:* Freshmen: 61% (263); all full-time undergraduates: 61% (1,033). *Average award:* Freshmen: $5589; Undergraduates: $5843. *Scholarships, grants, and awards:* Federal Pell, FSEOG, state, private, college/university gift aid from institutional funds.

GIFT AID (NON-NEED-BASED) *Total amount:* $4,645,183 (31% state, 42% institutional, 27% external sources). *Receiving aid:* Freshmen: 64% (272). Undergraduates: 47% (799). *Average award:* Freshmen: $3588. Undergraduates: $3578. *Scholarships, grants, and awards by category: Academic interests/achievement:* 1,797 awards ($1,064,508 total): business, communication, education, English, general academic interests/achievements, mathematics, physical sciences, pre-medicine, social sciences. *Creative arts/performance:* 53 awards ($90,828 total): art/fine arts, journalism/publications, music, theater/drama. *Special achievements/activities:* 12 awards ($5750 total): community service, general special achievements/activities, leadership. *Special characteristics:* 33 awards ($146,113 total): children of faculty/staff, veterans, veterans' children. *Tuition waivers:* Full or partial for employees or children of employees.

LOANS *Student loans:* $7,631,224 (39% need-based, 61% non-need-based). 89% of past graduating class borrowed through all loan programs. *Average indebtedness per student:* $21,176. *Average need-based loan:* Freshmen: $2600. Undergraduates: $3179. *Parent loans:* $765,191 (100% non-need-based). *Programs:* Federal Direct (Subsidized and Unsubsidized Stafford, PLUS), Perkins.

WORK-STUDY *Federal work-study:* Total amount: $324,859; 184 jobs averaging $1765.

ATHLETIC AWARDS Total amount: $1,576,604 (100% non-need-based).

APPLYING FOR FINANCIAL AID *Required financial aid forms:* FAFSA, institution's own form, state aid form, verification worksheet. *Financial aid deadline:* 4/15. *Notification date:* Continuous beginning 5/15. Students must reply within 3 weeks of notification.

CONTACT Tammy Brown, Director of Financial Aid, Concord University, PO Box 1000, Athens, WV 24712-1000, 304-384-5358 or toll-free 888-384-5249. *Fax:* 304-384-3084. *E-mail:* tbrown@concord.edu. *Website:* http://www.concord.edu/.

CONNECTICUT COLLEGE
New London, CT

Tuition & fees: $52,850	Average undergraduate aid package: $42,988

ABOUT THE INSTITUTION Independent, coed. *Awards:* bachelor's degrees. 42 undergraduate majors. *Total enrollment:* 1,817. Undergraduates: 1,817. Freshmen: 444. Both federal and institutional methodology are used as a basis for awarding need-based institutional aid.

UNDERGRADUATE EXPENSES for 2017–2018 *Comprehensive fee:* $67,440 includes full-time tuition ($52,530), mandatory fees ($320), and room and board ($14,590). *College room only:* $8420. *Part-time tuition:* $1563 per credit hour.

FRESHMAN FINANCIAL AID (Fall 2017, est.) 316 applied for aid; of those 86% were deemed to have need. 100% of freshmen with need received aid; of those 100% had need fully met. *Average percent of need met:* 100% (excluding resources awarded to replace EFC). *Average financial aid package:* $40,993 (excluding resources awarded to replace EFC). 24% of all full-time freshmen had no need and received non-need-based gift aid.

UNDERGRADUATE FINANCIAL AID (Fall 2017, est.) 1,122 applied for aid; of those 91% were deemed to have need. 100% of undergraduates with need received aid; of those 100% had need fully met. *Average percent of need met:* 100% (excluding resources awarded to replace EFC). *Average financial aid package:* $42,988 (excluding resources awarded to replace EFC). 6% of all full-time undergraduates had no need and received non-need-based gift aid.

GIFT AID (NEED-BASED) *Total amount:* $38,592,022 (4% federal, 94% institutional, 2% external sources). *Receiving aid:* Freshmen: 58% (260); all full-time undergraduates: 55% (977). *Average award:* Freshmen: $38,878; Undergraduates: $39,433. *Scholarships, grants, and awards:* Federal Pell, FSEOG, state, college/university gift aid from institutional funds.

GIFT AID (NON-NEED-BASED) *Total amount:* $2,835,226 (69% institutional, 31% external sources). *Receiving aid:* Freshmen: 11% (50). Undergraduates: 3% (50). *Average award:* Freshmen: $13,114. Undergraduates: $13,114. *Tuition waivers:* Full or partial for employees or children of employees.

LOANS *Student loans:* $8,248,849 (45% need-based, 55% non-need-based). 46% of past graduating class borrowed through all loan programs. *Average indebtedness per student:* $31,884. *Average need-based loan:* Freshmen: $3249. Undergraduates: $4383. *Parent loans:* $2,664,816 (100% non-need-based). *Programs:* Federal Direct (Subsidized and Unsubsidized Stafford, PLUS), college/university.

WORK-STUDY *Federal work-study:* Total amount: $1,605,598; jobs available.

APPLYING FOR FINANCIAL AID *Required financial aid forms:* FAFSA, CSS Financial Aid PROFILE, noncustodial (divorced/separated) parent's statement. *Financial aid deadline (priority):* 1/15. *Notification date:* 4/1. Students must reply by 5/1.

CONTACT Financial Aid Services Office, Connecticut College, 270 Mohegan Avenue, New London, CT 06320-4196, 860-439-2058. *Fax:* 860-439-5357. *E-mail:* finaid@conncoll.edu.
Website: http://www.conncoll.edu/.

CONSERVATORIO DE MUSICA DE PUERTO RICO
San Juan, PR

CONTACT Mr. Michael Rajaballey, Director of Financial Aid, Conservatorio de Musica de Puerto Rico, 951 Ave. Ponce de Leon, Miramar, San Juan, PR 00907, 787-751-0160 Ext. 231. *Fax:* 787-763-3886. *E-mail:* mrajaballey@cmpr.gobierno.pr. *Website:* http://www.cmpr.edu/.

CONVERSE COLLEGE
Spartanburg, SC

Tuition & fees: $18,030	Average undergraduate aid package: $14,724

ABOUT THE INSTITUTION Independent, undergraduate: women only; graduate: coed. *Awards:* certificates, bachelor's, and master's degrees. 49 undergraduate majors. *Total enrollment:* 1,319. Undergraduates: 870. Freshmen: 242. Federal methodology is used as a basis for awarding need-based institutional aid.

UNDERGRADUATE EXPENSES for 2018–2019 *Comprehensive fee:* $28,640 includes full-time tuition ($17,680), mandatory fees ($350), and room and board ($10,610). Full-time tuition and fees vary according to course load and program. Room and board charges vary according to board plan. *Part-time tuition:* $875 per credit. Part-time tuition and fees vary according to course load and program.

FRESHMAN FINANCIAL AID (Fall 2016) 231 applied for aid; of those 86% were deemed to have need. 99% of freshmen with need received aid; of those 17% had need fully met. *Average percent of need met:* 64% (excluding resources awarded to replace EFC). *Average financial aid package:* $15,526 (excluding resources awarded to replace EFC). 13% of all full-time freshmen had no need and received non-need-based gift aid.

UNDERGRADUATE FINANCIAL AID (Fall 2016) 772 applied for aid; of those 85% were deemed to have need. 98% of undergraduates with need received aid; of those 18% had need fully met. *Average percent of need met:* 62% (excluding resources awarded to replace EFC). *Average financial aid package:* $14,724

(excluding resources awarded to replace EFC). 16% of all full-time undergraduates had no need and received non-need-based gift aid.

GIFT AID (NEED-BASED) *Total amount:* $6,931,282 (25% federal, 42% state, 30% institutional, 3% external sources). *Receiving aid:* Freshmen: 63% (153); all full-time undergraduates: 62% (499). *Average award:* Freshmen: $12,688; Undergraduates: $11,504. *Scholarships, grants, and awards:* Federal Pell, FSEOG, state, private, college/university gift aid from institutional funds.

GIFT AID (NON-NEED-BASED) *Total amount:* $1,535,395 (42% state, 53% institutional, 5% external sources). *Receiving aid:* Freshmen: 10% (25). Undergraduates: 9% (74). *Average award:* Freshmen: $6225. Undergraduates: $5532. *Scholarships, grants, and awards by category:* Academic interests/achievement: 947 awards ($2,279,554 total): general academic interests/achievements. Creative arts/performance: 200 awards ($562,945 total): applied art and design, general creative arts/performance, music, theater/drama. Special characteristics: 6 awards ($27,060 total): children and siblings of alumni, children of faculty/staff. *Tuition waivers:* Full or partial for employees or children of employees. *ROTC:* Army cooperative.

LOANS *Student loans:* $8,354,234 (30% need-based, 70% non-need-based). 77% of past graduating class borrowed through all loan programs. *Average indebtedness per student:* $29,814. *Average need-based loan:* Freshmen: $3654. Undergraduates: $4352. *Parent loans:* $1,495,353 (100% non-need-based). *Programs:* Federal Direct (Subsidized and Unsubsidized Stafford, PLUS), Perkins, state.

WORK-STUDY *Federal work-study:* 62 jobs averaging $1339. *State or other work-study/employment:* Total amount: $148,754 (100% non-need-based). 90 part-time jobs averaging $1653.

ATHLETIC AWARDS Total amount: $830,290 (59% need-based, 41% non-need-based).

APPLYING FOR FINANCIAL AID *Required financial aid form:* FAFSA. *Financial aid deadline (priority):* 1/1. *Notification date:* Continuous beginning 3/15. Students must reply by 5/1 or within 2 weeks of notification.

CONTACT Mr. James W. Kellam, Director of Financial Planning, Converse College, 580 East Main Street, Spartanburg, SC 29302-0006, 864-596-9019 or toll-free 800-766-1125. *Fax:* 864-596-9749. *E-mail:* james.kellam@converse.edu. *Website:* http://www.converse.edu/.

COOPER UNION FOR THE ADVANCEMENT OF SCIENCE AND ART
New York, NY

Tuition & fees: N/R	Average undergraduate aid package: $47,735

ABOUT THE INSTITUTION Independent, coed. *Awards:* certificates, bachelor's, and master's degrees (also offers master's program primarily made up of currently-enrolled students). 7 undergraduate majors. *Total enrollment:* 941. Undergraduates: 867. Freshmen: 191. Federal methodology is used as a basis for awarding need-based institutional aid.

UNDERGRADUATE EXPENSES for 2018–2019 *Application fee:* $75. *Tuition:* part-time $1310 per credit hour. *Required fees:* $1075 per term. Full-time tuition and fees vary according to degree level and reciprocity agreements. Part-time tuition and fees vary according to degree level and reciprocity agreements. Room and board charges vary according to housing facility.

FRESHMAN FINANCIAL AID (Fall 2017, est.) 132 applied for aid; of those 77% were deemed to have need. 100% of freshmen with need received aid; of those 21% had need fully met. *Average percent of need met:* 74% (excluding resources awarded to replace EFC). *Average financial aid package:* $46,706 (excluding resources awarded to replace EFC). 47% of all full-time freshmen had no need and received non-need-based gift aid.

UNDERGRADUATE FINANCIAL AID (Fall 2017, est.) 497 applied for aid; of those 83% were deemed to have need. 100% of undergraduates with need received aid; of those 39% had need fully met. *Average percent of need met:* 76% (excluding resources awarded to replace EFC). *Average financial aid package:* $47,735 (excluding resources awarded to replace EFC). 51% of all full-time undergraduates had no need and received non-need-based gift aid.

GIFT AID (NEED-BASED) *Total amount:* $30,883,994 (4% federal, 1% state, 94% institutional, 1% external sources). *Receiving aid:* Freshmen: 53% (101); all full-time undergraduates: 49% (413). *Average award:* Freshmen: $24,749; Undergrad-

uates: $25,221. *Scholarships, grants, and awards:* Federal Pell, FSEOG, state, private, college/university gift aid from institutional funds.

GIFT AID (NON-NEED-BASED) *Total amount:* $8,973,770 (98% institutional, 2% external sources). *Receiving aid:* Freshmen: 53% (101). Undergraduates: 49% (413). *Average award:* Freshmen: $22,930. Undergraduates: $24,338. *Scholarships, grants, and awards by category:* Academic interests/achievement: 592 awards ($17,404,346 total): architecture, engineering/technologies. *Creative arts/performance:* 267 awards ($7,362,347 total): art/fine arts. *Tuition waivers:* Full or partial for employees or children of employees.

LOANS *Student loans:* $1,947,076 (64% need-based, 36% non-need-based). 18% of past graduating class borrowed through all loan programs. *Average indebtedness per student:* $17,037. *Average need-based loan:* Freshmen: $3434. Undergraduates: $4529. *Parent loans:* $449,648 (69% need-based, 31% non-need-based). *Programs:* Federal Direct (Subsidized and Unsubsidized Stafford, PLUS), Perkins.

WORK-STUDY *Federal work-study:* Total amount: $36,000; 37 jobs averaging $902. *State or other work-study/employment:* Part-time jobs available.

APPLYING FOR FINANCIAL AID *Required financial aid form:* FAFSA. *Financial aid deadline:* Continuous. *Notification date:* Continuous beginning 12/1. Students must reply by 12/20 or within 2 weeks of notification.

CONTACT Mr. Charlie Xu, Director of Financial Aid, Cooper Union for the Advancement of Science and Art, 30 Cooper Square, New York, NY 10003-7120, 212-353-4043. *Fax:* 212-353-4343. *E-mail:* cxu@cooper.edu. *Website:* http://www.cooper.edu/.

COPPIN STATE UNIVERSITY
Baltimore, MD

CONTACT Ms. Thelma Ross, Director of Financial Aid, Coppin State University, 2500 West North Avenue, Baltimore, MD 21216-3698, 410-951-3633 or toll-free 800-635-3674. *Fax:* 410-951-3637. *E-mail:* thross@coppin.edu. *Website:* http://www.coppin.edu/.

CORBAN UNIVERSITY
Salem, OR

Tuition & fees: $33,040	Average undergraduate aid package: $22,273

ABOUT THE INSTITUTION Independent Christian, coed. *Awards:* associate, bachelor's, master's, and doctoral degrees. 44 undergraduate majors. *Total enrollment:* 1,187. Undergraduates: 1,021. Freshmen: 197. Federal methodology is used as a basis for awarding need-based institutional aid.

UNDERGRADUATE EXPENSES for 2018–2019 *Application fee:* $40. *One-time required fee:* $150. *Comprehensive fee:* $43,271 includes full-time tuition ($32,380), mandatory fees ($660), and room and board ($10,231). *College room only:* $5852. Full-time tuition and fees vary according to course load, degree level, program, and reciprocity agreements. Room and board charges vary according to board plan. *Part-time tuition:* $1350 per credit hour. *Part-time fees:* $330 per term. Part-time tuition and fees vary according to course load, degree level, program, and reciprocity agreements.

FRESHMAN FINANCIAL AID (Fall 2016) 225 applied for aid; of those 91% were deemed to have need. 100% of freshmen with need received aid; of those 18% had need fully met. *Average percent of need met:* 71% (excluding resources awarded to replace EFC). *Average financial aid package:* $22,607 (excluding resources awarded to replace EFC). 7% of all full-time freshmen had no need and received non-need-based gift aid.

UNDERGRADUATE FINANCIAL AID (Fall 2016) 838 applied for aid; of those 91% were deemed to have need. 100% of undergraduates with need received aid; of those 17% had need fully met. *Average percent of need met:* 70% (excluding resources awarded to replace EFC). *Average financial aid package:* $22,273 (excluding resources awarded to replace EFC). 10% of all full-time undergraduates had no need and received non-need-based gift aid.

GIFT AID (NEED-BASED) *Total amount:* $9,465,309 (19% federal, 3% state, 69% institutional, 9% external sources). *Receiving aid:* Freshmen: 86% (204); all full-time undergraduates: 80% (755). *Average award:* Freshmen: $19,368; Undergrad-

uates: $18,636. *Scholarships, grants, and awards:* Federal Pell, FSEOG, state, private, college/university gift aid from institutional funds.

GIFT AID (NON-NEED-BASED) *Total amount:* $1,486,118 (3% federal, 76% institutional, 21% external sources). *Receiving aid:* Freshmen: 11% (26). Undergraduates: 8% (79). *Average award:* Freshmen: $11,756. Undergraduates: $10,522. *Scholarships, grants, and awards by category:* Academic interests/achievement: 448 awards ($4,360,984 total): business, communication, education, foreign languages, general academic interests/achievements, home economics, religion/biblical studies, social sciences. *Creative arts/performance:* 76 awards ($157,650 total): debating, journalism/publications, music, performing arts, theater/drama. *Special achievements/activities:* 297 awards ($329,248 total): general special achievements/activities, leadership, memberships. *Special characteristics:* 155 awards ($698,219 total): children and siblings of alumni, children of faculty/staff, international students, relatives of clergy, siblings of current students, veterans, veterans' children. *Tuition waivers:* Full or partial for children of alumni, employees or children of employees, senior citizens. *ROTC:* Army cooperative, Air Force cooperative.

LOANS *Student loans:* $7,108,125 (72% need-based, 28% non-need-based). 78% of past graduating class borrowed through all loan programs. *Average indebtedness per student:* $31,408. *Average need-based loan:* Freshmen: $3647. Undergraduates: $4289. *Parent loans:* $1,585,182 (62% need-based, 38% non-need-based). *Programs:* Federal Direct (Subsidized and Unsubsidized Stafford, PLUS).

WORK-STUDY *Federal work-study:* 226 jobs averaging $1494.

ATHLETIC AWARDS Total amount: $5,758,771 (69% need-based, 31% non-need-based).

APPLYING FOR FINANCIAL AID *Required financial aid form:* FAFSA. *Financial aid deadline:* Continuous. *Notification date:* Continuous beginning 12/5. Students must reply by 9/15.

CONTACT Ellen Zarfas, Director of Financial Aid, Corban University, 5000 Deer Park Drive, SE, Salem, OR 97317, 503-375-7106 or toll-free 800-845-3005. *Fax:* 503-585-4316. *E-mail:* financialaid@corban.edu. *Website:* http://www.corban.edu/.

CORNELL COLLEGE
Mount Vernon, IA

Tuition & fees: $42,299	Average undergraduate aid package: $30,999

ABOUT THE INSTITUTION Independent Methodist, coed. *Awards:* bachelor's degrees. 51 undergraduate majors. *Total enrollment:* 1,009. Undergraduates: 1,009. Freshmen: 300. Federal methodology is used as a basis for awarding need-based institutional aid.

UNDERGRADUATE EXPENSES for 2018–2019 *Application fee:* $30. *Comprehensive fee:* $51,683 includes full-time tuition ($41,874), mandatory fees ($425), and room and board ($9384). *College room only:* $4326. Room and board charges vary according to board plan and housing facility. *Part-time tuition:* $5232 per course. Part-time tuition and fees vary according to course load.

FRESHMAN FINANCIAL AID (Fall 2017, est.) 263 applied for aid; of those 80% were deemed to have need. 100% of freshmen with need received aid; of those 28% had need fully met. *Average percent of need met:* 84% (excluding resources awarded to replace EFC). *Average financial aid package:* $30,926 (excluding resources awarded to replace EFC). 26% of all full-time freshmen had no need and received non-need-based gift aid.

UNDERGRADUATE FINANCIAL AID (Fall 2017, est.) 799 applied for aid; of those 89% were deemed to have need. 100% of undergraduates with need received aid; of those 21% had need fully met. *Average percent of need met:* 80% (excluding resources awarded to replace EFC). *Average financial aid package:* $30,999 (excluding resources awarded to replace EFC). 28% of all full-time undergraduates had no need and received non-need-based gift aid.

GIFT AID (NEED-BASED) *Total amount:* $18,350,721 (7% federal, 3% state, 88% institutional, 2% external sources). *Receiving aid:* Freshmen: 64% (210); all full-time undergraduates: 70% (703). *Average award:* Freshmen: $27,868; Undergraduates: $26,977. *Scholarships, grants, and awards:* Federal Pell, FSEOG, state, college/university gift aid from institutional funds.

GIFT AID (NON-NEED-BASED) *Total amount:* $7,073,084 (1% state, 98% institutional, 1% external sources). *Receiving aid:* Freshmen: 14% (47). Undergraduates: 11% (108). *Average award:* Freshmen: $24,013. Undergraduates: $21,726. *Scholarships, grants, and awards by category:* Academic interests/

achievement: 966 awards ($18,865,935 total): general academic interests/achievements. *Creative arts/performance:* 174 awards ($923,666 total): art/fine arts, dance, music, performing arts, theater/drama. *Special characteristics:* 77 awards ($1,220,765 total): children and siblings of alumni, children of faculty/staff. *Tuition waivers:* Full or partial for employees or children of employees.

LOANS *Student loans:* $6,393,242 (69% need-based, 31% non-need-based). 70% of past graduating class borrowed through all loan programs. *Average indebtedness per student:* $34,130. *Average need-based loan:* Freshmen: $3444. Undergraduates: $4505. *Parent loans:* $1,897,175 (44% need-based, 56% non-need-based). *Programs:* Federal Direct (Subsidized and Unsubsidized Stafford, PLUS), college/university, McElory Loans, Sherman Loans, United Methodist Student Loans, private loans.

WORK-STUDY *Federal work-study:* Total amount: $579,147; 350 jobs averaging $1655. *State or other work-study/employment:* Total amount: $111,150 (100% non-need-based). 117 part-time jobs averaging $950.

APPLYING FOR FINANCIAL AID *Required financial aid form:* FAFSA. *Financial aid deadline (priority):* 3/1. *Notification date:* Continuous beginning 3/1. Students must reply by 5/1 or within 2 weeks of notification.

CONTACT Ms. Pam Perry, Director of Financial Assistance, Cornell College, 600 First Street South West, Mount Vernon, IA 52314-1098, 319-895-4216 or toll-free 800-747-1112. *Fax:* 319-895-4106. *E-mail:* pperry@cornellcollege.edu. *Website:* http://www.cornellcollege.edu/.

CORNELL UNIVERSITY
Ithaca, NY

Tuition & fees: $52,853	Average undergraduate aid package: $47,202

ABOUT THE INSTITUTION Independent, coed. *Awards:* bachelor's, master's, and doctoral degrees. 75 undergraduate majors. *Total enrollment:* 23,016. Undergraduates: 14,907. Freshmen: 3,349. Federal methodology is used as a basis for awarding need-based institutional aid.

UNDERGRADUATE EXPENSES for 2017–2018 *Application fee:* $80. *Comprehensive fee:* $67,233 includes full-time tuition ($52,612), mandatory fees ($241), and room and board ($14,380). *College room only:* $8564. Full-time tuition and fees vary according to degree level. Room and board charges vary according to board plan and housing facility.

FRESHMAN FINANCIAL AID (Fall 2017, est.) 1,852 applied for aid; of those 86% were deemed to have need. 100% of freshmen with need received aid; of those 100% had need fully met. *Average percent of need met:* 100% (excluding resources awarded to replace EFC). *Average financial aid package:* $47,860 (excluding resources awarded to replace EFC).

UNDERGRADUATE FINANCIAL AID (Fall 2017, est.) 7,642 applied for aid; of those 92% were deemed to have need. 100% of undergraduates with need received aid; of those 100% had need fully met. *Average percent of need met:* 100% (excluding resources awarded to replace EFC). *Average financial aid package:* $47,202 (excluding resources awarded to replace EFC).

GIFT AID (NEED-BASED) *Total amount:* $285,601,763 (6% federal, 2% state, 87% institutional, 5% external sources). *Receiving aid:* Freshmen: 46% (1,553); all full-time undergraduates: 45% (6,766). *Average award:* Freshmen: $42,053; Undergraduates: $40,540. *Scholarships, grants, and awards:* Federal Pell, FSEOG, state, private, college/university gift aid from institutional funds.

GIFT AID (NON-NEED-BASED) *Total amount:* $3,706,128 (100% external sources). *Tuition waivers:* Full or partial for employees or children of employees. **ROTC:** Army, Naval, Air Force.

LOANS *Student loans:* $40,736,316 (92% need-based, 8% non-need-based). 41% of past graduating class borrowed through all loan programs. *Average indebtedness per student:* $25,542. *Average need-based loan:* Freshmen: $4845. Undergraduates: $5158. *Parent loans:* $13,133,421 (100% need-based). *Programs:* Federal Direct (Subsidized and Unsubsidized Stafford, PLUS), Perkins, college/university.

WORK-STUDY *Federal work-study:* Total amount: $12,946,624; 5,318 jobs averaging $2434. *State or other work-study/employment:* Total amount: $1,709,977 (100% need-based). 743 part-time jobs averaging $2277.

APPLYING FOR FINANCIAL AID *Required financial aid forms:* FAFSA, CSS Financial Aid PROFILE, noncustodial (divorced/separated) parent's statement, business/farm supplement, federal income tax form(s). *Financial aid deadline:* 2/15. *Notification date:* 4/1. Students must reply by 5/1.

CONTACT Ms. Susan Hitchcock, Director of Financial Aid and Student Employment, Cornell University, 203 Day Hall, Ithaca, NY 14853-2488, 607-255-5145. *Website:* http://www.cornell.edu/.

CORNERSTONE UNIVERSITY
Grand Rapids, MI

Tuition & fees: $24,500	Average undergraduate aid package: $21,975

ABOUT THE INSTITUTION Independent nondenominational, coed. *Awards:* diplomas, associate, bachelor's, master's, and doctoral degrees. 59 undergraduate majors. *Total enrollment:* 2,361. Undergraduates: 1,755. Freshmen: 287. Federal methodology is used as a basis for awarding need-based institutional aid.

UNDERGRADUATE EXPENSES for 2018–2019 *Comprehensive fee:* $33,800 includes full-time tuition ($24,500) and room and board ($9300). Full-time tuition and fees vary according to course load and reciprocity agreements. Room and board charges vary according to board plan and housing facility. Part-time tuition and fees vary according to course load.

FRESHMAN FINANCIAL AID (Fall 2017, est.) 258 applied for aid; of those 89% were deemed to have need. 100% of freshmen with need received aid; of those 16% had need fully met. *Average percent of need met:* 72% (excluding resources awarded to replace EFC). *Average financial aid package:* $22,748 (excluding resources awarded to replace EFC). 18% of all full-time freshmen had no need and received non-need-based gift aid.

UNDERGRADUATE FINANCIAL AID (Fall 2017, est.) 904 applied for aid; of those 93% were deemed to have need. 100% of undergraduates with need received aid; of those 13% had need fully met. *Average percent of need met:* 70% (excluding resources awarded to replace EFC). *Average financial aid package:* $21,975 (excluding resources awarded to replace EFC). 20% of all full-time undergraduates had no need and received non-need-based gift aid.

GIFT AID (NEED-BASED) *Total amount:* $13,768,158 (14% federal, 8% state, 76% institutional, 2% external sources). *Receiving aid:* Freshmen: 82% (230); all full-time undergraduates: 80% (839). *Average award:* Freshmen: $18,753; Undergraduates: $17,455. *Scholarships, grants, and awards:* Federal Pell, FSEOG, state, private, college/university gift aid from institutional funds.

GIFT AID (NON-NEED-BASED) *Total amount:* $2,512,470 (97% institutional, 3% external sources). *Receiving aid:* Freshmen: 9% (24). Undergraduates: 6% (68). *Average award:* Freshmen: $11,755. Undergraduates: $10,381. *Scholarships, grants, and awards by category: Academic interests/achievement:* business, communication, education, English, general academic interests/achievements, home economics, humanities, mathematics, physical sciences, religion/biblical studies, social sciences. *Creative arts/performance:* music. *Special characteristics:* children of faculty/staff, ethnic background, international students, members of minority groups, relatives of clergy. *Tuition waivers:* Full or partial for employees or children of employees. **ROTC:** Army cooperative.

LOANS *Student loans:* $6,267,783 (49% need-based, 51% non-need-based). 81% of past graduating class borrowed through all loan programs. *Average indebtedness per student:* $33,729. *Average need-based loan:* Freshmen: $3264. Undergraduates: $4154. *Parent loans:* $1,147,858 (100% non-need-based). *Programs:* Federal Direct (Subsidized and Unsubsidized Stafford, PLUS).

WORK-STUDY *Federal work-study:* Total amount: $172,272; 183 jobs averaging $941.

ATHLETIC AWARDS Total amount: $1,642,205 (62% need-based, 38% non-need-based).

APPLYING FOR FINANCIAL AID *Required financial aid form:* FAFSA. *Financial aid deadline:* Continuous. *Notification date:* Continuous beginning 12/1. Students must reply within 4 weeks of notification.

CONTACT Mrs. Carol S. Carpenter, Director of Student Financial Services, Cornerstone University, 1001 East Beltline Avenue, NE, Grand Rapids, MI 49525-5897, 616-222-1424 or toll-free 800-787-9778. *Fax:* 616-222-1400. *E-mail:* carol.carpenter@cornerstone.edu. *Website:* http://www.cornerstone.edu/.

CORNISH COLLEGE OF THE ARTS
Seattle, WA

CONTACT Monique Theriault, Office of Financial Aid, Cornish College of the Arts, 1000 Lenora Street, Seattle, WA 98121, 206-726-5013 or toll-free 800-726-ARTS. *Fax:* 206-720-1011. *E-mail:* mtheriault@cornish.edu. *Website:* http://www.cornish.edu/.

COVENANT COLLEGE
Lookout Mountain, GA

Tuition & fees: $34,330	Average undergraduate aid package: $28,025

ABOUT THE INSTITUTION Independent Presbyterian Church in America, coed. *Awards:* bachelor's and master's degrees (master's degree in education only). 27 undergraduate majors. *Total enrollment:* 1,068. Undergraduates: 1,030. Freshmen: 263. Federal methodology is used as a basis for awarding need-based institutional aid.

UNDERGRADUATE EXPENSES for 2018–2019 *Application fee:* $35. *Comprehensive fee:* $44,590 includes full-time tuition ($33,360), mandatory fees ($970), and room and board ($10,260). *Part-time tuition:* $1430 per credit hour.

FRESHMAN FINANCIAL AID (Fall 2016) 231 applied for aid; of those 81% were deemed to have need. 100% of freshmen with need received aid; of those 39% had need fully met. *Average percent of need met:* 84% (excluding resources awarded to replace EFC). *Average financial aid package:* $29,124 (excluding resources awarded to replace EFC). 28% of all full-time freshmen had no need and received non-need-based gift aid.

UNDERGRADUATE FINANCIAL AID (Fall 2016) 736 applied for aid; of those 86% were deemed to have need. 100% of undergraduates with need received aid; of those 32% had need fully met. *Average percent of need met:* 81% (excluding resources awarded to replace EFC). *Average financial aid package:* $28,025 (excluding resources awarded to replace EFC). 33% of all full-time undergraduates had no need and received non-need-based gift aid.

GIFT AID (NEED-BASED) *Total amount:* $13,371,631 (9% federal, 5% state, 83% institutional, 3% external sources). *Receiving aid:* Freshmen: 69% (184); all full-time undergraduates: 64% (623). *Average award:* Freshmen: $23,438; Undergraduates: $21,383. *Scholarships, grants, and awards:* Federal Pell, FSEOG, state, private, college/university gift aid from institutional funds.

GIFT AID (NON-NEED-BASED) *Total amount:* $5,480,310 (4% state, 88% institutional, 8% external sources). *Receiving aid:* Freshmen: 15% (39). Undergraduates: 11% (105). *Average award:* Freshmen: $17,350. Undergraduates: $14,904. *Scholarships, grants, and awards by category:* Academic interests/achievement: general academic interests/achievements. Creative arts/performance: music. Special achievements/activities: leadership. Special characteristics: children of faculty/staff, international students, members of minority groups, religious affiliation. *ROTC:* Army cooperative.

LOANS *Student loans:* $3,952,780 (90% need-based, 10% non-need-based). 64% of past graduating class borrowed through all loan programs. *Average indebtedness per student:* $26,184. *Average need-based loan:* Freshmen: $5896. Undergraduates: $7002. *Parent loans:* $993,403 (87% need-based, 13% non-need-based). *Programs:* Perkins, state.

WORK-STUDY *Federal work-study:* jobs available. *State or other work-study/employment:* Total amount: $1,069,676 (70% need-based, 30% non-need-based). Part-time jobs available.

APPLYING FOR FINANCIAL AID *Required financial aid forms:* FAFSA, state aid form. *Financial aid deadline (priority):* 2/1. *Notification date:* Continuous beginning 3/15. Students must reply by 5/1.

CONTACT Mrs. Margaret Stewart, Assistant Director of Financial Aid, Covenant College, 14049 Scenic Highway, Lookout Mountain, GA 30750, 706-419-1152 or toll-free 888-451-2683. *Fax:* 706-820-2820. *E-mail:* margaret.stewart@covenant.edu. *Website:* http://www.covenant.edu/.

COX COLLEGE
Springfield, MO

Tuition & fees: $10,270	Average undergraduate aid package: $3422

ABOUT THE INSTITUTION Independent, coed, primarily women. *Awards:* certificates, associate, bachelor's, and master's degrees. 5 undergraduate majors. *Total enrollment:* 899. Undergraduates: 778. Federal methodology is used as a basis for awarding need-based institutional aid.

UNDERGRADUATE EXPENSES for 2017–2018 *Application fee:* $50. *One-time required fee:* $225. *Tuition:* full-time $8800; part-time $400 per credit hour. Full-time tuition and fees vary according to course load, degree level, and program. Part-time tuition and fees vary according to course load, degree level, and program.

FRESHMAN FINANCIAL AID (Fall 2016) 6 applied for aid; of those 100% were deemed to have need. 100% of freshmen with need received aid. *Average financial aid package:* $3375 (excluding resources awarded to replace EFC).

UNDERGRADUATE FINANCIAL AID (Fall 2016) 205 applied for aid; of those 100% were deemed to have need. 100% of undergraduates with need received aid. *Average financial aid package:* $3422 (excluding resources awarded to replace EFC).

GIFT AID (NEED-BASED) *Total amount:* $651,326 (7% federal, 34% state, 47% institutional, 12% external sources). *Receiving aid:* Freshmen: 83% (5); all full-time undergraduates: 33% (144). *Average award:* Freshmen: $1915; Undergraduates: $4390. *Scholarships, grants, and awards:* Federal Pell, FSEOG, state, private, college/university gift aid from institutional funds, United Negro College Fund, Federal Nursing.

GIFT AID (NON-NEED-BASED) *Scholarships, grants, and awards by category:* Academic interests/achievement: general academic interests/achievements, home economics.

LOANS *Student loans:* $4,393,255 (40% need-based, 60% non-need-based). *Average need-based loan:* Freshmen: $1. Undergraduates: $3422. *Parent loans:* $264,677 (100% need-based). *Programs:* Federal Direct (Subsidized and Unsubsidized Stafford, PLUS).

WORK-STUDY *Federal work-study:* 22 jobs averaging $2061. *State or other work-study/employment:* Part-time jobs available.

APPLYING FOR FINANCIAL AID *Required financial aid forms:* FAFSA, institution's own form. *Financial aid deadline (priority):* 2/1. *Notification date:* Continuous beginning 5/20.

CONTACT Leesa Taylor, Financial Aid Counselor, Cox College, 1423 North Jefferson Avenue, Springfield, MO 65802, 417-269-3160 or toll-free 866-898-5355 (in-state). *Fax:* 417-269-3586. *E-mail:* leesa.taylor@coxcollege.edu. *Website:* http://www.coxcollege.edu/.

CREATIVE CENTER
Omaha, NE

CONTACT Financial Aid Office, Creative Center, 10850 Emmet Street, Omaha, NE 68164, 402-898-1000 or toll-free 888-898-1789. *Website:* http://www.creativecenter.edu/.

CREIGHTON UNIVERSITY
Omaha, NE

Tuition & fees: $39,916	Average undergraduate aid package: $28,732

ABOUT THE INSTITUTION Independent Roman Catholic (Jesuit), coed. *Awards:* certificates, associate, bachelor's, master's, and doctoral degrees. 50 undergraduate majors. *Total enrollment:* 8,654. Undergraduates: 4,255. Freshmen: 1,120. Federal methodology is used as a basis for awarding need-based institutional aid.

UNDERGRADUATE EXPENSES for 2018–2019 *Application fee:* $40. *Comprehensive fee:* $50,952 includes full-time tuition ($38,200), mandatory fees ($1716), and room and board ($11,036). Full-time tuition and fees vary according to program. Room and board charges vary according to housing facility. *Part-time* tuition: $1195 per credit hour. *Part-time fees:* $168 per term. Part-time tuition and fees vary according to course load and program.

FRESHMAN FINANCIAL AID (Fall 2017, est.) 952 applied for aid; of those 71% were deemed to have need. 100% of freshmen with need received aid; of those 30% had need fully met. *Average percent of need met:* 83% (excluding resources awarded to replace EFC). *Average financial aid package:* $29,125 (excluding resources awarded to replace EFC). 38% of all full-time freshmen had no need and received non-need-based gift aid.

UNDERGRADUATE FINANCIAL AID (Fall 2017, est.) 2,693 applied for aid; of those 80% were deemed to have need. 100% of undergraduates with need received aid; of those 26% had need fully met. *Average percent of need met:* 79% (excluding resources awarded to replace EFC). *Average financial aid package:* $28,732 (excluding resources awarded to replace EFC). 40% of all full-time undergraduates had no need and received non-need-based gift aid.

GIFT AID (NEED-BASED) *Total amount:* $41,992,885 (8% federal, 89% institutional, 3% external sources). *Receiving aid:* Freshmen: 60% (672); all full-time undergraduates: 52% (2,087). *Average award:* Freshmen: $21,759; Undergraduates: $21,635. *Scholarships, grants, and awards:* Federal Pell, FSEOG, state, private, college/university gift aid from institutional funds.

GIFT AID (NON-NEED-BASED) *Total amount:* $30,407,864 (96% institutional, 4% external sources). *Receiving aid:* Freshmen: 16% (175). Undergraduates: 11% (421). *Average award:* Freshmen: $17,630. Undergraduates: $16,224. *Scholarships, grants, and awards by category:* Academic interests/achievement: 3,151 awards ($45,702,728 total): business, education, general academic interests/achievements, military science. *Creative arts/performance:* 19 awards ($76,000 total): art/fine arts, dance, music, performing arts, theater/drama. *Special characteristics:* 97 awards ($1,208,410 total): members of minority groups. *Tuition waivers:* Full or partial for employees or children of employees, adult students, senior citizens. *ROTC:* Army, Air Force cooperative.

LOANS *Student loans:* $29,426,544 (64% need-based, 36% non-need-based). 54% of past graduating class borrowed through all loan programs. *Average indebtedness per student:* $35,766. *Average need-based loan:* Freshmen: $5068. Undergraduates: $6411. *Parent loans:* $6,037,139 (31% need-based, 69% non-need-based). *Programs:* Federal Direct (Subsidized and Unsubsidized Stafford, PLUS), Perkins, Federal Nursing.

WORK-STUDY *Federal work-study:* Total amount: $1,826,215; 839 jobs averaging $2177.

ATHLETIC AWARDS Total amount: $4,116,697 (23% need-based, 77% non-need-based).

APPLYING FOR FINANCIAL AID *Required financial aid forms:* FAFSA, institution's own form. *Financial aid deadline (priority):* 1/15. *Notification date:* Continuous beginning 2/15. Students must reply within 4 weeks of notification.

CONTACT Ms. Paula S. Kohles, Director of Financial Aid, Creighton University, 2500 California Plaza, Omaha, NE 68178, 402-280-2731 or toll-free 800-282-5835. *Fax:* 402-280-2895. *E-mail:* paulakohles@creighton.edu.
Website: http://www.creighton.edu/.

CRISWELL COLLEGE
Dallas, TX

Tuition & fees: $10,710	Average undergraduate aid package: $7082

ABOUT THE INSTITUTION Independent Southern Baptist Convention, coed. *Awards:* associate, bachelor's, and master's degrees. 6 undergraduate majors. *Total enrollment:* 264. Undergraduates: 198. Freshmen: 17. Federal methodology is used as a basis for awarding need-based institutional aid.

UNDERGRADUATE EXPENSES for 2018–2019 *Application fee:* $35. *Tuition:* full-time $9960; part-time $415 per credit hour. *Required fees:* full-time $750; $750 per year. Full-time tuition and fees vary according to course load. Part-time tuition and fees vary according to course load.

FRESHMAN FINANCIAL AID (Fall 2016) 12 applied for aid; of those 83% were deemed to have need. 100% of freshmen with need received aid; of those 20% had need fully met. *Average percent of need met:* 58% (excluding resources awarded to replace EFC). *Average financial aid package:* $7824 (excluding resources awarded to replace EFC). 8% of all full-time freshmen had no need and received non-need-based gift aid.

UNDERGRADUATE FINANCIAL AID (Fall 2016) 112 applied for aid; of those 77% were deemed to have need. 100% of undergraduates with need received aid; of those 3% had need fully met. *Average percent of need met:* 33% (excluding resources awarded to replace EFC). *Average financial aid package:* $7082 (excluding resources awarded to replace EFC). 16% of all full-time undergraduates had no need and received non-need-based gift aid.

GIFT AID (NEED-BASED) *Total amount:* $414,540 (82% federal, 18% institutional). *Receiving aid:* Freshmen: 67% (8); all full-time undergraduates: 59% (74). *Average award:* Freshmen: $3222; Undergraduates: $3921. *Scholarships, grants, and awards:* Federal Pell, private, college/university gift aid from institutional funds.

GIFT AID (NON-NEED-BASED) *Total amount:* $265,109 (100% institutional). *Receiving aid:* Freshmen: 58% (7). Undergraduates: 40% (50). *Average award:* Freshmen: $15,370. Undergraduates: $5529. *Scholarships, grants, and awards by category:* Academic interests/achievement: general academic interests/achievements, religion/biblical studies. *Special achievements/activities:* religious involvement. *Tuition waivers:* Full or partial for employees or children of employees.

LOANS *Student loans:* $594,664 (56% need-based, 44% non-need-based). *Average need-based loan:* Freshmen: $3243. Undergraduates: $3776. *Parent loans:* $8618 (100% need-based). *Programs:* Federal Direct (Subsidized and Unsubsidized Stafford, PLUS).

WORK-STUDY *State or other work-study/employment:* Part-time jobs available.

APPLYING FOR FINANCIAL AID *Required financial aid forms:* FAFSA, institution's own form. *Financial aid deadline (priority):* 4/15. *Notification date:* Continuous. Students must reply within 6 weeks of notification.

CONTACT Jimmy Criswell, Director of Financial Aid, Criswell College, 4010 Gaston Avenue, Dallas, TX 75246, 214-818-1393 or toll-free 800-899-0012. *Fax:* 214-370-0497. *E-mail:* jcriswell@criswell.edu.
Website: http://www.criswell.edu/.

CROSSROADS BIBLE COLLEGE
Indianapolis, IN

Tuition & fees: N/R	Average undergraduate aid package: N/A

ABOUT THE INSTITUTION Independent Baptist, coed. 8 undergraduate majors. Institutional methodology is used as a basis for awarding need-based institutional aid.

GIFT AID (NEED-BASED) *Total amount:* $1,068,492 (46% federal, 42% state, 11% institutional, 1% external sources). *Scholarships, grants, and awards:* Federal Pell, FSEOG, state, college/university gift aid from institutional funds.

GIFT AID (NON-NEED-BASED) *Scholarships, grants, and awards by category:* Academic interests/achievement: religion/biblical studies. *Special achievements/activities:* 7 awards ($2631 total): religious involvement. *Special characteristics:* children of faculty/staff, married students, siblings of current students, spouses of current students.

LOANS *Student loans:* $1,150,019 (100% need-based). 100% of past graduating class borrowed through all loan programs. *Average indebtedness per student:* $37,497. *Parent loans:* $1458 (100% need-based). *Programs:* Federal Direct (Subsidized and Unsubsidized Stafford, PLUS).

WORK-STUDY *Federal work-study:* 6 jobs averaging $2393. *State or other work-study/employment:* Total amount: $45,212 (100% need-based). Part-time jobs available.

APPLYING FOR FINANCIAL AID *Required financial aid forms:* FAFSA, institution's own form. *Financial aid deadline:* 6/30 (priority: 5/31). *Notification date:* 7/31. Students must reply by 6/30 or within 2 weeks of notification.

CONTACT Mrs. Phyllis Dodson, Senior Director of Financial Aid, Crossroads Bible College, 601 North Shortridge Road, Indianapolis, IN 46219, 317-789-8250 or toll-free 800-822-3119. *Fax:* 317-789-8253. *E-mail:* pdodson@crossroads.edu.
Website: http://www.crossroads.edu/.

CROWLEY'S RIDGE COLLEGE

Paragould, AR

CONTACT Financial Aid Office, Crowley's Ridge College, 100 College Drive, Paragould, AR 72450-9731, 870-236-6901 or toll-free 800-264-1096. *Website:* http://www.crc.edu/.

CROWN COLLEGE

St. Bonifacius, MN

ABOUT THE INSTITUTION Independent The Christian and Missionary Alliance, coed. 34 undergraduate majors.

GIFT AID (NEED-BASED) *Scholarships, grants, and awards:* Federal Pell, FSEOG, state, private, college/university gift aid from institutional funds.

GIFT AID (NON-NEED-BASED) *Scholarships, grants, and awards by category:* **Academic interests/achievement:** general academic interests/achievements. *Creative arts/performance:* music. *Special achievements/activities:* leadership. *Special characteristics:* children and siblings of alumni, children of faculty/staff, international students, members of minority groups, relatives of clergy, siblings of current students.

LOANS *Programs:* Federal Direct (Subsidized and Unsubsidized Stafford, PLUS), Perkins, state, SELF Loans, CitiAssist Loans, Sallie Mae Signature Loans, alternative loans.

APPLYING FOR FINANCIAL AID *Required financial aid form:* FAFSA.

CONTACT Mrs. Judy Bedford, Interim Director of Financial Aid, Crown College, 8700 College View Drive, St. Bonifacius, MN 55375-9001, 952-446-4177 or toll-free 800-68-CROWN. *Fax:* 952-446-4178. *E-mail:* finaid@crown.edu. *Website:* http://www.crown.edu/.

THE CULINARY INSTITUTE OF AMERICA

Hyde Park, NY

Tuition & fees: $31,616	Average undergraduate aid package: $16,541

ABOUT THE INSTITUTION Independent, coed. *Awards:* certificates, associate, and bachelor's degrees. 5 undergraduate majors. *Total enrollment:* 3,131. Undergraduates: 3,116. Freshmen: 433. Federal methodology is used as a basis for awarding need-based institutional aid.

UNDERGRADUATE EXPENSES for 2017–2018 *Application fee:* $50. *Comprehensive fee:* $42,486 includes full-time tuition ($29,380), mandatory fees ($2236), and room and board ($10,870). *College room only:* $7320. Room and board charges vary according to board plan, housing facility, and location.

FRESHMAN FINANCIAL AID (Fall 2016) 439 applied for aid; of those 90% were deemed to have need. 100% of freshmen with need received aid; of those 9% had need fully met. *Average percent of need met:* 79% (excluding resources awarded to replace EFC). *Average financial aid package:* $18,382 (excluding resources awarded to replace EFC). 17% of all full-time freshmen had no need and received non-need-based gift aid.

UNDERGRADUATE FINANCIAL AID (Fall 2016) 1,924 applied for aid; of those 93% were deemed to have need. 100% of undergraduates with need received aid; of those 7% had need fully met. *Average percent of need met:* 71% (excluding resources awarded to replace EFC). *Average financial aid package:* $16,541 (excluding resources awarded to replace EFC). 5% of all full-time undergraduates had no need and received non-need-based gift aid.

GIFT AID (NEED-BASED) *Total amount:* $20,438,851 (16% federal, 2% state, 79% institutional, 3% external sources). *Receiving aid:* Freshmen: 73% (375); all full-time undergraduates: 59% (1,649). *Average award:* Freshmen: $13,950; Undergraduates: $12,031. *Scholarships, grants, and awards:* Federal Pell, FSEOG, state, private, college/university gift aid from institutional funds.

GIFT AID (NON-NEED-BASED) *Total amount:* $2,506,423 (1% state, 93% institutional, 6% external sources). *Receiving aid:* Freshmen: 66% (338). Undergraduates: 50% (1,375). *Average award:* Freshmen: $5695. Undergraduates: $6359. *Scholarships, grants, and awards by category:* **Academic interests/achievement:** 1,284 awards ($6,741,972 total): general academic interests/achieve-

ments. *Creative arts/performance:* 143 awards ($426,180 total): general creative arts/performance. *Special achievements/activities:* 73 awards ($62,264 total): general special achievements/activities. *Tuition waivers:* Full or partial for employees or children of employees.

LOANS *Student loans:* $19,984,458 (91% need-based, 9% non-need-based). 63% of past graduating class borrowed through all loan programs. *Average indebtedness per student:* $51,200. *Average need-based loan:* Freshmen: $3047. Undergraduates: $3825. *Parent loans:* $8,300,049 (100% non-need-based). *Programs:* Federal Direct (Subsidized and Unsubsidized Stafford, PLUS), Perkins, alternative loans.

WORK-STUDY *Federal work-study:* 1,045 jobs averaging $2238. *State or other work-study/employment:* Part-time jobs available.

APPLYING FOR FINANCIAL AID *Required financial aid forms:* FAFSA, state aid form. *Financial aid deadline:* Continuous. *Notification date:* Continuous beginning 12/15. Students must reply within 2 weeks of notification.

CONTACT Kathleen Gailor, Director of Student Financial Planning, The Culinary Institute of America, 1946 Campus Drive, Hyde Park, NY 12538-1499, 845-451-1500 or toll-free 800-CULINARY. *Fax:* 845-905-4030. *E-mail:* sfrs@culinary.edu. *Website:* http://www.ciachef.edu/.

CULINARY INSTITUTE OF VIRGINIA

Norfolk, VA

CONTACT Ms. Lynn Robinson, Director of Financial Aid, Culinary Institute of Virginia, 8 Abbott Park Place, Providence, RI 02903, 401-598-4648 or toll-free 866-619-CHEF. *Fax:* 401-598-1040. *E-mail:* fp@jwu.edu. *Website:* http://www.chefva.com/.

CULVER-STOCKTON COLLEGE

Canton, MO

Tuition & fees: $26,680	Average undergraduate aid package: $21,033

ABOUT THE INSTITUTION Independent Christian Church (Disciples of Christ), coed. *Awards:* bachelor's and master's degrees. 41 undergraduate majors. *Total enrollment:* 1,134. Undergraduates: 1,093. Freshmen: 305. Federal methodology is used as a basis for awarding need-based institutional aid.

UNDERGRADUATE EXPENSES for 2018–2019 *One-time required fee:* $210. *Comprehensive fee:* $35,200 includes full-time tuition ($26,255), mandatory fees ($425), and room and board ($8520). *College room only:* $3815. Room and board charges vary according to board plan and housing facility. *Part-time tuition:* $600 per credit hour. *Part-time fees:* $17.71 per credit hour.

FRESHMAN FINANCIAL AID (Fall 2017, est.) 292 applied for aid; of those 96% were deemed to have need. 100% of freshmen with need received aid; of those 19% had need fully met. *Average percent of need met:* 72% (excluding resources awarded to replace EFC). *Average financial aid package:* $21,156 (excluding resources awarded to replace EFC). 9% of all full-time freshmen had no need and received non-need-based gift aid.

UNDERGRADUATE FINANCIAL AID (Fall 2017, est.) 851 applied for aid; of those 93% were deemed to have need. 100% of undergraduates with need received aid; of those 16% had need fully met. *Average percent of need met:* 72% (excluding resources awarded to replace EFC). *Average financial aid package:* $21,033 (excluding resources awarded to replace EFC). 16% of all full-time undergraduates had no need and received non-need-based gift aid.

GIFT AID (NEED-BASED) *Total amount:* $10,669,946 (21% federal, 4% state, 73% institutional, 2% external sources). *Receiving aid:* Freshmen: 91% (279); all full-time undergraduates: 82% (787). *Average award:* Freshmen: $18,188; Undergraduates: $17,185. *Scholarships, grants, and awards:* Federal Pell, FSEOG, state, private, college/university gift aid from institutional funds.

GIFT AID (NON-NEED-BASED) *Total amount:* $1,877,350 (2% federal, 1% state, 94% institutional, 3% external sources). *Receiving aid:* Freshmen: 13% (39). Undergraduates: 10% (93). *Average award:* Freshmen: $10,018. Undergraduates: $9964. *Scholarships, grants, and awards by category:* **Academic interests/achievement:** 883 awards ($6,952,172 total): general academic interests/achievements. *Creative arts/performance:* 118 awards ($519,125 total): art/fine arts, dance, debating, music, theater/drama. *Special achievements/activities:* 127 awards ($287,696 total):

cheerleading/drum major, general special achievements/activities, leadership. *Special characteristics:* 125 awards ($764,136 total): children and siblings of alumni, children of faculty/staff, first-generation college students, international students, local/state students, religious affiliation, siblings of current students, veterans, veterans' children. *Tuition waivers:* Full or partial for employees or children of employees, senior citizens.

LOANS *Student loans:* $7,697,519 (75% need-based, 25% non-need-based). 85% of past graduating class borrowed through all loan programs. *Average indebtedness per student:* $29,105. *Average need-based loan:* Freshmen: $3402. Undergraduates: $4259. *Parent loans:* $2,024,469 (51% need-based, 49% non-need-based). *Programs:* Federal Direct (Subsidized and Unsubsidized Stafford, PLUS), Perkins, Federal Nursing, state, college/university.

WORK-STUDY *Federal work-study:* Total amount: $79,068; 72 jobs averaging $1146. *State or other work-study/employment:* Total amount: $428,024 (53% need-based, 47% non-need-based). 383 part-time jobs averaging $1117.

ATHLETIC AWARDS Total amount: $3,868,751 (70% need-based, 30% non-need-based).

APPLYING FOR FINANCIAL AID *Required financial aid form:* FAFSA. *Financial aid deadline:* 6/1 (priority: 1/1). *Notification date:* Continuous. Students must reply within 2 weeks of notification.

CONTACT Ms. Tina M. Wiseman, Director of Financial Aid, Culver-Stockton College, One College Hill, Canton, MO 63435, 573-288-6307 or toll-free 800-537-1883. *Fax:* 573-288-6308. *E-mail:* twiseman@culver.edu. *Website:* http://www.culver.edu/.

CUMBERLAND UNIVERSITY
Lebanon, TN

CONTACT Ms. Beatrice LaChance, Executive Director of Enrollment Services, Cumberland University, 1 Cumberland Square, Lebanon, TN 37087-3554, 615-444-2562 Ext. 1244 or toll-free 800-467-0562. *Fax:* 615-443-8424. *E-mail:* lvaughan@cumberland.edu. *Website:* http://www.cumberland.edu/.

CURRY COLLEGE
Milton, MA

Tuition & fees: $39,720	Average undergraduate aid package: $28,668

ABOUT THE INSTITUTION Independent, coed. *Awards:* certificates, bachelor's, and master's degrees. 26 undergraduate majors. *Total enrollment:* 2,799. Undergraduates: 2,565. Freshmen: 603. Federal methodology is used as a basis for awarding need-based institutional aid.

UNDERGRADUATE EXPENSES for 2018–2019 *Application fee:* $50. *One-time required fee:* $350. *Comprehensive fee:* $55,605 includes full-time tuition ($37,850), mandatory fees ($1870), and room and board ($15,885). *College room only:* $8535. Full-time tuition and fees vary according to class time, course load, location, and program. Room and board charges vary according to board plan and housing facility. *Part-time tuition:* $1262 per credit. *Part-time fees:* $420 per year. Part-time tuition and fees vary according to class time, course load, location, and program.

FRESHMAN FINANCIAL AID (Fall 2017, est.) 515 applied for aid; of those 100% were deemed to have need. 100% of freshmen with need received aid; of those 12% had need fully met. *Average percent of need met:* 72% (excluding resources awarded to replace EFC). *Average financial aid package:* $30,765 (excluding resources awarded to replace EFC). 14% of all full-time freshmen had no need and received non-need-based gift aid.

UNDERGRADUATE FINANCIAL AID (Fall 2017, est.) 1,632 applied for aid; of those 97% were deemed to have need. 100% of undergraduates with need received aid; of those 12% had need fully met. *Average percent of need met:* 69% (excluding resources awarded to replace EFC). *Average financial aid package:* $28,668 (excluding resources awarded to replace EFC). 18% of all full-time undergraduates had no need and received non-need-based gift aid.

GIFT AID (NEED-BASED) *Total amount:* $35,854,134 (8% federal, 2% state, 88% institutional, 2% external sources). *Receiving aid:* Freshmen: 86% (514); all full-

time undergraduates: 77% (1,583). *Average award:* Freshmen: $27,843; Undergraduates: $24,285. *Scholarships, grants, and awards:* Federal Pell, FSEOG, state, private, college/university gift aid from institutional funds, TEACH Grants.

GIFT AID (NON-NEED-BASED) *Total amount:* $7,451,012 (3% federal, 96% institutional, 1% external sources). *Receiving aid:* Freshmen: 8% (51). Undergraduates: 6% (133). *Average award:* Freshmen: $19,866. Undergraduates: $16,232. *Scholarships, grants, and awards by category:* Academic interests/achievement: 2,139 awards ($26,899,250 total): general academic interests/achievements. *Special characteristics:* 34 awards ($1,099,928 total): children and siblings of alumni, children of current students, children of faculty/staff, siblings of current students, spouses of current students. *Tuition waivers:* Full or partial for children of alumni, employees or children of employees. *ROTC:* Army cooperative.

LOANS *Student loans:* $20,669,337 (41% need-based, 59% non-need-based). 80% of past graduating class borrowed through all loan programs. *Average indebtedness per student:* $45,947. *Average need-based loan:* Freshmen: $3616. Undergraduates: $4394. *Parent loans:* $10,047,110 (100% non-need-based). *Programs:* Federal Direct (Subsidized and Unsubsidized Stafford, PLUS), Perkins, state.

WORK-STUDY *Federal work-study:* Total amount: $2,168,800; 923 jobs averaging $2338.

APPLYING FOR FINANCIAL AID *Required financial aid form:* FAFSA. *Financial aid deadline (priority):* 3/1. *Notification date:* Continuous beginning 12/1. Students must reply by 5/1 or within 2 weeks of notification.

CONTACT Linda Brennan, Director of Financial Aid, Curry College, 1071 Blue Hill Avenue, Milton, MA 02186-2395, 617-333-2354 or toll-free 800-669-0686. *Fax:* 617-333-2915. *E-mail:* fin-aid@curry.edu. *Website:* http://www.curry.edu/.

CURTIS INSTITUTE OF MUSIC
Philadelphia, PA

CONTACT Veronica McAuley, Director of Student Financial Assistance, Curtis Institute of Music, 1726 Locust Street, Philadelphia, PA 19103-6107, 215-717-3188. *E-mail:* veronica.mcauley@curtis.edu. *Website:* http://www.curtis.edu/.

DAEMEN COLLEGE
Amherst, NY

Tuition & fees: $27,990	Average undergraduate aid package: $28,324

ABOUT THE INSTITUTION Independent, coed. *Awards:* certificates, bachelor's, master's, and doctoral degrees. 38 undergraduate majors. *Total enrollment:* 2,636. Undergraduates: 1,802. Freshmen: 387. Federal methodology is used as a basis for awarding need-based institutional aid.

UNDERGRADUATE EXPENSES for 2017–2018 *Application fee:* $25. *Comprehensive fee:* $40,686 includes full-time tuition ($27,450), mandatory fees ($540), and room and board ($12,696). Full-time tuition and fees vary according to location and reciprocity agreements. Room and board charges vary according to board plan and housing facility. *Part-time tuition:* $915 per credit hour. *Part-time fees:* $7 per credit hour; $80 per term. Part-time tuition and fees vary according to course load, location, and reciprocity agreements.

FRESHMAN FINANCIAL AID (Fall 2017, est.) 364 applied for aid; of those 72% were deemed to have need. 100% of freshmen with need received aid; of those 16% had need fully met. *Average percent of need met:* 87% (excluding resources awarded to replace EFC). *Average financial aid package:* $30,169 (excluding resources awarded to replace EFC). 25% of all full-time freshmen had no need and received non-need-based gift aid.

UNDERGRADUATE FINANCIAL AID (Fall 2017, est.) 1,425 applied for aid; of those 67% were deemed to have need. 100% of undergraduates with need received aid; of those 12% had need fully met. *Average percent of need met:* 82% (excluding resources awarded to replace EFC). *Average financial aid package:* $28,324 (excluding resources awarded to replace EFC). 28% of all full-time undergraduates had no need and received non-need-based gift aid.

GIFT AID (NEED-BASED) *Total amount:* $10,977,211 (27% federal, 20% state, 53% institutional). *Receiving aid:* Freshmen: 68% (263); all full-time undergraduates: 61% (951). *Average award:* Freshmen: $13,765; Undergraduates: $11,058. *Scholarships, grants, and awards:* Federal Pell, FSEOG, state, private, college/university gift aid from institutional funds, New York State Nursing Grants.

GIFT AID (NON-NEED-BASED) *Total amount:* $15,888,577 (1% state, 93% institutional, 6% external sources). *Receiving aid:* Freshmen: 60% (234). Undergraduates: 55% (855). *Average award:* Freshmen: $11,376. Undergraduates: $11,119. *Scholarships, grants, and awards by category:* Academic interests/achievement: 1,438 awards ($13,429,686 total): education, general academic interests/achievements, home economics. *Creative arts/performance:* 14 awards ($46,000 total): art/fine arts. *Special achievements/activities:* 100 awards ($135,300 total): leadership. *Special characteristics:* 63 awards ($961,375 total): children and siblings of alumni, children of faculty/staff, international students, veterans. *Tuition waivers:* Full or partial for employees or children of employees, senior citizens. *ROTC:* Army cooperative.

LOANS *Student loans:* $11,951,623 (39% need-based, 61% non-need-based). 84% of past graduating class borrowed through all loan programs. *Average indebtedness per student:* $35,530. *Average need-based loan:* Freshmen: $3893. Undergraduates: $4630. *Parent loans:* $1,747,795 (72% need-based, 28% non-need-based). *Programs:* Federal Direct (Subsidized and Unsubsidized Stafford, PLUS), Perkins, alternative loans.

WORK-STUDY *Federal work-study:* Total amount: $1,869,553; 612 jobs averaging $2918. *State or other work-study/employment:* Total amount: $104,091 (100% non-need-based). 50 part-time jobs averaging $2040.

ATHLETIC AWARDS Total amount: $1,114,426 (33% need-based, 67% non-need-based).

APPLYING FOR FINANCIAL AID *Required financial aid forms:* FAFSA, state aid form. *Financial aid deadline:* Continuous. *Notification date:* Continuous beginning 11/15. Students must reply within 2 weeks of notification.

CONTACT Mr. Jeffrey Pagano, Director of Financial Aid, Daemen College, 4380 Main Street, Amherst, NY 14226-3592, 716-839-8254 or toll-free 800-462-7652. *Fax:* 716-839-8378. *E-mail:* jpagano@daemen.edu. *Website:* http://www.daemen.edu/.

DAKOTA STATE UNIVERSITY
Madison, SD

Tuition & fees (SD res): $9147	Average undergraduate aid package: $7954

ABOUT THE INSTITUTION State-supported, coed. *Awards:* certificates, associate, bachelor's, master's, and doctoral degrees. 29 undergraduate majors. *Total enrollment:* 3,307. Undergraduates: 2,962. Freshmen: 381. Federal methodology is used as a basis for awarding need-based institutional aid.

UNDERGRADUATE EXPENSES for 2017–2018 *Application fee:* $20. *Tuition, state resident:* full-time $7191; part-time $239.70 per credit hour. *Tuition, nonresident:* full-time $10,120; part-time $337.35 per credit hour. *Required fees:* full-time $1956; $39 per credit. Full-time tuition and fees vary according to location and reciprocity agreements. Part-time tuition and fees vary according to location and reciprocity agreements. *College room and board:* $6720; *Room only:* $3658. Room and board charges vary according to board plan and housing facility.

FRESHMAN FINANCIAL AID (Fall 2016) 288 applied for aid; of those 80% were deemed to have need. 100% of freshmen with need received aid; of those 9% had need fully met. *Average percent of need met:* 72% (excluding resources awarded to replace EFC). *Average financial aid package:* $7789 (excluding resources awarded to replace EFC). 15% of all full-time freshmen had no need and received non-need-based gift aid.

UNDERGRADUATE FINANCIAL AID (Fall 2016) 1,091 applied for aid; of those 82% were deemed to have need. 100% of undergraduates with need received aid; of those 10% had need fully met. *Average percent of need met:* 74% (excluding resources awarded to replace EFC). *Average financial aid package:* $7954 (excluding resources awarded to replace EFC). 9% of all full-time undergraduates had no need and received non-need-based gift aid.

GIFT AID (NEED-BASED) *Total amount:* $3,949,085 (75% federal, 4% state, 10% institutional, 11% external sources). *Receiving aid:* Freshmen: 45% (139); all full-time undergraduates: 41% (519). *Average award:* Freshmen: $4345; Undergraduates: $4333. *Scholarships, grants, and awards:* Federal Pell, FSEOG, state, private, college/university gift aid from institutional funds, Veterans Education Benefits (GI Bill).

GIFT AID (NON-NEED-BASED) *Total amount:* $427,282 (5% federal, 16% state, 39% institutional, 40% external sources). *Receiving aid:* Freshmen: 52% (160). Undergraduates: 32% (403). *Average award:* Freshmen: $3809. Undergraduates: $5095. *Scholarships, grants, and awards by category:* Academic interests/achievement: 389 awards ($519,325 total): biological sciences, business, communication, computer science, education, English, general academic interests/achievements, home economics, mathematics, physical sciences. *Creative arts/performance:* 12 awards ($5100 total): music. *Special characteristics:* 2 awards ($2050 total): veterans. *Tuition waivers:* Full or partial for employees or children of employees, senior citizens. *ROTC:* Army cooperative, Air Force cooperative.

LOANS *Student loans:* $12,495,730 (71% need-based, 29% non-need-based). 74% of past graduating class borrowed through all loan programs. *Average indebtedness per student:* $29,962. *Average need-based loan:* Freshmen: $3619. Undergraduates: $4167. *Parent loans:* $1,349,074 (71% need-based, 29% non-need-based). *Programs:* Federal Direct (Subsidized and Unsubsidized Stafford, PLUS), Perkins, alternative loans.

WORK-STUDY *Federal work-study:* 133 jobs averaging $2103. *State or other work-study/employment:* Total amount: $132,673 (100% non-need-based). 22 part-time jobs averaging $6031.

ATHLETIC AWARDS Total amount: $430,977 (71% need-based, 29% non-need-based).

APPLYING FOR FINANCIAL AID *Required financial aid forms:* FAFSA, institutional scholarship application form. *Financial aid deadline (priority):* 3/1. *Notification date:* Continuous beginning 4/1. Students must reply within 2 weeks of notification.

CONTACT Denise Grayson, Financial Aid Director, Dakota State University, 103 Heston Hall, 820 North Washington Avenue, Madison, SD 57042-1799, 605-256-5158 or toll-free 888-DSU-9988. *Fax:* 605-256-5020. *E-mail:* fa@dsu.edu. *Website:* http://www.dsu.edu/.

DAKOTA WESLEYAN UNIVERSITY
Mitchell, SD

ABOUT THE INSTITUTION Independent United Methodist, coed. 46 undergraduate majors.

GIFT AID (NEED-BASED) *Scholarships, grants, and awards:* Federal Pell, FSEOG, state, college/university gift aid from institutional funds.

GIFT AID (NON-NEED-BASED) *Scholarships, grants, and awards by category:* Academic interests/achievement: biological sciences, business, education, general academic interests/achievements, mathematics, premedicine. *Creative arts/performance:* art/fine arts, music, theater/drama. *Special achievements/activities:* cheerleading/drum major, general special achievements/activities. *Special characteristics:* children of faculty/staff, religious affiliation.

LOANS *Programs:* Federal Direct (Subsidized and Unsubsidized Stafford, PLUS), Perkins, private loans, United Methodist Student Loans (for members of Methodist Church).

CONTACT Mary Alexander, Director of Financial Aid, Dakota Wesleyan University, 1200 West University Avenue, Mitchell, SD 57301, 605-995-2663 or toll-free 800-333-8506. *Fax:* 605-995-2122. *E-mail:* maalexan@dwu.edu. *Website:* http://www.dwu.edu/.

DALLAS BAPTIST UNIVERSITY
Dallas, TX

Tuition & fees: $28,870	Average undergraduate aid package: $16,211

ABOUT THE INSTITUTION Independent Baptist General Convention of Texas, coed. *Awards:* certificates, associate, bachelor's, master's, and doctoral degrees. 47 undergraduate majors. *Total enrollment:* 5,067. Undergraduates: 3,161. Freshmen: 540. Federal methodology is used as a basis for awarding need-based institutional aid.

UNDERGRADUATE EXPENSES for 2018–2019 *Application fee:* $25. *Comprehensive fee:* $36,862 includes full-time tuition ($27,870), mandatory fees

($1000), and room and board ($7992). *College room only:* $3915. Full-time tuition and fees vary according to course load. Room and board charges vary according to board plan and housing facility. *Part-time tuition:* $929 per credit hour. *Part-time fees:* $500 per term. Part-time tuition and fees vary according to course load.

FRESHMAN FINANCIAL AID (Fall 2017, est.) 512 applied for aid; of those 77% were deemed to have need. 100% of freshmen with need received aid; of those 35% had need fully met. *Average percent of need met:* 61% (excluding resources awarded to replace EFC). *Average financial aid package:* $16,680 (excluding resources awarded to replace EFC). 22% of all full-time freshmen had no need and received non-need-based gift aid.

UNDERGRADUATE FINANCIAL AID (Fall 2017, est.) 1,973 applied for aid; of those 77% were deemed to have need. 99% of undergraduates with need received aid; of those 34% had need fully met. *Average percent of need met:* 57% (excluding resources awarded to replace EFC). *Average financial aid package:* $16,211 (excluding resources awarded to replace EFC). 21% of all full-time undergraduates had no need and received non-need-based gift aid.

GIFT AID (NEED-BASED) *Total amount:* $6,556,725 (59% federal, 41% state). *Receiving aid:* Freshmen: 47% (251); all full-time undergraduates: 40% (950). *Average award:* Freshmen: $4007; Undergraduates: $4095. *Scholarships, grants, and awards:* Federal Pell, FSEOG, state, private, college/university gift aid from institutional funds.

GIFT AID (NON-NEED-BASED) *Total amount:* $20,320,495 (89% institutional, 11% external sources). *Receiving aid:* Freshmen: 68% (368). Undergraduates: 56% (1,346). *Average award:* Freshmen: $9663. Undergraduates: $9490. *Scholarships, grants, and awards by category:* Academic interests/achievement: 942 awards ($2,869,316 total): biological sciences, business, communication, computer science, education, English, general academic interests/achievements, humanities, mathematics, physical sciences, premedicine, religion/biblical studies, social sciences. *Creative arts/performance:* 100 awards ($352,368 total): art/fine arts, music. *Special achievements/activities:* 1,764 awards ($9,100,584 total): community service, general special achievements/activities, leadership, memberships, religious involvement. *Special characteristics:* 266 awards ($894,731 total): children of faculty/staff, general special characteristics, relatives of clergy, religious affiliation, veterans, veterans' children. *Tuition waivers:* Full or partial for employees or children of employees. *ROTC:* Army cooperative, Air Force cooperative.

LOANS *Student loans:* $15,436,220 (32% need-based, 68% non-need-based). 84% of past graduating class borrowed through all loan programs. *Average indebtedness per student:* $24,805. *Average need-based loan:* Freshmen: $3422. Undergraduates: $4209. *Parent loans:* $3,802,979 (100% non-need-based). *Programs:* Federal Direct (Subsidized and Unsubsidized Stafford, PLUS), state.

WORK-STUDY *Federal work-study:* Total amount: $379,426; 122 jobs averaging $2304. *State or other work-study/employment:* Total amount: $33,000 (100% need-based). 9 part-time jobs averaging $2566.

ATHLETIC AWARDS Total amount: $2,063,881 (100% non-need-based).

APPLYING FOR FINANCIAL AID *Required financial aid forms:* FAFSA, institution's own form. *Financial aid deadline:* Continuous. *Notification date:* Continuous beginning 2/1.

CONTACT Mr. Justin Silcox, Director of Financial Aid, Dallas Baptist University, 3000 Mountain Creek Parkway, Dallas, TX 75211-9299, 214-333-5363 or toll-free 800-460-1328. *Fax:* 214-333-5586. *E-mail:* justin@dbu.edu. *Website:* http://www.dbu.edu/.

DALLAS CHRISTIAN COLLEGE
Dallas, TX

CONTACT Robin L. Walker, Director of Student Financial Aid, Dallas Christian College, 2700 Christian Parkway, Dallas, TX 75234-7299, 972-241-3371 Ext. 105 or toll-free 800-688-1029. *Fax:* 972-241-8021. *E-mail:* finaid@dallas.edu. *Website:* http://www.dallas.edu/.

DALTON STATE COLLEGE
Dalton, GA

CONTACT Holly Woods, Assistant Director of Financial Aid, Dalton State College, 650 College Drive, Dalton, GA 30720, 706-272-4545 or toll-free 800-829-4436. *Fax:* 706-272-2458. *E-mail:* finaid@daltonstate.edu. *Website:* http://www.daltonstate.edu/.

DARTMOUTH COLLEGE
Hanover, NH

Tuition & fees: $52,950	Average undergraduate aid package: $50,665

ABOUT THE INSTITUTION Independent, coed. *Awards:* bachelor's, master's, and doctoral degrees. 61 undergraduate majors. *Total enrollment:* 6,509. Undergraduates: 4,410. Freshmen: 1,215. Both federal and institutional methodology are used as a basis for awarding need-based institutional aid.

UNDERGRADUATE EXPENSES for 2017–2018 *Application fee:* $80. *One-time required fee:* $418. *Comprehensive fee:* $68,109 includes full-time tuition ($51,468), mandatory fees ($1482), and room and board ($15,159). *College room only:* $9144. Room and board charges vary according to board plan. *Payment plan:* Tuition prepayment.

FRESHMAN FINANCIAL AID (Fall 2017, est.) 691 applied for aid; of those 85% were deemed to have need. 100% of freshmen with need received aid; of those 100% had need fully met. *Average percent of need met:* 100% (excluding resources awarded to replace EFC). *Average financial aid package:* $52,069 (excluding resources awarded to replace EFC).

UNDERGRADUATE FINANCIAL AID (Fall 2017, est.) 2,494 applied for aid; of those 90% were deemed to have need. 100% of undergraduates with need received aid; of those 100% had need fully met. *Average percent of need met:* 100% (excluding resources awarded to replace EFC). *Average financial aid package:* $50,665 (excluding resources awarded to replace EFC).

GIFT AID (NEED-BASED) *Total amount:* $104,122,977 (4% federal, 93% institutional, 3% external sources). *Receiving aid:* Freshmen: 45% (549); all full-time undergraduates: 48% (2,138). *Average award:* Freshmen: $51,461; Undergraduates: $48,772. *Scholarships, grants, and awards:* Federal Pell, FSEOG, state, private, college/university gift aid from institutional funds.

GIFT AID (NON-NEED-BASED) *Total amount:* $885,163 (6% federal, 94% external sources). *ROTC:* Army cooperative.

LOANS *Student loans:* $8,955,406 (52% need-based, 48% non-need-based). 52% of past graduating class borrowed through all loan programs. *Average indebtedness per student:* $19,571. *Average need-based loan:* Freshmen: $4244. Undergraduates: $4569. *Parent loans:* $4,138,433 (100% non-need-based). *Programs:* Federal Direct (Subsidized and Unsubsidized Stafford, PLUS), Perkins, state, college/university.

WORK-STUDY *Federal work-study:* Total amount: $3,122,545; 1,397 jobs averaging $2199. *State or other work-study/employment:* Total amount: $1,244,882 (100% need-based). 547 part-time jobs averaging $2404.

APPLYING FOR FINANCIAL AID *Required financial aid forms:* FAFSA, CSS Financial Aid PROFILE, noncustodial (divorced/separated) parent's statement, business/farm supplement, current W-2 or federal tax returns. *Financial aid deadline:* 2/1. *Notification date:* 4/2. Students must reply by 5/1.

CONTACT Mr. Gordon D. Koff, Director of Financial Aid, Dartmouth College, 6024 McNutt Hall, Hanover, NH 03755, 603-646-2451. *Fax:* 603-646-1414. *E-mail:* gordon.d.koff@dartmouth.edu. *Website:* http://www.dartmouth.edu/.

DAVENPORT UNIVERSITY
Grand Rapids, MI

CONTACT David DeBoer, Executive Director of Financial Aid, Davenport University, 6191 Kraft Avenue SE, Grand Rapids, MI 49512, 616-732-1132 or toll-free 800-686-1600 (in-state), 866-686-1600 (out-of-state). *Fax:* 616-732-1167. *E-mail:* david.debore@davenport.edu. *Website:* http://www.davenport.edu/.

DAVIDSON COLLEGE
Davidson, NC

Tuition & fees: $49,949	Average undergraduate aid package: $47,803

ABOUT THE INSTITUTION Independent Presbyterian, coed. **Awards:** bachelor's degrees. 27 undergraduate majors. **Total enrollment:** 1,796. Undergraduates: 1,796. Freshmen: 514. Both federal and institutional methodology are used as a basis for awarding need-based institutional aid.

UNDERGRADUATE EXPENSES for 2017–2018 Application fee: $50. **Comprehensive fee:** $63,903 includes full-time tuition ($49,454), mandatory fees ($495), and room and board ($13,954). **College room only:** $7102. Room and board charges vary according to board plan.

FRESHMAN FINANCIAL AID (Fall 2017, est.) 365 applied for aid; of those 73% were deemed to have need. 100% of freshmen with need received aid; of those 100% had need fully met. **Average percent of need met:** 100% (excluding resources awarded to replace EFC). **Average financial aid package:** $47,564 (excluding resources awarded to replace EFC). 4% of all full-time freshmen had no need and received non-need-based gift aid.

UNDERGRADUATE FINANCIAL AID (Fall 2017, est.) 1,079 applied for aid; of those 84% were deemed to have need. 100% of undergraduates with need received aid; of those 100% had need fully met. **Average percent of need met:** 100% (excluding resources awarded to replace EFC). **Average financial aid package:** $47,803 (excluding resources awarded to replace EFC). 7% of all full-time undergraduates had no need and received non-need-based gift aid.

GIFT AID (NEED-BASED) Total amount: $40,398,279 (4% federal, 1% state, 93% institutional, 2% external sources). **Receiving aid:** Freshmen: 51% (266); all full-time undergraduates: 50% (899). **Average award:** Freshmen: $43,859; Undergraduates: $44,434. **Scholarships, grants, and awards:** Federal Pell, FSEOG, state, private, college/university gift aid from institutional funds, need-linked special talent scholarships.

GIFT AID (NON-NEED-BASED) Total amount: $4,998,850 (10% federal, 66% institutional, 24% external sources). **Receiving aid:** Freshmen: 18% (93). Undergraduates: 13% (234). **Average award:** Freshmen: $26,274. Undergraduates: $24,739. **Scholarships, grants, and awards by category:** Academic interests/achievement: biological sciences, business, education, foreign languages, general academic interests/achievements, international studies, mathematics, physical sciences, premedicine, social sciences. Creative arts/performance: art/fine arts, creative writing, music, performing arts, theater/drama. Special achievements/activities: community service, general special achievements/activities, leadership, religious involvement. Special characteristics: general special characteristics, out-of-state students, relatives of clergy, religious affiliation. **Tuition waivers:** Full or partial for employees or children of employees. **ROTC:** Army, Air Force cooperative.

LOANS Student loans: $2,645,604 (29% need-based, 71% non-need-based). 26% of past graduating class borrowed through all loan programs. **Average indebtedness per student:** $20,431. **Average need-based loan:** Freshmen: $2841. Undergraduates: $3770. **Parent loans:** $2,997,487 (100% non-need-based). **Programs:** Federal Direct (Subsidized and Unsubsidized Stafford, PLUS), alternative loans.

WORK-STUDY Federal work-study: Total amount: $716,457; 348 jobs averaging $2059. **State or other work-study/employment:** Total amount: $335,475 (100% need-based). 194 part-time jobs averaging $1729.

ATHLETIC AWARDS Total amount: $3,704,396 (10% need-based, 90% non-need-based).

APPLYING FOR FINANCIAL AID Required financial aid forms: FAFSA, CSS Financial Aid PROFILE, noncustodial (divorced/separated) parent's statement, business/farm supplement, federal income tax form(s), W-2 forms. **Financial aid deadline:** 2/15. **Notification date:** 4/1. Students must reply by 5/1.

CONTACT Mr. David R. Gelinas, Director of Financial Aid, Davidson College, 413 North Main Street, PO Box 7157, Davidson, NC 28035-7157, 704-894-2232 or toll-free 800-768-0380. *Fax:* 704-894-2845. *E-mail:* dagelinas@davidson.edu. *Website:* http://www.davidson.edu/.

DAVIS & ELKINS COLLEGE
Elkins, WV

CONTACT Susan M. George, Director of Financial Planning, Davis & Elkins College, 100 Campus Drive, Elkins, WV 26241-3996, 304-637-1373 or toll-free 800-624-3157. *Fax:* 304-637-1986. *E-mail:* ssw@davisandelkins.edu. *Website:* http://www.dewv.edu/.

DAVIS COLLEGE
Johnson City, NY

Tuition & fees: $16,300	Average undergraduate aid package: $9924

ABOUT THE INSTITUTION Independent nondenominational, coed. **Awards:** certificates, diplomas, associate, and bachelor's degrees. 8 undergraduate majors. **Total enrollment:** 216. Undergraduates: 216. Freshmen: 42. Federal methodology is used as a basis for awarding need-based institutional aid.

UNDERGRADUATE EXPENSES for 2017–2018 Application fee: $45. **One-time required fee:** $150. **Comprehensive fee:** $24,000 includes full-time tuition ($15,000), mandatory fees ($1300), and room and board ($7700). Full-time tuition and fees vary according to course load and location. Room and board charges vary according to board plan and housing facility. **Part-time tuition:** $500 per credit hour. **Part-time fees:** $650 per year. Part-time tuition and fees vary according to course load and location.

FRESHMAN FINANCIAL AID (Fall 2016) 35 applied for aid; of those 100% were deemed to have need. 100% of freshmen with need received aid. **Average percent of need met:** 60% (excluding resources awarded to replace EFC). **Average financial aid package:** $9924 (excluding resources awarded to replace EFC).

UNDERGRADUATE FINANCIAL AID (Fall 2016) 178 applied for aid; of those 100% were deemed to have need. 100% of undergraduates with need received aid. **Average percent of need met:** 74% (excluding resources awarded to replace EFC). **Average financial aid package:** $9924 (excluding resources awarded to replace EFC).

GIFT AID (NEED-BASED) Total amount: $950,962 (68% federal, 20% state, 12% institutional). **Receiving aid:** Freshmen: 97% (34); all full-time undergraduates: 99% (177). **Average award:** Freshmen: $9924; Undergraduates: $9924. **Scholarships, grants, and awards:** Federal Pell, FSEOG, state, private, college/university gift aid from institutional funds.

GIFT AID (NON-NEED-BASED) Total amount: $625,545 (11% state, 78% institutional, 11% external sources). **Scholarships, grants, and awards by category:** Academic interests/achievement: general academic interests/achievements, religion/biblical studies. Special achievements/activities: 5 awards ($7500 total): leadership. Special characteristics: children and siblings of alumni, children of educators, children of faculty/staff, general special characteristics, international students, married students, out-of-state students, relatives of clergy, siblings of current students, spouses of current students. **Tuition waivers:** Full or partial for employees or children of employees.

LOANS Student loans: $1,028,450 (47% need-based, 53% non-need-based). **Average indebtedness per student:** $9381. **Parent loans:** $150,800 (100% non-need-based). **Programs:** Federal Direct (Subsidized and Unsubsidized Stafford, PLUS), college/university.

WORK-STUDY Federal work-study: jobs available. **State or other work-study/employment:** Total amount: $80,914 (100% non-need-based). 11 part-time jobs averaging $1000.

APPLYING FOR FINANCIAL AID Required financial aid forms: FAFSA, institution's own form, state aid form. **Financial aid deadline:** 8/15 (priority: 7/15). **Notification date:** Continuous beginning 1/1. Students must reply within 2 weeks of notification.

CONTACT Sandra Conklin, Financial Aid Director, Davis College, 400 Riverside Drive, Johnson City, NY 13790, 607-729-1581 Ext. 331 or toll-free 877-949-3248. *Fax:* 607-798-7754. *E-mail:* financialaid@davisny.edu. *Website:* http://www.davisny.edu/.

DEAN COLLEGE
Franklin, MA

Tuition & fees: $39,434	Average undergraduate aid package: $27,345

ABOUT THE INSTITUTION Independent, coed. *Awards:* certificates, associate, and bachelor's degrees. 25 undergraduate majors. *Total enrollment:* 1,301. Undergraduates: 1,301. Freshmen: 497. Federal methodology is used as a basis for awarding need-based institutional aid.

UNDERGRADUATE EXPENSES for 2018–2019 *One-time required fee:* $300. *Comprehensive fee:* $56,270 includes full-time tuition ($39,234), mandatory fees ($200), and room and board ($16,836). *College room only:* $10,634. Full-time tuition and fees vary according to class time and course load. Room and board charges vary according to housing facility. *Part-time tuition:* $350 per credit hour. *Part-time fees:* $25 per term. Part-time tuition and fees vary according to class time and course load.

FRESHMAN FINANCIAL AID (Fall 2017, est.) 375 applied for aid; of those 93% were deemed to have need. 100% of freshmen with need received aid; of those 8% had need fully met. *Average percent of need met:* 61% (excluding resources awarded to replace EFC). *Average financial aid package:* $27,040 (excluding resources awarded to replace EFC). 20% of all full-time freshmen had no need and received non-need-based gift aid.

UNDERGRADUATE FINANCIAL AID (Fall 2017, est.) 947 applied for aid; of those 93% were deemed to have need. 100% of undergraduates with need received aid; of those 11% had need fully met. *Average percent of need met:* 61% (excluding resources awarded to replace EFC). *Average financial aid package:* $27,345 (excluding resources awarded to replace EFC). 22% of all full-time undergraduates had no need and received non-need-based gift aid.

GIFT AID (NEED-BASED) *Total amount:* $20,000,742 (11% federal, 3% state, 85% institutional, 1% external sources). *Receiving aid:* Freshmen: 66% (292); all full-time undergraduates: 65% (770). *Average award:* Freshmen: $9468; Undergraduates: $7605. *Scholarships, grants, and awards:* Federal Pell, FSEOG, state, private, college/university gift aid from institutional funds.

GIFT AID (NON-NEED-BASED) *Total amount:* $4,455,931 (100% institutional). *Receiving aid:* Freshmen: 78% (344). Undergraduates: 73% (870). *Average award:* Freshmen: $17,085. Undergraduates: $14,464. *Tuition waivers:* Full or partial for employees or children of employees.

LOANS *Student loans:* $9,971,428 (76% need-based, 24% non-need-based). 86% of past graduating class borrowed through all loan programs. *Average indebtedness per student:* $48,717. *Average need-based loan:* Freshmen: $3597. Undergraduates: $3926. *Parent loans:* $6,712,485 (72% need-based, 28% non-need-based). *Programs:* Federal Direct (Subsidized and Unsubsidized Stafford, PLUS), Perkins, Federal Nursing, state.

WORK-STUDY *Federal work-study:* Total amount: $185,214; jobs available.

APPLYING FOR FINANCIAL AID *Required financial aid form:* FAFSA. *Financial aid deadline (priority):* 3/1. *Notification date:* Continuous beginning 3/15. Students must reply by 5/1 or within 2 weeks of notification.

CONTACT Mr. Frank Dunning Mullen, Dean of Student Financial Planning and Services, Dean College, 99 Main Street, Franklin, MA 02038, 508-541-1518 or toll-free 877-TRY-DEAN. *Fax:* 508-541-1941. *E-mail:* fmullen@dean.edu. *Website:* http://www.dean.edu/.

DEFIANCE COLLEGE
Defiance, OH

Tuition & fees: $32,730	Average undergraduate aid package: $23,603

ABOUT THE INSTITUTION Independent United Church of Christ, coed. *Awards:* associate, bachelor's, and master's degrees. 33 undergraduate majors. *Total enrollment:* 630. Undergraduates: 599. Freshmen: 151. Federal methodology is used as a basis for awarding need-based institutional aid.

UNDERGRADUATE EXPENSES for 2018–2019 *Application fee:* $25. *Comprehensive fee:* $42,950 includes full-time tuition ($31,990), mandatory fees ($740), and room and board ($10,220). *College room only:* $5500. Full-time tuition and fees vary according to course load. Room and board charges vary according to board plan and housing facility. *Part-time tuition:* $495 per credit hour. *Part-time fees:* $100 per term. Part-time tuition and fees vary according to course load.

FRESHMAN FINANCIAL AID (Fall 2016) 135 applied for aid; of those 99% were deemed to have need. 100% of freshmen with need received aid; of those 11% had need fully met. *Average percent of need met:* 71% (excluding resources awarded to replace EFC). *Average financial aid package:* $23,953 (excluding resources awarded to replace EFC). 3% of all full-time freshmen had no need and received non-need-based gift aid.

UNDERGRADUATE FINANCIAL AID (Fall 2016) 481 applied for aid; of those 98% were deemed to have need. 100% of undergraduates with need received aid; of those 13% had need fully met. *Average percent of need met:* 67% (excluding resources awarded to replace EFC). *Average financial aid package:* $23,603 (excluding resources awarded to replace EFC). 8% of all full-time undergraduates had no need and received non-need-based gift aid.

GIFT AID (NEED-BASED) *Total amount:* $8,997,171 (14% federal, 3% state, 79% institutional, 4% external sources). *Receiving aid:* Freshmen: 97% (133); all full-time undergraduates: 91% (468). *Average award:* Freshmen: $19,639; Undergraduates: $18,809. *Scholarships, grants, and awards:* Federal Pell, FSEOG, state, private, college/university gift aid from institutional funds.

GIFT AID (NON-NEED-BASED) *Total amount:* $1,044,507 (92% institutional, 8% external sources). *Receiving aid:* Freshmen: 8% (11). Undergraduates: 8% (39). *Average award:* Freshmen: $15,433. Undergraduates: $17,479. *Scholarships, grants, and awards by category:* Academic interests/achievement: biological sciences, business, communication, education, English, general academic interests/achievements, humanities, international studies, mathematics, physical sciences, pre-medicine, religion/biblical studies, social sciences. *Creative arts/performance:* applied art and design, music. *Special achievements/activities:* community service, general special achievements/activities, leadership, religious involvement. *Special characteristics:* children and siblings of alumni, children of faculty/staff, international students, religious affiliation, veterans, veterans' children. *Tuition waivers:* Full or partial for employees or children of employees.

LOANS *Student loans:* $5,051,592 (80% need-based, 20% non-need-based). *Average need-based loan:* Freshmen: $3760. Undergraduates: $4590. *Parent loans:* $1,651,736 (61% need-based, 39% non-need-based). *Programs:* Federal Direct (Subsidized and Unsubsidized Stafford, PLUS), Perkins, alternative loans.

WORK-STUDY *Federal work-study:* jobs available. *State or other work-study/employment:* Part-time jobs available.

APPLYING FOR FINANCIAL AID *Required financial aid form:* FAFSA. *Financial aid deadline (priority):* 4/1. *Notification date:* Continuous beginning 12/15. Students must reply by 5/1 or within 2 weeks of notification.

CONTACT Amy Francis, Director of Financial Aid, Defiance College, 701 North Clinton Street, Defiance, OH 43512-1610, 419-783-2376 or toll-free 800-520-4632. *Fax:* 419-783-2579. *E-mail:* afrancis@defiance.edu. *Website:* http://www.defiance.edu/.

DELAWARE STATE UNIVERSITY
Dover, DE

Tuition & fees (DE res): $7868	Average undergraduate aid package: $11,234

ABOUT THE INSTITUTION State-supported, coed. *Awards:* certificates, bachelor's, master's, and doctoral degrees. 137 undergraduate majors. *Total enrollment:* 4,353. Undergraduates: 4,051. Freshmen: 951. Federal methodology is used as a basis for awarding need-based institutional aid.

UNDERGRADUATE EXPENSES for 2017–2018 *Application fee:* $35. *Tuition, state resident:* full-time $7868; part-time $280 per credit hour. *Tuition, nonresident:* full-time $16,904; part-time $638 per credit hour. *Required fees:* $300 per term. Full-time tuition and fees vary according to course load, reciprocity agreements, and student level. Part-time tuition and fees vary according to course load, reciprocity agreements, and student level. *College room and board:* $11,054; *Room only:* $6976. Room and board charges vary according to board plan and housing facility.

FRESHMAN FINANCIAL AID (Fall 2016) 893 applied for aid; of those 91% were deemed to have need. 99% of freshmen with need received aid; of those 8% had need fully met. *Average percent of need met:* 77% (excluding resources awarded to replace EFC). *Average financial aid package:* $11,863 (excluding resources

awarded to replace EFC). 3% of all full-time freshmen had no need and received non need-based gift aid.

UNDERGRADUATE FINANCIAL AID (Fall 2016) 3,301 applied for aid; of those 90% were deemed to have need. 98% of undergraduates with need received aid; of those 16% had need fully met. *Average percent of need met:* 77% (excluding resources awarded to replace EFC). *Average financial aid package:* $11,234 (excluding resources awarded to replace EFC). 3% of all full-time undergraduates had no need and received non-need-based gift aid.

GIFT AID (NEED-BASED) Total amount: $304,853 (29% federal, 69% state, 1% institutional, 1% external sources). *Receiving aid:* Freshmen: 60% (567); all full-time undergraduates: 58% (2,084). *Average award:* Freshmen: $5210; Undergraduates: $5250. *Scholarships, grants, and awards:* Federal Pell, FSEOG, state, college/university gift aid from institutional funds, Federal Nursing.

GIFT AID (NON-NEED-BASED) Total amount: $17,297,348 (33% state, 60% institutional, 7% external sources). *Receiving aid:* Freshmen: 62% (585). Undergraduates: 41% (1,483). *Average award:* Freshmen: $1144. Undergraduates: $4530. *Scholarships, grants, and awards by category:* Academic interests/achievement: general academic interests/achievements. *Creative arts/performance:* music. *Special achievements/activities:* general special achievements/activities. *Special characteristics:* out-of-state students. *Tuition waivers:* Full or partial for employees or children of employees, senior citizens. *ROTC:* Army, Air Force.

LOANS Student loans: $5,701,994 (1% need-based, 99% non-need-based). 87% of past graduating class borrowed through all loan programs. *Average indebtedness per student:* $36,812. *Average need-based loan:* Freshmen: $3262. Undergraduates: $3883. *Programs:* Federal Direct (Subsidized and Unsubsidized Stafford, PLUS), Perkins, Federal Nursing.

WORK-STUDY Federal work-study jobs available. *State or other work-study/employment:* Part-time jobs available.

ATHLETIC AWARDS Total amount: $1,064,396 (46% need-based, 54% non-need-based).

APPLYING FOR FINANCIAL AID *Required financial aid form:* FAFSA. *Financial aid deadline (priority):* 3/15. *Notification date:* Continuous beginning 4/1. Students must reply by 7/10.

CONTACT Office of Student Financial Aid Services, Delaware State University, 1200 North DuPont Highway, Dover, DE 19901-2277, 302-857-6250 or toll-free 800-845-2544. *E-mail:* faid@desu.edu.
Website: http://www.desu.edu/.

DELAWARE VALLEY UNIVERSITY
Doylestown, PA

Tuition & fees: $38,000	Average undergraduate aid package: $27,782

ABOUT THE INSTITUTION Independent, coed. *Awards:* certificates, bachelor's, master's, and doctoral degrees. 31 undergraduate majors. *Total enrollment:* 2,422. Undergraduates: 1,992. Freshmen: 412. Federal methodology is used as a basis for awarding need-based institutional aid.

UNDERGRADUATE EXPENSES for 2017–2018 *Application fee:* $50. *Comprehensive fee:* $51,950 includes full-time tuition ($35,610), mandatory fees ($2390), and room and board ($13,950). *College room only:* $6648. Full-time tuition and fees vary according to class time and program. Room and board charges vary according to board plan and housing facility. *Part-time tuition:* $982 per credit hour. *Part-time fees:* $116 per course. Part-time tuition and fees vary according to class time, course load, and program.

FRESHMAN FINANCIAL AID (Fall 2017, est.) 387 applied for aid; of those 90% were deemed to have need. 100% of freshmen with need received aid; of those 14% had need fully met. *Average percent of need met:* 70% (excluding resources awarded to replace EFC). *Average financial aid package:* $29,940 (excluding resources awarded to replace EFC). 15% of all full-time freshmen had no need and received non-need-based gift aid.

UNDERGRADUATE FINANCIAL AID (Fall 2017, est.) 1,552 applied for aid; of those 91% were deemed to have need. 99% of undergraduates with need received aid; of those 9% had need fully met. *Average percent of need met:* 66% (excluding resources awarded to replace EFC). *Average financial aid package:* $27,782 (excluding resources awarded to replace EFC). 18% of all full-time undergraduates had no need and received non-need-based gift aid.

GIFT AID (NEED-BASED) Total amount: $31,839,978 (10% federal, 5% state, 84% institutional, 1% external sources). *Receiving aid:* Freshmen: 84% (346); all full-

time undergraduates: 80% (1,100). *Average award:* Freshmen: $25,779; Undergraduates: $23,360. *Scholarships, grants, and awards:* Federal Pell, FSEOG, state, private, college/university gift aid from institutional funds.

GIFT AID (NON-NEED-BASED) Total amount: $6,739,967 (99% institutional, 1% external sources). *Receiving aid:* Freshmen: 9% (38). Undergraduates: 7% (122). *Average award:* Freshmen: $20,688. Undergraduates: $18,122. *Scholarships, grants, and awards by category:* Creative arts/performance: 27 awards ($25,200 total): music. Special achievements/activities: 52 awards ($52,639 total): general special achievements/activities. Special characteristics: 144 awards ($294,000 total): ethnic background, members of minority groups, siblings of current students, veterans. *Tuition waivers:* Full or partial for employees or children of employees.

LOANS Student loans: $16,214,281 (73% need-based, 27% non-need-based). 82% of past graduating class borrowed through all loan programs. *Average indebtedness per student:* $45,953. *Average need-based loan:* Freshmen: $3710. Undergraduates: $4578. *Parent loans:* $8,757,645 (60% need-based, 40% non-need-based). *Programs:* Federal Direct (Subsidized and Unsubsidized Stafford, PLUS), Perkins.

WORK-STUDY Federal work-study: Total amount: $199,255; 150 jobs averaging $1642.

APPLYING FOR FINANCIAL AID *Required financial aid forms:* FAFSA, state aid form. *Financial aid deadline (priority):* 4/17. *Notification date:* Continuous beginning 1/30. Students must reply by 5/1 or within 2 weeks of notification.

CONTACT Ms. Joan Hock, Director of Student Financial Aid, Delaware Valley University, 700 East Butler Avenue, Doylestown, PA 18901-2697, 215-489-2975 or toll-free 800-2DELVAL. *E-mail:* finaid@delval.edu.
Website: http://www.delval.edu/.

DELTA STATE UNIVERSITY
Cleveland, MS

ABOUT THE INSTITUTION State-supported, coed. 38 undergraduate majors.

GIFT AID (NEED-BASED) *Scholarships, grants, and awards:* Federal Pell, FSEOG, state, private, college/university gift aid from institutional funds.

GIFT AID (NON-NEED-BASED) *Scholarships, grants, and awards by category:* Academic interests/achievement: biological sciences, business, computer science, education, English, foreign languages, general academic interests/achievements, health fields, humanities, mathematics, physical sciences, premedicine, social sciences. *Creative arts/performance:* art/fine arts, creative writing, journalism/publications, music, performing arts. *Special achievements/activities:* cheerleading/drum major, general special achievements/activities, leadership, memberships. *Special characteristics:* children and siblings of alumni, children of faculty/staff, general special characteristics, out-of-state students.

LOANS Programs: Federal Direct (Subsidized and Unsubsidized Stafford, PLUS), Perkins.

APPLYING FOR FINANCIAL AID *Required financial aid forms:* FAFSA, institution's own form.

CONTACT Ms. Christie Rocconi, Director of Student Financial Assistance, Delta State University, Kent Wyatt Hall 144, Highway 8 West, Cleveland, MS 38733-0001, 662-846-4670 or toll-free 800-468-6378. *Fax:* 662-846-4683. *E-mail:* finaid@deltastate.edu.
Website: http://www.deltastate.edu/.

DENISON UNIVERSITY
Granville, OH

Tuition & fees: $50,440	Average undergraduate aid package: $44,138

ABOUT THE INSTITUTION Independent, coed. *Awards:* bachelor's degrees. 39 undergraduate majors. *Total enrollment:* 2,341. Undergraduates: 2,341. Freshmen: 617. Federal methodology is used as a basis for awarding need-based institutional aid.

UNDERGRADUATE EXPENSES for 2017–2018 *Comprehensive fee:* $62,770 includes full-time tuition ($49,310), mandatory fees ($1130), and room and board ($12,330). *College room only:* $6790. Room and board charges vary according to board plan and housing facility. *Part-time tuition:* $1541 per credit hour. Part-time tuition and fees vary according to course load.

FRESHMAN FINANCIAL AID (Fall 2017, est.) 458 applied for aid; of those 75% were deemed to have need. 100% of freshmen with need received aid; of those 79% had need fully met. *Average percent of need met:* 100% (excluding resources awarded to replace EFC). *Average financial aid package:* $47,566 (excluding resources awarded to replace EFC). 39% of all full-time freshmen had no need and received non-need-based gift aid.

UNDERGRADUATE FINANCIAL AID (Fall 2017, est.) 1,497 applied for aid; of those 84% were deemed to have need. 100% of undergraduates with need received aid; of those 47% had need fully met. *Average percent of need met:* 91% (excluding resources awarded to replace EFC). *Average financial aid package:* $44,138 (excluding resources awarded to replace EFC). 41% of all full-time undergraduates had no need and received non-need-based gift aid.

GIFT AID (NEED-BASED) *Total amount:* $43,729,860 (6% federal, 1% state, 92% institutional, 1% external sources). *Receiving aid:* Freshmen: 55% (342); all full-time undergraduates: 54% (1,257). *Average award:* Freshmen: $41,557; Undergraduates: $38,832. *Scholarships, grants, and awards:* Federal Pell, FSEOG, state, private, college/university gift aid from institutional funds.

GIFT AID (NON-NEED-BASED) *Total amount:* $25,987,946 (99% institutional, 1% external sources). *Receiving aid:* Freshmen: 11% (66). Undergraduates: 6% (142). *Average award:* Freshmen: $21,511. Undergraduates: $21,862. *Scholarships, grants, and awards by category: Academic interests/achievement:* biological sciences, English, foreign languages, mathematics, physical sciences. *Special characteristics:* children of faculty/staff, veterans. *Tuition waivers:* Full or partial for employees or children of employees. *ROTC:* Army cooperative.

LOANS *Student loans:* $8,373,141 (84% need-based, 16% non-need-based). 53% of past graduating class borrowed through all loan programs. *Average indebtedness per student:* $27,823. *Average need-based loan:* Freshmen: $3598. Undergraduates: $5161. *Parent loans:* $3,376,313 (72% need-based, 28% non-need-based). *Programs:* Federal Direct (Subsidized and Unsubsidized Stafford, PLUS), Perkins, college/university.

WORK-STUDY *Federal work-study:* Total amount: $1,691,286; jobs available. *State or other work-study/employment:* Total amount: $3,290,394 (32% need-based, 68% non-need-based). Part-time jobs available.

APPLYING FOR FINANCIAL AID *Required financial aid forms:* FAFSA, CSS Financial Aid PROFILE, noncustodial (divorced/separated) parent's statement. *Financial aid deadline (priority):* 1/15. *Notification date:* Continuous beginning 3/15. Students must reply by 5/1 or within 2 weeks of notification.

CONTACT Ms. Laura Meek, Director of Financial Aid, Denison University, PO Box M, Granville, OH 43023-0613, 740-587-6279 or toll-free 800-DENISON. *Fax:* 740-587-5706. *E-mail:* meekl@denison.edu.
Website: http://www.denison.edu/.

DENVER COLLEGE OF NURSING
Denver, CO

CONTACT Financial Aid Office, Denver College of Nursing, 1401 19th Street, Denver, CO 80202, 303-292-0015 or toll-free 888-479-5550.
Website: http://www.denvercollegeofnursing.edu/.

DEPAUL UNIVERSITY
Chicago, IL

Tuition & fees: $38,410	Average undergraduate aid package: $23,589

ABOUT THE INSTITUTION Independent Roman Catholic, coed. *Awards:* certificates, bachelor's, master's, and doctoral degrees. 98 undergraduate majors. *Total enrollment:* 22,769. Undergraduates: 14,816. Freshmen: 2,542. Federal methodology is used as a basis for awarding need-based institutional aid.

UNDERGRADUATE EXPENSES for 2017–2018 *Tuition:* full-time $38,410; part-time $615 per credit hour. Full-time tuition and fees vary according to course load and program. Part-time tuition and fees vary according to course load and program. Room and board charges vary according to board plan, housing facility, and location.

FRESHMAN FINANCIAL AID (Fall 2016) 2,077 applied for aid; of those 84% were deemed to have need. 100% of freshmen with need received aid; of those 16%

had need fully met. *Average percent of need met:* 67% (excluding resources awarded to replace EFC). *Average financial aid package:* $25,812 (excluding resources awarded to replace EFC). 25% of all full-time freshmen had no need and received non-need-based gift aid.

UNDERGRADUATE FINANCIAL AID (Fall 2016) 10,144 applied for aid; of those 89% were deemed to have need. 99% of undergraduates with need received aid; of those 10% had need fully met. *Average percent of need met:* 62% (excluding resources awarded to replace EFC). *Average financial aid package:* $23,589 (excluding resources awarded to replace EFC). 19% of all full-time undergraduates had no need and received non-need-based gift aid.

GIFT AID (NEED-BASED) *Total amount:* $104,535,974 (21% federal, 17% state, 62% institutional). *Receiving aid:* Freshmen: 63% (1,537); all full-time undergraduates: 59% (7,698). *Average award:* Freshmen: $11,045; Undergraduates: $12,156. *Scholarships, grants, and awards:* Federal Pell, FSEOG, state, private, college/university gift aid from institutional funds, TEACH Grants, veteran awards.

GIFT AID (NON-NEED-BASED) *Total amount:* $108,507,704 (7% federal, 91% institutional, 2% external sources). *Receiving aid:* Freshmen: 61% (1,486). Undergraduates: 47% (6,108). *Average award:* Freshmen: $16,447. Undergraduates: $15,348. *Scholarships, grants, and awards by category: Academic interests/achievement:* general academic interests/achievements. *Creative arts/performance:* art/fine arts, music, theater/drama. *Special achievements/activities:* community service, leadership. *Special characteristics:* children of faculty/staff, local/state students, veterans, veterans' children. *Tuition waivers:* Full or partial for employees or children of employees. *ROTC:* Army.

LOANS *Student loans:* $81,343,691 (41% need-based, 59% non-need-based). 65% of past graduating class borrowed through all loan programs. *Average indebtedness per student:* $30,115. *Average need-based loan:* Freshmen: $3257. Undergraduates: $4269. *Parent loans:* $61,806,707 (100% non-need-based). *Programs:* Federal Direct (Subsidized and Unsubsidized Stafford, PLUS), Perkins, private loans.

WORK-STUDY *Federal work-study:* 734 jobs averaging $3659. *State or other work-study/employment:* Total amount: $6,626,461 (100% non-need-based). 2,313 part-time jobs averaging $3005.

ATHLETIC AWARDS Total amount: $5,920,265 (100% non-need-based).

APPLYING FOR FINANCIAL AID *Required financial aid form:* FAFSA. *Financial aid deadline:* Continuous. *Notification date:* Continuous beginning 1/15. Students must reply by 5/1 or within 4 weeks of notification.

CONTACT DePaul Central, Office of Financial Aid, DePaul University, 1 East Jackson Boulevard, Chicago, IL 60604-2287, 312-362-8610 or toll-free 800-4DE-PAUL (out-of-state). *Fax:* 312-362-5748.
Website: http://www.depaul.edu/.

DEPAUW UNIVERSITY
Greencastle, IN

Tuition & fees: $47,838	Average undergraduate aid package: $42,206

ABOUT THE INSTITUTION Independent United Methodist Church, coed. *Awards:* bachelor's degrees. 44 undergraduate majors. *Total enrollment:* 2,158. Undergraduates: 2,153. Freshmen: 595. Federal methodology is used as a basis for awarding need-based institutional aid.

UNDERGRADUATE EXPENSES for 2017–2018 *Comprehensive fee:* $60,367 includes full-time tuition ($47,026), mandatory fees ($812), and room and board ($12,529). Room and board charges vary according to board plan. *Part-time tuition:* $1470 per credit hour.

FRESHMAN FINANCIAL AID (Fall 2017, est.) 481 applied for aid; of those 80% were deemed to have need. 100% of freshmen with need received aid; of those 32% had need fully met. *Average percent of need met:* 91% (excluding resources awarded to replace EFC). *Average financial aid package:* $42,524 (excluding resources awarded to replace EFC). 37% of all full-time freshmen had no need and received non-need-based gift aid.

UNDERGRADUATE FINANCIAL AID (Fall 2017, est.) 1,452 applied for aid; of those 87% were deemed to have need. 100% of undergraduates with need received aid; of those 28% had need fully met. *Average percent of need met:* 91% (excluding resources awarded to replace EFC). *Average financial aid package:* $42,206 (excluding resources awarded to replace EFC). 39% of all full-time undergraduates had no need and received non-need-based gift aid.

GIFT AID (NEED-BASED) *Total amount:* $46,779,128 (5% federal, 3% state, 85% institutional, 7% external sources). *Receiving aid:* Freshmen: 65% (387); all full-time undergraduates: 59% (1,255). *Average award:* Freshmen: $38,681; Undergraduates: $37,234. *Scholarships, grants, and awards:* Federal Pell, FSEOG, state, private, college/university gift aid from institutional funds.

GIFT AID (NON-NEED-BASED) *Total amount:* $21,909,554 (87% institutional, 13% external sources). *Receiving aid:* Freshmen: 16% (93). Undergraduates: 11% (236). *Average award:* Freshmen: $24,251. Undergraduates: $20,562. *Scholarships, grants, and awards by category: Academic interests/achievement:* general academic interests/achievements. *Special achievements/activities:* community service. *Special characteristics:* children and siblings of alumni. *Tuition waivers:* Full or partial for employees or children of employees. *ROTC:* Army cooperative, Air Force cooperative.

LOANS *Student loans:* $11,588,617 (60% need-based, 40% non-need-based). 66% of past graduating class borrowed through all loan programs. *Average indebtedness per student:* $23,635. *Average need-based loan:* Freshmen: $3812. Undergraduates: $4838. *Parent loans:* $4,416,285 (25% need-based, 75% non-need-based). *Programs:* Federal Direct (Subsidized and Unsubsidized Stafford, PLUS), Perkins, college/university.

WORK-STUDY *Federal work-study:* Total amount: $1,001,112; jobs available. *State or other work-study/employment:* Total amount: $1,133,986 (36% need-based, 64% non-need-based). Part-time jobs available.

APPLYING FOR FINANCIAL AID *Required financial aid forms:* FAFSA, CSS Financial Aid PROFILE. *Financial aid deadline:* 2/1 (priority: 12/15). *Notification date:* 2/1. Students must reply by 5/1.

CONTACT Office of Financial Aid, DePauw University, 200 East Seminary, Greencastle, IN 46135-0037, 765-658-4030 or toll-free 800-447-2495. *Fax:* 765-658-4137. *E-mail:* financialaid@depauw.edu.
Website: http://www.depauw.edu/.

DESALES UNIVERSITY
Center Valley, PA

Tuition & fees: $36,100	Average undergraduate aid package: $25,821

ABOUT THE INSTITUTION Independent Roman Catholic, coed. *Awards:* certificates, bachelor's, master's, and doctoral degrees. 47 undergraduate majors. *Total enrollment:* 3,315. Undergraduates: 2,345. Freshmen: 475. Federal methodology is used as a basis for awarding need-based institutional aid.

UNDERGRADUATE EXPENSES for 2017–2018 *Comprehensive fee:* $48,900 includes full-time tuition ($34,500), mandatory fees ($1600), and room and board ($12,800). Full-time tuition and fees vary according to class time and course load. Room and board charges vary according to board plan and housing facility. *Part-time tuition:* $1440 per credit hour. Part-time tuition and fees vary according to class time and course load.

FRESHMAN FINANCIAL AID (Fall 2017, est.) 396 applied for aid; of those 88% were deemed to have need. 100% of freshmen with need received aid; of those 25% had need fully met. *Average percent of need met:* 76% (excluding resources awarded to replace EFC). *Average financial aid package:* $27,969 (excluding resources awarded to replace EFC). 17% of all full-time freshmen had no need and received non-need-based gift aid.

UNDERGRADUATE FINANCIAL AID (Fall 2017, est.) 1,550 applied for aid; of those 90% were deemed to have need. 99% of undergraduates with need received aid; of those 21% had need fully met. *Average percent of need met:* 72% (excluding resources awarded to replace EFC). *Average financial aid package:* $25,821 (excluding resources awarded to replace EFC). 19% of all full-time undergraduates had no need and received non-need-based gift aid.

GIFT AID (NEED-BASED) *Total amount:* $26,238,856 (13% federal, 7% state, 79% institutional, 1% external sources). *Receiving aid:* Freshmen: 83% (348); all full-time undergraduates: 72% (1,309). *Average award:* Freshmen: $22,015; Undergraduates: $20,163. *Scholarships, grants, and awards:* Federal Pell, FSEOG, state, private, college/university gift aid from institutional funds.

GIFT AID (NON-NEED-BASED) *Total amount:* $7,903,314 (2% federal, 97% institutional, 1% external sources). *Receiving aid:* Freshmen: 78% (329). Undergraduates: 63% (1,149). *Average award:* Freshmen: $16,972. Undergraduates: $16,682. *Scholarships, grants, and awards by category: Academic interests/achievement:* 1,630 awards ($12,379,051 total): biological sciences, business, commu-

nication, computer science, education, English, foreign languages, general academic interests/achievements, health fields, home economics, humanities, mathematics, physical sciences, premedicine, religion/biblical studies, social sciences. *Creative arts/performance:* 168 awards ($324,574 total): cinema/film/broadcasting, dance, performing arts, theater/drama. *Special achievements/activities:* 311 awards ($1,027,761 total): leadership. *Special characteristics:* 40 awards ($202,631 total): ethnic background, international students, siblings of current students, veterans' children. *Tuition waivers:* Full or partial for employees or children of employees, adult students, senior citizens. *ROTC:* Army cooperative.

LOANS *Student loans:* $19,810,704 (64% need-based, 36% non-need-based). 79% of past graduating class borrowed through all loan programs. *Average indebtedness per student:* $42,536. *Average need-based loan:* Freshmen: $3597. Undergraduates: $4671. *Parent loans:* $4,940,485 (32% need-based, 68% non-need-based). *Programs:* Federal Direct (Subsidized and Unsubsidized Stafford, PLUS), Perkins, Federal Nursing.

WORK-STUDY *Federal work-study:* Total amount: $809,104; 440 jobs averaging $1988. *State or other work-study/employment:* Total amount: $592,000 (11% need-based, 89% non-need-based). 329 part-time jobs averaging $1997.

APPLYING FOR FINANCIAL AID *Required financial aid forms:* FAFSA, PHEAA form (PA residents only). *Financial aid deadline (priority):* 12/1. *Notification date:* Continuous beginning 12/1. Students must reply by 5/1.

CONTACT Mrs. Joyce Farmer, Director of Financial Aid, DeSales University, 2755 Station Avenue, Center Valley, PA 18034-9568, 610-282-1100 Ext. 1208. *Fax:* 610-282-0131. *E-mail:* joyce.farmer@desales.edu.
Website: http://www.desales.edu/.

DESIGN INSTITUTE OF SAN DIEGO
San Diego, CA

CONTACT Financial Aid Office, Design Institute of San Diego, 8555 Commerce Avenue, San Diego, CA 92121, 858-566-1200 or toll-free 800-619-4337.
Website: http://www.disd.edu/.

DEVRY COLLEGE OF NEW YORK–MIDTOWN MANHATTAN CAMPUS
New York, NY

CONTACT Elvira Senese, Dean of Student Finance, DeVry College of New York–Midtown Manhattan Campus, 30-20 Thomson Avenue, Long Island City, NY 11101, 718-472-2728 or toll-free 866-338-7934. *Fax:* 718-269-4284.
Website: http://www.devry.edu/.

DEVRY UNIVERSITY–ADDISON CAMPUS
Addison, IL

CONTACT Sejal Amin, Director of Student Finance, DeVry University–Addison Campus, 1221 North Swift Road, Addison, IL 60101-6106, 630-953-1300 or toll-free 866-338-7934.
Website: http://www.devry.edu/.

DEVRY UNIVERSITY–ALPHARETTA CAMPUS
Alpharetta, GA

CONTACT David Pickett, Assistant Director of Financial Aid, DeVry University–Alpharetta Campus, 2555 Northwinds Parkway, Alpharetta, GA 30004, 770-521-4900 or toll-free 866-338-7934. *Fax:* 770-664-8024.
Website: http://www.devry.edu/.

DEVRY UNIVERSITY–ARLINGTON CAMPUS
Arlington, VA

CONTACT Roberta McDevitt, Director of Student Finance, DeVry University–Arlington Campus, 2341 Jefferson Davis Highway, Arlington, VA 22202, 866-338-7932 or toll-free 866-338-7934. *Fax:* 703-414-4040.
Website: http://www.devry.edu/.

DEVRY UNIVERSITY–CHARLOTTE CAMPUS
Charlotte, NC

CONTACT Financial Aid Office, DeVry University–Charlotte Campus, 2015 Ayrsley Town Boulevard, Suite 109, Charlotte, NC 28273, 704-697-1020 or toll-free 866-338-7934.
Website: http://www.devry.edu/.

DEVRY UNIVERSITY–CHESAPEAKE CAMPUS
Chesapeake, VA

CONTACT Financial Aid Office, DeVry University–Chesapeake Campus, 1317 Executive Boulevard, Suite 100, Chesapeake, VA 23320, 757-382-5680 or toll-free 866-338-7934.
Website: http://www.devry.edu/.

DEVRY UNIVERSITY–CHICAGO CAMPUS
Chicago, IL

CONTACT Milena Dobrina, Director of Financial Aid, DeVry University–Chicago Campus, 3300 North Campbell Avenue, Chicago, IL 60618-5994, 773-929-8500 or toll-free 866-338-7934. *Fax:* 773-348-1780.
Website: http://www.devry.edu/.

DEVRY UNIVERSITY–CHICAGO LOOP CAMPUS
Chicago, IL

CONTACT Financial Aid Office, DeVry University–Chicago Loop Campus, 225 West Washington Street, Suite 100, Chicago, IL 60606, 312-372-4900 or toll-free 866-338-7934.
Website: http://www.devry.edu/.

DEVRY UNIVERSITY–CINCINNATI CAMPUS
Cincinnati, OH

CONTACT Financial Aid Office, DeVry University–Cincinnati Campus, 8800 Governors Hill Drive, Suite 100, Cincinnati, OH 45249, 513-583-5000 or toll-free 866-338-7934.
Website: http://www.devry.edu/.

DEVRY UNIVERSITY–COLUMBUS CAMPUS
Columbus, OH

CONTACT Student Finance Office, DeVry University–Columbus Campus, 1350 Alum Creek Drive, Columbus, OH 43209-2705, 614-253-7291 or toll-free 866-338-7934. *Fax:* 614-252-4108.
Website: http://www.devry.edu/.

DEVRY UNIVERSITY–DECATUR CAMPUS
Decatur, GA

CONTACT Student Finance Office, DeVry University–Decatur Campus, 1 West Court Square, Suite 100, Decatur, GA 30030-2556, 404-270-2702 or toll-free 866-338-7934.
Website: http://www.devry.edu/.

DEVRY UNIVERSITY–FOLSOM CAMPUS
Folsom, CA

CONTACT Financial Aid Office, DeVry University–Folsom Campus, 950 Iron Point Road, Folsom, CA 95630, 916-351-3700 or toll-free 866-338-7934.
Website: http://www.devry.edu/.

DEVRY UNIVERSITY–FREMONT CAMPUS
Fremont, CA

CONTACT Kim Kane, Director of Student Finance, DeVry University–Fremont Campus, 6600 Dumbarton Circle, Fremont, CA 94555, 510-574-1100 or toll-free 866-338-7934. *Fax:* 510-742-0868.
Website: http://www.devry.edu/.

DEVRY UNIVERSITY–FRESNO CAMPUS
Fresno, CA

CONTACT Financial Aid Office, DeVry University–Fresno Campus, 7575 North Fresno Street, Fresno, CA 93720, 559-439-8595 or toll-free 866-338-7934.
Website: http://www.devry.edu/.

DEVRY UNIVERSITY–FT. WASHINGTON CAMPUS
Fort Washington, PA

CONTACT Financial Aid Office, DeVry University–Ft. Washington Campus, 1140 Virginia Drive, Fort Washington, PA 19034, 215-591-5700 or toll-free 866-338-7934.
Website: http://www.devry.edu/.

DEVRY UNIVERSITY–HENDERSON CAMPUS
Henderson, NV

CONTACT Financial Aid Office, DeVry University–Henderson Campus, 2490 Paseo Verde Parkway, Suite 150, Henderson, NV 89074, 702-933-9700 or toll-free 866-338-7934.
Website: http://www.devry.edu/.

DEVRY UNIVERSITY–IRVING CAMPUS
Irving, TX

CONTACT Student Finance Office, DeVry University–Irving Campus, 4800 Regent Boulevard, Irving, TX 75063-2440, 972-929-9310 or toll-free 866-338-7934.
Website: http://www.devry.edu/.

DEVRY UNIVERSITY–JACKSONVILLE CAMPUS
Jacksonville, FL

CONTACT Financial Aid Office, DeVry University–Jacksonville Campus, 5200 Belfort Road, Suite 175, Jacksonville, FL 32256, 904-367-4942 or toll-free 866-338-7934.
Website: http://www.devry.edu/.

DEVRY UNIVERSITY–KANSAS CITY CAMPUS
Kansas City, MO

CONTACT Maureen Kelly, Senior Associate Director of Financial Aid, DeVry University–Kansas City Campus, 11224 Holmes Street, Kansas City, MO 64131-3698, 816-941-0430 or toll-free 866-338-7934.
Website: http://www.devry.edu/.

DEVRY UNIVERSITY–LONG BEACH CAMPUS
Long Beach, CA

CONTACT Kathy Odom, Director of Financial Aid, DeVry University–Long Beach Campus, 3880 Kilroy Airport Way, Long Beach, CA 90806, 562-427-0861 or toll-free 866-338-7934. *Fax:* 562-989-1578.
Website: http://www.devry.edu/.

DEVRY UNIVERSITY–MIRAMAR CAMPUS
Miramar, FL

CONTACT Office of Financial Aid, DeVry University–Miramar Campus, 2300 Southwest 145th Avenue, Miramar, FL 33027, 954-499-9700 or toll-free 866-338-7934.
Website: http://www.devry.edu/.

DEVRY UNIVERSITY–MORRISVILLE CAMPUS
Morrisville, NC

CONTACT Financial Aid Office, DeVry University–Morrisville Campus, 1600 Perimeter Park Drive, Suite 100, Morrisville, NC 27560, 919-463-1380 or toll-free 866-338-7934.
Website: http://www.devry.edu/.

DEVRY UNIVERSITY–NASHVILLE CAMPUS
Nashville, TN

CONTACT Financial Aid Office, DeVry University–Nashville Campus, 3343 Perimeter Hill Drive, Suite 200, Nashville, TN 37211, 615-445-3456 or toll-free 866-338-7934.
Website: http://www.devry.edu/.

DEVRY UNIVERSITY–NORTH BRUNSWICK CAMPUS
North Brunswick, NJ

CONTACT Student Finance Office, DeVry University–North Brunswick Campus, 630 U.S. Highway 1, North Brunswick, NJ 08902, 732-729-3777 or toll-free 866-338-7934.
Website: http://www.devry.edu/.

DEVRY UNIVERSITY–OKLAHOMA CITY CAMPUS
Oklahoma City, OK

CONTACT Financial Aid Office, DeVry University–Oklahoma City Campus, Lakepointe Towers, 4013 Northwest Expressway Street, Suite 100, Oklahoma City, OK 73116, 405-767-9516 or toll-free 866-338-7934.
Website: http://www.devry.edu/.

DEVRY UNIVERSITY ONLINE
Addison, IL

CONTACT Financial Aid Office, DeVry University Online, 1221 North Swift Road, Addison, IL 60101 or toll-free 866-338-7934.
Website: http://www.devry.edu/.

DEVRY UNIVERSITY–ORLANDO CAMPUS
Orlando, FL

CONTACT Estrella Velazquez-Domenech, Director of Student Finance, DeVry University–Orlando Campus, 4000 Millenia Boulevard, Orlando, FL 32839, 407-345-2816 or toll-free 866-338-7934. *Fax:* 407-355-4855.
Website: http://www.devry.edu/.

DEVRY UNIVERSITY–PHOENIX CAMPUS
Phoenix, AZ

CONTACT Student Finance Office, DeVry University Phoenix Campus, 2149 West Dunlap Avenue, Phoenix, AZ 85021-2995, 602-749-4545 or toll-free 866-338-7934. *Website:* http://www.devry.edu/.

DEVRY UNIVERSITY–POMONA CAMPUS
Pomona, CA

CONTACT Student Finance Office, DeVry University–Pomona Campus, 901 Corporate Center Drive, Pomona, CA 91768-2642, 909-622-8866 or toll-free 866-338-7934. *Website:* http://www.devry.edu/.

DEVRY UNIVERSITY–SAN ANTONIO CAMPUS
San Antonio, TX

CONTACT Financial Aid Office, DeVry University–San Antonio Campus, 618 NW Loop 410, Suite 202, San Antonio, TX 78216, 210-524-5400 or toll-free 866-338-7934. *Website:* http://www.devry.edu/.

DEVRY UNIVERSITY–SAN DIEGO CAMPUS
San Diego, CA

CONTACT Financial Aid Office, DeVry University–San Diego Campus, 2655 Camino Del Rio North, Suite 360, San Diego, CA 92108, 619-683-2446 or toll-free 866-338-7934. *Website:* http://www.devry.edu/.

DEVRY UNIVERSITY–SEVEN HILLS CAMPUS
Seven Hills, OH

CONTACT Financial Aid Office, DeVry University–Seven Hills Campus, 4141 Rockside Road, Suite 110, Seven Hills, OH 44131, 216-328-8754 or toll-free 866-338-7934. *Website:* http://www.devry.edu/.

DEVRY UNIVERSITY–SHERMAN OAKS CAMPUS
Sherman Oaks, CA

CONTACT Financial Aid Office, DeVry University–Sherman Oaks Campus, 15301 Ventura Boulevard, Building D-100, Sherman Oaks, CA 91403, 818-713-8111 or toll-free 866-338-7934. *Website:* http://www.devry.edu/.

DEVRY UNIVERSITY–TINLEY PARK CAMPUS
Tinley Park, IL

CONTACT Director of Student Finance, DeVry University–Tinley Park Campus, 18624 West Creek Drive, Tinley Park, IL 60477, 708-342-3300 or toll-free 866-338-7934. *Fax:* 708-342-3120. *Website:* http://www.devry.edu/.

DEVRY UNIVERSITY–WESTMINSTER CAMPUS
Westminster, CO

CONTACT Office of Financial Aid, DeVry University–Westminster Campus, 1870 West 122nd Avenue, Westminster, CO 80234-2010, 303-280-7400 or toll-free 866-338-7934. *Website:* http://www.devry.edu/.

DICKINSON COLLEGE
Carlisle, PA

Tuition & fees: $52,930 — **Average undergraduate aid package: $45,710**

ABOUT THE INSTITUTION Independent, coed. *Awards:* bachelor's degrees. 43 undergraduate majors. *Total enrollment:* 2,382. Undergraduates: 2,382. Freshmen: 607. Both federal and institutional methodology are used as a basis for awarding need-based institutional aid.

UNDERGRADUATE EXPENSES for 2017–2018 *Application fee:* $65. *One-time required fee:* $25. *Comprehensive fee:* $66,166 includes full-time tuition ($52,480), mandatory fees ($450), and room and board ($13,236). *College room only:* $6826. Room and board charges vary according to board plan and housing facility. *Part-time tuition:* $6560 per course. *Part-time fees:* $56 per course.

FRESHMAN FINANCIAL AID (Fall 2017, est.) 422 applied for aid; of those 89% were deemed to have need. 100% of freshmen with need received aid; of those 92% had need fully met. *Average percent of need met:* 99% (excluding resources awarded to replace EFC). *Average financial aid package:* $44,642 (excluding resources awarded to replace EFC). 11% of all full-time freshmen had no need and received non-need-based gift aid.

UNDERGRADUATE FINANCIAL AID (Fall 2017, est.) 1,428 applied for aid; of those 93% were deemed to have need. 100% of undergraduates with need received aid; of those 77% had need fully met. *Average percent of need met:* 98% (excluding resources awarded to replace EFC). *Average financial aid package:* $45,710 (excluding resources awarded to replace EFC). 15% of all full-time undergraduates had no need and received non-need-based gift aid.

GIFT AID (NEED-BASED) *Total amount:* $51,961,394 (3% federal, 1% state, 94% institutional, 2% external sources). *Receiving aid:* Freshmen: 60% (362); all full-time undergraduates: 56% (1,306). *Average award:* Freshmen: $40,052; Undergraduates: $39,595. *Scholarships, grants, and awards:* Federal Pell, FSEOG, state, private, college/university gift aid from institutional funds.

GIFT AID (NON-NEED-BASED) *Total amount:* $5,989,301 (26% federal, 66% institutional, 8% external sources). *Receiving aid:* Freshmen: 4% (22). Undergraduates: 3% (66). *Average award:* Freshmen: $11,343. Undergraduates: $10,287. *Scholarships, grants, and awards by category:* Academic interests/achievement: 877 awards ($12,905,615 total): general academic interests/achievements, military science. *Special characteristics:* 36 awards ($1,006,710 total): children and siblings of alumni, children of faculty/staff, veterans, veterans' children. *Tuition waivers:* Full or partial for employees or children of employees, senior citizens. *ROTC:* Army.

LOANS *Student loans:* $11,180,151 (60% need-based, 40% non-need-based). 54% of past graduating class borrowed through all loan programs. *Average indebtedness per student:* $25,881. *Average need-based loan:* Freshmen: $4032. Undergraduates: $4933. *Parent loans:* $3,414,074 (23% need-based, 77% non-need-based).

Programs: Federal Direct (Subsidized and Unsubsidized Stafford, PLUS), Perkins, college/university.

WORK-STUDY *Federal work-study:* Total amount: $2,260,809; 992 jobs averaging $2277. *State or other work-study/employment:* Total amount: $798,214 (74% need-based, 26% non-need-based). 217 part-time jobs averaging $3678.

APPLYING FOR FINANCIAL AID *Required financial aid forms:* FAFSA, CSS Financial Aid PROFILE, state aid form, noncustodial (divorced/separated) parent's statement. *Financial aid deadline:* 1/15 (priority: 11/15). *Notification date:* 3/23. Students must reply by 5/1 or within 2 weeks of notification.

CONTACT Rick A. Heckman, Director of Financial Aid, Dickinson College, PO Box 1773, Carlisle, PA 17013-2896, 717-245-1308 or toll-free 800-644-1773. *Fax:* 717-245-1972. *E-mail:* finaid@dickinson.edu.
Website: http://www.dickinson.edu/.

DICKINSON STATE UNIVERSITY
Dickinson, ND

ABOUT THE INSTITUTION State-supported, coed. *Awards:* certificates, associate, bachelor's, and master's degrees. 45 undergraduate majors. *Total enrollment:* 1,425. Undergraduates: 1,525. Freshmen: 194.

GIFT AID (NEED-BASED) *Scholarships, grants, and awards:* Federal Pell, FSEOG, state, private, college/university gift aid from institutional funds.

GIFT AID (NON-NEED-BASED) *Scholarships, grants, and awards by category:* Academic interests/achievement: agriculture, biological sciences, business, communication, computer science, education, English, foreign languages, general academic interests/achievements, health fields, humanities, mathematics, physical sciences, premedicine, social sciences. *Creative arts/performance:* art/fine arts, creative writing, journalism/publications, music, theater/drama. *Special achievements/activities:* cheerleading/drum major, leadership, rodeo. *Special characteristics:* children of faculty/staff, children with a deceased or disabled parent, ethnic background, general special characteristics, international students, members of minority groups, veterans, veterans' children.

LOANS *Programs:* Federal Direct (Subsidized and Unsubsidized Stafford, PLUS), Perkins, Federal Nursing, private loans, Alaska Loans.

APPLYING FOR FINANCIAL AID *Required financial aid form:* FAFSA.

CONTACT Mr. Chris Meek, Director of Financial Aid, Dickinson State University, 291 Campus Drive, Dickinson, ND 58601-4896, 701-483-2565 or toll-free 800-279-4295. *Fax:* 701-483-2720. *E-mail:* christopher.meek@dickinsonstate.edu.
Website: http://www.dickinsonstate.edu/.

DIGIPEN INSTITUTE OF TECHNOLOGY
Redmond, WA

Tuition & fees: $31,340	Average undergraduate aid package: $11,022

ABOUT THE INSTITUTION Proprietary, coed. *Awards:* bachelor's and master's degrees. 7 undergraduate majors. *Total enrollment:* 1,102. Undergraduates: 1,028. Both federal and institutional methodology are used as a basis for awarding need-based institutional aid.

UNDERGRADUATE EXPENSES for 2018–2019 *Application fee:* $60. *One-time required fee:* $150. *Tuition:* full-time $31,140; part-time $1005 per credit. Full-time tuition and fees vary according to course load, degree level, and program. Part-time tuition and fees vary according to course load, degree level, and program. Room and board charges vary according to board plan and housing facility.

FRESHMAN FINANCIAL AID (Fall 2016) 156 applied for aid; of those 76% were deemed to have need. 97% of freshmen with need received aid; of those 6% had need fully met. *Average percent of need met:* 35% (excluding resources awarded to replace EFC). *Average financial aid package:* $10,929 (excluding resources awarded to replace EFC). 9% of all full-time freshmen had no need and received non-need-based gift aid.

UNDERGRADUATE FINANCIAL AID (Fall 2016) 652 applied for aid; of those 84% were deemed to have need. 96% of undergraduates with need received aid; of those 6% had need fully met. *Average percent of need met:* 33% (excluding resources awarded to replace EFC). *Average financial aid package:* $11,022

(excluding resources awarded to replace EFC). 8% of all full-time undergraduates had no need and received non-need-based gift aid.

GIFT AID (NEED-BASED) *Receiving aid:* Freshmen: 31% (60); all full-time undergraduates: 30% (297). *Average award:* Freshmen: $9234; Undergraduates: $9352. *Scholarships, grants, and awards:* Federal Pell, FSEOG, state, private, college/university gift aid from institutional funds.

GIFT AID (NON-NEED-BASED) *Receiving aid:* Freshmen: 27% (52). Undergraduates: 14% (135). *Average award:* Freshmen: $9022. Undergraduates: $8987. *Scholarships, grants, and awards by category:* Academic interests/achievement: computer science, engineering/technologies, mathematics. *Creative arts/performance:* art/fine arts. *Special achievements/activities:* general special achievements/activities, leadership. *Tuition waivers:* Full or partial for employees or children of employees.

LOANS *Student loans:* 69% of past graduating class borrowed through all loan programs. *Average indebtedness per student:* $28,539. *Average need-based loan:* Freshmen: $3346. Undergraduates: $4179. *Programs:* Federal Direct (Subsidized and Unsubsidized Stafford, PLUS), private loans.

WORK-STUDY Federal work-study jobs available.

APPLYING FOR FINANCIAL AID *Required financial aid form:* FAFSA. *Financial aid deadline (priority):* 2/15. *Notification date:* Continuous beginning 11/15. Students must reply within 2 weeks of notification.

CONTACT Mrs. Trinity Huttner, Director of Financial Aid and Scholarships, DigiPen Institute of Technology, 9931 Willows Road, Redmond, WA 98052, 425-629-5096 or toll-free 866-478-5236. *Fax:* 425-558-0378. *E-mail:* kimking@digipen.edu.
Website: http://www.digipen.edu/.

DILLARD UNIVERSITY
New Orleans, LA

CONTACT Mr. Theodis Wright, Director of Financial Aid and Scholarships, Dillard University, 2601 Gentilly Boulevard, New Orleans, LA 70122-3097, 504-816-4677 or toll-free 800-216-8094. *Fax:* 504-816-5456. *E-mail:* twright@dillard.edu.
Website: http://www.dillard.edu/.

DIXIE STATE UNIVERSITY
St. George, UT

Tuition & fees (UT res): $5080	Average undergraduate aid package: $9950

ABOUT THE INSTITUTION State-supported, coed. *Awards:* certificates, diplomas, associate, and bachelor's degrees. 60 undergraduate majors. *Total enrollment:* 8,993. Undergraduates: 8,993. Freshmen: 2,166. Federal methodology is used as a basis for awarding need-based institutional aid.

UNDERGRADUATE EXPENSES for 2017–2018 *Tuition, state resident:* full-time $4308; part-time $179.50 per credit hour. *Tuition, nonresident:* full-time $13,776; part-time $574 per credit hour. *Required fees:* full-time $772; $32 per credit hour. Full-time tuition and fees vary according to course load. Part-time tuition and fees vary according to course load. *College room and board:* $6328. Room and board charges vary according to board plan, housing facility, and location.

FRESHMAN FINANCIAL AID (Fall 2016) 1,416 applied for aid; of those 88% were deemed to have need. 100% of freshmen with need received aid; of those 8% had need fully met. *Average percent of need met:* 46% (excluding resources awarded to replace EFC). *Average financial aid package:* $8655 (excluding resources awarded to replace EFC). 3% of all full-time freshmen had no need and received non-need-based gift aid.

UNDERGRADUATE FINANCIAL AID (Fall 2016) 4,007 applied for aid; of those 94% were deemed to have need. 100% of undergraduates with need received aid; of those 10% had need fully met. *Average percent of need met:* 50% (excluding resources awarded to replace EFC). *Average financial aid package:* $9950 (excluding resources awarded to replace EFC). 2% of all full-time undergraduates had no need and received non-need-based gift aid.

GIFT AID (NEED-BASED) *Total amount:* $24,501,975 (67% federal, 28% state, 3% institutional, 2% external sources). *Receiving aid:* Freshmen: 59% (1,123); all full-time undergraduates: 60% (3,330). *Average award:* Freshmen: $6344; Undergraduates: $6692. **Scholarships, grants, and awards:** Federal Pell, FSEOG, state, private, college/university gift aid from institutional funds.

GIFT AID (NON-NEED-BASED) Total amount: $887,563 (93% state, 4% institutional, 3% external sources). **Receiving aid:** Freshmen: 24% (457). Undergraduates: 22% (1,240). **Average award:** Freshmen: $1910. Undergraduates: $2141. **Scholarships, grants, and awards by category:** Academic interests/achievement: general academic interests/achievements. **Tuition waivers:** Full or partial for employees or children of employees, senior citizens. **ROTC:** Army.

LOANS Student loans: $51,681,099 (91% need-based, 9% non-need-based). 86% of past graduating class borrowed through all loan programs. Average indebtedness per student: $12,201. **Average need-based loan:** Freshmen: $3445. Undergraduates: $4259. **Parent loans:** $11,227,851 (84% need-based, 16% non-need-based). **Programs:** Federal Direct (Subsidized and Unsubsidized Stafford, PLUS), Perkins.

WORK-STUDY Federal work-study: jobs available. **State or other work-study/employment:** Total amount: $668,642 (81% need-based, 19% non-need-based). Part-time jobs available.

ATHLETIC AWARDS Total amount: $1,088,047 (92% need-based, 8% non-need-based).

APPLYING FOR FINANCIAL AID Required financial aid form: FAFSA. **Financial aid deadline:** 6/30 (priority: 5/1). **Notification date:** Continuous beginning 3/1. Students must reply within 2 weeks of notification.

CONTACT J. D. Robertson, Director of Financial Aid, Dixie State University, 225 South 700 East, St. George, UT 84770, 435-652-7575. Fax: 435-656-4087. E-mail: finaid@dixie.edu.
Website: http://www.dixie.edu/.

DOANE UNIVERSITY
Crete, NE

Tuition & fees: $32,250	Average undergraduate aid package: $25,179

ABOUT THE INSTITUTION Independent United Church of Christ, coed. **Awards:** certificates, bachelor's, master's, and doctoral degrees (non-traditional undergraduate programs and graduate programs offered at Lincoln campus). 47 undergraduate majors. **Total enrollment:** 1,069. Undergraduates: 1,069. Freshmen: 299. Both federal and institutional methodology are used as a basis for awarding need-based institutional aid.

UNDERGRADUATE EXPENSES for 2017–2018 Comprehensive fee: $41,340 includes full-time tuition ($31,450), mandatory fees ($800), and room and board ($9090). Full-time tuition and fees vary according to location. Room and board charges vary according to board plan, housing facility, and location. **Part-time tuition:** $1048 per credit hour. Part-time tuition and fees vary according to course load and location.

FRESHMAN FINANCIAL AID (Fall 2017, est.) 283 applied for aid; of those 83% were deemed to have need. 100% of freshmen with need received aid; of those 39% had need fully met. **Average percent of need met:** 97% (excluding resources awarded to replace EFC). **Average financial aid package:** $26,137 (excluding resources awarded to replace EFC). 5% of all full-time freshmen had no need and received non-need-based gift aid.

UNDERGRADUATE FINANCIAL AID (Fall 2017, est.) 912 applied for aid; of those 88% were deemed to have need. 100% of undergraduates with need received aid; of those 37% had need fully met. **Average percent of need met:** 87% (excluding resources awarded to replace EFC). **Average financial aid package:** $25,179 (excluding resources awarded to replace EFC). 8% of all full-time undergraduates had no need and received non-need-based gift aid.

GIFT AID (NEED-BASED) Total amount: $13,828,012 (12% federal, 3% state, 82% institutional, 3% external sources). **Receiving aid:** Freshmen: 79% (236); all full-time undergraduates: 75% (796). **Average award:** Freshmen: $23,554; Undergraduates: $21,182. **Scholarships, grants, and awards:** Federal Pell, FSEOG, state, private, college/university gift aid from institutional funds.

GIFT AID (NON-NEED-BASED) Total amount: $3,969,191 (5% federal, 91% institutional, 4% external sources). **Receiving aid:** Freshmen: 15% (44). Undergraduates: 12% (132). **Average award:** Freshmen: $17,162. Undergraduates: $17,710. **Scholarships, grants, and awards by category:** Academic interests/achievement: general academic interests/achievements. Creative arts/performance: art/fine arts, debating, music, performing arts, theater/drama. Special characteristics: children and siblings of alumni, children of faculty/staff, religious affiliation, siblings of

current students. **Tuition waivers:** Full or partial for employees or children of employees, senior citizens. **ROTC:** Army cooperative, Air Force cooperative.

LOANS Student loans: $7,441,560 (62% need-based, 38% non-need-based). 75% of past graduating class borrowed through all loan programs. Average indebtedness per student: $28,240. **Average need-based loan:** Freshmen: $3350. Undergraduates: $4554. **Parent loans:** $3,637,874 (76% need-based, 24% non-need-based). **Programs:** Federal Direct (Subsidized and Unsubsidized Stafford, PLUS), Perkins.

WORK-STUDY Federal work-study: Total amount: $426,641; jobs available. **State or other work-study/employment:** Total amount: $496,650 (100% non-need-based). Part-time jobs available.

ATHLETIC AWARDS Total amount: $3,875,082 (76% need-based, 24% non-need-based).

APPLYING FOR FINANCIAL AID Required financial aid form: FAFSA. **Financial aid deadline:** Continuous. **Notification date:** Continuous beginning 3/15. Students must reply within 4 weeks of notification.

CONTACT Ms. Peggy Tvrdy, Director of Financial Aid, Doane University, 1014 Boswell Avenue, Crete, NE 68333-2430, 402-826-8260 or toll-free 800-333-6263. Fax: 402-826-8600. E-mail: peggy.tvrdy@doane.edu.
Website: http://www.doane.edu/.

DOMINICAN COLLEGE
Orangeburg, NY

Tuition & fees: $29,000	Average undergraduate aid package: $23,168

ABOUT THE INSTITUTION Independent, coed. **Awards:** certificates, diplomas, associate, bachelor's, master's, and doctoral degrees. 31 undergraduate majors. **Total enrollment:** 1,954. Undergraduates: 1,425. Freshmen: 229. Federal methodology is used as a basis for awarding need-based institutional aid.

UNDERGRADUATE EXPENSES for 2018–2019 Application fee: $35. **Comprehensive fee:** $42,150 includes full-time tuition ($28,140), mandatory fees ($860), and room and board ($13,150). Full-time tuition and fees vary according to course load and degree level. Room and board charges vary according to board plan and housing facility. **Part-time tuition:** $851 per credit hour. **Part-time fees:** $200 per term. Part-time tuition and fees vary according to course load, degree level, and program.

FRESHMAN FINANCIAL AID (Fall 2017, est.) 224 applied for aid; of those 90% were deemed to have need. 100% of freshmen with need received aid; of those 12% had need fully met. **Average percent of need met:** 74% (excluding resources awarded to replace EFC). **Average financial aid package:** $26,111 (excluding resources awarded to replace EFC). 11% of all full-time freshmen had no need and received non-need-based gift aid.

UNDERGRADUATE FINANCIAL AID (Fall 2017, est.) 1,103 applied for aid; of those 91% were deemed to have need. 100% of undergraduates with need received aid; of those 13% had need fully met. **Average percent of need met:** 69% (excluding resources awarded to replace EFC). **Average financial aid package:** $23,168 (excluding resources awarded to replace EFC). 14% of all full-time undergraduates had no need and received non-need-based gift aid.

GIFT AID (NEED-BASED) Total amount: $42,331,497 (7% federal, 4% state, 39% institutional, 50% external sources). **Receiving aid:** Freshmen: 88% (201); all full-time undergraduates: 82% (990). **Average award:** Freshmen: $22,286; Undergraduates: $18,594. **Scholarships, grants, and awards:** Federal Pell, FSEOG, state, private, college/university gift aid from institutional funds.

GIFT AID (NON-NEED-BASED) Total amount: $4,148,938 (2% state, 47% institutional, 51% external sources). **Receiving aid:** Freshmen: 8% (18). Undergraduates: 8% (96). **Average award:** Freshmen: $10,500. Undergraduates: $9897. **Scholarships, grants, and awards by category:** Academic interests/achievement: education, general academic interests/achievements. Special characteristics: children of faculty/staff, general special characteristics, relatives of clergy. **Tuition waivers:** Full or partial for employees or children of employees, senior citizens.

LOANS Student loans: $8,593,530 (76% need-based, 24% non-need-based). 92% of past graduating class borrowed through all loan programs. Average indebtedness per student: $32,859. **Average need-based loan:** Freshmen: $3823. Undergraduates: $5017. **Parent loans:** $2,867,889 (61% need-based, 39% non-need-based). **Programs:** Federal Direct (Subsidized and Unsubsidized Stafford, PLUS), Perkins, Federal Nursing.

WORK STUDY *Federal work-study.* Total amount: $350,572; 220 jobs averaging $1500. *State or other work-study/employment:* Total amount: $298,825 (49% need-based, 51% non-need-based). Part-time jobs available.

ATHLETIC AWARDS Total amount: $3,020,358 (71% need-based, 29% non-need-based).

APPLYING FOR FINANCIAL AID *Required financial aid forms:* FAFSA, state aid form. *Financial aid deadline (priority):* 2/15. *Notification date:* Continuous beginning 11/1. Students must reply within 4 weeks of notification.

CONTACT Ms. Stacy Salinas, Director of Financial Aid, Dominican College, 470 Western Highway, Orangeburg, NY 10962-1210, 845-848-7818 or toll-free 866-432-4636. *Fax:* 845-359-4317. *E-mail:* stacy.salinas@dc.edu.
Website: http://www.dc.edu/.

DOMINICAN UNIVERSITY
River Forest, IL

Tuition & fees: $33,434	Average undergraduate aid package: $23,125

ABOUT THE INSTITUTION Independent Roman Catholic, coed. *Awards:* certificates, bachelor's, master's, and doctoral degrees. 65 undergraduate majors. *Total enrollment:* 3,127. Undergraduates: 2,171. Freshmen: 441. Federal methodology is used as a basis for awarding need-based institutional aid.

UNDERGRADUATE EXPENSES for 2018–2019 *Application fee:* $25. *One-time required fee:* $150. *Comprehensive fee:* $43,675 includes full-time tuition ($32,964), mandatory fees ($470), and room and board ($10,241). Full-time tuition and fees vary according to course load, program, and reciprocity agreements. Room and board charges vary according to board plan and housing facility. *Part-time tuition:* $1100 per credit hour. *Part-time fees:* $90 per term. Part-time tuition and fees vary according to course load, program, and reciprocity agreements.

FRESHMAN FINANCIAL AID (Fall 2017, est.) 464 applied for aid; of those 96% were deemed to have need. 100% of freshmen with need received aid; of those 12% had need fully met. *Average percent of need met:* 76% (excluding resources awarded to replace EFC). *Average financial aid package:* $25,099 (excluding resources awarded to replace EFC). 10% of all full-time freshmen had no need and received non-need-based gift aid.

UNDERGRADUATE FINANCIAL AID (Fall 2017, est.) 1,864 applied for aid; of those 94% were deemed to have need. 100% of undergraduates with need received aid; of those 10% had need fully met. *Average percent of need met:* 71% (excluding resources awarded to replace EFC). *Average financial aid package:* $23,125 (excluding resources awarded to replace EFC). 11% of all full-time undergraduates had no need and received non-need-based gift aid.

GIFT AID (NEED-BASED) *Total amount:* $34,077,493 (16% federal, 15% state, 67% institutional, 2% external sources). *Receiving aid:* Freshmen: 90% (444); all full-time undergraduates: 86% (1,717). *Average award:* Freshmen: $21,986; Undergraduates: $19,644. *Scholarships, grants, and awards:* Federal Pell, FSEOG, state, private, college/university gift aid from institutional funds.

GIFT AID (NON-NEED-BASED) *Total amount:* $4,689,721 (1% federal, 92% institutional, 7% external sources). *Receiving aid:* Freshmen: 9% (43). Undergraduates: 6% (129). *Average award:* Freshmen: $19,368. Undergraduates: $15,808. *Scholarships, grants, and awards by category:* Academic interests/achievement: general academic interests/achievements, home economics. Creative arts/performance: applied art and design, art/fine arts. Special characteristics: children and siblings of alumni, children of faculty/staff, siblings of current students. *Tuition waivers:* Full or partial for employees or children of employees.

LOANS *Student loans:* $14,149,118 (84% need-based, 16% non-need-based). 91% of past graduating class borrowed through all loan programs. *Average indebtedness per student:* $28,659. *Average need-based loan:* Freshmen: $3200. Undergraduates: $4266. *Parent loans:* $2,864,660 (47% need-based, 53% non-need-based). *Programs:* Federal Direct (Subsidized and Unsubsidized Stafford, PLUS).

WORK-STUDY *Federal work-study:* Total amount: $523,192; jobs available. *State or other work-study/employment:* Total amount: $160,802 (27% need-based, 73% non-need-based). Part-time jobs available.

APPLYING FOR FINANCIAL AID *Required financial aid form:* FAFSA. *Financial aid deadline (priority):* 2/15. *Notification date:* Continuous beginning 12/1. Students must reply within 2 weeks of notification.

CONTACT Victoria Spivak, Director of Financial Aid, Dominican University, 7900 West Division Street, River Forest, IL 60305-1099, 708-524-6950 or toll-free 800-828-8475. *Fax:* 708-366-6478. *E-mail:* vlamick@dom.edu.
Website: http://www.dom.edu/.

DOMINICAN UNIVERSITY OF CALIFORNIA
San Rafael, CA

Tuition & fees: $44,690	Average undergraduate aid package: $28,594

ABOUT THE INSTITUTION Independent Roman Catholic Church, coed. *Awards:* bachelor's and master's degrees. 24 undergraduate majors. *Total enrollment:* 1,750. Undergraduates: 1,302. Freshmen: 242. Federal methodology is used as a basis for awarding need-based institutional aid.

UNDERGRADUATE EXPENSES for 2018–2019 *Comprehensive fee:* $59,340 includes full-time tuition ($44,240), mandatory fees ($450), and room and board ($14,650). *College room only:* $8280. Full-time tuition and fees vary according to course load. Room and board charges vary according to board plan. *Part-time tuition:* $1850 per credit hour. *Part-time fees:* $150 per term. Part-time tuition and fees vary according to course load.

FRESHMAN FINANCIAL AID (Fall 2016) 238 applied for aid; of those 89% were deemed to have need. 100% of freshmen with need received aid; of those 17% had need fully met. *Average percent of need met:* 70% (excluding resources awarded to replace EFC). *Average financial aid package:* $30,693 (excluding resources awarded to replace EFC). 15% of all full-time freshmen had no need and received non-need-based gift aid.

UNDERGRADUATE FINANCIAL AID (Fall 2016) 1,043 applied for aid; of those 91% were deemed to have need. 100% of undergraduates with need received aid; of those 14% had need fully met. *Average percent of need met:* 67% (excluding resources awarded to replace EFC). *Average financial aid package:* $28,594 (excluding resources awarded to replace EFC). 18% of all full-time undergraduates had no need and received non-need-based gift aid.

GIFT AID (NEED-BASED) *Total amount:* $23,007,531 (8% federal, 12% state, 77% institutional, 3% external sources). *Receiving aid:* Freshmen: 79% (213); all full-time undergraduates: 77% (948). *Average award:* Freshmen: $27,496; Undergraduates: $24,123. *Scholarships, grants, and awards:* Federal Pell, FSEOG, state, private, college/university gift aid from institutional funds, Scholarships for Disadvantaged Students (SDS).

GIFT AID (NON-NEED-BASED) *Total amount:* $5,225,163 (97% institutional, 3% external sources). *Receiving aid:* Freshmen: 14% (37). Undergraduates: 10% (123). *Average award:* Freshmen: $20,171. Undergraduates: $17,006. *Scholarships, grants, and awards by category:* Academic interests/achievement: general academic interests/achievements, humanities. Creative arts/performance: dance, music. Special achievements/activities: community service, leadership. Special characteristics: adult students, children and siblings of alumni, children of faculty/staff, international students, members of minority groups, veterans, veterans' children. *Tuition waivers:* Full or partial for employees or children of employees.

LOANS *Student loans:* $9,851,666 (78% need-based, 22% non-need-based). 77% of past graduating class borrowed through all loan programs. *Average indebtedness per student:* $37,827. *Average need-based loan:* Freshmen: $3378. Undergraduates: $4603. *Parent loans:* $6,922,208 (53% need-based, 47% non-need-based). *Programs:* Federal Direct (Subsidized and Unsubsidized Stafford, PLUS), Perkins, private loans.

WORK-STUDY *Federal work-study:* 205 jobs averaging $1735. *State or other work-study/employment:* Total amount: $163,700 (80% need-based, 20% non-need-based). 12 part-time jobs averaging $13,650.

ATHLETIC AWARDS Total amount: $979,905 (68% need-based, 32% non-need-based).

APPLYING FOR FINANCIAL AID *Required financial aid forms:* FAFSA, institution's own form. *Financial aid deadline (priority):* 3/1. *Notification date:* Continuous beginning 3/15. Students must reply within 2 weeks of notification.

CONTACT Ms. Lauren Coburn, Associate Director of Financial Aid, Dominican University of California, 50 Acacia Avenue, San Rafael, CA 94901-2298, 415-257-1348 or toll-free 888-323-6763. *Fax:* 415-485-3294. *E-mail:* lauren.coburn@dominican.edu.
Website: http://www.dominican.edu/.

DORDT COLLEGE
Sioux Center, IA

Tuition & fees: N/R	Average undergraduate aid package: $25,109

ABOUT THE INSTITUTION Independent Christian Reformed, coed. 86 undergraduate majors. Federal methodology is used as a basis for awarding need-based institutional aid.

FRESHMAN FINANCIAL AID (Fall 2017, est.) 327 applied for aid; of those 82% were deemed to have need. 100% of freshmen with need received aid; of those 49% had need fully met. *Average percent of need met:* 81% (excluding resources awarded to replace EFC). *Average financial aid package:* $25,520 (excluding resources awarded to replace EFC). 22% of all full-time freshmen had no need and received non-need-based gift aid.

UNDERGRADUATE FINANCIAL AID (Fall 2017, est.) 1,053 applied for aid; of those 85% were deemed to have need. 100% of undergraduates with need received aid; of those 43% had need fully met. *Average percent of need met:* 80% (excluding resources awarded to replace EFC). *Average financial aid package:* $25,109 (excluding resources awarded to replace EFC). 22% of all full-time undergraduates had no need and received non-need-based gift aid.

GIFT AID (NEED-BASED) *Total amount:* $17,756,527 (9% federal, 8% state, 74% institutional, 9% external sources). *Receiving aid:* Freshmen: 67% (266); all full-time undergraduates: 67% (894). *Average award:* Freshmen: $19,387; Undergraduates: $17,569. *Scholarships, grants, and awards:* Federal Pell, FSEOG, state, private, college/university gift aid from institutional funds.

GIFT AID (NON-NEED-BASED) *Total amount:* $3,852,276 (91% institutional, 9% external sources). *Receiving aid:* Freshmen: 14% (55). Undergraduates: 11% (153). *Average award:* Freshmen: $23,530. Undergraduates: $22,291. *Scholarships, grants, and awards by category:* Academic interests/achievement: 1,075 awards ($8,329,589 total): agriculture, biological sciences, business, communication, computer science, education, engineering/technologies, English, foreign languages, general academic interests/achievements, humanities, mathematics, physical sciences, premedicine, religion/biblical studies, social sciences. Creative arts/performance: 313 awards ($1,101,770 total): debating, journalism/publications, music, theater/drama. Special achievements/activities: 52 awards ($81,880 total): community service, general special achievements/activities, leadership. Special characteristics: 1,147 awards ($1,841,984 total): children and siblings of alumni, children of faculty/staff, general special characteristics, handicapped students, international students, local/state students, members of minority groups, out-of-state students, religious affiliation.

LOANS *Student loans:* $10,094,084 (89% need-based, 11% non-need-based). 76% of past graduating class borrowed through all loan programs. *Average indebtedness per student:* $29,481. *Average need-based loan:* Freshmen: $4049. Undergraduates: $4765. *Parent loans:* $3,376,739 (87% need-based, 13% non-need-based). *Programs:* Federal Direct (Subsidized and Unsubsidized Stafford, PLUS), Perkins, state, college/university, alternative loans.

WORK-STUDY *Federal work-study:* Total amount: $1,246,523; 384 jobs averaging $2861. *State or other work-study/employment:* Total amount: $1,798,270 (84% need-based, 16% non-need-based). 546 part-time jobs averaging $3113.

ATHLETIC AWARDS Total amount: $3,310,251 (75% need-based, 25% non-need-based).

APPLYING FOR FINANCIAL AID *Required financial aid forms:* FAFSA, institution's own form. *Financial aid deadline:* Continuous. *Notification date:* Continuous beginning 1/1. Students must reply within 3 weeks of notification.

CONTACT Mr. Harlan Harmelink, Director of Financial Aid, Dordt College, 498 4th Avenue NE, Sioux Center, IA 51250-1697, 712-722-6082 or toll-free 800-343-6738. *Fax:* 712-722-6035. *E-mail:* harlan.harmelink@dordt.edu. *Website:* http://www.dordt.edu/.

DRAKE UNIVERSITY
Des Moines, IA

Tuition & fees: $41,396	Average undergraduate aid package: $28,868

ABOUT THE INSTITUTION Independent, coed. *Awards:* certificates, bachelor's, master's, and doctoral degrees. 66 undergraduate majors. *Total* enrollment: 4,904. Undergraduates: 3,098. Freshmen: 758. Federal methodology is used as a basis for awarding need-based institutional aid.

UNDERGRADUATE EXPENSES for 2018–2019 *Comprehensive fee:* $51,554 includes full-time tuition ($41,250), mandatory fees ($146), and room and board ($10,158). *College room only:* $5486. Full-time tuition and fees vary according to course load, degree level, program, and student level. Room and board charges vary according to board plan and housing facility. *Part-time tuition:* $775 per credit hour. Part-time tuition and fees vary according to class time, degree level, and program. *Payment plan:* Guaranteed tuition.

FRESHMAN FINANCIAL AID (Fall 2017, est.) 657 applied for aid; of those 80% were deemed to have need. 100% of freshmen with need received aid; of those 32% had need fully met. *Average percent of need met:* 76% (excluding resources awarded to replace EFC). *Average financial aid package:* $29,236 (excluding resources awarded to replace EFC). 26% of all full-time freshmen had no need and received non-need-based gift aid.

UNDERGRADUATE FINANCIAL AID (Fall 2017, est.) 2,119 applied for aid; of those 85% were deemed to have need. 100% of undergraduates with need received aid; of those 28% had need fully met. *Average percent of need met:* 77% (excluding resources awarded to replace EFC). *Average financial aid package:* $28,868 (excluding resources awarded to replace EFC). 32% of all full-time undergraduates had no need and received non-need-based gift aid.

GIFT AID (NEED-BASED) *Total amount:* $36,731,177 (10% federal, 5% state, 83% institutional, 2% external sources). *Receiving aid:* Freshmen: 68% (516); all full-time undergraduates: 60% (1,767). *Average award:* Freshmen: $22,855; Undergraduates: $20,625. *Scholarships, grants, and awards:* Federal Pell, FSEOG, state, private, college/university gift aid from institutional funds.

GIFT AID (NON-NEED-BASED) *Total amount:* $19,917,352 (3% federal, 94% institutional, 3% external sources). *Receiving aid:* Freshmen: 17% (128). Undergraduates: 11% (336). *Average award:* Freshmen: $19,146. Undergraduates: $15,950. *Scholarships, grants, and awards by category:* Academic interests/achievement: 2,457 awards ($33,994,576 total): general academic interests/achievements. Creative arts/performance: 327 awards ($2,714,947 total): art/fine arts, music, theater/drama. Special characteristics: 211 awards ($309,375 total): children and siblings of alumni, international students. *Tuition waivers:* Full or partial for children of alumni, employees or children of employees, senior citizens. *ROTC:* Army cooperative, Air Force cooperative.

LOANS *Student loans:* $28,745,001 (47% need-based, 53% non-need-based). 62% of past graduating class borrowed through all loan programs. *Average indebtedness per student:* $34,600. *Average need-based loan:* Freshmen: $3084. Undergraduates: $5573. *Parent loans:* $41,756,989 (22% need-based, 78% non-need-based). *Programs:* Federal Direct (Subsidized and Unsubsidized Stafford, PLUS), Perkins, college/university, Health Professions Student Loans (HPSL).

WORK-STUDY *Federal work-study:* Total amount: $2,791,308; 1,458 jobs averaging $1914.

ATHLETIC AWARDS Total amount: $4,450,466 (20% need-based, 80% non-need-based).

APPLYING FOR FINANCIAL AID *Required financial aid form:* FAFSA. *Financial aid deadline:* Continuous. *Notification date:* Continuous beginning 1/1. Students must reply by 5/1 or within 3 weeks of notification.

CONTACT Office of Student Financial Planning, Drake University, 2507 University Avenue, Des Moines, IA 50311-4516, 800-443-7253 Ext. 2905 or toll-free 800-44-DRAKE Ext. 3181. *Fax:* 515-271-4042. *E-mail:* financialaid@drake.edu. *Website:* http://www.drake.edu/.

DREW UNIVERSITY
Madison, NJ

Tuition & fees: $39,500	Average undergraduate aid package: $44,512

ABOUT THE INSTITUTION Independent United Methodist Church, coed. *Awards:* certificates, bachelor's, master's, and doctoral degrees. 33 undergraduate majors. *Total enrollment:* 2,117. Undergraduates: 1,537. Freshmen: 371. Federal methodology is used as a basis for awarding need-based institutional aid.

UNDERGRADUATE EXPENSES for 2018–2019 *Application fee:* $40. *Comprehensive fee:* $53,608 includes full-time tuition ($38,668), mandatory fees ($832), and room and board ($14,108). *College room only:* $8909. Room and board charges vary according to board plan and housing facility. *Part-time tuition:* $1612 per credit. Part-time tuition and fees vary according to course load. *Payment plan.* Tuition prepayment.

FRESHMAN FINANCIAL AID (Fall 2017, est.) 327 applied for aid; of those 91% were deemed to have need. 100% of freshmen with need received aid; of those 15% had need fully met. *Average percent of need met:* 85% (excluding resources awarded to replace EFC). *Average financial aid package:* $44,763 (excluding resources awarded to replace EFC). 18% of all full-time freshmen had no need and received non-need-based gift aid.

UNDERGRADUATE FINANCIAL AID (Fall 2017, est.) 1,054 applied for aid; of those 93% were deemed to have need. 100% of undergraduates with need received aid; of those 13% had need fully met. *Average percent of need met:* 83% (excluding resources awarded to replace EFC). *Average financial aid package:* $44,512 (excluding resources awarded to replace EFC). 24% of all full-time undergraduates had no need and received non-need-based gift aid.

GIFT AID (NEED-BASED) *Total amount:* $37,220,734 (6% federal, 8% state, 85% institutional, 1% external sources). *Receiving aid:* Freshmen: 80% (296); all full-time undergraduates: 70% (978). *Average award:* Freshmen: $40,105; Undergraduates: $38,899. *Scholarships, grants, and awards:* Federal Pell, FSEOG, state, private, college/university gift aid from institutional funds.

GIFT AID (NON-NEED-BASED) *Total amount:* $8,384,630 (99% institutional, 1% external sources). *Receiving aid:* Freshmen: 5% (20). Undergraduates: 4% (59). *Average award:* Freshmen: $21,288. Undergraduates: $22,610. *Scholarships, grants, and awards by category: Academic interests/achievement:* general academic interests/achievements. *Creative arts/performance:* art/fine arts, music, performing arts, theater/drama. *Special achievements/activities:* community service. *Tuition waivers:* Full or partial for employees or children of employees. *ROTC:* Army cooperative.

LOANS *Student loans:* $5,578,669 (59% need-based, 41% non-need-based). 68% of past graduating class borrowed through all loan programs. *Average indebtedness per student:* $24,058. *Average need-based loan:* Freshmen: $3475. Undergraduates: $4519. *Parent loans:* $5,156,257 (44% need-based, 56% non-need-based). *Programs:* Federal Direct (Subsidized and Unsubsidized Stafford, PLUS), Perkins, state.

WORK-STUDY *Federal work-study:* Total amount: $1,369,057; 709 jobs averaging $2000. *State or other work-study/employment:* Total amount: $415,203 (85% need-based, 15% non-need-based). Part-time jobs available.

APPLYING FOR FINANCIAL AID *Required financial aid form:* FAFSA. *Financial aid deadline (priority):* 2/15. *Notification date:* 3/25. Students must reply by 5/1.

CONTACT Colby McCarthy, Director of Financial Assistance, Drew University, 36 Madison Avenue, Madison, NJ 07940-1493, 973-408-3112. *Fax:* 973-408-3188. *E-mail:* finaid@drew.edu. *Website:* http://www.drew.edu/.

DREXEL UNIVERSITY
Philadelphia, PA

Tuition & fees: $52,002	Average undergraduate aid package: $37,744

ABOUT THE INSTITUTION Independent, coed. *Awards:* certificates, bachelor's, master's, and doctoral degrees. 81 undergraduate majors. *Total enrollment:* 24,190. Undergraduates: 15,498. Freshmen: 3,275. Federal methodology is used as a basis for awarding need-based institutional aid.

UNDERGRADUATE EXPENSES for 2018–2019 *Application fee:* $50. *Comprehensive fee:* $65,892 includes full-time tuition ($49,632), mandatory fees ($2370), and room and board ($13,890). *College room only:* $8205. Full-time tuition and fees vary according to course load, location, program, and student level. Room and board charges vary according to board plan and housing facility. *Part-time tuition:* $1116 per credit hour. *Part-time fees:* $150 per term. Part-time tuition and fees vary according to course load and program.

FRESHMAN FINANCIAL AID (Fall 2017, est.) 2,939 applied for aid; of those 84% were deemed to have need. 100% of freshmen with need received aid; of those 34% had need fully met. *Average percent of need met:* 82% (excluding resources awarded to replace EFC). *Average financial aid package:* $42,948 (excluding resources awarded to replace EFC). 24% of all full-time freshmen had no need and received non-need-based gift aid.

UNDERGRADUATE FINANCIAL AID (Fall 2017, est.) 9,584 applied for aid; of those 90% were deemed to have need. 99% of undergraduates with need received aid;

of those 23% had need fully met. *Average percent of need met:* 73% (excluding resources awarded to replace EFC). *Average financial aid package:* $37,744 (excluding resources awarded to replace EFC). 31% of all full-time undergraduates had no need and received non-need-based gift aid.

GIFT AID (NEED-BASED) *Total amount:* $223,479,987 (8% federal, 3% state, 88% institutional, 1% external sources). *Receiving aid:* Freshmen: 76% (2,474); all full-time undergraduates: 61% (8,206). *Average award:* Freshmen: $32,749; Undergraduates: $27,694. *Scholarships, grants, and awards:* Federal Pell, FSEOG, state, private, college/university gift aid from institutional funds, United Negro College Fund.

GIFT AID (NON-NEED-BASED) *Total amount:* $70,959,730 (99% institutional, 1% external sources). *Receiving aid:* Freshmen: 14% (459). Undergraduates: 7% (984). *Average award:* Freshmen: $15,736. Undergraduates: $15,018. *Scholarships, grants, and awards by category: Academic interests/achievement:* general academic interests/achievements. *Creative arts/performance:* dance, music, performing arts, theater/drama. *Special achievements/activities:* cheerleading/drum major. *Special characteristics:* children and siblings of alumni, siblings of current students, twins. *Tuition waivers:* Full or partial for employees or children of employees. *ROTC:* Army, Naval cooperative, Air Force cooperative.

LOANS *Student loans:* $96,318,278 (77% need-based, 23% non-need-based). *Average need-based loan:* Freshmen: $8448. Undergraduates: $11,000. *Parent loans:* $42,606,627 (100% non-need-based). *Programs:* Federal Direct (Subsidized and Unsubsidized Stafford, PLUS), Perkins, Federal Nursing, college/university.

WORK-STUDY *Federal work-study:* Total amount: $6,187,573; jobs available.

ATHLETIC AWARDS Total amount: $9,817,763 (26% need-based, 74% non-need-based).

APPLYING FOR FINANCIAL AID *Required financial aid forms:* FAFSA, CSS Financial Aid PROFILE. *Financial aid deadline:* 2/15. *Notification date:* Continuous beginning 4/1. Students must reply by 5/1.

CONTACT Helen Gourousis, Director of Financial Aid, Drexel University, 3141 Chestnut Street, Philadelphia, PA 19104-2875, 215-895-5928 or toll-free 800-2-DREXEL. *Fax:* 215-895-6903. *E-mail:* gouroush@drexel.edu. *Website:* http://www.drexel.edu/.

DRURY UNIVERSITY
Springfield, MO

Tuition & fees: $28,365	Average undergraduate aid package: $20,254

ABOUT THE INSTITUTION Independent, coed. *Awards:* bachelor's and master's degrees (also offers evening program with significant enrollment not reflected in profile). 21 undergraduate majors. *Total enrollment:* 1,659. Undergraduates: 1,425. Freshmen: 360. Federal methodology is used as a basis for awarding need-based institutional aid.

UNDERGRADUATE EXPENSES for 2018–2019 *One-time required fee:* $150. *Comprehensive fee:* $37,405 includes full-time tuition ($27,350), mandatory fees ($1015), and room and board ($9040). *College room only:* $6774. Full-time tuition and fees vary according to class time. Room and board charges vary according to board plan and housing facility. *Part-time fees:* $911 per credit hour. Part-time tuition and fees vary according to class time.

FRESHMAN FINANCIAL AID (Fall 2016) 295 applied for aid; of those 85% were deemed to have need. 100% of freshmen with need received aid; of those 25% had need fully met. *Average percent of need met:* 81% (excluding resources awarded to replace EFC). *Average financial aid package:* $21,933 (excluding resources awarded to replace EFC). 31% of all full-time freshmen had no need and received non-need-based gift aid.

UNDERGRADUATE FINANCIAL AID (Fall 2016) 1,007 applied for aid; of those 87% were deemed to have need. 100% of undergraduates with need received aid; of those 22% had need fully met. *Average percent of need met:* 75% (excluding resources awarded to replace EFC). *Average financial aid package:* $20,254 (excluding resources awarded to replace EFC). 31% of all full-time undergraduates had no need and received non-need-based gift aid.

GIFT AID (NEED-BASED) *Total amount:* $13,583,327 (13% federal, 7% state, 75% institutional, 5% external sources). *Receiving aid:* Freshmen: 69% (252); all full-time undergraduates: 67% (881). *Average award:* Freshmen: $18,391; Undergraduates: $16,645. *Scholarships, grants, and awards:* Federal Pell, FSEOG, state, private, college/university gift aid from institutional funds.

GIFT AID (NON-NEED-BASED) *Total amount:* $4,842,099 (3% state, 92% institutional, 5% external sources). *Receiving aid:* Freshmen: 14% (50). Undergraduates: 12% (152). *Average award:* Freshmen: $10,765. Undergraduates: $9409. *Scholarships, grants, and awards by category:* Academic interests/achievement: 1,234 awards ($9,502,866 total): architecture, biological sciences, business, communication, computer science, education, English, foreign languages, general academic interests/achievements, health fields, humanities, international studies, mathematics, physical sciences, premedicine, social sciences. *Creative arts/performance:* 139 awards ($384,600 total): art/fine arts, creative writing, debating, music, theater/drama. *Special achievements/activities:* 28 awards ($28,025 total): cheerleading/drum major, leadership, religious involvement. *Special characteristics:* 171 awards ($1,337,523 total): children and siblings of alumni, children of faculty/staff, ethnic background, international students, members of minority groups, relatives of clergy, religious affiliation, siblings of current students, veterans. *Tuition waivers:* Full or partial for minority students, children of alumni, employees or children of employees. *ROTC:* Army cooperative.

LOANS *Student loans:* $9,532,415 (59% need-based, 41% non-need-based). 64% of past graduating class borrowed through all loan programs. *Average indebtedness per student:* $31,137. *Average need-based loan:* Freshmen: $4135. Undergraduates: $4447. *Parent loans:* $2,085,557 (39% need-based, 61% non-need-based). *Programs:* Federal Direct (Subsidized and Unsubsidized Stafford, PLUS), state, alternative loans.

WORK-STUDY *Federal work-study:* 108 jobs averaging $2720. *State or other work-study/employment:* 340 part-time jobs averaging $1265.

ATHLETIC AWARDS Total amount: $3,196,502 (27% need-based, 73% non-need-based).

APPLYING FOR FINANCIAL AID *Required financial aid form:* FAFSA. *Financial aid deadline (priority):* 1/10. *Notification date:* Continuous beginning 2/15. Students must reply by 5/1.

CONTACT Ms. Becky Ahrens, Director of Financial Aid, Drury University, 900 North Benton Avenue, Springfield, MO 65802-3791, 417-873-7312 or toll-free 800-922-2274. *Fax:* 417-873-6906. *E-mail:* bahrens@drury.edu. *Website:* http://www.drury.edu/.

DUKE UNIVERSITY
Durham, NC

Tuition & fees: $53,500	Average undergraduate aid package: $52,745

ABOUT THE INSTITUTION Independent United Methodist Church, coed. *Awards:* certificates, bachelor's, master's, and doctoral degrees. 45 undergraduate majors. *Total enrollment:* 15,928. Undergraduates: 6,609. Freshmen: 1,723. Both federal and institutional methodology are used as a basis for awarding need-based institutional aid.

UNDERGRADUATE EXPENSES for 2017–2018 *Application fee:* $85. *Comprehensive fee:* $68,298 includes full-time tuition ($51,720), mandatory fees ($1780), and room and board ($14,798). *College room only:* $8494. Room and board charges vary according to board plan and housing facility. *Part-time tuition:* $1616 per credit hour. *Payment plan:* Tuition prepayment.

FRESHMAN FINANCIAL AID (Fall 2017, est.) 1,048 applied for aid; of those 79% were deemed to have need. 100% of freshmen with need received aid; of those 100% had need fully met. *Average percent of need met:* 100% (excluding resources awarded to replace EFC). *Average financial aid package:* $53,831 (excluding resources awarded to replace EFC). 2% of all full-time freshmen had no need and received non-need-based gift aid.

UNDERGRADUATE FINANCIAL AID (Fall 2017, est.) 3,461 applied for aid; of those 85% were deemed to have need. 100% of undergraduates with need received aid; of those 100% had need fully met. *Average percent of need met:* 100% (excluding resources awarded to replace EFC). *Average financial aid package:* $52,745 (excluding resources awarded to replace EFC). 3% of all full-time undergraduates had no need and received non-need-based gift aid.

GIFT AID (NEED-BASED) *Total amount:* $134,462,189 (4% federal, 1% state, 91% institutional, 4% external sources). *Receiving aid:* Freshmen: 46% (801); all full-time undergraduates: 41% (2,787). *Average award:* Freshmen: $49,174; Undergraduates: $47,556. *Scholarships, grants, and awards:* Federal Pell, FSEOG, state, private, college/university gift aid from institutional funds.

GIFT AID (NON-NEED-BASED) *Total amount:* $21,949,129 (69% institutional, 31% external sources). *Receiving aid:* Freshmen: 3% (52). Undergraduates: 4% (266). *Average award:* Freshmen: $71,491. Undergraduates: $69,506. *Scholarships, grants, and awards by category:* Academic interests/achievement: 116 awards ($7,733,101 total): general academic interests/achievements, mathematics. *Special achievements/activities:* 76 awards ($5,227,957 total): general special achievements/activities, leadership. *Special characteristics:* 65 awards ($4,517,222 total): children and siblings of alumni, ethnic background, international students, local/state students. *ROTC:* Army, Naval, Air Force.

LOANS *Student loans:* $17,327,720 (75% need-based, 25% non-need-based). 33% of past graduating class borrowed through all loan programs. *Average indebtedness per student:* $23,819. *Average need-based loan:* Freshmen: $2905. Undergraduates: $3289. *Parent loans:* $6,930,499 (79% need-based, 21% non-need-based). *Programs:* Federal Direct (Subsidized and Unsubsidized Stafford, PLUS), Perkins, college/university, alternative loans.

WORK-STUDY *Federal work-study:* Total amount: $3,921,029; 1,917 jobs averaging $2045. *State or other work-study/employment:* Total amount: $2,121,708 (55% need-based, 45% non-need-based). 540 part-time jobs averaging $1933.

ATHLETIC AWARDS Total amount: $21,236,330 (23% need-based, 77% non-need-based).

APPLYING FOR FINANCIAL AID *Required financial aid forms:* FAFSA, CSS Financial Aid PROFILE, noncustodial (divorced/separated) parent's statement, business/farm supplement, federal income tax form(s), W-2 forms. *Financial aid deadline:* 2/1. *Notification date:* 4/1. Students must reply by 5/1.

CONTACT Alison Rabil, Director of Financial Aid, Duke University, 2127 Campus Drive Addition, Box 90397, Durham, NC 27708-0397, 919-684-6225. *Fax:* 919-660-9811. *E-mail:* finaid@duke.edu. *Website:* http://www.duke.edu/.

DUNLAP-STONE UNIVERSITY
Phoenix, AZ

ABOUT THE INSTITUTION Proprietary, coed. 1 undergraduate major.
CONTACT Office of the Bursar, Dunlap-Stone University, 19820 North 7th Street, Suite #100, Phoenix, AZ 85024, 800-474-8013. *E-mail:* info@expandglobal.com. *Website:* http://www.dunlap-stone.edu/.

DUQUESNE UNIVERSITY
Pittsburgh, PA

Tuition & fees: $36,394	Average undergraduate aid package: $24,570

ABOUT THE INSTITUTION Independent Roman Catholic, coed. *Awards:* certificates, bachelor's, master's, and doctoral degrees. 71 undergraduate majors. *Total enrollment:* 9,190. Undergraduates: 5,942. Freshmen: 1,562. Federal methodology is used as a basis for awarding need-based institutional aid.

UNDERGRADUATE EXPENSES for 2017–2018 *Application fee:* $50. *Comprehensive fee:* $48,508 includes full-time tuition ($36,394) and room and board ($12,114). *College room only:* $6658. Full-time tuition and fees vary according to course load and program. Room and board charges vary according to board plan and housing facility. *Part-time tuition:* $1206 per credit hour. Part-time tuition and fees vary according to course load and program.

FRESHMAN FINANCIAL AID (Fall 2016) 1,369 applied for aid; of those 82% were deemed to have need. 100% of freshmen with need received aid; of those 24% had need fully met. *Average percent of need met:* 76% (excluding resources awarded to replace EFC). *Average financial aid package:* $25,928 (excluding resources awarded to replace EFC). 26% of all full-time freshmen had no need and received non-need-based gift aid.

UNDERGRADUATE FINANCIAL AID (Fall 2016) 4,620 applied for aid; of those 85% were deemed to have need. 100% of undergraduates with need received aid; of those 20% had need fully met. *Average percent of need met:* 72% (excluding resources awarded to replace EFC). *Average financial aid package:* $24,570 (excluding resources awarded to replace EFC). 28% of all full-time undergraduates had no need and received non-need-based gift aid.

GIFT AID (NEED-BASED) Total amount: $73,010,674 (7% federal, 7% state, 81% institutional, 5% external sources). **Receiving aid:** Freshmen: 72% (1,127); all full-time undergraduates: 66% (3,832). **Average award:** Freshmen: $22,873; Undergraduates: $21,218. **Scholarships, grants, and awards:** Federal Pell, FSEOG, state, private, college/university gift aid from institutional funds, United Negro College Fund.

GIFT AID (NON-NEED-BASED) Total amount: $23,208,765 (97% institutional, 3% external sources). **Receiving aid:** Freshmen: 72% (1,126). Undergraduates: 64% (3,741). **Average award:** Freshmen: $15,289. Undergraduates: $13,180. **Scholarships, grants, and awards by category:** Academic interests/achievement: 5,022 awards ($58,685,937 total): education, general academic interests/achievements. Creative arts/performance: 230 awards ($1,675,750 total): dance, music. Special characteristics: 1,088 awards ($13,132,800 total): children and siblings of alumni, children of faculty/staff, ethnic background, general special characteristics, international students, members of minority groups, relatives of clergy, religious affiliation, veterans, veterans' children. **Tuition waivers:** Full or partial for employees or children of employees, senior citizens. **ROTC:** Army, Naval cooperative, Air Force cooperative.

LOANS Student loans: $48,675,522 (87% need-based, 13% non-need-based). 61% of past graduating class borrowed through all loan programs. Average indebtedness per student: $43,637. **Average need-based loan:** Freshmen: $3819. Undergraduates: $4628. **Parent loans:** $22,158,713 (91% need-based, 9% non-need-based). **Programs:** Federal Direct (Subsidized and Unsubsidized Stafford, PLUS), Perkins, Federal Nursing, private loans.

WORK-STUDY Federal work-study: jobs available.

ATHLETIC AWARDS Total amount: $6,760,541 (46% need-based, 54% non-need-based).

APPLYING FOR FINANCIAL AID Required financial aid forms: FAFSA, institution's own form. **Financial aid deadline:** 5/1. **Notification date:** Continuous beginning 1/31. Students must reply by 5/1 or within 3 weeks of notification.

CONTACT Mr. Richard C. Esposito, Director of Financial Aid, Duquesne University, 600 Forbes Avenue, Pittsburgh, PA 15282-0299, 412-396-6607 or toll-free 800-456-0590. Fax: 412-396-5284. E-mail: esposito@duq.edu.
Website: http://www.duq.edu/.

D'YOUVILLE COLLEGE
Buffalo, NY

ABOUT THE INSTITUTION Independent, coed. **Awards:** certificates, bachelor's, master's, and doctoral degrees. 22 undergraduate majors. **Total enrollment:** 3,021. Undergraduates: 1,735. Freshmen: 277.

GIFT AID (NEED-BASED) Scholarships, grants, and awards: Federal Pell, FSEOG, state, private, college/university gift aid from institutional funds.

GIFT AID (NON-NEED-BASED) Scholarships, grants, and awards by category: Academic interests/achievement: biological sciences, business, education, English, general academic interests/achievements, health fields, humanities, international studies, mathematics, premedicine, social sciences. Special characteristics: children and siblings of alumni, children of faculty/staff, veterans.

LOANS Programs: Federal Direct (Subsidized and Unsubsidized Stafford, PLUS), Perkins, Federal Nursing.

APPLYING FOR FINANCIAL AID Required financial aid forms: FAFSA, state aid form.

CONTACT Mr. Matthew R. Metz, Director of Financial Aid, D'Youville College, 320 Porter Avenue, Buffalo, NY 14201-1084, 716-829-7500 or toll-free 800-777-3921. Fax: 716-829-7779. E-mail: metzm@dyc.edu.
Website: http://www.dyc.edu/.

EAGLE GATE COLLEGE
Layton, UT

CONTACT Financial Aid Office, Eagle Gate College, 915 North 400 West, Layton, UT 84041, 801-546-7500 or toll-free 866-29-EAGLE.
Website: http://eaglegatecollege.edu/.

EAGLE GATE COLLEGE
Murray, UT

CONTACT Financial Aid Office, Eagle Gate College, 5588 South Green Street, Murray, UT 84123, 801-333-8100 or toll-free 866-29-EAGLE.
Website: http://eaglegatecollege.edu/.

EARLHAM COLLEGE
Richmond, IN

Tuition & fees: $46,450	Average undergraduate aid package: $42,386

ABOUT THE INSTITUTION Independent Society of Friends, coed. **Awards:** certificates, bachelor's, and master's degrees. 36 undergraduate majors. **Total enrollment:** 1,126. Undergraduates: 1,067. Freshmen: 287. Federal methodology is used as a basis for awarding need-based institutional aid.

UNDERGRADUATE EXPENSES for 2018–2019 Comprehensive fee: $56,850 includes full-time tuition ($45,500), mandatory fees ($950), and room and board ($10,400). **College room only:** $5500. Full-time tuition and fees vary according to course load and program. Room and board charges vary according to board plan. **Part-time tuition:** $1517 per credit hour. Part-time tuition and fees vary according to course load and program.

FRESHMAN FINANCIAL AID (Fall 2017, est.) 277 applied for aid; of those 93% were deemed to have need. 100% of freshmen with need received aid; of those 55% had need fully met. **Average percent of need met:** 94% (excluding resources awarded to replace EFC). **Average financial aid package:** $43,032 (excluding resources awarded to replace EFC). 9% of all full-time freshmen had no need and received non-need-based gift aid.

UNDERGRADUATE FINANCIAL AID (Fall 2017, est.) 934 applied for aid; of those 96% were deemed to have need. 100% of undergraduates with need received aid; of those 50% had need fully met. **Average percent of need met:** 94% (excluding resources awarded to replace EFC). **Average financial aid package:** $42,386 (excluding resources awarded to replace EFC). 11% of all full-time undergraduates had no need and received non-need-based gift aid.

GIFT AID (NEED-BASED) Total amount: $33,083,897 (5% federal, 3% state, 92% institutional). **Receiving aid:** Freshmen: 90% (258); all full-time undergraduates: 87% (894). **Average award:** Freshmen: $38,564; Undergraduates: $37,896. **Scholarships, grants, and awards:** Federal Pell, FSEOG, state, private, college/university gift aid from institutional funds.

GIFT AID (NON-NEED-BASED) Total amount: $3,140,306 (99% institutional, 1% external sources). **Receiving aid:** Freshmen: 17% (49). Undergraduates: 18% (180). **Average award:** Freshmen: $25,203. Undergraduates: $22,981. **Scholarships, grants, and awards by category:** Academic interests/achievement: 118 awards ($2,711,758 total): general academic interests/achievements. Special achievements/activities: religious involvement. **Tuition waivers:** Full or partial for employees or children of employees.

LOANS Student loans: $3,879,986 (75% need-based, 25% non-need-based). 58% of past graduating class borrowed through all loan programs. Average indebtedness per student: $27,830. **Average need-based loan:** Freshmen: $2216. Undergraduates: $4974. **Parent loans:** $1,138,511 (24% need-based, 76% non-need-based). **Programs:** Federal Direct (Subsidized and Unsubsidized Stafford, PLUS), Perkins, college/university.

WORK-STUDY Federal work-study: Total amount: $923,642; 650 jobs averaging $2200. **State or other work-study/employment:** Total amount: $457,640 (100% need-based). Part-time jobs available.

APPLYING FOR FINANCIAL AID Required financial aid form: FAFSA. **Financial aid deadline:** 3/1. **Notification date:** Continuous beginning 3/1. Students must reply by 5/1 or within 3 weeks of notification.

CONTACT Kathy Gottschalk, Director of Financial Aid, Earlham College, National Road West, Richmond, IN 47374-4095, 765-983-1217 or toll-free 800-327-5426. Fax: 765-983-1299. E-mail: gottska@earlham.edu.
Website: http://www.earlham.edu/.

EAST CAROLINA UNIVERSITY
Greenville, NC

Tuition & fees (NC res): $7143	Average undergraduate aid package: $10,383

ABOUT THE INSTITUTION State-supported, coed. *Awards:* certificates, bachelor's, master's, and doctoral degrees. 75 undergraduate majors. *Total enrollment:* 29,131. Undergraduates: 23,265. Freshmen: 4,362. Federal methodology is used as a basis for awarding need-based institutional aid.

UNDERGRADUATE EXPENSES for 2017–2018 *Application fee:* $75. *Tuition, state resident:* full-time $4452; part-time $247 per credit hour. *Tuition, nonresident:* full-time $20,729; part-time $1151 per credit hour. *Required fees:* full-time $2691. Full-time tuition and fees vary according to location and program. Part-time tuition and fees vary according to course load, location, and program. *College room and board:* $9835; *Room only:* $5623. Room and board charges vary according to board plan and housing facility. *Payment plan:* Guaranteed tuition.

FRESHMAN FINANCIAL AID (Fall 2017, est.) 3,713 applied for aid; of those 75% were deemed to have need. 97% of freshmen with need received aid; of those 8% had need fully met. *Average percent of need met:* 57% (excluding resources awarded to replace EFC). *Average financial aid package:* $9640 (excluding resources awarded to replace EFC). 2% of all full-time freshmen had no need and received non-need-based gift aid.

UNDERGRADUATE FINANCIAL AID (Fall 2017, est.) 14,796 applied for aid; of those 82% were deemed to have need. 97% of undergraduates with need received aid; of those 9% had need fully met. *Average percent of need met:* 61% (excluding resources awarded to replace EFC). *Average financial aid package:* $10,383 (excluding resources awarded to replace EFC). 1% of all full-time undergraduates had no need and received non-need-based gift aid.

GIFT AID (NEED-BASED) *Total amount:* $82,793,944 (46% federal, 21% state, 29% institutional, 4% external sources). *Receiving aid:* Freshmen: 43% (1,839); all full-time undergraduates: 43% (8,515). *Average award:* Freshmen: $8272; Undergraduates: $7702. *Scholarships, grants, and awards:* Federal Pell, FSEOG, state, private, college/university gift aid from institutional funds, Federal Nursing.

GIFT AID (NON-NEED-BASED) *Total amount:* $615,610 (3% state, 49% institutional, 48% external sources). *Receiving aid:* Freshmen: 13% (542). Undergraduates: 10% (1,892). *Average award:* Freshmen: $3887. Undergraduates: $3884. *Scholarships, grants, and awards by category:* Academic interests/achievement: biological sciences, business, communication, computer science, education, engineering/technologies, English, foreign languages, general academic interests/achievements, health fields, home economics, humanities, international studies, library science, mathematics, military science, physical sciences, social sciences. *Creative arts/performance:* applied art and design, art/fine arts, dance, music, performing arts. *Special characteristics:* adult students, children and siblings of alumni, children of faculty/staff, ethnic background, general special characteristics, handicapped students. *Tuition waivers:* Full or partial for employees or children of employees. *ROTC:* Army, Air Force.

LOANS *Student loans:* $117,404,921 (96% need-based, 4% non-need-based). 69% of past graduating class borrowed through all loan programs. *Average indebtedness per student:* $28,918. *Average need-based loan:* Freshmen: $6012. Undergraduates: $7040. *Parent loans:* $27,653,960 (100% need-based). *Programs:* Federal Direct (Subsidized and Unsubsidized Stafford, PLUS), Perkins, Federal Nursing, state.

WORK-STUDY *Federal work-study:* Total amount: $1,390,303; 436 jobs averaging $3189. *State or other work-study/employment:* Part-time jobs available.

ATHLETIC AWARDS Total amount: $7,296,381 (93% need-based, 7% non-need-based).

APPLYING FOR FINANCIAL AID *Required financial aid form:* FAFSA. *Financial aid deadline (priority):* 3/1. *Notification date:* 4/1. Students must reply within 3 weeks of notification.

CONTACT Ms. Julie Poorman, Director of Financial Aid, East Carolina University, East 5th Street, Greenville, NC 27858-4353, 252-328-6610. *Fax:* 252-328-4347. *E-mail:* poormanj@ecu.edu.
Website: http://www.ecu.edu/.

EAST CENTRAL UNIVERSITY
Ada, OK

Tuition & fees (OK res): $6600	Average undergraduate aid package: $6226

ABOUT THE INSTITUTION State-supported, coed. *Awards:* certificates, bachelor's, and master's degrees. 72 undergraduate majors. *Total enrollment:* 3,639. Undergraduates: 3,029. Freshmen: 471. Federal methodology is used as a basis for awarding need-based institutional aid.

UNDERGRADUATE EXPENSES for 2017–2018 *Application fee:* $20. *Tuition, state resident:* full-time $5301; part-time $176.70 per semester hour. *Tuition, nonresident:* full-time $14,421; part-time $480.70 per semester hour. *Required fees:* full-time $1299; $43.30 per semester hour. *College room and board:* $6730; *Room only:* $3516. Room and board charges vary according to board plan and housing facility. *Payment plan:* Guaranteed tuition.

FRESHMAN FINANCIAL AID (Fall 2016) 412 applied for aid; of those 80% were deemed to have need. 100% of freshmen with need received aid; of those 31% had need fully met. *Average financial aid package:* $5792 (excluding resources awarded to replace EFC). 1% of all full-time freshmen had no need and received non-need-based gift aid.

UNDERGRADUATE FINANCIAL AID (Fall 2016) 2,228 applied for aid; of those 88% were deemed to have need. 100% of undergraduates with need received aid; of those 38% had need fully met. *Average financial aid package:* $6226 (excluding resources awarded to replace EFC). 1% of all full-time undergraduates had no need and received non-need-based gift aid.

GIFT AID (NEED-BASED) *Total amount:* $11,159,427 (56% federal, 29% state, 15% external sources). *Receiving aid:* Freshmen: 44% (256); all full-time undergraduates: 31% (881). *Average award:* Freshmen: $4034; Undergraduates: $3976. *Scholarships, grants, and awards:* Federal Pell, FSEOG, state, private, college/university gift aid from institutional funds.

GIFT AID (NON-NEED-BASED) *Total amount:* $1,656,326 (12% state, 71% institutional, 17% external sources). *Receiving aid:* Freshmen: 12% (71). Undergraduates: 16% (457). *Average award:* Freshmen: $825. Undergraduates: $1082. *Scholarships, grants, and awards by category:* Academic interests/achievement: communication, general academic interests/achievements. *Creative arts/performance:* music, performing arts, theater/drama. *Special achievements/activities:* cheerleading/drum major. *Special characteristics:* children of faculty/staff, general special characteristics, international students, members of minority groups, out-of-state students, veterans, veterans' children. *Tuition waivers:* Full or partial for employees or children of employees.

LOANS *Student loans:* $14,153,879 (100% need-based). 39% of past graduating class borrowed through all loan programs. *Average indebtedness per student:* $24,171. *Average need-based loan:* Freshmen: $5132. Undergraduates: $7097. *Parent loans:* $183,475 (100% need-based). *Programs:* Federal Direct (Subsidized and Unsubsidized Stafford, PLUS).

WORK-STUDY *Federal work-study:* jobs available. *State or other work-study/employment:* Part-time jobs available.

ATHLETIC AWARDS Total amount: $1,276,018 (100% non-need-based).

APPLYING FOR FINANCIAL AID *Required financial aid form:* FAFSA. *Financial aid deadline (priority):* 3/1. *Notification date:* Continuous beginning 4/15. Students must reply within 6 weeks of notification.

CONTACT Becky Isaacs, Director of Financial Aid, East Central University, 1100 East 14th Street, Ada, OK 74820-6999, 580-332-8000 Ext. 242. *Fax:* 580-436-5612. *E-mail:* bisaacs@ecok.edu.
Website: http://www.ecok.edu/.

EASTERN CONNECTICUT STATE UNIVERSITY
Willimantic, CT

ABOUT THE INSTITUTION State-supported, coed. 32 undergraduate majors.
GIFT AID (NEED-BASED) *Scholarships, grants, and awards:* Federal Pell, FSEOG, state, private, college/university gift aid from institutional funds.
GIFT AID (NON-NEED-BASED) *Scholarships, grants, and awards by category:* Academic interests/achievement: area/ethnic studies, biological sciences, business, communication, computer science, education, English, foreign languages,

general academic interests/achievements, home economics, international studies, mathematics, physical sciences, social sciences. *Creative arts/performance:* art/fine arts, general creative arts/performance, music, performing arts, theater/drama. *Special achievements/activities:* community service, leadership. *Special characteristics:* adult students, children of union members/company employees, ethnic background, handicapped students, local/state students, members of minority groups, religious affiliation, veterans.

LOANS *Programs:* Federal Direct (Subsidized and Unsubsidized Stafford, PLUS), Perkins, alternative loans.

APPLYING FOR FINANCIAL AID *Required financial aid form:* FAFSA.

CONTACT Jennifer Horner, Director of Financial Aid, Eastern Connecticut State University, 83 Windham Street, Wood SSC, Willimantic, CT 06226-2295, 860-465-5775. *E-mail:* hornerje@easternct.edu.
Website: http://www.easternct.edu/.

EASTERN ILLINOIS UNIVERSITY
Charleston, IL

Tuition & fees (IL res): $11,678	Average undergraduate aid package: $13,067

ABOUT THE INSTITUTION State-supported, coed. *Awards:* certificates, bachelor's, and master's degrees. 48 undergraduate majors. *Total enrollment:* 7,415. Undergraduates: 5,957. Freshmen: 772. Federal methodology is used as a basis for awarding need-based institutional aid.

UNDERGRADUATE EXPENSES for 2017–2018 *Application fee:* $30. *Tuition, state resident:* full-time $8760; part-time $292 per credit hour. *Tuition, nonresident:* full-time $10,950; part-time $365 per credit hour. *Required fees:* full-time $2918; $111 per credit hour. Full-time tuition and fees vary according to course load and student level. Part-time tuition and fees vary according to course load and student level. *College room and board:* $9736. Room and board charges vary according to board plan and housing facility. *Payment plan:* Guaranteed tuition.

FRESHMAN FINANCIAL AID (Fall 2017, est.) 593 applied for aid; of those 83% were deemed to have need. 99% of freshmen with need received aid; of those 8% had need fully met. *Average percent of need met:* 54% (excluding resources awarded to replace EFC). *Average financial aid package:* $13,760 (excluding resources awarded to replace EFC). 10% of all full-time freshmen had no need and received non-need-based gift aid.

UNDERGRADUATE FINANCIAL AID (Fall 2017, est.) 3,693 applied for aid; of those 82% were deemed to have need. 100% of undergraduates with need received aid; of those 10% had need fully met. *Average percent of need met:* 57% (excluding resources awarded to replace EFC). *Average financial aid package:* $13,067 (excluding resources awarded to replace EFC). 12% of all full-time undergraduates had no need and received non-need-based gift aid.

GIFT AID (NEED-BASED) *Total amount:* $24,621,907 (42% federal, 33% state, 20% institutional, 5% external sources). *Receiving aid:* Freshmen: 62% (395); all full-time undergraduates: 55% (2,355). *Average award:* Freshmen: $9503; Undergraduates: $8459. *Scholarships, grants, and awards:* Federal Pell, FSEOG, state, private, college/university gift aid from institutional funds.

GIFT AID (NON-NEED-BASED) *Total amount:* $2,485,870 (6% federal, 5% state, 67% institutional, 22% external sources). *Receiving aid:* Freshmen: 49% (311). Undergraduates: 36% (1,569). *Average award:* Freshmen: $4575. Undergraduates: $3671. *Scholarships, grants, and awards by category:* Academic interests/achievement: biological sciences, business, communication, computer science, education, engineering/technologies, English, foreign languages, general academic interests/achievements, health fields, home economics, humanities, international studies, mathematics, physical sciences, premedicine, social sciences. *Creative arts/performance:* applied art and design, art/fine arts, cinema/film/broadcasting, creative writing, debating, general creative arts/performance, journalism/publications, music, performing arts, theater/drama. *Special achievements/activities:* general special achievements/activities, leadership. *Tuition waivers:* Full or partial for employees or children of employees, senior citizens. *ROTC:* Army.

LOANS *Student loans:* $22,889,331 (87% need-based, 13% non-need-based). 77% of past graduating class borrowed through all loan programs. *Average indebtedness per student:* $30,695. *Average need-based loan:* Freshmen: $3468. Undergraduates: $4424. *Parent loans:* $3,924,100 (78% need-based, 22% non-need-based). *Programs:* Federal Direct (Subsidized and Unsubsidized Stafford, PLUS), Perkins.

WORK-STUDY *Federal work-study:* Total amount: $327,764; jobs available. *State or other work-study/employment:* Part-time jobs available.

ATHLETIC AWARDS Total amount: $3,057,952 (51% need based, 16% non-need-based).

APPLYING FOR FINANCIAL AID *Required financial aid form:* FAFSA. *Financial aid deadline (priority):* 3/1. *Notification date:* Continuous beginning 3/1. Students must reply within 2 weeks of notification.

CONTACT Mandi Starwalt, Interim Senior Associate Director of Financial Aid and Scholarships, Eastern Illinois University, 600 Lincoln Avenue, Charleston, IL 61920, 217-581-7812 or toll-free 877-581-2348. *Fax:* 217-581-6422. *E-mail:* finaid@eiu.edu. *Website:* http://www.eiu.edu/.

EASTERN KENTUCKY UNIVERSITY
Richmond, KY

Tuition & fees (KY res): $8996	Average undergraduate aid package: $11,620

ABOUT THE INSTITUTION State-supported, coed. 101 undergraduate majors. Both federal and institutional methodology are used as a basis for awarding need-based institutional aid.

UNDERGRADUATE EXPENSES for 2017–2018 *Tuition, state resident:* full-time $8996; part-time $375 per credit hour. *Tuition, nonresident:* full-time $18,774; part-time $782.25 per credit hour. Full-time tuition and fees vary according to degree level and location. Part-time tuition and fees vary according to course load. *College room and board:* $9728; *Room only:* $5484. Room and board charges vary according to board plan and housing facility.

FRESHMAN FINANCIAL AID (Fall 2017, est.) 2,349 applied for aid; of those 83% were deemed to have need. 100% of freshmen with need received aid; of those 31% had need fully met. *Average percent of need met:* 80% (excluding resources awarded to replace EFC). *Average financial aid package:* $12,365 (excluding resources awarded to replace EFC). 14% of all full-time freshmen had no need and received non-need-based gift aid.

UNDERGRADUATE FINANCIAL AID (Fall 2017, est.) 8,964 applied for aid; of those 86% were deemed to have need. 98% of undergraduates with need received aid; of those 30% had need fully met. *Average percent of need met:* 78% (excluding resources awarded to replace EFC). *Average financial aid package:* $11,620 (excluding resources awarded to replace EFC). 14% of all full-time undergraduates had no need and received non-need-based gift aid.

GIFT AID (NEED-BASED) *Total amount:* $58,466,176 (43% federal, 26% state, 29% institutional, 2% external sources). *Receiving aid:* Freshmen: 48% (1,221); all full-time undergraduates: 46% (4,941). *Average award:* Freshmen: $6413; Undergraduates: $6059. *Scholarships, grants, and awards:* Federal Pell, FSEOG, state, private, college/university gift aid from institutional funds.

GIFT AID (NON-NEED-BASED) *Total amount:* $12,268,193 (28% state, 69% institutional, 3% external sources). *Receiving aid:* Freshmen: 73% (1,836). Undergraduates: 49% (5,240). *Average award:* Freshmen: $6368. Undergraduates: $5845. *Scholarships, grants, and awards by category:* Academic interests/achievement: 3,954 awards ($20,036,566 total): general academic interests/achievements. Creative arts/performance: 141 awards ($386,103 total): music. *Special achievements/activities:* 48 awards ($25,484 total): cheerleading/drum major. *Special characteristics:* 475 awards ($2,099,823 total): children and siblings of alumni, children of faculty/staff, members of minority groups. *Tuition waivers:* Full or partial for employees or children of employees, senior citizens.

LOANS *Student loans:* $61,846,751 (88% need-based, 12% non-need-based). 72% of past graduating class borrowed through all loan programs. *Average indebtedness per student:* $33,102. *Average need-based loan:* Freshmen: $3069. Undergraduates: $3979. *Parent loans:* $10,430,046 (83% need-based, 17% non-need-based). *Programs:* Federal Direct (Subsidized and Unsubsidized Stafford, PLUS), Perkins, college/university.

WORK-STUDY *Federal work-study:* Total amount: $5,000,251; 1,200 jobs averaging $2400. *State or other work-study/employment:* Total amount: $3,229,248 (100% non-need-based). 1,200 part-time jobs averaging $2400.

ATHLETIC AWARDS Total amount: $4,549,086 (49% need-based, 51% non-need-based).

APPLYING FOR FINANCIAL AID *Required financial aid form:* FAFSA. *Financial aid deadline (priority):* 2/1. *Notification date:* Continuous beginning 4/1.

CONTACT Office of Financial Aid, Eastern Kentucky University, 521 Lancaster Avenue, Whitlock Building, CPO Box 59, Richmond, KY 40475-3102, 859-622-2361 or toll-free 800-465-9191. *Fax:* 859-622-2019. *E-mail:* finaid@eku.edu. *Website:* http://www.eku.edu/.

EASTERN MENNONITE UNIVERSITY
Harrisonburg, VA

Tuition & fees: $37,100	Average undergraduate aid package: $31,315

ABOUT THE INSTITUTION Independent Mennonite, coed. *Awards:* certificates, associate, bachelor's, and master's degrees. 38 undergraduate majors. *Total enrollment:* 1,530. Undergraduates: 1,098. Freshmen: 189. Federal methodology is used as a basis for awarding need-based institutional aid.

UNDERGRADUATE EXPENSES for 2018–2019 *Application fee:* $25. *Comprehensive fee:* $48,260 includes full-time tuition ($36,760), mandatory fees ($340), and room and board ($11,160). Room and board charges vary according to board plan and housing facility. *Part-time tuition:* $1400 per credit hour. Part-time tuition and fees vary according to course load.

FRESHMAN FINANCIAL AID (Fall 2016) 192 applied for aid; of those 94% were deemed to have need. 100% of freshmen with need received aid; of those 23% had need fully met. *Average percent of need met:* 79% (excluding resources awarded to replace EFC). *Average financial aid package:* $33,055 (excluding resources awarded to replace EFC). 16% of all full-time freshmen had no need and received non-need-based gift aid.

UNDERGRADUATE FINANCIAL AID (Fall 2016) 840 applied for aid; of those 92% were deemed to have need. 100% of undergraduates with need received aid; of those 17% had need fully met. *Average percent of need met:* 75% (excluding resources awarded to replace EFC). *Average financial aid package:* $31,315 (excluding resources awarded to replace EFC). 16% of all full-time undergraduates had no need and received non-need-based gift aid.

GIFT AID (NEED-BASED) *Total amount:* $15,084,208 (13% federal, 9% state, 73% institutional, 5% external sources). *Receiving aid:* Freshmen: 81% (180); all full-time undergraduates: 71% (764). *Average award:* Freshmen: $22,597; Undergraduates: $19,417. *Scholarships, grants, and awards:* Federal Pell, FSEOG, state, private, college/university gift aid from institutional funds, Federal Nursing.

GIFT AID (NON-NEED-BASED) *Total amount:* $3,786,087 (8% state, 80% institutional, 12% external sources). *Receiving aid:* Freshmen: 15% (33). Undergraduates: 9% (93). *Average award:* Freshmen: $17,609. Undergraduates: $15,317. *Scholarships, grants, and awards by category:* Academic interests/achievement: biological sciences, business, education, engineering/technologies, English, foreign languages, general academic interests/achievements, humanities, mathematics, physical sciences, premedicine, religion/biblical studies, social sciences. *Creative arts/performance:* art/fine arts, music. *Special achievements/activities:* general special achievements/activities, religious involvement. *Special characteristics:* children and siblings of alumni, children of faculty/staff, ethnic background, general special characteristics, international students, religious affiliation. *Tuition waivers:* Full or partial for employees or children of employees.

LOANS *Student loans:* $7,592,256 (85% need-based, 15% non-need-based). 72% of past graduating class borrowed through all loan programs. *Average indebtedness per student:* $39,845. *Average need-based loan:* Freshmen: $6213. Undergraduates: $8346. *Parent loans:* $2,032,103 (78% need-based, 22% non-need-based). *Programs:* Federal Direct (Subsidized and Unsubsidized Stafford, PLUS), Perkins, Federal Nursing.

WORK-STUDY *Federal work-study:* 316 jobs averaging $1266. *State or other work-study/employment:* Total amount: $71,189 (100% need-based). 49 part-time jobs averaging $1453.

APPLYING FOR FINANCIAL AID *Required financial aid forms:* FAFSA, state aid form. *Financial aid deadline (priority):* 4/15. *Notification date:* Continuous beginning 2/1. Students must reply within 5 weeks of notification.

CONTACT Ms. Michele Hensley, Director of Financial Assistance, Eastern Mennonite University, 1200 Park Road, Harrisonburg, VA 22802-2462, 540-432-4138 or toll-free 800-368-2665. *Fax:* 540-432-4081. *E-mail:* michele.hensley@emu.edu. *Website:* http://www.emu.edu/.

EASTERN MICHIGAN UNIVERSITY
Ypsilanti, MI

Tuition & fees (MI res): $13,649	Average undergraduate aid package: $10,030

ABOUT THE INSTITUTION State-supported, coed. *Awards:* certificates, bachelor's, master's, and doctoral degrees. 131 undergraduate majors. *Total enrollment:* 20,313. Undergraduates: 16,997. Freshmen: 2,815. Federal methodology is used as a basis for awarding need-based institutional aid.

UNDERGRADUATE EXPENSES for 2017–2018 *Application fee:* $35. *One-time required fee:* $323. *Tuition, state resident:* full-time $12,120; part-time $323 per credit hour. *Tuition, nonresident:* full-time $27,711; part-time $872.75 per credit hour. *Required fees:* full-time $1529; $47.30 per credit hour or $50 per credit hour. Full-time tuition and fees vary according to course level and reciprocity agreements. Part-time tuition and fees vary according to course level and reciprocity agreements. *College room and board:* $9672. Room and board charges vary according to board plan, housing facility, and location.

FRESHMAN FINANCIAL AID (Fall 2016) 2,554 applied for aid; of those 79% were deemed to have need. 99% of freshmen with need received aid; of those 6% had need fully met. *Average percent of need met:* 45% (excluding resources awarded to replace EFC). *Average financial aid package:* $10,667 (excluding resources awarded to replace EFC). 25% of all full-time freshmen had no need and received non-need-based gift aid.

UNDERGRADUATE FINANCIAL AID (Fall 2016) 10,503 applied for aid; of those 82% were deemed to have need. 98% of undergraduates with need received aid; of those 4% had need fully met. *Average percent of need met:* 47% (excluding resources awarded to replace EFC). *Average financial aid package:* $10,030 (excluding resources awarded to replace EFC). 19% of all full-time undergraduates had no need and received non-need-based gift aid.

GIFT AID (NEED-BASED) *Total amount:* $40,024,110 (75% federal, 3% state, 22% institutional). *Receiving aid:* Freshmen: 51% (1,422); all full-time undergraduates: 48% (6,165). *Average award:* Freshmen: $6850; Undergraduates: $5707. *Scholarships, grants, and awards:* Federal Pell, FSEOG, state, private, college/university gift aid from institutional funds, Federal Nursing.

GIFT AID (NON-NEED-BASED) *Total amount:* $31,740,195 (1% state, 93% institutional, 6% external sources). *Receiving aid:* Freshmen: 53% (1,475). Undergraduates: 33% (4,169). *Average award:* Freshmen: $5149. Undergraduates: $5413. *Scholarships, grants, and awards by category:* Academic interests/achievement: 6,252 awards ($24,981,404 total): agriculture, architecture, biological sciences, business, communication, computer science, education, engineering/technologies, English, foreign languages, general academic interests/achievements, health fields, home economics, humanities, mathematics, physical sciences, religion/biblical studies, social sciences. *Creative arts/performance:* 104 awards ($110,389 total): applied art and design, art/fine arts, cinema/film/broadcasting, creative writing, dance, debating, general creative arts/performance, music, performing arts, theater/drama. *Special achievements/activities:* 93 awards ($127,600 total): general special achievements/activities, leadership, memberships, religious involvement. *Special characteristics:* 323 awards ($4,185,765 total): children and siblings of alumni, ethnic background, international students, members of minority groups, out-of-state students, previous college experience, religious affiliation. *Tuition waivers:* Full or partial for employees or children of employees. *ROTC:* Army, Naval cooperative, Air Force cooperative.

LOANS *Student loans:* $81,549,704 (42% need-based, 58% non-need-based). 70% of past graduating class borrowed through all loan programs. *Average indebtedness per student:* $30,205. *Average need-based loan:* Freshmen: $3206. Undergraduates: $4080. *Parent loans:* $19,032,525 (100% non-need-based). *Programs:* Federal Direct (Subsidized and Unsubsidized Stafford, PLUS), Perkins, private loans.

WORK-STUDY *Federal work-study:* 595 jobs averaging $2302.

ATHLETIC AWARDS Total amount: $4,036,697 (100% non-need-based).

APPLYING FOR FINANCIAL AID *Required financial aid form:* FAFSA. *Financial aid deadline:* Continuous. *Notification date:* Continuous beginning 12/12.

CONTACT Donna Holubik, Director of Financial Aid, Eastern Michigan University, 403 Pierce Hall, Ypsilanti, MI 48197, 734-487-1048 or toll-free 800-GO TO EMU. *Fax:* 734-487-4281. *E-mail:* dholubik@emich.edu. *Website:* http://www.emich.edu/.

EASTERN NAZARENE COLLEGE
Quincy, MA

CONTACT Lisa Seals, Interim Director of Financial Aid, Eastern Nazarene College, 23 East Elm Avenue, Quincy, MA 02170, 617-745-3869 or toll-free 800-88-ENC88. *Fax:* 617-745-3992. *E-mail:* lisa.seals@enc.edu. *Website:* http://www.enc.edu/.

EASTERN NEW MEXICO UNIVERSITY
Portales, NM

CONTACT Mr. Brent Small, Director of Financial Aid, Eastern New Mexico University, Station 20, 1500 South Avenue K, Portales, NM 88130, 575-562-2194 or toll-free 800-367-3668. *Fax:* 575-562-2198. *E-mail:* brent.small@enmu.edu. *Website:* http://www.enmu.edu/.

EASTERN OREGON UNIVERSITY
La Grande, OR

Tuition & fees (OR res): $8362	Average undergraduate aid package: $9696

ABOUT THE INSTITUTION State-supported, coed. *Awards:* certificates, associate, bachelor's, and master's degrees. 22 undergraduate majors. *Total enrollment:* 3,016. Undergraduates: 2,737. Freshmen: 327. Federal methodology is used as a basis for awarding need-based institutional aid.

UNDERGRADUATE EXPENSES for 2017–2018 *Application fee:* $50. *One-time required fee:* $350. *Tuition, state resident:* full-time $6928; part-time $153.95 per credit hour. *Tuition, nonresident:* full-time $18,248; part-time $405.50 per credit hour. *Required fees:* full-time $1434; $466 per term. Full-time tuition and fees vary according to course load, location, and reciprocity agreements. Part-time tuition and fees vary according to course load, location, and reciprocity agreements. *College room and board:* $9250; *Room only:* $5500. Room and board charges vary according to board plan and housing facility.

FRESHMAN FINANCIAL AID (Fall 2016) 312 applied for aid; of those 76% were deemed to have need. 100% of freshmen with need received aid; of those 29% had need fully met. *Average percent of need met:* 67% (excluding resources awarded to replace EFC). *Average financial aid package:* $10,515 (excluding resources awarded to replace EFC). 19% of all full-time freshmen had no need and received non-need-based gift aid.

UNDERGRADUATE FINANCIAL AID (Fall 2016) 1,567 applied for aid; of those 86% were deemed to have need. 98% of undergraduates with need received aid; of those 13% had need fully met. *Average percent of need met:* 56% (excluding resources awarded to replace EFC). *Average financial aid package:* $9696 (excluding resources awarded to replace EFC). 8% of all full-time undergraduates had no need and received non-need-based gift aid.

GIFT AID (NEED-BASED) *Total amount:* $8,053,978 (74% federal, 17% state, 8% institutional, 1% external sources). *Receiving aid:* Freshmen: 67% (221); all full-time undergraduates: 71% (1,271). *Average award:* Freshmen: $7137; Undergraduates: $8126. *Scholarships, grants, and awards:* Federal Pell, FSEOG, state, private, college/university gift aid from institutional funds.

GIFT AID (NON-NEED-BASED) *Total amount:* $2,674,184 (44% institutional, 56% external sources). *Receiving aid:* Freshmen: 60% (196). Undergraduates: 36% (649). *Average award:* Freshmen: $2054. Undergraduates: $2112. *Scholarships, grants, and awards by category: Academic interests/achievement:* general academic interests/achievements. *Creative arts/performance:* art/fine arts, general creative arts/performance. *Special achievements/activities:* leadership. *Special characteristics:* local/state students, members of minority groups. *Tuition waivers:* Full or partial for employees or children of employees, senior citizens. *ROTC:* Army.

LOANS *Student loans:* $11,318,870 (46% need-based, 54% non-need-based). 67% of past graduating class borrowed through all loan programs. *Average indebtedness per student:* $31,314. *Average need-based loan:* Freshmen: $3139. Undergraduates: $4227. *Parent loans:* $2,396,020 (100% non-need-based). *Programs:* Federal Direct (Subsidized and Unsubsidized Stafford, PLUS), Perkins.

WORK-STUDY *Federal work-study:* jobs available.

ATHLETIC AWARDS Total amount: $969,585 (100% non-need-based).

APPLYING FOR FINANCIAL AID *Required financial aid form:* FAFSA. *Financial aid deadline (priority):* 2/1. *Notification date:* Continuous beginning 4/1. Students must reply within 4 weeks of notification.

CONTACT Financial Aid Office, Eastern Oregon University, One University Boulevard, Inlow Hall, Room 201, La Grande, OR 97850-2899, 541-962-3550 or toll-free 800-452-8639. *Fax:* 541-962-3661. *E-mail:* fao@eou.edu. *Website:* http://www.eou.edu/.

EASTERN UNIVERSITY
St. Davids, PA

Tuition & fees: $32,882	Average undergraduate aid package: $20,817

ABOUT THE INSTITUTION Independent Christian, coed. *Awards:* certificates, diplomas, associate, bachelor's, master's, and doctoral degrees. 37 undergraduate majors. *Total enrollment:* 3,291. Undergraduates: 1,887. Freshmen: 381. Both federal and institutional methodology are used as a basis for awarding need-based institutional aid.

UNDERGRADUATE EXPENSES for 2018–2019 *Application fee:* $35. *One-time required fee:* $65. *Comprehensive fee:* $44,136 includes full-time tuition ($32,492), mandatory fees ($390), and room and board ($11,254). *College room only:* $5986. Full-time tuition and fees vary according to course load, degree level, and program. Room and board charges vary according to housing facility and location. *Part-time tuition:* $712 per credit. *Part-time fees:* $195 per term. Part-time tuition and fees vary according to course load, degree level, and program.

FRESHMAN FINANCIAL AID (Fall 2016) 386 applied for aid; of those 90% were deemed to have need. 100% of freshmen with need received aid; of those 21% had need fully met. *Average percent of need met:* 80% (excluding resources awarded to replace EFC). *Average financial aid package:* $25,020 (excluding resources awarded to replace EFC). 9% of all full-time freshmen had no need and received non-need-based gift aid.

UNDERGRADUATE FINANCIAL AID (Fall 2016) 1,740 applied for aid; of those 93% were deemed to have need. 99% of undergraduates with need received aid; of those 26% had need fully met. *Average percent of need met:* 81% (excluding resources awarded to replace EFC). *Average financial aid package:* $20,817 (excluding resources awarded to replace EFC). 5% of all full-time undergraduates had no need and received non-need-based gift aid.

GIFT AID (NEED-BASED) *Total amount:* $9,872,775 (41% federal, 22% state, 37% institutional). *Receiving aid:* Freshmen: 71% (301); all full-time undergraduates: 70% (1,365). *Average award:* Freshmen: $8725; Undergraduates: $7123. *Scholarships, grants, and awards:* Federal Pell, FSEOG, state, private, college/university gift aid from institutional funds.

GIFT AID (NON-NEED-BASED) *Total amount:* $20,521,225 (96% institutional, 4% external sources). *Receiving aid:* Freshmen: 80% (337). Undergraduates: 66% (1,295). *Average award:* Freshmen: $15,372. Undergraduates: $13,445. *Scholarships, grants, and awards by category: Academic interests/achievement:* 67 awards ($153,000 total): engineering/technologies. *Creative arts/performance:* 36 awards ($97,500 total): music. *Special achievements/activities:* 464 awards ($1,982,528 total): leadership. *Special characteristics:* 283 awards ($1,047,784 total): children and siblings of alumni, children of faculty/staff, international students, previous college experience, relatives of clergy, siblings of current students, veterans, veterans' children. *Tuition waivers:* Full or partial for children of alumni, employees or children of employees. *ROTC:* Army cooperative, Air Force cooperative.

LOANS *Student loans:* $14,770,336 (37% need-based, 63% non-need-based). 75% of past graduating class borrowed through all loan programs. *Average indebtedness per student:* $37,225. *Average need-based loan:* Freshmen: $3530. Undergraduates: $4134. *Parent loans:* $3,189,390 (100% non-need-based). *Programs:* Federal Direct (Subsidized and Unsubsidized Stafford, PLUS), Perkins.

WORK-STUDY *Federal work-study:* 337 jobs averaging $1088. *State or other work-study/employment:* Part-time jobs available.

APPLYING FOR FINANCIAL AID *Required financial aid form:* FAFSA. *Financial aid deadline:* Continuous. *Notification date:* Continuous beginning 4/1.

CONTACT Andrea L. Ruth, Interim Financial Aid Director, Eastern University, 1300 Eagle Road, St. Davids, PA 19087-3696, 610-225-5102 or toll-free 800-452-0996. *Fax:* 610-225-5651. *E-mail:* finaid@eastern.edu. *Website:* http://www.eastern.edu/.

EASTERN WASHINGTON UNIVERSITY
Cheney, WA

Tuition & fees (WA res): $7109	Average undergraduate aid package: $13,055

ABOUT THE INSTITUTION State-supported, coed. *Awards:* certificates, bachelor's, master's, and doctoral degrees. 93 undergraduate majors. *Total enrollment:* 12,607. Undergraduates: 11,473. Freshmen: 1,634. Federal methodology is used as a basis for awarding need-based institutional aid.

UNDERGRADUATE EXPENSES for 2017–2018 Application fee: $50. *Tuition, state resident:* full-time $6242; part-time $208.07 per credit hour. *Tuition, nonresident:* full-time $22,995; part-time $766.51 per credit hour. *Required fees:* full-time $867. Full-time tuition and fees vary according to course load, degree level, location, and program. Part-time tuition and fees vary according to course load, degree level, location, and program. *College room and board:* $11,493; *Room only:* $6528. Room and board charges vary according to board plan and housing facility.

FRESHMAN FINANCIAL AID (Fall 2016) 1,485 applied for aid; of those 75% were deemed to have need. 80% of freshmen with need received aid; of those 7% had need fully met. *Average percent of need met:* 86% (excluding resources awarded to replace EFC). *Average financial aid package:* $12,429 (excluding resources awarded to replace EFC). 8% of all full-time freshmen had no need and received non-need-based gift aid.

UNDERGRADUATE FINANCIAL AID (Fall 2016) 7,553 applied for aid; of those 82% were deemed to have need. 85% of undergraduates with need received aid; of those 9% had need fully met. *Average percent of need met:* 59% (excluding resources awarded to replace EFC). *Average financial aid package:* $13,055 (excluding resources awarded to replace EFC). 5% of all full-time undergraduates had no need and received non-need-based gift aid.

GIFT AID (NEED-BASED) Total amount: $40,529,151 (45% federal, 41% state, 9% institutional, 5% external sources). *Receiving aid:* Freshmen: 46% (782); all full-time undergraduates: 44% (4,437). *Average award:* Freshmen: $7883; Undergraduates: $8019. *Scholarships, grants, and awards:* Federal Pell, FSEOG, state, private, college/university gift aid from institutional funds.

GIFT AID (NON-NEED-BASED) Total amount: $9,200,558 (2% institutional, 98% external sources). *Receiving aid:* Freshmen: 24% (401). Undergraduates: 12% (1,172). *Average award:* Freshmen: $3476. Undergraduates: $3710. *Scholarships, grants, and awards by category: Academic interests/achievement:* 681 awards ($1,084,940 total): area/ethnic studies, biological sciences, business, communication, computer science, education, engineering/technologies, English, foreign languages, general academic interests/achievements, home economics, humanities, international studies, mathematics, military science, physical sciences, premedicine, social sciences. *Creative arts/performance:* art/fine arts, cinema/film/broadcasting, creative writing, journalism/publications, music, theater/drama. *Special characteristics:* adult students, children and siblings of alumni, children of union members/company employees, ethnic background, first-generation college students, handicapped students, local/state students, married students, spouses of deceased or disabled public servants, veterans, veterans' children. *Tuition waivers:* Full or partial for employees or children of employees. *ROTC:* Army.

LOANS Student loans: $39,321,916 (84% need-based, 16% non-need-based). 52% of past graduating class borrowed through all loan programs. *Average indebtedness per student:* $27,961. *Average need-based loan:* Freshmen: $3183. Undergraduates: $4138. *Parent loans:* $5,483,914 (67% need-based, 33% non-need-based). *Programs:* Federal Direct (Subsidized and Unsubsidized Stafford, PLUS), Perkins, credit-based education loans from commercial lenders.

WORK-STUDY Federal work-study: 205 jobs averaging $2723. *State or other work-study/employment:* Total amount: $412,041 (100% need-based). 172 part-time jobs averaging $2620.

ATHLETIC AWARDS Total amount: $3,042,165 (37% need-based, 63% non-need-based).

APPLYING FOR FINANCIAL AID Required financial aid forms: FAFSA, Washington Application for Student Financial Aid (WASFA) for undocumented state residents and DACA students only. *Financial aid deadline (priority):* 2/1. *Notification date:* Continuous beginning 3/1. Students must reply within 4 weeks of notification.

CONTACT Mr. Bruce DeFrates, Director of Financial Aid and Scholarships, Eastern Washington University, 102 Sutton Hall, Cheney, WA 99004-2447, 509-359-2314. *Fax:* 509-359-4330. *E-mail:* bdefrates@ewu.edu. *Website:* http://www.ewu.edu/.

EAST STROUDSBURG UNIVERSITY OF PENNSYLVANIA
East Stroudsburg, PA

Tuition & fees (PA res): $10,298	Average undergraduate aid package: $8857

ABOUT THE INSTITUTION State-supported, coed. *Awards:* certificates, bachelor's, master's, and doctoral degrees. 42 undergraduate majors. *Total enrollment:* 6,742. Undergraduates: 6,051. Freshmen: 1,282. Federal methodology is used as a basis for awarding need-based institutional aid.

UNDERGRADUATE EXPENSES for 2017–2018 Application fee: $25. *Tuition, state resident:* full-time $7492; part-time $312 per credit hour. *Tuition, nonresident:* full-time $18,730; part-time $780 per credit hour. *Required fees:* full-time $2806; $151 per credit hour or $716 per term. Full-time tuition and fees vary according to course load, location, and program. Part-time tuition and fees vary according to location and program. *College room and board:* $8672; *Room only:* $6000. Room and board charges vary according to board plan and housing facility.

FRESHMAN FINANCIAL AID (Fall 2016) 1,242 applied for aid; of those 82% were deemed to have need. 97% of freshmen with need received aid; of those 47% had need fully met. *Average percent of need met:* 54% (excluding resources awarded to replace EFC). *Average financial aid package:* $8679 (excluding resources awarded to replace EFC).

UNDERGRADUATE FINANCIAL AID (Fall 2016) 3,838 applied for aid; of those 84% were deemed to have need. 97% of undergraduates with need received aid; of those 49% had need fully met. *Average percent of need met:* 68% (excluding resources awarded to replace EFC). *Average financial aid package:* $8857 (excluding resources awarded to replace EFC).

GIFT AID (NEED-BASED) Total amount: $33,423,017 (73% federal, 18% state, 9% institutional). *Receiving aid:* Freshmen: 72% (943); all full-time undergraduates: 50% (2,955). *Average award:* Freshmen: $7927; Undergraduates: $8374. *Scholarships, grants, and awards:* Federal Pell, FSEOG, state, private, college/university gift aid from institutional funds.

GIFT AID (NON-NEED-BASED) Total amount: $1,220,738 (100% external sources). *Receiving aid:* Freshmen: 71% (934). Undergraduates: 49% (2,899). *Tuition waivers:* Full or partial for employees or children of employees, senior citizens. *ROTC:* Army, Air Force cooperative.

LOANS Student loans: $51,291,721 (27% need-based, 73% non-need-based). 75% of past graduating class borrowed through all loan programs. *Average indebtedness per student:* $24,182. *Average need-based loan:* Freshmen: $3142. Undergraduates: $4116. *Parent loans:* $10,347,449 (100% non-need-based). *Programs:* Federal Direct (Subsidized and Unsubsidized Stafford, PLUS), Perkins, Federal Nursing.

WORK-STUDY Federal work-study: jobs available. *State or other work-study/employment:* Part-time jobs available.

ATHLETIC AWARDS Total amount: $1,079,071 (100% need-based).

APPLYING FOR FINANCIAL AID Required financial aid form: FAFSA. *Financial aid deadline (priority):* 2/17. *Notification date:* 3/17. Students must reply by 5/1 or within 3 weeks of notification.

CONTACT Aristalia Benitez, Office of Financial Aid, East Stroudsburg University of Pennsylvania, 200 Prospect Street, East Stroudsburg, PA 18301-2999, 570-422-2828 or toll-free 877-230-5547. *Fax:* 570-422-2849. *E-mail:* finaid@esu.edu. *Website:* http://www.esu.edu/.

EAST TENNESSEE STATE UNIVERSITY
Johnson City, TN

ABOUT THE INSTITUTION State-supported, coed. *Awards:* certificates, bachelor's, master's, and doctoral degrees. 49 undergraduate majors. *Total enrollment:* 14,353. Undergraduates: 11,323. Freshmen: 2,050.

GIFT AID (NEED-BASED) Scholarships, grants, and awards: Federal Pell, FSEOG, state, private, college/university gift aid from institutional funds, Federal Nursing.

GIFT AID (NON-NEED-BASED) Scholarships, grants, and awards by category: *Academic interests/achievement:* biological sciences, business, computer science, education, engineering/technologies, English, general academic interests/

achievements, health fields, mathematics, military science, social sciences. *Creative arts/performance:* art/fine arts, journalism/publications, music, theater/drama. *Special achievements/activities:* leadership, memberships. *Special characteristics:* children of union members/company employees, members of minority groups.

LOANS *Programs:* Federal Direct (Subsidized and Unsubsidized Stafford, PLUS), Perkins, Federal Nursing, state, college/university.

APPLYING FOR FINANCIAL AID *Required financial aid form:* FAFSA.

CONTACT Financial Aid Office, East Tennessee State University, PO Box 70722, 105 Burgin Dossett, Johnson City, TN 37614-1710, 423-439-4300 or toll-free 800-462-3878. *Fax:* 423-439-5855. *E-mail:* finaid@etsu.edu.

Website: http://www.etsu.edu/.

EAST TEXAS BAPTIST UNIVERSITY
Marshall, TX

Tuition & fees: $25,470	Average undergraduate aid package: $19,276

ABOUT THE INSTITUTION Independent Baptist, coed. *Awards:* certificates, bachelor's, and master's degrees. 43 undergraduate majors. *Total enrollment:* 1,533. Undergraduates: 1,421. Freshmen: 420. Federal methodology is used as a basis for awarding need-based institutional aid.

UNDERGRADUATE EXPENSES for 2017–2018 *Application fee:* $25. *Comprehensive fee:* $34,385 includes full-time tuition ($24,420), mandatory fees ($1050), and room and board ($8915). *College room only:* $4576. Room and board charges vary according to board plan and housing facility. *Part-time tuition:* $814 per credit hour. *Part-time fees:* $45 per credit hour.

FRESHMAN FINANCIAL AID (Fall 2016) 333 applied for aid; of those 89% were deemed to have need. 100% of freshmen with need received aid; of those 14% had need fully met. *Average percent of need met:* 29% (excluding resources awarded to replace EFC). *Average financial aid package:* $19,612 (excluding resources awarded to replace EFC). 14% of all full-time freshmen had no need and received non-need-based gift aid.

UNDERGRADUATE FINANCIAL AID (Fall 2016) 1,101 applied for aid; of those 91% were deemed to have need. 100% of undergraduates with need received aid; of those 13% had need fully met. *Average percent of need met:* 30% (excluding resources awarded to replace EFC). *Average financial aid package:* $19,276 (excluding resources awarded to replace EFC). 15% of all full-time undergraduates had no need and received non-need-based gift aid.

GIFT AID (NEED-BASED) *Total amount:* $4,482,987 (54% federal, 38% state, 8% institutional). *Receiving aid:* Freshmen: 63% (219); all full-time undergraduates: 63% (739). *Average award:* Freshmen: $6789; Undergraduates: $6424. *Scholarships, grants, and awards:* Federal Pell, FSEOG, state, private, college/university gift aid from institutional funds.

GIFT AID (NON-NEED-BASED) *Total amount:* $13,147,006 (1% state, 96% institutional, 3% external sources). *Receiving aid:* Freshmen: 85% (294). Undergraduates: 83% (979). *Average award:* Freshmen: $12,280. Undergraduates: $11,448. *Scholarships, grants, and awards by category: Academic interests/ achievement:* 982 awards ($6,735,857 total): biological sciences, business, communication, education, English, general academic interests/achievements, home economics, humanities, mathematics, physical sciences, religion/biblical studies, social sciences. *Creative arts/performance:* 88 awards ($219,496 total): music, theater/drama. *Special achievements/activities:* 849 awards ($2,437,080 total): cheerleading/drum major, general special achievements/activities, leadership, religious involvement, rodeo. *Special characteristics:* 171 awards ($1,018,142 total): adult students, children and siblings of alumni, children of faculty/staff, general special characteristics, international students, out-of-state students, previous college experience, religious affiliation, veterans. *Tuition waivers:* Full or partial for employees or children of employees.

LOANS *Student loans:* $7,608,297 (39% need-based, 61% non-need-based). 83% of past graduating class borrowed through all loan programs. *Average indebtedness per student:* $33,823. *Average need-based loan:* Freshmen: $3026. Undergraduates: $3884. *Parent loans:* $2,383,014 (100% non-need-based). *Programs:* Federal Direct (Subsidized and Unsubsidized Stafford, PLUS), Perkins, state.

WORK-STUDY *Federal work-study:* 83 jobs averaging $1512. *State or other work-study/employment:* Total amount: $391,565 (2% need-based, 98% non-need-based). 262 part-time jobs averaging $1480.

APPLYING FOR FINANCIAL AID *Required financial aid forms:* FAFSA, institution's own form. *Financial aid deadline (priority):* 6/1. *Notification date:* Continuous beginning 1/1.

CONTACT Mr. Nathan Flory, Director of Financial Aid, East Texas Baptist University, One Tiger Drive, Marshall, TX 75670-1498, 903-923-2137 or toll-free 800-804-ETBU. *Fax:* 903-934-8120. *E-mail:* nflory@etbu.edu.

Website: http://www.etbu.edu/.

EAST-WEST UNIVERSITY
Chicago, IL

CONTACT Cesar Campos, Director of Financial Aid, East-West University, 816 South Michigan Avenue, Chicago, IL 60605-2103, 312-939-0111 Ext. 1806. *Fax:* 312-939-0083. *E-mail:* cesar@eastwest.edu.

Website: http://www.eastwest.edu/.

ECCLESIA COLLEGE
Springdale, AR

CONTACT Financial Aid Office, Ecclesia College, 9653 Nations Drive, Springdale, AR 72762, 479-248-7236.

Website: http://www.ecollege.edu/.

ECKERD COLLEGE
St. Petersburg, FL

Tuition & fees: $43,044	Average undergraduate aid package: $36,810

ABOUT THE INSTITUTION Independent Presbyterian, coed. *Awards:* bachelor's degrees. 38 undergraduate majors. *Total enrollment:* 1,957. Undergraduates: 1,957. Freshmen: 561. Federal methodology is used as a basis for awarding need-based institutional aid.

UNDERGRADUATE EXPENSES for 2018–2019 *Application fee:* $40. *Comprehensive fee:* $55,206 includes full-time tuition ($42,428), mandatory fees ($616), and room and board ($12,162). *College room only:* $6362. Room and board charges vary according to board plan and housing facility.

FRESHMAN FINANCIAL AID (Fall 2017, est.) 466 applied for aid; of those 82% were deemed to have need. 100% of freshmen with need received aid; of those 47% had need fully met. *Average percent of need met:* 88% (excluding resources awarded to replace EFC). *Average financial aid package:* $35,564 (excluding resources awarded to replace EFC). 30% of all full-time freshmen had no need and received non-need-based gift aid.

UNDERGRADUATE FINANCIAL AID (Fall 2017, est.) 1,316 applied for aid; of those 88% were deemed to have need. 100% of undergraduates with need received aid; of those 47% had need fully met. *Average percent of need met:* 88% (excluding resources awarded to replace EFC). *Average financial aid package:* $36,810 (excluding resources awarded to replace EFC). 32% of all full-time undergraduates had no need and received non-need-based gift aid.

GIFT AID (NEED-BASED) *Total amount:* $28,402,341 (6% federal, 5% state, 87% institutional, 2% external sources). *Receiving aid:* Freshmen: 69% (383); all full-time undergraduates: 61% (1,155). *Average award:* Freshmen: $25,760; Undergraduates: $25,494. *Scholarships, grants, and awards:* Federal Pell, FSEOG, state, private, college/university gift aid from institutional funds.

GIFT AID (NON-NEED-BASED) *Total amount:* $14,530,025 (4% state, 93% institutional, 3% external sources). *Average award:* Freshmen: $16,285. Undergraduates: $17,555. *Scholarships, grants, and awards by category: Academic interests/achievement:* 1,739 awards ($24,766,838 total): general academic interests/ achievements. *Creative arts/performance:* 54 awards ($54,000 total): art/fine arts, creative writing, music, theater/drama. *Special characteristics:* children of faculty/staff, international students, local/state students, religious affiliation. *Tuition waivers:* Full or partial for employees or children of employees. *ROTC:* Army cooperative, Air Force cooperative.

LOANS *Student loans:* $12,278,703 (69% need-based, 31% non-need-based). 67% of past graduating class borrowed through all loan programs. *Average indebtedness per student:* $33,484. *Average need-based loan:* Freshmen: $3800. Undergraduates: $4476. *Parent loans:* $6,569,359 (46% need-based, 54% non-need-based). *Programs:* Federal Direct (Subsidized and Unsubsidized Stafford, PLUS), Perkins, college/university.

WORK-STUDY *Federal work-study:* Total amount: $1,814,026; 917 jobs averaging $2000. *State or other work-study/employment:* Total amount: $24,000 (100% non-need-based). Part-time jobs available.

ATHLETIC AWARDS Total amount: $2,562,887 (35% need-based, 65% non-need-based).

APPLYING FOR FINANCIAL AID *Required financial aid form:* FAFSA. *Financial aid deadline (priority):* 3/1. *Notification date:* Continuous beginning 10/15. Students must reply by 5/1.

CONTACT Dr. Pat Garrett Watkins, Director of Financial Aid, Eckerd College, 4200 54th Avenue, South, St. Petersburg, FL 33711, 727-864-8334 or toll-free 800-456-9009. *Fax:* 727-866-2304. *E-mail:* watkinpe@eckerd.edu.

Website: http://www.eckerd.edu/.

ECPI UNIVERSITY
Virginia Beach, VA

ABOUT THE INSTITUTION Proprietary, coed. *Awards:* certificates, diplomas, associate, bachelor's, and master's degrees. 28 undergraduate majors. *Total enrollment:* 11,739. Undergraduates: 11,745. Freshmen: 1,309.

GIFT AID (NEED-BASED) *Scholarships, grants, and awards:* Federal Pell, FSEOG, state, private, college/university gift aid from institutional funds.

GIFT AID (NON-NEED-BASED) *Scholarships, grants, and awards by category:* Academic interests/achievement: business, computer science, engineering/technologies, health fields, home economics. *Special achievements/activities:* community service, general special achievements/activities. *Special characteristics:* adult students, children and siblings of alumni, children of current students, children of faculty/staff, general special characteristics, parents of current students, veterans, veterans' children.

LOANS *Programs:* Federal Direct (Subsidized and Unsubsidized Stafford, PLUS), Perkins, college/university, private loans.

APPLYING FOR FINANCIAL AID *Required financial aid forms:* FAFSA, institution's own form.

CONTACT Mrs. Kathi Turner, Director of Financial Aid, ECPI University, 5555 Greenwich Road, Suite 300, Virginia Beach, VA 23462, 757-490-9090 or toll-free 844-611-0766. *Fax:* 757-671-8661. *E-mail:* kturner@ecpi.edu.

Website: http://www.ecpi.edu/.

EDGEWOOD COLLEGE
Madison, WI

Tuition & fees: $29,500	Average undergraduate aid package: $19,031

ABOUT THE INSTITUTION Independent Roman Catholic, coed. *Awards:* certificates, bachelor's, master's, and doctoral degrees. 57 undergraduate majors. *Total enrollment:* 2,221. Undergraduates: 1,564. Freshmen: 284. Federal methodology is used as a basis for awarding need-based institutional aid.

UNDERGRADUATE EXPENSES for 2018–2019 *Application fee:* $30. *Comprehensive fee:* $40,520 includes full-time tuition ($29,500) and room and board ($11,020). Full-time tuition and fees vary according to degree level. Room and board charges vary according to housing facility. *Part-time tuition:* $927 per credit. Part-time tuition and fees vary according to course load and degree level.

FRESHMAN FINANCIAL AID (Fall 2016) 240 applied for aid; of those 85% were deemed to have need. 100% of freshmen with need received aid; of those 12% had need fully met. *Average percent of need met:* 79% (excluding resources awarded to replace EFC). *Average financial aid package:* $22,039 (excluding resources awarded to replace EFC). 19% of all full-time freshmen had no need and received non-need-based gift aid.

UNDERGRADUATE FINANCIAL AID (Fall 2016) 1,197 applied for aid; of those 89% were deemed to have need. 100% of undergraduates with need received

aid; of those 13% had need fully met. *Average percent of need met:* 75% (excluding resources awarded to replace EFC). *Average financial aid package:* $19,031 (excluding resources awarded to replace EFC). 18% of all full-time undergraduates had no need and received non-need-based gift aid.

GIFT AID (NEED-BASED) *Total amount:* $15,791,731 (16% federal, 11% state, 59% institutional, 14% external sources). *Receiving aid:* Freshmen: 78% (205); all full-time undergraduates: 74% (1,040). *Average award:* Freshmen: $17,033; Undergraduates: $13,323. *Scholarships, grants, and awards:* Federal Pell, FSEOG, state, private, college/university gift aid from institutional funds.

GIFT AID (NON-NEED-BASED) *Total amount:* $3,025,876 (9% federal, 63% institutional, 28% external sources). *Receiving aid:* Freshmen: 7% (18). Undergraduates: 6% (84). *Average award:* Freshmen: $9270. Undergraduates: $6399. *Scholarships, grants, and awards by category:* Academic interests/achievement: 1,060 awards ($6,370,444 total): area/ethnic studies, foreign languages, general academic interests/achievements. *Creative arts/performance:* 163 awards ($150,600 total): art/fine arts, creative writing, music, performing arts, theater/drama. *Special achievements/activities:* 38 awards ($276,413 total): community service, religious involvement. *Special characteristics:* 74 awards ($735,245 total): children and siblings of alumni, children of faculty/staff. *Tuition waivers:* Full or partial for employees or children of employees. *ROTC:* Army cooperative, Naval cooperative, Air Force cooperative.

LOANS *Student loans:* $12,600,331 (70% need-based, 30% non-need-based). 79% of past graduating class borrowed through all loan programs. *Average indebtedness per student:* $35,300. *Average need-based loan:* Freshmen: $4004. Undergraduates: $5582. *Parent loans:* $1,928,037 (43% need-based, 57% non-need-based). *Programs:* Federal Direct (Subsidized and Unsubsidized Stafford, PLUS), Perkins, state.

WORK-STUDY *Federal work-study:* 567 jobs averaging $1972. *State or other work-study/employment:* Total amount: $1,411,935 (24% need-based, 76% non-need-based). 466 part-time jobs averaging $2022.

APPLYING FOR FINANCIAL AID *Required financial aid form:* FAFSA. *Financial aid deadline (priority):* 12/1. *Notification date:* Continuous beginning 12/15. Students must reply by 5/1 or within 2 weeks of notification.

CONTACT Ms. Kari J. Gribble, Director of Financial Aid and Edgewood Central, Edgewood College, 1000 Edgewood College Drive, Madison, WI 53711-1997, 608-663-4300 or toll-free 800-444-4861 Ext. 2294. *E-mail:* ecentral@edgewood.edu. *Website:* http://www.edgewood.edu/.

EDINBORO UNIVERSITY OF PENNSYLVANIA
Edinboro, PA

ABOUT THE INSTITUTION State-supported, coed. 39 undergraduate majors.

GIFT AID (NEED-BASED) *Scholarships, grants, and awards:* Federal Pell, FSEOG, state, private, college/university gift aid from institutional funds.

GIFT AID (NON-NEED-BASED) *Scholarships, grants, and awards by category:* Academic interests/achievement: biological sciences, business, communication, computer science, education, engineering/technologies, English, foreign languages, general academic interests/achievements, health fields, humanities, mathematics, military science, physical sciences, premedicine, religion/biblical studies, social sciences. *Creative arts/performance:* applied art and design, art/fine arts, cinema/film/broadcasting, creative writing, journalism/publications, music, theater/drama. *Special achievements/activities:* community service, general special achievements/activities, leadership, memberships. *Special characteristics:* adult students, children and siblings of alumni, children of faculty/staff, children of union members/company employees, children with a deceased or disabled parent, first-generation college students, general special characteristics, handicapped students, international students, local/state students, members of minority groups, out-of-state students, religious affiliation, veterans, veterans' children.

LOANS *Programs:* Federal Direct (Subsidized and Unsubsidized Stafford, PLUS), Perkins, Federal Nursing.

APPLYING FOR FINANCIAL AID *Required financial aid forms:* FAFSA, state aid form.

CONTACT Ms. Alyssa Dobson, Director of Financial Aid, Edinboro University of Pennsylvania, Hamilton Hall, Edinboro, PA 16444, 814-732-3500 or toll-free 888-846-2676. *Fax:* 814-732-2129. *E-mail:* finaid@edinboro.edu.

Website: http://www.edinboro.edu/.

EDP UNIVERSITY OF PUERTO RICO

Hato Rey, PR

CONTACT Yaitzaenid Gonzalez, Financial Aid Administrator, EDP University of Puerto Rico, PO Box 192303, San Juan, PR 00919-2303, 787-765-3560 Ext. 253. *Fax:* 787-777-0025. *E-mail:* ygonzalez@edpcollege.edu. *Website:* http://www.edpuniversity.edu/.

EDP UNIVERSITY OF PUERTO RICO– SAN SEBASTIAN

San Sebastian, PR

CONTACT Mrs. Yaitzaenid Gonzalez, Financial Aid Administrator, EDP University of Puerto Rico–San Sebastian, PO Box 192303, San Juan, PR 00919, 787-765-3560 Ext. 253. *Fax:* 787-777-0025. *E-mail:* ygonzalez@edpcollege.edu. *Website:* http://www.edpuniversity.edu/.

EDWARD WATERS COLLEGE

Jacksonville, FL

CONTACT Gabriel Mbomeh, Director of Financial Aid, Edward Waters College, 1658 Kings Road, Jacksonville, FL 32209-6199, 904-366-2528 or toll-free 888-898-3191. *Website:* http://www.ewc.edu/.

ELIZABETH CITY STATE UNIVERSITY

Elizabeth City, NC

ABOUT THE INSTITUTION State-supported, coed. *Awards:* bachelor's and master's degrees. 35 undergraduate majors. *Total enrollment:* 1,357. Undergraduates: 1,310. Freshmen: 203.
GIFT AID (NEED-BASED) *Scholarships, grants, and awards:* Federal Pell, FSEOG, state, college/university gift aid from institutional funds, Thurgood Marshall College Fund.
GIFT AID (NON-NEED-BASED) *Scholarships, grants, and awards by category:* Academic interests/achievement: computer science, education, general academic interests/achievements, mathematics, military science. *Creative arts/performance:* music, performing arts. *Special characteristics:* ethnic background, handicapped students, international students, members of minority groups, veterans, veterans' children.
LOANS *Programs:* Federal Direct (Subsidized and Unsubsidized Stafford, PLUS), Perkins, state, college/university.
WORK-STUDY *Federal work-study:* jobs available. *State or other work-study/employment:* Part-time jobs available.
APPLYING FOR FINANCIAL AID *Required financial aid form:* FAFSA.
CONTACT Jill Gable, Director of Financial Aid, Elizabeth City State University, 1704 Weeksville Road, Campus Box 914, Elizabeth City, NC 27909-7806, 252-335-3283 or toll-free 800-347-3278. *Fax:* 252-335-3716. *E-mail:* jegable@ecsu.edu. *Website:* http://www.ecsu.edu/.

ELIZABETHTOWN COLLEGE

Elizabethtown, PA

Tuition & fees: $46,940	Average undergraduate aid package: $33,166

ABOUT THE INSTITUTION Independent Church of the Brethren, coed. *Awards:* bachelor's and master's degrees. 40 undergraduate majors. *Total enrollment:* 1,735. Undergraduates: 1,671. Freshmen: 411. Both federal and institutional methodology are used as a basis for awarding need-based institutional aid.

UNDERGRADUATE EXPENSES for 2018–2019 *Application fee:* $30. *Comprehensive fee:* $58,310 includes full-time tuition ($46,940) and room and board ($11,370). *College room only:* $5630. Full-time tuition and fees vary according to course load. Room and board charges vary according to board plan and housing facility. *Part-time tuition:* $1100 per credit hour. Part-time tuition and fees vary according to course load.
FRESHMAN FINANCIAL AID (Fall 2017, est.) 382 applied for aid; of those 90% were deemed to have need. 100% of freshmen with need received aid; of those 29% had need fully met. *Average percent of need met:* 84% (excluding resources awarded to replace EFC). *Average financial aid package:* $34,258 (excluding resources awarded to replace EFC). 17% of all full-time freshmen had no need and received non-need-based gift aid.
UNDERGRADUATE FINANCIAL AID (Fall 2017, est.) 1,375 applied for aid; of those 92% were deemed to have need. 100% of undergraduates with need received aid; of those 23% had need fully met. *Average percent of need met:* 80% (excluding resources awarded to replace EFC). *Average financial aid package:* $33,166 (excluding resources awarded to replace EFC). 21% of all full-time undergraduates had no need and received non-need-based gift aid.
GIFT AID (NEED-BASED) *Total amount:* $36,081,267 (5% federal, 4% state, 84% institutional, 7% external sources). *Receiving aid:* Freshmen: 84% (344); all full-time undergraduates: 77% (1,260). *Average award:* Freshmen: $30,473; Undergraduates: $28,603. *Scholarships, grants, and awards:* Federal Pell, FSEOG, state, private, college/university gift aid from institutional funds.
GIFT AID (NON-NEED-BASED) *Total amount:* $11,781,144 (81% institutional, 19% external sources). *Receiving aid:* Freshmen: 18% (72). Undergraduates: 13% (220). *Average award:* Freshmen: $24,611. Undergraduates: $22,579. *Scholarships, grants, and awards by category:* Academic interests/achievement: biological sciences, business, communication, computer science, education, engineering/technologies, English, foreign languages, general academic interests/achievements, health fields, humanities, international studies, mathematics, physical sciences, premedicine, religion/biblical studies, social sciences. *Creative arts/performance:* art/fine arts, music, performing arts, theater/drama. *Special achievements/activities:* religious involvement. *Special characteristics:* children of faculty/staff, international students, local/state students, members of minority groups, religious affiliation, siblings of current students. *Tuition waivers:* Full or partial for employees or children of employees.
LOANS *Student loans:* $14,400,562 (61% need-based, 39% non-need-based). 77% of past graduating class borrowed through all loan programs. *Average indebtedness per student:* $42,316. *Average need-based loan:* Freshmen: $3707. Undergraduates: $4567. *Parent loans:* $4,828,251 (45% need-based, 55% non-need-based). *Programs:* Federal Direct (Subsidized and Unsubsidized Stafford, PLUS), Perkins.
WORK-STUDY *Federal work-study:* Total amount: $974,200; 679 jobs averaging $1263.
APPLYING FOR FINANCIAL AID *Required financial aid forms:* FAFSA, state aid form. *Financial aid deadline (priority):* 2/1. *Notification date:* Continuous beginning 11/1. Students must reply by 5/1 or within 2 weeks of notification.
CONTACT Ms. Melodie R. Jackson, Director of Financial Aid, Elizabethtown College, 1 Alpha Drive, Elizabethtown, PA 17022, 717-361-1404. *Fax:* 717-361-1514. *E-mail:* jacksonmr@etown.edu. *Website:* http://www.etown.edu/.

ELMHURST COLLEGE

Elmhurst, IL

Tuition & fees: $37,055	Average undergraduate aid package: $27,497

ABOUT THE INSTITUTION Independent United Church of Christ, coed. *Awards:* bachelor's and master's degrees. 70 undergraduate majors. *Total enrollment:* 3,483. Undergraduates: 2,875. Freshmen: 497. Federal methodology is used as a basis for awarding need-based institutional aid.
UNDERGRADUATE EXPENSES for 2018–2019 *Comprehensive fee:* $47,421 includes full-time tuition ($36,755), mandatory fees ($300), and room and board ($10,366). *College room only:* $6244. Room and board charges vary according to board plan and housing facility. *Part-time tuition:* $1045 per semester hour. Part-time tuition and fees vary according to course load.
FRESHMAN FINANCIAL AID (Fall 2017, est.) 455 applied for aid; of those 90% were deemed to have need. 100% of freshmen with need received aid; of those 26% had need fully met. *Average percent of need met:* 79% (excluding resources

awarded to replace EFC). *Average financial aid package:* $26,913 (excluding resources awarded to replace EFC). 9% of all full-time freshmen had no need and received non-need-based gift aid.

UNDERGRADUATE FINANCIAL AID (Fall 2017, est.) 2,306 applied for aid; of those 92% were deemed to have need. 100% of undergraduates with need received aid; of those 18% had need fully met. *Average percent of need met:* 73% (excluding resources awarded to replace EFC). *Average financial aid package:* $27,497 (excluding resources awarded to replace EFC). 6% of all full-time undergraduates had no need and received non-need-based gift aid.

GIFT AID (NEED-BASED) *Total amount:* $47,962,378 (10% federal, 9% state, 80% institutional, 1% external sources). *Receiving aid:* Freshmen: 82% (410); all full-time undergraduates: 77% (2,130). *Average award:* Freshmen: $23,787; Undergraduates: $22,917. *Scholarships, grants, and awards:* Federal Pell, FSEOG, state, private, college/university gift aid from institutional funds, Federal Nursing.

GIFT AID (NON-NEED-BASED) *Total amount:* $9,281,435 (96% institutional, 4% external sources). *Receiving aid:* Freshmen: 19% (92). Undergraduates: 9% (240). *Average award:* Freshmen: $17,122. Undergraduates: $15,901. *Scholarships, grants, and awards by category: Academic interests/achievement:* 2,565 awards ($41,648,252 total): biological sciences, business, communication, computer science, education, English, foreign languages, general academic interests/achievements, humanities, international studies, mathematics, physical sciences, premedicine, religion/biblical studies, social sciences. *Creative arts/performance:* 150 awards ($2,363,932 total): art/fine arts, music, theater/drama. *Special characteristics:* 1,001 awards ($3,569,552 total): children and siblings of alumni, children of current students, children with a deceased or disabled parent, ethnic background, members of minority groups, religious affiliation, siblings of current students, spouses of current students, veterans, veterans' children. *Tuition waivers:* Full or partial for employees or children of employees, senior citizens. *ROTC:* Army cooperative, Air Force cooperative.

LOANS *Student loans:* $16,002,725 (40% need-based, 60% non-need-based). 71% of past graduating class borrowed through all loan programs. *Average indebtedness per student:* $29,925. *Average need-based loan:* Freshmen: $3410. Undergraduates: $4417. *Parent loans:* $5,231,503 (89% need-based, 11% non-need-based). *Programs:* Federal Direct (Subsidized and Unsubsidized Stafford, PLUS), Perkins, alternative loans.

WORK-STUDY *Federal work-study:* Total amount: $217,411; 356 jobs averaging $611. *State or other work-study/employment:* Total amount: $447,776 (100% non-need-based). 328 part-time jobs averaging $1365.

APPLYING FOR FINANCIAL AID *Required financial aid form:* FAFSA. *Financial aid deadline (priority):* 12/15. *Notification date:* Continuous beginning 12/1. Students must reply within 3 weeks of notification.

CONTACT Ruth A. Pusich, Director of Student Financial Services, Elmhurst College, Goebel Hall 106A, 190 Prospect Avenue, Elmhurst, IL 60126-3296, 630-617-3080 or toll-free 800-697-1871. *Fax:* 630-617-3487. *E-mail:* ruthp@elmhurst.edu. *Website:* http://www.elmhurst.edu/.

ELMIRA COLLEGE
Elmira, NY

Tuition & fees: $41,900	Average undergraduate aid package: $32,512

ABOUT THE INSTITUTION Independent, coed. *Awards:* certificates, associate, bachelor's, and master's degrees. 48 undergraduate majors. *Total enrollment:* 1,187. Undergraduates: 1,101. Freshmen: 208. Federal methodology is used as a basis for awarding need-based institutional aid.

UNDERGRADUATE EXPENSES for 2017–2018 *Comprehensive fee:* $53,900 includes full-time tuition ($41,900) and room and board ($12,000). *College room only:* $6400. Full-time tuition and fees vary according to degree level. Room and board charges vary according to board plan and housing facility. *Part-time tuition:* $1200 per credit hour. Part-time tuition and fees vary according to course load and degree level. *Payment plan:* Tuition prepayment.

FRESHMAN FINANCIAL AID (Fall 2017, est.) 194 applied for aid; of those 90% were deemed to have need. 100% of freshmen with need received aid; of those 17% had need fully met. *Average percent of need met:* 76% (excluding resources awarded to replace EFC). *Average financial aid package:* $32,600 (excluding resources awarded to replace EFC). 14% of all full-time freshmen had no need and received non-need-based gift aid.

UNDERGRADUATE FINANCIAL AID (Fall 2017, est.) 738 applied for aid; of those 94% were deemed to have need. 100% of undergraduates with need received aid; of those 18% had need fully met. *Average percent of need met:* 77% (excluding resources awarded to replace EFC). *Average financial aid package:* $32,512 (excluding resources awarded to replace EFC). 15% of all full-time undergraduates had no need and received non-need-based gift aid.

GIFT AID (NEED-BASED) *Total amount:* $19,197,028 (9% federal, 4% state, 84% institutional, 3% external sources). *Receiving aid:* Freshmen: 86% (175); all full-time undergraduates: 83% (694). *Average award:* Freshmen: $29,550; Undergraduates: $28,475. *Scholarships, grants, and awards:* Federal Pell, FSEOG, state, private, college/university gift aid from institutional funds.

GIFT AID (NON-NEED-BASED) *Total amount:* $4,311,015 (1% federal, 1% state, 90% institutional, 8% external sources). *Receiving aid:* Freshmen: 12% (24). Undergraduates: 12% (98). *Average award:* Freshmen: $24,695. Undergraduates: $23,911. *Scholarships, grants, and awards by category: Academic interests/achievement:* 734 awards ($14,602,987 total): general academic interests/achievements. *Special achievements/activities:* 22 awards ($273,000 total): leadership. *Special characteristics:* 857 awards ($3,200,979 total): children and siblings of alumni, children of faculty/staff, general special characteristics, international students, local/state students, out-of-state students, previous college experience, siblings of current students, twins, veterans. *Tuition waivers:* Full or partial for employees or children of employees, adult students. *ROTC:* Army, Air Force cooperative.

LOANS *Student loans:* $7,439,175 (72% need-based, 28% non-need-based). 83% of past graduating class borrowed through all loan programs. *Average indebtedness per student:* $29,601. *Average need-based loan:* Freshmen: $3401. Undergraduates: $4592. *Parent loans:* $3,533,379 (52% need-based, 48% non-need-based). *Programs:* Federal Direct (Subsidized and Unsubsidized Stafford, PLUS), Perkins.

WORK-STUDY *Federal work-study:* Total amount: $147,621; 117 jobs averaging $1200. *State or other work-study/employment:* Total amount: $196,100 (30% need-based, 70% non-need-based). 151 part-time jobs averaging $1100.

APPLYING FOR FINANCIAL AID *Required financial aid forms:* FAFSA, state aid form. *Financial aid deadline:* Continuous. *Notification date:* Continuous beginning 11/15. Students must reply by 5/1 or within 3 weeks of notification.

CONTACT Dean Kathleen Lynne Cohen, Dean of Financial Aid, Elmira College, One Park Place, Elmira, NY 14901-2099, 607-735-1728 or toll-free 800-935-6472. *Fax:* 607-735-1718. *E-mail:* kcohen@elmira.edu. *Website:* http://www.elmira.edu/.

ELMS COLLEGE
Chicopee, MA

Tuition & fees: $35,788	Average undergraduate aid package: $22,746

ABOUT THE INSTITUTION Independent Roman Catholic, coed. *Awards:* certificates, associate, bachelor's, master's, and doctoral degrees. 31 undergraduate majors. *Total enrollment:* 1,580. Undergraduates: 1,174. Freshmen: 173. Federal methodology is used as a basis for awarding need-based institutional aid.

UNDERGRADUATE EXPENSES for 2018–2019 *Comprehensive fee:* $48,894 includes full-time tuition ($34,114), mandatory fees ($1674), and room and board ($13,106). Room and board charges vary according to board plan. *Part-time tuition:* $691 per credit hour. Part-time tuition and fees vary according to location and program.

FRESHMAN FINANCIAL AID (Fall 2017, est.) 165 applied for aid; of those 98% were deemed to have need. 100% of freshmen with need received aid; of those 9% had need fully met. *Average percent of need met:* 72% (excluding resources awarded to replace EFC). *Average financial aid package:* $28,556 (excluding resources awarded to replace EFC). 5% of all full-time freshmen had no need and received non-need-based gift aid.

UNDERGRADUATE FINANCIAL AID (Fall 2017, est.) 911 applied for aid; of those 96% were deemed to have need. 100% of undergraduates with need received aid; of those 7% had need fully met. *Average percent of need met:* 61% (excluding resources awarded to replace EFC). *Average financial aid package:* $22,746 (excluding resources awarded to replace EFC). 7% of all full-time undergraduates had no need and received non-need-based gift aid.

GIFT AID (NEED-BASED) *Total amount:* $15,973,743 (18% federal, 4% state, 73% institutional, 5% external sources). *Receiving aid:* Freshmen: 93% (161); all full-time undergraduates: 86% (836). *Average award:* Freshmen: $25,199; Undergrad-

uates: $18,925. **Scholarships, grants, and awards:** Federal Pell, FSEOG, state, private, college/university gift aid from institutional funds, Federal Nursing.

GIFT AID (NON-NEED-BASED) *Total amount:* $1,376,753 (1% state, 92% institutional, 7% external sources). *Receiving aid:* Freshmen: 5% (8). Undergraduates: 4% (34). *Average award:* Freshmen: $16,562. Undergraduates: $14,622. **Scholarships, grants, and awards by category:** *Academic interests/achievement:* 738 awards ($9,722,945 total): general academic interests/achievements. *Special characteristics:* 47 awards ($350,818 total): children of faculty/staff, general special characteristics, religious affiliation, siblings of current students. **Tuition waivers:** Full or partial for employees or children of employees, senior citizens. **ROTC:** Army cooperative, Air Force cooperative.

LOANS *Student loans:* $11,158,781 (86% need-based, 14% non-need-based). 73% of past graduating class borrowed through all loan programs. *Average indebtedness per student:* $38,539. *Average need-based loan:* Freshmen: $3475. Undergraduates: $4691. *Parent loans:* $3,080,450 (63% need-based, 37% non-need-based). *Programs:* Federal Direct (Subsidized and Unsubsidized Stafford, PLUS).

WORK-STUDY *Federal work-study:* Total amount: $110,032; 96 jobs averaging $1206. *State or other work-study/employment:* Total amount: $2400 (100% non-need-based). Part-time jobs available.

APPLYING FOR FINANCIAL AID *Required financial aid form:* FAFSA. *Financial aid deadline (priority):* 3/1. *Notification date:* Continuous beginning 12/15. Students must reply within 2 weeks of notification.

CONTACT Financial Aid Office, Elms College, 291 Springfield Street, Chicopee, MA 01013, 413-265-2249 or toll-free 800-255-ELMS. *E-mail:* finaid@elms.edu. *Website:* http://www.elms.edu/.

ELON UNIVERSITY
Elon, NC

Tuition & fees: $35,318	Average undergraduate aid package: $20,060

ABOUT THE INSTITUTION Independent United Church of Christ, coed. *Awards:* bachelor's, master's, and doctoral degrees. 76 undergraduate majors. *Total enrollment:* 6,791. Undergraduates: 6,045. Freshmen: 1,573. Institutional methodology is used as a basis for awarding need-based institutional aid.

UNDERGRADUATE EXPENSES for 2018–2019 *Application fee:* $50. *Comprehensive fee:* $47,548 includes full-time tuition ($34,850), mandatory fees ($468), and room and board ($12,230). *College room only:* $6020. Room and board charges vary according to board plan and housing facility. *Part-time tuition:* $1110 per credit hour. Part-time tuition and fees vary according to course load.

FRESHMAN FINANCIAL AID (Fall 2017, est.) 1,000 applied for aid; of those 62% were deemed to have need. 100% of freshmen with need received aid; of those 18% had need fully met. *Average percent of need met:* 63% (excluding resources awarded to replace EFC). *Average financial aid package:* $19,885 (excluding resources awarded to replace EFC). 28% of all full-time freshmen had no need and received non-need-based gift aid.

UNDERGRADUATE FINANCIAL AID (Fall 2017, est.) 2,685 applied for aid; of those 72% were deemed to have need. 99% of undergraduates with need received aid; of those 18% had need fully met. *Average percent of need met:* 62% (excluding resources awarded to replace EFC). *Average financial aid package:* $20,060 (excluding resources awarded to replace EFC). 23% of all full-time undergraduates had no need and received non-need-based gift aid.

GIFT AID (NEED-BASED) *Total amount:* $25,664,634 (10% federal, 6% state, 83% institutional, 1% external sources). *Receiving aid:* Freshmen: 35% (548); all full-time undergraduates: 30% (1,742). *Average award:* Freshmen: $14,644; Undergraduates: $15,476. *Scholarships, grants, and awards:* Federal Pell, FSEOG, state, private, college/university gift aid from institutional funds.

GIFT AID (NON-NEED-BASED) *Total amount:* $11,723,394 (99% institutional, 1% external sources). *Receiving aid:* Freshmen: 24% (382). Undergraduates: 17% (987). *Average award:* Freshmen: $8421. Undergraduates: $7889. **Scholarships, grants, and awards by category:** *Academic interests/achievement:* 2,919 awards ($15,025,438 total): biological sciences, business, communication, computer science, education, engineering/technologies, general academic interests/achievements, mathematics, military science, physical sciences, premedicine, religion/biblical studies, social sciences. *Creative arts/performance:* 143 awards ($465,881 total): art/fine arts, journalism/publications, music, performing arts, theater/drama. *Special achievements/activities:* 153 awards ($392,391 total): community service, general special achieve-

ments/activities, leadership, religious involvement. *Special characteristics:* 169 awards ($2,832,785 total): adult students, children of faculty/staff, ethnic background, first-generation college students, international students, members of minority groups, relatives of clergy, veterans. **Tuition waivers:** Full or partial for employees or children of employees. **ROTC:** Army, Air Force cooperative.

LOANS *Student loans:* $16,529,716 (65% need-based, 35% non-need-based). 38% of past graduating class borrowed through all loan programs. *Average indebtedness per student:* $30,458. *Average need-based loan:* Freshmen: $3367. Undergraduates: $4378. *Parent loans:* $13,712,260 (60% need-based, 40% non-need-based). *Programs:* Federal Direct (Subsidized and Unsubsidized Stafford, PLUS), Perkins, state, college/university, private loans.

WORK-STUDY *Federal work-study:* Total amount: $3,295,404; 1,341 jobs averaging $2369.

ATHLETIC AWARDS Total amount: $9,097,166 (32% need-based, 68% non-need-based).

APPLYING FOR FINANCIAL AID *Required financial aid forms:* FAFSA, CSS Financial Aid PROFILE. *Financial aid deadline (priority):* 2/15. *Notification date:* 3/30.

CONTACT Dr. Patrick Murphy, Director of Financial Planning, Elon University, 2725 Campus Box, Elon, NC 27244, 336-278-7640 or toll-free 800-334-8448. *Fax:* 336-278-7639. *E-mail:* finaid@elon.edu. *Website:* http://www.elon.edu/.

EMBRY-RIDDLE AERONAUTICAL UNIVERSITY–DAYTONA
Daytona Beach, FL

Tuition & fees: $35,714	Average undergraduate aid package: $16,996

ABOUT THE INSTITUTION Independent, coed. *Awards:* associate, bachelor's, master's, and doctoral degrees. 25 undergraduate majors. *Total enrollment:* 6,338. Undergraduates: 5,729. Freshmen: 1,357. Federal methodology is used as a basis for awarding need-based institutional aid.

UNDERGRADUATE EXPENSES for 2018–2019 *Application fee:* $50. *Comprehensive fee:* $47,152 includes full-time tuition ($34,292), mandatory fees ($1422), and room and board ($11,438). *College room only:* $6900. Room and board charges vary according to board plan, housing facility, and location. *Part-time tuition:* $1433 per credit hour. *Part-time fees:* $711 per term.

FRESHMAN FINANCIAL AID (Fall 2017, est.) 1,297 applied for aid; of those 66% were deemed to have need. 100% of freshmen with need received aid. *Average financial aid package:* $19,457 (excluding resources awarded to replace EFC).

UNDERGRADUATE FINANCIAL AID (Fall 2017, est.) 3,742 applied for aid; of those 81% were deemed to have need. 100% of undergraduates with need received aid. *Average financial aid package:* $16,996 (excluding resources awarded to replace EFC).

GIFT AID (NEED-BASED) *Total amount:* $77,819,143 (10% federal, 9% state, 67% institutional, 14% external sources). *Receiving aid:* Freshmen: 54% (725); all full-time undergraduates: 50% (2,678). *Average award:* Freshmen: $17,653; Undergraduates: $14,976. *Scholarships, grants, and awards:* Federal Pell, FSEOG, state, private, college/university gift aid from institutional funds.

GIFT AID (NON-NEED-BASED) *Receiving aid:* Freshmen: 42% (565). Undergraduates: 47% (2,529). **Scholarships, grants, and awards by category:** *Special achievements/activities:* leadership. **Tuition waivers:** Full or partial for employees or children of employees. **ROTC:** Army, Naval, Air Force.

LOANS *Student loans:* $38,158,565 (100% need-based). *Average need-based loan:* Freshmen: $3795. Undergraduates: $4487. *Parent loans:* $28,420,048 (100% need-based). *Programs:* Federal Direct (Subsidized and Unsubsidized Stafford, PLUS), Perkins.

WORK-STUDY *Federal work-study:* Total amount: $372,854; 187 jobs averaging $1909. *State or other work-study/employment:* Total amount: $3,753,774 (100% need-based). 1,206 part-time jobs averaging $2816.

ATHLETIC AWARDS Total amount: $3,785,061 (100% need-based).

APPLYING FOR FINANCIAL AID *Required financial aid form:* FAFSA. *Financial aid deadline (priority):* 3/1. *Notification date:* Continuous beginning 3/1. Students must reply within 4 weeks of notification.

CONTACT Financial Aid Office, Embry-Riddle Aeronautical University–Daytona, 600 South Clyde Morris Boulevard, Daytona Beach, FL 32114-3900, 386-226-6300 or toll-free 800-862-2416. *Fax:* 386-226-6307. *E-mail:* dbfinaid@erau.edu. *Website:* http://www.daytonabeach.erau.edu/.

EMBRY-RIDDLE AERONAUTICAL UNIVERSITY–PRESCOTT
Prescott, AZ

Tuition & fees: $34,662	Average undergraduate aid package: $16,671

ABOUT THE INSTITUTION Independent, coed. *Awards:* bachelor's, master's, and doctoral degrees. 21 undergraduate majors. *Total enrollment:* 2,439. Undergraduates: 2,377. Freshmen: 604. Federal methodology is used as a basis for awarding need-based institutional aid.
UNDERGRADUATE EXPENSES for 2017–2018 *Application fee:* $50. *Comprehensive fee:* $45,130 includes full-time tuition ($33,408), mandatory fees ($1254), and room and board ($10,468). *College room only:* $5860. Full-time tuition and fees vary according to course load. Room and board charges vary according to board plan, housing facility, location, and student level. *Part-time tuition:* $1392 per credit hour. *Part-time fees:* $627 per term. Part-time tuition and fees vary according to course load.
FRESHMAN FINANCIAL AID (Fall 2017, est.) 568 applied for aid; of those 64% were deemed to have need. 100% of freshmen with need received aid. *Average financial aid package:* $17,718 (excluding resources awarded to replace EFC). 16% of all full-time freshmen had no need and received non-need-based gift aid.
UNDERGRADUATE FINANCIAL AID (Fall 2017, est.) 1,656 applied for aid; of those 91% were deemed to have need. 100% of undergraduates with need received aid. *Average financial aid package:* $16,671 (excluding resources awarded to replace EFC). 19% of all full-time undergraduates had no need and received non-need-based gift aid.
GIFT AID (NEED-BASED) *Total amount:* $36,446,813 (8% federal, 79% institutional, 13% external sources). *Receiving aid:* Freshmen: 48% (324); all full-time undergraduates: 47% (1,219). *Average award:* Freshmen: $16,207; Undergraduates: $14,902. *Scholarships, grants, and awards:* Federal Pell, FSEOG, state, private, college/university gift aid from institutional funds.
GIFT AID (NON-NEED-BASED) *Receiving aid:* Freshmen: 37% (250). Undergraduates: 39% (1,007). *Average award:* Freshmen: $11,903. Undergraduates: $11,347. *Tuition waivers:* Full or partial for employees or children of employees. *ROTC:* Army, Air Force.
LOANS *Student loans:* $18,480,303 (100% need-based). *Average need-based loan:* Freshmen: $3524. Undergraduates: $4307. *Parent loans:* $10,347,515 (100% need-based). *Programs:* Federal Direct (Subsidized and Unsubsidized Stafford, PLUS), Perkins.
WORK-STUDY *Federal work-study:* Total amount: $86,647; 30 jobs averaging $2503. *State or other work-study/employment:* Total amount: $1,679,749 (100% need-based). 607 part-time jobs averaging $2643.
ATHLETIC AWARDS Total amount: $1,920,079 (100% need-based).
APPLYING FOR FINANCIAL AID *Required financial aid form:* FAFSA. *Financial aid deadline (priority):* 3/1. *Notification date:* Continuous beginning 3/1. Students must reply within 4 weeks of notification.
CONTACT Ms. Debra Hintz, Director of Financial Aid, Prescott Campus, Embry-Riddle Aeronautical University–Prescott, 3700 Willow Creek Road, Prescott, AZ 86301-3720, 928-777-3765 or toll-free 800-888-3728. *Fax:* 928-777-3893. *E-mail:* prfinaid@erau.edu. *Website:* http://www.prescott.erau.edu/.

EMBRY-RIDDLE AERONAUTICAL UNIVERSITY–WORLDWIDE
Daytona Beach, FL

Tuition & fees: $9076	Average undergraduate aid package: $5326

ABOUT THE INSTITUTION Independent, coed. *Awards:* certificates, associate, bachelor's, master's, and doctoral degrees (programs offered at 100 military bases worldwide). 17 undergraduate majors. *Total enrollment:* 15,457. Undergraduates: 11,137. Freshmen: 397. Federal methodology is used as a basis for awarding need-based institutional aid.
UNDERGRADUATE EXPENSES for 2017–2018 *Application fee:* $50. *Tuition:* full-time $9000; part-time $375 per credit hour. Full-time tuition and fees vary according to program. Part-time tuition and fees vary according to program. Room and board charges vary according to location.
FRESHMAN FINANCIAL AID (Fall 2017, est.) 39 applied for aid; of those 95% were deemed to have need. 100% of freshmen with need received aid. *Average financial aid package:* $8513 (excluding resources awarded to replace EFC).
UNDERGRADUATE FINANCIAL AID (Fall 2017, est.) 1,166 applied for aid; of those 96% were deemed to have need. 100% of undergraduates with need received aid. *Average financial aid package:* $5326 (excluding resources awarded to replace EFC).
GIFT AID (NEED-BASED) *Total amount:* $12,918,517 (91% federal, 1% state, 7% institutional, 1% external sources). *Receiving aid:* Freshmen: 32% (30); all full-time undergraduates: 32% (928). *Average award:* Freshmen: $4603; Undergraduates: $4534. *Scholarships, grants, and awards:* Federal Pell, FSEOG, state, private, college/university gift aid from institutional funds.
GIFT AID (NON-NEED-BASED) *Receiving aid:* Freshmen: 8% (8). Undergraduates: 15% (427). *Tuition waivers:* Full or partial for employees or children of employees.
LOANS *Student loans:* $12,720,319 (100% need-based). *Average need-based loan:* Freshmen: $3275. Undergraduates: $4402. *Parent loans:* $142,210 (100% need-based). *Programs:* Federal Direct (Subsidized and Unsubsidized Stafford, PLUS), Perkins.
APPLYING FOR FINANCIAL AID *Required financial aid form:* FAFSA. *Financial aid deadline (priority):* 3/1. *Notification date:* Continuous. Students must reply within 4 weeks of notification.
CONTACT Ms. Dagmar Bowen, Director of Financial Aid, Worldwide, Embry-Riddle Aeronautical University–Worldwide, 600 South Clyde Morris Boulevard, Daytona Beach, FL 32114-3900, 800-522-6787. *Fax:* 386-226-6915. *E-mail:* wwfinaid@erau.edu. *Website:* http://www.worldwide.erau.edu/.

EMERSON COLLEGE
Boston, MA

ABOUT THE INSTITUTION Independent, coed. *Awards:* certificates, bachelor's, master's, and doctoral degrees. 29 undergraduate majors. *Total enrollment:* 4,466. Undergraduates: 3,813. Freshmen: 932.
GIFT AID (NEED-BASED) *Scholarships, grants, and awards:* Federal Pell, FSEOG, state, private, college/university gift aid from institutional funds.
GIFT AID (NON-NEED-BASED) *Scholarships, grants, and awards by category: Academic interests/achievement:* general academic interests/achievements. *Creative arts/performance:* performing arts. *Special characteristics:* parents of current students.
LOANS *Programs:* Federal Direct (Subsidized and Unsubsidized Stafford, PLUS), Perkins, state.
WORK-STUDY *Federal work-study:* 383 jobs averaging $1980. *State or other work-study/employment:* Total amount: $1,031,948 (54% need-based, 46% non-need-based). 85 part-time jobs averaging $12,943.
APPLYING FOR FINANCIAL AID *Required financial aid forms:* FAFSA, CSS Financial Aid PROFILE, noncustodial (divorced/separated) parent's statement, business/farm supplement.
CONTACT Angela Grant, Director of Financial Aid, Emerson College, 120 Boylston Street, Boston, MA 02116-4624, 617-824-8655. *Fax:* 617-824-8619. *E-mail:* finaid@emerson.edu. *Website:* http://www.emerson.edu/.

EMMANUEL COLLEGE
Franklin Springs, GA

Tuition & fees: $19,710	Average undergraduate aid package: $16,046

ABOUT THE INSTITUTION Independent Pentecostal Holiness Church, coed. *Awards:* associate and bachelor's degrees. 25 undergraduate majors. *Total enrollment:* 952. Undergraduates: 952. Freshmen: 263. Federal methodology is used as a basis for awarding need-based institutional aid.

UNDERGRADUATE EXPENSES for 2017–2018 *Application fee:* $25. *Comprehensive fee:* $27,598 includes full-time tuition ($19,370), mandatory fees ($340), and room and board ($7888). Room and board charges vary according to housing facility. *Part-time tuition:* $815 per credit hour.

FRESHMAN FINANCIAL AID (Fall 2017, est.) 232 applied for aid; of those 90% were deemed to have need. 100% of freshmen with need received aid; of those 20% had need fully met. *Average percent of need met:* 67% (excluding resources awarded to replace EFC). *Average financial aid package:* $15,412 (excluding resources awarded to replace EFC). 6% of all full-time freshmen had no need and received non-need-based gift aid.

UNDERGRADUATE FINANCIAL AID (Fall 2017, est.) 672 applied for aid; of those 88% were deemed to have need. 100% of undergraduates with need received aid; of those 20% had need fully met. *Average percent of need met:* 69% (excluding resources awarded to replace EFC). *Average financial aid package:* $16,046 (excluding resources awarded to replace EFC). 11% of all full-time undergraduates had no need and received non-need-based gift aid.

GIFT AID (NEED-BASED) Total amount: $5,122,505 (32% federal, 22% state, 41% institutional, 5% external sources). *Receiving aid:* Freshmen: 83% (208); all full-time undergraduates: 78% (592). *Average award:* Freshmen: $12,174; Undergraduates: $12,524. *Scholarships, grants, and awards:* Federal Pell, FSEOG, state, college/university gift aid from institutional funds.

GIFT AID (NON-NEED-BASED) Total amount: $933,107 (48% state, 45% institutional, 7% external sources). *Receiving aid:* Freshmen: 11% (28). Undergraduates: 11% (81). *Average award:* Freshmen: $3976. Undergraduates: $4232. *Scholarships, grants, and awards by category:* Academic interests/achievement: 442 awards ($1,673,020 total): business, communication, education, English, general academic interests/achievements, health fields, religion/biblical studies. *Creative arts/performance:* 12 awards ($28,000 total): applied art and design, art/fine arts, creative writing, dance, general creative arts/performance, journalism/publications, music, performing arts, theater/drama. *Special achievements/activities:* 23 awards ($90,638 total): cheerleading/drum major, general special achievements/activities, hobbies/interests, leadership, memberships, religious involvement. *Special characteristics:* 238 awards ($724,344 total): adult students, children of current students, children of educators, children of faculty/staff, first-generation college students, general special characteristics, international students, local/state students, married students, parents of current students, relatives of clergy, religious affiliation, siblings of current students, spouses of current students, twins. *Tuition waivers:* Full or partial for employees or children of employees, senior citizens.

LOANS Student loans: $3,774,953 (79% need-based, 21% non-need-based). 73% of past graduating class borrowed through all loan programs. *Average indebtedness per student:* $24,840. *Average need-based loan:* Freshmen: $3028. Undergraduates: $3615. *Parent loans:* $2,371,838 (50% need-based, 50% non-need-based). *Programs:* Federal Direct (Subsidized and Unsubsidized Stafford, PLUS), state.

WORK-STUDY *Federal work-study:* Total amount: $397,228; 71 jobs averaging $849. *State or other work-study/employment:* 142 part-time jobs averaging $962.

ATHLETIC AWARDS Total amount: $4,127,342 (55% need-based, 45% non-need-based).

APPLYING FOR FINANCIAL AID *Required financial aid forms:* FAFSA, institution's own form, state aid form. *Financial aid deadline:* 6/15 (priority: 5/1). *Notification date:* Continuous beginning 3/1. Students must reply within 2 weeks of notification.

CONTACT Mrs. Niki Stinson, Director of Financial Aid, Emmanuel College, PO Box 129, Franklin Springs, GA 30639-0129, 706-245-2871 or toll-free 800-860-8800. *Fax:* 706-245-2846. *E-mail:* nstinson@ec.edu. *Website:* http://www.ec.edu/.

EMMANUEL COLLEGE
Boston, MA

Tuition & fees: $39,804	Average undergraduate aid package: $29,174

ABOUT THE INSTITUTION Independent Roman Catholic, coed. *Awards:* certificates, bachelor's, and master's degrees. 39 undergraduate majors. *Total enrollment:* 2,083. Undergraduates: 1,947. Freshmen: 474. Federal methodology is used as a basis for awarding need-based institutional aid.

UNDERGRADUATE EXPENSES for 2018–2019 *Application fee:* $60. *One-time required fee:* $350. *Comprehensive fee:* $54,798 includes full-time tuition ($39,544), mandatory fees ($260), and room and board ($14,994). Room and board charges vary according to board plan and housing facility. *Part-time tuition:* $1235.75 per credit hour.

FRESHMAN FINANCIAL AID (Fall 2017, est.) 445 applied for aid; of those 89% were deemed to have need. 100% of freshmen with need received aid; of those 30% had need fully met. *Average percent of need met:* 73% (excluding resources awarded to replace EFC). *Average financial aid package:* $29,383 (excluding resources awarded to replace EFC). 16% of all full-time freshmen had no need and received non-need-based gift aid.

UNDERGRADUATE FINANCIAL AID (Fall 2017, est.) 1,579 applied for aid; of those 91% were deemed to have need. 100% of undergraduates with need received aid; of those 32% had need fully met. *Average percent of need met:* 71% (excluding resources awarded to replace EFC). *Average financial aid package:* $29,174 (excluding resources awarded to replace EFC). 15% of all full-time undergraduates had no need and received non-need-based gift aid.

GIFT AID (NEED-BASED) Total amount: $35,925,214 (8% federal, 2% state, 87% institutional, 3% external sources). *Receiving aid:* Freshmen: 84% (398); all full-time undergraduates: 80% (1,443). *Average award:* Freshmen: $25,226; Undergraduates: $24,150. *Scholarships, grants, and awards:* Federal Pell, FSEOG, state, private, college/university gift aid from institutional funds.

GIFT AID (NON-NEED-BASED) Total amount: $4,375,397 (99% institutional, 1% external sources). *Receiving aid:* Freshmen: 84% (398). Undergraduates: 80% (1,443). *Average award:* Freshmen: $18,271. Undergraduates: $16,575. *Scholarships, grants, and awards by category:* Academic interests/achievement: 797 awards ($13,189,924 total): general academic interests/achievements. *Special achievements/activities:* general special achievements/activities. *Special characteristics:* 60 awards ($347,920 total): children of faculty/staff, siblings of current students, spouses of current students, veterans. *Tuition waivers:* Full or partial for employees or children of employees. *ROTC:* Army cooperative.

LOANS Student loans: $14,704,498 (94% need-based, 6% non-need-based). *Average need-based loan:* Freshmen: $3314. Undergraduates: $4529. *Parent loans:* $8,052,561 (100% non-need-based). *Programs:* Federal Direct (Subsidized and Unsubsidized Stafford, PLUS), Perkins, state.

WORK-STUDY *Federal work-study:* Total amount: $147,362; jobs available. *State or other work-study/employment:* Total amount: $1,488,788 (100% non-need-based). Part-time jobs available.

APPLYING FOR FINANCIAL AID *Required financial aid form:* FAFSA. *Financial aid deadline (priority):* 2/15. *Notification date:* Continuous beginning 2/1.

CONTACT Jennifer Porter, Associate Vice President for Student Financial Services, Emmanuel College, 400 The Fenway, Boston, MA 02115, 617-735-9938. *Fax:* 617-735-9939. *E-mail:* financialservices@emmanuel.edu. *Website:* http://www.emmanuel.edu/.

EMMAUS BIBLE COLLEGE
Dubuque, IA

CONTACT Steve Seeman, Financial Aid Director, Emmaus Bible College, 2570 Asbury Road, Dubuque, IA 52001-3097, 800-397-2425 Ext. 1309 or toll-free 800-397-2425. *Fax:* 563-588-1216. *E-mail:* financialaid@emmaus.edu. *Website:* http://www.emmaus.edu/.

EMORY & HENRY COLLEGE
Emory, VA

Tuition & fees: $35,050 | Average undergraduate aid package: $32,567

ABOUT THE INSTITUTION Independent United Methodist, coed. *Awards:* bachelor's, master's, and doctoral degrees. 66 undergraduate majors. *Total enrollment:* 1,226. Undergraduates: 1,000. Freshmen: 253. Federal methodology is used as a basis for awarding need-based institutional aid.

UNDERGRADUATE EXPENSES for 2017–2018 *Comprehensive fee:* $46,870 includes full-time tuition ($34,500), mandatory fees ($550), and room and board ($11,820). *College room only:* $6200. Full-time tuition and fees vary according to degree level, location, and student level. Room and board charges vary according to board plan and housing facility. *Part-time tuition:* $1300 per credit hour. *Part-time fees:* $50 per term. Part-time tuition and fees vary according to course load, degree level, location, and student level. *Payment plan:* Guaranteed tuition.

FRESHMAN FINANCIAL AID (Fall 2017, est.) 244 applied for aid; of those 95% were deemed to have need. 100% of freshmen with need received aid; of those 23% had need fully met. *Average percent of need met:* 81% (excluding resources awarded to replace EFC). *Average financial aid package:* $33,682 (excluding resources awarded to replace EFC). 7% of all full-time freshmen had no need and received non-need-based gift aid.

UNDERGRADUATE FINANCIAL AID (Fall 2017, est.) 883 applied for aid; of those 93% were deemed to have need. 100% of undergraduates with need received aid; of those 24% had need fully met. *Average percent of need met:* 82% (excluding resources awarded to replace EFC). *Average financial aid package:* $32,567 (excluding resources awarded to replace EFC). 14% of all full-time undergraduates had no need and received non-need-based gift aid.

GIFT AID (NEED-BASED) *Total amount:* $21,830,623 (10% federal, 8% state, 80% institutional, 2% external sources). *Receiving aid:* Freshmen: 90% (228); all full-time undergraduates: 85% (817). *Average award:* Freshmen: $29,025; Undergraduates: $27,203. *Scholarships, grants, and awards:* Federal Pell, FSEOG, state, private, college/university gift aid from institutional funds.

GIFT AID (NON-NEED-BASED) *Total amount:* $3,390,401 (12% state, 83% institutional, 5% external sources). *Receiving aid:* Freshmen: 10% (25). Undergraduates: 15% (140). *Average award:* Freshmen: $17,088. Undergraduates: $17,579. *Scholarships, grants, and awards by category:* Academic interests/achievement: 946 awards ($16,461,238 total): communication, general academic interests/achievements, premedicine. *Creative arts/performance:* 150 awards ($296,300 total): art/fine arts, music, performing arts, theater/drama. *Special achievements/activities:* 16 awards ($35,234 total): cheerleading/drum major, community service, religious involvement. *Special characteristics:* 496 awards ($1,727,437 total): children and siblings of alumni, children of educators, children of faculty/staff, out-of-state students, religious affiliation, siblings of current students. *Tuition waivers:* Full or partial for employees or children of employees.

LOANS *Student loans:* $5,962,283 (76% need-based, 24% non-need-based). 71% of past graduating class borrowed through all loan programs. *Average indebtedness per student:* $27,825. *Average need-based loan:* Freshmen: $3609. Undergraduates: $4659. *Parent loans:* $3,453,710 (45% need-based, 55% non-need-based). *Programs:* Federal Direct (Subsidized and Unsubsidized Stafford, PLUS), Perkins.

WORK-STUDY *Federal work-study:* Total amount: $705,435; 367 jobs averaging $1798. *State or other work-study/employment:* Total amount: $139,500 (100% need-based). Part-time jobs available.

APPLYING FOR FINANCIAL AID *Required financial aid forms:* FAFSA, state aid form. *Financial aid deadline (priority):* 3/1. *Notification date:* Continuous beginning 1/2. Students must reply within 2 weeks of notification.

CONTACT Ms. Scarlett C. Blevins, Director of Financial Aid, Emory & Henry College, PO Box 947, Emory, VA 24327-0010, 276-944-6940 or toll-free 800-848-5493. *Fax:* 276-944-6884. *E-mail:* scblevins@ehc.edu.
Website: http://www.ehc.edu/.

EMORY UNIVERSITY
Atlanta, GA

Tuition & fees: $51,306 | Average undergraduate aid package: $43,777

ABOUT THE INSTITUTION Independent Methodist, coed. *Awards:* certificates, bachelor's, master's, and doctoral degrees (enrollment figures include Emory University, Oxford College; application data for main campus only). 73 undergraduate majors. *Total enrollment:* 14,273. Undergraduates: 6,937. Freshmen: 1,388. Both federal and institutional methodology are used as a basis for awarding need-based institutional aid.

UNDERGRADUATE EXPENSES for 2018–2019 *Application fee:* $75. *Comprehensive fee:* $65,762 includes full-time tuition ($50,590), mandatory fees ($716), and room and board ($14,456). *College room only:* $8306. Room and board charges vary according to board plan and housing facility. *Part-time tuition:* $2108 per credit hour.

FRESHMAN FINANCIAL AID (Fall 2017, est.) 821 applied for aid; of those 80% were deemed to have need. 100% of freshmen with need received aid; of those 100% had need fully met. *Average percent of need met:* 100% (excluding resources awarded to replace EFC). *Average financial aid package:* $44,118 (excluding resources awarded to replace EFC). 4% of all full-time freshmen had no need and received non-need-based gift aid.

UNDERGRADUATE FINANCIAL AID (Fall 2017, est.) 3,409 applied for aid; of those 88% were deemed to have need. 100% of undergraduates with need received aid; of those 96% had need fully met. *Average percent of need met:* 99% (excluding resources awarded to replace EFC). *Average financial aid package:* $43,777 (excluding resources awarded to replace EFC). 5% of all full-time undergraduates had no need and received non-need-based gift aid.

GIFT AID (NEED-BASED) *Total amount:* $118,199,801 (7% federal, 2% state, 90% institutional, 1% external sources). *Receiving aid:* Freshmen: 45% (619); all full-time undergraduates: 43% (2,856). *Average award:* Freshmen: $41,305; Undergraduates: $39,571. *Scholarships, grants, and awards:* Federal Pell, FSEOG, state, private, college/university gift aid from institutional funds.

GIFT AID (NON-NEED-BASED) *Total amount:* $13,834,198 (11% state, 78% institutional, 11% external sources). *Receiving aid:* Freshmen: 16% (223). Undergraduates: 10% (693). *Average award:* Freshmen: $27,096. Undergraduates: $26,925. *Scholarships, grants, and awards by category:* Academic interests/achievement: business, general academic interests/achievements, humanities, physical sciences. *Creative arts/performance:* art/fine arts, cinema/film/broadcasting, debating, music, theater/drama. *Special achievements/activities:* leadership. *Special characteristics:* children of faculty/staff, local/state students, religious affiliation, veterans, veterans' children. *Tuition waivers:* Full or partial for employees or children of employees. *ROTC:* Army cooperative, Naval cooperative, Air Force cooperative.

LOANS *Student loans:* $25,865,703 (63% need-based, 37% non-need-based). 36% of past graduating class borrowed through all loan programs. *Average indebtedness per student:* $28,262. *Average need-based loan:* Freshmen: $3556. Undergraduates: $6154. *Parent loans:* $5,270,620 (17% need-based, 83% non-need-based). *Programs:* Federal Direct (Subsidized and Unsubsidized Stafford, PLUS), Perkins, Federal Nursing, state, college/university, alternative loans.

WORK-STUDY *Federal work-study:* Total amount: $5,799,515; jobs available. *State or other work-study/employment:* Total amount: $611,426 (22% need-based, 78% non-need-based). Part-time jobs available.

APPLYING FOR FINANCIAL AID *Required financial aid forms:* FAFSA, CSS Financial Aid PROFILE, noncustodial (divorced/separated) parent's statement. *Financial aid deadline:* 3/1 (priority: 2/15). *Notification date:* 4/1. Students must reply by 5/1.

CONTACT Mr. John Leach, Director of Financial Aid, Emory University, Boisfeuillet Jones Center, Suite 300, 200 Dowman Drive, Atlanta, GA 30322-1960, 404-727-6039 or toll-free 800-727-6036. *Fax:* 404-727-6709. *E-mail:* john.blanchard.leach@emory.edu.
Website: http://www.emory.edu/.

EMPORIA STATE UNIVERSITY
Emporia, KS

Tuition & fees (KS res): $6345 | Average undergraduate aid package: $9540

ABOUT THE INSTITUTION State-supported, coed. *Awards:* certificates, bachelor's, master's, and doctoral degrees. 34 undergraduate majors. *Total enrollment:* 5,732. Undergraduates: 3,605. Freshmen: 606. Federal methodology is used as a basis for awarding need-based institutional aid.

UNDERGRADUATE EXPENSES for 2017–2018 *Application fee:* $30. *Tuition, state resident:* full-time $5027; part-time $167.60 per credit hour. *Tuition, nonresident:* full-time $18,600; part-time $620 per credit hour. *Required fees:* full-time $1318; $80.95 per credit hour. Full-time tuition and fees vary according to course load, degree level, and location. Part-time tuition and fees vary according to course load, degree level, and location. *College room and board:* $8684; *Room only:* $5130. Room and board charges vary according to board plan, housing facility, and location.

FRESHMAN FINANCIAL AID (Fall 2017, est.) 543 applied for aid; of those 75% were deemed to have need. 100% of freshmen with need received aid; of those 15% had need fully met. *Average percent of need met:* 61% (excluding resources awarded to replace EFC). *Average financial aid package:* $9538 (excluding resources awarded to replace EFC). 24% of all full-time freshmen had no need and received non-need-based gift aid.

UNDERGRADUATE FINANCIAL AID (Fall 2017, est.) 2,561 applied for aid; of those 85% were deemed to have need. 99% of undergraduates with need received aid; of those 13% had need fully met. *Average percent of need met:* 60% (excluding resources awarded to replace EFC). *Average financial aid package:* $9540 (excluding resources awarded to replace EFC). 18% of all full-time undergraduates had no need and received non-need-based gift aid.

GIFT AID (NEED-BASED) *Total amount:* $10,958,005 (56% federal, 6% state, 26% institutional, 12% external sources). *Receiving aid:* Freshmen: 67% (403); all full-time undergraduates: 63% (2,074). *Average award:* Freshmen: $5468; Undergraduates: $5716. *Scholarships, grants, and awards:* Federal Pell, FSEOG, state, private, college/university gift aid from institutional funds, Jones Foundation Grants.

GIFT AID (NON-NEED-BASED) *Total amount:* $1,955,127 (1% state, 99% institutional). *Receiving aid:* Freshmen: 5% (33). Undergraduates: 3% (100). *Average award:* Freshmen: $2754. Undergraduates: $2982. *Scholarships, grants, and awards by category:* Academic interests/achievement: 1,418 awards ($3,441,760 total): biological sciences, business, communication, computer science, education, engineering/technologies, English, foreign languages, general academic interests/achievements, health fields, humanities, mathematics, physical sciences, pre-medicine, social sciences. *Creative arts/performance:* 145 awards ($154,588 total): art/fine arts, creative writing, debating, music, theater/drama. *Special achievements/activities:* 54 awards ($41,400 total): general special achievements/activities, leadership, memberships. *Special characteristics:* 84 awards ($86,698 total): children and siblings of alumni, children of faculty/staff, children of union members/company employees, first-generation college students, general special characteristics, handicapped students, international students, members of minority groups, religious affiliation, veterans, veterans' children. *Tuition waivers:* Full or partial for employees or children of employees, senior citizens.

LOANS *Student loans:* $16,736,895 (73% need-based, 27% non-need-based). 68% of past graduating class borrowed through all loan programs. *Average indebtedness per student:* $22,816. *Average need-based loan:* Freshmen: $5704. Undergraduates: $6670. *Parent loans:* $8,228,840 (27% need-based, 73% non-need-based). *Programs:* Federal Direct (Subsidized and Unsubsidized Stafford, PLUS), Perkins, alternative loans, Alaska Loans.

WORK-STUDY *Federal work-study:* Total amount: $404,894; 184 jobs averaging $2185. *State or other work-study/employment:* Total amount: $49,521 (73% need-based, 27% non-need-based). 18 part-time jobs averaging $2683.

ATHLETIC AWARDS Total amount: $1,430,930 (41% need-based, 59% non-need-based).

APPLYING FOR FINANCIAL AID *Required financial aid forms:* FAFSA, state aid form. *Financial aid deadline (priority):* 3/15. *Notification date:* Continuous beginning 3/15. Students must reply within 2 weeks of notification.

CONTACT Jaime Morris, Director of Financial Aid, Emporia State University, 1 Kellogg Circle, Emporia, KS 66801-5087, 620-341-5457 or toll-free 877-GOTOESU (in-state), 877-468-6378 (out-of-state). *Fax:* 620-341-6088. *E-mail:* jmorri12@emporia.edu. *Website:* http://www.emporia.edu/.

ENDICOTT COLLEGE
Beverly, MA

Tuition & fees: $33,050 | Average undergraduate aid package: $20,881

ABOUT THE INSTITUTION Independent, coed. *Awards:* certificates, associate, bachelor's, master's, and doctoral degrees. 38 undergraduate majors. *Total enrollment:* 5,058. Undergraduates: 3,482. Freshmen: 780. Federal methodology is used as a basis for awarding need-based institutional aid.

UNDERGRADUATE EXPENSES for 2018–2019 *Application fee:* $50. *Comprehensive fee:* $48,326 includes full-time tuition ($32,350), mandatory fees ($700), and room and board ($15,276). *College room only:* $10,530. Full-time tuition and fees vary according to location and program. Room and board charges vary according to housing facility. *Part-time tuition:* $994 per credit hour. Part-time tuition and fees vary according to location and program. *Payment plan:* Tuition prepayment.

FRESHMAN FINANCIAL AID (Fall 2017, est.) 676 applied for aid; of those 81% were deemed to have need. 100% of freshmen with need received aid; of those 9% had need fully met. *Average percent of need met:* 62% (excluding resources awarded to replace EFC). *Average financial aid package:* $21,066 (excluding resources awarded to replace EFC). 22% of all full-time freshmen had no need and received non-need-based gift aid.

UNDERGRADUATE FINANCIAL AID (Fall 2017, est.) 2,302 applied for aid; of those 84% were deemed to have need. 100% of undergraduates with need received aid; of those 10% had need fully met. *Average percent of need met:* 64% (excluding resources awarded to replace EFC). *Average financial aid package:* $20,881 (excluding resources awarded to replace EFC). 23% of all full-time undergraduates had no need and received non-need-based gift aid.

GIFT AID (NEED-BASED) *Total amount:* $30,204,544 (9% federal, 2% state, 89% institutional). *Receiving aid:* Freshmen: 70% (539); all full-time undergraduates: 64% (1,883). *Average award:* Freshmen: $16,668; Undergraduates: $15,942. *Scholarships, grants, and awards:* Federal Pell, FSEOG, state, private, college/university gift aid from institutional funds.

GIFT AID (NON-NEED-BASED) *Total amount:* $7,611,926 (94% institutional, 6% external sources). *Receiving aid:* Freshmen: 69% (528). Undergraduates: 61% (1,796). *Average award:* Freshmen: $9457. Undergraduates: $9693. *Scholarships, grants, and awards by category:* Academic interests/achievement: business, education, general academic interests/achievements, health fields. *Creative arts/performance:* art/fine arts, music, performing arts. *Special achievements/activities:* community service, general special achievements/activities, leadership, religious involvement. *Special characteristics:* children and siblings of alumni, children of educators, general special characteristics, international students, local/state students, religious affiliation. *Tuition waivers:* Full or partial for employees or children of employees. *ROTC:* Army cooperative.

LOANS *Student loans:* $25,772,388 (30% need-based, 70% non-need-based). 77% of past graduating class borrowed through all loan programs. *Average indebtedness per student:* $44,159. *Average need-based loan:* Freshmen: $3681. Undergraduates: $4698. *Parent loans:* $6,022,264 (100% non-need-based). *Programs:* Federal Direct (Subsidized and Unsubsidized Stafford, PLUS), Perkins.

WORK-STUDY *Federal work-study:* Total amount: $1,538,275; 787 jobs averaging $2000.

APPLYING FOR FINANCIAL AID *Required financial aid forms:* FAFSA, institution's own form. *Financial aid deadline (priority):* 3/15. *Notification date:* Continuous beginning 1/15. Students must reply within 2 weeks of notification.

CONTACT Ms. Marcia Toomey, Dean of Financial Aid, Endicott College, 376 Hale Street, Beverly, MA 01915-2096, 978-232-2060 or toll-free 800-325-1114. *Fax:* 978-232-2085. *E-mail:* mtoomey@endicott.edu. *Website:* http://www.endicott.edu/.

EPIC BIBLE COLLEGE
Sacramento, CA

CONTACT Financial Aid Office, Epic Bible College, 4330 Auburn Boulevard, Sacramento, CA 95841, 916-348-4689. *Website:* http://epic.edu/.

ERSKINE COLLEGE
Due West, SC

CONTACT Mrs. Becky Pressley, Director of Financial Aid, Erskine College, PO Box 337, Due West, SC 29639, 864-379-8832 or toll-free 800-241-8721. *Fax:* 864-379-2172. *E-mail:* pressley@erskine.edu.
Website: http://www.erskine.edu/.

ESCUELA DE ARTES PLASTICAS Y DISE&NNO DE PUERTO RICO
San Juan, PR

CONTACT Mr. Alfred Diaz Melendez, Financial Aid Administrator, Escuela de Artes Plasticas y Dise&nno de Puerto Rico, PO Box 9021112, San Juan, PR 00902-1112, 787-725-8120 Ext. 317. *Fax:* 787-725-3798. *E-mail:* adiaz@eap.edu.
Website: http://www.eap.edu/.

EUGENE LANG COLLEGE OF LIBERAL ARTS
New York, NY

Tuition & fees: $46,340	Average undergraduate aid package: $25,923

ABOUT THE INSTITUTION Independent, coed. *Awards:* bachelor's degrees. 30 undergraduate majors. *Total enrollment:* 1,738. Undergraduates: 1,738. Freshmen: 464. Federal methodology is used as a basis for awarding need-based institutional aid.

UNDERGRADUATE EXPENSES for 2017–2018 *Application fee:* $50. *Comprehensive fee:* $62,590 includes full-time tuition ($45,240), mandatory fees ($1100), and room and board ($16,250). *College room only:* $15,000. Room and board charges vary according to housing facility and location. *Part-time tuition:* $1540 per credit hour. *Part-time fees:* $550 per term. Part-time tuition and fees vary according to course load.

FRESHMAN FINANCIAL AID (Fall 2016) 364 applied for aid; of those 84% were deemed to have need. 100% of freshmen with need received aid; of those 10% had need fully met. *Average percent of need met:* 72% (excluding resources awarded to replace EFC). *Average financial aid package:* $26,201 (excluding resources awarded to replace EFC). 23% of all full-time freshmen had no need and received non-need-based gift aid.

UNDERGRADUATE FINANCIAL AID (Fall 2016) 1,001 applied for aid; of those 87% were deemed to have need. 100% of undergraduates with need received aid; of those 14% had need fully met. *Average percent of need met:* 82% (excluding resources awarded to replace EFC). *Average financial aid package:* $25,923 (excluding resources awarded to replace EFC). 25% of all full-time undergraduates had no need and received non-need-based gift aid.

GIFT AID (NEED-BASED) *Total amount:* $15,645,927 (15% federal, 3% state, 75% institutional, 7% external sources). *Receiving aid:* Freshmen: 52% (256); all full-time undergraduates: 49% (787). *Average award:* Freshmen: $14,131; Undergraduates: $16,078. *Scholarships, grants, and awards:* Federal Pell, FSEOG, state, private, college/university gift aid from institutional funds.

GIFT AID (NON-NEED-BASED) *Total amount:* $15,986,945 (97% institutional, 3% external sources). *Receiving aid:* Freshmen: 49% (239). Undergraduates: 47% (747). *Average award:* Freshmen: $15,531. Undergraduates: $11,242. *Scholarships, grants, and awards by category:* Special achievements/activities: general special achievements/activities, leadership. *Special characteristics:* local/state students, members of minority groups. *Tuition waivers:* Full or partial for employees or children of employees.

LOANS *Student loans:* $12,033,665 (45% need-based, 55% non-need-based). 58% of past graduating class borrowed through all loan programs. *Average indebtedness per student:* $62,290. *Average need-based loan:* Freshmen: $3462. Undergraduates: $4167. *Parent loans:* $2,664,575 (17% need-based, 83% non-need-based). *Programs:* Federal Direct (Subsidized and Unsubsidized Stafford, PLUS).

WORK-STUDY *Federal work-study:* 136 jobs averaging $3360. *State or other work-study/employment:* Part-time jobs available.

APPLYING FOR FINANCIAL AID *Required financial aid form:* FAFSA. *Financial aid deadline:* 2/1. *Notification date:* Continuous beginning 4/1. Students must reply within 4 weeks of notification.

CONTACT Office of Student Financial Services, Eugene Lang College of Liberal Arts, 72 Fifth Avenue, 2nd Floor, New York, NY 10011, 212-229-8930 or toll-free 800-292-3040. *E-mail:* sfs@newschool.edu.
Website: http://www.newschool.edu/lang.

EUREKA COLLEGE
Eureka, IL

Tuition & fees: $25,390	Average undergraduate aid package: $16,506

ABOUT THE INSTITUTION Independent Christian Church (Disciples of Christ), coed. *Awards:* bachelor's degrees. 23 undergraduate majors. *Total enrollment:* 672. Undergraduates: 672. Freshmen: 153. Both federal and institutional methodology are used as a basis for awarding need-based institutional aid.

UNDERGRADUATE EXPENSES for 2017–2018 *Comprehensive fee:* $34,760 includes full-time tuition ($25,150), mandatory fees ($240), and room and board ($9370). *College room only:* $4490. Full-time tuition and fees vary according to course load and program. Room and board charges vary according to board plan and housing facility. *Part-time tuition:* $700 per semester hour. *Part-time fees:* $120 per semester hour. Part-time tuition and fees vary according to course load and program.

FRESHMAN FINANCIAL AID (Fall 2017, est.) 102 applied for aid; of those 84% were deemed to have need. 100% of freshmen with need received aid; of those 12% had need fully met. *Average percent of need met:* 64% (excluding resources awarded to replace EFC). *Average financial aid package:* $17,273 (excluding resources awarded to replace EFC). 16% of all full-time freshmen had no need and received non-need-based gift aid.

UNDERGRADUATE FINANCIAL AID (Fall 2017, est.) 512 applied for aid; of those 88% were deemed to have need. 100% of undergraduates with need received aid; of those 8% had need fully met. *Average percent of need met:* 84% (excluding resources awarded to replace EFC). *Average financial aid package:* $16,506 (excluding resources awarded to replace EFC). 22% of all full-time undergraduates had no need and received non-need-based gift aid.

GIFT AID (NEED-BASED) *Total amount:* $5,992,214 (17% federal, 17% state, 64% institutional, 2% external sources). *Receiving aid:* Freshmen: 81% (86); all full-time undergraduates: 76% (449). *Average award:* Freshmen: $17,368; Undergraduates: $13,239. *Scholarships, grants, and awards:* Federal Pell, FSEOG, state, private, college/university gift aid from institutional funds.

GIFT AID (NON-NEED-BASED) *Total amount:* $1,084,507 (98% institutional, 2% external sources). *Average award:* Freshmen: $9742. Undergraduates: $8278. *Scholarships, grants, and awards by category:* Academic interests/achievement: $3,402,967 total: general academic interests/achievements. *Creative arts/performance:* $34,250 total: art/fine arts, music, performing arts, theater/drama. *Special achievements/activities:* $714,500 total: community service, leadership, religious involvement. *Special characteristics:* $191,184 total: children and siblings of alumni, children of faculty/staff, relatives of clergy, religious affiliation, siblings of current students. *Tuition waivers:* Full or partial for employees or children of employees, senior citizens.

LOANS *Student loans:* $3,974,691 (87% need-based, 13% non-need-based). 75% of past graduating class borrowed through all loan programs. *Average indebtedness per student:* $34,180. *Average need-based loan:* Freshmen: $2320. Undergraduates: $3267. *Parent loans:* $779,347 (88% need-based, 12% non-need-based). *Programs:* Federal Direct (Subsidized and Unsubsidized Stafford, PLUS), Perkins, alternative loans.

WORK-STUDY *Federal work-study:* Total amount: $73,907; 119 jobs averaging $1971. *State or other work-study/employment:* Total amount: $158,743 (100% non-need-based). Part-time jobs available.

APPLYING FOR FINANCIAL AID *Required financial aid form:* FAFSA. *Financial aid deadline (priority):* 10/1. *Notification date:* Continuous beginning 2/15. Students must reply within 2 weeks of notification.

CONTACT Mrs. Tammy Crothers, Director of Financial Aid, Eureka College, 300 East College Avenue, Eureka, IL 61530, 309-467-6311 or toll-free 888-4-EUREKA. *Fax:* 309-467-6897. *E-mail:* tcrothers@eureka.edu. *Website:* http://www.eureka.edu/.

EVANGEL UNIVERSITY
Springfield, MO

Tuition & fees: $23,421	Average undergraduate aid package: $18,255

ABOUT THE INSTITUTION Independent Assemblies of God, coed. *Awards:* associate, bachelor's, master's, and doctoral degrees. 48 undergraduate majors. *Total enrollment:* 2,112. Undergraduates: 1,631. Freshmen: 400. Federal methodology is used as a basis for awarding need-based institutional aid.

UNDERGRADUATE EXPENSES for 2018–2019 *Tuition:* full-time $22,146; part-time $896 per credit hour. Full-time tuition and fees vary according to course load. Part-time tuition and fees vary according to course load. Room and board charges vary according to board plan.

FRESHMAN FINANCIAL AID (Fall 2016) 376 applied for aid; of those 91% were deemed to have need. 100% of freshmen with need received aid; of those 14% had need fully met. *Average percent of need met:* 71% (excluding resources awarded to replace EFC). *Average financial aid package:* $18,494 (excluding resources awarded to replace EFC). 9% of all full-time freshmen had no need and received non-need-based gift aid.

UNDERGRADUATE FINANCIAL AID (Fall 2016) 1,384 applied for aid; of those 88% were deemed to have need. 100% of undergraduates with need received aid; of those 13% had need fully met. *Average percent of need met:* 70% (excluding resources awarded to replace EFC). *Average financial aid package:* $18,255 (excluding resources awarded to replace EFC). 13% of all full-time undergraduates had no need and received non-need-based gift aid.

GIFT AID (NEED-BASED) *Total amount:* $13,690,140 (23% federal, 1% state, 70% institutional, 6% external sources). *Receiving aid:* Freshmen: 89% (343); all full-time undergraduates: 83% (1,205). *Average award:* Freshmen: $14,226; Undergraduates: $13,273. *Scholarships, grants, and awards:* Federal Pell, FSEOG, state, private, college/university gift aid from institutional funds.

GIFT AID (NON-NEED-BASED) *Total amount:* $2,137,869 (90% institutional, 10% external sources). *Receiving aid:* Freshmen: 12% (45). Undergraduates: 9% (134). *Average award:* Freshmen: $10,424. Undergraduates: $8215. *Scholarships, grants, and awards by category:* Academic interests/achievement: 1,152 awards ($7,745,981 total): biological sciences, business, communication, computer science, education, engineering/technologies, English, foreign languages, general academic interests/achievements, home economics, humanities, international studies, mathematics, physical sciences, premedicine, religion/biblical studies, social sciences. *Creative arts/performance:* 153 awards ($91,988 total): art/fine arts, debating, music, theater/drama. *Special achievements/activities:* 229 awards ($125,125 total): cheerleading/drum major, general special achievements/activities, leadership, religious involvement. *Special characteristics:* 208 awards ($1,505,547 total): adult students, children and siblings of alumni, children of educators, children of faculty/staff, general special characteristics, out-of-state students, relatives of clergy, religious affiliation. *Tuition waivers:* Full or partial for employees or children of employees. *ROTC:* Army cooperative.

LOANS *Student loans:* $12,475,860 (75% need-based, 25% non-need-based). 83% of past graduating class borrowed through all loan programs. *Average indebtedness per student:* $30,443. *Average need-based loan:* Freshmen: $3775. Undergraduates: $4622. *Parent loans:* $2,681,481 (54% need-based, 46% non-need-based). *Programs:* Federal Direct (Subsidized and Unsubsidized Stafford, PLUS), Perkins, college/university.

WORK-STUDY *Federal work-study:* 964 jobs averaging $1835.

ATHLETIC AWARDS Total amount: $2,667,062 (66% need-based, 34% non-need-based).

APPLYING FOR FINANCIAL AID *Required financial aid form:* FAFSA. *Financial aid deadline (priority):* 3/1. *Notification date:* Continuous beginning 3/1.

CONTACT Mrs. Valerie Sharp, Director of Financial Aid, Evangel University, 1111 North Glenstone Avenue, Springfield, MO 65802-2191, 417-865-2811 Ext. 7302 or toll-free 800-382-6435. *Fax:* 417-575-5478. *E-mail:* sharpv@evangel.edu. *Website:* http://www.evangel.edu/.

EVERGLADES UNIVERSITY
Boca Raton, FL

ABOUT THE INSTITUTION Independent, coed. 11 undergraduate majors.

GIFT AID (NEED-BASED) *Scholarships, grants, and awards:* Federal Pell, FSEOG, state, private, college/university gift aid from institutional funds.

GIFT AID (NON-NEED-BASED) *Scholarships, grants, and awards by category:* Special characteristics: general special characteristics, local/state students, veterans.

LOANS *Programs:* Federal Direct (Subsidized and Unsubsidized Stafford, PLUS), Perkins.

APPLYING FOR FINANCIAL AID *Required financial aid forms:* FAFSA, institution's own form.

CONTACT Miss Seeta Singh Moonilall, Regional Director of Financial Aid, Everglades University, 5002 T-Rex Avenue, Suite 100, Boca Raton, FL 33431, 561-912-1211 or toll-free 888-772-6077. *Fax:* 516-912-1191. *E-mail:* smoonilall@evergladesuniversity.edu. *Website:* http://www.evergladesuniversity.edu/.

THE EVERGREEN STATE COLLEGE
Olympia, WA

Tuition & fees (WA res): $7416	Average undergraduate aid package: $12,210

ABOUT THE INSTITUTION State-supported, coed. *Awards:* bachelor's and master's degrees. 45 undergraduate majors. *Total enrollment:* 3,907. Undergraduates: 3,610. Freshmen: 521. Federal methodology is used as a basis for awarding need-based institutional aid.

UNDERGRADUATE EXPENSES for 2017–2018 *Application fee:* $50. *Tuition, state resident:* full-time $6678; part-time $226.60 per credit hour. *Tuition, nonresident:* full-time $24,138; part-time $804.60 per credit hour. *Required fees:* full-time $738; $9.25 per credit hour or $5 per term. Full-time tuition and fees vary according to course load, location, and program. Part-time tuition and fees vary according to course load, location, and program. *College room and board:* $9681; *Room only:* $6471. Room and board charges vary according to board plan, housing facility, location, and student level.

FRESHMAN FINANCIAL AID (Fall 2016) 474 applied for aid; of those 76% were deemed to have need. 95% of freshmen with need received aid; of those 10% had need fully met. *Average percent of need met:* 57% (excluding resources awarded to replace EFC). *Average financial aid package:* $10,879 (excluding resources awarded to replace EFC). 1% of all full-time freshmen had no need and received non-need-based gift aid.

UNDERGRADUATE FINANCIAL AID (Fall 2016) 2,664 applied for aid; of those 87% were deemed to have need. 94% of undergraduates with need received aid; of those 7% had need fully met. *Average percent of need met:* 62% (excluding resources awarded to replace EFC). *Average financial aid package:* $12,210 (excluding resources awarded to replace EFC). 1% of all full-time undergraduates had no need and received non-need-based gift aid.

GIFT AID (NEED-BASED) *Total amount:* $15,947,196 (49% federal, 41% state, 9% institutional, 1% external sources). *Receiving aid:* Freshmen: 58% (322); all full-time undergraduates: 58% (2,000). *Average award:* Freshmen: $8665; Undergraduates: $9456. *Scholarships, grants, and awards:* Federal Pell, FSEOG, state, private, college/university gift aid from institutional funds.

GIFT AID (NON-NEED-BASED) *Total amount:* $179,580 (41% state, 30% institutional, 29% external sources). *Receiving aid:* Freshmen: 3% (15). Undergraduates: 1% (32). *Average award:* Freshmen: $835. Undergraduates: $2504. *Scholarships, grants, and awards by category:* Academic interests/achievement: general academic interests/achievements. *Creative arts/performance:* general creative arts/performance. *Special achievements/activities:* general special achievements/activities. *Special characteristics:* adult students, ethnic background, first-generation college students, general special characteristics, local/state students, out-of-state students, veterans, veterans' children. *Tuition waivers:* Full or partial for employees or children of employees, senior citizens.

LOANS *Student loans:* $13,991,558 (88% need-based, 12% non-need-based). 57% of past graduating class borrowed through all loan programs. *Average indebtedness per student:* $21,147. *Average need-based loan:* Freshmen: $3381. Undergraduates: $4148. *Parent loans:* $3,809,360 (77% need-based, 23% non-need-based).

Programs: Federal Direct (Subsidized and Unsubsidized Stafford, PLUS), college/university.
WORK-STUDY *Federal work-study:* jobs available. *State or other work-study/employment:* Total amount: $685,656 (100% need-based). Part-time jobs available.
ATHLETIC AWARDS Total amount: $246,760 (59% need-based, 41% non-need-based).
APPLYING FOR FINANCIAL AID *Required financial aid form:* FAFSA. *Financial aid deadline (priority):* 2/1. *Notification date:* Continuous beginning 4/1. Students must reply within 6 weeks of notification.
CONTACT Tracy Hall, Director of Financial Aid, The Evergreen State College, 2700 Evergreen Parkway NW, Olympia, WA 98505, 360-867-6205. *Fax:* 360-866-6576. *E-mail:* finaid@evergreen.edu.
Website: http://www.evergreen.edu/.

EXCELSIOR COLLEGE
Albany, NY

Tuition & fees: N/R	Average undergraduate aid package: N/A

ABOUT THE INSTITUTION Independent, coed. *Awards:* certificates, associate, bachelor's, and master's degrees (offers only external degree programs). 43 undergraduate majors. *Total enrollment:* 31,095. Undergraduates: 28,384. Federal methodology is used as a basis for awarding need-based institutional aid.
UNDERGRADUATE EXPENSES for 2018–2019 *Application fee:* $50. *Tuition:* part-time $510 per credit. Part-time tuition and fees vary according to reciprocity agreements.
GIFT AID (NEED-BASED) *Total amount:* $14,054,046 (71% federal, 7% state, 3% institutional, 19% external sources). *Scholarships, grants, and awards:* Federal Pell, FSEOG, state, private, college/university gift aid from institutional funds, Federal Nursing, Veterans Education Benefits (GI Bill).
GIFT AID (NON-NEED-BASED) *Tuition waivers:* Full or partial for employees or children of employees.
LOANS *Student loans:* $24,861,315 (100% need-based). *Programs:* Federal Direct (Subsidized and Unsubsidized Stafford, PLUS), Federal Nursing.
APPLYING FOR FINANCIAL AID *Financial aid deadline:* Continuous. *Notification date:* Continuous.
CONTACT Office of Financial Aid, Excelsior College, 7 Columbia Circle, Albany, NY 12203-5159, 518-464-8500 or toll-free 888-647-2388. *Fax:* 518-464-8777. *Website:* http://www.excelsior.edu/.

FAIRFIELD UNIVERSITY
Fairfield, CT

Tuition & fees: $47,165	Average undergraduate aid package: $34,731

ABOUT THE INSTITUTION Independent Roman Catholic (Jesuit), coed. *Awards:* certificates, bachelor's, master's, and doctoral degrees. 45 undergraduate majors. *Total enrollment:* 5,192. Undergraduates: 4,113. Freshmen: 994. Both federal and institutional methodology are used as a basis for awarding need-based institutional aid.
UNDERGRADUATE EXPENSES for 2017–2018 *Application fee:* $60. *One-time required fee:* $300. *Comprehensive fee:* $61,445 includes full-time tuition ($46,490), mandatory fees ($675), and room and board ($14,280). *College room only:* $8750. Full-time tuition and fees vary according to class time, course level, course load, degree level, and program. Room and board charges vary according to board plan and housing facility. *Part-time tuition:* $725 per credit hour. *Part-time fees:* $60 per term. Part-time tuition and fees vary according to class time, course level, course load, degree level, and program.
FRESHMAN FINANCIAL AID (Fall 2017, est.) 746 applied for aid; of those 64% were deemed to have need. 100% of freshmen with need received aid; of those 33% had need fully met. *Average percent of need met:* 85% (excluding resources awarded to replace EFC). *Average financial aid package:* $34,178 (excluding resources awarded to replace EFC). 40% of all full-time freshmen had no need and received non-need-based gift aid.

UNDERGRADUATE FINANCIAL AID (Fall 2017, est.) 2,484 applied for aid; of those 71% were deemed to have need. 100% of undergraduates with need received aid; of those 34% had need fully met. *Average percent of need met:* 84% (excluding resources awarded to replace EFC). *Average financial aid package:* $34,731 (excluding resources awarded to replace EFC). 40% of all full-time undergraduates had no need and received non-need-based gift aid.
GIFT AID (NEED-BASED) *Total amount:* $49,117,520 (5% federal, 95% institutional). *Receiving aid:* Freshmen: 39% (389); all full-time undergraduates: 39% (1,511). *Average award:* Freshmen: $28,236; Undergraduates: $27,572. *Scholarships, grants, and awards:* Federal Pell, FSEOG, state, private, college/university gift aid from institutional funds, Federal Nursing.
GIFT AID (NON-NEED-BASED) *Total amount:* $25,303,219 (91% institutional, 9% external sources). *Receiving aid:* Freshmen: 44% (438). Undergraduates: 39% (1,523). *Average award:* Freshmen: $14,404. Undergraduates: $14,987. *Scholarships, grants, and awards by category:* Academic interests/achievement: 1,236 awards ($22,425,055 total): general academic interests/achievements. *Creative arts/performance:* 33 awards ($11,180 total): general creative arts/performance. *Special achievements/activities:* 16 awards ($95,700 total): general special achievements/activities. *Special characteristics:* 178 awards ($3,074,278 total): children and siblings of alumni, children of faculty/staff, children with a deceased or disabled parent, ethnic background, first-generation college students, general special characteristics, members of minority groups, veterans, veterans' children. *Tuition waivers:* Full or partial for employees or children of employees. *ROTC:* Army cooperative, Air Force cooperative.
LOANS *Student loans:* $22,806,400 (33% need-based, 67% non-need-based). 75% of past graduating class borrowed through all loan programs. *Average indebtedness per student:* $32,186. *Average need-based loan:* Freshmen: $3471. Undergraduates: $4863. *Parent loans:* $7,134,802 (100% non-need-based). *Programs:* Federal Direct (Subsidized and Unsubsidized Stafford, PLUS), Federal Nursing, state, private loans.
WORK-STUDY *Federal work-study:* Total amount: $634,723; 540 jobs averaging $1175.
ATHLETIC AWARDS Total amount: $6,458,516 (100% non-need-based).
APPLYING FOR FINANCIAL AID *Required financial aid forms:* FAFSA, CSS Financial Aid PROFILE, noncustodial (divorced/separated) parent's statement, business/farm supplement. *Financial aid deadline:* 1/15. *Notification date:* 4/1. Students must reply by 5/1.
CONTACT Diana Draper, Director of Financial Aid, Fairfield University, 1073 North Benson Road, Fairfield, CT 06824, 203-254-4125. *Fax:* 203-254-4008. *E-mail:* finaid@fairfield.edu.
Website: http://www.fairfield.edu/.

FAIRLEIGH DICKINSON UNIVERSITY, FLORHAM CAMPUS
Madison, NJ

Tuition & fees: $41,780	Average undergraduate aid package: $40,034

ABOUT THE INSTITUTION Independent, coed. *Awards:* certificates, bachelor's, master's, and doctoral degrees. 40 undergraduate majors. *Total enrollment:* 3,512. Undergraduates: 2,747. Freshmen: 802. Federal methodology is used as a basis for awarding need-based institutional aid.
UNDERGRADUATE EXPENSES for 2017–2018 *Application fee:* $40. *One-time required fee:* $810. *Comprehensive fee:* $54,910 includes full-time tuition ($40,752), mandatory fees ($1028), and room and board ($13,130). *College room only:* $8636. Full-time tuition and fees vary according to location and program. Room and board charges vary according to board plan, housing facility, and location. *Part-time tuition:* $987 per credit hour. *Part-time fees:* $414 per year. Part-time tuition and fees vary according to location and program.
FRESHMAN FINANCIAL AID (Fall 2017, est.) 767 applied for aid; of those 92% were deemed to have need. 100% of freshmen with need received aid; of those 16% had need fully met. *Average percent of need met:* 79% (excluding resources awarded to replace EFC). *Average financial aid package:* $41,927 (excluding resources awarded to replace EFC). 12% of all full-time freshmen had no need and received non-need-based gift aid.

UNDERGRADUATE FINANCIAL AID (Fall 2017, est.) 2,307 applied for aid; of those 93% were deemed to have need. 100% of undergraduates with need received aid; of those 13% had need fully met. *Average percent of need met:* 73% (excluding resources awarded to replace EFC). *Average financial aid package:* $40,034 (excluding resources awarded to replace EFC). 16% of all full-time undergraduates had no need and received non-need-based gift aid.

GIFT AID (NEED-BASED) *Total amount:* $62,437,457 (7% federal, 13% state, 79% institutional, 1% external sources). *Receiving aid:* Freshmen: 88% (708); all full-time undergraduates: 81% (2,141). *Average award:* Freshmen: $32,218; Undergraduates: $29,076. *Scholarships, grants, and awards:* Federal Pell, FSEOG, state, private, college/university gift aid from institutional funds, Federal Nursing.

GIFT AID (NON-NEED-BASED) *Total amount:* $11,696,336 (2% federal, 96% institutional, 2% external sources). *Receiving aid:* Freshmen: 12% (96). Undergraduates: 16% (432). *Average award:* Freshmen: $18,141. Undergraduates: $17,451. *Tuition waivers:* Full or partial for employees or children of employees, senior citizens. *ROTC:* Army cooperative, Air Force cooperative.

LOANS *Student loans:* $21,243,709 (73% need-based, 27% non-need-based). 85% of past graduating class borrowed through all loan programs. *Average indebtedness per student:* $42,122. *Average need-based loan:* Freshmen: $3307. Undergraduates: $4420. *Parent loans:* $7,341,678 (62% need-based, 38% non-need-based). *Programs:* Federal Direct (Subsidized and Unsubsidized Stafford, PLUS), Perkins, Federal Nursing, state, college/university, private loans.

WORK-STUDY *Federal work-study:* Total amount: $1,606,076; jobs available.

APPLYING FOR FINANCIAL AID *Required financial aid forms:* FAFSA, institution's own form. *Financial aid deadline:* 2/15 (priority: 1/1). *Notification date:* Continuous beginning 5/1. Students must reply by 5/1 or within 4 weeks of notification.

CONTACT Renee Volak, Financial Aid Office, Fairleigh Dickinson University, Florham Campus, 285 Madison Avenue, M-MSO-02, Madison, NJ 07940-1099, 973-443-8700 or toll-free 800-338-8803. *Fax:* 973-443-8534. *E-mail:* finaid@fdu.edu. *Website:* http://www.fdu.edu/.

FAIRLEIGH DICKINSON UNIVERSITY, METROPOLITAN CAMPUS
Teaneck, NJ

Tuition & fees: $39,446	Average undergraduate aid package: $36,702

ABOUT THE INSTITUTION Independent, coed. *Awards:* certificates, associate, bachelor's, master's, and doctoral degrees. 53 undergraduate majors. *Total enrollment:* 7,846. Undergraduates: 5,467. Freshmen: 710. Federal methodology is used as a basis for awarding need-based institutional aid.

UNDERGRADUATE EXPENSES for 2017–2018 *Application fee:* $40. *One-time required fee:* $810. *Comprehensive fee:* $52,532 includes full-time tuition ($38,418), mandatory fees ($1028), and room and board ($13,086). *College room only:* $8592. Full-time tuition and fees vary according to location and program. Room and board charges vary according to board plan and housing facility. *Part-time tuition:* $987 per credit hour. *Part-time fees:* $414 per year. Part-time tuition and fees vary according to location and program.

FRESHMAN FINANCIAL AID (Fall 2017, est.) 614 applied for aid; of those 97% were deemed to have need. 100% of freshmen with need received aid; of those 10% had need fully met. *Average percent of need met:* 73% (excluding resources awarded to replace EFC). *Average financial aid package:* $40,106 (excluding resources awarded to replace EFC). 10% of all full-time freshmen had no need and received non-need-based gift aid.

UNDERGRADUATE FINANCIAL AID (Fall 2017, est.) 2,019 applied for aid; of those 97% were deemed to have need. 100% of undergraduates with need received aid; of those 9% had need fully met. *Average percent of need met:* 65% (excluding resources awarded to replace EFC). *Average financial aid package:* $36,702 (excluding resources awarded to replace EFC). 11% of all full-time undergraduates had no need and received non-need-based gift aid.

GIFT AID (NEED-BASED) *Total amount:* $51,761,206 (16% federal, 22% state, 61% institutional, 1% external sources). *Receiving aid:* Freshmen: 89% (594); all full-time undergraduates: 80% (1,897). *Average award:* Freshmen: $31,575; Undergraduates: $26,806. *Scholarships, grants, and awards:* Federal Pell, FSEOG, state, private, college/university gift aid from institutional funds, Federal Nursing.

GIFT AID (NON-NEED-BASED) *Total amount:* $6,115,990 (6% federal, 91% institutional, 3% external sources). *Receiving aid:* Freshmen: 10% (65). Undergraduates: 11% (258). *Average award:* Freshmen: $18,370. Undergraduates: $15,540. *Tuition waivers:* Full or partial for employees or children of employees, senior citizens. *ROTC:* Army cooperative, Air Force cooperative.

LOANS *Student loans:* $19,491,346 (86% need-based, 14% non-need-based). 70% of past graduating class borrowed through all loan programs. *Average indebtedness per student:* $40,151. *Average need-based loan:* Freshmen: $3202. Undergraduates: $4152. *Parent loans:* $4,436,429 (75% need-based, 25% non-need-based). *Programs:* Federal Direct (Subsidized and Unsubsidized Stafford, PLUS), Perkins, Federal Nursing, state, private loans.

WORK-STUDY *Federal work-study:* Total amount: $1,060,899; jobs available.

ATHLETIC AWARDS Total amount: $4,028,625 (52% need-based, 48% non-need-based).

APPLYING FOR FINANCIAL AID *Required financial aid forms:* FAFSA, institution's own form. *Financial aid deadline:* 2/15 (priority: 1/1). *Notification date:* Continuous beginning 5/1. Students must reply within 2 weeks of notification.

CONTACT Ms. Renee Volak, University Director of Financial Aid, Fairleigh Dickinson University, Metropolitan Campus, 1000 River Road T-KB1-04, Teaneck, NJ 07666-1914, 201-692-2363 or toll-free 800-338-8803. *Fax:* 201-692-2364. *E-mail:* finaid@fdu.edu. *Website:* http://www.fdu.edu/.

FAIRMONT STATE UNIVERSITY
Fairmont, WV

Tuition & fees (WV res): $9066	Average undergraduate aid package: $9060

ABOUT THE INSTITUTION State-supported, coed. 42 undergraduate majors. Federal methodology is used as a basis for awarding need-based institutional aid.

UNDERGRADUATE EXPENSES for 2017–2018 *Tuition, state resident:* full-time $7296; part-time $296 per credit hour. *Tuition, nonresident:* full-time $15,398; part-time $634 per credit hour. *Required fees:* full-time $1770. Full-time tuition and fees vary according to location and reciprocity agreements. Part-time tuition and fees vary according to course load, location, and reciprocity agreements. *College room and board:* $9184; *Room only:* $5348. Room and board charges vary according to board plan and housing facility.

FRESHMAN FINANCIAL AID (Fall 2016) 764 applied for aid; of those 74% were deemed to have need. 99% of freshmen with need received aid; of those 13% had need fully met. *Average percent of need met:* 73% (excluding resources awarded to replace EFC). *Average financial aid package:* $9509 (excluding resources awarded to replace EFC). 14% of all full-time freshmen had no need and received non-need-based gift aid.

UNDERGRADUATE FINANCIAL AID (Fall 2016) 2,912 applied for aid; of those 78% were deemed to have need. 98% of undergraduates with need received aid; of those 9% had need fully met. *Average percent of need met:* 70% (excluding resources awarded to replace EFC). *Average financial aid package:* $9060 (excluding resources awarded to replace EFC). 9% of all full-time undergraduates had no need and received non-need-based gift aid.

GIFT AID (NEED-BASED) *Total amount:* $14,284,063 (48% federal, 42% state, 10% institutional). *Receiving aid:* Freshmen: 64% (503); all full-time undergraduates: 59% (1,934). *Average award:* Freshmen: $7362; Undergraduates: $6629. *Scholarships, grants, and awards:* Federal Pell, FSEOG, state, private, college/university gift aid from institutional funds.

GIFT AID (NON-NEED-BASED) *Total amount:* $686,998 (2% state, 98% institutional). *Receiving aid:* Freshmen: 27% (211). Undergraduates: 20% (649). *Average award:* Freshmen: $7603. Undergraduates: $7995. *Scholarships, grants, and awards by category: Academic interests/achievement:* architecture, biological sciences, business, computer science, education, engineering/technologies, English, general academic interests/achievements, health fields, humanities, international studies, mathematics, physical sciences, social sciences. *Creative arts/performance:* art/fine arts, creative writing, debating, general creative arts/performance, journalism/publications, music, theater/drama. *Special achievements/activities:* cheerleading/drum major, general special achievements/activities, leadership. *Special characteristics:* adult students, children and siblings of alumni, children of faculty/staff, ethnic background, first-generation college students, general special characteristics, handicapped students, international students, local/state students, members of minority groups, out-of-state students, previous college experience, veterans, veterans' children. *Tuition waivers:* Full or partial for employees or children of employees.

LOANS *Student loans:* $14,979,139 (39% need-based, 61% non-need-based). 67% of past graduating class borrowed through all loan programs. *Average indebtedness per student:* $25,291. *Average need-based loan:* Freshmen: $2929. Undergraduates: $3594. *Parent loans:* $2,303,841 (100% non-need-based). *Programs:* Federal Direct (Subsidized and Unsubsidized Stafford, PLUS).

WORK-STUDY *Federal work-study:* jobs available. *State or other work-study/employment:* Part-time jobs available.

ATHLETIC AWARDS Total amount: $1,604,990 (65% need-based, 35% non-need-based).

APPLYING FOR FINANCIAL AID *Required financial aid form:* FAFSA. *Financial aid deadline (priority):* 3/1. *Notification date:* Continuous beginning 12/1. Students must reply within 2 weeks of notification.

CONTACT Patricia Wiemer, Director of Financial Aid and Scholarships, Fairmont State University, 1201 Locust Avenue, Fairmont, WV 26554, 304-367-4892 or toll-free 800-641-5678. *Fax:* 304-367-4789. *E-mail:* patricia.weimer@fairmontstate.edu. *Website:* http://www.fairmontstate.edu/.

FAITH BAPTIST BIBLE COLLEGE AND THEOLOGICAL SEMINARY
Ankeny, IA

CONTACT Mr. Breck Appell, Director of Financial Assistance, Faith Baptist Bible College and Theological Seminary, 1900 Northwest 4th Street, Ankeny, IA 50021-2152, 515-964-0601 or toll-free 888-FAITH 4U. *Fax:* 515-964-1638. *Website:* http://www.faith.edu/.

FAITH THEOLOGICAL SEMINARY
Baltimore, MD

CONTACT Financial Aid Office, Faith Theological Seminary, 529 Walker Avenue, Baltimore, MD 21212, 410-323-6211. *Website:* http://www.fts.edu/.

FAMILY OF FAITH CHRISTIAN UNIVERSITY
Shawnee, OK

CONTACT Financial Aid Office, Family of Faith Christian University, 30 Kinville, Shawnee, OK 74802, 405-273-5331. *Website:* http://www.familyoffaith.edu/.

FARMINGDALE STATE COLLEGE
Farmingdale, NY

Tuition & fees (NY res): $8076	Average undergraduate aid package: $7950

ABOUT THE INSTITUTION State-supported, coed. *Awards:* certificates, associate, bachelor's, and master's degrees. 34 undergraduate majors. *Total enrollment:* 9,574. Undergraduates: 9,552. Freshmen: 1,291. Federal methodology is used as a basis for awarding need-based institutional aid.

UNDERGRADUATE EXPENSES for 2017–2018 *Application fee:* $50. *Tuition, state resident:* full-time $6670; part-time $278 per credit. *Tuition, nonresident:* full-time $16,320; part-time $680 per credit. *Required fees:* full-time $1406; $57.25 per credit or $10 per term. Full-time tuition and fees vary according to program. Part-time tuition and fees vary according to course load and program. *College room and board:* $12,892. *Room only:* $7852. Room and board charges vary according to board plan and housing facility.

FRESHMAN FINANCIAL AID (Fall 2016) 1,038 applied for aid; of those 71% were deemed to have need. 92% of freshmen with need received aid; of those 9% had

need fully met. *Average percent of need met:* 61% (excluding resources awarded to replace EFC). *Average financial aid package:* $8390 (excluding resources awarded to replace EFC). 2% of all full-time freshmen had no need and received non-need-based gift aid.

UNDERGRADUATE FINANCIAL AID (Fall 2016) 4,894 applied for aid; of those 76% were deemed to have need. 94% of undergraduates with need received aid; of those 8% had need fully met. *Average percent of need met:* 58% (excluding resources awarded to replace EFC). *Average financial aid package:* $7950 (excluding resources awarded to replace EFC). 2% of all full-time undergraduates had no need and received non-need-based gift aid.

GIFT AID (NEED-BASED) *Total amount:* $21,047,850 (53% federal, 45% state, 1% institutional, 1% external sources). *Receiving aid:* Freshmen: 49% (609); all full-time undergraduates: 44% (3,030). *Average award:* Freshmen: $7494; Undergraduates: $6575. *Scholarships, grants, and awards:* Federal Pell, FSEOG, state, private, college/university gift aid from institutional funds.

GIFT AID (NON-NEED-BASED) *Total amount:* $952,740 (35% state, 13% institutional, 52% external sources). *Receiving aid:* Freshmen: 1% (12). Undergraduates: 27. *Average award:* Freshmen: $4329. Undergraduates: $3221. *Tuition waivers:* Full or partial for employees or children of employees. *ROTC:* Army cooperative, Naval cooperative, Air Force.

LOANS *Student loans:* $19,890,351 (63% need-based, 37% non-need-based). 50% of past graduating class borrowed through all loan programs. *Average indebtedness per student:* $22,105. *Average need-based loan:* Freshmen: $3151. Undergraduates: $4029. *Parent loans:* $1,308,435 (28% need-based, 72% non-need-based). *Programs:* Federal Direct (Subsidized and Unsubsidized Stafford, PLUS), Perkins, alternative loans.

WORK-STUDY *Federal work-study:* jobs available. *State or other work-study/employment:* Total amount: $304,694 (24% need-based, 76% non-need-based). Part-time jobs available.

APPLYING FOR FINANCIAL AID *Required financial aid form:* FAFSA. *Financial aid deadline (priority):* 4/1. *Notification date:* Continuous beginning 3/1.

CONTACT Office of Financial Aid, Farmingdale State College, 2350 Broadhollow Road, Laffin Hall, Room 324, Farmingdale, NY 11735, 631-420-2578. *Fax:* 631-420-3662. *E-mail:* faoffice@farmingdale.edu. *Website:* http://www.farmingdale.edu/.

FASHION INSTITUTE OF TECHNOLOGY
New York, NY

Tuition & fees (NY res): $7463	Average undergraduate aid package: $11,880

ABOUT THE INSTITUTION State and locally supported, coed, primarily women. *Awards:* certificates, associate, bachelor's, and master's degrees. 23 undergraduate majors. *Total enrollment:* 8,846. Undergraduates: 8,661. Freshmen: 1,263. Federal methodology is used as a basis for awarding need-based institutional aid.

UNDERGRADUATE EXPENSES for 2017–2018 *Application fee:* $50. *Tuition, state resident:* full-time $6670; part-time $278 per credit hour. *Tuition, nonresident:* full-time $20,192; part-time $841 per credit hour. *Required fees:* full-time $793. Full-time tuition and fees vary according to degree level. Part-time tuition and fees vary according to degree level. *College room and board:* $13,945; *Room only:* $9291. Room and board charges vary according to board plan and housing facility.

FRESHMAN FINANCIAL AID (Fall 2016) 879 applied for aid; of those 75% were deemed to have need. 100% of freshmen with need received aid; of those 47% had need fully met. *Average percent of need met:* 72% (excluding resources awarded to replace EFC). *Average financial aid package:* $10,679 (excluding resources awarded to replace EFC). 8% of all full-time freshmen had no need and received non-need-based gift aid.

UNDERGRADUATE FINANCIAL AID (Fall 2016) 4,551 applied for aid; of those 81% were deemed to have need. 100% of undergraduates with need received aid; of those 46% had need fully met. *Average percent of need met:* 68% (excluding resources awarded to replace EFC). *Average financial aid package:* $11,880 (excluding resources awarded to replace EFC). 4% of all full-time undergraduates had no need and received non-need-based gift aid.

GIFT AID (NEED-BASED) *Total amount:* $17,042,941 (60% federal, 30% state, 9% institutional, 1% external sources). *Receiving aid:* Freshmen: 39% (484); all full-time undergraduates: 37% (2,752). *Average award:* Freshmen: $6065; Undergraduates: $6106. *Scholarships, grants, and awards:* Federal Pell, FSEOG, state, private, college/university gift aid from institutional funds.

GIFT AID (NON-NEED-BASED) *Total amount:* $537,233 (23% institutional, 77% external sources). *Receiving aid:* Freshmen: 14% (179). Undergraduates: 6% (408). *Average award:* Freshmen: $769. Undergraduates: $784. *Tuition waivers:* Full or partial for employees or children of employees.

LOANS *Student loans:* $30,604,338 (35% need-based, 65% non-need-based). 52% of past graduating class borrowed through all loan programs. *Average indebtedness per student:* $25,074. *Average need-based loan:* Freshmen: $2353. Undergraduates: $3195. *Parent loans:* $10,582,696 (100% non-need-based). *Programs:* Federal Direct (Subsidized and Unsubsidized Stafford, PLUS), Perkins, alternative loans.

WORK-STUDY *Federal work-study:* jobs available.

APPLYING FOR FINANCIAL AID *Required financial aid forms:* FAFSA, state aid form. *Financial aid deadline (priority):* 2/15. *Notification date:* Continuous beginning 4/1. Students must reply within 2 weeks of notification.

CONTACT Financial Aid Office, Fashion Institute of Technology, Seventh Avenue at 27th Street, New York, NY 10001-5992, 212-217-3560. *E-mail:* finaid@fitnyc.edu. *Website:* http://www.fitnyc.edu/.

FAULKNER UNIVERSITY
Montgomery, AL

Tuition & fees: $21,690	Average undergraduate aid package: $11,980

ABOUT THE INSTITUTION Independent Church of Christ, coed. *Awards:* associate, bachelor's, master's, and doctoral degrees. 48 undergraduate majors. *Total enrollment:* 3,350. Undergraduates: 2,672. Freshmen: 333. Federal methodology is used as a basis for awarding need-based institutional aid.

UNDERGRADUATE EXPENSES for 2018–2019 *Comprehensive fee:* $29,240 includes full-time tuition ($19,880), mandatory fees ($1810), and room and board ($7550). *College room only:* $3600. Full-time tuition and fees vary according to class time, course load, location, and program. Room and board charges vary according to board plan and housing facility. *Part-time tuition:* $675 per semester hour. *Part-time fees:* $375 per term. Part-time tuition and fees vary according to class time, course load, location, and program.

FRESHMAN FINANCIAL AID (Fall 2016) 241 applied for aid; of those 100% were deemed to have need. 94% of freshmen with need received aid; of those 8% had need fully met. *Average percent of need met:* 61% (excluding resources awarded to replace EFC). *Average financial aid package:* $15,296 (excluding resources awarded to replace EFC). 9% of all full-time freshmen had no need and received non-need-based gift aid.

UNDERGRADUATE FINANCIAL AID (Fall 2016) 1,482 applied for aid; of those 100% were deemed to have need. 95% of undergraduates with need received aid; of those 6% had need fully met. *Average percent of need met:* 52% (excluding resources awarded to replace EFC). *Average financial aid package:* $11,980 (excluding resources awarded to replace EFC). 5% of all full-time undergraduates had no need and received non-need-based gift aid.

GIFT AID (NEED-BASED) *Total amount:* $12,091,179 (49% federal, 7% state, 38% institutional, 6% external sources). *Receiving aid:* Freshmen: 52% (162); all full-time undergraduates: 60% (1,058). *Average award:* Freshmen: $5021; Undergraduates: $4691. *Scholarships, grants, and awards:* Federal Pell, FSEOG, state, private, college/university gift aid from institutional funds.

GIFT AID (NON-NEED-BASED) *Total amount:* $1,033,176 (10% state, 70% institutional, 20% external sources). *Receiving aid:* Freshmen: 57% (177). Undergraduates: 74% (1,316). *Average award:* Freshmen: $7566. Undergraduates: $6701. *Scholarships, grants, and awards by category:* Academic interests/achievement: general academic interests/achievements, religion/biblical studies. Creative arts/performance: journalism/publications, music, theater/drama. Special achievements/activities: cheerleading/drum major, leadership, religious involvement. Special characteristics: adult students, children and siblings of alumni, children of faculty/staff, local/state students, out-of-state students, relatives of clergy, religious affiliation, siblings of current students. *Tuition waivers:* Full or partial for employees or children of employees, adult students. *ROTC:* Army cooperative, Air Force cooperative.

LOANS *Student loans:* $13,512,655 (92% need-based, 8% non-need-based). 76% of past graduating class borrowed through all loan programs. *Average indebtedness per student:* $33,622. *Average need-based loan:* Freshmen: $3184. Undergraduates: $3789. *Parent loans:* $2,186,958 (65% need-based, 35% non-need-based). *Programs:* Federal Direct (Subsidized and Unsubsidized Stafford, PLUS), Perkins.

WORK-STUDY *Federal work-study:* 208 jobs averaging $1271. *State or other work-study/employment:* Total amount: $2930 (43% need-based, 57% non-need-based). Part-time jobs available.

ATHLETIC AWARDS Total amount: $3,341,355 (64% need-based, 36% non-need-based).

APPLYING FOR FINANCIAL AID *Required financial aid forms:* FAFSA, institution's own form, state aid form. *Financial aid deadline:* 8/1 (priority: 3/15). *Notification date:* 5/1. Students must reply within 3 weeks of notification.

CONTACT Mr. William G. Jackson II, Director of Financial Aid, Faulkner University, 5345 Atlanta Highway, Montgomery, AL 36109-3398, 334-386-7195 or toll-free 800-879-9816. *Fax:* 334-386-7201. *E-mail:* faid@faulkner.edu. *Website:* http://www.faulkner.edu/.

FAYETTEVILLE STATE UNIVERSITY
Fayetteville, NC

CONTACT Mr. Keith Townsend, Administrative Assistant, Fayetteville State University, 1200 Murchison Road, Fayetteville, NC 28301-4298, 910-672-1327 or toll-free 800-222-2594. *Fax:* 910-672-1423. *E-mail:* ktownse7@uncfsu.edu. *Website:* http://www.uncfsu.edu/.

FELICIAN UNIVERSITY
Lodi, NJ

Tuition & fees: $34,315	Average undergraduate aid package: $26,743

ABOUT THE INSTITUTION Independent Roman Catholic, coed. *Awards:* certificates, associate, bachelor's, master's, and doctoral degrees. 30 undergraduate majors. *Total enrollment:* 1,996. Undergraduates: 1,626. Freshmen: 308. Federal methodology is used as a basis for awarding need-based institutional aid.

UNDERGRADUATE EXPENSES for 2018–2019 *Application fee:* $30. *Comprehensive fee:* $47,200 includes full-time tuition ($31,915), mandatory fees ($2400), and room and board ($12,885). Full-time tuition and fees vary according to program. Room and board charges vary according to housing facility. *Part-time tuition:* $1055 per credit hour. *Part-time fees:* $475 per term. Part-time tuition and fees vary according to course load and program.

FRESHMAN FINANCIAL AID (Fall 2016) 308 applied for aid; of those 96% were deemed to have need. 100% of freshmen with need received aid; of those 10% had need fully met. *Average percent of need met:* 72% (excluding resources awarded to replace EFC). *Average financial aid package:* $30,379 (excluding resources awarded to replace EFC). 5% of all full-time freshmen had no need and received non-need-based gift aid.

UNDERGRADUATE FINANCIAL AID (Fall 2016) 1,345 applied for aid; of those 96% were deemed to have need. 99% of undergraduates with need received aid; of those 7% had need fully met. *Average percent of need met:* 65% (excluding resources awarded to replace EFC). *Average financial aid package:* $26,743 (excluding resources awarded to replace EFC). 5% of all full-time undergraduates had no need and received non-need-based gift aid.

GIFT AID (NEED-BASED) *Total amount:* $15,091,185 (28% federal, 45% state, 27% institutional). *Receiving aid:* Freshmen: 76% (240); all full-time undergraduates: 75% (1,069). *Average award:* Freshmen: $16,478; Undergraduates: $13,799. *Scholarships, grants, and awards:* Federal Pell, FSEOG, state, private, college/university gift aid from institutional funds.

GIFT AID (NON-NEED-BASED) *Total amount:* $14,931,359 (4% federal, 96% institutional). *Receiving aid:* Freshmen: 92% (292). Undergraduates: 79% (1,128). *Average award:* Freshmen: $14,225. Undergraduates: $13,431. *Scholarships, grants, and awards by category:* Academic interests/achievement: business, education, English, general academic interests/achievements, health fields, religion/biblical studies. Special characteristics: children of faculty/staff, siblings of current students.

Tuition waivers: Full or partial for employees or children of employees. **ROTC:** Army cooperative, Air Force cooperative.
LOANS Student loans: $11,088,435 (43% need-based, 57% non-need-based). **Average need-based loan:** Freshmen: $3267. Undergraduates: $4279. **Parent loans:** $3,147,826 (100% non-need-based). **Programs:** Federal Direct (Subsidized and Unsubsidized Stafford, PLUS), state.
WORK-STUDY Federal work-study: 49 jobs averaging $2236. **State or other work-study/employment:** Total amount: $247,743 (100% non-need-based). Part-time jobs available.
ATHLETIC AWARDS Total amount: $1,653,685 (100% non-need-based).
APPLYING FOR FINANCIAL AID Required financial aid forms: FAFSA, state aid form. **Financial aid deadline:** Continuous. **Notification date:** Continuous.
CONTACT Ms. Cynthia Montalvo, Executive Financial Aid Director, Felician University, 262 South Main Street, Lodi, NJ 07644, 201-559-6036. *Fax:* 201-559-6025. *E-mail:* montalvoc@felician.edu.
Website: http://www.felician.edu/.

FERRIS STATE UNIVERSITY
Big Rapids, MI

Tuition & fees (MI res): $12,180	Average undergraduate aid package: $11,610

ABOUT THE INSTITUTION State-supported, coed. **Awards:** certificates, associate, bachelor's, master's, and doctoral degrees. 114 undergraduate majors. **Total enrollment:** 13,798. Undergraduates: 12,504. Freshmen: 1,817. Federal methodology is used as a basis for awarding need-based institutional aid.
UNDERGRADUATE EXPENSES for 2017–2018 Tuition, state resident: full-time $12,180; part-time $406 per credit hour. **Tuition, nonresident:** full-time $18,270; part-time $609 per credit hour. Full-time tuition and fees vary according to location, program, and student level. Part-time tuition and fees vary according to location and student level. **College room and board:** $9894. Room and board charges vary according to board plan and housing facility.
FRESHMAN FINANCIAL AID (Fall 2017, est.) 1,683 applied for aid; of those 82% were deemed to have need. 100% of freshmen with need received aid; of those 17% had need fully met. **Average percent of need met:** 71% (excluding resources awarded to replace EFC). **Average financial aid package:** $13,160 (excluding resources awarded to replace EFC). 17% of all full-time freshmen had no need and received non-need-based gift aid.
UNDERGRADUATE FINANCIAL AID (Fall 2017, est.) 8,149 applied for aid; of those 78% were deemed to have need. 99% of undergraduates with need received aid; of those 16% had need fully met. **Average percent of need met:** 66% (excluding resources awarded to replace EFC). **Average financial aid package:** $11,610 (excluding resources awarded to replace EFC). 14% of all full-time undergraduates had no need and received non-need-based gift aid.
GIFT AID (NEED-BASED) Total amount: $26,691,230 (84% federal, 4% state, 12% institutional). **Receiving aid:** Freshmen: 64% (1,145); all full-time undergraduates: 57% (5,073). **Average award:** Freshmen: $5640; Undergraduates: $5130. **Scholarships, grants, and awards:** Federal Pell, FSEOG, state, private, college/university gift aid from institutional funds.
GIFT AID (NON-NEED-BASED) Total amount: $32,841,270 (1% federal, 27% state, 54% institutional, 18% external sources). **Receiving aid:** Freshmen: 68% (1,214). Undergraduates: 46% (4,130). **Average award:** Freshmen: $4380. Undergraduates: $4350. **Scholarships, grants, and awards by category:** Academic interests/achievement: 3,994 awards ($13,214,028 total): agriculture, architecture, biological sciences, business, communication, computer science, education, engineering/technologies, general academic interests/achievements, health fields, mathematics. Creative arts/performance: 510 awards ($1,505,100 total): applied art and design, art/fine arts, debating, general creative arts/performance, journalism/publications, music, theater/drama. Special achievements/activities: 105 awards ($40,634 total): general special achievements/activities, memberships. Special characteristics: 141 awards ($133,757 total): adult students, children and siblings of alumni, ethnic background, general special characteristics, international students, local/state students, members of minority groups, previous college experience, veterans. **Tuition waivers:** Full or partial for employees or children of employees. **ROTC:** Army cooperative.
LOANS Student loans: $60,232,110 (43% need-based, 57% non-need-based). 78% of past graduating class borrowed through all loan programs. *Average indebtedness*

per student: $35,600. **Average need-based loan:** Freshmen: $3520. Undergraduates: $4560. **Parent loans:** $8,553,420 (100% non-need-based). **Programs:** Federal Direct (Subsidized and Unsubsidized Stafford, PLUS), Perkins, Federal Nursing, college/university, alternative loans.
WORK-STUDY Federal work-study: Total amount: $1,002,490; 454 jobs averaging $2372. **State or other work-study/employment:** Total amount: $1,365,000 (100% non-need-based). 190 part-time jobs averaging $1935.
ATHLETIC AWARDS Total amount: $2,568,380 (100% non-need-based).
APPLYING FOR FINANCIAL AID Required financial aid form: FAFSA. **Financial aid deadline (priority):** 2/15. **Notification date:** Continuous beginning 3/15. Students must reply within 3 weeks of notification.
CONTACT Nancy Wencl, Assistant Director of Financial Aid, Ferris State University, 1201 South State Street, Big Rapids, MI 49307-2020, 231-591-2100 or toll-free 800-433-7747. *Fax:* 231-591-2950. *E-mail:* wencln@ferris.edu.
Website: http://www.ferris.edu/.

FERRUM COLLEGE
Ferrum, VA

ABOUT THE INSTITUTION Independent United Methodist, coed. 31 undergraduate majors.
GIFT AID (NEED-BASED) Scholarships, grants, and awards: Federal Pell, FSEOG, state, private, college/university gift aid from institutional funds.
GIFT AID (NON-NEED-BASED) Scholarships, grants, and awards by category: Academic interests/achievement: general academic interests/achievements. Special achievements/activities: general special achievements/activities, leadership, religious involvement. Special characteristics: children of faculty/staff, international students, local/state students, relatives of clergy, religious affiliation.
LOANS Programs: Federal Direct (Subsidized and Unsubsidized Stafford, PLUS), Perkins.
APPLYING FOR FINANCIAL AID Required financial aid forms: FAFSA, state aid form.
CONTACT Heather Hollandsworth, Director of Financial Aid, Ferrum College, PO Box 1000, Ferrum, VA 24088, 540-365-4282 or toll-free 800-868-9797. *Fax:* 540-365-4266. *E-mail:* hhollandsworth@ferrum.edu.
Website: http://www.ferrum.edu/.

FIDM/FASHION INSTITUTE OF DESIGN & MERCHANDISING, LOS ANGELES CAMPUS
Los Angeles, CA

Tuition & fees: $32,945	Average undergraduate aid package: N/A

ABOUT THE INSTITUTION Proprietary, coed. **Awards:** associate and bachelor's degrees (also includes Orange County Campus). 14 undergraduate majors. **Total enrollment:** 2,367. Undergraduates: 2,367. Freshmen: 372. Both federal and institutional methodology are used as a basis for awarding need-based institutional aid.
UNDERGRADUATE EXPENSES for 2018–2019 Application fee: $225. **Tuition:** full-time $31,760; part-time $685 per credit hour. Full-time tuition and fees vary according to course load, degree level, and program. Part-time tuition and fees vary according to course load, degree level, and program.
GIFT AID (NEED-BASED) Total amount: $11,536,144 (36% federal, 23% state, 39% institutional, 2% external sources). **Scholarships, grants, and awards:** Federal Pell, FSEOG, state, private, college/university gift aid from institutional funds.
GIFT AID (NON-NEED-BASED) Scholarships, grants, and awards by category: Creative arts/performance: applied art and design. **Tuition waivers:** Full or partial for employees or children of employees.
LOANS Student loans: $16,952,703 (100% need-based). **Parent loans:** $17,127,713 (100% need-based). **Programs:** Federal Direct (Subsidized and Unsubsidized Stafford, PLUS), Perkins, alternative loans.
WORK-STUDY Federal work-study: jobs available.
APPLYING FOR FINANCIAL AID Required financial aid forms: FAFSA, business/farm supplement, verification worksheet. **Financial aid deadline:** Con-

tinuous. **Notification date:** Continuous beginning 1/1. Students must reply within 1 week of notification.

CONTACT Mr. Chris Jennings, Director of Student Financial Services, FIDM/Fashion Institute of Design & Merchandising, Los Angeles Campus, 919 South Grand Avenue, Los Angeles, CA 90015, 213-624-1200 or toll-free 800-624-1200. *Website:* http://www.fidm.edu/.

FIDM/FASHION INSTITUTE OF DESIGN & MERCHANDISING, SAN FRANCISCO CAMPUS
San Francisco, CA

CONTACT Financial Aid Office, FIDM/Fashion Institute of Design & Merchandising, San Francisco Campus, 55 Stockton Street, San Francisco, CA 94108-5829, 415-675-5200 or toll-free 800-422-3436. *Website:* http://www.fidm.edu/.

FINLANDIA UNIVERSITY
Hancock, MI

CONTACT Sandra Turnquist, Director of Financial Aid, Finlandia University, 601 Quincy Street, Hancock, MI 49930, 906-487-7240 or toll-free 877-202-5491. *Fax:* 906-487-7383. *E-mail:* sandra.turnquist@finlandia.edu. *Website:* http://www.finlandia.edu/.

FISHER COLLEGE
Boston, MA

Tuition & fees: $31,384	Average undergraduate aid package: $21,050

ABOUT THE INSTITUTION Independent, coed. *Awards:* certificates, associate, bachelor's, and master's degrees. 31 undergraduate majors. *Total enrollment:* 1,923. Undergraduates: 1,882. Freshmen: 263. Federal methodology is used as a basis for awarding need-based institutional aid.

UNDERGRADUATE EXPENSES for 2018–2019 *Application fee:* $50. *Comprehensive fee:* $47,310 includes full-time tuition ($30,389), mandatory fees ($995), and room and board ($15,926). Room and board charges vary according to housing facility. *Part-time tuition:* $1143 per course. *Part-time fees:* $95 per course. Part-time tuition and fees vary according to course load.

FRESHMAN FINANCIAL AID (Fall 2016) 205 applied for aid; of those 96% were deemed to have need. 100% of freshmen with need received aid. *Average financial aid package:* $27,235 (excluding resources awarded to replace EFC). 13% of all full-time freshmen had no need and received non-need-based gift aid.

UNDERGRADUATE FINANCIAL AID (Fall 2016) 701 applied for aid; of those 98% were deemed to have need. 100% of undergraduates with need received aid. *Average financial aid package:* $21,050 (excluding resources awarded to replace EFC). 8% of all full-time undergraduates had no need and received non-need-based gift aid.

GIFT AID (NEED-BASED) *Total amount:* $7,778,351 (39% federal, 10% state, 51% institutional). *Receiving aid:* Freshmen: 87% (196); all full-time undergraduates: 78% (578). *Average award:* Freshmen: $21,658; Undergraduates: $12,480. *Scholarships, grants, and awards:* Federal Pell, FSEOG, state, private, college/university gift aid from institutional funds.

GIFT AID (NON-NEED-BASED) *Total amount:* $6,648,515 (99% institutional, 1% external sources). *Average award:* Freshmen: $9256. Undergraduates: $6534. *Scholarships, grants, and awards by category:* Academic interests/achievement: general academic interests/achievements. *Tuition waivers:* Full or partial for employees or children of employees. *ROTC:* Army cooperative.

LOANS *Student loans:* $8,973,558 (42% need-based, 58% non-need-based). 49% of past graduating class borrowed through all loan programs. *Average indebtedness per student:* $12,724. *Average need-based loan:* Freshmen: $3865. Undergrad-

uates: $4125. *Parent loans:* $3,536,854 (100% non-need-based). *Programs:* Federal Direct (Subsidized and Unsubsidized Stafford, PLUS), Perkins.

WORK-STUDY *Federal work-study:* 57 jobs averaging $1141.

APPLYING FOR FINANCIAL AID *Required financial aid form:* FAFSA. *Financial aid deadline:* 3/15. *Notification date:* Continuous beginning 1/1.

CONTACT Colleen Woods, Director of Title IV Compliance, Fisher College, 118 Beacon Street, Boston, MA 02116, 617-236-8821. *E-mail:* cwoods@fisher.edu. *Website:* http://www.fisher.edu/.

FISK UNIVERSITY
Nashville, TN

CONTACT Mary Chambliss, Director of Financial Aid, Fisk University, 1000 17th Avenue North, Nashville, TN 37208-3051, 615-329-8735 or toll-free 888-702-0022. *E-mail:* mchambliss@fisk.edu. *Website:* http://www.fisk.edu/.

FITCHBURG STATE UNIVERSITY
Fitchburg, MA

Tuition & fees (MA res): $10,155	Average undergraduate aid package: $10,255

ABOUT THE INSTITUTION State-supported, coed. *Awards:* certificates, bachelor's, and master's degrees. 61 undergraduate majors. *Total enrollment:* 7,075. Undergraduates: 4,117. Freshmen: 756. Federal methodology is used as a basis for awarding need-based institutional aid.

UNDERGRADUATE EXPENSES for 2017–2018 *Application fee:* $50. *Tuition, state resident:* full-time $970; part-time $40.42 per credit hour. *Tuition, nonresident:* full-time $7050; part-time $293.75 per credit hour. *Required fees:* full-time $9185; $382.72 per credit hour. Full-time tuition and fees vary according to class time and reciprocity agreements. Part-time tuition and fees vary according to class time and reciprocity agreements. *College room and board:* $10,676. Room and board charges vary according to board plan and housing facility.

FRESHMAN FINANCIAL AID (Fall 2016) 733 applied for aid; of those 75% were deemed to have need. 96% of freshmen with need received aid. *Average percent of need met:* 76% (excluding resources awarded to replace EFC). *Average financial aid package:* $10,177 (excluding resources awarded to replace EFC). 8% of all full-time freshmen had no need and received non-need-based gift aid.

UNDERGRADUATE FINANCIAL AID (Fall 2016) 3,002 applied for aid; of those 76% were deemed to have need. 96% of undergraduates with need received aid. *Average percent of need met:* 76% (excluding resources awarded to replace EFC). *Average financial aid package:* $10,255 (excluding resources awarded to replace EFC). 5% of all full-time undergraduates had no need and received non-need-based gift aid.

GIFT AID (NEED-BASED) *Total amount:* $11,001,010 (60% federal, 19% state, 21% institutional). *Receiving aid:* Freshmen: 53% (403); all full-time undergraduates: 47% (1,622). *Average award:* Freshmen: $7027; Undergraduates: $6611. *Scholarships, grants, and awards:* Federal Pell, FSEOG, state, private, college/university gift aid from institutional funds.

GIFT AID (NON-NEED-BASED) *Total amount:* $1,964,868 (28% state, 37% institutional, 35% external sources). *Receiving aid:* Freshmen: 35% (266). Undergraduates: 24% (830). *Average award:* Freshmen: $1417. Undergraduates: $1249. *Tuition waivers:* Full or partial for employees or children of employees, senior citizens. *ROTC:* Army.

LOANS *Student loans:* $23,332,437 (39% need-based, 61% non-need-based). 81% of past graduating class borrowed through all loan programs. *Average indebtedness per student:* $26,316. *Average need-based loan:* Freshmen: $3612. Undergraduates: $4489. *Parent loans:* $3,818,463 (100% non-need-based). *Programs:* Federal Direct (Subsidized and Unsubsidized Stafford, PLUS), Federal Nursing, state.

WORK-STUDY *Federal work-study:* 218 jobs averaging $1525.

APPLYING FOR FINANCIAL AID *Required financial aid form:* FAFSA. *Financial aid deadline (priority):* 3/1. *Notification date:* Continuous beginning 1/30.

CONTACT Office of Financial Aid, Fitchburg State University, 160 Pearl Street, Fitchburg, MA 01420, 978-665-3156 or toll-free 800-705-9692. *Fax:* 978-665-3559. *E-mail:* finaid@fitchburgstate.edu.
Website: http://www.fitchburgstate.edu/.

FIVE TOWNS COLLEGE
Dix Hills, NY

CONTACT Mr. Jason LaBonte, Financial Aid Director, Five Towns College, 305 North Service Road, Dix Hills, NY 11746-5871, 631-656-2113. *Fax:* 631-656-2191. *E-mail:* jason.labonte@ftc.edu.
Website: http://www.ftc.edu/.

FLAGLER COLLEGE
St. Augustine, FL

Tuition & fees: $18,950	Average undergraduate aid package: $12,755

ABOUT THE INSTITUTION Independent, coed. *Awards:* bachelor's and master's degrees. 33 undergraduate majors. *Total enrollment:* 2,689. Undergraduates: 2,676. Freshmen: 1,935. Federal methodology is used as a basis for awarding need-based institutional aid.

UNDERGRADUATE EXPENSES for 2018–2019 *Application fee:* $50. *Comprehensive fee:* $30,290 includes full-time tuition ($18,850), mandatory fees ($100), and room and board ($11,340). *College room only:* $5800. Full-time tuition and fees vary according to location. Room and board charges vary according to board plan and housing facility. *Part-time tuition:* $645 per credit hour. Part-time tuition and fees vary according to location.

FRESHMAN FINANCIAL AID (Fall 2017, est.) 635 applied for aid; of those 77% were deemed to have need. 100% of freshmen with need received aid; of those 16% had need fully met. *Average percent of need met:* 59% (excluding resources awarded to replace EFC). *Average financial aid package:* $13,239 (excluding resources awarded to replace EFC). 25% of all full-time freshmen had no need and received non-need-based gift aid.

UNDERGRADUATE FINANCIAL AID (Fall 2017, est.) 2,070 applied for aid; of those 81% were deemed to have need. 100% of undergraduates with need received aid; of those 15% had need fully met. *Average percent of need met:* 59% (excluding resources awarded to replace EFC). *Average financial aid package:* $12,755 (excluding resources awarded to replace EFC). 21% of all full-time undergraduates had no need and received non-need-based gift aid.

GIFT AID (NEED-BASED) *Total amount:* $14,230,510 (25% federal, 30% state, 43% institutional, 2% external sources). *Receiving aid:* Freshmen: 66% (490); all full-time undergraduates: 63% (1,646). *Average award:* Freshmen: $10,360; Undergraduates: $9197. *Scholarships, grants, and awards:* Federal Pell, FSEOG, state, private, college/university gift aid from institutional funds.

GIFT AID (NON-NEED-BASED) *Total amount:* $3,569,183 (1% federal, 48% state, 47% institutional, 4% external sources). *Receiving aid:* Freshmen: 5% (38). Undergraduates: 5% (132). *Average award:* Freshmen: $3047. Undergraduates: $2808. *Scholarships, grants, and awards by category:* Academic interests/achievement: business, communication, education, English, foreign languages, general academic interests/achievements, humanities, physical sciences, religion/biblical studies, social sciences. *Creative arts/performance:* applied art and design, art/fine arts, cinema/film/broadcasting, creative writing, performing arts, theater/drama. *Special achievements/activities:* community service, general special achievements/activities, leadership, memberships, religious involvement. *Special characteristics:* children of educators, children of faculty/staff, ethnic background, first-generation college students, general special characteristics, international students, local/state students, members of minority groups, out-of-state students. *Tuition waivers:* Full or partial for employees or children of employees.

LOANS *Student loans:* $16,675,204 (64% need-based, 36% non-need-based). 69% of past graduating class borrowed through all loan programs. *Average indebtedness per student:* $30,039. *Average need-based loan:* Freshmen: $3055. Undergraduates: $3875. *Parent loans:* $4,278,397 (46% need-based, 54% non-need-based). *Programs:* Federal Direct (Subsidized and Unsubsidized Stafford, PLUS), Perkins, state.

WORK-STUDY *Federal work-study:* Total amount: $303,293; jobs available. *State or other work-study/employment:* Total amount: $220,689 (8% need-based, 92% non-need-based). Part-time jobs available.

ATHLETIC AWARDS Total amount: $1,880,363 (45% need-based, 55% non-need-based).

APPLYING FOR FINANCIAL AID *Required financial aid forms:* FAFSA, state aid form. *Financial aid deadline (priority):* 3/1. *Notification date:* Continuous beginning 11/1. Students must reply by 5/1 or within 2 weeks of notification.

CONTACT Office of Financial Aid, Flagler College, PO Box 1027, St. Augustine, FL 32085-1027, 904-819-6225 or toll-free 800-304-4208. *Fax:* 904-819-6453. *E-mail:* financialaid@flagler.edu.
Website: http://www.flagler.edu/.

FLAGLER COLLEGE–TALLAHASSEE
Tallahassee, FL

CONTACT Financial Aid Office, Flagler College–Tallahassee, 444 Appleyard Drive, Tallahassee, FL 32304, 850-201-8070.
Website: http://www.flagler.edu/.

FLORIDA AGRICULTURAL AND MECHANICAL UNIVERSITY
Tallahassee, FL

Tuition & fees (FL res): $5785	Average undergraduate aid package: $13,408

ABOUT THE INSTITUTION State-supported, coed. *Awards:* certificates, associate, bachelor's, master's, and doctoral degrees. 50 undergraduate majors. *Total enrollment:* 9,913. Undergraduates: 8,024. Freshmen: 1,684. Federal methodology is used as a basis for awarding need-based institutional aid.

UNDERGRADUATE EXPENSES for 2018–2019 *Application fee:* $30. *Tuition, state resident:* full-time $5645; part-time $188 per credit hour. *Tuition, nonresident:* full-time $17,585. *Required fees:* full-time $140. *College room and board:* $10,594; *Room only:* $6012. Room and board charges vary according to board plan and housing facility. *Payment plan:* Tuition prepayment.

FRESHMAN FINANCIAL AID (Fall 2016) 1,274 applied for aid; of those 88% were deemed to have need. 100% of freshmen with need received aid; of those 16% had need fully met. *Average percent of need met:* 67% (excluding resources awarded to replace EFC). *Average financial aid package:* $14,953 (excluding resources awarded to replace EFC). 5% of all full-time freshmen had no need and received non-need-based gift aid.

UNDERGRADUATE FINANCIAL AID (Fall 2016) 6,306 applied for aid; of those 89% were deemed to have need. 100% of undergraduates with need received aid; of those 11% had need fully met. *Average percent of need met:* 62% (excluding resources awarded to replace EFC). *Average financial aid package:* $13,408 (excluding resources awarded to replace EFC). 2% of all full-time undergraduates had no need and received non-need-based gift aid.

GIFT AID (NEED-BASED) *Total amount:* $28,248,804 (80% federal, 9% state, 11% institutional). *Receiving aid:* Freshmen: 72% (932); all full-time undergraduates: 70% (4,621). *Average award:* Freshmen: $6226; Undergraduates: $5899. *Scholarships, grants, and awards:* Federal Pell, FSEOG, state, private, college/university gift aid from institutional funds, United Negro College Fund.

GIFT AID (NON-NEED-BASED) *Total amount:* $15,278,064 (24% state, 45% institutional, 31% external sources). *Receiving aid:* Freshmen: 52% (666). Undergraduates: 36% (2,374). *Average award:* Freshmen: $12,261. Undergraduates: $10,014. *Scholarships, grants, and awards by category:* Academic interests/achievement: agriculture, architecture, area/ethnic studies, biological sciences, business, communication, computer science, education, engineering/technologies, English, foreign languages, general academic interests/achievements, health fields, humanities, mathematics, military science, physical sciences, premedicine, social sciences. *Creative arts/performance:* applied art and design, art/fine arts, cinema/film/broadcasting, creative writing, dance, journalism/publications, music, performing arts, theater/drama. *Special achievements/activities:* cheerleading/drum major, community service, general special achievements/activities, leadership. *Special characteristics:* 435

awards ($216,741 total). ethnic background, first-generation college students, general special characteristics, local/state students. **Tuition waivers:** Full or partial for employees or children of employees, senior citizens. **ROTC:** Army, Naval, Air Force cooperative.

LOANS *Student loans:* $35,181,955 (49% need-based, 51% non-need-based). 49% of past graduating class borrowed through all loan programs. *Average indebtedness per student:* $7454. *Average need-based loan:* Freshmen: $3446. Undergraduates: $4036. *Parent loans:* $12,670,637 (100% non-need-based). *Programs:* Federal Direct (Subsidized and Unsubsidized Stafford, PLUS), Perkins, private loans.

WORK-STUDY *Federal work-study:* 240 jobs averaging $1913.

ATHLETIC AWARDS Total amount: $2,451,303 (100% non-need-based).

APPLYING FOR FINANCIAL AID *Required financial aid form:* FAFSA. *Financial aid deadline (priority):* 3/1. *Notification date:* Continuous beginning 4/15.

CONTACT Ms. Lisa A. Stewart, Director of Financial Aid, Florida Agricultural and Mechanical University, 101 Foote-Hilyer Administration Center, Tallahassee, FL 32307, 850-599-3730 or toll-free 866-642-1198.
Website: http://www.famu.edu/.

FLORIDA ATLANTIC UNIVERSITY
Boca Raton, FL

Tuition & fees (FL res): $6039	Average undergraduate aid package: $13,750

ABOUT THE INSTITUTION State-supported, coed. **Awards:** certificates, associate, bachelor's, master's, and doctoral degrees. 63 undergraduate majors. **Total enrollment:** 30,203. Undergraduates: 25,025. Freshmen: 2,768. Federal methodology is used as a basis for awarding need-based institutional aid.

UNDERGRADUATE EXPENSES for 2018–2019 Application fee: $30. *Tuition, state resident:* full-time $6039; part-time $105.07 per credit hour. *Tuition, nonresident:* full-time $21,595; part-time $598.93 per credit hour. *Required fees:* $96.22 per credit hour. Full-time tuition and fees vary according to course load. Part-time tuition and fees vary according to course load. *College room and board:* $10,388; *Room only:* $6730. Room and board charges vary according to board plan and housing facility.

FRESHMAN FINANCIAL AID (Fall 2017, est.) 2,306 applied for aid; of those 75% were deemed to have need. 99% of freshmen with need received aid; of those 18% had need fully met. *Average percent of need met:* 68% (excluding resources awarded to replace EFC). *Average financial aid package:* $13,295 (excluding resources awarded to replace EFC). 3% of all full-time freshmen had no need and received non-need-based gift aid.

UNDERGRADUATE FINANCIAL AID (Fall 2017, est.) 11,529 applied for aid; of those 85% were deemed to have need. 97% of undergraduates with need received aid; of those 13% had need fully met. *Average percent of need met:* 64% (excluding resources awarded to replace EFC). *Average financial aid package:* $13,750 (excluding resources awarded to replace EFC). 1% of all full-time undergraduates had no need and received non-need-based gift aid.

GIFT AID (NEED-BASED) *Total amount:* $73,146,628 (63% federal, 17% state, 17% institutional, 3% external sources). *Receiving aid:* Freshmen: 51% (1,425); all full-time undergraduates: 49% (7,811). *Average award:* Freshmen: $8735; Undergraduates: $7347. *Scholarships, grants, and awards:* Federal Pell, FSEOG, state, private, college/university gift aid from institutional funds, Federal Nursing.

GIFT AID (NON-NEED-BASED) *Total amount:* $10,301,859 (54% state, 18% institutional, 28% external sources). *Receiving aid:* Freshmen: 12% (344). Undergraduates: 6% (906). *Average award:* Freshmen: $4701. Undergraduates: $4220. *Scholarships, grants, and awards by category:* Academic interests/achievement: business, engineering/technologies, general academic interests/achievements, physical sciences, social sciences. Creative arts/performance: music, performing arts. *Tuition waivers:* Full or partial for employees or children of employees, senior citizens. *ROTC:* Army, Air Force cooperative.

LOANS *Student loans:* $128,195,042 (79% need-based, 21% non-need-based). 51% of past graduating class borrowed through all loan programs. *Average indebtedness per student:* $22,818. *Average need-based loan:* Freshmen: $5219. Undergraduates: $7070. *Parent loans:* $8,756,765 (49% need-based, 51% non-need-based). *Programs:* Federal Direct (Subsidized and Unsubsidized Stafford, PLUS), Perkins, Federal Nursing, college/university.

WORK-STUDY *Federal work-study:* Total amount: $917,550; 250 jobs averaging $2103. *State or other work-study/employment:* Total amount: $23,015 (100% need-based). 5 part-time jobs averaging $3331.

ATHLETIC AWARDS Total amount: $5,216,684 (26% need-based, 74% non-need-based).

APPLYING FOR FINANCIAL AID *Required financial aid form:* FAFSA. *Notification date:* Continuous.

CONTACT Tracy Boulukos, Director of Student Financial Aid, Florida Atlantic University, 777 Glades Road, Boca Raton, FL 33431-0991, 561-297-3528. *E-mail:* tbouluko@fau.edu.
Website: http://www.fau.edu/.

FLORIDA COLLEGE
Temple Terrace, FL

ABOUT THE INSTITUTION Independent, coed. **Awards:** associate and bachelor's degrees. 10 undergraduate majors. **Total enrollment:** 508. Undergraduates: 508. Freshmen: 127.

GIFT AID (NEED-BASED) *Scholarships, grants, and awards:* Federal Pell, FSEOG, state, private, college/university gift aid from institutional funds.

GIFT AID (NON-NEED-BASED) *Scholarships, grants, and awards by category:* Academic interests/achievement: business, communication, education, English, general academic interests/achievements, religion/biblical studies. Creative arts/performance: music. Special achievements/activities: general special achievements/activities. Special characteristics: children of faculty/staff.

LOANS *Programs:* Federal Direct (Subsidized and Unsubsidized Stafford, PLUS), Perkins.

APPLYING FOR FINANCIAL AID *Required financial aid form:* FAFSA.

CONTACT Stephen Blaylock, Director of Financial Aid, Florida College, 119 North Glen Arven Avenue, Temple Terrace, FL 33617, 813-988-5131 Ext. 130. *Fax:* 813-899-6772. *E-mail:* blaylocks@floridacollege.edu.
Website: http://www.floridacollege.edu/.

FLORIDA GULF COAST UNIVERSITY
Fort Myers, FL

Tuition & fees (FL res): $6118	Average undergraduate aid package: $9892

ABOUT THE INSTITUTION State-supported, coed. **Awards:** certificates, associate, bachelor's, master's, and doctoral degrees. 50 undergraduate majors. **Total enrollment:** 14,983. Undergraduates: 13,820. Freshmen: 2,632. Federal methodology is used as a basis for awarding need-based institutional aid.

UNDERGRADUATE EXPENSES for 2018–2019 Application fee: $30. *Tuition, state resident:* full-time $4191. *Tuition, nonresident:* full-time $22,328. *Required fees:* full-time $1927. Full-time tuition and fees vary according to course load. Part-time tuition and fees vary according to course load. *College room and board:* $8620; *Room only:* $4820. Room and board charges vary according to board plan.

FRESHMAN FINANCIAL AID (Fall 2016) 1,828 applied for aid; of those 75% were deemed to have need. 100% of freshmen with need received aid; of those 8% had need fully met. *Average percent of need met:* 46% (excluding resources awarded to replace EFC). *Average financial aid package:* $9419 (excluding resources awarded to replace EFC). 2% of all full-time freshmen had no need and received non-need-based gift aid.

UNDERGRADUATE FINANCIAL AID (Fall 2016) 7,440 applied for aid; of those 69% were deemed to have need. 100% of undergraduates with need received aid; of those 9% had need fully met. *Average percent of need met:* 57% (excluding resources awarded to replace EFC). *Average financial aid package:* $9892 (excluding resources awarded to replace EFC). 3% of all full-time undergraduates had no need and received non-need-based gift aid.

GIFT AID (NEED-BASED) *Total amount:* $29,146,887 (57% federal, 14% state, 25% institutional, 4% external sources). *Receiving aid:* Freshmen: 34% (876); all full-time undergraduates: 36% (3,814). *Average award:* Freshmen: $4315; Undergraduates: $5443. *Scholarships, grants, and awards:* Federal Pell, FSEOG, state, private, college/university gift aid from institutional funds.

GIFT AID (NON-NEED-BASED) *Total amount:* $3,966,760 (1% federal, 56% state, 27% institutional, 16% external sources). *Receiving aid:* Freshmen: 21% (547). Undergraduates: 13% (1,412). *Average award:* Freshmen: $2665. Undergraduates: $3297. *Scholarships, grants, and awards by category:* Academic interests/ achievement: biological sciences, business, education, engineering/technologies, general academic interests/achievements, health fields, humanities, mathematics, physical sciences, religion/biblical studies, social sciences. *Creative arts/performance:* art/fine arts, music. *Special achievements/activities:* community service, leadership. *Special characteristics:* adult students, ethnic background, handicapped students, international students, local/state students, members of minority groups, out-of-state students.

LOANS *Student loans:* $44,056,021 (75% need-based, 25% non-need-based). 51% of past graduating class borrowed through all loan programs. *Average indebtedness per student:* $24,879. *Average need-based loan:* Freshmen: $7352. Undergraduates: $7335. *Programs:* Federal Direct (Subsidized and Unsubsidized Stafford, PLUS).

WORK-STUDY *Federal work-study:* 258 jobs averaging $1627. *State or other work-study/employment:* Total amount: $4,570,436 (100% need-based). 9 part-time jobs averaging $18,531.

ATHLETIC AWARDS Total amount: $1,043,121 (100% non-need-based).

APPLYING FOR FINANCIAL AID *Required financial aid forms:* FAFSA, institution's own form, state aid form. *Financial aid deadline:* 6/30 (priority: 3/1). *Notification date:* Continuous beginning 3/15.

CONTACT Jorge Lopez-Rosado, Director of Student Financial Services, Florida Gulf Coast University, 10501 FGCU Boulevard South, Fort Myers, FL 33965, 239-590-1210 or toll-free 888-889-1095. *Fax:* 239-590-7923.

Website: http://www.fgcu.edu/.

FLORIDA INSTITUTE OF TECHNOLOGY
Melbourne, FL

Tuition & fees: $41,850	Average undergraduate aid package: $37,796

ABOUT THE INSTITUTION Independent, coed. *Awards:* certificates, bachelor's, master's, and doctoral degrees. 66 undergraduate majors. *Total enrollment:* 6,402. Undergraduates: 3,635. Freshmen: 721. Federal methodology is used as a basis for awarding need-based institutional aid.

UNDERGRADUATE EXPENSES for 2018–2019 *Comprehensive fee:* $54,730 includes full-time tuition ($41,100), mandatory fees ($750), and room and board ($12,880). *College room only:* $7000. Full-time tuition and fees vary according to course load and program. Room and board charges vary according to board plan and housing facility. *Part-time tuition:* $1170 per credit hour.

FRESHMAN FINANCIAL AID (Fall 2017, est.) 528 applied for aid; of those 87% were deemed to have need. 100% of freshmen with need received aid; of those 37% had need fully met. *Average percent of need met:* 86% (excluding resources awarded to replace EFC). *Average financial aid package:* $38,128 (excluding resources awarded to replace EFC). 28% of all full-time freshmen had no need and received non-need-based gift aid.

UNDERGRADUATE FINANCIAL AID (Fall 2017, est.) 1,871 applied for aid; of those 90% were deemed to have need. 100% of undergraduates with need received aid; of those 34% had need fully met. *Average percent of need met:* 84% (excluding resources awarded to replace EFC). *Average financial aid package:* $37,796 (excluding resources awarded to replace EFC). 31% of all full-time undergraduates had no need and received non-need-based gift aid.

GIFT AID (NEED-BASED) *Total amount:* $42,558,575 (15% federal, 11% state, 73% institutional, 1% external sources). *Receiving aid:* Freshmen: 64% (457); all full-time undergraduates: 51% (1,672). *Average award:* Freshmen: $27,222; Undergraduates: $26,815. *Scholarships, grants, and awards:* Federal Pell, FSEOG, state, private, college/university gift aid from institutional funds.

GIFT AID (NON-NEED-BASED) *Total amount:* $19,667,992 (4% federal, 5% state, 90% institutional, 1% external sources). *Receiving aid:* Freshmen: 59% (427). Undergraduates: 49% (1,589). *Average award:* Freshmen: $16,746. Undergraduates: $15,373. *Scholarships, grants, and awards by category:* Academic interests/ achievement: business, general academic interests/achievements, health fields, military science, premedicine. *Creative arts/performance:* music. *Special achievements/activ-*

ities: cheerleading/drum major, general special achievements/activities, hobbies/ interests, leadership, memberships. *Special characteristics:* children and siblings of alumni, children of faculty/staff, general special characteristics, international students, previous college experience, siblings of current students. *Tuition waivers:* Full or partial for employees or children of employees, senior citizens. *ROTC:* Army.

LOANS *Student loans:* $14,889,211 (89% need-based, 11% non-need-based). 47% of past graduating class borrowed through all loan programs. *Average indebtedness per student:* $33,135. *Average need-based loan:* Freshmen: $3602. Undergraduates: $5288. *Parent loans:* $10,159,857 (92% need-based, 8% non-need-based). *Programs:* Federal Direct (Subsidized and Unsubsidized Stafford, PLUS), Perkins, state, college/university.

WORK-STUDY *Federal work-study:* Total amount: $1,626,483; 363 jobs averaging $2500. *State or other work-study/employment:* 455 part-time jobs averaging $6342.

ATHLETIC AWARDS Total amount: $6,982,638 (49% need-based, 51% non-need-based).

APPLYING FOR FINANCIAL AID *Required financial aid forms:* FAFSA, state aid form. *Financial aid deadline (priority):* 3/1. *Notification date:* Continuous beginning 11/1. Students must reply by 5/1 or within 4 weeks of notification.

CONTACT Mr. John W. Duncan, Office of Financial Aid, Florida Institute of Technology, 150 West University Boulevard, Melbourne, FL 32901-6975, 321-674-8063 or toll-free 800-888-4348. *Fax:* 321-724-2778. *E-mail:* finaid@fit.edu. *Website:* http://www.fit.edu/.

FLORIDA INTERNATIONAL UNIVERSITY
Miami, FL

Tuition & fees (FL res): $6558	Average undergraduate aid package: $7885

ABOUT THE INSTITUTION State-supported, coed. *Awards:* certificates, bachelor's, master's, and doctoral degrees. 65 undergraduate majors. *Total enrollment:* 56,851. Undergraduates: 47,586. Freshmen: 4,298. Federal methodology is used as a basis for awarding need-based institutional aid.

UNDERGRADUATE EXPENSES for 2017–2018 *Application fee:* $30. *Tuition, state resident:* full-time $6168; part-time $205.57 per credit hour. *Tuition, nonresident:* full-time $18,566; part-time $618.87 per credit hour. *Required fees:* full-time $390. *College room and board:* $10,882; *Room only:* $6984. Room and board charges vary according to board plan and housing facility.

FRESHMAN FINANCIAL AID (Fall 2016) 3,129 applied for aid; of those 100% were deemed to have need. 95% of freshmen with need received aid; of those 8% had need fully met. *Average percent of need met:* 18% (excluding resources awarded to replace EFC). *Average financial aid package:* $7826 (excluding resources awarded to replace EFC). 23% of all full-time freshmen had no need and received non-need-based gift aid.

UNDERGRADUATE FINANCIAL AID (Fall 2016) 25,352 applied for aid; of those 98% were deemed to have need. 96% of undergraduates with need received aid; of those 9% had need fully met. *Average percent of need met:* 20% (excluding resources awarded to replace EFC). *Average financial aid package:* $7885 (excluding resources awarded to replace EFC). 4% of all full-time undergraduates had no need and received non-need-based gift aid.

GIFT AID (NEED-BASED) *Total amount:* $129,887,309 (69% federal, 9% state, 22% institutional). *Receiving aid:* Freshmen: 67% (2,345); all full-time undergraduates: 73% (19,600). *Average award:* Freshmen: $5431; Undergraduates: $5442. *Scholarships, grants, and awards:* Federal Pell, FSEOG, state, private, college/ university gift aid from institutional funds.

GIFT AID (NON-NEED-BASED) *Total amount:* $48,101,060 (7% federal, 21% state, 65% institutional, 7% external sources). *Receiving aid:* Freshmen: 71% (2,491). Undergraduates: 28% (7,351). *Average award:* Freshmen: $2241. Undergraduates: $2082. *Scholarships, grants, and awards by category:* Academic interests/ achievement: architecture, biological sciences, business, communication, computer science, education, engineering/technologies, English, foreign languages, general academic interests/achievements, health fields, humanities, mathematics, physical sciences, social sciences. *Creative arts/performance:* art/fine arts, dance, journalism/publications, music, performing arts, theater/drama. *Special characteristics:* first-generation college students, veterans, veterans' children. *Tuition waivers:* Full or partial for employees or children of employees. *ROTC:* Army, Air Force.

LOANS *Student loans:* $285,855,767 (25% need-based, 75% non-need-based). 47% of past graduating class borrowed through all loan programs. *Average indebtedness per student:* $20,022. *Average need-based loan:* Freshmen: $3278. Undergraduates: $4617. *Parent loans:* $5,134,388 (100% non-need-based). *Programs:* Federal Direct (Subsidized and Unsubsidized Stafford, PLUS), Perkins, college/university.

WORK-STUDY *Federal work-study:* jobs available. *State or other work-study/employment:* Total amount: $158,610 (100% need-based). Part-time jobs available.

ATHLETIC AWARDS Total amount: $5,809,362 (100% non-need-based).

APPLYING FOR FINANCIAL AID *Required financial aid form:* FAFSA. *Financial aid deadline:* 5/15 (priority: 3/1). *Notification date:* Continuous beginning 2/1. Students must reply by 5/1 or within 4 weeks of notification.

CONTACT Francisco Valines, Director of Financial Aid, Florida International University, 11200 SW 8th Street, PC 125, Miami, FL 33199, 305-348-7272. *Fax:* 305-348-2346. *E-mail:* francisco.valines@fiu.edu.
Website: http://www.fiu.edu/.

FLORIDA MEMORIAL UNIVERSITY
Miami-Dade, FL

CONTACT Brian Phillip, Director of Financial Aid, Florida Memorial University, 15800 Northwest 42nd Avenue, Miami, FL 33054, 305-626-3745 or toll-free 800-822-1362. *Fax:* 305-626-3106.
Website: http://www.fmuniv.edu/.

FLORIDA NATIONAL UNIVERSITY
Hialeah, FL

Tuition & fees: $13,850	Average undergraduate aid package: N/A

ABOUT THE INSTITUTION Proprietary, coed. *Awards:* certificates, diplomas, associate, bachelor's, and master's degrees. 31 undergraduate majors. *Total enrollment:* 4,169. Undergraduates: 4,023. Freshmen: 866. Institutional methodology is used as a basis for awarding need-based institutional aid.

UNDERGRADUATE EXPENSES for 2018–2019 *Tuition:* full-time $13,200; part-time $550 per credit hour. Full-time tuition and fees vary according to course level. Part-time tuition and fees vary according to course level. *Payment plans:* Guaranteed tuition, tuition prepayment.

FRESHMAN FINANCIAL AID (Fall 2016) 416 applied for aid; of those 92% were deemed to have need. 98% of freshmen with need received aid.

UNDERGRADUATE FINANCIAL AID (Fall 2016) 1,920 applied for aid; of those 95% were deemed to have need. 100% of undergraduates with need received aid.

GIFT AID (NEED-BASED) *Total amount:* $16,428,889 (81% federal, 4% state, 15% institutional). *Receiving aid:* Freshmen: 78% (368); all full-time undergraduates: 88% (1,788). *Average award:* Freshmen: $7011. *Scholarships, grants, and awards:* Federal Pell, FSEOG, state, private, college/university gift aid from institutional funds.

GIFT AID (NON-NEED-BASED) *Tuition waivers:* Full or partial for employees or children of employees.

LOANS *Student loans:* $23,809,850 (100% need-based). 95% of past graduating class borrowed through all loan programs. *Average indebtedness per student:* $10,982. *Parent loans:* $479,477 (100% need-based). *Programs:* Federal Direct (Subsidized and Unsubsidized Stafford, PLUS), Perkins.

WORK-STUDY *Federal work-study:* 19 jobs averaging $4500. *State or other work-study/employment:* Part-time jobs available.

ATHLETIC AWARDS Total amount: $413,992 (100% need-based).

APPLYING FOR FINANCIAL AID *Required financial aid form:* FAFSA. *Financial aid deadline:* Continuous. *Notification date:* Continuous.

CONTACT Mr. Omar Sanchez, Director of Financial Aid, Florida National University, 4425 West Jose Regueiro (20th) Avenue, Hialeah, FL 33012, 305-821-3333 Ext. 1003. *Fax:* 305-362-0595. *E-mail:* omarsnc@fnu.edu.
Website: http://www.fnu.edu/.

FLORIDA SOUTHERN COLLEGE
Lakeland, FL

Tuition & fees: $34,774	Average undergraduate aid package: $28,756

ABOUT THE INSTITUTION Independent United Methodist Church, coed. *Awards:* bachelor's, master's, and doctoral degrees. 63 undergraduate majors. *Total enrollment:* 3,073. Undergraduates: 2,633. Freshmen: 722. Federal methodology is used as a basis for awarding need-based institutional aid.

UNDERGRADUATE EXPENSES for 2017–2018 *Comprehensive fee:* $45,978 includes full-time tuition ($34,074), mandatory fees ($700), and room and board ($11,204). *College room only:* $6700. Room and board charges vary according to board plan and housing facility. *Part-time tuition:* $970 per credit hour. Part-time tuition and fees vary according to class time and course load.

FRESHMAN FINANCIAL AID (Fall 2017, est.) 654 applied for aid; of those 81% were deemed to have need. 100% of freshmen with need received aid; of those 33% had need fully met. *Average percent of need met:* 78% (excluding resources awarded to replace EFC). *Average financial aid package:* $29,865 (excluding resources awarded to replace EFC). 26% of all full-time freshmen had no need and received non-need-based gift aid.

UNDERGRADUATE FINANCIAL AID (Fall 2017, est.) 1,863 applied for aid; of those 85% were deemed to have need. 100% of undergraduates with need received aid; of those 28% had need fully met. *Average percent of need met:* 75% (excluding resources awarded to replace EFC). *Average financial aid package:* $28,756 (excluding resources awarded to replace EFC). 32% of all full-time undergraduates had no need and received non-need-based gift aid.

GIFT AID (NEED-BASED) *Total amount:* $38,523,941 (8% federal, 16% state, 74% institutional, 2% external sources). *Receiving aid:* Freshmen: 74% (532); all full-time undergraduates: 67% (1,571). *Average award:* Freshmen: $24,955; Undergraduates: $22,505. *Scholarships, grants, and awards:* Federal Pell, FSEOG, state, private, college/university gift aid from institutional funds, Federal Nursing.

GIFT AID (NON-NEED-BASED) *Total amount:* $14,162,696 (16% state, 79% institutional, 5% external sources). *Receiving aid:* Freshmen: 46% (331). Undergraduates: 46% (1,073). *Average award:* Freshmen: $21,247. Undergraduates: $21,720. *Scholarships, grants, and awards by category: Academic interests/achievement:* 1 award ($2203 total): agriculture, biological sciences, business, communication, education, general academic interests/achievements, health fields, physical sciences, religion/biblical studies, social sciences. *Creative arts/performance:* art/fine arts, music, theater/drama. *Special achievements/activities:* community service, general special achievements/activities, leadership. *Special characteristics:* children and siblings of alumni, children of faculty/staff, general special characteristics, local/state students, out-of-state students, relatives of clergy, religious affiliation, siblings of current students. *Tuition waivers:* Full or partial for children of alumni, employees or children of employees. *ROTC:* Army, Air Force cooperative.

LOANS *Student loans:* $16,688,939 (89% need-based, 11% non-need-based). 86% of past graduating class borrowed through all loan programs. *Average indebtedness per student:* $25,493. *Average need-based loan:* Freshmen: $5250. Undergraduates: $5466. *Parent loans:* $6,222,617 (92% need-based, 8% non-need-based). *Programs:* Federal Direct (Subsidized and Unsubsidized Stafford, PLUS), Perkins.

WORK-STUDY *Federal work-study:* Total amount: $305,245; 118 jobs averaging $2586. *State or other work-study/employment:* Total amount: $2203 (100% need-based). Part-time jobs available.

ATHLETIC AWARDS Total amount: $4,065,227 (45% need-based, 55% non-need-based).

APPLYING FOR FINANCIAL AID *Required financial aid forms:* FAFSA, institution's own form. *Financial aid deadline:* 7/1 (priority: 3/1). *Notification date:* Continuous beginning 3/1. Students must reply within 3 weeks of notification.

CONTACT Mr. William L. Healy, Director of Financial Aid, Florida Southern College, 111 Lake Hollingsworth Drive, Lakeland, FL 33801-5698, 863-680-4140 or toll-free 800-274-4131. *Fax:* 863-680-4567. *E-mail:* whealy@flsouthern.edu.
Website: http://www.flsouthern.edu/.

FLORIDA STATE UNIVERSITY
Tallahassee, FL

Tuition & fees (FL res): $6507	Average undergraduate aid package: $13,013

ABOUT THE INSTITUTION State-supported, coed. *Awards:* certificates, associate, bachelor's, master's, and doctoral degrees. 112 undergraduate majors. *Total enrollment:* 41,447. Undergraduates: 33,093. Freshmen: 6,494. Federal methodology is used as a basis for awarding need-based institutional aid.

UNDERGRADUATE EXPENSES for 2018–2019 *Application fee:* $30. *Tuition, state resident:* full-time $4640; part-time $215.55 per credit hour. *Tuition, nonresident:* full-time $19,806; part-time $721.10 per credit hour. *Required fees:* full-time $1867. Full-time tuition and fees vary according to course load, degree level, and location. Part-time tuition and fees vary according to course load, degree level, and location. *College room and board:* $10,458; *Room only:* $6380. Room and board charges vary according to board plan and housing facility. *Payment plan:* Tuition prepayment.

FRESHMAN FINANCIAL AID (Fall 2016) 5,139 applied for aid; of those 62% were deemed to have need. 98% of freshmen with need received aid; of those 21% had need fully met. *Average percent of need met:* 70% (excluding resources awarded to replace EFC). *Average financial aid package:* $14,486 (excluding resources awarded to replace EFC). 11% of all full-time freshmen had no need and received non-need-based gift aid.

UNDERGRADUATE FINANCIAL AID (Fall 2016) 20,291 applied for aid; of those 70% were deemed to have need. 98% of undergraduates with need received aid; of those 11% had need fully met. *Average percent of need met:* 65% (excluding resources awarded to replace EFC). *Average financial aid package:* $13,013 (excluding resources awarded to replace EFC). 15% of all full-time undergraduates had no need and received non-need-based gift aid.

GIFT AID (NEED-BASED) *Total amount:* $106,100,610 (38% federal, 28% state, 30% institutional, 4% external sources). *Receiving aid:* Freshmen: 47% (2,932); all full-time undergraduates: 43% (12,637). *Average award:* Freshmen: $13,458; Undergraduates: $10,859. *Scholarships, grants, and awards:* Federal Pell, FSEOG, state, private, college/university gift aid from institutional funds, Academic Competitiveness Grants, National SMART Grants.

GIFT AID (NON-NEED-BASED) *Total amount:* $14,026,363 (69% state, 22% institutional, 9% external sources). *Receiving aid:* Freshmen: 36% (2,228). Undergraduates: 27% (7,825). *Average award:* Freshmen: $5418. Undergraduates: $4987. *Scholarships, grants, and awards by category: Academic interests/achievement:* general academic interests/achievements. *Creative arts/performance:* cinema/film/broadcasting, dance, music, theater/drama. *Special characteristics:* local/state students. *Tuition waivers:* Full or partial for employees or children of employees, senior citizens. *ROTC:* Army, Naval cooperative, Air Force.

LOANS *Student loans:* $83,107,534 (78% need-based, 22% non-need-based). 50% of past graduating class borrowed through all loan programs. *Average indebtedness per student:* $23,679. *Average need-based loan:* Freshmen: $3435. Undergraduates: $4450. *Parent loans:* $13,069,334 (44% need-based, 56% non-need-based). *Programs:* Federal Direct (Subsidized and Unsubsidized Stafford, PLUS), Perkins, college/university.

WORK-STUDY *Federal work-study:* 855 jobs averaging $2400. *State or other work-study/employment:* Total amount: $60,678 (100% need-based). 21 part-time jobs averaging $2400.

ATHLETIC AWARDS Total amount: $6,002,731 (94% need-based, 6% non-need-based).

APPLYING FOR FINANCIAL AID *Required financial aid form:* FAFSA. *Financial aid deadline:* Continuous. *Notification date:* Continuous beginning 3/1.

CONTACT Darryl Marshall, Director of Financial Aid, Florida State University, University Center A4400, Tallahassee, FL 32306-2430, 850-644-5716. *Fax:* 850-644-6404. *E-mail:* ofacs@admin.fsu.edu.
Website: http://www.fsu.edu/.

FONTBONNE UNIVERSITY
St. Louis, MO

ABOUT THE INSTITUTION Independent Roman Catholic, coed. 38 undergraduate majors.

GIFT AID (NEED-BASED) *Scholarships, grants, and awards:* Federal Pell, FSEOG, state, private, college/university gift aid from institutional funds.

GIFT AID (NON-NEED-BASED) *Scholarships, grants, and awards by category: Academic interests/achievement:* computer science, English, general academic interests/achievements. *Creative arts/performance:* art/fine arts, creative writing, theater/drama. *Special achievements/activities:* community service, general special achievements/activities, leadership. *Special characteristics:* religious affiliation, siblings of current students.

LOANS *Programs:* Federal Direct (Subsidized and Unsubsidized Stafford, PLUS), Perkins, CitiAssist loans.

APPLYING FOR FINANCIAL AID *Required financial aid forms:* FAFSA, institution's own form.

CONTACT Dr. Matthew Kearney, Financial Aid Office, Fontbonne University, 6800 Wydown Boulevard, St. Louis, MO 63105-3098, 314-889-1414 or toll-free 800-205-5862. *Fax:* 314-889-1457. *E-mail:* fbufinaid@fontbonne.edu.
Website: http://www.fontbonne.edu/.

FORDHAM UNIVERSITY
New York, NY

Tuition & fees: $50,986	Average undergraduate aid package: $34,723

ABOUT THE INSTITUTION Independent Roman Catholic (Jesuit), coed. *Awards:* certificates, bachelor's, master's, and doctoral degrees (branch locations at Rose Hill and Lincoln Center). 69 undergraduate majors. *Total enrollment:* 16,037. Undergraduates: 9,599. Freshmen: 2,283. Both federal and institutional methodology are used as a basis for awarding need-based institutional aid.

UNDERGRADUATE EXPENSES for 2017–2018 *Application fee:* $70. *Comprehensive fee:* $68,431 includes full-time tuition ($49,645), mandatory fees ($1341), and room and board ($17,445). Room and board charges vary according to board plan, housing facility, and location. *Part-time tuition:* $1655 per credit hour. Part-time tuition and fees vary according to class time and course load.

FRESHMAN FINANCIAL AID (Fall 2016) 1,891 applied for aid; of those 69% were deemed to have need. 100% of freshmen with need received aid; of those 32% had need fully met. *Average percent of need met:* 80% (excluding resources awarded to replace EFC). *Average financial aid package:* $36,410 (excluding resources awarded to replace EFC). 26% of all full-time freshmen had no need and received non-need-based gift aid.

UNDERGRADUATE FINANCIAL AID (Fall 2016) 7,226 applied for aid; of those 75% were deemed to have need. 100% of undergraduates with need received aid; of those 27% had need fully met. *Average percent of need met:* 76% (excluding resources awarded to replace EFC). *Average financial aid package:* $34,723 (excluding resources awarded to replace EFC). 19% of all full-time undergraduates had no need and received non-need-based gift aid.

GIFT AID (NEED-BASED) *Total amount:* $130,407,622 (7% federal, 5% state, 84% institutional, 4% external sources). *Receiving aid:* Freshmen: 57% (1,252); all full-time undergraduates: 59% (5,191). *Average award:* Freshmen: $28,133; Undergraduates: $26,457. *Scholarships, grants, and awards:* Federal Pell, FSEOG, state, private, college/university gift aid from institutional funds.

GIFT AID (NON-NEED-BASED) *Total amount:* $43,467,583 (1% state, 89% institutional, 10% external sources). *Receiving aid:* Freshmen: 18% (396). Undergraduates: 13% (1,137). *Average award:* Freshmen: $18,451. Undergraduates: $17,059. *Scholarships, grants, and awards by category: Academic interests/achievement:* biological sciences, business, communication, foreign languages, general academic interests/achievements. *Creative arts/performance:* dance, music. *Special achievements/activities:* general special achievements/activities. *Special characteristics:* adult students, children and siblings of alumni, children of faculty/staff, children with a deceased or disabled parent, handicapped students. *Tuition waivers:* Full or partial for employees or children of employees. *ROTC:* Army, Naval cooperative, Air Force cooperative.

LOANS *Student loans:* $51,760,671 (61% need-based, 39% non-need-based). 60% of past graduating class borrowed through all loan programs. *Average indebtedness per student:* $35,735. *Average need-based loan:* Freshmen: $4999. Undergraduates: $8514. *Parent loans:* $26,434,481 (49% need-based, 51% non-need-based). *Programs:* Federal Direct (Subsidized and Unsubsidized Stafford, PLUS), Perkins.
WORK-STUDY *Federal work-study:* jobs available. *State or other work-study/employment:* Part-time jobs available.
ATHLETIC AWARDS Total amount: $13,124,045 (60% need-based, 40% non-need-based).
APPLYING FOR FINANCIAL AID *Required financial aid forms:* FAFSA, CSS Financial Aid PROFILE, state aid form, noncustodial (divorced/separated) parent's statement, business/farm supplement. *Financial aid deadline:* 2/1. *Notification date:* Continuous beginning 3/31. Students must reply by 5/1 or within 2 weeks of notification.
CONTACT Angela Van Dekker, Assistant Vice President of Student Financial Services, Fordham University, 441 East Fordham Road, Thebaud Hall, Room 208, New York, NY 10458, 718-817-3804 or toll-free 800-FORDHAM. *Fax:* 718-817-3817. *E-mail:* avandekker@fordham.edu.
Website: http://www.fordham.edu/.

FORT HAYS STATE UNIVERSITY
Hays, KS

Tuition & fees (KS res): $4007	Average undergraduate aid package: $7612

ABOUT THE INSTITUTION State-supported, coed. 66 undergraduate majors. Federal methodology is used as a basis for awarding need-based institutional aid.
UNDERGRADUATE EXPENSES for 2017–2018 *Tuition, state resident:* full-time $3120; part-time $166.95 per credit hour. *Tuition, nonresident:* full-time $10,979; part-time $494.39 per credit hour. *Required fees:* full-time $887; $36.95 per credit hour. Full-time tuition and fees vary according to course load. Part-time tuition and fees vary according to course load. *College room and board:* $7615; *Room only:* $3796. Room and board charges vary according to board plan and housing facility.
FRESHMAN FINANCIAL AID (Fall 2016) 452 applied for aid; of those 84% were deemed to have need. 96% of freshmen with need received aid; of those 8% had need fully met. *Average percent of need met:* 47% (excluding resources awarded to replace EFC). *Average financial aid package:* $7296 (excluding resources awarded to replace EFC). 17% of all full-time freshmen had no need and received non-need-based gift aid.
UNDERGRADUATE FINANCIAL AID (Fall 2016) 4,661 applied for aid; of those 84% were deemed to have need. 97% of undergraduates with need received aid; of those 9% had need fully met. *Average percent of need met:* 51% (excluding resources awarded to replace EFC). *Average financial aid package:* $7612 (excluding resources awarded to replace EFC). 10% of all full-time undergraduates had no need and received non-need-based gift aid.
GIFT AID (NEED-BASED) *Total amount:* $17,281,313 (74% federal, 5% state, 9% institutional, 12% external sources). *Receiving aid:* Freshmen: 43% (328); all full-time undergraduates: 55% (3,063). *Average award:* Freshmen: $5335; Undergraduates: $5165. *Scholarships, grants, and awards:* Federal Pell, FSEOG, state, private, college/university gift aid from institutional funds.
GIFT AID (NON-NEED-BASED) *Total amount:* $3,665,379 (1% state, 32% institutional, 67% external sources). *Receiving aid:* Freshmen: 2% (17). Undergraduates: 3% (165). *Average award:* Freshmen: $1160. Undergraduates: $1882. *Scholarships, grants, and awards by category:* *Academic interests/achievement:* agriculture, area/ethnic studies, biological sciences, business, communication, computer science, education, engineering/technologies, English, foreign languages, general academic interests/achievements, health fields, home economics, humanities, international studies, mathematics, military science, physical sciences, premedicine, social sciences. *Creative arts/performance:* applied art and design, art/fine arts, cinema/film/broadcasting, creative writing, dance, general creative arts/performance, journalism/publications, music, performing arts, theater/drama. *Special achievements/activities:* cheerleading/drum major, leadership, rodeo. *Special characteristics:* adult students, children and siblings of alumni, children of faculty/staff, general special characteristics, international students, veterans, veterans' children. *Tuition waivers:* Full or partial for employees or children of employees.
LOANS *Student loans:* $33,556,379 (79% need-based, 21% non-need-based). 67% of past graduating class borrowed through all loan programs. *Average indebtedness*

per student: $28,368. *Average need-based loan:* Freshmen: $2986. Undergraduates: $3982. *Parent loans:* $3,538,266 (28% need-based, 72% non-need-based). *Programs:* Federal Direct (Subsidized and Unsubsidized Stafford, PLUS), Perkins, college/university.
WORK-STUDY *Federal work-study:* jobs available. *State or other work-study/employment:* Total amount: $92,404 (63% need-based, 37% non-need-based). Part-time jobs available.
ATHLETIC AWARDS Total amount: $2,009,480 (50% need-based, 50% non-need-based).
APPLYING FOR FINANCIAL AID *Required financial aid forms:* FAFSA, institution's own form. *Financial aid deadline (priority):* 12/1. *Notification date:* Continuous beginning 12/1. Students must reply within 2 weeks of notification.
CONTACT Wendy Rohleder-Sook, Director of Financial Assistance, Fort Hays State University, Picken Hall, Room 202, 600 Park Street, Hays, KS 67601, 785-628-4408 or toll-free 800-628-FHSU. *Fax:* 785-628-4014. *E-mail:* finaid@fhsu.edu.
Website: http://www.fhsu.edu/.

FORT LEWIS COLLEGE
Durango, CO

Tuition & fees (CO res): $5609	Average undergraduate aid package: $16,444

ABOUT THE INSTITUTION State-supported, coed. *Awards:* certificates, bachelor's, and master's degrees. 55 undergraduate majors. *Total enrollment:* 3,331. Undergraduates: 3,299. Freshmen: 706. Federal methodology is used as a basis for awarding need-based institutional aid.
UNDERGRADUATE EXPENSES for 2017–2018 *Application fee:* $40. *Tuition, state resident:* full-time $3720; part-time $280 per credit hour. *Tuition, nonresident:* full-time $16,872; part-time $703 per credit hour. *Required fees:* full-time $1889; $62.95 per credit hour. Full-time tuition and fees vary according to course load and reciprocity agreements. Part-time tuition and fees vary according to course load and reciprocity agreements. *College room and board:* $9416; *Room only:* $4708. Room and board charges vary according to board plan and housing facility.
FRESHMAN FINANCIAL AID (Fall 2016) 569 applied for aid; of those 79% were deemed to have need. 100% of freshmen with need received aid; of those 15% had need fully met. *Average percent of need met:* 87% (excluding resources awarded to replace EFC). *Average financial aid package:* $15,593 (excluding resources awarded to replace EFC). 16% of all full-time freshmen had no need and received non-need-based gift aid.
UNDERGRADUATE FINANCIAL AID (Fall 2016) 2,110 applied for aid; of those 84% were deemed to have need. 99% of undergraduates with need received aid; of those 16% had need fully met. *Average percent of need met:* 90% (excluding resources awarded to replace EFC). *Average financial aid package:* $16,444 (excluding resources awarded to replace EFC). 15% of all full-time undergraduates had no need and received non-need-based gift aid.
GIFT AID (NEED-BASED) *Total amount:* $12,590,700 (41% federal, 11% state, 28% institutional, 20% external sources). *Receiving aid:* Freshmen: 54% (416); all full-time undergraduates: 50% (1,595). *Average award:* Freshmen: $4951; Undergraduates: $4959. *Scholarships, grants, and awards:* Federal Pell, FSEOG, state, private, college/university gift aid from institutional funds.
GIFT AID (NON-NEED-BASED) *Total amount:* $3,269,343 (1% state, 79% institutional, 20% external sources). *Receiving aid:* Freshmen: 3% (21). Undergraduates: 2% (78). *Average award:* Freshmen: $4687. Undergraduates: $4588. *Scholarships, grants, and awards by category:* *Academic interests/achievement:* area/ethnic studies, biological sciences, business, communication, education, English, general academic interests/achievements, humanities, mathematics, physical sciences, social sciences. *Creative arts/performance:* art/fine arts, journalism/publications, music, performing arts, theater/drama. *Special achievements/activities:* general special achievements/activities, leadership. *Special characteristics:* adult students, children and siblings of alumni, children of faculty/staff, ethnic background, first-generation college students, general special characteristics, handicapped students, international students, local/state students, out-of-state students, veterans' children. *Tuition waivers:* Full or partial for minority students, employees or children of employees, senior citizens.
LOANS *Student loans:* $16,018,868 (51% need-based, 49% non-need-based). 57% of past graduating class borrowed through all loan programs. *Average indebtedness per student:* $20,988. *Average need-based loan:* Freshmen: $3367. Undergrad-

uates: $3981. *Parent loans:* $17,600,878 (12% need-based, 88% non-need-based). *Programs:* Federal Direct (Subsidized and Unsubsidized Stafford, PLUS), Perkins. **WORK-STUDY** *Federal work-study:* 157 jobs averaging $1754. *State or other work-study/employment:* Total amount: $482,988 (86% need-based, 14% non-need-based). 250 part-time jobs averaging $1932. **ATHLETIC AWARDS** Total amount: $2,177,866 (42% need-based, 58% non-need-based).

APPLYING FOR FINANCIAL AID *Required financial aid form:* FAFSA. *Financial aid deadline (priority):* 11/15. *Notification date:* Continuous beginning 3/1. Students must reply by 9/16.

CONTACT Ms. Tracey Piccoli, Director of Financial Aid, Fort Lewis College, 1000 Rim Drive, 101 Miller Student Services Building, Durango, CO 81301, 800-352-7512 or toll-free 877-FLC-COLO. *Fax:* 970-247-7108. *E-mail:* finaid_off@fortlewis.edu. *Website:* http://www.fortlewis.edu/.

FORT VALLEY STATE UNIVERSITY
Fort Valley, GA

CONTACT Mr. James Stotts, Office of Financial Aid, Fort Valley State University, 1005 State University Drive, Fort Valley, GA 31030, 478-825-6182 or toll-free 877-462-3878. *Fax:* 478-825-6976. *E-mail:* parksc@tvsu.edu. *Website:* http://www.fvsu.edu/.

FRAMINGHAM STATE UNIVERSITY
Framingham, MA

Tuition & fees (MA res): $9920	Average undergraduate aid package: $9800

ABOUT THE INSTITUTION State-supported, coed. *Awards:* certificates, bachelor's, and master's degrees. 33 undergraduate majors. *Total enrollment:* 5,691. Undergraduates: 4,126. Freshmen: 764. Federal methodology is used as a basis for awarding need-based institutional aid.

UNDERGRADUATE EXPENSES for 2018–2019 *Application fee:* $50. *Tuition, state resident:* full-time $970; part-time $162 per course. *Tuition, nonresident:* full-time $7050; part-time $1175 per course. *Required fees:* full-time $8950; $1556 per course. Full-time tuition and fees vary according to class time and degree level. Part-time tuition and fees vary according to class time, course load, and degree level. *College room and board:* $11,820; *Room only:* $7690. Room and board charges vary according to board plan and housing facility. *Payment plan:* Tuition prepayment.

FRESHMAN FINANCIAL AID (Fall 2016) 634 applied for aid; of those 83% were deemed to have need. 100% of freshmen with need received aid; of those 27% had need fully met. *Average percent of need met:* 60% (excluding resources awarded to replace EFC). *Average financial aid package:* $9900 (excluding resources awarded to replace EFC). 6% of all full-time freshmen had no need and received non-need-based gift aid.

UNDERGRADUATE FINANCIAL AID (Fall 2016) 2,498 applied for aid; of those 79% were deemed to have need. 100% of undergraduates with need received aid; of those 35% had need fully met. *Average percent of need met:* 60% (excluding resources awarded to replace EFC). *Average financial aid package:* $9800 (excluding resources awarded to replace EFC). 6% of all full-time undergraduates had no need and received non-need-based gift aid.

GIFT AID (NEED-BASED) *Total amount:* $10,743,839 (54% federal, 21% state, 22% institutional, 3% external sources). *Receiving aid:* Freshmen: 61% (448); all full-time undergraduates: 43% (1,598). *Average award:* Freshmen: $5650; Undergraduates: $4600. *Scholarships, grants, and awards:* Federal Pell, FSEOG, state, private, college/university gift aid from institutional funds.

GIFT AID (NON-NEED-BASED) *Total amount:* $572,282 (6% state, 77% institutional, 17% external sources). *Receiving aid:* Freshmen: 9% (66). Undergraduates: 2% (85). *Average award:* Freshmen: $1200. Undergraduates: $2100. *Scholarships, grants, and awards by category:* Academic interests/achievement: biological sciences, education, engineering/technologies, English, general academic interests/achievements, home economics, mathematics, physical sciences. *Special characteristics:* children of faculty/staff, children of public servants, children of union members/

company employees, veterans. *Tuition waivers:* Full or partial for employees or children of employees, senior citizens.

LOANS *Student loans:* $22,858,033 (59% need-based, 41% non-need-based). 83% of past graduating class borrowed through all loan programs. *Average indebtedness per student:* $30,781. *Average need-based loan:* Freshmen: $4800. Undergraduates: $5150. *Parent loans:* $4,742,689 (41% need-based, 59% non-need-based). *Programs:* Federal Direct (Subsidized and Unsubsidized Stafford, PLUS), Perkins, state.

WORK-STUDY *Federal work-study:* jobs available. *State or other work-study/employment:* Total amount: $57,547 (100% need-based). Part-time jobs available.

APPLYING FOR FINANCIAL AID *Required financial aid form:* FAFSA. *Financial aid deadline (priority):* 3/1. *Notification date:* Continuous beginning 3/15. Students must reply by 5/1 or within 2 weeks of notification.

CONTACT Office of Financial Aid, Framingham State University, 100 State Street, PO Box 9101, Framingham, MA 01701-9101, 508-626-4534. *Fax:* 508-626-4598. *Website:* http://www.framingham.edu/.

FRANCISCAN MISSIONARIES OF OUR LADY UNIVERSITY
Baton Rouge, LA

CONTACT Tiffany D. Magee, Director of Financial Aid, Franciscan Missionaries of Our Lady University, 7434 Perkins Road, Baton Rouge, LA 70808, 225-768-1701. *Fax:* 225-490-1632. *E-mail:* tiffany.magee@ololcollege.edu. *Website:* http://www.franu.edu/.

FRANCISCAN UNIVERSITY OF STEUBENVILLE
Steubenville, OH

Tuition & fees: $26,430	Average undergraduate aid package: $17,301

ABOUT THE INSTITUTION Independent Roman Catholic, coed. *Awards:* associate, bachelor's, and master's degrees. 33 undergraduate majors. *Total enrollment:* 2,759. Undergraduates: 2,090. Freshmen: 456. Federal methodology is used as a basis for awarding need-based institutional aid.

UNDERGRADUATE EXPENSES for 2017–2018 *Application fee:* $20. *Comprehensive fee:* $34,830 includes full-time tuition ($25,970), mandatory fees ($460), and room and board ($8400). *College room only:* $4800. Room and board charges vary according to board plan. Part-time tuition and fees vary according to class time and course load.

FRESHMAN FINANCIAL AID (Fall 2017, est.) 370 applied for aid; of those 78% were deemed to have need. 100% of freshmen with need received aid; of those 18% had need fully met. *Average percent of need met:* 68% (excluding resources awarded to replace EFC). *Average financial aid package:* $17,368 (excluding resources awarded to replace EFC). 28% of all full-time freshmen had no need and received non-need-based gift aid.

UNDERGRADUATE FINANCIAL AID (Fall 2017, est.) 1,582 applied for aid; of those 81% were deemed to have need. 100% of undergraduates with need received aid; of those 17% had need fully met. *Average percent of need met:* 61% (excluding resources awarded to replace EFC). *Average financial aid package:* $17,301 (excluding resources awarded to replace EFC). 32% of all full-time undergraduates had no need and received non-need-based gift aid.

GIFT AID (NEED-BASED) *Total amount:* $15,331,865 (15% federal, 2% state, 67% institutional, 16% external sources). *Receiving aid:* Freshmen: 60% (287); all full-time undergraduates: 64% (1,275). *Average award:* Freshmen: $14,474; Undergraduates: $13,194. *Scholarships, grants, and awards:* Federal Pell, FSEOG, state, private, college/university gift aid from institutional funds.

GIFT AID (NON-NEED-BASED) *Receiving aid:* Freshmen: 8% (40). Undergraduates: 7% (136). *Average award:* Freshmen: $7126. Undergraduates: $6928. *Scholarships, grants, and awards by category:* Academic interests/achievement: general academic interests/achievements. *Special achievements/activ-*

ities: religious involvement. *Special characteristics:* children of faculty/staff, international students, local/state students, relatives of clergy, religious affiliation, siblings of current students. *Tuition waivers:* Full or partial for employees or children of employees. *ROTC:* Army, Air Force cooperative.
LOANS *Student loans:* $15,526,392 (61% need-based, 39% non-need-based). 89% of past graduating class borrowed through all loan programs. *Average indebtedness per student:* $34,222. *Average need-based loan:* Freshmen: $3340. Undergraduates: $4436. *Parent loans:* $3,618,181 (46% need-based, 54% non-need-based). *Programs:* Federal Direct (Subsidized and Unsubsidized Stafford, PLUS).
WORK-STUDY *Federal work-study:* Total amount: $144,812; jobs available. *State or other work-study/employment:* Total amount: $330,871 (51% need-based, 49% non-need-based). Part-time jobs available.
APPLYING FOR FINANCIAL AID *Required financial aid form:* FAFSA. *Financial aid deadline (priority):* 4/1. *Notification date:* Continuous beginning 11/15.
CONTACT Jody Peeler, Director of Financial Aid, Franciscan University of Steubenville, 1235 University Boulevard, Steubenville, OH 43952-1763, 740-284-5216 or toll-free 800-783-6220. *Fax:* 740-284-5469. *E-mail:* jpeeler@franciscan.edu. *Website:* http://www.franciscan.edu/.

children. *Tuition waivers:* Full or partial for employees or children of employees, senior citizens. *ROTC:* Army.
LOANS *Student loans:* $20,452,312 (86% need-based, 14% non-need-based). 80% of past graduating class borrowed through all loan programs. *Average indebtedness per student:* $36,082. *Average need-based loan:* Freshmen: $3308. Undergraduates: $4158. *Parent loans:* $4,409,813 (67% need-based, 33% non-need-based). *Programs:* Federal Direct (Subsidized and Unsubsidized Stafford, PLUS), Perkins, Federal Nursing, college/university.
WORK-STUDY *Federal work-study:* Total amount: $404,895; jobs available. *State or other work-study/employment:* Total amount: $247,832 (100% non-need-based). Part-time jobs available.
ATHLETIC AWARDS Total amount: $914,936 (52% need-based, 48% non-need-based).
APPLYING FOR FINANCIAL AID *Required financial aid form:* FAFSA. *Financial aid deadline (priority):* 3/1. *Notification date:* Continuous beginning 11/1.
CONTACT Kim Ellisor, Director of Financial Assistance, Francis Marion University, PO Box 100547, Florence, SC 29502-0547, 843-661-1190 or toll-free 800-368-7551. *Website:* http://www.fmarion.edu/.

FRANCIS MARION UNIVERSITY
Florence, SC

Tuition & fees (SC res): $10,742	Average undergraduate aid package: $12,437

ABOUT THE INSTITUTION State-supported, coed. *Awards:* certificates, bachelor's, and master's degrees. 33 undergraduate majors. *Total enrollment:* 3,786. Undergraduates: 3,460. Freshmen: 690. Federal methodology is used as a basis for awarding need-based institutional aid.
UNDERGRADUATE EXPENSES for 2017–2018 *Application fee:* $41. *Tuition, state resident:* full-time $10,178; part-time $508.90 per credit hour. *Tuition, nonresident:* full-time $20,354; part-time $1018 per credit hour. *Required fees:* full-time $564; $15.20 per credit hour or $87.80 per term. Full-time tuition and fees vary according to degree level and program. Part-time tuition and fees vary according to course load, degree level, and program. *College room and board:* $7948; *Room only:* $4490. Room and board charges vary according to board plan and housing facility.
FRESHMAN FINANCIAL AID (Fall 2017, est.) 631 applied for aid; of those 88% were deemed to have need. 100% of freshmen with need received aid; of those 10% had need fully met. *Average percent of need met:* 68% (excluding resources awarded to replace EFC). *Average financial aid package:* $13,021 (excluding resources awarded to replace EFC). 5% of all full-time freshmen had no need and received non-need-based gift aid.
UNDERGRADUATE FINANCIAL AID (Fall 2017, est.) 2,575 applied for aid; of those 90% were deemed to have need. 100% of undergraduates with need received aid; of those 10% had need fully met. *Average percent of need met:* 64% (excluding resources awarded to replace EFC). *Average financial aid package:* $12,437 (excluding resources awarded to replace EFC). 2% of all full-time undergraduates had no need and received non-need-based gift aid.
GIFT AID (NEED-BASED) *Total amount:* $17,132,692 (52% federal, 41% state, 5% institutional, 2% external sources). *Receiving aid:* Freshmen: 80% (550); all full-time undergraduates: 75% (2,206). *Average award:* Freshmen: $8900; Undergraduates: $7413. *Scholarships, grants, and awards:* Federal Pell, FSEOG, state, private, college/university gift aid from institutional funds, Federal Nursing.
GIFT AID (NON-NEED-BASED) *Total amount:* $1,877,398 (82% state, 13% institutional, 5% external sources). *Receiving aid:* Freshmen: 5% (37). Undergraduates: 3% (103). *Average award:* Freshmen: $2361. Undergraduates: $2230. *Scholarships, grants, and awards by category:* Academic interests/achievement: biological sciences, business, communication, computer science, education, engineering/technologies, English, foreign languages, general academic interests/achievements, home economics, humanities, mathematics, physical sciences, premedicine, social sciences. *Creative arts/performance:* art/fine arts, journalism/publications, music, performing arts, theater/drama. *Special achievements/activities:* cheerleading/drum major, community service, hobbies/interests, leadership, memberships. *Special characteristics:* adult students, children and siblings of alumni, children of faculty/staff, children of union members/company employees, handicapped students, international students, local/state students, members of minority groups, out-of-state students, public servants, spouses of deceased or disabled public servants, veterans, veterans'

FRANKLIN & MARSHALL COLLEGE
Lancaster, PA

Tuition & fees: $54,380	Average undergraduate aid package: $50,865

ABOUT THE INSTITUTION Independent, coed. *Awards:* bachelor's degrees. 41 undergraduate majors. *Total enrollment:* 2,283. Undergraduates: 2,289. Freshmen: 645. Institutional methodology is used as a basis for awarding need-based institutional aid.
UNDERGRADUATE EXPENSES for 2017–2018 *Application fee:* $60. *One-time required fee:* $200. *Comprehensive fee:* $67,960 includes full-time tuition ($54,280), mandatory fees ($100), and room and board ($13,580). *College room only:* $8030. Room and board charges vary according to board plan and housing facility. *Part-time tuition:* $6785 per course. Part-time tuition and fees vary according to course load.
FRESHMAN FINANCIAL AID (Fall 2017, est.) 459 applied for aid; of those 83% were deemed to have need. 100% of freshmen with need received aid; of those 100% had need fully met. *Average percent of need met:* 100% (excluding resources awarded to replace EFC). *Average financial aid package:* $52,315 (excluding resources awarded to replace EFC).
UNDERGRADUATE FINANCIAL AID (Fall 2017, est.) 1,400 applied for aid; of those 88% were deemed to have need. 100% of undergraduates with need received aid; of those 100% had need fully met. *Average percent of need met:* 100% (excluding resources awarded to replace EFC). *Average financial aid package:* $50,865 (excluding resources awarded to replace EFC). 1% of all full-time undergraduates had no need and received non-need-based gift aid.
GIFT AID (NEED-BASED) *Total amount:* $56,890,764 (4% federal, 1% state, 92% institutional, 3% external sources). *Receiving aid:* Freshmen: 59% (379); all full-time undergraduates: 54% (1,224). *Average award:* Freshmen: $48,311; Undergraduates: $46,102. *Scholarships, grants, and awards:* Federal Pell, FSEOG, state, private, college/university gift aid from institutional funds.
GIFT AID (NON-NEED-BASED) *Total amount:* $2,014,389 (1% federal, 32% institutional, 67% external sources). *Receiving aid:* Freshmen: 17% (109). Undergraduates: 15% (337). *Average award:* Undergraduates: $12,125. *Scholarships, grants, and awards by category:* Creative arts/performance: music. *Tuition waivers:* Full or partial for employees or children of employees.
LOANS *Student loans:* $9,776,975 (47% need-based, 53% non-need-based). 57% of past graduating class borrowed through all loan programs. *Average indebtedness per student:* $27,011. *Average need-based loan:* Freshmen: $2988. Undergraduates: $4107. *Parent loans:* $3,254,399 (4% need-based, 96% non-need-based). *Programs:* Federal Direct (Subsidized and Unsubsidized Stafford, PLUS), college/university.
WORK-STUDY *Federal work-study:* Total amount: $1,514,651; jobs available. *State or other work-study/employment:* Total amount: $449,160 (72% need-based, 28% non-need-based). Part-time jobs available.

APPLYING FOR FINANCIAL AID *Required financial aid forms:* FAFSA, CSS Financial Aid PROFILE, noncustodial (divorced/separated) parent's statement. *Financial aid deadline:* 2/1. *Notification date:* 4/1. Students must reply by 5/1.

CONTACT Mr. Clarke Paine, Director of Financial Aid, Franklin & Marshall College, PO Box 3003, Lancaster, PA 17604-3003, 717-358-3991 or toll-free 877-678-9111. *Fax:* 717-358-4462. *E-mail:* clarke.paine@fandm.edu. *Website:* http://www.fandm.edu/.

FRANKLIN COLLEGE
Franklin, IN

Tuition & fees: $30,920	Average undergraduate aid package: $22,129

ABOUT THE INSTITUTION Independent American Baptist Churches in the U.S.A., coed. *Awards:* bachelor's and master's degrees. 34 undergraduate majors. *Total enrollment:* 1,034. Undergraduates: 1,016. Freshmen: 267. Federal methodology is used as a basis for awarding need-based institutional aid.

UNDERGRADUATE EXPENSES for 2017–2018 *Application fee:* $40. *Comprehensive fee:* $40,135 includes full-time tuition ($30,735), mandatory fees ($185), and room and board ($9215). *College room only:* $5490. Full-time tuition and fees vary according to course load and degree level. Room and board charges vary according to board plan. *Part-time tuition:* $445 per credit hour. *Part-time fees:* $6 per credit hour. Part-time tuition and fees vary according to course load and degree level.

FRESHMAN FINANCIAL AID (Fall 2016) 232 applied for aid; of those 91% were deemed to have need. 100% of freshmen with need received aid; of those 15% had need fully met. *Average percent of need met:* 70% (excluding resources awarded to replace EFC). *Average financial aid package:* $22,156 (excluding resources awarded to replace EFC). 11% of all full-time freshmen had no need and received non-need-based gift aid.

UNDERGRADUATE FINANCIAL AID (Fall 2016) 906 applied for aid; of those 90% were deemed to have need. 100% of undergraduates with need received aid; of those 15% had need fully met. *Average percent of need met:* 72% (excluding resources awarded to replace EFC). *Average financial aid package:* $22,129 (excluding resources awarded to replace EFC). 15% of all full-time undergraduates had no need and received non-need-based gift aid.

GIFT AID (NEED-BASED) *Total amount:* $14,902,112 (10% federal, 16% state, 71% institutional, 3% external sources). *Receiving aid:* Freshmen: 89% (211); all full-time undergraduates: 84% (813). *Average award:* Freshmen: $19,557; Undergraduates: $18,625. *Scholarships, grants, and awards:* Federal Pell, FSEOG, state, private, college/university gift aid from institutional funds.

GIFT AID (NON-NEED-BASED) *Total amount:* $2,687,416 (1% state, 91% institutional, 8% external sources). *Receiving aid:* Freshmen: 13% (32). Undergraduates: 12% (116). *Average award:* Freshmen: $12,685. Undergraduates: $13,321. *Scholarships, grants, and awards by category: Academic interests/achievement:* general academic interests/achievements. *Creative arts/performance:* art/fine arts, journalism/publications, music, performing arts, theater/drama. *Special achievements/activities:* community service, general special achievements/activities, leadership, memberships, religious involvement. *Special characteristics:* children and siblings of alumni, children of current students, children of faculty/staff, ethnic background, first-generation college students, handicapped students, local/state students, members of minority groups, out-of-state students, relatives of clergy, religious affiliation, siblings of current students, spouses of current students, veterans, veterans' children. *Tuition waivers:* Full or partial for employees or children of employees, senior citizens. *ROTC:* Army cooperative.

LOANS *Student loans:* $6,920,362 (70% need-based, 30% non-need-based). 84% of past graduating class borrowed through all loan programs. *Average indebtedness per student:* $36,145. *Average need-based loan:* Freshmen: $3130. Undergraduates: $4294. *Parent loans:* $2,810,398 (43% need-based, 57% non-need-based). *Programs:* Federal Direct (Subsidized and Unsubsidized Stafford, PLUS), Perkins, college/university.

WORK-STUDY *Federal work-study:* jobs available. *State or other work-study/employment:* Total amount: $5200 (41% need-based, 59% non-need-based). Part-time jobs available.

APPLYING FOR FINANCIAL AID *Required financial aid form:* FAFSA. *Financial aid deadline (priority):* 12/1. *Notification date:* Continuous beginning 12/15. Students must reply by 5/1.

CONTACT Mr. James Vincent-Dunn, Director of Financial Aid, Franklin College, 101 Branigin Boulevard, Franklin, IN 46131-2598, 317-738-8073 or toll-free 800-852-0232. *Fax:* 317-738-8072. *E-mail:* jvincent-dunn@franklincollege.edu. *Website:* http://www.franklincollege.edu/.

FRANKLIN PIERCE UNIVERSITY
Rindge, NH

Tuition & fees: $34,995	Average undergraduate aid package: $27,928

ABOUT THE INSTITUTION Independent, coed. *Awards:* certificates, associate, bachelor's, master's, and doctoral degrees (profile does not reflect significant enrollment at 6 continuing education sites; master's degree is only offered at these sites). 47 undergraduate majors. *Total enrollment:* 2,311. Undergraduates: 1,711. Freshmen: 466. Federal methodology is used as a basis for awarding need-based institutional aid.

UNDERGRADUATE EXPENSES for 2017–2018 *Application fee:* $40. *Comprehensive fee:* $48,077 includes full-time tuition ($32,445), mandatory fees ($2550), and room and board ($13,082). *College room only:* $7622. Full-time tuition and fees vary according to course load, degree level, location, and program. Room and board charges vary according to board plan, housing facility, and student level. *Part-time tuition:* $1082 per credit hour. Part-time tuition and fees vary according to course load, degree level, location, and program.

FRESHMAN FINANCIAL AID (Fall 2017, est.) 397 applied for aid; of those 93% were deemed to have need. 100% of freshmen with need received aid; of those 23% had need fully met. *Average percent of need met:* 71% (excluding resources awarded to replace EFC). *Average financial aid package:* $26,482 (excluding resources awarded to replace EFC). 13% of all full-time freshmen had no need and received non-need-based gift aid.

UNDERGRADUATE FINANCIAL AID (Fall 2017, est.) 1,193 applied for aid; of those 93% were deemed to have need. 100% of undergraduates with need received aid; of those 20% had need fully met. *Average percent of need met:* 75% (excluding resources awarded to replace EFC). *Average financial aid package:* $27,928 (excluding resources awarded to replace EFC). 14% of all full-time undergraduates had no need and received non-need-based gift aid.

GIFT AID (NEED-BASED) *Total amount:* $31,583,852 (7% federal, 92% institutional, 1% external sources). *Receiving aid:* Freshmen: 85% (369); all full-time undergraduates: 8% (110). *Average award:* Freshmen: $23,255; Undergraduates: $23,562. *Scholarships, grants, and awards:* Federal Pell, FSEOG, state, private, college/university gift aid from institutional funds.

GIFT AID (NON-NEED-BASED) *Total amount:* $2,107,547 (100% institutional). *Receiving aid:* Freshmen: 17% (76). Undergraduates: 15% (193). *Average award:* Freshmen: $18,726. Undergraduates: $18,494. *Scholarships, grants, and awards by category: Academic interests/achievement:* communication, general academic interests/achievements. *Creative arts/performance:* performing arts, theater/drama. *Special achievements/activities:* general special achievements/activities, leadership. *Special characteristics:* adult students, children and siblings of alumni, children of current students, children of educators, children of faculty/staff, general special characteristics, international students, local/state students, married students, parents of current students, siblings of current students, spouses of current students. *Tuition waivers:* Full or partial for employees or children of employees, senior citizens. *ROTC:* Army cooperative, Air Force cooperative.

LOANS *Student loans:* $7,756,298 (54% need-based, 46% non-need-based). 84% of past graduating class borrowed through all loan programs. *Average indebtedness per student:* $41,661. *Average need-based loan:* Freshmen: $3383. Undergraduates: $4652. *Parent loans:* $6,476,009 (100% need-based). *Programs:* Federal Direct (Subsidized and Unsubsidized Stafford, PLUS), Perkins.

WORK-STUDY *Federal work-study:* Total amount: $928,825; jobs available. *State or other work-study/employment:* Part-time jobs available.

ATHLETIC AWARDS Total amount: $2,506,193 (100% non-need-based).

APPLYING FOR FINANCIAL AID *Required financial aid form:* FAFSA. *Financial aid deadline (priority):* 3/1. *Notification date:* Continuous beginning 12/1. Students must reply by 6/1.

CONTACT Kenneth Ferreira, Associate Vice President for Student Financial Services, Franklin Pierce University, 40 University Drive, Rindge, NH 03461-0060, 603-899-4180 or toll-free 800-437-0048. *Fax:* 603-899-4372. *E-mail:* ferreirak@ franklinpierce.edu.
Website: http://www.franklinpierce.edu/.

FRANKLIN UNIVERSITY
Columbus, OH

CONTACT Ms. Marlowe Collier, Financial Aid Assistant, Franklin University, 201 South Grant Avenue, Columbus, OH 43215-5399, 614-797-4700 or toll-free 877-341-6300. *Fax:* 614-220-8931. *E-mail:* finaid@franklin.edu.
Website: http://www.franklin.edu/.

FRANKLIN W. OLIN COLLEGE OF ENGINEERING
Needham, MA

Tuition & fees: $51,080	Average undergraduate aid package: $47,140

ABOUT THE INSTITUTION Independent, coed. *Awards:* bachelor's degrees. 3 undergraduate majors. *Total enrollment:* 380. Undergraduates: 380. Freshmen: 90. Federal methodology is used as a basis for awarding need-based institutional aid.

UNDERGRADUATE EXPENSES for 2018–2019 *Application fee:* $85. *One-time required fee:* $2656. *Comprehensive fee:* $67,380 includes full-time tuition ($50,400), mandatory fees ($680), and room and board ($16,300). *Part-time tuition:* $1575 per credit hour.

FRESHMAN FINANCIAL AID (Fall 2017, est.) 63 applied for aid; of those 79% were deemed to have need. 100% of freshmen with need received aid; of those 100% had need fully met. *Average percent of need met:* 100% (excluding resources awarded to replace EFC). *Average financial aid package:* $50,941 (excluding resources awarded to replace EFC). 44% of all full-time freshmen had no need and received non-need-based gift aid.

UNDERGRADUATE FINANCIAL AID (Fall 2017, est.) 187 applied for aid; of those 87% were deemed to have need. 100% of undergraduates with need received aid; of those 99% had need fully met. *Average percent of need met:* 99% (excluding resources awarded to replace EFC). *Average financial aid package:* $47,140 (excluding resources awarded to replace EFC). 53% of all full-time undergraduates had no need and received non-need-based gift aid.

GIFT AID (NEED-BASED) *Total amount:* $7,023,948 (3% federal, 96% institutional, 1% external sources). *Receiving aid:* Freshmen: 56% (50); all full-time undergraduates: 47% (162). *Average award:* Freshmen: $49,471; Undergraduates: $45,637. *Scholarships, grants, and awards:* Federal Pell, FSEOG, college/university gift aid from institutional funds.

GIFT AID (NON-NEED-BASED) *Total amount:* $5,078,122 (94% institutional, 6% external sources). *Receiving aid:* Freshmen: 56% (50). Undergraduates: 46% (161). *Average award:* Freshmen: $24,450. Undergraduates: $24,333. *Scholarships, grants, and awards by category:* Academic interests/achievement: 186 awards ($4,501,675 total): general academic interests/achievements.

LOANS *Student loans:* $545,969 (45% need-based, 55% non-need-based). 54% of past graduating class borrowed through all loan programs. *Average indebtedness per student:* $23,098. *Average need-based loan:* Freshmen: $3063. Undergraduates: $3122. *Parent loans:* $150,282 (100% non-need-based). *Programs:* Federal Direct (Subsidized and Unsubsidized Stafford, PLUS).

APPLYING FOR FINANCIAL AID *Required financial aid form:* FAFSA. *Financial aid deadline:* 2/15. *Notification date:* Continuous beginning 3/24. Students must reply by 5/1 or within 2 weeks of notification.

CONTACT Ms. Jean Ricker, Director of Financial Aid, Franklin W. Olin College of Engineering, 1000 Olin Way, Needham, MA 02492-1200, 781-292-2215. *E-mail:* finaid@olin.edu.
Website: http://www.olin.edu/.

FREED-HARDEMAN UNIVERSITY
Henderson, TN

ABOUT THE INSTITUTION Independent Church of Christ, coed. *Awards:* certificates, diplomas, bachelor's, master's, and doctoral degrees. 42 undergraduate majors. *Total enrollment:* 1,906. Undergraduates: 1,402. Freshmen: 325.

GIFT AID (NEED-BASED) *Scholarships, grants, and awards:* Federal Pell, FSEOG, state, private, college/university gift aid from institutional funds, Academic Competitiveness Grants, TEACH Grants.

LOANS *Programs:* Federal Direct (Subsidized and Unsubsidized Stafford, PLUS), Perkins, alternative loans.

WORK-STUDY *Federal work-study:* jobs available. *State or other work-study/employment:* Part-time jobs available.

APPLYING FOR FINANCIAL AID *Required financial aid forms:* FAFSA, institution's own form.

CONTACT Mrs. Summer Judd, Director of Financial Aid, Freed-Hardeman University, 158 East Main Street, Henderson, TN 38340-2399, 731-989-6662 or toll-free 800-FHU-FHU-1. *Fax:* 731-989-6775. *E-mail:* sjudd@fhu.edu.
Website: http://www.fhu.edu/.

FRESNO PACIFIC UNIVERSITY
Fresno, CA

ABOUT THE INSTITUTION Independent Mennonite Brethren Church, coed. *Awards:* certificates, associate, bachelor's, and master's degrees. 23 undergraduate majors. *Total enrollment:* 3,596. Undergraduates: 2,439. Freshmen: 201.

GIFT AID (NEED-BASED) *Scholarships, grants, and awards:* Federal Pell, FSEOG, state, private, college/university gift aid from institutional funds.

GIFT AID (NON-NEED-BASED) *Scholarships, grants, and awards by category:* Academic interests/achievement: business, general academic interests/achievements, humanities, social sciences. Creative arts/performance: music, performing arts, theater/drama. Special characteristics: children of faculty/staff, members of minority groups, relatives of clergy, religious affiliation, spouses of current students.

LOANS *Programs:* Federal Direct (Subsidized and Unsubsidized Stafford, PLUS), Perkins.

WORK-STUDY Federal work-study jobs available. *State or other work-study/ employment:* Part-time jobs available.

APPLYING FOR FINANCIAL AID *Required financial aid forms:* FAFSA, institution's own form.

CONTACT April Powell, Director of Financial Aid, Fresno Pacific University, 1717 South Chestnut Avenue, #2004, Fresno, CA 93702, 559-453-2041 or toll-free 800-660-6089. *Fax:* 559-453-5595. *E-mail:* sfs@fresno.edu.
Website: http://www.fresno.edu/.

FRIENDS UNIVERSITY
Wichita, KS

ABOUT THE INSTITUTION Independent Christian non-denominational, coed. *Awards:* bachelor's and master's degrees. 45 undergraduate majors. *Total enrollment:* 1,698. Undergraduates: 1,146. Freshmen: 176.

GIFT AID (NEED-BASED) *Scholarships, grants, and awards:* Federal Pell, FSEOG, state, private, college/university gift aid from institutional funds.

GIFT AID (NON-NEED-BASED) *Scholarships, grants, and awards by category:* Academic interests/achievement: general academic interests/achievements. Creative arts/performance: art/fine arts, dance, music, performing arts, theater/drama. Special achievements/activities: cheerleading/drum major, leadership, religious involvement. Special characteristics: children and siblings of alumni, children of faculty/staff, members of minority groups, relatives of clergy, religious affiliation.

LOANS *Programs:* Federal Direct (Subsidized and Unsubsidized Stafford, PLUS), Perkins.

APPLYING FOR FINANCIAL AID *Required financial aid form:* FAFSA.

CONTACT Tony Lubbers, Director of Financial Aid, Friends University, 2100 University Street, Wichita, KS 67213, 316-295-5599 or toll-free 800-794-6945. *Fax:* 316-295-5703. *E-mail:* lubberst@friends.edu.
Website: http://www.friends.edu/.

FROSTBURG STATE UNIVERSITY
Frostburg, MD

Tuition & fees (MD res): $8914	Average undergraduate aid package: $9993

ABOUT THE INSTITUTION State-supported, coed. **Awards:** bachelor's, master's, and doctoral degrees. 45 undergraduate majors. **Total enrollment:** 5,396. Undergraduates: 4,725. Freshmen: 774. Both federal and institutional methodology are used as a basis for awarding need-based institutional aid.

UNDERGRADUATE EXPENSES for 2018–2019 Application fee: $30. **Tuition, state resident:** full-time $6468; part-time $267 per credit hour. **Tuition, nonresident:** full-time $19,816; part-time $556 per credit hour. **Required fees:** full-time $2446; $115 per credit hour or $26 per term. Full-time tuition and fees vary according to location. Part-time tuition and fees vary according to course load and location. **College room and board:** $9210; **Room only:** $4520. Room and board charges vary according to board plan and housing facility.

FRESHMAN FINANCIAL AID (Fall 2017, est.) 741 applied for aid; of those 77% were deemed to have need. 100% of freshmen with need received aid; of those 17% had need fully met. **Average percent of need met:** 59% (excluding resources awarded to replace EFC). **Average financial aid package:** $10,469 (excluding resources awarded to replace EFC). 26% of all full-time freshmen had no need and received non-need-based gift aid.

UNDERGRADUATE FINANCIAL AID (Fall 2017, est.) 3,480 applied for aid; of those 77% were deemed to have need. 100% of undergraduates with need received aid; of those 14% had need fully met. **Average percent of need met:** 59% (excluding resources awarded to replace EFC). **Average financial aid package:** $9993 (excluding resources awarded to replace EFC). 21% of all full-time undergraduates had no need and received non-need-based gift aid.

GIFT AID (NEED-BASED) Total amount: $15,935,573 (53% federal, 24% state, 22% institutional, 1% external sources). **Receiving aid:** Freshmen: 56% (452); all full-time undergraduates: 50% (1,979). **Average award:** Freshmen: $8237; Undergraduates: $7651. **Scholarships, grants, and awards:** Federal Pell, FSEOG, state, private, college/university gift aid from institutional funds.

GIFT AID (NON-NEED-BASED) Total amount: $4,678,662 (1% federal, 12% state, 53% institutional, 34% external sources). **Receiving aid:** Freshmen: 26% (206). Undergraduates: 21% (853). **Average award:** Freshmen: $3498. Undergraduates: $3427. **Scholarships, grants, and awards by category:** Academic interests/achievement: biological sciences, business, communication, computer science, education, engineering/technologies, English, foreign languages, general academic interests/achievements, humanities, international studies, mathematics, physical sciences, premedicine, social sciences. Creative arts/performance: art/fine arts, creative writing, journalism/publications, music, performing arts, theater/drama. Special achievements/activities: community service, leadership. Special characteristics: adult students, children of union members/company employees, international students, local/state students, out-of-state students, veterans, veterans' children. **Tuition waivers:** Full or partial for employees or children of employees, senior citizens.

LOANS Student loans: $99,395,025 (87% need-based, 13% non-need-based). 78% of past graduating class borrowed through all loan programs. Average indebtedness per student: $29,802. **Average need-based loan:** Freshmen: $3112. Undergraduates: $3932. **Parent loans:** $5,880,150 (100% non-need-based). **Programs:** Federal Direct (Subsidized and Unsubsidized Stafford, PLUS), Perkins.

WORK-STUDY Federal work-study: Total amount: $87,616; 130 jobs averaging $674. **State or other work-study/employment:** Total amount: $375 (100% non-need-based). Part-time jobs available.

APPLYING FOR FINANCIAL AID Required financial aid form: FAFSA. **Financial aid deadline (priority):** 3/1. **Notification date:** Continuous beginning 3/15. Students must reply within 3 weeks of notification.

CONTACT Mrs. Angela Hovatter, Director of Financial Aid, Frostburg State University, 114 Pullen Hall, 101 Braddock Road, Frostburg, MD 21532-1099, 301-687-4301. Fax: 301-687-7074. E-mail: ahovatter@frostburg.edu. Website: http://www.frostburg.edu/.

FULL SAIL UNIVERSITY
Winter Park, FL

CONTACT Financial Aid Office, Full Sail University, 3300 University Boulevard, Winter Park, FL 32792, 800-575-1142 or toll-free 800-226-7625. Website: http://www.fullsail.edu/.

FURMAN UNIVERSITY
Greenville, SC

Tuition & fees: $48,348	Average undergraduate aid package: $39,679

ABOUT THE INSTITUTION Independent, coed. **Awards:** certificates, bachelor's, and master's degrees. 44 undergraduate majors. **Total enrollment:** 2,949. Undergraduates: 2,746. Freshmen: 702. Both federal and institutional methodology are used as a basis for awarding need-based institutional aid.

UNDERGRADUATE EXPENSES for 2017–2018 Application fee: $50. **Comprehensive fee:** $60,506 includes full-time tuition ($47,968), mandatory fees ($380), and room and board ($12,158). **College room only:** $6540. Room and board charges vary according to board plan and housing facility. **Part-time tuition:** $1499 per credit. Part-time tuition and fees vary according to course load.

FRESHMAN FINANCIAL AID (Fall 2017, est.) 499 applied for aid; of those 74% were deemed to have need. 100% of freshmen with need received aid; of those 40% had need fully met. **Average percent of need met:** 83% (excluding resources awarded to replace EFC). **Average financial aid package:** $38,887 (excluding resources awarded to replace EFC). 40% of all full-time freshmen had no need and received non-need-based gift aid.

UNDERGRADUATE FINANCIAL AID (Fall 2017, est.) 1,501 applied for aid; of those 82% were deemed to have need. 100% of undergraduates with need received aid; of those 39% had need fully met. **Average percent of need met:** 81% (excluding resources awarded to replace EFC). **Average financial aid package:** $39,679 (excluding resources awarded to replace EFC). 48% of all full-time undergraduates had no need and received non-need-based gift aid.

GIFT AID (NEED-BASED) Total amount: $35,498,029 (5% federal, 4% state, 87% institutional, 4% external sources). **Receiving aid:** Freshmen: 52% (362); all full-time undergraduates: 46% (1,204). **Average award:** Freshmen: $36,996; Undergraduates: $37,333. **Scholarships, grants, and awards:** Federal Pell, FSEOG, state, private, college/university gift aid from institutional funds.

GIFT AID (NON-NEED-BASED) Total amount: $28,948,635 (12% state, 82% institutional, 6% external sources). **Receiving aid:** Freshmen: 16% (110). Undergraduates: 14% (365). **Average award:** Freshmen: $16,603. Undergraduates: $18,601. **Scholarships, grants, and awards by category:** Academic interests/achievement: area/ethnic studies, biological sciences, business, communication, computer science, education, engineering/technologies, English, foreign languages, general academic interests/achievements, health fields, humanities, international studies, mathematics, military science, physical sciences, premedicine, religion/biblical studies, social sciences. Creative arts/performance: art/fine arts, creative writing, music, theater/drama. Special achievements/activities: community service, leadership, religious involvement. Special characteristics: children of faculty/staff, ethnic background, international students, local/state students, relatives of clergy, religious affiliation, veterans. **Tuition waivers:** Full or partial for employees or children of employees. **ROTC:** Army.

LOANS Student loans: $7,164,939 (88% need-based, 12% non-need-based). 39% of past graduating class borrowed through all loan programs. Average indebtedness per student: $32,919. **Average need-based loan:** Freshmen: $3280. Undergraduates: $4524. **Parent loans:** $3,820,344 (88% need-based, 12% non-need-based). **Programs:** Federal Direct (Subsidized and Unsubsidized Stafford, PLUS), Perkins, state, alternative loans.

WORK-STUDY Federal work-study: Total amount: $1,071,015; jobs available.

ATHLETIC AWARDS Total amount: $11,433,317 (37% need-based, 63% non-need-based).

APPLYING FOR FINANCIAL AID Required financial aid forms: FAFSA, CSS Financial Aid PROFILE, state aid form, business/farm supplement. **Financial aid deadline:** 3/1. **Notification date:** 4/1. Students must reply by 5/1 or within 2 weeks of notification.

CONTACT Mr. Forrest Stuart, Associate Vice President of Financial Aid, Furman University, 3300 Poinsett Highway, Greenville, SC 29613, 864-294-2204. *Fax:* 864-294-3127. *E-mail:* forrest.stuart@furman.edu.
Website: http://www.furman.edu/.

GALEN COLLEGE OF NURSING
Cincinnati, OH

CONTACT Financial Aid Office, Galen College of Nursing, 100 East Business Way, Suite 200, Cincinnati, OH 45241, 513-475-3600 or toll-free 877-223-7040.
Website: http://www.galencollege.edu/.

GALLAUDET UNIVERSITY
Washington, DC

ABOUT THE INSTITUTION Independent, coed. *Awards:* certificates, bachelor's, master's, and doctoral degrees (Undergraduate programs are open primarily to the students with hearing-impairments). 22 undergraduate majors. *Total enrollment:* 1,566. Undergraduates: 1,121. Freshmen: 245.

GIFT AID (NEED-BASED) *Scholarships, grants, and awards:* Federal Pell, FSEOG, state, private, college/university gift aid from institutional funds.

GIFT AID (NON-NEED-BASED) *Scholarships, grants, and awards by category: Academic interests/achievement:* general academic interests/achievements. *Special achievements/activities:* leadership. *Special characteristics:* members of minority groups.

LOANS *Programs:* Federal Direct (Subsidized and Unsubsidized Stafford, PLUS), Perkins.

WORK-STUDY *Federal work-study:* jobs available.

APPLYING FOR FINANCIAL AID *Required financial aid forms:* FAFSA, institution's own form.

CONTACT Shondra Dickson, Director of Financial Aid, Gallaudet University, Chapel Hall, Room G-02, 800 Florida Avenue, NE, Washington, DC 20002, 202-651-5290 or toll-free 800-995-0550. *Fax:* 202-651-5740. *E-mail:* financial.aid@gallaudet.edu.
Website: http://www.gallaudet.edu/.

GANNON UNIVERSITY
Erie, PA

Tuition & fees: N/R	Average undergraduate aid package: $25,829

ABOUT THE INSTITUTION Independent Roman Catholic, coed. *Awards:* certificates, associate, bachelor's, master's, and doctoral degrees. 65 undergraduate majors. *Total enrollment:* 4,149. Undergraduates: 3,076. Freshmen: 645. Federal methodology is used as a basis for awarding need-based institutional aid.

FRESHMAN FINANCIAL AID (Fall 2017, est.) 582 applied for aid; of those 91% were deemed to have need. 100% of freshmen with need received aid; of those 20% had need fully met. *Average percent of need met:* 75% (excluding resources awarded to replace EFC). *Average financial aid package:* $26,530 (excluding resources awarded to replace EFC). 12% of all full-time freshmen had no need and received non-need-based gift aid.

UNDERGRADUATE FINANCIAL AID (Fall 2017, est.) 2,131 applied for aid; of those 91% were deemed to have need. 100% of undergraduates with need received aid; of those 23% had need fully met. *Average percent of need met:* 74% (excluding resources awarded to replace EFC). *Average financial aid package:* $25,829 (excluding resources awarded to replace EFC). 17% of all full-time undergraduates had no need and received non-need-based gift aid.

GIFT AID (NEED-BASED) *Total amount:* $38,705,073 (10% federal, 7% state, 78% institutional, 5% external sources). *Receiving aid:* Freshmen: 82% (521); all full-time undergraduates: 76% (1,906). *Average award:* Freshmen: $23,126; Undergraduates: $21,750. *Scholarships, grants, and awards:* Federal Pell, FSEOG, state, private, college/university gift aid from institutional funds, Federal Nursing.

GIFT AID (NON-NEED-BASED) *Total amount:* $10,062,897 (65% institutional, 35% external sources). *Receiving aid:* Freshmen: 9% (59). Undergraduates:

10% (251). *Average award:* Freshmen: $17,677. Undergraduates: $15,285. *Scholarships, grants, and awards by category: Academic interests/achievement:* biological sciences, business, education, engineering/technologies, English, foreign languages, general academic interests/achievements, humanities, international studies, mathematics, premedicine, religion/biblical studies, social sciences. *Creative arts/performance:* music, performing arts, theater/drama. *Special achievements/activities:* community service, leadership. *Special characteristics:* adult students, ethnic background, international students, members of minority groups, religious affiliation, veterans. *ROTC:* Army.

LOANS *Student loans:* $12,688,766 (94% need-based, 6% non-need-based). *Average need-based loan:* Freshmen: $3383. Undergraduates: $4383. *Parent loans:* $5,594,150 (95% need-based, 5% non-need-based). *Programs:* Federal Direct (Subsidized and Unsubsidized Stafford, PLUS), Federal Nursing.

WORK-STUDY *Federal work-study:* Total amount: $788,077; jobs available. *State or other work-study/employment:* Total amount: $228,809 (100% non-need-based). Part-time jobs available.

ATHLETIC AWARDS Total amount: $4,137,578 (67% need-based, 33% non-need-based).

APPLYING FOR FINANCIAL AID *Required financial aid form:* FAFSA. *Financial aid deadline (priority):* 3/15. *Notification date:* Continuous beginning 11/1.

CONTACT Ms. Sharon Krahe, Director of Financial Aid, Gannon University, 109 University Square, Erie, PA 16541, 814-871-7670 or toll-free 800-GANNONU. *Fax:* 814-871-5826. *E-mail:* krahe001@gannon.edu.
Website: http://www.gannon.edu/.

GARDNER-WEBB UNIVERSITY
Boiling Springs, NC

Tuition & fees: $30,730	Average undergraduate aid package: $25,228

ABOUT THE INSTITUTION Independent Baptist, coed. *Awards:* certificates, associate, bachelor's, master's, and doctoral degrees. 65 undergraduate majors. *Total enrollment:* 3,884. Undergraduates: 2,343. Freshmen: 444. Federal methodology is used as a basis for awarding need-based institutional aid.

UNDERGRADUATE EXPENSES for 2017–2018 *Application fee:* $40. *Comprehensive fee:* $35,830 includes full-time tuition ($30,310), mandatory fees ($420), and room and board ($5100). *College room only:* $4980. Room and board charges vary according to board plan and housing facility. *Part-time tuition:* $482 per hour.

FRESHMAN FINANCIAL AID (Fall 2017, est.) 341 applied for aid; of those 89% were deemed to have need. 100% of freshmen with need received aid; of those 24% had need fully met. *Average percent of need met:* 80% (excluding resources awarded to replace EFC). *Average financial aid package:* $27,388 (excluding resources awarded to replace EFC). 19% of all full-time freshmen had no need and received non-need-based gift aid.

UNDERGRADUATE FINANCIAL AID (Fall 2017, est.) 1,180 applied for aid; of those 91% were deemed to have need. 100% of undergraduates with need received aid; of those 20% had need fully met. *Average percent of need met:* 75% (excluding resources awarded to replace EFC). *Average financial aid package:* $25,228 (excluding resources awarded to replace EFC). 23% of all full-time undergraduates had no need and received non-need-based gift aid.

GIFT AID (NEED-BASED) *Total amount:* $19,216,836 (14% federal, 15% state, 68% institutional, 3% external sources). *Receiving aid:* Freshmen: 64% (243); all full-time undergraduates: 59% (844). *Average award:* Freshmen: $8785; Undergraduates: $8063. *Scholarships, grants, and awards:* Federal Pell, FSEOG, state, private, college/university gift aid from institutional funds.

GIFT AID (NON-NEED-BASED) *Total amount:* $4,059,304 (99% institutional, 1% external sources). *Receiving aid:* Freshmen: 78% (297). Undergraduates: 70% (1,004). *Average award:* Freshmen: $13,806. Undergraduates: $12,416. *Scholarships, grants, and awards by category: Academic interests/achievement:* biological sciences, business, communication, computer science, education, English, foreign languages, general academic interests/achievements, health fields, humanities, mathematics, physical sciences, premedicine, religion/biblical studies, social sciences. *Creative arts/performance:* art/fine arts, music, theater/drama. *Special achievements/activities:* cheerleading/drum major, religious involvement. *Special characteristics:* children of faculty/staff, handicapped students, local/state students, members of minority groups, out-of-state students, previous college experience, relatives of clergy.

Tuition waivers: Full or partial for employees or children of employees. *ROTC:* Army, Air Force cooperative.

LOANS *Student loans:* $7,688,990 (92% need-based, 8% non-need-based). 69% of past graduating class borrowed through all loan programs. *Average indebtedness per student:* $31,926. *Average need-based loan:* Freshmen: $3210. Undergraduates: $4097. *Parent loans:* $4,710,874 (94% need-based, 6% non-need-based). *Programs:* Federal Direct (Subsidized and Unsubsidized Stafford, PLUS), Perkins, state, alternative loans.

WORK-STUDY *Federal work-study:* Total amount: $394,267; 297 jobs averaging $1341. *State or other work-study/employment:* Total amount: $36,402 (65% need-based, 35% non-need-based). 26 part-time jobs averaging $1402.

ATHLETIC AWARDS Total amount: $7,381,169 (49% need-based, 51% non-need-based).

APPLYING FOR FINANCIAL AID *Required financial aid forms:* FAFSA, state aid form. *Financial aid deadline (priority):* 3/15. *Notification date:* 3/1. Students must reply within 2 weeks of notification.

CONTACT Summer Nance, Assistant Vice President of Financial Planning, Gardner-Webb University, PO Box 955, Boiling Springs, NC 28017, 704-406-4243 or toll-free 800-253-6472. *Fax:* 704-406-4102.

Website: http://www.gardner-webb.edu/.

GENEVA COLLEGE
Beaver Falls, PA

Tuition & fees: $26,980	Average undergraduate aid package: $20,943

ABOUT THE INSTITUTION Independent Reformed Presbyterian Church of North America, coed. *Awards:* associate, bachelor's, and master's degrees (also offers non-traditional programs in Philadelphia and western Pennsylvania with significant enrollment not reflected in profile). 42 undergraduate majors. *Total enrollment:* 1,599. Undergraduates: 1,418. Freshmen: 303. Federal methodology is used as a basis for awarding need-based institutional aid.

UNDERGRADUATE EXPENSES for 2018–2019 *Application fee:* $40. *Comprehensive fee:* $37,150 includes full-time tuition ($26,730), mandatory fees ($250), and room and board ($10,170). Full-time tuition and fees vary according to course load. Room and board charges vary according to board plan. *Part-time tuition:* $900 per credit hour. Part-time tuition and fees vary according to course load.

FRESHMAN FINANCIAL AID (Fall 2016) 310 applied for aid; of those 89% were deemed to have need. 100% of freshmen with need received aid; of those 20% had need fully met. *Average percent of need met:* 75% (excluding resources awarded to replace EFC). *Average financial aid package:* $20,435 (excluding resources awarded to replace EFC). 14% of all full-time freshmen had no need and received non-need-based gift aid.

UNDERGRADUATE FINANCIAL AID (Fall 2016) 1,037 applied for aid; of those 91% were deemed to have need. 100% of undergraduates with need received aid; of those 23% had need fully met. *Average percent of need met:* 80% (excluding resources awarded to replace EFC). *Average financial aid package:* $20,943 (excluding resources awarded to replace EFC). 17% of all full-time undergraduates had no need and received non-need-based gift aid.

GIFT AID (NEED-BASED) *Total amount:* $14,883,261 (13% federal, 11% state, 72% institutional, 4% external sources). *Receiving aid:* Freshmen: 85% (277); all full-time undergraduates: 82% (941). *Average award:* Freshmen: $16,442; Undergraduates: $16,549. *Scholarships, grants, and awards:* Federal Pell, FSEOG, state, private, college/university gift aid from institutional funds.

GIFT AID (NON-NEED-BASED) *Total amount:* $2,915,976 (1% state, 91% institutional, 8% external sources). *Receiving aid:* Freshmen: 12% (39). Undergraduates: 12% (136). *Average award:* Freshmen: $11,466. Undergraduates: $10,965. *Scholarships, grants, and awards by category: Academic interests/achievement:* general academic interests/achievements. *Creative arts/performance:* music. *Special achievements/activities:* leadership, memberships, religious involvement. *Special characteristics:* children of faculty/staff, religious affiliation. *Tuition waivers:* Full or partial for employees or children of employees. *ROTC:* Army cooperative.

LOANS *Student loans:* $8,989,463 (62% need-based, 38% non-need-based). 80% of past graduating class borrowed through all loan programs. *Average indebtedness per student:* $35,440. *Average need-based loan:* Freshmen: $3824. Undergraduates: $4400. *Parent loans:* $1,696,774 (42% need-based, 58% non-need-based). *Programs:* Federal Direct (Subsidized and Unsubsidized Stafford, PLUS), Perkins.

WORK-STUDY *Federal work-study:* 198 jobs averaging $765. *State or other work-study/employment:* Part-time jobs available.

APPLYING FOR FINANCIAL AID *Required financial aid forms:* FAFSA, state aid form. *Financial aid deadline (priority):* 3/15. *Notification date:* Continuous beginning 12/15. Students must reply within 4 weeks of notification.

CONTACT Ms. Allyson Bentz, Director of Student Financial Services, Geneva College, 3200 College Avenue, Beaver Falls, PA 15010-3599, 724-847-6530 or toll-free 800-847-8255. *Fax:* 724-847-6776. *E-mail:* sfs@geneva.edu.

Website: http://www.geneva.edu/.

GEORGE FOX UNIVERSITY
Newberg, OR

Tuition & fees: $34,866	Average undergraduate aid package: $22,230

ABOUT THE INSTITUTION Independent Friends, coed. *Awards:* certificates, bachelor's, master's, and doctoral degrees. 46 undergraduate majors. *Total enrollment:* 3,899. Undergraduates: 2,569. Freshmen: 634. Federal methodology is used as a basis for awarding need-based institutional aid.

UNDERGRADUATE EXPENSES for 2017–2018 *Application fee:* $40. *Comprehensive fee:* $45,752 includes full-time tuition ($34,500), mandatory fees ($366), and room and board ($10,886). Full-time tuition and fees vary according to reciprocity agreements. Room and board charges vary according to board plan. Part-time tuition and fees vary according to course load.

FRESHMAN FINANCIAL AID (Fall 2017, est.) 586 applied for aid; of those 84% were deemed to have need. 100% of freshmen with need received aid; of those 42% had need fully met. *Average percent of need met:* 88% (excluding resources awarded to replace EFC). *Average financial aid package:* $24,100 (excluding resources awarded to replace EFC). 21% of all full-time freshmen had no need and received non-need-based gift aid.

UNDERGRADUATE FINANCIAL AID (Fall 2017, est.) 2,092 applied for aid; of those 89% were deemed to have need. 100% of undergraduates with need received aid; of those 35% had need fully met. *Average percent of need met:* 84% (excluding resources awarded to replace EFC). *Average financial aid package:* $22,230 (excluding resources awarded to replace EFC). 23% of all full-time undergraduates had no need and received non-need-based gift aid.

GIFT AID (NEED-BASED) *Total amount:* $34,121,067 (11% federal, 3% state, 81% institutional, 5% external sources). *Receiving aid:* Freshmen: 75% (481); all full-time undergraduates: 71% (1,790). *Average award:* Freshmen: $20,553; Undergraduates: $18,195. *Scholarships, grants, and awards:* Federal Pell, FSEOG, state, private, college/university gift aid from institutional funds, TEACH Grants.

GIFT AID (NON-NEED-BASED) *Total amount:* $8,953,778 (97% institutional, 3% external sources). *Receiving aid:* Freshmen: 7% (42). Undergraduates: 5% (122). *Average award:* Freshmen: $14,763. Undergraduates: $13,374. *Scholarships, grants, and awards by category: Academic interests/achievement:* biological sciences, business, communication, computer science, education, engineering/technologies, English, foreign languages, general academic interests/achievements, health fields, home economics, humanities, international studies, mathematics, physical sciences, religion/biblical studies, social sciences. *Creative arts/performance:* art/fine arts, cinema/film/broadcasting, debating, music, theater/drama. *Special achievements/activities:* leadership, religious involvement. *Special characteristics:* children and siblings of alumni, children of faculty/staff, ethnic background, international students, members of minority groups, out-of-state students, relatives of clergy, religious affiliation. *Tuition waivers:* Full or partial for employees or children of employees, senior citizens. *ROTC:* Air Force cooperative.

LOANS *Student loans:* $17,792,272 (76% need-based, 24% non-need-based). 68% of past graduating class borrowed through all loan programs. *Average indebtedness per student:* $29,207. *Average need-based loan:* Freshmen: $3130. Undergraduates: $3989. *Parent loans:* $7,180,494 (49% need-based, 51% non-need-based). *Programs:* Federal Direct (Subsidized and Unsubsidized Stafford, PLUS), Perkins, alternative loans.

WORK-STUDY *Federal work-study:* Total amount: $3,097,196; 1,399 jobs averaging $2214. *State or other work-study/employment:* Total amount: $880,950 (100% non-need-based). Part-time jobs available.

APPLYING FOR FINANCIAL AID *Required financial aid forms:* FAFSA, state aid form. *Financial aid deadline:* Continuous. *Notification date:* Continuous beginning 12/16. Students must reply by 5/1.

CONTACT Johanna Kaye, Director of Financial Aid, George Fox University, 414 North Meridian Street, Newberg, OR 97132-2697, 503-554-2235 or toll-free 800-765-4369. *Fax:* 503-554-3110. *E-mail:* kayej@georgefox.edu. *Website:* http://www.georgefox.edu/.

GEORGE MASON UNIVERSITY
Fairfax, VA

Tuition & fees (VA res): $11,724	Average undergraduate aid package: $12,989

ABOUT THE INSTITUTION State-supported, coed. *Awards:* certificates, bachelor's, master's, and doctoral degrees. 70 undergraduate majors. *Total enrollment:* 35,960. Undergraduates: 24,987. Freshmen: 3,489. Federal methodology is used as a basis for awarding need-based institutional aid.

UNDERGRADUATE EXPENSES for 2017–2018 *Application fee:* $70. *Tuition, state resident:* full-time $11,724; part-time $488.50 per credit hour. *Tuition, nonresident:* full-time $35,323; part-time $1423.75 per credit hour. Full-time tuition and fees vary according to course load. Part-time tuition and fees vary according to course load. Room and board charges vary according to board plan and housing facility.

FRESHMAN FINANCIAL AID (Fall 2016) 2,687 applied for aid; of those 72% were deemed to have need. 96% of freshmen with need received aid; of those 3% had need fully met. *Average percent of need met:* 62% (excluding resources awarded to replace EFC). *Average financial aid package:* $14,717 (excluding resources awarded to replace EFC). 13% of all full-time freshmen had no need and received non-need-based gift aid.

UNDERGRADUATE FINANCIAL AID (Fall 2016) 13,244 applied for aid; of those 82% were deemed to have need. 96% of undergraduates with need received aid; of those 2% had need fully met. *Average percent of need met:* 54% (excluding resources awarded to replace EFC). *Average financial aid package:* $12,989 (excluding resources awarded to replace EFC). 8% of all full-time undergraduates had no need and received non-need-based gift aid.

GIFT AID (NEED-BASED) *Total amount:* $61,912,932 (48% federal, 34% state, 18% institutional). *Receiving aid:* Freshmen: 52% (1,636); all full-time undergraduates: 47% (8,859). *Average award:* Freshmen: $7349; Undergraduates: $6408. *Scholarships, grants, and awards:* Federal Pell, FSEOG, state, private, college/university gift aid from institutional funds.

GIFT AID (NON-NEED-BASED) *Total amount:* $13,217,085 (73% institutional, 27% external sources). *Receiving aid:* Freshmen: 22% (704). Undergraduates: 11% (2,165). *Average award:* Freshmen: $4945. Undergraduates: $3968. *Scholarships, grants, and awards by category:* Academic interests/achievement: 3,114 awards ($10,069,641 total): general academic interests/achievements. *Creative arts/performance:* general creative arts/performance. *Special characteristics:* general special characteristics. *Tuition waivers:* Full or partial for employees or children of employees, senior citizens. *ROTC:* Army, Air Force cooperative.

LOANS *Student loans:* $100,645,190 (75% need-based, 25% non-need-based). 56% of past graduating class borrowed through all loan programs. *Average indebtedness per student:* $30,755. *Average need-based loan:* Freshmen: $3388. Undergraduates: $4453. *Parent loans:* $27,422,101 (57% need-based, 43% non-need-based). *Programs:* Federal Direct (Subsidized and Unsubsidized Stafford, PLUS), Perkins, Federal Nursing.

WORK-STUDY *Federal work-study:* 591 jobs averaging $2129.

ATHLETIC AWARDS Total amount: $5,944,484 (100% non-need-based).

APPLYING FOR FINANCIAL AID *Required financial aid form:* FAFSA. *Financial aid deadline (priority):* 3/1. *Notification date:* Continuous beginning 3/1. Students must reply within 3 weeks of notification.

CONTACT Office of Student Financial Aid, George Mason University, 1111 Student Union Building I, Mail Stop 3B5, Fairfax, VA 22030-4444, 703-993-2353 or toll-free 888-627-6612. *Fax:* 703-993-2350. *E-mail:* finaid@gmu.edu. *Website:* http://www.gmu.edu/.

GEORGETOWN COLLEGE
Georgetown, KY

Tuition & fees: $38,650	Average undergraduate aid package: $36,918

ABOUT THE INSTITUTION Independent Baptist Church, coed. *Awards:* certificates, diplomas, bachelor's, and master's degrees. 35 undergraduate majors. *Total enrollment:* 1,766. Undergraduates: 1,060. Freshmen: 305. Federal methodology is used as a basis for awarding need-based institutional aid.

UNDERGRADUATE EXPENSES for 2018–2019 *Comprehensive fee:* $48,430 includes full-time tuition ($38,650) and room and board ($9780). *College room only:* $4720. Full-time tuition and fees vary according to course load and degree level. Room and board charges vary according to board plan and housing facility. Part-time tuition and fees vary according to course load and degree level.

FRESHMAN FINANCIAL AID (Fall 2016) 292 applied for aid; of those 93% were deemed to have need. 100% of freshmen with need received aid; of those 100% had need fully met. *Average percent of need met:* 76% (excluding resources awarded to replace EFC). *Average financial aid package:* $37,938 (excluding resources awarded to replace EFC).

UNDERGRADUATE FINANCIAL AID (Fall 2016) 869 applied for aid; of those 86% were deemed to have need. 100% of undergraduates with need received aid; of those 100% had need fully met. *Average percent of need met:* 43% (excluding resources awarded to replace EFC). *Average financial aid package:* $36,918 (excluding resources awarded to replace EFC).

GIFT AID (NEED-BASED) *Total amount:* $21,160,515 (6% federal, 13% state, 80% institutional, 1% external sources). *Receiving aid:* Freshmen: 91% (272); all full-time undergraduates: 77% (741). *Average award:* Freshmen: $25,234; Undergraduates: $24,095. *Scholarships, grants, and awards:* Federal Pell, FSEOG, state, private, college/university gift aid from institutional funds.

GIFT AID (NON-NEED-BASED) *Total amount:* $75,187 (100% federal). *Receiving aid:* Freshmen: 1% (3). Undergraduates: 1% (7). *Scholarships, grants, and awards by category:* Academic interests/achievement: general academic interests/achievements, international studies. *Creative arts/performance:* art/fine arts, music, performing arts, theater/drama. *Special achievements/activities:* junior miss, religious involvement. *Special characteristics:* children and siblings of alumni, children of faculty/staff, local/state students, members of minority groups, out-of-state students, relatives of clergy, religious affiliation, veterans, veterans' children. *Tuition waivers:* Full or partial for employees or children of employees. *ROTC:* Army cooperative, Air Force cooperative.

LOANS *Student loans:* $7,404,575 (100% need-based). 80% of past graduating class borrowed through all loan programs. *Average indebtedness per student:* $31,267. *Average need-based loan:* Freshmen: $2911. Undergraduates: $3734. *Parent loans:* $2,263,069 (100% need-based). *Programs:* Federal Direct (Subsidized and Unsubsidized Stafford, PLUS), Perkins, college/university.

WORK-STUDY *Federal work-study:* jobs available.

ATHLETIC AWARDS Total amount: $5,223,993 (100% need-based).

APPLYING FOR FINANCIAL AID *Required financial aid forms:* FAFSA, institution's own form. *Financial aid deadline (priority):* 2/1. *Notification date:* Continuous beginning 3/1. Students must reply by 5/1 or within 3 weeks of notification.

CONTACT Mr. Bob Fultz, Director of Student Financial Planning, Georgetown College, 400 East College Street, Georgetown, KY 40324-1696, 502-863-8029 or toll-free 800-788-9985. *Fax:* 502-868-7733. *E-mail:* financialaid@georgetowncollege.edu. *Website:* http://www.georgetowncollege.edu/.

GEORGETOWN UNIVERSITY
Washington, DC

Tuition & fees: $52,300	Average undergraduate aid package: $46,571

ABOUT THE INSTITUTION Independent Roman Catholic (Jesuit), coed. *Awards:* certificates, bachelor's, master's, and doctoral degrees. 48 undergraduate majors. *Total enrollment:* 19,005. Undergraduates: 7,463. Freshmen: 1,597. Both federal and institutional methodology are used as a basis for awarding need-based institutional aid.

UNDERGRADUATE EXPENSES for 2017–2018 *Application fee:* $75. *Comprehensive fee:* $68,970 includes full-time tuition ($51,720), mandatory fees ($580), and room and board ($16,670). *College room only:* $11,000. Full-time tuition and fees vary according to course load and program. Room and board charges vary according to board plan and housing facility. *Part-time tuition:* $2155 per credit hour. Part-time tuition and fees vary according to course load and program.
FRESHMAN FINANCIAL AID (Fall 2017, est.) 943 applied for aid; of those 78% were deemed to have need. 100% of freshmen with need received aid; of those 100% had need fully met. *Average percent of need met:* 100% (excluding resources awarded to replace EFC). *Average financial aid package:* $46,703 (excluding resources awarded to replace EFC).
UNDERGRADUATE FINANCIAL AID (Fall 2017, est.) 3,564 applied for aid; of those 75% were deemed to have need. 100% of undergraduates with need received aid; of those 100% had need fully met. *Average percent of need met:* 100% (excluding resources awarded to replace EFC). *Average financial aid package:* $46,571 (excluding resources awarded to replace EFC).
GIFT AID (NEED-BASED) *Total amount:* $114,700,000 (5% federal, 92% institutional, 3% external sources). *Receiving aid:* Freshmen: 43% (692); all full-time undergraduates: 35% (2,488). *Average award:* Freshmen: $42,859; Undergraduates: $42,258. *Scholarships, grants, and awards:* Federal Pell, FSEOG, state, private, college/university gift aid from institutional funds.
GIFT AID (NON-NEED-BASED) *Total amount:* $2,200,000 (91% federal, 9% institutional). *Receiving aid:* Freshmen: 16% (250). Undergraduates: 11% (800). *Scholarships, grants, and awards by category:* Special characteristics: 144 awards ($4,453,882 total): children of faculty/staff. *ROTC:* Army, Naval cooperative, Air Force cooperative.
LOANS *Student loans:* $15,800,000 (44% need-based, 56% non-need-based). 38% of past graduating class borrowed through all loan programs. *Average indebtedness per student:* $23,387. *Average need-based loan:* Freshmen: $3415. Undergraduates: $4115. *Parent loans:* $9,600,000 (100% non-need-based). *Programs:* Federal Direct (Subsidized and Unsubsidized Stafford, PLUS), Perkins, Federal Nursing, alternative loans.
WORK-STUDY *Federal work-study:* Total amount: $7,500,000; 2,620 jobs averaging $2890.
ATHLETIC AWARDS Total amount: $8,800,000 (25% need-based, 75% non-need-based).
APPLYING FOR FINANCIAL AID *Required financial aid forms:* FAFSA, CSS Financial Aid PROFILE, federal income tax form(s). *Financial aid deadline:* 2/1. *Notification date:* 4/1. Students must reply by 5/1 or within 2 weeks of notification.
CONTACT Ms. Patricia A. McWade, Dean of Student Financial Services, Georgetown University, 37th and O Street, NW, Box 1252, Washington, DC 20057, 202-687-4547. *Fax:* 202-687-6542. *E-mail:* mcwadep@georgetown.edu.
Website: http://www.georgetown.edu/.

THE GEORGE WASHINGTON UNIVERSITY
Washington, DC

Tuition & fees: $53,518	Average undergraduate aid package: $45,233

ABOUT THE INSTITUTION Independent, coed. *Awards:* certificates, associate, bachelor's, master's, and doctoral degrees. 81 undergraduate majors. *Total enrollment:* 27,973. Undergraduates: 11,999. Freshmen: 2,610. Both federal and institutional methodology are used as a basis for awarding need-based institutional aid.
UNDERGRADUATE EXPENSES for 2017–2018 *Application fee:* $75. *Comprehensive fee:* $66,518 includes full-time tuition ($53,435), mandatory fees ($83), and room and board ($13,000). *College room only:* $8900. Full-time tuition and fees vary according to student level. Room and board charges vary according to housing facility. *Part-time tuition:* $1520 per credit hour. *Part-time fees:* $2.75 per credit hour. Part-time tuition and fees vary according to course load. *Payment plan:* Guaranteed tuition.
FRESHMAN FINANCIAL AID (Fall 2016) 1,632 applied for aid; of those 73% were deemed to have need. 98% of freshmen with need received aid; of those 51% had need fully met. *Average percent of need met:* 90% (excluding resources awarded to replace EFC). *Average financial aid package:* $46,348 (excluding resources

awarded to replace EFC). 29% of all full-time freshmen had no need and received non-need-based gift aid.
UNDERGRADUATE FINANCIAL AID (Fall 2016) 5,717 applied for aid; of those 83% were deemed to have need. 99% of undergraduates with need received aid; of those 49% had need fully met. *Average percent of need met:* 87% (excluding resources awarded to replace EFC). *Average financial aid package:* $45,233 (excluding resources awarded to replace EFC). 28% of all full-time undergraduates had no need and received non-need-based gift aid.
GIFT AID (NEED-BASED) *Total amount:* $147,123,803 (6% federal, 94% institutional). *Receiving aid:* Freshmen: 45% (1,136); all full-time undergraduates: 43% (4,398). *Average award:* Freshmen: $32,167; Undergraduates: $30,279. *Scholarships, grants, and awards:* Federal Pell, FSEOG, state, college/university gift aid from institutional funds.
GIFT AID (NON-NEED-BASED) *Total amount:* $48,620,171 (100% institutional). *Receiving aid:* Freshmen: 33% (832). Undergraduates: 23% (2,403). *Average award:* Freshmen: $20,188. Undergraduates: $19,846. *Scholarships, grants, and awards by category:* Academic interests/achievement: general academic interests/achievements. *Creative arts/performance:* general creative arts/performance. *Tuition waivers:* Full or partial for employees or children of employees. *ROTC:* Army cooperative, Naval, Air Force cooperative.
LOANS *Student loans:* $38,588,773 (73% need-based, 27% non-need-based). 46% of past graduating class borrowed through all loan programs. *Average indebtedness per student:* $33,305. *Average need-based loan:* Freshmen: $4389. Undergraduates: $5688. *Parent loans:* $27,008,259 (29% need-based, 71% non-need-based). *Programs:* Federal Direct (Subsidized and Unsubsidized Stafford, PLUS), Perkins.
WORK-STUDY *Federal work-study:* jobs available.
ATHLETIC AWARDS Total amount: $10,345,661 (37% need-based, 63% non-need-based).
APPLYING FOR FINANCIAL AID *Required financial aid forms:* FAFSA, CSS Financial Aid PROFILE, noncustodial (divorced/separated) parent's statement. *Financial aid deadline:* 2/1. *Notification date:* Continuous beginning 3/24. Students must reply by 5/1.
CONTACT Michelle Carmela Arcieri, Senior Associate Director of Student Financial Assistance, The George Washington University, 2121 I Street, NW, Rice Hall, Suite 301B, Washington, DC 21044, 202-994-5729. *Fax:* 202-994-0906. *E-mail:* finaid@gwu.edu.
Website: http://www.gwu.edu/.

GEORGIA COLLEGE & STATE UNIVERSITY
Milledgeville, GA

Tuition & fees (GA res): $9346	Average undergraduate aid package: $10,745

ABOUT THE INSTITUTION State-supported, coed. *Awards:* certificates, bachelor's, master's, and doctoral degrees. 36 undergraduate majors. *Total enrollment:* 6,952. Undergraduates: 5,987. Freshmen: 1,443. Federal methodology is used as a basis for awarding need-based institutional aid.
UNDERGRADUATE EXPENSES for 2017–2018 *Application fee:* $40. *Tuition, state resident:* full-time $7324. *Tuition, nonresident:* full-time $26,038. *Required fees:* full-time $2022. Full-time tuition and fees vary according to course load, location, and program. Part-time tuition and fees vary according to course load, location, and program. *College room and board:* $12,538; *Room only:* $6938. Room and board charges vary according to board plan and housing facility.
FRESHMAN FINANCIAL AID (Fall 2017, est.) 1,296 applied for aid; of those 61% were deemed to have need. 98% of freshmen with need received aid; of those 20% had need fully met. *Average percent of need met:* 63% (excluding resources awarded to replace EFC). *Average financial aid package:* $11,051 (excluding resources awarded to replace EFC). 2% of all full-time freshmen had no need and received non-need-based gift aid.
UNDERGRADUATE FINANCIAL AID (Fall 2017, est.) 4,202 applied for aid; of those 67% were deemed to have need. 97% of undergraduates with need received aid; of those 15% had need fully met. *Average percent of need met:* 58% (excluding resources awarded to replace EFC). *Average financial aid package:* $10,745 (excluding resources awarded to replace EFC). 4% of all full-time undergraduates had no need and received non-need-based gift aid.

GIFT AID (NEED-BASED) Total amount: $5,600,000 (96% federal, 4% institutional). Receiving aid: Freshmen: 18% (265); all full-time undergraduates: 20% (1,091). Average award: Freshmen: $4679; Undergraduates: $4577. Scholarships, grants, and awards: Federal Pell, FSEOG, state, college/university gift aid from institutional funds.

GIFT AID (NON-NEED-BASED) Total amount: $31,500,000 (92% state, 4% institutional, 4% external sources). Receiving aid: Freshmen: 51% (735). Undergraduates: 42% (2,264). Average award: Freshmen: $2862. Undergraduates: $2258. Scholarships, grants, and awards by category: Academic interests/ achievement: business, education, physical sciences, social sciences. Creative arts/performance: art/fine arts, journalism/publications, music. Special achievements/activities: general special achievements/activities. Special characteristics: adult students, children of faculty/staff, general special characteristics, local/state students, out-of-state students, public servants. Tuition waivers: Full or partial for employees or children of employees, senior citizens. ROTC: Army cooperative.

LOANS Student loans: $28,000,000 (32% need-based, 68% non-need-based). 47% of past graduating class borrowed through all loan programs. Average indebtedness per student: $30,407. Average need-based loan: Freshmen: $3986. Undergraduates: $4520. Parent loans: $6,000,000 (100% non-need-based). Programs: Federal Direct (Subsidized and Unsubsidized Stafford, PLUS).

WORK-STUDY Federal work-study: Total amount: $200,000; jobs available. State or other work-study/employment: Part-time jobs available.

ATHLETIC AWARDS Total amount: $700,000 (100% non-need-based).

APPLYING FOR FINANCIAL AID Required financial aid form: FAFSA. Financial aid deadline (priority): 3/1. Notification date: Continuous beginning 3/1. Students must reply within 2 weeks of notification.

CONTACT Ms. Cathy Crawley, Director of Financial Aid, Georgia College & State University, Campus Box 30, Milledgeville, GA 31061, 478-445-5149 or toll-free 800-342-0471. Fax: 478-445-0729. E-mail: cathy.crawley@gcsu.edu. Website: http://www.gcsu.edu/.

GEORGIA GWINNETT COLLEGE
Lawrenceville, GA

CONTACT Financial Aid Office, Georgia Gwinnett College, 1000 University Center Lane, Lawrenceville, GA 30043, 678-407-5000 or toll-free 877-704-4422. Website: http://www.ggc.edu/.

GEORGIA INSTITUTE OF TECHNOLOGY
Atlanta, GA

Tuition & fees (GA res): $12,418	Average undergraduate aid package: $13,016

ABOUT THE INSTITUTION State-supported, coed. Awards: bachelor's, master's, and doctoral degrees. 33 undergraduate majors. Total enrollment: 29,370. Undergraduates: 15,572. Freshmen: 2,860. Both federal and institutional methodology are used as a basis for awarding need-based institutional aid.

UNDERGRADUATE EXPENSES for 2017–2018 Application fee: $75. Tuition, state resident: full-time $10,008; part-time $2974 per term. Tuition, nonresident: full-time $30,604; part-time $9081 per term. Required fees: full-time $2410; $1205 per term. Part-time tuition and fees vary according to course load. College room and board: $14,126; Room only: $9286. Room and board charges vary according to board plan, housing facility, and student level.

FRESHMAN FINANCIAL AID (Fall 2016) 2,318 applied for aid; of those 51% were deemed to have need. 93% of freshmen with need received aid; of those 52% had need fully met. Average percent of need met: 66% (excluding resources awarded to replace EFC). Average financial aid package: $14,735 (excluding resources awarded to replace EFC). 8% of all full-time freshmen had no need and received non-need-based gift aid.

UNDERGRADUATE FINANCIAL AID (Fall 2016) 9,499 applied for aid; of those 64% were deemed to have need. 95% of undergraduates with need received aid; of those 40% had need fully met. Average percent of need met: 54% (excluding resources awarded to replace EFC). Average financial aid package: $13,016

(excluding resources awarded to replace EFC). 7% of all full-time undergraduates had no need and received non-need-based gift aid.

GIFT AID (NEED-BASED) Total amount: $57,560,968 (19% federal, 47% state, 32% institutional, 2% external sources). Receiving aid: Freshmen: 17% (489); all full-time undergraduates: 20% (3,162). Average award: Freshmen: $7831; Undergraduates: $7194. Scholarships, grants, and awards: Federal Pell, FSEOG, state, private, college/university gift aid from institutional funds.

GIFT AID (NON-NEED-BASED) Total amount: $41,145,376 (76% state, 21% institutional, 3% external sources). Receiving aid: Freshmen: 29% (820). Undergraduates: 24% (3,685). Average award: Freshmen: $5523. Undergraduates: $5690. Scholarships, grants, and awards by category: Academic interests/ achievement: 3,194 awards ($18,694,216 total): architecture, biological sciences, computer science, engineering/technologies, general academic interests/achievements, international studies, physical sciences. Special achievements/activities: 211 awards ($4,423,095 total): cheerleading/drum major, general special achievements/activities, leadership. Special characteristics: 6,866 awards ($58,801,071 total): children with a deceased or disabled parent, local/state students, members of minority groups, out-of-state students, veterans, veterans' children. Tuition waivers: Full or partial for employees or children of employees, senior citizens. ROTC: Army, Naval, Air Force.

LOANS Student loans: $45,039,694 (79% need-based, 21% non-need-based). 40% of past graduating class borrowed through all loan programs. Average indebtedness per student: $32,398. Average need-based loan: Freshmen: $3046. Undergraduates: $4046. Parent loans: $23,823,651 (77% need-based, 23% non-need-based). Programs: Federal Direct (Subsidized and Unsubsidized Stafford, PLUS), Perkins, college/university.

WORK-STUDY Federal work-study: 399 jobs averaging $1686.

ATHLETIC AWARDS Total amount: $7,763,225 (39% need-based, 61% non-need-based).

APPLYING FOR FINANCIAL AID Required financial aid forms: FAFSA, institution's own form, CSS Financial Aid PROFILE. Financial aid deadline: 1/31. Notification date: 4/15. Students must reply by 5/1.

CONTACT Ms. Marie Mons, Director of Student Financial Planning and Services, Georgia Institute of Technology, 225 North Avenue, NW, Atlanta, GA 30332-0460, 404-894-4160. Fax: 404-894-7412. E-mail: marie.mons@finaid.gatech.edu. Website: http://www.gatech.edu/.

GEORGIAN COURT UNIVERSITY
Lakewood, NJ

Tuition & fees: $32,260	Average undergraduate aid package: $28,824

ABOUT THE INSTITUTION Independent Roman Catholic, coed. Awards: certificates, bachelor's, and master's degrees. 30 undergraduate majors. Total enrollment: 2,390. Undergraduates: 1,613. Freshmen: 216. Federal methodology is used as a basis for awarding need-based institutional aid.

UNDERGRADUATE EXPENSES for 2017–2018 Application fee: $40. Comprehensive fee: $43,068 includes full-time tuition ($30,800), mandatory fees ($1460), and room and board ($10,808). Full-time tuition and fees vary according to location, program, and reciprocity agreements. Part-time tuition: $704 per credit hour. Part-time fees: $365 per term. Part-time tuition and fees vary according to location, program, and reciprocity agreements.

FRESHMAN FINANCIAL AID (Fall 2017, est.) 208 applied for aid; of those 93% were deemed to have need. 100% of freshmen with need received aid; of those 24% had need fully met. Average percent of need met: 82% (excluding resources awarded to replace EFC). Average financial aid package: $33,169 (excluding resources awarded to replace EFC). 11% of all full-time freshmen had no need and received non-need-based gift aid.

UNDERGRADUATE FINANCIAL AID (Fall 2017, est.) 1,192 applied for aid; of those 95% were deemed to have need. 100% of undergraduates with need received aid; of those 20% had need fully met. Average percent of need met: 74% (excluding resources awarded to replace EFC). Average financial aid package: $28,824 (excluding resources awarded to replace EFC). 12% of all full-time undergraduates had no need and received non-need-based gift aid.

GIFT AID (NEED-BASED) Total amount: $22,341,032 (15% federal, 22% state, 63% institutional). Receiving aid: Freshmen: 88% (190); all full-time undergraduates: 82% (1,099). Average award: Freshmen: $23,091; Undergraduates: $19,530. Schol-

arships, grants, and awards: Federal Pell, FSEOG, state, private, college/university gift aid from institutional funds.

GIFT AID (NON-NEED-BASED) *Total amount:* $2,744,038 (1% federal, 99% institutional). *Receiving aid:* Freshmen: 6% (12). Undergraduates: 4% (60). *Average award:* Freshmen: $13,913. Undergraduates: $14,344. *Scholarships, grants, and awards by category: Academic Interests/achievement:* biological sciences, business, communication, computer science, education, English, foreign languages, general academic interests/achievements, home economics, humanities, international studies, mathematics, physical sciences, premedicine, religion/biblical studies, social sciences. *Creative arts/performance:* applied art and design, art/fine arts, dance. *Special achievements/activities:* community service, general special achievements/activities, leadership, memberships, religious involvement. *Special characteristics:* adult students, children and siblings of alumni, children of faculty/staff, ethnic background, first-generation college students, local/state students, married students, members of minority groups, out-of-state students, previous college experience, religious affiliation, siblings of current students, veterans. *Tuition waivers:* Full or partial for children of alumni, employees or children of employees, senior citizens.

LOANS *Student loans:* $9,884,949 (81% need-based, 19% non-need-based). 78% of past graduating class borrowed through all loan programs. *Average indebtedness per student:* $39,006. *Average need-based loan:* Freshmen: $5564. Undergraduates: $6823. *Parent loans:* $1,682,738 (64% need-based, 36% non-need-based). *Programs:* Federal Direct (Subsidized and Unsubsidized Stafford, PLUS), state.

WORK-STUDY *Federal work-study:* Total amount: $319,800; 206 jobs averaging $1552. *State or other work-study/employment:* Total amount: $21,000 (4% need-based, 96% non-need-based). 15 part-time jobs averaging $1400.

ATHLETIC AWARDS Total amount: $1,853,605 (63% need-based, 37% non-need-based).

APPLYING FOR FINANCIAL AID *Required financial aid form:* FAFSA. *Financial aid deadline:* 7/1 (priority: 1/15). *Notification date:* Continuous beginning 12/1.

CONTACT Mr. Randy Brown, Director of Financial Aid, Georgian Court University, 900 Lakewood Avenue, Lakewood, NJ 08701-2697, 732-987-2258 or toll-free 800-458-8422. *Fax:* 732-987-2023. *E-mail:* rbrown@georgian.edu. *Website:* http://www.georgian.edu/.

GEORGIA SOUTHERN UNIVERSITY
Statesboro, GA

Tuition & fees (GA res): $6890	Average undergraduate aid package: $10,410

ABOUT THE INSTITUTION State-supported, coed. *Awards:* certificates, bachelor's, master's, and doctoral degrees. 56 undergraduate majors. *Total enrollment:* 20,418. Undergraduates: 17,759. Freshmen: 3,508. Federal methodology is used as a basis for awarding need-based institutional aid.

UNDERGRADUATE EXPENSES for 2017–2018 *Application fee:* $30. *Tuition, state resident:* full-time $4798; part-time $177.67 per credit hour. *Tuition, nonresident:* full-time $16,930; part-time $627.07 per credit hour. *Required fees:* full-time $2092; $1046 per term. Full-time tuition and fees vary according to course load, degree level, location, and program. Part-time tuition and fees vary according to course load, degree level, location, and program. *College room and board:* $9650; *Room only:* $5900. Room and board charges vary according to board plan and housing facility.

FRESHMAN FINANCIAL AID (Fall 2016) 3,357 applied for aid; of those 67% were deemed to have need. 97% of freshmen with need received aid; of those 15% had need fully met. *Average percent of need met:* 60% (excluding resources awarded to replace EFC). *Average financial aid package:* $10,636 (excluding resources awarded to replace EFC). 4% of all full-time freshmen had no need and received non-need-based gift aid.

UNDERGRADUATE FINANCIAL AID (Fall 2016) 14,429 applied for aid; of those 72% were deemed to have need. 97% of undergraduates with need received aid; of those 11% had need fully met. *Average percent of need met:* 55% (excluding resources awarded to replace EFC). *Average financial aid package:* $10,410 (excluding resources awarded to replace EFC). 2% of all full-time undergraduates had no need and received non-need-based gift aid.

GIFT AID (NEED-BASED) *Total amount:* $57,507,881 (53% federal, 43% state, 2% institutional, 2% external sources). *Receiving aid:* Freshmen: 56% (1,998); all full-time undergraduates: 53% (8,506). *Average award:* Freshmen: $7434; Undergrad-

uates: $6837. *Scholarships, grants, and awards:* Federal Pell, FSEOG, state, private, college/university gift aid from institutional funds, Hope Scholarships, TEACH Grants, Zell Miller Scholarships.

GIFT AID (NON-NEED-BASED) *Total amount:* $15,695,357 (90% state, 6% institutional, 4% external sources). *Receiving aid:* Freshmen: 2% (56). Undergraduates: 1% (161). *Average award:* Freshmen: $1734. Undergraduates: $1734. *Scholarships, grants, and awards by category: Academic interests/achievement:* 948 awards ($1,471,784 total): biological sciences, business, communication, computer science, education, engineering/technologies, English, foreign languages, general academic interests/achievements, health fields, home economics, humanities, international studies, mathematics, military science, social sciences. *Creative arts/performance:* 217 awards ($221,007 total): art/fine arts, cinema/film/broadcasting, creative writing, general creative arts/performance, music, theater/drama. *Special achievements/activities:* 215 awards ($261,100 total): cheerleading/drum major, community service, junior miss, leadership, memberships, religious involvement. *Special characteristics:* 167 awards ($274,665 total): adult students, children and siblings of alumni, children of public servants, first-generation college students, general special characteristics, handicapped students, married students, members of minority groups, religious affiliation, veterans, veterans' children. *Tuition waivers:* Full or partial for employees or children of employees, senior citizens. *ROTC:* Army.

LOANS *Student loans:* $82,225,906 (78% need-based, 22% non-need-based). 70% of past graduating class borrowed through all loan programs. *Average indebtedness per student:* $29,724. *Average need-based loan:* Freshmen: $4916. Undergraduates: $5594. *Parent loans:* $19,366,992 (77% need-based, 23% non-need-based). *Programs:* Federal Direct (Subsidized and Unsubsidized Stafford, PLUS), Perkins, state, Student Access Loans (SAL), alternative loans.

WORK-STUDY *Federal work-study:* 265 jobs averaging $1671.

ATHLETIC AWARDS Total amount: $5,299,419 (52% need-based, 48% non-need-based).

APPLYING FOR FINANCIAL AID *Required financial aid form:* FAFSA. *Financial aid deadline (priority):* 4/20. *Notification date:* Continuous beginning 4/20.

CONTACT Mrs. Tracey Mingo, Director of Financial Aid, Georgia Southern University, PO Box 8065, Statesboro, GA 30460-8065, 912-478-5413. *Fax:* 912-478-0573. *E-mail:* tmingo@georgiasouthern.edu. *Website:* http://www.georgiasouthern.edu/.

GEORGIA SOUTHERN UNIVERSITY– ARMSTRONG CAMPUS
Savannah, GA

ABOUT THE INSTITUTION State-supported, coed. *Awards:* certificates, associate, bachelor's, master's, and doctoral degrees. 42 undergraduate majors. *Total enrollment:* 7,041. Undergraduates: 6,281. Freshmen: 840.

GIFT AID (NEED-BASED) *Scholarships, grants, and awards:* Federal Pell, FSEOG, state, private, college/university gift aid from institutional funds, United Negro College Fund, Federal Nursing.

GIFT AID (NON-NEED-BASED) *Scholarships, grants, and awards by category: Academic interests/achievement:* biological sciences, computer science, education, engineering/technologies, English, foreign languages, general academic interests/ achievements, health fields, humanities, international studies, mathematics, military science, physical sciences. *Creative arts/performance:* art/fine arts, general creative arts/performance, music. *Special achievements/activities:* community service. *Special characteristics:* ethnic background, international students, religious affiliation.

LOANS *Programs:* Federal Direct (Subsidized and Unsubsidized Stafford, PLUS), state, alternative loans.

APPLYING FOR FINANCIAL AID *Required financial aid forms:* FAFSA, general scholarship application form.

CONTACT Office of Financial Aid, Georgia Southern University–Armstrong Campus, 11935 Abercorn Street, Victor Hall, 2nd Floor, Savannah, GA 31419-1997, 912-344-3266 or toll-free 800-633-2349. *Fax:* 912-344-3448. *E-mail:* fin.aid@armstrong.edu. *Website:* http://www.georgiasouthern.edu/.

GEORGIA SOUTHWESTERN STATE UNIVERSITY
Americus, GA

Tuition & fees (GA res): $6332	Average undergraduate aid package: $9680

ABOUT THE INSTITUTION State-supported, coed. **Awards:** certificates, bachelor's, and master's degrees. 24 undergraduate majors. **Total enrollment:** 3,052. Undergraduates: 2,606. Freshmen: 452. Federal methodology is used as a basis for awarding need-based institutional aid.

UNDERGRADUATE EXPENSES for 2017–2018 Application fee: $25. **Tuition, state resident:** full-time $4956; part-time $165.20 per credit hour. **Tuition, nonresident:** full-time $18,032; part-time $601.07 per credit hour. **Required fees:** full-time $1376. Full-time tuition and fees vary according to course load, location, and program. Part-time tuition and fees vary according to course load, location, and program. **College room and board:** $7910; **Room only:** $3970. Room and board charges vary according to board plan and housing facility.

FRESHMAN FINANCIAL AID (Fall 2017, est.) 415 applied for aid; of those 79% were deemed to have need. 99% of freshmen with need received aid; of those 14% had need fully met. **Average percent of need met:** 59% (excluding resources awarded to replace EFC). **Average financial aid package:** $10,015 (excluding resources awarded to replace EFC). 7% of all full-time freshmen had no need and received non-need-based gift aid.

UNDERGRADUATE FINANCIAL AID (Fall 2017, est.) 1,571 applied for aid; of those 82% were deemed to have need. 99% of undergraduates with need received aid; of those 12% had need fully met. **Average percent of need met:** 67% (excluding resources awarded to replace EFC). **Average financial aid package:** $9680 (excluding resources awarded to replace EFC). 6% of all full-time undergraduates had no need and received non-need-based gift aid.

GIFT AID (NEED-BASED) Total amount: $4,807,158 (100% federal). **Receiving aid:** Freshmen: 48% (213); all full-time undergraduates: 48% (849). **Average award:** Freshmen: $4724; Undergraduates: $4700. **Scholarships, grants, and awards:** Federal Pell, FSEOG, state, private, college/university gift aid from institutional funds.

GIFT AID (NON-NEED-BASED) Total amount: $4,127,128 (76% state, 19% institutional, 5% external sources). **Receiving aid:** Freshmen: 53% (234). Undergraduates: 38% (675). **Average award:** Freshmen: $1810. Undergraduates: $2083. **Scholarships, grants, and awards by category:** Academic interests/achievement: 159 awards ($306,575 total): general academic interests/achievements. Creative arts/performance: 42 awards ($34,925 total): art/fine arts, music, theater/drama. Special achievements/activities: 26 awards ($10,680 total): leadership. Special characteristics: children and siblings of alumni, general special characteristics, local/state students. **Tuition waivers:** Full or partial for senior citizens.

LOANS Student loans: $11,677,176 (44% need-based, 56% non-need-based). 74% of past graduating class borrowed through all loan programs. **Average indebtedness per student:** $25,775. **Average need-based loan:** Freshmen: $3235. Undergraduates: $3886. **Parent loans:** $801,663 (100% non-need-based). **Programs:** Federal Direct (Subsidized and Unsubsidized Stafford, PLUS), state.

WORK-STUDY Federal work-study: Total amount: $214,776; 115 jobs averaging $1868.

ATHLETIC AWARDS Total amount: $557,169 (100% non-need-based).

APPLYING FOR FINANCIAL AID Required financial aid form: FAFSA. **Financial aid deadline:** 6/15 (priority: 4/15). **Notification date:** Continuous beginning 5/1. Students must reply within 8 weeks of notification.

CONTACT Angela Bryant, Director of Financial Aid, Georgia Southwestern State University, 800 Georgia Southwestern State University Drive, Americus, GA 31709-4693, 229-928-1378 or toll-free 800-338-0082. *Fax:* 229-931-2061. *E-mail:* finaid@gsw.edu.
Website: http://www.gsw.edu/.

GEORGIA STATE UNIVERSITY
Atlanta, GA

Tuition & fees (GA res): $10,858	Average undergraduate aid package: $10,626

ABOUT THE INSTITUTION State-supported, coed. **Awards:** certificates, associate, bachelor's, master's, and doctoral degrees. 49 undergraduate majors. **Total enrollment:** 32,848. Undergraduates: 25,790. Freshmen: 4,270. Both federal and institutional methodology are used as a basis for awarding need-based institutional aid.

UNDERGRADUATE EXPENSES for 2017–2018 Application fee: $60. **Tuition, state resident:** full-time $8730; part-time $291 per credit hour. **Tuition, nonresident:** full-time $27,304; part-time $910 per credit hour. **Required fees:** full-time $2128; $1064 per term. Part-time tuition and fees vary according to course load. **College room and board:** $14,392; **Room only:** $10,560. Room and board charges vary according to board plan and housing facility.

FRESHMAN FINANCIAL AID (Fall 2016) 3,717 applied for aid; of those 88% were deemed to have need. 96% of freshmen with need received aid; of those 6% had need fully met. **Average percent of need met:** 54% (excluding resources awarded to replace EFC). **Average financial aid package:** $12,541 (excluding resources awarded to replace EFC).

UNDERGRADUATE FINANCIAL AID (Fall 2016) 22,320 applied for aid; of those 87% were deemed to have need. 97% of undergraduates with need received aid; of those 6% had need fully met. **Average percent of need met:** 53% (excluding resources awarded to replace EFC). **Average financial aid package:** $10,626 (excluding resources awarded to replace EFC).

GIFT AID (NEED-BASED) Total amount: $98,684,050 (97% federal, 3% institutional). **Receiving aid:** Freshmen: 54% (2,096); all full-time undergraduates: 55% (14,095). **Average award:** Freshmen: $5276; Undergraduates: $5109. **Scholarships, grants, and awards:** Federal Pell, FSEOG, state, private, college/university gift aid from institutional funds, United Negro College Fund.

GIFT AID (NON-NEED-BASED) Total amount: $82,596,966 (1% federal, 98% state, 1% institutional). **Receiving aid:** Freshmen: 73% (2,846). Undergraduates: 70% (17,735). **Tuition waivers:** Full or partial for employees or children of employees, senior citizens. **ROTC:** Army, Naval cooperative, Air Force cooperative.

LOANS Student loans: $152,761,082 (46% need-based, 54% non-need-based). 69% of past graduating class borrowed through all loan programs. **Average indebtedness per student:** $30,167. **Programs:** Federal Direct (Subsidized and Unsubsidized Stafford, PLUS), Perkins, Federal Nursing, state.

WORK-STUDY Federal work-study: jobs available. **State or other work-study/employment:** Part-time jobs available.

ATHLETIC AWARDS Total amount: $6,876,931 (100% non-need-based).

APPLYING FOR FINANCIAL AID Required financial aid form: FAFSA. **Financial aid deadline:** 4/1. **Notification date:** Continuous beginning 3/1. Students must reply by 4/1 or within 3 weeks of notification.

CONTACT Office of Student Financial Aid, Georgia State University, PO Box 4040, Atlanta, GA 30302, 404-413-2600. *Fax:* 404-413-2102. *E-mail:* onestopshop@gsu.edu. *Website:* http://www.gsu.edu/.

GETTYSBURG COLLEGE
Gettysburg, PA

Tuition & fees: $52,640	Average undergraduate aid package: $40,700

ABOUT THE INSTITUTION Independent Evangelical Lutheran Church in America, coed. **Awards:** bachelor's degrees. 82 undergraduate majors. **Total enrollment:** 2,409. Undergraduates: 2,409. Freshmen: 720. Both federal and institutional methodology are used as a basis for awarding need-based institutional aid.

UNDERGRADUATE EXPENSES for 2017–2018 Application fee: $60. **Comprehensive fee:** $65,210 includes full-time tuition ($52,640) and room and board ($12,570). **College room only:** $6740. Room and board charges vary according to board plan and housing facility.

FRESHMAN FINANCIAL AID (Fall 2017, est.) 567 applied for aid; of those 83% were deemed to have need. 99% of freshmen with need received aid; of those 90% had need fully met. **Average percent of need met:** 90% (excluding resources awarded to replace EFC). **Average financial aid package:** $40,147 (excluding resources

awarded to replace EFC). 18% of all full-time freshmen had no need and received non-need-based gift aid.

UNDERGRADUATE FINANCIAL AID (Fall 2017, est.) 1,837 applied for aid; of those 89% were deemed to have need. 97% of undergraduates with need received aid; of those 90% had need fully met. *Average percent of need met:* 90% (excluding resources awarded to replace EFC). *Average financial aid package:* $40,700 (excluding resources awarded to replace EFC). 18% of all full-time undergraduates had no need and received non-need-based gift aid.

GIFT AID (NEED-BASED) *Total amount:* $61,067,837 (4% federal, 1% state, 94% institutional, 1% external sources). *Receiving aid:* Freshmen: 64% (459); all full-time undergraduates: 60% (1,574). *Average award:* Freshmen: $36,718; Undergraduates: $36,153. *Scholarships, grants, and awards:* Federal Pell, FSEOG, state, private, college/university gift aid from institutional funds.

GIFT AID (NON-NEED-BASED) *Total amount:* $5,075,739 (27% federal, 65% institutional, 8% external sources). *Receiving aid:* Freshmen: 35% (255). Undergraduates: 31% (814). *Average award:* Freshmen: $16,727. Undergraduates: $13,256. *Scholarships, grants, and awards by category:* Academic interests/achievement: 1,132 awards ($14,263,000 total): general academic interests/achievements. Creative arts/performance: 19 awards ($185,000 total): music. *Tuition waivers:* Full or partial for employees or children of employees. *ROTC:* Army cooperative.

LOANS *Student loans:* $13,743,374 (68% need-based, 32% non-need-based). 62% of past graduating class borrowed through all loan programs. *Average indebtedness per student:* $31,323. *Average need-based loan:* Freshmen: $3626. Undergraduates: $4702. *Parent loans:* $6,340,792 (100% non-need-based). *Programs:* Federal Direct (Subsidized and Unsubsidized Stafford, PLUS), Perkins, college/university.

WORK-STUDY *Federal work-study:* Total amount: $273,019; 376 jobs averaging $958. *State or other work-study/employment:* Total amount: $964,130 (100% non-need-based). 1,180 part-time jobs averaging $1048.

APPLYING FOR FINANCIAL AID *Required financial aid forms:* FAFSA, CSS Financial Aid PROFILE, federal income tax form(s), verification worksheet. *Financial aid deadline:* 1/15. *Notification date:* 3/27. Students must reply by 5/1.

CONTACT Christina Gormley, Director of Financial Aid, Gettysburg College, 300 North Washington Street, Gettysburg, PA 17325, 717-337-6611 or toll-free 800-431-0803. *Fax:* 717-337-8555. *E-mail:* finaid@gettysburg.edu.
Website: http://www.gettysburg.edu/.

GLENVILLE STATE COLLEGE
Glenville, WV

Tuition & fees: N/R	Average undergraduate aid package: $14,539

ABOUT THE INSTITUTION State-supported, coed. 32 undergraduate majors. Federal methodology is used as a basis for awarding need-based institutional aid.

FRESHMAN FINANCIAL AID (Fall 2017, est.) 292 applied for aid; of those 89% were deemed to have need. 99% of freshmen with need received aid; of those 12% had need fully met. *Average percent of need met:* 70% (excluding resources awarded to replace EFC). *Average financial aid package:* $14,108 (excluding resources awarded to replace EFC). 2% of all full-time freshmen had no need and received non-need-based gift aid.

UNDERGRADUATE FINANCIAL AID (Fall 2017, est.) 1,002 applied for aid; of those 89% were deemed to have need. 99% of undergraduates with need received aid; of those 13% had need fully met. *Average percent of need met:* 73% (excluding resources awarded to replace EFC). *Average financial aid package:* $14,539 (excluding resources awarded to replace EFC). 3% of all full-time undergraduates had no need and received non-need-based gift aid.

GIFT AID (NEED-BASED) *Total amount:* $5,011,354 (74% federal, 26% state). *Receiving aid:* Freshmen: 72% (214); all full-time undergraduates: 73% (761). *Average award:* Freshmen: $6860; Undergraduates: $6571. *Scholarships, grants, and awards:* Federal Pell, FSEOG, state, private, college/university gift aid from institutional funds.

GIFT AID (NON-NEED-BASED) *Total amount:* $1,406,730 (44% state, 31% institutional, 25% external sources). *Receiving aid:* Freshmen: 64% (190). Undergraduates: 59% (614). *Average award:* Freshmen: $1700. Undergraduates: $2171. *Scholarships, grants, and awards by category:* Academic interests/achievement: 285 awards ($387,178 total): biological sciences, business, education,

English, general academic interests/achievements, international studies, mathematics, social sciences. *Creative arts/performance:* 128 awards ($66,984 total): art/fine arts, journalism/publications, music. *Special achievements/activities:* 5 awards ($1250 total): general special achievements/activities. *Special characteristics:* 281 awards ($1,142,663 total): children of faculty/staff, first-generation college students, out-of-state students, veterans, veterans' children.

LOANS *Student loans:* $5,789,986 (42% need-based, 58% non-need-based). 76% of past graduating class borrowed through all loan programs. *Average indebtedness per student:* $29,608. *Average need-based loan:* Freshmen: $2958. Undergraduates: $3740. *Parent loans:* $615,984 (100% non-need-based). *Programs:* Federal Direct (Subsidized and Unsubsidized Stafford, PLUS), private loans.

WORK-STUDY *Federal work-study:* Total amount: $138,842; 111 jobs averaging $1235. *State or other work-study/employment:* Total amount: $541,000 (100% non-need-based). 246 part-time jobs averaging $2080.

ATHLETIC AWARDS Total amount: $1,476,875 (100% non-need-based).

APPLYING FOR FINANCIAL AID *Required financial aid form:* FAFSA. *Financial aid deadline (priority):* 2/1. *Notification date:* Continuous beginning 3/1. Students must reply within 3 weeks of notification.

CONTACT Ms. Stephany Harper, Financial Aid Manager, Glenville State College, 200 High Street, Glenville, WV 26351-1200, 304-462-6171 or toll-free 800-924-2010. *Fax:* 304-462-4407. *E-mail:* stephany.harper@glenville.edu.
Website: http://www.glenville.edu/.

GODDARD COLLEGE
Plainfield, VT

ABOUT THE INSTITUTION Independent, coed. *Awards:* bachelor's and master's degrees. 53 undergraduate majors. *Total enrollment:* 505. Undergraduates: 194. Freshmen: 9.

GIFT AID (NEED-BASED) *Scholarships, grants, and awards:* Federal Pell, FSEOG, state, private, college/university gift aid from institutional funds.

GIFT AID (NON-NEED-BASED) *Scholarships, grants, and awards by category:* Creative arts/performance: art/fine arts, creative writing, dance, performing arts, theater/drama.

LOANS *Programs:* Federal Direct (Subsidized and Unsubsidized Stafford, PLUS), Perkins.

APPLYING FOR FINANCIAL AID *Required financial aid form:* FAFSA.

CONTACT Shannon Trainor, Associate Director of Financial Aid, Goddard College, 123 Pitkin Road, Plainfield, VT 05667, 802-454-8311 Ext. 303 or toll-free 800-906-8312. *Fax:* 802-322-1000. *E-mail:* shannon.trainor@goddard.edu.
Website: http://www.goddard.edu/.

GOD'S BIBLE SCHOOL AND COLLEGE
Cincinnati, OH

CONTACT Mrs. Lori Waggoner, Financial Aid Director, God's Bible School and College, 1810 Young Street, Cincinnati, OH 45202-6899, 513-721-7944 Ext. 205 or toll-free 800-486-4637. *Fax:* 513-721-1357. *E-mail:* lwaggoner@gbs.edu.
Website: http://www.gbs.edu/.

GOLDEN GATE UNIVERSITY
San Francisco, CA

CONTACT Kathleen Kelly, Interim Director of Financial Services, Golden Gate University, 536 Mission Street, San Francisco, CA 94105-2968, 415-442-7297 or toll-free 800-448-3381. *Fax:* 415-442-7819. *E-mail:* kkelly@ggu.edu.
Website: http://www.ggu.edu/.

GOLDEY-BEACOM COLLEGE
Wilmington, DE

CONTACT Jane H. Lysle, Dean of Enrollment Management, Goldey-Beacom College, 4701 Limestone Road, Wilmington, DE 19808-1999, 302-225-6274 or toll-free 800-833-4877. *Fax:* 302-998-8631. *E-mail:* lyslej@gbc.edu. *Website:* http://www.gbc.edu/.

GOLDFARB SCHOOL OF NURSING AT BARNES-JEWISH COLLEGE
St. Louis, MO

Tuition & fees: $20,188	Average undergraduate aid package: $4027

ABOUT THE INSTITUTION Independent, coed, primarily women. *Awards:* certificates, bachelor's, master's, and doctoral degrees. 1 undergraduate major. *Total enrollment:* 695. Undergraduates: 630. Federal methodology is used as a basis for awarding need-based institutional aid.

UNDERGRADUATE EXPENSES for 2018–2019 *Application fee:* $50. *Tuition:* full-time $19,058; part-time $733 per credit hour. *Required fees:* full-time $1130; $615 per term. Full-time tuition and fees vary according to course load and degree level. Part-time tuition and fees vary according to course load and degree level.

UNDERGRADUATE FINANCIAL AID (Fall 2016) 465 applied for aid; of those 95% were deemed to have need. 100% of undergraduates with need received aid. *Average financial aid package:* $4027 (excluding resources awarded to replace EFC). 1% of all full-time undergraduates had no need and received non-need-based gift aid.

GIFT AID (NEED-BASED) *Total amount:* $1,566,103 (54% federal, 13% state, 24% institutional, 9% external sources). *Receiving aid:* All full-time undergraduates: 30% (163). *Average award:* Undergraduates: $2750. *Scholarships, grants, and awards:* Federal Pell, FSEOG, state, private.

GIFT AID (NON-NEED-BASED) *Receiving aid:* Undergraduates: 9% (47). *Average award:* Undergraduates: $6250. *Scholarships, grants, and awards by category:* Academic interests/achievement: general academic interests/achievements.

LOANS *Student loans:* $7,516,929 (42% need-based, 58% non-need-based). *Average need-based loan:* Undergraduates: $4850. *Parent loans:* $963,349 (100% non-need-based). *Programs:* Federal Direct (Subsidized and Unsubsidized Stafford, PLUS).

WORK-STUDY *Federal work-study:* 29 jobs averaging $1164.

APPLYING FOR FINANCIAL AID *Required financial aid forms:* FAFSA, institution's own form. *Financial aid deadline (priority):* 4/1. *Notification date:* Continuous beginning 4/1. Students must reply within 2 weeks of notification.

CONTACT Michael Ward, Vice Dean, Student Affairs and Diversity, Goldfarb School of Nursing at Barnes-Jewish College, 4483 Duncan, St. Louis, MO 63110-1091, 314-362-9155 or toll-free 800-832-9009. *Fax:* 314-362-9222. *E-mail:* michael.ward@bjc.org. *Website:* http://www.barnesjewishcollege.edu/.

GONZAGA UNIVERSITY
Spokane, WA

Tuition & fees: $41,330	Average undergraduate aid package: $30,040

ABOUT THE INSTITUTION Independent Roman Catholic, coed. *Awards:* bachelor's, master's, and doctoral degrees. 56 undergraduate majors. *Total enrollment:* 7,506. Undergraduates: 5,209. Freshmen: 1,257. Federal methodology is used as a basis for awarding need-based institutional aid.

UNDERGRADUATE EXPENSES for 2017–2018 *Application fee:* $50. *Comprehensive fee:* $52,880 includes full-time tuition ($40,540), mandatory fees ($790), and room and board ($11,550). *College room only:* $5900. Full-time tuition and fees vary according to course load, location, program, reciprocity agreements, and student level. Room and board charges vary according to board plan, housing facility, and location. *Part-time tuition:* $1110 per credit. *Part-time fees:* $180 per term. Part-time tuition and fees vary according to course load, location, program, reciprocity agreements, and student level.

FRESHMAN FINANCIAL AID (Fall 2016) 1,091 applied for aid; of those 71% were deemed to have need. 100% of freshmen with need received aid; of those 29% had need fully met. *Average percent of need met:* 82% (excluding resources awarded to replace EFC). *Average financial aid package:* $27,736 (excluding resources awarded to replace EFC). 38% of all full-time freshmen had no need and received non-need-based gift aid.

UNDERGRADUATE FINANCIAL AID (Fall 2016) 3,404 applied for aid; of those 79% were deemed to have need. 100% of undergraduates with need received aid; of those 28% had need fully met. *Average percent of need met:* 80% (excluding resources awarded to replace EFC). *Average financial aid package:* $30,040 (excluding resources awarded to replace EFC). 44% of all full-time undergraduates had no need and received non-need-based gift aid.

GIFT AID (NEED-BASED) *Total amount:* $50,043,205 (7% federal, 5% state, 85% institutional, 3% external sources). *Receiving aid:* Freshmen: 62% (774); all full-time undergraduates: 54% (2,680). *Average award:* Freshmen: $21,414; Undergraduates: $22,206. *Scholarships, grants, and awards:* Federal Pell, FSEOG, state, private, college/university gift aid from institutional funds, Federal Nursing.

GIFT AID (NON-NEED-BASED) *Total amount:* $45,102,326 (94% institutional, 6% external sources). *Receiving aid:* Freshmen: 16% (196). Undergraduates: 12% (604). *Average award:* Freshmen: $15,510. Undergraduates: $15,837. *Scholarships, grants, and awards by category:* Academic interests/achievement: 193 awards ($890,555 total): business, engineering/technologies, military science. *Creative arts/performance:* 130 awards ($298,500 total): debating, music, performing arts. *Special achievements/activities:* 543 awards ($5,368,711 total): community service, general special achievements/activities, leadership, memberships. *Special characteristics:* 512 awards ($4,949,396 total): children and siblings of alumni, children of faculty/staff, international students, members of minority groups, siblings of current students. *Tuition waivers:* Full or partial for employees or children of employees, senior citizens. *ROTC:* Army.

LOANS *Student loans:* $21,665,213 (75% need-based, 25% non-need-based). 53% of past graduating class borrowed through all loan programs. *Average indebtedness per student:* $29,692. *Average need-based loan:* Freshmen: $4821. Undergraduates: $5578. *Parent loans:* $10,117,517 (75% need-based, 25% non-need-based). *Programs:* Federal Direct (Subsidized and Unsubsidized Stafford, PLUS), Perkins, Federal Nursing, college/university.

WORK-STUDY *Federal work-study:* 346 jobs averaging $2457. *State or other work-study/employment:* Total amount: $4,318,480 (38% need-based, 62% non-need-based). 188 part-time jobs averaging $2879.

ATHLETIC AWARDS Total amount: $4,949,895 (14% need-based, 86% non-need-based).

APPLYING FOR FINANCIAL AID *Required financial aid form:* FAFSA. *Financial aid deadline (priority):* 2/1. *Notification date:* Continuous beginning 3/1. Students must reply by 5/1.

CONTACT James White, Dean of Student Financial Services, Gonzaga University, 502 East Boone Avenue, Spokane, WA 99258-0072, 509-313-6568 or toll-free 800-322-2584 Ext. 6572. *Fax:* 509-313-5816. *E-mail:* whitej@gonzaga.edu. *Website:* http://www.gonzaga.edu/.

GORDON COLLEGE
Wenham, MA

Tuition & fees: $37,400	Average undergraduate aid package: $26,133

ABOUT THE INSTITUTION Independent nondenominational, coed. *Awards:* bachelor's and master's degrees. 37 undergraduate majors. *Total enrollment:* 1,963. Undergraduates: 1,591. Freshmen: 417. Federal methodology is used as a basis for awarding need-based institutional aid.

UNDERGRADUATE EXPENSES for 2018–2019 *Application fee:* $50. *Comprehensive fee:* $48,470 includes full-time tuition ($35,800), mandatory fees ($1600), and room and board ($11,070). *College room only:* $7000. Full-time tuition and fees vary according to course load and program. Room and board charges vary according to board plan and housing facility. *Part-time tuition:* $895 per credit. Part-time tuition and fees vary according to course load and program.

FRESHMAN FINANCIAL AID (Fall 2017, est.) 359 applied for aid; of those 86% were deemed to have need. 100% of freshmen with need received aid; of those 18%

had need fully met. *Average percent of need met:* 73% (excluding resources awarded to replace EFC). *Average financial aid package:* $27,047 (excluding resources awarded to replace EFC). 26% of all full-time freshmen had no need and received non-need-based gift aid.

UNDERGRADUATE FINANCIAL AID (Fall 2017, est.) 1,211 applied for aid; of those 87% were deemed to have need. 100% of undergraduates with need received aid; of those 19% had need fully met. *Average percent of need met:* 72% (excluding resources awarded to replace EFC). *Average financial aid package:* $26,133 (excluding resources awarded to replace EFC). 31% of all full-time undergraduates had no need and received non-need-based gift aid.

GIFT AID (NEED-BASED) *Total amount:* $6,427,156 (30% federal, 5% state, 30% institutional, 35% external sources). *Receiving aid:* Freshmen: 74% (308); all full-time undergraduates: 67% (1,047). *Average award:* Freshmen: $23,212; Undergraduates: $21,281. *Scholarships, grants, and awards:* Federal Pell, FSEOG, state, private, college/university gift aid from institutional funds.

GIFT AID (NON-NEED-BASED) *Total amount:* $9,891,742 (86% institutional, 14% external sources). *Receiving aid:* Freshmen: 10% (41). Undergraduates: 9% (140). *Average award:* Freshmen: $17,114. Undergraduates: $15,571. *Scholarships, grants, and awards by category:* Academic interests/achievement: 1,382 awards: general academic interests/achievements. Creative arts/performance: 134 awards: art/fine arts, music, theater/drama. Special achievements/activities: 185 awards: leadership. Special characteristics: 513 awards: children and siblings of alumni, children of faculty/staff, international students, relatives of clergy, veterans, veterans' children. *Tuition waivers:* Full or partial for employees or children of employees. *ROTC:* Army cooperative.

LOANS *Student loans:* $12,009,403 (67% need-based, 33% non-need-based). 82% of past graduating class borrowed through all loan programs. *Average indebtedness per student:* $37,780. *Average need-based loan:* Freshmen: $3663. Undergraduates: $4777. *Parent loans:* $3,931,700 (53% need-based, 47% non-need-based). *Programs:* Federal Direct (Subsidized and Unsubsidized Stafford, PLUS), Perkins, state.

WORK-STUDY *Federal work-study:* Total amount: $250,000; 395 jobs averaging $639.

APPLYING FOR FINANCIAL AID *Required financial aid form:* FAFSA. *Financial aid deadline (priority):* 3/1. *Notification date:* Continuous beginning 2/15. Students must reply by 5/1 or within 2 weeks of notification.

CONTACT Daniel O'Connell, Senior Director of Student Financial Services, Gordon College, 255 Grapevine Road, Wenham, MA 01984-1899, 978-867-4246 or toll-free 866-464-6736. *Fax:* 978-867-4657. *E-mail:* daniel.oconnell@gordon.edu. *Website:* http://www.gordon.edu/.

GOSHEN COLLEGE
Goshen, IN

Tuition & fees: $33,700	Average undergraduate aid package: $27,982

ABOUT THE INSTITUTION Independent Mennonite, coed. *Awards:* bachelor's and master's degrees. 57 undergraduate majors. *Total enrollment:* 950. Undergraduates: 883. Freshmen: 215. Federal methodology is used as a basis for awarding need-based institutional aid.

UNDERGRADUATE EXPENSES for 2018–2019 *Application fee:* $25. *Comprehensive fee:* $44,350 includes full-time tuition ($33,700) and room and board ($10,650). *College room only:* $5670. Full-time tuition and fees vary according to degree level and program. Room and board charges vary according to board plan and housing facility. *Part-time tuition:* $1380 per credit hour. Part-time tuition and fees vary according to course load, degree level, and program.

FRESHMAN FINANCIAL AID (Fall 2017, est.) 193 applied for aid; of those 94% were deemed to have need. 100% of freshmen with need received aid; of those 21% had need fully met. *Average percent of need met:* 85% (excluding resources awarded to replace EFC). *Average financial aid package:* $30,536 (excluding resources awarded to replace EFC). 15% of all full-time freshmen had no need and received non-need-based gift aid.

UNDERGRADUATE FINANCIAL AID (Fall 2017, est.) 662 applied for aid; of those 93% were deemed to have need. 100% of undergraduates with need received aid; of those 18% had need fully met. *Average percent of need met:* 83% (excluding resources awarded to replace EFC). *Average financial aid package:*

$27,982 (excluding resources awarded to replace EFC). 22% of all full-time undergraduates had no need and received non-need-based gift aid.

GIFT AID (NEED-BASED) *Total amount:* $12,702,921 (12% federal, 12% state, 65% institutional, 11% external sources). *Receiving aid:* Freshmen: 85% (182); all full-time undergraduates: 74% (602). *Average award:* Freshmen: $26,277; Undergraduates: $23,549. *Scholarships, grants, and awards:* Federal Pell, FSEOG, state, private, college/university gift aid from institutional funds.

GIFT AID (NON-NEED-BASED) *Total amount:* $3,905,844 (75% institutional, 25% external sources). *Receiving aid:* Freshmen: 18% (38). Undergraduates: 13% (106). *Average award:* Freshmen: $17,970. Undergraduates: $14,275. *Scholarships, grants, and awards by category:* Academic interests/achievement: business, communication, education, general academic interests/achievements. Creative arts/performance: music, theater/drama. Special achievements/activities: community service, junior miss. Special characteristics: children of educators, children of faculty/staff, ethnic background, international students, members of minority groups. *Tuition waivers:* Full or partial for employees or children of employees.

LOANS *Student loans:* $5,326,527 (75% need-based, 25% non-need-based). 63% of past graduating class borrowed through all loan programs. *Average indebtedness per student:* $27,062. *Average need-based loan:* Freshmen: $4364. Undergraduates: $5251. *Parent loans:* $676,793 (50% need-based, 50% non-need-based). *Programs:* Federal Direct (Subsidized and Unsubsidized Stafford, PLUS), Perkins, Federal Nursing.

WORK-STUDY *Federal work-study:* Total amount: $389,503; 341 jobs averaging $1066. *State or other work-study/employment:* Total amount: $94,400 (100% non-need-based). 55 part-time jobs averaging $1815.

ATHLETIC AWARDS Total amount: $1,431,885 (61% need-based, 39% non-need-based).

APPLYING FOR FINANCIAL AID *Required financial aid form:* FAFSA. *Financial aid deadline:* Continuous. *Notification date:* Continuous beginning 1/10.

CONTACT Mr. Joel D. Short, Director of Student Financial Aid, Goshen College, 1700 South Main Street, Goshen, IN 46526-4794, 574-535-7525 or toll-free 800-348-7422. *Fax:* 574-535-7654. *E-mail:* joelds@goshen.edu. *Website:* http://www.goshen.edu/.

GOUCHER COLLEGE
Baltimore, MD

Tuition & fees: $43,440	Average undergraduate aid package: $36,918

ABOUT THE INSTITUTION Independent, coed. *Awards:* certificates, bachelor's, and master's degrees. 34 undergraduate majors. *Total enrollment:* 2,172. Undergraduates: 1,473. Freshmen: 441. Federal methodology is used as a basis for awarding need-based institutional aid.

UNDERGRADUATE EXPENSES for 2017–2018 *Application fee:* $55. *Comprehensive fee:* $56,110 includes full-time tuition ($42,600), mandatory fees ($840), and room and board ($12,670). Room and board charges vary according to board plan and housing facility. *Part-time tuition:* $1420 per credit hour. *Payment plan:* Tuition prepayment.

FRESHMAN FINANCIAL AID (Fall 2017, est.) 360 applied for aid; of those 85% were deemed to have need. 100% of freshmen with need received aid; of those 25% had need fully met. *Average percent of need met:* 84% (excluding resources awarded to replace EFC). *Average financial aid package:* $37,562 (excluding resources awarded to replace EFC). 27% of all full-time freshmen had no need and received non-need-based gift aid.

UNDERGRADUATE FINANCIAL AID (Fall 2017, est.) 1,072 applied for aid; of those 89% were deemed to have need. 100% of undergraduates with need received aid; of those 23% had need fully met. *Average percent of need met:* 82% (excluding resources awarded to replace EFC). *Average financial aid package:* $36,918 (excluding resources awarded to replace EFC). 30% of all full-time undergraduates had no need and received non-need-based gift aid.

GIFT AID (NEED-BASED) *Total amount:* $31,313,942 (6% federal, 5% state, 85% institutional, 4% external sources). *Receiving aid:* Freshmen: 73% (306); all full-time undergraduates: 67% (958). *Average award:* Freshmen: $33,996; Undergraduates: $32,630. *Scholarships, grants, and awards:* Federal Pell, FSEOG, state, private, college/university gift aid from institutional funds.

GIFT AID (NON-NEED-BASED) *Total amount:* $10,087,070 (89% institutional, 11% external sources). *Receiving aid:* Freshmen: 9% (38). Undergraduates: 7% (102). *Average award:* Freshmen: $19,581. Undergraduates: $19,119. *Scholarships, grants, and awards by category: Creative arts/performance:* 41 awards ($621,250 total): art/fine arts, dance, music, performing arts, theater/drama. *Special achievements/activities:* 13 awards ($130,000 total): leadership. *Tuition waivers:* Full or partial for employees or children of employees. *ROTC:* Army cooperative, Air Force cooperative.

LOANS *Student loans:* $7,862,018 (69% need-based, 31% non-need-based). 64% of past graduating class borrowed through all loan programs. *Average indebtedness per student:* $33,702. *Average need-based loan:* Freshmen: $3156. Undergraduates: $4071. *Parent loans:* $3,296,900 (43% need-based, 57% non-need-based). *Programs:* Federal Direct (Subsidized and Unsubsidized Stafford, PLUS), Perkins.

WORK-STUDY *Federal work-study:* Total amount: $755,194; 397 jobs averaging $1863. *State or other work-study/employment:* Part-time jobs available.

APPLYING FOR FINANCIAL AID *Required financial aid form:* FAFSA. *Financial aid deadline (priority):* 2/1. *Notification date:* Continuous beginning 11/1. Students must reply by 5/1.

CONTACT Mrs. Stephanie Alford, Director of Student Financial Aid, Goucher College, 1021 Dulaney Valley Road, Baltimore, MD 21204-2794, 410-337-6141 or toll-free 800-468-2437. *Fax:* 410-337-6504. *E-mail:* stephanie.alford@goucher.edu. *Website:* http://www.goucher.edu/.

GOVERNORS STATE UNIVERSITY
University Park, IL

Tuition & fees (IL res): $11,746	Average undergraduate aid package: $11,536

ABOUT THE INSTITUTION State-supported, coed. *Awards:* certificates, bachelor's, master's, and doctoral degrees. 30 undergraduate majors. *Total enrollment:* 5,185. Undergraduates: 3,326. Freshmen: 199. Both federal and institutional methodology are used as a basis for awarding need-based institutional aid.

UNDERGRADUATE EXPENSES for 2018–2019 *Application fee:* $25. *Tuition, state resident:* full-time $9390; part-time $313 per credit hour. *Tuition, nonresident:* full-time $18,780; part-time $626 per credit hour. *Required fees:* full-time $2356; $76 per credit hour or $38 per term. Full-time tuition and fees vary according to course load, degree level, and reciprocity agreements. Part-time tuition and fees vary according to course load, degree level, and reciprocity agreements. *College room and board:* $10,104; *Room only:* $8104. Room and board charges vary according to board plan and housing facility. *Payment plan:* Guaranteed tuition.

FRESHMAN FINANCIAL AID (Fall 2016) 91% of freshmen with need received aid; of those 6% had need fully met. *Average percent of need met:* 57% (excluding resources awarded to replace EFC). *Average financial aid package:* $11,833 (excluding resources awarded to replace EFC). 57% of all full-time freshmen had no need and received non-need-based gift aid.

UNDERGRADUATE FINANCIAL AID (Fall 2016) 84% of undergraduates with need received aid; of those 6% had need fully met. *Average percent of need met:* 58% (excluding resources awarded to replace EFC). *Average financial aid package:* $11,536 (excluding resources awarded to replace EFC). 14% of all full-time undergraduates had no need and received non-need-based gift aid.

GIFT AID (NEED-BASED) *Total amount:* $20,154,302 (57% federal, 42% state, 1% institutional). *Receiving aid:* Freshmen: 71% (142); all full-time undergraduates: 66% (1,234). *Average award:* Freshmen: $9577; Undergraduates: $9223. *Scholarships, grants, and awards:* Federal Pell, FSEOG, state, private, college/university gift aid from institutional funds.

GIFT AID (NON-NEED-BASED) *Total amount:* $576,444 (65% institutional, 35% external sources). *Receiving aid:* Freshmen: 25% (50). Undergraduates: 7% (132). *Average award:* Freshmen: $2078. Undergraduates: $2526. *Scholarships, grants, and awards by category: Academic interests/achievement:* biological sciences, business, communication, education, English, general academic interests/achievements, health-fields, humanities, mathematics, physical sciences, social sciences. *Special characteristics:* children of faculty/staff, veterans. *Tuition waivers:* Full or partial for employees or children of employees, senior citizens. *ROTC:* Air Force cooperative.

LOANS *Student loans:* $21,503,809 (97% need-based, 3% non-need-based). *Average need-based loan:* Freshmen: $7764. Undergraduates: $8959. *Parent*

loans: $989,203 (100% non-need-based). *Programs:* Federal Direct (Subsidized and Unsubsidized Stafford, PLUS), Perkins.

WORK-STUDY *Federal work-study:* 141 jobs averaging $2248. *State or other work-study/employment:* Part-time jobs available.

ATHLETIC AWARDS Total amount: $285,190 (100% non-need-based).

APPLYING FOR FINANCIAL AID *Required financial aid form:* FAFSA. *Financial aid deadline:* 10/1 (priority: 5/1). *Notification date:* Continuous beginning 3/1. Students must reply within 2 weeks of notification.

CONTACT John Perry, Director of Financial Aid, Governors State University, 1 University Parkway, University Park, IL 60484, 708-534-5000 Ext. 4483 or toll-free 800-478-8478. *E-mail:* jperry@govst.edu. *Website:* http://www.govst.edu/.

GRACE BIBLE COLLEGE
Grand Rapids, MI

CONTACT Mr. Kurt Postma, Director of Financial Aid, Grace Bible College, 1011 Aldon Street, SW, Grand Rapids, MI 49509-1921, 616-538-2330 or toll-free 800-968-1887. *Fax:* 616-538-0599. *E-mail:* kpostma@gbcol.edu. *Website:* http://www.gbcol.edu/.

GRACE COLLEGE
Winona Lake, IN

CONTACT Charlette Sauders, Director of Financial Aid, Grace College, 200 Seminary Drive, Winona Lake, IN 46590-1294, 574-372-5100 Ext. 6161 or toll-free 800-54-GRACE. *Fax:* 574-372-5144. *E-mail:* charlette.sauders@grace.edu. *Website:* http://www.grace.edu/.

GRACE COLLEGE OF DIVINITY
Fayetteville, NC

CONTACT Financial Aid Office, Grace College of Divinity, 5117 Cliffdale Road, Fayetteville, NC 28314, 910-221-2224. *Website:* http://www.gcd.edu/.

GRACELAND UNIVERSITY
Lamoni, IA

Tuition & fees: $29,240	Average undergraduate aid package: $24,479

ABOUT THE INSTITUTION Independent Community of Christ, coed. *Awards:* certificates, bachelor's, master's, and doctoral degrees. 56 undergraduate majors. *Total enrollment:* 2,262. Undergraduates: 1,404. Freshmen: 255. Federal methodology is used as a basis for awarding need-based institutional aid.

UNDERGRADUATE EXPENSES for 2018–2019 *Comprehensive fee:* $38,000 includes full-time tuition ($28,600), mandatory fees ($640), and room and board ($8760). *College room only:* $3370. Full-time tuition and fees vary according to course load, degree level, location, and program. Room and board charges vary according to board plan, housing facility, and location. *Part-time tuition:* $800 per semester hour. *Part-time fees:* $320 per semester hour. Part-time tuition and fees vary according to course load, degree level, location, and program.

FRESHMAN FINANCIAL AID (Fall 2017, est.) 246 applied for aid; of those 93% were deemed to have need. 100% of freshmen with need received aid; of those 15% had need fully met. *Average percent of need met:* 78% (excluding resources awarded to replace EFC). *Average financial aid package:* $26,960 (excluding resources awarded to replace EFC). 5% of all full-time freshmen had no need and received non-need-based gift aid.

UNDERGRADUATE FINANCIAL AID (Fall 2017, est.) 993 applied for aid; of those 93% were deemed to have need. 97% of undergraduates with need received aid; of those 14% had need fully met. *Average percent of need met:* 74% (excluding

resources awarded to replace EFC). *Average financial aid package:* $24,479 (excluding resources awarded to replace EFC). 13% of all full-time undergraduates had no need and received non-need-based gift aid.

GIFT AID (NEED-BASED) *Total amount:* $15,403,521 (20% federal, 6% state, 72% institutional, 2% external sources). *Receiving aid:* Freshmen: 90% (229); all full-time undergraduates: 77% (867). *Average award:* Freshmen: $22,367; Undergraduates: $20,085. *Scholarships, grants, and awards:* Federal Pell, FSEOG, state, private, college/university gift aid from institutional funds.

GIFT AID (NON-NEED-BASED) *Total amount:* $2,253,645 (1% federal, 97% institutional, 2% external sources). *Receiving aid:* Freshmen: 31% (80). Undergraduates: 22% (250). *Average award:* Freshmen: $19,323. Undergraduates: $14,231. *Scholarships, grants, and awards by category:* Academic interests/achievement: 846 awards ($7,103,803 total): computer science, engineering/technologies, English, general academic interests/achievements, physical sciences. *Creative arts/performance:* 142 awards ($340,670 total): applied art and design, art/fine arts, creative writing, dance, music, theater/drama. *Special achievements/activities:* 134 awards ($182,578 total): cheerleading/drum major, general special achievements/activities, leadership, religious involvement. *Special characteristics:* 842 awards ($5,032,114 total): children and siblings of alumni, children of faculty/staff, first-generation college students, general special characteristics, international students, local/state students, members of minority groups, out-of-state students, religious affiliation. *Tuition waivers:* Full or partial for employees or children of employees, senior citizens.

LOANS *Student loans:* $8,281,550 (80% need-based, 20% non-need-based). 79% of past graduating class borrowed through all loan programs. *Average indebtedness per student:* $32,120. *Average need-based loan:* Freshmen: $3481. Undergraduates: $4562. *Parent loans:* $1,811,357 (55% need-based, 45% non-need-based). *Programs:* Federal Direct (Subsidized and Unsubsidized Stafford, PLUS), Perkins, college/university.

WORK-STUDY *Federal work-study:* Total amount: $713,093; 276 jobs averaging $905. *State or other work-study/employment:* Total amount: $522,807 (27% need-based, 73% non-need-based). 505 part-time jobs averaging $1148.

ATHLETIC AWARDS Total amount: $2,734,142 (74% need-based, 26% non-need-based).

APPLYING FOR FINANCIAL AID *Required financial aid form:* FAFSA. *Financial aid deadline:* Continuous. *Notification date:* Continuous beginning 2/1. Students must reply within 2 weeks of notification.

CONTACT Talia Brown, Executive Director for Enrollment Management, Graceland University, 1 University Place, Lamoni, IA 50140, 641-784-5117 or toll-free 866-GRACELAND. *Fax:* 641-784-5242. *E-mail:* talia.brown@graceland.edu. *Website:* http://www.graceland.edu/.

GRACE MISSION UNIVERSITY
Fullerton, CA

CONTACT Financial Aid Office, Grace Mission University, 1645 West Valencia Drive, Fullerton, CA 92833, 714-525-0088. *Website:* http://www.gm.edu/.

GRACE SCHOOL OF THEOLOGY
Conroe, TX

CONTACT Financial Aid Office, Grace School of Theology, 3705 College Park Drive Suite 140, Conroe, TX 77384-4894. *Website:* http://www.gsot.edu/.

GRAMBLING STATE UNIVERSITY
Grambling, LA

Tuition & fees (LA res): $7435	Average undergraduate aid package: $4045

ABOUT THE INSTITUTION State-supported, coed. *Awards:* certificates, bachelor's, master's, and doctoral degrees. 27 undergraduate majors. *Total*

enrollment: 5,188. Undergraduates: 4,089. Freshmen: 922. Federal methodology is used as a basis for awarding need-based institutional aid.

UNDERGRADUATE EXPENSES for 2018–2019 *Application fee:* $20. *Tuition, state resident:* full-time $5140. *Tuition, nonresident:* full-time $14,163. *Required fees:* full-time $2295. Full-time tuition and fees vary according to course load, degree level, and student level. Part-time tuition and fees vary according to course load, degree level, and student level. *College room and board:* $10,054; *Room only:* $6500. Room and board charges vary according to housing facility.

FRESHMAN FINANCIAL AID (Fall 2017, est.) 892 applied for aid; of those 88% were deemed to have need. 100% of freshmen with need received aid. *Average financial aid package:* $3744 (excluding resources awarded to replace EFC). 4% of all full-time freshmen had no need and received non-need-based gift aid.

UNDERGRADUATE FINANCIAL AID (Fall 2017, est.) 3,460 applied for aid; of those 87% were deemed to have need. 100% of undergraduates with need received aid. *Average financial aid package:* $4045 (excluding resources awarded to replace EFC). 1% of all full-time undergraduates had no need and received non-need-based gift aid.

GIFT AID (NEED-BASED) *Total amount:* $22,137,759 (92% federal, 4% state, 4% institutional). *Receiving aid:* Freshmen: 86% (782); all full-time undergraduates: 81% (3,013). *Average award:* Freshmen: $4309; Undergraduates: $4579. *Scholarships, grants, and awards:* Federal Pell, FSEOG, state, private, college/university gift aid from institutional funds.

GIFT AID (NON-NEED-BASED) *Total amount:* $949,019 (4% federal, 82% state, 14% external sources). *Receiving aid:* Freshmen: 83% (749). Undergraduates: 77% (2,888). *Average award:* Freshmen: $2594. Undergraduates: $2477. *Scholarships, grants, and awards by category:* Academic interests/achievement: biological sciences, business, communication, computer science, education, engineering/technologies, English, foreign languages, general academic interests/achievements, health fields, home economics, humanities, mathematics, military science, physical sciences, premedicine, social sciences. *Creative arts/performance:* dance, general creative arts/performance, music, performing arts, theater/drama. *Special achievements/activities:* cheerleading/drum major, junior miss, leadership. *Special characteristics:* children and siblings of alumni, children of faculty/staff, children of public servants, ethnic background, international students, local/state students, members of minority groups, out-of-state students, public servants, veterans, veterans' children. *Tuition waivers:* Full or partial for children of alumni, employees or children of employees, senior citizens. *ROTC:* Army, Air Force cooperative.

LOANS *Student loans:* $34,172,667 (30% need-based, 70% non-need-based). 92% of past graduating class borrowed through all loan programs. *Average indebtedness per student:* $47,162. *Average need-based loan:* Freshmen: $3482. Undergraduates: $4068. *Programs:* Federal Direct (Subsidized and Unsubsidized Stafford, PLUS), alternative loans.

WORK-STUDY *Federal work-study:* Total amount: $645,508; jobs available.

ATHLETIC AWARDS Total amount: $2,480,900 (100% non-need-based).

APPLYING FOR FINANCIAL AID *Required financial aid form:* FAFSA. *Financial aid deadline:* 6/1 (priority: 4/1). *Notification date:* Continuous beginning 3/1. Students must reply within 2 weeks of notification.

CONTACT Mr. Gavin Hamms, Director of Student Financial Aid and Scholarships, Grambling State University, PO Box 629, Grambling, LA 71245, 318-274-6328 or toll-free 800-569-4714. *Fax:* 318-274-3358. *E-mail:* hammsg@gram.edu. *Website:* http://www.gram.edu/.

GRAND CANYON UNIVERSITY
Phoenix, AZ

CONTACT Director of Financial Aid, Grand Canyon University, 3300 West Camelback Road, PO Box 11097, Phoenix, AZ 85017-3030, 800-800-9776 Ext. 2885 or toll-free 800-800-9776. *Fax:* 602-589-2044. *Website:* http://www.gcu.edu/.

GRAND VALLEY STATE UNIVERSITY
Allendale, MI

Tuition & fees (MI res): $11,994	Average undergraduate aid package: $10,093

ABOUT THE INSTITUTION State-supported, coed. *Awards:* certificates, bachelor's, master's, and doctoral degrees. 113 undergraduate majors. *Total enrollment:* 25,049. Undergraduates: 21,937. Freshmen: 4,117. Federal methodology is used as a basis for awarding need-based institutional aid.

UNDERGRADUATE EXPENSES for 2017–2018 *Application fee:* $30. *Tuition, state resident:* full-time $11,994; part-time $525 per credit hour. *Tuition, nonresident:* full-time $17,064; part-time $736 per credit hour. Full-time tuition and fees vary according to course level, course load, program, and student level. Part-time tuition and fees vary according to course level, course load, program, and student level. *College room and board:* $9000. Room and board charges vary according to board plan and housing facility.

FRESHMAN FINANCIAL AID (Fall 2017, est.) 3,173 applied for aid; of those 83% were deemed to have need. 98% of freshmen with need received aid; of those 16% had need fully met. *Average percent of need met:* 66% (excluding resources awarded to replace EFC). *Average financial aid package:* $10,902 (excluding resources awarded to replace EFC). 17% of all full-time freshmen had no need and received non-need-based gift aid.

UNDERGRADUATE FINANCIAL AID (Fall 2017, est.) 15,729 applied for aid; of those 73% were deemed to have need. 99% of undergraduates with need received aid; of those 18% had need fully met. *Average percent of need met:* 67% (excluding resources awarded to replace EFC). *Average financial aid package:* $10,093 (excluding resources awarded to replace EFC). 17% of all full-time undergraduates had no need and received non-need-based gift aid.

GIFT AID (NEED-BASED) *Total amount:* $69,129,282 (44% federal, 6% state, 46% institutional, 4% external sources). *Receiving aid:* Freshmen: 55% (2,246); all full-time undergraduates: 38% (7,451). *Average award:* Freshmen: $8257; Undergraduates: $5409. *Scholarships, grants, and awards:* Federal Pell, FSEOG, state, private, college/university gift aid from institutional funds.

GIFT AID (NON-NEED-BASED) *Total amount:* $12,104,191 (1% state, 88% institutional, 11% external sources). *Receiving aid:* Freshmen: 4% (161). Undergraduates: 3% (561). *Average award:* Freshmen: $3649. Undergraduates: $3440. *Scholarships, grants, and awards by category: Academic interests/achievement:* business, communication, computer science, education, engineering/technologies, English, foreign languages, general academic interests/achievements, health fields, humanities, international studies, mathematics, physical sciences, premedicine, social sciences. *Creative arts/performance:* applied art and design, art/fine arts, cinema/film/broadcasting, dance, journalism/publications, music, theater/drama. *Special characteristics:* adult students, children and siblings of alumni, children of faculty/staff, children of union members/company employees, children of workers in trades, general special characteristics, handicapped students, international students, local/state students, out-of-state students, public servants, spouses of deceased or disabled public servants, veterans, veterans' children. *Tuition waivers:* Full or partial for employees or children of employees.

LOANS *Student loans:* $113,569,048 (40% need-based, 60% non-need-based). 71% of past graduating class borrowed through all loan programs. *Average indebtedness per student:* $29,675. *Average need-based loan:* Freshmen: $3533. Undergraduates: $4296. *Parent loans:* $72,397,887 (100% non-need-based). *Programs:* Federal Direct (Subsidized and Unsubsidized Stafford, PLUS), Perkins, Federal Nursing.

WORK-STUDY *Federal work-study:* Total amount: $3,963,238; 1,376 jobs averaging $2880. *State or other work-study/employment:* Part-time jobs available.

ATHLETIC AWARDS Total amount: $3,733,423 (36% need-based, 64% non-need-based).

APPLYING FOR FINANCIAL AID *Required financial aid form:* FAFSA. *Financial aid deadline (priority):* 3/1. *Notification date:* Continuous beginning 1/16. Students must reply by 5/1 or within 4 weeks of notification.

CONTACT Michelle Rhodes, Office of Financial Aid, Grand Valley State University, 100 Student Services Building, Allendale, MI 49401, 616-331-3234 or toll-free 800-748-0246. *Fax:* 616-331-3180. *E-mail:* rhodesmi@gvsu.edu. *Website:* http://www.gvsu.edu/.

GRAND VIEW UNIVERSITY
Des Moines, IA

ABOUT THE INSTITUTION Independent Evangelical Lutheran Church in America, coed. *Awards:* certificates, bachelor's, and master's degrees. 44 undergraduate majors. *Total enrollment:* 1,836. Undergraduates: 1,788. Freshmen: 331.

GIFT AID (NEED-BASED) *Scholarships, grants, and awards:* Federal Pell, FSEOG, state, private, college/university gift aid from institutional funds.

GIFT AID (NON-NEED-BASED) *Scholarships, grants, and awards by category: Academic interests/achievement:* biological sciences, business, communication, education, English, general academic interests/achievements, international studies, mathematics, physical sciences, religion/biblical studies, social sciences. *Creative arts/performance:* applied art and design, art/fine arts, dance, music, theater/drama. *Special achievements/activities:* cheerleading/drum major, community service, junior miss, memberships, religious involvement. *Special characteristics:* adult students, children and siblings of alumni, children of educators, children of faculty/staff, ethnic background, first-generation college students, general special characteristics, international students, out-of-state students, religious affiliation, veterans.

LOANS *Programs:* Federal Direct (Subsidized and Unsubsidized Stafford, PLUS), Perkins, college/university, private loans.

WORK-STUDY *Federal work-study:* 336 jobs averaging $1354. *State or other work-study/employment:* Part-time jobs available.

CONTACT Ms. Michele Dunne, Director of Financial Aid, Grand View University, 1200 Grandview Avenue, Des Moines, IA 50316-1599, 515-263-2820 or toll-free 800-444-6083. *Fax:* 515-263-6191. *E-mail:* mdunne@grandview.edu. *Website:* http://www.grandview.edu/.

GRANTHAM UNIVERSITY
Lenexa, KS

CONTACT Financial Aid Office, Grantham University, 16025 West 113th Street, Lenexa, KS 66219 or toll-free 800-955-2527. *Website:* http://www.grantham.edu/.

GREAT LAKES CHRISTIAN COLLEGE
Lansing, MI

CONTACT Financial Aid Officer, Great Lakes Christian College, 6211 West Willow Highway, Lansing, MI 48917-1299, 517-321-0242 or toll-free 800-YES-GLCC. *Website:* http://www.glcc.edu/.

GREEN MOUNTAIN COLLEGE
Poultney, VT

CONTACT Wendy J. Ellis, Director of Student Financial Services, Green Mountain College, One Brennan Circle, Poultney, VT 05764-1199, 800-776-6675 Ext. 8209 or toll-free 800-776-6675. *Fax:* 802-287-8096. *E-mail:* ellisw@greenmtn.edu. *Website:* http://www.greenmtn.edu/.

GREENSBORO COLLEGE
Greensboro, NC

CONTACT Lindsay Latham, Director of Financial Aid, Greensboro College, 815 West Market Street, Greensboro, NC 27401-1875, 336-272-7102 Ext. 217 or toll-free 800-346-8226. *Fax:* 336-230-9622. *E-mail:* dvanarsdale@greensborocollege.edu. *Website:* http://www.greensboro.edu/.

GREENVILLE UNIVERSITY
Greenville, IL

Tuition & fees: $27,108	Average undergraduate aid package: $20,558

ABOUT THE INSTITUTION Independent Free Methodist, coed. **Awards:** bachelor's and master's degrees. 52 undergraduate majors. **Total enrollment:** 1,235. Undergraduates: 985. Freshmen: 220. Federal methodology is used as a basis for awarding need-based institutional aid.

UNDERGRADUATE EXPENSES for 2018–2019 Comprehensive fee: $36,556 includes full-time tuition ($26,778), mandatory fees ($330), and room and board ($9448). **College room only:** $4798. Full-time tuition and fees vary according to degree level and program. Room and board charges vary according to housing facility. **Part-time tuition:** $434 per credit hour. Part-time tuition and fees vary according to course load, degree level, and program.

FRESHMAN FINANCIAL AID (Fall 2016) 229 applied for aid; of those 89% were deemed to have need. 100% of freshmen with need received aid; of those 9% had need fully met. **Average percent of need met:** 72% (excluding resources awarded to replace EFC). **Average financial aid package:** $20,921 (excluding resources awarded to replace EFC). 22% of all full-time freshmen had no need and received non-need-based gift aid.

UNDERGRADUATE FINANCIAL AID (Fall 2016) 816 applied for aid; of those 92% were deemed to have need. 100% of undergraduates with need received aid; of those 12% had need fully met. **Average percent of need met:** 73% (excluding resources awarded to replace EFC). **Average financial aid package:** $20,558 (excluding resources awarded to replace EFC). 16% of all full-time undergraduates had no need and received non-need-based gift aid.

GIFT AID (NEED-BASED) Total amount: $12,691,699 (14% federal, 10% state, 73% institutional, 3% external sources). **Receiving aid:** Freshmen: 78% (203); all full-time undergraduates: 82% (738). **Average award:** Freshmen: $18,110; Undergraduates: $17,065. **Scholarships, grants, and awards:** Federal Pell, FSEOG, state, private, college/university gift aid from institutional funds.

GIFT AID (NON-NEED-BASED) Total amount: $2,067,569 (91% institutional, 9% external sources). **Receiving aid:** Freshmen: 6% (16). Undergraduates: 7% (66). **Average award:** Freshmen: $10,775. Undergraduates: $10,918. **Scholarships, grants, and awards by category:** Academic interests/achievement: biological sciences, engineering/technologies, mathematics, physical sciences. Creative arts/performance: applied art and design, art/fine arts, music, performing arts. Special achievements/activities: cheerleading/drum major, leadership, memberships, religious involvement. Special characteristics: children and siblings of alumni, children of faculty/staff, international students, local/state students, out-of-state students, religious affiliation, siblings of current students. **Tuition waivers:** Full or partial for employees or children of employees, senior citizens.

LOANS Student loans: $5,804,437 (81% need-based, 19% non-need-based). 84% of past graduating class borrowed through all loan programs. Average indebtedness per student: $28,724. **Average need-based loan:** Freshmen: $3291. Undergraduates: $4163. **Parent loans:** $2,672,316 (38% need-based, 62% non-need-based). **Programs:** Federal Direct (Subsidized and Unsubsidized Stafford, PLUS), Perkins, college/university.

WORK-STUDY Federal work-study: 143 jobs averaging $1354. **State or other work-study/employment:** Part-time jobs available.

APPLYING FOR FINANCIAL AID Required financial aid form: FAFSA. **Financial aid deadline (priority):** 11/1. **Notification date:** Continuous beginning 11/1. Students must reply within 3 weeks of notification.

CONTACT David Kessinger, Director of Financial Aid, Greenville University, 315 East College Avenue, Greenville, IL 62246-0159, 618-664-7108 or toll-free 800-345-4440. Fax: 618-664-7198. E-mail: david.kessinger@greenville.edu. Website: http://www.greenville.edu/.

GRINNELL COLLEGE
Grinnell, IA

Tuition & fees: $52,392	Average undergraduate aid package: $47,561

ABOUT THE INSTITUTION Independent, coed. **Awards:** bachelor's degrees. 27 undergraduate majors. **Total enrollment:** 1,712. Undergraduates: 1,712. Freshmen: 447. Both federal and institutional methodology are used as a basis for awarding need-based institutional aid.

UNDERGRADUATE EXPENSES for 2018–2019 Comprehensive fee: $65,202 includes full-time tuition ($51,924), mandatory fees ($468), and room and board ($12,810). **College room only:** $6050. Room and board charges vary according to board plan and housing facility. **Part-time tuition:** $1571 per credit hour.

FRESHMAN FINANCIAL AID (Fall 2017, est.) 363 applied for aid; of those 80% were deemed to have need. 100% of freshmen with need received aid; of those 100% had need fully met. **Average percent of need met:** 100% (excluding resources awarded to replace EFC). **Average financial aid package:** $47,058 (excluding resources awarded to replace EFC). 21% of all full-time freshmen had no need and received non-need-based gift aid.

UNDERGRADUATE FINANCIAL AID (Fall 2017, est.) 1,198 applied for aid; of those 90% were deemed to have need. 100% of undergraduates with need received aid; of those 100% had need fully met. **Average percent of need met:** 100% (excluding resources awarded to replace EFC). **Average financial aid package:** $47,561 (excluding resources awarded to replace EFC). 20% of all full-time undergraduates had no need and received non-need-based gift aid.

GIFT AID (NEED-BASED) Total amount: $44,144,499 (4% federal, 1% state, 93% institutional, 2% external sources). **Receiving aid:** Freshmen: 65% (290); all full-time undergraduates: 65% (1,078). **Average award:** Freshmen: $41,902; Undergraduates: $41,344. **Scholarships, grants, and awards:** Federal Pell, FSEOG, state, private, college/university gift aid from institutional funds, National Merit Scholarships, Dollars for Scholars Matching Funds.

GIFT AID (NON-NEED-BASED) Total amount: $6,962,231 (90% institutional, 10% external sources). **Receiving aid:** Freshmen: 9% (39). Undergraduates: 8% (126). **Average award:** Freshmen: $20,075. Undergraduates: $18,444. **Scholarships, grants, and awards by category:** Academic interests/achievement: general academic interests/achievements. **Tuition waivers:** Full or partial for employees or children of employees.

LOANS Student loans: $4,633,250 (92% need-based, 8% non-need-based). 55% of past graduating class borrowed through all loan programs. Average indebtedness per student: $19,392. **Average need-based loan:** Freshmen: $3068. Undergraduates: $4129. **Programs:** Federal Direct (Subsidized and Unsubsidized Stafford, PLUS), state, college/university.

WORK-STUDY Federal work-study: Total amount: $216,208; 562 jobs averaging $1928. **State or other work-study/employment:** Total amount: $2,431,592 (91% need-based, 9% non-need-based). 581 part-time jobs averaging $2078.

APPLYING FOR FINANCIAL AID Required financial aid forms: FAFSA, CSS Financial Aid PROFILE, noncustodial (divorced/separated) parent's statement. **Financial aid deadline:** 1/15. **Notification date:** 4/1. Students must reply by 5/1.

CONTACT Mr. Brad Lindberg, Assistant Vice President of Enrollment/Director of Financial Aid, Grinnell College, 1103 Park Street, Grinnell, IA 50112-1690, 641-269-3250 or toll-free 800-247-0113. Fax: 641-269-4937. E-mail: lindbergb@grinnell.edu. Website: http://www.grinnell.edu/.

GROVE CITY COLLEGE
Grove City, PA

Tuition & fees: $17,254	Average undergraduate aid package: $7424

ABOUT THE INSTITUTION Independent Presbyterian, coed. **Awards:** bachelor's degrees. 51 undergraduate majors. **Total enrollment:** 2,373. Undergraduates: 2,373. Freshmen: 636. Institutional methodology is used as a basis for awarding need-based institutional aid.

UNDERGRADUATE EXPENSES for 2017–2018 Application fee: $50. **Comprehensive fee:** $26,654 includes full-time tuition ($17,254) and room and board

($9100). Room and board charges vary according to housing facility. **Part-time tuition:** $560 per credit hour.
FRESHMAN FINANCIAL AID (Fall 2017, est.) 462 applied for aid; of those 71% were deemed to have need. 100% of freshmen with need received aid; of those 13% had need fully met. **Average percent of need met:** 53% (excluding resources awarded to replace EFC). **Average financial aid package:** $7989 (excluding resources awarded to replace EFC). 9% of all full-time freshmen had no need and received non-need-based gift aid.
UNDERGRADUATE FINANCIAL AID (Fall 2017, est.) 1,337 applied for aid; of those 80% were deemed to have need. 99% of undergraduates with need received aid; of those 9% had need fully met. **Average percent of need met:** 50% (excluding resources awarded to replace EFC). **Average financial aid package:** $7424 (excluding resources awarded to replace EFC). 18% of all full-time undergraduates had no need and received non-need-based gift aid.
GIFT AID (NEED-BASED) Total amount: $7,802,240 (13% state, 77% institutional, 10% external sources). **Receiving aid:** Freshmen: 51% (326); all full-time undergraduates: 46% (1,057). **Average award:** Freshmen: $7989; Undergraduates: $7424. **Scholarships, grants, and awards:** state, private, college/university gift aid from institutional funds.
GIFT AID (NON-NEED-BASED) Total amount: $2,368,571 (1% state, 55% institutional, 44% external sources). **Receiving aid:** Freshmen: 6% (40). Undergraduates: 4% (90). **Average award:** Freshmen: $7670. Undergraduates: $2936. **Scholarships, grants, and awards by category:** Academic interests/achievement: 715 awards ($1,734,372 total): biological sciences, business, communication, education, engineering/technologies, English, foreign languages, general academic interests/achievements, humanities, international studies, mathematics, physical sciences, religion/biblical studies, social sciences. Creative arts/performance: 6 awards ($9200 total): creative writing, music. Special achievements/activities: 33 awards ($120,702 total): community service, general special achievements/activities, leadership, memberships, religious involvement. Special characteristics: 18 awards ($114,708 total): ethnic background, first-generation college students, general special characteristics, handicapped students, members of minority groups. **Tuition waivers:** Full or partial for employees or children of employees.
LOANS Student loans: $13,719,644 (39% need-based, 61% non-need-based). 59% of past graduating class borrowed through all loan programs. Average indebtedness per student: $40,747. **Programs:** state, private loans.
APPLYING FOR FINANCIAL AID Required financial aid form: institution's own form. **Financial aid deadline:** 4/15. **Notification date:** Continuous beginning 3/15. Students must reply by 5/1.
CONTACT Mr. Thomas G. Ball, Director of Financial Aid, Grove City College, 100 Campus Drive, Grove City, PA 16127-2104, 724-458-3300. Fax: 724-450-4040. E-mail: financialaid@gcc.edu.
Website: http://www.gcc.edu/.

GUILFORD COLLEGE
Greensboro, NC

Tuition & fees: $34,215	Average undergraduate aid package: $25,481

ABOUT THE INSTITUTION Independent Society of Friends, coed. **Awards:** certificates, bachelor's, and master's degrees. 48 undergraduate majors. **Total enrollment:** 1,680. Undergraduates: 1,674. Freshmen: 343. Federal methodology is used as a basis for awarding need-based institutional aid.
UNDERGRADUATE EXPENSES for 2017–2018 Comprehensive fee: $44,437 includes full-time tuition ($33,710), mandatory fees ($505), and room and board ($10,222). **College room only:** $5000. Full-time tuition and fees vary according to degree level and program. Room and board charges vary according to board plan and housing facility. **Part-time tuition:** $1032 per credit hour. **Part-time fees:** $205 per term. Part-time tuition and fees vary according to degree level and program. **Payment plan:** Guaranteed tuition.
FRESHMAN FINANCIAL AID (Fall 2016) 396 applied for aid; of those 85% were deemed to have need. 100% of freshmen with need received aid; of those 67% had need fully met. **Average percent of need met:** 90% (excluding resources awarded to replace EFC). **Average financial aid package:** $29,257 (excluding resources awarded to replace EFC). 14% of all full-time freshmen had no need and received non-need-based gift aid.
UNDERGRADUATE FINANCIAL AID (Fall 2016) 1,206 applied for aid; of those 89% were deemed to have need. 100% of undergraduates with need received

aid; of those 56% had need fully met. **Average percent of need met:** 74% (excluding resources awarded to replace EFC). **Average financial aid package:** $25,481 (excluding resources awarded to replace EFC). 9% of all full-time undergraduates had no need and received non-need-based gift aid.
GIFT AID (NEED-BASED) Total amount: $22,817,910 (14% federal, 10% state, 72% institutional, 4% external sources). **Receiving aid:** Freshmen: 79% (333); all full-time undergraduates: 71% (1,028). **Average award:** Freshmen: $4565; Undergraduates: $4418. **Scholarships, grants, and awards:** Federal Pell, FSEOG, state, private, college/university gift aid from institutional funds.
GIFT AID (NON-NEED-BASED) Total amount: $5,828,887 (93% institutional, 7% external sources). **Receiving aid:** Freshmen: 80% (335). Undergraduates: 59% (863). **Average award:** Freshmen: $11,543. Undergraduates: $9961. **Scholarships, grants, and awards by category:** Academic interests/achievement: general academic interests/achievements. **Tuition waivers:** Full or partial for employees or children of employees. **ROTC:** Army cooperative, Air Force cooperative.
LOANS Student loans: $9,056,853 (93% need-based, 7% non-need-based). 65% of past graduating class borrowed through all loan programs. Average indebtedness per student: $35,392. **Average need-based loan:** Freshmen: $3135. Undergraduates: $3773. **Parent loans:** $3,054,328 (92% need-based, 8% non-need-based). **Programs:** Federal Direct (Subsidized and Unsubsidized Stafford, PLUS), Perkins.
WORK-STUDY Federal work-study: jobs available. **State or other work-study/employment:** Total amount: $425,447 (52% need-based, 48% non-need-based). Part-time jobs available.
APPLYING FOR FINANCIAL AID Required financial aid form: FAFSA. **Financial aid deadline (priority):** 2/15. **Notification date:** Continuous beginning 3/1. Students must reply within 2 weeks of notification.
CONTACT Mr. Brian DeYoung, Director of Financial Aid, Guilford College, 5800 West Friendly Avenue, Greensboro, NC 27410, 336-316-2410 or toll-free 800-992-7759. Fax: 336-316-2942. E-mail: deyoungbk@guilford.edu.
Website: http://www.guilford.edu/.

GUSTAVUS ADOLPHUS COLLEGE
St. Peter, MN

Tuition & fees: $45,100	Average undergraduate aid package: $37,892

ABOUT THE INSTITUTION Independent Evangelical Lutheran Church in America, coed. **Awards:** bachelor's degrees. 67 undergraduate majors. **Total enrollment:** 2,201. Undergraduates: 2,201. Freshmen: 589. Both federal and institutional methodology are used as a basis for awarding need-based institutional aid.
UNDERGRADUATE EXPENSES for 2018–2019 One-time required fee: $490. **Comprehensive fee:** $55,010 includes full-time tuition ($44,900), mandatory fees ($200), and room and board ($9910). **College room only:** $6300. Room and board charges vary according to board plan and housing facility. **Part-time tuition:** $7680 per course. **Payment plan:** Tuition prepayment.
FRESHMAN FINANCIAL AID (Fall 2017, est.) 518 applied for aid; of those 86% were deemed to have need. 100% of freshmen with need received aid; of those 60% had need fully met. **Average percent of need met:** 92% (excluding resources awarded to replace EFC). **Average financial aid package:** $38,506 (excluding resources awarded to replace EFC). 20% of all full-time freshmen had no need and received non-need-based gift aid.
UNDERGRADUATE FINANCIAL AID (Fall 2017, est.) 1,675 applied for aid; of those 92% were deemed to have need. 100% of undergraduates with need received aid; of those 29% had need fully met. **Average percent of need met:** 92% (excluding resources awarded to replace EFC). **Average financial aid package:** $37,892 (excluding resources awarded to replace EFC). 28% of all full-time undergraduates had no need and received non-need-based gift aid.
GIFT AID (NEED-BASED) Total amount: $45,739,135 (6% federal, 9% state, 83% institutional, 2% external sources). **Receiving aid:** Freshmen: 76% (446); all full-time undergraduates: 69% (1,529). **Average award:** Freshmen: $32,990; Undergraduates: $32,482. **Scholarships, grants, and awards:** Federal Pell, FSEOG, state, private, college/university gift aid from institutional funds.
GIFT AID (NON-NEED-BASED) Total amount: $17,996,015 (96% institutional, 4% external sources). **Receiving aid:** Freshmen: 13% (74). Undergraduates: 8% (186). **Average award:** Freshmen: $23,581. Undergraduates: $22,283. **Scholarships, grants, and awards by category:** Academic interests/achievement: general academic interests/achievements. Creative arts/performance: art/fine arts,

dance, debating, music, theater/drama. *Special achievements/activities:* junior miss. *Special characteristics:* children and siblings of alumni, ethnic background, first-generation college students, international students, members of minority groups, out-of-state students, siblings of current students. *Tuition waivers:* Full or partial for employees or children of employees. *ROTC:* Army cooperative.

LOANS *Student loans:* $14,738,394 (37% need-based, 63% non-need-based). *Average need-based loan:* Freshmen: $3537. Undergraduates: $3480. *Parent loans:* $2,293,564 (100% non-need-based). *Programs:* Federal Direct (Subsidized and Unsubsidized Stafford, PLUS), Perkins, state.

WORK-STUDY *Federal work-study:* Total amount: $2,290,442; jobs available. *State or other work-study/employment:* Total amount: $1,420,186 (98% need-based, 2% non-need-based). Part-time jobs available.

APPLYING FOR FINANCIAL AID *Required financial aid form:* FAFSA. *Financial aid deadline:* 4/15 (priority: 2/15). *Notification date:* Continuous beginning 12/15. Students must reply by 5/1 or within 2 weeks of notification.

CONTACT Mr. Doug Minter, Dean of Financial Aid, Gustavus Adolphus College, 800 West College Avenue, St. Peter, MN 56082-1498, 507-933-7527 or toll-free 800-GUSTAVU(S). *Fax:* 507-933-7727. *E-mail:* finaid@gustavus.edu. *Website:* http://www.gustavus.edu/.

GUTENBERG COLLEGE
Eugene, OR

CONTACT Financial Aid Office, Gutenberg College, 1883 University Street, Eugene, OR 97403, 541-683-5141.
Website: http://www.gutenberg.edu/.

GWYNEDD MERCY UNIVERSITY
Gwynedd Valley, PA

Tuition & fees: $33,520	Average undergraduate aid package: $22,116

ABOUT THE INSTITUTION Independent Roman Catholic, coed. *Awards:* certificates, bachelor's, master's, and doctoral degrees. 38 undergraduate majors. *Total enrollment:* 2,807. Undergraduates: 2,081. Freshmen: 266. Federal methodology is used as a basis for awarding need-based institutional aid.

UNDERGRADUATE EXPENSES for 2018–2019 *Comprehensive fee:* $45,500 includes full-time tuition ($32,820), mandatory fees ($700), and room and board ($11,980). *College room only:* $5360. Full-time tuition and fees vary according to location and program. Room and board charges vary according to board plan and housing facility. *Part-time tuition:* $725 per credit hour. Part-time tuition and fees vary according to location and program.

FRESHMAN FINANCIAL AID (Fall 2017, est.) 257 applied for aid; of those 93% were deemed to have need. 100% of freshmen with need received aid; of those 14% had need fully met. *Average percent of need met:* 71% (excluding resources awarded to replace EFC). *Average financial aid package:* $26,574 (excluding resources awarded to replace EFC). 8% of all full-time freshmen had no need and received non-need-based gift aid.

UNDERGRADUATE FINANCIAL AID (Fall 2017, est.) 1,551 applied for aid; of those 92% were deemed to have need. 98% of undergraduates with need received aid; of those 11% had need fully met. *Average percent of need met:* 60% (excluding resources awarded to replace EFC). *Average financial aid package:* $22,116 (excluding resources awarded to replace EFC). 9% of all full-time undergraduates had no need and received non-need-based gift aid.

GIFT AID (NEED-BASED) *Total amount:* $25,256,965 (13% federal, 10% state, 71% institutional, 6% external sources). *Receiving aid:* Freshmen: 92% (240); all full-time undergraduates: 74% (1,276). *Average award:* Freshmen: $22,734; Undergraduates: $19,869. *Scholarships, grants, and awards:* Federal Pell, FSEOG, state, private, college/university gift aid from institutional funds.

GIFT AID (NON-NEED-BASED) *Total amount:* $3,070,474 (1% federal, 88% institutional, 11% external sources). *Receiving aid:* Freshmen: 10% (26). Undergraduates: 7% (117). *Average award:* Freshmen: $17,691. Undergraduates: $13,795. *Scholarships, grants, and awards by category:* Academic interests/achievement: 1,324 awards ($1,877,432 total): general academic interests/achievements. *Special achievements/activities:* 548 awards ($544,607 total): general special

---

achievements/activities. *Special characteristics:* 99 awards ($630,766 total): children and siblings of alumni, children of faculty/staff, siblings of current students, veterans, veterans' children. *Tuition waivers:* Full or partial for employees or children of employees.

LOANS *Student loans:* $19,293,367 (76% need-based, 24% non-need-based). 87% of past graduating class borrowed through all loan programs. *Average indebtedness per student:* $46,139. *Average need-based loan:* Freshmen: $3348. Undergraduates: $4172. *Parent loans:* $3,245,455 (58% need-based, 42% non-need-based). *Programs:* Federal Direct (Subsidized and Unsubsidized Stafford, PLUS), Perkins, Federal Nursing, alternative loans.

WORK-STUDY *Federal work-study:* Total amount: $560,712; 397 jobs averaging $1418. *State or other work-study/employment:* Part-time jobs available.

APPLYING FOR FINANCIAL AID *Required financial aid forms:* FAFSA, institution's own form. *Financial aid deadline:* 5/1 (priority: 3/15). *Notification date:* Continuous beginning 2/15. Students must reply by 5/1 or within 2 weeks of notification.

CONTACT Mrs. Elizabeth R. Howard, Director of Student Financial Aid, Gwynedd Mercy University, PO Box 901, Gwynedd Valley, PA 19437-0901, 215-646-7300 Ext. 483 or toll-free 800-342-5462. *Fax:* 215-641-5556. *E-mail:* howard.e@gmercyu.edu. *Website:* http://www.gmercyu.edu/.

HALLMARK UNIVERSITY
San Antonio, TX

CONTACT Financial Aid Office, Hallmark University, 10401 IH 10 West, San Antonio, TX 78230, 210-690-9000 or toll-free 800-880-6600.
Website: http://www.hallmarkuniversity.edu/.

HAMILTON COLLEGE
Clinton, NY

Tuition & fees: $52,770	Average undergraduate aid package: $47,372

ABOUT THE INSTITUTION Independent, coed. *Awards:* bachelor's degrees. 42 undergraduate majors. *Total enrollment:* 1,897. Undergraduates: 1,897. Freshmen: 480. Both federal and institutional methodology are used as a basis for awarding need-based institutional aid.

UNDERGRADUATE EXPENSES for 2017–2018 *Application fee:* $60. *Comprehensive fee:* $66,170 includes full-time tuition ($52,250), mandatory fees ($520), and room and board ($13,400). *College room only:* $7320. Room and board charges vary according to board plan. *Part-time tuition:* $6531 per course.

FRESHMAN FINANCIAL AID (Fall 2017, est.) 292 applied for aid; of those 95% were deemed to have need. 100% of freshmen with need received aid; of those 100% had need fully met. *Average percent of need met:* 100% (excluding resources awarded to replace EFC). *Average financial aid package:* $46,050 (excluding resources awarded to replace EFC).

UNDERGRADUATE FINANCIAL AID (Fall 2017, est.) 994 applied for aid; of those 96% were deemed to have need. 100% of undergraduates with need received aid; of those 100% had need fully met. *Average percent of need met:* 100% (excluding resources awarded to replace EFC). *Average financial aid package:* $47,372 (excluding resources awarded to replace EFC).

GIFT AID (NEED-BASED) *Total amount:* $42,337,216 (3% federal, 2% state, 93% institutional, 2% external sources). *Receiving aid:* Freshmen: 58% (276); all full-time undergraduates: 51% (954). *Average award:* Freshmen: $42,570; Undergraduates: $42,968. *Scholarships, grants, and awards:* Federal Pell, FSEOG, state, private, college/university gift aid from institutional funds.

GIFT AID (NON-NEED-BASED) *Total amount:* $732,940 (8% state, 22% institutional, 70% external sources). *Tuition waivers:* Full or partial for employees or children of employees. *ROTC:* Army cooperative, Air Force cooperative.

LOANS *Student loans:* $3,056,226 (100% need-based). 43% of past graduating class borrowed through all loan programs. *Average indebtedness per student:* $19,281. *Average need-based loan:* Freshmen: $3254. Undergraduates: $4264. *Programs:* Federal Direct (Subsidized and Unsubsidized Stafford, PLUS), state, college/university.

WORK STUDY *Federal work-study.* Total amount: $1,112,399, 613 jobs averaging $1815. *State or other work-study/employment:* Total amount: $100,000 (100% need-based). 53 part-time jobs averaging $1887.

APPLYING FOR FINANCIAL AID *Required financial aid forms:* FAFSA, institution's own form, CSS Financial Aid PROFILE, state aid form, noncustodial (divorced/separated) parent's statement, business/farm supplement. *Financial aid deadline:* 1/15. *Notification date:* 4/1. Students must reply by 12/1.

CONTACT Office of Financial Aid, Hamilton College, 198 College Hill Road, Clinton, NY 13323, 315-859-4434 or toll-free 800-843-2655. *Fax:* 315-859-4962. *E-mail:* finaid@hamilton.edu.
Website: http://www.hamilton.edu/.

HAMILTON TECHNICAL COLLEGE
Davenport, IA

CONTACT Ms. Lisa Boyd, Executive Vice President/Director of Financial Aid, Hamilton Technical College, 1011 East 53rd Street, Davenport, IA 52807-2653, 563-386-3570 Ext. 33 or toll-free 866-966-4825. *Fax:* 563-386-6756.
Website: http://www.hamiltontechcollege.edu/.

HAMLINE UNIVERSITY
St. Paul, MN

Tuition & fees: $41,298	Average undergraduate aid package: $29,877

ABOUT THE INSTITUTION Independent United Methodist Church, coed. *Awards:* certificates, bachelor's, master's, and doctoral degrees. 54 undergraduate majors. *Total enrollment:* 3,734. Undergraduates: 2,168. Freshmen: 535. Federal methodology is used as a basis for awarding need-based institutional aid.

UNDERGRADUATE EXPENSES for 2018–2019 *Comprehensive fee:* $51,656 includes full-time tuition ($40,284), mandatory fees ($1014), and room and board ($10,358). *College room only:* $5100. Room and board charges vary according to board plan and housing facility. *Part-time tuition:* $1259 per credit hour. *Part-time fees:* $788 per year. Part-time tuition and fees vary according to course load.

FRESHMAN FINANCIAL AID (Fall 2016) 522 applied for aid; of those 93% were deemed to have need. 100% of freshmen with need received aid; of those 22% had need fully met. *Average percent of need met:* 85% (excluding resources awarded to replace EFC). *Average financial aid package:* $32,000 (excluding resources awarded to replace EFC). 10% of all full-time freshmen had no need and received non-need-based gift aid.

UNDERGRADUATE FINANCIAL AID (Fall 2016) 1,861 applied for aid; of those 93% were deemed to have need. 100% of undergraduates with need received aid; of those 17% had need fully met. *Average percent of need met:* 79% (excluding resources awarded to replace EFC). *Average financial aid package:* $29,877 (excluding resources awarded to replace EFC). 15% of all full-time undergraduates had no need and received non-need-based gift aid.

GIFT AID (NEED-BASED) *Total amount:* $40,095,007 (9% federal, 11% state, 79% institutional, 1% external sources). *Receiving aid:* Freshmen: 89% (485); all full-time undergraduates: 83% (1,725). *Average award:* Freshmen: $25,648; Undergraduates: $23,426. *Scholarships, grants, and awards:* Federal Pell, FSEOG, state, private, college/university gift aid from institutional funds, Academic Competitiveness Grants, National SMART Grants, TEACH Grants, United Methodist Scholarships.

GIFT AID (NON-NEED-BASED) *Total amount:* $7,365,322 (1% federal, 97% institutional, 2% external sources). *Receiving aid:* Freshmen: 16% (86). Undergraduates: 10% (211). *Average award:* Freshmen: $19,965. Undergraduates: $16,630. *Scholarships, grants, and awards by category:* Academic interests/achievement: biological sciences, business, communication, education, English, foreign languages, general academic interests/achievements, humanities, mathematics, physical sciences, premedicine, religion/biblical studies, social sciences. *Creative arts/performance:* applied art and design, art/fine arts, creative writing, general creative arts/performance, journalism/publications, music, theater/drama. *Special achievements/activities:* community service, general special achievements/activities, leadership, memberships. *Special characteristics:* children and siblings of alumni, first-generation college students, general special characteristics, international students, local/state stu-

dents, members of minority groups, out-of-state students, previous college experience, relatives of clergy, religious affiliation, veterans. *Tuition waivers:* Full or partial for employees or children of employees. *ROTC:* Army cooperative, Air Force cooperative.

LOANS *Student loans:* $15,332,958 (72% need-based, 28% non-need-based). 80% of past graduating class borrowed through all loan programs. *Average indebtedness per student:* $34,935. *Average need-based loan:* Freshmen: $3484. Undergraduates: $4748. *Parent loans:* $5,545,772 (45% need-based, 55% non-need-based). *Programs:* Federal Direct (Subsidized and Unsubsidized Stafford, PLUS), state, alternative loans, United Methodist Student Loans.

WORK-STUDY *Federal work-study:* jobs available. *State or other work-study/employment:* Total amount: $2,612,026 (66% need-based, 34% non-need-based). Part-time jobs available.

APPLYING FOR FINANCIAL AID *Required financial aid form:* FAFSA. *Financial aid deadline (priority):* 2/1. *Notification date:* Continuous beginning 1/1. Students must reply by 5/1 or within 2 weeks of notification.

CONTACT Ms. Lynette Wahl, Office of Financial Aid, Hamline University, 1536 Hewitt Avenue, MS C1915, St. Paul, MN 55104, 651-523-3000 or toll-free 800-753-9753. *Fax:* 651-523-2585. *E-mail:* finaid@hamline.edu.
Website: http://www.hamline.edu/.

HAMPDEN-SYDNEY COLLEGE
Hampden-Sydney, VA

Tuition & fees: $45,852	Average undergraduate aid package: $33,875

ABOUT THE INSTITUTION Independent Presbyterian Church (U.S.A.), men only. *Awards:* bachelor's degrees. 26 undergraduate majors. *Total enrollment:* 1,046. Undergraduates: 1,046. Freshmen: 312. Federal methodology is used as a basis for awarding need-based institutional aid.

UNDERGRADUATE EXPENSES for 2018–2019 *Application fee:* $30. *Comprehensive fee:* $59,410 includes full-time tuition ($43,446), mandatory fees ($2406), and room and board ($13,558). *College room only:* $6150. Full-time tuition and fees vary according to course load and student level. Room and board charges vary according to board plan and housing facility. *Part-time tuition:* $1360 per credit hour. Part-time tuition and fees vary according to course load and student level.

FRESHMAN FINANCIAL AID (Fall 2017, est.) 274 applied for aid; of those 84% were deemed to have need. 100% of freshmen with need received aid; of those 26% had need fully met. *Average percent of need met:* 79% (excluding resources awarded to replace EFC). *Average financial aid package:* $33,456 (excluding resources awarded to replace EFC). 26% of all full-time freshmen had no need and received non-need-based gift aid.

UNDERGRADUATE FINANCIAL AID (Fall 2017, est.) 792 applied for aid; of those 87% were deemed to have need. 100% of undergraduates with need received aid; of those 23% had need fully met. *Average percent of need met:* 79% (excluding resources awarded to replace EFC). *Average financial aid package:* $33,875 (excluding resources awarded to replace EFC). 33% of all full-time undergraduates had no need and received non-need-based gift aid.

GIFT AID (NEED-BASED) *Receiving aid:* Freshmen: 73% (229); all full-time undergraduates: 66% (686). *Average award:* Freshmen: $29,916; Undergraduates: $29,908. *Scholarships, grants, and awards:* Federal Pell, FSEOG, state, private, college/university gift aid from institutional funds.

GIFT AID (NON-NEED-BASED) *Receiving aid:* Freshmen: 14% (44). Undergraduates: 11% (117). *Average award:* Freshmen: $16,826. Undergraduates: $17,872. *Scholarships, grants, and awards by category:* Academic interests/achievement: 881 awards ($11,699,446 total): biological sciences, business, education, general academic interests/achievements, home economics, international studies, premedicine. *Special achievements/activities:* 697 awards ($2,358,233 total): general special achievements/activities, leadership. *Special characteristics:* 124 awards ($1,178,568 total): children of faculty/staff, international students, out-of-state students, veterans, veterans' children. *Tuition waivers:* Full or partial for employees or children of employees. *ROTC:* Army cooperative.

LOANS *Student loans:* 65% of past graduating class borrowed through all loan programs. *Average indebtedness per student:* $35,921. *Average need-based loan:* Freshmen: $3810. Undergraduates: $4698. *Programs:* Federal Direct (Subsidized and Unsubsidized Stafford, PLUS), Perkins, college/university.

WORK-STUDY *Federal work-study:* 175 jobs averaging $1395.

APPLYING FOR FINANCIAL AID *Required financial aid forms:* FAFSA, state aid form. *Financial aid deadline (priority):* 3/1. *Notification date:* 3/15. Students must reply by 5/1 or within 2 weeks of notification.

CONTACT Ms. Zita Marie Barree, Director of Financial Aid, Hampden-Sydney College, PO Box 726, Hampden-Sydney, VA 23943-0726, 434-223-6119 or toll-free 800-755-0733. *Fax:* 434-223-6075. *E-mail:* hsfinaid@hsc.edu. *Website:* http://www.hsc.edu/.

HAMPSHIRE COLLEGE
Amherst, MA

ABOUT THE INSTITUTION Independent, coed. *Awards:* bachelor's degrees. 57 undergraduate majors. *Total enrollment:* 1,268. Undergraduates: 1,268. Freshmen: 325.

GIFT AID (NEED-BASED) *Scholarships, grants, and awards:* Federal Pell, FSEOG, state, private, college/university gift aid from institutional funds.

GIFT AID (NON-NEED-BASED) *Scholarships, grants, and awards by category:* Academic interests/achievement: biological sciences, English, general academic interests/achievements, humanities, international studies, mathematics, physical sciences, social sciences. *Creative arts/performance:* creative writing. *Special achievements/activities:* community service, leadership. *Special characteristics:* children of faculty/staff.

LOANS *Programs:* Federal Direct (Subsidized and Unsubsidized Stafford, PLUS), Perkins.

WORK-STUDY *Federal work-study:* 575 jobs averaging $2900. *State or other work-study/employment:* Total amount: $487,351 (23% need-based, 77% non-need-based). 253 part-time jobs averaging $2900.

APPLYING FOR FINANCIAL AID *Required financial aid forms:* FAFSA, CSS Financial Aid PROFILE, noncustodial (divorced/separated) parent's statement.

CONTACT Ms. Jennifer Garratt Lawton, Director of Financial Aid, Hampshire College, 893 West Street, Amherst, MA 01002, 413-559-5484 or toll-free 877-937-4267. *Fax:* 413-559-5585. *E-mail:* financialaid@hampshire.edu. *Website:* http://www.hampshire.edu/.

HAMPTON UNIVERSITY
Hampton, VA

Tuition & fees: $25,442	Average undergraduate aid package: $5803

ABOUT THE INSTITUTION Independent, coed. *Awards:* certificates, associate, bachelor's, master's, and doctoral degrees. 76 undergraduate majors. *Total enrollment:* 4,619. Undergraduates: 3,799. Freshmen: 1,018. Federal methodology is used as a basis for awarding need-based institutional aid.

UNDERGRADUATE EXPENSES for 2017–2018 *Application fee:* $35. *Comprehensive fee:* $36,660 includes full-time tuition ($22,630), mandatory fees ($2812), and room and board ($11,218). *College room only:* $5834. Full-time tuition and fees vary according to course load, degree level, location, program, and reciprocity agreements. Room and board charges vary according to board plan, housing facility, and location. *Part-time tuition:* $575 per credit hour. Part-time tuition and fees vary according to class time, course load, location, and reciprocity agreements.

FRESHMAN FINANCIAL AID (Fall 2016) 887 applied for aid; of those 81% were deemed to have need. 95% of freshmen with need received aid; of those 42% had need fully met. *Average percent of need met:* 43% (excluding resources awarded to replace EFC). *Average financial aid package:* $5975 (excluding resources awarded to replace EFC). 3% of all full-time freshmen had no need and received non-need-based gift aid.

UNDERGRADUATE FINANCIAL AID (Fall 2016) 2,356 applied for aid; of those 77% were deemed to have need. 96% of undergraduates with need received aid; of those 44% had need fully met. *Average percent of need met:* 44% (excluding resources awarded to replace EFC). *Average financial aid package:* $5803 (excluding resources awarded to replace EFC). 24% of all full-time undergraduates had no need and received non-need-based gift aid.

GIFT AID (NEED-BASED) *Total amount:* $8,679,971 (93% federal, 1% state, 3% institutional, 3% external sources). *Receiving aid:* Freshmen: 62% (676); all full-

time undergraduates: 54% (1,730). *Average award:* Freshmen: $5361; Undergraduates: $5322. *Scholarships, grants, and awards:* Federal Pell, FSEOG, state, private, college/university gift aid from institutional funds, United Negro College Fund.

GIFT AID (NON-NEED-BASED) *Total amount:* $25,364,474 (4% federal, 9% state, 69% institutional, 18% external sources). *Receiving aid:* Freshmen: 52% (572). Undergraduates: 39% (1,256). *Average award:* Freshmen: $4275. Undergraduates: $9947. *Scholarships, grants, and awards by category:* Academic interests/achievement: 169 awards ($2,207,170 total): architecture, biological sciences, business, communication, computer science, education, engineering/technologies, general academic interests/achievements, health fields, physical sciences. *Creative arts/performance:* 5 awards ($41,500 total): music. *Special achievements/activities:* 9 awards ($22,500 total): leadership. *Special characteristics:* 773 awards ($2,928,955 total): adult students, children of faculty/staff, international students, members of minority groups, veterans, veterans' children. *Tuition waivers:* Full or partial for employees or children of employees. *ROTC:* Army, Naval.

LOANS *Student loans:* $45,905,819 (22% need-based, 78% non-need-based). 75% of past graduating class borrowed through all loan programs. *Average indebtedness per student:* $34,131. *Average need-based loan:* Freshmen: $5503. Undergraduates: $5575. *Parent loans:* $38,632,468 (100% non-need-based). *Programs:* Federal Direct (Subsidized and Unsubsidized Stafford, PLUS), Perkins, Federal Nursing.

WORK-STUDY *Federal work-study:* 264 jobs averaging $1249. *State or other work-study/employment:* Total amount: $228,881 (82% need-based, 18% non-need-based). Part-time jobs available.

ATHLETIC AWARDS Total amount: $6,036,683 (100% non-need-based).

APPLYING FOR FINANCIAL AID *Required financial aid forms:* FAFSA, state aid form (VA residents only). *Financial aid deadline:* 4/15 (priority: 2/15). *Notification date:* Continuous beginning 4/15. Students must reply within 2 weeks of notification.

CONTACT Mr. Martin Miles, Director of Financial Aid, Hampton University, Whipple Barn, 2nd Floor, Hampton, VA 23668, 757-727-5332 or toll-free 800-624-3328. *Fax:* 757-728-6567. *E-mail:* martin.miles@hamptonu.edu. *Website:* http://www.hamptonu.edu/.

HANNIBAL-LAGRANGE UNIVERSITY
Hannibal, MO

CONTACT Brice Baumgardner, Director of Financial Aid, Hannibal-LaGrange University, 2800 Palmyra Road, Hannibal, MO 63401-1940, 573-629-3279 Ext. 3279 or toll-free 800-HLG-1119. *Fax:* 573-248-0954. *E-mail:* bbaumgardner@hlg.edu. *Website:* http://www.hlg.edu/.

HANOVER COLLEGE
Hanover, IN

Tuition & fees: $36,520	Average undergraduate aid package: $29,314

ABOUT THE INSTITUTION Independent Presbyterian, coed. *Awards:* bachelor's degrees. 38 undergraduate majors. *Total enrollment:* 1,090. Undergraduates: 1,090. Freshmen: 308. Federal methodology is used as a basis for awarding need-based institutional aid.

UNDERGRADUATE EXPENSES for 2017–2018 *One-time required fee:* $350. *Comprehensive fee:* $47,750 includes full-time tuition ($35,750), mandatory fees ($770), and room and board ($11,230). *College room only:* $5600. Full-time tuition and fees vary according to reciprocity agreements. Room and board charges vary according to housing facility. *Part-time tuition:* $3972 per unit. Part-time tuition and fees vary according to course load and reciprocity agreements.

FRESHMAN FINANCIAL AID (Fall 2016) 314 applied for aid; of those 65% were deemed to have need. 100% of freshmen with need received aid; of those 36% had need fully met. *Average percent of need met:* 86% (excluding resources awarded to replace EFC). *Average financial aid package:* $29,008 (excluding resources awarded to replace EFC). 12% of all full-time freshmen had no need and received non-need-based gift aid.

UNDERGRADUATE FINANCIAL AID (Fall 2016) 929 applied for aid; of those 90% were deemed to have need. 100% of undergraduates with need received aid; of those 27% had need fully met. *Average percent of need met:* 82% (excluding resources awarded to replace EFC). *Average financial aid package:* $29,314 (excluding resources awarded to replace EFC). 22% of all full-time undergraduates had no need and received non-need-based gift aid.

GIFT AID (NEED-BASED) *Total amount:* $20,818,771 (7% federal, 8% state, 81% institutional, 4% external sources). *Receiving aid:* Freshmen: 64% (204); all full-time undergraduates: 78% (840). *Average award:* Freshmen: $26,222; Undergraduates: $25,419. *Scholarships, grants, and awards:* Federal Pell, FSEOG, state, private, college/university gift aid from institutional funds.

GIFT AID (NON-NEED-BASED) *Total amount:* $6,531,658 (1% state, 94% institutional, 5% external sources). *Receiving aid:* Freshmen: 20% (63). Undergraduates: 15% (167). *Average award:* Freshmen: $23,193. Undergraduates: $20,679. *Scholarships, grants, and awards by category:* Academic interests/achievement: general academic interests/achievements. *Special characteristics:* children and siblings of alumni, children of faculty/staff, international students, members of minority groups, out-of-state students, religious affiliation, siblings of current students. *Tuition waivers:* Full or partial for employees or children of employees, senior citizens.

LOANS *Student loans:* $6,909,915 (64% need-based, 36% non-need-based). 72% of past graduating class borrowed through all loan programs. *Average indebtedness per student:* $30,835. *Average need-based loan:* Freshmen: $3097. Undergraduates: $4212. *Parent loans:* $4,166,437 (38% need-based, 62% non-need-based). *Programs:* Federal Direct (Subsidized and Unsubsidized Stafford, PLUS), college/university.

WORK-STUDY *Federal work-study:* 347 jobs averaging $1513.

APPLYING FOR FINANCIAL AID *Required financial aid form:* FAFSA. *Financial aid deadline (priority):* 3/1. *Notification date:* Continuous beginning 3/1. Students must reply by 5/1.

CONTACT Mr. Richard A. Nash, Director of Financial Aid, Hanover College, 517 Ball Drive, Hanover, IN 47243-0108, 800-213-2178 Ext. 7029 or toll-free 800-213-2178. *Fax:* 812-866-7284. *E-mail:* finaid@hanover.edu. *Website:* http://www.hanover.edu/.

GIFT AID (NON-NEED-BASED) *Total amount:* $11,846,334 (7% state, 74% institutional, 19% external sources). *Receiving aid:* Freshmen: 10% (104). Undergraduates: 7% (283). *Average award:* Freshmen: $6669. Undergraduates: $7000. *Scholarships, grants, and awards by category:* Academic interests/achievement: 3,646 awards ($24,357,854 total): communication, computer science, engineering/technologies, English, general academic interests/achievements, health fields, religion/biblical studies. *Creative arts/performance:* art/fine arts, cinema/film/broadcasting, debating, general creative arts/performance, journalism/publications, music. *Special achievements/activities:* cheerleading/drum major, general special achievements/activities, leadership, religious involvement. *Special characteristics:* children of faculty/staff, children with a deceased or disabled parent, general special characteristics, international students, relatives of clergy, siblings of current students. *Tuition waivers:* Full or partial for employees or children of employees, senior citizens. *ROTC:* Army cooperative.

LOANS *Student loans:* $21,768,597 (87% need-based, 13% non-need-based). 65% of past graduating class borrowed through all loan programs. *Average indebtedness per student:* $31,007. *Average need-based loan:* Freshmen: $4840. Undergraduates: $5204. *Parent loans:* $8,606,770 (86% need-based, 14% non-need-based). *Programs:* Federal Direct (Subsidized and Unsubsidized Stafford, PLUS), Perkins, Federal Nursing, state, college/university.

WORK-STUDY *Federal work-study:* 600 jobs averaging $929. *State or other work-study/employment:* Total amount: $1,786,805 (60% need-based, 40% non-need-based). 1,455 part-time jobs averaging $1281.

ATHLETIC AWARDS Total amount: $2,718,032 (57% need-based, 43% non-need-based).

APPLYING FOR FINANCIAL AID *Required financial aid form:* FAFSA. *Financial aid deadline (priority):* 4/15. *Notification date:* Continuous. Students must reply within 2 weeks of notification.

CONTACT Dr. Jonathan C. Roberts, Director of Student Financial Services, Harding University, PO Box 12282, Searcy, AR 72149-2282, 501-279-4257 or toll-free 800-477-4407. *Fax:* 501-279-4129. *E-mail:* jroberts@harding.edu. *Website:* http://www.harding.edu/.

HARDING UNIVERSITY
Searcy, AR

Tuition & fees: $19,190	Average undergraduate aid package: $12,882

ABOUT THE INSTITUTION Independent Church of Christ, coed. *Awards:* certificates, bachelor's, master's, and doctoral degrees. 85 undergraduate majors. *Total enrollment:* 5,539. Undergraduates: 4,182. Freshmen: 945. Federal methodology is used as a basis for awarding need-based institutional aid.

UNDERGRADUATE EXPENSES for 2017–2018 *Application fee:* $50. *Comprehensive fee:* $26,084 includes full-time tuition ($18,690), mandatory fees ($500), and room and board ($6894). *College room only:* $3592. Full-time tuition and fees vary according to course load. Room and board charges vary according to board plan and housing facility. *Part-time tuition:* $623 per credit hour. *Part-time fees:* $25 per credit hour. Part-time tuition and fees vary according to course load. *Payment plan:* Tuition prepayment.

FRESHMAN FINANCIAL AID (Fall 2016) 887 applied for aid; of those 75% were deemed to have need. 99% of freshmen with need received aid; of those 22% had need fully met. *Average percent of need met:* 82% (excluding resources awarded to replace EFC). *Average financial aid package:* $12,898 (excluding resources awarded to replace EFC). 31% of all full-time freshmen had no need and received non-need-based gift aid.

UNDERGRADUATE FINANCIAL AID (Fall 2016) 3,177 applied for aid; of those 81% were deemed to have need. 99% of undergraduates with need received aid; of those 16% had need fully met. *Average percent of need met:* 78% (excluding resources awarded to replace EFC). *Average financial aid package:* $12,882 (excluding resources awarded to replace EFC). 30% of all full-time undergraduates had no need and received non-need-based gift aid.

GIFT AID (NEED-BASED) *Total amount:* $23,021,402 (23% federal, 9% state, 64% institutional, 4% external sources). *Receiving aid:* Freshmen: 63% (637); all full-time undergraduates: 57% (2,358). *Average award:* Freshmen: $9954; Undergraduates: $9508. *Scholarships, grants, and awards:* Federal Pell, FSEOG, state, private, college/university gift aid from institutional funds.

HARDIN-SIMMONS UNIVERSITY
Abilene, TX

Tuition & fees: $28,990	Average undergraduate aid package: $24,855

ABOUT THE INSTITUTION Independent Baptist, coed. *Awards:* certificates, bachelor's, master's, and doctoral degrees. 58 undergraduate majors. *Total enrollment:* 2,252. Undergraduates: 1,749. Freshmen: 457. Federal methodology is used as a basis for awarding need-based institutional aid.

UNDERGRADUATE EXPENSES for 2018–2019 *Comprehensive fee:* $37,070 includes full-time tuition ($27,290), mandatory fees ($1700), and room and board ($8080). *College room only:* $4080. Full-time tuition and fees vary according to program. Room and board charges vary according to board plan and housing facility. *Part-time tuition:* $810 per credit hour. *Part-time fees:* $400 per term. Part-time tuition and fees vary according to course load and program. *Payment plan:* Guaranteed tuition.

FRESHMAN FINANCIAL AID (Fall 2017, est.) 453 applied for aid; of those 84% were deemed to have need. 100% of freshmen with need received aid; of those 23% had need fully met. *Average percent of need met:* 78% (excluding resources awarded to replace EFC). *Average financial aid package:* $24,488 (excluding resources awarded to replace EFC). 16% of all full-time freshmen had no need and received non-need-based gift aid.

UNDERGRADUATE FINANCIAL AID (Fall 2017, est.) 1,564 applied for aid; of those 76% were deemed to have need. 100% of undergraduates with need received aid; of those 19% had need fully met. *Average percent of need met:* 68% (excluding resources awarded to replace EFC). *Average financial aid package:* $24,855 (excluding resources awarded to replace EFC). 24% of all full-time undergraduates had no need and received non-need-based gift aid.

GIFT AID (NEED-BASED) *Total amount:* $8,048,291 (60% federal, 23% state, 17% institutional). *Receiving aid:* Freshmen: 67% (303); all full-time undergraduates: 59% (929). *Average award:* Freshmen: $6165; Undergraduates: $6018. *Scholarships, grants, and awards:* Federal Pell, FSEOG, state, private, college/university gift aid from institutional funds.

GIFT AID (NON-NEED-BASED) *Total amount:* $31,993,396 (98% institutional, 2% external sources). *Receiving aid:* Freshmen: 84% (382). Undergraduates:

74% (1,170). *Average award:* Freshmen: $15,249. Undergraduates: $12,914. *Scholarships, grants, and awards by category:* Academic interests/achievement: biological sciences, business, communication, computer science, education, English, foreign languages, general academic interests/achievements, health fields, humanities, mathematics, physical sciences, premedicine, religion/biblical studies, social sciences. *Creative arts/performance:* applied art and design, art/fine arts, creative writing, journalism/publications, music, performing arts, theater/drama. *Special achievements/activities:* general special achievements/activities. *Special characteristics:* children and siblings of alumni, children of educators, children of faculty/staff, ethnic background, general special characteristics, handicapped students, out-of-state students, public servants, relatives of clergy, religious affiliation, siblings of current students, veterans, veterans' children. *Tuition waivers:* Full or partial for employees or children of employees.

LOANS *Student loans:* $21,101,576 (30% need-based, 70% non-need-based). 68% of past graduating class borrowed through all loan programs. *Average indebtedness per student:* $51,346. *Average need-based loan:* Freshmen: $3220. Undergraduates: $4142. *Parent loans:* $3,200,750 (100% non-need-based). *Programs:* Federal Direct (Subsidized and Unsubsidized Stafford, PLUS), Perkins, Federal Nursing, state, college/university.

WORK-STUDY *Federal work-study:* Total amount: $152,214; jobs available. *State or other work-study/employment:* Total amount: $13,239 (100% need-based). Part-time jobs available.

APPLYING FOR FINANCIAL AID *Required financial aid form:* FAFSA. *Financial aid deadline (priority):* 3/1. *Notification date:* Continuous beginning 12/1. Students must reply by 6/1 or within 2 weeks of notification.

CONTACT Mrs. Bridget Moore, Director of Financial Aid and Scholarships, Hardin-Simmons University, Box 16050, Abilene, TX 79698, 325-670-1482 or toll-free 877-464-7889. *Fax:* 325-670-5822. *E-mail:* bnmoore@hsutx.edu. *Website:* http://www.hsutx.edu/.

HARRISBURG UNIVERSITY OF SCIENCE AND TECHNOLOGY
Harrisburg, PA

Tuition & fees: $23,900	Average undergraduate aid package: $21,651

ABOUT THE INSTITUTION Independent, coed. *Awards:* bachelor's, master's, and doctoral degrees. 8 undergraduate majors. *Total enrollment:* 4,071. Undergraduates: 511. Freshmen: 178. Federal methodology is used as a basis for awarding need-based institutional aid.

UNDERGRADUATE EXPENSES for 2018–2019 *Tuition:* full-time $23,900; part-time $1000 per semester hour. Full-time tuition and fees vary according to class time, course level, course load, degree level, location, program, reciprocity agreements, and student level. Part-time tuition and fees vary according to class time, course level, course load, degree level, location, program, reciprocity agreements, and student level. Room and board charges vary according to housing facility.

FRESHMAN FINANCIAL AID (Fall 2017, est.) 203 applied for aid; of those 98% were deemed to have need. 100% of freshmen with need received aid; of those 17% had need fully met. *Average percent of need met:* 69% (excluding resources awarded to replace EFC). *Average financial aid package:* $21,553 (excluding resources awarded to replace EFC). 9% of all full-time freshmen had no need and received non-need-based gift aid.

UNDERGRADUATE FINANCIAL AID (Fall 2017, est.) 414 applied for aid; of those 97% were deemed to have need. 100% of undergraduates with need received aid; of those 18% had need fully met. *Average percent of need met:* 69% (excluding resources awarded to replace EFC). *Average financial aid package:* $21,651 (excluding resources awarded to replace EFC). 7% of all full-time undergraduates had no need and received non-need-based gift aid.

GIFT AID (NEED-BASED) *Receiving aid:* Freshmen: 90% (197); all full-time undergraduates: 92% (398). *Average award:* Freshmen: $19,218; Undergraduates: $18,890. *Scholarships, grants, and awards:* Federal Pell, FSEOG, state, private, college/university gift aid from institutional funds.

GIFT AID (NON-NEED-BASED) *Receiving aid:* Freshmen: 13% (29). Undergraduates: 14% (61). *Average award:* Freshmen: $15,777. Undergraduates: $15,238. *Scholarships, grants, and awards by category:* Academic interests/achievement: biological sciences, business, computer science, physical sciences.

LOANS *Student loans:* 94% of past graduating class borrowed through all loan programs. *Average indebtedness per student:* $34,547. *Average need-based loan:* Freshmen: $3568. Undergraduates: $3985. *Programs:* Federal Direct (Subsidized and Unsubsidized Stafford, PLUS).

WORK-STUDY *Federal work-study:* 11 jobs averaging $1636.

APPLYING FOR FINANCIAL AID *Required financial aid form:* FAFSA. *Financial aid deadline:* Continuous. *Notification date:* Continuous. Students must reply within 2 weeks of notification.

CONTACT Mr. Vince P. Frank, Director of Financial Aid Services, Harrisburg University of Science and Technology, 326 Market Street, Harrisburg, PA 17101-2208, 717-901-5115 or toll-free 866-HBG-UNIV. *Fax:* 717-901-3115. *E-mail:* vfrank@harrisburgu.edu. *Website:* http://www.HarrisburgU.edu/.

HARRISON COLLEGE
Indianapolis, IN

CONTACT Financial Aid Office, Harrison College, 550 East Washington Street, Indianapolis, IN 46204, 317-447-6200 or toll-free 888-544-4422. *Website:* http://www.harrison.edu/.

HARRISON COLLEGE
Grove City, OH

CONTACT Financial Aid Office, Harrison College, 3880 Jackpot Road, Grove City, OH 43123, 614-539-8800 or toll-free 888-544-4422. *Website:* http://www.harrison.edu/.

HARRIS-STOWE STATE UNIVERSITY
St. Louis, MO

Tuition & fees (MO res): $5340	Average undergraduate aid package: $9247

ABOUT THE INSTITUTION State-supported, coed. *Awards:* certificates and bachelor's degrees. 22 undergraduate majors. *Total enrollment:* 1,442. Undergraduates: 1,442. Freshmen: 270. Federal methodology is used as a basis for awarding need-based institutional aid.

UNDERGRADUATE EXPENSES for 2017–2018 *Application fee:* $20. *Tuition, state resident:* full-time $4896; part-time $204 per credit hour. *Tuition, nonresident:* full-time $9529; part-time $397 per credit hour. *Required fees:* full-time $444; $222 per term. Full-time tuition and fees vary according to course load. *Room only:* $6500. Room and board charges vary according to housing facility.

FRESHMAN FINANCIAL AID (Fall 2016) 340 applied for aid; of those 95% were deemed to have need. 98% of freshmen with need received aid; of those 61% had need fully met. *Average percent of need met:* 87% (excluding resources awarded to replace EFC). *Average financial aid package:* $11,146 (excluding resources awarded to replace EFC). 5% of all full-time freshmen had no need and received non-need-based gift aid.

UNDERGRADUATE FINANCIAL AID (Fall 2016) 1,157 applied for aid; of those 87% were deemed to have need. 86% of undergraduates with need received aid; of those 66% had need fully met. *Average percent of need met:* 76% (excluding resources awarded to replace EFC). *Average financial aid package:* $9247 (excluding resources awarded to replace EFC). 4% of all full-time undergraduates had no need and received non-need-based gift aid.

GIFT AID (NEED-BASED) *Total amount:* $3,697,125 (89% federal, 11% state). *Receiving aid:* Freshmen: 52% (176); all full-time undergraduates: 72% (832). *Average award:* Freshmen: $6406; Undergraduates: $5198. *Scholarships, grants, and awards:* Federal Pell, FSEOG, state, private, college/university gift aid from institutional funds.

GIFT AID (NON-NEED-BASED) *Total amount:* $281,394 (83% institutional, 17% external sources). *Receiving aid:* Freshmen: 38% (128). Undergraduates: 25% (295). *Average award:* Freshmen: $2672. Undergraduates: $2462. *Scholarships, grants, and awards by category:* Academic interests/achievement: general academic interests/achievements. *Creative arts/performance:* music, theater/drama. *Tuition waivers:* Full or partial for employees or children of employees. *ROTC:* Army cooperative.

LOANS *Student loans:* $5,432,491 (48% need-based, 52% non-need-based). *Average need-based loan:* Freshmen: $3301. Undergraduates: $4016. *Parent loans:* $620,377 (100% need-based). *Programs:* Federal Direct (Subsidized and Unsubsidized Stafford, PLUS), college/university.

WORK-STUDY *Federal work-study:* jobs available. *State or other work-study/employment:* Total amount: $14,528 (100% need-based). Part-time jobs available.

ATHLETIC AWARDS Total amount: $220,399 (100% need-based).

APPLYING FOR FINANCIAL AID *Required financial aid forms:* FAFSA, institution's own form. *Financial aid deadline:* Continuous. *Notification date:* Continuous beginning 4/1.

CONTACT Regina Blackshear, Director of Financial Aid, Harris-Stowe State University, 3026 Laclede Avenue, St. Louis, MO 63103-2136, 314-340-3502. *Fax:* 314-340-3503.

Website: http://www.hssu.edu/.

HARTWICK COLLEGE
Oneonta, NY

Tuition & fees: $45,510	Average undergraduate aid package: $36,253

ABOUT THE INSTITUTION Independent, coed. *Awards:* bachelor's degrees. 37 undergraduate majors. *Total enrollment:* 1,201. Undergraduates: 1,201. Freshmen: 351. Federal methodology is used as a basis for awarding need-based institutional aid.

UNDERGRADUATE EXPENSES for 2018–2019 *One-time required fee:* $400. *Comprehensive fee:* $57,970 includes full-time tuition ($44,650), mandatory fees ($860), and room and board ($12,460). *College room only:* $6460. Full-time tuition and fees vary according to course load. Room and board charges vary according to board plan and housing facility. *Part-time tuition:* $1435 per credit hour. Part-time tuition and fees vary according to course load.

FRESHMAN FINANCIAL AID (Fall 2017, est.) 331 applied for aid; of those 96% were deemed to have need. 100% of freshmen with need received aid; of those 15% had need fully met. *Average percent of need met:* 83% (excluding resources awarded to replace EFC). *Average financial aid package:* $39,511 (excluding resources awarded to replace EFC). 10% of all full-time freshmen had no need and received non-need-based gift aid.

UNDERGRADUATE FINANCIAL AID (Fall 2017, est.) 1,036 applied for aid; of those 95% were deemed to have need. 100% of undergraduates with need received aid; of those 13% had need fully met. *Average percent of need met:* 79% (excluding resources awarded to replace EFC). *Average financial aid package:* $36,253 (excluding resources awarded to replace EFC). 15% of all full-time undergraduates had no need and received non-need-based gift aid.

GIFT AID (NEED-BASED) *Total amount:* $28,893,481 (8% federal, 5% state, 85% institutional, 2% external sources). *Receiving aid:* Freshmen: 90% (316); all full-time undergraduates: 82% (969). *Average award:* Freshmen: $33,774; Undergraduates: $30,823. *Scholarships, grants, and awards:* Federal Pell, FSEOG, state, private, college/university gift aid from institutional funds.

GIFT AID (NON-NEED-BASED) *Total amount:* $5,586,989 (98% institutional, 2% external sources). *Receiving aid:* Freshmen: 14% (49). Undergraduates: 15% (178). *Average award:* Freshmen: $28,127. Undergraduates: $24,021. *Scholarships, grants, and awards by category:* Academic interests/achievement: 182 awards: general academic interests/achievements. *Creative arts/performance:* art/fine arts, music. *Special characteristics:* children and siblings of alumni, children of faculty/staff, international students, siblings of current students, veterans. *Tuition waivers:* Full or partial for employees or children of employees.

LOANS *Student loans:* $10,945,619 (72% need-based, 28% non-need-based). 82% of past graduating class borrowed through all loan programs. *Average indebtedness per student:* $27,653. *Average need-based loan:* Freshmen: $5122. Undergraduates: $5130. *Parent loans:* $13,559,059 (43% need-based, 57% non-need-based). *Programs:* Federal Direct (Subsidized and Unsubsidized Stafford, PLUS), Perkins, Federal Nursing, college/university, alternative loans.

WORK-STUDY *Federal work-study:* Total amount: $1,522,361; 850 jobs averaging $2000.

ATHLETIC AWARDS Total amount: $887,083 (4% need-based, 96% non-need-based).

APPLYING FOR FINANCIAL AID *Required financial aid form:* FAFSA. *Financial aid deadline:* Continuous. *Notification date:* Continuous beginning 12/22. Students must reply by 5/1 or within 2 weeks of notification.

CONTACT Mrs. Melissa Allen, Director of Financial Aid, Hartwick College, One Hartwick Drive, Oneonta, NY 13820, 607-431-4130 or toll-free 888-HARTWICK. *Fax:* 607-431-4006. *E-mail:* finaid@hartwick.edu.

Website: http://www.hartwick.edu/.

HARVARD UNIVERSITY
Cambridge, MA

Tuition & fees: $48,949	Average undergraduate aid package: $53,730

ABOUT THE INSTITUTION Independent, coed. *Awards:* bachelor's, master's, and doctoral degrees. 47 undergraduate majors. *Total enrollment:* 11,168. Undergraduates: 6,766. Freshmen: 1,685. Institutional methodology is used as a basis for awarding need-based institutional aid.

UNDERGRADUATE EXPENSES for 2017–2018 *Application fee:* $75. *Comprehensive fee:* $65,609 includes full-time tuition ($44,990), mandatory fees ($3959), and room and board ($16,660). *College room only:* $10,300. *Payment plan:* Tuition prepayment.

FRESHMAN FINANCIAL AID (Fall 2016) 1,077 applied for aid; of those 85% were deemed to have need. 100% of freshmen with need received aid; of those 100% had need fully met. *Average percent of need met:* 100% (excluding resources awarded to replace EFC). *Average financial aid package:* $55,354 (excluding resources awarded to replace EFC). 1% of all full-time freshmen had no need and received non-need-based gift aid.

UNDERGRADUATE FINANCIAL AID (Fall 2016) 3,987 applied for aid; of those 92% were deemed to have need. 100% of undergraduates with need received aid; of those 100% had need fully met. *Average percent of need met:* 100% (excluding resources awarded to replace EFC). *Average financial aid package:* $53,730 (excluding resources awarded to replace EFC). 1% of all full-time undergraduates had no need and received non-need-based gift aid.

GIFT AID (NEED-BASED) *Total amount:* $185,987,860 (4% federal, 93% institutional, 3% external sources). *Receiving aid:* Freshmen: 55% (918); all full-time undergraduates: 55% (3,675). *Average award:* Freshmen: $53,120; Undergraduates: $50,699. *Scholarships, grants, and awards:* Federal Pell, FSEOG, state, private, college/university gift aid from institutional funds.

GIFT AID (NON-NEED-BASED) *Total amount:* $6,656,954 (20% federal, 4% institutional, 76% external sources). *Average award:* Freshmen: $5000. Undergraduates: $20,064. *ROTC:* Army, Naval, Air Force.

LOANS *Student loans:* $5,286,550 (64% need-based, 36% non-need-based). 20% of past graduating class borrowed through all loan programs. *Average indebtedness per student:* $15,114. *Average need-based loan:* Freshmen: $3712. Undergraduates: $4270. *Parent loans:* $6,617,022 (100% non-need-based). *Programs:* Federal Direct (Subsidized and Unsubsidized Stafford, PLUS), state, college/university.

WORK-STUDY *Federal work-study:* 880 jobs averaging $2803. *State or other work-study/employment:* Total amount: $6,162,825 (88% need-based, 12% non-need-based). 2,146 part-time jobs averaging $2872.

APPLYING FOR FINANCIAL AID *Required financial aid forms:* FAFSA, CSS Financial Aid PROFILE, noncustodial (divorced/separated) parent's statement, business/farm supplement, federal income tax form(s). *Financial aid deadline (priority):* 3/1. *Notification date:* 4/1. Students must reply by 5/1 or within 2 weeks of notification.

CONTACT Financial Aid Office, Harvard University, 86 Brattle Street, Cambridge, MA 02138, 617-495-1581.

Website: http://www.harvard.edu/.

HARVEY MUDD COLLEGE
Claremont, CA

Tuition & fees: $54,636	Average undergraduate aid package: $43,248

ABOUT THE INSTITUTION Independent, coed. *Awards:* bachelor's degrees. 7 undergraduate majors. *Total enrollment:* 844. Undergraduates: 844. Freshmen: 225. Both federal and institutional methodology are used as a basis for awarding need-based institutional aid.

UNDERGRADUATE EXPENSES for 2017–2018 *Application fee:* $70. *One-time required fee:* $250. *Comprehensive fee:* $72,228 includes full-time tuition ($54,347), mandatory fees ($289), and room and board ($17,592). *College room only:* $9554. Room and board charges vary according to board plan. *Part-time tuition:* $1698 per unit. Part-time tuition and fees vary according to course load.

FRESHMAN FINANCIAL AID (Fall 2016) 151 applied for aid; of those 79% were deemed to have need. 100% of freshmen with need received aid; of those 100% had need fully met. *Average percent of need met:* 100% (excluding resources awarded to replace EFC). *Average financial aid package:* $42,654 (excluding resources awarded to replace EFC). 17% of all full-time freshmen had no need and received non-need-based gift aid.

UNDERGRADUATE FINANCIAL AID (Fall 2016) 483 applied for aid; of those 86% were deemed to have need. 100% of undergraduates with need received aid; of those 100% had need fully met. *Average percent of need met:* 100% (excluding resources awarded to replace EFC). *Average financial aid package:* $43,248 (excluding resources awarded to replace EFC). 19% of all full-time undergraduates had no need and received non-need-based gift aid.

GIFT AID (NEED-BASED) *Total amount:* $16,302,844 (4% federal, 4% state, 89% institutional, 3% external sources). *Receiving aid:* Freshmen: 52% (113); all full-time undergraduates: 48% (401). *Average award:* Freshmen: $41,649; Undergraduates: $40,138. *Scholarships, grants, and awards:* Federal Pell, FSEOG, state, private, college/university gift aid from institutional funds.

GIFT AID (NON-NEED-BASED) *Total amount:* $2,604,599 (91% institutional, 9% external sources). *Receiving aid:* Freshmen: 20% (44). Undergraduates: 21% (176). *Average award:* Freshmen: $11,251. Undergraduates: $12,696. *Scholarships, grants, and awards by category:* Academic interests/achievement: 289 awards ($3,972,269 total): general academic interests/achievements. *Special characteristics:* 3 awards ($125,000 total): international students. *Tuition waivers:* Full or partial for employees or children of employees. *ROTC:* Army cooperative, Air Force cooperative.

LOANS *Student loans:* $3,026,966 (83% need-based, 17% non-need-based). 49% of past graduating class borrowed through all loan programs. *Average indebtedness per student:* $25,041. *Average need-based loan:* Freshmen: $4176. Undergraduates: $5657. *Parent loans:* $1,607,224 (67% need-based, 33% non-need-based). *Programs:* Federal Direct (Subsidized and Unsubsidized Stafford, PLUS), college/university, private loans.

WORK-STUDY *Federal work-study:* 121 jobs averaging $839. *State or other work-study/employment:* Total amount: $194,572 (57% need-based, 43% non-need-based). 25 part-time jobs averaging $7783.

APPLYING FOR FINANCIAL AID *Required financial aid forms:* FAFSA, CSS Financial Aid PROFILE, state aid form, noncustodial (divorced/separated) parent's statement, business/farm supplement. *Financial aid deadline:* 2/1. *Notification date:* 4/1. Students must reply by 5/1.

CONTACT Mrs. Gilma Lopez, Director of Financial Aid, Harvey Mudd College, 301 Platt Boulevard, Claremont, CA 91711-5994, 909-621-8055. *Fax:* 909-607-4494. *E-mail:* financial_aid@hmc.edu. *Website:* http://www.hmc.edu/.

HASKELL INDIAN NATIONS UNIVERSITY
Lawrence, KS

CONTACT Reta Brewer, Director of Financial Aid, Haskell Indian Nations University, 155 Indian Avenue, Box 5027, Lawrence, KS 66046-4800, 785-749-8468. *Fax:* 785-832-6617. *Website:* http://www.haskell.edu/.

HASTINGS COLLEGE
Hastings, NE

CONTACT Mrs. Traci Noelle Boeve, Director of Student Financial Aid, Hastings College, 710 North Turner Avenue, Hastings, NE 68901, 402-461-7431 or toll-free 800-532-7642. *Fax:* 402-461-7714. *E-mail:* tboeve@hastings.edu. *Website:* http://www.hastings.edu/.

HAVERFORD COLLEGE
Haverford, PA

Tuition & fees: $52,754	Average undergraduate aid package: $51,271

ABOUT THE INSTITUTION Independent, coed. *Awards:* bachelor's degrees. 38 undergraduate majors. *Total enrollment:* 1,296. Undergraduates: 1,296. Freshmen: 349. Institutional methodology is used as a basis for awarding need-based institutional aid.

UNDERGRADUATE EXPENSES for 2017–2018 *Application fee:* $65. *One-time required fee:* $240. *Comprehensive fee:* $68,712 includes full-time tuition ($52,278), mandatory fees ($476), and room and board ($15,958). *College room only:* $9120.

FRESHMAN FINANCIAL AID (Fall 2017, est.) 199 applied for aid; of those 83% were deemed to have need. 100% of freshmen with need received aid; of those 100% had need fully met. *Average percent of need met:* 100% (excluding resources awarded to replace EFC). *Average financial aid package:* $49,905 (excluding resources awarded to replace EFC).

UNDERGRADUATE FINANCIAL AID (Fall 2017, est.) 663 applied for aid; of those 92% were deemed to have need. 100% of undergraduates with need received aid; of those 100% had need fully met. *Average percent of need met:* 100% (excluding resources awarded to replace EFC). *Average financial aid package:* $51,271 (excluding resources awarded to replace EFC).

GIFT AID (NEED-BASED) *Total amount:* $29,879,980 (3% federal, 1% state, 94% institutional, 2% external sources). *Receiving aid:* Freshmen: 48% (166); all full-time undergraduates: 47% (609). *Average award:* Freshmen: $46,673; Undergraduates: $48,895. *Scholarships, grants, and awards:* Federal Pell, FSEOG, state, college/university gift aid from institutional funds.

GIFT AID (NON-NEED-BASED) *Receiving aid:* Freshmen: 7% (26). Undergraduates: 4% (56). *Tuition waivers:* Full or partial for employees or children of employees. *ROTC:* Air Force cooperative.

LOANS *Student loans:* $1,586,815 (36% need-based, 64% non-need-based). 23% of past graduating class borrowed through all loan programs. *Average indebtedness per student:* $15,000. *Average need-based loan:* Freshmen: $2679. Undergraduates: $3418. *Parent loans:* $1,247,993 (100% non-need-based). *Programs:* Federal Direct (Subsidized and Unsubsidized Stafford, PLUS), college/university.

WORK-STUDY *Federal work-study:* Total amount: $496,663; jobs available. *State or other work-study/employment:* Total amount: $569,017 (4% need-based, 96% non-need-based). Part-time jobs available.

APPLYING FOR FINANCIAL AID *Required financial aid forms:* FAFSA, CSS Financial Aid PROFILE, noncustodial (divorced/separated) parent's statement, business/farm supplement. *Financial aid deadline (priority):* 2/1. *Notification date:* 3/25. Students must reply by 5/1.

CONTACT Mr. Michael Colahan, Director of Financial Aid, Haverford College, 370 Lancaster Avenue, Haverford, PA 19041-1392, 610-896-1350. *Fax:* 610-896-1338. *E-mail:* finaid@haverford.edu. *Website:* http://www.haverford.edu/.

HAWAII PACIFIC UNIVERSITY
Honolulu, HI

Tuition & fees: $25,980	Average undergraduate aid package: $14,367

ABOUT THE INSTITUTION Independent, coed. *Awards:* certificates, associate, bachelor's, master's, and doctoral degrees. 37 undergraduate majors. *Total*

enrollment: 4,116. Undergraduates: 3,560. Freshmen: 500. Federal methodology is used as a basis for awarding need-based institutional aid.

UNDERGRADUATE EXPENSES for 2018–2019 Application fee: $50. **Comprehensive fee:** $40,780 includes full-time tuition ($25,630), mandatory fees ($350), and room and board ($14,800). Full-time tuition and fees vary according to course level, course load, degree level, location, program, and student level. Room and board charges vary according to board plan, housing facility, and location. **Part-time tuition:** $855 per credit. **Part-time fees:** $25 per term. Part-time tuition and fees vary according to course level, course load, degree level, location, program, and student level.

FRESHMAN FINANCIAL AID (Fall 2017, est.) 404 applied for aid; of those 88% were deemed to have need. 100% of freshmen with need received aid; of those 10% had need fully met. **Average percent of need met:** 50% (excluding resources awarded to replace EFC). **Average financial aid package:** $19,107 (excluding resources awarded to replace EFC). 23% of all full-time freshmen had no need and received non-need-based gift aid.

UNDERGRADUATE FINANCIAL AID (Fall 2017, est.) 1,537 applied for aid; of those 91% were deemed to have need. 99% of undergraduates with need received aid; of those 7% had need fully met. **Average percent of need met:** 56% (excluding resources awarded to replace EFC). **Average financial aid package:** $14,367 (excluding resources awarded to replace EFC). 26% of all full-time undergraduates had no need and received non-need-based gift aid.

GIFT AID (NEED-BASED) Total amount: $14,692,017 (28% federal, 68% institutional, 4% external sources). **Receiving aid:** Freshmen: 74% (353); all full-time undergraduates: 54% (1,309). **Average award:** Freshmen: $3134; Undergraduates: $3072. **Scholarships, grants, and awards:** Federal Pell, FSEOG, private, college/university gift aid from institutional funds.

GIFT AID (NON-NEED-BASED) Total amount: $4,824,410 (94% institutional, 6% external sources). **Receiving aid:** Freshmen: 72% (344). Undergraduates: 46% (1,115). **Average award:** Freshmen: $9068. Undergraduates: $6936. **Scholarships, grants, and awards by category:** Academic interests/achievement: business, education, general academic interests/achievements. **Creative arts/performance:** dance, debating, journalism/publications, music, performing arts. **Special achievements/activities:** cheerleading/drum major, community service, hobbies/interests, leadership, memberships, religious involvement. **Special characteristics:** ethnic background, international students, local/state students, out-of-state students, previous college experience, relatives of clergy, religious affiliation. **Tuition waivers:** Full or partial for employees or children of employees. **ROTC:** Army cooperative, Air Force cooperative.

LOANS Student loans: $13,764,154 (84% need-based, 16% non-need-based). 59% of past graduating class borrowed through all loan programs. **Average indebtedness per student:** $27,481. **Average need-based loan:** Freshmen: $5912. Undergraduates: $5662. **Parent loans:** $6,737,570 (54% need-based, 46% non-need-based). **Programs:** Federal Direct (Subsidized and Unsubsidized Stafford, PLUS), Perkins, Federal Nursing.

WORK-STUDY Federal work-study: Total amount: $1,670,128; 604 jobs averaging $2765.

ATHLETIC AWARDS Total amount: $3,121,778 (35% need-based, 65% non-need-based).

APPLYING FOR FINANCIAL AID Required financial aid form: FAFSA. **Financial aid deadline (priority):** 3/1. **Notification date:** Continuous beginning 12/15. Students must reply within 3 weeks of notification.

CONTACT James M. Oshiro, Executive Director of Financial Aid, Hawaii Pacific University, 1164 Bishop Street, Suite 201, Honolulu, HI 96813-2785, 808-544-0253 or toll-free 866-225-5478. Fax: 808-544-0884. E-mail: financialaid@hpu.edu. Website: http://www.hpu.edu/.

HEBREW THEOLOGICAL COLLEGE
Skokie, IL

CONTACT Ms. Rhoda Morris, Financial Aid Administrator, Hebrew Theological College, 7135 Carpenter Road, Skokie, IL 60077-3263, 847-982-2500. Fax: 847-674-6381.
Website: http://www.htc.edu/.

HEIDELBERG UNIVERSITY
Tiffin, OH

Tuition & fees: $31,000	Average undergraduate aid package: $22,421

ABOUT THE INSTITUTION Independent United Church of Christ, coed. **Awards:** bachelor's and master's degrees. 44 undergraduate majors. **Total enrollment:** 1,209. Undergraduates: 1,059. Freshmen: 319. Federal methodology is used as a basis for awarding need-based institutional aid.

UNDERGRADUATE EXPENSES for 2018–2019 Comprehensive fee: $41,400 includes full-time tuition ($30,400), mandatory fees ($600), and room and board ($10,400). **College room only:** $5300. Room and board charges vary according to board plan and housing facility. **Part-time tuition:** $900 per contact hour.

FRESHMAN FINANCIAL AID (Fall 2016) 364 applied for aid; of those 91% were deemed to have need. 100% of freshmen with need received aid; of those 22% had need fully met. **Average percent of need met:** 81% (excluding resources awarded to replace EFC). **Average financial aid package:** $24,888 (excluding resources awarded to replace EFC). 8% of all full-time freshmen had no need and received non-need-based gift aid.

UNDERGRADUATE FINANCIAL AID (Fall 2016) 1,035 applied for aid; of those 92% were deemed to have need. 100% of undergraduates with need received aid; of those 30% had need fully met. **Average percent of need met:** 79% (excluding resources awarded to replace EFC). **Average financial aid package:** $22,421 (excluding resources awarded to replace EFC). 14% of all full-time undergraduates had no need and received non-need-based gift aid.

GIFT AID (NEED-BASED) Total amount: $24,830,752 (8% federal, 3% state, 87% institutional, 2% external sources). **Receiving aid:** Freshmen: 90% (333); all full-time undergraduates: 89% (948). **Average award:** Freshmen: $19,650; Undergraduates: $19,536. **Scholarships, grants, and awards:** Federal Pell, FSEOG, state, private, college/university gift aid from institutional funds.

GIFT AID (NON-NEED-BASED) Total amount: $2,778,131 (98% institutional, 2% external sources). **Receiving aid:** Freshmen: 9% (32). Undergraduates: 14% (147). **Average award:** Freshmen: $14,166. Undergraduates: $13,998. **Scholarships, grants, and awards by category:** Academic interests/achievement: 763 awards ($9,590,465 total): general academic interests/achievements. **Creative arts/performance:** 58 awards ($93,925 total): music, performing arts, theater/drama. **Special characteristics:** 250 awards ($1,025,340 total): children and siblings of alumni, children of faculty/staff, out-of-state students, relatives of clergy, religious affiliation. **Tuition waivers:** Full or partial for employees or children of employees. **ROTC:** Army cooperative, Air Force cooperative.

LOANS Student loans: $9,010,985 (95% need-based, 5% non-need-based). 86% of past graduating class borrowed through all loan programs. **Average indebtedness per student:** $35,872. **Average need-based loan:** Freshmen: $3950. Undergraduates: $4854. **Parent loans:** $4,513,137 (97% need-based, 3% non-need-based). **Programs:** Federal Direct (Subsidized and Unsubsidized Stafford, PLUS), Perkins.

WORK-STUDY Federal work-study: 703 jobs averaging $2000. **State or other work-study/employment:** Total amount: $82,045 (100% non-need-based). 61 part-time jobs averaging $1000.

APPLYING FOR FINANCIAL AID Required financial aid form: FAFSA. **Financial aid deadline:** Continuous. **Notification date:** Continuous beginning 12/15. Students must reply by 5/1.

CONTACT Ms. Juli L. Weininger, Director of Financial Aid, Heidelberg University, 310 East Market Street, Tiffin, OH 44883-2462, 419-448-2293 or toll-free 800-434-3352. Fax: 419-448-2296.
Website: http://www.heidelberg.edu/.

HELLENIC AMERICAN UNIVERSITY
Nashua, NH

CONTACT Financial Aid Office, Hellenic American University, 505 Amherst Street, Nashua, NH 03063, 603-577-8700.
Website: http://www.hauniv.edu/.

HELLENIC COLLEGE
Brookline, MA

ABOUT THE INSTITUTION Independent Greek Orthodox, coed. 6 undergraduate majors.

GIFT AID (NEED-BASED) *Scholarships, grants, and awards:* Federal Pell, FSEOG, state, private, college/university gift aid from institutional funds.

GIFT AID (NON-NEED-BASED) *Scholarships, grants, and awards by category: Academic interests/achievement:* religion/biblical studies. *Special achievements/activities:* religious involvement.

LOANS *Programs:* Federal Direct (Subsidized and Unsubsidized Stafford, PLUS), state.

APPLYING FOR FINANCIAL AID *Required financial aid forms:* FAFSA, institution's own form.

CONTACT Michael Kirchmaier, Director of Financial Aid, Hellenic College, 50 Goddard Avenue, Brookline, MA 02146-7496, 617-850-1239 or toll-free 866-424-2338. *Fax:* 617-850-1240. *E-mail:* mkirchmaier@hchc.edu. *Website:* http://www.hchc.edu/.

HENDERSON STATE UNIVERSITY
Arkadelphia, AR

Tuition & fees (AR res): $8311	Average undergraduate aid package: $10,091

ABOUT THE INSTITUTION State-supported, coed. *Awards:* certificates, bachelor's, and master's degrees. 40 undergraduate majors. *Total enrollment:* 3,565. Undergraduates: 3,066. Freshmen: 746. Both federal and institutional methodology are used as a basis for awarding need-based institutional aid.

UNDERGRADUATE EXPENSES for 2017–2018 *Tuition, state resident:* full-time $6630; part-time $221 per credit hour. *Tuition, nonresident:* full-time $8280; part-time $276 per credit hour. *Required fees:* full-time $1681. Full-time tuition and fees vary according to course load. Part-time tuition and fees vary according to course load. *College room and board:* $7320. Room and board charges vary according to board plan and housing facility.

FRESHMAN FINANCIAL AID (Fall 2017, est.) 578 applied for aid; of those 87% were deemed to have need. 100% of freshmen with need received aid; of those 13% had need fully met. *Average percent of need met:* 45% (excluding resources awarded to replace EFC). *Average financial aid package:* $9279 (excluding resources awarded to replace EFC). 13% of all full-time freshmen had no need and received non-need-based gift aid.

UNDERGRADUATE FINANCIAL AID (Fall 2017, est.) 2,213 applied for aid; of those 87% were deemed to have need. 100% of undergraduates with need received aid; of those 14% had need fully met. *Average percent of need met:* 58% (excluding resources awarded to replace EFC). *Average financial aid package:* $10,091 (excluding resources awarded to replace EFC). 12% of all full-time undergraduates had no need and received non-need-based gift aid.

GIFT AID (NEED-BASED) *Total amount:* $6,739,451 (98% federal, 2% state). *Receiving aid:* Freshmen: 56% (344); all full-time undergraduates: 53% (1,356). *Average award:* Freshmen: $4800; Undergraduates: $4815. *Scholarships, grants, and awards:* Federal Pell, FSEOG, state, private.

GIFT AID (NON-NEED-BASED) *Total amount:* $12,297,742 (33% state, 54% institutional, 13% external sources). *Receiving aid:* Freshmen: 77% (475). Undergraduates: 52% (1,339). *Average award:* Freshmen: $7185. Undergraduates: $7068. *Scholarships, grants, and awards by category: Academic interests/achievement:* biological sciences, education, general academic interests/achievements, international studies, mathematics. *Creative arts/performance:* art/fine arts, cinema/film/broadcasting, dance, debating, journalism/publications, music, performing arts, theater/drama. *Special achievements/activities:* cheerleading/drum major, general special achievements/activities, leadership. *Special characteristics:* children and siblings of alumni, children of faculty/staff, international students, out-of-state students. *Tuition waivers:* Full or partial for children of alumni, employees or children of employees, senior citizens. *ROTC:* Army cooperative.

LOANS *Student loans:* $9,414,340 (46% need-based, 54% non-need-based). 77% of past graduating class borrowed through all loan programs. *Average indebtedness per student:* $20,638. *Average need-based loan:* Freshmen: $3000. Undergraduates: $3860. *Parent loans:* $2,760,416 (45% need-based, 55% non-need-based). *Programs:* Federal Direct (Subsidized and Unsubsidized Stafford, PLUS), Perkins.

WORK-STUDY *Federal work-study:* Total amount: $137,576; jobs available. *State or other work-study/employment:* Total amount: $196,937 (100% need-based). Part-time jobs available.

ATHLETIC AWARDS Total amount: $2,466,834 (72% need-based, 28% non-need-based).

APPLYING FOR FINANCIAL AID *Required financial aid form:* FAFSA. *Financial aid deadline (priority):* 6/1. *Notification date:* Continuous beginning 4/15.

CONTACT Ms. Christina Jones, Director of Financial Aid, Henderson State University, 1100 Henderson Street, HSU Box 7812, Arkadelphia, AR 71999-0001, 870-230-5138 or toll-free 800-228-7333. *Fax:* 870-230-5481. *E-mail:* jonesc@hsu.edu. *Website:* http://www.hsu.edu/.

HENDRIX COLLEGE
Conway, AR

Tuition & fees: $45,790	Average undergraduate aid package: $38,736

ABOUT THE INSTITUTION Independent United Methodist, coed. *Awards:* bachelor's and master's degrees. 30 undergraduate majors. *Total enrollment:* 1,249. Undergraduates: 1,238. Freshmen: 338. Federal methodology is used as a basis for awarding need-based institutional aid.

UNDERGRADUATE EXPENSES for 2018–2019 *Application fee:* $40. *Comprehensive fee:* $58,074 includes full-time tuition ($45,440), mandatory fees ($350), and room and board ($12,284). *College room only:* $6324. Full-time tuition and fees vary according to course load. Room and board charges vary according to board plan and housing facility. *Part-time tuition:* $5466 per course. Part-time tuition and fees vary according to course load.

FRESHMAN FINANCIAL AID (Fall 2017, est.) 325 applied for aid; of those 86% were deemed to have need. 100% of freshmen with need received aid; of those 32% had need fully met. *Average percent of need met:* 90% (excluding resources awarded to replace EFC). *Average financial aid package:* $41,885 (excluding resources awarded to replace EFC). 17% of all full-time freshmen had no need and received non-need-based gift aid.

UNDERGRADUATE FINANCIAL AID (Fall 2017, est.) 1,063 applied for aid; of those 84% were deemed to have need. 100% of undergraduates with need received aid; of those 34% had need fully met. *Average percent of need met:* 87% (excluding resources awarded to replace EFC). *Average financial aid package:* $38,736 (excluding resources awarded to replace EFC). 26% of all full-time undergraduates had no need and received non-need-based gift aid.

GIFT AID (NEED-BASED) *Total amount:* $29,539,412 (6% federal, 6% state, 87% institutional, 1% external sources). *Receiving aid:* Freshmen: 83% (280); all full-time undergraduates: 73% (888). *Average award:* Freshmen: $37,973; Undergraduates: $34,649. *Scholarships, grants, and awards:* Federal Pell, FSEOG, state, private, college/university gift aid from institutional funds.

GIFT AID (NON-NEED-BASED) *Total amount:* $11,503,317 (12% state, 86% institutional, 2% external sources). *Receiving aid:* Freshmen: 20% (66). Undergraduates: 19% (226). *Average award:* Freshmen: $27,460. Undergraduates: $2553. *Scholarships, grants, and awards by category: Academic interests/achievement:* general academic interests/achievements. *Creative arts/performance:* art/fine arts, dance, music, theater/drama. *Special achievements/activities:* community service, general special achievements/activities, leadership, religious involvement. *Special characteristics:* children of faculty/staff, international students, previous college experience, relatives of clergy. *Tuition waivers:* Full or partial for employees or children of employees. *ROTC:* Army cooperative.

LOANS *Student loans:* $4,943,991 (67% need-based, 33% non-need-based). 58% of past graduating class borrowed through all loan programs. *Average indebtedness per student:* $27,786. *Average need-based loan:* Freshmen: $3203. Undergraduates: $3624. *Parent loans:* $2,127,523 (27% need-based, 73% non-need-based). *Programs:* Federal Direct (Subsidized and Unsubsidized Stafford, PLUS), Perkins, United Methodist Student Loans.

WORK-STUDY *Federal work-study:* Total amount: $1,151,670; jobs available. *State or other work-study/employment:* Total amount: $496,132 (26% need-based, 74% non-need-based). Part-time jobs available.

APPLYING FOR FINANCIAL AID *Required financial aid forms:* FAFSA, state aid form. *Financial aid deadline (priority):* 3/1. *Notification date:* Continuous beginning 12/1. Students must reply by 5/1 or within 4 weeks of notification.
CONTACT Ms. Kristina Burford, Associate Vice President for Enrollment and Director of Financial Aid, Hendrix College, 1600 Washington Avenue, Conway, AR 72032, 501-450-1368 or toll-free 800-277-9017. *Fax:* 501-450-3871. *E-mail:* burford@hendrix.edu.
Website: http://www.hendrix.edu/.

HENLEY-PUTNAM UNIVERSITY
San Jose, CA

CONTACT Financial Aid Office, Henley-Putnam University, 2107 N. First Street, Suite 210, San Jose, CA 95131, 408-453-9900 or toll-free 888-852-8746.
Website: http://www.henley-putnam.edu/.

HERITAGE BIBLE COLLEGE
Dunn, NC

ABOUT THE INSTITUTION Independent Pentecostal Free Will Baptist, coed. *Awards:* associate and bachelor's degrees. 2 undergraduate majors. *Total enrollment:* 69. Undergraduates: 69. Freshmen: 10.
GIFT AID (NEED-BASED) *Scholarships, grants, and awards:* Federal Pell, FSEOG, private, college/university gift aid from institutional funds.
GIFT AID (NON-NEED-BASED) *Scholarships, grants, and awards by category:* Academic interests/achievement: religion/biblical studies. Special achievements/activities: leadership, religious involvement.
LOANS *Programs:* Federal Direct (Subsidized and Unsubsidized Stafford, PLUS).
APPLYING FOR FINANCIAL AID *Required financial aid forms:* FAFSA, institution's own form, verification worksheet.
CONTACT Ms. Kayla Bullard, Director of Financial Aid, Heritage Bible College, PO Box 1628, Dunn, NC 28335, 910-892-3178 Ext. 232 or toll-free 800-297-6351. *Fax:* 910-891-1660. *E-mail:* ksutton@heritagebiblecollege.edu.
Website: http://www.heritagebiblecollege.edu/.

HERITAGE CHRISTIAN UNIVERSITY
Florence, AL

CONTACT Mechelle R. Thompson, Associate Director of Financial Aid, Heritage Christian University, PO Box HCU, Florence, AL 35630, 800-367-3565 Ext. 303 or toll-free 800-367-3565. *Fax:* 256-716-8021. *E-mail:* mthompson@hcu.edu.
Website: http://www.hcu.edu/.

HERITAGE UNIVERSITY
Toppenish, WA

CONTACT Mr. Norberto Espindola, Director of Enrollment Management Services, Heritage University, 3240 Fort Road, Toppenish, WA 98948-9599, 509-865-8500 or toll-free 888-272-6190. *Fax:* 509-865-8659. *E-mail:* financial_aid@heritage.edu.
Website: http://www.heritage.edu/.

HERZING UNIVERSITY
Birmingham, AL

CONTACT Financial Aid Office, Herzing University, 280 West Valley Avenue, Birmingham, AL 35209, 205-916-2800 or toll-free 800-596-0724.
Website: http://www.herzing.edu/birmingham/.

HERZING UNIVERSITY
Winter Park, FL

CONTACT Financial Aid Office, Herzing University, 1865 SR 436, Winter Park, FL 32792, 407-641-5227 or toll-free 800-596-0724.
Website: http://www.herzing.edu/orlando.

HERZING UNIVERSITY
Atlanta, GA

CONTACT Financial Aid Office, Herzing University, 3393 Peachtree Road, Suite 1003, Atlanta, GA 30326, 404-816-4533 or toll-free 800-596-0724.
Website: http://www.herzing.edu/atlanta/.

HERZING UNIVERSITY
Kenner, LA

CONTACT Financial Aid Office, Herzing University, 2500 Williams Boulevard, Kenner, LA 70062, 504-733-0074 or toll-free 800-596-0724.
Website: http://www.herzing.edu/new-orleans.

HERZING UNIVERSITY
Brookfield, WI

CONTACT Financial Aid Office, Herzing University, 555 South Executive Drive, Brookfield, WI 53005, 262-649-1710 or toll-free 800-596-0724.
Website: http://www.herzing.edu/brookfield.

HERZING UNIVERSITY
Kenosha, WI

CONTACT Financial Aid Office, Herzing University, 4006 Washington Road, Kenosha, WI 53144, 262-671-0675 or toll-free 800-596-0724.
Website: http://www.herzing.edu/kenosha.

HERZING UNIVERSITY
Madison, WI

CONTACT Financial Aid Office, Herzing University, 5218 East Terrace Drive, Madison, WI 53718, 608-249-6611 or toll-free 800-596-0724.
Website: http://www.herzing.edu/madison/.

HERZING UNIVERSITY ONLINE
Menomonee Falls, WI

CONTACT Financial Aid Office, Herzing University Online, W140N8917 Lilly Road, Menomonee Falls, WI 53051, 866-508-0748.
Website: http://www.herzingonline.edu/.

HIGH POINT UNIVERSITY
High Point, NC

Tuition & fees: $35,118	Average undergraduate aid package: $15,723

ABOUT THE INSTITUTION Independent United Methodist, coed. **Awards:** certificates, bachelor's, master's, and doctoral degrees. 48 undergraduate majors. **Total enrollment:** 4,951. Undergraduates: 4,467. Freshmen: 1,111. Institutional methodology is used as a basis for awarding need-based institutional aid.

UNDERGRADUATE EXPENSES for 2018–2019 Application fee: $50. **Comprehensive fee:** $49,248 includes full-time tuition ($30,748), mandatory fees ($4370), and room and board ($14,130). Full-time tuition and fees vary according to course load and reciprocity agreements. Room and board charges vary according to board plan and housing facility. **Part-time tuition:** $955 per credit hour. **Part-time fees:** $2102 per term. Part-time tuition and fees vary according to course load and reciprocity agreements.

FRESHMAN FINANCIAL AID (Fall 2016) 863 applied for aid; of those 73% were deemed to have need. 100% of freshmen with need received aid; of those 10% had need fully met. **Average percent of need met:** 52% (excluding resources awarded to replace EFC). **Average financial aid package:** $15,623 (excluding resources awarded to replace EFC). 33% of all full-time freshmen had no need and received non-need-based gift aid.

UNDERGRADUATE FINANCIAL AID (Fall 2016) 2,417 applied for aid; of those 77% were deemed to have need. 100% of undergraduates with need received aid; of those 10% had need fully met. **Average percent of need met:** 51% (excluding resources awarded to replace EFC). **Average financial aid package:** $15,723 (excluding resources awarded to replace EFC). 33% of all full-time undergraduates had no need and received non-need-based gift aid.

GIFT AID (NEED-BASED) Total amount: $20,323,133 (10% federal, 7% state, 71% institutional, 12% external sources). **Receiving aid:** Freshmen: 46% (629); all full-time undergraduates: 40% (1,811). **Average award:** Freshmen: $12,637; Undergraduates: $11,884. **Scholarships, grants, and awards:** Federal Pell, FSEOG, state, private, college/university gift aid from institutional funds.

GIFT AID (NON-NEED-BASED) Total amount: $13,875,944 (83% institutional, 17% external sources). **Receiving aid:** Freshmen: 39% (540). Undergraduates: 33% (1,499). **Average award:** Freshmen: $7238. Undergraduates: $7416. **Scholarships, grants, and awards by category:** Academic interests/achievement: biological sciences, business, communication, education, English, foreign languages, general academic interests/achievements, humanities, international studies, mathematics, physical sciences, premedicine, religion/biblical studies. Creative arts/performance: art/fine arts, music, theater/drama. Special achievements/activities: general special achievements/activities, leadership, religious involvement. Special characteristics: children of faculty/staff, first-generation college students, relatives of clergy, veterans. **Tuition waivers:** Full or partial for employees or children of employees. **ROTC:** Army cooperative, Air Force cooperative.

LOANS Student loans: $27,422,580 (22% need-based, 78% non-need-based). 65% of past graduating class borrowed through all loan programs. Average indebtedness per student: $37,025. **Average need-based loan:** Freshmen: $3335. Undergraduates: $4252. **Parent loans:** $18,379,710 (100% non-need-based). **Programs:** Federal Direct (Subsidized and Unsubsidized Stafford, PLUS), Perkins.

WORK-STUDY Federal work-study: 228 jobs averaging $1128. **State or other work-study/employment:** Part-time jobs available.

ATHLETIC AWARDS Total amount: $5,738,804 (25% need-based, 75% non-need-based).

APPLYING FOR FINANCIAL AID Required financial aid forms: FAFSA, state aid form. **Financial aid deadline (priority):** 3/1. **Notification date:** Continuous beginning 3/1. Students must reply by 5/1 or within 3 weeks of notification.

CONTACT Mr. Ron Elmore, Director of Student Financial Planning, High Point University, Box 3232, University Station, One University Parkway, High Point, NC 27268, 336-841-9128 or toll-free 800-345-6993. Fax: 336-884-0221. E-mail: relmore@highpoint.edu.
Website: http://www.highpoint.edu/.

HILBERT COLLEGE
Hamburg, NY

Tuition & fees: $22,350	Average undergraduate aid package: $15,839

ABOUT THE INSTITUTION Independent Roman Catholic, coed. **Awards:** associate, bachelor's, and master's degrees. 23 undergraduate majors. **Total enrollment:** 792. Undergraduates: 746. Freshmen: 169. Federal methodology is used as a basis for awarding need-based institutional aid.

UNDERGRADUATE EXPENSES for 2018–2019 Application fee: $25. **One-time required fee:** $50. **Comprehensive fee:** $31,700 includes full-time tuition ($21,750), mandatory fees ($600), and room and board ($9350). Room and board charges vary according to board plan and housing facility. **Part-time tuition:** $560 per credit hour. **Part-time fees:** $13 per credit hour; $55 per term.

FRESHMAN FINANCIAL AID (Fall 2017, est.) 165 applied for aid; of those 93% were deemed to have need. 99% of freshmen with need received aid; of those 19% had need fully met. **Average percent of need met:** 76% (excluding resources awarded to replace EFC). **Average financial aid package:** $16,942 (excluding resources awarded to replace EFC). 7% of all full-time freshmen had no need and received non-need-based gift aid.

UNDERGRADUATE FINANCIAL AID (Fall 2017, est.) 658 applied for aid; of those 91% were deemed to have need. 100% of undergraduates with need received aid; of those 20% had need fully met. **Average percent of need met:** 74% (excluding resources awarded to replace EFC). **Average financial aid package:** $15,839 (excluding resources awarded to replace EFC). 10% of all full-time undergraduates had no need and received non-need-based gift aid.

GIFT AID (NEED-BASED) Total amount: $7,047,431 (23% federal, 14% state, 53% institutional, 10% external sources). **Receiving aid:** Freshmen: 91% (152); all full-time undergraduates: 86% (585). **Average award:** Freshmen: $13,668; Undergraduates: $11,962. **Scholarships, grants, and awards:** Federal Pell, FSEOG, state, private, college/university gift aid from institutional funds.

GIFT AID (NON-NEED-BASED) Total amount: $691,616 (1% state, 79% institutional, 20% external sources). **Receiving aid:** Freshmen: 7% (11). Undergraduates: 8% (51). **Average award:** Freshmen: $7729. Undergraduates: $6024. **Scholarships, grants, and awards by category:** Academic interests/achievement: general academic interests/achievements. Special achievements/activities: leadership. Special characteristics: children and siblings of alumni, members of minority groups, siblings of current students. **Tuition waivers:** Full or partial for minority students, children of alumni, employees or children of employees, adult students, senior citizens. **ROTC:** Army cooperative.

LOANS Student loans: $5,081,320 (72% need-based, 28% non-need-based). 81% of past graduating class borrowed through all loan programs. Average indebtedness per student: $19,613. **Average need-based loan:** Freshmen: $3865. Undergraduates: $4996. **Parent loans:** $1,008,421 (49% need-based, 51% non-need-based). **Programs:** Federal Direct (Subsidized and Unsubsidized Stafford, PLUS), Perkins.

WORK-STUDY Federal work-study: Total amount: $71,621; jobs available.

APPLYING FOR FINANCIAL AID Required financial aid forms: FAFSA, state aid form. **Financial aid deadline (priority):** 12/1. **Notification date:** Continuous beginning 2/1. Students must reply within 2 weeks of notification.

CONTACT Laura Worley, Director of Financial Aid, Hilbert College, 5200 South Park Avenue, Hamburg, NY 14075-1597, 716-649-7900 Ext. 414 or toll-free 800-649-8003. Fax: 716-649-1152. E-mail: lworley@hilbert.edu.
Website: http://www.hilbert.edu/.

HILLSDALE COLLEGE
Hillsdale, MI

Tuition & fees: $26,742	Average undergraduate aid package: $19,939

ABOUT THE INSTITUTION Independent, coed. **Awards:** bachelor's, master's, and doctoral degrees. 38 undergraduate majors. **Total enrollment:** 1,556. Undergraduates: 1,512. Freshmen: 369. Federal methodology is used as a basis for awarding need-based institutional aid.

UNDERGRADUATE EXPENSES for 2017–2018 Application fee: $35. **One-time required fee:** $325. **Comprehensive fee:** $37,352 includes full-time tuition

($25,540), mandatory fees ($1202), and room and board ($10,610). *College room only:* $5240. Full-time tuition and fees vary according to degree level. Room and board charges vary according to board plan. *Part-time tuition:* $1020 per credit hour. *Part-time fees:* $85 per credit hour; $1202 per year. Part-time tuition and fees vary according to degree level.

FRESHMAN FINANCIAL AID (Fall 2017, est.) 221 applied for aid; of those 82% were deemed to have need. 98% of freshmen with need received aid; of those 36% had need fully met. *Average percent of need met:* 65% (excluding resources awarded to replace EFC). *Average financial aid package:* $19,899 (excluding resources awarded to replace EFC). 44% of all full-time freshmen had no need and received non-need-based gift aid.

UNDERGRADUATE FINANCIAL AID (Fall 2017, est.) 809 applied for aid; of those 96% were deemed to have need. 97% of undergraduates with need received aid; of those 43% had need fully met. *Average percent of need met:* 68% (excluding resources awarded to replace EFC). *Average financial aid package:* $19,939 (excluding resources awarded to replace EFC). 44% of all full-time undergraduates had no need and received non-need-based gift aid.

GIFT AID (NEED-BASED) *Total amount:* $3,890,891 (99% institutional, 1% external sources). *Receiving aid:* Freshmen: 26% (96); all full-time undergraduates: 33% (488). *Average award:* Freshmen: $6735; Undergraduates: $8471. *Scholarships, grants, and awards:* private, college/university gift aid from institutional funds.

GIFT AID (NON-NEED-BASED) *Total amount:* $18,705,988 (98% institutional, 2% external sources). *Receiving aid:* Freshmen: 46% (168). Undergraduates: 47% (685). *Average award:* Freshmen: $15,396. Undergraduates: $14,430. *Scholarships, grants, and awards by category:* Academic interests/achievement: 956 awards ($19,211,668 total): biological sciences, business, communication, education, engineering/technologies, English, foreign languages, general academic interests/achievements, mathematics, physical sciences, premedicine, social sciences. *Creative arts/performance:* 183 awards ($631,806 total): art/fine arts, debating, journalism/publications, music, theater/drama. *Special achievements/activities:* 41 awards ($202,161 total): community service, leadership. *Special characteristics:* 163 awards ($2,599,336 total): children and siblings of alumni, children of educators, children of faculty/staff, first-generation college students, international students, veterans. *Tuition waivers:* Full or partial for children of alumni, employees or children of employees.

LOANS *Student loans:* $5,677,853 (47% need-based, 53% non-need-based). 53% of past graduating class borrowed through all loan programs. *Average indebtedness per student:* $28,171. *Average need-based loan:* Freshmen: $5825. Undergraduates: $5996. *Programs:* college/university, private loans.

ATHLETIC AWARDS *Total amount:* $181,168 (100% non-need-based).

APPLYING FOR FINANCIAL AID *Required financial aid form:* institution's own form. *Financial aid deadline (priority):* 5/1. *Notification date:* Continuous beginning 12/1. Students must reply within 4 weeks of notification.

CONTACT Mr. Rich Moeggengberg, Director of Student Financial Aid, Hillsdale College, 33 East College Street, Hillsdale, MI 49242-1298, 517-607-2350. *Fax:* 517-607-2298. *E-mail:* rmoeggenberg@hillsdale.edu. *Website:* http://www.hillsdale.edu/.

HIRAM COLLEGE
Hiram, OH

Tuition & fees: $34,300	Average undergraduate aid package: N/A

ABOUT THE INSTITUTION Independent, coed. *Awards:* bachelor's and master's degrees. 36 undergraduate majors. *Total enrollment:* 1,221. Undergraduates: 1,210. Freshmen: 258. Both federal and institutional methodology are used as a basis for awarding need-based institutional aid.

UNDERGRADUATE EXPENSES for 2017–2018 *Application fee:* $25. *Comprehensive fee:* $44,590 includes full-time tuition ($32,700), mandatory fees ($1600), and room and board ($10,290). *College room only:* $5150. Room and board charges vary according to housing facility. *Part-time tuition:* $475 per credit hour. *Part-time fees:* $125 per term. *Payment plan:* Guaranteed tuition.

GIFT AID (NEED-BASED) *Scholarships, grants, and awards:* Federal Pell, FSEOG, state, private, college/university gift aid from institutional funds.

GIFT AID (NON-NEED-BASED) *Scholarships, grants, and awards by category:* Academic interests/achievement: general academic interests/achievements, humanities, physical sciences, religion/biblical studies, social sciences. *Creative arts/performance:* music. *Special achievements/activities:* memberships. *Special character-

istics: children and siblings of alumni, general special characteristics, members of minority groups, relatives of clergy, religious affiliation. *Tuition waivers:* Full or partial for employees or children of employees. *ROTC:* Army cooperative, Air Force cooperative.

LOANS *Programs:* Federal Direct (Subsidized and Unsubsidized Stafford, PLUS), Perkins.

WORK-STUDY Federal work-study jobs available. *State or other work-study/employment:* Part-time jobs available.

APPLYING FOR FINANCIAL AID *Required financial aid form:* FAFSA. *Financial aid deadline (priority):* 2/15. *Notification date:* Continuous.

CONTACT Linda Shirey, Interim Director of Financial Aid, Hiram College, Box 67, Hiram, OH 44234-0067, 330-569-5107 or toll-free 800-362-5280. *Fax:* 330-569-5499. *Website:* http://www.hiram.edu/.

HOBART AND WILLIAM SMITH COLLEGES
Geneva, NY

Tuition & fees: $55,255	Average undergraduate aid package: $36,758

ABOUT THE INSTITUTION Independent, coed. *Awards:* certificates, bachelor's, and master's degrees. 47 undergraduate majors. *Total enrollment:* 2,244. Undergraduates: 2,237. Freshmen: 634. Both federal and institutional methodology are used as a basis for awarding need-based institutional aid.

UNDERGRADUATE EXPENSES for 2018–2019 *Comprehensive fee:* $69,290 includes full-time tuition ($54,060), mandatory fees ($1195), and room and board ($14,035). Room and board charges vary according to board plan. *Payment plan:* Tuition prepayment.

FRESHMAN FINANCIAL AID (Fall 2016) 434 applied for aid; of those 83% were deemed to have need. 100% of freshmen with need received aid; of those 64% had need fully met. *Average percent of need met:* 79% (excluding resources awarded to replace EFC). *Average financial aid package:* $36,231 (excluding resources awarded to replace EFC). 32% of all full-time freshmen had no need and received non-need-based gift aid.

UNDERGRADUATE FINANCIAL AID (Fall 2016) 1,494 applied for aid; of those 86% were deemed to have need. 99% of undergraduates with need received aid; of those 67% had need fully met. *Average percent of need met:* 78% (excluding resources awarded to replace EFC). *Average financial aid package:* $36,758 (excluding resources awarded to replace EFC). 35% of all full-time undergraduates had no need and received non-need-based gift aid.

GIFT AID (NEED-BASED) *Total amount:* $41,353,213 (5% federal, 3% state, 87% institutional, 5% external sources). *Receiving aid:* Freshmen: 65% (356); all full-time undergraduates: 63% (1,271). *Average award:* Freshmen: $33,012; Undergraduates: $32,528. *Scholarships, grants, and awards:* Federal Pell, FSEOG, state, private, college/university gift aid from institutional funds.

GIFT AID (NON-NEED-BASED) *Total amount:* $14,373,881 (91% institutional, 9% external sources). *Receiving aid:* Freshmen: 11% (63). Undergraduates: 10% (208). *Average award:* Freshmen: $14,507. Undergraduates: $16,040. *Scholarships, grants, and awards by category:* Academic interests/achievement: 561 awards ($11,318,944 total): general academic interests/achievements, premedicine. *Creative arts/performance:* 106 awards ($1,041,250 total): art/fine arts, creative writing, dance, music, performing arts. *Special achievements/activities:* 211 awards ($2,990,273 total): community service, leadership. *Special characteristics:* 237 awards ($1,285,363 total): children and siblings of alumni, relatives of clergy, veterans' children. *Tuition waivers:* Full or partial for employees or children of employees. *ROTC:* Army cooperative, Air Force cooperative.

LOANS *Student loans:* $12,295,601 (57% need-based, 43% non-need-based). 61% of past graduating class borrowed through all loan programs. *Average indebtedness per student:* $33,600. *Average need-based loan:* Freshmen: $3247. Undergraduates: $3975. *Parent loans:* $5,520,818 (41% need-based, 59% non-need-based). *Programs:* Federal Direct (Subsidized and Unsubsidized Stafford, PLUS), Perkins, college/university.

WORK-STUDY *Federal work-study:* 864 jobs averaging $1953. *State or other work-study/employment:* Total amount: $1,211,660 (17% need-based, 83% non-need-based). 485 part-time jobs averaging $1892.

APPLYING FOR FINANCIAL AID *Required financial aid forms:* FAFSA, CSS Financial Aid PROFILE, state aid form, noncustodial (divorced/separated) parent's statement. *Financial aid deadline:* 2/1. *Notification date:* 4/1. Students must reply by 5/1.

CONTACT Beth Nepa, Director of Financial Aid, Hobart and William Smith Colleges, Demarest Hall, 300 Pulteney Street, Geneva, NY 14456-3397, 315-781-3315 or toll-free 800-852-2256. *Fax:* 315-781-4048. *E-mail:* nepa@hws.edu. *Website:* http://www.hws.edu/.

HOBE SOUND BIBLE COLLEGE
Hobe Sound, FL

CONTACT Director of Financial Aid, Hobe Sound Bible College, PO Box 1065, Hobe Sound, FL 33475-1065, 561-546-5534. *Fax:* 561-545-1422. *Website:* http://www.hsbc.edu/.

HODGES UNIVERSITY
Naples, FL

CONTACT Mr. Joe Gilchrist, Vice President of Financial Aid, Hodges University, 2655 Northbrooke Drive, Naples, FL 34119, 239-598-6116 or toll-free 800-466-8017. *Fax:* 239-598-6257. *E-mail:* jgilchrist@hodges.edu. *Website:* http://www.hodges.edu/.

HOFSTRA UNIVERSITY
Hempstead, NY

Tuition & fees: $43,960	Average undergraduate aid package: $31,000

ABOUT THE INSTITUTION Independent, coed. *Awards:* certificates, bachelor's, master's, and doctoral degrees. 135 undergraduate majors. *Total enrollment:* 11,131. Undergraduates: 6,861. Freshmen: 1,638. Federal methodology is used as a basis for awarding need-based institutional aid.

UNDERGRADUATE EXPENSES for 2017–2018 *Application fee:* $70. *Comprehensive fee:* $58,890 includes full-time tuition ($42,900), mandatory fees ($1060), and room and board ($14,930). *College room only:* $10,020. Full-time tuition and fees vary according to course load. Room and board charges vary according to board plan and housing facility. *Part-time tuition:* $1438 per credit hour. *Part-time fees:* $155 per term. Part-time tuition and fees vary according to course load. *Payment plan:* Guaranteed tuition.

FRESHMAN FINANCIAL AID (Fall 2017, est.) 1,423 applied for aid; of those 86% were deemed to have need. 100% of freshmen with need received aid; of those 26% had need fully met. *Average percent of need met:* 72% (excluding resources awarded to replace EFC). *Average financial aid package:* $33,000 (excluding resources awarded to replace EFC). 20% of all full-time freshmen had no need and received non-need-based gift aid.

UNDERGRADUATE FINANCIAL AID (Fall 2017, est.) 4,923 applied for aid; of those 85% were deemed to have need. 100% of undergraduates with need received aid; of those 24% had need fully met. *Average percent of need met:* 67% (excluding resources awarded to replace EFC). *Average financial aid package:* $31,000 (excluding resources awarded to replace EFC). 25% of all full-time undergraduates had no need and received non-need-based gift aid.

GIFT AID (NEED-BASED) *Total amount:* $84,410,000 (9% federal, 5% state, 84% institutional, 2% external sources). *Receiving aid:* Freshmen: 74% (1,209); all full-time undergraduates: 62% (3,993). *Average award:* Freshmen: $23,000; Undergraduates: $21,000. *Scholarships, grants, and awards:* Federal Pell, FSEOG, state, private, college/university gift aid from institutional funds, United Negro College Fund.

GIFT AID (NON-NEED-BASED) *Total amount:* $38,230,000 (1% federal, 1% state, 96% institutional, 2% external sources). *Receiving aid:* Freshmen: 16% (268). Undergraduates: 11% (689). *Average award:* Freshmen: $20,000. Undergraduates: $19,000. *Scholarships, grants, and awards by category:* Academic interests/achievement: 6,423 awards ($92,822,000 total): communication, engineering/technologies, general academic interests/achievements. Creative arts/performance: 230

awards ($799,000 total): applied art and design, art/fine arts, cinema/film/broadcasting, dance, journalism/publications, music, performing arts, theater/drama. *Special achievements/activities:* 238 awards ($6,450,000 total): cheerleading/drum major, general special achievements/activities, leadership. *Special characteristics:* 457 awards ($9,631,000 total): children and siblings of alumni, children of faculty/staff, children of union members/company employees, general special characteristics, handicapped students, local/state students, members of minority groups, public servants, veterans, veterans' children. *Tuition waivers:* Full or partial for employees or children of employees. *ROTC:* Army.

LOANS *Student loans:* $43,100,000 (72% need-based, 28% non-need-based). 64% of past graduating class borrowed through all loan programs. *Average need-based loan:* Freshmen: $4000. Undergraduates: $4000. *Parent loans:* $36,800,000 (58% need-based, 42% non-need-based). *Programs:* Federal Direct (Subsidized and Unsubsidized Stafford, PLUS), state, college/university.

WORK-STUDY *Federal work-study:* Total amount: $4,900,000; 1,611 jobs averaging $3000. *State or other work-study/employment:* Total amount: $4,800,000 (21% need-based, 79% non-need-based). 1,465 part-time jobs averaging $3200.

ATHLETIC AWARDS Total amount: $6,460,000 (46% need-based, 54% non-need-based).

APPLYING FOR FINANCIAL AID *Required financial aid forms:* FAFSA, state aid form. *Financial aid deadline (priority):* 11/15. *Notification date:* Continuous beginning 1/15. Students must reply by 5/1 or within 2 weeks of notification.

CONTACT Sandra Filbry-Mervius, Director of Financial Aid, Hofstra University, 126 Hofstra University, Hempstead, NY 11549, 516-463-4335 or toll-free 800-HOFSTRA. *Fax:* 516-463-4936. *E-mail:* sandra.a.filbry@hofstra.edu. *Website:* http://www.hofstra.edu/.

HOLLINS UNIVERSITY
Roanoke, VA

Tuition & fees: $39,035	Average undergraduate aid package: $36,843

ABOUT THE INSTITUTION Independent, undergraduate: women only; graduate: coed. *Awards:* certificates, bachelor's, and master's degrees. 28 undergraduate majors. *Total enrollment:* 790. Undergraduates: 654. Freshmen: 155. Federal methodology is used as a basis for awarding need-based institutional aid.

UNDERGRADUATE EXPENSES for 2018–2019 *Comprehensive fee:* $52,555 includes full-time tuition ($38,400), mandatory fees ($635), and room and board ($13,520). Room and board charges vary according to housing facility. Part-time tuition and fees vary according to course load. *Payment plan:* Tuition prepayment.

FRESHMAN FINANCIAL AID (Fall 2017, est.) 144 applied for aid; of those 87% were deemed to have need. 100% of freshmen with need received aid; of those 25% had need fully met. *Average percent of need met:* 85% (excluding resources awarded to replace EFC). *Average financial aid package:* $36,595 (excluding resources awarded to replace EFC). 19% of all full-time freshmen had no need and received non-need-based gift aid.

UNDERGRADUATE FINANCIAL AID (Fall 2017, est.) 536 applied for aid; of those 93% were deemed to have need. 100% of undergraduates with need received aid; of those 24% had need fully met. *Average percent of need met:* 84% (excluding resources awarded to replace EFC). *Average financial aid package:* $36,843 (excluding resources awarded to replace EFC). 19% of all full-time undergraduates had no need and received non-need-based gift aid.

GIFT AID (NEED-BASED) *Total amount:* $15,087,203 (9% federal, 5% state, 85% institutional, 1% external sources). *Receiving aid:* Freshmen: 81% (125); all full-time undergraduates: 80% (497). *Average award:* Freshmen: $33,368; Undergraduates: $32,377. *Scholarships, grants, and awards:* Federal Pell, FSEOG, state, private, college/university gift aid from institutional funds.

GIFT AID (NON-NEED-BASED) *Total amount:* $4,624,646 (5% state, 94% institutional, 1% external sources). *Receiving aid:* Freshmen: 81% (125). Undergraduates: 80% (497). *Average award:* Freshmen: $32,288. Undergraduates: $29,506. *Scholarships, grants, and awards by category:* Academic interests/achievement: general academic interests/achievements. Creative arts/performance: creative writing, dance, music, theater/drama. Special achievements/activities: community service, general special achievements/activities, hobbies/interests, leadership. Special characteristics: adult students, children and siblings of alumni, children of faculty/staff, international students, local/state students, out-of-state students, previous college experience, veterans. **Tuition waivers:** Full or partial for employees or children of employees.

LOANS Student loans: $4,126,859 (76% need-based, 24% non-need-based). 74% of past graduating class borrowed through all loan programs. *Average indebtedness per student:* $31,211. **Average need-based loan:** Freshmen: $3866. Undergraduates: $4982. **Parent loans:** $1,763,318 (48% need-based, 52% non-need-based). **Programs:** Federal Direct (Subsidized and Unsubsidized Stafford, PLUS), college/university.

WORK-STUDY Federal work-study: Total amount: $158,750; 105 jobs averaging $1500. **State or other work-study/employment:** Total amount: $346,200 (39% need-based, 61% non-need-based). 186 part-time jobs averaging $1500.

APPLYING FOR FINANCIAL AID Required financial aid forms: FAFSA, state aid form. **Financial aid deadline (priority):** 2/15. **Notification date:** Continuous beginning 2/8. Students must reply by 5/1.

CONTACT Mrs. MaryJean Sullivan, Director of Scholarships and Financial Assistance, Hollins University, 7916 Williamson Road, Box 9718, Roanoke, VA 24020, 540-362-6332 or toll-free 800-456-9595. *Fax:* 540-362-6093. *E-mail:* sfa@hollins.edu. *Website:* http://www.hollins.edu/.

HOLY CROSS COLLEGE
Notre Dame, IN

CONTACT Robert Benjamin, Director of Financial Aid, Holy Cross College, PO Box 308, Notre Dame, IN 46556, 574-239-8362. *E-mail:* rbenjamin@hcc-nd.edu. *Website:* http://www.hcc-nd.edu/.

HOLY FAMILY UNIVERSITY
Philadelphia, PA

Tuition & fees: $30,346	Average undergraduate aid package: $21,883

ABOUT THE INSTITUTION Independent Roman Catholic, coed. *Awards:* certificates, associate, bachelor's, master's, and doctoral degrees. 43 undergraduate majors. *Total enrollment:* 3,081. Undergraduates: 2,093. Freshmen: 361. Federal methodology is used as a basis for awarding need-based institutional aid.

UNDERGRADUATE EXPENSES for 2018–2019 Application fee: $25. **One-time required fee:** $504. **Comprehensive fee:** $43,922 includes full-time tuition ($29,338), mandatory fees ($1008), and room and board ($13,576). **College room only:** $7140. Full-time tuition and fees vary according to class time, course level, course load, degree level, program, and reciprocity agreements. Room and board charges vary according to board plan and housing facility. **Part-time tuition:** $627 per credit hour. **Part-time fees:** $112 per term. Part-time tuition and fees vary according to class time, course level, course load, degree level, program, and reciprocity agreements.

FRESHMAN FINANCIAL AID (Fall 2017, est.) 349 applied for aid; of those 90% were deemed to have need. 100% of freshmen with need received aid; of those 16% had need fully met. **Average percent of need met:** 81% (excluding resources awarded to replace EFC). **Average financial aid package:** $25,350 (excluding resources awarded to replace EFC). 9% of all full-time freshmen had no need and received non-need-based gift aid.

UNDERGRADUATE FINANCIAL AID (Fall 2017, est.) 1,371 applied for aid; of those 92% were deemed to have need. 99% of undergraduates with need received aid; of those 13% had need fully met. **Average percent of need met:** 72% (excluding resources awarded to replace EFC). **Average financial aid package:** $21,883 (excluding resources awarded to replace EFC). 11% of all full-time undergraduates had no need and received non-need-based gift aid.

GIFT AID (NEED-BASED) Total amount: $23,095,155 (14% federal, 12% state, 71% institutional, 3% external sources). **Receiving aid:** Freshmen: 87% (312); all full-time undergraduates: 76% (1,237). **Average award:** Freshmen: $21,294; Undergraduates: $17,716. **Scholarships, grants, and awards:** Federal Pell, FSEOG, state, private, college/university gift aid from institutional funds, United Negro College Fund, Federal Nursing.

GIFT AID (NON-NEED-BASED) Total amount: $2,905,025 (95% institutional, 5% external sources). **Receiving aid:** Freshmen: 87% (311). Undergraduates: 73% (1,182). **Average award:** Freshmen: $16,074. Undergraduates: $12,972. **Scholar-**

ships, grants, and awards by category. Academic interests/achievement. 1,379 awards ($17,558,113 total): general academic interests/achievements. **Tuition waivers:** Full or partial for employees or children of employees, senior citizens. **ROTC:** Army cooperative.

LOANS Student loans: $21,791,769 (87% need-based, 13% non-need-based). 89% of past graduating class borrowed through all loan programs. *Average indebtedness per student:* $36,609. **Average need-based loan:** Freshmen: $2775. Undergraduates: $3756. **Parent loans:** $2,378,437 (89% need-based, 11% non-need-based). **Programs:** Federal Direct (Subsidized and Unsubsidized Stafford, PLUS), Perkins, Federal Nursing.

WORK-STUDY Federal work-study: Total amount: $312,985; 293 jobs averaging $1069.

ATHLETIC AWARDS Total amount: $1,071,204 (77% need-based, 23% non-need-based).

APPLYING FOR FINANCIAL AID Required financial aid form: FAFSA. **Financial aid deadline (priority):** 3/1. **Notification date:** Continuous beginning 3/15. Students must reply by 8/15.

CONTACT Ms. Janice Hetrick, Director of Financial Aid, Holy Family University, 9801 Frankford Avenue, Philadelphia, PA 19114-2094, 215-637-7700 Ext. 3233. *Fax:* 215-599-1694. *E-mail:* finaid@holyfamily.edu. *Website:* http://www.holyfamily.edu/.

HOLY NAMES UNIVERSITY
Oakland, CA

CONTACT Christina Miller, Director of Financial Aid, Holy Names University, 3500 Mountain Boulevard, Oakland, CA 94619-1699, 510-436-1327 or toll-free 800-430-1321. *Fax:* 510-436-1199. *E-mail:* miller@hnu.edu. *Website:* http://www.hnu.edu/.

HOOD COLLEGE
Frederick, MD

Tuition & fees: $39,492	Average undergraduate aid package: $30,919

ABOUT THE INSTITUTION Independent, coed. *Awards:* certificates, bachelor's, master's, and doctoral degrees (also offers adult program with significant enrollment not reflected in profile). 33 undergraduate majors. *Total enrollment:* 2,112. Undergraduates: 1,128. Freshmen: 256. Federal methodology is used as a basis for awarding need-based institutional aid.

UNDERGRADUATE EXPENSES for 2018–2019 Comprehensive fee: $52,192 includes full-time tuition ($38,910), mandatory fees ($582), and room and board ($12,700). **College room only:** $6600. Room and board charges vary according to board plan. **Part-time tuition:** $1134 per credit hour. **Part-time fees:** $188 per term.

FRESHMAN FINANCIAL AID (Fall 2017, est.) 237 applied for aid; of those 91% were deemed to have need. 100% of freshmen with need received aid; of those 12% had need fully met. **Average percent of need met:** 78% (excluding resources awarded to replace EFC). **Average financial aid package:** $34,658 (excluding resources awarded to replace EFC). 13% of all full-time freshmen had no need and received non-need-based gift aid.

UNDERGRADUATE FINANCIAL AID (Fall 2017, est.) 936 applied for aid; of those 93% were deemed to have need. 100% of undergraduates with need received aid; of those 18% had need fully met. **Average percent of need met:** 73% (excluding resources awarded to replace EFC). **Average financial aid package:** $30,919 (excluding resources awarded to replace EFC). 15% of all full-time undergraduates had no need and received non-need-based gift aid.

GIFT AID (NEED-BASED) Total amount: $22,936,492 (10% federal, 7% state, 79% institutional, 4% external sources). **Receiving aid:** Freshmen: 85% (216); all full-time undergraduates: 83% (866). **Average award:** Freshmen: $30,793; Undergraduates: $26,886. **Scholarships, grants, and awards:** Federal Pell, FSEOG, state, private, college/university gift aid from institutional funds.

GIFT AID (NON-NEED-BASED) Total amount: $4,338,740 (1% state, 84% institutional, 15% external sources). **Receiving aid:** Freshmen: 9% (22). Undergraduates: 13% (138). **Average award:** Freshmen: $18,523. Undergraduates: $17,472.

Scholarships, grants, and awards by category: Academic interests/ achievement: biological sciences, business, communication, computer science, education, English, foreign languages, general academic interests/achievements, humanities, mathematics, religion/biblical studies, social sciences. *Creative arts/performance:* art/ fine arts, music. *Special achievements/activities:* leadership. *Special characteristics:* children and siblings of alumni, children of faculty/staff, ethnic background, first-generation college students, international students, local/state students, out-of-state students, previous college experience, religious affiliation, siblings of current students, veterans, veterans' children. *Tuition waivers:* Full or partial for employees or children of employees, senior citizens. *ROTC:* Army.

LOANS *Student loans:* $7,501,731 (78% need-based, 22% non-need-based). 73% of past graduating class borrowed through all loan programs. *Average indebtedness per student:* $35,823. *Average need-based loan:* Freshmen: $4248. Undergraduates: $4568. *Parent loans:* $2,484,446 (49% need-based, 51% non-need-based). *Programs:* Federal Direct (Subsidized and Unsubsidized Stafford, PLUS), Perkins.

WORK-STUDY *Federal work-study:* Total amount: $197,480; jobs available. *State or other work-study/employment:* Total amount: $231,450 (54% need-based, 46% non-need-based). Part-time jobs available.

APPLYING FOR FINANCIAL AID *Required financial aid forms:* FAFSA, institution's own form. *Financial aid deadline (priority):* 2/15. *Notification date:* Continuous beginning 11/15. Students must reply by 5/1 or within 4 weeks of notification.

CONTACT Ms. Melena Verity, Interim Director of Financial Aid, Hood College, 401 Rosemont Avenue, Frederick, MD 21701-8575, 301-696-3411 or toll-free 800-922-1599. *Fax:* 301-696-3812. *E-mail:* verity@hood.edu.
Website: http://www.hood.edu/.

HOPE COLLEGE
Holland, MI

Tuition & fees: $34,010	Average undergraduate aid package: $26,952

ABOUT THE INSTITUTION Independent Reformed Church in America, coed. *Awards:* bachelor's degrees. 63 undergraduate majors. *Total enrollment:* 3,150. Undergraduates: 3,150. Freshmen: 779. Federal methodology is used as a basis for awarding need-based institutional aid.

UNDERGRADUATE EXPENSES for 2018–2019 *Application fee:* $35. *Comprehensive fee:* $44,320 includes full-time tuition ($33,700), mandatory fees ($310), and room and board ($10,310). *College room only:* $4730. Room and board charges vary according to board plan. Part-time tuition and fees vary according to course load and program.

FRESHMAN FINANCIAL AID (Fall 2017, est.) 660 applied for aid; of those 80% were deemed to have need. 100% of freshmen with need received aid; of those 25% had need fully met. *Average percent of need met:* 82% (excluding resources awarded to replace EFC). *Average financial aid package:* $27,577 (excluding resources awarded to replace EFC). 26% of all full-time freshmen had no need and received non-need-based gift aid.

UNDERGRADUATE FINANCIAL AID (Fall 2017, est.) 2,059 applied for aid; of those 84% were deemed to have need. 100% of undergraduates with need received aid; of those 25% had need fully met. *Average percent of need met:* 81% (excluding resources awarded to replace EFC). *Average financial aid package:* $26,952 (excluding resources awarded to replace EFC). 27% of all full-time undergraduates had no need and received non-need-based gift aid.

GIFT AID (NEED-BASED) *Total amount:* $29,172,755 (9% federal, 6% state, 84% institutional, 1% external sources). *Receiving aid:* Freshmen: 60% (467); all full-time undergraduates: 50% (1,493). *Average award:* Freshmen: $22,340; Undergraduates: $20,276. *Scholarships, grants, and awards:* Federal Pell, FSEOG, state, private, college/university gift aid from institutional funds.

GIFT AID (NON-NEED-BASED) *Total amount:* $10,749,114 (4% federal, 89% institutional, 7% external sources). *Receiving aid:* Freshmen: 61% (475). Undergraduates: 44% (1,329). *Average award:* Freshmen: $9539. Undergraduates: $8812. *Scholarships, grants, and awards by category: Academic interests/ achievement:* 1,938 awards ($14,475,492 total): general academic interests/achievements. *Creative arts/performance:* 133 awards ($343,200 total): art/fine arts, creative writing, dance, music, theater/drama. *Special characteristics:* 455 awards ($2,205,270 total): children and siblings of alumni, ethnic background, religious affiliation, siblings of

current students. *Tuition waivers:* Full or partial for employees or children of employees. *ROTC:* Army cooperative.

LOANS *Student loans:* $14,336,483 (48% need-based, 52% non-need-based). 62% of past graduating class borrowed through all loan programs. *Average indebtedness per student:* $33,033. *Average need-based loan:* Freshmen: $3917. Undergraduates: $5287. *Parent loans:* $4,727,596 (100% non-need-based). *Programs:* Federal Direct (Subsidized and Unsubsidized Stafford, PLUS), Perkins.

WORK-STUDY *Federal work-study:* Total amount: $321,855; 136 jobs averaging $2370. *State or other work-study/employment:* 588 part-time jobs averaging $1103.

APPLYING FOR FINANCIAL AID *Required financial aid forms:* FAFSA, institution's own form. *Financial aid deadline (priority):* 3/1. *Notification date:* Continuous beginning 3/15. Students must reply within 2 weeks of notification.

CONTACT Ms. Jill Nutt, Director of Financial Aid, Hope College, 141 East 12th Street, Holland, MI 49422-9000, 616-395-7765 or toll-free 800-968-7850. *Fax:* 616-395-7160. *E-mail:* nutt@hope.edu.
Website: http://www.hope.edu/.

HOPE INTERNATIONAL UNIVERSITY
Fullerton, CA

Tuition & fees: $31,800	Average undergraduate aid package: $11,197

ABOUT THE INSTITUTION Independent Christian Churches and Churches of Christ, coed. *Awards:* certificates, associate, bachelor's, and master's degrees. 17 undergraduate majors. *Total enrollment:* 1,162. Undergraduates: 726. Freshmen: 96. Federal methodology is used as a basis for awarding need-based institutional aid.

UNDERGRADUATE EXPENSES for 2017–2018 *Application fee:* $40. *Comprehensive fee:* $41,730 includes full-time tuition ($30,700), mandatory fees ($1100), and room and board ($9930). *College room only:* $4900. Full-time tuition and fees vary according to course level, course load, degree level, location, program, and reciprocity agreements. Room and board charges vary according to board plan. *Part-time tuition:* $1395 per credit hour. Part-time tuition and fees vary according to course level, course load, degree level, location, program, and reciprocity agreements.

FRESHMAN FINANCIAL AID (Fall 2016) 93 applied for aid; of those 86% were deemed to have need. 100% of freshmen with need received aid; of those 2% had need fully met. *Average percent of need met:* 28% (excluding resources awarded to replace EFC). *Average financial aid package:* $13,008 (excluding resources awarded to replace EFC). 2% of all full-time freshmen had no need and received non-need-based gift aid.

UNDERGRADUATE FINANCIAL AID (Fall 2016) 447 applied for aid; of those 91% were deemed to have need. 100% of undergraduates with need received aid; of those 4% had need fully met. *Average percent of need met:* 36% (excluding resources awarded to replace EFC). *Average financial aid package:* $11,197 (excluding resources awarded to replace EFC). 3% of all full-time undergraduates had no need and received non-need-based gift aid.

GIFT AID (NEED-BASED) *Total amount:* $3,270,888 (48% federal, 38% state, 14% institutional). *Receiving aid:* Freshmen: 56% (55); all full-time undergraduates: 54% (263). *Average award:* Freshmen: $14,561; Undergraduates: $14,974. *Scholarships, grants, and awards:* Federal Pell, FSEOG, state, private, college/university gift aid from institutional funds.

GIFT AID (NON-NEED-BASED) *Total amount:* $2,398,441 (96% institutional, 4% external sources). *Receiving aid:* Freshmen: 62% (61). Undergraduates: 63% (306). *Average award:* Freshmen: $17,000. Undergraduates: $13,408. *Scholarships, grants, and awards by category: Academic interests/achievement:* general academic interests/achievements. *Creative arts/performance:* music. *Special achievements/activities:* cheerleading/drum major, leadership. *Special characteristics:* children of faculty/staff, veterans. *Tuition waivers:* Full or partial for employees or children of employees. *ROTC:* Army cooperative.

LOANS *Student loans:* $2,525,476 (53% need-based, 47% non-need-based). 80% of past graduating class borrowed through all loan programs. *Average indebtedness per student:* $26,733. *Average need-based loan:* Freshmen: $2505. Undergraduates: $3626. *Parent loans:* $1,184,113 (100% non-need-based). *Programs:* Federal Direct (Subsidized and Unsubsidized Stafford, PLUS).

WORK-STUDY *Federal work-study:* jobs available. *State or other work-study/employment:* Total amount: $81,224 (100% non-need-based). Part-time jobs available.

ATHLETIC AWARDS Total amount: $3,860,985 (100% non-need-based).

APPLYING FOR FINANCIAL AID *Required financial aid forms:* FAFSA, institution's own form. *Financial aid deadline (priority):* 3/2. *Notification date:* Continuous beginning 1/1. Students must reply within 2 weeks of notification.

CONTACT Ms. Shannon O'Shields, Director of Student Financial Services, Hope International University, 2500 East Nutwood Avenue, Fullerton, CA 92831, 714-879-3901 Ext. 2207 or toll-free 866-722-HOPE. *Fax:* 714-681-7421. *E-mail:* soshields@hiu.edu.

Website: http://www.hiu.edu/.

HORIZON UNIVERSITY
Indianapolis, IN

CONTACT Financial Aid Office, Horizon University, 7700 Indian Lake Road, Indianapolis, IN 46236, 858-695-8587 or toll-free 800-553-HORIZON.
Website: http://www.horizonuniversity.edu/.

HOUGHTON COLLEGE
Houghton, NY

ABOUT THE INSTITUTION Independent Wesleyan, coed. *Awards:* associate, bachelor's, and master's degrees. 66 undergraduate majors. *Total enrollment:* 1,059. Undergraduates: 1,043. Freshmen: 257.

GIFT AID (NEED-BASED) *Scholarships, grants, and awards:* Federal Pell, FSEOG, state, private, college/university gift aid from institutional funds.

GIFT AID (NON-NEED-BASED) *Scholarships, grants, and awards by category:* Academic interests/achievement: biological sciences, business, communication, education, English, general academic interests/achievements, international studies, mathematics, physical sciences, religion/biblical studies. *Creative arts/performance:* art/fine arts, music, performing arts. *Special achievements/activities:* community service, general special achievements/activities, leadership, memberships, religious involvement. *Special characteristics:* adult students, children and siblings of alumni, children of faculty/staff, general special characteristics, handicapped students, international students, local/state students, relatives of clergy, religious affiliation, siblings of current students, veterans.

LOANS *Programs:* Federal Direct (Subsidized and Unsubsidized Stafford, PLUS), Perkins, state.

WORK-STUDY *Federal work-study:* 477 jobs averaging $1861. *State or other work-study/employment:* Total amount: $236,132 (36% need-based, 64% non-need-based). 123 part-time jobs averaging $1945.

APPLYING FOR FINANCIAL AID *Required financial aid forms:* FAFSA, noncustodial (divorced/separated) parent's statement.

CONTACT Mrs. Marianne Loper, Director of Financial Aid, Houghton College, One Willard Avenue, Houghton, NY 14744, 585-567-9328 or toll-free 800-777-2556. *Fax:* 585-567-9610. *E-mail:* sfso@houghton.edu.

Website: http://www.houghton.edu/.

HOUSTON BAPTIST UNIVERSITY
Houston, TX

Tuition & fees: $32,530	Average undergraduate aid package: $27,234

ABOUT THE INSTITUTION Independent Baptist, coed. *Awards:* bachelor's, master's, and doctoral degrees. 55 undergraduate majors. *Total enrollment:* 3,325. Undergraduates: 2,316. Freshmen: 519. Federal methodology is used as a basis for awarding need-based institutional aid.

UNDERGRADUATE EXPENSES for 2018–2019 *Comprehensive fee:* $41,344 includes full-time tuition ($30,480), mandatory fees ($2050), and room and board ($8814). *College room only:* $4800. Room and board charges vary according to board plan and housing facility. *Part-time tuition:* $1270 per semester hour.

Part-time fees: $1025 per term. Part-time tuition and fees vary according to course load.

FRESHMAN FINANCIAL AID (Fall 2017, est.) 442 applied for aid; of those 92% were deemed to have need. 100% of freshmen with need received aid; of those 10% had need fully met. *Average percent of need met:* 70% (excluding resources awarded to replace EFC). *Average financial aid package:* $27,336 (excluding resources awarded to replace EFC). 20% of all full-time freshmen had no need and received non-need-based gift aid.

UNDERGRADUATE FINANCIAL AID (Fall 2017, est.) 1,619 applied for aid; of those 94% were deemed to have need. 100% of undergraduates with need received aid; of those 14% had need fully met. *Average percent of need met:* 69% (excluding resources awarded to replace EFC). *Average financial aid package:* $27,234 (excluding resources awarded to replace EFC). 25% of all full-time undergraduates had no need and received non-need-based gift aid.

GIFT AID (NEED-BASED) *Total amount:* $27,865,607 (18% federal, 10% state, 70% institutional, 2% external sources). *Receiving aid:* Freshmen: 80% (406); all full-time undergraduates: 71% (1,496). *Average award:* Freshmen: $21,703; Undergraduates: $20,468. *Scholarships, grants, and awards:* Federal Pell, FSEOG, state, college/university gift aid from institutional funds.

GIFT AID (NON-NEED-BASED) *Total amount:* $8,059,714 (98% institutional, 2% external sources). *Receiving aid:* Freshmen: 79% (403). Undergraduates: 67% (1,411). *Average award:* Freshmen: $14,978. Undergraduates: $14,111. *Scholarships, grants, and awards by category:* Academic interests/achievement: 2,457 awards ($24,240,546 total): general academic interests/achievements. *Creative arts/performance:* 58 awards ($226,856 total): art/fine arts, music. *Special achievements/activities:* 133 awards ($171,044 total): cheerleading/drum major, religious involvement. *Special characteristics:* 126 awards ($847,746 total): children of faculty/staff, relatives of clergy, religious affiliation. *Tuition waivers:* Full or partial for employees or children of employees, senior citizens. *ROTC:* Army cooperative, Naval cooperative, Air Force cooperative.

LOANS *Student loans:* $15,862,420 (77% need-based, 23% non-need-based). 60% of past graduating class borrowed through all loan programs. *Average indebtedness per student:* $31,767. *Average need-based loan:* Freshmen: $3856. Undergraduates: $4471. *Parent loans:* $3,910,833 (4% need-based, 96% non-need-based). *Programs:* Federal Direct (Subsidized and Unsubsidized Stafford, PLUS), state.

WORK-STUDY *Federal work-study:* Total amount: $909,577; 924 jobs averaging $985.

ATHLETIC AWARDS Total amount: $8,331,586 (42% need-based, 58% non-need-based).

APPLYING FOR FINANCIAL AID *Required financial aid form:* FAFSA. *Financial aid deadline (priority):* 3/1. *Notification date:* Continuous beginning 3/1. Students must reply within 4 weeks of notification.

CONTACT Ms. Veronica Jene Gabbard, Senior Director of Financial Aid and Scholarships, Houston Baptist University, 7502 Fondren Road, Houston, TX 77074-3298, 281-649-3747 or toll-free 800-696-3210. *Fax:* 281-649-3298. *E-mail:* financialaid@hbu.edu.

Website: http://www.hbu.edu/.

HOWARD PAYNE UNIVERSITY
Brownwood, TX

Tuition & fees: $28,090	Average undergraduate aid package: $20,390

ABOUT THE INSTITUTION Independent Baptist General Convention of Texas, coed. *Awards:* certificates, bachelor's, and master's degrees. 69 undergraduate majors. *Total enrollment:* 1,081. Undergraduates: 990. Freshmen: 262. Federal methodology is used as a basis for awarding need-based institutional aid.

UNDERGRADUATE EXPENSES for 2018–2019 *Comprehensive fee:* $36,476 includes full-time tuition ($25,290), mandatory fees ($2800), and room and board ($8386). Full-time tuition and fees vary according to course load, location, and program. Room and board charges vary according to board plan and housing facility. *Part-time tuition:* $845 per credit hour. Part-time tuition and fees vary according to location and program.

FRESHMAN FINANCIAL AID (Fall 2016) 311 applied for aid; of those 93% were deemed to have need. 100% of freshmen with need received aid; of those 18% had need fully met. *Average percent of need met:* 78% (excluding resources awarded to replace EFC). *Average financial aid package:* $19,362 (excluding resources

awarded to replace EFC). 8% of all full-time freshmen had no need and received non-need-based gift aid.

UNDERGRADUATE FINANCIAL AID (Fall 2016) 871 applied for aid; of those 93% were deemed to have need. 100% of undergraduates with need received aid; of those 20% had need fully met. *Average percent of need met:* 78% (excluding resources awarded to replace EFC). *Average financial aid package:* $20,390 (excluding resources awarded to replace EFC). 15% of all full-time undergraduates had no need and received non-need-based gift aid.

GIFT AID (NEED-BASED) *Total amount:* $13,003,297 (16% federal, 11% state, 70% institutional, 3% external sources). *Receiving aid:* Freshmen: 88% (286); all full-time undergraduates: 84% (801). *Average award:* Freshmen: $15,777; Undergraduates: $16,195. *Scholarships, grants, and awards:* Federal Pell, FSEOG, state, private, college/university gift aid from institutional funds.

GIFT AID (NON-NEED-BASED) *Total amount:* $2,569,614 (96% institutional, 4% external sources). *Receiving aid:* Freshmen: 12% (39). Undergraduates: 11% (103). *Average award:* Freshmen: $11,327. Undergraduates: $12,984. *Scholarships, grants, and awards by category: Academic interests/achievement:* biological sciences, business, communication, education, English, general academic interests/achievements, mathematics, physical sciences, premedicine, religion/biblical studies, social sciences. *Creative arts/performance:* art/fine arts, music, theater/drama. *Special achievements/activities:* community service, leadership, religious involvement. *Special characteristics:* children and siblings of alumni, children of faculty/staff, local/state students, relatives of clergy, religious affiliation, siblings of current students. *Tuition waivers:* Full or partial for employees or children of employees.

LOANS *Student loans:* $7,645,088 (67% need-based, 33% non-need-based). 73% of past graduating class borrowed through all loan programs. *Average indebtedness per student:* $34,875. *Average need-based loan:* Freshmen: $4476. Undergraduates: $5129. *Parent loans:* $1,189,522 (55% need-based, 45% non-need-based). *Programs:* Federal Direct (Subsidized and Unsubsidized Stafford, PLUS), Perkins, state.

WORK-STUDY *Federal work-study:* jobs available. *State or other work-study/employment:* Total amount: $9047 (100% need-based). Part-time jobs available.

APPLYING FOR FINANCIAL AID *Required financial aid forms:* FAFSA, institution's own form, Core Residency Form. *Financial aid deadline (priority):* 3/15. *Notification date:* Continuous beginning 2/1. Students must reply within 2 weeks of notification.

CONTACT Mrs. Glenda Huff, Director of Financial Aid, Howard Payne University, 1000 Fisk Avenue, Brownwood, TX 76801, 325-649-8014 or toll-free 800-880-4478. *Fax:* 325-649-8973. *E-mail:* ghuff@hputx.edu. *Website:* http://www.hputx.edu/.

HOWARD UNIVERSITY
Washington, DC

ABOUT THE INSTITUTION Independent, coed. 65 undergraduate majors.

GIFT AID (NEED-BASED) *Scholarships, grants, and awards:* Federal Pell, FSEOG, state, private, college/university gift aid from institutional funds, Federal Nursing.

GIFT AID (NON-NEED-BASED) *Scholarships, grants, and awards by category: Academic interests/achievement:* architecture, biological sciences, business, communication, computer science, education, engineering/technologies, English, foreign languages, health fields, humanities, international studies, mathematics, military science, physical sciences, premedicine, religion/biblical studies, social sciences. *Creative arts/performance:* applied art and design, art/fine arts, cinema/film/broadcasting, dance, journalism/publications, music, performing arts, theater/drama. *Special achievements/activities:* cheerleading/drum major, general special achievements/activities, leadership, memberships, religious involvement. *Special characteristics:* adult students, ethnic background, first-generation college students, handicapped students, international students, local/state students, married students, members of minority groups, previous college experience, religious affiliation.

LOANS *Programs:* Federal Direct (Subsidized and Unsubsidized Stafford, PLUS), Perkins, Federal Nursing, district, college/university.

APPLYING FOR FINANCIAL AID *Required financial aid form:* FAFSA.

CONTACT Office of Financial Aid, Howard University, 2400 Sixth Street, NW, Washington, DC 20059, 202-806-2864 or toll-free 800-822-6363. *Fax:* 202-806-2818. *Website:* http://www.howard.edu/.

HULT INTERNATIONAL BUSINESS SCHOOL
Cambridge, MA

Tuition & fees: N/R	Average undergraduate aid package: $12,180

ABOUT THE INSTITUTION Independent, coed. 1 undergraduate major. Institutional methodology is used as a basis for awarding need-based institutional aid.

FRESHMAN FINANCIAL AID (Fall 2017, est.) 108 applied for aid; of those 100% were deemed to have need. 100% of freshmen with need received aid. *Average financial aid package:* $11,442 (excluding resources awarded to replace EFC). 10% of all full-time freshmen had no need and received non-need-based gift aid.

UNDERGRADUATE FINANCIAL AID (Fall 2017, est.) 334 applied for aid; of those 96% were deemed to have need. 100% of undergraduates with need received aid. *Average financial aid package:* $12,180 (excluding resources awarded to replace EFC). 9% of all full-time undergraduates had no need and received non-need-based gift aid.

GIFT AID (NEED-BASED) *Total amount:* $3,825,911 (3% federal, 97% institutional). *Receiving aid:* Freshmen: 56% (108); all full-time undergraduates: 69% (322). *Average award:* Freshmen: $11,138; Undergraduates: $11,877. *Scholarships, grants, and awards:* college/university gift aid from institutional funds.

GIFT AID (NON-NEED-BASED) *Total amount:* $1,190,126 (100% institutional). *Receiving aid:* Freshmen: 27% (52). Undergraduates: 37% (173). *Average award:* Freshmen: $7060. Undergraduates: $6360. *Scholarships, grants, and awards by category: Academic interests/achievement:* business.

LOANS *Student loans:* $359,948 (28% need-based, 72% non-need-based). *Average indebtedness per student:* $12,343. *Parent loans:* $94,672 (100% non-need-based).

APPLYING FOR FINANCIAL AID *Required financial aid form:* institution's own form. *Financial aid deadline:* Continuous. *Notification date:* Continuous beginning 11/15. Students must reply by 5/1.

CONTACT Karen Van Dyne, Director of Financial Aid, Hult International Business School, 1 Education Street, Cambridge, MA 02141, 617-619-1097. *E-mail:* karen.vandyne@hult.edu. *Website:* http://www.hult.edu/.

HUMBOLDT STATE UNIVERSITY
Arcata, CA

Tuition & fees (CA res): $7492	Average undergraduate aid package: $14,037

ABOUT THE INSTITUTION State-supported, coed. *Awards:* certificates, bachelor's, and master's degrees. 67 undergraduate majors. *Total enrollment:* 8,347. Undergraduates: 7,774. Freshmen: 1,210. Federal methodology is used as a basis for awarding need-based institutional aid.

UNDERGRADUATE EXPENSES for 2018–2019 *Application fee:* $55. *Tuition, state resident:* full-time $5742; part-time $3330 per term. *Tuition, non-resident:* full-time $17,622; part-time $396 per credit hour. *Required fees:* full-time $1750; $1314 per term. Full-time tuition and fees vary according to degree level. Part-time tuition and fees vary according to course load and degree level. *College room and board:* $13,056; *Room only:* $6610. Room and board charges vary according to board plan and housing facility.

FRESHMAN FINANCIAL AID (Fall 2017, est.) 1,090 applied for aid; of those 83% were deemed to have need. 98% of freshmen with need received aid; of those 8% had need fully met. *Average percent of need met:* 69% (excluding resources awarded to replace EFC). *Average financial aid package:* $13,988 (excluding resources awarded to replace EFC). 7% of all full-time freshmen had no need and received non-need-based gift aid.

UNDERGRADUATE FINANCIAL AID (Fall 2017, est.) 6,376 applied for aid; of those 90% were deemed to have need. 98% of undergraduates with need received aid; of those 7% had need fully met. *Average percent of need met:* 67% (excluding resources awarded to replace EFC). *Average financial aid package:* $14,037 (excluding resources awarded to replace EFC). 4% of all full-time undergraduates had no need and received non-need-based gift aid.

GIFT AID (NEED-BASED) *Total amount:* $52,976,150 (41% federal, 28% state, 27% institutional, 4% external sources). *Receiving aid:* Freshmen: 71% (841); all full-

time undergraduates: 74% (5,368). *Average award:* Freshmen: $9724; Undergraduates: $9141. *Scholarships, grants, and awards:* Federal Pell, FSEOG, state, private, college/university gift aid from institutional funds.
GIFT AID (NON-NEED-BASED) *Total amount:* $745,290 (32% state, 11% institutional, 57% external sources). *Receiving aid:* Freshmen: 2% (18). Undergraduates: 1% (91). *Average award:* Freshmen: $749. Undergraduates: $912. *Scholarships, grants, and awards by category:* Academic interests/achievement: general academic interests/achievements. *Tuition waivers:* Full or partial for employees or children of employees.
LOANS *Student loans:* $30,211,158 (85% need-based, 15% non-need-based). 74% of past graduating class borrowed through all loan programs. *Average indebtedness per student:* $24,638. *Average need-based loan:* Freshmen: $5861. Undergraduates: $7165. *Parent loans:* $3,452,323 (31% need-based, 69% non-need-based). *Programs:* Federal Direct (Subsidized and Unsubsidized Stafford, PLUS), Perkins, college/university.
WORK-STUDY *Federal work-study:* Total amount: $787,162; jobs available.
ATHLETIC AWARDS Total amount: $829,366 (65% need-based, 35% non-need-based).
APPLYING FOR FINANCIAL AID *Required financial aid form:* FAFSA. *Financial aid deadline (priority):* 3/2. *Notification date:* Continuous beginning 4/15. Students must reply within 4 weeks of notification.
CONTACT Peggy Metzger, Director of Financial Aid, Humboldt State University, 1 Harpst Street, Arcata, CA 95521-8299, 707-826-4321 or toll-free 866-850-9556. *E-mail:* pmetzger@humboldt.edu.
Website: http://www.humboldt.edu/.

HUMPHREYS UNIVERSITY
Stockton, CA

CONTACT Rita Franco, Director of Financial Aid, Humphreys University, 6650 Inglewood Avenue, Stockton, CA 95207-3896, 209-478-0800. *Fax:* 209-235-2983. *Website:* http://www.humphreys.edu/.

HUNTER COLLEGE OF THE CITY UNIVERSITY OF NEW YORK
New York, NY

Tuition & fees (NY res): $6980	Average undergraduate aid package: $8126

ABOUT THE INSTITUTION State and locally supported, coed. *Awards:* certificates, bachelor's, master's, and doctoral degrees. 63 undergraduate majors. *Total enrollment:* 23,005. Undergraduates: 16,844. Freshmen: 2,337. Federal methodology is used as a basis for awarding need-based institutional aid.
UNDERGRADUATE EXPENSES for 2017–2018 *Application fee:* $65. *Tuition, state resident:* full-time $6530; part-time $285 per credit hour. *Tuition, nonresident:* full-time $17,400; part-time $580 per credit hour. *Required fees:* full-time $450; $132.55 per term. Full-time tuition and fees vary according to course load, degree level, and program. Part-time tuition and fees vary according to course load, degree level, and program. *Room only:* $4857. Room and board charges vary according to housing facility and location.
FRESHMAN FINANCIAL AID (Fall 2017, est.) 2,167 applied for aid; of those 87% were deemed to have need. 97% of freshmen with need received aid; of those 32% had need fully met. *Average percent of need met:* 94% (excluding resources awarded to replace EFC). *Average financial aid package:* $9039 (excluding resources awarded to replace EFC). 5% of all full-time freshmen had no need and received non-need-based gift aid.
UNDERGRADUATE FINANCIAL AID (Fall 2017, est.) 10,550 applied for aid; of those 90% were deemed to have need. 99% of undergraduates with need received aid; of those 53% had need fully met. *Average percent of need met:* 79% (excluding resources awarded to replace EFC). *Average financial aid package:* $8126 (excluding resources awarded to replace EFC). 3% of all full-time undergraduates had no need and received non-need-based gift aid.
GIFT AID (NEED-BASED) *Total amount:* $66,906,914 (58% federal, 42% state). *Receiving aid:* Freshmen: 71% (1,652); all full-time undergraduates: 65% (8,186). *Average award:* Freshmen: $8983; Undergraduates: $7789. *Scholarships, grants,*

and awards: Federal Pell, FSEOG, state, private, college/university gift aid from institutional funds.
GIFT AID (NON-NEED-BASED) *Total amount:* $10,702,049 (33% state, 57% institutional, 10% external sources). *Receiving aid:* Freshmen: 63% (1,461). Undergraduates: 34% (4,251). *Average award:* Freshmen: $4173. Undergraduates: $4179. *Scholarships, grants, and awards by category:* Academic interests/achievement: 5,257 awards ($10,702,050 total): general academic interests/achievements.
LOANS *Student loans:* $11,449,892 (45% need-based, 55% non-need-based). 15% of past graduating class borrowed through all loan programs. *Average indebtedness per student:* $12,122. *Average need-based loan:* Freshmen: $3129. Undergraduates: $4068. *Parent loans:* $1,003,788 (100% non-need-based). *Programs:* Federal Direct (Subsidized and Unsubsidized Stafford, PLUS), Perkins.
WORK-STUDY *Federal work-study:* Total amount: $1,350,568; 1,067 jobs averaging $1266. *State or other work-study/employment:* Total amount: $1,331,248 (100% non-need-based). Part-time jobs available.
APPLYING FOR FINANCIAL AID *Required financial aid forms:* FAFSA, state aid form. *Financial aid deadline (priority):* 4/1. *Notification date:* Continuous beginning 5/15.
CONTACT Dzelika Daniel, Director of Financial Aid, Hunter College of the City University of New York, 695 Park Avenue, New York, NY 10065-5085, 212-772-4400. *Fax:* 212-650-3666. *E-mail:* dd1611@hunter.cuny.edu. *Website:* http://www.hunter.cuny.edu/.

HUNTINGDON COLLEGE
Montgomery, AL

Tuition & fees: $26,400	Average undergraduate aid package: $19,156

ABOUT THE INSTITUTION Independent United Methodist, coed. *Awards:* bachelor's degrees. 34 undergraduate majors. *Total enrollment:* 1,102. Undergraduates: 1,102. Freshmen: 294. Both federal and institutional methodology are used as a basis for awarding need-based institutional aid.
UNDERGRADUATE EXPENSES for 2017–2018 *Comprehensive fee:* $35,900 includes full-time tuition ($24,900), mandatory fees ($1500), and room and board ($9500). Full-time tuition and fees vary according to course load and program. Room and board charges vary according to housing facility. *Part-time tuition:* $1040 per credit hour. Part-time tuition and fees vary according to course load and program.
FRESHMAN FINANCIAL AID (Fall 2017, est.) 273 applied for aid; of those 89% were deemed to have need. 100% of freshmen with need received aid; of those 15% had need fully met. *Average percent of need met:* 67% (excluding resources awarded to replace EFC). *Average financial aid package:* $19,451 (excluding resources awarded to replace EFC). 17% of all full-time freshmen had no need and received non-need-based gift aid.
UNDERGRADUATE FINANCIAL AID (Fall 2017, est.) 755 applied for aid; of those 89% were deemed to have need. 100% of undergraduates with need received aid; of those 13% had need fully met. *Average percent of need met:* 67% (excluding resources awarded to replace EFC). *Average financial aid package:* $19,156 (excluding resources awarded to replace EFC). 22% of all full-time undergraduates had no need and received non-need-based gift aid.
GIFT AID (NEED-BASED) *Total amount:* $10,987,772 (22% federal, 3% state, 69% institutional, 6% external sources). *Receiving aid:* Freshmen: 83% (243); all full-time undergraduates: 77% (674). *Average award:* Freshmen: $16,478; Undergraduates: $15,593. *Scholarships, grants, and awards:* Federal Pell, FSEOG, state, private, college/university gift aid from institutional funds.
GIFT AID (NON-NEED-BASED) *Total amount:* $3,402,043 (3% state, 76% institutional, 21% external sources). *Receiving aid:* Freshmen: 11% (32). Undergraduates: 9% (75). *Average award:* Freshmen: $12,207. Undergraduates: $11,673. *Scholarships, grants, and awards by category:* Academic interests/achievement: 294 awards ($3,666,015 total): biological sciences, computer science, general academic interests/achievements, mathematics. *Creative arts/performance:* 93 awards ($738,908 total): dance, music, performing arts. *Special achievements/activities:* 12 awards ($104,040 total): cheerleading/drum major, community service. *Special characteristics:* 240 awards ($2,206,187 total): children and siblings of alumni, children of faculty/staff, children of workers in trades, local/state students, spouses of current

students, veterans, veterans' children. *Tuition waivers:* Full or partial for employees or children of employees. *ROTC:* Army cooperative, Air Force cooperative.

LOANS *Student loans:* $6,873,860 (78% need-based, 22% non-need-based). 85% of past graduating class borrowed through all loan programs. *Average indebtedness per student:* $32,201. *Average need-based loan:* Freshmen: $3423. Undergraduates: $4197. *Parent loans:* $2,587,435 (57% need-based, 43% non-need-based). *Programs:* Federal Direct (Subsidized and Unsubsidized Stafford, PLUS), Perkins.

WORK-STUDY *Federal work-study:* Total amount: $103,117; 149 jobs averaging $910.

APPLYING FOR FINANCIAL AID *Required financial aid form:* FAFSA. *Financial aid deadline (priority):* 3/1. *Notification date:* Continuous beginning 3/1. Students must reply by 5/1 or within 2 weeks of notification.

CONTACT Ms. Brittany Davis, Director of Financial Aid, Huntingdon College, 1500 East Fairview Avenue, Montgomery, AL 36106-2148, 334-833-4428 or toll-free 800-763-0313. *Fax:* 334-833-4235. *E-mail:* finaid@hawks.huntingdon.edu. *Website:* http://www.huntingdon.edu/.

HUNTINGTON UNIVERSITY
Huntington, IN

Tuition & fees: $25,540	Average undergraduate aid package: $19,060

ABOUT THE INSTITUTION Independent Church of the United Brethren in Christ, coed. *Awards:* associate, bachelor's, master's, and doctoral degrees. 87 undergraduate majors. *Total enrollment:* 1,295. Undergraduates: 996. Freshmen: 196. Both federal and institutional methodology are used as a basis for awarding need-based institutional aid.

UNDERGRADUATE EXPENSES for 2017–2018 *Application fee:* $20. *Comprehensive fee:* $33,996 includes full-time tuition ($24,694), mandatory fees ($846), and room and board ($8456). *College room only:* $3980. Full-time tuition and fees vary according to course load, degree level, and program. Room and board charges vary according to board plan. *Part-time fees:* $420 per credit hour. Part-time tuition and fees vary according to course load, degree level, and program.

FRESHMAN FINANCIAL AID (Fall 2017, est.) 205 applied for aid; of those 71% were deemed to have need. 100% of freshmen with need received aid; of those 3% had need fully met. *Average percent of need met:* 71% (excluding resources awarded to replace EFC). *Average financial aid package:* $20,385 (excluding resources awarded to replace EFC). 16% of all full-time freshmen had no need and received non-need-based gift aid.

UNDERGRADUATE FINANCIAL AID (Fall 2017, est.) 598 applied for aid; of those 90% were deemed to have need. 100% of undergraduates with need received aid; of those 7% had need fully met. *Average percent of need met:* 87% (excluding resources awarded to replace EFC). *Average financial aid package:* $19,060 (excluding resources awarded to replace EFC). 32% of all full-time undergraduates had no need and received non-need-based gift aid.

GIFT AID (NEED-BASED) *Total amount:* $9,738,006 (17% federal, 20% state, 59% institutional, 4% external sources). *Receiving aid:* Freshmen: 69% (146); all full-time undergraduates: 62% (526). *Average award:* Freshmen: $16,094; Undergraduates: $14,851. *Scholarships, grants, and awards:* Federal Pell, FSEOG, state, private, college/university gift aid from institutional funds.

GIFT AID (NON-NEED-BASED) *Total amount:* $1,641,467 (98% institutional, 2% external sources). *Receiving aid:* Freshmen: 10% (22). Undergraduates: 9% (74). *Average award:* Freshmen: $9670. Undergraduates: $9626. *Scholarships, grants, and awards by category: Academic interests/achievement:* agriculture, business, communication, general academic interests/achievements. *Creative arts/performance:* applied art and design, art/fine arts, cinema/film/broadcasting, creative writing, journalism/publications, music, performing arts, theater/drama. *Special achievements/activities:* cheerleading/drum major, leadership, memberships, religious involvement. *Special characteristics:* children and siblings of alumni, children of faculty/staff, ethnic background, international students, local/state students, relatives of clergy, religious affiliation. *Tuition waivers:* Full or partial for minority students, children of alumni, employees or children of employees.

LOANS *Student loans:* $5,301,879 (80% need-based, 20% non-need-based). 74% of past graduating class borrowed through all loan programs. *Average indebtedness per student:* $32,515. *Average need-based loan:* Freshmen: $3614. Undergraduates: $4562. *Parent loans:* $1,478,512 (79% need-based, 21% non-need-based). *Programs:* Federal Direct (Subsidized and Unsubsidized Stafford, PLUS), Perkins.

WORK-STUDY *Federal work-study:* Total amount: $100,000; jobs available.

ATHLETIC AWARDS Total amount: $1,063,613 (60% need-based, 40% non-need-based).

APPLYING FOR FINANCIAL AID *Required financial aid form:* FAFSA. *Financial aid deadline (priority):* 4/15. *Notification date:* Continuous beginning 12/10. Students must reply by 5/1 or within 2 weeks of notification.

CONTACT Lisa Montany, Director of Financial Aid, Huntington University, 2303 College Avenue, Huntington, IN 46750, 260-359-4014 or toll-free 800-642-6493. *Fax:* 260-358-3699. *E-mail:* finaid@huntington.edu. *Website:* http://www.huntington.edu/.

HUNTSVILLE BIBLE COLLEGE
Huntsville, AL

CONTACT Financial Aid Office, Huntsville Bible College, 904 Oakwood Avenue, Huntsville, AL 35811-1632, 256-539-0834. *Website:* http://www.huntsvillebiblecollege.org/.

HUSSIAN COLLEGE, SCHOOL OF ART
Philadelphia, PA

CONTACT Financial Aid Office, Hussian College, School of Art, The Bourse - Suite 300, 111 South Independence Mall East, Philadelphia, PA 19106, 215-981-0900. *Website:* http://www.hussiancollege.edu/.

HUSSON UNIVERSITY
Bangor, ME

Tuition & fees: $17,600	Average undergraduate aid package: $15,074

ABOUT THE INSTITUTION Independent, coed. *Awards:* certificates, associate, bachelor's, master's, and doctoral degrees. 46 undergraduate majors. *Total enrollment:* 3,640. Undergraduates: 2,763. Freshmen: 577. Federal methodology is used as a basis for awarding need-based institutional aid.

UNDERGRADUATE EXPENSES for 2018–2019 *Application fee:* $40. *One-time required fee:* $150. *Comprehensive fee:* $27,430 includes full-time tuition ($17,100), mandatory fees ($500), and room and board ($9830). *College room only:* $4950. Full-time tuition and fees vary according to class time and location. Room and board charges vary according to board plan and housing facility. *Part-time tuition:* $570 per credit. *Part-time fees:* $120 per year. Part-time tuition and fees vary according to class time, course load, and location. *Payment plan:* Tuition prepayment.

FRESHMAN FINANCIAL AID (Fall 2017, est.) 553 applied for aid; of those 89% were deemed to have need. 100% of freshmen with need received aid; of those 12% had need fully met. *Average percent of need met:* 65% (excluding resources awarded to replace EFC). *Average financial aid package:* $15,351 (excluding resources awarded to replace EFC). 17% of all full-time freshmen had no need and received non-need-based gift aid.

UNDERGRADUATE FINANCIAL AID (Fall 2017, est.) 2,111 applied for aid; of those 90% were deemed to have need. 100% of undergraduates with need received aid; of those 9% had need fully met. *Average percent of need met:* 67% (excluding resources awarded to replace EFC). *Average financial aid package:* $15,074 (excluding resources awarded to replace EFC). 14% of all full-time undergraduates had no need and received non-need-based gift aid.

GIFT AID (NEED-BASED) *Total amount:* $19,410,752 (29% federal, 5% state, 60% institutional, 6% external sources). *Receiving aid:* Freshmen: 75% (426); all full-time undergraduates: 69% (1,588). *Average award:* Freshmen: $10,579; Undergraduates: $8919. *Scholarships, grants, and awards:* Federal Pell, FSEOG, state, private, college/university gift aid from institutional funds.

GIFT AID (NON-NEED-BASED) *Total amount:* $1,607,513 (90% institutional, 10% external sources). *Receiving aid:* Freshmen: 75% (427). Undergraduates: 58% (1,334). *Average award:* Freshmen: $4945. Undergraduates: $3793. *Scholarships,* grants, and awards by category: Academic interests/achievement: general academic interests/achievements. Special achievements/activities: leadership. Special characteristics: children and siblings of alumni, children of faculty/staff, children of union members/company employees, ethnic background, international students, members of minority groups, out-of-state students. **Tuition waivers:** Full or partial for employees or children of employees, senior citizens. **ROTC:** Army, Naval cooperative.

LOANS *Student loans:* $18,534,234 (77% need-based, 23% non-need-based). 88% of past graduating class borrowed through all loan programs. *Average indebtedness per student:* $33,412. **Average need-based loan:** Freshmen: $2864. Undergraduates: $4287. **Parent loans:** $3,453,707 (44% need-based, 56% non-need-based). **Programs:** Federal Direct (Subsidized and Unsubsidized Stafford, PLUS), Perkins, state, alternative loans.

WORK-STUDY *Federal work-study:* Total amount: $1,961,141; 413 jobs averaging $1600.

APPLYING FOR FINANCIAL AID *Required financial aid form:* FAFSA. *Financial aid deadline:* 4/15. *Notification date:* Continuous beginning 12/1. Students must reply by 5/1 or within 2 weeks of notification.

CONTACT Anne Tabor, Director of Financial Aid, Husson University, 1 College Circle, Bangor, ME 04401, 207-941-7156 or toll-free 800-4-HUSSON. *Fax:* 207-941-7932. *E-mail:* tabora@husson.edu. *Website:* http://www.husson.edu/.

HUSTON-TILLOTSON UNIVERSITY
Austin, TX

ABOUT THE INSTITUTION Independent interdenominational, coed. *Awards:* associate, bachelor's, and master's degrees. 26 undergraduate majors. *Total enrollment:* 1,103. Undergraduates: 1,053. Freshmen: 183.

GIFT AID (NEED-BASED) *Scholarships, grants, and awards:* Federal Pell, FSEOG, state, private, college/university gift aid from institutional funds, United Negro College Fund.

GIFT AID (NON-NEED-BASED) *Scholarships, grants, and awards by category:* Academic interests/achievement: general academic interests/achievements. Creative arts/performance: music. Special characteristics: general special characteristics.

LOANS *Programs:* Federal Direct (Subsidized and Unsubsidized Stafford, PLUS), state, private loans.

APPLYING FOR FINANCIAL AID *Required financial aid forms:* FAFSA, institution's own form.

CONTACT Office of Financial Aid, Huston-Tillotson University, 900 Chicon Street, Austin, TX 78702, 512-505-3031. *Fax:* 512-505-3192. *Website:* http://www.htu.edu/.

IDAHO STATE UNIVERSITY
Pocatello, ID

Tuition & fees (ID res): $7166	Average undergraduate aid package: $8733

ABOUT THE INSTITUTION State-supported, coed. *Awards:* certificates, bachelor's, master's, and doctoral degrees. 98 undergraduate majors. *Total enrollment:* 12,643. Undergraduates: 10,683. Freshmen: 1,364. Federal methodology is used as a basis for awarding need-based institutional aid.

UNDERGRADUATE EXPENSES for 2017–2018 *Application fee:* $50. *Tuition, state resident:* full-time $5425; part-time $359 per credit hour. *Tuition, nonresident:* full-time $20,201; part-time $599 per credit hour. *Required fees:* full-time $1741. Full-time tuition and fees vary according to course load, program, and reciprocity agreements. Part-time tuition and fees vary according to course load. *College room and board:* $7024; *Room only:* $2790. Room and board charges vary according to board plan, housing facility, and location. *Payment plan:* Guaranteed tuition.

FRESHMAN FINANCIAL AID (Fall 2016) 994 applied for aid; of those 82% were deemed to have need. 99% of freshmen with need received aid; of those 7% had need fully met. *Average percent of need met:* 49% (excluding resources awarded to replace EFC). *Average financial aid package:* $8422 (excluding resources

awarded to replace EFC). 12% of all full-time freshmen had no need and received non-need-based gift aid.

UNDERGRADUATE FINANCIAL AID (Fall 2016) 4,909 applied for aid; of those 87% were deemed to have need. 99% of undergraduates with need received aid; of those 5% had need fully met. *Average percent of need met:* 47% (excluding resources awarded to replace EFC). *Average financial aid package:* $8733 (excluding resources awarded to replace EFC). 8% of all full-time undergraduates had no need and received non-need-based gift aid.

GIFT AID (NEED-BASED) *Total amount:* $20,300,894 (73% federal, 6% state, 17% institutional, 4% external sources). *Receiving aid:* Freshmen: 51% (627); all full-time undergraduates: 49% (3,176). *Average award:* Freshmen: $4691; Undergraduates: $4803. *Scholarships, grants, and awards:* Federal Pell, FSEOG, state, private, college/university gift aid from institutional funds, Federal Nursing.

GIFT AID (NON-NEED-BASED) *Total amount:* $2,751,314 (9% state, 72% institutional, 19% external sources). *Receiving aid:* Freshmen: 36% (442). Undergraduates: 29% (1,909). *Average award:* Freshmen: $2420. Undergraduates: $2338. *Scholarships, grants, and awards by category:* Academic interests/achievement: architecture, biological sciences, business, communication, computer science, education, engineering/technologies, English, foreign languages, general academic interests/achievements, home economics, humanities, international studies, mathematics, military science, physical sciences, premedicine, social sciences. Creative arts/performance: art/fine arts, dance, debating, journalism/publications, music, performing arts, theater/drama. Special achievements/activities: cheerleading/drum major, general special achievements/activities. Special characteristics: children of faculty/staff, children with a deceased or disabled parent, ethnic background, first-generation college students, general special characteristics, handicapped students, international students, local/state students, members of minority groups, out-of-state students. **Tuition waivers:** Full or partial for employees or children of employees, senior citizens. **ROTC:** Army.

LOANS *Student loans:* $30,923,649 (94% need-based, 6% non-need-based). 61% of past graduating class borrowed through all loan programs. *Average indebtedness per student:* $29,340. **Average need-based loan:** Freshmen: $3056. Undergraduates: $3793. **Parent loans:** $1,199,668 (87% need-based, 13% non-need-based). **Programs:** Federal Direct (Subsidized and Unsubsidized Stafford, PLUS), Perkins, Federal Nursing.

WORK-STUDY *Federal work-study:* jobs available. **State or other work-study/employment:** Total amount: $312,296 (100% need-based). Part-time jobs available.

ATHLETIC AWARDS Total amount: $2,195,660 (29% need-based, 71% non-need-based).

APPLYING FOR FINANCIAL AID *Required financial aid form:* FAFSA. *Financial aid deadline (priority):* 3/1. *Notification date:* Continuous beginning 4/1.

CONTACT Mr. James R. Martin, Director of Financial Aid, Idaho State University, 921 South 8th Avenue, Museum Building 337, Stop 8077, Pocatello, ID 83209-8077, 208-282-2756. *Fax:* 208-282-4755. *E-mail:* finaidem@isu.edu. *Website:* http://www.isu.edu/.

IGLOBAL UNIVERSITY
Vienna, VA

CONTACT Financial Aid Office, IGlobal University, 8133 Leesburg Pike, #230, Vienna, VA 22182, 703-941-2020. *Website:* http://www.igu.edu/.

ILLINOIS COLLEGE
Jacksonville, IL

Tuition & fees: $33,090	Average undergraduate aid package: $27,933

ABOUT THE INSTITUTION Independent interdenominational, coed. *Awards:* bachelor's and master's degrees. 44 undergraduate majors. *Total enrollment:* 959. Undergraduates: 959. Freshmen: 258. Federal methodology is used as a basis for awarding need-based institutional aid.

UNDERGRADUATE EXPENSES for 2018–2019 *Comprehensive fee:* $42,370 includes full-time tuition ($32,540), mandatory fees ($550), and room and board ($9280). Room and board charges vary according to board plan and housing facility. *Part-time tuition:* $990 per credit hour. Part-time tuition and fees vary according to course load.

FRESHMAN FINANCIAL AID (Fall 2016) 271 applied for aid; of those 93% were deemed to have need. 100% of freshmen with need received aid; of those 27% had need fully met. *Average percent of need met:* 90% (excluding resources awarded to replace EFC). *Average financial aid package:* $29,646 (excluding resources awarded to replace EFC). 13% of all full-time freshmen had no need and received non-need-based gift aid.

UNDERGRADUATE FINANCIAL AID (Fall 2016) 866 applied for aid; of those 92% were deemed to have need. 100% of undergraduates with need received aid; of those 24% had need fully met. *Average percent of need met:* 87% (excluding resources awarded to replace EFC). *Average financial aid package:* $27,933 (excluding resources awarded to replace EFC). 16% of all full-time undergraduates had no need and received non-need-based gift aid.

GIFT AID (NEED-BASED) *Total amount:* $18,518,771 (10% federal, 10% state, 77% institutional, 3% external sources). *Receiving aid:* Freshmen: 86% (253); all full-time undergraduates: 84% (798). *Average award:* Freshmen: $25,391; Undergraduates: $23,190. *Scholarships, grants, and awards:* Federal Pell, FSEOG, state, private, college/university gift aid from institutional funds.

GIFT AID (NON-NEED-BASED) *Total amount:* $3,645,991 (97% institutional, 3% external sources). *Receiving aid:* Freshmen: 14% (40). Undergraduates: 13% (120). *Average award:* Freshmen: $19,085. Undergraduates: $17,694. *Scholarships, grants, and awards by category:* Academic interests/achievement: general academic interests/achievements. Creative arts/performance: art/fine arts, music, theater/drama. Special characteristics: children and siblings of alumni, children of faculty/staff, international students, previous college experience, siblings of current students. *Tuition waivers:* Full or partial for employees or children of employees.

LOANS *Student loans:* $7,215,404 (68% need-based, 32% non-need-based). 86% of past graduating class borrowed through all loan programs. *Average indebtedness per student:* $32,740. *Average need-based loan:* Freshmen: $3969. Undergraduates: $4566. *Parent loans:* $1,905,512 (30% need-based, 70% non-need-based). *Programs:* Federal Direct (Subsidized and Unsubsidized Stafford, PLUS).

WORK-STUDY *Federal work-study:* jobs available.

APPLYING FOR FINANCIAL AID *Required financial aid form:* FAFSA. *Financial aid deadline (priority):* 10/31. *Notification date:* Continuous beginning 12/15. Students must reply within 2 weeks of notification.

CONTACT Office of Student Financial Services, Illinois College, 1101 West College Avenue, Jacksonville, IL 62650-2299, 217-245-3035 or toll-free 866-464-5265. *Fax:* 217-245-3274. *E-mail:* sfs@ic.edu. *Website:* http://www.ic.edu/.

THE ILLINOIS INSTITUTE OF ART–CHICAGO
Chicago, IL

Financial Aid Office, The Illinois Institute of Art–Chicago, 350 North Orleans Street, Suite 136, Chicago, IL 60654-1593, 800-351-3450.

THE ILLINOIS INSTITUTE OF ART–SCHAUMBURG
Schaumburg, IL

CONTACT Financial Aid Office, The Illinois Institute of Art–Schaumburg, 1000 North Plaza Drive, Suite 100, Schaumburg, IL 60173, 847-619-3450 or toll-free 800-314-3450. *Website:* http://www.artinstitutes.edu/schaumburg/.

ILLINOIS INSTITUTE OF TECHNOLOGY
Chicago, IL

Tuition & fees: N/R	Average undergraduate aid package: $38,963

ABOUT THE INSTITUTION Independent, coed. 38 undergraduate majors. Federal methodology is used as a basis for awarding need-based institutional aid.

FRESHMAN FINANCIAL AID (Fall 2016) 387 applied for aid; of those 93% were deemed to have need. 100% of freshmen with need received aid; of those 22% had need fully met. *Average percent of need met:* 85% (excluding resources awarded to replace EFC). *Average financial aid package:* $41,478 (excluding resources awarded to replace EFC). 28% of all full-time freshmen had no need and received non-need-based gift aid.

UNDERGRADUATE FINANCIAL AID (Fall 2016) 1,703 applied for aid; of those 96% were deemed to have need. 100% of undergraduates with need received aid; of those 13% had need fully met. *Average percent of need met:* 77% (excluding resources awarded to replace EFC). *Average financial aid package:* $38,963 (excluding resources awarded to replace EFC). 36% of all full-time undergraduates had no need and received non-need-based gift aid.

GIFT AID (NEED-BASED) *Total amount:* $54,716,678 (11% federal, 5% state, 83% institutional, 1% external sources). *Receiving aid:* Freshmen: 71% (356); all full-time undergraduates: 62% (1,626). *Average award:* Freshmen: $35,496; Undergraduates: $33,045. *Scholarships, grants, and awards:* Federal Pell, FSEOG, state, private, college/university gift aid from institutional funds.

GIFT AID (NON-NEED-BASED) *Total amount:* $26,706,762 (2% federal, 97% institutional, 1% external sources). *Receiving aid:* Freshmen: 14% (70). Undergraduates: 7% (190). *Average award:* Freshmen: $25,683. Undergraduates: $24,787. *Scholarships, grants, and awards by category:* Academic interests/achievement: architecture, biological sciences, business, communication, computer science, engineering/technologies, general academic interests/achievements, humanities, mathematics, premedicine, social sciences. Creative arts/performance: applied art and design. Special achievements/activities: community service, general special achievements/activities, hobbies/interests, leadership, memberships. Special characteristics: children and siblings of alumni, children of faculty/staff, children of public servants, general special characteristics, international students, local/state students, previous college experience, veterans, veterans' children.

LOANS *Student loans:* $12,821,318 (81% need-based, 19% non-need-based). 54% of past graduating class borrowed through all loan programs. *Average indebtedness per student:* $32,671. *Average need-based loan:* Freshmen: $4027. Undergraduates: $5308. *Parent loans:* $5,930,700 (46% need-based, 54% non-need-based).

WORK-STUDY *Federal work-study:* jobs available. *State or other work-study/employment:* Part-time jobs available.

APPLYING FOR FINANCIAL AID *Required financial aid form:* FAFSA. *Financial aid deadline (priority):* 1/1. *Notification date:* Continuous beginning 2/15.

CONTACT Abby McGrath, Director of Financial Aid, Illinois Institute of Technology, 3300 South Federal Street, Chicago, IL 60616, 312-567-5730 or toll-free 800-448-2329. *Fax:* 312-567-3982. *E-mail:* finaid@iit.edu. *Website:* http://www.iit.edu/.

ILLINOIS STATE UNIVERSITY
Normal, IL

ABOUT THE INSTITUTION State-supported, coed. *Awards:* certificates, bachelor's, master's, and doctoral degrees. 73 undergraduate majors. *Total enrollment:* 20,784. Undergraduates: 18,330. Freshmen: 3,352.

GIFT AID (NEED-BASED) *Scholarships, grants, and awards:* Federal Pell, FSEOG, state, private, college/university gift aid from institutional funds, Federal Nursing.

GIFT AID (NON-NEED-BASED) *Scholarships, grants, and awards by category:* Academic interests/achievement: agriculture, biological sciences, business, communication, computer science, education, engineering/technologies, English, foreign languages, general academic interests/achievements, health fields, home economics, humanities, international studies, library science, mathematics, military science, physical sciences, premedicine, social sciences. Creative arts/performance:

applied art and design, art/fine arts, cinema/film/broadcasting, creative writing, debating, general creative arts/performance, music, performing arts, theater/drama. *Special achievements/activities:* community service, leadership. *Special characteristics:* children and siblings of alumni, children of faculty/staff, children of union members/company employees, children with a deceased or disabled parent, first-generation college students, general special characteristics, local/state students, members of minority groups, previous college experience, religious affiliation.

LOANS *Programs:* Federal Direct (Subsidized and Unsubsidized Stafford, PLUS), Perkins, Federal Nursing.

APPLYING FOR FINANCIAL AID *Required financial aid form:* FAFSA.

CONTACT Mr. David Krueger, Associate Director of Financial Aid, Illinois State University, Campus Box 2320, Normal, IL 61790-2320, 309-438-2231 or toll-free 800-366-2478. *Fax:* 309-438-3755. *E-mail:* financialaid@illinoisstate.edu. *Website:* http://www.illinoisstate.edu/.

ILLINOIS WESLEYAN UNIVERSITY
Bloomington, IL

Tuition & fees: $47,636	Average undergraduate aid package: $34,735

ABOUT THE INSTITUTION Independent, coed. *Awards:* bachelor's degrees. 49 undergraduate majors. *Total enrollment:* 1,649. Undergraduates: 1,649. Freshmen: 378. Both federal and institutional methodology are used as a basis for awarding need-based institutional aid.

UNDERGRADUATE EXPENSES for 2018–2019 *Comprehensive fee:* $58,620 includes full-time tuition ($47,434), mandatory fees ($202), and room and board ($10,984). *College room only:* $6878. Room and board charges vary according to housing facility. *Part-time tuition:* $1482 per credit hour.

FRESHMAN FINANCIAL AID (Fall 2017, est.) 332 applied for aid; of those 85% were deemed to have need. 100% of freshmen with need received aid; of those 20% had need fully met. *Average percent of need met:* 87% (excluding resources awarded to replace EFC). *Average financial aid package:* $36,363 (excluding resources awarded to replace EFC). 24% of all full-time freshmen had no need and received non-need-based gift aid.

UNDERGRADUATE FINANCIAL AID (Fall 2017, est.) 1,264 applied for aid; of those 84% were deemed to have need. 100% of undergraduates with need received aid; of those 18% had need fully met. *Average percent of need met:* 85% (excluding resources awarded to replace EFC). *Average financial aid package:* $34,735 (excluding resources awarded to replace EFC). 33% of all full-time undergraduates had no need and received non-need-based gift aid.

GIFT AID (NEED-BASED) *Total amount:* $29,038,979 (6% federal, 7% state, 86% institutional, 1% external sources). *Receiving aid:* Freshmen: 73% (283); all full-time undergraduates: 65% (1,065). *Average award:* Freshmen: $30,758; Undergraduates: $27,990. *Scholarships, grants, and awards:* Federal Pell, FSEOG, state, private, college/university gift aid from institutional funds.

GIFT AID (NON-NEED-BASED) *Total amount:* $11,285,893 (100% institutional). *Receiving aid:* Freshmen: 8% (30). Undergraduates: 6% (91). *Average award:* Freshmen: $22,311. Undergraduates: $19,202. *Scholarships, grants, and awards by category:* Academic interests/achievement: general academic interests/achievements. Creative arts/performance: art/fine arts, general creative arts/performance, music, theater/drama. Special characteristics: children of faculty/staff, general special characteristics, international students. *Tuition waivers:* Full or partial for employees or children of employees. *ROTC:* Army cooperative.

LOANS *Student loans:* $9,935,403 (50% need-based, 50% non-need-based). 69% of past graduating class borrowed through all loan programs. *Average indebtedness per student:* $36,036. *Average need-based loan:* Freshmen: $4469. Undergraduates: $5853. *Parent loans:* $4,503,971 (100% non-need-based). *Programs:* Federal Direct (Subsidized and Unsubsidized Stafford, PLUS), Perkins, Federal Nursing, college/university.

WORK-STUDY *Federal work-study:* Total amount: $332,770; jobs available. *State or other work-study/employment:* Total amount: $1,124,273 (80% need-based, 20% non-need-based). Part-time jobs available.

APPLYING FOR FINANCIAL AID *Required financial aid forms:* FAFSA, institution's own form. *Financial aid deadline (priority):* 3/1. *Notification date:* Continuous beginning 3/1. Students must reply by 5/1.

CONTACT Mr. Scott Seibring, Director of Financial Aid, Illinois Wesleyan University, 1312 North Park Street, PO Box 2900, Bloomington, IL 61702-2900, 309-556-3393 or toll-free 800-332-2498. *Fax:* 309-556-3833. *E-mail:* seibring@iwu.edu. *Website:* http://www.iwu.edu/.

IMMACULATA UNIVERSITY
Immaculata, PA

CONTACT Mr. Robert Forest, Director of Student Financial Aid, Immaculata University, 1145 King Road, Box 500, Immaculata, PA 19345, 610-647-4400 Ext. 3026 or toll-free 877-428-6329. *Fax:* 610-640-0836. *E-mail:* rforest@immaculata.edu. *Website:* http://www.immaculata.edu/.

INDEPENDENCE UNIVERSITY
Salt Lake City, UT

CONTACT Financial Aid Director, Independence University, 2423 Hoover Avenue, National City, CA 91950-6605, 619-477-4800 or toll-free 800-917-6391. *Fax:* 619-477-5202. *Website:* http://www.independence.edu/.

INDIANA STATE UNIVERSITY
Terre Haute, IN

Tuition & fees (IN res): $8916	Average undergraduate aid package: $11,078

ABOUT THE INSTITUTION State-supported, coed. *Awards:* certificates, bachelor's, master's, and doctoral degrees. 75 undergraduate majors. *Total enrollment:* 13,771. Undergraduates: 11,591. Freshmen: 2,688. Federal methodology is used as a basis for awarding need-based institutional aid.

UNDERGRADUATE EXPENSES for 2017–2018 *Application fee:* $25. *Tuition, state resident:* full-time $8716; part-time $316 per credit hour. *Tuition, nonresident:* full-time $19,252; part-time $682 per credit hour. *Required fees:* full-time $200; $100 per term. Full-time tuition and fees vary according to reciprocity agreements. Part-time tuition and fees vary according to course load and reciprocity agreements. *College room and board:* $9883. Room and board charges vary according to board plan, housing facility, and student level.

FRESHMAN FINANCIAL AID (Fall 2016) 2,318 applied for aid; of those 85% were deemed to have need. 96% of freshmen with need received aid; of those 15% had need fully met. *Average percent of need met:* 82% (excluding resources awarded to replace EFC). *Average financial aid package:* $11,415 (excluding resources awarded to replace EFC). 8% of all full-time freshmen had no need and received non-need-based gift aid.

UNDERGRADUATE FINANCIAL AID (Fall 2016) 8,090 applied for aid; of those 85% were deemed to have need. 96% of undergraduates with need received aid; of those 15% had need fully met. *Average percent of need met:* 81% (excluding resources awarded to replace EFC). *Average financial aid package:* $11,078 (excluding resources awarded to replace EFC). 8% of all full-time undergraduates had no need and received non-need-based gift aid.

GIFT AID (NEED-BASED) *Total amount:* $26,058,334 (77% federal, 16% state, 7% institutional). *Receiving aid:* Freshmen: 52% (1,258); all full-time undergraduates: 46% (4,309). *Average award:* Freshmen: $5815; Undergraduates: $5783. *Scholarships, grants, and awards:* Federal Pell, FSEOG, state, private, college/university gift aid from institutional funds.

GIFT AID (NON-NEED-BASED) *Total amount:* $29,169,470 (59% state, 32% institutional, 9% external sources). *Receiving aid:* Freshmen: 51% (1,251). Undergraduates: 38% (3,557). *Average award:* Freshmen: $4831. Undergraduates: $4914. *Scholarships, grants, and awards by category:* Academic interests/achievement: area/ethnic studies, biological sciences, business, communication, computer science, education, engineering/technologies, English, foreign languages, general academic interests/achievements, health fields, humanities, mathematics, physical sciences, premedicine, social sciences. Creative arts/performance: applied art and design, art/fine arts, music, performing arts, theater/drama. Special characteristics: children and siblings of alumni, children of faculty/staff, members of minority groups, previous college experience, veterans. *Tuition waivers:* Full or partial for employees or children of employees, senior citizens. *ROTC:* Army, Air Force.

LOANS *Student loans:* $49,288,130 (43% need-based, 57% non-need-based). 74% of past graduating class borrowed through all loan programs. *Average indebtedness per student:* $28,092. *Average need-based loan:* Freshmen: $3164. Undergraduates: $3942. *Parent loans:* $11,700,372 (100% non-need-based). *Programs:* Federal Direct (Subsidized and Unsubsidized Stafford, PLUS), Perkins.

WORK-STUDY *Federal work-study:* jobs available.

ATHLETIC AWARDS Total amount: $4,468,204 (100% non-need-based).

APPLYING FOR FINANCIAL AID *Required financial aid form:* FAFSA. *Financial aid deadline:* 7/1 (priority: 3/1). *Notification date:* Continuous beginning 3/15.

CONTACT Crystal Baker, Director of Student Financial Aid, Indiana State University, 150 Tirey Hall, Terre Haute, IN 47809-1401, 812-237-2215 or toll-free 800-468-6478. *Fax:* 812-237-4330. *E-mail:* isu-finaid@mail.indstate.edu. *Website:* http://www.indstate.edu/.

INDIANA TECH
Fort Wayne, IN

Tuition & fees: N/R	Average undergraduate aid package: $17,004

ABOUT THE INSTITUTION Independent, coed. *Awards:* associate, bachelor's, master's, and doctoral degrees. 31 undergraduate majors. *Total enrollment:* 7,996. Undergraduates: 6,870. Freshmen: 1,320. Federal methodology is used as a basis for awarding need-based institutional aid.

UNDERGRADUATE EXPENSES for 2018–2019 *Tuition:* part-time $520 per credit hour. *Required fees:* $165 per term. Full-time tuition and fees vary according to course load and program. Part-time tuition and fees vary according to course load and program. Room and board charges vary according to board plan and housing facility. *Payment plan:* Guaranteed tuition.

FRESHMAN FINANCIAL AID (Fall 2016) 830 applied for aid; of those 96% were deemed to have need. 100% of freshmen with need received aid; of those 26% had need fully met. *Average percent of need met:* 33% (excluding resources awarded to replace EFC). *Average financial aid package:* $20,059 (excluding resources awarded to replace EFC). 2% of all full-time freshmen had no need and received non-need-based gift aid.

UNDERGRADUATE FINANCIAL AID (Fall 2016) 3,701 applied for aid; of those 95% were deemed to have need. 99% of undergraduates with need received aid; of those 33% had need fully met. *Average percent of need met:* 39% (excluding resources awarded to replace EFC). *Average financial aid package:* $17,004 (excluding resources awarded to replace EFC). 1% of all full-time undergraduates had no need and received non-need-based gift aid.

GIFT AID (NEED-BASED) *Total amount:* $36,165,695 (50% federal, 25% state, 24% institutional, 1% external sources). *Receiving aid:* Freshmen: 76% (675); all full-time undergraduates: 68% (2,868). *Average award:* Freshmen: $10,568; Undergraduates: $9535. *Scholarships, grants, and awards:* Federal Pell, FSEOG, state, private, college/university gift aid from institutional funds.

GIFT AID (NON-NEED-BASED) *Receiving aid:* Freshmen: 34% (308). Undergraduates: 18% (756). *Average award:* Freshmen: $11,068. Undergraduates: $9494. *Scholarships, grants, and awards by category:* Academic interests/achievement: 1,066 awards ($8,734,484 total): computer science, education, engineering/technologies, general academic interests/achievements. Special characteristics: 369 awards ($1,286,399 total): children of current students, children of faculty/staff, local/state students, married students, siblings of current students, spouses of current students, veterans, veterans' children. *Tuition waivers:* Full or partial for minority students, children of alumni, employees or children of employees, adult students, senior citizens. *ROTC:* Army cooperative.

LOANS *Student loans:* $42,875,072 (40% need-based, 60% non-need-based). 74% of past graduating class borrowed through all loan programs. *Average indebtedness per student:* $41,844. *Average need-based loan:* Freshmen: $3120. Undergraduates: $3129. *Parent loans:* $2,985,202 (100% non-need-based). *Programs:* Federal Direct (Subsidized and Unsubsidized Stafford, PLUS).

WORK-STUDY *Federal work-study:* 88 jobs averaging $1401.

ATHLETIC AWARDS Total amount: $5,853,598 (100% non-need-based).

APPLYING FOR FINANCIAL AID *Required financial aid form:* FAFSA. *Financial aid deadline:* Continuous. *Notification date:* Continuous beginning 11/15. Students must reply within 2 weeks of notification.

CONTACT Mrs. Lisa Claudette Green, Financial Aid Systems Analyst, Indiana Tech, 1600 East Washington Boulevard, Fort Wayne, IN 46803-1297, 800-937-2448 Ext. 2334 or toll-free 800-937-2448. *Fax:* 219-422-1578. *E-mail:* financialaid@indianatech.edu. *Website:* http://www.indianatech.edu/.

INDIANA UNIVERSITY BLOOMINGTON
Bloomington, IN

Tuition & fees (IN res): $10,681	Average undergraduate aid package: $13,500

ABOUT THE INSTITUTION State-supported, coed. *Awards:* certificates, associate, bachelor's, master's, and doctoral degrees. 109 undergraduate majors. *Total enrollment:* 43,710. Undergraduates: 33,429. Freshmen: 8,001. Federal methodology is used as a basis for awarding need-based institutional aid.

UNDERGRADUATE EXPENSES for 2018–2019 *Application fee:* $65. *Tuition, state resident:* full-time $9342; part-time $291.89 per credit hour. *Tuition, nonresident:* full-time $34,117; part-time $1066.15 per credit hour. *Required fees:* full-time $1339. Full-time tuition and fees vary according to location and program. Part-time tuition and fees vary according to course load, location, and program. Room and board charges vary according to board plan and housing facility.

FRESHMAN FINANCIAL AID (Fall 2016) 5,580 applied for aid; of those 63% were deemed to have need. 95% of freshmen with need received aid; of those 33% had need fully met. *Average percent of need met:* 71% (excluding resources awarded to replace EFC). *Average financial aid package:* $14,159 (excluding resources awarded to replace EFC). 25% of all full-time freshmen had no need and received non-need-based gift aid.

UNDERGRADUATE FINANCIAL AID (Fall 2016) 18,747 applied for aid; of those 70% were deemed to have need. 96% of undergraduates with need received aid; of those 26% had need fully met. *Average percent of need met:* 69% (excluding resources awarded to replace EFC). *Average financial aid package:* $13,500 (excluding resources awarded to replace EFC). 32% of all full-time undergraduates had no need and received non-need-based gift aid.

GIFT AID (NEED-BASED) *Total amount:* $120,541,817 (23% federal, 31% state, 41% institutional, 5% external sources). *Receiving aid:* Freshmen: 37% (2,860); all full-time undergraduates: 34% (10,761). *Average award:* Freshmen: $12,629; Undergraduates: $11,445. *Scholarships, grants, and awards:* Federal Pell, FSEOG, state, private, college/university gift aid from institutional funds.

GIFT AID (NON-NEED-BASED) *Total amount:* $78,268,610 (1% federal, 3% state, 83% institutional, 13% external sources). *Receiving aid:* Freshmen: 10% (730). Undergraduates: 7% (2,304). *Average award:* Freshmen: $7384. Undergraduates: $5626. *Tuition waivers:* Full or partial for employees or children of employees. *ROTC:* Army, Air Force.

LOANS *Student loans:* $103,428,667 (56% need-based, 44% non-need-based). 45% of past graduating class borrowed through all loan programs. *Average indebtedness per student:* $28,792. *Average need-based loan:* Freshmen: $3262. Undergraduates: $4454. *Parent loans:* $41,606,526 (34% need-based, 66% non-need-based). *Programs:* Federal Direct (Subsidized and Unsubsidized Stafford, PLUS), Perkins, Federal Nursing, college/university.

WORK-STUDY *Federal work-study:* 555 jobs averaging $1967. *State or other work-study/employment:* Total amount: $41,729 (70% need-based, 30% non-need-based). Part-time jobs available.

ATHLETIC AWARDS Total amount: $12,827,678 (32% need-based, 68% non-need-based).

APPLYING FOR FINANCIAL AID *Required financial aid form:* FAFSA. *Financial aid deadline (priority):* 4/15. *Notification date:* Continuous beginning 2/15.

CONTACT Jackie Kennedy-Fletcher, Director of Student Financial Assistance, Indiana University Bloomington, 408 North Union Street, Bloomington, IN 47405, 812-855-6500. *Fax:* 812-855-7615. *E-mail:* rsvposfa@indiana.edu. *Website:* http://www.iub.edu/.

INDIANA UNIVERSITY EAST
Richmond, IN

Tuition & fees (IN res): $7344	Average undergraduate aid package: $8822

ABOUT THE INSTITUTION State-supported, coed. **Awards:** certificates, bachelor's, and master's degrees. 26 undergraduate majors. **Total enrollment:** 3,490. Undergraduates: 3,292. Freshmen: 396. Federal methodology is used as a basis for awarding need-based institutional aid.

UNDERGRADUATE EXPENSES for 2018–2019 Application fee: $35. **Tuition, state resident:** full-time $6727; part-time $224.23 per credit hour. **Tuition, nonresident:** full-time $18,783; part-time $626.08 per credit hour. **Required fees:** full-time $617. Full-time tuition and fees vary according to course load, location, program, and reciprocity agreements. Part-time tuition and fees vary according to course load, location, program, and reciprocity agreements.

FRESHMAN FINANCIAL AID (Fall 2016) 327 applied for aid; of those 79% were deemed to have need. 98% of freshmen with need received aid; of those 20% had need fully met. **Average percent of need met:** 68% (excluding resources awarded to replace EFC). **Average financial aid package:** $8755 (excluding resources awarded to replace EFC). 7% of all full-time freshmen had no need and received non-need-based gift aid.

UNDERGRADUATE FINANCIAL AID (Fall 2016) 1,669 applied for aid; of those 85% were deemed to have need. 97% of undergraduates with need received aid; of those 18% had need fully met. **Average percent of need met:** 68% (excluding resources awarded to replace EFC). **Average financial aid package:** $8822 (excluding resources awarded to replace EFC). 7% of all full-time undergraduates had no need and received non-need-based gift aid.

GIFT AID (NEED-BASED) Total amount: $9,491,137 (54% federal, 34% state, 8% institutional, 4% external sources). **Receiving aid:** Freshmen: 69% (239); all full-time undergraduates: 64% (1,189). **Average award:** Freshmen: $7466; Undergraduates: $7046. **Scholarships, grants, and awards:** Federal Pell, FSEOG, state, private, college/university gift aid from institutional funds.

GIFT AID (NON-NEED-BASED) Total amount: $897,363 (12% federal, 12% state, 40% institutional, 36% external sources). **Receiving aid:** Freshmen: 10% (35). Undergraduates: 7% (136). **Average award:** Freshmen: $1486. Undergraduates: $2009. **Tuition waivers:** Full or partial for employees or children of employees.

LOANS Student loans: $11,011,612 (75% need-based, 25% non-need-based). 74% of past graduating class borrowed through all loan programs. **Average indebtedness per student:** $22,392. **Average need-based loan:** Freshmen: $2891. Undergraduates: $3867. **Parent loans:** $217,244 (13% need-based, 87% non-need-based). **Programs:** Federal Direct (Subsidized and Unsubsidized Stafford, PLUS), Perkins, college/university.

WORK-STUDY Federal work-study: 50 jobs averaging $2355. **State or other work-study/employment:** Part-time jobs available.

ATHLETIC AWARDS Total amount: $481,660 (45% need-based, 55% non-need-based).

APPLYING FOR FINANCIAL AID Required financial aid forms: FAFSA, institution's own form. **Financial aid deadline (priority):** 3/10. **Notification date:** Continuous beginning 5/1. Students must reply within 2 weeks of notification.

CONTACT Sarah Soper, Director of Financial Aid and Scholarships, Indiana University East, Whitewater Hall 112, 2325 Chester Boulevard, Richmond, IN 47374-1289, 765-973-8206 or toll-free 800-959-EAST. **Fax:** 765-973-8288. **E-mail:** eaosfa@iue.edu.
Website: http://www.iue.edu/.

INDIANA UNIVERSITY KOKOMO
Kokomo, IN

Tuition & fees (IN res): $7344	Average undergraduate aid package: $8575

ABOUT THE INSTITUTION State-supported, coed. **Awards:** certificates, associate, bachelor's, and master's degrees. 33 undergraduate majors. **Total enrollment:** 3,029. Undergraduates: 2,876. Freshmen: 605. Federal methodology is used as a basis for awarding need-based institutional aid.

UNDERGRADUATE EXPENSES for 2018–2019 Application fee: $35. **Tuition, state resident:** full-time $6727; part-time $224.23 per credit hour.

Tuition, nonresident: full-time $18,783; part-time $626.08 per credit hour. **Required fees:** full-time $617. Full-time tuition and fees vary according to course load, location, and program. Part-time tuition and fees vary according to course load, location, and program.

FRESHMAN FINANCIAL AID (Fall 2016) 445 applied for aid; of those 77% were deemed to have need. 93% of freshmen with need received aid; of those 18% had need fully met. **Average percent of need met:** 65% (excluding resources awarded to replace EFC). **Average financial aid package:** $7844 (excluding resources awarded to replace EFC). 6% of all full-time freshmen had no need and received non-need-based gift aid.

UNDERGRADUATE FINANCIAL AID (Fall 2016) 1,842 applied for aid; of those 80% were deemed to have need. 95% of undergraduates with need received aid; of those 16% had need fully met. **Average percent of need met:** 67% (excluding resources awarded to replace EFC). **Average financial aid package:** $8575 (excluding resources awarded to replace EFC). 7% of all full-time undergraduates had no need and received non-need-based gift aid.

GIFT AID (NEED-BASED) Total amount: $9,875,802 (50% federal, 42% state, 5% institutional, 3% external sources). **Receiving aid:** Freshmen: 58% (280); all full-time undergraduates: 58% (1,204). **Average award:** Freshmen: $7178; Undergraduates: $7246. **Scholarships, grants, and awards:** Federal Pell, FSEOG, state, private, college/university gift aid from institutional funds.

GIFT AID (NON-NEED-BASED) Total amount: $1,033,569 (14% federal, 23% state, 27% institutional, 36% external sources). **Receiving aid:** Freshmen: 8% (36). Undergraduates: 6% (120). **Average award:** Freshmen: $1928. Undergraduates: $1414. **Tuition waivers:** Full or partial for employees or children of employees. **ROTC:** Army.

LOANS Student loans: $8,997,502 (68% need-based, 32% non-need-based). 73% of past graduating class borrowed through all loan programs. **Average indebtedness per student:** $23,664. **Average need-based loan:** Freshmen: $2622. Undergraduates: $3552. **Parent loans:** $281,745 (20% need-based, 80% non-need-based). **Programs:** Federal Direct (Subsidized and Unsubsidized Stafford, PLUS), Perkins, Federal Nursing, college/university.

WORK-STUDY Federal work-study: 99 jobs averaging $1877. **State or other work-study/employment:** Total amount: $4893 (31% need-based, 69% non-need-based). Part-time jobs available.

ATHLETIC AWARDS Total amount: $111,950 (59% need-based, 41% non-need-based).

APPLYING FOR FINANCIAL AID Required financial aid form: FAFSA. **Financial aid deadline:** 6/30 (priority: 3/10). **Notification date:** Continuous beginning 1/10.

CONTACT Dara Johnson, Director of Financial Aid, Indiana University Kokomo, Kelley Student Center, Room 230, 2300 South Washington Street, Kokomo, IN 46904-9003, 765-455-9216 or toll-free 888-875-4485. **Fax:** 765-455-9537. **E-mail:** finaidko@iuk.edu.
Website: http://www.iuk.edu/.

INDIANA UNIVERSITY NORTHWEST
Gary, IN

Tuition & fees (IN res): $7344	Average undergraduate aid package: $8390

ABOUT THE INSTITUTION State-supported, coed. **Awards:** certificates, associate, bachelor's, and master's degrees. 44 undergraduate majors. **Total enrollment:** 4,055. Undergraduates: 3,700. Freshmen: 606. Federal methodology is used as a basis for awarding need-based institutional aid.

UNDERGRADUATE EXPENSES for 2018–2019 Application fee: $35. **Tuition, state resident:** full-time $6727; part-time $224.23 per credit hour. **Tuition, nonresident:** full-time $18,783; part-time $626.08 per credit hour. **Required fees:** full-time $617. Full-time tuition and fees vary according to course load, location, and program. Part-time tuition and fees vary according to course load, location, and program.

FRESHMAN FINANCIAL AID (Fall 2016) 504 applied for aid; of those 72% were deemed to have need. 93% of freshmen with need received aid; of those 16% had need fully met. **Average percent of need met:** 67% (excluding resources awarded to replace EFC). **Average financial aid package:** $8104 (excluding resources awarded to replace EFC). 11% of all full-time freshmen had no need and received non-need-based gift aid.

UNDERGRADUATE FINANCIAL AID (Fall 2016) 2,342 applied for aid; of those 80% were deemed to have need. 95% of undergraduates with need received aid; of those 14% had need fully met. *Average percent of need met:* 65% (excluding resources awarded to replace EFC). *Average financial aid package:* $8390 (excluding resources awarded to replace EFC). 8% of all full-time undergraduates had no need and received non-need-based gift aid.

GIFT AID (NEED-BASED) *Total amount:* $11,876,956 (56% federal, 32% state, 8% institutional, 4% external sources). *Receiving aid:* Freshmen: 51% (287); all full-time undergraduates: 53% (1,463). *Average award:* Freshmen: $7648; Undergraduates: $7259. *Scholarships, grants, and awards:* Federal Pell, FSEOG, state, private, college/university gift aid from institutional funds, United Negro College Fund, Federal Nursing, Illiana Scholarships, transfer scholarships.

GIFT AID (NON-NEED-BASED) *Total amount:* $1,299,340 (8% federal, 9% state, 70% institutional, 13% external sources). *Receiving aid:* Freshmen: 5% (30). Undergraduates: 3% (94). *Average award:* Freshmen: $3706. Undergraduates: $3379. *Tuition waivers:* Full or partial for employees or children of employees. *ROTC:* Army.

LOANS *Student loans:* $12,413,522 (69% need-based, 31% non-need-based). 68% of past graduating class borrowed through all loan programs. *Average indebtedness per student:* $28,241. *Average need-based loan:* Freshmen: $3020. Undergraduates: $3611. *Parent loans:* $444,792 (11% need-based, 89% non-need-based). *Programs:* Federal Direct (Subsidized and Unsubsidized Stafford, PLUS), Perkins, college/university.

WORK-STUDY *Federal work-study:* 76 jobs averaging $1769. *State or other work-study/employment:* Part-time jobs available.

ATHLETIC AWARDS Total amount: $58,050 (61% need-based, 39% non-need-based).

APPLYING FOR FINANCIAL AID *Required financial aid form:* FAFSA. *Financial aid deadline (priority):* 3/10. *Notification date:* Continuous beginning 4/15. Students must reply by 6/30.

CONTACT Harold Burtley, Director of Scholarships and Financial Aid, Indiana University Northwest, 3400 Broadway, Hawthorn Hall, Room 111, Gary, IN 46408, 219-980-6778 or toll-free 800-968-7486. *Fax:* 219-981-5622. *E-mail:* finaidnw@iun.edu.
Website: http://www.iun.edu/.

INDIANA UNIVERSITY OF PENNSYLVANIA
Indiana, PA

Tuition & fees (PA res): $12,146	Average undergraduate aid package: $10,314

ABOUT THE INSTITUTION State-supported, coed. *Awards:* certificates, associate, bachelor's, master's, and doctoral degrees. 62 undergraduate majors. *Total enrollment:* 12,316. Undergraduates: 10,143. Freshmen: 2,333. Federal methodology is used as a basis for awarding need-based institutional aid.

UNDERGRADUATE EXPENSES for 2017–2018 *Application fee:* $25. *Tuition, state resident:* full-time $9000; part-time $300 per credit hour. *Tuition, nonresident:* full-time $18,720; part-time $780 per credit hour. *Required fees:* full-time $3146; $116 per credit hour or $50 per term. Full-time tuition and fees vary according to course load and reciprocity agreements. Part-time tuition and fees vary according to course load and reciprocity agreements. *College room and board:* $12,488; *Room only:* $8950. Room and board charges vary according to board plan, housing facility, and location.

FRESHMAN FINANCIAL AID (Fall 2016) 2,090 applied for aid; of those 83% were deemed to have need. 99% of freshmen with need received aid; of those 9% had need fully met. *Average percent of need met:* 58% (excluding resources awarded to replace EFC). *Average financial aid package:* $11,469 (excluding resources awarded to replace EFC). 5% of all full-time freshmen had no need and received non-need-based gift aid.

UNDERGRADUATE FINANCIAL AID (Fall 2016) 8,468 applied for aid; of those 83% were deemed to have need. 98% of undergraduates with need received aid; of those 8% had need fully met. *Average percent of need met:* 55% (excluding resources awarded to replace EFC). *Average financial aid package:* $10,314 (excluding resources awarded to replace EFC). 4% of all full-time undergraduates had no need and received non-need-based gift aid.

GIFT AID (NEED-BASED) *Total amount:* $37,493,852 (48% federal, 30% state, 14% institutional, 8% external sources). *Receiving aid:* Freshmen: 55% (1,211); all full-time undergraduates: 47% (4,652). *Average award:* Freshmen: $6747; Undergraduates: $6170. *Scholarships, grants, and awards:* Federal Pell, FSEOG, state, private, college/university gift aid from institutional funds, United Negro College Fund.

GIFT AID (NON-NEED-BASED) *Total amount:* $2,263,298 (12% state, 64% institutional, 24% external sources). *Receiving aid:* Freshmen: 43% (941). Undergraduates: 40% (3,940). *Average award:* Freshmen: $3061. Undergraduates: $2452. *Scholarships, grants, and awards by category:* Academic interests/achievement: 5,229 awards ($11,690,707 total): area/ethnic studies, biological sciences, business, communication, computer science, education, engineering/technologies, English, foreign languages, general academic interests/achievements, health fields, home economics, humanities, international studies, mathematics, military science, physical sciences, premedicine, religion/biblical studies, social sciences. *Creative arts/performance:* applied art and design, art/fine arts, dance, general creative arts/performance, journalism/publications, music, performing arts, theater/drama. *Special achievements/activities:* community service, general special achievements/activities, hobbies/interests, leadership. *Special characteristics:* adult students, children of faculty/staff, ethnic background, first-generation college students, international students, local/state students, married students. *Tuition waivers:* Full or partial for employees or children of employees, senior citizens. *ROTC:* Army.

LOANS *Student loans:* $75,467,367 (70% need-based, 30% non-need-based). 83% of past graduating class borrowed through all loan programs. *Average indebtedness per student:* $39,833. *Average need-based loan:* Freshmen: $3616. Undergraduates: $4236. *Parent loans:* $22,162,231 (55% need-based, 45% non-need-based). *Programs:* Federal Direct (Subsidized and Unsubsidized Stafford, PLUS), Perkins.

WORK-STUDY *Federal work-study:* 953 jobs averaging $1876. *State or other work-study/employment:* Total amount: $1,002,935 (100% non-need-based). Part-time jobs available.

ATHLETIC AWARDS Total amount: $1,555,569 (54% need-based, 46% non-need-based).

APPLYING FOR FINANCIAL AID *Required financial aid forms:* FAFSA, state aid form. *Financial aid deadline (priority):* 10/1. *Notification date:* Continuous beginning 12/15.

CONTACT Ms. Ragan Griffin, Director of Financial Aid, Indiana University of Pennsylvania, 1090 South Drive, 200 Clark Hall, Indiana, PA 15705, 724-357-2218 or toll-free 800-442-6830. *Fax:* 724-357-2094. *E-mail:* financial-aid@iup.edu.
Website: http://www.iup.edu/.

INDIANA UNIVERSITY–PURDUE UNIVERSITY FORT WAYNE
Fort Wayne, IN

ABOUT THE INSTITUTION State-supported, coed. 103 undergraduate majors.

GIFT AID (NEED-BASED) *Scholarships, grants, and awards:* Federal Pell, FSEOG, state, private, college/university gift aid from institutional funds.

GIFT AID (NON-NEED-BASED) *Scholarships, grants, and awards by category:* Academic interests/achievement: biological sciences, engineering/technologies, general academic interests/achievements, premedicine. *Creative arts/performance:* art/fine arts, music, theater/drama. *Special achievements/activities:* leadership. *Special characteristics:* children and siblings of alumni, general special characteristics, local/state students.

LOANS *Programs:* Federal Direct (Subsidized and Unsubsidized Stafford, PLUS), Perkins.

APPLYING FOR FINANCIAL AID *Required financial aid forms:* FAFSA, general scholarship application form.

CONTACT Mr. David Peterson, Director of Financial Aid, Indiana University–Purdue University Fort Wayne, 2101 East Coliseum Boulevard, Fort Wayne, IN 46805-1499, 260-481-6240 or toll-free 800-324-4739. *E-mail:* finaid@ipfw.edu.
Website: http://www.ipfw.edu/.

INDIANA UNIVERSITY–PURDUE UNIVERSITY INDIANAPOLIS
Indianapolis, IN

Tuition & fees (IN res): $9465	Average undergraduate aid package: $11,003

ABOUT THE INSTITUTION State-supported, coed. *Awards:* certificates, associate, bachelor's, master's, and doctoral degrees. 86 undergraduate majors. *Total enrollment:* 29,791. Undergraduates: 21,610. Freshmen: 4,093. Federal methodology is used as a basis for awarding need-based institutional aid.

UNDERGRADUATE EXPENSES for 2018–2019 *Application fee:* $65. *Tuition, state resident:* full-time $8371; part-time $279.03 per credit hour. *Tuition, nonresident:* full-time $28,727; part-time $957.58 per credit hour. *Required fees:* full-time $1094. Full-time tuition and fees vary according to course load, location, and program. Part-time tuition and fees vary according to course load, location, and program. Room and board charges vary according to board plan and housing facility.

FRESHMAN FINANCIAL AID (Fall 2016) 3,525 applied for aid; of those 76% were deemed to have need. 97% of freshmen with need received aid; of those 25% had need fully met. *Average percent of need met:* 70% (excluding resources awarded to replace EFC). *Average financial aid package:* $11,684 (excluding resources awarded to replace EFC). 11% of all full-time freshmen had no need and received non-need-based gift aid.

UNDERGRADUATE FINANCIAL AID (Fall 2016) 14,280 applied for aid; of those 81% were deemed to have need. 97% of undergraduates with need received aid; of those 20% had need fully met. *Average percent of need met:* 67% (excluding resources awarded to replace EFC). *Average financial aid package:* $11,003 (excluding resources awarded to replace EFC). 12% of all full-time undergraduates had no need and received non-need-based gift aid.

GIFT AID (NEED-BASED) *Total amount:* $91,850,998 (37% federal, 38% state, 22% institutional, 3% external sources). *Receiving aid:* Freshmen: 59% (2,255); all full-time undergraduates: 54% (9,339). *Average award:* Freshmen: $10,507; Undergraduates: $9382. *Scholarships, grants, and awards:* Federal Pell, FSEOG, state, private, college/university gift aid from institutional funds.

GIFT AID (NON-NEED-BASED) *Total amount:* $31,086,322 (4% federal, 6% state, 44% institutional, 46% external sources). *Receiving aid:* Freshmen: 10% (396). Undergraduates: 7% (1,221). *Average award:* Freshmen: $7450. Undergraduates: $5269. *Tuition waivers:* Full or partial for employees or children of employees. *ROTC:* Army, Air Force cooperative.

LOANS *Student loans:* $79,317,796 (68% need-based, 32% non-need-based). 70% of past graduating class borrowed through all loan programs. *Average indebtedness per student:* $29,065. *Average need-based loan:* Freshmen: $3158. Undergraduates: $4030. *Parent loans:* $10,335,651 (26% need-based, 74% non-need-based). *Programs:* Federal Direct (Subsidized and Unsubsidized Stafford, PLUS), Perkins, Federal Nursing, college/university.

WORK-STUDY *Federal work-study:* 455 jobs averaging $2408. *State or other work-study/employment:* Total amount: $33,598 (59% need-based, 41% non-need-based). Part-time jobs available.

ATHLETIC AWARDS Total amount: $2,514,763 (30% need-based, 70% non-need-based).

APPLYING FOR FINANCIAL AID *Required financial aid form:* FAFSA. *Financial aid deadline (priority):* 3/10. *Notification date:* Continuous beginning 4/1.

CONTACT Marvin Smith, Director of Student Financial Services, Indiana University–Purdue University Indianapolis, 420 University Boulevard, CE 250, Indianapolis, IN 46202-5145, 317-274-4162. *Fax:* 317-274-3664. *E-mail:* finaid@iupui.edu. *Website:* http://www.iupui.edu/.

INDIANA UNIVERSITY SOUTH BEND
South Bend, IN

Tuition & fees (IN res): $7344	Average undergraduate aid package: $8881

ABOUT THE INSTITUTION State-supported, coed. *Awards:* certificates, diplomas, associate, bachelor's, and master's degrees. 60 undergraduate majors. *Total enrollment:* 5,385. Undergraduates: 4,876. Freshmen: 982. Federal methodology is used as a basis for awarding need-based institutional aid.

UNDERGRADUATE EXPENSES for 2018–2019 *Application fee:* $35. *Tuition, state resident:* full-time $6727; part-time $224.23 per credit hour. *Tuition, nonresident:* full-time $18,783; part-time $626.08 per credit hour. *Required fees:* full-time $617. Full-time tuition and fees vary according to course load, location, and program. Part-time tuition and fees vary according to course load, location, and program. Room and board charges vary according to housing facility.

FRESHMAN FINANCIAL AID (Fall 2016) 779 applied for aid; of those 80% were deemed to have need. 94% of freshmen with need received aid; of those 17% had need fully met. *Average percent of need met:* 64% (excluding resources awarded to replace EFC). *Average financial aid package:* $8201 (excluding resources awarded to replace EFC). 11% of all full-time freshmen had no need and received non-need-based gift aid.

UNDERGRADUATE FINANCIAL AID (Fall 2016) 3,235 applied for aid; of those 84% were deemed to have need. 95% of undergraduates with need received aid; of those 16% had need fully met. *Average percent of need met:* 67% (excluding resources awarded to replace EFC). *Average financial aid package:* $8881 (excluding resources awarded to replace EFC). 8% of all full-time undergraduates had no need and received non-need-based gift aid.

GIFT AID (NEED-BASED) *Total amount:* $17,824,968 (50% federal, 37% state, 11% institutional, 2% external sources). *Receiving aid:* Freshmen: 60% (520); all full-time undergraduates: 59% (2,233). *Average award:* Freshmen: $7242; Undergraduates: $7297. *Scholarships, grants, and awards:* Federal Pell, FSEOG, state, private, college/university gift aid from institutional funds.

GIFT AID (NON-NEED-BASED) *Total amount:* $2,238,664 (9% federal, 8% state, 42% institutional, 41% external sources). *Receiving aid:* Freshmen: 8% (66). Undergraduates: 6% (239). *Average award:* Freshmen: $1794. Undergraduates: $2203. *Tuition waivers:* Full or partial for employees or children of employees. *ROTC:* Army cooperative, Naval cooperative, Air Force cooperative.

LOANS *Student loans:* $15,127,184 (70% need-based, 30% non-need-based). 74% of past graduating class borrowed through all loan programs. *Average indebtedness per student:* $25,780. *Average need-based loan:* Freshmen: $2825. Undergraduates: $3649. *Parent loans:* $866,151 (23% need-based, 77% non-need-based). *Programs:* Federal Direct (Subsidized and Unsubsidized Stafford, PLUS), Perkins, state.

WORK-STUDY *Federal work-study:* 229 jobs averaging $1973. *State or other work-study/employment:* Total amount: $2713 (100% need-based). Part-time jobs available.

ATHLETIC AWARDS Total amount: $152,325 (56% need-based, 44% non-need-based).

APPLYING FOR FINANCIAL AID *Required financial aid forms:* FAFSA, institution's own form. *Financial aid deadline (priority):* 3/10. *Notification date:* Continuous beginning 5/1.

CONTACT Jill Bertrand, Director of Financial Aid and Scholarships, Indiana University South Bend, 1002 South Esther Street, PO Box 7111, South Bend, IN 46634-7111, 574-520-4357 or toll-free 877-GO-2-IUSB. *Fax:* 574-520-5561. *E-mail:* sbfinaid@iusb.edu. *Website:* http://www.iusb.edu/.

INDIANA UNIVERSITY SOUTHEAST
New Albany, IN

Tuition & fees (IN res): $7344	Average undergraduate aid package: $8245

ABOUT THE INSTITUTION State-supported, coed. *Awards:* certificates, associate, bachelor's, and master's degrees. 41 undergraduate majors. *Total enrollment:* 5,238. Undergraduates: 4,823. Freshmen: 927. Federal methodology is used as a basis for awarding need-based institutional aid.

UNDERGRADUATE EXPENSES for 2018–2019 *Application fee:* $35. *Tuition, state resident:* full-time $6727; part-time $224.23 per credit hour. *Tuition, nonresident:* full-time $18,783; part-time $626.08 per credit hour. *Required fees:* full-time $617. Full-time tuition and fees vary according to course load, location, program, and reciprocity agreements. Part-time tuition and fees vary according to course load, location, program, and reciprocity agreements. Room and board charges vary according to board plan and housing facility.

FRESHMAN FINANCIAL AID (Fall 2016) 790 applied for aid; of those 74% were deemed to have need. 94% of freshmen with need received aid; of those 12% had need fully met. *Average percent of need met:* 61% (excluding resources awarded to

replace EFC). *Average financial aid package:* $8008 (excluding resources awarded to replace EFC). 8% of all full-time freshmen had no need and received non-need-based gift aid.

UNDERGRADUATE FINANCIAL AID (Fall 2016) 2,780 applied for aid; of those 79% were deemed to have need. 94% of undergraduates with need received aid; of those 12% had need fully met. *Average percent of need met:* 63% (excluding resources awarded to replace EFC). *Average financial aid package:* $8245 (excluding resources awarded to replace EFC). 7% of all full-time undergraduates had no need and received non-need-based gift aid.

GIFT AID (NEED-BASED) *Total amount:* $13,812,994 (55% federal, 33% state, 7% institutional, 5% external sources). *Receiving aid:* Freshmen: 56% (486); all full-time undergraduates: 54% (1,769). *Average award:* Freshmen: $7063; Undergraduates: $6727. *Scholarships, grants, and awards:* Federal Pell, FSEOG, state, private, college/university gift aid from institutional funds.

GIFT AID (NON-NEED-BASED) *Total amount:* $1,758,598 (13% federal, 17% state, 32% institutional, 38% external sources). *Receiving aid:* Freshmen: 6% (49). Undergraduates: 4% (131). *Average award:* Freshmen: $1772. Undergraduates: $1706. *Tuition waivers:* Full or partial for employees or children of employees. *ROTC:* Army cooperative, Air Force cooperative.

LOANS *Student loans:* $13,614,648 (70% need-based, 30% non-need-based). 64% of past graduating class borrowed through all loan programs. *Average indebtedness per student:* $23,845. *Average need-based loan:* Freshmen: $3063. Undergraduates: $3750. *Parent loans:* $734,781 (28% need-based, 72% non-need-based). *Programs:* Federal Direct (Subsidized and Unsubsidized Stafford, PLUS), Perkins, college/university.

WORK-STUDY *Federal work-study:* 134 jobs averaging $1494. *State or other work-study/employment:* Total amount: $6781 (42% need-based, 58% non-need-based). Part-time jobs available.

ATHLETIC AWARDS Total amount: $132,250 (62% need-based, 38% non-need-based).

APPLYING FOR FINANCIAL AID *Required financial aid form:* FAFSA. *Financial aid deadline (priority):* 8/1. *Notification date:* Continuous beginning 2/10. Students must reply within 2 weeks of notification.

CONTACT Traci Armes, Director of Financial Aid, Indiana University Southeast, University Center, South Room 105, New Albany, IN 47150, 812-941-2246 or toll-free 800-852-8835. *Fax:* 812-941-2546. *E-mail:* financialaid@ius.edu.
Website: http://www.ius.edu/.

INDIANA WESLEYAN UNIVERSITY
Marion, IN

Tuition & fees: $25,980	Average undergraduate aid package: $29,681

ABOUT THE INSTITUTION Independent Wesleyan, coed. *Awards:* certificates, associate, bachelor's, master's, and doctoral degrees (also offers adult program with significant enrollment not reflected in profile). 86 undergraduate majors. *Total enrollment:* 3,071. Undergraduates: 2,799. Freshmen: 787. Both federal and institutional methodology are used as a basis for awarding need-based institutional aid.

UNDERGRADUATE EXPENSES for 2018–2019 *Comprehensive fee:* $34,292 includes full-time tuition ($25,980) and room and board ($8312). *College room only:* $4154. Full-time tuition and fees vary according to course load and degree level. Room and board charges vary according to board plan. *Part-time tuition:* $555 per credit hour. Part-time tuition and fees vary according to course load and degree level.

FRESHMAN FINANCIAL AID (Fall 2017, est.) 749 applied for aid; of those 87% were deemed to have need. 100% of freshmen with need received aid; of those 62% had need fully met. *Average percent of need met:* 92% (excluding resources awarded to replace EFC). *Average financial aid package:* $30,090 (excluding resources awarded to replace EFC). 13% of all full-time freshmen had no need and received non-need-based gift aid.

UNDERGRADUATE FINANCIAL AID (Fall 2017, est.) 2,323 applied for aid; of those 88% were deemed to have need. 100% of undergraduates with need received aid; of those 58% had need fully met. *Average percent of need met:* 92% (excluding resources awarded to replace EFC). *Average financial aid package:* $29,681 (excluding resources awarded to replace EFC). 10% of all full-time undergraduates had no need and received non-need-based gift aid.

GIFT AID (NEED-BASED) *Total amount:* $29,026,603 (26% federal, 14% state, 55% institutional, 5% external sources). *Receiving aid:* Freshmen: 65% (508); all full-time undergraduates: 63% (1,653). *Average award:* Freshmen: $3490; Undergraduates: $3548. *Scholarships, grants, and awards:* Federal Pell, FSEOG, state, private, college/university gift aid from institutional funds.

GIFT AID (NON-NEED-BASED) *Total amount:* $14,003,919 (9% state, 82% institutional, 9% external sources). *Receiving aid:* Freshmen: 83% (650). Undergraduates: 45% (1,198). *Average award:* Freshmen: $11,045. Undergraduates: $9802. *Scholarships, grants, and awards by category: Academic interests/achievement:* biological sciences, business, communication, computer science, education, English, foreign languages, general academic interests/achievements, health fields, international studies, mathematics, physical sciences, premedicine, religion/biblical studies, social sciences. *Creative arts/performance:* art/fine arts, music, theater/drama. *Special achievements/activities:* cheerleading/drum major, community service, hobbies/interests, religious involvement. *Special characteristics:* children and siblings of alumni, children of faculty/staff, relatives of clergy, religious affiliation, siblings of current students, veterans. *Tuition waivers:* Full or partial for employees or children of employees. *ROTC:* Army.

LOANS *Student loans:* $20,260,714 (58% need-based, 42% non-need-based). 73% of past graduating class borrowed through all loan programs. *Average indebtedness per student:* $30,355. *Average need-based loan:* Freshmen: $3213. Undergraduates: $4009. *Parent loans:* $25,582,439 (44% need-based, 56% non-need-based). *Programs:* Federal Direct (Subsidized and Unsubsidized Stafford, PLUS), Perkins, college/university.

WORK-STUDY *Federal work-study:* Total amount: $2,952,289; jobs available.

ATHLETIC AWARDS Total amount: $1,880,050 (53% need-based, 47% non-need-based).

APPLYING FOR FINANCIAL AID *Required financial aid forms:* FAFSA, institution's own form. *Financial aid deadline (priority):* 3/1. *Notification date:* Continuous beginning 9/1.

CONTACT Emily Mattison, Financial Aid Office, Indiana Wesleyan University, 4201 South Washington Street, Marion, IN 46953-4999, 765-677-2839 or toll-free 866-468-6498. *Fax:* 765-677-2809. *E-mail:* finaid@indwes.edu.
Website: http://www.indwes.edu/.

INDIAN RIVER STATE COLLEGE
Fort Pierce, FL

ABOUT THE INSTITUTION State-supported, coed. 92 undergraduate majors.

GIFT AID (NEED-BASED) *Scholarships, grants, and awards:* Federal Pell, FSEOG, state, private, college/university gift aid from institutional funds.

LOANS *Programs:* Federal Direct (Subsidized and Unsubsidized Stafford, PLUS).

WORK-STUDY Federal work-study jobs available.

APPLYING FOR FINANCIAL AID *Required financial aid forms:* FAFSA, institution's own form.

CONTACT Mary Lewis, Director of Financial Aid, Indian River State College, W Building, Main Campus, Fort Pierce, FL 34981, 772-462-7450 or toll-free 866-792-4772. *E-mail:* financialaid-info@irsc.edu.
Website: http://www.irsc.edu/.

INSTE BIBLE COLLEGE
Ankeny, IA

CONTACT Financial Aid Office, INSTE Bible College, 2302 SW 3rd Street, Ankeny, IA 50023, 515-289-9200.
Website: http://www.inste.edu/.

INSTITUTE OF AMERICAN INDIAN ARTS
Santa Fe, NM

CONTACT Lala M. Gallegos, Director of Financial Aid, Institute of American Indian Arts, 83 Avan Nu Po Road, Santa Fe, NM 87508, 505-424-5724. *Fax:* 505-424-0909. *E-mail:* lgallegos@iaia.edu.
Website: http://www.iaia.edu/.

INTER AMERICAN UNIVERSITY OF PUERTO RICO, AGUADILLA CAMPUS
Aguadilla, PR

CONTACT Mr. Juan Gonzalez, Director of Financial Aid, Inter American University of Puerto Rico, Aguadilla Campus, PO Box 20000, Aguadilla, PR 00605, 787-891-0925 Ext. 2108. *Fax:* 787-882-3020.
Website: http://www.aguadilla.inter.edu/.

INTER AMERICAN UNIVERSITY OF PUERTO RICO, ARECIBO CAMPUS
Arecibo, PR

CONTACT Ramón O. de Jesús, Financial Aid Director, Inter American University of Puerto Rico, Arecibo Campus, PO Box 4050, Arecibo, PR 00614-4050, 787-878-5475 Ext. 2275. *Fax:* 787-880-1624.
Website: http://www.arecibo.inter.edu/.

INTER AMERICAN UNIVERSITY OF PUERTO RICO, BARRANQUITAS CAMPUS
Barranquitas, PR

CONTACT Mr. Eduardo Fontanez Colon, Financial Aid Officer, Inter American University of Puerto Rico, Barranquitas Campus, Box 517, Barranquitas, PR 00794, 787-857-3600 Ext. 2049. *Fax:* 787-857-2244.
Website: http://www.br.inter.edu/.

INTER AMERICAN UNIVERSITY OF PUERTO RICO, BAYAMÓN CAMPUS
Bayamón, PR

Tuition & fees: $5178	Average undergraduate aid package: $3615

ABOUT THE INSTITUTION Independent, coed. *Awards:* certificates, associate, bachelor's, and master's degrees. 36 undergraduate majors. *Total enrollment:* 4,612. Undergraduates: 4,507. Freshmen: 1,044. Institutional methodology is used as a basis for awarding need-based institutional aid.
UNDERGRADUATE EXPENSES for 2018–2019 *Comprehensive fee:* $11,292 includes full-time tuition ($4488), mandatory fees ($690), and room and board ($6114). *College room only:* $3113. Full-time tuition and fees vary according to course load and program. *Part-time tuition:* $1122 per credit hour. *Part-time fees:* $187 per credit hour; $305 per semester hour. Part-time tuition and fees vary according to course load and program.
FRESHMAN FINANCIAL AID (Fall 2017, est.) 1,182 applied for aid; of those 98% were deemed to have need. 96% of freshmen with need received aid; of those .2% had need fully met. *Average percent of need met:* 9% (excluding resources awarded to replace EFC). *Average financial aid package:* $1379 (excluding resources awarded to replace EFC).
UNDERGRADUATE FINANCIAL AID (Fall 2017, est.) 2,554 applied for aid; of those 99% were deemed to have need. 99% of undergraduates with need received aid; of those .2% had need fully met. *Average percent of need met:* 30% (excluding resources awarded to replace EFC). *Average financial aid package:* $3615 (excluding resources awarded to replace EFC).
GIFT AID (NEED-BASED) *Total amount:* $1,034,340 (15% federal, 29% state, 56% institutional). *Receiving aid:* Freshmen: 92% (1,105); all full-time undergraduates: 90% (2,387). *Average award:* Freshmen: $1411; Undergraduates: $3110. *Scholarships, grants, and awards:* Federal Pell, state, college/university gift aid from institutional funds.
GIFT AID (NON-NEED-BASED) *ROTC:* Army cooperative.
LOANS *Student loans:* $2,913,304 (100% need-based). *Average need-based loan:* Freshmen: $170. Undergraduates: $2844. *Parent loans:* $447,259 (100% need-based). *Programs:* Perkins.
WORK-STUDY *Federal work-study:* Total amount: $146,439; jobs available.
APPLYING FOR FINANCIAL AID *Required financial aid form:* FAFSA. *Notification date:* Continuous.
CONTACT Mrs. Aurelis Baez, Director of Student Services, Inter American University of Puerto Rico, Bayamón Campus, 500 Dr. John Will Harris Road, Bayamon, PR 00957, 787-279-1912 Ext. 2017. *E-mail:* abaez@bayamon.inter.edu.
Website: http://bayamon.inter.edu/.

INTER AMERICAN UNIVERSITY OF PUERTO RICO, FAJARDO CAMPUS
Fajardo, PR

CONTACT Financial Aid Director, Inter American University of Puerto Rico, Fajardo Campus, Call Box 700003, Fajardo, PR 00738-7003, 787-863-2390 Ext. 2208.
Website: http://www.fajardo.inter.edu/.

INTER AMERICAN UNIVERSITY OF PUERTO RICO, GUAYAMA CAMPUS
Guayama, PR

ABOUT THE INSTITUTION Independent, coed. *Awards:* certificates, associate, bachelor's, and master's degrees. 18 undergraduate majors. *Total enrollment:* 1,927. Undergraduates: 1,815. Freshmen: 245.
GIFT AID (NEED-BASED) *Scholarships, grants, and awards:* Federal Pell, FSEOG, state, college/university gift aid from institutional funds.
LOANS *Programs:* Federal Direct (Subsidized and Unsubsidized Stafford, PLUS).
APPLYING FOR FINANCIAL AID *Required financial aid form:* FAFSA.
CONTACT Mr. Jose A. Vechini, Director of Financial Aid, Inter American University of Puerto Rico, Guayama Campus, Call Box 10004, Guayama, PR 00785, 787-864-2222 Ext. 2206. *Fax:* 787-864-8232. *E-mail:* jose.vechini@guayama.inter.edu.
Website: http://www.guayama.inter.edu/.

INTER AMERICAN UNIVERSITY OF PUERTO RICO, METROPOLITAN CAMPUS
San Juan, PR

CONTACT Mrs. Luz M. Medina, Acting Director of Financial Aid, Inter American University of Puerto Rico, Metropolitan Campus, PO Box 191293, San Juan, PR 00919-1293, 787-758-2891. *Fax:* 787-250-0782.
Website: http://metro.inter.edu/.

INTER AMERICAN UNIVERSITY OF PUERTO RICO, PONCE CAMPUS
Mercedita, PR

Tuition & fees: N/R	Average undergraduate aid package: N/A

ABOUT THE INSTITUTION Independent, coed. **Awards:** certificates, associate, bachelor's, master's, and doctoral degrees. 44 undergraduate majors. **Total enrollment:** 5,288. Undergraduates: 4,868. Freshmen: 894. Both federal and institutional methodology are used as a basis for awarding need-based institutional aid.

FRESHMAN FINANCIAL AID (Fall 2016) 2,306 applied for aid; of those 99% were deemed to have need. 95% of freshmen with need received aid. **Average percent of need met:** 1% (excluding resources awarded to replace EFC).

UNDERGRADUATE FINANCIAL AID (Fall 2016) 11,837 applied for aid; of those 99% were deemed to have need. 93% of undergraduates with need received aid. **Average percent of need met:** 10% (excluding resources awarded to replace EFC).

GIFT AID (NEED-BASED) Total amount: $10,892,820 (95% federal, 1% state, 4% institutional). **Receiving aid:** Freshmen: 94% (2,183); all full-time undergraduates: 91% (10,951). **Average award:** Freshmen: $752; Undergraduates: $3852. **Scholarships, grants, and awards:** Federal Pell, FSEOG, state, college/university gift aid from institutional funds, Federal Nursing.

LOANS Student loans: $1,725,838 (100% need-based). 16% of past graduating class borrowed through all loan programs. **Parent loans:** $284,800 (100% need-based). **Programs:** Federal Direct (Subsidized and Unsubsidized Stafford, PLUS), Perkins.

WORK-STUDY Federal work-study: jobs available.

APPLYING FOR FINANCIAL AID Required financial aid form: FAFSA. **Financial aid deadline:** Continuous. **Notification date:** Continuous.

CONTACT Karen Caquias, Financial Aid Officer, Inter American University of Puerto Rico, Ponce Campus, 104 Turpeaux Industrial Park, Mercedita, PR 00715-2201, 787-284-1912 Ext. 2161. *Fax:* 787-841-0103. *E-mail:* kcaquias@ponce.inter.edu. *Website:* http://www.ponce.inter.edu/.

INTER AMERICAN UNIVERSITY OF PUERTO RICO, SAN GERMÁN CAMPUS
San Germán, PR

CONTACT Ms. Maria I. Lugo, Financial Aid Director, Inter American University of Puerto Rico, San Germán Campus, PO Box 5100, San German, PR 00683-5008, 787-264-1912 Ext. 7252 or toll-free 800-981-8075 (in-state). *Fax:* 787-892-6350. *Website:* http://www.sg.inter.edu/.

INTERIOR DESIGNERS INSTITUTE
Newport Beach, CA

CONTACT Office of Financial Aid, Interior Designers Institute, 1061 Camelback Road, Newport Beach, CA 92660, 949-675-4451. *Website:* http://www.idi.edu/.

INTERNATIONAL BAPTIST COLLEGE AND SEMINARY
Chandler, AZ

CONTACT Financial Aid Office, International Baptist College and Seminary, 2211 West Germann Road, Chandler, AZ 85286, 480-838-7070 Ext. 268 or toll-free 800-422-4858. *Fax:* 480-838-5432. *E-mail:* financialaid@ibconline.edu. *Website:* http://www.ibcs.edu/.

INTERNATIONAL BUSINESS COLLEGE
Fort Wayne, IN

CONTACT Financial Aid Office, International Business College, 5699 Coventry Lane, Fort Wayne, IN 46804, 260-459-4500 or toll-free 800-589-6363. *Website:* http://www.ibcfortwayne.edu/.

IONA COLLEGE
New Rochelle, NY

Tuition & fees: $37,682	Average undergraduate aid package: $26,300

ABOUT THE INSTITUTION Independent Roman Catholic Church, coed. **Awards:** certificates, bachelor's, and master's degrees. 50 undergraduate majors. **Total enrollment:** 3,792. Undergraduates: 3,178. Freshmen: 860. Federal methodology is used as a basis for awarding need-based institutional aid.

UNDERGRADUATE EXPENSES for 2017–2018 Application fee: $50. **Comprehensive fee:** $52,514 includes full-time tuition ($35,482), mandatory fees ($2200), and room and board ($14,832). Room and board charges vary according to board plan. **Part-time tuition:** $1176 per credit hour. **Part-time fees:** $540 per term. Part-time tuition and fees vary according to course load.

FRESHMAN FINANCIAL AID (Fall 2017, est.) 860 applied for aid; of those 91% were deemed to have need. 100% of freshmen with need received aid; of those 14% had need fully met. **Average percent of need met:** 13% (excluding resources awarded to replace EFC). **Average financial aid package:** $26,200 (excluding resources awarded to replace EFC). 9% of all full-time freshmen had no need and received non-need-based gift aid.

UNDERGRADUATE FINANCIAL AID (Fall 2017, est.) 2,890 applied for aid; of those 87% were deemed to have need. 100% of undergraduates with need received aid; of those 19% had need fully met. **Average percent of need met:** 16% (excluding resources awarded to replace EFC). **Average financial aid package:** $26,300 (excluding resources awarded to replace EFC). 12% of all full-time undergraduates had no need and received non-need-based gift aid.

GIFT AID (NEED-BASED) Total amount: $51,095,234 (10% federal, 6% state, 82% institutional, 2% external sources). **Receiving aid:** Freshmen: 40% (341); all full-time undergraduates: 36% (1,072). **Average award:** Freshmen: $5370; Undergraduates: $5720. **Scholarships, grants, and awards:** Federal Pell, FSEOG, state, private, college/university gift aid from institutional funds.

GIFT AID (NON-NEED-BASED) Total amount: $8,781,813 (96% institutional, 4% external sources). **Receiving aid:** Freshmen: 91% (780). Undergraduates: 84% (2,489). **Average award:** Freshmen: $20,001. Undergraduates: $19,100. **Scholarships, grants, and awards by category:** Academic interests/achievement: 1,792 awards ($15,796,188 total): general academic interests/achievements. Creative arts/performance: 19 awards ($84,000 total): music. Special achievements/activities: 6 awards ($88,992 total): community service. Special characteristics: 332 awards ($1,330,978 total): children and siblings of alumni, religious affiliation, siblings of current students, veterans, veterans' children. **Tuition waivers:** Full or partial for children of alumni, employees or children of employees. **ROTC:** Army cooperative, Air Force cooperative.

LOANS Student loans: $18,061,153 (74% need-based, 26% non-need-based). 74% of past graduating class borrowed through all loan programs. **Average indebtedness per student:** $32,487. **Average need-based loan:** Freshmen: $2952. Undergraduates: $3835. **Parent loans:** $13,313,769 (56% need-based, 44% non-need-based). **Programs:** Federal Direct (Subsidized and Unsubsidized Stafford, PLUS), Perkins.

WORK-STUDY Federal work-study: Total amount: $538,275; 409 jobs averaging $1412. **State or other work-study/employment:** Part-time jobs available.

ATHLETIC AWARDS Total amount: $4,499,504 (60% need-based, 40% non-need-based).

APPLYING FOR FINANCIAL AID Required financial aid forms: FAFSA, state aid form. **Financial aid deadline:** 4/15. **Notification date:** Continuous beginning 3/1. Students must reply by 5/1 or within 2 weeks of notification.

CONTACT Mary Grant, Director of Financial Aid, Iona College, 715 North Avenue, New Rochelle, NY 10801-1890, 914-633-2676 or toll-free 800-231-IONA. *Fax:* 914-633-2486. *E-mail:* mgrant@iona.edu. *Website:* http://www.iona.edu/.

IOWA STATE UNIVERSITY OF SCIENCE AND TECHNOLOGY
Ames, IA

Tuition & fees (IA res): $8636	Average undergraduate aid package: $12,456

ABOUT THE INSTITUTION State-supported, coed. **Awards:** certificates, bachelor's, master's, and doctoral degrees. 168 undergraduate majors. **Total enrollment:** 35,993. Undergraduates: 30,406. Freshmen: 5,944. Federal methodology is used as a basis for awarding need-based institutional aid.

UNDERGRADUATE EXPENSES for 2017–2018 Application fee: $40. **Tuition, state resident:** full-time $7456; part-time $311 per credit hour. **Tuition, nonresident:** full-time $21,292; part-time $888 per credit hour. **Required fees:** full-time $1180. Full-time tuition and fees vary according to class time, degree level, program, and student level. Part-time tuition and fees vary according to class time, course load, degree level, program, and student level. **College room and board:** $8546; **Room only:** $4562. Room and board charges vary according to board plan and housing facility.

FRESHMAN FINANCIAL AID (Fall 2016) 5,171 applied for aid; of those 60% were deemed to have need. 99% of freshmen with need received aid; of those 20% had need fully met. **Average percent of need met:** 83% (excluding resources awarded to replace EFC). **Average financial aid package:** $13,195 (excluding resources awarded to replace EFC). 38% of all full-time freshmen had no need and received non-need-based gift aid.

UNDERGRADUATE FINANCIAL AID (Fall 2016) 21,603 applied for aid; of those 66% were deemed to have need. 98% of undergraduates with need received aid; of those 21% had need fully met. **Average percent of need met:** 79% (excluding resources awarded to replace EFC). **Average financial aid package:** $12,456 (excluding resources awarded to replace EFC). 35% of all full-time undergraduates had no need and received non-need-based gift aid.

GIFT AID (NEED-BASED) Total amount: $103,837,187 (29% federal, 1% state, 65% institutional, 5% external sources). **Receiving aid:** Freshmen: 50% (3,060); all full-time undergraduates: 48% (13,736). **Average award:** Freshmen: $8974; Undergraduates: $7606. **Scholarships, grants, and awards:** Federal Pell, FSEOG, state, college/university gift aid from institutional funds.

GIFT AID (NON-NEED-BASED) Total amount: $48,812,344 (6% federal, 1% state, 75% institutional, 18% external sources). **Receiving aid:** Freshmen: 24% (1,504). Undergraduates: 22% (6,204). **Average award:** Freshmen: $4332. Undergraduates: $3463. **Scholarships, grants, and awards by category:** Academic interests/achievement: agriculture, architecture, area/ethnic studies, biological sciences, business, communication, computer science, education, engineering/technologies, English, foreign languages, general academic interests/achievements, health fields, home economics, humanities, international studies, library science, mathematics, military science, physical sciences, premedicine, social sciences. Creative arts/performance: applied art and design, art/fine arts, journalism/publications, music, theater/drama. Special achievements/activities: community service, general special achievements/activities, leadership. Special characteristics: adult students, children and siblings of alumni, ethnic background, first-generation college students, general special characteristics, international students, local/state students, members of minority groups, out-of-state students, veterans, veterans' children. **ROTC:** Army, Naval, Air Force.

LOANS Student loans: $128,555,165 (57% need-based, 43% non-need-based). 59% of past graduating class borrowed through all loan programs. Average indebtedness per student: $27,643. **Average need-based loan:** Freshmen: $3423. Undergraduates: $4408. **Parent loans:** $34,555,693 (26% need-based, 74% non-need-based). **Programs:** Federal Direct (Subsidized and Unsubsidized Stafford, PLUS), Perkins, state, college/university, private loans.

WORK-STUDY Federal work-study: 1,336 jobs averaging $1079. **State or other work-study/employment:** Total amount: $1,181,639 (100% need-based). Part-time jobs available.

ATHLETIC AWARDS Total amount: $8,197,047 (41% need-based, 59% non-need-based).

APPLYING FOR FINANCIAL AID Required financial aid form: FAFSA. **Financial aid deadline (priority):** 12/1. **Notification date:** Continuous beginning 1/30. Students must reply by 5/1.

CONTACT Ms. Roberta Johnson, Director of Financial Aid, Iowa State University of Science and Technology, 0210 Beardshear Hall, 515 Morrill Road, Ames, IA 50011-2103, 515-294-2223 or toll-free 800-262-3810. Fax: 515-294-3622. E-mail: rljohns@iastate.edu.
Website: http://www.iastate.edu/.

IOWA WESLEYAN UNIVERSITY
Mount Pleasant, IA

Tuition & fees: $30,500	Average undergraduate aid package: $21,546

ABOUT THE INSTITUTION Independent United Methodist, coed. **Awards:** bachelor's degrees. 25 undergraduate majors. **Total enrollment:** 473. Undergraduates: 473. Freshmen: 75. Federal methodology is used as a basis for awarding need-based institutional aid.

UNDERGRADUATE EXPENSES for 2017–2018 Application fee: $20. **Comprehensive fee:** $41,000 includes full-time tuition ($29,500), mandatory fees ($1000), and room and board ($10,500). **College room only:** $4000. Room and board charges vary according to housing facility. **Part-time tuition:** $745 per credit hour. Part-time tuition and fees vary according to class time, course load, and location.

FRESHMAN FINANCIAL AID (Fall 2016) 150 applied for aid; of those 100% were deemed to have need. 100% of freshmen with need received aid; of those 13% had need fully met. **Average percent of need met:** 72% (excluding resources awarded to replace EFC). **Average financial aid package:** $25,803 (excluding resources awarded to replace EFC). 3% of all full-time freshmen had no need and received non-need-based gift aid.

UNDERGRADUATE FINANCIAL AID (Fall 2016) 448 applied for aid; of those 100% were deemed to have need. 100% of undergraduates with need received aid; of those 11% had need fully met. **Average percent of need met:** 68% (excluding resources awarded to replace EFC). **Average financial aid package:** $21,546 (excluding resources awarded to replace EFC). 3% of all full-time undergraduates had no need and received non-need-based gift aid.

GIFT AID (NEED-BASED) Total amount: $8,374,208 (14% federal, 7% state, 78% institutional, 1% external sources). **Receiving aid:** Freshmen: 73% (110); all full-time undergraduates: 62% (280). **Average award:** Freshmen: $13,827; Undergraduates: $13,646. **Scholarships, grants, and awards:** Federal Pell, FSEOG, state, private, college/university gift aid from institutional funds.

GIFT AID (NON-NEED-BASED) Receiving aid: Freshmen: 99% (149). Undergraduates: 93% (417). **Average award:** Freshmen: $13,638. Undergraduates: $15,437. **Scholarships, grants, and awards by category:** Academic interests/achievement: 351 awards ($2,953,931 total): business, education, English, general academic interests/achievements, health fields, social sciences. Creative arts/performance: 29 awards ($53,623 total): art/fine arts, music. Special characteristics: 60 awards ($228,371 total): children and siblings of alumni, children of faculty/staff, international students, out-of-state students, siblings of current students. **Tuition waivers:** Full or partial for employees or children of employees.

LOANS Student loans: $2,836,876 (45% need-based, 55% non-need-based). 75% of past graduating class borrowed through all loan programs. Average indebtedness per student: $33,152. **Average need-based loan:** Freshmen: $2056. Undergraduates: $2382. **Parent loans:** $714,044 (100% non-need-based). **Programs:** Federal Direct (Subsidized and Unsubsidized Stafford, PLUS), alternative loans.

WORK-STUDY Federal work-study: 84 jobs averaging $800. **State or other work-study/employment:** Total amount: $7786 (100% need-based). Part-time jobs available.

APPLYING FOR FINANCIAL AID Required financial aid form: FAFSA. **Financial aid deadline:** Continuous. **Notification date:** Continuous beginning 3/15.

CONTACT Kristy J. Johnson, Director of Financial Aid, Iowa Wesleyan University, 601 North Main Street, Mount Pleasant, IA 52641-1398, 319-385-6241 or toll-free 800-582-2383. Fax: 319-385-6203. E-mail: kristy.johnson@iw.edu.
Website: http://www.iw.edu/.

ITHACA COLLEGE
Ithaca, NY

Tuition & fees: $43,978	Average undergraduate aid package: $37,506

ABOUT THE INSTITUTION Independent, coed. **Awards:** certificates, bachelor's, master's, and doctoral degrees. 108 undergraduate majors. **Total enrollment:** 6,516. Undergraduates: 6,059. Freshmen: 1,622. Institutional methodology is used as a basis for awarding need-based institutional aid.

UNDERGRADUATE EXPENSES for 2018–2019 *Application fee:* $60. *Comprehensive fee:* $59,540 includes full-time tuition ($43,978) and room and board ($15,562). *College room only:* $8568. Room and board charges vary according to board plan and housing facility. *Part-time tuition:* $1466 per credit hour.

FRESHMAN FINANCIAL AID (Fall 2017, est.) 1,427 applied for aid; of those 79% were deemed to have need. 100% of freshmen with need received aid; of those 57% had need fully met. *Average percent of need met:* 92% (excluding resources awarded to replace EFC). *Average financial aid package:* $38,729 (excluding resources awarded to replace EFC). 26% of all full-time freshmen had no need and received non-need-based gift aid.

UNDERGRADUATE FINANCIAL AID (Fall 2017, est.) 4,648 applied for aid; of those 87% were deemed to have need. 100% of undergraduates with need received aid; of those 41% had need fully met. *Average percent of need met:* 86% (excluding resources awarded to replace EFC). *Average financial aid package:* $37,506 (excluding resources awarded to replace EFC). 25% of all full-time undergraduates had no need and received non-need-based gift aid.

GIFT AID (NEED-BASED) *Total amount:* $111,028,193 (6% federal, 3% state, 89% institutional, 2% external sources). *Receiving aid:* Freshmen: 68% (1,105); all full-time undergraduates: 67% (3,990). *Average award:* Freshmen: $28,655; Undergraduates: $27,622. *Scholarships, grants, and awards:* Federal Pell, FSEOG, state, private, college/university gift aid from institutional funds.

GIFT AID (NON-NEED-BASED) *Total amount:* $29,800,538 (3% federal, 1% state, 92% institutional, 4% external sources). *Receiving aid:* Freshmen: 23% (377). Undergraduates: 11% (637). *Average award:* Freshmen: $15,972. Undergraduates: $15,712. *Scholarships, grants, and awards by category: Academic interests/achievement:* 4,545 awards ($67,667,216 total): communication, general academic interests/achievements. *Creative arts/performance:* 188 awards ($636,925 total): cinema/film/broadcasting, dance, journalism/publications, music, performing arts, theater/drama. *Special achievements/activities:* 275 awards ($1,507,500 total): leadership. *Special characteristics:* 797 awards ($4,752,837 total): children and siblings of alumni, children of faculty/staff, general special characteristics, members of minority groups, siblings of current students. *Tuition waivers:* Full or partial for children of alumni, employees or children of employees. *ROTC:* Army cooperative, Air Force cooperative.

LOANS *Student loans:* $30,901,010 (76% need-based, 24% non-need-based). 69% of past graduating class borrowed through all loan programs. *Average indebtedness per student:* $42,016. *Average need-based loan:* Freshmen: $5512. Undergraduates: $6512. *Parent loans:* $32,559,172 (39% need-based, 61% non-need-based). *Programs:* Federal Direct (Subsidized and Unsubsidized Stafford, PLUS), Perkins, alternative loans.

WORK-STUDY *Federal work-study:* Total amount: $1,500,000; jobs available. *State or other work-study/employment:* Total amount: $9,417,350 (64% need-based, 36% non-need-based). 1,677 part-time jobs averaging $2402.

APPLYING FOR FINANCIAL AID *Required financial aid forms:* FAFSA, CSS Financial Aid PROFILE. *Financial aid deadline (priority):* 2/1. *Notification date:* Continuous beginning 2/1. Students must reply by 5/1.

CONTACT Ms. Lisa Hoskey, Director of Student Financial Services, Ithaca College, 953 Danby Road, Ithaca, NY 14850-7002, 800-429-4275 or toll-free 800-429-4274. *Fax:* 607-274-1895. *E-mail:* finaid@ithaca.edu. *Website:* http://www.ithaca.edu/.

JACKSON STATE UNIVERSITY
Jackson, MS

Tuition & fees (MS res): $7946	Average undergraduate aid package: $11,286

ABOUT THE INSTITUTION State-supported, coed. *Awards:* certificates, bachelor's, master's, and doctoral degrees. 43 undergraduate majors. *Total enrollment:* 8,558. Undergraduates: 6,500. Freshmen: 933. Federal methodology is used as a basis for awarding need-based institutional aid.

UNDERGRADUATE EXPENSES for 2018–2019 *Tuition, state resident:* full-time $7876; part-time $329 per hour. *Tuition, nonresident:* full-time $19,104; part-time $797 per hour. *Required fees:* full-time $70. Full-time tuition and fees vary according to course level, course load, degree level, and student level. Part-time tuition and fees vary according to course level, degree level, and student level. *College room*

---

and board: $9552; *Room only:* $5784. Room and board charges vary according to housing facility.

FRESHMAN FINANCIAL AID (Fall 2017, est.) 853 applied for aid; of those 90% were deemed to have need. 80% of freshmen with need received aid; of those 10% had need fully met. *Average percent of need met:* 54% (excluding resources awarded to replace EFC). *Average financial aid package:* $12,592 (excluding resources awarded to replace EFC). 2% of all full-time freshmen had no need and received non-need-based gift aid.

UNDERGRADUATE FINANCIAL AID (Fall 2017, est.) 5,548 applied for aid; of those 91% were deemed to have need. 95% of undergraduates with need received aid; of those 9% had need fully met. *Average percent of need met:* 51% (excluding resources awarded to replace EFC). *Average financial aid package:* $11,286 (excluding resources awarded to replace EFC). 2% of all full-time undergraduates had no need and received non-need-based gift aid.

GIFT AID (NEED-BASED) *Total amount:* $21,863,363 (95% federal, 5% state). *Receiving aid:* Freshmen: 56% (518); all full-time undergraduates: 65% (3,883). *Average award:* Freshmen: $5609; Undergraduates: $5179. *Scholarships, grants, and awards:* Federal Pell, FSEOG, state, college/university gift aid from institutional funds.

GIFT AID (NON-NEED-BASED) *Total amount:* $16,088,349 (94% institutional, 6% external sources). *Receiving aid:* Freshmen: 37% (345). Undergraduates: 29% (1,745). *Average award:* Freshmen: $10,059. Undergraduates: $9903. *Scholarships, grants, and awards by category: Academic interests/achievement:* 1,338 awards ($11,169,021 total): general academic interests/achievements. *Creative arts/performance:* 191 awards ($699,606 total): music. *Special achievements/activities:* 87 awards ($86,000 total): leadership. *Special characteristics:* children and siblings of alumni, children of faculty/staff. *Tuition waivers:* Full or partial for children of alumni, employees or children of employees. *ROTC:* Army, Air Force.

LOANS *Student loans:* $39,259,357 (45% need-based, 55% non-need-based). 80% of past graduating class borrowed through all loan programs. *Average indebtedness per student:* $29,864. *Average need-based loan:* Freshmen: $3417. Undergraduates: $4200. *Parent loans:* $12,861,710 (100% non-need-based). *Programs:* Federal Direct (Subsidized and Unsubsidized Stafford, PLUS), Perkins.

WORK-STUDY *Federal work-study:* Total amount: $2,190,209; 1,104 jobs averaging $2097.

ATHLETIC AWARDS Total amount: $2,845,658 (100% non-need-based).

APPLYING FOR FINANCIAL AID *Required financial aid form:* FAFSA. *Financial aid deadline (priority):* 4/15. *Notification date:* Continuous beginning 5/1.

CONTACT Mrs. Glenda Lattimore, Director of Financial Aid, Jackson State University, 1400 J.R. Lynch Street, PO Box 17065, Jackson, MS 39217, 601-979-2227 or toll-free 800-848-6817. *Fax:* 601-979-2237. *E-mail:* glenda.s.lattimore@jsums.edu. *Website:* http://www.jsums.edu/.

JACKSONVILLE STATE UNIVERSITY
Jacksonville, AL

Tuition & fees (AL res): $10,020	Average undergraduate aid package: $9800

ABOUT THE INSTITUTION State-supported, coed. *Awards:* certificates, bachelor's, master's, and doctoral degrees. 63 undergraduate majors. *Total enrollment:* 8,514. Undergraduates: 7,561. Freshmen: 1,320. Federal methodology is used as a basis for awarding need-based institutional aid.

UNDERGRADUATE EXPENSES for 2017–2018 *Application fee:* $35. *Tuition, state resident:* full-time $9270; part-time $309 per credit hour. *Tuition, nonresident:* full-time $18,540; part-time $618 per credit hour. *Required fees:* full-time $750; $750 per year. *College room and board:* $7898. Room and board charges vary according to board plan and housing facility.

FRESHMAN FINANCIAL AID (Fall 2016) 1,233 applied for aid; of those 98% were deemed to have need. 100% of freshmen with need received aid. *Average financial aid package:* $10,352 (excluding resources awarded to replace EFC).

UNDERGRADUATE FINANCIAL AID (Fall 2016) 4,911 applied for aid; of those 98% were deemed to have need. 100% of undergraduates with need received aid. *Average financial aid package:* $9800 (excluding resources awarded to replace EFC).

GIFT AID (NEED-BASED) *Total amount:* $34,394,731 (37% federal, 1% state, 59% institutional, 3% external sources). *Receiving aid:* Freshmen: 41% (526); all full-

time undergraduates. 45% (2,432). *Average award:* Freshmen: $4652; Undergraduates: $4602. *Scholarships, grants, and awards:* Federal Pell, FSEOG, state, private, college/university gift aid from institutional funds.

GIFT AID (NON-NEED-BASED) *Receiving aid:* Freshmen: 70% (901). Undergraduates: 48% (2,622). *Scholarships, grants, and awards by category: Academic interests/achievement:* biological sciences, business, communication, computer science, education, English, general academic interests/achievements, health fields, home economics, humanities, mathematics, military science, physical sciences, social sciences. *Creative arts/performance:* art/fine arts, journalism/publications, music, theater/drama. *Special achievements/activities:* general special achievements/activities, leadership. *Special characteristics:* children and siblings of alumni, local/state students. *Tuition waivers:* Full or partial for employees or children of employees. *ROTC:* Army.

LOANS *Student loans:* $35,315,533 (39% need-based, 61% non-need-based). *Average need-based loan:* Freshmen: $1000. Undergraduates: $1000. *Parent loans:* $3,394,388 (100% non-need-based). *Programs:* Federal Direct (Subsidized and Unsubsidized Stafford, PLUS), state, college/university.

WORK-STUDY *Federal work-study:* jobs available. *State or other work-study/employment:* Total amount: $2,974,779 (100% non-need-based). Part-time jobs available.

ATHLETIC AWARDS Total amount: $4,858,303 (100% non-need-based).

APPLYING FOR FINANCIAL AID *Required financial aid form:* FAFSA. *Financial aid deadline (priority):* 3/15. *Notification date:* Continuous beginning 4/16. Students must reply within 2 weeks of notification.

CONTACT Ms. Vickie Adams, Director of Financial Aid, Jacksonville State University, 700 Pelham Road North, Jacksonville, AL 36265-9982, 256-782-5006 Ext. 8399 or toll-free 800-231-5291. *Fax:* 256-782-5476. *E-mail:* finaid@jsu.edu. *Website:* http://www.jsu.edu/.

JACKSONVILLE UNIVERSITY
Jacksonville, FL

Tuition & fees: $35,260	Average undergraduate aid package: $26,452

ABOUT THE INSTITUTION Independent, coed. *Awards:* certificates, bachelor's, master's, and doctoral degrees. 84 undergraduate majors. *Total enrollment:* 4,222. Undergraduates: 2,877. Freshmen: 576. Federal methodology is used as a basis for awarding need-based institutional aid.

UNDERGRADUATE EXPENSES for 2017–2018 *Application fee:* $30. *Comprehensive fee:* $49,210 includes full-time tuition ($35,260) and room and board ($13,950). *College room only:* $9150. Full-time tuition and fees vary according to course level, course load, degree level, and program. Room and board charges vary according to board plan and housing facility. *Part-time tuition:* $1175 per credit hour. *Part-time fees:* $580 per credit hour. Part-time tuition and fees vary according to course level, course load, degree level, and program.

FRESHMAN FINANCIAL AID (Fall 2017, est.) 574 applied for aid; of those 89% were deemed to have need. 100% of freshmen with need received aid; of those 24% had need fully met. *Average percent of need met:* 89% (excluding resources awarded to replace EFC). *Average financial aid package:* $31,030 (excluding resources awarded to replace EFC). 8% of all full-time freshmen had no need and received non-need-based gift aid.

UNDERGRADUATE FINANCIAL AID (Fall 2017, est.) 2,098 applied for aid; of those 75% were deemed to have need. 100% of undergraduates with need received aid; of those 28% had need fully met. *Average percent of need met:* 75% (excluding resources awarded to replace EFC). *Average financial aid package:* $26,452 (excluding resources awarded to replace EFC). 14% of all full-time undergraduates had no need and received non-need-based gift aid.

GIFT AID (NEED-BASED) *Total amount:* $30,862,461 (13% federal, 14% state, 73% institutional). *Receiving aid:* Freshmen: 84% (511); all full-time undergraduates: 73% (1,578). *Average award:* Freshmen: $25,992; Undergraduates: $19,345. *Scholarships, grants, and awards:* Federal Pell, FSEOG, state, private, college/university gift aid from institutional funds.

GIFT AID (NON-NEED-BASED) *Total amount:* $5,570,992 (13% state, 87% institutional). *Receiving aid:* Freshmen: 10% (63). Undergraduates: 24% (527). *Average award:* Freshmen: $16,757. Undergraduates: $15,448. *Scholarships, grants, and awards by category: Academic interests/achievement:* general academic interests/achievements. *Creative arts/performance:* art/fine arts, general cre-

ative arts/performance, music, theater/drama. *Special achievements/activities:* general special achievements/activities, leadership. *Special characteristics:* children of educators, children of faculty/staff, international students. *Tuition waivers:* Full or partial for employees or children of employees. *ROTC:* Army, Naval.

LOANS *Student loans:* $15,047,777 (89% need-based, 11% non-need-based). *Average need-based loan:* Freshmen: $2497. Undergraduates: $3369. *Parent loans:* $4,820,315 (94% need-based, 6% non-need-based). *Programs:* Federal Direct (Subsidized and Unsubsidized Stafford, PLUS), Perkins.

WORK-STUDY *Federal work-study:* Total amount: $225,243; 252 jobs averaging $894. *State or other work-study/employment:* Total amount: $70,646 (48% need-based, 52% non-need-based). 70 part-time jobs averaging $491.

ATHLETIC AWARDS Total amount: $5,552,858 (66% need-based, 34% non-need-based).

APPLYING FOR FINANCIAL AID *Required financial aid forms:* FAFSA, institution's own form, proof of medical insurance coverage and waiver form. *Financial aid deadline (priority):* 3/31. *Notification date:* Continuous beginning 2/20.

CONTACT Chip Moore, Director of Financial Aid, Jacksonville University, 2800 University Boulevard North, Jacksonville, FL 32211, 904-256-7062 or toll-free 800-225-2027. *Fax:* 904-256-7148. *E-mail:* cmoore@ju.edu. *Website:* http://www.ju.edu/.

JAMES MADISON UNIVERSITY
Harrisonburg, VA

Tuition & fees (VA res): $10,830	Average undergraduate aid package: $8945

ABOUT THE INSTITUTION State-supported, coed. *Awards:* bachelor's, master's, and doctoral degrees (also offers specialist in education degree). 46 undergraduate majors. *Total enrollment:* 21,836. Undergraduates: 19,974. Freshmen: 4,668. Federal methodology is used as a basis for awarding need-based institutional aid.

UNDERGRADUATE EXPENSES for 2017–2018 *Application fee:* $70. *Tuition, state resident:* full-time $6250; part-time $208 per credit hour. *Tuition, nonresident:* full-time $22,614; part-time $735 per credit hour. *Required fees:* full-time $4580. *College room and board:* $9822; *Room only:* $5114. Room and board charges vary according to board plan.

FRESHMAN FINANCIAL AID (Fall 2017, est.) 3,360 applied for aid; of those 65% were deemed to have need. 87% of freshmen with need received aid; of those 86% had need fully met. *Average percent of need met:* 37% (excluding resources awarded to replace EFC). *Average financial aid package:* $8547 (excluding resources awarded to replace EFC). 2% of all full-time freshmen had no need and received non-need-based gift aid.

UNDERGRADUATE FINANCIAL AID (Fall 2017, est.) 11,329 applied for aid; of those 70% were deemed to have need. 91% of undergraduates with need received aid; of those 72% had need fully met. *Average percent of need met:* 41% (excluding resources awarded to replace EFC). *Average financial aid package:* $8945 (excluding resources awarded to replace EFC). 1% of all full-time undergraduates had no need and received non-need-based gift aid.

GIFT AID (NEED-BASED) *Total amount:* $36,089,595 (39% federal, 21% state, 31% institutional, 9% external sources). *Receiving aid:* Freshmen: 25% (1,146); all full-time undergraduates: 22% (4,064). *Average award:* Freshmen: $8415; Undergraduates: $7487. *Scholarships, grants, and awards:* Federal Pell, FSEOG, state, private, college/university gift aid from institutional funds.

GIFT AID (NON-NEED-BASED) *Total amount:* $5,982,025 (2% state, 92% institutional, 6% external sources). *Receiving aid:* Freshmen: 4% (165). Undergraduates: 4% (719). *Average award:* Freshmen: $6601. Undergraduates: $5219. *Scholarships, grants, and awards by category: Academic interests/achievement:* architecture, biological sciences, business, computer science, education, engineering/technologies, English, general academic interests/achievements, health fields, humanities, international studies, mathematics, military science, physical sciences, premedicine, religion/biblical studies, social sciences. *Creative arts/performance:* art/fine arts, cinema/film/broadcasting, dance, journalism/publications, music, theater/drama. *Special achievements/activities:* cheerleading/drum major, general special achievements/activities, leadership. *Special characteristics:* children and siblings of alumni, children of faculty/staff, handicapped students, international students, local/state students, members of minority groups, out-of-state students, siblings of current students. *Tuition waivers:* Full or partial for employees or children of employees. *ROTC:* Army, Air Force cooperative.

LOANS *Student loans:* $71,149,579 (33% need-based, 67% non-need-based). 50% of past graduating class borrowed through all loan programs. *Average indebtedness per student:* $27,656. *Average need-based loan:* Freshmen: $3501. Undergraduates: $4320. *Parent loans:* $46,891,278 (100% non-need-based). *Programs:* Federal Direct (Subsidized and Unsubsidized Stafford, PLUS), Perkins.

WORK-STUDY *Federal work-study:* Total amount: $507,780; jobs available. *State or other work-study/employment:* Total amount: $6,895,350 (100% non-need-based). Part-time jobs available.

ATHLETIC AWARDS Total amount: $7,068,497 (100% non-need-based).

APPLYING FOR FINANCIAL AID *Required financial aid form:* FAFSA. *Financial aid deadline (priority):* 3/1. *Notification date:* Continuous beginning 4/1. Students must reply within 4 weeks of notification.

CONTACT Lisa L. Turner, Director of Financial Aid and Scholarships, James Madison University, 800 South Main Street, MSC 3519, Harrisonburg, VA 22807, 540-568-7820. *Fax:* 540-568-7994. *E-mail:* fin_aid@jmu.edu. *Website:* http://www.jmu.edu/.

JARVIS CHRISTIAN COLLEGE
Hawkins, TX

CONTACT Alice Copeland, Director of Financial Aid, Jarvis Christian College, PO Box 1470, Hawkins, TX 75765, 903-730-4890 Ext. 2402. *Fax:* 903-730-4891. *E-mail:* alice.copeland@jarvis.edu. *Website:* http://www.jarvis.edu/.

JEFFERSON COLLEGE OF HEALTH SCIENCES
Roanoke, VA

Tuition & fees: $26,866	Average undergraduate aid package: N/A

ABOUT THE INSTITUTION Independent, coed. *Awards:* certificates, associate, bachelor's, master's, and doctoral degrees. 12 undergraduate majors. *Total enrollment:* 1,062. Undergraduates: 800. Freshmen: 133. Federal methodology is used as a basis for awarding need-based institutional aid.

UNDERGRADUATE EXPENSES for 2018–2019 *Application fee:* $35. *Comprehensive fee:* $36,380 includes full-time tuition ($26,416), mandatory fees ($450), and room and board ($9514). Full-time tuition and fees vary according to course load. Room and board charges vary according to location. *Part-time tuition:* $765 per credit hour. *Part-time fees:* $150 per year. Part-time tuition and fees vary according to course load.

FRESHMAN FINANCIAL AID (Fall 2016) 41 applied for aid; of those 95% were deemed to have need. 100% of freshmen with need received aid.

UNDERGRADUATE FINANCIAL AID (Fall 2016) 582 applied for aid; of those 96% were deemed to have need. 100% of undergraduates with need received aid.

GIFT AID (NEED-BASED) *Total amount:* $6,732,752 (16% federal, 24% state, 46% institutional, 14% external sources). *Receiving aid:* Freshmen: 93% (39); all full-time undergraduates: 91% (559). *Scholarships, grants, and awards:* Federal Pell, FSEOG, state, private, college/university gift aid from institutional funds.

GIFT AID (NON-NEED-BASED) *Total amount:* $72,760 (100% institutional). *Receiving aid:* Undergraduates: 1% (5). *Scholarships, grants, and awards by category:* Academic interests/achievement: biological sciences. *Special characteristics:* local/state students. *Tuition waivers:* Full or partial for employees or children of employees.

LOANS *Student loans:* $6,902,823 (34% need-based, 66% non-need-based). *Parent loans:* $2,035,470 (100% non-need-based). *Programs:* Federal Direct (Subsidized and Unsubsidized Stafford, PLUS), alternative loans.

WORK-STUDY *Federal work-study:* jobs available. *State or other work-study/employment:* Total amount: $10,320 (100% non-need-based). Part-time jobs available.

APPLYING FOR FINANCIAL AID *Required financial aid forms:* FAFSA, state aid form. *Financial aid deadline (priority):* 5/1. *Notification date:* Continuous beginning 5/1.

CONTACT Debra A. Johnson, Director of Financial Aid, Jefferson College of Health Sciences, 101 Elm Avenue SE, Roanoke, VA 24013-2222, 540-985-8492 or toll-free 888-985-8483. *Fax:* 540-224-6916. *E-mail:* djjohnson@jchs.edu. *Website:* http://www.jchs.edu/.

THE JEWISH THEOLOGICAL SEMINARY
New York, NY

CONTACT Linda Levine, Registrar/Director of Financial Aid, The Jewish Theological Seminary, 3080 Broadway, New York, NY 10027-4649, 212-678-8007. *Fax:* 212-678-8947. *E-mail:* financialaid@jtsa.edu. *Website:* http://www.jtsa.edu/.

JOHN BROWN UNIVERSITY
Siloam Springs, AR

Tuition & fees: $26,928	Average undergraduate aid package: $19,535

ABOUT THE INSTITUTION Independent interdenominational, coed. *Awards:* certificates, associate, bachelor's, and master's degrees. 35 undergraduate majors. *Total enrollment:* 2,613. Undergraduates: 1,972. Freshmen: 326. Federal methodology is used as a basis for awarding need-based institutional aid.

UNDERGRADUATE EXPENSES for 2018–2019 *Application fee:* $25. *Comprehensive fee:* $36,152 includes full-time tuition ($25,750), mandatory fees ($1178), and room and board ($9224). *College room only:* $4424. Full-time tuition and fees vary according to course load and degree level. Room and board charges vary according to board plan and housing facility. *Part-time tuition:* $833 per credit hour. *Part-time fees:* $286 per term. Part-time tuition and fees vary according to course load and degree level.

FRESHMAN FINANCIAL AID (Fall 2016) 268 applied for aid; of those 82% were deemed to have need. 100% of freshmen with need received aid; of those 20% had need fully met. *Average percent of need met:* 78% (excluding resources awarded to replace EFC). *Average financial aid package:* $21,504 (excluding resources awarded to replace EFC). 64% of all full-time freshmen had no need and received non-need-based gift aid.

UNDERGRADUATE FINANCIAL AID (Fall 2016) 1,217 applied for aid; of those 86% were deemed to have need. 100% of undergraduates with need received aid; of those 16% had need fully met. *Average percent of need met:* 67% (excluding resources awarded to replace EFC). *Average financial aid package:* $19,535 (excluding resources awarded to replace EFC). 50% of all full-time undergraduates had no need and received non-need-based gift aid.

GIFT AID (NEED-BASED) *Total amount:* $12,858,129 (19% federal, 9% state, 69% institutional, 3% external sources). *Receiving aid:* Freshmen: 59% (190); all full-time undergraduates: 60% (908). *Average award:* Freshmen: $17,406; Undergraduates: $14,636. *Scholarships, grants, and awards:* Federal Pell, FSEOG, state, private, college/university gift aid from institutional funds.

GIFT AID (NON-NEED-BASED) *Total amount:* $7,669,785 (3% state, 67% institutional, 30% external sources). *Receiving aid:* Freshmen: 62% (200). Undergraduates: 52% (790). *Average award:* Freshmen: $15,252. Undergraduates: $15,114. *Scholarships, grants, and awards by category:* Academic interests/achievement: general academic interests/achievements. Creative arts/performance: art/fine arts, journalism/publications, music, theater/drama. *Tuition waivers:* Full or partial for employees or children of employees. *ROTC:* Army cooperative, Air Force cooperative.

LOANS *Student loans:* $6,836,724 (70% need-based, 30% non-need-based). 59% of past graduating class borrowed through all loan programs. *Average indebtedness per student:* $24,467. *Average need-based loan:* Freshmen: $4540. Undergraduates: $4582. *Parent loans:* $1,991,541 (22% need-based, 78% non-need-based). *Programs:* Federal Direct (Subsidized and Unsubsidized Stafford, PLUS), Perkins, college/university.

WORK-STUDY *Federal work-study:* jobs available. *State or other work-study/employment:* Total amount: $691,110 (86% need-based, 14% non-need-based). Part-time jobs available.

ATHLETIC AWARDS Total amount: $1,059,513 (39% need-based, 61% non-need-based).

APPLYING FOR FINANCIAL AID *Required financial aid forms:* FAFSA, institution's own form, state aid form. *Financial aid deadline (priority):* 3/1. *Notification date:* Continuous beginning 3/1. Students must reply by 5/1.

CONTACT Mr. Kim Eldridge, Director of Student Financial Aid, John Brown University, 2000 West University Street, Siloam Springs, AR 72761-2121, 479-524-7424 or toll-free 877-JBU-INFO. *Fax:* 479-524-7405. *E-mail:* keldridg@jbu.edu. *Website:* http://www.jbu.edu/.

JOHN CARROLL UNIVERSITY
University Heights, OH

Tuition & fees: $39,790	Average undergraduate aid package: $31,771

ABOUT THE INSTITUTION Independent Roman Catholic (Jesuit), coed. *Awards:* certificates, bachelor's, and master's degrees. 53 undergraduate majors. *Total enrollment:* 3,523. Undergraduates: 3,026. Freshmen: 717. Federal methodology is used as a basis for awarding need-based institutional aid.

UNDERGRADUATE EXPENSES for 2017–2018 *One-time required fee:* $325. *Comprehensive fee:* $51,370 includes full-time tuition ($38,490), mandatory fees ($1300), and room and board ($11,580). Full-time tuition and fees vary according to degree level. Room and board charges vary according to board plan and housing facility. *Part-time tuition:* $1283 per credit hour. Part-time tuition and fees vary according to course load and degree level.

FRESHMAN FINANCIAL AID (Fall 2017, est.) 697 applied for aid; of those 81% were deemed to have need. 100% of freshmen with need received aid; of those 23% had need fully met. *Average percent of need met:* 80% (excluding resources awarded to replace EFC). *Average financial aid package:* $31,209 (excluding resources awarded to replace EFC). 25% of all full-time freshmen had no need and received non-need-based gift aid.

UNDERGRADUATE FINANCIAL AID (Fall 2017, est.) 2,449 applied for aid; of those 84% were deemed to have need. 100% of undergraduates with need received aid; of those 23% had need fully met. *Average percent of need met:* 80% (excluding resources awarded to replace EFC). *Average financial aid package:* $31,771 (excluding resources awarded to replace EFC). 27% of all full-time undergraduates had no need and received non-need-based gift aid.

GIFT AID (NEED-BASED) *Total amount:* $52,377,417 (8% federal, 2% state, 89% institutional, 1% external sources). *Receiving aid:* Freshmen: 73% (550); all full-time undergraduates: 70% (2,023). *Average award:* Freshmen: $25,341; Undergraduates: $25,049. *Scholarships, grants, and awards:* Federal Pell, FSEOG, state, private, college/university gift aid from institutional funds.

GIFT AID (NON-NEED-BASED) *Total amount:* $20,156,815 (1% state, 99% institutional). *Receiving aid:* Freshmen: 73% (550). Undergraduates: 70% (2,023). *Average award:* Freshmen: $21,118. Undergraduates: $20,191. *Scholarships, grants, and awards by category:* Academic interests/achievement: biological sciences, business, communication, computer science, education, English, foreign languages, health fields, mathematics, military science, physical sciences, premedicine, religion/biblical studies, social sciences. *Special achievements/activities:* community service, leadership. *Special characteristics:* children of educators, children of faculty/staff, local/state students, veterans, veterans' children. *Tuition waivers:* Full or partial for employees or children of employees, senior citizens. *ROTC:* Army.

LOANS *Student loans:* $17,458,888 (86% need-based, 14% non-need-based). 71% of past graduating class borrowed through all loan programs. *Average indebtedness per student:* $30,860. *Average need-based loan:* Freshmen: $2078. Undergraduates: $3857. *Parent loans:* $6,164,114 (81% need-based, 19% non-need-based). *Programs:* Federal Direct (Subsidized and Unsubsidized Stafford, PLUS), Perkins.

WORK-STUDY *Federal work-study:* Total amount: $1,143,974; jobs available.

APPLYING FOR FINANCIAL AID *Required financial aid form:* FAFSA. *Financial aid deadline (priority):* 2/15. *Notification date:* Continuous beginning 2/15. Students must reply by 5/1 or within 4 weeks of notification.

CONTACT Office of Enrollment and Financial Assistance, John Carroll University, 20700 North Park Boulevard, University Heights, OH 44118-4581, 216-397-4248 or toll-free 888-335-6800. *Fax:* 216-397-3098. *E-mail:* enrollment@jcu.edu. *Website:* http://www.jcu.edu/.

JOHN F. KENNEDY UNIVERSITY
Pleasant Hill, CA

CONTACT Mindy Bergeron, Director of Financial Aid, John F. Kennedy University, 100 Ellinwood Way, Pleasant Hill, CA 94523, 925-969-3385 or toll-free 800-696-JFKU. *Fax:* 925-969-3390. *E-mail:* bergeron@jfku.edu. *Website:* http://www.jfku.edu/.

JOHN JAY COLLEGE OF CRIMINAL JUSTICE OF THE CITY UNIVERSITY OF NEW YORK
New York, NY

Tuition & fees (NY res): $7070	Average undergraduate aid package: $8610

ABOUT THE INSTITUTION State and locally supported, coed. *Awards:* certificates, bachelor's, and master's degrees. 29 undergraduate majors. *Total enrollment:* 14,834. Undergraduates: 12,916. Freshmen: 1,844. Federal methodology is used as a basis for awarding need-based institutional aid.

UNDERGRADUATE EXPENSES for 2017–2018 *Application fee:* $65. *Tuition, state resident:* full-time $6530; part-time $285 per credit hour. *Tuition, nonresident:* full-time $13,920; part-time $580 per credit hour. *Required fees:* full-time $540; $183 per term. *College room and board:* $20,007.

FRESHMAN FINANCIAL AID (Fall 2016) 3,058 applied for aid; of those 92% were deemed to have need. 92% of freshmen with need received aid. *Average percent of need met:* 85% (excluding resources awarded to replace EFC). *Average financial aid package:* $8610 (excluding resources awarded to replace EFC).

UNDERGRADUATE FINANCIAL AID (Fall 2016) 10,236 applied for aid; of those 96% were deemed to have need. 85% of undergraduates with need received aid. *Average percent of need met:* 85% (excluding resources awarded to replace EFC). *Average financial aid package:* $8610 (excluding resources awarded to replace EFC).

GIFT AID (NEED-BASED) *Total amount:* $63,804,956 (52% federal, 42% state, 2% institutional, 4% external sources). *Receiving aid:* Freshmen: 61% (2,389); all full-time undergraduates: 61% (7,707). *Average award:* Freshmen: $2693; Undergraduates: $2693. *Scholarships, grants, and awards:* Federal Pell, FSEOG, state, private, college/university gift aid from institutional funds.

GIFT AID (NON-NEED-BASED) *Receiving aid:* Freshmen: 5% (214). Undergraduates: 2% (226). *Scholarships, grants, and awards by category:* Academic interests/achievement: general academic interests/achievements.

LOANS *Student loans:* $23,179,697 (28% need-based, 72% non-need-based). *Average need-based loan:* Freshmen: $3903. Undergraduates: $3903. *Parent loans:* $1,291,894 (100% non-need-based). *Programs:* Federal Direct (Subsidized and Unsubsidized Stafford, PLUS), Perkins, college/university.

WORK-STUDY *Federal work-study:* jobs available. *State or other work-study/employment:* Part-time jobs available.

APPLYING FOR FINANCIAL AID *Required financial aid forms:* FAFSA, state aid form. *Financial aid deadline:* Continuous. *Notification date:* Continuous beginning 4/1. Students must reply within 2 weeks of notification.

CONTACT Sylvia C. Lopez-Crespo, Director of Financial Aid, John Jay College of Criminal Justice of the City University of New York, 524 West 59th Street, New York, NY 10019-1093, 212-237-8897 or toll-free 877-JOHNJAY. *Fax:* 212-237-8936. *E-mail:* sylopez@jjay.cuny.edu. *Website:* http://www.jjay.cuny.edu/.

JOHN PAUL THE GREAT CATHOLIC UNIVERSITY
Escondido, CA

Tuition & fees: $26,100	Average undergraduate aid package: $16,979

ABOUT THE INSTITUTION Independent Roman Catholic Church, coed. *Awards:* certificates, bachelor's, and master's degrees. 3 undergraduate majors. *Total enrollment:* 329. Undergraduates: 260. Freshmen: 77. Both federal and institutional methodology are used as a basis for awarding need-based institutional aid.

UNDERGRADUATE EXPENSES for 2018–2019 *Application fee:* $50. *Tuition:* full-time $25,200; part-time $667 per credit. Full-time tuition and fees vary according to degree level. Part-time tuition and fees vary according to degree level. Room and board charges vary according to housing facility. *Payment plan:* Guaranteed tuition.

FRESHMAN FINANCIAL AID (Fall 2016) 67 applied for aid; of those 88% were deemed to have need. 100% of freshmen with need received aid; of those 2% had need fully met. *Average percent of need met:* 35% (excluding resources awarded to replace EFC). *Average financial aid package:* $14,238 (excluding resources awarded to replace EFC). 8% of all full-time freshmen had no need and received non-need-based gift aid.

UNDERGRADUATE FINANCIAL AID (Fall 2016) 143 applied for aid; of those 100% were deemed to have need. 100% of undergraduates with need received aid; of those 8% had need fully met. *Average percent of need met:* 43% (excluding resources awarded to replace EFC). *Average financial aid package:* $16,979 (excluding resources awarded to replace EFC). 20% of all full-time undergraduates had no need and received non-need-based gift aid.

GIFT AID (NEED-BASED) *Total amount:* $1,973,064 (13% federal, 8% state, 78% institutional, 1% external sources). *Receiving aid:* Freshmen: 81% (59); all full-time undergraduates: 68% (143). *Average award:* Freshmen: $11,936; Undergraduates: $13,798. *Scholarships, grants, and awards:* Federal Pell, FSEOG, state, private, college/university gift aid from institutional funds.

GIFT AID (NON-NEED-BASED) *Total amount:* $754,293 (100% institutional). *Receiving aid:* Freshmen: 5% (4). Undergraduates: 4% (8). *Average award:* Freshmen: $6083. Undergraduates: $8312. *Scholarships, grants, and awards by category:* Academic interests/achievement: general academic interests/achievements. Creative arts/performance: general creative arts/performance. Special achievements/activities: leadership.

LOANS *Student loans:* $1,251,247 (87% need-based, 13% non-need-based). *Average need-based loan:* Freshmen: $2917. Undergraduates: $3907. *Parent loans:* $786,561 (61% need-based, 39% non-need-based). *Programs:* Federal Direct (Subsidized and Unsubsidized Stafford, PLUS).

WORK-STUDY *Federal work-study:* jobs available.

APPLYING FOR FINANCIAL AID *Required financial aid forms:* FAFSA, institution's own form. *Financial aid deadline (priority):* 4/15. *Notification date:* Continuous beginning 10/1. Students must reply by 5/1 or within 2 weeks of notification.

CONTACT Lisa Williams, Director of Financial Aid, John Paul the Great Catholic University, 220 West Grand Avenue, Escondido, CA 92025, 858-653-6740 Ext. 1303. *Fax:* 858-653-3791. *E-mail:* lwilliams@jpcatholic.com. *Website:* http://www.jpcatholic.edu/.

JOHNS HOPKINS UNIVERSITY
Baltimore, MD

CONTACT Mr. Tom McDermott, Director of Student Financial Services, Johns Hopkins University, 146 Garland Hall, Baltimore, MD 21218, 410-516-8028. *Fax:* 410-516-6015. *E-mail:* tmcderm1@jhu.edu. *Website:* http://www.jhu.edu/.

JOHNSON & WALES UNIVERSITY
Denver, CO

CONTACT Ms. Lynn Robinson, Executive Director of Student Financial Services, Johnson & Wales University, 8 Abbott Park Place, Providence, RI 02903, 401-598-4648 or toll-free 877-598-3368. *Fax:* 401-598-1040. *E-mail:* fp@jwu.edu. *Website:* http://www.jwu.edu/denver/.

JOHNSON & WALES UNIVERSITY
North Miami, FL

CONTACT Ms. Lynn Robinson, Executive Director of Student Financial Services, Johnson & Wales University, 8 Abbott Park Place, Providence, RI 02903, 401-598-4648 or toll-free 866-598-3567. *Fax:* 401-598-1040. *E-mail:* fp@jwu.edu. *Website:* http://www.jwu.edu/northmiami/.

JOHNSON & WALES UNIVERSITY
Charlotte, NC

CONTACT Ms. Lynn Robinson, Executive Director of Student Financial Services, Johnson & Wales University, 8 Abbott Park Place, Providence, RI 02903, 401-598-1648 or toll-free 866-598-2427. *Fax:* 401-598-4751. *E-mail:* fp@jwu.edu. *Website:* http://www.jwu.edu/charlotte/.

JOHNSON & WALES UNIVERSITY
Providence, RI

CONTACT Ms. Lynn Robinson, Executive Director of Student Financial Services, Johnson & Wales University, 8 Abbott Park Place, Providence, RI 02903, 401-598-4648 or toll-free 800-342-5598. *Fax:* 401-598-1040. *E-mail:* fp@jwu.edu. *Website:* http://www.jwu.edu/providence/.

JOHNSON C. SMITH UNIVERSITY
Charlotte, NC

Tuition & fees: $18,236	Average undergraduate aid package: $15,658

ABOUT THE INSTITUTION Independent, coed. *Awards:* bachelor's and master's degrees. 24 undergraduate majors. *Total enrollment:* 1,483. Undergraduates: 1,394. Freshmen: 339. Federal methodology is used as a basis for awarding need-based institutional aid.

UNDERGRADUATE EXPENSES for 2017–2018 *Application fee:* $25. *Comprehensive fee:* $25,336 includes full-time tuition ($18,236) and room and board ($7100). *College room only:* $4086. Full-time tuition and fees vary according to course load. Room and board charges vary according to board plan and housing facility. *Part-time tuition:* $418 per credit hour. Part-time tuition and fees vary according to course load.

FRESHMAN FINANCIAL AID (Fall 2016) 291 applied for aid; of those 95% were deemed to have need. 100% of freshmen with need received aid; of those 4% had need fully met. *Average percent of need met:* 58% (excluding resources awarded to replace EFC). *Average financial aid package:* $16,143 (excluding resources awarded to replace EFC). 5% of all full-time freshmen had no need and received non-need-based gift aid.

UNDERGRADUATE FINANCIAL AID (Fall 2016) 1,222 applied for aid; of those 97% were deemed to have need. 99% of undergraduates with need received aid; of those 5% had need fully met. *Average percent of need met:* 58% (excluding resources awarded to replace EFC). *Average financial aid package:* $15,658 (excluding resources awarded to replace EFC). 6% of all full-time undergraduates had no need and received non-need-based gift aid.

GIFT AID (NEED-BASED) *Total amount:* $12,316,983 (41% federal, 21% state, 34% institutional, 4% external sources). *Receiving aid:* Freshmen: 87% (261); all full-time undergraduates: 88% (1,127). *Average award:* Freshmen: $13,405; Undergraduates: $11,855. *Scholarships, grants, and awards:* Federal Pell, FSEOG, state, private, college/university gift aid from institutional funds, United Negro College Fund.

GIFT AID (NON-NEED-BASED) *Total amount:* $1,268,329 (3% state, 92% institutional, 5% external sources). *Receiving aid:* Freshmen: 3% (9). Undergraduates: 3% (43). *Average award:* Freshmen: $13,707. Undergraduates: $14,336. *Scholarships, grants, and awards by category: Academic interests/achievement:* biological sciences, computer science, engineering/technologies, general academic interests/achievements, mathematics. *Creative arts/performance:* music. *Special achievements/activities:* general special achievements/activities. *Special characteristics:* children of faculty/staff, ethnic background, general special characteristics, international students, out-of-state students, siblings of current students. *Tuition waivers:* Full or partial for employees or children of employees.

LOANS *Student loans:* $9,471,823 (93% need-based, 7% non-need-based). 79% of past graduating class borrowed through all loan programs. *Average indebtedness per student:* $35,769. *Average need-based loan:* Freshmen: $3476. Undergraduates: $4036. *Parent loans:* $5,531,349 (77% need-based, 23% non-need-based). *Programs:* Federal Direct (Subsidized and Unsubsidized Stafford, PLUS).

WORK-STUDY *Federal work-study:* jobs available. *State or other work-study/employment:* Total amount: $282,810 (68% need-based, 32% non-need-based). Part-time jobs available.

ATHLETIC AWARDS Total amount: $1,774,402 (65% need-based, 35% non-need-based).

APPLYING FOR FINANCIAL AID *Required financial aid forms:* FAFSA, state aid form. *Financial aid deadline:* 4/1 (priority: 3/1). *Notification date:* Continuous beginning 3/15.

CONTACT Shelline Warren, Office of Financial Aid, Johnson C. Smith University, 100 Beatties Ford Road, Charlotte, NC 28216, 704-378-1498 or toll-free 800-782-7303. *Fax:* 704-378-1292.
Website: http://www.jcsu.edu/.

JOHNSON UNIVERSITY
Knoxville, TN

Tuition & fees: $16,060	Average undergraduate aid package: $11,438

ABOUT THE INSTITUTION Independent Christian Churches and Churches of Christ, coed. *Awards:* certificates, associate, bachelor's, master's, and doctoral degrees. 12 undergraduate majors. *Total enrollment:* 1,158. Undergraduates: 814. Freshmen: 153. Federal methodology is used as a basis for awarding need-based institutional aid.

UNDERGRADUATE EXPENSES for 2018–2019 *Application fee:* $35. *Comprehensive fee:* $22,760 includes full-time tuition ($14,880), mandatory fees ($1180), and room and board ($6700). *College room only:* $3000. Full-time tuition and fees vary according to class time, course load, degree level, location, and program. Room and board charges vary according to board plan, housing facility, and location. *Part-time tuition:* $470 per credit hour. Part-time tuition and fees vary according to class time, course load, degree level, location, and program.

FRESHMAN FINANCIAL AID (Fall 2017, est.) 174 applied for aid; of those 86% were deemed to have need. 99% of freshmen with need received aid; of those 11% had need fully met. *Average percent of need met:* 63% (excluding resources awarded to replace EFC). *Average financial aid package:* $11,285 (excluding resources awarded to replace EFC). 13% of all full-time freshmen had no need and received non-need-based gift aid.

UNDERGRADUATE FINANCIAL AID (Fall 2017, est.) 655 applied for aid; of those 85% were deemed to have need. 100% of undergraduates with need received aid; of those 12% had need fully met. *Average percent of need met:* 64% (excluding resources awarded to replace EFC). *Average financial aid package:* $11,438 (excluding resources awarded to replace EFC). 14% of all full-time undergraduates had no need and received non-need-based gift aid.

GIFT AID (NEED-BASED) *Total amount:* $4,510,922 (34% federal, 16% state, 38% institutional, 12% external sources). *Receiving aid:* Freshmen: 82% (148); all full-time undergraduates: 77% (527). *Average award:* Freshmen: $8376; Undergraduates: $8142. *Scholarships, grants, and awards:* Federal Pell, FSEOG, state, private, college/university gift aid from institutional funds.

GIFT AID (NON-NEED-BASED) *Total amount:* $958,377 (16% state, 58% institutional, 26% external sources). *Receiving aid:* Freshmen: 8% (15). Undergraduates: 8% (57). *Average award:* Freshmen: $3120. Undergraduates: $4772. *Scholarships, grants, and awards by category: Academic interests/achievement:* business, communication, education, general academic interests/achievements, religion/biblical studies. *Creative arts/performance:* art/fine arts, general creative arts/performance, music. *Special achievements/activities:* community service, general special achievements/activities, leadership, religious involvement. *Special characteristics:* children of current students, children of educators, children of faculty/staff, ethnic background, general special characteristics, international students, married students, members of minority groups, parents of current students, relatives of clergy, religious affiliation, siblings of current students, spouses of current students. *Tuition waivers:* Full or partial for employees or children of employees.

LOANS *Student loans:* $4,018,621 (77% need-based, 23% non-need-based). 73% of past graduating class borrowed through all loan programs. *Average indebtedness per student:* $24,353. *Average need-based loan:* Freshmen: $3752. Undergraduates: $4320. *Parent loans:* $1,594,291 (36% need-based, 64% non-need-based). *Programs:* Federal Direct (Subsidized and Unsubsidized Stafford, PLUS), alternative loans.

WORK-STUDY *Federal work-study:* Total amount: $137,554; jobs available. *State or other work-study/employment:* Part-time jobs available.

APPLYING FOR FINANCIAL AID *Required financial aid forms:* FAFSA, institution's own form. *Financial aid deadline:* Continuous. *Notification date:* Continuous beginning 12/1. Students must reply within 4 weeks of notification.

CONTACT Office of Student Financial Aid, Johnson University, 7900 Johnson Drive, Knoxville, TN 37998, 865-251-2303 or toll-free 800-827-2122. *Fax:* 865-251-2337. *E-mail:* financialaid@johnsonu.edu.
Website: http://www.johnsonu.edu/.

JOHNSON UNIVERSITY FLORIDA
Kissimmee, FL

Tuition & fees: $16,060	Average undergraduate aid package: $11,929

ABOUT THE INSTITUTION Independent Christian Churches and Churches of Christ, coed. *Awards:* certificates, associate, bachelor's, and master's degrees. 11 undergraduate majors. *Total enrollment:* 185. Undergraduates: 180. Freshmen: 56. Federal methodology is used as a basis for awarding need-based institutional aid.

UNDERGRADUATE EXPENSES for 2018–2019 *Application fee:* $35. *Comprehensive fee:* $22,760 includes full-time tuition ($14,880), mandatory fees ($1180), and room and board ($6700). *College room only:* $3000. Full-time tuition and fees vary according to course load and degree level. *Part-time tuition:* $470 per credit hour. Part-time tuition and fees vary according to degree level.

FRESHMAN FINANCIAL AID (Fall 2017, est.) 69 applied for aid; of those 91% were deemed to have need. 100% of freshmen with need received aid; of those 13% had need fully met. *Average percent of need met:* 64% (excluding resources awarded to replace EFC). *Average financial aid package:* $11,487 (excluding resources awarded to replace EFC). 9% of all full-time freshmen had no need and received non-need-based gift aid.

UNDERGRADUATE FINANCIAL AID (Fall 2017, est.) 162 applied for aid; of those 93% were deemed to have need. 100% of undergraduates with need received aid; of those 13% had need fully met. *Average percent of need met:* 66% (excluding resources awarded to replace EFC). *Average financial aid package:* $11,929 (excluding resources awarded to replace EFC). 7% of all full-time undergraduates had no need and received non-need-based gift aid.

GIFT AID (NEED-BASED) *Total amount:* $1,351,993 (40% federal, 35% state, 20% institutional, 5% external sources). *Receiving aid:* Freshmen: 85% (63); all full-time undergraduates: 89% (148). *Average award:* Freshmen: $9311; Undergraduates: $8960. *Scholarships, grants, and awards:* Federal Pell, FSEOG, state, private, college/university gift aid from institutional funds.

GIFT AID (NON-NEED-BASED) *Total amount:* $162,798 (4% federal, 42% state, 38% institutional, 16% external sources). *Receiving aid:* Freshmen: 11% (8). Undergraduates: 11% (18). *Average award:* Freshmen: $6162. Undergraduates: $4757. *Scholarships, grants, and awards by category: Academic interests/achievement:* education, religion/biblical studies. *Creative arts/performance:* music. *Special characteristics:* children and siblings of alumni, children of faculty/staff, relatives of clergy, religious affiliation, spouses of current students. *Tuition waivers:* Full or partial for employees or children of employees.

LOANS *Student loans:* $862,903 (87% need-based, 13% non-need-based). 86% of past graduating class borrowed through all loan programs. *Average indebtedness per student:* $28,906. *Average need-based loan:* Freshmen: $2993. Undergraduates: $3660. *Parent loans:* $176,125 (45% need-based, 55% non-need-based). *Programs:* Federal Direct (Subsidized and Unsubsidized Stafford, PLUS), alternative loans, Sallie Mae Loans.

WORK-STUDY *Federal work-study:* Total amount: $35,479; jobs available. *State or other work-study/employment:* Total amount: $11,590 (100% need-based). Part-time jobs available.

APPLYING FOR FINANCIAL AID *Required financial aid forms:* FAFSA, institution's own form. *Financial aid deadline:* Continuous. *Notification date:* Continuous beginning 12/1. Students must reply within 4 weeks of notification.

CONTACT Office of Student Financial Aid, Johnson University Florida, 1011 Bill Beck Boulevard, Kissimmee, FL 34744-5301, 407-569-1353 or toll-free 888-468-6322. *Fax:* 321-206-2007. *E-mail:* financialaidfl@johnsonu.edu. *Website:* http://www.johnsonu.edu/.

JOHN WESLEY UNIVERSITY
High Point, NC

ABOUT THE INSTITUTION Independent interdenominational, coed. *Awards:* certificates, associate, bachelor's, master's, and doctoral degrees. 7 undergraduate majors. *Total enrollment:* 159. Undergraduates: 136. Freshmen: 31.

GIFT AID (NEED-BASED) *Scholarships, grants, and awards:* Federal Pell, FSEOG, state, private, college/university gift aid from institutional funds.

GIFT AID (NON-NEED-BASED) *Scholarships, grants, and awards by category:* Academic interests/achievement: business, education, general academic interests/achievements, religion/biblical studies. *Creative arts/performance:* music. *Special achievements/activities:* leadership. *Special characteristics:* children of faculty/staff, general special characteristics, married students, spouses of current students.

LOANS *Programs:* Federal Direct (Subsidized and Unsubsidized Stafford, PLUS).

WORK-STUDY *Federal work-study:* 7 jobs averaging $1671. *State or other work-study/employment:* Total amount: $20,936 (100% need-based). 13 part-time jobs averaging $1610.

APPLYING FOR FINANCIAL AID *Required financial aid form:* FAFSA.

CONTACT Mrs. Mary Emily Kennon, Assistant Director of Business Affairs, John Wesley University, 1215 Eastchester Drive, High Point, NC 27265, 336-887-3000 or toll-free 855-528-7358. *Fax:* 336-889-2261. *E-mail:* mkennon@johnwesley.edu. *Website:* http://www.johnwesley.edu/.

JOSE MARIA VARGAS UNIVERSITY
Pembroke Pines, FL

CONTACT Financial Aid Office, Jose Maria Vargas University, 10131 Pines Boulevard, Pembroke Pines, FL 33026, 954-322-4446. *Website:* http://www.jmvu.edu/.

JUDSON COLLEGE
Marion, AL

ABOUT THE INSTITUTION Independent Baptist, coed, primarily women. 22 undergraduate majors.

GIFT AID (NEED-BASED) *Scholarships, grants, and awards:* Federal Pell, FSEOG, state, private, college/university gift aid from institutional funds, Academic Competitiveness Grants, National SMART Grants, TEACH Grants.

GIFT AID (NON-NEED-BASED) *Scholarships, grants, and awards by category:* Academic interests/achievement: biological sciences, general academic interests/achievements, premedicine. *Creative arts/performance:* art/fine arts, music. *Special achievements/activities:* general special achievements/activities. *Special characteristics:* children of educators, children of faculty/staff, relatives of clergy, religious affiliation.

LOANS *Programs:* Perkins, college/university.

APPLYING FOR FINANCIAL AID *Required financial aid forms:* FAFSA, state aid form.

CONTACT Mrs. Melena Verity, Acting Director of Financial Aid, Judson College, 302 Bibb Street, Marion, AL 36756, 334-683-5170 or toll-free 800-447-9472. *Fax:* 334-683-5282. *E-mail:* mverity@judson.edu. *Website:* http://www.judson.edu/.

JUDSON UNIVERSITY
Elgin, IL

Tuition & fees: $29,860	Average undergraduate aid package: $23,674

ABOUT THE INSTITUTION Independent Baptist, coed. *Awards:* certificates, associate, bachelor's, master's, and doctoral degrees. 41 undergraduate majors. *Total enrollment:* 1,283. Undergraduates: 1,081. Freshmen: 181. Federal methodology is used as a basis for awarding need-based institutional aid.

UNDERGRADUATE EXPENSES for 2018–2019 *Application fee:* $50. *One-time required fee:* $100. *Comprehensive fee:* $39,848 includes full-time tuition ($28,834), mandatory fees ($1026), and room and board ($9988). *College room only:* $7764. Full-time tuition and fees vary according to class time, course load, degree level, and program. Room and board charges vary according to board plan. *Part-time tuition:* $1185 per credit hour. Part-time tuition and fees vary according to class time, course load, degree level, and program.

FRESHMAN FINANCIAL AID (Fall 2017, est.) 153 applied for aid; of those 91% were deemed to have need. 100% of freshmen with need received aid; of those 14% had need fully met. *Average percent of need met:* 63% (excluding resources awarded to replace EFC). *Average financial aid package:* $25,767 (excluding resources awarded to replace EFC). 8% of all full-time freshmen had no need and received non-need-based gift aid.

UNDERGRADUATE FINANCIAL AID (Fall 2017, est.) 614 applied for aid; of those 92% were deemed to have need. 100% of undergraduates with need received aid; of those 20% had need fully met. *Average percent of need met:* 60% (excluding resources awarded to replace EFC). *Average financial aid package:* $23,674 (excluding resources awarded to replace EFC). 8% of all full-time undergraduates had no need and received non-need-based gift aid.

GIFT AID (NEED-BASED) *Total amount:* $4,740,157 (45% federal, 27% state, 28% institutional). *Receiving aid:* Freshmen: 11% (19); all full-time undergraduates: 37% (387). *Average award:* Freshmen: $7877; Undergraduates: $7943. *Scholarships, grants, and awards:* Federal Pell, FSEOG, state, private, college/university gift aid from institutional funds.

GIFT AID (NON-NEED-BASED) *Total amount:* $6,800,917 (98% institutional, 2% external sources). *Receiving aid:* Freshmen: 83% (139). Undergraduates: 53% (552). *Average award:* Freshmen: $15,183. Undergraduates: $11,724. *Scholarships, grants, and awards by category:* Academic interests/achievement: general academic interests/achievements. *Creative arts/performance:* art/fine arts, music, theater/drama. *Special achievements/activities:* 17 awards ($157,831 total): leadership. *Special characteristics:* 6 awards ($23,000 total): members of minority groups. *Tuition waivers:* Full or partial for employees or children of employees, adult students, senior citizens. *ROTC:* Army cooperative.

LOANS *Student loans:* $361,494 (100% need-based). 72% of past graduating class borrowed through all loan programs. *Average indebtedness per student:* $39,021. *Average need-based loan:* Freshmen: $5503. Undergraduates: $4854. *Parent loans:* $983,312 (100% non-need-based). *Programs:* Federal Direct (Subsidized and Unsubsidized Stafford, PLUS), Perkins.

WORK-STUDY *Federal work-study:* Total amount: $474,342; 311 jobs averaging $1525. *State or other work-study/employment:* Part-time jobs available.

ATHLETIC AWARDS Total amount: $2,678,420 (100% non-need-based).

APPLYING FOR FINANCIAL AID *Required financial aid form:* FAFSA. *Financial aid deadline:* 8/1 (priority: 3/1). *Notification date:* Continuous beginning 3/1. Students must reply by 5/1 or within 4 weeks of notification.

CONTACT Diana Winton, Director of Financial Aid, Judson University, 1151 North State Street, Elgin, IL 60123-1498, 847-628-2532 or toll-free 800-879-5376. *Fax:* 847-628-2533. *E-mail:* diana.winton@judsonu.edu. *Website:* http://www.judsonu.edu/.

THE JUILLIARD SCHOOL
New York, NY

Tuition & fees: $43,520	Average undergraduate aid package: $35,281

ABOUT THE INSTITUTION Independent, coed. *Awards:* certificates, diplomas, bachelor's, master's, and doctoral degrees. 4 undergraduate majors. *Total enrollment:* 927. Undergraduates: 566. Freshmen: 110. Federal methodology is used as a basis for awarding need-based institutional aid.

UNDERGRADUATE EXPENSES for 2017–2018 *Application fee:* $110. *Comprehensive fee:* $59,510 includes full-time tuition ($43,170), mandatory fees ($350), and room and board ($15,990).

FRESHMAN FINANCIAL AID (Fall 2017, est.) 103 applied for aid; of those 85% were deemed to have need. 100% of freshmen with need received aid; of those 33% had need fully met. *Average percent of need met:* 82% (excluding resources awarded to replace EFC). *Average financial aid package:* $38,790 (excluding resources awarded to replace EFC). 9% of all full-time freshmen had no need and received non-need-based gift aid.

UNDERGRADUATE FINANCIAL AID (Fall 2017, est.) 421 applied for aid; of those 85% were deemed to have need. 100% of undergraduates with need received aid; of those 31% had need fully met. *Average percent of need met:* 77% (excluding resources awarded to replace EFC). *Average financial aid package:* $35,281 (excluding resources awarded to replace EFC). 12% of all full-time undergraduates had no need and received non-need-based gift aid.

GIFT AID (NEED-BASED) *Total amount:* $10,917,740 (5% federal, 92% institutional, 3% external sources). *Receiving aid:* Freshmen: 80% (88); all full-time undergraduates: 72% (350). *Average award:* Freshmen: $34,726; Undergraduates: $30,721. *Scholarships, grants, and awards:* Federal Pell, FSEOG, state, private, college/university gift aid from institutional funds.

GIFT AID (NON-NEED-BASED) *Total amount:* $2,741,833 (99% institutional, 1% external sources). *Receiving aid:* Freshmen: 5% (6). Undergraduates: 2% (9). *Average award:* Freshmen: $19,017. Undergraduates: $21,139. *Scholarships, grants, and awards by category:* Creative arts/performance: dance, music, performing arts, theater/drama. *Tuition waivers:* Full or partial for employees or children of employees.

LOANS *Student loans:* $2,501,494 (84% need-based, 16% non-need-based). 49% of past graduating class borrowed through all loan programs. *Average indebtedness per student:* $33,025. *Average need-based loan:* Freshmen: $3819. Undergraduates: $4802. *Parent loans:* $2,501,494 (84% need-based, 16% non-need-based). *Programs:* Federal Direct (Subsidized and Unsubsidized Stafford, PLUS).

WORK-STUDY *Federal work-study:* Total amount: $320,872; 167 jobs averaging $1921. *State or other work-study/employment:* Total amount: $586,000 (64% need-based, 36% non-need-based). 294 part-time jobs averaging $1993.

APPLYING FOR FINANCIAL AID *Required financial aid forms:* FAFSA, CSS Financial Aid PROFILE. *Financial aid deadline:* 3/1. *Notification date:* 4/1. Students must reply by 5/1.

CONTACT Ms. Tina Gonzalez, Director of Financial Aid, The Juilliard School, 60 Lincoln Center Plaza, New York, NY 10023, 212-799-5000 Ext. 211. *Fax:* 212-358-2594. *E-mail:* financialaid@juilliard.edu. *Website:* http://www.juilliard.edu/.

JUNIATA COLLEGE
Huntingdon, PA

Tuition & fees: $45,597	Average undergraduate aid package: $36,787

ABOUT THE INSTITUTION Independent Church of the Brethren, coed. *Awards:* bachelor's and master's degrees. 63 undergraduate majors. *Total enrollment:* 1,495. Undergraduates: 1,485. Freshmen: 341. Federal methodology is used as a basis for awarding need-based institutional aid.

UNDERGRADUATE EXPENSES for 2018–2019 *Comprehensive fee:* $58,118 includes full-time tuition ($44,772), mandatory fees ($825), and room and board ($12,521). *College room only:* $6666. Full-time tuition and fees vary according to course load, degree level, and program. Room and board charges vary according to board plan and housing facility. Part-time tuition and fees vary according to course load and degree level.

FRESHMAN FINANCIAL AID (Fall 2017, est.) 312 applied for aid; of those 88% were deemed to have need. 98% of freshmen with need received aid; of those 16% had need fully met. *Average percent of need met:* 84% (excluding resources awarded to replace EFC). *Average financial aid package:* $37,720 (excluding resources awarded to replace EFC). 21% of all full-time freshmen had no need and received non-need-based gift aid.

UNDERGRADUATE FINANCIAL AID (Fall 2017, est.) 1,137 applied for aid; of those 92% were deemed to have need. 98% of undergraduates with need received aid; of those 17% had need fully met. *Average percent of need met:* 83% (excluding resources awarded to replace EFC). *Average financial aid package:* $36,787 (excluding resources awarded to replace EFC). 24% of all full-time undergraduates had no need and received non-need-based gift aid.

GIFT AID (NEED-BASED) *Total amount:* $31,088,818 (6% federal, 5% state, 88% institutional, 1% external sources). *Receiving aid:* Freshmen: 75% (269); all full-time undergraduates: 74% (1,024). *Average award:* Freshmen: $32,238; Undergraduates: $30,389. *Scholarships, grants, and awards:* Federal Pell, FSEOG, state, private, college/university gift aid from institutional funds.

GIFT AID (NON-NEED-BASED) *Total amount:* $8,613,846 (99% institutional, 1% external sources). *Receiving aid:* Freshmen: 75% (269). Undergraduates: 74% (1,024). *Average award:* Freshmen: $24,402. Undergraduates: $22,987. *Scholarships, grants, and awards by category:* Academic interests/achievement: biological sciences, business, communication, computer science, education, foreign languages, general academic interests/achievements, home economics, humanities, international studies, mathematics, physical sciences, premedicine, social sciences. *Creative arts/performance:* art/fine arts, music, performing arts, theater/drama. *Special achievements/activities:* community service, general special achievements/activities, leadership. *Special characteristics:* children and siblings of alumni, children of faculty/staff, ethnic background, first-generation college students, international students, local/state students, siblings of current students. *Tuition waivers:* Full or partial for employees or children of employees, senior citizens.

LOANS *Student loans:* $10,184,981 (67% need-based, 33% non-need-based). 70% of past graduating class borrowed through all loan programs. *Average indebtedness per student:* $38,478. *Average need-based loan:* Freshmen: $4859. Undergraduates: $5950. *Parent loans:* $2,977,502 (51% need-based, 49% non-need-based). *Programs:* Federal Direct (Subsidized and Unsubsidized Stafford, PLUS), Perkins, college/university.

WORK-STUDY *Federal work-study:* Total amount: $1,083,885; 334 jobs averaging $480. *State or other work-study/employment:* Total amount: $745,100 (15% need-based, 85% non-need-based). 739 part-time jobs averaging $875.

APPLYING FOR FINANCIAL AID *Required financial aid form:* FAFSA. *Financial aid deadline (priority):* 2/15. *Notification date:* Continuous beginning 3/1. Students must reply by 5/1 or within 2 weeks of notification.

CONTACT Tracie Patrick, Director of Student Financial Planning, Juniata College, 1700 Moore Street, Huntingdon, PA 16652-2119, 814-641-3140 or toll-free 877-JUNIATA. *Fax:* 814-641-5311. *E-mail:* patrict@juniata.edu. *Website:* http://www.juniata.edu/.

KALAMAZOO COLLEGE
Kalamazoo, MI

Tuition & fees: $48,516	Average undergraduate aid package: $40,877

ABOUT THE INSTITUTION Independent American Baptist Churches in the U.S.A., coed. *Awards:* bachelor's degrees. 30 undergraduate majors. *Total enrollment:* 1,436. Undergraduates: 1,436. Freshmen: 448. Both federal and institutional methodology are used as a basis for awarding need-based institutional aid.

UNDERGRADUATE EXPENSES for 2018–2019 *Comprehensive fee:* $58,272 includes full-time tuition ($48,162), mandatory fees ($354), and room and board ($9756). *College room only:* $4746. Full-time tuition and fees vary according to course load. Room and board charges vary according to board plan and housing facility. Part-time tuition and fees vary according to course load.

FRESHMAN FINANCIAL AID (Fall 2017, est.) 418 applied for aid; of those 85% were deemed to have need. 100% of freshmen with need received aid; of those 54% had need fully met. *Average percent of need met:* 96% (excluding resources awarded to replace EFC). *Average financial aid package:* $42,907 (excluding resources awarded to replace EFC). 20% of all full-time freshmen had no need and received non-need-based gift aid.

UNDERGRADUATE FINANCIAL AID (Fall 2017, est.) 1,120 applied for aid; of those 90% were deemed to have need. 100% of undergraduates with need received aid; of those 42% had need fully met. *Average percent of need met:* 93% (excluding resources awarded to replace EFC). *Average financial aid package:* $40,877 (excluding resources awarded to replace EFC). 26% of all full-time undergraduates had no need and received non-need-based gift aid.

GIFT AID (NEED-BASED) *Total amount:* $32,478,202 (6% federal, 2% state, 89% institutional, 3% external sources). *Receiving aid:* Freshmen: 78% (350); all full-time undergraduates: 70% (991). *Average award:* Freshmen: $34,678; Undergraduates: $32,723. *Scholarships, grants, and awards:* Federal Pell, FSEOG, state, private, college/university gift aid from institutional funds.

GIFT AID (NON-NEED-BASED) *Total amount:* $11,491,852 (84% institutional, 16% external sources). *Receiving aid:* Freshmen: 22% (97). Undergraduates: 13% (187). *Average award:* Freshmen: $26,548. Undergraduates: $22,143. *Scholarships, grants, and awards by category: Academic interests/achievement:* general academic interests/achievements. *Creative arts/performance:* art/fine arts, music, performing arts. *Special achievements/activities:* leadership. *Special characteristics:* children and siblings of alumni. *Tuition waivers:* Full or partial for employees or children of employees. *ROTC:* Army cooperative.

LOANS *Student loans:* $8,918,518 (66% need-based, 34% non-need-based). 78% of past graduating class borrowed through all loan programs. *Average indebtedness per student:* $31,789. *Average need-based loan:* Freshmen: $4321. Undergraduates: $5815. *Parent loans:* $1,879,798 (100% non-need-based). *Programs:* Federal Direct (Subsidized and Unsubsidized Stafford, PLUS), Perkins.

WORK-STUDY *Federal work-study:* Total amount: $1,482,975; jobs available. *State or other work-study/employment:* Total amount: $177,000 (100% need-based). Part-time jobs available.

APPLYING FOR FINANCIAL AID *Required financial aid form:* FAFSA. *Financial aid deadline (priority):* 11/15. *Notification date:* Continuous beginning 1/15. Students must reply by 5/1.

CONTACT Office of Financial Aid, Kalamazoo College, 1200 Academy Street, Kalamazoo, MI 49006-3295, 269-337-7192 or toll-free 800-253-3602. *Fax:* 269-337-7390. *E-mail:* finaid@kzoo.edu. *Website:* http://www.kzoo.edu/.

KANSAS CITY ART INSTITUTE
Kansas City, MO

Tuition & fees: $37,550	Average undergraduate aid package: $27,003

ABOUT THE INSTITUTION Independent, coed. *Awards:* certificates and bachelor's degrees. 12 undergraduate majors. *Total enrollment:* 663. Undergraduates: 663. Freshmen: 171. Both federal and institutional methodology are used as a basis for awarding need-based institutional aid.

UNDERGRADUATE EXPENSES for 2017–2018 *Application fee:* $45. *Comprehensive fee:* $47,950 includes full-time tuition ($37,400), mandatory fees ($150), and room and board ($10,400). Full-time tuition and fees vary according to reciprocity agreements. *Part-time tuition:* $1510 per credit hour. Part-time tuition and fees vary according to reciprocity agreements.

FRESHMAN FINANCIAL AID (Fall 2017, est.) 165 applied for aid; of those 87% were deemed to have need. 100% of freshmen with need received aid; of those 18% had need fully met. *Average percent of need met:* 64% (excluding resources awarded to replace EFC). 15% of all full-time freshmen had no need and received non-need-based gift aid.

UNDERGRADUATE FINANCIAL AID (Fall 2017, est.) 605 applied for aid; of those 92% were deemed to have need. 100% of undergraduates with need received aid; of those 12% had need fully met. *Average percent of need met:* 64% (excluding resources awarded to replace EFC). *Average financial aid package:* $27,003 (excluding resources awarded to replace EFC). 14% of all full-time undergraduates had no need and received non-need-based gift aid.

GIFT AID (NEED-BASED) *Total amount:* $12,494,168 (12% federal, 2% state, 80% institutional, 6% external sources). *Receiving aid:* Freshmen: 84% (144); all full-time undergraduates: 85% (554). *Average award:* Freshmen: $24,079; Undergraduates: $22,499. *Scholarships, grants, and awards:* Federal Pell, FSEOG, state, private, college/university gift aid from institutional funds.

GIFT AID (NON-NEED-BASED) *Total amount:* $2,328,351 (87% institutional, 13% external sources). *Receiving aid:* Freshmen: 13% (22). Undergraduates: 7%

(44). *Average award:* Freshmen: $19,115. Undergraduates: $18,295. *Scholarships, grants, and awards by category: Creative arts/performance:* art/fine arts. *Tuition waivers:* Full or partial for employees or children of employees.

LOANS *Student loans:* $4,974,361 (83% need-based, 17% non-need-based). 85% of past graduating class borrowed through all loan programs. *Average indebtedness per student:* $25,000. *Average need-based loan:* Freshmen: $3357. Undergraduates: $4780. *Parent loans:* $2,037,775 (69% need-based, 31% non-need-based). *Programs:* Federal Direct (Subsidized and Unsubsidized Stafford, PLUS), Perkins, alternative loans.

WORK-STUDY *Federal work-study:* Total amount: $110,472; jobs available. *State or other work-study/employment:* Total amount: $192,793 (59% need-based, 41% non-need-based). Part-time jobs available.

APPLYING FOR FINANCIAL AID *Required financial aid form:* FAFSA. *Financial aid deadline (priority):* 3/15. *Notification date:* Continuous beginning 3/15. Students must reply within 2 weeks of notification.

CONTACT Mrs. Lori Lynn Baer, Financial Aid Director, Kansas City Art Institute, 4415 Warwick Boulevard, Kansas City, MO 64111-1874, 816-802-3337 or toll-free 800-522-5224. *Fax:* 816-802-3453. *E-mail:* financialaid@kcai.edu. *Website:* http://www.kcai.edu/.

KANSAS STATE UNIVERSITY
Manhattan, KS

Tuition & fees (KS res): $10,135	Average undergraduate aid package: $13,182

ABOUT THE INSTITUTION State-supported, coed. *Awards:* certificates, associate, bachelor's, master's, and doctoral degrees. 87 undergraduate majors. *Total enrollment:* 22,795. Undergraduates: 18,488. Freshmen: 3,350. Federal methodology is used as a basis for awarding need-based institutional aid.

UNDERGRADUATE EXPENSES for 2017–2018 *Application fee:* $40. *Tuition, state resident:* full-time $9273. *Tuition, nonresident:* full-time $24,630. *Required fees:* full-time $862. Full-time tuition and fees vary according to course level, course load, degree level, location, program, and reciprocity agreements. Part-time tuition and fees vary according to course level, course load, degree level, location, program, and reciprocity agreements. *College room and board:* $9430. Room and board charges vary according to board plan, housing facility, and location.

FRESHMAN FINANCIAL AID (Fall 2016) 2,692 applied for aid; of those 68% were deemed to have need. 99% of freshmen with need received aid; of those 24% had need fully met. *Average percent of need met:* 81% (excluding resources awarded to replace EFC). *Average financial aid package:* $13,500 (excluding resources awarded to replace EFC). 12% of all full-time freshmen had no need and received non-need-based gift aid.

UNDERGRADUATE FINANCIAL AID (Fall 2016) 11,643 applied for aid; of those 75% were deemed to have need. 98% of undergraduates with need received aid; of those 19% had need fully met. *Average percent of need met:* 78% (excluding resources awarded to replace EFC). *Average financial aid package:* $13,182 (excluding resources awarded to replace EFC). 9% of all full-time undergraduates had no need and received non-need-based gift aid.

GIFT AID (NEED-BASED) *Total amount:* $53,611,010 (34% federal, 5% state, 52% institutional, 9% external sources). *Receiving aid:* Freshmen: 19% (999); all full-time undergraduates: 28% (5,003). *Average award:* Freshmen: $4535; Undergraduates: $4299. *Scholarships, grants, and awards:* Federal Pell, FSEOG, state, private, college/university gift aid from institutional funds.

GIFT AID (NON-NEED-BASED) *Total amount:* $10,751,632 (1% federal, 81% institutional, 18% external sources). *Receiving aid:* Freshmen: 27% (1,454). Undergraduates: 27% (4,787). *Average award:* Freshmen: $4922. Undergraduates: $4421. *Tuition waivers:* Full or partial for employees or children of employees. *ROTC:* Army, Air Force.

LOANS *Student loans:* $72,474,492 (69% need-based, 31% non-need-based). 57% of past graduating class borrowed through all loan programs. *Average indebtedness per student:* $28,318. *Average need-based loan:* Freshmen: $3658. Undergraduates: $4454. *Parent loans:* $32,021,644 (31% need-based, 69% non-need-based). *Programs:* Federal Direct (Subsidized and Unsubsidized Stafford, PLUS), Perkins, college/university.

WORK-STUDY *Federal work-study:* jobs available. *State or other work-study/employment:* Total amount: $13,116,845 (82% need-based, 18% non-need-based). Part-time jobs available.

ATHLETIC AWARDS Total amount: $6,725,779 (00% need-based, 12% non-need-based).

APPLYING FOR FINANCIAL AID *Required financial aid form:* FAFSA. *Financial aid deadline (priority):* 12/1. *Notification date:* Continuous beginning 1/15. Students must reply within 2 weeks of notification.

CONTACT Mr. Larry Moeder, Executive Director of Undergraduate Admissions and Student Financial Assistance, Kansas State University, 104 Fairchild Hall, Manhattan, KS 66506, 785-532-6420 or toll-free 800-432-8270. *E-mail:* larrym@ksu.edu. *Website:* http://www.k-state.edu/.

KANSAS WESLEYAN UNIVERSITY
Salina, KS

Tuition & fees: $29,500	Average undergraduate aid package: $21,316

ABOUT THE INSTITUTION Independent United Methodist, coed. *Awards:* associate, bachelor's, and master's degrees. 62 undergraduate majors. *Total enrollment:* 791. Undergraduates: 693. Freshmen: 184. Federal methodology is used as a basis for awarding need-based institutional aid.

UNDERGRADUATE EXPENSES for 2018–2019 *Application fee:* $20. *One-time required fee:* $300. *Comprehensive fee:* $39,000 includes full-time tuition ($29,500) and room and board ($9500). Room and board charges vary according to housing facility. *Part-time tuition:* $3000 per term. Part-time tuition and fees vary according to course load.

FRESHMAN FINANCIAL AID (Fall 2016) 161 applied for aid; of those 86% were deemed to have need. 100% of freshmen with need received aid; of those 13% had need fully met. *Average percent of need met:* 62% (excluding resources awarded to replace EFC). *Average financial aid package:* $20,665 (excluding resources awarded to replace EFC). 14% of all full-time freshmen had no need and received non-need-based gift aid.

UNDERGRADUATE FINANCIAL AID (Fall 2016) 657 applied for aid; of those 85% were deemed to have need. 100% of undergraduates with need received aid; of those 19% had need fully met. *Average percent of need met:* 68% (excluding resources awarded to replace EFC). *Average financial aid package:* $21,316 (excluding resources awarded to replace EFC). 12% of all full-time undergraduates had no need and received non-need-based gift aid.

GIFT AID (NEED-BASED) *Total amount:* $6,818,935 (21% federal, 7% state, 72% institutional). *Receiving aid:* Freshmen: 75% (122); all full-time undergraduates: 78% (515). *Average award:* Freshmen: $7193; Undergraduates: $7695. *Scholarships, grants, and awards:* Federal Pell, FSEOG, state, private, college/university gift aid from institutional funds, United Negro College Fund.

GIFT AID (NON-NEED-BASED) *Total amount:* $969,742 (2% federal, 25% institutional, 73% external sources). *Receiving aid:* Freshmen: 79% (128). Undergraduates: 78% (517). *Average award:* Freshmen: $12,250. Undergraduates: $11,252. *Scholarships, grants, and awards by category: Academic interests/achievement:* $4,285,612 total: biological sciences, business, communication, computer science, education, English, foreign languages, general academic interests/achievements, home economics, humanities, mathematics, physical sciences, premedicine, religion/biblical studies, social sciences. *Creative arts/performance:* $381,785 total: applied art and design, art/fine arts, cinema/film/broadcasting, dance, debating, journalism/publications, music, performing arts, theater/drama. *Special achievements/activities:* $244,081 total: cheerleading/drum major, junior miss, memberships, religious involvement. *Special characteristics:* $842,226 total: children and siblings of alumni, children of current students, children of educators, children of faculty/staff, general special characteristics, international students, local/state students, previous college experience, religious affiliation, siblings of current students, spouses of current students, veterans, veterans' children. *Tuition waivers:* Full or partial for children of alumni, employees or children of employees, senior citizens.

LOANS *Student loans:* $5,105,986 (45% need-based, 55% non-need-based). 87% of past graduating class borrowed through all loan programs. *Average indebtedness per student:* $34,526. *Average need-based loan:* Freshmen: $3189. Undergraduates: $4294. *Parent loans:* $2,655,222 (100% non-need-based). *Programs:* Federal Direct (Subsidized and Unsubsidized Stafford, PLUS), Perkins, private loans.

WORK-STUDY *Federal work-study:* 98 jobs averaging $1488. *State or other work-study/employment:* Total amount: $519,973 (95% need-based, 5% non-need-based). 31 part-time jobs averaging $828.

ATHLETIC AWARDS Total amount: $2,827,049 (100% non-need-based).

APPLYING FOR FINANCIAL AID *Required financial aid form:* FAFSA. *Financial aid deadline (priority):* 3/15. *Notification date:* Continuous beginning 10/15.

CONTACT Mrs. Lois Elizabeth Madsen, Director of Student Financial Planning, Kansas Wesleyan University, 100 East Claflin, Hall of the Pioneers, Room 285, Salina, KS 67401-6196, 785-833-4315 or toll-free 800-874-1154 Ext. 1285. *Fax:* 785-827-0927. *E-mail:* lois.madsen@kwu.edu. *Website:* http://www.kwu.edu/.

KAPLAN UNIVERSITY, AUGUSTA
Augusta, ME

CONTACT Financial Aid Office, Kaplan University, Augusta, 14 Marketplace Drive, Augusta, ME 04330, 207-213-2500 or toll-free 888-561-4343. *Website:* http://www.kaplanuniversity.edu/.

KAPLAN UNIVERSITY, DAVENPORT
Davenport, IA

CONTACT Financial Aid Office, Kaplan University, Davenport, 1801 East Kimberly Road, Suite 1, Davenport, IA 52807, 563-355-3500 or toll-free 800-987-7734. *Website:* http://www.kaplanuniversity.edu/.

KAPLAN UNIVERSITY, MASON CITY
Mason City, IA

CONTACT Financial Aid Office, Kaplan University, Mason City, 2570 4th Street, SW, Mason City, IA 50401, 641-423-2530 or toll-free 800-987-7734. *Website:* http://www.kaplanuniversity.edu/.

KEAN UNIVERSITY
Union, NJ

Tuition & fees (NJ res): $12,107	Average undergraduate aid package: $11,052

ABOUT THE INSTITUTION State-supported, coed. *Awards:* certificates, bachelor's, master's, and doctoral degrees. 47 undergraduate majors. *Total enrollment:* 14,226. Undergraduates: 11,984. Freshmen: 1,784. Federal methodology is used as a basis for awarding need-based institutional aid.

UNDERGRADUATE EXPENSES for 2017–2018 *Application fee:* $75. *Tuition, state resident:* full-time $7909; part-time $308 per credit. *Tuition, nonresident:* full-time $14,811; part-time $523 per credit. *Required fees:* full-time $4198; $154 per credit. Part-time tuition and fees vary according to course load. *College room and board:* $13,513. Room and board charges vary according to board plan, housing facility, and location.

FRESHMAN FINANCIAL AID (Fall 2017, est.) 1,637 applied for aid; of those 87% were deemed to have need. 93% of freshmen with need received aid; of those 1% had need fully met. *Average percent of need met:* 81% (excluding resources awarded to replace EFC). *Average financial aid package:* $10,551 (excluding resources awarded to replace EFC). 3% of all full-time freshmen had no need and received non-need-based gift aid.

UNDERGRADUATE FINANCIAL AID (Fall 2017, est.) 7,837 applied for aid; of those 89% were deemed to have need. 96% of undergraduates with need received aid; of those 1% had need fully met. *Average percent of need met:* 84% (excluding resources awarded to replace EFC). *Average financial aid package:* $11,052 (excluding resources awarded to replace EFC). 1% of all full-time undergraduates had no need and received non-need-based gift aid.

GIFT AID (NEED-BASED) *Total amount:* $46,849,443 (56% federal, 37% state, 6% institutional, 1% external sources). *Receiving aid:* Freshmen: 56% (987); all full-time undergraduates: 53% (4,985). *Average award:* Freshmen: $9356; Undergrad-

uates: $8690. **Scholarships, grants, and awards:** Federal Pell, FSEOG, state, private, college/university gift aid from institutional funds.

GIFT AID (NON-NEED-BASED) Total amount: $30,680 (100% state). **Receiving aid:** Freshmen: 20% (357). Undergraduates: 12% (1,109). **Average award:** Freshmen: $2464. Undergraduates: $3237. **Scholarships, grants, and awards by category:** Academic interests/achievement: architecture, area/ethnic studies, biological sciences, business, communication, computer science, education, engineering/technologies, English, foreign languages, general academic interests/achievements, home economics, humanities, international studies, mathematics, physical sciences, premedicine, social sciences. Creative arts/performance: applied art and design, art/fine arts, cinema/film/broadcasting, dance, general creative arts/performance, music, performing arts, theater/drama. Special achievements/activities: community service, general special achievements/activities, leadership, memberships. Special characteristics: adult students, first-generation college students, general special characteristics, local/state students, previous college experience, veterans. **Tuition waivers:** Full or partial for employees or children of employees, senior citizens. **ROTC:** Army cooperative, Air Force cooperative.

LOANS Student loans: $61,675,703 (43% need-based, 57% non-need-based). 76% of past graduating class borrowed through all loan programs. Average indebtedness per student: $32,277. **Average need-based loan:** Freshmen: $3417. Undergraduates: $4444. **Parent loans:** $9,996,917 (100% non-need-based). **Programs:** Federal Direct (Subsidized and Unsubsidized Stafford, PLUS), Perkins.

WORK-STUDY Federal work-study: Total amount: $836,794; 288 jobs averaging $2409.

APPLYING FOR FINANCIAL AID Required financial aid form: FAFSA. **Financial aid deadline (priority):** 4/15. **Notification date:** Continuous beginning 11/1. Students must reply by 5/1.

CONTACT Ms. Sherrell Watson Hall, Director of Financial Aid, Kean University, 1000 Morris Avenue, Union, NJ 07083, 908-737-3190. Fax: 908-737-3200. E-mail: finaid@kean.edu.

Website: http://www.kean.edu/.

KEENE STATE COLLEGE
Keene, NH

Tuition & fees (NH res): $13,868	Average undergraduate aid package: $12,701

ABOUT THE INSTITUTION State-supported, coed. **Awards:** certificates, bachelor's, and master's degrees. 64 undergraduate majors. **Total enrollment:** 3,866. Undergraduates: 3,780. Freshmen: 931. Federal methodology is used as a basis for awarding need-based institutional aid.

UNDERGRADUATE EXPENSES for 2017–2018 Application fee: $50. **Tuition, state resident:** full-time $11,188; part-time $466 per credit hour. **Tuition, nonresident:** full-time $19,934; part-time $514 per credit hour. **Required fees:** full-time $2680; $106 per credit hour. Part-time tuition and fees vary according to course load. **College room and board:** $10,736. Room and board charges vary according to board plan and housing facility.

FRESHMAN FINANCIAL AID (Fall 2016) 965 applied for aid; of those 79% were deemed to have need. 99% of freshmen with need received aid; of those 14% had need fully met. **Average percent of need met:** 64% (excluding resources awarded to replace EFC). **Average financial aid package:** $12,507 (excluding resources awarded to replace EFC). 22% of all full-time freshmen had no need and received non-need-based gift aid.

UNDERGRADUATE FINANCIAL AID (Fall 2016) 3,312 applied for aid; of those 79% were deemed to have need. 100% of undergraduates with need received aid; of those 14% had need fully met. **Average percent of need met:** 65% (excluding resources awarded to replace EFC). **Average financial aid package:** $12,701 (excluding resources awarded to replace EFC). 17% of all full-time undergraduates had no need and received non-need-based gift aid.

GIFT AID (NEED-BASED) Total amount: $13,757,238 (31% federal, 2% state, 59% institutional, 8% external sources). **Receiving aid:** Freshmen: 56% (590); all full-time undergraduates: 48% (1,904). **Average award:** Freshmen: $5692; Undergraduates: $7089. **Scholarships, grants, and awards:** Federal Pell, FSEOG, state, private, college/university gift aid from institutional funds.

GIFT AID (NON-NEED-BASED) Total amount: $11,027,883 (93% institutional, 7% external sources). **Receiving aid:** Freshmen: 57% (600). Undergraduates: 37% (1,494). **Average award:** Freshmen: $5562. Undergraduates: $4677. **Scholar-**

ships, grants, and awards by category: Academic interests/achievement: 1,954 awards ($8,598,266 total): general academic interests/achievements. Creative arts/performance: 19 awards ($68,700 total): applied art and design, art/fine arts, cinema/film/broadcasting, dance, general creative arts/performance, music, theater/drama. Special achievements/activities: 27 awards ($50,000 total): general special achievements/activities, leadership. Special characteristics: children and siblings of alumni. **Tuition waivers:** Full or partial for employees or children of employees, senior citizens. **ROTC:** Army cooperative, Air Force cooperative.

LOANS Student loans: $33,415,760 (29% need-based, 71% non-need-based). 82% of past graduating class borrowed through all loan programs. Average indebtedness per student: $40,195. **Average need-based loan:** Freshmen: $3191. Undergraduates: $4241. **Parent loans:** $9,514,806 (100% non-need-based). **Programs:** Federal Direct (Subsidized and Unsubsidized Stafford, PLUS), Perkins, college/university.

WORK-STUDY Federal work-study: 1,061 jobs averaging $2311. **State or other work-study/employment:** Total amount: $758,539 (100% non-need-based). 608 part-time jobs averaging $1246.

APPLYING FOR FINANCIAL AID Required financial aid form: FAFSA. **Financial aid deadline:** 3/1. **Notification date:** Continuous. Students must reply within 4 weeks of notification.

CONTACT Ms. Catherine Mullins, Director, Financial Aid, Keene State College, 229 Main Street, Keene, NH 03435-2606, 603-358-2280 or toll-free 800-KSC-1909. Fax: 603-358-2794. E-mail: financialaid@keene.edu.

Website: http://www.keene.edu/.

KEHILATH YAKOV RABBINICAL SEMINARY
Ossining, NY

CONTACT Financial Aid Office, Kehilath Yakov Rabbinical Seminary, 206 Wilson Street, Brooklyn, NY 11211-7207, 718-963-1212.

Website: http://kehilathyakov.com/.

KEISER UNIVERSITY
Fort Lauderdale, FL

Tuition & fees: N/R	Average undergraduate aid package: $6219

ABOUT THE INSTITUTION Independent, coed. **Awards:** certificates, associate, bachelor's, master's, and doctoral degrees (profile includes data from campuses located in Daytona Beach, Fort Lauderdale, Fort Myers, Jacksonville, Lakeland, Melbourne, Miami, Orlando, Pembroke Pines, Port St. Lucie, Sarasota, Tallahassee, Tampa, and West Palm Beach; not all programs offered at all locations, but many classes offered 100% online). 59 undergraduate majors. **Total enrollment:** 17,129. Undergraduates: 16,039. Freshmen: 2,289. Federal methodology is used as a basis for awarding need-based institutional aid.

FRESHMAN FINANCIAL AID (Fall 2016) 4,007 applied for aid; of those 100% were deemed to have need. 100% of freshmen with need received aid; of those 100% had need fully met. **Average percent of need met:** 90% (excluding resources awarded to replace EFC). **Average financial aid package:** $6831 (excluding resources awarded to replace EFC). 14% of all full-time freshmen had no need and received non-need-based gift aid.

UNDERGRADUATE FINANCIAL AID (Fall 2016) 14,381 applied for aid; of those 100% were deemed to have need. 100% of undergraduates with need received aid; of those 100% had need fully met. **Average percent of need met:** 84% (excluding resources awarded to replace EFC). **Average financial aid package:** $6219 (excluding resources awarded to replace EFC).

GIFT AID (NEED-BASED) Total amount: $89,849,313 (49% federal, 17% state, 34% institutional). **Receiving aid:** Freshmen: 86% (3,858); all full-time undergraduates: 84% (14,381). **Average award:** Freshmen: $6831; Undergraduates: $6219. **Scholarships, grants, and awards:** Federal Pell, FSEOG, state, private, college/university gift aid from institutional funds.

GIFT AID (NON-NEED-BASED) Receiving aid: Freshmen: 14% (614). **Average award:** Freshmen: $2734.

LOANS Student loans: $151,011,360 (100% need-based). *Average need-based loan:* Freshmen: $10,496. Undergraduates: $10,560. *Parent loans:* $12,619,224 (100% need-based). *Programs:* Federal Direct (Subsidized and Unsubsidized Stafford, PLUS), Perkins.

WORK-STUDY *Federal work-study:* 34 jobs averaging $3236.

ATHLETIC AWARDS Total amount: $2,008,065 (100% need-based).

APPLYING FOR FINANCIAL AID *Required financial aid form:* FAFSA. *Financial aid deadline:* Continuous. *Notification date:* Continuous. Students must reply within 2 weeks of notification.

CONTACT Mr. Fred Pfeffer, Associate Vice Chancellor for Student Financial Services, Keiser University, 1500 West Commercial Boulevard, Fort Lauderdale, FL 33309, 954-776-4456 or toll-free 888-534-7379. *Fax:* 954-749-4456. *E-mail:* fredp@keiseruniversity.edu.
Website: http://www.keiseruniversity.edu/.

KENDALL COLLEGE
Chicago, IL

ABOUT THE INSTITUTION Proprietary, coed. *Awards:* associate and bachelor's degrees. 5 undergraduate majors. *Total enrollment:* 1,200. Undergraduates: 1,200. Freshmen: 58.

GIFT AID (NEED-BASED) *Scholarships, grants, and awards:* Federal Pell, FSEOG, state, private, college/university gift aid from institutional funds.

GIFT AID (NON-NEED-BASED) *Scholarships, grants, and awards by category:* Academic interests/achievement: business, education, general academic interests/achievements. Special characteristics: children of faculty/staff, international students, out-of-state students, veterans, veterans' children.

LOANS *Programs:* Federal Direct (Subsidized and Unsubsidized Stafford, PLUS), Perkins, alternative loans.

WORK-STUDY *Federal work-study:* jobs available. *State or other work-study/employment:* Total amount: $21,084 (100% non-need-based).

APPLYING FOR FINANCIAL AID *Required financial aid form:* FAFSA.

CONTACT Lauren Walker, Director of Financial Aid, Kendall College, 900 N. North Branch Street, Chicago, IL 60642, 312-752-2267 or toll-free 888-90-KENDALL. *E-mail:* financial_aid@kendall.edu.
Website: http://www.kendall.edu/.

KENNESAW STATE UNIVERSITY
Kennesaw, GA

Tuition & fees (GA res): $7432	Average undergraduate aid package: $9525

ABOUT THE INSTITUTION State-supported, coed. *Awards:* certificates, bachelor's, master's, and doctoral degrees. 87 undergraduate majors. *Total enrollment:* 35,846. Undergraduates: 32,945. Freshmen: 5,238. Federal methodology is used as a basis for awarding need-based institutional aid.

UNDERGRADUATE EXPENSES for 2017–2018 *Application fee:* $40. *Tuition, state resident:* full-time $5426; part-time $181 per credit hour. *Tuition, nonresident:* full-time $19,152; part-time $638 per credit hour. *Required fees:* full-time $2006; $1003 per term. Full-time tuition and fees vary according to course load, degree level, location, program, and student level. Part-time tuition and fees vary according to course load, degree level, location, program, and student level. *College room and board:* $11,467. Room and board charges vary according to board plan, housing facility, and student level.

FRESHMAN FINANCIAL AID (Fall 2017, est.) 4,715 applied for aid; of those 73% were deemed to have need. 99% of freshmen with need received aid; of those 9% had need fully met. *Average percent of need met:* 18% (excluding resources awarded to replace EFC). *Average financial aid package:* $9659 (excluding resources awarded to replace EFC). 1% of all full-time freshmen had no need and received non-need-based gift aid.

UNDERGRADUATE FINANCIAL AID (Fall 2017, est.) 20,909 applied for aid; of those 80% were deemed to have need. 98% of undergraduates with need received aid; of those 7% had need fully met. *Average percent of need met:* 31% (excluding resources awarded to replace EFC). *Average financial aid package:* $9525 (excluding resources awarded to replace EFC). 1% of all full-time undergraduates had no need and received non-need-based gift aid.

GIFT AID (NEED-BASED) *Total amount:* $38,841,768 (99% federal, 1% institutional). *Receiving aid:* Freshmen: 33% (1,670); all full-time undergraduates: 39% (9,585). *Average award:* Freshmen: $4851; Undergraduates: $4553. *Scholarships, grants, and awards:* Federal Pell, FSEOG, state, private, college/university gift aid from institutional funds, United Negro College Fund.

GIFT AID (NON-NEED-BASED) *Total amount:* $72,905,343 (97% state, 2% institutional, 1% external sources). *Receiving aid:* Freshmen: 56% (2,846). Undergraduates: 39% (9,599). *Average award:* Freshmen: $1807. Undergraduates: $1572. *Scholarships, grants, and awards by category:* Academic interests/achievement: biological sciences, business, communication, computer science, education, engineering/technologies, English, foreign languages, general academic interests/achievements, health fields, humanities, international studies, mathematics, physical sciences, premedicine, social sciences. Creative arts/performance: art/fine arts, dance, music, performing arts, theater/drama. Special achievements/activities: community service, leadership, memberships. Special characteristics: children and siblings of alumni, children of union members/company employees, children of workers in trades, ethnic background, general special characteristics, handicapped students, international students, local/state students, members of minority groups, religious affiliation, veterans, veterans' children. *Tuition waivers:* Full or partial for employees or children of employees, senior citizens. *ROTC:* Army cooperative, Air Force cooperative.

LOANS *Student loans:* $204,251,562 (1% need-based, 99% non-need-based). *Average need-based loan:* Freshmen: $3031. Undergraduates: $3826. *Parent loans:* $19,215,276 (100% non-need-based). *Programs:* Federal Direct (Subsidized and Unsubsidized Stafford, PLUS), Perkins, college/university.

WORK-STUDY *Federal work-study:* Total amount: $832,547; jobs available.

ATHLETIC AWARDS Total amount: $3,880,158 (100% non-need-based).

APPLYING FOR FINANCIAL AID *Required financial aid form:* FAFSA. *Financial aid deadline:* 6/1 (priority: 3/1). *Notification date:* Continuous beginning 12/1.

CONTACT Mr. Ron H. Day, Director of Student Financial Aid, Kennesaw State University, 585 Cobb Avenue, NW, Mail Drop #0119, Kennesaw, GA 30144-5591, 770-423-6074. *Fax:* 470-578-9096. *E-mail:* finaid@kennesaw.edu.
Website: http://www.kennesaw.edu/.

KENT STATE UNIVERSITY
Kent, OH

Tuition & fees (OH res): $10,012	Average undergraduate aid package: $10,715

ABOUT THE INSTITUTION State-supported, coed. *Awards:* certificates, bachelor's, master's, and doctoral degrees. 101 undergraduate majors. *Total enrollment:* 28,972. Undergraduates: 23,178. Freshmen: 4,292. Federal methodology is used as a basis for awarding need-based institutional aid.

UNDERGRADUATE EXPENSES for 2018–2019 *Application fee:* $50. *One-time required fee:* $150. *Tuition, state resident:* full-time $10,012; part-time $456 per credit hour. *Tuition, nonresident:* full-time $18,544; part-time $818 per credit hour. Full-time tuition and fees vary according to course load. Part-time tuition and fees vary according to course load. *College room and board:* $10,916; *Room only:* $6876. Room and board charges vary according to board plan and housing facility.

FRESHMAN FINANCIAL AID (Fall 2017, est.) 3,819 applied for aid; of those 77% were deemed to have need. 100% of freshmen with need received aid; of those 16% had need fully met. *Average percent of need met:* 63% (excluding resources awarded to replace EFC). *Average financial aid package:* $11,138 (excluding resources awarded to replace EFC). 18% of all full-time freshmen had no need and received non-need-based gift aid.

UNDERGRADUATE FINANCIAL AID (Fall 2017, est.) 15,181 applied for aid; of those 82% were deemed to have need. 100% of undergraduates with need received aid; of those 13% had need fully met. *Average percent of need met:* 59% (excluding resources awarded to replace EFC). *Average financial aid package:* $10,715 (excluding resources awarded to replace EFC). 10% of all full-time undergraduates had no need and received non-need-based gift aid.

GIFT AID (NEED-BASED) *Total amount:* $82,054,650 (37% federal, 10% state, 49% institutional, 4% external sources). *Receiving aid:* Freshmen: 35% (1,494); all full-time undergraduates: 34% (6,625). *Average award:* Freshmen: $5807; Undergraduates: $5472. *Scholarships, grants, and awards:* Federal Pell, FSEOG, state, private, college/university gift aid from institutional funds.

GIFT AID (NON-NEED-BASED) *Total amount:* $27,279,399 (4% state, 88% institutional, 8% external sources). *Receiving aid:* Freshmen: 56% (2,392). Undergraduates: 40% (7,799). *Average award:* Freshmen: $5843. Undergraduates: $5348. *Scholarships, grants, and awards by category: Academic interests/achievement:* architecture, area/ethnic studies, biological sciences, business, communication, computer science, education, engineering/technologies, English, foreign languages, general academic interests/achievements, health fields, home economics, humanities, international studies, library science, mathematics, military science, physical sciences, premedicine, religion/biblical studies, social sciences. *Creative arts/performance:* applied art and design, art/fine arts, cinema/film/broadcasting, creative writing, dance, general creative arts/performance, journalism/publications, music, performing arts, theater/drama. *Special achievements/activities:* community service, general special achievements/activities, leadership. *Special characteristics:* adult students, children and siblings of alumni, children of faculty/staff, children of union members/company employees, ethnic background, first-generation college students, handicapped students, international students, local/state students, members of minority groups, out-of-state students, previous college experience, veterans, veterans' children. *Tuition waivers:* Full or partial for employees or children of employees, senior citizens. *ROTC:* Army, Air Force.
LOANS *Student loans:* $96,552,813 (80% need-based, 20% non-need-based). 74% of past graduating class borrowed through all loan programs. *Average indebtedness per student:* $32,790. *Average need-based loan:* Freshmen: $3811. Undergraduates: $4664. *Parent loans:* $37,637,823 (47% need-based, 53% non-need-based). *Programs:* Federal Direct (Subsidized and Unsubsidized Stafford, PLUS), Perkins, Federal Nursing, state, college/university, alternative loans.
WORK-STUDY *Federal work-study:* Total amount: $1,011,452; 371 jobs averaging $3140.
ATHLETIC AWARDS Total amount: $6,640,261 (32% need-based, 68% non-need-based).
APPLYING FOR FINANCIAL AID *Required financial aid form:* FAFSA. *Financial aid deadline (priority):* 2/1. *Notification date:* Continuous beginning 1/15. Students must reply within 2 weeks of notification.
CONTACT Mark A. Evans, Executive Director of Student Financial Aid, Kent State University, 103 Schwartz Center, Kent, OH 44242-0001, 330-672-0507 or toll-free 800-988-KENT. *Fax:* 330-672-4036. *E-mail:* mevans@kent.edu.
Website: http://www.kent.edu/.

KENT STATE UNIVERSITY AT GEAUGA
Burton, OH

Tuition & fees (OH res): $5664	Average undergraduate aid package: $6911

ABOUT THE INSTITUTION State-supported, coed. *Awards:* certificates, associate, bachelor's, and master's degrees. 10 undergraduate majors. *Total enrollment:* 2,248. Undergraduates: 2,247. Freshmen: 265. Federal methodology is used as a basis for awarding need-based institutional aid.
UNDERGRADUATE EXPENSES for 2017–2018 *Application fee:* $40. *One-time required fee:* $150. *Tuition, state resident:* full-time $5664; part-time $258 per credit hour. *Tuition, nonresident:* full-time $14,028; part-time $620 per credit hour. Full-time tuition and fees vary according to course level and course load. Part-time tuition and fees vary according to course level and course load.
FRESHMAN FINANCIAL AID (Fall 2017, est.) 168 applied for aid; of those 74% were deemed to have need. 97% of freshmen with need received aid; of those 7% had need fully met. *Average percent of need met:* 56% (excluding resources awarded to replace EFC). *Average financial aid package:* $6284 (excluding resources awarded to replace EFC). 4% of all full-time freshmen had no need and received non-need-based gift aid.
UNDERGRADUATE FINANCIAL AID (Fall 2017, est.) 441 applied for aid; of those 79% were deemed to have need. 98% of undergraduates with need received aid; of those 6% had need fully met. *Average percent of need met:* 57% (excluding resources awarded to replace EFC). *Average financial aid package:* $6911 (excluding resources awarded to replace EFC). 3% of all full-time undergraduates had no need and received non-need-based gift aid.
GIFT AID (NEED-BASED) *Total amount:* $2,170,999 (85% federal, 3% state, 4% institutional, 8% external sources). *Receiving aid:* Freshmen: 38% (85); all full-time undergraduates: 41% (243). *Average award:* Freshmen: $4803; Undergraduates: $4848. *Scholarships, grants, and awards:* Federal Pell, FSEOG, state, private, college/university gift aid from institutional funds.
GIFT AID (NON-NEED-BASED) *Total amount:* $325,621 (2% federal, 4% state, 6% institutional, 88% external sources). *Receiving aid:* Freshmen: 8% (17). Undergraduates: 7% (44). *Average award:* Freshmen: $1143. Undergraduates: $1175. *Scholarships, grants, and awards by category: Academic interests/achievement:* business, education, general academic interests/achievements, home economics, humanities. *Special characteristics:* children of faculty/staff, out-of-state students. *Tuition waivers:* Full or partial for employees or children of employees, senior citizens.
LOANS *Student loans:* $4,632,259 (79% need-based, 21% non-need-based). *Average need-based loan:* Freshmen: $3375. Undergraduates: $3816. *Parent loans:* $118,201 (62% need-based, 38% non-need-based). *Programs:* Federal Direct (Subsidized and Unsubsidized Stafford, PLUS), Perkins, Federal Nursing, state, college/university, alternative loans.
WORK-STUDY *Federal work-study:* Total amount: $33,262; 15 jobs averaging $2260.
APPLYING FOR FINANCIAL AID *Required financial aid form:* FAFSA. *Financial aid deadline (priority):* 2/1. *Notification date:* Continuous beginning 1/15. Students must reply within 2 weeks of notification.
CONTACT Donna Holcomb, Financial Aid Representative, Kent State University at Geauga, 14111 Claridon-Troy Road, Burton, OH 44021, 440-834-4187. *Fax:* 440-834-8846. *E-mail:* dholcomb@kent.edu.
Website: http://www.geauga.kent.edu/.

KENT STATE UNIVERSITY AT STARK
Canton, OH

Tuition & fees (OH res): $5664	Average undergraduate aid package: $7045

ABOUT THE INSTITUTION State-supported, coed. *Awards:* associate, bachelor's, and master's degrees. 17 undergraduate majors. *Total enrollment:* 5,030. Undergraduates: 4,995. Freshmen: 652. Federal methodology is used as a basis for awarding need-based institutional aid.
UNDERGRADUATE EXPENSES for 2017–2018 *Application fee:* $40. *One-time required fee:* $150. *Tuition, state resident:* full-time $5664; part-time $258 per credit hour. *Tuition, nonresident:* full-time $14,028; part-time $620 per credit hour. Full-time tuition and fees vary according to course level and course load. Part-time tuition and fees vary according to course level and course load.
FRESHMAN FINANCIAL AID (Fall 2017, est.) 452 applied for aid; of those 76% were deemed to have need. 98% of freshmen with need received aid; of those 15% had need fully met. *Average percent of need met:* 66% (excluding resources awarded to replace EFC). *Average financial aid package:* $6470 (excluding resources awarded to replace EFC). 10% of all full-time freshmen had no need and received non-need-based gift aid.
UNDERGRADUATE FINANCIAL AID (Fall 2017, est.) 1,765 applied for aid; of those 83% were deemed to have need. 99% of undergraduates with need received aid; of those 12% had need fully met. *Average percent of need met:* 62% (excluding resources awarded to replace EFC). *Average financial aid package:* $7045 (excluding resources awarded to replace EFC). 5% of all full-time undergraduates had no need and received non-need-based gift aid.
GIFT AID (NEED-BASED) *Total amount:* $7,640,196 (78% federal, 3% state, 9% institutional, 10% external sources). *Receiving aid:* Freshmen: 41% (224); all full-time undergraduates: 46% (1,006). *Average award:* Freshmen: $4647; Undergraduates: $4636. *Scholarships, grants, and awards:* Federal Pell, FSEOG, state, private, college/university gift aid from institutional funds.
GIFT AID (NON-NEED-BASED) *Total amount:* $887,692 (1% federal, 12% state, 41% institutional, 46% external sources). *Receiving aid:* Freshmen: 24% (133). Undergraduates: 16% (353). *Average award:* Freshmen: $2847. Undergraduates: $2465. *Scholarships, grants, and awards by category: Academic interests/achievement:* business, communication, education, foreign languages, general academic interests/achievements, home economics, social sciences. *Creative arts/performance:* journalism/publications, music, performing arts, theater/drama. *Special achievements/activities:* community service. *Special characteristics:* adult students, children and siblings of alumni, children of faculty/staff, first-generation college students, general special characteristics, members of minority groups, out-of-state students, public servants,

veterans. **Tuition waivers:** Full or partial for employees or children of employees, senior citizens. **ROTC:** Army cooperative, Air Force cooperative.

LOANS *Student loans:* $13,611,918 (78% need-based, 22% non-need-based). **Average need-based loan:** Freshmen: $3187. Undergraduates: $3878. **Parent loans:** $297,144 (27% need-based, 73% non-need-based). **Programs:** Federal Direct (Subsidized and Unsubsidized Stafford, PLUS), Perkins, Federal Nursing, state, college/university, alternative loans.

WORK-STUDY *Federal work-study:* Total amount: $108,166; 57 jobs averaging $2390.

APPLYING FOR FINANCIAL AID *Required financial aid form:* FAFSA. **Financial aid deadline (priority):** 2/1. **Notification date:** Continuous beginning 1/15. Students must reply within 2 weeks of notification.

CONTACT Amber Wallace, Assistant Director of Enrollment Management and Student Services, Kent State University at Stark, 132 Main Hall, North Canton, OH 44720, 330-244-3257. *Fax:* 330-499-0301. *E-mail:* awalla13@kent.edu. *Website:* http://www.stark.kent.edu/.

KENTUCKY CHRISTIAN UNIVERSITY
Grayson, KY

CONTACT Mrs. Jennie M. Bender, Director of Financial Aid, Kentucky Christian University, 100 Academic Parkway, Grayson, KY 41143-2205, 606-474-3226 or toll-free 800-522-3181. *Fax:* 606-474-3268. *E-mail:* jbender@kcu.edu. *Website:* http://www.kcu.edu/.

KENTUCKY MOUNTAIN BIBLE COLLEGE
Jackson, KY

ABOUT THE INSTITUTION Independent interdenominational, coed. **Awards:** associate and bachelor's degrees. 9 undergraduate majors. **Total enrollment:** 83. Undergraduates: 83. Freshmen: 16.

GIFT AID (NEED-BASED) *Scholarships, grants, and awards:* Federal Pell, FSEOG, state, private, college/university gift aid from institutional funds.

GIFT AID (NON-NEED-BASED) *Scholarships, grants, and awards by category:* Academic interests/achievement: general academic interests/achievements. Creative arts/performance: music, theater/drama. Special characteristics: children of faculty/staff.

LOANS *Programs:* college/university.

APPLYING FOR FINANCIAL AID *Required financial aid forms:* FAFSA, institution's own form.

CONTACT Mrs. Adelle Semrow, Director of Financial Aid, Kentucky Mountain Bible College, 855 Highway 541, Jackson, KY 41339, 800-879-KMBC Ext. 175 or toll-free 800-879-KMBC. *Fax:* 800-659-4324. *E-mail:* finaid@kmbc.edu. *Website:* http://www.kmbc.edu/.

KENTUCKY STATE UNIVERSITY
Frankfort, KY

Tuition & fees (KY res): $7796	Average undergraduate aid package: $12,829

ABOUT THE INSTITUTION State-related, coed. **Awards:** certificates, associate, bachelor's, master's, and doctoral degrees. 28 undergraduate majors. **Total enrollment:** 1,925. Undergraduates: 1,757. Freshmen: 318. Federal methodology is used as a basis for awarding need-based institutional aid.

UNDERGRADUATE EXPENSES for 2018–2019 *Tuition, state resident:* full-time $7406; part-time $325 per credit hour. **Tuition, nonresident:** full-time $18,314; part-time $802 per credit hour. **Required fees:** full-time $390. Full-time tuition and fees vary according to course load. Part-time tuition and fees vary according to course load. **College room and board:** $6690; **Room only:** $3340. Room and board charges vary according to board plan and housing facility.

FRESHMAN FINANCIAL AID (Fall 2017, est.) 281 applied for aid; of those 93% were deemed to have need. 100% of freshmen with need received aid; of those 13% had need fully met. **Average percent of need met:** 77% (excluding resources awarded to replace EFC). **Average financial aid package:** $12,640 (excluding resources awarded to replace EFC). 6% of all full-time freshmen had no need and received non-need-based gift aid.

UNDERGRADUATE FINANCIAL AID (Fall 2017, est.) 1,066 applied for aid; of those 91% were deemed to have need. 100% of undergraduates with need received aid; of those 15% had need fully met. **Average percent of need met:** 80% (excluding resources awarded to replace EFC). **Average financial aid package:** $12,829 (excluding resources awarded to replace EFC). 8% of all full-time undergraduates had no need and received non-need-based gift aid.

GIFT AID (NEED-BASED) *Total amount:* $8,560,112 (52% federal, 10% state, 34% institutional, 4% external sources). **Receiving aid:** Freshmen: 89% (260); all full-time undergraduates: 86% (968). **Average award:** Freshmen: $9348; Undergraduates: $9162. **Scholarships, grants, and awards:** Federal Pell, FSEOG, state, private, college/university gift aid from institutional funds.

GIFT AID (NON-NEED-BASED) *Total amount:* $640,220 (11% state, 69% institutional, 20% external sources). **Receiving aid:** Freshmen: 5% (15). Undergraduates: 6% (62). **Average award:** Freshmen: $3290. Undergraduates: $4570. **Scholarships, grants, and awards by category:** Academic interests/achievement: 57 awards ($296,178 total): general academic interests/achievements. Creative arts/performance: 91 awards ($559,233 total): art/fine arts, music, performing arts. Special achievements/activities: 10 awards ($10,000 total): cheerleading/drum major, general special achievements/activities. Special characteristics: 44 awards ($236,138 total): adult students, children of faculty/staff, children of union members/company employees, children with a deceased or disabled parent, ethnic background, local/state students, public servants, veterans. **Tuition waivers:** Full or partial for employees or children of employees, senior citizens. **ROTC:** Army cooperative, Air Force cooperative.

LOANS *Student loans:* $6,921,134 (92% need-based, 8% non-need-based). 73% of past graduating class borrowed through all loan programs. *Average indebtedness per student:* $29,553. **Average need-based loan:** Freshmen: $3397. Undergraduates: $4085. **Parent loans:** $2,591,299 (88% need-based, 12% non-need-based). **Programs:** Federal Direct (Subsidized and Unsubsidized Stafford, PLUS), private loans.

WORK-STUDY *Federal work-study:* Total amount: $471,887; 129 jobs averaging $3658. **State or other work-study/employment:** Total amount: $108,201 (53% need-based, 47% non-need-based). 41 part-time jobs averaging $2639.

ATHLETIC AWARDS Total amount: $1,011,978 (87% need-based, 13% non-need-based).

APPLYING FOR FINANCIAL AID *Required financial aid form:* FAFSA. **Financial aid deadline (priority):** 4/15. **Notification date:** Continuous beginning 3/15. Students must reply within 4 weeks of notification.

CONTACT Ms. Russelle Keese, Director of Financial Aid, Kentucky State University, 400 East Main Street, Academic Services Building Room 353, Frankfort, KY 40601, 502-597-5759 or toll-free 877-367-5978. *Fax:* 502-597-5950. *E-mail:* russelle.keese@kysu.edu. *Website:* http://www.kysu.edu/.

KENTUCKY WESLEYAN COLLEGE
Owensboro, KY

ABOUT THE INSTITUTION Independent Methodist, coed. **Awards:** bachelor's degrees. 31 undergraduate majors. **Total enrollment:** 785. Undergraduates: 785. Freshmen: 194.

GIFT AID (NEED-BASED) *Scholarships, grants, and awards:* Federal Pell, FSEOG, state, private, college/university gift aid from institutional funds.

GIFT AID (NON-NEED-BASED) *Scholarships, grants, and awards by category:* Academic interests/achievement: general academic interests/achievements. Creative arts/performance: art/fine arts, creative writing, general creative arts/performance, music, performing arts. Special achievements/activities: general special achievements/activities, junior miss, leadership. Special characteristics: children and siblings of alumni, children of faculty/staff, general special characteristics, local/state students, out-of-state students, relatives of clergy, religious affiliation, veterans.

LOANS *Programs:* Federal Direct (Subsidized and Unsubsidized Stafford, PLUS), Perkins.

APPLYING FOR FINANCIAL AID *Required financial aid form:* FAFSA.

CONTACT Mrs. Crystal Hamilton, Director of Financial Aid, Kentucky Wesleyan College, 3000 Frederica Street, Owensboro, KY 42301, 270-852-3130 or toll-free 800-999-0592 (in-state), 800-990-0592 (out-of-state). *Fax:* 270-852-3133. *E-mail:* cLhamilton@kwc.edu.
Website: http://www.kwc.edu/.

KENYON COLLEGE
Gambier, OH

Tuition & fees: $55,930	Average undergraduate aid package: $46,069

ABOUT THE INSTITUTION Independent, coed. *Awards:* bachelor's degrees. 36 undergraduate majors. *Total enrollment:* 1,677. Undergraduates: 1,677. Freshmen: 453. Institutional methodology is used as a basis for awarding need-based institutional aid.
UNDERGRADUATE EXPENSES for 2018–2019 *Comprehensive fee:* $68,440 includes full-time tuition ($53,830), mandatory fees ($2100), and room and board ($12,510). *College room only:* $5470. Full-time tuition and fees vary according to reciprocity agreements. Room and board charges vary according to housing facility and student level. Part-time tuition and fees vary according to reciprocity agreements.
FRESHMAN FINANCIAL AID (Fall 2017, est.) 270 applied for aid; of those 74% were deemed to have need. 100% of freshmen with need received aid; of those 100% had need fully met. *Average percent of need met:* 100% (excluding resources awarded to replace EFC). *Average financial aid package:* $45,275 (excluding resources awarded to replace EFC). 16% of all full-time freshmen had no need and received non-need-based gift aid.
UNDERGRADUATE FINANCIAL AID (Fall 2017, est.) 865 applied for aid; of those 84% were deemed to have need. 100% of undergraduates with need received aid; of those 100% had need fully met. *Average percent of need met:* 100% (excluding resources awarded to replace EFC). *Average financial aid package:* $46,069 (excluding resources awarded to replace EFC). 13% of all full-time undergraduates had no need and received non-need-based gift aid.
GIFT AID (NEED-BASED) *Total amount:* $30,094,349 (3% federal, 1% state, 93% institutional, 3% external sources). *Receiving aid:* Freshmen: 43% (193); all full-time undergraduates: 43% (716). *Average award:* Freshmen: $43,775; Undergraduates: $42,031. *Scholarships, grants, and awards:* Federal Pell, FSEOG, state, private, college/university gift aid from institutional funds.
GIFT AID (NON-NEED-BASED) *Total amount:* $6,167,960 (78% institutional, 22% external sources). *Receiving aid:* Freshmen: 17% (78). Undergraduates: 12% (190). *Average award:* Freshmen: $14,855. Undergraduates: $16,649. *Scholarships, grants, and awards by category:* Academic interests/achievement: 415 awards ($6,247,593 total): biological sciences, computer science, English, foreign languages, general academic interests/achievements, humanities, mathematics, social sciences. *Creative arts/performance:* 34 awards ($510,000 total): art/fine arts, creative writing, music. *Tuition waivers:* Full or partial for employees or children of employees.
LOANS *Student loans:* $5,504,320 (57% need-based, 43% non-need-based). 38% of past graduating class borrowed through all loan programs. *Average indebtedness per student:* $21,404. *Average need-based loan:* Freshmen: $2705. Undergraduates: $4164. *Parent loans:* $2,425,980 (8% need-based, 92% non-need-based). *Programs:* Federal Direct (Subsidized and Unsubsidized Stafford, PLUS), college/university.
WORK-STUDY *Federal work-study:* Total amount: $437,724; 324 jobs averaging $1797. *State or other work-study/employment:* Total amount: $383,416 (100% need-based). 196 part-time jobs averaging $1811.
APPLYING FOR FINANCIAL AID *Required financial aid forms:* FAFSA, CSS Financial Aid PROFILE, noncustodial (divorced/separated) parent's statement, federal income tax form(s), W-2 forms. *Financial aid deadline (priority):* 1/15. *Notification date:* 3/25. Students must reply by 5/1.
CONTACT Mr. Craig Alan Slaughter, Director of Financial Aid, Kenyon College, 105 College-Park Street, Gambier, OH 43022-9623, 740-427-5430 or toll-free 800-848-2468. *Fax:* 740-427-5240. *E-mail:* slaughterc@kenyon.edu.
Website: http://www.kenyon.edu/.

KETTERING COLLEGE
Kettering, OH

CONTACT Financial Aid Office, Kettering College, 3737 Southern Boulevard, Kettering, OH 45429-1299, 937-395-8601 or toll-free 800-433-5262.
Website: http://www.kc.edu/.

KETTERING UNIVERSITY
Flint, MI

CONTACT Diane Bice, Director of Financial Aid, Kettering University, 1700 University Avenue, Flint, MI 48504, 800-955-4464 Ext. 7859 or toll-free 800-955-4464 Ext. 7865 (in-state), 800-955-4464 (out-of-state). *Fax:* 810-762-9807. *E-mail:* finaid@kettering.edu.
Website: http://www.kettering.edu/.

KEUKA COLLEGE
Keuka Park, NY

Tuition & fees: $30,946	Average undergraduate aid package: $20,000

ABOUT THE INSTITUTION Independent American Baptist Churches in the U.S.A., coed. *Awards:* bachelor's and master's degrees. 35 undergraduate majors. *Total enrollment:* 2,003. Undergraduates: 1,730. Freshmen: 365. Federal methodology is used as a basis for awarding need-based institutional aid.
UNDERGRADUATE EXPENSES for 2017–2018 *One-time required fee:* $225. *Comprehensive fee:* $42,398 includes full-time tuition ($29,926), mandatory fees ($1020), and room and board ($11,452). *College room only:* $5520. Full-time tuition and fees vary according to course load, degree level, location, program, and reciprocity agreements. Room and board charges vary according to housing facility. *Part-time tuition:* $999 per credit hour. *Part-time fees:* $650 per year. Part-time tuition and fees vary according to course load, degree level, location, program, and reciprocity agreements.
FRESHMAN FINANCIAL AID (Fall 2017, est.) 300 applied for aid; of those 97% were deemed to have need. 100% of freshmen with need received aid; of those 9% had need fully met. *Average financial aid package:* $26,000 (excluding resources awarded to replace EFC). 7% of all full-time freshmen had no need and received non-need-based gift aid.
UNDERGRADUATE FINANCIAL AID (Fall 2017, est.) 1,200 applied for aid; of those 92% were deemed to have need. 100% of undergraduates with need received aid; of those 9% had need fully met. *Average financial aid package:* $20,000 (excluding resources awarded to replace EFC). 3% of all full-time undergraduates had no need and received non-need-based gift aid.
GIFT AID (NEED-BASED) *Total amount:* $6,759,021 (48% federal, 30% state, 9% institutional, 13% external sources). *Receiving aid:* Freshmen: 80% (240); all full-time undergraduates: 67% (900). *Average award:* Freshmen: $9000; Undergraduates: $8000. *Scholarships, grants, and awards:* Federal Pell, FSEOG, state, college/university gift aid from institutional funds.
GIFT AID (NON-NEED-BASED) *Receiving aid:* Freshmen: 93% (280). Undergraduates: 56% (750). *Average award:* Freshmen: $14,000. Undergraduates: $12,000. *Scholarships, grants, and awards by category:* Academic interests/achievement: education, general academic interests/achievements. *Special achievements/activities:* community service, leadership. *Special characteristics:* children and siblings of alumni, children of faculty/staff, first-generation college students, international students, members of minority groups, religious affiliation, siblings of current students, veterans, veterans' children. *Tuition waivers:* Full or partial for employees or children of employees.
LOANS *Student loans:* $14,500,000 (100% need-based). *Average need-based loan:* Freshmen: $3000. Undergraduates: $4300. *Parent loans:* $2,000,000 (100% need-based). *Programs:* Federal Direct (Subsidized and Unsubsidized Stafford, PLUS), Perkins.
WORK-STUDY *Federal work-study:* Total amount: $138,712; jobs available. *State or other work-study/employment:* Total amount: $361,288 (100% need-based). Part-time jobs available.

APPLYING FOR FINANCIAL AID *Required financial aid form:* FAFSA. *Financial aid deadline (priority):* 11/1. *Notification date:* Continuous beginning 11/1. Students must reply by 5/1 or within 2 weeks of notification.
CONTACT Jennifer Bates, Executive Director of Financial Aid, Keuka College, 141 Central Avenue, Keuka Park, NY 14478-0098, 315-279-5232 or toll-free 800-33-KEUKA. *Fax:* 315-536-5327. *E-mail:* jbates@keuka.edu.
Website: http://www.keuka.edu/.

KEYSTONE COLLEGE
La Plume, PA

CONTACT Director of Financial Assistance and Planning, Keystone College, One College Green, La Plume, PA 18440, 570-945-8134 or toll-free 877-4-COLLEGE. *Fax:* 570-945-8134. *E-mail:* financialaid@keystone.edu.
Website: http://www.keystone.edu/.

THE KING'S COLLEGE
New York, NY

Tuition & fees: $36,450	Average undergraduate aid package: $25,583

ABOUT THE INSTITUTION Independent nondenominational, coed. *Awards:* bachelor's degrees. 6 undergraduate majors. *Total enrollment:* 555. Undergraduates: 554. Freshmen: 149. Federal methodology is used as a basis for awarding need-based institutional aid.
UNDERGRADUATE EXPENSES for 2018–2019 *Application fee:* $30. *Tuition:* full-time $36,000; part-time $1460 per credit hour. *Required fees:* full-time $450; $225 per term. Part-time tuition and fees vary according to course load. Room and board charges vary according to location.
FRESHMAN FINANCIAL AID (Fall 2016) 141 applied for aid; of those 86% were deemed to have need. 100% of freshmen with need received aid; of those 16% had need fully met. *Average percent of need met:* 69% (excluding resources awarded to replace EFC). *Average financial aid package:* $26,538 (excluding resources awarded to replace EFC). 25% of all full-time freshmen had no need and received non-need-based gift aid.
UNDERGRADUATE FINANCIAL AID (Fall 2016) 416 applied for aid; of those 87% were deemed to have need. 100% of undergraduates with need received aid; of those 15% had need fully met. *Average percent of need met:* 67% (excluding resources awarded to replace EFC). *Average financial aid package:* $25,583 (excluding resources awarded to replace EFC). 29% of all full-time undergraduates had no need and received non-need-based gift aid.
GIFT AID (NEED-BASED) *Total amount:* $7,815,831 (9% federal, 1% state, 87% institutional, 3% external sources). *Receiving aid:* Freshmen: 75% (121); all full-time undergraduates: 71% (362). *Average award:* Freshmen: $22,093; Undergraduates: $20,736. *Scholarships, grants, and awards:* Federal Pell, FSEOG, state, private, college/university gift aid from institutional funds.
GIFT AID (NON-NEED-BASED) *Total amount:* $2,361,152 (98% institutional, 2% external sources). *Receiving aid:* Freshmen: 32% (51). Undergraduates: 35% (179). *Average award:* Freshmen: $14,444. Undergraduates: $15,629. *Scholarships, grants, and awards by category:* Academic interests/achievement: 142 awards ($1,798,395 total): general academic interests/achievements. *Special achievements/activities:* 97 awards ($195,125 total): general special achievements/activities, leadership. *Special characteristics:* 23 awards ($12,750 total): children and siblings of alumni, international students. *Tuition waivers:* Full or partial for employees or children of employees. *ROTC:* Army cooperative.
LOANS *Student loans:* $3,762,379 (90% need-based, 10% non-need-based). 67% of past graduating class borrowed through all loan programs. *Average indebtedness per student:* $34,271. *Average need-based loan:* Freshmen: $3027. Undergraduates: $3639. *Parent loans:* $2,226,854 (90% need-based, 10% non-need-based). *Programs:* Federal Direct (Subsidized and Unsubsidized Stafford, PLUS), private loans.
APPLYING FOR FINANCIAL AID *Required financial aid form:* FAFSA. *Financial aid deadline:* Continuous. *Notification date:* Continuous beginning 11/15.

CONTACT Noah Hunter, Director of Admissions and New Student Financial Aid, The King's College, 56 Broadway, New York, NY 10004, 212-659-3610 or toll-free 888-969-7200 Ext. 3610. *E-mail:* financialservices@tkc.edu.
Website: http://www.tkc.edu/.

KING'S COLLEGE
Wilkes-Barre, PA

Tuition & fees: $35,830	Average undergraduate aid package: $25,469

ABOUT THE INSTITUTION Independent Roman Catholic, coed. *Awards:* certificates, bachelor's, and master's degrees. 42 undergraduate majors. *Total enrollment:* 2,468. Undergraduates: 2,197. Freshmen: 624. Federal methodology is used as a basis for awarding need-based institutional aid.
UNDERGRADUATE EXPENSES for 2017–2018 *Application fee:* $30. *Comprehensive fee:* $48,240 includes full-time tuition ($34,630), mandatory fees ($1200), and room and board ($12,410). *College room only:* $6240. Room and board charges vary according to board plan. *Part-time tuition:* $566 per credit hour.
FRESHMAN FINANCIAL AID (Fall 2017, est.) 565 applied for aid; of those 90% were deemed to have need. 100% of freshmen with need received aid; of those 21% had need fully met. *Average percent of need met:* 76% (excluding resources awarded to replace EFC). *Average financial aid package:* $26,789 (excluding resources awarded to replace EFC). 15% of all full-time freshmen had no need and received non-need-based gift aid.
UNDERGRADUATE FINANCIAL AID (Fall 2017, est.) 1,757 applied for aid; of those 90% were deemed to have need. 100% of undergraduates with need received aid; of those 19% had need fully met. *Average percent of need met:* 73% (excluding resources awarded to replace EFC). *Average financial aid package:* $25,469 (excluding resources awarded to replace EFC). 15% of all full-time undergraduates had no need and received non-need-based gift aid.
GIFT AID (NEED-BASED) *Total amount:* $32,445,563 (9% federal, 7% state, 83% institutional, 1% external sources). *Receiving aid:* Freshmen: 81% (507); all full-time undergraduates: 79% (1,590). *Average award:* Freshmen: $21,701; Undergraduates: $19,645. *Scholarships, grants, and awards:* Federal Pell, FSEOG, state, private, college/university gift aid from institutional funds.
GIFT AID (NON-NEED-BASED) *Total amount:* $6,555,259 (1% federal, 97% institutional, 2% external sources). *Receiving aid:* Freshmen: 12% (73). Undergraduates: 10% (197). *Average award:* Freshmen: $17,460. Undergraduates: $16,259. *Scholarships, grants, and awards by category:* Academic interests/achievement: 1,656 awards ($20,889,259 total): biological sciences, business, communication, computer science, education, engineering/technologies, English, foreign languages, general academic interests/achievements, humanities, international studies, mathematics, physical sciences, premedicine, religion/biblical studies, social sciences. *Special achievements/activities:* 1,103 awards ($4,592,474 total): community service, general special achievements/activities, leadership, religious involvement. *Special characteristics:* 392 awards ($3,450,290 total): children and siblings of alumni, children of educators, children of faculty/staff, general special characteristics, international students, relatives of clergy, siblings of current students, veterans. *Tuition waivers:* Full or partial for employees or children of employees, senior citizens. *ROTC:* Army, Air Force cooperative.
LOANS *Student loans:* $19,537,440 (66% need-based, 34% non-need-based). 77% of past graduating class borrowed through all loan programs. *Average indebtedness per student:* $38,625. *Average need-based loan:* Freshmen: $3879. Undergraduates: $5059. *Parent loans:* $5,737,044 (54% need-based, 46% non-need-based). *Programs:* Federal Direct (Subsidized and Unsubsidized Stafford, PLUS), Perkins, private loans.
WORK-STUDY *Federal work-study:* Total amount: $325,000; 269 jobs averaging $1910. *State or other work-study/employment:* Total amount: $204,000 (100% non-need-based). 253 part-time jobs averaging $1046.
APPLYING FOR FINANCIAL AID *Required financial aid form:* FAFSA. *Financial aid deadline (priority):* 2/15. *Notification date:* Continuous beginning 3/1. Students must reply by 5/1 or within 2 weeks of notification.
CONTACT Mr. Jared Menghini, Director of Financial Aid, King's College, 133 North River Street, Wilkes-Barre, PA 18711-0801, 570-208-5868 or toll-free 888-KINGSPA. *Fax:* 570-208-6015. *E-mail:* finaid@kings.edu.
Website: http://www.kings.edu/.

THE KING'S UNIVERSITY
Southlake, TX

Tuition & fees: N/R	Average undergraduate aid package: N/A

ABOUT THE INSTITUTION Independent International Church of the Foursquare Gospel, coed. 1 undergraduate major. Federal methodology is used as a basis for awarding need-based institutional aid.

GIFT AID (NEED-BASED) Scholarships, grants, and awards: Federal Pell, FSEOG, private, college/university gift aid from institutional funds.

LOANS Programs: Federal Direct (Subsidized and Unsubsidized Stafford, PLUS).

WORK-STUDY Federal work-study jobs available.

APPLYING FOR FINANCIAL AID Required financial aid forms: FAFSA, institution's own form. **Financial aid deadline:** Continuous. **Notification date:** Continuous.

CONTACT Mr. Travis Termin, Financial Aid Officer, The King's University, 2121 East Southlake Boulevard, Southlake, TX 76092, 817-722-1730 or toll-free 888-779-8040. *Fax:* 817-722-1766. *E-mail:* financialaid@tku.edu.
Website: http://www.tku.edu/.

KING UNIVERSITY
Bristol, TN

Tuition & fees: $29,714	Average undergraduate aid package: $16,036

ABOUT THE INSTITUTION Independent Presbyterian Church (U.S.A.), coed. **Awards:** certificates, associate, bachelor's, master's, and doctoral degrees. 41 undergraduate majors. **Total enrollment:** 2,162. Undergraduates: 1,799. Freshmen: 170. Federal methodology is used as a basis for awarding need-based institutional aid.

UNDERGRADUATE EXPENSES for 2018–2019 One-time required fee: $125. **Comprehensive fee:** $34,114 includes full-time tuition ($28,104), mandatory fees ($1610), and room and board ($4400). **College room only:** $4362. Full-time tuition and fees vary according to class time, course load, degree level, location, and program. Room and board charges vary according to board plan and housing facility. **Part-time tuition:** $600 per semester hour. **Part-time fees:** $120 per term. Part-time tuition and fees vary according to class time, course load, degree level, location, and program.

FRESHMAN FINANCIAL AID (Fall 2017, est.) 168 applied for aid; of those 90% were deemed to have need. 100% of freshmen with need received aid; of those 15% had need fully met. **Average percent of need met:** 79% (excluding resources awarded to replace EFC). **Average financial aid package:** $24,806 (excluding resources awarded to replace EFC). 12% of all full-time freshmen had no need and received non-need-based gift aid.

UNDERGRADUATE FINANCIAL AID (Fall 2017, est.) 1,442 applied for aid; of those 92% were deemed to have need. 99% of undergraduates with need received aid; of those 13% had need fully met. **Average percent of need met:** 68% (excluding resources awarded to replace EFC). **Average financial aid package:** $16,036 (excluding resources awarded to replace EFC). 7% of all full-time undergraduates had no need and received non-need-based gift aid.

GIFT AID (NEED-BASED) Total amount: $12,912,953 (33% federal, 14% state, 50% institutional, 3% external sources). **Receiving aid:** Freshmen: 78% (149); all full-time undergraduates: 72% (1,120). **Average award:** Freshmen: $20,503; Undergraduates: $13,202. **Scholarships, grants, and awards:** Federal Pell, FSEOG, state, private, college/university gift aid from institutional funds.

GIFT AID (NON-NEED-BASED) Total amount: $1,602,109 (14% state, 77% institutional, 9% external sources). **Receiving aid:** Freshmen: 7% (14). Undergraduates: 6% (95). **Average award:** Freshmen: $11,813. Undergraduates: $10,261. **Scholarships, grants, and awards by category:** Academic interests/achievement: 646 awards ($5,650,579 total): general academic interests/achievements. Creative arts/performance: 29 awards ($98,000 total): art/fine arts, music, performing arts, theater/drama. Special achievements/activities: 56 awards ($54,000 total): general special achievements/activities. Special characteristics: 242 awards ($809,297 total): children of faculty/staff, out-of-state students, veterans, veterans' children. **Tuition waivers:** Full or partial for employees or children of employees, senior citizens.

LOANS Student loans: $14,368,157 (82% need-based, 18% non-need-based). 83% of past graduating class borrowed through all loan programs. *Average indebtedness per student:* $24,370. **Average need-based loan:** Freshmen: $3936. Undergraduates: $4676. **Parent loans:** $905,866 (52% need-based, 48% non-need-based). **Programs:** Federal Direct (Subsidized and Unsubsidized Stafford, PLUS), Perkins.

WORK-STUDY Federal work-study: Total amount: $142,857; 137 jobs averaging $1036. **State or other work-study/employment:** Total amount: $215,265 (100% non-need-based). 115 part-time jobs averaging $1236.

ATHLETIC AWARDS Total amount: $2,912,427 (66% need-based, 34% non-need-based).

APPLYING FOR FINANCIAL AID Required financial aid form: FAFSA. **Financial aid deadline (priority):** 1/1. **Notification date:** Continuous beginning 12/15. Students must reply within 4 weeks of notification.

CONTACT Richard J. Brand, Director of Financial Aid, King University, 1350 King College Road, Bristol, TN 37620-2699, 423-652-4728 or toll-free 800-362-0014. *Fax:* 423-652-6039. *E-mail:* rjbrand@king.edu.
Website: http://www.king.edu/.

KNOX COLLEGE
Galesburg, IL

Tuition & fees: $46,554	Average undergraduate aid package: $35,746

ABOUT THE INSTITUTION Independent, coed. **Awards:** bachelor's degrees. 42 undergraduate majors. **Total enrollment:** 1,356. Undergraduates: 1,356. Freshmen: 358. Both federal and institutional methodology are used as a basis for awarding need-based institutional aid.

UNDERGRADUATE EXPENSES for 2018–2019 Application fee: $50. **Comprehensive fee:** $56,424 includes full-time tuition ($45,783), mandatory fees ($771), and room and board ($9870). **College room only:** $4941. Full-time tuition and fees vary according to course load. Room and board charges vary according to housing facility. **Part-time tuition:** $5087 per credit. Part-time tuition and fees vary according to course load.

FRESHMAN FINANCIAL AID (Fall 2017, est.) 336 applied for aid; of those 91% were deemed to have need. 100% of freshmen with need received aid; of those 33% had need fully met. **Average percent of need met:** 90% (excluding resources awarded to replace EFC). **Average financial aid package:** $38,565 (excluding resources awarded to replace EFC). 14% of all full-time freshmen had no need and received non-need-based gift aid.

UNDERGRADUATE FINANCIAL AID (Fall 2017, est.) 1,215 applied for aid; of those 93% were deemed to have need. 100% of undergraduates with need received aid; of those 34% had need fully met. **Average percent of need met:** 86% (excluding resources awarded to replace EFC). **Average financial aid package:** $35,746 (excluding resources awarded to replace EFC). 13% of all full-time undergraduates had no need and received non-need-based gift aid.

GIFT AID (NEED-BASED) Total amount: $36,389,855 (6% federal, 4% state, 88% institutional, 2% external sources). **Receiving aid:** Freshmen: 84% (302); all full-time undergraduates: 84% (1,126). **Average award:** Freshmen: $31,323; Undergraduates: $28,374. **Scholarships, grants, and awards:** Federal Pell, FSEOG, state, private, college/university gift aid from institutional funds.

GIFT AID (NON-NEED-BASED) Total amount: $4,001,492 (95% institutional, 5% external sources). **Receiving aid:** Freshmen: 13% (45). Undergraduates: 9% (122). **Average award:** Freshmen: $24,600. Undergraduates: $21,835. **Scholarships, grants, and awards by category:** Academic interests/achievement: general academic interests/achievements, mathematics. Creative arts/performance: art/fine arts, creative writing, dance, music, theater/drama. Special achievements/activities: community service. Special characteristics: children of faculty/staff, veterans. **Tuition waivers:** Full or partial for employees or children of employees.

LOANS Student loans: $7,880,616 (64% need-based, 36% non-need-based). 60% of past graduating class borrowed through all loan programs. *Average indebtedness per student:* $31,235. **Average need-based loan:** Freshmen: $3473. Undergraduates: $4280. **Parent loans:** $1,718,906 (100% non-need-based). **Programs:** Federal Direct (Subsidized and Unsubsidized Stafford, PLUS), Perkins, college/university, private loans.

WORK-STUDY Federal work-study: Total amount: $1,499,252; 681 jobs averaging $2200. **State or other work-study/employment:** Total amount: $388,500 (100% need-based). Part-time jobs available.

APPLYING FOR FINANCIAL AID Required financial aid forms: FAFSA, institution's own form. *Financial aid deadline (priority):* 10/1. *Notification date:* Continuous beginning 12/15. Students must reply by 5/1 or within 2 weeks of notification.

CONTACT Ms. Leigh T. Brinson, Director of Financial Aid, Knox College, 2 East South Street, Galesburg, IL 61401, 309-341-7149 or toll-free 800-678-KNOX. *Fax:* 309-341-7453. *E-mail:* ltbrinson@knox.edu.

Website: http://www.knox.edu/.

KUTZTOWN UNIVERSITY OF PENNSYLVANIA
Kutztown, PA

Tuition & fees (PA res): $9987	Average undergraduate aid package: $8860

ABOUT THE INSTITUTION State-supported, coed. *Awards:* certificates, bachelor's, master's, and doctoral degrees. 42 undergraduate majors. *Total enrollment:* 8,329. Undergraduates: 7,489. Freshmen: 1,605. Federal methodology is used as a basis for awarding need-based institutional aid.

UNDERGRADUATE EXPENSES for 2017–2018 *Application fee:* $35. *One-time required fee:* $108. *Tuition, state resident:* full-time $7492; part-time $312 per credit. *Tuition, nonresident:* full-time $11,238; part-time $468 per credit. *Required fees:* full-time $2495; $104.62 per credit. Full-time tuition and fees vary according to course load. Part-time tuition and fees vary according to course load. *College room and board:* $10,282. Room and board charges vary according to board plan and housing facility.

FRESHMAN FINANCIAL AID (Fall 2016) 1,594 applied for aid; of those 78% were deemed to have need. 98% of freshmen with need received aid; of those 7% had need fully met. *Average percent of need met:* 40% (excluding resources awarded to replace EFC). *Average financial aid package:* $8384 (excluding resources awarded to replace EFC). 11% of all full-time freshmen had no need and received non-need-based gift aid.

UNDERGRADUATE FINANCIAL AID (Fall 2016) 6,321 applied for aid; of those 82% were deemed to have need. 98% of undergraduates with need received aid; of those 7% had need fully met. *Average percent of need met:* 46% (excluding resources awarded to replace EFC). *Average financial aid package:* $8860 (excluding resources awarded to replace EFC). 4% of all full-time undergraduates had no need and received non-need-based gift aid.

GIFT AID (NEED-BASED) *Total amount:* $23,484,117 (49% federal, 36% state, 8% institutional, 7% external sources). *Receiving aid:* Freshmen: 45% (768); all full-time undergraduates: 45% (3,284). *Average award:* Freshmen: $5888; Undergraduates: $5741. *Scholarships, grants, and awards:* Federal Pell, FSEOG, state, private, college/university gift aid from institutional funds.

GIFT AID (NON-NEED-BASED) *Total amount:* $955,239 (18% state, 37% institutional, 45% external sources). *Receiving aid:* Freshmen: 43% (732). Undergraduates: 19% (1,408). *Average award:* Freshmen: $919. Undergraduates: $1169. *Scholarships, grants, and awards by category:* Academic interests/achievement: 399 awards ($1,391,548 total): biological sciences, business, communication, computer science, education, English, foreign languages, general academic interests/achievements, humanities, international studies, library science, mathematics, physical sciences. *Creative arts/performance:* 34 awards ($39,940 total): applied art and design, art/fine arts, dance, music. *Special achievements/activities:* 258 awards ($610,502 total): community service, general special achievements/activities, leadership, religious involvement. *Special characteristics:* 113 awards ($916,720 total): children of faculty/staff, children of union members/company employees, first-generation college students, handicapped students, local/state students. *Tuition waivers:* Full or partial for employees or children of employees, senior citizens. *ROTC:* Army cooperative.

LOANS *Student loans:* $57,639,758 (81% need-based, 19% non-need-based). 82% of past graduating class borrowed through all loan programs. *Average indebtedness per student:* $40,084. *Average need-based loan:* Freshmen: $3356. Undergraduates: $4172. *Parent loans:* $15,141,894 (84% need-based, 16% non-need-based). *Programs:* Federal Direct (Subsidized and Unsubsidized Stafford, PLUS), Perkins.

WORK-STUDY *Federal work-study:* 468 jobs averaging $2572.

ATHLETIC AWARDS Total amount: $674,417 (70% need-based, 30% non-need-based).

KUYPER COLLEGE
Grand Rapids, MI

Tuition & fees: $21,090	Average undergraduate aid package: $18,369

ABOUT THE INSTITUTION Independent Christian, coed. *Awards:* certificates, associate, and bachelor's degrees. 25 undergraduate majors. *Total enrollment:* 208. Undergraduates: 208. Freshmen: 38. Federal methodology is used as a basis for awarding need-based institutional aid.

UNDERGRADUATE EXPENSES for 2017–2018 *One-time required fee:* $544. *Comprehensive fee:* $28,344 includes full-time tuition ($20,506), mandatory fees ($584), and room and board ($7254). Full-time tuition and fees vary according to course load and reciprocity agreements. Room and board charges vary according to board plan, housing facility, and student level. *Part-time tuition:* $950 per credit hour. *Part-time fees:* $295 per year. Part-time tuition and fees vary according to course load and reciprocity agreements.

FRESHMAN FINANCIAL AID (Fall 2017, est.) 27 applied for aid; of those 96% were deemed to have need. 100% of freshmen with need received aid; of those 8% had need fully met. *Average percent of need met:* 69% (excluding resources awarded to replace EFC). *Average financial aid package:* $16,518 (excluding resources awarded to replace EFC). 4% of all full-time freshmen had no need and received non-need-based gift aid.

UNDERGRADUATE FINANCIAL AID (Fall 2017, est.) 137 applied for aid; of those 91% were deemed to have need. 100% of undergraduates with need received aid; of those 4% had need fully met. *Average percent of need met:* 77% (excluding resources awarded to replace EFC). *Average financial aid package:* $18,369 (excluding resources awarded to replace EFC). 10% of all full-time undergraduates had no need and received non-need-based gift aid.

GIFT AID (NEED-BASED) *Total amount:* $1,418,919 (24% federal, 13% state, 60% institutional, 3% external sources). *Receiving aid:* Freshmen: 93% (26); all full-time undergraduates: 85% (125). *Average award:* Freshmen: $12,498; Undergraduates: $12,426. *Scholarships, grants, and awards:* Federal Pell, FSEOG, state, private, college/university gift aid from institutional funds.

GIFT AID (NON-NEED-BASED) *Total amount:* $289,197 (1% federal, 98% institutional, 1% external sources). *Receiving aid:* Freshmen: 4% (1). Undergraduates: 3% (5). *Average award:* Freshmen: $500. Undergraduates: $4644. *Scholarships, grants, and awards by category:* Academic interests/achievement: $396,794 total: business, communication, general academic interests/achievements. *Creative arts/performance:* $1113 total: music. *Special achievements/activities:* $3500 total: leadership. *Special characteristics:* $82,921 total: children and siblings of alumni, children of faculty/staff, handicapped students, international students, relatives of clergy, siblings of current students. *Tuition waivers:* Full or partial for employees or children of employees. *ROTC:* Army cooperative.

LOANS *Student loans:* $862,391 (82% need-based, 18% non-need-based). 69% of past graduating class borrowed through all loan programs. *Average indebtedness per student:* $36,147. *Average need-based loan:* Freshmen: $5723. Undergraduates: $7496. *Parent loans:* $84,375 (36% need-based, 64% non-need-based). *Programs:* Federal Direct (Subsidized and Unsubsidized Stafford, PLUS), alternative loans.

WORK-STUDY *Federal work-study:* Total amount: $33,382; jobs available. *State or other work-study/employment:* Total amount: $300,000 (100% non-need-based). Part-time jobs available.

APPLYING FOR FINANCIAL AID Required financial aid form: FAFSA. *Financial aid deadline (priority):* 3/1. *Notification date:* Continuous beginning 3/20. Students must reply within 2 weeks of notification.

CONTACT Ms. Agnes Russell, Director of Financial Aid, Kuyper College, 3333 East Beltline NE, Grand Rapids, MI 49525-9749, 616-222-3000 Ext. 656. *Fax:* 616-222-3045. *E-mail:* arussell@kuyper.edu.

Website: http://www.kuyper.edu/.

APPLYING FOR FINANCIAL AID Required financial aid form: FAFSA. *Financial aid deadline (priority):* 3/1. *Notification date:* Continuous beginning 3/30. Students must reply by 5/1 or within 4 weeks of notification.

CONTACT Mr. Bernard McCree, Director of Financial Aid, Kutztown University of Pennsylvania, 209 Stratton Administration Center, Kutztown, PA 19530-0730, 610-683-4032 or toll-free 877-628-1915. *Fax:* 610-683-1380. *E-mail:* mccree@kutztown.edu.

Website: http://www.kutztown.edu/.

LAFAYETTE COLLEGE
Easton, PA

Tuition & fees: $50,850	Average undergraduate aid package: $49,361

ABOUT THE INSTITUTION Independent Presbyterian Church (U.S.A.), coed. **Awards:** bachelor's degrees. 35 undergraduate majors. **Total enrollment:** 2,594. Undergraduates: 2,594. Freshmen: 680. Both federal and institutional methodology are used as a basis for awarding need-based institutional aid.

UNDERGRADUATE EXPENSES for 2017–2018 Application fee: $65. **One-time required fee:** $740. **Comprehensive fee:** $65,890 includes full-time tuition ($50,400), mandatory fees ($450), and room and board ($15,040). **College room only:** $9300.

FRESHMAN FINANCIAL AID (Fall 2017, est.) 446 applied for aid; of those 55% were deemed to have need. 100% of freshmen with need received aid; of those 100% had need fully met. **Average percent of need met:** 100% (excluding resources awarded to replace EFC). **Average financial aid package:** $49,946 (excluding resources awarded to replace EFC). 4% of all full-time freshmen had no need and received non-need-based gift aid.

UNDERGRADUATE FINANCIAL AID (Fall 2017, est.) 1,339 applied for aid; of those 57% were deemed to have need. 100% of undergraduates with need received aid; of those 100% had need fully met. **Average percent of need met:** 100% (excluding resources awarded to replace EFC). **Average financial aid package:** $49,361 (excluding resources awarded to replace EFC). 8% of all full-time undergraduates had no need and received non-need-based gift aid.

GIFT AID (NEED-BASED) Total amount: $32,124,215 (5% federal, 94% institutional, 1% external sources). **Receiving aid:** Freshmen: 35% (239); all full-time undergraduates: 29% (733). **Average award:** Freshmen: $44,113; Undergraduates: $43,399. **Scholarships, grants, and awards:** Federal Pell, FSEOG, state, private, college/university gift aid from institutional funds.

GIFT AID (NON-NEED-BASED) Total amount: $7,805,179 (82% institutional, 18% external sources). **Receiving aid:** Freshmen: 6% (43). Undergraduates: 5% (126). **Average award:** Freshmen: $26,759. Undergraduates: $28,900. **Scholarships, grants, and awards by category:** Academic interests/achievement: general academic interests/achievements. **Creative arts/performance:** applied art and design, art/fine arts, cinema/film/broadcasting, creative writing, dance, general creative arts/performance, music, performing arts, theater/drama. **Tuition waivers:** Full or partial for employees or children of employees. **ROTC:** Army cooperative.

LOANS Student loans: $6,357,485 (48% need-based, 52% non-need-based). 45% of past graduating class borrowed through all loan programs. **Average indebtedness per student:** $32,974. **Average need-based loan:** Freshmen: $3337. Undergraduates: $4099. **Parent loans:** $3,542,441 (1% need-based, 99% non-need-based). **Programs:** Federal Direct (Subsidized and Unsubsidized Stafford, PLUS), Perkins, college/university.

WORK-STUDY Federal work-study: Total amount: $649,222; 516 jobs averaging $1258. **State or other work-study/employment:** Total amount: $1,340,582 (35% need-based, 65% non-need-based). Part-time jobs available.

ATHLETIC AWARDS Total amount: $10,184,420 (7% need-based, 93% non-need-based).

APPLYING FOR FINANCIAL AID Required financial aid forms: FAFSA, CSS Financial Aid PROFILE, noncustodial (divorced/separated) parent's statement, federal income tax form(s). **Financial aid deadline:** 1/15. **Notification date:** 4/1. Students must reply by 5/1.

CONTACT Ms. Ashley Bianchi, Director of Financial Aid, Lafayette College, 730 High Street, 107 Markle Hall, Easton, PA 18042-1777, 610-330-5055. Fax: 610-330-5758. E-mail: bianchia@lafayette.edu.
Website: http://www.lafayette.edu/.

LAGRANGE COLLEGE
LaGrange, GA

Tuition & fees: $29,480	Average undergraduate aid package: $25,146

ABOUT THE INSTITUTION Independent United Methodist, coed. **Awards:** bachelor's and master's degrees. 28 undergraduate majors. **Total enrollment:** 1,049. Undergraduates: 937. Freshmen: 274. Federal methodology is used as a basis for awarding need-based institutional aid.

UNDERGRADUATE EXPENSES for 2017–2018 One-time required fee: $150. **Comprehensive fee:** $41,110 includes full-time tuition ($29,150), mandatory fees ($330), and room and board ($11,630). **College room only:** $6430. Full-time tuition and fees vary according to class time, course load, degree level, and program. Room and board charges vary according to board plan and housing facility. **Part-time tuition:** $1200 per semester hour. Part-time tuition and fees vary according to class time, course load, degree level, and program.

FRESHMAN FINANCIAL AID (Fall 2016) 228 applied for aid; of those 93% were deemed to have need. 100% of freshmen with need received aid; of those 17% had need fully met. **Average percent of need met:** 93% (excluding resources awarded to replace EFC). **Average financial aid package:** $24,446 (excluding resources awarded to replace EFC). 7% of all full-time freshmen had no need and received non-need-based gift aid.

UNDERGRADUATE FINANCIAL AID (Fall 2016) 802 applied for aid; of those 93% were deemed to have need. 100% of undergraduates with need received aid; of those 16% had need fully met. **Average percent of need met:** 90% (excluding resources awarded to replace EFC). **Average financial aid package:** $25,146 (excluding resources awarded to replace EFC). 6% of all full-time undergraduates had no need and received non-need-based gift aid.

GIFT AID (NEED-BASED) Total amount: $4,664,184 (36% federal, 64% institutional). **Receiving aid:** Freshmen: 83% (195); all full-time undergraduates: 69% (622). **Average award:** Freshmen: $6606; Undergraduates: $6763. **Scholarships, grants, and awards:** Federal Pell, FSEOG, private, college/university gift aid from institutional funds.

GIFT AID (NON-NEED-BASED) Total amount: $10,702,804 (19% state, 79% institutional, 2% external sources). **Receiving aid:** Freshmen: 90% (212). Undergraduates: 81% (734). **Average award:** Freshmen: $14,803. Undergraduates: $14,715. **Scholarships, grants, and awards by category:** Academic interests/achievement: education, general academic interests/achievements. **Creative arts/performance:** art/fine arts, music, theater/drama. **Special achievements/activities:** leadership. **Special characteristics:** children of faculty/staff, ethnic background, first-generation college students, relatives of clergy, religious affiliation. **Tuition waivers:** Full or partial for employees or children of employees, senior citizens.

LOANS Student loans: $8,471,191 (36% need-based, 64% non-need-based). 81% of past graduating class borrowed through all loan programs. **Average indebtedness per student:** $35,580. **Average need-based loan:** Freshmen: $3100. Undergraduates: $4046. **Parent loans:** $1,528,920 (100% non-need-based). **Programs:** Federal Direct (Subsidized and Unsubsidized Stafford, PLUS), state.

WORK-STUDY Federal work-study: jobs available. **State or other work-study/employment:** Total amount: $381,785 (100% non-need-based). Part-time jobs available.

APPLYING FOR FINANCIAL AID Required financial aid forms: FAFSA, state aid form. **Financial aid deadline (priority):** 3/1. **Notification date:** Continuous beginning 3/15. Students must reply within 4 weeks of notification.

CONTACT Michelle Reeves, Assistant Director, LaGrange College, 601 Broad Street, LaGrange, GA 30240-2999, 888-253-9918 or toll-free 800-593-2885. Fax: 706-880-8348. E-mail: mreeves@lagrange.edu.
Website: http://www.lagrange.edu/.

LAGUNA COLLEGE OF ART & DESIGN
Laguna Beach, CA

Tuition & fees: $30,700	Average undergraduate aid package: N/A

ABOUT THE INSTITUTION Independent, coed. **Awards:** certificates, bachelor's, and master's degrees. 14 undergraduate majors. **Total enrollment:** 612. Undergraduates: 567. Federal methodology is used as a basis for awarding need-based institutional aid.

UNDERGRADUATE EXPENSES for 2018–2019 Application fee: $45. **Tuition:** full-time $30,700; part-time $1267 per unit. Full-time tuition and fees vary according to course load and degree level. Part-time tuition and fees vary according to course load and degree level.

FRESHMAN FINANCIAL AID (Fall 2016) 84 applied for aid; of those 100% were deemed to have need. 100% of freshmen with need received aid.

UNDERGRADUATE FINANCIAL AID (Fall 2016) 553 applied for aid; of those 100% were deemed to have need. 100% of undergraduates with need received aid.

GIFT AID (NEED-BASED) *Total amount:* $3,181,263 (17% federal, 11% state, 71% institutional, 1% external sources). *Scholarships, grants, and awards:* Federal Pell, FSEOG, state, private, college/university gift aid from institutional funds.
GIFT AID (NON-NEED-BASED) *Scholarships, grants, and awards by category: Academic interests/achievement:* general academic interests/achievements. *Creative arts/performance:* 568 awards: applied art and design, art/fine arts. *Tuition waivers:* Full or partial for employees or children of employees.
LOANS *Student loans:* $2,671,329 (44% need-based, 56% non-need-based). 90% of past graduating class borrowed through all loan programs. *Average indebtedness per student:* $38,000. *Parent loans:* $2,588,113 (100% need-based). *Programs:* Federal Direct (Subsidized and Unsubsidized Stafford, PLUS).
WORK-STUDY *Federal work-study:* 33 jobs averaging $1496.
APPLYING FOR FINANCIAL AID *Required financial aid form:* FAFSA. *Financial aid deadline:* Continuous. *Notification date:* Continuous beginning 2/1.
CONTACT Christopher Brown, Director of Admissions and Financial Aid, Laguna College of Art & Design, 2825 Laguna Canyon Road, Laguna Beach, CA 92651-1136, 949-376-6000 or toll-free 800-255-0762. *Fax:* 949-715-4084. *E-mail:* cbrown@lcad.edu.
Website: http://www.lcad.edu/.

LAKE ERIE COLLEGE
Painesville, OH

ABOUT THE INSTITUTION Independent, coed. *Awards:* certificates, bachelor's, and master's degrees. 35 undergraduate majors. *Total enrollment:* 1,201. Undergraduates: 955. Freshmen: 219.
GIFT AID (NEED-BASED) *Scholarships, grants, and awards:* Federal Pell, FSEOG, state, private, college/university gift aid from institutional funds.
GIFT AID (NON-NEED-BASED) *Scholarships, grants, and awards by category: Academic interests/achievement:* biological sciences, business, communication, education, English, foreign languages, general academic interests/achievements, humanities, international studies, mathematics, physical sciences, social sciences. *Creative arts/performance:* art/fine arts, dance, general creative arts/performance, music, performing arts, theater/drama. *Special achievements/activities:* community service, general special achievements/activities, hobbies/interests. *Special characteristics:* children of faculty/staff, twins, veterans, veterans' children.
LOANS *Programs:* Federal Direct (Subsidized and Unsubsidized Stafford, PLUS), Perkins.
WORK-STUDY *Federal work-study:* jobs available.
APPLYING FOR FINANCIAL AID *Required financial aid form:* FAFSA.
CONTACT Tricia Pangonis, Director of Financial Aid, Lake Erie College, 391 West Washington Street, Painesville, OH 44077-3389, 440-375-7102 or toll-free 800-916-0904. *Fax:* 440-375-7103. *E-mail:* finaid@lec.edu.
Website: http://www.lec.edu/.

LAKE FOREST COLLEGE
Lake Forest, IL

CONTACT Mr. Jerry Cebrzynski, Director of Financial Aid, Lake Forest College, 555 North Sheridan Road, Lake Forest, IL 60045-2399, 847-735-5104 or toll-free 800-828-4751. *Fax:* 847-735-6271. *E-mail:* cebrzynski@lakeforest.edu.
Website: http://www.lakeforest.edu/.

LAKELAND UNIVERSITY
Plymouth, WI

CONTACT Ms. Patty Taylor, Director of Financial Aid, Lakeland University, PO Box 359, Sheboygan, WI 53082-0359, 920-565-1214 or toll-free 800-569-2166. *Fax:* 920-565-1470.
Website: http://www.lakeland.edu/.

LAKE SUPERIOR STATE UNIVERSITY
Sault Sainte Marie, MI

Tuition & fees: N/R	Average undergraduate aid package: $11,557

ABOUT THE INSTITUTION State-supported, coed. 70 undergraduate majors. Both federal and institutional methodology are used as a basis for awarding need-based institutional aid.
FRESHMAN FINANCIAL AID (Fall 2017, est.) 330 applied for aid; of those 80% were deemed to have need. 98% of freshmen with need received aid; of those 24% had need fully met. *Average percent of need met:* 83% (excluding resources awarded to replace EFC). *Average financial aid package:* $12,640 (excluding resources awarded to replace EFC). 5% of all full-time freshmen had no need and received non-need-based gift aid.
UNDERGRADUATE FINANCIAL AID (Fall 2017, est.) 1,450 applied for aid; of those 82% were deemed to have need. 98% of undergraduates with need received aid; of those 18% had need fully met. *Average percent of need met:* 68% (excluding resources awarded to replace EFC). *Average financial aid package:* $11,557 (excluding resources awarded to replace EFC). 10% of all full-time undergraduates had no need and received non-need-based gift aid.
GIFT AID (NEED-BASED) *Total amount:* $10,932,120 (32% federal, 26% state, 36% institutional, 6% external sources). *Receiving aid:* Freshmen: 66% (245); all full-time undergraduates: 56% (1,018). *Average award:* Freshmen: $10,359; Undergraduates: $8582. *Scholarships, grants, and awards:* Federal Pell, FSEOG, state, private, college/university gift aid from institutional funds, Federal Nursing, Academic Competitiveness Grants, National SMART Grants.
GIFT AID (NON-NEED-BASED) *Average award:* Freshmen: $6693. Undergraduates: $6614. *Scholarships, grants, and awards by category: Academic interests/achievement:* general academic interests/achievements.
LOANS *Student loans:* $10,237,678 (46% need-based, 54% non-need-based). 74% of past graduating class borrowed through all loan programs. *Average indebtedness per student:* $27,405. *Average need-based loan:* Freshmen: $3599. Undergraduates: $4613. *Parent loans:* $2,259,363 (100% non-need-based). *Programs:* Federal Direct (Subsidized and Unsubsidized Stafford, PLUS), Perkins, Federal Nursing, alternative loans.
WORK-STUDY *Federal work-study:* Total amount: $307,611; jobs available. *State or other work-study/employment:* Total amount: $650,454 (3% need-based, 97% non-need-based). Part-time jobs available.
ATHLETIC AWARDS Total amount: $1,391,091 (100% need-based).
APPLYING FOR FINANCIAL AID *Required financial aid form:* FAFSA. *Financial aid deadline (priority):* 3/1. *Notification date:* Continuous beginning 10/1. Students must reply by 5/1 or within 3 weeks of notification.
CONTACT Deborah Faust, Director of Financial Aid, Lake Superior State University, 650 West Easterday Avenue, Sault Sainte Marie, MI 49783, 906-635-2678 or toll-free 888-800-LSSU Ext. 2231. *Fax:* 906-635-6669. *E-mail:* finaid@lssu.edu.
Website: http://www.lssu.edu/.

LAKEVIEW COLLEGE OF NURSING
Danville, IL

Tuition & fees: $15,610	Average undergraduate aid package: $22,950

ABOUT THE INSTITUTION Independent, coed, primarily women. *Awards:* bachelor's degrees. 1 undergraduate major. *Total enrollment:* 236. Undergraduates: 236. Federal methodology is used as a basis for awarding need-based institutional aid.
UNDERGRADUATE EXPENSES for 2017–2018 *Application fee:* $100. *Tuition:* full-time $13,200; part-time $440 per credit hour. *Required fees:* full-time $2410; $65 per credit hour. Full-time tuition and fees vary according to course level, course load, and location. Part-time tuition and fees vary according to course level, course load, and location.
UNDERGRADUATE FINANCIAL AID (Fall 2017, est.) 384 applied for aid; of those 97% were deemed to have need. 99% of undergraduates with need received aid. *Average percent of need met:* 82% (excluding resources awarded to replace EFC). *Average financial aid package:* $22,950 (excluding resources awarded to replace EFC).

GIFT AID (NEED-BASED) *Total amount:* $941,450 (76% federal, 24% state). *Receiving aid:* All full-time undergraduates: 36% (145). *Average award:* Undergraduates: $5750. *Scholarships, grants, and awards:* Federal Pell, state, private, college/university gift aid from institutional funds.

GIFT AID (NON-NEED-BASED) *Total amount:* $162,000 (54% institutional, 46% external sources). *Receiving aid:* Undergraduates: 11% (45). *Tuition waivers:* Full or partial for employees or children of employees. **ROTC:** Army cooperative, Air Force cooperative.

LOANS *Student loans:* $2,800,000 (82% need-based, 18% non-need-based). 52% of past graduating class borrowed through all loan programs. *Average need-based loan:* Undergraduates: $5500. *Parent loans:* $400,000 (100% non-need-based). *Programs:* Federal Direct (Subsidized and Unsubsidized Stafford, PLUS).

APPLYING FOR FINANCIAL AID *Required financial aid forms:* FAFSA, institution's own form. *Financial aid deadline:* 10/1 (priority: 3/1). *Notification date:* Continuous beginning 3/1. Students must reply by 10/1.

CONTACT Ms. Tammy Garza, Assistant Director of Financial Aid, Lakeview College of Nursing, 903 North Logan Avenue, Danville, IL 61832, 217-709-0928. *Fax:* 217-709-0956. *E-mail:* tgarza@lakeviewcol.edu. *Website:* http://www.lakeviewcol.edu/.

LAMAR UNIVERSITY
Beaumont, TX

Tuition & fees (TX res): $10,111	Average undergraduate aid package: $5125

ABOUT THE INSTITUTION State-supported, coed. *Awards:* certificates, bachelor's, master's, and doctoral degrees. 52 undergraduate majors. *Total enrollment:* 14,506. Undergraduates: 9,234. Freshmen: 1,447. Federal methodology is used as a basis for awarding need-based institutional aid.

UNDERGRADUATE EXPENSES for 2017–2018 *Application fee:* $25. *One-time required fee:* $10. *Tuition, state resident:* full-time $7290; part-time $243 per credit hour. *Tuition, nonresident:* full-time $19,740; part-time $658 per credit hour. *Required fees:* full-time $2821; $392 per credit hour. Full-time tuition and fees vary according to course load, location, and program. Part-time tuition and fees vary according to course load, location, and program. *College room and board:* $8740; *Room only:* $5540. Room and board charges vary according to board plan. *Payment plan:* Guaranteed tuition.

FRESHMAN FINANCIAL AID (Fall 2016) 1,263 applied for aid; of those 79% were deemed to have need. 95% of freshmen with need received aid; of those 16% had need fully met. *Average percent of need met:* 22% (excluding resources awarded to replace EFC). *Average financial aid package:* $5395 (excluding resources awarded to replace EFC). 8% of all full-time freshmen had no need and received non-need-based gift aid.

UNDERGRADUATE FINANCIAL AID (Fall 2016) 5,280 applied for aid; of those 84% were deemed to have need. 97% of undergraduates with need received aid; of those 11% had need fully met. *Average percent of need met:* 23% (excluding resources awarded to replace EFC). *Average financial aid package:* $5125 (excluding resources awarded to replace EFC). 9% of all full-time undergraduates had no need and received non-need-based gift aid.

GIFT AID (NEED-BASED) *Total amount:* $28,405,675 (54% federal, 40% state, 6% institutional). *Receiving aid:* Freshmen: 55% (810); all full-time undergraduates: 52% (3,628). *Average award:* Freshmen: $7776; Undergraduates: $6660. *Scholarships, grants, and awards:* Federal Pell, FSEOG, state, private, college/university gift aid from institutional funds, United Negro College Fund.

GIFT AID (NON-NEED-BASED) *Total amount:* $7,040,280 (77% institutional, 23% external sources). *Receiving aid:* Freshmen: 23% (343). Undergraduates: 15% (1,049). *Average award:* Freshmen: $2348. Undergraduates: $2491. *Scholarships, grants, and awards by category:* Academic interests/achievement: general academic interests/achievements. Creative arts/performance: general creative arts/performance. Special achievements/activities: general special achievements/activities. *Tuition waivers:* Full or partial for employees or children of employees, senior citizens. **ROTC:** Air Force cooperative.

LOANS *Student loans:* $34,218,296 (41% need-based, 59% non-need-based). 57% of past graduating class borrowed through all loan programs. *Average indebtedness per student:* $35,651. *Average need-based loan:* Freshmen: $3221. Undergrad-

uates: $3909. *Parent loans:* $4,258,909 (100% non-need-based). *Programs:* Federal Direct (Subsidized and Unsubsidized Stafford, PLUS), Perkins, Federal Nursing, state.

WORK-STUDY *Federal work-study:* 274 jobs averaging $2852. *State or other work-study/employment:* Total amount: $128,829 (100% need-based). 101 part-time jobs averaging $1276.

APPLYING FOR FINANCIAL AID *Required financial aid forms:* FAFSA, institution's own form. *Notification date:* Continuous. Students must reply within 2 weeks of notification.

CONTACT Student Financial Assistance Office, Lamar University, PO Box 10042, Beaumont, TX 77710, 409-880-8450. *Fax:* 409-880-8934. *E-mail:* financialaid@lamar.edu. *Website:* http://www.lamar.edu/.

LANCASTER BIBLE COLLEGE
Lancaster, PA

Tuition & fees: N/R	Average undergraduate aid package: $16,958

ABOUT THE INSTITUTION Independent nondenominational, coed. 17 undergraduate majors. Federal methodology is used as a basis for awarding need-based institutional aid.

FRESHMAN FINANCIAL AID (Fall 2017, est.) 198 applied for aid; of those 84% were deemed to have need. 100% of freshmen with need received aid; of those 30% had need fully met. *Average percent of need met:* 85% (excluding resources awarded to replace EFC). *Average financial aid package:* $19,703 (excluding resources awarded to replace EFC). 22% of all full-time freshmen had no need and received non-need-based gift aid.

UNDERGRADUATE FINANCIAL AID (Fall 2017, est.) 917 applied for aid; of those 87% were deemed to have need. 100% of undergraduates with need received aid; of those 24% had need fully met. *Average percent of need met:* 72% (excluding resources awarded to replace EFC). *Average financial aid package:* $16,958 (excluding resources awarded to replace EFC). 21% of all full-time undergraduates had no need and received non-need-based gift aid.

GIFT AID (NEED-BASED) *Total amount:* $8,027,716 (22% federal, 13% state, 61% institutional, 4% external sources). *Receiving aid:* Freshmen: 78% (165); all full-time undergraduates: 78% (783). *Average award:* Freshmen: $17,246; Undergraduates: $14,238. *Scholarships, grants, and awards:* Federal Pell, FSEOG, state, private, college/university gift aid from institutional funds, Office of Vocational Rehabilitation Awards, Blindness and Visual Services Awards.

GIFT AID (NON-NEED-BASED) *Total amount:* $1,691,340 (96% institutional, 4% external sources). *Receiving aid:* Freshmen: 77% (164). Undergraduates: 65% (653). *Average award:* Freshmen: $6802. Undergraduates: $6674. *Scholarships, grants, and awards by category:* Academic interests/achievement: 530 awards ($1,792,525 total): general academic interests/achievements. Creative arts/performance: 62 awards ($164,700 total): general creative arts/performance, music. Special achievements/activities: 133 awards ($161,505 total): general special achievements/activities, leadership, religious involvement. Special characteristics: 261 awards ($1,275,195 total): children and siblings of alumni, children of current students, children of faculty/staff, international students, relatives of clergy, siblings of current students.

LOANS *Student loans:* $5,736,312 (74% need-based, 26% non-need-based). 71% of past graduating class borrowed through all loan programs. *Average indebtedness per student:* $33,818. *Average need-based loan:* Freshmen: $3209. Undergraduates: $4248. *Parent loans:* $1,074,582 (60% need-based, 40% non-need-based). *Programs:* Federal Direct (Subsidized and Unsubsidized Stafford, PLUS), state, college/university, alternative loans.

WORK-STUDY *Federal work-study:* Total amount: $96,180; 68 jobs averaging $1500.

APPLYING FOR FINANCIAL AID *Required financial aid forms:* FAFSA, state aid form. *Financial aid deadline (priority):* 5/1. *Notification date:* Continuous beginning 11/1. Students must reply within 3 weeks of notification.

CONTACT Mrs. Karen Fox, Director of Financial Aid, Lancaster Bible College, 901 Eden Road, Lancaster, PA 17601, 717-560-8254 Ext. 5352 or toll-free 800-544-7335. *Fax:* 717-560-8216. *E-mail:* kfox@lbc.edu. *Website:* http://www.lbc.edu/.

LANDER UNIVERSITY
Greenwood, SC

CONTACT Director of Financial Aid, Lander University, 320 Stanley Avenue, Greenwood, SC 29649, 864-388-8340 or toll-free 888-452-6337. *Fax:* 864-388-8811. *E-mail:* fhardin@lander.edu.
Website: http://www.lander.edu/.

LANE COLLEGE
Jackson, TN

ABOUT THE INSTITUTION Independent Christian Methodist Episcopal Church, coed. *Awards:* bachelor's degrees. 16 undergraduate majors. *Total enrollment:* 1,427. Undergraduates: 1,427. Freshmen: 403.
GIFT AID (NEED-BASED) *Scholarships, grants, and awards:* Federal Pell, FSEOG, state, private, college/university gift aid from institutional funds, United Negro College Fund.
LOANS *Programs:* Federal Direct (Subsidized and Unsubsidized Stafford, PLUS).
WORK-STUDY *Federal work-study:* jobs available.
APPLYING FOR FINANCIAL AID *Required financial aid form:* FAFSA.
CONTACT Mr. Tony Calhoun, Director of Financial Aid, Lane College, 545 Lane Avenue, Jackson, TN 38301, 731-426-7558 or toll-free 800-960-7533. *Fax:* 731-426-7652. *E-mail:* tcalhoun@lanecollege.edu.
Website: http://www.lanecollege.edu/.

LANGSTON UNIVERSITY
Langston, OK

ABOUT THE INSTITUTION State-supported, coed. *Awards:* associate, bachelor's, master's, and doctoral degrees. 28 undergraduate majors. *Total enrollment:* 2,222. Undergraduates: 2,013. Freshmen: 633.
GIFT AID (NEED-BASED) *Scholarships, grants, and awards:* Federal Pell, FSEOG, state.
GIFT AID (NON-NEED-BASED) *Scholarships, grants, and awards by category:* *Academic interests/achievement:* agriculture, business, education, engineering/technologies, general academic interests/achievements, health fields. *Creative arts/performance:* music. *Special achievements/activities:* cheerleading/drum major, leadership. *Special characteristics:* ethnic background.
LOANS *Programs:* Federal Direct (Subsidized and Unsubsidized Stafford, PLUS).
APPLYING FOR FINANCIAL AID *Required financial aid forms:* FAFSA, institution's own form.
CONTACT Sheila Mcgill, Director of Financial Aid, Langston University, Success Center, Langston, OK 73050, 405-466-3287. *Fax:* 405-466-2986. *E-mail:* smcgill@langston.edu.
Website: http://www.langston.edu/.

LA ROCHE COLLEGE
Pittsburgh, PA

Tuition & fees: $28,564	Average undergraduate aid package: $30,310

ABOUT THE INSTITUTION Independent Roman Catholic Church, coed. *Awards:* certificates, associate, bachelor's, master's, and doctoral degrees. 35 undergraduate majors. *Total enrollment:* 1,535. Undergraduates: 1,378. Freshmen: 227. Federal methodology is used as a basis for awarding need-based institutional aid.
UNDERGRADUATE EXPENSES for 2018–2019 *Application fee:* $50. *Comprehensive fee:* $40,120 includes full-time tuition ($27,714), mandatory fees ($850), and room and board ($11,556). *College room only:* $7316. Room and board charges vary according to board plan and housing facility. *Part-time tuition:* $700 per credit hour. *Part-time fees:* $40 per term.
FRESHMAN FINANCIAL AID (Fall 2017, est.) 189 applied for aid; of those 96% were deemed to have need. 100% of freshmen with need received aid; of those 37%

had need fully met. *Average percent of need met:* 93% (excluding resources awarded to replace EFC). *Average financial aid package:* $32,879 (excluding resources awarded to replace EFC). 3% of all full-time freshmen had no need and received non-need-based gift aid.
UNDERGRADUATE FINANCIAL AID (Fall 2017, est.) 850 applied for aid; of those 94% were deemed to have need. 100% of undergraduates with need received aid; of those 37% had need fully met. *Average percent of need met:* 94% (excluding resources awarded to replace EFC). *Average financial aid package:* $30,310 (excluding resources awarded to replace EFC). 4% of all full-time undergraduates had no need and received non-need-based gift aid.
GIFT AID (NEED-BASED) *Total amount:* $5,894,633 (41% federal, 28% state, 31% institutional). *Receiving aid:* Freshmen: 63% (142); all full-time undergraduates: 51% (589). *Average award:* Freshmen: $8712; Undergraduates: $8593. *Scholarships, grants, and awards:* Federal Pell, FSEOG, state, private, college/university gift aid from institutional funds.
GIFT AID (NON-NEED-BASED) *Total amount:* $10,800,509 (93% institutional, 7% external sources). *Receiving aid:* Freshmen: 81% (182). Undergraduates: 60% (699). *Average award:* Freshmen: $14,928. Undergraduates: $19,408. *Scholarships, grants, and awards by category:* *Academic interests/achievement:* 955 awards ($9,264,125 total): general academic interests/achievements. *Tuition waivers:* Full or partial for employees or children of employees, senior citizens.
ROTC: Army cooperative, Air Force cooperative.
LOANS *Student loans:* $7,524,558 (43% need-based, 57% non-need-based). 74% of past graduating class borrowed through all loan programs. *Average indebtedness per student:* $27,298. *Average need-based loan:* Freshmen: $3433. Undergraduates: $7400. *Parent loans:* $2,187,781 (100% non-need-based). *Programs:* Federal Direct (Subsidized and Unsubsidized Stafford, PLUS), Perkins, state.
WORK-STUDY *Federal work-study:* Total amount: $394,000; 136 jobs averaging $1544.
APPLYING FOR FINANCIAL AID *Required financial aid form:* FAFSA. *Financial aid deadline (priority):* 5/1. *Notification date:* Continuous beginning 11/1. Students must reply within 2 weeks of notification.
CONTACT Mrs. Sharon E. Platt, Director of Financial Aid, La Roche College, 9000 Babcock Boulevard, Pittsburgh, PA 15237-5898, 412-536-1125 or toll-free 800-838-4LRC. *Fax:* 412-536-1072. *E-mail:* sharon.platt@laroche.edu.
Website: http://www.laroche.edu/.

LA SALLE UNIVERSITY
Philadelphia, PA

Tuition & fees: $29,500	Average undergraduate aid package: $32,236

ABOUT THE INSTITUTION Independent Roman Catholic, coed. *Awards:* certificates, associate, bachelor's, master's, and doctoral degrees. 55 undergraduate majors. *Total enrollment:* 5,197. Undergraduates: 3,821. Freshmen: 1,052. Federal methodology is used as a basis for awarding need-based institutional aid.
UNDERGRADUATE EXPENSES for 2018–2019 *One-time required fee:* $250. *Comprehensive fee:* $44,190 includes full-time tuition ($28,800), mandatory fees ($700), and room and board ($14,690). *College room only:* $7530. Full-time tuition and fees vary according to course load and program. Room and board charges vary according to board plan and housing facility. *Part-time tuition:* $585 per credit hour. *Part-time fees:* $250 per term. Part-time tuition and fees vary according to course load and program.
FRESHMAN FINANCIAL AID (Fall 2016) 809 applied for aid; of those 94% were deemed to have need. 100% of freshmen with need received aid; of those 14% had need fully met. *Average percent of need met:* 73% (excluding resources awarded to replace EFC). *Average financial aid package:* $32,533 (excluding resources awarded to replace EFC). 11% of all full-time freshmen had no need and received non-need-based gift aid.
UNDERGRADUATE FINANCIAL AID (Fall 2016) 2,765 applied for aid; of those 94% were deemed to have need. 100% of undergraduates with need received aid; of those 14% had need fully met. *Average percent of need met:* 75% (excluding resources awarded to replace EFC). *Average financial aid package:* $32,236 (excluding resources awarded to replace EFC). 15% of all full-time undergraduates had no need and received non-need-based gift aid.
GIFT AID (NEED-BASED) *Total amount:* $66,178,822 (12% federal, 6% state, 81% institutional, 1% external sources). *Receiving aid:* Freshmen: 87% (753); all full-time undergraduates: 81% (2,559). *Average award:* Freshmen: $26,235; Undergrad-

uates: $25,432. **Scholarships, grants, and awards:** Federal Pell, FSEOG, state, private, college/university gift aid from institutional funds, Federal Nursing.

GIFT AID (NON-NEED-BASED) Total amount: $11,508,229 (97% institutional, 3% external sources). **Receiving aid:** Freshmen: 8% (68). Undergraduates: 7% (211). **Average award:** Freshmen: $20,598. Undergraduates: $19,520. **Scholarships, grants, and awards by category:** Academic interests/achievement: 2,751 awards ($48,214,821 total): general academic interests/achievements. Special achievements/activities: 14 awards ($140,000 total): community service. Special characteristics: 92 awards ($3,183,801 total): children of faculty/staff, children with a deceased or disabled parent, relatives of clergy, veterans. **Tuition waivers:** Full or partial for employees or children of employees. **ROTC:** Army cooperative, Air Force cooperative.

LOANS Student loans: $28,207,030 (73% need-based, 27% non-need-based). 77% of past graduating class borrowed through all loan programs. Average indebtedness per student: $37,002. **Average need-based loan:** Freshmen: $3895. Undergraduates: $4822. **Parent loans:** $10,058,896 (56% need-based, 44% non-need-based). **Programs:** Federal Direct (Subsidized and Unsubsidized Stafford, PLUS), Perkins, Federal Nursing.

WORK-STUDY Federal work-study: 364 jobs averaging $1837.

ATHLETIC AWARDS Total amount: $6,254,022 (43% need-based, 57% non-need-based).

APPLYING FOR FINANCIAL AID Required financial aid form: FAFSA. **Financial aid deadline (priority):** 1/1. **Notification date:** Continuous beginning 2/1. Students must reply by 5/1 or within 2 weeks of notification.

CONTACT Joseph Alaimo, Financial Aid Director, La Salle University, 1900 West Olney Avenue, Philadelphia, PA 19141-1199, 215-951-1070 or toll-free 800-328-1910. Fax: 215-951-5098.

Website: http://www.lasalle.edu/.

LASELL COLLEGE
Newton, MA

Tuition & fees: $36,000	Average undergraduate aid package: $28,275

ABOUT THE INSTITUTION Independent, coed. **Awards:** bachelor's and master's degrees. 34 undergraduate majors. **Total enrollment:** 2,100. Undergraduates: 1,731. Freshmen: 411. Federal methodology is used as a basis for awarding need-based institutional aid.

UNDERGRADUATE EXPENSES for 2018–2019 Application fee: $40. **Comprehensive fee:** $51,400 includes full-time tuition ($34,700), mandatory fees ($1300), and room and board ($15,400). Room and board charges vary according to housing facility. **Part-time tuition:** $1155 per credit hour. **Part-time fees:** $325 per term. Part-time tuition and fees vary according to course load.

FRESHMAN FINANCIAL AID (Fall 2017, est.) 365 applied for aid; of those 93% were deemed to have need. 100% of freshmen with need received aid; of those 13% had need fully met. **Average percent of need met:** 73% (excluding resources awarded to replace EFC). **Average financial aid package:** $29,059 (excluding resources awarded to replace EFC). 12% of all full-time freshmen had no need and received non-need-based gift aid.

UNDERGRADUATE FINANCIAL AID (Fall 2017, est.) 1,395 applied for aid; of those 93% were deemed to have need. 100% of undergraduates with need received aid; of those 14% had need fully met. **Average percent of need met:** 73% (excluding resources awarded to replace EFC). **Average financial aid package:** $28,275 (excluding resources awarded to replace EFC). 14% of all full-time undergraduates had no need and received non-need-based gift aid.

GIFT AID (NEED-BASED) Total amount: $30,763,219 (8% federal, 2% state, 87% institutional, 3% external sources). **Receiving aid:** Freshmen: 83% (341); all full-time undergraduates: 78% (1,302). **Average award:** Freshmen: $25,345; Undergraduates: $23,648. **Scholarships, grants, and awards:** Federal Pell, FSEOG, state, private, college/university gift aid from institutional funds.

GIFT AID (NON-NEED-BASED) Total amount: $4,831,974 (72% institutional, 28% external sources). **Receiving aid:** Freshmen: 6% (25). Undergraduates: 7% (123). **Average award:** Freshmen: $9832. Undergraduates: $11,954. **Scholarships, grants, and awards by category:** Academic interests/achievement: general academic interests/achievements. Special achievements/activities: general special achievements/activities. Special characteristics: children and siblings of alumni, children of

faculty/staff, siblings of current students, veterans, veterans' children. **Tuition waivers:** Full or partial for children of alumni, employees or children of employees.

LOANS Student loans: $13,980,315 (70% need-based, 30% non-need-based). 88% of past graduating class borrowed through all loan programs. Average indebtedness per student: $41,455. **Average need-based loan:** Freshmen: $3132. Undergraduates: $4240. **Parent loans:** $6,488,821 (53% need-based, 47% non-need-based). **Programs:** Federal Direct (Subsidized and Unsubsidized Stafford, PLUS).

WORK-STUDY Federal work-study: Total amount: $210,000; jobs available.

APPLYING FOR FINANCIAL AID Required financial aid form: FAFSA. **Financial aid deadline (priority):** 11/20. **Notification date:** Continuous beginning 12/1. Students must reply by 5/1 or within 2 weeks of notification.

CONTACT Michele R. Kosboth, Director of Student Financial Planning, Lasell College, 1844 Commonwealth Avenue, Newton, MA 02466-2709, 617-243-2227 or toll-free 888-LASELL-4. Fax: 617-243-2326. E-mail: finaid@lasell.edu. Website: http://www.lasell.edu/.

LA SIERRA UNIVERSITY
Riverside, CA

Tuition & fees: $32,130	Average undergraduate aid package: $22,896

ABOUT THE INSTITUTION Independent Seventh-day Adventist, coed. **Awards:** certificates, bachelor's, master's, and doctoral degrees. 54 undergraduate majors. **Total enrollment:** 2,418. Undergraduates: 1,935. Freshmen: 421. Federal methodology is used as a basis for awarding need-based institutional aid.

UNDERGRADUATE EXPENSES for 2018–2019 Comprehensive fee: $40,380 includes full-time tuition ($31,140), mandatory fees ($990), and room and board ($8250). Full-time tuition and fees vary according to course load, degree level, location, and program. Room and board charges vary according to board plan and housing facility. **Part-time tuition:** $865 per quarter hour. Part-time tuition and fees vary according to course load, degree level, location, and program.

FRESHMAN FINANCIAL AID (Fall 2017, est.) 401 applied for aid; of those 82% were deemed to have need. 99% of freshmen with need received aid; of those 10% had need fully met. **Average percent of need met:** 76% (excluding resources awarded to replace EFC). **Average financial aid package:** $25,608 (excluding resources awarded to replace EFC). 17% of all full-time freshmen had no need and received non-need-based gift aid.

UNDERGRADUATE FINANCIAL AID (Fall 2017, est.) 1,661 applied for aid; of those 78% were deemed to have need. 99% of undergraduates with need received aid; of those 13% had need fully met. **Average percent of need met:** 69% (excluding resources awarded to replace EFC). **Average financial aid package:** $22,896 (excluding resources awarded to replace EFC). 20% of all full-time undergraduates had no need and received non-need-based gift aid.

GIFT AID (NEED-BASED) Total amount: $23,345,139 (23% federal, 24% state, 51% institutional, 2% external sources). **Receiving aid:** Freshmen: 80% (325); all full-time undergraduates: 76% (1,292). **Average award:** Freshmen: $21,802; Undergraduates: $18,520. **Scholarships, grants, and awards:** Federal Pell, FSEOG, state, private, college/university gift aid from institutional funds.

GIFT AID (NON-NEED-BASED) Receiving aid: Freshmen: 9% (38). Undergraduates: 6% (107). **Average award:** Freshmen: $13,091. Undergraduates: $10,030. **Scholarships, grants, and awards by category:** Academic interests/achievement: biological sciences, business, education, English, foreign languages, general academic interests/achievements, religion/biblical studies. Creative arts/performance: applied art and design, art/fine arts, music, theater/drama. Special achievements/activities: leadership. Special characteristics: adult students, children of faculty/staff, public servants, relatives of clergy, religious affiliation, siblings of current students. **Tuition waivers:** Full or partial for employees or children of employees.

LOANS Student loans: $5,266,408 (100% need-based). **Average need-based loan:** Freshmen: $3286. Undergraduates: $4278. **Parent loans:** $5,408,734 (100% need-based). **Programs:** Federal Direct (Subsidized and Unsubsidized Stafford, PLUS), Perkins, state.

WORK-STUDY Federal work-study: Total amount: $1,208,638; jobs available.

ATHLETIC AWARDS Total amount: $324,178 (100% need-based).

APPLYING FOR FINANCIAL AID Required financial aid forms: FAFSA, state aid form. **Financial aid deadline:** 8/15 (priority: 3/2). **Notification date:** Continuous beginning 4/15. Students must reply by 8/5 or within 2 weeks of notification.

LAWRENCE TECHNOLOGICAL UNIVERSITY
Southfield, MI

Tuition & fees: $32,130	Average undergraduate aid package: $24,840

ABOUT THE INSTITUTION Independent, coed. *Awards:* certificates, associate, bachelor's, master's, and doctoral degrees. 44 undergraduate majors. *Total enrollment:* 3,069. Undergraduates: 2,191. Freshmen: 373. Federal methodology is used as a basis for awarding need-based institutional aid.

UNDERGRADUATE EXPENSES for 2017–2018 *Application fee:* $30. *Comprehensive fee:* $41,630 includes full-time tuition ($31,410), mandatory fees ($720), and room and board ($9500). *College room only:* $6700. Full-time tuition and fees vary according to course level, degree level, location, program, and student level. Room and board charges vary according to board plan and housing facility. *Part-time tuition:* $1047 per credit hour. *Part-time fees:* $360 per term. Part-time tuition and fees vary according to course level, degree level, location, program, and student level.

FRESHMAN FINANCIAL AID (Fall 2016) 351 applied for aid; of those 76% were deemed to have need. 100% of freshmen with need received aid; of those 24% had need fully met. *Average percent of need met:* 74% (excluding resources awarded to replace EFC). *Average financial aid package:* $24,490 (excluding resources awarded to replace EFC). 21% of all full-time freshmen had no need and received non-need-based gift aid.

UNDERGRADUATE FINANCIAL AID (Fall 2016) 1,408 applied for aid; of those 72% were deemed to have need. 100% of undergraduates with need received aid; of those 16% had need fully met. *Average percent of need met:* 69% (excluding resources awarded to replace EFC). *Average financial aid package:* $24,840 (excluding resources awarded to replace EFC). 21% of all full-time undergraduates had no need and received non-need-based gift aid.

GIFT AID (NEED-BASED) *Total amount:* $16,453,986 (14% federal, 8% state, 76% institutional, 2% external sources). *Receiving aid:* Freshmen: 72% (264); all full-time undergraduates: 58% (983). *Average award:* Freshmen: $17,684; Undergraduates: $15,970. *Scholarships, grants, and awards:* Federal Pell, FSEOG, state, private, college/university gift aid from institutional funds, Michigan National Guard and ROTC Scholarships.

GIFT AID (NON-NEED-BASED) *Total amount:* $5,508,149 (99% institutional, 1% external sources). *Receiving aid:* Freshmen: 67% (247). Undergraduates: 49% (834). *Average award:* Freshmen: $16,938. Undergraduates: $15,440. *Tuition waivers:* Full or partial for employees or children of employees. *ROTC:* Air Force cooperative.

LOANS *Student loans:* $7,011,559 (96% need-based, 4% non-need-based). 69% of past graduating class borrowed through all loan programs. *Average indebtedness per student:* $32,572. *Average need-based loan:* Freshmen: $5817. Undergraduates: $7009. *Parent loans:* $7,443,514 (93% need-based, 7% non-need-based). *Programs:* Federal Direct (Subsidized and Unsubsidized Stafford, PLUS), Perkins, state, college/university, private loans.

WORK-STUDY *Federal work-study:* 80 jobs averaging $1378. *State or other work-study/employment:* Part-time jobs available.

ATHLETIC AWARDS Total amount: $2,866,288 (100% non-need-based).

APPLYING FOR FINANCIAL AID *Required financial aid form:* FAFSA. *Financial aid deadline (priority):* 4/1. *Notification date:* Continuous beginning 4/1. Students must reply within 2 weeks of notification.

CONTACT Susie Poli Smith, Director of Financial Aid, Lawrence Technological University, 21000 West Ten Mile Road, Southfield, MI 48075-1058, 248-204-2126 or toll-free 800-225-5588. *Fax:* 248-204-2228. *E-mail:* spolismit@ltu.edu. *Website:* http://www.ltu.edu/.

LAWRENCE UNIVERSITY
Appleton, WI

Tuition & fees: $46,101	Average undergraduate aid package: $39,869

ABOUT THE INSTITUTION Independent, coed. *Awards:* bachelor's degrees. 37 undergraduate majors. *Total enrollment:* 1,473. Undergraduates: 1,473. Freshmen: 353. Institutional methodology is used as a basis for awarding need-based institutional aid.

UNDERGRADUATE EXPENSES for 2017–2018 *Comprehensive fee:* $56,133 includes full-time tuition ($45,801), mandatory fees ($300), and room and board ($10,032). *College room only:* $4989.

FRESHMAN FINANCIAL AID (Fall 2017, est.) 300 applied for aid; of those 81% were deemed to have need. 99% of freshmen with need received aid; of those 59% had need fully met. *Average percent of need met:* 96% (excluding resources awarded to replace EFC). *Average financial aid package:* $41,820 (excluding resources awarded to replace EFC). 30% of all full-time freshmen had no need and received non-need-based gift aid.

UNDERGRADUATE FINANCIAL AID (Fall 2017, est.) 1,016 applied for aid; of those 86% were deemed to have need. 99% of undergraduates with need received aid; of those 47% had need fully met. *Average percent of need met:* 94% (excluding resources awarded to replace EFC). *Average financial aid package:* $39,869 (excluding resources awarded to replace EFC). 36% of all full-time undergraduates had no need and received non-need-based gift aid.

GIFT AID (NEED-BASED) *Total amount:* $29,446,081 (5% federal, 2% state, 90% institutional, 3% external sources). *Receiving aid:* Freshmen: 67% (238); all full-time undergraduates: 60% (857). *Average award:* Freshmen: $36,619; Undergraduates: $33,921. *Scholarships, grants, and awards:* Federal Pell, FSEOG, state, private, college/university gift aid from institutional funds.

GIFT AID (NON-NEED-BASED) *Total amount:* $11,769,222 (1% state, 96% institutional, 3% external sources). *Average award:* Freshmen: $23,151. Undergraduates: $22,044. *Scholarships, grants, and awards by category:* Academic interests/achievement: 766 awards ($14,496,937 total): general academic interests/achievements. Creative arts/performance: 65 awards ($506,373 total): music, performing arts, theater/drama. Special achievements/activities: 565 awards ($1,221,862 total): community service, general special achievements/activities, leadership. Special characteristics: 362 awards ($6,156,558 total): children and siblings of alumni, general special characteristics, international students, siblings of current students, veterans, veterans' children. *Tuition waivers:* Full or partial for employees or children of employees.

LOANS *Student loans:* $7,471,995 (55% need-based, 45% non-need-based). 60% of past graduating class borrowed through all loan programs. *Average indebtedness per student:* $32,488. *Average need-based loan:* Freshmen: $4932. Undergraduates: $5657. *Parent loans:* $1,339,240 (100% non-need-based). *Programs:* Federal Direct (Subsidized and Unsubsidized Stafford, PLUS), private loans.

WORK-STUDY *Federal work-study:* Total amount: $1,144,107; 545 jobs averaging $2100. *State or other work-study/employment:* Total amount: $824,324 (100% non-need-based). 415 part-time jobs averaging $2000.

APPLYING FOR FINANCIAL AID *Required financial aid forms:* FAFSA, CSS Financial Aid PROFILE, noncustodial (divorced/separated) parent's statement, federal income tax form(s). *Financial aid deadline (priority):* 12/1. *Notification date:* Continuous beginning 1/15. Students must reply by 5/1.

CONTACT Mrs. Sara Beth Holman, Director of Financial Aid, Lawrence University, 711 East Boldt Way, SPC 32, Appleton, WI 54911, 920-832-6583 or toll-free 800-227-0982. *Fax:* 920-832-6582. *E-mail:* sara.b.holman@lawrence.edu. *Website:* http://www.lawrence.edu/.

LEBANON VALLEY COLLEGE
Annville, PA

Tuition & fees: $43,650	Average undergraduate aid package: $33,826

ABOUT THE INSTITUTION Independent United Methodist, coed. *Awards:* certificates, bachelor's, master's, and doctoral degrees. 43 undergraduate majors. *Total enrollment:* 1,910. Undergraduates: 1,756. Freshmen: 466. Federal methodology is used as a basis for awarding need-based institutional aid.

UNDERGRADUATE EXPENSES for 2018–2019 *Comprehensive fee:* $55,510 includes full-time tuition ($42,420), mandatory fees ($1230), and room and board ($11,860). *College room only:* $5720. Room and board charges vary according to board plan and housing facility. *Part-time tuition:* $698 per credit hour. Part-time tuition and fees vary according to class time and degree level.
FRESHMAN FINANCIAL AID (Fall 2017, est.) 446 applied for aid; of those 90% were deemed to have need. 100% of freshmen with need received aid; of those 17% had need fully met. *Average percent of need met:* 82% (excluding resources awarded to replace EFC). *Average financial aid package:* $35,396 (excluding resources awarded to replace EFC). 14% of all full-time freshmen had no need and received non-need-based gift aid.
UNDERGRADUATE FINANCIAL AID (Fall 2017, est.) 1,522 applied for aid; of those 91% were deemed to have need. 100% of undergraduates with need received aid; of those 55% had need fully met. *Average percent of need met:* 81% (excluding resources awarded to replace EFC). *Average financial aid package:* $33,826 (excluding resources awarded to replace EFC). 13% of all full-time undergraduates had no need and received non-need-based gift aid.
GIFT AID (NEED-BASED) *Total amount:* $36,805,568 (5% federal, 6% state, 89% institutional). *Receiving aid:* Freshmen: 86% (400); all full-time undergraduates: 85% (1,375). *Average award:* Freshmen: $28,114; Undergraduates: $27,423. *Scholarships, grants, and awards:* Federal Pell, FSEOG, state, private, college/university gift aid from institutional funds, TEACH Grants.
GIFT AID (NON-NEED-BASED) *Total amount:* $6,719,676 (1% federal, 84% institutional, 15% external sources). *Receiving aid:* Freshmen: 8% (38). Undergraduates: 9% (147). *Average award:* Freshmen: $21,402. Undergraduates: $19,852. *Scholarships, grants, and awards by category:* Academic interests/achievement: 1,522 awards ($28,063,627 total): biological sciences, English, general academic interests/achievements, mathematics, physical sciences, religion/biblical studies, social sciences. *Creative arts/performance:* 78 awards ($161,424 total): creative writing, music. *Special achievements/activities:* 2 awards ($4380 total): general special achievements/activities. *Special characteristics:* 122 awards ($1,113,902 total): children and siblings of alumni, children of faculty/staff, general special characteristics, international students, veterans. *Tuition waivers:* Full or partial for employees or children of employees, senior citizens.
LOANS *Student loans:* $14,875,608 (37% need-based, 63% non-need-based). 80% of past graduating class borrowed through all loan programs. *Average indebtedness per student:* $43,588. *Average need-based loan:* Freshmen: $3982. Undergraduates: $4548. *Parent loans:* $5,771,124 (100% non-need-based). *Programs:* Federal Direct (Subsidized and Unsubsidized Stafford, PLUS), Perkins.
WORK-STUDY *Federal work-study:* Total amount: $1,552,542; 1,472 jobs averaging $1023.
APPLYING FOR FINANCIAL AID *Required financial aid form:* FAFSA. *Financial aid deadline (priority):* 2/15. *Notification date:* Continuous beginning 3/1. Students must reply by 5/1 or within 2 weeks of notification.
CONTACT Mrs. Kendra M. Feigert, Director of Financial Aid, Lebanon Valley College, 101 North College Avenue, Annville, PA 17003, 717-867-6126 or toll-free 866-LVC-4ADM. *Fax:* 717-867-6027. *E-mail:* feigert@lvc.edu.
Website: http://www.lvc.edu/.

LEES-MCRAE COLLEGE
Banner Elk, NC

| Tuition & fees: $26,198 | Average undergraduate aid package: $25,260 |

ABOUT THE INSTITUTION Independent Presbyterian Church (U.S.A.), coed. *Awards:* bachelor's degrees. 24 undergraduate majors. *Total enrollment:* 991. Undergraduates: 991. Freshmen: 187. Both federal and institutional methodology are used as a basis for awarding need-based institutional aid.
UNDERGRADUATE EXPENSES for 2017–2018 *Application fee:* $35. *Comprehensive fee:* $36,956 includes full-time tuition ($24,878), mandatory fees ($1320), and room and board ($10,758). *College room only:* $5142. Full-time tuition and fees vary according to course load, location, and reciprocity agreements. Room and board charges vary according to housing facility. *Part-time tuition:* $710 per credit hour. Part-time tuition and fees vary according to course load, location, and reciprocity agreements. *Payment plan:* Guaranteed tuition.
FRESHMAN FINANCIAL AID (Fall 2017, est.) 193 applied for aid; of those 91% were deemed to have need. 100% of freshmen with need received aid. *Average*

percent of need met: 68% (excluding resources awarded to replace EFC). *Average financial aid package:* $24,172 (excluding resources awarded to replace EFC). 5% of all full-time freshmen had no need and received non-need-based gift aid.
UNDERGRADUATE FINANCIAL AID (Fall 2017, est.) 748 applied for aid; of those 91% were deemed to have need. 100% of undergraduates with need received aid; of those 1% had need fully met. *Average percent of need met:* 73% (excluding resources awarded to replace EFC). *Average financial aid package:* $25,260 (excluding resources awarded to replace EFC). 9% of all full-time undergraduates had no need and received non-need-based gift aid.
GIFT AID (NEED-BASED) *Total amount:* $11,376,900 (18% federal, 15% state, 65% institutional, 2% external sources). *Receiving aid:* Freshmen: 74% (151); all full-time undergraduates: 66% (586). *Average award:* Freshmen: $10,860; Undergraduates: $8625. *Scholarships, grants, and awards:* Federal Pell, FSEOG, state, private, college/university gift aid from institutional funds, Federal Nursing.
GIFT AID (NON-NEED-BASED) *Receiving aid:* Freshmen: 86% (176). Undergraduates: 67% (600). *Average award:* Freshmen: $8480. Undergraduates: $5910. *Scholarships, grants, and awards by category:* Academic interests/achievement: general academic interests/achievements. *Creative arts/performance:* performing arts, theater/drama. *Special achievements/activities:* general special achievements/activities. *Special characteristics:* children and siblings of alumni, children of faculty/staff, children with a deceased or disabled parent, local/state students, religious affiliation, siblings of current students, veterans, veterans' children. *Tuition waivers:* Full or partial for employees or children of employees.
LOANS *Student loans:* $5,099,193 (100% need-based). *Average need-based loan:* Freshmen: $3500. Undergraduates: $4180. *Parent loans:* $2,116,028 (100% need-based). *Programs:* Federal Direct (Subsidized and Unsubsidized Stafford, PLUS), Perkins, state.
WORK-STUDY *Federal work-study:* Total amount: $162,280; jobs available. *State or other work-study/employment:* Total amount: $6400 (100% need-based). Part-time jobs available.
ATHLETIC AWARDS Total amount: $1,747,948 (100% need-based).
APPLYING FOR FINANCIAL AID *Required financial aid forms:* FAFSA, state aid form. *Financial aid deadline (priority):* 3/31. *Notification date:* Continuous beginning 12/15. Students must reply within 2 weeks of notification.
CONTACT Cathy Shell, Director of Financial Aid, Lees-McRae College, PO Box 128, Banner Elk, NC 28604-0128, 828-898-8740 or toll-free 800-280-4562. *Fax:* 828-898-8746. *E-mail:* shell@lmc.edu.
Website: http://www.lmc.edu/.

LEE UNIVERSITY
Cleveland, TN

| Tuition & fees: $17,690 | Average undergraduate aid package: $12,666 |

ABOUT THE INSTITUTION Independent Church of God, coed. *Awards:* certificates, bachelor's, and master's degrees. 82 undergraduate majors. *Total enrollment:* 5,370. Undergraduates: 4,860. Freshmen: 901. Federal methodology is used as a basis for awarding need-based institutional aid.
UNDERGRADUATE EXPENSES for 2018–2019 *Application fee:* $25. *Comprehensive fee:* $25,990 includes full-time tuition ($17,040), mandatory fees ($650), and room and board ($8300). *College room only:* $4530. Full-time tuition and fees vary according to course load, location, and program. Room and board charges vary according to board plan and housing facility. *Part-time tuition:* $710 per credit hour. *Part-time fees:* $35 per term. Part-time tuition and fees vary according to course load, location, and program.
FRESHMAN FINANCIAL AID (Fall 2017, est.) 837 applied for aid; of those 79% were deemed to have need. 100% of freshmen with need received aid; of those 25% had need fully met. *Average percent of need met:* 65% (excluding resources awarded to replace EFC). *Average financial aid package:* $13,944 (excluding resources awarded to replace EFC). 19% of all full-time freshmen had no need and received non-need-based gift aid.
UNDERGRADUATE FINANCIAL AID (Fall 2017, est.) 3,357 applied for aid; of those 83% were deemed to have need. 100% of undergraduates with need received aid; of those 18% had need fully met. *Average percent of need met:* 55% (excluding resources awarded to replace EFC). *Average financial aid package:* $12,666 (excluding resources awarded to replace EFC). 15% of all full-time undergraduates had no need and received non-need-based gift aid.

GIFT AID (NEED-BASED) Total amount: $23,367,928 (34% federal, 19% state, 44% institutional, 3% external sources). **Receiving aid:** Freshmen: 70% (624); all full-time undergraduates: 65% (2,508). **Average award:** Freshmen: $12,058; Undergraduates: $9970. **Scholarships, grants, and awards:** Federal Pell, FSEOG, state, private, college/university gift aid from institutional funds.

GIFT AID (NON-NEED-BASED) Total amount: $7,248,711 (1% federal, 24% state, 71% institutional, 4% external sources). **Receiving aid:** Freshmen: 13% (113). Undergraduates: 9% (332). **Average award:** Freshmen: $9663. Undergraduates: $7177. **Scholarships, grants, and awards by category:** Academic interests/achievement: biological sciences, business, communication, education, general academic interests/achievements, religion/biblical studies. Creative arts/performance: music, theater/drama. Special achievements/activities: cheerleading/drum major, leadership, religious involvement. Special characteristics: children of faculty/staff, local/state students, siblings of current students, spouses of current students. **Tuition waivers:** Full or partial for employees or children of employees, senior citizens.

LOANS Student loans: $26,345,280 (72% need-based, 28% non-need-based). 63% of past graduating class borrowed through all loan programs. Average indebtedness per student: $32,792. **Average need-based loan:** Freshmen: $3158. Undergraduates: $4214. **Parent loans:** $6,236,539 (54% need-based, 46% non-need-based). **Programs:** Federal Direct (Subsidized and Unsubsidized Stafford, PLUS), Perkins.

WORK-STUDY Federal work-study: Total amount: $409,064; 235 jobs averaging $1980. **State or other work-study/employment:** Total amount: $7484 (40% need-based, 60% non-need-based). 675 part-time jobs averaging $1484.

ATHLETIC AWARDS Total amount: $2,493,972 (43% need-based, 57% non-need-based).

APPLYING FOR FINANCIAL AID Required financial aid form: FAFSA. **Financial aid deadline (priority):** 3/15. **Notification date:** Continuous beginning 2/1.

CONTACT Mrs. Marian Dill, Director of Student Financial Aid, Lee University, 1120 North Ocoee Street, Cleveland, TN 37311, 423-614-8300 or toll-free 800-533-9930. Fax: 423-614-8308. E-mail: finaid@leeuniversity.edu. Website: http://www.leeuniversity.edu/.

LEHIGH UNIVERSITY
Bethlehem, PA

Tuition & fees: $50,740	Average undergraduate aid package: $46,861

ABOUT THE INSTITUTION Independent, coed. **Awards:** certificates, bachelor's, master's, and doctoral degrees. 69 undergraduate majors. **Total enrollment:** 7,017. Undergraduates: 5,075. Freshmen: 1,234. Both federal and institutional methodology are used as a basis for awarding need-based institutional aid.

UNDERGRADUATE EXPENSES for 2017–2018 Application fee: $70. **Comprehensive fee:** $63,860 includes full-time tuition ($50,320), mandatory fees ($420), and room and board ($13,120). **College room only:** $7590. Room and board charges vary according to board plan and housing facility. **Part-time tuition:** $2100 per credit hour. **Payment plan:** Tuition prepayment.

FRESHMAN FINANCIAL AID (Fall 2017, est.) 815 applied for aid; of those 71% were deemed to have need. 100% of freshmen with need received aid; of those 75% had need fully met. **Average percent of need met:** 96% (excluding resources awarded to replace EFC). **Average financial aid package:** $46,421 (excluding resources awarded to replace EFC). 4% of all full-time freshmen had no need and received non-need-based gift aid.

UNDERGRADUATE FINANCIAL AID (Fall 2017, est.) 2,699 applied for aid; of those 78% were deemed to have need. 100% of undergraduates with need received aid; of those 76% had need fully met. **Average percent of need met:** 97% (excluding resources awarded to replace EFC). **Average financial aid package:** $46,861 (excluding resources awarded to replace EFC). 5% of all full-time undergraduates had no need and received non-need-based gift aid.

GIFT AID (NEED-BASED) Total amount: $77,366,179 (5% federal, 2% state, 93% institutional). **Receiving aid:** Freshmen: 42% (524); all full-time undergraduates: 39% (1,961). **Average award:** Freshmen: $41,234; Undergraduates: $40,472. **Scholarships, grants, and awards:** Federal Pell, FSEOG, state, private, college/university gift aid from institutional funds.

GIFT AID (NON-NEED-BASED) Total amount: $7,593,785 (49% institutional, 51% external sources). **Receiving aid:** Freshmen: 7% (85). Undergraduates: 7% (361). **Average award:** Freshmen: $13,964. Undergraduates: $12,724. Scholar-

ships, grants, and awards by category: Academic interests/achievement: 169 awards ($1,488,495 total): business, communication, engineering/technologies, general academic interests/achievements, international studies, military science. Creative arts/performance: 66 awards ($68,220 total): general creative arts/performance, journalism/publications, music, performing arts, theater/drama. Special achievements/activities: 13 awards ($28,500 total): general special achievements/activities. Special characteristics: 101 awards ($4,801,048 total): children of faculty/staff, members of minority groups. **Tuition waivers:** Full or partial for employees or children of employees. **ROTC:** Army.

LOANS Student loans: $24,803,597 (35% need-based, 65% non-need-based). 51% of past graduating class borrowed through all loan programs. Average indebtedness per student: $35,440. **Average need-based loan:** Freshmen: $3366. Undergraduates: $4073. **Parent loans:** $6,342,476 (100% non-need-based). **Programs:** Federal Direct (Subsidized and Unsubsidized Stafford, PLUS), Perkins, college/university.

WORK-STUDY Federal work-study: Total amount: $2,854,280; 1,233 jobs averaging $1930. **State or other work-study/employment:** Total amount: $1,071,819 (16% need-based, 84% non-need-based). 89 part-time jobs averaging $1696.

ATHLETIC AWARDS Total amount: $12,303,065 (1% need-based, 99% non-need-based).

APPLYING FOR FINANCIAL AID Required financial aid forms: FAFSA, CSS Financial Aid PROFILE, noncustodial (divorced/separated) parent's statement, business/farm supplement. **Financial aid deadline:** 2/15. **Notification date:** 3/30. Students must reply by 5/1 or within 3 weeks of notification.

CONTACT Jennifer Mertz, Director of Financial Aid, Lehigh University, 27 Memorial Drive West, Bethlehem, PA 18015-3094, 610-758-3181. Fax: 610-758-6211. E-mail: jlm207@lehigh.edu. Website: http://www.lehigh.edu/.

LEHMAN COLLEGE OF THE CITY UNIVERSITY OF NEW YORK
Bronx, NY

Tuition & fees (NY res): $7010	Average undergraduate aid package: $9448

ABOUT THE INSTITUTION State and locally supported, coed. **Awards:** certificates, bachelor's, and master's degrees. 52 undergraduate majors. **Total enrollment:** 13,829. Undergraduates: 11,671. Freshmen: 944. Federal methodology is used as a basis for awarding need-based institutional aid.

UNDERGRADUATE EXPENSES for 2017–2018 Application fee: $65. **Tuition, state resident:** full-time $6330; part-time $285 per credit hour. **Tuition, nonresident:** full-time $13,440; part-time $580 per credit hour. **Required fees:** full-time $680; $130 per term. Full-time tuition and fees vary according to course load. Part-time tuition and fees vary according to course load.

FRESHMAN FINANCIAL AID (Fall 2016) 867 applied for aid; of those 95% were deemed to have need. 96% of freshmen with need received aid; of those 1% had need fully met. **Average percent of need met:** 76% (excluding resources awarded to replace EFC). **Average financial aid package:** $11,322 (excluding resources awarded to replace EFC). 1% of all full-time freshmen had no need and received non-need-based gift aid.

UNDERGRADUATE FINANCIAL AID (Fall 2016) 6,606 applied for aid; of those 97% were deemed to have need. 96% of undergraduates with need received aid; of those 1% had need fully met. **Average percent of need met:** 54% (excluding resources awarded to replace EFC). **Average financial aid package:** $9448 (excluding resources awarded to replace EFC). 1% of all full-time undergraduates had no need and received non-need-based gift aid.

GIFT AID (NEED-BASED) Total amount: $47,511,760 (56% federal, 43% state, 1% institutional). **Receiving aid:** Freshmen: 82% (754); all full-time undergraduates: 80% (5,773). **Average award:** Freshmen: $10,360; Undergraduates: $8116. **Scholarships, grants, and awards:** Federal Pell, FSEOG, state, college/university gift aid from institutional funds.

GIFT AID (NON-NEED-BASED) Total amount: $1,404,308 (73% state, 27% institutional). **Receiving aid:** Freshmen: 63% (575). Undergraduates: 20% (1,420). **Average award:** Freshmen: $5776. Undergraduates: $3450. **Tuition waivers:** Full or partial for employees or children of employees. **ROTC:** Army cooperative.

LOANS Student loans: $14,809,026 (57% need-based, 43% non-need-based). 4% of past graduating class borrowed through all loan programs. Average indebtedness per student: $4410. **Average need-based loan:** Freshmen: $2768. Undergraduates:

$4063. **Parent loans:** $33,357 (100% non-need-based). **Programs:** Federal Direct (Subsidized and Unsubsidized Stafford, PLUS), Perkins.

WORK-STUDY *Federal work-study:* 448 jobs averaging $1846. **State or other work-study/employment:** Part-time jobs available.

APPLYING FOR FINANCIAL AID *Required financial aid forms:* FAFSA, state aid form. **Financial aid deadline:** Continuous. **Notification date:** Continuous beginning 1/15. Students must reply by 5/1.

CONTACT Financial Aid Office, Lehman College of the City University of New York, 250 Bedford Park Boulevard West, Bronx, NY 10468-1589, 718-960-8000 or toll-free 877-LEHMAN1.

Website: http://www.lehman.cuny.edu/.

LE MOYNE COLLEGE
Syracuse, NY

Tuition & fees: $34,625	Average undergraduate aid package: $26,170

ABOUT THE INSTITUTION Independent Roman Catholic (Jesuit), coed. **Awards:** certificates, bachelor's, and master's degrees. 55 undergraduate majors. **Total enrollment:** 3,431. Undergraduates: 2,788. Freshmen: 545. Both federal and institutional methodology are used as a basis for awarding need-based institutional aid.

UNDERGRADUATE EXPENSES for 2018–2019 Comprehensive fee: $48,405 includes full-time tuition ($33,560), mandatory fees ($1065), and room and board ($13,780). **College room only:** $8590. Room and board charges vary according to board plan and housing facility. **Part-time tuition:** $704 per credit hour. Part-time tuition and fees vary according to class time and course load.

FRESHMAN FINANCIAL AID (Fall 2016) 602 applied for aid; of those 88% were deemed to have need. 100% of freshmen with need received aid; of those 28% had need fully met. **Average percent of need met:** 81% (excluding resources awarded to replace EFC). **Average financial aid package:** $27,000 (excluding resources awarded to replace EFC). 12% of all full-time freshmen had no need and received non-need-based gift aid.

UNDERGRADUATE FINANCIAL AID (Fall 2016) 2,292 applied for aid; of those 91% were deemed to have need. 100% of undergraduates with need received aid; of those 26% had need fully met. **Average percent of need met:** 78% (excluding resources awarded to replace EFC). **Average financial aid package:** $26,170 (excluding resources awarded to replace EFC). 13% of all full-time undergraduates had no need and received non-need-based gift aid.

GIFT AID (NEED-BASED) Total amount: $44,042,128 (9% federal, 7% state, 81% institutional, 3% external sources). **Receiving aid:** Freshmen: 84% (529); all full-time undergraduates: 82% (2,081). **Average award:** Freshmen: $22,747; Undergraduates: $21,366. **Scholarships, grants, and awards:** Federal Pell, FSEOG, state, private, college/university gift aid from institutional funds.

GIFT AID (NON-NEED-BASED) Total amount: $5,555,004 (1% state, 94% institutional, 5% external sources). **Receiving aid:** Freshmen: 13% (80). Undergraduates: 13% (318). **Average award:** Freshmen: $16,061. Undergraduates: $14,365. **Scholarships, grants, and awards by category:** Academic interests/achievement: 968 awards ($16,584,331 total): general academic interests/achievements. Creative arts/performance: 30 awards ($8669 total): music. Special achievements/activities: 308 awards ($3,696,100 total): leadership. Special characteristics: 179 awards ($705,250 total): children and siblings of alumni, members of minority groups. **Tuition waivers:** Full or partial for employees or children of employees. **ROTC:** Army cooperative, Air Force cooperative.

LOANS *Student loans:* $22,163,340 (94% need-based, 6% non-need-based). 85% of past graduating class borrowed through all loan programs. *Average indebtedness per student:* $35,209. **Average need-based loan:** Freshmen: $3758. Undergraduates: $4676. **Parent loans:** $5,790,564 (94% need-based, 6% non-need-based). **Programs:** Federal Direct (Subsidized and Unsubsidized Stafford, PLUS), Perkins.

WORK-STUDY *Federal work-study:* 358 jobs averaging $1405. **State or other work-study/employment:** 453 part-time jobs averaging $1658.

ATHLETIC AWARDS Total amount: $2,558,480 (65% need-based, 35% non-need-based).

APPLYING FOR FINANCIAL AID *Required financial aid forms:* FAFSA, state aid form. **Financial aid deadline (priority):** 2/15. **Notification date:** 2/15. Students must reply by 5/1 or within 2 weeks of notification.

CONTACT Mrs. Sharon J. Halpin, Director of Financial Aid, Le Moyne College, 1419 Salt Springs Road, Syracuse, NY 13214-1301, 315-445-4400 or toll-free 800-333-4733. *Fax:* 315-445-4182. *E-mail:* halpins@lemoyne.edu. *Website:* http://www.lemoyne.edu/.

LEMOYNE-OWEN COLLEGE
Memphis, TN

CONTACT Office of Student Financial Services, LeMoyne-Owen College, 807 Walker Avenue, Memphis, TN 38126-6595, 901-435-1552 or toll-free 800-737-7778. *Fax:* 901-435-1574. *Website:* http://www.loc.edu/.

LENOIR-RHYNE UNIVERSITY
Hickory, NC

Tuition & fees: $35,350	Average undergraduate aid package: $28,898

ABOUT THE INSTITUTION Independent Lutheran, coed. **Awards:** bachelor's, master's, and doctoral degrees. 51 undergraduate majors. **Total enrollment:** 2,557. Undergraduates: 1,699. Freshmen: 408. Federal methodology is used as a basis for awarding need-based institutional aid.

UNDERGRADUATE EXPENSES for 2017–2018 Application fee: $35. **Comprehensive fee:** $47,500 includes full-time tuition ($35,350) and room and board ($12,150). Room and board charges vary according to board plan. **Part-time tuition:** $1460 per credit.

FRESHMAN FINANCIAL AID (Fall 2016) 447 applied for aid; of those 93% were deemed to have need. 100% of freshmen with need received aid; of those 18% had need fully met. **Average percent of need met:** 79% (excluding resources awarded to replace EFC). **Average financial aid package:** $30,392 (excluding resources awarded to replace EFC). 11% of all full-time freshmen had no need and received non-need-based gift aid.

UNDERGRADUATE FINANCIAL AID (Fall 2016) 1,332 applied for aid; of those 93% were deemed to have need. 100% of undergraduates with need received aid; of those 16% had need fully met. **Average percent of need met:** 73% (excluding resources awarded to replace EFC). **Average financial aid package:** $28,898 (excluding resources awarded to replace EFC). 14% of all full-time undergraduates had no need and received non-need-based gift aid.

GIFT AID (NEED-BASED) Total amount: $27,355,715 (12% federal, 13% state, 73% institutional, 2% external sources). **Receiving aid:** Freshmen: 89% (414); all full-time undergraduates: 86% (1,231). **Average award:** Freshmen: $26,804; Undergraduates: $24,324. **Scholarships, grants, and awards:** Federal Pell, FSEOG, state, private, college/university gift aid from institutional funds.

GIFT AID (NON-NEED-BASED) Total amount: $4,587,816 (93% institutional, 7% external sources). **Receiving aid:** Freshmen: 12% (56). Undergraduates: 10% (145). **Average award:** Freshmen: $19,779. Undergraduates: $17,497. **Scholarships, grants, and awards by category:** Academic interests/achievement: general academic interests/achievements. Creative arts/performance: music. Special achievements/activities: cheerleading/drum major, leadership. Special characteristics: children and siblings of alumni, children of faculty/staff, ethnic background, local/state students, members of minority groups, relatives of clergy, religious affiliation, siblings of current students. **Tuition waivers:** Full or partial for employees or children of employees, senior citizens.

LOANS *Student loans:* $8,536,632 (84% need-based, 16% non-need-based). 85% of past graduating class borrowed through all loan programs. *Average indebtedness per student:* $28,485. **Average need-based loan:** Freshmen: $3133. Undergraduates: $4315. **Parent loans:** $5,359,177 (60% need-based, 40% non-need-based). **Programs:** Federal Direct (Subsidized and Unsubsidized Stafford, PLUS), Perkins, state.

WORK-STUDY *Federal work-study:* jobs available. **State or other work-study/employment:** Part-time jobs available.

ATHLETIC AWARDS Total amount: $4,331,501 (62% need-based, 38% non-need-based).

APPLYING FOR FINANCIAL AID *Required financial aid form:* FAFSA. *Financial aid deadline:* Continuous. *Notification date:* Continuous beginning 3/1. Students must reply within 3 weeks of notification.

CONTACT Financial Aid Office, Lenoir-Rhyne University, PO Box 7227, Hickory, NC 28603, 828-328-7301 or toll-free 800-277-5721. *Fax:* 828-328-7039. *E-mail:* finaid@lr.edu.

Website: http://www.lr.edu/.

LESLEY UNIVERSITY
Cambridge, MA

Tuition & fees: $27,600	Average undergraduate aid package: $17,580

ABOUT THE INSTITUTION Independent, coed, primarily women. *Awards:* certificates, associate, bachelor's, master's, and doctoral degrees. 22 undergraduate majors. *Total enrollment:* 4,732. Undergraduates: 2,096. Freshmen: 383. Federal methodology is used as a basis for awarding need-based institutional aid.

UNDERGRADUATE EXPENSES for 2018–2019 *Comprehensive fee:* $43,830 includes full-time tuition ($27,600) and room and board ($16,230). *College room only:* $9830. Full-time tuition and fees vary according to class time, course level, course load, degree level, location, program, and reciprocity agreements. Room and board charges vary according to board plan. *Part-time tuition:* $920 per credit hour.

FRESHMAN FINANCIAL AID (Fall 2017, est.) 338 applied for aid; of those 84% were deemed to have need. 100% of freshmen with need received aid; of those 9% had need fully met. *Average percent of need met:* 80% (excluding resources awarded to replace EFC). *Average financial aid package:* $19,144 (excluding resources awarded to replace EFC). 13% of all full-time freshmen had no need and received non-need-based gift aid.

UNDERGRADUATE FINANCIAL AID (Fall 2017, est.) 1,319 applied for aid; of those 87% were deemed to have need. 100% of undergraduates with need received aid; of those 6% had need fully met. *Average percent of need met:* 70% (excluding resources awarded to replace EFC). *Average financial aid package:* $17,580 (excluding resources awarded to replace EFC). 26% of all full-time undergraduates had no need and received non-need-based gift aid.

GIFT AID (NEED-BASED) *Total amount:* $14,094,549 (22% federal, 4% state, 71% institutional, 3% external sources). *Receiving aid:* Freshmen: 75% (283); all full-time undergraduates: 68% (1,113). *Average award:* Freshmen: $14,222; Undergraduates: $12,324. *Scholarships, grants, and awards:* Federal Pell, FSEOG, state, private, college/university gift aid from institutional funds.

GIFT AID (NON-NEED-BASED) *Total amount:* $5,682,542 (100% institutional). *Receiving aid:* Freshmen: 5% (19). Undergraduates: 4% (74). *Average award:* Freshmen: $10,896. Undergraduates: $10,209. *Scholarships, grants, and awards by category:* Special achievements/activities: general special achievements/activities. Special characteristics: ethnic background. *Tuition waivers:* Full or partial for employees or children of employees.

LOANS *Student loans:* $11,234,153 (51% need-based, 49% non-need-based). 80% of past graduating class borrowed through all loan programs. *Average indebtedness per student:* $23,000. *Average need-based loan:* Freshmen: $3735. Undergraduates: $4685. *Parent loans:* $5,460,484 (100% non-need-based). *Programs:* Federal Direct (Subsidized and Unsubsidized Stafford, PLUS), Perkins.

WORK-STUDY *Federal work-study:* Total amount: $500,000; jobs available. *State or other work-study/employment:* Part-time jobs available.

APPLYING FOR FINANCIAL AID *Required financial aid form:* FAFSA. *Financial aid deadline (priority):* 2/15. *Notification date:* Continuous beginning 2/1.

CONTACT Scott A. Jewell, Director of Student Financial Services, Lesley University, 29 Everett Street, Cambridge, MA 02138-2790, 617-349-8714 or toll-free 800-999-1959 Ext. 8800. *Fax:* 617-349-8667. *E-mail:* sjewell@lesley.edu.

Website: http://www.lesley.edu/.

LETOURNEAU UNIVERSITY
Longview, TX

Tuition & fees: $30,210	Average undergraduate aid package: $23,366

ABOUT THE INSTITUTION Independent nondenominational, coed. *Awards:* associate, bachelor's, and master's degrees. 66 undergraduate majors. *Total enrollment:* 3,003. Undergraduates: 2,611. Freshmen: 303. Both federal and institutional methodology are used as a basis for awarding need-based institutional aid.

UNDERGRADUATE EXPENSES for 2018–2019 *Comprehensive fee:* $40,180 includes full-time tuition ($29,630), mandatory fees ($580), and room and board ($9970). Full-time tuition and fees vary according to course level, course load, location, and program. Room and board charges vary according to board plan and housing facility. Part-time tuition and fees vary according to course level, course load, location, and program.

FRESHMAN FINANCIAL AID (Fall 2017, est.) 253 applied for aid; of those 85% were deemed to have need. 100% of freshmen with need received aid; of those 17% had need fully met. *Average percent of need met:* 78% (excluding resources awarded to replace EFC). *Average financial aid package:* $25,705 (excluding resources awarded to replace EFC). 24% of all full-time freshmen had no need and received non-need-based gift aid.

UNDERGRADUATE FINANCIAL AID (Fall 2017, est.) 1,001 applied for aid; of those 90% were deemed to have need. 99% of undergraduates with need received aid; of those 14% had need fully met. *Average percent of need met:* 70% (excluding resources awarded to replace EFC). *Average financial aid package:* $23,366 (excluding resources awarded to replace EFC). 24% of all full-time undergraduates had no need and received non-need-based gift aid.

GIFT AID (NEED-BASED) *Total amount:* $18,422,448 (20% federal, 9% state, 69% institutional, 2% external sources). *Receiving aid:* Freshmen: 75% (214); all full-time undergraduates: 69% (871). *Average award:* Freshmen: $20,378; Undergraduates: $17,806. *Scholarships, grants, and awards:* Federal Pell, FSEOG, state, private, college/university gift aid from institutional funds, United Negro College Fund.

GIFT AID (NON-NEED-BASED) *Total amount:* $2,654,389 (3% federal, 91% institutional, 6% external sources). *Receiving aid:* Freshmen: 11% (31). Undergraduates: 7% (84). *Average award:* Freshmen: $15,668. Undergraduates: $14,058. *Tuition waivers:* Full or partial for employees or children of employees.

LOANS *Student loans:* $14,596,581 (81% need-based, 19% non-need-based). 66% of past graduating class borrowed through all loan programs. *Average indebtedness per student:* $36,704. *Average need-based loan:* Freshmen: $4380. Undergraduates: $5279. *Parent loans:* $1,815,193 (54% need-based, 46% non-need-based). *Programs:* Federal Direct (Subsidized and Unsubsidized Stafford, PLUS), Perkins, state, private loans.

WORK-STUDY *Federal work-study:* Total amount: $330,923; jobs available. *State or other work-study/employment:* Total amount: $7831 (100% need-based). Part-time jobs available.

APPLYING FOR FINANCIAL AID *Required financial aid form:* FAFSA. *Financial aid deadline:* 8/1 (priority: 11/1). *Notification date:* Continuous beginning 11/30. Students must reply within 2 weeks of notification.

CONTACT Financial Aid Office, LeTourneau University, PO Box 7001, Longview, TX 75607, 903-233-4312 or toll-free 800-759-8811. *Fax:* 903-233-4302. *E-mail:* financialaid@letu.edu.

Website: http://www.letu.edu/.

LEWIS & CLARK COLLEGE
Portland, OR

Tuition & fees: $48,988	Average undergraduate aid package: $40,854

ABOUT THE INSTITUTION Independent, coed. *Awards:* certificates, bachelor's, master's, and doctoral degrees. 35 undergraduate majors. *Total enrollment:* 3,419. Undergraduates: 2,134. Freshmen: 506. Both federal and institutional methodology are used as a basis for awarding need-based institutional aid.

UNDERGRADUATE EXPENSES for 2017–2018 *Comprehensive fee:* $61,084 includes full-time tuition ($48,628), mandatory fees ($360), and room and board ($12,096). *College room only:* $6728. Room and board charges vary according to board plan and housing facility. *Part-time tuition:* $2431 per credit hour. *Part-time fees:* $18 per credit hour. Part-time tuition and fees vary according to course load.

FRESHMAN FINANCIAL AID (Fall 2017, est.) 441 applied for aid; of those 79% were deemed to have need. 100% of freshmen with need received aid; of those 45% had need fully met. *Average percent of need met:* 88% (excluding resources awarded to replace EFC). *Average financial aid package:* $39,084 (excluding resources awarded to replace EFC). 28% of all full-time freshmen had no need and received non-need-based gift aid.

UNDERGRADUATE FINANCIAL AID (Fall 2017, est.) 1,412 applied for aid; of those 86% were deemed to have need. 100% of undergraduates with need received aid; of those 41% had need fully met. *Average percent of need met:* 87% (excluding resources awarded to replace EFC). *Average financial aid package:* $40,854 (excluding resources awarded to replace EFC). 34% of all full-time undergraduates had no need and received non-need-based gift aid.

GIFT AID (NEED-BASED) *Total amount:* $39,543,885 (6% federal, 89% institutional, 5% external sources). *Receiving aid:* Freshmen: 65% (339); all full-time undergraduates: 59% (1,191). *Average award:* Freshmen: $32,156; Undergraduates: $33,162. *Scholarships, grants, and awards:* Federal Pell, FSEOG, state, private, college/university gift aid from institutional funds.

GIFT AID (NON-NEED-BASED) *Total amount:* $12,069,351 (98% institutional, 2% external sources). *Receiving aid:* Freshmen: 17% (91). Undergraduates: 8% (153). *Average award:* Freshmen: $18,713. Undergraduates: $16,695. *Scholarships, grants, and awards by category:* Academic interests/achievement: general academic interests/achievements. *Creative arts/performance:* debating, music. *Special achievements/activities:* community service, leadership. *Special characteristics:* children of faculty/staff, first-generation college students. *Tuition waivers:* Full or partial for employees or children of employees. *ROTC:* Army cooperative.

LOANS *Student loans:* $7,408,034 (95% need-based, 5% non-need-based). 50% of past graduating class borrowed through all loan programs. *Average indebtedness per student:* $27,591. *Average need-based loan:* Freshmen: $3320. Undergraduates: $4381. *Parent loans:* $10,615,034 (66% need-based, 34% non-need-based). *Programs:* Federal Direct (Subsidized and Unsubsidized Stafford, PLUS), Perkins.

WORK-STUDY *Federal work-study:* Total amount: $2,317,285; 944 jobs averaging $2455. *State or other work-study/employment:* Total amount: $929,444 (47% need-based, 53% non-need-based). 156 part-time jobs averaging $2140.

APPLYING FOR FINANCIAL AID *Required financial aid forms:* FAFSA, CSS Financial Aid PROFILE. *Financial aid deadline (priority):* 1/15. *Notification date:* Continuous beginning 1/30. Students must reply by 7/1 or within 2 weeks of notification.

CONTACT Anastacia Dillon, Director of Financial Aid, Lewis & Clark College, Templeton Campus Center, MSC 56, Portland, OR 97219-7899, 503-768-7090 or toll-free 800-444-4111. *Fax:* 503-768-7074. *E-mail:* fao@lclark.edu.
Website: http://www.lclark.edu/.

LEWIS-CLARK STATE COLLEGE
Lewiston, ID

Tuition & fees: N/R	Average undergraduate aid package: $8277

ABOUT THE INSTITUTION State-supported, coed. 50 undergraduate majors. Federal methodology is used as a basis for awarding need-based institutional aid.

FRESHMAN FINANCIAL AID (Fall 2016) 512 applied for aid; of those 75% were deemed to have need. 100% of freshmen with need received aid; of those 14% had need fully met. *Average percent of need met:* 75% (excluding resources awarded to replace EFC). *Average financial aid package:* $7809 (excluding resources awarded to replace EFC). 13% of all full-time freshmen had no need and received non-need-based gift aid.

UNDERGRADUATE FINANCIAL AID (Fall 2016) 2,389 applied for aid; of those 77% were deemed to have need. 98% of undergraduates with need received aid; of those 28% had need fully met. *Average percent of need met:* 80% (excluding resources awarded to replace EFC). *Average financial aid package:* $8277 (excluding resources awarded to replace EFC). 13% of all full-time undergraduates had no need and received non-need-based gift aid.

GIFT AID (NEED-BASED) *Total amount:* $13,430,129 (44% federal, 56% state). *Receiving aid:* Freshmen: 50% (262); all full-time undergraduates: 50% (1,300). *Average award:* Freshmen: $4337; Undergraduates: $4501. *Scholarships, grants,*

and awards: Federal Pell, FSEOG, state, private, college/university gift aid from institutional funds.

GIFT AID (NON-NEED-BASED) *Total amount:* $2,705,050 (2% federal, 1% state, 50% institutional, 47% external sources). *Receiving aid:* Freshmen: 48% (251). Undergraduates: 33% (855). *Average award:* Freshmen: $3647. Undergraduates: $4015. *Scholarships, grants, and awards by category:* Academic interests/achievement: 40 awards ($38,500 total): biological sciences, business, communication, education, engineering/technologies, English, general academic interests/achievements, health fields, home economics, humanities, mathematics, physical sciences, social sciences. *Creative arts/performance:* 6 awards ($29,000 total): art/fine arts, creative writing, debating, music, theater/drama. *Special achievements/activities:* 110 awards ($147,975 total): community service, general special achievements/activities, junior miss, leadership, memberships, rodeo. *Special characteristics:* adult students, children and siblings of alumni, children of faculty/staff, ethnic background, first-generation college students, general special characteristics, members of minority groups, out-of-state students, previous college experience.

LOANS *Student loans:* $12,498,933 (46% need-based, 54% non-need-based). 77% of past graduating class borrowed through all loan programs. *Average indebtedness per student:* $27,370. *Average need-based loan:* Freshmen: $1995. Undergraduates: $3718. *Parent loans:* $577,983 (100% non-need-based). *Programs:* Federal Direct (Subsidized and Unsubsidized Stafford, PLUS), Perkins, Federal Nursing.

WORK-STUDY *Federal work-study:* 62 jobs averaging $1569. *State or other work-study/employment:* Total amount: $149,452 (63% need-based, 37% non-need-based). 89 part-time jobs averaging $1690.

ATHLETIC AWARDS Total amount: $2,022,513 (100% non-need-based).

APPLYING FOR FINANCIAL AID *Required financial aid form:* FAFSA. *Financial aid deadline (priority):* 3/1. *Notification date:* Continuous beginning 4/15. Students must reply within 2 weeks of notification.

CONTACT Ms. Laura Hughes, Director of Financial Aid, Lewis-Clark State College, 500 8th Avenue, Lewiston, ID 83501-2698, 208-792-2224 or toll-free 800-933-5272. *Fax:* 208-792-2063. *E-mail:* lhughes@lcsc.edu.
Website: http://www.lcsc.edu/.

LEWIS UNIVERSITY
Romeoville, IL

Tuition & fees: $32,450	Average undergraduate aid package: $25,119

ABOUT THE INSTITUTION Independent Roman Catholic Church, coed. *Awards:* certificates, associate, bachelor's, master's, and doctoral degrees. 73 undergraduate majors. *Total enrollment:* 6,506. Undergraduates: 4,506. Freshmen: 609. Federal methodology is used as a basis for awarding need-based institutional aid.

UNDERGRADUATE EXPENSES for 2018–2019 *Application fee:* $40. *Comprehensive fee:* $43,028 includes full-time tuition ($32,300), mandatory fees ($150), and room and board ($10,578). Full-time tuition and fees vary according to course load, location, and program. Room and board charges vary according to board plan and housing facility. *Part-time tuition:* $948 per credit hour. *Part-time fees:* $75 per term. Part-time tuition and fees vary according to course load, location, and program.

FRESHMAN FINANCIAL AID (Fall 2017, est.) 564 applied for aid; of those 87% were deemed to have need. 100% of freshmen with need received aid; of those 25% had need fully met. *Average percent of need met:* 92% (excluding resources awarded to replace EFC). *Average financial aid package:* $28,160 (excluding resources awarded to replace EFC). 17% of all full-time freshmen had no need and received non-need-based gift aid.

UNDERGRADUATE FINANCIAL AID (Fall 2017, est.) 3,134 applied for aid; of those 90% were deemed to have need. 100% of undergraduates with need received aid; of those 20% had need fully met. *Average percent of need met:* 86% (excluding resources awarded to replace EFC). *Average financial aid package:* $25,119 (excluding resources awarded to replace EFC). 16% of all full-time undergraduates had no need and received non-need-based gift aid.

GIFT AID (NEED-BASED) *Total amount:* $41,865,500 (15% federal, 14% state, 70% institutional, 1% external sources). *Receiving aid:* Freshmen: 80% (489); all full-time undergraduates: 73% (2,674). *Average award:* Freshmen: $19,706; Undergraduates: $15,882. *Scholarships, grants, and awards:* Federal Pell, FSEOG, state, private, college/university gift aid from institutional funds.

GIFT AID (NON-NEED-BASED) *Total amount:* $8,372,696 (99% institutional, 1% external sources). *Receiving aid:* Freshmen: 14% (87). Undergraduates: 9%

(320), *Average award:* Freshmen: $14,406. Undergraduates: $11,661. *Scholarships, grants, and awards by category: Academic interests/achievement:* general academic interests/achievements. *Creative arts/performance:* art/fine arts, music, theater/drama. *Special achievements/activities:* cheerleading/drum major, community service, general special achievements/activities, leadership, memberships, religious involvement. *Special characteristics:* children and siblings of alumni, children of faculty/staff, previous college experience, religious affiliation, veterans, veterans' children. *Tuition waivers:* Full or partial for children of alumni, employees or children of employees. *ROTC:* Army cooperative, Air Force cooperative.

LOANS *Student loans:* $33,052,521 (72% need-based, 28% non-need-based). 79% of past graduating class borrowed through all loan programs. *Average indebtedness per student:* $34,006. *Average need-based loan:* Freshmen: $3361. Undergraduates: $4425. *Parent loans:* $8,099,387 (44% need-based, 56% non-need-based). *Programs:* Federal Direct (Subsidized and Unsubsidized Stafford, PLUS), Perkins.

WORK-STUDY *Federal work-study:* Total amount: $3,987,611; jobs available. *State or other work-study/employment:* Total amount: $1,331,967 (35% need-based, 65% non-need-based). Part-time jobs available.

ATHLETIC AWARDS Total amount: $3,564,015 (46% need-based, 54% non-need-based).

APPLYING FOR FINANCIAL AID *Required financial aid form:* FAFSA. *Financial aid deadline:* 5/1 (priority: 10/31). *Notification date:* Continuous beginning 11/1. Students must reply by 5/1 or within 2 weeks of notification.

CONTACT Ms. Janeen Decharinte, Director of Financial Aid Services, Lewis University, One University Parkway, Romeoville, IL 60446, 815-836-5263 or toll-free 800-897-9000. *Fax:* 815-836-5135. *E-mail:* decharja@lewisu.edu. *Website:* http://www.lewisu.edu/.

LIBERTY UNIVERSITY
Lynchburg, VA

Tuition & fees: $23,940	Average undergraduate aid package: $15,024

ABOUT THE INSTITUTION Independent nondenominational, coed. *Awards:* certificates, associate, bachelor's, master's, and doctoral degrees (also offers external degree program with significant enrollment not reflected in profile). 91 undergraduate majors. *Total enrollment:* 15,549. Undergraduates: 13,785. Freshmen: 2,816. Federal methodology is used as a basis for awarding need-based institutional aid.

UNDERGRADUATE EXPENSES for 2017–2018 *Application fee:* $50. *Comprehensive fee:* $33,790 includes full-time tuition ($22,880), mandatory fees ($1060), and room and board ($9850). *College room only:* $6210. Full-time tuition and fees vary according to course load. Room and board charges vary according to housing facility. *Part-time tuition:* $780 per credit hour. Part-time tuition and fees vary according to course load.

FRESHMAN FINANCIAL AID (Fall 2017, est.) 2,680 applied for aid; of those 79% were deemed to have need. 100% of freshmen with need received aid; of those 11% had need fully met. *Average percent of need met:* 55% (excluding resources awarded to replace EFC). *Average financial aid package:* $14,553 (excluding resources awarded to replace EFC). 19% of all full-time freshmen had no need and received non-need-based gift aid.

UNDERGRADUATE FINANCIAL AID (Fall 2017, est.) 12,158 applied for aid; of those 81% were deemed to have need. 100% of undergraduates with need received aid; of those 11% had need fully met. *Average percent of need met:* 56% (excluding resources awarded to replace EFC). *Average financial aid package:* $15,024 (excluding resources awarded to replace EFC). 17% of all full-time undergraduates had no need and received non-need-based gift aid.

GIFT AID (NEED-BASED) *Total amount:* $107,434,467 (16% federal, 7% state, 73% institutional, 4% external sources). *Receiving aid:* Freshmen: 76% (2,112); all full-time undergraduates: 73% (9,727). *Average award:* Freshmen: $11,182; Undergraduates: $10,905. *Scholarships, grants, and awards:* Federal Pell, FSEOG, state, private, college/university gift aid from institutional funds.

GIFT AID (NON-NEED-BASED) *Total amount:* $31,989,047 (9% state, 87% institutional, 4% external sources). *Receiving aid:* Freshmen: 14% (390). Undergraduates: 14% (1,794). *Average award:* Freshmen: $7042. Undergraduates: $7540. *Scholarships, grants, and awards by category: Academic interests/achievement:* biological sciences, business, communication, computer science, education, engineering/technologies, English, general academic interests/achievements, mathematics, premedicine, religion/biblical studies. *Creative arts/performance:* cinema/

film/broadcasting, debating, journalism/publications, music, performing arts. *Special achievements/activities:* cheerleading/drum major, leadership. *Special characteristics:* children of faculty/staff, international students, local/state students, religious affiliation, veterans. *Tuition waivers:* Full or partial for employees or children of employees. *ROTC:* Army, Air Force cooperative.

LOANS *Student loans:* $72,788,458 (84% need-based, 16% non-need-based). 61% of past graduating class borrowed through all loan programs. *Average indebtedness per student:* $21,875. *Average need-based loan:* Freshmen: $3472. Undergraduates: $4331. *Parent loans:* $30,777,126 (83% need-based, 17% non-need-based). *Programs:* Federal Direct (Subsidized and Unsubsidized Stafford, PLUS), state, college/university, Canadian federal and provincial loans.

WORK-STUDY *Federal work-study:* Total amount: $2,236,831; jobs available. *State or other work-study/employment:* Part-time jobs available.

ATHLETIC AWARDS Total amount: $7,003,331 (60% need-based, 40% non-need-based).

APPLYING FOR FINANCIAL AID *Required financial aid forms:* FAFSA, state aid form. *Financial aid deadline:* 3/1. *Notification date:* Continuous beginning 3/15. Students must reply within 3 weeks of notification.

CONTACT Robert Ritz, Office of Financial Aid, Liberty University, 1971 University Boulevard, Lynchburg, VA 24515, 434-582-2270 or toll-free 800-543-5317. *Fax:* 434-582-2053. *E-mail:* financialaid@liberty.edu. *Website:* http://www.liberty.edu/.

LIFE PACIFIC COLLEGE
San Dimas, CA

CONTACT Mrs. Luci Perez, Director of Financial Aid, Life Pacific College, 1100 Covina Boulevard, San Dimas, CA 91773-3298, 909-599-5433 Ext. 322 or toll-free 877-886-5433 Ext. 314. *Fax:* 909-706-3031. *E-mail:* lperez@lifepacific.edu. *Website:* http://www.lifepacific.edu/.

LIFE UNIVERSITY
Marietta, GA

Tuition & fees: $11,715	Average undergraduate aid package: $11,000

ABOUT THE INSTITUTION Independent, coed. *Awards:* certificates, associate, bachelor's, master's, and doctoral degrees. 11 undergraduate majors. *Total enrollment:* 2,619. Undergraduates: 755. Freshmen: 115. Federal methodology is used as a basis for awarding need-based institutional aid.

UNDERGRADUATE EXPENSES for 2017–2018 *Application fee:* $50. *Comprehensive fee:* $26,115 includes full-time tuition ($10,665), mandatory fees ($1050), and room and board ($14,400). *College room only:* $5100. Full-time tuition and fees vary according to course load. Room and board charges vary according to housing facility. *Part-time tuition:* $237 per credit hour.

FRESHMAN FINANCIAL AID (Fall 2017, est.) 92 applied for aid; of those 89% were deemed to have need. 100% of freshmen with need received aid. *Average percent of need met:* 29% (excluding resources awarded to replace EFC). *Average financial aid package:* $11,000 (excluding resources awarded to replace EFC). 5% of all full-time freshmen had no need and received non-need-based gift aid.

UNDERGRADUATE FINANCIAL AID (Fall 2017, est.) 526 applied for aid; of those 94% were deemed to have need. 100% of undergraduates with need received aid. *Average percent of need met:* 29% (excluding resources awarded to replace EFC). *Average financial aid package:* $11,000 (excluding resources awarded to replace EFC). 1% of all full-time undergraduates had no need and received non-need-based gift aid.

GIFT AID (NEED-BASED) *Total amount:* $1,834,000 (100% federal). *Receiving aid:* Freshmen: 51% (58); all full-time undergraduates: 46% (316). *Average award:* Freshmen: $5100; Undergraduates: $5300. *Scholarships, grants, and awards:* Federal Pell, FSEOG.

GIFT AID (NON-NEED-BASED) *Total amount:* $451,000 (36% state, 64% institutional). *Receiving aid:* Freshmen: 69% (78). Undergraduates: 49% (335). *Average award:* Freshmen: $1700. Undergraduates: $1800. *Scholarships, grants, and awards by category: Academic interests/achievement:* general academic interests/achievements. *Special achievements/activities:* general special achievements/

activities, leadership. *Special characteristics:* children and siblings of alumni, general special characteristics, international students, local/state students, members of minority groups. *Tuition waivers:* Full or partial for employees or children of employees.

LOANS *Student loans:* $2,200,000 (55% need-based, 45% non-need-based). 67% of past graduating class borrowed through all loan programs. *Average indebtedness per student:* $29,500. *Average need-based loan:* Freshmen: $3700. Undergraduates: $5300. *Parent loans:* $440,000 (100% need-based). *Programs:* Federal Direct (Subsidized and Unsubsidized Stafford, PLUS), Perkins, state, college/university, alternative loans.

WORK-STUDY *Federal work-study:* Total amount: $120,000; jobs available. *State or other work-study/employment:* Total amount: $13,500 (100% non-need-based). Part-time jobs available.

ATHLETIC AWARDS Total amount: $610,000 (100% non-need-based).

APPLYING FOR FINANCIAL AID *Required financial aid form:* FAFSA. *Financial aid deadline (priority):* 3/15. *Notification date:* Continuous beginning 4/1.

CONTACT Melissa Waters, Director of Financial Aid, Life University, 1269 Barclay Circle, Marietta, GA 30060, 770-426-2901 or toll-free 800-543-3202. *Fax:* 770-426-2926. *E-mail:* finaid@life.edu. *Website:* http://www.life.edu/.

LIM COLLEGE
New York, NY

Tuition & fees: N/R	Average undergraduate aid package: N/A

ABOUT THE INSTITUTION Proprietary, coed, primarily women. *Awards:* certificates, bachelor's, and master's degrees. 5 undergraduate majors. *Total enrollment:* 161. Undergraduates: 1,402. Freshmen: 253. Both federal and institutional methodology are used as a basis for awarding need-based institutional aid.

UNDERGRADUATE EXPENSES for 2018–2019 *Application fee:* $40. *Tuition:* part-time $870 per credit. Room and board charges vary according to housing facility.

FRESHMAN FINANCIAL AID (Fall 2016) 255 applied for aid; of those 65% were deemed to have need. 99% of freshmen with need received aid; of those 2% had need fully met. *Average percent of need met:* 37% (excluding resources awarded to replace EFC). *Average financial aid package:* $10,352 (excluding resources awarded to replace EFC). 9% of all full-time freshmen had no need and received non-need-based gift aid.

GIFT AID (NEED-BASED) *Total amount:* $4,170,866 (51% federal, 11% state, 37% institutional, 1% external sources). *Receiving aid:* Freshmen: 38% (96). *Average award:* Freshmen: $7112. *Scholarships, grants, and awards:* Federal Pell, FSEOG, state, private, college/university gift aid from institutional funds.

GIFT AID (NON-NEED-BASED) *Total amount:* $3,404,838 (8% federal, 1% state, 87% institutional, 4% external sources). *Receiving aid:* Freshmen: 54% (137). *Average award:* Freshmen: $3979. *Scholarships, grants, and awards by category:* Academic interests/achievement: general academic interests/achievements. *Special achievements/activities:* leadership, memberships. *Special characteristics:* children of faculty/staff, local/state students, siblings of current students. *Tuition waivers:* Full or partial for employees or children of employees.

LOANS *Student loans:* $10,602,805 (32% need-based, 68% non-need-based). 72% of past graduating class borrowed through all loan programs. *Average indebtedness per student:* $35,716. *Average need-based loan:* Freshmen: $3313. *Parent loans:* $9,867,071 (100% non-need-based). *Programs:* Federal Direct (Subsidized and Unsubsidized Stafford, PLUS).

WORK-STUDY Federal work-study jobs available.

APPLYING FOR FINANCIAL AID *Required financial aid forms:* FAFSA, institution's own form. *Financial aid deadline (priority):* 3/1. *Notification date:* Continuous.

CONTACT Office of Student Financial Services, LIM College, 12 East 53rd Street, New York, NY 10022-5268, 212-310-0632 Ext. 389 or toll-free 800-677-1323. *Fax:* 212-750-3452. *E-mail:* sfs@limcollege.edu. *Website:* http://www.limcollege.edu/.

LIMESTONE COLLEGE
Gaffney, SC

CONTACT Mr. Bobby Greer, Director of Financial Aid, Limestone College, 1115 College Drive, Gaffney, SC 29340-3799, 864-488-4567 or toll-free 800-795-7151. *Fax:* 864-487-8706. *E-mail:* bgreer@llmestone.edu. *Website:* http://www.limestone.edu/.

LINCOLN CHRISTIAN UNIVERSITY
Lincoln, IL

ABOUT THE INSTITUTION Independent Christian Churches and Churches of Christ, coed. *Awards:* associate, bachelor's, master's, and doctoral degrees. 12 undergraduate majors. *Total enrollment:* 787. Undergraduates: 464. Freshmen: 82.

GIFT AID (NEED-BASED) *Scholarships, grants, and awards:* Federal Pell, FSEOG, state, private, college/university gift aid from institutional funds.

GIFT AID (NON-NEED-BASED) *Scholarships, grants, and awards by category:* Academic interests/achievement: general academic interests/achievements. *Special characteristics:* children of faculty/staff, international students, relatives of clergy.

LOANS *Programs:* Federal Direct (Subsidized and Unsubsidized Stafford, PLUS), Perkins, alternative loans.

APPLYING FOR FINANCIAL AID *Required financial aid form:* FAFSA.

CONTACT Nancy Siddens, Director of Financial Aid, Lincoln Christian University, 100 Campus View Drive, Lincoln, IL 62656, 217-732-3168 Ext. 2250 or toll-free 888-522-5228. *Fax:* 217-732-4199. *E-mail:* finaid@lincolnchristian.edu. *Website:* http://www.lincolnchristian.edu/.

LINCOLN COLLEGE
Lincoln, IL

CONTACT Financial Aid Office, Lincoln College, 300 Keokuk Street, Lincoln, IL 62656-1699, 217-732-3155 or toll-free 800-569-0558. *Website:* http://www.lincolncollege.edu/.

LINCOLN COLLEGE OF NEW ENGLAND
Southington, CT

CONTACT Financial Aid Office, Lincoln College of New England, 2279 Mount Vernon Road, Southington, CT 06489-1057, 860-628-4751 or toll-free 800-825-0087. *Website:* http://www.lincolncollegene.edu/.

LINCOLN MEMORIAL UNIVERSITY
Harrogate, TN

Tuition & fees: N/R	Average undergraduate aid package: $22,114

ABOUT THE INSTITUTION Independent, coed. *Awards:* certificates, associate, bachelor's, master's, and doctoral degrees. 43 undergraduate majors. *Total enrollment:* 4,770. Undergraduates: 1,919. Freshmen: 346. Federal methodology is used as a basis for awarding need-based institutional aid.

FRESHMAN FINANCIAL AID (Fall 2016) 254 applied for aid; of those 90% were deemed to have need. 100% of freshmen with need received aid; of those 34% had need fully met. *Average percent of need met:* 87% (excluding resources awarded to replace EFC). *Average financial aid package:* $24,123 (excluding resources awarded to replace EFC). 6% of all full-time freshmen had no need and received non-need-based gift aid.

UNDERGRADUATE FINANCIAL AID (Fall 2016) 1,050 applied for aid, of those 89% were deemed to have need. 100% of undergraduates with need received aid; of those 32% had need fully met. *Average percent of need met:* 83% (excluding resources awarded to replace EFC). *Average financial aid package:* $22,114 (excluding resources awarded to replace EFC). 7% of all full-time undergraduates had no need and received non-need-based gift aid.

GIFT AID (NEED-BASED) *Total amount:* $16,803,411 (19% federal, 15% state, 61% institutional, 5% external sources). *Receiving aid:* Freshmen: 84% (227); all full-time undergraduates: 82% (929). *Average award:* Freshmen: $16,547; Undergraduates: $14,876. *Scholarships, grants, and awards:* Federal Pell, FSEOG, state, private, college/university gift aid from institutional funds.

GIFT AID (NON-NEED-BASED) *Total amount:* $2,750,499 (7% state, 81% institutional, 12% external sources). *Receiving aid:* Freshmen: 9% (25). Undergraduates: 10% (113). *Average award:* Freshmen: $11,927. Undergraduates: $9788. *Scholarships, grants, and awards by category: Academic interests/achievement:* general academic interests/achievements. *Creative arts/performance:* music. *Special achievements/activities:* cheerleading/drum major. *Special characteristics:* children and siblings of alumni, children of faculty/staff, local/state students, members of minority groups. *Tuition waivers:* Full or partial for employees or children of employees. *ROTC:* Army cooperative.

LOANS *Student loans:* $7,943,170 (77% need-based, 23% non-need-based). 75% of past graduating class borrowed through all loan programs. *Average indebtedness per student:* $18,038. *Average need-based loan:* Freshmen: $4107. Undergraduates: $6522. *Parent loans:* $1,019,859 (54% need-based, 46% non-need-based). *Programs:* Federal Direct (Subsidized and Unsubsidized Stafford, PLUS), Perkins.

WORK-STUDY *Federal work-study:* jobs available. *State or other work-study/employment:* Total amount: $127,843 (54% need-based, 46% non-need-based). Part-time jobs available.

ATHLETIC AWARDS Total amount: $3,025,260 (44% need-based, 56% non-need-based).

APPLYING FOR FINANCIAL AID *Required financial aid form:* FAFSA. *Financial aid deadline (priority):* 2/15. *Notification date:* Continuous beginning 3/1. Students must reply within 3 weeks of notification.

CONTACT Tammy Tomfohrde, Executive Director of Financial Aid, Lincoln Memorial University, 6965 Cumberland Gap Parkway, Harrogate, TN 37752-1901, 423-869-6465 or toll-free 800-325-0900. *Fax:* 423-869-6347. *E-mail:* tammy.tomfohrde@lmunet.edu.
Website: http://www.lmunet.edu/.

LINCOLN UNIVERSITY
Oakland, CA

CONTACT Financial Aid Office, Lincoln University, 401 15th Street, Oakland, CA 94612, 510-628-8010 or toll-free 888-810-9998.
Website: http://www.lincolnuca.edu/.

LINCOLN UNIVERSITY
Jefferson City, MO

Tuition & fees (MO res): $7632	Average undergraduate aid package: $14,660

ABOUT THE INSTITUTION State-supported, coed. *Awards:* certificates, associate, bachelor's, and master's degrees. 39 undergraduate majors. *Total enrollment:* 2,619. Undergraduates: 2,512. Freshmen: 475. Federal methodology is used as a basis for awarding need-based institutional aid.

UNDERGRADUATE EXPENSES for 2017–2018 *Tuition, state resident:* full-time $6270; part-time $209 per credit hour. *Tuition, nonresident:* full-time $12,810; part-time $427 per credit hour. *Required fees:* full-time $1362; $10 per credit hour or $531 per term. Full-time tuition and fees vary according to course load, location, and reciprocity agreements. Part-time tuition and fees vary according to course load, location, and reciprocity agreements. *College room and board:* $6770; *Room only:* $3510. Room and board charges vary according to board plan and housing facility.

FRESHMAN FINANCIAL AID (Fall 2017, est.) 437 applied for aid; of those 95% were deemed to have need. 97% of freshmen with need received aid; of those 3% had

need fully met. *Average percent of need met:* 61% (excluding resources awarded to replace EFC). *Average financial aid package:* $17,962 (excluding resources awarded to replace EFC).

UNDERGRADUATE FINANCIAL AID (Fall 2017, est.) 1,621 applied for aid; of those 89% were deemed to have need. 98% of undergraduates with need received aid; of those 4% had need fully met. *Average percent of need met:* 68% (excluding resources awarded to replace EFC). *Average financial aid package:* $14,660 (excluding resources awarded to replace EFC). 1% of all full-time undergraduates had no need and received non-need-based gift aid.

GIFT AID (NEED-BASED) *Total amount:* $9,315,970 (73% federal, 8% state, 12% institutional, 7% external sources). *Receiving aid:* Freshmen: 79% (367); all full-time undergraduates: 72% (1,280). *Average award:* Freshmen: $3854; Undergraduates: $4024. *Scholarships, grants, and awards:* Federal Pell, FSEOG, state, private, college/university gift aid from institutional funds.

GIFT AID (NON-NEED-BASED) *Total amount:* $452,702 (10% federal, 4% state, 25% institutional, 61% external sources). *Receiving aid:* Freshmen: 53% (245). Undergraduates: 39% (697). *Average award:* Undergraduates: $3000. *Scholarships, grants, and awards by category: Academic interests/achievement:* 116 awards ($814,806 total): agriculture, general academic interests/achievements, military science. *Creative arts/performance:* 83 awards ($157,930 total): art/fine arts, journalism/publications, music, performing arts, theater/drama. *Special achievements/activities:* 7 awards ($1565 total): cheerleading/drum major. *Special characteristics:* 532 awards ($3,098,508 total): adult students, children of faculty/staff, international students, out-of-state students. *Tuition waivers:* Full or partial for employees or children of employees, senior citizens. *ROTC:* Army.

LOANS *Student loans:* $11,428,522 (45% need-based, 55% non-need-based). 70% of past graduating class borrowed through all loan programs. *Average indebtedness per student:* $32,928. *Average need-based loan:* Freshmen: $3472. Undergraduates: $4112. *Parent loans:* $2,903,852 (100% non-need-based). *Programs:* Federal Direct (Subsidized and Unsubsidized Stafford, PLUS), private loans.

WORK-STUDY *Federal work-study:* Total amount: $245,060; 188 jobs averaging $984. *State or other work-study/employment:* Total amount: $49,436 (100% non-need-based). 33 part-time jobs averaging $1780.

ATHLETIC AWARDS Total amount: $1,125,688 (100% need-based).

APPLYING FOR FINANCIAL AID *Required financial aid form:* FAFSA. *Financial aid deadline (priority):* 3/1. *Notification date:* Continuous beginning 2/15. Students must reply within 2 weeks of notification.

CONTACT Mr. Alfred Robinson, Director of Student Financial Aid, Lincoln University, 820 Chestnut Street, Jefferson City, MO 65102-0029, 573-681-6156. *Fax:* 573-681-5871. *E-mail:* robinsona@lincolnu.edu.
Website: http://www.lincolnu.edu/.

LINCOLN UNIVERSITY
Lincoln University, PA

Tuition & fees (PA res): $10,636	Average undergraduate aid package: $12,397

ABOUT THE INSTITUTION State-related, coed. *Awards:* certificates, bachelor's, and master's degrees. 32 undergraduate majors. *Total enrollment:* 2,266. Undergraduates: 2,002. Freshmen: 664. Federal methodology is used as a basis for awarding need-based institutional aid.

UNDERGRADUATE EXPENSES for 2018–2019 *One-time required fee:* $216. *Tuition, state resident:* full-time $7866. *Tuition, nonresident:* full-time $13,002. *Required fees:* full-time $2770. Full-time tuition and fees vary according to course load, degree level, location, program, and student level. Part-time tuition and fees vary according to course load, degree level, location, program, and student level. *College room and board:* $9738. Room and board charges vary according to board plan and housing facility. *Payment plan:* Guaranteed tuition.

FRESHMAN FINANCIAL AID (Fall 2016) 498 applied for aid; of those 95% were deemed to have need. 100% of freshmen with need received aid; of those 4% had need fully met. *Average percent of need met:* 35% (excluding resources awarded to replace EFC). *Average financial aid package:* $11,744 (excluding resources awarded to replace EFC). 3% of all full-time freshmen had no need and received non-need-based gift aid.

UNDERGRADUATE FINANCIAL AID (Fall 2016) 1,598 applied for aid; of those 94% were deemed to have need. 99% of undergraduates with need received aid; of those 6% had need fully met. *Average percent of need met:* 38% (excluding

resources awarded to replace EFC). *Average financial aid package:* $12,397 (excluding resources awarded to replace EFC). 3% of all full-time undergraduates had no need and received non-need-based gift aid.

GIFT AID (NEED-BASED) *Total amount:* $33,708,308 (77% federal, 5% state, 12% institutional, 6% external sources). *Receiving aid:* Freshmen: 87% (449); all full-time undergraduates: 89% (1,492). *Average award:* Freshmen: $6896; Undergraduates: $6797. *Scholarships, grants, and awards:* Federal Pell, FSEOG, state, private, college/university gift aid from institutional funds, United Negro College Fund.

GIFT AID (NON-NEED-BASED) *Total amount:* $1,560,784 (66% federal, 24% institutional, 10% external sources). *Receiving aid:* Freshmen: 60% (311). Undergraduates: 54% (896). *Average award:* Freshmen: $6315. Undergraduates: $5821. *Scholarships, grants, and awards by category: Academic interests/achievement:* 636 awards ($2,773,128 total): general academic interests/achievements. *Creative arts/performance:* 162 awards ($205,472 total): art/fine arts, music. *Special characteristics:* 125 awards ($341,198 total): children and siblings of alumni, children of faculty/staff. *Tuition waivers:* Full or partial for children of alumni, employees or children of employees. *ROTC:* Army cooperative.

LOANS *Student loans:* $13,381,957 (96% need-based, 4% non-need-based). 86% of past graduating class borrowed through all loan programs. *Average indebtedness per student:* $41,630. *Average need-based loan:* Freshmen: $3663. Undergraduates: $4192. *Parent loans:* $8,635,476 (93% need-based, 7% non-need-based). *Programs:* Federal Direct (Subsidized and Unsubsidized Stafford, PLUS), Perkins, private loans.

WORK-STUDY *Federal work-study:* 202 jobs averaging $1037. *State or other work-study/employment:* Total amount: $23,951 (100% need-based). Part-time jobs available.

ATHLETIC AWARDS Total amount: $781,668 (93% need-based, 7% non-need-based).

APPLYING FOR FINANCIAL AID *Required financial aid form:* FAFSA. *Financial aid deadline (priority):* 4/1. *Notification date:* Continuous beginning 2/20. Students must reply within 2 weeks of notification.

CONTACT Ms. Kim Anderson, Director of Financial Aid, Lincoln University, 1570 Baltimore Pike, Lincoln University, PA 19352, 800-561-2606 or toll-free 800-790-0191. *Fax:* 484-365-8198. *E-mail:* kanderson@lincoln.edu. *Website:* http://www.lincoln.edu/.

LINDENWOOD UNIVERSITY
St. Charles, MO

Tuition & fees: $16,960	Average undergraduate aid package: $12,478

ABOUT THE INSTITUTION Independent Presbyterian, coed. *Awards:* certificates, bachelor's, master's, and doctoral degrees. 86 undergraduate majors. *Total enrollment:* 10,045. Undergraduates: 6,948. Freshmen: 949. Federal methodology is used as a basis for awarding need-based institutional aid.

UNDERGRADUATE EXPENSES for 2017–2018 *Application fee:* $30. *Comprehensive fee:* $25,760 includes full-time tuition ($16,300), mandatory fees ($660), and room and board ($8800). Full-time tuition and fees vary according to class time. Room and board charges vary according to board plan. *Part-time tuition:* $460 per credit hour. *Part-time fees:* $305 per term. Part-time tuition and fees vary according to course load.

FRESHMAN FINANCIAL AID (Fall 2017, est.) 938 applied for aid; of those 58% were deemed to have need. 100% of freshmen with need received aid; of those 17% had need fully met. *Average percent of need met:* 60% (excluding resources awarded to replace EFC). *Average financial aid package:* $15,902 (excluding resources awarded to replace EFC). 40% of all full-time freshmen had no need and received non-need-based gift aid.

UNDERGRADUATE FINANCIAL AID (Fall 2017, est.) 6,081 applied for aid; of those 62% were deemed to have need. 95% of undergraduates with need received aid; of those 9% had need fully met. *Average percent of need met:* 42% (excluding resources awarded to replace EFC). *Average financial aid package:* $12,478 (excluding resources awarded to replace EFC). 31% of all full-time undergraduates had no need and received non-need-based gift aid.

GIFT AID (NEED-BASED) *Receiving aid:* Freshmen: 52% (490); all full-time undergraduates: 51% (3,159). *Average award:* Freshmen: $6630; Undergraduates: $4974. *Scholarships, grants, and awards:* Federal Pell, FSEOG, state, private, college/university gift aid from institutional funds.

GIFT AID (NON-NEED-BASED) *Receiving aid:* Freshmen: 48% (453). Undergraduates: 27% (1,672). *Average award:* Freshmen: $7380. Undergraduates: $7185. *Scholarships, grants, and awards by category: Academic interests/achievement:* biological sciences, business, communication, computer science, education, engineering/technologies, English, foreign languages, general academic interests/achievements, health fields, humanities, international studies, library science, mathematics, military science, physical sciences, premedicine, religion/biblical studies, social sciences. *Creative arts/performance:* applied art and design, art/fine arts, cinema/film/broadcasting, dance, debating, general creative arts/performance, journalism/publications, music, performing arts, theater/drama. *Special achievements/activities:* cheerleading/drum major, community service, general special achievements/activities, junior miss, leadership. *Special characteristics:* children and siblings of alumni, children of faculty/staff, children of union members/company employees, public servants, veterans, veterans' children. *Tuition waivers:* Full or partial for employees or children of employees, senior citizens. *ROTC:* Army cooperative, Air Force cooperative.

LOANS *Student loans:* $38,000,000 (45% need-based, 55% non-need-based). 61% of past graduating class borrowed through all loan programs. *Average indebtedness per student:* $32,774. *Average need-based loan:* Freshmen: $3446. Undergraduates: $4138. *Parent loans:* $7,300,000 (100% non-need-based). *Programs:* Federal Direct (Subsidized and Unsubsidized Stafford, PLUS), Perkins.

WORK-STUDY *Federal work-study:* Total amount: $674,000; 169 jobs averaging $2850. *State or other work-study/employment:* Total amount: $3,600,000 (100% non-need-based). Part-time jobs available.

ATHLETIC AWARDS Total amount: $4,600,000 (100% non-need-based).

APPLYING FOR FINANCIAL AID *Required financial aid form:* FAFSA. *Financial aid deadline:* Continuous. *Notification date:* Continuous. Students must reply within 2 weeks of notification.

CONTACT Ms. Lori Bode, Director, Financial Aid, Lindenwood University, 209 South Kingshighway, St. Charles, MO 63301-1695, 636-949-4925. *Fax:* 636-949-4924. *E-mail:* lbode@lindenwood.edu. *Website:* http://www.lindenwood.edu/.

LINDSEY WILSON COLLEGE
Columbia, KY

Tuition & fees: $24,850	Average undergraduate aid package: N/A

ABOUT THE INSTITUTION Independent United Methodist, coed. *Awards:* associate, bachelor's, master's, and doctoral degrees. 34 undergraduate majors. *Total enrollment:* 2,565. Undergraduates: 2,068. Freshmen: 547. Federal methodology is used as a basis for awarding need-based institutional aid.

UNDERGRADUATE EXPENSES for 2018–2019 *Comprehensive fee:* $34,235 includes full-time tuition ($24,600), mandatory fees ($250), and room and board ($9385). *College room only:* $3400. Full-time tuition and fees vary according to class time, degree level, and location. *Part-time tuition:* $1025 per credit hour. *Part-time fees:* $50 per term. Part-time tuition and fees vary according to class time, degree level, and location.

FRESHMAN FINANCIAL AID (Fall 2017, est.) 542 applied for aid; of those 96% were deemed to have need. 100% of freshmen with need received aid; of those 25% had need fully met.

UNDERGRADUATE FINANCIAL AID (Fall 2017, est.) 1,893 applied for aid; of those 95% were deemed to have need. 100% of undergraduates with need received aid; of those 23% had need fully met.

GIFT AID (NEED-BASED) *Total amount:* $34,268,683 (17% federal, 19% state, 61% institutional, 3% external sources). *Receiving aid:* Freshmen: 96% (520); all full-time undergraduates: 93% (1,771). *Average award:* Freshmen: $22,324; Undergraduates: $19,576. *Scholarships, grants, and awards:* Federal Pell, FSEOG, state, private, college/university gift aid from institutional funds.

GIFT AID (NON-NEED-BASED) *Scholarships, grants, and awards by category: Academic interests/achievement:* biological sciences, business, education, English, general academic interests/achievements, mathematics, premedicine, religion/biblical studies. *Creative arts/performance:* applied art and design, music. *Special achievements/activities:* cheerleading/drum major, general special achievements/activities, junior miss, leadership, religious involvement. *Special characteristics:* children and siblings of alumni, children of faculty/staff, relatives of clergy, religious affiliation. *Tuition waivers:* Full or partial for employees or children of employees, senior citizens.

LOANS *Student loans:* $9,312,488 (100% need-based). 72% of past graduating class borrowed through all loan programs. *Average indebtedness per student:* $28,870. *Average need-based loan:* Freshmen: $8284. Undergraduates: $4183. *Parent loans:* $893,066 (100% need-based). *Programs:* Federal Direct (Subsidized and Unsubsidized Stafford, PLUS), Perkins, college/university.
WORK-STUDY *Federal work-study:* Total amount: $492,808; 225 jobs averaging $2178. *State or other work-study/employment:* Total amount: $37,500 (100% need-based). 23 part-time jobs averaging $2479.
ATHLETIC AWARDS Total amount: $2,235,344 (100% need-based).
APPLYING FOR FINANCIAL AID *Required financial aid form:* FAFSA. *Financial aid deadline (priority):* 4/1. *Notification date:* Continuous beginning 4/15. Students must reply within 2 weeks of notification.
CONTACT Ms. Marilyn D. Radford, Director of Student Financial Services, Lindsey Wilson College, 210 Lindsey Wilson Street, Columbia, KY 42728, 270-384-8022 or toll-free 800-264-0138. *Fax:* 270-384-8591. *E-mail:* radfordm@lindsey.edu. *Website:* http://www.lindsey.edu/.

LINFIELD COLLEGE
McMinnville, OR

Tuition & fees: $41,576	Average undergraduate aid package: $34,716

ABOUT THE INSTITUTION Independent American Baptist Churches in the USA, coed. *Awards:* certificates and bachelor's degrees (Linfield College includes the Linfield College McMinnville Campus in McMinnville, Oregon; the Linfield-Good Samaritan School of Nursing in Portland, Oregon(Portland Campus) and the Linfield College Adult Degree Program online). 49 undergraduate majors. *Total enrollment:* 1,535. Undergraduates: 1,535. Freshmen: 400. Federal methodology is used as a basis for awarding need-based institutional aid.
UNDERGRADUATE EXPENSES for 2017–2018 *Comprehensive fee:* $53,346 includes full-time tuition ($41,100), mandatory fees ($476), and room and board ($11,770). *College room only:* $6400. Full-time tuition and fees vary according to course load, location, and program. Room and board charges vary according to board plan, housing facility, and location. *Part-time tuition:* $1285 per semester hour. *Part-time fees:* $132 per term. Part-time tuition and fees vary according to course load, location, and program.
FRESHMAN FINANCIAL AID (Fall 2017, est.) 376 applied for aid; of those 88% were deemed to have need. 100% of freshmen with need received aid; of those 25% had need fully met. *Average percent of need met:* 85% (excluding resources awarded to replace EFC). *Average financial aid package:* $36,595 (excluding resources awarded to replace EFC). 12% of all full-time freshmen had no need and received non-need-based gift aid.
UNDERGRADUATE FINANCIAL AID (Fall 2017, est.) 1,289 applied for aid; of those 90% were deemed to have need. 100% of undergraduates with need received aid; of those 23% had need fully met. *Average percent of need met:* 82% (excluding resources awarded to replace EFC). *Average financial aid package:* $34,716 (excluding resources awarded to replace EFC). 20% of all full-time undergraduates had no need and received non-need-based gift aid.
GIFT AID (NEED-BASED) *Total amount:* $30,664,447 (7% federal, 2% state, 88% institutional, 3% external sources). *Receiving aid:* Freshmen: 67% (267); all full-time undergraduates: 64% (942). *Average award:* Freshmen: $31,393; Undergraduates: $28,935. *Scholarships, grants, and awards:* Federal Pell, FSEOG, state, private, college/university gift aid from institutional funds.
GIFT AID (NON-NEED-BASED) *Total amount:* $7,015,824 (97% institutional, 3% external sources). *Receiving aid:* Freshmen: 81% (323). Undergraduates: 75% (1,105). *Average award:* Freshmen: $21,043. Undergraduates: $19,043. *Scholarships, grants, and awards by category: Academic interests/achievement:* 1,227 awards ($20,746,555 total): biological sciences, business, communication, computer science, education, English, foreign languages, general academic interests/achievements, humanities, international studies, mathematics, physical sciences, religion/biblical studies, social sciences. *Creative arts/performance:* 65 awards ($183,455 total): debating, music, theater/drama. *Special achievements/activities:* 32 awards ($55,400 total): community service, leadership. *Special characteristics:* 747 awards ($7,313,537 total): children and siblings of alumni, children of faculty/staff, international students, members of minority groups, previous college experience, siblings of current students, veterans. *Tuition waivers:* Full or partial for employees or children of employees, senior citizens. *ROTC:* Air Force cooperative.

LOANS *Student loans:* $9,813,537 (72% need-based, 28% non-need-based). 72% of past graduating class borrowed through all loan programs. *Average indebtedness per student:* $34,244. *Average need-based loan:* Freshmen: $3503. Undergraduates: $4497. *Parent loans:* $4,447,236 (41% need-based, 59% non-need-based). *Programs:* Federal Direct (Subsidized and Unsubsidized Stafford, PLUS), Perkins, private loans.
WORK-STUDY *Federal work-study:* Total amount: $2,275,313; 557 jobs averaging $1379. *State or other work-study/employment:* Total amount: $1,634,464 (9% need-based, 91% non-need-based). 340 part-time jobs averaging $1114.
APPLYING FOR FINANCIAL AID *Required financial aid form:* FAFSA. *Financial aid deadline (priority):* 2/1. *Notification date:* 4/1. Students must reply by 5/1 or within 2 weeks of notification.
CONTACT Ms. Keri Burke, Director of Financial Aid, Linfield College, 900 Southeast Baker Street, A484, McMinnville, OR 97128-6894, 503-883-2269 or toll-free 800-640-2287. *Fax:* 503-883-2486. *E-mail:* finaid@linfield.edu. *Website:* http://www.linfield.edu/.

LIPSCOMB UNIVERSITY
Nashville, TN

Tuition & fees: $32,144	Average undergraduate aid package: $26,236

ABOUT THE INSTITUTION Independent Church of Christ, coed. *Awards:* certificates, associate, bachelor's, master's, and doctoral degrees. 103 undergraduate majors. *Total enrollment:* 4,642. Undergraduates: 2,987. Freshmen: 641. Federal methodology is used as a basis for awarding need-based institutional aid.
UNDERGRADUATE EXPENSES for 2018–2019 *Application fee:* $50. *Comprehensive fee:* $44,796 includes full-time tuition ($29,676), mandatory fees ($2468), and room and board ($12,652). *College room only:* $7164. Full-time tuition and fees vary according to course load. Room and board charges vary according to board plan and housing facility. *Part-time tuition:* $1240 per credit hour. Part-time tuition and fees vary according to course load.
FRESHMAN FINANCIAL AID (Fall 2017, est.) 640 applied for aid; of those 71% were deemed to have need. 100% of freshmen with need received aid; of those 21% had need fully met. *Average percent of need met:* 67% (excluding resources awarded to replace EFC). *Average financial aid package:* $24,038 (excluding resources awarded to replace EFC). 29% of all full-time freshmen had no need and received non-need-based gift aid.
UNDERGRADUATE FINANCIAL AID (Fall 2017, est.) 2,626 applied for aid; of those 66% were deemed to have need. 100% of undergraduates with need received aid; of those 22% had need fully met. *Average percent of need met:* 64% (excluding resources awarded to replace EFC). *Average financial aid package:* $26,236 (excluding resources awarded to replace EFC). 29% of all full-time undergraduates had no need and received non-need-based gift aid.
GIFT AID (NEED-BASED) *Total amount:* $31,894,102 (11% federal, 15% state, 66% institutional, 8% external sources). *Receiving aid:* Freshmen: 71% (455); all full-time undergraduates: 63% (1,710). *Average award:* Freshmen: $21,805; Undergraduates: $23,054. *Scholarships, grants, and awards:* Federal Pell, FSEOG, state, private, college/university gift aid from institutional funds.
GIFT AID (NON-NEED-BASED) *Total amount:* $12,156,214 (11% state, 85% institutional, 4% external sources). *Receiving aid:* Freshmen: 71% (452). Undergraduates: 55% (1,483). *Average award:* Freshmen: $13,815. Undergraduates: $15,436. *Scholarships, grants, and awards by category: Academic interests/achievement:* biological sciences, business, communication, education, engineering/technologies, English, general academic interests/achievements, home economics, mathematics, premedicine, religion/biblical studies. *Creative arts/performance:* art/fine arts, journalism/publications, music, theater/drama. *Special achievements/activities:* cheerleading/drum major, community service, general special achievements/activities, leadership, religious involvement. *Special characteristics:* adult students, children of educators, children of faculty/staff, children with a deceased or disabled parent, international students, local/state students, members of minority groups, out-of-state students, relatives of clergy, religious affiliation. *Tuition waivers:* Full or partial for employees or children of employees. *ROTC:* Army cooperative, Air Force cooperative.
LOANS *Student loans:* $12,408,631 (89% need-based, 11% non-need-based). 59% of past graduating class borrowed through all loan programs. *Average indebtedness per student:* $29,673. *Average need-based loan:* Freshmen: $3664. Undergrad-

uates: $5682. *Parent loans:* $5,777,289 (88% need-based, 12% non-need-based). *Programs:* Federal Direct (Subsidized and Unsubsidized Stafford, PLUS), Perkins.

WORK-STUDY *Federal work-study:* Total amount: $437,986; 195 jobs averaging $2320.

ATHLETIC AWARDS Total amount: $31,770,658 (94% need-based, 6% non-need-based).

APPLYING FOR FINANCIAL AID *Required financial aid form:* FAFSA. *Financial aid deadline (priority):* 3/1. *Notification date:* Continuous beginning 3/1.

CONTACT Ms. Tiffany Summers, Director of Financial Aid, Lipscomb University, One University Park Drive, Nashville, TN 37204-3951, 615-966-1791 or toll-free 877-582-4766. *Fax:* 615-966-7640. *E-mail:* tiffany.summers@lipscomb.edu. *Website:* http://www.lipscomb.edu/.

LIVING ARTS COLLEGE
Raleigh, NC

CONTACT Financial Aid Office, Living Arts College, 3000 Wakefield Crossing Drive, Raleigh, NC 27614, 919-488-8500 or toll-free 800-288-7442. *Website:* http://www.living-arts-college.edu/.

LIVINGSTONE COLLEGE
Salisbury, NC

CONTACT Mrs. Terry Jefferies, Financial Aid Director, Livingstone College, 701 West Monroe Street, Price Building, Salisbury, NC 28144-5298, 704-216-6069 or toll-free 800-835-3435. *Fax:* 704-216-6319. *E-mail:* tjefferies@livingstone.edu. *Website:* http://www.livingstone.edu/.

LOCK HAVEN UNIVERSITY OF PENNSYLVANIA
Lock Haven, PA

Tuition & fees (PA res): $10,576	Average undergraduate aid package: $9582

ABOUT THE INSTITUTION State-supported, coed. *Awards:* associate, bachelor's, and master's degrees. 40 undergraduate majors. *Total enrollment:* 3,827. Undergraduates: 3,472. Freshmen: 790. Federal methodology is used as a basis for awarding need-based institutional aid.

UNDERGRADUATE EXPENSES for 2017–2018 *Application fee:* $25. *Tuition, state resident:* full-time $7492; part-time $312 per credit hour. *Tuition, nonresident:* full-time $16,730; part-time $697 per credit hour. *Required fees:* full-time $3084; $162.80 per credit hour. Full-time tuition and fees vary according to course load, location, and program. Part-time tuition and fees vary according to course load, location, and program. *College room and board:* $9968; *Room only:* $6328. Room and board charges vary according to board plan and housing facility.

FRESHMAN FINANCIAL AID (Fall 2017, est.) 779 applied for aid; of those 86% were deemed to have need. 99% of freshmen with need received aid; of those 96% had need fully met. *Average percent of need met:* 85% (excluding resources awarded to replace EFC). *Average financial aid package:* $11,774 (excluding resources awarded to replace EFC). 1% of all full-time freshmen had no need and received non-need-based gift aid.

UNDERGRADUATE FINANCIAL AID (Fall 2017, est.) 3,095 applied for aid; of those 85% were deemed to have need. 98% of undergraduates with need received aid; of those 94% had need fully met. *Average percent of need met:* 86% (excluding resources awarded to replace EFC). *Average financial aid package:* $9582 (excluding resources awarded to replace EFC). 1% of all full-time undergraduates had no need and received non-need-based gift aid.

GIFT AID (NEED-BASED) *Total amount:* $11,380,693 (57% federal, 36% state, 7% institutional). *Receiving aid:* Freshmen: 57% (470); all full-time undergraduates: 52% (1,827). *Average award:* Freshmen: $7697; Undergraduates: $5780. *Scholar-*

ships, grants, and awards: Federal Pell, FSEOG, state, private, college/university gift aid from institutional funds.

GIFT AID (NON-NEED-BASED) *Total amount:* $1,454,433 (2% federal, 37% institutional, 61% external sources). *Receiving aid:* Freshmen: 20% (165). Undergraduates: 9% (317). *Average award:* Freshmen: $1816. Undergraduates: $2283. *Scholarships, grants, and awards by category: Academic interests/achievement:* biological sciences, business, communication, computer science, education, English, foreign languages, general academic interests/achievements, health fields, international studies, library science, mathematics, physical sciences, premedicine, social sciences. *Creative arts/performance:* art/fine arts, journalism/publications, music, performing arts. *Special achievements/activities:* community service, general special achievements/activities, leadership, memberships. *Special characteristics:* adult students, ethnic background, handicapped students, international students, local/state students, married students, members of minority groups, previous college experience. *Tuition waivers:* Full or partial for minority students, employees or children of employees, senior citizens. *ROTC:* Army.

LOANS *Student loans:* $34,904,817 (30% need-based, 70% non-need-based). 95% of past graduating class borrowed through all loan programs. *Average indebtedness per student:* $34,863. *Average need-based loan:* Freshmen: $3388. Undergraduates: $4397. *Parent loans:* $7,465,924 (100% non-need-based). *Programs:* Federal Direct (Subsidized and Unsubsidized Stafford, PLUS), Perkins, college/university, alternative loans.

WORK-STUDY *Federal work-study:* Total amount: $201,746; jobs available. *State or other work-study/employment:* Total amount: $250,000 (100% non-need-based). Part-time jobs available.

ATHLETIC AWARDS Total amount: $587,278 (100% non-need-based).

APPLYING FOR FINANCIAL AID *Required financial aid forms:* FAFSA, state aid form. *Financial aid deadline (priority):* 3/15. *Notification date:* Continuous beginning 3/20. Students must reply within 2 weeks of notification.

CONTACT Robert Fryer, Director of Financial Aid, Lock Haven University of Pennsylvania, 401 North Fairview Street, 223 Ulmer Hall, Lock Haven, PA 17745-2390, 570-484-2452 or toll-free 800-332-8900 (in-state), 800-233-8978 (out-of-state). *Fax:* 570-484-2918. *E-mail:* rcf138@lockhaven.edu. *Website:* http://www.lockhaven.edu/.

LOGAN UNIVERSITY
Chesterfield, MO

Tuition & fees: $8400	Average undergraduate aid package: $11,002

ABOUT THE INSTITUTION Independent, coed. *Awards:* bachelor's, master's, and doctoral degrees. 2 undergraduate majors. *Total enrollment:* 1,371. Undergraduates: 126. Entering class: 28. Federal methodology is used as a basis for awarding need-based institutional aid.

UNDERGRADUATE EXPENSES for 2017–2018 *Application fee:* $25. *Tuition:* full-time $8250; part-time $275 per credit hour. *Required fees:* full-time $150; $80 per term. Full-time tuition and fees vary according to course load, degree level, and program. Part-time tuition and fees vary according to course load, degree level, and program.

UNDERGRADUATE FINANCIAL AID (Fall 2017, est.) 46 applied for aid; of those 100% were deemed to have need. 100% of undergraduates with need received aid; of those 2% had need fully met. *Average percent of need met:* 43% (excluding resources awarded to replace EFC). *Average financial aid package:* $11,002 (excluding resources awarded to replace EFC).

GIFT AID (NEED-BASED) *Total amount:* $258,375 (91% federal, 2% state, 5% institutional, 2% external sources). *Receiving aid:* Entering class: 50% (4); all full-time undergraduates: 71% (35). *Average award:* Freshmen: $4763; Undergraduates: $5525. *Scholarships, grants, and awards:* Federal Pell, FSEOG, state, private.

GIFT AID (NON-NEED-BASED) *Total amount:* $750 (100% external sources). *Receiving aid:* Undergraduates: 14% (7). *Tuition waivers:* Full or partial for employees or children of employees.

LOANS *Student loans:* $766,067 (94% need-based, 6% non-need-based). *Average need-based loan:* Freshmen: $7200. Undergraduates: $2818. *Parent loans:* $27,527 (54% need-based, 46% non-need-based). *Programs:* Federal Direct (Subsidized and Unsubsidized Stafford, PLUS), Perkins.

WORK-STUDY *Federal work-study:* Total amount: $2880; jobs available.

APPLYING FOR FINANCIAL AID *Required financial aid form:* FAFSA. *Financial aid deadline:* Continuous. *Notification date:* Continuous beginning 8/1. Students must reply within 2 weeks of notification.

CONTACT Kerry R. Hallahan, Director of Financial Aid, Logan University, 1851 Schoettler Road, Chesterfield, MO 63017, 636-230-1741 or toll-free 800-533-9210. *E-mail:* kerry.hallahan@logan.edu. *Website:* http://www.logan.edu/.

LOMA LINDA UNIVERSITY
Loma Linda, CA

CONTACT Verdell Schaefer, Director of Financial Aid, Loma Linda University, 11139 Anderson Street, Loma Linda, CA 92350, 909-558-4509 or toll-free 800-422-4558. *Fax:* 909-558-4879. *E-mail:* finaid@univ.llu.edu. *Website:* http://www.llu.edu/.

LONG ISLAND UNIVERSITY–LIU BROOKLYN
Brooklyn, NY

Tuition & fees: $36,978	Average undergraduate aid package: $20,824

ABOUT THE INSTITUTION Independent, coed. *Awards:* certificates, associate, bachelor's, master's, and doctoral degrees. 58 undergraduate majors. *Total enrollment:* 6,982. Undergraduates: 3,945. Freshmen: 674. Both federal and institutional methodology are used as a basis for awarding need-based institutional aid.

UNDERGRADUATE EXPENSES for 2017–2018 *Application fee:* $50. *Comprehensive fee:* $50,698 includes full-time tuition ($35,038), mandatory fees ($1940), and room and board ($13,720). Room and board charges vary according to board plan and housing facility. *Part-time tuition:* $1093 per credit. *Part-time fees:* $460 per term.

FRESHMAN FINANCIAL AID (Fall 2017, est.) 638 applied for aid; of those 93% were deemed to have need. 99% of freshmen with need received aid; of those 2% had need fully met. *Average percent of need met:* 63% (excluding resources awarded to replace EFC). *Average financial aid package:* $25,945 (excluding resources awarded to replace EFC). 5% of all full-time freshmen had no need and received non-need-based gift aid.

UNDERGRADUATE FINANCIAL AID (Fall 2017, est.) 3,128 applied for aid; of those 93% were deemed to have need. 99% of undergraduates with need received aid; of those 2% had need fully met. *Average percent of need met:* 48% (excluding resources awarded to replace EFC). *Average financial aid package:* $20,824 (excluding resources awarded to replace EFC). 4% of all full-time undergraduates had no need and received non-need-based gift aid.

GIFT AID (NEED-BASED) *Total amount:* $29,640,466 (38% federal, 29% state, 33% institutional). *Receiving aid:* Freshmen: 72% (483); all full-time undergraduates: 70% (2,378). *Average award:* Freshmen: $11,292; Undergraduates: $9976. *Scholarships, grants, and awards:* Federal Pell, FSEOG, state, private, college/university gift aid from institutional funds, United Negro College Fund, Federal Nursing, Scholarships for Disadvantaged Students (SDS).

GIFT AID (NON-NEED-BASED) *Total amount:* $21,428,140 (98% institutional, 2% external sources). *Receiving aid:* Freshmen: 58% (389). Undergraduates: 50% (1,680). *Average award:* Freshmen: $21,205. Undergraduates: $15,289. *Scholarships, grants, and awards by category:* Academic interests/achievement: general academic interests/achievements, home economics, international studies. Creative arts/performance: art/fine arts, cinema/film/broadcasting, creative writing, dance, journalism/publications, music, performing arts, theater/drama. Special achievements/activities: cheerleading/drum major, general special achievements/activities. Special characteristics: children and siblings of alumni, children of current students, children of faculty/staff, general special characteristics, handicapped students, international students, siblings of current students, twins, veterans, veterans' children. *Tuition waivers:* Full or partial for employees or children of employees. *ROTC:* Army cooperative.

LOANS *Student loans:* $27,906,464 (41% need-based, 59% non-need-based). 82% of past graduating class borrowed through all loan programs. *Average indebtedness*

per student: $46,578. *Average need-based loan:* Freshmen: $2444. Undergraduates: $3447. *Parent loans:* $17,008,474 (100% non-need-based). *Programs:* Federal Direct (Subsidized and Unsubsidized Stafford, PLUS), Perkins, Health Professions Student Loans (HPSL).

WORK-STUDY *Federal work-study:* Total amount: $1,171,107; 449 jobs averaging $2602.

ATHLETIC AWARDS Total amount: $7,599,154 (100% non-need-based).

APPLYING FOR FINANCIAL AID *Required financial aid forms:* FAFSA, state aid form. *Financial aid deadline:* Continuous. *Notification date:* Continuous beginning 2/15. Students must reply by 5/1 or within 2 weeks of notification.

CONTACT Ms. Margaret Nelson, Executive Director of Enrollment Services, Long Island University–LIU Brooklyn, 1 University Plaza, Brooklyn, NY 11201-8423, 718-488-1037 or toll-free 800-LIU-PLAN. *Fax:* 718-488-3343. *E-mail:* brooklyn-enrollmentservices@liu.edu. *Website:* http://www.liu.edu/.

LONG ISLAND UNIVERSITY–LIU POST
Brookville, NY

Tuition & fees: $36,978	Average undergraduate aid package: $24,166

ABOUT THE INSTITUTION Independent, coed. *Awards:* certificates, associate, bachelor's, master's, and doctoral degrees. 76 undergraduate majors. *Total enrollment:* 8,499. Undergraduates: 6,316. Freshmen: 694. Federal methodology is used as a basis for awarding need-based institutional aid.

UNDERGRADUATE EXPENSES for 2017–2018 *Application fee:* $50. *Comprehensive fee:* $50,698 includes full-time tuition ($35,038), mandatory fees ($1940), and room and board ($13,720). Room and board charges vary according to board plan and housing facility. *Part-time tuition:* $1093 per credit. *Part-time fees:* $460 per term.

FRESHMAN FINANCIAL AID (Fall 2017, est.) 652 applied for aid; of those 85% were deemed to have need. 100% of freshmen with need received aid; of those 6% had need fully met. *Average percent of need met:* 77% (excluding resources awarded to replace EFC). *Average financial aid package:* $28,850 (excluding resources awarded to replace EFC). 14% of all full-time freshmen had no need and received non-need-based gift aid.

UNDERGRADUATE FINANCIAL AID (Fall 2017, est.) 2,391 applied for aid; of those 86% were deemed to have need. 99% of undergraduates with need received aid; of those 4% had need fully met. *Average percent of need met:* 62% (excluding resources awarded to replace EFC). *Average financial aid package:* $24,166 (excluding resources awarded to replace EFC). 10% of all full-time undergraduates had no need and received non-need-based gift aid.

GIFT AID (NEED-BASED) *Total amount:* $14,664,084 (40% federal, 25% state, 35% institutional). *Receiving aid:* Freshmen: 44% (306); all full-time undergraduates: 48% (1,339). *Average award:* Freshmen: $5000; Undergraduates: $6177. *Scholarships, grants, and awards:* Federal Pell, FSEOG, state, private, college/university gift aid from institutional funds, United Negro College Fund, Federal Nursing, Scholarships for Disadvantaged Students (SDS).

GIFT AID (NON-NEED-BASED) *Total amount:* $32,971,849 (1% state, 97% institutional, 2% external sources). *Receiving aid:* Freshmen: 70% (485). Undergraduates: 57% (1,588). *Average award:* Freshmen: $20,054. Undergraduates: $15,714. *Scholarships, grants, and awards by category:* Academic interests/achievement: general academic interests/achievements, home economics, international studies. Creative arts/performance: art/fine arts, cinema/film/broadcasting, creative writing, dance, journalism/publications, music, performing arts, theater/drama. Special achievements/activities: cheerleading/drum major, general special achievements/activities. Special characteristics: children and siblings of alumni, children of current students, children of faculty/staff, general special characteristics, handicapped students, international students, siblings of current students, twins, veterans, veterans' children. *Tuition waivers:* Full or partial for employees or children of employees. *ROTC:* Army cooperative.

LOANS *Student loans:* $19,295,138 (36% need-based, 64% non-need-based). 65% of past graduating class borrowed through all loan programs. *Average indebtedness per student:* $36,533. *Average need-based loan:* Freshmen: $2104. Undergraduates: $3097. *Parent loans:* $14,442,656 (100% non-need-based). *Programs:* Federal Direct (Subsidized and Unsubsidized Stafford, PLUS), Perkins.

WORK-STUDY *Federal work-study:* Total amount: $1,238,050; 535 jobs averaging $2255.

ATHLETIC AWARDS Total amount: $6,238,668 (100% non-need-based).
APPLYING FOR FINANCIAL AID *Required financial aid forms:* FAFSA, state aid form. *Financial aid deadline:* Continuous. *Notification date:* Continuous beginning 2/15. Students must reply by 5/1 or within 2 weeks of notification.

CONTACT Ms. Joanne Graziano, Executive Director of Enrollment Services, Long Island University LIU Post, 720 Northern Boulevard, Brookville, NY 11548-1300, 516-299-2553 or toll-free 800-LIU-PLAN. *Fax:* 516-299-3833. *E-mail:* post-enrollmentservices@liu.edu.
Website: http://www.liu.edu/.

LONGWOOD UNIVERSITY
Farmville, VA

Tuition & fees (VA res): $13,080	Average undergraduate aid package: $14,965

ABOUT THE INSTITUTION State-supported, coed. *Awards:* certificates, bachelor's, and master's degrees. 25 undergraduate majors. *Total enrollment:* 4,883. Undergraduates: 4,386. Freshmen: 929. Federal methodology is used as a basis for awarding need-based institutional aid.
UNDERGRADUATE EXPENSES for 2018–2019 *Application fee:* $50. *Tuition, state resident:* full-time $8280; part-time $276 per credit hour. *Tuition, nonresident:* full-time $22,800; part-time $760 per credit hour. *Required fees:* full-time $4800. Full-time tuition and fees vary according to course load and program. Part-time tuition and fees vary according to course load and program. *College room and board:* $10,732; *Room only:* $7336. Room and board charges vary according to board plan, housing facility, and location.
FRESHMAN FINANCIAL AID (Fall 2016) 808 applied for aid; of those 75% were deemed to have need. *Average percent of need met:* 79% (excluding resources awarded to replace EFC). *Average financial aid package:* $14,609 (excluding resources awarded to replace EFC). 5% of all full-time freshmen had no need and received non-need-based gift aid.
UNDERGRADUATE FINANCIAL AID (Fall 2016) 2,933 applied for aid; of those 93% were deemed to have need. *Average percent of need met:* 80% (excluding resources awarded to replace EFC). *Average financial aid package:* $14,965 (excluding resources awarded to replace EFC). 5% of all full-time undergraduates had no need and received non-need-based gift aid.
GIFT AID (NEED-BASED) *Total amount:* $13,681,802 (33% federal, 37% state, 25% institutional, 5% external sources). *Receiving aid:* Freshmen: 51% (483); all full-time undergraduates: 39% (1,705). *Average award:* Freshmen: $7735; Undergraduates: $7712. *Scholarships, grants, and awards:* Federal Pell, FSEOG, state, private, college/university gift aid from institutional funds.
GIFT AID (NON-NEED-BASED) *Total amount:* $2,669,414 (3% federal, 5% state, 64% institutional, 28% external sources). *Receiving aid:* Freshmen: 4% (40). Undergraduates: 3% (110). *Average award:* Freshmen: $3860. Undergraduates: $5016. *Scholarships, grants, and awards by category: Academic interests/ achievement:* biological sciences, business, computer science, education, English, general academic interests/achievements, humanities, international studies, mathematics, military science, social sciences. *Creative arts/performance:* art/fine arts, music, theater/drama. *Special achievements/activities:* community service, leadership, memberships. *Special characteristics:* children and siblings of alumni, general special characteristics, local/state students. *Tuition waivers:* Full or partial for employees or children of employees, senior citizens. *ROTC:* Army.
LOANS *Student loans:* $22,055,618 (63% need-based, 37% non-need-based). 69% of past graduating class borrowed through all loan programs. *Average indebtedness per student:* $28,376. *Average need-based loan:* Freshmen: $3334. Undergraduates: $4348. *Parent loans:* $15,393,734 (35% need-based, 65% non-need-based). *Programs:* Federal Direct (Subsidized and Unsubsidized Stafford, PLUS), Perkins, private loans.
WORK-STUDY *Federal work-study:* jobs available. *State or other work-study/employment:* Part-time jobs available.
ATHLETIC AWARDS Total amount: $2,780,841 (35% need-based, 65% non-need-based).
APPLYING FOR FINANCIAL AID *Required financial aid form:* FAFSA. *Financial aid deadline (priority):* 3/1. *Notification date:* Continuous beginning 3/1. Students must reply within 4 weeks of notification.

CONTACT Mrs. Gayle Covington, Interim Director, Longwood University, 201 High Street, Farmville, VA 23909, 434-395-2077 or toll-free 800-281-4677. *Fax:* 434-395-2829. *E-mail:* covingtonjj@longwood.edu.
Website: http://www.longwood.edu/.

LORAS COLLEGE
Dubuque, IA

Tuition & fees: $34,184	Average undergraduate aid package: $27,733

ABOUT THE INSTITUTION Independent Roman Catholic, coed. *Awards:* certificates, bachelor's, and master's degrees. 35 undergraduate majors. *Total enrollment:* 1,467. Undergraduates: 1,397. Freshmen: 337. Federal methodology is used as a basis for awarding need-based institutional aid.
UNDERGRADUATE EXPENSES for 2018–2019 *Comprehensive fee:* $42,459 includes full-time tuition ($32,524), mandatory fees ($1660), and room and board ($8275). *College room only:* $4000. Full-time tuition and fees vary according to course load and degree level. Room and board charges vary according to board plan and housing facility. *Part-time tuition:* $725 per credit hour. *Part-time fees:* $42 per credit hour.
FRESHMAN FINANCIAL AID (Fall 2017, est.) 326 applied for aid; of those 85% were deemed to have need. 100% of freshmen with need received aid; of those 32% had need fully met. *Average percent of need met:* 90% (excluding resources awarded to replace EFC). *Average financial aid package:* $28,297 (excluding resources awarded to replace EFC). 18% of all full-time freshmen had no need and received non-need-based gift aid.
UNDERGRADUATE FINANCIAL AID (Fall 2017, est.) 1,157 applied for aid; of those 87% were deemed to have need. 100% of undergraduates with need received aid; of those 33% had need fully met. *Average percent of need met:* 89% (excluding resources awarded to replace EFC). *Average financial aid package:* $27,733 (excluding resources awarded to replace EFC). 24% of all full-time undergraduates had no need and received non-need-based gift aid.
GIFT AID (NEED-BASED) *Total amount:* $21,412,711 (8% federal, 6% state, 85% institutional, 1% external sources). *Receiving aid:* Freshmen: 82% (276); all full-time undergraduates: 75% (1,005). *Average award:* Freshmen: $22,697; Undergraduates: $21,256. *Scholarships, grants, and awards:* Federal Pell, FSEOG, state, private, college/university gift aid from institutional funds.
GIFT AID (NON-NEED-BASED) *Total amount:* $7,520,391 (98% institutional, 2% external sources). *Receiving aid:* Freshmen: 17% (57). Undergraduates: 15% (198). *Average award:* Freshmen: $17,816. Undergraduates: $18,242. *Scholarships, grants, and awards by category: Academic interests/achievement:* 1,291 awards ($21,370,620 total): biological sciences, business, communication, computer science, education, engineering/technologies, English, general academic interests/ achievements, home economics, mathematics, physical sciences, premedicine, religion/ biblical studies. *Creative arts/performance:* 73 awards ($80,325 total): music. *Special achievements/activities:* 208 awards ($1,297,349 total): leadership, religious involvement. *Special characteristics:* 343 awards ($882,430 total): first-generation college students, local/state students, out-of-state students, religious affiliation. *Tuition waivers:* Full or partial for employees or children of employees. *ROTC:* Army cooperative.
LOANS *Student loans:* $8,009,866 (47% need-based, 53% non-need-based). 73% of past graduating class borrowed through all loan programs. *Average indebtedness per student:* $34,156. *Average need-based loan:* Freshmen: $3932. Undergraduates: $4968. *Parent loans:* $1,561,887 (100% non-need-based). *Programs:* Federal Direct (Subsidized and Unsubsidized Stafford, PLUS), Perkins, college/university.
WORK-STUDY *Federal work-study:* Total amount: $1,316,670; 563 jobs averaging $2339. *State or other work-study/employment:* Total amount: $12,500 (100% non-need-based). 10 part-time jobs averaging $1250.
APPLYING FOR FINANCIAL AID *Required financial aid form:* FAFSA. *Financial aid deadline (priority):* 3/1. *Notification date:* Continuous beginning 3/1. Students must reply within 3 weeks of notification.
CONTACT Ms. Julie A. Dunn, Director of Financial Planning, Loras College, 1450 Alta Vista Street, Dubuque, IA 52001-4327, 563-588-7136 or toll-free 800-245-6727. *Fax:* 563-588-7119. *E-mail:* julie.dunn@loras.edu.
Website: http://www.loras.edu/.

LOS ANGELES FILM SCHOOL
Hollywood, CA

CONTACT Financial Aid Office, Los Angeles Film School, 6363 Sunset Boulevard, Hollywood, CA 90028, 323-860-0789 or toll-free 877-952-3456. *Website:* http://www.lafilm.edu/.

LOUISIANA COLLEGE
Pineville, LA

Tuition & fees: $16,000	Average undergraduate aid package: $13,440

ABOUT THE INSTITUTION Independent Southern Baptist, coed. *Awards:* certificates, associate, bachelor's, and master's degrees. 59 undergraduate majors. *Total enrollment:* 1,198. Undergraduates: 989. Freshmen: 306. Federal methodology is used as a basis for awarding need-based institutional aid.

UNDERGRADUATE EXPENSES for 2018–2019 *Application fee:* $25. *Comprehensive fee:* $21,274 includes full-time tuition ($16,000) and room and board ($5274). *College room only:* $2132. Full-time tuition and fees vary according to program. Room and board charges vary according to board plan and housing facility. *Part-time tuition:* $500 per credit hour. Part-time tuition and fees vary according to course load and program.

FRESHMAN FINANCIAL AID (Fall 2017, est.) 275 applied for aid; of those 84% were deemed to have need. 100% of freshmen with need received aid; of those 24% had need fully met. *Average percent of need met:* 74% (excluding resources awarded to replace EFC). *Average financial aid package:* $14,112 (excluding resources awarded to replace EFC). 17% of all full-time freshmen had no need and received non-need-based gift aid.

UNDERGRADUATE FINANCIAL AID (Fall 2017, est.) 806 applied for aid; of those 85% were deemed to have need. 100% of undergraduates with need received aid; of those 22% had need fully met. *Average percent of need met:* 67% (excluding resources awarded to replace EFC). *Average financial aid package:* $13,440 (excluding resources awarded to replace EFC). 16% of all full-time undergraduates had no need and received non-need-based gift aid.

GIFT AID (NEED-BASED) *Total amount:* $7,426,064 (29% federal, 19% state, 47% institutional, 5% external sources). *Receiving aid:* Freshmen: 74% (231); all full-time undergraduates: 77% (664). *Average award:* Freshmen: $11,873; Undergraduates: $11,170. *Scholarships, grants, and awards:* Federal Pell, FSEOG, state, private, college/university gift aid from institutional funds.

GIFT AID (NON-NEED-BASED) *Total amount:* $2,226,682 (1% federal, 38% state, 52% institutional, 9% external sources). *Receiving aid:* Freshmen: 17% (53). Undergraduates: 16% (137). *Average award:* Freshmen: $8052. Undergraduates: $6552. *Scholarships, grants, and awards by category:* Academic interests/achievement: business, communication, English, general academic interests/achievements, health fields, home economics, humanities, mathematics, religion/biblical studies, social sciences. *Creative arts/performance:* art/fine arts, journalism/publications, music, performing arts, theater/drama. *Special achievements/activities:* cheerleading/drum major, leadership. *Special characteristics:* children of faculty/staff. *Tuition waivers:* Full or partial for employees or children of employees, senior citizens.

LOANS *Student loans:* $4,213,802 (77% need-based, 23% non-need-based). 71% of past graduating class borrowed through all loan programs. *Average indebtedness per student:* $26,285. *Average need-based loan:* Freshmen: $293. Undergraduates: $3327. *Parent loans:* $891,650 (54% need-based, 46% non-need-based). *Programs:* Federal Direct (Subsidized and Unsubsidized Stafford, PLUS).

WORK-STUDY *Federal work-study:* Total amount: $109,278; 119 jobs averaging $750.

APPLYING FOR FINANCIAL AID *Required financial aid forms:* FAFSA, institution's own form. *Financial aid deadline (priority):* 5/1. *Notification date:* Continuous beginning 2/1. Students must reply by 7/1 or within 2 weeks of notification.

CONTACT Mr. Jeremy N. Treme, Director of Financial Aid, Louisiana College, 1140 College Drive, Pineville, LA 71359-0001, 318-487-7387 or toll-free 800-487-1906. *Fax:* 318-487-7449. *E-mail:* jeremy.treme@lacollege.edu. *Website:* http://www.lacollege.edu/.

LOUISIANA STATE UNIVERSITY AND AGRICULTURAL & MECHANICAL COLLEGE
Baton Rouge, LA

Tuition & fees (LA res): $11,374	Average undergraduate aid package: $15,278

ABOUT THE INSTITUTION State-supported, coed. *Awards:* certificates, bachelor's, master's, and doctoral degrees. 69 undergraduate majors. *Total enrollment:* 30,861. Undergraduates: 25,444. Freshmen: 4,917. Federal methodology is used as a basis for awarding need-based institutional aid.

UNDERGRADUATE EXPENSES for 2017–2018 *Application fee:* $50. *Tuition, state resident:* full-time $8038. *Tuition, nonresident:* full-time $24,715. *Required fees:* full-time $3336. Full-time tuition and fees vary according to course load. Part-time tuition and fees vary according to course load. *College room and board:* $11,750; *Room only:* $7740. Room and board charges vary according to board plan and housing facility.

FRESHMAN FINANCIAL AID (Fall 2016) 4,397 applied for aid; of those 72% were deemed to have need. 100% of freshmen with need received aid; of those 22% had need fully met. *Average percent of need met:* 67% (excluding resources awarded to replace EFC). *Average financial aid package:* $15,330 (excluding resources awarded to replace EFC). 21% of all full-time freshmen had no need and received non-need-based gift aid.

UNDERGRADUATE FINANCIAL AID (Fall 2016) 15,768 applied for aid; of those 74% were deemed to have need. 98% of undergraduates with need received aid; of those 19% had need fully met. *Average percent of need met:* 63% (excluding resources awarded to replace EFC). *Average financial aid package:* $15,278 (excluding resources awarded to replace EFC). 18% of all full-time undergraduates had no need and received non-need-based gift aid.

GIFT AID (NEED-BASED) *Total amount:* $103,930,718 (24% federal, 39% state, 35% institutional, 2% external sources). *Receiving aid:* Freshmen: 55% (3,030); all full-time undergraduates: 45% (10,294). *Average award:* Freshmen: $10,228; Undergraduates: $10,104. *Scholarships, grants, and awards:* Federal Pell, FSEOG, state, private, college/university gift aid from institutional funds.

GIFT AID (NON-NEED-BASED) *Total amount:* $62,090,073 (4% federal, 56% state, 30% institutional, 10% external sources). *Receiving aid:* Freshmen: 3% (137). Undergraduates: 2% (347). *Average award:* Freshmen: $4321. Undergraduates: $4063. *Scholarships, grants, and awards by category:* Academic interests/achievement: 1,726 awards ($3,851,118 total): agriculture, architecture, biological sciences, business, computer science, education, engineering/technologies, English, foreign languages, general academic interests/achievements, health fields, humanities, mathematics, physical sciences. *Creative arts/performance:* 175 awards ($306,720 total): applied art and design, art/fine arts, journalism/publications, music, performing arts, theater/drama. *Special characteristics:* 1,427 awards ($15,007,931 total): children with a deceased or disabled parent, general special characteristics, out-of-state students, veterans. *Tuition waivers:* Full or partial for employees or children of employees. *ROTC:* Army, Naval cooperative, Air Force.

LOANS *Student loans:* $88,487,943 (71% need-based, 29% non-need-based). 42% of past graduating class borrowed through all loan programs. *Average indebtedness per student:* $24,933. *Average need-based loan:* Freshmen: $5716. Undergraduates: $6845. *Parent loans:* $50,973,399 (46% need-based, 54% non-need-based). *Programs:* Federal Direct (Subsidized and Unsubsidized Stafford, PLUS), Perkins, college/university.

WORK-STUDY *Federal work-study:* 1,035 jobs averaging $2000. *State or other work-study/employment:* Total amount: $10,555,308 (39% need-based, 61% non-need-based). 3,995 part-time jobs averaging $2300.

ATHLETIC AWARDS Total amount: $13,255,530 (35% need-based, 65% non-need-based).

APPLYING FOR FINANCIAL AID *Required financial aid forms:* FAFSA, institution's own form. *Financial aid deadline (priority):* 4/1. *Notification date:* Continuous beginning 11/15. Students must reply by 5/1.

CONTACT Ms. Amy Marix, Director of Financial Aid and Scholarships, Louisiana State University and Agricultural & Mechanical College, 1146 Pleasant Hall, Baton Rouge, LA 70803, 225-578-3103. *Fax:* 225-578-6300. *E-mail:* financialaid@lsu.edu. *Website:* http://www.lsu.edu/.

LOUISIANA STATE UNIVERSITY AT ALEXANDRIA

Alexandria, LA

CONTACT Financial Aid Office, Louisiana State University at Alexandria, 8100 Highway 71 South, Alexandria, LA 71302-9121, 318-445-3672 or toll-free 888-473-6417.
Website: http://www.lsua.edu/.

LOUISIANA STATE UNIVERSITY HEALTH SCIENCES CENTER

New Orleans, LA

CONTACT Mr. Patrick Gorman, Director of Financial Aid, Louisiana State University Health Sciences Center, 433 Bolivar Street, New Orleans, LA 70112, 504-568-4821. *Fax:* 504-599-1390.
Website: http://www.lsuhsc.edu/.

LOUISIANA STATE UNIVERSITY IN SHREVEPORT

Shreveport, LA

ABOUT THE INSTITUTION State-supported, coed. 32 undergraduate majors.
GIFT AID (NEED-BASED) *Scholarships, grants, and awards:* Federal Pell, FSEOG, state, private, college/university gift aid from institutional funds.
GIFT AID (NON-NEED-BASED) *Scholarships, grants, and awards by category: Academic interests/achievement:* biological sciences, business, computer science, education, English, general academic interests/achievements, humanities, physical sciences, premedicine, social sciences.
LOANS *Programs:* Federal Direct (Subsidized and Unsubsidized Stafford, PLUS).
APPLYING FOR FINANCIAL AID *Required financial aid form:* FAFSA.

CONTACT Office of Student Financial Aid, Louisiana State University in Shreveport, One University Place, Shreveport, LA 71115-2399, 318-797-5363 or toll-free 800-229-5957. *Fax:* 318-797-5366. *E-mail:* finaid@lsus.edu.
Website: http://www.lsus.edu/.

LOUISIANA TECH UNIVERSITY

Ruston, LA

Tuition & fees (LA res): $9645	Average undergraduate aid package: $11,358

ABOUT THE INSTITUTION State-supported, coed. *Awards:* certificates, associate, bachelor's, master's, and doctoral degrees. 79 undergraduate majors. *Total enrollment:* 12,672. Undergraduates: 11,281. Freshmen: 2,018. Federal methodology is used as a basis for awarding need-based institutional aid.
UNDERGRADUATE EXPENSES for 2017–2018 *Application fee:* $20. *Tuition, state resident:* full-time $6400; part-time $402 per credit hour. *Tuition, nonresident:* full-time $15,313; part-time $773 per credit hour. *Required fees:* full-time $3245. Full-time tuition and fees vary according to course load, location, and program. Part-time tuition and fees vary according to course load, location, and program. *College room and board:* $6360; *Room only:* $2910. Room and board charges vary according to board plan and housing facility.
FRESHMAN FINANCIAL AID (Fall 2016) 1,885 applied for aid; of those 69% were deemed to have need. 99% of freshmen with need received aid; of those 23% had need fully met. *Average percent of need met:* 82% (excluding resources awarded to replace EFC). *Average financial aid package:* $11,667 (excluding resources awarded to replace EFC). 26% of all full-time freshmen had no need and received non-need-based gift aid.
UNDERGRADUATE FINANCIAL AID (Fall 2016) 6,346 applied for aid; of those 70% were deemed to have need. 98% of undergraduates with need received aid;

of those 20% had need fully met. *Average percent of need met:* 80% (excluding resources awarded to replace EFC). *Average financial aid package:* $11,358 (excluding resources awarded to replace EFC). 23% of all full-time undergraduates had no need and received non-need-based gift aid.
GIFT AID (NEED-BASED) *Total amount:* $28,911,002 (36% federal, 36% state, 25% institutional, 3% external sources). *Receiving aid:* Freshmen: 63% (1,265); all full-time undergraduates: 55% (4,108). *Average award:* Freshmen: $10,079; Undergraduates: $9484. *Scholarships, grants, and awards:* Federal Pell, FSEOG, state, private, college/university gift aid from institutional funds.
GIFT AID (NON-NEED-BASED) *Total amount:* $19,056,009 (44% state, 49% institutional, 7% external sources). *Receiving aid:* Freshmen: 14% (281). Undergraduates: 10% (774). *Average award:* Freshmen: $4363. Undergraduates: $4502. *Scholarships, grants, and awards by category: Academic interests/achievement:* agriculture, architecture, biological sciences, business, computer science, education, engineering/technologies, English, foreign languages, general academic interests/achievements, health fields, home economics, international studies, mathematics, military science, physical sciences, social sciences. *Creative arts/performance:* applied art and design, art/fine arts, creative writing, debating, general creative arts/performance, journalism/publications, music, performing arts, theater/drama. *Special achievements/activities:* cheerleading/drum major, junior miss. *Special characteristics:* children and siblings of alumni, children of faculty/staff, children of public servants, handicapped students, international students, members of minority groups, out-of-state students, spouses of deceased or disabled public servants, veterans, veterans' children. *Tuition waivers:* Full or partial for children of alumni, employees or children of employees, senior citizens. *ROTC:* Army cooperative, Air Force.
LOANS *Student loans:* $24,973,573 (70% need-based, 30% non-need-based). 49% of past graduating class borrowed through all loan programs. *Average indebtedness per student:* $22,262. *Average need-based loan:* Freshmen: $3079. Undergraduates: $3668. *Parent loans:* $9,452,786 (36% need-based, 64% non-need-based). *Programs:* Federal Direct (Subsidized and Unsubsidized Stafford, PLUS), Perkins, private loans.
WORK-STUDY *Federal work-study:* 327 jobs averaging $1969. *State or other work-study/employment:* Total amount: $2,606,076 (100% non-need-based). 1,251 part-time jobs averaging $2083.
ATHLETIC AWARDS Total amount: $5,002,254 (50% need-based, 50% non-need-based).
APPLYING FOR FINANCIAL AID *Required financial aid forms:* FAFSA, institution's own form. *Financial aid deadline (priority):* 4/15. *Notification date:* Continuous beginning 3/1. Students must reply within 3 weeks of notification.

CONTACT Aimee D. Baxter, Office of Financial Aid, Louisiana Tech University, PO Box 7925, Ruston, LA 71272, 318-257-2641 or toll-free 800-528-3241. *Fax:* 318-257-2628. *E-mail:* techaid@latech.edu.
Website: http://www.latech.edu/.

LOURDES UNIVERSITY

Sylvania, OH

CONTACT Deb LaJeunesse, Director of Financial Aid, Lourdes University, 6832 Convent Boulevard, Sylvania, OH 43560-2898, 419-824-3732 or toll-free 800-878-3210. *Fax:* 419-517-8866. *E-mail:* finaid@lourdes.edu.
Website: http://www.lourdes.edu/.

LOYOLA MARYMOUNT UNIVERSITY

Los Angeles, CA

Tuition & fees: $46,136	Average undergraduate aid package: $29,281

ABOUT THE INSTITUTION Independent Roman Catholic, coed. *Awards:* certificates, bachelor's, master's, and doctoral degrees. 50 undergraduate majors. *Total enrollment:* 9,618. Undergraduates: 6,391. Freshmen: 1,446. Both federal and institutional methodology are used as a basis for awarding need-based institutional aid.
UNDERGRADUATE EXPENSES for 2017–2018 *Application fee:* $60. *One-time required fee:* $250. *Comprehensive fee:* $60,826 includes full-time tuition ($45,460), mandatory fees ($676), and room and board ($14,690). *College room*

only: $10,290. Full-time tuition and fees vary according to reciprocity agreements. Room and board charges vary according to board plan and housing facility. **Part-time tuition:** $1897 per credit hour. **Part-time fees:** $8 per unit; $64 per term. Part-time tuition and fees vary according to course load.

FRESHMAN FINANCIAL AID (Fall 2016) 1,027 applied for aid; of those 65% were deemed to have need. 99% of freshmen with need received aid; of those 27% had need fully met. **Average percent of need met:** 68% (excluding resources awarded to replace EFC). **Average financial aid package:** $28,854 (excluding resources awarded to replace EFC). 35% of all full-time freshmen had no need and received non-need-based gift aid.

UNDERGRADUATE FINANCIAL AID (Fall 2016) 4,322 applied for aid; of those 75% were deemed to have need. 99% of undergraduates with need received aid; of those 21% had need fully met. **Average percent of need met:** 65% (excluding resources awarded to replace EFC). **Average financial aid package:** $29,281 (excluding resources awarded to replace EFC). 27% of all full-time undergraduates had no need and received non-need-based gift aid.

GIFT AID (NEED-BASED) Total amount: $64,242,169 (9% federal, 12% state, 78% institutional, 1% external sources). **Receiving aid:** Freshmen: 47% (625); all full-time undergraduates: 51% (3,066). **Average award:** Freshmen: $21,349; Undergraduates: $20,916. **Scholarships, grants, and awards:** Federal Pell, FSEOG, state, private, college/university gift aid from institutional funds.

GIFT AID (NON-NEED-BASED) Total amount: $23,412,101 (78% institutional, 22% external sources). **Receiving aid:** Freshmen: 11% (142). Undergraduates: 8% (453). **Average award:** Freshmen: $12,034. Undergraduates: $11,113. **Scholarships, grants, and awards by category:** Academic interests/achievement: area/ethnic studies, biological sciences, business, communication, computer science, education, engineering/technologies, English, foreign languages, general academic interests/achievements, health fields, home economics, humanities, international studies, mathematics, physical sciences, religion/biblical studies, social sciences. Creative arts/performance: applied art and design, art/fine arts, cinema/film/broadcasting, creative writing, dance, debating, general creative arts/performance, journalism/publications, music, performing arts, theater/drama. Special achievements/activities: community service, general special achievements/activities, leadership, memberships, religious involvement. Special characteristics: adult students, children and siblings of alumni, children of faculty/staff, ethnic background, first-generation college students, general special characteristics, handicapped students, international students, local/state students, members of minority groups, out-of-state students, previous college experience, religious affiliation, veterans, veterans' children. **Tuition waivers:** Full or partial for employees or children of employees. **ROTC:** Army cooperative, Air Force.

LOANS Student loans: $24,979,020 (74% need-based, 26% non-need-based). 53% of past graduating class borrowed through all loan programs. Average indebtedness per student: $32,560. **Average need-based loan:** Freshmen: $4721. Undergraduates: $5688. **Parent loans:** $25,411,627 (50% need-based, 50% non-need-based). **Programs:** Federal Direct (Subsidized and Unsubsidized Stafford, PLUS), college/university.

WORK-STUDY Federal work-study: 1,384 jobs averaging $1949. **State or other work-study/employment:** Total amount: $4,692,189 (28% need-based, 72% non-need-based). 2,285 part-time jobs averaging $2053.

ATHLETIC AWARDS Total amount: $8,416,096 (44% need-based, 56% non-need-based).

APPLYING FOR FINANCIAL AID Required financial aid form: FAFSA. **Financial aid deadline (priority):** 2/1. **Notification date:** Continuous beginning 12/15. Students must reply by 5/1.

CONTACT Dr. Maureen Weatherall, Vice Provost for Enrollment Management, Loyola Marymount University, One LMU Drive, Suite 270, Los Angeles, CA 90045-2659, 310-338-2753 or toll-free 800-LMU-INFO. Fax: 310-338-2793. E-mail: finaid@lmu.edu.

Website: http://www.lmu.edu/.

LOYOLA UNIVERSITY CHICAGO
Chicago, IL

Tuition & fees: $43,808	Average undergraduate aid package: $34,844

ABOUT THE INSTITUTION Independent Roman Catholic (Jesuit), coed. **Awards:** certificates, associate, bachelor's, master's, and doctoral degrees (also offers adult part-time program with significant enrollment not reflected in profile). 85 under-

graduate majors. **Total enrollment:** 16,673. Undergraduates: 11,420. Freshmen: 2,654. Federal methodology is used as a basis for awarding need-based institutional aid.

UNDERGRADUATE EXPENSES for 2018–2019 Tuition: full-time $42,720; part-time $788 per credit hour. **Required fees:** full-time $1088; $350 per year. Full-time tuition and fees vary according to degree level, location, program, and student level. Part-time tuition and fees vary according to course load. Room and board charges vary according to board plan, housing facility, and location.

FRESHMAN FINANCIAL AID (Fall 2017, est.) 2,261 applied for aid; of those 81% were deemed to have need. 100% of freshmen with need received aid; of those 18% had need fully met. **Average percent of need met:** 82% (excluding resources awarded to replace EFC). **Average financial aid package:** $36,370 (excluding resources awarded to replace EFC). 29% of all full-time freshmen had no need and received non-need-based gift aid.

UNDERGRADUATE FINANCIAL AID (Fall 2017, est.) 7,797 applied for aid; of those 88% were deemed to have need. 100% of undergraduates with need received aid; of those 14% had need fully met. **Average percent of need met:** 81% (excluding resources awarded to replace EFC). **Average financial aid package:** $34,844 (excluding resources awarded to replace EFC). 29% of all full-time undergraduates had no need and received non-need-based gift aid.

GIFT AID (NEED-BASED) Total amount: $140,563,096 (12% federal, 7% state, 79% institutional, 2% external sources). **Receiving aid:** Freshmen: 68% (1,810); all full-time undergraduates: 62% (6,542). **Average award:** Freshmen: $23,423; Undergraduates: $21,420. **Scholarships, grants, and awards:** Federal Pell, FSEOG, state, private, college/university gift aid from institutional funds.

GIFT AID (NON-NEED-BASED) Total amount: $59,744,419 (4% federal, 94% institutional, 2% external sources). **Receiving aid:** Freshmen: 10% (275). Undergraduates: 6% (663). **Average award:** Freshmen: $18,733. Undergraduates: $16,444. **Scholarships, grants, and awards by category:** Academic interests/achievement: 7,664 awards ($131,465,681 total): general academic interests/achievements. Creative arts/performance: 39 awards ($116,600 total): art/fine arts, debating, journalism/publications, music, theater/drama. Special achievements/activities: 527 awards ($4,191,468 total): community service, general special achievements/activities, leadership, memberships. Special characteristics: 1,387 awards ($3,911,894 total): adult students, general special characteristics, religious affiliation. **Tuition waivers:** Full or partial for employees or children of employees, senior citizens. **ROTC:** Army, Naval cooperative, Air Force cooperative.

LOANS Student loans: $67,151,374 (75% need-based, 25% non-need-based). 67% of past graduating class borrowed through all loan programs. Average indebtedness per student: $34,973. **Average need-based loan:** Freshmen: $3897. Undergraduates: $4617. **Parent loans:** $50,204,242 (56% need-based, 44% non-need-based). **Programs:** Federal Direct (Subsidized and Unsubsidized Stafford, PLUS), Perkins, Federal Nursing.

WORK-STUDY Federal work-study: Total amount: $14,556,685; 5,021 jobs averaging $2790.

ATHLETIC AWARDS Total amount: $4,793,851 (26% need-based, 74% non-need-based).

APPLYING FOR FINANCIAL AID Required financial aid form: FAFSA. **Financial aid deadline:** Continuous. **Notification date:** Continuous beginning 2/15. Students must reply within 3 weeks of notification.

CONTACT Mr. Tobyn Friar, Director of Financial Aid, Loyola University Chicago, 6525 North Sheridan Road, Chicago, IL 60660, 773-508-7704 or toll-free 800-262-2373. Fax: 773-508-3397. E-mail: nmerz@luc.edu.

Website: http://www.luc.edu/.

LOYOLA UNIVERSITY MARYLAND
Baltimore, MD

Tuition & fees: $47,725	Average undergraduate aid package: $32,414

ABOUT THE INSTITUTION Independent Roman Catholic (Jesuit), coed. **Awards:** certificates, bachelor's, master's, and doctoral degrees. 35 undergraduate majors. **Total enrollment:** 6,084. Undergraduates: 4,104. Freshmen: 1,095. Institutional methodology is used as a basis for awarding need-based institutional aid.

UNDERGRADUATE EXPENSES for 2017–2018 Application fee: $60. **One-time required fee:** $1240. **Comprehensive fee:** $61,875 includes full-time tuition ($46,160), mandatory fees ($1565), and room and board ($14,150). Full-time tuition and fees vary according to course load. Room and board charges vary according to board plan and housing facility. *Part-time tuition:* $745 per credit. Part-time tuition and fees vary according to course load.

FRESHMAN FINANCIAL AID (Fall 2016) 866 applied for aid; of those 72% were deemed to have need. 98% of freshmen with need received aid; of those 90% had need fully met. *Average percent of need met:* 89% (excluding resources awarded to replace EFC). *Average financial aid package:* $32,616 (excluding resources awarded to replace EFC). 32% of all full-time freshmen had no need and received non-need-based gift aid.

UNDERGRADUATE FINANCIAL AID (Fall 2016) 2,657 applied for aid; of those 82% were deemed to have need. 99% of undergraduates with need received aid; of those 89% had need fully met. *Average percent of need met:* 90% (excluding resources awarded to replace EFC). *Average financial aid package:* $32,414 (excluding resources awarded to replace EFC). 23% of all full-time undergraduates had no need and received non-need-based gift aid.

GIFT AID (NEED-BASED) *Total amount:* $57,332,369 (6% federal, 1% state, 92% institutional, 1% external sources). *Receiving aid:* Freshmen: 39% (424); all full-time undergraduates: 39% (1,578). *Average award:* Freshmen: $19,718; Undergraduates: $21,593. *Scholarships, grants, and awards:* Federal Pell, FSEOG, state, private, college/university gift aid from institutional funds.

GIFT AID (NON-NEED-BASED) *Total amount:* $18,914,448 (8% federal, 90% institutional, 2% external sources). *Receiving aid:* Freshmen: 42% (462). Undergraduates: 30% (1,214). *Average award:* Freshmen: $18,137. Undergraduates: $17,650. *Scholarships, grants, and awards by category:* Academic interests/achievement: general academic interests/achievements. *Tuition waivers:* Full or partial for employees or children of employees. *ROTC:* Army, Air Force cooperative.

LOANS *Student loans:* $24,210,630 (83% need-based, 17% non-need-based). 62% of past graduating class borrowed through all loan programs. *Average indebtedness per student:* $33,969. *Average need-based loan:* Freshmen: $4002. Undergraduates: $4908. *Parent loans:* $17,964,055 (100% non-need-based). *Programs:* Federal Direct (Subsidized and Unsubsidized Stafford, PLUS), Perkins, college/university.

WORK-STUDY *Federal work-study:* jobs available. *State or other work-study/employment:* Total amount: $1,099,050 (73% need-based, 27% non-need-based). Part-time jobs available.

ATHLETIC AWARDS Total amount: $6,272,545 (22% need-based, 78% non-need-based).

APPLYING FOR FINANCIAL AID *Required financial aid forms:* FAFSA, CSS Financial Aid PROFILE, noncustodial (divorced/separated) parent's statement. *Financial aid deadline:* 1/15. *Notification date:* 3/15. Students must reply by 5/1.

CONTACT Office of Financial Aid, Loyola University Maryland, Knott Humanities Center 211A, Baltimore, MD 21210, 410-617-2576 or toll-free 800-221-9107. *Fax:* 410-617-5149. *E-mail:* financialaid@loyola.edu. *Website:* http://www.loyola.edu/.

LOYOLA UNIVERSITY NEW ORLEANS
New Orleans, LA

Tuition & fees: $39,692	Average undergraduate aid package: $33,676

ABOUT THE INSTITUTION Independent Roman Catholic (Jesuit), coed. *Awards:* certificates, bachelor's, master's, and doctoral degrees. 63 undergraduate majors. *Total enrollment:* 3,759. Undergraduates: 2,602. Freshmen: 803. Federal methodology is used as a basis for awarding need-based institutional aid.

UNDERGRADUATE EXPENSES for 2018–2019 *One-time required fee:* $250. *Comprehensive fee:* $53,072 includes full-time tuition ($38,126), mandatory fees ($1566), and room and board ($13,380). *College room only:* $7430. Full-time tuition and fees vary according to class time, course load, and degree level. Room and board charges vary according to board plan and housing facility. *Part-time tuition:* $1073 per credit hour. *Part-time fees:* $402 per term. Part-time tuition and fees vary according to class time and degree level.

FRESHMAN FINANCIAL AID (Fall 2017, est.) 752 applied for aid; of those 88% were deemed to have need. 100% of freshmen with need received aid; of those 15% had need fully met. *Average percent of need met:* 83% (excluding resources awarded to replace EFC). *Average financial aid package:* $35,842 (excluding resources awarded to replace EFC). 16% of all full-time freshmen had no need and received non-need-based gift aid.

UNDERGRADUATE FINANCIAL AID (Fall 2017, est.) 2,052 applied for aid; of those 89% were deemed to have need. 100% of undergraduates with need received aid; of those 17% had need fully met. *Average percent of need met:* 79% (excluding resources awarded to replace EFC). *Average financial aid package:* $33,676 (excluding resources awarded to replace EFC). 22% of all full-time undergraduates had no need and received non-need-based gift aid.

GIFT AID (NEED-BASED) *Total amount:* $51,364,739 (8% federal, 7% state, 83% institutional, 2% external sources). *Receiving aid:* Freshmen: 83% (661); all full-time undergraduates: 75% (1,805). *Average award:* Freshmen: $32,173; Undergraduates: $29,558. *Scholarships, grants, and awards:* Federal Pell, FSEOG, state, private, college/university gift aid from institutional funds, United Negro College Fund.

GIFT AID (NON-NEED-BASED) *Total amount:* $11,881,395 (9% state, 88% institutional, 3% external sources). *Receiving aid:* Freshmen: 11% (86). Undergraduates: 10% (249). *Average award:* Freshmen: $18,586. Undergraduates: $16,800. *Scholarships, grants, and awards by category:* Academic interests/achievement: general academic interests/achievements. *Creative arts/performance:* art/fine arts, general creative arts/performance. *Special achievements/activities:* leadership. *Special characteristics:* children and siblings of alumni, children of faculty/staff, veterans' children. *Tuition waivers:* Full or partial for employees or children of employees, senior citizens. *ROTC:* Army cooperative, Naval cooperative, Air Force cooperative.

LOANS *Student loans:* $15,147,903 (72% need-based, 28% non-need-based). 71% of past graduating class borrowed through all loan programs. *Average indebtedness per student:* $29,946. *Average need-based loan:* Freshmen: $3182. Undergraduates: $4402. *Parent loans:* $6,565,329 (46% need-based, 54% non-need-based). *Programs:* Federal Direct (Subsidized and Unsubsidized Stafford, PLUS), Perkins.

WORK-STUDY *Federal work-study:* Total amount: $1,128,037; 767 jobs averaging $1600.

ATHLETIC AWARDS Total amount: $2,057,539 (54% need-based, 46% non-need-based).

APPLYING FOR FINANCIAL AID *Required financial aid form:* FAFSA. *Financial aid deadline (priority):* 2/15. *Notification date:* Continuous beginning 3/1. Students must reply within 2 weeks of notification.

CONTACT Ms. Carrie E. Glass, Director of Scholarships and Financial Aid, Loyola University New Orleans, 6363 St. Charles Avenue, New Orleans, LA 70118-6195, 504-865-3231 or toll-free 800-4-LOYOLA. *Fax:* 504-865-3233. *E-mail:* finaid@loyno.edu. *Website:* http://www.loyno.edu/.

LUBBOCK CHRISTIAN UNIVERSITY
Lubbock, TX

Tuition & fees: $21,794	Average undergraduate aid package: $15,700

ABOUT THE INSTITUTION Independent Church of Christ, coed. *Awards:* bachelor's and master's degrees. 60 undergraduate majors. *Total enrollment:* 1,883. Undergraduates: 1,484. Freshmen: 310. Federal methodology is used as a basis for awarding need-based institutional aid.

UNDERGRADUATE EXPENSES for 2017–2018 *Application fee:* $25. *Comprehensive fee:* $29,272 includes full-time tuition ($21,794) and room and board ($7478). Full-time tuition and fees vary according to degree level and program. Room and board charges vary according to board plan and housing facility. *Part-time tuition:* $705 per credit hour. *Part-time fees:* $60 per term. Part-time tuition and fees vary according to course load, degree level, and program.

FRESHMAN FINANCIAL AID (Fall 2017, est.) 263 applied for aid; of those 83% were deemed to have need. 100% of freshmen with need received aid; of those 11% had need fully met. *Average percent of need met:* 65% (excluding resources awarded to replace EFC). *Average financial aid package:* $15,012 (excluding resources awarded to replace EFC). 18% of all full-time freshmen had no need and received non-need-based gift aid.

UNDERGRADUATE FINANCIAL AID (Fall 2017, est.) 1,101 applied for aid; of those 87% were deemed to have need. 100% of undergraduates with need received aid; of those 10% had need fully met. *Average percent of need met:* 64% (excluding resources awarded to replace EFC). *Average financial aid package:* $15,700 (excluding resources awarded to replace EFC). 16% of all full-time undergraduates had no need and received non-need-based gift aid.

GIFT AID (NEED-BASED) Total amount: $30,330,222 (82% federal, 5% state, 10% institutional, 3% external sources). Receiving aid: Freshmen: 69% (215); all full-time undergraduates: 71% (908). Average award: Freshmen: $11,124; Undergraduates: $11,316. Scholarships, grants, and awards: Federal Pell, FSEOG, state, college/university gift aid from institutional funds.

GIFT AID (NON-NEED-BASED) Total amount: $1,954,634 (1% federal, 78% institutional, 21% external sources). Receiving aid: Freshmen: 7% (22). Undergraduates: 7% (92). Average award: Freshmen: $5289. Undergraduates: $6550. Scholarships, grants, and awards by category: Academic interests/achievement: 816 awards ($3,749,974 total): agriculture, business, communication, computer science, education, English, foreign languages, general academic interests/achievements, humanities, physical sciences, religion/biblical studies, social sciences. Creative arts/performance: 59 awards ($81,874 total): art/fine arts, journalism/publications, music, performing arts, theater/drama. Special achievements/activities: 55 awards ($79,250 total): leadership. Special characteristics: 206 awards ($845,345 total): children and siblings of alumni, children of faculty/staff, siblings of current students, spouses of current students. Tuition waivers: Full or partial for employees or children of employees. ROTC: Army cooperative, Air Force cooperative.

LOANS Student loans: $11,197,775 (72% need-based, 28% non-need-based). 70% of past graduating class borrowed through all loan programs. Average indebtedness per student: $35,879. Average need-based loan: Freshmen: $3430. Undergraduates: $4469. Parent loans: $3,971,256 (43% need-based, 57% non-need-based). Programs: Federal Direct (Subsidized and Unsubsidized Stafford, PLUS), Perkins, state.

WORK-STUDY Federal work-study: Total amount: $907,949; 630 jobs averaging $1714. State or other work-study/employment: Total amount: $5594 (58% need-based, 42% non-need-based). 15 part-time jobs averaging $776.

ATHLETIC AWARDS Total amount: $2,129,147 (69% need-based, 31% non-need-based).

APPLYING FOR FINANCIAL AID Required financial aid forms: FAFSA, institution's own form. Financial aid deadline (priority): 6/1. Notification date: Continuous beginning 10/15.

CONTACT Mrs. Amy Hardesty, Director of Financial Aid, Lubbock Christian University, 5601 19th Street, Lubbock, TX 79407, 806-720-7176 or toll-free 800-933-7601. Fax: 806-720-7185. E-mail: amy.hardesty@lcu.edu.
Website: http://www.lcu.edu/.

LUTHER COLLEGE
Decorah, IA

Tuition & fees: $42,290	Average undergraduate aid package: $35,397

ABOUT THE INSTITUTION Independent Evangelical Lutheran Church in America, coed. Awards: bachelor's degrees. 41 undergraduate majors. Total enrollment: 2,053. Undergraduates: 2,053. Freshmen: 517. Federal methodology is used as a basis for awarding need-based institutional aid.

UNDERGRADUATE EXPENSES for 2018–2019 Comprehensive fee: $51,750 includes full-time tuition ($41,950), mandatory fees ($340), and room and board ($9460). College room only: $4420. Full-time tuition and fees vary according to course load. Room and board charges vary according to board plan and housing facility. Part-time tuition: $1498 per credit hour. Part-time tuition and fees vary according to course load.

FRESHMAN FINANCIAL AID (Fall 2017, est.) 485 applied for aid; of those 87% were deemed to have need. 100% of freshmen with need received aid; of those 39% had need fully met. Average percent of need met: 92% (excluding resources awarded to replace EFC). Average financial aid package: $38,605 (excluding resources awarded to replace EFC). 19% of all full-time freshmen had no need and received non-need-based gift aid.

UNDERGRADUATE FINANCIAL AID (Fall 2017, est.) 1,749 applied for aid; of those 89% were deemed to have need. 100% of undergraduates with need received aid; of those 38% had need fully met. Average percent of need met: 89% (excluding resources awarded to replace EFC). Average financial aid package: $35,397 (excluding resources awarded to replace EFC). 22% of all full-time undergraduates had no need and received non-need-based gift aid.

GIFT AID (NEED-BASED) Total amount: $42,529,893 (5% federal, 3% state, 84% institutional, 8% external sources). Receiving aid: Freshmen: 81% (420); all full-time undergraduates: 78% (1,559). Average award: Freshmen: $30,804; Undergrad-

uates: $27,778. Scholarships, grants, and awards: Federal Pell, FSEOG, state, private, college/university gift aid from institutional funds.

GIFT AID (NON-NEED-BASED) Total amount: $11,119,840 (93% institutional, 7% external sources). Receiving aid: Freshmen: 16% (82). Undergraduates: 13% (268). Average award: Freshmen: $25,334. Undergraduates: $21,053. Scholarships, grants, and awards by category: Academic interests/achievement: 1,691 awards ($28,498,151 total): general academic interests/achievements. Creative arts/performance: 706 awards ($2,976,586 total): music. Special characteristics: 601 awards ($1,026,415 total): children and siblings of alumni, members of minority groups, religious affiliation. Tuition waivers: Full or partial for employees or children of employees.

LOANS Student loans: $9,908,081 (77% need-based, 23% non-need-based). 71% of past graduating class borrowed through all loan programs. Average indebtedness per student: $36,685. Average need-based loan: Freshmen: $7118. Undergraduates: $7319. Parent loans: $5,297,575 (31% need-based, 69% non-need-based). Programs: Federal Direct (Subsidized and Unsubsidized Stafford, PLUS), Perkins, college/university.

WORK-STUDY Federal work-study: Total amount: $1,579,975; 770 jobs averaging $2055. State or other work-study/employment: Total amount: $1,919,151 (38% need-based, 62% non-need-based). 897 part-time jobs averaging $1769.

APPLYING FOR FINANCIAL AID Required financial aid forms: FAFSA, institution's own form. Financial aid deadline (priority): 3/1. Notification date: Continuous beginning 3/15. Students must reply by 5/1.

CONTACT Ms. Janice Cordell, Director of Financial Aid, Luther College, 700 College Drive, Decorah, IA 52101-1045, 563-387-1018 or toll-free 800-458-8437. Fax: 563-387-2241. E-mail: cordellj@luther.edu.
Website: http://www.luther.edu/.

LUTHER RICE COLLEGE & SEMINARY
Lithonia, GA

CONTACT Mr. Casey Kuffrey, Financial Aid Director, Luther Rice College & Seminary, 3038 Evans Mill Road, Lithonia, GA 30038-2418, 770-484-1204 Ext. 5284 or toll-free 800-442-1577. Fax: 678-990-5388. E-mail: casey.kuffrey@lutherrice.edu.
Website: http://www.lutherrice.edu/.

LYCOMING COLLEGE
Williamsport, PA

Tuition & fees: $40,090	Average undergraduate aid package: $37,279

ABOUT THE INSTITUTION Independent United Methodist, coed. Awards: bachelor's degrees. 51 undergraduate majors. Total enrollment: 1,223. Undergraduates: 1,223. Freshmen: 282. Federal methodology is used as a basis for awarding need-based institutional aid.

UNDERGRADUATE EXPENSES for 2018–2019 One-time required fee: $225. Comprehensive fee: $52,658 includes full-time tuition ($39,360), mandatory fees ($730), and room and board ($12,568). Room and board charges vary according to board plan and housing facility. Part-time tuition: $1230 per credit hour. Part-time tuition and fees vary according to course load.

FRESHMAN FINANCIAL AID (Fall 2017, est.) 260 applied for aid; of those 95% were deemed to have need. 100% of freshmen with need received aid; of those 13% had need fully met. Average percent of need met: 84% (excluding resources awarded to replace EFC). Average financial aid package: $39,141 (excluding resources awarded to replace EFC). 12% of all full-time freshmen had no need and received non-need-based gift aid.

UNDERGRADUATE FINANCIAL AID (Fall 2017, est.) 1,065 applied for aid; of those 95% were deemed to have need. 100% of undergraduates with need received aid; of those 26% had need fully met. Average percent of need met: 84% (excluding resources awarded to replace EFC). Average financial aid package: $37,279 (excluding resources awarded to replace EFC). 15% of all full-time undergraduates had no need and received non-need-based gift aid.

GIFT AID (NEED-BASED) Total amount: $32,579,899 (8% federal, 4% state, 86% institutional, 2% external sources). Receiving aid: Freshmen: 87% (246); all full-time undergraduates: 85% (1,009). Average award: Freshmen: $33,058; Undergrad-

uates: $31,590. **Scholarships, grants, and awards:** Federal Pell, FSEOG, state, private, college/university gift aid from institutional funds.
GIFT AID (NON-NEED-BASED) Total amount: $3,420,115 (97% institutional, 3% external sources). **Receiving aid:** Freshmen: 6% (17). Undergraduates: 9% (102). **Average award:** Freshmen: $28,502. Undergraduates: $24,770. **Scholarships, grants, and awards by category: Academic interests/achievement:** biological sciences, business, communication, computer science, education, engineering/technologies, English, foreign languages, general academic interests/achievements, health fields, humanities, international studies, mathematics, physical sciences, premedicine, religion/biblical studies, social sciences. **Creative arts/performance:** applied art and design, art/fine arts, creative writing, music, theater/drama. **Special achievements/activities:** community service, general special achievements/activities, leadership. **Special characteristics:** children of educators, children of faculty/staff, local/state students, relatives of clergy. **Tuition waivers:** Full or partial for employees or children of employees. **ROTC:** Army cooperative.
LOANS Student loans: $9,557,114 (71% need-based, 29% non-need-based). **Average need-based loan:** Freshmen: $3652. Undergraduates: $4751. **Parent loans:** $3,180,454 (40% need-based, 60% non-need-based). **Programs:** Federal Direct (Subsidized and Unsubsidized Stafford, PLUS), Perkins, college/university.
WORK-STUDY Federal work-study: Total amount: $200,495; jobs available.
APPLYING FOR FINANCIAL AID Required financial aid form: FAFSA. **Financial aid deadline (priority):** 5/1. **Notification date:** Continuous beginning 3/1. Students must reply by 5/1.
CONTACT Mr. James S. Lakis, Director of Financial Aid, Lycoming College, 700 College Place, Williamsport, PA 17701-5192, 570-321-4040 or toll-free 800-345-3920 Ext. 4026. Fax: 570-321-4993. E-mail: lakis@lycoming.edu.
Website: http://www.lycoming.edu/.

LYNCHBURG COLLEGE
Lynchburg, VA

Tuition & fees: $37,690	Average undergraduate aid package: $28,781

ABOUT THE INSTITUTION Independent Christian Church (Disciples of Christ), coed. **Awards:** certificates, bachelor's, master's, and doctoral degrees. 38 undergraduate majors. **Total enrollment:** 2,808. Undergraduates: 2,048. Freshmen: 544. Federal methodology is used as a basis for awarding need-based institutional aid.
UNDERGRADUATE EXPENSES for 2018–2019 Application fee: $30. **Comprehensive fee:** $48,370 includes full-time tuition ($36,720), mandatory fees ($970), and room and board ($10,680). **College room only:** $5470. Room and board charges vary according to board plan and housing facility. **Part-time tuition:** $510 per credit hour. Part-time tuition and fees vary according to course load. **Payment plan:** Tuition prepayment.
FRESHMAN FINANCIAL AID (Fall 2017, est.) 499 applied for aid; of those 86% were deemed to have need. 100% of freshmen with need received aid; of those 27% had need fully met. **Average percent of need met:** 81% (excluding resources awarded to replace EFC). **Average financial aid package:** $29,360 (excluding resources awarded to replace EFC). 19% of all full-time freshmen had no need and received non-need-based gift aid.
UNDERGRADUATE FINANCIAL AID (Fall 2017, est.) 1,646 applied for aid; of those 91% were deemed to have need. 100% of undergraduates with need received aid; of those 22% had need fully met. **Average percent of need met:** 78% (excluding resources awarded to replace EFC). **Average financial aid package:** $28,781 (excluding resources awarded to replace EFC). 22% of all full-time undergraduates had no need and received non-need-based gift aid.
GIFT AID (NEED-BASED) Total amount: $37,025,589 (8% federal, 8% state, 82% institutional, 2% external sources). **Receiving aid:** Freshmen: 80% (431); all full-time undergraduates: 78% (1,496). **Average award:** Freshmen: $26,691; Undergraduates: $25,227. **Scholarships, grants, and awards:** Federal Pell, FSEOG, state, private, college/university gift aid from institutional funds.
GIFT AID (NON-NEED-BASED) Total amount: $11,341,122 (12% state, 85% institutional, 3% external sources). **Receiving aid:** Freshmen: 18% (97). Undergraduates: 13% (259). **Average award:** Freshmen: $20,157. Undergraduates: $18,983. **Scholarships, grants, and awards by category: Academic interests/achievement:** general academic interests/achievements. **Creative arts/performance:** art/fine arts, music, theater/drama. **Tuition waivers:** Full or partial for employees or children of employees, adult students, senior citizens.

LOANS Student loans: $15,075,293 (57% need-based, 43% non-need-based). 80% of past graduating class borrowed through all loan programs. **Average indebtedness per student:** $35,290. **Average need-based loan:** Freshmen: $2436. Undergraduates: $3587. **Parent loans:** $4,937,153 (61% need-based, 39% non-need-based). **Programs:** Federal Direct (Subsidized and Unsubsidized Stafford, PLUS), Perkins, alternative loans.
WORK-STUDY Federal work-study: Total amount: $274,297; 187 jobs averaging $1347. **State or other work-study/employment:** Total amount: $377,882 (24% need-based, 76% non-need-based). 513 part-time jobs averaging $1300.
APPLYING FOR FINANCIAL AID Required financial aid forms: FAFSA, state aid form. **Financial aid deadline (priority):** 11/1. **Notification date:** Continuous beginning 12/1. Students must reply by 5/1 or within 2 weeks of notification.
CONTACT Mrs. Michelle G. Davis, Associate Director of Financial Aid, Lynchburg College, 1501 Lakeside Drive, Lynchburg, VA 24501, 434-544-8228 or toll-free 800-426-8101. Fax: 434-544-8653. E-mail: davis@lynchburg.edu.
Website: http://www.lynchburg.edu/.

LYNN UNIVERSITY
Boca Raton, FL

Tuition & fees: $38,210	Average undergraduate aid package: $22,741

ABOUT THE INSTITUTION Independent, coed. **Awards:** certificates, associate, bachelor's, master's, and doctoral degrees. 33 undergraduate majors. **Total enrollment:** 3,010. Undergraduates: 2,182. Freshmen: 482. Federal methodology is used as a basis for awarding need-based institutional aid.
UNDERGRADUATE EXPENSES for 2018–2019 Application fee: $45. **One-time required fee:** $1000. **Comprehensive fee:** $50,380 includes full-time tuition ($35,960), mandatory fees ($2250), and room and board ($12,170). Full-time tuition and fees vary according to degree level and program. Room and board charges vary according to board plan and housing facility. **Part-time tuition:** $1040 per credit hour. Part-time tuition and fees vary according to course load and program.
FRESHMAN FINANCIAL AID (Fall 2017, est.) 440 applied for aid; of those 50% were deemed to have need. 100% of freshmen with need received aid; of those 100% had need fully met. **Average percent of need met:** 52% (excluding resources awarded to replace EFC). **Average financial aid package:** $22,362 (excluding resources awarded to replace EFC). 40% of all full-time freshmen had no need and received non-need-based gift aid.
UNDERGRADUATE FINANCIAL AID (Fall 2017, est.) 1,550 applied for aid; of those 49% were deemed to have need. 100% of undergraduates with need received aid; of those 100% had need fully met. **Average percent of need met:** 52% (excluding resources awarded to replace EFC). **Average financial aid package:** $22,741 (excluding resources awarded to replace EFC). 29% of all full-time undergraduates had no need and received non-need-based gift aid.
GIFT AID (NEED-BASED) Total amount: $13,073,879 (19% federal, 10% state, 69% institutional, 2% external sources). **Receiving aid:** Freshmen: 41% (192); all full-time undergraduates: 37% (673). **Average award:** Freshmen: $10,538; Undergraduates: $10,401. **Scholarships, grants, and awards:** Federal Pell, FSEOG, state, private, college/university gift aid from institutional funds.
GIFT AID (NON-NEED-BASED) Total amount: $8,490,949 (7% state, 90% institutional, 3% external sources). **Receiving aid:** Freshmen: 43% (202). Undergraduates: 37% (673). **Average award:** Freshmen: $10,549. Undergraduates: $10,810. **Scholarships, grants, and awards by category: Academic interests/achievement:** 430 awards ($5,486,680 total): biological sciences, business, communication, general academic interests/achievements, international studies. **Creative arts/performance:** 43 awards ($1,160,102 total): music. **Special achievements/activities:** 4 awards ($20,000 total): leadership. **Special characteristics:** 332 awards ($2,368,621 total): children and siblings of alumni, children of educators, children of faculty/staff, out-of-state students, siblings of current students, veterans. **Tuition waivers:** Full or partial for employees or children of employees. **ROTC:** Air Force cooperative.
LOANS Student loans: $6,329,170 (86% need-based, 14% non-need-based). 39% of past graduating class borrowed through all loan programs. **Average indebtedness per student:** $32,533. **Average need-based loan:** Freshmen: $4069. Undergraduates: $4751. **Parent loans:** $8,531,235 (93% need-based, 7% non-need-based). **Programs:** Federal Direct (Subsidized and Unsubsidized Stafford, PLUS), Perkins.

WORK STUDY *Federal work-study.* Total amount: $460,322, 224 jobs averaging $2055. *State or other work-study/employment:* Total amount: $297,070 (65% need-based, 35% non-need-based). 35 part-time jobs averaging $8516.

ATHLETIC AWARDS Total amount: $3,174,321 (46% need-based, 54% non-need-based).

APPLYING FOR FINANCIAL AID *Required financial aid form:* FAFSA. *Financial aid deadline (priority):* 3/1. *Notification date:* Continuous beginning 11/1. Students must reply within 2 weeks of notification.

CONTACT Mr. John Chambers, Director of Student Financial Assistance, Lynn University, 3601 North Military Trail, Boca Raton, FL 33431-5598, 561-237-7973 or toll-free 800-888-5966. *Fax:* 561-237-7189. *E-mail:* jchambers@lynn.edu. *Website:* http://www.lynn.edu/.

LYON COLLEGE
Batesville, AR

Tuition & fees: $27,340	Average undergraduate aid package: $22,842

ABOUT THE INSTITUTION Independent Presbyterian, coed. *Awards:* bachelor's degrees. 14 undergraduate majors. *Total enrollment:* 672. Undergraduates: 672. Freshmen: 190. Federal methodology is used as a basis for awarding need-based institutional aid.

UNDERGRADUATE EXPENSES for 2017–2018 *Comprehensive fee:* $36,120 includes full-time tuition ($27,100), mandatory fees ($240), and room and board ($8780). *College room only:* $2499. Full-time tuition and fees vary according to course load. Room and board charges vary according to board plan and housing facility. *Part-time tuition:* $895 per credit hour. *Part-time fees:* $450 per credit hour.

FRESHMAN FINANCIAL AID (Fall 2017, est.) 188 applied for aid; of those 86% were deemed to have need. 99% of freshmen with need received aid; of those 25% had need fully met. *Average percent of need met:* 74% (excluding resources awarded to replace EFC). *Average financial aid package:* $23,396 (excluding resources awarded to replace EFC). 14% of all full-time freshmen had no need and received non-need-based gift aid.

UNDERGRADUATE FINANCIAL AID (Fall 2017, est.) 552 applied for aid; of those 88% were deemed to have need. 100% of undergraduates with need received aid; of those 25% had need fully met. *Average percent of need met:* 73% (excluding resources awarded to replace EFC). *Average financial aid package:* $22,842 (excluding resources awarded to replace EFC). 15% of all full-time undergraduates had no need and received non-need-based gift aid.

GIFT AID (NEED-BASED) *Total amount:* $6,781,572 (17% federal, 12% state, 68% institutional, 3% external sources). *Receiving aid:* Freshmen: 84% (159); all full-time undergraduates: 74% (483). *Average award:* Freshmen: $20,992; Undergraduates: $20,053. *Scholarships, grants, and awards:* Federal Pell, FSEOG, state, private, college/university gift aid from institutional funds.

GIFT AID (NON-NEED-BASED) *Total amount:* $4,971,853 (12% state, 37% institutional, 51% external sources). *Receiving aid:* Freshmen: 18% (35). Undergraduates: 15% (100). *Average award:* Freshmen: $14,268. Undergraduates: $15,710. *Scholarships, grants, and awards by category:* Academic interests/achievement: business, general academic interests/achievements. *Creative arts/performance;* art/fine arts, music, theater/drama. *Special achievements/activities:* cheerleading/drum major, general special achievements/activities. *Special characteristics:* children and siblings of alumni, children of faculty/staff, ethnic background, first-generation college students, local/state students, members of minority groups, religious affiliation. *Tuition waivers:* Full or partial for employees or children of employees.

LOANS *Student loans:* $3,245,756 (69% need-based, 31% non-need-based). 74% of past graduating class borrowed through all loan programs. *Average indebtedness per student:* $26,353. *Average need-based loan:* Freshmen: $3862. Undergraduates: $4207. *Parent loans:* $877,300 (43% need-based, 57% non-need-based). *Programs:* Federal Direct (Subsidized and Unsubsidized Stafford, PLUS), Perkins.

WORK-STUDY *Federal work-study:* Total amount: $1000; jobs available. *State or other work-study/employment:* Part-time jobs available.

ATHLETIC AWARDS Total amount: $4,453,687 (63% need-based, 37% non-need-based).

APPLYING FOR FINANCIAL AID *Required financial aid forms:* FAFSA, state aid form. *Financial aid deadline (priority):* 3/15. *Notification date:* Continuous beginning 12/1. Students must reply by 8/1.

CONTACT Office of Student Assistance, Lyon College, 2300 Highland Road, Batesville, AR 72501, 870-307-7257 or toll-free 800-423-2542. *Fax:* 870-307-7542. *E-mail:* financialaid@lyon.edu. *Website:* http://www.lyon.edu/.

MACALESTER COLLEGE
St. Paul, MN

Tuition & fees: $54,344	Average undergraduate aid package: $45,680

ABOUT THE INSTITUTION Independent, coed. *Awards:* bachelor's degrees. 37 undergraduate majors. *Total enrollment:* 2,136. Undergraduates: 2,136. Both federal and institutional methodology are used as a basis for awarding need-based institutional aid.

UNDERGRADUATE EXPENSES for 2018–2019 *Application fee:* $40. *Comprehensive fee:* $66,500 includes full-time tuition ($54,114), mandatory fees ($230), and room and board ($12,156). *College room only:* $6526. Full-time tuition and fees vary according to course load. Room and board charges vary according to board plan and housing facility. *Part-time tuition:* $1691 per credit. Part-time tuition and fees vary according to course load.

FRESHMAN FINANCIAL AID (Fall 2017, est.) 434 applied for aid; of those 89% were deemed to have need. 100% of freshmen with need received aid; of those 100% had need fully met. *Average percent of need met:* 100% (excluding resources awarded to replace EFC). *Average financial aid package:* $47,580 (excluding resources awarded to replace EFC). 12% of all full-time freshmen had no need and received non-need-based gift aid.

UNDERGRADUATE FINANCIAL AID (Fall 2017, est.) 1,597 applied for aid; of those 91% were deemed to have need. 100% of undergraduates with need received aid; of those 100% had need fully met. *Average percent of need met:* 100% (excluding resources awarded to replace EFC). *Average financial aid package:* $45,680 (excluding resources awarded to replace EFC). 12% of all full-time undergraduates had no need and received non-need-based gift aid.

GIFT AID (NEED-BASED) *Total amount:* $56,433,786 (3% federal, 1% state, 94% institutional, 2% external sources). *Receiving aid:* Freshmen: 70% (382); all full-time undergraduates: 69% (1,438). *Average award:* Freshmen: $42,208; Undergraduates: $39,177. *Scholarships, grants, and awards:* Federal Pell, FSEOG, state, private, college/university gift aid from institutional funds.

GIFT AID (NON-NEED-BASED) *Total amount:* $4,173,752 (90% institutional, 10% external sources). *Receiving aid:* Freshmen: 6% (30). Undergraduates: 4% (84). *Average award:* Freshmen: $16,733. Undergraduates: $15,258. *Scholarships, grants, and awards by category:* Academic interests/achievement: general academic interests/achievements. *Special characteristics:* ethnic background. *Tuition waivers:* Full or partial for employees or children of employees. *ROTC:* Army cooperative, Naval cooperative, Air Force cooperative.

LOANS *Student loans:* $8,247,896 (92% need-based, 8% non-need-based). 61% of past graduating class borrowed through all loan programs. *Average indebtedness per student:* $24,381. *Average need-based loan:* Freshmen: $4237. Undergraduates: $5040. *Parent loans:* $1,477,917 (100% non-need-based). *Programs:* Federal Direct (Subsidized and Unsubsidized Stafford, PLUS), Perkins, state, college/university.

WORK-STUDY *Federal work-study:* Total amount: $500,972; jobs available. *State or other work-study/employment:* Total amount: $3,133,951 (96% need-based, 4% non-need-based). Part-time jobs available.

APPLYING FOR FINANCIAL AID *Required financial aid forms:* FAFSA, CSS Financial Aid PROFILE, noncustodial (divorced/separated) parent's statement, federal income tax form(s). *Financial aid deadline (priority):* 2/1. *Notification date:* 4/1. Students must reply by 5/1.

CONTACT Financial Aid Office, Macalester College, 1600 Grand Avenue, St. Paul, MN 55105, 651-696-6214 or toll-free 800-231-7974. *Fax:* 651-696-6866. *E-mail:* financialaid@macalester.edu. *Website:* http://www.macalester.edu/.

MACHZIKEI HADATH RABBINICAL COLLEGE
Brooklyn, NY

CONTACT Rabbi Baruch Rozmarin, Director of Financial Aid, Machzikei Hadath Rabbinical College, 5407 16th Avenue, Brooklyn, NY 11204-1805, 718-854-8777.

MACMURRAY COLLEGE
Jacksonville, IL

ABOUT THE INSTITUTION Independent United Methodist, coed. *Awards:* associate and bachelor's degrees. 19 undergraduate majors. *Total enrollment:* 552. Undergraduates: 552. Freshmen: 147.

GIFT AID (NEED-BASED) *Scholarships, grants, and awards:* Federal Pell, FSEOG, state, private, college/university gift aid from institutional funds.

GIFT AID (NON-NEED-BASED) *Scholarships, grants, and awards by category:* Academic interests/achievement: general academic interests/achievements. *Special achievements/activities:* leadership, religious involvement. *Special characteristics:* children and siblings of alumni, children of faculty/staff, first-generation college students, general special characteristics, out-of-state students, veterans.

LOANS *Programs:* Federal Direct (Subsidized and Unsubsidized Stafford, PLUS), Perkins.

WORK-STUDY *Federal work-study:* 313 jobs averaging $1510.

APPLYING FOR FINANCIAL AID *Required financial aid form:* FAFSA.

CONTACT Mrs. Laci N. Engelbrecht, Director of One-Stop Student Services, MacMurray College, 447 East College Avenue, Jacksonville, IL 62650, 217-479-7041 or toll-free 800-252-7485. *Fax:* 217-479-7013. *E-mail:* one-stop@mac.edu. *Website:* http://www.mac.edu/.

MADONNA UNIVERSITY
Livonia, MI

CONTACT Cathy Durham, Financial Aid Secretary, Madonna University, 36600 Schoolcraft Road, Livonia, MI 48150-1173, 734-432-5663 or toll-free 800-852-4951. *Fax:* 734-432-5344. *E-mail:* finaid@madonna.edu. *Website:* http://www.madonna.edu/.

MAHARISHI UNIVERSITY OF MANAGEMENT
Fairfield, IA

CONTACT Mr. Bill Christensen, Director of Financial Aid, Maharishi University of Management, 1000 North 4th Street, DB 1127, Fairfield, IA 52557-1127, 641-472-1156 or toll-free 800-369-6480. *Fax:* 641-472-1133. *E-mail:* bchrist@mum.edu. *Website:* http://www.mum.edu/.

MAINE COLLEGE OF ART
Portland, ME

CONTACT Adrienne J. Amari, Director of Financial Aid, Maine College of Art, 522 Congress Street, Portland, ME 04101-3987, 207-775-3052 Ext. 5073 or toll-free 800-699-1509. *Fax:* 207-772-5069. *E-mail:* aamari@meca.edu. *Website:* http://www.meca.edu/.

MAINE MARITIME ACADEMY
Castine, ME

CONTACT Mrs. Kathy S. Heath, Director of Financial Aid, Maine Maritime Academy, Pleasant Street, Castine, ME 04420, 207-326-2205 or toll-free 800-464-6565 (in-state), 800-227-8465 (out-of-state). *Fax:* 207-326-2515. *E-mail:* bbayle@mma.edu. *Website:* http://www.mainemaritime.edu/.

MALONE UNIVERSITY
Canton, OH

Tuition & fees: $30,860	Average undergraduate aid package: $25,724

ABOUT THE INSTITUTION Independent Evangelical Friends Church–Eastern Region, coed. *Awards:* bachelor's and master's degrees. 47 undergraduate majors. *Total enrollment:* 1,729. Undergraduates: 1,333. Freshmen: 338. Institutional methodology is used as a basis for awarding need-based institutional aid.

UNDERGRADUATE EXPENSES for 2018–2019 *Application fee:* $20. *Comprehensive fee:* $40,360 includes full-time tuition ($29,900), mandatory fees ($960), and room and board ($9500). *College room only:* $4700. Room and board charges vary according to board plan. *Part-time tuition:* $500 per credit hour. *Part-time fees:* $240 per term. Part-time tuition and fees vary according to course load.

FRESHMAN FINANCIAL AID (Fall 2017, est.) 325 applied for aid; of those 90% were deemed to have need. 100% of freshmen with need received aid; of those 15% had need fully met. *Average percent of need met:* 82% (excluding resources awarded to replace EFC). *Average financial aid package:* $27,995 (excluding resources awarded to replace EFC). 13% of all full-time freshmen had no need and received non-need-based gift aid.

UNDERGRADUATE FINANCIAL AID (Fall 2017, est.) 956 applied for aid; of those 94% were deemed to have need. 100% of undergraduates with need received aid; of those 20% had need fully met. *Average percent of need met:* 80% (excluding resources awarded to replace EFC). *Average financial aid package:* $25,724 (excluding resources awarded to replace EFC). 13% of all full-time undergraduates had no need and received non-need-based gift aid.

GIFT AID (NEED-BASED) *Total amount:* $16,393,835 (13% federal, 6% state, 78% institutional, 3% external sources). *Receiving aid:* Freshmen: 87% (292); all full-time undergraduates: 86% (897). *Average award:* Freshmen: $24,250; Undergraduates: $21,814. *Scholarships, grants, and awards:* Federal Pell, FSEOG, state, private, college/university gift aid from institutional funds.

GIFT AID (NON-NEED-BASED) *Total amount:* $2,097,719 (1% federal, 1% state, 91% institutional, 7% external sources). *Receiving aid:* Freshmen: 11% (36). Undergraduates: 12% (121). *Average award:* Freshmen: $14,850. Undergraduates: $12,106. *Scholarships, grants, and awards by category:* Academic interests/achievement: biological sciences, business, communication, education, general academic interests/achievements, health fields, mathematics, premedicine, religion/biblical studies, social sciences. Creative arts/performance: creative writing, debating, journalism/publications, music, theater/drama. *Special achievements/activities:* cheerleading/drum major, general special achievements/activities, leadership, religious involvement. *Special characteristics:* children and siblings of alumni, handicapped students, international students, local/state students, members of minority groups, relatives of clergy, religious affiliation, veterans. *Tuition waivers:* Full or partial for employees or children of employees, senior citizens.

LOANS *Student loans:* $7,141,937 (76% need-based, 24% non-need-based). 83% of past graduating class borrowed through all loan programs. *Average indebtedness per student:* $33,330. *Average need-based loan:* Freshmen: $3513. Undergraduates: $4212. *Parent loans:* $2,870,064 (42% need-based, 58% non-need-based). *Programs:* Federal Direct (Subsidized and Unsubsidized Stafford, PLUS), Perkins, Federal Nursing, state, college/university, private loans.

WORK-STUDY *Federal work-study:* Total amount: $505,026; 363 jobs averaging $1862. *State or other work-study/employment:* 106 part-time jobs averaging $1922.

ATHLETIC AWARDS Total amount: $3,924,699 (69% need-based, 31% non-need-based).

APPLYING FOR FINANCIAL AID *Required financial aid forms:* FAFSA, CSS Financial Aid PROFILE. *Financial aid deadline:* 7/31 (priority: 3/1). *Notifi-*

cation data: Continuous beginning 10/15. Students must reply within 2 weeks of notification.

CONTACT Mrs. Pamela S. Pustay, Director of Financial Aid, Malone University, 2600 Cleveland Avenue NW, Canton, OH 44709, 330-471-8161 or toll-free 800-521-1146. *Fax:* 330-471-8652. *E-mail:* ppustay@malone.edu.
Website: http://www.malone.edu/.

MANCHESTER UNIVERSITY
North Manchester, IN

Tuition & fees: $32,758	Average undergraduate aid package: $30,161

ABOUT THE INSTITUTION Independent Church of the Brethren, coed. *Awards:* associate, bachelor's, master's, and doctoral degrees. 90 undergraduate majors. *Total enrollment:* 1,572. Undergraduates: 1,262. Freshmen: 397. Federal methodology is used as a basis for awarding need-based institutional aid.

UNDERGRADUATE EXPENSES for 2018–2019 *Application fee:* $25. *One-time required fee:* $250. *Comprehensive fee:* $42,338 includes full-time tuition ($31,500), mandatory fees ($1258), and room and board ($9580). *College room only:* $5250. Room and board charges vary according to board plan and housing facility. *Part-time tuition:* $725 per credit hour. *Part-time fees:* $35 per credit hour. Part-time tuition and fees vary according to course load.

FRESHMAN FINANCIAL AID (Fall 2017, est.) 378 applied for aid; of those 93% were deemed to have need. 100% of freshmen with need received aid; of those 22% had need fully met. *Average percent of need met:* 87% (excluding resources awarded to replace EFC). *Average financial aid package:* $31,221 (excluding resources awarded to replace EFC). 6% of all full-time freshmen had no need and received non-need-based gift aid.

UNDERGRADUATE FINANCIAL AID (Fall 2017, est.) 1,132 applied for aid; of those 92% were deemed to have need. 100% of undergraduates with need received aid; of those 12% had need fully met. *Average percent of need met:* 86% (excluding resources awarded to replace EFC). *Average financial aid package:* $30,161 (excluding resources awarded to replace EFC). 6% of all full-time undergraduates had no need and received non-need-based gift aid.

GIFT AID (NEED-BASED) *Total amount:* $23,686,935 (10% federal, 16% state, 72% institutional, 2% external sources). *Receiving aid:* Freshmen: 89% (353); all full-time undergraduates: 86% (1,041). *Average award:* Freshmen: $25,868; Undergraduates: $24,312. *Scholarships, grants, and awards:* Federal Pell, FSEOG, state, private, college/university gift aid from institutional funds.

GIFT AID (NON-NEED-BASED) *Total amount:* $5,919,172 (1% state, 98% institutional, 1% external sources). *Receiving aid:* Freshmen: 19% (77). Undergraduates: 10% (127). *Average award:* Freshmen: $18,558. Undergraduates: $17,676. *Scholarships, grants, and awards by category:* Academic interests/achievement: general academic interests/achievements. *Creative arts/performance:* music. *Special characteristics:* children and siblings of alumni, children of faculty/staff, international students, members of minority groups, out-of-state students, parents of current students, religious affiliation, siblings of current students, spouses of current students. *Tuition waivers:* Full or partial for employees or children of employees.

LOANS *Student loans:* $7,336,008 (72% need-based, 28% non-need-based). 85% of past graduating class borrowed through all loan programs. *Average indebtedness per student:* $32,920. *Average need-based loan:* Freshmen: $3025. Undergraduates: $3907. *Parent loans:* $2,265,342 (61% need-based, 39% non-need-based). *Programs:* Federal Direct (Subsidized and Unsubsidized Stafford, PLUS).

WORK-STUDY *Federal work-study:* Total amount: $1,052,882; jobs available.

APPLYING FOR FINANCIAL AID *Required financial aid form:* FAFSA. *Financial aid deadline (priority):* 3/1. *Notification date:* Continuous beginning 12/15. Students must reply by 5/1 or within 3 weeks of notification.

CONTACT Mrs. Sherri Shockey, Director of Student Financial Services, Manchester University, 604 East College Avenue, North Manchester, IN 46962-1225, 260-982-5066 or toll-free 800-852-3648. *Fax:* 260-982-5043. *E-mail:* slshockey@manchester.edu.
Website: http://www.manchester.edu/.

MANHATTAN CHRISTIAN COLLEGE
Manhattan, KS

CONTACT Mrs. Margaret Carlisle, Director of Financial Aid, Manhattan Christian College, 1415 Anderson Avenue, Manhattan, KS 66502-4081, 785-539-3571 or toll-free 877-246-4622. *E-mail:* carlisle@mccks.edu.
Website: http://www.mccks.edu/.

MANHATTAN COLLEGE
Riverdale, NY

Tuition & fees: $42,087	Average undergraduate aid package: $25,262

ABOUT THE INSTITUTION Independent Roman Catholic Church, coed. *Awards:* certificates, bachelor's, and master's degrees. 44 undergraduate majors. *Total enrollment:* 4,242. Undergraduates: 3,664. Freshmen: 765. Both federal and institutional methodology are used as a basis for awarding need-based institutional aid.

UNDERGRADUATE EXPENSES for 2017–2018 *Application fee:* $60. *Comprehensive fee:* $57,687 includes full-time tuition ($38,200), mandatory fees ($3887), and room and board ($15,600). Full-time tuition and fees vary according to course load, program, and student level. Room and board charges vary according to board plan. *Part-time tuition:* $980 per credit. Part-time tuition and fees vary according to course load.

FRESHMAN FINANCIAL AID (Fall 2016) 765 applied for aid; of those 95% were deemed to have need. 100% of freshmen with need received aid. *Average percent of need met:* 80% (excluding resources awarded to replace EFC). *Average financial aid package:* $25,262 (excluding resources awarded to replace EFC). 28% of all full-time freshmen had no need and received non-need-based gift aid.

UNDERGRADUATE FINANCIAL AID (Fall 2016) 2,997 applied for aid; of those 90% were deemed to have need. 92% of undergraduates with need received aid. *Average percent of need met:* 65% (excluding resources awarded to replace EFC). *Average financial aid package:* $25,262 (excluding resources awarded to replace EFC). 22% of all full-time undergraduates had no need and received non-need-based gift aid.

GIFT AID (NEED-BASED) *Total amount:* $57,196,362 (9% federal, 5% state, 85% institutional, 1% external sources). *Receiving aid:* Freshmen: 78% (635); all full-time undergraduates: 34% (1,246). *Average award:* Freshmen: $25,262; Undergraduates: $17,892. *Scholarships, grants, and awards:* Federal Pell, FSEOG, state, private, college/university gift aid from institutional funds.

GIFT AID (NON-NEED-BASED) *Total amount:* $2,968,876 (17% state, 83% institutional). *Receiving aid:* Freshmen: 68% (550). Undergraduates: 42% (1,533). *Average award:* Freshmen: $10,963. Undergraduates: $6585. *Scholarships, grants, and awards by category:* Academic interests/achievement: biological sciences, business, computer science, engineering/technologies, foreign languages, general academic interests/achievements, mathematics, military science. *Creative arts/performance:* music. *Special achievements/activities:* community service, leadership. *Special characteristics:* children of faculty/staff. *Tuition waivers:* Full or partial for employees or children of employees. *ROTC:* Army cooperative, Air Force.

LOANS *Student loans:* $23,247,731 (62% need-based, 38% non-need-based). 76% of past graduating class borrowed through all loan programs. *Average indebtedness per student:* $39,443. *Parent loans:* $16,491,793 (100% non-need-based). *Programs:* Federal Direct (Subsidized and Unsubsidized Stafford, PLUS), Perkins.

WORK-STUDY *Federal work-study:* jobs available. *State or other work-study/employment:* Part-time jobs available.

ATHLETIC AWARDS Total amount: $6,383,831 (100% non-need-based).

APPLYING FOR FINANCIAL AID *Required financial aid forms:* FAFSA, institution's own form, state aid form. *Financial aid deadline (priority):* 3/1. *Notification date:* 4/1. Students must reply by 5/1.

CONTACT Mr. Denise Scalzo, Director of Financial Aid, Manhattan College, 4513 Manhattan College Parkway, Riverdale, NY 10471, 718-862-7100 or toll-free 800-622-9235. *Fax:* 718-862-8027. *E-mail:* dcsalzo01@manhattan.edu.
Website: http://www.manhattan.edu/.

MANHATTAN SCHOOL OF MUSIC
New York, NY

CONTACT Ms. Amy Anderson, Assistant Dean for Enrollment Management, Manhattan School of Music, 120 Claremont Avenue, New York, NY 10027-4698, 212-749-2802 Ext. 4501. *Fax:* 212-749-3025. *E-mail:* aanderson@msmnyc.edu. *Website:* http://www.msmnyc.edu/.

MANHATTANVILLE COLLEGE
Purchase, NY

Tuition & fees: $38,820	Average undergraduate aid package: $28,326

ABOUT THE INSTITUTION Independent, coed. *Awards:* certificates, bachelor's, master's, and doctoral degrees. 47 undergraduate majors. *Total enrollment:* 2,682. Undergraduates: 1,725. Freshmen: 416. Federal methodology is used as a basis for awarding need-based institutional aid.

UNDERGRADUATE EXPENSES for 2018–2019 *Application fee:* $50. *Comprehensive fee:* $53,340 includes full-time tuition ($37,370), mandatory fees ($1450), and room and board ($14,520). *College room only:* $8680. Full-time tuition and fees vary according to course load. Room and board charges vary according to board plan. *Part-time tuition:* $845 per credit hour. *Part-time fees:* $60 per course. Part-time tuition and fees vary according to course load and program.

FRESHMAN FINANCIAL AID (Fall 2017, est.) 367 applied for aid; of those 86% were deemed to have need. 100% of freshmen with need received aid; of those 11% had need fully met. *Average percent of need met:* 70% (excluding resources awarded to replace EFC). *Average financial aid package:* $28,326 (excluding resources awarded to replace EFC). 22% of all full-time freshmen had no need and received non-need-based gift aid.

UNDERGRADUATE FINANCIAL AID (Fall 2017, est.) 1,316 applied for aid; of those 93% were deemed to have need. 100% of undergraduates with need received aid; of those 12% had need fully met. *Average percent of need met:* 70% (excluding resources awarded to replace EFC). *Average financial aid package:* $28,326 (excluding resources awarded to replace EFC). 24% of all full-time undergraduates had no need and received non-need-based gift aid.

GIFT AID (NEED-BASED) *Total amount:* $34,251,073 (8% federal, 5% state, 87% institutional). *Receiving aid:* Freshmen: 63% (261); all full-time undergraduates: 59% (960). *Average award:* Freshmen: $6852; Undergraduates: $5526. *Scholarships, grants, and awards:* Federal Pell, FSEOG, state, private, college/university gift aid from institutional funds.

GIFT AID (NON-NEED-BASED) *Total amount:* $5,211,078 (1% state, 95% institutional, 4% external sources). *Receiving aid:* Freshmen: 75% (314). Undergraduates: 73% (1,191). *Average award:* Freshmen: $18,575. Undergraduates: $18,648. *Scholarships, grants, and awards by category: Academic interests/achievement:* 1,524 awards ($29,192,206 total): general academic interests/achievements. *Creative arts/performance:* 16 awards ($103,000 total): art/fine arts, creative writing, dance, music, performing arts, theater/drama. *Special achievements/activities:* 398 awards ($705,500 total): community service. *Special characteristics:* children of faculty/staff, general special characteristics, previous college experience, veterans. *Tuition waivers:* Full or partial for children of alumni, employees or children of employees.

LOANS *Student loans:* $7,542,382 (49% need-based, 51% non-need-based). 77% of past graduating class borrowed through all loan programs. *Average indebtedness per student:* $33,850. *Average need-based loan:* Freshmen: $3685. Undergraduates: $4619. *Parent loans:* $4,698,022 (100% non-need-based). *Programs:* Federal Direct (Subsidized and Unsubsidized Stafford, PLUS).

WORK-STUDY *Federal work-study:* Total amount: $953,714; 535 jobs averaging $1665. *State or other work-study/employment:* Part-time jobs available.

APPLYING FOR FINANCIAL AID *Required financial aid forms:* FAFSA, state aid form. *Financial aid deadline (priority):* 3/1. *Notification date:* Continuous beginning 11/15. Students must reply by 5/1 or within 2 weeks of notification.

CONTACT Mr. Robert Gilmore, Director of Financial Aid, Manhattanville College, 2900 Purchase Street, Purchase, NY 10577-2132, 914-323-5357 or toll-free 800-328-4553. *Fax:* 914-323-5382. *E-mail:* robert.gilmore@mville.edu. *Website:* http://www.mville.edu/.

MANSFIELD UNIVERSITY OF PENNSYLVANIA
Mansfield, PA

Tuition & fees (PA res): $12,316	Average undergraduate aid package: $10,205

ABOUT THE INSTITUTION State-supported, coed. *Awards:* certificates, associate, bachelor's, and master's degrees. 51 undergraduate majors. *Total enrollment:* 1,897. Undergraduates: 1,836. Freshmen: 406. Federal methodology is used as a basis for awarding need-based institutional aid.

UNDERGRADUATE EXPENSES for 2017–2018 *Application fee:* $25. *Tuition, state resident:* full-time $9450; part-time $315 per credit hour. *Tuition, nonresident:* full-time $18,900; part-time $630 per credit hour. *Required fees:* full-time $2866. *College room and board:* $11,928; *Room only:* $8468. Room and board charges vary according to board plan.

FRESHMAN FINANCIAL AID (Fall 2016) 435 applied for aid; of those 71% were deemed to have need. 100% of freshmen with need received aid; of those 40% had need fully met. *Average percent of need met:* 37% (excluding resources awarded to replace EFC). *Average financial aid package:* $10,164 (excluding resources awarded to replace EFC). 13% of all full-time freshmen had no need and received non-need-based gift aid.

UNDERGRADUATE FINANCIAL AID (Fall 2016) 1,808 applied for aid; of those 64% were deemed to have need. 100% of undergraduates with need received aid; of those 48% had need fully met. *Average percent of need met:* 43% (excluding resources awarded to replace EFC). *Average financial aid package:* $10,205 (excluding resources awarded to replace EFC). 8% of all full-time undergraduates had no need and received non-need-based gift aid.

GIFT AID (NEED-BASED) *Total amount:* $7,496,531 (54% federal, 29% state, 17% institutional). *Receiving aid:* Freshmen: 51% (228); all full-time undergraduates: 47% (898). *Average award:* Freshmen: $6859; Undergraduates: $6658. *Scholarships, grants, and awards:* Federal Pell, FSEOG, state, private, college/university gift aid from institutional funds.

GIFT AID (NON-NEED-BASED) *Total amount:* $2,708,418 (8% state, 74% institutional, 18% external sources). *Receiving aid:* Freshmen: 40% (180). Undergraduates: 23% (437). *Average award:* Freshmen: $2770. Undergraduates: $2046. *Scholarships, grants, and awards by category: Academic interests/achievement:* biological sciences, communication, education, general academic interests/achievements, health fields, mathematics, physical sciences. *Creative arts/performance:* art/fine arts, journalism/publications, music. *Special achievements/activities:* leadership. *Special characteristics:* children and siblings of alumni, local/state students, members of minority groups, religious affiliation. *Tuition waivers:* Full or partial for employees or children of employees, senior citizens. *ROTC:* Army cooperative.

LOANS *Student loans:* $17,560,109 (36% need-based, 64% non-need-based). 85% of past graduating class borrowed through all loan programs. *Average indebtedness per student:* $36,624. *Average need-based loan:* Freshmen: $3496. Undergraduates: $4433. *Parent loans:* $4,799,089 (100% non-need-based). *Programs:* Federal Direct (Subsidized and Unsubsidized Stafford, PLUS), Perkins.

WORK-STUDY *Federal work-study:* jobs available. *State or other work-study/employment:* Total amount: $56,874 (100% non-need-based). Part-time jobs available.

ATHLETIC AWARDS Total amount: $418,568 (6% need-based, 94% non-need-based).

APPLYING FOR FINANCIAL AID *Required financial aid forms:* FAFSA, state aid form. *Financial aid deadline:* 6/30 (priority: 2/15). *Notification date:* Continuous beginning 2/17. Students must reply within 4 weeks of notification.

CONTACT Mr. Charles M. Scheetz, Director of Financial Aid, Mansfield University of Pennsylvania, 224 South Hall, 71 South Academy Street, Mansfield, PA 16933, 570-662-4129 or toll-free 800-577-6826. *Fax:* 570-662-4136. *Website:* http://www.mansfield.edu/.

MAPLE SPRINGS BAPTIST BIBLE COLLEGE AND SEMINARY
Capitol Heights, MD

CONTACT Ms. Fannie G. Thompson, Director of Business Affairs, Maple Springs Baptist Bible College and Seminary, 4130 Belt Road, Capitol Heights, MD 20743, 301-736-3631. *Fax:* 301-735-6507. *Website:* http://www.msbbcs.edu/.

MARANATHA BAPTIST UNIVERSITY
Watertown, WI

ABOUT THE INSTITUTION Independent Baptist, coed. *Awards:* certificates, associate, bachelor's, master's, and doctoral degrees. 31 undergraduate majors. *Total enrollment:* 1,139. Undergraduates: 925. Freshmen: 146.

GIFT AID (NEED-BASED) *Scholarships, grants, and awards:* Federal Pell, FSEOG, state, private, college/university gift aid from institutional funds.

GIFT AID (NON-NEED-BASED) *Scholarships, grants, and awards by category:* Academic interests/achievement: business, general academic interests/achievements, religion/biblical studies. *Creative arts/performance:* music. *Special characteristics:* children and siblings of alumni, children of educators, children of faculty/staff, relatives of clergy, spouses of current students.

LOANS *Programs:* Federal Direct (Subsidized and Unsubsidized Stafford, PLUS), state, alternative loans.

APPLYING FOR FINANCIAL AID *Required financial aid form:* FAFSA.

CONTACT Mr. Bruce Roth, Associate Director of Financial Aid, Maranatha Baptist University, 745 West Main Street, Watertown, WI 53094, 920-206-2318 or toll-free 800-622-2947. *Fax:* 920-261-9109. *E-mail:* financialaid@mbu.edu. *Website:* http://www.mbu.edu/.

MARCONI INTERNATIONAL UNIVERSITY
Pembroke Pines, FL

CONTACT Financial Aid Office, Marconi International University, 1806 Flamingo Road, Suite 120, Pembroke Pines, FL 33028, 954-374-4701. *Website:* http://www.marconiinternationaluniversity.edu/.

MARIA COLLEGE
Albany, NY

ABOUT THE INSTITUTION Independent, coed. *Awards:* certificates, associate, and bachelor's degrees. 8 undergraduate majors. *Total enrollment:* 849. Undergraduates: 849. Freshmen: 41.

GIFT AID (NEED-BASED) *Scholarships, grants, and awards:* Federal Pell, FSEOG, state, private, college/university gift aid from institutional funds.

GIFT AID (NON-NEED-BASED) *Scholarships, grants, and awards by category:* Academic interests/achievement: communication, general academic interests/achievements, home economics.

LOANS *Programs:* Federal Direct (Subsidized and Unsubsidized Stafford, PLUS), Perkins.

WORK-STUDY *Federal work-study:* 36 jobs averaging $1198.

APPLYING FOR FINANCIAL AID *Required financial aid forms:* FAFSA, state aid form.

CONTACT Ms. Donna Myers, Director of Financial Aid, Maria College, 700 New Scotland, Albany, NY 12208, 518-438-3111. *E-mail:* dmyers01@mariacollege.edu. *Website:* http://www.mariacollege.edu/.

MARIAN UNIVERSITY
Indianapolis, IN

CONTACT Mr. John E. Shelton, Dean of Financial Aid, Marian University, 3200 Cold Spring Road, Indianapolis, IN 46222-1997, 317-955-6040 or toll-free 800-772-7264 (in-state). *Fax:* 317-955-6424. *E-mail:* jshelton@marian.edu. *Website:* http://www.marian.edu/.

MARIAN UNIVERSITY
Fond du Lac, WI

ABOUT THE INSTITUTION Independent Roman Catholic, coed. *Awards:* certificates, bachelor's, master's, and doctoral degrees. 43 undergraduate majors. *Total enrollment:* 1,971. Undergraduates: 1,462. Freshmen: 351.

GIFT AID (NEED-BASED) *Scholarships, grants, and awards:* Federal Pell, FSEOG, state, private, college/university gift aid from institutional funds, endowed and restricted scholarships and grants.

GIFT AID (NON-NEED-BASED) *Scholarships, grants, and awards by category:* Academic interests/achievement: general academic interests/achievements. *Creative arts/performance:* music. *Special characteristics:* children of faculty/staff, children of union members/company employees, children with a deceased or disabled parent, local/state students, out-of-state students, siblings of current students, veterans.

LOANS *Programs:* Federal Direct (Subsidized and Unsubsidized Stafford, PLUS), Perkins, Federal Nursing.

APPLYING FOR FINANCIAL AID *Required financial aid forms:* FAFSA, institution's own form.

CONTACT Mr. John Smith, Interim Director of Financial Aid, Marian University, 45 South National Avenue, Fond du Lac, WI 54935-4699, 920-923-7614 or toll-free 800-2-MARIAN. *Fax:* 920-923-8767. *E-mail:* jrsmith49@marianuniversity.edu. *Website:* http://www.marianuniversity.edu/.

MARIETTA COLLEGE
Marietta, OH

Tuition & fees: $36,040	Average undergraduate aid package: $31,373

ABOUT THE INSTITUTION Independent, coed. *Awards:* certificates, associate, bachelor's, and master's degrees. 43 undergraduate majors. *Total enrollment:* 1,145. Undergraduates: 1,065. Freshmen: 272. Federal methodology is used as a basis for awarding need-based institutional aid.

UNDERGRADUATE EXPENSES for 2018–2019 *Comprehensive fee:* $47,360 includes full-time tuition ($35,030), mandatory fees ($1010), and room and board ($11,320). Full-time tuition and fees vary according to course load. Room and board charges vary according to board plan and housing facility. *Part-time tuition:* $1170 per credit hour. Part-time tuition and fees vary according to course load.

FRESHMAN FINANCIAL AID (Fall 2016) 238 applied for aid; of those 94% were deemed to have need. 100% of freshmen with need received aid; of those 42% had need fully met. *Average percent of need met:* 81% (excluding resources awarded to replace EFC). *Average financial aid package:* $34,019 (excluding resources awarded to replace EFC). 8% of all full-time freshmen had no need and received non-need-based gift aid.

UNDERGRADUATE FINANCIAL AID (Fall 2016) 721 applied for aid; of those 92% were deemed to have need. 100% of undergraduates with need received aid; of those 43% had need fully met. *Average percent of need met:* 79% (excluding resources awarded to replace EFC). *Average financial aid package:* $31,373 (excluding resources awarded to replace EFC). 13% of all full-time undergraduates had no need and received non-need-based gift aid.

GIFT AID (NEED-BASED) *Total amount:* $4,567,172 (34% federal, 12% state, 45% institutional, 9% external sources). *Receiving aid:* Freshmen: 69% (187); all full-time undergraduates: 57% (562). *Average award:* Freshmen: $3855; Undergraduates: $2909. *Scholarships, grants, and awards:* Federal Pell, FSEOG, state, private, college/university gift aid from institutional funds.

GIFT AID (NON-NEED-BASED) *Total amount:* $18,532,684 (83% institutional, 17% external sources). *Receiving aid:* Freshmen: 13% (36). Undergraduates:

10% (102). *Average award:* Freshmen: $20,812. Undergraduates: $19,323. *Scholarships, grants, and awards by category:* Academic interests/achievement: 1,800 awards ($11,539,710 total): general academic interests/achievements. *Creative arts/performance:* art/fine arts, music, performing arts, theater/drama. *Special characteristics:* 50 awards ($158,450 total): children and siblings of alumni, members of minority groups. *Tuition waivers:* Full or partial for employees or children of employees.

LOANS *Student loans:* $6,326,253 (52% need-based, 48% non-need-based). 78% of past graduating class borrowed through all loan programs. *Average indebtedness per student:* $40,196. *Average need-based loan:* Freshmen: $4392. Undergraduates: $5840. *Parent loans:* $2,723,678 (100% non-need-based). *Programs:* Federal Direct (Subsidized and Unsubsidized Stafford, PLUS), Perkins.

WORK-STUDY *Federal work-study:* 706 jobs averaging $1909.

APPLYING FOR FINANCIAL AID *Required financial aid form:* FAFSA. *Financial aid deadline (priority):* 2/15. *Notification date:* 1/1. Students must reply by 5/1 or within 2 weeks of notification.

CONTACT Mrs. Emily Schuck, Assistant Vice President for Enrollment Management, Marietta College, 215 Fifth Street, Marietta, OH 45750-4000, 740-376-4712 or toll-free 800-331-7896. *Fax:* 740-376-4990. *E-mail:* finaid@marietta.edu. *Website:* http://www.marietta.edu/.

MARIST COLLEGE
Poughkeepsie, NY

Tuition & fees: $36,680	Average undergraduate aid package: $26,750

ABOUT THE INSTITUTION Independent, coed. *Awards:* certificates, bachelor's, and master's degrees. 50 undergraduate majors. *Total enrollment:* 6,657. Undergraduates: 5,699. Freshmen: 1,285. Federal methodology is used as a basis for awarding need-based institutional aid.

UNDERGRADUATE EXPENSES for 2017–2018 *Application fee:* $50. *One-time required fee:* $100. *Comprehensive fee:* $52,580 includes full-time tuition ($36,100), mandatory fees ($580), and room and board ($15,900). *College room only:* $11,150. Full-time tuition and fees vary according to course load and location. Room and board charges vary according to board plan, housing facility, and location. *Part-time tuition:* $675 per credit. *Part-time fees:* $40 per term. Part-time tuition and fees vary according to course load.

FRESHMAN FINANCIAL AID (Fall 2017, est.) 1,052 applied for aid; of those 73% were deemed to have need. 100% of freshmen with need received aid; of those 26% had need fully met. *Average percent of need met:* 72% (excluding resources awarded to replace EFC). *Average financial aid package:* $27,579 (excluding resources awarded to replace EFC). 31% of all full-time freshmen had no need and received non-need-based gift aid.

UNDERGRADUATE FINANCIAL AID (Fall 2017, est.) 3,582 applied for aid; of those 80% were deemed to have need. 100% of undergraduates with need received aid; of those 25% had need fully met. *Average percent of need met:* 67% (excluding resources awarded to replace EFC). *Average financial aid package:* $26,750 (excluding resources awarded to replace EFC). 28% of all full-time undergraduates had no need and received non-need-based gift aid.

GIFT AID (NEED-BASED) *Total amount:* $45,471,030 (10% federal, 4% state, 85% institutional, 1% external sources). *Receiving aid:* Freshmen: 58% (749); all full-time undergraduates: 56% (2,766). *Average award:* Freshmen: $18,130; Undergraduates: $16,425. *Scholarships, grants, and awards:* Federal Pell, FSEOG, state, private, college/university gift aid from institutional funds.

GIFT AID (NON-NEED-BASED) *Total amount:* $15,957,455 (3% state, 88% institutional, 9% external sources). *Receiving aid:* Freshmen: 9% (115). Undergraduates: 6% (305). *Average award:* Freshmen: $9150. Undergraduates: $9085. *Scholarships, grants, and awards by category:* Academic interests/achievement: 3,533 awards ($33,010,368 total): general academic interests/achievements. *Creative arts/performance:* 107 awards ($203,000 total): music, theater/drama. *Special characteristics:* 120 awards ($558,750 total): local/state students. *Tuition waivers:* Full or partial for employees or children of employees, adult students. *ROTC:* Army.

LOANS *Student loans:* $32,364,311 (62% need-based, 38% non-need-based). 63% of past graduating class borrowed through all loan programs. *Average indebtedness per student:* $37,681. *Average need-based loan:* Freshmen: $3421. Undergrad-

uates: $5044. *Parent loans:* $13,104,128 (26% need-based, 74% non-need-based). *Programs:* Federal Direct (Subsidized and Unsubsidized Stafford, PLUS), Perkins.

WORK-STUDY *Federal work-study:* Total amount: $3,950,288; 1,503 jobs averaging $2687. *State or other work-study/employment:* Total amount: $956,500 (9% need-based, 91% non-need-based). 423 part-time jobs averaging $2000.

ATHLETIC AWARDS Total amount: $5,307,392 (44% need-based, 56% non-need-based).

APPLYING FOR FINANCIAL AID *Required financial aid form:* FAFSA. *Financial aid deadline:* 5/1 (priority: 11/15). *Notification date:* Continuous beginning 3/31. Students must reply by 5/1 or within 2 weeks of notification.

CONTACT Joseph R. Weglarz, Executive Director of Student Financial Services, Marist College, 3399 North Road, Poughkeepsie, NY 12601, 845-575-3230 or toll-free 800-436-5483. *Fax:* 845-575-3099. *E-mail:* joseph.weglarz@marist.edu. *Website:* http://www.marist.edu/.

MARLBORO COLLEGE
Marlboro, VT

Tuition & fees: $40,840	Average undergraduate aid package: $39,880

ABOUT THE INSTITUTION Independent, coed. *Awards:* bachelor's and master's degrees. 138 undergraduate majors. *Total enrollment:* 241. Undergraduates: 183. Freshmen: 28. Federal methodology is used as a basis for awarding need-based institutional aid.

UNDERGRADUATE EXPENSES for 2018–2019 *Application fee:* $50. *Comprehensive fee:* $53,225 includes full-time tuition ($39,870), mandatory fees ($970), and room and board ($12,385). *College room only:* $7142. Full-time tuition and fees vary according to reciprocity agreements. Room and board charges vary according to board plan. *Part-time tuition:* $1329 per credit hour. *Part-time fees:* $105 per term. Part-time tuition and fees vary according to course load.

FRESHMAN FINANCIAL AID (Fall 2017, est.) 24 applied for aid; of those 88% were deemed to have need. 100% of freshmen with need received aid; of those 33% had need fully met. *Average percent of need met:* 72% (excluding resources awarded to replace EFC). *Average financial aid package:* $44,049 (excluding resources awarded to replace EFC). 25% of all full-time freshmen had no need and received non-need-based gift aid.

UNDERGRADUATE FINANCIAL AID (Fall 2017, est.) 147 applied for aid; of those 95% were deemed to have need. 100% of undergraduates with need received aid; of those 34% had need fully met. *Average percent of need met:* 74% (excluding resources awarded to replace EFC). *Average financial aid package:* $39,880 (excluding resources awarded to replace EFC). 16% of all full-time undergraduates had no need and received non-need-based gift aid.

GIFT AID (NEED-BASED) *Total amount:* $5,234,937 (10% federal, 1% state, 88% institutional, 1% external sources). *Receiving aid:* Freshmen: 75% (21); all full-time undergraduates: 81% (140). *Average award:* Freshmen: $40,587; Undergraduates: $32,707. *Scholarships, grants, and awards:* Federal Pell, FSEOG, state, private, college/university gift aid from institutional funds.

GIFT AID (NON-NEED-BASED) *Receiving aid:* Freshmen: 21% (6). Undergraduates: 16% (27). *Average award:* Freshmen: $31,844. Undergraduates: $22,756. *Scholarships, grants, and awards by category:* Academic interests/achievement: general academic interests/achievements. *Creative arts/performance:* art/fine arts, general creative arts/performance. *Special achievements/activities:* leadership. *Tuition waivers:* Full or partial for employees or children of employees.

LOANS *Student loans:* $1,354,078 (68% need-based, 32% non-need-based). 77% of past graduating class borrowed through all loan programs. *Average indebtedness per student:* $31,747. *Average need-based loan:* Freshmen: $3500. Undergraduates: $4411. *Parent loans:* $164,065 (100% need-based). *Programs:* Federal Direct (Subsidized and Unsubsidized Stafford, PLUS).

WORK-STUDY *Federal work-study:* Total amount: $253,684; jobs available. *State or other work-study/employment:* Part-time jobs available.

APPLYING FOR FINANCIAL AID *Required financial aid form:* FAFSA. *Financial aid deadline:* 3/1. *Notification date:* Continuous beginning 3/1. Students must reply by 5/1 or within 2 weeks of notification.

CONTACT Cathy Fuller, Financial Aid Office, Marlboro College, PO Box A; 2582 South Road, Marlboro, VT 05344-0300, 802-258-9237 or toll-free 800-343-0049. *Fax:* 802-258-9300. *E-mail:* finaid@marlboro.edu. *Website:* http://www.marlboro.edu/.

MARQUETTE UNIVERSITY
Milwaukee, WI

Tuition & fees: $39,900	Average undergraduate aid package: $29,472

ABOUT THE INSTITUTION Independent Roman Catholic (Jesuit), coed. *Awards:* certificates, bachelor's, master's, and doctoral degrees. 78 undergraduate majors. *Total enrollment:* 11,426. Undergraduates: 8,335. Freshmen: 2,023. Federal methodology is used as a basis for awarding need-based institutional aid.

UNDERGRADUATE EXPENSES for 2017–2018 *Comprehensive fee:* $51,790 includes full-time tuition ($39,330), mandatory fees ($570), and room and board ($11,890). *College room only:* $4180. Full-time tuition and fees vary according to course load and program. Room and board charges vary according to housing facility. *Part-time tuition:* $1025 per credit hour. Part-time tuition and fees vary according to program.

FRESHMAN FINANCIAL AID (Fall 2017, est.) 1,654 applied for aid; of those 78% were deemed to have need. 100% of freshmen with need received aid; of those 22% had need fully met. *Average percent of need met:* 76% (excluding resources awarded to replace EFC). *Average financial aid package:* $29,812 (excluding resources awarded to replace EFC). 35% of all full-time freshmen had no need and received non-need-based gift aid.

UNDERGRADUATE FINANCIAL AID (Fall 2017, est.) 5,721 applied for aid; of those 81% were deemed to have need. 100% of undergraduates with need received aid; of those 24% had need fully met. *Average percent of need met:* 79% (excluding resources awarded to replace EFC). *Average financial aid package:* $29,472 (excluding resources awarded to replace EFC). 38% of all full-time undergraduates had no need and received non-need-based gift aid.

GIFT AID (NEED-BASED) *Total amount:* $100,414,492 (9% federal, 3% state, 83% institutional, 5% external sources). *Receiving aid:* Freshmen: 63% (1,277); all full-time undergraduates: 58% (4,578). *Average award:* Freshmen: $24,753; Undergraduates: $22,290. *Scholarships, grants, and awards:* Federal Pell, FSEOG, state, private, college/university gift aid from institutional funds, Federal Nursing, Veterans Education Benefits (GI Bill).

GIFT AID (NON-NEED-BASED) *Total amount:* $47,015,149 (92% institutional, 8% external sources). *Receiving aid:* Freshmen: 8% (157). Undergraduates: 7% (526). *Average award:* Freshmen: $15,206. Undergraduates: $13,065. *Scholarships, grants, and awards by category: Academic interests/achievement:* biological sciences, business, communication, education, engineering/technologies, English, foreign languages, general academic interests/achievements, home economics, mathematics, physical sciences. *Creative arts/performance:* theater/drama. *Special characteristics:* children of faculty/staff. *Tuition waivers:* Full or partial for employees or children of employees, senior citizens. *ROTC:* Army, Naval, Air Force.

LOANS *Student loans:* $49,200,453 (64% need-based, 36% non-need-based). 59% of past graduating class borrowed through all loan programs. *Average indebtedness per student:* $37,713. *Average need-based loan:* Freshmen: $3603. Undergraduates: $6920. *Parent loans:* $18,259,359 (38% need-based, 62% non-need-based). *Programs:* Federal Direct (Subsidized and Unsubsidized Stafford, PLUS), Perkins, Federal Nursing, state, college/university, private loans.

WORK-STUDY *Federal work-study:* Total amount: $4,206,241; jobs available. *State or other work-study/employment:* Part-time jobs available.

ATHLETIC AWARDS Total amount: $6,278,223 (29% need-based, 71% non-need-based).

APPLYING FOR FINANCIAL AID *Required financial aid form:* FAFSA. *Financial aid deadline:* Continuous. *Notification date:* Continuous beginning 1/9.

CONTACT Susan Teerink, Director of Financial Aid, Marquette University, Zilber Hall, 1250 West Wisconsin Avenue, Milwaukee, WI 53201-1881, 414-288-4000 or toll-free 800-222-6544. *Fax:* 414-288-1718. *E-mail:* financialaid@marquette.edu. *Website:* http://www.marquette.edu/.

MARSHALL UNIVERSITY
Huntington, WV

Tuition & fees (WV res): $7798	Average undergraduate aid package: $11,101

ABOUT THE INSTITUTION State-supported, coed. *Awards:* certificates, associate, bachelor's, master's, and doctoral degrees. 55 undergraduate majors. *Total enrollment:* 13,246. Undergraduates: 9,489. Freshmen: 1,801. Federal methodology is used as a basis for awarding need-based institutional aid.

UNDERGRADUATE EXPENSES for 2017–2018 *Application fee:* $30. *Tuition, state resident:* full-time $6676; part-time $278.25 per credit hour. *Tuition, nonresident:* full-time $16,734; part-time $697.50 per credit hour. *Required fees:* full-time $1122; $47 per credit hour. Full-time tuition and fees vary according to degree level, location, program, and reciprocity agreements. Part-time tuition and fees vary according to course load, degree level, location, program, and reciprocity agreements. *College room and board:* $10,126; *Room only:* $6266. Room and board charges vary according to board plan and housing facility.

FRESHMAN FINANCIAL AID (Fall 2017, est.) 1,735 applied for aid; of those 78% were deemed to have need. 99% of freshmen with need received aid; of those 25% had need fully met. *Average percent of need met:* 49% (excluding resources awarded to replace EFC). *Average financial aid package:* $12,330 (excluding resources awarded to replace EFC). 17% of all full-time freshmen had no need and received non-need-based gift aid.

UNDERGRADUATE FINANCIAL AID (Fall 2017, est.) 6,913 applied for aid; of those 81% were deemed to have need. 98% of undergraduates with need received aid; of those 20% had need fully met. *Average percent of need met:* 48% (excluding resources awarded to replace EFC). *Average financial aid package:* $11,101 (excluding resources awarded to replace EFC). 13% of all full-time undergraduates had no need and received non-need-based gift aid.

GIFT AID (NEED-BASED) *Total amount:* $29,453,831 (64% federal, 29% state, 7% institutional). *Receiving aid:* Freshmen: 62% (1,113); all full-time undergraduates: 56% (4,352). *Average award:* Freshmen: $7217; Undergraduates: $6459. *Scholarships, grants, and awards:* Federal Pell, FSEOG, state, private, college/university gift aid from institutional funds, Federal Nursing.

GIFT AID (NON-NEED-BASED) *Total amount:* $20,993,681 (45% state, 40% institutional, 15% external sources). *Receiving aid:* Freshmen: 50% (889). Undergraduates: 36% (2,803). *Average award:* Freshmen: $3202. Undergraduates: $2707. *Scholarships, grants, and awards by category: Academic interests/achievement:* general academic interests/achievements. *Creative arts/performance:* art/fine arts, general creative arts/performance. *Special characteristics:* children and siblings of alumni, children of faculty/staff, local/state students, members of minority groups. *Tuition waivers:* Full or partial for children of alumni, employees or children of employees, senior citizens. *ROTC:* Army.

LOANS *Student loans:* $38,221,173 (79% need-based, 21% non-need-based). 67% of past graduating class borrowed through all loan programs. *Average indebtedness per student:* $28,095. *Average need-based loan:* Freshmen: $5435. Undergraduates: $6896. *Parent loans:* $6,901,315 (100% non-need-based). *Programs:* Federal Direct (Subsidized and Unsubsidized Stafford, PLUS), Perkins, Federal Nursing.

WORK-STUDY *Federal work-study:* Total amount: $602,646; jobs available. *State or other work-study/employment:* Part-time jobs available.

ATHLETIC AWARDS Total amount: $5,643,844 (100% non-need-based).

APPLYING FOR FINANCIAL AID *Required financial aid forms:* FAFSA, state aid form. *Financial aid deadline (priority):* 3/1. *Notification date:* 4/1.

CONTACT Ms. Nadine Hamrick, Interim Director of Student Financial Aid, Marshall University, One John Marshall Drive, Huntington, WV 25755, 304-696-2280 or toll-free 800-642-3499. *Fax:* 304-696-3242. *E-mail:* hamrick@marshall.edu. *Website:* http://www.marshall.edu/.

MARS HILL UNIVERSITY
Mars Hill, NC

CONTACT Amanda Randolph, Director of Financial Aid, Mars Hill University, PO Box 370, Mars Hill, NC 28754, 828-689-1123 or toll-free 866-648-4968. *Fax:* 828-689-1300. *E-mail:* arandolph@mhc.edu. *Website:* http://www.mhu.edu/.

MARTIN LUTHER COLLEGE
New Ulm, MN

Tuition & fees: $14,680	Average undergraduate aid package: $12,279

ABOUT THE INSTITUTION Independent Wisconsin Evangelical Lutheran Synod, coed. **Awards:** certificates, diplomas, bachelor's, and master's degrees. 14 undergraduate majors. **Total enrollment:** 937. Undergraduates: 859. Freshmen: 196. Federal methodology is used as a basis for awarding need-based institutional aid.

UNDERGRADUATE EXPENSES for 2017–2018 Comprehensive fee: $20,470 includes full-time tuition ($14,680) and room and board ($5790). **Part-time tuition:** $310 per credit.

FRESHMAN FINANCIAL AID (Fall 2016) 167 applied for aid; of those 86% were deemed to have need. 100% of freshmen with need received aid; of those 17% had need fully met. **Average percent of need met:** 79% (excluding resources awarded to replace EFC). **Average financial aid package:** $12,508 (excluding resources awarded to replace EFC). 12% of all full-time freshmen had no need and received non-need-based gift aid.

UNDERGRADUATE FINANCIAL AID (Fall 2016) 602 applied for aid; of those 87% were deemed to have need. 100% of undergraduates with need received aid; of those 17% had need fully met. **Average percent of need met:** 73% (excluding resources awarded to replace EFC). **Average financial aid package:** $12,279 (excluding resources awarded to replace EFC). 16% of all full-time undergraduates had no need and received non-need-based gift aid.

GIFT AID (NEED-BASED) Total amount: $4,285,665 (20% federal, 6% state, 55% institutional, 19% external sources). **Receiving aid:** Freshmen: 80% (143); all full-time undergraduates: 78% (516). **Average award:** Freshmen: $9170; Undergraduates: $8218. **Scholarships, grants, and awards:** Federal Pell, FSEOG, state, private, college/university gift aid from institutional funds.

GIFT AID (NON-NEED-BASED) Total amount: $621,566 (50% institutional, 50% external sources). **Receiving aid:** Freshmen: 7% (13). Undergraduates: 5% (33). **Average award:** Freshmen: $3157. Undergraduates: $2707. **Scholarships, grants, and awards by category:** Academic interests/achievement: general academic interests/achievements. Creative arts/performance: music.

LOANS Student loans: $4,623,928 (69% need-based, 31% non-need-based). 75% of past graduating class borrowed through all loan programs. **Average indebtedness per student:** $23,239. **Average need-based loan:** Freshmen: $3733. Undergraduates: $4390. **Parent loans:** $169,203 (26% need-based, 74% non-need-based). **Programs:** Federal Direct (Subsidized and Unsubsidized Stafford, PLUS), Perkins, state, college/university, alternative loans.

WORK-STUDY Federal work-study: jobs available. **State or other work-study/employment:** Total amount: $26,019 (79% need-based, 21% non-need-based). Part-time jobs available.

APPLYING FOR FINANCIAL AID Required financial aid forms: FAFSA, institution's own form. **Financial aid deadline:** 4/17. **Notification date:** Continuous beginning 1/30.

CONTACT Mr. Mark Bauer, Director of Financial Aid, Martin Luther College, 1995 Luther Court, New Ulm, MN 56073, 507-354-8221 or toll-free 877-MLC-1995. Fax: 507-354-8225. E-mail: bauermd@mlc-wels.edu. Website: http://www.mlc-wels.edu/.

MARTIN METHODIST COLLEGE
Pulaski, TN

CONTACT Ms. Anita Beecham, Financial Aid Assistant, Martin Methodist College, 433 West Madison Street, Pulaski, TN 38478-2716, 931-363-9808 or toll-free 800-467-1273. Fax: 931-363-9818. E-mail: abeecham@martinmethodist.edu. Website: http://www.martinmethodist.edu/.

MARTIN UNIVERSITY
Indianapolis, IN

CONTACT Berdia Marshall, Director of Financial Aid, Martin University, 2171 Avondale Place, Indianapolis, IN 46218-3867, 317-543-3670. Fax: 317-543-4790. E-mail: bmarshall@martin.edu. Website: http://www.martin.edu/.

MARY BALDWIN UNIVERSITY
Staunton, VA

Tuition & fees: $31,085	Average undergraduate aid package: $26,009

ABOUT THE INSTITUTION Independent, coed, primarily women. **Awards:** certificates, bachelor's, master's, and doctoral degrees. 26 undergraduate majors. **Total enrollment:** 1,654. Undergraduates: 1,137. Freshmen: 109. Federal methodology is used as a basis for awarding need-based institutional aid.

UNDERGRADUATE EXPENSES for 2018–2019 Comprehensive fee: $40,495 includes full-time tuition ($30,690), mandatory fees ($395), and room and board ($9410). Room and board charges vary according to housing facility and student level. **Part-time tuition:** $460 per semester hour. **Part-time fees:** $60 per term.

FRESHMAN FINANCIAL AID (Fall 2017, est.) 105 applied for aid; of those 96% were deemed to have need. 100% of freshmen with need received aid; of those 17% had need fully met. **Average percent of need met:** 84% (excluding resources awarded to replace EFC). **Average financial aid package:** $31,700 (excluding resources awarded to replace EFC). 4% of all full-time freshmen had no need and received non-need-based gift aid.

UNDERGRADUATE FINANCIAL AID (Fall 2017, est.) 670 applied for aid; of those 96% were deemed to have need. 100% of undergraduates with need received aid; of those 12% had need fully met. **Average percent of need met:** 74% (excluding resources awarded to replace EFC). **Average financial aid package:** $26,009 (excluding resources awarded to replace EFC). 3% of all full-time undergraduates had no need and received non-need-based gift aid.

GIFT AID (NEED-BASED) Total amount: $14,546,334 (18% federal, 8% state, 69% institutional, 5% external sources). **Receiving aid:** Freshmen: 95% (101); all full-time undergraduates: 93% (637). **Average award:** Freshmen: $28,433; Undergraduates: $22,046. **Scholarships, grants, and awards:** Federal Pell, FSEOG, state, private, college/university gift aid from institutional funds.

GIFT AID (NON-NEED-BASED) Total amount: $403,314 (13% state, 86% institutional, 1% external sources). **Average award:** Freshmen: $19,188. Undergraduates: $15,189. **Scholarships, grants, and awards by category:** Academic interests/achievement: 543 awards ($8,257,706 total): general academic interests/achievements. Special characteristics: 18 awards ($310,818 total): children of educators, children of faculty/staff. **Tuition waivers:** Full or partial for employees or children of employees. **ROTC:** Army cooperative, Naval cooperative, Air Force cooperative.

LOANS Student loans: $6,649,252 (96% need-based, 4% non-need-based). 92% of past graduating class borrowed through all loan programs. **Average indebtedness per student:** $32,679. **Average need-based loan:** Freshmen: $3356. Undergraduates: $4475. **Parent loans:** $766,738 (95% need-based, 5% non-need-based). **Programs:** Federal Direct (Subsidized and Unsubsidized Stafford, PLUS), alternative loans.

WORK-STUDY Federal work-study: Total amount: $302,337; 188 jobs averaging $1608. **State or other work-study/employment:** Total amount: $181,380 (93% need-based, 7% non-need-based). 97 part-time jobs averaging $1870.

APPLYING FOR FINANCIAL AID Required financial aid forms: FAFSA, state aid form. **Financial aid deadline (priority):** 3/1. **Notification date:** Continuous beginning 11/15. Students must reply within 3 weeks of notification.

CONTACT Mrs. Robin Dietrich, Director of Financial Aid, Mary Baldwin University, PO Box 1500, Staunton, VA 24402, 540-887-7025 or toll-free 800-468-2262. Fax: 540-887-7229. E-mail: rdietric@marybaldwin.edu. Website: http://www.marybaldwin.edu/.

MARYLAND INSTITUTE COLLEGE OF ART

Baltimore, MD

CONTACT Ms. Diane Prengaman, Associate Vice President for Financial Aid, Maryland Institute College of Art, 1300 Mount Royal Avenue, Baltimore, MD 21217, 410-225-2285. *Fax:* 410-225-2337. *E-mail:* dprengam@mica.edu.
Website: http://www.mica.edu/.

MARYMOUNT CALIFORNIA UNIVERSITY

Rancho Palos Verdes, CA

Tuition & fees: $35,884	Average undergraduate aid package: $34,826

ABOUT THE INSTITUTION Independent Roman Catholic, coed. *Awards:* associate, bachelor's, and master's degrees. 7 undergraduate majors. *Total enrollment:* 973. Undergraduates: 935. Freshmen: 236. Federal methodology is used as a basis for awarding need-based institutional aid.

UNDERGRADUATE EXPENSES for 2018–2019 *Application fee:* $50. *One-time required fee:* $300. *Comprehensive fee:* $50,296 includes full-time tuition ($34,134), mandatory fees ($1750), and room and board ($14,412). *College room only:* $9004. Room and board charges vary according to board plan and housing facility. *Part-time tuition:* $1475 per credit hour. *Part-time fees:* $600 per year.

FRESHMAN FINANCIAL AID (Fall 2017, est.) 168 applied for aid; of those 99% were deemed to have need. 100% of freshmen with need received aid; of those 30% had need fully met. *Average percent of need met:* 93% (excluding resources awarded to replace EFC). *Average financial aid package:* $35,846 (excluding resources awarded to replace EFC). 3% of all full-time freshmen had no need and received non-need-based gift aid.

UNDERGRADUATE FINANCIAL AID (Fall 2017, est.) 631 applied for aid; of those 99% were deemed to have need. 100% of undergraduates with need received aid; of those 25% had need fully met. *Average percent of need met:* 81% (excluding resources awarded to replace EFC). *Average financial aid package:* $34,826 (excluding resources awarded to replace EFC). 2% of all full-time undergraduates had no need and received non-need-based gift aid.

GIFT AID (NEED-BASED) *Total amount:* $9,020,126 (23% federal, 24% state, 52% institutional, 1% external sources). *Receiving aid:* Freshmen: 72% (166); all full-time undergraduates: 70% (626). *Average award:* Freshmen: $24,782; Undergraduates: $23,634. *Scholarships, grants, and awards:* Federal Pell, FSEOG, state, private, college/university gift aid from institutional funds.

GIFT AID (NON-NEED-BASED) *Total amount:* $3,622,798 (89% institutional, 11% external sources). *Receiving aid:* Freshmen: 57% (132). Undergraduates: 58% (516). *Average award:* Freshmen: $13,685. Undergraduates: $14,142. *Scholarships, grants, and awards by category:* Creative arts/performance: 9 awards ($48,000 total): applied art and design. *Tuition waivers:* Full or partial for employees or children of employees, senior citizens.

LOANS *Student loans:* $5,074,696 (44% need-based, 56% non-need-based). 75% of past graduating class borrowed through all loan programs. *Average indebtedness per student:* $31,562. *Average need-based loan:* Freshmen: $3508. Undergraduates: $4396. *Parent loans:* $2,801,496 (100% non-need-based). *Programs:* Federal Direct (Subsidized and Unsubsidized Stafford, PLUS), alternative loans.

WORK-STUDY Federal work-study jobs available. *State or other work-study/employment:* Total amount: $895,558 (100% non-need-based). Part-time jobs available.

ATHLETIC AWARDS Total amount: $4,172,272 (100% non-need-based).

APPLYING FOR FINANCIAL AID *Required financial aid form:* FAFSA. *Financial aid deadline:* 2/15. *Notification date:* Continuous beginning 3/1. Students must reply by 8/1 or within 3 weeks of notification.

CONTACT Mr. Eunice Cho, Director of Financial Aid, Marymount California University, 30800 Palos Verdes Drive East, Rancho Palos Verdes, CA 90275, 310-377-5501 Ext. 7285. *Fax:* 310-303-7270. *E-mail:* echo@marymountcalifornia.edu.
Website: http://www.marymountcalifornia.edu/.

MARYMOUNT MANHATTAN COLLEGE

New York, NY

Tuition & fees: $33,778	Average undergraduate aid package: $17,829

ABOUT THE INSTITUTION Independent, coed. *Awards:* associate and bachelor's degrees. 53 undergraduate majors. *Total enrollment:* 2,150. Undergraduates: 2,150. Freshmen: 546. Both federal and institutional methodology are used as a basis for awarding need-based institutional aid.

UNDERGRADUATE EXPENSES for 2018–2019 *Application fee:* $60. *Comprehensive fee:* $50,610 includes full-time tuition ($32,210), mandatory fees ($1568), and room and board ($16,832). *College room only:* $14,832. Full-time tuition and fees vary according to course load and program. Room and board charges vary according to board plan. *Part-time tuition:* $1075 per credit hour. *Part-time fees:* $571 per term. Part-time tuition and fees vary according to course load and program.

FRESHMAN FINANCIAL AID (Fall 2016) 451 applied for aid; of those 88% were deemed to have need. 99% of freshmen with need received aid; of those 7% had need fully met. *Average percent of need met:* 52% (excluding resources awarded to replace EFC). *Average financial aid package:* $19,019 (excluding resources awarded to replace EFC). 9% of all full-time freshmen had no need and received non-need-based gift aid.

UNDERGRADUATE FINANCIAL AID (Fall 2016) 1,445 applied for aid; of those 87% were deemed to have need. 100% of undergraduates with need received aid; of those 9% had need fully met. *Average percent of need met:* 54% (excluding resources awarded to replace EFC). *Average financial aid package:* $17,829 (excluding resources awarded to replace EFC). 8% of all full-time undergraduates had no need and received non-need-based gift aid.

GIFT AID (NEED-BASED) *Total amount:* $18,944,285 (14% federal, 6% state, 78% institutional, 2% external sources). *Receiving aid:* Freshmen: 74% (393); all full-time undergraduates: 67% (1,244). *Average award:* Freshmen: $16,402; Undergraduates: $14,526. *Scholarships, grants, and awards:* Federal Pell, FSEOG, state, private, college/university gift aid from institutional funds.

GIFT AID (NON-NEED-BASED) *Total amount:* $4,786,490 (8% federal, 91% institutional, 1% external sources). *Average award:* Freshmen: $9754. Undergraduates: $9243. *Scholarships, grants, and awards by category:* Academic interests/achievement: 1,331 awards ($10,835,050 total): biological sciences, general academic interests/achievements. Creative arts/performance: 384 awards ($1,385,317 total): art/fine arts, dance, performing arts, theater/drama. Special achievements/activities: 34 awards ($67,000 total): leadership. Special characteristics: 99 awards ($614,168 total): general special characteristics, international students, local/state students, out-of-state students, veterans, veterans' children. *Tuition waivers:* Full or partial for employees or children of employees, senior citizens.

LOANS *Student loans:* $4,592,296 (83% need-based, 17% non-need-based). 64% of past graduating class borrowed through all loan programs. *Average indebtedness per student:* $26,742. *Average need-based loan:* Freshmen: $3371. Undergraduates: $4152. *Parent loans:* $13,273,405 (100% non-need-based). *Programs:* Federal Direct (Subsidized and Unsubsidized Stafford, PLUS).

WORK-STUDY *Federal work-study:* 123 jobs averaging $3139.

APPLYING FOR FINANCIAL AID *Required financial aid forms:* FAFSA, state aid form. *Financial aid deadline:* Continuous. *Notification date:* Continuous beginning 2/15. Students must reply by 5/1 or within 2 weeks of notification.

CONTACT Christina Bennett, Director of Financial Aid, Marymount Manhattan College, 221 East 71st Street, New York, NY 10021, 212-517-0556 or toll-free 800-627-9668. *E-mail:* cbennett@mmm.edu.
Website: http://www.mmm.edu/.

MARYMOUNT UNIVERSITY

Arlington, VA

Tuition & fees: $30,425	Average undergraduate aid package: $20,543

ABOUT THE INSTITUTION Independent Roman Catholic Church, coed. *Awards:* certificates, bachelor's, master's, and doctoral degrees. 26 undergraduate majors. **Total enrollment:** 3,375. Undergraduates: 2,305. Freshmen: 405. Both federal and institutional methodology are used as a basis for awarding need-based institutional aid.

UNDERGRADUATE EXPENSES for 2017–2018 *Application fee:* $40. *One-time required fee:* $450. *Comprehensive fee:* $43,230 includes full-time tuition ($29,950), mandatory fees ($475), and room and board ($12,805). Room and board charges vary according to housing facility. *Part-time tuition:* $975 per credit hour. *Part-time fees:* $11 per credit hour.

FRESHMAN FINANCIAL AID (Fall 2017, est.) 328 applied for aid; of those 88% were deemed to have need. 100% of freshmen with need received aid; of those 18% had need fully met. *Average percent of need met:* 72% (excluding resources awarded to replace EFC). *Average financial aid package:* $24,030 (excluding resources awarded to replace EFC). 26% of all full-time freshmen had no need and received non-need-based gift aid.

UNDERGRADUATE FINANCIAL AID (Fall 2017, est.) 1,382 applied for aid; of those 91% were deemed to have need. 100% of undergraduates with need received aid; of those 13% had need fully met. *Average percent of need met:* 60% (excluding resources awarded to replace EFC). *Average financial aid package:* $20,543 (excluding resources awarded to replace EFC). 21% of all full-time undergraduates had no need and received non-need-based gift aid.

GIFT AID (NEED-BASED) Total amount: $6,021,573 (50% federal, 1% state, 49% institutional). *Receiving aid:* Freshmen: 43% (173); all full-time undergraduates: 39% (800). *Average award:* Freshmen: $5729; Undergraduates: $6828. *Scholarships, grants, and awards:* Federal Pell, FSEOG, state, private, college/university gift aid from institutional funds.

GIFT AID (NON-NEED-BASED) Total amount: $21,005,978 (1% federal, 11% state, 87% institutional, 1% external sources). *Receiving aid:* Freshmen: 72% (287). Undergraduates: 52% (1,070). *Average award:* Freshmen: $13,981. Undergraduates: $13,216. *Scholarships, grants, and awards by category: Academic interests/achievement:* 1,495 awards ($15,929,966 total): biological sciences, business, computer science, general academic interests/achievements, home economics, humanities, mathematics, social sciences. *Special achievements/activities:* 163 awards ($605,465 total): community service, general special achievements/activities, leadership, memberships, religious involvement. *Special characteristics:* 779 awards ($1,457,865 total): children and siblings of alumni, children of faculty/staff, general special characteristics, local/state students, out-of-state students, religious affiliation, veterans, veterans' children. *Tuition waivers:* Full or partial for employees or children of employees, senior citizens. *ROTC:* Army cooperative, Air Force cooperative.

LOANS Student loans: $13,448,683 (32% need-based, 68% non-need-based). 63% of past graduating class borrowed through all loan programs. *Average indebtedness per student:* $34,051. *Average need-based loan:* Freshmen: $3497. Undergraduates: $4468. *Parent loans:* $7,528,289 (100% non-need-based). *Programs:* Federal Direct (Subsidized and Unsubsidized Stafford, PLUS).

WORK-STUDY *Federal work-study:* Total amount: $1,407,278; 668 jobs averaging $2044.

APPLYING FOR FINANCIAL AID *Required financial aid form:* FAFSA. *Financial aid deadline (priority):* 3/1. *Notification date:* Continuous beginning 1/15. Students must reply within 3 weeks of notification.

CONTACT Mrs. Debbie A. Raines, Director of Financial Aid, Marymount University, 2807 North Glebe Road, Arlington, VA 22207-4299, 703-284-1530 or toll-free 800-548-7638. *Fax:* 703-516-4771. *E-mail:* financial.aid@marymount.edu. *Website:* http://www.marymount.edu/.

MARYVILLE COLLEGE
Maryville, TN

Tuition & fees: $34,880	Average undergraduate aid package: $32,881

ABOUT THE INSTITUTION Independent Presbyterian, coed. *Awards:* bachelor's degrees. 55 undergraduate majors. *Total enrollment:* 1,181. Undergraduates: 1,181. Freshmen: 301. Federal methodology is used as a basis for awarding need-based institutional aid.

UNDERGRADUATE EXPENSES for 2018–2019 *Comprehensive fee:* $46,304 includes full-time tuition ($34,070), mandatory fees ($810), and room and board ($11,424). *College room only:* $5674. Room and board charges vary according to board plan and housing facility. *Part-time tuition:* $876 per credit

hour. *Part-time fees:* $15 per credit hour; $195 per term. Part-time tuition and fees vary according to course load.

FRESHMAN FINANCIAL AID (Fall 2017, est.) 301 applied for aid; of those 87% were deemed to have need. 100% of freshmen with need received aid; of those 10% had need fully met. *Average percent of need met:* 79% (excluding resources awarded to replace EFC). *Average financial aid package:* $33,305 (excluding resources awarded to replace EFC). 13% of all full-time freshmen had no need and received non-need-based gift aid.

UNDERGRADUATE FINANCIAL AID (Fall 2017, est.) 1,158 applied for aid; of those 85% were deemed to have need. 100% of undergraduates with need received aid; of those 22% had need fully met. *Average percent of need met:* 80% (excluding resources awarded to replace EFC). *Average financial aid package:* $32,881 (excluding resources awarded to replace EFC). 15% of all full-time undergraduates had no need and received non-need-based gift aid.

GIFT AID (NEED-BASED) Total amount: $26,114,244 (13% federal, 9% state, 77% institutional, 1% external sources). *Receiving aid:* Freshmen: 87% (263); all full-time undergraduates: 85% (986). *Average award:* Freshmen: $27,352; Undergraduates: $26,451. *Scholarships, grants, and awards:* Federal Pell, FSEOG, state, private, college/university gift aid from institutional funds.

GIFT AID (NON-NEED-BASED) Total amount: $6,015,324 (2% federal, 10% state, 86% institutional, 2% external sources). *Receiving aid:* Freshmen: 23% (68). Undergraduates: 24% (274). *Average award:* Freshmen: $22,534. Undergraduates: $22,292. *Scholarships, grants, and awards by category: Academic interests/achievement:* general academic interests/achievements. *Creative arts/performance:* art/fine arts, music, theater/drama. *Special achievements/activities:* community service, leadership. *Special characteristics:* children and siblings of alumni, children of faculty/staff, members of minority groups, religious affiliation, veterans. *Tuition waivers:* Full or partial for employees or children of employees.

LOANS Student loans: $7,430,992 (76% need-based, 24% non-need-based). 76% of past graduating class borrowed through all loan programs. *Average indebtedness per student:* $27,889. *Average need-based loan:* Freshmen: $3732. Undergraduates: $4797. *Parent loans:* $2,546,572 (100% non-need-based). *Programs:* Federal Direct (Subsidized and Unsubsidized Stafford, PLUS), Perkins.

WORK-STUDY *Federal work-study:* Total amount: $1,101,721; 643 jobs averaging $1713. *State or other work-study/employment:* Part-time jobs available.

APPLYING FOR FINANCIAL AID *Required financial aid form:* FAFSA. *Financial aid deadline (priority):* 3/1. *Notification date:* Continuous beginning 3/15. Students must reply within 4 weeks of notification.

CONTACT Ms. Alayne Bowman, Director of Financial Aid, Maryville College, 502 East Lamar Alexander Parkway, Maryville, TN 37804-5907, 865-981-8087 or toll-free 800-597-2687. *Fax:* 865-981-8084. *E-mail:* alayne.bowman@maryvillecollege.edu. *Website:* http://www.maryvillecollege.edu/.

MARYVILLE UNIVERSITY OF SAINT LOUIS
St. Louis, MO

Tuition & fees: $28,470	Average undergraduate aid package: $15,811

ABOUT THE INSTITUTION Independent, coed. *Awards:* certificates, bachelor's, master's, and doctoral degrees. 58 undergraduate majors. *Total enrollment:* 7,689. Undergraduates: 3,183. Freshmen: 604. Both federal and institutional methodology are used as a basis for awarding need-based institutional aid.

UNDERGRADUATE EXPENSES for 2018–2019 *Comprehensive fee:* $38,558 includes full-time tuition ($26,070), mandatory fees ($2400), and room and board ($10,088). Full-time tuition and fees vary according to course load, degree level, and program. Room and board charges vary according to board plan and housing facility. *Part-time tuition:* $781 per credit hour. *Part-time fees:* $450 per term. Part-time tuition and fees vary according to class time, degree level, and program.

FRESHMAN FINANCIAL AID (Fall 2017, est.) 532 applied for aid; of those 90% were deemed to have need. 100% of freshmen with need received aid; of those 13% had need fully met. *Average percent of need met:* 59% (excluding resources awarded to replace EFC). *Average financial aid package:* $20,091 (excluding resources awarded to replace EFC). 18% of all full-time freshmen had no need and received non-need-based gift aid.

UNDERGRADUATE FINANCIAL AID (Fall 2017, est.) 2,217 applied for aid, of those 90% were deemed to have need. 100% of undergraduates with need received aid; of those 9% had need fully met. *Average percent of need met:* 54% (excluding resources awarded to replace EFC). *Average financial aid package:* $15,811 (excluding resources awarded to replace EFC). 20% of all full-time undergraduates had no need and received non-need-based gift aid.

GIFT AID (NEED-BASED) *Total amount:* $26,262,014 (14% federal, 4% state, 81% institutional, 1% external sources). *Receiving aid:* Freshmen: 79% (476); all full-time undergraduates: 82% (1,952). *Average award:* Freshmen: $18,186; Undergraduates: $13,542. *Scholarships, grants, and awards:* Federal Pell, FSEOG, state, private, college/university gift aid from institutional funds, United Negro College Fund, Academic Competitiveness Grants, National SMART Grants, TEACH Grants.

GIFT AID (NON-NEED-BASED) *Total amount:* $10,033,482 (1% state, 98% institutional, 1% external sources). *Receiving aid:* Freshmen: 10% (58). Undergraduates: 6% (154). *Average award:* Freshmen: $17,829. Undergraduates: $15,421. *Scholarships, grants, and awards by category:* Academic interests/achievement: 2,458 awards ($23,369,489 total): biological sciences, business, education, English, general academic interests/achievements, health fields, home economics, international studies, mathematics, social sciences. *Creative arts/performance:* 91 awards ($216,188 total): applied art and design, art/fine arts, music. *Special achievements/activities:* 557 awards ($4,183,871 total): cheerleading/drum major, community service, general special achievements/activities, leadership, religious involvement. *Special characteristics:* 380 awards ($2,447,624 total): adult students, children and siblings of alumni, ethnic background, first-generation college students, general special characteristics, international students, members of minority groups, out-of-state students, parents of current students. *Tuition waivers:* Full or partial for employees or children of employees, senior citizens. *ROTC:* Army cooperative.

LOANS *Student loans:* $14,613,251 (75% need-based, 25% non-need-based). 66% of past graduating class borrowed through all loan programs. *Average indebtedness per student:* $29,849. *Average need-based loan:* Freshmen: $2738. Undergraduates: $3841. *Parent loans:* $5,842,207 (53% need-based, 47% non-need-based). *Programs:* Federal Direct (Subsidized and Unsubsidized Stafford, PLUS), private loans.

WORK-STUDY *Federal work-study:* Total amount: $458,400; 361 jobs averaging $945. *State or other work-study/employment:* Total amount: $493,743 (62% need-based, 38% non-need-based). 350 part-time jobs averaging $490.

ATHLETIC AWARDS Total amount: $2,892,831 (50% need-based, 50% non-need-based).

APPLYING FOR FINANCIAL AID *Required financial aid form:* FAFSA. *Financial aid deadline (priority):* 12/1. *Notification date:* Continuous beginning 12/5. Students must reply by 5/1 or within 2 weeks of notification.

CONTACT Ms. Martha Harbaugh, Director of Financial Aid, Maryville University of Saint Louis, 650 Maryville University Drive, St. Louis, MO 63141-7299, 800-627-9855 Ext. 9361 or toll-free 800-627-9855. *Fax:* 314-529-9199. *E-mail:* mharbaugh@maryville.edu.
Website: http://www.maryville.edu/.

MARYWOOD UNIVERSITY
Scranton, PA

Tuition & fees: $34,910	Average undergraduate aid package: $26,010

ABOUT THE INSTITUTION Independent Roman Catholic, coed. *Awards:* certificates, bachelor's, master's, and doctoral degrees. 67 undergraduate majors. *Total enrollment:* 2,950. Undergraduates: 1,964. Freshmen: 449. Both federal and institutional methodology are used as a basis for awarding need-based institutional aid.

UNDERGRADUATE EXPENSES for 2018–2019 *Application fee:* $35. *Comprehensive fee:* $48,810 includes full-time tuition ($33,160), mandatory fees ($1750), and room and board ($13,900). *College room only:* $7822. Full-time tuition and fees vary according to course load. Room and board charges vary according to board plan and housing facility. Part-time tuition and fees vary according to course load.

FRESHMAN FINANCIAL AID (Fall 2017, est.) 431 applied for aid; of those 93% were deemed to have need. 100% of freshmen with need received aid; of those 21% had need fully met. *Average percent of need met:* 77% (excluding resources awarded to replace EFC). *Average financial aid package:* $28,187 (excluding resources awarded to replace EFC). 10% of all full-time freshmen had no need and received non-need-based gift aid.

UNDERGRADUATE FINANCIAL AID (Fall 2017, est.) 1,578 applied for aid; of those 93% were deemed to have need. 100% of undergraduates with need received aid; of those 20% had need fully met. *Average percent of need met:* 72% (excluding resources awarded to replace EFC). *Average financial aid package:* $26,010 (excluding resources awarded to replace EFC). 16% of all full-time undergraduates had no need and received non-need-based gift aid.

GIFT AID (NEED-BASED) *Total amount:* $30,255,300 (9% federal, 8% state, 82% institutional, 1% external sources). *Receiving aid:* Freshmen: 90% (400); all full-time undergraduates: 84% (1,455). *Average award:* Freshmen: $23,380; Undergraduates: $20,937. *Scholarships, grants, and awards:* Federal Pell, FSEOG, state, college/university gift aid from institutional funds.

GIFT AID (NON-NEED-BASED) *Total amount:* $5,094,327 (96% institutional, 4% external sources). *Receiving aid:* Freshmen: 17% (75). Undergraduates: 12% (206). *Average award:* Freshmen: $18,616. Undergraduates: $13,525. *Scholarships, grants, and awards by category:* Academic interests/achievement: architecture, biological sciences, business, communication, computer science, education, English, foreign languages, general academic interests/achievements, health fields, home economics, mathematics, premedicine, religion/biblical studies, social sciences. *Creative arts/performance:* art/fine arts, music. *Special achievements/activities:* community service, general special achievements/activities, leadership. *Tuition waivers:* Full or partial for employees or children of employees, senior citizens. *ROTC:* Army cooperative, Air Force cooperative.

LOANS *Student loans:* $13,577,461 (71% need-based, 29% non-need-based). 87% of past graduating class borrowed through all loan programs. *Average indebtedness per student:* $41,880. *Average need-based loan:* Freshmen: $3663. Undergraduates: $4434. *Parent loans:* $4,379,299 (48% need-based, 52% non-need-based). *Programs:* Federal Direct (Subsidized and Unsubsidized Stafford, PLUS), Perkins.

WORK-STUDY *Federal work-study:* Total amount: $1,213,665; 597 jobs averaging $1998.

APPLYING FOR FINANCIAL AID *Required financial aid forms:* FAFSA, state aid form. *Financial aid deadline (priority):* 2/15. *Notification date:* Continuous beginning 12/15. Students must reply by 5/1 or within 3 weeks of notification.

CONTACT Barbara Schmitt, Director of Financial Aid, Marywood University, 2300 Adams Avenue, Scranton, PA 18509-1598, 570-348-6225 or toll-free 866-279-9663. *Fax:* 570-961-4739. *E-mail:* schmitt@marywood.edu.
Website: http://www.marywood.edu/.

MASSACHUSETTS COLLEGE OF ART AND DESIGN
Boston, MA

Tuition & fees (MA res): $13,200	Average undergraduate aid package: $10,436

ABOUT THE INSTITUTION State-supported, coed. *Awards:* certificates, bachelor's, and master's degrees. 18 undergraduate majors. *Total enrollment:* 2,065. Undergraduates: 1,931. Freshmen: 424. Federal methodology is used as a basis for awarding need-based institutional aid.

UNDERGRADUATE EXPENSES for 2018–2019 *Application fee:* $70. *Tuition, state resident:* full-time $13,200. *Tuition, nonresident:* full-time $36,400. *College room and board:* $13,500. Room and board charges vary according to board plan and housing facility.

FRESHMAN FINANCIAL AID (Fall 2017, est.) 269 applied for aid; of those 90% were deemed to have need. 100% of freshmen with need received aid. *Average financial aid package:* $11,504 (excluding resources awarded to replace EFC). 13% of all full-time freshmen had no need and received non-need-based gift aid.

UNDERGRADUATE FINANCIAL AID (Fall 2017, est.) 1,603 applied for aid; of those 94% were deemed to have need. 100% of undergraduates with need received aid. *Average financial aid package:* $10,436 (excluding resources awarded to replace EFC). 29% of all full-time undergraduates had no need and received non-need-based gift aid.

GIFT AID (NEED-BASED) *Total amount:* $8,886,011 (31% federal, 9% state, 60% institutional). *Receiving aid:* Freshmen: 50% (213); all full-time undergraduates: 72% (1,201). *Average award:* Freshmen: $8004; Undergraduates: $7298. *Scholarships, grants, and awards:* Federal Pell, FSEOG, state, private, college/university gift aid from institutional funds.

GIFT AID (NON-NEED-BASED) *Total amount:* $3,111,978 (4% federal, 79% institutional, 17% external sources). *Receiving aid:* Freshmen: 5% (21). Undergraduates: 9% (149). *Average award:* Freshmen: $1024. Undergraduates: $4245. *Scholarships, grants, and awards by category:* Special characteristics: children of faculty/staff, children of union members/company employees, veterans.
LOANS *Student loans:* $11,761,361 (34% need-based, 66% non-need-based). 76% of past graduating class borrowed through all loan programs. *Average indebtedness per student:* $26,792. *Average need-based loan:* Freshmen: $3347. Undergraduates: $4189. *Parent loans:* $3,069,515 (100% non-need-based). *Programs:* Federal Direct (Subsidized and Unsubsidized Stafford, PLUS), Perkins, state, alternative loans.
WORK-STUDY *Federal work-study:* Total amount: $266,928; jobs available. *State or other work-study/employment:* Part-time jobs available.
APPLYING FOR FINANCIAL AID *Required financial aid form:* FAFSA. *Financial aid deadline (priority):* 3/1. *Notification date:* Continuous beginning 3/15. Students must reply within 3 weeks of notification.
CONTACT Auelio Ramirez, Director of Student Financial Assistance, Massachusetts College of Art and Design, 621 Huntington Avenue, Boston, MA 02115-5882, 617-879-7850. *Fax:* 617-879-7880. *E-mail:* aurelio.ramirez@massart.edu. *Website:* http://www.massart.edu/.

MASSACHUSETTS COLLEGE OF LIBERAL ARTS
North Adams, MA

Tuition & fees (MA res): $10,135	Average undergraduate aid package: $15,345

ABOUT THE INSTITUTION State-supported, coed. *Awards:* certificates, bachelor's, and master's degrees. 43 undergraduate majors. *Total enrollment:* 1,588. Undergraduates: 1,407. Freshmen: 289. Federal methodology is used as a basis for awarding need-based institutional aid.
UNDERGRADUATE EXPENSES for 2017–2018 *Tuition, state resident:* full-time $1030; part-time $42.92 per credit. *Tuition, nonresident:* full-time $9975; part-time $415.63 per credit. *Required fees:* full-time $9105; $308.75 per credit. Full-time tuition and fees vary according to reciprocity agreements. Part-time tuition and fees vary according to course load and reciprocity agreements. *College room and board:* $10,724. Room and board charges vary according to board plan and housing facility.
FRESHMAN FINANCIAL AID (Fall 2017, est.) 286 applied for aid; of those 85% were deemed to have need. 99% of freshmen with need received aid; of those 81% had need fully met. *Average percent of need met:* 76% (excluding resources awarded to replace EFC). *Average financial aid package:* $15,219 (excluding resources awarded to replace EFC). 10% of all full-time freshmen had no need and received non-need-based gift aid.
UNDERGRADUATE FINANCIAL AID (Fall 2017, est.) 1,115 applied for aid; of those 85% were deemed to have need. 98% of undergraduates with need received aid; of those 80% had need fully met. *Average percent of need met:* 76% (excluding resources awarded to replace EFC). *Average financial aid package:* $15,345 (excluding resources awarded to replace EFC). 7% of all full-time undergraduates had no need and received non-need-based gift aid.
GIFT AID (NEED-BASED) *Total amount:* $6,500,268 (47% federal, 14% state, 31% institutional, 8% external sources). *Receiving aid:* Freshmen: 66% (189); all full-time undergraduates: 63% (762). *Average award:* Freshmen: $6784; Undergraduates: $6475. *Scholarships, grants, and awards:* Federal Pell, FSEOG, state, private, college/university gift aid from institutional funds.
GIFT AID (NON-NEED-BASED) *Total amount:* $302,934 (3% state, 78% institutional, 19% external sources). *Receiving aid:* Freshmen: 54% (155). Undergraduates: 31% (375). *Average award:* Freshmen: $3652. Undergraduates: $3362. *Scholarships, grants, and awards by category:* Academic interests/achievement: biological sciences, business, communication, computer science, education, English, general academic interests/achievements, health fields, humanities, mathematics, physical sciences, social sciences. Creative arts/performance: applied art and design, art/fine arts, cinema/film/broadcasting, journalism/publications, music, performing arts, theater/drama. Special achievements/activities: general special achievements/activities, leadership, memberships. *Tuition waivers:* Full or partial for employees or children of employees, senior citizens.

LOANS *Student loans:* $8,416,273 (91% need-based, 9% non-need-based). 81% of past graduating class borrowed through all loan programs. *Average indebtedness per student:* $27,883. *Average need-based loan:* Freshmen: $3126. Undergraduates: $4006. *Parent loans:* $1,083,563 (92% need-based, 8% non-need-based). *Programs:* Federal Direct (Subsidized and Unsubsidized Stafford, PLUS), Perkins, state.
WORK-STUDY *Federal work-study:* Total amount: $315,512; jobs available. *State or other work-study/employment:* Part-time jobs available.
APPLYING FOR FINANCIAL AID *Required financial aid form:* FAFSA. *Financial aid deadline (priority):* 3/1. *Notification date:* Continuous beginning 3/1. Students must reply by 5/1 or within 2 weeks of notification.
CONTACT Mrs. Elizabeth M. Petri, Director of Financial Aid, Massachusetts College of Liberal Arts, 375 Church Street, North Adams, MA 01247, 413-662-5219 or toll-free 800-989-MCLA. *Fax:* 413-662-5105. *E-mail:* e.petri@mcla.edu. *Website:* http://www.mcla.edu/.

MASSACHUSETTS INSTITUTE OF TECHNOLOGY
Cambridge, MA

Tuition & fees: $51,832	Average undergraduate aid package: $47,451

ABOUT THE INSTITUTION Independent, coed. *Awards:* bachelor's, master's, and doctoral degrees. 41 undergraduate majors. *Total enrollment:* 11,466. Undergraduates: 4,547. Freshmen: 1,097. Institutional methodology is used as a basis for awarding need-based institutional aid.
UNDERGRADUATE EXPENSES for 2018–2019 *Application fee:* $75. *Comprehensive fee:* $67,342 includes full-time tuition ($51,520), mandatory fees ($312), and room and board ($15,510). *College room only:* $9890. Room and board charges vary according to board plan and housing facility. Part-time tuition and fees vary according to course load.
FRESHMAN FINANCIAL AID (Fall 2016) 866 applied for aid; of those 79% were deemed to have need. 100% of freshmen with need received aid; of those 100% had need fully met. *Average percent of need met:* 100% (excluding resources awarded to replace EFC). *Average financial aid package:* $47,524 (excluding resources awarded to replace EFC).
UNDERGRADUATE FINANCIAL AID (Fall 2016) 2,912 applied for aid; of those 89% were deemed to have need. 100% of undergraduates with need received aid; of those 100% had need fully met. *Average percent of need met:* 100% (excluding resources awarded to replace EFC). *Average financial aid package:* $47,451 (excluding resources awarded to replace EFC).
GIFT AID (NEED-BASED) *Total amount:* $118,932,285 (5% federal, 91% institutional, 4% external sources). *Receiving aid:* Freshmen: 60% (668); all full-time undergraduates: 56% (2,517). *Average award:* Freshmen: $45,215; Undergraduates: $45,570. *Scholarships, grants, and awards:* Federal Pell, FSEOG, state, private, college/university gift aid from institutional funds, United Negro College Fund.
GIFT AID (NON-NEED-BASED) *Total amount:* $7,221,762 (14% federal, 86% external sources). *Receiving aid:* Freshmen: 2% (23). Undergraduates: 1% (49). *Tuition waivers:* Full or partial for employees or children of employees. *ROTC:* Army, Naval, Air Force.
LOANS *Student loans:* $6,551,297 (42% need-based, 58% non-need-based). 29% of past graduating class borrowed through all loan programs. *Average indebtedness per student:* $20,048. *Average need-based loan:* Freshmen: $3028. Undergraduates: $3591. *Parent loans:* $4,017,387 (6% need-based, 94% non-need-based). *Programs:* Federal Direct (Subsidized and Unsubsidized Stafford, PLUS), Perkins, college/university.
WORK-STUDY *Federal work-study:* 567 jobs averaging $2365. *State or other work-study/employment:* Total amount: $3,588,594 (82% need-based, 18% non-need-based). 1,331 part-time jobs averaging $2696.
APPLYING FOR FINANCIAL AID *Required financial aid forms:* FAFSA, CSS Financial Aid PROFILE, noncustodial (divorced/separated) parent's statement, parent's complete federal income tax form(s) and W-2s from 2 years ago. *Financial aid deadline:* 2/15. *Notification date:* 3/17.
CONTACT Stuart Schmill, Dean of Admissions and Student Financial Services, Massachusetts Institute of Technology, 77 Massachusetts Avenue, Room 11-120, Cambridge, MA 02139-4307, 617-258-5529. *Fax:* 617-648-9968. *E-mail:* sfs@mit.edu. *Website:* http://www.mit.edu/.

MASSACHUSETTS MARITIME ACADEMY
Buzzards Bay, MA

Tuition & fees (MA res): $8398	Average undergraduate aid package: $15,186

ABOUT THE INSTITUTION State-supported, coed. *Awards:* bachelor's and master's degrees. 7 undergraduate majors. *Total enrollment:* 1,780. Undergraduates: 1,688. Freshmen: 392. Federal methodology is used as a basis for awarding need-based institutional aid.

UNDERGRADUATE EXPENSES for 2017–2018 *Application fee:* $50. *Tuition, state resident:* full-time $1714; part-time $71 per credit. *Tuition, nonresident:* full-time $19,140; part-time $798 per credit. *Required fees:* full-time $6684; $267 per credit. Full-time tuition and fees vary according to program and reciprocity agreements. Part-time tuition and fees vary according to program and reciprocity agreements. *College room and board:* $12,306; *Room only:* $7340.

FRESHMAN FINANCIAL AID (Fall 2016) 356 applied for aid; of those 74% were deemed to have need. 95% of freshmen with need received aid; of those 31% had need fully met. *Average percent of need met:* 74% (excluding resources awarded to replace EFC). *Average financial aid package:* $17,027 (excluding resources awarded to replace EFC). 8% of all full-time freshmen had no need and received non-need-based gift aid.

UNDERGRADUATE FINANCIAL AID (Fall 2016) 1,350 applied for aid; of those 70% were deemed to have need. 95% of undergraduates with need received aid; of those 36% had need fully met. *Average percent of need met:* 77% (excluding resources awarded to replace EFC). *Average financial aid package:* $15,186 (excluding resources awarded to replace EFC). 6% of all full-time undergraduates had no need and received non-need-based gift aid.

GIFT AID (NEED-BASED) *Total amount:* $5,530,929 (21% federal, 10% state, 68% institutional, 1% external sources). *Receiving aid:* Freshmen: 42% (168); all full-time undergraduates: 37% (616). *Average award:* Freshmen: $12,431; Undergraduates: $9929. *Scholarships, grants, and awards:* Federal Pell, FSEOG, state, private, college/university gift aid from institutional funds.

GIFT AID (NON-NEED-BASED) *Total amount:* $1,547,357 (19% state, 21% institutional, 60% external sources). *Receiving aid:* Freshmen: 8% (34). Undergraduates: 8% (126). *Average award:* Freshmen: $3586. Undergraduates: $3160. *Scholarships, grants, and awards by category:* Academic interests/achievement: 19 awards ($245,775 total): general academic interests/achievements. *Special achievements/activities:* 19 awards ($245,775 total): leadership. *Special characteristics:* ethnic background. *Tuition waivers:* Full or partial for employees or children of employees. *ROTC:* Army cooperative.

LOANS *Student loans:* $13,088,217 (25% need-based, 75% non-need-based). 79% of past graduating class borrowed through all loan programs. *Average indebtedness per student:* $37,414. *Average need-based loan:* Freshmen: $3375. Undergraduates: $4165. *Parent loans:* $2,324,990 (100% non-need-based). *Programs:* Federal Direct (Subsidized and Unsubsidized Stafford, PLUS).

WORK-STUDY *Federal work-study:* 244 jobs averaging $1490.

APPLYING FOR FINANCIAL AID *Required financial aid form:* FAFSA. *Financial aid deadline (priority):* 3/1. *Notification date:* Continuous beginning 1/15.

CONTACT Ms. Catherine Kedski, Director of Financial Aid, Massachusetts Maritime Academy, 101 Academy Drive, Buzzards Bay, MA 02532, 508-830-5042 or toll-free 800-544-3411. *Fax:* 508-830-5077. *E-mail:* ckedski@maritime.edu. *Website:* http://www.maritime.edu/.

THE MASTER'S UNIVERSITY
Santa Clarita, CA

ABOUT THE INSTITUTION Independent nondenominational, coed. *Awards:* bachelor's, master's, and doctoral degrees. 45 undergraduate majors. *Total enrollment:* 1,908. Undergraduates: 1,340. Freshmen: 164.

GIFT AID (NEED-BASED) *Scholarships, grants, and awards:* Federal Pell, FSEOG, state, private, college/university gift aid from institutional funds.

GIFT AID (NON-NEED-BASED) *Scholarships, grants, and awards by category:* Academic interests/achievement: biological sciences, business, communication, computer science, education, general academic interests/achievements, mathematics, physical sciences, religion/biblical studies, social sciences. *Creative arts/performance:* music. *Special achievements/activities:* leadership. *Special characteristics:* children and siblings of alumni, children of faculty/staff, general special characteristics, international students, relatives of clergy, veterans, veterans' children.

LOANS *Programs:* Federal Direct (Subsidized and Unsubsidized Stafford, PLUS), alternative loans.

APPLYING FOR FINANCIAL AID *Required financial aid forms:* FAFSA, institution's own form, state aid form.

CONTACT Mr. Gary Edwards, Director of Financial Aid, The Master's University, 21726 Placerita Canyon Road, Santa Clarita, CA 91321-1200, 661-362-2291 or toll-free 800-568-6248. *Fax:* 661-362-2693. *E-mail:* gedwards@masters.edu. *Website:* http://www.masters.edu/.

MAYVILLE STATE UNIVERSITY
Mayville, ND

ABOUT THE INSTITUTION State-supported, coed. 36 undergraduate majors.

GIFT AID (NEED-BASED) *Scholarships, grants, and awards:* Federal Pell, FSEOG, state, private, college/university gift aid from institutional funds.

GIFT AID (NON-NEED-BASED) *Scholarships, grants, and awards by category:* Academic interests/achievement: biological sciences, business, communication, computer science, education, English, general academic interests/achievements, health fields, library science, mathematics, physical sciences, premedicine, social sciences. *Creative arts/performance:* music, theater/drama. *Special characteristics:* children of faculty/staff, international students, local/state students, members of minority groups, out-of-state students, veterans' children.

LOANS *Programs:* Federal Direct (Subsidized and Unsubsidized Stafford, PLUS), Perkins, Federal Nursing, college/university.

APPLYING FOR FINANCIAL AID *Required financial aid form:* FAFSA.

CONTACT Ms. Shirley Hanson, Director of Financial Aid, Mayville State University, 330 3rd Street NE, Mayville, ND 58257-1299, 701-788-4767 or toll-free 800-437-4104. *Fax:* 701-788-4818. *E-mail:* shirley.m.hanson@mayvillestate.edu. *Website:* http://www.mayvillestate.edu/.

MCDANIEL COLLEGE
Westminster, MD

Tuition & fees: $41,800	Average undergraduate aid package: $36,984

ABOUT THE INSTITUTION Independent, coed. *Awards:* certificates, bachelor's, and master's degrees. 34 undergraduate majors. *Total enrollment:* 2,845. Undergraduates: 1,577. Freshmen: 450. Federal methodology is used as a basis for awarding need-based institutional aid.

UNDERGRADUATE EXPENSES for 2017–2018 *Application fee:* $50. *Comprehensive fee:* $52,910 includes full-time tuition ($41,800) and room and board ($11,110). *College room only:* $5100. Full-time tuition and fees vary according to course load. Room and board charges vary according to board plan and housing facility. *Part-time tuition:* $1306 per credit hour. Part-time tuition and fees vary according to course load and reciprocity agreements.

FRESHMAN FINANCIAL AID (Fall 2017, est.) 416 applied for aid; of those 92% were deemed to have need. 100% of freshmen with need received aid; of those 24% had need fully met. *Average percent of need met:* 88% (excluding resources awarded to replace EFC). *Average financial aid package:* $39,191 (excluding resources awarded to replace EFC). 14% of all full-time freshmen had no need and received non-need-based gift aid.

UNDERGRADUATE FINANCIAL AID (Fall 2017, est.) 1,317 applied for aid; of those 93% were deemed to have need. 100% of undergraduates with need received aid; of those 22% had need fully met. *Average percent of need met:* 85% (excluding resources awarded to replace EFC). *Average financial aid package:* $36,984 (excluding resources awarded to replace EFC). 19% of all full-time undergraduates had no need and received non-need-based gift aid.

GIFT AID (NEED-BASED) *Total amount:* $38,118,665 (7% federal, 7% state, 84% institutional, 2% external sources). *Receiving aid:* Freshmen: 85% (383); all full-time undergraduates: 79% (1,228). *Average award:* Freshmen: $35,998; Undergraduates: $32,586. *Scholarships, grants, and awards:* Federal Pell, FSEOG, state, private, college/university gift aid from institutional funds, TEACH Grants.

GIFT AID (NON-NEED-BASED) *Total amount:* $7,953,409 (6% federal, 93% institutional, 1% external sources). *Receiving aid:* Freshmen: 14% (63). Undergraduates: 11% (173). *Average award:* Freshmen: $21,775. Undergraduates: $18,680. *Scholarships, grants, and awards by category:* Academic interests/ achievement: general academic interests/achievements. *Special achievements/activities:* leadership. *Special characteristics:* children of educators, general special characteristics, local/state students, previous college experience, siblings of current students, veterans. *Tuition waivers:* Full or partial for employees or children of employees. *ROTC:* Army.

LOANS *Student loans:* $9,022,535 (73% need-based, 27% non-need-based). 73% of past graduating class borrowed through all loan programs. *Average indebtedness per student:* $34,099. *Average need-based loan:* Freshmen: $3982. Undergraduates: $3306. *Parent loans:* $3,637,110 (40% need-based, 60% non-need-based). *Programs:* Federal Direct (Subsidized and Unsubsidized Stafford, PLUS), Perkins.

WORK-STUDY *Federal work-study:* Total amount: $1,012,519; jobs available. *State or other work-study/employment:* Part-time jobs available.

APPLYING FOR FINANCIAL AID *Required financial aid form:* FAFSA. *Financial aid deadline:* 4/1 (priority: 11/15). *Notification date:* Continuous beginning 12/15. Students must reply by 5/1 or within 2 weeks of notification.

CONTACT Ms. Zhanna Goltser, Financial Aid Office, McDaniel College, 2 College Hill, Westminster, MD 21157-4390, 410-857-2233 or toll-free 800-638-5005. *Fax:* 410-857-2729. *E-mail:* finaid@mcdaniel.edu. *Website:* http://www.mcdaniel.edu/.

MCKENDREE UNIVERSITY
Lebanon, IL

Tuition & fees: $30,520	Average undergraduate aid package: $21,099

ABOUT THE INSTITUTION Independent United Methodist Church, coed. *Awards:* certificates, associate, bachelor's, master's, and doctoral degrees. 44 undergraduate majors. *Total enrollment:* 2,676. Undergraduates: 2,104. Freshmen: 364. Federal methodology is used as a basis for awarding need-based institutional aid.

UNDERGRADUATE EXPENSES for 2018–2019 *Comprehensive fee:* $40,440 includes full-time tuition ($29,420), mandatory fees ($1100); and room and board ($9920). *College room only:* $5120. Full-time tuition and fees vary according to course load, degree level, and location. Room and board charges vary according to board plan and housing facility. *Part-time tuition:* $960 per credit hour. Part-time tuition and fees vary according to course load, degree level, and location.

FRESHMAN FINANCIAL AID (Fall 2016) 409 applied for aid; of those 90% were deemed to have need. 99% of freshmen with need received aid; of those 26% had need fully met. *Average percent of need met:* 75% (excluding resources awarded to replace EFC). *Average financial aid package:* $21,989 (excluding resources awarded to replace EFC). 15% of all full-time freshmen had no need and received non-need-based gift aid.

UNDERGRADUATE FINANCIAL AID (Fall 2016) 1,580 applied for aid; of those 91% were deemed to have need. 97% of undergraduates with need received aid; of those 19% had need fully met. *Average percent of need met:* 71% (excluding resources awarded to replace EFC). *Average financial aid package:* $21,099 (excluding resources awarded to replace EFC). 17% of all full-time undergraduates had no need and received non-need-based gift aid.

GIFT AID (NEED-BASED) *Total amount:* $22,559,219 (15% federal, 12% state, 69% institutional, 4% external sources). *Receiving aid:* Freshmen: 82% (367); all full-time undergraduates: 76% (1,371). *Average award:* Freshmen: $19,280; Undergraduates: $18,025. *Scholarships, grants, and awards:* Federal Pell, FSEOG, state, private, college/university gift aid from institutional funds.

GIFT AID (NON-NEED-BASED) *Total amount:* $4,659,024 (91% institutional, 9% external sources). *Receiving aid:* Freshmen: 16% (71). Undergraduates: 11% (191). *Average award:* Freshmen: $14,110. Undergraduates: $11,530. *Scholarships, grants, and awards by category:* Academic interests/achievement: 1,177 awards ($9,542,854 total): biological sciences, business, general academic interests/ achievements, religion/biblical studies. *Creative arts/performance:* 119 awards ($428,713 total): dance, debating, music. *Special achievements/activities:* 538 awards ($2,258,395 total): cheerleading/drum major, community service, leadership. *Special characteristics:* 254 awards ($1,066,523 total): children and siblings of alumni, children of faculty/staff, general special characteristics, international students, religious affili-

ation, veterans, veterans' children. *Tuition waivers:* Full or partial for children of alumni, employees or children of employees. *ROTC:* Army cooperative, Air Force cooperative.

LOANS *Student loans:* $10,544,662 (71% need-based, 29% non-need-based). 77% of past graduating class borrowed through all loan programs. *Average indebtedness per student:* $28,375. *Average need-based loan:* Freshmen: $3592. Undergraduates: $4321. *Parent loans:* $4,355,081 (41% need-based, 59% non-need-based). *Programs:* Federal Direct (Subsidized and Unsubsidized Stafford, PLUS), Perkins.

WORK-STUDY *Federal work-study:* jobs available. *State or other work-study/employment:* Total amount: $31,309 (7% need-based, 93% non-need-based). 67 part-time jobs averaging $1138.

ATHLETIC AWARDS Total amount: $5,195,038 (45% need-based, 55% non-need-based).

APPLYING FOR FINANCIAL AID *Required financial aid form:* FAFSA. *Financial aid deadline (priority):* 5/31. *Notification date:* Continuous beginning 3/1.

CONTACT Elizabeth L. Juehne, Director of Financial Aid, McKendree University, 701 College Road, Lebanon, IL 62254-1299, 618-537-6532 or toll-free 800-232-7228. *Fax:* 618-537-6530. *E-mail:* bjuehne@mckendree.edu. *Website:* http://www.mckendree.edu/.

MCMURRY UNIVERSITY
Abilene, TX

Tuition & fees: $26,712	Average undergraduate aid package: $21,941

ABOUT THE INSTITUTION Independent United Methodist, coed. *Awards:* bachelor's and master's degrees. 46 undergraduate majors. *Total enrollment:* 1,108. Undergraduates: 1,105. Freshmen: 246. Federal methodology is used as a basis for awarding need-based institutional aid.

UNDERGRADUATE EXPENSES for 2017–2018 *Application fee:* $25. *One-time required fee:* $175. *Comprehensive fee:* $35,036 includes full-time tuition ($26,622), mandatory fees ($90), and room and board ($8324). *College room only:* $4104. Full-time tuition and fees vary according to course load. Room and board charges vary according to board plan and housing facility. *Part-time tuition:* $887 per credit hour. *Part-time fees:* $3 per credit hour. Part-time tuition and fees vary according to course load.

FRESHMAN FINANCIAL AID (Fall 2017, est.) 223 applied for aid; of those 94% were deemed to have need. 100% of freshmen with need received aid; of those 10% had need fully met. *Average percent of need met:* 72% (excluding resources awarded to replace EFC). *Average financial aid package:* $21,967 (excluding resources awarded to replace EFC). 10% of all full-time freshmen had no need and received non-need-based gift aid.

UNDERGRADUATE FINANCIAL AID (Fall 2017, est.) 823 applied for aid; of those 94% were deemed to have need. 100% of undergraduates with need received aid; of those 12% had need fully met. *Average percent of need met:* 72% (excluding resources awarded to replace EFC). *Average financial aid package:* $21,941 (excluding resources awarded to replace EFC). 11% of all full-time undergraduates had no need and received non-need-based gift aid.

GIFT AID (NEED-BASED) *Total amount:* $13,231,697 (20% federal, 8% state, 67% institutional, 5% external sources). *Receiving aid:* Freshmen: 85% (209); all full-time undergraduates: 81% (774). *Average award:* Freshmen: $17,759; Undergraduates: $16,829. *Scholarships, grants, and awards:* Federal Pell, FSEOG, state, private, college/university gift aid from institutional funds.

GIFT AID (NON-NEED-BASED) *Total amount:* $1,876,992 (1% federal, 89% institutional, 10% external sources). *Receiving aid:* Freshmen: 8% (19). Undergraduates: 8% (73). *Average award:* Freshmen: $11,978. Undergraduates: $11,582. *Scholarships, grants, and awards by category:* Academic interests/ achievement: biological sciences, business, computer science, education, English, foreign languages, general academic interests/achievements, mathematics, physical sciences, premedicine, religion/biblical studies, social sciences. *Creative arts/performance:* art/fine arts, music, theater/drama. *Special achievements/activities:* general special achievements/activities, religious involvement. *Special characteristics:* adult students, children of faculty/staff, ethnic background, first-generation college students, general special characteristics, international students, local/state students, members of minority groups, out-of-state students, previous college experience, relatives of clergy, religious affiliation, veterans, veterans' children. **Tuition waivers:** Full or partial for employees or children of employees.

LOANS *Student loans:* $7,290,000 (78% need-based, 22% non-need-based). 90% of past graduating class borrowed through all loan programs. *Average indebtedness per student:* $31,350. **Average need-based loan:** Freshmen: $3148. Undergraduates: $4260. **Parent loans:** $2,079,939 (60% need-based, 40% non-need-based). **Programs:** Federal Direct (Subsidized and Unsubsidized Stafford, PLUS), Perkins, state, private loans, United Methodist Student Loans.

WORK-STUDY *Federal work-study:* Total amount: $1,043,716; 130 jobs averaging $975. **State or other work-study/employment:** Total amount: $140,369 (15% need-based, 85% non-need-based). 40 part-time jobs averaging $1106.

APPLYING FOR FINANCIAL AID *Required financial aid forms:* FAFSA, institution's own form. *Financial aid deadline (priority):* 3/15. **Notification date:** Continuous beginning 11/15. Students must reply within 3 weeks of notification.

CONTACT Mr. Tim Sechrist, Director of Student Financial Services, McMurry University, #1 McMurry University Box 908, Abilene, TX 79697, 325-793-4978 or toll-free 800-460-2392. *Fax:* 325-793-4718. *E-mail:* financialaid@mcm.edu. *Website:* http://www.mcm.edu/.

MCNEESE STATE UNIVERSITY
Lake Charles, LA

CONTACT Ms. Taina J. Savoit, Director of Financial Aid, McNeese State University, PO Box 93260, Lake Charles, LA 70609-3260, 337-475-5065 or toll-free 800-622-3352. *Fax:* 337-475-5068. *E-mail:* financialaid@mcneese.edu. *Website:* http://www.mcneese.edu/.

MCPHERSON COLLEGE
McPherson, KS

ABOUT THE INSTITUTION Independent Church of the Brethren, coed. *Awards:* bachelor's and master's degrees. 41 undergraduate majors. **Total enrollment:** 733. Undergraduates: 725. Freshmen: 202.

GIFT AID (NEED-BASED) *Scholarships, grants, and awards:* Federal Pell, FSEOG, state, private, college/university gift aid from institutional funds.

GIFT AID (NON-NEED-BASED) *Scholarships, grants, and awards by category:* Academic interests/achievement: general academic interests/achievements. *Creative arts/performance:* art/fine arts, music, performing arts, theater/drama. *Special achievements/activities:* cheerleading/drum major. *Special characteristics:* children and siblings of alumni, children of faculty/staff, international students, religious affiliation.

LOANS *Programs:* Federal Direct (Subsidized and Unsubsidized Stafford, PLUS), Perkins.

WORK-STUDY *Federal work-study:* jobs available. **State or other work-study/employment:** Part-time jobs available.

APPLYING FOR FINANCIAL AID *Required financial aid form:* FAFSA.

CONTACT Ms. Sara Brubaker, Director of Financial Aid and Admissions Operations, McPherson College, 1600 East Euclid, McPherson, KS 67460-1402, 620-242-0400 or toll-free 800-365-7402. *Fax:* 620-241-8443. *E-mail:* krehbieb2@mcpherson.edu. *Website:* http://www.mcpherson.edu/.

MCPHS UNIVERSITY
Boston, MA

Tuition & fees: $32,705	Average undergraduate aid package: $8116

ABOUT THE INSTITUTION Independent, coed. *Awards:* certificates, bachelor's, master's, and doctoral degrees. 12 undergraduate majors. **Total enrollment:** 7,208. Undergraduates: 3,882. Freshmen: 769. Federal methodology is used as a basis for awarding need-based institutional aid.

UNDERGRADUATE EXPENSES for 2018–2019 *Comprehensive fee:* $49,105 includes full-time tuition ($31,600), mandatory fees ($1105), and room and board ($16,400). **College room only:** $13,126. Full-time tuition and fees vary according to course load, degree level, location, program, and student level. Room and board charges vary according to board plan, housing facility, and location.

FRESHMAN FINANCIAL AID (Fall 2017, est.) 594 applied for aid; of those 90% were deemed to have need. 100% of freshmen with need received aid; of those 40% had need fully met. **Average percent of need met:** 24% (excluding resources awarded to replace EFC). **Average financial aid package:** $9948 (excluding resources awarded to replace EFC). 28% of all full-time freshmen had no need and received non-need-based gift aid.

UNDERGRADUATE FINANCIAL AID (Fall 2017, est.) 2,640 applied for aid; of those 93% were deemed to have need. 100% of undergraduates with need received aid; of those 34% had need fully met. **Average percent of need met:** 21% (excluding resources awarded to replace EFC). **Average financial aid package:** $8116 (excluding resources awarded to replace EFC). 26% of all full-time undergraduates had no need and received non-need-based gift aid.

GIFT AID (NEED-BASED) *Total amount:* $6,857,810 (47% federal, 7% state, 46% institutional). **Receiving aid:** Freshmen: 72% (536); all full-time undergraduates: 74% (2,467). **Average award:** Freshmen: $7511; Undergraduates: $5748. **Scholarships, grants, and awards:** Federal Pell, FSEOG, state, private, college/university gift aid from institutional funds, United Negro College Fund, Federal Nursing.

GIFT AID (NON-NEED-BASED) *Total amount:* $10,864,271 (93% institutional, 7% external sources). **Receiving aid:** Undergraduates: 8. **Average award:** Freshmen: $5888. Undergraduates: $6122. **Scholarships, grants, and awards by category:** Academic interests/achievement: general academic interests/achievements. *Tuition waivers:* Full or partial for employees or children of employees.

LOANS *Student loans:* $28,039,511 (25% need-based, 75% non-need-based). 81% of past graduating class borrowed through all loan programs. *Average indebtedness per student:* $58,012. **Average need-based loan:** Freshmen: $2480. Undergraduates: $2941. **Parent loans:** $9,591,973 (100% non-need-based). **Programs:** Federal Direct (Subsidized and Unsubsidized Stafford, PLUS), Perkins, state, college/university, alternative loans.

WORK-STUDY *Federal work-study:* Total amount: $347,209; jobs available.

APPLYING FOR FINANCIAL AID *Required financial aid form:* FAFSA. *Financial aid deadline:* Continuous. **Notification date:** Continuous beginning 12/15.

CONTACT Elizabeth Goreham, Director of Student Financial Services, MCPHS University, 179 Longwood Avenue, Boston, MA 02115-5896, 617-879-5986. *E-mail:* elizabeth.goreham@mcphs.edu. *Website:* http://www.mcphs.edu/.

MEDAILLE COLLEGE
Buffalo, NY

CONTACT Ms. Catherine Buzanski, Director of Financial Aid, Medaille College, 18 Agassiz Circle, Buffalo, NY 14214-2695, 716-880-2179 or toll-free 800-292-1582. *Fax:* 716-884-0291. *E-mail:* cbuzanski@medaille.edu. *Website:* http://www.medaille.edu/.

MEDGAR EVERS COLLEGE OF THE CITY UNIVERSITY OF NEW YORK
Brooklyn, NY

Tuition & fees (NY res): $6650	Average undergraduate aid package: $9209

ABOUT THE INSTITUTION State and locally supported, coed. *Awards:* certificates, associate, and bachelor's degrees. 15 undergraduate majors. **Total enrollment:** 6,652. Undergraduates: 6,652. Freshmen: 1,186. Federal methodology is used as a basis for awarding need-based institutional aid.

UNDERGRADUATE EXPENSES for 2018–2019 *Application fee:* $65. *Tuition, state resident:* full-time $6330; part-time $275 per credit. *Tuition, nonresident:* full-time $16,800; part-time $560 per credit. *Required fees:* full-time $320; $100.85 per term. Full-time tuition and fees vary according to course load. Part-time tuition and fees vary according to course load.

FRESHMAN FINANCIAL AID (Fall 2017, est.) 1,141 applied for aid. of those 3% had need fully met. **Average financial aid package:** $8900 (excluding resources awarded to replace EFC).

UNDERGRADUATE FINANCIAL AID (Fall 2017, est.) 4,432 applied for aid. of those 2% had need fully met. *Average financial aid package:* $9209 (excluding resources awarded to replace EFC).

GIFT AID (NEED-BASED) *Total amount:* $41,822,120 (63% federal, 34% state, 3% institutional). *Receiving aid:* Freshmen: 88% (1,010); all full-time undergraduates: 83% (3,977). *Average award:* Freshmen: $8170; Undergraduates: $8014. *Scholarships, grants, and awards:* Federal Pell, FSEOG, state, private, college/university gift aid from institutional funds, Thurgood Marshall Scholarship Fund.

GIFT AID (NON-NEED-BASED) *Receiving aid:* Freshmen: 10% (118). Undergraduates: 10% (483). *Scholarships, grants, and awards by category:* Academic interests/achievement: general academic interests/achievements.

LOANS *Student loans:* $6,484,416 (100% need-based). *Average need-based loan:* Freshmen: $2317. Undergraduates: $3432. *Programs:* Federal Direct (Subsidized and Unsubsidized Stafford, PLUS), Perkins.

WORK-STUDY *Federal work-study:* Total amount: $287,999; jobs available. *State or other work-study/employment:* Part-time jobs available.

APPLYING FOR FINANCIAL AID *Required financial aid forms:* FAFSA, state aid form, University Financial Aid Information Supplemental Request (FASIR). *Financial aid deadline (priority):* 1/2. *Notification date:* Continuous beginning 4/1. Students must reply within 3 weeks of notification.

CONTACT Nigel Thompson, Director of Financial Aid, Medgar Evers College of the City University of New York, 1650 Bedford Avenue, Brooklyn, NY 11225, 718-270-6038. *Fax:* 718-270-6194. *E-mail:* nigel.thompson@mec.cuny.edu. *Website:* http://www.mec.cuny.edu/.

MEDICAL UNIVERSITY OF SOUTH CAROLINA
Charleston, SC

Tuition & fees: N/R	Average undergraduate aid package: $11,145

ABOUT THE INSTITUTION State-supported, coed. 2 undergraduate majors. Federal methodology is used as a basis for awarding need-based institutional aid.

UNDERGRADUATE FINANCIAL AID (Fall 2016) 253 applied for aid; of those 92% were deemed to have need. 97% of undergraduates with need received aid; of those 4% had need fully met. *Average percent of need met:* 35% (excluding resources awarded to replace EFC). *Average financial aid package:* $11,145 (excluding resources awarded to replace EFC). 2% of all full-time undergraduates had no need and received non-need-based gift aid.

GIFT AID (NEED-BASED) *Total amount:* $566,824 (36% federal, 8% state, 55% institutional, 1% external sources). *Receiving aid:* All full-time undergraduates: 34% (105). *Average award:* Undergraduates: $5398. *Scholarships, grants, and awards:* Federal Pell, FSEOG, state, private, college/university gift aid from institutional funds, Federal Nursing, Scholarships for Disadvantaged Students (SDS).

GIFT AID (NON-NEED-BASED) *Total amount:* $589,022 (8% federal, 38% state, 39% institutional, 15% external sources). *Receiving aid:* Undergraduates: 17% (53). *Average award:* Undergraduates: $8207. *Scholarships, grants, and awards by category:* Academic interests/achievement: general academic interests/achievements, home economics. *Special characteristics:* ethnic background, general special characteristics, local/state students, members of minority groups.

LOANS *Student loans:* $3,828,743 (32% need-based, 68% non-need-based). *Average need-based loan:* Undergraduates: $6667. *Parent loans:* $128,858 (100% non-need-based). *Programs:* Federal Direct (Subsidized and Unsubsidized Stafford, PLUS), Perkins, Federal Nursing, state, alternative loans, Health Professions Student Loans (HPSL), Loans for Disadvantaged Students, Primary Care Loans.

WORK-STUDY *Federal work-study:* jobs available.

APPLYING FOR FINANCIAL AID *Required financial aid form:* FAFSA. *Notification date:* Continuous.

CONTACT Mr. Joseph M. DuRant, Director for Student Financial Aid Services, Medical University of South Carolina, 45 Courtenay Drive, MSC 203, Charleston, SC 29425, 843-792-2252. *Fax:* 843-792-6356. *E-mail:* durantjm@musc.edu. *Website:* http://www.musc.edu/.

MENLO COLLEGE
Atherton, CA

CONTACT Jessica Ayers, Director of Financial Aid, Menlo College, 1000 El Camino Real, Atherton, CA 94027-4301, 650-543-3880 or toll-free 800-556-3656. *Fax:* 650-543-4103. *E-mail:* financialaid@menlo.edu. *Website:* http://www.menlo.edu/.

MERCER UNIVERSITY
Macon, GA

Tuition & fees: $36,000	Average undergraduate aid package: $35,680

ABOUT THE INSTITUTION Independent Baptist, coed. *Awards:* certificates, bachelor's, master's, and doctoral degrees. 61 undergraduate majors. *Total enrollment:* 7,130. Undergraduates: 3,224. Freshmen: 890. Federal methodology is used as a basis for awarding need-based institutional aid.

UNDERGRADUATE EXPENSES for 2017–2018 *Application fee:* $50. *Comprehensive fee:* $48,153 includes full-time tuition ($35,700), mandatory fees ($300), and room and board ($12,153). *College room only:* $6174. Full-time tuition and fees vary according to location. Room and board charges vary according to board plan, housing facility, location, and student level. *Part-time tuition:* $1190 per credit hour. *Part-time fees:* $10 per credit hour. Part-time tuition and fees vary according to course load and location.

FRESHMAN FINANCIAL AID (Fall 2017, est.) 887 applied for aid; of those 75% were deemed to have need. 100% of freshmen with need received aid; of those 44% had need fully met. *Average percent of need met:* 89% (excluding resources awarded to replace EFC). *Average financial aid package:* $37,448 (excluding resources awarded to replace EFC). 24% of all full-time freshmen had no need and received non-need-based gift aid.

UNDERGRADUATE FINANCIAL AID (Fall 2017, est.) 3,166 applied for aid; of those 70% were deemed to have need. 100% of undergraduates with need received aid; of those 39% had need fully met. *Average percent of need met:* 85% (excluding resources awarded to replace EFC). *Average financial aid package:* $35,680 (excluding resources awarded to replace EFC). 27% of all full-time undergraduates had no need and received non-need-based gift aid.

GIFT AID (NEED-BASED) *Total amount:* $51,196,821 (9% federal, 12% state, 77% institutional, 2% external sources). *Receiving aid:* Freshmen: 75% (664); all full-time undergraduates: 70% (2,212). *Average award:* Freshmen: $26,433; Undergraduates: $25,059. *Scholarships, grants, and awards:* Federal Pell, FSEOG, state, college/university gift aid from institutional funds, Federal Nursing.

GIFT AID (NON-NEED-BASED) *Total amount:* $26,346,690 (17% state, 81% institutional, 2% external sources). *Receiving aid:* Freshmen: 22% (199). Undergraduates: 19% (589). *Average award:* Freshmen: $21,260. Undergraduates: $20,044. *Scholarships, grants, and awards by category:* Academic interests/achievement: biological sciences, business, education, engineering/technologies, English, foreign languages, general academic interests/achievements, international studies, military science, religion/biblical studies. *Creative arts/performance:* art/fine arts, debating, music, theater/drama. *Special achievements/activities:* community service, general special achievements/activities, leadership. *Special characteristics:* adult students, children of faculty/staff, children of public servants, general special characteristics, international students, relatives of clergy, siblings of current students. *Tuition waivers:* Full or partial for employees or children of employees. *ROTC:* Army.

LOANS *Student loans:* $14,597,181 (72% need-based, 28% non-need-based). 68% of past graduating class borrowed through all loan programs. *Average indebtedness per student:* $26,429. *Average need-based loan:* Freshmen: $9705. Undergraduates: $10,276. *Parent loans:* $4,003,948 (41% need-based, 59% non-need-based). *Programs:* Federal Direct (Subsidized and Unsubsidized Stafford, PLUS), Perkins, Federal Nursing, college/university.

WORK-STUDY *Federal work-study:* Total amount: $1,623,102; 789 jobs averaging $2032.

ATHLETIC AWARDS Total amount: $8,474,827 (44% need-based, 56% non-need-based).

APPLYING FOR FINANCIAL AID *Required financial aid forms:* FAFSA, institution's own form, state aid form (GA residents only). *Financial aid deadline*

(priority): 2/1. **Notification date:** Continuous. Students must reply within 2 weeks of notification.

CONTACT Ms. Maria Hammett, Associate Vice President, Mercer University, Office of Financial Planning, Macon, GA 31207-0003, 478-301-2226 or toll-free 800-MERCER-U. *Fax:* 478-301-2671. *E-mail:* hammett_ma@mercer.edu. *Website:* http://www.mercer.edu/.

MERCY COLLEGE
Dobbs Ferry, NY

Tuition & fees: $18,713	Average undergraduate aid package: $13,811

ABOUT THE INSTITUTION Independent Roman Catholic Church, coed. *Awards:* certificates, associate, bachelor's, master's, and doctoral degrees. 36 undergraduate majors. *Total enrollment:* 9,506. Undergraduates: 6,864. Freshmen: 910. Federal methodology is used as a basis for awarding need-based institutional aid.

UNDERGRADUATE EXPENSES for 2017–2018 Application fee: $40. *Comprehensive fee:* $32,613 includes full-time tuition ($18,083), mandatory fees ($630), and room and board ($13,900). *College room only:* $9350. Full-time tuition and fees vary according to course load. Room and board charges vary according to board plan. *Part-time tuition:* $761 per credit. *Part-time fees:* $158 per term. Part-time tuition and fees vary according to course load.

FRESHMAN FINANCIAL AID (Fall 2016) 891 applied for aid; of those 93% were deemed to have need. 96% of freshmen with need received aid; of those 2% had need fully met. *Average percent of need met:* 55% (excluding resources awarded to replace EFC). *Average financial aid package:* $15,270 (excluding resources awarded to replace EFC). 4% of all full-time freshmen had no need and received non-need-based gift aid.

UNDERGRADUATE FINANCIAL AID (Fall 2016) 4,577 applied for aid; of those 94% were deemed to have need. 96% of undergraduates with need received aid; of those 2% had need fully met. *Average percent of need met:* 50% (excluding resources awarded to replace EFC). *Average financial aid package:* $13,811 (excluding resources awarded to replace EFC). 2% of all full-time undergraduates had no need and received non-need-based gift aid.

GIFT AID (NEED-BASED) Total amount: $39,725,305 (40% federal, 22% state, 38% institutional). *Receiving aid:* Freshmen: 79% (719); all full-time undergraduates: 77% (3,773). *Average award:* Freshmen: $12,472; Undergraduates: $10,218. *Scholarships, grants, and awards:* Federal Pell, FSEOG, state, private, college/university gift aid from institutional funds, Federal Nursing.

GIFT AID (NON-NEED-BASED) Total amount: $5,241,668 (10% state, 87% institutional, 3% external sources). *Receiving aid:* Freshmen: 36% (332). Undergraduates: 24% (1,192). *Average award:* Freshmen: $6090. Undergraduates: $4684. *Scholarships, grants, and awards by category: Academic interests/achievement:* business, general academic interests/achievements. *Special characteristics:* children of faculty/staff. *Tuition waivers:* Full or partial for employees or children of employees, senior citizens. *ROTC:* Army cooperative, Air Force cooperative.

LOANS Student loans: $33,360,287 (42% need-based, 58% non-need-based). 81% of past graduating class borrowed through all loan programs. *Average indebtedness per student:* $30,258. *Average need-based loan:* Freshmen: $3119. Undergraduates: $4040. *Parent loans:* $5,620,203 (100% non-need-based). *Programs:* Federal Direct (Subsidized and Unsubsidized Stafford, PLUS), Federal Nursing.

WORK-STUDY Federal work-study: jobs available.

ATHLETIC AWARDS Total amount: $1,277,431 (100% non-need-based).

APPLYING FOR FINANCIAL AID Required financial aid forms: FAFSA, state aid form. *Financial aid deadline (priority):* 2/15. *Notification date:* Continuous beginning 2/15. Students must reply by 5/1 or within 2 weeks of notification.

CONTACT Margaret M. McGrail, Vice President of Enrollment Services, Mercy College, 555 Broadway, Dobbs Ferry, NY 10522, 877-637-2946 or toll-free 877-MERCY-GO (out-of-state). *Fax:* 914-674-7382. *E-mail:* admissions@mercy.edu. *Website:* http://www.mercy.edu/.

MERCY COLLEGE OF HEALTH SCIENCES
Des Moines, IA

CONTACT Lisa Croat, Financial Aid Director, Mercy College of Health Sciences, 921 Sixth Avenue, Des Moines, IA 50309, 515-643-6636 or toll-free 800-637-2994. *Fax:* 515-643-6747. *E-mail:* financialaid@mchs.edu. *Website:* http://www.mchs.edu/.

MERCY COLLEGE OF OHIO
Toledo, OH

ABOUT THE INSTITUTION Independent Roman Catholic Church, coed, primarily women. *Awards:* certificates, associate, bachelor's, and master's degrees. 7 undergraduate majors. *Total enrollment:* 1,416. Undergraduates: 1,404. Freshmen: 66.

GIFT AID (NEED-BASED) Scholarships, grants, and awards: Federal Pell, FSEOG, state, private, college/university gift aid from institutional funds, Federal Nursing.

GIFT AID (NON-NEED-BASED) Scholarships, grants, and awards by category: Academic interests/achievement: general academic interests/achievements, home economics, premedicine. *Special characteristics:* first-generation college students.

LOANS Programs: Federal Direct (Subsidized and Unsubsidized Stafford, PLUS), state, college/university.

APPLYING FOR FINANCIAL AID Required financial aid form: FAFSA.

CONTACT Julie Leslie, Director of Financial Aid, Mercy College of Ohio, 2221 Madison Avenue, Toledo, OH 43604, 419-251-1598 or toll-free 888-80-MERCY. *Fax:* 419-251-0969. *E-mail:* julie.leslie@mercycollege.edu. *Website:* http://www.mercycollege.edu/.

MERCYHURST UNIVERSITY
Erie, PA

CONTACT Carrie Newman, Director of Student Financial Services, Mercyhurst University, 501 East 38th Street, Erie, PA 16546, 814-824-2288 or toll-free 800-825-1926. *Fax:* 814-824-2300. *E-mail:* sfs@mercyhurst.edu. *Website:* http://www.mercyhurst.edu/.

MEREDITH COLLEGE
Raleigh, NC

Tuition & fees: $35,916	Average undergraduate aid package: $27,707

ABOUT THE INSTITUTION Independent, undergraduate: women only; graduate: coed. *Awards:* certificates, bachelor's, and master's degrees. 41 undergraduate majors. *Total enrollment:* 1,981. Undergraduates: 1,682. Freshmen: 395. Both federal and institutional methodology are used as a basis for awarding need-based institutional aid.

UNDERGRADUATE EXPENSES for 2017–2018 Application fee: $40. *Comprehensive fee:* $46,634 includes full-time tuition ($35,816), mandatory fees ($100), and room and board ($10,718). Full-time tuition and fees vary according to course load. Room and board charges vary according to board plan and housing facility. *Part-time tuition:* $889 per credit hour. *Part-time fees:* $100 per year. Part-time tuition and fees vary according to course load.

FRESHMAN FINANCIAL AID (Fall 2017, est.) 357 applied for aid; of those 86% were deemed to have need. 100% of freshmen with need received aid; of those 16% had need fully met. *Average percent of need met:* 77% (excluding resources awarded to replace EFC). *Average financial aid package:* $28,267 (excluding resources awarded to replace EFC). 12% of all full-time freshmen had no need and received non-need-based gift aid.

UNDERGRADUATE FINANCIAL AID (Fall 2017, est.) 1,274 applied for aid; of those 89% were deemed to have need. 100% of undergraduates with need received aid; of those 18% had need fully met. *Average percent of need met:* 75% (excluding resources awarded to replace EFC). *Average financial aid package:* $27,707 (excluding resources awarded to replace EFC). 8% of all full-time undergraduates had no need and received non-need-based gift aid.
GIFT AID (NEED-BASED) *Total amount:* $26,719,482 (11% federal, 14% state, 68% institutional, 7% external sources). *Receiving aid:* Freshmen: 78% (306); all full-time undergraduates: 74% (1,136). *Average award:* Freshmen: $24,941; Undergraduates: $23,453. *Scholarships, grants, and awards:* Federal Pell, FSEOG, state, private, college/university gift aid from institutional funds.
GIFT AID (NON-NEED-BASED) *Total amount:* $7,186,228 (1% state, 88% institutional, 11% external sources). *Average award:* Freshmen: $17,223. Undergraduates: $16,687. *Scholarships, grants, and awards by category:* Academic interests/achievement: biological sciences, business, computer science, education, English, foreign languages, general academic interests/achievements, mathematics, physical sciences, religion/biblical studies. *Creative arts/performance:* applied art and design, art/fine arts, creative writing, music, theater/drama. *Special achievements/activities:* community service, leadership. *Special characteristics:* adult students, children of faculty/staff, ethnic background, first-generation college students, international students, members of minority groups, out-of-state students, previous college experience, religious affiliation. *Tuition waivers:* Full or partial for employees or children of employees. *ROTC:* Army cooperative, Air Force cooperative.
LOANS *Student loans:* $10,774,633 (91% need-based, 9% non-need-based). 69% of past graduating class borrowed through all loan programs. *Average indebtedness per student:* $34,959. *Average need-based loan:* Freshmen: $3144. Undergraduates: $4083. *Parent loans:* $6,613,739 (46% need-based, 54% non-need-based). *Programs:* Federal Direct (Subsidized and Unsubsidized Stafford, PLUS), Perkins, college/university.
WORK-STUDY *Federal work-study:* Total amount: $637,360; jobs available. *State or other work-study/employment:* Part-time jobs available.
APPLYING FOR FINANCIAL AID *Required financial aid form:* FAFSA. *Financial aid deadline (priority):* 2/15. *Notification date:* Continuous beginning 3/15. Students must reply by 5/1 or within 2 weeks of notification.
CONTACT Mr. Kevin Michaelsen, Director of Financial Assistance, Meredith College, 3800 Hillsborough Street, Raleigh, NC 27607-5298, 919-760-8565 or toll-free 800-MEREDITH. *Fax:* 919-760-2375. *E-mail:* michaelsen@meredith.edu.
Website: http://www.meredith.edu/.

MERRIMACK COLLEGE
North Andover, MA

Tuition & fees: $40,190	Average undergraduate aid package: $23,808

ABOUT THE INSTITUTION Independent Roman Catholic, coed. *Awards:* certificates, bachelor's, and master's degrees. 64 undergraduate majors. *Total enrollment:* 4,171. Undergraduates: 3,515. Freshmen: 855. Federal methodology is used as a basis for awarding need-based institutional aid.
UNDERGRADUATE EXPENSES for 2017–2018 *Comprehensive fee:* $55,415 includes full-time tuition ($37,910), mandatory fees ($2280), and room and board ($15,225). Full-time tuition and fees vary according to degree level. Room and board charges vary according to board plan and housing facility. *Part-time tuition:* $1360 per credit. Part-time tuition and fees vary according to class time, course load, and degree level.
FRESHMAN FINANCIAL AID (Fall 2017, est.) 764 applied for aid; of those 88% were deemed to have need. 100% of freshmen with need received aid; of those 12% had need fully met. *Average percent of need met:* 64% (excluding resources awarded to replace EFC). *Average financial aid package:* $24,754 (excluding resources awarded to replace EFC). 18% of all full-time freshmen had no need and received non-need-based gift aid.
UNDERGRADUATE FINANCIAL AID (Fall 2017, est.) 2,656 applied for aid; of those 90% were deemed to have need. 100% of undergraduates with need received aid; of those 11% had need fully met. *Average percent of need met:* 63% (excluding resources awarded to replace EFC). *Average financial aid package:* $23,808 (excluding resources awarded to replace EFC). 23% of all full-time undergraduates had no need and received non-need-based gift aid.

GIFT AID (NEED-BASED) *Total amount:* $42,977,621 (8% federal, 2% state, 89% institutional, 1% external sources). *Receiving aid:* Freshmen: 79% (675); all full-time undergraduates: 70% (2,347). *Average award:* Freshmen: $21,901; Undergraduates: $20,182. *Scholarships, grants, and awards:* Federal Pell, FSEOG, state, private, college/university gift aid from institutional funds.
GIFT AID (NON-NEED-BASED) *Total amount:* $11,452,037 (99% institutional, 1% external sources). *Receiving aid:* Freshmen: 9% (75). Undergraduates: 7% (239). *Average award:* Freshmen: $14,176. Undergraduates: $13,184. *Scholarships, grants, and awards by category:* Academic interests/achievement: general academic interests/achievements. *Special achievements/activities:* leadership. *Special characteristics:* children of faculty/staff, international students, relatives of clergy, religious affiliation, siblings of current students, veterans. *Tuition waivers:* Full or partial for employees or children of employees, senior citizens. *ROTC:* Air Force cooperative.
LOANS *Student loans:* $31,321,282 (65% need-based, 35% non-need-based). *Average need-based loan:* Freshmen: $3412. Undergraduates: $4436. *Parent loans:* $9,216,129 (52% need-based, 48% non-need-based). *Programs:* Federal Direct (Subsidized and Unsubsidized Stafford, PLUS), Perkins, state, college/university.
WORK-STUDY *Federal work-study:* Total amount: $247,666; jobs available. *State or other work-study/employment:* Part-time jobs available.
ATHLETIC AWARDS Total amount: $8,801,339 (45% need-based, 55% non-need-based).
APPLYING FOR FINANCIAL AID *Required financial aid form:* FAFSA. *Financial aid deadline (priority):* 2/15. *Notification date:* Continuous beginning 3/15.
CONTACT Adrienne Montgomery, Director of Financial Aid, Merrimack College, 315 Turnpike Street, North Andover, MA 01845, 978-837-5186. *Fax:* 978-837-5067. *E-mail:* montgomerya@merrimack.edu.
Website: http://www.merrimack.edu/.

MESIVTA OF EASTERN PARKWAY– YESHIVA ZICHRON MEILECH
Brooklyn, NY

CONTACT Rabbi Joseph Halberstadt, Dean, Mesivta of Eastern Parkway–Yeshiva Zichron Meilech, 510 Dahill Road, Brooklyn, NY 11218-5559, 718-438-1002.

MESIVTA TORAH VODAATH RABBINICAL SEMINARY
Brooklyn, NY

CONTACT Mrs. Kayla Goldring, Director of Financial Aid, Mesivta Torah Vodaath Rabbinical Seminary, 425 East Ninth Street, Brooklyn, NY 11218-5209, 718-941-8000. *Website:* http://www.torahvodaath.org/.

MESIVTHA TIFERETH JERUSALEM OF AMERICA
New York, NY

CONTACT Rabbi Dickstein, Director of Financial Aid, Mesivtha Tifereth Jerusalem of America, 141 East Broadway, New York, NY 10002-6301, 212-964-2830.

MESSENGER COLLEGE
Euless, TX

CONTACT Patricia J. Pentecost, Director of Financial Aid, Messenger College, 300 East 50th Street, Joplin, MO 64804, 417-624-7070 Ext. 104 or toll-free 800-385-8940. *Fax:* 417-624-5070. *E-mail:* ppentecost@messengercollege.edu. *Website:* http://www.messengercollege.edu/.

MESSIAH COLLEGE
Mechanicsburg, PA

Tuition & fees: $35,160 | **Average undergraduate aid package: $24,287**

ABOUT THE INSTITUTION Independent interdenominational, coed. *Awards:* certificates, bachelor's, master's, and doctoral degrees. 79 undergraduate majors. *Total enrollment:* 3,331. Undergraduates: 2,759. Freshmen: 665. Federal methodology is used as a basis for awarding need-based institutional aid.

UNDERGRADUATE EXPENSES for 2018–2019 *Application fee:* $50. *Comprehensive fee:* $45,680 includes full-time tuition ($34,320), mandatory fees ($840), and room and board ($10,520). *College room only:* $5570. Room and board charges vary according to board plan and housing facility. *Part-time tuition:* $1430 per credit hour.

FRESHMAN FINANCIAL AID (Fall 2017, est.) 608 applied for aid; of those 88% were deemed to have need. 100% of freshmen with need received aid; of those 17% had need fully met. *Average percent of need met:* 73% (excluding resources awarded to replace EFC). *Average financial aid package:* $25,467 (excluding resources awarded to replace EFC). 19% of all full-time freshmen had no need and received non-need-based gift aid.

UNDERGRADUATE FINANCIAL AID (Fall 2017, est.) 2,185 applied for aid; of those 89% were deemed to have need. 100% of undergraduates with need received aid; of those 17% had need fully met. *Average percent of need met:* 71% (excluding resources awarded to replace EFC). *Average financial aid package:* $24,287 (excluding resources awarded to replace EFC). 26% of all full-time undergraduates had no need and received non-need-based gift aid.

GIFT AID (NEED-BASED) *Total amount:* $35,803,896 (9% federal, 7% state, 81% institutional, 3% external sources). *Receiving aid:* Freshmen: 80% (535); all full-time undergraduates: 72% (1,925). *Average award:* Freshmen: $20,360; Undergraduates: $18,561. *Scholarships, grants, and awards:* Federal Pell, FSEOG, state, private, college/university gift aid from institutional funds, Federal Nursing.

GIFT AID (NON-NEED-BASED) *Total amount:* $12,432,576 (3% federal, 94% institutional, 3% external sources). *Receiving aid:* Freshmen: 11% (71). Undergraduates: 9% (231). *Average award:* Freshmen: $14,751. Undergraduates: $14,659. *Scholarships, grants, and awards by category:* Academic interests/achievement: 2,111 awards ($23,456,115 total): general academic interests/achievements, humanities. Creative arts/performance: 119 awards ($696,801 total): art/fine arts, dance, music, theater/drama. Special achievements/activities: 487 awards ($6,105,862 total): leadership. Special characteristics: 160 awards ($1,869,443 total): adult students, children of faculty/staff, local/state students, religious affiliation. *Tuition waivers:* Full or partial for employees or children of employees, adult students, senior citizens.

LOANS *Student loans:* $20,501,352 (67% need-based, 33% non-need-based). 72% of past graduating class borrowed through all loan programs. *Average indebtedness per student:* $37,399. *Average need-based loan:* Freshmen: $3786. Undergraduates: $4763. *Parent loans:* $4,868,148 (50% need-based, 50% non-need-based). *Programs:* Federal Direct (Subsidized and Unsubsidized Stafford, PLUS), Perkins, Federal Nursing.

WORK-STUDY *Federal work-study:* Total amount: $1,544,140; 711 jobs averaging $2181. *State or other work-study/employment:* Total amount: $2,800,129 (20% need-based, 80% non-need-based). 932 part-time jobs averaging $1965.

APPLYING FOR FINANCIAL AID *Required financial aid form:* FAFSA. *Financial aid deadline (priority):* 4/1. *Notification date:* Continuous beginning 12/1. Students must reply by 5/1 or within 4 weeks of notification.

CONTACT Mr. Michael Strite, Assistant Director of Financial Aid, Messiah College, One College Avenue, Suite 3006, Mechanicsburg, PA 17055, 717-691-6007 or toll-free 800-233-4220. *Fax:* 717-796-4791. *E-mail:* mstrite@messiah.edu. *Website:* http://www.messiah.edu/.

METHODIST UNIVERSITY
Fayetteville, NC

Tuition & fees: $32,860 | **Average undergraduate aid package: $22,474**

ABOUT THE INSTITUTION Independent United Methodist, coed. 57 undergraduate majors. Federal methodology is used as a basis for awarding need-based institutional aid.

UNDERGRADUATE EXPENSES for 2017–2018 *Comprehensive fee:* $45,155 includes full-time tuition ($32,500), mandatory fees ($360), and room and board ($12,295). *College room only:* $6180. Full-time tuition and fees vary according to class time. Room and board charges vary according to housing facility. Part-time tuition and fees vary according to class time and course load.

FRESHMAN FINANCIAL AID (Fall 2016) 405 applied for aid; of those 95% were deemed to have need. 100% of freshmen with need received aid; of those 10% had need fully met. *Average percent of need met:* 65% (excluding resources awarded to replace EFC). *Average financial aid package:* $24,664 (excluding resources awarded to replace EFC). 18% of all full-time freshmen had no need and received non-need-based gift aid.

UNDERGRADUATE FINANCIAL AID (Fall 2016) 1,576 applied for aid; of those 94% were deemed to have need. 99% of undergraduates with need received aid; of those 8% had need fully met. *Average percent of need met:* 61% (excluding resources awarded to replace EFC). *Average financial aid package:* $22,474 (excluding resources awarded to replace EFC). 17% of all full-time undergraduates had no need and received non-need-based gift aid.

GIFT AID (NEED-BASED) *Total amount:* $26,011,860 (14% federal, 12% state, 70% institutional, 4% external sources). *Receiving aid:* Freshmen: 81% (382); all full-time undergraduates: 75% (1,457). *Average award:* Freshmen: $21,061; Undergraduates: $18,142. *Scholarships, grants, and awards:* Federal Pell, FSEOG, state, private, college/university gift aid from institutional funds.

GIFT AID (NON-NEED-BASED) *Total amount:* $9,325,165 (72% institutional, 28% external sources). *Receiving aid:* Freshmen: 7% (32). Undergraduates: 4% (82). *Average award:* Freshmen: $25,027. Undergraduates: $18,523. *Scholarships, grants, and awards by category:* Academic interests/achievement: 764 awards ($9,941,104 total): education, English, general academic interests/achievements, military science. Creative arts/performance: 60 awards ($434,301 total): dance, debating, music. Special achievements/activities: 26 awards ($23,575 total): cheerleading/drum major, leadership. Special characteristics: 584 awards ($5,050,019 total): children and siblings of alumni, children of faculty/staff, international students, local/state students, relatives of clergy, religious affiliation, siblings of current students. *Tuition waivers:* Full or partial for senior citizens.

LOANS *Student loans:* $11,224,032 (86% need-based, 14% non-need-based). 74% of past graduating class borrowed through all loan programs. *Average indebtedness per student:* $33,978. *Average need-based loan:* Freshmen: $4305. Undergraduates: $5777. *Parent loans:* $6,262,507 (72% need-based, 28% non-need-based). *Programs:* Federal Direct (Subsidized and Unsubsidized Stafford, PLUS), Perkins, college/university.

WORK-STUDY *Federal work-study:* 472 jobs averaging $536. *State or other work-study/employment:* Total amount: $247,100 (1% need-based, 99% non-need-based). 168 part-time jobs averaging $1250.

APPLYING FOR FINANCIAL AID *Required financial aid form:* FAFSA. *Financial aid deadline (priority):* 6/1. *Notification date:* Continuous beginning 12/6. Students must reply within 2 weeks of notification.

CONTACT Bonnie Adamson, Financial Aid Office, Methodist University, 5400 Ramsey Street, Fayetteville, NC 28311-1420, 910-630-7307 or toll-free 800-488-7110 Ext. 7027. *Fax:* 910-630-7285. *E-mail:* adamson@methodist.edu. *Website:* http://www.methodist.edu/.

METHODIST COLLEGE
Peoria, IL

CONTACT Financial Aid Office, Methodist College, 415 St. Mark Court, Peoria, IL 61603, 309-672-5513. *Website:* http://www.methodistcol.edu/.

METROPOLITAN COLLEGE OF NEW YORK
New York, NY

Tuition & fees: $19,180	Average undergraduate aid package: $17,286

ABOUT THE INSTITUTION Independent, coed. *Awards:* certificates, associate, bachelor's, and master's degrees. 7 undergraduate majors. *Total enrollment:* 1,113. Undergraduates: 777. Freshmen: 99. Federal methodology is used as a basis for awarding need-based institutional aid.

UNDERGRADUATE EXPENSES for 2017–2018 *Application fee:* $30. *Tuition:* full-time $18,330; part-time $766 per credit. Full-time tuition and fees vary according to degree level and program. Part-time tuition and fees vary according to degree level and program. *Payment plan:* Guaranteed tuition.

FRESHMAN FINANCIAL AID (Fall 2017, est.) 89 applied for aid; of those 100% were deemed to have need. 97% of freshmen with need received aid; of those 2% had need fully met. *Average percent of need met:* 42% (excluding resources awarded to replace EFC). *Average financial aid package:* $13,461 (excluding resources awarded to replace EFC). 3% of all full-time freshmen had no need and received non-need-based gift aid.

UNDERGRADUATE FINANCIAL AID (Fall 2017, est.) 638 applied for aid; of those 100% were deemed to have need. 99% of undergraduates with need received aid; of those 1% had need fully met. *Average percent of need met:* 46% (excluding resources awarded to replace EFC). *Average financial aid package:* $17,286 (excluding resources awarded to replace EFC). 2% of all full-time undergraduates had no need and received non-need-based gift aid.

GIFT AID (NEED-BASED) *Total amount:* $8,352,000 (45% federal, 26% state, 22% institutional, 7% external sources). *Receiving aid:* Freshmen: 90% (86); all full-time undergraduates: 92% (626). *Average award:* Freshmen: $10,691; Undergraduates: $12,710. *Scholarships, grants, and awards:* Federal Pell, FSEOG, state, private, college/university gift aid from institutional funds.

GIFT AID (NON-NEED-BASED) *Total amount:* $601,893 (15% institutional, 85% external sources). *Receiving aid:* Freshmen: 2% (2). Undergraduates: 1% (4). *Average award:* Freshmen: $2000. Undergraduates: $2931. *Scholarships, grants, and awards by category:* Academic interests/achievement: general academic interests/achievements. *Tuition waivers:* Full or partial for employees or children of employees.

LOANS *Student loans:* $7,686,507 (98% need-based, 2% non-need-based). *Average need-based loan:* Freshmen: $3421. Undergraduates: $4917. *Parent loans:* $146,651 (92% need-based, 8% non-need-based). *Programs:* Federal Direct (Subsidized and Unsubsidized Stafford, PLUS).

WORK-STUDY *Federal work-study:* Total amount: $134,071; jobs available. *State or other work-study/employment:* Part-time jobs available.

APPLYING FOR FINANCIAL AID *Required financial aid form:* FAFSA. *Financial aid deadline:* Continuous. *Notification date:* Continuous.

CONTACT Mr. Douane Campbell, Director of Financial Aid, Metropolitan College of New York, 60 West Street, New York, NY 10006, 212-343-1234 Ext. 5004 or toll-free 800-33-THINK Ext. 5001. *Fax:* 212-343-7399. *E-mail:* fa@mcny.edu. *Website:* http://www.mcny.edu/.

METROPOLITAN STATE UNIVERSITY
St. Paul, MN

CONTACT Dr. Lois J. Larson, Director of Financial Aid, Metropolitan State University, 700 East 7th Street, St. Paul, MN 55106-5000, 651-793-1411. *Fax:* 651-642-0636. *E-mail:* financial.aid@metrostate.edu. *Website:* http://www.metrostate.edu/.

METROPOLITAN STATE UNIVERSITY OF DENVER
Denver, CO

Tuition & fees (CO res): $7352	Average undergraduate aid package: $9130

ABOUT THE INSTITUTION State-supported, coed. *Awards:* certificates, bachelor's, and master's degrees. 70 undergraduate majors. *Total enrollment:* 20,304. Undergraduates: 19,666. Freshmen: 2,548. Federal methodology is used as a basis for awarding need-based institutional aid.

UNDERGRADUATE EXPENSES for 2017–2018 *Application fee:* $25. *Tuition, state resident:* full-time $6062. *Tuition, nonresident:* full-time $18,859. *Required fees:* full-time $1290. Full-time tuition and fees vary according to course load and location. Part-time tuition and fees vary according to course load and location.

FRESHMAN FINANCIAL AID (Fall 2016) 1,609 applied for aid; of those 80% were deemed to have need. 92% of freshmen with need received aid; of those 5% had need fully met. *Average percent of need met:* 51% (excluding resources awarded to replace EFC). *Average financial aid package:* $7475 (excluding resources awarded to replace EFC). 5% of all full-time freshmen had no need and received non-need-based gift aid.

UNDERGRADUATE FINANCIAL AID (Fall 2016) 9,539 applied for aid; of those 85% were deemed to have need. 94% of undergraduates with need received aid; of those 6% had need fully met. *Average percent of need met:* 56% (excluding resources awarded to replace EFC). *Average financial aid package:* $9130 (excluding resources awarded to replace EFC). 5% of all full-time undergraduates had no need and received non-need-based gift aid.

GIFT AID (NEED-BASED) *Total amount:* $53,311,548 (51% federal, 31% state, 15% institutional, 3% external sources). *Receiving aid:* Freshmen: 54% (1,039); all full-time undergraduates: 52% (6,466). *Average award:* Freshmen: $6298; Undergraduates: $6697. *Scholarships, grants, and awards:* Federal Pell, FSEOG, state, private, college/university gift aid from institutional funds.

GIFT AID (NON-NEED-BASED) *Total amount:* $1,885,649 (2% state, 80% institutional, 18% external sources). *Receiving aid:* Freshmen: 3% (64). Undergraduates: 6% (698). *Average award:* Freshmen: $1932. Undergraduates: $1779. *Scholarships, grants, and awards by category:* Academic interests/achievement: biological sciences, business, communication, computer science, education, engineering/technologies, English, foreign languages, general academic interests/achievements, home economics, humanities, mathematics, physical sciences, social sciences. *Creative arts/performance:* music, performing arts, theater/drama. *Special achievements/activities:* leadership. *Special characteristics:* adult students, first-generation college students, local/state students, veterans. *Tuition waivers:* Full or partial for senior citizens. *ROTC:* Army, Air Force cooperative.

LOANS *Student loans:* $72,407,663 (86% need-based, 14% non-need-based). 64% of past graduating class borrowed through all loan programs. *Average indebtedness per student:* $25,805. *Average need-based loan:* Freshmen: $3251. Undergraduates: $4089. *Parent loans:* $2,364,511 (52% need-based, 48% non-need-based). *Programs:* Federal Direct (Subsidized and Unsubsidized Stafford, PLUS), Perkins.

WORK-STUDY *Federal work-study:* 157 jobs averaging $3585. *State or other work-study/employment:* Total amount: $3,021,287 (87% need-based, 13% non-need-based). 698 part-time jobs averaging $3555.

ATHLETIC AWARDS Total amount: $1,815,408 (48% need-based, 52% non-need-based).

APPLYING FOR FINANCIAL AID *Required financial aid form:* FAFSA. *Financial aid deadline:* Continuous. *Notification date:* Continuous beginning 11/1.

CONTACT Office of Financial Aid, Metropolitan State University of Denver, PO Box 173362, Denver, CO 80217-3362, 303-556-8593. *Fax:* 303-556-4927. *Website:* http://www.msudenver.edu/.

MIAMI INTERNATIONAL UNIVERSITY OF ART & DESIGN

Miami, FL

Financial Aid Office, Miami International University of Art & Design, 1737 Bayshore Drive, Miami, FL 33132, 800-225-9023 Ext. 125 or toll-free 800-225-9023. *Fax:* 305-374-7946.

MIAMI REGIONAL UNIVERSITY

Miami Springs, FL

CONTACT Financial Aid Office, Miami Regional University, 700 South Royal Poinciana Boulevard, Miami Springs, FL 33166, 305-442-9223. *Website:* http://www.mru.edu/.

MIAMI UNIVERSITY

Oxford, OH

Tuition & fees (OH res): $14,578	Average undergraduate aid package: $15,056

ABOUT THE INSTITUTION State-related, coed. *Awards:* certificates, associate, bachelor's, master's, and doctoral degrees. 106 undergraduate majors. *Total enrollment:* 19,700. Undergraduates: 17,147. Freshmen: 3,822. Federal methodology is used as a basis for awarding need-based institutional aid.

UNDERGRADUATE EXPENSES for 2017–2018 *Application fee:* $50. *Tuition, state resident:* full-time $13,772. *Tuition, nonresident:* full-time $31,962. *Required fees:* full-time $806. Full-time tuition and fees vary according to location, program, and student level. Part-time tuition and fees vary according to course load, location, program, and student level. *College room and board:* $12,725; *Room only:* $7833. Room and board charges vary according to board plan, housing facility, and student level. *Payment plan:* Guaranteed tuition.

FRESHMAN FINANCIAL AID (Fall 2017, est.) 2,763 applied for aid; of those 58% were deemed to have need. 98% of freshmen with need received aid; of those 29% had need fully met. *Average percent of need met:* 64% (excluding resources awarded to replace EFC). *Average financial aid package:* $16,002 (excluding resources awarded to replace EFC). 28% of all full-time freshmen had no need and received non-need-based gift aid.

UNDERGRADUATE FINANCIAL AID (Fall 2017, est.) 8,490 applied for aid; of those 66% were deemed to have need. 99% of undergraduates with need received aid; of those 24% had need fully met. *Average percent of need met:* 64% (excluding resources awarded to replace EFC). *Average financial aid package:* $15,056 (excluding resources awarded to replace EFC). 31% of all full-time undergraduates had no need and received non-need-based gift aid.

GIFT AID (NEED-BASED) *Total amount:* $50,689,753 (20% federal, 3% state, 77% institutional). *Receiving aid:* Freshmen: 34% (1,358); all full-time undergraduates: 30% (4,782). *Average award:* Freshmen: $12,867; Undergraduates: $11,276. *Scholarships, grants, and awards:* Federal Pell, FSEOG, state, private, college/university gift aid from institutional funds.

GIFT AID (NON-NEED-BASED) *Total amount:* $54,576,121 (94% institutional, 6% external sources). *Receiving aid:* Freshmen: 9% (338). Undergraduates: 5% (870). *Average award:* Freshmen: $9622. Undergraduates: $8931. *Scholarships, grants, and awards by category: Academic interests/achievement:* architecture, education, engineering/technologies, general academic interests/achievements. *Creative arts/performance:* art/fine arts, music, theater/drama. *Special achievements/activities:* general special achievements/activities, leadership. *Special characteristics:* children of faculty/staff, local/state students, members of minority groups, out-of-state students. *Tuition waivers:* Full or partial for employees or children of employees. **ROTC:** Army cooperative, Naval, Air Force.

LOANS *Student loans:* $57,661,730 (30% need-based, 70% non-need-based). 49% of past graduating class borrowed through all loan programs. *Average indebtedness per student:* $29,434. *Average need-based loan:* Freshmen: $4115. Undergraduates: $5187. *Parent loans:* $24,078,770 (100% non-need-based). *Programs:* Federal Direct (Subsidized and Unsubsidized Stafford, PLUS), Perkins, college/university, private loans.

WORK-STUDY Federal work-study. Total amount: $3,398,141, 2,823 jobs averaging $1087.

ATHLETIC AWARDS Total amount: $10,036,754 (100% non-need-based).

APPLYING FOR FINANCIAL AID *Required financial aid form:* FAFSA. *Financial aid deadline (priority):* 2/15. *Notification date:* Continuous beginning 3/20. Students must reply by 5/1 or within 3 weeks of notification.

CONTACT Mr. Brent Shock, Office of Student Financial Aid, Miami University, Campus Avenue Building, Oxford, OH 45056-3427, 513-529-0001. *Fax:* 513-529-8713. *E-mail:* financialaid@miamioh.edu. *Website:* http://miamioh.edu/.

MIAMI UNIVERSITY HAMILTON

Hamilton, OH

CONTACT Financial Aid Office, Miami University Hamilton, 1601 Peck Boulevard, Hamilton, OH 45011-3399, 513-785-3000. *Website:* http://regionals.miamioh.edu/.

MIAMI UNIVERSITY MIDDLETOWN

Middletown, OH

CONTACT Financial Aid Office, Miami University Middletown, 4200 East University Boulevard, Middletown, OH 45042-3497, 513-727-3200 or toll-free 866-426-4643. *Website:* http://regionals.miamioh.edu/.

MICHIGAN STATE UNIVERSITY

East Lansing, MI

Tuition & fees (MI res): $14,460	Average undergraduate aid package: $13,466

ABOUT THE INSTITUTION State-supported, coed. *Awards:* certificates, bachelor's, master's, and doctoral degrees. 156 undergraduate majors. *Total enrollment:* 50,019. Undergraduates: 38,996. Freshmen: 8,366. Federal methodology is used as a basis for awarding need-based institutional aid.

UNDERGRADUATE EXPENSES for 2017–2018 *Application fee:* $65. *Tuition, state resident:* full-time $14,460; part-time $482 per credit hour. *Tuition, nonresident:* full-time $39,405; part-time $1314 per credit hour. Full-time tuition and fees vary according to course load, program, and student level. Part-time tuition and fees vary according to course load, program, and student level. *College room and board:* $9976; *Room only:* $4120. Room and board charges vary according to board plan and housing facility.

FRESHMAN FINANCIAL AID (Fall 2017, est.) 5,868 applied for aid; of those 67% were deemed to have need. 94% of freshmen with need received aid; of those 17% had need fully met. *Average percent of need met:* 61% (excluding resources awarded to replace EFC). *Average financial aid package:* $14,029 (excluding resources awarded to replace EFC). 9% of all full-time freshmen had no need and received non-need-based gift aid.

UNDERGRADUATE FINANCIAL AID (Fall 2017, est.) 21,893 applied for aid; of those 78% were deemed to have need. 97% of undergraduates with need received aid; of those 14% had need fully met. *Average percent of need met:* 59% (excluding resources awarded to replace EFC). *Average financial aid package:* $13,466 (excluding resources awarded to replace EFC). 9% of all full-time undergraduates had no need and received non-need-based gift aid.

GIFT AID (NEED-BASED) *Total amount:* $136,593,777 (31% federal, 5% state, 64% institutional). *Receiving aid:* Freshmen: 31% (2,518); all full-time undergraduates: 34% (12,130). *Average award:* Freshmen: $11,792; Undergraduates: $10,593. *Scholarships, grants, and awards:* Federal Pell, FSEOG, state, private, college/university gift aid from institutional funds, United Negro College Fund.

GIFT AID (NON-NEED-BASED) *Total amount:* $89,445,688 (3% federal, 69% institutional, 28% external sources). *Receiving aid:* Freshmen: 21% (1,708). Undergraduates: 16% (5,545). *Average award:* Freshmen: $10,242. Undergraduates: $10,493. *Scholarships, grants, and awards by category: Academic interests/achievement:* agriculture, biological sciences, business, communication, computer science, education, engineering/technologies, English, foreign languages, general academic interests/achievements, health fields, home economics, international studies, mathematics, military science, physical sciences, social sciences. *Creative arts/performance:* art/fine arts, creative writing, debating, journalism/publications, music, performing arts, theater/drama. *Special achievements/activities:* community service, general special achievements/activities, hobbies/interests, leadership, memberships, rodeo. *Special characteristics:* children and siblings of alumni, children of faculty/staff, children of union members/company employees, first-generation college students, handicapped students, international students, local/state students, out-of-state students, spouses of deceased or disabled public servants, veterans. *Tuition waivers:* Full or partial for employees or children of employees. *ROTC:* Army, Air Force.

LOANS *Student loans:* $135,680,860 (38% need-based, 62% non-need-based). 49% of past graduating class borrowed through all loan programs. *Average indebtedness per student:* $32,310. *Average need-based loan:* Freshmen: $3138. Undergraduates: $4020. *Parent loans:* $79,014,715 (100% non-need-based). *Programs:* Federal Direct (Subsidized and Unsubsidized Stafford, PLUS), college/university.

WORK-STUDY *Federal work-study:* Total amount: $3,521,125; 1,620 jobs averaging $2174.

ATHLETIC AWARDS Total amount: $14,026,307 (38% need-based, 62% non-need-based).

APPLYING FOR FINANCIAL AID *Required financial aid form:* FAFSA. *Financial aid deadline:* Continuous. *Notification date:* Continuous beginning 1/1. Students must reply within 4 weeks of notification.

CONTACT Mr. Keith Williams, Associate Director of Financial Aid, Michigan State University, 252 Student Services Building, East Lansing, MI 48824-1113, 517-353-5940. *Fax:* 517-432-1155. *E-mail:* willi398@msu.edu.
Website: http://www.msu.edu/.

MICHIGAN TECHNOLOGICAL UNIVERSITY
Houghton, MI

Tuition & fees (MI res): $15,074	Average undergraduate aid package: $15,463

ABOUT THE INSTITUTION State-supported, coed. *Awards:* certificates, associate, bachelor's, master's, and doctoral degrees. 56 undergraduate majors. *Total enrollment:* 7,319. Undergraduates: 5,917. Freshmen: 1,323. Federal methodology is used as a basis for awarding need-based institutional aid.

UNDERGRADUATE EXPENSES for 2017–2018 *Tuition, state resident:* full-time $14,774; part-time $558 per credit hour. *Tuition, nonresident:* full-time $32,018; part-time $1186 per credit hour. *Required fees:* full-time $300; $150 per term. Full-time tuition and fees vary according to program and student level. Part-time tuition and fees vary according to course load, program, and student level. *College room and board:* $10,477; *Room only:* $5827. Room and board charges vary according to board plan and housing facility.

FRESHMAN FINANCIAL AID (Fall 2017, est.) 1,218 applied for aid; of those 74% were deemed to have need. 100% of freshmen with need received aid; of those 18% had need fully met. *Average percent of need met:* 79% (excluding resources awarded to replace EFC). *Average financial aid package:* $16,495 (excluding resources awarded to replace EFC). 27% of all full-time freshmen had no need and received non-need-based gift aid.

UNDERGRADUATE FINANCIAL AID (Fall 2017, est.) 4,472 applied for aid; of those 81% were deemed to have need. 100% of undergraduates with need received aid; of those 15% had need fully met. *Average percent of need met:* 71% (excluding resources awarded to replace EFC). *Average financial aid package:* $15,463 (excluding resources awarded to replace EFC). 25% of all full-time undergraduates had no need and received non-need-based gift aid.

GIFT AID (NEED-BASED) *Total amount:* $40,458,160 (16% federal, 7% state, 72% institutional, 5% external sources). *Receiving aid:* Freshmen: 58% (766); all full-time undergraduates: 51% (2,836). *Average award:* Freshmen: $8040; Undergraduates: $7481. *Scholarships, grants, and awards:* Federal Pell, FSEOG, state, private, college/university gift aid from institutional funds.

GIFT AID (NON-NEED-BASED) *Total amount:* $9,251,618 (1% state, 90% institutional, 9% external sources). *Receiving aid:* Freshmen: 59% (779). Undergraduates: 54% (2,957). *Average award:* Freshmen: $5507. Undergraduates: $5679. *Scholarships, grants, and awards by category:* Academic interests/achievement: 27 awards ($103,632 total): business. *Creative arts/performance:* 27 awards ($44,000 total): art/fine arts, performing arts, theater/drama. *Special achievements/activities:* 31 awards ($269,000 total): general special achievements/activities. *Special characteristics:* 1,171 awards ($4,360,852 total): children and siblings of alumni, children of faculty/staff, veterans, veterans' children. *Tuition waivers:* Full or partial for children of alumni, employees or children of employees, senior citizens. *ROTC:* Army, Air Force.

LOANS *Student loans:* $37,552,781 (82% need-based, 18% non-need-based). 69% of past graduating class borrowed through all loan programs. *Average indebtedness per student:* $35,834. *Average need-based loan:* Freshmen: $3331. Undergraduates: $4739. *Parent loans:* $7,778,222 (87% need-based, 13% non-need-based). *Programs:* Federal Direct (Subsidized and Unsubsidized Stafford, PLUS), Perkins, college/university.

WORK-STUDY *Federal work-study:* Total amount: $286,104; 196 jobs averaging $1589.

ATHLETIC AWARDS Total amount: $3,313,816 (33% need-based, 67% non-need-based).

APPLYING FOR FINANCIAL AID *Required financial aid form:* FAFSA. *Financial aid deadline (priority):* 3/1. *Notification date:* Continuous beginning 2/1. Students must reply by 5/1.

CONTACT Mr. Joseph Cooper, Director of Student Financial Services Center, Michigan Technological University, 1400 Townsend Drive, Houghton, MI 49931-1295, 906-487-2622 or toll-free 888-MTU-1885. *Fax:* 906-487-3042. *E-mail:* jjcooper@mtu.edu.
Website: http://www.mtu.edu/.

MID-AMERICA CHRISTIAN UNIVERSITY
Oklahoma City, OK

CONTACT Mr. Todd Martin, Director of Financial Aid, Mid-America Christian University, 3500 Southwest 119th Street, Oklahoma City, OK 73170-4504, 405-691-3800 or toll-free 888-436-3035. *Fax:* 405-692-3165. *E-mail:* tmartin@mabc.edu.
Website: http://www.macu.edu/.

MIDAMERICA NAZARENE UNIVERSITY
Olathe, KS

Tuition & fees: $30,736	Average undergraduate aid package: $25,027

ABOUT THE INSTITUTION Independent Church of the Nazarene, coed. *Awards:* certificates, associate, bachelor's, and master's degrees. 53 undergraduate majors. *Total enrollment:* 1,888. Undergraduates: 1,308. Freshmen: 223. Federal methodology is used as a basis for awarding need-based institutional aid.

UNDERGRADUATE EXPENSES for 2018–2019 *Comprehensive fee:* $39,444 includes full-time tuition ($29,986), mandatory fees ($750), and room and board ($8708). *College room only:* $4834. Full-time tuition and fees vary according to course load, degree level, program, and reciprocity agreements. Room and board charges vary according to board plan and housing facility. *Part-time tuition:* $1119 per credit hour. Part-time tuition and fees vary according to course load, degree level, program, and reciprocity agreements.

FRESHMAN FINANCIAL AID (Fall 2016) 164 applied for aid; of those 93% were deemed to have need. 100% of freshmen with need received aid; of those 75% had need fully met. *Average percent of need met:* 76% (excluding resources awarded to replace EFC). *Average financial aid package:* $25,049 (excluding resources awarded to replace EFC). 15% of all full-time freshmen had no need and received non-need-based gift aid.

UNDERGRADUATE FINANCIAL AID (Fall 2016) 839 applied for aid; of those 95% were deemed to have need. 99% of undergraduates with need received aid; of those 31% had need fully met. *Average percent of need met:* 75% (excluding resources awarded to replace EFC). *Average financial aid package:* $25,027 (excluding resources awarded to replace EFC). 15% of all full-time undergraduates had no need and received non-need-based gift aid.

GIFT AID (NEED-BASED) Total amount: $10,360,977 (19% federal, 5% state, 74% institutional, 2% external sources). **Receiving aid:** Freshmen: 85% (152); all full-time undergraduates: 73% (722). **Average award:** Freshmen: $19,342; Undergraduates: $17,239. **Scholarships, grants, and awards:** Federal Pell, FSEOG, state, private, college/university gift aid from institutional funds.

GIFT AID (NON-NEED-BASED) **Total amount:** $1,694,413 (97% institutional, 3% external sources). **Receiving aid:** Freshmen: 21% (38). Undergraduates: 12% (123). **Average award:** Freshmen: $19,549. Undergraduates: $17,631. **Scholarships, grants, and awards by category:** *Academic interests/achievement:* 820 awards ($6,200,050 total): general academic interests/achievements, religion/biblical studies. *Creative arts/performance:* 56 awards ($128,500 total): art/fine arts, music. *Special achievements/activities:* 435 awards ($3,684,171 total): cheerleading/drum major, general special achievements/activities, leadership. *Special characteristics:* 276 awards ($402,533 total): children of educators, children of faculty/staff, members of minority groups, relatives of clergy, religious affiliation, veterans. **Tuition waivers:** Full or partial for employees or children of employees, senior citizens. **ROTC:** Army cooperative, Air Force cooperative.

LOANS **Student loans:** $8,694,308 (85% need-based, 15% non-need-based). 80% of past graduating class borrowed through all loan programs. *Average indebtedness per student:* $33,018. **Average need-based loan:** Freshmen: $5833. Undergraduates: $7772. **Parent loans:** $1,631,812 (51% need-based, 49% non-need-based). **Programs:** Federal Direct (Subsidized and Unsubsidized Stafford, PLUS), Perkins, college/university.

WORK-STUDY *Federal work-study:* 100 jobs averaging $1370.

ATHLETIC AWARDS Total amount: $3,402,422 (56% need-based, 44% non-need-based).

APPLYING FOR FINANCIAL AID *Required financial aid form:* FAFSA. *Financial aid deadline (priority):* 3/1. *Notification date:* Continuous beginning 11/1. Students must reply within 2 weeks of notification.

CONTACT Cathy Colaipetro, Director of Student Financial Services, MidAmerica Nazarene University, 2030 East College Way, Olathe, KS 66062-1899, 913-971-3298 or toll-free 800-800-8887. *Fax:* 913-971-3482. *E-mail:* ccolaipetro@mnu.edu. *Website:* http://www.mnu.edu/.

MID-ATLANTIC CHRISTIAN UNIVERSITY
Elizabeth City, NC

ABOUT THE INSTITUTION Independent Christian, coed. *Awards:* certificates, associate, and bachelor's degrees. 13 undergraduate majors. **Total enrollment:** 192. Undergraduates: 192. Freshmen: 54.

GIFT AID (NEED-BASED) *Scholarships, grants, and awards:* Federal Pell, FSEOG, state, private, college/university gift aid from institutional funds.

GIFT AID (NON-NEED-BASED) *Scholarships, grants, and awards by category:* *Academic interests/achievement:* general academic interests/achievements, religion/biblical studies. *Special achievements/activities:* general special achievements/activities, religious involvement. *Special characteristics:* children and siblings of alumni, children of faculty/staff, general special characteristics, handicapped students, international students, married students, spouses of current students.

LOANS *Programs:* Federal Direct (Subsidized and Unsubsidized Stafford, PLUS), private loans.

APPLYING FOR FINANCIAL AID *Required financial aid forms:* FAFSA, institution's own form.

CONTACT Jenny Rowland, Financial Aid Administrator, Mid-Atlantic Christian University, 715 North Poindexter Street, Elizabeth City, NC 27909, 252-334-2020 or toll-free 866-996-MACU. *Fax:* 252-334-2064. *E-mail:* jenny.rowland@macuniversity.edu. *Website:* http://www.macuniversity.edu/.

MIDDLEBURY COLLEGE
Middlebury, VT

Tuition & fees: $52,496	Average undergraduate aid package: $50,792

ABOUT THE INSTITUTION Independent, coed. *Awards:* bachelor's, master's, and doctoral degrees. 48 undergraduate majors. **Total enrollment:** 2,603. Undergraduates: 2,561. Freshmen: 635. Both federal and institutional methodology are used as a basis for awarding need-based institutional aid.

UNDERGRADUATE EXPENSES for 2017–2018 *Application fee:* $65. **Comprehensive fee:** $67,464 includes full-time tuition ($52,080), mandatory fees ($416), and room and board ($14,968). **Payment plan:** Tuition prepayment.

FRESHMAN FINANCIAL AID (Fall 2017, est.) 367 applied for aid; of those 79% were deemed to have need. 100% of freshmen with need received aid; of those 100% had need fully met. **Average percent of need met:** 100% (excluding resources awarded to replace EFC). **Average financial aid package:** $50,113 (excluding resources awarded to replace EFC). 1% of all full-time freshmen had no need and received non-need-based gift aid.

UNDERGRADUATE FINANCIAL AID (Fall 2017, est.) 1,344 applied for aid; of those 85% were deemed to have need. 100% of undergraduates with need received aid; of those 100% had need fully met. **Average percent of need met:** 100% (excluding resources awarded to replace EFC). **Average financial aid package:** $50,792 (excluding resources awarded to replace EFC). 1% of all full-time undergraduates had no need and received non-need-based gift aid.

GIFT AID (NEED-BASED) **Total amount:** $55,661,825 (4% federal, 94% institutional, 2% external sources). **Receiving aid:** Freshmen: 46% (290); all full-time undergraduates: 44% (1,114). **Average award:** Freshmen: $47,092; Undergraduates: $47,439. **Scholarships, grants, and awards:** Federal Pell, FSEOG, state, private, college/university gift aid from institutional funds.

GIFT AID (NON-NEED-BASED) **Total amount:** $25,000 (100% institutional). **Average award:** Freshmen: $5000. Undergraduates: $5000. **Tuition waivers:** Full or partial for employees or children of employees. **ROTC:** Army cooperative.

LOANS **Student loans:** $5,166,563 (44% need-based, 56% non-need-based). 46% of past graduating class borrowed through all loan programs. *Average indebtedness per student:* $19,382. **Average need-based loan:** Freshmen: $3118. Undergraduates: $3637. **Parent loans:** $2,300,000 (100% non-need-based). **Programs:** Federal Direct (Subsidized and Unsubsidized Stafford, PLUS), college/university.

WORK-STUDY *Federal work-study:* Total amount: $391,574; jobs available. *State or other work-study/employment:* Total amount: $2,043,624 (26% need-based, 74% non-need-based). Part-time jobs available.

APPLYING FOR FINANCIAL AID *Required financial aid forms:* FAFSA, institution's own form, CSS Financial Aid PROFILE, noncustodial (divorced/separated) parent's statement. *Financial aid deadline:* 2/1 (priority: 11/15). *Notification date:* 4/1. Students must reply by 5/1.

CONTACT Ms. Heidi Sullivan, Student Financial Services Counselor, Middlebury College, Service Building 104, Middlebury, VT 05753, 802-443-5158. *Fax:* 802-443-2065. *E-mail:* studentfinancialservices@middlebury.edu. *Website:* http://www.middlebury.edu/.

MIDDLE GEORGIA STATE UNIVERSITY
Macon, GA

Tuition & fees (GA res): $4608	Average undergraduate aid package: N/A

ABOUT THE INSTITUTION State-supported, coed. *Awards:* certificates, associate, bachelor's, and master's degrees. 27 undergraduate majors. **Total enrollment:** 7,341. Undergraduates: 7,221. Freshmen: 2,209. Federal methodology is used as a basis for awarding need-based institutional aid.

UNDERGRADUATE EXPENSES for 2018–2019 *Application fee:* $30. **Tuition, state resident:** full-time $3326; part-time $110.87 per credit hour. **Tuition, nonresident:** full-time $12,286; part-time $409.54 per credit hour. **Required fees:** full-time $1282. Full-time tuition and fees vary according to program. Part-time tuition and fees vary according to program. **College room and board:** $7614; **Room only:** $5390. Room and board charges vary according to board plan, housing facility, and location.

GIFT AID (NEED-BASED) *Total amount:* $15,266,835 (100% federal). *Scholarships, grants, and awards:* Federal Pell, FSEOG, state, private, college/university gift aid from institutional funds, Zell Miller Scholarships, HOPE Scholarships.
GIFT AID (NON-NEED-BASED) *Total amount:* $3,877,799 (100% state). *Scholarships, grants, and awards by category:* Academic interests/achievement: biological sciences, business, communication, education, engineering/technologies, general academic interests/achievements, health fields, social sciences. *Creative arts/performance:* journalism/publications. *Special characteristics:* local/state students. *Tuition waivers:* Full or partial for employees or children of employees, senior citizens.
LOANS *Student loans:* $26,697,152 (48% need-based, 52% non-need-based). *Parent loans:* $5,441,924 (100% non-need-based). *Programs:* Federal Direct (Subsidized and Unsubsidized Stafford, PLUS), state, college/university.
WORK-STUDY *Federal work-study:* Total amount: $155,390; jobs available. *State or other work-study/employment:* Part-time jobs available.
ATHLETIC AWARDS Total amount: $515,860 (100% non-need-based).
APPLYING FOR FINANCIAL AID *Required financial aid forms:* FAFSA, state aid form. *Financial aid deadline (priority):* 3/15. *Notification date:* 4/20. Students must reply within 2 weeks of notification.
CONTACT Lee Ann Kirkland, Office of Financial Aid, Middle Georgia State University, 100 University Parkway, Macon, GA 31206, 877-238-8664. *Fax:* 478-471-2790. *E-mail:* fainfo@mga.edu.
Website: http://www.mga.edu/.

MIDDLE TENNESSEE STATE UNIVERSITY
Murfreesboro, TN

Tuition & fees (TN res): $8948	Average undergraduate aid package: $10,111

ABOUT THE INSTITUTION State-supported, coed. *Awards:* certificates, bachelor's, master's, and doctoral degrees. 68 undergraduate majors. *Total enrollment:* 21,913. Undergraduates: 19,523. Freshmen: 3,016. Federal methodology is used as a basis for awarding need-based institutional aid.
UNDERGRADUATE EXPENSES for 2017–2018 *Application fee:* $25. *Tuition, state resident:* full-time $7176; part-time $285 per credit hour. *Tuition, nonresident:* full-time $25,806; part-time $1024 per credit hour. *Required fees:* full-time $1772; $74 per credit hour. Full-time tuition and fees vary according to course load. Part-time tuition and fees vary according to course load. *College room and board:* $6408; *Room only:* $5304. Room and board charges vary according to board plan and housing facility.
FRESHMAN FINANCIAL AID (Fall 2017, est.) 2,641 applied for aid; of those 77% were deemed to have need. 99% of freshmen with need received aid; of those 12% had need fully met. *Average percent of need met:* 67% (excluding resources awarded to replace EFC). *Average financial aid package:* $11,039 (excluding resources awarded to replace EFC). 20% of all full-time freshmen had no need and received non-need-based gift aid.
UNDERGRADUATE FINANCIAL AID (Fall 2017, est.) 13,528 applied for aid; of those 80% were deemed to have need. 99% of undergraduates with need received aid; of those 11% had need fully met. *Average percent of need met:* 63% (excluding resources awarded to replace EFC). *Average financial aid package:* $10,111 (excluding resources awarded to replace EFC). 13% of all full-time undergraduates had no need and received non-need-based gift aid.
GIFT AID (NEED-BASED) *Total amount:* $46,768,483 (76% federal, 24% state). *Receiving aid:* Freshmen: 48% (1,312); all full-time undergraduates: 49% (7,092). *Average award:* Freshmen: $6910; Undergraduates: $6170. *Scholarships, grants, and awards:* Federal Pell, FSEOG, state, private, college/university gift aid from institutional funds.
GIFT AID (NON-NEED-BASED) *Total amount:* $54,701,631 (10% federal, 46% state, 26% institutional, 18% external sources). *Receiving aid:* Freshmen: 63% (1,728). Undergraduates: 44% (6,431). *Average award:* Freshmen: $7823. Undergraduates: $8161. *Scholarships, grants, and awards by category:* Academic interests/achievement: 673 awards ($1,128,600 total): agriculture, area/ethnic studies, biological sciences, business, communication, computer science, education, engineering/technologies, English, foreign languages, health fields, home economics, humanities, international studies, mathematics, military science, physical sciences,

premedicine, social sciences. *Creative arts/performance:* 561 awards ($922,673 total): art/fine arts, creative writing, dance, debating, journalism/publications, music, performing arts, theater/drama. *Special achievements/activities:* 2,440 awards ($7,790,097 total): cheerleading/drum major, general special achievements/activities, hobbies/interests, leadership, memberships. *Special characteristics:* 2,687 awards ($3,587,506 total): adult students, children and siblings of alumni, ethnic background, first-generation college students, general special characteristics, handicapped students, international students, local/state students, members of minority groups. *Tuition waivers:* Full or partial for employees or children of employees. *ROTC:* Army, Air Force cooperative.
LOANS *Student loans:* $65,359,250 (47% need-based, 53% non-need-based). 63% of past graduating class borrowed through all loan programs. *Average indebtedness per student:* $25,717. *Average need-based loan:* Freshmen: $3157. Undergraduates: $4001. *Parent loans:* $11,175,083 (100% non-need-based). *Programs:* Federal Direct (Subsidized and Unsubsidized Stafford, PLUS), Perkins, state, college/university.
WORK-STUDY *Federal work-study:* Total amount: $707,096; 336 jobs averaging $2095.
ATHLETIC AWARDS Total amount: $7,638,721 (100% non-need-based).
APPLYING FOR FINANCIAL AID *Required financial aid form:* FAFSA. *Financial aid deadline (priority):* 1/17. *Notification date:* Continuous beginning 2/15. Students must reply by 6/1.
CONTACT Stephen White, Director of Financial Aid, Middle Tennessee State University, SSAC 260, 1301 East Main Street, Murfreesboro, TN 37132, 615-898-5454 or toll-free 800-331-MTSU. *Fax:* 615-898-5167. *E-mail:* stephen.white@mtsu.edu. *Website:* http://www.mtsu.edu/.

MIDLAND COLLEGE
Midland, TX

ABOUT THE INSTITUTION State and locally supported, coed. *Awards:* certificates, associate, and bachelor's degrees. 27 undergraduate majors. *Total enrollment:* 5,564. Undergraduates: 5,564. Freshmen: 780.
GIFT AID (NEED-BASED) *Scholarships, grants, and awards:* Federal Pell, FSEOG, state, private, college/university gift aid from institutional funds.
WORK-STUDY Federal work-study jobs available. *State or other work-study/employment:* Part-time jobs available.
APPLYING FOR FINANCIAL AID *Required financial aid form:* FAFSA.
CONTACT Yolanda Ramos, Director of Financial Aid, Midland College, 3600 North Garfield, Midland, TX 79705, 432-685-5511. *Fax:* 432-685-6451. *E-mail:* finaid@midland.edu.
Website: http://www.midland.edu/.

MIDLAND UNIVERSITY
Fremont, NE

CONTACT Penny James, Director of Financial Aid, Midland University, 900 North Clarkson Street, Fremont, NE 68025-4200, 402-721-5480 Ext. 6520 or toll-free 800-642-8382 Ext. 6501. *Fax:* 402-721-0250. *E-mail:* finaid@mlc.edu.
Website: http://www.midlandu.edu/.

MID-SOUTH CHRISTIAN COLLEGE
Memphis, TN

Tuition & fees: $6658	Average undergraduate aid package: $6000

ABOUT THE INSTITUTION Independent, coed. Federal methodology is used as a basis for awarding need-based institutional aid.
UNDERGRADUATE EXPENSES for 2017–2018 *One-time required fee:* $365. *Comprehensive fee:* $10,058 includes full-time tuition ($5568), mandatory fees ($1090), and room and board ($3400). *College room only:* $1800. Full-time tuition and fees vary according to course load and program. Room and board charges

vary according to board plan and housing facility. *Part-time tuition:* $174 per credit hour. *Part-time fees:* $20 per credit hour; $225 per term. Part-time tuition and fees vary according to course load. *Payment plan:* Guaranteed tuition.

FRESHMAN FINANCIAL AID (Fall 2017, est.) 6 applied for aid; of those 100% were deemed to have need. 100% of freshmen with need received aid; of those 67% had need fully met. *Average percent of need met:* 90% (excluding resources awarded to replace EFC). *Average financial aid package:* $6000 (excluding resources awarded to replace EFC).

UNDERGRADUATE FINANCIAL AID (Fall 2017, est.) 18 applied for aid; of those 100% were deemed to have need. 100% of undergraduates with need received aid; of those 61% had need fully met. *Average percent of need met:* 90% (excluding resources awarded to replace EFC). *Average financial aid package:* $6000 (excluding resources awarded to replace EFC).

GIFT AID (NEED-BASED) Total amount: $22,957 (100% federal). *Receiving aid:* Freshmen: 100% (6); all full-time undergraduates: 100% (18). *Average award:* Freshmen: $6000; Undergraduates: $6000. *Scholarships, grants, and awards:* Federal Pell, FSEOG.

GIFT AID (NON-NEED-BASED) Total amount: $14,644 (100% institutional). *Tuition waivers:* Full or partial for employees or children of employees.

WORK-STUDY Federal work-study jobs available. *State or other work-study/employment:* Total amount: $53,072 (100% need-based). 11 part-time jobs averaging $2400.

APPLYING FOR FINANCIAL AID *Required financial aid form:* FAFSA. *Financial aid deadline:* Continuous. *Notification date:* Continuous beginning 6/15.

CONTACT Mrs. Mary Jackson, Director of Financial Aid, Mid-South Christian College, PO Box 181056, Memphis, TN 38181, 901-375-4400. *Fax:* 901-375-4085. *E-mail:* info@midsouthchristian.edu.
Website: http://www.midsouthchristian.edu/.

MIDSTATE COLLEGE
Peoria, IL

CONTACT Financial Aid Office, Midstate College, 411 West Northmoor Road, Peoria, IL 61614, 309-692-4092 or toll-free 800-251-4299.
Website: http://www.midstate.edu/.

MIDWAY UNIVERSITY
Midway, KY

ABOUT THE INSTITUTION Independent Christian Church (Disciples of Christ), coed. 26 undergraduate majors.

GIFT AID (NEED-BASED) *Scholarships, grants, and awards:* Federal Pell, FSEOG, state, private, college/university gift aid from institutional funds.

GIFT AID (NON-NEED-BASED) *Scholarships, grants, and awards by category:* Academic interests/achievement: agriculture, business, general academic interests/achievements, premedicine. *Creative arts/performance:* music. *Special achievements/activities:* cheerleading/drum major, general special achievements/activities, junior miss, leadership, religious involvement. *Special characteristics:* adult students, children and siblings of alumni, children of faculty/staff, members of minority groups, previous college experience, relatives of clergy, religious affiliation, veterans.

LOANS *Programs:* Federal Direct (Subsidized and Unsubsidized Stafford, PLUS), Perkins.

APPLYING FOR FINANCIAL AID *Required financial aid forms:* FAFSA, institution's own form.

CONTACT Justin Cristello, Director of Student Financial Planning, Midway University, 512 East Stephens Street, Midway, KY 40347-1120, 859-846-5340 or toll-free 800-755-0031. *Fax:* 859-846-5751. *E-mail:* faid@midway.edu.
Website: http://www.midway.edu/.

MIDWESTERN STATE UNIVERSITY
Wichita Falls, TX

Tuition & fees: N/R	Average undergraduate aid package: $10,091

ABOUT THE INSTITUTION State-supported, coed. 73 undergraduate majors. Federal methodology is used as a basis for awarding need-based institutional aid.

FRESHMAN FINANCIAL AID (Fall 2017, est.) 697 applied for aid; of those 76% were deemed to have need. 100% of freshmen with need received aid; of those 44% had need fully met. *Average percent of need met:* 67% (excluding resources awarded to replace EFC). *Average financial aid package:* $11,228 (excluding resources awarded to replace EFC). 14% of all full-time freshmen had no need and received non-need-based gift aid.

UNDERGRADUATE FINANCIAL AID (Fall 2017, est.) 3,587 applied for aid; of those 73% were deemed to have need. 100% of undergraduates with need received aid; of those 49% had need fully met. *Average percent of need met:* 62% (excluding resources awarded to replace EFC). *Average financial aid package:* $10,091 (excluding resources awarded to replace EFC). 18% of all full-time undergraduates had no need and received non-need-based gift aid.

GIFT AID (NEED-BASED) Total amount: $18,421,306 (55% federal, 22% state, 21% institutional, 2% external sources). *Receiving aid:* Freshmen: 60% (487); all full-time undergraduates: 55% (2,304). *Average award:* Freshmen: $8452; Undergraduates: $7239. *Scholarships, grants, and awards:* Federal Pell, FSEOG, state, private, college/university gift aid from institutional funds, state nursing scholarships.

GIFT AID (NON-NEED-BASED) Total amount: $2,366,362 (1% federal, 86% institutional, 13% external sources). *Receiving aid:* Freshmen: 5% (41). Undergraduates: 4% (167). *Average award:* Freshmen: $2151. Undergraduates: $2342. *Scholarships, grants, and awards by category:* Academic interests/achievement: biological sciences, business, communication, computer science, education, engineering/technologies, English, foreign languages, general academic interests/achievements, health fields, humanities, international studies, mathematics, physical sciences, premedicine, social sciences. *Creative arts/performance:* art/fine arts, creative writing, general creative arts/performance, journalism/publications, music, theater/drama. *Special achievements/activities:* cheerleading/drum major, general special achievements/activities, leadership. *Special characteristics:* children and siblings of alumni, children of faculty/staff, children of union members/company employees, children of workers in trades, children with a deceased or disabled parent, first-generation college students, handicapped students, international students, members of minority groups, veterans, veterans' children.

LOANS *Student loans:* $24,780,380 (82% need-based, 18% non-need-based). 66% of past graduating class borrowed through all loan programs. *Average indebtedness per student:* $28,468. *Average need-based loan:* Freshmen: $5808. Undergraduates: $7240. *Parent loans:* $7,273,904 (57% need-based, 43% non-need-based). *Programs:* Federal Direct (Subsidized and Unsubsidized Stafford, PLUS), state, college/university, private loans.

WORK-STUDY *Federal work-study:* Total amount: $254,304; jobs available. *State or other work-study/employment:* Part-time jobs available.

ATHLETIC AWARDS Total amount: $1,501,176 (50% need-based, 50% non-need-based).

APPLYING FOR FINANCIAL AID *Required financial aid forms:* FAFSA, institution's own form, verification documents including tax transcript and verification worksheet. *Financial aid deadline (priority):* 3/1. *Notification date:* Continuous beginning 4/15. Students must reply within 4 weeks of notification.

CONTACT Ms. Kathy Browning, Director of Financial Aid, Midwestern State University, 3410 Taft Boulevard, Wichita Falls, TX 76308, 940-397-4214 or toll-free 800-842-1922. *Fax:* 940-397-4852. *E-mail:* financial-aid@mwsu.edu.
Website: http://www.mwsu.edu/.

MIDWEST UNIVERSITY
Wentzville, MO

CONTACT Financial Aid Office, Midwest University, 851 Parr Road, Wentzville, MO 63385, 636-327-4645.
Website: http://www.midwest.edu/.

MIDWIVES COLLEGE OF UTAH
Salt Lake City, UT

CONTACT Financial Aid Office, Midwives College of Utah, 1174 East 2700 South, Suite 2, Salt Lake City, UT 84106, 801-764-9068 or toll-free 866-680-2756. *Website:* http://www.midwifery.edu/.

MILES COLLEGE
Fairfield, AL

CONTACT P. N. Lanier, Financial Aid Administrator, Miles College, PO Box 3800, Birmingham, AL 35208, 205-929-1663 or toll-free 800-445-0708 (out-of-state). *Fax:* 205-929-1668. *E-mail:* pnlani@netscape.net. *Website:* http://www.miles.edu/.

MILLENNIA ATLANTIC UNIVERSITY
Doral, FL

Tuition & fees: N/R	Average undergraduate aid package: $23,660

ABOUT THE INSTITUTION Proprietary, coed. 8 undergraduate majors. Federal methodology is used as a basis for awarding need-based institutional aid.

UNDERGRADUATE FINANCIAL AID (Fall 2017, est.) 10 applied for aid; of those 100% were deemed to have need. 100% of undergraduates with need received aid. *Average percent of need met:* 100% (excluding resources awarded to replace EFC). *Average financial aid package:* $23,660 (excluding resources awarded to replace EFC).

GIFT AID (NEED-BASED) *Total amount:* $9193 (74% federal, 26% state). *Receiving aid:* All full-time undergraduates: 20% (2). *Average award:* Undergraduates: $9244. *Scholarships, grants, and awards:* Federal Pell, FSEOG, state, college/university gift aid from institutional funds.

LOANS *Student loans:* $61,819 (100% need-based). *Average need-based loan:* Undergraduates: $14,028. *Programs:* Federal Direct (Subsidized and Unsubsidized Stafford, PLUS), private loans.

WORK-STUDY *Federal work-study:* Total amount: $7045; 1 job averaging $7045.

APPLYING FOR FINANCIAL AID *Required financial aid forms:* FAFSA, institution's own form. *Financial aid deadline:* Continuous. *Notification date:* Continuous beginning 7/1. Students must reply by 8/1 or within 2 weeks of notification.

CONTACT Mrs. Maria C. Velar, Financial Aid Manager, Millennia Atlantic University, 3801 NW 97th Avenue, Suite 100, Doral, FL 33178, 785-331-1000 Ext. 202. *E-mail:* mvelar@maufl.edu. *Website:* http://www.maufl.edu/.

MILLERSVILLE UNIVERSITY OF PENNSYLVANIA
Millersville, PA

Tuition & fees (PA res): $11,858	Average undergraduate aid package: $8467

ABOUT THE INSTITUTION State-supported, coed. *Awards:* certificates, associate, bachelor's, master's, and doctoral degrees. 38 undergraduate majors. *Total enrollment:* 7,720. Undergraduates: 6,758. Freshmen: 1,351. Federal methodology is used as a basis for awarding need-based institutional aid.

UNDERGRADUATE EXPENSES for 2017–2018 *Application fee:* $50. *Tuition, state resident:* full-time $9270; part-time $309 per credit. *Tuition, nonresident:* full-time $18,730; part-time $780 per credit. *Required fees:* full-time $2588; $88.50 per credit or $20 per credit. Full-time tuition and fees vary according to course load. Part-time tuition and fees vary according to course load. *College room and board:* $13,440. Room and board charges vary according to board plan and housing facility.

FRESHMAN FINANCIAL AID (Fall 2016) 1,204 applied for aid; of those 77% were deemed to have need. 97% of freshmen with need received aid; of those 6% had need fully met. *Average percent of need met:* 54% (excluding resources awarded to replace EFC). *Average financial aid package:* $7836 (excluding resources awarded to replace EFC). 7% of all full-time freshmen had no need and received non-need-based gift aid.

UNDERGRADUATE FINANCIAL AID (Fall 2016) 4,918 applied for aid; of those 83% were deemed to have need. 97% of undergraduates with need received aid; of those 4% had need fully met. *Average percent of need met:* 58% (excluding resources awarded to replace EFC). *Average financial aid package:* $8467 (excluding resources awarded to replace EFC). 4% of all full-time undergraduates had no need and received non-need-based gift aid.

GIFT AID (NEED-BASED) *Total amount:* $17,723,377 (47% federal, 34% state, 14% institutional, 5% external sources). *Receiving aid:* Freshmen: 50% (647); all full-time undergraduates: 48% (2,854). *Average award:* Freshmen: $5615; Undergraduates: $5884. *Scholarships, grants, and awards:* Federal Pell, FSEOG, state, private, college/university gift aid from institutional funds, Schock Scholarships.

GIFT AID (NON-NEED-BASED) *Total amount:* $3,010,558 (1% federal, 9% state, 54% institutional, 36% external sources). *Receiving aid:* Freshmen: 16% (204). Undergraduates: 8% (458). *Average award:* Freshmen: $2960. Undergraduates: $2867. *Scholarships, grants, and awards by category: Academic interests/ achievement:* 970 awards ($2,636,895 total): biological sciences, business, communication, computer science, education, English, foreign languages, general academic interests/achievements, home economics, humanities, mathematics, physical sciences, social sciences. *Creative arts/performance:* 40 awards ($43,846 total): art/fine arts, music. *Special achievements/activities:* 4 awards ($7641 total): community service. *Special characteristics:* 107 awards ($782,546 total): children of union members/ company employees, international students. *Tuition waivers:* Full or partial for employees or children of employees, senior citizens. *ROTC:* Army.

LOANS *Student loans:* $35,221,247 (42% need-based, 58% non-need-based). 72% of past graduating class borrowed through all loan programs. *Average indebtedness per student:* $31,476. *Average need-based loan:* Freshmen: $3292. Undergraduates: $4085. *Parent loans:* $12,225,660 (100% non-need-based). *Programs:* Federal Direct (Subsidized and Unsubsidized Stafford, PLUS), college/university, private loans.

WORK-STUDY *Federal work-study:* 231 jobs averaging $1367. *State or other work-study/employment:* Total amount: $1,999,119 (100% non-need-based). 1,452 part-time jobs averaging $1377.

ATHLETIC AWARDS Total amount: $575,278 (37% need-based, 63% non-need-based).

APPLYING FOR FINANCIAL AID *Required financial aid form:* FAFSA. *Financial aid deadline (priority):* 3/15. *Notification date:* Continuous beginning 3/19. Students must reply within 2 weeks of notification.

CONTACT Mr. Dwight G. Horsey, Director of Financial Aid, Millersville University of Pennsylvania, PO Box 1002, Millersville, PA 17551-0302, 717-871-5100 or toll-free 800-MU-ADMIT. *Fax:* 717-871-7980. *E-mail:* dwight.horsey@millersville.edu. *Website:* http://www.millersville.edu/.

MILLIGAN COLLEGE
Milligan College, TN

Tuition & fees: $33,700	Average undergraduate aid package: $24,449

ABOUT THE INSTITUTION Independent Christian, coed. *Awards:* bachelor's, master's, and doctoral degrees. 26 undergraduate majors. *Total enrollment:* 1,171. Undergraduates: 859. Freshmen: 204. Federal methodology is used as a basis for awarding need-based institutional aid.

UNDERGRADUATE EXPENSES for 2018–2019 *Application fee:* $30. *Comprehensive fee:* $40,800 includes full-time tuition ($32,500), mandatory fees ($1200), and room and board ($7100). *College room only:* $3550. Full-time tuition and fees vary according to course load and degree level. Room and board charges vary according to housing facility. *Part-time fees:* $905 per semester hour; $375 per term. Part-time tuition and fees vary according to course load and degree level.

FRESHMAN FINANCIAL AID (Fall 2017, est.) 181 applied for aid; of those 88% were deemed to have need. 100% of freshmen with need received aid; of those 29% had need fully met. *Average percent of need met:* 79% (excluding resources awarded to replace EFC). *Average financial aid package:* $25,604 (excluding

resources awarded to replace EFC). 15% of all full-time freshmen had no need and received non-need-based gift aid.

UNDERGRADUATE FINANCIAL AID (Fall 2017, est.) 713 applied for aid; of those 88% were deemed to have need. 100% of undergraduates with need received aid; of those 26% had need fully met. *Average percent of need met:* 77% (excluding resources awarded to replace EFC). *Average financial aid package:* $24,449 (excluding resources awarded to replace EFC). 15% of all full-time undergraduates had no need and received non-need-based gift aid.

GIFT AID (NEED-BASED) *Total amount:* $9,039,460 (13% federal, 14% state, 69% institutional, 4% external sources). *Receiving aid:* Freshmen: 83% (160); all full-time undergraduates: 82% (626). *Average award:* Freshmen: $22,314; Undergraduates: $20,974. *Scholarships, grants, and awards:* Federal Pell, FSEOG, state, private, college/university gift aid from institutional funds.

GIFT AID (NON-NEED-BASED) *Total amount:* $2,234,484 (19% state, 73% institutional, 8% external sources). *Receiving aid:* Freshmen: 21% (40). Undergraduates: 16% (125). *Average award:* Freshmen: $12,252. Undergraduates: $11,258. *Scholarships, grants, and awards by category: Academic interests/achievement:* 580 awards ($6,488,282 total): engineering/technologies, general academic interests/achievements. *Creative arts/performance:* 54 awards ($310,350 total): art/fine arts, cinema/film/broadcasting, dance, music, theater/drama. *Special achievements/activities:* 49 awards ($250,750 total): cheerleading/drum major, community service. *Special characteristics:* 28 awards ($781,419 total): children of faculty/staff. *Tuition waivers:* Full or partial for employees or children of employees.

LOANS *Student loans:* $4,089,640 (73% need-based, 27% non-need-based). 64% of past graduating class borrowed through all loan programs. *Average indebtedness per student:* $29,277. *Average need-based loan:* Freshmen: $4963. Undergraduates: $4760. *Parent loans:* $1,323,856 (45% need-based, 55% non-need-based). *Programs:* Federal Direct (Subsidized and Unsubsidized Stafford, PLUS), Perkins, alternative loans.

WORK-STUDY *Federal work-study:* Total amount: $136,085; 113 jobs averaging $1200. *State or other work-study/employment:* Total amount: $198,601 (13% need-based, 87% non-need-based). 132 part-time jobs averaging $1504.

ATHLETIC AWARDS Total amount: $4,701,070 (68% need-based, 32% non-need-based).

APPLYING FOR FINANCIAL AID *Required financial aid form:* FAFSA. *Financial aid deadline (priority):* 12/1. *Notification date:* Continuous beginning 12/1. Students must reply within 2 weeks of notification.

CONTACT Diane Keasling, Coordinator of Financial Aid, Milligan College, PO Box 250, Milligan College, TN 37682, 423-461-8968 or toll-free 800-262-8337. *Fax:* 423-929-2368. *E-mail:* dlkeasling@milligan.edu. *Website:* http://www.milligan.edu/.

MILLIKIN UNIVERSITY
Decatur, IL

Tuition & fees: $33,066	Average undergraduate aid package: $24,841

ABOUT THE INSTITUTION Independent Presbyterian Church (U.S.A.), coed. *Awards:* certificates, bachelor's, master's, and doctoral degrees. 57 undergraduate majors. *Total enrollment:* 2,040. Undergraduates: 1,950. Freshmen: 474. Federal methodology is used as a basis for awarding need-based institutional aid.

UNDERGRADUATE EXPENSES for 2017–2018 *Comprehensive fee:* $44,148 includes full-time tuition ($32,274), mandatory fees ($792), and room and board ($11,082). *College room only:* $8356. Room and board charges vary according to board plan, housing facility, and student level. *Part-time tuition:* $465 per credit hour. *Part-time fees:* $22 per credit hour.

FRESHMAN FINANCIAL AID (Fall 2016) 424 applied for aid; of those 88% were deemed to have need. 100% of freshmen with need received aid; of those 35% had need fully met. *Average percent of need met:* 86% (excluding resources awarded to replace EFC). *Average financial aid package:* $27,477 (excluding resources awarded to replace EFC). 11% of all full-time freshmen had no need and received non-need-based gift aid.

UNDERGRADUATE FINANCIAL AID (Fall 2016) 1,636 applied for aid; of those 91% were deemed to have need. 100% of undergraduates with need received aid; of those 37% had need fully met. *Average percent of need met:* 85% (excluding resources awarded to replace EFC). *Average financial aid package:* $24,841 (excluding resources awarded to replace EFC). 8% of all full-time undergraduates had no need and received non-need-based gift aid.

GIFT AID (NEED BASED) *Total amount:* $11,211,220 (29% federal, 28% state, 43% institutional). *Receiving aid:* Freshmen: 70% (310); all full-time undergraduates: 71% (1,273). *Average award:* Freshmen: $8345; Undergraduates: $8596. *Scholarships, grants, and awards:* Federal Pell, FSEOG, state, private, college/university gift aid from institutional funds.

GIFT AID (NON-NEED-BASED) *Total amount:* $24,767,563 (97% institutional, 3% external sources). *Receiving aid:* Freshmen: 84% (374). Undergraduates: 79% (1,411). *Average award:* Freshmen: $18,468. Undergraduates: $16,300. *Scholarships, grants, and awards by category: Academic interests/achievement:* 1,867 awards ($22,214,161 total): biological sciences, business, communication, education, English, foreign languages, general academic interests/achievements, home economics, humanities, international studies, mathematics, physical sciences, premedicine. *Creative arts/performance:* 466 awards ($1,186,650 total): art/fine arts, creative writing, dance, music, theater/drama. *Special achievements/activities:* 50 awards ($95,293 total): community service, general special achievements/activities, leadership. *Special characteristics:* 208 awards ($858,317 total): children and siblings of alumni, children of faculty/staff, children of union members/company employees, children with a deceased or disabled parent, general special characteristics, international students, parents of current students, previous college experience, relatives of clergy, siblings of current students, veterans. *Tuition waivers:* Full or partial for employees or children of employees.

LOANS *Student loans:* $12,508,098 (45% need-based, 55% non-need-based). 83% of past graduating class borrowed through all loan programs. *Average indebtedness per student:* $33,146. *Average need-based loan:* Freshmen: $4556. Undergraduates: $4644. *Parent loans:* $4,398,199 (100% non-need-based). *Programs:* Federal Direct (Subsidized and Unsubsidized Stafford, PLUS), Perkins, private loans.

WORK-STUDY *Federal work-study:* 439 jobs averaging $1013. *State or other work-study/employment:* Total amount: $289,616 (100% non-need-based). 440 part-time jobs averaging $658.

APPLYING FOR FINANCIAL AID *Required financial aid form:* FAFSA. *Financial aid deadline (priority):* 1/15. *Notification date:* Continuous beginning 1/15. Students must reply by 5/1 or within 4 weeks of notification.

CONTACT Cheryl Howerton, Director of Financial Aid, Millikin University, 1184 West Main Street, Decatur, IL 62522-2084, 217-424-6317 or toll-free 800-373-7733. *Fax:* 217-424-5070. *E-mail:* studentfinancialservices@millikin.edu. *Website:* http://www.millikin.edu/.

MILLSAPS COLLEGE
Jackson, MS

Tuition & fees: $39,910	Average undergraduate aid package: $34,823

ABOUT THE INSTITUTION Independent United Methodist, coed. *Awards:* bachelor's and master's degrees. 31 undergraduate majors. *Total enrollment:* 859. Undergraduates: 807. Freshmen: 229. Federal methodology is used as a basis for awarding need-based institutional aid.

UNDERGRADUATE EXPENSES for 2018–2019 *Comprehensive fee:* $53,640 includes full-time tuition ($37,290), mandatory fees ($2620), and room and board ($13,730). *College room only:* $7680. Room and board charges vary according to board plan and housing facility. *Part-time tuition:* $1150 per semester hour. *Part-time fees:* $38 per semester hour.

FRESHMAN FINANCIAL AID (Fall 2016) 205 applied for aid; of those 86% were deemed to have need. 100% of freshmen with need received aid; of those 23% had need fully met. *Average percent of need met:* 78% (excluding resources awarded to replace EFC). *Average financial aid package:* $35,521 (excluding resources awarded to replace EFC). 23% of all full-time freshmen had no need and received non-need-based gift aid.

UNDERGRADUATE FINANCIAL AID (Fall 2016) 586 applied for aid; of those 88% were deemed to have need. 100% of undergraduates with need received aid; of those 20% had need fully met. *Average percent of need met:* 77% (excluding resources awarded to replace EFC). *Average financial aid package:* $34,823 (excluding resources awarded to replace EFC). 34% of all full-time undergraduates had no need and received non-need-based gift aid.

GIFT AID (NEED-BASED) *Total amount:* $14,631,477 (9% federal, 3% state, 87% institutional, 1% external sources). *Receiving aid:* Freshmen: 76% (175); all full-time undergraduates: 65% (515). *Average award:* Freshmen: $29,260; Undergraduates: $28,403. *Scholarships, grants, and awards:* Federal Pell, FSEOG, state, private, college/university gift aid from institutional funds.

GIFT AID (NON-NEED-BASED) *Total amount:* $7,674,658 (2% state, 96% institutional, 2% external sources). *Receiving aid:* Freshmen: 15% (35). Undergraduates: 10% (80). *Average award:* Freshmen: $27,240. Undergraduates: $24,511. *Scholarships, grants, and awards by category: Academic interests/ achievement:* business, general academic interests/achievements. *Creative arts/performance:* art/fine arts, music, theater/drama. *Special achievements/activities:* community service, general special achievements/activities, hobbies/interests, leadership, religious involvement. *Special characteristics:* adult students, children of faculty/staff, ethnic background, first-generation college students, local/state students, religious affiliation. *Tuition waivers:* Full or partial for employees or children of employees. *ROTC:* Army cooperative, Air Force cooperative.

LOANS *Student loans:* $4,499,772 (70% need-based, 30% non-need-based). 58% of past graduating class borrowed through all loan programs. *Average indebtedness per student:* $33,569. *Average need-based loan:* Freshmen: $3421. Undergraduates: $4671. *Parent loans:* $2,725,189 (43% need-based, 57% non-need-based). *Programs:* Federal Direct (Subsidized and Unsubsidized Stafford, PLUS), Perkins.

WORK-STUDY *Federal work-study:* jobs available.

APPLYING FOR FINANCIAL AID *Required financial aid form:* FAFSA. *Financial aid deadline (priority):* 3/1. *Notification date:* Continuous beginning 3/15. Students must reply by 5/1 or within 2 weeks of notification.

CONTACT Isabelle Higbee, Director of Financial Aid, Millsaps College, 1701 North State Street, Jackson, MS 39210-0001, 601-974-1220 or toll-free 800-352-1050. *Fax:* 601-974-1224. *E-mail:* financialaid@millsaps.edu. *Website:* http://www.millsaps.edu/.

MILLS COLLEGE
Oakland, CA

Tuition & fees: $30,257	Average undergraduate aid package: $43,655

ABOUT THE INSTITUTION Independent, undergraduate: women only; graduate: coed. *Awards:* certificates, bachelor's, master's, and doctoral degrees. 31 undergraduate majors. *Total enrollment:* 1,309. Undergraduates: 768. Freshmen: 174. Federal methodology is used as a basis for awarding need-based institutional aid.

UNDERGRADUATE EXPENSES for 2018–2019 *Application fee:* $50. *Comprehensive fee:* $43,705 includes full-time tuition ($28,765), mandatory fees ($1492), and room and board ($13,448). *College room only:* $7064. Full-time tuition and fees vary according to course load. Room and board charges vary according to board plan and housing facility. *Part-time tuition:* $1199 per semester hour. Part-time tuition and fees vary according to course load.

FRESHMAN FINANCIAL AID (Fall 2017, est.) 163 applied for aid; of those 94% were deemed to have need. 100% of freshmen with need received aid; of those 18% had need fully met. *Average percent of need met:* 85% (excluding resources awarded to replace EFC). *Average financial aid package:* $49,500 (excluding resources awarded to replace EFC). 8% of all full-time freshmen had no need and received non-need-based gift aid.

UNDERGRADUATE FINANCIAL AID (Fall 2017, est.) 666 applied for aid; of those 95% were deemed to have need. 100% of undergraduates with need received aid; of those 10% had need fully met. *Average percent of need met:* 78% (excluding resources awarded to replace EFC). *Average financial aid package:* $43,655 (excluding resources awarded to replace EFC). 5% of all full-time undergraduates had no need and received non-need-based gift aid.

GIFT AID (NEED-BASED) *Total amount:* $22,439,186 (9% federal, 11% state, 79% institutional, 1% external sources). *Receiving aid:* Freshmen: 82% (141); all full-time undergraduates: 80% (586). *Average award:* Freshmen: $44,523; Undergraduates: $38,265. *Scholarships, grants, and awards:* Federal Pell, FSEOG, state, private, college/university gift aid from institutional funds.

GIFT AID (NON-NEED-BASED) *Total amount:* $614,603 (100% institutional). *Receiving aid:* Freshmen: 88% (151). Undergraduates: 85% (623). *Average award:* Freshmen: $21,528. Undergraduates: $19,571. *Scholarships, grants, and awards by category: Academic interests/achievement:* biological sciences, computer science, general academic interests/achievements, mathematics, physical sciences, premedicine. *Creative arts/performance:* music. *Special achievements/activities:* leadership. *Tuition waivers:* Full or partial for employees or children of employees. *ROTC:* Army cooperative.

LOANS *Student loans:* $4,523,769 (99% need-based, 1% non-need-based). 75% of past graduating class borrowed through all loan programs. *Average indebtedness per student:* $29,954. *Average need-based loan:* Freshmen: $4760. Undergraduates: $7481. *Parent loans:* $1,287,118 (97% need-based, 3% non-need-based). *Programs:* Federal Direct (Subsidized and Unsubsidized Stafford, PLUS), Perkins, college/university.

WORK-STUDY *Federal work-study:* Total amount: $446,597; 191 jobs averaging $2338. *State or other work-study/employment:* Part-time jobs available.

APPLYING FOR FINANCIAL AID *Required financial aid forms:* FAFSA, state aid form. *Financial aid deadline:* 2/15 (priority: 2/1). *Notification date:* Continuous beginning 3/1. Students must reply by 5/1 or within 4 weeks of notification.

CONTACT Mr. Dustin Smith-Salinas, Director of Financial Aid, Mills College, 5000 MacArthur Boulevard, Oakland, CA 94613, 510-430-2039 or toll-free 800-87-MILLS. *Fax:* 510-430-2003. *E-mail:* dsmithsalinas@mills.edu. *Website:* http://www.mills.edu/.

MILWAUKEE INSTITUTE OF ART AND DESIGN
Milwaukee, WI

CONTACT Carol Masse, Director of Financial Aid, Milwaukee Institute of Art and Design, 273 East Erie Street, Milwaukee, WI 53202-6003, 414-291-3272 or toll-free 888-749-MIAD. *Fax:* 414-291-8077. *E-mail:* carolmasse@miad.edu. *Website:* http://www.miad.edu/.

MILWAUKEE SCHOOL OF ENGINEERING
Milwaukee, WI

Tuition & fees: $40,749	Average undergraduate aid package: $28,577

ABOUT THE INSTITUTION Independent, coed, primarily men. *Awards:* bachelor's and master's degrees. 16 undergraduate majors. *Total enrollment:* 2,823. Undergraduates: 2,610. Freshmen: 513. Federal methodology is used as a basis for awarding need-based institutional aid.

UNDERGRADUATE EXPENSES for 2018–2019 *Comprehensive fee:* $50,157 includes full-time tuition ($39,039), mandatory fees ($1710), and room and board ($9408). *College room only:* $5889. Full-time tuition and fees vary according to course load. Room and board charges vary according to board plan and housing facility. *Part-time tuition:* $678 per credit hour. *Part-time fees:* $12.50 per credit hour. Part-time tuition and fees vary according to course load.

FRESHMAN FINANCIAL AID (Fall 2016) 509 applied for aid; of those 88% were deemed to have need. 100% of freshmen with need received aid; of those 21% had need fully met. *Average percent of need met:* 84% (excluding resources awarded to replace EFC). *Average financial aid package:* $30,726 (excluding resources awarded to replace EFC). 17% of all full-time freshmen had no need and received non-need-based gift aid.

UNDERGRADUATE FINANCIAL AID (Fall 2016) 2,184 applied for aid; of those 91% were deemed to have need. 100% of undergraduates with need received aid; of those 22% had need fully met. *Average percent of need met:* 77% (excluding resources awarded to replace EFC). *Average financial aid package:* $28,577 (excluding resources awarded to replace EFC). 16% of all full-time undergraduates had no need and received non-need-based gift aid.

GIFT AID (NEED-BASED) *Total amount:* $49,312,512 (6% federal, 5% state, 84% institutional, 5% external sources). *Receiving aid:* Freshmen: 82% (450); all full-time undergraduates: 77% (1,983). *Average award:* Freshmen: $27,930; Undergraduates: $24,940. *Scholarships, grants, and awards:* Federal Pell, FSEOG, state, private, college/university gift aid from institutional funds.

GIFT AID (NON-NEED-BASED) *Total amount:* $8,905,620 (1% federal, 92% institutional, 7% external sources). *Receiving aid:* Freshmen: 12% (66). Undergraduates: 12% (309). *Average award:* Freshmen: $14,803. Undergraduates: $13,893. *Scholarships, grants, and awards by category: Academic interests/achievement:* 2,468 awards ($33,471,250 total): business, communication, computer science, engineering/technologies, home economics, mathematics. *Special character istics:* 37 awards ($988,637 total): children of faculty/staff. *Tuition waivers:* Full or partial for employees or children of employees. *ROTC:* Army cooperative, Naval cooperative, Air Force cooperative.

LOANS *Student loans:* $20,292,396 (68% need-based, 32% non-need-based). 76% of past graduating class borrowed through all loan programs. *Average indebtedness per student:* $38,421. *Average need-based loan:* Freshmen: $3304. Undergraduates: $4267. *Parent loans:* $7,959,414 (18% need-based, 82% non-need-based). *Programs:* Federal Direct (Subsidized and Unsubsidized Stafford, PLUS), Perkins, state, college/university.

WORK-STUDY *Federal work-study:* 269 jobs averaging $1248.

APPLYING FOR FINANCIAL AID *Required financial aid form:* FAFSA. *Financial aid deadline (priority):* 1/1. *Notification date:* Continuous beginning 1/15. Students must reply within 2 weeks of notification.

CONTACT Steve Midthun, Associate Director of Financial Aid, Milwaukee School of Engineering, 1025 North Broadway, Milwaukee, WI 53202-3109, 414-277-7223 or toll-free 800-332-6763. *Fax:* 414-277-6952. *E-mail:* finaid@msoe.edu. *Website:* http://www.msoe.edu/.

MINNEAPOLIS COLLEGE OF ART AND DESIGN
Minneapolis, MN

CONTACT Ms. Laura Link, Director of Financial Aid, Minneapolis College of Art and Design, 2501 Stevens Avenue South, Minneapolis, MN 55404-4347, 612-874-3733 or toll-free 800-874-6223. *Fax:* 612-874-3701. *E-mail:* laura_link@mead.edu. *Website:* http://www.mcad.edu/.

MINNESOTA STATE UNIVERSITY MANKATO
Mankato, MN

Tuition & fees (MN res): $8663	Average undergraduate aid package: $9505

ABOUT THE INSTITUTION State-supported, coed. *Awards:* certificates, associate, bachelor's, master's, and doctoral degrees. 108 undergraduate majors. *Total enrollment:* 15,407. Undergraduates: 13,459. Freshmen: 2,456. Federal methodology is used as a basis for awarding need-based institutional aid.

UNDERGRADUATE EXPENSES for 2017–2018 *Tuition, state resident:* full-time $7678; part-time $280.75 per credit hour. *Tuition, nonresident:* full-time $15,230; part-time $603.70 per credit hour. *Required fees:* full-time $985; $40.93 per credit hour. Full-time tuition and fees vary according to course load, location, program, and reciprocity agreements. Part-time tuition and fees vary according to course load, location, program, and reciprocity agreements. *College room and board:* $8475; *Room only:* $5524. Room and board charges vary according to board plan and housing facility.

FRESHMAN FINANCIAL AID (Fall 2017, est.) 2,566 applied for aid; of those 71% were deemed to have need. 99% of freshmen with need received aid; of those 15% had need fully met. *Average percent of need met:* 68% (excluding resources awarded to replace EFC). *Average financial aid package:* $9733 (excluding resources awarded to replace EFC). 14% of all full-time freshmen had no need and received non-need-based gift aid.

UNDERGRADUATE FINANCIAL AID (Fall 2017, est.) 8,082 applied for aid; of those 71% were deemed to have need. 99% of undergraduates with need received aid; of those 18% had need fully met. *Average percent of need met:* 70% (excluding resources awarded to replace EFC). *Average financial aid package:* $9505 (excluding resources awarded to replace EFC). 10% of all full-time undergraduates had no need and received non-need-based gift aid.

GIFT AID (NEED-BASED) *Total amount:* $26,852,425 (57% federal, 31% state, 6% institutional, 6% external sources). *Receiving aid:* Freshmen: 48% (1,499); all full-time undergraduates: 43% (4,563). *Average award:* Freshmen: $6255; Undergraduates: $5975. *Scholarships, grants, and awards:* Federal Pell, FSEOG, state, private, college/university gift aid from institutional funds.

GIFT AID (NON-NEED BASED) *Total amount:* $10,359,760 (5% federal, 59% institutional, 36% external sources). *Receiving aid:* Freshmen: 3% (96). Undergraduates: 3% (298). *Average award:* Freshmen: $5118. Undergraduates: $5664. *Scholarships, grants, and awards by category:* Academic interests/achievement: general academic interests/achievements. Creative arts/performance: art/fine arts, general creative arts/performance. Special achievements/activities: leadership. *Special characteristics:* members of minority groups. *Tuition waivers:* Full or partial for employees or children of employees, senior citizens. *ROTC:* Army.

LOANS *Student loans:* $71,595,152 (57% need-based, 43% non-need-based). 73% of past graduating class borrowed through all loan programs. *Average indebtedness per student:* $31,483. *Average need-based loan:* Freshmen: $3970. Undergraduates: $4350. *Parent loans:* $5,030,467 (18% need-based, 82% non-need-based). *Programs:* Federal Direct (Subsidized and Unsubsidized Stafford, PLUS), Perkins, state, college/university, alternative loans.

WORK-STUDY *Federal work-study:* Total amount: $1,492,442; 328 jobs averaging $4336. *State or other work-study/employment:* Total amount: $1,440,779 (100% need-based). 338 part-time jobs averaging $4087.

ATHLETIC AWARDS Total amount: $2,902,423 (31% need-based, 69% non-need-based).

APPLYING FOR FINANCIAL AID *Required financial aid form:* FAFSA. *Financial aid deadline (priority):* 3/15. *Notification date:* Continuous beginning 3/30.

CONTACT Tyler Heu, Director of Financial Aid, Minnesota State University Mankato, 120 Wigley Administration Center, Mankato, MN 56001, 507-389-1866 or toll-free 800-722-0544. *Fax:* 507-389-6410. *E-mail:* campushub@mnsu.edu. *Website:* http://www.mnsu.edu/.

MINNESOTA STATE UNIVERSITY MOORHEAD
Moorhead, MN

Tuition & fees (MN res): $8496	Average undergraduate aid package: $3211

ABOUT THE INSTITUTION State-supported, coed. *Awards:* certificates, bachelor's, master's, and doctoral degrees. 83 undergraduate majors. *Total enrollment:* 6,019. Undergraduates: 5,147. Freshmen: 844. Federal methodology is used as a basis for awarding need-based institutional aid.

UNDERGRADUATE EXPENSES for 2018–2019 *Application fee:* $20. *Tuition, state resident:* full-time $7410; part-time $239 per credit hour. *Tuition, nonresident:* full-time $14,820; part-time $478 per credit hour. *Required fees:* full-time $1086; $45.22 per credit hour or $543 per term. Full-time tuition and fees vary according to course load and reciprocity agreements. Part-time tuition and fees vary according to reciprocity agreements. *College room and board:* $9280; *Room only:* $5950. Room and board charges vary according to board plan and housing facility.

FRESHMAN FINANCIAL AID (Fall 2017, est.) 753 applied for aid; of those 75% were deemed to have need. 99% of freshmen with need received aid. *Average financial aid package:* $2706 (excluding resources awarded to replace EFC).

UNDERGRADUATE FINANCIAL AID (Fall 2017, est.) 3,307 applied for aid; of those 77% were deemed to have need. 98% of undergraduates with need received aid. *Average financial aid package:* $3211 (excluding resources awarded to replace EFC).

GIFT AID (NEED-BASED) *Total amount:* $9,722,337 (64% federal, 33% state, 1% institutional, 2% external sources). *Receiving aid:* Freshmen: 44% (364); all full-time undergraduates: 40% (1,685). *Average award:* Freshmen: $2500; Undergraduates: $2716. *Scholarships, grants, and awards:* Federal Pell, FSEOG, state, private, college/university gift aid from institutional funds, TEACH Grants.

GIFT AID (NON-NEED-BASED) *Total amount:* $3,929,638 (15% federal, 4% state, 53% institutional, 28% external sources). *Receiving aid:* Freshmen: 48% (402). Undergraduates: 24% (1,011). *Scholarships, grants, and awards by category:* Academic interests/achievement: biological sciences, business, communication, computer science, education, engineering/technologies, English, general academic interests/ achievements, home economics, international studies, mathematics, physical sciences, premedicine, social sciences. Creative arts/performance: art/fine arts, cinema/film/ broadcasting, creative writing, music, theater/drama. Special achievements/activities: community service, general special achievements/activities. Special characteristics:

adult students, children of faculty/staff, first-generation college students, members of minority groups, out-of-state students. *Tuition waivers:* Full or partial for employees or children of employees, senior citizens. *ROTC:* Army cooperative, Air Force cooperative.

LOANS *Student loans:* $24,703,370 (36% need-based, 64% non-need-based). 84% of past graduating class borrowed through all loan programs. *Average indebtedness per student:* $32,713. *Average need-based loan:* Freshmen: $3213. Undergraduates: $3940. *Parent loans:* $520,044 (100% non-need-based). *Programs:* Federal Direct (Subsidized and Unsubsidized Stafford, PLUS), Perkins, state, private loans.

WORK-STUDY *Federal work-study:* Total amount: $511,536; 238 jobs averaging $2555. *State or other work-study/employment:* Total amount: $3,380,011 (11% need-based, 89% non-need-based). 163 part-time jobs averaging $2385.

ATHLETIC AWARDS Total amount: $961,938 (100% non-need-based).

APPLYING FOR FINANCIAL AID *Required financial aid form:* FAFSA. *Financial aid deadline:* Continuous. *Notification date:* Continuous beginning 6/1.

CONTACT Ms. Melissa Dingmann, Director of Financial Aid, Minnesota State University Moorhead, 1104 7th Avenue South, Moorhead, MN 56563, 218-477-2251 or toll-free 800-593-7246. *Fax:* 218-477-2058. *E-mail:* finaid@mnstate.edu. *Website:* http://www.mnstate.edu/.

MINOT STATE UNIVERSITY
Minot, ND

Tuition & fees (ND res): $6810	Average undergraduate aid package: $10,424

ABOUT THE INSTITUTION State-supported, coed. *Awards:* certificates, associate, bachelor's, and master's degrees. 58 undergraduate majors. *Total enrollment:* 3,216. Undergraduates: 2,956. Freshmen: 373. Federal methodology is used as a basis for awarding need-based institutional aid.

UNDERGRADUATE EXPENSES for 2017–2018 *Application fee:* $35. *Tuition, state resident:* full-time $5400; part-time $225 per credit hour. *Tuition, nonresident:* full-time $5400; part-time $225 per credit hour. *Required fees:* full-time $1410; $58.72 per credit hour. Full-time tuition and fees vary according to class time, course load, degree level, location, program, and reciprocity agreements. Part-time tuition and fees vary according to class time, course load, degree level, location, program, and reciprocity agreements. *College room and board:* $6140; *Room only:* $2246. Room and board charges vary according to board plan and housing facility.

FRESHMAN FINANCIAL AID (Fall 2016) 229 applied for aid; of those 55% were deemed to have need. 95% of freshmen with need received aid; of those 34% had need fully met. *Average percent of need met:* 67% (excluding resources awarded to replace EFC). *Average financial aid package:* $9946 (excluding resources awarded to replace EFC). 19% of all full-time freshmen had no need and received non-need-based gift aid.

UNDERGRADUATE FINANCIAL AID (Fall 2016) 1,324 applied for aid; of those 68% were deemed to have need. 96% of undergraduates with need received aid; of those 34% had need fully met. *Average percent of need met:* 68% (excluding resources awarded to replace EFC). *Average financial aid package:* $10,424 (excluding resources awarded to replace EFC). 16% of all full-time undergraduates had no need and received non-need-based gift aid.

GIFT AID (NEED-BASED) *Total amount:* $4,102,940 (63% federal, 19% state, 9% institutional, 9% external sources). *Receiving aid:* Freshmen: 38% (117); all full-time undergraduates: 38% (765). *Average award:* Freshmen: $6284; Undergraduates: $5412. *Scholarships, grants, and awards:* Federal Pell, FSEOG, state, private, college/university gift aid from institutional funds.

GIFT AID (NON-NEED-BASED) *Total amount:* $1,121,765 (22% state, 42% institutional, 36% external sources). *Receiving aid:* Freshmen: 4% (14). Undergraduates: 3% (55). *Average award:* Freshmen: $1116. Undergraduates: $1372. *Scholarships, grants, and awards by category:* Academic interests/achievement: biological sciences, business, communication, computer science, education, English, foreign languages, general academic interests/achievements, health fields, home economics, humanities, mathematics, social sciences. *Creative arts/performance:* art/fine arts, cinema/film/broadcasting, music, performing arts, theater/drama. *Special characteristics:* children and siblings of alumni, children of faculty/staff, ethnic background, international students, local/state students, members of minority groups, out-of-state

students, veterans, veterans' children. *Tuition waivers:* Full or partial for minority students, children of alumni, employees or children of employees, senior citizens.

LOANS *Student loans:* $8,166,445 (58% need-based, 42% non-need-based). 47% of past graduating class borrowed through all loan programs. *Average indebtedness per student:* $23,400. *Average need-based loan:* Freshmen: $4401. Undergraduates: $6045. *Parent loans:* $122,304 (12% need-based, 88% non-need-based). *Programs:* Federal Direct (Subsidized and Unsubsidized Stafford, PLUS), Federal Nursing, state, alternative loans.

WORK-STUDY *Federal work-study:* 77 jobs averaging $1532.

ATHLETIC AWARDS Total amount: $1,042,518 (81% need-based, 19% non-need-based).

APPLYING FOR FINANCIAL AID *Required financial aid forms:* FAFSA, institutional scholarship application form. *Financial aid deadline (priority):* 4/15. *Notification date:* Continuous beginning 3/15. Students must reply within 4 weeks of notification.

CONTACT Ms. Laurie Weber, Director of Financial Aid, Minot State University, 500 University Avenue, West, Minot, ND 58707-0002, 701-858-3875 or toll-free 800-777-0750 Ext. 3350. *Fax:* 701-858-4310. *E-mail:* laurie.weber@minotstateu.edu. *Website:* http://www.minotstateu.edu/.

MIRRER YESHIVA CENTRAL INSTITUTE
Brooklyn, NY

CONTACT Financial Aid Office, Mirrer Yeshiva Central Institute, 1795 Ocean Parkway, Brooklyn, NY 11223-2010, 718-645-0536.

MISERICORDIA UNIVERSITY
Dallas, PA

Tuition & fees: $33,240	Average undergraduate aid package: $24,313

ABOUT THE INSTITUTION Independent Roman Catholic, coed. *Awards:* certificates, bachelor's, master's, and doctoral degrees. 33 undergraduate majors. *Total enrollment:* 2,764. Undergraduates: 2,146. Freshmen: 440. Federal methodology is used as a basis for awarding need-based institutional aid.

UNDERGRADUATE EXPENSES for 2018–2019 *Application fee:* $35. *Comprehensive fee:* $47,200 includes full-time tuition ($31,530), mandatory fees ($1710), and room and board ($13,960). *College room only:* $7600. Full-time tuition and fees vary according to degree level. Room and board charges vary according to board plan and housing facility. *Part-time tuition:* $610 per credit. Part-time tuition and fees vary according to class time and location.

FRESHMAN FINANCIAL AID (Fall 2017, est.) 415 applied for aid; of those 88% were deemed to have need. 100% of freshmen with need received aid; of those 26% had need fully met. *Average percent of need met:* 83% (excluding resources awarded to replace EFC). *Average financial aid package:* $25,752 (excluding resources awarded to replace EFC). 11% of all full-time freshmen had no need and received non-need-based gift aid.

UNDERGRADUATE FINANCIAL AID (Fall 2017, est.) 1,534 applied for aid; of those 89% were deemed to have need. 100% of undergraduates with need received aid; of those 26% had need fully met. *Average percent of need met:* 81% (excluding resources awarded to replace EFC). *Average financial aid package:* $24,313 (excluding resources awarded to replace EFC). 10% of all full-time undergraduates had no need and received non-need-based gift aid.

GIFT AID (NEED-BASED) *Total amount:* $24,594,124 (11% federal, 7% state, 81% institutional, 1% external sources). *Receiving aid:* Freshmen: 84% (367); all full-time undergraduates: 82% (1,356). *Average award:* Freshmen: $19,908; Undergraduates: $17,695. *Scholarships, grants, and awards:* Federal Pell, FSEOG, state, private, college/university gift aid from institutional funds.

GIFT AID (NON-NEED-BASED) *Total amount:* $5,888,284 (97% institutional, 3% external sources). *Receiving aid:* Freshmen: 17% (76). Undergraduates: 14% (229). *Average award:* Freshmen: $16,750. Undergraduates: $14,098. *Scholarships, grants, and awards by category:* Academic interests/achievement: $17,246,797 total: general academic interests/achievements. *Special achievements/*

activities; $2,757,083 total: community service, general special achievements/activities, leadership. *Special characteristics:* $2,871,612 total: children and siblings of alumni, children of current students, children of faculty/staff, general special characteristics, members of minority groups, out-of-state students, previous college experience, relatives of clergy, siblings of current students. *Tuition waivers:* Full or partial for employees or children of employees. *ROTC:* Army cooperative, Air Force cooperative.

LOANS *Student loans:* $16,445,251 (64% need-based, 36% non-need-based). 86% of past graduating class borrowed through all loan programs. *Average indebtedness per student:* $47,764. *Average need-based loan:* Freshmen: $7364. Undergraduates: $8593. *Parent loans:* $4,297,947 (41% need-based, 59% non-need-based). *Programs:* Federal Direct (Subsidized and Unsubsidized Stafford, PLUS), Perkins, Federal Nursing, state.

WORK-STUDY Federal work-study jobs available.

APPLYING FOR FINANCIAL AID *Required financial aid form:* FAFSA. *Financial aid deadline:* 5/1 (priority: 3/1). *Notification date:* 3/15. Students must reply within 2 weeks of notification.

CONTACT Susan Fronzoni, Director of Student Financial Services, Misericordia University, 301 Lake Street, Dallas, PA 18612-1098, 866-262-6363. *E-mail:* finaid@misericordia.edu.
Website: http://www.misericordia.edu/.

MISSISSIPPI COLLEGE
Clinton, MS

ABOUT THE INSTITUTION Independent Southern Baptist, coed. 59 undergraduate majors.

GIFT AID (NEED-BASED) *Scholarships, grants, and awards:* Federal Pell, FSEOG, state, private, college/university gift aid from institutional funds, Federal Nursing.

GIFT AID (NON-NEED-BASED) *Scholarships, grants, and awards by category:* Academic interests/achievement: general academic interests/achievements. *Creative arts/performance:* applied art and design, art/fine arts, music. *Special achievements/activities:* general special achievements/activities, leadership, religious involvement. *Special characteristics:* children and siblings of alumni, children of faculty/staff, general special characteristics, relatives of clergy.

LOANS *Programs:* Federal Direct (Subsidized and Unsubsidized Stafford, PLUS), Perkins, Federal Nursing, college/university.

WORK-STUDY *Federal work-study:* 185 jobs averaging $929.

APPLYING FOR FINANCIAL AID *Required financial aid forms:* FAFSA, state aid form.

CONTACT Mrs. Karon Q. McMillan, Director of Financial Aid, Mississippi College, Box 4035, 200 South Capitol Street, Clinton, MS 39058-0001, 601-925-3249 or toll-free 800-738-1236. *Fax:* 601-925-3950. *E-mail:* kmcmilla@mc.edu.
Website: http://www.mc.edu/.

MISSISSIPPI STATE UNIVERSITY
Mississippi State, MS

Tuition & fees (MS res): $8318	Average undergraduate aid package: $14,785

ABOUT THE INSTITUTION State-supported, coed. *Awards:* certificates, associate, bachelor's, master's, and doctoral degrees. 76 undergraduate majors. *Total enrollment:* 21,883. Undergraduates: 18,312. Freshmen: 3,435. Federal methodology is used as a basis for awarding need-based institutional aid.

UNDERGRADUATE EXPENSES for 2017–2018 *Application fee:* $40. *One-time required fee:* $55. *Tuition, state resident:* full-time $8318; part-time $346.59 per credit hour. *Tuition, nonresident:* full-time $22,358; part-time $931.59 per credit hour. Full-time tuition and fees vary according to degree level and location. Part-time tuition and fees vary according to course load, degree level, and location. *College room and board:* $9614; *Room only:* $6044. Room and board charges vary according to board plan, housing facility, and student level. *Payment plan:* Tuition prepayment.

FRESHMAN FINANCIAL AID (Fall 2016) 3,061 applied for aid; of those 83% were deemed to have need. 99% of freshmen with need received aid; of those 30% had

need fully met. *Average percent of need met:* 61% (excluding resources awarded to replace EFC). *Average financial aid package:* $16,612 (excluding resources awarded to replace EFC). 29% of all full-time freshmen had no need and received non-need-based gift aid.

UNDERGRADUATE FINANCIAL AID (Fall 2016) 12,236 applied for aid; of those 86% were deemed to have need. 98% of undergraduates with need received aid; of those 25% had need fully met. *Average percent of need met:* 60% (excluding resources awarded to replace EFC). *Average financial aid package:* $14,785 (excluding resources awarded to replace EFC). 22% of all full-time undergraduates had no need and received non-need-based gift aid.

GIFT AID (NEED-BASED) *Total amount:* $60,597,045 (44% federal, 13% state, 34% institutional, 9% external sources). *Receiving aid:* Freshmen: 67% (2,443); all full-time undergraduates: 55% (9,195). *Average award:* Freshmen: $6352; Undergraduates: $6091. *Scholarships, grants, and awards:* Federal Pell, FSEOG, state, private, college/university gift aid from institutional funds, United Negro College Fund.

GIFT AID (NON-NEED-BASED) *Total amount:* $24,117,304 (10% state, 84% institutional, 6% external sources). *Receiving aid:* Freshmen: 10% (364). Undergraduates: 5% (788). *Average award:* Freshmen: $4036. Undergraduates: $4568. *Scholarships, grants, and awards by category:* Academic interests/achievement: agriculture, architecture, area/ethnic studies, biological sciences, business, communication, computer science, education, engineering/technologies, English, foreign languages, general academic interests/achievements, health fields, home economics, humanities, international studies, library science, mathematics, military science, physical sciences, premedicine, religion/biblical studies, social sciences. *Creative arts/performance:* applied art and design, art/fine arts, cinema/film/broadcasting, creative writing, dance, debating, general creative arts/performance, journalism/publications, music, performing arts, theater/drama. *Special achievements/activities:* cheerleading/drum major, general special achievements/activities, junior miss, leadership, memberships. *Special characteristics:* adult students, children and siblings of alumni, children of educators, children of faculty/staff, children of public servants, first-generation college students, handicapped students, local/state students, out-of-state students, previous college experience, spouses of deceased or disabled public servants. *Tuition waivers:* Full or partial for children of alumni, employees or children of employees, senior citizens. *ROTC:* Army, Air Force.

LOANS *Student loans:* $107,577,437 (82% need-based, 18% non-need-based). 56% of past graduating class borrowed through all loan programs. *Average indebtedness per student:* $30,721. *Average need-based loan:* Freshmen: $3337. Undergraduates: $3871. *Parent loans:* $22,887,089 (68% need-based, 32% non-need-based). *Programs:* Federal Direct (Subsidized and Unsubsidized Stafford, PLUS), Perkins, college/university.

WORK-STUDY *Federal work-study:* 950 jobs averaging $3450.

ATHLETIC AWARDS Total amount: $8,859,941 (100% non-need-based).

APPLYING FOR FINANCIAL AID *Required financial aid forms:* FAFSA, state aid form, general scholarship application. *Financial aid deadline (priority):* 3/1. *Notification date:* Continuous beginning 12/1. Students must reply by 5/1.

CONTACT Mr. Kenneth Paul McKinney, Director of Financial Aid, Mississippi State University, PO Box 6035, Mississippi State, MS 39762, 662-325-7428. *Fax:* 662-325-0702. *E-mail:* financialaid@saffairs.msstate.edu.
Website: http://www.msstate.edu/.

MISSISSIPPI UNIVERSITY FOR WOMEN
Columbus, MS

CONTACT Ms. Nicole Patrick, Director of Financial Aid, Mississippi University for Women, 1100 College Street, MUW 1614, Columbus, MS 39701-4044, 662-329-7114 or toll-free 877-GO 2 THE W. *Fax:* 662-329-7325. *E-mail:* jnpatrick@muw.edu.
Website: http://www.muw.edu/.

MISSISSIPPI VALLEY STATE UNIVERSITY
Itta Bena, MS

CONTACT Margaret Sherrer, Director of Student Financial Aid, Mississippi Valley State University, 14000 Highway 82W #7268, Itta Bena, MS 38941-1400, 662-254-3335 or toll-free 800-844-6885 (in-state). *Fax:* 662-254-7900. *E-mail:* margaret.sherrer@mvsu.edu.
Website: http://www.mvsu.edu/.

MISSOURI BAPTIST UNIVERSITY
St. Louis, MO

Tuition & fees: $26,020	Average undergraduate aid package: $18,252

ABOUT THE INSTITUTION Independent Southern Baptist, coed. *Awards:* certificates, associate, bachelor's, master's, and doctoral degrees. 56 undergraduate majors. *Total enrollment:* 5,488. Undergraduates: 4,508. Freshmen: 283. Federal methodology is used as a basis for awarding need-based institutional aid.
UNDERGRADUATE EXPENSES for 2017–2018 *Application fee:* $35. *Comprehensive fee:* $36,400 includes full-time tuition ($24,764), mandatory fees ($1256), and room and board ($10,380). Full-time tuition and fees vary according to course load and location. Room and board charges vary according to board plan and housing facility. *Part-time tuition:* $857 per credit hour. *Part-time fees:* $27 per credit hour. Part-time tuition and fees vary according to course load and location.
FRESHMAN FINANCIAL AID (Fall 2017, est.) 245 applied for aid; of those 84% were deemed to have need. 100% of freshmen with need received aid; of those 40% had need fully met. *Average financial aid package:* $23,313 (excluding resources awarded to replace EFC). 14% of all full-time freshmen had no need and received non-need-based gift aid.
UNDERGRADUATE FINANCIAL AID (Fall 2017, est.) 1,332 applied for aid; of those 91% were deemed to have need. 100% of undergraduates with need received aid; of those 27% had need fully met. *Average financial aid package:* $18,252 (excluding resources awarded to replace EFC). 3% of all full-time undergraduates had no need and received non-need-based gift aid.
GIFT AID (NEED-BASED) *Total amount:* $16,453,243 (43% federal, 7% state, 41% institutional, 9% external sources). *Receiving aid:* Freshmen: 60% (166); all full-time undergraduates: 65% (966). *Average award:* Freshmen: $5768; Undergraduates: $5197. *Scholarships, grants, and awards:* Federal Pell, FSEOG, state, private, college/university gift aid from institutional funds.
GIFT AID (NON-NEED-BASED) *Total amount:* $712,351 (1% federal, 1% state, 92% institutional, 6% external sources). *Receiving aid:* Freshmen: 75% (206). Undergraduates: 60% (897). *Average award:* Freshmen: $8463. Undergraduates: $8179. *Scholarships, grants, and awards by category:* Academic interests/achievement: general academic interests/achievements, religion/biblical studies. Creative arts/performance: music, theater/drama. Special achievements/activities: cheerleading/drum major, memberships, religious involvement. Special characteristics: adult students, children and siblings of alumni, children of current students, children of faculty/staff, first-generation college students, parents of current students, public servants, relatives of clergy, religious affiliation, siblings of current students, spouses of current students, veterans, veterans' children. *Tuition waivers:* Full or partial for children of alumni, employees or children of employees, senior citizens. *ROTC:* Army cooperative.
LOANS *Student loans:* $21,201,407 (95% need-based, 5% non-need-based). 93% of past graduating class borrowed through all loan programs. *Average indebtedness per student:* $27,951. *Average need-based loan:* Freshmen: $3535. Undergraduates: $4353. *Parent loans:* $5,063,976 (92% need-based, 8% non-need-based). *Programs:* Federal Direct (Subsidized and Unsubsidized Stafford, PLUS).
WORK-STUDY *Federal work-study:* Total amount: $2,191,015; 516 jobs averaging $2148. *State or other work-study/employment:* Part-time jobs available.
ATHLETIC AWARDS Total amount: $17,322,410 (89% need-based, 11% non-need-based).
APPLYING FOR FINANCIAL AID *Required financial aid forms:* FAFSA, institution's own form. *Financial aid deadline (priority):* 4/1. *Notification date:* Continuous beginning 4/15. Students must reply within 2 weeks of notification.

CONTACT Mr. Zach Greenlee, Director of Student Financial Services, Missouri Baptist University, One College Park Drive, St. Louis, MO 63141, 314-392-2398 or toll-free 877-434-1115 Ext. 2290. *Fax:* 314-744-5320. *E-mail:* greenleez@mobap.edu. *Website:* http://www.mobap.edu/.

MISSOURI SOUTHERN STATE UNIVERSITY
Joplin, MO

Tuition & fees (MO res): $6067	Average undergraduate aid package: $9471

ABOUT THE INSTITUTION State-supported, coed. 51 undergraduate majors. Institutional methodology is used as a basis for awarding need-based institutional aid.
UNDERGRADUATE EXPENSES for 2017–2018 *Tuition, state resident:* full-time $5501; part-time $183.37 per credit hour. *Tuition, nonresident:* full-time $11,002; part-time $366.74 per credit hour. *Required fees:* full-time $566; $168 per term.
FRESHMAN FINANCIAL AID (Fall 2017, est.) 948 applied for aid; of those 81% were deemed to have need. 98% of freshmen with need received aid; of those 17% had need fully met. *Average percent of need met:* 42% (excluding resources awarded to replace EFC). *Average financial aid package:* $8972 (excluding resources awarded to replace EFC). 15% of all full-time freshmen had no need and received non-need-based gift aid.
UNDERGRADUATE FINANCIAL AID (Fall 2017, est.) 4,137 applied for aid; of those 83% were deemed to have need. 98% of undergraduates with need received aid; of those 19% had need fully met. *Average percent of need met:* 45% (excluding resources awarded to replace EFC). *Average financial aid package:* $9471 (excluding resources awarded to replace EFC). 10% of all full-time undergraduates had no need and received non-need-based gift aid.
GIFT AID (NEED-BASED) *Total amount:* $14,832,749 (83% federal, 17% state). *Receiving aid:* Freshmen: 63% (609); all full-time undergraduates: 61% (2,674). *Average award:* Freshmen: $5080; Undergraduates: $5044. *Scholarships, grants, and awards:* Federal Pell, FSEOG, state, private, college/university gift aid from institutional funds, TEACH Grants.
GIFT AID (NON-NEED-BASED) *Total amount:* $5,955,819 (3% state, 80% institutional, 17% external sources). *Receiving aid:* Freshmen: 53% (509). Undergraduates: 38% (1,650). *Average award:* Freshmen: $2770. Undergraduates: $2770. *Scholarships, grants, and awards by category:* Academic interests/achievement: general academic interests/achievements. Creative arts/performance: art/fine arts, journalism/publications, music, theater/drama. Special achievements/activities: cheerleading/drum major, general special achievements/activities, leadership. Special characteristics: veterans.
LOANS *Student loans:* $18,597,740 (46% need-based, 54% non-need-based). 64% of past graduating class borrowed through all loan programs. *Average indebtedness per student:* $25,314. *Average need-based loan:* Freshmen: $2790. Undergraduates: $3497. *Parent loans:* $400,318 (100% non-need-based). *Programs:* Federal Direct (Subsidized and Unsubsidized Stafford, PLUS), Perkins.
WORK-STUDY *Federal work-study:* Total amount: $192,510; jobs available. *State or other work-study/employment:* Total amount: $719,736 (100% non-need-based). Part-time jobs available.
ATHLETIC AWARDS Total amount: $1,717,763 (100% non-need-based).
APPLYING FOR FINANCIAL AID *Required financial aid form:* FAFSA. *Financial aid deadline:* Continuous. *Notification date:* Continuous beginning 3/15. Students must reply by 5/1.

CONTACT Becca L. Diskin, Director of Financial Aid, Missouri Southern State University, 3950 Newman Road, Joplin, MO 64801-1595, 417-659-5422 or toll-free 866-818-MSSU. *Fax:* 417-659-4474. *E-mail:* diskin-b@mssu.edu. *Website:* http://www.mssu.edu/.

MISSOURI STATE UNIVERSITY
Springfield, MO

Tuition & fees (MO res): $7306	Average undergraduate aid package: $9224

ABOUT THE INSTITUTION State-supported, coed. *Awards:* certificates, bachelor's, master's, and doctoral degrees. 97 undergraduate majors. *Total enrollment:* 23,697. Undergraduates: 20,364. Freshmen: 3,238. Federal methodology is used as a basis for awarding need-based institutional aid.

UNDERGRADUATE EXPENSES for 2017–2018 *Application fee:* $35. *Tuition, state resident:* full-time $6300; part-time $210 per credit hour. *Tuition, nonresident:* full-time $13,740; part-time $458 per credit hour. *Required fees:* full-time $1006. Full-time tuition and fees vary according to course level, course load, and program. Part-time tuition and fees vary according to course level, course load, and program. *College room and board:* $8537. Room and board charges vary according to board plan, housing facility, and location.

FRESHMAN FINANCIAL AID (Fall 2017, est.) 2,811 applied for aid; of those 70% were deemed to have need. 98% of freshmen with need received aid; of those 18% had need fully met. *Average percent of need met:* 57% (excluding resources awarded to replace EFC). *Average financial aid package:* $9294 (excluding resources awarded to replace EFC). 18% of all full-time freshmen had no need and received non-need-based gift aid.

UNDERGRADUATE FINANCIAL AID (Fall 2017, est.) 11,947 applied for aid; of those 78% were deemed to have need. 97% of undergraduates with need received aid; of those 15% had need fully met. *Average percent of need met:* 55% (excluding resources awarded to replace EFC). *Average financial aid package:* $9224 (excluding resources awarded to replace EFC). 12% of all full-time undergraduates had no need and received non-need-based gift aid.

GIFT AID (NEED-BASED) *Total amount:* $47,127,445 (57% federal, 21% state, 18% institutional, 4% external sources). *Receiving aid:* Freshmen: 51% (1,657); all full-time undergraduates: 48% (7,379). *Average award:* Freshmen: $6204; Undergraduates: $5942. *Scholarships, grants, and awards:* Federal Pell, FSEOG, state, private, college/university gift aid from institutional funds.

GIFT AID (NON-NEED-BASED) *Total amount:* $12,775,002 (7% federal, 13% state, 53% institutional, 27% external sources). *Receiving aid:* Freshmen: 9% (290). Undergraduates: 5% (730). *Average award:* Freshmen: $2881. Undergraduates: $3302. *Scholarships, grants, and awards by category:* Academic interests/achievement: general academic interests/achievements. Creative arts/performance: general creative arts/performance. Special achievements/activities: leadership. Special characteristics: children and siblings of alumni, local/state students, members of minority groups. *Tuition waivers:* Full or partial for children of alumni, employees or children of employees, senior citizens. *ROTC:* Army.

LOANS *Student loans:* $79,075,906 (65% need-based, 35% non-need-based). 65% of past graduating class borrowed through all loan programs. *Average indebtedness per student:* $25,714. *Average need-based loan:* Freshmen: $3314. Undergraduates: $4203. *Parent loans:* $9,811,779 (37% need-based, 63% non-need-based). *Programs:* Federal Direct (Subsidized and Unsubsidized Stafford, PLUS), Perkins.

WORK-STUDY *Federal work-study:* Total amount: $992,174; jobs available.

ATHLETIC AWARDS Total amount: $4,436,038 (21% need-based, 79% non-need-based).

APPLYING FOR FINANCIAL AID *Required financial aid form:* FAFSA. *Financial aid deadline (priority):* 3/31. *Notification date:* Continuous beginning 3/31.

CONTACT Vicki Mattocks, Director of Financial Aid, Missouri State University, 901 South National Avenue, Springfield, MO 65804, 417-836-5262 or toll-free 800-492-7900. *E-mail:* financialaid@missouristate.edu.
Website: http://www.missouristate.edu/.

MISSOURI UNIVERSITY OF SCIENCE AND TECHNOLOGY
Rolla, MO

Tuition & fees (MO res): $8460	Average undergraduate aid package: $15,065

ABOUT THE INSTITUTION State-supported, coed. *Awards:* certificates, bachelor's, master's, and doctoral degrees. 39 undergraduate majors. *Total enrollment:* 8,884. Undergraduates: 6,920. Freshmen: 1,426. Federal methodology is used as a basis for awarding need-based institutional aid.

UNDERGRADUATE EXPENSES for 2018–2019 *Application fee:* $50. *Tuition, state resident:* full-time $8460; part-time $282 per credit hour. *Tuition, nonresident:* full-time $26,322; part-time $877.40 per credit hour. Full-time tuition and fees vary according to course load, degree level, program, and student level. Part-time tuition and fees vary according to course load, degree level, program, and student level. *College room and board:* $10,094. Room and board charges vary according to board plan, housing facility, and location.

FRESHMAN FINANCIAL AID (Fall 2016) 854 applied for aid; of those 99% were deemed to have need. 100% of freshmen with need received aid; of those 14% had need fully met. *Average percent of need met:* 40% (excluding resources awarded to replace EFC). *Average financial aid package:* $16,722 (excluding resources awarded to replace EFC). 19% of all full-time freshmen had no need and received non-need-based gift aid.

UNDERGRADUATE FINANCIAL AID (Fall 2016) 3,567 applied for aid; of those 99% were deemed to have need. 100% of undergraduates with need received aid; of those 30% had need fully met. *Average percent of need met:* 48% (excluding resources awarded to replace EFC). *Average financial aid package:* $15,065 (excluding resources awarded to replace EFC). 11% of all full-time undergraduates had no need and received non-need-based gift aid.

GIFT AID (NEED-BASED) *Total amount:* $11,564,511 (62% federal, 27% state, 11% institutional). *Receiving aid:* Freshmen: 54% (794); all full-time undergraduates: 52% (3,219). *Average award:* Freshmen: $10,079; Undergraduates: $7978. *Scholarships, grants, and awards:* Federal Pell, FSEOG, state, private, college/university gift aid from institutional funds, ROTC (Army and Air Force) Scholarships.

GIFT AID (NON-NEED-BASED) *Total amount:* $35,673,732 (10% state, 68% institutional, 22% external sources). *Receiving aid:* Freshmen: 17% (251). Undergraduates: 23% (1,399). *Average award:* Freshmen: $6129. Undergraduates: $5550. *Scholarships, grants, and awards by category:* Academic interests/achievement: biological sciences, business, communication, computer science, education, engineering/technologies, English, general academic interests/achievements, humanities, international studies, mathematics, military science, physical sciences, pre-medicine, social sciences. Creative arts/performance: music, theater/drama. Special characteristics: children and siblings of alumni, children of faculty/staff, children of union members/company employees, members of minority groups, out-of-state students. *Tuition waivers:* Full or partial for employees or children of employees. *ROTC:* Army, Air Force.

LOANS *Student loans:* $28,673,991 (42% need-based, 58% non-need-based). 66% of past graduating class borrowed through all loan programs. *Average indebtedness per student:* $27,500. *Average need-based loan:* Freshmen: $6880. Undergraduates: $7584. *Parent loans:* $12,604,852 (100% non-need-based). *Programs:* Perkins, state, college/university, alternative loans.

WORK-STUDY *Federal work-study:* jobs available. *State or other work-study/employment:* Total amount: $2,912,747 (1% need-based, 99% non-need-based). Part-time jobs available.

ATHLETIC AWARDS Total amount: $3,055,229 (100% non-need-based).

APPLYING FOR FINANCIAL AID *Required financial aid form:* FAFSA. *Financial aid deadline (priority):* 2/1. *Notification date:* Continuous beginning 4/1. Students must reply within 3 weeks of notification.

CONTACT Ms. Bridgette Betz, Director of Student Financial Assistance, Missouri University of Science and Technology, G1 Parker Hall, Rolla, MO 65409, 573-341-4282 or toll-free 800-522-0938. *Fax:* 573-341-4274. *E-mail:* berry@mst.edu.
Website: http://www.mst.edu/.

MISSOURI VALLEY COLLEGE
Marshall, MO

Tuition & fees: $20,600	Average undergraduate aid package: $21,370

ABOUT THE INSTITUTION Independent Presbyterian Church, coed. *Awards:* associate, bachelor's, and master's degrees. 59 undergraduate majors. *Total enrollment:* 1,820. Undergraduates: 1,798. Freshmen: 392. Both federal and institutional methodology are used as a basis for awarding need-based institutional aid.

UNDERGRADUATE EXPENSES for 2018–2019 *Comprehensive fee:* $29,750 includes full-time tuition ($19,300), mandatory fees ($1300), and room and board ($9150). *College room only:* $4850. Full-time tuition and fees vary according to program. Room and board charges vary according to board plan, gender, housing facility, location, and student level. *Part-time tuition:* $350 per credit hour. Part-time tuition and fees vary according to program. *Payment plan:* Tuition prepayment.

FRESHMAN FINANCIAL AID (Fall 2016) 449 applied for aid; of those 96% were deemed to have need. 100% of freshmen with need received aid; of those 3% had need fully met. *Average percent of need met:* 83% (excluding resources awarded to replace EFC). *Average financial aid package:* $17,674 (excluding resources awarded to replace EFC). 4% of all full-time freshmen had no need and received non-need-based gift aid.

UNDERGRADUATE FINANCIAL AID (Fall 2016) 1,265 applied for aid; of those 88% were deemed to have need. 100% of undergraduates with need received aid; of those 2% had need fully met. *Average percent of need met:* 86% (excluding resources awarded to replace EFC). *Average financial aid package:* $21,370 (excluding resources awarded to replace EFC). 9% of all full-time undergraduates had no need and received non-need-based gift aid.

GIFT AID (NEED-BASED) *Total amount:* $5,437,691 (56% federal, 10% state, 34% institutional). *Receiving aid:* Freshmen: 96% (431); all full-time undergraduates: 62% (1,107). *Average award:* Freshmen: $12,200; Undergraduates: $12,599. *Scholarships, grants, and awards:* Federal Pell, FSEOG, state, private, college/university gift aid from institutional funds.

GIFT AID (NON-NEED-BASED) *Total amount:* $4,479,597 (95% institutional, 5% external sources). *Receiving aid:* Freshmen: 14% (62). Undergraduates: 12% (211). *Average award:* Freshmen: $9501. Undergraduates: $12,551. *Scholarships, grants, and awards by category: Academic interests/achievement:* biological sciences, business, communication, computer science, education, English, general academic interests/achievements, health fields, humanities, mathematics, military science, physical sciences, premedicine, social sciences. *Creative arts/performance:* applied art and design, art/fine arts, cinema/film/broadcasting, dance, journalism/publications, music, performing arts, theater/drama. *Special achievements/activities:* cheerleading/drum major, community service, general special achievements/activities, hobbies/interests, junior miss, leadership, rodeo. *Special characteristics:* children and siblings of alumni, children of faculty/staff. *Tuition waivers:* Full or partial for children of alumni, employees or children of employees. *ROTC:* Army cooperative.

LOANS *Student loans:* $7,703,496 (41% need-based, 59% non-need-based). 74% of past graduating class borrowed through all loan programs. *Average indebtedness per student:* $31,508. *Average need-based loan:* Freshmen: $4961. Undergraduates: $6481. *Parent loans:* $2,442,399 (100% non-need-based). *Programs:* Federal Direct (Subsidized and Unsubsidized Stafford, PLUS), Perkins.

WORK-STUDY *Federal work-study:* jobs available. *State or other work-study/employment:* Total amount: $362,316 (100% non-need-based). Part-time jobs available.

ATHLETIC AWARDS Total amount: $11,649,482 (100% non-need-based).

APPLYING FOR FINANCIAL AID *Required financial aid form:* FAFSA. *Financial aid deadline (priority):* 2/1. *Notification date:* Continuous beginning 10/30. Students must reply within 4 weeks of notification.

CONTACT Office of Financial Aid, Missouri Valley College, 500 East College, Marshall, MO 65340-3197, 660-831-4171. *Fax:* 660-831-4003. *E-mail:* financialaid@moval.edu.
Website: http://www.moval.edu/.

MISSOURI WESTERN STATE UNIVERSITY
St. Joseph, MO

Tuition & fees (MO res): $6842	Average undergraduate aid package: N/A

ABOUT THE INSTITUTION State-supported, coed. *Awards:* certificates, associate, bachelor's, and master's degrees. 52 undergraduate majors. *Total enrollment:* 5,533. Undergraduates: 5,292. Freshmen: 979. Federal methodology is used as a basis for awarding need-based institutional aid.

UNDERGRADUATE EXPENSES for 2017–2018 *Tuition, state resident:* full-time $6124; part-time $204.14 per credit hour. *Tuition, nonresident:* full-time $12,632; part-time $421.05 per credit hour. *Required fees:* full-time $718; $99.10 per credit hour. Full-time tuition and fees vary according to course load and program. Part-time tuition and fees vary according to course load and program. *College room and board:* $8102; *Room only:* $4644. Room and board charges vary according to board plan and housing facility.

GIFT AID (NEED-BASED) *Scholarships, grants, and awards:* Federal Pell, FSEOG, state, private, college/university gift aid from institutional funds.

GIFT AID (NON-NEED-BASED) *Scholarships, grants, and awards by category: Academic interests/achievement:* architecture, biological sciences, business, communication, computer science, education, engineering/technologies, English, foreign languages, general academic interests/achievements, home economics, humanities, mathematics, military science, physical sciences, premedicine, religion/biblical studies, social sciences. *Creative arts/performance:* art/fine arts, cinema/film/broadcasting, creative writing, dance, journalism/publications, music, performing arts, theater/drama. *Special achievements/activities:* cheerleading/drum major, community service, general special achievements/activities, leadership, memberships, religious involvement. *Special characteristics:* adult students, children and siblings of alumni, children of public servants, children of union members/company employees, children of workers in trades, first-generation college students, general special characteristics, international students, local/state students, out-of-state students, previous college experience, public servants, religious affiliation, veterans. *Tuition waivers:* Full or partial for employees or children of employees, senior citizens. *ROTC:* Army.

LOANS *Programs:* Federal Direct (Subsidized and Unsubsidized Stafford, PLUS), Perkins.

WORK-STUDY *Federal work-study:* 325 jobs averaging $1428. *State or other work-study/employment:* 664 part-time jobs averaging $2071.

APPLYING FOR FINANCIAL AID *Required financial aid forms:* FAFSA, institutional scholarship application form. *Financial aid deadline:* Continuous. *Notification date:* Continuous beginning 4/15. Students must reply within 2 weeks of notification.

CONTACT Marilyn Baker, Director of Financial Aid, Missouri Western State University, 4525 Downs Drive, Saint Joseph, MO 64507-2294, 816-271-5986 or toll-free 800-662-7041. *Fax:* 816-271-5879. *E-mail:* mbaker3@missouriwestern.edu. *Website:* http://www.missouriwestern.edu/.

MITCHELL COLLEGE
New London, CT

Tuition & fees: N/R	Average undergraduate aid package: $23,370

ABOUT THE INSTITUTION Independent, coed. 14 undergraduate majors. Federal methodology is used as a basis for awarding need-based institutional aid.

FRESHMAN FINANCIAL AID (Fall 2016) 102 applied for aid; of those 87% were deemed to have need. 100% of freshmen with need received aid; of those 6% had need fully met. *Average percent of need met:* 60% (excluding resources awarded to replace EFC). *Average financial aid package:* $22,393 (excluding resources awarded to replace EFC). 183% of all full-time freshmen had no need and received non-need-based gift aid.

UNDERGRADUATE FINANCIAL AID (Fall 2016) 428 applied for aid; of those 87% were deemed to have need. 100% of undergraduates with need received aid; of those 9% had need fully met. *Average percent of need met:* 61% (excluding resources awarded to replace EFC). *Average financial aid package:* $23,370 (excluding resources awarded to replace EFC). 61% of all full-time undergraduates had no need and received non-need-based gift aid.

GIFT AID (NEED-BASED) Total amount: $10,017,723 (13% federal, 6% state, 77% institutional, 4% external sources). **Receiving aid:** Freshmen: 82% (89); all full-time undergraduates: 70% (374). **Average award:** Freshmen: $19,245; Undergraduates: $19,756. **Scholarships, grants, and awards:** Federal Pell, FSEOG, state, private, college/university gift aid from institutional funds.

GIFT AID (NON-NEED-BASED) Total amount: $2,492,152 (3% state, 69% institutional, 28% external sources). **Receiving aid:** Freshmen: 82% (89). Undergraduates: 67% (359). **Average award:** Freshmen: $8551. Undergraduates: $9311. **Scholarships, grants, and awards by category:** Special achievements/activities: general special achievements/activities, leadership. **Special characteristics:** siblings of current students.

LOANS Student loans: $4,687,731 (75% need-based, 25% non-need-based). 75% of past graduating class borrowed through all loan programs. **Average indebtedness per student:** $36,430. **Average need-based loan:** Freshmen: $3457. Undergraduates: $3916. **Parent loans:** $2,411,049 (68% need-based, 32% non-need-based). **Programs:** Federal Direct (Subsidized and Unsubsidized Stafford, PLUS), Perkins, alternative loans.

WORK-STUDY Federal work-study: jobs available.

APPLYING FOR FINANCIAL AID Required financial aid form: FAFSA. **Financial aid deadline:** Continuous. **Notification date:** Continuous beginning 1/3. Students must reply by 5/1 or within 2 weeks of notification.

CONTACT Dan Brewer, Director of Financial Aid, Mitchell College, 437 Pequot Avenue, New London, CT 06320-4498, 800-629-6047 or toll-free 800-443-2811. *Fax:* 860-444-1209. *E-mail:* brewer_d@mitchell.edu. *Website:* http://www.mitchell.edu/.

MOLLOY COLLEGE
Rockville Centre, NY

Tuition & fees: $30,310	Average undergraduate aid package: $16,123

ABOUT THE INSTITUTION Independent, coed. **Awards:** certificates, associate, bachelor's, master's, and doctoral degrees. 43 undergraduate majors. **Total enrollment:** 4,980. Undergraduates: 3,534. Freshmen: 514. Federal methodology is used as a basis for awarding need-based institutional aid.

UNDERGRADUATE EXPENSES for 2017–2018 Application fee: $40. **Comprehensive fee:** $45,022 includes full-time tuition ($29,110), mandatory fees ($1200), and room and board ($14,712). Full-time tuition and fees vary according to degree level. Room and board charges vary according to board plan. **Part-time tuition:** $965 per credit hour. Part-time tuition and fees vary according to degree level.

FRESHMAN FINANCIAL AID (Fall 2016) 539 applied for aid; of those 88% were deemed to have need. 100% of freshmen with need received aid; of those 11% had need fully met. **Average percent of need met:** 57% (excluding resources awarded to replace EFC). **Average financial aid package:** $19,410 (excluding resources awarded to replace EFC). 9% of all full-time freshmen had no need and received non-need-based gift aid.

UNDERGRADUATE FINANCIAL AID (Fall 2016) 2,630 applied for aid; of those 90% were deemed to have need. 100% of undergraduates with need received aid; of those 9% had need fully met. **Average percent of need met:** 46% (excluding resources awarded to replace EFC). **Average financial aid package:** $16,123 (excluding resources awarded to replace EFC). 8% of all full-time undergraduates had no need and received non-need-based gift aid.

GIFT AID (NEED-BASED) Total amount: $26,701,641 (19% federal, 12% state, 67% institutional, 2% external sources). **Receiving aid:** Freshmen: 83% (467); all full-time undergraduates: 76% (2,212). **Average award:** Freshmen: $15,007; Undergraduates: $12,441. **Scholarships, grants, and awards:** Federal Pell, FSEOG, state, private, college/university gift aid from institutional funds, Federal Nursing, TEACH Grants, TRiO Grants.

GIFT AID (NON-NEED-BASED) Total amount: $3,726,878 (7% state, 92% institutional, 1% external sources). **Receiving aid:** Freshmen: 7% (41). Undergraduates: 5% (151). **Average award:** Freshmen: $12,848. Undergraduates: $9906. **Scholarships, grants, and awards by category:** Academic interests/achievement: 1,610 awards ($12,938,125 total): biological sciences, business, communication, education, English, general academic interests/achievements, humanities, international studies, mathematics, social sciences. Creative arts/performance: 58 awards ($142,750 total): art/fine arts, creative writing, music, performing arts, theater/drama. Special achievements/activities: 601 awards ($2,562,533 total): community service, general special achievements/activities, leadership, memberships, religious involvement. Special characteristics: 72 awards ($100,163 total): ethnic background, members of minority groups, religious affiliation, siblings of current students, veterans. **Tuition waivers:** Full or partial for employees or children of employees, senior citizens. **ROTC:** Army cooperative, Naval cooperative.

LOANS Student loans: $27,753,638 (82% need-based, 18% non-need-based). 76% of past graduating class borrowed through all loan programs. **Average indebtedness per student:** $33,197. **Average need-based loan:** Freshmen: $3162. Undergraduates: $4152. **Parent loans:** $13,710,438 (62% need-based, 38% non-need-based). **Programs:** Federal Direct (Subsidized and Unsubsidized Stafford, PLUS), Perkins, Federal Nursing, private loans.

WORK-STUDY Federal work-study: 197 jobs averaging $1501.

ATHLETIC AWARDS Total amount: $1,830,483 (73% need-based, 27% non-need-based).

APPLYING FOR FINANCIAL AID Required financial aid forms: FAFSA, state aid form. **Financial aid deadline:** 5/1 (priority: 4/15). **Notification date:** Continuous beginning 1/20. Students must reply within 5 weeks of notification.

CONTACT Ana C. Lockward, Director of Financial Aid, Molloy College, 1000 Hempstead Avenue, Rockville Centre, NY 11571, 516-323-4200 or toll-free 888-4MOLLOY. *Fax:* 516-323-4213. *E-mail:* alockward@molloy.edu. *Website:* http://www.molloy.edu/.

MONMOUTH COLLEGE
Monmouth, IL

Tuition & fees: $37,674	Average undergraduate aid package: $34,091

ABOUT THE INSTITUTION Independent Presbyterian Church, coed. **Awards:** bachelor's degrees. 36 undergraduate majors. **Total enrollment:** 1,033. Undergraduates: 1,033. Federal methodology is used as a basis for awarding need-based institutional aid.

UNDERGRADUATE EXPENSES for 2018–2019 Comprehensive fee: $46,640 includes full-time tuition ($37,674) and room and board ($8966). **College room only:** $5054. Room and board charges vary according to housing facility. **Part-time tuition:** $4709 per course.

FRESHMAN FINANCIAL AID (Fall 2017, est.) 273 applied for aid; of those 93% were deemed to have need. 100% of freshmen with need received aid; of those 29% had need fully met. **Average percent of need met:** 92% (excluding resources awarded to replace EFC). **Average financial aid package:** $35,129 (excluding resources awarded to replace EFC). 10% of all full-time freshmen had no need and received non-need-based gift aid.

UNDERGRADUATE FINANCIAL AID (Fall 2017, est.) 903 applied for aid; of those 94% were deemed to have need. 100% of undergraduates with need received aid; of those 24% had need fully met. **Average percent of need met:** 89% (excluding resources awarded to replace EFC). **Average financial aid package:** $34,091 (excluding resources awarded to replace EFC). 15% of all full-time undergraduates had no need and received non-need-based gift aid.

GIFT AID (NEED-BASED) Total amount: $24,197,850 (8% federal, 9% state, 81% institutional, 2% external sources). **Receiving aid:** Freshmen: 90% (253); all full-time undergraduates: 84% (851). **Average award:** Freshmen: $29,547; Undergraduates: $28,485. **Scholarships, grants, and awards:** Federal Pell, FSEOG, state, private, college/university gift aid from institutional funds.

GIFT AID (NON-NEED-BASED) Total amount: $4,081,710 (95% institutional, 5% external sources). **Receiving aid:** Freshmen: 19% (52). Undergraduates: 15% (148). **Average award:** Freshmen: $23,241. Undergraduates: $21,863. **Scholarships, grants, and awards by category:** Academic interests/achievement: foreign languages, general academic interests/achievements. Creative arts/performance: art/fine arts, debating, music, theater/drama. Special achievements/activities: general special achievements/activities, religious involvement. Special characteristics: international students, veterans. **Tuition waivers:** Full or partial for employees or children of employees. **ROTC:** Army cooperative.

LOANS Student loans: $6,215,507 (49% need-based, 51% non-need-based). 96% of past graduating class borrowed through all loan programs. **Average indebtedness per student:** $33,333. **Average need-based loan:** Freshmen: $4249. Undergraduates: $4832. **Parent loans:** $28,944,702 (100% non-need-based). **Programs:** Federal Direct (Subsidized and Unsubsidized Stafford, PLUS), Perkins.

WORK-STUDY *Federal work-study:* Total amount: $637,429; 456 jobs averaging $1341. *State or other work-study/employment:* Part-time jobs available.
APPLYING FOR FINANCIAL AID *Required financial aid form:* FAFSA. *Financial aid deadline (priority):* 10/15. *Notification date:* Continuous beginning 11/15. Students must reply by 5/1.
CONTACT Mrs. Jayne A. Schreck, Associate Vice President for Financial Aid, Monmouth College, 700 East Broadway, Monmouth, IL 61462-1998, 309-457-2129 or toll-free 800-747-2687. *Fax:* 309-457-2373. *E-mail:* jayne@monmouthcollege.edu. *Website:* http://www.monmouthcollege.edu/.

MONMOUTH UNIVERSITY
West Long Branch, NJ

Tuition & fees: $36,732	Average undergraduate aid package: $27,389

ABOUT THE INSTITUTION Independent, coed. *Awards:* certificates, bachelor's, master's, and doctoral degrees. 34 undergraduate majors. *Total enrollment:* 6,371. Undergraduates: 4,707. Freshmen: 1,089. Federal methodology is used as a basis for awarding need-based institutional aid.
UNDERGRADUATE EXPENSES for 2017–2018 *Application fee:* $50. *One-time required fee:* $200. *Comprehensive fee:* $50,284 includes full-time tuition ($36,032), mandatory fees ($700), and room and board ($13,552). *College room only:* $7784. Room and board charges vary according to board plan and housing facility. *Part-time tuition:* $1043 per credit hour. *Part-time fees:* $175 per term. Part-time tuition and fees vary according to course load.
FRESHMAN FINANCIAL AID (Fall 2017, est.) 991 applied for aid; of those 86% were deemed to have need. 100% of freshmen with need received aid; of those 94% had need fully met. *Average percent of need met:* 70% (excluding resources awarded to replace EFC). *Average financial aid package:* $28,429 (excluding resources awarded to replace EFC). 20% of all full-time freshmen had no need and received non-need-based gift aid.
UNDERGRADUATE FINANCIAL AID (Fall 2017, est.) 3,719 applied for aid; of those 87% were deemed to have need. 100% of undergraduates with need received aid; of those 97% had need fully met. *Average percent of need met:* 66% (excluding resources awarded to replace EFC). *Average financial aid package:* $27,389 (excluding resources awarded to replace EFC). 26% of all full-time undergraduates had no need and received non-need-based gift aid.
GIFT AID (NEED-BASED) *Total amount:* $60,748,616 (12% federal, 19% state, 66% institutional, 3% external sources). *Receiving aid:* Freshmen: 65% (705); all full-time undergraduates: 58% (2,739). *Average award:* Freshmen: $14,099; Undergraduates: $12,962. *Scholarships, grants, and awards:* Federal Pell, FSEOG, state, private, college/university gift aid from institutional funds, Federal Nursing.
GIFT AID (NON-NEED-BASED) *Total amount:* $12,220,555 (94% institutional, 6% external sources). *Receiving aid:* Freshmen: 65% (705). Undergraduates: 58% (2,739). *Average award:* Freshmen: $11,854. Undergraduates: $9517. *Scholarships, grants, and awards by category:* Academic interests/achievement: 4,386 awards ($40,354,546 total): biological sciences, business, communication, computer science, education, English, foreign languages, general academic interests/achievements, home economics, humanities, mathematics, physical sciences, social sciences. *Special achievements/activities:* 1 award ($2500 total): leadership. *Special characteristics:* 804 awards ($5,394,824 total): adult students, children and siblings of alumni, children of faculty/staff, children of public servants, first-generation college students, general special characteristics, international students, local/state students, members of minority groups, out-of-state students, previous college experience, veterans, veterans' children. *Tuition waivers:* Full or partial for employees or children of employees, senior citizens. *ROTC:* Army cooperative, Air Force cooperative.
LOANS *Student loans:* $25,819,660 (47% need-based, 53% non-need-based). 72% of past graduating class borrowed through all loan programs. *Average indebtedness per student:* $30,985. *Average need-based loan:* Freshmen: $3435. Undergraduates: $4689. *Parent loans:* $15,758,651 (100% non-need-based). *Programs:* Federal Direct (Subsidized and Unsubsidized Stafford, PLUS), Perkins, state, college/university, private loans.
WORK-STUDY *Federal work-study:* Total amount: $3,846,739; 2,022 jobs averaging $1965.
ATHLETIC AWARDS Total amount: $9,351,514 (62% need-based, 38% non-need-based).

APPLYING FOR FINANCIAL AID *Required financial aid form:* FAFSA. *Financial aid deadline:* Continuous. *Notification date:* Continuous beginning 12/15. Students must reply within 2 weeks of notification.
CONTACT Ms. Claire Alasio, Associate Vice President and Director of Financial Aid, Monmouth University, 400 Cedar Avenue, West Long Branch, NJ 07764-1898, 732-571-3463 or toll-free 800-543-9671. *Fax:* 732-923-4791. *E-mail:* finaid@monmouth.edu. *Website:* http://www.monmouth.edu/.

MONROE COLLEGE
Bronx, NY

CONTACT Mr. Daniel Sharon, Director of Student Financial Services, Monroe College, 2501 Jerome Avenue, Bronx, NY 10468, 646-393-8257 or toll-free 800-55MONROE. *Fax:* 718-817-8401. *E-mail:* dsharon@monroecollege.edu. *Website:* http://www.monroecollege.edu/.

MONTANA BIBLE COLLEGE
Bozeman, MT

CONTACT Financial Aid Office, Montana Bible College, 3625 South 19th Avenue, Bozeman, MT 59718, 406-586-3585 or toll-free 888-462-2463. *Website:* http://www.montanabiblecollege.edu/.

MONTANA STATE UNIVERSITY
Bozeman, MT

Tuition & fees (MT res): $7223	Average undergraduate aid package: $11,308

ABOUT THE INSTITUTION State-supported, coed. *Awards:* certificates, associate, bachelor's, master's, and doctoral degrees. 59 undergraduate majors. *Total enrollment:* 16,440. Undergraduates: 14,400. Freshmen: 3,503. Federal methodology is used as a basis for awarding need-based institutional aid.
UNDERGRADUATE EXPENSES for 2017–2018 *Application fee:* $30. *Tuition, state resident:* full-time $5490; part-time $229 per credit hour. *Tuition, nonresident:* full-time $22,194; part-time $925 per credit hour. *Required fees:* full-time $1733; $113 per credit hour. Full-time tuition and fees vary according to course load, degree level, location, and program. Part-time tuition and fees vary according to course load, degree level, location, and program. *College room and board:* $9250. Room and board charges vary according to board plan and housing facility.
FRESHMAN FINANCIAL AID (Fall 2016) 1,995 applied for aid; of those 59% were deemed to have need. 95% of freshmen with need received aid; of those 41% had need fully met. *Average percent of need met:* 76% (excluding resources awarded to replace EFC). *Average financial aid package:* $1154 (excluding resources awarded to replace EFC). 16% of all full-time freshmen had no need and received non-need-based gift aid.
UNDERGRADUATE FINANCIAL AID (Fall 2016) 7,706 applied for aid; of those 70% were deemed to have need. 96% of undergraduates with need received aid; of those 32% had need fully met. *Average percent of need met:* 74% (excluding resources awarded to replace EFC). *Average financial aid package:* $11,308 (excluding resources awarded to replace EFC). 10% of all full-time undergraduates had no need and received non-need-based gift aid.
GIFT AID (NEED-BASED) *Total amount:* $20,916,722 (70% federal, 2% state, 15% institutional, 13% external sources). *Receiving aid:* Freshmen: 34% (861); all full-time undergraduates: 32% (3,767). *Average award:* Freshmen: $4967; Undergraduates: $4905. *Scholarships, grants, and awards:* Federal Pell, FSEOG, state, private, college/university gift aid from institutional funds, Federal Nursing.
GIFT AID (NON-NEED-BASED) *Total amount:* $5,710,747 (8% state, 46% institutional, 46% external sources). *Receiving aid:* Freshmen: 3% (73). Undergraduates: 1% (173). *Average award:* Freshmen: $1798. Undergraduates: $2012. *Scholarships, grants, and awards by category:* Academic interests/achievement: agriculture, architecture, area/ethnic studies, biological sciences, business, communi-

ration, computer science, education, engineering/technologies, English, foreign languages, general academic interests/achievements, health fields, home economics, humanities, mathematics, military science, physical sciences, social sciences. *Creative arts/performance:* art/fine arts, cinema/film/broadcasting, dance, music, theater/drama. *Special achievements/activities:* general special achievements/activities, leadership. *Special characteristics:* children and siblings of alumni, general special characteristics, local/state students, members of minority groups. *Tuition waivers:* Full or partial for minority students, employees or children of employees, senior citizens. *ROTC:* Army, Air Force.

LOANS *Student loans:* $50,594,541 (70% need-based, 30% non-need-based). 55% of past graduating class borrowed through all loan programs. *Average indebtedness per student:* $27,254. *Average need-based loan:* Freshmen: $6560. Undergraduates: $7269. *Parent loans:* $28,961,839 (31% need-based, 69% non-need-based). *Programs:* Federal Direct (Subsidized and Unsubsidized Stafford, PLUS), Perkins, Federal Nursing, college/university.

WORK-STUDY *Federal work-study:* jobs available. *State or other work-study/employment:* Total amount: $483,181 (100% need-based). Part-time jobs available.

ATHLETIC AWARDS Total amount: $1,727,811 (21% need-based, 79% non-need-based).

APPLYING FOR FINANCIAL AID *Required financial aid form:* FAFSA. *Financial aid deadline (priority):* 3/1. *Notification date:* Continuous beginning 4/1.

CONTACT Brandi Payne, Director of Financial Aid, Montana State University, PO Box 174160, Bozeman, MT 59717-4160, 406-994-2845 or toll-free 888-MSU-CATS. *Fax:* 406-994-6962. *E-mail:* bpayne@montana.edu. *Website:* http://www.montana.edu/.

ogies, English, foreign languages, general academic interests/achievements, health fields, humanities, mathematics, physical sciences, premedicine, social sciences. *Creative arts/performance:* art/fine arts, music, theater/drama. *Special achievements/activities:* cheerleading/drum major, general special achievements/activities. *Special characteristics:* adult students, children and siblings of alumni, children of faculty/staff, children of union members/company employees, ethnic background, first-generation college students, local/state students, members of minority groups, out-of-state students, veterans. *Tuition waivers:* Full or partial for employees or children of employees, senior citizens. *ROTC:* Army.

LOANS *Student loans:* $13,012,806 (75% need-based, 25% non-need-based). 68% of past graduating class borrowed through all loan programs. *Average indebtedness per student:* $26,780. *Average need-based loan:* Freshmen: $5454. Undergraduates: $6113. *Parent loans:* $2,589,496 (17% need-based, 83% non-need-based). *Programs:* Federal Direct (Subsidized and Unsubsidized Stafford, PLUS), college/university.

WORK-STUDY *Federal work-study:* jobs available. *State or other work-study/employment:* Total amount: $297,189 (95% need-based, 5% non-need-based). Part-time jobs available.

ATHLETIC AWARDS Total amount: $767,025 (40% need-based, 60% non-need-based).

APPLYING FOR FINANCIAL AID *Required financial aid form:* FAFSA. *Financial aid deadline:* Continuous. *Notification date:* Continuous beginning 3/1.

CONTACT Emily Williamson, Director of Financial Aid and Scholarships, Montana State University Billings, 1500 University Drive, Billings, MT 59101, 406-657-1617 or toll-free 800-565-6782. *Fax:* 406-657-1789. *E-mail:* finaid@msubillings.edu. *Website:* http://www.msubillings.edu/.

MONTANA STATE UNIVERSITY BILLINGS
Billings, MT

Tuition & fees (MT res): $5826	Average undergraduate aid package: $10,006

ABOUT THE INSTITUTION State-supported, coed. *Awards:* certificates, associate, bachelor's, and master's degrees. 70 undergraduate majors. *Total enrollment:* 4,388. Undergraduates: 3,972. Federal methodology is used as a basis for awarding need-based institutional aid.

UNDERGRADUATE EXPENSES for 2017–2018 *Application fee:* $30. *Tuition, state resident:* full-time $4397; part-time $183.20 per credit hour. *Tuition, nonresident:* full-time $16,662; part-time $715.10 per credit hour. *Required fees:* full-time $1429. Full-time tuition and fees vary according to course load, location, and program. Part-time tuition and fees vary according to course load, location, and program. *College room and board:* $7510. Room and board charges vary according to board plan, housing facility, and location.

FRESHMAN FINANCIAL AID (Fall 2016) 481 applied for aid; of those 74% were deemed to have need. 99% of freshmen with need received aid; of those 34% had need fully met. *Average percent of need met:* 74% (excluding resources awarded to replace EFC). *Average financial aid package:* $9959 (excluding resources awarded to replace EFC). 9% of all full-time freshmen had no need and received non-need-based gift aid.

UNDERGRADUATE FINANCIAL AID (Fall 2016) 1,848 applied for aid; of those 80% were deemed to have need. 99% of undergraduates with need received aid; of those 34% had need fully met. *Average percent of need met:* 75% (excluding resources awarded to replace EFC). *Average financial aid package:* $10,006 (excluding resources awarded to replace EFC). 6% of all full-time undergraduates had no need and received non-need-based gift aid.

GIFT AID (NEED-BASED) *Total amount:* $6,748,863 (75% federal, 1% state, 18% institutional, 6% external sources). *Receiving aid:* Freshmen: 56% (314); all full-time undergraduates: 50% (1,241). *Average award:* Freshmen: $4512; Undergraduates: $4468. *Scholarships, grants, and awards:* Federal Pell, FSEOG, private, college/university gift aid from institutional funds, Montana Tuition Waiver Awards.

GIFT AID (NON-NEED-BASED) *Total amount:* $678,242 (6% state, 65% institutional, 29% external sources). *Receiving aid:* Freshmen: 3% (15). Undergraduates: 2% (39). *Average award:* Freshmen: $2136. Undergraduates: $2625. *Scholarships, grants, and awards by category:* Academic interests/achievement: biological sciences, business, communication, computer science, education, engineering/technol-

---

MONTANA STATE UNIVERSITY– NORTHERN
Havre, MT

CONTACT Cindy Small, Director of Financial Aid, Montana State University–Northern, PO Box 7751, Havre, MT 59501, 406-265-3787 or toll-free 800-662-6132. *Website:* http://www.msun.edu/.

MONTANA TECH OF THE UNIVERSITY OF MONTANA
Butte, MT

Tuition & fees (MT res): $7411	Average undergraduate aid package: $11,025

ABOUT THE INSTITUTION State-supported, coed. *Awards:* certificates, diplomas, associate, bachelor's, master's, and doctoral degrees. 40 undergraduate majors. *Total enrollment:* 2,678. Undergraduates: 2,428. Freshmen: 384. Federal methodology is used as a basis for awarding need-based institutional aid.

UNDERGRADUATE EXPENSES for 2018–2019 *Application fee:* $30. *Tuition, state resident:* full-time $5707. *Tuition, nonresident:* full-time $20,870. *Required fees:* full-time $1704. Full-time tuition and fees vary according to course load, degree level, location, and program. Part-time tuition and fees vary according to course load, degree level, location, and program. *College room and board:* $9828; *Room only:* $4366. Room and board charges vary according to board plan.

FRESHMAN FINANCIAL AID (Fall 2016) 287 applied for aid; of those 70% were deemed to have need. 100% of freshmen with need received aid; of those 22% had need fully met. *Average percent of need met:* 67% (excluding resources awarded to replace EFC). *Average financial aid package:* $10,327 (excluding resources awarded to replace EFC). 14% of all full-time freshmen had no need and received non-need-based gift aid.

UNDERGRADUATE FINANCIAL AID (Fall 2016) 1,421 applied for aid; of those 79% were deemed to have need. 100% of undergraduates with need received aid; of those 13% had need fully met. *Average percent of need met:* 59% (excluding resources awarded to replace EFC). *Average financial aid package:* $11,025 (excluding resources awarded to replace EFC). 13% of all full-time undergraduates had no need and received non-need-based gift aid.

GIFT AID (NEED-BASED) *Total amount:* $5,682,880 (64% federal, 1% state, 27% institutional, 8% external sources). *Receiving aid:* Freshmen: 51% (174); all full-time undergraduates: 45% (930). *Average award:* Freshmen: $5777; Undergraduates: $5768. *Scholarships, grants, and awards:* Federal Pell, FSEOG, state, private, college/university gift aid from institutional funds.

GIFT AID (NON-NEED-BASED) *Total amount:* $1,927,578 (7% state, 66% institutional, 27% external sources). *Receiving aid:* Freshmen: 9% (30). Undergraduates: 4% (75). *Average award:* Freshmen: $3862. Undergraduates: $3784. *Scholarships, grants, and awards by category:* Academic interests/achievement: biological sciences, business, communication, computer science, engineering/technologies, general academic interests/achievements, home economics, humanities, mathematics, physical sciences. *Special achievements/activities:* community service, general special achievements/activities, hobbies/interests, leadership, memberships. *Special characteristics:* children and siblings of alumni, children of faculty/staff, first-generation college students, general special characteristics, local/state students, married students, out-of-state students, veterans. *Tuition waivers:* Full or partial for minority students, employees or children of employees, senior citizens.

LOANS *Student loans:* $7,458,575 (77% need-based, 23% non-need-based). 54% of past graduating class borrowed through all loan programs. *Average indebtedness per student:* $27,926. *Average need-based loan:* Freshmen: $3325. Undergraduates: $3992. *Parent loans:* $1,846,127 (34% need-based, 66% non-need-based). *Programs:* Federal Direct (Subsidized and Unsubsidized Stafford, PLUS).

WORK-STUDY *Federal work-study:* jobs available. *State or other work-study/employment:* Total amount: $11,250 (100% need-based). Part-time jobs available.

ATHLETIC AWARDS Total amount: $982,963 (50% need-based, 50% non-need-based).

APPLYING FOR FINANCIAL AID *Required financial aid form:* FAFSA. *Financial aid deadline (priority):* 12/1. *Notification date:* Continuous beginning 2/15. Students must reply within 2 weeks of notification.

CONTACT Shauna Savage, Assistant Director of Financial Aid, Montana Tech of The University of Montana, 1300 West Park Street, Butte, MT 59701-8997, 406-496-4256 or toll-free 800-445-TECH. *Fax:* 406-496-4710. *E-mail:* financialaid@mtech.edu. *Website:* http://www.mtech.edu/.

MONTCLAIR STATE UNIVERSITY
Montclair, NJ

Tuition & fees (NJ res): $12,455	Average undergraduate aid package: $9931

ABOUT THE INSTITUTION State-supported, coed. *Awards:* certificates, bachelor's, master's, and doctoral degrees. 64 undergraduate majors. *Total enrollment:* 21,013. Undergraduates: 16,852. Freshmen: 3,004. Federal methodology is used as a basis for awarding need-based institutional aid.

UNDERGRADUATE EXPENSES for 2017–2018 *Application fee:* $65. *Tuition, state resident:* full-time $10,808; part-time $360 per credit. *Tuition, nonresident:* full-time $18,920; part-time $631 per credit. *Required fees:* full-time $1647; $55 per credit. *College room and board:* $13,466. Room and board charges vary according to board plan and housing facility.

FRESHMAN FINANCIAL AID (Fall 2016) 2,757 applied for aid; of those 84% were deemed to have need. 92% of freshmen with need received aid; of those 12% had need fully met. *Average percent of need met:* 66% (excluding resources awarded to replace EFC). *Average financial aid package:* $9632 (excluding resources awarded to replace EFC). 4% of all full-time freshmen had no need and received non-need-based gift aid.

UNDERGRADUATE FINANCIAL AID (Fall 2016) 12,347 applied for aid; of those 87% were deemed to have need. 95% of undergraduates with need received aid; of those 12% had need fully met. *Average percent of need met:* 67% (excluding resources awarded to replace EFC). *Average financial aid package:* $9931 (excluding resources awarded to replace EFC). 3% of all full-time undergraduates had no need and received non-need-based gift aid.

GIFT AID (NEED-BASED) *Total amount:* $60,596,839 (54% federal, 46% state). *Receiving aid:* Freshmen: 49% (1,460); all full-time undergraduates: 41% (6,887). *Average award:* Freshmen: $9457; Undergraduates: $8536. *Scholarships, grants, and awards:* Federal Pell, FSEOG, state, private, college/university gift aid from institutional funds.

GIFT AID (NON-NEED-BASED) *Total amount:* $4,636,002 (5% state, 56% institutional, 39% external sources). *Receiving aid:* Freshmen: 4% (105). Undergraduates: 3% (445). *Average award:* Freshmen: $3175. Undergraduates: $4899. *Scholarships, grants, and awards by category:* Academic interests/achievement: biological sciences, business, communication, education, English, foreign languages, general academic interests/achievements, home economics, humanities, international studies, mathematics, physical sciences, religion/biblical studies, social sciences. *Creative arts/performance:* art/fine arts, cinema/film/broadcasting, dance, music, performing arts, theater/drama. *Special achievements/activities:* community service, general special achievements/activities, leadership. *Special characteristics:* children and siblings of alumni, international students. *Tuition waivers:* Full or partial for employees or children of employees, senior citizens.

LOANS *Student loans:* $90,829,540 (39% need-based, 61% non-need-based). 71% of past graduating class borrowed through all loan programs. *Average indebtedness per student:* $28,070. *Average need-based loan:* Freshmen: $3325. Undergraduates: $4229. *Parent loans:* $23,381,887 (100% non-need-based). *Programs:* Federal Direct (Subsidized and Unsubsidized Stafford, PLUS), Perkins, state, private loans.

WORK-STUDY *Federal work-study:* 533 jobs averaging $1362. *State or other work-study/employment:* Total amount: $5,960,178 (100% non-need-based). Part-time jobs available.

APPLYING FOR FINANCIAL AID *Required financial aid forms:* FAFSA, state aid form. *Financial aid deadline (priority):* 2/1. *Notification date:* Continuous beginning 2/15. Students must reply within 2 weeks of notification.

CONTACT Mr. James T. Anderson, Director of Financial Aid, Montclair State University, College Hall, Room 222, Montclair, NJ 07043, 973-655-7022. *Fax:* 973-655-7712. *E-mail:* financialaid@montclair.edu. *Website:* http://www.montclair.edu/.

MONTREAT COLLEGE
Montreat, NC

Tuition & fees: N/R	Average undergraduate aid package: $20,747

ABOUT THE INSTITUTION Independent Presbyterian Church (U.S.A.), coed. 19 undergraduate majors. Federal methodology is used as a basis for awarding need-based institutional aid.

FRESHMAN FINANCIAL AID (Fall 2016) 170 applied for aid; of those 91% were deemed to have need. 100% of freshmen with need received aid; of those 8% had need fully met. *Average percent of need met:* 66% (excluding resources awarded to replace EFC). *Average financial aid package:* $21,786 (excluding resources awarded to replace EFC). 5% of all full-time freshmen had no need and received non-need-based gift aid.

UNDERGRADUATE FINANCIAL AID (Fall 2016) 457 applied for aid; of those 91% were deemed to have need. 100% of undergraduates with need received aid; of those 10% had need fully met. *Average percent of need met:* 66% (excluding resources awarded to replace EFC). *Average financial aid package:* $20,747 (excluding resources awarded to replace EFC). 11% of all full-time undergraduates had no need and received non-need-based gift aid.

GIFT AID (NEED-BASED) *Total amount:* $4,966,547 (30% federal, 20% state, 33% institutional, 17% external sources). *Receiving aid:* Freshmen: 82% (154); all full-time undergraduates: 80% (409). *Average award:* Freshmen: $17,306; Undergraduates: $16,318. *Scholarships, grants, and awards:* Federal Pell, FSEOG, state, private, college/university gift aid from institutional funds.

GIFT AID (NON-NEED-BASED) *Total amount:* $717,866 (71% institutional, 29% external sources). *Receiving aid:* Freshmen: 3% (5). Undergraduates: 4% (21). *Average award:* Freshmen: $5551. Undergraduates: $8786. *Scholarships, grants, and awards by category:* Academic interests/achievement: computer science, general academic interests/achievements. *Creative arts/performance:* music. *Special achievements/activities:* leadership. *Special characteristics:* children and siblings of alumni, children of faculty/staff, first-generation college students, international students, local/state students, relatives of clergy, religious affiliation, veterans, veterans' children.

LOANS *Student loans:* $4,308,389 (84% need-based, 16% non-need-based). 78% of past graduating class borrowed through all loan programs. *Average indebtedness per student:* $21,802. *Average need-based loan:* Freshmen: $4749. Undergrad-

uates: $4787. **Parent loans:** $1,058,297 (73% need-based, 27% non-need-based).
Programs: Federal Direct (Subsidized and Unsubsidized Stafford, PLUS), Perkins.
WORK-STUDY *Federal work-study:* 46 jobs averaging $1800. ***State or other work-study/employment:*** Total amount: $63,500 (83% need-based, 17% non-need-based). 29 part-time jobs averaging $1800.
ATHLETIC AWARDS Total amount: $2,684,631 (77% need-based, 23% non-need-based).
APPLYING FOR FINANCIAL AID *Required financial aid form:* FAFSA. *Financial aid deadline (priority):* 3/1. *Notification date:* Continuous beginning 1/15. Students must reply within 2 weeks of notification.
CONTACT MacKenzie May, Financial Aid Counselor, Montreat College, PO Box 1267, Montreat, NC 28757, 828-669-8012 or toll-free 800-622-6968. *Fax:* 828-412-0257. *E-mail:* financialaid@montreat.edu.
Website: http://www.montreat.edu/.

MONTSERRAT COLLEGE OF ART
Beverly, MA

CONTACT Emma Puglisi, Director of Financial Aid, Montserrat College of Art, 23 Essex Street, PO Box 26, Beverly, MA 01915, 978-922-8222 Ext. 1155 or toll-free 800-836-0487. *Fax:* 978-922-4268. *E-mail:* finaid@montserrat.edu.
Website: http://www.montserrat.edu/.

MOODY BIBLE INSTITUTE
Chicago, IL

Tuition & fees: N/R	Average undergraduate aid package: $5816

ABOUT THE INSTITUTION Independent nondenominational, coed. 8 undergraduate majors. Federal methodology is used as a basis for awarding need-based institutional aid.
FRESHMAN FINANCIAL AID (Fall 2017, est.) 243 applied for aid; of those 82% were deemed to have need. 98% of freshmen with need received aid; of those 13% had need fully met. *Average percent of need met:* 57% (excluding resources awarded to replace EFC). *Average financial aid package:* $5045 (excluding resources awarded to replace EFC). 14% of all full-time freshmen had no need and received non-need-based gift aid.
UNDERGRADUATE FINANCIAL AID (Fall 2017, est.) 1,769 applied for aid; of those 87% were deemed to have need. 97% of undergraduates with need received aid; of those 14% had need fully met. *Average percent of need met:* 57% (excluding resources awarded to replace EFC). *Average financial aid package:* $5816 (excluding resources awarded to replace EFC). 9% of all full-time undergraduates had no need and received non-need-based gift aid.
GIFT AID (NEED-BASED) *Total amount:* $13,800,073 (28% federal, 68% institutional, 4% external sources). *Receiving aid:* Freshmen: 70% (191); all full-time undergraduates: 68% (1,460). *Average award:* Freshmen: $8846; Undergraduates: $9012. *Scholarships, grants, and awards:* Federal Pell, FSEOG, private, college/university gift aid from institutional funds.
GIFT AID (NON-NEED-BASED) *Total amount:* $5,393,115 (94% institutional, 6% external sources). *Receiving aid:* Freshmen: 8% (22). Undergraduates: 7% (157). *Average award:* Freshmen: $9866. Undergraduates: $8925.
LOANS *Student loans:* $6,213,840 (90% need-based, 10% non-need-based). 24% of past graduating class borrowed through all loan programs. *Average indebtedness per student:* $15,715. *Average need-based loan:* Freshmen: $3279. Undergraduates: $4033. *Parent loans:* $353,168 (91% need-based, 9% non-need-based). *Programs:* Federal Direct (Subsidized and Unsubsidized Stafford, PLUS), alternative loans, institutional loans for aviation students.
WORK-STUDY *Federal work-study:* Total amount: $109,222; 62 jobs averaging $1876.
APPLYING FOR FINANCIAL AID *Required financial aid forms:* FAFSA, institution's own form. *Financial aid deadline (priority):* 9/1. *Notification date:* Continuous beginning 3/29. Students must reply by 9/1.

CONTACT Moody Central, Moody Bible Institute, 820 North LaSalle Boulevard, Chicago, IL 60610-3284, 312-329-4184 or toll-free 800-967-4MBI. *Fax:* 312-329-4274. *E-mail:* financial.aid@moody.edu.
Website: http://www.moody.edu/.

MOORE COLLEGE OF ART & DESIGN
Philadelphia, PA

CONTACT Michelle Shonleber, Director of Financial Aid, Moore College of Art & Design, 20th and the Parkway, Philadelphia, PA 19103-1179, 215-965-4042 or toll-free 800-523-2025. *Fax:* 215-568-1773. *E-mail:* mshonleber@moore.edu.
Website: http://www.moore.edu/.

MORAVIAN COLLEGE
Bethlehem, PA

Tuition & fees: $43,636	Average undergraduate aid package: $30,834

ABOUT THE INSTITUTION Independent Moravian Church, coed. *Awards:* certificates, bachelor's, master's, and doctoral degrees. 34 undergraduate majors. *Total enrollment:* 2,463. Undergraduates: 2,033. Freshmen: 477. Federal methodology is used as a basis for awarding need-based institutional aid.
UNDERGRADUATE EXPENSES for 2018–2019 *One-time required fee:* $140. *Comprehensive fee:* $57,014 includes full-time tuition ($41,905), mandatory fees ($1731), and room and board ($13,378). *College room only:* $7538. Full-time tuition and fees vary according to class time and program. Room and board charges vary according to board plan and housing facility. *Part-time tuition:* $1548 per credit. Part-time tuition and fees vary according to class time.
FRESHMAN FINANCIAL AID (Fall 2017, est.) 483 applied for aid; of those 92% were deemed to have need. 100% of freshmen with need received aid; of those 16% had need fully met. *Average percent of need met:* 76% (excluding resources awarded to replace EFC). *Average financial aid package:* $32,824 (excluding resources awarded to replace EFC). 14% of all full-time freshmen had no need and received non-need-based gift aid.
UNDERGRADUATE FINANCIAL AID (Fall 2017, est.) 1,585 applied for aid; of those 94% were deemed to have need. 100% of undergraduates with need received aid; of those 15% had need fully met. *Average percent of need met:* 73% (excluding resources awarded to replace EFC). *Average financial aid package:* $30,834 (excluding resources awarded to replace EFC). 18% of all full-time undergraduates had no need and received non-need-based gift aid.
GIFT AID (NEED-BASED) *Total amount:* $36,874,183 (8% federal, 6% state, 84% institutional, 2% external sources). *Receiving aid:* Freshmen: 82% (444); all full-time undergraduates: 79% (1,476). *Average award:* Freshmen: $27,562; Undergraduates: $25,346. *Scholarships, grants, and awards:* Federal Pell, FSEOG, state, private, college/university gift aid from institutional funds, United Negro College Fund, Federal Nursing.
GIFT AID (NON-NEED-BASED) *Total amount:* $6,117,170 (94% institutional, 6% external sources). *Receiving aid:* Freshmen: 10% (54). Undergraduates: 8% (150). *Average award:* Freshmen: $20,297. Undergraduates: $14,331. *Scholarships, grants, and awards by category:* Academic interests/achievement: area/ethnic studies, biological sciences, business, communication, computer science, education, engineering/technologies, English, foreign languages, general academic interests/achievements, home economics, humanities, international studies, library science, mathematics, military science, physical sciences, premedicine, religion/biblical studies, social sciences. Creative arts/performance: art/fine arts, music. Special achievements/activities: community service, leadership, religious involvement. Special characteristics: adult students, children and siblings of alumni, children of educators, children of faculty/staff, children of union members/company employees, first-generation college students, international students, out-of-state students, relatives of clergy, religious affiliation, siblings of current students, veterans, veterans' children. *Tuition waivers:* Full or partial for employees or children of employees. *ROTC:* Army cooperative.
LOANS *Student loans:* $17,638,407 (69% need-based, 31% non-need-based). 86% of past graduating class borrowed through all loan programs. *Average indebtedness per student:* $33,096. *Average need-based loan:* Freshmen: $372. Undergraduates: $4433. *Parent loans:* $7,534,338 (54% need-based, 46% non-need-based).

Programs: Federal Direct (Subsidized and Unsubsidized Stafford, PLUS), Perkins, Federal Nursing, state.
WORK-STUDY *Federal work-study:* Total amount: $2,314,517; jobs available. *State or other work-study/employment:* Total amount: $83,050 (30% need-based, 70% non-need-based). Part-time jobs available.
APPLYING FOR FINANCIAL AID *Required financial aid form:* FAFSA. *Financial aid deadline:* Continuous. *Notification date:* Continuous beginning 11/20. Students must reply by 5/1.
CONTACT Dr. Dennis P. Levy, Director of Financial Aid Services, Moravian College, 1200 Main Street, Bethlehem, PA 18018-6650, 610-861-1330 or toll-free 800-441-3191. *Fax:* 610-861-1346. *E-mail:* levyd@moravian.edu.
Website: http://www.moravian.edu/.

MOREHEAD STATE UNIVERSITY
Morehead, KY

Tuition & fees (KY res): $8950	Average undergraduate aid package: $11,532

ABOUT THE INSTITUTION State-supported, coed. *Awards:* certificates, associate, bachelor's, master's, and doctoral degrees. 50 undergraduate majors. *Total enrollment:* 10,584. Undergraduates: 9,665. Freshmen: 1,271. Federal methodology is used as a basis for awarding need-based institutional aid.
UNDERGRADUATE EXPENSES for 2017–2018 *Application fee:* $30. *Tuition, state resident:* full-time $8950; part-time $374 per credit hour. *Tuition, nonresident:* full-time $13,426; part-time $561 per credit hour. Full-time tuition and fees vary according to course load, degree level, location, reciprocity agreements, and student level. Part-time tuition and fees vary according to course load, degree level, location, reciprocity agreements, and student level. *College room and board:* $9436; *Room only:* $5270. Room and board charges vary according to board plan and housing facility.
FRESHMAN FINANCIAL AID (Fall 2017, est.) 1,276 applied for aid; of those 85% were deemed to have need. 100% of freshmen with need received aid; of those 19% had need fully met. *Average percent of need met:* 64% (excluding resources awarded to replace EFC). *Average financial aid package:* $12,594 (excluding resources awarded to replace EFC). 15% of all full-time freshmen had no need and received non-need-based gift aid.
UNDERGRADUATE FINANCIAL AID (Fall 2017, est.) 4,858 applied for aid; of those 88% were deemed to have need. 99% of undergraduates with need received aid; of those 17% had need fully met. *Average percent of need met:* 61% (excluding resources awarded to replace EFC). *Average financial aid package:* $11,532 (excluding resources awarded to replace EFC). 15% of all full-time undergraduates had no need and received non-need-based gift aid.
GIFT AID (NEED-BASED) *Total amount:* $18,239,927 (77% federal, 22% state, 1% institutional). *Receiving aid:* Freshmen: 53% (711); all full-time undergraduates: 51% (2,879). *Average award:* Freshmen: $5836; Undergraduates: $5783. *Scholarships, grants, and awards:* Federal Pell, FSEOG, state, private, college/university gift aid from institutional funds.
GIFT AID (NON-NEED-BASED) *Total amount:* $22,350,143 (26% state, 65% institutional, 9% external sources). *Receiving aid:* Freshmen: 45% (594). Undergraduates: 52% (2,916). *Average award:* Freshmen: $7229. Undergraduates: $7684. *Scholarships, grants, and awards by category:* Academic interests/achievement: 1,802 awards ($9,227,041 total): agriculture, biological sciences, business, communication, education, engineering/technologies, general academic interests/achievements, health fields, international studies, military science, physical sciences, social sciences. *Creative arts/performance:* 89 awards ($183,149 total): applied art and design, art/fine arts, journalism/publications, music, theater/drama. *Special achievements/activities:* 287 awards ($916,704 total): cheerleading/drum major, community service, general special achievements/activities, junior miss, leadership. *Special characteristics:* 1,123 awards ($3,107,431 total): adult students, children and siblings of alumni, ethnic background, general special characteristics, handicapped students, international students, local/state students, members of minority groups, out-of-state students, previous college experience, veterans, veterans' children. *Tuition waivers:* Full or partial for minority students, children of alumni, employees or children of employees, senior citizens. *ROTC:* Army.
LOANS *Student loans:* $30,901,633 (42% need-based, 58% non-need-based). 71% of past graduating class borrowed through all loan programs. *Average indebtedness per student:* $26,623. *Average need-based loan:* Freshmen: $3165. Undergrad-

uates: $3769. *Parent loans:* $3,626,640 (100% non-need-based). *Programs:* Federal Direct (Subsidized and Unsubsidized Stafford, PLUS), Perkins, college/university.
WORK-STUDY *Federal work-study:* Total amount: $801,778; 341 jobs averaging $2327. *State or other work-study/employment:* Total amount: $2,070,639 (100% non-need-based). 765 part-time jobs averaging $2659.
ATHLETIC AWARDS Total amount: $2,465,397 (100% non-need-based).
APPLYING FOR FINANCIAL AID *Required financial aid form:* FAFSA. *Financial aid deadline (priority):* 3/15. *Notification date:* Continuous.
CONTACT Denise Trusty, Director of Financial Aid, Morehead State University, 205 Enrollment Services Center, Morehead, KY 40351, 606-783-2011 or toll-free 800-585-6781. *Fax:* 606-783-2293. *E-mail:* dmtrusty@moreheadstate.edu.
Website: http://www.moreheadstate.edu/.

MOREHOUSE COLLEGE
Atlanta, GA

Tuition & fees: $27,574	Average undergraduate aid package: $23,565

ABOUT THE INSTITUTION Independent, men only. *Awards:* bachelor's degrees. 27 undergraduate majors. *Total enrollment:* 2,202. Undergraduates: 2,202. Freshmen: 617. Both federal and institutional methodology are used as a basis for awarding need-based institutional aid.
UNDERGRADUATE EXPENSES for 2018–2019 *Application fee:* $50. *Comprehensive fee:* $41,012 includes full-time tuition ($25,368), mandatory fees ($2206), and room and board ($13,438). *College room only:* $7510. Full-time tuition and fees vary according to course load. Room and board charges vary according to board plan and housing facility. Part-time tuition and fees vary according to course load.
FRESHMAN FINANCIAL AID (Fall 2017, est.) 597 applied for aid; of those 89% were deemed to have need. 99% of freshmen with need received aid. *Average financial aid package:* $23,454 (excluding resources awarded to replace EFC). 1% of all full-time freshmen had no need and received non-need-based gift aid.
UNDERGRADUATE FINANCIAL AID (Fall 2017, est.) 1,956 applied for aid; of those 88% were deemed to have need. 100% of undergraduates with need received aid. *Average financial aid package:* $23,565 (excluding resources awarded to replace EFC). 1% of all full-time undergraduates had no need and received non-need-based gift aid.
GIFT AID (NEED-BASED) *Total amount:* $31,968,186 (19% federal, 3% state, 59% institutional, 19% external sources). *Receiving aid:* Freshmen: 84% (520); all full-time undergraduates: 80% (1,674). *Average award:* Freshmen: $20,361; Undergraduates: $20,851. *Scholarships, grants, and awards:* Federal Pell, FSEOG, state, private, college/university gift aid from institutional funds, United Negro College Fund.
GIFT AID (NON-NEED-BASED) *Total amount:* $826,536 (21% institutional, 79% external sources). *Average award:* Freshmen: $10,680. Undergraduates: $28,810. *Scholarships, grants, and awards by category:* Academic interests/achievement: biological sciences, business, computer science, engineering/technologies, general academic interests/achievements, mathematics, military science. *Creative arts/performance:* art/fine arts, music. *Special achievements/activities:* cheerleading/drum major, community service, leadership, religious involvement. *Special characteristics:* children and siblings of alumni, children of faculty/staff, local/state students. *Tuition waivers:* Full or partial for employees or children of employees. *ROTC:* Army, Naval, Air Force cooperative.
LOANS *Student loans:* $15,496,202 (40% need-based, 60% non-need-based). 80% of past graduating class borrowed through all loan programs. *Average indebtedness per student:* $31,833. *Average need-based loan:* Freshmen: $3856. Undergraduates: $4349. *Parent loans:* $26,944,815 (100% non-need-based). *Programs:* Federal Direct (Subsidized and Unsubsidized Stafford, PLUS), Perkins, state.
WORK-STUDY *Federal work-study:* Total amount: $979,123; jobs available. *State or other work-study/employment:* Total amount: $126,803 (100% need-based). Part-time jobs available.
ATHLETIC AWARDS Total amount: $2,125,576 (100% need-based).
APPLYING FOR FINANCIAL AID *Required financial aid forms:* FAFSA, institution's own form, CSS Financial Aid PROFILE, state aid form. *Financial aid deadline:* 4/1 (priority: 2/15). *Notification date:* Continuous beginning 3/1. Students must reply by 5/1 or within 2 weeks of notification.

CONTACT Sheryl T. Spivey, Director of Financial Aid, Morehouse College, 830 Westview Drive, SW, Atlanta, GA 30314, 404-653-7750 or toll-free 800-851-1254. *Fax:* 404-215-2711. *E-mail:* sheryl.spivey@morehouse.edu. *Website:* http://www.morehouse.edu/.

MORGAN STATE UNIVERSITY
Baltimore, MD

Tuition & fees (MD res): $7767	Average undergraduate aid package: $11,374

ABOUT THE INSTITUTION State-supported, coed. 55 undergraduate majors. Both federal and institutional methodology are used as a basis for awarding need-based institutional aid.

UNDERGRADUATE EXPENSES for 2017–2018 *Tuition, state resident:* full-time $5264; part-time $240 per credit. *Tuition, nonresident:* full-time $15,330; part-time $604 per credit. *Required fees:* full-time $2503; $80 per credit. *College room and board:* $10,650. Room and board charges vary according to board plan and housing facility.

FRESHMAN FINANCIAL AID (Fall 2017, est.) 1,130 applied for aid; of those 98% were deemed to have need. 100% of freshmen with need received aid; of those 7% had need fully met. *Average percent of need met:* 42% (excluding resources awarded to replace EFC). *Average financial aid package:* $11,310 (excluding resources awarded to replace EFC). 10% of all full-time freshmen had no need and received non-need-based gift aid.

UNDERGRADUATE FINANCIAL AID (Fall 2017, est.) 4,967 applied for aid; of those 95% were deemed to have need. 100% of undergraduates with need received aid; of those 7% had need fully met. *Average percent of need met:* 40% (excluding resources awarded to replace EFC). *Average financial aid package:* $11,374 (excluding resources awarded to replace EFC). 9% of all full-time undergraduates had no need and received non-need-based gift aid.

GIFT AID (NEED-BASED) *Total amount:* $29,120,871 (61% federal, 15% state, 19% institutional, 5% external sources). *Receiving aid:* Freshmen: 74% (882); all full-time undergraduates: 58% (3,379). *Average award:* Freshmen: $7561; Undergraduates: $7183. *Scholarships, grants, and awards:* Federal Pell, FSEOG, state, private, college/university gift aid from institutional funds.

GIFT AID (NON-NEED-BASED) *Total amount:* $7,377,665 (3% federal, 8% state, 80% institutional, 9% external sources). *Receiving aid:* Freshmen: 25% (299). Undergraduates: 19% (1,090). *Average award:* Freshmen: $6947. Undergraduates: $6029. *Scholarships, grants, and awards by category: Academic interests/ achievement:* 728 awards ($5,802,670 total): general academic interests/achievements. *Tuition waivers:* Full or partial for employees or children of employees.

LOANS *Student loans:* $34,793,990 (55% need-based, 45% non-need-based). 83% of past graduating class borrowed through all loan programs. *Average indebtedness per student:* $34,578. *Average need-based loan:* Freshmen: $4419. Undergraduates: $5010. *Parent loans:* $13,395,204 (100% need-based). *Programs:* Federal Direct (Subsidized and Unsubsidized Stafford, PLUS), Perkins.

WORK-STUDY *Federal work-study:* Total amount: $563,739; 260 jobs averaging $2168. *State or other work-study/employment:* Part-time jobs available.

ATHLETIC AWARDS Total amount: $4,109,307 (100% non-need-based).

APPLYING FOR FINANCIAL AID *Required financial aid forms:* FAFSA, institution's own form, federal income tax form(s). *Financial aid deadline (priority):* 4/1. *Notification date:* Continuous beginning 6/1. Students must reply within 2 weeks of notification.

CONTACT Tanya Wilkerson, Director of Financial Aid, Morgan State University, 1700 East Cold Spring Lane, Baltimore, MD 21251, 443-885-3170 or toll-free 800-332-6674. *Fax:* 443-885-8272. *Website:* http://www.morgan.edu/.

MORNINGSIDE COLLEGE
Sioux City, IA

Tuition & fees: $30,390	Average undergraduate aid package: $24,135

ABOUT THE INSTITUTION Independent United Methodist Church, coed. *Awards:* certificates, bachelor's, and master's degrees. 44 undergraduate majors. *Total enrollment:* 2,788. Undergraduates: 1,322. Freshmen: 354. Federal methodology is used as a basis for awarding need-based institutional aid.

UNDERGRADUATE EXPENSES for 2017–2018 *Comprehensive fee:* $39,780 includes full-time tuition ($28,890), mandatory fees ($1500), and room and board ($9390). *College room only:* $5090. Full-time tuition and fees vary according to program. Room and board charges vary according to housing facility. *Part-time tuition:* $910 per credit hour. Part-time tuition and fees vary according to course load and program.

FRESHMAN FINANCIAL AID (Fall 2017, est.) 338 applied for aid; of those 90% were deemed to have need. 100% of freshmen with need received aid; of those 23% had need fully met. *Average percent of need met:* 77% (excluding resources awarded to replace EFC). *Average financial aid package:* $25,670 (excluding resources awarded to replace EFC). 14% of all full-time freshmen had no need and received non-need-based gift aid.

UNDERGRADUATE FINANCIAL AID (Fall 2017, est.) 1,107 applied for aid; of those 90% were deemed to have need. 100% of undergraduates with need received aid; of those 24% had need fully met. *Average percent of need met:* 74% (excluding resources awarded to replace EFC). *Average financial aid package:* $24,135 (excluding resources awarded to replace EFC). 21% of all full-time undergraduates had no need and received non-need-based gift aid.

GIFT AID (NEED-BASED) *Total amount:* $4,195,026 (41% federal, 48% state, 11% institutional). *Receiving aid:* Freshmen: 59% (208); all full-time undergraduates: 51% (640). *Average award:* Freshmen: $6022; Undergraduates: $6366. *Scholarships, grants, and awards:* Federal Pell, FSEOG, state, private, college/university gift aid from institutional funds.

GIFT AID (NON-NEED-BASED) *Total amount:* $17,374,721 (5% federal, 1% state, 90% institutional, 4% external sources). *Receiving aid:* Freshmen: 86% (304). Undergraduates: 79% (994). *Average award:* Freshmen: $15,810. Undergraduates: $15,529. *Scholarships, grants, and awards by category: Academic interests/ achievement:* 1,519 awards ($11,395,748 total): general academic interests/achievements. *Creative arts/performance:* 212 awards ($803,295 total): art/fine arts, creative writing, dance, music, theater/drama. *Special achievements/activities:* 1 award ($250 total): cheerleading/drum major. *Special characteristics:* 107 awards ($2,510,549 total): children and siblings of alumni, children of faculty/staff, international students. *Tuition waivers:* Full or partial for children of alumni, employees or children of employees, senior citizens. *ROTC:* Army cooperative.

LOANS *Student loans:* $8,750,480 (42% need-based, 58% non-need-based). 84% of past graduating class borrowed through all loan programs. *Average indebtedness per student:* $36,449. *Average need-based loan:* Freshmen: $3881. Undergraduates: $4635. *Parent loans:* $2,121,750 (100% non-need-based). *Programs:* Federal Direct (Subsidized and Unsubsidized Stafford, PLUS), Perkins, college/university, private loans.

WORK-STUDY *Federal work-study:* Total amount: $729,583; 542 jobs averaging $1346. *State or other work-study/employment:* Total amount: $529,975 (100% non-need-based). 265 part-time jobs averaging $2000.

ATHLETIC AWARDS Total amount: $2,828,079 (100% non-need-based).

APPLYING FOR FINANCIAL AID *Required financial aid form:* FAFSA. *Financial aid deadline:* Continuous. *Notification date:* 11/24.

CONTACT Karen K. Gagnon, Associate Vice President for Institutional Research/ Director of Student Financial Planning, Morningside College, 1501 Morningside Avenue, Sioux City, IA 51106, 712-274-5272 or toll-free 800-831-0806 Ext. 5111. *Fax:* 712-274-5605. *E-mail:* gagnon@morningside.edu. *Website:* http://www.morningside.edu/.

MORRIS COLLEGE
Sumter, SC

CONTACT Ms. Sandra S. Gibson, Director of Financial Aid, Morris College, 100 West College Street, Sumter, SC 29150-3599, 803-934-3238 or toll-free 866-853-1345. *Fax:* 803-773-3687.
Website: http://www.morris.edu/.

MORRISVILLE STATE COLLEGE
Morrisville, NY

Tuition & fees (NY res): $8309	Average undergraduate aid package: $10,227

ABOUT THE INSTITUTION State-supported, coed. *Awards:* certificates, associate, and bachelor's degrees. 94 undergraduate majors. *Total enrollment:* 3,003. Undergraduates: 3,003. Freshmen: 912. Federal methodology is used as a basis for awarding need-based institutional aid.

UNDERGRADUATE EXPENSES for 2017–2018 *Application fee:* $50. *Tuition, state resident:* full-time $6670; part-time $278 per credit hour. *Tuition, nonresident:* full-time $11,300; part-time $472 per credit hour. *Required fees:* full-time $1639; $67.10 per credit hour. Full-time tuition and fees vary according to course level, degree level, location, and program. Part-time tuition and fees vary according to class time, course level, course load, degree level, location, and program. *College room and board:* $13,238; *Room only:* $7648. Room and board charges vary according to board plan, housing facility, and location.

FRESHMAN FINANCIAL AID (Fall 2017, est.) 873 applied for aid; of those 92% were deemed to have need. 99% of freshmen with need received aid; of those .3% had need fully met. *Average percent of need met:* 44% (excluding resources awarded to replace EFC). *Average financial aid package:* $10,586 (excluding resources awarded to replace EFC). 15% of all full-time freshmen had no need and received non-need-based gift aid.

UNDERGRADUATE FINANCIAL AID (Fall 2017, est.) 2,426 applied for aid; of those 91% were deemed to have need. 99% of undergraduates with need received aid; of those 1% had need fully met. *Average percent of need met:* 46% (excluding resources awarded to replace EFC). *Average financial aid package:* $10,227 (excluding resources awarded to replace EFC). 12% of all full-time undergraduates had no need and received non-need-based gift aid.

GIFT AID (NEED-BASED) *Total amount:* $14,828,829 (51% federal, 49% state). *Receiving aid:* Freshmen: 76% (686); all full-time undergraduates: 71% (1,824). *Average award:* Freshmen: $7431; Undergraduates: $7144. *Scholarships, grants, and awards:* Federal Pell, FSEOG, state, college/university gift aid from institutional funds.

GIFT AID (NON-NEED-BASED) *Total amount:* $2,297,974 (7% state, 58% institutional, 35% external sources). *Receiving aid:* Freshmen: 41% (373). Undergraduates: 28% (722). *Average award:* Freshmen: $2229. Undergraduates: $2162. *Scholarships, grants, and awards by category: Academic interests/achievement:* general academic interests/achievements. *Special achievements/activities:* leadership, memberships. *Special characteristics:* children of faculty/staff, local/state students, members of minority groups, out-of-state students. *Tuition waivers:* Full or partial for minority students, children of alumni, employees or children of employees, senior citizens. *ROTC:* Army cooperative, Air Force cooperative.

LOANS *Student loans:* $17,354,413 (43% need-based, 57% non-need-based). 85% of past graduating class borrowed through all loan programs. *Average indebtedness per student:* $28,402. *Average need-based loan:* Freshmen: $3235. Undergraduates: $3813. *Parent loans:* $8,689,698 (100% non-need-based). *Programs:* Federal Direct (Subsidized and Unsubsidized Stafford, PLUS), Perkins, Federal Nursing.

WORK-STUDY *Federal work-study:* Total amount: $259,172; jobs available.

APPLYING FOR FINANCIAL AID *Required financial aid forms:* FAFSA, state aid form. *Financial aid deadline (priority):* 3/1. *Notification date:* Continuous beginning 3/15. Students must reply by 5/1.

CONTACT Financial Aid Office, Morrisville State College, PO Box 901, Morrisville, NY 13408-0901, 315-684-6289 or toll-free 800-258-0111. *Fax:* 315-684-6628. *E-mail:* finaid@morrisville.edu.
Website: http://www.morrisville.edu/.

MORTHLAND COLLEGE
West Frankfort, IL

CONTACT Financial Aid Office, Morthland College, 202 East Oak Street, West Frankfort, IL 62896, 618-937-2127.
Website: http://www.morthland.edu/.

MOUNT ALOYSIUS COLLEGE
Cresson, PA

Tuition & fees: $22,430	Average undergraduate aid package: $13,500

ABOUT THE INSTITUTION Independent Roman Catholic, coed. *Awards:* certificates, associate, bachelor's, and master's degrees. 25 undergraduate majors. *Total enrollment:* 1,740. Undergraduates: 1,688. Freshmen: 267. Federal methodology is used as a basis for awarding need-based institutional aid.

UNDERGRADUATE EXPENSES for 2017–2018 *Application fee:* $30. *Comprehensive fee:* $32,768 includes full-time tuition ($21,230), mandatory fees ($1200), and room and board ($10,338). *College room only:* $5200. *Part-time tuition:* $800 per credit hour.

FRESHMAN FINANCIAL AID (Fall 2017, est.) 261 applied for aid; of those 81% were deemed to have need. 100% of freshmen with need received aid. *Average percent of need met:* 37% (excluding resources awarded to replace EFC). *Average financial aid package:* $15,500 (excluding resources awarded to replace EFC). 19% of all full-time freshmen had no need and received non-need-based gift aid.

UNDERGRADUATE FINANCIAL AID (Fall 2017, est.) 990 applied for aid; of those 78% were deemed to have need. 100% of undergraduates with need received aid. *Average percent of need met:* 36% (excluding resources awarded to replace EFC). *Average financial aid package:* $13,500 (excluding resources awarded to replace EFC). 22% of all full-time undergraduates had no need and received non-need-based gift aid.

GIFT AID (NEED-BASED) *Total amount:* $11,465,767 (18% federal, 14% state, 66% institutional, 2% external sources). *Receiving aid:* Freshmen: 81% (211); all full-time undergraduates: 78% (776). *Average award:* Freshmen: $3000; Undergraduates: $2800. *Scholarships, grants, and awards:* Federal Pell, FSEOG, state, private.

GIFT AID (NON-NEED-BASED) *Receiving aid:* Freshmen: 19% (50). Undergraduates: 22% (214). *Average award:* Freshmen: $7000. Undergraduates: $5000. *Scholarships, grants, and awards by category: Academic interests/achievement:* general academic interests/achievements. *Creative arts/performance:* music, performing arts. *Special achievements/activities:* leadership. *Special characteristics:* children of current students, parents of current students, religious affiliation, siblings of current students, spouses of current students, twins.

LOANS *Student loans:* $7,181,315 (100% need-based). 86% of past graduating class borrowed through all loan programs. *Average indebtedness per student:* $36,899. *Average need-based loan:* Freshmen: $3800. Undergraduates: $4200. *Parent loans:* $3,255,672 (100% need-based). *Programs:* Federal Direct (Subsidized and Unsubsidized Stafford, PLUS), Federal Nursing, alternative loans.

WORK-STUDY *Federal work-study:* Total amount: $290,039; jobs available.

APPLYING FOR FINANCIAL AID *Required financial aid form:* FAFSA. *Financial aid deadline (priority):* 4/1. *Notification date:* Continuous beginning 2/15. Students must reply within 2 weeks of notification.

CONTACT Mrs. Stacy L. Schenk, Director of Financial Aid, Mount Aloysius College, 7373 Admiral Peary Highway, Cresson, PA 16630-1900, 814-886-6357 or toll-free 888-823-2220. *Fax:* 814-886-6463. *E-mail:* sschenk@mtaloy.edu.
Website: http://www.mtaloy.edu/.

MOUNT ANGEL SEMINARY
Saint Benedict, OR

CONTACT Dorene Preis, Director of Student Financial Aid/Registrar, Mount Angel Seminary, 1 Abbey Drive, Saint Benedict, OR 97373, 503-845-3951. *Fax:* 503-845-3126. *E-mail:* dpreis@mtangel.edu.
Website: http://www.mountangelabbey.org/seminary/.

MOUNT CARMEL COLLEGE OF NURSING
Columbus, OH

Tuition & fees: $13,442	Average undergraduate aid package: $10,326

ABOUT THE INSTITUTION Independent, coed, primarily women. **Awards:** certificates, bachelor's, master's, and doctoral degrees. 1 undergraduate major. **Total enrollment:** 1,069. Undergraduates: 880. Freshmen: 95. Federal methodology is used as a basis for awarding need-based institutional aid.

UNDERGRADUATE EXPENSES for 2017–2018 *Application fee:* $30. *One-time required fee:* $225. *Tuition:* full-time $12,927; part-time $417 per semester hour. *Required fees:* full-time $515; $417 per semester hour. Full-time tuition and fees vary according to course level, course load, program, and student level. Part-time tuition and fees vary according to course level, course load, program, and student level.

FRESHMAN FINANCIAL AID (Fall 2017, est.) 90 applied for aid; of those 86% were deemed to have need. 95% of freshmen with need received aid; of those 8% had need fully met. *Average percent of need met:* 36% (excluding resources awarded to replace EFC). *Average financial aid package:* $5984 (excluding resources awarded to replace EFC). 11% of all full-time freshmen had no need and received non-need-based gift aid.

UNDERGRADUATE FINANCIAL AID (Fall 2017, est.) 575 applied for aid; of those 89% were deemed to have need. 95% of undergraduates with need received aid; of those 6% had need fully met. *Average percent of need met:* 40% (excluding resources awarded to replace EFC). *Average financial aid package:* $10,326 (excluding resources awarded to replace EFC). 4% of all full-time undergraduates had no need and received non-need-based gift aid.

GIFT AID (NEED-BASED) *Total amount:* $3,568,503 (27% federal, 11% state, 16% institutional, 46% external sources). *Receiving aid:* Freshmen: 60% (60); all full-time undergraduates: 41% (356). *Average award:* Freshmen: $4579; Undergraduates: $8995. *Scholarships, grants, and awards:* Federal Pell, FSEOG, state, private, Federal Nursing.

GIFT AID (NON-NEED-BASED) *Total amount:* $2,086,692 (5% institutional, 95% external sources). *Receiving aid:* Freshmen: 3% (3). Undergraduates: 2% (18). *Average award:* Freshmen: $1752. Undergraduates: $2950. *Scholarships, grants, and awards by category:* Academic interests/achievement: general academic interests/achievements. Special achievements/activities: community service. Special characteristics: children of faculty/staff, members of minority groups. **Tuition waivers:** Full or partial for employees or children of employees. **ROTC:** Army cooperative, Naval cooperative, Air Force cooperative.

LOANS *Student loans:* $6,125,875 (77% need-based, 23% non-need-based). 66% of past graduating class borrowed through all loan programs. *Average indebtedness per student:* $36,309. *Average need-based loan:* Freshmen: $2835. Undergraduates: $4332. *Parent loans:* $1,454,075 (61% need-based, 39% non-need-based). *Programs:* Federal Direct (Subsidized and Unsubsidized Stafford, PLUS), Federal Nursing, state, college/university.

WORK-STUDY *State or other work-study/employment:* Total amount: $7812 (66% need-based, 34% non-need-based). Part-time jobs available.

APPLYING FOR FINANCIAL AID *Required financial aid form:* FAFSA. *Financial aid deadline (priority):* 3/1. *Notification date:* Continuous beginning 3/1. Students must reply within 2 weeks of notification.

CONTACT Dr. Todd A. Everett, Director of Financial Aid, Mount Carmel College of Nursing, 127 South Davis Avenue, Columbus, OH 43222, 614-234-5169 Ext. 5177 or toll-free 800-556-6942. *Fax:* 614-234-5427. *E-mail:* teverett@mccn.edu.
Website: http://www.mccn.edu/.

MOUNT HOLYOKE COLLEGE
South Hadley, MA

Tuition & fees: $49,998	Average undergraduate aid package: $40,769

ABOUT THE INSTITUTION Independent, women only. **Awards:** certificates, bachelor's, and master's degrees. 50 undergraduate majors. **Total enrollment:** 2,334. Undergraduates: 2,210. Freshmen: 529. Both federal and institutional methodology are used as a basis for awarding need-based institutional aid.

UNDERGRADUATE EXPENSES for 2018–2019 *Application fee:* $60. *Comprehensive fee:* $64,658 includes full-time tuition ($49,780), mandatory fees ($218), and room and board ($14,660). *College room only:* $7160.

FRESHMAN FINANCIAL AID (Fall 2017, est.) 396 applied for aid; of those 84% were deemed to have need. 100% of freshmen with need received aid; of those 100% had need fully met. *Average percent of need met:* 100% (excluding resources awarded to replace EFC). *Average financial aid package:* $41,558 (excluding resources awarded to replace EFC). 15% of all full-time freshmen had no need and received non-need-based gift aid.

UNDERGRADUATE FINANCIAL AID (Fall 2017, est.) 1,551 applied for aid; of those 92% were deemed to have need. 100% of undergraduates with need received aid; of those 100% had need fully met. *Average percent of need met:* 100% (excluding resources awarded to replace EFC). *Average financial aid package:* $40,769 (excluding resources awarded to replace EFC). 13% of all full-time undergraduates had no need and received non-need-based gift aid.

GIFT AID (NEED-BASED) *Total amount:* $49,103,117 (5% federal, 1% state, 92% institutional, 2% external sources). *Receiving aid:* Freshmen: 63% (331); all full-time undergraduates: 65% (1,416). *Average award:* Freshmen: $37,011; Undergraduates: $35,067. *Scholarships, grants, and awards:* Federal Pell, FSEOG, state, private, college/university gift aid from institutional funds.

GIFT AID (NON-NEED-BASED) *Total amount:* $8,580,888 (89% institutional, 11% external sources). *Receiving aid:* Freshmen: 12% (61). Undergraduates: 10% (224). *Average award:* Freshmen: $19,213. Undergraduates: $21,064. *Scholarships, grants, and awards by category:* Academic interests/achievement: general academic interests/achievements. Special characteristics: general special characteristics. **Tuition waivers:** Full or partial for employees or children of employees. **ROTC:** Army cooperative, Air Force cooperative.

LOANS *Student loans:* $8,938,836 (76% need-based, 24% non-need-based). 66% of past graduating class borrowed through all loan programs. *Average indebtedness per student:* $23,872. *Average need-based loan:* Freshmen: $3106. Undergraduates: $4595. *Parent loans:* $3,368,164 (100% non-need-based). *Programs:* Federal Direct (Subsidized and Unsubsidized Stafford, PLUS), state, college/university.

WORK-STUDY *Federal work-study:* Total amount: $1,822,181; 826 jobs averaging $2123. *State or other work-study/employment:* Total amount: $714,890 (100% need-based). 325 part-time jobs averaging $2135.

APPLYING FOR FINANCIAL AID *Required financial aid forms:* FAFSA, CSS Financial Aid PROFILE, noncustodial (divorced/separated) parent's statement, federal income tax form(s), W-2 forms. *Financial aid deadline:* 3/1 (priority: 2/1). *Notification date:* 4/1. Students must reply by 5/1.

CONTACT Ms. Kathryn Blaisdell, Director of Student Financial Services, Mount Holyoke College, 50 College Street, South Hadley, MA 01075-1492, 413-538-2291. *Fax:* 413-538-2512. *E-mail:* kblaisde@mtholyoke.edu.
Website: http://www.mtholyoke.edu/.

MOUNT MARTY COLLEGE
Yankton, SD

Tuition & fees: $26,310	Average undergraduate aid package: $27,350

ABOUT THE INSTITUTION Independent Roman Catholic, coed. **Awards:** certificates, associate, bachelor's, master's, and doctoral degrees. 31 undergraduate majors. **Total enrollment:** 1,048. Undergraduates: 876. Freshmen: 121. Federal methodology is used as a basis for awarding need-based institutional aid.

UNDERGRADUATE EXPENSES for 2017–2018 *Application fee:* $35. *Comprehensive fee:* $34,156 includes full-time tuition ($24,160), mandatory fees ($2150), and room and board ($7846). Full-time tuition and fees vary according to degree level, location, and program. Room and board charges vary according to board plan. *Part-time tuition:* $530 per credit hour. *Part-time fees:* $45 per credit hour. Part-time tuition and fees vary according to course load, degree level, location, and program.

FRESHMAN FINANCIAL AID (Fall 2017, est.) 106 applied for aid; of those 95% were deemed to have need. 100% of freshmen with need received aid; of those 56% had need fully met. *Average percent of need met:* 93% (excluding resources awarded to replace EFC). *Average financial aid package:* $29,970 (excluding resources awarded to replace EFC). 6% of all full-time freshmen had no need and received non-need-based gift aid.

UNDERGRADUATE FINANCIAL AID (Fall 2017, est.) 423 applied for aid; of those 88% were deemed to have need. 99% of undergraduates with need received aid; of those 45% had need fully met. *Average percent of need met:* 86% (excluding resources awarded to replace EFC). *Average financial aid package:* $27,350 (excluding resources awarded to replace EFC). 10% of all full-time undergraduates had no need and received non-need-based gift aid.

GIFT AID (NEED-BASED) *Total amount:* $5,486,032 (20% federal, 1% state, 76% institutional, 3% external sources). *Receiving aid:* Freshmen: 91% (99); all full-time undergraduates: 80% (358). *Average award:* Freshmen: $20,344; Undergraduates: $16,832. *Scholarships, grants, and awards:* Federal Pell, FSEOG, state, private, college/university gift aid from institutional funds.

GIFT AID (NON-NEED-BASED) *Total amount:* $491,787 (4% state, 95% institutional, 1% external sources). *Average award:* Freshmen: $12,750. Undergraduates: $10,339. *Scholarships, grants, and awards by category: Academic interests/achievement:* general academic interests/achievements. *Creative arts/performance:* art/fine arts, music, performing arts, theater/drama. *Special achievements/activities:* community service, general special achievements/activities, leadership, religious involvement. *Special characteristics:* children of current students, children of faculty/staff, international students, parents of current students, religious affiliation, siblings of current students, spouses of current students. *Tuition waivers:* Full or partial for employees or children of employees. *ROTC:* Army cooperative.

LOANS *Student loans:* $2,100,087 (97% need-based, 3% non-need-based). 78% of past graduating class borrowed through all loan programs. *Average indebtedness per student:* $32,744. *Average need-based loan:* Freshmen: $4221. Undergraduates: $5198. *Parent loans:* $656,174 (95% need-based, 5% non-need-based). *Programs:* Federal Direct (Subsidized and Unsubsidized Stafford, PLUS), Perkins, Federal Nursing, state, college/university.

WORK-STUDY *Federal work-study:* Total amount: $229,155; 127 jobs averaging $1758. *State or other work-study/employment:* Total amount: $99,000 (71% need-based, 29% non-need-based). 55 part-time jobs averaging $1784.

ATHLETIC AWARDS Total amount: $1,084,884 (88% need-based, 12% non-need-based).

APPLYING FOR FINANCIAL AID *Required financial aid forms:* FAFSA, institution's own form. *Financial aid deadline (priority):* 3/1. *Notification date:* Continuous beginning 3/15. Students must reply within 2 weeks of notification.

CONTACT Mr. Ken Kocer, Director of Financial Assistance, Mount Marty College, 1105 West 8th Street, Yankton, SD 57078-3724, 605-668-1589 or toll-free 800-658-4552. *Fax:* 605-668-1585. *E-mail:* kkocer@mtmc.edu. *Website:* http://www.mtmc.edu/.

MOUNT MARY UNIVERSITY
Milwaukee, WI

Tuition & fees: $30,100	Average undergraduate aid package: $25,609

ABOUT THE INSTITUTION Independent Roman Catholic, undergraduate: women only; graduate: coed. *Awards:* certificates, bachelor's, master's, and doctoral degrees. 44 undergraduate majors. *Total enrollment:* 1,358. Undergraduates: 735. Freshmen: 123. Federal methodology is used as a basis for awarding need-based institutional aid.

UNDERGRADUATE EXPENSES for 2018–2019 *Comprehensive fee:* $38,700 includes full-time tuition ($29,510), mandatory fees ($590), and room and board ($8600). Full-time tuition and fees vary according to degree level and program. Room and board charges vary according to board plan. *Part-time tuition:* $895 per credit hour. *Part-time fees:* $370 per year. Part-time tuition and fees vary according to course load, degree level, and program.

FRESHMAN FINANCIAL AID (Fall 2017, est.) 121 applied for aid; of those 96% were deemed to have need. 100% of freshmen with need received aid; of those 6% had

need fully met. *Average percent of need met:* 76% (excluding resources awarded to replace EFC). *Average financial aid package:* $27,799 (excluding resources awarded to replace EFC). 5% of all full-time freshmen had no need and received non-need-based gift aid.

UNDERGRADUATE FINANCIAL AID (Fall 2017, est.) 602 applied for aid; of those 97% were deemed to have need. 100% of undergraduates with need received aid; of those 9% had need fully met. *Average percent of need met:* 72% (excluding resources awarded to replace EFC). *Average financial aid package:* $25,609 (excluding resources awarded to replace EFC). 6% of all full-time undergraduates had no need and received non-need-based gift aid.

GIFT AID (NEED-BASED) *Total amount:* $12,536,256 (16% federal, 12% state, 70% institutional, 2% external sources). *Receiving aid:* Freshmen: 95% (116); all full-time undergraduates: 86% (581). *Average award:* Freshmen: $23,817; Undergraduates: $20,645. *Scholarships, grants, and awards:* Federal Pell, FSEOG, state, private, college/university gift aid from institutional funds.

GIFT AID (NON-NEED-BASED) *Total amount:* $940,801 (1% federal, 97% institutional, 2% external sources). *Receiving aid:* Freshmen: 6% (7). Undergraduates: 6% (43). *Average award:* Freshmen: $20,230. Undergraduates: $13,909. *Scholarships, grants, and awards by category: Academic interests/achievement:* 602 awards ($4,418,090 total): business, communication, education, English, general academic interests/achievements, humanities, mathematics, social sciences. *Creative arts/performance:* 58 awards ($64,725 total): applied art and design, art/fine arts, music. *Special achievements/activities:* 6 awards ($57,420 total): general special achievements/activities, leadership. *Special characteristics:* 24 awards ($205,928 total): children and siblings of alumni, children of faculty/staff, international students, siblings of current students, veterans. *Tuition waivers:* Full or partial for employees or children of employees, senior citizens.

LOANS *Student loans:* $5,363,747 (89% need-based, 11% non-need-based). 79% of past graduating class borrowed through all loan programs. *Average indebtedness per student:* $27,308. *Average need-based loan:* Freshmen: $3040. Undergraduates: $4647. *Parent loans:* $463,599 (65% need-based, 35% non-need-based). *Programs:* Federal Direct (Subsidized and Unsubsidized Stafford, PLUS), Perkins.

WORK-STUDY *Federal work-study:* Total amount: $130,000; 90 jobs averaging $1444. *State or other work-study/employment:* Total amount: $170,000 (100% non-need-based). 100 part-time jobs averaging $1700.

APPLYING FOR FINANCIAL AID *Required financial aid form:* FAFSA. *Financial aid deadline (priority):* 12/1. *Notification date:* Continuous beginning 12/15. Students must reply within 2 weeks of notification.

CONTACT Debra Duff, Director of Financial Aid, Mount Mary University, 2900 North Menomonee River Parkway, Milwaukee, WI 53222-4597, 414-930-3163 or toll-free 800-321-6265. *Fax:* 414-930-3709. *E-mail:* finaid@mtmary.edu. *Website:* http://www.mtmary.edu/.

MOUNT MERCY UNIVERSITY
Cedar Rapids, IA

Tuition & fees: $31,998	Average undergraduate aid package: $24,022

ABOUT THE INSTITUTION Independent Roman Catholic, coed. *Awards:* bachelor's, master's, and doctoral degrees. 49 undergraduate majors. *Total enrollment:* 1,848. Undergraduates: 1,517. Freshmen: 239. Federal methodology is used as a basis for awarding need-based institutional aid.

UNDERGRADUATE EXPENSES for 2018–2019 *Comprehensive fee:* $41,532 includes full-time tuition ($31,598), mandatory fees ($400), and room and board ($9534). Full-time tuition and fees vary according to course load. Room and board charges vary according to board plan and housing facility. *Part-time tuition:* $958 per credit hour. *Part-time fees:* $200 per year. Part-time tuition and fees vary according to course load.

FRESHMAN FINANCIAL AID (Fall 2016) 233 applied for aid; of those 90% were deemed to have need. 98% of freshmen with need received aid; of those 23% had need fully met. *Average percent of need met:* 79% (excluding resources awarded to replace EFC). *Average financial aid package:* $25,722 (excluding resources awarded to replace EFC). 12% of all full-time freshmen had no need and received non-need-based gift aid.

UNDERGRADUATE FINANCIAL AID (Fall 2016) 999 applied for aid; of those 92% were deemed to have need. 99% of undergraduates with need received aid; of those 19% had need fully met. *Average percent of need met:* 75% (excluding resources awarded to replace EFC) *Average financial aid package:* $24,022 (excluding resources awarded to replace EFC). 15% of all full-time undergraduates had no need and received non-need-based gift aid.

GIFT AID (NEED-BASED) *Total amount:* $19,241,573 (12% federal, 17% state, 67% institutional, 4% external sources). *Receiving aid:* Freshmen: 61% (206); all full-time undergraduates: 76% (906). *Average award:* Freshmen: $22,701; Undergraduates: $20,438. *Scholarships, grants, and awards:* Federal Pell, FSEOG, state, private, college/university gift aid from institutional funds.

GIFT AID (NON-NEED-BASED) *Total amount:* $3,610,556 (7% state, 88% institutional, 5% external sources). *Receiving aid:* Freshmen: 11% (38). Undergraduates: 10% (120). *Average award:* Freshmen: $16,258. Undergraduates: $13,346. *Scholarships, grants, and awards by category:* Academic interests/achievement: 1,563 awards ($12,493,908 total): general academic interests/achievements. *Creative arts/performance:* 110 awards ($239,665 total): art/fine arts, creative writing, music, theater/drama. *Special characteristics:* 347 awards ($662,405 total): children and siblings of alumni, international students, out-of-state students, previous college experience, siblings of current students, veterans. *Tuition waivers:* Full or partial for employees or children of employees.

LOANS *Student loans:* $8,778,335 (74% need-based, 26% non-need-based). 79% of past graduating class borrowed through all loan programs. *Average indebtedness per student:* $25,739. *Average need-based loan:* Freshmen: $2869. Undergraduates: $3857. *Parent loans:* $2,524,603 (44% need-based, 56% non-need-based). *Programs:* Federal Direct (Subsidized and Unsubsidized Stafford, PLUS), Perkins, state, college/university.

WORK-STUDY *Federal work-study:* jobs available. *State or other work-study/employment:* Total amount: $213,172 (43% need-based, 57% non-need-based). Part-time jobs available.

APPLYING FOR FINANCIAL AID *Required financial aid form:* FAFSA. *Financial aid deadline (priority):* 3/1. *Notification date:* Continuous beginning 3/15. Students must reply by 5/1 or within 3 weeks of notification.

CONTACT Bethany Rinderknecht, Director of Financial Aid, Mount Mercy University, 1330 Elmhurst Drive NE, Cedar Rapids, IA 52402-4797, 319-368-6467 Ext. 1545 or toll-free 800-248-4504. *Fax:* 319-364-3546. *E-mail:* brinderknecht@mtmercy.edu.
Website: http://www.mtmercy.edu/.

MOUNT ST. JOSEPH UNIVERSITY
Cincinnati, OH

Tuition & fees: $30,100	Average undergraduate aid package: $22,394

ABOUT THE INSTITUTION Independent Roman Catholic, coed. *Awards:* certificates, associate, bachelor's, master's, and doctoral degrees. 48 undergraduate majors. *Total enrollment:* 2,010. Undergraduates: 1,318. Freshmen: 277. Federal methodology is used as a basis for awarding need-based institutional aid.

UNDERGRADUATE EXPENSES for 2018–2019 *Application fee:* $25. *Comprehensive fee:* $39,542 includes full-time tuition ($29,100), mandatory fees ($1000), and room and board ($9442). Full-time tuition and fees vary according to course load, location, and reciprocity agreements. Room and board charges vary according to board plan, housing facility, and location. *Part-time tuition:* $540 per credit hour. *Part-time fees:* $540 per credit hour. Part-time tuition and fees vary according to course load, location, and reciprocity agreements.

FRESHMAN FINANCIAL AID (Fall 2017, est.) 271 applied for aid; of those 93% were deemed to have need. 100% of freshmen with need received aid; of those 18% had need fully met. *Average percent of need met:* 83% (excluding resources awarded to replace EFC). *Average financial aid package:* $24,612 (excluding resources awarded to replace EFC). 9% of all full-time freshmen had no need and received non-need-based gift aid.

UNDERGRADUATE FINANCIAL AID (Fall 2017, est.) 914 applied for aid; of those 90% were deemed to have need. 100% of undergraduates with need received aid; of those 16% had need fully met. *Average percent of need met:* 77% (excluding resources awarded to replace EFC). *Average financial aid package:* $22,394 (excluding resources awarded to replace EFC). 15% of all full-time undergraduates had no need and received non-need-based gift aid.

GIFT AID (NEED-BASED) *Total amount:* $14,838,719 (16% federal, 6% state, 76% institutional, 2% external sources). *Receiving aid:* Freshmen: 91% (250); all full-time undergraduates: 82% (817). *Average award:* Freshmen: $19,404; Undergrad-

state. $17,776. *Scholarships, grants, and awards.* Federal Pell, FSEOG, state, private, college/university gift aid from institutional funds.

GIFT AID (NON-NEED-BASED) *Total amount:* $1,751,352 (1% federal, 98% institutional, 1% external sources). *Receiving aid:* Freshmen: 11% (31). Undergraduates: 9% (87). *Average award:* Freshmen: $12,323. Undergraduates: $11,293. *Scholarships, grants, and awards by category:* Academic interests/achievement: 93 awards ($968,500 total): general academic interests/achievements. *Creative arts/performance:* 8 awards ($11,500 total): art/fine arts, music. *Special achievements/activities:* community service, leadership. *Special characteristics:* 11 awards ($267,075 total): adult students, children and siblings of alumni, children of faculty/staff. *Tuition waivers:* Full or partial for employees or children of employees, senior citizens. *ROTC:* Army cooperative, Air Force cooperative.

LOANS *Student loans:* $4,334,313 (85% need-based, 15% non-need-based). *Average need-based loan:* Freshmen: $4292. Undergraduates: $4125. *Parent loans:* $2,750,051 (91% need-based, 9% non-need-based). *Programs:* Federal Direct (Subsidized and Unsubsidized Stafford, PLUS), Perkins.

WORK-STUDY *Federal work-study:* Total amount: $349,590; 235 jobs averaging $1488. *State or other work-study/employment:* Total amount: $202,600 (99% need-based, 1% non-need-based). 138 part-time jobs averaging $1468.

APPLYING FOR FINANCIAL AID *Required financial aid form:* FAFSA. *Financial aid deadline:* Continuous. *Notification date:* Continuous beginning 1/31. Students must reply by 5/1 or within 4 weeks of notification.

CONTACT Ms. Kathryn Kelly, Director of Student Administrative Services, Mount St. Joseph University, 5701 Delhi Road, Cincinnati, OH 45233-1670, 513-244-4418 or toll-free 800-654-9314. *Fax:* 513-244-4201. *E-mail:* kathryn.kelly@msj.edu. *Website:* http://www.msj.edu/.

MOUNT SAINT MARY COLLEGE
Newburgh, NY

Tuition & fees: $31,118	Average undergraduate aid package: $20,126

ABOUT THE INSTITUTION Independent, coed. *Awards:* certificates, bachelor's, and master's degrees. 25 undergraduate majors. *Total enrollment:* 2,365. Undergraduates: 2,036. Freshmen: 401. Federal methodology is used as a basis for awarding need-based institutional aid.

UNDERGRADUATE EXPENSES for 2018–2019 *Application fee:* $45. *Comprehensive fee:* $46,226 includes full-time tuition ($30,046), mandatory fees ($1072), and room and board ($15,108). *College room only:* $8752. Full-time tuition and fees vary according to class time, course load, location, and program. Room and board charges vary according to board plan and housing facility. *Part-time tuition:* $1002 per credit. *Part-time fees:* $86 per year. Part-time tuition and fees vary according to class time, course load, location, and program.

FRESHMAN FINANCIAL AID (Fall 2017, est.) 394 applied for aid; of those 90% were deemed to have need. 100% of freshmen with need received aid; of those 19% had need fully met. *Average percent of need met:* 75% (excluding resources awarded to replace EFC). *Average financial aid package:* $23,758 (excluding resources awarded to replace EFC). 11% of all full-time freshmen had no need and received non-need-based gift aid.

UNDERGRADUATE FINANCIAL AID (Fall 2017, est.) 1,544 applied for aid; of those 89% were deemed to have need. 100% of undergraduates with need received aid; of those 16% had need fully met. *Average percent of need met:* 64% (excluding resources awarded to replace EFC). *Average financial aid package:* $20,126 (excluding resources awarded to replace EFC). 15% of all full-time undergraduates had no need and received non-need-based gift aid.

GIFT AID (NEED-BASED) *Total amount:* $21,380,709 (16% federal, 8% state, 75% institutional, 1% external sources). *Receiving aid:* Freshmen: 88% (350); all full-time undergraduates: 76% (1,320). *Average award:* Freshmen: $18,614; Undergraduates: $15,747. *Scholarships, grants, and awards:* Federal Pell, FSEOG, state, private, college/university gift aid from institutional funds, Federal Nursing, Academic Competitiveness Grants, National SMART Grants.

GIFT AID (NON-NEED-BASED) *Total amount:* $3,903,652 (2% state, 96% institutional, 2% external sources). *Receiving aid:* Freshmen: 13% (52). Undergraduates: 8% (145). *Average award:* Freshmen: $14,886. Undergraduates: $11,056. *Scholarships, grants, and awards by category:* Academic interests/achievement: 1,433 awards ($13,317,124 total): general academic interests/achievements. *Special achievements/activities:* 14 awards ($35,000 total): leadership. *Special* *characteristics:* 28 awards ($759,308 total): children of faculty/staff. **Tuition waivers:** Full or partial for employees or children of employees. **ROTC:** Army cooperative.

LOANS *Student loans:* $14,057,314 (94% need-based, 6% non-need-based). 84% of past graduating class borrowed through all loan programs. *Average indebtedness per student:* $28,313. *Average need-based loan:* Freshmen: $3000. Undergraduates: $4265. *Parent loans:* $11,137,520 (100% need-based). *Programs:* Federal Direct (Subsidized and Unsubsidized Stafford, PLUS), Perkins, Federal Nursing.

WORK-STUDY *Federal work-study:* Total amount: $520,000; 360 jobs averaging $1444. *State or other work-study/employment:* Part-time jobs available.

APPLYING FOR FINANCIAL AID *Required financial aid form:* FAFSA. *Financial aid deadline:* 3/1 (priority: 2/15). *Notification date:* Continuous beginning 3/15. Students must reply by 5/1.

CONTACT Jason Franky, Director of Financial Aid, Mount Saint Mary College, 330 Powell Avenue, Newburgh, NY 12550-3494, 845-561-3394 or toll-free 888-937-6762. *Fax:* 845-569-3302. *E-mail:* jason.franky@msmc.edu. *Website:* http://www.msmc.edu/.

MOUNT SAINT MARY'S UNIVERSITY
Los Angeles, CA

Tuition & fees: $41,170	Average undergraduate aid package: $27,877

ABOUT THE INSTITUTION Independent Roman Catholic, coed, primarily women. *Awards:* certificates, associate, bachelor's, master's, and doctoral degrees. 47 undergraduate majors. *Total enrollment:* 679. Undergraduates: 2,601. Freshmen: 496. Both federal and institutional methodology are used as a basis for awarding need-based institutional aid.

UNDERGRADUATE EXPENSES for 2018–2019 *Comprehensive fee:* $53,405 includes full-time tuition ($40,018), mandatory fees ($1152), and room and board ($12,235). Full-time tuition and fees vary according to course load, degree level, and program. Room and board charges vary according to board plan and housing facility. Part-time tuition and fees vary according to course load, degree level, and program.

FRESHMAN FINANCIAL AID (Fall 2017, est.) 475 applied for aid; of those 97% were deemed to have need. 100% of freshmen with need received aid; of those 6% had need fully met. *Average percent of need met:* 47% (excluding resources awarded to replace EFC). *Average financial aid package:* $34,579 (excluding resources awarded to replace EFC). 5% of all full-time freshmen had no need and received non-need-based gift aid.

UNDERGRADUATE FINANCIAL AID (Fall 2017, est.) 2,375 applied for aid; of those 97% were deemed to have need. 97% of undergraduates with need received aid; of those 9% had need fully met. *Average percent of need met:* 41% (excluding resources awarded to replace EFC). *Average financial aid package:* $27,877 (excluding resources awarded to replace EFC). 6% of all full-time undergraduates had no need and received non-need-based gift aid.

GIFT AID (NEED-BASED) *Total amount:* $47,334,090 (15% federal, 19% state, 65% institutional, 1% external sources). *Receiving aid:* Freshmen: 94% (456); all full-time undergraduates: 71% (1,820). *Average award:* Freshmen: $21,914; Undergraduates: $19,318. *Scholarships, grants, and awards:* Federal Pell, FSEOG, state, private, college/university gift aid from institutional funds.

GIFT AID (NON-NEED-BASED) *Total amount:* $3,256,928 (99% institutional, 1% external sources). *Receiving aid:* Freshmen: 4% (20). Undergraduates: 5% (120). *Average award:* Freshmen: $17,739. Undergraduates: $11,774. *Scholarships, grants, and awards by category:* Academic interests/achievement: general academic interests/achievements. *Creative arts/performance:* music. *Special achievements/activities:* community service, leadership. *Special characteristics:* children and siblings of alumni. *Tuition waivers:* Full or partial for employees or children of employees.

LOANS *Student loans:* $14,382,774 (91% need-based, 9% non-need-based). 92% of past graduating class borrowed through all loan programs. *Average indebtedness per student:* $35,161. *Average need-based loan:* Freshmen: $3478. Undergraduates: $4384. *Parent loans:* $6,750,438 (95% need-based, 5% non-need-based). *Programs:* Federal Direct (Subsidized and Unsubsidized Stafford, PLUS), Federal Nursing, college/university.

WORK-STUDY *Federal work-study:* Total amount: $1,344,422; jobs available. *State or other work-study/employment:* Part-time jobs available.

APPLYING FOR FINANCIAL AID *Required financial aid form:* FAFSA. *Financial aid deadline:* Continuous. *Notification date:* Continuous beginning 2/15. Students must reply by 5/1 or within 3 weeks of notification.

CONTACT La Royce Housley, Director of Financial Aid, Mount Saint Mary's University, 12001 Chalon Road, Los Angeles, CA 90049, 310-954-4192 or toll-free 800-999-9893. *Website:* http://www.msmu.edu/.

MOUNT ST. MARY'S UNIVERSITY
Emmitsburg, MD

Tuition & fees: $40,550	Average undergraduate aid package: $29,515

ABOUT THE INSTITUTION Independent Roman Catholic, coed. *Awards:* certificates, bachelor's, and master's degrees. 33 undergraduate majors. *Total enrollment:* 2,323. Undergraduates: 1,817. Freshmen: 524. Federal methodology is used as a basis for awarding need-based institutional aid.

UNDERGRADUATE EXPENSES for 2017–2018 *Application fee:* $45. *Comprehensive fee:* $53,380 includes full-time tuition ($39,200), mandatory fees ($1350), and room and board ($12,830). *College room only:* $6500. Full-time tuition and fees vary according to location and program. Room and board charges vary according to housing facility. *Part-time tuition:* $1275 per credit hour. Part-time tuition and fees vary according to location and program.

FRESHMAN FINANCIAL AID (Fall 2017, est.) 482 applied for aid; of those 90% were deemed to have need. 100% of freshmen with need received aid; of those 23% had need fully met. *Average percent of need met:* 78% (excluding resources awarded to replace EFC). *Average financial aid package:* $32,667 (excluding resources awarded to replace EFC). 16% of all full-time freshmen had no need and received non-need-based gift aid.

UNDERGRADUATE FINANCIAL AID (Fall 2017, est.) 1,378 applied for aid; of those 90% were deemed to have need. 100% of undergraduates with need received aid; of those 23% had need fully met. *Average percent of need met:* 74% (excluding resources awarded to replace EFC). *Average financial aid package:* $29,515 (excluding resources awarded to replace EFC). 23% of all full-time undergraduates had no need and received non-need-based gift aid.

GIFT AID (NEED-BASED) *Total amount:* $28,744,387 (9% federal, 6% state, 82% institutional, 3% external sources). *Receiving aid:* Freshmen: 83% (434); all full-time undergraduates: 73% (1,232). *Average award:* Freshmen: $28,001; Undergraduates: $24,811. *Scholarships, grants, and awards:* Federal Pell, FSEOG, state, private, college/university gift aid from institutional funds.

GIFT AID (NON-NEED-BASED) *Total amount:* $10,411,299 (6% federal, 86% institutional, 8% external sources). *Receiving aid:* Freshmen: 16% (82). Undergraduates: 13% (215). *Average award:* Freshmen: $20,831. Undergraduates: $18,997. *Scholarships, grants, and awards by category:* Academic interests/achievement: 1,583 awards ($28,151,047 total): general academic interests/achievements. *Creative arts/performance:* 8 awards ($32,000 total): art/fine arts. *Special achievements/activities:* 22 awards ($148,000 total): religious involvement. *Special characteristics:* 83 awards ($765,997 total): children of faculty/staff, siblings of current students. *Tuition waivers:* Full or partial for employees or children of employees. *ROTC:* Army cooperative.

LOANS *Student loans:* $13,417,519 (64% need-based, 36% non-need-based). 76% of past graduating class borrowed through all loan programs. *Average indebtedness per student:* $36,112. *Average need-based loan:* Freshmen: $4345. Undergraduates: $4723. *Parent loans:* $7,179,798 (53% need-based, 47% non-need-based). *Programs:* Federal Direct (Subsidized and Unsubsidized Stafford, PLUS), Perkins.

WORK-STUDY *Federal work-study:* Total amount: $210,000; 107 jobs averaging $1970. *State or other work-study/employment:* Total amount: $715,000 (84% need-based, 16% non-need-based). 522 part-time jobs averaging $1473.

ATHLETIC AWARDS Total amount: $3,829,494 (44% need-based, 56% non-need-based).

APPLYING FOR FINANCIAL AID *Required financial aid form:* FAFSA. *Financial aid deadline:* 3/1. *Notification date:* Continuous beginning 2/15. Students must reply by 5/1.

CONTACT Mr. David C. Reeder, Director of Financial Aid, Mount St. Mary's University, 16300 Old Emmitsburg Road, Emmitsburg, MD 21727-7799, 301-447-5207 or toll-free 800-448-4347. *Fax:* 301-447-5915. *E-mail:* reeder@msmary.edu. *Website:* http://www.msmary.edu/.

MT. SIERRA COLLEGE
Monrovia, CA

ABOUT THE INSTITUTION Proprietary, coed. 8 undergraduate majors.
GIFT AID (NEED-BASED) *Scholarships, grants, and awards:* Federal Pell, FSEOG, private, college/university gift aid from institutional funds.
LOANS *Programs:* Federal Direct (Subsidized and Unsubsidized Stafford, PLUS).
WORK-STUDY *Federal work-study:* 13 jobs averaging $2700.
APPLYING FOR FINANCIAL AID *Required financial aid forms:* FAFSA, institution's own form.
CONTACT Financial Aid Office, Mt. Sierra College, 800 Royal Oaks Drive, Suite 101, Monrovia, CA 91016, 888-828-8800 or toll-free 888-828-8000.
Website: http://www.mtsierra.edu/.

MOUNT VERNON NAZARENE UNIVERSITY
Mount Vernon, OH

Tuition & fees: $29,194	Average undergraduate aid package: $21,072

ABOUT THE INSTITUTION Independent Nazarene, coed. *Awards:* associate, bachelor's, and master's degrees. 72 undergraduate majors. *Total enrollment:* 2,222. Undergraduates: 1,828. Freshmen: 344. Federal methodology is used as a basis for awarding need-based institutional aid.
UNDERGRADUATE EXPENSES for 2018–2019 *Application fee:* $25. *Comprehensive fee:* $37,364 includes full-time tuition ($28,944), mandatory fees ($250), and room and board ($8170). *College room only:* $4564. Full-time tuition and fees vary according to program. *Part-time tuition:* $803 per credit hour. Part-time tuition and fees vary according to course load and program.
FRESHMAN FINANCIAL AID (Fall 2017, est.) 322 applied for aid; of those 92% were deemed to have need. 100% of freshmen with need received aid; of those 53% had need fully met. *Average percent of need met:* 68% (excluding resources awarded to replace EFC). *Average financial aid package:* $25,284 (excluding resources awarded to replace EFC). 11% of all full-time freshmen had no need and received non-need-based gift aid.
UNDERGRADUATE FINANCIAL AID (Fall 2017, est.) 1,184 applied for aid; of those 92% were deemed to have need. 100% of undergraduates with need received aid; of those 54% had need fully met. *Average percent of need met:* 64% (excluding resources awarded to replace EFC). *Average financial aid package:* $21,072 (excluding resources awarded to replace EFC). 33% of all full-time undergraduates had no need and received non-need-based gift aid.
GIFT AID (NEED-BASED) *Total amount:* $17,028,406 (14% federal, 5% state, 77% institutional, 4% external sources). *Receiving aid:* Freshmen: 89% (295); all full-time undergraduates: 67% (1,088). *Average award:* Freshmen: $20,312; Undergraduates: $18,449. *Scholarships, grants, and awards:* Federal Pell, FSEOG, state, private, college/university gift aid from institutional funds.
GIFT AID (NON-NEED-BASED) *Total amount:* $2,597,848 (2% state, 96% institutional, 2% external sources). *Receiving aid:* Freshmen: 47% (156). Undergraduates: 36% (586). *Average award:* Freshmen: $13,906. Undergraduates: $11,569. *Scholarships, grants, and awards by category:* Academic interests/achievement: general academic interests/achievements. Creative arts/performance: art/fine arts, music. Special achievements/activities: general special achievements/activities, religious involvement. Special characteristics: children of faculty/staff, international students, members of minority groups, relatives of clergy, religious affiliation. Tuition waivers: Full or partial for employees or children of employees, senior citizens.
LOANS *Student loans:* $7,658,584 (94% need-based, 6% non-need-based). 78% of past graduating class borrowed through all loan programs. *Average indebtedness per student:* $25,745. *Average need-based loan:* Freshmen: $3512. Undergraduates: $4159. *Parent loans:* $1,694,855 (82% need-based, 18% non-need-based). *Programs:* Federal Direct (Subsidized and Unsubsidized Stafford, PLUS), Perkins, Federal Nursing, state, college/university, Charles E. Schell Foundation loans.
WORK-STUDY *Federal work-study:* Total amount: $126,029; jobs available. *State or other work-study/employment:* Part-time jobs available.
ATHLETIC AWARDS Total amount: $959,570 (68% need-based, 32% non-need-based).

APPLYING FOR FINANCIAL AID *Required financial aid form:* FAFSA. *Financial aid deadline (priority):* 3/1. *Notification date:* Continuous beginning 11/15.
CONTACT Office of Student Financial Services, Mount Vernon Nazarene University, 800 Martinsburg Road, Mount Vernon, OH 43050-9500, 866-686-8243 or toll-free 866-462-6868. *Fax:* 740-399-8682. *E-mail:* finaid@mvnu.edu.
Website: http://www.mvnu.edu/.

MUHLENBERG COLLEGE
Allentown, PA

Tuition & fees: $50,830	Average undergraduate aid package: $36,168

ABOUT THE INSTITUTION Independent Lutheran Church, coed. *Awards:* certificates, associate, and bachelor's degrees. 37 undergraduate majors. *Total enrollment:* 2,408. Undergraduates: 2,408. Freshmen: 593. Institutional methodology is used as a basis for awarding need-based institutional aid.
UNDERGRADUATE EXPENSES for 2017–2018 *Application fee:* $50. *One-time required fee:* $120. *Comprehensive fee:* $62,250 includes full-time tuition ($50,095), mandatory fees ($735), and room and board ($11,420). *College room only:* $6205. Room and board charges vary according to board plan, housing facility, and location. *Part-time tuition:* $5890 per course. *Part-time fees:* $367.50 per term. Part-time tuition and fees vary according to program.
FRESHMAN FINANCIAL AID (Fall 2017, est.) 439 applied for aid; of those 81% were deemed to have need. 100% of freshmen with need received aid; of those 27% had need fully met. *Average percent of need met:* 87% (excluding resources awarded to replace EFC). *Average financial aid package:* $37,050 (excluding resources awarded to replace EFC). 29% of all full-time freshmen had no need and received non-need-based gift aid.
UNDERGRADUATE FINANCIAL AID (Fall 2017, est.) 1,503 applied for aid; of those 86% were deemed to have need. 99% of undergraduates with need received aid; of those 25% had need fully met. *Average percent of need met:* 87% (excluding resources awarded to replace EFC). *Average financial aid package:* $36,168 (excluding resources awarded to replace EFC). 32% of all full-time undergraduates had no need and received non-need-based gift aid.
GIFT AID (NEED-BASED) *Total amount:* $37,834,000 (4% federal, 2% state, 94% institutional). *Receiving aid:* Freshmen: 63% (356); all full-time undergraduates: 56% (1,266). *Average award:* Freshmen: $33,460; Undergraduates: $32,257. *Scholarships, grants, and awards:* Federal Pell, FSEOG, state, private, college/university gift aid from institutional funds, United Negro College Fund.
GIFT AID (NON-NEED-BASED) *Total amount:* $11,163,000 (96% institutional, 4% external sources). *Receiving aid:* Freshmen: 12% (69). Undergraduates: 9% (197). *Average award:* Freshmen: $13,936. Undergraduates: $13,264. *Scholarships, grants, and awards by category:* Academic interests/achievement: general academic interests/achievements. Creative arts/performance: art/fine arts, cinema/film/broadcasting, dance, music, performing arts, theater/drama. Special characteristics: relatives of clergy, veterans' children. Tuition waivers: Full or partial for employees or children of employees. ROTC: Army cooperative.
LOANS *Student loans:* $11,002,000 (55% need-based, 45% non-need-based). 59% of past graduating class borrowed through all loan programs. *Average indebtedness per student:* $32,241. *Average need-based loan:* Freshmen: $3709. Undergraduates: $4634. *Parent loans:* $4,501,000 (18% need-based, 82% non-need-based). *Programs:* Federal Direct (Subsidized and Unsubsidized Stafford, PLUS), Perkins.
WORK-STUDY *Federal work-study:* Total amount: $230,000; jobs available. *State or other work-study/employment:* Total amount: $181,000 (27% need-based, 73% non-need-based). Part-time jobs available.
APPLYING FOR FINANCIAL AID *Required financial aid forms:* FAFSA, institution's own form, CSS Financial Aid PROFILE, noncustodial (divorced/separated) parent's statement. *Financial aid deadline:* 3/1. *Notification date:* 4/1. Students must reply by 5/1.
CONTACT Mr. Greg Mitton, Director of Financial Aid, Muhlenberg College, 2400 Chew Street, Allentown, PA 18104-5586, 484-664-3175. *Fax:* 484-664-3234. *E-mail:* gregmitton@muhlenberg.edu.
Website: http://www.muhlenberg.edu/.

MULTNOMAH UNIVERSITY
Portland, OR

CONTACT Mrs. Mary J. McGlothlan, Director of Financial Aid, Multnomah University, 8435 NE Glisan Street, Portland, OR 97220-5898, 503-251-5337 or toll-free 877-251-6560. *Fax:* 503-445-5199. *E-mail:* mmcglothlan@multnomah.edu. *Website:* http://www.multnomah.edu/.

MURRAY STATE UNIVERSITY
Murray, KY

Tuition & fees (KY res): $8340	Average undergraduate aid package: $12,274

ABOUT THE INSTITUTION State-supported, coed. *Awards:* certificates, bachelor's, master's, and doctoral degrees. 65 undergraduate majors. *Total enrollment:* 10,495. Undergraduates: 8,886. Freshmen: 1,502. Federal methodology is used as a basis for awarding need-based institutional aid.

UNDERGRADUATE EXPENSES for 2017–2018 Application fee: $40. *Tuition, state resident:* full-time $8340; part-time $367.50 per credit hour. *Tuition, nonresident:* full-time $22,728; part-time $992.50 per credit hour. Full-time tuition and fees vary according to course load and reciprocity agreements. Part-time tuition and fees vary according to reciprocity agreements. *College room and board:* $8906; *Room only:* $5246. Room and board charges vary according to board plan and housing facility.

FRESHMAN FINANCIAL AID (Fall 2017, est.) 1,423 applied for aid; of those 72% were deemed to have need. 100% of freshmen with need received aid; of those 22% had need fully met. *Average percent of need met:* 39% (excluding resources awarded to replace EFC). *Average financial aid package:* $11,656 (excluding resources awarded to replace EFC). 18% of all full-time freshmen had no need and received non-need-based gift aid.

UNDERGRADUATE FINANCIAL AID (Fall 2017, est.) 6,040 applied for aid; of those 76% were deemed to have need. 100% of undergraduates with need received aid; of those 25% had need fully met. *Average percent of need met:* 34% (excluding resources awarded to replace EFC). *Average financial aid package:* $12,274 (excluding resources awarded to replace EFC). 11% of all full-time undergraduates had no need and received non-need-based gift aid.

GIFT AID (NEED-BASED) Total amount: $25,829,586 (45% federal, 22% state, 28% institutional, 5% external sources). *Receiving aid:* Freshmen: 63% (950); all full-time undergraduates: 57% (3,933). *Average award:* Freshmen: $7023; Undergraduates: $6258. *Scholarships, grants, and awards:* Federal Pell, FSEOG, state, private, college/university gift aid from institutional funds, Federal Nursing.

GIFT AID (NON-NEED-BASED) Total amount: $11,676,864 (2% federal, 18% state, 44% institutional, 36% external sources). *Receiving aid:* Freshmen: 10% (151). Undergraduates: 6% (435). *Average award:* Freshmen: $6085. Undergraduates: $5487. *Scholarships, grants, and awards by category:* Academic interests/achievement: 2,067 awards ($5,748,515 total): agriculture, biological sciences, business, communication, computer science, education, engineering/technologies, English, general academic interests/achievements, health fields, home economics, humanities, international studies, mathematics, military science, physical sciences, pre-medicine, social sciences. *Creative arts/performance:* 93 awards ($146,940 total): art/fine arts, dance, journalism/publications, music, theater/drama. *Special achievements/activities:* 186 awards ($855,600 total): community service, memberships, rodeo. *Special characteristics:* 470 awards ($1,477,210 total): adult students, children of faculty/staff, general special characteristics, local/state students, married students, members of minority groups, out-of-state students, veterans, veterans' children. *Tuition waivers:* Full or partial for employees or children of employees, senior citizens. *ROTC:* Army.

LOANS Student loans: $31,434,344 (76% need-based, 24% non-need-based). 51% of past graduating class borrowed through all loan programs. *Average indebtedness per student:* $27,564. *Average need-based loan:* Freshmen: $5280. Undergraduates: $6428. *Parent loans:* $5,806,319 (41% need-based, 59% non-need-based). *Programs:* Federal Direct (Subsidized and Unsubsidized Stafford, PLUS), Perkins, Federal Nursing, college/university.

WORK-STUDY Federal work-study: Total amount: $554,762; 442 jobs averaging $1375. *State or other work-study/employment:* Total amount: $3,629,760 (40% need-based, 60% non-need-based). Part-time jobs available.

ATHLETIC AWARDS Total amount: $4,417,025 (54% need-based, 46% non-need-based).

APPLYING FOR FINANCIAL AID *Required financial aid forms:* FAFSA, general scholarship application form, summer term institutional loan application. *Financial aid deadline:* Continuous. *Notification date:* Continuous beginning 12/15. Students must reply by 5/1.

CONTACT Wendy Cain, Bursar/Interim Director of Student Financial Services, Murray State University, 120 Sparks Hall, Murray, KY 42071-0009, 270-809-2273 or toll-free 800-272-4678. *Fax:* 270-809-3116. *E-mail:* wcain@murraystate.edu. *Website:* http://www.murraystate.edu/.

MUSICIANS INSTITUTE
Hollywood, CA

CONTACT Director of Financial Aid, Musicians Institute, 1655 North McCadden Place, Hollywood, CA 90028, 323-462-1384 or toll-free 800-255-PLAY. *Website:* http://www.mi.edu/.

MUSKINGUM UNIVERSITY
New Concord, OH

Tuition & fees: $28,516	Average undergraduate aid package: $24,239

ABOUT THE INSTITUTION Independent Presbyterian Church (U.S.A.), coed. *Awards:* bachelor's and master's degrees. 73 undergraduate majors. *Total enrollment:* 2,371. Undergraduates: 1,557. Freshmen: 383. Federal methodology is used as a basis for awarding need-based institutional aid.

UNDERGRADUATE EXPENSES for 2018–2019 One-time required fee: $250. *Comprehensive fee:* $39,996 includes full-time tuition ($27,500), mandatory fees ($1016), and room and board ($11,480). *College room only:* $5860. *Part-time tuition:* $610 per credit hour. Part-time tuition and fees vary according to course load.

FRESHMAN FINANCIAL AID (Fall 2016) 300 applied for aid; of those 95% were deemed to have need. 100% of freshmen with need received aid; of those 26% had need fully met. *Average percent of need met:* 79% (excluding resources awarded to replace EFC). *Average financial aid package:* $25,880 (excluding resources awarded to replace EFC). 10% of all full-time freshmen had no need and received non-need-based gift aid.

UNDERGRADUATE FINANCIAL AID (Fall 2016) 1,156 applied for aid; of those 95% were deemed to have need. 100% of undergraduates with need received aid; of those 17% had need fully met. *Average percent of need met:* 77% (excluding resources awarded to replace EFC). *Average financial aid package:* $24,239 (excluding resources awarded to replace EFC). 14% of all full-time undergraduates had no need and received non-need-based gift aid.

GIFT AID (NEED-BASED) Total amount: $20,804,862 (15% federal, 6% state, 77% institutional, 2% external sources). *Receiving aid:* Freshmen: 89% (284); all full-time undergraduates: 85% (1,093). *Average award:* Freshmen: $20,701; Undergraduates: $19,222. *Scholarships, grants, and awards:* Federal Pell, FSEOG, state, private, college/university gift aid from institutional funds.

GIFT AID (NON-NEED-BASED) Total amount: $2,843,381 (1% state, 97% institutional, 2% external sources). *Receiving aid:* Freshmen: 83% (265). Undergraduates: 77% (994). *Average award:* Freshmen: $14,490. Undergraduates: $13,018. *Scholarships, grants, and awards by category:* Academic interests/achievement: 658 awards ($8,787,425 total): biological sciences, computer science, engineering/technologies, general academic interests/achievements, mathematics, physical sciences, premedicine. *Creative arts/performance:* 121 awards ($187,570 total): applied art and design, art/fine arts, debating, journalism/publications, music, theater/drama. *Special achievements/activities:* 240 awards ($222,950 total): community service, junior miss, leadership. *Special characteristics:* 861 awards ($1,838,401 total): children and siblings of alumni, ethnic background, international students, local/state students, members of minority groups, previous college experience, relatives of clergy, religious affiliation, siblings of current students. *Tuition waivers:* Full or partial for children of alumni, employees or children of employees.

LOANS Student loans: $12,586,238 (76% need-based, 24% non-need-based). 78% of past graduating class borrowed through all loan programs. *Average indebtedness* per student: $33,490. *Average need based loans* Freshmen: $1501. Undergraduates: $5331. *Parent loans:* $3,444,710 (46% need-based, 54% non-need-based). *Programs:* Federal Direct (Subsidized and Unsubsidized Stafford, PLUS), Perkins, Federal Nursing, college/university.

WORK-STUDY *Federal work-study:* 394 jobs averaging $1000. *State or other work-study/employment:* Total amount: $320,000 (94% need-based, 6% non-need-based). Part-time jobs available.

APPLYING FOR FINANCIAL AID *Required financial aid form:* FAFSA. *Financial aid deadline (priority):* 3/1. *Notification date:* Continuous beginning 12/1. Students must reply by 5/1 or within 2 weeks of notification.

CONTACT Mrs. Beth DaLonzo, Senior Director of Admission and Student Financial Services, Muskingum University, 163 Stormont Street, New Concord, OH 43762, 740-826-8139 or toll-free 800-752-6082. *Fax:* 740-826-8100. *E-mail:* bdalonzo@muskingum.edu.
Website: http://www.muskingum.edu/.

NAROPA UNIVERSITY
Boulder, CO

CONTACT Ms. Nancy Morrell, Director of Student Financial Services, Naropa University, 2130 Arapahoe Avenue, Boulder, CO 80302-6697, 303-546-3534 or toll-free 800-772-6951. *Fax:* 303-546-3536. *E-mail:* finaid@naropa.edu.
Website: http://www.naropa.edu/.

NATIONAL AMERICAN UNIVERSITY
Centennial, CO

CONTACT Financial Aid Office, National American University, 8242 South University Boulevard, Suite 100, Centennial, CO 80122, 303-542-7000 or toll-free 877-628-5211.
Website: http://www.national.edu/.

NATIONAL AMERICAN UNIVERSITY
Colorado Springs, CO

CONTACT Financial Aid Office, National American University, 1079 Space Center Drive, Suite 140, Colorado Springs, CO 80915, 719-208-3800 or toll-free 855-369-9397.
Website: http://www.national.edu/.

NATIONAL AMERICAN UNIVERSITY
Colorado Springs, CO

CONTACT Financial Aid Coordinator, National American University, 2577 North Chelton Road, Colorado Springs, CO 80909, 719-471-4205 or toll-free 855-369-9397.
Website: http://www.national.edu/.

NATIONAL AMERICAN UNIVERSITY
Indianapolis, IN

CONTACT Financial Aid Office, National American University, 3600 Woodview Trace, Suite 200, Indianapolis, IN 46268, 317-810-8100 or toll-free 800-609-1430.
Website: http://www.national.edu/.

NATIONAL AMERICAN UNIVERSITY
Overland Park, KS

CONTACT Financial Aid Office, National American University, 10310 Mastin Street, Overland Park, KS 66212, 913-981-8700 or toll-free 866-628-1288.
Website: http://www.national.edu/.

NATIONAL AMERICAN UNIVERSITY
Wichita, KS

CONTACT Financial Aid Office, National American University, 7309 East 21st Street, Suite G40, Wichita, KS 67206, 316-681-3050 or toll-free 877-628-9424.
Website: http://www.national.edu/.

NATIONAL AMERICAN UNIVERSITY
Wichita, KS

CONTACT Financial Aid Office, National American University, 8428 West 13th Street North, Suite 120, Wichita, KS 67212 or toll-free 877-628-9424.
Website: http://www.national.edu/.

NATIONAL AMERICAN UNIVERSITY
Bloomington, MN

CONTACT Financial Aid Office, National American University, 7801 Metro Parkway, Suite 200, Bloomington, MN 55425, 952-356-3600 or toll-free 866-628-6387.
Website: http://www.national.edu/.

NATIONAL AMERICAN UNIVERSITY
Brooklyn Center, MN

CONTACT Financial Aid Office, National American University, 6200 Shingle Creek Parkway, Suite 130, Brooklyn Center, MN 55430, 763-852-7500 or toll-free 866-628-6387.
Website: http://www.national.edu/.

NATIONAL AMERICAN UNIVERSITY
Burnsville, MN

CONTACT Financial Aid Office, National American University, 513 West Travelers Trail, Burnsville, MN 55337, 952-563-1250 or toll-free 866-628-6387.
Website: http://www.national.edu/.

NATIONAL AMERICAN UNIVERSITY
Roseville, MN

CONTACT Financial Aid Office, National American University, 1550 West Highway 36, Roseville, MN 55113, 651-855-6300 or toll-free 866-628-6387.
Website: http://www.national.edu/.

NATIONAL AMERICAN UNIVERSITY
Independence, MO

CONTACT Financial Aid Office, National American University, 3620 Arowhead Avenue, Independence, MO 64057, 816-412-7700 or toll-free 866-628-1288. *Website:* http://www.national.edu/.

NATIONAL AMERICAN UNIVERSITY
Kansas City, MO

CONTACT Mary Anderson, Coordinator of Financial Aid, National American University, 4200 Blue Ridge, Kansas City, MO 64133, 816-353-4554 or toll-free 866-628-1288. *Fax:* 816-353-1176.
Website: http://www.national.edu/.

NATIONAL AMERICAN UNIVERSITY
Lee's Summit, MO

CONTACT Financial Aid Office, National American University, 401 NW Murray Road, Lee's Summit, MO 64081, 816-600-3900 or toll-free 866-628-1288. *Website:* http://www.national.edu/.

NATIONAL AMERICAN UNIVERSITY
Bellevue, NE

CONTACT Financial Aid Office, National American University, 3604 Summit Plaza Drive, Bellevue, NE 68123, 402-972-4250.
Website: http://www.national.edu/.

NATIONAL AMERICAN UNIVERSITY
Albuquerque, NM

CONTACT Financial Aid Office, National American University, 10131 Coors Boulevard NW, Suite I-01, Albuquerque, NM 87114, 505-348-3750 or toll-free 800-895-9904.
Website: http://www.national.edu/.

NATIONAL AMERICAN UNIVERSITY
Albuquerque, NM

CONTACT Director of Financial Aid, National American University, 321 Kansas City Street, Rapid City, SD 57701, 605-394-4800 or toll-free 800-895-9904.
Website: http://www.national.edu/.

NATIONAL AMERICAN UNIVERSITY
Tulsa, OK

CONTACT Financial Aid Office, National American University, 8040 South Sheridan Road, Tulsa, OK 74133, 918-879-8400 or toll-free 800-209-0338.
Website: http://www.national.edu/.

NATIONAL AMERICAN UNIVERSITY
Ellsworth AFB, SD

CONTACT Financial Aid Office, National American University, 1000 Ellsworth Street, Rushmore Center, Suite 2400B, Ellsworth AFB, SD 57706, 605-718-6550. *Website:* http://www.national.edu/.

NATIONAL AMERICAN UNIVERSITY
Rapid City, SD

CONTACT Financial Aid Director, National American University, PO Box 1780, Rapid City, SD 57709-1780, 605-721-5213 or toll-free 800-209-0490.
Website: http://www.national.edu/.

NATIONAL AMERICAN UNIVERSITY
Sioux Falls, SD

CONTACT Ms. Rhonda Kohnen, Financial Aid Coordinator, National American University, 2801 South Kiwanis Avenue, Suite 100, Sioux Falls, SD 57105-4293, 605-334-5430 or toll-free 800-388-5430. *Fax:* 605-334-1575. *E-mail:* rkohnen@national.edu.
Website: http://www.national.edu/.

NATIONAL AMERICAN UNIVERSITY
Austin, TX

CONTACT Financial Aid Office, National American University, 13801 Burnet Road, Suite 300, Austin, TX 78727, 512-651-4100 or toll-free 888-628-8392.
Website: http://www.national.edu/.

NATIONAL AMERICAN UNIVERSITY
Georgetown, TX

CONTACT Financial Aid Office, National American University, 1015 West University Avenue, Suite 700, Georgetown, TX 78628, 512-942-6750 or toll-free 888-628-8392.
Website: http://www.national.edu/.

NATIONAL AMERICAN UNIVERSITY
Houston, TX

CONTACT Financial Aid Office, National American University, 11511 Katy Freeway, Suite 200, Houston, TX 77079, 832-619-7300 or toll-free 855-455-8029.
Website: http://www.national.edu/.

NATIONAL AMERICAN UNIVERSITY
Lewisville, TX

CONTACT Financial Aid Office, National American University, 475 State Highway 121 Bypass, Suite 150, Lewisville, TX 75067, 972-829-2150 or toll-free 800-548-0605.
Website: http://www.national.edu/.

NATIONAL AMERICAN UNIVERSITY
Mesquite, TX

CONTACT Financial Aid Office, National American University, 18600 LBJ Freeway, Mesquite, TX 75150, 972-773-8800 or toll-free 800-548-0605. *Website:* http://www.national.edu/.

NATIONAL AMERICAN UNIVERSITY
Richardson, TX

CONTACT Financial Aid Office, National American University, 300 North Coit Road, Suite 225, Richardson, TX 75080, 972-773-8650 or toll-free 800-548-0605. *Website:* http://www.national.edu/.

NATIONAL LOUIS UNIVERSITY
Chicago, IL

CONTACT Janet Jazwiec, Assistant Director of Student Finance, National Louis University, 1000 Capitol Drive, Wheeling, IL 60090, 847-947-5453 or toll-free 888-658-8632. *Fax:* 847-947-5453. *E-mail:* jjazwiec@nl.edu. *Website:* http://www.nl.edu/.

NATIONAL PARALEGAL COLLEGE
Phoenix, AZ

CONTACT Financial Aid Office, National Paralegal College, 717 East Maryland Avenue, Phoenix, AZ 85014, 845-371-9101 or toll-free 800-371-6105. *Website:* http://nationalparalegal.edu/.

NATIONAL UNIVERSITY
La Jolla, CA

ABOUT THE INSTITUTION Independent, coed. *Awards:* certificates, associate, bachelor's, and master's degrees. 54 undergraduate majors. *Total enrollment:* 17,097. Undergraduates: 7,877. Freshmen: 146.
GIFT AID (NEED-BASED) *Scholarships, grants, and awards:* Federal Pell, FSEOG, state, college/university gift aid from institutional funds.
GIFT AID (NON-NEED-BASED) *Scholarships, grants, and awards by category:* Academic interests/achievement: general academic interests/achievements. *Special achievements/activities:* leadership.
LOANS *Programs:* Federal Direct (Subsidized and Unsubsidized Stafford, PLUS), Perkins, college/university.
APPLYING FOR FINANCIAL AID *Required financial aid forms:* FAFSA, institution's own form.
CONTACT Valerie Ryan, Director of Financial Aid, National University, 9980 Carroll Canyon, San Diego, CA 92131, 858-642-8500 or toll-free 800-628-8648. *Fax:* 858-642-8720. *E-mail:* vryan@nu.edu. *Website:* http://www.nu.edu/.

NATIONAL UNIVERSITY COLLEGE
Arecibo, PR

CONTACT Financial Aid Office, National University College, Calle Manuel Pérez Avilés, Avenida Vctor Rojas, Arecibo, PR 00612. *Website:* http://www.nuc.edu/.

NATIONAL UNIVERSITY COLLEGE
Bayamón, PR

CONTACT Ms. Elizabeth Cruz, Institutional Director of Financial Aid, National University College, PO Box 2036, Bayamon, PR 00961, 787-780-5134 Ext. 4021 or toll-free 800-780-5134. *E-mail:* ecruz@nuc.edu. *Website:* http://www.nuc.edu/.

NATIONAL UNIVERSITY COLLEGE
Caguas, PR

CONTACT Financial Aid Office, National University College, 190 Avenida Gautier Benitez Esquina Avenida Federico Degatau, Caguas, PR 00725, 787-653-4733 or toll-free 800-780-5134. *Website:* http://www.nuc.edu/.

NATIONAL UNIVERSITY COLLEGE
Ponce, PR

CONTACT Financial Aid Office, National University College, PO Box 801243, Ponce, PR 00716, 787-840-4474. *Website:* http://www.nuc.edu/.

NATIONAL UNIVERSITY COLLEGE
Rio Grande, PR

CONTACT Financial Aid Office, National University College, Carretera #3 Km. 22.1, Bo. Ciénaga Baja, Rio Grande, PR 00745, 787-809-5100 or toll-free 800-981-0812. *Website:* http://www.nuc.edu/.

NAVAJO TECHNICAL UNIVERSITY
Crownpoint, NM

CONTACT Office of Financial Aid, Navajo Technical University, PO Box 849, Crownpoint, NM 87313, 505-786-4309. *Website:* http://www.navajotech.edu/.

NAZARENE BIBLE COLLEGE
Lenexa, KS

CONTACT Miss Jenny Madsen, Director of Financial Aid, Nazarene Bible College, 1111 Academy Park Loop, Colorado Springs, CO 80910-3717, 719-884-5051 or toll-free 800-873-3873. *Fax:* 719-884-5199. *Website:* http://www.nbc.edu/.

NAZARETH COLLEGE OF ROCHESTER
Rochester, NY

Tuition & fees: $33,324	Average undergraduate aid package: $27,685

ABOUT THE INSTITUTION Independent, coed. *Awards:* certificates, bachelor's, master's, and doctoral degrees. 75 undergraduate majors. *Total enrollment:* 2,900. Undergraduates: 2,194. Freshmen: 550. Federal methodology is used as a basis for awarding need-based institutional aid.
UNDERGRADUATE EXPENSES for 2018–2019 *Application fee:* $45. *One-time required fee:* $550. *Comprehensive fee:* $46,734 includes full-time tuition

($31,924), mandatory fees ($1400), and room and board ($13,410). Full-time tuition and fees vary according to course load, program, and reciprocity agreements. Room and board charges vary according to board plan and housing facility. **Part-time tuition:** $760 per credit hour.

FRESHMAN FINANCIAL AID (Fall 2017, est.) 532 applied for aid; of those 89% were deemed to have need. 100% of freshmen with need received aid; of those 37% had need fully met. **Average percent of need met:** 83% (excluding resources awarded to replace EFC). **Average financial aid package:** $28,120 (excluding resources awarded to replace EFC). 14% of all full-time freshmen had no need and received non-need-based gift aid.

UNDERGRADUATE FINANCIAL AID (Fall 2017, est.) 1,926 applied for aid; of those 91% were deemed to have need. 100% of undergraduates with need received aid; of those 30% had need fully met. **Average percent of need met:** 80% (excluding resources awarded to replace EFC). **Average financial aid package:** $27,685 (excluding resources awarded to replace EFC). 16% of all full-time undergraduates had no need and received non-need-based gift aid.

GIFT AID (NEED-BASED) Total amount: $31,309,097 (10% federal, 8% state, 79% institutional, 3% external sources). **Receiving aid:** Freshmen: 86% (474); all full-time undergraduates: 84% (1,755). **Average award:** Freshmen: $19,456; Undergraduates: $17,736. **Scholarships, grants, and awards:** Federal Pell, FSEOG, state, private, college/university gift aid from institutional funds, Federal Nursing.

GIFT AID (NON-NEED-BASED) Total amount: $5,587,824 (1% state, 92% institutional, 7% external sources). **Receiving aid:** Freshmen: 36% (198). Undergraduates: 28% (591). **Average award:** Freshmen: $20,933. Undergraduates: $18,299. **Scholarships, grants, and awards by category:** Academic interests/achievement: $19,243,680 total: biological sciences, business, communication, education, English, foreign languages, general academic interests/achievements, home economics, humanities, international studies, mathematics, physical sciences, premedicine, religion/biblical studies, social sciences. Creative arts/performance: $1,138,150 total: applied art and design, art/fine arts, dance, music, performing arts, theater/drama. Special achievements/activities: $67,250 total: leadership. Special characteristics: $5,782,267 total: children and siblings of alumni, children of faculty/staff, ethnic background, general special characteristics, out-of-state students, siblings of current students, veterans. **Tuition waivers:** Full or partial for minority students, children of alumni, employees or children of employees. **ROTC:** Army cooperative, Air Force cooperative.

LOANS Student loans: $19,052,325 (81% need-based, 19% non-need-based). 80% of past graduating class borrowed through all loan programs. Average indebtedness per student: $40,958. **Average need-based loan:** Freshmen: $3559. Undergraduates: $4570. **Parent loans:** $7,388,129 (56% need-based, 44% non-need-based). **Programs:** Federal Direct (Subsidized and Unsubsidized Stafford, PLUS), Perkins, Federal Nursing.

WORK-STUDY Federal work-study: Total amount: $2,480,928; 1,127 jobs averaging $2148.

APPLYING FOR FINANCIAL AID Required financial aid forms: FAFSA, state aid form. **Financial aid deadline (priority):** 2/1. **Notification date:** Continuous beginning 1/15. Students must reply by 5/1 or within 2 weeks of notification.

CONTACT Janice Scheutzow, Director of Financial Aid, Nazareth College of Rochester, 4245 East Avenue, Rochester, NY 14618-3790, 585-389-2310 or toll-free 800-462-3944. Fax: 585-389-2317. E-mail: jscheut1@naz.edu. Website: http://www.naz.edu/.

NEBRASKA CHRISTIAN COLLEGE OF HOPE INTERNATIONAL UNIVERSITY
Papillion, NE

Tuition & fees: $16,830	Average undergraduate aid package: $8472

ABOUT THE INSTITUTION Independent Christian Churches and Churches of Christ, coed. **Awards:** certificates, associate, bachelor's, and master's degrees. 6 undergraduate majors. **Total enrollment:** 145. Undergraduates: 145. Freshmen: 46. Federal methodology is used as a basis for awarding need-based institutional aid.

UNDERGRADUATE EXPENSES for 2017–2018 Application fee: $40. **Comprehensive fee:** $25,960 includes full-time tuition ($16,530), mandatory fees ($300), and room and board ($9130). Full-time tuition and fees vary according to course load. Room and board charges vary according to board plan and housing facility. **Part-time**

tuition: $710 per credit hour. Part-time tuition and fees vary according to course load.

FRESHMAN FINANCIAL AID (Fall 2016) 20 applied for aid; of those 75% were deemed to have need. 100% of freshmen with need received aid; of those 7% had need fully met. **Average percent of need met:** 35% (excluding resources awarded to replace EFC). **Average financial aid package:** $10,227 (excluding resources awarded to replace EFC). 25% of all full-time freshmen had no need and received non-need-based gift aid.

UNDERGRADUATE FINANCIAL AID (Fall 2016) 87 applied for aid; of those 90% were deemed to have need. 100% of undergraduates with need received aid; of those 5% had need fully met. **Average percent of need met:** 34% (excluding resources awarded to replace EFC). **Average financial aid package:** $8472 (excluding resources awarded to replace EFC). 6% of all full-time undergraduates had no need and received non-need-based gift aid.

GIFT AID (NEED-BASED) Total amount: $309,600 (83% federal, 10% state, 7% institutional). **Receiving aid:** Freshmen: 45% (9); all full-time undergraduates: 42% (42). **Average award:** Freshmen: $9299; Undergraduates: $7535. **Scholarships, grants, and awards:** Federal Pell, FSEOG, state, private, college/university gift aid from institutional funds.

GIFT AID (NON-NEED-BASED) Total amount: $714,081 (81% institutional, 19% external sources). **Receiving aid:** Freshmen: 30% (6). Undergraduates: 28% (28). **Average award:** Freshmen: $5667. Undergraduates: $11,046. **Scholarships, grants, and awards by category:** Academic interests/achievement: general academic interests/achievements, religion/biblical studies. Special characteristics: children of faculty/staff, international students, relatives of clergy. **Tuition waivers:** Full or partial for employees or children of employees.

LOANS Student loans: $441,025 (59% need-based, 41% non-need-based). 83% of past graduating class borrowed through all loan programs. Average indebtedness per student: $18,479. **Average need-based loan:** Freshmen: $2700. Undergraduates: $2851. **Parent loans:** $152,373 (100% non-need-based). **Programs:** Federal Direct (Subsidized and Unsubsidized Stafford, PLUS), private loans.

WORK-STUDY Federal work-study: jobs available. **State or other work-study/employment:** Total amount: $18,072 (100% non-need-based). Part-time jobs available.

APPLYING FOR FINANCIAL AID Required financial aid forms: FAFSA, institution's own form. **Financial aid deadline (priority):** 1/1. **Notification date:** Continuous beginning 1/1. Students must reply within 2 weeks of notification.

CONTACT Kelli Sprouse, Office of Financial Aid, Nebraska Christian College of Hope International University, 12550 South 114th Street, Papillion, NE 68046, 402-935-9400. Fax: 402-935-9500. E-mail: kelli.sprouse@nechristian.edu. Website: http://www.nechristian.edu/.

NEBRASKA METHODIST COLLEGE
Omaha, NE

Tuition & fees: $15,980	Average undergraduate aid package: $9579

ABOUT THE INSTITUTION Independent United Methodist Church, coed. **Awards:** certificates, associate, bachelor's, master's, and doctoral degrees. 10 undergraduate majors. **Total enrollment:** 1,167. Undergraduates: 881. Freshmen: 45. Federal methodology is used as a basis for awarding need-based institutional aid.

UNDERGRADUATE EXPENSES for 2018–2019 Application fee: $25. **Tuition:** full-time $15,660; part-time $580 per credit hour. **Required fees:** full-time $320; $160 per term. Full-time tuition and fees vary according to course load, degree level, and program. Part-time tuition and fees vary according to course load, degree level, and program.

FRESHMAN FINANCIAL AID (Fall 2017, est.) 38 applied for aid; of those 74% were deemed to have need. 100% of freshmen with need received aid; of those 14% had need fully met. **Average percent of need met:** 49% (excluding resources awarded to replace EFC). **Average financial aid package:** $11,629 (excluding resources awarded to replace EFC). 26% of all full-time freshmen had no need and received non-need-based gift aid.

UNDERGRADUATE FINANCIAL AID (Fall 2017, est.) 414 applied for aid; of those 88% were deemed to have need. 99% of undergraduates with need received aid; of those 4% had need fully met. **Average percent of need met:** 34% (excluding resources awarded to replace EFC). **Average financial aid package:** $9579

(excluding resources awarded to replace EFC). 13% of all full-time undergraduates had no need and received non-need-based gift aid.

GIFT AID (NEED-BASED) *Total amount:* $3,134,090 (41% federal, 7% state, 41% institutional, 11% external sources). *Receiving aid:* Freshmen: 74% (28); all full-time undergraduates: 76% (323). *Average award:* Freshmen: $8089; Undergraduates: $6117. *Scholarships, grants, and awards:* Federal Pell, FSEOG, state, private, college/university gift aid from institutional funds, Federal Nursing.

GIFT AID (NON-NEED-BASED) *Total amount:* $358,465 (83% institutional, 17% external sources). *Receiving aid:* Freshmen: 8% (3). Undergraduates: 2% (9). *Average award:* Freshmen: $5100. Undergraduates: $4390. *Scholarships, grants, and awards by category: Academic interests/achievement:* general academic interests/achievements, home economics. *Special achievements/activities:* general special achievements/activities, leadership, memberships. *Special characteristics:* children of faculty/staff, religious affiliation. *Tuition waivers:* Full or partial for employees or children of employees. *ROTC:* Air Force cooperative.

LOANS *Student loans:* $6,521,859 (87% need-based, 13% non-need-based). 100% of past graduating class borrowed through all loan programs. *Average indebtedness per student:* $37,215. *Average need-based loan:* Freshmen: $4136. Undergraduates: $4690. *Parent loans:* $1,124,465 (58% need-based, 42% non-need-based). *Programs:* Federal Direct (Subsidized and Unsubsidized Stafford, PLUS), Federal Nursing, private loans.

WORK-STUDY *Federal work-study:* Total amount: $44,520; 22 jobs averaging $2050.

APPLYING FOR FINANCIAL AID *Required financial aid forms:* FAFSA, institution's own form. *Financial aid deadline (priority):* 3/1. *Notification date:* Continuous beginning 3/15. Students must reply within 3 weeks of notification.

CONTACT Ms. Penny James, Director of Financial Aid, Nebraska Methodist College, The Josie Harper Campus, 720 North 87th Street, Omaha, NE 68114-3426, 402-354-7225 or toll-free 800-335-5510. *Fax:* 402-354-7020. *E-mail:* penny.james@methodistcollege.edu.
Website: http://www.methodistcollege.edu/.

NEBRASKA WESLEYAN UNIVERSITY
Lincoln, NE

CONTACT Mr. Thomas J. Ochsner, Director of Scholarships and Financial Aid, Nebraska Wesleyan University, 5000 Saint Paul Avenue, Lincoln, NE 68504, 402-465-2212 or toll-free 800-541-3818. *Fax:* 402-465-2194. *E-mail:* tjo@nebrwesleyan.edu.
Website: http://www.nebrwesleyan.edu/.

NER ISRAEL RABBINICAL COLLEGE
Baltimore, MD

CONTACT Mr. Moshe Pelberg, Financial Aid Administrator, Ner Israel Rabbinical College, 400 Mount Wilson Lane, Baltimore, MD 21208, 410-484-7200.

NEUMANN UNIVERSITY
Aston, PA

Tuition & fees: $30,050	Average undergraduate aid package: $16,953

ABOUT THE INSTITUTION Independent Roman Catholic, coed. *Awards:* certificates, associate, bachelor's, master's, and doctoral degrees. 22 undergraduate majors. *Total enrollment:* 2,715. Undergraduates: 2,085. Freshmen: 360. Both federal and institutional methodology are used as a basis for awarding need-based institutional aid.

UNDERGRADUATE EXPENSES for 2017–2018 *Application fee:* $35. *One-time required fee:* $100. *Comprehensive fee:* $42,570 includes full-time tuition ($28,710), mandatory fees ($1340), and room and board ($12,520). *College room only:* $7530. Full-time tuition and fees vary according to degree level. Room and board charges vary according to board plan and housing facility. *Part-time tuition:* $655 per credit hour. *Part-time fees:* $90 per term. Part-time tuition and fees vary according to degree level and program.

FRESHMAN FINANCIAL AID (Fall 2016) 356 applied for aid; of those 91% were deemed to have need. 100% of freshmen with need received aid; of those 59% had need fully met. *Average percent of need met:* 70% (excluding resources awarded to replace EFC). *Average financial aid package:* $23,372 (excluding resources awarded to replace EFC). 13% of all full-time freshmen had no need and received non-need-based gift aid.

UNDERGRADUATE FINANCIAL AID (Fall 2016) 1,486 applied for aid; of those 91% were deemed to have need. 100% of undergraduates with need received aid; of those 65% had need fully met. *Average percent of need met:* 70% (excluding resources awarded to replace EFC). *Average financial aid package:* $16,953 (excluding resources awarded to replace EFC). 15% of all full-time undergraduates had no need and received non-need-based gift aid.

GIFT AID (NEED-BASED) *Total amount:* $23,365,720 (17% federal, 9% state, 72% institutional, 2% external sources). *Receiving aid:* Freshmen: 53% (200); all full-time undergraduates: 54% (873). *Average award:* Freshmen: $12,806; Undergraduates: $7540. *Scholarships, grants, and awards:* Federal Pell, FSEOG, state, private, college/university gift aid from institutional funds.

GIFT AID (NON-NEED-BASED) *Receiving aid:* Freshmen: 85% (317). Undergraduates: 80% (1,285). *Average award:* Freshmen: $10,588. Undergraduates: $9017. *Scholarships, grants, and awards by category: Academic interests/achievement:* general academic interests/achievements. *Tuition waivers:* Full or partial for employees or children of employees. *ROTC:* Army cooperative, Air Force cooperative.

LOANS *Student loans:* $17,335,927 (100% need-based). 88% of past graduating class borrowed through all loan programs. *Average indebtedness per student:* $39,694. *Average need-based loan:* Freshmen: $3115. Undergraduates: $4116. *Parent loans:* $5,442,375 (100% need-based). *Programs:* Federal Direct (Subsidized and Unsubsidized Stafford, PLUS), Federal Nursing.

WORK-STUDY *Federal work-study:* jobs available. *State or other work-study/employment:* Part-time jobs available.

APPLYING FOR FINANCIAL AID *Required financial aid forms:* FAFSA, state aid form. *Financial aid deadline:* Continuous. *Notification date:* Continuous beginning 3/1. Students must reply by 5/1 or within 2 weeks of notification.

CONTACT Ms. Eileen M. Tucker, Director of Financial Assistance, Neumann University, One Neumann Drive, Aston, PA 19014-1298, 610-558-5521 or toll-free 800-963-8626. *E-mail:* tuckere@neumann.edu.
Website: http://www.neumann.edu/.

NEUMONT COLLEGE OF COMPUTER SCIENCE
Salt Lake City, UT

Tuition & fees: $24,750	Average undergraduate aid package: N/A

ABOUT THE INSTITUTION Proprietary, coed. *Awards:* bachelor's degrees. 2 undergraduate majors. *Total enrollment:* 431. Undergraduates: 431. Freshmen: 178. Both federal and institutional methodology are used as a basis for awarding need-based institutional aid.

UNDERGRADUATE EXPENSES for 2018–2019 *Application fee:* $35. *One-time required fee:* $2500. *Tuition:* full-time $22,950. Full-time tuition and fees vary according to course load, degree level, and program. Part-time tuition and fees vary according to course load, degree level, and program. Room and board charges vary according to housing facility.

GIFT AID (NEED-BASED) *Scholarships, grants, and awards:* Federal Pell, FSEOG, private, college/university gift aid from institutional funds.

GIFT AID (NON-NEED-BASED) *Scholarships, grants, and awards by category: Special achievements/activities:* community service, religious involvement. *Special characteristics:* 47 awards ($631,010 total): children of faculty/staff, international students, local/state students, veterans. *Tuition waivers:* Full or partial for employees or children of employees.

LOANS *Student loans:* 91% of past graduating class borrowed through all loan programs. *Average indebtedness per student:* $39,623. *Programs:* Federal Direct (Subsidized and Unsubsidized Stafford, PLUS), college/university, private loans.

APPLYING FOR FINANCIAL AID *Required financial aid forms:* FAFSA, institution's own form. *Financial aid deadline:* 7/30. *Notification date:* Continuous beginning 5/15.

CONTACT Mr. Nate Blanchard, Director of Financial Aid, Neumont College of Computer Science, 143 South Main Street, Salt Lake City, UT 84111, 801-302-2873 or toll-free 888-NEUMONT. *Fax:* 801-302-2834. *E-mail:* nate.blanchard@neumont.edu. *Website:* http://www.neumont.edu/.

NEVADA STATE COLLEGE
Henderson, NV

CONTACT Anthony Morrone, Director of Financial Aid, Nevada State College, 1124 Nevada State Drive, Henderson, NV 89002, 702-992-2150. *Fax:* 702-992-2151. *E-mail:* finaid@nsc.edu.
Website: http://www.nsc.edu/.

NEWBERRY COLLEGE
Newberry, SC

Tuition & fees: $26,424	Average undergraduate aid package: $22,269

ABOUT THE INSTITUTION Independent Evangelical Lutheran, coed. *Awards:* bachelor's degrees. 34 undergraduate majors. *Total enrollment:* 1,181. Undergraduates: 1,181. Freshmen: 353. Federal methodology is used as a basis for awarding need-based institutional aid.

UNDERGRADUATE EXPENSES for 2018–2019 *Comprehensive fee:* $37,090 includes full-time tuition ($24,174), mandatory fees ($2250), and room and board ($10,666). Full-time tuition and fees vary according to course load. Room and board charges vary according to board plan and housing facility. *Part-time tuition:* $820 per credit hour. *Part-time fees:* $70 per credit hour. Part-time tuition and fees vary according to course load.

FRESHMAN FINANCIAL AID (Fall 2016) 266 applied for aid; of those 92% were deemed to have need. 100% of freshmen with need received aid; of those 11% had need fully met. *Average percent of need met:* 72% (excluding resources awarded to replace EFC). *Average financial aid package:* $22,497 (excluding resources awarded to replace EFC). 14% of all full-time freshmen had no need and received non-need-based gift aid.

UNDERGRADUATE FINANCIAL AID (Fall 2016) 986 applied for aid; of those 91% were deemed to have need. 100% of undergraduates with need received aid; of those 17% had need fully met. *Average percent of need met:* 74% (excluding resources awarded to replace EFC). *Average financial aid package:* $22,269 (excluding resources awarded to replace EFC). 15% of all full-time undergraduates had no need and received non-need-based gift aid.

GIFT AID (NEED-BASED) *Total amount:* $15,590,733 (15% federal, 20% state, 61% institutional, 4% external sources). *Receiving aid:* Freshmen: 86% (245); all full-time undergraduates: 85% (896). *Average award:* Freshmen: $19,866; Undergraduates: $19,229. *Scholarships, grants, and awards:* Federal Pell, FSEOG, state, private, college/university gift aid from institutional funds.

GIFT AID (NON-NEED-BASED) *Total amount:* $3,032,282 (1% federal, 27% state, 67% institutional, 5% external sources). *Receiving aid:* Freshmen: 9% (27). Undergraduates: 14% (145). *Average award:* Freshmen: $9836. Undergraduates: $10,686. *Scholarships, grants, and awards by category:* Academic interests/achievement: biological sciences, business, communication, education, foreign languages, general academic interests/achievements, humanities, mathematics, physical sciences, religion/biblical studies, social sciences. *Creative arts/performance:* music, theater/drama. *Special achievements/activities:* cheerleading/drum major, religious involvement. *Special characteristics:* children and siblings of alumni, children of faculty/staff, international students, local/state students, relatives of clergy, religious affiliation, siblings of current students. *Tuition waivers:* Full or partial for employees or children of employees. *ROTC:* Army.

LOANS *Student loans:* $6,756,393 (71% need-based, 29% non-need-based). 90% of past graduating class borrowed through all loan programs. *Average indebtedness per student:* $22,380. *Average need-based loan:* Freshmen: $3067. Undergraduates: $3846. *Parent loans:* $2,633,379 (68% need-based, 32% non-need-based). *Programs:* Federal Direct (Subsidized and Unsubsidized Stafford, PLUS), Perkins.

WORK-STUDY *Federal work-study:* jobs available.

ATHLETIC AWARDS Total amount: $2,899,978 (57% need-based, 43% non-need-based).

APPLYING FOR FINANCIAL AID *Required financial aid form:* FAFSA. *Financial aid deadline (priority):* 3/15. *Notification date:* Continuous beginning 3/15. Students must reply by 8/20.

CONTACT Danielle Bell, Director of Financial Aid, Newberry College, 2100 College Street, Newberry, SC 29108, 803-321-5128 or toll-free 800-845-4955. *Fax:* 803-321-5627. *E-mail:* danielle.bell@newberry.edu.
Website: http://www.newberry.edu/.

NEWBURY COLLEGE
Brookline, MA

CONTACT Elreo Campbell, Executive Director of Student Financial Services, Newbury College, 129 Fisher Avenue, Brookline, MA 02445-5796, 617-730-7100 or toll-free 800-NEWBURY. *Fax:* 617-730-7108.
Website: http://www.newbury.edu/.

NEW COLLEGE OF FLORIDA
Sarasota, FL

Tuition & fees (FL res): $6916	Average undergraduate aid package: $14,822

ABOUT THE INSTITUTION State-supported, coed. *Awards:* bachelor's and master's degrees. 46 undergraduate majors. *Total enrollment:* 859. Undergraduates: 835. Freshmen: 199. Federal methodology is used as a basis for awarding need-based institutional aid.

UNDERGRADUATE EXPENSES for 2017–2018 *Application fee:* $30. *Tuition, state resident:* full-time $6916. *Tuition, nonresident:* full-time $29,944. *College room and board:* $9264; *Room only:* $6603. Room and board charges vary according to board plan and housing facility.

FRESHMAN FINANCIAL AID (Fall 2017, est.) 184 applied for aid; of those 66% were deemed to have need. 100% of freshmen with need received aid; of those 26% had need fully met. *Average percent of need met:* 90% (excluding resources awarded to replace EFC). *Average financial aid package:* $16,063 (excluding resources awarded to replace EFC). 35% of all full-time freshmen had no need and received non-need-based gift aid.

UNDERGRADUATE FINANCIAL AID (Fall 2017, est.) 673 applied for aid; of those 71% were deemed to have need. 99% of undergraduates with need received aid; of those 31% had need fully met. *Average percent of need met:* 86% (excluding resources awarded to replace EFC). *Average financial aid package:* $14,822 (excluding resources awarded to replace EFC). 34% of all full-time undergraduates had no need and received non-need-based gift aid.

GIFT AID (NEED-BASED) *Total amount:* $4,356,278 (30% federal, 31% state, 37% institutional, 2% external sources). *Receiving aid:* Freshmen: 55% (109); all full-time undergraduates: 52% (438). *Average award:* Freshmen: $11,802; Undergraduates: $9932. *Scholarships, grants, and awards:* Federal Pell, FSEOG, state, private, college/university gift aid from institutional funds.

GIFT AID (NON-NEED-BASED) *Total amount:* $2,173,287 (64% state, 34% institutional, 2% external sources). *Receiving aid:* Freshmen: 8% (16). Undergraduates: 7% (60). *Average award:* Freshmen: $2289. Undergraduates: $2514. *Scholarships, grants, and awards by category:* Academic interests/achievement: 1,094 awards ($4,208,954 total): general academic interests/achievements. *Special achievements/activities:* 31 awards ($61,250 total): general special achievements/activities. *Special characteristics:* 353 awards ($3,005,140 total): out-of-state students.

LOANS *Student loans:* $3,549,690 (52% need-based, 48% non-need-based). 34% of past graduating class borrowed through all loan programs. *Average indebtedness per student:* $16,297. *Average need-based loan:* Freshmen: $2653. Undergraduates: $3600. *Parent loans:* $427,586 (33% need-based, 67% non-need-based). *Programs:* Federal Direct (Subsidized and Unsubsidized Stafford, PLUS), alternative loans.

WORK-STUDY *Federal work-study:* Total amount: $27,700; 30 jobs averaging $1156. *State or other work-study/employment:* Part-time jobs available.

APPLYING FOR FINANCIAL AID *Required financial aid form:* FAFSA. *Financial aid deadline (priority):* 11/1. *Notification date:* Continuous beginning 2/1. Students must reply by 5/1 or within 2 weeks of notification.

CONTACT Tara Karas, Director of Financial Aid, New College of Florida, 5000 Bay Shore Road, Sarasota, FL 34243-2109, 941-487-5000. *Fax:* 941-487-5010. *E-mail:* tkaras@ncf.edu.
Website: http://www.ncf.edu/.

NEW ENGLAND COLLEGE
Henniker, NH

Tuition & fees: $36,954	Average undergraduate aid package: $23,463

ABOUT THE INSTITUTION Independent, coed. *Awards:* associate, bachelor's, master's, and doctoral degrees. 35 undergraduate majors. *Total enrollment:* 2,625. Undergraduates: 1,756. Freshmen: 353. Both federal and institutional methodology are used as a basis for awarding need-based institutional aid.

UNDERGRADUATE EXPENSES for 2017–2018 *Application fee:* $35. *Comprehensive fee:* $50,828 includes full-time tuition ($35,858), mandatory fees ($1096), and room and board ($13,874). *College room only:* $6274. Full-time tuition and fees vary according to class time, course load, location, program, and reciprocity agreements. Room and board charges vary according to board plan and housing facility. *Part-time tuition:* $439 per credit hour. Part-time tuition and fees vary according to class time, course load, location, and program.

FRESHMAN FINANCIAL AID (Fall 2017, est.) 484 applied for aid; of those 90% were deemed to have need. 100% of freshmen with need received aid; of those 4% had need fully met. *Average percent of need met:* 62% (excluding resources awarded to replace EFC). *Average financial aid package:* $27,668 (excluding resources awarded to replace EFC). 7% of all full-time freshmen had no need and received non-need-based gift aid.

UNDERGRADUATE FINANCIAL AID (Fall 2017, est.) 1,585 applied for aid; of those 99% were deemed to have need. 93% of undergraduates with need received aid; of those 7% had need fully met. *Average percent of need met:* 74% (excluding resources awarded to replace EFC). *Average financial aid package:* $23,463 (excluding resources awarded to replace EFC). 6% of all full-time undergraduates had no need and received non-need-based gift aid.

GIFT AID (NEED-BASED) *Total amount:* $23,337,174 (20% federal, 80% institutional). *Receiving aid:* Freshmen: 82% (426); all full-time undergraduates: 75% (1,342). *Average award:* Freshmen: $22,785; Undergraduates: $17,182. *Scholarships, grants, and awards:* Federal Pell, FSEOG, state, private, college/university gift aid from institutional funds.

GIFT AID (NON-NEED-BASED) *Total amount:* $2,277,075 (100% institutional). *Average award:* Freshmen: $22,309. Undergraduates: $19,847. *Scholarships, grants, and awards by category:* Academic interests/achievement: 966 awards ($14,875,735 total): biological sciences, business, communication, computer science, education, general academic interests/achievements, humanities, international studies, social sciences. *Creative arts/performance:* 1 award ($10,000 total): applied art and design, art/fine arts, creative writing, theater/drama. *Special achievements/activities:* 30 awards ($97,888 total): community service, leadership. *Special characteristics:* 359 awards ($821,552 total): children and siblings of alumni, children of educators, children of faculty/staff, ethnic background, international students, local/state students, parents of current students, siblings of current students, veterans, veterans' children. *Tuition waivers:* Full or partial for children of alumni, employees or children of employees, adult students, senior citizens. *ROTC:* Army cooperative, Air Force cooperative.

LOANS *Student loans:* $8,348,223 (67% need-based, 33% non-need-based). 85% of past graduating class borrowed through all loan programs. *Average indebtedness per student:* $37,450. *Average need-based loan:* Freshmen: $4609. Undergraduates: $4616. *Parent loans:* $5,641,160 (98% need-based, 2% non-need-based). *Programs:* Federal Direct (Subsidized and Unsubsidized Stafford, PLUS), Perkins, state.

WORK-STUDY *Federal work-study:* Total amount: $691,822; jobs available. *State or other work-study/employment:* Part-time jobs available.

APPLYING FOR FINANCIAL AID *Required financial aid form:* FAFSA. *Financial aid deadline (priority):* 4/1. *Notification date:* Continuous beginning 2/1. Students must reply by 9/7 or within 4 weeks of notification.

CONTACT Kristen Blase, Student Financial Services Director, New England College, 15 Main Street, Henniker, NH 03242-3293, 603-428-2226 or toll-free 800-521-7642. *Fax:* 603-428-2404. *E-mail:* rstein@nec.edu.
Website: http://www.nec.edu/.

NEW ENGLAND COLLEGE OF BUSINESS AND FINANCE
Boston, MA

CONTACT Financial Aid Office, New England College of Business and Finance, 10 High Street, Suite 204, Boston, MA 02111-2645, 617-951-2350 or toll-free 800-997-1673.
Website: http://necb.edu/.

NEW ENGLAND CONSERVATORY OF MUSIC
Boston, MA

Tuition & fees: $46,930	Average undergraduate aid package: $28,118

ABOUT THE INSTITUTION Independent, coed. 9 undergraduate majors. Federal methodology is used as a basis for awarding need-based institutional aid.

UNDERGRADUATE EXPENSES for 2017–2018 *Comprehensive fee:* $62,630 includes full-time tuition ($46,100), mandatory fees ($830), and room and board ($15,700). Room and board charges vary according to board plan. *Part-time tuition:* $1480 per credit. *Part-time fees:* $800 per year.

FRESHMAN FINANCIAL AID (Fall 2016) 73 applied for aid; of those 79% were deemed to have need. 100% of freshmen with need received aid; of those 31% had need fully met. *Average percent of need met:* 69% (excluding resources awarded to replace EFC). *Average financial aid package:* $28,909 (excluding resources awarded to replace EFC). 50% of all full-time freshmen had no need and received non-need-based gift aid.

UNDERGRADUATE FINANCIAL AID (Fall 2016) 213 applied for aid; of those 77% were deemed to have need. 100% of undergraduates with need received aid; of those 20% had need fully met. *Average percent of need met:* 63% (excluding resources awarded to replace EFC). *Average financial aid package:* $28,118 (excluding resources awarded to replace EFC). 51% of all full-time freshmen had no need and received non-need-based gift aid.

GIFT AID (NEED-BASED) *Total amount:* $3,871,845 (10% federal, 1% state, 77% institutional, 12% external sources). *Receiving aid:* Freshmen: 48% (58); all full-time undergraduates: 44% (165). *Average award:* Freshmen: $25,712; Undergraduates: $23,465. *Scholarships, grants, and awards:* Federal Pell, FSEOG, state, private, college/university gift aid from institutional funds.

GIFT AID (NON-NEED-BASED) *Total amount:* $3,921,156 (85% institutional, 15% external sources). *Receiving aid:* Freshmen: 14% (17). Undergraduates: 8% (30). *Average award:* Freshmen: $17,597. Undergraduates: $16,407. *Scholarships, grants, and awards by category:* Creative arts/performance: 370 awards ($6,408,148 total): music. *Tuition waivers:* Full or partial for employees or children of employees.

LOANS *Student loans:* $1,480,101 (74% need-based, 26% non-need-based). 49% of past graduating class borrowed through all loan programs. *Average indebtedness per student:* $33,003. *Average need-based loan:* Freshmen: $3929. Undergraduates: $5045. *Parent loans:* $461,330 (68% need-based, 32% non-need-based). *Programs:* Federal Direct (Subsidized and Unsubsidized Stafford, PLUS), state.

WORK-STUDY *Federal work-study:* 211 jobs averaging $1818.

APPLYING FOR FINANCIAL AID *Required financial aid forms:* FAFSA, institution's own form. *Financial aid deadline (priority):* 2/15. *Notification date:* 4/1. Students must reply by 5/1.

CONTACT Ms. Lauren Gayle Urbanek, Associate Dean for Financial Aid, New England Conservatory of Music, 290 Huntington Avenue, Boston, MA 02115, 617-585-1110. *Fax:* 617-585-1115. *E-mail:* finaid@necmusic.edu.
Website: http://necmusic.edu/.

NEW ENGLAND INSTITUTE OF TECHNOLOGY
East Greenwich, RI

CONTACT Financial Aid Office, New England Institute of Technology, One New England Tech Boulevard, East Greenwich, RI 02818, 401-467-7744 or toll-free 800-736-7744.
Website: http://www.neit.edu/.

NEW HAMPSHIRE INSTITUTE OF ART
Manchester, NH

CONTACT Linda Lavallee, Director of Financial Aid, New Hampshire Institute of Art, 148 Concord Street, Manchester, NH 03104-4858, 603-623-0313 Ext. 577 or toll-free 866-241-4918. *Fax:* 603-647-0658. *E-mail:* llavallee@nhia.edu.
Website: http://www.nhia.edu/.

NEW HOPE CHRISTIAN COLLEGE
Eugene, OR

CONTACT Nathan Icenhower, Financial Aid Administrator, New Hope Christian College, 2155 Bailey Hill Road, Eugene, OR 97405-1194, 541-485-1780 Ext. 3106 or toll-free 800-322-2638. *Fax:* 541-343-5801. *E-mail:* finaid@newhope.edu.
Website: http://www.newhope.edu/.

NEW JERSEY CITY UNIVERSITY
Jersey City, NJ

Tuition & fees (NJ res): $11,431	Average undergraduate aid package: $10,636

ABOUT THE INSTITUTION State-supported, coed. *Awards:* certificates, bachelor's, master's, and doctoral degrees. 31 undergraduate majors. *Total enrollment:* 8,284. Undergraduates: 6,509. Freshmen: 991. Federal methodology is used as a basis for awarding need-based institutional aid.
UNDERGRADUATE EXPENSES for 2017–2018 *Application fee:* $50. *Tuition, state resident:* full-time $8115; part-time $278.30 per credit hour. *Tuition, nonresident:* full-time $17,142; part-time $587.95 per credit hour. *Required fees:* full-time $3316; $111.15 per credit hour. Part-time tuition and fees vary according to course load. *College room and board:* $12,446. Room and board charges vary according to board plan and housing facility.
FRESHMAN FINANCIAL AID (Fall 2016) 930 applied for aid; of those 94% were deemed to have need. 97% of freshmen with need received aid; of those 2% had need fully met. *Average percent of need met:* 53% (excluding resources awarded to replace EFC). *Average financial aid package:* $12,419 (excluding resources awarded to replace EFC). 4% of all full-time freshmen had no need and received non-need-based gift aid.
UNDERGRADUATE FINANCIAL AID (Fall 2016) 4,701 applied for aid; of those 94% were deemed to have need. 97% of undergraduates with need received aid; of those 3% had need fully met. *Average percent of need met:* 47% (excluding resources awarded to replace EFC). *Average financial aid package:* $10,636 (excluding resources awarded to replace EFC). 2% of all full-time undergraduates had no need and received non-need-based gift aid.
GIFT AID (NEED-BASED) *Total amount:* $30,971,469 (56% federal, 44% state). *Receiving aid:* Freshmen: 77% (735); all full-time undergraduates: 69% (3,532). *Average award:* Freshmen: $9953; Undergraduates: $8436. *Scholarships, grants, and awards:* Federal Pell, FSEOG, state, college/university gift aid from institutional funds.
GIFT AID (NON-NEED-BASED) *Total amount:* $5,682,310 (3% state, 87% institutional, 10% external sources). *Receiving aid:* Freshmen: 37% (357). Undergraduates: 20% (1,015). *Average award:* Freshmen: $8474. Undergraduates: $7980. *Scholarships, grants, and awards by category:* Academic interests/

achievement: general academic interests/achievements. *Tuition waivers:* Full or partial for employees or children of employees, senior citizens. *ROTC:* Army cooperative, Naval cooperative.
LOANS *Student loans:* $26,422,449 (45% need-based, 55% non-need-based). 68% of past graduating class borrowed through all loan programs. *Average indebtedness per student:* $27,173. *Average need-based loan:* Freshmen: $3335. Undergraduates: $4046. *Parent loans:* $2,193,136 (100% non-need-based). *Programs:* Federal Direct (Subsidized and Unsubsidized Stafford, PLUS), Perkins, state.
WORK-STUDY *Federal work-study:* jobs available.
APPLYING FOR FINANCIAL AID *Required financial aid form:* FAFSA. *Financial aid deadline (priority):* 3/15. *Notification date:* 5/15.
CONTACT Mr. Robert Macauley, Director of Financial Aid, New Jersey City University, 2039 Kennedy Boulevard, Jersey City, NJ 07305-1597, 201-200-3171 or toll-free 888-441-NJCU.
Website: http://www.njcu.edu/.

NEW JERSEY INSTITUTE OF TECHNOLOGY
Newark, NJ

Tuition & fees (NJ res): $16,898	Average undergraduate aid package: $13,104

ABOUT THE INSTITUTION State-supported, coed. *Awards:* certificates, bachelor's, master's, and doctoral degrees. 41 undergraduate majors. *Total enrollment:* 11,446. Undergraduates: 8,483. Freshmen: 1,114. Federal methodology is used as a basis for awarding need-based institutional aid.
UNDERGRADUATE EXPENSES for 2017–2018 *Application fee:* $75. *Tuition, state resident:* full-time $13,906; part-time $529 per credit. *Tuition, nonresident:* full-time $28,926; part-time $1237 per credit. *Required fees:* full-time $2992; $176 per credit. Full-time tuition and fees vary according to course load and degree level. Part-time tuition and fees vary according to course load and degree level. *College room and board:* $13,300; *Room only:* $8680. Room and board charges vary according to board plan and housing facility.
FRESHMAN FINANCIAL AID (Fall 2016) 929 applied for aid; of those 80% were deemed to have need. 97% of freshmen with need received aid; of those 17% had need fully met. *Average percent of need met:* 51% (excluding resources awarded to replace EFC). *Average financial aid package:* $13,628 (excluding resources awarded to replace EFC). 19% of all full-time freshmen had no need and received non-need-based gift aid.
UNDERGRADUATE FINANCIAL AID (Fall 2016) 4,925 applied for aid; of those 89% were deemed to have need. 96% of undergraduates with need received aid; of those 9% had need fully met. *Average percent of need met:* 41% (excluding resources awarded to replace EFC). *Average financial aid package:* $13,104 (excluding resources awarded to replace EFC). 12% of all full-time undergraduates had no need and received non-need-based gift aid.
GIFT AID (NEED-BASED) *Total amount:* $43,831,437 (29% federal, 42% state, 28% institutional, 1% external sources). *Receiving aid:* Freshmen: 69% (721); all full-time undergraduates: 68% (4,207). *Average award:* Freshmen: $12,671; Undergraduates: $12,484. *Scholarships, grants, and awards:* Federal Pell, FSEOG, state, private, college/university gift aid from institutional funds, United Negro College Fund.
GIFT AID (NON-NEED-BASED) *Total amount:* $12,170,759 (99% institutional, 1% external sources). *Receiving aid:* Freshmen: 47% (498). Undergraduates: 27% (1,686). *Average award:* Freshmen: $14,272. Undergraduates: $16,181. *Scholarships, grants, and awards by category:* Academic interests/achievement: 692 awards ($9,353,191 total): architecture, area/ethnic studies, biological sciences, business, communication, computer science, education, engineering/technologies, general academic interests/achievements, humanities, international studies, mathematics, physical sciences, premedicine. *Creative arts/performance:* 69 awards ($622,342 total): applied art and design, art/fine arts, journalism/publications, performing arts, theater/drama. *Special achievements/activities:* community service, general special achievements/activities, hobbies/interests, leadership, religious involvement. *Special characteristics:* adult students, children of faculty/staff, children of union members/company employees, ethnic background, first-generation college students, general special characteristics, handicapped students, international students, local/state students, members of minority groups, out-of-state students, relatives of clergy, religious affiliation, siblings of current students, veterans, veterans' children.

Tuition waivers: Full or partial for employees or children of employees. *ROTC:* Army cooperative, Air Force.

LOANS *Student loans:* $37,091,031 (37% need-based, 63% non-need-based). 62% of past graduating class borrowed through all loan programs. *Average indebtedness per student:* $40,979. *Average need-based loan:* Freshmen: $3322. Undergraduates: $4392. *Parent loans:* $4,643,263 (100% non-need-based). *Programs:* Federal Direct (Subsidized and Unsubsidized Stafford, PLUS), state, alternative loans.

WORK-STUDY *Federal work-study:* 276 jobs averaging $1710. *State or other work-study/employment:* Total amount: $1,745,279 (100% non-need-based). 821 part-time jobs averaging $2126.

ATHLETIC AWARDS Total amount: $4,251,474 (36% need-based, 64% non-need-based).

APPLYING FOR FINANCIAL AID *Required financial aid forms:* FAFSA, institution's own form. *Financial aid deadline:* 2/15. *Notification date:* Continuous beginning 11/1. Students must reply by 5/1 or within 2 weeks of notification.

CONTACT Ivon Nunez, Director of Financial Aid Services, New Jersey Institute of Technology, Student Mall, University Heights, Newark, NJ 07102, 973-596-3476 or toll-free 800-925-NJIT. *Fax:* 973-596-6471. *E-mail:* ivon.nunez@njit.edu. *Website:* http://www.njit.edu/.

NEWMAN UNIVERSITY
Wichita, KS

Tuition & fees: $30,564	Average undergraduate aid package: $12,560

ABOUT THE INSTITUTION Independent Roman Catholic, coed. *Awards:* associate, bachelor's, and master's degrees. 42 undergraduate majors. *Total enrollment:* 1,766. Undergraduates: 1,198. Freshmen: 212. Federal methodology is used as a basis for awarding need-based institutional aid.

UNDERGRADUATE EXPENSES for 2018–2019 *Comprehensive fee:* $38,970 includes full-time tuition ($29,260), mandatory fees ($1304), and room and board ($8406). *College room only:* $4484. Room and board charges vary according to board plan and housing facility. *Part-time tuition:* $976 per credit hour. Part-time tuition and fees vary according to course load.

FRESHMAN FINANCIAL AID (Fall 2016) 155 applied for aid; of those 67% were deemed to have need. 100% of freshmen with need received aid; of those 29% had need fully met. *Average percent of need met:* 41% (excluding resources awarded to replace EFC). *Average financial aid package:* $14,494 (excluding resources awarded to replace EFC). 92% of all full-time freshmen had no need and received non-need-based gift aid.

UNDERGRADUATE FINANCIAL AID (Fall 2016) 781 applied for aid; of those 79% were deemed to have need. 100% of undergraduates with need received aid; of those 24% had need fully met. *Average percent of need met:* 37% (excluding resources awarded to replace EFC). *Average financial aid package:* $12,560 (excluding resources awarded to replace EFC). 88% of all full-time undergraduates had no need and received non-need-based gift aid.

GIFT AID (NEED-BASED) *Total amount:* $1,921,162 (45% federal, 25% state, 30% institutional). *Receiving aid:* Freshmen: 56% (100); all full-time undergraduates: 59% (566). *Average award:* Freshmen: $5064; Undergraduates: $3438. *Scholarships, grants, and awards:* Federal Pell, FSEOG, state, private, college/university gift aid from institutional funds.

GIFT AID (NON-NEED-BASED) *Total amount:* $5,600,878 (91% institutional, 9% external sources). *Receiving aid:* Freshmen: 57% (102). Undergraduates: 61% (586). *Average award:* Freshmen: $5997. Undergraduates: $5731. *Scholarships, grants, and awards by category:* Academic interests/achievement: general academic interests/achievements. *Creative arts/performance:* art/fine arts, journalism/publications, music, theater/drama. *Special achievements/activities:* community service, leadership, memberships, religious involvement. *Special characteristics:* children and siblings of alumni, children of current students, children of faculty/staff, international students, married students, siblings of current students, spouses of current students. *Tuition waivers:* Full or partial for employees or children of employees.

LOANS *Student loans:* $2,121,046 (47% need-based, 53% non-need-based). 60% of past graduating class borrowed through all loan programs. *Average indebtedness per student:* $25,963. *Average need-based loan:* Undergraduates: $2216. *Parent loans:* $311,858 (100% non-need-based). *Programs:* Federal Direct (Subsidized and Unsubsidized Stafford, PLUS), Perkins.

WORK-STUDY *Federal work-study:* jobs available. *State or other work-study/employment:* Total amount: $126,533 (100% need-based). Part-time jobs available.

ATHLETIC AWARDS Total amount: $1,539,985 (100% non-need-based).

APPLYING FOR FINANCIAL AID *Required financial aid form:* FAFSA. *Financial aid deadline (priority):* 12/1. *Notification date:* Continuous beginning 12/15.

CONTACT Myra Pfannenstiel, Director of Financial Aid, Newman University, 3100 McCormick Avenue, Wichita, KS 67213, 316-942-4291 Ext. 2132 or toll-free 877-NEWMANU. *Fax:* 316-942-4483. *E-mail:* pfannenstielm@newmanu.edu. *Website:* http://www.newmanu.edu/.

NEW MEXICO HIGHLANDS UNIVERSITY
Las Vegas, NM

Tuition & fees (NM res): $6454	Average undergraduate aid package: $9183

ABOUT THE INSTITUTION State-supported, coed. *Awards:* certificates, bachelor's, and master's degrees. 44 undergraduate majors. *Total enrollment:* 3,471. Undergraduates: 2,181. Freshmen: 316. Both federal and institutional methodology are used as a basis for awarding need-based institutional aid.

UNDERGRADUATE EXPENSES for 2017–2018 *One-time required fee:* $15. *Tuition, state resident:* full-time $4748; part-time $177 per credit hour. *Tuition, nonresident:* full-time $8117; part-time $316 per credit hour. *Required fees:* full-time $1706; $64.85 per term. Full-time tuition and fees vary according to course load and location. Part-time tuition and fees vary according to course load and location. *College room and board:* $7654; *Room only:* $3740. Room and board charges vary according to board plan and housing facility.

FRESHMAN FINANCIAL AID (Fall 2016) 289 applied for aid; of those 87% were deemed to have need. 100% of freshmen with need received aid; of those 6% had need fully met. *Average percent of need met:* 56% (excluding resources awarded to replace EFC). *Average financial aid package:* $8591 (excluding resources awarded to replace EFC). 9% of all full-time freshmen had no need and received non-need-based gift aid.

UNDERGRADUATE FINANCIAL AID (Fall 2016) 1,198 applied for aid; of those 91% were deemed to have need. 100% of undergraduates with need received aid; of those 3% had need fully met. *Average percent of need met:* 54% (excluding resources awarded to replace EFC). *Average financial aid package:* $9183 (excluding resources awarded to replace EFC). 7% of all full-time undergraduates had no need and received non-need-based gift aid.

GIFT AID (NEED-BASED) *Total amount:* $8,024,671 (69% federal, 18% state, 6% institutional, 7% external sources). *Receiving aid:* Freshmen: 79% (246); all full-time undergraduates: 72% (1,035). *Average award:* Freshmen: $7224; Undergraduates: $6914. *Scholarships, grants, and awards:* Federal Pell, FSEOG, state, private, college/university gift aid from institutional funds.

GIFT AID (NON-NEED-BASED) *Total amount:* $819,238 (15% federal, 39% state, 35% institutional, 11% external sources). *Receiving aid:* Freshmen: 9% (29). Undergraduates: 7% (96). *Average award:* Freshmen: $1903. Undergraduates: $2163. *Scholarships, grants, and awards by category:* Academic interests/achievement: biological sciences, business, communication, computer science, education, engineering/technologies, English, foreign languages, general academic interests/achievements, health fields, humanities, mathematics, physical sciences, social sciences. *Creative arts/performance:* art/fine arts, music, performing arts. *Tuition waivers:* Full or partial for employees or children of employees, senior citizens.

LOANS *Student loans:* $4,973,511 (50% need-based, 50% non-need-based). 54% of past graduating class borrowed through all loan programs. *Average indebtedness per student:* $19,391. *Average need-based loan:* Freshmen: $3030. Undergraduates: $4011. *Parent loans:* $76,086 (100% non-need-based). *Programs:* Federal Direct (Subsidized and Unsubsidized Stafford, PLUS), Perkins.

WORK-STUDY *Federal work-study:* jobs available. *State or other work-study/employment:* Total amount: $334,206 (82% need-based, 18% non-need-based). Part-time jobs available.

ATHLETIC AWARDS Total amount: $614,901 (61% need-based, 39% non-need-based).

APPLYING FOR FINANCIAL AID *Required financial aid form:* FAFSA. *Financial aid deadline (priority):* 3/1. *Notification date:* Continuous beginning 3/15. Students must reply within 4 weeks of notification.

CONTACT Eileen Sedillo, Director of Financial Aid, New Mexico Highlands University, PO Box 9000, Las Vegas, NM 87701, 505-454-3430 or toll-free 800-338-6648. *Fax:* 505-454-3398. *E-mail:* sedillo_e@nmhu.edu. *Website:* http://www.nmhu.edu/.

NEW MEXICO INSTITUTE OF MINING AND TECHNOLOGY
Socorro, NM

Tuition & fees (NM res): $7183	Average undergraduate aid package: $12,524

ABOUT THE INSTITUTION State-supported, coed. *Awards:* associate, bachelor's, master's, and doctoral degrees. 23 undergraduate majors. *Total enrollment:* 2,009. Undergraduates: 1,471. Freshmen: 240. Federal methodology is used as a basis for awarding need-based institutional aid.

UNDERGRADUATE EXPENSES for 2017–2018 *Application fee:* $15. *Tuition, state resident:* full-time $6133; part-time $255.54 per credit hour. *Tuition, nonresident:* full-time $19,941; part-time $830.87 per credit hour. *Required fees:* full-time $1050; $17 per credit hour or $309 per term. Full-time tuition and fees vary according to reciprocity agreements. Part-time tuition and fees vary according to course load. *College room and board:* $8202. Room and board charges vary according to board plan and housing facility.

FRESHMAN FINANCIAL AID (Fall 2017, est.) 235 applied for aid; of those 58% were deemed to have need. 98% of freshmen with need received aid; of those 20% had need fully met. *Average percent of need met:* 81% (excluding resources awarded to replace EFC). *Average financial aid package:* $11,791 (excluding resources awarded to replace EFC). 36% of all full-time freshmen had no need and received non-need-based gift aid.

UNDERGRADUATE FINANCIAL AID (Fall 2017, est.) 1,159 applied for aid; of those 60% were deemed to have need. 97% of undergraduates with need received aid; of those 21% had need fully met. *Average percent of need met:* 78% (excluding resources awarded to replace EFC). *Average financial aid package:* $12,524 (excluding resources awarded to replace EFC). 32% of all full-time undergraduates had no need and received non-need-based gift aid.

GIFT AID (NEED-BASED) *Total amount:* $2,815,988 (85% federal, 13% state, 2% external sources). *Receiving aid:* Freshmen: 27% (73); all full-time undergraduates: 33% (427). *Average award:* Freshmen: $5739; Undergraduates: $6059. *Scholarships, grants, and awards:* Federal Pell, FSEOG, state, private, college/university gift aid from institutional funds.

GIFT AID (NON-NEED-BASED) *Total amount:* $5,095,505 (39% state, 52% institutional, 9% external sources). *Receiving aid:* Freshmen: 48% (129). Undergraduates: 35% (456). *Average award:* Freshmen: $5601. Undergraduates: $5656. *Scholarships, grants, and awards by category:* Academic interests/achievement: general academic interests/achievements. *Tuition waivers:* Full or partial for employees or children of employees, senior citizens.

LOANS *Student loans:* $3,459,324 (46% need-based, 54% non-need-based). 42% of past graduating class borrowed through all loan programs. *Average indebtedness per student:* $26,817. *Average need-based loan:* Freshmen: $3512. Undergraduates: $4408. *Parent loans:* $177,542 (100% non-need-based). *Programs:* Federal Direct (Subsidized and Unsubsidized Stafford, PLUS), Perkins.

WORK-STUDY *Federal work-study:* Total amount: $530,504; jobs available. *State or other work-study/employment:* Total amount: $152,496 (48% need-based, 52% non-need-based). Part-time jobs available.

APPLYING FOR FINANCIAL AID *Required financial aid form:* FAFSA. *Financial aid deadline (priority):* 5/1. *Notification date:* Continuous beginning 5/1. Students must reply within 2 weeks of notification.

CONTACT Mr. Kenneth Aerts, Director of Financial Aid, New Mexico Institute of Mining and Technology, 801 Leroy Place, Socorro, NM 87801, 575-835-5333 or toll-free 800-428-TECH. *Fax:* 575-835-5959. *E-mail:* kenneth.aerts@nmt.edu. *Website:* http://www.nmt.edu/.

NEW MEXICO STATE UNIVERSITY
Las Cruces, NM

Tuition & fees (NM res): $6461	Average undergraduate aid package: $12,018

ABOUT THE INSTITUTION State-supported, coed. *Awards:* certificates, associate, bachelor's, master's, and doctoral degrees. 82 undergraduate majors. *Total enrollment:* 14,432. Undergraduates: 11,713. Freshmen: 2,042. Federal methodology is used as a basis for awarding need-based institutional aid.

UNDERGRADUATE EXPENSES for 2017–2018 *Application fee:* $20. *One-time required fee:* $165. *Tuition, state resident:* full-time $5323; part-time $221.80 per credit hour. *Tuition, nonresident:* full-time $19,884; part-time $828.50 per credit hour. *Required fees:* full-time $1138; $47.40 per credit hour. Full-time tuition and fees vary according to course load and reciprocity agreements. Part-time tuition and fees vary according to course load and reciprocity agreements. *College room and board:* $8686; *Room only:* $4886. Room and board charges vary according to board plan and housing facility.

FRESHMAN FINANCIAL AID (Fall 2016) 1,574 applied for aid; of those 82% were deemed to have need. 100% of freshmen with need received aid; of those 14% had need fully met. *Average percent of need met:* 69% (excluding resources awarded to replace EFC). *Average financial aid package:* $12,054 (excluding resources awarded to replace EFC). 21% of all full-time freshmen had no need and received non-need-based gift aid.

UNDERGRADUATE FINANCIAL AID (Fall 2016) 7,186 applied for aid; of those 87% were deemed to have need. 100% of undergraduates with need received aid; of those 9% had need fully met. *Average percent of need met:* 65% (excluding resources awarded to replace EFC). *Average financial aid package:* $12,018 (excluding resources awarded to replace EFC). 13% of all full-time undergraduates had no need and received non-need-based gift aid.

GIFT AID (NEED-BASED) *Total amount:* $41,233,851 (53% federal, 27% state, 15% institutional, 5% external sources). *Receiving aid:* Freshmen: 70% (1,271); all full-time undergraduates: 62% (6,079). *Average award:* Freshmen: $9924; Undergraduates: $9202. *Scholarships, grants, and awards:* Federal Pell, FSEOG, state, private, college/university gift aid from institutional funds.

GIFT AID (NON-NEED-BASED) *Total amount:* $11,653,065 (2% federal, 55% state, 35% institutional, 8% external sources). *Receiving aid:* Freshmen: 7% (121). Undergraduates: 4% (366). *Average award:* Freshmen: $3584. Undergraduates: $2578. *Scholarships, grants, and awards by category:* Academic interests/achievement: 597 awards ($576,905 total): agriculture, area/ethnic studies, biological sciences, business, communication, computer science, education, engineering/technologies, English, foreign languages, general academic interests/achievements, health fields, home economics, humanities, mathematics, military science, physical sciences, social sciences. *Creative arts/performance:* 46 awards ($37,462 total): applied art and design, art/fine arts, cinema/film/broadcasting, creative writing, dance, general creative arts/performance, journalism/publications, music, performing arts, theater/drama. *Special achievements/activities:* 21 awards ($17,578 total): cheerleading/drum major, general special achievements/activities, hobbies/interests, junior miss, leadership, memberships, rodeo. *Special characteristics:* 597 awards ($740,608 total): adult students, children and siblings of alumni, children of current students, children of faculty/staff, children of public servants, children of union members/company employees, children of workers in trades, children with a deceased or disabled parent, ethnic background, handicapped students, international students, local/state students, married students, members of minority groups, out-of-state students, previous college experience, public servants, spouses of current students, spouses of deceased or disabled public servants, veterans, veterans' children. *Tuition waivers:* Full or partial for employees or children of employees, senior citizens. *ROTC:* Army, Air Force.

LOANS *Student loans:* $30,731,225 (83% need-based, 17% non-need-based). 53% of past graduating class borrowed through all loan programs. *Average indebtedness per student:* $21,019. *Average need-based loan:* Freshmen: $2487. Undergraduates: $3507. *Parent loans:* $977,140 (52% need-based, 48% non-need-based). *Programs:* Federal Direct (Subsidized and Unsubsidized Stafford, PLUS), Perkins, state.

WORK-STUDY *Federal work-study:* 247 jobs averaging $2734. *State or other work-study/employment:* Total amount: $1,973,227 (78% need-based, 22% non-need-based). 338 part-time jobs averaging $5916.

ATHLETIC AWARDS Total amount: $4,248,842 (28% need-based, 72% non-need-based).

APPLYING FOR FINANCIAL AID *Required financial aid form:* FAFSA. *Financial aid deadline:* 6/30 (priority: 1/1). *Notification date:* Continuous beginning 1/1.

CONTACT Dr. Vandeen McKenzie, Director of Financial Aid, New Mexico State University, Box 30001, MSC 5100, Las Cruces, NM 88003-8001, 575-646-4105 or toll-free 800-662-6678. *Fax:* 575-646-7381. *E-mail:* financialaid@nmsu.edu. *Website:* http://www.nmsu.edu/.

NEW ORLEANS BAPTIST THEOLOGICAL SEMINARY
New Orleans, LA

CONTACT Owen Nease, Financial Aid Office, New Orleans Baptist Theological Seminary, 3939 Gentilly Boulevard, New Orleans, LA 70126-4858, 504-282-4455 Ext. 3348 or toll-free 800-662-8701. *Fax:* 504-816-8437. *E-mail:* financialaid@nobts.edu. *Website:* http://www.nobts.edu/.

NEW SAINT ANDREWS COLLEGE
Moscow, ID

CONTACT Brenda Schlect, College Bursars Office, New Saint Andrews College, 405 South Main Street, PO Box 9025, Moscow, ID 83843, 208-882-1566 Ext. 113. *Fax:* 208-882-4297. *E-mail:* bschlect@nsa.edu. *Website:* http://www.nsa.edu/.

THE NEW SCHOOL COLLEGE OF PERFORMING ARTS
New York, NY

Tuition & fees: $46,340	Average undergraduate aid package: $18,407

ABOUT THE INSTITUTION Independent, coed. *Awards:* diplomas, bachelor's, and master's degrees. 8 undergraduate majors. *Total enrollment:* 895. Undergraduates: 594. Freshmen: 167. Federal methodology is used as a basis for awarding need-based institutional aid.

UNDERGRADUATE EXPENSES for 2017–2018 Application fee: $50. *Comprehensive fee:* $62,590 includes full-time tuition ($45,240), mandatory fees ($1100), and room and board ($16,250). *College room only:* $15,000. Room and board charges vary according to housing facility and location. *Part-time tuition:* $1540 per credit hour. *Part-time fees:* $550 per term. Part-time tuition and fees vary according to course load.

FRESHMAN FINANCIAL AID (Fall 2016) 86 applied for aid; of those 86% were deemed to have need. 100% of freshmen with need received aid; of those 4% had need fully met. *Average percent of need met:* 74% (excluding resources awarded to replace EFC). *Average financial aid package:* $16,338 (excluding resources awarded to replace EFC). 28% of all full-time freshmen had no need and received non-need-based gift aid.

UNDERGRADUATE FINANCIAL AID (Fall 2016) 246 applied for aid; of those 88% were deemed to have need. 100% of undergraduates with need received aid; of those 13% had need fully met. *Average percent of need met:* 78% (excluding resources awarded to replace EFC). *Average financial aid package:* $18,407 (excluding resources awarded to replace EFC). 32% of all full-time undergraduates had no need and received non-need-based gift aid.

GIFT AID (NEED-BASED) *Total amount:* $2,111,464 (34% federal, 4% state, 48% institutional, 14% external sources). *Receiving aid:* Freshmen: 17% (24); all full-time undergraduates: 23% (127). *Average award:* Freshmen: $6879; Undergraduates: $7141. *Scholarships, grants, and awards:* Federal Pell, FSEOG, state, private, college/university gift aid from institutional funds.

GIFT AID (NON-NEED-BASED) *Total amount:* $7,814,686 (95% institutional, 5% external sources). *Receiving aid:* Freshmen: 38% (54). Undergraduates: 31% (172). *Average award:* Freshmen: $15,125. Undergraduates: $17,173. *Tuition waivers:* Full or partial for employees or children of employees.

LOANS *Student loans:* $4,621,578 (30% need-based, 70% non-need-based). 43% of past graduating class borrowed through all loan programs. *Average indebtedness per student:* $77,353. *Average need-based loan:* Freshmen: $3250. Undergrad-

uates: $4149. *Parent loans:* $955,525 (6% need based, 94% non need based). *Programs:* Federal Direct (Subsidized and Unsubsidized Stafford, PLUS).

WORK-STUDY *Federal work-study:* 36 jobs averaging $3194. *State or other work-study/employment:* Part-time jobs available.

APPLYING FOR FINANCIAL AID *Required financial aid form:* FAFSA. *Financial aid deadline:* 2/1. *Notification date:* Continuous beginning 4/1. Students must reply within 4 weeks of notification.

CONTACT Office of Student Financial Services, The New School College of Performing Arts, 72 Fifth Avenue, 2nd Floor, New York, NY 10011, 212-229-8930 or toll-free 800-292-3040. *E-mail:* sfs@newschool.edu. *Website:* http://www.newschool.edu/performing-arts/.

THE NEW SCHOOL FOR PUBLIC ENGAGEMENT
New York, NY

Tuition & fees: $30,860	Average undergraduate aid package: $18,122

ABOUT THE INSTITUTION Independent, coed. *Awards:* certificates, bachelor's, master's, and doctoral degrees. 9 undergraduate majors. *Total enrollment:* 1,448. Undergraduates: 471. Freshmen: 13. Federal methodology is used as a basis for awarding need-based institutional aid.

UNDERGRADUATE EXPENSES for 2017–2018 Application fee: $50. *Comprehensive fee:* $47,110 includes full-time tuition ($29,760), mandatory fees ($1100), and room and board ($16,250). *College room only:* $15,000. Room and board charges vary according to housing facility and location. *Part-time tuition:* $1240 per credit hour. *Part-time fees:* $550 per term. Part-time tuition and fees vary according to course load.

FRESHMAN FINANCIAL AID (Fall 2016) 4 applied for aid; of those 75% were deemed to have need. 100% of freshmen with need received aid. *Average percent of need met:* 67% (excluding resources awarded to replace EFC). *Average financial aid package:* $19,538 (excluding resources awarded to replace EFC). 29% of all full-time freshmen had no need and received non-need-based gift aid.

UNDERGRADUATE FINANCIAL AID (Fall 2016) 145 applied for aid; of those 89% were deemed to have need. 100% of undergraduates with need received aid; of those 7% had need fully met. *Average percent of need met:* 65% (excluding resources awarded to replace EFC). *Average financial aid package:* $18,122 (excluding resources awarded to replace EFC). 24% of all full-time undergraduates had no need and received non-need-based gift aid.

GIFT AID (NEED-BASED) *Total amount:* $2,944,969 (19% federal, 2% state, 66% institutional, 13% external sources). *Receiving aid:* Freshmen: 43% (3); all full-time undergraduates: 52% (127). *Average award:* Freshmen: $11,955; Undergraduates: $11,648. *Scholarships, grants, and awards:* Federal Pell, FSEOG, state, private, college/university gift aid from institutional funds.

GIFT AID (NON-NEED-BASED) *Total amount:* $874,464 (97% institutional, 3% external sources). *Receiving aid:* Freshmen: 43% (3). Undergraduates: 40% (99). *Average award:* Freshmen: $1500. Undergraduates: $2950. *Scholarships, grants, and awards by category:* Academic interests/achievement: general academic interests/achievements. *Tuition waivers:* Full or partial for employees or children of employees.

LOANS *Student loans:* $2,507,003 (76% need-based, 24% non-need-based). *Average need-based loan:* Freshmen: $4833. Undergraduates: $4379. *Parent loans:* $477,420 (100% non-need-based). *Programs:* Federal Direct (Subsidized and Unsubsidized Stafford, PLUS).

WORK-STUDY *Federal work-study:* 6 jobs averaging $3333.

APPLYING FOR FINANCIAL AID *Required financial aid form:* FAFSA. *Financial aid deadline:* 2/1. *Notification date:* Continuous beginning 4/1. Students must reply within 4 weeks of notification.

CONTACT Office of Financial Aid, The New School for Public Engagement, 72 Fifth Avenue, New York, NY 10003, 212-229-8930 or toll-free 800-292-3040. *E-mail:* sfs@newschool.edu. *Website:* http://www.newschool.edu/public-engagement/.

NEWSCHOOL OF ARCHITECTURE AND DESIGN
San Diego, CA

ABOUT THE INSTITUTION Proprietary, coed, primarily men. 9 undergraduate majors.

GIFT AID (NEED-BASED) *Scholarships, grants, and awards:* Federal Pell, FSEOG, state, private, college/university gift aid from institutional funds.

GIFT AID (NON-NEED-BASED) *Scholarships, grants, and awards by category: Academic interests/achievement:* architecture, general academic interests/achievements. *Creative arts/performance:* general creative arts/performance. *Special characteristics:* children of faculty/staff, international students, veterans.

LOANS *Programs:* Federal Direct (Subsidized and Unsubsidized Stafford, PLUS), alternative loans.

APPLYING FOR FINANCIAL AID *Required financial aid forms:* FAFSA, institution's own form.

CONTACT Bryan Charbonneau, Director of Financial Aid, NewSchool of Architecture and Design, 1249 F Street, San Diego, CA 92101-6634, 619-684-8774 or toll-free 800-490-7081. *Fax:* 619-684-8880. *E-mail:* bcharbonneau@newschoolarch.edu.
Website: http://www.newschoolarch.edu/.

NEW WORLD SCHOOL OF THE ARTS
Miami, FL

CONTACT Financial Aid Office, New World School of the Arts, 300 NE 2nd Avenue, Miami, FL 33132, 305-237-3135.
Website: http://www.mdc.edu/nwsa/.

NEW YORK CITY COLLEGE OF TECHNOLOGY OF THE CITY UNIVERSITY OF NEW YORK
Brooklyn, NY

CONTACT Sandra Higgins, Director of Financial Aid, New York City College of Technology of the City University of New York, 300 Jay Street, Namm Hall, Room G-13, Brooklyn, NY 11201, 718-260-5700. *Fax:* 718-254-8525. *E-mail:* financialaid@citytech.cuny.edu.
Website: http://www.citytech.cuny.edu/.

NEW YORK COLLEGE OF HEALTH PROFESSIONS
Syosset, NY

CONTACT Financial Aid Office, New York College of Health Professions, 6801 Jericho Turnpike, Syosset, NY 11791-4413, 516-364-0808 or toll-free 800-922-7337 Ext. 351.
Website: http://www.nycollege.edu/.

NEW YORK FILM ACADEMY
Burbank, CA

CONTACT Financial Aid Office, New York Film Academy, 3300 Riverside Drive, Burbank, CA 91505, 818-333-3558.
Website: http://www.nyfa.edu/.

NEW YORK INSTITUTE OF TECHNOLOGY
Old Westbury, NY

Tuition & fees: $36,890	Average undergraduate aid package: $26,036

ABOUT THE INSTITUTION Independent, coed. *Awards:* certificates, diplomas, associate, bachelor's, master's, and doctoral degrees. 40 undergraduate majors. *Total enrollment:* 7,422. Undergraduates: 3,688. Freshmen: 894. Federal methodology is used as a basis for awarding need-based institutional aid.

UNDERGRADUATE EXPENSES for 2018–2019 *Application fee:* $50. *Comprehensive fee:* $51,180 includes full-time tuition ($35,585), mandatory fees ($1305), and room and board ($14,290). *College room only:* $9320. Full-time tuition and fees vary according to program. Room and board charges vary according to housing facility and location. *Part-time tuition:* $1205 per credit. *Part-time fees:* $540 per term. Part-time tuition and fees vary according to course load and program.

FRESHMAN FINANCIAL AID (Fall 2017, est.) 779 applied for aid; of those 91% were deemed to have need. 100% of freshmen with need received aid. *Average financial aid package:* $29,280 (excluding resources awarded to replace EFC). 16% of all full-time freshmen had no need and received non-need-based gift aid.

UNDERGRADUATE FINANCIAL AID (Fall 2017, est.) 2,608 applied for aid; of those 92% were deemed to have need. 100% of undergraduates with need received aid. *Average financial aid package:* $26,036 (excluding resources awarded to replace EFC). 14% of all full-time undergraduates had no need and received non-need-based gift aid.

GIFT AID (NEED-BASED) *Total amount:* $20,490,811 (38% federal, 20% state, 42% institutional). *Receiving aid:* Freshmen: 66% (562); all full-time undergraduates: 63% (2,025). *Average award:* Freshmen: $10,423; Undergraduates: $9511. *Scholarships, grants, and awards:* Federal Pell, FSEOG, state, private, college/university gift aid from institutional funds.

GIFT AID (NON-NEED-BASED) *Total amount:* $41,164,458 (3% federal, 1% state, 94% institutional, 2% external sources). *Receiving aid:* Freshmen: 81% (690). Undergraduates: 65% (2,102). *Average award:* Freshmen: $19,274. Undergraduates: $15,279. *Scholarships, grants, and awards by category: Academic interests/achievement:* general academic interests/achievements. *Special characteristics:* children of faculty/staff, previous college experience, veterans. *Tuition waivers:* Full or partial for employees or children of employees, senior citizens. *ROTC:* Army cooperative, Air Force cooperative.

LOANS *Student loans:* $17,340,689 (40% need-based, 60% non-need-based). *Average need-based loan:* Freshmen: $3440. Undergraduates: $4304. *Parent loans:* $13,753,346 (100% non-need-based). *Programs:* Federal Direct (Subsidized and Unsubsidized Stafford, PLUS), Perkins, alternative loans.

WORK-STUDY *Federal work-study:* Total amount: $1,354,396; jobs available. *State or other work-study/employment:* Total amount: $710,289 (100% non-need-based). Part-time jobs available.

ATHLETIC AWARDS Total amount: $3,221,963 (100% non-need-based).

APPLYING FOR FINANCIAL AID *Required financial aid form:* FAFSA. *Financial aid deadline (priority):* 2/14. *Notification date:* Continuous. Students must reply within 4 weeks of notification.

CONTACT Ms. Doreen Meyer, Director of Financial Aid, New York Institute of Technology, PO Box 8000, Old Westbury, NY 11568-8000, 516-686-1083 or toll-free 800-345-NYIT. *Fax:* 516-686-7997. *E-mail:* dmeyer@nyit.edu.
Website: http://www.nyit.edu/.

NEW YORK SCHOOL OF INTERIOR DESIGN
New York, NY

Tuition & fees: N/R	Average undergraduate aid package: $13,278

ABOUT THE INSTITUTION Independent, coed, primarily women. 1 undergraduate major. Federal methodology is used as a basis for awarding need-based institutional aid.

FRESHMAN FINANCIAL AID (Fall 2017, est.) 4 applied for aid; of those 100% were deemed to have need. 100% of freshmen with need received aid. *Average percent of need met:* 26% (excluding resources awarded to replace EFC). *Average financial aid package:* $11,321 (excluding resources awarded to replace EFC). 33% of all full-time freshmen had no need and received non-need-based gift aid.

UNDERGRADUATE FINANCIAL AID (Fall 2017, est.) 48 applied for aid; of those 94% were deemed to have need. 100% of undergraduates with need received aid. *Average percent of need met:* 32% (excluding resources awarded to replace EFC). *Average financial aid package:* $13,278 (excluding resources awarded to replace EFC). 19% of all full-time undergraduates had no need and received non-need-based gift aid.

GIFT AID (NEED-BASED) Total amount: $632,961 (38% federal, 7% state, 53% institutional, 2% external sources). *Receiving aid:* Freshmen: 67% (4); all full-time undergraduates: 59% (35). *Average award:* Freshmen: $8696; Undergraduates: $11,747. *Scholarships, grants, and awards:* Federal Pell, FSEOG, state, private, college/university gift aid from institutional funds.

GIFT AID (NON-NEED-BASED) Total amount: $103,644 (99% institutional, 1% external sources). *Average award:* Freshmen: $11,000. Undergraduates: $7936.

LOANS Student loans: $1,100,488 (86% need-based, 14% non-need-based). 46% of past graduating class borrowed through all loan programs. *Average indebtedness per student:* $65,401. *Average need-based loan:* Freshmen: $3500. Undergraduates: $4368. *Parent loans:* $564,200 (59% need-based, 41% non-need-based). *Programs:* Federal Direct (Subsidized and Unsubsidized Stafford, PLUS).

WORK-STUDY Federal work-study: Total amount: $22,000; 13 jobs averaging $2926.

APPLYING FOR FINANCIAL AID Required financial aid forms: FAFSA, state aid form. *Financial aid deadline (priority):* 8/1. *Notification date:* Continuous beginning 4/15. Students must reply within 2 weeks of notification.

CONTACT Mrs. Rashmi H. Wadhvani, Financial Aid Consultant, New York School of Interior Design, 170 East 70th Street, New York, NY 10021-5110, 212-472-1500 Ext. 204 or toll-free 800-336-9743 Ext. 205. *Fax:* 212-472-1867. *E-mail:* rwadhvani@nysid.edu.

Website: http://www.nysid.edu/.

NEW YORK UNIVERSITY
New York, NY

ABOUT THE INSTITUTION Independent, coed. *Awards:* certificates, associate, bachelor's, master's, and doctoral degrees. 116 undergraduate majors. *Total enrollment:* 51,123. Undergraduates: 26,417. Freshmen: 6,022.

GIFT AID (NEED-BASED) Scholarships, grants, and awards: Federal Pell, FSEOG, state, private, college/university gift aid from institutional funds, Federal Nursing.

GIFT AID (NON-NEED-BASED) Scholarships, grants, and awards by category: *Academic interests/achievement:* general academic interests/achievements. *Creative arts/performance:* general creative arts/performance.

LOANS Programs: Federal Direct (Subsidized and Unsubsidized Stafford, PLUS), Perkins, Federal Nursing, college/university.

APPLYING FOR FINANCIAL AID Required financial aid forms: FAFSA, CSS Financial Aid PROFILE, state aid form, noncustodial (divorced/separated) parent's statement.

CONTACT Office of Financial Aid, New York University, 25 West Fourth Street, New York, NY 10012-1199, 212-998-4444. *Fax:* 212-995-4661. *E-mail:* financial.aid@nyu.edu.

Website: http://www.nyu.edu/.

NIAGARA UNIVERSITY
Niagara Falls, NY

Tuition & fees: $33,500	Average undergraduate aid package: $26,503

ABOUT THE INSTITUTION Independent Roman Catholic Church, coed. *Awards:* certificates, associate, bachelor's, master's, and doctoral degrees. 54 undergraduate majors. *Total enrollment:* 3,949. Undergraduates: 2,994. Freshmen: 590. Federal methodology is used as a basis for awarding need-based institutional aid.

UNDERGRADUATE EXPENSES for 2018–2019 Comprehensive fee: $46,700 includes full-time tuition ($31,700), mandatory fees ($1800), and room and board ($13,200). Full-time tuition and fees vary according to program. Room and board charges vary according to housing facility. Part-time tuition and fees vary according to program.

FRESHMAN FINANCIAL AID (Fall 2017, est.) 534 applied for aid; of those 88% were deemed to have need. 100% of freshmen with need received aid; of those 56% had need fully met. *Average percent of need met:* 85% (excluding resources awarded to replace EFC). *Average financial aid package:* $28,761 (excluding resources awarded to replace EFC). 18% of all full-time freshmen had no need and received non-need-based gift aid.

UNDERGRADUATE FINANCIAL AID (Fall 2017, est.) 2,173 applied for aid; of those 91% were deemed to have need. 100% of undergraduates with need received aid; of those 51% had need fully met. *Average percent of need met:* 82% (excluding resources awarded to replace EFC). *Average financial aid package:* $26,503 (excluding resources awarded to replace EFC). 17% of all full-time undergraduates had no need and received non-need-based gift aid.

GIFT AID (NEED-BASED) Total amount: $44,544,961 (13% federal, 7% state, 79% institutional, 1% external sources). *Receiving aid:* Freshmen: 80% (462); all full-time undergraduates: 70% (1,951). *Average award:* Freshmen: $24,682; Undergraduates: $22,246. *Scholarships, grants, and awards:* Federal Pell, FSEOG, state, private, college/university gift aid from institutional funds.

GIFT AID (NON-NEED-BASED) Total amount: $7,967,322 (7% federal, 92% institutional, 1% external sources). *Receiving aid:* Freshmen: 66% (383). Undergraduates: 56% (1,569). *Average award:* Freshmen: $17,096. Undergraduates: $15,547. *Scholarships, grants, and awards by category:* *Academic interests/achievement:* 2,367 awards ($32,173,268 total): general academic interests/achievements. *Creative arts/performance:* 65 awards ($294,808 total): theater/drama. *Special achievements/activities:* 18 awards ($90,000 total): community service. *Special characteristics:* 89 awards ($2,413,255 total): children of faculty/staff, relatives of clergy. *Tuition waivers:* Full or partial for employees or children of employees. *ROTC:* Army.

LOANS Student loans: $18,020,103 (94% need-based, 6% non-need-based). 81% of past graduating class borrowed through all loan programs. *Average indebtedness per student:* $34,214. *Average need-based loan:* Freshmen: $4250. Undergraduates: $4941. *Parent loans:* $4,841,453 (92% need-based, 8% non-need-based). *Programs:* Federal Direct (Subsidized and Unsubsidized Stafford, PLUS), Perkins, Federal Nursing.

WORK-STUDY Federal work-study: Total amount: $1,296,449; 377 jobs averaging $3655. *State or other work-study/employment:* Total amount: $240,418 (100% non-need-based). 39 part-time jobs averaging $6308.

ATHLETIC AWARDS Total amount: $4,552,491 (44% need-based, 56% non-need-based).

APPLYING FOR FINANCIAL AID Required financial aid forms: FAFSA, state aid form. *Financial aid deadline (priority):* 2/15. *Notification date:* Continuous beginning 2/1. Students must reply by 5/1.

CONTACT Ms. Katie L. Kocsis, Director of Financial Aid, Niagara University, PO Box 2010, Niagara University, NY 14109, 716-286-8686 or toll-free 800-462-2111. *Fax:* 716-286-8678. *E-mail:* kkocsis@niagara.edu.

Website: http://www.niagara.edu/.

NICHOLLS STATE UNIVERSITY
Thibodaux, LA

Tuition & fees (LA res): $7886	Average undergraduate aid package: $9900

ABOUT THE INSTITUTION State-supported, coed. 37 undergraduate majors. Federal methodology is used as a basis for awarding need-based institutional aid.

UNDERGRADUATE EXPENSES for 2017–2018 Tuition, state resident: full-time $4922. *Tuition, nonresident:* full-time $6015. *Required fees:* full-time $2964. Full-time tuition and fees vary according to location and program. Part-time tuition and fees vary according to course load, location, and program. *College room and board:* $9790. Room and board charges vary according to board plan, housing facility, and location.

FRESHMAN FINANCIAL AID (Fall 2016) 1,023 applied for aid; of those 73% were deemed to have need. 99% of freshmen with need received aid; of those 13% had need fully met. *Average percent of need met:* 64% (excluding resources awarded to replace EFC). *Average financial aid package:* $10,845 (excluding resources

awarded to replace EFC). 10% of all full-time freshmen had no need and received non-need-based gift aid.

UNDERGRADUATE FINANCIAL AID (Fall 2016) 4,096 applied for aid; of those 72% were deemed to have need. 99% of undergraduates with need received aid; of those 12% had need fully met. *Average percent of need met:* 59% (excluding resources awarded to replace EFC). *Average financial aid package:* $9900 (excluding resources awarded to replace EFC). 8% of all full-time undergraduates had no need and received non-need-based gift aid.

GIFT AID (NEED-BASED) *Total amount:* $17,890,563 (54% federal, 29% state, 10% institutional, 7% external sources). *Receiving aid:* Freshmen: 65% (703); all full-time undergraduates: 58% (2,653). *Average award:* Freshmen: $7750; Undergraduates: $6506. *Scholarships, grants, and awards:* Federal Pell, FSEOG, state, private, college/university gift aid from institutional funds.

GIFT AID (NON-NEED-BASED) *Total amount:* $5,982,135 (6% federal, 57% state, 26% institutional, 11% external sources). *Receiving aid:* Freshmen: 7% (73). Undergraduates: 6% (262). *Average award:* Freshmen: $2601. Undergraduates: $3990. *Scholarships, grants, and awards by category: Academic interests/achievement:* 669 awards ($1,762,337 total): general academic interests/achievements. *Creative arts/performance:* 162 awards ($162,430 total): dance, music. *Special achievements/activities:* 62 awards ($36,350 total): cheerleading/drum major, leadership. *Special characteristics:* 761 awards ($2,794,974 total): children of faculty/staff, general special characteristics, local/state students, members of minority groups, out-of-state students, previous college experience, public servants, veterans. *Tuition waivers:* Full or partial for employees or children of employees, senior citizens.

LOANS *Student loans:* $15,803,100 (67% need-based, 33% non-need-based). *Average need-based loan:* Freshmen: $2665. Undergraduates: $3481. *Parent loans:* $3,304,874 (62% need-based, 38% non-need-based). *Programs:* Federal Direct (Subsidized and Unsubsidized Stafford, PLUS).

WORK-STUDY *Federal work-study:* 90 jobs averaging $1692. *State or other work-study/employment:* Total amount: $360,847 (77% need-based, 23% non-need-based). 57 part-time jobs averaging $3244.

ATHLETIC AWARDS Total amount: $2,293,739 (57% need-based, 43% non-need-based).

APPLYING FOR FINANCIAL AID *Required financial aid forms:* FAFSA, institution's own form, state aid form, noncustodial (divorced/separated) parent's statement. *Financial aid deadline:* 6/30 (priority: 4/15). *Notification date:* Continuous.

CONTACT Casie Triche, Director of Financial Aid, Nicholls State University, PO Box 2005, Thibodaux, LA 70310, 985-448-4077 or toll-free 877-NICHOLLS. *Fax:* 985-448-4124. *E-mail:* finaid@nicholls.edu.
Website: http://www.nicholls.edu/.

NICHOLS COLLEGE
Dudley, MA

Tuition & fees: $34,000	Average undergraduate aid package: $30,653

ABOUT THE INSTITUTION Independent, coed. *Awards:* bachelor's and master's degrees. 20 undergraduate majors. *Total enrollment:* 1,533. Undergraduates: 1,301. Freshmen: 373. Federal methodology is used as a basis for awarding need-based institutional aid.

UNDERGRADUATE EXPENSES for 2018–2019 *Comprehensive fee:* $47,800 includes full-time tuition ($33,600), mandatory fees ($400), and room and board ($13,800). Room and board charges vary according to housing facility. *Part-time tuition:* $1120 per credit. *Part-time fees:* $200 per term. Part-time tuition and fees vary according to class time, course load, and location.

FRESHMAN FINANCIAL AID (Fall 2017, est.) 370 applied for aid; of those 85% were deemed to have need. 100% of freshmen with need received aid; of those 24% had need fully met. *Average percent of need met:* 92% (excluding resources awarded to replace EFC). *Average financial aid package:* $32,635 (excluding resources awarded to replace EFC). 15% of all full-time freshmen had no need and received non-need-based gift aid.

UNDERGRADUATE FINANCIAL AID (Fall 2017, est.) 1,044 applied for aid; of those 87% were deemed to have need. 100% of undergraduates with need received aid; of those 26% had need fully met. *Average percent of need met:* 81% (excluding resources awarded to replace EFC). *Average financial aid package:*

$30,653 (excluding resources awarded to replace EFC). 25% of all full-time undergraduates had no need and received non-need-based gift aid.

GIFT AID (NEED-BASED) *Total amount:* $20,688,008 (10% federal, 2% state, 87% institutional, 1% external sources). *Receiving aid:* Freshmen: 85% (316); all full-time undergraduates: 75% (909). *Average award:* Freshmen: $23,082; Undergraduates: $19,407. *Scholarships, grants, and awards:* Federal Pell, FSEOG, state, private, college/university gift aid from institutional funds.

GIFT AID (NON-NEED-BASED) *Total amount:* $2,474,000 (100% institutional). *Receiving aid:* Freshmen: 5% (17). Undergraduates: 13% (162). *Average award:* Freshmen: $19,615. Undergraduates: $17,915. *Scholarships, grants, and awards by category: Academic interests/achievement:* general academic interests/achievements. *Special achievements/activities:* community service, general special achievements/activities, leadership. *Special characteristics:* children and siblings of alumni, children of faculty/staff, siblings of current students. *Tuition waivers:* Full or partial for employees or children of employees.

LOANS *Student loans:* $9,405,154 (89% need-based, 11% non-need-based). 84% of past graduating class borrowed through all loan programs. *Average indebtedness per student:* $34,873. *Average need-based loan:* Freshmen: $3194. Undergraduates: $4346. *Parent loans:* $4,961,982 (88% need-based, 12% non-need-based). *Programs:* Federal Direct (Subsidized Stafford, PLUS), state.

WORK-STUDY *Federal work-study:* Total amount: $401,531; jobs available.

APPLYING FOR FINANCIAL AID *Required financial aid form:* FAFSA. *Financial aid deadline (priority):* 3/1. *Notification date:* Continuous beginning 12/1. Students must reply within 2 weeks of notification.

CONTACT Mrs. Jennifer Bianco, Director of Financial Assistance, Nichols College, PO Box 5000, Dudley, MA 01571, 508-213-2340 or toll-free 800-470-3379. *Fax:* 508-213-2118. *E-mail:* jennifer.bianco@nichols.edu.
Website: http://www.nichols.edu/.

NORFOLK STATE UNIVERSITY
Norfolk, VA

CONTACT Mr. Kevin Burns, Director of Financial Aid, Norfolk State University, 700 Park Avenue, Norfolk, VA 23504-3907, 757-823-8381 or toll-free 800-274-1821. *Fax:* 757-823-9059. *E-mail:* kburns@nsu.edu.
Website: http://www.nsu.edu/.

NORTH AMERICAN UNIVERSITY
Stafford, TX

CONTACT Financial Aid Office, North American University, 11929 West Airport Boulevard, Stafford, TX 77477, 832-230-5555.
Website: http://www.na.edu/.

NORTH CAROLINA AGRICULTURAL AND TECHNICAL STATE UNIVERSITY
Greensboro, NC

Tuition & fees (NC res): $6526	Average undergraduate aid package: $11,092

ABOUT THE INSTITUTION State-supported, coed. 92 undergraduate majors. Both federal and institutional methodology are used as a basis for awarding need-based institutional aid.

UNDERGRADUATE EXPENSES for 2017–2018 *Tuition, state resident:* full-time $3540. *Tuition, nonresident:* full-time $16,430. *Required fees:* full-time $2986. Full-time tuition and fees vary according to course load, degree level, and program. Part-time tuition and fees vary according to course load, degree level, and program. *College room and board:* $7260; *Room only:* $3400. Room and board charges vary according to board plan and housing facility.

FRESHMAN FINANCIAL AID (Fall 2016) 1,875 applied for aid; of those 91% were deemed to have need. 99% of freshmen with need received aid; of those 9% had need fully met. *Average percent of need met:* 61% (excluding resources awarded

to replace EFC) *Average financial aid package:* $11,444 (excluding resources awarded to replace EFC). 2% of all full-time freshmen had no need and received non-need-based gift aid.

UNDERGRADUATE FINANCIAL AID (Fall 2016) 8,221 applied for aid; of those 91% were deemed to have need. 99% of undergraduates with need received aid; of those 7% had need fully met. *Average percent of need met:* 59% (excluding resources awarded to replace EFC). *Average financial aid package:* $11,092 (excluding resources awarded to replace EFC). 2% of all full-time undergraduates had no need and received non-need-based gift aid.

GIFT AID (NEED-BASED) *Total amount:* $63,434,134 (42% federal, 34% state, 14% institutional, 10% external sources). *Receiving aid:* Freshmen: 78% (1,487); all full-time undergraduates: 72% (6,193). *Average award:* Freshmen: $7693; Undergraduates: $8240. *Scholarships, grants, and awards:* Federal Pell, FSEOG, state, private, college/university gift aid from institutional funds.

GIFT AID (NON-NEED-BASED) *Total amount:* $872,206 (1% federal, 13% state, 44% institutional, 42% external sources). *Receiving aid:* Freshmen: 34% (642). Undergraduates: 26% (2,255). *Average award:* Freshmen: $4763. Undergraduates: $5372. *Scholarships, grants, and awards by category: Academic interests/ achievement:* agriculture, business, engineering/technologies, general academic interests/achievements. *Creative arts/performance:* music.

LOANS *Student loans:* $78,694,219 (96% need-based, 4% non-need-based). 90% of past graduating class borrowed through all loan programs. *Average indebtedness per student:* $34,379. *Average need-based loan:* Freshmen: $3319. Undergraduates: $4004. *Parent loans:* $28,226,597 (82% need-based, 18% non-need-based). *Programs:* Federal Direct (Subsidized and Unsubsidized Stafford, PLUS), Perkins.

WORK-STUDY *Federal work-study:* jobs available.

ATHLETIC AWARDS Total amount: $5,299,599 (96% need-based, 4% non-need-based).

APPLYING FOR FINANCIAL AID *Required financial aid form:* FAFSA. *Financial aid deadline (priority):* 3/15. *Notification date:* 4/15. Students must reply within 2 weeks of notification.

CONTACT Mrs. Sherri Avent, Director of Student Financial Aid, North Carolina Agricultural and Technical State University, Dowdy Administration Building, Room 100, 1601 East Market Street, Greensboro, NC 27411, 336-334-7973 or toll-free 800-443-8964 (in-state). *Fax:* 336-334-7954. *E-mail:* avent@ncat.edu. *Website:* http://www.ncat.edu/.

NORTH CAROLINA CENTRAL UNIVERSITY
Durham, NC

CONTACT Mrs. Sharon J. Oliver, Director of Financial Aid, North Carolina Central University, 106 Student Services Building, Durham, NC 27707-3129, 919-530-5313 or toll-free 877-667-7533. *Fax:* 919-530-7959. *E-mail:* soliver@nccu.edu. *Website:* http://www.nccu.edu/.

NORTH CAROLINA STATE UNIVERSITY
Raleigh, NC

Tuition & fees (NC res): $9100	Average undergraduate aid package: $13,108

ABOUT THE INSTITUTION State-supported, coed. *Awards:* certificates, associate, bachelor's, master's, and doctoral degrees. 93 undergraduate majors. *Total enrollment:* 34,432. Undergraduates: 24,150. Freshmen: 4,799. Federal methodology is used as a basis for awarding need-based institutional aid.

UNDERGRADUATE EXPENSES for 2018–2019 *Application fee:* $85. *Tuition, state resident:* full-time $6535. *Tuition, nonresident:* full-time $25,879. *Required fees:* full-time $2565. Full-time tuition and fees vary according to course level, degree level, location, program, and reciprocity agreements. Part-time tuition and fees vary according to course level, course load, degree level, location, program, and reciprocity agreements. *College room and board:* $11,078; *Room only:* $6714. Room and board charges vary according to board plan and housing facility. *Payment plan:* Guaranteed tuition.

FRESHMAN FINANCIAL AID (Fall 2017, est.) 3,902 applied for aid; of those 62% were deemed to have need. 98% of freshmen with need received aid; of those 23% had need fully met. *Average percent of need met:* 77% (excluding resources awarded to replace EFC). *Average financial aid package:* $13,222 (excluding resources awarded to replace EFC). 4% of all full-time freshmen had no need and received non-need-based gift aid.

UNDERGRADUATE FINANCIAL AID (Fall 2017, est.) 14,729 applied for aid; of those 71% were deemed to have need. 98% of undergraduates with need received aid; of those 22% had need fully met. *Average percent of need met:* 75% (excluding resources awarded to replace EFC). *Average financial aid package:* $13,108 (excluding resources awarded to replace EFC). 5% of all full-time undergraduates had no need and received non-need-based gift aid.

GIFT AID (NEED-BASED) *Total amount:* $97,933,381 (23% federal, 18% state, 55% institutional, 4% external sources). *Receiving aid:* Freshmen: 47% (2,248); all full-time undergraduates: 45% (9,546). *Average award:* Freshmen: $10,144; Undergraduates: $9974. *Scholarships, grants, and awards:* Federal Pell, FSEOG, state, private, college/university gift aid from institutional funds, United Negro College Fund.

GIFT AID (NON-NEED-BASED) *Total amount:* $17,119,009 (1% federal, 4% state, 57% institutional, 38% external sources). *Receiving aid:* Freshmen: 9% (435). Undergraduates: 6% (1,322). *Average award:* Freshmen: $5766. Undergraduates: $5591. *Scholarships, grants, and awards by category: Academic interests/ achievement:* 3,816 awards ($15,508,848 total): agriculture, architecture, biological sciences, business, computer science, education, engineering/technologies, general academic interests/achievements, humanities, mathematics, military science, physical sciences, social sciences. *Special achievements/activities:* cheerleading/drum major, general special achievements/activities, leadership. *Special characteristics:* children and siblings of alumni, children of faculty/staff, general special characteristics, local/state students. *Tuition waivers:* Full or partial for employees or children of employees. *ROTC:* Army, Naval, Air Force.

LOANS *Student loans:* $73,160,839 (64% need-based, 36% non-need-based). 52% of past graduating class borrowed through all loan programs. *Average indebtedness per student:* $24,053. *Average need-based loan:* Freshmen: $3470. Undergraduates: $4033. *Parent loans:* $15,640,582 (20% need-based, 80% non-need-based). *Programs:* Federal Direct (Subsidized and Unsubsidized Stafford, PLUS), Perkins, state, college/university.

WORK-STUDY *Federal work-study:* Total amount: $1,407,776; 873 jobs averaging $1608. *State or other work-study/employment:* Total amount: $2,495,956 (35% need-based, 65% non-need-based). Part-time jobs available.

ATHLETIC AWARDS Total amount: $9,399,184 (29% need-based, 71% non-need-based).

APPLYING FOR FINANCIAL AID *Required financial aid form:* FAFSA. *Financial aid deadline (priority):* 3/1. *Notification date:* Continuous beginning 4/1.

CONTACT Ms. Krista Ringler, Director of Scholarships and Financial Aid, North Carolina State University, 2016 Harris Hall, Box 7302, Raleigh, NC 27695-7302, 919-515-2421. *Fax:* 919-515-8422. *E-mail:* krista_ringler@ncsu.edu. *Website:* http://www.ncsu.edu/.

NORTH CAROLINA WESLEYAN COLLEGE
Rocky Mount, NC

CONTACT Leah Hill, Director of Financial Aid, North Carolina Wesleyan College, 3400 North Wesleyan Boulevard, Rocky Mount, NC 27804, 252-985-5200 or toll-free 800-488-6292. *Fax:* 252-985-5295. *E-mail:* lhill@ncwc.edu. *Website:* http://www.ncwc.edu/.

NORTH CENTRAL COLLEGE
Naperville, IL

Tuition & fees: $37,749	Average undergraduate aid package: $27,601

ABOUT THE INSTITUTION Independent United Methodist, coed. *Awards:* certificates, bachelor's, and master's degrees. 73 undergraduate majors. *Total*

enrollment: 2,965. Undergraduates: 2,769. Freshmen: 603. Federal methodology is used as a basis for awarding need-based institutional aid.

UNDERGRADUATE EXPENSES for 2017–2018 *Application fee:* $25. *Comprehensive fee:* $48,399 includes full-time tuition ($37,569), mandatory fees ($180), and room and board ($10,650). *College room only:* $7317. Room and board charges vary according to housing facility. *Part-time tuition:* $1044 per credit hour. *Part-time fees:* $20 per term. Part-time tuition and fees vary according to course load.

FRESHMAN FINANCIAL AID (Fall 2017, est.) 552 applied for aid; of those 87% were deemed to have need. 100% of freshmen with need received aid; of those 21% had need fully met. *Average percent of need met:* 83% (excluding resources awarded to replace EFC). *Average financial aid package:* $28,633 (excluding resources awarded to replace EFC). 20% of all full-time freshmen had no need and received non-need-based gift aid.

UNDERGRADUATE FINANCIAL AID (Fall 2017, est.) 2,266 applied for aid; of those 90% were deemed to have need. 100% of undergraduates with need received aid; of those 19% had need fully met. *Average percent of need met:* 79% (excluding resources awarded to replace EFC). *Average financial aid package:* $27,601 (excluding resources awarded to replace EFC). 22% of all full-time undergraduates had no need and received non-need-based gift aid.

GIFT AID (NEED-BASED) *Total amount:* $46,090,669 (6% federal, 9% state, 83% institutional, 2% external sources). *Receiving aid:* Freshmen: 80% (481); all full-time undergraduates: 77% (2,039). *Average award:* Freshmen: $24,522; Undergraduates: $22,447. *Scholarships, grants, and awards:* Federal Pell, FSEOG, state, private, college/university gift aid from institutional funds.

GIFT AID (NON-NEED-BASED) *Total amount:* $12,959,228 (97% institutional, 3% external sources). *Receiving aid:* Freshmen: 14% (87). Undergraduates: 10% (276). *Average award:* Freshmen: $20,561. Undergraduates: $18,225. *Scholarships, grants, and awards by category: Academic interests/achievement:* biological sciences, business, communication, computer science, education, English, foreign languages, general academic interests/achievements, humanities, international studies, mathematics, physical sciences, premedicine, religion/biblical studies, social sciences. *Creative arts/performance:* art/fine arts, cinema/film/broadcasting, debating, journalism/publications, music, theater/drama. *Special achievements/activities:* community service, religious involvement. *Special characteristics:* adult students, children of faculty/staff, general special characteristics, international students, relatives of clergy. *Tuition waivers:* Full or partial for employees or children of employees, senior citizens. *ROTC:* Army cooperative, Air Force cooperative.

LOANS *Student loans:* $19,156,518 (69% need-based, 31% non-need-based). 77% of past graduating class borrowed through all loan programs. *Average indebtedness per student:* $38,267. *Average need-based loan:* Freshmen: $3259. Undergraduates: $4564. *Parent loans:* $6,517,021 (38% need-based, 62% non-need-based). *Programs:* Federal Direct (Subsidized and Unsubsidized Stafford, PLUS), Perkins, college/university.

WORK-STUDY *Federal work-study:* Total amount: $355,550; 1,527 jobs averaging $233. *State or other work-study/employment:* Part-time jobs available.

APPLYING FOR FINANCIAL AID *Required financial aid form:* FAFSA. *Financial aid deadline:* Continuous. *Notification date:* Continuous beginning 2/1. Students must reply within 4 weeks of notification.

CONTACT Kristina Bonn, Director of Financial Aid, North Central College, 30 North Brainard Street, Naperville, IL 60540, 630-637-5600 or toll-free 800-411-1861. *Fax:* 630-637-5608. *E-mail:* klbonn@noctrl.edu. *Website:* http://www.northcentralcollege.edu/.

NORTHCENTRAL UNIVERSITY
San Diego, CA

CONTACT Financial Aid Office, Northcentral University, 2488 Historic Decatur Road, Suite 100, San Diego, CA 92106 or toll-free 866-776-0331. *Website:* http://www.ncu.edu/.

NORTH CENTRAL UNIVERSITY
Minneapolis, MN

CONTACT Mrs. Donna Jager, Director of Financial Aid, North Central University, 910 Elliot Avenue, Minneapolis, MN 55404-1322, 612-343-4485 or toll-free 800-289-6222. *Fax:* 612-343-8067. *E-mail:* finaid@northcentral.edu. *Website:* http://www.northcentral.edu/.

NORTH DAKOTA STATE UNIVERSITY
Fargo, ND

CONTACT Jeanne Enebo, Director of Financial Aid, North Dakota State University, PO Box 5315, Fargo, ND 58105, 701-231-7537 or toll-free 800-488-6378. *Fax:* 701-231-6126. *E-mail:* j.enebo@ndsu.edu. *Website:* http://www.ndsu.edu/.

NORTHEAST CATHOLIC COLLEGE
Warner, NH

Tuition & fees: N/R	Average undergraduate aid package: $19,398

ABOUT THE INSTITUTION Independent Roman Catholic, coed. 1 undergraduate major. Institutional methodology is used as a basis for awarding need-based institutional aid.

FRESHMAN FINANCIAL AID (Fall 2016) 21 applied for aid; of those 100% were deemed to have need. 100% of freshmen with need received aid; of those 90% had need fully met. *Average percent of need met:* 90% (excluding resources awarded to replace EFC). *Average financial aid package:* $17,581 (excluding resources awarded to replace EFC). 13% of all full-time freshmen had no need and received non-need-based gift aid.

UNDERGRADUATE FINANCIAL AID (Fall 2016) 100% of undergraduates with need received aid; of those 85% had need fully met. *Average percent of need met:* 85% (excluding resources awarded to replace EFC). *Average financial aid package:* $19,398 (excluding resources awarded to replace EFC). 30% of all full-time undergraduates had no need and received non-need-based gift aid.

GIFT AID (NEED-BASED) *Total amount:* $567,828 (34% federal, 1% state, 65% institutional). *Receiving aid:* Freshmen: 88% (21); all full-time undergraduates: 73% (66). *Average award:* Freshmen: $8734; Undergraduates: $15,610. *Scholarships, grants, and awards:* Federal Pell, state, private, college/university gift aid from institutional funds.

GIFT AID (NON-NEED-BASED) *Total amount:* $1,020,956 (99% institutional, 1% external sources). *Receiving aid:* Freshmen: 79% (19). Undergraduates: 56% (50). *Average award:* Freshmen: $8000. Undergraduates: $6575. *Scholarships, grants, and awards by category: Academic interests/achievement:* 63 awards ($1,014,456 total): English, general academic interests/achievements, humanities, religion/biblical studies.

LOANS *Student loans:* $363,242 (100% need-based). 71% of past graduating class borrowed through all loan programs. *Average indebtedness per student:* $18,186. *Average need-based loan:* Freshmen: $3288. Undergraduates: $3134. *Parent loans:* $18,306 (100% need-based). *Programs:* Federal Direct (Subsidized and Unsubsidized Stafford, PLUS), alternative loans.

APPLYING FOR FINANCIAL AID *Required financial aid form:* FAFSA. *Financial aid deadline:* Continuous. *Notification date:* Continuous beginning 1/1.

CONTACT Marie A. Lasher, Financial Aid Director, Northeast Catholic College, 511 Kearsarge Mountain Road, Warner, NH 03278, 603-456-4136 or toll-free 877-498-1723. *Fax:* 603-456-2660. *E-mail:* mlasher@northeastcatholic.edu. *Website:* http://www.magdalen.edu/.

NORTHEASTERN ILLINOIS UNIVERSITY
Chicago, IL

Tuition & fees (IL res): $13,420	Average undergraduate aid package: $9950

ABOUT THE INSTITUTION State-supported, coed. **Awards:** certificates, bachelor's, and master's degrees. 41 undergraduate majors. **Total enrollment:** 9,538. Undergraduates: 7,665. Freshmen: 801. Federal methodology is used as a basis for awarding need-based institutional aid.

UNDERGRADUATE EXPENSES for 2017–2018 Application fee: $30. **Tuition, state resident:** full-time $11,320; part-time $377 per credit hour. **Tuition, nonresident:** full-time $22,639; part-time $755 per credit hour. **Required fees:** full-time $2100; $69.80 per credit hour or $3 per term. Full-time tuition and fees vary according to course load, degree level, and program. Part-time tuition and fees vary according to course load, degree level, and program. **College room and board:** $11,424; **Room only:** $8424. Room and board charges vary according to housing facility. **Payment plan:** Guaranteed tuition.

FRESHMAN FINANCIAL AID (Fall 2017, est.) 740 applied for aid; of those 81% were deemed to have need. 92% of freshmen with need received aid; of those 5% had need fully met. **Average financial aid package:** $10,174 (excluding resources awarded to replace EFC). 1% of all full-time freshmen had no need and received non-need-based gift aid.

UNDERGRADUATE FINANCIAL AID (Fall 2017, est.) 3,300 applied for aid; of those 81% were deemed to have need. 89% of undergraduates with need received aid; of those 8% had need fully met. **Average financial aid package:** $9950 (excluding resources awarded to replace EFC). 2% of all full-time undergraduates had no need and received non-need-based gift aid.

GIFT AID (NEED-BASED) Total amount: $33,935,483 (60% federal, 37% state, 2% institutional, 1% external sources). **Receiving aid:** Freshmen: 69% (549); all full-time undergraduates: 52% (2,154). **Average award:** Freshmen: $8534; Undergraduates: $7826. **Scholarships, grants, and awards:** Federal Pell, FSEOG, state, private, college/university gift aid from institutional funds.

GIFT AID (NON-NEED-BASED) Total amount: $791,036 (37% state, 38% institutional, 25% external sources). **Average award:** Freshmen: $1825. Undergraduates: $2328. **Scholarships, grants, and awards by category:** Academic interests/achievement: biological sciences, business, communication, computer science, education, English, foreign languages, general academic interests/achievements, mathematics, physical sciences, social sciences. Creative arts/performance: art/fine arts, creative writing, dance, journalism/publications, music, performing arts, theater/drama. Special achievements/activities: leadership. Special characteristics: adult students, children of faculty/staff, children of union members/company employees, general special characteristics. **Tuition waivers:** Full or partial for employees or children of employees, senior citizens. **ROTC:** Army cooperative, Air Force cooperative.

LOANS Student loans: $34,185,841 (46% need-based, 54% non-need-based). 53% of past graduating class borrowed through all loan programs. **Average indebtedness per student:** $15,819. **Average need-based loan:** Freshmen: $2344. Undergraduates: $3087. **Parent loans:** $9,915,398 (100% non-need-based). **Programs:** Federal Direct (Subsidized and Unsubsidized Stafford, PLUS), Perkins.

WORK-STUDY Federal work-study: Total amount: $49,449; jobs available. **State or other work-study/employment:** Total amount: $402,719 (100% non-need-based). Part-time jobs available.

APPLYING FOR FINANCIAL AID Required financial aid form: FAFSA. **Financial aid deadline (priority):** 2/15. **Notification date:** Continuous beginning 12/1. Students must reply within 2 weeks of notification.

CONTACT Office of Financial Aid, Northeastern Illinois University, 5500 North St. Louis Avenue, Chicago, IL 60625, 773-442-5010. Fax: 773-442-5040. E-mail: financial-aid@neiu.edu. Website: http://www.neiu.edu/.

NORTHEASTERN STATE UNIVERSITY
Tahlequah, OK

Tuition & fees (OK res): $6334	Average undergraduate aid package: $12,937

ABOUT THE INSTITUTION State-supported, coed. **Awards:** certificates, bachelor's, master's, and doctoral degrees. 60 undergraduate majors. **Total enrollment:** 7,906. Undergraduates: 6,818. Freshmen: 840. Federal methodology is used as a basis for awarding need-based institutional aid.

UNDERGRADUATE EXPENSES for 2017–2018 Application fee: $25. **Tuition, state resident:** full-time $5212; part-time $173.75 per credit hour. **Tuition, nonresident:** full-time $12,900; part-time $430 per credit hour. **Required fees:** full-time $1122; $37.40 per credit hour. Full-time tuition and fees vary according to course load and program. Part-time tuition and fees vary according to course load and program. **College room and board:** $7020; **Room only:** $3100. Room and board charges vary according to board plan and housing facility. **Payment plan:** Guaranteed tuition.

FRESHMAN FINANCIAL AID (Fall 2017, est.) 800 applied for aid; of those 70% were deemed to have need. 99% of freshmen with need received aid; of those 83% had need fully met. **Average percent of need met:** 98% (excluding resources awarded to replace EFC). **Average financial aid package:** $11,859 (excluding resources awarded to replace EFC). 8% of all full-time freshmen had no need and received non-need-based gift aid.

UNDERGRADUATE FINANCIAL AID (Fall 2017, est.) 4,066 applied for aid; of those 80% were deemed to have need. 99% of undergraduates with need received aid; of those 67% had need fully met. **Average percent of need met:** 94% (excluding resources awarded to replace EFC). **Average financial aid package:** $12,937 (excluding resources awarded to replace EFC). 4% of all full-time undergraduates had no need and received non-need-based gift aid.

GIFT AID (NEED-BASED) Total amount: $21,435,244 (68% federal, 23% state, 2% institutional, 7% external sources). **Receiving aid:** Freshmen: 60% (509); all full-time undergraduates: 59% (2,807). **Average award:** Freshmen: $7417; Undergraduates: $7011. **Scholarships, grants, and awards:** Federal Pell, FSEOG, state, private, college/university gift aid from institutional funds, United Negro College Fund.

GIFT AID (NON-NEED-BASED) Total amount: $1,895,328 (1% federal, 2% state, 38% institutional, 59% external sources). **Receiving aid:** Freshmen: 21% (178). Undergraduates: 12% (556). **Average award:** Freshmen: $2660. Undergraduates: $2886. **Scholarships, grants, and awards by category:** Academic interests/achievement: biological sciences, business, communication, computer science, education, English, foreign languages, general academic interests/achievements, health fields, home economics, humanities, library science, mathematics, physical sciences, premedicine, social sciences. Creative arts/performance: applied art and design, art/fine arts, dance, debating, journalism/publications, music, performing arts, theater/drama. Special achievements/activities: cheerleading/drum major, community service, junior miss, leadership. Special characteristics: children and siblings of alumni, children of faculty/staff, children with a deceased or disabled parent, local/state students, members of minority groups, out-of-state students, religious affiliation, spouses of deceased or disabled public servants. **Tuition waivers:** Full or partial for employees or children of employees. **ROTC:** Army.

LOANS Student loans: $33,053,938 (77% need-based, 23% non-need-based). 61% of past graduating class borrowed through all loan programs. **Average indebtedness per student:** $21,268. **Average need-based loan:** Freshmen: $5793. Undergraduates: $7412. **Parent loans:** $11,578,912 (19% need-based, 81% non-need-based). **Programs:** Federal Direct (Subsidized and Unsubsidized Stafford, PLUS), Perkins.

WORK-STUDY Federal work-study: Total amount: $825,094; 272 jobs averaging $2726. **State or other work-study/employment:** Total amount: $1,919,791 (100% need-based). 430 part-time jobs averaging $1711.

ATHLETIC AWARDS Total amount: $1,142,803 (17% need-based, 83% non-need-based).

APPLYING FOR FINANCIAL AID Required financial aid form: FAFSA. **Financial aid deadline:** Continuous. **Notification date:** Continuous beginning 11/1.

CONTACT Dr. Teri Cochran, Director of Student Financial Services, Northeastern State University, 715 North Grand Avenue, Tahlequah, OK 74464-2399, 918-444-3410 or toll-free 800-722-9614. Fax: 918-458-2510. E-mail: cochrant@nsuok.edu. Website: http://www.nsuok.edu/.

NORTHEASTERN UNIVERSITY
Boston, MA

Tuition & fees: $49,497	Average undergraduate aid package: $34,461

ABOUT THE INSTITUTION Independent, coed. *Awards:* certificates, bachelor's, master's, and doctoral degrees. 65 undergraduate majors. *Total enrollment:* 26,660. Undergraduates: 18,269. Freshmen: 3,108. Institutional methodology is used as a basis for awarding need-based institutional aid.

UNDERGRADUATE EXPENSES for 2017–2018 *Application fee:* $75. *Comprehensive fee:* $65,737 includes full-time tuition ($48,560), mandatory fees ($937), and room and board ($16,240). *College room only:* $8680. Room and board charges vary according to board plan and housing facility.

FRESHMAN FINANCIAL AID (Fall 2017, est.) 2,170 applied for aid; of those 63% were deemed to have need. 100% of freshmen with need received aid; of those 100% had need fully met. *Average percent of need met:* 100% (excluding resources awarded to replace EFC). *Average financial aid package:* $39,377 (excluding resources awarded to replace EFC). 28% of all full-time freshmen had no need and received non-need-based gift aid.

UNDERGRADUATE FINANCIAL AID (Fall 2017, est.) 8,757 applied for aid; of those 71% were deemed to have need. 99% of undergraduates with need received aid; of those 42% had need fully met. *Average percent of need met:* 86% (excluding resources awarded to replace EFC). *Average financial aid package:* $34,461 (excluding resources awarded to replace EFC). 27% of all full-time undergraduates had no need and received non-need-based gift aid.

GIFT AID (NEED-BASED) *Total amount:* $178,282,123 (7% federal, 1% state, 90% institutional, 2% external sources). *Receiving aid:* Freshmen: 43% (1,322); all full-time undergraduates: 33% (5,898). *Average award:* Freshmen: $35,423; Undergraduates: $30,469. *Scholarships, grants, and awards:* Federal Pell, FSEOG, state, private, college/university gift aid from institutional funds.

GIFT AID (NON-NEED-BASED) *Total amount:* $117,941,931 (14% federal, 77% institutional, 9% external sources). *Receiving aid:* Freshmen: 20% (634). Undergraduates: 14% (2,555). *Average award:* Freshmen: $19,358. Undergraduates: $15,221. *Tuition waivers:* Full or partial for employees or children of employees. *ROTC:* Army, Naval cooperative, Air Force cooperative.

LOANS *Student loans:* $76,643,006 (45% need-based, 55% non-need-based). *Average need-based loan:* Freshmen: $4212. Undergraduates: $4586. *Parent loans:* $13,587,876 (14% need-based, 86% non-need-based). *Programs:* Federal Direct (Subsidized and Unsubsidized Stafford, PLUS), Perkins, Federal Nursing, state.

WORK-STUDY *Federal work-study:* Total amount: $8,229,485; jobs available.

ATHLETIC AWARDS Total amount: $13,108,577 (14% need-based, 86% non-need-based).

APPLYING FOR FINANCIAL AID *Required financial aid forms:* FAFSA, CSS Financial Aid PROFILE, noncustodial (divorced/separated) parent's statement. *Financial aid deadline (priority):* 2/15. *Notification date:* 4/1. Students must reply by 5/1.

CONTACT Mr. James Slattery, Interim Dean of Student Financial Services, Northeastern University, 360 Huntington Avenue, Boston, MA 02115, 617-373-3190. *Fax:* 617-373-8735. *E-mail:* sfs@northeastern.edu. *Website:* http://www.northeastern.edu/.

NORTHERN ARIZONA UNIVERSITY
Flagstaff, AZ

Tuition & fees (AZ res): $11,060	Average undergraduate aid package: $12,003

ABOUT THE INSTITUTION State-supported, coed. *Awards:* certificates, bachelor's, master's, and doctoral degrees. 67 undergraduate majors. *Total enrollment:* 31,057. Undergraduates: 27,086. Freshmen: 5,900. Federal methodology is used as a basis for awarding need-based institutional aid.

UNDERGRADUATE EXPENSES for 2017–2018 *Application fee:* $25. *Tuition, state resident:* full-time $10,038; part-time $717 per credit hour. *Tuition, nonresident:* full-time $23,820; part-time $993 per credit hour. *Required fees:* full-time $1022; $14 per credit hour or $343 per term. Full-time tuition and fees vary according to course load, location, and reciprocity agreements. Part-time tuition and fees vary according to course load, location, and reciprocity agreements. *College room and board:* $9944; *Room only:* $5408. Room and board charges vary according to board plan and housing facility. *Payment plan:* Guaranteed tuition.

FRESHMAN FINANCIAL AID (Fall 2016) 4,481 applied for aid; of those 78% were deemed to have need. 98% of freshmen with need received aid; of those 13% had need fully met. *Average percent of need met:* 66% (excluding resources awarded to replace EFC). *Average financial aid package:* $13,241 (excluding resources awarded to replace EFC). 22% of all full-time freshmen had no need and received non-need-based gift aid.

UNDERGRADUATE FINANCIAL AID (Fall 2016) 16,002 applied for aid; of those 83% were deemed to have need. 98% of undergraduates with need received aid; of those 11% had need fully met. *Average percent of need met:* 61% (excluding resources awarded to replace EFC). *Average financial aid package:* $12,003 (excluding resources awarded to replace EFC). 17% of all full-time undergraduates had no need and received non-need-based gift aid.

GIFT AID (NEED-BASED) *Total amount:* $125,048,153 (35% federal, 2% state, 59% institutional, 4% external sources). *Receiving aid:* Freshmen: 46% (2,366); all full-time undergraduates: 42% (9,079). *Average award:* Freshmen: $7547; Undergraduates: $6941. *Scholarships, grants, and awards:* Federal Pell, FSEOG, state, private, college/university gift aid from institutional funds, Federal Nursing, TEACH Grants, tribal grants.

GIFT AID (NON-NEED-BASED) *Total amount:* $26,273,931 (1% federal, 94% institutional, 5% external sources). *Receiving aid:* Freshmen: 52% (2,644). Undergraduates: 35% (7,436). *Average award:* Freshmen: $6572. Undergraduates: $6610. *Scholarships, grants, and awards by category:* Academic interests/achievement: general academic interests/achievements. *Creative arts/performance:* art/fine arts, music, theater/drama. *Special achievements/activities:* leadership. *Special characteristics:* children and siblings of alumni, local/state students, members of minority groups. *Tuition waivers:* Full or partial for employees or children of employees. *ROTC:* Army, Air Force.

LOANS *Student loans:* $104,801,549 (84% need-based, 16% non-need-based). 59% of past graduating class borrowed through all loan programs. *Average indebtedness per student:* $24,413. *Average need-based loan:* Freshmen: $3402. Undergraduates: $4237. *Parent loans:* $46,571,290 (75% need-based, 25% non-need-based). *Programs:* Federal Direct (Subsidized and Unsubsidized Stafford, PLUS), Perkins, Federal Nursing, state, college/university.

WORK-STUDY *Federal work-study:* jobs available. *State or other work-study/employment:* Total amount: $11,819,676 (63% need-based, 37% non-need-based). Part-time jobs available.

ATHLETIC AWARDS Total amount: $4,902,100 (44% need-based, 56% non-need-based).

APPLYING FOR FINANCIAL AID *Required financial aid form:* FAFSA. *Financial aid deadline (priority):* 11/15. *Notification date:* Continuous beginning 2/1.

CONTACT Office of Financial Aid, Northern Arizona University, PO Box 4108, Flagstaff, AZ 86011, 928-523-4951 or toll-free 888-628-2968. *Fax:* 928-523-1551. *E-mail:* financial.aid@nau.edu. *Website:* http://www.nau.edu/.

NORTHERN ILLINOIS UNIVERSITY
De Kalb, IL

Tuition & fees (IL res): $12,262	Average undergraduate aid package: $12,759

ABOUT THE INSTITUTION State-supported, coed. *Awards:* bachelor's, master's, and doctoral degrees. 65 undergraduate majors. *Total enrollment:* 18,042. Undergraduates: 13,454. Freshmen: 1,852. Federal methodology is used as a basis for awarding need-based institutional aid.

UNDERGRADUATE EXPENSES for 2017–2018 *Application fee:* $40. *Tuition, state resident:* full-time $9466; part-time $440 per credit hour. *Tuition, nonresident:* full-time $18,931; part-time $793 per credit hour. *Required fees:* full-time $2796; $94 per credit hour or $125 per term. Part-time tuition and fees vary according to course load and location. *College room and board:* $10,880. Room and board charges vary according to student level.

FRESHMAN FINANCIAL AID (Fall 2016) 1,661 applied for aid; of those 84% were deemed to have need. 99% of freshmen with need received aid; of those 9% had need fully met. *Average percent of need met:* 65% (excluding resources awarded

to replace EFC). *Average financial aid package:* $14,067 (excluding resources awarded to replace EFC). 14% of all full-time freshmen had no need and received non-need-based gift aid.

UNDERGRADUATE FINANCIAL AID (Fall 2016) 10,723 applied for aid; of those 87% were deemed to have need. 99% of undergraduates with need received aid; of those 7% had need fully met. *Average percent of need met:* 61% (excluding resources awarded to replace EFC). *Average financial aid package:* $12,759 (excluding resources awarded to replace EFC). 9% of all full-time undergraduates had no need and received non-need-based gift aid.

GIFT AID (NEED-BASED) *Total amount:* $63,644,553 (44% federal, 33% state, 20% institutional, 3% external sources). *Receiving aid:* Freshmen: 72% (1,322); all full-time undergraduates: 59% (7,643). *Average award:* Freshmen: $9337; Undergraduates: $8232. *Scholarships, grants, and awards:* Federal Pell, FSEOG, state, private, college/university gift aid from institutional funds, TEACH Grants.

GIFT AID (NON-NEED-BASED) *Total amount:* $7,843,261 (13% federal, 10% state, 68% institutional, 9% external sources). *Receiving aid:* Freshmen: 4% (75). Undergraduates: 2% (249). *Average award:* Freshmen: $4819. Undergraduates: $4194. *Scholarships, grants, and awards by category: Academic interests/achievement:* area/ethnic studies, biological sciences, business, communication, computer science, education, engineering/technologies, English, foreign languages, general academic interests/achievements, health fields, humanities, international studies, library science, mathematics, military science, physical sciences, social sciences. *Creative arts/performance:* applied art and design, art/fine arts, creative writing, dance, debating, journalism/publications, music, performing arts, theater/drama. *Special achievements/activities:* cheerleading/drum major, community service, general special achievements/activities, leadership, memberships. *Special characteristics:* adult students, children and siblings of alumni, children of faculty/staff, children with a deceased or disabled parent, ethnic background, first-generation college students, handicapped students, international students, members of minority groups, veterans, veterans' children. *Tuition waivers:* Full or partial for employees or children of employees, senior citizens. *ROTC:* Army, Air Force cooperative.

LOANS *Student loans:* $83,872,548 (79% need-based, 21% non-need-based). 76% of past graduating class borrowed through all loan programs. *Average indebtedness per student:* $34,708. *Average need-based loan:* Freshmen: $3598. Undergraduates: $4662. *Parent loans:* $18,843,426 (50% need-based, 50% non-need-based). *Programs:* Federal Direct (Subsidized and Unsubsidized Stafford, PLUS).

WORK-STUDY *Federal work-study:* 5,830 jobs averaging $2641.

ATHLETIC AWARDS Total amount: $6,981,186 (30% need-based, 70% non-need-based).

APPLYING FOR FINANCIAL AID *Required financial aid form:* FAFSA. *Notification date:* Continuous beginning 3/1.

CONTACT Ms. Rebecca A. Babel, Director of Student Financial Aid, Northern Illinois University, Swen Parson Hall, Room 245, De Kalb, IL 60115, 815-753-1395 or toll-free 800-892-3050. *Fax:* 815-753-9475. *E-mail:* finaid@niu.edu. *Website:* http://www.niu.edu/.

awarded to replace EFC). 18% of all full-time freshmen had no need and received non-need-based gift aid.

UNDERGRADUATE FINANCIAL AID (Fall 2016) 7,260 applied for aid; of those 81% were deemed to have need. 99% of undergraduates with need received aid; of those 21% had need fully met. *Average percent of need met:* 64% (excluding resources awarded to replace EFC). *Average financial aid package:* $10,941 (excluding resources awarded to replace EFC). 13% of all full-time undergraduates had no need and received non-need-based gift aid.

GIFT AID (NEED-BASED) *Total amount:* $22,901,545 (79% federal, 17% state, 4% institutional). *Receiving aid:* Freshmen: 41% (815); all full-time undergraduates: 37% (3,443). *Average award:* Freshmen: $5960; Undergraduates: $5623. *Scholarships, grants, and awards:* Federal Pell, FSEOG, state, private, college/university gift aid from institutional funds.

GIFT AID (NON-NEED-BASED) *Total amount:* $32,261,105 (2% federal, 21% state, 66% institutional, 11% external sources). *Receiving aid:* Freshmen: 57% (1,154). Undergraduates: 36% (3,364). *Average award:* Freshmen: $6608. Undergraduates: $7085. *Scholarships, grants, and awards by category: Academic interests/achievement:* biological sciences, business, communication, computer science, education, engineering/technologies, English, foreign languages, general academic interests/achievements, health fields, home economics, international studies, mathematics, physical sciences, premedicine, social sciences. *Creative arts/performance:* art/fine arts, music, theater/drama. *Special achievements/activities:* cheerleading/drum major, community service, general special achievements/activities, leadership. *Special characteristics:* adult students, children and siblings of alumni, children of faculty/staff, children of public servants, children with a deceased or disabled parent, general special characteristics, handicapped students, local/state students, members of minority groups, spouses of deceased or disabled public servants, veterans, veterans' children. *Tuition waivers:* Full or partial for children of alumni, employees or children of employees, senior citizens. *ROTC:* Army cooperative, Air Force cooperative.

LOANS *Student loans:* $69,086,729 (39% need-based, 61% non-need-based). 64% of past graduating class borrowed through all loan programs. *Average indebtedness per student:* $27,612. *Average need-based loan:* Freshmen: $3617. Undergraduates: $4506. *Parent loans:* $58,867,679 (100% non-need-based). *Programs:* Federal Direct (Subsidized and Unsubsidized Stafford, PLUS), Perkins, Federal Nursing, college/university.

WORK-STUDY *Federal work-study:* jobs available. *State or other work-study/employment:* Total amount: $3,577,581 (100% non-need-based). Part-time jobs available.

ATHLETIC AWARDS Total amount: $3,075,751 (100% non-need-based).

APPLYING FOR FINANCIAL AID *Required financial aid form:* FAFSA. *Financial aid deadline:* Continuous. *Notification date:* Continuous beginning 3/15.

CONTACT Leah Stewart, Director of Student Financial Assistance, Northern Kentucky University, 416 Administrative Center, Highland Heights, KY 41099, 859-572-5144 or toll-free 800-637-9948. *Fax:* 859-572-6997. *E-mail:* ofa@nku.edu. *Website:* http://www.nku.edu/.

NORTHERN KENTUCKY UNIVERSITY
Highland Heights, KY

Tuition & fees (KY res): $9744	Average undergraduate aid package: $10,941

ABOUT THE INSTITUTION State-supported, coed. *Awards:* certificates, bachelor's, master's, and doctoral degrees. 70 undergraduate majors. *Total enrollment:* 14,474. Undergraduates: 12,347. Freshmen: 2,145. Federal methodology is used as a basis for awarding need-based institutional aid.

UNDERGRADUATE EXPENSES for 2017–2018 *Application fee:* $40. *Tuition, state resident:* full-time $9360; part-time $390 per credit hour. *Tuition, nonresident:* full-time $18,720; part-time $780 per credit hour. *Required fees:* full-time $384; $16 per credit hour. Full-time tuition and fees vary according to course load, program, and reciprocity agreements. Part-time tuition and fees vary according to course load, program, and reciprocity agreements. *College room and board:* $9732. Room and board charges vary according to board plan and housing facility.

FRESHMAN FINANCIAL AID (Fall 2016) 1,762 applied for aid; of those 79% were deemed to have need. 99% of freshmen with need received aid; of those 24% had need fully met. *Average percent of need met:* 69% (excluding resources awarded to replace EFC). *Average financial aid package:* $11,887 (excluding resources

NORTHERN MICHIGAN UNIVERSITY
Marquette, MI

Tuition & fees (MI res): $10,490	Average undergraduate aid package: $9747

ABOUT THE INSTITUTION State-supported, coed. *Awards:* certificates, associate, bachelor's, master's, and doctoral degrees. 146 undergraduate majors. *Total enrollment:* 7,612. Undergraduates: 7,018. Freshmen: 1,501. Federal methodology is used as a basis for awarding need-based institutional aid.

UNDERGRADUATE EXPENSES for 2018–2019 *Application fee:* $35. *Tuition, state resident:* full-time $9528; part-time $397 per credit hour. *Tuition, nonresident:* full-time $15,024; part-time $626 per credit hour. *Required fees:* full-time $962. *College room and board:* $10,328; *Room only:* $5498. Room and board charges vary according to board plan, housing facility, and student level.

FRESHMAN FINANCIAL AID (Fall 2016) 1,162 applied for aid; of those 77% were deemed to have need. 99% of freshmen with need received aid; of those 19% had need fully met. *Average percent of need met:* 68% (excluding resources awarded to replace EFC). *Average financial aid package:* $9613 (excluding resources awarded to replace EFC). 15% of all full-time freshmen had no need and received non-need-based gift aid.

UNDERGRADUATE FINANCIAL AID (Fall 2016) 5,037 applied for aid; of those 82% were deemed to have need. 98% of undergraduates with need received aid; of those 15% had need fully met. *Average percent of need met:* 64% (excluding resources awarded to replace EFC). *Average financial aid package:* $9747 (excluding resources awarded to replace EFC). 10% of all full-time undergraduates had no need and received non-need-based gift aid.

GIFT AID (NEED-BASED) *Total amount:* $13,775,925 (74% federal, 3% state, 21% institutional, 2% external sources). *Receiving aid:* Freshmen: 47% (627); all full-time undergraduates: 45% (2,839). *Average award:* Freshmen: $4599; Undergraduates: $4774. *Scholarships, grants, and awards:* Federal Pell, FSEOG, state, private, college/university gift aid from institutional funds.

GIFT AID (NON-NEED-BASED) *Total amount:* $15,577,925 (1% federal, 26% state, 64% institutional, 9% external sources). *Receiving aid:* Freshmen: 54% (719). Undergraduates: 42% (2,662). *Average award:* Freshmen: $2406. Undergraduates: $2809. *Scholarships, grants, and awards by category: Academic interests/achievement:* biological sciences, business, communication, computer science, education, engineering/technologies, English, foreign languages, general academic interests/achievements, health fields, home economics, humanities, international studies, mathematics, military science, physical sciences, premedicine, social sciences. *Creative arts/performance:* applied art and design, journalism/publications, music, theater/drama. *Special achievements/activities:* cheerleading/drum major, leadership, memberships. *Special characteristics:* children and siblings of alumni, children of faculty/staff, children of union members/company employees, international students, local/state students, members of minority groups, out-of-state students. *Tuition waivers:* Full or partial for employees or children of employees. *ROTC:* Army.

LOANS *Student loans:* $36,100,416 (40% need-based, 60% non-need-based). 74% of past graduating class borrowed through all loan programs. *Average indebtedness per student:* $31,075. *Average need-based loan:* Freshmen: $3405. Undergraduates: $4225. *Parent loans:* $5,108,155 (100% non-need-based). *Programs:* Federal Direct (Subsidized and Unsubsidized Stafford, PLUS), Perkins, state, alternative loans.

WORK-STUDY *Federal work-study:* 518 jobs averaging $1860.

ATHLETIC AWARDS Total amount: $3,509,429 (100% non-need-based).

APPLYING FOR FINANCIAL AID *Required financial aid form:* FAFSA. *Financial aid deadline (priority):* 3/1. *Notification date:* Continuous beginning 12/15.

CONTACT Michael Rotundo, Director of Financial Aid, Northern Michigan University, 1401 Presque Isle Avenue, Marquette, MI 49855, 906-227-2327 or toll-free 800-682-9797. *Fax:* 906-227-2321. *E-mail:* fao@nmu.edu.
Website: http://www.nmu.edu/.

NORTHERN NEW MEXICO COLLEGE
Espa&nnola, NM

CONTACT Financial Aid Office, Northern New Mexico College, 921 Paseo de O&nnate, Espa&nnola, NM 87532, 505-747-2100.
Website: http://www.nnmc.edu/.

NORTHERN STATE UNIVERSITY
Aberdeen, SD

Tuition & fees (SD res): $8280	Average undergraduate aid package: $10,864

ABOUT THE INSTITUTION State-supported, coed. *Awards:* certificates, associate, bachelor's, and master's degrees. 44 undergraduate majors. *Total enrollment:* 3,611. Undergraduates: 3,162. Freshmen: 324. Federal methodology is used as a basis for awarding need-based institutional aid.

UNDERGRADUATE EXPENSES for 2018–2019 *Application fee:* $20. *Tuition, state resident:* full-time $7191; part-time $240 per credit hour. *Tuition, nonresident:* full-time $10,120; part-time $337 per credit hour. *Required fees:* full-time $1089; $36.30 per credit hour. Full-time tuition and fees vary according to course load, program, and reciprocity agreements. Part-time tuition and fees vary according to course load, program, and reciprocity agreements. *College room and board:* $7844; *Room only:* $3640. Room and board charges vary according to board plan and housing facility.

FRESHMAN FINANCIAL AID (Fall 2017, est.) 280 applied for aid; of those 74% were deemed to have need. 100% of freshmen with need received aid; of those 34% had need fully met. *Average percent of need met:* 74% (excluding resources awarded to replace EFC). *Average financial aid package:* $10,057 (excluding resources awarded to replace EFC). 18% of all full-time freshmen had no need and received non-need-based gift aid.

UNDERGRADUATE FINANCIAL AID (Fall 2017, est.) 1,001 applied for aid; of those 79% were deemed to have need. 100% of undergraduates with need received aid; of those 28% had need fully met. *Average percent of need met:* 74% (excluding resources awarded to replace EFC). *Average financial aid package:* $10,864 (excluding resources awarded to replace EFC). 10% of all full-time undergraduates had no need and received non-need-based gift aid.

GIFT AID (NEED-BASED) *Total amount:* $3,594,706 (71% federal, 2% state, 14% institutional, 13% external sources). *Receiving aid:* Freshmen: 62% (192); all full-time undergraduates: 54% (673). *Average award:* Freshmen: $4719; Undergraduates: $4862. *Scholarships, grants, and awards:* Federal Pell, FSEOG, state, private, college/university gift aid from institutional funds, South Dakota Education Access Foundation Grants.

GIFT AID (NON-NEED-BASED) *Total amount:* $769,042 (4% federal, 11% state, 61% institutional, 24% external sources). *Receiving aid:* Freshmen: 4% (12). Undergraduates: 2% (26). *Average award:* Freshmen: $1339. Undergraduates: $1623. *Scholarships, grants, and awards by category: Academic interests/achievement:* 600 awards ($788,685 total): agriculture, biological sciences, business, communication, computer science, education, English, foreign languages, general academic interests/achievements, humanities, international studies, mathematics, physical sciences, social sciences. *Creative arts/performance:* 100 awards ($112,500 total): art/fine arts, music, theater/drama. *Special achievements/activities:* 7 awards ($4000 total): leadership. *Special characteristics:* 47 awards ($50,250 total): adult students, ethnic background, handicapped students, international students, local/state students, members of minority groups. *Tuition waivers:* Full or partial for employees or children of employees, senior citizens.

LOANS *Student loans:* $6,854,537 (64% need-based, 36% non-need-based). 73% of past graduating class borrowed through all loan programs. *Average indebtedness per student:* $29,968. *Average need-based loan:* Freshmen: $4879. Undergraduates: $5593. *Parent loans:* $493,107 (41% need-based, 59% non-need-based). *Programs:* Federal Direct (Subsidized and Unsubsidized Stafford, PLUS), Perkins, college/university, alternative loans.

WORK-STUDY *Federal work-study:* Total amount: $738,835; 302 jobs averaging $2484. *State or other work-study/employment:* Total amount: $365,498 (100% non-need-based). 339 part-time jobs averaging $1078.

ATHLETIC AWARDS Total amount: $1,378,132 (43% need-based, 57% non-need-based).

APPLYING FOR FINANCIAL AID *Required financial aid form:* FAFSA. *Financial aid deadline (priority):* 3/1. *Notification date:* 4/15. Students must reply within 2 weeks of notification.

CONTACT Sharon Kienow, Director of Financial Aid, Northern State University, 1200 South Jay Street, Aberdeen, SD 57401-7198, 605-626-2640 or toll-free 800-678-5330. *Fax:* 605-626-2587. *E-mail:* finaid@northern.edu.
Website: http://www.northern.edu/.

NORTHERN VERMONT UNIVERSITY–JOHNSON
Johnson, VT

CONTACT Ms. Kimberly Goodell, Financial Aid Officer, Northern Vermont University–Johnson, 337 College Hill, Johnson, VT 05656-9405, 802-635-2356 or toll-free 800-635-2356. *Fax:* 802-635-1463. *E-mail:* goodellk@badger.jsc.vsc.edu.
Website: http://www.northernvermont.edu/.

NORTHERN VERMONT UNIVERSITY–LYNDON
Lyndonville, VT

CONTACT Student Services Consultant, Northern Vermont University–Lyndon, 1001 College Road, Lyndonville, VT 05851, 802-626-6396 or toll-free 800-225-1998. *Fax:* 802-626-9770. *E-mail:* financialaid@lyndonstate.edu. *Website:* http://www.northernvermont.edu/.

NORTH GREENVILLE UNIVERSITY
Tigerville, SC

CONTACT Mike Jordan, Director of Financial Aid, North Greenville University, PO Box 1892, Tigerville, SC 29688, 864-977-7058 or toll-free 800-468-6642 Ext. 7001. *Fax:* 864-977-7177. *E-mail:* mjordan@ngu.edu. *Website:* http://www.ngu.edu/.

NORTHLAND COLLEGE
Ashland, WI

Tuition & fees: $36,183	Average undergraduate aid package: $30,526

ABOUT THE INSTITUTION Independent United Church of Christ, coed. *Awards:* bachelor's degrees. 31 undergraduate majors. *Total enrollment:* 635. Undergraduates: 635. Freshmen: 189. Federal methodology is used as a basis for awarding need-based institutional aid.

UNDERGRADUATE EXPENSES for 2018–2019 *Comprehensive fee:* $45,359 includes full-time tuition ($34,666), mandatory fees ($1517), and room and board ($9176). *College room only:* $4234. Full-time tuition and fees vary according to course load. Room and board charges vary according to board plan and housing facility. *Part-time tuition:* $670 per credit. Part-time tuition and fees vary according to course load.

FRESHMAN FINANCIAL AID (Fall 2017, est.) 186 applied for aid; of those 92% were deemed to have need. 99% of freshmen with need received aid; of those 12% had need fully met. *Average percent of need met:* 82% (excluding resources awarded to replace EFC). *Average financial aid package:* $32,280 (excluding resources awarded to replace EFC). 9% of all full-time freshmen had no need and received non-need-based gift aid.

UNDERGRADUATE FINANCIAL AID (Fall 2017, est.) 565 applied for aid; of those 91% were deemed to have need. 99% of undergraduates with need received aid; of those 20% had need fully met. *Average percent of need met:* 84% (excluding resources awarded to replace EFC). *Average financial aid package:* $30,526 (excluding resources awarded to replace EFC). 13% of all full-time undergraduates had no need and received non-need-based gift aid.

GIFT AID (NEED-BASED) *Total amount:* $12,943,326 (9% federal, 4% state, 86% institutional, 1% external sources). *Receiving aid:* Freshmen: 90% (170); all full-time undergraduates: 84% (500). *Average award:* Freshmen: $27,975; Undergraduates: $25,259. *Scholarships, grants, and awards:* Federal Pell, FSEOG, state, private, college/university gift aid from institutional funds.

GIFT AID (NON-NEED-BASED) *Total amount:* $1,554,944 (98% institutional, 2% external sources). *Receiving aid:* Freshmen: 16% (31). Undergraduates: 12% (69). *Average award:* Freshmen: $20,469. Undergraduates: $19,101. *Tuition waivers:* Full or partial for employees or children of employees.

LOANS *Student loans:* $4,096,274 (43% need-based, 57% non-need-based). 77% of past graduating class borrowed through all loan programs. *Average indebtedness per student:* $28,731. *Average need-based loan:* Freshmen: $3792. Undergraduates: $4801. *Parent loans:* $469,068 (96% need-based, 4% non-need-based). *Programs:* Federal Direct (Subsidized and Unsubsidized Stafford, PLUS), Perkins.

WORK-STUDY *Federal work-study:* Total amount: $548,573; 313 jobs averaging $1741. *State or other work-study/employment:* Total amount: $366,099 (100% non-need-based). 231 part-time jobs averaging $1572.

APPLYING FOR FINANCIAL AID *Required financial aid form:* FAFSA. *Financial aid deadline:* Continuous. *Notification date:* Continuous beginning 3/1. Students must reply by 5/1 or within 4 weeks of notification.

CONTACT Kelly Dunn, Director of Financial Aid, Northland College, 1411 Ellis Avenue, Ashland, WI 54806, 715-682-1255 or toll-free 800-753-1840 (in-state), 800-753-1040 (out-of-state). *Fax:* 715-682-1368. *E-mail:* finaid@northland.edu. *Website:* http://www.northland.edu/.

NORTH PARK UNIVERSITY
Chicago, IL

CONTACT Dr. Lucy Shaker, Director of Financial Aid, North Park University, 3225 West Foster Avenue, Chicago, IL 60625-4895, 773-244-5526 or toll-free 800-888-NPC8. *Fax:* 773-244-4953. *Website:* http://www.northpark.edu/.

NORTHPOINT BIBLE COLLEGE
Haverhill, MA

CONTACT Financial Aid Office, Northpoint Bible College, 320 South Main Street, Haverhill, MA 01835, 978-478-3400 or toll-free 800-356-4014. *Website:* http://northpoint.edu/.

NORTHWEST CHRISTIAN UNIVERSITY
Eugene, OR

Tuition & fees: $28,680	Average undergraduate aid package: $21,511

ABOUT THE INSTITUTION Independent Christian, coed. *Awards:* certificates, associate, bachelor's, and master's degrees. 26 undergraduate majors. *Total enrollment:* 798. Undergraduates: 605. Freshmen: 102. Federal methodology is used as a basis for awarding need-based institutional aid.

UNDERGRADUATE EXPENSES for 2017–2018 *Comprehensive fee:* $37,480 includes full-time tuition ($28,500), mandatory fees ($180), and room and board ($8800). Full-time tuition and fees vary according to course load. Room and board charges vary according to housing facility. *Part-time tuition:* $950 per credit hour. *Part-time fees:* $180 per year. Part-time tuition and fees vary according to course load.

FRESHMAN FINANCIAL AID (Fall 2017, est.) 98 applied for aid; of those 91% were deemed to have need. 100% of freshmen with need received aid; of those 26% had need fully met. *Average percent of need met:* 80% (excluding resources awarded to replace EFC). *Average financial aid package:* $24,111 (excluding resources awarded to replace EFC). 13% of all full-time freshmen had no need and received non-need-based gift aid.

UNDERGRADUATE FINANCIAL AID (Fall 2017, est.) 397 applied for aid; of those 90% were deemed to have need. 99% of undergraduates with need received aid; of those 16% had need fully met. *Average percent of need met:* 70% (excluding resources awarded to replace EFC). *Average financial aid package:* $21,511 (excluding resources awarded to replace EFC). 15% of all full-time undergraduates had no need and received non-need-based gift aid.

GIFT AID (NEED-BASED) *Total amount:* $5,783,444 (23% federal, 5% state, 66% institutional, 6% external sources). *Receiving aid:* Freshmen: 87% (89); all full-time undergraduates: 78% (346). *Average award:* Freshmen: $20,945; Undergraduates: $17,800. *Scholarships, grants, and awards:* Federal Pell, FSEOG, state, private, college/university gift aid from institutional funds.

GIFT AID (NON-NEED-BASED) *Total amount:* $867,768 (2% federal, 92% institutional, 6% external sources). *Receiving aid:* Freshmen: 16% (16). Undergraduates: 8% (35). *Average award:* Freshmen: $12,077. Undergraduates: $9148. *Scholarships, grants, and awards by category:* Academic interests/achievement: 280 awards ($2,155,722 total): general academic interests/achievements, religion/biblical studies. *Creative arts/performance:* 48 awards ($141,659 total): music. *Special achievements/activities:* 310 awards ($259,758 total): community service, leadership, religious involvement. *Special characteristics:* 108 awards ($383,615 total): children of faculty/staff, international students, relatives of clergy, religious affiliation, siblings of current students. *Tuition waivers:* Full or partial for employees or children of employees.

LOANS *Student loans:* $3,133,283 (76% need-based, 24% non-need-based). 84% of past graduating class borrowed through all loan programs. *Average indebtedness per student:* $28,740. *Average need-based loan:* Freshmen: $3044. Undergraduates: $4245. *Parent loans:* $817,053 (59% need-based, 41% non-need-based). *Programs:* Federal Direct (Subsidized and Unsubsidized Stafford, PLUS).

WORK-STUDY *Federal work-study:* Total amount: $264,309; 118 jobs averaging $2750. *State or other work-study/employment:* Total amount: $13,717 (21% need-based, 79% non-need-based). 8 part-time jobs averaging $2750.

ATHLETIC AWARDS Total amount: $1,009,915 (66% need-based, 34% non-need-based).

APPLYING FOR FINANCIAL AID *Required financial aid form:* FAFSA. *Financial aid deadline (priority):* 1/1. *Notification date:* Continuous beginning 1/15. Students must reply within 2 weeks of notification.

CONTACT Jocelyn Hubbs, Director of Financial Aid, Northwest Christian University, 828 East 11th Avenue, Eugene, OR 97401-3745, 541-684-7291 or toll-free 877-463-6622. *Fax:* 541-684-7300. *E-mail:* jhubbs@nwcu.edu.

Website: http://www.nwcu.edu/.

NORTHWEST COLLEGE OF ART & DESIGN
Tacoma, WA

Tuition & fees: $20,600	Average undergraduate aid package: $12,093

ABOUT THE INSTITUTION Proprietary, coed. *Awards:* bachelor's degrees. 1 undergraduate major. *Total enrollment:* 114. Undergraduates: 114. Both federal and institutional methodology are used as a basis for awarding need-based institutional aid.

UNDERGRADUATE EXPENSES for 2017–2018 *Tuition:* full-time $20,500; part-time $870 per credit hour. *Required fees:* full-time $100; $100 per year. Full-time tuition and fees vary according to degree level. Part-time tuition and fees vary according to course load.

UNDERGRADUATE FINANCIAL AID (Fall 2016) 91 applied for aid; of those 100% were deemed to have need. 100% of undergraduates with need received aid; of those 79% had need fully met. *Average percent of need met:* 63% (excluding resources awarded to replace EFC). *Average financial aid package:* $12,093 (excluding resources awarded to replace EFC).

GIFT AID (NEED-BASED) *Total amount:* $441,961 (45% federal, 55% state). *Receiving aid:* All full-time undergraduates: 45% (44). *Average award:* Undergraduates: $10,549. *Scholarships, grants, and awards:* Federal Pell, state, private, college/university gift aid from institutional funds.

GIFT AID (NON-NEED-BASED) *Total amount:* $33,441 (100% institutional). *Receiving aid:* Undergraduates: 7% (7). *Average award:* Undergraduates: $1413. *Scholarships, grants, and awards by category: Creative arts/performance:* applied art and design, art/fine arts. *Tuition waivers:* Full or partial for children of alumni, employees or children of employees.

LOANS *Student loans:* $969,896 (36% need-based, 64% non-need-based). *Average need-based loan:* Undergraduates: $7995. *Parent loans:* $361,814 (100% non-need-based). *Programs:* Federal Direct (Subsidized and Unsubsidized Stafford, PLUS), Sallie Mae Smart Option Loans.

APPLYING FOR FINANCIAL AID *Required financial aid form:* FAFSA. *Financial aid deadline:* Continuous. *Notification date:* Continuous.

CONTACT Julie Perigard, Financial Aid Officer, Northwest College of Art & Design, 1126 Pacific Avenue, Suite 101, Tacoma, WA 98402, 253-272-1126 or toll-free 800-769-ARTS. *Fax:* 360-572-9058. *E-mail:* jperigard@ncad.edu.

Website: http://www.ncad.edu/.

NORTHWESTERN COLLEGE
Orange City, IA

Tuition & fees: $31,100	Average undergraduate aid package: $25,672

ABOUT THE INSTITUTION Independent Reformed Church in America, coed. *Awards:* certificates, bachelor's, and master's degrees. 47 undergraduate majors. *Total enrollment:* 1,251. Undergraduates: 1,049. Freshmen: 281. Federal methodology is used as a basis for awarding need-based institutional aid.

UNDERGRADUATE EXPENSES for 2018–2019 *Comprehensive fee:* $40,300 includes full-time tuition ($30,900), mandatory fees ($200), and room and board ($9200). Room and board charges vary according to board plan and housing facility. *Part-time tuition:* $650 per credit hour. *Part-time fees:* $75 per term. Part-time tuition and fees vary according to course load. *Payment plan:* Tuition prepayment.

FRESHMAN FINANCIAL AID (Fall 2017, est.) 262 applied for aid; of those 87% were deemed to have need. 100% of freshmen with need received aid; of those 65% had need fully met. *Average percent of need met:* 96% (excluding resources awarded to replace EFC). *Average financial aid package:* $25,084 (excluding resources awarded to replace EFC). 18% of all full-time freshmen had no need and received non-need-based gift aid.

UNDERGRADUATE FINANCIAL AID (Fall 2017, est.) 845 applied for aid; of those 87% were deemed to have need. 100% of undergraduates with need received aid; of those 60% had need fully met. *Average percent of need met:* 93% (excluding resources awarded to replace EFC). *Average financial aid package:* $25,672 (excluding resources awarded to replace EFC). 25% of all full-time undergraduates had no need and received non-need-based gift aid.

GIFT AID (NEED-BASED) *Total amount:* $6,030,617 (23% federal, 27% state, 50% institutional). *Receiving aid:* Freshmen: 72% (203); all full-time undergraduates: 69% (683). *Average award:* Freshmen: $6246; Undergraduates: $7244. *Scholarships, grants, and awards:* Federal Pell, FSEOG, state, private, college/university gift aid from institutional funds.

GIFT AID (NON-NEED-BASED) *Total amount:* $11,689,931 (1% federal, 93% institutional, 6% external sources). *Receiving aid:* Freshmen: 80% (224). Undergraduates: 73% (723). *Average award:* Freshmen: $12,648. Undergraduates: $12,162. *Scholarships, grants, and awards by category: Academic interests/achievement:* 955 awards ($10,394,875 total): biological sciences, business, communication, computer science, education, English, foreign languages, general academic interests/achievements, humanities, mathematics, physical sciences, premedicine, religion/biblical studies, social sciences. *Creative arts/performance:* 171 awards ($501,333 total): art/fine arts, dance, music, performing arts, theater/drama. *Special characteristics:* 570 awards ($1,725,560 total): children and siblings of alumni, children of faculty/staff, ethnic background, first-generation college students, handicapped students, international students, religious affiliation, siblings of current students, veterans. *Tuition waivers:* Full or partial for employees or children of employees.

LOANS *Student loans:* $5,896,986 (45% need-based, 55% non-need-based). 78% of past graduating class borrowed through all loan programs. *Average indebtedness per student:* $32,164. *Average need-based loan:* Freshmen: $3860. Undergraduates: $4947. *Parent loans:* $1,220,998 (100% non-need-based). *Programs:* Federal Direct (Subsidized and Unsubsidized Stafford, PLUS), Perkins, college/university, alternative loans.

WORK-STUDY *Federal work-study:* Total amount: $223,218; 144 jobs averaging $1550. *State or other work-study/employment:* Total amount: $725,256 (100% non-need-based). 666 part-time jobs averaging $1089.

ATHLETIC AWARDS Total amount: $3,054,545 (100% non-need-based).

APPLYING FOR FINANCIAL AID *Required financial aid form:* FAFSA. *Financial aid deadline (priority):* 4/15. *Notification date:* Continuous beginning 12/1. Students must reply within 3 weeks of notification.

CONTACT Mr. Eric Anderson, Director of Financial Aid, Northwestern College, 101 Seventh Street, SW, Orange City, IA 51041-1996, 712-707-7131 or toll-free 800-747-4757. *Fax:* 712-707-7164. *E-mail:* finaid@nwciowa.edu.

Website: http://www.nwciowa.edu/.

NORTHWESTERN OKLAHOMA STATE UNIVERSITY
Alva, OK

CONTACT Rita J. Castleberry, Director of Financial Aid, Northwestern Oklahoma State University, 709 Oklahoma Boulevard, Alva, OK 73717-2799, 580-327-8542. *Fax:* 580-327-8177. *E-mail:* rjcastleberry@nwosu.edu. *Website:* http://www.nwosu.edu/.

NORTHWESTERN STATE UNIVERSITY OF LOUISIANA
Natchitoches, LA

ABOUT THE INSTITUTION State-supported, coed. *Awards:* certificates, associate, bachelor's, master's, and doctoral degrees. 35 undergraduate majors. *Total enrollment:* 10,572. Undergraduates: 9,452. Freshmen: 1,542.

GIFT AID (NEED-BASED) *Scholarships, grants, and awards:* Federal Pell, FSEOG, state, private, college/university gift aid from institutional funds.

GIFT AID (NON-NEED-BASED) *Scholarships, grants, and awards by category:* *Academic interests/achievement:* biological sciences, business, communication, education, engineering/technologies, English, general academic interests/achievements, health fields, humanities, mathematics, military science, social sciences. *Creative arts/performance:* art/fine arts, cinema/film/broadcasting, creative writing, dance, general creative arts/performance, music, performing arts, theater/drama. *Special achievements/activities:* cheerleading/drum major, general special achievements/activities, leadership, memberships. *Special characteristics:* adult students, children of faculty/staff, children of public servants, general special characteristics, international students, married students, out-of-state students, public servants, veterans, veterans' children.

LOANS *Programs:* Federal Direct (Subsidized and Unsubsidized Stafford, PLUS), Perkins, Federal Nursing, state, college/university, alternative loans.

APPLYING FOR FINANCIAL AID *Required financial aid forms:* FAFSA, institution's own form.

CONTACT Ms. Lauren Jackson, Director of Financial Aid, Northwestern State University of Louisiana, 212 Student Services Center, Natchitoches, LA 71497, 318-357-5961 or toll-free 800-327-1903. *Fax:* 318-357-5488. *E-mail:* nsufinaid@nsula.edu. *Website:* http://www.nsula.edu/.

NORTHWESTERN UNIVERSITY
Evanston, IL

Tuition & fees: $52,678	Average undergraduate aid package: $49,030

ABOUT THE INSTITUTION Independent, coed. *Awards:* certificates, bachelor's, master's, and doctoral degrees. 112 undergraduate majors. *Total enrollment:* 21,474. Undergraduates: 8,278. Freshmen: 1,903. Federal methodology is used as a basis for awarding need-based institutional aid.

UNDERGRADUATE EXPENSES for 2017–2018 *Application fee:* $75. *Comprehensive fee:* $68,725 includes full-time tuition ($52,239), mandatory fees ($439), and room and board ($16,047). Room and board charges vary according to board plan and housing facility.

FRESHMAN FINANCIAL AID (Fall 2017, est.) 1,178 applied for aid; of those 80% were deemed to have need. 100% of freshmen with need received aid; of those 100% had need fully met. *Average percent of need met:* 100% (excluding resources awarded to replace EFC). *Average financial aid package:* $50,668 (excluding resources awarded to replace EFC). 4% of all full-time freshmen had no need and received non-need-based gift aid.

UNDERGRADUATE FINANCIAL AID (Fall 2017, est.) 4,174 applied for aid; of those 89% were deemed to have need. 100% of undergraduates with need received aid; of those 100% had need fully met. *Average percent of need met:* 100% (excluding resources awarded to replace EFC). *Average financial aid package:* $49,030 (excluding resources awarded to replace EFC). 4% of all full-time undergraduates had no need and received non-need-based gift aid.

GIFT AID (NEED-BASED) *Total amount:* $177,167,315 (5% federal, 1% state, 91% institutional, 3% external sources). *Receiving aid:* Freshmen: 48% (922); all full-time undergraduates: 44% (3,647). *Average award:* Freshmen: $49,645; Undergraduates: $46,720. *Scholarships, grants, and awards:* Federal Pell, FSEOG, state, college/university gift aid from institutional funds.

GIFT AID (NON-NEED-BASED) *Average award:* Freshmen: $6659. Undergraduates: $4923. *Scholarships, grants, and awards by category:* *Creative arts/performance:* music. *Special characteristics:* international students. **ROTC:** Army cooperative, Naval, Air Force cooperative.

LOANS *Student loans:* $13,457,946 (44% need-based, 56% non-need-based). 37% of past graduating class borrowed through all loan programs. *Average indebtedness per student:* $19,718. *Average need-based loan:* Freshmen: $3054. Undergraduates: $4339. *Parent loans:* $10,249,246 (100% non-need-based). *Programs:* Federal Direct (Subsidized and Unsubsidized Stafford, PLUS), Perkins, college/university.

WORK-STUDY *Federal work-study:* Total amount: $3,400,000; jobs available. *State or other work-study/employment:* Total amount: $2,868,934 (100% need-based). Part-time jobs available.

ATHLETIC AWARDS Total amount: $17,714,100 (100% non-need-based).

APPLYING FOR FINANCIAL AID *Required financial aid forms:* FAFSA, CSS Financial Aid PROFILE, noncustodial (divorced/separated) parent's statement, parent and student income tax forms. *Financial aid deadline:* 3/5. *Notification date:* 4/15. Students must reply by 5/1 or within 2 weeks of notification.

CONTACT Office of Financial Aid, Northwestern University, 1801 Hinman Avenue, Evanston, IL 60204-1270, 847-491-7400. *E-mail:* undergradaid@u.northwestern.edu. *Website:* http://www.northwestern.edu/.

NORTHWEST MISSOURI STATE UNIVERSITY
Maryville, MO

Tuition & fees (MO res): $9571	Average undergraduate aid package: $9727

ABOUT THE INSTITUTION State-supported, coed. *Awards:* certificates, bachelor's, and master's degrees. 64 undergraduate majors. *Total enrollment:* 6,338. Undergraduates: 5,474. Freshmen: 1,216. Federal methodology is used as a basis for awarding need-based institutional aid.

UNDERGRADUATE EXPENSES for 2017–2018 *Application fee:* $25. *Tuition, state resident:* full-time $5626; part-time $187.55 per credit hour. *Tuition, nonresident:* full-time $12,190; part-time $406.35 per credit hour. *Required fees:* full-time $3945; $131.50 per credit hour. Full-time tuition and fees vary according to course load, location, program, and reciprocity agreements. Part-time tuition and fees vary according to course load and location. *College room and board:* $9770; *Room only:* $6200. Room and board charges vary according to board plan and housing facility.

FRESHMAN FINANCIAL AID (Fall 2016) 1,224 applied for aid; of those 77% were deemed to have need. 100% of freshmen with need received aid; of those 48% had need fully met. *Average percent of need met:* 62% (excluding resources awarded to replace EFC). *Average financial aid package:* $11,144 (excluding resources awarded to replace EFC). 13% of all full-time freshmen had no need and received non-need-based gift aid.

UNDERGRADUATE FINANCIAL AID (Fall 2016) 4,157 applied for aid; of those 79% were deemed to have need. 99% of undergraduates with need received aid; of those 30% had need fully met. *Average percent of need met:* 62% (excluding resources awarded to replace EFC). *Average financial aid package:* $9727 (excluding resources awarded to replace EFC). 8% of all full-time undergraduates had no need and received non-need-based gift aid.

GIFT AID (NEED-BASED) *Total amount:* $14,853,464 (50% federal, 20% state, 26% institutional, 4% external sources). *Receiving aid:* Freshmen: 65% (863); all full-time undergraduates: 57% (2,759). *Average award:* Freshmen: $6536; Undergraduates: $5951. *Scholarships, grants, and awards:* Federal Pell, FSEOG, state, private, college/university gift aid from institutional funds.

GIFT AID (NON-NEED-BASED) *Total amount:* $4,570,523 (1% federal, 5% state, 87% institutional, 7% external sources). *Receiving aid:* Freshmen: 48% (640). Undergraduates: 24% (1,181). *Average award:* Freshmen: $3687. Undergraduates: $2910. *Scholarships, grants, and awards by category:* *Academic interests/achievement:* agriculture, biological sciences, business, communication, computer science, education, English, foreign languages, general academic interests/achievements, health fields, home economics, humanities, mathematics, physical sciences, social sciences. *Creative arts/performance:* art/fine arts, cinema/film/broadcasting, dance, debating, journalism/publications, music, theater/drama. *Special achievements/activities:* cheerleading/drum major, general special achievements/activities, leadership, memberships. *Special characteristics:* children and siblings of alumni, children of faculty/staff, general special characteristics, members of minority groups, out-of-state students, previous college experience. *Tuition waivers:* Full or partial for employees or children of employees, senior citizens.

LOANS *Student loans:* $28,723,813 (58% need-based, 42% non-need-based). 71% of past graduating class borrowed through all loan programs. *Average indebtedness per student:* $28,332. *Average need-based loan:* Freshmen: $3341. Undergraduates: $3880. *Parent loans:* $7,652,468 (32% need-based, 68% non-need-based). *Programs:* Federal Direct (Subsidized and Unsubsidized Stafford, PLUS), Perkins.

WORK-STUDY *Federal work-study:* 386 jobs averaging $1253. *State or other work-study/employment:* Total amount: $1,406,485 (25% need-based, 75% non-need-based). 1,048 part-time jobs averaging $1661.

ATHLETIC AWARDS Total amount: $2,237,134 (29% need-based, 71% non-need-based).

APPLYING FOR FINANCIAL AID *Required financial aid form:* FAFSA. *Financial aid deadline:* Continuous. *Notification date:* Continuous beginning 3/15.

CONTACT Mr. Charles Mayfield, Director of Financial Assistance, Northwest Missouri State University, 800 University Drive, Maryville, MO 64468-6001, 660-562-1138 or toll-free 800-633-1175.
Website: http://www.nwmissouri.edu/.

NORTHWEST NAZARENE UNIVERSITY
Nampa, ID

Tuition & fees: $29,300	Average undergraduate aid package: $23,634

ABOUT THE INSTITUTION Independent Church of the Nazarene, coed. *Awards:* certificates, associate, bachelor's, master's, and doctoral degrees. 72 undergraduate majors. *Total enrollment:* 2,223. Undergraduates: 1,530. Freshmen: 289. Federal methodology is used as a basis for awarding need-based institutional aid.

UNDERGRADUATE EXPENSES for 2018–2019 *Comprehensive fee:* $36,700 includes full-time tuition ($29,300) and room and board ($7400). *College room only:* $3550. Full-time tuition and fees vary according to class time, course load, degree level, location, program, and reciprocity agreements. Room and board charges vary according to board plan. *Part-time tuition:* $1200 per credit hour. Part-time tuition and fees vary according to class time, location, and program.

FRESHMAN FINANCIAL AID (Fall 2017, est.) 257 applied for aid; of those 88% were deemed to have need. 100% of freshmen with need received aid; of those 26% had need fully met. *Average percent of need met:* 86% (excluding resources awarded to replace EFC). *Average financial aid package:* $25,716 (excluding resources awarded to replace EFC). 16% of all full-time freshmen had no need and received non-need-based gift aid.

UNDERGRADUATE FINANCIAL AID (Fall 2017, est.) 1,101 applied for aid; of those 81% were deemed to have need. 100% of undergraduates with need received aid; of those 22% had need fully met. *Average percent of need met:* 81% (excluding resources awarded to replace EFC). *Average financial aid package:* $23,634 (excluding resources awarded to replace EFC). 16% of all full-time undergraduates had no need and received non-need-based gift aid.

GIFT AID (NEED-BASED) *Total amount:* $5,303,970 (50% federal, 50% institutional). *Receiving aid:* Freshmen: 60% (163); all full-time undergraduates: 58% (668). *Average award:* Freshmen: $9943; Undergraduates: $7489. *Scholarships, grants, and awards:* Federal Pell, FSEOG, state, private, college/university gift aid from institutional funds.

GIFT AID (NON-NEED-BASED) *Total amount:* $15,024,771 (92% institutional, 8% external sources). *Receiving aid:* Freshmen: 81% (220). Undergraduates: 70% (809). *Average award:* Freshmen: $15,329. Undergraduates: $12,903. *Scholarships, grants, and awards by category:* Academic interests/achievement: biological sciences, business, communication, computer science, education, engineering/technologies, English, general academic interests/achievements, home economics, mathematics, military science, physical sciences, premedicine, religion/biblical studies,

social sciences. *Creative arts/performance:* debating, music, theater/drama. *Special achievements/activities:* leadership, religious involvement. *Special characteristics:* children and siblings of alumni, children of faculty/staff, international students, relatives of clergy, religious affiliation. *Tuition waivers:* Full or partial for employees or children of employees, senior citizens. *ROTC:* Army.

LOANS *Student loans:* $3,639,025 (100% need-based). 73% of past graduating class borrowed through all loan programs. *Average indebtedness per student:* $34,288. *Average need-based loan:* Freshmen: $4001. Undergraduates: $5137. *Parent loans:* $1,058,539 (92% need-based, 8% non-need-based). *Programs:* Federal Direct (Subsidized and Unsubsidized Stafford, PLUS), Perkins, college/university.

WORK-STUDY Federal work-study jobs available.

ATHLETIC AWARDS Total amount: $2,250,832 (100% non-need-based).

APPLYING FOR FINANCIAL AID *Required financial aid form:* FAFSA. *Financial aid deadline (priority):* 2/1. *Notification date:* Continuous beginning 12/1.

CONTACT Mrs. Ann Crabb, Director of Financial Aid, Northwest Nazarene University, 623 South University Boulevard, Nampa, ID 83686, 208-467-8638 or toll-free 877-668-4968. *Fax:* 208-467-8375. *E-mail:* atcrabb@nnu.edu.
Website: http://www.nnu.edu/.

NORTHWEST UNIVERSITY
Kirkland, WA

Tuition & fees: $31,540	Average undergraduate aid package: $17,638

ABOUT THE INSTITUTION Independent Assemblies of God, coed. *Awards:* certificates, diplomas, associate, bachelor's, master's, and doctoral degrees. 69 undergraduate majors. *Total enrollment:* 2,583. Undergraduates: 1,871. Freshmen: 215. Federal methodology is used as a basis for awarding need-based institutional aid.

UNDERGRADUATE EXPENSES for 2018–2019 *Application fee:* $30. *Comprehensive fee:* $40,170 includes full-time tuition ($31,100), mandatory fees ($440), and room and board ($8630). *College room only:* $4315. Full-time tuition and fees vary according to class time, course load, location, program, and reciprocity agreements. Room and board charges vary according to housing facility and location. *Part-time tuition:* $1250 per credit hour. *Part-time fees:* $120 per term. Part-time tuition and fees vary according to class time, course load, and location.

FRESHMAN FINANCIAL AID (Fall 2016) 225 applied for aid; of those 85% were deemed to have need. 99% of freshmen with need received aid; of those 16% had need fully met. *Average percent of need met:* 70% (excluding resources awarded to replace EFC). *Average financial aid package:* $16,561 (excluding resources awarded to replace EFC). 14% of all full-time freshmen had no need and received non-need-based gift aid.

UNDERGRADUATE FINANCIAL AID (Fall 2016) 1,107 applied for aid; of those 88% were deemed to have need. 99% of undergraduates with need received aid; of those 14% had need fully met. *Average percent of need met:* 71% (excluding resources awarded to replace EFC). *Average financial aid package:* $17,638 (excluding resources awarded to replace EFC). 14% of all full-time undergraduates had no need and received non-need-based gift aid.

GIFT AID (NEED-BASED) *Total amount:* $12,623,665 (19% federal, 15% state, 63% institutional, 3% external sources). *Receiving aid:* Freshmen: 67% (160); all full-time undergraduates: 71% (867). *Average award:* Freshmen: $15,502; Undergraduates: $15,035. *Scholarships, grants, and awards:* Federal Pell, FSEOG, state, private, college/university gift aid from institutional funds.

GIFT AID (NON-NEED-BASED) *Total amount:* $2,455,298 (94% institutional, 6% external sources). *Receiving aid:* Freshmen: 8% (20). Undergraduates: 7% (85). *Average award:* Freshmen: $9413. Undergraduates: $10,384. *Scholarships, grants, and awards by category:* Academic interests/achievement: 540 awards ($4,423,650 total): general academic interests/achievements. *Creative arts/performance:* 119 awards ($481,775 total): debating, music. *Special achievements/activities:* 128 awards ($908,398 total): leadership, religious involvement. *Special characteristics:* 60 awards ($1,070,237 total): children of current students, children of educators, children of faculty/staff, general special characteristics, international students, married students, parents of current students, relatives of clergy, religious affiliation, siblings of current students, spouses of current students. *Tuition waivers:* Full or partial for employees or children of employees. *ROTC:* Army cooperative, Air Force cooperative.

LOANS *Student loans:* $8,828,998 (76% need-based, 24% non need based). 02% of past graduating class borrowed through all loan programs. *Average indebtedness per student:* $24,930. *Average need-based loan:* Freshmen: $2977. Undergraduates: $3866. *Parent loans:* $1,841,862 (44% need-based, 56% non-need-based). *Programs:* Federal Direct (Subsidized and Unsubsidized Stafford, PLUS), Perkins, alternative loans.

WORK-STUDY *Federal work-study:* 9 jobs averaging $3551. *State or other work-study/employment:* Total amount: $1292 (100% need-based). 5 part-time jobs averaging $2642.

ATHLETIC AWARDS Total amount: $1,160,692 (53% need-based, 47% non-need-based).

APPLYING FOR FINANCIAL AID *Required financial aid form:* FAFSA. *Financial aid deadline:* Continuous. *Notification date:* Continuous beginning 12/1. Students must reply within 4 weeks of notification.

CONTACT Mr. Roger Wilson, Director of Financial Aid, Northwest University, PO Box 579, Kirkland, WA 98083-0579, 425-889-5336 or toll-free 800-669-3781. *Fax:* 425-889-5224. *E-mail:* roger.wilson@northwestu.edu. *Website:* http://www.northwestu.edu/.

NORTHWOOD UNIVERSITY, MICHIGAN CAMPUS
Midland, MI

Tuition & fees: $26,080	Average undergraduate aid package: $18,932

ABOUT THE INSTITUTION Independent, coed. *Awards:* associate, bachelor's, and master's degrees. 18 undergraduate majors. *Total enrollment:* 1,927. Undergraduates: 1,442. Freshmen: 321. Federal methodology is used as a basis for awarding need-based institutional aid.

UNDERGRADUATE EXPENSES for 2017–2018 *Application fee:* $30. *Comprehensive fee:* $36,250 includes full-time tuition ($24,770), mandatory fees ($1310), and room and board ($10,170). *College room only:* $5300. Full-time tuition and fees vary according to course load and location. Room and board charges vary according to board plan. *Part-time tuition:* $953 per semester hour. Part-time tuition and fees vary according to course load and location.

FRESHMAN FINANCIAL AID (Fall 2017, est.) 226 applied for aid; of those 84% were deemed to have need. 100% of freshmen with need received aid; of those 29% had need fully met. *Average percent of need met:* 61% (excluding resources awarded to replace EFC). *Average financial aid package:* $20,656 (excluding resources awarded to replace EFC). 14% of all full-time freshmen had no need and received non-need-based gift aid.

UNDERGRADUATE FINANCIAL AID (Fall 2017, est.) 950 applied for aid; of those 87% were deemed to have need. 100% of undergraduates with need received aid; of those 21% had need fully met. *Average percent of need met:* 63% (excluding resources awarded to replace EFC). *Average financial aid package:* $18,932 (excluding resources awarded to replace EFC). 19% of all full-time undergraduates had no need and received non-need-based gift aid.

GIFT AID (NEED-BASED) *Total amount:* $9,632,162 (17% federal, 14% state, 67% institutional, 2% external sources). *Receiving aid:* Freshmen: 54% (141); all full-time undergraduates: 53% (678). *Average award:* Freshmen: $5996; Undergraduates: $6001. *Scholarships, grants, and awards:* Federal Pell, FSEOG, state, private, college/university gift aid from institutional funds.

GIFT AID (NON-NEED-BASED) *Total amount:* $3,316,047 (97% institutional, 3% external sources). *Receiving aid:* Freshmen: 36% (94). Undergraduates: 27% (341). *Average award:* Freshmen: $10,527. Undergraduates: $7541. *Scholarships, grants, and awards by category:* Academic interests/achievement: 1,071 awards ($8,014,788 total): business, general academic interests/achievements. *Special achievements/activities:* cheerleading/drum major. *Special characteristics:* 83 awards ($467,777 total): children and siblings of alumni, children of faculty/staff, siblings of current students. *Tuition waivers:* Full or partial for employees or children of employees.

LOANS *Student loans:* $8,987,388 (68% need-based, 32% non-need-based). 72% of past graduating class borrowed through all loan programs. *Average indebtedness per student:* $31,992. *Average need-based loan:* Freshmen: $3316. Undergraduates: $4422. *Parent loans:* $3,747,602 (54% need-based, 46% non-need-based). *Programs:* Federal Direct (Subsidized and Unsubsidized Stafford, PLUS), private loans.

WORK-STUDY *Federal work-study:* Total amount: $281,439; 136 jobs averaging $1531.

ATHLETIC AWARDS Total amount: $3,856,462 (47% need-based, 53% non-need-based).

APPLYING FOR FINANCIAL AID *Required financial aid form:* FAFSA. *Financial aid deadline:* Continuous. *Notification date:* Continuous beginning 1/1.

CONTACT Mark Martin, Financial Aid Director, Northwood University, Michigan Campus, 4000 Whiting Drive, Midland, MI 48640-2398, 989-837-4230 or toll-free 800-457-7878. *Fax:* 989-837-4130. *E-mail:* mi.finaid@northwood.edu. *Website:* http://www.northwood.edu/.

NORWICH UNIVERSITY
Northfield, VT

CONTACT Ms. Jana Cox, Director of Student Financial Planning, Norwich University, 158 Harmon Drive, Northfield, VT 05663, 802-485-2015 or toll-free 800-468-6679. *Fax:* 802-485-2024. *E-mail:* jcox1@norwich.edu. *Website:* http://www.norwich.edu/.

NOSSI COLLEGE OF ART
Nashville, TN

CONTACT Ms. Mary P. Kidd, Director of Financial Aid, Nossi College of Art, 590 Cheron Road, Nashville, TN 37115, 615-514-2787 or toll-free 888-986-ARTS. *Fax:* 615-514-2788. *E-mail:* financialaid@nossi.edu. *Website:* http://www.nossi.edu/.

NOTRE DAME COLLEGE
South Euclid, OH

CONTACT Ms. Dianna Roberts, Assistant Director of Financial Aid, Notre Dame College, 4545 College Road, South Euclid, OH 44118, 216-373-5213 or toll-free 877-NDC-OHIO. *Fax:* 216-373-5243. *E-mail:* droberts@ndc.edu. *Website:* http://www.notredamecollege.edu/.

NOTRE DAME DE NAMUR UNIVERSITY
Belmont, CA

CONTACT Wilbert Lleses, Director of Financial Aid, Notre Dame de Namur University, 1500 Ralston Avenue, Belmont, CA 94002, 650-508-3441 or toll-free 800-263-0545. *Fax:* 650-508-3635. *E-mail:* wlleses@ndnu.edu. *Website:* http://www.ndnu.edu/.

NOTRE DAME OF MARYLAND UNIVERSITY
Baltimore, MD

CONTACT Audrey Brooks, Director of Financial Aid, Notre Dame of Maryland University, 4701 North Charles Street, Baltimore, MD 21210-2404, 410-532-5369 or toll-free 800-435-0200. *Fax:* 410-532-6287. *E-mail:* finaid@ndm.edu. *Website:* http://www.ndm.edu/.

NOVA SOUTHEASTERN UNIVERSITY
Fort Lauderdale, FL

Tuition & fees: $29,940	Average undergraduate aid package: $30,300

ABOUT THE INSTITUTION Independent, coed. **Awards:** certificates, associate, bachelor's, master's, and doctoral degrees. 49 undergraduate majors. **Total enrollment:** 20,793. Undergraduates: 4,497. Freshmen: 984. Federal methodology is used as a basis for awarding need-based institutional aid.

UNDERGRADUATE EXPENSES for 2017–2018 Application fee: $50. **Comprehensive fee:** $42,490 includes full-time tuition ($28,980), mandatory fees ($960), and room and board ($12,550). Full-time tuition and fees vary according to program. Room and board charges vary according to board plan and housing facility. **Part-time tuition:** $966 per credit hour. Part-time tuition and fees vary according to course load and program.

FRESHMAN FINANCIAL AID (Fall 2017, est.) 853 applied for aid; of those 84% were deemed to have need. 100% of freshmen with need received aid; of those 17% had need fully met. **Average percent of need met:** 87% (excluding resources awarded to replace EFC). **Average financial aid package:** $32,899 (excluding resources awarded to replace EFC). 25% of all full-time freshmen had no need and received non-need-based gift aid.

UNDERGRADUATE FINANCIAL AID (Fall 2017, est.) 2,559 applied for aid; of those 88% were deemed to have need. 99% of undergraduates with need received aid; of those 13% had need fully met. **Average percent of need met:** 73% (excluding resources awarded to replace EFC). **Average financial aid package:** $30,300 (excluding resources awarded to replace EFC). 23% of all full-time undergraduates had no need and received non-need-based gift aid.

GIFT AID (NEED-BASED) Total amount: $46,300,943 (22% federal, 23% state, 50% institutional, 5% external sources). **Receiving aid:** Freshmen: 73% (715); all full-time undergraduates: 69% (2,167). **Average award:** Freshmen: $21,577; Undergraduates: $17,639. **Scholarships, grants, and awards:** Federal Pell, FSEOG, state, private, college/university gift aid from institutional funds, United Negro College Fund.

GIFT AID (NON-NEED-BASED) Total amount: $12,231,405 (11% state, 86% institutional, 3% external sources). **Receiving aid:** Freshmen: 6% (58). Undergraduates: 5% (155). **Average award:** Freshmen: $13,447. Undergraduates: $12,165. **Scholarships, grants, and awards by category:** Academic interests/achievement: 2,501 awards ($31,741,753 total): general academic interests/achievements. Creative arts/performance: 34 awards ($84,200 total): general creative arts/performance. Special achievements/activities: 268 awards ($3,470,900 total): general special achievements/activities. Special characteristics: 61 awards ($384,216 total): children of faculty/staff, veterans. **Tuition waivers:** Full or partial for employees or children of employees.

LOANS Student loans: $27,120,624 (94% need-based, 6% non-need-based). 53% of past graduating class borrowed through all loan programs. **Average indebtedness per student:** $32,127. **Average need-based loan:** Freshmen: $2365. Undergraduates: $3305. **Parent loans:** $9,090,261 (91% need-based, 9% non-need-based). **Programs:** Federal Direct (Subsidized and Unsubsidized Stafford, PLUS), Perkins.

WORK-STUDY Federal work-study: Total amount: $8,476,068; 1,144 jobs averaging $6106. **State or other work-study/employment:** Total amount: $507,946 (65% need-based, 35% non-need-based). 458 part-time jobs averaging $1061.

ATHLETIC AWARDS Total amount: $4,777,369 (38% need-based, 62% non-need-based).

APPLYING FOR FINANCIAL AID Required financial aid forms: FAFSA, state aid form. **Financial aid deadline (priority):** 4/15. **Notification date:** Continuous.

CONTACT Dr. Stephanie G. Brown, Vice President for Enrollment and Student Services, Nova Southeastern University, 3301 College Avenue, Fort Lauderdale, FL 33314, 954-262-7456 or toll-free 800-541-NOVA. Fax: 954-262-3967. E-mail: browstep@nova.edu.
Website: http://www.nova.edu/.

NYACK COLLEGE
Nyack, NY

CONTACT Steve Phillips, Director of Student Financial Services, Nyack College, 1 South Boulevard, Nyack, NY 10960-3698, 845-675-4747 or toll-free 800-33-NYACK. Fax: 845-358-7016. E-mail: nyacksfs@nyack.edu.
Website: http://www.nyack.edu/.

OAK HILLS CHRISTIAN COLLEGE
Bemidji, MN

CONTACT Daniel Hovestol, Financial Aid Director, Oak Hills Christian College, 1600 Oak Hills Road, SW, Bemidji, MN 56601-8832, 218-751-8671 Ext. 1220 or toll-free 888-751-8670 Ext. 1285. Fax: 218-444-1311. E-mail: ohfinaid@oakhills.edu.
Website: http://www.oakhills.edu/.

OAKLAND CITY UNIVERSITY
Oakland City, IN

Tuition & fees: $24,000	Average undergraduate aid package: $21,053

ABOUT THE INSTITUTION Independent General Baptist, coed. **Awards:** certificates, associate, bachelor's, master's, and doctoral degrees. 28 undergraduate majors. **Total enrollment:** 1,303. Undergraduates: 1,113. Freshmen: 99. Both federal and institutional methodology are used as a basis for awarding need-based institutional aid.

UNDERGRADUATE EXPENSES for 2018–2019 Application fee: $35. **Comprehensive fee:** $33,900 includes full-time tuition ($24,000) and room and board ($9900). Full-time tuition and fees vary according to degree level. Room and board charges vary according to board plan and housing facility. **Part-time tuition:** $800 per credit hour.

FRESHMAN FINANCIAL AID (Fall 2016) 80 applied for aid; of those 100% were deemed to have need. 100% of freshmen with need received aid. **Average percent of need met:** 93% (excluding resources awarded to replace EFC). **Average financial aid package:** $23,488 (excluding resources awarded to replace EFC).

UNDERGRADUATE FINANCIAL AID (Fall 2016) 435 applied for aid; of those 100% were deemed to have need. 100% of undergraduates with need received aid. **Average percent of need met:** 34% (excluding resources awarded to replace EFC). **Average financial aid package:** $21,053 (excluding resources awarded to replace EFC).

GIFT AID (NEED-BASED) Total amount: $6,482,307 (34% federal, 12% state, 52% institutional, 2% external sources). **Receiving aid:** Freshmen: 76% (65); all full-time undergraduates: 30% (377). **Average award:** Freshmen: $15,343; Undergraduates: $11,567. **Scholarships, grants, and awards:** Federal Pell, FSEOG, state, private, college/university gift aid from institutional funds.

GIFT AID (NON-NEED-BASED) Total amount: $1,148,597 (100% federal). **Scholarships, grants, and awards by category:** Academic interests/achievement: general academic interests/achievements. Creative arts/performance: art/fine arts, music. Special achievements/activities: religious involvement. Special characteristics: children and siblings of alumni, children of faculty/staff, ethnic background, international students, members of minority groups, religious affiliation. **Tuition waivers:** Full or partial for employees or children of employees.

LOANS Student loans: $2,379,932 (49% need-based, 51% non-need-based). **Parent loans:** $249,320 (100% non-need-based). **Programs:** Federal Direct (Subsidized and Unsubsidized Stafford, PLUS), Perkins, college/university.

WORK-STUDY Federal work-study: jobs available. **State or other work-study/employment:** Part-time jobs available.

ATHLETIC AWARDS Total amount: $1,103,447 (100% need-based).

APPLYING FOR FINANCIAL AID Required financial aid form: FAFSA. **Financial aid deadline (priority):** 3/10. **Notification date:** Continuous beginning 5/15.

CONTACT Nicole Sharp, Director of Financial Aid, Oakland City University, 138 North Lucretia Street, Oakland City, IN 47660-1099, 812-749-1225 or toll-free 800-737-5125. Fax: 812-749-1438. E-mail: nsharp@oak.edu.
Website: http://www.oak.edu/.

OAKLAND UNIVERSITY
Rochester, MI

ABOUT THE INSTITUTION State-supported, coed. **Awards:** certificates, bachelor's, master's, and doctoral degrees. 95 undergraduate majors. **Total enrollment:** 19,333. Undergraduates: 15,901. Freshmen: 2,456.

GIFT AID (NEED-BASED) *Scholarships, grants, and awards:* Federal Pell, FSEOG, state, private, college/university gift aid from institutional funds.

GIFT AID (NON-NEED-BASED) *Scholarships, grants, and awards by category:* Academic interests/achievement: humanities.

LOANS *Programs:* Federal Direct (Subsidized and Unsubsidized Stafford, PLUS), Perkins, private loans.

APPLYING FOR FINANCIAL AID *Required financial aid form:* FAFSA.

CONTACT Ms. Cindy Hermsen, Director of Financial Aid, Oakland University, 120 North Foundation Hall, Rochester, MI 48309-4401, 248-370-2550 or toll-free 800-OAK-UNIV. *E-mail:* finaid@oakland.edu. *Website:* http://www.oakland.edu/.

OAKWOOD UNIVERSITY
Huntsville, AL

CONTACT Financial Aid Director, Oakwood University, 7000 Adventist Boulevard, Huntsville, AL 35896, 256-726-7210 or toll-free 800-824-5312. *Website:* http://www.oakwood.edu/.

OBERLIN COLLEGE
Oberlin, OH

Tuition & fees: $53,460	Average undergraduate aid package: $43,251

ABOUT THE INSTITUTION Independent, coed. **Awards:** certificates, diplomas, bachelor's, and master's degrees. 55 undergraduate majors. **Total enrollment:** 2,853. Undergraduates: 2,827. Freshmen: 728. Both federal and institutional methodology are used as a basis for awarding need-based institutional aid.

UNDERGRADUATE EXPENSES for 2017–2018 **Comprehensive fee:** $67,862 includes full-time tuition ($52,762), mandatory fees ($698), and room and board ($14,402). **College room only:** $7482. Room and board charges vary according to board plan and housing facility. **Part-time tuition:** $2220 per credit. Part-time tuition and fees vary according to course load.

FRESHMAN FINANCIAL AID (Fall 2016) 468 applied for aid; of those 84% were deemed to have need. 100% of freshmen with need received aid; of those 100% had need fully met. **Average percent of need met:** 100% (excluding resources awarded to replace EFC). **Average financial aid package:** $42,825 (excluding resources awarded to replace EFC). 46% of all full-time freshmen had no need and received non-need-based gift aid.

UNDERGRADUATE FINANCIAL AID (Fall 2016) 1,615 applied for aid; of those 87% were deemed to have need. 100% of undergraduates with need received aid; of those 100% had need fully met. **Average percent of need met:** 100% (excluding resources awarded to replace EFC). **Average financial aid package:** $43,251 (excluding resources awarded to replace EFC). 40% of all full-time undergraduates had no need and received non-need-based gift aid.

GIFT AID (NEED-BASED) **Total amount:** $52,939,277 (3% federal, 93% institutional, 4% external sources). **Receiving aid:** Freshmen: 52% (375); all full-time undergraduates: 42% (1,184). **Average award:** Freshmen: $37,998; Undergraduates: $38,289. **Scholarships, grants, and awards:** Federal Pell, FSEOG, state, private, college/university gift aid from institutional funds.

GIFT AID (NON-NEED-BASED) **Total amount:** $16,823,717 (87% institutional, 13% external sources). **Receiving aid:** Freshmen: 44% (323). Undergraduates: 40% (1,124). **Average award:** Freshmen: $16,847. Undergraduates: $16,047. **Scholarships, grants, and awards by category:** Academic interests/achievement: 1,728 awards ($23,921,218 total): general academic interests/achievements, physical sciences. Creative arts/performance: 526 awards ($9,434,998 total): music. **Tuition waivers:** Full or partial for employees or children of employees.

LOANS **Student loans:** $8,571,378 (89% need-based, 11% non-need-based). 42% of past graduating class borrowed through all loan programs. *Average indebtedness*

per student: $29,781. **Average need-based loan:** Freshmen: $4533. Undergraduates: $5112. **Parent loans:** $2,938,116 (80% need-based, 20% non-need-based). **Programs:** Federal Direct (Subsidized and Unsubsidized Stafford, PLUS).

WORK-STUDY *Federal work-study:* 1,200 jobs averaging $2400. *State or other work-study/employment:* Total amount: $1,075,536 (80% need-based, 20% non-need-based). 800 part-time jobs averaging $2400.

APPLYING FOR FINANCIAL AID *Required financial aid forms:* FAFSA, CSS Financial Aid PROFILE, institution's own non-custodial form. **Financial aid deadline (priority):** 2/15. **Notification date:** 3/25. Students must reply by 5/1.

CONTACT Mr. Robert A. Reddy Jr., Director of Financial Aid, Oberlin College, Carnegie Building #123, 52 West Lorain Street, Oberlin, OH 44074, 440-775-8142 or toll-free 800-622-OBIE. *Fax:* 440-775-8249. *E-mail:* financial.aid@oberlin.edu. *Website:* http://www.oberlin.edu/.

OCCIDENTAL COLLEGE
Los Angeles, CA

Tuition & fees: $52,838	Average undergraduate aid package: $47,741

ABOUT THE INSTITUTION Independent, coed. **Awards:** diplomas, bachelor's, and master's degrees. 33 undergraduate majors. **Total enrollment:** 2,055. Undergraduates: 2,055. Freshmen: 564. Both federal and institutional methodology are used as a basis for awarding need-based institutional aid.

UNDERGRADUATE EXPENSES for 2017–2018 **Application fee:** $65. **Comprehensive fee:** $67,806 includes full-time tuition ($52,260), mandatory fees ($578), and room and board ($14,968). **College room only:** $8518. Room and board charges vary according to board plan. **Part-time tuition:** $2177 per unit. **Part-time fees:** $578 per year. Part-time tuition and fees vary according to course load. **Payment plan:** Tuition prepayment.

FRESHMAN FINANCIAL AID (Fall 2016) 353 applied for aid; of those 81% were deemed to have need. 100% of freshmen with need received aid; of those 100% had need fully met. **Average percent of need met:** 100% (excluding resources awarded to replace EFC). **Average financial aid package:** $48,188 (excluding resources awarded to replace EFC). 12% of all full-time freshmen had no need and received non-need-based gift aid.

UNDERGRADUATE FINANCIAL AID (Fall 2016) 1,320 applied for aid; of those 86% were deemed to have need. 100% of undergraduates with need received aid; of those 100% had need fully met. **Average percent of need met:** 100% (excluding resources awarded to replace EFC). **Average financial aid package:** $47,741 (excluding resources awarded to replace EFC). 12% of all full-time undergraduates had no need and received non-need-based gift aid.

GIFT AID (NEED-BASED) **Total amount:** $43,323,967 (4% federal, 5% state, 88% institutional, 3% external sources). **Receiving aid:** Freshmen: 56% (283); all full-time undergraduates: 55% (1,132). **Average award:** Freshmen: $41,801; Undergraduates: $40,172. **Scholarships, grants, and awards:** Federal Pell, FSEOG, state, private, college/university gift aid from institutional funds.

GIFT AID (NON-NEED-BASED) **Total amount:** $5,138,907 (90% institutional, 10% external sources). **Receiving aid:** Freshmen: 31% (155). Undergraduates: 28% (576). **Average award:** Freshmen: $12,737. Undergraduates: $11,614. **Scholarships, grants, and awards by category:** Academic interests/achievement: 493 awards ($6,115,983 total): general academic interests/achievements. Creative arts/performance: 32 awards ($20,814 total): music. Special achievements/activities: 28 awards ($420,000 total): leadership. Special characteristics: 57 awards ($1,458,409 total): children of educators, children of faculty/staff, veterans, veterans' children. **Tuition waivers:** Full or partial for employees or children of employees. **ROTC:** Army cooperative, Air Force cooperative.

LOANS **Student loans:** $9,933,050 (58% need-based, 42% non-need-based). 57% of past graduating class borrowed through all loan programs. *Average indebtedness per student:* $32,008. **Average need-based loan:** Freshmen: $4718. Undergraduates: $6074. **Parent loans:** $3,029,684 (100% non-need-based). **Programs:** Federal Direct (Subsidized and Unsubsidized Stafford, PLUS), Perkins, college/university, alternative loans.

WORK-STUDY *Federal work-study:* 776 jobs averaging $2747. *State or other work-study/employment:* Total amount: $931,870 (68% need-based, 32% non-need-based). 170 part-time jobs averaging $1364.

APPLYING FOR FINANCIAL AID *Required financial aid forms:* FAFSA, CSS Financial Aid PROFILE, state aid form, noncustodial (divorced/separated) parent's statement. *Financial aid deadline:* 1/15. *Notification date:* 3/25. Students must reply by 5/1.

CONTACT Gina Becerril, Director of Financial Aid, Occidental College, 1600 Campus Road, Los Angeles, CA 90041, 323-259-2548 or toll-free 800-825-5262. *Fax:* 323-341-4961. *E-mail:* finaid@oxy.edu. *Website:* http://www.oxy.edu/.

OGLALA LAKOTA COLLEGE
Kyle, SD

CONTACT Financial Aid Director, Oglala Lakota College, 490 Piya Wiconi Road, Kyle, SD 57752-0490, 605-455-6000. *Website:* http://www.olc.edu/.

OGLETHORPE UNIVERSITY
Atlanta, GA

Tuition & fees: $36,825	Average undergraduate aid package: $31,801

ABOUT THE INSTITUTION Independent, coed. *Awards:* bachelor's degrees. 32 undergraduate majors. *Total enrollment:* 1,250. Undergraduates: 1,250. Freshmen: 334. Federal methodology is used as a basis for awarding need-based institutional aid.

UNDERGRADUATE EXPENSES for 2017–2018 *Application fee:* $50. *Comprehensive fee:* $49,785 includes full-time tuition ($36,400), mandatory fees ($425), and room and board ($12,960). *College room only:* $4210. Full-time tuition and fees vary according to degree level. Room and board charges vary according to housing facility and location. *Part-time tuition:* $1525 per credit hour. Part-time tuition and fees vary according to class time, course load, and degree level. *Payment plan:* Tuition prepayment.

FRESHMAN FINANCIAL AID (Fall 2017, est.) 308 applied for aid; of those 89% were deemed to have need. 100% of freshmen with need received aid; of those 19% had need fully met. *Average percent of need met:* 79% (excluding resources awarded to replace EFC). *Average financial aid package:* $33,750 (excluding resources awarded to replace EFC). 17% of all full-time freshmen had no need and received non-need-based gift aid.

UNDERGRADUATE FINANCIAL AID (Fall 2017, est.) 944 applied for aid; of those 93% were deemed to have need. 99% of undergraduates with need received aid; of those 17% had need fully met. *Average percent of need met:* 75% (excluding resources awarded to replace EFC). *Average financial aid package:* $31,801 (excluding resources awarded to replace EFC). 25% of all full-time undergraduates had no need and received non-need-based gift aid.

GIFT AID (NEED-BASED) *Total amount:* $23,582,766 (11% federal, 10% state, 78% institutional, 1% external sources). *Receiving aid:* Freshmen: 83% (275); all full-time undergraduates: 74% (865). *Average award:* Freshmen: $29,648; Undergraduates: $27,055. *Scholarships, grants, and awards:* Federal Pell, FSEOG, state, private, college/university gift aid from institutional funds.

GIFT AID (NON-NEED-BASED) *Total amount:* $7,491,021 (6% state, 94% institutional). *Receiving aid:* Freshmen: 12% (39). Undergraduates: 10% (116). *Average award:* Freshmen: $24,179. Undergraduates: $21,483. *Scholarships, grants, and awards by category:* Academic interests/achievement: biological sciences, business, communication, English, foreign languages, general academic interests/achievements, humanities, international studies, mathematics, social sciences. *Creative arts/performance:* art/fine arts, journalism/publications, music, performing arts, theater/drama. *Special achievements/activities:* community service, leadership, memberships, religious involvement. *Special characteristics:* children of faculty/staff, siblings of current students. *Tuition waivers:* Full or partial for employees or children of employees. *ROTC:* Army cooperative, Naval cooperative, Air Force cooperative.

LOANS *Student loans:* $7,665,496 (77% need-based, 23% non-need-based). 69% of past graduating class borrowed through all loan programs. *Average indebtedness per student:* $28,495. *Average need-based loan:* Freshmen: $3353. Undergraduates: $4199. *Parent loans:* $2,402,552 (56% need-based, 44% non-need-based). *Programs:* Federal Direct (Subsidized and Unsubsidized Stafford, PLUS), Perkins, state.

WORK-STUDY *Federal work-study:* Total amount: $167,121; 101 jobs averaging $1713.

APPLYING FOR FINANCIAL AID *Required financial aid form:* FAFSA. *Financial aid deadline (priority):* 2/15. *Notification date:* Continuous beginning 11/1. Students must reply by 5/1.

CONTACT Mr. Chris Summers, Director of Financial Aid, Oglethorpe University, 4484 Peachtree Road NE, Atlanta, GA 30319, 404-364-8355 or toll-free 800-428-4484. *Fax:* 404-364-8359. *E-mail:* csummers@oglethorpe.edu. *Website:* http://www.oglethorpe.edu/.

OHIO CHRISTIAN UNIVERSITY
Circleville, OH

CONTACT Michael Fracassa, Assistant Vice President of Finance, Ohio Christian University, 1476 Lancaster Pike, PO Box 458, Circleville, OH 43113-9487, 740-477-7758 or toll-free 877-762-8669. *Fax:* 740-477-5921. *E-mail:* mfracassa@ohiochristian.edu. *Website:* http://www.ohiochristian.edu/.

OHIO DOMINICAN UNIVERSITY
Columbus, OH

CONTACT Ms. Cynthia A. Hahn, Director of Financial Aid, Ohio Dominican University, 1216 Sunbury Road, Columbus, OH 43219, 614-251-4778 or toll-free 800-955-6446. *Fax:* 614-251-4456. *E-mail:* fin-aid@ohiodominican.edu. *Website:* http://www.ohiodominican.edu/.

OHIO NORTHERN UNIVERSITY
Ada, OH

Tuition & fees: $32,260	Average undergraduate aid package: $27,756

ABOUT THE INSTITUTION Independent United Methodist Church, coed. *Awards:* certificates, bachelor's, master's, and doctoral degrees. 127 undergraduate majors. *Total enrollment:* 3,088. Undergraduates: 2,312. Freshmen: 640. Federal methodology is used as a basis for awarding need-based institutional aid.

UNDERGRADUATE EXPENSES for 2018–2019 *Comprehensive fee:* $43,910 includes full-time tuition ($31,350), mandatory fees ($910), and room and board ($11,650). Full-time tuition and fees vary according to course load, degree level, and program. Room and board charges vary according to board plan, housing facility, and student level. *Part-time tuition:* $1310 per credit hour. Part-time tuition and fees vary according to course load, degree level, and program.

FRESHMAN FINANCIAL AID (Fall 2017, est.) 621 applied for aid; of those 89% were deemed to have need. 100% of freshmen with need received aid; of those 24% had need fully met. *Average percent of need met:* 24% (excluding resources awarded to replace EFC). *Average financial aid package:* $27,782 (excluding resources awarded to replace EFC). 12% of all full-time freshmen had no need and received non-need-based gift aid.

UNDERGRADUATE FINANCIAL AID (Fall 2017, est.) 1,881 applied for aid; of those 90% were deemed to have need. 100% of undergraduates with need received aid; of those 23% had need fully met. *Average percent of need met:* 23% (excluding resources awarded to replace EFC). *Average financial aid package:* $27,756 (excluding resources awarded to replace EFC). 16% of all full-time undergraduates had no need and received non-need-based gift aid.

GIFT AID (NEED-BASED) *Total amount:* $37,832,758 (7% federal, 4% state, 86% institutional, 3% external sources). *Receiving aid:* Freshmen: 86% (552); all full-time undergraduates: 81% (1,679). *Average award:* Freshmen: $24,714; Undergraduates: $23,399. *Scholarships, grants, and awards:* Federal Pell, FSEOG, state, private, college/university gift aid from institutional funds.

GIFT AID (NON-NEED-BASED) *Total amount:* $5,202,583 (1% state, 98% institutional, 1% external sources). *Average award:* Freshmen: $16,538. Undergraduates: $14,791. *Scholarships, grants, and awards by category:* Academic interests/achievement: biological sciences, business, communication, computer science, education, engineering/technologies, English, foreign languages, general academic interests/achievements, health fields, humanities, international studies, mathematics, physical sciences, premedicine, religion/biblical studies, social sciences. *Creative arts/performance:* applied art and design, art/fine arts, creative writing, dance, journalism/publications, music, performing arts, theater/drama. *Special achievements/activities:* community service, general special achievements/activities, junior miss, leadership. *Special characteristics:* children and siblings of alumni, children of faculty/staff, ethnic background, international students, out-of-state students, relatives of clergy, religious affiliation, siblings of current students, veterans. *Tuition waivers:* Full or partial for minority students, children of alumni, employees or children of employees. **ROTC:** Army cooperative, Air Force cooperative.

LOANS *Student loans:* $15,823,900 (41% need-based, 59% non-need-based). *Average need-based loan:* Freshmen: $4024. Undergraduates: $5458. *Parent loans:* $4,426,757 (100% non-need-based). *Programs:* Federal Direct (Subsidized and Unsubsidized Stafford, PLUS), Perkins, state, college/university, Health Professions Student Loans (HPSL).

WORK-STUDY *Federal work-study:* Total amount: $292,186; jobs available. *State or other work-study/employment:* Total amount: $243,010 (100% need-based). Part-time jobs available.

APPLYING FOR FINANCIAL AID *Required financial aid form:* FAFSA. *Financial aid deadline (priority):* 3/1. *Notification date:* Continuous beginning 12/1. Students must reply within 2 weeks of notification.

CONTACT Melanie Weaver, Director of Financial Aid, Ohio Northern University, 525 South Main Street, Ada, OH 45810, 419-772-2272 or toll-free 888-408-4ONU. *Fax:* 419-772-2313. *E-mail:* m-weaver.2@onu.edu. *Website:* http://www.onu.edu/.

economics, humanities, international studies, mathematics, military science, physical sciences, premedicine, social sciences. *Creative arts/performance:* creative writing, dance, journalism/publications, music, performing arts, theater/drama. *Special achievements/activities:* cheerleading/drum major, hobbies/interests, leadership, memberships. *Special characteristics:* adult students, children and siblings of alumni, children of faculty/staff, children of public servants, children of union members/company employees, children of workers in trades, ethnic background, handicapped students, members of minority groups, out-of-state students, previous college experience. *Tuition waivers:* Full or partial for employees or children of employees, senior citizens. **ROTC:** Army, Naval, Air Force.

LOANS *Student loans:* $197,825,607 (60% need-based, 40% non-need-based). 53% of past graduating class borrowed through all loan programs. *Average indebtedness per student:* $28,158. *Average need-based loan:* Freshmen: $3566. Undergraduates: $4767. *Parent loans:* $48,336,349 (100% non-need-based). *Programs:* Federal Direct (Subsidized and Unsubsidized Stafford, PLUS), Perkins, Federal Nursing, state, college/university.

WORK-STUDY *Federal work-study:* Total amount: $5,260,224; 1,821 jobs averaging $2889. *State or other work-study/employment:* Total amount: $2500 (100% non-need-based). 1 part-time job averaging $2500.

ATHLETIC AWARDS Total amount: $19,247,665 (100% non-need-based).

APPLYING FOR FINANCIAL AID *Required financial aid form:* FAFSA. *Financial aid deadline (priority):* 2/1. *Notification date:* 3/15. Students must reply by 5/1 or within 4 weeks of notification.

CONTACT Ms. Diane Corbett, Executive Director of Student Financial Aid, The Ohio State University, 281 West Lane Avenue, 4th Floor, Columbus, OH 43210, 614-292-8595. *E-mail:* buckeyelink@osu.edu. *Website:* http://www.osu.edu/.

THE OHIO STATE UNIVERSITY
Columbus, OH

Tuition & fees (OH res): $10,591	Average undergraduate aid package: $13,960

ABOUT THE INSTITUTION State-supported, coed. *Awards:* certificates, diplomas, associate, bachelor's, master's, and doctoral degrees. 159 undergraduate majors. *Total enrollment:* 59,837. Undergraduates: 45,946. Freshmen: 7,209. Federal methodology is used as a basis for awarding need-based institutional aid.

UNDERGRADUATE EXPENSES for 2017–2018 *Application fee:* $60. *Tuition, state resident:* full-time $10,591; part-time $480.10 per credit hour. *Tuition, nonresident:* full-time $29,695; part-time $1276 per credit hour. Full-time tuition and fees vary according to course load, degree level, location, program, reciprocity agreements, and student level. Part-time tuition and fees vary according to course load, degree level, location, program, reciprocity agreements, and student level. *College room and board:* $12,252. Room and board charges vary according to board plan, housing facility, and location. *Payment plan:* Guaranteed tuition.

FRESHMAN FINANCIAL AID (Fall 2017, est.) 5,869 applied for aid; of those 59% were deemed to have need. 99% of freshmen with need received aid; of those 24% had need fully met. *Average percent of need met:* 73% (excluding resources awarded to replace EFC). *Average financial aid package:* $14,976 (excluding resources awarded to replace EFC). 26% of all full-time freshmen had no need and received non-need-based gift aid.

UNDERGRADUATE FINANCIAL AID (Fall 2017, est.) 27,918 applied for aid; of those 71% were deemed to have need. 99% of undergraduates with need received aid; of those 19% had need fully met. *Average percent of need met:* 70% (excluding resources awarded to replace EFC). *Average financial aid package:* $13,960 (excluding resources awarded to replace EFC). 19% of all full-time undergraduates had no need and received non-need-based gift aid.

GIFT AID (NEED-BASED) *Total amount:* $177,839,167 (25% federal, 6% state, 64% institutional, 5% external sources). *Receiving aid:* Freshmen: 45% (3,236); all full-time undergraduates: 41% (17,285). *Average award:* Freshmen: $11,497; Undergraduates: $10,325. *Scholarships, grants, and awards:* Federal Pell, FSEOG, state, private, college/university gift aid from institutional funds.

GIFT AID (NON-NEED-BASED) *Total amount:* $87,454,209 (1% federal, 2% state, 85% institutional, 12% external sources). *Receiving aid:* Freshmen: 4% (288). Undergraduates: 2% (864). *Average award:* Freshmen: $6886. Undergraduates: $7189. *Scholarships, grants, and awards by category:* Academic interests/achievement: agriculture, architecture, area/ethnic studies, biological sciences, business, communication, computer science, education, engineering/technologies, English, foreign languages, general academic interests/achievements, health fields, home

OHIO UNIVERSITY
Athens, OH

Tuition & fees (OH res): $11,896	Average undergraduate aid package: $8870

ABOUT THE INSTITUTION State-supported, coed. *Awards:* certificates, associate, bachelor's, master's, and doctoral degrees. 116 undergraduate majors. *Total enrollment:* 29,525. Undergraduates: 23,323. Freshmen: 4,056. Institutional methodology is used as a basis for awarding need-based institutional aid.

UNDERGRADUATE EXPENSES for 2017–2018 *Application fee:* $50. *Tuition, state resident:* full-time $11,896; part-time $563 per semester hour. *Tuition, nonresident:* full-time $21,360; part-time $1029 per semester hour. Full-time tuition and fees vary according to degree level, location, program, and reciprocity agreements. Part-time tuition and fees vary according to course load, degree level, location, program, and reciprocity agreements. *College room and board:* $11,498; *Room only:* $6822. Room and board charges vary according to board plan. *Payment plan:* Guaranteed tuition.

FRESHMAN FINANCIAL AID (Fall 2017, est.) 3,299 applied for aid; of those 75% were deemed to have need. 100% of freshmen with need received aid; of those 41% had need fully met. *Average percent of need met:* 56% (excluding resources awarded to replace EFC). *Average financial aid package:* $9672 (excluding resources awarded to replace EFC). 7% of all full-time freshmen had no need and received non-need-based gift aid.

UNDERGRADUATE FINANCIAL AID (Fall 2017, est.) 12,550 applied for aid; of those 80% were deemed to have need. 100% of undergraduates with need received aid; of those 36% had need fully met. *Average percent of need met:* 48% (excluding resources awarded to replace EFC). *Average financial aid package:* $8870 (excluding resources awarded to replace EFC). 9% of all full-time undergraduates had no need and received non-need-based gift aid.

GIFT AID (NEED-BASED) *Total amount:* $66,028,990 (39% federal, 7% state, 49% institutional, 5% external sources). *Receiving aid:* Freshmen: 56% (2,242); all full-time undergraduates: 45% (7,847). *Average award:* Freshmen: $6847; Undergraduates: $6200. *Scholarships, grants, and awards:* Federal Pell, FSEOG, state, private, college/university gift aid from institutional funds.

GIFT AID (NON-NEED-BASED) *Total amount:* $10,477,455 (1% federal, 3% state, 91% institutional, 5% external sources). *Receiving aid:* Freshmen: 7% (288). Undergraduates: 9% (1,579). *Average award:* Freshmen: $4017. Undergraduates: $4432. *Scholarships, grants, and awards by category:* Academic interests/achievement: area/ethnic studies, biological sciences, business, communication, computer science, education, engineering/technologies, English, foreign languages, general academic interests/achievements, health fields, home economics, humanities, international studies, mathematics, military science, physical sciences, premedicine, social sciences. *Creative arts/performance:* applied art and design, art/fine arts, cinema/film/broadcasting, creative writing, dance, debating, journalism/publications, music, performing arts, theater/drama. *Special characteristics:* children and siblings of alumni, children of faculty/staff, first-generation college students. *Tuition waivers:* Full or partial for employees or children of employees, senior citizens. *ROTC:* Army, Air Force.

LOANS *Student loans:* $116,409,827 (89% need-based, 11% non-need-based). 67% of past graduating class borrowed through all loan programs. *Average indebtedness per student:* $27,993. *Average need-based loan:* Freshmen: $3294. Undergraduates: $3064. *Parent loans:* $37,166,933 (45% need-based, 55% non-need-based). *Programs:* Federal Direct (Subsidized and Unsubsidized Stafford, PLUS), Perkins, state, college/university.

WORK-STUDY *Federal work-study:* Total amount: $1,335,037; 681 jobs averaging $1839. *State or other work-study/employment:* Total amount: $16,476,926 (100% non-need-based). Part-time jobs available.

ATHLETIC AWARDS Total amount: $7,879,777 (28% need-based, 72% non-need-based).

APPLYING FOR FINANCIAL AID *Required financial aid form:* FAFSA. *Financial aid deadline (priority):* 1/15. *Notification date:* 2/1.

CONTACT Ms. Valerie K. Miller, Director of Financial Aid, Ohio University, 020 Chubb Hall, Athens, OH 45701-2979, 740-593-9853. *Fax:* 740-593-4140. *E-mail:* millerv@ohio.edu.
Website: http://www.ohio.edu/.

OHIO UNIVERSITY–CHILLICOTHE
Chillicothe, OH

Tuition & fees: N/R	Average undergraduate aid package: $6088

ABOUT THE INSTITUTION State-supported, coed. 22 undergraduate majors. Federal methodology is used as a basis for awarding need-based institutional aid.

FRESHMAN FINANCIAL AID (Fall 2017, est.) 234 applied for aid; of those 83% were deemed to have need. 100% of freshmen with need received aid; of those 13% had need fully met. *Average percent of need met:* 52% (excluding resources awarded to replace EFC). *Average financial aid package:* $6471 (excluding resources awarded to replace EFC). 1% of all full-time freshmen had no need and received non-need-based gift aid.

UNDERGRADUATE FINANCIAL AID (Fall 2017, est.) 759 applied for aid; of those 87% were deemed to have need. 100% of undergraduates with need received aid; of those 14% had need fully met. *Average percent of need met:* 42% (excluding resources awarded to replace EFC). *Average financial aid package:* $6088 (excluding resources awarded to replace EFC). 1% of all full-time undergraduates had no need and received non-need-based gift aid.

GIFT AID (NEED-BASED) *Total amount:* $4,508,270 (81% federal, 1% state, 14% institutional, 4% external sources). *Receiving aid:* Freshmen: 55% (169); all full-time undergraduates: 53% (554). *Average award:* Freshmen: $5436; Undergraduates: $4718. *Scholarships, grants, and awards:* Federal Pell, FSEOG, state, private, college/university gift aid from institutional funds.

GIFT AID (NON-NEED-BASED) *Total amount:* $108,037 (3% federal, 8% state, 56% institutional, 33% external sources). *Receiving aid:* Freshmen: 1% (2). Undergraduates: 3. *Average award:* Freshmen: $3433. Undergraduates: $4042. *Scholarships, grants, and awards by category:* Academic interests/achievement: area/ethnic studies, biological sciences, business, communication, computer science, education, engineering/technologies, English, foreign languages, general academic interests/achievements, health fields, home economics, humanities, mathematics, military science, physical sciences, premedicine, social sciences. *Creative arts/performance:* applied art and design, art/fine arts, cinema/film/broadcasting, creative writing, dance, debating, journalism/publications, music, performing arts, theater/drama. *Special characteristics:* children and siblings of alumni, children of faculty/staff, first-generation college students.

LOANS *Student loans:* $4,292,320 (94% need-based, 6% non-need-based). 67% of past graduating class borrowed through all loan programs. *Average indebtedness per student:* $27,993. *Average need-based loan:* Freshmen: $2660. Undergraduates: $2865. *Parent loans:* $78,999 (13% need-based, 87% non-need-based). *Programs:*

Federal Direct (Subsidized and Unsubsidized Stafford, PLUS), Perkins, state, college/university.

WORK-STUDY *Federal work-study:* Total amount: $37,398; 19 jobs averaging $1615.

APPLYING FOR FINANCIAL AID *Required financial aid form:* FAFSA. *Financial aid deadline (priority):* 1/15. *Notification date:* 2/1.

CONTACT Ms. Valerie K. Miller, Director of Financial Aid, Ohio University–Chillicothe, 020 Chubb Hall, Athens, OH 45701-2979, 740-593-4141 or toll-free 877-462-6824. *Fax:* 740-593-4140. *E-mail:* millerv@ohio.edu.
Website: http://www.chillicothe.ohiou.edu/.

OHIO UNIVERSITY–EASTERN
St. Clairsville, OH

Tuition & fees (OH res): $5050	Average undergraduate aid package: $6031

ABOUT THE INSTITUTION State-supported, coed. *Awards:* associate, bachelor's, and master's degrees (also offers some graduate courses). 11 undergraduate majors. *Total enrollment:* 751. Undergraduates: 751. Federal methodology is used as a basis for awarding need-based institutional aid.

UNDERGRADUATE EXPENSES for 2017–2018 *Application fee:* $20. *Tuition, state resident:* full-time $4984; part-time $219 per credit hour. *Tuition, nonresident:* full-time $6652; part-time $305 per credit hour. *Required fees:* full-time $66; $3 per credit hour. Full-time tuition and fees vary according to course load, location, program, reciprocity agreements, and student level. Part-time tuition and fees vary according to course load, location, program, reciprocity agreements, and student level.

FRESHMAN FINANCIAL AID (Fall 2017, est.) 69 applied for aid; of those 72% were deemed to have need. 100% of freshmen with need received aid; of those 10% had need fully met. *Average percent of need met:* 44% (excluding resources awarded to replace EFC). *Average financial aid package:* $5787 (excluding resources awarded to replace EFC).

UNDERGRADUATE FINANCIAL AID (Fall 2017, est.) 243 applied for aid; of those 79% were deemed to have need. 100% of undergraduates with need received aid; of those 13% had need fully met. *Average percent of need met:* 42% (excluding resources awarded to replace EFC). *Average financial aid package:* $6031 (excluding resources awarded to replace EFC).

GIFT AID (NEED-BASED) *Total amount:* $1,231,854 (75% federal, 22% institutional, 3% external sources). *Receiving aid:* Freshmen: 41% (45); all full-time undergraduates: 47% (170). *Average award:* Freshmen: $5069; Undergraduates: $4637. *Scholarships, grants, and awards:* Federal Pell, FSEOG, state, college/university gift aid from institutional funds.

GIFT AID (NON-NEED-BASED) *Total amount:* $43,436 (73% institutional, 27% external sources). *Scholarships, grants, and awards by category:* Academic interests/achievement: area/ethnic studies, biological sciences, business, communication, computer science, education, engineering/technologies, English, foreign languages, general academic interests/achievements, health fields, home economics, humanities, international studies, mathematics, military science, physical sciences, premedicine, social sciences. *Creative arts/performance:* applied art and design, art/fine arts, cinema/film/broadcasting, creative writing, dance, debating, journalism/publications, music, performing arts, theater/drama. *Special characteristics:* children and siblings of alumni, children of faculty/staff, first-generation college students. *Tuition waivers:* Full or partial for employees or children of employees, senior citizens.

LOANS *Student loans:* $940,028 (99% need-based, 1% non-need-based). 67% of past graduating class borrowed through all loan programs. *Average indebtedness per student:* $27,993. *Average need-based loan:* Freshmen: $3025. Undergraduates: $3025. *Parent loans:* $3426 (100% need-based). *Programs:* Federal Direct (Subsidized and Unsubsidized Stafford, PLUS), Perkins, state, college/university.

WORK-STUDY *Federal work-study:* Total amount: $19,413; 11 jobs averaging $1467.

APPLYING FOR FINANCIAL AID *Required financial aid form:* FAFSA. *Financial aid deadline (priority):* 1/15. *Notification date:* 2/1.

CONTACT Ms. Valerie K. Miller, Director of Financial Aid, Ohio University–Eastern, 020 Chubb Hall, Athens, OH 45701-2979, 740-593-4141 or toll-free 800-648-3331. *Fax:* 740-593-4140. *E-mail:* millerv@ohio.edu.
Website: http://www.eastern.ohiou.edu/.

OHIO UNIVERSITY–LANCASTER
Lancaster, OH

Tuition & fees: N/R	Average undergraduate aid package: $5519

ABOUT THE INSTITUTION State-supported, coed. 14 undergraduate majors. Federal methodology is used as a basis for awarding need-based institutional aid.

FRESHMAN FINANCIAL AID (Fall 2017, est.) 228 applied for aid; of those 77% were deemed to have need. 100% of freshmen with need received aid; of those 18% had need fully met. *Average percent of need met:* 45% (excluding resources awarded to replace EFC). *Average financial aid package:* $5511 (excluding resources awarded to replace EFC).

UNDERGRADUATE FINANCIAL AID (Fall 2017, est.) 668 applied for aid; of those 83% were deemed to have need. 100% of undergraduates with need received aid; of those 15% had need fully met. *Average percent of need met:* 41% (excluding resources awarded to replace EFC). *Average financial aid package:* $5519 (excluding resources awarded to replace EFC).

GIFT AID (NEED-BASED) Total amount: $3,251,401 (83% federal, 15% institutional, 2% external sources). *Receiving aid:* Freshmen: 42% (149); all full-time undergraduates: 44% (436). *Average award:* Freshmen: $4795; Undergraduates: $4365. *Scholarships, grants, and awards:* Federal Pell, FSEOG, state, private, college/university gift aid from institutional funds.

GIFT AID (NON-NEED-BASED) Total amount: $77,648 (6% state, 69% institutional, 25% external sources). *Scholarships, grants, and awards by category:* Academic interests/achievement: area/ethnic studies, biological sciences, business, communication, computer science, education, engineering/technologies, English, foreign languages, general academic interests/achievements, health fields, home economics, humanities, international studies, mathematics, military science, physical sciences, premedicine, social sciences. *Creative arts/performance:* applied art and design, art/fine arts, cinema/film/broadcasting, creative writing, dance, debating, journalism/publications, music, performing arts, theater/drama. *Special characteristics:* children and siblings of alumni, children of faculty/staff, first-generation college students.

LOANS Student loans: $3,279,905 (96% need-based, 4% non-need-based). 67% of past graduating class borrowed through all loan programs. *Average indebtedness per student:* $27,993. *Average need-based loan:* Freshmen: $2490. Undergraduates: $2804. *Parent loans:* $94,038 (34% need-based, 66% non-need-based). *Programs:* Federal Direct (Subsidized and Unsubsidized Stafford, PLUS), Perkins, state, college/university.

WORK-STUDY Federal work-study: Total amount: $25,940; 8 jobs averaging $1452.

APPLYING FOR FINANCIAL AID Required financial aid form: FAFSA. *Financial aid deadline (priority):* 1/15. *Notification date:* 2/1.

CONTACT Ms. Valerie K. Miller, Director of Financial Aid, Ohio University–Lancaster, 020 Chubb Hall, Athens, OH 45701-2979, 740-593-4141 or toll-free 888-446-4468. *Fax:* 740-593-4140. *E-mail:* millerv@ohio.edu. *Website:* http://www.ohiou.edu/lancaster/.

OHIO UNIVERSITY–SOUTHERN CAMPUS
Ironton, OH

Tuition & fees: N/R	Average undergraduate aid package: $5787

ABOUT THE INSTITUTION State-supported, coed. 17 undergraduate majors. Both federal and institutional methodology are used as a basis for awarding need-based institutional aid.

FRESHMAN FINANCIAL AID (Fall 2017, est.) 158 applied for aid; of those 83% were deemed to have need. 100% of freshmen with need received aid; of those 15% had need fully met. *Average percent of need met:* 52% (excluding resources awarded to replace EFC). *Average financial aid package:* $5725 (excluding resources awarded to replace EFC).

UNDERGRADUATE FINANCIAL AID (Fall 2017, est.) 759 applied for aid; of those 88% were deemed to have need. 100% of undergraduates with need received aid; of those 15% had need fully met. *Average percent of need met:* 44% (excluding resources awarded to replace EFC). *Average financial aid package:* $5787 (excluding resources awarded to replace EFC).

GIFT AID (NEED-BASED) Total amount: $4,151,124 (81% federal, 17% institutional, 2% external sources). *Receiving aid:* Freshmen: 63% (125); all full-time undergraduates: 67% (615). *Average award:* Freshmen: $4383; Undergraduates: $4125. *Scholarships, grants, and awards:* Federal Pell, FSEOG, state, private, college/university gift aid from institutional funds.

GIFT AID (NON-NEED-BASED) Total amount: $72,299 (3% federal, 87% institutional, 10% external sources). *Scholarships, grants, and awards by category:* Academic interests/achievement: area/ethnic studies, biological sciences, business, communication, computer science, education, engineering/technologies, English, foreign languages, general academic interests/achievements, health fields, home economics, humanities, international studies, mathematics, military science, physical sciences, premedicine, social sciences. *Creative arts/performance:* applied art and design, art/fine arts, cinema/film/broadcasting, creative writing, dance, debating, journalism/publications, music, performing arts, theater/drama. *Special characteristics:* children and siblings of alumni, children of faculty/staff, first-generation college students.

LOANS Student loans: $3,773,662 (95% need-based, 5% non-need-based). 67% of past graduating class borrowed through all loan programs. *Average indebtedness per student:* $27,993. *Average need-based loan:* Freshmen: $2806. Undergraduates: $3090. *Parent loans:* $89,013 (28% need-based, 72% non-need-based). *Programs:* Federal Direct (Subsidized and Unsubsidized Stafford, PLUS), Perkins, state, college/university.

WORK-STUDY Federal work-study: Total amount: $31,777; 18 jobs averaging $1764.

APPLYING FOR FINANCIAL AID Required financial aid form: FAFSA. *Financial aid deadline (priority):* 1/15. *Notification date:* 2/1.

CONTACT Ms. Valerie K. Miller, Director of Financial Aid, Ohio University–Southern Campus, 020 Chubb Hall, Athens, OH 45701-2979, 740-593-4141 or toll-free 800-626-0513. *Fax:* 740-593-4140. *E-mail:* millerv@ohio.edu. *Website:* http://www.ohiou.edu/.

OHIO UNIVERSITY–ZANESVILLE
Zanesville, OH

Tuition & fees (OH res): $5076	Average undergraduate aid package: $5805

ABOUT THE INSTITUTION State-supported, coed. *Awards:* associate and bachelor's degrees (offers first 2 years of most bachelor's degree programs available at the main campus in Athens; also offers several bachelor's degree programs that can be completed at this campus; also offers some graduate courses). 5 undergraduate majors. *Total enrollment:* 1,878. Undergraduates: 1,878. Freshmen: 228. Federal methodology is used as a basis for awarding need-based institutional aid.

UNDERGRADUATE EXPENSES for 2017–2018 Application fee: $20. *Tuition, state resident:* full-time $4984; part-time $234 per semester hour. *Tuition, nonresident:* full-time $8624; part-time $413 per semester hour. *Required fees:* full-time $92. Full-time tuition and fees vary according to course load and student level. Part-time tuition and fees vary according to course load and student level.

FRESHMAN FINANCIAL AID (Fall 2017, est.) 162 applied for aid; of those 80% were deemed to have need. 100% of freshmen with need received aid; of those 11% had need fully met. *Average percent of need met:* 51% (excluding resources awarded to replace EFC). *Average financial aid package:* $5835 (excluding resources awarded to replace EFC).

UNDERGRADUATE FINANCIAL AID (Fall 2017, est.) 633 applied for aid; of those 81% were deemed to have need. 100% of undergraduates with need received aid; of those 14% had need fully met. *Average percent of need met:* 43% (excluding resources awarded to replace EFC). *Average financial aid package:* $5805 (excluding resources awarded to replace EFC).

GIFT AID (NEED-BASED) Total amount: $3,012,751 (80% federal, 16% institutional, 4% external sources). *Receiving aid:* Freshmen: 53% (111); all full-time undergraduates: 54% (434). *Average award:* Freshmen: $4953; Undergraduates: $4478. *Scholarships, grants, and awards:* Federal Pell, FSEOG, state, private, college/university gift aid from institutional funds.

GIFT AID (NON-NEED-BASED) Total amount: $24,570 (29% state, 71% institutional). *Scholarships, grants, and awards by category:* Academic interests/achievement: area/ethnic studies, biological sciences, business, communication, computer science, education, engineering/technologies, English, foreign languages, general academic interests/achievements, health fields, home economics, humanities, international studies, mathematics, military science, physical sciences, premedicine, social sciences. *Creative arts/performance:* applied art and design, art/fine arts, cinema/film/broadcasting, creative writing, dance, debating, journalism/publications, music, performing arts, theater/drama. *Special characteristics:* children and siblings of alumni, children of faculty/staff, first-generation college students. *Tuition waivers:* Full or partial for employees or children of employees, senior citizens.

LOANS *Student loans:* $2,938,918 (96% need-based, 4% non-need-based). 67% of past graduating class borrowed through all loan programs. *Average indebtedness per student:* $27,993. *Average need-based loan:* Freshmen: $2594. Undergraduates: $2911. *Parent loans:* $55,543 (76% need-based, 24% non-need-based). *Programs:* Federal Direct (Subsidized and Unsubsidized Stafford, PLUS), Perkins, state, college/university.

WORK-STUDY *Federal work-study:* Total amount: $17,278; 8 jobs averaging $1579.

APPLYING FOR FINANCIAL AID *Required financial aid form:* FAFSA. *Financial aid deadline (priority):* 1/15. *Notification date:* 2/1.

CONTACT Ms. Valerie K. Miller, Director of Financial Aid, Ohio University–Zanesville, 020 Chubb Hall, Athens, OH 45701-2979, 740-593-4141. *Fax:* 740-593-4140. *E-mail:* millerv@ohio.edu.
Website: http://www.ohio.edu/zanesville/.

OHIO VALLEY UNIVERSITY
Vienna, WV

Tuition & fees: $21,100	Average undergraduate aid package: $15,748

ABOUT THE INSTITUTION Independent Church of Christ, coed. *Awards:* certificates, associate, bachelor's, and master's degrees. 16 undergraduate majors. *Total enrollment:* 433. Undergraduates: 403. Freshmen: 116. Federal methodology is used as a basis for awarding need-based institutional aid.

UNDERGRADUATE EXPENSES for 2017–2018 *Comprehensive fee:* $28,800 includes full-time tuition ($21,100) and room and board ($7700). *College room only:* $3850. Full-time tuition and fees vary according to course load. Room and board charges vary according to board plan, housing facility, and location. *Part-time tuition:* $825 per credit hour. Part-time tuition and fees vary according to course load.

FRESHMAN FINANCIAL AID (Fall 2016) 109 applied for aid; of those 92% were deemed to have need. 95% of freshmen with need received aid; of those 15% had need fully met. *Average percent of need met:* 52% (excluding resources awarded to replace EFC). *Average financial aid package:* $13,511 (excluding resources awarded to replace EFC). 24% of all full-time freshmen had no need and received non-need-based gift aid.

UNDERGRADUATE FINANCIAL AID (Fall 2016) 535 applied for aid; of those 70% were deemed to have need. 86% of undergraduates with need received aid; of those 19% had need fully met. *Average percent of need met:* 58% (excluding resources awarded to replace EFC). *Average financial aid package:* $15,748 (excluding resources awarded to replace EFC). 13% of all full-time undergraduates had no need and received non-need-based gift aid.

GIFT AID (NEED-BASED) *Total amount:* $2,748,239 (32% federal, 7% state, 57% institutional, 4% external sources). *Receiving aid:* Freshmen: 83% (90); all full-time undergraduates: 59% (316). *Average award:* Freshmen: $13,381; Undergraduates: $12,900. *Scholarships, grants, and awards:* Federal Pell, FSEOG, state, private, college/university gift aid from institutional funds.

GIFT AID (NON-NEED-BASED) *Total amount:* $615,515 (8% state, 83% institutional, 9% external sources). *Receiving aid:* Freshmen: 11% (12). Undergraduates: 9% (50). *Average award:* Freshmen: $3978. Undergraduates: $5617. *Scholarships, grants, and awards by category:* Academic interests/achievement: business, computer science, education, English, general academic interests/achievements, mathematics, religion/biblical studies. *Creative arts/performance:* general creative arts/performance, journalism/publications, music, performing arts, theater/drama. *Special achievements/activities:* community service, general special achievements/activities, leadership, religious involvement. *Special characteristics:* adult students, children of faculty/staff, ethnic background, general special characteristics, international students, local/state students, relatives of clergy, religious affiliation. *Tuition waivers:* Full or partial for employees or children of employees.

LOANS *Student loans:* $1,949,154 (80% need-based, 20% non-need-based). 80% of past graduating class borrowed through all loan programs. *Average need-based loan:* Freshmen: $2866. Undergraduates: $3566. *Parent loans:* $433,665 (65% need-based, 35% non-need-based). *Programs:* Federal Direct (Subsidized and Unsubsidized Stafford, PLUS), Perkins.

WORK-STUDY *Federal work-study:* jobs available. *State or other work-study/employment:* Part-time jobs available.

ATHLETIC AWARDS Total amount: $1,328,343 (100% need-based).

APPLYING FOR FINANCIAL AID *Required financial aid form:* FAFSA. *Financial aid deadline (priority):* 3/1. *Notification date:* Continuous beginning 1/1. Students must reply within 4 weeks of notification.

CONTACT Lindsay Cole, Director of Financial Aid, Ohio Valley University, 1 Campus View Drive, Vienna, WV 26105-8000, 304-865-6077 or toll-free 877-446-8668. *Fax:* 304-865-6001. *E-mail:* lindsay.cole@ovu.edu.
Website: http://www.ovu.edu/.

OHIO WESLEYAN UNIVERSITY
Delaware, OH

Tuition & fees: $45,740	Average undergraduate aid package: $36,326

ABOUT THE INSTITUTION Independent United Methodist, coed. *Awards:* bachelor's degrees. 87 undergraduate majors. *Total enrollment:* 1,565. Undergraduates: 1,565. Freshmen: 453. Federal methodology is used as a basis for awarding need-based institutional aid.

UNDERGRADUATE EXPENSES for 2018–2019 *Comprehensive fee:* $58,170 Includes full-time tuition ($45,500), mandatory fees ($240), and room and board ($12,430). *College room only:* $6800. Full-time tuition and fees vary according to course load. Room and board charges vary according to board plan and housing facility. *Part-time tuition:* $2720 per credit hour. Part-time tuition and fees vary according to course load.

FRESHMAN FINANCIAL AID (Fall 2016) 431 applied for aid; of those 88% were deemed to have need. 100% of freshmen with need received aid; of those 16% had need fully met. *Average percent of need met:* 79% (excluding resources awarded to replace EFC). *Average financial aid package:* $36,981 (excluding resources awarded to replace EFC). 22% of all full-time freshmen had no need and received non-need-based gift aid.

UNDERGRADUATE FINANCIAL AID (Fall 2016) 1,294 applied for aid; of those 89% were deemed to have need. 100% of undergraduates with need received aid; of those 20% had need fully met. *Average percent of need met:* 79% (excluding resources awarded to replace EFC). *Average financial aid package:* $36,326 (excluding resources awarded to replace EFC). 28% of all full-time undergraduates had no need and received non-need-based gift aid.

GIFT AID (NEED-BASED) *Total amount:* $35,534,678 (7% federal, 1% state, 91% institutional, 1% external sources). *Receiving aid:* Freshmen: 78% (381); all full-time undergraduates: 71% (1,156). *Average award:* Freshmen: $32,215; Undergraduates: $30,716. *Scholarships, grants, and awards:* Federal Pell, FSEOG, state, private, college/university gift aid from institutional funds.

GIFT AID (NON-NEED-BASED) *Total amount:* $12,441,937 (99% institutional, 1% external sources). *Receiving aid:* Freshmen: 12% (57). Undergraduates: 12% (191). *Average award:* Freshmen: $22,909. Undergraduates: $23,369. *Scholarships, grants, and awards by category:* Academic interests/achievement: business, education, general academic interests/achievements. *Creative arts/performance:* applied art and design, art/fine arts, dance, music, performing arts, theater/drama. *Special achievements/activities:* general special achievements/activities, leadership. *Special characteristics:* children and siblings of alumni, international students, local/state students, members of minority groups, relatives of clergy, religious affiliation, twins. *Tuition waivers:* Full or partial for employees or children of employees. *ROTC:* Army cooperative, Air Force cooperative.

LOANS *Student loans:* $11,920,916 (67% need-based, 33% non-need-based). 70% of past graduating class borrowed through all loan programs. *Average indebtedness per student:* $35,221. *Average need-based loan:* Freshmen: $3723. Undergraduates: $4850. *Parent loans:* $4,538,303 (42% need-based, 58% non-need-based). *Programs:* Federal Direct (Subsidized and Unsubsidized Stafford, PLUS), college/university.

WORK-STUDY *Federal work-study:* jobs available. *State or other work-study/employment:* Total amount: $641,010 (13% need-based, 87% non-need-based). Part-time jobs available.

APPLYING FOR FINANCIAL AID *Required financial aid form:* FAFSA. *Financial aid deadline (priority):* 12/1. *Notification date:* Continuous beginning 2/15. Students must reply by 5/1 or within 2 weeks of notification.

CONTACT Mr. Kevin Paskvan, Director of Financial Aid, Ohio Wesleyan University, 61 South Sandusky Street, Delaware, OH 43015, 740-368-3050 or toll-free 800-922-8953. *Fax:* 740-368-3066. *E-mail:* financialaid@owu.edu. *Website:* http://www.owu.edu/.

OHR HAMEIR THEOLOGICAL SEMINARY
Cortlandt Manor, NY

CONTACT Financial Aid Office, Ohr Hameir Theological Seminary, Furnace Woods Road, Peekskill, NY 10566, 914-736-1500.

OHR SOMAYACH/JOSEPH TANENBAUM EDUCATIONAL CENTER
Monsey, NY

CONTACT Financial Aid Office, Ohr Somayach/Joseph Tanenbaum Educational Center, PO Box 334244, Route 306, Monsey, NY 10952-0334, 914-425-1370. *Website:* http://ohr.edu/.

OKLAHOMA BAPTIST UNIVERSITY
Shawnee, OK

Tuition & fees: $28,258	Average undergraduate aid package: $23,506

ABOUT THE INSTITUTION Independent Southern Baptist, coed. *Awards:* associate, bachelor's, and master's degrees. 68 undergraduate majors. *Total enrollment:* 2,085. Undergraduates: 1,972. Freshmen: 570. Federal methodology is used as a basis for awarding need-based institutional aid.

UNDERGRADUATE EXPENSES for 2018–2019 *Comprehensive fee:* $35,608 includes full-time tuition ($25,138), mandatory fees ($3120), and room and board ($7350). *College room only:* $3310. Room and board charges vary according to housing facility. Part-time tuition and fees vary according to course load.

FRESHMAN FINANCIAL AID (Fall 2016) 526 applied for aid; of those 90% were deemed to have need. 100% of freshmen with need received aid; of those 26% had need fully met. *Average percent of need met:* 85% (excluding resources awarded to replace EFC). *Average financial aid package:* $24,504 (excluding resources awarded to replace EFC). 16% of all full-time freshmen had no need and received non-need-based gift aid.

UNDERGRADUATE FINANCIAL AID (Fall 2016) 1,486 applied for aid; of those 92% were deemed to have need. 100% of undergraduates with need received aid; of those 24% had need fully met. *Average percent of need met:* 81% (excluding resources awarded to replace EFC). *Average financial aid package:* $23,506 (excluding resources awarded to replace EFC). 23% of all full-time undergraduates had no need and received non-need-based gift aid.

GIFT AID (NEED-BASED) *Total amount:* $27,738,285 (14% federal, 5% state, 73% institutional, 8% external sources). *Receiving aid:* Freshmen: 63% (355); all full-time undergraduates: 55% (1,010). *Average award:* Freshmen: $7710; Undergraduates: $6904. *Scholarships, grants, and awards:* Federal Pell, FSEOG, state, private, college/university gift aid from institutional funds, TEACH Grants.

GIFT AID (NON-NEED-BASED) *Total amount:* $6,193,757 (97% institutional, 3% external sources). *Receiving aid:* Freshmen: 84% (474). Undergraduates: 71% (1,298). *Average award:* Freshmen: $11,069. Undergraduates: $10,725. *Scholarships, grants, and awards by category: Academic interests/achievement:* biological sciences, business, computer science, education, English, foreign languages, general academic interests/achievements, health fields, humanities, mathematics, physical sciences, premedicine, religion/biblical studies, social sciences. *Creative arts/performance:* applied art and design, art/fine arts, music, performing arts, theater/drama. *Special achievements/activities:* cheerleading/drum major, leadership, religious

involvement. *Special characteristics:* adult students, children and siblings of alumni, children of faculty/staff, general special characteristics, international students, local/state students, members of minority groups, out-of-state students, relatives of clergy, religious affiliation, veterans. *Tuition waivers:* Full or partial for employees or children of employees, senior citizens. *ROTC:* Air Force cooperative.

LOANS *Student loans:* $8,261,701 (62% need-based, 38% non-need-based). 58% of past graduating class borrowed through all loan programs. *Average indebtedness per student:* $24,451. *Average need-based loan:* Freshmen: $3359. Undergraduates: $4542. *Parent loans:* $2,484,772 (60% need-based, 40% non-need-based). *Programs:* Federal Direct (Subsidized and Unsubsidized Stafford, PLUS), Perkins.

WORK-STUDY *Federal work-study:* jobs available. *State or other work-study/employment:* Total amount: $7,977,379 (44% need-based, 56% non-need-based). Part-time jobs available.

ATHLETIC AWARDS Total amount: $4,632,244 (11% need-based, 89% non-need-based).

APPLYING FOR FINANCIAL AID *Required financial aid form:* FAFSA. *Financial aid deadline:* Continuous. *Notification date:* Continuous beginning 10/31. Students must reply by 3/1 or within 2 weeks of notification.

CONTACT Jonna Raney, Director of Student Financial Services, Oklahoma Baptist University, 500 West University, Shawnee, OK 74804, 405-585-5020 or toll-free 800-654-3285. *Fax:* 405-585-5030. *E-mail:* jonna.raney@okbu.edu. *Website:* http://www.okbu.edu/.

OKLAHOMA CHRISTIAN UNIVERSITY
Oklahoma City, OK

Tuition & fees: $22,760	Average undergraduate aid package: $23,007

ABOUT THE INSTITUTION Independent Church of Christ, coed. *Awards:* certificates, bachelor's, and master's degrees. 61 undergraduate majors. *Total enrollment:* 2,470. Undergraduates: 1,986. Freshmen: 515. Federal methodology is used as a basis for awarding need-based institutional aid.

UNDERGRADUATE EXPENSES for 2018–2019 *Application fee:* $25. *Comprehensive fee:* $30,950 includes full-time tuition ($22,460), mandatory fees ($300), and room and board ($8190). Full-time tuition and fees vary according to course load and reciprocity agreements. Room and board charges vary according to board plan and housing facility. *Part-time tuition:* $935 per credit hour. Part-time tuition and fees vary according to course load and reciprocity agreements.

FRESHMAN FINANCIAL AID (Fall 2016) 382 applied for aid; of those 80% were deemed to have need. 100% of freshmen with need received aid; of those 48% had need fully met. *Average percent of need met:* 59% (excluding resources awarded to replace EFC). *Average financial aid package:* $23,205 (excluding resources awarded to replace EFC). 33% of all full-time freshmen had no need and received non-need-based gift aid.

UNDERGRADUATE FINANCIAL AID (Fall 2016) 1,392 applied for aid; of those 85% were deemed to have need. 100% of undergraduates with need received aid; of those 43% had need fully met. *Average percent of need met:* 66% (excluding resources awarded to replace EFC). *Average financial aid package:* $23,007 (excluding resources awarded to replace EFC). 31% of all full-time undergraduates had no need and received non-need-based gift aid.

GIFT AID (NEED-BASED) *Total amount:* $14,500,436 (16% federal, 4% state, 72% institutional, 8% external sources). *Receiving aid:* Freshmen: 35% (161); all full-time undergraduates: 39% (714). *Average award:* Freshmen: $2995; Undergraduates: $3258. *Scholarships, grants, and awards:* Federal Pell, FSEOG, state, private, college/university gift aid from institutional funds.

GIFT AID (NON-NEED-BASED) *Total amount:* $7,129,396 (2% state, 87% institutional, 11% external sources). *Receiving aid:* Freshmen: 61% (283). Undergraduates: 54% (1,000). *Average award:* Freshmen: $7185. Undergraduates: $7552. *Scholarships, grants, and awards by category: Academic interests/achievement:* engineering/technologies, general academic interests/achievements, religion/biblical studies. *Creative arts/performance:* applied art and design, journalism/publications, music, theater/drama. *Special achievements/activities:* cheerleading/drum major. *Special characteristics:* children of faculty/staff, international students. *Tuition waivers:* Full or partial for employees or children of employees. *ROTC:* Army cooperative, Air Force cooperative.

LOANS *Student loans:* $8,586,610 (71% need-based, 29% non-need-based). 62% of past graduating class borrowed through all loan programs. *Average indebtedness*

per student: $28,438. **Average need-based loan:** Freshmen: $2252. Undergraduates: $2269. **Parent loans:** $2,979,150 (33% need-based, 67% non-need-based). **Programs:** Federal Direct (Subsidized and Unsubsidized Stafford, PLUS), Perkins, alternative loans.
WORK-STUDY Federal work-study: jobs available.
ATHLETIC AWARDS Total amount: $2,158,717 (34% need-based, 66% non-need-based).
APPLYING FOR FINANCIAL AID Required financial aid form: FAFSA. **Financial aid deadline (priority):** 4/1. **Notification date:** Continuous beginning 3/1. Students must reply within 4 weeks of notification.
CONTACT Clint LaRue, Director of Financial Services, Oklahoma Christian University, Box 11000, Oklahoma City, OK 73136-1100, 405-425-5190 or toll-free 800-877-5010. *Fax:* 405-425-5197. *E-mail:* clint.larue@oc.edu.
Website: http://www.oc.edu/.

OKLAHOMA CITY UNIVERSITY
Oklahoma City, OK

Tuition & fees: $31,026	Average undergraduate aid package: $21,635

ABOUT THE INSTITUTION Independent United Methodist, coed. **Awards:** bachelor's, master's, and doctoral degrees. 69 undergraduate majors. **Total enrollment:** 2,821. Undergraduates: 1,692. Freshmen: 296. Federal methodology is used as a basis for awarding need-based institutional aid.
UNDERGRADUATE EXPENSES for 2018–2019 Application fee: $55. **One-time required fee:** $360. **Comprehensive fee:** $39,922 includes full-time tuition ($27,276), mandatory fees ($3750), and room and board ($8896). **College room only:** $4100. Full-time tuition and fees vary according to course level, course load, and program. Room and board charges vary according to board plan and housing facility. **Part-time tuition:** $925. **Part-time fees:** $125 per credit hour. Part-time tuition and fees vary according to course level and program.
FRESHMAN FINANCIAL AID (Fall 2017, est.) 208 applied for aid; of those 81% were deemed to have need. 91% of freshmen with need received aid; of those 86% had need fully met. **Average percent of need met:** 61% (excluding resources awarded to replace EFC). **Average financial aid package:** $23,951 (excluding resources awarded to replace EFC). 10% of all full-time freshmen had no need and received non-need-based gift aid.
UNDERGRADUATE FINANCIAL AID (Fall 2017, est.) 749 applied for aid; of those 89% were deemed to have need. 90% of undergraduates with need received aid; of those 88% had need fully met. **Average percent of need met:** 59% (excluding resources awarded to replace EFC). **Average financial aid package:** $21,635 (excluding resources awarded to replace EFC). 5% of all full-time undergraduates had no need and received non-need-based gift aid.
GIFT AID (NEED-BASED) Total amount: $2,253,645 (42% federal, 8% state, 34% institutional, 16% external sources). **Receiving aid:** Freshmen: 46% (151); all full-time undergraduates: 35% (573). **Average award:** Freshmen: $19,925; Undergraduates: $17,773. **Scholarships, grants, and awards:** Federal Pell, FSEOG, state, private, college/university gift aid from institutional funds, United Negro College Fund, Federal Nursing, Native American Grants.
GIFT AID (NON-NEED-BASED) Total amount: $106,176 (2% federal, 5% state, 34% institutional, 59% external sources). **Receiving aid:** Freshmen: 6% (21). Undergraduates: 4% (67). **Average award:** Freshmen: $16,508. Undergraduates: $14,043. **Scholarships, grants, and awards by category:** Academic interests/achievement: 971 awards: business, communication, education, general academic interests/achievements, home economics, religion/biblical studies. Creative arts/performance: 528 awards: applied art and design, art/fine arts, dance, debating, music, performing arts, theater/drama. Special achievements/activities: 68 awards: general special achievements/activities, junior miss, leadership, religious involvement. Special characteristics: 67 awards: children of faculty/staff, relatives of clergy, religious affiliation. **Tuition waivers:** Full or partial for employees or children of employees. **ROTC:** Army cooperative, Air Force cooperative.
LOANS Student loans: $4,017,250 (82% need-based, 18% non-need-based). 56% of past graduating class borrowed through all loan programs. *Average indebtedness per student:* $27,209. **Average need-based loan:** Freshmen: $3714. Undergraduates: $4338. **Parent loans:** $3,295,335 (68% need-based, 32% non-need-based). **Programs:** Federal Direct (Subsidized and Unsubsidized Stafford, PLUS), Perkins, Federal Nursing.

WORK-STUDY Federal work-study: Total amount: $177,136; 227 jobs averaging $1407. **State or other work-study/employment:** Total amount: $275,646 (100% non-need-based). 256 part-time jobs averaging $1383.
ATHLETIC AWARDS Total amount: $2,908,313 (92% need-based, 8% non-need-based).
APPLYING FOR FINANCIAL AID Required financial aid form: FAFSA. **Financial aid deadline (priority):** 3/1. **Notification date:** Continuous beginning 1/15. Students must reply within 4 weeks of notification.
CONTACT Denise Flis, Senior Director of Student Financial Services, Oklahoma City University, 2501 North Blackwelder, Oklahoma City, OK 73106-1493, 405-208-5848 or toll-free 800-633-7242. *Fax:* 405-208-5466. *E-mail:* dflis@okcu.edu.
Website: http://www.okcu.edu/.

OKLAHOMA PANHANDLE STATE UNIVERSITY
Goodwell, OK

ABOUT THE INSTITUTION State-supported, coed. 28 undergraduate majors.
GIFT AID (NEED-BASED) Scholarships, grants, and awards: Federal Pell, FSEOG, state, private, college/university gift aid from institutional funds.
GIFT AID (NON-NEED-BASED) Scholarships, grants, and awards by category: Academic interests/achievement: agriculture, biological sciences, business, computer science, education, English, general academic interests/achievements, health fields, home economics, mathematics, physical sciences. Creative arts/performance: art/fine arts, debating, music, performing arts, theater/drama. Special achievements/activities: cheerleading/drum major, general special achievements/activities, rodeo. Special characteristics: children and siblings of alumni, children of faculty/staff, general special characteristics, local/state students, out-of-state students, veterans, veterans' children.
LOANS Programs: Perkins.
APPLYING FOR FINANCIAL AID Required financial aid form: FAFSA.
CONTACT Ms. Lori Ferguson, Director of Financial Aid, Oklahoma Panhandle State University, PO Box 430, Goodwell, OK 73939-0430, 580-349-1582 or toll-free 800-664-6778. *E-mail:* lorif@opsu.edu.
Website: http://www.opsu.edu/.

OKLAHOMA STATE UNIVERSITY
Stillwater, OK

Tuition & fees (OK res): $8738	Average undergraduate aid package: $14,543

ABOUT THE INSTITUTION State-supported, coed. **Awards:** certificates, bachelor's, master's, and doctoral degrees. 85 undergraduate majors. **Total enrollment:** 25,254. Undergraduates: 20,978. Freshmen: 4,220. Federal methodology is used as a basis for awarding need-based institutional aid.
UNDERGRADUATE EXPENSES for 2017–2018 Application fee: $40. **One-time required fee:** $95. **Tuition, state resident:** full-time $5190; part-time $173 per credit hour. **Tuition, nonresident:** full-time $20,228; part-time $674.25 per credit hour. **Required fees:** full-time $3548; $118.25 per credit hour. Full-time tuition and fees vary according to program. Part-time tuition and fees vary according to course load and program. **College room and board:** $8558; **Room only:** $4758. Room and board charges vary according to board plan and housing facility. **Payment plan:** Guaranteed tuition.
FRESHMAN FINANCIAL AID (Fall 2016) 3,208 applied for aid; of those 70% were deemed to have need. 97% of freshmen with need received aid; of those 17% had need fully met. **Average percent of need met:** 79% (excluding resources awarded to replace EFC). **Average financial aid package:** $14,954 (excluding resources awarded to replace EFC). 27% of all full-time freshmen had no need and received non-need-based gift aid.
UNDERGRADUATE FINANCIAL AID (Fall 2016) 12,232 applied for aid; of those 77% were deemed to have need. 98% of undergraduates with need received aid; of those 11% had need fully met. **Average percent of need met:** 75% (excluding resources awarded to replace EFC). **Average financial aid package:** $14,543

(excluding resources awarded to replace EFC). 28% of all full-time undergraduates had no need and received non-need-based gift aid.

GIFT AID (NEED-BASED) Total amount: $56,865,456 (42% federal, 24% state, 21% institutional, 13% external sources). **Receiving aid:** Freshmen: 44% (1,721); all full-time undergraduates: 38% (7,033). **Average award:** Freshmen: $8007; Undergraduates: $7349. **Scholarships, grants, and awards:** Federal Pell, FSEOG, state, private, college/university gift aid from institutional funds, TEACH Grants.

GIFT AID (NON-NEED-BASED) Total amount: $14,517,933 (10% state, 48% institutional, 42% external sources). **Receiving aid:** Freshmen: 6% (233). Undergraduates: 3% (538). **Average award:** Freshmen: $7533. Undergraduates: $6484. **Scholarships, grants, and awards by category:** Academic interests/achievement: agriculture, architecture, area/ethnic studies, biological sciences, business, communication, computer science, education, engineering/technologies, English, foreign languages, general academic interests/achievements, home economics, humanities, international studies, mathematics, military science, physical sciences, premedicine, social sciences. Creative arts/performance: art/fine arts, creative writing, general creative arts/performance, journalism/publications, music, theater/drama. Special achievements/activities: cheerleading/drum major, community service, general special achievements/activities, leadership, memberships, rodeo. Special characteristics: adult students, children and siblings of alumni, children of faculty/staff, ethnic background, first-generation college students, general special characteristics, handicapped students, international students, local/state students, out-of-state students, previous college experience. Tuition waivers: Full or partial for children of alumni, employees or children of employees, senior citizens. ROTC: Army, Air Force.

LOANS Student loans: $67,620,862 (72% need-based, 28% non-need-based). 49% of past graduating class borrowed through all loan programs. Average indebtedness per student: $23,790. Average need-based loan: Freshmen: $3297. Undergraduates: $4064. Parent loans: $44,718,286 (37% need-based, 63% non-need-based). **Programs:** Federal Direct (Subsidized and Unsubsidized Stafford, PLUS), Perkins.

WORK-STUDY Federal work-study: 333 jobs averaging $2547. **State or other work-study/employment:** Total amount: $13,673,242 (100% non-need-based). 4,296 part-time jobs averaging $2972.

ATHLETIC AWARDS Total amount: $6,458,583 (25% need-based, 75% non-need-based).

APPLYING FOR FINANCIAL AID Required financial aid form: FAFSA. **Financial aid deadline:** Continuous. **Notification date:** Continuous beginning 12/1. Students must reply within 2 weeks of notification.

CONTACT Office of Scholarships and Financial Aid, Oklahoma State University, 119 Student Union, Stillwater, OK 74078-5061, 405-744-6604 or toll-free 800-233-5019. Fax: 405-744-6438. E-mail: finaid@okstate.edu. Website: http://www.okstate.edu/.

OKLAHOMA WESLEYAN UNIVERSITY
Bartlesville, OK

ABOUT THE INSTITUTION Independent Wesleyan Church, coed. 39 undergraduate majors.

GIFT AID (NEED-BASED) Scholarships, grants, and awards: Federal Pell, FSEOG, state, private, college/university gift aid from institutional funds.

GIFT AID (NON-NEED-BASED) Scholarships, grants, and awards by category: Academic interests/achievement: biological sciences, business, computer science, education, general academic interests/achievements, health fields, religion/biblical studies. Creative arts/performance: music. Special achievements/activities: leadership, religious involvement. Special characteristics: children and siblings of alumni, children of educators, children of faculty/staff, international students, relatives of clergy, religious affiliation, siblings of current students.

LOANS Programs: Federal Direct (Subsidized and Unsubsidized Stafford, PLUS), Perkins, college/university.

WORK-STUDY Federal work-study: 129 jobs averaging $1633. **State or other work-study/employment:** Total amount: $44,960 (66% need-based, 34% non-need-based). 30 part-time jobs averaging $1489.

APPLYING FOR FINANCIAL AID Required financial aid forms: FAFSA, institution's own form.

CONTACT Mrs. Kandi Lyn Molder, Director of Student Financial Services, Oklahoma Wesleyan University, 2201 Silver Lake Road, Bartlesville, OK 74006, 918-335-6282 or toll-free 866-222-8226. Fax: 918-335-6811. E-mail: financialaid@okwu.edu. Website: http://www.okwu.edu/.

OLD DOMINION UNIVERSITY
Norfolk, VA

Tuition & fees (VA res): $10,350	Average undergraduate aid package: $11,059

ABOUT THE INSTITUTION State-supported, coed. **Awards:** certificates, bachelor's, master's, and doctoral degrees. 51 undergraduate majors. **Total enrollment:** 24,375. Undergraduates: 19,540. Freshmen: 2,938. Federal methodology is used as a basis for awarding need-based institutional aid.

UNDERGRADUATE EXPENSES for 2017–2018 Application fee: $50. **Tuition, state resident:** full-time $10,050; part-time $335 per credit hour. **Tuition, nonresident:** full-time $27,900; part-time $930 per credit hour. **Required fees:** full-time $300; $66 per term. **College room and board:** $11,268; **Room only:** $6278. Room and board charges vary according to board plan, housing facility, location, and student level.

FRESHMAN FINANCIAL AID (Fall 2017, est.) 2,660 applied for aid; of those 82% were deemed to have need. 96% of freshmen with need received aid; of those 19% had need fully met. **Average percent of need met:** 49% (excluding resources awarded to replace EFC). **Average financial aid package:** $12,247 (excluding resources awarded to replace EFC). 9% of all full-time freshmen had no need and received non-need-based gift aid.

UNDERGRADUATE FINANCIAL AID (Fall 2017, est.) 12,100 applied for aid; of those 86% were deemed to have need. 96% of undergraduates with need received aid; of those 15% had need fully met. **Average percent of need met:** 47% (excluding resources awarded to replace EFC). **Average financial aid package:** $11,059 (excluding resources awarded to replace EFC). 6% of all full-time undergraduates had no need and received non-need-based gift aid.

GIFT AID (NEED-BASED) Total amount: $64,997,162 (57% federal, 33% state, 10% institutional). **Receiving aid:** Freshmen: 62% (1,810); all full-time undergraduates: 53% (7,986). **Average award:** Freshmen: $7999; Undergraduates: $7369. **Scholarships, grants, and awards:** Federal Pell, FSEOG, state, private, college/university gift aid from institutional funds, United Negro College Fund, Federal Nursing.

GIFT AID (NON-NEED-BASED) Total amount: $13,120,866 (12% state, 73% institutional, 15% external sources). **Receiving aid:** Freshmen: 27% (780). Undergraduates: 14% (2,050). **Average award:** Freshmen: $5351. Undergraduates: $5170. **Scholarships, grants, and awards by category:** Academic interests/achievement: 2,853 awards ($10,556,436 total): area/ethnic studies, biological sciences, business, communication, computer science, education, engineering/technologies, English, foreign languages, general academic interests/achievements, health fields, humanities, international studies, library science, mathematics, military science, physical sciences, social sciences. Creative arts/performance: 180 awards ($176,792 total): applied art and design, art/fine arts, cinema/film/broadcasting, creative writing, dance, general creative arts/performance, journalism/publications, music, performing arts, theater/drama. Special achievements/activities: 26 awards ($35,500 total): cheerleading/drum major, community service, leadership, memberships. Special characteristics: 195 awards ($538,400 total): children of faculty/staff, international students, local/state students, previous college experience, veterans' children. Tuition waivers: Full or partial for employees or children of employees, senior citizens. ROTC: Army, Naval.

LOANS Student loans: $93,385,320 (43% need-based, 57% non-need-based). 72% of past graduating class borrowed through all loan programs. Average indebtedness per student: $32,092. Average need-based loan: Freshmen: $3493. Undergraduates: $4361. Parent loans: $18,933,984 (100% non-need-based). **Programs:** Federal Direct (Subsidized and Unsubsidized Stafford, PLUS), Perkins, Federal Nursing, college/university.

WORK-STUDY Federal work-study: Total amount: $4,358,828; 200 jobs averaging $2400.

ATHLETIC AWARDS Total amount: $6,779,070 (100% non-need-based).

APPLYING FOR FINANCIAL AID Required financial aid form: FAFSA. **Financial aid deadline (priority):** 2/1. **Notification date:** Continuous beginning 3/1. Students must reply within 2 weeks of notification.

CONTACT Office of Financial Aid, Old Dominion University, 2000 Rollins Hall, Norfolk, VA 23529, 757-683-3683 or toll-free 800-348-7926. Fax: 757-683-5920. E-mail: finaid@odu.edu. Website: http://www.odu.edu/.

OLIVET COLLEGE
Olivet, MI

Tuition & fees: N/R	Average undergraduate aid package: $18,615

ABOUT THE INSTITUTION Independent Congregational Christian Church, coed. *Awards:* bachelor's and master's degrees. 34 undergraduate majors. *Total enrollment:* 1,078. Undergraduates: 1,045. Freshmen: 351. Federal methodology is used as a basis for awarding need-based institutional aid.

FRESHMAN FINANCIAL AID (Fall 2016) 345 applied for aid; of those 99% were deemed to have need. 100% of freshmen with need received aid; of those 14% had need fully met. *Average percent of need met:* 80% (excluding resources awarded to replace EFC). *Average financial aid package:* $19,120 (excluding resources awarded to replace EFC). 14% of all full-time freshmen had no need and received non-need-based gift aid.

UNDERGRADUATE FINANCIAL AID (Fall 2016) 1,014 applied for aid; of those 88% were deemed to have need. 100% of undergraduates with need received aid; of those 18% had need fully met. *Average percent of need met:* 80% (excluding resources awarded to replace EFC). *Average financial aid package:* $18,615 (excluding resources awarded to replace EFC). 9% of all full-time undergraduates had no need and received non-need-based gift aid.

GIFT AID (NEED-BASED) *Total amount:* $13,070,215 (22% federal, 8% state, 68% institutional, 2% external sources). *Receiving aid:* Freshmen: 89% (311); all full-time undergraduates: 81% (846). *Average award:* Freshmen: $16,000; Undergraduates: $14,100. *Scholarships, grants, and awards:* Federal Pell, FSEOG, state, private, college/university gift aid from institutional funds.

GIFT AID (NON-NEED-BASED) *Total amount:* $1,414,505 (99% institutional, 1% external sources). *Receiving aid:* Freshmen: 14% (49). Undergraduates: 7% (68). *Average award:* Freshmen: $13,650. Undergraduates: $13,315. *Scholarships, grants, and awards by category: Academic interests/achievement:* 745 awards ($6,851,329 total): business, communication, education, English, foreign languages, general academic interests/achievements. *Creative arts/performance:* 24 awards ($31,850 total): art/fine arts, journalism/publications, music. *Special achievements/activities:* 159 awards ($1,238,915 total): community service, leadership, memberships. *Special characteristics:* 67 awards ($891,284 total): children and siblings of alumni, children of faculty/staff, international students, religious affiliation, siblings of current students. *ROTC:* Air Force cooperative.

LOANS *Student loans:* $8,017,664 (62% need-based, 38% non-need-based). 87% of past graduating class borrowed through all loan programs. *Average indebtedness per student:* $26,872. *Average need-based loan:* Freshmen: $3520. Undergraduates: $5155. *Parent loans:* $3,288,579 (38% need-based, 62% non-need-based). *Programs:* Federal Direct (Subsidized and Unsubsidized Stafford, PLUS), Perkins, alternative loans, CitiAssist Loans, Sallie Mae Smart Option Loans.

WORK-STUDY *Federal work-study:* 196 jobs averaging $908.

APPLYING FOR FINANCIAL AID *Required financial aid form:* FAFSA. *Financial aid deadline:* Continuous. *Notification date:* Continuous beginning 3/1.

CONTACT Ms. Libby M. Jean, Director of Student Services, Olivet College, 320 South Main Street, Olivet, MI 49076-9701, 269-749-7655 or toll-free 800-456-7189. *Fax:* 269-749-3821. *E-mail:* ljean@olivetcollege.edu. *Website:* http://www.olivetcollege.edu/.

OLIVET NAZARENE UNIVERSITY
Bourbonnais, IL

Tuition & fees: $34,940	Average undergraduate aid package: $29,045

ABOUT THE INSTITUTION Independent Church of the Nazarene, coed. *Awards:* bachelor's, master's, and doctoral degrees. 70 undergraduate majors. *Total enrollment:* 4,986. Undergraduates: 3,371. Freshmen: 752. Federal methodology is used as a basis for awarding need-based institutional aid.

UNDERGRADUATE EXPENSES for 2017–2018 *Application fee:* $25. *Comprehensive fee:* $42,840 includes full-time tuition ($33,950), mandatory fees ($990), and room and board ($7900). Full-time tuition and fees vary according to course load.

Room and board charges vary according to board plan. *Part-time tuition:* $1415 per semester hour. Part-time tuition and fees vary according to course load.

FRESHMAN FINANCIAL AID (Fall 2017, est.) 721 applied for aid; of those 91% were deemed to have need. 99% of freshmen with need received aid; of those 22% had need fully met. *Average percent of need met:* 85% (excluding resources awarded to replace EFC). *Average financial aid package:* $30,970 (excluding resources awarded to replace EFC). 13% of all full-time freshmen had no need and received non-need-based gift aid.

UNDERGRADUATE FINANCIAL AID (Fall 2017, est.) 2,597 applied for aid; of those 92% were deemed to have need. 100% of undergraduates with need received aid; of those 28% had need fully met. *Average percent of need met:* 85% (excluding resources awarded to replace EFC). *Average financial aid package:* $29,045 (excluding resources awarded to replace EFC). 18% of all full-time undergraduates had no need and received non-need-based gift aid.

GIFT AID (NEED-BASED) *Total amount:* $53,241,947 (11% federal, 6% state, 82% institutional, 1% external sources). *Receiving aid:* Freshmen: 87% (654); all full-time undergraduates: 81% (2,370). *Average award:* Freshmen: $26,780; Undergraduates: $23,977. *Scholarships, grants, and awards:* Federal Pell, FSEOG, state, private, college/university gift aid from institutional funds.

GIFT AID (NON-NEED-BASED) *Total amount:* $12,112,739 (6% federal, 91% institutional, 3% external sources). *Receiving aid:* Freshmen: 15% (112). Undergraduates: 16% (462). *Average award:* Freshmen: $16,688. Undergraduates: $15,977. *Scholarships, grants, and awards by category: Academic interests/achievement:* general academic interests/achievements, military science. *Creative arts/performance:* art/fine arts, music, performing arts, theater/drama. *Special achievements/activities:* cheerleading/drum major. *Special characteristics:* children of faculty/staff, general special characteristics, relatives of clergy, religious affiliation, veterans. *Tuition waivers:* Full or partial for employees or children of employees. *ROTC:* Army.

LOANS *Student loans:* $18,858,671 (66% need-based, 34% non-need-based). 80% of past graduating class borrowed through all loan programs. *Average indebtedness per student:* $33,847. *Average need-based loan:* Freshmen: $3606. Undergraduates: $4363. *Parent loans:* $5,976,898 (31% need-based, 69% non-need-based). *Programs:* Federal Direct (Subsidized and Unsubsidized Stafford, PLUS), Perkins, private loans.

WORK-STUDY *Federal work-study:* Total amount: $465,035; jobs available. *State or other work-study/employment:* Total amount: $671,394 (33% need-based, 67% non-need-based). Part-time jobs available.

ATHLETIC AWARDS Total amount: $4,709,025 (55% need-based, 45% non-need-based).

APPLYING FOR FINANCIAL AID *Required financial aid form:* FAFSA. *Financial aid deadline (priority):* 3/1. *Notification date:* Continuous beginning 11/1. Students must reply within 2 weeks of notification.

CONTACT Mr. Greg Bruner, Director of Financial Aid, Olivet Nazarene University, One University Avenue, Bourbonnais, IL 60914, 815-939-5249 or toll-free 800-648-1463. *Fax:* 815-939-5074. *E-mail:* gbruner@olivet.edu. *Website:* http://www.olivet.edu/.

O'MORE COLLEGE OF DESIGN
Franklin, TN

ABOUT THE INSTITUTION Independent, coed. *Awards:* bachelor's degrees. 4 undergraduate majors. *Total enrollment:* 148. Undergraduates: 148. Freshmen: 16.

GIFT AID (NEED-BASED) *Scholarships, grants, and awards:* Federal Pell, FSEOG, state, college/university gift aid from institutional funds.

GIFT AID (NON-NEED-BASED) *Scholarships, grants, and awards by category: Academic interests/achievement:* general academic interests/achievements. *Creative arts/performance:* art/fine arts, general creative arts/performance. *Special achievements/activities:* general special achievements/activities, leadership, memberships. *Special characteristics:* children of faculty/staff, international students.

LOANS *Programs:* Federal Direct (Subsidized and Unsubsidized Stafford, PLUS).

APPLYING FOR FINANCIAL AID *Required financial aid form:* FAFSA.

CONTACT Sara Martin, Financial Aid Director, O'More College of Design, 423 South Margin Street, Franklin, TN 37064-2816, 615-794-4254 Ext. 226 or toll-free 888-662-1970. *Fax:* 615-790-1662. *E-mail:* financialaid@omorecollege.edu. *Website:* http://www.omorecollege.edu/.

ORAL ROBERTS UNIVERSITY
Tulsa, OK

Tuition & fees: $27,728	Average undergraduate aid package: $25,595

ABOUT THE INSTITUTION Independent interdenominational, coed. **Awards:** certificates, diplomas, bachelor's, master's, and doctoral degrees. 75 undergraduate majors. **Total enrollment:** 538. Undergraduates: 3,371. Freshmen: 622. Federal methodology is used as a basis for awarding need-based institutional aid.

UNDERGRADUATE EXPENSES for 2018–2019 Application fee: $35. **Comprehensive fee:** $37,178 includes full-time tuition ($26,700), mandatory fees ($1028), and room and board ($9450). **College room only:** $4390. Full-time tuition and fees vary according to course load, degree level, and location. Room and board charges vary according to board plan and housing facility. **Part-time tuition:** $1115 per contact hour. Part-time tuition and fees vary according to course load, degree level, and location.

FRESHMAN FINANCIAL AID (Fall 2017, est.) 646 applied for aid; of those 89% were deemed to have need. 100% of freshmen with need received aid; of those 49% had need fully met. **Average percent of need met:** 90% (excluding resources awarded to replace EFC). **Average financial aid package:** $27,859 (excluding resources awarded to replace EFC). 21% of all full-time freshmen had no need and received non-need-based gift aid.

UNDERGRADUATE FINANCIAL AID (Fall 2017, est.) 2,264 applied for aid; of those 91% were deemed to have need. 100% of undergraduates with need received aid; of those 43% had need fully met. **Average percent of need met:** 90% (excluding resources awarded to replace EFC). **Average financial aid package:** $25,595 (excluding resources awarded to replace EFC). 23% of all full-time undergraduates had no need and received non-need-based gift aid.

GIFT AID (NEED-BASED) Total amount: $32,797,466 (19% federal, 3% state, 76% institutional, 2% external sources). **Receiving aid:** Freshmen: 77% (573); all full-time undergraduates: 70% (2,014). **Average award:** Freshmen: $19,767; Undergraduates: $17,721. **Scholarships, grants, and awards:** Federal Pell, FSEOG, state, private, college/university gift aid from institutional funds.

GIFT AID (NON-NEED-BASED) Total amount: $9,097,278 (96% institutional, 4% external sources). **Receiving aid:** Freshmen: 22% (166). Undergraduates: 26% (751). **Average award:** Freshmen: $15,409. Undergraduates: $13,540. **Scholarships, grants, and awards by category:** Academic interests/achievement: biological sciences, business, communication, education, engineering/technologies, general academic interests/achievements, health fields, religion/biblical studies. Creative arts/performance: applied art and design, art/fine arts, cinema/film/broadcasting, journalism/publications, music. Special achievements/activities: cheerleading/drum major, community service, general special achievements/activities, leadership, memberships, religious involvement. Special characteristics: children and siblings of alumni, children of faculty/staff, general special characteristics, international students, relatives of clergy, siblings of current students. **Tuition waivers:** Full or partial for employees or children of employees. **ROTC:** Air Force cooperative.

LOANS Student loans: $18,093,378 (61% need-based, 39% non-need-based). Average indebtedness per student: $32,745. **Average need-based loan:** Freshmen: $7288. Undergraduates: $7891. **Parent loans:** $6,485,324 (54% need-based, 46% non-need-based). **Programs:** Federal Direct (Subsidized and Unsubsidized Stafford, PLUS), Perkins.

WORK-STUDY Federal work-study: Total amount: $845,455; jobs available. **State or other work-study/employment:** Total amount: $1,099,961 (49% need-based, 51% non-need-based). Part-time jobs available.

ATHLETIC AWARDS Total amount: $4,394,846 (38% need-based, 62% non-need-based).

APPLYING FOR FINANCIAL AID Required financial aid form: FAFSA. **Financial aid deadline:** Continuous. **Notification date:** Continuous beginning 12/1. Students must reply by 5/1.

CONTACT Office of Financial Aid, Oral Roberts University, 7777 South Lewis Avenue, Tulsa, OK 74171, 918-495-6510 or toll-free 800-678-8876. Fax: 918-495-6803.
Website: http://www.oru.edu/.

OREGON COLLEGE OF ART AND CRAFT
Portland, OR

ABOUT THE INSTITUTION Independent, coed. **Awards:** certificates, bachelor's, and master's degrees. 2 undergraduate majors. **Total enrollment:** 163. Undergraduates: 123. Freshmen: 27.

GIFT AID (NEED-BASED) Scholarships, grants, and awards: Federal Pell, FSEOG, state, private, college/university gift aid from institutional funds.

GIFT AID (NON-NEED-BASED) Scholarships, grants, and awards by category: Academic interests/achievement: general academic interests/achievements. Creative arts/performance: art/fine arts.

LOANS Programs: Federal Direct (Subsidized and Unsubsidized Stafford, PLUS), private loans.

APPLYING FOR FINANCIAL AID Required financial aid forms: FAFSA, scholarship application.

CONTACT Ms. Linda L. Anderson, Director of Financial Aid, Oregon College of Art and Craft, 8245 Southwest Barnes Road, Portland, OR 97225, 971-255-4224 or toll-free 800-390-0632. Fax: 503-297-9651. E-mail: landerson@ocac.edu.
Website: http://www.ocac.edu/.

OREGON HEALTH & SCIENCE UNIVERSITY
Portland, OR

Tuition & fees (OR res): $19,602	Average undergraduate aid package: $15,336

ABOUT THE INSTITUTION State-related, coed. 2 undergraduate majors. Federal methodology is used as a basis for awarding need-based institutional aid.

UNDERGRADUATE EXPENSES for 2017–2018 Tuition, state resident: full-time $13,644; part-time $379 per credit hour. **Tuition, nonresident:** full-time $25,020; part-time $695 per credit hour. **Required fees:** full-time $5958; $1744.94 per term. Full-time tuition and fees vary according to course load, location, program, and reciprocity agreements. Part-time tuition and fees vary according to course load, location, program, and reciprocity agreements. **Payment plan:** Guaranteed tuition.

UNDERGRADUATE FINANCIAL AID (Fall 2017, est.) 377 applied for aid; of those 93% were deemed to have need. 100% of undergraduates with need received aid; of those 7% had need fully met. **Average percent of need met:** 31% (excluding resources awarded to replace EFC). **Average financial aid package:** $15,336 (excluding resources awarded to replace EFC).

GIFT AID (NEED-BASED) Total amount: $4,035,909 (49% federal, 8% state, 9% institutional, 34% external sources). **Receiving aid:** All full-time undergraduates: 54% (215). **Average award:** Undergraduates: $13,035. **Scholarships, grants, and awards:** Federal Pell, FSEOG, state, private, college/university gift aid from institutional funds.

GIFT AID (NON-NEED-BASED) Total amount: $45,637 (25% federal, 33% institutional, 42% external sources). **Receiving aid:** Undergraduates: 1% (3). **Scholarships, grants, and awards by category:** Academic interests/achievement: 44 awards ($429,860 total): home economics. **Tuition waivers:** Full or partial for employees or children of employees.

LOANS Student loans: $10,630,698 (92% need-based, 8% non-need-based). **Average need-based loan:** Undergraduates: $7814. **Parent loans:** $437,579 (65% need-based, 35% non-need-based). **Programs:** Federal Direct (Subsidized and Unsubsidized Stafford, PLUS), Perkins, Federal Nursing, college/university, alternative loans.

WORK-STUDY Federal work-study: Total amount: $24,949; 23 jobs averaging $1085.

APPLYING FOR FINANCIAL AID Notification date: Continuous.

CONTACT Becca Moore, Administrative Coordinator, Oregon Health & Science University, 3181 SW Sam Jackson Park Road, Mail Code L109, Portland, OR 97239-3089, 503-494-7800. Fax: 503-494-4629. E-mail: glawatz@ohsu.edu.
Website: http://www.ohsu.edu/.

OREGON INSTITUTE OF TECHNOLOGY
Klamath Falls, OR

CONTACT Tracey Lehman, Director of Financial Aid, Oregon Institute of Technology, 3201 Campus Drive, Klamath Falls, OR 97601, 541-885-1280 or toll-free 800-422-2017. *Fax:* 541-885-1024. *E-mail:* tracey.lehman@oit.edu. *Website:* http://www.oit.edu/.

OREGON STATE UNIVERSITY
Corvallis, OR

Tuition & fees (OR res): $10,797	Average undergraduate aid package: $13,177

ABOUT THE INSTITUTION State-supported, coed. *Awards:* certificates, bachelor's, master's, and doctoral degrees. 81 undergraduate majors. *Total enrollment:* 30,896. Undergraduates: 25,838. Freshmen: 3,819. Federal methodology is used as a basis for awarding need-based institutional aid.

UNDERGRADUATE EXPENSES for 2017–2018 Application fee: $60. *One-time required fee:* $350. *Tuition, state resident:* full-time $9075; part-time $195 per credit hour. *Tuition, nonresident:* full-time $27,735; part-time $594 per credit hour. *Required fees:* full-time $1722; $528.90 per term. Full-time tuition and fees vary according to course load, location, and program. Part-time tuition and fees vary according to course load, location, and program. *College room and board:* $12,540; *Room only:* $8610. Room and board charges vary according to board plan and housing facility.

FRESHMAN FINANCIAL AID (Fall 2016) 3,013 applied for aid; of those 66% were deemed to have need. 99% of freshmen with need received aid; of those 13% had need fully met. *Average percent of need met:* 70% (excluding resources awarded to replace EFC). *Average financial aid package:* $12,911 (excluding resources awarded to replace EFC). 26% of all full-time freshmen had no need and received non-need-based gift aid.

UNDERGRADUATE FINANCIAL AID (Fall 2016) 12,517 applied for aid; of those 78% were deemed to have need. 99% of undergraduates with need received aid; of those 9% had need fully met. *Average percent of need met:* 66% (excluding resources awarded to replace EFC). *Average financial aid package:* $13,177 (excluding resources awarded to replace EFC). 16% of all full-time undergraduates had no need and received non-need-based gift aid.

GIFT AID (NEED-BASED) Total amount: $75,343,035 (41% federal, 13% state, 37% institutional, 9% external sources). *Receiving aid:* Freshmen: 48% (1,676); all full-time undergraduates: 41% (7,575). *Average award:* Freshmen: $8506; Undergraduates: $7366. *Scholarships, grants, and awards:* Federal Pell, FSEOG, state, private, college/university gift aid from institutional funds.

GIFT AID (NON-NEED-BASED) Total amount: $17,127,025 (9% federal, 77% institutional, 14% external sources). *Receiving aid:* Freshmen: 1% (40). Undergraduates: 1% (189). *Average award:* Freshmen: $5577. Undergraduates: $4952. *Scholarships, grants, and awards by category: Academic interests/achievement:* general academic interests/achievements. *Special achievements/activities:* leadership. *Special characteristics:* children and siblings of alumni, local/state students, members of minority groups. *Tuition waivers:* Full or partial for employees or children of employees. *ROTC:* Army, Naval, Air Force.

LOANS Student loans: $104,506,944 (85% need-based, 15% non-need-based). 58% of past graduating class borrowed through all loan programs. *Average indebtedness per student:* $26,749. *Average need-based loan:* Freshmen: $4423. Undergraduates: $4940. *Parent loans:* $31,223,313 (80% need-based, 20% non-need-based). *Programs:* Federal Direct (Subsidized and Unsubsidized Stafford, PLUS), Perkins, college/university.

WORK-STUDY Federal work-study: 553 jobs averaging $2951.

ATHLETIC AWARDS Total amount: $9,565,436 (33% need-based, 67% non-need-based).

APPLYING FOR FINANCIAL AID Required financial aid form: FAFSA. *Financial aid deadline (priority):* 2/28. *Notification date:* Continuous beginning 4/1. Students must reply within 4 weeks of notification.

CONTACT Keith Raab, Director of Financial Aid and Scholarships, Oregon State University, 218 Kerr Administration Building, Corvallis, OR 97331-2120, 541-737-2241 or toll-free 800-291-4192. *E-mail:* financial.aid@oregonstate.edu. *Website:* http://www.oregonstate.edu/.

OREGON STATE UNIVERSITY–CASCADES
Bend, OR

CONTACT Financial Aid Office, Oregon State University–Cascades, 2600 Northwest College Way, Bend, OR 97701, 541-322-3100. *Website:* http://www.osucascades.edu/.

OTIS COLLEGE OF ART AND DESIGN
Los Angeles, CA

CONTACT Jessika Huerta, Director of Financial Aid, Otis College of Art and Design, 9045 Lincoln Boulevard, Los Angeles, CA 90045-9785, 310-665-6898 or toll-free 800-527-OTIS. *Fax:* 310-665-6884. *E-mail:* jhuerta@otis.edu. *Website:* http://www.otis.edu/.

OTTAWA UNIVERSITY
Ottawa, KS

CONTACT Financial Aid Coordinator, Ottawa University, 1001 South Cedar, Ottawa, KS 66067-3399, 785-242-5200 or toll-free 800-755-5200. *E-mail:* finaid@ottawa.edu. *Website:* http://www.ottawa.edu/.

OTTERBEIN UNIVERSITY
Westerville, OH

ABOUT THE INSTITUTION Independent United Methodist, coed. *Awards:* certificates, bachelor's, master's, and doctoral degrees. 48 undergraduate majors. *Total enrollment:* 2,936. Undergraduates: 2,480. Freshmen: 609.

GIFT AID (NEED-BASED) Scholarships, grants, and awards: Federal Pell, FSEOG, state, private, college/university gift aid from institutional funds, Federal Nursing.

GIFT AID (NON-NEED-BASED) Scholarships, grants, and awards by category: Academic interests/achievement: general academic interests/achievements. *Creative arts/performance:* art/fine arts, music, theater/drama. *Special achievements/activities:* community service, leadership. *Special characteristics:* children and siblings of alumni, children of faculty/staff, general special characteristics, international students, members of minority groups, previous college experience, relatives of clergy, siblings of current students, veterans.

LOANS Programs: Federal Direct (Subsidized and Unsubsidized Stafford, PLUS), Perkins, Federal Nursing, state, college/university.

APPLYING FOR FINANCIAL AID Required financial aid form: FAFSA.

CONTACT Mr. Thomas V. Yarnell, Director of Student Financial Services, Otterbein University, One Otterbein College, Westerville, OH 43081-2006, 614-823-1502 or toll-free 800-488-8144. *Fax:* 614-823-1588. *E-mail:* tyarnell@otterbein.edu. *Website:* http://www.otterbein.edu/.

OUACHITA BAPTIST UNIVERSITY
Arkadelphia, AR

Tuition & fees: $26,790 | Average undergraduate aid package: $23,850

ABOUT THE INSTITUTION Independent Baptist, coed. *Awards:* associate and bachelor's degrees. 54 undergraduate majors. *Total enrollment:* 1,545. Undergraduates: 1,545. Freshmen: 468. Both federal and institutional methodology are used as a basis for awarding need-based institutional aid.

UNDERGRADUATE EXPENSES for 2018–2019 *Comprehensive fee:* $34,670 includes full-time tuition ($26,200), mandatory fees ($590), and room and board ($7880). Full-time tuition and fees vary according to degree level and location. Room and board charges vary according to housing facility. *Part-time tuition:* $725 per semester hour. Part-time tuition and fees vary according to degree level and location.

FRESHMAN FINANCIAL AID (Fall 2017, est.) 434 applied for aid; of those 78% were deemed to have need. 100% of freshmen with need received aid; of those 37% had need fully met. *Average percent of need met:* 83% (excluding resources awarded to replace EFC). *Average financial aid package:* $23,214 (excluding resources awarded to replace EFC). 26% of all full-time freshmen had no need and received non-need-based gift aid.

UNDERGRADUATE FINANCIAL AID (Fall 2017, est.) 1,198 applied for aid; of those 83% were deemed to have need. 100% of undergraduates with need received aid; of those 36% had need fully met. *Average percent of need met:* 85% (excluding resources awarded to replace EFC). *Average financial aid package:* $23,850 (excluding resources awarded to replace EFC). 30% of all full-time undergraduates had no need and received non-need-based gift aid.

GIFT AID (NEED-BASED) *Total amount:* $16,080,951 (14% federal, 7% state, 74% institutional, 5% external sources). *Receiving aid:* Freshmen: 71% (331); all full-time undergraduates: 65% (967). *Average award:* Freshmen: $16,591; Undergraduates: $16,576. *Scholarships, grants, and awards:* Federal Pell, FSEOG, state, private, college/university gift aid from institutional funds.

GIFT AID (NON-NEED-BASED) *Total amount:* $9,362,478 (21% state, 74% institutional, 5% external sources). *Receiving aid:* Freshmen: 24% (112). Undergraduates: 20% (302). *Average award:* Freshmen: $15,139. Undergraduates: $13,091. *Scholarships, grants, and awards by category: Academic interests/ achievement:* area/ethnic studies, biological sciences, business, communication, computer science, education, engineering/technologies, English, foreign languages, general academic interests/achievements, health fields, home economics, humanities, international studies, mathematics, physical sciences, premedicine, religion/biblical studies, social sciences. *Creative arts/performance:* art/fine arts, journalism/publications, music, performing arts, theater/drama. *Special achievements/activities:* cheerleading/ drum major, general special achievements/activities. *Special characteristics:* children and siblings of alumni, children of faculty/staff, ethnic background, first-generation college students, general special characteristics, handicapped students, international students, local/state students, married students, members of minority groups, out-of-state students, previous college experience, relatives of clergy, religious affiliation, twins. *Tuition waivers:* Full or partial for employees or children of employees. *ROTC:* Army.

LOANS *Student loans:* $7,170,153 (59% need-based, 41% non-need-based). 52% of past graduating class borrowed through all loan programs. *Average indebtedness per student:* $28,406. *Average need-based loan:* Freshmen: $3234. Undergraduates: $4024. *Parent loans:* $2,134,656 (36% need-based, 64% non-need-based). *Programs:* Federal Direct (Subsidized and Unsubsidized Stafford, PLUS), Perkins, college/university.

WORK-STUDY *Federal work-study:* Total amount: $662,130; jobs available. *State or other work-study/employment:* Total amount: $239,782 (60% need-based, 40% non-need-based). Part-time jobs available.

ATHLETIC AWARDS Total amount: $2,620,395 (63% need-based, 37% non-need-based).

APPLYING FOR FINANCIAL AID *Required financial aid forms:* FAFSA, state aid form. *Financial aid deadline:* 5/1 (priority: 12/1). *Notification date:* Continuous beginning 10/1.

CONTACT Ms. Susan Hurst, Director of Financial Aid, Ouachita Baptist University, PO Box 3774, Arkadelphia, AR 71998-0001, 870-245-5570 or toll-free 800-342-5628. *Fax:* 870-245-5318. *E-mail:* hursts@obu.edu. *Website:* http://www.obu.edu/.

OUR LADY OF THE LAKE UNIVERSITY
San Antonio, TX

Tuition & fees: $28,740 | Average undergraduate aid package: $22,549

ABOUT THE INSTITUTION Independent Roman Catholic, coed. *Awards:* bachelor's, master's, and doctoral degrees. 32 undergraduate majors. *Total enrollment:* 3,212. Undergraduates: 1,342. Freshmen: 338. Both federal and institutional methodology are used as a basis for awarding need-based institutional aid.

UNDERGRADUATE EXPENSES for 2018–2019 *Application fee:* $35. *Comprehensive fee:* $38,342 includes full-time tuition ($27,912), mandatory fees ($828), and room and board ($9602). *College room only:* $5814. Full-time tuition and fees vary according to course load and location. Room and board charges vary according to board plan and housing facility. *Part-time tuition:* $895 per credit hour. *Part-time fees:* $414 per term. Part-time tuition and fees vary according to course load and location.

FRESHMAN FINANCIAL AID (Fall 2016) 204 applied for aid; of those 91% were deemed to have need. 100% of freshmen with need received aid; of those 38% had need fully met. *Average percent of need met:* 87% (excluding resources awarded to replace EFC). *Average financial aid package:* $23,250 (excluding resources awarded to replace EFC). 11% of all full-time freshmen had no need and received non-need-based gift aid.

UNDERGRADUATE FINANCIAL AID (Fall 2016) 1,084 applied for aid; of those 94% were deemed to have need. 100% of undergraduates with need received aid; of those 41% had need fully met. *Average percent of need met:* 84% (excluding resources awarded to replace EFC). *Average financial aid package:* $22,549 (excluding resources awarded to replace EFC). 9% of all full-time undergraduates had no need and received non-need-based gift aid.

GIFT AID (NEED-BASED) *Total amount:* $15,414,238 (25% federal, 20% state, 53% institutional, 2% external sources). *Receiving aid:* Freshmen: 87% (185); all full-time undergraduates: 85% (997). *Average award:* Freshmen: $17,813; Undergraduates: $15,648. *Scholarships, grants, and awards:* Federal Pell, FSEOG, state, private, college/university gift aid from institutional funds.

GIFT AID (NON-NEED-BASED) *Total amount:* $2,208,956 (100% institutional). *Receiving aid:* Freshmen: 31% (65). Undergraduates: 31% (364). *Average award:* Freshmen: $9723. Undergraduates: $8806. *Scholarships, grants, and awards by category: Academic interests/achievement:* general academic interests/ achievements. *Special characteristics:* children of faculty/staff, religious affiliation. *Tuition waivers:* Full or partial for employees or children of employees. *ROTC:* Army cooperative.

LOANS *Student loans:* $9,539,183 (67% need-based, 33% non-need-based). 85% of past graduating class borrowed through all loan programs. *Average indebtedness per student:* $34,224. *Average need-based loan:* Freshmen: $3408. Undergraduates: $4785. *Parent loans:* $1,922,642 (22% need-based, 78% non-need-based). *Programs:* Federal Direct (Subsidized and Unsubsidized Stafford, PLUS), Perkins, state, private loans.

WORK-STUDY *Federal work-study:* jobs available. *State or other work-study/employment:* Total amount: $29,784 (100% need-based). Part-time jobs available.

ATHLETIC AWARDS Total amount: $852,108 (26% need-based, 74% non-need-based).

APPLYING FOR FINANCIAL AID *Required financial aid forms:* FAFSA, institution's own form. *Financial aid deadline (priority):* 5/1. *Notification date:* Continuous beginning 3/1.

CONTACT Esmeralda Flores, Director of Financial Aid, Our Lady of the Lake University, 411 Southwest 24th Street, San Antonio, TX 78207-4689, 210-434-6711 Ext. 2558 or toll-free 800-436-6558. *Fax:* 210-431-3958. *E-mail:* emflores@ lake.ollusa.edu. *Website:* http://www.ollusa.edu/.

OZARK CHRISTIAN COLLEGE
Joplin, MO

Tuition & fees: N/R	Average undergraduate aid package: N/A

ABOUT THE INSTITUTION Independent Christian, coed. 7 undergraduate majors. Federal methodology is used as a basis for awarding need-based institutional aid.

GIFT AID (NEED-BASED) *Total amount:* $1,253,499 (87% federal, 13% institutional). *Scholarships, grants, and awards:* Federal Pell, FSEOG, private, college/university gift aid from institutional funds.

GIFT AID (NON-NEED-BASED) *Total amount:* $2,507,111 (64% institutional, 36% external sources). *Scholarships, grants, and awards by category: Academic interests/achievement:* education, general academic interests/achievements, international studies, religion/biblical studies. *Creative arts/performance:* music, theater/drama. *Special achievements/activities:* religious involvement. *Special characteristics:* children of faculty/staff, international students, relatives of clergy, religious affiliation, spouses of current students.

LOANS *Student loans:* $3,197,836 (45% need-based, 55% non-need-based). 50% of past graduating class borrowed through all loan programs. *Parent loans:* $152,822 (100% non-need-based). *Programs:* Federal Direct (Subsidized and Unsubsidized Stafford, PLUS).

WORK-STUDY *Federal work-study:* 22 jobs averaging $1606.

APPLYING FOR FINANCIAL AID *Required financial aid form:* FAFSA. *Financial aid deadline:* Continuous. *Notification date:* Continuous beginning 2/1.

CONTACT Rebecca Morrow, Financial Aid Counselor, Ozark Christian College, 1111 North Main Street, Joplin, MO 64801-4804, 417-624-2518 Ext. 2027 or toll-free 800-299-4622. *Fax:* 417-624-0090. *E-mail:* morrow.becky@occ.edu. *Website:* http://www.occ.edu/.

PACE UNIVERSITY
New York, NY

CONTACT Financial Aid Office, Pace University, 1 Pace Plaza, New York, NY 10038, 877-672-1830 or toll-free 800-874-7223. *Fax:* 212-346-1750. *E-mail:* financialaid@pace.edu. *Website:* http://www.pace.edu/nyc.

PACE UNIVERSITY, PLEASANTVILLE CAMPUS
Pleasantville, NY

CONTACT Financial Aid Office, Pace University, Pleasantville Campus, 861 Bedford Road, Pleasantville, NY 10570, 914-773-3200 or toll-free 800-874-PACE. *Website:* http://www.pace.edu/westchester.

PACIFIC COLLEGE
Costa Mesa, CA

CONTACT Financial Aid Office, Pacific College, 3160 Red Hill Avenue, Costa Mesa, CA 92626, 714-662-4402. *Website:* http://www.pacific-college.edu/.

PACIFIC ISLANDS UNIVERSITY
Mangilao, GU

CONTACT Financial Aid Office, Pacific Islands University, 172 Kinney's Road, Mangilao, GU 96913, 671-734-1812. *Website:* http://www.piu.edu/.

PACIFIC LUTHERAN UNIVERSITY
Tacoma, WA

Tuition & fees: $40,722	Average undergraduate aid package: $32,706

ABOUT THE INSTITUTION Independent Evangelical Lutheran Church in America, coed. *Awards:* certificates, bachelor's, master's, and doctoral degrees. 40 undergraduate majors. *Total enrollment:* 3,064. Undergraduates: 2,709. Freshmen: 535. Federal methodology is used as a basis for awarding need-based institutional aid.

UNDERGRADUATE EXPENSES for 2017–2018 *Application fee:* $40. *Comprehensive fee:* $51,242 includes full-time tuition ($40,352), mandatory fees ($370), and room and board ($10,520). *College room only:* $4940. Full-time tuition and fees vary according to course load and degree level. Room and board charges vary according to board plan and housing facility. *Part-time tuition:* $1261 per semester hour. *Part-time fees:* $370 per year. Part-time tuition and fees vary according to course load and degree level.

FRESHMAN FINANCIAL AID (Fall 2017, est.) 496 applied for aid; of those 85% were deemed to have need. 100% of freshmen with need received aid; of those 26% had need fully met. *Average percent of need met:* 90% (excluding resources awarded to replace EFC). *Average financial aid package:* $34,019 (excluding resources awarded to replace EFC). 4% of all full-time freshmen had no need and received non-need-based gift aid.

UNDERGRADUATE FINANCIAL AID (Fall 2017, est.) 2,174 applied for aid; of those 90% were deemed to have need. 100% of undergraduates with need received aid; of those 24% had need fully met. *Average percent of need met:* 85% (excluding resources awarded to replace EFC). *Average financial aid package:* $32,706 (excluding resources awarded to replace EFC). 4% of all full-time undergraduates had no need and received non-need-based gift aid.

GIFT AID (NEED-BASED) *Total amount:* $15,421,730 (26% federal, 18% state, 47% institutional, 9% external sources). *Receiving aid:* Freshmen: 57% (303); all full-time undergraduates: 55% (1,444). *Average award:* Freshmen: $13,194; Undergraduates: $11,768. *Scholarships, grants, and awards:* Federal Pell, FSEOG, state, private, college/university gift aid from institutional funds, Federal Nursing, ROTC Scholarships.

GIFT AID (NON-NEED-BASED) *Total amount:* $46,304,993 (5% federal, 94% institutional, 1% external sources). *Receiving aid:* Freshmen: 75% (401). Undergraduates: 70% (1,841). *Average award:* Freshmen: $12,809. Undergraduates: $12,719. *Scholarships, grants, and awards by category: Academic interests/achievement:* 2,578 awards ($46,696,282 total): general academic interests/achievements. *Creative arts/performance:* 224 awards ($823,166 total): art/fine arts, dance, debating, music, theater/drama. *Special achievements/activities:* 60 awards ($107,000 total): leadership. *Special characteristics:* 908 awards ($2,184,272 total): children and siblings of alumni, children of faculty/staff, international students, out-of-state students, relatives of clergy, religious affiliation. *Tuition waivers:* Full or partial for children of alumni, employees or children of employees. *ROTC:* Army.

LOANS *Student loans:* $18,430,496 (66% need-based, 34% non-need-based). 70% of past graduating class borrowed through all loan programs. *Average indebtedness per student:* $26,379. *Average need-based loan:* Freshmen: $3782. Undergraduates: $5547. *Parent loans:* $4,821,177 (100% non-need-based). *Programs:* Federal Direct (Subsidized and Unsubsidized Stafford, PLUS), Perkins, Federal Nursing, state.

WORK-STUDY *Federal work-study:* Total amount: $512,881; jobs available. *State or other work-study/employment:* Total amount: $38,481 (100% need-based). Part-time jobs available.

APPLYING FOR FINANCIAL AID *Required financial aid form:* FAFSA. *Financial aid deadline (priority):* 12/1. *Notification date:* Continuous beginning 12/16. Students must reply by 5/1.

CONTACT Lorie J. Staab, Student Financial Services, Pacific Lutheran University, Hauge Administration Building, Room 130, Tacoma, WA 98447, 253-535-7461 or toll-free 800-274-6758. *Fax:* 253-535-8406. *E-mail:* sfs@plu.edu. *Website:* http://www.plu.edu/.

PACIFIC NORTHWEST COLLEGE OF ART

Portland, OR

CONTACT Peggy Burgus, Director of Financial Aid, Pacific Northwest College of Art, 1241 Northwest Johnson Street, Portland, OR 97209, 503-821-8976. *Fax:* 503-821-8978.
Website: http://www.pnca.edu/.

PACIFIC OAKS COLLEGE

Pasadena, CA

CONTACT Rosie Tristan, Financial Aid Specialist, Pacific Oaks College, 5 Westmoreland Place, Pasadena, CA 91103, 626-397-1350 or toll-free 877-314-2380. *Fax:* 626-577-6144. *E-mail:* financial@pacificoaks.edu.
Website: http://www.pacificoaks.edu/.

PACIFIC RIM CHRISTIAN UNIVERSITY

Honolulu, HI

CONTACT Financial Aid Office, Pacific Rim Christian University, 2223 Ho'one'e Place, Honolulu, HI 96819, 808-518-4791.
Website: http://www.pacrim.edu/.

PACIFIC UNION COLLEGE

Angwin, CA

ABOUT THE INSTITUTION Independent Seventh-day Adventist, coed. 40 undergraduate majors.
GIFT AID (NEED-BASED) *Scholarships, grants, and awards:* Federal Pell, FSEOG, state, private, college/university gift aid from institutional funds.
GIFT AID (NON-NEED-BASED) *Scholarships, grants, and awards by category: Academic interests/achievement:* education, religion/biblical studies. *Creative arts/performance:* art/fine arts, music, theater/drama. *Special achievements/activities:* community service, leadership, religious involvement. *Special characteristics:* children and siblings of alumni, siblings of current students, spouses of current students, veterans.
LOANS *Programs:* Federal Direct (Subsidized and Unsubsidized Stafford, PLUS), Perkins, college/university.
WORK-STUDY *Federal work-study:* jobs available.
APPLYING FOR FINANCIAL AID *Required financial aid forms:* FAFSA, institution's own form.
CONTACT Laurie Wheeler, Director of Student Financial Services, Pacific Union College, One Angwin Avenue, Angwin, CA 94508, 707-965-7321 or toll-free 800-862-7080. *Fax:* 707-965-6595. *E-mail:* llwheeler@puc.edu.
Website: http://www.puc.edu/.

PACIFIC UNIVERSITY

Forest Grove, OR

Tuition & fees: N/R	Average undergraduate aid package: $31,952

ABOUT THE INSTITUTION Independent, coed. 50 undergraduate majors. Federal methodology is used as a basis for awarding need-based institutional aid.
FRESHMAN FINANCIAL AID (Fall 2017, est.) 411 applied for aid; of those 85% were deemed to have need. 100% of freshmen with need received aid; of those 17% had need fully met. *Average percent of need met:* 80% (excluding resources awarded to replace EFC). *Average financial aid package:* $34,829 (excluding resources awarded to replace EFC). 17% of all full-time freshmen had no need and received non-need-based gift aid.

UNDERGRADUATE FINANCIAL AID (Fall 2017, est.) 1,545 applied for aid; of those 91% were deemed to have need. 100% of undergraduates with need received aid; of those 13% had need fully met. *Average percent of need met:* 73% (excluding resources awarded to replace EFC). *Average financial aid package:* $31,952 (excluding resources awarded to replace EFC). 18% of all full-time undergraduates had no need and received non-need-based gift aid.
GIFT AID (NEED-BASED) *Total amount:* $35,868,892 (8% federal, 1% state, 88% institutional, 3% external sources). *Receiving aid:* Freshmen: 57% (240); all full-time undergraduates: 57% (999). *Average award:* Freshmen: $11,802; Undergraduates: $10,672. *Scholarships, grants, and awards:* Federal Pell, FSEOG, state, private, college/university gift aid from institutional funds.
GIFT AID (NON-NEED-BASED) *Total amount:* $7,514,176 (98% institutional, 2% external sources). *Receiving aid:* Freshmen: 78% (330). Undergraduates: 74% (1,294). *Average award:* Freshmen: $20,238. Undergraduates: $19,877. *Scholarships, grants, and awards by category: Academic interests/achievement:* biological sciences, business, communication, education, English, foreign languages, general academic interests/achievements, health fields, humanities, mathematics, physical sciences, premedicine, social sciences. *Creative arts/performance:* art/fine arts, debating, journalism/publications, music, theater/drama. *Special achievements/activities:* community service, memberships, religious involvement. *Special characteristics:* children and siblings of alumni, children of faculty/staff, ethnic background, first-generation college students, general special characteristics, international students, relatives of clergy, veterans.
LOANS *Student loans:* $8,389,859 (81% need-based, 19% non-need-based). 79% of past graduating class borrowed through all loan programs. *Average indebtedness per student:* $36,001. *Average need-based loan:* Freshmen: $2411. Undergraduates: $2869. *Parent loans:* $2,671,459 (67% need-based, 33% non-need-based). *Programs:* Federal Direct (Subsidized and Unsubsidized Stafford, PLUS), Perkins, private loans.
WORK-STUDY *Federal work-study:* Total amount: $1,953,253; jobs available. *State or other work-study/employment:* Part-time jobs available.
APPLYING FOR FINANCIAL AID *Required financial aid form:* FAFSA. *Financial aid deadline (priority):* 3/1. *Notification date:* Continuous beginning 3/1.
CONTACT Office of Financial Aid, Pacific University, 2043 College Way, Forest Grove, OR 97116-1797, 503-352-2222 or toll-free 877-722-8648. *E-mail:* financialaid@pacificu.edu.
Website: http://www.pacificu.edu/.

PAIER COLLEGE OF ART, INC.

Hamden, CT

CONTACT Mr. John DeRose, Director of Financial Aid, Paier College of Art, Inc., 20 Gorham Avenue, Hamden, CT 06514-3902, 203-287-3034. *Fax:* 203-287-3021. *E-mail:* paier.art@snet.net.
Website: http://www.paiercollegeofart.edu/.

PAINE COLLEGE

Augusta, GA

CONTACT Ms. Gerri Bogan, Director of Financial Aid, Paine College, 1235 15th Street, Augusta, GA 30901, 706-821-8262 or toll-free 800-476-7703. *Fax:* 706-821-8691. *E-mail:* bogang@mail.paine.edu.
Website: http://www.paine.edu/.

PALM BEACH ATLANTIC UNIVERSITY

West Palm Beach, FL

Tuition & fees: $31,450	Average undergraduate aid package: $21,938

ABOUT THE INSTITUTION Independent nondenominational, coed. *Awards:* bachelor's, master's, and doctoral degrees. 53 undergraduate majors. *Total*

enrollment: 3,839. Undergraduates: 3,003. Freshmen: 533. Federal methodology is used as a basis for awarding need-based institutional aid.

UNDERGRADUATE EXPENSES for 2018–2019 *Application fee:* $50. *Comprehensive fee:* $41,580 includes full-time tuition ($30,990), mandatory fees ($460), and room and board ($10,130). *College room only:* $5370. Full-time tuition and fees vary according to course load, location, and program. Room and board charges vary according to board plan and housing facility. *Part-time tuition:* $745 per credit hour. *Part-time fees:* $145 per term. Part-time tuition and fees vary according to course load, location, and program.

FRESHMAN FINANCIAL AID (Fall 2017, est.) 492 applied for aid; of those 86% were deemed to have need. 100% of freshmen with need received aid; of those 18% had need fully met. *Average percent of need met:* 68% (excluding resources awarded to replace EFC). *Average financial aid package:* $23,523 (excluding resources awarded to replace EFC). 21% of all full-time freshmen had no need and received non-need-based gift aid.

UNDERGRADUATE FINANCIAL AID (Fall 2017, est.) 1,945 applied for aid; of those 87% were deemed to have need. 100% of undergraduates with need received aid; of those 16% had need fully met. *Average percent of need met:* 63% (excluding resources awarded to replace EFC). *Average financial aid package:* $21,938 (excluding resources awarded to replace EFC). 25% of all full-time undergraduates had no need and received non-need-based gift aid.

GIFT AID (NEED-BASED) *Total amount:* $30,674,166 (14% federal, 15% state, 62% institutional, 9% external sources). *Receiving aid:* Freshmen: 79% (424); all full-time undergraduates: 72% (1,678). *Average award:* Freshmen: $21,135; Undergraduates: $19,029. *Scholarships, grants, and awards:* Federal Pell, FSEOG, state, private, college/university gift aid from institutional funds, United Negro College Fund.

GIFT AID (NON-NEED-BASED) *Total amount:* $10,820,916 (17% state, 77% institutional, 6% external sources). *Receiving aid:* Freshmen: 12% (66). Undergraduates: 10% (227). *Average award:* Freshmen: $13,237. Undergraduates: $12,397. *Scholarships, grants, and awards by category:* Academic interests/achievement: 2,130 awards ($27,129,573 total): general academic interests/achievements. Creative arts/performance: 137 awards ($456,467 total): dance, music, theater/drama. Special achievements/activities: 209 awards ($294,450 total): leadership. Special characteristics: 109 awards ($1,216,119 total): adult students, children and siblings of alumni, children of current students, children of educators, children of faculty/staff, previous college experience, veterans. *Tuition waivers:* Full or partial for children of alumni, employees or children of employees. *ROTC:* Army cooperative.

LOANS *Student loans:* $11,444,121 (78% need-based, 22% non-need-based). 52% of past graduating class borrowed through all loan programs. *Average indebtedness per student:* $26,907. *Average need-based loan:* Freshmen: $3307. Undergraduates: $3868. *Parent loans:* $4,441,636 (58% need-based, 42% non-need-based). *Programs:* Federal Direct (Subsidized and Unsubsidized Stafford, PLUS), private loans.

WORK-STUDY *Federal work-study:* Total amount: $499,586; 205 jobs averaging $3186. *State or other work-study/employment:* Total amount: $32,129 (100% need-based). 12 part-time jobs averaging $3010.

ATHLETIC AWARDS Total amount: $2,113,087 (42% need-based, 58% non-need-based).

APPLYING FOR FINANCIAL AID *Required financial aid forms:* FAFSA, state aid form. *Financial aid deadline (priority):* 5/1. *Notification date:* Continuous beginning 10/15. Students must reply by 5/1.

CONTACT Mrs. Jennifer McMahon, Director of Financial Aid, Palm Beach Atlantic University, PO Box 24708, West Palm Beach, FL 33416-4708, 561-803-2000 or toll-free 888-GO-TO-PBA. *Fax:* 561-803-2130. *E-mail:* finaid@pba.edu. *Website:* http://www.pba.edu/.

PALM BEACH STATE COLLEGE
Lake Worth, FL

CONTACT Financial Aid Office, Palm Beach State College, 4200 Congress Avenue, Lake Worth, FL 33461-4796, 561-967-7222. *Website:* http://www.palmbeachstate.edu/.

PALO ALTO UNIVERSITY
Palo Alto, CA

CONTACT Financial Aid Office, Palo Alto University, 1791 Arastradero Road, Palo Alto, CA 94304, 650-433-3800 or toll-free 800-818-6136. *Website:* http://www.paloaltou.edu/.

PARK UNIVERSITY
Parkville, MO

Tuition & fees: N/R	Average undergraduate aid package: N/A

ABOUT THE INSTITUTION Independent, coed. 44 undergraduate majors. Both federal and institutional methodology are used as a basis for awarding need-based institutional aid.

GIFT AID (NEED-BASED) *Scholarships, grants, and awards:* Federal Pell, FSEOG, state, private, college/university gift aid from institutional funds.

GIFT AID (NON-NEED-BASED) *Scholarships, grants, and awards by category:* Academic interests/achievement: general academic interests/achievements. Creative arts/performance: art/fine arts, music, theater/drama. Special characteristics: children of faculty/staff, religious affiliation, siblings of current students, veterans.

LOANS *Programs:* Federal Direct (Subsidized and Unsubsidized Stafford, PLUS), Perkins, college/university.

WORK-STUDY Federal work-study jobs available. *State or other work-study/employment:* Part-time jobs available.

APPLYING FOR FINANCIAL AID *Required financial aid forms:* FAFSA, institution's own form. *Financial aid deadline:* Continuous. *Notification date:* Continuous beginning 4/1. Students must reply by 8/1 or within 4 weeks of notification.

CONTACT Brynn Bologna, Director, Student Financial Services, Park University, 8700 NW River Park Drive, Parkville, MO 64152, 816-584-6714 or toll-free 800-745-7275. *E-mail:* cathy.colapietro@park.edu. *Website:* http://www.park.edu/.

PARSONS SCHOOL OF DESIGN
New York, NY

Tuition & fees: $47,920	Average undergraduate aid package: $23,960

ABOUT THE INSTITUTION Independent, coed. *Awards:* certificates, associate, bachelor's, and master's degrees. 14 undergraduate majors. *Total enrollment:* 5,278. Undergraduates: 4,291. Freshmen: 917. Federal methodology is used as a basis for awarding need-based institutional aid.

UNDERGRADUATE EXPENSES for 2017–2018 *Application fee:* $50. *Comprehensive fee:* $62,920 includes full-time tuition ($46,820), mandatory fees ($1100), and room and board ($15,000). *College room only:* $16,250. Full-time tuition and fees vary according to degree level and location. Room and board charges vary according to board plan, housing facility, and location. *Part-time tuition:* $1590 per credit hour. *Part-time fees:* $550 per term. Part-time tuition and fees vary according to degree level and location.

FRESHMAN FINANCIAL AID (Fall 2016) 422 applied for aid; of those 81% were deemed to have need. 100% of freshmen with need received aid; of those 11% had need fully met. *Average percent of need met:* 70% (excluding resources awarded to replace EFC). *Average financial aid package:* $25,388 (excluding resources awarded to replace EFC). 36% of all full-time freshmen had no need and received non-need-based gift aid.

UNDERGRADUATE FINANCIAL AID (Fall 2016) 1,426 applied for aid; of those 88% were deemed to have need. 100% of undergraduates with need received aid; of those 16% had need fully met. *Average percent of need met:* 79% (excluding resources awarded to replace EFC). *Average financial aid package:* $23,960 (excluding resources awarded to replace EFC). 48% of all full-time undergraduates had no need and received non-need-based gift aid.

GIFT AID (NEED-BASED) *Total amount:* $25,304,919 (15% federal, 4% state, 76% institutional, 5% external sources). *Receiving aid:* Freshmen: 35% (319); all full-time undergraduates: 31% (1,185). *Average award:* Freshmen: $16,094; Undergrad-

uates: $16,503. *Scholarships, grants, and awards:* Federal Pell, FSEOG, state, private, college/university gift aid from institutional funds.

GIFT AID (NON-NEED-BASED) *Total amount:* $28,106,362 (97% institutional, 3% external sources). *Receiving aid:* Freshmen: 23% (211). Undergraduates: 28% (1,047). *Average award:* Freshmen: $11,241. Undergraduates: $7449. *Scholarships, grants, and awards by category:* Special achievements/activities: leadership. *Tuition waivers:* Full or partial for employees or children of employees.

LOANS *Student loans:* $20,214,701 (43% need-based, 57% non-need-based). 33% of past graduating class borrowed through all loan programs. *Average indebtedness per student:* $70,361. *Average need-based loan:* Freshmen: $3350. Undergraduates: $4281. *Parent loans:* $5,777,130 (17% need-based, 83% non-need-based). *Programs:* Federal Direct (Subsidized and Unsubsidized Stafford, PLUS).

WORK-STUDY *Federal work-study:* 146 jobs averaging $3026. *State or other work-study/employment:* Part-time jobs available.

APPLYING FOR FINANCIAL AID *Required financial aid form:* FAFSA. *Financial aid deadline:* 2/1. *Notification date:* Continuous beginning 4/1. Students must reply within 4 weeks of notification.

CONTACT Office of Student Financial Services, Parsons School of Design, 72 Fifth Avenue, 2nd Floor, New York, NY 10011, 212-229-8930 or toll-free 800-292-3040. *E-mail:* sfs@newschool.edu.

Website: http://www.newschool.edu/parsons/.

PATRICK HENRY COLLEGE
Purcellville, VA

ABOUT THE INSTITUTION Independent nondenominational, coed. *Awards:* bachelor's degrees. 7 undergraduate majors. *Total enrollment:* 277. Undergraduates: 277. Freshmen: 51.

GIFT AID (NEED-BASED) *Scholarships, grants, and awards:* private, college/university gift aid from institutional funds.

GIFT AID (NON-NEED-BASED) *Scholarships, grants, and awards by category:* Academic interests/achievement: general academic interests/achievements. Creative arts/performance: debating, journalism/publications, music. Special achievements/activities: community service, leadership, memberships, religious involvement. Special characteristics: children of faculty/staff, children of public servants, public servants, relatives of clergy, veterans.

LOANS *Programs:* private loans.

APPLYING FOR FINANCIAL AID *Required financial aid form:* CSS Financial Aid PROFILE.

CONTACT Mr. William K. Kellaris, Director of Financial Aid, Patrick Henry College, 10 Patrick Henry Circle, Purcellville, VA 20132, 540-441-8140 or toll-free 888-338-1776. *Fax:* 540-441-8149. *E-mail:* financialaid@phc.edu.

Website: http://www.phc.edu/.

PATTEN UNIVERSITY
Oakland, CA

CONTACT Mr. Robert A. Olivera, Dean of Enrollment Services, Patten University, 2433 Coolidge Avenue, Oakland, CA 94601-2699, 510-261-8500 Ext. 783 or toll-free 877-4PATTEN. *Fax:* 510-534-8969. *E-mail:* oliverob@patten.edu.

Website: http://patten.edu/.

PAUL QUINN COLLEGE
Dallas, TX

ABOUT THE INSTITUTION Independent African Methodist Episcopal, coed. 9 undergraduate majors.

GIFT AID (NEED-BASED) *Scholarships, grants, and awards:* Federal Pell, FSEOG, state, private, college/university gift aid from institutional funds, United Negro College Fund.

GIFT AID (NON-NEED-BASED) *Scholarships, grants, and awards by category:* Creative arts/performance: music, performing arts. Special characteristics: first-generation college students, local/state students.

LOANS *Programs:* Federal Direct (Subsidized and Unsubsidized Stafford, PLUS), alternative loans.

WORK-STUDY *Federal work-study:* 100 jobs averaging $2000. *State or other work-study/employment:* 204 part-time jobs averaging $5000.

APPLYING FOR FINANCIAL AID *Required financial aid form:* FAFSA.

CONTACT Mildred Martinez, Financial Aid Officer I, Paul Quinn College, 3837 Simpson Stuart Road, Dallas, TX 75241, 214-379-5438 or toll-free 877-346-1063. *Fax:* 214-379-5448. *E-mail:* mmartinez@pqc.edu.

Website: http://www.pqc.edu/.

PAUL SMITH'S COLLEGE
Paul Smiths, NY

ABOUT THE INSTITUTION Independent, coed. 12 undergraduate majors.

GIFT AID (NEED-BASED) *Scholarships, grants, and awards:* Federal Pell, FSEOG, state, private, college/university gift aid from institutional funds.

GIFT AID (NON-NEED-BASED) *Scholarships, grants, and awards by category:* Academic interests/achievement: general academic interests/achievements, social sciences. Special achievements/activities: leadership, memberships. Special characteristics: veterans, veterans' children.

LOANS *Programs:* Federal Direct (Subsidized and Unsubsidized Stafford, PLUS), Perkins.

WORK-STUDY *Federal work-study:* jobs available. *State or other work-study/employment:* Total amount: $1,595,101 (100% need-based). Part-time jobs available.

APPLYING FOR FINANCIAL AID *Required financial aid forms:* FAFSA, state aid form.

CONTACT Mary Ellen Chamberlain, Director of Financial Aid, Paul Smith's College, Routes 86 and 30, Paul Smiths, NY 12970, 518-327-6119 or toll-free 800-421-2605. *Fax:* 518-327-6055. *E-mail:* mchamberlain@paulsmiths.edu.

Website: http://www.paulsmiths.edu/.

PEABODY CONSERVATORY OF THE JOHNS HOPKINS UNIVERSITY
Baltimore, MD

Tuition & fees: N/R	Average undergraduate aid package: $7422

ABOUT THE INSTITUTION Independent, coed. 10 undergraduate majors. Federal methodology is used as a basis for awarding need-based institutional aid.

FRESHMAN FINANCIAL AID (Fall 2017, est.) 49 applied for aid; of those 86% were deemed to have need. 100% of freshmen with need received aid; of those 33% had need fully met. *Average percent of need met:* 17% (excluding resources awarded to replace EFC). *Average financial aid package:* $7095 (excluding resources awarded to replace EFC). 9% of all full-time freshmen had no need and received non-need-based gift aid.

UNDERGRADUATE FINANCIAL AID (Fall 2017, est.) 146 applied for aid; of those 80% were deemed to have need. 98% of undergraduates with need received aid; of those 49% had need fully met. *Average percent of need met:* 18% (excluding resources awarded to replace EFC). *Average financial aid package:* $7422 (excluding resources awarded to replace EFC). 7% of all full-time undergraduates had no need and received non-need-based gift aid.

GIFT AID (NEED-BASED) *Total amount:* $5,686,519 (4% federal, 94% institutional, 2% external sources). *Receiving aid:* Freshmen: 29% (23); all full-time undergraduates: 23% (65). *Average award:* Freshmen: $2903; Undergraduates: $4854. *Scholarships, grants, and awards:* Federal Pell, FSEOG, state, private, college/university gift aid from institutional funds.

GIFT AID (NON-NEED-BASED) *Receiving aid:* Freshmen: 48% (38). Undergraduates: 31% (89). *Average award:* Freshmen: $16,285. Undergraduates: $17,931. *Scholarships, grants, and awards by category:* Creative arts/performance: music.

LOANS *Student loans:* $1,044,474 (47% need-based, 53% non-need-based). 49% of past graduating class borrowed through all loan programs. *Average indebtedness per student:* $30,737. *Average need-based loan:* Freshmen: $3734. Undergrad-

uates: $5439. *Parent loans:* $1,348,644 (100% non-need-based). *Programs:* Federal Direct (Subsidized and Unsubsidized Stafford, PLUS), Perkins, college/university.

WORK-STUDY *Federal work-study:* Total amount: $130,358; 71 jobs averaging $1836.

APPLYING FOR FINANCIAL AID *Required financial aid form:* FAFSA. *Financial aid deadline (priority):* 3/1. *Notification date:* 4/1. Students must reply by 5/1.

CONTACT Rebecca Polgar, Director of Financial Aid, Peabody Conservatory of The Johns Hopkins University, 1 East Mount Vernon Place, Baltimore, MD 21202-2397, 667-208-6590 or toll-free 800-368-2521 (out-of-state). *Fax:* 410-659-8102. *E-mail:* finaid@peabody.jhu.edu.
Website: http://www.peabody.jhu.edu/.

PEIRCE COLLEGE
Philadelphia, PA

Tuition & fees: $15,060	Average undergraduate aid package: N/A

ABOUT THE INSTITUTION Independent, coed, primarily women. *Awards:* certificates, associate, bachelor's, and master's degrees. 10 undergraduate majors. *Total enrollment:* 1,478. Undergraduates: 1,389. Freshmen: 87. Federal methodology is used as a basis for awarding need-based institutional aid.

UNDERGRADUATE EXPENSES for 2017–2018 *Application fee:* $50. *Tuition:* full-time $14,400; part-time $600 per credit. Full-time tuition and fees vary according to course load and reciprocity agreements. Part-time tuition and fees vary according to course load and reciprocity agreements.

GIFT AID (NEED-BASED) *Scholarships, grants, and awards:* Federal Pell, FSEOG, state, private, college/university gift aid from institutional funds.

GIFT AID (NON-NEED-BASED) *Scholarships, grants, and awards by category:* Academic interests/achievement: business, computer science, general academic interests/achievements, health fields. *Special achievements/activities:* leadership, memberships. *Special characteristics:* children and siblings of alumni, children of faculty/staff, children of public servants, international students, public servants, siblings of current students, veterans, veterans' children. *Tuition waivers:* Full or partial for children of alumni, employees or children of employees.

LOANS *Programs:* Federal Direct (Subsidized and Unsubsidized Stafford, PLUS).

WORK-STUDY Federal work-study jobs available.

APPLYING FOR FINANCIAL AID *Required financial aid form:* FAFSA. *Financial aid deadline:* Continuous. *Notification date:* Continuous beginning 5/1.

CONTACT Chanel Greene, Manager of Financial Aid, Peirce College, 1420 Pine Street, Philadelphia, PA 19102, 215-670-9330 or toll-free 888-467-3472. *Fax:* 215-545-3671. *E-mail:* cgreene1@peirce.edu.
Website: http://www.peirce.edu/.

PENN STATE ABINGTON
Abington, PA

Tuition & fees (PA res): $14,516	Average undergraduate aid package: $10,195

ABOUT THE INSTITUTION State-related, coed. *Awards:* certificates, associate, and bachelor's degrees (enrollment figures include students enrolled at The Graduate School at Penn State who are taking courses at this location). 118 undergraduate majors. *Total enrollment:* 3,893. Undergraduates: 3,888. Freshmen: 1,056. Federal methodology is used as a basis for awarding need-based institutional aid.

UNDERGRADUATE EXPENSES for 2017–2018 *Application fee:* $65. *Tuition, state resident:* full-time $13,540; part-time $557 per credit hour. *Tuition, nonresident:* full-time $21,582; part-time $899 per credit hour. *Required fees:* full-time $976. Full-time tuition and fees vary according to course level, degree level, location, program, and student level. Part-time tuition and fees vary according to course level, course load, degree level, location, program, and student level.

FRESHMAN FINANCIAL AID (Fall 2016) 702 applied for aid; of those 84% were deemed to have need. 98% of freshmen with need received aid; of those 11% had need fully met. *Average percent of need met:* 56% (excluding resources awarded to replace EFC). *Average financial aid package:* $10,966 (excluding resources

awarded to replace EFC). 10% of all full-time freshmen had no need and received non-need-based gift aid.

UNDERGRADUATE FINANCIAL AID (Fall 2016) 2,465 applied for aid; of those 88% were deemed to have need. 98% of undergraduates with need received aid; of those 13% had need fully met. *Average percent of need met:* 56% (excluding resources awarded to replace EFC). *Average financial aid package:* $10,195 (excluding resources awarded to replace EFC). 6% of all full-time undergraduates had no need and received non-need-based gift aid.

GIFT AID (NEED-BASED) *Total amount:* $15,532,788 (48% federal, 29% state, 22% institutional, 1% external sources). *Receiving aid:* Freshmen: 44% (384); all full-time undergraduates: 46% (1,406). *Average award:* Freshmen: $6074; Undergraduates: $5482. *Scholarships, grants, and awards:* Federal Pell, FSEOG, state, private, college/university gift aid from institutional funds.

GIFT AID (NON-NEED-BASED) *Total amount:* $1,032,506 (3% state, 84% institutional, 13% external sources). *Receiving aid:* Freshmen: 55% (482). Undergraduates: 52% (1,570). *Average award:* Freshmen: $4175. Undergraduates: $4134. *Scholarships, grants, and awards by category:* Academic interests/achievement: general academic interests/achievements. *Special characteristics:* children and siblings of alumni, general special characteristics. *Tuition waivers:* Full or partial for employees or children of employees, senior citizens. *ROTC:* Army cooperative, Air Force cooperative.

LOANS *Student loans:* $16,607,803 (86% need-based, 14% non-need-based). 78% of past graduating class borrowed through all loan programs. *Average indebtedness per student:* $31,007. *Average need-based loan:* Freshmen: $3322. Undergraduates: $4016. *Parent loans:* $2,800,091 (88% need-based, 12% non-need-based). *Programs:* Federal Direct (Subsidized and Unsubsidized Stafford, PLUS), Perkins, college/university, private loans.

WORK-STUDY *Federal work-study:* jobs available.

APPLYING FOR FINANCIAL AID *Required financial aid form:* FAFSA. *Financial aid deadline (priority):* 2/15. *Notification date:* Continuous.

CONTACT Student Aid Office, Penn State Abington, 1600 Woodland Road, Abington, PA 19001-3990, 215-881-7348. *Fax:* 215-881-7655.
Website: http://www.abington.psu.edu/.

PENN STATE ALTOONA
Altoona, PA

Tuition & fees (PA res): $15,190	Average undergraduate aid package: $9995

ABOUT THE INSTITUTION State-related, coed. *Awards:* certificates, associate, and bachelor's degrees (enrollment figures include students enrolled at The Graduate School at Penn State who are taking courses at this location). 125 undergraduate majors. *Total enrollment:* 3,482. Undergraduates: 3,482. Freshmen: 1,274. Federal methodology is used as a basis for awarding need-based institutional aid.

UNDERGRADUATE EXPENSES for 2017–2018 *Application fee:* $65. *Tuition, state resident:* full-time $14,214; part-time $592 per credit hour. *Tuition, nonresident:* full-time $22,716; part-time $947 per credit hour. *Required fees:* full-time $976. Full-time tuition and fees vary according to course level, degree level, location, program, and student level. Part-time tuition and fees vary according to course level, course load, degree level, location, program, and student level. *College room and board:* $11,280; *Room only:* $6180. Room and board charges vary according to board plan, housing facility, and location.

FRESHMAN FINANCIAL AID (Fall 2016) 968 applied for aid; of those 80% were deemed to have need. 97% of freshmen with need received aid; of those 26% had need fully met. *Average percent of need met:* 65% (excluding resources awarded to replace EFC). *Average financial aid package:* $9941 (excluding resources awarded to replace EFC). 8% of all full-time freshmen had no need and received non-need-based gift aid.

UNDERGRADUATE FINANCIAL AID (Fall 2016) 2,656 applied for aid; of those 84% were deemed to have need. 97% of undergraduates with need received aid; of those 24% had need fully met. *Average percent of need met:* 63% (excluding resources awarded to replace EFC). *Average financial aid package:* $9995 (excluding resources awarded to replace EFC). 7% of all full-time undergraduates had no need and received non-need-based gift aid.

GIFT AID (NEED-BASED) *Total amount:* $12,720,579 (41% federal, 25% state, 29% institutional, 5% external sources). *Receiving aid:* Freshmen: 32% (386); all full-time undergraduates: 32% (1,071). *Average award:* Freshmen: $5267; Undergrad-

uates: $5479. *Scholarships, grants, and awards:* Federal Pell, FSEOG, state, private, college/university gift aid from institutional funds.

GIFT AID (NON-NEED-BASED) *Total amount:* $897,082 (3% state, 83% institutional, 14% external sources). *Receiving aid:* Freshmen: 47% (557). Undergraduates: 43% (1,433). *Average award:* Freshmen: $3654. Undergraduates: $3299. *Scholarships, grants, and awards by category:* Academic interests/achievement: general academic interests/achievements. *Special characteristics:* children and siblings of alumni, general special characteristics. *Tuition waivers:* Full or partial for employees or children of employees, senior citizens. *ROTC:* Army cooperative, Air Force cooperative.

LOANS *Student loans:* $23,338,384 (84% need-based, 16% non-need-based). 77% of past graduating class borrowed through all loan programs. *Average indebtedness per student:* $41,629. *Average need-based loan:* Freshmen: $3452. Undergraduates: $3997. *Parent loans:* $9,255,865 (86% need-based, 14% non-need-based). *Programs:* Federal Direct (Subsidized and Unsubsidized Stafford, PLUS), Perkins, college/university, private loans.

WORK-STUDY *Federal work-study:* jobs available.

APPLYING FOR FINANCIAL AID *Required financial aid form:* FAFSA. *Financial aid deadline (priority):* 2/15. *Notification date:* Continuous beginning 3/1.

CONTACT Mr. David Pearlman, Director of Student Aid, Penn State Altoona, W113 Smith Building, Altoona, PA 16601-3760, 814-949-5055 or toll-free 800-848-9843. *Fax:* 814-949-5536. *E-mail:* dpp1@psu.edu.
Website: http://www.altoona.psu.edu/.

PENN STATE BEAVER
Monaca, PA

Tuition & fees (PA res): $13,694	Average undergraduate aid package: $10,943

ABOUT THE INSTITUTION State-related, coed. *Awards:* certificates and bachelor's degrees. 118 undergraduate majors. *Total enrollment:* 655. Undergraduates: 655. Freshmen: 184. Federal methodology is used as a basis for awarding need-based institutional aid.

UNDERGRADUATE EXPENSES for 2017–2018 *Application fee:* $65. *Tuition, state resident:* full-time $12,718; part-time $524 per credit hour. *Tuition, nonresident:* full-time $20,352; part-time $848 per credit hour. *Required fees:* full-time $976. Full-time tuition and fees vary according to course level, degree level, location, program, and student level. Part-time tuition and fees vary according to course level, course load, degree level, location, program, and student level. *College room and board:* $11,280; *Room only:* $6180. Room and board charges vary according to board plan, housing facility, and location.

FRESHMAN FINANCIAL AID (Fall 2016) 213 applied for aid; of those 84% were deemed to have need. 99% of freshmen with need received aid; of those 30% had need fully met. *Average percent of need met:* 73% (excluding resources awarded to replace EFC). *Average financial aid package:* $11,325 (excluding resources awarded to replace EFC). 15% of all full-time freshmen had no need and received non-need-based gift aid.

UNDERGRADUATE FINANCIAL AID (Fall 2016) 565 applied for aid; of those 84% were deemed to have need. 98% of undergraduates with need received aid; of those 28% had need fully met. *Average percent of need met:* 70% (excluding resources awarded to replace EFC). *Average financial aid package:* $10,943 (excluding resources awarded to replace EFC). 12% of all full-time undergraduates had no need and received non-need-based gift aid.

GIFT AID (NEED-BASED) *Total amount:* $3,518,344 (35% federal, 22% state, 36% institutional, 7% external sources). *Receiving aid:* Freshmen: 42% (93); all full-time undergraduates: 40% (252). *Average award:* Freshmen: $6022; Undergraduates: $5679. *Scholarships, grants, and awards:* Federal Pell, FSEOG, state, private, college/university gift aid from institutional funds.

GIFT AID (NON-NEED-BASED) *Total amount:* $322,011 (98% institutional, 2% external sources). *Receiving aid:* Freshmen: 71% (158). Undergraduates: 59% (366). *Average award:* Freshmen: $5472. Undergraduates: $4185. *Scholarships, grants, and awards by category:* Academic interests/achievement: general academic interests/achievements. *Special characteristics:* children and siblings of alumni. *Tuition waivers:* Full or partial for employees or children of employees, senior citizens.

LOANS *Student loans:* $3,753,929 (86% need-based, 14% non-need-based). 78% of past graduating class borrowed through all loan programs. *Average indebtedness per student:* $35,924. *Average need-based loan:* Freshmen: $3272. Undergraduates: $3984. *Parent loans:* $1,770,478 (88% need-based, 12% non-need-based). *Programs:* Federal Direct (Subsidized and Unsubsidized Stafford, PLUS), Perkins, college/university, private loans.

WORK-STUDY *Federal work-study:* jobs available. *State or other work-study/employment:* Part-time jobs available.

APPLYING FOR FINANCIAL AID *Required financial aid form:* FAFSA. *Financial aid deadline (priority):* 2/15. *Notification date:* Continuous beginning 3/1.

CONTACT Gail Gray, Student Aid and Veterans Coordinator, Penn State Beaver, 113 Student Union Building, 100 University Drive, Monaca, PA 15061, 724-773-3803. *E-mail:* gailgray@psu.edu.
Website: http://www.br.psu.edu/.

PENN STATE BERKS
Reading, PA

Tuition & fees (PA res): $15,190	Average undergraduate aid package: $9706

ABOUT THE INSTITUTION State-related, coed. *Awards:* certificates, associate, and bachelor's degrees (enrollment figures include students enrolled at The Graduate School at Penn State who are taking courses at this location). 129 undergraduate majors. *Total enrollment:* 2,719. Undergraduates: 2,719. Freshmen: 694. Federal methodology is used as a basis for awarding need-based institutional aid.

UNDERGRADUATE EXPENSES for 2017–2018 *Application fee:* $65. *Tuition, state resident:* full-time $14,214; part-time $592 per credit hour. *Tuition, nonresident:* full-time $22,716; part-time $947 per credit hour. *Required fees:* full-time $976. Full-time tuition and fees vary according to course level, degree level, location, program, and student level. Part-time tuition and fees vary according to course level, course load, degree level, location, program, and student level. *College room and board:* $12,400; *Room only:* $7300. Room and board charges vary according to board plan, housing facility, and location.

FRESHMAN FINANCIAL AID (Fall 2016) 640 applied for aid; of those 82% were deemed to have need. 96% of freshmen with need received aid; of those 25% had need fully met. *Average percent of need met:* 64% (excluding resources awarded to replace EFC). *Average financial aid package:* $9582 (excluding resources awarded to replace EFC). 6% of all full-time freshmen had no need and received non-need-based gift aid.

UNDERGRADUATE FINANCIAL AID (Fall 2016) 2,168 applied for aid; of those 85% were deemed to have need. 97% of undergraduates with need received aid; of those 24% had need fully met. *Average percent of need met:* 62% (excluding resources awarded to replace EFC). *Average financial aid package:* $9706 (excluding resources awarded to replace EFC). 5% of all full-time undergraduates had no need and received non-need-based gift aid.

GIFT AID (NEED-BASED) *Total amount:* $10,960,381 (42% federal, 29% state, 24% institutional, 5% external sources). *Receiving aid:* Freshmen: 37% (266); all full-time undergraduates: 39% (981). *Average award:* Freshmen: $5465; Undergraduates: $5269. *Scholarships, grants, and awards:* Federal Pell, FSEOG, state, private, college/university gift aid from institutional funds.

GIFT AID (NON-NEED-BASED) *Total amount:* $531,123 (5% state, 80% institutional, 15% external sources). *Receiving aid:* Freshmen: 51% (370). Undergraduates: 48% (1,208). *Average award:* Freshmen: $3448. Undergraduates: $3186. *Scholarships, grants, and awards by category:* Academic interests/achievement: general academic interests/achievements. *Special characteristics:* children and siblings of alumni. *Tuition waivers:* Full or partial for employees or children of employees, senior citizens. *ROTC:* Army cooperative.

LOANS *Student loans:* $17,850,997 (85% need-based, 15% non-need-based). 77% of past graduating class borrowed through all loan programs. *Average indebtedness per student:* $39,022. *Average need-based loan:* Freshmen: $3429. Undergraduates: $4187. *Parent loans:* $7,086,187 (89% need-based, 11% non-need-based). *Programs:* Federal Direct (Subsidized and Unsubsidized Stafford, PLUS), Perkins, college/university, private loans.

WORK-STUDY *Federal work-study:* jobs available.

APPLYING FOR FINANCIAL AID *Required financial aid form:* FAFSA. *Financial aid deadline (priority):* 2/15. *Notification date:* Continuous beginning 3/1.

CONTACT Judith A. Rile, Financial Aid Coordinator, Penn State Berks, Perkins Student Center, Room 6, Reading, PA 19610-6009, 610-396-6070. *Fax:* 610-396-6316. *E-mail:* jar38@psu.edu.
Website: http://www.bk.psu.edu/.

PENN STATE BRANDYWINE
Media, PA

Tuition & fees (PA res): $14,460	Average undergraduate aid package: $10,446

ABOUT THE INSTITUTION State-related, coed. *Awards:* certificates, associate, and bachelor's degrees. 120 undergraduate majors. *Total enrollment:* 1,438. Undergraduates: 1,438. Freshmen: 430. Federal methodology is used as a basis for awarding need-based institutional aid.

UNDERGRADUATE EXPENSES for 2017–2018 *Application fee:* $65. *Tuition, state resident:* full-time $13,484; part-time $555 per credit hour. *Tuition, nonresident:* full-time $21,402; part-time $892 per credit hour. *Required fees:* full-time $976. Full-time tuition and fees vary according to course level, degree level, location, program, and student level. Part-time tuition and fees vary according to course level, course load, degree level, location, program, and student level. *College room and board:* $11,860; *Room only:* $6760. Room and board charges vary according to board plan.

FRESHMAN FINANCIAL AID (Fall 2016) 295 applied for aid; of those 80% were deemed to have need. 99% of freshmen with need received aid; of those 18% had need fully met. *Average percent of need met:* 58% (excluding resources awarded to replace EFC). *Average financial aid package:* $10,512 (excluding resources awarded to replace EFC). 10% of all full-time freshmen had no need and received non-need-based gift aid.

UNDERGRADUATE FINANCIAL AID (Fall 2016) 947 applied for aid; of those 83% were deemed to have need. 97% of undergraduates with need received aid; of those 16% had need fully met. *Average percent of need met:* 58% (excluding resources awarded to replace EFC). *Average financial aid package:* $10,446 (excluding resources awarded to replace EFC). 8% of all full-time undergraduates had no need and received non-need-based gift aid.

GIFT AID (NEED-BASED) *Total amount:* $5,756,856 (42% federal, 26% state, 29% institutional, 3% external sources). *Receiving aid:* Freshmen: 39% (127); all full-time undergraduates: 42% (478). *Average award:* Freshmen: $5891; Undergraduates: $5587. *Scholarships, grants, and awards:* Federal Pell, FSEOG, state, private, college/university gift aid from institutional funds.

GIFT AID (NON-NEED-BASED) *Total amount:* $535,653 (2% federal, 76% institutional, 22% external sources). *Receiving aid:* Freshmen: 58% (188). Undergraduates: 49% (563). *Average award:* Freshmen: $5045. Undergraduates: $4510. *Scholarships, grants, and awards by category:* Academic interests/achievement: general academic interests/achievements. *Special characteristics:* children and siblings of alumni. *Tuition waivers:* Full or partial for employees or children of employees, senior citizens. *ROTC:* Army cooperative, Air Force cooperative.

LOANS *Student loans:* $5,606,573 (82% need-based, 18% non-need-based). 80% of past graduating class borrowed through all loan programs. *Average indebtedness per student:* $34,353. *Average need-based loan:* Freshmen: $3352. Undergraduates: $3945. *Parent loans:* $1,465,270 (79% need-based, 21% non-need-based). *Programs:* Federal Direct (Subsidized and Unsubsidized Stafford, PLUS), Perkins, college/university, private loans.

WORK-STUDY *Federal work-study:* jobs available. *State or other work-study/employment:* Part-time jobs available.

APPLYING FOR FINANCIAL AID *Required financial aid form:* FAFSA. *Financial aid deadline (priority):* 2/15. *Notification date:* Continuous beginning 3/1.

CONTACT Student Financial Aid Office, Penn State Brandywine, 105 Main Building, 25 Yearsley Mill Road, Media, PA 19063, 610-892-1260. *E-mail:* bw-financial@psu.edu. *Website:* http://www.brandywine.psu.edu/.

PENN STATE ERIE, THE BEHREND COLLEGE
Erie, PA

Tuition & fees (PA res): $15,190	Average undergraduate aid package: $10,632

ABOUT THE INSTITUTION State-related, coed. *Awards:* certificates, associate, bachelor's, and master's degrees. 129 undergraduate majors. *Total enrollment:* 4,502. Undergraduates: 4,345. Freshmen: 1,052. Federal methodology is used as a basis for awarding need-based institutional aid.

UNDERGRADUATE EXPENSES for 2017–2018 *Application fee:* $65. *Tuition, state resident:* full-time $14,214; part-time $592 per credit hour. *Tuition, nonresident:* full-time $22,716; part-time $947 per credit hour. *Required fees:* full-time $976. Full-time tuition and fees vary according to course level, degree level, location, program, and student level. Part-time tuition and fees vary according to course level, course load, degree level, location, program, and student level. *College room and board:* $11,280; *Room only:* $6180. Room and board charges vary according to board plan, housing facility, and location.

FRESHMAN FINANCIAL AID (Fall 2016) 878 applied for aid; of those 82% were deemed to have need. 98% of freshmen with need received aid; of those 32% had need fully met. *Average percent of need met:* 69% (excluding resources awarded to replace EFC). *Average financial aid package:* $10,282 (excluding resources awarded to replace EFC). 6% of all full-time freshmen had no need and received non-need-based gift aid.

UNDERGRADUATE FINANCIAL AID (Fall 2016) 3,227 applied for aid; of those 86% were deemed to have need. 98% of undergraduates with need received aid; of those 28% had need fully met. *Average percent of need met:* 67% (excluding resources awarded to replace EFC). *Average financial aid package:* $10,632 (excluding resources awarded to replace EFC). 6% of all full-time undergraduates had no need and received non-need-based gift aid.

GIFT AID (NEED-BASED) *Total amount:* $17,614,808 (34% federal, 27% state, 31% institutional, 8% external sources). *Receiving aid:* Freshmen: 29% (338); all full-time undergraduates: 32% (1,315). *Average award:* Freshmen: $5510; Undergraduates: $5687. *Scholarships, grants, and awards:* Federal Pell, FSEOG, state, private, college/university gift aid from institutional funds.

GIFT AID (NON-NEED-BASED) *Total amount:* $1,289,441 (73% institutional, 27% external sources). *Receiving aid:* Freshmen: 48% (554). Undergraduates: 46% (1,921). *Average award:* Freshmen: $3663. Undergraduates: $3891. *Scholarships, grants, and awards by category:* Academic interests/achievement: general academic interests/achievements. *Special characteristics:* children and siblings of alumni. *Tuition waivers:* Full or partial for employees or children of employees, senior citizens. *ROTC:* Army cooperative.

LOANS *Student loans:* $28,911,293 (88% need-based, 12% non-need-based). 73% of past graduating class borrowed through all loan programs. *Average indebtedness per student:* $39,977. *Average need-based loan:* Freshmen: $3495. Undergraduates: $4418. *Parent loans:* $10,749,450 (90% need-based, 10% non-need-based). *Programs:* Federal Direct (Subsidized and Unsubsidized Stafford, PLUS), Perkins, college/university, private loans.

WORK-STUDY *Federal work-study:* jobs available.

APPLYING FOR FINANCIAL AID *Required financial aid form:* FAFSA. *Financial aid deadline (priority):* 2/15. *Notification date:* Continuous beginning 3/1.

CONTACT Ms. Jane Brady, Associate Director of Financial Aid, Penn State Erie, The Behrend College, 4851 College Drive, Metzgar Admissions and Alumni Center, Erie, PA 16563, 814-898-6162 or toll-free 866-374-3378. *Fax:* 814-898-7595. *E-mail:* jub9@psu.edu.
Website: http://www.psbehrend.psu.edu/.

PENN STATE GREATER ALLEGHENY
McKeesport, PA

Tuition & fees (PA res): $13,694	Average undergraduate aid package: $12,245

ABOUT THE INSTITUTION State-related, coed. *Awards:* certificates, associate, and bachelor's degrees. 119 undergraduate majors. *Total enrollment:* 497. Undergraduates: 497. Freshmen: 115. Federal methodology is used as a basis for awarding need-based institutional aid.

UNDERGRADUATE EXPENSES for 2017–2018 *Application fee:* $65. *Tuition, state resident:* full-time $12,718; part-time $524 per credit hour. *Tuition, nonresident:* full-time $20,352; part-time $848 per credit hour. *Required fees:* full-time $976. Full-time tuition and fees vary according to course level, degree level, location, program, and student level. Part-time tuition and fees vary according to course level, course load, degree level, location, program, and student level. *College room and board:* $11,280; *Room only:* $6180. Room and board charges vary according to board plan, housing facility, and location.

FRESHMAN FINANCIAL AID (Fall 2016) 146 applied for aid; of those 88% were deemed to have need. 98% of freshmen with need received aid; of those 25% had need fully met. *Average percent of need met:* 72% (excluding resources awarded to replace EFC). *Average financial aid package:* $13,195 (excluding resources awarded to replace EFC). 13% of all full-time freshmen had no need and received non-need-based gift aid.

UNDERGRADUATE FINANCIAL AID (Fall 2016) 439 applied for aid; of those 89% were deemed to have need. 97% of undergraduates with need received aid; of those 21% had need fully met. *Average percent of need met:* 68% (excluding resources awarded to replace EFC). *Average financial aid package:* $12,245 (excluding resources awarded to replace EFC). 8% of all full-time undergraduates had no need and received non-need-based gift aid.

GIFT AID (NEED-BASED) *Total amount:* $3,349,491 (36% federal, 24% state, 26% institutional, 14% external sources). *Receiving aid:* Freshmen: 50% (79); all full-time undergraduates: 52% (251). *Average award:* Freshmen: $6296; Undergraduates: $5631. *Scholarships, grants, and awards:* Federal Pell, FSEOG, state, private, college/university gift aid from institutional funds.

GIFT AID (NON-NEED-BASED) *Total amount:* $243,254 (2% state, 79% institutional, 19% external sources). *Receiving aid:* Freshmen: 69% (109). Undergraduates: 62% (300). *Average award:* Freshmen: $5679. Undergraduates: $4918. *Tuition waivers:* Full or partial for employees or children of employees, senior citizens.

LOANS *Student loans:* $2,975,638 (87% need-based, 13% non-need-based). 77% of past graduating class borrowed through all loan programs. *Average indebtedness per student:* $37,163. *Average need-based loan:* Freshmen: $3370. Undergraduates: $3970. *Parent loans:* $812,572 (80% need-based, 20% non-need-based). *Programs:* Federal Direct (Subsidized and Unsubsidized Stafford, PLUS), Perkins, college/university, private loans.

WORK-STUDY *Federal work-study:* jobs available. *State or other work-study/employment:* Part-time jobs available.

APPLYING FOR FINANCIAL AID *Required financial aid form:* FAFSA. *Financial aid deadline (priority):* 2/15. *Notification date:* Continuous beginning 3/1.

CONTACT Student Aid Office, Penn State Greater Allegheny, 4000 University Drive, McKeesport, PA 15132-7698, 412-675-9160. *Fax:* 412-675-9036. *Website:* http://www.ga.psu.edu/.

PENN STATE HARRISBURG
Middletown, PA

Tuition & fees (PA res): $15,190	Average undergraduate aid package: $9771

ABOUT THE INSTITUTION State-related, coed. *Awards:* certificates, associate, bachelor's, master's, and doctoral degrees. 29 undergraduate majors. *Total enrollment:* 5,077. Undergraduates: 4,286. Freshmen: 962. Federal methodology is used as a basis for awarding need-based institutional aid.

UNDERGRADUATE EXPENSES for 2017–2018 *Application fee:* $65. *Tuition, state resident:* full-time $14,214; part-time $592 per credit hour. *Tuition, nonresident:* full-time $22,716; part-time $947 per credit hour. *Required fees:*

full-time $976. Full-time tuition and fees vary according to course level, degree level, location, program, and student level. Part-time tuition and fees vary according to course level, course load, degree level, location, program, and student level. *College room and board:* $12,940; *Room only:* $7840. Room and board charges vary according to board plan, housing facility, and location.

FRESHMAN FINANCIAL AID (Fall 2016) 618 applied for aid; of those 80% were deemed to have need. 95% of freshmen with need received aid; of those 23% had need fully met. *Average percent of need met:* 63% (excluding resources awarded to replace EFC). *Average financial aid package:* $10,055 (excluding resources awarded to replace EFC). 9% of all full-time freshmen had no need and received non-need-based gift aid.

UNDERGRADUATE FINANCIAL AID (Fall 2016) 2,688 applied for aid; of those 86% were deemed to have need. 97% of undergraduates with need received aid; of those 19% had need fully met. *Average percent of need met:* 59% (excluding resources awarded to replace EFC). *Average financial aid package:* $9771 (excluding resources awarded to replace EFC). 8% of all full-time undergraduates had no need and received non-need-based gift aid.

GIFT AID (NEED-BASED) *Total amount:* $13,965,796 (44% federal, 25% state, 27% institutional, 4% external sources). *Receiving aid:* Freshmen: 24% (240); all full-time undergraduates: 32% (1,204). *Average award:* Freshmen: $5938; Undergraduates: $5437. *Scholarships, grants, and awards:* Federal Pell, FSEOG, state, private, college/university gift aid from institutional funds.

GIFT AID (NON-NEED-BASED) *Total amount:* $843,219 (2% state, 85% institutional, 13% external sources). *Receiving aid:* Freshmen: 40% (401). Undergraduates: 42% (1,576). *Average award:* Freshmen: $2398. Undergraduates: $2404. *Scholarships, grants, and awards by category: Academic interests/achievement:* general academic interests/achievements. *Special characteristics:* children and siblings of alumni, general special characteristics. *Tuition waivers:* Full or partial for employees or children of employees, senior citizens. *ROTC:* Army cooperative.

LOANS *Student loans:* $23,596,363 (87% need-based, 13% non-need-based). 60% of past graduating class borrowed through all loan programs. *Average indebtedness per student:* $42,315. *Average need-based loan:* Freshmen: $3469. Undergraduates: $4372. *Parent loans:* $7,957,442 (89% need-based, 11% non-need-based). *Programs:* Federal Direct (Subsidized and Unsubsidized Stafford, PLUS), Perkins, college/university, private loans.

WORK-STUDY *Federal work-study:* jobs available.

APPLYING FOR FINANCIAL AID *Required financial aid form:* FAFSA. *Financial aid deadline (priority):* 2/15. *Notification date:* Continuous beginning 3/1.

CONTACT Student Aid Office, Penn State Harrisburg, 777 West Harrisburg Pike, Middletown, PA 17057-4898, 717-948-6307 or toll-free 800-222-2056. *Fax:* 717-948-6008. *E-mail:* hbgfinaid@psu.edu. *Website:* http://www.harrisburg.psu.edu/.

PENN STATE HAZLETON
Hazleton, PA

Tuition & fees (PA res): $14,460	Average undergraduate aid package: $11,673

ABOUT THE INSTITUTION State-related, coed. *Awards:* certificates, associate, and bachelor's degrees. 125 undergraduate majors. *Total enrollment:* 755. Undergraduates: 755. Freshmen: 204. Federal methodology is used as a basis for awarding need-based institutional aid.

UNDERGRADUATE EXPENSES for 2017–2018 *Application fee:* $65. *Tuition, state resident:* full-time $13,484; part-time $555 per credit hour. *Tuition, nonresident:* full-time $21,402; part-time $892 per credit hour. *Required fees:* full-time $976. Full-time tuition and fees vary according to course level, degree level, location, program, and student level. Part-time tuition and fees vary according to course level, course load, degree level, location, program, and student level. *College room and board:* $11,280; *Room only:* $6180. Room and board charges vary according to board plan, housing facility, and location.

FRESHMAN FINANCIAL AID (Fall 2016) 283 applied for aid; of those 88% were deemed to have need. 98% of freshmen with need received aid; of those 24% had need fully met. *Average percent of need met:* 69% (excluding resources awarded to replace EFC). *Average financial aid package:* $12,610 (excluding resources awarded to replace EFC). 12% of all full-time freshmen had no need and received non-need-based gift aid.

UNDERGRADUATE FINANCIAL AID (Fall 2016) 682 applied for aid; of those 91% were deemed to have need. 98% of undergraduates with need received aid; of those 23% had need fully met. *Average percent of need met:* 67% (excluding resources awarded to replace EFC). *Average financial aid package:* $11,673 (excluding resources awarded to replace EFC). 8% of all full-time undergraduates had no need and received non-need-based gift aid.

GIFT AID (NEED-BASED) *Total amount:* $5,065,849 (35% federal, 19% state, 43% institutional, 3% external sources). *Receiving aid:* Freshmen: 48% (145); all full-time undergraduates: 47% (360). *Average award:* Freshmen: $5644; Undergraduates: $5862. *Scholarships, grants, and awards:* Federal Pell, FSEOG, state, private, college/university gift aid from institutional funds.

GIFT AID (NON-NEED-BASED) *Total amount:* $319,561 (1% state, 93% institutional, 6% external sources). *Receiving aid:* Freshmen: 70% (210). Undergraduates: 62% (474). *Average award:* Freshmen: $5803. Undergraduates: $4771. *Scholarships, grants, and awards by category:* Academic interests/achievement: general academic interests/achievements. Special characteristics: children and siblings of alumni. *Tuition waivers:* Full or partial for employees or children of employees, senior citizens. *ROTC:* Air Force cooperative.

LOANS *Student loans:* $4,758,625 (91% need-based, 9% non-need-based). 86% of past graduating class borrowed through all loan programs. *Average indebtedness per student:* $45,703. *Average need-based loan:* Freshmen: $3321. Undergraduates: $3903. *Parent loans:* $2,322,222 (92% need-based, 8% non-need-based). *Programs:* Federal Direct (Subsidized and Unsubsidized Stafford, PLUS), Perkins, college/university, private loans.

WORK-STUDY *Federal work-study:* jobs available. *State or other work-study/employment:* Part-time jobs available.

APPLYING FOR FINANCIAL AID *Required financial aid form:* FAFSA. *Financial aid deadline (priority):* 2/15. *Notification date:* Continuous beginning 3/1.

CONTACT Mrs. Sarah Evancho, Student Aid Coordinator, Penn State Hazleton, Administration Building, Room 222, Hazleton, PA 18201-1291, 570-450-3163 or toll-free 800-279-8495. *E-mail:* sjw37@psu.edu.
Website: http://www.hn.psu.edu/.

PENN STATE LEHIGH VALLEY
Center Valley, PA

Tuition & fees (PA res): $14,460	Average undergraduate aid package: $10,598

ABOUT THE INSTITUTION State-related, coed. *Awards:* certificates, associate, and bachelor's degrees (enrollment figures include students enrolled at The Graduate School at Penn State who are taking courses at this location). 119 undergraduate majors. *Total enrollment:* 919. Undergraduates: 900. Freshmen: 247. Federal methodology is used as a basis for awarding need-based institutional aid.

UNDERGRADUATE EXPENSES for 2017–2018 *Application fee:* $65. *Tuition, state resident:* full-time $13,484; part-time $555 per credit hour. *Tuition, nonresident:* full-time $21,402; part-time $892 per credit hour. *Required fees:* full-time $976. Full-time tuition and fees vary according to course level, degree level, location, program, and student level. Part-time tuition and fees vary according to course level, course load, degree level, location, program, and student level.

FRESHMAN FINANCIAL AID (Fall 2016) 202 applied for aid; of those 81% were deemed to have need. 99% of freshmen with need received aid; of those 14% had need fully met. *Average percent of need met:* 57% (excluding resources awarded to replace EFC). *Average financial aid package:* $10,837 (excluding resources awarded to replace EFC). 14% of all full-time freshmen had no need and received non-need-based gift aid.

UNDERGRADUATE FINANCIAL AID (Fall 2016) 560 applied for aid; of those 83% were deemed to have need. 97% of undergraduates with need received aid; of those 14% had need fully met. *Average percent of need met:* 57% (excluding resources awarded to replace EFC). *Average financial aid package:* $10,598 (excluding resources awarded to replace EFC). 9% of all full-time undergraduates had no need and received non-need-based gift aid.

GIFT AID (NEED-BASED) *Total amount:* $3,430,999 (44% federal, 29% state, 26% institutional, 1% external sources). *Receiving aid:* Freshmen: 44% (98); all full-time undergraduates: 44% (299). *Average award:* Freshmen: $5795; Undergraduates: $5490. *Scholarships, grants, and awards:* Federal Pell, FSEOG, state, private, college/university gift aid from institutional funds.

GIFT AID (NON-NEED-BASED) *Total amount:* $248,970 (5% federal, 2% state, 82% institutional, 11% external sources). *Receiving aid:* Freshmen: 63% (141). Undergraduates: 52% (353). *Average award:* Freshmen: $4363. Undergraduates: $3106. *Scholarships, grants, and awards by category:* Academic interests/achievement: general academic interests/achievements. Special characteristics: general special characteristics. *Tuition waivers:* Full or partial for employees or children of employees, senior citizens. *ROTC:* Army cooperative.

LOANS *Student loans:* $3,350,009 (83% need-based, 17% non-need-based). 69% of past graduating class borrowed through all loan programs. *Average indebtedness per student:* $38,922. *Average need-based loan:* Freshmen: $3402. Undergraduates: $4055. *Parent loans:* $599,757 (81% need-based, 19% non-need-based). *Programs:* Federal Direct (Subsidized and Unsubsidized Stafford, PLUS), Perkins, college/university, private loans.

WORK-STUDY *Federal work-study:* jobs available. *State or other work-study/employment:* Part-time jobs available.

APPLYING FOR FINANCIAL AID *Required financial aid form:* FAFSA. *Financial aid deadline:* Continuous. *Notification date:* Continuous beginning 3/1.

CONTACT Maryann Hubick, Student Aid Coordinator, Penn State Lehigh Valley, 8380 Mohr Lane, Fogelsville, PA 18051, 610-285-5033. *Fax:* 610-285-5220. *E-mail:* mxh61@psu.edu.
Website: http://www.lv.psu.edu/.

PENN STATE NEW KENSINGTON
New Kensington, PA

Tuition & fees (PA res): $13,694	Average undergraduate aid package: $9896

ABOUT THE INSTITUTION State-related, coed. *Awards:* certificates, associate, and bachelor's degrees. 124 undergraduate majors. *Total enrollment:* 595. Undergraduates: 595. Freshmen: 132. Federal methodology is used as a basis for awarding need-based institutional aid.

UNDERGRADUATE EXPENSES for 2017–2018 *Application fee:* $65. *Tuition, state resident:* full-time $12,718; part-time $524 per credit hour. *Tuition, nonresident:* full-time $20,352; part-time $848 per credit hour. *Required fees:* full-time $976. Full-time tuition and fees vary according to course level, degree level, location, program, and student level. Part-time tuition and fees vary according to course level, course load, degree level, location, program, and student level.

FRESHMAN FINANCIAL AID (Fall 2016) 178 applied for aid; of those 84% were deemed to have need. 97% of freshmen with need received aid; of those 20% had need fully met. *Average percent of need met:* 67% (excluding resources awarded to replace EFC). *Average financial aid package:* $10,178 (excluding resources awarded to replace EFC). 14% of all full-time freshmen had no need and received non-need-based gift aid.

UNDERGRADUATE FINANCIAL AID (Fall 2016) 449 applied for aid; of those 83% were deemed to have need. 98% of undergraduates with need received aid; of those 22% had need fully met. *Average percent of need met:* 64% (excluding resources awarded to replace EFC). *Average financial aid package:* $9896 (excluding resources awarded to replace EFC). 9% of all full-time undergraduates had no need and received non-need-based gift aid.

GIFT AID (NEED-BASED) *Total amount:* $2,572,282 (35% federal, 30% state, 28% institutional, 7% external sources). *Receiving aid:* Freshmen: 43% (83); all full-time undergraduates: 37% (195). *Average award:* Freshmen: $4991; Undergraduates: $5227. *Scholarships, grants, and awards:* Federal Pell, FSEOG, state, private, college/university gift aid from institutional funds.

GIFT AID (NON-NEED-BASED) *Total amount:* $182,256 (4% state, 87% institutional, 9% external sources). *Receiving aid:* Freshmen: 64% (125). Undergraduates: 54% (280). *Average award:* Freshmen: $3150. Undergraduates: $3406. *Scholarships, grants, and awards by category:* Academic interests/achievement: general academic interests/achievements. Special characteristics: children and siblings of alumni. *Tuition waivers:* Full or partial for employees or children of employees, senior citizens. *ROTC:* Air Force cooperative.

LOANS *Student loans:* $3,006,381 (87% need-based, 13% non-need-based). 75% of past graduating class borrowed through all loan programs. *Average indebtedness per student:* $38,989. *Average need-based loan:* Freshmen: $3374. Undergraduates: $3889. *Parent loans:* $721,071 (81% need-based, 19% non-need-based). *Pro-

grams: Federal Direct (Subsidized and Unsubsidized Stafford, PLUS), Perkins, college/university, private loans.
WORK-STUDY *Federal work-study:* jobs available. *State or other work-study/employment:* Part-time jobs available.
APPLYING FOR FINANCIAL AID *Required financial aid form:* FAFSA. *Financial aid deadline (priority):* 2/15. *Notification date:* Continuous beginning 3/1.
CONTACT Office of Student Aid, Penn State New Kensington, Administrative Building, 3550 Seventh Street Road, New Kensington, PA 15068, 724-334-6047 or toll-free 888-968-7297. *Fax:* 724-334-6111. *E-mail:* nk-finaid@psu.edu.
Website: http://www.nk.psu.edu/.

PENN STATE SCHUYLKILL
Schuylkill Haven, PA

Tuition & fees (PA res): $14,398	Average undergraduate aid package: $11,387

ABOUT THE INSTITUTION State-related, coed. *Awards:* certificates, associate, and bachelor's degrees (bachelor's degree programs completed at the Harrisburg campus). 124 undergraduate majors. *Total enrollment:* 732. Undergraduates: 732. Freshmen: 178. Federal methodology is used as a basis for awarding need-based institutional aid.
UNDERGRADUATE EXPENSES for 2017–2018 *Application fee:* $65. *Tuition, state resident:* full-time $13,484; part-time $555 per credit hour. *Tuition, nonresident:* full-time $21,402; part-time $892 per credit hour. *Required fees:* full-time $914. Full-time tuition and fees vary according to course level, degree level, location, program, and student level. Part-time tuition and fees vary according to course level, course load, degree level, location, program, and student level. *College room and board:* $8426; *Room only:* $6426. Room and board charges vary according to board plan, housing facility, and location.
FRESHMAN FINANCIAL AID (Fall 2016) 194 applied for aid; of those 90% were deemed to have need. 99% of freshmen with need received aid; of those 19% had need fully met. *Average percent of need met:* 64% (excluding resources awarded to replace EFC). *Average financial aid package:* $11,653 (excluding resources awarded to replace EFC). 8% of all full-time freshmen had no need and received non-need-based gift aid.
UNDERGRADUATE FINANCIAL AID (Fall 2016) 586 applied for aid; of those 93% were deemed to have need. 99% of undergraduates with need received aid; of those 21% had need fully met. *Average percent of need met:* 67% (excluding resources awarded to replace EFC). *Average financial aid package:* $11,387 (excluding resources awarded to replace EFC). 5% of all full-time undergraduates had no need and received non-need-based gift aid.
GIFT AID (NEED-BASED) *Total amount:* $4,362,082 (40% federal, 24% state, 33% institutional, 3% external sources). *Receiving aid:* Freshmen: 59% (119); all full-time undergraduates: 58% (358). *Average award:* Freshmen: $5241; Undergraduates: $5436. *Scholarships, grants, and awards:* Federal Pell, FSEOG, state, private, college/university gift aid from institutional funds.
GIFT AID (NON-NEED-BASED) *Total amount:* $166,649 (4% state, 88% institutional, 8% external sources). *Receiving aid:* Freshmen: 79% (160). Undergraduates: 70% (437). *Average award:* Freshmen: $3998. Undergraduates: $4421. *Scholarships, grants, and awards by category:* Academic interests/achievement: general academic interests/achievements. Special characteristics: general special characteristics. *Tuition waivers:* Full or partial for employees or children of employees, senior citizens.
LOANS *Student loans:* $4,426,543 (90% need-based, 10% non-need-based). 88% of past graduating class borrowed through all loan programs. *Average indebtedness per student:* $38,360. *Average need-based loan:* Freshmen: $3227. Undergraduates: $4032. *Parent loans:* $1,712,419 (96% need-based, 4% non-need-based). *Programs:* Federal Direct (Subsidized and Unsubsidized Stafford, PLUS), Perkins, college/university, private loans.
WORK-STUDY *Federal work-study:* jobs available. *State or other work-study/employment:* Part-time jobs available.
APPLYING FOR FINANCIAL AID *Required financial aid form:* FAFSA. *Financial aid deadline (priority):* 2/15. *Notification date:* Continuous beginning 3/1.

CONTACT Student Aid and Admissions Office, Penn State Schuylkill, 200 University Drive, Schuylkill Haven, PA 17972-2208, 570-385-6244. *Fax:* 570-385-6272. *E-mail:* sl-financialaid@psu.edu.
Website: http://www.sl.psu.edu/.

PENN STATE SHENANGO
Sharon, PA

Tuition & fees (PA res): $13,324	Average undergraduate aid package: $13,129

ABOUT THE INSTITUTION State-related, coed. *Awards:* certificates, associate, and bachelor's degrees. 124 undergraduate majors. *Total enrollment:* 490. Undergraduates: 490. Freshmen: 65. Federal methodology is used as a basis for awarding need-based institutional aid.
UNDERGRADUATE EXPENSES for 2017–2018 *Application fee:* $65. *Tuition, state resident:* full-time $12,474; part-time $504 per credit hour. *Tuition, nonresident:* full-time $19,960; part-time $832 per credit hour. *Required fees:* full-time $850. Full-time tuition and fees vary according to course level, degree level, location, program, and student level. Part-time tuition and fees vary according to course level, course load, degree level, location, program, and student level.
FRESHMAN FINANCIAL AID (Fall 2016) 57 applied for aid; of those 91% were deemed to have need. 100% of freshmen with need received aid; of those 23% had need fully met. *Average percent of need met:* 58% (excluding resources awarded to replace EFC). *Average financial aid package:* $11,549 (excluding resources awarded to replace EFC). 7% of all full-time freshmen had no need and received non-need-based gift aid.
UNDERGRADUATE FINANCIAL AID (Fall 2016) 214 applied for aid; of those 94% were deemed to have need. 100% of undergraduates with need received aid; of those 14% had need fully met. *Average percent of need met:* 57% (excluding resources awarded to replace EFC). *Average financial aid package:* $13,129 (excluding resources awarded to replace EFC). 7% of all full-time undergraduates had no need and received non-need-based gift aid.
GIFT AID (NEED-BASED) *Total amount:* $2,446,369 (38% federal, 14% state, 47% institutional, 1% external sources). *Receiving aid:* Freshmen: 50% (30); all full-time undergraduates: 71% (161). *Average award:* Freshmen: $6585; Undergraduates: $5934. *Scholarships, grants, and awards:* Federal Pell, FSEOG, state, private, college/university gift aid from institutional funds.
GIFT AID (NON-NEED-BASED) *Total amount:* $128,042 (1% state, 97% institutional, 2% external sources). *Receiving aid:* Freshmen: 83% (50). Undergraduates: 78% (177). *Average award:* Freshmen: $3425. Undergraduates: $4055. *Scholarships, grants, and awards by category:* Academic interests/achievement: general academic interests/achievements. Special characteristics: children and siblings of alumni. *Tuition waivers:* Full or partial for employees or children of employees, senior citizens.
LOANS *Student loans:* $2,185,622 (95% need-based, 5% non-need-based). 94% of past graduating class borrowed through all loan programs. *Average indebtedness per student:* $45,746. *Average need-based loan:* Freshmen: $3224. Undergraduates: $3856. *Parent loans:* $89,812 (79% need-based, 21% non-need-based). *Programs:* Federal Direct (Subsidized and Unsubsidized Stafford, PLUS), Perkins, college/university, private loans.
WORK-STUDY *Federal work-study:* jobs available. *State or other work-study/employment:* Part-time jobs available.
APPLYING FOR FINANCIAL AID *Required financial aid form:* FAFSA. *Financial aid deadline (priority):* 2/15. *Notification date:* Continuous beginning 3/1.
CONTACT Shawn O'Neill, Financial Aid Coordinator, Penn State Shenango, Lecture Hall, Room 225, 147 Shenango Avenue, Sharon, PA 16146, 724-983-2804. *E-mail:* swo3@psu.edu.
Website: http://www.shenango.psu.edu/.

PENN STATE UNIVERSITY PARK
State College, PA

Tuition & fees (PA res): $18,436	Average undergraduate aid package: $10,783

ABOUT THE INSTITUTION State-related, coed. *Awards:* certificates, associate, bachelor's, master's, and doctoral degrees. 120 undergraduate majors. *Total enrollment:* 47,119. Undergraduates: 40,835. Freshmen: 7,863. Federal methodology is used as a basis for awarding need-based institutional aid.

UNDERGRADUATE EXPENSES for 2017–2018 *Application fee:* $65. *Tuition, state resident:* full-time $17,416; part-time $726 per credit hour. *Tuition, nonresident:* full-time $32,644; part-time $1360 per credit hour. *Required fees:* full-time $1020. Full-time tuition and fees vary according to course level, degree level, location, program, and student level. Part-time tuition and fees vary according to course level, course load, degree level, location, program, and student level. *College room and board:* $11,280; *Room only:* $6180. Room and board charges vary according to board plan, housing facility, and location.

FRESHMAN FINANCIAL AID (Fall 2016) 6,266 applied for aid; of those 65% were deemed to have need. 91% of freshmen with need received aid; of those 34% had need fully met. *Average percent of need met:* 64% (excluding resources awarded to replace EFC). *Average financial aid package:* $9620 (excluding resources awarded to replace EFC). 6% of all full-time freshmen had no need and received non-need-based gift aid.

UNDERGRADUATE FINANCIAL AID (Fall 2016) 23,987 applied for aid; of those 77% were deemed to have need. 95% of undergraduates with need received aid; of those 30% had need fully met. *Average percent of need met:* 63% (excluding resources awarded to replace EFC). *Average financial aid package:* $10,783 (excluding resources awarded to replace EFC). 9% of all full-time undergraduates had no need and received non-need-based gift aid.

GIFT AID (NEED-BASED) *Total amount:* $104,188,678 (29% federal, 18% state, 46% institutional, 7% external sources). *Receiving aid:* Freshmen: 16% (1,335); all full-time undergraduates: 18% (7,301). *Average award:* Freshmen: $6536; Undergraduates: $6629. *Scholarships, grants, and awards:* Federal Pell, FSEOG, state, private, college/university gift aid from institutional funds, United Negro College Fund.

GIFT AID (NON-NEED-BASED) *Total amount:* $22,582,019 (83% institutional, 17% external sources). *Receiving aid:* Freshmen: 28% (2,392). Undergraduates: 26% (10,546). *Average award:* Freshmen: $5649. Undergraduates: $5195. *Scholarships, grants, and awards by category: Academic interests/achievement:* general academic interests/achievements. *Tuition waivers:* Full or partial for employees or children of employees, senior citizens. *ROTC:* Army, Naval, Air Force.

LOANS *Student loans:* $226,918,793 (80% need-based, 20% non-need-based). 54% of past graduating class borrowed through all loan programs. *Average indebtedness per student:* $37,307. *Average need-based loan:* Freshmen: $3552. Undergraduates: $4681. *Parent loans:* $125,798,876 (85% need-based, 15% non-need-based). *Programs:* Federal Direct (Subsidized and Unsubsidized Stafford, PLUS), Perkins, college/university, private loans.

WORK-STUDY *Federal work-study:* 557 jobs averaging $2200.

ATHLETIC AWARDS Total amount: $19,176,388 (67% need-based, 33% non-need-based).

APPLYING FOR FINANCIAL AID *Required financial aid form:* FAFSA. *Financial aid deadline (priority):* 2/15. *Notification date:* Continuous beginning 3/1.

CONTACT Ms. Melissa J. Kunes, Executive Director for Student Aid, Penn State University Park, 301 Shields Building, University Park, PA 16802, 814-863-0507. *Fax:* 814-863-0322. *Website:* http://www.psu.edu/.

PENN STATE WILKES-BARRE
Lehman, PA

Tuition & fees (PA res): $13,568	Average undergraduate aid package: $9665

ABOUT THE INSTITUTION State-related, coed. *Awards:* certificates, associate, and bachelor's degrees (enrollment figures include students enrolled at The Graduate School at Penn State who are taking courses at this location). 122 undergraduate majors. *Total enrollment:* 467. Undergraduates: 456. Freshmen: 103. Federal methodology is used as a basis for awarding need-based institutional aid.

UNDERGRADUATE EXPENSES for 2017–2018 *Application fee:* $65. *Tuition, state resident:* full-time $12,718; part-time $524 per credit hour. *Tuition, nonresident:* full-time $20,352; part-time $848 per credit hour. *Required fees:* full-time $850. Full-time tuition and fees vary according to course level, degree level, location, program, and student level. Part-time tuition and fees vary according to course level, course load, degree level, location, program, and student level.

FRESHMAN FINANCIAL AID (Fall 2016) 120 applied for aid; of those 82% were deemed to have need. 98% of freshmen with need received aid; of those 22% had need fully met. *Average percent of need met:* 67% (excluding resources awarded to replace EFC). *Average financial aid package:* $10,504 (excluding resources awarded to replace EFC). 13% of all full-time freshmen had no need and received non-need-based gift aid.

UNDERGRADUATE FINANCIAL AID (Fall 2016) 378 applied for aid; of those 84% were deemed to have need. 99% of undergraduates with need received aid; of those 24% had need fully met. *Average percent of need met:* 62% (excluding resources awarded to replace EFC). *Average financial aid package:* $9665 (excluding resources awarded to replace EFC). 8% of all full-time undergraduates had no need and received non-need-based gift aid.

GIFT AID (NEED-BASED) *Total amount:* $2,052,371 (36% federal, 27% state, 34% institutional, 3% external sources). *Receiving aid:* Freshmen: 51% (63); all full-time undergraduates: 43% (179). *Average award:* Freshmen: $5510; Undergraduates: $5606. *Scholarships, grants, and awards:* Federal Pell, FSEOG, state, private, college/university gift aid from institutional funds.

GIFT AID (NON-NEED-BASED) *Total amount:* $111,493 (92% institutional, 8% external sources). *Receiving aid:* Freshmen: 63% (78). Undergraduates: 54% (225). *Average award:* Freshmen: $3205. Undergraduates: $2933. *Tuition waivers:* Full or partial for employees or children of employees, senior citizens. *ROTC:* Army cooperative, Air Force cooperative.

LOANS *Student loans:* $2,320,966 (87% need-based, 13% non-need-based). 86% of past graduating class borrowed through all loan programs. *Average indebtedness per student:* $34,805. *Average need-based loan:* Freshmen: $3329. Undergraduates: $3991. *Parent loans:* $689,523 (90% need-based, 10% non-need-based). *Programs:* Federal Direct (Subsidized and Unsubsidized Stafford, PLUS), Perkins, college/university, private loans.

WORK-STUDY *Federal work-study:* jobs available. *State or other work-study/employment:* Part-time jobs available.

APPLYING FOR FINANCIAL AID *Required financial aid form:* FAFSA. *Financial aid deadline (priority):* 2/15. *Notification date:* Continuous beginning 3/1.

CONTACT Stacey Zelinka, Financial Aid Coordinator, Penn State Wilkes-Barre, Old Route 115, PO Box PSU, Lehman, PA 18627, 570-675-9238. *Fax:* 570-675-9113. *E-mail:* saz3@psu.edu. *Website:* http://www.wb.psu.edu/.

PENN STATE WORTHINGTON SCRANTON
Dunmore, PA

Tuition & fees (PA res): $14,460	Average undergraduate aid package: $10,309

ABOUT THE INSTITUTION State-related, coed. *Awards:* certificates, associate, and bachelor's degrees. 119 undergraduate majors. *Total enrollment:* 1,029. Undergraduates: 1,029. Freshmen: 261. Federal methodology is used as a basis for awarding need-based institutional aid.

UNDERGRADUATE EXPENSES for 2017–2018 *Application fee:* $65. *Tuition, state resident:* full-time $13,484; part-time $555 per credit hour. *Tuition, nonresident:* full-time $21,402; part-time $892 per credit hour. *Required fees:* full-time $976. Full-time tuition and fees vary according to course level, degree level, location, program, and student level. Part-time tuition and fees vary according to course level, course load, degree level, location, program, and student level.

FRESHMAN FINANCIAL AID (Fall 2016) 232 applied for aid; of those 90% were deemed to have need. 99% of freshmen with need received aid; of those 18% had need fully met. *Average percent of need met:* 61% (excluding resources awarded to

replace EFC). *Average financial aid package:* $10,717 (excluding resources awarded to replace EFC). 6% of all full-time freshmen had no need and received non-need-based gift aid.

UNDERGRADUATE FINANCIAL AID (Fall 2016) 774 applied for aid; of those 91% were deemed to have need. 98% of undergraduates with need received aid; of those 17% had need fully met. *Average percent of need met:* 59% (excluding resources awarded to replace EFC). *Average financial aid package:* $10,309 (excluding resources awarded to replace EFC). 4% of all full-time undergraduates had no need and received non-need-based gift aid.

GIFT AID (NEED-BASED) *Total amount:* $5,040,733 (45% federal, 32% state, 22% institutional, 1% external sources). *Receiving aid:* Freshmen: 58% (140); all full-time undergraduates: 56% (471). *Average award:* Freshmen: $5241; Undergraduates: $5201. *Scholarships, grants, and awards:* Federal Pell, FSEOG, state, private, college/university gift aid from institutional funds.

GIFT AID (NON-NEED-BASED) *Total amount:* $155,142 (91% institutional, 9% external sources). *Receiving aid:* Freshmen: 70% (169). Undergraduates: 62% (522). *Average award:* Freshmen: $5613. Undergraduates: $3869. *Tuition waivers:* Full or partial for employees or children of employees, senior citizens. *ROTC:* Army cooperative, Air Force cooperative.

LOANS *Student loans:* $5,604,240 (89% need-based, 11% non-need-based). 88% of past graduating class borrowed through all loan programs. *Average indebtedness per student:* $41,945. *Average need-based loan:* Freshmen: $3365. Undergraduates: $3916. *Parent loans:* $874,703 (88% need-based, 12% non-need-based). *Programs:* Federal Direct (Subsidized and Unsubsidized Stafford, PLUS), Perkins, college/university, private loans.

WORK-STUDY *Federal work-study:* jobs available. *State or other work-study/employment:* Part-time jobs available.

APPLYING FOR FINANCIAL AID *Required financial aid form:* FAFSA. *Financial aid deadline:* Continuous. *Notification date:* Continuous beginning 3/1.

CONTACT Financial Aid Office, Penn State Worthington Scranton, Room 21, Study Learning Center, 120 Ridge View Drive, Dunmore, PA 18512, 570-963-2690. *Fax:* 570-963-2683.
Website: http://www.sn.psu.edu/.

PENN STATE YORK
York, PA

Tuition & fees (PA res): $14,460	Average undergraduate aid package: $9753

ABOUT THE INSTITUTION State-related, coed. *Awards:* certificates, associate, bachelor's, and master's degrees (also offers up to 2 years of most bachelor's degree programs offered at University Park campus). 126 undergraduate majors. *Total enrollment:* 983. Undergraduates: 967. Freshmen: 287. Federal methodology is used as a basis for awarding need-based institutional aid.

UNDERGRADUATE EXPENSES for 2017–2018 *Application fee:* $65. *Tuition, state resident:* full-time $13,484; part-time $555 per credit hour. *Tuition, nonresident:* full-time $21,402; part-time $892 per credit hour. *Required fees:* full-time $976. Full-time tuition and fees vary according to course level, degree level, location, program, and student level. Part-time tuition and fees vary according to course level, course load, degree level, location, program, and student level.

FRESHMAN FINANCIAL AID (Fall 2016) 207 applied for aid; of those 75% were deemed to have need. 95% of freshmen with need received aid; of those 16% had need fully met. *Average percent of need met:* 56% (excluding resources awarded to replace EFC). *Average financial aid package:* $9757 (excluding resources awarded to replace EFC). 17% of all full-time freshmen had no need and received non-need-based gift aid.

UNDERGRADUATE FINANCIAL AID (Fall 2016) 587 applied for aid; of those 80% were deemed to have need. 96% of undergraduates with need received aid; of those 18% had need fully met. *Average percent of need met:* 58% (excluding resources awarded to replace EFC). *Average financial aid package:* $9753 (excluding resources awarded to replace EFC). 13% of all full-time undergraduates had no need and received non-need-based gift aid.

GIFT AID (NEED-BASED) *Total amount:* $3,174,613 (42% federal, 23% state, 32% institutional, 3% external sources). *Receiving aid:* Freshmen: 30% (85); all full-time undergraduates: 34% (284). *Average award:* Freshmen: $5287; Undergraduates: $5197. *Scholarships, grants, and awards:* Federal Pell, FSEOG, state, private, college/university gift aid from institutional funds.

GIFT AID (NON-NEED-BASED) *Total amount:* $416,643 (3% federal, 4% state, 81% institutional, 12% external sources). *Receiving aid:* Freshmen: 40% (115). Undergraduates: 40% (333). *Average award:* Freshmen: $3456. Undergraduates: $3147. *Scholarships, grants, and awards by category:* Academic interests/achievement: general academic interests/achievements. *Special characteristics:* children and siblings of alumni. *Tuition waivers:* Full or partial for employees or children of employees, senior citizens.

LOANS *Student loans:* $4,212,169 (79% need-based, 21% non-need-based). 73% of past graduating class borrowed through all loan programs. *Average indebtedness per student:* $39,091. *Average need-based loan:* Freshmen: $3155. Undergraduates: $3864. *Parent loans:* $901,399 (77% need-based, 23% non-need-based). *Programs:* Federal Direct (Subsidized and Unsubsidized Stafford, PLUS), Perkins, college/university, private loans.

WORK-STUDY *Federal work-study:* jobs available. *State or other work-study/employment:* Part-time jobs available.

APPLYING FOR FINANCIAL AID *Required financial aid form:* FAFSA. *Financial aid deadline (priority):* 2/15. *Notification date:* Continuous beginning 3/1.

CONTACT Financial Aid Office, Penn State York, 1031 Edgecomb Avenue, York, PA 17403-3326, 717-771-4045 or toll-free 800-778-6227. *E-mail:* yorkfinaid@yk.psu.edu. *Website:* http://www.york.psu.edu/.

PENNSYLVANIA ACADEMY OF THE FINE ARTS
Philadelphia, PA

Tuition & fees: N/R	Average undergraduate aid package: N/A

ABOUT THE INSTITUTION Independent, coed. 1 undergraduate major. Federal methodology is used as a basis for awarding need-based institutional aid.

GIFT AID (NEED-BASED) *Total amount:* $2,450,338 (13% federal, 4% state, 63% institutional, 20% external sources). *Scholarships, grants, and awards:* Federal Pell, FSEOG, state, college/university gift aid from institutional funds.

GIFT AID (NON-NEED-BASED) *Total amount:* $290,503 (84% institutional, 16% external sources).

LOANS *Student loans:* $341,235 (32% need-based, 68% non-need-based). *Parent loans:* $345,176 (71% need-based, 29% non-need-based). *Programs:* Federal Direct (Subsidized and Unsubsidized Stafford, PLUS).

WORK-STUDY *Federal work-study:* jobs available.

APPLYING FOR FINANCIAL AID *Notification date:* Continuous.

CONTACT Celeste Franklin, Director of Financial Aid, Pennsylvania Academy of the Fine Arts, 128 North Broad Street, Philadelphia, PA 19102, 215-972-2019. *Fax:* 215-972-0839. *E-mail:* finaid@pafa.edu.
Website: http://www.pafa.edu/.

PENNSYLVANIA COLLEGE OF ART & DESIGN
Lancaster, PA

CONTACT J. David Hershey, Registrar/Director of Financial Aid, Pennsylvania College of Art & Design, 204 North Prince Street, PO Box 59, Lancaster, PA 17608-0059, 717-396-7833 Ext. 13 or toll-free 800-689-0379 Ext. 1001. *Fax:* 717-396-1339. *E-mail:* finaid@pcad.edu.
Website: http://www.pcad.edu/.

PENNSYLVANIA COLLEGE OF HEALTH SCIENCES
Lancaster, PA

CONTACT Financial Aid Office, Pennsylvania College of Health Sciences, 850 Greenfield Road, Lancaster, PA 17601, 717-544-4912 or toll-free 800-622-5443. *Website:* http://www.pacollege.edu/.

PENNSYLVANIA COLLEGE OF TECHNOLOGY
Williamsport, PA

Tuition & fees (PA res): $18,840	Average undergraduate aid package: $12,768

ABOUT THE INSTITUTION State-related, coed. *Awards:* certificates, associate, bachelor's, and master's degrees. 74 undergraduate majors. *Total enrollment:* 5,382. Undergraduates: 5,382. Freshmen: 1,225. Federal methodology is used as a basis for awarding need-based institutional aid.

UNDERGRADUATE EXPENSES for 2018–2019 *Tuition, state resident:* full-time $16,350. *Tuition, nonresident:* full-time $23,280. *Required fees:* full-time $2490. Full-time tuition and fees vary according to course load and program. Part-time tuition and fees vary according to course load and program. *College room and board:* $11,340; *Room only:* $6456. Room and board charges vary according to board plan and housing facility.

FRESHMAN FINANCIAL AID (Fall 2016) 1,203 applied for aid; of those 94% were deemed to have need. 100% of freshmen with need received aid. *Average percent of need met:* 24% (excluding resources awarded to replace EFC). *Average financial aid package:* $12,300 (excluding resources awarded to replace EFC).

UNDERGRADUATE FINANCIAL AID (Fall 2016) 4,330 applied for aid; of those 96% were deemed to have need. 100% of undergraduates with need received aid. *Average percent of need met:* 23% (excluding resources awarded to replace EFC). *Average financial aid package:* $12,768 (excluding resources awarded to replace EFC).

GIFT AID (NEED-BASED) *Total amount:* $32,145,972 (28% federal, 22% state, 6% institutional, 44% external sources). *Receiving aid:* Freshmen: 71% (860); all full-time undergraduates: 68% (3,117). *Average award:* Freshmen: $7659; Undergraduates: $8452. *Scholarships, grants, and awards:* Federal Pell, FSEOG, state, private, college/university gift aid from institutional funds.

GIFT AID (NON-NEED-BASED) *Tuition waivers:* Full or partial for employees or children of employees. *ROTC:* Army.

LOANS *Student loans:* $46,016,761 (100% need-based). 87% of past graduating class borrowed through all loan programs. *Average indebtedness per student:* $7218. *Average need-based loan:* Freshmen: $3178. Undergraduates: $2267. *Parent loans:* $17,443,947 (100% need-based). *Programs:* Federal Direct (Subsidized and Unsubsidized Stafford, PLUS).

WORK-STUDY *Federal work-study:* 113 jobs averaging $1537.

APPLYING FOR FINANCIAL AID *Required financial aid forms:* FAFSA, institution's own form. *Financial aid deadline (priority):* 3/1. *Notification date:* Continuous beginning 12/1. Students must reply within 2 weeks of notification.

CONTACT Mr. Dennis Correll, Associate Dean for Enrollment Management, Pennsylvania College of Technology, One College Avenue, Williamsport, PA 17701, 570-326-4766 or toll-free 800-367-9222. *Fax:* 570-321-5552. *E-mail:* dcorrell@pct.edu. *Website:* http://www.pct.edu/.

PENSACOLA CHRISTIAN COLLEGE
Pensacola, FL

CONTACT Financial Aid Office, Pensacola Christian College, 250 Brent Lane, Pensacola, FL 32503-2267, 850-478-8496 or toll-free 800-722-4636. *Website:* http://www.pcci.edu/.

PEPPERDINE UNIVERSITY
Malibu, CA

Tuition & fees: $53,932	Average undergraduate aid package: $40,510

ABOUT THE INSTITUTION Independent Church of Christ, coed. *Awards:* bachelor's, master's, and doctoral degrees. 60 undergraduate majors. *Total enrollment:* 7,710. Undergraduates: 3,604. Freshmen: 862. Federal methodology is used as a basis for awarding need-based institutional aid.

UNDERGRADUATE EXPENSES for 2018–2019 *Application fee:* $65. *Comprehensive fee:* $69,252 includes full-time tuition ($53,680), mandatory fees ($252), and room and board ($15,320). Room and board charges vary according to board plan and housing facility. *Part-time tuition:* $1685 per credit hour.

FRESHMAN FINANCIAL AID (Fall 2017, est.) 859 applied for aid; of those 61% were deemed to have need. 100% of freshmen with need received aid; of those 16% had need fully met. *Average percent of need met:* 74% (excluding resources awarded to replace EFC). *Average financial aid package:* $39,938 (excluding resources awarded to replace EFC). 27% of all full-time freshmen had no need and received non-need-based gift aid.

UNDERGRADUATE FINANCIAL AID (Fall 2017, est.) 3,236 applied for aid; of those 52% were deemed to have need. 100% of undergraduates with need received aid; of those 17% had need fully met. *Average percent of need met:* 74% (excluding resources awarded to replace EFC). *Average financial aid package:* $40,510 (excluding resources awarded to replace EFC). 28% of all full-time undergraduates had no need and received non-need-based gift aid.

GIFT AID (NEED-BASED) *Total amount:* $58,232,992 (6% federal, 6% state, 85% institutional, 3% external sources). *Receiving aid:* Freshmen: 61% (527); all full-time undergraduates: 51% (1,680). *Average award:* Freshmen: $37,244; Undergraduates: $36,718. *Scholarships, grants, and awards:* Federal Pell, FSEOG, state, private, college/university gift aid from institutional funds, United Negro College Fund.

GIFT AID (NON-NEED-BASED) *Total amount:* $17,473,651 (3% federal, 91% institutional, 6% external sources). *Average award:* Freshmen: $15,158. Undergraduates: $17,846. *Tuition waivers:* Full or partial for employees or children of employees. *ROTC:* Army cooperative, Air Force cooperative.

LOANS *Student loans:* $13,349,111 (89% need-based, 11% non-need-based). 56% of past graduating class borrowed through all loan programs. *Average indebtedness per student:* $31,410. *Average need-based loan:* Freshmen: $4159. Undergraduates: $5867. *Parent loans:* $17,699,059 (88% need-based, 12% non-need-based). *Programs:* Federal Direct (Subsidized and Unsubsidized Stafford, PLUS), Perkins, college/university.

WORK-STUDY *Federal work-study:* Total amount: $205,418; jobs available. *State or other work-study/employment:* Total amount: $70,818 (57% need-based, 43% non-need-based). Part-time jobs available.

ATHLETIC AWARDS Total amount: $16,661,529 (72% need-based, 28% non-need-based).

APPLYING FOR FINANCIAL AID *Required financial aid form:* FAFSA. *Financial aid deadline (priority):* 2/15. *Notification date:* 4/15. Students must reply by 5/1.

CONTACT Ms. Janet Lockhart, Director of Financial Assistance, Pepperdine University, 24255 Pacific Coast Highway, Malibu, CA 90263-4301, 310-506-4301. *Fax:* 310-506-4746. *E-mail:* janet.lockhart@pepperdine.edu. *Website:* http://www.pepperdine.edu/.

PERU STATE COLLEGE
Peru, NE

CONTACT Diana Lind, Director of Financial Aid, Peru State College, PO Box 10, Peru, NE 68421, 402-872-2228 or toll-free 800-742-4412 (in-state), 800-741-4412 (out-of-state). *Fax:* 402-872-2419. *E-mail:* finaid@oakmail.peru.edu. *Website:* http://www.peru.edu/.

PFEIFFER UNIVERSITY
Misenheimer, NC

Tuition & fees: $29,574	Average undergraduate aid package: $23,786

ABOUT THE INSTITUTION Independent United Methodist, coed. *Awards:* certificates, bachelor's, and master's degrees. 45 undergraduate majors. *Total enrollment:* 1,306. Undergraduates: 813. Freshmen: 277. Federal methodology is used as a basis for awarding need-based institutional aid.

UNDERGRADUATE EXPENSES for 2017–2018 *Comprehensive fee:* $40,532 includes full-time tuition ($28,560), mandatory fees ($1014), and room and board ($10,958). *College room only:* $5836. Full-time tuition and fees vary according to course load. Room and board charges vary according to board plan and housing facility. *Part-time tuition:* $450 per semester hour. *Part-time fees:* $210 per term. Part-time tuition and fees vary according to course load.

FRESHMAN FINANCIAL AID (Fall 2016) 170 applied for aid; of those 92% were deemed to have need. 100% of freshmen with need received aid; of those 12% had need fully met. *Average percent of need met:* 68% (excluding resources awarded to replace EFC). *Average financial aid package:* $21,854 (excluding resources awarded to replace EFC). 11% of all full-time freshmen had no need and received non-need-based gift aid.

UNDERGRADUATE FINANCIAL AID (Fall 2016) 567 applied for aid; of those 93% were deemed to have need. 100% of undergraduates with need received aid; of those 15% had need fully met. *Average percent of need met:* 72% (excluding resources awarded to replace EFC). *Average financial aid package:* $23,786 (excluding resources awarded to replace EFC). 15% of all full-time undergraduates had no need and received non-need-based gift aid.

GIFT AID (NEED-BASED) *Total amount:* $9,986,080 (15% federal, 16% state, 61% institutional, 8% external sources). *Receiving aid:* Freshmen: 75% (134); all full-time undergraduates: 71% (527). *Average award:* Freshmen: $19,136; Undergraduates: $20,281. *Scholarships, grants, and awards:* Federal Pell, FSEOG, state, private, college/university gift aid from institutional funds.

GIFT AID (NON-NEED-BASED) *Total amount:* $1,727,518 (1% state, 91% institutional, 8% external sources). *Receiving aid:* Freshmen: 7% (13). Undergraduates: 8% (59). *Average award:* Freshmen: $13,789. Undergraduates: $12,602. *Scholarships, grants, and awards by category:* Academic interests/achievement: general academic interests/achievements. *Creative arts/performance:* music. *Special achievements/activities:* leadership, religious involvement. *Special characteristics:* children and siblings of alumni, children of educators, children of faculty/staff. *Tuition waivers:* Full or partial for employees or children of employees. *ROTC:* Army cooperative.

LOANS *Student loans:* $4,225,883 (79% need-based, 21% non-need-based). 77% of past graduating class borrowed through all loan programs. *Average indebtedness per student:* $15,939. *Average need-based loan:* Freshmen: $2924. Undergraduates: $3795. *Parent loans:* $1,672,208 (57% need-based, 43% non-need-based). *Programs:* Federal Direct (Subsidized and Unsubsidized Stafford, PLUS), Perkins, state.

WORK-STUDY *Federal work-study:* jobs available.

ATHLETIC AWARDS Total amount: $1,613,289 (48% need-based, 52% non-need-based).

APPLYING FOR FINANCIAL AID *Required financial aid forms:* FAFSA, state aid form, noncustodial (divorced/separated) parent's statement. *Financial aid deadline:* 7/1 (priority: 1/1). *Notification date:* Continuous beginning 4/1.

CONTACT Frances King, Director of Financial Aid, Pfeiffer University, PO Box 960, Misenheimer, NC 28109, 704-463-1360 Ext. 3037 or toll-free 800-338-2060. *Fax:* 704-463-1363. *E-mail:* frances.king@pfeiffer.edu. *Website:* http://www.pfeiffer.edu/.

PHILANDER SMITH COLLEGE
Little Rock, AR

Tuition & fees: $12,714	Average undergraduate aid package: $13,134

ABOUT THE INSTITUTION Independent United Methodist, coed. *Awards:* bachelor's degrees. 19 undergraduate majors. *Total enrollment:* 765. Undergraduates: 765. Freshmen: 289. Federal methodology is used as a basis for awarding need-based institutional aid.

UNDERGRADUATE EXPENSES for 2017–2018 *Application fee:* $25. *One-time required fee:* $235. *Comprehensive fee:* $17,906 includes full-time tuition ($11,804), mandatory fees ($910), and room and board ($5192). *College room only:* $3058. Full-time tuition and fees vary according to program. Room and board charges vary according to board plan and housing facility. *Part-time tuition:* $245 per credit hour. *Part-time fees:* $910 per year; $405 per term. Part-time tuition and fees vary according to course load.

FRESHMAN FINANCIAL AID (Fall 2016) 287 applied for aid; of those 97% were deemed to have need. 100% of freshmen with need received aid; of those 4% had need fully met. *Average percent of need met:* 51% (excluding resources awarded to replace EFC). *Average financial aid package:* $12,704 (excluding resources awarded to replace EFC). 3% of all full-time freshmen had no need and received non-need-based gift aid.

UNDERGRADUATE FINANCIAL AID (Fall 2016) 690 applied for aid; of those 97% were deemed to have need. 100% of undergraduates with need received aid; of those 5% had need fully met. *Average percent of need met:* 51% (excluding resources awarded to replace EFC). *Average financial aid package:* $13,134 (excluding resources awarded to replace EFC). 4% of all full-time undergraduates had no need and received non-need-based gift aid.

GIFT AID (NEED-BASED) *Total amount:* $6,293,413 (50% federal, 3% state, 38% institutional, 9% external sources). *Receiving aid:* Freshmen: 95% (275); all full-time undergraduates: 90% (644). *Average award:* Freshmen: $9748; Undergraduates: $9917. *Scholarships, grants, and awards:* Federal Pell, FSEOG, state, private, college/university gift aid from institutional funds, United Negro College Fund.

GIFT AID (NON-NEED-BASED) *Total amount:* $610,376 (1% federal, 2% state, 85% institutional, 12% external sources). *Receiving aid:* Freshmen: 2% (6). Undergraduates: 2% (17). *Average award:* Freshmen: $12,302. Undergraduates: $13,673. *Scholarships, grants, and awards by category:* Academic interests/achievement: 399 awards ($3,204,881 total): general academic interests/achievements. *Creative arts/performance:* 31 awards ($68,767 total): music. *Special achievements/activities:* 92 awards ($212,970 total): community service, religious involvement. *Special characteristics:* 9 awards ($51,900 total): children of faculty/staff. *Tuition waivers:* Full or partial for employees or children of employees. *ROTC:* Army cooperative.

LOANS *Student loans:* $4,937,357 (95% need-based, 5% non-need-based). 78% of past graduating class borrowed through all loan programs. *Average indebtedness per student:* $46,965. *Average need-based loan:* Freshmen: $3180. Undergraduates: $3653. *Parent loans:* $1,740,965 (88% need-based, 12% non-need-based). *Programs:* Federal Direct (Subsidized and Unsubsidized Stafford, PLUS).

WORK-STUDY *Federal work-study:* 88 jobs averaging $2600.

ATHLETIC AWARDS Total amount: $236,338 (89% need-based, 11% non-need-based).

APPLYING FOR FINANCIAL AID *Required financial aid form:* FAFSA. *Financial aid deadline (priority):* 3/1. *Notification date:* Continuous beginning 3/1.

CONTACT K. Michael Francois, Director of Financial Aid, Philander Smith College, 900 Daisy Bates Drive, Little Rock, AR 72202-3799, 501-370-5350 or toll-free 800-446-6772. *Fax:* 501-370-5357. *E-mail:* kmfrancois@philander.edu. *Website:* http://www.philander.edu/.

PIEDMONT COLLEGE
Demorest, GA

Tuition & fees: $24,464	Average undergraduate aid package: $20,522

ABOUT THE INSTITUTION Independent United Church of Christ, coed. *Awards:* certificates, bachelor's, master's, and doctoral degrees. 50 undergraduate majors. *Total enrollment:* 2,361. Undergraduates: 1,281. Freshmen: 291. Both federal and institutional methodology are used as a basis for awarding need-based institutional aid.

UNDERGRADUATE EXPENSES for 2017–2018 *Comprehensive fee:* $34,334 includes full-time tuition ($24,264), mandatory fees ($200), and room and board ($9870). *College room only:* $5502. Full-time tuition and fees vary according to course load, degree level, location, and program. Room and board charges vary according to board plan. *Part-time tuition:* $1011 per credit hour. *Part-time* fees: $100 per term. Part-time tuition and fees vary according to course load, degree level, location, and program.

FRESHMAN FINANCIAL AID (Fall 2017, est.) 281 applied for aid; of those 89% were deemed to have need. 100% of freshmen with need received aid; of those 20% had need fully met. *Average percent of need met:* 75% (excluding resources awarded to replace EFC). *Average financial aid package:* $22,356 (excluding resources awarded to replace EFC). 14% of all full-time freshmen had no need and received non-need-based gift aid.

UNDERGRADUATE FINANCIAL AID (Fall 2017, est.) 1,061 applied for aid; of those 89% were deemed to have need. 100% of undergraduates with need received aid; of those 17% had need fully met. *Average percent of need met:* 69% (excluding resources awarded to replace EFC). *Average financial aid package:* $20,522 (excluding resources awarded to replace EFC). 15% of all full-time undergraduates had no need and received non-need-based gift aid.

GIFT AID (NEED-BASED) *Total amount:* $15,901,509 (18% federal, 17% state, 64% institutional, 1% external sources). *Receiving aid:* Freshmen: 86% (249); all full-time undergraduates: 82% (944). *Average award:* Freshmen: $18,824; Undergraduates: $16,583. *Scholarships, grants, and awards:* Federal Pell, FSEOG, state, private, college/university gift aid from institutional funds.

GIFT AID (NON-NEED-BASED) *Total amount:* $3,135,070 (18% state, 80% institutional, 2% external sources). *Receiving aid:* Freshmen: 14% (41). Undergraduates: 9% (108). *Average award:* Freshmen: $12,974. Undergraduates: $10,583. *Scholarships, grants, and awards by category: Academic interests/ achievement:* 1,420 awards ($9,875,256 total): biological sciences, business, communication, education, English, foreign languages, general academic interests/achievements, health fields, home economics, humanities, mathematics, physical sciences, premedicine, religion/biblical studies, social sciences. *Creative arts/performance:* 178 awards ($194,736 total): applied art and design, art/fine arts, cinema/film/broadcasting, debating, journalism/publications, music, performing arts, theater/drama. *Special achievements/activities:* 19 awards ($156,134 total): community service, leadership, religious involvement. *Special characteristics:* 160 awards ($1,346,910 total): adult students, children of faculty/staff, international students, out-of-state students, siblings of current students, veterans, veterans' children. *Tuition waivers:* Full or partial for employees or children of employees.

LOANS *Student loans:* $7,731,383 (80% need-based, 20% non-need-based). 75% of past graduating class borrowed through all loan programs. *Average indebtedness per student:* $29,160. *Average need-based loan:* Freshmen: $3418. Undergraduates: $4375. *Parent loans:* $1,956,376 (39% need-based, 61% non-need-based). *Programs:* Federal Direct (Subsidized and Unsubsidized Stafford, PLUS), state.

WORK-STUDY *Federal work-study:* Total amount: $177,297; 81 jobs averaging $2189. *State or other work-study/employment:* Total amount: $664,856 (39% need-based, 61% non-need-based). 267 part-time jobs averaging $2534.

APPLYING FOR FINANCIAL AID *Required financial aid forms:* FAFSA, institution's own form, state aid form. *Financial aid deadline (priority):* 3/1. *Notification date:* Continuous beginning 1/1. Students must reply within 4 weeks of notification.

CONTACT Mr. David Richmond McMillion, Director of Financial Aid, Piedmont College, PO Box 10, Demorest, GA 30535-0010, 706-778-3000 Ext. 1191 or toll-free 800-277-7020. *Fax:* 706-778-0708. *E-mail:* dmcmillion@piedmont.edu. *Website:* http://www.piedmont.edu/.

PIEDMONT INTERNATIONAL UNIVERSITY
Winston-Salem, NC

Tuition & fees: $10,100	Average undergraduate aid package: $8834

ABOUT THE INSTITUTION Independent Baptist, coed. *Awards:* certificates, associate, bachelor's, master's, and doctoral degrees. 15 undergraduate majors. *Total enrollment:* 384. Undergraduates: 197. Freshmen: 33. Federal methodology is used as a basis for awarding need-based institutional aid.

UNDERGRADUATE EXPENSES for 2017–2018 *Application fee:* $55. *Comprehensive fee:* $17,285 includes full-time tuition ($9300), mandatory fees ($800), and room and board ($7185). Full-time tuition and fees vary according to location and program. Room and board charges vary according to board plan. *Part-time tuition:*

$325 per credit hour. *Part-time fees:* $60 per course; $100 per term. Part-time tuition and fees vary according to program.

FRESHMAN FINANCIAL AID (Fall 2017, est.) 64 applied for aid; of those 94% were deemed to have need. 98% of freshmen with need received aid; of those 5% had need fully met. *Average percent of need met:* 40% (excluding resources awarded to replace EFC). *Average financial aid package:* $8055 (excluding resources awarded to replace EFC). 6% of all full-time freshmen had no need and received non-need-based gift aid.

UNDERGRADUATE FINANCIAL AID (Fall 2017, est.) 250 applied for aid; of those 91% were deemed to have need. 99% of undergraduates with need received aid; of those 3% had need fully met. *Average percent of need met:* 36% (excluding resources awarded to replace EFC). *Average financial aid package:* $8834 (excluding resources awarded to replace EFC). 9% of all full-time undergraduates had no need and received non-need-based gift aid.

GIFT AID (NEED-BASED) *Total amount:* $1,730,908 (59% federal, 41% institutional). *Receiving aid:* Freshmen: 91% (59); all full-time undergraduates: 85% (223). *Average award:* Freshmen: $5776; Undergraduates: $6397. *Scholarships, grants, and awards:* Federal Pell, FSEOG, college/university gift aid from institutional funds.

GIFT AID (NON-NEED-BASED) *Total amount:* $93,703 (96% institutional, 4% external sources). *Receiving aid:* Freshmen: 3% (2). Undergraduates: 2% (5). *Average award:* Freshmen: $2708. Undergraduates: $3201. *Scholarships, grants, and awards by category: Academic interests/achievement:* 28 awards ($49,572 total): general academic interests/achievements. *Special achievements/activities:* 3 awards ($7540 total): religious involvement. *Special characteristics:* 11 awards ($20,210 total): children and siblings of alumni, children of faculty/staff, ethnic background, general special characteristics, international students, members of minority groups, relatives of clergy, spouses of current students, veterans. *Tuition waivers:* Full or partial for employees or children of employees.

LOANS *Student loans:* $1,464,209 (90% need-based, 10% non-need-based). *Average need-based loan:* Freshmen: $3447. Undergraduates: $4120. *Parent loans:* $246,203 (66% need-based, 34% non-need-based). *Programs:* Federal Direct (Subsidized and Unsubsidized Stafford, PLUS).

WORK-STUDY Federal work-study jobs available.

APPLYING FOR FINANCIAL AID *Required financial aid forms:* FAFSA, institution's own form. *Financial aid deadline (priority):* 3/1. *Notification date:* Continuous beginning 3/15. Students must reply within 2 weeks of notification.

CONTACT Mandy McLain, Director of Financial Aid, Piedmont International University, 420 South Broad Street, Winston-Salem, NC 27101-5197, 336-714-7878 or toll-free 800-937-5097. *Fax:* 336-714-7820. *E-mail:* financialaid@piedmontu.edu. *Website:* http://www.piedmontu.edu/.

PILLAR COLLEGE
Newark, NJ

CONTACT Financial Aid Office, Pillar College, 60 Park Place, Suite 701, Newark, NJ 07102, 973-803-5000 or toll-free 800-234-9305. *Website:* http://www.pillar.edu/.

PINE MANOR COLLEGE
Chestnut Hill, MA

Tuition & fees: $30,860	Average undergraduate aid package: $25,335

ABOUT THE INSTITUTION Independent, coed. *Awards:* associate, bachelor's, and master's degrees. 12 undergraduate majors. *Total enrollment:* 450. Undergraduates: 419. Freshmen: 76. Federal methodology is used as a basis for awarding need-based institutional aid.

UNDERGRADUATE EXPENSES for 2017–2018 *Application fee:* $25. *Comprehensive fee:* $44,290 includes full-time tuition ($29,860), mandatory fees ($1000), and room and board ($13,430). Full-time tuition and fees vary according to course load. Room and board charges vary according to housing facility. *Part-time tuition:* $930 per credit hour. *Part-time fees:* $1000 per year. Part-time tuition and fees vary according to course load.

FRESHMAN FINANCIAL AID (Fall 2016) 90 applied for aid; of those 100% were deemed to have need. 100% of freshmen with need received aid; of those 6% had need fully met. **Average percent of need met:** 76% (excluding resources awarded to replace EFC). **Average financial aid package:** $26,900 (excluding resources awarded to replace EFC). 2% of all full-time freshmen had no need and received non-need-based gift aid.

UNDERGRADUATE FINANCIAL AID (Fall 2016) 264 applied for aid; of those 100% were deemed to have need. 100% of undergraduates with need received aid; of those 4% had need fully met. **Average percent of need met:** 69% (excluding resources awarded to replace EFC). **Average financial aid package:** $25,335 (excluding resources awarded to replace EFC). 9% of all full-time undergraduates had no need and received non-need-based gift aid.

GIFT AID (NEED-BASED) Total amount: $5,742,860 (18% federal, 3% state, 77% institutional, 2% external sources). **Receiving aid:** Freshmen: 98% (90); all full-time undergraduates: 90% (264). **Average award:** Freshmen: $22,777; Undergraduates: $20,700. **Scholarships, grants, and awards:** Federal Pell, FSEOG, state, private, college/university gift aid from institutional funds.

GIFT AID (NON-NEED-BASED) Total amount: $457,567 (82% institutional, 18% external sources). **Receiving aid:** Freshmen: 9% (8). Undergraduates: 9% (25). **Average award:** Freshmen: $21,500. Undergraduates: $14,485. **Scholarships, grants, and awards by category:** Academic interests/achievement: 122 awards ($997,607 total): general academic interests/achievements. Special characteristics: 8 awards ($91,670 total): children and siblings of alumni, children of faculty/staff. **Tuition waivers:** Full or partial for children of alumni, employees or children of employees.

LOANS Student loans: $1,954,389 (95% need-based, 5% non-need-based). 81% of past graduating class borrowed through all loan programs. Average indebtedness per student: $34,970. **Average need-based loan:** Freshmen: $2932. Undergraduates: $3654. **Parent loans:** $967,652 (100% need-based). **Programs:** Federal Direct (Subsidized and Unsubsidized Stafford, PLUS), state, alternative loans.

WORK-STUDY Federal work-study: 258 jobs averaging $825.

APPLYING FOR FINANCIAL AID Required financial aid form: FAFSA. **Financial aid deadline:** Continuous. **Notification date:** Continuous beginning 2/1. Students must reply by 5/1 or within 2 weeks of notification.

CONTACT Ms. Deborah A. Gravel, Director of Financial Aid, Pine Manor College, 400 Heath Street, Chestnut Hill, MA 02467, 617-731-7628 or toll-free 800-762-1357. *Fax:* 617-731-7102. *E-mail:* dgravel@pmc.edu. *Website:* http://www.pmc.edu/.

PIONEER PACIFIC COLLEGE
Wilsonville, OR

CONTACT Financial Aid Office, Pioneer Pacific College, 27501 Southwest Parkway Avenue, Wilsonville, OR 97070, 503-682-3903 or toll-free 866-PPC-INFO. *Website:* http://www.pioneerpacific.edu/.

PITTSBURG STATE UNIVERSITY
Pittsburg, KS

Tuition & fees (KS res): $7100	Average undergraduate aid package: $7092

ABOUT THE INSTITUTION State-supported, coed. **Awards:** certificates, associate, bachelor's, master's, and doctoral degrees. 62 undergraduate majors. **Total enrollment:** 6,907. Undergraduates: 5,706. Freshmen: 979. Federal methodology is used as a basis for awarding need-based institutional aid.

UNDERGRADUATE EXPENSES for 2017–2018 Application fee: $30. **Tuition, state resident:** full-time $5548; part-time $185 per credit hour. **Tuition, nonresident:** full-time $16,600; part-time $554 per credit hour. **Required fees:** full-time $1552; $66 per credit hour. **College room and board:** $7700. Room and board charges vary according to board plan.

FRESHMAN FINANCIAL AID (Fall 2016) Average financial aid package: $6013 (excluding resources awarded to replace EFC). 58% of all full-time freshmen had no need and received non-need-based gift aid.

UNDERGRADUATE FINANCIAL AID (Fall 2016) Average financial aid package: $7092 (excluding resources awarded to replace EFC). 38% of all full-time undergraduates had no need and received non-need-based gift aid.

GIFT AID (NEED-BASED) Total amount: $10,386,662 (90% federal, 7% state, 3% institutional). **Receiving aid:** Freshmen: 39% (393); all full-time undergraduates:

42% (2,181). **Average award:** Freshmen: $4369; Undergraduates: $4542. **Scholarships, grants, and awards:** Federal Pell, FSEOG, state, private, college/university gift aid from institutional funds.

GIFT AID (NON-NEED-BASED) Total amount: $9,947,996 (9% federal, 3% state, 55% institutional, 33% external sources). **Receiving aid:** Freshmen: 60% (602). Undergraduates: 42% (2,216). **Average award:** Freshmen: $2231. Undergraduates: $2521. **Scholarships, grants, and awards by category:** Academic interests/achievement: biological sciences, business, communication, computer science, education, engineering/technologies, English, foreign languages, general academic interests/achievements, health fields, home economics, mathematics, military science, physical sciences, social sciences. Creative arts/performance: music. Special characteristics: children and siblings of alumni, general special characteristics. **Tuition waivers:** Full or partial for employees or children of employees. **ROTC:** Army.

LOANS Student loans: $24,496,591 (44% need-based, 56% non-need-based). 68% of past graduating class borrowed through all loan programs. Average indebtedness per student: $24,389. **Average need-based loan:** Freshmen: $3196. Undergraduates: $3990. **Programs:** Federal Direct (Subsidized and Unsubsidized Stafford, PLUS), Perkins, Federal Nursing, college/university.

WORK-STUDY Federal work-study: jobs available. **State or other work-study/employment:** Total amount: $137,771 (100% non-need-based). Part-time jobs available.

APPLYING FOR FINANCIAL AID Required financial aid forms: FAFSA, state aid form. **Financial aid deadline (priority):** 3/1. **Notification date:** Continuous beginning 3/1. Students must reply within 2 weeks of notification.

CONTACT Tammy Higgins, Director of Student Financial Assistance, Pittsburg State University, 1701 South Broadway Street, Pittsburg, KS 66762-7534, 620-235-4238 or toll-free 800-854-7488. *Fax:* 620-235-4078. *E-mail:* thiggins@pittstate.edu. *Website:* http://www.pittstate.edu/.

PITZER COLLEGE
Claremont, CA

Tuition & fees: $52,236	Average undergraduate aid package: $18,929

ABOUT THE INSTITUTION Independent, coed. **Awards:** bachelor's degrees. 50 undergraduate majors. **Total enrollment:** 1,112. Undergraduates: 1,112. Freshmen: 262. Both federal and institutional methodology are used as a basis for awarding need-based institutional aid.

UNDERGRADUATE EXPENSES for 2017–2018 Application fee: $70. **Comprehensive fee:** $68,500 includes full-time tuition ($51,964), mandatory fees ($272), and room and board ($16,264). Room and board charges vary according to board plan. Part-time tuition and fees vary according to course load.

FRESHMAN FINANCIAL AID (Fall 2017, est.) 143 applied for aid; of those 74% were deemed to have need. 99% of freshmen with need received aid; of those 100% had need fully met. **Average percent of need met:** 100% (excluding resources awarded to replace EFC). **Average financial aid package:** $46,934 (excluding resources awarded to replace EFC). 1% of all full-time freshmen had no need and received non-need-based gift aid.

UNDERGRADUATE FINANCIAL AID (Fall 2017, est.) 530 applied for aid; of those 82% were deemed to have need. 98% of undergraduates with need received aid; of those 100% had need fully met. **Average percent of need met:** 100% (excluding resources awarded to replace EFC). **Average financial aid package:** $18,929 (excluding resources awarded to replace EFC). 1% of all full-time undergraduates had no need and received non-need-based gift aid.

GIFT AID (NEED-BASED) Total amount: $18,699,151 (5% federal, 4% state, 91% institutional). **Receiving aid:** Freshmen: 40% (105); all full-time undergraduates: 40% (422). **Average award:** Freshmen: $43,050; Undergraduates: $44,048. **Scholarships, grants, and awards:** Federal Pell, FSEOG, state, private, college/university gift aid from institutional funds, United World College Scholarships.

GIFT AID (NON-NEED-BASED) Total amount: $56,500 (100% institutional). **Receiving aid:** Freshmen: 1% (2). Undergraduates: 2% (17). **Average award:** Freshmen: $3833. Undergraduates: $4708. **Scholarships, grants, and awards by category:** Academic interests/achievement: general academic interests/achievements. **Tuition waivers:** Full or partial for employees or children of employees. **ROTC:** Army cooperative, Air Force cooperative.

LOANS Student loans: $2,094,076 (59% need-based, 41% non-need-based). 32% of past graduating class borrowed through all loan programs. Average indebtedness per student: $20,947. **Average need-based loan:** Freshmen: $3162. Undergraduates: $4117. **Parent loans:** $1,825,259 (1% need-based, 99% non-need-based). **Programs:** Federal Direct (Subsidized and Unsubsidized Stafford, PLUS), Perkins, college/university.

WORK-STUDY *Federal work-study:* Total amount: $876,107; jobs available. *State or other work-study/employment:* Total amount: $31,177 (100% need-based). Part-time jobs available.

APPLYING FOR FINANCIAL AID *Required financial aid forms:* FAFSA, institution's own form, CSS Financial Aid PROFILE, state aid form, noncustodial (divorced/separated) parent's statement, business/farm supplement. **Financial aid deadline:** 1/1. **Notification date:** Continuous beginning 3/15. Students must reply by 5/1.

CONTACT Robin Thompson, Director of Financial Aid, Pitzer College, 1050 North Mills Avenue, Claremont, CA 91711-6101, 909-621-8208 or toll-free 800-748-9371. *Fax:* 909-607-1205. *E-mail:* robin_thompson@pitzer.edu. *Website:* http://www.pitzer.edu/.

PLATT COLLEGE
Riverside, CA

CONTACT Financial Aid Office, Platt College, 6465 Sycamore Canyon Boulevard, Suite 100, Riverside, CA 92507, 951-572-4300 or toll-free 888-807-5288. *Website:* http://www.plattcollege.edu/.

PLATT COLLEGE
Aurora, CO

Tuition & fees: N/R	Average undergraduate aid package: $6095

ABOUT THE INSTITUTION Proprietary, coed. 2 undergraduate majors. Federal methodology is used as a basis for awarding need-based institutional aid.

FRESHMAN FINANCIAL AID (Fall 2017, est.) 2 applied for aid; of those 100% were deemed to have need. 100% of freshmen with need received aid. **Average percent of need met:** 50% (excluding resources awarded to replace EFC). **Average financial aid package:** $6095 (excluding resources awarded to replace EFC).

UNDERGRADUATE FINANCIAL AID (Fall 2017, est.) 192 applied for aid; of those 100% were deemed to have need. 100% of undergraduates with need received aid. **Average percent of need met:** 75% (excluding resources awarded to replace EFC). **Average financial aid package:** $6095 (excluding resources awarded to replace EFC).

GIFT AID (NEED-BASED) Total amount: $1,895,675 (99% federal, 1% external sources). **Receiving aid:** Freshmen: 50% (1); all full-time undergraduates: 40% (86). **Average award:** Freshmen: $2000; Undergraduates: $2000. **Scholarships, grants, and awards:** Federal Pell, FSEOG, private.

GIFT AID (NON-NEED-BASED) Total amount: $1,535,964 (100% federal).

LOANS *Student loans:* $3,725,808 (30% need-based, 70% non-need-based). 96% of past graduating class borrowed through all loan programs. *Average indebtedness per student:* $43,477. *Average need-based loan:* Freshmen: $4750. Undergraduates: $4750. *Parent loans:* $58,518 (100% non-need-based). **Programs:** Federal Direct (Subsidized and Unsubsidized Stafford, PLUS).

APPLYING FOR FINANCIAL AID *Required financial aid forms:* FAFSA, institution's own form. **Financial aid deadline:** Continuous. **Notification date:** Continuous beginning 1/1.

CONTACT Ms. Laura Kellogg, Director of Financial Aid, Platt College, 3100 South Parker Road, #200, Aurora, CO 80014, 303-369-5151 Ext. 233. *Fax:* 303-745-1433. *E-mail:* laura.kellogg@plattcolorado.edu. *Website:* http://www.plattcolorado.edu/.

PLATT COLLEGE SAN DIEGO
San Diego, CA

CONTACT Matilde Aguilar, Student Accounts Coordinator, Platt College San Diego, 6250 El Cajon Boulevard, San Diego, CA 92115, 619-265-0107 Ext. 12 or toll-free 866-752-8826. *Fax:* 619-265-8655. *E-mail:* maguilar@platt.edu. *Website:* http://www.platt.edu/.

PLYMOUTH STATE UNIVERSITY
Plymouth, NH

Tuition & fees: N/R	Average undergraduate aid package: $11,652

ABOUT THE INSTITUTION State-supported, coed. **Awards:** certificates, bachelor's, master's, and doctoral degrees. 54 undergraduate majors. **Total enrollment:** 5,050. Undergraduates: 4,125. Freshmen: 1,144. Federal methodology is used as a basis for awarding need-based institutional aid.

FRESHMAN FINANCIAL AID (Fall 2016) 1,028 applied for aid; of those 80% were deemed to have need. 100% of freshmen with need received aid; of those 17% had need fully met. **Average percent of need met:** 58% (excluding resources awarded to replace EFC). **Average financial aid package:** $9992 (excluding resources awarded to replace EFC). 23% of all full-time freshmen had no need and received non-need-based gift aid.

UNDERGRADUATE FINANCIAL AID (Fall 2016) 3,355 applied for aid; of those 82% were deemed to have need. 100% of undergraduates with need received aid; of those 17% had need fully met. **Average percent of need met:** 58% (excluding resources awarded to replace EFC). **Average financial aid package:** $11,652 (excluding resources awarded to replace EFC). 20% of all full-time undergraduates had no need and received non-need-based gift aid.

GIFT AID (NEED-BASED) Total amount: $19,399,492 (29% federal, 1% state, 62% institutional, 8% external sources). **Receiving aid:** Freshmen: 64% (820); all full-time undergraduates: 63% (2,503). **Average award:** Freshmen: $7112; Undergraduates: $6988. **Scholarships, grants, and awards:** Federal Pell, FSEOG, state, private, college/university gift aid from institutional funds.

GIFT AID (NON-NEED-BASED) Total amount: $4,104,644 (92% institutional, 8% external sources). **Receiving aid:** Freshmen: 19% (245). Undergraduates: 13% (514). **Average award:** Freshmen: $4602. Undergraduates: $4352. **Scholarships, grants, and awards by category:** *Academic interests/achievement:* 2,733 awards ($11,399,966 total): biological sciences, computer science, engineering/technologies, general academic interests/achievements, mathematics, premedicine. *Creative arts/performance:* 62 awards ($97,328 total): creative writing, dance, music, theater/drama. *Special characteristics:* 55 awards ($199,914 total): children of faculty/staff, international students. *ROTC:* Army cooperative, Air Force cooperative.

LOANS *Student loans:* $31,752,377 (33% need-based, 67% non-need-based). 81% of past graduating class borrowed through all loan programs. *Average indebtedness per student:* $39,319. *Average need-based loan:* Freshmen: $3147. Undergraduates: $3971. *Parent loans:* $8,456,531 (100% non-need-based). **Programs:** Federal Direct (Subsidized and Unsubsidized Stafford, PLUS), Perkins.

WORK-STUDY *Federal work-study:* 1,858 jobs averaging $2273.

APPLYING FOR FINANCIAL AID *Required financial aid form:* FAFSA. **Financial aid deadline (priority):** 3/1. **Notification date:** Continuous beginning 11/30. Students must reply by 5/1.

CONTACT Crystal Gaff, Director of Financial Aid, Plymouth State University, 17 High Street, Plymouth, NH 03264-1595, 603-535-2338 or toll-free 800-842-6900. *Fax:* 603-535-2627. *E-mail:* clgaff@plymouth.edu. *Website:* http://www.plymouth.edu/.

POINT LOMA NAZARENE UNIVERSITY
San Diego, CA

Tuition & fees: $35,700	Average undergraduate aid package: $22,975

ABOUT THE INSTITUTION Independent Nazarene, coed. *Awards:* certificates, bachelor's, master's, and doctoral degrees. 65 undergraduate majors. *Total enrollment:* 4,467. Undergraduates: 3,150. Freshmen: 618. Federal methodology is used as a basis for awarding need-based institutional aid.

UNDERGRADUATE EXPENSES for 2018–2019 *Application fee:* $55. *Comprehensive fee:* $46,150 includes full-time tuition ($35,100), mandatory fees ($600), and room and board ($10,450). Full-time tuition and fees vary according to course load and program. Room and board charges vary according to board plan. *Part-time tuition:* $1465 per credit hour. Part-time tuition and fees vary according to course load and program.

FRESHMAN FINANCIAL AID (Fall 2016) 530 applied for aid; of those 77% were deemed to have need. 100% of freshmen with need received aid; of those 19% had need fully met. *Average percent of need met:* 67% (excluding resources awarded to replace EFC). *Average financial aid package:* $23,148 (excluding resources awarded to replace EFC). 20% of all full-time freshmen had no need and received non-need-based gift aid.

UNDERGRADUATE FINANCIAL AID (Fall 2016) 2,012 applied for aid; of those 84% were deemed to have need. 100% of undergraduates with need received aid; of those 14% had need fully met. *Average percent of need met:* 62% (excluding resources awarded to replace EFC). *Average financial aid package:* $22,975 (excluding resources awarded to replace EFC). 21% of all full-time undergraduates had no need and received non-need-based gift aid.

GIFT AID (NEED-BASED) *Total amount:* $27,585,724 (14% federal, 19% state, 55% institutional, 12% external sources). *Receiving aid:* Freshmen: 68% (404); all full-time undergraduates: 62% (1,619). *Average award:* Freshmen: $18,033; Undergraduates: $17,171. *Scholarships, grants, and awards:* Federal Pell, FSEOG, state, private, college/university gift aid from institutional funds.

GIFT AID (NON-NEED-BASED) *Total amount:* $8,340,656 (77% institutional, 23% external sources). *Receiving aid:* Freshmen: 8% (47). Undergraduates: 5% (140). *Average award:* Freshmen: $11,369. Undergraduates: $10,421. *Scholarships, grants, and awards by category:* Academic interests/achievement: biological sciences, business, communication, computer science, education, engineering/technologies, English, foreign languages, general academic interests/achievements, home economics, international studies, mathematics, physical sciences, religion/biblical studies, social sciences. *Creative arts/performance:* art/fine arts, debating, music, theater/drama. *Tuition waivers:* Full or partial for employees or children of employees, senior citizens. *ROTC:* Army cooperative, Naval cooperative, Air Force cooperative.

LOANS *Student loans:* $19,283,111 (76% need-based, 24% non-need-based). 64% of past graduating class borrowed through all loan programs. *Average indebtedness per student:* $35,414. *Average need-based loan:* Freshmen: $3462. Undergraduates: $4874. *Parent loans:* $9,362,479 (47% need-based, 53% non-need-based). *Programs:* Federal Direct (Subsidized and Unsubsidized Stafford, PLUS), Perkins, Federal Nursing.

WORK-STUDY *Federal work-study:* jobs available.

ATHLETIC AWARDS Total amount: $2,520,899 (45% need-based, 55% non-need-based).

APPLYING FOR FINANCIAL AID *Required financial aid form:* FAFSA. *Financial aid deadline (priority):* 3/2. *Notification date:* Continuous beginning 12/15. Students must reply by 5/15.

CONTACT Pam Macias, Director of Financial Aid, Point Loma Nazarene University, 3900 Lomaland Drive, San Diego, CA 92106, 619-849-2538 or toll-free 800-733-7770. *Fax:* 619-849-7078. *E-mail:* sfs@pointloma.edu.
Website: http://www.pointloma.edu/.

POINT PARK UNIVERSITY
Pittsburgh, PA

Tuition & fees: $30,130	Average undergraduate aid package: $25,353

ABOUT THE INSTITUTION Independent, coed. *Awards:* certificates, associate, bachelor's, master's, and doctoral degrees. 57 undergraduate majors. *Total enrollment:* 4,224. Undergraduates: 3,281. Freshmen: 640. Federal methodology is used as a basis for awarding need-based institutional aid.

UNDERGRADUATE EXPENSES for 2017–2018 *Application fee:* $40. *Comprehensive fee:* $42,090 includes full-time tuition ($28,860), mandatory fees ($1270), and room and board ($11,960). *College room only:* $5220. Full-time tuition and fees vary according to program. Room and board charges vary according to board plan and housing facility. *Part-time tuition:* $819 per credit. *Part-time fees:* $55 per credit. Part-time tuition and fees vary according to program.

FRESHMAN FINANCIAL AID (Fall 2017, est.) 620 applied for aid; of those 91% were deemed to have need. 100% of freshmen with need received aid; of those 14% had need fully met. *Average percent of need met:* 76% (excluding resources awarded to replace EFC). *Average financial aid package:* $28,190 (excluding resources awarded to replace EFC). 9% of all full-time freshmen had no need and received non-need-based gift aid.

UNDERGRADUATE FINANCIAL AID (Fall 2017, est.) 2,516 applied for aid; of those 93% were deemed to have need. 100% of undergraduates with need received aid; of those 13% had need fully met. *Average percent of need met:* 71% (excluding resources awarded to replace EFC). *Average financial aid package:* $25,353 (excluding resources awarded to replace EFC). 6% of all full-time undergraduates had no need and received non-need-based gift aid.

GIFT AID (NEED-BASED) *Total amount:* $45,263,220 (14% federal, 8% state, 72% institutional, 6% external sources). *Receiving aid:* Freshmen: 91% (563); all full-time undergraduates: 92% (2,305). *Average award:* Freshmen: $23,101; Undergraduates: $19,916. *Scholarships, grants, and awards:* Federal Pell, FSEOG, state, private, college/university gift aid from institutional funds.

GIFT AID (NON-NEED-BASED) *Total amount:* $3,481,058 (1% state, 87% institutional, 12% external sources). *Receiving aid:* Freshmen: 8% (50). Undergraduates: 8% (191). *Average award:* Freshmen: $13,082. Undergraduates: $13,043. *Scholarships, grants, and awards by category:* Academic interests/achievement: biological sciences, business, communication, computer science, education, engineering/technologies, English, general academic interests/achievements, health fields, humanities, international studies, mathematics, physical sciences, premedicine, social sciences. *Creative arts/performance:* cinema/film/broadcasting, dance, performing arts, theater/drama. *Special achievements/activities:* community service, memberships. *Special characteristics:* children of faculty/staff, international students, previous college experience, siblings of current students. *Tuition waivers:* Full or partial for employees or children of employees. *ROTC:* Army cooperative, Air Force cooperative.

LOANS *Student loans:* $23,706,160 (78% need-based, 22% non-need-based). 76% of past graduating class borrowed through all loan programs. *Average indebtedness per student:* $27,924. *Average need-based loan:* Freshmen: $4712. Undergraduates: $5380. *Parent loans:* $5,022,484 (93% need-based, 7% non-need-based). *Programs:* Federal Direct (Subsidized and Unsubsidized Stafford, PLUS), Perkins.

WORK-STUDY *Federal work-study:* Total amount: $372,000; jobs available. *State or other work-study/employment:* Total amount: $1,166,005 (57% need-based, 43% non-need-based). Part-time jobs available.

ATHLETIC AWARDS Total amount: $1,916,474 (85% need-based, 15% non-need-based).

APPLYING FOR FINANCIAL AID *Required financial aid form:* FAFSA. *Financial aid deadline (priority):* 3/15. *Notification date:* Continuous beginning 10/15. Students must reply within 2 weeks of notification.

CONTACT George Santucci, Director of Financial Aid, Point Park University, 201 Wood Street, Pittsburgh, PA 15222-1984, 412-392-3930 or toll-free 800-321-0129. *E-mail:* financialaid@pointpark.edu.
Website: http://www.pointpark.edu/.

POINT UNIVERSITY
West Point, GA

CONTACT Blair Walker, Director of Financial Aid, Point University, 2605 Ben Hill Road, East Point, GA 30344, 404-761-8861 or toll-free 855-37-POINT. *Fax:* 404-669-2024. *E-mail:* blairw@acc.edu. *Website:* http://point.edu/.

POLK STATE COLLEGE
Winter Haven, FL

CONTACT Lenora Burnett, Financial Aid Supervisor, Polk State College, 999 Avenue H, NE, Winter Haven, FL 33881, 863-297-5269. *E-mail:* lburnett@polk.edu. *Website:* http://www.polk.edu/.

POLYTECHNIC UNIVERSITY OF PUERTO RICO
Hato Rey, PR

ABOUT THE INSTITUTION Independent, coed. *Awards:* associate, bachelor's, master's, and doctoral degrees. 21 undergraduate majors. *Total enrollment:* 4,317. Undergraduates: 3,494.

GIFT AID (NEED-BASED) *Scholarships, grants, and awards:* Federal Pell, FSEOG, state, private, college/university gift aid from institutional funds.

LOANS *Programs:* Federal Direct (Subsidized and Unsubsidized Stafford, PLUS).

APPLYING FOR FINANCIAL AID *Required financial aid form:* FAFSA.

CONTACT Sergio E. Villoldo, Financial Aid Director, Polytechnic University of Puerto Rico, 377 Ponce de Leon Avenue, Hato Rey, PR 00918, 787-754-8000 Ext. 253. *Fax:* 787-766-1163. *E-mail:* svilloldo@pupr.edu. *Website:* http://www.pupr.edu/.

POLYTECHNIC UNIVERSITY OF PUERTO RICO, MIAMI CAMPUS
Miami, FL

CONTACT Maria Victoria Shehadeh, Administrative Affairs Coordinator/Financial Aid Officer, Polytechnic University of Puerto Rico, Miami Campus, 8180 Northwest 36th Street, Suite 401, Miami, FL 33166, 305-418-8000 Ext. 204 or toll-free 888-729-7659. *E-mail:* mshehadeh@pupr.edu. *Website:* http://www.pupr.edu/miami/.

POLYTECHNIC UNIVERSITY OF PUERTO RICO, ORLANDO CAMPUS
Orlando, FL

CONTACT Mrs. Ileana Diaz, Financial Aid Officer, Polytechnic University of Puerto Rico, Orlando Campus, 550 North Econlockhatchee Trail, Orlando, FL 32825, 407-677-7000 Ext. 806 or toll-free 888-577-POLY. *Fax:* 407-677-5082. *E-mail:* idiaz@pupr.edu. *Website:* http://www.pupr.edu/orlando/.

POMONA COLLEGE
Claremont, CA

Tuition & fees: $52,780	Average undergraduate aid package: $52,173

ABOUT THE INSTITUTION Independent, coed. *Awards:* bachelor's degrees. 49 undergraduate majors. *Total enrollment:* 1,704. Undergraduates: 1,704. Freshmen: 412. Both federal and institutional methodology are used as a basis for awarding need-based institutional aid.

UNDERGRADUATE EXPENSES for 2018–2019 *Application fee:* $70. *Comprehensive fee:* $69,496 includes full-time tuition ($52,412), mandatory fees ($368), and room and board ($16,716). Room and board charges vary according to board plan.

FRESHMAN FINANCIAL AID (Fall 2016) 274 applied for aid; of those 86% were deemed to have need. 100% of freshmen with need received aid; of those 100% had need fully met. *Average percent of need met:* 100% (excluding resources awarded to replace EFC). *Average financial aid package:* $52,748 (excluding resources awarded to replace EFC). 1% of all full-time freshmen had no need and received non-need-based gift aid.

UNDERGRADUATE FINANCIAL AID (Fall 2016) 997 applied for aid; of those 92% were deemed to have need. 100% of undergraduates with need received aid; of those 100% had need fully met. *Average percent of need met:* 100% (excluding resources awarded to replace EFC). *Average financial aid package:* $52,173 (excluding resources awarded to replace EFC). 1% of all full-time undergraduates had no need and received non-need-based gift aid.

GIFT AID (NEED-BASED) *Total amount:* $45,007,792 (5% federal, 2% state, 91% institutional, 2% external sources). *Receiving aid:* Freshmen: 57% (235); all full-time undergraduates: 56% (918). *Average award:* Freshmen: $50,686; Undergraduates: $50,069. *Scholarships, grants, and awards:* Federal Pell, FSEOG, state, private, college/university gift aid from institutional funds.

GIFT AID (NON-NEED-BASED) *Total amount:* $284,902 (26% federal, 5% institutional, 69% external sources). *Receiving aid:* Freshmen: 1. Undergraduates: 3. *Average award:* Freshmen: $5000. Undergraduates: $5000. *Tuition waivers:* Full or partial for employees or children of employees. *ROTC:* Army cooperative, Air Force cooperative.

LOANS *Student loans:* $2,224,611 (100% non-need-based). 31% of past graduating class borrowed through all loan programs. *Average indebtedness per student:* $17,408. *Parent loans:* $1,445,848 (100% non-need-based). *Programs:* Federal Direct (Subsidized and Unsubsidized Stafford, PLUS), Perkins, college/university.

WORK-STUDY *Federal work-study:* jobs available. *State or other work-study/employment:* Total amount: $1,847,751 (98% need-based, 2% non-need-based). Part-time jobs available.

APPLYING FOR FINANCIAL AID *Required financial aid forms:* FAFSA, CSS Financial Aid PROFILE, state aid form, noncustodial (divorced/separated) parent's statement, business/farm supplement. *Financial aid deadline:* 3/1. *Notification date:* 4/1. Students must reply by 5/1.

CONTACT Office of Financial Aid, Pomona College, 333 North College Way, Sumner Hall, Claremont, CA 91711, 909-621-8205. *Fax:* 909-607-7941. *E-mail:* financial_aid@pomadm.pomona.edu. *Website:* http://www.pomona.edu/.

PONTIFICAL CATHOLIC UNIVERSITY OF PUERTO RICO
Ponce, PR

CONTACT Mrs. Rosalia Martinez, Director of Financial Aid, Pontifical Catholic University of Puerto Rico, 2250 Las Americas Avenue, Suite 549, Ponce, PR 00717-9777, 787-841-2000 Ext. 1065 or toll-free 800-961-7696. *Fax:* 787-651-2041. *E-mail:* rosalia.martinez@email.pucpr.edu. *Website:* http://www.pucpr.edu/.

PONTIFICAL CATHOLIC UNIVERSITY OF PUERTO RICO–ARECIBO CAMPUS
Arecibo, PR

CONTACT Financial Aid Office, Pontifical Catholic University of Puerto Rico–Arecibo Campus, PO Box 144045, Arecibo, PR 00614-4045, 787-881-1212 Ext.6000. *Website:* http://www.pucpr.edu/arecibo/.

PONTIFICAL CATHOLIC UNIVERSITY OF PUERTO RICO–MAYAGUEZ CAMPUS
Mayaguez, PR

CONTACT Financial Aid Office, Pontifical Catholic University of Puerto Rico–Mayaguez Campus, 482 Sur Calle Ramon Emerito Betances, Mayaguez, PR 00680. *Website:* http://www.pucpr.edu/mayaguez/.

PONTIFICAL COLLEGE JOSEPHINUM
Columbus, OH

CONTACT Marky Leichtnam, Financial Aid Director, Pontifical College Josephinum, 7625 North High Street, Columbus, OH 43235-1498, 614-985-2212 or toll-free 888-252-5812. *Fax:* 614-885-2307. *E-mail:* mleichtnam@pcj.edu. *Website:* http://www.pcj.edu/.

PORTLAND STATE UNIVERSITY
Portland, OR

Tuition & fees (OR res): $8783	Average undergraduate aid package: $10,562

ABOUT THE INSTITUTION State-supported, coed. *Awards:* certificates, bachelor's, master's, and doctoral degrees. 80 undergraduate majors. *Total enrollment:* 27,305. Undergraduates: 21,725. Freshmen: 1,827. Federal methodology is used as a basis for awarding need-based institutional aid.

UNDERGRADUATE EXPENSES for 2017–2018 *Application fee:* $50. *Tuition, state resident:* full-time $7403; part-time $164.50 per credit hour. *Tuition, nonresident:* full-time $24,750; part-time $550 per credit hour. *Required fees:* full-time $1380; $136 per credit hour or $460 per term. Full-time tuition and fees vary according to program and reciprocity agreements. Part-time tuition and fees vary according to program and reciprocity agreements. *College room and board:* $12,831; *Room only:* $9204. Room and board charges vary according to board plan and housing facility.

FRESHMAN FINANCIAL AID (Fall 2017, est.) 1,516 applied for aid; of those 83% were deemed to have need. 98% of freshmen with need received aid; of those 7% had need fully met. *Average percent of need met:* 57% (excluding resources awarded to replace EFC). *Average financial aid package:* $10,928 (excluding resources awarded to replace EFC). 1% of all full-time freshmen had no need and received non-need-based gift aid.

UNDERGRADUATE FINANCIAL AID (Fall 2017, est.) 10,347 applied for aid; of those 90% were deemed to have need. 96% of undergraduates with need received aid; of those 5% had need fully met. *Average percent of need met:* 51% (excluding resources awarded to replace EFC). *Average financial aid package:* $10,562 (excluding resources awarded to replace EFC). 1% of all full-time undergraduates had no need and received non-need-based gift aid.

GIFT AID (NEED-BASED) *Total amount:* $55,170,461 (70% federal, 21% state, 3% institutional, 6% external sources). *Receiving aid:* Freshmen: 56% (953); all full-time undergraduates: 49% (6,867). *Average award:* Freshmen: $7202; Undergraduates: $7066. *Scholarships, grants, and awards:* Federal Pell, FSEOG, state, private, college/university gift aid from institutional funds, United Negro College Fund.

GIFT AID (NON-NEED-BASED) *Total amount:* $1,179,033 (9% federal, 1% state, 24% institutional, 66% external sources). *Receiving aid:* Freshmen: 2% (38).

Undergraduates. 1% (111). *Average award:* Freshmen: $2934. Undergraduates: $3337. *Scholarships, grants, and awards by category:* Academic interests/achievement: architecture, area/ethnic studies, business, computer science, education, engineering/technologies, foreign languages, general academic interests/achievements, humanities, international studies, physical sciences, social sciences. *Creative arts/performance:* art/fine arts, general creative arts/performance, music, theater/drama. *Special achievements/activities:* community service, general special achievements/activities, leadership, memberships. *Special characteristics:* adult students, ethnic background, handicapped students, international students, members of minority groups, out-of-state students, veterans. *Tuition waivers:* Full or partial for employees or children of employees, senior citizens. *ROTC:* Army cooperative, Air Force cooperative.

LOANS *Student loans:* $78,762,831 (88% need-based, 12% non-need-based). 60% of past graduating class borrowed through all loan programs. *Average indebtedness per student:* $26,867. *Average need-based loan:* Freshmen: $3350. Undergraduates: $4513. *Parent loans:* $10,328,901 (51% need-based, 49% non-need-based). *Programs:* Federal Direct (Subsidized and Unsubsidized Stafford, PLUS), Perkins.

WORK-STUDY *Federal work-study:* Total amount: $2,333,376; jobs available. *State or other work-study/employment:* Part-time jobs available.

ATHLETIC AWARDS Total amount: $1,552,179 (36% need-based, 64% non-need-based).

APPLYING FOR FINANCIAL AID *Required financial aid form:* FAFSA. *Financial aid deadline:* Continuous. *Notification date:* Continuous beginning 3/15.

CONTACT G. Michael Johnson, Director of Financial Aid, Portland State University, PO Box 851, Portland, OR 97207, 800-547-8887. *Fax:* 503-725-5965. *E-mail:* askfa@pdx.edu. *Website:* http://www.pdx.edu/.

POST UNIVERSITY
Waterbury, CT

Tuition & fees: $29,550	Average undergraduate aid package: N/A

ABOUT THE INSTITUTION Independent, coed. *Awards:* certificates, associate, bachelor's, and master's degrees. 22 undergraduate majors. *Total enrollment:* 8,540. Undergraduates: 7,844. Freshmen: 747. Federal methodology is used as a basis for awarding need-based institutional aid.

UNDERGRADUATE EXPENSES for 2018–2019 *Comprehensive fee:* $40,150 includes full-time tuition ($28,250), mandatory fees ($1300), and room and board ($10,600). Full-time tuition and fees vary according to class time, course level, course load, degree level, location, program, and student level. Room and board charges vary according to housing facility. *Part-time tuition:* $945 per credit hour. Part-time tuition and fees vary according to class time, course level, course load, degree level, location, program, and student level. *Payment plan:* Tuition prepayment.

GIFT AID (NEED-BASED) *Total amount:* $30,686,211 (64% federal, 36% institutional). *Scholarships, grants, and awards:* Federal Pell, FSEOG, state, private, college/university gift aid from institutional funds.

GIFT AID (NON-NEED-BASED) *Scholarships, grants, and awards by category:* Academic interests/achievement: $582,875 total: agriculture, biological sciences, business, communication, computer science, education, general academic interests/achievements, humanities, international studies, social sciences. *Special characteristics:* $297,727 total: children and siblings of alumni, children of faculty/staff, local/state students, spouses of current students, veterans, veterans' children. *Tuition waivers:* Full or partial for employees or children of employees, senior citizens.

LOANS *Student loans:* $11,967,213 (90% need-based, 10% non-need-based). 84% of past graduating class borrowed through all loan programs. *Average indebtedness per student:* $20,246. *Parent loans:* $3,756,164 (100% non-need-based). *Programs:* Federal Direct (Subsidized and Unsubsidized Stafford, PLUS), college/university.

WORK-STUDY *Federal work-study* jobs available. *State or other work-study/employment:* Part-time jobs available.

ATHLETIC AWARDS Total amount: $1,744,199 (67% need-based, 33% non-need-based).

APPLYING FOR FINANCIAL AID *Required financial aid form:* FAFSA. *Financial aid deadline (priority):* 3/1. *Notification date:* Continuous beginning 4/1. Students must reply within 2 weeks of notification.

CONTACT Ms. Michael Greer, Director of Financial Aid, Post University, 800 Country Club Road, Waterbury, CT 06723-2540, 203-591-5615 or toll-free 800-345-2562. *Fax:* 203-596-4599. *E-mail:* mgreer@post.edu. *Website:* http://www.post.edu/.

PRAIRIE VIEW A&M UNIVERSITY
Prairie View, TX

Tuition & fees (TX res): $10,533	Average undergraduate aid package: $15,507

ABOUT THE INSTITUTION State-supported, coed. *Awards:* certificates, bachelor's, master's, and doctoral degrees. 38 undergraduate majors. *Total enrollment:* 9,125. Undergraduates: 8,026. Freshmen: 2,051. Federal methodology is used as a basis for awarding need-based institutional aid.

UNDERGRADUATE EXPENSES for 2018–2019 Application fee: $40. *One-time required fee:* $40. *Tuition, state resident:* full-time $6790. *Tuition, non-resident:* full-time $21,100. *Required fees:* full-time $3743. Full-time tuition and fees vary according to course load, degree level, program, and reciprocity agreements. Part-time tuition and fees vary according to course load, degree level, program, and reciprocity agreements. *College room and board:* $8743; *Room only:* $5774. Room and board charges vary according to board plan, housing facility, and student level. *Payment plan:* Guaranteed tuition.

FRESHMAN FINANCIAL AID (Fall 2016) 1,758 applied for aid; of those 93% were deemed to have need. 97% of freshmen with need received aid; of those 7% had need fully met. *Average percent of need met:* 76% (excluding resources awarded to replace EFC). *Average financial aid package:* $16,636 (excluding resources awarded to replace EFC). 3% of all full-time freshmen had no need and received non-need-based gift aid.

UNDERGRADUATE FINANCIAL AID (Fall 2016) 6,351 applied for aid; of those 93% were deemed to have need. 98% of undergraduates with need received aid; of those 11% had need fully met. *Average percent of need met:* 73% (excluding resources awarded to replace EFC). *Average financial aid package:* $15,507 (excluding resources awarded to replace EFC). 3% of all full-time undergraduates had no need and received non-need-based gift aid.

GIFT AID (NEED-BASED) *Total amount:* $40,344,107 (62% federal, 31% state, 7% institutional). *Receiving aid:* Freshmen: 76% (1,379); all full-time undergraduates: 72% (4,889). *Average award:* Freshmen: $9905; Undergraduates: $7745. *Scholarships, grants, and awards:* Federal Pell, FSEOG, state, private, college/university gift aid from institutional funds, United Negro College Fund, Federal Nursing.

GIFT AID (NON-NEED-BASED) *Total amount:* $19,371,429 (92% institutional, 8% external sources). *Receiving aid:* Freshmen: 48% (882). Undergraduates: 48% (3,240). *Average award:* Freshmen: $6887. Undergraduates: $5773. *Tuition waivers:* Full or partial for employees or children of employees, senior citizens. *ROTC:* Army, Naval, Air Force cooperative.

LOANS Student loans: $41,369,186 (78% need-based, 22% non-need-based). 86% of past graduating class borrowed through all loan programs. *Average indebtedness per student:* $37,209. *Average need-based loan:* Freshmen: $6557. Undergraduates: $7575. *Parent loans:* $11,044,970 (100% non-need-based). *Programs:* Federal Direct (Subsidized and Unsubsidized Stafford, PLUS), state, alternative loans.

WORK-STUDY Federal work-study: 420 jobs averaging $2754. *State or other work-study/employment:* Total amount: $70,919 (100% need-based). 32 part-time jobs averaging $2216.

ATHLETIC AWARDS Total amount: $3,309,993 (100% non-need-based).

APPLYING FOR FINANCIAL AID Required financial aid form: FAFSA. *Financial aid deadline:* 3/15. *Notification date:* 6/1. Students must reply by 8/1.

CONTACT Mr. Ralph Perri, Director of Student Financial Aid and Scholarships, Prairie View A&M University, PO Box 519, Mail Stop 1005, Prairie View, TX 77446, 936-261-1000. *E-mail:* finaidscholarships@pvamu.edu. *Website:* http://www.pvamu.edu/.

PRATT INSTITUTE
Brooklyn, NY

Tuition & fees: $51,870	Average undergraduate aid package: $30,560

ABOUT THE INSTITUTION Independent, coed. *Awards:* certificates, associate, bachelor's, and master's degrees. 25 undergraduate majors. *Total enrollment:* 4,829. Undergraduates: 3,439. Freshmen: 693. Federal methodology is used as a basis for awarding need-based institutional aid.

UNDERGRADUATE EXPENSES for 2018–2019 Application fee: $50. *Comprehensive fee:* $64,492 includes full-time tuition ($49,810), mandatory fees ($2060), and room and board ($12,622). *College room only:* $8862. Room and board charges vary according to board plan and housing facility. *Part-time tuition:* $1607 per credit hour.

FRESHMAN FINANCIAL AID (Fall 2016) 376 applied for aid; of those 81% were deemed to have need. 100% of freshmen with need received aid; of those 13% had need fully met. *Average percent of need met:* 58% (excluding resources awarded to replace EFC). *Average financial aid package:* $29,698 (excluding resources awarded to replace EFC). 32% of all full-time freshmen had no need and received non-need-based gift aid.

UNDERGRADUATE FINANCIAL AID (Fall 2016) 1,712 applied for aid; of those 88% were deemed to have need. 100% of undergraduates with need received aid; of those 9% had need fully met. *Average percent of need met:* 57% (excluding resources awarded to replace EFC). *Average financial aid package:* $30,560 (excluding resources awarded to replace EFC). 33% of all full-time undergraduates had no need and received non-need-based gift aid.

GIFT AID (NEED-BASED) *Total amount:* $4,693,909 (79% federal, 16% state, 5% institutional). *Receiving aid:* Freshmen: 19% (131); all full-time undergraduates: 24% (785). *Average award:* Freshmen: $5868; Undergraduates: $5790. *Scholarships, grants, and awards:* Federal Pell, FSEOG, state, college/university gift aid from institutional funds.

GIFT AID (NON-NEED-BASED) *Total amount:* $49,614,497 (4% state, 95% institutional, 1% external sources). *Receiving aid:* Freshmen: 44% (306). Undergraduates: 45% (1,489). *Average award:* Freshmen: $19,113. Undergraduates: $17,724. *Scholarships, grants, and awards by category:* Academic interests/achievement: general academic interests/achievements. *ROTC:* Army cooperative.

LOANS Student loans: $16,164,677 (100% need-based). 58% of past graduating class borrowed through all loan programs. *Average indebtedness per student:* $37,926. *Average need-based loan:* Freshmen: $6857. Undergraduates: $10,133. *Parent loans:* $30,861,560 (100% need-based). *Programs:* Federal Direct (Subsidized and Unsubsidized Stafford, PLUS), Perkins.

WORK-STUDY Federal work-study: jobs available. *State or other work-study/employment:* Part-time jobs available.

APPLYING FOR FINANCIAL AID Required financial aid forms: FAFSA, state aid form. *Financial aid deadline:* 3/1. *Notification date:* Continuous beginning 3/15. Students must reply by 5/1 or within 2 weeks of notification.

CONTACT Mr. Nedzad Goga, Director of Financial Aid, Pratt Institute, 200 Willoughby Avenue, Myrtle Hall, Room 6E-9, Brooklyn, NY 11205-3899, 718-636-3563 or toll-free 800-331-0834. *Fax:* 718-636-3739. *E-mail:* finaid@pratt.edu. *Website:* http://www.pratt.edu/.

PRESBYTERIAN COLLEGE
Clinton, SC

Tuition & fees: $37,842	Average undergraduate aid package: $36,465

ABOUT THE INSTITUTION Independent Presbyterian Church (U.S.A.), coed. *Awards:* bachelor's and doctoral degrees. 29 undergraduate majors. *Total enrollment:* 1,282. Undergraduates: 1,016. Freshmen: 276. Federal methodology is used as a basis for awarding need-based institutional aid.

UNDERGRADUATE EXPENSES for 2017–2018 Comprehensive fee: $48,140 includes full-time tuition ($34,982), mandatory fees ($2860), and room and board ($10,298). *College room only:* $4992. Full-time tuition and fees vary according to course load and reciprocity agreements. Room and board charges vary according to board plan and housing facility. *Part-time tuition:* $1457 per credit hour. *Part-time fees:* $77 per credit hour; $25 per term. Part-time tuition and fees vary according to course load and program.

FRESHMAN FINANCIAL AID (Fall 2017, est.) 255 applied for aid; of those 86% were deemed to have need. 100% of freshmen with need received aid; of those 34% had need fully met. *Average percent of need met:* 86% (excluding resources awarded to replace EFC). *Average financial aid package:* $36,977 (excluding resources awarded to replace EFC). 19% of all full-time freshmen had no need and received non-need-based gift aid.

UNDERGRADUATE FINANCIAL AID (Fall 2017, est.) 812 applied for aid; of those 87% were deemed to have need. 100% of undergraduates with need received aid; of those 39% had need fully met. *Average percent of need met:* 86% (excluding resources awarded to replace EFC). *Average financial aid package:* $36,465 (excluding resources awarded to replace EFC). 24% of all full-time undergraduates had no need and received non-need-based gift aid.

GIFT AID (NEED-BASED) *Total amount:* $18,090,375 (8% federal, 21% state, 69% institutional, 2% external sources). *Receiving aid:* Freshmen: 80% (220); all full-time undergraduates: 75% (709). *Average award:* Freshmen: $31,642; Undergraduates: $29,804. *Scholarships, grants, and awards:* Federal Pell, FSEOG, state, private, college/university gift aid from institutional funds.

GIFT AID (NON-NEED-BASED) *Total amount:* $6,104,761 (8% state, 85% institutional, 7% external sources). *Receiving aid:* Freshmen: 23% (63). Undergraduates: 25% (238). *Average award:* Freshmen: $18,289. Undergraduates: $16,805. *Scholarships, grants, and awards by category:* Academic interests/achievement: general academic interests/achievements. Creative arts/performance: music. Special characteristics: children of faculty/staff, relatives of clergy. *Tuition waivers:* Full or partial for employees or children of employees, senior citizens. **ROTC:** Army.

LOANS *Student loans:* $4,127,723 (66% need-based, 34% non-need-based). *Average need-based loan:* Freshmen: $3239. Undergraduates: $4408. *Parent loans:* $2,391,018 (44% need-based, 56% non-need-based). *Programs:* Federal Direct (Subsidized and Unsubsidized Stafford, PLUS), Perkins, state.

WORK-STUDY *Federal work-study:* Total amount: $401,696; jobs available. *State or other work-study/employment:* Total amount: $225,390 (1% need-based, 99% non-need-based). Part-time jobs available.

ATHLETIC AWARDS Total amount: $5,886,442 (50% need-based, 50% non-need-based).

APPLYING FOR FINANCIAL AID *Required financial aid form:* FAFSA. *Financial aid deadline (priority):* 3/1. *Notification date:* Continuous beginning 1/1. Students must reply by 5/1.

CONTACT Mr. Brian J. Fortman, Director of Financial Aid, Presbyterian College, 503 South Broad Street, Clinton, SC 29325, 864-833-8287 or toll-free 800-476-7272. *E-mail:* bjfortman@presby.edu.
Website: http://www.presby.edu/.

PRESCOTT COLLEGE
Prescott, AZ

ABOUT THE INSTITUTION Independent, coed. *Awards:* certificates, bachelor's, master's, and doctoral degrees. 30 undergraduate majors. *Total enrollment:* 703. Undergraduates: 356. Freshmen: 47.

GIFT AID (NEED-BASED) *Scholarships, grants, and awards:* Federal Pell, FSEOG, state, private, college/university gift aid from institutional funds.

GIFT AID (NON-NEED-BASED) *Scholarships, grants, and awards by category:* Academic interests/achievement: general academic interests/achievements. Special achievements/activities: general special achievements/activities, leadership.

LOANS *Programs:* Federal Direct (Subsidized and Unsubsidized Stafford, PLUS).

WORK-STUDY *Federal work-study:* jobs available. *State or other work-study/employment:* Part-time jobs available.

APPLYING FOR FINANCIAL AID *Required financial aid form:* FAFSA.

CONTACT Mary Frances Causey, Director of Financial Aid, Prescott College, 220 Grove Avenue, Prescott, AZ 86301, 928-350-1111 or toll-free 877-350-2100. *Fax:* 928-350-1120. *E-mail:* finaid@prescott.edu.
Website: http://www.prescott.edu/.

PRESENTATION COLLEGE
Aberdeen, SD

CONTACT Ms. Janel Wagner, Director of Financial Aid, Presentation College, 1500 North Main Street, Aberdeen, SD 57401-1299, 605-229-8427 or toll-free 800-437-6060. *Fax:* 605-229-8537. *E-mail:* janel.wagner@presentation.edu.
Website: http://www.presentation.edu/.

PRINCETON UNIVERSITY
Princeton, NJ

Tuition & fees: $49,330	Average undergraduate aid package: $53,415

ABOUT THE INSTITUTION Independent, coed. *Awards:* bachelor's, master's, and doctoral degrees. 38 undergraduate majors. *Total enrollment:* 8,273. Undergraduates: 5,394. Freshmen: 1,305. Both federal and institutional methodology are used as a basis for awarding need-based institutional aid.

UNDERGRADUATE EXPENSES for 2018–2019 *Application fee:* $65. *One-time required fee:* $890. *Comprehensive fee:* $65,620 includes full-time tuition ($49,330) and room and board ($16,290). *College room only:* $9450. Room and board charges vary according to board plan. *Part-time tuition:* $5892 per year. *Part-time fees:* $25 per term.

FRESHMAN FINANCIAL AID (Fall 2017, est.) 930 applied for aid; of those 86% were deemed to have need. 100% of freshmen with need received aid; of those 100% had need fully met. *Average percent of need met:* 100% (excluding resources awarded to replace EFC). *Average financial aid package:* $54,310 (excluding resources awarded to replace EFC).

UNDERGRADUATE FINANCIAL AID (Fall 2017, est.) 3,378 applied for aid; of those 93% were deemed to have need. 100% of undergraduates with need received aid; of those 100% had need fully met. *Average percent of need met:* 100% (excluding resources awarded to replace EFC). *Average financial aid package:* $53,415 (excluding resources awarded to replace EFC).

GIFT AID (NEED-BASED) *Total amount:* $161,800,000 (4% federal, 94% institutional, 2% external sources). *Receiving aid:* Freshmen: 61% (798); all full-time undergraduates: 60% (3,155). *Average award:* Freshmen: $52,800; Undergraduates: $51,365. *Scholarships, grants, and awards:* Federal Pell, FSEOG, state, private, college/university gift aid from institutional funds.

GIFT AID (NON-NEED-BASED) *Tuition waivers:* Full or partial for employees or children of employees. **ROTC:** Army, Naval cooperative, Air Force cooperative.

LOANS *Student loans:* 17% of past graduating class borrowed through all loan programs. *Average indebtedness per student:* $9005. *Programs:* Federal Direct (Subsidized and Unsubsidized Stafford, PLUS), Perkins, college/university.

WORK-STUDY *Federal work-study:* Total amount: $850,000; jobs available. *State or other work-study/employment:* Total amount: $3,050,000 (100% need-based). Part-time jobs available.

APPLYING FOR FINANCIAL AID *Required financial aid forms:* FAFSA, institution's own form. *Financial aid deadline (priority):* 2/1. *Notification date:* 4/1. Students must reply by 5/1.

CONTACT Robin Moscato, Director of Financial Aid, Princeton University, PO Box 591, Princeton, NJ 08542, 609-258-3330. *Fax:* 609-258-3558. *E-mail:* pfaa@princeton.edu.
Website: http://www.princeton.edu/.

PRINCIPIA COLLEGE
Elsah, IL

Tuition & fees: $29,470	Average undergraduate aid package: $31,771

ABOUT THE INSTITUTION Independent Christian Science, coed. *Awards:* bachelor's degrees. 22 undergraduate majors. *Total enrollment:* 455. Undergraduates: 455. Freshmen: 85. Institutional methodology is used as a basis for awarding need-based institutional aid.

UNDERGRADUATE EXPENSES for 2018–2019 *Comprehensive fee:* $41,080 includes full-time tuition ($28,770), mandatory fees ($700), and room and board ($11,610). **College room only:** $5510. Full-time tuition and fees vary according to course load. Room and board charges vary according to board plan. **Part-time tuition:** $944 per credit hour. Part-time tuition and fees vary according to course load.

FRESHMAN FINANCIAL AID (Fall 2017, est.) 60 applied for aid; of those 97% were deemed to have need. 100% of freshmen with need received aid; of those 48% had need fully met. **Average percent of need met:** 92% (excluding resources awarded to replace EFC). **Average financial aid package:** $33,381 (excluding resources awarded to replace EFC). 28% of all full-time freshmen had no need and received non-need-based gift aid.

UNDERGRADUATE FINANCIAL AID (Fall 2017, est.) 325 applied for aid; of those 98% were deemed to have need. 100% of undergraduates with need received aid; of those 54% had need fully met. **Average percent of need met:** 93% (excluding resources awarded to replace EFC). **Average financial aid package:** $31,771 (excluding resources awarded to replace EFC). 22% of all full-time undergraduates had no need and received non-need-based gift aid.

GIFT AID (NEED-BASED) Total amount: $9,351,370 (100% institutional). **Receiving aid:** Freshmen: 68% (58); all full-time undergraduates: 72% (318). **Average award:** Freshmen: $29,795; Undergraduates: $28,101. **Scholarships, grants, and awards:** private, college/university gift aid from institutional funds.

GIFT AID (NON-NEED-BASED) Total amount: $2,740,777 (100% institutional). **Receiving aid:** Freshmen: 60% (51). Undergraduates: 52% (229). **Average award:** Freshmen: $22,145. Undergraduates: $22,714. **Scholarships, grants, and awards by category:** Academic interests/achievement: 106 awards ($1,631,250 total): general academic interests/achievements. Special achievements/activities: 360 awards ($3,562,139 total): community service, general special achievements/activities, leadership, religious involvement. Special characteristics: 60 awards ($263,250 total): children and siblings of alumni, children of faculty/staff. **Tuition waivers:** Full or partial for employees or children of employees.

LOANS Student loans: $2,443,948 (50% need-based, 50% non-need-based). 65% of past graduating class borrowed through all loan programs. Average indebtedness per student: $18,335. Average need-based loan: Freshmen: $5481. Undergraduates: $5558. **Programs:** college/university.

APPLYING FOR FINANCIAL AID Required financial aid forms: CSS Financial Aid PROFILE, noncustodial (divorced/separated) parent's statement, federal income tax form(s). **Financial aid deadline (priority):** 3/1. **Notification date:** Continuous beginning 3/1. Students must reply by 5/1 or within 4 weeks of notification.

CONTACT Katie Schiele, Assistant Director of Financial Aid, Principia College, 1 Maybeck Place, Elsah, IL 62028-9799, 618-374-5628 or toll-free 800-277-4648 Ext. 2804. Fax: 618-374-4000. E-mail: kaite.schiele@principia.edu. Website: http://www.principiacollege.edu/.

PROVIDENCE CHRISTIAN COLLEGE
Pasadena, CA

CONTACT Financial Aid Office, Providence Christian College, 1539 East Howard Street, Pasadena, CA 91124, 626-696-4000. Website: http://www.providencecc.edu/.

PROVIDENCE COLLEGE
Providence, RI

Tuition & fees: $48,764	Average undergraduate aid package: $31,565

ABOUT THE INSTITUTION Independent Roman Catholic, coed. **Awards:** certificates, bachelor's, and master's degrees. 67 undergraduate majors. **Total enrollment:** 4,874. Undergraduates: 4,306. Freshmen: 1,064. Both federal and institutional methodology are used as a basis for awarding need-based institutional aid.

UNDERGRADUATE EXPENSES for 2017–2018 Application fee: $65. **Comprehensive fee:** $63,004 includes full-time tuition ($47,870), mandatory fees ($894), and room and board ($14,240). **College room only:** $8210. Full-time tuition and fees vary according to class time and degree level. Room and board charges vary according to board plan and housing facility. **Part-time tuition:** $1709.64 per credit hour. Part-time tuition and fees vary according to class time and degree level.

FRESHMAN FINANCIAL AID (Fall 2017, est.) 793 applied for aid; of those 72% were deemed to have need. 100% of freshmen with need received aid; of those 27% had need fully met. **Average percent of need met:** 86% (excluding resources awarded to replace EFC). **Average financial aid package:** $32,640 (excluding resources awarded to replace EFC). 20% of all full-time freshmen had no need and received non-need-based gift aid.

UNDERGRADUATE FINANCIAL AID (Fall 2017, est.) 2,579 applied for aid; of those 73% were deemed to have need. 100% of undergraduates with need received aid; of those 23% had need fully met. **Average percent of need met:** 83% (excluding resources awarded to replace EFC). **Average financial aid package:** $31,565 (excluding resources awarded to replace EFC). 20% of all full-time undergraduates had no need and received non-need-based gift aid.

GIFT AID (NEED-BASED) Total amount: $55,165,363 (6% federal, 1% state, 91% institutional, 2% external sources). **Receiving aid:** Freshmen: 51% (539); all full-time undergraduates: 46% (1,874). **Average award:** Freshmen: $27,732; Undergraduates: $27,621. **Scholarships, grants, and awards:** Federal Pell, FSEOG, state, private, college/university gift aid from institutional funds, Academic Competitiveness Grants, National SMART Grants.

GIFT AID (NON-NEED-BASED) Total amount: $15,565,485 (88% institutional, 12% external sources). **Receiving aid:** Freshmen: 4% (47). Undergraduates: 3% (119). **Average award:** Freshmen: $16,055. Undergraduates: $17,350. **Scholarships, grants, and awards by category:** Academic interests/achievement: business, general academic interests/achievements, military science, premedicine. Creative arts/performance: theater/drama. Special achievements/activities: community service. Special characteristics: siblings of current students. **Tuition waivers:** Full or partial for employees or children of employees. **ROTC:** Army.

LOANS Student loans: $25,578,916 (56% need-based, 44% non-need-based). 68% of past graduating class borrowed through all loan programs. Average indebtedness per student: $41,383. Average need-based loan: Freshmen: $4846. Undergraduates: $5084. **Parent loans:** $9,209,126 (20% need-based, 80% non-need-based). **Programs:** Federal Direct (Subsidized and Unsubsidized Stafford, PLUS), Perkins.

WORK-STUDY Federal work-study: Total amount: $1,500,000; jobs available. **State or other work-study/employment:** Total amount: $1,300,000 (100% non-need-based). Part-time jobs available.

ATHLETIC AWARDS Total amount: $9,575,238 (9% need-based, 91% non-need-based).

APPLYING FOR FINANCIAL AID Required financial aid forms: FAFSA, CSS Financial Aid PROFILE, federal income tax form(s). **Financial aid deadline:** 2/1. **Notification date:** 3/15. Students must reply by 5/1.

CONTACT Ms. Sandra J. Oliveira, Executive Director of Financial Aid, Providence College, One Cunningham Square, Providence, RI 02918, 401-865-2286 or toll-free 800-721-6444. Fax: 401-865-1186. E-mail: solivei6@providence.edu. Website: http://www.providence.edu/.

PURCHASE COLLEGE, STATE UNIVERSITY OF NEW YORK
Purchase, NY

ABOUT THE INSTITUTION State-supported, coed. **Awards:** certificates, bachelor's, and master's degrees. 43 undergraduate majors. **Total enrollment:** 4,224. Undergraduates: 4,121. Freshmen: 732.

GIFT AID (NEED-BASED) Scholarships, grants, and awards: Federal Pell, FSEOG, state, private, college/university gift aid from institutional funds.

GIFT AID (NON-NEED-BASED) Scholarships, grants, and awards by category: Academic interests/achievement: area/ethnic studies, biological sciences, computer science, English, general academic interests/achievements, humanities, mathematics, social sciences. Creative arts/performance: art/fine arts, cinema/film/broadcasting, creative writing, dance, general creative arts/performance, music, performing arts, theater/drama.

LOANS Programs: Federal Direct (Subsidized and Unsubsidized Stafford, PLUS), Perkins.

WORK-STUDY Federal work-study: jobs available. **State or other work-study/employment:** Total amount: $666,135 (4% need-based, 96% non-need-based). Part-time jobs available.

APPLYING FOR FINANCIAL AID Required financial aid forms: FAFSA, state aid form.

CONTACT Ms. Corey York, Director of Student Financial Services, Purchase College, State University of New York, 735 Anderson Hill Road, Purchase, NY 10577-1400, 914-251-6085. *Fax:* 914-251-6099. *E-mail:* corey.york@purchase.edu. *Website:* http://www.purchase.edu/.

PURDUE UNIVERSITY
West Lafayette, IN

Tuition & fees (IN res): $9992	Average undergraduate aid package: $13,942

ABOUT THE INSTITUTION State-supported, coed. *Awards:* certificates, associate, bachelor's, master's, and doctoral degrees. 142 undergraduate majors. *Total enrollment:* 41,573. Undergraduates: 31,006. Freshmen: 7,566. Federal methodology is used as a basis for awarding need-based institutional aid.

UNDERGRADUATE EXPENSES for 2018–2019 *Application fee:* $60. *Tuition, state resident:* full-time $9208; part-time $330 per credit hour. *Tuition, nonresident:* full-time $28,010; part-time $930 per credit hour. *Required fees:* full-time $784; $18 per credit hour. Full-time tuition and fees vary according to course load and program. Part-time tuition and fees vary according to course load. *College room and board:* $10,030; *Room only:* $4860. Room and board charges vary according to board plan and housing facility.

FRESHMAN FINANCIAL AID (Fall 2017, est.) 5,295 applied for aid; of those 68% were deemed to have need. 95% of freshmen with need received aid; of those 40% had need fully met. *Average percent of need met:* 76% (excluding resources awarded to replace EFC). *Average financial aid package:* $13,452 (excluding resources awarded to replace EFC). 13% of all full-time freshmen had no need and received non-need-based gift aid.

UNDERGRADUATE FINANCIAL AID (Fall 2017, est.) 16,796 applied for aid; of those 72% were deemed to have need. 97% of undergraduates with need received aid; of those 33% had need fully met. *Average percent of need met:* 77% (excluding resources awarded to replace EFC). *Average financial aid package:* $13,942 (excluding resources awarded to replace EFC). 15% of all full-time undergraduates had no need and received non-need-based gift aid.

GIFT AID (NEED-BASED) *Total amount:* $98,577,908 (23% federal, 24% state, 49% institutional, 4% external sources). *Receiving aid:* Freshmen: 34% (2,456); all full-time undergraduates: 31% (8,910). *Average award:* Freshmen: $12,990; Undergraduates: $12,782. *Scholarships, grants, and awards:* Federal Pell, FSEOG, state, private, college/university gift aid from institutional funds.

GIFT AID (NON-NEED-BASED) *Total amount:* $48,389,910 (14% federal, 5% state, 64% institutional, 17% external sources). *Receiving aid:* Freshmen: 18% (1,318). Undergraduates: 14% (3,876). *Average award:* Freshmen: $5392. Undergraduates: $5344. *Scholarships, grants, and awards by category:* Academic interests/achievement: agriculture, computer science, education, engineering/technologies, general academic interests/achievements, health fields, humanities, mathematics, military science, physical sciences. *Creative arts/performance:* music. *Special achievements/activities:* leadership. *Special characteristics:* children of faculty/staff. *Tuition waivers:* Full or partial for employees or children of employees, senior citizens. *ROTC:* Army, Naval, Air Force.

LOANS *Student loans:* $86,727,613 (60% need-based, 40% non-need-based). 42% of past graduating class borrowed through all loan programs. *Average indebtedness per student:* $27,617. *Average need-based loan:* Freshmen: $4402. Undergraduates: $5059. *Parent loans:* $38,194,981 (34% need-based, 66% non-need-based). *Programs:* Federal Direct (Subsidized and Unsubsidized Stafford, PLUS), Perkins, college/university.

WORK-STUDY *Federal work-study:* Total amount: $1,521,031; jobs available. *State or other work-study/employment:* Total amount: $22,246,602 (23% need-based, 77% non-need-based). Part-time jobs available.

ATHLETIC AWARDS Total amount: $10,343,326 (30% need-based, 70% non-need-based).

APPLYING FOR FINANCIAL AID *Required financial aid form:* FAFSA. *Financial aid deadline (priority):* 3/1. *Notification date:* 4/15.

CONTACT Theodore E. Malone, Division of Financial Aid, Purdue University, Schleman Hall of Student Services, Room 305, West Lafayette, IN 47907-2050, 765-494-5056. *Fax:* 765-496-3918. *Website:* http://www.purdue.edu/.

PURDUE UNIVERSITY NORTHWEST
Hammond, IN

CONTACT Ms. Mary Ann Bishel, Executive Director of Financial Aid, Purdue University Northwest, 2200 169th Street, Hammond, IN 46323-2094, 219-989-2301 or toll-free 800-447-8738. *Fax:* 219-989-2141. *E-mail:* finaid2@purduecal.edu. *Website:* http://www.pnw.edu/.

QUEENS COLLEGE OF THE CITY UNIVERSITY OF NEW YORK
Queens, NY

Tuition & fees (NY res): $7138	Average undergraduate aid package: $6475

ABOUT THE INSTITUTION State and locally supported, coed. *Awards:* certificates, bachelor's, and master's degrees. 83 undergraduate majors. *Total enrollment:* 19,866. Undergraduates: 16,680. Freshmen: 1,672. Federal methodology is used as a basis for awarding need-based institutional aid.

UNDERGRADUATE EXPENSES for 2017–2018 *Application fee:* $65. *Tuition, state resident:* full-time $6530; part-time $285 per credit. *Tuition, nonresident:* full-time $17,400; part-time $580 per credit. *Required fees:* full-time $608; $208.85 per term. Full-time tuition and fees vary according to course load. Part-time tuition and fees vary according to course load. *College room and board:* $15,352; *Room only:* $12,020. Room and board charges vary according to board plan and housing facility.

FRESHMAN FINANCIAL AID (Fall 2017, est.) 1,378 applied for aid; of those 85% were deemed to have need. 99% of freshmen with need received aid; of those 3% had need fully met. *Average percent of need met:* 57% (excluding resources awarded to replace EFC). *Average financial aid package:* $5503 (excluding resources awarded to replace EFC). 2% of all full-time freshmen had no need and received non-need-based gift aid.

UNDERGRADUATE FINANCIAL AID (Fall 2017, est.) 9,400 applied for aid; of those 92% were deemed to have need. 96% of undergraduates with need received aid; of those 3% had need fully met. *Average percent of need met:* 49% (excluding resources awarded to replace EFC). *Average financial aid package:* $6475 (excluding resources awarded to replace EFC). 1% of all full-time undergraduates had no need and received non-need-based gift aid.

GIFT AID (NEED-BASED) *Total amount:* $60,304,638 (61% federal, 39% state). *Receiving aid:* Freshmen: 65% (1,066); all full-time undergraduates: 63% (7,632). *Average award:* Freshmen: $8877; Undergraduates: $7486. *Scholarships, grants, and awards:* Federal Pell, FSEOG, state, private, college/university gift aid from institutional funds.

GIFT AID (NON-NEED-BASED) *Total amount:* $4,252,147 (51% state, 27% institutional, 22% external sources). *Receiving aid:* Freshmen: 53% (871). Undergraduates: 19% (2,255). *Average award:* Freshmen: $5433. Undergraduates: $6045. *Scholarships, grants, and awards by category:* Academic interests/achievement: 3,666 awards ($11,143,061 total): general academic interests/achievements. *Tuition waivers:* Full or partial for employees or children of employees, senior citizens. *ROTC:* Army cooperative.

LOANS *Student loans:* $11,314,640 (51% need-based, 49% non-need-based). 15% of past graduating class borrowed through all loan programs. *Average indebtedness per student:* $14,738. *Average need-based loan:* Freshmen: $3306. Undergraduates: $4132. *Parent loans:* $866,338 (100% non-need-based). *Programs:* Federal Direct (Subsidized and Unsubsidized Stafford, PLUS), Perkins.

WORK-STUDY *Federal work-study:* Total amount: $920,332; 531 jobs averaging $1733.

ATHLETIC AWARDS Total amount: $427,366 (100% non-need-based).

APPLYING FOR FINANCIAL AID *Required financial aid forms:* FAFSA, state aid form. *Financial aid deadline:* Continuous. *Notification date:* Continuous beginning 3/1. Students must reply within 3 weeks of notification.

CONTACT Mr. Clifford Couloute, Director of Financial Aid, Queens College of the City University of New York, 65-30 Kissena Boulevard, Queens, NY 11367-1597, 718-997-5109. *Fax:* 718-997-5122. *E-mail:* qc.finaid@qc.cuny.edu. *Website:* http://www.qc.cuny.edu/.

QUEENS UNIVERSITY OF CHARLOTTE
Charlotte, NC

ABOUT THE INSTITUTION Independent Presbyterian, coed. 40 undergraduate majors.

GIFT AID (NEED-BASED) *Scholarships, grants, and awards:* Federal Pell, FSEOG, state, private, college/university gift aid from institutional funds.

GIFT AID (NON-NEED-BASED) *Scholarships, grants, and awards by category: Academic interests/achievement:* business, communication, education, general academic interests/achievements, home economics, humanities, social sciences. *Creative arts/performance:* art/fine arts, music, theater/drama. *Special achievements/activities:* cheerleading/drum major, community service, general special achievements/activities, leadership, memberships, religious involvement. *Special characteristics:* adult students, children and siblings of alumni, children of current students, children of faculty/staff, first-generation college students, international students, relatives of clergy, religious affiliation, siblings of current students, veterans, veterans' children.

LOANS *Programs:* Federal Direct (Subsidized and Unsubsidized Stafford, PLUS), state.

APPLYING FOR FINANCIAL AID *Required financial aid form:* FAFSA.

CONTACT Nancy Buchanan, Senior Director of Financial Aid, Queens University of Charlotte, 1900 Selwyn Avenue, Charlotte, NC 28274-0002, 704-337-2713 or toll-free 800-849-0202. *Fax:* 704-337-2416. *E-mail:* buchanann@queens.edu. *Website:* http://www.queens.edu/.

QUINCY UNIVERSITY
Quincy, IL

CONTACT Lisa Flack, Director of Financial Aid, Quincy University, 1800 College Avenue, Quincy, IL 62301-2699, 217-228-5260 or toll-free 800-688-4295. *Fax:* 217-228-5635. *E-mail:* financialaid@quincy.edu. *Website:* http://www.quincy.edu/.

QUINNIPIAC UNIVERSITY
Hamden, CT

Tuition & fees: $47,960	Average undergraduate aid package: $28,707

ABOUT THE INSTITUTION Independent, coed. *Awards:* certificates, bachelor's, master's, and doctoral degrees. 67 undergraduate majors. *Total enrollment:* 10,200. Undergraduates: 7,305. Federal methodology is used as a basis for awarding need-based institutional aid.

UNDERGRADUATE EXPENSES for 2018–2019 *Application fee:* $65. *One-time required fee:* $1045. *Comprehensive fee:* $62,950 includes full-time tuition ($45,540), mandatory fees ($2420), and room and board ($14,990). Room and board charges vary according to board plan and housing facility. *Part-time tuition:* $1045 per credit hour. *Part-time fees:* $45 per credit hour. Part-time tuition and fees vary according to class time and course load.

FRESHMAN FINANCIAL AID (Fall 2017, est.) 1,665 applied for aid; of those 83% were deemed to have need. 100% of freshmen with need received aid; of those 17% had need fully met. *Average percent of need met:* 67% (excluding resources awarded to replace EFC). *Average financial aid package:* $28,944 (excluding resources awarded to replace EFC). 27% of all full-time freshmen had no need and received non-need-based gift aid.

UNDERGRADUATE FINANCIAL AID (Fall 2017, est.) 5,136 applied for aid; of those 86% were deemed to have need. 100% of undergraduates with need received aid; of those 16% had need fully met. *Average percent of need met:* 65% (excluding resources awarded to replace EFC). *Average financial aid package:* $28,707 (excluding resources awarded to replace EFC). 26% of all full-time undergraduates had no need and received non-need-based gift aid.

GIFT AID (NEED-BASED) *Total amount:* $91,534,308 (6% federal, 1% state, 88% institutional, 5% external sources). *Receiving aid:* Freshmen: 69% (1,352); all full-time undergraduates: 62% (4,334). *Average award:* Freshmen: $23,375; Undergraduates: $22,734. *Scholarships, grants, and awards:* Federal Pell, FSEOG, state, private, college/university gift aid from institutional funds.

GIFT AID (NON-NEED-BASED) *Total amount:* $41,517,086 (96% institutional, 4% external sources). *Receiving aid:* Freshmen: 60% (1,174). Undergraduates: 46% (3,194). *Average award:* Freshmen: $16,331. Undergraduates: $16,877. *Scholarships, grants, and awards by category: Academic interests/achievement:* 4,471 awards ($78,546,638 total): general academic interests/achievements. *Special characteristics:* 397 awards ($4,796,561 total): children of faculty/staff, international students, siblings of current students. *Tuition waivers:* Full or partial for employees or children of employees. *ROTC:* Army cooperative, Air Force cooperative.

LOANS *Student loans:* $58,554,920 (72% need-based, 28% non-need-based). 68% of past graduating class borrowed through all loan programs. *Average indebtedness per student:* $48,894. *Average need-based loan:* Freshmen: $3417. Undergraduates: $4429. *Parent loans:* $28,315,752 (100% non-need-based). *Programs:* Federal Direct (Subsidized and Unsubsidized Stafford, PLUS).

WORK-STUDY *Federal work-study:* Total amount: $3,658,515; 1,745 jobs averaging $2062.

ATHLETIC AWARDS Total amount: $11,566,166 (100% non-need-based).

APPLYING FOR FINANCIAL AID *Required financial aid form:* FAFSA. *Financial aid deadline (priority):* 3/1. *Notification date:* Continuous beginning 1/15. Students must reply by 5/1 or within 2 weeks of notification.

CONTACT Mr. Dominic Yoia, Associate Vice President and University Director of Financial Aid, Quinnipiac University, 275 Mount Carmel Avenue, Hamden, CT 06518, 203-582-5224 or toll-free 800-462-1944. *Fax:* 203-582-5238. *E-mail:* finaid@quinnipiac.edu. *Website:* http://www.qu.edu/.

RABBI JACOB JOSEPH SCHOOL
Edison, NJ

CONTACT Financial Aid Office, Rabbi Jacob Joseph School, One Plainfield Ave, Edison, NJ 08817, 732-985-6533.

RABBINICAL ACADEMY MESIVTA RABBI CHAIM BERLIN
Brooklyn, NY

CONTACT Office of Financial Aid, Rabbinical Academy Mesivta Rabbi Chaim Berlin, 1605 Coney Island Avenue, Brooklyn, NY 11230-4715, 718-377-0777.

RABBINICAL COLLEGE BETH SHRAGA
Monsey, NY

CONTACT Financial Aid Office, Rabbinical College Beth Shraga, 28 Saddle River Road, Monsey, NY 10952-3035, 914-356-1980.

RABBINICAL COLLEGE BOBOVER YESHIVA B'NEI ZION
Brooklyn, NY

CONTACT Financial Aid Office, Rabbinical College Bobover Yeshiva B'nei Zion, 1577 48th Street, Brooklyn, NY 11219, 718-438-2018.

RABBINICAL COLLEGE OF AMERICA
Morristown, NJ

CONTACT Financial Aid Office, Rabbinical College of America, 226 Sussex Avenue, Morristown, NJ 07960, 973-267-9404. *Fax:* 973-267-5208. *Website:* http://www.rca.edu/.

RABBINICAL COLLEGE OF LONG ISLAND
Long Beach, NY

CONTACT Rabbi Cone, Financial Aid Administrator, Rabbinical College of Long Island, 201 Magnolia Boulevard, Long Beach, NY 11561-3305, 516-431-7414.

RABBINICAL COLLEGE OF OHR SHIMON YISROEL
Brooklyn, NY

CONTACT Financial Aid Office, Rabbinical College of Ohr Shimon Yisroel, 215-217 Hewes Street, Brooklyn, NY 11211, 718-855-4092.

RABBINICAL COLLEGE OF TELSHE
Wickliffe, OH

CONTACT Financial Aid Office, Rabbinical College of Telshe, 28400 Euclid Avenue, Wickliffe, OH 44092-2523, 216-943-5300.

RABBINICAL COLLEGE OHR YISROEL
Brooklyn, NY

CONTACT Financial Aid Office, Rabbinical College Ohr Yisroel, 8800 Seaview Avenue, Brooklyn, NY 11236.
Website: http://www.rabbinicalcollegeohryisroel.com/.

RABBINICAL SEMINARY OF AMERICA
Flushing, NY

CONTACT Ms. Leah Eisenstein, Director of Financial Aid, Rabbinical Seminary of America, 92-15 69th Avenue, Forest Hills, NY 11375, 718-268-4700. *Fax:* 718-268-4684.

RADFORD UNIVERSITY
Radford, VA

Tuition & fees (VA res): $10,627	Average undergraduate aid package: $10,054

ABOUT THE INSTITUTION State-supported, coed. *Awards:* certificates, bachelor's, master's, and doctoral degrees. 38 undergraduate majors. *Total enrollment:* 9,418. Undergraduates: 8,418. Freshmen: 1,848. Federal methodology is used as a basis for awarding need-based institutional aid.
UNDERGRADUATE EXPENSES for 2017–2018 *Tuition, state resident:* full-time $7407; part-time $308 per credit hour. *Tuition, nonresident:* full-time $19,042; part-time $793 per credit hour. *Required fees:* full-time $3220; $135 per credit hour. Full-time tuition and fees vary according to course load. Part-time tuition and fees vary according to course load. *College room and board:* $9131; *Room only:* $5026. Room and board charges vary according to board plan and housing facility.
FRESHMAN FINANCIAL AID (Fall 2017, est.) 1,658 applied for aid; of those 79% were deemed to have need. 96% of freshmen with need received aid; of those 25% had need fully met. *Average percent of need met:* 78% (excluding resources awarded to replace EFC). *Average financial aid package:* $9960 (excluding resources awarded to replace EFC). 6% of all full-time freshmen had no need and received non-need-based gift aid.

UNDERGRADUATE FINANCIAL AID (Fall 2017, est.) 6,378 applied for aid; of those 81% were deemed to have need. 96% of undergraduates with need received aid; of those 22% had need fully met. *Average percent of need met:* 77% (excluding resources awarded to replace EFC). *Average financial aid package:* $10,054 (excluding resources awarded to replace EFC). 4% of all full-time undergraduates had no need and received non-need-based gift aid.
GIFT AID (NEED-BASED) *Total amount:* $30,023,825 (49% federal, 32% state, 15% institutional, 4% external sources). *Receiving aid:* Freshmen: 46% (843); all full-time undergraduates: 42% (3,372). *Average award:* Freshmen: $7794; Undergraduates: $7452. *Scholarships, grants, and awards:* Federal Pell, FSEOG, state, private, college/university gift aid from institutional funds.
GIFT AID (NON-NEED-BASED) *Total amount:* $1,660,618 (8% federal, 4% state, 74% institutional, 14% external sources). *Receiving aid:* Freshmen: 19% (350). Undergraduates: 12% (990). *Average award:* Freshmen: $3280. Undergraduates: $4056. *Scholarships, grants, and awards by category: Academic interests/achievement:* 521 awards ($1,706,626 total): general academic interests/achievements. *Tuition waivers:* Full or partial for employees or children of employees, senior citizens. *ROTC:* Army.
LOANS *Student loans:* $47,885,228 (82% need-based, 18% non-need-based). 71% of past graduating class borrowed through all loan programs. *Average indebtedness per student:* $31,463. *Average need-based loan:* Freshmen: $3408. Undergraduates: $4084. *Parent loans:* $13,897,850 (78% need-based, 22% non-need-based). *Programs:* Federal Direct (Subsidized and Unsubsidized Stafford, PLUS), Perkins, Federal Nursing, state, college/university.
WORK-STUDY *Federal work-study:* Total amount: $668,580; 272 jobs averaging $2458. *State or other work-study/employment:* Total amount: $803,545 (61% need-based, 39% non-need-based). 329 part-time jobs averaging $2442.
ATHLETIC AWARDS Total amount: $3,071,768 (80% need-based, 20% non-need-based).
APPLYING FOR FINANCIAL AID *Required financial aid form:* FAFSA. *Financial aid deadline (priority):* 2/15. *Notification date:* Continuous beginning 4/15. Students must reply within 2 weeks of notification.
CONTACT Mrs. Barbara Porter, Director of Financial Aid, Radford University, PO Box 6905, Radford, VA 24142, 540-831-5408. *Fax:* 540-831-5138. *E-mail:* finaid@radford.edu.
Website: http://www.radford.edu/.

RAMAPO COLLEGE OF NEW JERSEY
Mahwah, NJ

Tuition & fees (NJ res): $14,080	Average undergraduate aid package: $10,489

ABOUT THE INSTITUTION State-supported, coed. *Awards:* certificates, bachelor's, and master's degrees. 36 undergraduate majors. *Total enrollment:* 6,120. Undergraduates: 5,618. Freshmen: 913. Federal methodology is used as a basis for awarding need-based institutional aid.
UNDERGRADUATE EXPENSES for 2017–2018 *Application fee:* $65. *Tuition, state resident:* full-time $11,640; part-time $363.75 per credit hour. *Tuition, nonresident:* full-time $20,774; part-time $649.20 per credit hour. *Required fees:* full-time $2440; $76.25 per credit hour. Full-time tuition and fees vary according to reciprocity agreements. Part-time tuition and fees vary according to reciprocity agreements. *College room and board:* $12,180; *Room only:* $8460. Room and board charges vary according to board plan and housing facility.
FRESHMAN FINANCIAL AID (Fall 2016) 868 applied for aid; of those 67% were deemed to have need. 92% of freshmen with need received aid; of those 3% had need fully met. *Average percent of need met:* 53% (excluding resources awarded to replace EFC). *Average financial aid package:* $11,418 (excluding resources awarded to replace EFC). 13% of all full-time freshmen had no need and received non-need-based gift aid.
UNDERGRADUATE FINANCIAL AID (Fall 2016) 4,063 applied for aid; of those 67% were deemed to have need. 96% of undergraduates with need received aid; of those 5% had need fully met. *Average percent of need met:* 53% (excluding resources awarded to replace EFC). *Average financial aid package:* $10,489 (excluding resources awarded to replace EFC). 11% of all full-time undergraduates had no need and received non-need-based gift aid.
GIFT AID (NEED-BASED) *Total amount:* $13,146,783 (48% federal, 44% state, 8% institutional). *Receiving aid:* Freshmen: 29% (274); all full-time undergraduates: 28% (1,397). *Average award:* Freshmen: $12,314; Undergraduates: $9240. *Schol-*

arships, grants, and awards: Federal Pell, FSEOG, state, private, college/university gift aid from institutional funds, Federal Nursing.

GIFT AID (NON-NEED-BASED) *Total amount:* $10,357,777 (3% state, 93% institutional, 4% external sources). *Receiving aid:* Freshmen: 15% (141). Undergraduates: 11% (548). *Average award:* Freshmen: $11,082. Undergraduates: $10,394. *Scholarships, grants, and awards by category: Academic interests/achievement:* general academic interests/achievements. *Special characteristics:* children of faculty/staff, international students, out-of-state students. **Tuition waivers:** Full or partial for employees or children of employees, senior citizens. **ROTC:** Army cooperative, Air Force cooperative.

LOANS *Student loans:* $32,044,512 (31% need-based, 69% non-need-based). 49% of past graduating class borrowed through all loan programs. *Average indebtedness per student:* $10,082. *Average need-based loan:* Freshmen: $3314. Undergraduates: $4298. *Parent loans:* $7,481,923 (100% non-need-based). *Programs:* Federal Direct (Subsidized and Unsubsidized Stafford, PLUS), state.

WORK-STUDY *Federal work-study:* jobs available. *State or other work-study/employment:* Total amount: $1,639,386 (100% non-need-based). Part-time jobs available.

APPLYING FOR FINANCIAL AID *Required financial aid form:* FAFSA. *Financial aid deadline (priority):* 3/1. *Notification date:* Continuous beginning 4/1. Students must reply by 5/1 or within 2 weeks of notification.

CONTACT F. Shawn O'Neill, Director of Financial Aid, Ramapo College of New Jersey, 505 Ramapo Valley Road, Mahwah, NJ 07430-1680, 201-684-7550 or toll-free 800-9RAMAPO. *Fax:* 201-684-7085. *E-mail:* finaid@ramapo.edu.
Website: http://www.ramapo.edu/.

RANDALL UNIVERSITY
Moore, OK

ABOUT THE INSTITUTION Independent Free Will Baptist, coed. 24 undergraduate majors.

GIFT AID (NEED-BASED) *Scholarships, grants, and awards:* Federal Pell, FSEOG, state, private, college/university gift aid from institutional funds, Bureau of Indian Affairs Grants.

GIFT AID (NON-NEED-BASED) *Scholarships, grants, and awards by category: Academic interests/achievement:* business, education, English, general academic interests/achievements, health fields, religion/biblical studies. *Creative arts/performance:* music, theater/drama. *Special achievements/activities:* religious involvement. *Special characteristics:* children and siblings of alumni, children of faculty/staff, general special characteristics, local/state students, relatives of clergy, religious affiliation, veterans, veterans' children.

LOANS *Programs:* Federal Direct (Subsidized and Unsubsidized Stafford, PLUS).

WORK-STUDY *Federal work-study:* 23 jobs averaging $1935.

APPLYING FOR FINANCIAL AID *Required financial aid forms:* FAFSA, institution's own form.

CONTACT Denise Conklin, Director of Financial Aid, Randall University, PO Box 7208, Moore, OK 73153-1208, 405-912-9012. *Fax:* 405-912-9050. *E-mail:* dconklin@hc.edu.
Website: http://www.hc.edu/.

RANDOLPH COLLEGE
Lynchburg, VA

Tuition & fees: $39,695	Average undergraduate aid package: $32,962

ABOUT THE INSTITUTION Independent Methodist, coed. *Awards:* bachelor's and master's degrees. 37 undergraduate majors. *Total enrollment:* 684. Undergraduates: 663. Freshmen: 202. Federal methodology is used as a basis for awarding need-based institutional aid.

UNDERGRADUATE EXPENSES for 2018–2019 *Comprehensive fee:* $53,275 includes full-time tuition ($39,000), mandatory fees ($695), and room and board ($13,580). *Part-time tuition:* $1565 per credit hour. Part-time tuition and fees vary according to course load.

FRESHMAN FINANCIAL AID (Fall 2017, est.) 192 applied for aid; of those 91% were deemed to have need. 100% of freshmen with need received aid; of those 20%

had need fully met. *Average percent of need met:* 77% (excluding resources awarded to replace EFC). *Average financial aid package:* $34,868 (excluding resources awarded to replace EFC). 17% of all full-time freshmen had no need and received non-need-based gift aid.

UNDERGRADUATE FINANCIAL AID (Fall 2017, est.) 556 applied for aid; of those 92% were deemed to have need. 100% of undergraduates with need received aid; of those 18% had need fully met. *Average percent of need met:* 76% (excluding resources awarded to replace EFC). *Average financial aid package:* $32,962 (excluding resources awarded to replace EFC). 20% of all full-time undergraduates had no need and received non-need-based gift aid.

GIFT AID (NEED-BASED) *Total amount:* $14,186,321 (9% federal, 8% state, 81% institutional, 2% external sources). *Receiving aid:* Freshmen: 44% (89); all full-time undergraduates: 79% (509). *Average award:* Freshmen: $30,826; Undergraduates: $28,380. *Scholarships, grants, and awards:* Federal Pell, FSEOG, state, private, college/university gift aid from institutional funds.

GIFT AID (NON-NEED-BASED) *Total amount:* $3,716,586 (1% federal, 9% state, 90% institutional). *Receiving aid:* Freshmen: 11% (22). Undergraduates: 9% (59). *Average award:* Freshmen: $23,718. Undergraduates: $23,376. *Scholarships, grants, and awards by category: Academic interests/achievement:* biological sciences, education, English, general academic interests/achievements, mathematics, physical sciences, premedicine, social sciences. *Special achievements/activities:* community service, general special achievements/activities, leadership. *Special characteristics:* adult students, children of faculty/staff, international students, local/state students, relatives of clergy, religious affiliation, twins. **Tuition waivers:** Full or partial for employees or children of employees, adult students.

LOANS *Student loans:* $5,049,990 (71% need-based, 29% non-need-based). 69% of past graduating class borrowed through all loan programs. *Average indebtedness per student:* $33,830. *Average need-based loan:* Freshmen: $3909. Undergraduates: $4742. *Parent loans:* $2,216,389 (57% need-based, 43% non-need-based). *Programs:* Federal Direct (Subsidized and Unsubsidized Stafford, PLUS), Perkins, college/university, alternative loans.

WORK-STUDY *Federal work-study:* Total amount: $267,047; jobs available. *State or other work-study/employment:* Total amount: $92,000 (2% need-based, 98% non-need-based). Part-time jobs available.

APPLYING FOR FINANCIAL AID *Required financial aid forms:* FAFSA, noncustodial (divorced/separated) parent's statement. *Financial aid deadline (priority):* 3/1. *Notification date:* Continuous beginning 10/1. Students must reply within 2 weeks of notification.

CONTACT Debi Woodall-Stevens, Director of Student Financial Services, Randolph College, 2500 Rivermont Avenue, Lynchburg, VA 24503, 434-947-8128 or toll-free 800-745-7692. *Fax:* 434-947-8996. *E-mail:* dwstevens@randolphcollege.edu.
Website: http://www.randolphcollege.edu/.

RANDOLPH-MACON COLLEGE
Ashland, VA

Tuition & fees: $41,300	Average undergraduate aid package: $29,069

ABOUT THE INSTITUTION Independent United Methodist, coed. *Awards:* bachelor's degrees. 34 undergraduate majors. *Total enrollment:* 1,453. Undergraduates: 1,453. Freshmen: 374. Federal methodology is used as a basis for awarding need-based institutional aid.

UNDERGRADUATE EXPENSES for 2018–2019 *Application fee:* $30. *One-time required fee:* $100. *Comprehensive fee:* $53,160 includes full-time tuition ($40,000), mandatory fees ($1300), and room and board ($11,860). *College room only:* $6600. Full-time tuition and fees vary according to reciprocity agreements. Room and board charges vary according to board plan and housing facility.

FRESHMAN FINANCIAL AID (Fall 2017, est.) 350 applied for aid; of those 81% were deemed to have need. 100% of freshmen with need received aid; of those 29% had need fully met. *Average percent of need met:* 80% (excluding resources awarded to replace EFC). *Average financial aid package:* $29,326 (excluding resources awarded to replace EFC). 24% of all full-time freshmen had no need and received non-need-based gift aid.

UNDERGRADUATE FINANCIAL AID (Fall 2017, est.) 1,249 applied for aid; of those 84% were deemed to have need. 100% of undergraduates with need received aid; of those 29% had need fully met. *Average percent of need met:* 79% (excluding resources awarded to replace EFC). *Average financial aid package:*

$29,069 (excluding resources awarded to replace EFC). 26% of all full-time undergraduates had no need and received non-need-based gift aid.

GIFT AID (NEED-BASED) *Total amount:* $26,819,121 (5% federal, 8% state, 82% institutional, 5% external sources). *Receiving aid:* Freshmen: 76% (283); all full-time undergraduates: 74% (1,052). *Average award:* Freshmen: $26,710; Undergraduates: $25,777. *Scholarships, grants, and awards:* Federal Pell, FSEOG, state, private, college/university gift aid from institutional funds.

GIFT AID (NON-NEED-BASED) *Total amount:* $11,356,442 (12% state, 78% institutional, 10% external sources). *Receiving aid:* Freshmen: 20% (74). Undergraduates: 18% (261). *Average award:* Freshmen: $20,925. Undergraduates: $19,033. *Scholarships, grants, and awards by category:* Academic interests/achievement: general academic interests/achievements, religion/biblical studies. *Special achievements/activities:* general special achievements/activities, religious involvement. *Special characteristics:* children and siblings of alumni, children of faculty/staff, ethnic background, out-of-state students, relatives of clergy, siblings of current students, veterans, veterans' children. *Tuition waivers:* Full or partial for employees or children of employees. *ROTC:* Army cooperative.

LOANS *Student loans:* $8,565,177 (60% need-based, 40% non-need-based). 74% of past graduating class borrowed through all loan programs. *Average indebtedness per student:* $34,660. *Average need-based loan:* Freshmen: $3157. Undergraduates: $4048. *Parent loans:* $6,260,749 (37% need-based, 63% non-need-based). *Programs:* Federal Direct (Subsidized and Unsubsidized Stafford, PLUS), Perkins, college/university.

WORK-STUDY *Federal work-study:* Total amount: $548,728; 334 jobs averaging $2098.

APPLYING FOR FINANCIAL AID *Required financial aid forms:* FAFSA, state aid form. *Financial aid deadline:* 3/1 (priority: 2/15). *Notification date:* 3/1. Students must reply by 5/1 or within 2 weeks of notification.

CONTACT Ms. Mary Neal, Director of Financial Aid, Randolph-Macon College, PO Box 5005, Ashland, VA 23005-5505, 804-752-7259 or toll-free 800-888-1762. *Fax:* 804-752-3719. *E-mail:* mneal@rmc.edu.

Website: http://www.rmc.edu/.

RASMUSSEN COLLEGE AURORA
Aurora, IL

CONTACT Financial Aid Office, Rasmussen College Aurora, 2363 Sequoia Drive, Aurora, IL 60506, 630-888-3500 or toll-free 888-549-6755.

Website: http://www.rasmussen.edu/.

RASMUSSEN COLLEGE BLAINE
Blaine, MN

CONTACT Financial Aid Office, Rasmussen College Blaine, 3629 95th Avenue NE, Blaine, MN 55014, 763-795-4720 or toll-free 888-549-6755.

Website: http://www.rasmussen.edu/.

RASMUSSEN COLLEGE BLOOMINGTON
Bloomington, MN

CONTACT Financial Aid Office, Rasmussen College Bloomington, 4400 West 78th Street, Bloomington, MN 55435, 952-545-2000 or toll-free 888-549-6755.

Website: http://www.rasmussen.edu/.

RASMUSSEN COLLEGE EAGAN
Eagan, MN

CONTACT Financial Aid Office, Rasmussen College Eagan, 3500 Federal Drive, Eagan, MN 55122, 651-687-9000 or toll-free 888-549-6755.

Website: http://www.rasmussen.edu/.

RASMUSSEN COLLEGE FARGO
Fargo, ND

CONTACT Financial Aid Office, Rasmussen College Fargo, 4012 19th Avenue South, Fargo, ND 58103, 701-277-3889 or toll-free 888-549-6755.

Website: http://www.rasmussen.edu/.

RASMUSSEN COLLEGE FORT MYERS
Fort Myers, FL

CONTACT Financial Aid Office, Rasmussen College Fort Myers, 9160 Forum Corporate Parkway, Suite 100, Fort Myers, FL 33905, 239-477-2100 or toll-free 888-549-6755.

Website: http://www.rasmussen.edu/.

RASMUSSEN COLLEGE GREEN BAY
Green Bay, WI

CONTACT Financial Aid Office, Rasmussen College Green Bay, 904 South Taylor Street, Suite 100, Green Bay, WI 54303, 920-593-8400 or toll-free 888-549-6755.

Website: http://www.rasmussen.edu/.

RASMUSSEN COLLEGE KANSAS CITY/OVERLAND PARK
Overland Park, KS

CONTACT Financial Aid Office, Rasmussen College Kansas City/Overland Park, 11600 College Boulevard, Overland Park, KS 66210, 913-491-7870 or toll-free 888-549-6755.

Website: http://www.rasmussen.edu/.

RASMUSSEN COLLEGE LAKE ELMO/WOODBURY
Lake Elmo, MN

CONTACT Financial Aid Office, Rasmussen College Lake Elmo/Woodbury, 8565 Eagle Point Circle, Lake Elmo, MN 55042, 651-259-6600 or toll-free 888-549-6755.

Website: http://www.rasmussen.edu/.

RASMUSSEN COLLEGE LAND O' LAKES
Land O' Lakes, FL

CONTACT Financial Aid Office, Rasmussen College Land O' Lakes, 18600 Fernview Street, Land O' Lakes, FL 34638, 813-435-3601 or toll-free 888-549-6755.

Website: http://www.rasmussen.edu/.

RASMUSSEN COLLEGE MANKATO
Mankato, MN

CONTACT Financial Aid Office, Rasmussen College Mankato, 1400 Madison Avenue, Mankato, MN 56001, 507-625-6556 or toll-free 888-549-6755.

Website: http://www.rasmussen.edu/.

RASMUSSEN COLLEGE MOKENA/ TINLEY PARK

Mokena, IL

CONTACT Financial Aid Office, Rasmussen College Mokena/Tinley Park, 8650 West Spring Lake Road, Mokena, IL 60448, 815-534-3300 or toll-free 888-549-6755.
Website: http://www.rasmussen.edu/.

RASMUSSEN COLLEGE MOORHEAD

Moorhead, MN

CONTACT Financial Aid Office, Rasmussen College Moorhead, 1250 29th Avenue South, Moorhead, MN 56560, 218-304-6200 or toll-free 888-549-6755.
Website: http://www.rasmussen.edu/.

RASMUSSEN COLLEGE NEW PORT RICHEY

New Port Richey, FL

CONTACT Financial Aid Office, Rasmussen College New Port Richey, 8661 Citizens Drive, New Port Richey, FL 34654, 727-942-0069 or toll-free 888-549-6755.
Website: http://www.rasmussen.edu/.

RASMUSSEN COLLEGE OCALA

Ocala, FL

CONTACT Financial Aid Office, Rasmussen College Ocala, 4755 SW 46th Court, Ocala, FL 34474, 352-629-1941 or toll-free 888-549-6755.
Website: http://www.rasmussen.edu/.

RASMUSSEN COLLEGE OCALA SCHOOL OF NURSING

Ocala, FL

CONTACT Financial Aid Office, Rasmussen College Ocala School of Nursing, 2100 SW 22nd Place, Ocala, FL 34471, 352-291-8560 or toll-free 888-549-6755.
Website: http://www.rasmussen.edu/.

RASMUSSEN COLLEGE ROCKFORD

Rockford, IL

CONTACT Financial Aid Office, Rasmussen College Rockford, 6000 East State Street, Fourth Floor, Rockford, IL 61108, 815-316-4800 or toll-free 888-549-6755.
Website: http://www.rasmussen.edu/.

RASMUSSEN COLLEGE ROMEOVILLE/ JOLIET

Romeoville, IL

CONTACT Financial Aid Office, Rasmussen College Romeoville/Joliet, 1400 West Normantown Road, Romeoville, IL 60446, 815-306-2600 or toll-free 888-549-6755.
Website: http://www.rasmussen.edu/.

RASMUSSEN COLLEGE ST. CLOUD

St. Cloud, MN

CONTACT Financial Aid Office, Rasmussen College St. Cloud, 226 Park Avenue South, St. Cloud, MN 56301, 320-251-5600 or toll-free 888-549-6755.
Website: http://www.rasmussen.edu/.

RASMUSSEN COLLEGE TAMPA/ BRANDON

Tampa, FL

CONTACT Financial Aid Office, Rasmussen College Tampa/Brandon, 4042 Park Oaks Boulevard, Suite 100, Tampa, FL 33610, 813-246-7600 or toll-free 888-549-6755.
Website: http://www.rasmussen.edu/.

RASMUSSEN COLLEGE TOPEKA

Topeka, KS

CONTACT Financial Aid Office, Rasmussen College Topeka, 620 SW Governor View, Topeka, KS 66606, 785-228-7320 or toll-free 888-549-6755.
Website: http://www.rasmussen.edu/.

RASMUSSEN COLLEGE WAUSAU

Wausau, WI

CONTACT Financial Aid Office, Rasmussen College Wausau, 1101 Westwood Drive, Wausau, WI 54401, 715-841-8000 or toll-free 888-549-6755.
Website: http://www.rasmussen.edu/.

REED COLLEGE

Portland, OR

Tuition & fees: $54,200	Average undergraduate aid package: $43,875

ABOUT THE INSTITUTION Independent, coed. *Awards:* bachelor's and master's degrees. 35 undergraduate majors. *Total enrollment:* 1,470. Undergraduates: 1,447. Freshmen: 411. Both federal and institutional methodology are used as a basis for awarding need-based institutional aid.

UNDERGRADUATE EXPENSES for 2017–2018 *Comprehensive fee:* $67,870 includes full-time tuition ($53,900), mandatory fees ($300), and room and board ($13,670). Full-time tuition and fees vary according to degree level. Room and board charges vary according to board plan and housing facility. Part-time tuition and fees vary according to course load and degree level.

FRESHMAN FINANCIAL AID (Fall 2017, est.) 258 applied for aid; of those 83% were deemed to have need. 96% of freshmen with need received aid; of those 94% had need fully met. *Average percent of need met:* 100% (excluding resources awarded to replace EFC). *Average financial aid package:* $42,917 (excluding resources awarded to replace EFC).

UNDERGRADUATE FINANCIAL AID (Fall 2017, est.) 819 applied for aid; of those 91% were deemed to have need. 98% of undergraduates with need received aid; of those 85% had need fully met. *Average percent of need met:* 100% (excluding resources awarded to replace EFC). *Average financial aid package:* $43,875 (excluding resources awarded to replace EFC).

GIFT AID (NEED-BASED) *Total amount:* $29,746,320 (6% federal, 93% institutional, 1% external sources). *Receiving aid:* Freshmen: 50% (205); all full-time undergraduates: 52% (732). *Average award:* Freshmen: $39,129; Undergraduates: $38,994. *Scholarships, grants, and awards:* Federal Pell, FSEOG, state, private, college/university gift aid from institutional funds.

GIFT AID (NON-NEED-BASED) *Tuition waivers:* Full or partial for employees or children of employees.

LOANS *Student loans:* $4,576,716 (87% need-based, 13% non-need-based). 50% of past graduating class borrowed through all loan programs. *Average indebtedness per student:* $17,467. *Average need-based loan:* Freshmen: $2060. Undergraduates: $3124. *Parent loans:* $1,688,936 (100% non-need-based). *Programs:* Federal Direct (Subsidized and Unsubsidized Stafford, PLUS), Perkins, college/university.
WORK-STUDY *Federal work-study:* Total amount: $625,867; jobs available. *State or other work-study/employment:* Total amount: $426,443 (100% need-based). Part-time jobs available.
APPLYING FOR FINANCIAL AID *Required financial aid forms:* FAFSA, CSS Financial Aid PROFILE, noncustodial (divorced/separated) parent's statement. *Financial aid deadline:* 2/1. *Notification date:* 4/1. Students must reply by 5/1 or within 2 weeks of notification.
CONTACT Office of Financial Aid, Reed College, 3203 Southeast Woodstock Boulevard, Portland, OR 97202-8199, 503-777-7223 or toll-free 800-547-4750. *Fax:* 503-788-6682. *E-mail:* financial.aid@reed.edu.
Website: http://www.reed.edu/.

REGENT UNIVERSITY
Virginia Beach, VA

Tuition & fees: $17,478	Average undergraduate aid package: $10,819

ABOUT THE INSTITUTION Independent Christian, coed. *Awards:* certificates, associate, bachelor's, master's, and doctoral degrees. 34 undergraduate majors. *Total enrollment:* 10,187. Undergraduates: 4,660. Freshmen: 487. Federal methodology is used as a basis for awarding need-based institutional aid.
UNDERGRADUATE EXPENSES for 2017–2018 *Application fee:* $50. *Comprehensive fee:* $25,728 includes full-time tuition ($16,650), mandatory fees ($828), and room and board ($8250). *College room only:* $5730. Full-time tuition and fees vary according to course load. Room and board charges vary according to board plan and housing facility. *Part-time tuition:* $555 per credit hour. *Part-time fees:* $564 per term. Part-time tuition and fees vary according to course load.
FRESHMAN FINANCIAL AID (Fall 2017, est.) 260 applied for aid; of those 87% were deemed to have need. 100% of freshmen with need received aid; of those 21% had need fully met. *Average percent of need met:* 55% (excluding resources awarded to replace EFC). *Average financial aid package:* $13,920 (excluding resources awarded to replace EFC). 15% of all full-time freshmen had no need and received non-need-based gift aid.
UNDERGRADUATE FINANCIAL AID (Fall 2017, est.) 2,030 applied for aid; of those 92% were deemed to have need. 100% of undergraduates with need received aid; of those 9% had need fully met. *Average percent of need met:* 60% (excluding resources awarded to replace EFC). *Average financial aid package:* $10,819 (excluding resources awarded to replace EFC). 13% of all full-time undergraduates had no need and received non-need-based gift aid.
GIFT AID (NEED-BASED) *Total amount:* $18,591,618 (60% federal, 10% state, 29% institutional, 1% external sources). *Receiving aid:* Freshmen: 77% (219); all full-time undergraduates: 72% (1,701). *Average award:* Freshmen: $11,475; Undergraduates: $8566. *Scholarships, grants, and awards:* Federal Pell, state, private, college/university gift aid from institutional funds.
GIFT AID (NON-NEED-BASED) *Total amount:* $2,943,214 (1% federal, 24% state, 70% institutional, 5% external sources). *Receiving aid:* Freshmen: 16% (46). Undergraduates: 6% (143). *Average award:* Freshmen: $10,322. Undergraduates: $7253. *Scholarships, grants, and awards by category:* Special achievements/activities: 181 awards ($167,838 total): leadership, memberships, religious involvement. *Special characteristics:* 576 awards ($1,042,197 total): children and siblings of alumni, children of faculty/staff, children of public servants, public servants, religious affiliation, siblings of current students, spouses of current students, veterans, veterans' children. *Tuition waivers:* Full or partial for employees or children of employees. *ROTC:* Army cooperative, Naval cooperative.
LOANS *Student loans:* $27,440,542 (40% need-based, 60% non-need-based). 76% of past graduating class borrowed through all loan programs. *Average indebtedness per student:* $28,035. *Average need-based loan:* Freshmen: $3231. Undergraduates: $3703. *Parent loans:* $13,859,383 (44% need-based, 56% non-need-based). *Programs:* Federal Direct (Subsidized and Unsubsidized Stafford, PLUS).
ATHLETIC AWARDS Total amount: $47,348 (96% need-based, 4% non-need-based).

APPLYING FOR FINANCIAL AID *Required financial aid forms:* FAFSA, state aid form. *Financial aid deadline (priority):* 3/15. *Notification date:* Continuous beginning 3/15. Students must reply within 2 weeks of notification.
CONTACT Mrs. Rachael Moser, Assistant Director, Regent University, 1000 Regent University Drive, Virginia Beach, VA 23464, 757-352-4125 or toll-free 800-373-5504. *Fax:* 757-352-4118. *E-mail:* finaid@regent.edu.
Website: http://www.regent.edu/.

REGIS COLLEGE
Weston, MA

CONTACT Bonnie L. Quinn, Director of Financial Aid, Regis College, Box 81, Weston, MA 02493, 781-768-7270 or toll-free 866-438-7344. *Fax:* 781-768-7225. *E-mail:* finaid@regiscollege.edu.
Website: http://www.regiscollege.edu/.

REGIS UNIVERSITY
Denver, CO

Tuition & fees: $36,810	Average undergraduate aid package: $28,259

ABOUT THE INSTITUTION Independent Roman Catholic (Jesuit), coed. *Awards:* certificates, bachelor's, master's, and doctoral degrees. 39 undergraduate majors. *Total enrollment:* 8,131. Undergraduates: 3,874. Freshmen: 540. Federal methodology is used as a basis for awarding need-based institutional aid.
UNDERGRADUATE EXPENSES for 2018–2019 *Comprehensive fee:* $48,370 includes full-time tuition ($36,460), mandatory fees ($350), and room and board ($11,560). *College room only:* $6600. Full-time tuition and fees vary according to class time, course level, course load, degree level, location, program, reciprocity agreements, and student level. Room and board charges vary according to board plan and housing facility. *Part-time tuition:* $1139 per semester hour. Part-time tuition and fees vary according to class time, course level, course load, degree level, location, program, reciprocity agreements, and student level.
FRESHMAN FINANCIAL AID (Fall 2016) 410 applied for aid; of those 84% were deemed to have need. 100% of freshmen with need received aid; of those 20% had need fully met. *Average percent of need met:* 86% (excluding resources awarded to replace EFC). *Average financial aid package:* $32,981 (excluding resources awarded to replace EFC). 27% of all full-time freshmen had no need and received non-need-based gift aid.
UNDERGRADUATE FINANCIAL AID (Fall 2016) 1,789 applied for aid; of those 88% were deemed to have need. 99% of undergraduates with need received aid; of those 15% had need fully met. *Average percent of need met:* 78% (excluding resources awarded to replace EFC). *Average financial aid package:* $28,259 (excluding resources awarded to replace EFC). 23% of all full-time undergraduates had no need and received non-need-based gift aid.
GIFT AID (NEED-BASED) *Total amount:* $27,526,959 (16% federal, 9% state, 71% institutional, 4% external sources). *Receiving aid:* Freshmen: 70% (342); all full-time undergraduates: 58% (1,369). *Average award:* Freshmen: $23,634; Undergraduates: $18,816. *Scholarships, grants, and awards:* Federal Pell, FSEOG, state, private, college/university gift aid from institutional funds.
GIFT AID (NON-NEED-BASED) *Total amount:* $9,741,278 (96% institutional, 4% external sources). *Receiving aid:* Freshmen: 11% (55). Undergraduates: 8% (180). *Average award:* Freshmen: $15,556. Undergraduates: $14,934. *Scholarships, grants, and awards by category:* Academic interests/achievement: 874 awards ($11,216,658 total): biological sciences, general academic interests/achievements, mathematics, physical sciences. *Creative arts/performance:* 33 awards ($127,770 total): debating, music. *Special achievements/activities:* 53 awards ($437,000 total): leadership. *Special characteristics:* 19 awards ($370,580 total): adult students, children of faculty/staff, local/state students, public servants. *Tuition waivers:* Full or partial for employees or children of employees. *ROTC:* Army cooperative, Naval cooperative, Air Force cooperative.
LOANS *Student loans:* $21,559,401 (79% need-based, 21% non-need-based). 62% of past graduating class borrowed through all loan programs. *Average indebtedness per student:* $28,153. *Average need-based loan:* Freshmen: $3954. Undergraduates: $4405. *Parent loans:* $4,918,666 (34% need-based, 66% non-need-based).

Programs: Federal Direct (Subsidized and Unsubsidized Stafford, PLUS), Perkins, Federal Nursing.
WORK-STUDY Federal work-study: 407 jobs averaging $1873. **State or other work-study/employment:** Total amount: $1,197,496 (40% need-based, 60% non-need-based). 663 part-time jobs averaging $2573.
ATHLETIC AWARDS Total amount: $2,594,903 (29% need-based, 71% non-need-based).
APPLYING FOR FINANCIAL AID Required financial aid form: FAFSA. **Financial aid deadline (priority):** 5/31. **Notification date:** Continuous beginning 11/15.
CONTACT Ellie Miller, Director of Financial Aid, Regis University, 3333 Regis Boulevard, Denver, CO 80221-1099, 303-964-5758 or toll-free 800-388-2366 Ext. 4900. **Fax:** 303-964-5449. **E-mail:** emiller@regis.edu.
Website: http://www.regis.edu/.

REINHARDT UNIVERSITY
Waleska, GA

CONTACT Angela D. Harlow, Director of Financial Aid, Reinhardt University, 7300 Reinhardt College Circle, Waleska, GA 30183-2981, 770-720-5603. **Fax:** 770-720-9126.
Website: http://www.reinhardt.edu/.

RENSSELAER POLYTECHNIC INSTITUTE
Troy, NY

Tuition & fees: $53,880	Average undergraduate aid package: $40,405

ABOUT THE INSTITUTION Independent, coed. **Awards:** bachelor's, master's, and doctoral degrees. 40 undergraduate majors. **Total enrollment:** 7,633. Undergraduates: 6,366. Freshmen: 1,663. Both federal and institutional methodology are used as a basis for awarding need-based institutional aid.
UNDERGRADUATE EXPENSES for 2018–2019 Application fee: $70. **Comprehensive fee:** $69,140 includes full-time tuition ($52,550), mandatory fees ($1330), and room and board ($15,260). **College room only:** $8650. Room and board charges vary according to board plan and location. **Part-time tuition:** $1640 per credit hour.
FRESHMAN FINANCIAL AID (Fall 2017, est.) 1,229 applied for aid; of those 81% were deemed to have need. 100% of freshmen with need received aid; of those 22% had need fully met. **Average percent of need met:** 84% (excluding resources awarded to replace EFC). **Average financial aid package:** $40,705 (excluding resources awarded to replace EFC). 22% of all full-time freshmen had no need and received non-need-based gift aid.
UNDERGRADUATE FINANCIAL AID (Fall 2017, est.) 4,144 applied for aid; of those 89% were deemed to have need. 100% of undergraduates with need received aid; of those 17% had need fully met. **Average percent of need met:** 80% (excluding resources awarded to replace EFC). **Average financial aid package:** $40,405 (excluding resources awarded to replace EFC). 26% of all full-time undergraduates had no need and received non-need-based gift aid.
GIFT AID (NEED-BASED) Total amount: $130,241,211 (10% federal, 2% state, 86% institutional, 2% external sources). **Receiving aid:** Freshmen: 60% (991); all full-time undergraduates: 58% (3,684). **Average award:** Freshmen: $36,478; Undergraduates: $34,894. **Scholarships, grants, and awards:** Federal Pell, FSEOG, state, private, college/university gift aid from institutional funds, Academic Competitiveness Grants, National SMART Grants, Gates Millennium Scholarships.
GIFT AID (NON-NEED-BASED) Total amount: $40,177,694 (4% federal, 1% state, 93% institutional, 2% external sources). **Receiving aid:** Freshmen: 11% (183). Undergraduates: 7% (433). **Average award:** Freshmen: $20,777. Undergraduates: $19,331. **Scholarships, grants, and awards by category:** Academic interests/achievement: general academic interests/achievements, humanities, mathematics, military science. Creative arts/performance: general creative arts/performance. Special achievements/activities: general special achievements/activities. Special characteristics: children and siblings of alumni, children of faculty/staff, ethnic background, general

special characteristics, members of minority groups. **Tuition waivers:** Full or partial for employees or children of employees. **ROTC:** Army, Naval, Air Force.
LOANS Student loans: $40,771,507 (60% need-based, 40% non-need-based). 65% of past graduating class borrowed through all loan programs. **Average need-based loan:** Freshmen: $3602. Undergraduates: $5227. **Parent loans:** $10,855,668 (24% need-based, 76% non-need-based). **Programs:** Federal Direct (Subsidized and Unsubsidized Stafford, PLUS), Perkins, college/university.
WORK-STUDY Federal work-study: Total amount: $1,497,127; 830 jobs averaging $1980.
ATHLETIC AWARDS Total amount: $2,389,201 (100% non-need-based).
APPLYING FOR FINANCIAL AID Required financial aid forms: FAFSA, CSS Financial Aid PROFILE. **Financial aid deadline (priority):** 2/1. **Notification date:** 3/15.
CONTACT Mr. Martin Daniels, Director of Financial Aid, Rensselaer Polytechnic Institute, Academy Hall, Troy, NY 12180-3590, 518-276-6813. **Fax:** 518-276-4797. **E-mail:** financial_aid@rpi.edu.
Website: http://www.rpi.edu/.

RESEARCH COLLEGE OF NURSING
Kansas City, MO

ABOUT THE INSTITUTION Independent, coed, primarily women. **Awards:** certificates, bachelor's, and master's degrees (bachelor's degree offered jointly with Rockhurst College). 1 undergraduate major. **Total enrollment:** 415. Undergraduates: 264. Freshmen: 78.
GIFT AID (NEED-BASED) Scholarships, grants, and awards: Federal Pell, FSEOG, state, private, college/university gift aid from institutional funds.
GIFT AID (NON-NEED-BASED) Scholarships, grants, and awards by category: Academic interests/achievement: general academic interests/achievements, health fields. Special characteristics: children and siblings of alumni, children of educators, children of faculty/staff, siblings of current students.
LOANS Programs: Federal Direct (Subsidized and Unsubsidized Stafford, PLUS), Federal Nursing.
APPLYING FOR FINANCIAL AID Required financial aid form: FAFSA.
CONTACT Ms. Stacie Withers, Director of Financial Aid, Research College of Nursing, 2525 East Meyer Boulevard, Kansas City, MO 64132, 816-995-2832. **Fax:** 816-995-2833. **E-mail:** stacie.withers@researchcollege.edu.
Website: http://www.researchcollege.edu/.

RESURRECTION UNIVERSITY
Chicago, IL

Tuition & fees: $38,448	Average undergraduate aid package: $23,000

ABOUT THE INSTITUTION Independent, coed. **Awards:** certificates, bachelor's, master's, and doctoral degrees. 3 undergraduate majors. **Total enrollment:** 709. Undergraduates: 602. Both federal and institutional methodology are used as a basis for awarding need-based institutional aid.
UNDERGRADUATE EXPENSES for 2018–2019 Application fee: $50. **One-time required fee:** $150. **Tuition:** full-time $37,578. Full-time tuition and fees vary according to course load, degree level, and program. Part-time tuition and fees vary according to course load, degree level, and program.
UNDERGRADUATE FINANCIAL AID (Fall 2017, est.) 459 applied for aid; of those 100% were deemed to have need. 100% of undergraduates with need received aid. **Average percent of need met:** 30% (excluding resources awarded to replace EFC). **Average financial aid package:** $23,000 (excluding resources awarded to replace EFC). 2% of all full-time undergraduates had no need and received non-need-based gift aid.
GIFT AID (NEED-BASED) Total amount: $2,681,526 (50% federal, 34% state, 16% institutional). **Receiving aid:** All full-time undergraduates: 68% (330). **Average award:** Undergraduates: $5960. **Scholarships, grants, and awards:** Federal Pell, FSEOG, state, private, college/university gift aid from institutional funds.

GIFT AID (NON-NEED-BASED) *Total amount:* $342,600 (86% institutional, 14% external sources). *Receiving aid:* Undergraduates: 68% (330). *Average award:* Undergraduates: $2000.

LOANS *Student loans:* $5,749,128 (46% need-based, 54% non-need-based). *Average need-based loan:* Undergraduates: $5500. *Parent loans:* $895,868 (100% non-need-based). *Programs:* Federal Direct (Subsidized and Unsubsidized Stafford, PLUS).

WORK-STUDY *Federal work-study:* Total amount: $27,407; jobs available.

APPLYING FOR FINANCIAL AID *Notification date:* Continuous.

CONTACT Ms. Shirley Howell, Financial Aid Officer, Resurrection University, 1431 North Claremont Avenue, Chicago, IL 60622, 773-252-5125. *Fax:* 773-227-5134. *E-mail:* shirley.howell@resu.edu.
Website: http://www.resu.edu/.

RHODE ISLAND COLLEGE
Providence, RI

Tuition & fees (RI res): $8776	Average undergraduate aid package: $9745

ABOUT THE INSTITUTION State-supported, coed. *Awards:* certificates, bachelor's, master's, and doctoral degrees. 108 undergraduate majors. *Total enrollment:* 8,174. Undergraduates: 7,079. Freshmen: 1,040. Both federal and institutional methodology are used as a basis for awarding need-based institutional aid.

UNDERGRADUATE EXPENSES for 2017–2018 *Application fee:* $50. *Tuition, state resident:* full-time $7637; part-time $300 per credit. *Tuition, nonresident:* full-time $20,150; part-time $740 per credit. *Required fees:* full-time $1139; $39 per credit. Part-time tuition and fees vary according to course load. *College room and board:* $11,335; *Room only:* $6582. Room and board charges vary according to housing facility.

FRESHMAN FINANCIAL AID (Fall 2017, est.) 971 applied for aid; of those 83% were deemed to have need. 96% of freshmen with need received aid; of those 13% had need fully met. *Average percent of need met:* 70% (excluding resources awarded to replace EFC). *Average financial aid package:* $11,033 (excluding resources awarded to replace EFC). 4% of all full-time freshmen had no need and received non-need-based gift aid.

UNDERGRADUATE FINANCIAL AID (Fall 2017, est.) 4,584 applied for aid; of those 84% were deemed to have need. 96% of undergraduates with need received aid; of those 20% had need fully met. *Average percent of need met:* 68% (excluding resources awarded to replace EFC). *Average financial aid package:* $9745 (excluding resources awarded to replace EFC). 2% of all full-time undergraduates had no need and received non-need-based gift aid.

GIFT AID (NEED-BASED) *Total amount:* $25,114,651 (61% federal, 8% state, 26% institutional, 5% external sources). *Receiving aid:* Freshmen: 68% (692); all full-time undergraduates: 60% (3,225). *Average award:* Freshmen: $8597; Undergraduates: $7016. *Scholarships, grants, and awards:* Federal Pell, FSEOG, state, private, college/university gift aid from institutional funds.

GIFT AID (NON-NEED-BASED) *Total amount:* $651,157 (65% institutional, 35% external sources). *Receiving aid:* Freshmen: 2% (20). Undergraduates: 2% (91). *Average award:* Freshmen: $2647. Undergraduates: $2441. *Scholarships, grants, and awards by category: Academic interests/achievement:* general academic interests/achievements. *Creative arts/performance:* art/fine arts, cinema/film/broadcasting, dance, journalism/publications, music, theater/drama. *Special characteristics:* children and siblings of alumni. *Tuition waivers:* Full or partial for employees or children of employees. *ROTC:* Army cooperative.

LOANS *Student loans:* $29,728,609 (72% need-based, 28% non-need-based). 71% of past graduating class borrowed through all loan programs. *Average indebtedness per student:* $25,791. *Average need-based loan:* Freshmen: $3314. Undergraduates: $3958. *Parent loans:* $1,731,362 (43% need-based, 57% non-need-based). *Programs:* Federal Direct (Subsidized and Unsubsidized Stafford, PLUS), Perkins.

WORK-STUDY *Federal work-study:* Total amount: $1,988,754; jobs available.

APPLYING FOR FINANCIAL AID *Required financial aid forms:* FAFSA, institution's own form. *Financial aid deadline (priority):* 2/1. *Notification date:* Continuous beginning 2/15. Students must reply within 3 weeks of notification.

CONTACT Mr. Kenneth Ferus, Director of Financial Aid, Rhode Island College, 600 Mount Pleasant Avenue, Providence, RI 02908, 401-456-8033 or toll-free 800-669-5760. *Fax:* 401-456-8686. *E-mail:* kferus@ric.edu.
Website: http://www.ric.edu/.

RHODE ISLAND SCHOOL OF DESIGN
Providence, RI

ABOUT THE INSTITUTION Independent, coed. *Awards:* bachelor's and master's degrees. 16 undergraduate majors. *Total enrollment:* 2,440. Undergraduates: 1,976. Freshmen: 450.

GIFT AID (NEED-BASED) *Scholarships, grants, and awards:* Federal Pell, FSEOG, state, private, college/university gift aid from institutional funds.

GIFT AID (NON-NEED-BASED) *Scholarships, grants, and awards by category: Creative arts/performance:* applied art and design, art/fine arts. *Special characteristics:* children of faculty/staff.

LOANS *Programs:* Federal Direct (Subsidized and Unsubsidized Stafford, PLUS), Perkins.

WORK-STUDY *Federal work-study:* jobs available. *State or other work-study/employment:* Total amount: $1,500,000 (100% need-based). Part-time jobs available.

APPLYING FOR FINANCIAL AID *Required financial aid forms:* FAFSA, CSS Financial Aid PROFILE.

CONTACT Anthony Gallonio, Assistant Vice President of Enrollment Services, Rhode Island School of Design, 2 College Street, Providence, RI 02903-2784, 401-454-6661 or toll-free 800-364-7473. *Fax:* 401-454-6412. *E-mail:* financialaid@risd.edu.
Website: http://www.risd.edu/.

RHODES COLLEGE
Memphis, TN

Tuition & fees: $46,504	Average undergraduate aid package: $38,952

ABOUT THE INSTITUTION Independent, coed. *Awards:* bachelor's and master's degrees (master's degree in accounting only). 34 undergraduate majors. *Total enrollment:* 2,010. Undergraduates: 1,988. Freshmen: 512. Both federal and institutional methodology are used as a basis for awarding need-based institutional aid.

UNDERGRADUATE EXPENSES for 2018–2019 *Comprehensive fee:* $57,794 includes full-time tuition ($46,194), mandatory fees ($310), and room and board ($11,290). *College room only:* $5373. Room and board charges vary according to board plan and housing facility. *Part-time tuition:* $1930 per credit hour. Part-time tuition and fees vary according to course load.

FRESHMAN FINANCIAL AID (Fall 2017, est.) 441 applied for aid; of those 70% were deemed to have need. 100% of freshmen with need received aid; of those 51% had need fully met. *Average percent of need met:* 94% (excluding resources awarded to replace EFC). *Average financial aid package:* $39,190 (excluding resources awarded to replace EFC). 35% of all full-time freshmen had no need and received non-need-based gift aid.

UNDERGRADUATE FINANCIAL AID (Fall 2017, est.) 1,320 applied for aid; of those 73% were deemed to have need. 100% of undergraduates with need received aid; of those 44% had need fully met. *Average percent of need met:* 90% (excluding resources awarded to replace EFC). *Average financial aid package:* $38,952 (excluding resources awarded to replace EFC). 44% of all full-time undergraduates had no need and received non-need-based gift aid.

GIFT AID (NEED-BASED) *Total amount:* $30,525,886 (5% federal, 5% state, 89% institutional, 1% external sources). *Receiving aid:* Freshmen: 60% (305); all full-time undergraduates: 49% (961). *Average award:* Freshmen: $31,593; Undergraduates: $31,751. *Scholarships, grants, and awards:* Federal Pell, FSEOG, state, private, college/university gift aid from institutional funds.

GIFT AID (NON-NEED-BASED) *Total amount:* $24,804,510 (1% federal, 4% state, 90% institutional, 5% external sources). *Receiving aid:* Freshmen: 29% (148). Undergraduates: 17% (327). *Average award:* Freshmen: $23,484. Undergraduates: $22,626. *Scholarships, grants, and awards by category: Academic interests/achievement:* general academic interests/achievements, physical sciences. *Creative arts/performance:* art/fine arts, general creative arts/performance, music, theater/drama. *Special characteristics:* children of faculty/staff, members of minority groups, relatives of clergy, religious affiliation. *Tuition waivers:* Full or partial for employees or children of employees. *ROTC:* Army cooperative, Naval cooperative, Air Force cooperative.

LOANS *Student loans:* $7,458,919 (43% need-based, 57% non-need-based). 48% of past graduating class borrowed through all loan programs. *Average indebtedness per student:* $27,576. *Average need-based loan:* Freshmen: $1710. Undergrad-

uates: $3303. *Parent loans:* $2,344,790 (18% need-based, 82% non-need-based). *Programs:* Federal Direct (Subsidized and Unsubsidized Stafford, PLUS), Perkins.
WORK-STUDY *Federal work-study:* Total amount: $640,018; jobs available. *State or other work-study/employment:* Total amount: $889,087 (32% need-based, 68% non-need-based). Part-time jobs available.
APPLYING FOR FINANCIAL AID *Required financial aid forms:* FAFSA, CSS Financial Aid PROFILE, noncustodial (divorced/separated) parent's statement. *Financial aid deadline:* 3/1. *Notification date:* 4/15. Students must reply by 5/1.
CONTACT Mr. Michael Morgan, Director of Financial Aid, Rhodes College, 2000 North Parkway, Memphis, TN 38112-1690, 901-843-3808 or toll-free 800-844-5969. *Fax:* 901-843-3435. *E-mail:* morganm@rhodes.edu.
Website: http://www.rhodes.edu/.

RICE UNIVERSITY
Houston, TX

Tuition & fees: $45,608	Average undergraduate aid package: $44,799

ABOUT THE INSTITUTION Independent, coed. *Awards:* bachelor's, master's, and doctoral degrees. 58 undergraduate majors. *Total enrollment:* 7,022. Undergraduates: 4,001. Freshmen: 1,046. Both federal and institutional methodology are used as a basis for awarding need-based institutional aid.
UNDERGRADUATE EXPENSES for 2017–2018 *Application fee:* $75. *One-time required fee:* $625. *Comprehensive fee:* $59,458 includes full-time tuition ($44,900), mandatory fees ($708), and room and board ($13,850). *College room only:* $9490. Room and board charges vary according to board plan. *Part-time tuition:* $1871 per credit hour.
FRESHMAN FINANCIAL AID (Fall 2017, est.) 841 applied for aid; of those 52% were deemed to have need. 100% of freshmen with need received aid; of those 100% had need fully met. *Average percent of need met:* 100% (excluding resources awarded to replace EFC). *Average financial aid package:* $46,077 (excluding resources awarded to replace EFC). 11% of all full-time freshmen had no need and received non-need-based gift aid.
UNDERGRADUATE FINANCIAL AID (Fall 2017, est.) 2,818 applied for aid; of those 54% were deemed to have need. 100% of undergraduates with need received aid; of those 100% had need fully met. *Average percent of need met:* 100% (excluding resources awarded to replace EFC). *Average financial aid package:* $44,799 (excluding resources awarded to replace EFC). 11% of all full-time undergraduates had no need and received non-need-based gift aid.
GIFT AID (NEED-BASED) *Total amount:* $60,775,035 (5% federal, 3% state, 92% institutional). *Receiving aid:* Freshmen: 41% (430); all full-time undergraduates: 38% (1,506). *Average award:* Freshmen: $41,573; Undergraduates: $40,285. *Scholarships, grants, and awards:* Federal Pell, FSEOG, state, private, college/university gift aid from institutional funds.
GIFT AID (NON-NEED-BASED) *Total amount:* $12,665,824 (3% federal, 76% institutional, 21% external sources). *Receiving aid:* Freshmen: 2% (17). Undergraduates: 1% (52). *Average award:* Freshmen: $26,283. Undergraduates: $20,779. *Scholarships, grants, and awards by category: Academic interests/ achievement:* engineering/technologies, general academic interests/achievements. *Creative arts/performance:* art/fine arts, music. *Special achievements/activities:* general special achievements/activities, leadership. *Special characteristics:* local/state students, members of minority groups. *Tuition waivers:* Full or partial for employees or children of employees. *ROTC:* Army cooperative, Naval, Air Force cooperative.
LOANS *Student loans:* $4,983,565 (34% need-based, 66% non-need-based). 25% of past graduating class borrowed through all loan programs. *Average indebtedness per student:* $26,556. *Average need-based loan:* Freshmen: $2913. Undergraduates: $3237. *Parent loans:* $2,415,454 (100% non-need-based). *Programs:* Federal Direct (Subsidized and Unsubsidized Stafford, PLUS), Perkins, state.
WORK-STUDY *Federal work-study:* Total amount: $2,443,620; jobs available. *State or other work-study/employment:* Part-time jobs available.
ATHLETIC AWARDS Total amount: $12,326,525 (4% need-based, 96% non-need-based).
APPLYING FOR FINANCIAL AID *Required financial aid forms:* FAFSA, CSS Financial Aid PROFILE, noncustodial (divorced/separated) parent's statement, business/farm supplement, federal income tax form(s), W-2 forms. *Financial aid deadline:* 4/15 (priority: 2/15). *Notification date:* Continuous beginning 4/1. Students must reply by 5/1.

CONTACT Office of Student Financial Services, Rice University, 116 Allen Center, MS 12, Houston, TX 77005, 713-348-4958. *Fax:* 713-348-2139. *E-mail:* fina@rice.edu. *Website:* http://www.rice.edu/.

RIDER UNIVERSITY
Lawrenceville, NJ

Tuition & fees: $41,310	Average undergraduate aid package: $30,642

ABOUT THE INSTITUTION Independent, coed. *Awards:* certificates, associate, bachelor's, master's, and doctoral degrees. 65 undergraduate majors. *Total enrollment:* 5,073. Undergraduates: 4,094. Federal methodology is used as a basis for awarding need-based institutional aid.
UNDERGRADUATE EXPENSES for 2018–2019 *Application fee:* $50. *Comprehensive fee:* $56,010 includes full-time tuition ($40,570), mandatory fees ($740), and room and board ($14,700). *College room only:* $9640.
FRESHMAN FINANCIAL AID (Fall 2017, est.) 928 applied for aid; of those 92% were deemed to have need. 100% of freshmen with need received aid; of those 14% had need fully met. *Average percent of need met:* 78% (excluding resources awarded to replace EFC). *Average financial aid package:* $34,344 (excluding resources awarded to replace EFC). 13% of all full-time freshmen had no need and received non-need-based gift aid.
UNDERGRADUATE FINANCIAL AID (Fall 2017, est.) 3,084 applied for aid; of those 92% were deemed to have need. 100% of undergraduates with need received aid; of those 15% had need fully met. *Average percent of need met:* 75% (excluding resources awarded to replace EFC). *Average financial aid package:* $30,642 (excluding resources awarded to replace EFC). 19% of all full-time undergraduates had no need and received non-need-based gift aid.
GIFT AID (NEED-BASED) *Total amount:* $69,800,099 (9% federal, 13% state, 77% institutional, 1% external sources). *Receiving aid:* Freshmen: 85% (853); all full-time undergraduates: 75% (2,789). *Average award:* Freshmen: $29,812; Undergraduates: $26,595. *Scholarships, grants, and awards:* Federal Pell, FSEOG, state, private, college/university gift aid from institutional funds.
GIFT AID (NON-NEED-BASED) *Total amount:* $15,948,486 (3% federal, 96% institutional, 1% external sources). *Receiving aid:* Freshmen: 11% (109). Undergraduates: 11% (399). *Average award:* Freshmen: $19,539. Undergraduates: $18,887. *Scholarships, grants, and awards by category: Academic interests/ achievement:* general academic interests/achievements. *Creative arts/performance:* theater/drama. *Special characteristics:* members of minority groups. *ROTC:* Army cooperative.
LOANS *Student loans:* $33,876,212 (68% need-based, 32% non-need-based). 74% of past graduating class borrowed through all loan programs. *Average indebtedness per student:* $35,332. *Average need-based loan:* Freshmen: $3144. Undergraduates: $3705. *Parent loans:* $12,536,245 (57% need-based, 43% non-need-based). *Programs:* Federal Direct (Subsidized and Unsubsidized Stafford, PLUS), Perkins.
WORK-STUDY *Federal work-study:* Total amount: $3,936,399; jobs available.
ATHLETIC AWARDS Total amount: $4,646,630 (44% need-based, 56% non-need-based).
APPLYING FOR FINANCIAL AID *Required financial aid form:* FAFSA. *Financial aid deadline (priority):* 2/1. *Notification date:* Continuous beginning 2/1.
CONTACT Mr. Drew Aromando, Office of Financial Aid, Rider University, 2083 Lawrenceville Road, Lawrenceville, NJ 08648-3001, 609-896-5360 or toll-free 800-257-9026. *Fax:* 609-219-4487. *E-mail:* finaid@rider.edu.
Website: http://www.rider.edu/.

RINGLING COLLEGE OF ART AND DESIGN
Sarasota, FL

Tuition & fees: $46,420	Average undergraduate aid package: $25,765

ABOUT THE INSTITUTION Independent, coed. **Awards:** bachelor's degrees. 11 undergraduate majors. **Total enrollment:** 1,456. Undergraduates: 1,456. Freshmen: 367. Federal methodology is used as a basis for awarding need-based institutional aid.

UNDERGRADUATE EXPENSES for 2018–2019 **Application fee:** $70. **Comprehensive fee:** $61,090 includes full-time tuition ($42,330), mandatory fees ($4090), and room and board ($14,670). Full-time tuition and fees vary according to course load, program, and student level. Room and board charges vary according to board plan and housing facility. **Part-time tuition:** $1972 per credit hour. Part-time tuition and fees vary according to program and student level.

FRESHMAN FINANCIAL AID (Fall 2017, est.) 295 applied for aid; of those 83% were deemed to have need. 100% of freshmen with need received aid; of those 9% had need fully met. **Average percent of need met:** 50% (excluding resources awarded to replace EFC). **Average financial aid package:** $24,796 (excluding resources awarded to replace EFC). 29% of all full-time freshmen had no need and received non-need-based gift aid.

UNDERGRADUATE FINANCIAL AID (Fall 2017, est.) 977 applied for aid; of those 91% were deemed to have need. 100% of undergraduates with need received aid; of those 5% had need fully met. **Average percent of need met:** 50% (excluding resources awarded to replace EFC). **Average financial aid package:** $25,765 (excluding resources awarded to replace EFC). 27% of all full-time undergraduates had no need and received non-need-based gift aid.

GIFT AID (NEED-BASED) Total amount: $15,278,438 (14% federal, 11% state, 70% institutional, 5% external sources). **Receiving aid:** Freshmen: 66% (244); all full-time undergraduates: 63% (883). **Average award:** Freshmen: $18,055; Undergraduates: $16,733. **Scholarships, grants, and awards:** Federal Pell, FSEOG, state, private, college/university gift aid from institutional funds.

GIFT AID (NON-NEED-BASED) Total amount: $5,099,861 (6% state, 89% institutional, 5% external sources). **Receiving aid:** Freshmen: 3% (12). Undergraduates: 2% (33). **Average award:** Freshmen: $9970. Undergraduates: $11,845. **Scholarships, grants, and awards by category:** Academic interests/achievement: general academic interests/achievements. Creative arts/performance: applied art and design, art/fine arts, cinema/film/broadcasting. Special achievements/activities: community service. **Tuition waivers:** Full or partial for employees or children of employees.

LOANS Student loans: $10,778,557 (85% need-based, 15% non-need-based). 61% of past graduating class borrowed through all loan programs. Average indebtedness per student: $46,575. **Average need-based loan:** Freshmen: $6399. Undergraduates: $8302. **Parent loans:** $12,860,775 (80% need-based, 20% non-need-based). **Programs:** Federal Direct (Subsidized and Unsubsidized Stafford, PLUS).

WORK-STUDY Federal work-study: Total amount: $143,434; jobs available. **State or other work-study/employment:** Total amount: $298,000 (5% need-based, 95% non-need-based). Part-time jobs available.

APPLYING FOR FINANCIAL AID Required financial aid form: FAFSA. **Financial aid deadline (priority):** 3/1. **Notification date:** Continuous beginning 2/1.

CONTACT Mr. Lee Harrell, Director of Financial Aid, Ringling College of Art and Design, 2700 North Tamiami Trail, Sarasota, FL 34243, 941-359-7532 or toll-free 800-255-7695. Fax: 941-359-6107. E-mail: lharrell@ringling.edu. Website: http://www.ringling.edu/.

RIO GRANDE BIBLE INSTITUTE
Edinburg, TX

CONTACT Financial Aid Office, Rio Grande Bible Institute, 4300 S US Hwy 281, Edinburg, TX 78539, 956-380-8100. Website: http://www.riogrande.edu/.

RIPON COLLEGE
Ripon, WI

CONTACT Mr. Leigh D. Mlodzik, Dean of Admission and Financial Aid, Ripon College, 300 Seward Street, Ripon, WI 54971, 920-748-8704 or toll-free 800-947-4766. Fax: 920-748-8335. E-mail: financialaid@ripon.edu. Website: http://www.ripon.edu/.

RIVIER UNIVERSITY
Nashua, NH

CONTACT Valerie Patnaude, Director of Financial Aid, Rivier University, 420 Main Street, Nashua, NH 03060-5086, 603-897-8533 or toll-free 800-44RIVIER. Fax: 603-897-8810. E-mail: vpatnaude@rivier.edu. Website: http://www.rivier.edu/.

ROANOKE COLLEGE
Salem, VA

Tuition & fees: $44,030	Average undergraduate aid package: $34,319

ABOUT THE INSTITUTION Independent Evangelical Lutheran Church in America, coed. **Awards:** bachelor's degrees. 34 undergraduate majors. **Total enrollment:** 2,037. Undergraduates: 2,037. Freshmen: 557. Federal methodology is used as a basis for awarding need-based institutional aid.

UNDERGRADUATE EXPENSES for 2018–2019 **Application fee:** $30. **One-time required fee:** $125. **Comprehensive fee:** $57,720 includes full-time tuition ($42,446), mandatory fees ($1584), and room and board ($13,690). **College room only:** $6356. Room and board charges vary according to board plan and housing facility. **Part-time tuition:** $2028 per course. **Part-time fees:** $60 per term. Part-time tuition and fees vary according to course load and reciprocity agreements.

FRESHMAN FINANCIAL AID (Fall 2017, est.) 508 applied for aid; of those 87% were deemed to have need. 100% of freshmen with need received aid; of those 19% had need fully met. **Average percent of need met:** 84% (excluding resources awarded to replace EFC). **Average financial aid package:** $36,817 (excluding resources awarded to replace EFC). 20% of all full-time freshmen had no need and received non-need-based gift aid.

UNDERGRADUATE FINANCIAL AID (Fall 2017, est.) 1,639 applied for aid; of those 90% were deemed to have need. 100% of undergraduates with need received aid; of those 16% had need fully met. **Average percent of need met:** 81% (excluding resources awarded to replace EFC). **Average financial aid package:** $34,319 (excluding resources awarded to replace EFC). 25% of all full-time undergraduates had no need and received non-need-based gift aid.

GIFT AID (NEED-BASED) Total amount: $43,310,565 (6% federal, 6% state, 85% institutional, 3% external sources). **Receiving aid:** Freshmen: 80% (444); all full-time undergraduates: 75% (1,472). **Average award:** Freshmen: $31,080; Undergraduates: $28,109. **Scholarships, grants, and awards:** Federal Pell, FSEOG, state, private, college/university gift aid from institutional funds.

GIFT AID (NON-NEED-BASED) Total amount: $11,779,039 (5% state, 90% institutional, 5% external sources). **Receiving aid:** Freshmen: 79% (442). Undergraduates: 74% (1,454). **Average award:** Freshmen: $22,607. Undergraduates: $20,257. **Scholarships, grants, and awards by category:** Academic interests/achievement: general academic interests/achievements. Creative arts/performance: art/fine arts, music. **Tuition waivers:** Full or partial for employees or children of employees, adult students, senior citizens.

LOANS Student loans: $13,822,808 (91% need-based, 9% non-need-based). 76% of past graduating class borrowed through all loan programs. Average indebtedness per student: $41,187. **Average need-based loan:** Freshmen: $3980. Undergraduates: $4877. **Parent loans:** $4,852,580 (94% need-based, 6% non-need-based). **Programs:** Federal Direct (Subsidized and Unsubsidized Stafford, PLUS), Perkins, college/university, alternative loans.

WORK-STUDY Federal work-study: Total amount: $1,595,086; jobs available.

APPLYING FOR FINANCIAL AID Required financial aid forms: FAFSA, state aid form. **Financial aid deadline (priority):** 3/1. **Notification date:** Continuous beginning 10/1. Students must reply within 2 weeks of notification.

CONTACT Mr. Thomas S. Blair Jr., Director of Financial Aid, Roanoke College, 221 College Lane, Salem, VA 24153-3794, 540-375-2235 or toll-free 800-388-2276. *E-mail:* finaid@roanoke.edu. *Website:* http://www.roanoke.edu/.

ROBERT MORRIS UNIVERSITY
Moon Township, PA

Tuition & fees: $29,420	Average undergraduate aid package: $22,897

ABOUT THE INSTITUTION Independent, coed. *Awards:* certificates, bachelor's, master's, and doctoral degrees. 32 undergraduate majors. *Total enrollment:* 5,076. Undergraduates: 4,243. Freshmen: 871. Federal methodology is used as a basis for awarding need-based institutional aid.

UNDERGRADUATE EXPENSES for 2017–2018 *Application fee:* $30. *Comprehensive fee:* $40,600 includes full-time tuition ($28,210), mandatory fees ($1210), and room and board ($11,180). *College room only:* $6220. Full-time tuition and fees vary according to degree level and program. Room and board charges vary according to board plan and housing facility. *Part-time tuition:* $905 per credit hour. *Part-time fees:* $80 per credit hour. Part-time tuition and fees vary according to course load, degree level, and program.

FRESHMAN FINANCIAL AID (Fall 2017, est.) 782 applied for aid; of those 89% were deemed to have need. 100% of freshmen with need received aid; of those 12% had need fully met. *Average percent of need met:* 76% (excluding resources awarded to replace EFC). *Average financial aid package:* $25,418 (excluding resources awarded to replace EFC). 16% of all full-time freshmen had no need and received non-need-based gift aid.

UNDERGRADUATE FINANCIAL AID (Fall 2017, est.) 2,996 applied for aid; of those 90% were deemed to have need. 100% of undergraduates with need received aid; of those 13% had need fully met. *Average percent of need met:* 71% (excluding resources awarded to replace EFC). *Average financial aid package:* $22,897 (excluding resources awarded to replace EFC). 17% of all full-time undergraduates had no need and received non-need-based gift aid.

GIFT AID (NEED-BASED) *Total amount:* $42,096,676 (16% federal, 12% state, 68% institutional, 4% external sources). *Receiving aid:* Freshmen: 80% (697); all full-time undergraduates: 68% (2,647). *Average award:* Freshmen: $19,385; Undergraduates: $16,555. *Scholarships, grants, and awards:* Federal Pell, FSEOG, state, private, college/university gift aid from institutional funds.

GIFT AID (NON-NEED-BASED) *Total amount:* $11,259,593 (9% federal, 1% state, 87% institutional, 3% external sources). *Receiving aid:* Freshmen: 9% (74). Undergraduates: 7% (263). *Average award:* Freshmen: $14,405. Undergraduates: $12,841. *Scholarships, grants, and awards by category:* Academic interests/achievement: general academic interests/achievements. Special characteristics: children of faculty/staff, veterans. *Tuition waivers:* Full or partial for employees or children of employees. *ROTC:* Army, Naval cooperative, Air Force cooperative.

LOANS *Student loans:* $32,120,396 (70% need-based, 30% non-need-based). 76% of past graduating class borrowed through all loan programs. *Average indebtedness per student:* $39,856. *Average need-based loan:* Freshmen: $5292. Undergraduates: $6650. *Parent loans:* $14,006,821 (54% need-based, 46% non-need-based). *Programs:* Federal Direct (Subsidized and Unsubsidized Stafford, PLUS), Perkins, private loans.

WORK-STUDY *Federal work-study:* Total amount: $2,469,868; jobs available. *State or other work-study/employment:* Total amount: $65,000 (16% need-based, 84% non-need-based). Part-time jobs available.

ATHLETIC AWARDS Total amount: $3,562,929 (37% need-based, 63% non-need-based).

APPLYING FOR FINANCIAL AID *Required financial aid form:* FAFSA. *Financial aid deadline:* Continuous. *Notification date:* Continuous beginning 11/15. Students must reply within 2 weeks of notification.

CONTACT Ms. Stephanie Hendershot, Director of Financial Aid, Robert Morris University, 6001 University Boulevard, Moon Township, PA 15108-1189, 412-397-6250 or toll-free 800-762-0097. *Fax:* 412-397-2200. *E-mail:* finaid@rmu.edu. *Website:* http://www.rmu.edu/.

ROBERT MORRIS UNIVERSITY ILLINOIS
Chicago, IL

Tuition & fees: $28,530	Average undergraduate aid package: $17,114

ABOUT THE INSTITUTION Independent, coed. *Awards:* associate, bachelor's, and master's degrees. 16 undergraduate majors. *Total enrollment:* 2,307. Undergraduates: 2,003. Freshmen: 427. Federal methodology is used as a basis for awarding need-based institutional aid.

UNDERGRADUATE EXPENSES for 2018–2019 *Application fee:* $20. *Tuition:* full-time $28,050; part-time $775 per quarter hour. Part-time tuition and fees vary according to course load.

FRESHMAN FINANCIAL AID (Fall 2016) 531 applied for aid; of those 98% were deemed to have need. 98% of freshmen with need received aid; of those 6% had need fully met. *Average percent of need met:* 51% (excluding resources awarded to replace EFC). *Average financial aid package:* $17,401 (excluding resources awarded to replace EFC). 3% of all full-time freshmen had no need and received non-need-based gift aid.

UNDERGRADUATE FINANCIAL AID (Fall 2016) 2,653 applied for aid; of those 97% were deemed to have need. 95% of undergraduates with need received aid; of those 5% had need fully met. *Average percent of need met:* 56% (excluding resources awarded to replace EFC). *Average financial aid package:* $17,114 (excluding resources awarded to replace EFC). 3% of all full-time undergraduates had no need and received non-need-based gift aid.

GIFT AID (NEED-BASED) *Total amount:* $18,368,809 (48% federal, 24% state, 28% institutional). *Receiving aid:* Freshmen: 91% (498); all full-time undergraduates: 87% (2,437). *Average award:* Freshmen: $13,004; Undergraduates: $13,866. *Scholarships, grants, and awards:* Federal Pell, FSEOG, state, private, college/university gift aid from institutional funds.

GIFT AID (NON-NEED-BASED) *Total amount:* $13,592,867 (100% institutional). *Receiving aid:* Freshmen: 76% (415). Undergraduates: 83% (2,322). *Average award:* Freshmen: $18,239. Undergraduates: $18,623. *Scholarships, grants, and awards by category:* Academic interests/achievement: general academic interests/ achievements. *Creative arts/performance:* applied art and design, dance, journalism/ publications, music, performing arts, theater/drama. *Special achievements/activities:* cheerleading/drum major, community service, general special achievements/activities, leadership. *Special characteristics:* adult students, children of current students, children of faculty/staff, children of public servants, general special characteristics, local/state students, out-of-state students, veterans. *Tuition waivers:* Full or partial for employees or children of employees. *ROTC:* Army cooperative.

LOANS *Student loans:* $20,204,575 (97% need-based, 3% non-need-based). 62% of past graduating class borrowed through all loan programs. *Average indebtedness per student:* $34,382. *Average need-based loan:* Freshmen: $3908. Undergraduates: $4198. *Parent loans:* $6,154,316 (89% need-based, 11% non-need-based). *Programs:* Federal Direct (Subsidized and Unsubsidized Stafford, PLUS), Perkins.

WORK-STUDY *Federal work-study:* 146 jobs averaging $2239.

ATHLETIC AWARDS Total amount: $8,626,535 (88% need-based, 12% non-need-based).

APPLYING FOR FINANCIAL AID *Required financial aid form:* FAFSA. *Financial aid deadline:* Continuous. *Notification date:* Continuous.

CONTACT Michelle Hayes, Director of Financial Services, Robert Morris University Illinois, 401 South State Street, Suite 135, Chicago, IL 60605, 312-935-4106 or toll-free 800-762-5960. *Fax:* 312-935-4043. *E-mail:* mhayes@robertmorris.edu. *Website:* http://www.robertmorris.edu/.

ROBERTS WESLEYAN COLLEGE
Rochester, NY

Tuition & fees: $30,936	Average undergraduate aid package: $22,228

ABOUT THE INSTITUTION Independent Free Methodist Church of North America, coed. *Awards:* bachelor's, master's, and doctoral degrees. 62 undergraduate

majors. **Total enrollment:** 1,740. Undergraduates: 1,321. Freshmen: 219. Federal methodology is used as a basis for awarding need-based institutional aid.
UNDERGRADUATE EXPENSES for 2018–2019 One-time required fee: $250. **Comprehensive fee:** $41,366 includes full-time tuition ($29,600), mandatory fees ($1336), and room and board ($10,430). **College room only:** $6548. Room and board charges vary according to board plan and housing facility. Part-time tuition and fees vary according to course load.
FRESHMAN FINANCIAL AID (Fall 2017, est.) 203 applied for aid; of those 88% were deemed to have need. 100% of freshmen with need received aid; of those 20% had need fully met. **Average percent of need met:** 78% (excluding resources awarded to replace EFC). **Average financial aid package:** $25,757 (excluding resources awarded to replace EFC). 17% of all full-time freshmen had no need and received non-need-based gift aid.
UNDERGRADUATE FINANCIAL AID (Fall 2017, est.) 1,073 applied for aid; of those 94% were deemed to have need. 100% of undergraduates with need received aid; of those 13% had need fully met. **Average percent of need met:** 71% (excluding resources awarded to replace EFC). **Average financial aid package:** $22,228 (excluding resources awarded to replace EFC). 14% of all full-time undergraduates had no need and received non-need-based gift aid.
GIFT AID (NEED-BASED) Total amount: $15,778,947 (14% federal, 8% state, 65% institutional, 13% external sources). **Receiving aid:** Freshmen: 82% (179); all full-time undergraduates: 80% (966). **Average award:** Freshmen: $20,770; Undergraduates: $17,073. **Scholarships, grants, and awards:** Federal Pell, FSEOG, state, private, college/university gift aid from institutional funds, Academic Competitiveness Grants, National SMART Grants, TEACH Grants.
GIFT AID (NON-NEED-BASED) Total amount: $3,305,817 (1% federal, 73% institutional, 26% external sources). **Receiving aid:** Freshmen: 15% (32). Undergraduates: 9% (103). **Average award:** Freshmen: $13,710. Undergraduates: $11,437. **Scholarships, grants, and awards by category:** Academic interests/achievement: 585 awards ($6,500,287 total): general academic interests/achievements. Creative arts/performance: 93 awards ($522,596 total): art/fine arts, music. Special achievements/activities: 159 awards ($440,625 total): general special achievements/activities, junior miss, religious involvement. Special characteristics: 341 awards ($1,433,465 total): children and siblings of alumni, children of faculty/staff, international students, out-of-state students, relatives of clergy, religious affiliation. **Tuition waivers:** Full or partial for employees or children of employees, senior citizens. **ROTC:** Army cooperative, Air Force cooperative.
LOANS Student loans: $9,042,491 (84% need-based, 16% non-need-based). 84% of past graduating class borrowed through all loan programs. Average indebtedness per student: $34,679. **Average need-based loan:** Freshmen: $4997. Undergraduates: $5738. **Parent loans:** $2,103,277 (59% need-based, 41% non-need-based). **Programs:** Federal Direct (Subsidized and Unsubsidized Stafford, PLUS), Perkins.
WORK-STUDY Federal work-study: Total amount: $296,296; 618 jobs averaging $479. **State or other work-study/employment:** Total amount: $85,000 (100% non-need-based), 46 part-time jobs averaging $1891.
ATHLETIC AWARDS Total amount: $1,493,505 (56% need-based, 44% non-need-based).
APPLYING FOR FINANCIAL AID Required financial aid forms: FAFSA, state aid form. **Financial aid deadline (priority):** 3/15. **Notification date:** Continuous beginning 11/1. Students must reply by 5/1 or within 2 weeks of notification.
CONTACT Mr. Stephen Field, Executive Director of Student Financial Services, Roberts Wesleyan College, 2301 Westside Drive, Rochester, NY 14624-1997, 585-594-6150 or toll-free 800-777-4RWC. Fax: 585-594-6036. E-mail: finaid@roberts.edu. Website: http://www.roberts.edu/.

ROCHESTER COLLEGE
Rochester Hills, MI

CONTACT Student Financial Services, Rochester College, 800 West Avon Road, Rochester Hills, MI 48307, 248-218-2038 or toll-free 800-521-6010. Fax: 248-218-2065.
Website: http://www.rc.edu/.

ROCHESTER INSTITUTE OF TECHNOLOGY
Rochester, NY

Tuition & fees: $40,068	Average undergraduate aid package: $28,000

ABOUT THE INSTITUTION Independent, coed. **Awards:** certificates, associate, bachelor's, master's, and doctoral degrees. 113 undergraduate majors. **Total enrollment:** 16,584. Undergraduates: 13,515. Freshmen: 2,758. Both federal and institutional methodology are used as a basis for awarding need-based institutional aid.
UNDERGRADUATE EXPENSES for 2017–2018 Application fee: $65. **Comprehensive fee:** $52,734 includes full-time tuition ($39,506), mandatory fees ($562), and room and board ($12,666). **College room only:** $7376. Full-time tuition and fees vary according to course load. Room and board charges vary according to board plan and housing facility. **Part-time tuition:** $1463 per credit hour. **Part-time fees:** $70 per term. Part-time tuition and fees vary according to class time and course load. **Payment plan:** Tuition prepayment.
FRESHMAN FINANCIAL AID (Fall 2016) 2,297 applied for aid; of those 84% were deemed to have need. 100% of freshmen with need received aid; of those 77% had need fully met. **Average percent of need met:** 87% (excluding resources awarded to replace EFC). **Average financial aid package:** $28,468 (excluding resources awarded to replace EFC). 17% of all full-time freshmen had no need and received non-need-based gift aid.
UNDERGRADUATE FINANCIAL AID (Fall 2016) 10,091 applied for aid; of those 89% were deemed to have need. 100% of undergraduates with need received aid; of those 81% had need fully met. **Average percent of need met:** 87% (excluding resources awarded to replace EFC). **Average financial aid package:** $28,000 (excluding resources awarded to replace EFC). 15% of all full-time undergraduates had no need and received non-need-based gift aid.
GIFT AID (NEED-BASED) Total amount: $164,203,917 (10% federal, 5% state, 85% institutional). **Receiving aid:** Freshmen: 71% (1,851); all full-time undergraduates: 70% (8,593). **Average award:** Freshmen: $23,968; Undergraduates: $22,200. **Scholarships, grants, and awards:** Federal Pell, FSEOG, state, private, college/university gift aid from institutional funds, National Science Foundation Grants.
GIFT AID (NON-NEED-BASED) Total amount: $49,146,816 (19% federal, 25% state, 48% institutional, 8% external sources). **Receiving aid:** Freshmen: 17% (446). Undergraduates: 25% (3,015). **Average award:** Freshmen: $11,343. Undergraduates: $10,200. **Scholarships, grants, and awards by category:** Academic interests/achievement: biological sciences, business, communication, computer science, engineering/technologies, general academic interests/achievements, home economics, humanities, international studies, mathematics, military science, physical sciences, premedicine, social sciences. Creative arts/performance: applied art and design, art/fine arts, cinema/film/broadcasting. Special achievements/activities: community service, leadership. Special characteristics: children of faculty/staff, veterans. **Tuition waivers:** Full or partial for employees or children of employees. **ROTC:** Army, Naval cooperative, Air Force.
LOANS Student loans: $80,602,260 (50% need-based, 50% non-need-based). 76% of past graduating class borrowed through all loan programs. Average indebtedness per student: $38,927. **Average need-based loan:** Freshmen: $4600. Undergraduates: $6500. **Parent loans:** $25,242,646 (41% need-based, 59% non-need-based). **Programs:** Federal Direct (Subsidized and Unsubsidized Stafford, PLUS).
WORK-STUDY Federal work-study: jobs available. **State or other work-study/employment:** Total amount: $14,756,813 (100% non-need-based). Part-time jobs available.
APPLYING FOR FINANCIAL AID Required financial aid forms: FAFSA, state aid form. **Financial aid deadline (priority):** 3/1. **Notification date:** Continuous beginning 3/15. Students must reply by 5/1.
CONTACT Mr. Larry Chambers, Associate Vice President for Financial Aid and Scholarships, Rochester Institute of Technology, 56 Lomb Memorial Drive, Rochester, NY 14623-5604, 585-475-2186. Fax: 585-475-7270. E-mail: larry.chambers@rit.edu. Website: http://www.rit.edu/.

ROCKFORD UNIVERSITY
Rockford, IL

Tuition & fees: $30,930	Average undergraduate aid package: $20,212

ABOUT THE INSTITUTION Independent, coed. *Awards:* certificates, bachelor's, and master's degrees. 50 undergraduate majors. *Total enrollment:* 1,261. Undergraduates: 1,061. Freshmen: 152. Federal methodology is used as a basis for awarding need-based institutional aid.

UNDERGRADUATE EXPENSES for 2018–2019 *Comprehensive fee:* $39,590 includes full-time tuition ($30,800), mandatory fees ($130), and room and board ($8660). *College room only:* $4700. Full-time tuition and fees vary according to course load. Room and board charges vary according to board plan and housing facility. *Part-time tuition:* $795 per credit hour. Part-time tuition and fees vary according to course load.

FRESHMAN FINANCIAL AID (Fall 2016) 154 applied for aid; of those 94% were deemed to have need. 100% of freshmen with need received aid; of those 8% had need fully met. *Average percent of need met:* 73% (excluding resources awarded to replace EFC). *Average financial aid package:* $23,142 (excluding resources awarded to replace EFC). 8% of all full-time freshmen had no need and received non-need-based gift aid.

UNDERGRADUATE FINANCIAL AID (Fall 2016) 837 applied for aid; of those 94% were deemed to have need. 100% of undergraduates with need received aid; of those 10% had need fully met. *Average percent of need met:* 65% (excluding resources awarded to replace EFC). *Average financial aid package:* $20,212 (excluding resources awarded to replace EFC). 10% of all full-time undergraduates had no need and received non-need-based gift aid.

GIFT AID (NEED-BASED) *Total amount:* $12,576,083 (17% federal, 15% state, 66% institutional, 2% external sources). *Receiving aid:* Freshmen: 91% (143); all full-time undergraduates: 88% (776). *Average award:* Freshmen: $19,735; Undergraduates: $15,734. *Scholarships, grants, and awards:* Federal Pell, FSEOG, state, private, college/university gift aid from institutional funds.

GIFT AID (NON-NEED-BASED) *Total amount:* $1,699,472 (91% institutional, 9% external sources). *Receiving aid:* Freshmen: 7% (11). Undergraduates: 9% (76). *Average award:* Freshmen: $13,992. Undergraduates: $11,202. *Scholarships, grants, and awards by category:* Academic interests/achievement: 826 awards ($7,732,199 total): biological sciences, business, computer science, education, English, foreign languages, general academic interests/achievements, mathematics, physical sciences, premedicine, social sciences. *Creative arts/performance:* 32 awards ($144,875 total): art/fine arts, dance, music, performing arts, theater/drama. *Special achievements/activities:* 7 awards ($15,345 total): community service, leadership. *Special characteristics:* 164 awards ($942,800 total): children and siblings of alumni, children of current students, children of educators, children of faculty/staff, general special characteristics, international students, out-of-state students, parents of current students, siblings of current students. *Tuition waivers:* Full or partial for employees or children of employees.

LOANS *Student loans:* $7,977,082 (85% need-based, 15% non-need-based). 90% of past graduating class borrowed through all loan programs. *Average indebtedness per student:* $38,951. *Average need-based loan:* Freshmen: $3883. Undergraduates: $4937. *Parent loans:* $1,764,986 (55% need-based, 45% non-need-based). *Programs:* Federal Direct (Subsidized and Unsubsidized Stafford, PLUS), Perkins, college/university, alternative loans.

WORK-STUDY *Federal work-study:* 142 jobs averaging $630. *State or other work-study/employment:* Total amount: $314,006 (19% need-based, 81% non-need-based). 149 part-time jobs averaging $2083.

APPLYING FOR FINANCIAL AID *Required financial aid form:* FAFSA. *Financial aid deadline (priority):* 3/1. *Notification date:* Continuous beginning 3/15. Students must reply within 4 weeks of notification.

CONTACT Todd M. Fischer-Free, Assistant Vice President of Student Administrative Services, Rockford University, 5050 East State Street, Rockford, IL 61108, 815-226-3385 or toll-free 800-892-2984. *Fax:* 815-394-5174. *E-mail:* tfree@rockford.edu. *Website:* http://www.rockford.edu/.

ROCKHURST UNIVERSITY
Kansas City, MO

Tuition & fees: $36,590	Average undergraduate aid package: $29,079

ABOUT THE INSTITUTION Independent Roman Catholic (Jesuit), coed. *Awards:* certificates, bachelor's, master's, and doctoral degrees. 32 undergraduate majors. *Total enrollment:* 3,043. Undergraduates: 2,208. Freshmen: 430. Federal methodology is used as a basis for awarding need-based institutional aid.

UNDERGRADUATE EXPENSES for 2017–2018 *Comprehensive fee:* $46,560 includes full-time tuition ($35,800), mandatory fees ($790), and room and board ($9970). *College room only:* $6120. Full-time tuition and fees vary according to class time and course load. Room and board charges vary according to board plan and housing facility. *Part-time tuition:* $597 per credit hour. *Part-time fees:* $25 per credit hour. Part-time tuition and fees vary according to class time and course load.

FRESHMAN FINANCIAL AID (Fall 2016) 363 applied for aid; of those 87% were deemed to have need. 100% of freshmen with need received aid; of those 29% had need fully met. *Average percent of need met:* 86% (excluding resources awarded to replace EFC). *Average financial aid package:* $30,058 (excluding resources awarded to replace EFC). 17% of all full-time freshmen had no need and received non-need-based gift aid.

UNDERGRADUATE FINANCIAL AID (Fall 2016) 1,393 applied for aid; of those 70% were deemed to have need. 100% of undergraduates with need received aid; of those 28% had need fully met. *Average percent of need met:* 84% (excluding resources awarded to replace EFC). *Average financial aid package:* $29,079 (excluding resources awarded to replace EFC). 16% of all full-time undergraduates had no need and received non-need-based gift aid.

GIFT AID (NEED-BASED) *Total amount:* $21,690,965 (6% federal, 4% state, 89% institutional, 1% external sources). *Receiving aid:* Freshmen: 78% (314); all full-time undergraduates: 69% (973). *Average award:* Freshmen: $24,644; Undergraduates: $23,642. *Scholarships, grants, and awards:* Federal Pell, FSEOG, state, private, college/university gift aid from institutional funds, United Negro College Fund.

GIFT AID (NON-NEED-BASED) *Total amount:* $9,726,917 (1% state, 98% institutional, 1% external sources). *Receiving aid:* Freshmen: 17% (68). Undergraduates: 13% (187). *Average award:* Freshmen: $21,323. Undergraduates: $20,682. *Scholarships, grants, and awards by category:* Academic interests/achievement: biological sciences, business, communication, computer science, education, engineering/technologies, English, foreign languages, general academic interests/achievements, home economics, humanities, international studies, mathematics, physical sciences, premedicine, religion/biblical studies, social sciences. *Creative arts/performance:* creative writing, music, performing arts, theater/drama. *Special achievements/activities:* community service, leadership. *Special characteristics:* children of faculty/staff, siblings of current students. *Tuition waivers:* Full or partial for employees or children of employees, senior citizens. *ROTC:* Army cooperative.

LOANS *Student loans:* $7,341,917 (68% need-based, 32% non-need-based). 66% of past graduating class borrowed through all loan programs. *Average indebtedness per student:* $26,198. *Average need-based loan:* Freshmen: $3732. Undergraduates: $4115. *Parent loans:* $2,550,877 (38% need-based, 62% non-need-based). *Programs:* Federal Direct (Subsidized and Unsubsidized Stafford, PLUS), Perkins.

WORK-STUDY *Federal work-study:* jobs available. *State or other work-study/employment:* Part-time jobs available.

ATHLETIC AWARDS Total amount: $3,036,910 (28% need-based, 72% non-need-based).

APPLYING FOR FINANCIAL AID *Required financial aid form:* FAFSA. *Financial aid deadline (priority):* 1/1. *Notification date:* Continuous beginning 1/1. Students must reply by 6/1 or within 4 weeks of notification.

CONTACT Maureen McKinnon, Director of Financial Aid, Rockhurst University, 1100 Rockhurst Road, Kansas City, MO 64110-2561, 816-501-4831 or toll-free 800-842-6776. *Fax:* 816-501-3139. *E-mail:* maureen.mckinnon@rockhurst.edu. *Website:* http://www.rockhurst.edu/.

ROCKY MOUNTAIN COLLEGE
Billings, MT

Tuition & fees: $28,512	Average undergraduate aid package: $24,480

ABOUT THE INSTITUTION Independent interdenominational, coed. *Awards:* associate, bachelor's, and master's degrees. 48 undergraduate majors. *Total enrollment:* 992. Undergraduates: 899. Freshmen: 247. Federal methodology is used as a basis for awarding need-based institutional aid.

UNDERGRADUATE EXPENSES for 2018–2019 *Application fee:* $35. *Comprehensive fee:* $36,842 includes full-time tuition ($27,982), mandatory fees ($530), and room and board ($8330). *College room only:* $4018. Full-time tuition and fees vary according to course load, degree level, and program. Room and board charges vary according to board plan and housing facility. *Part-time tuition:* $1166 per credit. *Part-time fees:* $160 per term. Part-time tuition and fees vary according to course load, degree level, and program.

FRESHMAN FINANCIAL AID (Fall 2017, est.) 226 applied for aid; of those 90% were deemed to have need. 100% of freshmen with need received aid; of those 17% had need fully met. *Average percent of need met:* 73% (excluding resources awarded to replace EFC). *Average financial aid package:* $24,276 (excluding resources awarded to replace EFC). 5% of all full-time freshmen had no need and received non-need-based gift aid.

UNDERGRADUATE FINANCIAL AID (Fall 2017, est.) 722 applied for aid; of those 91% were deemed to have need. 100% of undergraduates with need received aid; of those 18% had need fully met. *Average percent of need met:* 77% (excluding resources awarded to replace EFC). *Average financial aid package:* $24,480 (excluding resources awarded to replace EFC). 4% of all full-time undergraduates had no need and received non-need-based gift aid.

GIFT AID (NEED-BASED) *Total amount:* $12,771,403 (12% federal, 76% institutional, 12% external sources). *Receiving aid:* Freshmen: 82% (203); all full-time undergraduates: 76% (655). *Average award:* Freshmen: $20,428; Undergraduates: $19,625. *Scholarships, grants, and awards:* Federal Pell, FSEOG, state, private, college/university gift aid from institutional funds.

GIFT AID (NON-NEED-BASED) *Total amount:* $1,489,311 (75% institutional, 25% external sources). *Receiving aid:* Freshmen: 14% (35). Undergraduates: 13% (116). *Average award:* Freshmen: $13,808. Undergraduates: $13,358. *Scholarships, grants, and awards by category:* Academic interests/achievement: 732 awards ($8,665,786 total): general academic interests/achievements. *Creative arts/performance:* 16 awards ($24,500 total): music. *Special achievements/activities:* 16 awards ($38,750 total): cheerleading/drum major. *Special characteristics:* 46 awards ($481,421 total): children of faculty/staff, veterans. *Tuition waivers:* Full or partial for employees or children of employees. *ROTC:* Army cooperative.

LOANS *Student loans:* $4,794,470 (72% need-based, 28% non-need-based). 73% of past graduating class borrowed through all loan programs. *Average indebtedness per student:* $29,452. *Average need-based loan:* Freshmen: $3247. Undergraduates: $3894. *Parent loans:* $880,929 (46% need-based, 54% non-need-based). *Programs:* Federal Direct (Subsidized and Unsubsidized Stafford, PLUS), Perkins.

WORK-STUDY *Federal work-study:* Total amount: $145,638; 315 jobs averaging $462. *State or other work-study/employment:* Total amount: $165,138 (51% need-based, 49% non-need-based). 188 part-time jobs averaging $878.

ATHLETIC AWARDS Total amount: $3,038,815 (89% need-based, 11% non-need-based).

APPLYING FOR FINANCIAL AID *Required financial aid form:* FAFSA. *Financial aid deadline:* Continuous. *Notification date:* Continuous beginning 2/15. Students must reply within 4 weeks of notification.

CONTACT Jessica Francischetti, Director of Financial Assistance, Rocky Mountain College, 1511 Poly Drive, Billings, MT 59102-1796, 406-657-1031 or toll-free 800-877-6259. *Fax:* 406-657-1169. *E-mail:* finaid@rocky.edu. *Website:* http://www.rocky.edu/.

ROCKY MOUNTAIN COLLEGE OF ART + DESIGN
Lakewood, CO

CONTACT Michael Dulay, Director of Financial Aid, Rocky Mountain College of Art + Design, 1600 Pierce Street, Lakewood, CO 80214, 303-753-6046 or toll-free 800-888-ARTS. *Fax:* 303-567-7280. *E-mail:* mdulay@rmcad.edu. *Website:* http://www.rmcad.edu/.

ROGERS STATE UNIVERSITY
Claremore, OK

Tuition & fees (OK res): $6870	Average undergraduate aid package: $9771

ABOUT THE INSTITUTION State-supported, coed. *Awards:* associate, bachelor's, and master's degrees. 25 undergraduate majors. *Total enrollment:* 3,723. Undergraduates: 3,694. Freshmen: 524. Federal methodology is used as a basis for awarding need-based institutional aid.

UNDERGRADUATE EXPENSES for 2017–2018 *Application fee:* $20. *Tuition, state resident:* full-time $4170. *Tuition, nonresident:* full-time $12,510. *Required fees:* full-time $2700. Full-time tuition and fees vary according to course level, course load, location, program, and student level. Part-time tuition and fees vary according to course level, course load, location, program, and student level. *College room and board:* $8050; *Room only:* $4600. Room and board charges vary according to housing facility.

FRESHMAN FINANCIAL AID (Fall 2017, est.) 260 applied for aid; of those 87% were deemed to have need. 96% of freshmen with need received aid; of those 5% had need fully met. *Average percent of need met:* 51% (excluding resources awarded to replace EFC). *Average financial aid package:* $9422 (excluding resources awarded to replace EFC). 2% of all full-time freshmen had no need and received non-need-based gift aid.

UNDERGRADUATE FINANCIAL AID (Fall 2017, est.) 1,755 applied for aid; of those 86% were deemed to have need. 98% of undergraduates with need received aid; of those 11% had need fully met. *Average percent of need met:* 52% (excluding resources awarded to replace EFC). *Average financial aid package:* $9771 (excluding resources awarded to replace EFC). 8% of all full-time undergraduates had no need and received non-need-based gift aid.

GIFT AID (NEED-BASED) *Total amount:* $10,359,878 (63% federal, 18% state, 11% institutional, 8% external sources). *Receiving aid:* Freshmen: 69% (198); all full-time undergraduates: 66% (1,335). *Average award:* Freshmen: $7169; Undergraduates: $7294. *Scholarships, grants, and awards:* Federal Pell, FSEOG, state, private, college/university gift aid from institutional funds.

GIFT AID (NON-NEED-BASED) *Total amount:* $1,667,513 (10% state, 73% institutional, 17% external sources). *Receiving aid:* Freshmen: 2% (5). Undergraduates: 5% (100). *Average award:* Freshmen: $1788. Undergraduates: $6019. *Scholarships, grants, and awards by category:* Academic interests/achievement: business, general academic interests/achievements, military science, premedicine. *Creative arts/performance:* art/fine arts, dance, music, theater/drama. *Special achievements/activities:* cheerleading/drum major, junior miss, leadership. *Special characteristics:* adult students, out-of-state students, veterans. *Tuition waivers:* Full or partial for employees or children of employees, senior citizens.

LOANS *Student loans:* $16,569,362 (84% need-based, 16% non-need-based). 51% of past graduating class borrowed through all loan programs. *Average indebtedness per student:* $16,164. *Average need-based loan:* Freshmen: $3277. Undergraduates: $3762. *Parent loans:* $390,685 (43% need-based, 57% non-need-based). *Programs:* Federal Direct (Subsidized and Unsubsidized Stafford, PLUS), alternative loans.

WORK-STUDY *Federal work-study:* Total amount: $90,822; jobs available. *State or other work-study/employment:* Part-time jobs available.

ATHLETIC AWARDS Total amount: $805,527 (32% need-based, 68% non-need-based).

APPLYING FOR FINANCIAL AID *Required financial aid form:* FAFSA. *Financial aid deadline (priority):* 5/1. *Notification date:* Continuous beginning 3/15. Students must reply within 2 weeks of notification.

CONTACT Ms. Heidi Hoskinson, Vice President of Enrollment Management, Rogers State University, 1701 West Will Rogers Boulevard, Claremore, OK 74017-3252, 918-343-7553 or toll-free 800-256-7511. *Fax:* 918-343-7598. *E-mail:* finaid@rsu.edu. *Website:* http://www.rsu.edu/.

ROGER WILLIAMS UNIVERSITY
Bristol, RI

Tuition & fees: $32,510	Average undergraduate aid package: $22,130

ABOUT THE INSTITUTION Independent, coed. *Awards:* certificates, associate, bachelor's, master's, and doctoral degrees. 69 undergraduate majors. *Total enrollment:* 5,024. Undergraduates: 4,703. Freshmen: 1,135. Both federal and institutional methodology are used as a basis for awarding need-based institutional aid.

UNDERGRADUATE EXPENSES for 2018–2019 *Application fee:* $50. *Comprehensive fee:* $48,074 includes full-time tuition ($30,326), mandatory fees ($2184), and room and board ($15,564). *College room only:* $8310. Full-time tuition and fees vary according to class time, course load, degree level, and program. Room and board charges vary according to board plan and housing facility. Part-time tuition and fees vary according to class time, course load, degree level, and program. *Payment plan:* Guaranteed tuition.

FRESHMAN FINANCIAL AID (Fall 2017, est.) 1,017 applied for aid; of those 81% were deemed to have need. 99% of freshmen with need received aid; of those 11% had need fully met. *Average percent of need met:* 84% (excluding resources awarded to replace EFC). *Average financial aid package:* $19,985 (excluding resources awarded to replace EFC). 16% of all full-time freshmen had no need and received non-need-based gift aid.

UNDERGRADUATE FINANCIAL AID (Fall 2017, est.) 3,168 applied for aid; of those 82% were deemed to have need. 97% of undergraduates with need received aid; of those 12% had need fully met. *Average percent of need met:* 88% (excluding resources awarded to replace EFC). *Average financial aid package:* $22,130 (excluding resources awarded to replace EFC). 13% of all full-time undergraduates had no need and received non-need-based gift aid.

GIFT AID (NEED-BASED) *Total amount:* $39,948,796 (6% federal, 1% state, 91% institutional, 2% external sources). *Receiving aid:* Freshmen: 33% (375); all full-time undergraduates: 40% (1,600). *Average award:* Freshmen: $14,297; Undergraduates: $14,413. *Scholarships, grants, and awards:* Federal Pell, FSEOG, state, private, college/university gift aid from institutional funds.

GIFT AID (NON-NEED-BASED) *Total amount:* $7,049,992 (99% institutional, 1% external sources). *Receiving aid:* Freshmen: 72% (819). Undergraduates: 58% (2,338). *Average award:* Freshmen: $13,516. Undergraduates: $12,898. *Scholarships, grants, and awards by category: Academic interests/achievement:* 3,654 awards ($41,789,000 total): general academic interests/achievements. *Tuition waivers:* Full or partial for employees or children of employees. *ROTC:* Army.

LOANS *Student loans:* $16,324,025 (85% need-based, 15% non-need-based). 61% of past graduating class borrowed through all loan programs. *Average indebtedness per student:* $44,225. *Average need-based loan:* Freshmen: $3169. Undergraduates: $4533. *Parent loans:* $10,473,432 (94% need-based, 6% non-need-based). *Programs:* Federal Direct (Subsidized and Unsubsidized Stafford, PLUS), Perkins.

WORK-STUDY *Federal work-study:* Total amount: $506,728; jobs available.

APPLYING FOR FINANCIAL AID *Required financial aid form:* FAFSA. *Financial aid deadline:* 2/1. *Notification date:* Continuous beginning 12/15. Students must reply by 5/1 or within 2 weeks of notification.

CONTACT Diane Usher, Associate Director of Student Financial Aid and Planning, Roger Williams University, One Old Ferry Road, Bristol, RI 02809, 401-254-3100 or toll-free 800-458-7144. *Fax:* 401-254-3356. *E-mail:* finaid@rwu.edu. *Website:* http://www.rwu.edu/.

ROLLINS COLLEGE
Winter Park, FL

Tuition & fees: $49,760	Average undergraduate aid package: $39,094

ABOUT THE INSTITUTION Independent, coed. *Awards:* bachelor's, master's, and doctoral degrees. 36 undergraduate majors. *Total enrollment:* 2,650. Undergraduates: 1,984. Freshmen: 530. Federal methodology is used as a basis for awarding need-based institutional aid.

UNDERGRADUATE EXPENSES for 2018–2019 *Application fee:* $50. *Comprehensive fee:* $64,500 includes full-time tuition ($49,760) and room and board ($14,740). *College room only:* $8720. Room and board charges vary according to housing facility.

FRESHMAN FINANCIAL AID (Fall 2017, est.) 373 applied for aid; of those 85% were deemed to have need. 99% of freshmen with need received aid; of those 32% had need fully met. *Average percent of need met:* 81% (excluding resources awarded to replace EFC). *Average financial aid package:* $40,224 (excluding resources awarded to replace EFC). 30% of all full-time freshmen had no need and received non-need-based gift aid.

UNDERGRADUATE FINANCIAL AID (Fall 2017, est.) 1,167 applied for aid; of those 89% were deemed to have need. 100% of undergraduates with need received aid; of those 28% had need fully met. *Average percent of need met:* 80% (excluding resources awarded to replace EFC). *Average financial aid package:* $39,094 (excluding resources awarded to replace EFC). 32% of all full-time undergraduates had no need and received non-need-based gift aid.

GIFT AID (NEED-BASED) *Total amount:* $31,111,095 (10% federal, 15% state, 74% institutional, 1% external sources). *Receiving aid:* Freshmen: 59% (315); all full-time undergraduates: 52% (1,032). *Average award:* Freshmen: $35,408; Undergraduates: $33,915. *Scholarships, grants, and awards:* FSEOG, state, private, college/university gift aid from institutional funds.

GIFT AID (NON-NEED-BASED) *Total amount:* $22,212,380 (9% state, 90% institutional, 1% external sources). *Receiving aid:* Freshmen: 13% (68). Undergraduates: 8% (166). *Average award:* Freshmen: $26,363. Undergraduates: $25,295. *Scholarships, grants, and awards by category: Academic interests/achievement:* 128 awards ($685,694 total): computer science, engineering/technologies, general academic interests/achievements, mathematics, physical sciences. *Creative arts/performance:* 61 awards ($423,400 total): art/fine arts, music, theater/drama. *Tuition waivers:* Full or partial for employees or children of employees.

LOANS *Student loans:* $6,468,924 (76% need-based, 24% non-need-based). 45% of past graduating class borrowed through all loan programs. *Average indebtedness per student:* $32,700. *Average need-based loan:* Freshmen: $3132. Undergraduates: $4252. *Parent loans:* $4,626,646 (55% need-based, 45% non-need-based). *Programs:* Federal Direct (Subsidized and Unsubsidized Stafford, PLUS).

WORK-STUDY *Federal work-study:* Total amount: $504,014; 232 jobs averaging $2172. *State or other work-study/employment:* Total amount: $6250 (100% need-based). 1 part-time job averaging $6250.

ATHLETIC AWARDS Total amount: $4,262,639 (32% need-based, 68% non-need-based).

APPLYING FOR FINANCIAL AID *Required financial aid form:* FAFSA. *Financial aid deadline (priority):* 3/1. *Notification date:* Continuous beginning 1/1. Students must reply by 5/1.

CONTACT Mr. Steve Booker, Director of Financial Aid, Rollins College, 1000 Holt Avenue, #2721, Winter Park, FL 32789-4499, 407-646-2395. *Fax:* 407-646-2173. *E-mail:* sbooker@rollins.edu. *Website:* http://www.rollins.edu/.

ROOSEVELT UNIVERSITY
Chicago, IL

CONTACT Office of Financial Aid, Roosevelt University, 430 South Michigan Avenue, Chicago, IL 60605-1394, 866-421-0935 or toll-free 877-APPLYRU. *Fax:* 312-341-3545. *E-mail:* fao@roosevelt.edu. *Website:* http://www.roosevelt.edu/.

ROSE-HULMAN INSTITUTE OF TECHNOLOGY
Terre Haute, IN

Tuition & fees: $45,762	Average undergraduate aid package: $30,070

ABOUT THE INSTITUTION Independent, coed, primarily men. *Awards:* bachelor's and master's degrees. 16 undergraduate majors. *Total enrollment:* 2,245. Undergraduates: 2,168. Freshmen: 557. Federal methodology is used as a basis for awarding need-based institutional aid.

UNDERGRADUATE EXPENSES for 2017–2018 *Application fee:* $50. *One-time required fee:* $2250. *Comprehensive fee:* $59,823 includes full-time tuition ($44,847), mandatory fees ($915), and room and board ($14,061). *College room only:* $8559. Full-time tuition and fees vary according to course load. Room and board charges vary according to board plan. *Part-time tuition:* $1309 per credit hour. Part-time tuition and fees vary according to course load. *Payment plan:* Tuition prepayment.

FRESHMAN FINANCIAL AID (Fall 2017, est.) 416 applied for aid; of those 81% were deemed to have need. 100% of freshmen with need received aid; of those 76% had need fully met. *Average percent of need met:* 71% (excluding resources awarded to replace EFC). *Average financial aid package:* $31,203 (excluding resources awarded to replace EFC). 39% of all full-time freshmen had no need and received non-need-based gift aid.

UNDERGRADUATE FINANCIAL AID (Fall 2017, est.) 1,431 applied for aid; of those 87% were deemed to have need. 100% of undergraduates with need received aid; of those 80% had need fully met. *Average percent of need met:* 69% (excluding resources awarded to replace EFC). *Average financial aid package:* $30,070 (excluding resources awarded to replace EFC). 41% of all full-time undergraduates had no need and received non-need-based gift aid.

GIFT AID (NEED-BASED) *Total amount:* $31,413,379 (4% federal, 4% state, 92% institutional). *Receiving aid:* Freshmen: 61% (339); all full-time undergraduates: 58% (1,236). *Average award:* Freshmen: $29,035; Undergraduates: $26,898. *Scholarships, grants, and awards:* Federal Pell, FSEOG, state, college/university gift aid from institutional funds.

GIFT AID (NON-NEED-BASED) *Total amount:* $12,727,513 (83% institutional, 17% external sources). *Receiving aid:* Freshmen: 47% (264). Undergraduates: 48% (1,014). *Average award:* Freshmen: $10,862. Undergraduates: $12,343. *Tuition waivers:* Full or partial for employees or children of employees. *ROTC:* Army, Air Force.

LOANS *Student loans:* $13,572,192 (93% need-based, 7% non-need-based). 60% of past graduating class borrowed through all loan programs. *Average indebtedness per student:* $45,345. *Average need-based loan:* Freshmen: $4796. Undergraduates: $5716. *Parent loans:* $6,306,484 (96% need-based, 4% non-need-based). *Programs:* Federal Direct (Subsidized and Unsubsidized Stafford, PLUS), Perkins.

WORK-STUDY *Federal work-study:* Total amount: $964,825; 742 jobs averaging $1272. *State or other work-study/employment:* Part-time jobs available.

APPLYING FOR FINANCIAL AID *Required financial aid form:* FAFSA. *Financial aid deadline (priority):* 3/10. *Notification date:* 1/15. Students must reply by 5/1.

CONTACT Mrs. Melinda L. Middleton, Director of Financial Aid, Rose-Hulman Institute of Technology, 5500 Wabash Avenue, CM 5, Terre Haute, IN 47803, 812-877-8259 or toll-free 800-248-7448. *Fax:* 812-877-8746. *E-mail:* melinda.middleton@rose-hulman.edu.
Website: http://www.rose-hulman.edu/.

ROSEMONT COLLEGE
Rosemont, PA

Tuition & fees: $19,486	Average undergraduate aid package: $18,852

ABOUT THE INSTITUTION Independent Roman Catholic, coed. *Awards:* certificates, bachelor's, and master's degrees. 24 undergraduate majors. *Total enrollment:* 1,008. Undergraduates: 635. Freshmen: 143. Federal methodology is used as a basis for awarding need-based institutional aid.

UNDERGRADUATE EXPENSES for 2017–2018 *Comprehensive fee:* $31,446 includes full-time tuition ($18,500), mandatory fees ($986), and room and board ($11,960). Full-time tuition and fees vary according to course load and degree level. Room and board charges vary according to board plan and housing facility. *Part-time tuition:* $700 per credit hour. *Part-time fees:* $342 per term. Part-time tuition and fees vary according to course load and degree level.

FRESHMAN FINANCIAL AID (Fall 2016) 169 applied for aid; of those 92% were deemed to have need. 100% of freshmen with need received aid; of those 3% had need fully met. *Average percent of need met:* 67% (excluding resources awarded to replace EFC). *Average financial aid package:* $17,578 (excluding resources awarded to replace EFC). 13% of all full-time freshmen had no need and received non-need-based gift aid.

UNDERGRADUATE FINANCIAL AID (Fall 2016) 466 applied for aid; of those 93% were deemed to have need. 100% of undergraduates with need received aid; of those 8% had need fully met. *Average percent of need met:* 72% (excluding resources awarded to replace EFC). *Average financial aid package:* $18,852 (excluding resources awarded to replace EFC). 13% of all full-time undergraduates had no need and received non-need-based gift aid.

GIFT AID (NEED-BASED) *Total amount:* $3,618,506 (43% federal, 24% state, 30% institutional, 3% external sources). *Receiving aid:* Freshmen: 86% (155); all full-time undergraduates: 84% (432). *Average award:* Freshmen: $14,313; Undergraduates: $14,887. *Scholarships, grants, and awards:* Federal Pell, FSEOG, state, private, college/university gift aid from institutional funds, Academic Competitiveness Grants, National SMART Grants.

GIFT AID (NON-NEED-BASED) *Total amount:* $3,412,656 (100% institutional). *Receiving aid:* Freshmen: 2% (4). Undergraduates: 4% (19). *Average award:* Freshmen: $4897. Undergraduates: $4789. *Scholarships, grants, and awards by category:* Academic interests/achievement: 516 awards ($2,661,754 total): general academic interests/achievements. Creative arts/performance: 1 award ($500 total): art/fine arts. *Tuition waivers:* Full or partial for employees or children of employees.

LOANS *Student loans:* $3,895,270 (48% need-based, 52% non-need-based). 84% of past graduating class borrowed through all loan programs. *Average indebtedness per student:* $30,437. *Average need-based loan:* Freshmen: $3290. Undergraduates: $4082. *Parent loans:* $1,161,150 (90% need-based, 10% non-need-based). *Programs:* Federal Direct (Subsidized and Unsubsidized Stafford, PLUS), Perkins, alternative loans.

WORK-STUDY *Federal work-study:* 123 jobs averaging $849. *State or other work-study/employment:* Total amount: $12,353 (100% need-based). 13 part-time jobs averaging $950.

APPLYING FOR FINANCIAL AID *Required financial aid form:* FAFSA. *Financial aid deadline:* Continuous. *Notification date:* Continuous beginning 3/15. Students must reply by 5/1 or within 4 weeks of notification.

CONTACT Mrs. Deborah E. Scheiner, Assistant Director of Financial Aid, Rosemont College, 1400 Montgomery Avenue, Rosemont, PA 19010, 610-527-0200 Ext. 2220 or toll-free 888-2-ROSEMONT. *Fax:* 610-526-2971. *E-mail:* deborah.scheiner@rosemont.edu.
Website: http://www.rosemont.edu/.

ROWAN UNIVERSITY
Glassboro, NJ

Tuition & fees (NJ res): $13,108	Average undergraduate aid package: $10,064

ABOUT THE INSTITUTION State-supported, coed. *Awards:* certificates, bachelor's, master's, and doctoral degrees. 78 undergraduate majors. *Total enrollment:* 18,484. Undergraduates: 15,401. Freshmen: 2,387. Both federal and institutional methodology are used as a basis for awarding need-based institutional aid.

UNDERGRADUATE EXPENSES for 2017–2018 *Application fee:* $65. *Tuition, state resident:* full-time $9434; part-time $362 per credit hour. *Tuition, nonresident:* full-time $17,704; part-time $682 per credit hour. *Required fees:* full-time $3674; $157 per credit hour. Full-time tuition and fees vary according to course load, degree level, location, and program. Part-time tuition and fees vary according to course load, degree level, location, and program. *College room and board:* $11,688; *Room only:* $7608. Room and board charges vary according to board plan and housing facility.

FRESHMAN FINANCIAL AID (Fall 2016) 2,120 applied for aid; of those 74% were deemed to have need. 94% of freshmen with need received aid; of those 16% had need fully met. *Average percent of need met:* 67% (excluding resources awarded to replace EFC). *Average financial aid package:* $9618 (excluding resources awarded to replace EFC). 10% of all full-time freshmen had no need and received non-need-based gift aid.

UNDERGRADUATE FINANCIAL AID (Fall 2016) 10,428 applied for aid; of those 80% were deemed to have need. 96% of undergraduates with need received aid; of those 17% had need fully met. *Average percent of need met:* 68% (excluding resources awarded to replace EFC). *Average financial aid package:* $10,064 (excluding resources awarded to replace EFC). 9% of all full-time undergraduates had no need and received non-need-based gift aid.

GIFT AID (NEED-BASED) *Total amount:* $53,353,270 (37% federal, 37% state, 23% institutional, 3% external sources). *Receiving aid:* Freshmen: 31% (710); all full-time undergraduates: 35% (4,439). *Average award:* Freshmen: $9710; Undergraduates: $8598. *Scholarships, grants, and awards:* Federal Pell, FSEOG, state, private, college/university gift aid from institutional funds.

GIFT AID (NON-NEED-BASED) *Total amount:* $10,122,171 (95% institutional, 5% external sources). *Receiving aid:* Freshmen: 27% (626). Undergraduates: 18% (2,291). *Average award:* Freshmen: $6009. Undergraduates: $8105. *Scholarships, grants, and awards by category:* Academic interests/achievement: general academic interests/achievements. Creative arts/performance: general creative arts/performance, music. *Tuition waivers:* Full or partial for employees or children of employees. *ROTC:* Army cooperative.

LOANS *Student loans:* $87,496,289 (93% need-based, 7% non-need-based). 68% of past graduating class borrowed through all loan programs. *Average indebtedness per student:* $31,900. *Average need-based loan:* Freshmen: $3264. Undergraduates: $4272. *Parent loans:* $24,155,617 (100% need-based). *Programs:* Federal Direct (Subsidized and Unsubsidized Stafford, PLUS), state.

WORK-STUDY *Federal work-study:* 437 jobs averaging $1587. *State or other work-study/employment:* Total amount: $2,764,451 (66% need-based, 34% non-need-based). Part-time jobs available.

APPLYING FOR FINANCIAL AID *Required financial aid form:* FAFSA. *Financial aid deadline (priority):* 3/16. *Notification date:* Continuous beginning 3/16. Students must reply by 5/1.

CONTACT Pamela Gordy, Director of the Office of Financial Aid, Rowan University, 201 Mullica Hill Road, Glassboro, NJ 08028-1701, 856-256-4281 or toll-free 800-447-1165 (in-state), 800-447-1165N (out-of-state). *E-mail:* gordy@rowan.edu. *Website:* http://www.rowan.edu/.

RUSH UNIVERSITY
Chicago, IL

CONTACT Mike Frechette, Director of Student Financial Aid, Rush University, 600 South Paulina Street, Suite 440, Chicago, IL 60612-3832, 312-942-6256. *Fax:* 312-942-2732. *E-mail:* michael_frechette@rush.edu. *Website:* http://www.rushu.rush.edu/.

RUST COLLEGE
Holly Springs, MS

CONTACT Mrs. Helen L. Street, Director of Financial Aid, Rust College, 150 Rust Avenue, Holly Springs, MS 38635, 662-252-8000 Ext. 4061 or toll-free 888-886-8492 Ext. 4065. *Fax:* 662-252-8895. *Website:* http://www.rustcollege.edu/.

RUTGERS UNIVERSITY–CAMDEN
Camden, NJ

Tuition & fees (NJ res): $14,501	Average undergraduate aid package: $12,663

ABOUT THE INSTITUTION State-supported, coed. *Awards:* certificates, bachelor's, master's, and doctoral degrees. 39 undergraduate majors. *Total*

enrollment: 6,853. Undergraduates: 5,489. Freshmen: 758. Both federal and institutional methodology are used as a basis for awarding need-based institutional aid.

UNDERGRADUATE EXPENSES for 2017–2018 *Application fee:* $70. *Tuition, state resident:* full-time $11,619; part-time $374 per credit hour. *Tuition, nonresident:* full-time $27,042; part-time $878 per credit hour. *Required fees:* full-time $2882; $590.50 per term. Full-time tuition and fees vary according to program. Part-time tuition and fees vary according to course load and program. *College room and board:* $12,094; *Room only:* $8422. Room and board charges vary according to board plan and housing facility.

FRESHMAN FINANCIAL AID (Fall 2016) 602 applied for aid; of those 92% were deemed to have need. 100% of freshmen with need received aid; of those 5% had need fully met. *Average percent of need met:* 52% (excluding resources awarded to replace EFC). *Average financial aid package:* $15,736 (excluding resources awarded to replace EFC). 3% of all full-time freshmen had no need and received non-need-based gift aid.

UNDERGRADUATE FINANCIAL AID (Fall 2016) 3,533 applied for aid; of those 93% were deemed to have need. 100% of undergraduates with need received aid; of those 2% had need fully met. *Average percent of need met:* 47% (excluding resources awarded to replace EFC). *Average financial aid package:* $12,663 (excluding resources awarded to replace EFC). 2% of all full-time undergraduates had no need and received non-need-based gift aid.

GIFT AID (NEED-BASED) *Total amount:* $25,388,010 (37% federal, 43% state, 20% institutional). *Receiving aid:* Freshmen: 66% (431); all full-time undergraduates: 62% (2,492). *Average award:* Freshmen: $12,136; Undergraduates: $9796. *Scholarships, grants, and awards:* Federal Pell, FSEOG, state, private, college/university gift aid from institutional funds, Federal Nursing.

GIFT AID (NON-NEED-BASED) *Total amount:* $5,296,046 (92% institutional, 8% external sources). *Receiving aid:* Freshmen: 49% (321). Undergraduates: 20% (792). *Average award:* Freshmen: $3857. Undergraduates: $3905. *Tuition waivers:* Full or partial for employees or children of employees. *ROTC:* Army cooperative, Air Force cooperative.

LOANS *Student loans:* $30,760,012 (42% need-based, 58% non-need-based). 75% of past graduating class borrowed through all loan programs. *Average indebtedness per student:* $32,781. *Average need-based loan:* Freshmen: $3857. Undergraduates: $4590. *Parent loans:* $3,227,618 (100% non-need-based). *Programs:* Federal Direct (Subsidized and Unsubsidized Stafford, PLUS), Perkins, Federal Nursing, state, college/university, alternative loans.

WORK-STUDY *Federal work-study:* 277 jobs averaging $1858. *State or other work-study/employment:* Total amount: $1,539,251 (100% non-need-based). 588 part-time jobs averaging $2759.

APPLYING FOR FINANCIAL AID *Required financial aid form:* FAFSA. *Financial aid deadline (priority):* 3/15. *Notification date:* Continuous beginning 3/1. Students must reply within 2 weeks of notification.

CONTACT Ms. Carolann Pierre, Senior Funds Management Specialist, Rutgers University–Camden, 620 George Street, New Brunswick, NJ 08901, 848-932-2603. *Fax:* 732-932-0516. *E-mail:* carolann.pierre@ofa.rutgers.edu. *Website:* http://www.camden.rutgers.edu/.

RUTGERS UNIVERSITY–NEWARK
Newark, NJ

Tuition & fees (NJ res): $14,085	Average undergraduate aid package: $13,928

ABOUT THE INSTITUTION State-supported, coed. *Awards:* certificates, bachelor's, master's, and doctoral degrees. 63 undergraduate majors. *Total enrollment:* 12,768. Undergraduates: 8,551. Freshmen: 1,325. Federal methodology is used as a basis for awarding need-based institutional aid.

UNDERGRADUATE EXPENSES for 2017–2018 *Application fee:* $70. *Tuition, state resident:* full-time $11,619; part-time $374 per credit hour. *Tuition, nonresident:* full-time $27,560; part-time $894 per credit hour. *Required fees:* full-time $2466; $474.75 per term. Full-time tuition and fees vary according to program. Part-time tuition and fees vary according to course load and program. *College room and board:* $13,266; *Room only:* $8216. Room and board charges vary according to board plan and housing facility.

FRESHMAN FINANCIAL AID (Fall 2016) 1,077 applied for aid; of those 93% were deemed to have need. 100% of freshmen with need received aid; of those 3% had need fully met. *Average percent of need met:* 54% (excluding resources awarded

to replace EFC). *Average financial aid package:* $15,122 (excluding resources awarded to replace EFC). 1% of all full-time freshmen had no need and received non-need-based gift aid.

UNDERGRADUATE FINANCIAL AID (Fall 2016) 5,463 applied for aid; of those 95% were deemed to have need. 100% of undergraduates with need received aid; of those 2% had need fully met. *Average percent of need met:* 51% (excluding resources awarded to replace EFC). *Average financial aid package:* $13,928 (excluding resources awarded to replace EFC). 1% of all full-time undergraduates had no need and received non-need-based gift aid.

GIFT AID (NEED-BASED) *Total amount:* $51,601,708 (37% federal, 46% state, 17% institutional). *Receiving aid:* Freshmen: 64% (859); all full-time undergraduates: 66% (4,373). *Average award:* Freshmen: $12,415; Undergraduates: $11,465. *Scholarships, grants, and awards:* Federal Pell, FSEOG, state, private, college/university gift aid from institutional funds.

GIFT AID (NON-NEED-BASED) *Total amount:* $6,234,919 (87% institutional, 13% external sources). *Receiving aid:* Freshmen: 15% (207). Undergraduates: 8% (553). *Average award:* Freshmen: $8011. Undergraduates: $8046. *Tuition waivers:* Full or partial for employees or children of employees. *ROTC:* Army, Naval, Air Force.

LOANS *Student loans:* $35,565,695 (48% need-based, 52% non-need-based). 63% of past graduating class borrowed through all loan programs. *Average indebtedness per student:* $29,077. *Average need-based loan:* Freshmen: $4154. Undergraduates: $4594. *Parent loans:* $4,196,023 (100% non-need-based). *Programs:* Federal Direct (Subsidized and Unsubsidized Stafford, PLUS), Perkins, state, college/university, alternative loans.

WORK-STUDY *Federal work-study:* 563 jobs averaging $2018. *State or other work-study/employment:* Total amount: $2,481,009 (100% non-need-based). 948 part-time jobs averaging $2617.

APPLYING FOR FINANCIAL AID *Required financial aid form:* FAFSA. *Financial aid deadline (priority):* 3/15. *Notification date:* Continuous beginning 3/1. Students must reply within 4 weeks of notification.

CONTACT Ms. Carolann Pierre, Senior Funds Management Specialist, Rutgers University–Newark, 620 George Street, New Brunswick, NJ 08901, 848-932-2603. *Fax:* 732-932-0516. *E-mail:* carolann.pierre@ofa.rutgers.edu. *Website:* http://www.newark.rutgers.edu/.

RUTGERS UNIVERSITY–NEW BRUNSWICK
Piscataway, NJ

Tuition & fees (NJ res): $14,638	Average undergraduate aid package: $13,747

ABOUT THE INSTITUTION State-supported, coed. *Awards:* certificates, diplomas, associate, bachelor's, master's, and doctoral degrees. 150 undergraduate majors. *Total enrollment:* 49,577. Undergraduates: 35,641. Freshmen: 6,268. Federal methodology is used as a basis for awarding need-based institutional aid.

UNDERGRADUATE EXPENSES for 2017–2018 *Application fee:* $70. *Tuition, state resident:* full-time $11,619; part-time $374 per credit hour. *Tuition, nonresident:* full-time $27,560; part-time $894 per credit hour. *Required fees:* full-time $3019; $433.50 per term. Full-time tuition and fees vary according to program. Part-time tuition and fees vary according to course load and program. *College room and board:* $12,452; *Room only:* $7602. Room and board charges vary according to board plan and housing facility.

FRESHMAN FINANCIAL AID (Fall 2016) 4,323 applied for aid; of those 79% were deemed to have need. 100% of freshmen with need received aid; of those 6% had need fully met. *Average percent of need met:* 52% (excluding resources awarded to replace EFC). *Average financial aid package:* $15,044 (excluding resources awarded to replace EFC). 6% of all full-time freshmen had no need and received non-need-based gift aid.

UNDERGRADUATE FINANCIAL AID (Fall 2016) 21,143 applied for aid; of those 86% were deemed to have need. 100% of undergraduates with need received aid; of those 4% had need fully met. *Average percent of need met:* 48% (excluding resources awarded to replace EFC). *Average financial aid package:* $13,747 (excluding resources awarded to replace EFC). 2% of all full-time undergraduates had no need and received non-need-based gift aid.

GIFT AID (NEED-BASED) *Total amount:* $146,366,638 (35% federal, 45% state, 20% institutional). *Receiving aid:* Freshmen: 35% (2,233); all full-time under-

---

graduates: 38% (12,756). *Average award:* Freshmen: $12,943; Undergraduates: $11,124. *Scholarships, grants, and awards:* Federal Pell, FSEOG, state, private, college/university gift aid from institutional funds, Federal Nursing.

GIFT AID (NON-NEED-BASED) *Total amount:* $66,404,185 (93% institutional, 7% external sources). *Receiving aid:* Freshmen: 15% (995). Undergraduates: 9% (3,149). *Average award:* Freshmen: $11,601. Undergraduates: $10,461. *Tuition waivers:* Full or partial for employees or children of employees. *ROTC:* Army, Naval, Air Force.

LOANS *Student loans:* $181,006,796 (39% need-based, 61% non-need-based). 59% of past graduating class borrowed through all loan programs. *Average indebtedness per student:* $32,601. *Average need-based loan:* Freshmen: $4053. Undergraduates: $4688. *Parent loans:* $40,965,389 (100% non-need-based). *Programs:* Federal Direct (Subsidized and Unsubsidized Stafford, PLUS), Perkins, Federal Nursing, state, college/university, alternative loans.

WORK-STUDY *Federal work-study:* 3,163 jobs averaging $1952. *State or other work-study/employment:* Total amount: $15,115,915 (100% non-need-based). 7,461 part-time jobs averaging $2026.

ATHLETIC AWARDS Total amount: $13,222,229 (100% non-need-based).

APPLYING FOR FINANCIAL AID *Required financial aid form:* FAFSA. *Financial aid deadline (priority):* 3/15. *Notification date:* Continuous beginning 3/1. Students must reply within 2 weeks of notification.

CONTACT Ms. Carolann Pierre, Senior Funds Management Specialist, Rutgers University–New Brunswick, 620 George Street, New Brunswick, NJ 08901, 848-932-2603. *Fax:* 732-932-0516. *E-mail:* carolann.pierre@ofa.rutgers.edu. *Website:* http://newbrunswick.rutgers.edu/.

SACRED HEART MAJOR SEMINARY
Detroit, MI

CONTACT Financial Aid Office, Sacred Heart Major Seminary, 2701 Chicago Boulevard, Detroit, MI 48206-1799, 313-883-8534. *Fax:* 313-868-7025. *E-mail:* financialaid@shms.edu. *Website:* http://www.shms.edu/.

SACRED HEART UNIVERSITY
Fairfield, CT

Tuition & fees: $39,820	Average undergraduate aid package: $20,729

ABOUT THE INSTITUTION Independent Roman Catholic, coed. *Awards:* certificates, bachelor's, master's, and doctoral degrees (also offers part-time program with significant enrollment not reflected in profile). 45 undergraduate majors. *Total enrollment:* 8,543. Undergraduates: 5,603. Freshmen: 1,387. Both federal and institutional methodology are used as a basis for awarding need-based institutional aid.

UNDERGRADUATE EXPENSES for 2017–2018 *Application fee:* $50. *Comprehensive fee:* $54,590 includes full-time tuition ($39,570), mandatory fees ($250), and room and board ($14,770). *College room only:* $10,100. Room and board charges vary according to board plan and housing facility. *Part-time tuition:* $600 per credit hour. *Part-time fees:* $115 per term. Part-time tuition and fees vary according to course load.

FRESHMAN FINANCIAL AID (Fall 2017, est.) 1,231 applied for aid; of those 82% were deemed to have need. 100% of freshmen with need received aid; of those 15% had need fully met. *Average percent of need met:* 57% (excluding resources awarded to replace EFC). *Average financial aid package:* $20,600 (excluding resources awarded to replace EFC). 26% of all full-time freshmen had no need and received non-need-based gift aid.

UNDERGRADUATE FINANCIAL AID (Fall 2017, est.) 3,959 applied for aid; of those 84% were deemed to have need. 100% of undergraduates with need received aid; of those 16% had need fully met. *Average percent of need met:* 57% (excluding resources awarded to replace EFC). *Average financial aid package:* $20,729 (excluding resources awarded to replace EFC). 96% of all full-time undergraduates had no need and received non-need-based gift aid.

GIFT AID (NEED-BASED) *Total amount:* $51,325,650 (9% federal, 1% state, 83% institutional, 7% external sources). *Receiving aid:* Freshmen: 73% (1,010); all full-time undergraduates: 67% (3,326). *Average award:* Freshmen: $16,566; Undergraduates: $16,376. **Scholarships, grants, and awards:** Federal Pell, FSEOG, state, private, college/university gift aid from institutional funds.

GIFT AID (NON-NEED-BASED) Total amount: $23,668,832 (5% federal, 88% institutional, 7% external sources). **Receiving aid:** Freshmen: 10% (140). Undergraduates: 9% (459). **Average award:** Freshmen: $13,114. Undergraduates: $12,447. **Scholarships, grants, and awards by category:** Academic interests/ achievement: 4,488 awards ($47,996,269 total): biological sciences, business, computer science, education, English, general academic interests/achievements, health fields, humanities, mathematics, physical sciences, premedicine. Creative arts/performance: 991 awards ($2,096,116 total): applied art and design, art/fine arts, cinema/film/ broadcasting, creative writing, dance, music, performing arts, theater/drama. Special achievements/activities: 2,298 awards ($9,001,314 total): community service, general special achievements/activities, hobbies/interests, leadership, memberships, religious involvement. Special characteristics: 552 awards ($4,851,394 total): adult students, children and siblings of alumni, children of current students, children of faculty/staff, children of union members/company employees, ethnic background, general special characteristics, handicapped students, international students, local/state students, members of minority groups, out-of-state students, religious affiliation, siblings of current students, twins, veterans, veterans' children. **Tuition waivers:** Full or partial for employees or children of employees. **ROTC:** Air Force cooperative.

LOANS Student loans: $40,853,146 (67% need-based, 33% non-need-based). 72% of past graduating class borrowed through all loan programs. Average indebtedness per student: $42,033. **Average need-based loan:** Freshmen: $4167. Undergraduates: $4952. **Parent loans:** $22,506,536 (55% need-based, 45% non-need-based). **Programs:** Federal Direct (Subsidized and Unsubsidized Stafford, PLUS), Perkins, state.

WORK-STUDY Federal work-study: Total amount: $1,411,925; 1,037 jobs averaging $1679. **State or other work-study/employment:** Total amount: $1,010,950 (12% need-based, 88% non-need-based). 650 part-time jobs averaging $1281.

ATHLETIC AWARDS Total amount: $8,919,852 (42% need-based, 58% non-need-based).

APPLYING FOR FINANCIAL AID Required financial aid forms: FAFSA, CSS Financial Aid PROFILE, noncustodial (divorced/separated) parent's statement. **Financial aid deadline (priority):** 2/15. **Notification date:** Continuous beginning 3/1. Students must reply within 2 weeks of notification.

CONTACT Ms. Julie B. Savino, Executive Director of University Financial Assistance, Sacred Heart University, 5151 Park Avenue, Fairfield, CT 06825, 203-371-7980. Fax: 203-365-7608. E-mail: savinoj@sacredheart.edu.
Website: http://www.sacredheart.edu/.

SAE EXPRESSION COLLEGE
Emeryville, CA

CONTACT Financial Aid Office, SAE Expression College, 6601 Shellmound Street, Emeryville, CA 94608, 510-654-2934 or toll-free 877-833-8800.
Website: http://www.sae.edu/.

THE SAGE COLLEGES
Troy, NY

Tuition & fees: $30,857   **Average undergraduate aid package:** N/A

ABOUT THE INSTITUTION Independent, coed. **Awards:** certificates, bachelor's, master's, and doctoral degrees. 24 undergraduate majors. **Total enrollment:** 2,525. Undergraduates: 1,320. Freshmen: 202. Both federal and institutional methodology are used as a basis for awarding need-based institutional aid.

UNDERGRADUATE EXPENSES for 2018–2019 Application fee: $30. **Comprehensive fee:** $43,475 includes full-time tuition ($29,357), mandatory fees ($1500), and room and board ($12,618). **College room only:** $6430. Room and board charges vary according to board plan.

FRESHMAN FINANCIAL AID (Fall 2017, est.) 200 applied for aid; of those 96% were deemed to have need. 100% of freshmen with need received aid. 3% of all full-time freshmen had no need and received non-need-based gift aid.

UNDERGRADUATE FINANCIAL AID (Fall 2017, est.) 1,157 applied for aid; of those 94% were deemed to have need. 100% of undergraduates with need received

aid. 4% of all full-time undergraduates had no need and received non-need-based gift aid.

GIFT AID (NEED-BASED) Total amount: $18,816,209 (11% federal, 12% state, 77% institutional). **Receiving aid:** Freshmen: 75% (150); all full-time undergraduates: 69% (839). **Average award:** Freshmen: $12,523; Undergraduates: $12,243. **Scholarships, grants, and awards:** Federal Pell, FSEOG, state, private, college/university gift aid from institutional funds.

GIFT AID (NON-NEED-BASED) Total amount: $1,675,282 (1% state, 90% institutional, 9% external sources). **Receiving aid:** Freshmen: 64% (129). Undergraduates: 57% (696). **Average award:** Freshmen: $14,384. Undergraduates: $10,073. **Scholarships, grants, and awards by category:** Academic interests/ achievement: business, education, English, general academic interests/achievements, home economics. Creative arts/performance: art/fine arts, performing arts, theater/ drama. Special achievements/activities: community service, general special achievements/activities, leadership. Special characteristics: adult students, children and siblings of alumni, ethnic background, first-generation college students, general special characteristics, members of minority groups, veterans. **Tuition waivers:** Full or partial for employees or children of employees. **ROTC:** Army cooperative, Air Force cooperative.

LOANS Student loans: $7,105,105 (58% need-based, 42% non-need-based). 94% of past graduating class borrowed through all loan programs. Average indebtedness per student: $30,905. **Average need-based loan:** Freshmen: $3453. Undergraduates: $4307. **Parent loans:** $2,286,906 (100% non-need-based). **Programs:** Federal Direct (Subsidized and Unsubsidized Stafford, PLUS).

WORK-STUDY Federal work-study: Total amount: $633,001; jobs available. **State or other work-study/employment:** Total amount: $166,290 (100% non-need-based). Part-time jobs available.

APPLYING FOR FINANCIAL AID Required financial aid forms: FAFSA, state aid form. **Financial aid deadline (priority):** 2/15. **Notification date:** Continuous beginning 11/15. Students must reply by 5/1 or within 2 weeks of notification.

CONTACT Office of Financial Aid, The Sage Colleges, 65 First Street, Troy, NY 12180, 518-244-4525. Fax: 518-244-2460. E-mail: finaid@sage.edu.
Website: http://www.sage.edu/.

SAGINAW VALLEY STATE UNIVERSITY
University Center, MI

Tuition & fees (MI res): $9819   **Average undergraduate aid package:** N/A

ABOUT THE INSTITUTION State-supported, coed. **Awards:** certificates, bachelor's, master's, and doctoral degrees. 83 undergraduate majors. **Total enrollment:** 8,662. Undergraduates: 7,893. Freshmen: 1,230. Federal methodology is used as a basis for awarding need-based institutional aid.

UNDERGRADUATE EXPENSES for 2017–2018 Application fee: $30. **Tuition, state resident:** full-time $9381; part-time $312.70 per credit hour. **Tuition, nonresident:** full-time $22,624; part-time $754.15 per credit hour. **Required fees:** full-time $438; $14.60 per credit hour. Full-time tuition and fees vary according to course level, degree level, location, and program. Part-time tuition and fees vary according to course level, degree level, location, and program. **College room and board:** $9465; **Room only:** $4592. Room and board charges vary according to board plan and housing facility.

FRESHMAN FINANCIAL AID (Fall 2017, est.) 1,054 applied for aid; of those 81% were deemed to have need. 100% of freshmen with need received aid. 17% of all full-time freshmen had no need and received non-need-based gift aid.

UNDERGRADUATE FINANCIAL AID (Fall 2017, est.) 4,973 applied for aid; of those 86% were deemed to have need. 100% of undergraduates with need received aid. 14% of all full-time undergraduates had no need and received non-need-based gift aid.

GIFT AID (NEED-BASED) Total amount: $24,446,873 (50% federal, 7% state, 32% institutional, 11% external sources). **Receiving aid:** Freshmen: 66% (805); all full-time undergraduates: 56% (3,593). **Average award:** Freshmen: $7535; Undergraduates: $6421. **Scholarships, grants, and awards:** Federal Pell, FSEOG, state, private, college/university gift aid from institutional funds.

GIFT AID (NON-NEED-BASED) Total amount: $11,962,429 (3% state, 52% institutional, 45% external sources). **Receiving aid:** Freshmen: 6% (79). Undergraduates: 4% (276) **Average award:** Freshmen: $3283. Undergraduates: $6272. **Scholarships, grants, and awards by category:** *Academic interests/achievement:* biological sciences, business, computer science, education, engineering/technologies, general academic interests/achievements, health fields, mathematics, physical sciences. *Creative arts/performance:* art/fine arts, music, theater/drama. *Special achievements/activities:* community service, leadership. *Special characteristics:* adult students, local/state students, members of minority groups, veterans, veterans' children. **Tuition waivers:** Full or partial for employees or children of employees.

LOANS Student loans: $36,422,810 (74% need-based, 26% non-need-based). 68% of past graduating class borrowed through all loan programs. *Average indebtedness per student:* $31,695. **Parent loans:** $7,006,006 (41% need-based, 59% non-need-based). **Programs:** Federal Direct (Subsidized and Unsubsidized Stafford, PLUS), private loans.

WORK-STUDY Federal work-study jobs available. **State or other work-study/employment:** Total amount: $368,310 (40% need-based, 60% non-need-based). Part-time jobs available.

ATHLETIC AWARDS Total amount: $2,378,021 (45% need-based, 55% non-need-based).

APPLYING FOR FINANCIAL AID Required financial aid forms: FAFSA, institution's own form, CSS Financial Aid PROFILE. **Financial aid deadline:** Continuous. **Notification date:** Continuous beginning 3/1.

CONTACT Robert Lemuel, Director of Scholarships and Financial Aid, Saginaw Valley State University, 7400 Bay Road, University Center, MI 48710, 989-964-4900 or toll-free 800-968-9500. *Fax:* 989-790-0180. *E-mail:* cfsc@svsu.edu. *Website:* http://www.svsu.edu/.

ST. AMBROSE UNIVERSITY
Davenport, IA

Tuition & fees: $30,894	Average undergraduate aid package: $22,886

ABOUT THE INSTITUTION Independent Roman Catholic, coed. **Awards:** certificates, bachelor's, master's, and doctoral degrees. 49 undergraduate majors. **Total enrollment:** 3,118. Undergraduates: 2,370. Freshmen: 550. Federal methodology is used as a basis for awarding need-based institutional aid.

UNDERGRADUATE EXPENSES for 2018–2019 Comprehensive fee: $41,364 includes full-time tuition ($30,614), mandatory fees ($280), and room and board ($10,470). **College room only:** $6384. Full-time tuition and fees vary according to course load and location. Room and board charges vary according to board plan and housing facility. **Part-time tuition:** $942 per credit hour. **Part-time fees:** $280 per term. Part-time tuition and fees vary according to course load and location.

FRESHMAN FINANCIAL AID (Fall 2016) 519 applied for aid; of those 88% were deemed to have need. 100% of freshmen with need received aid; of those 25% had need fully met. **Average percent of need met:** 71% (excluding resources awarded to replace EFC). **Average financial aid package:** $23,589 (excluding resources awarded to replace EFC). 16% of all full-time freshmen had no need and received non-need-based gift aid.

UNDERGRADUATE FINANCIAL AID (Fall 2016) 1,870 applied for aid; of those 89% were deemed to have need. 100% of undergraduates with need received aid; of those 23% had need fully met. **Average percent of need met:** 77% (excluding resources awarded to replace EFC). **Average financial aid package:** $22,886 (excluding resources awarded to replace EFC). 19% of all full-time undergraduates had no need and received non-need-based gift aid.

GIFT AID (NEED-BASED) Total amount: $27,654,759 (11% federal, 7% state, 79% institutional, 3% external sources). **Receiving aid:** Freshmen: 84% (456); all full-time undergraduates: 74% (1,649). **Average award:** Freshmen: $19,197; Undergraduates: $17,899. **Scholarships, grants, and awards:** Federal Pell, FSEOG, state, private, college/university gift aid from institutional funds.

GIFT AID (NON-NEED-BASED) Total amount: $5,786,819 (98% institutional, 2% external sources). **Receiving aid:** Freshmen: 26% (144). Undergraduates: 20% (435). **Average award:** Freshmen: $14,455. Undergraduates: $13,462. **Scholarships, grants, and awards by category:** *Academic interests/achievement:* biological sciences, communication, engineering/technologies, foreign languages, general academic interests/achievements, health fields, international studies, religion/biblical studies. *Creative arts/performance:* art/fine arts, dance, journalism/publications, music, theater/drama. *Special achievements/activities:* cheerleading/drum major, leadership.

Special characteristics: adult students, children and siblings of alumni, children of educators, children of faculty/staff, international students, members of minority groups, out-of-state students, previous college experience, religious affiliation, veterans. **Tuition waivers:** Full or partial for employees or children of employees.

LOANS Student loans: $17,613,942 (91% need-based, 9% non-need-based). **Average need-based loan:** Freshmen: $3471. Undergraduates: $4423. **Parent loans:** $5,049,493 (93% need-based, 7% non-need-based). **Programs:** Federal Direct (Subsidized and Unsubsidized Stafford, PLUS), Perkins.

WORK-STUDY Federal work-study: jobs available. **State or other work-study/employment:** Total amount: $413,792 (86% need-based, 14% non-need-based). Part-time jobs available.

ATHLETIC AWARDS Total amount: $2,702,474 (73% need-based, 27% non-need-based).

APPLYING FOR FINANCIAL AID Required financial aid form: FAFSA. **Financial aid deadline:** Continuous. **Notification date:** Continuous beginning 12/16.

CONTACT Ms. Julie Haack, Director of Financial Aid, St. Ambrose University, 518 West Locust Street, Davenport, IA 52803, 563-333-5775 or toll-free 800-383-2627. *Fax:* 563-333-6243. *E-mail:* haackjuliea@sau.edu. *Website:* http://www.sau.edu/.

ST. ANDREWS UNIVERSITY
Laurinburg, NC

Tuition & fees: $25,618	Average undergraduate aid package: $21,123

ABOUT THE INSTITUTION Independent Presbyterian, coed. **Awards:** diplomas, bachelor's, and master's degrees. 16 undergraduate majors. **Total enrollment:** 655. Undergraduates: 627. Freshmen: 187. Federal methodology is used as a basis for awarding need-based institutional aid.

UNDERGRADUATE EXPENSES for 2018–2019 Application fee: $35. **Tuition:** full-time $25,618; part-time $288 per credit. Full-time tuition and fees vary according to course load and location. Part-time tuition and fees vary according to location. Room and board charges vary according to housing facility.

FRESHMAN FINANCIAL AID (Fall 2016) 195 applied for aid; of those 97% were deemed to have need. 99% of freshmen with need received aid; of those 10% had need fully met. **Average percent of need met:** 70% (excluding resources awarded to replace EFC). **Average financial aid package:** $21,097 (excluding resources awarded to replace EFC). 8% of all full-time freshmen had no need and received non-need-based gift aid.

UNDERGRADUATE FINANCIAL AID (Fall 2016) 483 applied for aid; of those 94% were deemed to have need. 99% of undergraduates with need received aid; of those 10% had need fully met. **Average percent of need met:** 70% (excluding resources awarded to replace EFC). **Average financial aid package:** $21,123 (excluding resources awarded to replace EFC). 14% of all full-time undergraduates had no need and received non-need-based gift aid.

GIFT AID (NEED-BASED) Total amount: $4,974,733 (24% federal, 16% state, 52% institutional, 8% external sources). **Receiving aid:** Freshmen: 83% (188); all full-time undergraduates: 73% (449). **Average award:** Freshmen: $17,970; Undergraduates: $17,187. **Scholarships, grants, and awards:** Federal Pell, FSEOG, state, private, college/university gift aid from institutional funds.

GIFT AID (NON-NEED-BASED) Total amount: $1,020,638 (97% institutional, 3% external sources). **Receiving aid:** Freshmen: 7% (16). Undergraduates: 6% (37). **Average award:** Freshmen: $10,005. Undergraduates: $10,894. **Scholarships, grants, and awards by category:** *Academic interests/achievement:* business, general academic interests/achievements. *Creative arts/performance:* general creative arts/performance, performing arts, theater/drama. *Special achievements/activities:* community service, general special achievements/activities, leadership. **Tuition waivers:** Full or partial for employees or children of employees, adult students, senior citizens.

LOANS Student loans: $3,422,985 (82% need-based, 18% non-need-based). 69% of past graduating class borrowed through all loan programs. *Average indebtedness per student:* $26,209. **Average need-based loan:** Freshmen: $3594. Undergraduates: $4538. **Parent loans:** $2,212,688 (53% need-based, 47% non-need-based). **Programs:** Federal Direct (Subsidized and Unsubsidized Stafford, PLUS), state.

WORK-STUDY Federal work-study: jobs available. **State or other work-study/employment:** Part-time jobs available.

ATHLETIC AWARDS Total amount: $3,252,784 (82% need-based, 18% non-need-based).

APPLYING FOR FINANCIAL AID *Required financial aid form:* FAFSA. *Financial aid deadline:* Continuous. *Notification date:* Continuous beginning 2/1. Students must reply within 2 weeks of notification.

CONTACT Shawn Caulder, Director of Financial Aid, St. Andrews University, 1700 Dogwood Mile, Laurinburg, NC 28352, 910-277-5562 or toll-free 800-763-0198. *Fax:* 910-277-5206.

Website: http://www.sa.edu/.

SAINT ANSELM COLLEGE
Manchester, NH

Tuition & fees: $41,200	Average undergraduate aid package: $28,108

ABOUT THE INSTITUTION Independent Roman Catholic, coed. *Awards:* bachelor's degrees. 42 undergraduate majors. *Total enrollment:* 1,964. Undergraduates: 1,964. Freshmen: 546. Both federal and institutional methodology are used as a basis for awarding need-based institutional aid.

UNDERGRADUATE EXPENSES for 2018–2019 *Application fee:* $50. *Comprehensive fee:* $55,700 includes full-time tuition ($39,900), mandatory fees ($1300), and room and board ($14,500). Full-time tuition and fees vary according to program. Room and board charges vary according to housing facility. *Part-time tuition:* $1000 per credit. *Part-time fees:* $600 per term.

FRESHMAN FINANCIAL AID (Fall 2017, est.) 495 applied for aid; of those 85% were deemed to have need. 100% of freshmen with need received aid; of those 27% had need fully met. *Average percent of need met:* 79% (excluding resources awarded to replace EFC). *Average financial aid package:* $28,104 (excluding resources awarded to replace EFC). 20% of all full-time freshmen had no need and received non-need-based gift aid.

UNDERGRADUATE FINANCIAL AID (Fall 2017, est.) 1,597 applied for aid; of those 88% were deemed to have need. 100% of undergraduates with need received aid; of those 23% had need fully met. *Average percent of need met:* 79% (excluding resources awarded to replace EFC). *Average financial aid package:* $28,108 (excluding resources awarded to replace EFC). 23% of all full-time undergraduates had no need and received non-need-based gift aid.

GIFT AID (NEED-BASED) *Total amount:* $30,535,149 (5% federal, 93% institutional, 2% external sources). *Receiving aid:* Freshmen: 75% (422); all full-time undergraduates: 72% (1,398). *Average award:* Freshmen: $24,780; Undergraduates: $23,682. *Scholarships, grants, and awards:* Federal Pell, FSEOG, state, private, college/university gift aid from institutional funds.

GIFT AID (NON-NEED-BASED) *Total amount:* $8,660,947 (96% institutional, 4% external sources). *Receiving aid:* Freshmen: 17% (94). Undergraduates: 12% (241). *Average award:* Freshmen: $15,990. Undergraduates: $15,587. *Scholarships, grants, and awards by category:* Academic interests/achievement: 1,273 awards ($18,848,625 total): general academic interests/achievements. *Creative arts/performance:* 304 awards ($4,790,225 total): general creative arts/performance. *Special characteristics:* 288 awards ($4,220,269 total): children and siblings of alumni, children of educators, children of faculty/staff, relatives of clergy, siblings of current students. *Tuition waivers:* Full or partial for employees or children of employees. *ROTC:* Army cooperative.

LOANS *Student loans:* $15,660,474 (53% need-based, 47% non-need-based). 84% of past graduating class borrowed through all loan programs. *Average indebtedness per student:* $36,567. *Average need-based loan:* Freshmen: $2931. Undergraduates: $4152. *Parent loans:* $5,665,492 (31% need-based, 69% non-need-based). *Programs:* Federal Direct (Subsidized and Unsubsidized Stafford, PLUS).

WORK-STUDY *Federal work-study:* Total amount: $1,606,568; 1,084 jobs averaging $1482. *State or other work-study/employment:* Total amount: $17,500 (100% need-based). 9 part-time jobs averaging $1944.

ATHLETIC AWARDS Total amount: $2,395,691 (38% need-based, 62% non-need-based).

APPLYING FOR FINANCIAL AID *Required financial aid forms:* FAFSA, CSS Financial Aid PROFILE, noncustodial (divorced/separated) parent's statement, parent and student federal income tax form(s), W-2 forms. *Financial aid deadline:* 2/15. *Notification date:* Continuous beginning 2/1. Students must reply by 5/1 or within 2 weeks of notification.

CONTACT Elizabeth Keuffel, Director of Financial Aid, Saint Anselm College, 100 Saint Anselm Drive, Manchester, NH 03102-1310, 603-641-7110 or toll-free 888-4ANSELM. *Fax:* 603-656-6015. *E-mail:* financial_aid@anselm.edu.

Website: http://www.anselm.edu/.

SAINT ANTHONY COLLEGE OF NURSING
Rockford, IL

ABOUT THE INSTITUTION Independent Roman Catholic, coed, primarily women. *Awards:* certificates, bachelor's, master's, and doctoral degrees. 1 undergraduate major. *Total enrollment:* 321. Undergraduates: 238.

GIFT AID (NEED-BASED) *Scholarships, grants, and awards:* Federal Pell, state, private, college/university gift aid from institutional funds.

LOANS *Programs:* Federal Direct (Subsidized and Unsubsidized Stafford, PLUS), alternative loans.

APPLYING FOR FINANCIAL AID *Required financial aid form:* FAFSA.

CONTACT Serrita Woods, Financial Aid Coordinator, Saint Anthony College of Nursing, 5658 East State Street, Rockford, IL 61108, 815-395-5089. *Fax:* 815-227-2730. *E-mail:* serritawoods@sacn.edu.

Website: http://www.sacn.edu/.

ST. AUGUSTINE COLLEGE
Chicago, IL

CONTACT Mrs. Maria Zambonino, Director of Financial Aid, St. Augustine College, 1345 W Angyle, Chicago, IL 60640, 773-878-3813. *Fax:* 773-878-9032. *E-mail:* mzambonino@hotmail.com.

Website: http://www.staugustine.edu/.

SAINT AUGUSTINE'S UNIVERSITY
Raleigh, NC

Tuition & fees: $17,890	Average undergraduate aid package: $10,315

ABOUT THE INSTITUTION Independent Episcopal, coed. *Awards:* bachelor's degrees. 22 undergraduate majors. *Total enrollment:* 944. Undergraduates: 944. Freshmen: 347. Federal methodology is used as a basis for awarding need-based institutional aid.

UNDERGRADUATE EXPENSES for 2017–2018 *Application fee:* $50. *Comprehensive fee:* $25,582 includes full-time tuition ($12,890), mandatory fees ($5000), and room and board ($7692). *College room only:* $3182. Full-time tuition and fees vary according to course load. Room and board charges vary according to housing facility. *Part-time tuition:* $537 per credit hour. *Part-time fees:* $208 per credit hour. Part-time tuition and fees vary according to course load.

FRESHMAN FINANCIAL AID (Fall 2016) 349 applied for aid; of those 100% were deemed to have need. 100% of freshmen with need received aid. *Average percent of need met:* 46% (excluding resources awarded to replace EFC). *Average financial aid package:* $10,315 (excluding resources awarded to replace EFC). 1% of all full-time freshmen had no need and received non-need-based gift aid.

UNDERGRADUATE FINANCIAL AID (Fall 2016) 950 applied for aid; of those 100% were deemed to have need. 100% of undergraduates with need received aid. *Average percent of need met:* 46% (excluding resources awarded to replace EFC). *Average financial aid package:* $10,315 (excluding resources awarded to replace EFC). 4% of all full-time undergraduates had no need and received non-need-based gift aid.

GIFT AID (NEED-BASED) *Total amount:* $9,722,265 (48% federal, 24% state, 24% institutional, 4% external sources). *Receiving aid:* Freshmen: 99% (349); all full-time undergraduates: 82% (814). *Average award:* Freshmen: $2679; Undergraduates: $4670. *Scholarships, grants, and awards:* Federal Pell, FSEOG, state, private, college/university gift aid from institutional funds, United Negro College Fund.

GIFT AID (NON-NEED BASED) *Receiving aid:* Freshmen: 99% (349). Undergraduates: 93% (916). *Average award:* Freshmen: $3154. Undergraduates: $3750. *Scholarships, grants, and awards by category:* Academic interests/achievement: biological sciences, general academic interests/achievements, military science. *Creative arts/performance:* music, performing arts. *Special characteristics:* children of faculty/staff, local/state students. *Tuition waivers:* Full or partial for children of alumni, employees or children of employees. *ROTC:* Army, Air Force cooperative.

LOANS *Student loans:* $7,483,805 (100% need-based). 93% of past graduating class borrowed through all loan programs. *Average indebtedness per student:* $19,500. *Parent loans:* $2,584,524 (100% need-based). *Programs:* Federal Direct (Subsidized and Unsubsidized Stafford, PLUS), Perkins.

WORK-STUDY *Federal work-study:* 462 jobs averaging $1887.

ATHLETIC AWARDS Total amount: $1,077,214 (100% need-based).

APPLYING FOR FINANCIAL AID *Required financial aid forms:* FAFSA, institution's own form. *Financial aid deadline (priority):* 3/15. *Notification date:* Continuous beginning 3/15. Students must reply within 2 weeks of notification.

CONTACT Ms. Barbara Grimm, Director of Financial Aid, Saint Augustine's University, 1315 Oakwood Avenue, Raleigh, NC 27610-2298, 919-516-4128 or toll-free 800-948-1126. *Fax:* 919-516-4431. *E-mail:* bgrimm@st-aug.edu. *Website:* http://www.st-aug.edu/.

ST. BONAVENTURE UNIVERSITY
St. Bonaventure, NY

Tuition & fees: $33,331	Average undergraduate aid package: $22,673

ABOUT THE INSTITUTION Independent Roman Catholic Church, coed. *Awards:* certificates, associate, bachelor's, and master's degrees. 33 undergraduate majors. *Total enrollment:* 2,089. Undergraduates: 1,627. Freshmen: 439. Federal methodology is used as a basis for awarding need-based institutional aid.

UNDERGRADUATE EXPENSES for 2017–2018 *One-time required fee:* $100. *Comprehensive fee:* $45,146 includes full-time tuition ($32,366), mandatory fees ($965), and room and board ($11,815). *College room only:* $6230. Room and board charges vary according to board plan and housing facility. *Part-time tuition:* $962 per credit hour. *Part-time fees:* $962 per credit hour. Part-time tuition and fees vary according to course load.

FRESHMAN FINANCIAL AID (Fall 2016) 386 applied for aid; of those 87% were deemed to have need. 100% of freshmen with need received aid; of those 23% had need fully met. *Average percent of need met:* 78% (excluding resources awarded to replace EFC). *Average financial aid package:* $29,259 (excluding resources awarded to replace EFC). 12% of all full-time freshmen had no need and received non-need-based gift aid.

UNDERGRADUATE FINANCIAL AID (Fall 2016) 1,340 applied for aid; of those 88% were deemed to have need. 100% of undergraduates with need received aid; of those 34% had need fully met. *Average percent of need met:* 75% (excluding resources awarded to replace EFC). *Average financial aid package:* $22,673 (excluding resources awarded to replace EFC). 44% of all full-time undergraduates had no need and received non-need-based gift aid.

GIFT AID (NEED-BASED) *Total amount:* $22,864,347 (11% federal, 8% state, 79% institutional, 2% external sources). *Receiving aid:* Freshmen: 56% (243); all full-time undergraduates: 54% (870). *Average award:* Freshmen: $17,554; Undergraduates: $11,290. *Scholarships, grants, and awards:* Federal Pell, FSEOG, state, private, college/university gift aid from institutional funds.

GIFT AID (NON-NEED-BASED) *Total amount:* $5,492,875 (13% federal, 86% institutional, 1% external sources). *Receiving aid:* Freshmen: 70% (300). Undergraduates: 49% (786). *Average award:* Freshmen: $2657. Undergraduates: $2951. *Scholarships, grants, and awards by category:* Academic interests/achievement: 1,378 awards ($17,639,293 total): business, education, general academic interests/achievements. *Creative arts/performance:* 78 awards ($94,617 total): journalism/publications, music, performing arts. *Special characteristics:* 481 awards ($2,695,092 total): children of faculty/staff, local/state students, members of minority groups, out-of-state students, relatives of clergy, religious affiliation, siblings of current students. *Tuition waivers:* Full or partial for employees or children of employees, senior citizens. *ROTC:* Army.

LOANS *Student loans:* $11,130,441 (92% need-based, 8% non-need-based). 63% of past graduating class borrowed through all loan programs. *Average indebtedness*

per student: $15,101. *Average need-based loan:* Freshmen: $3333. Undergraduates: $4338. *Parent loans:* $4,893,802 (94% need-based, 6% non-need-based). *Programs:* Federal Direct (Subsidized and Unsubsidized Stafford, PLUS), Perkins, college/university.

WORK-STUDY *Federal work-study:* 271 jobs averaging $927. *State or other work-study/employment:* 374 part-time jobs averaging $910.

ATHLETIC AWARDS Total amount: $3,382,724 (52% need-based, 48% non-need-based).

APPLYING FOR FINANCIAL AID *Required financial aid forms:* FAFSA, state aid form. *Financial aid deadline (priority):* 2/15. *Notification date:* Continuous beginning 3/1. Students must reply by 5/1 or within 2 weeks of notification.

CONTACT Mr. Bernard Valento, Vice President of Enrollment, St. Bonaventure University, 3261 West State Road, St. Bonaventure, NY 14778-2284, 716-375-2128 or toll-free 800-462-5050. *Fax:* 716-375-2087. *E-mail:* bvalento@sbu.edu. *Website:* http://www.sbu.edu/.

ST. CATHERINE UNIVERSITY
St. Paul, MN

Tuition & fees: $38,349	Average undergraduate aid package: $36,000

ABOUT THE INSTITUTION Independent Roman Catholic, undergraduate: women only; graduate: coed. *Awards:* certificates, associate, bachelor's, master's, and doctoral degrees. 80 undergraduate majors. *Total enrollment:* 4,724. Undergraduates: 5,258. Freshmen: 399. Federal methodology is used as a basis for awarding need-based institutional aid.

UNDERGRADUATE EXPENSES for 2017–2018 *Comprehensive fee:* $47,545 includes full-time tuition ($37,590), mandatory fees ($759), and room and board ($9196). *College room only:* $5400. Full-time tuition and fees vary according to degree level. Room and board charges vary according to board plan and housing facility. *Part-time tuition:* $1253 per credit hour. *Part-time fees:* $322 per term. Part-time tuition and fees vary according to degree level.

FRESHMAN FINANCIAL AID (Fall 2017, est.) 386 applied for aid; of those 89% were deemed to have need. 100% of freshmen with need received aid; of those 37% had need fully met. *Average percent of need met:* 93% (excluding resources awarded to replace EFC). *Average financial aid package:* $38,300 (excluding resources awarded to replace EFC). 11% of all full-time freshmen had no need and received non-need-based gift aid.

UNDERGRADUATE FINANCIAL AID (Fall 2017, est.) 1,740 applied for aid; of those 86% were deemed to have need. 100% of undergraduates with need received aid; of those 39% had need fully met. *Average percent of need met:* 90% (excluding resources awarded to replace EFC). *Average financial aid package:* $36,000 (excluding resources awarded to replace EFC). 13% of all full-time undergraduates had no need and received non-need-based gift aid.

GIFT AID (NEED-BASED) *Total amount:* $12,912,000 (42% federal, 36% state, 16% institutional, 6% external sources). *Receiving aid:* Freshmen: 75% (292); all full-time undergraduates: 65% (1,140). *Average award:* Freshmen: $11,200; Undergraduates: $9600. *Scholarships, grants, and awards:* Federal Pell, FSEOG, state, private, college/university gift aid from institutional funds.

GIFT AID (NON-NEED-BASED) *Total amount:* $32,373,100 (100% institutional). *Receiving aid:* Freshmen: 89% (343). Undergraduates: 83% (1,465). *Average award:* Freshmen: $23,400. Undergraduates: $19,000. *Scholarships, grants, and awards by category:* Academic interests/achievement: business, education, English, foreign languages, general academic interests/achievements, health fields, home economics, humanities, mathematics, physical sciences, premedicine, social sciences. *Creative arts/performance:* art/fine arts, music. *Special achievements/activities:* community service, general special achievements/activities, leadership, memberships. *Special characteristics:* adult students, children and siblings of alumni, children of current students, children of educators, children of faculty/staff, ethnic background, general special characteristics, international students, local/state students, out-of-state students, religious affiliation, siblings of current students, spouses of current students. *Tuition waivers:* Full or partial for employees or children of employees, senior citizens. *ROTC:* Army cooperative, Air Force cooperative.

LOANS *Student loans:* $19,012,100 (42% need-based, 58% non-need-based). 84% of past graduating class borrowed through all loan programs. *Average indebtedness per student:* $38,199. *Average need-based loan:* Freshmen: $3600. Undergraduates: $5200. *Parent loans:* $3,711,400 (100% non-need-based). *Programs:* Federal

Direct (Subsidized and Unsubsidized Stafford, PLUS), Perkins, Federal Nursing, state, alternative loans.

WORK-STUDY Federal work-study jobs available. *State or other work-study/ employment:* Part-time jobs available.

APPLYING FOR FINANCIAL AID *Required financial aid forms:* FAFSA, institution's own form. *Financial aid deadline (priority):* 4/15. *Notification date:* Continuous beginning 4/15. Students must reply within 2 weeks of notification.

CONTACT Katie Zmudzien, Associate Director of Admissions and Financial Aid, St. Catherine University, 2004 Randolph Avenue, St. Paul, MN 55105, 651-690-6934 or toll-free 800-945-4599. *Fax:* 651-690-6765. *E-mail:* finaid@stkate.edu. *Website:* http://www.stkate.edu/.

SAINT CHARLES BORROMEO SEMINARY, OVERBROOK
Wynnewood, PA

CONTACT Ms. Nora M. Downey, Coordinator of Financial Aid, Saint Charles Borromeo Seminary, Overbrook, 100 East Wynnewood Road, Wynnewood, PA 19096-3099, 610-785-6582. *Fax:* 610-667-3971. *E-mail:* ndowney@scs.edu. *Website:* http://www.scs.edu/.

ST. CLOUD STATE UNIVERSITY
St. Cloud, MN

ABOUT THE INSTITUTION State-supported, coed. *Awards:* certificates, diplomas, associate, bachelor's, master's, and doctoral degrees. 98 undergraduate majors. *Total enrollment:* 15,092. Undergraduates: 13,236. Freshmen: 1,800.

GIFT AID (NEED-BASED) *Scholarships, grants, and awards:* Federal Pell, FSEOG, state, private, college/university gift aid from institutional funds.

GIFT AID (NON-NEED-BASED) *Scholarships, grants, and awards by category:* Academic interests/achievement: biological sciences, business, communication, computer science, education, engineering/technologies, English, general academic interests/achievements, health fields, international studies, mathematics, physical sciences, social sciences. *Creative arts/performance:* applied art and design, art/fine arts, cinema/film/broadcasting, creative writing, journalism/publications, music, performing arts, theater/drama. *Special achievements/activities:* community service, general special achievements/activities. *Special characteristics:* children of faculty/staff, children of union members/company employees, members of minority groups, out-of-state students.

LOANS *Programs:* Federal Direct (Subsidized and Unsubsidized Stafford, PLUS), state.

APPLYING FOR FINANCIAL AID *Required financial aid form:* FAFSA.

CONTACT Office of Financial Aid, St. Cloud State University, 720 4th Avenue South, St. Cloud, MN 56301, 320-308-2047 or toll-free 877-654-7278. *Fax:* 320-308-5424. *E-mail:* financialaid@stcloudstate.edu. *Website:* http://www.stcloudstate.edu/.

ST. EDWARD'S UNIVERSITY
Austin, TX

Tuition & fees: $43,050	Average undergraduate aid package: $34,850

ABOUT THE INSTITUTION Independent Roman Catholic, coed. *Awards:* certificates, bachelor's, and master's degrees. 56 undergraduate majors. *Total enrollment:* 4,601. Undergraduates: 4,056. Freshmen: 864. Federal methodology is used as a basis for awarding need-based institutional aid.

UNDERGRADUATE EXPENSES for 2017–2018 *Application fee:* $50. *One-time required fee:* $250. *Comprehensive fee:* $55,990 includes full-time tuition ($42,550), mandatory fees ($500), and room and board ($12,940). Full-time tuition and fees vary according to degree level. Room and board charges vary according to board plan and housing facility. *Part-time tuition:* $1419 per credit hour. *Part-time fees:*

$150 per year. Part-time tuition and fees vary according to course load and degree level.

FRESHMAN FINANCIAL AID (Fall 2017, est.) 686 applied for aid; of those 91% were deemed to have need. 100% of freshmen with need received aid; of those 13% had need fully met. *Average percent of need met:* 72% (excluding resources awarded to replace EFC). *Average financial aid package:* $37,627 (excluding resources awarded to replace EFC). 6% of all full-time freshmen had no need and received non-need-based gift aid.

UNDERGRADUATE FINANCIAL AID (Fall 2017, est.) 2,664 applied for aid; of those 93% were deemed to have need. 100% of undergraduates with need received aid; of those 10% had need fully met. *Average percent of need met:* 68% (excluding resources awarded to replace EFC). *Average financial aid package:* $34,850 (excluding resources awarded to replace EFC). 4% of all full-time undergraduates had no need and received non-need-based gift aid.

GIFT AID (NEED-BASED) *Total amount:* $51,925,594 (14% federal, 8% state, 78% institutional). *Receiving aid:* Freshmen: 71% (558); all full-time undergraduates: 64% (2,250). *Average award:* Freshmen: $24,131; Undergraduates: $21,938. *Scholarships, grants, and awards:* Federal Pell, FSEOG, state, private, college/university gift aid from institutional funds.

GIFT AID (NON-NEED-BASED) *Total amount:* $35,468,462 (6% federal, 88% institutional, 6% external sources). *Receiving aid:* Freshmen: 55% (435). Undergraduates: 49% (1,733). *Average award:* Freshmen: $19,354. Undergraduates: $17,083. *Scholarships, grants, and awards by category:* Academic interests/achievement: 1,932 awards ($27,736,686 total): biological sciences, business, communication, computer science, education, English, foreign languages, general academic interests/achievements, home economics, humanities, international studies, mathematics, military science, physical sciences, premedicine, religion/biblical studies, social sciences. *Creative arts/performance:* 41 awards ($100,175 total): art/fine arts, journalism/publications, theater/drama. *Special achievements/activities:* 47 awards ($140,264 total): cheerleading/drum major, community service, general special achievements/activities, leadership. *Special characteristics:* 234 awards ($2,727,974 total): adult students, children of faculty/staff, local/state students, out-of-state students, religious affiliation, veterans, veterans' children. *Tuition waivers:* Full or partial for employees or children of employees. *ROTC:* Army cooperative, Air Force cooperative.

LOANS *Student loans:* $23,662,131 (40% need-based, 60% non-need-based). 69% of past graduating class borrowed through all loan programs. *Average indebtedness per student:* $34,812. *Average need-based loan:* Freshmen: $3707. Undergraduates: $4726. *Parent loans:* $6,173,182 (100% non-need-based). *Programs:* Federal Direct (Subsidized and Unsubsidized Stafford, PLUS), Perkins, state, private loans.

WORK-STUDY *Federal work-study:* Total amount: $527,649; 267 jobs averaging $1976. *State or other work-study/employment:* Total amount: $39,340 (100% need-based). 18 part-time jobs averaging $2067.

ATHLETIC AWARDS Total amount: $4,045,911 (100% non-need-based).

APPLYING FOR FINANCIAL AID *Required financial aid form:* FAFSA. *Financial aid deadline (priority):* 2/1. *Notification date:* Continuous beginning 2/1. Students must reply by 5/1 or within 2 weeks of notification.

CONTACT Office of Student Financial Services, St. Edward's University, 3001 South Congress Avenue, Austin, TX 78704-6489, 512-448-8523 or toll-free 800-555-0164. *Fax:* 512-416-5837. *E-mail:* seu.finaid@stedwards.edu. *Website:* http://www.stedwards.edu/.

ST. FRANCIS COLLEGE
Brooklyn Heights, NY

CONTACT Ms. Hellitz Lopez, Director of Student Financial Services, St. Francis College, 180 Remsen Street, Brooklyn Heights, NY 11201-4398, 718-489-5346. *Fax:* 718-643-0076. *E-mail:* hlopez@sfc.edu. *Website:* http://www.sfc.edu/.

SAINT FRANCIS MEDICAL CENTER COLLEGE OF NURSING
Peoria, IL

Tuition & fees: $21,057	Average undergraduate aid package: $10,953

ABOUT THE INSTITUTION Independent Roman Catholic, coed, primarily women. *Awards:* certificates, bachelor's, master's, and doctoral degrees. 1 undergraduate major. *Total enrollment:* 645. Undergraduates: 402. Federal methodology is used as a basis for awarding need-based institutional aid.

UNDERGRADUATE EXPENSES for 2018–2019 *Application fee:* $50. *Tuition:* full-time $20,020; part-time $616 per semester hour. *Required fees:* full-time $1037; $215 per term. Full-time tuition and fees vary according to course load, degree level, program, and student level. Part-time tuition and fees vary according to course load, degree level, program, and student level.

UNDERGRADUATE FINANCIAL AID (Fall 2017, est.) 265 applied for aid; of those 79% were deemed to have need. 100% of undergraduates with need received aid; of those 4% had need fully met. *Average percent of need met:* 41% (excluding resources awarded to replace EFC). *Average financial aid package:* $10,953 (excluding resources awarded to replace EFC). 8% of all full-time undergraduates had no need and received non-need-based gift aid.

GIFT AID (NEED-BASED) *Total amount:* $1,311,887 (35% federal, 48% state, 9% institutional, 8% external sources). *Receiving aid:* All full-time undergraduates: 50% (157). *Average award:* Undergraduates: $7143. *Scholarships, grants, and awards:* Federal Pell, state, private, college/university gift aid from institutional funds.

GIFT AID (NON-NEED-BASED) *Total amount:* $130,514 (20% state, 54% institutional, 26% external sources). *Receiving aid:* Undergraduates: 1% (2). *Average award:* Undergraduates: $2522. *Scholarships, grants, and awards by category:* Academic interests/achievement: 25 awards ($25,000 total): general academic interests/achievements, health fields. *Tuition waivers:* Full or partial for employees or children of employees.

LOANS *Student loans:* $3,255,198 (77% need-based, 23% non-need-based). *Average need-based loan:* Undergraduates: $5721. *Parent loans:* $668,565 (57% need-based, 43% non-need-based). *Programs:* Federal Direct (Subsidized and Unsubsidized Stafford, PLUS), college/university.

APPLYING FOR FINANCIAL AID *Required financial aid forms:* FAFSA, institution's own form. *Financial aid deadline (priority):* 3/1. *Notification date:* Continuous beginning 5/1.

CONTACT Ms. Nancy Perryman, Coordinator for Student Financial Assistance, Saint Francis Medical Center College of Nursing, 511 Northeast Greenleaf Street, Peoria, IL 61603-3783, 309-655-4119. *Fax:* 309-655-3962. *E-mail:* nancy.s.perryman@osfhealthcare.org. *Website:* http://www.sfmccon.edu/.

SAINT FRANCIS UNIVERSITY
Loretto, PA

CONTACT Mr. Jamie Kosh, Director of Financial Aid, Saint Francis University, PO Box 600, Loretto, PA 15931, 814-472-3010 or toll-free 866-DIAL-SFU. *Fax:* 814-472-3999. *E-mail:* jkosh@francis.edu. *Website:* http://www.francis.edu/.

ST. GREGORY THE GREAT SEMINARY
Seward, NE

CONTACT Financial Aid Office, St. Gregory the Great Seminary, 800 Fletcher Road, Seward, NE 67434, 402-643-4052. *Website:* http://www.stgregoryseminary.edu/.

ST. JOHN FISHER COLLEGE
Rochester, NY

Tuition & fees: $33,120	Average undergraduate aid package: $23,140

ABOUT THE INSTITUTION Independent Roman Catholic Church, coed. *Awards:* certificates, bachelor's, master's, and doctoral degrees. 40 undergraduate majors. *Total enrollment:* 3,782. Undergraduates: 2,759. Freshmen: 626. Federal methodology is used as a basis for awarding need-based institutional aid.

UNDERGRADUATE EXPENSES for 2017–2018 *Comprehensive fee:* $45,270 includes full-time tuition ($32,540), mandatory fees ($580), and room and board ($12,150). *College room only:* $7780. Full-time tuition and fees vary according to program. Room and board charges vary according to board plan. *Part-time tuition:* $885 per credit hour. *Part-time fees:* $10 per credit hour. Part-time tuition and fees vary according to course load and program.

FRESHMAN FINANCIAL AID (Fall 2017, est.) 604 applied for aid; of those 90% were deemed to have need. 100% of freshmen with need received aid; of those 38% had need fully met. *Average percent of need met:* 73% (excluding resources awarded to replace EFC). *Average financial aid package:* $24,214 (excluding resources awarded to replace EFC). 13% of all full-time freshmen had no need and received non-need-based gift aid.

UNDERGRADUATE FINANCIAL AID (Fall 2017, est.) 2,337 applied for aid; of those 93% were deemed to have need. 100% of undergraduates with need received aid; of those 33% had need fully met. *Average percent of need met:* 69% (excluding resources awarded to replace EFC). *Average financial aid package:* $23,140 (excluding resources awarded to replace EFC). 17% of all full-time undergraduates had no need and received non-need-based gift aid.

GIFT AID (NEED-BASED) *Total amount:* $38,331,996 (11% federal, 8% state, 79% institutional, 2% external sources). *Receiving aid:* Freshmen: 87% (542); all full-time undergraduates: 82% (2,158). *Average award:* Freshmen: $20,277; Undergraduates: $18,096. *Scholarships, grants, and awards:* Federal Pell, FSEOG, state, private, college/university gift aid from institutional funds, Federal Nursing.

GIFT AID (NON-NEED-BASED) *Total amount:* $5,369,742 (98% institutional, 2% external sources). *Receiving aid:* Freshmen: 67% (417). Undergraduates: 65% (1,706). *Average award:* Freshmen: $13,847. Undergraduates: $12,151. *Scholarships, grants, and awards by category:* Academic interests/achievement: 1,434 awards ($17,668,375 total): biological sciences, business, English, foreign languages, general academic interests/achievements, humanities, mathematics, physical sciences, social sciences. *Special achievements/activities:* 88 awards ($1,830,584 total): community service. *Special characteristics:* 368 awards ($2,886,678 total): children and siblings of alumni, children of faculty/staff, ethnic background, first-generation college students, local/state students, members of minority groups. *Tuition waivers:* Full or partial for employees or children of employees. *ROTC:* Army cooperative, Naval cooperative, Air Force cooperative.

LOANS *Student loans:* $23,519,857 (95% need-based, 5% non-need-based). 79% of past graduating class borrowed through all loan programs. *Average indebtedness per student:* $38,639. *Average need-based loan:* Freshmen: $3705. Undergraduates: $4810. *Parent loans:* $14,489,649 (91% need-based, 9% non-need-based). *Programs:* Federal Direct (Subsidized and Unsubsidized Stafford, PLUS), Perkins.

WORK-STUDY *Federal work-study:* Total amount: $2,018,223; 1,345 jobs averaging $1500.

APPLYING FOR FINANCIAL AID *Required financial aid forms:* FAFSA, state aid form. *Financial aid deadline (priority):* 1/15. *Notification date:* Continuous beginning 2/21. Students must reply by 5/1 or within 3 weeks of notification.

CONTACT Mrs. Angela Monnat, Director of Financial Aid, St. John Fisher College, 3690 East Avenue, Rochester, NY 14618-3597, 585-385-8042 or toll-free 800-444-4640. *Fax:* 585-385-8044. *E-mail:* amonnat@sjfc.edu. *Website:* http://www.sjfc.edu/.

ST. JOHN'S COLLEGE
Springfield, IL

CONTACT Mary M. Deatherage, Financial Aid Officer, St. John's College, 421 North Ninth Street, Springfield, IL 62702, 217-544-6464 Ext. 44705. *Fax:* 217-757-6870. *E-mail:* mdeather@st-johns.org. *Website:* http://www.sjcs.edu/.

ST. JOHN'S COLLEGE
Annapolis, MD

Tuition & fees: $51,670	Average undergraduate aid package: $41,116

ABOUT THE INSTITUTION Independent, coed. **Awards:** bachelor's and master's degrees. 1 undergraduate major. **Total enrollment:** 513. Undergraduates: 458. Freshmen: 122. Both federal and institutional methodology are used as a basis for awarding need-based institutional aid.

UNDERGRADUATE EXPENSES for 2017–2018 One-time required fee: $125. **Comprehensive fee:** $63,904 includes full-time tuition ($51,200), mandatory fees ($470), and room and board ($12,234). **College room only:** $5984. Room and board charges vary according to board plan and housing facility. **Payment plan:** Tuition prepayment.

FRESHMAN FINANCIAL AID (Fall 2017, est.) 103 applied for aid; of those 88% were deemed to have need. 100% of freshmen with need received aid; of those 23% had need fully met. **Average percent of need met:** 88% (excluding resources awarded to replace EFC). **Average financial aid package:** $42,027 (excluding resources awarded to replace EFC). 23% of all full-time freshmen had no need and received non-need-based gift aid.

UNDERGRADUATE FINANCIAL AID (Fall 2017, est.) 360 applied for aid; of those 88% were deemed to have need. 100% of undergraduates with need received aid; of those 25% had need fully met. **Average percent of need met:** 87% (excluding resources awarded to replace EFC). **Average financial aid package:** $41,116 (excluding resources awarded to replace EFC). 24% of all full-time undergraduates had no need and received non-need-based gift aid.

GIFT AID (NEED-BASED) Total amount: $11,484,730 (4% federal, 1% state, 91% institutional, 4% external sources). **Receiving aid:** Freshmen: 74% (89); all full-time undergraduates: 74% (314). **Average award:** Freshmen: $38,747; Undergraduates: $36,575. **Scholarships, grants, and awards:** Federal Pell, FSEOG, state, private, college/university gift aid from institutional funds.

GIFT AID (NON-NEED-BASED) Total amount: $2,736,071 (1% state, 86% institutional, 13% external sources). **Receiving aid:** Freshmen: 12% (15). Undergraduates: 15% (62). **Average award:** Freshmen: $20,503. Undergraduates: $19,170. **Scholarships, grants, and awards by category:** Academic interests/achievement: general academic interests/achievements. **Tuition waivers:** Full or partial for employees or children of employees.

LOANS Student loans: $2,686,012 (69% need-based, 31% non-need-based). 74% of past graduating class borrowed through all loan programs. **Average need-based loan:** Freshmen: $3773. Undergraduates: $4734. **Parent loans:** $895,420 (16% need-based, 84% non-need-based). **Programs:** Federal Direct (Subsidized and Unsubsidized Stafford, PLUS), college/university.

WORK-STUDY Federal work-study: Total amount: $130,000; 55 jobs averaging $2700. **State or other work-study/employment:** Total amount: $181,889 (74% need-based, 26% non-need-based). 125 part-time jobs averaging $2700.

APPLYING FOR FINANCIAL AID Required financial aid forms: FAFSA, state aid form. **Financial aid deadline (priority):** 2/1. **Notification date:** Continuous beginning 12/15. Students must reply by 5/1 or within 2 weeks of notification.

CONTACT Mr. Steven Bell, Director of Financial Aid, St. John's College, 60 College Avenue, Annapolis, MD 21401, 410-626-2502 or toll-free 800-727-9238. Fax: 410-626-2885. E-mail: skbell@sjc.edu. Website: http://www.sjc.edu/.

ST. JOHN'S COLLEGE
Santa Fe, NM

Tuition & fees: $53,218	Average undergraduate aid package: $42,100

ABOUT THE INSTITUTION Independent, coed. **Awards:** bachelor's and master's degrees. 1 undergraduate major. **Total enrollment:** 383. Undergraduates: 322. Freshmen: 70. Both federal and institutional methodology are used as a basis for awarding need-based institutional aid.

UNDERGRADUATE EXPENSES for 2018–2019 Comprehensive fee: $65,366 includes full-time tuition ($52,734), mandatory fees ($484), and room and board ($12,148). Full-time tuition and fees vary according to location. Room and board charges vary according to board plan, housing facility, and location. **Part-time tuition:** $1551 per credit.

FRESHMAN FINANCIAL AID (Fall 2017, est.) 92 applied for aid; of those 98% were deemed to have need. 100% of freshmen with need received aid; of those 32% had need fully met. **Average percent of need met:** 87% (excluding resources awarded to replace EFC). **Average financial aid package:** $45,500 (excluding resources awarded to replace EFC). 12% of all full-time freshmen had no need and received non-need-based gift aid.

UNDERGRADUATE FINANCIAL AID (Fall 2017, est.) 309 applied for aid; of those 98% were deemed to have need. 100% of undergraduates with need received aid; of those 44% had need fully met. **Average percent of need met:** 89% (excluding resources awarded to replace EFC). **Average financial aid package:** $42,100 (excluding resources awarded to replace EFC). 12% of all full-time undergraduates had no need and received non-need-based gift aid.

GIFT AID (NEED-BASED) Total amount: $6,679,073 (10% federal, 90% institutional). **Receiving aid:** Freshmen: 87% (90); all full-time undergraduates: 89% (303). **Average award:** Freshmen: $32,000; Undergraduates: $33,500. **Scholarships, grants, and awards:** Federal Pell, FSEOG, state, private, college/university gift aid from institutional funds.

GIFT AID (NON-NEED-BASED) Total amount: $5,695,332 (2% federal, 94% institutional, 4% external sources). **Receiving aid:** Freshmen: 87% (90). Undergraduates: 89% (303). **Average award:** Freshmen: $20,032. Undergraduates: $19,583. **Scholarships, grants, and awards by category:** Special characteristics: 4 awards ($80,766 total): children of faculty/staff, veterans. **Tuition waivers:** Full or partial for employees or children of employees.

LOANS Student loans: $1,806,453 (60% need-based, 40% non-need-based). 78% of past graduating class borrowed through all loan programs. **Average indebtedness per student:** $26,990. **Average need-based loan:** Freshmen: $4650. Undergraduates: $7450. **Parent loans:** $460,955 (100% non-need-based). **Programs:** Federal Direct (Subsidized and Unsubsidized Stafford, PLUS), Perkins, college/university.

WORK-STUDY Federal work-study: Total amount: $210,344; 76 jobs averaging $2791. **State or other work-study/employment:** Total amount: $282,705 (4% need-based, 96% non-need-based). 100 part-time jobs averaging $2827.

APPLYING FOR FINANCIAL AID Required financial aid forms: FAFSA, CSS Financial Aid PROFILE. **Financial aid deadline (priority):** 2/15. **Notification date:** Continuous beginning 12/15. Students must reply by 5/1 or within 2 weeks of notification.

CONTACT Michael R. Rodriguez, Director of Financial Aid, St. John's College, 1160 Camino Cruz Blanca, Santa Fe, NM 87505, 505-984-6058 or toll-free 800-331-5232. Fax: 505-984-6164. E-mail: mrodriguez@sjc.edu. Website: http://www.sjc.edu/.

SAINT JOHN'S UNIVERSITY
Collegeville, MN

Tuition & fees: $43,356	Average undergraduate aid package: $33,379

ABOUT THE INSTITUTION Independent Roman Catholic, undergraduate: men only; graduate: coed. **Awards:** bachelor's and master's degrees (coordinate with College of Saint Benedict for women). 46 undergraduate majors. **Total enrollment:** 1,815. Undergraduates: 1,720. Freshmen: 465. Federal methodology is used as a basis for awarding need-based institutional aid.

UNDERGRADUATE EXPENSES for 2017–2018 Comprehensive fee: $53,472 includes full-time tuition ($42,574), mandatory fees ($782), and room and board ($10,116). **College room only:** $5070. Room and board charges vary according to board plan and housing facility. **Part-time tuition:** $1774 per credit hour. Part-time tuition and fees vary according to course load.

FRESHMAN FINANCIAL AID (Fall 2017, est.) 401 applied for aid; of those 85% were deemed to have need. 100% of freshmen with need received aid; of those 36% had need fully met. **Average percent of need met:** 92% (excluding resources awarded to replace EFC). **Average financial aid package:** $35,367 (excluding resources awarded to replace EFC). 22% of all full-time freshmen had no need and received non-need-based gift aid.

UNDERGRADUATE FINANCIAL AID (Fall 2017, est.) 1,340 applied for aid; of those 88% were deemed to have need. 100% of undergraduates with need received aid; of those 33% had need fully met. **Average percent of need met:** 90% (excluding resources awarded to replace EFC). **Average financial aid package:**

$33,379 (excluding resources awarded to replace EFC). 25% of all full-time undergraduates had no need and received non-need-based gift aid.

GIFT AID (NEED-BASED) Total amount: $35,386,383 (6% federal, 6% state, 85% institutional, 3% external sources). **Receiving aid:** Freshmen: 73% (338); all full-time undergraduates: 68% (1,159). **Average award:** Freshmen: $31,180; Undergraduates: $29,686. **Scholarships, grants, and awards:** Federal Pell, FSEOG, state, private, college/university gift aid from institutional funds.

GIFT AID (NON-NEED-BASED) Total amount: $11,515,938 (83% institutional, 17% external sources). **Receiving aid:** Freshmen: 72% (334). Undergraduates: 65% (1,101). **Average award:** Freshmen: $18,314. Undergraduates: $17,270. **Scholarships, grants, and awards by category:** Academic interests/achievement: 1,675 awards ($24,025,521 total): general academic interests/achievements. Creative arts/performance: 112 awards ($334,687 total): art/fine arts, music, theater/drama. Special characteristics: 307 awards ($1,167,320 total): out-of-state students. **Tuition waivers:** Full or partial for employees or children of employees. **ROTC:** Army.

LOANS Student loans: $11,254,280 (90% need-based, 10% non-need-based). 72% of past graduating class borrowed through all loan programs. Average indebtedness per student: $41,698. **Average need-based loan:** Freshmen: $2479. Undergraduates: $3296. **Parent loans:** $1,221,358 (93% need-based, 7% non-need-based). **Programs:** Federal Direct (Subsidized and Unsubsidized Stafford, PLUS), Perkins, state, alternative loans.

WORK-STUDY Federal work-study: Total amount: $423,188; 171 jobs averaging $3400. **State or other work-study/employment:** Total amount: $2,739,866 (79% need-based, 21% non-need-based). 875 part-time jobs averaging $3400.

APPLYING FOR FINANCIAL AID Required financial aid forms: FAFSA, institution's own form. **Financial aid deadline (priority):** 3/15. **Notification date:** Continuous beginning 3/15. Students must reply by 5/1 or within 3 weeks of notification.

CONTACT Mrs. Kari Vogt, Financial Aid Counselor, Saint John's University, PO Box 5000, Collegeville, MN 56321-5000, 320-363-3664 or toll-free 800-544-1489. Fax: 320-363-3102. E-mail: kvogt@csbsju.edu.
Website: http://www.csbsju.edu/.

GIFT AID (NON-NEED-BASED) Total amount: $191,244,515 (95% institutional, 5% external sources). **Receiving aid:** Freshmen: 81% (2,609). Undergraduates: 74% (8,544). **Average award:** Freshmen: $22,761. Undergraduates: $21,098. **Scholarships, grants, and awards by category:** Academic interests/achievement: 7,242 awards ($119,419,881 total): biological sciences, business, communication, computer science, English, foreign languages, general academic interests/achievements, health fields, humanities, mathematics, military science, physical sciences, premedicine, social sciences. Creative arts/performance: 117 awards ($352,240 total): art/fine arts, cinema/film/broadcasting, creative writing, dance, debating, journalism/publications, music. Special achievements/activities: 317 awards ($1,236,932 total): cheerleading/drum major, community service, general special achievements/activities, hobbies/interests, leadership, religious involvement. Special characteristics: 3,159 awards ($12,042,644 total): children of faculty/staff, general special characteristics, local/state students, previous college experience, public servants, relatives of clergy, religious affiliation, veterans, veterans' children. **Tuition waivers:** Full or partial for employees or children of employees, adult students, senior citizens. **ROTC:** Army.

LOANS Student loans: $46,645,189 (58% need-based, 42% non-need-based). 68% of past graduating class borrowed through all loan programs. Average indebtedness per student: $32,831. **Average need-based loan:** Freshmen: $3928. Undergraduates: $4609. **Parent loans:** $66,023,692 (100% non-need-based). **Programs:** Federal Direct (Subsidized and Unsubsidized Stafford, PLUS), Perkins.

WORK-STUDY Federal work-study: 822 jobs averaging $2484. **State or other work-study/employment:** Part-time jobs available.

ATHLETIC AWARDS Total amount: $7,474,836 (100% non-need-based).

APPLYING FOR FINANCIAL AID Required financial aid forms: FAFSA, state aid form. **Financial aid deadline (priority):** 12/15. **Notification date:** Continuous beginning 2/15. Students must reply by 5/1 or within 2 weeks of notification.

CONTACT Mrs. Maryanne Twomey, Director for Institutional Programs and Research, St. John's University, 8000 Utopia Parkway, Queens, NY 11439, 718-990-2000 or toll-free 888-9STJOHNS. Fax: 718-990-5945. E-mail: studentfinancialserv@stjohns.edu.
Website: http://www.stjohns.edu/.

ST. JOHN'S UNIVERSITY
Queens, NY

Tuition & fees: $40,520	Average undergraduate aid package: $28,656

ABOUT THE INSTITUTION Independent Roman Catholic Church, coed. **Awards:** certificates, bachelor's, master's, and doctoral degrees. 66 undergraduate majors. **Total enrollment:** 21,346. Undergraduates: 16,766. Freshmen: 2,967. Institutional methodology is used as a basis for awarding need-based institutional aid.

UNDERGRADUATE EXPENSES for 2017–2018 One-time required fee: $250. **Comprehensive fee:** $57,540 includes full-time tuition ($39,690), mandatory fees ($830), and room and board ($17,020). **College room only:** $10,670. Full-time tuition and fees vary according to course load, location, program, reciprocity agreements, and student level. Room and board charges vary according to board plan, housing facility, and location. **Part-time tuition:** $1323 per credit. **Part-time fees:** $312.50 per term. Part-time tuition and fees vary according to course load, location, program, and student level.

FRESHMAN FINANCIAL AID (Fall 2016) 2,904 applied for aid; of those 90% were deemed to have need. 100% of freshmen with need received aid; of those 16% had need fully met. **Average percent of need met:** 74% (excluding resources awarded to replace EFC). **Average financial aid package:** $30,684 (excluding resources awarded to replace EFC). 9% of all full-time freshmen had no need and received non-need-based gift aid.

UNDERGRADUATE FINANCIAL AID (Fall 2016) 9,639 applied for aid; of those 93% were deemed to have need. 100% of undergraduates with need received aid; of those 12% had need fully met. **Average percent of need met:** 66% (excluding resources awarded to replace EFC). **Average financial aid package:** $28,656 (excluding resources awarded to replace EFC). 6% of all full-time undergraduates had no need and received non-need-based gift aid.

GIFT AID (NEED-BASED) Total amount: $57,776,521 (39% federal, 22% state, 39% institutional). **Receiving aid:** Freshmen: 60% (1,930); all full-time undergraduates: 59% (6,809). **Average award:** Freshmen: $8770; Undergraduates: $8725. **Scholarships, grants, and awards:** Federal Pell, FSEOG, state, private, college/university gift aid from institutional funds.

ST. JOHN VIANNEY COLLEGE SEMINARY
Miami, FL

CONTACT Ms. Bonnie DeAngulo, Director of Financial Aid, St. John Vianney College Seminary, 2900 Southwest 87th Avenue, Miami, FL 33165-3244, 305-223-4561 Ext. 10. Website: http://www.sjvcs.edu/.

ST. JOSEPH'S COLLEGE, LONG ISLAND CAMPUS
Patchogue, NY

Tuition & fees: $26,560	Average undergraduate aid package: $13,862

ABOUT THE INSTITUTION Independent, coed. **Awards:** certificates, bachelor's, and master's degrees. 41 undergraduate majors. **Total enrollment:** 3,966. Undergraduates: 3,059. Freshmen: 402. Federal methodology is used as a basis for awarding need-based institutional aid.

UNDERGRADUATE EXPENSES for 2017–2018 Application fee: $25. **Tuition:** full-time $25,930; part-time $840 per credit. Full-time tuition and fees vary according to course load, location, and program. Part-time tuition and fees vary according to course load, location, and program.

FRESHMAN FINANCIAL AID (Fall 2016) 413 applied for aid; of those 81% were deemed to have need. 100% of freshmen with need received aid; of those 38% had need fully met. **Average percent of need met:** 73% (excluding resources awarded to replace EFC). **Average financial aid package:** $17,996 (excluding resources awarded to replace EFC). 18% of all full-time freshmen had no need and received non-need-based gift aid.

UNDERGRADUATE FINANCIAL AID (Fall 2016) 2,465 applied for aid; of those 80% were deemed to have need. 99% of undergraduates with need received aid; of those 28% had need fully met. **Average percent of need met:** 63% (excluding

resources awarded to replace EFC). *Average financial aid package:* $13,862 (excluding resources awarded to replace EFC). 15% of all full-time undergraduates had no need and received non-need-based gift aid.

GIFT AID (NEED-BASED) *Total amount:* $23,337,214 (23% federal, 10% state, 67% institutional). *Receiving aid:* Freshmen: 79% (329); all full-time undergraduates: 69% (1,891). *Average award:* Freshmen: $14,007; Undergraduates: $11,540. *Scholarships, grants, and awards:* Federal Pell, FSEOG, state, private, college/university gift aid from institutional funds.

GIFT AID (NON-NEED-BASED) *Total amount:* $4,473,213 (2% state, 93% institutional, 5% external sources). *Receiving aid:* Freshmen: 77% (321). Undergraduates: 62% (1,705). *Average award:* Freshmen: $10,836. Undergraduates: $9494. *Scholarships, grants, and awards by category: Academic interests/ achievement:* 1,909 awards ($16,233,351 total): general academic interests/achievements. *Special achievements/activities:* 1 award ($1250 total): community service, leadership. *Special characteristics:* 225 awards ($642,221 total): children and siblings of alumni, children of faculty/staff, parents of current students, public servants, siblings of current students, spouses of current students, twins. *Tuition waivers:* Full or partial for employees or children of employees. *ROTC:* Army cooperative.

LOANS *Student loans:* $13,319,195 (89% need-based, 11% non-need-based). 65% of past graduating class borrowed through all loan programs. *Average indebtedness per student:* $30,358. *Average need-based loan:* Freshmen: $3070. Undergraduates: $4294. *Parent loans:* $4,038,248 (86% need-based, 14% non-need-based). *Programs:* Federal Direct (Subsidized and Unsubsidized Stafford, PLUS), Perkins.

WORK-STUDY *Federal work-study:* 93 jobs averaging $2568. *State or other work-study/employment:* Total amount: $313,425 (65% need-based, 35% non-need-based). 89 part-time jobs averaging $3697.

APPLYING FOR FINANCIAL AID *Required financial aid forms:* FAFSA, state aid form. *Financial aid deadline (priority):* 2/25. *Notification date:* Continuous beginning 3/15. Students must reply by 5/1 or within 2 weeks of notification.

CONTACT Amy Thompson, Director of Financial Aid, St. Joseph's College, Long Island Campus, 155 West Roe Boulevard, Patchogue, NY 11772-2399, 631-687-2600. *Fax:* 631-650-2525. *E-mail:* financialaid.li@sjcny.edu.

Website: http://www.sjcny.edu/.

ST. JOSEPH'S COLLEGE, NEW YORK
Brooklyn, NY

Tuition & fees: $26,550	Average undergraduate aid package: $17,201

ABOUT THE INSTITUTION Independent, coed. *Awards:* certificates, bachelor's, and master's degrees. 41 undergraduate majors. *Total enrollment:* 1,176. Undergraduates: 929. Freshmen: 172. Federal methodology is used as a basis for awarding need-based institutional aid.

UNDERGRADUATE EXPENSES for 2017–2018 *Application fee:* $25. *Tuition:* full-time $25,930; part-time $840 per credit. Full-time tuition and fees vary according to course load and program. Part-time tuition and fees vary according to course load and program.

FRESHMAN FINANCIAL AID (Fall 2016) 195 applied for aid; of those 89% were deemed to have need. 99% of freshmen with need received aid; of those 24% had need fully met. *Average percent of need met:* 71% (excluding resources awarded to replace EFC). *Average financial aid package:* $18,764 (excluding resources awarded to replace EFC). 11% of all full-time freshmen had no need and received non-need-based gift aid.

UNDERGRADUATE FINANCIAL AID (Fall 2016) 761 applied for aid; of those 85% were deemed to have need. 99% of undergraduates with need received aid; of those 19% had need fully met. *Average percent of need met:* 66% (excluding resources awarded to replace EFC). *Average financial aid package:* $17,201 (excluding resources awarded to replace EFC). 13% of all full-time undergraduates had no need and received non-need-based gift aid.

GIFT AID (NEED-BASED) *Total amount:* $10,321,320 (30% federal, 12% state, 58% institutional). *Receiving aid:* Freshmen: 88% (172); all full-time undergraduates: 81% (634). *Average award:* Freshmen: $15,492; Undergraduates: $15,207. *Scholarships, grants, and awards:* Federal Pell, FSEOG, state, private, college/university gift aid from institutional funds.

GIFT AID (NON-NEED-BASED) *Total amount:* $1,377,025 (3% state, 89% institutional, 8% external sources). *Receiving aid:* Freshmen: 87% (169). Undergrad-

uates: 75% (585). *Average award:* Freshmen: $11,755. Undergraduates: $11,591. *Scholarships, grants, and awards by category: Academic interests/ achievement:* 417 awards ($3,776,158 total): general academic interests/achievements. *Special achievements/activities:* community service, leadership. *Special characteristics:* 63 awards ($110,034 total): children and siblings of alumni, children of faculty/staff, parents of current students, public servants, siblings of current students, spouses of current students, twins. *Tuition waivers:* Full or partial for employees or children of employees.

LOANS *Student loans:* $3,517,023 (92% need-based, 8% non-need-based). 54% of past graduating class borrowed through all loan programs. *Average indebtedness per student:* $21,123. *Average need-based loan:* Freshmen: $2764. Undergraduates: $3825. *Parent loans:* $1,096,795 (88% need-based, 12% non-need-based). *Programs:* Federal Direct (Subsidized and Unsubsidized Stafford, PLUS), Perkins.

WORK-STUDY *Federal work-study:* 96 jobs averaging $2594. *State or other work-study/employment:* Total amount: $18,829 (100% need-based). Part-time jobs available.

APPLYING FOR FINANCIAL AID *Required financial aid forms:* FAFSA, state aid form. *Financial aid deadline (priority):* 2/25. *Notification date:* Continuous beginning 3/15. Students must reply by 5/1 or within 2 weeks of notification.

CONTACT Ms. Amy Thompson, Director of Financial Aid, St. Joseph's College, New York, 245 Clinton Avenue, Brooklyn, NY 11205-3688, 718-940-5700. *Fax:* 718-636-6827. *E-mail:* financialaid.bk@sjcny.edu.

Website: http://www.sjcny.edu/.

SAINT JOSEPH'S COLLEGE OF MAINE
Standish, ME

CONTACT Office of Financial Aid, Saint Joseph's College of Maine, 278 Whites Bridge Road, Standish, ME 04084-5263, 800-752-1266 or toll-free 800-338-7057. *Fax:* 207-893-6699. *E-mail:* finaid@sjcme.edu.

Website: http://www.sjcme.edu/.

SAINT JOSEPH SEMINARY COLLEGE
Saint Benedict, LA

CONTACT Katie F. Plude, Director of Student Financial Aid, Saint Joseph Seminary College, 75376 River Road, Saint Benedict, LA 70457, 985-867-2248. *Fax:* 985-867-2270. *E-mail:* kplude@sjasc.edu.

Website: http://www.sjasc.edu/.

SAINT JOSEPH'S UNIVERSITY
Philadelphia, PA

Tuition & fees: $43,880	Average undergraduate aid package: $29,634

ABOUT THE INSTITUTION Independent Roman Catholic (Jesuit), coed. *Awards:* certificates, associate, bachelor's, master's, and doctoral degrees. 70 undergraduate majors. *Total enrollment:* 8,086. Undergraduates: 5,145. Freshmen: 1,077. Federal methodology is used as a basis for awarding need-based institutional aid.

UNDERGRADUATE EXPENSES for 2017–2018 *Application fee:* $50. *Comprehensive fee:* $58,720 includes full-time tuition ($43,700), mandatory fees ($180), and room and board ($14,840). *College room only:* $9424. Full-time tuition and fees vary according to course load. Room and board charges vary according to board plan and housing facility. *Part-time tuition:* $584 per credit. Part-time tuition and fees vary according to course load.

FRESHMAN FINANCIAL AID (Fall 2017, est.) 927 applied for aid; of those 80% were deemed to have need. 100% of freshmen with need received aid; of those 23% had need fully met. *Average percent of need met:* 79% (excluding resources awarded to replace EFC). *Average financial aid package:* $30,645 (excluding resources awarded to replace EFC). 25% of all full-time freshmen had no need and received non-need-based gift aid.

UNDERGRADUATE FINANCIAL AID (Fall 2017, est.) 3,100 applied for aid, of those 84% were deemed to have need. 100% of undergraduates with need received aid; of those 23% had need fully met. *Average percent of need met:* 76% (excluding resources awarded to replace EFC). *Average financial aid package:* $29,634 (excluding resources awarded to replace EFC). 33% of all full-time undergraduates had no need and received non-need-based gift aid.

GIFT AID (NEED-BASED) *Total amount:* $66,293,563 (5% federal, 2% state, 92% institutional, 1% external sources). *Receiving aid:* Freshmen: 68% (727); all full-time undergraduates: 58% (2,585). *Average award:* Freshmen: $24,981; Undergraduates: $23,091. *Scholarships, grants, and awards:* Federal Pell, FSEOG, state, private, college/university gift aid from institutional funds, United Negro College Fund.

GIFT AID (NON-NEED-BASED) *Total amount:* $25,914,671 (97% institutional, 3% external sources). *Receiving aid:* Freshmen: 12% (124). Undergraduates: 8% (376). *Average award:* Freshmen: $15,594. Undergraduates: $13,435. *Scholarships, grants, and awards by category: Academic interests/achievement:* biological sciences, computer science, general academic interests/achievements, mathematics, physical sciences, premedicine. *Creative arts/performance:* debating, general creative arts/performance, theater/drama. *Special achievements/activities:* community service, general special achievements/activities. *Special characteristics:* children and siblings of alumni, children of faculty/staff, members of minority groups, siblings of current students, veterans, veterans' children. *Tuition waivers:* Full or partial for employees or children of employees. *ROTC:* Army cooperative, Naval cooperative, Air Force.

LOANS *Student loans:* $30,849,951 (58% need-based, 42% non-need-based). *Average need-based loan:* Freshmen: $3377. Undergraduates: $4441. *Parent loans:* $14,905,079 (40% need-based, 60% non-need-based). *Programs:* Federal Direct (Subsidized and Unsubsidized Stafford, PLUS).

WORK-STUDY *Federal work-study:* Total amount: $2,022,382; jobs available.

ATHLETIC AWARDS Total amount: $7,143,940 (37% need-based, 63% non-need-based).

APPLYING FOR FINANCIAL AID *Required financial aid form:* FAFSA. *Financial aid deadline (priority):* 12/1. *Notification date:* Continuous beginning 3/31. Students must reply by 5/1.

CONTACT Elizabeth Rihl Lewinsky, Director of Financial Aid, Saint Joseph's University, 5600 City Avenue, Philadelphia, PA 19131-1395, 610-660-1346 or toll-free 888-BE-A-HAWK (in-state), 800-BE-A-HAWK (out-of-state). *Fax:* 610-660-1342. *E-mail:* lewinsky@sju.edu.
Website: http://www.sju.edu/.

ST. LAWRENCE UNIVERSITY
Canton, NY

Tuition & fees: $54,846	Average undergraduate aid package: $44,793

ABOUT THE INSTITUTION Independent, coed. *Awards:* certificates, bachelor's, and master's degrees. 34 undergraduate majors. *Total enrollment:* 2,493. Undergraduates: 2,414. Freshmen: 695. Both federal and institutional methodology are used as a basis for awarding need-based institutional aid.

UNDERGRADUATE EXPENSES for 2018–2019 *Application fee:* $60. *Comprehensive fee:* $68,980 includes full-time tuition ($54,454), mandatory fees ($392), and room and board ($14,134). *College room only:* $7614. Room and board charges vary according to board plan. *Payment plan:* Tuition prepayment.

FRESHMAN FINANCIAL AID (Fall 2017, est.) 540 applied for aid; of those 87% were deemed to have need. 100% of freshmen with need received aid; of those 22% had need fully met. *Average percent of need met:* 88% (excluding resources awarded to replace EFC). *Average financial aid package:* $45,856 (excluding resources awarded to replace EFC). 30% of all full-time freshmen had no need and received non-need-based gift aid.

UNDERGRADUATE FINANCIAL AID (Fall 2017, est.) 1,813 applied for aid; of those 84% were deemed to have need. 100% of undergraduates with need received aid; of those 27% had need fully met. *Average percent of need met:* 87% (excluding resources awarded to replace EFC). *Average financial aid package:* $44,793 (excluding resources awarded to replace EFC). 33% of all full-time undergraduates had no need and received non-need-based gift aid.

GIFT AID (NEED-BASED) *Total amount:* $55,490,557 (4% federal, 3% state, 93% institutional). *Receiving aid:* Freshmen: 68% (472); all full-time undergraduates: 64% (1,526). *Average award:* Freshmen: $39,769; Undergraduates: $37,572. *Schol-

urships, grants, and awards:* Federal Pell, FSEOG, state, private, college/university gift aid from institutional funds.

GIFT AID (NON-NEED-BASED) *Total amount:* $19,286,472 (89% institutional, 11% external sources). *Receiving aid:* Freshmen: 53% (371). Undergraduates: 47% (1,110). *Average award:* Freshmen: $18,541. Undergraduates: $18,912. *Scholarships, grants, and awards by category: Academic interests/achievement:* general academic interests/achievements. *Special achievements/activities:* community service, leadership. *Special characteristics:* children and siblings of alumni, siblings of current students, veterans' children. *Tuition waivers:* Full or partial for employees or children of employees. *ROTC:* Army cooperative, Air Force cooperative.

LOANS *Student loans:* $11,798,603 (45% need-based, 55% non-need-based). 60% of past graduating class borrowed through all loan programs. *Average indebtedness per student:* $32,627. *Average need-based loan:* Freshmen: $3364. Undergraduates: $4492. *Parent loans:* $3,886,913 (100% non-need-based). *Programs:* Federal Direct (Subsidized and Unsubsidized Stafford, PLUS), Perkins, college/university.

WORK-STUDY *Federal work-study:* Total amount: $1,477,662; 905 jobs averaging $1633. *State or other work-study/employment:* Total amount: $486,967 (100% non-need-based). 297 part-time jobs averaging $1640.

ATHLETIC AWARDS Total amount: $2,256,132 (100% non-need-based).

APPLYING FOR FINANCIAL AID *Required financial aid forms:* FAFSA, noncustodial (divorced/separated) parent's statement. *Financial aid deadline:* 2/1. *Notification date:* 3/20. Students must reply by 5/1 or within 2 weeks of notification.

CONTACT Mrs. Patricia J.B. Farmer, Director of Financial Aid, St. Lawrence University, Payson Hall, 23 Romoda Drive, Canton, NY 13617-1455, 315-229-5265 or toll-free 800-285-1856. *Fax:* 315-229-7418. *E-mail:* pfarmer@stlawu.edu. *Website:* http://www.stlawu.edu/.

SAINT LEO UNIVERSITY
Saint Leo, FL

Tuition & fees: $21,970	Average undergraduate aid package: $22,237

ABOUT THE INSTITUTION Independent Roman Catholic, coed. *Awards:* certificates, associate, bachelor's, master's, and doctoral degrees. 34 undergraduate majors. *Total enrollment:* 5,898. Undergraduates: 2,264. Freshmen: 610. Federal methodology is used as a basis for awarding need-based institutional aid.

UNDERGRADUATE EXPENSES for 2017–2018 *Application fee:* $40. *Comprehensive fee:* $32,540 includes full-time tuition ($21,600), mandatory fees ($370), and room and board ($10,570). *College room only:* $5620. Room and board charges vary according to board plan and housing facility.

FRESHMAN FINANCIAL AID (Fall 2017, est.) 476 applied for aid; of those 89% were deemed to have need. 100% of freshmen with need received aid; of those 16% had need fully met. *Average percent of need met:* 74% (excluding resources awarded to replace EFC). *Average financial aid package:* $22,815 (excluding resources awarded to replace EFC). 20% of all full-time freshmen had no need and received non-need-based gift aid.

UNDERGRADUATE FINANCIAL AID (Fall 2017, est.) 1,690 applied for aid; of those 89% were deemed to have need. 100% of undergraduates with need received aid; of those 18% had need fully met. *Average percent of need met:* 73% (excluding resources awarded to replace EFC). *Average financial aid package:* $22,237 (excluding resources awarded to replace EFC). 25% of all full-time undergraduates had no need and received non-need-based gift aid.

GIFT AID (NEED-BASED) *Total amount:* $24,073,782 (21% federal, 19% state, 58% institutional, 2% external sources). *Receiving aid:* Freshmen: 80% (426); all full-time undergraduates: 73% (1,494). *Average award:* Freshmen: $18,309; Undergraduates: $16,931. *Scholarships, grants, and awards:* Federal Pell, FSEOG, state, private, college/university gift aid from institutional funds, United Negro College Fund.

GIFT AID (NON-NEED-BASED) *Total amount:* $5,245,995 (14% state, 76% institutional, 10% external sources). *Receiving aid:* Freshmen: 5% (29). Undergraduates: 4% (90). *Average award:* Freshmen: $6854. Undergraduates: $7317. *Scholarships, grants, and awards by category: Academic interests/achievement:* $11,218,437 total: business, general academic interests/achievements, military science. *Special achievements/activities:* $331,226 total: leadership, religious involvement. *Special characteristics:* $30,500 total: siblings of current students. *Tuition waivers:* Full or partial for employees or children of employees. *ROTC:* Army, Air Force.

LOANS *Student loans:* $13,280,711 (77% need-based, 23% non-need-based). 73% of past graduating class borrowed through all loan programs. *Average indebtedness per student:* $40,359. *Average need-based loan:* Freshmen: $3336. Undergraduates: $4111. *Parent loans:* $4,067,530 (73% need-based, 27% non-need-based). *Programs:* Federal Direct (Subsidized and Unsubsidized Stafford, PLUS), state.

WORK-STUDY *Federal work-study:* Total amount: $1,808,057; 425 jobs averaging $4254. *State or other work-study/employment:* Total amount: $22,300 (100% need-based). 5 part-time jobs averaging $4460.

ATHLETIC AWARDS Total amount: $3,064,226 (34% need-based, 66% non-need-based).

APPLYING FOR FINANCIAL AID *Required financial aid forms:* FAFSA, state aid form. *Financial aid deadline:* Continuous. *Notification date:* Continuous beginning 12/1.

CONTACT Ms. Melinda Clark, Associate Vice President of Financial Aid, Saint Leo University, PO Box 6665, MC 2228, Saint Leo, FL 33574-6665, 800-240-7658 or toll-free 800-334-5532. *Fax:* 866-708-7770. *E-mail:* finaid@saintleo.edu. *Website:* http://www.saintleo.edu/.

SAINT LOUIS CHRISTIAN COLLEGE
Florissant, MO

CONTACT Mrs. Catherine Wilhoit, Director of Financial Aid, Saint Louis Christian College, 1360 Grandview Drive, Florissant, MO 63033-6499, 314-837-6777 Ext. 1101 or toll-free 800-887-SLCC. *Fax:* 314-837-8291. *Website:* http://www.stlchristian.edu/.

ST. LOUIS COLLEGE OF PHARMACY
St. Louis, MO

Tuition & fees: $30,010	Average undergraduate aid package: $17,366

ABOUT THE INSTITUTION Independent, coed. *Awards:* bachelor's and doctoral degrees. 2 undergraduate majors. *Total enrollment:* 1,309. Undergraduates: 448. Freshmen: 106. Federal methodology is used as a basis for awarding need-based institutional aid.

UNDERGRADUATE EXPENSES for 2018–2019 *Application fee:* $55. *Comprehensive fee:* $42,295 includes full-time tuition ($28,450), mandatory fees ($1560), and room and board ($12,285). *College room only:* $6685. Full-time tuition and fees vary according to program and student level. Room and board charges vary according to board plan and housing facility. *Part-time tuition:* $1015 per credit hour. *Part-time fees:* $1560 per year.

FRESHMAN FINANCIAL AID (Fall 2016) 109 applied for aid; of those 94% were deemed to have need. 100% of freshmen with need received aid; of those 19% had need fully met. *Average percent of need met:* 52% (excluding resources awarded to replace EFC). *Average financial aid package:* $17,193 (excluding resources awarded to replace EFC). 15% of all full-time freshmen had no need and received non-need-based gift aid.

UNDERGRADUATE FINANCIAL AID (Fall 2016) 453 applied for aid; of those 91% were deemed to have need. 100% of undergraduates with need received aid; of those 12% had need fully met. *Average percent of need met:* 49% (excluding resources awarded to replace EFC). *Average financial aid package:* $17,366 (excluding resources awarded to replace EFC). 16% of all full-time undergraduates had no need and received non-need-based gift aid.

GIFT AID (NEED-BASED) *Total amount:* $4,796,605 (19% federal, 5% state, 71% institutional, 5% external sources). *Receiving aid:* Freshmen: 82% (98); all full-time undergraduates: 71% (377). *Average award:* Freshmen: $13,793; Undergraduates: $12,993. *Scholarships, grants, and awards:* Federal Pell, FSEOG, state, private, college/university gift aid from institutional funds.

GIFT AID (NON-NEED-BASED) *Total amount:* $1,327,918 (3% state, 90% institutional, 7% external sources). *Receiving aid:* Freshmen: 12% (14). Undergraduates: 6% (32). *Average award:* Freshmen: $12,781. Undergraduates: $12,128. *Scholarships, grants, and awards by category:* Academic interests/achievement: 442 awards ($4,808,032 total): general academic interests/achievements. *Special achievements/activities:* 20 awards ($59,150 total): community service, general

---

special achievements/activities, leadership. *Special characteristics:* 1 award ($27,400 total): children of faculty/staff. *Tuition waivers:* Full or partial for employees or children of employees. *ROTC:* Army cooperative, Naval cooperative, Air Force cooperative.

LOANS *Student loans:* $5,690,876 (78% need-based, 22% non-need-based). 86% of past graduating class borrowed through all loan programs. *Average need-based loan:* Freshmen: $4769. Undergraduates: $5779. *Parent loans:* $2,160,071 (64% need-based, 36% non-need-based). *Programs:* Federal Direct (Subsidized and Unsubsidized Stafford, PLUS), Perkins, Health Professions Student Loans (HPSL).

WORK-STUDY *Federal work-study:* 138 jobs averaging $951. *State or other work-study/employment:* Part-time jobs available.

ATHLETIC AWARDS Total amount: $194,552 (75% need-based, 25% non-need-based).

APPLYING FOR FINANCIAL AID *Required financial aid form:* FAFSA. *Financial aid deadline (priority):* 3/15. *Notification date:* Continuous beginning 3/15. Students must reply within 2 weeks of notification.

CONTACT Mr. Dan Stiffler, Director of Financial Aid, St. Louis College of Pharmacy, 4588 Parkview Place, St. Louis, MO 63110, 314-367-8700 Ext. 4001 or toll-free 800-278-5267. *Fax:* 314-446-8310. *E-mail:* financialaid@stlcop.edu. *Website:* http://www.stlcop.edu/.

SAINT LOUIS UNIVERSITY
St. Louis, MO

Tuition & fees: $42,166	Average undergraduate aid package: $29,810

ABOUT THE INSTITUTION Independent Roman Catholic (Jesuit), coed. *Awards:* certificates, bachelor's, master's, and doctoral degrees. 75 undergraduate majors. *Total enrollment:* 12,098. Undergraduates: 7,411. Freshmen: 1,633. Federal methodology is used as a basis for awarding need-based institutional aid.

UNDERGRADUATE EXPENSES for 2017–2018 *Comprehensive fee:* $53,162 includes full-time tuition ($41,540), mandatory fees ($626), and room and board ($10,996). *College room only:* $6124. Full-time tuition and fees vary according to course load, degree level, location, and program. Room and board charges vary according to board plan, housing facility, and location. *Part-time tuition:* $1450 per credit hour. *Part-time fees:* $198 per term. Part-time tuition and fees vary according to course load, degree level, location, and program.

FRESHMAN FINANCIAL AID (Fall 2016) 1,246 applied for aid; of those 77% were deemed to have need. 100% of freshmen with need received aid; of those 51% had need fully met. *Average percent of need met:* 86% (excluding resources awarded to replace EFC). *Average financial aid package:* $32,013 (excluding resources awarded to replace EFC). 33% of all full-time freshmen had no need and received non-need-based gift aid.

UNDERGRADUATE FINANCIAL AID (Fall 2016) 4,715 applied for aid; of those 85% were deemed to have need. 100% of undergraduates with need received aid; of those 34% had need fully met. *Average percent of need met:* 78% (excluding resources awarded to replace EFC). *Average financial aid package:* $29,810 (excluding resources awarded to replace EFC). 34% of all full-time undergraduates had no need and received non-need-based gift aid.

GIFT AID (NEED-BASED) *Total amount:* $107,963,969 (10% federal, 2% state, 86% institutional, 2% external sources). *Receiving aid:* Freshmen: 60% (932); all full-time undergraduates: 51% (3,796). *Average award:* Freshmen: $34,048; Undergraduates: $27,300. *Scholarships, grants, and awards:* Federal Pell, FSEOG, state, private, college/university gift aid from institutional funds, Federal Nursing.

GIFT AID (NON-NEED-BASED) *Total amount:* $38,513,187 (9% federal, 2% state, 65% institutional, 24% external sources). *Receiving aid:* Freshmen: 11% (166). Undergraduates: 8% (560). *Average award:* Freshmen: $19,212. Undergraduates: $17,447. *Scholarships, grants, and awards by category:* Academic interests/achievement: 5,719 awards ($88,049,862 total): agriculture, area/ethnic studies, biological sciences, business, communication, computer science, education, engineering/technologies, English, foreign languages, general academic interests/achievements, home economics, humanities, international studies, mathematics, military science, physical sciences, premedicine, religion/biblical studies, social sciences. *Creative arts/performance:* 156 awards ($258,565 total): art/fine arts, music, performing arts, theater/drama. *Special achievements/activities:* 690 awards ($7,026,263 total): cheerleading/drum major, community service, general special achievements/activities, leadership, memberships, religious involvement. *Special characteristics:* 1,460 awards

---

($20,998,731 total); children of faculty/staff, first generation college students, international students, members of minority groups, previous college experience, religious affiliation, siblings of current students, spouses of current students, veterans. *Tuition waivers:* Full or partial for employees or children of employees. *ROTC:* Army cooperative, Air Force.

LOANS *Student loans:* $41,663,558 (36% need-based, 64% non-need-based). 55% of past graduating class borrowed through all loan programs. *Average indebtedness per student:* $21,292. *Average need-based loan:* Freshmen: $3365. Undergraduates: $5303. *Parent loans:* $13,261,256 (100% non-need-based). *Programs:* Federal Direct (Subsidized and Unsubsidized Stafford, PLUS), Federal Nursing, state, college/university.

WORK-STUDY *Federal work-study:* 638 jobs averaging $1762. *State or other work-study/employment:* Total amount: $539,933 (100% non-need-based). 231 part-time jobs averaging $2337.

ATHLETIC AWARDS Total amount: $5,533,715 (29% need-based, 71% non-need-based).

APPLYING FOR FINANCIAL AID *Required financial aid form:* FAFSA. *Financial aid deadline (priority):* 2/1. *Notification date:* Continuous beginning 2/1. Students must reply by 5/1 or within 4 weeks of notification.

CONTACT Cari S. Wickliffe, Director of Student Financial Services, Saint Louis University, One Grand Boulevard, DuBourg Hall, Room 121, St. Louis, MO 63103, 314-977-2350 or toll-free 800-758-3678. *Fax:* 314-977-3437. *E-mail:* sfs@slu.edu. *Website:* http://www.slu.edu/.

SAINT LUKE'S COLLEGE OF HEALTH SCIENCES
Kansas City, MO

Tuition & fees: N/R	Average undergraduate aid package: $13,000

ABOUT THE INSTITUTION Independent Episcopal, coed, primarily women. 1 undergraduate major. Both federal and institutional methodology are used as a basis for awarding need-based institutional aid.

UNDERGRADUATE FINANCIAL AID (Fall 2016) 373 applied for aid; of those 99% were deemed to have need. 100% of undergraduates with need received aid; of those 5% had need fully met. *Average percent of need met:* 60% (excluding resources awarded to replace EFC). *Average financial aid package:* $13,000 (excluding resources awarded to replace EFC).

GIFT AID (NEED-BASED) *Total amount:* $924,811 (57% federal, 14% state, 29% institutional). *Receiving aid:* All full-time undergraduates: 47% (232). *Average award:* Undergraduates: $2000. *Scholarships, grants, and awards:* Federal Pell, FSEOG, state, private, college/university gift aid from institutional funds.

GIFT AID (NON-NEED-BASED) *Total amount:* $124,798 (100% external sources). *Receiving aid:* Undergraduates: 6% (29).

LOANS *Average need-based loan:* Undergraduates: $5500. *Parent loans:* $864,881 (100% non-need-based). *Programs:* Federal Direct (Subsidized and Unsubsidized Stafford, PLUS), Perkins, Federal Nursing, college/university.

WORK-STUDY *Federal work-study:* 8 jobs averaging $2200.

APPLYING FOR FINANCIAL AID *Required financial aid form:* FAFSA. *Financial aid deadline:* Continuous. *Notification date:* Continuous beginning 4/1.

CONTACT Jennifer Wright, Director of Financial Aid, Saint Luke's College of Health Sciences, 624 Westport Road, Kansas City, MO 64111, 816-936-8730. *Fax:* 816-936-8760. *E-mail:* finaid@saintlukescollege.edu. *Website:* http://www.saintlukescollege.edu/.

SAINT MARTIN'S UNIVERSITY
Lacey, WA

Tuition & fees: $37,356	Average undergraduate aid package: $27,128

ABOUT THE INSTITUTION Independent Roman Catholic, coed. *Awards:* certificates, bachelor's, and master's degrees. 26 undergraduate majors. *Total*

enrollment: 1,565. Undergraduates: 1,310. Freshmen: 278. Federal methodology is used as a basis for awarding need-based institutional aid.

UNDERGRADUATE EXPENSES for 2018–2019 *Comprehensive fee:* $48,801 includes full-time tuition ($36,950), mandatory fees ($406), and room and board ($11,445). *College room only:* $5550. Full-time tuition and fees vary according to degree level, location, and program. Room and board charges vary according to board plan and housing facility. *Part-time tuition:* $1240 per credit. Part-time tuition and fees vary according to course load, degree level, location, and program.

FRESHMAN FINANCIAL AID (Fall 2016) 164 applied for aid; of those 89% were deemed to have need. 100% of freshmen with need received aid; of those 23% had need fully met. *Average percent of need met:* 78% (excluding resources awarded to replace EFC). *Average financial aid package:* $28,575 (excluding resources awarded to replace EFC). 15% of all full-time freshmen had no need and received non-need-based gift aid.

UNDERGRADUATE FINANCIAL AID (Fall 2016) 869 applied for aid; of those 92% were deemed to have need. 100% of undergraduates with need received aid; of those 22% had need fully met. *Average percent of need met:* 76% (excluding resources awarded to replace EFC). *Average financial aid package:* $27,128 (excluding resources awarded to replace EFC). 14% of all full-time undergraduates had no need and received non-need-based gift aid.

GIFT AID (NEED-BASED) *Total amount:* $17,943,858 (12% federal, 13% state, 60% institutional, 15% external sources). *Receiving aid:* Freshmen: 83% (146); all full-time undergraduates: 83% (793). *Average award:* Freshmen: $26,248; Undergraduates: $24,061. *Scholarships, grants, and awards:* Federal Pell, FSEOG, state, private, college/university gift aid from institutional funds.

GIFT AID (NON-NEED-BASED) *Total amount:* $2,908,295 (3% state, 80% institutional, 17% external sources). *Receiving aid:* Freshmen: 14% (25). Undergraduates: 14% (134). *Average award:* Freshmen: $15,645. Undergraduates: $13,883. *Scholarships, grants, and awards by category:* Academic interests/achievement: business, education, engineering/technologies, general academic interests/achievements, international studies, premedicine. *Creative arts/performance:* music, theater/drama. *Special achievements/activities:* community service, general special achievements/activities, hobbies/interests, leadership, religious involvement. *Special characteristics:* children and siblings of alumni, children of faculty/staff, ethnic background, general special characteristics, international students, local/state students, members of minority groups, out-of-state students, siblings of current students, veterans, veterans' children. *Tuition waivers:* Full or partial for children of alumni, employees or children of employees. *ROTC:* Army cooperative, Air Force cooperative.

LOANS *Student loans:* $5,985,412 (75% need-based, 25% non-need-based). 80% of past graduating class borrowed through all loan programs. *Average indebtedness per student:* $30,744. *Average need-based loan:* Freshmen: $3016. Undergraduates: $4022. *Parent loans:* $1,667,540 (47% need-based, 53% non-need-based). *Programs:* Federal Direct (Subsidized and Unsubsidized Stafford, PLUS), Perkins, state, private loans.

WORK-STUDY *Federal work-study:* 132 jobs averaging $1647. *State or other work-study/employment:* Total amount: $29,288 (84% need-based, 16% non-need-based). 22 part-time jobs averaging $7506.

ATHLETIC AWARDS Total amount: $1,601,168 (56% need-based, 44% non-need-based).

APPLYING FOR FINANCIAL AID *Required financial aid form:* FAFSA. *Financial aid deadline (priority):* 1/15. *Notification date:* Continuous beginning 11/21. Students must reply within 3 weeks of notification.

CONTACT Mr. Michael Grosso, Director of Financial Aid, Saint Martin's University, 5000 Abbey Way SE, Lacey, WA 98503-7500, 360-438-4389 or toll-free 800-368-8803. *Fax:* 360-412-6190. *E-mail:* finaid@stmartin.edu. *Website:* http://www.stmartin.edu/.

SAINT MARY-OF-THE-WOODS COLLEGE
Saint Mary of the Woods, IN

Tuition & fees: $29,510	Average undergraduate aid package: $21,973

ABOUT THE INSTITUTION Independent Roman Catholic, coed, primarily women. *Awards:* certificates, associate, bachelor's, and master's degrees (also offers external degree program with significant enrollment not reflected in profile). 37 undergraduate majors. **Total enrollment:** 952. Undergraduates: 756. Freshmen: 135. Both federal and institutional methodology are used as a basis for awarding need-based institutional aid.

UNDERGRADUATE EXPENSES for 2018–2019 *Comprehensive fee:* $40,424 includes full-time tuition ($29,510) and room and board ($10,914). *College room only:* $6614. Full-time tuition and fees vary according to location, program, and student level. Room and board charges vary according to housing facility. *Part-time tuition:* $496 per credit hour. Part-time tuition and fees vary according to course load, location, program, and student level. *Payment plan:* Guaranteed tuition.

FRESHMAN FINANCIAL AID (Fall 2016) 77 applied for aid; of those 100% were deemed to have need. 100% of freshmen with need received aid. *Average financial aid package:* $28,166 (excluding resources awarded to replace EFC).

UNDERGRADUATE FINANCIAL AID (Fall 2016) 398 applied for aid; of those 100% were deemed to have need. 100% of undergraduates with need received aid. *Average financial aid package:* $21,973 (excluding resources awarded to replace EFC).

GIFT AID (NEED-BASED) *Total amount:* $7,201,353 (17% federal, 17% state, 65% institutional, 1% external sources). *Receiving aid:* Freshmen: 97% (77); all full-time undergraduates: 96% (392). *Average award:* Freshmen: $25,295; Undergraduates: $18,000. *Scholarships, grants, and awards:* Federal Pell, FSEOG, state, private, college/university gift aid from institutional funds.

GIFT AID (NON-NEED-BASED) *Total amount:* $315,554 (100% external sources). *Scholarships, grants, and awards by category:* Academic interests/achievement: general academic interests/achievements. Creative arts/performance: applied art and design, art/fine arts, creative writing, dance, general creative arts/performance, journalism/publications, performing arts. Special achievements/activities: community service, general special achievements/activities, memberships, religious involvement. Special characteristics: adult students, children and siblings of alumni, children of current students, children of faculty/staff, ethnic background, first-generation college students, general special characteristics, international students, out-of-state students, parents of current students, siblings of current students, spouses of current students. *Tuition waivers:* Full or partial for employees or children of employees. *ROTC:* Army cooperative, Naval cooperative, Air Force cooperative.

LOANS *Student loans:* $3,711,220 (37% need-based, 63% non-need-based). *Average need-based loan:* Freshmen: $3113. Undergraduates: $3987. *Parent loans:* $579,985 (100% non-need-based). *Programs:* Federal Direct (Subsidized and Unsubsidized Stafford, PLUS), Perkins.

WORK-STUDY *Federal work-study:* jobs available.

ATHLETIC AWARDS Total amount: $615,467 (100% need-based).

APPLYING FOR FINANCIAL AID *Required financial aid form:* FAFSA. *Financial aid deadline:* 3/10. *Notification date:* Continuous beginning 12/1. Students must reply by 5/1.

CONTACT Ms. Darla Hopper, Executive Director of Financial Aid, Saint Mary-of-the-Woods College, Rooney Library, 1 St Mary of Woods College, Saint Mary-of-the-Woods, IN 47876, 812-535-5110 or toll-free 800-926-SMWC. *Fax:* 812-535-4900. *E-mail:* dhopper@smwc.edu.
Website: http://www.smwc.edu/.

SAINT MARY'S COLLEGE
Notre Dame, IN

Tuition & fees: $40,800	Average undergraduate aid package: $35,934

ABOUT THE INSTITUTION Independent Roman Catholic, women only. **Awards:** bachelor's, master's, and doctoral degrees. 37 undergraduate majors. **Total enrollment:** 1,701. Undergraduates: 1,625. Freshmen: 427. Federal methodology is used as a basis for awarding need-based institutional aid.

UNDERGRADUATE EXPENSES for 2017–2018 *One-time required fee:* $150. *Comprehensive fee:* $52,900 includes full-time tuition ($39,980), mandatory fees ($820), and room and board ($12,100). *College room only:* $7500. Full-time tuition and fees vary according to course load. Room and board charges vary according to board plan and housing facility. *Part-time tuition:* $1500 per credit hour. Part-time tuition and fees vary according to course load.

FRESHMAN FINANCIAL AID (Fall 2017, est.) 347 applied for aid; of those 79% were deemed to have need. 100% of freshmen with need received aid; of those 17% had need fully met. *Average percent of need met:* 88% (excluding resources

awarded to replace EFC). *Average financial aid package:* $34,444 (excluding resources awarded to replace EFC). 20% of all full-time freshmen had no need and received non-need-based gift aid.

UNDERGRADUATE FINANCIAL AID (Fall 2017, est.) 1,475 applied for aid; of those 72% were deemed to have need. 100% of undergraduates with need received aid; of those 19% had need fully met. *Average percent of need met:* 86% (excluding resources awarded to replace EFC). *Average financial aid package:* $35,934 (excluding resources awarded to replace EFC). 27% of all full-time undergraduates had no need and received non-need-based gift aid.

GIFT AID (NEED-BASED) *Total amount:* $30,212,746 (6% federal, 4% state, 90% institutional). *Receiving aid:* Freshmen: 78% (272); all full-time undergraduates: 69% (1,030). *Average award:* Freshmen: $32,211; Undergraduates: $29,333. *Scholarships, grants, and awards:* Federal Pell, FSEOG, state, private, college/university gift aid from institutional funds.

GIFT AID (NON-NEED-BASED) *Total amount:* $6,016,805 (100% institutional). *Receiving aid:* Freshmen: 20% (71). Undergraduates: 27% (393). *Average award:* Freshmen: $17,246. Undergraduates: $15,305. *Scholarships, grants, and awards by category:* Academic interests/achievement: 1,405 awards ($33,207,242 total): general academic interests/achievements. Creative arts/performance: 12 awards ($16,000 total): music. Special characteristics: 55 awards ($211,347 total): siblings of current students, veterans. *Tuition waivers:* Full or partial for employees or children of employees. *ROTC:* Army cooperative, Naval cooperative, Air Force cooperative.

LOANS *Student loans:* $8,777,122 (91% need-based, 9% non-need-based). 71% of past graduating class borrowed through all loan programs. *Average indebtedness per student:* $33,698. *Average need-based loan:* Freshmen: $5464. Undergraduates: $6737. *Parent loans:* $3,555,010 (84% need-based, 16% non-need-based). *Programs:* Federal Direct (Subsidized and Unsubsidized Stafford, PLUS), Perkins.

WORK-STUDY *Federal work-study:* Total amount: $441,690; 275 jobs averaging $1606. *State or other work-study/employment:* Total amount: $2000 (100% need-based). 3 part-time jobs averaging $2000.

APPLYING FOR FINANCIAL AID *Required financial aid form:* FAFSA. *Financial aid deadline:* 3/1. *Notification date:* Continuous beginning 12/15.

CONTACT Kathleen M. Brown, Director of Financial Aid, Saint Mary's College, 141 Le Mans Hall, Notre Dame, IN 46556, 574-284-4557 or toll-free 800-551-7621. *Fax:* 574-284-4818. *E-mail:* kbrown@saintmarys.edu.
Website: http://www.saintmarys.edu/.

SAINT MARY'S COLLEGE OF CALIFORNIA
Moraga, CA

Tuition & fees: $47,280	Average undergraduate aid package: $31,609

ABOUT THE INSTITUTION Independent Roman Catholic, coed. **Awards:** bachelor's, master's, and doctoral degrees. 64 undergraduate majors. **Total enrollment:** 3,913. Undergraduates: 2,780. Entering class: 23. Federal methodology is used as a basis for awarding need-based institutional aid.

UNDERGRADUATE EXPENSES for 2018–2019 *Application fee:* $60. *Comprehensive fee:* $62,650 includes full-time tuition ($47,130), mandatory fees ($150), and room and board ($15,370). Room and board charges vary according to board plan and housing facility. *Part-time tuition:* $5906 per course. *Part-time fees:* $75 per term.

UNDERGRADUATE FINANCIAL AID (Fall 2016) 2,035 applied for aid; of those 89% were deemed to have need. 100% of undergraduates with need received aid; of those .2% had need fully met. *Average percent of need met:* 62% (excluding resources awarded to replace EFC). *Average financial aid package:* $31,609 (excluding resources awarded to replace EFC). 19% of all full-time undergraduates had no need and received non-need-based gift aid.

GIFT AID (NEED-BASED) *Total amount:* $43,184,211 (8% federal, 11% state, 80% institutional, 1% external sources). *Receiving aid:* Entering class: 67% (376); all full-time undergraduates: 66% (1,764). *Average award:* Freshmen: $26,247; Undergraduates: $24,496. *Scholarships, grants, and awards:* Federal Pell, FSEOG, state, private, college/university gift aid from institutional funds.

GIFT AID (NON-NEED-BASED) *Total amount:* $8,295,974 (99% institutional, 1% external sources). *Receiving aid:* Freshmen: 50% (282). Undergraduates: 40% (1,056). *Average award:* Freshmen: $17,608. Undergraduates: $16,842. *Scholar-*

ships, grants, and awards by category. Academic interests/achievement: English, general academic interests/achievements, humanities, international studies, mathematics, physical sciences, religion/biblical studies. Creative arts/performance: cinema/film/broadcasting, dance, debating, music, performing arts, theater/drama. Special achievements/activities: leadership, memberships. Special characteristics: children and siblings of alumni, children of educators, children of faculty/staff, general special characteristics, relatives of clergy, veterans, veterans' children. Tuition waivers: Full or partial for employees or children of employees. ROTC: Army cooperative.

LOANS Student loans: $16,333,405 (96% need-based, 4% non-need-based). 78% of past graduating class borrowed through all loan programs. Average indebtedness per student: $31,356. Average need-based loan: Freshmen: $6129. Undergraduates: $6353. Parent loans: $11,016,531 (97% need-based, 3% non-need-based). Programs: Federal Direct (Subsidized and Unsubsidized Stafford, PLUS), Perkins.

WORK-STUDY Federal work-study: jobs available.

ATHLETIC AWARDS Total amount: $5,969,738 (40% need-based, 60% non-need-based).

APPLYING FOR FINANCIAL AID Required financial aid form: FAFSA. Financial aid deadline (priority): 2/15. Notification date: Continuous beginning 12/16. Students must reply by 5/1 or within 2 weeks of notification.

CONTACT Wilbert Lleses, Dean of Financial Aid, Saint Mary's College of California, 1928 St. Mary's Road, PMB 4530, Moraga, CA 94575, 925-631-4522 or toll-free 800-800-4SMC. Fax: 925-376-2965. E-mail: finaid@stmarys-ca.edu. Website: http://www.stmarys-ca.edu/.

ST. MARY'S COLLEGE OF MARYLAND
St. Mary's City, MD

Tuition & fees (MD res): $14,496	Average undergraduate aid package: $12,454

ABOUT THE INSTITUTION State-supported, coed. Awards: bachelor's and master's degrees. 26 undergraduate majors. Total enrollment: 1,598. Undergraduates: 1,570. Freshmen: 342. Federal methodology is used as a basis for awarding need-based institutional aid.

UNDERGRADUATE EXPENSES for 2018–2019 Application fee: $50. Tuition, state resident: full-time $11,646; part-time $200 per credit hour. Tuition, nonresident: full-time $27,097; part-time $200 per credit hour. Required fees: full-time $2850. Full-time tuition and fees vary according to course load. Part-time tuition and fees vary according to course load. College room and board: $12,816; Room only: $7400. Room and board charges vary according to board plan and housing facility.

FRESHMAN FINANCIAL AID (Fall 2016) 284 applied for aid; of those 63% were deemed to have need. 99% of freshmen with need received aid; of those 5% had need fully met. Average percent of need met: 72% (excluding resources awarded to replace EFC). Average financial aid package: $15,606 (excluding resources awarded to replace EFC). 29% of all full-time freshmen had no need and received non-need-based gift aid.

UNDERGRADUATE FINANCIAL AID (Fall 2016) 1,126 applied for aid; of those 73% were deemed to have need. 99% of undergraduates with need received aid; of those 4% had need fully met. Average percent of need met: 68% (excluding resources awarded to replace EFC). Average financial aid package: $12,454 (excluding resources awarded to replace EFC). 26% of all full-time undergraduates had no need and received non-need-based gift aid.

GIFT AID (NEED-BASED) Total amount: $7,696,938 (19% federal, 18% state, 60% institutional, 3% external sources). Receiving aid: Freshmen: 49% (162); all full-time undergraduates: 48% (753). Average award: Freshmen: $11,527; Undergraduates: $10,240. Scholarships, grants, and awards: Federal Pell, FSEOG, state, private, college/university gift aid from institutional funds.

GIFT AID (NON-NEED-BASED) Total amount: $1,697,301 (8% state, 87% institutional, 5% external sources). Average award: Freshmen: $3651. Undergraduates: $4084. Scholarships, grants, and awards by category: Academic interests/achievement: 800 awards ($2,821,164 total): education, general academic interests/achievements. Special characteristics: 10 awards ($92,144 total): children of faculty/staff. Tuition waivers: Full or partial for employees or children of employees, senior citizens.

LOANS Student loans: $5,937,840 (78% need-based, 22% non-need-based). 53% of past graduating class borrowed through all loan programs. Average indebtedness

per student: $21,911. Average need-based loan: Freshmen: $3187. Undergraduates: $4272. Parent loans: $5,129,610 (71% need-based, 29% non-need-based). Programs: Federal Direct (Subsidized and Unsubsidized Stafford, PLUS), Perkins.

WORK-STUDY Federal work-study: 177 jobs averaging $960. State or other work-study/employment: Total amount: $48,342 (100% need-based). Part-time jobs available.

APPLYING FOR FINANCIAL AID Required financial aid form: FAFSA. Financial aid deadline (priority): 2/28. Notification date: Continuous beginning 11/15. Students must reply by 5/1.

CONTACT Mr. Robert W Maddox, Director of Financial Aid, St. Mary's College of Maryland, 18952 East Fisher Road, St. Mary's City, MD 20686-3001, 240-895-3000 or toll-free 800-492-7181. Fax: 240-895-4959. E-mail: finaid@smcm.edu. Website: http://www.smcm.edu/.

ST. MARY'S UNIVERSITY
San Antonio, TX

Tuition & fees: $30,600	Average undergraduate aid package: $25,624

ABOUT THE INSTITUTION Independent Roman Catholic, coed. Awards: bachelor's, master's, and doctoral degrees. 41 undergraduate majors. Total enrollment: 3,649. Undergraduates: 2,327. Freshmen: 643. Federal methodology is used as a basis for awarding need-based institutional aid.

UNDERGRADUATE EXPENSES for 2018–2019 Comprehensive fee: $41,390 includes full-time tuition ($29,710), mandatory fees ($890), and room and board ($10,790). College room only: $6800. Full-time tuition and fees vary according to course level, course load, degree level, and program. Room and board charges vary according to board plan, housing facility, and student level. Part-time tuition: $925 per credit hour. Part-time fees: $260 per term. Part-time tuition and fees vary according to course level, course load, degree level, and program.

FRESHMAN FINANCIAL AID (Fall 2016) 499 applied for aid; of those 93% were deemed to have need. 99% of freshmen with need received aid; of those 12% had need fully met. Average percent of need met: 73% (excluding resources awarded to replace EFC). Average financial aid package: $26,401 (excluding resources awarded to replace EFC). 17% of all full-time freshmen had no need and received non-need-based gift aid.

UNDERGRADUATE FINANCIAL AID (Fall 2016) 1,658 applied for aid; of those 94% were deemed to have need. 99% of undergraduates with need received aid; of those 11% had need fully met. Average percent of need met: 71% (excluding resources awarded to replace EFC). Average financial aid package: $25,624 (excluding resources awarded to replace EFC). 20% of all full-time undergraduates had no need and received non-need-based gift aid.

GIFT AID (NEED-BASED) Total amount: $30,175,719 (17% federal, 14% state, 67% institutional, 2% external sources). Receiving aid: Freshmen: 78% (456); all full-time undergraduates: 70% (1,521). Average award: Freshmen: $21,579; Undergraduates: $19,727. Scholarships, grants, and awards: Federal Pell, FSEOG, state, private, college/university gift aid from institutional funds.

GIFT AID (NON-NEED-BASED) Total amount: $8,781,870 (99% institutional, 1% external sources). Receiving aid: Freshmen: 6% (36). Undergraduates: 5% (103). Average award: Freshmen: $18,388. Undergraduates: $18,516. Scholarships, grants, and awards by category: Academic interests/achievement: 3,020 awards ($23,496,741 total): general academic interests/achievements, military science. Creative arts/performance: 88 awards ($260,601 total): music. Special achievements/activities: 22 awards ($47,700 total): cheerleading/drum major. Special characteristics: 264 awards ($4,648,430 total): children of faculty/staff, veterans, veterans' children. Tuition waivers: Full or partial for employees or children of employees. ROTC: Army, Air Force cooperative.

LOANS Student loans: $13,681,173 (83% need-based, 17% non-need-based). 77% of past graduating class borrowed through all loan programs. Average indebtedness per student: $37,866. Average need-based loan: Freshmen: $3473. Undergraduates: $4378. Parent loans: $2,176,547 (59% need-based, 41% non-need-based). Programs: Federal Direct (Subsidized and Unsubsidized Stafford, PLUS), state.

WORK-STUDY Federal work-study: 426 jobs averaging $2131. State or other work-study/employment: Total amount: $177,640 (23% need-based, 77% non-need-based). 81 part-time jobs averaging $2193.

ATHLETIC AWARDS Total amount: $2,497,112 (32% need-based, 68% non-need-based).

APPLYING FOR FINANCIAL AID *Required financial aid form:* FAFSA. *Financial aid deadline:* 6/1 (priority: 3/1). *Notification date:* Continuous beginning 10/1. Students must reply within 2 weeks of notification.

CONTACT Mr. David R. Krause, Director of Financial Assistance, St. Mary's University, One Camino Santa Maria, San Antonio, TX 78228-8541, 210-436-3141 or toll-free 800-367-7868. *Fax:* 210-431-2221. *E-mail:* dkrause@stmarytx.edu. *Website:* http://www.stmarytx.edu/.

SAINT MARY'S UNIVERSITY OF MINNESOTA
Winona, MN

Tuition & fees: $35,140	Average undergraduate aid package: $27,927

ABOUT THE INSTITUTION Independent Roman Catholic, coed. *Awards:* certificates, diplomas, bachelor's, master's, and doctoral degrees. 56 undergraduate majors. *Total enrollment:* 5,754. Undergraduates: 1,503. Freshmen: 300. Federal methodology is used as a basis for awarding need-based institutional aid.

UNDERGRADUATE EXPENSES for 2018–2019 *Application fee:* $25. *Comprehensive fee:* $44,220 includes full-time tuition ($34,500), mandatory fees ($640), and room and board ($9080). *College room only:* $5080. Full-time tuition and fees vary according to course load and location. Room and board charges vary according to board plan and housing facility. *Part-time tuition:* $1150 per credit. Part-time tuition and fees vary according to course load and location.

FRESHMAN FINANCIAL AID (Fall 2017, est.) 273 applied for aid; of those 86% were deemed to have need. 100% of freshmen with need received aid; of those 24% had need fully met. *Average percent of need met:* 76% (excluding resources awarded to replace EFC). *Average financial aid package:* $27,733 (excluding resources awarded to replace EFC). 12% of all full-time freshmen had no need and received non-need-based gift aid.

UNDERGRADUATE FINANCIAL AID (Fall 2017, est.) 835 applied for aid; of those 99% were deemed to have need. 98% of undergraduates with need received aid; of those 18% had need fully met. *Average percent of need met:* 74% (excluding resources awarded to replace EFC). *Average financial aid package:* $27,927 (excluding resources awarded to replace EFC). 8% of all full-time undergraduates had no need and received non-need-based gift aid.

GIFT AID (NEED-BASED) *Total amount:* $19,289,179 (10% federal, 7% state, 81% institutional, 2% external sources). *Receiving aid:* Freshmen: 78% (233); all full-time undergraduates: 65% (729). *Average award:* Freshmen: $21,341; Undergraduates: $18,713. *Scholarships, grants, and awards:* Federal Pell, FSEOG, state, college/university gift aid from institutional funds.

GIFT AID (NON-NEED-BASED) *Average award:* Freshmen: $19,763. Undergraduates: $20,405. *Scholarships, grants, and awards by category:* Academic interests/achievement: 803 awards ($10,551,100 total): general academic interests/achievements. *Creative arts/performance:* 131 awards ($238,625 total): art/fine arts, music, theater/drama. *Special achievements/activities:* 120 awards ($239,000 total): leadership. *Special characteristics:* 261 awards ($1,210,890 total): children and siblings of alumni, children of faculty/staff, ethnic background, international students, local/state students, members of minority groups. *Tuition waivers:* Full or partial for employees or children of employees. *ROTC:* Army cooperative.

LOANS *Student loans:* $7,031,100 (100% need-based). 77% of past graduating class borrowed through all loan programs. *Average indebtedness per student:* $39,917. *Average need-based loan:* Freshmen: $3171. Undergraduates: $4311. *Parent loans:* $1,349,998 (100% need-based). *Programs:* Federal Direct (Subsidized and Unsubsidized Stafford, PLUS), Perkins, state.

WORK-STUDY *Federal work-study:* Total amount: $368,899; jobs available. *State or other work-study/employment:* Total amount: $530,266 (100% need-based). Part-time jobs available.

APPLYING FOR FINANCIAL AID *Required financial aid form:* FAFSA. *Financial aid deadline (priority):* 12/1. *Notification date:* Continuous beginning 1/1. Students must reply within 3 weeks of notification.

CONTACT Ms. Joy Rockwell, Associate Director of Financial Aid, Saint Mary's University of Minnesota, 700 Terrace Heights #5, Winona, MN 55987-1399, 507-457-1472 or toll-free 800-635-5987. *Fax:* 507-457-6698. *E-mail:* jrockwel@smumn.edu. *Website:* http://www.smumn.edu/.

SAINT MICHAEL'S COLLEGE
Colchester, VT

Tuition & fees: $45,375	Average undergraduate aid package: $32,102

ABOUT THE INSTITUTION Independent Roman Catholic, coed. *Awards:* certificates, bachelor's, and master's degrees. 35 undergraduate majors. *Total enrollment:* 2,077. Undergraduates: 1,792. Freshmen: 409. Federal methodology is used as a basis for awarding need-based institutional aid.

UNDERGRADUATE EXPENSES for 2018–2019 *Application fee:* $50. *Comprehensive fee:* $57,595 includes full-time tuition ($45,050), mandatory fees ($325), and room and board ($12,220). Full-time tuition and fees vary according to course load. Room and board charges vary according to board plan and housing facility. *Part-time tuition:* $1445 per credit hour. Part-time tuition and fees vary according to course load.

FRESHMAN FINANCIAL AID (Fall 2017, est.) 357 applied for aid; of those 87% were deemed to have need. 100% of freshmen with need received aid; of those 25% had need fully met. *Average percent of need met:* 85% (excluding resources awarded to replace EFC). *Average financial aid package:* $35,838 (excluding resources awarded to replace EFC). 23% of all full-time freshmen had no need and received non-need-based gift aid.

UNDERGRADUATE FINANCIAL AID (Fall 2017, est.) 1,269 applied for aid; of those 89% were deemed to have need. 100% of undergraduates with need received aid; of those 26% had need fully met. *Average percent of need met:* 78% (excluding resources awarded to replace EFC). *Average financial aid package:* $32,102 (excluding resources awarded to replace EFC). 33% of all full-time undergraduates had no need and received non-need-based gift aid.

GIFT AID (NEED-BASED) *Total amount:* $27,921,643 (6% federal, 1% state, 90% institutional, 3% external sources). *Receiving aid:* Freshmen: 75% (308); all full-time undergraduates: 64% (1,122). *Average award:* Freshmen: $27,821; Undergraduates: $25,274. *Scholarships, grants, and awards:* Federal Pell, FSEOG, state, private, college/university gift aid from institutional funds.

GIFT AID (NON-NEED-BASED) *Total amount:* $12,625,207 (95% institutional, 5% external sources). *Receiving aid:* Freshmen: 13% (55). Undergraduates: 11% (199). *Average award:* Freshmen: $18,883. Undergraduates: $17,739. *Scholarships, grants, and awards by category:* Academic interests/achievement: general academic interests/achievements. *Creative arts/performance:* art/fine arts, performing arts, theater/drama. *Special characteristics:* members of minority groups, out-of-state students, siblings of current students, veterans, veterans' children. *Tuition waivers:* Full or partial for employees or children of employees, senior citizens. *ROTC:* Army cooperative, Air Force cooperative.

LOANS *Student loans:* $9,922,311 (53% need-based, 47% non-need-based). 77% of past graduating class borrowed through all loan programs. *Average indebtedness per student:* $40,009. *Average need-based loan:* Freshmen: $5248. Undergraduates: $5529. *Parent loans:* $3,541,657 (56% need-based, 44% non-need-based). *Programs:* Federal Direct (Subsidized and Unsubsidized Stafford, PLUS).

WORK-STUDY *Federal work-study:* Total amount: $577,195; 250 jobs averaging $1750. *State or other work-study/employment:* Total amount: $480,916 (83% need-based, 17% non-need-based). 280 part-time jobs averaging $1750.

ATHLETIC AWARDS Total amount: $1,128,161 (10% need-based, 90% non-need-based).

APPLYING FOR FINANCIAL AID *Required financial aid form:* FAFSA. *Financial aid deadline (priority):* 2/1. *Notification date:* Continuous beginning 2/1. Students must reply by 5/1 or within 2 weeks of notification.

CONTACT Matthew DeSorgher, Director of Student Financial Services, Saint Michael's College, One Winooski Park, Colchester, VT 05439, 802-654-3243 or toll-free 800-762-8000. *Fax:* 802-654-2591. *E-mail:* finaid@smcvt.edu. *Website:* http://www.smcvt.edu/.

ST. NORBERT COLLEGE
De Pere, WI

Tuition & fees: $38,129	Average undergraduate aid package: $26,100

ABOUT THE INSTITUTION Independent Roman Catholic, coed. *Awards:* bachelor's and master's degrees. 35 undergraduate majors. *Total enrollment:* 2,165. Undergraduates: 2,067. Freshmen: 526. Federal methodology is used as a basis for awarding need-based institutional aid.

UNDERGRADUATE EXPENSES for 2018–2019 *Comprehensive fee:* $48,083 includes full-time tuition ($37,314), mandatory fees ($815), and room and board ($9954). *College room only:* $5536. Full-time tuition and fees vary according to course load. Room and board charges vary according to board plan and housing facility. *Part-time tuition:* $1166 per credit hour. Part-time tuition and fees vary according to course load.

FRESHMAN FINANCIAL AID (Fall 2016) 532 applied for aid; of those 84% were deemed to have need. 100% of freshmen with need received aid; of those 22% had need fully met. *Average percent of need met:* 80% (excluding resources awarded to replace EFC). *Average financial aid package:* $25,972 (excluding resources awarded to replace EFC). 23% of all full-time freshmen had no need and received non-need-based gift aid.

UNDERGRADUATE FINANCIAL AID (Fall 2016) 1,733 applied for aid; of those 87% were deemed to have need. 100% of undergraduates with need received aid; of those 26% had need fully met. *Average percent of need met:* 82% (excluding resources awarded to replace EFC). *Average financial aid package:* $26,100 (excluding resources awarded to replace EFC). 25% of all full-time undergraduates had no need and received non-need-based gift aid.

GIFT AID (NEED-BASED) *Total amount:* $30,810,309 (7% federal, 7% state, 81% institutional, 5% external sources). *Receiving aid:* Freshmen: 76% (441); all full-time undergraduates: 72% (1,466). *Average award:* Freshmen: $21,250; Undergraduates: $20,136. *Scholarships, grants, and awards:* Federal Pell, FSEOG, state, private, college/university gift aid from institutional funds.

GIFT AID (NON-NEED-BASED) *Total amount:* $7,199,334 (1% federal, 91% institutional, 8% external sources). *Receiving aid:* Freshmen: 2% (13). Undergraduates: 2% (47). *Average award:* Freshmen: $13,978. Undergraduates: $12,873. *Scholarships, grants, and awards by category:* Academic interests/achievement: general academic interests/achievements. *Creative arts/performance:* art/fine arts, music, theater/drama. *Special characteristics:* children of faculty/staff, international students. *Tuition waivers:* Full or partial for employees or children of employees. *ROTC:* Army.

LOANS *Student loans:* $17,444,074 (96% need-based, 4% non-need-based). 72% of past graduating class borrowed through all loan programs. *Average indebtedness per student:* $33,794. *Average need-based loan:* Freshmen: $3861. Undergraduates: $4737. *Parent loans:* $4,374,148 (94% need-based, 6% non-need-based). *Programs:* Federal Direct (Subsidized and Unsubsidized Stafford, PLUS), Perkins, state, college/university.

WORK-STUDY *Federal work-study:* 373 jobs averaging $1238. *State or other work-study/employment:* Total amount: $800,545 (65% need-based, 35% non-need-based). Part-time jobs available.

APPLYING FOR FINANCIAL AID *Required financial aid form:* FAFSA. *Financial aid deadline (priority):* 1/1. *Notification date:* Continuous beginning 1/1. Students must reply within 2 weeks of notification.

CONTACT Ms. Jessica Rafeld, Director of Financial Aid, St. Norbert College, 100 Grant Street, De Pere, WI 54115-2099, 920-403-3071 or toll-free 800-236-4878. *Fax:* 920-403-3062. *E-mail:* financialaid@snc.edu.
Website: http://www.snc.edu/.

ST. OLAF COLLEGE
Northfield, MN

Tuition & fees: $47,840	Average undergraduate aid package: $40,769

ABOUT THE INSTITUTION Independent Lutheran, coed. *Awards:* bachelor's degrees. 46 undergraduate majors. *Total enrollment:* 3,035. Undergraduates: 3,035. Freshmen: 786. Both federal and institutional methodology are used as a basis for awarding need-based institutional aid.

UNDERGRADUATE EXPENSES for 2018–2019 *Comprehensive fee:* $53,040 includes full-time tuition ($47,840) and room and board ($5200). *College room only:* $5650. Room and board charges vary according to board plan. *Part-time tuition:* $5980 per course. Part-time tuition and fees vary according to course load.

FRESHMAN FINANCIAL AID (Fall 2017, est.) 689 applied for aid; of those 91% were deemed to have need. 100% of freshmen with need received aid; of those 93% had need fully met. *Average percent of need met:* 100% (excluding resources awarded to replace EFC). *Average financial aid package:* $41,392 (excluding resources awarded to replace EFC). 18% of all full-time freshmen had no need and received non-need-based gift aid.

UNDERGRADUATE FINANCIAL AID (Fall 2017, est.) 2,330 applied for aid; of those 95% were deemed to have need. 100% of undergraduates with need received aid; of those 74% had need fully met. *Average percent of need met:* 96% (excluding resources awarded to replace EFC). *Average financial aid package:* $40,769 (excluding resources awarded to replace EFC). 20% of all full-time undergraduates had no need and received non-need-based gift aid.

GIFT AID (NEED-BASED) *Total amount:* $72,740,817 (4% federal, 3% state, 93% institutional). *Receiving aid:* Freshmen: 80% (628); all full-time undergraduates: 74% (2,203). *Average award:* Freshmen: $35,083; Undergraduates: $33,553. *Scholarships, grants, and awards:* Federal Pell, FSEOG, state, private, college/university gift aid from institutional funds.

GIFT AID (NON-NEED-BASED) *Total amount:* $12,608,273 (81% institutional, 19% external sources). *Receiving aid:* Freshmen: 29% (229). Undergraduates: 20% (608). *Average award:* Freshmen: $17,307. Undergraduates: $16,237. *Scholarships, grants, and awards by category:* Academic interests/achievement: 622 awards ($9,923,190 total): general academic interests/achievements. *Creative arts/performance:* 132 awards ($880,840 total): art/fine arts, dance, music, theater/drama. *Special achievements/activities:* 84 awards ($567,715 total): community service, leadership, religious involvement. *Tuition waivers:* Full or partial for employees or children of employees, senior citizens.

LOANS *Student loans:* $16,598,188 (41% need-based, 59% non-need-based). 57% of past graduating class borrowed through all loan programs. *Average indebtedness per student:* $27,002. *Average need-based loan:* Freshmen: $1997. Undergraduates: $3167. *Parent loans:* $2,272,130 (100% non-need-based). *Programs:* Federal Direct (Subsidized and Unsubsidized Stafford, PLUS), Perkins, Federal Nursing, state, college/university.

WORK-STUDY *Federal work-study:* Total amount: $811,902; 374 jobs averaging $2170. *State or other work-study/employment:* Total amount: $4,156,479 (93% need-based, 7% non-need-based). 1,949 part-time jobs averaging $2133.

APPLYING FOR FINANCIAL AID *Required financial aid forms:* FAFSA, CSS Financial Aid PROFILE, noncustodial (divorced/separated) parent's statement. *Financial aid deadline:* 3/1 (priority: 2/1). *Notification date:* 4/1. Students must reply by 5/1.

CONTACT Ms. Carly Eichhorst, Director of Student Financial Aid, St. Olaf College, 1520 Saint Olaf Avenue, Northfield, MN 55057-1098, 507-786-3019 or toll-free 800-800-3025. *Fax:* 507-786-6688. *E-mail:* finaid@stolaf.edu.
Website: http://www.stolaf.edu/.

ST. PETERSBURG COLLEGE
St. Petersburg, FL

ABOUT THE INSTITUTION State and locally supported, coed. *Awards:* certificates, diplomas, associate, and bachelor's degrees. 48 undergraduate majors. *Total enrollment:* 29,835. Undergraduates: 29,835. Freshmen: 2,827.

GIFT AID (NEED-BASED) *Scholarships, grants, and awards:* Federal Pell, FSEOG, state, college/university gift aid from institutional funds, Federal Nursing.

LOANS *Programs:* Federal Direct (Subsidized and Unsubsidized Stafford, PLUS), college/university.

APPLYING FOR FINANCIAL AID *Required financial aid form:* FAFSA.

CONTACT Office of Financial Aid, St. Petersburg College, 6605 Fifth Avenue N, St. Petersburg, FL 33710, 727-341-7907.
Website: http://www.spcollege.edu/.

SAINT PETER'S UNIVERSITY
Jersey City, NJ

Tuition & fees: N/R	Average undergraduate aid package: $32,097

ABOUT THE INSTITUTION Independent Roman Catholic (Jesuit), coed. *Awards:* certificates, associate, bachelor's, master's, and doctoral degrees. 45 undergraduate majors. *Total enrollment:* 3,524. Undergraduates: 2,637. Freshmen: 651. Federal methodology is used as a basis for awarding need-based institutional aid.
FRESHMAN FINANCIAL AID (Fall 2017, est.) 651 applied for aid; of those 92% were deemed to have need. 100% of freshmen with need received aid; of those 7% had need fully met. *Average percent of need met:* 81% (excluding resources awarded to replace EFC). *Average financial aid package:* $33,384 (excluding resources awarded to replace EFC). 8% of all full-time freshmen had no need and received non-need-based gift aid.
UNDERGRADUATE FINANCIAL AID (Fall 2017, est.) 2,257 applied for aid; of those 92% were deemed to have need. 100% of undergraduates with need received aid; of those 6% had need fully met. *Average percent of need met:* 79% (excluding resources awarded to replace EFC). *Average financial aid package:* $32,097 (excluding resources awarded to replace EFC). 8% of all full-time undergraduates had no need and received non-need-based gift aid.
GIFT AID (NEED-BASED) *Total amount:* $63,389,468 (13% federal, 26% state, 61% institutional). *Receiving aid:* Freshmen: 91% (591); all full-time undergraduates: 91% (2,060). *Average award:* Freshmen: $31,748; Undergraduates: $29,853. *Scholarships, grants, and awards:* Federal Pell, FSEOG, state, private, college/university gift aid from institutional funds, Federal Nursing.
GIFT AID (NON-NEED-BASED) *Total amount:* $5,416,073 (100% institutional). *Receiving aid:* Freshmen: 6% (41). Undergraduates: 6% (135). *Average award:* Freshmen: $24,382. Undergraduates: $21,252. *Scholarships, grants, and awards by category: Academic interests/achievement:* general academic interests/achievements. *Special achievements/activities:* leadership. *Special characteristics:* children of faculty/staff, general special characteristics, relatives of clergy, religious affiliation. *ROTC:* Army cooperative.
LOANS *Student loans:* $18,612,283 (83% need-based, 17% non-need-based). 73% of past graduating class borrowed through all loan programs. *Average indebtedness per student:* $22,317. *Average need-based loan:* Freshmen: $3288. Undergraduates: $4048. *Parent loans:* $5,130,642 (59% need-based, 41% non-need-based). *Programs:* Federal Direct (Subsidized and Unsubsidized Stafford, PLUS).
WORK-STUDY *Federal work-study:* Total amount: $504,252; jobs available.
ATHLETIC AWARDS Total amount: $2,962,324 (61% need-based, 39% non-need-based).
APPLYING FOR FINANCIAL AID *Required financial aid forms:* FAFSA, noncustodial (divorced/separated) parent's statement. *Financial aid deadline (priority):* 3/15. *Notification date:* Continuous beginning 2/15. Students must reply by 5/1 or within 2 weeks of notification.
CONTACT Jennifer Ragsdale, Acting Director of Financial Aid, Saint Peter's University, 2641 Kennedy Boulevard, Jersey City, NJ 07306, 201-761-6071 or toll-free 888-SPC-9933. *Fax:* 201-761-6073. *E-mail:* jragsdale@spc.edu. *Website:* http://www.saintpeters.edu/.

ST. THOMAS AQUINAS COLLEGE
Sparkill, NY

Tuition & fees: $30,750	Average undergraduate aid package: $18,100

ABOUT THE INSTITUTION Independent, coed. *Awards:* certificates, associate, bachelor's, and master's degrees. 43 undergraduate majors. *Total enrollment:* 1,915. Undergraduates: 1,778. Freshmen: 246. Federal methodology is used as a basis for awarding need-based institutional aid.
UNDERGRADUATE EXPENSES for 2017–2018 *Application fee:* $30. *Comprehensive fee:* $43,500 includes full-time tuition ($29,950), mandatory fees ($800), and room and board ($12,750). *College room only:* $6880. Room and board charges vary according to board plan and housing facility. *Part-time tuition:* $955 per credit hour. *Part-time fees:* $200 per term.

FRESHMAN FINANCIAL AID (Fall 2017, est.) 230 applied for aid; of those 86% were deemed to have need. 99% of freshmen with need received aid; of those 18% had need fully met. *Average percent of need met:* 34% (excluding resources awarded to replace EFC). *Average financial aid package:* $16,500 (excluding resources awarded to replace EFC). 22% of all full-time freshmen had no need and received non-need-based gift aid.
UNDERGRADUATE FINANCIAL AID (Fall 2017, est.) 1,020 applied for aid; of those 82% were deemed to have need. 95% of undergraduates with need received aid; of those 22% had need fully met. *Average percent of need met:* 38% (excluding resources awarded to replace EFC). *Average financial aid package:* $18,100 (excluding resources awarded to replace EFC). 21% of all full-time undergraduates had no need and received non-need-based gift aid.
GIFT AID (NEED-BASED) *Total amount:* $5,722,672 (33% federal, 20% state, 42% institutional, 5% external sources). *Receiving aid:* Freshmen: 80% (196); all full-time undergraduates: 69% (756). *Average award:* Freshmen: $12,000; Undergraduates: $11,500. *Scholarships, grants, and awards:* Federal Pell, FSEOG, state, private, college/university gift aid from institutional funds.
GIFT AID (NON-NEED-BASED) *Total amount:* $8,295,111 (1% state, 98% institutional, 1% external sources). *Receiving aid:* Freshmen: 50% (124). Undergraduates: 52% (562). *Average award:* Freshmen: $14,200. Undergraduates: $13,800. *Scholarships, grants, and awards by category: Academic interests/achievement:* business, communication, computer science, education, engineering/technologies, English, foreign languages, general academic interests/achievements, humanities, mathematics, religion/biblical studies, social sciences. *Creative arts/performance:* creative writing. *Special achievements/activities:* community service, leadership. *Special characteristics:* siblings of current students, spouses of current students, twins, veterans. *Tuition waivers:* Full or partial for employees or children of employees. *ROTC:* Air Force cooperative.
LOANS *Student loans:* $5,846,403 (42% need-based, 58% non-need-based). 78% of past graduating class borrowed through all loan programs. *Average indebtedness per student:* $28,750. *Average need-based loan:* Freshmen: $3500. Undergraduates: $4800. *Parent loans:* $4,230,889 (85% need-based, 15% non-need-based). *Programs:* Federal Direct (Subsidized and Unsubsidized Stafford, PLUS), Perkins, state, alternative loans.
WORK-STUDY *Federal work-study:* Total amount: $165,684; 114 jobs averaging $1453.
ATHLETIC AWARDS Total amount: $2,307,096 (100% non-need-based).
APPLYING FOR FINANCIAL AID *Required financial aid forms:* FAFSA, state aid form. *Financial aid deadline (priority):* 2/15. *Notification date:* Continuous beginning 3/1. Students must reply by 5/1 or within 2 weeks of notification.
CONTACT Mrs. Jean Marie Mohr, Director of Financial Aid, St. Thomas Aquinas College, 125 Route 340, Sparkill, NY 10976, 845-398-4106. *Fax:* 845-398-4114. *E-mail:* jmohr@stac.edu. *Website:* http://www.stac.edu/.

ST. THOMAS UNIVERSITY
Miami Gardens, FL

Tuition & fees: $31,080	Average undergraduate aid package: N/A

ABOUT THE INSTITUTION Independent Roman Catholic, coed. *Awards:* certificates, bachelor's, master's, and doctoral degrees. 33 undergraduate majors. *Total enrollment:* 4,549. Undergraduates: 2,912. Freshmen: 229. Both federal and institutional methodology are used as a basis for awarding need-based institutional aid.
UNDERGRADUATE EXPENSES for 2018–2019 *Application fee:* $40. *Comprehensive fee:* $42,780 includes full-time tuition ($30,900), mandatory fees ($180), and room and board ($11,700). *College room only:* $7200. Full-time tuition and fees vary according to course load and program. Room and board charges vary according to board plan and housing facility. *Part-time tuition:* $618 per credit hour. *Part-time fees:* $75 per course; $120 per course. Part-time tuition and fees vary according to course load and program.
GIFT AID (NEED-BASED) *Scholarships, grants, and awards:* Federal Pell, FSEOG, state, private, college/university gift aid from institutional funds.
GIFT AID (NON-NEED-BASED) *Scholarships, grants, and awards by category: Academic interests/achievement:* general academic interests/achievements. *Special achievements/activities:* leadership. *Tuition waivers:* Full or partial for employees or children of employees. *ROTC:* Air Force cooperative.

LOANS *Programs:* Federal Direct (Subsidized and Unsubsidized Stafford, PLUS), Perkins.

WORK-STUDY Federal work-study jobs available.

APPLYING FOR FINANCIAL AID *Required financial aid form:* FAFSA. *Financial aid deadline (priority):* 4/1. *Notification date:* Continuous beginning 3/1.

CONTACT Ms. Yamirka Rial, Director of Financial Aid, St. Thomas University, 16401 Northwest 37th Avenue, Miami Gardens, FL 33054, 305-474-6965 or toll-free 800-367-9010. *Fax:* 305-474-6930. *E-mail:* yrial@stu.edu.
Website: http://www.stu.edu/.

SAINT VINCENT COLLEGE
Latrobe, PA

Tuition & fees: $34,830	Average undergraduate aid package: $29,423

ABOUT THE INSTITUTION Independent Roman Catholic, coed. *Awards:* certificates, bachelor's, master's, and doctoral degrees. 50 undergraduate majors. *Total enrollment:* 1,859. Undergraduates: 1,666. Freshmen: 456. Federal methodology is used as a basis for awarding need-based institutional aid.

UNDERGRADUATE EXPENSES for 2017–2018 *Application fee:* $25. *Comprehensive fee:* $46,229 includes full-time tuition ($33,516), mandatory fees ($1314), and room and board ($11,399). *College room only:* $6113. Full-time tuition and fees vary according to course load and degree level. Room and board charges vary according to board plan and housing facility. *Part-time tuition:* $1048 per credit hour. Part-time tuition and fees vary according to course load and degree level.

FRESHMAN FINANCIAL AID (Fall 2017, est.) 431 applied for aid; of those 92% were deemed to have need. 100% of freshmen with need received aid; of those 24% had need fully met. *Average percent of need met:* 85% (excluding resources awarded to replace EFC). *Average financial aid package:* $32,283 (excluding resources awarded to replace EFC). 13% of all full-time freshmen had no need and received non-need-based gift aid.

UNDERGRADUATE FINANCIAL AID (Fall 2017, est.) 1,389 applied for aid; of those 99% were deemed to have need. 100% of undergraduates with need received aid; of those 23% had need fully met. *Average percent of need met:* 85% (excluding resources awarded to replace EFC). *Average financial aid package:* $29,423 (excluding resources awarded to replace EFC). 19% of all full-time undergraduates had no need and received non-need-based gift aid.

GIFT AID (NEED-BASED) *Total amount:* $32,929,106 (7% federal, 7% state, 84% institutional, 2% external sources). *Receiving aid:* Freshmen: 77% (350); all full-time undergraduates: 72% (1,161). *Average award:* Freshmen: $7651; Undergraduates: $6688. *Scholarships, grants, and awards:* Federal Pell, FSEOG, state, private, college/university gift aid from institutional funds, United Negro College Fund.

GIFT AID (NON-NEED-BASED) *Total amount:* $5,809,053 (99% institutional, 1% external sources). *Receiving aid:* Freshmen: 87% (396). Undergraduates: 86% (1,372). *Average award:* Freshmen: $20,326. Undergraduates: $19,173. *Scholarships, grants, and awards by category:* Academic interests/achievement: biological sciences, business, general academic interests/achievements, home economics, mathematics, physical sciences. *Special characteristics:* children of faculty/staff, first-generation college students, general special characteristics, out-of-state students, previous college experience, religious affiliation. *Tuition waivers:* Full or partial for employees or children of employees. *ROTC:* Army cooperative, Air Force cooperative.

LOANS *Student loans:* $11,502,668 (31% need-based, 69% non-need-based). 82% of past graduating class borrowed through all loan programs. *Average indebtedness per student:* $46,794. *Average need-based loan:* Freshmen: $3827. Undergraduates: $4667. *Parent loans:* $4,499,385 (6% need-based, 94% non-need-based). *Programs:* Federal Direct (Subsidized and Unsubsidized Stafford, PLUS), Perkins, private loans.

WORK-STUDY *Federal work-study:* Total amount: $193,027; jobs available. *State or other work-study/employment:* Total amount: $398,565 (100% need-based). Part-time jobs available.

APPLYING FOR FINANCIAL AID *Required financial aid form:* FAFSA. *Financial aid deadline (priority):* 5/1. *Notification date:* Continuous beginning 10/1.

CONTACT Mrs. Mary Gazal, Director of Financial Aid, Saint Vincent College, 300 Fraser Purchase Road, Latrobe, PA 15650, 724-805-2555 or toll-free 800-782-5549. *Fax:* 724-805-2953. *E-mail:* financialaid@stvincent.edu.
Website: http://www.stvincent.edu/.

SAINT XAVIER UNIVERSITY
Chicago, IL

CONTACT Ms. Susan Swisher, Director of Financial Aid, Saint Xavier University, 3700 West 103rd Street, Chicago, IL 60655-3105, 773-298-3073 or toll-free 800-462-9288. *Fax:* 773-298-3033. *E-mail:* swisher@sxu.edu.
Website: http://www.sxu.edu/.

SALEM COLLEGE
Winston-Salem, NC

Tuition & fees: $28,566	Average undergraduate aid package: N/A

ABOUT THE INSTITUTION Independent Moravian, coed, primarily women. 30 undergraduate majors. Federal methodology is used as a basis for awarding need-based institutional aid.

UNDERGRADUATE EXPENSES for 2017–2018 *Comprehensive fee:* $40,206 includes full-time tuition ($28,100), mandatory fees ($466), and room and board ($11,640). *College room only:* $5960. Room and board charges vary according to housing facility. *Part-time tuition:* $400 per semester hour. *Part-time fees:* $250 per year.

FRESHMAN FINANCIAL AID (Fall 2016) 187 applied for aid; of those 89% were deemed to have need. 100% of freshmen with need received aid.

UNDERGRADUATE FINANCIAL AID (Fall 2016) 817 applied for aid; of those 91% were deemed to have need. 100% of undergraduates with need received aid.

GIFT AID (NEED-BASED) *Total amount:* $2,650,068 (19% federal, 15% state, 66% institutional). *Scholarships, grants, and awards:* Federal Pell, FSEOG, state, private, college/university gift aid from institutional funds.

GIFT AID (NON-NEED-BASED) *Total amount:* $2,591,626 (94% institutional, 6% external sources). *Scholarships, grants, and awards by category:* Academic interests/achievement: general academic interests/achievements. *Creative arts/performance:* music. *Special achievements/activities:* leadership. *Special characteristics:* children of educators, children of faculty/staff, relatives of clergy. *Tuition waivers:* Full or partial for employees or children of employees.

LOANS *Student loans:* $947,524 (62% need-based, 38% non-need-based). 76% of past graduating class borrowed through all loan programs. *Parent loans:* $237,332 (100% non-need-based). *Programs:* Federal Direct (Subsidized and Unsubsidized Stafford, PLUS).

WORK-STUDY *Federal work-study:* 75 jobs averaging $341. *State or other work-study/employment:* Total amount: $139,200 (100% non-need-based). 138 part-time jobs averaging $1009.

APPLYING FOR FINANCIAL AID *Required financial aid forms:* FAFSA, state aid form. *Financial aid deadline (priority):* 3/1. *Notification date:* Continuous beginning 3/1. Students must reply by 5/1 or within 2 weeks of notification.

CONTACT Paul J. Coscia, Assistant Vice President for Financial Aid, Salem College, 601 South Church Street, Winston-Salem, NC 27101, 336-917-5577 or toll-free 800-327-2536. *Fax:* 336-917-5584. *E-mail:* paul.coscia@salem.edu.
Website: http://www.salem.edu/.

SALEM INTERNATIONAL UNIVERSITY
Salem, WV

ABOUT THE INSTITUTION Independent, coed. 9 undergraduate majors.

GIFT AID (NEED-BASED) *Scholarships, grants, and awards:* Federal Pell, FSEOG, state, private, college/university gift aid from institutional funds.

GIFT AID (NON-NEED-BASED) *Scholarships, grants, and awards by category:* Academic interests/achievement: business, education, general academic interests/achievements, humanities. *Special characteristics:* out-of-state students, religious affiliation.

LOANS *Programs:* Perkins, alternative loans.
APPLYING FOR FINANCIAL AID *Required financial aid form:* FAFSA.

CONTACT Donald Ronan, Director of Financial Aid and Compliance, Salem International University, 615 West Carmel Drive, Suite 140, Carmel, IN 46032, 317-805-1793 or toll-free 888-235-5024. *Fax:* 317-573-8997. *E-mail:* dronan@salemu.edu. *Website:* http://www.salemu.edu/.

SALEM STATE UNIVERSITY
Salem, MA

CONTACT Mary Benda, Director of Financial Aid, Salem State University, 352 Lafayette Street, Salem, MA 01970-5353, 978-542-6139. *Fax:* 978-542-6876. *Website:* http://www.salemstate.edu/.

SALISBURY UNIVERSITY
Salisbury, MD

Tuition & fees (MD res): $9582	Average undergraduate aid package: $8186

ABOUT THE INSTITUTION State-supported, coed. *Awards:* certificates, bachelor's, master's, and doctoral degrees. 49 undergraduate majors. *Total enrollment:* 8,714. Undergraduates: 7,782. Freshmen: 1,328. Federal methodology is used as a basis for awarding need-based institutional aid.

UNDERGRADUATE EXPENSES for 2017–2018 *Application fee:* $50. *Tuition, state resident:* full-time $6982; part-time $287 per credit hour. *Tuition, nonresident:* full-time $16,022; part-time $662 per credit hour. *Required fees:* full-time $2600; $92 per credit hour. *College room and board:* $11,550; *Room only:* $6750. Room and board charges vary according to board plan and housing facility.

FRESHMAN FINANCIAL AID (Fall 2016) 1,083 applied for aid; of those 69% were deemed to have need. 100% of freshmen with need received aid; of those 14% had need fully met. *Average percent of need met:* 57% (excluding resources awarded to replace EFC). *Average financial aid package:* $8990 (excluding resources awarded to replace EFC). 24% of all full-time freshmen had no need and received non-need-based gift aid.

UNDERGRADUATE FINANCIAL AID (Fall 2016) 5,373 applied for aid; of those 74% were deemed to have need. 100% of undergraduates with need received aid; of those 12% had need fully met. *Average percent of need met:* 53% (excluding resources awarded to replace EFC). *Average financial aid package:* $8186 (excluding resources awarded to replace EFC). 8% of all full-time undergraduates had no need and received non-need-based gift aid.

GIFT AID (NEED-BASED) *Total amount:* $18,661,276 (43% federal, 22% state, 26% institutional, 9% external sources). *Receiving aid:* Freshmen: 49% (646); all full-time undergraduates: 44% (3,167). *Average award:* Freshmen: $7605; Undergraduates: $6190. *Scholarships, grants, and awards:* Federal Pell, FSEOG, state, private, college/university gift aid from institutional funds.

GIFT AID (NON-NEED-BASED) *Total amount:* $4,033,462 (9% state, 70% institutional, 21% external sources). *Average award:* Freshmen: $2693. Undergraduates: $2612. *Scholarships, grants, and awards by category:* Academic interests/achievement: 1,887 awards ($4,727,041 total). *Tuition waivers:* Full or partial for employees or children of employees, senior citizens. *ROTC:* Army, Air Force cooperative.

LOANS *Student loans:* $35,612,521 (62% need-based, 38% non-need-based). 59% of past graduating class borrowed through all loan programs. *Average indebtedness per student:* $26,940. *Average need-based loan:* Freshmen: $3150. Undergraduates: $4017. *Parent loans:* $21,132,480 (39% need-based, 61% non-need-based). *Programs:* Federal Direct (Subsidized and Unsubsidized Stafford, PLUS), Perkins.

WORK-STUDY *Federal work-study:* 76 jobs averaging $1817.

APPLYING FOR FINANCIAL AID *Required financial aid form:* FAFSA. *Financial aid deadline (priority):* 3/1. *Notification date:* Continuous beginning 3/15. Students must reply by 5/1.

CONTACT Justin Rummel, Director of Financial Aid, Salisbury University, 1101 Camden Avenue, Salisbury, MD 21801, 410-543-6165 or toll-free 888-543-0148. *Fax:* 410-543-6138. *E-mail:* finaid@salisbury.edu. *Website:* http://www.salisbury.edu/.

SALVE REGINA UNIVERSITY
Newport, RI

Tuition & fees: $38,986	Average undergraduate aid package: $27,756

ABOUT THE INSTITUTION Independent Roman Catholic, coed. *Awards:* certificates, associate, bachelor's, master's, and doctoral degrees. 47 undergraduate majors. *Total enrollment:* 2,823. Undergraduates: 2,180. Freshmen: 603. Federal methodology is used as a basis for awarding need-based institutional aid.

UNDERGRADUATE EXPENSES for 2017–2018 *Application fee:* $50. *Comprehensive fee:* $53,046 includes full-time tuition ($38,386), mandatory fees ($600), and room and board ($14,060). Full-time tuition and fees vary according to course load and location. Room and board charges vary according to board plan and housing facility. *Part-time tuition:* $1280 per credit. *Part-time fees:* $60 per term. Part-time tuition and fees vary according to course load and location.

FRESHMAN FINANCIAL AID (Fall 2017, est.) 536 applied for aid; of those 90% were deemed to have need. 100% of freshmen with need received aid; of those 12% had need fully met. *Average percent of need met:* 70% (excluding resources awarded to replace EFC). *Average financial aid package:* $29,388 (excluding resources awarded to replace EFC). 17% of all full-time freshmen had no need and received non-need-based gift aid.

UNDERGRADUATE FINANCIAL AID (Fall 2017, est.) 1,685 applied for aid; of those 91% were deemed to have need. 100% of undergraduates with need received aid; of those 12% had need fully met. *Average percent of need met:* 67% (excluding resources awarded to replace EFC). *Average financial aid package:* $27,756 (excluding resources awarded to replace EFC). 19% of all full-time undergraduates had no need and received non-need-based gift aid.

GIFT AID (NEED-BASED) *Total amount:* $13,436,234 (19% federal, 1% state, 76% institutional, 4% external sources). *Receiving aid:* Freshmen: 82% (481); all full-time undergraduates: 73% (1,526). *Average award:* Freshmen: $25,375; Undergraduates: $22,799. *Scholarships, grants, and awards:* Federal Pell, FSEOG, state, private, college/university gift aid from institutional funds.

GIFT AID (NON-NEED-BASED) *Total amount:* $29,929,718 (98% institutional, 2% external sources). *Receiving aid:* Freshmen: 81% (480). Undergraduates: 73% (1,530). *Average award:* Freshmen: $15,470. Undergraduates: $14,854. *Scholarships, grants, and awards by category:* Academic interests/achievement: general academic interests/achievements. *Creative arts/performance:* art/fine arts. *Special characteristics:* children and siblings of alumni. *Tuition waivers:* Full or partial for employees or children of employees. *ROTC:* Army cooperative.

LOANS *Student loans:* $11,909,831 (54% need-based, 46% non-need-based). 65% of past graduating class borrowed through all loan programs. *Average indebtedness per student:* $37,464. *Average need-based loan:* Freshmen: $3398. Undergraduates: $4436. *Parent loans:* $5,234,781 (100% non-need-based). *Programs:* Federal Direct (Subsidized and Unsubsidized Stafford, PLUS), Perkins, Federal Nursing, alternative loans.

WORK-STUDY *Federal work-study:* Total amount: $2,509,329; jobs available. *State or other work-study/employment:* Part-time jobs available.

APPLYING FOR FINANCIAL AID *Required financial aid form:* FAFSA. *Financial aid deadline (priority):* 3/1. *Notification date:* Continuous beginning 1/3. Students must reply by 5/1 or within 2 weeks of notification.

CONTACT Mrs. Anne McDermott, Director of Financial Aid, Salve Regina University, 100 Ochre Point Avenue, Newport, RI 02840-4192, 401-341-2901 or toll-free 888-GO SALVE. *Fax:* 401-341-2928. *E-mail:* financial_aid@salve.edu. *Website:* http://www.salve.edu/.

SAMFORD UNIVERSITY
Birmingham, AL

Tuition & fees: $31,650	Average undergraduate aid package: $19,523

ABOUT THE INSTITUTION Independent Baptist, coed. **Awards:** certificates, bachelor's, master's, and doctoral degrees. 74 undergraduate majors. **Total enrollment:** 5,509. Undergraduates: 3,373. Freshmen: 857. Federal methodology is used as a basis for awarding need-based institutional aid.

UNDERGRADUATE EXPENSES for 2018–2019 Application fee: $40. **Comprehensive fee:** $42,200 includes full-time tuition ($30,800), mandatory fees ($850), and room and board ($10,550). **College room only:** $5686. Full-time tuition and fees vary according to course load and program. Room and board charges vary according to board plan and housing facility. **Part-time tuition:** $1030 per credit hour. **Part-time fees:** $355 per term. Part-time tuition and fees vary according to course load and program.

FRESHMAN FINANCIAL AID (Fall 2016) 695 applied for aid; of those 61% were deemed to have need. 100% of freshmen with need received aid; of those 24% had need fully met. **Average percent of need met:** 75% (excluding resources awarded to replace EFC). **Average financial aid package:** $19,155 (excluding resources awarded to replace EFC). 46% of all full-time freshmen had no need and received non-need-based gift aid.

UNDERGRADUATE FINANCIAL AID (Fall 2016) 1,828 applied for aid; of those 70% were deemed to have need. 100% of undergraduates with need received aid; of those 21% had need fully met. **Average percent of need met:** 69% (excluding resources awarded to replace EFC). **Average financial aid package:** $19,523 (excluding resources awarded to replace EFC). 47% of all full-time undergraduates had no need and received non-need-based gift aid.

GIFT AID (NEED-BASED) Total amount: $16,453,105 (12% federal, 2% state, 82% institutional, 4% external sources). **Receiving aid:** Freshmen: 46% (424); all full-time undergraduates: 39% (1,235). **Average award:** Freshmen: $15,638; Undergraduates: $15,859. **Scholarships, grants, and awards:** Federal Pell, FSEOG, state, private, college/university gift aid from institutional funds, United Negro College Fund, Federal Nursing.

GIFT AID (NON-NEED-BASED) Total amount: $18,649,825 (2% state, 93% institutional, 5% external sources). **Receiving aid:** Freshmen: 11% (103). Undergraduates: 8% (256). **Average award:** Freshmen: $11,527. Undergraduates: $10,848. **Scholarships, grants, and awards by category:** Academic interests/achievement: 2,478 awards ($22,760,659 total): architecture, biological sciences, business, communication, computer science, education, English, foreign languages, general academic interests/achievements, health fields, home economics, humanities, international studies, mathematics, physical sciences, premedicine, religion/biblical studies, social sciences. Creative arts/performance: 233 awards ($1,250,336 total): art/fine arts, cinema/film/broadcasting, debating, journalism/publications, music, performing arts, theater/drama. Special achievements/activities: 1,060 awards ($2,076,474 total): cheerleading/drum major, community service, leadership, religious involvement. Special characteristics: 161 awards ($2,570,501 total): children and siblings of alumni, children of faculty/staff, ethnic background, members of minority groups, relatives of clergy, religious affiliation, siblings of current students, spouses of current students, veterans, veterans' children. **Tuition waivers:** Full or partial for employees or children of employees. **ROTC:** Army cooperative, Air Force.

LOANS Student loans: $12,694,065 (65% need-based, 35% non-need-based). 34% of past graduating class borrowed through all loan programs. Average indebtedness per student: $27,539. **Average need-based loan:** Freshmen: $3394. Undergraduates: $3936. **Parent loans:** $8,720,002 (38% need-based, 62% non-need-based). **Programs:** Federal Direct (Subsidized and Unsubsidized Stafford, PLUS), Perkins, Federal Nursing, college/university.

WORK-STUDY Federal work-study: 412 jobs averaging $2091. **State or other work-study/employment:** Total amount: $1,066,149 (29% need-based, 71% non-need-based). 715 part-time jobs averaging $1535.

ATHLETIC AWARDS Total amount: $7,979,045 (42% need-based, 58% non-need-based).

APPLYING FOR FINANCIAL AID Required financial aid forms: FAFSA, state aid form. **Financial aid deadline (priority):** 3/1. **Notification date:** 4/1. Students must reply by 5/1.

CONTACT Lane Smith, Director of Financial Aid, Samford University, 800 Lakeshore Drive, Birmingham, AL 35229, 205-726-2905 or toll-free 800-888-7218. Fax: 205-726-2738. E-mail: lsmith1@samford.edu. Website: http://www.samford.edu/.

SAM HOUSTON STATE UNIVERSITY
Huntsville, TX

Tuition & fees (TX res): $9890	Average undergraduate aid package: $11,263

ABOUT THE INSTITUTION State-supported, coed. **Awards:** certificates, bachelor's, master's, and doctoral degrees. 104 undergraduate majors. **Total enrollment:** 20,938. Undergraduates: 18,416. Freshmen: 2,873. Federal methodology is used as a basis for awarding need-based institutional aid.

UNDERGRADUATE EXPENSES for 2017–2018 Application fee: $45. **Tuition, state resident:** full-time $6840; part-time $228 per credit hour. **Tuition, nonresident:** full-time $19,290; part-time $643 per credit hour. **Required fees:** full-time $3050. Full-time tuition and fees vary according to course load and location. Part-time tuition and fees vary according to course load and location. **College room and board:** $9180; **Room only:** $5238. Room and board charges vary according to board plan and housing facility. **Payment plan:** Guaranteed tuition.

FRESHMAN FINANCIAL AID (Fall 2016) 2,208 applied for aid; of those 79% were deemed to have need. 99% of freshmen with need received aid; of those 11% had need fully met. **Average percent of need met:** 77% (excluding resources awarded to replace EFC). **Average financial aid package:** $11,276 (excluding resources awarded to replace EFC). 7% of all full-time freshmen had no need and received non-need-based gift aid.

UNDERGRADUATE FINANCIAL AID (Fall 2016) 11,217 applied for aid; of those 85% were deemed to have need. 97% of undergraduates with need received aid; of those 10% had need fully met. **Average percent of need met:** 77% (excluding resources awarded to replace EFC). **Average financial aid package:** $11,263 (excluding resources awarded to replace EFC). 3% of all full-time undergraduates had no need and received non-need-based gift aid.

GIFT AID (NEED-BASED) Total amount: $62,980,120 (49% federal, 39% state, 5% institutional, 7% external sources). **Receiving aid:** Freshmen: 56% (1,489); all full-time undergraduates: 55% (7,921). **Average award:** Freshmen: $8668; Undergraduates: $7560. **Scholarships, grants, and awards:** Federal Pell, FSEOG, state, college/university gift aid from institutional funds.

GIFT AID (NON-NEED-BASED) Total amount: $4,577,477 (43% institutional, 57% external sources). **Receiving aid:** Freshmen: 4% (105). Undergraduates: 3% (423). **Average award:** Freshmen: $2599. Undergraduates: $2624. **Scholarships, grants, and awards by category:** Academic interests/achievement: agriculture, biological sciences, business, communication, computer science, education, engineering/technologies, English, foreign languages, general academic interests/achievements, health fields, home economics, humanities, library science, mathematics, military science, physical sciences, social sciences. Creative arts/performance: art/fine arts, cinema/film/broadcasting, dance, journalism/publications, music, performing arts, theater/drama. Special achievements/activities: general special achievements/activities, leadership, rodeo. Special characteristics: children of union members/company employees, ethnic background, first-generation college students, members of minority groups, veterans. **Tuition waivers:** Full or partial for employees or children of employees. **ROTC:** Army.

LOANS Student loans: $107,108,698 (76% need-based, 24% non-need-based). 68% of past graduating class borrowed through all loan programs. Average indebtedness per student: $27,920. **Average need-based loan:** Freshmen: $5818. Undergraduates: $7582. **Parent loans:** $54,008,000 (46% need-based, 54% non-need-based). **Programs:** Federal Direct (Subsidized and Unsubsidized Stafford, PLUS), Perkins, state.

WORK-STUDY Federal work-study: jobs available. **State or other work-study/employment:** Total amount: $161,751 (100% need-based). Part-time jobs available.

ATHLETIC AWARDS Total amount: $4,348,914 (43% need-based, 57% non-need-based).

APPLYING FOR FINANCIAL AID Required financial aid form: FAFSA. **Financial aid deadline (priority):** 3/15. **Notification date:** Continuous beginning 4/1. Students must reply within 4 weeks of notification.

CONTACT Lydia Hall, Director of Financial Aid, Sam Houston State University, 1903 University, Estill 201, Box 2328, Huntsville, TX 77341-2328, 936-294-1750 or toll-free 866-232-7528 Ext. 1828. Fax: 936-294-3668. E-mail: lth003@shsu.edu. Website: http://www.shsu.edu/.

SAMUEL MERRITT UNIVERSITY
Oakland, CA

Tuition & fees: N/R	Average undergraduate aid package: $11,861

ABOUT THE INSTITUTION Independent, coed, primarily women. *Awards:* certificates, bachelor's, master's, and doctoral degrees (bachelor's degree offered jointly with Saint Mary's College of California). 1 undergraduate major. *Total enrollment:* 2,141. Undergraduates: 919. Entering class: 224. Federal methodology is used as a basis for awarding need-based institutional aid.

UNDERGRADUATE FINANCIAL AID (Fall 2016) 678 applied for aid; of those 98% were deemed to have need. 100% of undergraduates with need received aid. *Average percent of need met:* 19% (excluding resources awarded to replace EFC). *Average financial aid package:* $11,861 (excluding resources awarded to replace EFC).

GIFT AID (NEED-BASED) *Total amount:* $5,906,096 (16% federal, 10% state, 72% institutional, 2% external sources). *Receiving aid:* All full-time undergraduates: 35% (264). *Average award:* Undergraduates: $13,002. *Scholarships, grants, and awards:* Federal Pell, FSEOG, state, private, college/university gift aid from institutional funds, Federal Nursing.

LOANS *Student loans:* $20,255,687 (20% need-based, 80% non-need-based). *Average need-based loan:* Undergraduates: $6110. *Parent loans:* $2,651,447 (100% non-need-based). *Programs:* Federal Direct (Subsidized and Unsubsidized Stafford, PLUS), Perkins, Federal Nursing.

WORK-STUDY *Federal work-study:* 138 jobs averaging $1903. *State or other work-study/employment:* Part-time jobs available.

APPLYING FOR FINANCIAL AID *Required financial aid form:* FAFSA. *Financial aid deadline (priority):* 3/2. *Notification date:* Continuous beginning 4/15. Students must reply within 2 weeks of notification.

CONTACT Saeng Saephanh, Financial Aid Technician, Samuel Merritt University, 3100 Telegraph Avenue, Peralta Medical Office Building, Oakland, CA 94609, 510-869-1527 or toll-free 800-607-6377. *Fax:* 510-869-1529. *E-mail:* ssaephanh@samuelmerritt.edu.
Website: http://www.samuelmerritt.edu/.

SAN DIEGO CHRISTIAN COLLEGE
Santee, CA

ABOUT THE INSTITUTION Independent nondenominational, coed. 28 undergraduate majors.

GIFT AID (NEED-BASED) *Scholarships, grants, and awards:* Federal Pell, FSEOG, state, private, college/university gift aid from institutional funds.

GIFT AID (NON-NEED-BASED) *Scholarships, grants, and awards by category:* *Academic interests/achievement:* general academic interests/achievements. *Creative arts/performance:* music, performing arts, theater/drama. *Special achievements/activities:* general special achievements/activities, leadership, memberships, religious involvement. *Special characteristics:* children and siblings of alumni, children of faculty/staff, out-of-state students, relatives of clergy, religious affiliation, siblings of current students, veterans, veterans' children.

LOANS *Programs:* Federal Direct (Subsidized and Unsubsidized Stafford, PLUS), Perkins.

WORK-STUDY *Federal work-study:* 65 jobs averaging $2400. *State or other work-study/employment:* Total amount: $65,000 (100% need-based). 29 part-time jobs averaging $2400.

APPLYING FOR FINANCIAL AID *Required financial aid form:* FAFSA.

CONTACT Mr. Daniel Reed, Director of Financial Aid, San Diego Christian College, 200 Riverview Parkway, Santee, CA 92071, 619-201-8730 or toll-free 800-676-2242. *Fax:* 619-201-8797. *E-mail:* daniel.reed@sdcc.edu.
Website: http://www.sdcc.edu/.

SAN DIEGO STATE UNIVERSITY
San Diego, CA

Tuition & fees (CA res): $7460	Average undergraduate aid package: $9700

ABOUT THE INSTITUTION State-supported, coed. *Awards:* certificates, bachelor's, master's, and doctoral degrees. 105 undergraduate majors. *Total enrollment:* 34,828. Undergraduates: 30,165. Freshmen: 5,366. Federal methodology is used as a basis for awarding need-based institutional aid.

UNDERGRADUATE EXPENSES for 2017–2018 *Application fee:* $55. *Tuition, state resident:* full-time $5742. *Tuition, nonresident:* full-time $17,622. *Required fees:* full-time $1718. Full-time tuition and fees vary according to course load, degree level, and location. Part-time tuition and fees vary according to course load, degree level, and location. *College room and board:* $15,966. Room and board charges vary according to board plan and housing facility.

FRESHMAN FINANCIAL AID (Fall 2017, est.) 3,800 applied for aid; of those 66% were deemed to have need. 96% of freshmen with need received aid; of those 8% had need fully met. *Average percent of need met:* 65% (excluding resources awarded to replace EFC). *Average financial aid package:* $9700 (excluding resources awarded to replace EFC). 3% of all full-time freshmen had no need and received non-need-based gift aid.

UNDERGRADUATE FINANCIAL AID (Fall 2017, est.) 18,000 applied for aid; of those 81% were deemed to have need. 97% of undergraduates with need received aid; of those 20% had need fully met. *Average percent of need met:* 67% (excluding resources awarded to replace EFC). *Average financial aid package:* $9700 (excluding resources awarded to replace EFC). 6% of all full-time undergraduates had no need and received non-need-based gift aid.

GIFT AID (NEED-BASED) *Total amount:* $108,341,000 (44% federal, 30% state, 26% institutional). *Receiving aid:* Freshmen: 30% (1,500); all full-time undergraduates: 39% (10,500). *Average award:* Freshmen: $9500; Undergraduates: $9500. *Scholarships, grants, and awards:* Federal Pell, FSEOG, state, private, college/university gift aid from institutional funds.

GIFT AID (NON-NEED-BASED) *Total amount:* $12,592,000 (28% state, 48% institutional, 24% external sources). *Receiving aid:* Freshmen: 24% (1,200). Undergraduates: 18% (5,000). *Average award:* Freshmen: $3300. Undergraduates: $2000. *Scholarships, grants, and awards by category:* *Academic interests/achievement:* area/ethnic studies, biological sciences, business, communication, computer science, education, engineering/technologies, English, foreign languages, general academic interests/achievements, health fields, home economics, humanities, international studies, mathematics, military science, physical sciences, religion/biblical studies, social sciences. *Creative arts/performance:* applied art and design, art/fine arts, cinema/film/broadcasting, creative writing, dance, debating, journalism/publications, music, performing arts, theater/drama. *Special achievements/activities:* cheerleading/drum major, hobbies/interests, leadership, memberships. *Special characteristics:* adult students, children and siblings of alumni, children of faculty/staff, children of workers in trades, first-generation college students, handicapped students, local/state students, previous college experience, veterans, veterans' children. *Tuition waivers:* Full or partial for employees or children of employees. *ROTC:* Army, Naval, Air Force.

LOANS *Student loans:* $129,501,000 (72% need-based, 28% non-need-based). 47% of past graduating class borrowed through all loan programs. *Average indebtedness per student:* $19,633. *Average need-based loan:* Freshmen: $3100. Undergraduates: $4100. *Parent loans:* $104,408,000 (27% need-based, 73% non-need-based). *Programs:* Federal Direct (Subsidized and Unsubsidized Stafford, PLUS), college/university.

WORK-STUDY *Federal work-study:* Total amount: $1,691,000; 770 jobs averaging $2200.

ATHLETIC AWARDS Total amount: $8,268,000 (100% non-need-based).

APPLYING FOR FINANCIAL AID *Required financial aid forms:* FAFSA, state aid form. *Financial aid deadline:* 3/2. *Notification date:* Continuous beginning 3/15.

CONTACT Mrs. Rose Pasenelli, Director of Financial Aid and Scholarships, San Diego State University, 5500 Campanile Drive, SSW-3605, San Diego, CA 92182-7436, 619-594-6323 or toll-free 855-594-6336 (in-state), 855-594-3983 (out-of-state). *E-mail:* rpasenel@mail.sdsu.edu.
Website: http://www.sdsu.edu/.

SAN FRANCISCO ART INSTITUTE
San Francisco, CA

Tuition & fees: $46,534	Average undergraduate aid package: $16,140

ABOUT THE INSTITUTION Independent, coed. **Awards:** certificates, bachelor's, and master's degrees. 8 undergraduate majors. **Total enrollment:** 433. Undergraduates: 299. Freshmen: 53. Both federal and institutional methodology are used as a basis for awarding need-based institutional aid.

UNDERGRADUATE EXPENSES for 2018–2019 Application fee: $75. **One-time required fee:** $200. **Comprehensive fee:** $62,243 includes full-time tuition ($45,664), mandatory fees ($870), and room and board ($15,709). **College room only:** $11,650. Full-time tuition and fees vary according to degree level. Room and board charges vary according to housing facility. **Part-time tuition:** $2000 per credit. Part-time tuition and fees vary according to degree level.

FRESHMAN FINANCIAL AID (Fall 2017, est.) 37 applied for aid; of those 78% were deemed to have need. 100% of freshmen with need received aid; of those 10% had need fully met. **Average percent of need met:** 41% (excluding resources awarded to replace EFC). **Average financial aid package:** $16,709 (excluding resources awarded to replace EFC). 40% of all full-time freshmen had no need and received non-need-based gift aid.

UNDERGRADUATE FINANCIAL AID (Fall 2017, est.) 182 applied for aid; of those 87% were deemed to have need. 100% of undergraduates with need received aid; of those 11% had need fully met. **Average percent of need met:** 49% (excluding resources awarded to replace EFC). **Average financial aid package:** $16,140 (excluding resources awarded to replace EFC). 40% of all full-time undergraduates had no need and received non-need-based gift aid.

GIFT AID (NEED-BASED) Total amount: $3,059,232 (10% federal, 3% state, 82% institutional, 5% external sources). **Receiving aid:** Freshmen: 48% (25); all full-time undergraduates: 47% (129). **Average award:** Freshmen: $5649; Undergraduates: $5679. **Scholarships, grants, and awards:** Federal Pell, FSEOG, state, private, college/university gift aid from institutional funds.

GIFT AID (NON-NEED-BASED) Receiving aid: Freshmen: 54% (28). Undergraduates: 57% (157). **Average award:** Freshmen: $10,563. Undergraduates: $8361. **Scholarships, grants, and awards by category:** Academic interests/achievement: general academic interests/achievements. Creative arts/performance: art/fine arts. **Special characteristics:** children and siblings of alumni, first-generation college students. **Tuition waivers:** Full or partial for employees or children of employees.

LOANS Student loans: $770,447 (100% need-based). 46% of past graduating class borrowed through all loan programs. **Average indebtedness per student:** $27,137. **Average need-based loan:** Freshmen: $1750. Undergraduates: $2416. **Parent loans:** $631,264 (100% need-based). **Programs:** Federal Direct (Subsidized and Unsubsidized Stafford, PLUS).

WORK-STUDY Federal work-study: Total amount: $89,333; jobs available. **State or other work-study/employment:** Part-time jobs available.

APPLYING FOR FINANCIAL AID Required financial aid form: FAFSA. **Financial aid deadline (priority):** 3/1. **Notification date:** Continuous beginning 3/1. Students must reply within 2 weeks of notification.

CONTACT Annita Alldredge, Director of Financial Aid, San Francisco Art Institute, 800 Chestnut Street, San Francisco, CA 94133, 415-749-4560 or toll-free 800-345-SFAI. Fax: 415-351-3503. E-mail: aalldredge@sfai.edu. Website: http://www.sfai.edu/.

SAN FRANCISCO CONSERVATORY OF MUSIC
San Francisco, CA

Tuition & fees: $44,810	Average undergraduate aid package: $35,000

ABOUT THE INSTITUTION Independent, coed. **Awards:** certificates, diplomas, bachelor's, and master's degrees. 9 undergraduate majors. **Total enrollment:** 414. Undergraduates: 205. Freshmen: 61. Both federal and institutional methodology are used as a basis for awarding need-based institutional aid.

UNDERGRADUATE EXPENSES for 2017–2018 **Application fee:** $110. **One-time required fee:** $50. **Comprehensive fee:** $60,970 includes full-time tuition ($43,700), mandatory fees ($1110), and room and board ($16,160). **College room only:** $12,460. Room and board charges vary according to board plan and housing facility. **Part-time tuition:** $1924 per credit. **Part-time fees:** $1110 per year. Part-time tuition and fees vary according to course load.

FRESHMAN FINANCIAL AID (Fall 2017, est.) 48 applied for aid; of those 90% were deemed to have need. 100% of freshmen with need received aid; of those 26% had need fully met. **Average percent of need met:** 75% (excluding resources awarded to replace EFC). **Average financial aid package:** $27,500 (excluding resources awarded to replace EFC). 11% of all full-time freshmen had no need and received non-need-based gift aid.

UNDERGRADUATE FINANCIAL AID (Fall 2017, est.) 182 applied for aid; of those 93% were deemed to have need. 100% of undergraduates with need received aid; of those 9% had need fully met. **Average percent of need met:** 75% (excluding resources awarded to replace EFC). **Average financial aid package:** $35,000 (excluding resources awarded to replace EFC). 10% of all full-time undergraduates had no need and received non-need-based gift aid.

GIFT AID (NEED-BASED) Total amount: $4,480,774 (7% federal, 5% state, 87% institutional, 1% external sources). **Receiving aid:** Freshmen: 70% (43); all full-time undergraduates: 83% (170). **Average award:** Freshmen: $25,000; Undergraduates: $23,000. **Scholarships, grants, and awards:** Federal Pell, FSEOG, state, college/university gift aid from institutional funds.

GIFT AID (NON-NEED-BASED) Total amount: $688,520 (100% institutional). **Receiving aid:** Freshmen: 43% (26). Undergraduates: 8% (16). **Average award:** Freshmen: $21,600. Undergraduates: $18,300. **Scholarships, grants, and awards by category:** Creative arts/performance: 24 awards ($360,000 total): music. **Tuition waivers:** Full or partial for employees or children of employees.

LOANS Student loans: $968,810 (92% need-based, 8% non-need-based). 42% of past graduating class borrowed through all loan programs. **Average indebtedness per student:** $42,000. **Average need-based loan:** Freshmen: $4620. Undergraduates: $7500. **Parent loans:** $1,052,087 (69% need-based, 31% non-need-based). **Programs:** Federal Direct (Subsidized and Unsubsidized Stafford, PLUS), Perkins.

WORK-STUDY Federal work-study: Total amount: $67,875; 23 jobs averaging $2500. **State or other work-study/employment:** Part-time jobs available.

APPLYING FOR FINANCIAL AID Required financial aid forms: FAFSA, institution's own form, CSS Financial Aid PROFILE, state aid form, noncustodial (divorced/separated) parent's statement. **Financial aid deadline:** 3/1 (priority: 2/15). **Notification date:** Continuous beginning 4/1. Students must reply within 2 weeks of notification.

CONTACT Doris Howard, Director of Financial Aid, San Francisco Conservatory of Music, 50 Oak Street, San Francisco, CA 94102-6011, 415-503-6214. Fax: 415-503-6299. E-mail: finaid@sfcm.edu. Website: http://www.sfcm.edu/.

SAN FRANCISCO STATE UNIVERSITY
San Francisco, CA

Tuition & fees (CA res): $7254	Average undergraduate aid package: $15,520

ABOUT THE INSTITUTION State-supported, coed. **Awards:** certificates, bachelor's, master's, and doctoral degrees. 91 undergraduate majors. **Total enrollment:** 29,607. Undergraduates: 26,617. Freshmen: 4,323. Federal methodology is used as a basis for awarding need-based institutional aid.

UNDERGRADUATE EXPENSES for 2017–2018 **Application fee:** $55. **Tuition, state resident:** full-time $5742; part-time $1665 per term. **Tuition, nonresident:** full-time $17,622; part-time $4041 per term. **Required fees:** full-time $1512; $756 per term. Full-time tuition and fees vary according to course load. Part-time tuition and fees vary according to course load. **College room and board:** $13,248; **Room only:** $8752. Room and board charges vary according to board plan and housing facility.

FRESHMAN FINANCIAL AID (Fall 2017, est.) 3,157 applied for aid; of those 84% were deemed to have need. 97% of freshmen with need received aid; of those 27% had need fully met. **Average percent of need met:** 71% (excluding resources awarded to replace EFC). **Average financial aid package:** $17,230 (excluding resources awarded to replace EFC). 1% of all full-time freshmen had no need and received non-need-based gift aid.

UNDERGRADUATE FINANCIAL AID (Fall 2017, est.) 17,449 applied for aid; of those 91% were deemed to have need. 96% of undergraduates with need received aid; of those 18% had need fully met. *Average percent of need met:* 64% (excluding resources awarded to replace EFC). *Average financial aid package:* $15,520 (excluding resources awarded to replace EFC). 1% of all full-time undergraduates had no need and received non-need-based gift aid.

GIFT AID (NEED-BASED) *Total amount:* $153,213,327 (40% federal, 58% state, 1% institutional, 1% external sources). *Receiving aid:* Freshmen: 69% (2,465); all full-time undergraduates: 65% (14,399). *Average award:* Freshmen: $9477; Undergraduates: $8871. *Scholarships, grants, and awards:* Federal Pell, FSEOG, state, private, college/university gift aid from institutional funds.

GIFT AID (NON-NEED-BASED) *Total amount:* $53,401 (3% institutional, 97% external sources). *Receiving aid:* Freshmen: 20% (703). Undergraduates: 10% (2,182). *Average award:* Freshmen: $4262. Undergraduates: $2535. *Tuition waivers:* Full or partial for employees or children of employees, senior citizens. **ROTC:** Army cooperative, Air Force cooperative.

LOANS *Student loans:* $64,027,869 (94% need-based, 6% non-need-based). 45% of past graduating class borrowed through all loan programs. *Average indebtedness per student:* $19,347. *Average need-based loan:* Freshmen: $3349. Undergraduates: $4353. *Parent loans:* $32,846,442 (100% need-based). *Programs:* Federal Direct (Subsidized and Unsubsidized Stafford, PLUS), Perkins.

WORK-STUDY *Federal work-study:* Total amount: $1,600,000; jobs available.

ATHLETIC AWARDS Total amount: $641,468 (100% need-based).

APPLYING FOR FINANCIAL AID *Required financial aid form:* FAFSA. *Financial aid deadline (priority):* 3/2. *Notification date:* Continuous beginning 4/15. Students must reply within 2 weeks of notification.

CONTACT Jimmie Wilder, Associate Director of Financial Aid, San Francisco State University, 1600 Holloway Avenue, San Francisco, CA 94132-1722, 415-338-7000. *Fax:* 415-338-0949. *E-mail:* finaid@sfsu.edu.
Website: http://www.sfsu.edu/.

SAN IGNACIO UNIVERSITY
Doral, FL

CONTACT Financial Aid Office, San Ignacio University, 10395 NW 41st Street, Suite 125, Doral, FL 33178.
Website: http://www.sanignaciouniversity.edu/.

SAN JOSE STATE UNIVERSITY
San Jose, CA

Tuition & fees (CA res): $7417	Average undergraduate aid package: $18,791

ABOUT THE INSTITUTION State-supported, coed. 88 undergraduate majors. Federal methodology is used as a basis for awarding need-based institutional aid.

UNDERGRADUATE EXPENSES for 2017–2018 *Tuition, state resident:* full-time $5472; part-time $1665 per term. *Tuition, nonresident:* full-time $14,400; part-time $3897 per term. *Required fees:* full-time $1945; $1946 per year. *College room and board:* $14,107; *Room only:* $9427. Room and board charges vary according to board plan, housing facility, and location.

FRESHMAN FINANCIAL AID (Fall 2017, est.) 3,551 applied for aid; of those 82% were deemed to have need. 98% of freshmen with need received aid; of those 72% had need fully met. *Average percent of need met:* 92% (excluding resources awarded to replace EFC). *Average financial aid package:* $19,745 (excluding resources awarded to replace EFC). 1% of all full-time freshmen had no need and received non-need-based gift aid.

UNDERGRADUATE FINANCIAL AID (Fall 2017, est.) 16,510 applied for aid; of those 93% were deemed to have need. 98% of undergraduates with need received aid; of those 69% had need fully met. *Average percent of need met:* 89% (excluding resources awarded to replace EFC). *Average financial aid package:* $18,791 (excluding resources awarded to replace EFC). 1% of all full-time undergraduates had no need and received non-need-based gift aid.

GIFT AID (NEED-BASED) *Total amount:* $135,391,501 (42% federal, 56% state, 1% institutional, 1% external sources). *Receiving aid:* Freshmen: 63% (2,727); all full-time undergraduates: 63% (14,473). *Average award:* Freshmen: $12,461;

Undergraduates: $10,793. *Scholarships, grants, and awards:* Federal Pell, FSEOG, state, private, college/university gift aid from institutional funds.

GIFT AID (NON-NEED-BASED) *Total amount:* $132,335 (41% institutional, 59% external sources). *Receiving aid:* Freshmen: 7% (289). Undergraduates: 4% (905). *Average award:* Freshmen: $1052. Undergraduates: $1489. *Scholarships, grants, and awards by category: Academic interests/achievement:* architecture, biological sciences, business, education, engineering/technologies, general academic interests/achievements, home economics, humanities, international studies, mathematics, physical sciences, religion/biblical studies, social sciences. *Creative arts/performance:* applied art and design, cinema/film/broadcasting, dance, journalism/publications, music, theater/drama. *Special achievements/activities:* community service, leadership. *Special characteristics:* adult students, children of faculty/staff, children with a deceased or disabled parent, ethnic background, first-generation college students, international students, local/state students, members of minority groups, veterans. *Tuition waivers:* Full or partial for employees or children of employees.

LOANS *Student loans:* $48,713,735 (88% need-based, 12% non-need-based). 47% of past graduating class borrowed through all loan programs. *Average indebtedness per student:* $19,303. *Average need-based loan:* Freshmen: $3433. Undergraduates: $4234. *Parent loans:* $14,760,613 (72% need-based, 28% non-need-based). *Programs:* Federal Direct (Subsidized and Unsubsidized Stafford, PLUS), Perkins, state.

WORK-STUDY *Federal work-study:* Total amount: $1,492,906; jobs available.

ATHLETIC AWARDS Total amount: $6,779,163 (86% need-based, 14% non-need-based).

APPLYING FOR FINANCIAL AID *Required financial aid forms:* FAFSA, state aid form. *Financial aid deadline:* 4/28 (priority: 3/2). *Notification date:* Continuous beginning 3/1.

CONTACT Coleetta McElroy, Director of Financial Aid and Scholarship Office, San Jose State University, One Washington Square, San Jose, CA 95192-0036, 408-283-7500. *E-mail:* coleetta.mcelroy@sjsu.edu.
Website: http://www.sjsu.edu/.

SANTA BARBARA BUSINESS COLLEGE
Ventura, CA

CONTACT Financial Aid Office, Santa Barbara Business College, 4839 Market Street, Ventura, CA 93003, 805-339-2999.
Website: http://www.sbbcollege.edu/.

SANTA CLARA UNIVERSITY
Santa Clara, CA

Tuition & fees: $49,858	Average undergraduate aid package: $37,051

ABOUT THE INSTITUTION Independent Roman Catholic (Jesuit), coed. *Awards:* certificates, bachelor's, master's, and doctoral degrees. 55 undergraduate majors. *Total enrollment:* 8,629. Undergraduates: 5,499. Freshmen: 1,404. Both federal and institutional methodology are used as a basis for awarding need-based institutional aid.

UNDERGRADUATE EXPENSES for 2017–2018 *Application fee:* $60. *Comprehensive fee:* $64,345 includes full-time tuition ($49,233), mandatory fees ($625), and room and board ($14,487). Room and board charges vary according to board plan and housing facility. *Part-time tuition:* $1368 per unit. Part-time tuition and fees vary according to course load.

FRESHMAN FINANCIAL AID (Fall 2017, est.) 938 applied for aid; of those 67% were deemed to have need. 97% of freshmen with need received aid; of those 43% had need fully met. *Average percent of need met:* 84% (excluding resources awarded to replace EFC). *Average financial aid package:* $38,585 (excluding resources awarded to replace EFC). 27% of all full-time freshmen had no need and received non-need-based gift aid.

UNDERGRADUATE FINANCIAL AID (Fall 2017, est.) 3,175 applied for aid; of those 76% were deemed to have need. 81% of undergraduates with need received aid; of those 37% had need fully met. *Average percent of need met:* 77% (excluding resources awarded to replace EFC). *Average financial aid package:* $37,051

(excluding resources awarded to replace EFC). 28% of all full-time undergraduates had no need and received non-need-based gift aid.

GIFT AID (NEED-BASED) *Total amount:* $64,358,850 (4% federal, 7% state, 87% institutional, 2% external sources). *Receiving aid:* Freshmen: 38% (537); all full-time undergraduates: 32% (1,772). *Average award:* Freshmen: $3051; Undergraduates: $28,976. *Scholarships, grants, and awards:* Federal Pell, FSEOG, state, private, college/university gift aid from institutional funds.

GIFT AID (NON-NEED-BASED) *Total amount:* $28,601,549 (96% institutional, 4% external sources). *Receiving aid:* Freshmen: 22% (302). Undergraduates: 16% (853). *Average award:* Freshmen: $16,012. Undergraduates: $16,185. *Scholarships, grants, and awards by category: Academic interests/achievement:* 2,517 awards ($40,876,928 total): business, engineering/technologies, general academic interests/achievements, military science. *Creative arts/performance:* 99 awards ($300,054 total): dance, debating, music, theater/drama. *Special characteristics:* 82 awards ($1,251,742 total): children and siblings of alumni, children of faculty/staff, children with a deceased or disabled parent, handicapped students. *Tuition waivers:* Full or partial for employees or children of employees. *ROTC:* Army, Air Force cooperative.

LOANS *Student loans:* $9,290,845 (85% need-based, 15% non-need-based). 42% of past graduating class borrowed through all loan programs. *Average indebtedness per student:* $28,808. *Average need-based loan:* Freshmen: $3340. Undergraduates: $4563. *Parent loans:* $9,589,191 (77% need-based, 23% non-need-based). *Programs:* Federal Direct (Subsidized and Unsubsidized Stafford, PLUS), private loans.

WORK-STUDY *Federal work-study:* Total amount: $756,966; 325 jobs averaging $3208. *State or other work-study/employment:* Part-time jobs available.

ATHLETIC AWARDS Total amount: $6,384,605 (23% need-based, 77% non-need-based).

APPLYING FOR FINANCIAL AID *Required financial aid forms:* FAFSA, CSS Financial Aid PROFILE. *Financial aid deadline (priority):* 2/1. *Notification date:* 4/1. Students must reply by 5/1 or within 2 weeks of notification.

CONTACT Mrs. Nancy Merz, Dean of Financial Aid, Santa Clara University, 500 El Camino Real, Santa Clara, CA 95053, 408-551-1000. *Fax:* 408-554-2154. *E-mail:* nmerz@scu.edu.
Website: http://www.scu.edu/.

SANTA FE COLLEGE
Gainesville, FL

CONTACT Financial Aid Office, Santa Fe College, 3000 Northwest 83rd Street, Gainesville, FL 32606, 352-395-5000.
Website: http://www.sfcollege.edu/.

SARAH LAWRENCE COLLEGE
Bronxville, NY

Tuition & fees: $54,010	Average undergraduate aid package: $34,955

ABOUT THE INSTITUTION Independent, coed. *Awards:* bachelor's and master's degrees. 60 undergraduate majors. *Total enrollment:* 1,696. Undergraduates: 1,399. Freshmen: 393. Both federal and institutional methodology are used as a basis for awarding need-based institutional aid.

UNDERGRADUATE EXPENSES for 2017–2018 *Application fee:* $60. *Comprehensive fee:* $68,866 includes full-time tuition ($52,600), mandatory fees ($1410), and room and board ($14,856). *College room only:* $9830. Full-time tuition and fees vary according to course load. Room and board charges vary according to board plan. *Part-time tuition:* $1753.33 per credit hour. *Part-time fees:* $570 per term. Part-time tuition and fees vary according to course load.

FRESHMAN FINANCIAL AID (Fall 2017, est.) 316 applied for aid; of those 84% were deemed to have need. 98% of freshmen with need received aid; of those 18% had need fully met. *Average percent of need met:* 76% (excluding resources awarded to replace EFC). *Average financial aid package:* $36,059 (excluding resources awarded to replace EFC). 20% of all full-time freshmen had no need and received non-need-based gift aid.

UNDERGRADUATE FINANCIAL AID (Fall 2017, est.) 961 applied for aid; of those 88% were deemed to have need. 99% of undergraduates with need received aid; of those 13% had need fully met. *Average percent of need met:* 76% (excluding resources awarded to replace EFC). *Average financial aid package:* $34,955 (excluding resources awarded to replace EFC). 19% of all full-time undergraduates had no need and received non-need-based gift aid.

GIFT AID (NEED-BASED) *Total amount:* $28,856,788 (4% federal, 1% state, 93% institutional, 2% external sources). *Receiving aid:* Freshmen: 65% (255); all full-time undergraduates: 59% (821). *Average award:* Freshmen: $34,059; Undergraduates: $34,955. *Scholarships, grants, and awards:* Federal Pell, FSEOG, state, private, college/university gift aid from institutional funds.

GIFT AID (NON-NEED-BASED) *Total amount:* $5,741,381 (1% state, 91% institutional, 8% external sources). *Receiving aid:* Freshmen: 11% (45). Undergraduates: 8% (104). *Average award:* Freshmen: $17,758. Undergraduates: $16,523. *Scholarships, grants, and awards by category: Academic interests/achievement:* 401 awards ($5,168,996 total): general academic interests/achievements. *Tuition waivers:* Full or partial for employees or children of employees. *ROTC:* Air Force cooperative.

LOANS *Student loans:* $6,078,580 (62% need-based, 38% non-need-based). 37% of past graduating class borrowed through all loan programs. *Average indebtedness per student:* $19,610. *Average need-based loan:* Freshmen: $2178. Undergraduates: $2976. *Parent loans:* $3,420,550 (55% need-based, 45% non-need-based). *Programs:* Federal Direct (Subsidized and Unsubsidized Stafford, PLUS), Perkins, private loans.

WORK-STUDY *Federal work-study:* Total amount: $1,221,558; 571 jobs averaging $2313. *State or other work-study/employment:* Total amount: $69,750 (49% need-based, 51% non-need-based). 83 part-time jobs averaging $2627.

APPLYING FOR FINANCIAL AID *Required financial aid forms:* FAFSA, state aid form, noncustodial (divorced/separated) parent's statement. *Financial aid deadline:* 2/1. *Notification date:* 4/1. Students must reply by 5/1.

CONTACT Ms. Deborah McCue, Director of Enrollment Operations and Systems, Sarah Lawrence College, One Mead Way, Bronxville, NY 10708, 914-395-2520 or toll-free 800-888-2858. *Fax:* 914-395-2515. *E-mail:* dmccue@sarahlawrence.edu.
Website: http://www.sarahlawrence.edu/.

SAVANNAH COLLEGE OF ART AND DESIGN
Savannah, GA

Tuition & fees: $36,630	Average undergraduate aid package: $18,094

ABOUT THE INSTITUTION Independent, coed. *Awards:* certificates, bachelor's, and master's degrees. 30 undergraduate majors. *Total enrollment:* 13,842. Undergraduates: 11,324. Freshmen: 2,534. Federal methodology is used as a basis for awarding need-based institutional aid.

UNDERGRADUATE EXPENSES for 2018–2019 *Application fee:* $70. *One-time required fee:* $500. *Comprehensive fee:* $51,180 includes full-time tuition ($36,630) and room and board ($14,550). *College room only:* $9591. Full-time tuition and fees vary according to course load and degree level. Room and board charges vary according to board plan, housing facility, and location. *Part-time tuition:* $4070 per course. Part-time tuition and fees vary according to course load and degree level.

FRESHMAN FINANCIAL AID (Fall 2016) 1,520 applied for aid; of those 82% were deemed to have need. 100% of freshmen with need received aid; of those 10% had need fully met. *Average percent of need met:* 43% (excluding resources awarded to replace EFC). *Average financial aid package:* $17,140 (excluding resources awarded to replace EFC). 41% of all full-time freshmen had no need and received non-need-based gift aid.

UNDERGRADUATE FINANCIAL AID (Fall 2016) 5,114 applied for aid; of those 86% were deemed to have need. 99% of undergraduates with need received aid; of those 8% had need fully met. *Average percent of need met:* 43% (excluding resources awarded to replace EFC). *Average financial aid package:* $18,094 (excluding resources awarded to replace EFC). 43% of all full-time undergraduates had no need and received non-need-based gift aid.

GIFT AID (NEED-BASED) *Total amount:* $67,334,587 (16% federal, 6% state, 77% institutional, 1% external sources). *Receiving aid:* Freshmen: 56% (1,237); all full-time undergraduates: 48% (4,271). *Average award:* Freshmen: $14,051; Undergraduates: $14,225. **Scholarships, grants, and awards:** Federal Pell, FSEOG, state, private, college/university gift aid from institutional funds, United Negro College Fund.

GIFT AID (NON-NEED-BASED) Total amount: $50,409,522 (2% state, 93% institutional, 5% external sources). **Receiving aid:** Freshmen: 5% (122). Undergraduates: 4% (336). **Average award:** Freshmen: $10,531. Undergraduates: $10,720. **Scholarships, grants, and awards by category:** Academic interests/achievement: architecture, general academic interests/achievements. Creative arts/performance: applied art and design, art/fine arts, cinema/film/broadcasting, creative writing, dance, debating, general creative arts/performance, journalism/publications, music, performing arts, theater/drama. Special achievements/activities: general special achievements/activities. Special characteristics: general special characteristics, veterans, veterans' children. **Tuition waivers:** Full or partial for employees or children of employees.

LOANS Student loans: $56,116,530 (76% need-based, 24% non-need-based). 54% of past graduating class borrowed through all loan programs. **Average indebtedness per student:** $39,022. **Average need-based loan:** Freshmen: $3266. Undergraduates: $4284. **Parent loans:** $63,398,447 (66% need-based, 34% non-need-based). **Programs:** Federal Direct (Subsidized and Unsubsidized Stafford, PLUS), state, alternative loans.

WORK-STUDY Federal work-study: 384 jobs averaging $1495. **State or other work-study/employment:** Total amount: $1,309,901 (100% need-based). 810 part-time jobs averaging $1617.

ATHLETIC AWARDS Total amount: $5,974,580 (33% need-based, 67% non-need-based).

APPLYING FOR FINANCIAL AID Required financial aid forms: FAFSA, state aid form. **Financial aid deadline:** Continuous. **Notification date:** Continuous beginning 3/1. Students must reply within 4 weeks of notification.

CONTACT Ms. Kim Beveridge, Director of Financial Aid, Savannah College of Art and Design, PO Box 3146, Savannah, GA 31402-3146, 800-859-7223 or toll-free 800-869-7223. E-mail: admission@scad.edu. Website: http://www.scad.edu/.

SAVANNAH STATE UNIVERSITY
Savannah, GA

ABOUT THE INSTITUTION State-supported, coed. 29 undergraduate majors.
GIFT AID (NEED-BASED) Scholarships, grants, and awards: Federal Pell, FSEOG, state, private, college/university gift aid from institutional funds.
GIFT AID (NON-NEED-BASED) Scholarships, grants, and awards by category: Academic interests/achievement: biological sciences, business, computer science, engineering/technologies, English, general academic interests/achievements, humanities, mathematics, military science, physical sciences, social sciences.
LOANS Programs: Federal Direct (Subsidized and Unsubsidized Stafford, PLUS), Perkins, state, college/university.
APPLYING FOR FINANCIAL AID Required financial aid form: FAFSA.
CONTACT Mr. Kenneth Wilson, Director of Financial Aid, Savannah State University, PO Box 20523, Savannah, GA 31404, 912-358-4162 or toll-free 800-788-0478. Fax: 912-358-3167. E-mail: finaid@savannahstate.edu. Website: http://www.savannahstate.edu/.

SCHILLER INTERNATIONAL UNIVERSITY
Largo, FL

CONTACT Financial Aid Office, Schiller International University, 8560 Ulmerton Road, Largo, FL 33771, 727-736-5082 or toll-free 800-261-9571 (in-state), 800-261-9751 (out-of-state). Website: http://www.schiller.edu/.

SCHOOL OF THE ART INSTITUTE OF CHICAGO
Chicago, IL

Tuition & fees: $47,420	Average undergraduate aid package: N/A

ABOUT THE INSTITUTION Independent, coed. **Awards:** certificates, bachelor's, and master's degrees. 33 undergraduate majors. **Total enrollment:** 3,570. Undergraduates: 2,849. Freshmen: 634. Federal methodology is used as a basis for awarding need-based institutional aid.

UNDERGRADUATE EXPENSES for 2017–2018 Application fee: $65. **Comprehensive fee:** $62,910 includes full-time tuition ($46,560), mandatory fees ($860), and room and board ($15,490). **College room only:** $11,900. Full-time tuition and fees vary according to course load, degree level, and program. Room and board charges vary according to board plan and housing facility. **Part-time tuition:** $1552 per credit hour. **Part-time fees:** $295 per term. Part-time tuition and fees vary according to course load, degree level, and program.

GIFT AID (NEED-BASED) Scholarships, grants, and awards: Federal Pell, FSEOG, state, private, college/university gift aid from institutional funds.
GIFT AID (NON-NEED-BASED) Scholarships, grants, and awards by category: Academic interests/achievement: general academic interests/achievements. Creative arts/performance: art/fine arts. **Tuition waivers:** Full or partial for employees or children of employees.
LOANS Programs: Federal Direct (Subsidized and Unsubsidized Stafford, PLUS).
WORK-STUDY Federal work-study jobs available. **State or other work-study/employment:** Part-time jobs available.
APPLYING FOR FINANCIAL AID Required financial aid form: FAFSA. **Financial aid deadline (priority):** 3/1. **Notification date:** Continuous beginning 4/1.
CONTACT Mr. Patrick James, Student Financial Services Office, School of the Art Institute of Chicago, 36 South Wabash, Suite 1218, Chicago, IL 60603-3103, 312-629-6600 or toll-free 800-232-SAIC. Fax: 312-629-6601. E-mail: finaid@saic.edu. Website: http://www.saic.edu/.

SCHOOL OF VISUAL ARTS
New York, NY

Tuition & fees: $39,900	Average undergraduate aid package: $19,523

ABOUT THE INSTITUTION Proprietary, coed. **Awards:** bachelor's and master's degrees. 15 undergraduate majors. **Total enrollment:** 4,395. Undergraduates: 3,752. Freshmen: 699. Federal methodology is used as a basis for awarding need-based institutional aid.

UNDERGRADUATE EXPENSES for 2018–2019 Application fee: $50. **Comprehensive fee:** $60,300 includes full-time tuition ($39,900) and room and board ($20,400). **College room only:** $17,500. Room and board charges vary according to housing facility. **Part-time tuition:** $1335 per credit hour.

FRESHMAN FINANCIAL AID (Fall 2017, est.) 350 applied for aid; of those 89% were deemed to have need. 98% of freshmen with need received aid; of those 5% had need fully met. **Average percent of need met:** 39% (excluding resources awarded to replace EFC). **Average financial aid package:** $19,728 (excluding resources awarded to replace EFC). 14% of all full-time freshmen had no need and received non-need-based gift aid.

UNDERGRADUATE FINANCIAL AID (Fall 2017, est.) 1,475 applied for aid; of those 93% were deemed to have need. 97% of undergraduates with need received aid; of those 2% had need fully met. **Average percent of need met:** 33% (excluding resources awarded to replace EFC). **Average financial aid package:** $19,523 (excluding resources awarded to replace EFC). 9% of all full-time undergraduates had no need and received non-need-based gift aid.

GIFT AID (NEED-BASED) Total amount: $17,337,039 (25% federal, 6% state, 67% institutional, 2% external sources). **Receiving aid:** Freshmen: 39% (271); all full-time undergraduates: 33% (1,131). **Average award:** Freshmen: $14,676; Undergraduates: $14,542. **Scholarships, grants, and awards:** Federal Pell, FSEOG, state, private, college/university gift aid from institutional funds.

GIFT AID (NON-NEED-BASED) *Total amount:* $4,059,123 (5% federal, 89% institutional, 6% external sources). *Receiving aid:* Freshmen: 26% (179). Undergraduates: 17% (575). *Average award:* Freshmen: $11,099. Undergraduates: $12,123. *Scholarships, grants, and awards by category: Creative arts/performance:* art/fine arts.
LOANS *Student loans:* $15,324,636 (91% need-based, 9% non-need-based). 52% of past graduating class borrowed through all loan programs. *Average indebtedness per student:* $47,989. *Average need-based loan:* Freshmen: $3878. Undergraduates: $4833. *Parent loans:* $14,175,422 (94% need-based, 6% non-need-based). *Programs:* Federal Direct (Subsidized and Unsubsidized Stafford, PLUS), Perkins, alternative loans.
WORK-STUDY *Federal work-study:* Total amount: $750,358; jobs available. *State or other work-study/employment:* Total amount: $603,100 (61% need-based, 39% non-need-based). Part-time jobs available.
APPLYING FOR FINANCIAL AID *Required financial aid forms:* FAFSA, state aid form. *Financial aid deadline:* 3/1 (priority: 2/1). *Notification date:* Continuous beginning 2/15. Students must reply within 4 weeks of notification.
CONTACT Mr. William Berrios, Financial Aid Office, School of Visual Arts, 209 East 23rd Street, New York, NY 10010, 212-592-2030 or toll-free 800-436-4204. *Fax:* 212-592-2029. *E-mail:* fa@sva.edu.
Website: http://www.sva.edu/.

SCHREINER UNIVERSITY
Kerrville, TX

Tuition & fees: $26,900	Average undergraduate aid package: $19,518

ABOUT THE INSTITUTION Independent Presbyterian, coed. *Awards:* certificates, associate, bachelor's, and master's degrees. 36 undergraduate majors. *Total enrollment:* 1,308. Undergraduates: 1,237. Freshmen: 302. Federal methodology is used as a basis for awarding need-based institutional aid.
UNDERGRADUATE EXPENSES for 2017–2018 *Application fee:* $25. *Comprehensive fee:* $37,052 includes full-time tuition ($24,990), mandatory fees ($1910), and room and board ($10,152). *College room only:* $4980. Full-time tuition and fees vary according to course load, location, and program. Room and board charges vary according to board plan and housing facility. *Part-time tuition:* $1069 per credit hour. *Part-time fees:* $1155 per year. Part-time tuition and fees vary according to course load and program.
FRESHMAN FINANCIAL AID (Fall 2017, est.) 310 applied for aid; of those 86% were deemed to have need. 100% of freshmen with need received aid; of those 14% had need fully met. *Average percent of need met:* 68% (excluding resources awarded to replace EFC). *Average financial aid package:* $19,144 (excluding resources awarded to replace EFC). 25% of all full-time freshmen had no need and received non-need-based gift aid.
UNDERGRADUATE FINANCIAL AID (Fall 2017, est.) 928 applied for aid; of those 88% were deemed to have need. 100% of undergraduates with need received aid; of those 12% had need fully met. *Average percent of need met:* 68% (excluding resources awarded to replace EFC). *Average financial aid package:* $19,518 (excluding resources awarded to replace EFC). 21% of all full-time undergraduates had no need and received non-need-based gift aid.
GIFT AID (NEED-BASED) *Total amount:* $13,433,667 (15% federal, 13% state, 55% institutional, 17% external sources). *Receiving aid:* Freshmen: 73% (266); all full-time undergraduates: 75% (814). *Average award:* Freshmen: $16,491; Undergraduates: $16,266. *Scholarships, grants, and awards:* Federal Pell, FSEOG, state, private, college/university gift aid from institutional funds.
GIFT AID (NON-NEED-BASED) *Total amount:* $3,795,849 (2% state, 71% institutional, 27% external sources). *Receiving aid:* Freshmen: 10% (36). Undergraduates: 7% (81). *Average award:* Freshmen: $10,232. Undergraduates: $10,118. *Scholarships, grants, and awards by category: Academic interests/achievement:* biological sciences, business, communication, education, English, general academic interests/achievements, mathematics, physical sciences, premedicine, religion/biblical studies, social sciences. *Creative arts/performance:* applied art and design, art/fine arts, journalism/publications, music, theater/drama. *Special achievements/activities:* community service, leadership, memberships, religious involvement. *Special characteristics:* children of faculty/staff, general special characteristics, international students, local/state students, relatives of clergy, religious affiliation, siblings of current

students, veterans. *Tuition waivers:* Full or partial for employees or children of employees.
LOANS *Student loans:* $8,846,260 (68% need-based, 32% non-need-based). 76% of past graduating class borrowed through all loan programs. *Average indebtedness per student:* $29,746. *Average need-based loan:* Freshmen: $3140. Undergraduates: $3761. *Parent loans:* $1,524,498 (57% need-based, 43% non-need-based). *Programs:* Federal Direct (Subsidized and Unsubsidized Stafford, PLUS), state, alternative loans.
WORK-STUDY *Federal work-study:* Total amount: $86,716; jobs available. *State or other work-study/employment:* Total amount: $8563 (74% need-based, 26% non-need-based). Part-time jobs available.
APPLYING FOR FINANCIAL AID *Required financial aid form:* FAFSA. *Financial aid deadline:* 5/15 (priority: 5/1). *Notification date:* Continuous beginning 2/15. Students must reply within 2 weeks of notification.
CONTACT Ms. Natalie Sandoval, Director of Financial Aid, Schreiner University, 2100 Memorial Boulevard, Kerrville, TX 78028, 830-792-7217 or toll-free 800-343-4919. *Fax:* 830-792-7226. *E-mail:* tlbryant@schreiner.edu.
Website: http://www.schreiner.edu/.

SCRIPPS COLLEGE
Claremont, CA

Tuition & fees: $52,966	Average undergraduate aid package: $46,503

ABOUT THE INSTITUTION Independent, women only. *Awards:* certificates and bachelor's degrees. 58 undergraduate majors. *Total enrollment:* 1,077. Undergraduates: 1,059. Freshmen: 327. Both federal and institutional methodology are used as a basis for awarding need-based institutional aid.
UNDERGRADUATE EXPENSES for 2017–2018 *Application fee:* $60. *Comprehensive fee:* $69,260 includes full-time tuition ($52,748), mandatory fees ($218), and room and board ($16,294). *College room only:* $8872. Full-time tuition and fees vary according to course load and degree level. Room and board charges vary according to board plan. *Part-time tuition:* $6594 per course. Part-time tuition and fees vary according to course load and degree level. *Payment plan:* Tuition prepayment.
FRESHMAN FINANCIAL AID (Fall 2016) 162 applied for aid; of those 59% were deemed to have need. 100% of freshmen with need received aid; of those 100% had need fully met. *Average percent of need met:* 100% (excluding resources awarded to replace EFC). *Average financial aid package:* $46,467 (excluding resources awarded to replace EFC). 14% of all full-time freshmen had no need and received non-need-based gift aid.
UNDERGRADUATE FINANCIAL AID (Fall 2016) 482 applied for aid; of those 77% were deemed to have need. 100% of undergraduates with need received aid; of those 100% had need fully met. *Average percent of need met:* 100% (excluding resources awarded to replace EFC). *Average financial aid package:* $46,503 (excluding resources awarded to replace EFC). 21% of all full-time undergraduates had no need and received non-need-based gift aid.
GIFT AID (NEED-BASED) *Total amount:* $13,887,791 (5% federal, 3% state, 91% institutional, 1% external sources). *Receiving aid:* Freshmen: 35% (95); all full-time undergraduates: 36% (370). *Average award:* Freshmen: $38,332; Undergraduates: $37,532. *Scholarships, grants, and awards:* Federal Pell, FSEOG, state, private, college/university gift aid from institutional funds.
GIFT AID (NON-NEED-BASED) *Total amount:* $3,848,785 (91% institutional, 9% external sources). *Receiving aid:* Freshmen: 1% (2). Undergraduates: 1% (7). *Average award:* Freshmen: $16,083. Undergraduates: $16,667. *Scholarships, grants, and awards by category: Academic interests/achievement:* general academic interests/achievements. *Tuition waivers:* Full or partial for employees or children of employees. *ROTC:* Army cooperative, Air Force cooperative.
LOANS *Student loans:* $2,180,553 (80% need-based, 20% non-need-based). 41% of past graduating class borrowed through all loan programs. *Average indebtedness per student:* $19,639. *Average need-based loan:* Freshmen: $3338. Undergraduates: $3625. *Parent loans:* $1,387,317 (70% need-based, 30% non-need-based). *Programs:* Federal Direct (Subsidized and Unsubsidized Stafford, PLUS), Perkins, college/university.
WORK-STUDY *Federal work-study:* jobs available. *State or other work-study/employment:* Total amount: $9600 (77% need-based, 23% non-need-based). Part-time jobs available.

APPLYING FOR FINANCIAL AID *Required financial aid forms:* FAFSA, CSS Financial Aid PROFILE, state aid form, noncustodial (divorced/separated) parent's statement, business/farm supplement. *Financial aid deadline:* 2/1. *Notification date:* 5/1.

CONTACT Patrick Moore, Director of Financial Aid, Scripps College, 1030 Columbia Avenue, Claremont, CA 91711-3948, 909-621-8275 or toll-free 800-770-1333. *Fax:* 909-607-7742. *E-mail:* finaid@scrippscollege.edu. *Website:* http://www.scrippscollege.edu/.

SEATTLE PACIFIC UNIVERSITY
Seattle, WA

Tuition & fees: $40,902	Average undergraduate aid package: $34,345

ABOUT THE INSTITUTION Independent Free Methodist, coed. *Awards:* certificates, bachelor's, master's, and doctoral degrees. 51 undergraduate majors. *Total enrollment:* 3,813. Undergraduates: 2,911. Freshmen: 647. Federal methodology is used as a basis for awarding need-based institutional aid.

UNDERGRADUATE EXPENSES for 2017–2018 *Application fee:* $50. *Comprehensive fee:* $52,080 includes full-time tuition ($40,464), mandatory fees ($438), and room and board ($11,178). *College room only:* $6093. Room and board charges vary according to board plan and housing facility. *Part-time tuition:* $1124 per credit hour. Part-time tuition and fees vary according to course load.

FRESHMAN FINANCIAL AID (Fall 2017, est.) 577 applied for aid; of those 84% were deemed to have need. 99% of freshmen with need received aid; of those 10% had need fully met. *Average percent of need met:* 81% (excluding resources awarded to replace EFC). *Average financial aid package:* $34,500 (excluding resources awarded to replace EFC). 19% of all full-time freshmen had no need and received non-need-based gift aid.

UNDERGRADUATE FINANCIAL AID (Fall 2017, est.) 2,199 applied for aid; of those 87% were deemed to have need. 100% of undergraduates with need received aid; of those 7% had need fully met. *Average percent of need met:* 78% (excluding resources awarded to replace EFC). *Average financial aid package:* $34,345 (excluding resources awarded to replace EFC). 24% of all full-time undergraduates had no need and received non-need-based gift aid.

GIFT AID (NEED-BASED) *Total amount:* $53,621,651 (8% federal, 7% state, 78% institutional, 7% external sources). *Receiving aid:* Freshmen: 76% (484); all full-time undergraduates: 70% (1,905). *Average award:* Freshmen: $34,604; Undergraduates: $33,723. *Scholarships, grants, and awards:* Federal Pell, FSEOG, state, private, college/university gift aid from institutional funds.

GIFT AID (NON-NEED-BASED) *Total amount:* $16,095,599 (1% state, 82% institutional, 17% external sources). *Average award:* Freshmen: $24,752. Undergraduates: $23,152. *Scholarships, grants, and awards by category: Academic interests/achievement:* 565 awards ($8,531,254 total): engineering/technologies, general academic interests/achievements. *Creative arts/performance:* 42 awards ($60,000 total): art/fine arts, performing arts. *Special characteristics:* 235 awards ($1,149,869 total): children and siblings of alumni, children of faculty/staff, general special characteristics, international students, relatives of clergy, religious affiliation, veterans, veterans' children. *Tuition waivers:* Full or partial for employees or children of employees, senior citizens. *ROTC:* Army cooperative, Naval cooperative, Air Force cooperative.

LOANS *Student loans:* $14,784,835 (92% need-based, 8% non-need-based). 71% of past graduating class borrowed through all loan programs. *Average indebtedness per student:* $28,646. *Average need-based loan:* Freshmen: $4291. Undergraduates: $5157. *Parent loans:* $8,461,848 (92% need-based, 8% non-need-based). *Programs:* Federal Direct (Subsidized and Unsubsidized Stafford, PLUS), Perkins, Federal Nursing, state, college/university.

WORK-STUDY *Federal work-study:* Total amount: $1,042,955; 436 jobs averaging $2392. *State or other work-study/employment:* Total amount: $319,453 (100% need-based). 109 part-time jobs averaging $2931.

ATHLETIC AWARDS Total amount: $2,185,503 (47% need-based, 53% non-need-based).

APPLYING FOR FINANCIAL AID *Required financial aid form:* FAFSA. *Financial aid deadline (priority):* 3/15. *Notification date:* Continuous beginning 3/15. Students must reply by 5/1 or within 4 weeks of notification.

CONTACT Mr. Jordan Grant, Director of Student Financial Services, Seattle Pacific University, 3307 Third Avenue West, Seattle, WA 98119-1997, 206-281-2469 or toll-free 800-366-3344. *E-mail:* grantj@spu.edu. *Website:* http://www.spu.edu/.

SEATTLE UNIVERSITY
Seattle, WA

Tuition & fees: $42,885	Average undergraduate aid package: $36,167

ABOUT THE INSTITUTION Independent Roman Catholic, coed. *Awards:* certificates, bachelor's, master's, and doctoral degrees. 71 undergraduate majors. *Total enrollment:* 7,278. Undergraduates: 4,647. Freshmen: 957. Federal methodology is used as a basis for awarding need-based institutional aid.

UNDERGRADUATE EXPENSES for 2017–2018 *Application fee:* $55. *Comprehensive fee:* $54,957 includes full-time tuition ($42,120), mandatory fees ($765), and room and board ($12,072). *College room only:* $7272. Full-time tuition and fees vary according to course load. Room and board charges vary according to board plan and housing facility. *Part-time tuition:* $936 per credit hour. Part-time tuition and fees vary according to course load.

FRESHMAN FINANCIAL AID (Fall 2017, est.) 820 applied for aid; of those 77% were deemed to have need. 100% of freshmen with need received aid; of those 14% had need fully met. *Average percent of need met:* 67% (excluding resources awarded to replace EFC). *Average financial aid package:* $35,825 (excluding resources awarded to replace EFC). 10% of all full-time freshmen had no need and received non-need-based gift aid.

UNDERGRADUATE FINANCIAL AID (Fall 2017, est.) 3,066 applied for aid; of those 82% were deemed to have need. 100% of undergraduates with need received aid; of those 13% had need fully met. *Average percent of need met:* 65% (excluding resources awarded to replace EFC). *Average financial aid package:* $36,167 (excluding resources awarded to replace EFC). 4% of all full-time undergraduates had no need and received non-need-based gift aid.

GIFT AID (NEED-BASED) *Total amount:* $76,270,143 (7% federal, 5% state, 84% institutional, 4% external sources). *Receiving aid:* Freshmen: 59% (562); all full-time undergraduates: 52% (2,294). *Average award:* Freshmen: $24,853; Undergraduates: $25,021. *Scholarships, grants, and awards:* Federal Pell, FSEOG, state, private, college/university gift aid from institutional funds, Federal Nursing.

GIFT AID (NON-NEED-BASED) *Total amount:* $16,422,813 (27% federal, 72% institutional, 1% external sources). *Receiving aid:* Freshmen: 46% (433). Undergraduates: 30% (1,301). *Average award:* Freshmen: $17,043. Undergraduates: $14,628. *Scholarships, grants, and awards by category: Academic interests/achievement:* general academic interests/achievements. *Creative arts/performance:* art/fine arts, music, theater/drama. *Special achievements/activities:* leadership. *Special characteristics:* children and siblings of alumni, children of educators, children of faculty/staff, members of minority groups, religious affiliation. *Tuition waivers:* Full or partial for employees or children of employees. *ROTC:* Army, Naval cooperative, Air Force cooperative.

LOANS *Student loans:* $25,477,851 (67% need-based, 33% non-need-based). 67% of past graduating class borrowed through all loan programs. *Average indebtedness per student:* $28,848. *Average need-based loan:* Freshmen: $4148. Undergraduates: $6746. *Parent loans:* $10,206,168 (39% need-based, 61% non-need-based). *Programs:* Federal Direct (Subsidized and Unsubsidized Stafford, PLUS), Perkins, Federal Nursing.

WORK-STUDY *Federal work-study:* Total amount: $1,622,078; 506 jobs averaging $3657. *State or other work-study/employment:* Total amount: $2,082,437 (100% need-based). 531 part-time jobs averaging $4742.

ATHLETIC AWARDS Total amount: $4,956,456 (100% non-need-based).

APPLYING FOR FINANCIAL AID *Required financial aid form:* FAFSA. *Financial aid deadline (priority):* 2/1. *Notification date:* 3/1. Students must reply by 5/1 or within 2 weeks of notification.

CONTACT Mr. Jeff Scofield, Director of Student Financial Services, Seattle University, 901 12th Avenue, PO Box 222000, Seattle, WA 98122-1090, 206-296-2000 or toll-free 800-542-0833 (in-state), 800-426-7123 (out-of-state). *Fax:* 206-296-5755. *E-mail:* financial-aid@seattleu.edu. *Website:* http://www.seattleu.edu/.

SELMA UNIVERSITY
Selma, AL

CONTACT Financial Aid Office, Selma University, 1501 Lapsley Street, Selma, AL 36701-5299, 334-872-2533.
Website: http://www.selmauniversity.edu/.

SENTARA COLLEGE OF HEALTH SCIENCES
Chesapeake, VA

CONTACT Financial Aid Office, Sentara College of Health Sciences, 1441 Crossways Boulevard, Crossways 1, Suite 105, Chesapeake, VA 23320, 757-388-2900.
Website: http://www.sentara.edu/.

SETON HALL UNIVERSITY
South Orange, NJ

CONTACT Office of Enrollment Services, Seton Hall University, 400 South Orange Avenue, South Orange, NJ 07079, 973-761-9350 or toll-free 800-THE HALL. *Fax:* 973-275-2040. *E-mail:* thehall@shu.edu.
Website: http://www.shu.edu/.

SETON HILL UNIVERSITY
Greensburg, PA

Tuition & fees: $34,660	Average undergraduate aid package: $24,918

ABOUT THE INSTITUTION Independent Roman Catholic, coed. **Awards:** certificates, bachelor's, and master's degrees. 74 undergraduate majors. **Total enrollment:** 2,048. Undergraduates: 1,676. Freshmen: 427. Federal methodology is used as a basis for awarding need-based institutional aid.
UNDERGRADUATE EXPENSES for 2017–2018 *Application fee:* $35. *Comprehensive fee:* $45,940 includes full-time tuition ($33,910), mandatory fees ($750), and room and board ($11,280). Full-time tuition and fees vary according to course load, degree level, and program. Room and board charges vary according to board plan and housing facility. *Part-time tuition:* $910 per credit. *Part-time fees:* $25 per credit. Part-time tuition and fees vary according to course load, degree level, and program.
FRESHMAN FINANCIAL AID (Fall 2016) 370 applied for aid; of those 85% were deemed to have need. 100% of freshmen with need received aid; of those 22% had need fully met. *Average percent of need met:* 73% (excluding resources awarded to replace EFC). *Average financial aid package:* $25,565 (excluding resources awarded to replace EFC). 15% of all full-time freshmen had no need and received non-need-based gift aid.
UNDERGRADUATE FINANCIAL AID (Fall 2016) 1,370 applied for aid; of those 92% were deemed to have need. 100% of undergraduates with need received aid; of those 18% had need fully met. *Average percent of need met:* 71% (excluding resources awarded to replace EFC). *Average financial aid package:* $24,918 (excluding resources awarded to replace EFC). 15% of all full-time undergraduates had no need and received non-need-based gift aid.
GIFT AID (NEED-BASED) *Total amount:* $22,142,229 (10% federal, 9% state, 79% institutional, 2% external sources). *Receiving aid:* Freshmen: 84% (316); all full-time undergraduates: 84% (1,262). *Average award:* Freshmen: $21,514; Undergraduates: $19,632. *Scholarships, grants, and awards:* Federal Pell, FSEOG, state, private, college/university gift aid from institutional funds.
GIFT AID (NON-NEED-BASED) *Total amount:* $4,092,339 (1% state, 96% institutional, 3% external sources). *Receiving aid:* Freshmen: 14% (52). Undergraduates: 11% (163). *Average award:* Freshmen: $15,494. Undergraduates: $13,974. *Scholarships, grants, and awards by category:* Academic interests/achievement: general academic interests/achievements. Creative arts/performance: applied art and design, art/fine arts, dance, music, performing arts, theater/drama.

Special achievements/activities: cheerleading/drum major, general special achievements/activities. *Special characteristics:* children and siblings of alumni, children of faculty/staff, international students, siblings of current students. *Tuition waivers:* Full or partial for employees or children of employees. *ROTC:* Army cooperative.
LOANS *Student loans:* $12,507,132 (72% need-based, 28% non-need-based). 81% of past graduating class borrowed through all loan programs. *Average indebtedness per student:* $35,356. *Average need-based loan:* Freshmen: $5201. Undergraduates: $6154. *Parent loans:* $4,093,184 (59% need-based, 41% non-need-based). *Programs:* Federal Direct (Subsidized and Unsubsidized Stafford, PLUS), Perkins, college/university.
WORK-STUDY *Federal work-study:* jobs available. *State or other work-study/employment:* Total amount: $261,340 (16% need-based, 84% non-need-based). Part-time jobs available.
ATHLETIC AWARDS Total amount: $3,991,196 (54% need-based, 46% non-need-based).
APPLYING FOR FINANCIAL AID *Required financial aid forms:* FAFSA, institution's own form. *Financial aid deadline:* Continuous. *Notification date:* Continuous beginning 11/30. Students must reply by 5/1.
CONTACT Tracey Snyder de Baez, Director of Financial Aid, Seton Hill University, 1 Seton Hill Drive, Greensburg, PA 15601, 724-830-1010 or toll-free 800-826-6234. *Fax:* 724-830-1194. *E-mail:* snyderdebaez@setonhill.edu.
Website: http://www.setonhill.edu/.

SEWANEE: THE UNIVERSITY OF THE SOUTH
Sewanee, TN

Tuition & fees: $45,120	Average undergraduate aid package: $34,591

ABOUT THE INSTITUTION Independent Episcopal, coed. **Awards:** certificates, bachelor's, master's, and doctoral degrees. 37 undergraduate majors. **Total enrollment:** 1,778. Undergraduates: 1,702. Freshmen: 448. Both federal and institutional methodology are used as a basis for awarding need-based institutional aid.
UNDERGRADUATE EXPENSES for 2018–2019 *Comprehensive fee:* $58,000 includes full-time tuition ($44,848), mandatory fees ($272), and room and board ($12,880). *College room only:* $6675. *Part-time tuition:* $1425 per credit hour.
FRESHMAN FINANCIAL AID (Fall 2017, est.) 330 applied for aid; of those 75% were deemed to have need. 100% of freshmen with need received aid; of those 35% had need fully met. *Average percent of need met:* 92% (excluding resources awarded to replace EFC). *Average financial aid package:* $37,018 (excluding resources awarded to replace EFC). 35% of all full-time freshmen had no need and received non-need-based gift aid.
UNDERGRADUATE FINANCIAL AID (Fall 2017, est.) 1,013 applied for aid; of those 80% were deemed to have need. 100% of undergraduates with need received aid; of those 34% had need fully met. *Average percent of need met:* 91% (excluding resources awarded to replace EFC). *Average financial aid package:* $34,591 (excluding resources awarded to replace EFC). 38% of all full-time undergraduates had no need and received non-need-based gift aid.
GIFT AID (NEED-BASED) *Total amount:* $22,897,913 (7% federal, 4% state, 88% institutional, 1% external sources). *Receiving aid:* Freshmen: 54% (243); all full-time undergraduates: 47% (786). *Average award:* Freshmen: $31,211; Undergraduates: $28,853. *Scholarships, grants, and awards:* Federal Pell, FSEOG, state, private, college/university gift aid from institutional funds.
GIFT AID (NON-NEED-BASED) *Total amount:* $10,369,623 (4% state, 94% institutional, 2% external sources). *Receiving aid:* Freshmen: 14% (63). Undergraduates: 11% (186). *Average award:* Freshmen: $15,415. Undergraduates: $14,019. *Scholarships, grants, and awards by category:* Academic interests/achievement: general academic interests/achievements. Creative arts/performance: general creative arts/performance. Special achievements/activities: general special achievements/activities. Special characteristics: general special characteristics. *Tuition waivers:* Full or partial for employees or children of employees.
LOANS *Student loans:* $3,638,500 (71% need-based, 29% non-need-based). 40% of past graduating class borrowed through all loan programs. *Average indebtedness per student:* $26,772. *Average need-based loan:* Freshmen: $3136. Undergraduates: $4287. *Parent loans:* $3,077,449 (17% need-based, 83% non-need-based).

Programs: Federal Direct (Subsidized and Unsubsidized Stafford, PLUS), Perkins, private loans.

WORK-STUDY *Federal work-study:* Total amount: $740,246; 453 jobs averaging $1634. *State or other work-study/employment:* Total amount: $479,250 (30% need-based, 70% non-need-based). 152 part-time jobs averaging $3153.

APPLYING FOR FINANCIAL AID *Required financial aid forms:* FAFSA, CSS Financial Aid PROFILE. *Financial aid deadline (priority):* 12/1. *Notification date:* Continuous beginning 2/1. Students must reply by 5/1 or within 2 weeks of notification.

CONTACT Ms. Beth A. Cragar, Associate Dean of Admission for Financial Aid, Sewanee: The University of the South, 735 University Avenue, Sewanee, TN 37383-1000, 931-598-1312 or toll-free 800-522-2234. *Fax:* 931-598-3273. *E-mail:* finaid@sewanee.edu.

Website: http://www.sewanee.edu/.

SHASTA BIBLE COLLEGE
Redding, CA

ABOUT THE INSTITUTION Independent nondenominational, coed. 3 undergraduate majors.

GIFT AID (NEED-BASED) *Scholarships, grants, and awards:* Federal Pell, FSEOG, state, private, college/university gift aid from institutional funds.

GIFT AID (NON-NEED-BASED) *Scholarships, grants, and awards by category:* Academic interests/achievement: education. Creative arts/performance: music. Special achievements/activities: general special achievements/activities. Special characteristics: relatives of clergy, veterans.

LOANS *Programs:* Federal Direct (Subsidized and Unsubsidized Stafford, PLUS).

WORK-STUDY Federal work-study jobs available. *State or other work-study/employment:* Part-time jobs available.

APPLYING FOR FINANCIAL AID *Required financial aid forms:* FAFSA, institution's own form, state aid form.

CONTACT Linda Iles, Financial Aid Administrator, Shasta Bible College, 2951 Goodwater Avenue, Redding, CA 96002, 530-221-4275 Ext. 32 or toll-free 800-800-4SBC. *Fax:* 530-221-6929. *E-mail:* finaid@shasta.edu.

Website: http://www.shasta.edu/.

SHAWNEE STATE UNIVERSITY
Portsmouth, OH

Tuition & fees (OH res): $8556	Average undergraduate aid package: $8972

ABOUT THE INSTITUTION State-supported, coed. *Awards:* certificates, associate, bachelor's, and master's degrees. 49 undergraduate majors. *Total enrollment:* 3,582. Undergraduates: 3,406. Freshmen: 700. Federal methodology is used as a basis for awarding need-based institutional aid.

UNDERGRADUATE EXPENSES for 2018–2019 *Tuition, state resident:* full-time $8556; part-time $260.45 per credit hour. *Tuition, nonresident:* full-time $14,714; part-time $502.46 per credit hour. *Required fees:* $46.39 per credit hour. Full-time tuition and fees vary according to course load, program, and reciprocity agreements. Part-time tuition and fees vary according to course load, program, and reciprocity agreements. *College room and board:* $10,864; *Room only:* $6896. Room and board charges vary according to board plan and housing facility. *Payment plan:* Guaranteed tuition.

FRESHMAN FINANCIAL AID (Fall 2016) 817 applied for aid; of those 72% were deemed to have need. 100% of freshmen with need received aid; of those 5% had need fully met. *Average percent of need met:* 44% (excluding resources awarded to replace EFC). *Average financial aid package:* $8662 (excluding resources awarded to replace EFC). 14% of all full-time freshmen had no need and received non-need-based gift aid.

UNDERGRADUATE FINANCIAL AID (Fall 2016) 2,874 applied for aid; of those 66% were deemed to have need. 100% of undergraduates with need received aid; of those 5% had need fully met. *Average percent of need met:* 45% (excluding resources awarded to replace EFC). *Average financial aid package:* $8972 (excluding resources awarded to replace EFC). 13% of all full-time undergraduates had no need and received non-need-based gift aid.

GIFT AID (NEED-BASED) *Total amount:* $13,163,279 (61% federal, 14% state, 18% institutional, 7% external sources). *Receiving aid:* Freshmen: 50% (425); all full-time undergraduates: 46% (1,417). *Average award:* Freshmen: $5954; Undergraduates: $5855. *Scholarships, grants, and awards:* Federal Pell, FSEOG, state, private, college/university gift aid from institutional funds.

GIFT AID (NON-NEED-BASED) *Total amount:* $736,498 (3% state, 75% institutional, 22% external sources). *Receiving aid:* Freshmen: 37% (310). Undergraduates: 22% (665). *Average award:* Freshmen: $3522. Undergraduates: $3875. *Scholarships, grants, and awards by category:* Academic interests/achievement: 158 awards ($554,464 total): general academic interests/achievements. Special characteristics: 80 awards ($614,519 total): children of faculty/staff, out-of-state students, veterans. *Tuition waivers:* Full or partial for employees or children of employees, senior citizens.

LOANS *Student loans:* $16,844,770 (79% need-based, 21% non-need-based). 79% of past graduating class borrowed through all loan programs. *Average indebtedness per student:* $30,554. *Average need-based loan:* Freshmen: $3360. Undergraduates: $3964. *Parent loans:* $3,564,890 (66% need-based, 34% non-need-based). *Programs:* Federal Direct (Subsidized and Unsubsidized Stafford, PLUS), private loans.

WORK-STUDY *Federal work-study:* 60 jobs averaging $1854.

ATHLETIC AWARDS Total amount: $562,288 (48% need-based, 52% non-need-based).

APPLYING FOR FINANCIAL AID *Required financial aid form:* FAFSA. *Financial aid deadline:* Continuous. *Notification date:* Continuous beginning 12/15.

CONTACT Ms. Charlotte Hardy, Assistant Director of Financial Aid, Shawnee State University, 940 Second Street, Portsmouth, OH 45662-4344, 740-351-3548 or toll-free 800-959-2778. *Fax:* 740-351-3435. *E-mail:* chardy@shawnee.edu. *Website:* http://www.shawnee.edu/.

SHAW UNIVERSITY
Raleigh, NC

CONTACT Rochelle King, Director of Financial Aid, Shaw University, 118 East South Street, Raleigh, NC 27601-2399, 919-546-8565 or toll-free 800-214-6683. *Fax:* 919-546-8356. *E-mail:* rking@shawu.edu.

Website: http://www.shawu.edu/.

SHENANDOAH UNIVERSITY
Winchester, VA

Tuition & fees: $32,530	Average undergraduate aid package: $18,768

ABOUT THE INSTITUTION Independent United Methodist, coed. *Awards:* certificates, bachelor's, master's, and doctoral degrees. 39 undergraduate majors. *Total enrollment:* 3,844. Undergraduates: 2,066. Freshmen: 438. Federal methodology is used as a basis for awarding need-based institutional aid.

UNDERGRADUATE EXPENSES for 2018–2019 *Application fee:* $30. *Comprehensive fee:* $42,900 includes full-time tuition ($31,280), mandatory fees ($1250), and room and board ($10,370). Full-time tuition and fees vary according to course load and program. Room and board charges vary according to board plan and housing facility. *Part-time tuition:* $910. *Part-time fees:* $90 per term. Part-time tuition and fees vary according to course load and program.

FRESHMAN FINANCIAL AID (Fall 2016) 387 applied for aid; of those 84% were deemed to have need. 100% of freshmen with need received aid; of those 10% had need fully met. *Average percent of need met:* 63% (excluding resources awarded to replace EFC). *Average financial aid package:* $19,644 (excluding resources awarded to replace EFC). 18% of all full-time freshmen had no need and received non-need-based gift aid.

UNDERGRADUATE FINANCIAL AID (Fall 2016) 1,882 applied for aid; of those 89% were deemed to have need. 100% of undergraduates with need received aid; of those 11% had need fully met. *Average percent of need met:* 59% (excluding resources awarded to replace EFC). *Average financial aid package:* $18,768 (excluding resources awarded to replace EFC). 21% of all full-time undergraduates had no need and received non-need-based gift aid.

GIFT AID (NEED-BASED) *Total amount:* $8,593,667 (31% federal, 69% institutional). *Receiving aid:* Freshmen: 55% (243); all full-time undergraduates: 66% (1,309). *Average award:* Freshmen: $6691; Undergraduates: $6265. *Scholarships, grants, and awards:* Federal Pell, FSEOG, state, college/university gift aid from institutional funds.

GIFT AID (NON-NEED-BASED) *Total amount:* $20,581,630 (15% state, 83% institutional, 2% external sources). *Receiving aid:* Freshmen: 75% (327). Undergraduates: 82% (1,638). *Average award:* Freshmen: $11,009. Undergraduates: $10,168. *Scholarships, grants, and awards by category: Academic interests/ achievement:* 2,048 awards ($15,210,323 total): biological sciences, business, communication, computer science, education, English, foreign languages, general academic interests/achievements, home economics, humanities, international studies, mathematics, physical sciences, religion/biblical studies, social sciences. *Creative arts/performance:* 428 awards ($4,160,076 total): dance, music, performing arts, theater/drama. *Special achievements/activities:* 70 awards ($140,510 total): religious involvement. *Special characteristics:* 1,073 awards ($4,077,264 total): children of faculty/staff, local/ state students. *Tuition waivers:* Full or partial for employees or children of employees.

LOANS *Student loans:* $18,653,387 (33% need-based, 67% non-need-based). 87% of past graduating class borrowed through all loan programs. *Average indebtedness per student:* $34,121. *Average need-based loan:* Freshmen: $3255. Undergraduates: $4329. *Parent loans:* $8,583,840 (100% non-need-based). *Programs:* Federal Direct (Subsidized and Unsubsidized Stafford, PLUS), Perkins, Federal Nursing.

WORK-STUDY *Federal work-study:* 640 jobs averaging $2300. *State or other work-study/employment:* Total amount: $1,081,024 (100% non-need-based). 483 part-time jobs averaging $2300.

APPLYING FOR FINANCIAL AID *Required financial aid forms:* FAFSA, state aid form. *Financial aid deadline:* Continuous. *Notification date:* Continuous beginning 3/15. Students must reply within 4 weeks of notification.

CONTACT Ms. Karen Bucher, Director of Financial Aid, Shenandoah University, 1460 University Drive, Winchester, VA 22601-5195, 540-665-4538 or toll-free 800-432-2266. *Fax:* 540-665-4939. *E-mail:* kbucher@su.edu.
Website: http://www.su.edu/.

SHEPHERD UNIVERSITY
Shepherdstown, WV

Tuition & fees (WV res): $7548	Average undergraduate aid package: $12,802

ABOUT THE INSTITUTION State-supported, coed. *Awards:* bachelor's, master's, and doctoral degrees. 28 undergraduate majors. *Total enrollment:* 3,736. Undergraduates: 3,420. Freshmen: 598. Federal methodology is used as a basis for awarding need-based institutional aid.

UNDERGRADUATE EXPENSES for 2018–2019 *Application fee:* $45. *Tuition, state resident:* full-time $7548; part-time $315 per credit hour. *Tuition, nonresident:* full-time $18,052; part-time $752 per credit hour. Full-time tuition and fees vary according to program and reciprocity agreements. Part-time tuition and fees vary according to program. *College room and board:* $10,500. Room and board charges vary according to board plan and housing facility.

FRESHMAN FINANCIAL AID (Fall 2017, est.) 585 applied for aid; of those 69% were deemed to have need. 99% of freshmen with need received aid; of those 37% had need fully met. *Average percent of need met:* 81% (excluding resources awarded to replace EFC). *Average financial aid package:* $12,978 (excluding resources awarded to replace EFC). 26% of all full-time freshmen had no need and received non-need-based gift aid.

UNDERGRADUATE FINANCIAL AID (Fall 2017, est.) 2,511 applied for aid; of those 70% were deemed to have need. 98% of undergraduates with need received aid; of those 31% had need fully met. *Average percent of need met:* 76% (excluding resources awarded to replace EFC). *Average financial aid package:* $12,802 (excluding resources awarded to replace EFC). 22% of all full-time undergraduates had no need and received non-need-based gift aid.

GIFT AID (NEED-BASED) *Total amount:* $7,097,270 (72% federal, 24% state, 4% institutional). *Receiving aid:* Freshmen: 47% (280); all full-time undergraduates: 45% (1,186). *Average award:* Freshmen: $6159; Undergraduates: $5611. *Scholarships, grants, and awards:* Federal Pell, FSEOG, state, private, college/university gift aid from institutional funds.

GIFT AID (NON-NEED-BASED) *Total amount:* $6,686,282 (35% state, 59% institutional, 6% external sources). *Receiving aid:* Freshmen: 41% (246). Undergraduates: 28% (737). *Average award:* Freshmen: $10,109. Undergraduates: $10,904. *Scholarships, grants, and awards by category: Academic interests/ achievement:* biological sciences, business, communication, computer science, education, engineering/technologies, English, general academic interests/achievements, health fields, home economics, humanities, mathematics, physical sciences, premedicine, social sciences. *Creative arts/performance:* applied art and design, art/fine arts, music, performing arts, theater/drama. *Special achievements/activities:* leadership. *Special characteristics:* ethnic background, handicapped students, local/state students, members of minority groups, out-of-state students, previous college experience. *Tuition waivers:* Full or partial for minority students, employees or children of employees, senior citizens. *ROTC:* Air Force cooperative.

LOANS *Student loans:* $11,745,791 (43% need-based, 57% non-need-based). 68% of past graduating class borrowed through all loan programs. *Average indebtedness per student:* $27,686. *Average need-based loan:* Freshmen: $3306. Undergraduates: $4048. *Parent loans:* $4,078,956 (100% non-need-based). *Programs:* Federal Direct (Subsidized and Unsubsidized Stafford, PLUS), Perkins, private loans.

WORK-STUDY *Federal work-study:* Total amount: $211,268; 116 jobs averaging $1130. *State or other work-study/employment:* Total amount: $647,975 (100% non-need-based). 428 part-time jobs averaging $1514.

ATHLETIC AWARDS Total amount: $1,347,295 (100% non-need-based).

APPLYING FOR FINANCIAL AID *Required financial aid forms:* FAFSA, state aid form. *Financial aid deadline (priority):* 3/1. *Notification date:* Continuous beginning 2/28. Students must reply within 2 weeks of notification.

CONTACT Ms. Joyce Cabral, Director of Financial Aid, Shepherd University, PO Box 5000, Shepherdstown, WV 25443-5000, 304-876-5470 or toll-free 800-344-5231. *Fax:* 304-876-5238. *E-mail:* faoweb@shepherd.edu.
Website: http://www.shepherd.edu/.

SHILOH UNIVERSITY
Kalona, IA

CONTACT Financial Aid Office, Shiloh University, 100 Shiloh Drive, Kalona, IA 52247, 319-656-2447.
Website: http://www.shilohuniversity.edu/.

SHIPPENSBURG UNIVERSITY OF PENNSYLVANIA
Shippensburg, PA

Tuition & fees (PA res): $12,086	Average undergraduate aid package: $9429

ABOUT THE INSTITUTION State-supported, coed. *Awards:* certificates, bachelor's, master's, and doctoral degrees. 41 undergraduate majors. *Total enrollment:* 6,581. Undergraduates: 5,585. Freshmen: 1,219. Federal methodology is used as a basis for awarding need-based institutional aid.

UNDERGRADUATE EXPENSES for 2017–2018 *Application fee:* $45. *Tuition, state resident:* full-time $9000; part-time $300 per credit hour. *Tuition, nonresident:* full-time $16,858; part-time $702 per credit hour. *Required fees:* full-time $3086; $129 per credit hour. *College room and board:* $12,010; *Room only:* $7880. Room and board charges vary according to board plan and housing facility.

FRESHMAN FINANCIAL AID (Fall 2017, est.) 1,142 applied for aid; of those 82% were deemed to have need. 99% of freshmen with need received aid; of those 7% had need fully met. *Average percent of need met:* 52% (excluding resources awarded to replace EFC). *Average financial aid package:* $9796 (excluding resources awarded to replace EFC). 8% of all full-time freshmen had no need and received non-need-based gift aid.

UNDERGRADUATE FINANCIAL AID (Fall 2017, est.) 4,448 applied for aid; of those 83% were deemed to have need. 99% of undergraduates with need received aid; of those 10% had need fully met. *Average percent of need met:* 55% (excluding resources awarded to replace EFC). *Average financial aid package:* $9429 (excluding resources awarded to replace EFC). 7% of all full-time undergraduates had no need and received non-need-based gift aid.

GIFT AID (NEED-BASED) *Total amount:* $18,334,478 (45% federal, 32% state, 15% institutional, 8% external sources). *Receiving aid:* Freshmen: 62% (747); all full-time undergraduates: 53% (2,738). *Average award:* Freshmen: $7672; Undergraduates: $6963. *Scholarships, grants, and awards:* Federal Pell, FSEOG, state, private, college/university gift aid from institutional funds.

GIFT AID (NON-NEED-BASED) *Total amount:* $1,297,573 (6% state, 17% institutional, 77% external sources). *Receiving aid:* Freshmen: 4% (47). Undergraduates: 3% (180). *Average award:* Freshmen: $4153. Undergraduates: $5376. *Scholarships, grants, and awards by category:* Academic interests/achievement: biological sciences, business, communication, computer science, education, English, foreign languages, general academic interests/achievements, humanities, mathematics, physical sciences, social sciences. Creative arts/performance: art/fine arts, music, theater/drama. Special achievements/activities: community service, general special achievements/activities, leadership. Special characteristics: children and siblings of alumni, general special characteristics, handicapped students, local/state students. *Tuition waivers:* Full or partial for employees or children of employees, senior citizens. *ROTC:* Army.

LOANS *Student loans:* $43,491,289 (67% need-based, 33% non-need-based). 80% of past graduating class borrowed through all loan programs. *Average indebtedness per student:* $33,839. *Average need-based loan:* Freshmen: $3540. Undergraduates: $4058. *Parent loans:* $12,090,249 (49% need-based, 51% non-need-based). *Programs:* Federal Direct (Subsidized and Unsubsidized Stafford, PLUS), Perkins, alternative loans.

WORK-STUDY *Federal work-study:* Total amount: $144,280; 111 jobs averaging $1300. *State or other work-study/employment:* Total amount: $997,522 (29% need-based, 71% non-need-based). 578 part-time jobs averaging $1726.

ATHLETIC AWARDS Total amount: $1,158,909 (55% need-based, 45% non-need-based).

APPLYING FOR FINANCIAL AID *Required financial aid form:* FAFSA. *Financial aid deadline (priority):* 3/15. *Notification date:* Continuous. Students must reply within 2 weeks of notification.

CONTACT Mrs. Trina M. Snyder, Director of Financial Aid and Scholarships, Shippensburg University of Pennsylvania, 1871 Old Main Drive, Shippensburg, PA 17257-2299, 717-477-1131 or toll-free 800-822-8028 (in-state). *Fax:* 717-477-4028. *E-mail:* finaid@ship.edu.
Website: http://www.ship.edu/.

SHORTER UNIVERSITY
Rome, GA

CONTACT Ms. Tara Jones, Director of Financial Aid, Shorter University, 315 Shorter Avenue, Rome, GA 30165, 706-233-7227 or toll-free 800-868-6980. *Fax:* 706-233-7314. *E-mail:* tjones@shorter.edu.
Website: http://www.shorter.edu/.

SH'OR YOSHUV RABBINICAL COLLEGE
Lawrence, NY

CONTACT Office of Financial Aid, Sh'or Yoshuv Rabbinical College, 1526 Central Avenue, Far Rockaway, NY 11691-4002, 718-327-2048.

SIENA COLLEGE
Loudonville, NY

Tuition & fees: $36,975	Average undergraduate aid package: $29,350

ABOUT THE INSTITUTION Independent Roman Catholic, coed. *Awards:* certificates, bachelor's, and master's degrees. 34 undergraduate majors. *Total enrollment:* 3,236. Undergraduates: 3,174. Freshmen: 776. Federal methodology is used as a basis for awarding need-based institutional aid.

UNDERGRADUATE EXPENSES for 2018–2019 *Application fee:* $50. *One-time required fee:* $625. *Comprehensive fee:* $51,975 includes full-time tuition ($36,675), mandatory fees ($300), and room and board ($15,000). *College room only:* $8895. Full-time tuition and fees vary according to course load. Room and board charges vary according to board plan and housing facility. *Part-time tuition:* $675 per credit hour. *Part-time fees:* $80 per term. Part-time tuition and fees vary according to course load.

FRESHMAN FINANCIAL AID (Fall 2016) 696 applied for aid; of those 87% were deemed to have need. 100% of freshmen with need received aid; of those 27% had need fully met. *Average percent of need met:* 75% (excluding resources awarded to replace EFC). *Average financial aid package:* $30,196 (excluding resources awarded to replace EFC). 17% of all full-time freshmen had no need and received non-need-based gift aid.

UNDERGRADUATE FINANCIAL AID (Fall 2016) 2,558 applied for aid; of those 90% were deemed to have need. 100% of undergraduates with need received aid; of those 27% had need fully met. *Average percent of need met:* 75% (excluding resources awarded to replace EFC). *Average financial aid package:* $29,350 (excluding resources awarded to replace EFC). 17% of all full-time undergraduates had no need and received non-need-based gift aid.

GIFT AID (NEED-BASED) *Total amount:* $53,639,119 (8% federal, 5% state, 87% institutional). *Receiving aid:* Freshmen: 78% (606); all full-time undergraduates: 75% (2,289). *Average award:* Freshmen: $23,538; Undergraduates: $22,275. *Scholarships, grants, and awards:* Federal Pell, FSEOG, state, private, college/university gift aid from institutional funds, Siena Grants, Franciscan Community Grants.

GIFT AID (NON-NEED-BASED) *Total amount:* $9,003,275 (1% federal, 1% state, 84% institutional, 14% external sources). *Receiving aid:* Freshmen: 75% (580). Undergraduates: 71% (2,156). *Average award:* Freshmen: $13,337. Undergraduates: $11,837. *Scholarships, grants, and awards by category:* Academic interests/achievement: biological sciences, business, communication, computer science, education, English, foreign languages, general academic interests/achievements, home economics, humanities, international studies, mathematics, military science, physical sciences, premedicine, religion/biblical studies, social sciences. Creative arts/performance: creative writing, journalism/publications, music, performing arts, theater/drama. Special achievements/activities: community service, general special achievements/activities, hobbies/interests, leadership, memberships, religious involvement. Special characteristics: adult students, children and siblings of alumni, children of faculty/staff, children of public servants, children of union members/company employees, children of workers in trades, children with a deceased or disabled parent, ethnic background, general special characteristics, local/state students, out-of-state students, previous college experience, relatives of clergy, religious affiliation, veterans' children. *Tuition waivers:* Full or partial for employees or children of employees. *ROTC:* Army, Air Force cooperative.

LOANS *Student loans:* $22,421,559 (83% need-based, 17% non-need-based). 80% of past graduating class borrowed through all loan programs. *Average indebtedness per student:* $35,827. *Average need-based loan:* Freshmen: $3489. Undergraduates: $4419. *Parent loans:* $7,808,808 (75% need-based, 25% non-need-based). *Programs:* Federal Direct (Subsidized and Unsubsidized Stafford, PLUS), Perkins.

WORK-STUDY *Federal work-study:* 380 jobs averaging $1000.

ATHLETIC AWARDS Total amount: $5,408,049 (40% need-based, 60% non-need-based).

APPLYING FOR FINANCIAL AID *Required financial aid forms:* FAFSA, state aid form. *Financial aid deadline:* 2/15 (priority: 10/15). *Notification date:* 12/15. Students must reply by 5/1.

CONTACT Mary Lawyer, Associate Vice President for Enrollment Management, Siena College, 515 Loudon Road, Loudonville, NY 12211-1462, 518-783-2427 or toll-free 888-AT-SIENA. *Fax:* 518-783-2410. *E-mail:* aid@siena.edu.
Website: http://www.siena.edu/.

SIENA HEIGHTS UNIVERSITY
Adrian, MI

CONTACT Office of Financial Aid, Siena Heights University, 1247 East Siena Heights Drive, Adrian, MI 49221, 517-264-7130 or toll-free 800-521-0009.
Website: http://www.sienaheights.edu/.

SIERRA NEVADA COLLEGE
Incline Village, NV

CONTACT Nicole D. Ferguson, Director of Financial Aid, Sierra Nevada College, 999 Tahoe Boulevard, Incline Village, NV 89451, 775-831-1314 Ext. 7404. *Fax:* 775-832-1678. *E-mail:* nferguson@sierranevada.edu. *Website:* http://www.sierranevada.edu/.

SILVER LAKE COLLEGE OF THE HOLY FAMILY
Manitowoc, WI

CONTACT Ms. Michelle Leider, Associate Director of Financial Aid, Silver Lake College of the Holy Family, 2406 South Alverno Road, Manitowoc, WI 54220-9319, 920-686-6122 or toll-free 800-236-4752 Ext. 175. *Fax:* 920-684-7082. *E-mail:* financialaid@sl.edu. *Website:* http://www.sl.edu/.

SIMMONS COLLEGE
Boston, MA

Tuition & fees: $40,800	Average undergraduate aid package: $31,887

ABOUT THE INSTITUTION Independent, undergraduate: women only; graduate: coed. *Awards:* certificates, bachelor's, master's, and doctoral degrees. 55 undergraduate majors. *Total enrollment:* 6,402. Undergraduates: 1,763. Freshmen: 405. Federal methodology is used as a basis for awarding need-based institutional aid.

UNDERGRADUATE EXPENSES for 2018–2019 *Application fee:* $55. *Comprehensive fee:* $56,000 includes full-time tuition ($39,660), mandatory fees ($1140), and room and board ($15,200). Full-time tuition and fees vary according to course load and program. Room and board charges vary according to board plan and location. *Part-time tuition:* $1360 per credit hour. *Part-time fees:* $260 per term. Part-time tuition and fees vary according to course load and program.

FRESHMAN FINANCIAL AID (Fall 2017, est.) 364 applied for aid; of those 91% were deemed to have need. 100% of freshmen with need received aid; of those 12% had need fully met. *Average percent of need met:* 78% (excluding resources awarded to replace EFC). *Average financial aid package:* $32,115 (excluding resources awarded to replace EFC). 15% of all full-time freshmen had no need and received non-need-based gift aid.

UNDERGRADUATE FINANCIAL AID (Fall 2017, est.) 1,277 applied for aid; of those 93% were deemed to have need. 100% of undergraduates with need received aid; of those 12% had need fully met. *Average percent of need met:* 76% (excluding resources awarded to replace EFC). *Average financial aid package:* $31,887 (excluding resources awarded to replace EFC). 20% of all full-time undergraduates had no need and received non-need-based gift aid.

GIFT AID (NEED-BASED) *Total amount:* $35,238,984 (8% federal, 1% state, 89% institutional, 2% external sources). *Receiving aid:* Freshmen: 83% (332); all full-time undergraduates: 76% (1,177). *Average award:* Freshmen: $29,218; Undergraduates: $28,339. *Scholarships, grants, and awards:* Federal Pell, FSEOG, state, private, college/university gift aid from institutional funds.

GIFT AID (NON-NEED-BASED) *Total amount:* $7,293,988 (96% institutional, 4% external sources). *Receiving aid:* Freshmen: 8% (30). Undergraduates: 5% (83). *Average award:* Freshmen: $20,792. Undergraduates: $19,131. *Scholarships, grants, and awards by category:* Academic interests/achievement: general academic interests/achievements. *Special achievements/activities:* community service, general special achievements/activities. *Special characteristics:* children and siblings of alumni, general special characteristics. *Tuition waivers:* Full or partial for employees or children of employees. *ROTC:* Army cooperative.

LOANS *Student loans:* $13,018,211 (35% need-based, 65% non-need-based). 80% of past graduating class borrowed through all loan programs. *Average indebtedness per student:* $39,942. *Average need-based loan:* Freshmen: $3031. Undergraduates: $4032. *Parent loans:* $3,868,498 (100% non-need-based). *Programs:* Federal Direct (Subsidized and Unsubsidized Stafford, PLUS), Perkins, college/university.

WORK-STUDY *Federal work-study:* Total amount: $1,967,030; 829 jobs averaging $2373.

APPLYING FOR FINANCIAL AID *Required financial aid forms:* FAFSA, institution's own form. *Financial aid deadline (priority):* 3/1. *Notification date:* Continuous beginning 3/15.

CONTACT Amanda Galban, Senior Associate Director of Financial Aid, Simmons College, 300 The Fenway, Boston, MA 02115, 617-521-2001 or toll-free 800-345-8468. *Fax:* 617-521-3195. *E-mail:* amanda.galban@simmons.edu. *Website:* http://www.simmons.edu/.

SIMMONS COLLEGE OF KENTUCKY
Louisville, KY

CONTACT Financial Aid Office, Simmons College of Kentucky, 1018 South 7th Street, Louisville, KY 40203, 502-776-1443. *Website:* http://www.simmonscollegeky.edu/.

SIMPSON COLLEGE
Indianola, IA

Tuition & fees: $39,144	Average undergraduate aid package: $29,443

ABOUT THE INSTITUTION Independent United Methodist, coed. *Awards:* certificates, bachelor's, and master's degrees. 61 undergraduate majors. *Total enrollment:* 1,479. Undergraduates: 1,432. Freshmen: 298. Federal methodology is used as a basis for awarding need-based institutional aid.

UNDERGRADUATE EXPENSES for 2018–2019 *One-time required fee:* $200. *Comprehensive fee:* $47,524 includes full-time tuition ($38,412), mandatory fees ($732), and room and board ($8380). *College room only:* $4062. Full-time tuition and fees vary according to class time, course load, degree level, and program. Room and board charges vary according to board plan and housing facility. *Part-time tuition:* $375 per credit hour. *Part-time fees:* $6 per credit hour. Part-time tuition and fees vary according to class time, course load, degree level, and program.

FRESHMAN FINANCIAL AID (Fall 2017, est.) 296 applied for aid; of those 86% were deemed to have need. 100% of freshmen with need received aid; of those 29% had need fully met. *Average percent of need met:* 84% (excluding resources awarded to replace EFC). *Average financial aid package:* $31,851 (excluding resources awarded to replace EFC). 13% of all full-time freshmen had no need and received non-need-based gift aid.

UNDERGRADUATE FINANCIAL AID (Fall 2017, est.) 1,272 applied for aid; of those 83% were deemed to have need. 100% of undergraduates with need received aid; of those 22% had need fully met. *Average percent of need met:* 80% (excluding resources awarded to replace EFC). *Average financial aid package:* $29,443 (excluding resources awarded to replace EFC). 15% of all full-time undergraduates had no need and received non-need-based gift aid.

GIFT AID (NEED-BASED) *Total amount:* $24,714,203 (8% federal, 12% state, 77% institutional, 3% external sources). *Receiving aid:* Freshmen: 85% (253); all full-time undergraduates: 81% (1,032). *Average award:* Freshmen: $26,115; Undergraduates: $23,867. *Scholarships, grants, and awards:* Federal Pell, FSEOG, state, private, college/university gift aid from institutional funds.

GIFT AID (NON-NEED-BASED) *Total amount:* $5,739,451 (2% federal, 93% institutional, 5% external sources). *Receiving aid:* Freshmen: 18% (52). Undergraduates: 11% (143). *Average award:* Freshmen: $22,897. Undergraduates: $21,045. *Scholarships, grants, and awards by category:* Academic interests/achievement: $14,256,508 total: general academic interests/achievements. *Creative arts/performance:* $600,882 total: art/fine arts, debating, music, performing arts, theater/drama. *Special achievements/activities:* $202,000 total: community service, leadership, religious involvement. *Special characteristics:* $3,599,100 total: adult students, children and siblings of alumni, children of educators, children of faculty/staff, ethnic background, first-generation college students, international students, members of minority groups, out-of-state students, relatives of clergy, religious affiliation, siblings of current students, twins, veterans, veterans' children. *Tuition waivers:* Full or partial for children of alumni, employees or children of employees, senior citizens.

LOANS *Student loans:* $9,674,795 (70% need-based, 30% non-need-based). 81% of past graduating class borrowed through all loan programs. *Average indebtedness*

per student: $38,155. **Average need-based loan:** Freshmen: $4342. Undergraduates: $4950. **Parent loans:** $2,194,481 (41% need-based, 59% non-need-based). **Programs:** Federal Direct (Subsidized and Unsubsidized Stafford, PLUS), Perkins, college/university, alternative loans.

WORK-STUDY **Federal work-study:** Total amount: $374,843; 295 jobs averaging $1377. **State or other work-study/employment:** Total amount: $692,925 (39% need-based, 61% non-need-based). 490 part-time jobs averaging $1473.

APPLYING FOR FINANCIAL AID **Required financial aid form:** FAFSA. **Financial aid deadline (priority):** 2/1. **Notification date:** Continuous beginning 12/15. Students must reply by 5/1 or within 3 weeks of notification.

CONTACT Tracie Lynn Pavon, Assistant Vice President for Enrollment and Financial Assistance, Simpson College, 701 North C Street, Indianola, IA 50125-1297, 515-961-1630 Ext. 1596 or toll-free 800-362-2454. Fax: 515-961-1300. E-mail: tracie.pavon@simpson.edu.

Website: http://www.simpson.edu/.

SIMPSON UNIVERSITY
Redding, CA

ABOUT THE INSTITUTION Independent The Christian and Missionary Alliance, coed. **Awards:** certificates, associate, bachelor's, and master's degrees. 31 undergraduate majors. **Total enrollment:** 1,012. Undergraduates: 790. Freshmen: 118.

GIFT AID (NEED-BASED) **Scholarships, grants, and awards:** Federal Pell, FSEOG, state, private, college/university gift aid from institutional funds.

GIFT AID (NON-NEED-BASED) **Scholarships, grants, and awards by category:** Academic interests/achievement: business, communication, general academic interests/achievements. Creative arts/performance: music. Special achievements/activities: community service, leadership, religious involvement. Special characteristics: children and siblings of alumni, children of faculty/staff, ethnic background, general special characteristics, members of minority groups, out-of-state students, relatives of clergy, religious affiliation, siblings of current students, spouses of current students, veterans, veterans' children.

LOANS **Programs:** Federal Direct (Subsidized and Unsubsidized Stafford, PLUS), Perkins, private loans.

WORK-STUDY **Federal work-study:** 58 jobs averaging $1229.

APPLYING FOR FINANCIAL AID **Required financial aid forms:** FAFSA, state aid form.

CONTACT Miss Kari Meyers, Associate Director of Financial Aid, Simpson University, 2211 College View Drive, Redding, CA 96003-8606, 530-226-4621 or toll-free 888-9-SIMPSON. Fax: 530-226-4855. E-mail: financialaid@simpsonu.edu.

Website: http://www.simpsonu.edu/.

SINTE GLESKA UNIVERSITY
Mission, SD

CONTACT Office of Financial Aid, Sinte Gleska University, PO Box 105, Mission, SD 5755504105, 605-856-8197 Ext. 8477. Fax: 605-856-5874. E-mail: bhay@sintegleska.edu.

Website: http://www.sintegleska.edu/.

SITTING BULL COLLEGE
Fort Yates, ND

CONTACT Donna M. Seaboy, Financial Aid Director, Sitting Bull College, 9299 Highway 24, Fort Yates, ND 58538, 701-854-8013. Fax: 701-854-3403. E-mail: donnas@sbci.edu.

Website: http://www.sittingbull.edu/.

SKIDMORE COLLEGE
Saratoga Springs, NY

Tuition & fees: $52,446	Average undergraduate aid package: $49,300

ABOUT THE INSTITUTION Independent, coed. **Awards:** bachelor's degrees. 41 undergraduate majors. **Total enrollment:** 2,684. Undergraduates: 2,680. Freshmen: 661. Both federal and institutional methodology are used as a basis for awarding need-based institutional aid.

UNDERGRADUATE EXPENSES for 2017–2018 **Application fee:** $65. **One-time required fee:** $150. **Comprehensive fee:** $66,450 includes full-time tuition ($51,456), mandatory fees ($990), and room and board ($14,004). **College room only:** $8278. Full-time tuition and fees vary according to course load. Room and board charges vary according to board plan and housing facility. **Part-time tuition:** $1715 per credit. **Part-time fees:** $25 per term. Part-time tuition and fees vary according to course load. **Payment plan:** Tuition prepayment.

FRESHMAN FINANCIAL AID (Fall 2017, est.) 337 applied for aid; of those 81% were deemed to have need. 100% of freshmen with need received aid; of those 100% had need fully met. **Average percent of need met:** 100% (excluding resources awarded to replace EFC). **Average financial aid package:** $47,700 (excluding resources awarded to replace EFC). 1% of all full-time freshmen had no need and received non-need-based gift aid.

UNDERGRADUATE FINANCIAL AID (Fall 2017, est.) 1,360 applied for aid; of those 82% were deemed to have need. 100% of undergraduates with need received aid; of those 94% had need fully met. **Average percent of need met:** 94% (excluding resources awarded to replace EFC). **Average financial aid package:** $49,300 (excluding resources awarded to replace EFC). 1% of all full-time undergraduates had no need and received non-need-based gift aid.

GIFT AID (NEED-BASED) **Total amount:** $48,840,000 (5% federal, 3% state, 92% institutional). **Receiving aid:** Freshmen: 41% (272); all full-time undergraduates: 42% (1,111). **Average award:** Freshmen: $45,900; Undergraduates: $44,600. **Scholarships, grants, and awards:** Federal Pell, FSEOG, state, private, college/university gift aid from institutional funds.

GIFT AID (NON-NEED-BASED) **Total amount:** $1,819,000 (9% state, 31% institutional, 60% external sources). **Receiving aid:** Freshmen: 2% (10). Undergraduates: 2% (42). **Average award:** Freshmen: $15,000. Undergraduates: $13,250. **Scholarships, grants, and awards by category:** Academic interests/achievement: biological sciences, computer science, mathematics, physical sciences. Creative arts/performance: music. Special characteristics: children of faculty/staff. **Tuition waivers:** Full or partial for employees or children of employees, senior citizens. **ROTC:** Army cooperative, Air Force cooperative.

LOANS **Student loans:** $5,400,000 (44% need-based, 56% non-need-based). 39% of past graduating class borrowed through all loan programs. **Average indebtedness per student:** $23,916. **Average need-based loan:** Freshmen: $3100. Undergraduates: $4200. **Parent loans:** $2,600,000 (100% non-need-based). **Programs:** Federal Direct (Subsidized and Unsubsidized Stafford, PLUS), Perkins, state.

WORK-STUDY **Federal work-study:** Total amount: $750,000; jobs available. **State or other work-study/employment:** Total amount: $800,000 (100% non-need-based). Part-time jobs available.

APPLYING FOR FINANCIAL AID **Required financial aid forms:** CSS Financial Aid PROFILE, noncustodial (divorced/separated) parent's statement. **Financial aid deadline:** 2/1. **Notification date:** 4/1. Students must reply by 5/1.

CONTACT Ms. Beth A. Post, Director of Financial Aid, Skidmore College, 815 North Broadway, Saratoga Springs, NY 12866, 518-580-5750 or toll-free 800-867-6007. Fax: 518-580-5752. E-mail: finaid@skidmore.edu.

Website: http://www.skidmore.edu/.

SLIPPERY ROCK UNIVERSITY OF PENNSYLVANIA
Slippery Rock, PA

Tuition & fees (PA res): $10,205	Average undergraduate aid package: $9352

ABOUT THE INSTITUTION State-supported, coed. *Awards:* certificates, bachelor's, master's, and doctoral degrees. 51 undergraduate majors. *Total enrollment:* 8,895. Undergraduates: 7,638. Freshmen: 1,597. Federal methodology is used as a basis for awarding need-based institutional aid.

UNDERGRADUATE EXPENSES for 2017–2018 *Application fee:* $30. *Tuition, state resident:* full-time $7492; part-time $312 per credit hour. *Tuition, nonresident:* full-time $11,238; part-time $468 per credit hour. *Required fees:* full-time $2713; $113.04 per credit hour. Full-time tuition and fees vary according to course load. Part-time tuition and fees vary according to course load. *College room and board:* $10,312; *Room only:* $6742. Room and board charges vary according to board plan and housing facility.

FRESHMAN FINANCIAL AID (Fall 2017, est.) 1,535 applied for aid; of those 78% were deemed to have need. 99% of freshmen with need received aid; of those 8% had need fully met. *Average percent of need met:* 55% (excluding resources awarded to replace EFC). *Average financial aid package:* $8777 (excluding resources awarded to replace EFC). 10% of all full-time freshmen had no need and received non-need-based gift aid.

UNDERGRADUATE FINANCIAL AID (Fall 2017, est.) 6,224 applied for aid; of those 80% were deemed to have need. 98% of undergraduates with need received aid; of those 7% had need fully met. *Average percent of need met:* 58% (excluding resources awarded to replace EFC). *Average financial aid package:* $9352 (excluding resources awarded to replace EFC). 8% of all full-time undergraduates had no need and received non-need-based gift aid.

GIFT AID (NEED-BASED) *Total amount:* $20,013,051 (55% federal, 39% state, 6% institutional). *Receiving aid:* Freshmen: 49% (775); all full-time undergraduates: 45% (3,217). *Average award:* Freshmen: $6230; Undergraduates: $6066. *Scholarships, grants, and awards:* Federal Pell, FSEOG, state, private, college/university gift aid from institutional funds.

GIFT AID (NON-NEED-BASED) *Total amount:* $6,450,839 (10% state, 55% institutional, 35% external sources). *Receiving aid:* Freshmen: 34% (536). Undergraduates: 20% (1,418). *Average award:* Freshmen: $2842. Undergraduates: $2713. *Scholarships, grants, and awards by category:* Academic interests/achievement: biological sciences, business, communication, computer science, education, engineering/technologies, English, foreign languages, general academic interests/achievements, home economics, mathematics, military science, physical sciences, social sciences. *Creative arts/performance:* applied art and design, art/fine arts, dance, music, performing arts, theater/drama. *Special achievements/activities:* community service, general special achievements/activities, leadership. *Special characteristics:* children and siblings of alumni, children of faculty/staff, children of union members/company employees, ethnic background, general special characteristics, local/state students, members of minority groups, out-of-state students, previous college experience. *Tuition waivers:* Full or partial for minority students, employees or children of employees, senior citizens. *ROTC:* Army.

LOANS *Student loans:* $53,931,444 (38% need-based, 62% non-need-based). 85% of past graduating class borrowed through all loan programs. *Average indebtedness per student:* $34,300. *Average need-based loan:* Freshmen: $3712. Undergraduates: $4497. *Parent loans:* $12,114,680 (100% non-need-based). *Programs:* Federal Direct (Subsidized and Unsubsidized Stafford, PLUS), Perkins.

WORK-STUDY *Federal work-study:* Total amount: $670,781; 584 jobs averaging $1589. *State or other work-study/employment:* Total amount: $1,737,682 (100% non-need-based). 957 part-time jobs averaging $1889.

ATHLETIC AWARDS Total amount: $1,124,556 (100% non-need-based).

APPLYING FOR FINANCIAL AID *Required financial aid form:* FAFSA. *Financial aid deadline (priority):* 5/1. *Notification date:* Continuous beginning 12/15.

CONTACT Ms. Alyssa Dobson, Director of Financial Aid and Scholarships, Slippery Rock University of Pennsylvania, 108 Maltby Center, Suite 107, Slippery Rock, PA 16057, 724-738-2044 or toll-free 800-SRU-9111. *Fax:* 724-738-2922. *E-mail:* alyssa.dobson@sru.edu.
Website: http://www.sru.edu/.

SMITH COLLEGE
Northampton, MA

Tuition & fees: $50,044	Average undergraduate aid package: $51,046

ABOUT THE INSTITUTION Independent, undergraduate: women only; graduate: coed. *Awards:* certificates, bachelor's, master's, and doctoral degrees. 53 undergraduate majors. *Total enrollment:* 2,918. Undergraduates: 2,521. Freshmen: 638. Both federal and institutional methodology are used as a basis for awarding need-based institutional aid.

UNDERGRADUATE EXPENSES for 2017–2018 *Comprehensive fee:* $66,774 includes full-time tuition ($49,760), mandatory fees ($284), and room and board ($16,730). *Part-time tuition:* $1560 per credit hour. *Payment plan:* Tuition prepayment.

FRESHMAN FINANCIAL AID (Fall 2017, est.) 484 applied for aid; of those 77% were deemed to have need. 100% of freshmen with need received aid; of those 100% had need fully met. *Average percent of need met:* 100% (excluding resources awarded to replace EFC). *Average financial aid package:* $50,844 (excluding resources awarded to replace EFC). 11% of all full-time freshmen had no need and received non-need-based gift aid.

UNDERGRADUATE FINANCIAL AID (Fall 2017, est.) 1,802 applied for aid; of those 86% were deemed to have need. 100% of undergraduates with need received aid; of those 100% had need fully met. *Average percent of need met:* 100% (excluding resources awarded to replace EFC). *Average financial aid package:* $51,046 (excluding resources awarded to replace EFC). 7% of all full-time undergraduates had no need and received non-need-based gift aid.

GIFT AID (NEED-BASED) *Total amount:* $70,993,552 (4% federal, 1% state, 93% institutional, 2% external sources). *Receiving aid:* Freshmen: 58% (367); all full-time undergraduates: 61% (1,534). *Average award:* Freshmen: $48,185; Undergraduates: $45,819. *Scholarships, grants, and awards:* Federal Pell, FSEOG, state, private, college/university gift aid from institutional funds.

GIFT AID (NON-NEED-BASED) *Total amount:* $4,172,922 (2% federal, 78% institutional, 20% external sources). *Receiving aid:* Freshmen: 3% (18). Undergraduates: 1% (29). *Average award:* Freshmen: $16,095. Undergraduates: $16,278. *Scholarships, grants, and awards by category:* Academic interests/achievement: general academic interests/achievements. *Special characteristics:* local/state students. *Tuition waivers:* Full or partial for employees or children of employees. *ROTC:* Army cooperative, Air Force cooperative.

LOANS *Student loans:* $7,956,875 (68% need-based, 32% non-need-based). 58% of past graduating class borrowed through all loan programs. *Average indebtedness per student:* $24,501. *Average need-based loan:* Freshmen: $3023. Undergraduates: $4350. *Parent loans:* $3,249,102 (83% need-based, 17% non-need-based). *Programs:* Federal Direct (Subsidized and Unsubsidized Stafford, PLUS), Perkins, college/university.

WORK-STUDY *Federal work-study:* Total amount: $2,563,207; jobs available. *State or other work-study/employment:* Total amount: $1,464,637 (81% need-based, 19% non-need-based). Part-time jobs available.

APPLYING FOR FINANCIAL AID *Required financial aid forms:* FAFSA, institution's own form, CSS Financial Aid PROFILE, noncustodial (divorced/separated) parent's statement, student/parent tax returns. *Financial aid deadline:* 1/25. *Notification date:* 4/1. Students must reply by 5/1.

CONTACT David Belanger, Director of Student Financial Services, Smith College, College Hall 106, 10 Elm Street, Northampton, MA 01063, 413-585-2530 or toll-free 800-383-3232. *Fax:* 413-585-2566. *E-mail:* sfs@smith.edu.
Website: http://www.smith.edu/.

SOKA UNIVERSITY OF AMERICA
Aliso Viejo, CA

Tuition & fees: $32,980	Average undergraduate aid package: $36,220

ABOUT THE INSTITUTION Independent, coed. *Awards:* bachelor's and master's degrees. 1 undergraduate major. *Total enrollment:* 427. Undergraduates: 412. Freshmen: 107. Both federal and institutional methodology are used as a basis for awarding need-based institutional aid.

UNDERGRADUATE EXPENSES for 2018–2019 *Application fee:* $45. *Comprehensive fee:* $45,510 includes full-time tuition ($31,310), mandatory fees ($1670), and room and board ($12,530). Full-time tuition and fees vary according to class time, course level, course load, and program. Room and board charges vary according to board plan. *Part-time tuition:* $1305 per credit hour. Part-time tuition and fees vary according to class time, course level, course load, and program.

FRESHMAN FINANCIAL AID (Fall 2017, est.) 106 applied for aid; of those 84% were deemed to have need. 100% of freshmen with need received aid; of those 63% had need fully met. *Average percent of need met:* 100% (excluding resources awarded to replace EFC). *Average financial aid package:* $35,003 (excluding resources awarded to replace EFC). 7% of all full-time freshmen had no need and received non-need-based gift aid.

UNDERGRADUATE FINANCIAL AID (Fall 2017, est.) 411 applied for aid; of those 85% were deemed to have need. 100% of undergraduates with need received aid; of those 71% had need fully met. *Average percent of need met:* 88% (excluding resources awarded to replace EFC). *Average financial aid package:* $36,220 (excluding resources awarded to replace EFC). 5% of all full-time undergraduates had no need and received non-need-based gift aid.

GIFT AID (NEED-BASED) *Total amount:* $9,411,577 (5% federal, 4% state, 91% institutional). *Receiving aid:* Freshmen: 84% (89); all full-time undergraduates: 85% (350). *Average award:* Freshmen: $23,938; Undergraduates: $24,414. *Scholarships, grants, and awards:* Federal Pell, FSEOG, state, private, college/university gift aid from institutional funds, Hispanic Educational Endowment Fund (HEEF) STEM Scholarships through Southern California Edison.

GIFT AID (NON-NEED-BASED) *Total amount:* $4,234,117 (99% institutional, 1% external sources). *Receiving aid:* Freshmen: 84% (89). Undergraduates: 85% (350). *Average award:* Freshmen: $13,785. Undergraduates: $11,409. *Scholarships, grants, and awards by category:* Academic interests/achievement: general academic interests/achievements. *Special achievements/activities:* leadership. *Tuition waivers:* Full or partial for employees or children of employees.

LOANS *Student loans:* $1,126,970 (89% need-based, 11% non-need-based). 62% of past graduating class borrowed through all loan programs. *Average indebtedness per student:* $23,441. *Average need-based loan:* Freshmen: $3122. Undergraduates: $4092. *Parent loans:* $215,930 (100% non-need-based). *Programs:* Federal Direct (Subsidized and Unsubsidized Stafford, PLUS), college/university.

WORK-STUDY *Federal work-study:* Total amount: $66,962; 34 jobs averaging $1969. *State or other work-study/employment:* Part-time jobs available.

ATHLETIC AWARDS Total amount: $442,640 (100% non-need-based).

APPLYING FOR FINANCIAL AID *Required financial aid forms:* FAFSA, institution's own form, state aid form, Soka Dream Financial Aid Application. *Financial aid deadline:* 3/2 (priority: 2/15). *Notification date:* 3/15. Students must reply by 5/1 or within 1 week of notification.

CONTACT Dr. Andrew Woolsey, Director of Enrollment Services, Soka University of America, 1 University Drive, Aliso Viejo, CA 92656, 949-480-4112 or toll-free 888-600-SOKA. *Fax:* 949-480-4151. *E-mail:* awoolsey@soka.edu. *Website:* http://www.soka.edu/.

SONOMA STATE UNIVERSITY
Rohnert Park, CA

Tuition & fees (CA res): $7724	Average undergraduate aid package: $10,616

ABOUT THE INSTITUTION State-supported, coed. *Awards:* bachelor's and master's degrees. 63 undergraduate majors. *Total enrollment:* 9,223. Undergraduates: 8,551. Freshmen: 1,784. Federal methodology is used as a basis for awarding need-based institutional aid.

UNDERGRADUATE EXPENSES for 2017–2018 *Application fee:* $55. *Tuition, area resident:* part-time $3330 per year. *Tuition, state resident:* full-time $5742. *Tuition, nonresident:* full-time $17,622. *Required fees:* full-time $1982. Full-time tuition and fees vary according to course load and degree level. Part-time tuition and fees vary according to course load and degree level. *College room and board:* $13,554. Room and board charges vary according to board plan and housing facility.

FRESHMAN FINANCIAL AID (Fall 2017, est.) 1,529 applied for aid; of those 75% were deemed to have need. 95% of freshmen with need received aid; of those 4% had need fully met. *Average percent of need met:* 54% (excluding resources awarded to replace EFC). *Average financial aid package:* $10,986 (excluding

resources awarded to replace EFC). 1% of all full-time freshmen had no need and received non-need-based gift aid.

UNDERGRADUATE FINANCIAL AID (Fall 2017, est.) 5,735 applied for aid; of those 82% were deemed to have need. 95% of undergraduates with need received aid; of those 5% had need fully met. *Average percent of need met:* 51% (excluding resources awarded to replace EFC). *Average financial aid package:* $10,616 (excluding resources awarded to replace EFC). 1% of all full-time undergraduates had no need and received non-need-based gift aid.

GIFT AID (NEED-BASED) *Total amount:* $35,130,407 (41% federal, 59% state). *Receiving aid:* Freshmen: 46% (807); all full-time undergraduates: 43% (3,320). *Average award:* Freshmen: $10,637; Undergraduates: $10,045. *Scholarships, grants, and awards:* Federal Pell, FSEOG, state, private, college/university gift aid from institutional funds.

GIFT AID (NON-NEED-BASED) *Total amount:* $4,035,673 (48% state, 12% institutional, 40% external sources). *Receiving aid:* Freshmen: 27% (466). Undergraduates: 17% (1,362). *Average award:* Freshmen: $2050. Undergraduates: $2374. *Scholarships, grants, and awards by category:* Academic interests/achievement: area/ethnic studies, biological sciences, business, communication, computer science, education, engineering/technologies, English, foreign languages, general academic interests/achievements, health fields, humanities, mathematics, physical sciences, premedicine, social sciences. Creative arts/performance: applied art and design, art/fine arts, cinema/film/broadcasting, creative writing, dance, journalism/publications, music, performing arts, theater/drama. Special achievements/activities: community service, leadership, memberships. Special characteristics: adult students, children and siblings of alumni, children of educators, children of faculty/staff, children of public servants, children of union members/company employees, children of workers in trades, ethnic background, first-generation college students, general special characteristics, handicapped students, international students, local/state students, married students, members of minority groups, out-of-state students, previous college experience, veterans. *Tuition waivers:* Full or partial for employees or children of employees. **ROTC:** Army cooperative, Air Force cooperative.

LOANS *Student loans:* $22,612,479 (49% need-based, 51% non-need-based). 59% of past graduating class borrowed through all loan programs. *Average indebtedness per student:* $20,797. *Average need-based loan:* Freshmen: $2562. Undergraduates: $3112. *Parent loans:* $13,182,045 (100% non-need-based). *Programs:* Federal Direct (Subsidized and Unsubsidized Stafford, PLUS).

WORK-STUDY *Federal work-study:* Total amount: $674,069; jobs available. *State or other work-study/employment:* Total amount: $1,600,000 (100% non-need-based). Part-time jobs available.

ATHLETIC AWARDS Total amount: $607,569 (100% non-need-based).

APPLYING FOR FINANCIAL AID *Required financial aid form:* FAFSA. *Financial aid deadline (priority):* 11/30. *Notification date:* Continuous beginning 3/1. Students must reply within 2 weeks of notification.

CONTACT Susan Gutierrez, Director of Financial Aid, Sonoma State University, 1801 East Cotati Avenue, Rohnert Park, CA 94928-3609, 707-664-2287. *Fax:* 707-664-4242. *E-mail:* susan.gutierrez@sonoma.edu. *Website:* http://www.sonoma.edu/.

SOUTH CAROLINA STATE UNIVERSITY
Orangeburg, SC

CONTACT Sandra S. Davis, Director of Financial Aid, South Carolina State University, 300 College Street Northeast, Orangeburg, SC 29117, 803-536-7067 or toll-free 800-260-5956. *Fax:* 803-536-8420. *E-mail:* sdavis@scsu.edu. *Website:* http://www.scsu.edu/.

SOUTH COLLEGE
Knoxville, TN

CONTACT Financial Aid Office, South College, 720 North Fifth Avenue, Knoxville, TN 37917, 865-524-3043. *Website:* http://www.southcollegetn.edu/.

SOUTH DAKOTA SCHOOL OF MINES AND TECHNOLOGY
Rapid City, SD

ABOUT THE INSTITUTION State-supported, coed. **Awards:** certificates, associate, bachelor's, master's, and doctoral degrees. 17 undergraduate majors. **Total enrollment:** 2,859. Undergraduates: 2,485. Freshmen: 497.

GIFT AID (NEED-BASED) **Scholarships, grants, and awards:** Federal Pell, FSEOG, state, private, college/university gift aid from institutional funds.

GIFT AID (NON-NEED-BASED) **Scholarships, grants, and awards by category:** *Academic interests/achievement:* biological sciences, computer science, engineering/technologies, mathematics, military science, physical sciences. *Special characteristics:* adult students, ethnic background, international students, local/state students, married students, members of minority groups, out-of-state students.

LOANS **Programs:** Federal Direct (Subsidized and Unsubsidized Stafford, PLUS), Perkins.

APPLYING FOR FINANCIAL AID *Required financial aid form:* FAFSA.

CONTACT David W. Martin, Director of Financial Aid, South Dakota School of Mines and Technology, 501 East Saint Joseph Street, Rapid City, SD 57701-3995, 605-394-2274 or toll-free 800-544-8162. *Fax:* 605-394-1979. *E-mail:* david.martin@sdsmt.edu.
Website: http://www.sdsmt.edu/.

SOUTH DAKOTA STATE UNIVERSITY
Brookings, SD

Tuition & fees (SD res): $8460	Average undergraduate aid package: N/A

ABOUT THE INSTITUTION State-supported, coed. **Awards:** certificates, associate, bachelor's, master's, and doctoral degrees. 81 undergraduate majors. **Total enrollment:** 12,613. Undergraduates: 10,959. Freshmen: 2,273. Federal methodology is used as a basis for awarding need-based institutional aid.

UNDERGRADUATE EXPENSES for 2017–2018 **Application fee:** $20. **Tuition, state resident:** full-time $7200; part-time $240 per credit hour. **Tuition, nonresident:** full-time $10,440; part-time $348 per credit hour. **Required fees:** full-time $1260; $42 per credit hour. Full-time tuition and fees vary according to course level, course load, degree level, location, program, and reciprocity agreements. Part-time tuition and fees vary according to course level, course load, degree level, location, program, and reciprocity agreements. **College room and board:** $7110; **Room only:** $3710. Room and board charges vary according to board plan and housing facility.

GIFT AID (NEED-BASED) **Total amount:** $23,255,461 (44% federal, 9% state, 26% institutional, 21% external sources). **Scholarships, grants, and awards:** Federal Pell, FSEOG, state, private, college/university gift aid from institutional funds.

GIFT AID (NON-NEED-BASED) **Scholarships, grants, and awards by category:** *Academic interests/achievement:* agriculture, area/ethnic studies, biological sciences, business, communication, computer science, education, engineering/technologies, English, foreign languages, general academic interests/achievements, health fields, home economics, humanities, international studies, mathematics, military science, physical sciences, premedicine, social sciences. *Creative arts/performance:* art/fine arts, debating, general creative arts/performance, journalism/publications, music, performing arts, theater/drama. *Special achievements/activities:* community service, general special achievements/activities, hobbies/interests, junior miss, leadership, memberships, rodeo. *Special characteristics:* adult students, children of faculty/staff, children of workers in trades, ethnic background, first-generation college students, general special characteristics, handicapped students, international students, members of minority groups, veterans, veterans' children. **Tuition waivers:** Full or partial for children of alumni, employees or children of employees, senior citizens. **ROTC:** Army, Air Force.

LOANS **Student loans:** $78,151,515 (39% need-based, 61% non-need-based). *Average indebtedness per student:* $31,131. **Parent loans:** $6,494,264 (100% non-need-based). **Programs:** Federal Direct (Subsidized and Unsubsidized Stafford, PLUS), Perkins, Federal Nursing.

WORK-STUDY **Federal work-study:** jobs available. **State or other work-study/employment:** Total amount: $14,018,890 (100% need-based). Part-time jobs available.

APPLYING FOR FINANCIAL AID *Required financial aid form:* FAFSA. *Financial aid deadline (priority):* 3/15. **Notification date:** Continuous.

CONTACT Carolyn Halgerson, Director of Financial Aid, South Dakota State University, Administration 100, PO Box 2201, Brookings, SD 57007, 605-688-4695 or toll-free 800-952-3541. *Fax:* 605-688-5882. *E-mail:* carolyn.halgerson@sdstate.edu. *Website:* http://www.sdstate.edu/.

SOUTHEASTERN BAPTIST COLLEGE
Laurel, MS

CONTACT Financial Aid Officer, Southeastern Baptist College, 4229 Highway 15 North, Laurel, MS 39440-1096, 601-426-6346.
Website: http://www.southeasternbaptist.edu/.

SOUTHEASTERN BAPTIST THEOLOGICAL SEMINARY
Wake Forest, NC

CONTACT Financial Aid Office, Southeastern Baptist Theological Seminary, 120 South Wingate Street, Wake Forest, NC 27587, 919-761-2100 or toll-free 800-284-6317.
Website: http://www.sebts.edu/.

SOUTHEASTERN LOUISIANA UNIVERSITY
Hammond, LA

Tuition & fees (LA res): $8153	Average undergraduate aid package: $9450

ABOUT THE INSTITUTION State-supported, coed. **Awards:** certificates, associate, bachelor's, master's, and doctoral degrees. 37 undergraduate majors. **Total enrollment:** 14,308. Undergraduates: 13,340. Freshmen: 2,736. Federal methodology is used as a basis for awarding need-based institutional aid.

UNDERGRADUATE EXPENSES for 2017–2018 **Application fee:** $20. **Tuition, state resident:** full-time $5777; part-time $340 per credit hour. **Tuition, nonresident:** full-time $18,255; part-time $340 per credit hour. **Required fees:** full-time $2376. Full-time tuition and fees vary according to course load. Part-time tuition and fees vary according to course load. **College room and board:** $8340; **Room only:** $4940. Room and board charges vary according to board plan and housing facility. **Payment plan:** Guaranteed tuition.

FRESHMAN FINANCIAL AID (Fall 2016) 1,793 applied for aid; of those 74% were deemed to have need. 100% of freshmen with need received aid; of those 11% had need fully met. *Average financial aid package:* $9407 (excluding resources awarded to replace EFC). 17% of all full-time freshmen had no need and received non-need-based gift aid.

UNDERGRADUATE FINANCIAL AID (Fall 2016) 7,264 applied for aid; of those 78% were deemed to have need. 100% of undergraduates with need received aid; of those 9% had need fully met. *Average financial aid package:* $9450 (excluding resources awarded to replace EFC). 9% of all full-time undergraduates had no need and received non-need-based gift aid.

GIFT AID (NEED-BASED) **Total amount:** $23,048,338 (86% federal, 13% state, 1% institutional). **Receiving aid:** Freshmen: 43% (873); all full-time undergraduates: 43% (3,842). **Average award:** Freshmen: $5016; Undergraduates: $5198. **Scholarships, grants, and awards:** Federal Pell, FSEOG, state, private, college/university gift aid from institutional funds.

GIFT AID (NON-NEED-BASED) **Total amount:** $22,420,050 (74% state, 21% institutional, 5% external sources). **Receiving aid:** Freshmen: 49% (984). Undergraduates: 33% (2,970). **Average award:** Freshmen: $1370. Undergraduates: $1561. **Scholarships, grants, and awards by category:** *Academic interests/achievement:* business, communication, computer science, education, English, foreign languages, general academic interests/achievements, humanities, mathematics, premedicine, social sciences. *Creative arts/performance:* art/fine arts, music, theater/drama.

Special achievements/activities: cheerleading/drum major, leadership, memberships. *Special characteristics:* adult students, children and siblings of alumni, children of faculty/staff, first-generation college students, out-of-state students, veterans, veterans' children. *Tuition waivers:* Full or partial for employees or children of employees. **ROTC:** Army.

LOANS *Student loans:* $36,331,903 (45% need-based, 55% non-need-based). 56% of past graduating class borrowed through all loan programs. *Average indebtedness per student:* $20,164. *Average need-based loan:* Freshmen: $3057. Undergraduates: $3779. *Parent loans:* $3,126,214 (100% non-need-based). *Programs:* Federal Direct (Subsidized and Unsubsidized Stafford, PLUS), Perkins, college/university.

WORK-STUDY *Federal work-study:* 168 jobs averaging $1992. *State or other work-study/employment:* Total amount: $1,722,632 (100% non-need-based). 854 part-time jobs averaging $1907.

ATHLETIC AWARDS Total amount: $3,078,689 (100% non-need-based).

APPLYING FOR FINANCIAL AID *Required financial aid form:* FAFSA. *Financial aid deadline (priority):* 5/1. *Notification date:* Continuous beginning 4/1. Students must reply within 2 weeks of notification.

CONTACT Mr. Charles Cambre, Director of Financial Aid, Southeastern Louisiana University, SLU 10768, Hammond, LA 70402, 985-549-2244 or toll-free 800-222-7358. *Fax:* 985-549-5077. *E-mail:* finaid@selu.edu.

Website: http://www.southeastern.edu/.

SOUTHEASTERN OKLAHOMA STATE UNIVERSITY
Durant, OK

Tuition & fees (OK res): $6750	Average undergraduate aid package: $11,735

ABOUT THE INSTITUTION State-supported, coed. *Awards:* certificates, bachelor's, and master's degrees. 41 undergraduate majors. *Total enrollment:* 3,724. Undergraduates: 3,132. Freshmen: 517. Federal methodology is used as a basis for awarding need-based institutional aid.

UNDERGRADUATE EXPENSES for 2017–2018 *Application fee:* $20. *Tuition, state resident:* full-time $6240; part-time $208 per credit hour. *Tuition, nonresident:* full-time $14,880; part-time $496 per credit hour. *Required fees:* full-time $510; $17 per credit hour. Full-time tuition and fees vary according to course level, course load, degree level, location, and program. Part-time tuition and fees vary according to course level, course load, degree level, location, and program. *College room and board:* $6568; *Room only:* $3368. Room and board charges vary according to board plan, housing facility, and student level. *Payment plan:* Guaranteed tuition.

FRESHMAN FINANCIAL AID (Fall 2016) 407 applied for aid; of those 86% were deemed to have need. 97% of freshmen with need received aid; of those 12% had need fully met. *Average percent of need met:* 5% (excluding resources awarded to replace EFC). *Average financial aid package:* $13,097 (excluding resources awarded to replace EFC). 3% of all full-time freshmen had no need and received non-need-based gift aid.

UNDERGRADUATE FINANCIAL AID (Fall 2016) 1,713 applied for aid; of those 89% were deemed to have need. 96% of undergraduates with need received aid; of those 10% had need fully met. *Average percent of need met:* 6% (excluding resources awarded to replace EFC). *Average financial aid package:* $11,735 (excluding resources awarded to replace EFC). 1% of all full-time undergraduates had no need and received non-need-based gift aid.

GIFT AID (NEED-BASED) *Total amount:* $8,670,385 (70% federal, 30% state). *Receiving aid:* Freshmen: 50% (232); all full-time undergraduates: 49% (1,057). *Average award:* Freshmen: $2075; Undergraduates: $2002. *Scholarships, grants, and awards:* Federal Pell, FSEOG, state, private, college/university gift aid from institutional funds.

GIFT AID (NON-NEED-BASED) *Total amount:* $3,382,970 (4% state, 20% institutional, 76% external sources). *Receiving aid:* Freshmen: 40% (184). Undergraduates: 25% (530). *Average award:* Freshmen: $609. Undergraduates: $720. *Scholarships, grants, and awards by category: Academic interests/achievement:* biological sciences, business, communication, computer science, education, engineering/technologies, English, general academic interests/achievements, mathematics, physical sciences, social sciences. *Creative arts/performance:* art/fine arts, dance, debating, music, performing arts, theater/drama. *Special achievements/*

activities: cheerleading/drum major, leadership, rodeo. *Special characteristics:* children and siblings of alumni, out-of-state students. *Tuition waivers:* Full or partial for minority students, children of alumni, employees or children of employees, adult students, senior citizens.

LOANS *Student loans:* $11,571,827 (35% need-based, 65% non-need-based). 61% of past graduating class borrowed through all loan programs. *Average indebtedness per student:* $16,542. *Average need-based loan:* Freshmen: $1467. Undergraduates: $2093. *Parent loans:* $562,623 (100% non-need-based). *Programs:* Federal Direct (Subsidized and Unsubsidized Stafford, PLUS).

WORK-STUDY *Federal work-study:* jobs available. *State or other work-study/employment:* Part-time jobs available.

ATHLETIC AWARDS Total amount: $1,921,233 (100% non-need-based).

APPLYING FOR FINANCIAL AID *Required financial aid forms:* FAFSA, institution's own form. *Financial aid deadline (priority):* 12/1. *Notification date:* Continuous beginning 3/1. Students must reply within 2 weeks of notification.

CONTACT Tony Lehrling, Director of Student Financial Aid, Southeastern Oklahoma State University, 1405 North 4th Avenue, Durant, OK 74701-0609, 580-745-2186 or toll-free 800-435-1327. *Fax:* 580-745-7469. *E-mail:* shudson@se.edu. *Website:* http://www.se.edu/.

SOUTHEASTERN UNIVERSITY
Lakeland, FL

Tuition & fees: $25,360	Average undergraduate aid package: $15,554

ABOUT THE INSTITUTION Independent Assemblies of God, coed. *Awards:* certificates, associate, bachelor's, master's, and doctoral degrees. 59 undergraduate majors. *Total enrollment:* 7,163. Undergraduates: 6,240. Freshmen: 1,225. Federal methodology is used as a basis for awarding need-based institutional aid.

UNDERGRADUATE EXPENSES for 2018–2019 *Application fee:* $40. *Comprehensive fee:* $34,910 includes full-time tuition ($24,360), mandatory fees ($1000), and room and board ($9550). Full-time tuition and fees vary according to class time, degree level, location, and reciprocity agreements. Room and board charges vary according to board plan and housing facility. *Part-time tuition:* $1015 per credit hour. *Part-time fees:* $200 per term. Part-time tuition and fees vary according to class time, course load, degree level, location, and reciprocity agreements.

FRESHMAN FINANCIAL AID (Fall 2017, est.) 1,030 applied for aid; of those 85% were deemed to have need. 100% of freshmen with need received aid; of those 14% had need fully met. *Average percent of need met:* 60% (excluding resources awarded to replace EFC). *Average financial aid package:* $15,729 (excluding resources awarded to replace EFC). 20% of all full-time freshmen had no need and received non-need-based gift aid.

UNDERGRADUATE FINANCIAL AID (Fall 2017, est.) 3,734 applied for aid; of those 89% were deemed to have need. 100% of undergraduates with need received aid; of those 13% had need fully met. *Average percent of need met:* 61% (excluding resources awarded to replace EFC). *Average financial aid package:* $15,554 (excluding resources awarded to replace EFC). 19% of all full-time undergraduates had no need and received non-need-based gift aid.

GIFT AID (NEED-BASED) *Total amount:* $38,287,358 (28% federal, 18% state, 52% institutional, 2% external sources). *Receiving aid:* Freshmen: 56% (626); all full-time undergraduates: 59% (2,513). *Average award:* Freshmen: $5959; Undergraduates: $6252. *Scholarships, grants, and awards:* Federal Pell, FSEOG, state, private, college/university gift aid from institutional funds.

GIFT AID (NON-NEED-BASED) *Total amount:* $5,672,202 (24% state, 71% institutional, 5% external sources). *Receiving aid:* Freshmen: 78% (875). Undergraduates: 77% (3,291). *Average award:* Freshmen: $8444. Undergraduates: $9024. *Scholarships, grants, and awards by category: Academic interests/achievement:* communication, education, general academic interests/achievements, religion/biblical studies. *Creative arts/performance:* art/fine arts, cinema/film/broadcasting, journalism/publications, music, performing arts. *Special achievements/activities:* cheerleading/drum major, general special achievements/activities, leadership, religious involvement. *Special characteristics:* children of educators, children of faculty/staff, international students, religious affiliation. *Tuition waivers:* Full or partial for employees or children of employees. **ROTC:** Army cooperative.

LOANS *Student loans:* $24,260,369 (91% need-based, 9% non-need-based). 91% of past graduating class borrowed through all loan programs. *Average indebtedness per student:* $29,810. *Average need-based loan:* Freshmen: $3391. Undergrad-

uates; $4107. *Parent loans:* $15,588,482 (85% need-based, 15% non-need-based).
Programs: Federal Direct (Subsidized and Unsubsidized Stafford, PLUS), Perkins,
WORK-STUDY *Federal work-study:* Total amount: $174,527; 86 jobs averaging $2029.
ATHLETIC AWARDS Total amount: $2,907,187 (71% need-based, 29% non-need-based).
APPLYING FOR FINANCIAL AID *Required financial aid form:* FAFSA. *Financial aid deadline (priority):* 2/15. *Notification date:* Continuous beginning 3/15. Students must reply by 5/1 or within 6 weeks of notification.
CONTACT Mr. Michael E. Yohe, Executive Director of Student Financial Services, Southeastern University, 1000 Longfellow Boulevard, Lakeland, FL 33801-6099, 863-667-5000 or toll-free 800-500-8760. *Fax:* 863-667-5200. *E-mail:* meyohe@seu.edu. *Website:* http://www.seu.edu/.

SOUTHEAST MISSOURI STATE UNIVERSITY
Cape Girardeau, MO

Tuition & fees (MO res): $7185	Average undergraduate aid package: $9234

ABOUT THE INSTITUTION State-supported, coed. *Awards:* certificates, associate, bachelor's, and master's degrees. 63 undergraduate majors. *Total enrollment:* 11,502. Undergraduates: 10,458. Freshmen: 1,803. Both federal and institutional methodology are used as a basis for awarding need-based institutional aid.
UNDERGRADUATE EXPENSES for 2017–2018 *Application fee:* $30. *Tuition, state resident:* full-time $6183; part-time $206.10 per credit hour. *Tuition, nonresident:* full-time $11,718; part-time $390.60 per credit hour. *Required fees:* full-time $1002; $33.40 per credit hour. Full-time tuition and fees vary according to course load and location. Part-time tuition and fees vary according to course load and location. *College room and board:* $8715. Room and board charges vary according to board plan and housing facility.
FRESHMAN FINANCIAL AID (Fall 2016) 1,562 applied for aid; of those 73% were deemed to have need. 99% of freshmen with need received aid; of those 17% had need fully met. *Average percent of need met:* 62% (excluding resources awarded to replace EFC). *Average financial aid package:* $9718 (excluding resources awarded to replace EFC). 26% of all full-time freshmen had no need and received non-need-based gift aid.
UNDERGRADUATE FINANCIAL AID (Fall 2016) 6,069 applied for aid; of those 78% were deemed to have need. 98% of undergraduates with need received aid; of those 15% had need fully met. *Average percent of need met:* 59% (excluding resources awarded to replace EFC). *Average financial aid package:* $9234 (excluding resources awarded to replace EFC). 19% of all full-time undergraduates had no need and received non-need-based gift aid.
GIFT AID (NEED-BASED) *Total amount:* $27,638,417 (49% federal, 18% state, 30% institutional, 3% external sources). *Receiving aid:* Freshmen: 62% (1,078); all full-time undergraduates: 53% (4,105). *Average award:* Freshmen: $7040; Undergraduates: $6269. *Scholarships, grants, and awards:* Federal Pell, FSEOG, state, private, college/university gift aid from institutional funds.
GIFT AID (NON-NEED-BASED) *Total amount:* $10,455,458 (4% federal, 21% state, 70% institutional, 5% external sources). *Receiving aid:* Freshmen: 8% (146). Undergraduates: 5% (389). *Average award:* Freshmen: $4649. Undergraduates: $4188. *Scholarships, grants, and awards by category: Academic interests/ achievement:* 3,420 awards ($10,242,459 total): agriculture, biological sciences, business, communication, computer science, education, engineering/technologies, English, foreign languages, general academic interests/achievements, health fields, home economics, humanities, international studies, mathematics, military science, physical sciences, premedicine, religion/biblical studies, social sciences. *Creative arts/performance:* 339 awards ($338,650 total): dance, music, performing arts, theater/drama. *Special achievements/activities:* 1,841 awards ($4,667,835 total): cheerleading/drum major, general special achievements/activities, leadership, memberships. *Special characteristics:* 1,173 awards ($3,706,875 total): children of faculty/staff, first-generation college students, general special characteristics, international students, members of minority groups, out-of-state students, previous college experience, veterans. *Tuition waivers:* Full or partial for employees or children of employees, senior citizens. **ROTC:** Air Force.
LOANS *Student loans:* $32,936,219 (70% need-based, 30% non-need-based). 64% of past graduating class borrowed through all loan programs. *Average indebtedness*

per student: $27,991. *Average need-based loan:* Freshmen: $3463. Undergraduates: $4167. *Parent loans:* $6,668,884 (32% need-based, 68% non-need-based).
Programs: Federal Direct (Subsidized and Unsubsidized Stafford, PLUS), Perkins.
WORK-STUDY *Federal work-study:* 216 jobs averaging $1671. *State or other work-study/employment:* Total amount: $3,738,900 (100% non-need-based). 1,695 part-time jobs averaging $2084.
ATHLETIC AWARDS Total amount: $3,382,622 (48% need-based, 52% non-need-based).
APPLYING FOR FINANCIAL AID *Required financial aid form:* FAFSA. *Financial aid deadline (priority):* 2/1. *Notification date:* Continuous beginning 12/1. Students must reply within 3 weeks of notification.
CONTACT Ms. Karen Walker, Director of Financial Aid, Southeast Missouri State University, One University Plaza, Cape Girardeau, MO 63701, 573-651-2253. *Fax:* 573-986-6431. *E-mail:* sfs@semo.edu. *Website:* http://www.semo.edu/.

SOUTHERN ADVENTIST UNIVERSITY
Collegedale, TN

Tuition & fees: $21,950	Average undergraduate aid package: $16,298

ABOUT THE INSTITUTION Independent Seventh-day Adventist, coed. *Awards:* certificates, associate, bachelor's, master's, and doctoral degrees. 82 undergraduate majors. *Total enrollment:* 3,035. Undergraduates: 2,564. Freshmen: 567. Federal methodology is used as a basis for awarding need-based institutional aid.
UNDERGRADUATE EXPENSES for 2018–2019 *Application fee:* $25. *Comprehensive fee:* $28,890 includes full-time tuition ($21,100), mandatory fees ($850), and room and board ($6940). *College room only:* $4400. Full-time tuition and fees vary according to course load. Room and board charges vary according to board plan. *Part-time tuition:* $890 per credit hour. *Part-time fees:* $850 per term. Part-time tuition and fees vary according to course load.
FRESHMAN FINANCIAL AID (Fall 2017, est.) 473 applied for aid; of those 80% were deemed to have need. 100% of freshmen with need received aid; of those 2% had need fully met. *Average percent of need met:* 69% (excluding resources awarded to replace EFC). *Average financial aid package:* $16,593 (excluding resources awarded to replace EFC). 30% of all full-time freshmen had no need and received non-need-based gift aid.
UNDERGRADUATE FINANCIAL AID (Fall 2017, est.) 1,704 applied for aid; of those 86% were deemed to have need. 100% of undergraduates with need received aid; of those 2% had need fully met. *Average percent of need met:* 68% (excluding resources awarded to replace EFC). *Average financial aid package:* $16,298 (excluding resources awarded to replace EFC). 27% of all full-time undergraduates had no need and received non-need-based gift aid.
GIFT AID (NEED-BASED) *Total amount:* $19,556,532 (22% federal, 6% state, 54% institutional, 18% external sources). *Receiving aid:* Freshmen: 65% (365); all full-time undergraduates: 64% (1,380). *Average award:* Freshmen: $11,033; Undergraduates: $10,702. *Scholarships, grants, and awards:* Federal Pell, FSEOG, state, private, college/university gift aid from institutional funds.
GIFT AID (NON-NEED-BASED) *Total amount:* $6,414,408 (3% state, 67% institutional, 30% external sources). *Receiving aid:* Freshmen: 1% (6). Undergraduates: 1% (22). *Average award:* Freshmen: $8593. Undergraduates: $7645. *Scholarships, grants, and awards by category: Academic interests/achievement:* biological sciences, business, communication, computer science, education, English, foreign languages, general academic interests/achievements, home economics, humanities, mathematics, physical sciences, premedicine, religion/biblical studies, social sciences. *Creative arts/performance:* art/fine arts, journalism/publications, music, theater/drama. *Special achievements/activities:* community service, general special achievements/activities, leadership, religious involvement. *Special characteristics:* children and siblings of alumni, ethnic background, general special characteristics, international students, local/state students, members of minority groups, out-of-state students, religious affiliation, veterans. *Tuition waivers:* Full or partial for senior citizens.
LOANS *Student loans:* $11,232,347 (88% need-based, 12% non-need-based). 70% of past graduating class borrowed through all loan programs. *Average indebtedness per student:* $33,445. *Average need-based loan:* Freshmen: $4011. Undergraduates: $4660. *Parent loans:* $2,745,559 (86% need-based, 14% non-need-based).
Programs: Federal Direct (Subsidized and Unsubsidized Stafford, PLUS), Federal Nursing, college/university.

WORK-STUDY *Federal work-study:* Total amount: $2,622,866; 801 jobs averaging $2500. *State or other work-study/employment:* Part-time jobs available.
APPLYING FOR FINANCIAL AID *Required financial aid form:* FAFSA. *Financial aid deadline (priority):* 11/30. *Notification date:* Continuous beginning 11/1. Students must reply within 2 weeks of notification.
CONTACT Mr. Fred McClanahan, Prospective Students Financial Adviser, Southern Adventist University, PO Box 370, Collegedale, TN 37315-0370, 423-236-2844 or toll-free 800-768-8437. *Fax:* 423-236-1844. *E-mail:* prospectivefinance@southern.edu. *Website:* http://www.southern.edu/.

SOUTHERN ARKANSAS UNIVERSITY–MAGNOLIA
Magnolia, AR

Tuition & fees (AR res): $8346	Average undergraduate aid package: $12,305

ABOUT THE INSTITUTION State-supported, coed. *Awards:* certificates, associate, bachelor's, and master's degrees. 40 undergraduate majors. *Total enrollment:* 4,643. Undergraduates: 3,475. Freshmen: 870. Federal methodology is used as a basis for awarding need-based institutional aid.
UNDERGRADUATE EXPENSES for 2017–2018 *Tuition, state resident:* full-time $6840; part-time $228 per credit hour. *Tuition, nonresident:* full-time $10,650; part-time $355 per credit hour. *Required fees:* full-time $1506. Full-time tuition and fees vary according to course load. Part-time tuition and fees vary according to course load. *College room and board:* $6028; *Room only:* $2988. Room and board charges vary according to board plan and housing facility.
FRESHMAN FINANCIAL AID (Fall 2016) 814 applied for aid; of those 87% were deemed to have need. 100% of freshmen with need received aid; of those 42% had need fully met. *Average percent of need met:* 60% (excluding resources awarded to replace EFC). *Average financial aid package:* $12,154 (excluding resources awarded to replace EFC). 15% of all full-time freshmen had no need and received non-need-based gift aid.
UNDERGRADUATE FINANCIAL AID (Fall 2016) 2,547 applied for aid; of those 88% were deemed to have need. 99% of undergraduates with need received aid; of those 40% had need fully met. *Average percent of need met:* 56% (excluding resources awarded to replace EFC). *Average financial aid package:* $12,305 (excluding resources awarded to replace EFC). 16% of all full-time undergraduates had no need and received non-need-based gift aid.
GIFT AID (NEED-BASED) *Total amount:* $8,002,016 (97% federal, 3% state). *Receiving aid:* Freshmen: 58% (490); all full-time undergraduates: 57% (1,595). *Average award:* Freshmen: $4809; Undergraduates: $4705. *Scholarships, grants, and awards:* Federal Pell, FSEOG, state, private, college/university gift aid from institutional funds.
GIFT AID (NON-NEED-BASED) *Total amount:* $13,131,077 (25% state, 57% institutional, 18% external sources). *Receiving aid:* Freshmen: 69% (584). Undergraduates: 56% (1,567). *Average award:* Freshmen: $5548. Undergraduates: $5286. *Scholarships, grants, and awards by category:* Academic interests/achievement: 1,247 awards ($6,681,978 total): agriculture, biological sciences, business, computer science, education, English, foreign languages, general academic interests/achievements, health fields, library science, mathematics, physical sciences, social sciences. Creative arts/performance: 198 awards ($634,296 total): art/fine arts, dance, music, theater/drama. Special achievements/activities: 68 awards ($239,259 total): cheerleading/drum major, leadership, rodeo. Special characteristics: 866 awards ($2,816,357 total): adult students, children and siblings of alumni, children of faculty/staff, out-of-state students. *Tuition waivers:* Full or partial for children of alumni, employees or children of employees, senior citizens.
LOANS *Student loans:* $12,709,708 (45% need-based, 55% non-need-based). 54% of past graduating class borrowed through all loan programs. *Average indebtedness per student:* $22,616. *Average need-based loan:* Freshmen: $3081. Undergraduates: $3796. *Parent loans:* $1,845,123 (100% non-need-based). *Programs:* Federal Direct (Subsidized and Unsubsidized Stafford, PLUS), Perkins.
WORK-STUDY *Federal work-study:* 548 jobs averaging $1716. *State or other work-study/employment:* Total amount: $718,638 (100% non-need-based). 474 part-time jobs averaging $3015.
ATHLETIC AWARDS Total amount: $1,280,789 (100% non-need-based).

APPLYING FOR FINANCIAL AID *Required financial aid forms:* FAFSA, state aid form. *Financial aid deadline (priority):* 5/1. *Notification date:* Continuous beginning 2/1.
CONTACT Ms. Marcela D. McRae-Brunson, Director of Student Aid, Southern Arkansas University–Magnolia, MSC 9344, Magnolia, AR 71753, 870-235-4023 or toll-free 800-332-7286. *Fax:* 870-235-4913. *E-mail:* mdbrunson@saumag.edu. *Website:* http://www.saumag.edu/.

THE SOUTHERN BAPTIST THEOLOGICAL SEMINARY
Louisville, KY

CONTACT Mrs. Erin Joiner, Manager of Financial Aid, The Southern Baptist Theological Seminary, 2825 Lexington Road, Louisville, KY 40280, 502-897-4206. *Fax:* 502-897-4031. *E-mail:* financialaid@sbts.edu. *Website:* http://www.sbts.edu/.

SOUTHERN CALIFORNIA INSTITUTE OF ARCHITECTURE
Los Angeles, CA

Tuition & fees: N/R	Average undergraduate aid package: $18,445

ABOUT THE INSTITUTION Independent, coed. 1 undergraduate major. Federal methodology is used as a basis for awarding need-based institutional aid.
FRESHMAN FINANCIAL AID (Fall 2017, est.) 9 applied for aid; of those 100% were deemed to have need. 100% of freshmen with need received aid; of those 22% had need fully met. *Average percent of need met:* 37% (excluding resources awarded to replace EFC). *Average financial aid package:* $17,318 (excluding resources awarded to replace EFC). 57% of all full-time freshmen had no need and received non-need-based gift aid.
UNDERGRADUATE FINANCIAL AID (Fall 2017, est.) 85 applied for aid; of those 98% were deemed to have need. 100% of undergraduates with need received aid; of those 2% had need fully met. *Average percent of need met:* 30% (excluding resources awarded to replace EFC). *Average financial aid package:* $18,445 (excluding resources awarded to replace EFC). 31% of all full-time undergraduates had no need and received non-need-based gift aid.
GIFT AID (NEED-BASED) *Total amount:* $1,186,703 (23% federal, 14% state, 62% institutional, 1% external sources). *Receiving aid:* Freshmen: 38% (8); all full-time undergraduates: 57% (69). *Average award:* Freshmen: $17,453; Undergraduates: $17,297. *Scholarships, grants, and awards:* Federal Pell, FSEOG, state, private, college/university gift aid from institutional funds.
GIFT AID (NON-NEED-BASED) *Total amount:* $801,403 (100% institutional). *Receiving aid:* Freshmen: 5% (1). Undergraduates: 1% (1). *Average award:* Freshmen: $24,479. Undergraduates: $20,301. *Scholarships, grants, and awards by category:* Academic interests/achievement: architecture.
LOANS *Student loans:* $1,301,563 (99% need-based, 1% non-need-based). 87% of past graduating class borrowed through all loan programs. *Average indebtedness per student:* $39,287. *Average need-based loan:* Freshmen: $2000. Undergraduates: $3930. *Parent loans:* $1,130,578 (81% need-based, 19% non-need-based). *Programs:* Federal Direct (Subsidized and Unsubsidized Stafford, PLUS), alternative loans.
WORK-STUDY *Federal work-study:* Total amount: $46,597; jobs available.
APPLYING FOR FINANCIAL AID *Required financial aid forms:* FAFSA, institution's own form. *Financial aid deadline (priority):* 3/2. *Notification date:* 4/1. Students must reply by 10/1 or within 4 weeks of notification.
CONTACT Marisela De La Torre, Financial Aid Manager, Southern California Institute of Architecture, 960 East 3rd Street, Los Angeles, CA 90013, 213-613-2200 Ext. 376. *Fax:* 213-613-2260. *E-mail:* financialaid@sciarc.edu. *Website:* http://www.sciarc.edu/.

SOUTHERN CALIFORNIA INSTITUTE OF TECHNOLOGY

Anaheim, CA

CONTACT Financial Aid Office, Southern California Institute of Technology, 525 North Muller Street, Anaheim, CA 92801, 714-520-5552. *Website:* http://www.scitech.edu/.

SOUTHERN CALIFORNIA SEMINARY

El Cajon, CA

CONTACT Financial Aid Office, Southern California Seminary, 2075 East Madison Avenue, El Cajon, CA 92019, 619-201-8999 or toll-free 888-389-7244 (out-of-state). *Website:* http://www.socalsem.edu/.

SOUTHERN CONNECTICUT STATE UNIVERSITY

New Haven, CT

ABOUT THE INSTITUTION State-supported, coed. *Awards:* certificates, bachelor's, master's, and doctoral degrees. 43 undergraduate majors. *Total enrollment:* 10,320. Undergraduates: 7,963. Freshmen: 1,404.

GIFT AID (NEED-BASED) *Scholarships, grants, and awards:* Federal Pell, FSEOG, state, private, college/university gift aid from institutional funds.

GIFT AID (NON-NEED-BASED) *Scholarships, grants, and awards by category: Special characteristics:* children of faculty/staff, veterans.

LOANS *Programs:* Federal Direct (Subsidized and Unsubsidized Stafford, PLUS), Perkins.

WORK-STUDY *Federal work-study:* 96 jobs averaging $4196. *State or other work-study/employment:* Total amount: $92,000 (100% non-need-based). Part-time jobs available.

APPLYING FOR FINANCIAL AID *Required financial aid form:* FAFSA.

CONTACT Mrs. Gloria Lee, Director of Financial Aid, Southern Connecticut State University, Wintergreen Building, New Haven, CT 06515-1355, 203-392-5445. *Fax:* 203-392-5229. *E-mail:* leeg1@southernct.edu. *Website:* http://www.southernct.edu/.

SOUTHERN ILLINOIS UNIVERSITY CARBONDALE

Carbondale, IL

Tuition & fees (IL res): $13,936	Average undergraduate aid package: $15,046

ABOUT THE INSTITUTION State-supported, coed. *Awards:* certificates, associate, bachelor's, master's, and doctoral degrees. 81 undergraduate majors. *Total enrollment:* 14,554. Undergraduates: 10,987. Freshmen: 1,319. Federal methodology is used as a basis for awarding need-based institutional aid.

UNDERGRADUATE EXPENSES for 2017–2018 *Application fee:* $40. *Tuition, state resident:* full-time $9450; part-time $315 per credit hour. *Tuition, nonresident:* full-time $23,625; part-time $787.50 per credit hour. *Required fees:* full-time $4486; $1001.33 per credit hour. Full-time tuition and fees vary according to course load, location, program, reciprocity agreements, and student level. Part-time tuition and fees vary according to course load, location, program, reciprocity agreements, and student level. *College room and board:* $10,622. Room and board charges vary according to board plan and housing facility. *Payment plan:* Guaranteed tuition.

FRESHMAN FINANCIAL AID (Fall 2016) 1,278 applied for aid; of those 85% were deemed to have need. 99% of freshmen with need received aid; of those 13% had need fully met. *Average percent of need met:* 63% (excluding resources awarded to replace EFC). *Average financial aid package:* $17,101 (excluding resources awarded to replace EFC). 8% of all full-time freshmen had no need and received non-need-based gift aid.

UNDERGRADUATE FINANCIAL AID (Fall 2016) 7,562 applied for aid; of those 88% were deemed to have need. 99% of undergraduates with need received aid; of those 10% had need fully met. *Average percent of need met:* 61% (excluding resources awarded to replace EFC). *Average financial aid package:* $15,046 (excluding resources awarded to replace EFC). 4% of all full-time undergraduates had no need and received non-need-based gift aid.

GIFT AID (NEED-BASED) *Total amount:* $40,667,947 (46% federal, 31% state, 20% institutional, 3% external sources). *Receiving aid:* Freshmen: 57% (740); all full-time undergraduates: 47% (4,410). *Average award:* Freshmen: $8629; Undergraduates: $7904. *Scholarships, grants, and awards:* Federal Pell, FSEOG, state, private, college/university gift aid from institutional funds.

GIFT AID (NON-NEED-BASED) *Total amount:* $8,679,452 (9% federal, 50% institutional, 41% external sources). *Receiving aid:* Freshmen: 37% (476). Undergraduates: 24% (2,269). *Average award:* Freshmen: $6968. Undergraduates: $6693. *Scholarships, grants, and awards by category: Academic interests/achievement:* agriculture, architecture, area/ethnic studies, biological sciences, business, communication, computer science, education, engineering/technologies, English, foreign languages, general academic interests/achievements, health fields, home economics, humanities, international studies, mathematics, military science, physical sciences, premedicine, social sciences. *Creative arts/performance:* applied art and design, art/fine arts, cinema/film/broadcasting, creative writing, dance, debating, general creative arts/performance, journalism/publications, music, performing arts, theater/drama. *Special achievements/activities:* cheerleading/drum major, community service, general special achievements/activities, leadership. *Special characteristics:* children and siblings of alumni, children of educators, children of faculty/staff, children of public servants, children with a deceased or disabled parent, first-generation college students, general special characteristics, handicapped students, international students, local/state students, members of minority groups, public servants, spouses of deceased or disabled public servants, veterans, veterans' children. *Tuition waivers:* Full or partial for children of alumni, employees or children of employees, senior citizens. *ROTC:* Army, Air Force.

LOANS *Student loans:* $52,823,296 (77% need-based, 23% non-need-based). 66% of past graduating class borrowed through all loan programs. *Average indebtedness per student:* $29,637. *Average need-based loan:* Freshmen: $3384. Undergraduates: $4693. *Parent loans:* $7,717,961 (34% need-based, 66% non-need-based). *Programs:* Federal Direct (Subsidized and Unsubsidized Stafford, PLUS), Perkins.

WORK-STUDY *Federal work-study:* 1,382 jobs averaging $1291.

ATHLETIC AWARDS Total amount: $2,415,136 (35% need-based, 65% non-need-based).

APPLYING FOR FINANCIAL AID *Required financial aid form:* FAFSA. *Financial aid deadline (priority):* 4/1. *Notification date:* Continuous beginning 3/15.

CONTACT Terri R. Harfst, Director of Financial Aid, Southern Illinois University Carbondale, Student Services Building, 1263 Lincoln Drive, 2nd Floor, Carbondale, IL 62901-4702, 618-453-3102. *Fax:* 618-453-4606. *E-mail:* fao@siu.edu. *Website:* http://www.siu.edu/.

SOUTHERN ILLINOIS UNIVERSITY EDWARDSVILLE

Edwardsville, IL

ABOUT THE INSTITUTION State-supported, coed. *Awards:* certificates, bachelor's, master's, and doctoral degrees. 47 undergraduate majors. *Total enrollment:* 13,796. Undergraduates: 11,402. Freshmen: 1,797.

GIFT AID (NEED-BASED) *Scholarships, grants, and awards:* Federal Pell, FSEOG, state, private, college/university gift aid from institutional funds, Federal Nursing.

GIFT AID (NON-NEED-BASED) *Scholarships, grants, and awards by category: Academic interests/achievement:* business, education, general academic interests/achievements, home economics. *Creative arts/performance:* art/fine arts, dance, music, theater/drama. *Special characteristics:* children of faculty/staff.

LOANS *Programs:* Federal Direct (Subsidized and Unsubsidized Stafford, PLUS), Perkins, Federal Nursing, college/university, alternative loans.

APPLYING FOR FINANCIAL AID *Required financial aid form:* FAFSA.

CONTACT Sally Mullen, Director of Financial Aid, Southern Illinois University Edwardsville, Campus Box 1060, Edwardsville, IL 62026-1060, 618-650-3834 or toll-free 800-447-SIUE. *Fax:* 618-650-3885. *E-mail:* smullen@siue.edu.
Website: http://www.siue.edu/.

SOUTHERN METHODIST UNIVERSITY
Dallas, TX

Tuition & fees: $54,493	Average undergraduate aid package: $44,049

ABOUT THE INSTITUTION Independent United Methodist Church, coed. *Awards:* certificates, bachelor's, master's, and doctoral degrees. 70 undergraduate majors. *Total enrollment:* 11,789. Undergraduates: 6,452. Freshmen: 1,423. Both federal and institutional methodology are used as a basis for awarding need-based institutional aid.

UNDERGRADUATE EXPENSES for 2018–2019 *Application fee:* $60. *Comprehensive fee:* $71,338 includes full-time tuition ($48,365), mandatory fees ($6128), and room and board ($16,845). Room and board charges vary according to board plan and housing facility. *Part-time tuition:* $2020 per credit hour. Part-time tuition and fees vary according to course load. *Payment plan:* Tuition prepayment.

FRESHMAN FINANCIAL AID (Fall 2017, est.) 729 applied for aid; of those 67% were deemed to have need. 100% of freshmen with need received aid; of those 49% had need fully met. *Average percent of need met:* 87% (excluding resources awarded to replace EFC). *Average financial aid package:* $43,715 (excluding resources awarded to replace EFC). 41% of all full-time freshmen had no need and received non-need-based gift aid.

UNDERGRADUATE FINANCIAL AID (Fall 2017, est.) 2,442 applied for aid; of those 81% were deemed to have need. 99% of undergraduates with need received aid; of those 37% had need fully met. *Average percent of need met:* 87% (excluding resources awarded to replace EFC). *Average financial aid package:* $44,049 (excluding resources awarded to replace EFC). 37% of all full-time undergraduates had no need and received non-need-based gift aid.

GIFT AID (NEED-BASED) *Total amount:* $66,418,642 (6% federal, 4% state, 88% institutional, 2% external sources). *Receiving aid:* Freshmen: 21% (300); all full-time undergraduates: 23% (1,440). *Average award:* Freshmen: $19,090; Undergraduates: $22,487. *Scholarships, grants, and awards:* Federal Pell, FSEOG, state, private, college/university gift aid from institutional funds.

GIFT AID (NON-NEED-BASED) *Total amount:* $55,821,055 (96% institutional, 4% external sources). *Receiving aid:* Freshmen: 26% (374). Undergraduates: 22% (1,366). *Average award:* Freshmen: $27,407. Undergraduates: $25,304. *Tuition waivers:* Full or partial for employees or children of employees. *ROTC:* Army, Air Force cooperative.

LOANS *Student loans:* $21,082,013 (53% need-based, 47% non-need-based). 36% of past graduating class borrowed through all loan programs. *Average indebtedness per student:* $32,468. *Average need-based loan:* Freshmen: $3373. Undergraduates: $4343. *Parent loans:* $15,480,766 (19% need-based, 81% non-need-based). *Programs:* Federal Direct (Subsidized and Unsubsidized Stafford, PLUS), Perkins, state, college/university.

WORK-STUDY *Federal work-study:* Total amount: $4,678,537; jobs available. *State or other work-study/employment:* Total amount: $214,500 (25% need-based, 75% non-need-based). Part-time jobs available.

ATHLETIC AWARDS Total amount: $15,575,487 (35% need-based, 65% non-need-based).

APPLYING FOR FINANCIAL AID *Required financial aid forms:* FAFSA, CSS Financial Aid PROFILE, noncustodial (divorced/separated) parent's statement. *Financial aid deadline (priority):* 11/1. *Notification date:* Continuous beginning 1/20. Students must reply by 5/1.

CONTACT Marc Peterson, Director of Financial Aid, Southern Methodist University, PO Box 750181, Dallas, TX 75275, 214-768-3417 or toll-free 800-323-0672. *Fax:* 214-768-3878. *E-mail:* enrol_serv@smu.edu.
Website: http://www.smu.edu/.

SOUTHERN NAZARENE UNIVERSITY
Bethany, OK

CONTACT Diana Lee, Director of Financial Assistance, Southern Nazarene University, 6729 Northwest 39th Expressway, Bethany, OK 73008, 405-491-6310 or toll-free 800-648-9899. *Fax:* 405-717-6271. *E-mail:* dlee@snu.edu.
Website: http://www.snu.edu/.

SOUTHERN NEW HAMPSHIRE UNIVERSITY
Manchester, NH

Tuition & fees: $31,136	Average undergraduate aid package: $22,185

ABOUT THE INSTITUTION Independent, coed. *Awards:* certificates, associate, bachelor's, master's, and doctoral degrees. 47 undergraduate majors. *Total enrollment:* 4,092. Undergraduates: 3,020. Freshmen: 768. Federal methodology is used as a basis for awarding need-based institutional aid.

UNDERGRADUATE EXPENSES for 2017–2018 *Application fee:* $40. *Comprehensive fee:* $43,414 includes full-time tuition ($30,756), mandatory fees ($380), and room and board ($12,278). *College room only:* $8799. Full-time tuition and fees vary according to course load. Room and board charges vary according to board plan and housing facility. *Part-time tuition:* $1282 per credit hour.

FRESHMAN FINANCIAL AID (Fall 2016) 704 applied for aid; of those 88% were deemed to have need. 100% of freshmen with need received aid; of those 15% had need fully met. *Average percent of need met:* 62% (excluding resources awarded to replace EFC). *Average financial aid package:* $22,182 (excluding resources awarded to replace EFC). 17% of all full-time freshmen had no need and received non-need-based gift aid.

UNDERGRADUATE FINANCIAL AID (Fall 2016) 2,322 applied for aid; of those 91% were deemed to have need. 100% of undergraduates with need received aid; of those 15% had need fully met. *Average percent of need met:* 63% (excluding resources awarded to replace EFC). *Average financial aid package:* $22,185 (excluding resources awarded to replace EFC). 20% of all full-time undergraduates had no need and received non-need-based gift aid.

GIFT AID (NEED-BASED) *Total amount:* $38,520,808 (9% federal, 1% state, 89% institutional, 1% external sources). *Receiving aid:* Freshmen: 49% (373); all full-time undergraduates: 43% (1,257). *Average award:* Freshmen: $5603; Undergraduates: $6130. *Scholarships, grants, and awards:* Federal Pell, FSEOG, state, private, college/university gift aid from institutional funds.

GIFT AID (NON-NEED-BASED) *Total amount:* $2,839,088 (99% institutional, 1% external sources). *Receiving aid:* Freshmen: 81% (618). Undergraduates: 69% (2,026). *Average award:* Freshmen: $12,128. Undergraduates: $12,451. *Scholarships, grants, and awards by category:* Academic interests/achievement: business, computer science, education, general academic interests/achievements, social sciences. Creative arts/performance: music. Special achievements/activities: community service, general special achievements/activities, hobbies/interests, leadership, memberships. Special characteristics: children and siblings of alumni, children of educators, handicapped students, international students, local/state students, previous college experience, siblings of current students, twins, veterans. *Tuition waivers:* Full or partial for employees or children of employees, senior citizens. *ROTC:* Army cooperative, Air Force cooperative.

LOANS *Student loans:* $25,117,045 (93% need-based, 7% non-need-based). 70% of past graduating class borrowed through all loan programs. *Average indebtedness per student:* $40,327. *Average need-based loan:* Freshmen: $3202. Undergraduates: $4138. *Parent loans:* $9,130,113 (96% need-based, 4% non-need-based). *Programs:* Federal Direct (Subsidized and Unsubsidized Stafford, PLUS).

WORK-STUDY *Federal work-study:* jobs available.

ATHLETIC AWARDS Total amount: $2,936,161 (93% need-based, 7% non-need-based).

APPLYING FOR FINANCIAL AID *Required financial aid form:* FAFSA. *Financial aid deadline:* 6/30 (priority: 3/15). *Notification date:* Continuous beginning 3/15.

CONTACT Student Financial Services, Southern New Hampshire University, 2500 North River Road, Manchester, NH 03106, 603-645-9645 or toll-free 888-327-7648. *Fax:* 603-645-9639. *E-mail:* sfscampus@snhu.edu. *Website:* http://www.snhu.edu/.

SOUTHERN OREGON UNIVERSITY
Ashland, OR

Tuition & fees (OR res): $9286	Average undergraduate aid package: $10,995

ABOUT THE INSTITUTION State-supported, coed. *Awards:* certificates, bachelor's, and master's degrees. 39 undergraduate majors. *Total enrollment:* 5,916. Undergraduates: 5,314. Freshmen: 675. Federal methodology is used as a basis for awarding need-based institutional aid.

UNDERGRADUATE EXPENSES for 2017–2018 *Application fee:* $60. *Tuition, state resident:* full-time $7426; part-time $165 per credit hour. *Tuition, nonresident:* full-time $22,770; part-time $506 per credit hour. *Required fees:* full-time $1860; $76 per credit hour. Full-time tuition and fees vary according to course load, program, and reciprocity agreements. Part-time tuition and fees vary according to course load, program, and reciprocity agreements. *College room and board:* $12,831; *Room only:* $7191. Room and board charges vary according to board plan and housing facility.

FRESHMAN FINANCIAL AID (Fall 2017, est.) 662 applied for aid; of those 71% were deemed to have need. 95% of freshmen with need received aid; of those 12% had need fully met. *Average percent of need met:* 88% (excluding resources awarded to replace EFC). *Average financial aid package:* $8651 (excluding resources awarded to replace EFC).

UNDERGRADUATE FINANCIAL AID (Fall 2017, est.) 2,712 applied for aid; of those 80% were deemed to have need. 96% of undergraduates with need received aid; of those 12% had need fully met. *Average percent of need met:* 88% (excluding resources awarded to replace EFC). *Average financial aid package:* $10,995 (excluding resources awarded to replace EFC).

GIFT AID (NEED-BASED) *Total amount:* $11,759,714 (70% federal, 17% state, 13% institutional). *Receiving aid:* Freshmen: 41% (300); all full-time undergraduates: 47% (1,584). *Average award:* Freshmen: $6401; Undergraduates: $6661. *Scholarships, grants, and awards:* Federal Pell, FSEOG, state, private, college/university gift aid from institutional funds.

GIFT AID (NON-NEED-BASED) *Total amount:* $578,235 (2% federal, 26% state, 72% institutional). *Receiving aid:* Freshmen: 10% (70). Undergraduates: 9% (312). *Scholarships, grants, and awards by category: Academic interests/achievement:* biological sciences, business, education, English, foreign languages, general academic interests/achievements, health fields, mathematics, physical sciences, social sciences. *Creative arts/performance:* art/fine arts, creative writing, journalism/publications, music, theater/drama. *Special achievements/activities:* community service, general special achievements/activities, hobbies/interests, leadership, memberships. *Special characteristics:* adult students, international students, members of minority groups, out-of-state students, previous college experience, veterans, veterans' children. *Tuition waivers:* Full or partial for employees or children of employees, senior citizens. *ROTC:* Army.

LOANS *Student loans:* $14,956,870 (94% need-based, 6% non-need-based). 72% of past graduating class borrowed through all loan programs. *Average indebtedness per student:* $23,603. *Average need-based loan:* Freshmen: $5867. Undergraduates: $7488. *Parent loans:* $7,170,338 (25% need-based, 75% non-need-based). *Programs:* Federal Direct (Subsidized and Unsubsidized Stafford, PLUS), Perkins.

WORK-STUDY *Federal work-study:* Total amount: $355,655; jobs available.

ATHLETIC AWARDS Total amount: $386,485 (58% need-based, 42% non-need-based).

APPLYING FOR FINANCIAL AID *Financial aid deadline (priority):* 3/1. *Notification date:* Continuous beginning 12/1.

CONTACT Enrollment Services Center, Southern Oregon University, 1250 Siskiyou Boulevard, Ashland, OR 97520, 541-552-6600 or toll-free 855-470-3377 (out-of-state). *Fax:* 541-552-6614. *E-mail:* esc@sou.edu. *Website:* http://www.sou.edu/.

SOUTHERN TECHNICAL COLLEGE
Fort Myers, FL

CONTACT Financial Aid Office, Southern Technical College, 1685 Medical Lane, Fort Myers, FL 33907, 239-939-4766 or toll-free 877-347-5492. *Website:* http://www.southerntech.edu/locations/ft-myers/.

SOUTHERN UNIVERSITY AND AGRICULTURAL AND MECHANICAL COLLEGE
Baton Rouge, LA

CONTACT Mr. Phillip Rodgers Sr., Director of Financial Aid, Southern University and Agricultural and Mechanical College, PO Box 9961, Baton Rouge, LA 70813, 225-771-2790. *Fax:* 225-771-5898. *E-mail:* phillip_rodgers@cxs.subr.edu. *Website:* http://www.subr.edu/.

SOUTHERN UNIVERSITY AT NEW ORLEANS
New Orleans, LA

CONTACT La'Charlotte C. Garrett, Director of Financial Aid, Southern University at New Orleans, 6400 Press Drive, New Orleans, LA 70126, 504-286-5435. *Fax:* 504-286-5213. *E-mail:* lgarrett@suno.edu. *Website:* http://www.suno.edu/.

SOUTHERN UTAH UNIVERSITY
Cedar City, UT

Tuition & fees (UT res): $6676	Average undergraduate aid package: $9187

ABOUT THE INSTITUTION State-supported, coed. *Awards:* certificates, diplomas, associate, bachelor's, and master's degrees. 74 undergraduate majors. *Total enrollment:* 9,468. Undergraduates: 8,550. Freshmen: 1,899. Federal methodology is used as a basis for awarding need-based institutional aid.

UNDERGRADUATE EXPENSES for 2017–2018 *Application fee:* $50. *Tuition, state resident:* full-time $5918; part-time $278 per credit. *Tuition, nonresident:* full-time $19,530; part-time $919 per credit. *Required fees:* full-time $758; $379 per term. Full-time tuition and fees vary according to program. Part-time tuition and fees vary according to course load and program. *College room and board:* $7067; *Room only:* $3167. Room and board charges vary according to board plan and housing facility.

FRESHMAN FINANCIAL AID (Fall 2016) 1,176 applied for aid; of those 79% were deemed to have need. 99% of freshmen with need received aid; of those 20% had need fully met. *Average percent of need met:* 62% (excluding resources awarded to replace EFC). *Average financial aid package:* $8984 (excluding resources awarded to replace EFC). 31% of all full-time freshmen had no need and received non-need-based gift aid.

UNDERGRADUATE FINANCIAL AID (Fall 2016) 4,132 applied for aid; of those 87% were deemed to have need. 99% of undergraduates with need received aid; of those 11% had need fully met. *Average percent of need met:* 59% (excluding resources awarded to replace EFC). *Average financial aid package:* $9187 (excluding resources awarded to replace EFC). 25% of all full-time undergraduates had no need and received non-need-based gift aid.

GIFT AID (NEED-BASED) *Total amount:* $12,542,645 (99% federal, 1% state). *Receiving aid:* Freshmen: 33% (488); all full-time undergraduates: 44% (2,517). *Average award:* Freshmen: $4192; Undergraduates: $4397. *Scholarships, grants, and awards:* Federal Pell, FSEOG, state, private, college/university gift aid from institutional funds.

GIFT AID (NON-NEED-BASED) *Total amount:* $23,186,032 (4% state, 92% institutional, 4% external sources). *Receiving aid:* Freshmen: 29% (424). Undergrad-

uates: 22% (1,276). *Average award:* Freshmen: $6060. Undergraduates: $6517. *Scholarships, grants, and awards by category:* Academic interests/achievement: general academic interests/achievements. *Creative arts/performance:* art/fine arts, music, theater/drama. *Special achievements/activities:* general special achievements/activities, leadership. *Special characteristics:* children and siblings of alumni, local/state students, members of minority groups. *Tuition waivers:* Full or partial for children of alumni, employees or children of employees, senior citizens. ROTC: Army.
LOANS *Student loans:* $17,990,344 (44% need-based, 56% non-need-based). 52% of past graduating class borrowed through all loan programs. *Average indebtedness per student:* $16,824. *Average need-based loan:* Freshmen: $2893. Undergraduates: $3659. *Parent loans:* $557,420 (100% non-need-based). *Programs:* Federal Direct (Subsidized and Unsubsidized Stafford, PLUS), Perkins, college/university.
WORK-STUDY *Federal work-study:* jobs available. *State or other work-study/employment:* Total amount: $70,357 (100% need-based). Part-time jobs available.
ATHLETIC AWARDS Total amount: $299,723 (100% non-need-based).
APPLYING FOR FINANCIAL AID *Required financial aid forms:* FAFSA, institution's own form. *Financial aid deadline:* Continuous. *Notification date:* Continuous beginning 3/14.
CONTACT Jayson Matlock, Counselor, Southern Utah University, 351 West University Boulevard, Cedar City, UT 84720-2498, 435-586-7735. *Fax:* 435-586-7736. *E-mail:* finaid@suu.edu.
Website: http://www.suu.edu/.

SOUTHERN VERMONT COLLEGE
Bennington, VT

| Tuition & fees: $25,511 | Average undergraduate aid package: $16,000 |

ABOUT THE INSTITUTION Independent, coed. *Awards:* certificates, associate, and bachelor's degrees. 15 undergraduate majors. *Total enrollment:* 361. Undergraduates: 361. Freshmen: 84. Federal methodology is used as a basis for awarding need-based institutional aid.
UNDERGRADUATE EXPENSES for 2018–2019 *Application fee:* $30. *One-time required fee:* $100. *Comprehensive fee:* $36,511 includes full-time tuition ($25,236), mandatory fees ($275), and room and board ($11,000). Room and board charges vary according to board plan and housing facility. *Part-time tuition:* $1052 per credit hour. Part-time tuition and fees vary according to course load.
FRESHMAN FINANCIAL AID (Fall 2017, est.) 76 applied for aid; of those 100% were deemed to have need. 100% of freshmen with need received aid. *Average percent of need met:* 46% (excluding resources awarded to replace EFC). *Average financial aid package:* $17,500 (excluding resources awarded to replace EFC). 10% of all full-time freshmen had no need and received non-need-based gift aid.
UNDERGRADUATE FINANCIAL AID (Fall 2017, est.) 307 applied for aid; of those 100% were deemed to have need. 100% of undergraduates with need received aid. *Average percent of need met:* 42% (excluding resources awarded to replace EFC). *Average financial aid package:* $16,000 (excluding resources awarded to replace EFC). 9% of all full-time undergraduates had no need and received non-need-based gift aid.
GIFT AID (NEED-BASED) *Total amount:* $4,667,435 (19% federal, 3% state, 75% institutional, 3% external sources). *Receiving aid:* Freshmen: 90% (76); all full-time undergraduates: 84% (307). *Average award:* Freshmen: $17,500; Undergraduates: $16,000. *Scholarships, grants, and awards:* Federal Pell, FSEOG, state, private, college/university gift aid from institutional funds.
GIFT AID (NON-NEED-BASED) *Total amount:* $376,047 (92% institutional, 8% external sources). *Receiving aid:* Freshmen: 90% (76). Undergraduates: 84% (307). *Average award:* Freshmen: $14,000. Undergraduates: $12,000. *Scholarships, grants, and awards by category:* Academic interests/achievement: $347,199 total: general academic interests/achievements. *Special achievements/activities:* community service, leadership. *Special characteristics:* children of faculty/staff. *Tuition waivers:* Full or partial for employees or children of employees, senior citizens.
LOANS *Student loans:* $2,665,676 (99% need-based, 1% non-need-based). 82% of past graduating class borrowed through all loan programs. *Average indebtedness per student:* $35,728. *Average need-based loan:* Freshmen: $3500. Undergraduates:

$4500. *Parent loans:* $728,173 (95% need-based, 5% non-need-based). *Programs:* Federal Direct (Subsidized and Unsubsidized Stafford, PLUS).
WORK-STUDY *Federal work-study:* Total amount: $102,944; 99 jobs averaging $1500. *State or other work-study/employment:* Total amount: $10,000 (100% non-need-based). 6 part-time jobs averaging $1500.
APPLYING FOR FINANCIAL AID *Required financial aid form:* FAFSA. *Financial aid deadline (priority):* 1/1. *Notification date:* Continuous beginning 12/15. Students must reply by 5/1.
CONTACT Phylle Lentz, Associate Director of Financial Aid, Southern Vermont College, 982 Mansion Drive, Bennington, VT 05201, 802-447-6331. *Fax:* 802-447-6329. *E-mail:* plentz@svc.edu.
Website: http://www.svc.edu/.

SOUTHERN VIRGINIA UNIVERSITY
Buena Vista, VA

CONTACT Darin Hassell, Financial Aid Specialist, Southern Virginia University, One University Hill Drive, Buena Vista, VA 24416, 540-261-4351 or toll-free 800-229-8420. *Fax:* 540-261-8559. *E-mail:* finaid@svu.edu.
Website: http://www.svu.edu/.

SOUTHERN WESLEYAN UNIVERSITY
Central, SC

CONTACT Mrs. Laura Hedden, Financial Aid Associate, Southern Wesleyan University, 907 Wesleyan Drive, Central, SC 29630-1020, 800-282-8798 Ext. 5517 or toll-free 800-CU-AT-SWU. *Fax:* 864-644-5970. *E-mail:* finaid@swu.edu.
Website: http://www.swu.edu/.

SOUTH FLORIDA BIBLE COLLEGE AND THEOLOGICAL SEMINARY
Deerfield Beach, FL

CONTACT Financial Aid Office, South Florida Bible College and Theological Seminary, 2200 SW 10th Street, Deerfield Beach, FL 33442, 954-428-8980.
Website: http://www.sfbc.edu/.

SOUTH UNIVERSITY
Montgomery, AL

CONTACT Financial Aid Office, South University, 5355 Vaughn Road, Montgomery, AL 36116-1120, 334-395-8800 or toll-free 866-629-2962.
Website: http://www.southuniversity.edu/montgomery/.

SOUTH UNIVERSITY
Royal Palm Beach, FL

Financial Aid Office, South University, University Centre, 9801 Belvedere Road, Royal Palm Beach, FL 33411, 561-273-6500 or toll-free 866-629-2902.

SOUTH UNIVERSITY
Tampa, FL

CONTACT Financial Aid Office, South University, 4401 North Himes Avenue, Suite 175, Tampa, FL 33614, 813-393-3800 or toll-free 800-846-1472.
Website: http://www.southuniversity.edu/tampa/.

SOUTH UNIVERSITY
Savannah, GA

CONTACT Financial Aid Office, South University, 709 Mall Boulevard, Savannah, GA 31406, 912-201-8000 or toll-free 866-629-2901. *Website:* http://www.southuniversity.edu/savannah/.

SOUTH UNIVERSITY
Novi, MI

CONTACT Financial Aid Office, South University, 41555 Twelve Mile Road, Novi, MI 48377, 248-675-0200 or toll-free 877-693-2085. *Website:* http://www.southuniversity.edu/novi.aspx.

SOUTH UNIVERSITY
High Point, NC

CONTACT Financial Aid Office, South University, 3975 Premier Drive, High Point, NC 27265, 336-812-7200 or toll-free 855-268-2187. *Website:* http://www.southuniversity.edu/high-point.aspx.

SOUTH UNIVERSITY
Cleveland, OH

CONTACT Financial Aid Office, South University, 4743 Richmond Road, Cleveland, OH 44128, 216-755-5000 or toll-free 855-398-9280. *Website:* http://www.southuniversity.edu/cleveland.aspx.

SOUTH UNIVERSITY
Columbia, SC

CONTACT Financial Aid Office, South University, 9 Science Court, Columbia, SC 29203, 803-799-9082 or toll-free 866-629-3031. *Website:* http://www.southuniversity.edu/columbia/.

SOUTH UNIVERSITY
Round Rock, TX

CONTACT Financial Aid Office, South University, 1220 West Louis Henna Boulevard, Round Rock, TX 78681, 512-516-8800 or toll-free 877-659-5706. *Website:* http://www.southuniversity.edu/austin.aspx.

SOUTH UNIVERSITY
Glen Allen, VA

CONTACT Financial Aid Office, South University, 2151 Old Brick Road, Glen Allen, VA 23060, 804-727-6800 or toll-free 888-422-5076. *Website:* http://www.southuniversity.edu/richmond.

SOUTH UNIVERSITY
Virginia Beach, VA

CONTACT Financial Aid Office, South University, 301 Bendix Road, Suite 100, Virginia Beach, VA 23452, 757-493-6900 or toll-free 877-206-1845. *Website:* http://www.southuniversity.edu/virginia-beach.

SOUTHWEST BAPTIST UNIVERSITY
Bolivar, MO

Tuition & fees: $24,010	Average undergraduate aid package: $19,846

ABOUT THE INSTITUTION Independent Southern Baptist, coed. *Awards:* certificates, associate, bachelor's, master's, and doctoral degrees. 56 undergraduate majors. *Total enrollment:* 3,592. Undergraduates: 2,822. Freshmen: 474. Both federal and institutional methodology are used as a basis for awarding need-based institutional aid.

UNDERGRADUATE EXPENSES for 2018–2019 *Application fee:* $30. *Comprehensive fee:* $31,730 includes full-time tuition ($23,100), mandatory fees ($910), and room and board ($7720). *College room only:* $3400. Full-time tuition and fees vary according to course load, degree level, and location. Room and board charges vary according to board plan and housing facility. *Part-time tuition:* $870 per credit hour. *Part-time fees:* $185 per term. Part-time tuition and fees vary according to course load and location.

FRESHMAN FINANCIAL AID (Fall 2017, est.) 433 applied for aid; of those 90% were deemed to have need. 100% of freshmen with need received aid; of those 25% had need fully met. *Average percent of need met:* 81% (excluding resources awarded to replace EFC). *Average financial aid package:* $23,107 (excluding resources awarded to replace EFC). 11% of all full-time freshmen had no need and received non-need-based gift aid.

UNDERGRADUATE FINANCIAL AID (Fall 2017, est.) 1,608 applied for aid; of those 92% were deemed to have need. 100% of undergraduates with need received aid; of those 19% had need fully met. *Average percent of need met:* 71% (excluding resources awarded to replace EFC). *Average financial aid package:* $19,846 (excluding resources awarded to replace EFC). 13% of all full-time undergraduates had no need and received non-need-based gift aid.

GIFT AID (NEED-BASED) *Total amount:* $8,975,981 (53% federal, 14% state, 33% institutional). *Receiving aid:* Freshmen: 74% (337); all full-time undergraduates: 69% (1,244). *Average award:* Freshmen: $6299; Undergraduates: $6299. *Scholarships, grants, and awards:* Federal Pell, FSEOG, state, private, college/university gift aid from institutional funds, Federal Nursing.

GIFT AID (NON-NEED-BASED) *Total amount:* $13,886,564 (1% state, 94% institutional, 5% external sources). *Receiving aid:* Freshmen: 86% (391). Undergraduates: 82% (1,475). *Average award:* Freshmen: $10,662. Undergraduates: $9933. *Scholarships, grants, and awards by category: Academic interests/achievement:* 1,236 awards ($10,041,910 total): general academic interests/achievements. *Creative arts/performance:* 149 awards ($320,730 total): art/fine arts, debating, music, theater/drama. *Special achievements/activities:* 110 awards ($211,000 total): religious involvement. *Special characteristics:* 387 awards ($467,750 total): general special characteristics, handicapped students, international students, local/state students, relatives of clergy, religious affiliation, siblings of current students. *Tuition waivers:* Full or partial for employees or children of employees. *ROTC:* Army cooperative.

LOANS *Student loans:* $9,579,137 (45% need-based, 55% non-need-based). 71% of past graduating class borrowed through all loan programs. *Average indebtedness per student:* $29,429. *Average need-based loan:* Freshmen: $3253. Undergraduates: $3391. *Parent loans:* $1,042,381 (100% non-need-based). *Programs:* Federal Direct (Subsidized and Unsubsidized Stafford, PLUS), Federal Nursing, state, alternative loans.

WORK-STUDY *Federal work-study:* Total amount: $642,850; 342 jobs averaging $1880.

ATHLETIC AWARDS Total amount: $3,143,945 (100% non-need-based).

APPLYING FOR FINANCIAL AID *Required financial aid form:* FAFSA. *Financial aid deadline (priority):* 2/1. *Notification date:* Continuous beginning 12/15. Students must reply within 2 weeks of notification.

CONTACT Mr. Brad Gamble, Director of Financial Aid, Southwest Baptist University, 1600 University Avenue, Bolivar, MO 65613-2597, 417-328-1823 or toll-free 800-526-5859. *Fax:* 417-328-1514. *E-mail:* bgamble@sbuniv.edu. *Website:* http://www.sbuniv.edu/.

SOUTHWESTERN ADVENTIST UNIVERSITY
Keene, TX

CONTACT Student Financial Services, Southwestern Adventist University, PO Box 567, Keene, TX 76059, 817-645-3921 Ext. 262 or toll-free 800-433-2240. *Fax:* 817-556-4744.
Website: http://www.swau.edu/.

SOUTHWESTERN ASSEMBLIES OF GOD UNIVERSITY
Waxahachie, TX

CONTACT Financial Aid Office, Southwestern Assemblies of God University, 1200 Sycamore Street, Waxahachie, TX 75165-2397, 972-825-4730 or toll-free 888-937-7248. *Fax:* 972-937-4001. *E-mail:* finaid@sagu.edu.
Website: http://www.sagu.edu/.

SOUTHWESTERN CHRISTIAN COLLEGE
Terrell, TX

Tuition & fees: N/R	Average undergraduate aid package: $12,194

ABOUT THE INSTITUTION Independent Church of Christ, coed. 2 undergraduate majors. Federal methodology is used as a basis for awarding need-based institutional aid.

FRESHMAN FINANCIAL AID (Fall 2016) 56 applied for aid; of those 100% were deemed to have need. 100% of freshmen with need received aid; of those 62% had need fully met. *Average percent of need met:* 48% (excluding resources awarded to replace EFC). *Average financial aid package:* $12,194 (excluding resources awarded to replace EFC). 14% of all full-time freshmen had no need and received non-need-based gift aid.

UNDERGRADUATE FINANCIAL AID (Fall 2016) 79 applied for aid; of those 82% were deemed to have need. 100% of undergraduates with need received aid; of those 65% had need fully met. *Average percent of need met:* 48% (excluding resources awarded to replace EFC). *Average financial aid package:* $12,194 (excluding resources awarded to replace EFC). 6% of all full-time undergraduates had no need and received non-need-based gift aid.

GIFT AID (NEED-BASED) *Total amount:* $755,892 (70% federal, 14% state, 14% institutional, 2% external sources). *Receiving aid:* Freshmen: 86% (56); all full-time undergraduates: 45% (65). *Average award:* Freshmen: $4238; Undergraduates: $4238. *Scholarships, grants, and awards:* Federal Pell, FSEOG, state, college/university gift aid from institutional funds.

GIFT AID (NON-NEED-BASED) *Total amount:* $184,427. *Receiving aid:* Freshmen: 86% (56). Undergraduates: 45% (65). *Average award:* Freshmen: $11,974. Undergraduates: $11,974. *Scholarships, grants, and awards by category:* Academic interests/achievement: 2 awards ($24,388 total): general academic interests/achievements. Creative arts/performance: music. Special characteristics: 9 awards ($39,412 total): children of faculty/staff, local/state students.

LOANS *Student loans:* $342,722 (60% need-based, 40% non-need-based). *Average need-based loan:* Freshmen: $1858. Undergraduates: $1858. *Parent loans:* $44,858 (100% need-based). *Programs:* Federal Direct (Subsidized and Unsubsidized Stafford, PLUS).

WORK-STUDY *Federal work-study:* 56 jobs averaging $1400. *State or other work-study/employment:* Total amount: $919 (100% need-based). 1 part-time job averaging $919.

ATHLETIC AWARDS Total amount: $223,355 (100% need-based).

APPLYING FOR FINANCIAL AID *Required financial aid form:* FAFSA. *Financial aid deadline (priority):* 6/1. *Notification date:* Continuous.

CONTACT Ms. Kim Smith, Financial Aid Counselor, Southwestern Christian College, PO Box 10, 200 Bowser Circle, Terrell, TX 75160, 972-524-3341 Ext. 124. *Fax:* 972-563-7133. *E-mail:* ksmit@swcc.edu.
Website: http://www.swcc.edu/.

SOUTHWESTERN CHRISTIAN UNIVERSITY
Bethany, OK

CONTACT Mrs. Billie Stewart, Financial Aid Director, Southwestern Christian University, PO Box 340, Bethany, OK 73008, 405-789-7661 Ext. 3456. *Fax:* 405-495-0078. *E-mail:* billie.stewart@swcu.edu.
Website: http://www.swcu.edu/.

SOUTHWESTERN COLLEGE
Winfield, KS

Tuition & fees: $30,150	Average undergraduate aid package: $23,291

ABOUT THE INSTITUTION Independent United Methodist, coed. *Awards:* certificates, bachelor's, master's, and doctoral degrees. 56 undergraduate majors. *Total enrollment:* 1,306. Undergraduates: 1,147. Freshmen: 189. Federal methodology is used as a basis for awarding need-based institutional aid.

UNDERGRADUATE EXPENSES for 2018–2019 *Application fee:* $25. *Comprehensive fee:* $37,910 includes full-time tuition ($30,000), mandatory fees ($150), and room and board ($7760). *College room only:* $3620. Full-time tuition and fees vary according to course load, degree level, location, and program. Room and board charges vary according to board plan and housing facility. *Part-time tuition:* $1250 per credit hour. Part-time tuition and fees vary according to course load, degree level, location, and program.

FRESHMAN FINANCIAL AID (Fall 2016) 169 applied for aid; of those 90% were deemed to have need. 100% of freshmen with need received aid; of those 15% had need fully met. *Average percent of need met:* 79% (excluding resources awarded to replace EFC). *Average financial aid package:* $23,788 (excluding resources awarded to replace EFC). 14% of all full-time freshmen had no need and received non-need-based gift aid.

UNDERGRADUATE FINANCIAL AID (Fall 2016) 433 applied for aid; of those 92% were deemed to have need. 100% of undergraduates with need received aid; of those 16% had need fully met. *Average percent of need met:* 77% (excluding resources awarded to replace EFC). *Average financial aid package:* $23,291 (excluding resources awarded to replace EFC). 16% of all full-time undergraduates had no need and received non-need-based gift aid.

GIFT AID (NEED-BASED) *Total amount:* $6,372,429 (29% federal, 5% state, 61% institutional, 5% external sources). *Receiving aid:* Freshmen: 84% (152); all full-time undergraduates: 78% (395). *Average award:* Freshmen: $18,524; Undergraduates: $17,112. *Scholarships, grants, and awards:* Federal Pell, FSEOG, state, private, college/university gift aid from institutional funds.

GIFT AID (NON-NEED-BASED) *Total amount:* $1,475,328 (58% institutional, 42% external sources). *Receiving aid:* Freshmen: 9% (17). Undergraduates: 7% (36). *Average award:* Freshmen: $15,052. Undergraduates: $9839. *Scholarships, grants, and awards by category:* Academic interests/achievement: 554 awards ($2,444,419 total): biological sciences, business, communication, computer science, education, English, foreign languages, general academic interests/achievements, home economics, humanities, mathematics, physical sciences, premedicine, religion/biblical studies, social sciences. Creative arts/performance: 51 awards ($212,249 total): cinema/film/broadcasting, creative writing, dance, journalism/publications, music, performing arts, theater/drama. Special achievements/activities: 65 awards ($272,639 total): cheerleading/drum major, community service, general special achievements/activities, leadership, memberships, religious involvement. Special characteristics: 196 awards ($331,272 total): adult students, children of faculty/staff, international students, local/state students, members of minority groups, religious affiliation, veterans. *Tuition waivers:* Full or partial for employees or children of employees, senior citizens.

LOANS *Student loans:* $5,233,010 (87% need-based, 13% non need based), 86% of past graduating class borrowed through all loan programs. *Average indebtedness per student:* $39,231. *Average need-based loan:* Freshmen: $5063. Undergraduates: $5825. *Parent loans:* $1,703,009 (40% need-based, 60% non-need-based). *Programs:* Federal Direct (Subsidized and Unsubsidized Stafford, PLUS), Perkins.

WORK-STUDY *Federal work-study:* 145 jobs averaging $1583. *State or other work-study/employment:* Total amount: $105,639 (30% need-based, 70% non-need-based). 74 part-time jobs averaging $1435.

ATHLETIC AWARDS Total amount: $1,574,669 (81% need-based, 19% non-need-based).

APPLYING FOR FINANCIAL AID *Required financial aid form:* FAFSA. *Financial aid deadline (priority):* 4/1. *Notification date:* Continuous beginning 2/1. Students must reply within 4 weeks of notification.

CONTACT Mrs. Brenda D. Hicks, Director of Financial Aid, Southwestern College, 100 College Street, Winfield, KS 67156-2499, 620-229-6215 or toll-free 800-846-1543. *Fax:* 620-229-6245. *E-mail:* finaid@sckans.edu. *Website:* http://www.sckans.edu/.

SOUTHWESTERN OKLAHOMA STATE UNIVERSITY
Weatherford, OK

Tuition & fees (OK res): $7005	Average undergraduate aid package: $5333

ABOUT THE INSTITUTION State-supported, coed. *Awards:* certificates, associate, bachelor's, master's, and doctoral degrees. 43 undergraduate majors. *Total enrollment:* 5,320. Undergraduates: 4,510. Freshmen: 990. Both federal and institutional methodology are used as a basis for awarding need-based institutional aid.

UNDERGRADUATE EXPENSES for 2017–2018 *Application fee:* $15. *One-time required fee:* $100. *Tuition, state resident:* full-time $5610; part-time $187 per credit hour. *Tuition, nonresident:* full-time $12,510; part-time $417 per credit hour. *Required fees:* full-time $1395; $46.50 per credit hour. Full-time tuition and fees vary according to degree level, location, and program. Part-time tuition and fees vary according to degree level, location, and program. *College room and board:* $5500; *Room only:* $2300. Room and board charges vary according to board plan and housing facility.

FRESHMAN FINANCIAL AID (Fall 2017, est.) 926 applied for aid; of those 79% were deemed to have need. 100% of freshmen with need received aid; of those 16% had need fully met. *Average percent of need met:* 62% (excluding resources awarded to replace EFC). *Average financial aid package:* $5769 (excluding resources awarded to replace EFC). 16% of all full-time freshmen had no need and received non-need-based gift aid.

UNDERGRADUATE FINANCIAL AID (Fall 2017, est.) 3,173 applied for aid; of those 78% were deemed to have need. 100% of undergraduates with need received aid; of those 17% had need fully met. *Average percent of need met:* 62% (excluding resources awarded to replace EFC). *Average financial aid package:* $5333 (excluding resources awarded to replace EFC). 11% of all full-time undergraduates had no need and received non-need-based gift aid.

GIFT AID (NEED-BASED) *Total amount:* $12,156,952 (61% federal, 39% state). *Receiving aid:* Freshmen: 73% (723); all full-time undergraduates: 66% (2,437). *Average award:* Freshmen: $3828; Undergraduates: $3557. *Scholarships, grants, and awards:* Federal Pell, FSEOG, state, private, college/university gift aid from institutional funds.

GIFT AID (NON-NEED-BASED) *Total amount:* $4,102,440 (22% federal, 11% state, 33% institutional, 34% external sources). *Receiving aid:* Freshmen: 41% (410). Undergraduates: 24% (880). *Average award:* Freshmen: $1661. Undergraduates: $1540. *Scholarships, grants, and awards by category:* Academic interests/achievement: biological sciences, business, communication, computer science, education, engineering/technologies, English, foreign languages, general academic interests/achievements, mathematics, physical sciences, social sciences. *Creative arts/performance:* applied art and design, art/fine arts, music, theater/drama. *Special achievements/activities:* cheerleading/drum major, leadership, rodeo. *Special characteristics:* children and siblings of alumni, children of faculty/staff, local/state students, out-of-state students. *Tuition waivers:* Full or partial for children of alumni, employees or children of employees, senior citizens.

LOANS *Student loans:* $17,764,876 (40% need-based, 60% non-need-based). 52% of past graduating class borrowed through all loan programs. *Average indebtedness*

per student: $18,520. *Average need-based loan:* Freshmen: $1594. Undergraduates: $1990. *Parent loans:* $10,833,222 (100% non-need-based). *Programs:* Federal Direct (Subsidized and Unsubsidized Stafford, PLUS).

WORK-STUDY *Federal work-study:* Total amount: $1,995,702; jobs available.

ATHLETIC AWARDS Total amount: $1,731,990 (100% non-need-based).

APPLYING FOR FINANCIAL AID *Required financial aid forms:* FAFSA, institution's own form. *Financial aid deadline:* 3/1. *Notification date:* Continuous beginning 3/15.

CONTACT Mr. Jerome Wichert, Director of Student Financial Services, Southwestern Oklahoma State University, 100 Campus Drive, Weatherford, OK 73096, 580-774-3786. *Fax:* 580-774-7066. *E-mail:* jerome.wichert@swosu.edu. *Website:* http://www.swosu.edu/.

SOUTHWESTERN UNIVERSITY
Georgetown, TX

Tuition & fees: $42,000	Average undergraduate aid package: $36,217

ABOUT THE INSTITUTION Independent Methodist, coed. *Awards:* bachelor's degrees. 36 undergraduate majors. *Total enrollment:* 1,387. Undergraduates: 1,387. Freshmen: 362. Federal methodology is used as a basis for awarding need-based institutional aid.

UNDERGRADUATE EXPENSES for 2018–2019 *Comprehensive fee:* $54,000 includes full-time tuition ($42,000) and room and board ($12,000). *College room only:* $6480. Room and board charges vary according to board plan and housing facility. *Part-time tuition:* $1750 per credit hour. Part-time tuition and fees vary according to course load.

FRESHMAN FINANCIAL AID (Fall 2017, est.) 324 applied for aid; of those 78% were deemed to have need. 100% of freshmen with need received aid; of those 23% had need fully met. *Average percent of need met:* 88% (excluding resources awarded to replace EFC). *Average financial aid package:* $35,991 (excluding resources awarded to replace EFC). 30% of all full-time freshmen had no need and received non-need-based gift aid.

UNDERGRADUATE FINANCIAL AID (Fall 2017, est.) 1,016 applied for aid; of those 87% were deemed to have need. 100% of undergraduates with need received aid; of those 23% had need fully met. *Average percent of need met:* 86% (excluding resources awarded to replace EFC). *Average financial aid package:* $36,217 (excluding resources awarded to replace EFC). 34% of all full-time undergraduates had no need and received non-need-based gift aid.

GIFT AID (NEED-BASED) *Total amount:* $26,442,853 (8% federal, 6% state, 81% institutional, 5% external sources). *Receiving aid:* Freshmen: 69% (248); all full-time undergraduates: 64% (870). *Average award:* Freshmen: $31,462; Undergraduates: $30,483. *Scholarships, grants, and awards:* Federal Pell, FSEOG, state, private, college/university gift aid from institutional funds.

GIFT AID (NON-NEED-BASED) *Total amount:* $10,275,852 (96% institutional, 4% external sources). *Receiving aid:* Freshmen: 68% (247). Undergraduates: 63% (858). *Average award:* Freshmen: $22,395. Undergraduates: $21,445. *Scholarships, grants, and awards by category:* Academic interests/achievement: 1,605 awards ($27,296,721 total): business, general academic interests/achievements, humanities, international studies, mathematics, premedicine, social sciences. *Creative arts/performance:* 112 awards ($1,775,940 total): art/fine arts, music, theater/drama. *Special achievements/activities:* 4 awards ($4000 total): leadership. *Special characteristics:* 125 awards ($1,328,735 total): children of faculty/staff, ethnic background, general special characteristics, members of minority groups, relatives of clergy, religious affiliation, veterans, veterans' children. *Tuition waivers:* Full or partial for employees or children of employees. *ROTC:* Air Force cooperative.

LOANS *Student loans:* $6,938,252 (91% need-based, 9% non-need-based). 58% of past graduating class borrowed through all loan programs. *Average indebtedness per student:* $34,788. *Average need-based loan:* Freshmen: $3906. Undergraduates: $5005. *Parent loans:* $4,717,155 (88% need-based, 12% non-need-based). *Programs:* Federal Direct (Subsidized and Unsubsidized Stafford, PLUS), state, college/university.

WORK-STUDY *Federal work-study:* Total amount: $483,964; 227 jobs averaging $2097. *State or other work-study/employment:* Total amount: $1,011,750 (57% need-based, 43% non-need-based). 469 part-time jobs averaging $2475.

APPLYING FOR FINANCIAL AID *Required financial aid form:* FAFSA. *Financial aid deadline (priority):* 3/1. *Notification date:* Continuous beginning 12/1. Students must reply by 5/1 or within 2 weeks of notification.
CONTACT Mr. James P. Gaeta, Associate Dean of Enrollment Services, Southwestern University, PO Box 770, Georgetown, TX 78627-0770, 512-863-1259 or toll-free 800-252-3166. *Fax:* 512-863-1507. *E-mail:* gaetaj@southwestern.edu. *Website:* http://www.southwestern.edu/.

SOUTHWEST MINNESOTA STATE UNIVERSITY
Marshall, MN

CONTACT Mr. David Vikander, Director of Financial Aid, Southwest Minnesota State University, 1501 State Street, Marshall, MN 56258, 507-537-6281 or toll-free 800-642-0684. *Fax:* 507-537-6275. *E-mail:* vikander@smsu.edu. *Website:* http://www.smsu.edu/.

SOUTHWEST UNIVERSITY
Kenner, LA

CONTACT Financial Aid Office, Southwest University, 2200 Veterans Memorial Boulevard, Kenner, LA 70062, 504-468-2900 or toll-free 800-433-5923. *Website:* http://www.southwest.edu/.

SOUTHWEST UNIVERSITY AT EL PASO
El Paso, TX

CONTACT Financial Aid Office, Southwest University at El Paso, 1414 Geronimo Drive, El Paso, TX 79925, 915-778-4001. *Website:* http://southwestuniversity.edu/.

SOUTHWEST UNIVERSITY OF VISUAL ARTS
Tucson, AZ

CONTACT Financial Aid Office, Southwest University of Visual Arts, 2525 North Country Club Road, Tucson, AZ 85716-2505, 520-325-0123 or toll-free 800-825-8753. *Website:* http://www.suva.edu/.

SPALDING UNIVERSITY
Louisville, KY

CONTACT Director of Student Financial Services, Spalding University, 851 South Fourth Street, Louisville, KY 40203, 502-588-7185 or toll-free 800-896-8941. *Fax:* 502-585-7128. *E-mail:* onestop@spalding.edu. *Website:* http://www.spalding.edu/.

SPELMAN COLLEGE
Atlanta, GA

Tuition & fees: $28,181	Average undergraduate aid package: $17,443

ABOUT THE INSTITUTION Independent, women only. *Awards:* bachelor's degrees. 31 undergraduate majors. *Total enrollment:* 2,137. Undergraduates: 2,137. Freshmen: 548. Federal methodology is used as a basis for awarding need-based institutional aid.
UNDERGRADUATE EXPENSES for 2017–2018 *Application fee:* $35. *One-time required fee:* $250. *Comprehensive fee:* $41,642 includes full-time tuition ($24,382), mandatory fees ($3799), and room and board ($13,461). Full-time tuition and fees vary according to course load. Room and board charges vary according to board plan and housing facility. *Part-time tuition:* $1010 per credit hour. *Part-time fees:* $1010 per credit hour; $1900 per term. Part-time tuition and fees vary according to course load.
FRESHMAN FINANCIAL AID (Fall 2017, est.) 529 applied for aid; of those 89% were deemed to have need. 100% of freshmen with need received aid; of those 46% had need fully met. *Average percent of need met:* 32% (excluding resources awarded to replace EFC). *Average financial aid package:* $15,660 (excluding resources awarded to replace EFC). 10% of all full-time freshmen had no need and received non-need-based gift aid.
UNDERGRADUATE FINANCIAL AID (Fall 2017, est.) 1,884 applied for aid; of those 91% were deemed to have need. 100% of undergraduates with need received aid; of those 49% had need fully met. *Average percent of need met:* 35% (excluding resources awarded to replace EFC). *Average financial aid package:* $17,443 (excluding resources awarded to replace EFC). 8% of all full-time undergraduates had no need and received non-need-based gift aid.
GIFT AID (NEED-BASED) *Total amount:* $23,981,601 (23% federal, 7% state, 57% institutional, 13% external sources). *Receiving aid:* Freshmen: 85% (465); all full-time undergraduates: 72% (1,504). *Average award:* Freshmen: $12,119; Undergraduates: $14,406. *Scholarships, grants, and awards:* Federal Pell, FSEOG, state, private, college/university gift aid from institutional funds, United Negro College Fund.
GIFT AID (NON-NEED-BASED) *Total amount:* $1,592,664 (2% state, 91% institutional, 7% external sources). *Receiving aid:* Freshmen: 1% (8). Undergraduates: 1% (31). *Average award:* Freshmen: $45,405. Undergraduates: $39,108. *Tuition waivers:* Full or partial for employees or children of employees. *ROTC:* Army cooperative, Naval cooperative, Air Force cooperative.
LOANS *Student loans:* $24,585,511 (63% need-based, 37% non-need-based). 80% of past graduating class borrowed through all loan programs. *Average indebtedness per student:* $32,427. *Average need-based loan:* Freshmen: $3682. Undergraduates: $4773. *Parent loans:* $46,385,715 (100% non-need-based). *Programs:* Federal Direct (Subsidized and Unsubsidized Stafford, PLUS), Perkins, state.
WORK-STUDY *Federal work-study:* Total amount: $330,008; 182 jobs averaging $1813.
APPLYING FOR FINANCIAL AID *Required financial aid form:* FAFSA. *Financial aid deadline (priority):* 2/1. *Notification date:* Continuous beginning 12/15.
CONTACT Ms. Lenora Jackson, Director of Financial Aid, Spelman College, 350 Spelman Lane, SW, Atlanta, GA 30314-4399, 404-270-5212 or toll-free 800-982-2411. *Fax:* 404-270-5220. *E-mail:* lenoraj@spelman.edu. *Website:* http://www.spelman.edu/.

SPRING ARBOR UNIVERSITY
Spring Arbor, MI

ABOUT THE INSTITUTION Independent Free Methodist, coed. 62 undergraduate majors.
GIFT AID (NEED-BASED) *Scholarships, grants, and awards:* Federal Pell, FSEOG, private, college/university gift aid from institutional funds.
GIFT AID (NON-NEED-BASED) *Scholarships, grants, and awards by category:* Academic interests/achievement: general academic interests/achievements. Creative arts/performance: art/fine arts. Special achievements/activities: junior miss. Special characteristics: adult students, children of faculty/staff, general special characteristics, international students, members of minority groups, relatives of clergy, religious affiliation.

LOANS *Programs:* Federal Direct (Subsidized and Unsubsidized Stafford, PLUS), Perkins.

WORK-STUDY *Federal work-study:* jobs available.

APPLYING FOR FINANCIAL AID *Required financial aid form:* FAFSA.

CONTACT Herbert Rotich, Director of Financial Aid, Spring Arbor University, 106 East Main Street, Spring Arbor, MI 49283-9799, 517-750-6463 or toll-free 800-968-0011. *Fax:* 517-750-6620. *E-mail:* hrotich@arbor.edu. *Website:* http://www.arbor.edu/.

SPRINGFIELD COLLEGE
Springfield, MA

Tuition & fees: N/R	Average undergraduate aid package: $28,115

ABOUT THE INSTITUTION Independent, coed. 38 undergraduate majors. Federal methodology is used as a basis for awarding need-based institutional aid.

FRESHMAN FINANCIAL AID (Fall 2017, est.) 650 applied for aid; of those 92% were deemed to have need. 100% of freshmen with need received aid; of those 12% had need fully met. *Average percent of need met:* 75% (excluding resources awarded to replace EFC). *Average financial aid package:* $28,265 (excluding resources awarded to replace EFC). 12% of all full-time freshmen had no need and received non-need-based gift aid.

UNDERGRADUATE FINANCIAL AID (Fall 2017, est.) 1,990 applied for aid; of those 92% were deemed to have need. 100% of undergraduates with need received aid; of those 10% had need fully met. *Average percent of need met:* 74% (excluding resources awarded to replace EFC). *Average financial aid package:* $28,115 (excluding resources awarded to replace EFC). 12% of all full-time undergraduates had no need and received non-need-based gift aid.

GIFT AID (NEED-BASED) *Total amount:* $40,543,446 (6% federal, 2% state, 89% institutional, 3% external sources). *Receiving aid:* Freshmen: 91% (597); all full-time undergraduates: 84% (1,828). *Average award:* Freshmen: $23,785; Undergraduates: $22,534. *Scholarships, grants, and awards:* Federal Pell, FSEOG, state, private, college/university gift aid from institutional funds.

GIFT AID (NON-NEED-BASED) *Total amount:* $4,636,092 (92% institutional, 8% external sources). *Receiving aid:* Freshmen: 10% (65). Undergraduates: 6% (141). *Average award:* Freshmen: $16,083. Undergraduates: $13,345. *Scholarships, grants, and awards by category: Academic interests/achievement:* general academic interests/achievements. *Special characteristics:* children and siblings of alumni, children of current students, children of faculty/staff, siblings of current students.

LOANS *Student loans:* $20,726,466 (70% need-based, 30% non-need-based). 87% of past graduating class borrowed through all loan programs. *Average indebtedness per student:* $42,329. *Average need-based loan:* Freshmen: $3812. Undergraduates: $4535. *Parent loans:* $6,849,039 (50% need-based, 50% non-need-based). *Programs:* Federal Direct (Subsidized and Unsubsidized Stafford, PLUS).

WORK-STUDY *Federal work-study:* Total amount: $1,973,745; jobs available. *State or other work-study/employment:* Total amount: $839,564 (83% need-based, 17% non-need-based). Part-time jobs available.

APPLYING FOR FINANCIAL AID *Required financial aid form:* FAFSA. *Financial aid deadline:* Continuous. *Notification date:* Continuous beginning 11/10. Students must reply by 5/1.

CONTACT Ms. Kinser Cancelmo, Assistant Director of Financial Aid, Springfield College, 263 Alden Street, Springfield, MA 01109-3797, 413-748-3108 or toll-free 800-343-1257. *Fax:* 413-748-3462. *E-mail:* financialaid@springfieldcollege.edu. *Website:* http://www.springfield.edu/.

SPRING HILL COLLEGE
Mobile, AL

Tuition & fees: $37,584	Average undergraduate aid package: $33,589

ABOUT THE INSTITUTION Independent Roman Catholic (Jesuit), coed. *Awards:* certificates, bachelor's, and master's degrees. 48 undergraduate majors.

Total enrollment: 1,501. Undergraduates: 1,393. Freshmen: 393. Federal methodology is used as a basis for awarding need-based institutional aid.

UNDERGRADUATE EXPENSES for 2017–2018 *Application fee:* $25. *Comprehensive fee:* $50,654 includes full-time tuition ($35,312), mandatory fees ($2272), and room and board ($13,070). *College room only:* $6900. Full-time tuition and fees vary according to course load. Room and board charges vary according to board plan and housing facility. *Part-time tuition:* $1104 per credit hour. *Part-time fees:* $57 per credit hour. Part-time tuition and fees vary according to course load.

FRESHMAN FINANCIAL AID (Fall 2017, est.) 323 applied for aid; of those 94% were deemed to have need. 100% of freshmen with need received aid; of those 25% had need fully met. *Average percent of need met:* 84% (excluding resources awarded to replace EFC). *Average financial aid package:* $36,147 (excluding resources awarded to replace EFC). 16% of all full-time freshmen had no need and received non-need-based gift aid.

UNDERGRADUATE FINANCIAL AID (Fall 2017, est.) 1,090 applied for aid; of those 87% were deemed to have need. 100% of undergraduates with need received aid; of those 24% had need fully met. *Average percent of need met:* 82% (excluding resources awarded to replace EFC). *Average financial aid package:* $33,589 (excluding resources awarded to replace EFC). 25% of all full-time undergraduates had no need and received non-need-based gift aid.

GIFT AID (NEED-BASED) *Total amount:* $27,175,681 (9% federal, 1% state, 89% institutional, 1% external sources). *Receiving aid:* Freshmen: 65% (255); all full-time undergraduates: 58% (802). *Average award:* Freshmen: $9283; Undergraduates: $8275. *Scholarships, grants, and awards:* Federal Pell, FSEOG, state, private, college/university gift aid from institutional funds, TEACH Grants.

GIFT AID (NON-NEED-BASED) *Total amount:* $9,921,861 (1% state, 99% institutional). *Receiving aid:* Freshmen: 77% (303). Undergraduates: 69% (947). *Average award:* Freshmen: $27,109. Undergraduates: $23,594. *Scholarships, grants, and awards by category: Academic interests/achievement:* general academic interests/achievements. *Special achievements/activities:* community service. *Special characteristics:* children of faculty/staff, siblings of current students. *Tuition waivers:* Full or partial for employees or children of employees. *ROTC:* Army cooperative, Air Force cooperative.

LOANS *Student loans:* $6,553,117 (71% need-based, 29% non-need-based). *Average need-based loan:* Freshmen: $3366. Undergraduates: $4418. *Parent loans:* $3,446,940 (46% need-based, 54% non-need-based). *Programs:* Federal Direct (Subsidized and Unsubsidized Stafford, PLUS), Perkins, alternative loans.

WORK-STUDY *Federal work-study:* Total amount: $299,471; jobs available. *State or other work-study/employment:* Total amount: $59,500 (100% non-need-based). Part-time jobs available.

ATHLETIC AWARDS Total amount: $1,625,411 (39% need-based, 61% non-need-based).

APPLYING FOR FINANCIAL AID *Required financial aid forms:* FAFSA, state aid form. *Financial aid deadline (priority):* 3/1. *Notification date:* Continuous beginning 2/15. Students must reply by 5/1 or within 2 weeks of notification.

CONTACT Mrs. Melinda N. McCall, Director of Financial Aid, Spring Hill College, 4000 Dauphin Street, Mobile, AL 36608, 251-380-2253 or toll-free 800-SHC-6704. *Fax:* 251-460-2176. *E-mail:* mmccall@shc.edu. *Website:* http://www.shc.edu/.

STANBRIDGE UNIVERSITY
Irvine, CA

CONTACT Financial Aid Office, Stanbridge University, 2041 Business Center Drive, Irvine, CA 92612, 949-794-9090. *Website:* http://www.stanbridge.edu/.

STANFORD UNIVERSITY
Stanford, CA

Tuition & fees: $49,617	Average undergraduate aid package: $51,729

ABOUT THE INSTITUTION Independent, coed. *Awards:* certificates, bachelor's, master's, and doctoral degrees. 72 undergraduate majors. *Total*

enrollment: 16,914. Undergraduates: 7,034. Freshmen: 1,738. Both federal and institutional methodology are used as a basis for awarding need-based institutional aid.
UNDERGRADUATE EXPENSES for 2017–2018 *Application fee:* $90. *Comprehensive fee:* $64,729 includes full-time tuition ($48,987), mandatory fees ($630), and room and board ($15,112). Room and board charges vary according to board plan.
FRESHMAN FINANCIAL AID (Fall 2016) 1,012 applied for aid; of those 80% were deemed to have need. 98% of freshmen with need received aid; of those 95% had need fully met. *Average percent of need met:* 100% (excluding resources awarded to replace EFC). *Average financial aid package:* $53,337 (excluding resources awarded to replace EFC). 1% of all full-time freshmen had no need and received non-need-based gift aid.
UNDERGRADUATE FINANCIAL AID (Fall 2016) 3,714 applied for aid; of those 91% were deemed to have need. 99% of undergraduates with need received aid; of those 92% had need fully met. *Average percent of need met:* 100% (excluding resources awarded to replace EFC). *Average financial aid package:* $51,729 (excluding resources awarded to replace EFC). 1% of all full-time undergraduates had no need and received non-need-based gift aid.
GIFT AID (NEED-BASED) *Total amount:* $156,248,759 (4% federal, 2% state, 91% institutional, 3% external sources). *Receiving aid:* Freshmen: 45% (776); all full-time undergraduates: 47% (3,252). *Average award:* Freshmen: $50,234; Undergraduates: $48,039. *Scholarships, grants, and awards:* Federal Pell, FSEOG, state, private, college/university gift aid from institutional funds.
GIFT AID (NON-NEED-BASED) *Total amount:* $7,134,085 (5% federal, 18% institutional, 77% external sources). *Receiving aid:* Freshmen: 1% (23). Undergraduates: 2% (126). *Average award:* Freshmen: $1431. Undergraduates: $10,434. *Tuition waivers:* Full or partial for employees or children of employees. *ROTC:* Army cooperative, Naval cooperative, Air Force cooperative.
LOANS *Student loans:* $6,442,138 (25% need-based, 75% non-need-based). 18% of past graduating class borrowed through all loan programs. *Average indebtedness per student:* $20,205. *Average need-based loan:* Freshmen: $2359. Undergraduates: $3059. *Parent loans:* $4,038,947 (100% non-need-based). *Programs:* Federal Direct (Subsidized and Unsubsidized Stafford, PLUS), Perkins.
WORK-STUDY *Federal work-study:* 549 jobs averaging $2358. *State or other work-study/employment:* Total amount: $4,102,717 (86% need-based, 14% non-need-based). 1,782 part-time jobs averaging $2296.
ATHLETIC AWARDS Total amount: $23,359,875 (13% need-based, 87% non-need-based).
APPLYING FOR FINANCIAL AID *Required financial aid forms:* FAFSA, CSS Financial Aid PROFILE. *Financial aid deadline (priority):* 2/15. *Notification date:* Continuous beginning 4/1. Students must reply by 5/1.
CONTACT Financial Aid Office, Stanford University, Montag Hall, 355 Galvez Street, Stanford, CA 94305-3021, 650-723-3058. *Fax:* 650-725-0540. *E-mail:* financialaid@stanford.edu.
Website: http://www.stanford.edu/.

STATE COLLEGE OF FLORIDA MANATEE-SARASOTA
Bradenton, FL

CONTACT Financial Aid Office, State College of Florida Manatee-Sarasota, 5840 26th Street West, PO Box 1849, Bradenton, FL 34206-7046, 941-752-5000. *Website:* http://www.scf.edu/.

STATE UNIVERSITY OF NEW YORK AT FREDONIA
Fredonia, NY

Tuition & fees (NY res): $8288	Average undergraduate aid package: $11,791

ABOUT THE INSTITUTION State-supported, coed. *Awards:* certificates, bachelor's, and master's degrees. 71 undergraduate majors. *Total enrollment:* 4,631. Undergraduates: 4,392. Freshmen: 1,129. Federal methodology is used as a basis for awarding need-based institutional aid.

UNDERGRADUATE EXPENSES for 2018–2019 *Application fee:* $50. *Tuition, state resident:* full-time $6670; part-time $278 per credit hour. *Tuition, nonresident:* full-time $16,320; part-time $680 per credit hour. *Required fees:* full-time $1618; $67.15 per credit hour. *College room and board:* $12,490; *Room only:* $7500. Room and board charges vary according to board plan and housing facility.
FRESHMAN FINANCIAL AID (Fall 2017, est.) 1,061 applied for aid; of those 84% were deemed to have need. 99% of freshmen with need received aid; of those 23% had need fully met. *Average percent of need met:* 69% (excluding resources awarded to replace EFC). *Average financial aid package:* $13,113 (excluding resources awarded to replace EFC). 14% of all full-time freshmen had no need and received non-need-based gift aid.
UNDERGRADUATE FINANCIAL AID (Fall 2017, est.) 3,765 applied for aid; of those 83% were deemed to have need. 99% of undergraduates with need received aid; of those 19% had need fully met. *Average percent of need met:* 66% (excluding resources awarded to replace EFC). *Average financial aid package:* $11,791 (excluding resources awarded to replace EFC). 9% of all full-time undergraduates had no need and received non-need-based gift aid.
GIFT AID (NEED-BASED) *Total amount:* $23,507,405 (37% federal, 44% state, 17% institutional, 2% external sources). *Receiving aid:* Freshmen: 64% (719); all full-time undergraduates: 57% (2,428). *Average award:* Freshmen: $7425; Undergraduates: $6752. *Scholarships, grants, and awards:* Federal Pell, FSEOG, state, private, college/university gift aid from institutional funds, TEACH Grants.
GIFT AID (NON-NEED-BASED) *Total amount:* $296,965 (100% federal). *Receiving aid:* Freshmen: 44% (497). Undergraduates: 27% (1,149). *Average award:* Freshmen: $3813. Undergraduates: $3352. *Scholarships, grants, and awards by category:* Academic interests/achievement: 343 awards ($471,326 total): biological sciences, business, communication, computer science, education, English, foreign languages, general academic interests/achievements, humanities, international studies, mathematics, physical sciences, social sciences. *Creative arts/performance:* 127 awards ($119,280 total): applied art and design, art/fine arts, dance, music, performing arts, theater/drama. *Special achievements/activities:* 21 awards ($59,725 total): general special achievements/activities, leadership. *Special characteristics:* 146 awards ($430,973 total): children and siblings of alumni, ethnic background, general special characteristics, international students, local/state students, members of minority groups, out-of-state students, parents of current students, previous college experience.
LOANS *Student loans:* $30,593,728 (42% need-based, 58% non-need-based). 86% of past graduating class borrowed through all loan programs. *Average indebtedness per student:* $27,586. *Average need-based loan:* Freshmen: $5855. Undergraduates: $5448. *Parent loans:* $4,330,511 (100% non-need-based). *Programs:* Federal Direct (Subsidized and Unsubsidized Stafford, PLUS), Perkins, alternative loans.
WORK-STUDY *Federal work-study:* Total amount: $325,595; 173 jobs averaging $2025.
APPLYING FOR FINANCIAL AID *Required financial aid forms:* FAFSA, state aid form. *Financial aid deadline:* Continuous. *Notification date:* Continuous beginning 12/1. Students must reply by 5/1.
CONTACT Mark Zaffalon, Financial Aid Counselor, State University of New York at Fredonia, 209 Maytum Hall, Fredonia, NY 14063, 716-673-3253 or toll-free 800-252-1212. *Fax:* 716-673-3785. *E-mail:* mark.zaffalon@fredonia.edu. *Website:* http://www.fredonia.edu/.

STATE UNIVERSITY OF NEW YORK AT NEW PALTZ
New Paltz, NY

Tuition & fees (NY res): $7975	Average undergraduate aid package: $11,568

ABOUT THE INSTITUTION State-supported, coed. *Awards:* certificates, bachelor's, and master's degrees. 67 undergraduate majors. *Total enrollment:* 7,565. Undergraduates: 6,733. Freshmen: 1,105. Federal methodology is used as a basis for awarding need-based institutional aid.
UNDERGRADUATE EXPENSES for 2018–2019 *Application fee:* $50. *Tuition, state resident:* full-time $6670. *Tuition, nonresident:* full-time $16,320. *Required fees:* full-time $1305. *College room and board:* $12,642; *Room only:* $8480. Room and board charges vary according to board plan.

FRESHMAN FINANCIAL AID (Fall 2017, est.) 1,012 applied for aid; of those 72% were deemed to have need. 99% of freshmen with need received aid; of those 7% had need fully met. *Average percent of need met:* 60% (excluding resources awarded to replace EFC). *Average financial aid package:* $12,457 (excluding resources awarded to replace EFC). 1% of all full-time freshmen had no need and received non-need-based gift aid.

UNDERGRADUATE FINANCIAL AID (Fall 2017, est.) 4,918 applied for aid; of those 78% were deemed to have need. 99% of undergraduates with need received aid; of those 8% had need fully met. *Average percent of need met:* 58% (excluding resources awarded to replace EFC). *Average financial aid package:* $11,568 (excluding resources awarded to replace EFC). 1% of all full-time undergraduates had no need and received non-need-based gift aid.

GIFT AID (NEED-BASED) *Total amount:* $21,587,643 (55% federal, 45% state). *Receiving aid:* Freshmen: 40% (433); all full-time undergraduates: 37% (2,277). *Average award:* Freshmen: $5381; Undergraduates: $5106. *Scholarships, grants, and awards:* Federal Pell, FSEOG, state, private, college/university gift aid from institutional funds.

GIFT AID (NON-NEED-BASED) *Total amount:* $1,439,163 (5% federal, 27% state, 24% institutional, 44% external sources). *Receiving aid:* Freshmen: 18% (198). Undergraduates: 11% (704). *Average award:* Freshmen: $7078. Undergraduates: $3653. *Scholarships, grants, and awards by category: Academic interests/achievement:* area/ethnic studies, biological sciences, business, communication, education, engineering/technologies, English, foreign languages, general academic interests/achievements, international studies, mathematics, physical sciences. *Creative arts/performance:* art/fine arts, music, theater/drama. *Special characteristics:* children of faculty/staff, ethnic background, first-generation college students, local/state students, members of minority groups.

LOANS *Student loans:* $27,793,603 (50% need-based, 50% non-need-based). 60% of past graduating class borrowed through all loan programs. *Average indebtedness per student:* $26,385. *Average need-based loan:* Freshmen: $3368. Undergraduates: $4252. *Parent loans:* $22,570,933 (100% non-need-based). *Programs:* Federal Direct (Subsidized and Unsubsidized Stafford, PLUS).

WORK-STUDY *Federal work-study:* Total amount: $1,690,471; jobs available. *State or other work-study/employment:* Total amount: $1,065,980 (100% non-need-based). Part-time jobs available.

APPLYING FOR FINANCIAL AID *Required financial aid forms:* FAFSA, state aid form. *Financial aid deadline (priority):* 3/1. *Notification date:* Continuous beginning 2/15.

CONTACT Mrs. Maureen Lohan-Bremer, Director of Financial Aid, State University of New York at New Paltz, 200 Hawk Drive, New Paltz, NY 12561-2437, 845-257-3250 or toll-free 877-MY-NP-411 (in-state). *Fax:* 845-257-3568. *E-mail:* fao@newpaltz.edu. *Website:* http://www.newpaltz.edu/.

STATE UNIVERSITY OF NEW YORK AT OSWEGO
Oswego, NY

Tuition & fees (NY res): $8191	Average undergraduate aid package: $11,491

ABOUT THE INSTITUTION State-supported, coed. *Awards:* certificates, bachelor's, and master's degrees. 68 undergraduate majors. *Total enrollment:* 8,026. Undergraduates: 7,125. Freshmen: 1,463. Federal methodology is used as a basis for awarding need-based institutional aid.

UNDERGRADUATE EXPENSES for 2017-2018 *Application fee:* $50. *Tuition, state resident:* full-time $6670; part-time $278 per credit hour. *Tuition, nonresident:* full-time $16,320; part-time $680 per credit hour. *Required fees:* full-time $1521; $47.91 per credit hour. Part-time tuition and fees vary according to course load. *College room and board:* $13,740; *Room only:* $8590. Room and board charges vary according to board plan and housing facility.

FRESHMAN FINANCIAL AID (Fall 2017, est.) 1,320 applied for aid; of those 79% were deemed to have need. 99% of freshmen with need received aid; of those 7% had need fully met. *Average percent of need met:* 82% (excluding resources awarded to replace EFC). *Average financial aid package:* $12,201 (excluding resources awarded to replace EFC). 17% of all full-time freshmen had no need and received non-need-based gift aid.

UNDERGRADUATE FINANCIAL AID (Fall 2017, est.) 5,750 applied for aid; of those 82% were deemed to have need. 99% of undergraduates with need received aid; of those 9% had need fully met. *Average percent of need met:* 81% (excluding resources awarded to replace EFC). *Average financial aid package:* $11,491 (excluding resources awarded to replace EFC). 12% of all full-time undergraduates had no need and received non-need-based gift aid.

GIFT AID (NEED-BASED) *Total amount:* $33,203,032 (44% federal, 40% state, 14% institutional, 2% external sources). *Receiving aid:* Freshmen: 68% (994); all full-time undergraduates: 63% (4,109). *Average award:* Freshmen: $8433; Undergraduates: $7880. *Scholarships, grants, and awards:* Federal Pell, FSEOG, state, private, college/university gift aid from institutional funds.

GIFT AID (NON-NEED-BASED) *Total amount:* $2,252,853 (1% federal, 5% state, 82% institutional, 12% external sources). *Receiving aid:* Freshmen: 17% (251). Undergraduates: 12% (760). *Average award:* Freshmen: $2028. Undergraduates: $2413. *Scholarships, grants, and awards by category: Academic interests/achievement:* area/ethnic studies, biological sciences, business, communication, computer science, education, English, foreign languages, general academic interests/achievements, humanities, international studies, mathematics, physical sciences, premedicine, social sciences. *ROTC:* Army cooperative, Air Force cooperative.

LOANS *Student loans:* $44,583,669 (81% need-based, 19% non-need-based). 79% of past graduating class borrowed through all loan programs. *Average indebtedness per student:* $28,429. *Average need-based loan:* Freshmen: $4175. Undergraduates: $4494. *Parent loans:* $15,176,268 (74% need-based, 26% non-need-based). *Programs:* Federal Direct (Subsidized and Unsubsidized Stafford, PLUS), Perkins.

WORK-STUDY *Federal work-study:* Total amount: $849,363; 612 jobs averaging $1332. *State or other work-study/employment:* Total amount: $953,785 (72% need-based, 28% non-need-based). Part-time jobs available.

APPLYING FOR FINANCIAL AID *Required financial aid forms:* FAFSA, state aid form. *Financial aid deadline (priority):* 2/15. *Notification date:* Continuous beginning 1/15. Students must reply by 5/1 or within 3 weeks of notification.

CONTACT Dr. Mark C. Humbert, Director of Financial Aid, State University of New York at Oswego, 206 Culkin Hall, Oswego, NY 13126, 315-312-2248. *Fax:* 315-312-3696. *E-mail:* finaid@oswego.edu. *Website:* http://www.oswego.edu/.

STATE UNIVERSITY OF NEW YORK AT PLATTSBURGH
Plattsburgh, NY

Tuition & fees (NY res): $8164	Average undergraduate aid package: $13,822

ABOUT THE INSTITUTION State-supported, coed. *Awards:* certificates, bachelor's, and master's degrees. 58 undergraduate majors. *Total enrollment:* 5,719. Undergraduates: 5,351. Freshmen: 1,110. Federal methodology is used as a basis for awarding need-based institutional aid.

UNDERGRADUATE EXPENSES for 2018-2019 *Application fee:* $50. *Tuition, state resident:* full-time $6670; part-time $278 per credit hour. *Tuition, nonresident:* full-time $16,320; part-time $680 per credit hour. *Required fees:* full-time $1494; $63.70 per credit hour. Full-time tuition and fees vary according to course load and location. Part-time tuition and fees vary according to course load and location. *College room and board:* $12,988; *Room only:* $8258. Room and board charges vary according to board plan and housing facility.

FRESHMAN FINANCIAL AID (Fall 2016) 893 applied for aid; of those 77% were deemed to have need. 98% of freshmen with need received aid; of those 22% had need fully met. *Average percent of need met:* 83% (excluding resources awarded to replace EFC). *Average financial aid package:* $14,667 (excluding resources awarded to replace EFC). 22% of all full-time freshmen had no need and received non-need-based gift aid.

UNDERGRADUATE FINANCIAL AID (Fall 2016) 3,838 applied for aid; of those 80% were deemed to have need. 98% of undergraduates with need received aid; of those 20% had need fully met. *Average percent of need met:* 76% (excluding resources awarded to replace EFC). *Average financial aid package:* $13,822 (excluding resources awarded to replace EFC). 15% of all full-time undergraduates had no need and received non-need-based gift aid.

GIFT AID (NEED-BASED) *Total amount:* $20,811,089 (42% federal, 33% state, 23% institutional, 2% external sources). *Receiving aid:* Freshmen: 60% (616); all full-

time undergraduates: 54% (2,613). *Average award:* Freshmen: $9101; Undergraduates: $7694. *Scholarships, grants, and awards:* Federal Pell, FSEOG, state, private, college/university gift aid from institutional funds.

GIFT AID (NON-NEED-BASED) *Total amount:* $4,293,676 (2% federal, 4% state, 90% institutional, 4% external sources). *Receiving aid:* Freshmen: 23% (236). Undergraduates: 16% (788). *Average award:* Freshmen: $6264. Undergraduates: $5261. *Scholarships, grants, and awards by category:* Academic interests/achievement: 4,699 awards ($8,353,211 total): area/ethnic studies, biological sciences, business, communication, computer science, education, engineering/technologies, English, general academic interests/achievements, health fields, home economics, humanities, international studies, mathematics, physical sciences, premedicine, social sciences. *Creative arts/performance:* 313 awards ($518,178 total): art/fine arts, journalism/publications, music, theater/drama. *Special achievements/activities:* 12 awards ($16,500 total): community service, general special achievements/activities, leadership. *Special characteristics:* 946 awards ($3,344,354 total): international students, out-of-state students.

LOANS *Student loans:* $25,624,281 (81% need-based, 19% non-need-based). 75% of past graduating class borrowed through all loan programs. *Average indebtedness per student:* $29,865. *Average need-based loan:* Freshmen: $7303. Undergraduates: $8065. *Parent loans:* $5,267,655 (76% need-based, 24% non-need-based). *Programs:* Federal Direct (Subsidized and Unsubsidized Stafford, PLUS), Perkins, Federal Nursing, private loans.

WORK-STUDY *Federal work-study:* 358 jobs averaging $2684. *State or other work-study/employment:* Part-time jobs available.

APPLYING FOR FINANCIAL AID *Required financial aid forms:* FAFSA, state aid form. *Financial aid deadline:* Continuous. *Notification date:* Continuous beginning 12/1. Students must reply by 5/1.

CONTACT Mr. Todd Moravec, Director of Financial Aid, State University of New York at Plattsburgh, 101 Broad Street, Plattsburgh, NY 12901-2681, 518-564-2072 or toll-free 888-673-0012. *Fax:* 518-564-4079. *E-mail:* todd.moravec@plattsburgh.edu. *Website:* http://www.plattsburgh.edu/.

STATE UNIVERSITY OF NEW YORK COLLEGE AT CORTLAND
Cortland, NY

Tuition & fees (NY res): $8300	Average undergraduate aid package: $14,832

ABOUT THE INSTITUTION State-supported, coed. *Awards:* certificates, bachelor's, and master's degrees. 57 undergraduate majors. *Total enrollment:* 6,913. Undergraduates: 6,346. Freshmen: 1,288. Federal methodology is used as a basis for awarding need-based institutional aid.

UNDERGRADUATE EXPENSES for 2017–2018 *Application fee:* $50. *Tuition, state resident:* full-time $6670; part-time $278 per credit hour. *Tuition, nonresident:* full-time $16,320; part-time $680 per credit hour. *Required fees:* full-time $1630. Full-time tuition and fees vary according to course load and degree level. Part-time tuition and fees vary according to course load and degree level. *College room and board:* $12,410; *Room only:* $7900. Room and board charges vary according to board plan and housing facility.

FRESHMAN FINANCIAL AID (Fall 2016) 966 applied for aid; of those 70% were deemed to have need. 96% of freshmen with need received aid; of those 12% had need fully met. *Average percent of need met:* 67% (excluding resources awarded to replace EFC). *Average financial aid package:* $14,939 (excluding resources awarded to replace EFC). 5% of all full-time freshmen had no need and received non-need-based gift aid.

UNDERGRADUATE FINANCIAL AID (Fall 2016) 4,882 applied for aid; of those 76% were deemed to have need. 97% of undergraduates with need received aid; of those 11% had need fully met. *Average percent of need met:* 67% (excluding resources awarded to replace EFC). *Average financial aid package:* $14,832 (excluding resources awarded to replace EFC). 5% of all full-time undergraduates had no need and received non-need-based gift aid.

GIFT AID (NEED-BASED) *Total amount:* $13,602,198 (56% federal, 43% state, 1% institutional). *Receiving aid:* Freshmen: 42% (429); all full-time undergraduates: 45% (2,663). *Average award:* Freshmen: $5215; Undergraduates: $5854. *Scholarships, grants, and awards:* Federal Pell, FSEOG, state, private, college/university gift aid from institutional funds.

GIFT AID (NON-NEED-BASED) *Total amount:* $5,657,786 (19% federal, 44% institutional, 37% external sources). *Receiving aid:* Freshmen: 26% (269). Undergraduates: 17% (1,015). *Average award:* Freshmen: $3357. Undergraduates: $3616. *Scholarships, grants, and awards by category:* Academic interests/achievement: education, general academic interests/achievements, international studies, mathematics, physical sciences. *Creative arts/performance:* art/fine arts, music. *Special achievements/activities:* community service, general special achievements/activities, hobbies/interests, leadership. *Special characteristics:* adult students, local/state students, members of minority groups. *Tuition waivers:* Full or partial for employees or children of employees. *ROTC:* Army cooperative, Air Force cooperative.

LOANS *Student loans:* $35,262,108 (38% need-based, 62% non-need-based). 75% of past graduating class borrowed through all loan programs. *Average indebtedness per student:* $29,111. *Average need-based loan:* Freshmen: $3657. Undergraduates: $3616. *Parent loans:* $9,328,008 (100% non-need-based). *Programs:* Federal Direct (Subsidized and Unsubsidized Stafford, PLUS), Perkins.

WORK-STUDY *Federal work-study:* jobs available. *State or other work-study/employment:* Total amount: $948,402 (100% non-need-based). Part-time jobs available.

APPLYING FOR FINANCIAL AID *Required financial aid forms:* FAFSA, state aid form. *Financial aid deadline (priority):* 3/1. *Notification date:* Continuous beginning 3/15. Students must reply by 5/1 or within 4 weeks of notification.

CONTACT Karen Gallagher, Director of Financial Advisement, State University of New York College at Cortland, PO Box 2000, Cortland, NY 13045, 607-753-4717. *Fax:* 607-753-5990. *E-mail:* finaid@cortland.edu. *Website:* http://www.cortland.edu/.

STATE UNIVERSITY OF NEW YORK COLLEGE AT GENESEO
Geneseo, NY

Tuition & fees (NY res): $8408	Average undergraduate aid package: $9946

ABOUT THE INSTITUTION State-supported, coed. *Awards:* bachelor's and master's degrees. 43 undergraduate majors. *Total enrollment:* 5,591. Undergraduates: 5,495. Freshmen: 1,340. Federal methodology is used as a basis for awarding need-based institutional aid.

UNDERGRADUATE EXPENSES for 2017–2018 *Application fee:* $50. *Tuition, state resident:* full-time $6670; part-time $278 per credit hour. *Tuition, nonresident:* full-time $16,320; part-time $680 per credit hour. *Required fees:* full-time $1738; $72.25 per credit hour. Part-time tuition and fees vary according to course load. *College room and board:* $13,214; *Room only:* $7890. Room and board charges vary according to board plan and housing facility.

FRESHMAN FINANCIAL AID (Fall 2017, est.) 1,203 applied for aid; of those 64% were deemed to have need. 100% of freshmen with need received aid; of those 11% had need fully met. *Average percent of need met:* 34% (excluding resources awarded to replace EFC). *Average financial aid package:* $9567 (excluding resources awarded to replace EFC). 9% of all full-time freshmen had no need and received non-need-based gift aid.

UNDERGRADUATE FINANCIAL AID (Fall 2017, est.) 4,037 applied for aid; of those 70% were deemed to have need. 100% of undergraduates with need received aid; of those 13% had need fully met. *Average percent of need met:* 36% (excluding resources awarded to replace EFC). *Average financial aid package:* $9946 (excluding resources awarded to replace EFC). 7% of all full-time undergraduates had no need and received non-need-based gift aid.

GIFT AID (NEED-BASED) *Total amount:* $12,322,301 (48% federal, 40% state, 12% institutional). *Receiving aid:* Freshmen: 44% (587); all full-time undergraduates: 41% (2,209). *Average award:* Freshmen: $2181; Undergraduates: $2398. *Scholarships, grants, and awards:* Federal Pell, FSEOG, state.

GIFT AID (NON-NEED-BASED) *Total amount:* $8,675,692 (1% federal, 45% state, 40% institutional, 14% external sources). *Receiving aid:* Freshmen: 12% (166). Undergraduates: 13% (708). *Average award:* Freshmen: $2137. Undergraduates: $2773. *Scholarships, grants, and awards by category:* Academic interests/achievement: area/ethnic studies, biological sciences, business, communication, education, English, foreign languages, general academic interests/achievements, humanities, international studies, mathematics, physical sciences, premedicine, social sciences. *Cre-*

ative arts/performance: applied art and design, art/fine arts, creative writing, dance, general creative arts/performance, journalism/publications, music, performing arts, theater/drama. *Special achievements/activities:* community service, general special achievements/activities, leadership, memberships. *Special characteristics:* adult students, ethnic background, first-generation college students, general special characteristics, handicapped students, international students, local/state students, members of minority groups, religious affiliation, veterans. *ROTC:* Army cooperative, Air Force cooperative.

LOANS *Student loans:* $20,716,573 (46% need-based, 54% non-need-based). 60% of past graduating class borrowed through all loan programs. *Average indebtedness per student:* $25,148. *Average need-based loan:* Freshmen: $2938. Undergraduates: $3663. *Parent loans:* $9,340,277 (100% non-need-based). *Programs:* Federal Direct (Subsidized and Unsubsidized Stafford, PLUS).

WORK-STUDY *Federal work-study:* Total amount: $662,931; 408 jobs averaging $1539.

APPLYING FOR FINANCIAL AID *Required financial aid forms:* FAFSA, state aid form. *Financial aid deadline (priority):* 2/1. *Notification date:* Continuous beginning 3/15. Students must reply by 5/1.

CONTACT Susan Romano, Director of Financial Aid, State University of New York College at Geneseo, 1 College Circle, Erwin Hall 104, Geneseo, NY 14454, 585-245-5731 or toll-free 866-245-5211. *Fax:* 585-245-5717. *E-mail:* finaid@geneseo.edu. *Website:* http://www.geneseo.edu/.

STATE UNIVERSITY OF NEW YORK COLLEGE AT OLD WESTBURY
Old Westbury, NY

CONTACT Ms. Vivian Mendonis, Financial Aid Assistant, State University of New York College at Old Westbury, PO Box 210, Old Westbury, NY 11568-0210, 516-876-3223. *Fax:* 516-876-3008. *E-mail:* finaid@oldwestbury.edu. *Website:* http://www.oldwestbury.edu/.

STATE UNIVERSITY OF NEW YORK COLLEGE AT ONEONTA
Oneonta, NY

ABOUT THE INSTITUTION State-supported, coed. *Awards:* certificates, bachelor's, and master's degrees. 68 undergraduate majors. *Total enrollment:* 6,358. Undergraduates: 5,940. Freshmen: 1,381.

GIFT AID (NEED-BASED) *Scholarships, grants, and awards:* Federal Pell, FSEOG, state, private, college/university gift aid from institutional funds.

GIFT AID (NON-NEED-BASED) *Scholarships, grants, and awards by category:* Academic interests/achievement: biological sciences, business, computer science, education, English, general academic interests/achievements, home economics, physical sciences, premedicine, social sciences. *Creative arts/performance:* music, theater/drama. *Special achievements/activities:* community service, general special achievements/activities, leadership. *Special characteristics:* general special characteristics, international students, local/state students.

LOANS *Programs:* Federal Direct (Subsidized and Unsubsidized Stafford, PLUS), Perkins.

WORK-STUDY *Federal work-study:* jobs available. *State or other work-study/employment:* Part-time jobs available.

APPLYING FOR FINANCIAL AID *Required financial aid forms:* FAFSA, noncustodial (divorced/separated) parent's statement.

CONTACT Mr. Bill Goodhue, Director of Financial Aid, State University of New York College at Oneonta, 108 Ravine Parkway, Oneonta, NY 13820, 607-436-2992 or toll-free 800-SUNY-123. *Fax:* 607-436-2659. *E-mail:* bill.goodhue@oneonta.edu. *Website:* http://www.oneonta.edu/.

STATE UNIVERSITY OF NEW YORK COLLEGE AT POTSDAM
Potsdam, NY

Tuition & fees (NY res): $8221	Average undergraduate aid package: $16,750

ABOUT THE INSTITUTION State-supported, coed. *Awards:* certificates, bachelor's, and master's degrees. 40 undergraduate majors. *Total enrollment:* 3,587. Undergraduates: 3,321. Freshmen: 783. Federal methodology is used as a basis for awarding need-based institutional aid.

UNDERGRADUATE EXPENSES for 2017–2018 *Application fee:* $50. *Tuition, state resident:* full-time $6670; part-time $278 per credit hour. *Tuition, nonresident:* full-time $16,320; part-time $680 per credit hour. *Required fees:* full-time $1551; $82.85 per credit hour. Full-time tuition and fees vary according to course load. Part-time tuition and fees vary according to course load. *College room and board:* $12,830; *Room only:* $7360. Room and board charges vary according to board plan and housing facility.

FRESHMAN FINANCIAL AID (Fall 2017, est.) 760 applied for aid; of those 86% were deemed to have need. 100% of freshmen with need received aid; of those 6% had need fully met. *Average percent of need met:* 95% (excluding resources awarded to replace EFC). *Average financial aid package:* $18,264 (excluding resources awarded to replace EFC). 9% of all full-time freshmen had no need and received non-need-based gift aid.

UNDERGRADUATE FINANCIAL AID (Fall 2017, est.) 3,040 applied for aid; of those 82% were deemed to have need. 100% of undergraduates with need received aid; of those 8% had need fully met. *Average percent of need met:* 94% (excluding resources awarded to replace EFC). *Average financial aid package:* $16,750 (excluding resources awarded to replace EFC). 9% of all full-time undergraduates had no need and received non-need-based gift aid.

GIFT AID (NEED-BASED) *Total amount:* $21,735,387 (41% federal, 40% state, 17% institutional, 2% external sources). *Receiving aid:* Freshmen: 71% (553); all full-time undergraduates: 65% (2,091). *Average award:* Freshmen: $9278; Undergraduates: $8424. *Scholarships, grants, and awards:* Federal Pell, FSEOG, state, private, college/university gift aid from institutional funds, ACCES-VR, TEACH Grants.

GIFT AID (NON-NEED-BASED) *Total amount:* $1,419,676 (1% federal, 6% state, 82% institutional, 11% external sources). *Receiving aid:* Freshmen: 35% (274). Undergraduates: 30% (974). *Average award:* Freshmen: $3380. Undergraduates: $3178. *Scholarships, grants, and awards by category:* Academic interests/achievement: 389 awards ($576,147 total): biological sciences, business, communication, computer science, education, engineering/technologies, English, foreign languages, general academic interests/achievements, humanities, mathematics, physical sciences, social sciences. *Creative arts/performance:* 237 awards ($409,252 total): art/fine arts, dance, music, performing arts, theater/drama. *Special achievements/activities:* 960 awards ($2,328,042 total): community service, general special achievements/activities, leadership. *Special characteristics:* 112 awards ($244,460 total): adult students, children and siblings of alumni, children of faculty/staff, ethnic background, handicapped students, local/state students, members of minority groups, previous college experience. *Tuition waivers:* Full or partial for employees or children of employees. *ROTC:* Army cooperative, Air Force cooperative.

LOANS *Student loans:* $19,842,829 (76% need-based, 24% non-need-based). 79% of past graduating class borrowed through all loan programs. *Average indebtedness per student:* $28,797. *Average need-based loan:* Freshmen: $3936. Undergraduates: $4597. *Parent loans:* $17,270,080 (37% need-based, 63% non-need-based). *Programs:* Federal Direct (Subsidized and Unsubsidized Stafford, PLUS), Perkins.

WORK-STUDY *Federal work-study:* Total amount: $275,390; 165 jobs averaging $1652.

APPLYING FOR FINANCIAL AID *Required financial aid forms:* FAFSA, state aid form. *Financial aid deadline (priority):* 1/1. *Notification date:* Continuous beginning 1/1. Students must reply by 5/1 or within 4 weeks of notification.

CONTACT Susan E. Godreau, Director of Financial Aid, State University of New York College at Potsdam, 44 Pierrepont Avenue, Potsdam, NY 13676, 315-267-2162 or toll-free 877-POTSDAM. *Fax:* 315-267-3067. *E-mail:* finaid@potsdam.edu. *Website:* http://www.potsdam.edu/.

STATE UNIVERSITY OF NEW YORK COLLEGE OF AGRICULTURE AND TECHNOLOGY AT COBLESKILL
Cobleskill, NY

Tuition & fees (NY res): $8139	Average undergraduate aid package: $7614

ABOUT THE INSTITUTION State-supported, coed. **Awards:** certificates, associate, and bachelor's degrees. 52 undergraduate majors. **Total enrollment:** 2,298. Undergraduates: 2,298. Freshmen: 705. Federal methodology is used as a basis for awarding need-based institutional aid.

UNDERGRADUATE EXPENSES for 2017–2018 Application fee: $50. **Tuition, state resident:** full-time $6670; part-time $277.92 per credit hour. **Tuition, nonresident:** full-time $16,320; part-time $680 per credit hour. **Required fees:** full-time $1469; $63.30 per credit hour. Full-time tuition and fees vary according to course level and degree level. Part-time tuition and fees vary according to course level and degree level. **College room and board:** $13,182; **Room only:** $7878. Room and board charges vary according to board plan and housing facility.

FRESHMAN FINANCIAL AID (Fall 2016) 635 applied for aid; of those 87% were deemed to have need. 99% of freshmen with need received aid; of those 1% had need fully met. **Average percent of need met:** 63% (excluding resources awarded to replace EFC). **Average financial aid package:** $8392 (excluding resources awarded to replace EFC). 4% of all full-time freshmen had no need and received non-need-based gift aid.

UNDERGRADUATE FINANCIAL AID (Fall 2016) 2,058 applied for aid; of those 90% were deemed to have need. 99% of undergraduates with need received aid; of those 1% had need fully met. **Average percent of need met:** 60% (excluding resources awarded to replace EFC). **Average financial aid package:** $7614 (excluding resources awarded to replace EFC). 3% of all full-time undergraduates had no need and received non-need-based gift aid.

GIFT AID (NEED-BASED) Total amount: $10,267,461 (51% federal, 49% state). **Receiving aid:** Freshmen: 72% (480); all full-time undergraduates: 64% (1,492). **Average award:** Freshmen: $5227; Undergraduates: $4333. **Scholarships, grants, and awards:** Federal Pell, FSEOG, state, private, college/university gift aid from institutional funds.

GIFT AID (NON-NEED-BASED) Total amount: $1,555,142 (18% federal, 31% institutional, 51% external sources). **Receiving aid:** Freshmen: 24% (159). Undergraduates: 20% (480). **Average award:** Freshmen: $2864. Undergraduates: $2623. **Scholarships, grants, and awards by category:** Academic interests/achievement: general academic interests/achievements. Special achievements/activities: leadership. Special characteristics: children and siblings of alumni, local/state students, members of minority groups. **Tuition waivers:** Full or partial for senior citizens.

LOANS Student loans: $12,404,857 (44% need-based, 56% non-need-based). 69% of past graduating class borrowed through all loan programs. Average indebtedness per student: $29,645. **Average need-based loan:** Freshmen: $2166. Undergraduates: $2279. **Parent loans:** $4,394,340 (100% non-need-based). **Programs:** Federal Direct (Subsidized and Unsubsidized Stafford, PLUS), Perkins.

WORK-STUDY Federal work-study: 97 jobs averaging $1166. **State or other work-study/employment:** 353 part-time jobs averaging $1506.

APPLYING FOR FINANCIAL AID Required financial aid forms: FAFSA, institution's own form, state aid form. **Financial aid deadline (priority):** 2/15. **Notification date:** Continuous beginning 3/10. Students must reply within 2 weeks of notification.

CONTACT Mr. Brian Smith, Office of Financial Aid, State University of New York College of Agriculture and Technology at Cobleskill, 118B Knapp Hall, Cobleskill, NY 12043, 518-255-5623 or toll-free 800-295-8988. *Fax:* 518-255-5844. *E-mail:* financialaid@cobleskill.edu.
Website: http://www.cobleskill.edu/.

STATE UNIVERSITY OF NEW YORK COLLEGE OF ENVIRONMENTAL SCIENCE AND FORESTRY
Syracuse, NY

Tuition & fees (NY res): $8568	Average undergraduate aid package: $10,160

ABOUT THE INSTITUTION State-supported, coed. **Awards:** certificates, associate, bachelor's, master's, and doctoral degrees. 27 undergraduate majors. **Total enrollment:** 2,219. Undergraduates: 1,796. Freshmen: 328. Federal methodology is used as a basis for awarding need-based institutional aid.

UNDERGRADUATE EXPENSES for 2018–2019 Application fee: $50. **One-time required fee:** $278. **Tuition, state resident:** full-time $6670; part-time $278 per credit hour. **Tuition, nonresident:** full-time $16,320; part-time $680 per credit hour. **Required fees:** full-time $1898; $76.13 per credit hour or $14.55 per term. Full-time tuition and fees vary according to location. Part-time tuition and fees vary according to course load and location. **College room and board:** $16,140; **Room only:** $8300. Room and board charges vary according to board plan, housing facility, and location.

FRESHMAN FINANCIAL AID (Fall 2017, est.) 315 applied for aid; of those 71% were deemed to have need. 100% of freshmen with need received aid; of those 35% had need fully met. **Average percent of need met:** 70% (excluding resources awarded to replace EFC). **Average financial aid package:** $11,625 (excluding resources awarded to replace EFC). 21% of all full-time freshmen had no need and received non-need-based gift aid.

UNDERGRADUATE FINANCIAL AID (Fall 2017, est.) 1,467 applied for aid; of those 73% were deemed to have need. 100% of undergraduates with need received aid; of those 48% had need fully met. **Average percent of need met:** 66% (excluding resources awarded to replace EFC). **Average financial aid package:** $10,160 (excluding resources awarded to replace EFC). 21% of all full-time undergraduates had no need and received non-need-based gift aid.

GIFT AID (NEED-BASED) Total amount: $8,026,484 (30% federal, 22% state, 44% institutional, 4% external sources). **Receiving aid:** Freshmen: 67% (219); all full-time undergraduates: 55% (981). **Average award:** Freshmen: $7510; Undergraduates: $6648. **Scholarships, grants, and awards:** Federal Pell, FSEOG, state, private, college/university gift aid from institutional funds, United Negro College Fund.

GIFT AID (NON-NEED-BASED) Total amount: $1,990,249 (35% state, 45% institutional, 20% external sources). **Receiving aid:** Freshmen: 49% (162). Undergraduates: 39% (697). **Average award:** Freshmen: $3716. Undergraduates: $3246. **Scholarships, grants, and awards by category:** Academic interests/achievement: agriculture, architecture, biological sciences, engineering/technologies, general academic interests/achievements, physical sciences, premedicine. Special achievements/activities: community service, general special achievements/activities, leadership, memberships. Special characteristics: children and siblings of alumni, general special characteristics, international students, local/state students, members of minority groups, out-of-state students. **ROTC:** Army cooperative, Air Force cooperative.

LOANS Student loans: $6,992,973 (43% need-based, 57% non-need-based). 68% of past graduating class borrowed through all loan programs. Average indebtedness per student: $26,679. **Average need-based loan:** Freshmen: $4642. Undergraduates: $4675. **Parent loans:** $2,306,028 (35% need-based, 65% non-need-based). **Programs:** Federal Direct (Subsidized and Unsubsidized Stafford, PLUS).

WORK-STUDY Federal work-study: Total amount: $330,000; 180 jobs averaging $1790. **State or other work-study/employment:** Total amount: $347,035 (55% need-based, 45% non-need-based). 217 part-time jobs averaging $886.

APPLYING FOR FINANCIAL AID Required financial aid forms: FAFSA, state aid form. **Financial aid deadline (priority):** 2/1. **Notification date:** Continuous beginning 2/1. Students must reply by 5/1 or within 2 weeks of notification.

CONTACT Mr. Mark J. Hill, Director of Financial Aid, State University of New York College of Environmental Science and Forestry, One Forestry Drive, Syracuse, NY 13210-2779, 315-470-6673. *Fax:* 315-470-4734. *E-mail:* mjhill@esf.edu.
Website: http://www.esf.edu/.

STATE UNIVERSITY OF NEW YORK COLLEGE OF TECHNOLOGY AT CANTON
Canton, NY

Tuition & fees (NY res): $8129	Average undergraduate aid package: $10,650

ABOUT THE INSTITUTION State-supported, coed. **Awards:** certificates, associate, and bachelor's degrees. 39 undergraduate majors. **Total enrollment:** 3,180. Undergraduates: 3,180. Freshmen: 692. Federal methodology is used as a basis for awarding need-based institutional aid.

UNDERGRADUATE EXPENSES for 2017–2018 **Application fee:** $50. **One-time required fee:** $120. **Tuition, state resident:** full-time $6670; part-time $278 per credit hour. **Tuition, nonresident:** full-time $16,320; part-time $680 per credit hour. **Required fees:** full-time $1459; $59 per credit hour or $5 per term. Full-time tuition and fees vary according to degree level. Part-time tuition and fees vary according to degree level. **College room and board:** $12,450; **Room only:** $7350. Room and board charges vary according to board plan and housing facility.

FRESHMAN FINANCIAL AID (Fall 2016) 674 applied for aid; of those 90% were deemed to have need. 99% of freshmen with need received aid; of those 19% had need fully met. **Average percent of need met:** 19% (excluding resources awarded to replace EFC). **Average financial aid package:** $11,077 (excluding resources awarded to replace EFC). 3% of all full-time freshmen had no need and received non-need-based gift aid.

UNDERGRADUATE FINANCIAL AID (Fall 2016) 2,438 applied for aid; of those 90% were deemed to have need. 99% of undergraduates with need received aid; of those 16% had need fully met. **Average percent of need met:** 16% (excluding resources awarded to replace EFC). **Average financial aid package:** $10,650 (excluding resources awarded to replace EFC). 2% of all full-time undergraduates had no need and received non-need-based gift aid.

GIFT AID (NEED-BASED) Total amount: $16,628,495 (51% federal, 43% state, 4% institutional, 2% external sources). **Receiving aid:** Freshmen: 76% (525); all full-time undergraduates: 70% (1,854). **Average award:** Freshmen: $8397; Undergraduates: $7852. **Scholarships, grants, and awards:** Federal Pell, FSEOG, state, college/university gift aid from institutional funds, Bureau of Indian Affairs Grants.

GIFT AID (NON-NEED-BASED) Receiving aid: Freshmen: 1% (7). Undergraduates: 1% (32). **Average award:** Freshmen: $2107. Undergraduates: $2071. **Tuition waivers:** Full or partial for employees or children of employees. **ROTC:** Army cooperative, Air Force cooperative.

LOANS Student loans: $14,938,648 (52% need-based, 48% non-need-based). 87% of past graduating class borrowed through all loan programs. **Average indebtedness per student:** $31,499. **Average need-based loan:** Freshmen: $3516. Undergraduates: $3904. **Parent loans:** $4,945,882 (100% need-based). **Programs:** Federal Direct (Subsidized and Unsubsidized Stafford, PLUS), Perkins.

WORK-STUDY Federal work-study: 190 jobs averaging $1280. **State or other work-study/employment:** Total amount: $355,540 (100% need-based). 12 part-time jobs averaging $1050.

APPLYING FOR FINANCIAL AID Required financial aid forms: FAFSA, state aid form. **Financial aid deadline (priority):** 3/1. **Notification date:** Continuous beginning 12/1. Students must reply within 4 weeks of notification.

CONTACT Ms. Kerrie Cooper, Director of Financial Aid, State University of New York College of Technology at Canton, Student Service Center, Canton, NY 13617, 315-386-7616 or toll-free 800-388-7123. Fax: 315-386-7930. E-mail: cooper@canton.edu.
Website: http://www.canton.edu/.

STATE UNIVERSITY OF NEW YORK COLLEGE OF TECHNOLOGY AT DELHI
Delhi, NY

ABOUT THE INSTITUTION State-supported, coed. **Awards:** certificates, associate, bachelor's, and master's degrees. 39 undergraduate majors. **Total enrollment:** 3,515. Undergraduates: 3,469. Freshmen: 966.

GIFT AID (NEED-BASED) Scholarships, grants, and awards: Federal Pell, FSEOG, state, private, college/university gift aid from institutional funds.

GIFT AID (NON-NEED-BASED) Scholarships, grants, and awards by category: Academic interests/achievement: general academic interests/achievements. Special achievements/activities: community service.

LOANS Programs: Federal Direct (Subsidized and Unsubsidized Stafford, PLUS), Perkins.

APPLYING FOR FINANCIAL AID Required financial aid forms: FAFSA, state aid form.

CONTACT Nancy B. Hughes, Director of Financial Aid, State University of New York College of Technology at Delhi, 158 Bush Hall, Delhi, NY 13753, 607-746-4570 or toll-free 800-96-DELHI. Fax: 607-746-4104.
Website: http://www.delhi.edu/.

STATE UNIVERSITY OF NEW YORK DOWNSTATE MEDICAL CENTER
Brooklyn, NY

CONTACT Financial Aid Office, State University of New York Downstate Medical Center, 450 Clarkson Avenue, Brooklyn, NY 11203-2098, 718-270-2488. Fax: 718-270-7592. E-mail: finaid1@downstate.edu.
Website: http://www.downstate.edu/.

STATE UNIVERSITY OF NEW YORK EMPIRE STATE COLLEGE
Saratoga Springs, NY

CONTACT Financial Aid Office, State University of New York Empire State College, 2 Union Avenue, Saratoga Springs, NY 12866-4391, 518-587-2100 or toll-free 800-847-3000.
Website: http://www.esc.edu/.

STATE UNIVERSITY OF NEW YORK MARITIME COLLEGE
Throggs Neck, NY

Tuition & fees (NY res): $8074	Average undergraduate aid package: $4667

ABOUT THE INSTITUTION State-supported, coed. **Awards:** certificates, associate, bachelor's, and master's degrees. 10 undergraduate majors. **Total enrollment:** 1,794. Undergraduates: 1,641. Freshmen: 342. Federal methodology is used as a basis for awarding need-based institutional aid.

UNDERGRADUATE EXPENSES for 2017–2018 **Application fee:** $50. **Tuition, state resident:** full-time $6670; part-time $278 per credit hour. **Tuition, nonresident:** full-time $16,320; part-time $680 per credit hour. **Required fees:** full-time $1404. Full-time tuition and fees vary according to course load. Part-time tuition and fees vary according to course load. **College room and board:** $12,134; **Room only:** $7714. Room and board charges vary according to board plan and housing facility.

FRESHMAN FINANCIAL AID (Fall 2017, est.) 305 applied for aid; of those 61% were deemed to have need. 98% of freshmen with need received aid. **Average percent of need met:** 27% (excluding resources awarded to replace EFC). **Average financial aid package:** $4278 (excluding resources awarded to replace EFC). 8% of all full-time freshmen had no need and received non-need-based gift aid.

UNDERGRADUATE FINANCIAL AID (Fall 2017, est.) 1,202 applied for aid; of those 70% were deemed to have need. 99% of undergraduates with need received aid; of those 1% had need fully met. **Average percent of need met:** 29% (excluding resources awarded to replace EFC). **Average financial aid package:** $4667 (excluding resources awarded to replace EFC). 6% of all full-time undergraduates had no need and received non-need-based gift aid.

GIFT AID (NEED-BASED) Total amount: $5,651,691 (32% federal, 34% state, 25% institutional, 9% external sources). **Receiving aid:** Freshmen: 37% (128); all full-time undergraduates: 40% (625). **Average award:** Freshmen: $3962; Undergraduates: $3630. **Scholarships, grants, and awards:** Federal Pell, FSEOG, state, private, college/university gift aid from institutional funds, Educational Opportunity Program (EOP).

GIFT AID (NON-NEED-BASED) Total amount: $922,551 (41% federal, 59% institutional). **Average award:** Freshmen: $1759. Undergraduates: $1833. **Scholarships, grants, and awards by category:** Academic interests/achievement: general academic interests/achievements. Special achievements/activities: leadership. **ROTC:** Army cooperative, Naval.

LOANS Student loans: $9,281,028 (33% need-based, 67% non-need-based). 62% of past graduating class borrowed through all loan programs. Average indebtedness per student: $36,503. **Average need-based loan:** Freshmen: $1773. Undergraduates: $2202. **Parent loans:** $12,335,764 (100% non-need-based). **Programs:** Federal Direct (Subsidized and Unsubsidized Stafford, PLUS), Perkins, alternative loans.

WORK-STUDY Federal work-study: Total amount: $55,466; jobs available. **State or other work-study/employment:** Total amount: $518,364 (100% non-need-based). Part-time jobs available.

APPLYING FOR FINANCIAL AID Required financial aid form: FAFSA. **Financial aid deadline (priority):** 2/1. **Notification date:** Continuous beginning 2/15. Students must reply by 5/1.

CONTACT Ms. Andrea Damar, Director of Financial Aid, State University of New York Maritime College, 6 Pennyfield Avenue, Throgs Neck, NY 10465-4198, 718-409-7227. Fax: 718-409-7275. E-mail: adamar@sunymaritime.edu. Website: http://www.sunymaritime.edu/.

STATE UNIVERSITY OF NEW YORK POLYTECHNIC INSTITUTE
Utica, NY

Tuition & fees (NY res): $7998	Average undergraduate aid package: $11,381

ABOUT THE INSTITUTION State-supported, coed. **Awards:** certificates, bachelor's, master's, and doctoral degrees. 25 undergraduate majors. **Total enrollment:** 2,933. Undergraduates: 2,184. Freshmen: 463. Federal methodology is used as a basis for awarding need-based institutional aid.

UNDERGRADUATE EXPENSES for 2017–2018 Application fee: $50. **Tuition, state resident:** full-time $6670; part-time $278 per credit hour. **Tuition, nonresident:** full-time $16,320; part-time $680 per credit hour. **Required fees:** full-time $1328; $55.20 per credit hour. Full-time tuition and fees vary according to course load, degree level, and location. Part-time tuition and fees vary according to course load, degree level, and location. **College room and board:** $12,440. Room and board charges vary according to board plan and location.

FRESHMAN FINANCIAL AID (Fall 2017, est.) 433 applied for aid; of those 80% were deemed to have need. 100% of freshmen with need received aid; of those 100% had need fully met. **Average percent of need met:** 100% (excluding resources awarded to replace EFC). **Average financial aid package:** $12,153 (excluding resources awarded to replace EFC). 21% of all full-time freshmen had no need and received non-need-based gift aid.

UNDERGRADUATE FINANCIAL AID (Fall 2017, est.) 1,563 applied for aid; of those 84% were deemed to have need. 100% of undergraduates with need received aid; of those 99% had need fully met. **Average percent of need met:** 98% (excluding resources awarded to replace EFC). **Average financial aid package:** $11,381 (excluding resources awarded to replace EFC). 15% of all full-time undergraduates had no need and received non-need-based gift aid.

GIFT AID (NEED-BASED) Total amount: $10,045,259 (39% federal, 34% state, 24% institutional, 3% external sources). **Receiving aid:** Freshmen: 72% (334); all full-time undergraduates: 66% (1,171). **Average award:** Freshmen: $9458; Undergraduates: $8321. **Scholarships, grants, and awards:** Federal Pell, FSEOG, state, private, college/university gift aid from institutional funds.

GIFT AID (NON-NEED-BASED) Total amount: $1,492,564 (15% state, 78% institutional, 7% external sources). **Receiving aid:** Freshmen: 53% (247). Undergraduates: 32% (572). **Average award:** Freshmen: $3492. Undergraduates: $4413. **Scholarships, grants, and awards by category:** Special characteristics: local/state students, members of minority groups, previous college experience. **ROTC:** Army cooperative, Air Force cooperative.

LOANS Student loans: $10,796,295 (84% need-based, 16% non-need-based). **Average need-based loan:** Freshmen: $3606. Undergraduates: $4358. **Parent**

---

loans: $6,651,717 (74% need-based, 26% non-need-based). **Programs:** Federal Direct (Subsidized and Unsubsidized Stafford, PLUS), Perkins, Federal Nursing.

WORK-STUDY Federal work-study: Total amount: $495,087; 152 jobs averaging $1500. **State or other work-study/employment:** Total amount: $292,448 (66% need-based, 34% non-need-based). Part-time jobs available.

APPLYING FOR FINANCIAL AID Required financial aid forms: FAFSA, state aid form. **Financial aid deadline (priority):** 12/1. **Notification date:** Continuous beginning 1/2. Students must reply within 2 weeks of notification.

CONTACT Financial Aid Office, State University of New York Polytechnic Institute, 100 Seymour Road, Utica, NY 13502, 315-792-7210 or toll-free 866-278-6948. Fax: 315-792-7220. E-mail: finaid@sunyit.edu. Website: http://www.sunypoly.edu/.

STATE UNIVERSITY OF NEW YORK UPSTATE MEDICAL UNIVERSITY
Syracuse, NY

CONTACT Michael Pede, Office of Financial Aid, State University of New York Upstate Medical University, Weiskotten Hall, Room 1213, 766 Irving Avenue, Syracuse, NY 13210-2375, 315-464-4329 or toll-free 800-736-2171. E-mail: finaid@upstate.edu. Website: http://www.upstate.edu/.

STEPHEN F. AUSTIN STATE UNIVERSITY
Nacogdoches, TX

Tuition & fees (TX res): $9537	Average undergraduate aid package: $12,338

ABOUT THE INSTITUTION State-supported, coed. **Awards:** bachelor's, master's, and doctoral degrees. 68 undergraduate majors. **Total enrollment:** 12,614. Undergraduates: 10,985. Freshmen: 2,150. Federal methodology is used as a basis for awarding need-based institutional aid.

UNDERGRADUATE EXPENSES for 2017–2018 Application fee: $45. **Tuition, state resident:** full-time $7260; part-time $242 per credit hour. **Tuition, nonresident:** full-time $19,710; part-time $657 per credit hour. **Required fees:** full-time $2277; $157.50 per credit hour. Full-time tuition and fees vary according to course load, degree level, and location. Part-time tuition and fees vary according to course load, degree level, and location. **College room and board:** $8868. Room and board charges vary according to board plan and housing facility. **Payment plan:** Guaranteed tuition.

FRESHMAN FINANCIAL AID (Fall 2016) 1,901 applied for aid; of those 77% were deemed to have need. 100% of freshmen with need received aid; of those 17% had need fully met. **Average percent of need met:** 61% (excluding resources awarded to replace EFC). **Average financial aid package:** $12,423 (excluding resources awarded to replace EFC). 11% of all full-time freshmen had no need and received non-need-based gift aid.

UNDERGRADUATE FINANCIAL AID (Fall 2016) 8,179 applied for aid; of those 81% were deemed to have need. 100% of undergraduates with need received aid; of those 17% had need fully met. **Average percent of need met:** 61% (excluding resources awarded to replace EFC). **Average financial aid package:** $12,338 (excluding resources awarded to replace EFC). 8% of all full-time undergraduates had no need and received non-need-based gift aid.

GIFT AID (NEED-BASED) Total amount: $35,896,274 (56% federal, 25% state, 19% institutional). **Receiving aid:** Freshmen: 48% (1,039); all full-time undergraduates: 49% (5,034). **Average award:** Freshmen: $9316; Undergraduates: $7504. **Scholarships, grants, and awards:** Federal Pell, FSEOG, state, private, college/university gift aid from institutional funds, TEACH Grants.

GIFT AID (NON-NEED-BASED) Total amount: $13,430,072 (2% federal, 1% state, 68% institutional, 29% external sources). **Receiving aid:** Freshmen: 36% (787). Undergraduates: 25% (2,514). **Average award:** Freshmen: $3040. Undergraduates: $2911. **Scholarships, grants, and awards by category:** Academic interests/achievement: agriculture, biological sciences, business, communication, computer science, education, general academic interests/achievements, health fields, home economics, mathematics, military science, physical sciences, premedicine. *Creative arts/ performance*: journalism/publications, music, theater/drama. *Special achievements/ activities*: cheerleading/drum major, general special achievements/activities, hobbies/ interests, leadership, rodeo. *Special characteristics*: adult students, children and siblings of alumni, children of faculty/staff, children of union members/company employees, first-generation college students, general special characteristics, local/state students, previous college experience, veterans, veterans' children. *Tuition waivers*: Full or partial for employees or children of employees, senior citizens. *ROTC*: Army.

LOANS *Student loans*: $64,532,574 (35% need-based, 65% non-need-based). 69% of past graduating class borrowed through all loan programs. *Average indebtedness per student*: $30,101. *Average need-based loan*: Freshmen: $3792. Undergraduates: $4704. *Parent loans*: $24,733,215 (100% non-need-based). *Programs*: Federal Direct (Subsidized and Unsubsidized Stafford, PLUS), Perkins, state, college/ university.

WORK-STUDY *Federal work-study*: jobs available. *State or other work-study/employment*: Total amount: $87,760 (100% need-based). Part-time jobs available.

ATHLETIC AWARDS Total amount: $4,076,331 (100% non-need-based).

APPLYING FOR FINANCIAL AID *Required financial aid form*: FAFSA. *Financial aid deadline (priority)*: 3/15. *Notification date*: Continuous beginning 3/15.

CONTACT H. Rachele Garrett, Office of Financial Aid, Stephen F. Austin State University, PO Box 13052, Nacogdoches, TX 75962, 936-468-2403 or toll-free 800-731-2902. *Fax*: 936-468-1048. *E-mail*: finaid@sfasu.edu. *Website*: http://www.sfasu.edu/.

STEPHENS COLLEGE
Columbia, MO

ABOUT THE INSTITUTION Independent, undergraduate: women only; graduate: coed. *Awards*: certificates, associate, bachelor's, and master's degrees. 23 undergraduate majors. *Total enrollment*: 891. Undergraduates: 706. Freshmen: 191.

GIFT AID (NEED-BASED) *Scholarships, grants, and awards*: Federal Pell, FSEOG, state, private, college/university gift aid from institutional funds, Academic Competitiveness Grants, National SMART Grants.

GIFT AID (NON-NEED-BASED) *Scholarships, grants, and awards by category*: *Academic interests/achievement*: English, general academic interests/achievements. *Creative arts/performance*: dance, music, performing arts, theater/drama. *Special achievements/activities*: leadership, memberships. *Special characteristics*: children of faculty/staff, children of union members/company employees, parents of current students, siblings of current students, veterans, veterans' children.

LOANS *Programs*: Federal Direct (Subsidized and Unsubsidized Stafford, PLUS), Perkins, alternative loans.

APPLYING FOR FINANCIAL AID *Required financial aid form*: FAFSA.

CONTACT Mrs. Kim Stonecipher-Fisher, Director of Financial Aid, Stephens College, 1200 East Broadway, Columbia, MO 65215-0002, 800-876-7207. *Fax*: 573-876-2320. *E-mail*: finaid@stephens.edu. *Website*: http://www.stephens.edu/.

STERLING COLLEGE
Sterling, KS

Tuition & fees: $24,485	Average undergraduate aid package: $22,982

ABOUT THE INSTITUTION Independent Presbyterian, coed. *Awards*: bachelor's degrees. 20 undergraduate majors. *Total enrollment*: 650. Undergraduates: 650. Freshmen: 128. Federal methodology is used as a basis for awarding need-based institutional aid.

UNDERGRADUATE EXPENSES for 2017–2018 *Application fee*: $25. *One-time required fee*: $100. *Comprehensive fee*: $33,065 includes full-time tuition ($23,985), mandatory fees ($500), and room and board ($8580). Full-time tuition and fees vary according to course load. Room and board charges vary according to board plan and housing facility. *Part-time tuition*: $448 per credit hour. Part-time tuition and fees vary according to course load.

FRESHMAN FINANCIAL AID (Fall 2017, est.) 181 applied for aid; of those 88% were deemed to have need. 100% of freshmen with need received aid; of those 14% had need fully met. *Average percent of need met*: 68% (excluding resources awarded to replace EFC). *Average financial aid package*: $20,964 (excluding resources awarded to replace EFC). 7% of all full-time freshmen had no need and received non-need-based gift aid.

UNDERGRADUATE FINANCIAL AID (Fall 2017, est.) 581 applied for aid; of those 87% were deemed to have need. 100% of undergraduates with need received aid; of those 24% had need fully met. *Average percent of need met*: 79% (excluding resources awarded to replace EFC). *Average financial aid package*: $22,982 (excluding resources awarded to replace EFC). 10% of all full-time undergraduates had no need and received non-need-based gift aid.

GIFT AID (NEED-BASED) *Total amount*: $5,000,208 (28% federal, 10% state, 62% institutional). *Receiving aid*: Freshmen: 82% (150); all full-time undergraduates: 82% (482). *Average award*: Freshmen: $8080; Undergraduates: $10,583. *Scholarships, grants, and awards*: Federal Pell, FSEOG, state, private, college/university gift aid from institutional funds.

GIFT AID (NON-NEED-BASED) *Total amount*: $695,673 (66% institutional, 34% external sources). *Average award*: Freshmen: $10,510. Undergraduates: $9942. *Scholarships, grants, and awards by category*: *Academic interests/ achievement*: 399 awards ($2,552,431 total): general academic interests/achievements. *Creative arts/performance*: 103 awards ($236,523 total): art/fine arts, cinema/film/ broadcasting, creative writing, debating, general creative arts/performance, journalism/ publications, music, performing arts, theater/drama. *Special achievements/activities*: 27 awards ($78,955 total): cheerleading/drum major, religious involvement. *Special characteristics*: 73 awards ($392,626 total): children and siblings of alumni, children of faculty/staff, public servants, siblings of current students, twins, veterans' children. *Tuition waivers*: Full or partial for employees or children of employees, senior citizens.

LOANS *Student loans*: $3,859,043 (68% need-based, 32% non-need-based). 81% of past graduating class borrowed through all loan programs. *Average indebtedness per student*: $28,221. *Average need-based loan*: Freshmen: $4998. Undergraduates: $5861. *Parent loans*: $1,562,692 (100% non-need-based). *Programs*: Federal Direct (Subsidized and Unsubsidized Stafford, PLUS), Perkins, college/university.

WORK-STUDY *Federal work-study*: Total amount: $292,927; 344 jobs averaging $854.

ATHLETIC AWARDS Total amount: $3,213,992 (86% need-based, 14% non-need-based).

APPLYING FOR FINANCIAL AID *Required financial aid form*: FAFSA. *Financial aid deadline (priority)*: 1/15. *Notification date*: Continuous beginning 2/1. Students must reply within 2 weeks of notification.

CONTACT Ms. Mitzi Suhler, Director of Financial Aid, Sterling College, 125 West Cooper, Sterling, KS 67579, 620-278-4226 or toll-free 800-346-1017. *Fax*: 620-869-9033. *E-mail*: msuhler@sterling.edu. *Website*: http://www.sterling.edu/.

STERLING COLLEGE
Craftsbury Common, VT

CONTACT Barbara Stuart, Director of Financial Aid, Sterling College, PO Box 72, Craftsbury Common, VT 05827, 800-648-3591 Ext. 3 or toll-free 800-648-3591 Ext. 100. *Fax*: 802-586-2596. *E-mail*: bstuart@sterlingcollege.edu. *Website*: http://www.sterlingcollege.edu/.

STETSON UNIVERSITY
DeLand, FL

Tuition & fees: $46,030	Average undergraduate aid package: $36,776

ABOUT THE INSTITUTION Independent, coed. *Awards*: certificates, bachelor's, master's, and doctoral degrees. 55 undergraduate majors. *Total enrollment*: 4,268. Undergraduates: 3,081. Freshmen: 864. Federal methodology is used as a basis for awarding need-based institutional aid.

UNDERGRADUATE EXPENSES for 2018–2019 *Application fee*: $50. *Comprehensive fee*: $59,082 includes full-time tuition ($45,670), mandatory fees ($360), and room and board ($13,052). *College room only:* $7512. Room and board charges vary according to board plan. *Part-time tuition:* $1150 per credit hour.

FRESHMAN FINANCIAL AID (Fall 2017, est.) 756 applied for aid; of those 86% were deemed to have need. 100% of freshmen with need received aid; of those 25% had need fully met. *Average percent of need met:* 77% (excluding resources awarded to replace EFC). *Average financial aid package:* $36,918 (excluding resources awarded to replace EFC). 20% of all full-time freshmen had no need and received non-need-based gift aid.

UNDERGRADUATE FINANCIAL AID (Fall 2017, est.) 2,299 applied for aid; of those 89% were deemed to have need. 100% of undergraduates with need received aid; of those 21% had need fully met. *Average percent of need met:* 76% (excluding resources awarded to replace EFC). *Average financial aid package:* $36,776 (excluding resources awarded to replace EFC). 26% of all full-time undergraduates had no need and received non-need-based gift aid.

GIFT AID (NEED-BASED) *Total amount:* $59,194,564 (9% federal, 12% state, 79% institutional). *Receiving aid:* Freshmen: 74% (643); all full-time undergraduates: 67% (2,034). *Average award:* Freshmen: $31,065; Undergraduates: $29,996. *Scholarships, grants, and awards:* Federal Pell, FSEOG, state, private, college/university gift aid from institutional funds.

GIFT AID (NON-NEED-BASED) *Total amount:* $28,283,589 (13% state, 86% institutional, 1% external sources). *Receiving aid:* Freshmen: 18% (155). Undergraduates: 12% (365). *Average award:* Freshmen: $26,810. Undergraduates: $24,126. *Scholarships, grants, and awards by category: Academic interests/achievement:* area/ethnic studies, biological sciences, business, communication, computer science, education, English, foreign languages, general academic interests/achievements, humanities, mathematics, military science, physical sciences, premedicine, religion/biblical studies, social sciences. *Creative arts/performance:* applied art and design, art/fine arts, music, theater/drama. *Special achievements/activities:* cheerleading/drum major, community service, general special achievements/activities, junior miss, leadership, religious involvement. *Special characteristics:* children and siblings of alumni, children of faculty/staff, ethnic background, first-generation college students, general special characteristics, international students, local/state students, members of minority groups, out-of-state students, veterans, veterans' children. *Tuition waivers:* Full or partial for employees or children of employees. *ROTC:* Army cooperative.

LOANS *Student loans:* $16,711,172 (76% need-based, 24% non-need-based). 70% of past graduating class borrowed through all loan programs. *Average indebtedness per student:* $31,457. *Average need-based loan:* Freshmen: $3897. Undergraduates: $5110. *Parent loans:* $8,907,579 (65% need-based, 35% non-need-based). *Programs:* Federal Direct (Subsidized and Unsubsidized Stafford, PLUS), Perkins.

WORK-STUDY *Federal work-study:* Total amount: $695,462; 286 jobs averaging $2432. *State or other work-study/employment:* Total amount: $260,560 (40% need-based, 60% non-need-based). 68 part-time jobs averaging $3832.

ATHLETIC AWARDS Total amount: $6,155,970 (31% need-based, 69% non-need-based).

APPLYING FOR FINANCIAL AID *Required financial aid form:* FAFSA. *Financial aid deadline (priority):* 11/1. *Notification date:* 3/1. Students must reply within 2 weeks of notification.

CONTACT Beth Kieft, Director of Financial Aid, Stetson University, 421 North Woodland Boulevard, DeLand, FL 32723, 386-822-7120 or toll-free 800-688-0101. *Fax:* 386-822-7126. *E-mail:* finaid@stetson.edu. *Website:* http://www.stetson.edu/.

STEVENS-HENAGER COLLEGE
Boise, ID

CONTACT Ms. Jaime L. Davis, Training and Project Development, Stevens-Henager College, 1444 South Entertainment Avenue, Boise, ID 83709, 208-383-4540 Ext. 1875 or toll-free 800-622-2640. *Fax:* 208-345-6999. *E-mail:* jaime.davis@stevenshenager.edu. *Website:* http://www.stevenshenager.edu/.

STEVENS-HENAGER COLLEGE
Idaho Falls, ID

CONTACT Financial Aid Office, Stevens-Henager College, 901 Pier View Drive, Suite 105, Idaho Falls, ID 83402, 208-522-0887 or toll-free 800-622-2640. *Website:* http://www.stevenshenager.edu/.

STEVENS-HENAGER COLLEGE
Logan, UT

CONTACT Financial Aid Office, Stevens-Henager College, 755 South Main Street, Logan, UT 84321, 435-752-0903 or toll-free 800-622-2640. *Website:* http://www.stevenshenager.edu/.

STEVENS-HENAGER COLLEGE
Orem, UT

CONTACT Financial Aid Office, Stevens-Henager College, 1476 South Sandhill Road, Orem, UT 84058, 801-373-0285 or toll-free 800-622-2640. *Website:* http://www.stevenshenager.edu/.

STEVENS-HENAGER COLLEGE
St. George, UT

CONTACT Financial Aid Office, Stevens-Henager College, 720 South River Road, Suite C-130, St. George, UT 84790, 435-628-9150 or toll-free 800-622-2640. *Website:* http://www.stevenshenager.edu/.

STEVENS-HENAGER COLLEGE
Salt Lake City, UT

CONTACT Financial Aid Office, Stevens-Henager College, 383 West Vine Street, Salt Lake City, UT 84123, 801-531-1180 or toll-free 800-622-2640. *Website:* http://www.stevenshenager.edu/.

STEVENS-HENAGER COLLEGE
West Haven, UT

CONTACT Financial Aid Office, Stevens-Henager College, 1890 South 1350 West, West Haven, UT 84401, 801-392-1471 or toll-free 800-622-2640. *Website:* http://www.stevenshenager.edu/.

STEVENS INSTITUTE OF TECHNOLOGY
Hoboken, NJ

Tuition & fees: $52,202	Average undergraduate aid package: $29,336

ABOUT THE INSTITUTION Independent, coed. *Awards:* certificates, bachelor's, master's, and doctoral degrees. 42 undergraduate majors. *Total enrollment:* 6,916. Undergraduates: 3,123. Freshmen: 762. Both federal and institutional methodology are used as a basis for awarding need-based institutional aid.

UNDERGRADUATE EXPENSES for 2018–2019 *Application fee:* $70. *Comprehensive fee:* $67,446 includes full-time tuition ($50,370), mandatory fees ($1832), and room and board ($15,244). Full-time tuition and fees vary according to course load. Room and board charges vary according to board plan and housing facility. *Part-time tuition:* $1679 per credit. *Part-time fees:* $916 per term. Part-time tuition and fees vary according to course load.

FRESHMAN FINANCIAL AID (Fall 2016) 671 applied for aid; of those 78% were deemed to have need. 99% of freshmen with need received aid; of those 17% had need fully met. *Average percent of need met:* 71% (excluding resources awarded to replace EFC). *Average financial aid package:* $31,639 (excluding resources awarded to replace EFC). 26% of all full-time freshmen had no need and received non-need-based gift aid.

UNDERGRADUATE FINANCIAL AID (Fall 2016) 2,948 applied for aid; of those 69% were deemed to have need. 98% of undergraduates with need received aid; of those 18% had need fully met. *Average percent of need met:* 69% (excluding resources awarded to replace EFC). *Average financial aid package:* $29,336 (excluding resources awarded to replace EFC). 34% of all full-time undergraduates had no need and received non-need-based gift aid.

GIFT AID (NEED-BASED) *Total amount:* $15,437,068 (17% federal, 16% state, 67% institutional). *Receiving aid:* Freshmen: 48% (357); all full-time undergraduates: 39% (1,198). *Average award:* Freshmen: $13,787; Undergraduates: $12,741. *Scholarships, grants, and awards:* Federal Pell, FSEOG, state, private, college/university gift aid from institutional funds, United Negro College Fund.

GIFT AID (NON-NEED-BASED) *Total amount:* $51,712,385 (98% institutional, 2% external sources). *Receiving aid:* Freshmen: 70% (518). Undergraduates: 60% (1,868). *Average award:* Freshmen: $18,399. Undergraduates: $18,074. *Scholarships, grants, and awards by category:* Academic interests/achievement: general academic interests/achievements. *Tuition waivers:* Full or partial for employees or children of employees. *ROTC:* Army cooperative, Air Force cooperative.

LOANS *Student loans:* $11,651,707 (56% need-based, 44% non-need-based). 69% of past graduating class borrowed through all loan programs. *Average indebtedness per student:* $38,402. *Average need-based loan:* Freshmen: $3364. Undergraduates: $4466. *Parent loans:* $6,309,367 (100% non-need-based). *Programs:* Federal Direct (Subsidized and Unsubsidized Stafford, PLUS), Perkins, state.

WORK-STUDY *Federal work-study:* 443 jobs averaging $1139.

APPLYING FOR FINANCIAL AID *Required financial aid forms:* FAFSA, CSS Financial Aid PROFILE. *Financial aid deadline (priority):* 2/15. *Notification date:* Continuous.

CONTACT Ms. Susan Gross, Director of Financial Aid, Stevens Institute of Technology, Castle Point on Hudson, Hoboken, NJ 07030, 201-216-8142 or toll-free 800-458-5323. *Fax:* 201-216-8050. *E-mail:* susan.gross@stevens.edu. *Website:* http://www.stevens.edu/.

STEVENSON UNIVERSITY
Stevenson, MD

Tuition & fees: $36,182	Average undergraduate aid package: $23,636

ABOUT THE INSTITUTION Independent, coed. *Awards:* certificates, bachelor's, and master's degrees. 34 undergraduate majors. *Total enrollment:* 3,876. Undergraduates: 3,397. Freshmen: 688. Federal methodology is used as a basis for awarding need-based institutional aid.

UNDERGRADUATE EXPENSES for 2018–2019 *Application fee:* $40. *Comprehensive fee:* $49,312 includes full-time tuition ($33,690), mandatory fees ($2492), and room and board ($13,130). *College room only:* $8492. Full-time tuition and fees vary according to course load and degree level. Room and board charges vary according to board plan and housing facility. *Part-time tuition:* $835 per credit hour. *Part-time fees:* $75 per term. Part-time tuition and fees vary according to degree level.

FRESHMAN FINANCIAL AID (Fall 2017, est.) 653 applied for aid; of those 91% were deemed to have need. 99% of freshmen with need received aid; of those 21% had need fully met. *Average percent of need met:* 69% (excluding resources awarded to replace EFC). *Average financial aid package:* $25,847 (excluding resources awarded to replace EFC). 12% of all full-time freshmen had no need and received non-need-based gift aid.

UNDERGRADUATE FINANCIAL AID (Fall 2017, est.) 2,544 applied for aid; of those 92% were deemed to have need. 100% of undergraduates with need received aid; of those 11% had need fully met. *Average percent of need met:* 66% (excluding resources awarded to replace EFC). *Average financial aid package:*

$23,636 (excluding resources awarded to replace EFC). 17% of all full-time undergraduates had no need and received non-need-based gift aid.

GIFT AID (NEED-BASED) *Total amount:* $45,652,221 (10% federal, 10% state, 78% institutional, 2% external sources). *Receiving aid:* Freshmen: 86% (593); all full-time undergraduates: 78% (2,290). *Average award:* Freshmen: $23,308; Undergraduates: $20,387. *Scholarships, grants, and awards:* Federal Pell, FSEOG, state, private, college/university gift aid from institutional funds, Federal Nursing.

GIFT AID (NON-NEED-BASED) *Total amount:* $9,999,632 (1% state, 95% institutional, 4% external sources). *Receiving aid:* Freshmen: 14% (96). Undergraduates: 9% (253). *Average award:* Freshmen: $18,600. Undergraduates: $14,939. *Scholarships, grants, and awards by category:* Academic interests/achievement: 2,509 awards ($36,656,093 total): general academic interests/achievements. Creative arts/performance: 17 awards ($60,250 total): art/fine arts. *Tuition waivers:* Full or partial for employees or children of employees. *ROTC:* Army cooperative, Air Force cooperative.

LOANS *Student loans:* $16,885,804 (72% need-based, 28% non-need-based). 76% of past graduating class borrowed through all loan programs. *Average indebtedness per student:* $37,000. *Average need-based loan:* Freshmen: $3214. Undergraduates: $4294. *Parent loans:* $18,213,120 (58% need-based, 42% non-need-based). *Programs:* Federal Direct (Subsidized and Unsubsidized Stafford, PLUS).

WORK-STUDY *Federal work-study:* Total amount: $312,576; 156 jobs averaging $2043.

APPLYING FOR FINANCIAL AID *Required financial aid form:* FAFSA. *Financial aid deadline (priority):* 2/15. *Notification date:* Continuous beginning 2/1. Students must reply by 5/1 or within 2 weeks of notification.

CONTACT Ms. Liesl M. Flanagan, Office of Financial Aid, Stevenson University, 100 Campus Circle, Owings Mills, MD 21117, 443-352-4366 or toll-free 877-468-6852 (in-state), 877-468-3852 (out-of-state). *Fax:* 443-352-4248. *E-mail:* blmiller@stevenson.edu. *Website:* http://www.stevenson.edu/.

STEVENS–THE INSTITUTE OF BUSINESS & ARTS
St. Louis, MO

CONTACT Financial Aid Office, Stevens–The Institute of Business & Arts, 1521 Washington Avenue, St. Louis, MO 63102, 314-421-0949 or toll-free 800-871-0949. *Website:* http://www.siba.edu/.

STILLMAN COLLEGE
Tuscaloosa, AL

ABOUT THE INSTITUTION Independent Presbyterian Church (U.S.A.), coed. 14 undergraduate majors.

GIFT AID (NEED-BASED) *Scholarships, grants, and awards:* Federal Pell, FSEOG, state, private, college/university gift aid from institutional funds, United Negro College Fund.

GIFT AID (NON-NEED-BASED) *Scholarships, grants, and awards by category:* Academic interests/achievement: education, general academic interests/achievements. Creative arts/performance: music. Special achievements/activities: leadership. Special characteristics: children of faculty/staff.

LOANS *Programs:* Federal Direct (Subsidized and Unsubsidized Stafford, PLUS), Perkins.

WORK-STUDY *Federal work-study:* 173 jobs averaging $1152. *State or other work-study/employment:* 173 part-time jobs averaging $1152.

APPLYING FOR FINANCIAL AID *Required financial aid forms:* FAFSA, state aid form.

CONTACT Christy G. Jackson, Financial Aid Counselor, Stillman College, PO Box 1430, Tuscaloosa, AL 35403, 205-366-8950 or toll-free 800-841-5722. *Fax:* 205-247-8107. *E-mail:* cjackson@stillman.edu. *Website:* http://www.stillman.edu/.

STOCKTON UNIVERSITY
Galloway, NJ

Tuition & fees (NJ res): $13,404	Average undergraduate aid package: $16,756

ABOUT THE INSTITUTION State-supported, coed. *Awards:* certificates, bachelor's, master's, and doctoral degrees. 31 undergraduate majors. *Total enrollment:* 9,216. Undergraduates: 8,275. Freshmen: 1,569. Federal methodology is used as a basis for awarding need-based institutional aid.

UNDERGRADUATE EXPENSES for 2017–2018 *Application fee:* $50. *Tuition, state resident:* full-time $8646; part-time $332.52 per credit. *Tuition, nonresident:* full-time $15,599; part-time $599.98 per credit. *Required fees:* full-time $4758; $182.99 per credit or $110 per term. Part-time tuition and fees vary according to course load. *College room and board:* $12,120; *Room only:* $8070. Room and board charges vary according to board plan and housing facility.

FRESHMAN FINANCIAL AID (Fall 2017, est.) 1,469 applied for aid; of those 80% were deemed to have need. 98% of freshmen with need received aid; of those 26% had need fully met. *Average percent of need met:* 74% (excluding resources awarded to replace EFC). *Average financial aid package:* $17,797 (excluding resources awarded to replace EFC). 6% of all full-time freshmen had no need and received non-need-based gift aid.

UNDERGRADUATE FINANCIAL AID (Fall 2017, est.) 6,838 applied for aid; of those 83% were deemed to have need. 98% of undergraduates with need received aid; of those 26% had need fully met. *Average percent of need met:* 67% (excluding resources awarded to replace EFC). *Average financial aid package:* $16,756 (excluding resources awarded to replace EFC). 7% of all full-time undergraduates had no need and received non-need-based gift aid.

GIFT AID (NEED-BASED) *Total amount:* $45,046,733 (35% federal, 30% state, 33% institutional, 2% external sources). *Receiving aid:* Freshmen: 56% (882); all full-time undergraduates: 46% (3,579). *Average award:* Freshmen: $9220; Undergraduates: $9059. *Scholarships, grants, and awards:* Federal Pell, FSEOG, state, private, college/university gift aid from institutional funds.

GIFT AID (NON-NEED-BASED) *Total amount:* $1,848,197 (5% state, 75% institutional, 20% external sources). *Receiving aid:* Freshmen: 19% (295). Undergraduates: 20% (1,561). *Average award:* Freshmen: $6134. Undergraduates: $6175. *Scholarships, grants, and awards by category:* Academic interests/achievement: area/ethnic studies, biological sciences, business, communication, computer science, education, general academic interests/achievements, health fields, home economics, humanities, mathematics, physical sciences, social sciences. *Creative arts/performance:* applied art and design, art/fine arts, creative writing, dance, journalism/publications, music, performing arts, theater/drama. *Special achievements/activities:* community service, general special achievements/activities, leadership. *Special characteristics:* adult students, children of faculty/staff, children of union members/company employees, ethnic background, first-generation college students, general special characteristics, international students, local/state students, members of minority groups, previous college experience. *Tuition waivers:* Full or partial for employees or children of employees, senior citizens. *ROTC:* Army cooperative.

LOANS *Student loans:* $53,337,863 (75% need-based, 25% non-need-based). 77% of past graduating class borrowed through all loan programs. *Average indebtedness per student:* $33,629. *Average need-based loan:* Freshmen: $3415. Undergraduates: $4467. *Parent loans:* $9,882,380 (73% need-based, 27% non-need-based). *Programs:* Federal Direct (Subsidized and Unsubsidized Stafford, PLUS), state.

WORK-STUDY *Federal work-study:* Total amount: $562,050; 260 jobs averaging $1780. *State or other work-study/employment:* Total amount: $1,673,110 (100% non-need-based). 911 part-time jobs averaging $1837.

APPLYING FOR FINANCIAL AID *Required financial aid forms:* FAFSA, state aid form. *Financial aid deadline (priority):* 3/1. *Notification date:* Continuous beginning 4/1. Students must reply within 2 weeks of notification.

CONTACT Mrs. Jeanne S. Lewis, Director of Financial Aid, Stockton University, 101 Vera King Farris Drive, Galloway, NJ 08205-9441, 609-652-4203. *Fax:* 609-626-5517. *E-mail:* jeanne.lewis@stockton.edu. *Website:* http://www.stockton.edu/.

STONEHILL COLLEGE
Easton, MA

Tuition & fees: $41,300	Average undergraduate aid package: $30,891

ABOUT THE INSTITUTION Independent Roman Catholic, coed. *Awards:* bachelor's and master's degrees. 45 undergraduate majors. *Total enrollment:* 2,498. Undergraduates: 2,498. Freshmen: 667. Institutional methodology is used as a basis for awarding need-based institutional aid.

UNDERGRADUATE EXPENSES for 2017–2018 *Application fee:* $60. *Comprehensive fee:* $57,060 includes full-time tuition ($41,300) and room and board ($15,760). *College room only:* $9657. Room and board charges vary according to board plan. *Part-time tuition:* $1377 per credit hour. Part-time tuition and fees vary according to course load. *Payment plan:* Tuition prepayment.

FRESHMAN FINANCIAL AID (Fall 2017, est.) 562 applied for aid; of those 72% were deemed to have need. 100% of freshmen with need received aid; of those 46% had need fully met. *Average percent of need met:* 88% (excluding resources awarded to replace EFC). *Average financial aid package:* $28,838 (excluding resources awarded to replace EFC). 37% of all full-time freshmen had no need and received non-need-based gift aid.

UNDERGRADUATE FINANCIAL AID (Fall 2017, est.) 1,967 applied for aid; of those 84% were deemed to have need. 100% of undergraduates with need received aid; of those 47% had need fully met. *Average percent of need met:* 90% (excluding resources awarded to replace EFC). *Average financial aid package:* $30,891 (excluding resources awarded to replace EFC). 29% of all full-time undergraduates had no need and received non-need-based gift aid.

GIFT AID (NEED-BASED) *Total amount:* $37,391,755 (6% federal, 2% state, 90% institutional, 2% external sources). *Receiving aid:* Freshmen: 60% (401); all full-time undergraduates: 65% (1,615). *Average award:* Freshmen: $23,901; Undergraduates: $25,209. *Scholarships, grants, and awards:* Federal Pell, FSEOG, state, private, college/university gift aid from institutional funds.

GIFT AID (NON-NEED-BASED) *Total amount:* $17,423,688 (1% federal, 98% institutional, 1% external sources). *Receiving aid:* Freshmen: 17% (111). Undergraduates: 17% (410). *Average award:* Freshmen: $19,471. Undergraduates: $18,442. *Scholarships, grants, and awards by category:* Academic interests/achievement: general academic interests/achievements. *Special characteristics:* children of faculty/staff, children of union members/company employees, relatives of clergy, siblings of current students, veterans, veterans' children. *Tuition waivers:* Full or partial for employees or children of employees. *ROTC:* Army.

LOANS *Student loans:* $17,824,786 (44% need-based, 56% non-need-based). 77% of past graduating class borrowed through all loan programs. *Average indebtedness per student:* $36,502. *Average need-based loan:* Freshmen: $3918. Undergraduates: $4781. *Parent loans:* $8,446,070 (17% need-based, 83% non-need-based). *Programs:* Federal Direct (Subsidized and Unsubsidized Stafford, PLUS), Perkins, state.

WORK-STUDY *Federal work-study:* Total amount: $785,944; jobs available. *State or other work-study/employment:* Total amount: $322,560 (2% need-based, 98% non-need-based). Part-time jobs available.

ATHLETIC AWARDS Total amount: $2,761,057 (28% need-based, 72% non-need-based).

APPLYING FOR FINANCIAL AID *Required financial aid forms:* FAFSA, CSS Financial Aid PROFILE, noncustodial (divorced/separated) parent's statement. *Financial aid deadline (priority):* 12/1. *Notification date:* 4/1. Students must reply by 5/1.

CONTACT Rhonda Nickley, Office Manager, Stonehill College, 320 Washington Street, Easton, MA 02357, 508-565-1088. *Fax:* 508-565-1426. *E-mail:* finaid@stonehill.edu. *Website:* http://www.stonehill.edu/.

STONY BROOK UNIVERSITY, STATE UNIVERSITY OF NEW YORK
Stony Brook, NY

Tuition & fees (NY res): $9257	Average undergraduate aid package: $13,292

ABOUT THE INSTITUTION State-supported, coed. *Awards:* certificates, bachelor's, master's, and doctoral degrees. 61 undergraduate majors. *Total enrollment:* 25,989. Undergraduates: 17,364. Freshmen: 3,167. Federal methodology is used as a basis for awarding need-based institutional aid.

UNDERGRADUATE EXPENSES for 2017–2018 *Application fee:* $50. *Tuition, state resident:* full-time $6670; part-time $278 per credit hour. *Tuition, nonresident:* full-time $24,180; part-time $1008 per credit hour. *Required fees:* full-time $2587; $128.25 per credit hour. Full-time tuition and fees vary according to course load and program. Part-time tuition and fees vary according to course load and program. *College room and board:* $13,446; *Room only:* $8402. Room and board charges vary according to board plan, housing facility, and location.

FRESHMAN FINANCIAL AID (Fall 2016) 2,211 applied for aid; of those 73% were deemed to have need. 99% of freshmen with need received aid; of those 16% had need fully met. *Average percent of need met:* 70% (excluding resources awarded to replace EFC). *Average financial aid package:* $14,202 (excluding resources awarded to replace EFC). 19% of all full-time freshmen had no need and received non-need-based gift aid.

UNDERGRADUATE FINANCIAL AID (Fall 2016) 10,468 applied for aid; of those 82% were deemed to have need. 98% of undergraduates with need received aid; of those 19% had need fully met. *Average percent of need met:* 67% (excluding resources awarded to replace EFC). *Average financial aid package:* $13,292 (excluding resources awarded to replace EFC). 10% of all full-time undergraduates had no need and received non-need-based gift aid.

GIFT AID (NEED-BASED) *Total amount:* $64,252,188 (41% federal, 34% state, 24% institutional, 1% external sources). *Receiving aid:* Freshmen: 51% (1,493); all full-time undergraduates: 46% (7,271). *Average award:* Freshmen: $10,601; Undergraduates: $8641. *Scholarships, grants, and awards:* Federal Pell, FSEOG, state, private, college/university gift aid from institutional funds.

GIFT AID (NON-NEED-BASED) *Total amount:* $12,394,896 (2% federal, 11% state, 76% institutional, 11% external sources). *Receiving aid:* Freshmen: 7% (200). Undergraduates: 3% (514). *Average award:* Freshmen: $5620. Undergraduates: $5378. *Scholarships, grants, and awards by category: Academic interests/achievement:* area/ethnic studies, biological sciences, business, computer science, engineering/technologies, English, foreign languages, general academic interests/achievements, health fields, international studies, mathematics, physical sciences, social sciences. *Creative arts/performance:* cinema/film/broadcasting, journalism/publications, music. *Special achievements/activities:* community service, leadership. *Special characteristics:* ethnic background, general special characteristics. *ROTC:* Army, Naval cooperative, Air Force cooperative.

LOANS *Student loans:* $83,866,940 (71% need-based, 29% non-need-based). 54% of past graduating class borrowed through all loan programs. *Average indebtedness per student:* $26,219. *Average need-based loan:* Freshmen: $3467. Undergraduates: $4763. *Parent loans:* $6,504,770 (44% need-based, 56% non-need-based). *Programs:* Federal Direct (Subsidized and Unsubsidized Stafford, PLUS), Perkins.

WORK-STUDY *Federal work-study:* 382 jobs averaging $2584. *State or other work-study/employment:* Total amount: $9,949,483 (35% need-based, 65% non-need-based). 2,687 part-time jobs averaging $3703.

ATHLETIC AWARDS Total amount: $6,514,484 (41% need-based, 59% non-need-based).

APPLYING FOR FINANCIAL AID *Required financial aid forms:* FAFSA, state aid form. *Financial aid deadline (priority):* 3/1. *Notification date:* Continuous beginning 4/1. Students must reply by 5/1.

CONTACT Office of Student Financial Aid and Scholarship Services, Stony Brook University, State University of New York, Administration Building, Room 180, Stony Brook, NY 11794, 631-632-6840. *Fax:* 631-632-9525. *E-mail:* finaid@stonybrook.edu. *Website:* http://www.stonybrook.edu/.

STRATFORD UNIVERSITY
Baltimore, MD

CONTACT Lesley Otterbein, Student Accounts Manager, Stratford University, 17 Commerce Street, Baltimore, MD 21202, 410-752-0490 or toll-free 800-624-9926 (in-state), 800-624-9926 Ext. 120 (out-of-state). *Fax:* 410-752-3730. *E-mail:* studentaccounts@stratford.edu. *Website:* http://www.stratford.edu/.

STRATFORD UNIVERSITY
Alexandria, VA

CONTACT Financial Aid Office, Stratford University, 2900 Eisenhower Avenue, Alexandria, VA 22314, 571-699-3200 or toll-free 800-444-0804. *Website:* http://www.stratford.edu/.

STRATFORD UNIVERSITY
Falls Church, VA

CONTACT Imane Babsiri, Student Account Manager, Stratford University, 7777 Leesburg Pike, Falls Church, VA 22043, 703-821-8570 Ext. 3401 or toll-free 800-444-0804. *E-mail:* ibabsiri@stratford.edu. *Website:* http://www.stratford.edu/.

STRATFORD UNIVERSITY
Glen Allen, VA

CONTACT Noshuo Rivers, Student Account Manager, Stratford University, 11104 West Broad Street, Glen Allen, VA 23060, 804-290-4231 or toll-free 877-373-5173. *E-mail:* studentaccounts@stratford.edu. *Website:* http://www.stratford.edu/.

STRATFORD UNIVERSITY
Newport News, VA

CONTACT Sheryl Kimberly, Student Accounts Manager, Stratford University, 836 J. Clyde Morris Boulevard, Newport News, VA 23601, 757-873-4235 or toll-free 855-873-4235. *E-mail:* skimberly@stratford.edu. *Website:* http://www.stratford.edu/.

STRATFORD UNIVERSITY
Virginia Beach, VA

CONTACT Financial Aid Office, Stratford University, 555 South Independence Boulevard, Virginia Beach, VA 23452, 757-497-4466 or toll-free 866-528-8363. *Website:* http://www.stratford.edu/.

STRATFORD UNIVERSITY
Woodbridge, VA

CONTACT Sherrese Whiting, Student Account Manager, Stratford University, 14349 Gideon Drive, Woodbridge, VA 22192, 703-897-1982 or toll-free 888-546-1250. *E-mail:* studentaccounts@stratford.edu. *Website:* http://www.stratford.edu/.

STRAYER UNIVERSITY–ALEXANDRIA CAMPUS

Alexandria, VA

CONTACT Financial Aid Office, Strayer University–Alexandria Campus, 2730 Eisenhower Avenue, Alexandria, VA 22314, 703-329-9100 or toll-free 888-311-0355. *Website:* http://www.strayer.edu/virginia/alexandria/.

STRAYER UNIVERSITY–ALLENTOWN CAMPUS

Center Valley, PA

CONTACT Financial Aid Office, Strayer University–Allentown Campus, 3800 Sierra Circle, Suite 300, Center Valley, PA 18034, 484-809-7770 or toll-free 888-311-0355. *Website:* http://www.strayer.edu/pennsylvania/allentown/.

STRAYER UNIVERSITY–ANNE ARUNDEL CAMPUS

Millersville, MD

CONTACT Financial Aid Office, Strayer University–Anne Arundel Campus, 1520 Jabez Run, Suite 100, Millersville, MD 21108, 410-923-4500 or toll-free 888-311-0355. *Website:* http://www.strayer.edu/maryland/anne-arundel/.

STRAYER UNIVERSITY–ARLINGTON CAMPUS

Arlington, VA

CONTACT Financial Aid Office, Strayer University–Arlington Campus, 2121 15th Street North, Arlington, VA 22201, 703-892-5100 or toll-free 888-311-0355. *Website:* http://www.strayer.edu/virginia/arlington/.

STRAYER UNIVERSITY–AUGUSTA CAMPUS

Augusta, GA

CONTACT Financial Aid Office, Strayer University–Augusta Campus, 1330 Augusta West Parkway, Augusta, GA 30909, 706-855-8233 or toll-free 888-311-0355. *Website:* http://www.strayer.edu/georgia/augusta/.

STRAYER UNIVERSITY–BAYMEADOWS CAMPUS

Jacksonville, FL

CONTACT Financial Aid Office, Strayer University–Baymeadows Campus, 8375 Dix Ellis Trail, Suite 200, Jacksonville, FL 32256, 904-538-1000 or toll-free 888-311-0355. *Website:* http://www.strayer.edu/florida/baymeadows/.

STRAYER UNIVERSITY–BIRMINGHAM CAMPUS

Birmingham, AL

CONTACT Financial Aid Office, Strayer University–Birmingham Campus, 3570 Grandview Parkway, Suite 200, Birmingham, AL 35243, 205-453-6300 or toll-free 888-311-0355. *Website:* http://www.strayer.edu/alabama/birmingham/.

STRAYER UNIVERSITY–CENTER CITY CAMPUS

Philadelphia, PA

CONTACT Financial Aid Office, Strayer University–Center City Campus, 1601 Cherry Street, Suite 100, Philadelphia, PA 19102, 267-256-0200 or toll-free 888-311-0355. *Website:* http://www.strayer.edu/pennsylvania/center-city/.

STRAYER UNIVERSITY–CHAMBLEE CAMPUS

Atlanta, GA

CONTACT Financial Aid Office, Strayer University–Chamblee Campus, 3355 Northeast Expressway, Suite 100, Atlanta, GA 30341, 770-454-9270 or toll-free 888-311-0355. *Website:* http://www.strayer.edu/georgia/chamblee/.

STRAYER UNIVERSITY–CHARLESTON CAMPUS

North Charleston, SC

CONTACT Financial Aid Office, Strayer University–Charleston Campus, 5010 Wetland Crossing, North Charleston, SC 29418, 843-746-5100 or toll-free 888-311-0355. *Website:* http://www.strayer.edu/south-carolina/charleston/.

STRAYER UNIVERSITY–CHERRY HILL CAMPUS

Cherry Hill, NJ

CONTACT Financial Aid Office, Strayer University–Cherry Hill Campus, 2201 Route 38, Suite 100, Cherry Hill, NJ 08002, 856-482-4200 or toll-free 888-311-0355. *Website:* http://www.strayer.edu/new-jersey/cherry-hill/.

STRAYER UNIVERSITY–CHESAPEAKE CAMPUS

Chesapeake, VA

CONTACT Financial Aid Office, Strayer University–Chesapeake Campus, 676 Independence Parkway, Suite 300, Chesapeake, VA 23320, 757-382-9900 or toll-free 888-311-0355. *Website:* http://www.strayer.edu/virginia/chesapeake/.

STRAYER UNIVERSITY–CHESTERFIELD CAMPUS
Midlothian, VA

CONTACT Financial Aid Office, Strayer University–Chesterfield Campus, 15521 Midlothian Turnpike, Suite 401, Midlothian, VA 23113, 804-794-2033 or toll-free 888-311-0355.
Website: http://www.strayer.edu/virginia/chesterfield/.

STRAYER UNIVERSITY–CHRISTIANA CAMPUS
Newark, DE

CONTACT Financial Aid Office, Strayer University–Christiana Campus, 240 Continental Drive, Suite 108, Newark, DE 19713, 302-292-6100 or toll-free 888-311-0355.
Website: http://www.strayer.edu/delaware/christiana/.

STRAYER UNIVERSITY–COBB COUNTY CAMPUS
Atlanta, GA

CONTACT Financial Aid Office, Strayer University–Cobb County Campus, 3101 Towercreek Parkway, SE, Suite 700, Atlanta, GA 30339, 770-612-2170 or toll-free 888-311-0355.
Website: http://www.strayer.edu/georgia/cobb-county/.

STRAYER UNIVERSITY–COLUMBIA CAMPUS
Columbia, SC

CONTACT Financial Aid Office, Strayer University–Columbia Campus, 200 Center Point Circle, Suite 300, Columbia, SC 29210, 803-750-2500 or toll-free 888-311-0355.
Website: http://www.strayer.edu/south-carolina/columbia/.

STRAYER UNIVERSITY–DELAWARE COUNTY CAMPUS
Springfield, PA

CONTACT Financial Aid Office, Strayer University–Delaware County Campus, 760 West Sproul Road, Suite 200, Springfield, PA 19064, 610-604-7700 or toll-free 888-311-0355.
Website: http://www.strayer.edu/pennsylvania/delaware-county/.

STRAYER UNIVERSITY–DOUGLASVILLE CAMPUS
Douglasville, GA

CONTACT Financial Aid Office, Strayer University–Douglasville Campus, 4655 Timber Ridge Drive, Douglasville, GA 30135, 678-715-2200 or toll-free 888-311-0355.
Website: http://www.strayer.edu/georgia/douglasville/.

STRAYER UNIVERSITY–FORT LAUDERDALE CAMPUS
Fort Lauderdale, FL

CONTACT Financial Aid Office, Strayer University–Fort Lauderdale Campus, 2307 West Broward Boulevard, Suite 100, Fort Lauderdale, FL 33312, 954-745-6960 or toll-free 888-311-0355.
Website: http://www.strayer.edu/florida/fort-lauderdale/.

STRAYER UNIVERSITY–FREDERICKSBURG CAMPUS
Fredericksburg, VA

CONTACT Financial Aid Office, Strayer University–Fredericksburg Campus, 150 Riverside Parkway, Suite 100, Fredericksburg, VA 22406, 540-374-4300 or toll-free 888-311-0355.
Website: http://www.strayer.edu/virginia/fredericksburg/.

STRAYER UNIVERSITY–GREENSBORO CAMPUS
Greensboro, NC

CONTACT Financial Aid Office, Strayer University–Greensboro Campus, 4900 Koger Boulevard, Suite 400, Greensboro, NC 27407, 336-315-7800 or toll-free 888-311-0355.
Website: http://www.strayer.edu/north-carolina/greensboro/.

STRAYER UNIVERSITY–GREENVILLE CAMPUS
Greenville, SC

CONTACT Financial Aid Office, Strayer University–Greenville Campus, 555 North Pleasantburg Drive, Suite 300, Greenville, SC 29607, 864-250-7000 or toll-free 888-311-0355.
Website: http://www.strayer.edu/south-carolina/greenville/.

STRAYER UNIVERSITY–HENRICO CAMPUS
Glen Allen, VA

CONTACT Financial Aid Office, Strayer University–Henrico Campus, 11501 Nuckols Road, Glen Allen, VA 23059, 804-527-1000 or toll-free 888-311-0355.
Website: http://www.strayer.edu/virginia/henrico/.

STRAYER UNIVERSITY–HUNTERSVILLE CAMPUS
Huntersville, NC

CONTACT Financial Aid Office, Strayer University–Huntersville Campus, 13620 Reese Boulevard, Suite 310, Huntersville, NC 28078, 704-379-6800 or toll-free 888-311-0355.
Website: http://www.strayer.edu/north-carolina/huntersville/.

STRAYER UNIVERSITY–HUNTSVILLE CAMPUS
Huntsville, AL

CONTACT Financial Aid Office, Strayer University–Huntsville Campus, 4955 Corporate Drive, NW, Suite 200, Huntsville, AL 35805, 256-665-9800 or toll-free 888-311-0355.
Website: http://www.strayer.edu/alabama/huntsville/.

STRAYER UNIVERSITY–IRVING CAMPUS
Irving, TX

CONTACT Financial Aid Office, Strayer University–Irving Campus, 7701 Las Colinas Ridge, Suite 450, Irving, TX 75063, 214-429-3900 or toll-free 888-311-0355.
Website: http://www.strayer.edu/texas/irving/.

STRAYER UNIVERSITY–JACKSON CAMPUS
Jackson, MS

CONTACT Financial Aid Office, Strayer University–Jackson Campus, 460 Briarwood Drive, Suite 200, Jackson, MS 39206, 601-718-5900 or toll-free 888-311-0355.
Website: http://www.strayer.edu/mississippi/jackson/.

STRAYER UNIVERSITY–KNOXVILLE CAMPUS
Knoxville, TN

CONTACT Financial Aid Office, Strayer University–Knoxville Campus, 10118 Parkside Drive, Suite 200, Knoxville, TN 37922, 865-288-6000 or toll-free 888-311-0355.
Website: http://www.strayer.edu/tennessee/knoxville/.

STRAYER UNIVERSITY–LITHONIA CAMPUS
Lithonia, GA

CONTACT Financial Aid Office, Strayer University–Lithonia Campus, 3120 Stonecrest Boulevard, Suite 200, Lithonia, GA 30038, 678-323-7700 or toll-free 888-311-0355.
Website: http://www.strayer.edu/georgia/lithonia/.

STRAYER UNIVERSITY–LITTLE ROCK CAMPUS
Little Rock, AR

CONTACT Financial Aid Office, Strayer University–Little Rock Campus, 10825 Financial Centre Parkway, Suite 400, Little Rock, AR 72211, 501-708-0600 or toll-free 888-311-0355.
Website: http://www.strayer.edu/arkansas/little-rock/.

STRAYER UNIVERSITY–LOUDOUN CAMPUS
Ashburn, VA

CONTACT Financial Aid Office, Strayer University–Loudoun Campus, 45150 Russell Branch Parkway, Suite 200, Ashburn, VA 20147, 703-729-8800 or toll-free 888-311-0355.
Website: http://www.strayer.edu/virginia/loudoun/.

STRAYER UNIVERSITY–LOWER BUCKS COUNTY CAMPUS
Trevose, PA

CONTACT Financial Aid Office, Strayer University–Lower Bucks County Campus, 3800 Horizon Boulevard, Suite 100, Trevose, PA 19053, 215-354-2700 or toll-free 888-311-0355.
Website: http://www.strayer.edu/pennsylvania/lower-bucks-county/.

STRAYER UNIVERSITY–MAITLAND CAMPUS
Maitland, FL

CONTACT Financial Aid Office, Strayer University–Maitland Campus, 901 North Lake Destiny Road, Suite 370, Maitland, FL 32751, 407-618-5900 or toll-free 888-311-0355.
Website: http://www.strayer.edu/florida/maitland/.

STRAYER UNIVERSITY–MANASSAS CAMPUS
Manassas, VA

CONTACT Financial Aid Office, Strayer University–Manassas Campus, 9990 Battleview Parkway, Manassas, VA 20109, 703-330-8400 or toll-free 888-311-0355.
Website: http://www.strayer.edu/virginia/manassas/.

STRAYER UNIVERSITY–MIRAMAR CAMPUS
Hollywood, FL

CONTACT Financial Aid Office, Strayer University–Miramar Campus, 15620 Southwest 29th Street, Hollywood, FL 33027, 954-378-2400 or toll-free 888-311-0355.
Website: http://www.strayer.edu/florida/miramar/.

STRAYER UNIVERSITY–MORRISVILLE CAMPUS
Morrisville, NC

CONTACT Financial Aid Office, Strayer University–Morrisville Campus, 4 Copley Parkway, Morrisville, NC 27560, 919-466-4400 or toll-free 888-311-0355.
Website: http://www.strayer.edu/north-carolina/morrisville.

STRAYER UNIVERSITY–MORROW CAMPUS

Morrow, GA

CONTACT Financial Aid Office, Strayer University–Morrow Campus, 3000 Corporate Center Drive, Suite 100, Morrow, GA 30260, 678-422-4100 or toll-free 888-311-0355.
Website: http://www.strayer.edu/georgia/morrow/.

STRAYER UNIVERSITY–NASHVILLE CAMPUS

Nashville, TN

CONTACT Financial Aid Office, Strayer University–Nashville Campus, 1809 Dabbs Avenue, Nashville, TN 37210, 615-871-2260 or toll-free 888-311-0355.
Website: http://www.strayer.edu/tennessee/nashville/.

STRAYER UNIVERSITY–NEWPORT NEWS CAMPUS

Newport News, VA

CONTACT Financial Aid Office, Strayer University–Newport News Campus, 99 Old Oyster Point Road, Unit 1, Newport News, VA 23602, 757-881-5100 or toll-free 888-311-0355.
Website: http://www.strayer.edu/virginia/newport-news/.

STRAYER UNIVERSITY–NORTH AUSTIN CAMPUS

Austin, TX

CONTACT Financial Aid Office, Strayer University–North Austin Campus, 8501 North Mopac Expressway, Suite 100, Austin, TX 78759, 512-568-3300 or toll-free 888-311-0355.
Website: http://www.strayer.edu/texas/north-austin/.

STRAYER UNIVERSITY–NORTH CHARLOTTE CAMPUS

Concord, NC

CONTACT Financial Aid Office, Strayer University–North Charlotte Campus, 7870 Commons Park Circle NW, Concord, NC 28027, 704-886-6500 or toll-free 888-311-0355.
Website: http://www.strayer.edu/north-carolina/north-charlotte/.

STRAYER UNIVERSITY–NORTH DALLAS CAMPUS

Dallas, TX

CONTACT Financial Aid Office, Strayer University–North Dallas Campus, 8111 LBJ Freeway, Suite 1100, Dallas, TX 75251, 972-773-8300.
Website: http://www.strayer.edu/texas/north-dallas.

STRAYER UNIVERSITY–NORTH RALEIGH CAMPUS

Raleigh, NC

CONTACT Financial Aid Office, Strayer University–North Raleigh Campus, 8701 Wadford Drive, Raleigh, NC 27616, 919-301-6500 or toll-free 888-311-0355.
Website: http://www.strayer.edu/north-carolina/north-raleigh/.

STRAYER UNIVERSITY–NORTHWEST HOUSTON CAMPUS

Houston, TX

CONTACT Financial Aid Office, Strayer University–Northwest Houston Campus, 10940 West Sam Houston Parkway North, Suite 200, Houston, TX 77064, 281-949-1800 or toll-free 888-311-0355.
Website: http://www.strayer.edu/texas/northwest-houston/.

STRAYER UNIVERSITY–ORLANDO EAST CAMPUS

Orlando, FL

CONTACT Financial Aid Office, Strayer University–Orlando East Campus, 2200 North Alafaya Trail, Suite 500, Orlando, FL 32826, 407-926-2000 or toll-free 888-311-0355.
Website: http://www.strayer.edu/florida/orlando-east/.

STRAYER UNIVERSITY–OWINGS MILLS CAMPUS

Owings Mills, MD

CONTACT Financial Aid Office, Strayer University–Owings Mills Campus, 500 Redland Court, Suite 100, Owings Mills, MD 21117, 443-394-3339 or toll-free 888-311-0355.
Website: http://www.strayer.edu/maryland/owings-mills/.

STRAYER UNIVERSITY–PALM BEACH GARDENS CAMPUS

West Palm Beach, FL

CONTACT Financial Aid Office, Strayer University–Palm Beach Gardens Campus, 11025 RCA Center Drive, Suite 200, West Palm Beach, FL 33410, 561-904-3000 or toll-free 888-311-0355.
Website: http://www.strayer.edu/florida/palm-beach-gardens/.

STRAYER UNIVERSITY–PISCATAWAY CAMPUS

Piscataway, NJ

CONTACT Financial Aid Office, Strayer University–Piscataway Campus, 242 Old New Brunswick Road, Suite 220, Piscataway, NJ 08854, 732-743-3800 or toll-free 888-311-0355.
Website: http://www.strayer.edu/new-jersey/piscataway/.

STRAYER UNIVERSITY–PRINCE GEORGE'S CAMPUS
Suitland, MD

CONTACT Financial Aid Office, Strayer University–Prince George's Campus, 5110 Auth Way, Suitland, MD 20746, 301-505-3300 or toll-free 888-311-0355.
Website: http://www.strayer.edu/maryland/prince-georges/.

STRAYER UNIVERSITY–ROCKVILLE CAMPUS
Rockville, MD

CONTACT Financial Aid Office, Strayer University–Rockville Campus, 1803 Research Boulevard, Suite 110, Rockville, MD 20850, 301-838-4700 or toll-free 888-311-0355.
Website: http://www.strayer.edu/maryland/rockville/.

STRAYER UNIVERSITY–ROSWELL CAMPUS
Roswell, GA

CONTACT Financial Aid Office, Strayer University–Roswell Campus, 100 Mansell Court East, Suite 100, Roswell, GA 30076, 770-650-3000 or toll-free 888-311-0355.
Website: http://www.strayer.edu/georgia/roswell/.

STRAYER UNIVERSITY–SAN ANTONIO CAMPUS
San Antonio, TX

CONTACT Financial Aid Office, Strayer University–San Antonio Campus, 40 NE Loop 410, Suite 500, San Antonio, TX 78216, 210-202-3700.
Website: http://www.strayer.edu/texas/san-antonio.

STRAYER UNIVERSITY–SAND LAKE CAMPUS
Orlando, FL

CONTACT Financial Aid Office, Strayer University–Sand Lake Campus, 8541 South Park Circle, Building 900, Orlando, FL 32819, 407-264-9400 or toll-free 888-311-0355.
Website: http://www.strayer.edu/florida/sand-lake/.

STRAYER UNIVERSITY–SAVANNAH CAMPUS
Savannah, GA

CONTACT Financial Aid Office, Strayer University–Savannah Campus, 20 Martin Court, Savannah, GA 31419, 912-921-2900 or toll-free 888-311-0355.
Website: http://www.strayer.edu/georgia/savannah/.

STRAYER UNIVERSITY–SHELBY CAMPUS
Memphis, TN

CONTACT Financial Aid Office, Strayer University–Shelby Campus, 7275 Appling Farms Parkway, Memphis, TN 38133, 901-251-7100 or toll-free 888-311-0355.
Website: http://www.strayer.edu/tennessee/shelby/.

STRAYER UNIVERSITY–SOUTH CHARLOTTE CAMPUS
Charlotte, NC

CONTACT Financial Aid Office, Strayer University–South Charlotte Campus, 9101 Kings Parade Boulevard, Suite 200, Charlotte, NC 28273, 704-499-9200 or toll-free 888-311-0355.
Website: http://www.strayer.edu/north-carolina/south-charlotte/.

STRAYER UNIVERSITY–SOUTH RALEIGH CAMPUS
Raleigh, NC

CONTACT Financial Aid Office, Strayer University–South Raleigh Campus, 3421 Olympia Drive, Raleigh, NC 27603, 919-890-7500 or toll-free 888-311-0355.
Website: http://www.strayer.edu/north-carolina/south-raleigh/.

STRAYER UNIVERSITY–STAFFORD CAMPUS
Stafford, TX

CONTACT Financial Aid Office, Strayer University–Stafford Campus, 12603 Southwest Freeway, Suite 400, Stafford, TX 77477, 281-201-3800.
Website: http://www.strayer.edu/texas/stafford.

STRAYER UNIVERSITY–TAKOMA PARK CAMPUS
Washington, DC

CONTACT Financial Aid Office, Strayer University–Takoma Park Campus, 6830 Laurel Street, NW, Washington, DC 20012, 202-722-8100 or toll-free 888-311-0355.
Website: http://www.strayer.edu/district-columbia/takoma-park/.

STRAYER UNIVERSITY–TAMPA EAST CAMPUS
Tampa, FL

CONTACT Financial Aid Office, Strayer University–Tampa East Campus, 5650 Breckenridge Park Drive, Suite 300, Tampa, FL 33610, 813-663-0100 or toll-free 888-311-0355.
Website: http://www.strayer.edu/florida/tampa-east/.

STRAYER UNIVERSITY–TAMPA WESTSHORE CAMPUS

Tampa, FL

CONTACT Financial Aid Office, Strayer University–Tampa Westshore Campus, 4902 Eisenhower Boulevard, Suite 100, Tampa, FL 33634, 813-882-0100 or toll-free 888-311-0355.
Website: http://www.strayer.edu/florida/tampa-westshore/.

STRAYER UNIVERSITY–TEAYS VALLEY CAMPUS

Scott Depot, WV

CONTACT Financial Aid Office, Strayer University–Teays Valley Campus, 3 Corporate Center Drive, Scott Depot, WV 25560, 304-760-1700 or toll-free 888-311-0355.
Website: http://www.strayer.edu/west-virginia/teays-valley/.

STRAYER UNIVERSITY–THOUSAND OAKS CAMPUS

Memphis, TN

CONTACT Financial Aid Office, Strayer University–Thousand Oaks Campus, 2620 Thousand Oaks Boulevard, Suite 1100, Memphis, TN 38118, 901-370-5200 or toll-free 888-311-0355.
Website: http://www.strayer.edu/tennessee/thousand-oaks/.

STRAYER UNIVERSITY–VIRGINIA BEACH CAMPUS

Virginia Beach, VA

CONTACT Financial Aid Office, Strayer University–Virginia Beach Campus, 249 Central Park Avenue, Suite 350, Virginia Beach, VA 23462, 757-493-6000 or toll-free 888-311-0355.
Website: http://www.strayer.edu/virginia/virginia-beach/.

STRAYER UNIVERSITY–WARRENDALE CAMPUS

Warrendale, PA

CONTACT Financial Aid Office, Strayer University–Warrendale Campus, 802 Warrendale Village Drive, Warrendale, PA 15086, 724-799-2900 or toll-free 888-311-0355.
Website: http://www.strayer.edu/pennsylvania/warrendale/.

STRAYER UNIVERSITY–WASHINGTON CAMPUS

Washington, DC

CONTACT Financial Aid Office, Strayer University–Washington Campus, 1133 15th Street, NW, Washington, DC 20025, 202-408-2400 or toll-free 888-311-0355.
Website: http://www.strayer.edu/district-columbia/washington/.

STRAYER UNIVERSITY–WHITE MARSH CAMPUS

Baltimore, MD

CONTACT Financial Aid Office, Strayer University–White Marsh Campus, 9920 Franklin Square Drive, Suite 200, Baltimore, MD 21236, 410-238-9000 or toll-free 888-311-0355.
Website: http://www.strayer.edu/maryland/white-marsh/.

STRAYER UNIVERSITY–WILLINGBORO CAMPUS

Willingboro, NJ

CONTACT Financial Aid Office, Strayer University–Willingboro Campus, 300 Willingboro Parkway, Willingboro Town Center, Suite 125, Willingboro, NJ 08046, 609-835-6000 or toll-free 888-311-0355.
Website: http://www.strayer.edu/new-jersey/willingboro/.

STRAYER UNIVERSITY–WOODBRIDGE CAMPUS

Woodbridge, VA

CONTACT Financial Aid Office, Strayer University–Woodbridge Campus, 13385 Minnieville Road, Woodbridge, VA 22192, 703-878-2800 or toll-free 888-311-0355.
Website: http://www.strayer.edu/virginia/woodbridge/.

STUDIO SCHOOL

Los Angeles, CA

CONTACT Financial Aid Office, Studio School, 1201 West 5th Street, Los Angeles, CA 90017.
Website: http://www.studioschool.org/.

SUFFOLK UNIVERSITY

Boston, MA

Tuition & fees: $38,566	Average undergraduate aid package: $31,688

ABOUT THE INSTITUTION Independent, coed. *Awards:* certificates, diplomas, associate, bachelor's, master's, and doctoral degrees (doctoral degree in law). 54 undergraduate majors. *Total enrollment:* 7,288. Undergraduates: 5,117. Freshmen: 1,087. Federal methodology is used as a basis for awarding need-based institutional aid.
UNDERGRADUATE EXPENSES for 2018–2019 *Application fee:* $50. *Tuition:* full-time $38,420; part-time $1130 per credit hour. *Required fees:* full-time $146; $19 per credit hour. Full-time tuition and fees vary according to course level and reciprocity agreements. Part-time tuition and fees vary according to course level, course load, and reciprocity agreements. Room and board charges vary according to board plan and housing facility.
FRESHMAN FINANCIAL AID (Fall 2017, est.) 802 applied for aid; of those 100% were deemed to have need. 97% of freshmen with need received aid; of those 33% had need fully met. *Average percent of need met:* 80% (excluding resources awarded to replace EFC). *Average financial aid package:* $31,817 (excluding resources awarded to replace EFC). 23% of all full-time freshmen had no need and received non-need-based gift aid.
UNDERGRADUATE FINANCIAL AID (Fall 2017, est.) 3,006 applied for aid; of those 100% were deemed to have need. 98% of undergraduates with need received aid; of those 30% had need fully met. *Average percent of need met:* 78% (excluding resources awarded to replace EFC). *Average financial aid package:*

$31,688 (excluding resources awarded to replace EFC). 27% of all full-time undergraduates had no need and received non-need-based gift aid.

GIFT AID (NEED-BASED) *Total amount:* $20,481,880 (33% federal, 8% state, 55% institutional, 4% external sources). *Receiving aid:* Freshmen: 64% (695); all full-time undergraduates: 49% (2,362). *Average award:* Freshmen: $7993; Undergraduates: $8150. *Scholarships, grants, and awards:* Federal Pell, FSEOG, state, private, college/university gift aid from institutional funds.

GIFT AID (NON-NEED-BASED) *Total amount:* $59,411,117 (100% institutional). *Receiving aid:* Freshmen: 60% (653). Undergraduates: 52% (2,499). *Average award:* Freshmen: $13,343. Undergraduates: $13,994. *Scholarships, grants, and awards by category:* Academic interests/achievement: 5,222 awards ($58,103,370 total): business, engineering/technologies, foreign languages, general academic interests/achievements, mathematics. *Creative arts/performance:* 2 awards ($3310 total): general creative arts/performance, journalism/publications. *Special achievements/activities:* 818 awards ($770,532 total): community service, general special achievements/activities, leadership. *Special characteristics:* 167 awards ($1,390,771 total): children and siblings of alumni, children of faculty/staff, general special characteristics, siblings of current students, veterans. *Tuition waivers:* Full or partial for children of alumni, employees or children of employees, senior citizens. **ROTC:** Army cooperative.

LOANS *Student loans:* $28,108,287 (41% need-based, 59% non-need-based). 74% of past graduating class borrowed through all loan programs. *Average indebtedness per student:* $28,859. *Average need-based loan:* Freshmen: $3660. Undergraduates: $4446. *Parent loans:* $9,457,263 (100% need-based). *Programs:* Federal Direct (Subsidized and Unsubsidized Stafford, PLUS), Perkins, state, college/university.

WORK-STUDY *Federal work-study:* Total amount: $1,958,950; 814 jobs averaging $2356. *State or other work-study/employment:* Total amount: $1,890,003 (100% non-need-based). 433 part-time jobs averaging $4056.

APPLYING FOR FINANCIAL AID *Required financial aid form:* FAFSA. *Financial aid deadline:* 6/30 (priority: 3/1). *Notification date:* Continuous beginning 2/5. Students must reply by 5/1 or within 2 weeks of notification.

CONTACT Ms. Jennifer H. Ricciardi, Director of Student Financial Services, Suffolk University, 8 Ashburton Place, Boston, MA 02108, 617-573-8470 or toll-free 800-6-SUFFOLK. *Fax:* 617-720-3579. *E-mail:* finaid@suffolk.edu. *Website:* http://www.suffolk.edu/.

SULLIVAN UNIVERSITY
Louisville, KY

CONTACT Charlene Geiser, Financial Planning Office, Sullivan University, 3101 Bardstown Road, Louisville, KY 40205, 502-456-6504 Ext. 311 or toll-free 800-844-1354. *Fax:* 502-456-0040. *E-mail:* cgeiser@sullivan.edu. *Website:* http://www.sullivan.edu/.

SUL ROSS STATE UNIVERSITY
Alpine, TX

CONTACT Mickey Corbett, Director of Financial Aid, Sul Ross State University, Box C-2, Lawrence Hall, Alpine, TX 79832, 432-837-8055 or toll-free 888-722-7778. *Fax:* 432-837-8411. *E-mail:* fa@sulross.edu. *Website:* http://www.sulross.edu/.

SUM BIBLE COLLEGE & THEOLOGICAL SEMINARY
Oakland, CA

CONTACT Financial Aid Office, SUM Bible College & Theological Seminary, 735 105th Avenue, Oakland, CA 94603, 510-567-6174 or toll-free 888-567-6174. *Website:* http://www.sum.edu/.

SUSQUEHANNA UNIVERSITY
Selinsgrove, PA

Tuition & fees: $45,470	Average undergraduate aid package: $36,552

ABOUT THE INSTITUTION Independent Evangelical Lutheran Church in America, coed. *Awards:* bachelor's degrees (also offers evening associate degree program limited to local adult students). 53 undergraduate majors. *Total enrollment:* 2,266. Undergraduates: 2,267. Freshmen: 634. Federal methodology is used as a basis for awarding need-based institutional aid.

UNDERGRADUATE EXPENSES for 2017–2018 *Comprehensive fee:* $57,560 includes full-time tuition ($44,890), mandatory fees ($580), and room and board ($12,090). *College room only:* $6320. Room and board charges vary according to board plan. *Part-time tuition:* $1430 per credit hour. *Payment plan:* Tuition prepayment.

FRESHMAN FINANCIAL AID (Fall 2017, est.) 594 applied for aid; of those 91% were deemed to have need. 100% of freshmen with need received aid; of those 23% had need fully met. *Average percent of need met:* 85% (excluding resources awarded to replace EFC). *Average financial aid package:* $37,399 (excluding resources awarded to replace EFC). 15% of all full-time freshmen had no need and received non-need-based gift aid.

UNDERGRADUATE FINANCIAL AID (Fall 2017, est.) 1,961 applied for aid; of those 92% were deemed to have need. 100% of undergraduates with need received aid; of those 18% had need fully met. *Average percent of need met:* 82% (excluding resources awarded to replace EFC). *Average financial aid package:* $36,552 (excluding resources awarded to replace EFC). 20% of all full-time undergraduates had no need and received non-need-based gift aid.

GIFT AID (NEED-BASED) *Total amount:* $55,381,519 (6% federal, 4% state, 88% institutional, 2% external sources). *Receiving aid:* Freshmen: 85% (539); all full-time undergraduates: 79% (1,795). *Average award:* Freshmen: $33,781; Undergraduates: $31,799. *Scholarships, grants, and awards:* Federal Pell, FSEOG, state, private, college/university gift aid from institutional funds.

GIFT AID (NON-NEED-BASED) *Total amount:* $13,276,273 (2% federal, 92% institutional, 6% external sources). *Receiving aid:* Freshmen: 16% (102). Undergraduates: 11% (260). *Average award:* Freshmen: $25,557. Undergraduates: $22,119. *Scholarships, grants, and awards by category:* Academic interests/achievement: business, education, general academic interests/achievements. *Creative arts/performance:* creative writing, music, theater/drama. *Special achievements/activities:* general special achievements/activities, leadership. *Special characteristics:* children and siblings of alumni, children of faculty/staff, relatives of clergy, veterans. *Tuition waivers:* Full or partial for employees or children of employees. **ROTC:** Army cooperative.

LOANS *Student loans:* $17,957,761 (67% need-based, 33% non-need-based). 82% of past graduating class borrowed through all loan programs. *Average indebtedness per student:* $33,757. *Average need-based loan:* Freshmen: $3197. Undergraduates: $4314. *Parent loans:* $6,952,898 (48% need-based, 52% non-need-based). *Programs:* Federal Direct (Subsidized and Unsubsidized Stafford, PLUS), college/university.

WORK-STUDY *Federal work-study:* Total amount: $1,824,183; 1,265 jobs averaging $2023. *State or other work-study/employment:* Total amount: $648,476 (49% need-based, 51% non-need-based). Part-time jobs available.

APPLYING FOR FINANCIAL AID *Required financial aid forms:* FAFSA, federal income tax form(s). *Financial aid deadline:* 2/1 (priority: 11/1). *Notification date:* Continuous beginning 12/1. Students must reply by 5/1.

CONTACT Ms. Erin M. Wolfe, Director of Student Financial Services, Susquehanna University, 514 University Avenue, Selinsgrove, PA 17870, 570-372-4450 or toll-free 800-326-9672. *Fax:* 570-372-2722. *E-mail:* wolfeerin@susqu.edu. *Website:* http://www.susqu.edu/.

SWARTHMORE COLLEGE
Swarthmore, PA

Tuition & fees: $50,822	Average undergraduate aid package: $50,361

ABOUT THE INSTITUTION Independent, coed. *Awards:* bachelor's degrees. 48 undergraduate majors. *Total enrollment:* 1,620. Undergraduates: 1,620. Freshmen: 415. Institutional methodology is used as a basis for awarding need-based institutional aid.

UNDERGRADUATE EXPENSES for 2017–2018 *Comprehensive fee:* $65,774 includes full-time tuition ($50,424), mandatory fees ($398), and room and board ($14,952). *College room only:* $7670. Room and board charges vary according to board plan.

FRESHMAN FINANCIAL AID (Fall 2017, est.) 263 applied for aid; of those 83% were deemed to have need. 100% of freshmen with need received aid; of those 100% had need fully met. *Average percent of need met:* 100% (excluding resources awarded to replace EFC). *Average financial aid package:* $52,104 (excluding resources awarded to replace EFC). 1% of all full-time freshmen had no need and received non-need-based gift aid.

UNDERGRADUATE FINANCIAL AID (Fall 2017, est.) 981 applied for aid; of those 92% were deemed to have need. 100% of undergraduates with need received aid; of those 100% had need fully met. *Average percent of need met:* 100% (excluding resources awarded to replace EFC). *Average financial aid package:* $50,361 (excluding resources awarded to replace EFC). 1% of all full-time undergraduates had no need and received non-need-based gift aid.

GIFT AID (NEED-BASED) *Total amount:* $43,787,569 (4% federal, 94% institutional, 2% external sources). *Receiving aid:* Freshmen: 56% (219); all full-time undergraduates: 56% (905). *Average award:* Freshmen: $50,505; Undergraduates: $48,661. *Scholarships, grants, and awards:* Federal Pell, FSEOG, state, private, college/university gift aid from institutional funds.

GIFT AID (NON-NEED-BASED) *Total amount:* $917,148 (88% institutional, 12% external sources). *Average award:* Freshmen: $50,424. Undergraduates: $50,424. *Scholarships, grants, and awards by category: Special characteristics:* 16 awards ($806,984 total): local/state students. *ROTC:* Army cooperative, Naval cooperative, Air Force cooperative.

LOANS *Student loans:* $1,517,920 (100% non-need-based). 27% of past graduating class borrowed through all loan programs. *Average indebtedness per student:* $20,209. *Parent loans:* $1,991,794 (100% non-need-based). *Programs:* Federal Direct (Subsidized and Unsubsidized Stafford, PLUS), college/university.

WORK-STUDY *Federal work-study:* Total amount: $965,555; 781 jobs averaging $1970. *State or other work-study/employment:* Total amount: $905,146 (89% need-based, 11% non-need-based). Part-time jobs available.

APPLYING FOR FINANCIAL AID *Required financial aid forms:* FAFSA, CSS Financial Aid PROFILE, noncustodial (divorced/separated) parent's statement, federal income tax form(s), W-2 forms. *Financial aid deadline:* 1/1. *Notification date:* 4/1. Students must reply by 5/1.

CONTACT Varo L. Duffins, Director of Financial Aid, Swarthmore College, 500 College Avenue, Swarthmore, PA 19081-1397, 610-328-8358 or toll-free 800-667-3110. *Fax:* 610-690-5751. *E-mail:* finaid@swarthmore.edu. *Website:* http://www.swarthmore.edu/.

SWEDISH INSTITUTE, COLLEGE OF HEALTH SCIENCES
New York, NY

CONTACT Financial Aid Office, Swedish Institute, College of Health Sciences, 226 West 26th Street, New York, NY 10001-6700, 212-924-5900. *Website:* http://www.swedishinstitute.edu/.

SWEET BRIAR COLLEGE
Sweet Briar, VA

Tuition & fees: $21,000	Average undergraduate aid package: $34,064

ABOUT THE INSTITUTION Independent, women only. *Awards:* bachelor's and master's degrees. 32 undergraduate majors. *Total enrollment:* 322. Undergraduates: 319. Freshmen: 79. Federal methodology is used as a basis for awarding need-based institutional aid.

UNDERGRADUATE EXPENSES for 2018–2019 *Comprehensive fee:* $34,000 includes full-time tuition ($21,000) and room and board ($13,000). Room and board charges vary according to board plan.

FRESHMAN FINANCIAL AID (Fall 2016) 123 applied for aid; of those 90% were deemed to have need. 100% of freshmen with need received aid; of those 31% had need fully met. *Average percent of need met:* 82% (excluding resources awarded to replace EFC). *Average financial aid package:* $34,928 (excluding resources awarded to replace EFC). 8% of all full-time freshmen had no need and received non-need-based gift aid.

UNDERGRADUATE FINANCIAL AID (Fall 2016) 281 applied for aid; of those 91% were deemed to have need. 100% of undergraduates with need received aid; of those 24% had need fully met. *Average percent of need met:* 81% (excluding resources awarded to replace EFC). *Average financial aid package:* $34,064 (excluding resources awarded to replace EFC). 6% of all full-time undergraduates had no need and received non-need-based gift aid.

GIFT AID (NEED-BASED) *Total amount:* $7,231,626 (8% federal, 4% state, 86% institutional, 2% external sources). *Receiving aid:* Freshmen: 83% (111); all full-time undergraduates: 81% (255). *Average award:* Freshmen: $28,753; Undergraduates: $28,297. *Scholarships, grants, and awards:* Federal Pell, FSEOG, state, private, college/university gift aid from institutional funds, United Negro College Fund.

GIFT AID (NON-NEED-BASED) *Total amount:* $1,777,414 (8% state, 90% institutional, 2% external sources). *Receiving aid:* Freshmen: 26% (35). Undergraduates: 21% (66). *Average award:* Freshmen: $27,205. Undergraduates: $29,940. *Scholarships, grants, and awards by category: Academic interests/achievement:* premedicine. *Creative arts/performance:* music. *Tuition waivers:* Full or partial for employees or children of employees, adult students, senior citizens.

LOANS *Student loans:* $1,734,480 (78% need-based, 22% non-need-based). 79% of past graduating class borrowed through all loan programs. *Average indebtedness per student:* $31,269. *Average need-based loan:* Freshmen: $6228. Undergraduates: $7457. *Parent loans:* $645,537 (49% need-based, 51% non-need-based). *Programs:* Federal Direct (Subsidized and Unsubsidized Stafford, PLUS), Perkins, college/university.

WORK-STUDY *Federal work-study:* jobs available. *State or other work-study/employment:* Total amount: $29,071 (100% need-based). Part-time jobs available.

APPLYING FOR FINANCIAL AID *Required financial aid forms:* FAFSA, noncustodial (divorced/separated) parent's statement. *Notification date:* Continuous.

CONTACT Wanda Spradley, Director of Financial Aid, Sweet Briar College, Box 1095, Sweet Briar, VA 24595, 800-381-6156 or toll-free 800-381-6142. *Fax:* 434-381-6450. *E-mail:* spradley@sbc.edu. *Website:* http://www.sbc.edu/.

SYRACUSE UNIVERSITY
Syracuse, NY

Tuition & fees: $46,755	Average undergraduate aid package: $38,870

ABOUT THE INSTITUTION Independent, coed. *Awards:* certificates, bachelor's, master's, and doctoral degrees. 138 undergraduate majors. *Total enrollment:* 22,484. Undergraduates: 15,252. Freshmen: 3,649. Both federal and institutional methodology are used as a basis for awarding need-based institutional aid.

UNDERGRADUATE EXPENSES for 2017–2018 *Application fee:* $75. *Comprehensive fee:* $62,313 includes full-time tuition ($45,150), mandatory fees ($1605), and room and board ($15,558). *College room only:* $8268. Full-time tuition and fees vary according to course load. Room and board charges vary according to board plan and housing facility. *Part-time tuition:* $1966 per credit hour. Part-time tuition and fees vary according to course load. *Payment plan:* Tuition prepayment.

FRESHMAN FINANCIAL AID (Fall 2017, est.) 2,416 applied for aid; of those 66% were deemed to have need. 100% of freshmen with need received aid; of those 55% had need fully met. *Average percent of need met:* 96% (excluding resources awarded to replace EFC). *Average financial aid package:* $38,450 (excluding resources awarded to replace EFC). 27% of all full-time freshmen had no need and received non-need-based gift aid.

UNDERGRADUATE FINANCIAL AID (Fall 2017, est.) 8,860 applied for aid; of those 76% were deemed to have need. 100% of undergraduates with need received aid; of those 45% had need fully met. *Average percent of need met:* 93% (excluding resources awarded to replace EFC). *Average financial aid package:* $38,870 (excluding resources awarded to replace EFC). 20% of all full-time undergraduates had no need and received non-need-based gift aid.

GIFT AID (NEED-BASED) *Total amount:* $235,719,640 (9% federal, 3% state, 86% institutional, 2% external sources). *Receiving aid:* Freshmen: 41% (1,494); all full-time undergraduates: 44% (6,308). *Average award:* Freshmen: $31,030; Undergraduates: $31,062. *Scholarships, grants, and awards:* Federal Pell, FSEOG, state, private, college/university gift aid from institutional funds.

GIFT AID (NON-NEED-BASED) *Total amount:* $33,496,331 (7% federal, 1% state, 87% institutional, 5% external sources). *Receiving aid:* Freshmen: 5% (185). Undergraduates: 4% (542). *Average award:* Freshmen: $9770. Undergraduates: $12,470. *Scholarships, grants, and awards by category: Academic interests/achievement:* general academic interests/achievements. *Creative arts/performance:* art/fine arts, music, theater/drama. *Tuition waivers:* Full or partial for employees or children of employees. *ROTC:* Army, Air Force.

LOANS *Student loans:* $78,508,977 (88% need-based, 12% non-need-based). 59% of past graduating class borrowed through all loan programs. *Average indebtedness per student:* $38,918. *Average need-based loan:* Freshmen: $4490. Undergraduates: $5750. *Parent loans:* $40,411,917 (86% need-based, 14% non-need-based). *Programs:* Federal Direct (Subsidized and Unsubsidized Stafford, PLUS).

WORK-STUDY *Federal work-study:* Total amount: $13,337,657; 5,292 jobs averaging $2585.

ATHLETIC AWARDS Total amount: $17,167,499 (40% need-based, 60% non-need-based).

APPLYING FOR FINANCIAL AID *Required financial aid forms:* FAFSA, CSS Financial Aid PROFILE, noncustodial (divorced/separated) parent's statement. *Financial aid deadline:* 1/1. *Notification date:* 3/15. Students must reply by 5/1.

CONTACT Office of Financial Aid and Scholarship Programs, Syracuse University, 200 Bowne Hall, Syracuse, NY 13244-1200, 315-443-1513. *Website:* http://www.syracuse.edu/.

TABOR COLLEGE
Hillsboro, KS

CONTACT Sommer Smith, Director of Student Financial Assistance, Tabor College, 400 South Jefferson, Hillsboro, KS 67063, 620-947-3121 Ext. 1726 or toll-free 800-822-6799. *Fax:* 620-947-6276. *E-mail:* sommersmith@tabor.edu. *Website:* http://www.tabor.edu/.

TALLADEGA COLLEGE
Talladega, AL

CONTACT K. Michael Francois, Director of Financial Aid, Talladega College, 627 West Battle Street, Talladega, AL 35160, 256-761-6341 or toll-free 866-540-3956. *Fax:* 256-761-6462. *Website:* http://www.talladega.edu/.

TALMUDICAL ACADEMY OF NEW JERSEY
Adelphia, NJ

CONTACT Office of Financial Aid, Talmudical Academy of New Jersey, Route 524, Adelphia, NJ 07710, 732-431-1600.

TALMUDICAL INSTITUTE OF UPSTATE NEW YORK
Rochester, NY

CONTACT Mrs. Ella Berenstein, Financial Aid Administrator, Talmudical Institute of Upstate New York, 769 Park Avenue, Rochester, NY 14607-3046, 585-473-2810. *Website:* http://www.tiuny.org/.

TALMUDICAL SEMINARY OF BOBOV
Brooklyn, NY

CONTACT Financial Aid Office, Talmudical Seminary of Bobov, 5120 New Utrecht Avenue, Brooklyn, NY 11219, 718-436-2122.

TALMUDICAL SEMINARY OHOLEI TORAH
Brooklyn, NY

CONTACT Financial Aid Administrator, Talmudical Seminary Oholei Torah, 667 Eastern Parkway, Brooklyn, NY 11213-3310, 718-774-5050.

TALMUDICAL YESHIVA OF PHILADELPHIA
Philadelphia, PA

CONTACT Director of Student Financial Aid/Registrar, Talmudical Yeshiva of Philadelphia, 6063 Drexel Road, Philadelphia, PA 19131-1296, 215-473-1212.

TALMUDIC UNIVERSITY
Miami Beach, FL

CONTACT Rabbi Ira Hill, Director of Financial Aid, Talmudic University, 1910 Alton Road, Miami Beach, FL 33139, 305-534-7050. *Fax:* 305-534-8444. *Website:* http://www.talmudicu.edu/.

TARLETON STATE UNIVERSITY
Stephenville, TX

Tuition & fees (TX res): $9078	Average undergraduate aid package: $9445

ABOUT THE INSTITUTION State-supported, coed. *Awards:* certificates, associate, bachelor's, master's, and doctoral degrees. 76 undergraduate majors. *Total enrollment:* 13,019. Undergraduates: 11,288. Freshmen: 1,754. Federal methodology is used as a basis for awarding need-based institutional aid.

UNDERGRADUATE EXPENSES for 2018–2019 *Application fee:* $45. *Tuition, state resident:* full-time $5012; part-time $167 per credit hour. *Tuition,*

nonresident: full-time $17,200; part-time $573 per credit hour. **Required fees:** full-time $4066. Full-time tuition and fees vary according to course load, degree level, program, and student level. Part-time tuition and fees vary according to course load, degree level, program, and student level. **College room and board:** $9872; **Room only:** $6220. Room and board charges vary according to board plan and housing facility. **Payment plan:** Guaranteed tuition.

FRESHMAN FINANCIAL AID (Fall 2017, est.) 1,682 applied for aid; of those 75% were deemed to have need. 100% of freshmen with need received aid; of those 3% had need fully met. **Average percent of need met:** 62% (excluding resources awarded to replace EFC). **Average financial aid package:** $10,478 (excluding resources awarded to replace EFC).

UNDERGRADUATE FINANCIAL AID (Fall 2017, est.) 6,688 applied for aid; of those 82% were deemed to have need. 99% of undergraduates with need received aid; of those 3% had need fully met. **Average percent of need met:** 54% (excluding resources awarded to replace EFC). **Average financial aid package:** $9445 (excluding resources awarded to replace EFC).

GIFT AID (NEED-BASED) Total amount: $41,399,454 (51% federal, 25% state, 17% institutional, 7% external sources). **Receiving aid:** Freshmen: 59% (1,116); all full-time undergraduates: 55% (4,623). **Average award:** Freshmen: $8987; Undergraduates: $7256. **Scholarships, grants, and awards:** Federal Pell, FSEOG, state, private, college/university gift aid from institutional funds.

GIFT AID (NON-NEED-BASED) Total amount: $4000 (100% state). **Receiving aid:** Undergraduates: 2. **Scholarships, grants, and awards by category:** Academic interests/achievement: general academic interests/achievements. Creative arts/performance: music, theater/drama. Special achievements/activities: general special achievements/activities. Special characteristics: children of educators, children of faculty/staff, veterans, veterans' children. **ROTC:** Army, Air Force cooperative.

LOANS Student loans: $59,356,134 (40% need-based, 60% non-need-based). 74% of past graduating class borrowed through all loan programs. **Average indebtedness per student:** $24,695. **Average need-based loan:** Freshmen: $3036. Undergraduates: $4040. **Parent loans:** $38,101,756 (100% non-need-based). **Programs:** Federal Direct (Subsidized and Unsubsidized Stafford, PLUS), state.

WORK-STUDY Federal work-study: Total amount: $582,871; jobs available. **State or other work-study/employment:** Total amount: $88,231 (100% need-based). Part-time jobs available.

ATHLETIC AWARDS Total amount: $2,081,113 (100% need-based).

APPLYING FOR FINANCIAL AID Required financial aid form: FAFSA. **Financial aid deadline:** 11/1 (priority: 3/15). **Notification date:** Continuous beginning 5/1. Students must reply within 2 weeks of notification.

CONTACT Ms. Kathy Purvis, Executive Director, Tarleton State University, Box T-0310, Stephenville, TX 76402, 254-968-9070 or toll-free 800-687-8236. *Fax:* 254-968-9600. *E-mail:* finaid@tarleton.edu.
Website: http://www.tarleton.edu/.

TAYLOR UNIVERSITY
Upland, IN

Tuition & fees: $32,885	Average undergraduate aid package: $23,875

ABOUT THE INSTITUTION Independent interdenominational, coed. **Awards:** diplomas, bachelor's, and master's degrees. 70 undergraduate majors. **Total enrollment:** 2,145. Undergraduates: 2,110. Freshmen: 448. Federal methodology is used as a basis for awarding need-based institutional aid.

UNDERGRADUATE EXPENSES for 2017–2018 Application fee: $25. **Comprehensive fee:** $42,130 includes full-time tuition ($32,640), mandatory fees ($245), and room and board ($9245). **College room only:** $4860. Full-time tuition and fees vary according to course load. Room and board charges vary according to board plan and housing facility. **Part-time tuition:** $1150 per credit hour. **Part-time fees:** $40 per term. Part-time tuition and fees vary according to course load.

FRESHMAN FINANCIAL AID (Fall 2017, est.) 371 applied for aid; of those 80% were deemed to have need. 100% of freshmen with need received aid; of those 33% had need fully met. **Average percent of need met:** 79% (excluding resources awarded to replace EFC). **Average financial aid package:** $25,071 (excluding resources awarded to replace EFC). 27% of all full-time freshmen had no need and received non-need-based gift aid.

UNDERGRADUATE FINANCIAL AID (Fall 2017, est.) 1,344 applied for aid; of those 85% were deemed to have need. 100% of undergraduates with need received

aid; of those 28% had need fully met. **Average percent of need met:** 76% (excluding resources awarded to replace EFC). **Average financial aid package:** $23,875 (excluding resources awarded to replace EFC). 29% of all full-time undergraduates had no need and received non-need-based gift aid.

GIFT AID (NEED-BASED) Total amount: $19,606,789 (10% federal, 8% state, 78% institutional, 4% external sources). **Receiving aid:** Freshmen: 66% (295); all full-time undergraduates: 62% (1,133). **Average award:** Freshmen: $21,503; Undergraduates: $19,706. **Scholarships, grants, and awards:** Federal Pell, FSEOG, state, private, college/university gift aid from institutional funds.

GIFT AID (NON-NEED-BASED) Total amount: $10,049,105 (1% state, 90% institutional, 9% external sources). **Receiving aid:** Freshmen: 16% (70). Undergraduates: 11% (196). **Average award:** Freshmen: $13,850. Undergraduates: $12,528. **Scholarships, grants, and awards by category:** Academic interests/achievement: 1,474 awards ($14,572,595 total): general academic interests/achievements. Creative arts/performance: 109 awards ($308,610 total): music, theater/drama. Special achievements/activities: 476 awards ($1,198,951 total): leadership. Special characteristics: 871 awards ($3,961,396 total): children and siblings of alumni, children of faculty/staff, ethnic background, international students, religious affiliation. **Tuition waivers:** Full or partial for employees or children of employees, senior citizens.

LOANS Student loans: $10,136,046 (63% need-based, 37% non-need-based). 43% of past graduating class borrowed through all loan programs. **Average indebtedness per student:** $28,094. **Average need-based loan:** Freshmen: $3999. Undergraduates: $4600. **Parent loans:** $20,201,106 (29% need-based, 71% non-need-based). **Programs:** Federal Direct (Subsidized and Unsubsidized Stafford, PLUS), college/university.

WORK-STUDY Federal work-study: Total amount: $524,987; 882 jobs averaging $639.

ATHLETIC AWARDS Total amount: $2,668,888 (56% need-based, 44% non-need-based).

APPLYING FOR FINANCIAL AID Required financial aid form: FAFSA. **Financial aid deadline:** 4/15 (priority: 2/15). **Notification date:** Continuous beginning 11/1. Students must reply by 5/1.

CONTACT Mr. Timothy A. Nace, Associate Vice President of Financial Aid, Taylor University, 236 West Reade Avenue, Upland, IN 46989-1001, 765-998-5358 or toll-free 800-882-3456. *Fax:* 765-998-4910. *E-mail:* tmnace@taylor.edu.
Website: http://www.taylor.edu/.

TELSHE YESHIVA–CHICAGO
Chicago, IL

CONTACT Office of Financial Aid, Telshe Yeshiva–Chicago, 3535 West Foster Avenue, Chicago, IL 60625-5598, 773-463-7738.

TEMPLE UNIVERSITY
Philadelphia, PA

Tuition & fees (PA res): $16,658	Average undergraduate aid package: $18,627

ABOUT THE INSTITUTION State-related, coed. **Awards:** certificates, diplomas, associate, bachelor's, master's, and doctoral degrees. 120 undergraduate majors. **Total enrollment:** 39,948. Undergraduates: 29,550. Freshmen: 5,171. Federal methodology is used as a basis for awarding need-based institutional aid.

UNDERGRADUATE EXPENSES for 2017–2018 Application fee: $55. **Tuition, state resident:** full-time $15,768; part-time $657 per credit hour. **Tuition, nonresident:** full-time $27,528; part-time $1147 per credit hour. **Required fees:** full-time $890. Full-time tuition and fees vary according to course load, degree level, location, program, reciprocity agreements, and student level. Part-time tuition and fees vary according to course load, degree level, location, program, reciprocity agreements, and student level. **College room and board:** $11,566; **Room only:** $7752. Room and board charges vary according to board plan and housing facility.

FRESHMAN FINANCIAL AID (Fall 2016) 4,406 applied for aid; of those 81% were deemed to have need. 99% of freshmen with need received aid; of those 30% had need fully met. **Average percent of need met:** 68% (excluding resources awarded to replace EFC). **Average financial aid package:** $19,406 (excluding resources

awarded to replace EFC). 18% of all full-time freshmen had no need and received non-need-based gift aid.

UNDERGRADUATE FINANCIAL AID (Fall 2016) 20,385 applied for aid; of those 87% were deemed to have need. 99% of undergraduates with need received aid; of those 24% had need fully met. *Average percent of need met:* 64% (excluding resources awarded to replace EFC). *Average financial aid package:* $18,627 (excluding resources awarded to replace EFC). 18% of all full-time undergraduates had no need and received non-need-based gift aid.

GIFT AID (NEED-BASED) *Total amount:* $95,610,964 (42% federal, 27% state, 31% institutional). *Receiving aid:* Freshmen: 55% (2,836); all full-time undergraduates: 54% (14,100). *Average award:* Freshmen: $7362; Undergraduates: $6439. *Scholarships, grants, and awards:* Federal Pell, FSEOG, state, private, college/university gift aid from institutional funds, United Negro College Fund, Federal Nursing.

GIFT AID (NON-NEED-BASED) *Total amount:* $98,367,024 (81% institutional, 19% external sources). *Receiving aid:* Freshmen: 42% (2,177). Undergraduates: 41% (10,623). *Average award:* Freshmen: $9702. Undergraduates: $6557. *Scholarships, grants, and awards by category: Academic interests/ achievement:* 9,606 awards ($64,061,103 total): general academic interests/achievements. *Creative arts/performance:* 307 awards ($1,011,181 total): art/fine arts, dance, general creative arts/performance, music, performing arts, theater/drama. *Special achievements/activities:* 208 awards ($263,170 total): cheerleading/drum major. *Special characteristics:* 431 awards ($8,162,745 total): children of faculty/staff. *Tuition waivers:* Full or partial for employees or children of employees. *ROTC:* Army, Naval cooperative, Air Force cooperative.

LOANS *Student loans:* $197,600,571 (76% need-based, 24% non-need-based). 67% of past graduating class borrowed through all loan programs. *Average indebtedness per student:* $38,108. *Average need-based loan:* Freshmen: $3733. Undergraduates: $4500. *Parent loans:* $63,123,984 (100% non-need-based). *Programs:* Federal Direct (Subsidized and Unsubsidized Stafford, PLUS), Perkins, Federal Nursing, state, college/university.

WORK-STUDY *Federal work-study:* 1,163 jobs averaging $1461.

ATHLETIC AWARDS Total amount: $10,119,229 (100% non-need-based).

APPLYING FOR FINANCIAL AID *Required financial aid form:* FAFSA. *Financial aid deadline (priority):* 3/1. *Notification date:* Continuous beginning 2/1. Students must reply by 5/1 or within 3 weeks of notification.

CONTACT Emilie Van Trieste, Director of Student Financial Services, Temple University, Conwell Hall, Ground Floor, Philadelphia, PA 19122-6096, 215-204-8760 or toll-free 888-340-2222. *Fax:* 215-204-5897. *E-mail:* emilie.vantrieste@temple.edu. *Website:* http://www.temple.edu/.

TENNESSEE STATE UNIVERSITY
Nashville, TN

ABOUT THE INSTITUTION State-supported, coed. *Awards:* certificates, associate, bachelor's, master's, and doctoral degrees. 58 undergraduate majors. *Total enrollment:* 8,753. Undergraduates: 7,007. Freshmen: 1,300.

GIFT AID (NEED-BASED) *Scholarships, grants, and awards:* Federal Pell, FSEOG, state, private, college/university gift aid from institutional funds.

GIFT AID (NON-NEED-BASED) *Scholarships, grants, and awards by category: Academic interests/achievement:* general academic interests/achievements. *Creative arts/performance:* music. *Special achievements/activities:* general special achievements/activities. *Special characteristics:* local/state students, members of minority groups.

LOANS *Programs:* Federal Direct (Subsidized and Unsubsidized Stafford, PLUS), Perkins.

APPLYING FOR FINANCIAL AID *Required financial aid form:* FAFSA.

CONTACT Amy Wood, Director of Financial Aid, Tennessee State University, 3500 John A. Merritt Boulevard, Nashville, TN 37209-1561, 615-963-7548. *Fax:* 615-963-7540. *E-mail:* awood7@tnstate.edu. *Website:* http://www.tnstate.edu/.

TENNESSEE TECHNOLOGICAL UNIVERSITY
Cookeville, TN

Tuition & fees (TN res): $8513	Average undergraduate aid package: $10,151

ABOUT THE INSTITUTION State-supported, coed. *Awards:* certificates, bachelor's, master's, and doctoral degrees. 80 undergraduate majors. *Total enrollment:* 10,504. Undergraduates: 9,365. Freshmen: 1,761. Federal methodology is used as a basis for awarding need-based institutional aid.

UNDERGRADUATE EXPENSES for 2017–2018 *Application fee:* $25. *Tuition, state resident:* full-time $8513; part-time $379 per credit hour. *Tuition, nonresident:* full-time $24,337; part-time $1040 per credit hour. Full-time tuition and fees vary according to program. Part-time tuition and fees vary according to program. *College room and board:* $9274; *Room only:* $4920. Room and board charges vary according to board plan and housing facility.

FRESHMAN FINANCIAL AID (Fall 2016) 1,456 applied for aid; of those 76% were deemed to have need. 100% of freshmen with need received aid; of those 13% had need fully met. *Average percent of need met:* 64% (excluding resources awarded to replace EFC). *Average financial aid package:* $11,596 (excluding resources awarded to replace EFC). 23% of all full-time freshmen had no need and received non-need-based gift aid.

UNDERGRADUATE FINANCIAL AID (Fall 2016) 7,301 applied for aid; of those 80% were deemed to have need. 99% of undergraduates with need received aid; of those 9% had need fully met. *Average percent of need met:* 60% (excluding resources awarded to replace EFC). *Average financial aid package:* $10,151 (excluding resources awarded to replace EFC). 17% of all full-time undergraduates had no need and received non-need-based gift aid.

GIFT AID (NEED-BASED) *Total amount:* $18,771,182 (74% federal, 24% state, 2% institutional). *Receiving aid:* Freshmen: 37% (594); all full-time undergraduates: 34% (3,176). *Average award:* Freshmen: $6336; Undergraduates: $5694. *Scholarships, grants, and awards:* Federal Pell, FSEOG, state, private, college/university gift aid from institutional funds, United Negro College Fund.

GIFT AID (NON-NEED-BASED) *Total amount:* $37,019,872 (56% state, 31% institutional, 13% external sources). *Receiving aid:* Freshmen: 66% (1,049). Undergraduates: 45% (4,231). *Average award:* Freshmen: $9004. Undergraduates: $9264. *Scholarships, grants, and awards by category: Academic interests/ achievement:* 2,516 awards ($5,498,608 total): agriculture, biological sciences, business, communication, computer science, education, engineering/technologies, English, foreign languages, general academic interests/achievements, health fields, home economics, humanities, international studies, mathematics, military science, physical sciences, premedicine, social sciences. *Creative arts/performance:* 254 awards ($548,690 total): art/fine arts, debating, music. *Special achievements/activities:* 1,035 awards ($4,304,644 total): cheerleading/drum major, general special achievements/ activities. *Special characteristics:* 232 awards ($919,697 total): children and siblings of alumni, children of educators, children of faculty/staff, children of public servants, ethnic background, first-generation college students, local/state students, members of minority groups, out-of-state students, public servants. *Tuition waivers:* Full or partial for employees or children of employees, senior citizens. *ROTC:* Army, Air Force cooperative.

LOANS *Student loans:* $26,327,706 (52% need-based, 48% non-need-based). 55% of past graduating class borrowed through all loan programs. *Average indebtedness per student:* $22,018. *Average need-based loan:* Freshmen: $3153. Undergraduates: $4029. *Parent loans:* $3,022,194 (100% non-need-based). *Programs:* Federal Direct (Subsidized and Unsubsidized Stafford, PLUS), Perkins, state, college/university.

WORK-STUDY *Federal work-study:* 456 jobs averaging $963. *State or other work-study/employment:* Part-time jobs available.

ATHLETIC AWARDS Total amount: $4,579,950 (100% non-need-based).

APPLYING FOR FINANCIAL AID *Required financial aid form:* FAFSA. *Financial aid deadline (priority):* 3/15. *Notification date:* Continuous beginning 3/1. Students must reply within 2 weeks of notification.

CONTACT Mr. Lester Clyde McKenzie III, Director of Financial Aid, Tennessee Technological University, PO Box 5076, 805 Quadrangle, Cookeville, TN 38501, 931-372-3073 or toll-free 800-255-8881. *Fax:* 931-372-6309. *E-mail:* lmckenzie@tntech.edu. *Website:* http://www.tntech.edu/.

TENNESSEE WESLEYAN UNIVERSITY
Athens, TN

Tuition & fees: $23,800 | Average undergraduate aid package: $17,516

ABOUT THE INSTITUTION Independent United Methodist, coed. *Awards:* bachelor's and master's degrees (profile includes information for both the main and branch campuses). 43 undergraduate majors. *Total enrollment:* 951. Undergraduates: 935. Freshmen: 208. Federal methodology is used as a basis for awarding need-based institutional aid.

UNDERGRADUATE EXPENSES for 2017–2018 *Comprehensive fee:* $31,550 includes full-time tuition ($22,800), mandatory fees ($1000), and room and board ($7750). *College room only:* $2230. Full-time tuition and fees vary according to class time and degree level. Room and board charges vary according to board plan and housing facility. *Part-time tuition:* $580 per credit hour. *Part-time fees:* $10 per credit hour. Part-time tuition and fees vary according to class time, course load, degree level, location, and program.

FRESHMAN FINANCIAL AID (Fall 2016) 334 applied for aid; of those 89% were deemed to have need. 97% of freshmen with need received aid; of those 24% had need fully met. *Average percent of need met:* 66% (excluding resources awarded to replace EFC). *Average financial aid package:* $16,549 (excluding resources awarded to replace EFC). 16% of all full-time freshmen had no need and received non-need-based gift aid.

UNDERGRADUATE FINANCIAL AID (Fall 2016) 1,019 applied for aid; of those 90% were deemed to have need. 98% of undergraduates with need received aid; of those 21% had need fully met. *Average percent of need met:* 67% (excluding resources awarded to replace EFC). *Average financial aid package:* $17,516 (excluding resources awarded to replace EFC). 14% of all full-time undergraduates had no need and received non-need-based gift aid.

GIFT AID (NEED-BASED) *Total amount:* $10,673,079 (22% federal, 21% state, 43% institutional, 14% external sources). *Receiving aid:* Freshmen: 57% (286); all full-time undergraduates: 66% (875). *Average award:* Freshmen: $14,833; Undergraduates: $15,404. *Scholarships, grants, and awards:* Federal Pell, FSEOG, state, private, college/university gift aid from institutional funds.

GIFT AID (NON-NEED-BASED) *Total amount:* $3,108,358 (1% federal, 16% state, 60% institutional, 23% external sources). *Receiving aid:* Freshmen: 12% (61). Undergraduates: 12% (160). *Average award:* Freshmen: $7799. Undergraduates: $7756. *Scholarships, grants, and awards by category: Academic interests/achievement:* general academic interests/achievements. *Creative arts/performance:* music. *Special achievements/activities:* cheerleading/drum major, general special achievements/activities, junior miss, memberships. *Special characteristics:* children and siblings of alumni, children of faculty/staff, general special characteristics, out-of-state students, relatives of clergy, religious affiliation, siblings of current students. *Tuition waivers:* Full or partial for employees or children of employees.

LOANS *Student loans:* $1,672,169 (26% need-based, 74% non-need-based). 68% of past graduating class borrowed through all loan programs. *Average indebtedness per student:* $18,540. *Average need-based loan:* Freshmen: $3109. Undergraduates: $3927. *Parent loans:* $943,569 (47% need-based, 53% non-need-based). *Programs:* Federal Direct (Subsidized and Unsubsidized Stafford, PLUS).

WORK-STUDY *Federal work-study:* jobs available. *State or other work-study/employment:* Total amount: $28,882 (3% need-based, 97% non-need-based). Part-time jobs available.

ATHLETIC AWARDS Total amount: $4,531,117 (66% need-based, 34% non-need-based).

APPLYING FOR FINANCIAL AID *Required financial aid forms:* FAFSA, institution's own form. *Financial aid deadline:* Continuous. *Notification date:* Continuous beginning 2/15. Students must reply within 2 weeks of notification.

CONTACT Mrs. Lacey Weese, Director of Financial Aid, Tennessee Wesleyan University, 204 East College Street, Athens, TN 37303, 423-746-5209 or toll-free 800-PICK-TWU. *Fax:* 423-744-9968. *E-mail:* lweese@tnwesleyan.edu. *Website:* http://www.tnwesleyan.edu/.

TEXAS A&M INTERNATIONAL UNIVERSITY
Laredo, TX

Tuition & fees (TX res): $8320 | Average undergraduate aid package: $9553

ABOUT THE INSTITUTION State-supported, coed. *Awards:* bachelor's, master's, and doctoral degrees. 22 undergraduate majors. *Total enrollment:* 7,640. Undergraduates: 6,799. Freshmen: 1,148. Federal methodology is used as a basis for awarding need-based institutional aid.

UNDERGRADUATE EXPENSES for 2017–2018 *Tuition, state resident:* full-time $4773. *Tuition, nonresident:* full-time $17,223. *Required fees:* full-time $3547. Full-time tuition and fees vary according to course load. Part-time tuition and fees vary according to course load and reciprocity agreements. *College room and board:* $8160; *Room only:* $5340. Room and board charges vary according to board plan and housing facility. *Payment plan:* Guaranteed tuition.

FRESHMAN FINANCIAL AID (Fall 2017, est.) 1,116 applied for aid; of those 89% were deemed to have need. 100% of freshmen with need received aid; of those 1% had need fully met. *Average percent of need met:* 68% (excluding resources awarded to replace EFC). *Average financial aid package:* $10,388 (excluding resources awarded to replace EFC). 9% of all full-time freshmen had no need and received non-need-based gift aid.

UNDERGRADUATE FINANCIAL AID (Fall 2017, est.) 5,016 applied for aid; of those 87% were deemed to have need. 99% of undergraduates with need received aid; of those .4% had need fully met. *Average percent of need met:* 67% (excluding resources awarded to replace EFC). *Average financial aid package:* $9553 (excluding resources awarded to replace EFC). 7% of all full-time undergraduates had no need and received non-need-based gift aid.

GIFT AID (NEED-BASED) *Total amount:* $33,406,382 (56% federal, 33% state, 11% institutional). *Receiving aid:* Freshmen: 88% (979); all full-time undergraduates: 83% (4,146). *Average award:* Freshmen: $8280; Undergraduates: $6936. *Scholarships, grants, and awards:* Federal Pell, FSEOG, state, college/university gift aid from institutional funds, Federal Nursing.

GIFT AID (NON-NEED-BASED) *Total amount:* $2,630,472 (9% state, 43% institutional, 48% external sources). *Receiving aid:* Freshmen: 37% (417). Undergraduates: 29% (1,478). *Average award:* Freshmen: $3919. Undergraduates: $3924. *Scholarships, grants, and awards by category: Academic interests/achievement:* business, communication, education, engineering/technologies, English, foreign languages, general academic interests/achievements, health fields, international studies, mathematics, physical sciences, premedicine, social sciences. *Creative arts/performance:* art/fine arts, dance, music, performing arts. *Tuition waivers:* Full or partial for senior citizens. *ROTC:* Army.

LOANS *Student loans:* $13,066,425 (62% need-based, 38% non-need-based). 74% of past graduating class borrowed through all loan programs. *Average indebtedness per student:* $17,394. *Average need-based loan:* Freshmen: $3756. Undergraduates: $2845. *Parent loans:* $267,724 (100% non-need-based). *Programs:* Federal Direct (Subsidized and Unsubsidized Stafford, PLUS), state, college/university, Hinson-Hazelwood Loan Program.

WORK-STUDY *Federal work-study:* Total amount: $23,785; 104 jobs averaging $1951. *State or other work-study/employment:* Total amount: $58,022 (72% need-based, 28% non-need-based). 26 part-time jobs averaging $1757.

ATHLETIC AWARDS Total amount: $816,867 (100% non-need-based).

APPLYING FOR FINANCIAL AID *Required financial aid form:* FAFSA. *Financial aid deadline:* 7/30 (priority: 3/15). *Notification date:* Continuous beginning 3/2. Students must reply within 6 weeks of notification.

CONTACT Mrs. Laura Elizondo, Director of Financial Aid, Texas A&M International University, 5201 University Boulevard, Laredo, TX 78041, 956-326-2225 or toll-free 888-489-2648. *Fax:* 956-326-2224. *E-mail:* laura@tamiu.edu. *Website:* http://www.tamiu.edu/.

TEXAS A&M UNIVERSITY
College Station, TX

Tuition & fees (TX res): $10,403	Average undergraduate aid package: $16,695

ABOUT THE INSTITUTION State-supported, coed. **Awards:** certificates, bachelor's, master's, and doctoral degrees. 109 undergraduate majors. **Total enrollment:** 67,580. Undergraduates: 53,065. Freshmen: 11,639. Both federal and institutional methodology are used as a basis for awarding need-based institutional aid.

UNDERGRADUATE EXPENSES for 2018–2019 Application fee: $75. **Tuition, state resident:** full-time $7052; part-time $235.07 per credit hour. **Tuition, nonresident:** full-time $33,803; part-time $1126.78 per credit hour. **Required fees:** full-time $3351. Full-time tuition and fees vary according to program. Part-time tuition and fees vary according to program. **College room and board:** $12,250. Room and board charges vary according to board plan, housing facility, and location. **Payment plan:** Guaranteed tuition.

FRESHMAN FINANCIAL AID (Fall 2017, est.) 7,877 applied for aid; of those 63% were deemed to have need. 95% of freshmen with need received aid; of those 25% had need fully met. **Average percent of need met:** 76% (excluding resources awarded to replace EFC). **Average financial aid package:** $18,142 (excluding resources awarded to replace EFC). 12% of all full-time freshmen had no need and received non-need-based gift aid.

UNDERGRADUATE FINANCIAL AID (Fall 2017, est.) 29,196 applied for aid; of those 73% were deemed to have need. 95% of undergraduates with need received aid; of those 22% had need fully met. **Average percent of need met:** 72% (excluding resources awarded to replace EFC). **Average financial aid package:** $16,695 (excluding resources awarded to replace EFC). 10% of all full-time undergraduates had no need and received non-need-based gift aid.

GIFT AID (NEED-BASED) Total amount: $175,058,358 (31% federal, 23% state, 33% institutional, 13% external sources). **Receiving aid:** Freshmen: 44% (4,451); all full-time undergraduates: 37% (17,498). **Average award:** Freshmen: $12,201; Undergraduates: $10,569. **Scholarships, grants, and awards:** Federal Pell, FSEOG, state, private, college/university gift aid from institutional funds.

GIFT AID (NON-NEED-BASED) Total amount: $40,354,216 (1% federal, 6% state, 52% institutional, 41% external sources). **Receiving aid:** Freshmen: 5% (499). Undergraduates: 3% (1,445). **Average award:** Freshmen: $4193. Undergraduates: $3987. **Scholarships, grants, and awards by category:** Academic interests/achievement: agriculture, architecture, biological sciences, business, computer science, education, engineering/technologies, general academic interests/achievements, health fields, mathematics, physical sciences, premedicine. Creative arts/performance: journalism/publications, performing arts, theater/drama. Special achievements/activities: community service, general special achievements/activities, leadership, memberships, rodeo. Special characteristics: children of faculty/staff, first-generation college students, general special characteristics, international students, local/state students, veterans, veterans' children. ROTC: Army, Naval, Air Force.

LOANS Student loans: $133,488,286 (64% need-based, 36% non-need-based). 43% of past graduating class borrowed through all loan programs. Average indebtedness per student: $23,505. **Average need-based loan:** Freshmen: $7418. Undergraduates: $8173. **Parent loans:** $76,113,847 (29% need-based, 71% non-need-based). **Programs:** Federal Direct (Subsidized and Unsubsidized Stafford, PLUS), Perkins, Federal Nursing, state, college/university.

WORK-STUDY Federal work-study: Total amount: $2,527,939; jobs available. **State or other work-study/employment:** Total amount: $344,500 (100% need-based). Part-time jobs available.

ATHLETIC AWARDS Total amount: $3,705,008 (28% need-based, 72% non-need-based).

APPLYING FOR FINANCIAL AID Required financial aid forms: FAFSA, scholarships section of the ApplyTexas application. **Financial aid deadline (priority):** 12/15. **Notification date:** Continuous beginning 2/25. Students must reply by 5/1.

CONTACT Scholarships and Financial Aid Office, Texas A&M University, The Pavilion 200, Spence Street, 1252 TAMU, College Station, TX 77842-3016, 979-845-3236. Fax: 979-847-9061. E-mail: financialaid@tamu.edu. Website: http://www.tamu.edu/.

TEXAS A&M UNIVERSITY–CENTRAL TEXAS
Killeen, TX

CONTACT Financial Aid Office, Texas A&M University–Central Texas, 1001 Leadership Place, Killeen, TX 76549, 254-519-5400. Website: http://www.tamuct.edu/.

TEXAS A&M UNIVERSITY–COMMERCE
Commerce, TX

Tuition & fees (TX res): $8748	Average undergraduate aid package: $9974

ABOUT THE INSTITUTION State-supported, coed. **Awards:** certificates, bachelor's, master's, and doctoral degrees. 51 undergraduate majors. **Total enrollment:** 12,490. Undergraduates: 8,031. Freshmen: 940. Federal methodology is used as a basis for awarding need-based institutional aid.

UNDERGRADUATE EXPENSES for 2018–2019 Tuition, state resident: full-time $4790; part-time $160 per credit hour. **Tuition, nonresident:** full-time $17,240; part-time $575 per credit hour. **Required fees:** full-time $3958. Full-time tuition and fees vary according to course load, degree level, location, program, and reciprocity agreements. Part-time tuition and fees vary according to course load, degree level, location, program, and reciprocity agreements. **College room and board:** $8326; **Room only:** $4426. Room and board charges vary according to board plan and housing facility.

FRESHMAN FINANCIAL AID (Fall 2017, est.) 904 applied for aid; of those 85% were deemed to have need. 97% of freshmen with need received aid; of those 7% had need fully met. **Average percent of need met:** 66% (excluding resources awarded to replace EFC). **Average financial aid package:** $11,948 (excluding resources awarded to replace EFC). 7% of all full-time freshmen had no need and received non-need-based gift aid.

UNDERGRADUATE FINANCIAL AID (Fall 2017, est.) 5,041 applied for aid; of those 89% were deemed to have need. 97% of undergraduates with need received aid; of those 6% had need fully met. **Average percent of need met:** 55% (excluding resources awarded to replace EFC). **Average financial aid package:** $9974 (excluding resources awarded to replace EFC). 1% of all full-time undergraduates had no need and received non-need-based gift aid.

GIFT AID (NEED-BASED) Total amount: $31,713,329 (53% federal, 28% state, 16% institutional, 3% external sources). **Receiving aid:** Freshmen: 74% (737); all full-time undergraduates: 68% (4,064). **Average award:** Freshmen: $11,120; Undergraduates: $8496. **Scholarships, grants, and awards:** Federal Pell, FSEOG, state, private, college/university gift aid from institutional funds.

GIFT AID (NON-NEED-BASED) Total amount: $2,754,911 (3% federal, 86% institutional, 11% external sources). **Average award:** Freshmen: $2397. Undergraduates: $2398. **Scholarships, grants, and awards by category:** Academic interests/achievement: 266 awards ($4,858,039 total): agriculture, biological sciences, business, communication, computer science, education, engineering/technologies, English, foreign languages, general academic interests/achievements, health fields, humanities, international studies, mathematics, physical sciences, premedicine, social sciences. Creative arts/performance: 40 awards ($480,973 total): applied art and design, art/fine arts, journalism/publications, music, performing arts, theater/drama. Special achievements/activities: 94 awards ($2,449,157 total): cheerleading/drum major, general special achievements/activities, junior miss, leadership, memberships, rodeo. Special characteristics: 13 awards ($28,330 total): adult students, children and siblings of alumni, first-generation college students, general special characteristics, out-of-state students, previous college experience, veterans, veterans' children. **Tuition waivers:** Full or partial for employees or children of employees, senior citizens. **ROTC:** Air Force cooperative.

LOANS Student loans: $33,325,473 (91% need-based, 9% non-need-based). 67% of past graduating class borrowed through all loan programs. Average indebtedness per student: $27,961. **Average need-based loan:** Freshmen: $2865. Undergraduates: $3682. **Parent loans:** $5,989,554 (77% need-based, 23% non-need-based). **Programs:** Federal Direct (Subsidized and Unsubsidized Stafford, PLUS), Perkins, state.

WORK-STUDY *Federal work-study:* Total amount: $383,509; 146 jobs averaging $2458. *State or other work-study/employment:* Total amount: $84,652 (100% need-based). 27 part-time jobs averaging $3011.
ATHLETIC AWARDS Total amount: $829,133 (67% need-based, 33% non-need-based).
APPLYING FOR FINANCIAL AID *Required financial aid form:* FAFSA. *Financial aid deadline (priority):* 4/1. *Notification date:* Continuous beginning 5/1. Students must reply within 4 weeks of notification.
CONTACT Ms. Maria Ramos, Director of Financial Aid and Scholarships, Texas A&M University–Commerce, PO Box 3011, Commerce, TX 75429, 903-886-5091 or toll-free 888-868-2682. *Fax:* 903-886-5098. *E-mail:* maria.ramos@tamuc.edu. *Website:* http://www.tamuc.edu/.

TEXAS A&M UNIVERSITY–CORPUS CHRISTI
Corpus Christi, TX

Tuition & fees (TX res): $8969	Average undergraduate aid package: $9651

ABOUT THE INSTITUTION State-supported, coed. *Awards:* bachelor's, master's, and doctoral degrees. 42 undergraduate majors. *Total enrollment:* 12,236. Undergraduates: 10,174. Freshmen: 2,074. Federal methodology is used as a basis for awarding need-based institutional aid.
UNDERGRADUATE EXPENSES for 2017–2018 *Application fee:* $50. *Tuition, state resident:* full-time $4994. *Tuition, nonresident:* full-time $8658. *Required fees:* full-time $3975; $1061 per term. Full-time tuition and fees vary according to course load, degree level, location, program, and student level. Part-time tuition and fees vary according to course load, degree level, location, program, and student level. *College room and board:* $10,410; *Room only:* $6890. Room and board charges vary according to board plan and housing facility. *Payment plan:* Guaranteed tuition.
FRESHMAN FINANCIAL AID (Fall 2017, est.) 1,875 applied for aid; of those 79% were deemed to have need. 96% of freshmen with need received aid; of those 2% had need fully met. *Average percent of need met:* 57% (excluding resources awarded to replace EFC). *Average financial aid package:* $10,193 (excluding resources awarded to replace EFC). 2% of all full-time freshmen had no need and received non-need-based gift aid.
UNDERGRADUATE FINANCIAL AID (Fall 2017, est.) 6,439 applied for aid; of those 83% were deemed to have need. 96% of undergraduates with need received aid; of those 2% had need fully met. *Average percent of need met:* 53% (excluding resources awarded to replace EFC). *Average financial aid package:* $9651 (excluding resources awarded to replace EFC). 4% of all full-time undergraduates had no need and received non-need-based gift aid.
GIFT AID (NEED-BASED) *Total amount:* $31,261,635 (63% federal, 33% state, 4% institutional). *Receiving aid:* Freshmen: 52% (1,141); all full-time undergraduates: 48% (3,964). *Average award:* Freshmen: $8750; Undergraduates: $7167. *Scholarships, grants, and awards:* Federal Pell, FSEOG, state, private, college/university gift aid from institutional funds.
GIFT AID (NON-NEED-BASED) *Total amount:* $4,435,401 (68% institutional, 32% external sources). *Receiving aid:* Freshmen: 5% (120). Undergraduates: 7% (610). *Average award:* Freshmen: $3397. Undergraduates: $2787. *Scholarships, grants, and awards by category:* Academic interests/achievement: 210 awards ($732,900 total): general academic interests/achievements. *Creative arts/performance:* 34 awards ($75,250 total): art/fine arts, general creative arts/performance. *Special achievements/activities:* 10 awards ($3850 total): general special achievements/activities. *Special characteristics:* 92 awards ($92,000 total): first-generation college students, international students. *Tuition waivers:* Full or partial for senior citizens. *ROTC:* Army.
LOANS *Student loans:* $42,003,263 (45% need-based, 55% non-need-based). 65% of past graduating class borrowed through all loan programs. *Average indebtedness per student:* $16,998. *Average need-based loan:* Freshmen: $3360. Undergraduates: $4091. *Parent loans:* $22,864,364 (100% non-need-based). *Programs:* Federal Direct (Subsidized and Unsubsidized Stafford, PLUS), Perkins, state, college/university.
WORK-STUDY *Federal work-study:* Total amount: $520,586; 148 jobs averaging $3254. *State or other work-study/employment:* Total amount: $970,919 (100% need-based). 256 part-time jobs averaging $3515.

ATHLETIC AWARDS Total amount: $2,172,683 (100% non-need-based).
APPLYING FOR FINANCIAL AID *Required financial aid form:* FAFSA. *Financial aid deadline (priority):* 3/31. *Notification date:* Continuous beginning 4/1. Students must reply by 4/30 or within 2 weeks of notification.
CONTACT Jeannie Gage, Director of Financial Assistance, Texas A&M University–Corpus Christi, 6300 Ocean Drive, Corpus Christi, TX 78412-5503, 361-825-2332 or toll-free 800-482-6822. *Fax:* 361-825-6095. *E-mail:* faoweb@tamucc.edu. *Website:* http://www.tamucc.edu/.

TEXAS A&M UNIVERSITY–KINGSVILLE
Kingsville, TX

Tuition & fees (TX res): $8462	Average undergraduate aid package: $14,131

ABOUT THE INSTITUTION State-supported, coed. *Awards:* certificates, bachelor's, master's, and doctoral degrees. 52 undergraduate majors. *Total enrollment:* 8,674. Undergraduates: 6,775. Freshmen: 1,114. Federal methodology is used as a basis for awarding need-based institutional aid.
UNDERGRADUATE EXPENSES for 2017–2018 *Application fee:* $25. *Tuition, state resident:* full-time $8462; part-time $120 per credit hour. *Tuition, nonresident:* full-time $22,034; part-time $465 per credit hour. Full-time tuition and fees vary according to course load and degree level. Part-time tuition and fees vary according to course load and degree level. *College room and board:* $8760. Room and board charges vary according to board plan and housing facility. *Payment plan:* Guaranteed tuition.
FRESHMAN FINANCIAL AID (Fall 2016) 1,130 applied for aid; of those 86% were deemed to have need. 95% of freshmen with need received aid; of those 29% had need fully met. *Average percent of need met:* 76% (excluding resources awarded to replace EFC). *Average financial aid package:* $14,537 (excluding resources awarded to replace EFC). 1% of all full-time freshmen had no need and received non-need-based gift aid.
UNDERGRADUATE FINANCIAL AID (Fall 2016) 4,333 applied for aid; of those 90% were deemed to have need. 95% of undergraduates with need received aid; of those 23% had need fully met. *Average percent of need met:* 73% (excluding resources awarded to replace EFC). *Average financial aid package:* $14,131 (excluding resources awarded to replace EFC). 1% of all full-time undergraduates had no need and received non-need-based gift aid.
GIFT AID (NEED-BASED) *Total amount:* $20,280,301 (70% federal, 30% state). *Receiving aid:* Freshmen: 75% (867); all full-time undergraduates: 76% (3,454). *Average award:* Freshmen: $7296; Undergraduates: $6692. *Scholarships, grants, and awards:* Federal Pell, FSEOG, state, private, college/university gift aid from institutional funds.
GIFT AID (NON-NEED-BASED) *Total amount:* $1,802,429 (100% institutional). *Receiving aid:* Freshmen: 4% (49). Undergraduates: 5% (217). *Average award:* Freshmen: $3417. Undergraduates: $3656. *Scholarships, grants, and awards by category:* Special achievements/activities: rodeo. *Special characteristics:* general special characteristics. *Tuition waivers:* Full or partial for employees or children of employees, senior citizens. *ROTC:* Army.
LOANS *Student loans:* $23,108,018 (100% need-based). 71% of past graduating class borrowed through all loan programs. *Average indebtedness per student:* $28,347. *Average need-based loan:* Freshmen: $2111. Undergraduates: $2890. *Parent loans:* $5,309,604 (100% need-based). *Programs:* Federal Direct (Subsidized and Unsubsidized Stafford, PLUS), Perkins, state, alternative loans.
WORK-STUDY *Federal work-study:* jobs available. *State or other work-study/employment:* Total amount: $50,734 (100% need-based). Part-time jobs available.
APPLYING FOR FINANCIAL AID *Required financial aid form:* FAFSA. *Financial aid deadline (priority):* 3/15. *Notification date:* Continuous beginning 11/1. Students must reply within 2 weeks of notification.
CONTACT Mr. Arnold Trejo, Executive Director of Student Financial Aid, Texas A&M University–Kingsville, 700 University Boulevard, Kingsville, TX 78363, 361-593-3911 or toll-free 800-687-6000. *Fax:* 361-593-3026. *E-mail:* financial.aid@tamuk.edu. *Website:* http://www.tamuk.edu/.

TEXAS A&M UNIVERSITY–SAN ANTONIO
San Antonio, TX

CONTACT Financial Aid Office, Texas A&M University–San Antonio, One University Way, San Antonio, TX 78224, 210-784-1000.
Website: http://www.tamusa.edu/.

TEXAS A&M UNIVERSITY–TEXARKANA
Texarkana, TX

Tuition & fees (TX res): $7634	Average undergraduate aid package: $10,222

ABOUT THE INSTITUTION State-supported, coed. *Awards:* bachelor's, master's, and doctoral degrees. 20 undergraduate majors. *Total enrollment:* 2,066. Undergraduates: 1,644. Entering class: 74. Federal methodology is used as a basis for awarding need-based institutional aid.

UNDERGRADUATE EXPENSES for 2017–2018 *Application fee:* $30. *One-time required fee:* $30. *Tuition, state resident:* full-time $5569; part-time $218.28 per credit hour. *Tuition, nonresident:* full-time $19,835; part-time $693.68 per credit hour. *Required fees:* full-time $2065; $109.56 per credit hour or $150 per term. Full-time tuition and fees vary according to course load, degree level, location, reciprocity agreements, and student level. Part-time tuition and fees vary according to course load, degree level, location, reciprocity agreements, and student level. *College room and board:* $7462; *Room only:* $4400. Room and board charges vary according to board plan. *Payment plan:* Guaranteed tuition.

UNDERGRADUATE FINANCIAL AID (Fall 2016) 879 applied for aid; of those 88% were deemed to have need. 98% of undergraduates with need received aid; of those 7% had need fully met. *Average percent of need met:* 69% (excluding resources awarded to replace EFC). *Average financial aid package:* $10,222 (excluding resources awarded to replace EFC). 10% of all full-time undergraduates had no need and received non-need-based gift aid.

GIFT AID (NEED-BASED) *Total amount:* $4,891,917 (66% federal, 23% state, 8% institutional, 3% external sources). *Receiving aid:* Entering class: 58% (106); all full-time undergraduates: 67% (716). *Average award:* Freshmen: $11,386; Undergraduates: $8154. *Scholarships, grants, and awards:* Federal Pell, FSEOG, state, private, college/university gift aid from institutional funds.

GIFT AID (NON-NEED-BASED) *Total amount:* $262,857 (4% federal, 86% institutional, 10% external sources). *Average award:* Freshmen: $2235. Undergraduates: $2321. *Scholarships, grants, and awards by category:* Academic interests/achievement: biological sciences, business, communication, computer science, education, engineering/technologies, English, general academic interests/achievements, home economics, international studies, mathematics, social sciences. *Special achievements/activities:* community service, general special achievements/activities, leadership, memberships. *Special characteristics:* veterans, veterans' children. *Tuition waivers:* Full or partial for employees or children of employees, senior citizens.

LOANS *Student loans:* $8,109,983 (90% need-based, 10% non-need-based). 60% of past graduating class borrowed through all loan programs. *Average indebtedness per student:* $19,410. *Average need-based loan:* Freshmen: $2755. Undergraduates: $3698. *Parent loans:* $501,342 (69% need-based, 31% non-need-based). *Programs:* Federal Direct (Subsidized and Unsubsidized Stafford, PLUS), state, college/university.

WORK-STUDY *Federal work-study:* 22 jobs averaging $2076. *State or other work-study/employment:* Part-time jobs available.

ATHLETIC AWARDS Total amount: $107,350 (63% need-based, 37% non-need-based).

APPLYING FOR FINANCIAL AID *Required financial aid form:* FAFSA. *Financial aid deadline (priority):* 3/15. *Notification date:* Continuous beginning 2/15. Students must reply within 2 weeks of notification.

CONTACT Michael G. Fuller, Director of Financial Aid and Veteran Services, Texas A&M University–Texarkana, 7101 University Avenue, Texarkana, TX 75503, 903-223-3060. *Fax:* 903-223-3140. *E-mail:* mfuller@tamut.edu. *Website:* http://www.tamut.edu/.

TEXAS CHRISTIAN UNIVERSITY
Fort Worth, TX

Tuition & fees: $44,760	Average undergraduate aid package: $30,763

ABOUT THE INSTITUTION Independent Christian Church (Disciples of Christ), coed. *Awards:* certificates, diplomas, bachelor's, master's, and doctoral degrees. 98 undergraduate majors. *Total enrollment:* 10,489. Undergraduates: 9,011. Freshmen: 1,955. Both federal and institutional methodology are used as a basis for awarding need-based institutional aid.

UNDERGRADUATE EXPENSES for 2017–2018 *Application fee:* $50. *Comprehensive fee:* $57,120 includes full-time tuition ($44,670), mandatory fees ($90), and room and board ($12,360). *College room only:* $7520. Room and board charges vary according to board plan and housing facility. *Part-time tuition:* $1890 per credit hour. *Part-time fees:* $45 per term. Part-time tuition and fees vary according to course load.

FRESHMAN FINANCIAL AID (Fall 2017, est.) 1,199 applied for aid; of those 66% were deemed to have need. 99% of freshmen with need received aid; of those 36% had need fully met. *Average percent of need met:* 71% (excluding resources awarded to replace EFC). *Average financial aid package:* $30,307 (excluding resources awarded to replace EFC). 30% of all full-time freshmen had no need and received non-need-based gift aid.

UNDERGRADUATE FINANCIAL AID (Fall 2017, est.) 4,360 applied for aid; of those 78% were deemed to have need. 98% of undergraduates with need received aid; of those 27% had need fully met. *Average percent of need met:* 65% (excluding resources awarded to replace EFC). *Average financial aid package:* $30,763 (excluding resources awarded to replace EFC). 28% of all full-time undergraduates had no need and received non-need-based gift aid.

GIFT AID (NEED-BASED) *Total amount:* $82,660,846 (8% federal, 4% state, 86% institutional, 2% external sources). *Receiving aid:* Freshmen: 38% (733); all full-time undergraduates: 36% (3,169). *Average award:* Freshmen: $28,394; Undergraduates: $27,790. *Scholarships, grants, and awards:* Federal Pell, FSEOG, state, private, college/university gift aid from institutional funds.

GIFT AID (NON-NEED-BASED) *Total amount:* $51,759,431 (98% institutional, 2% external sources). *Receiving aid:* Freshmen: 30% (579). Undergraduates: 26% (2,254). *Average award:* Freshmen: $16,868. Undergraduates: $17,963. *Scholarships, grants, and awards by category:* Academic interests/achievement: 3,989 awards ($59,078,400 total): agriculture, biological sciences, business, communication, education, engineering/technologies, English, foreign languages, general academic interests/achievements, health fields, humanities, international studies, mathematics, military science, physical sciences, premedicine, religion/biblical studies, social sciences. *Creative arts/performance:* 677 awards ($5,315,167 total): applied art and design, art/fine arts, cinema/film/broadcasting, creative writing, dance, general creative arts/performance, journalism/publications, music, performing arts, theater/drama. *Special achievements/activities:* 880 awards ($9,729,354 total): community service, general special achievements/activities, leadership, memberships, religious involvement. *Special characteristics:* 867 awards ($19,317,960 total): adult students, children of educators, children of faculty/staff, children of union members/company employees, children of workers in trades, ethnic background, general special characteristics, handicapped students, international students, local/state students, members of minority groups, previous college experience, relatives of clergy, religious affiliation, veterans, veterans' children. *Tuition waivers:* Full or partial for employees or children of employees. *ROTC:* Army, Air Force.

LOANS *Student loans:* $52,209,053 (53% need-based, 47% non-need-based). 36% of past graduating class borrowed through all loan programs. *Average indebtedness per student:* $42,212. *Average need-based loan:* Freshmen: $3166. Undergraduates: $4511. *Parent loans:* $20,554,297 (30% need-based, 70% non-need-based). *Programs:* Federal Direct (Subsidized and Unsubsidized Stafford, PLUS), Perkins, Federal Nursing, state.

WORK-STUDY *Federal work-study:* Total amount: $3,130,918; 1,325 jobs averaging $2065. *State or other work-study/employment:* Part-time jobs available.

ATHLETIC AWARDS Total amount: $17,456,829 (39% need-based, 61% non-need-based).

APPLYING FOR FINANCIAL AID *Required financial aid forms:* FAFSA, CSS Financial Aid PROFILE, noncustodial (divorced/separated) parent's statement. *Financial aid deadline:* 5/1 (priority: 2/15). *Notification date:* Continuous beginning 12/15.

CONTACT Michael Scott, Director of Scholarships and Student Financial Aid, Texas Christian University, PO Box 297012, Fort Worth, TX 76129-0002, 817-257-7858 or toll-free 800-828-3764. *Fax:* 817-257-7462. *E-mail:* m.scott@tcu.edu. *Website:* http://www.tcu.edu/.

TEXAS COLLEGE
Tyler, TX

CONTACT Ms. Cecelia K. Jones, Director of Financial Aid, Texas College, 2404 North Grand Avenue, Tyler, TX 75702, 903-593-8311 Ext. 2241 or toll-free 800-306-6299. *Fax:* 903-593-9607. *E-mail:* ckjones@texascollege.edu. *Website:* http://www.texascollege.edu/.

TEXAS LUTHERAN UNIVERSITY
Seguin, TX

Tuition & fees: $29,960	Average undergraduate aid package: $25,526

ABOUT THE INSTITUTION Independent Evangelical Lutheran Church, coed. *Awards:* bachelor's and master's degrees. 39 undergraduate majors. *Total enrollment:* 1,394. Undergraduates: 1,359. Freshmen: 417. Federal methodology is used as a basis for awarding need-based institutional aid.

UNDERGRADUATE EXPENSES for 2018–2019 *One-time required fee:* $300. *Comprehensive fee:* $40,110 includes full-time tuition ($29,650), mandatory fees ($310), and room and board ($10,150). *College room only:* $5750. Full-time tuition and fees vary according to course load. Room and board charges vary according to board plan and housing facility. *Part-time tuition:* $980 per semester hour. *Part-time fees:* $980 per semester hour; $155 per term.

FRESHMAN FINANCIAL AID (Fall 2017, est.) 394 applied for aid; of those 90% were deemed to have need. 100% of freshmen with need received aid; of those 28% had need fully met. *Average percent of need met:* 85% (excluding resources awarded to replace EFC). *Average financial aid package:* $26,587 (excluding resources awarded to replace EFC). 17% of all full-time freshmen had no need and received non-need-based gift aid.

UNDERGRADUATE FINANCIAL AID (Fall 2017, est.) 1,193 applied for aid; of those 90% were deemed to have need. 100% of undergraduates with need received aid; of those 20% had need fully met. *Average percent of need met:* 83% (excluding resources awarded to replace EFC). *Average financial aid package:* $25,526 (excluding resources awarded to replace EFC). 18% of all full-time undergraduates had no need and received non-need-based gift aid.

GIFT AID (NEED-BASED) *Total amount:* $23,347,563 (11% federal, 9% state, 79% institutional, 1% external sources). *Receiving aid:* Freshmen: 85% (354); all full-time undergraduates: 81% (1,056). *Average award:* Freshmen: $22,639; Undergraduates: $21,262. *Scholarships, grants, and awards:* Federal Pell, FSEOG, state, private, college/university gift aid from institutional funds, TEACH Grants.

GIFT AID (NON-NEED-BASED) *Total amount:* $2,020,562 (1% federal, 97% institutional, 2% external sources). *Receiving aid:* Freshmen: 10% (40). Undergraduates: 14% (180). *Average award:* Freshmen: $16,404. Undergraduates: $15,918. *Scholarships, grants, and awards by category: Academic interests/ achievement:* 1,114 awards ($17,870,791 total): biological sciences, business, communication, computer science, education, general academic interests/achievements, mathematics. *Creative arts/performance:* 160 awards ($1,668,760 total): journalism/ publications, music, performing arts, theater/drama. *Special achievements/activities:* 157 awards ($307,900 total): junior miss, leadership, religious involvement. *Special characteristics:* 148 awards ($795,842 total): children and siblings of alumni, children of educators, children of faculty/staff, local/state students, relatives of clergy, religious affiliation, veterans, veterans' children. *Tuition waivers:* Full or partial for children of alumni, employees or children of employees. *ROTC:* Army cooperative, Air Force cooperative.

LOANS *Student loans:* $6,914,925 (45% need-based, 55% non-need-based). 78% of past graduating class borrowed through all loan programs. *Average indebtedness per student:* $32,437. *Average need-based loan:* Freshmen: $3716. Undergraduates: $4286. *Parent loans:* $2,619,949 (100% non-need-based). *Programs:* Federal Direct (Subsidized and Unsubsidized Stafford, PLUS), Perkins, state, private loans.

WORK-STUDY *Federal work-study:* Total amount: $273,635; 137 jobs averaging $2317. *State or other work-study/employment:* Total amount: $6000 (100% need-based). 4 part-time jobs averaging $2318.

APPLYING FOR FINANCIAL AID *Required financial aid forms:* FAFSA, TASFA. *Financial aid deadline (priority):* 3/1. *Notification date:* Continuous beginning 5/1. Students must reply by 8/15.

CONTACT Bonnie Trevino, Director of Financial Aid, Texas Lutheran University, 1000 West Court Street, Seguin, TX 78155-5999, 830-372-8078 or toll-free 800-771-8521. *Fax:* 830-372-8179. *E-mail:* btrevino@tlu.edu. *Website:* http://www.tlu.edu/.

TEXAS SOUTHERN UNIVERSITY
Houston, TX

Tuition & fees: N/R	Average undergraduate aid package: $18,738

ABOUT THE INSTITUTION State-supported, coed. 49 undergraduate majors. Federal methodology is used as a basis for awarding need-based institutional aid.

FRESHMAN FINANCIAL AID (Fall 2017, est.) 2,543 applied for aid; of those 86% were deemed to have need. 99% of freshmen with need received aid; of those 100% had need fully met. *Average percent of need met:* 100% (excluding resources awarded to replace EFC). *Average financial aid package:* $21,430 (excluding resources awarded to replace EFC).

UNDERGRADUATE FINANCIAL AID (Fall 2017, est.) 5,822 applied for aid; of those 100% were deemed to have need. 100% of undergraduates with need received aid; of those 86% had need fully met. *Average percent of need met:* 86% (excluding resources awarded to replace EFC). *Average financial aid package:* $18,738 (excluding resources awarded to replace EFC).

GIFT AID (NEED-BASED) *Total amount:* $39,493,241 (59% federal, 22% state, 16% institutional, 3% external sources). *Receiving aid:* Freshmen: 80% (2,154); all full-time undergraduates: 79% (5,294). *Average award:* Freshmen: $4285; Undergraduates: $6300. *Scholarships, grants, and awards:* Federal Pell, FSEOG, state, private, college/university gift aid from institutional funds, United Negro College Fund, Federal Nursing.

LOANS *Student loans:* $39,279,877 (100% need-based). 97% of past graduating class borrowed through all loan programs. *Average indebtedness per student:* $36,580. *Average need-based loan:* Freshmen: $2800. Undergraduates: $3793. *Parent loans:* $15,328,871 (100% need-based). *Programs:* Federal Direct (Subsidized and Unsubsidized Stafford, PLUS), state, college/university.

WORK-STUDY *Federal work-study:* Total amount: $319,866; 174 jobs averaging $4000. *State or other work-study/employment:* Total amount: $32,326 (100% need-based). 17 part-time jobs averaging $4000.

ATHLETIC AWARDS Total amount: $2,950,025 (100% need-based).

APPLYING FOR FINANCIAL AID *Required financial aid forms:* FAFSA, institution's own form. *Financial aid deadline (priority):* 4/15. *Notification date:* Continuous beginning 4/15.

CONTACT Office of Financial Aid, Texas Southern University, 3100 Cleburne Street, Houston, TX 77004-4584, 713-313-7802. *Fax:* 713-313-1858. *Website:* http://www.tsu.edu/.

TEXAS STATE UNIVERSITY
San Marcos, TX

Tuition & fees (TX res): $10,621	Average undergraduate aid package: $11,616

ABOUT THE INSTITUTION State-supported, coed. *Awards:* certificates, bachelor's, master's, and doctoral degrees. 88 undergraduate majors. *Total enrollment:* 38,666. Undergraduates: 34,180. Freshmen: 5,874. Federal methodology is used as a basis for awarding need-based institutional aid.

UNDERGRADUATE EXPENSES for 2017–2018 *Application fee:* $75. *Tuition, state resident:* full-time $8087; part-time $270 per credit hour. *Tuition, nonresident:* full-time $20,537; part-time $685 per credit hour. *Required fees:* full-time $2534; $58.74 per credit hour or $446 per term. Full-time tuition and fees vary according to course load and degree level. Part-time tuition and fees vary according to course load and degree level. **College room and board:** $8100; **Room only:** $5390. Room and board charges vary according to board plan and housing facility. **Payment plans:** Guaranteed tuition, tuition prepayment.

FRESHMAN FINANCIAL AID (Fall 2017, est.) 5,298 applied for aid; of those 71% were deemed to have need. 97% of freshmen with need received aid; of those 23% had need fully met. **Average percent of need met:** 70% (excluding resources awarded to replace EFC). **Average financial aid package:** $12,458 (excluding resources awarded to replace EFC). 4% of all full-time freshmen had no need and received non-need-based gift aid.

UNDERGRADUATE FINANCIAL AID (Fall 2017, est.) 23,924 applied for aid; of those 70% were deemed to have need. 97% of undergraduates with need received aid; of those 20% had need fully met. **Average percent of need met:** 65% (excluding resources awarded to replace EFC). **Average financial aid package:** $11,616 (excluding resources awarded to replace EFC). 3% of all full-time undergraduates had no need and received non-need-based gift aid.

GIFT AID (NEED-BASED) Total amount: $108,209,114 (50% federal, 47% state, 1% institutional, 2% external sources). **Receiving aid:** Freshmen: 54% (3,085); all full-time undergraduates: 48% (13,435). **Average award:** Freshmen: $8631; Undergraduates: $7404. **Scholarships, grants, and awards:** Federal Pell, FSEOG, state, private, college/university gift aid from institutional funds.

GIFT AID (NON-NEED-BASED) Total amount: $12,003,638 (1% federal, 40% institutional, 59% external sources). **Receiving aid:** Freshmen: 9% (536). Undergraduates: 5% (1,383). **Average award:** Freshmen: $4291. Undergraduates: $4056. **Scholarships, grants, and awards by category:** Academic interests/achievement: 1,214 awards ($4,212,728 total): agriculture, biological sciences, business, communication, computer science, education, engineering/technologies, English, foreign languages, general academic interests/achievements, health fields, home economics, humanities, international studies, mathematics, military science, physical sciences, social sciences. Creative arts/performance: 468 awards ($1,393,087 total): applied art and design, art/fine arts, dance, journalism/publications, music, theater/drama. Special achievements/activities: 66 awards ($107,230 total): leadership. Special characteristics: 1,648 awards ($7,787,750 total): international students, spouses of deceased or disabled public servants, veterans, veterans' children. **Tuition waivers:** Full or partial for employees or children of employees. **ROTC:** Army, Air Force.

LOANS Student loans: $111,121,131 (76% need-based, 24% non-need-based). 66% of past graduating class borrowed through all loan programs. Average indebtedness per student: $26,568. **Average need-based loan:** Freshmen: $3102. Undergraduates: $3965. **Parent loans:** $56,691,853 (27% need-based, 73% non-need-based). **Programs:** Federal Direct (Subsidized and Unsubsidized Stafford, PLUS), Perkins, state, college/university, short-term emergency loans.

WORK-STUDY Federal work-study: Total amount: $5,910,763; 1,783 jobs averaging $3322. **State or other work-study/employment:** Total amount: $499,688 (100% need-based). 153 part-time jobs averaging $3290.

ATHLETIC AWARDS Total amount: $3,819,562 (2% need-based, 98% non-need-based).

APPLYING FOR FINANCIAL AID Required financial aid form: FAFSA. **Financial aid deadline (priority):** 1/15. **Notification date:** Continuous beginning 5/1. Students must reply within 3 weeks of notification.

CONTACT Dr. Chris Murr, Director of Financial Aid, Texas State University, 601 University Drive, San Marcos, TX 78666-4602, 512-245-2315. Fax: 512-245-7920. E-mail: cm18@txstate.edu.

Website: http://www.txstate.edu/.

time tuition and fees vary according to course load, location, program, and reciprocity agreements. **College room and board:** $5956; **Room only:** $3428. Room and board charges vary according to board plan and housing facility.

FRESHMAN FINANCIAL AID (Fall 2016) 3,113 applied for aid; of those 74% were deemed to have need. 100% of freshmen with need received aid; of those 15% had need fully met. **Average percent of need met:** 68% (excluding resources awarded to replace EFC). **Average financial aid package:** $14,477 (excluding resources awarded to replace EFC). 15% of all full-time freshmen had no need and received non-need-based gift aid.

UNDERGRADUATE FINANCIAL AID (Fall 2016) 16,239 applied for aid; of those 82% were deemed to have need. 100% of undergraduates with need received aid; of those 8% had need fully met. **Average percent of need met:** 67% (excluding resources awarded to replace EFC). **Average financial aid package:** $15,085 (excluding resources awarded to replace EFC). 12% of all full-time undergraduates had no need and received non-need-based gift aid.

GIFT AID (NEED-BASED) Total amount: $89,421,541 (39% federal, 20% state, 31% institutional, 10% external sources). **Receiving aid:** Freshmen: 44% (2,044); all full-time undergraduates: 42% (11,281). **Average award:** Freshmen: $8228; Undergraduates: $7786. **Scholarships, grants, and awards:** Federal Pell, FSEOG, state, private, college/university gift aid from institutional funds.

GIFT AID (NON-NEED-BASED) Total amount: $14,502,484 (78% institutional, 22% external sources). **Receiving aid:** Freshmen: 26% (1,229). Undergraduates: 17% (4,546). **Average award:** Freshmen: $3866. Undergraduates: $3564. **Scholarships, grants, and awards by category:** Academic interests/achievement: agriculture, architecture, biological sciences, business, communication, computer science, education, engineering/technologies, English, foreign languages, general academic interests/achievements, home economics, humanities, international studies, mathematics, military science, physical sciences, premedicine, social sciences. Creative arts/performance: applied art and design, art/fine arts, dance, journalism/publications, music, performing arts, theater/drama. Special achievements/activities: community service, general special achievements/activities, hobbies/interests, leadership, memberships, rodeo. Special characteristics: children of faculty/staff, first-generation college students, handicapped students, out-of-state students, veterans, veterans' children. **Tuition waivers:** Full- or partial for employees or children of employees, senior citizens. **ROTC:** Army, Air Force.

LOANS Student loans: $127,732,084 (80% need-based, 20% non-need-based). 55% of past graduating class borrowed through all loan programs. Average indebtedness per student: $30,759. **Average need-based loan:** Freshmen: $4655. Undergraduates: $5307. **Parent loans:** $24,616,110 (77% need-based, 23% non-need-based). **Programs:** Federal Direct (Subsidized and Unsubsidized Stafford, PLUS), Perkins, state, college/university, private loans.

WORK-STUDY Federal work-study: 360 jobs averaging $2520. **State or other work-study/employment:** Total amount: $7774 (100% need-based). 6 part-time jobs averaging $1296.

ATHLETIC AWARDS Total amount: $5,786,672 (44% need-based, 56% non-need-based).

APPLYING FOR FINANCIAL AID Required financial aid form: FAFSA. **Financial aid deadline (priority):** 3/15. **Notification date:** Continuous. Students must reply within 2 weeks of notification.

CONTACT Shannon Crossland, Interim Director of Student Financial Aid, Texas Tech University, PO Box 45011, Lubbock, TX 79409-5011, 806-742-3681. Fax: 806-742-0880.

Website: http://www.ttu.edu/.

TEXAS TECH UNIVERSITY
Lubbock, TX

Tuition & fees (TX res): $10,772	Average undergraduate aid package: $15,085

ABOUT THE INSTITUTION State-supported, coed. **Awards:** certificates, bachelor's, master's, and doctoral degrees. 88 undergraduate majors. **Total enrollment:** 36,996. Undergraduates: 30,737. Freshmen: 5,883. Federal methodology is used as a basis for awarding need-based institutional aid.

UNDERGRADUATE EXPENSES for 2017–2018 Application fee: $75. **Tuition, state resident:** full-time $8040; part-time $268 per credit hour. **Tuition, nonresident:** full-time $20,280; part-time $676 per credit hour. **Required fees:** full-time $2732; $50.50 per credit hour or $608 per term. Full-time tuition and fees vary according to course load, location, program, and reciprocity agreements. Part-

---

TEXAS WESLEYAN UNIVERSITY
Fort Worth, TX

Tuition & fees: $27,800	Average undergraduate aid package: $23,340

ABOUT THE INSTITUTION Independent United Methodist, coed. **Awards:** bachelor's, master's, and doctoral degrees. 41 undergraduate majors. **Total enrollment:** 2,619. Undergraduates: 1,905. Freshmen: 301. Federal methodology is used as a basis for awarding need-based institutional aid.

UNDERGRADUATE EXPENSES for 2017–2018 Comprehensive fee: $37,338 includes full-time tuition ($24,178), mandatory fees ($3622), and room and board ($9538). **College room only:** $5592. Full-time tuition and fees vary according to course level, course load, degree level, and program. Room and board charges vary

according to housing facility. **Part-time tuition:** $828 per credit hour. Part-time tuition and fees vary according to course level, course load, degree level, and program.
FRESHMAN FINANCIAL AID (Fall 2016) 264 applied for aid; of those 92% were deemed to have need. 100% of freshmen with need received aid; of those 13% had need fully met. **Average percent of need met:** 70% (excluding resources awarded to replace EFC). **Average financial aid package:** $24,949 (excluding resources awarded to replace EFC). 19% of all full-time freshmen had no need and received non-need-based gift aid.
UNDERGRADUATE FINANCIAL AID (Fall 2016) 1,192 applied for aid; of those 92% were deemed to have need. 100% of undergraduates with need received aid; of those 11% had need fully met. **Average percent of need met:** 66% (excluding resources awarded to replace EFC). **Average financial aid package:** $23,340 (excluding resources awarded to replace EFC). 18% of all full-time undergraduates had no need and received non-need-based gift aid.
GIFT AID (NEED-BASED) Total amount: $19,149,883 (20% federal, 14% state, 65% institutional, 1% external sources). **Receiving aid:** Freshmen: 80% (242); all full-time undergraduates: 73% (1,086). **Average award:** Freshmen: $20,526; Undergraduates: $17,945. **Scholarships, grants, and awards:** Federal Pell, FSEOG, state, private, college/university gift aid from institutional funds, Federal Nursing.
GIFT AID (NON-NEED-BASED) Total amount: $4,275,529 (2% federal, 3% state, 94% institutional, 1% external sources). **Receiving aid:** Freshmen: 22% (66). Undergraduates: 19% (277). **Average award:** Freshmen: $11,953. Undergraduates: $11,241. **Scholarships, grants, and awards by category:** Academic interests/achievement: biological sciences, business, communication, education, English, foreign languages, general academic interests/achievements, health fields, humanities, international studies, mathematics, military science, physical sciences, premedicine, religion/biblical studies, social sciences. Creative arts/performance: art/fine arts, creative writing, dance, debating, journalism/publications, music, performing arts, theater/drama. Special achievements/activities: cheerleading/drum major, community service, leadership, memberships, religious involvement. Special characteristics: adult students, children and siblings of alumni, children of current students, children of educators, children of faculty/staff, children of public servants, children of union members/company employees, children with a deceased or disabled parent, ethnic background, first-generation college students, general special characteristics, handicapped students, international students, local/state students, married students, members of minority groups, out-of-state students, parents of current students, previous college experience, public servants, relatives of clergy, religious affiliation, siblings of current students, spouses of current students, spouses of deceased or disabled public servants, twins, veterans, veterans' children. **Tuition waivers:** Full or partial for employees or children of employees. **ROTC:** Army cooperative, Air Force cooperative.
LOANS Student loans: $11,831,232 (87% need-based, 13% non-need-based). 57% of past graduating class borrowed through all loan programs. **Average indebtedness per student:** $12,360. **Average need-based loan:** Freshmen: $3202. Undergraduates: $3966. **Parent loans:** $1,426,509 (76% need-based, 24% non-need-based). **Programs:** Federal Direct (Subsidized and Unsubsidized Stafford, PLUS), state.
WORK-STUDY Federal work-study: 87 jobs averaging $4000. **State or other work-study/employment:** Total amount: $12,454 (91% need-based, 9% non-need-based). 4 part-time jobs averaging $4000.
ATHLETIC AWARDS Total amount: $1,802,255 (48% need-based, 52% non-need-based).
APPLYING FOR FINANCIAL AID Required financial aid form: FAFSA. **Financial aid deadline (priority):** 3/1. **Notification date:** Continuous beginning 3/1. Students must reply by 3/1.
CONTACT Laurie Rosenkrantz, Office of Financial Aid, Texas Wesleyan University, 1201 Wesleyan Street, Fort Worth, TX 76105-1536, 817-531-4420 or toll-free 800-580-8980. Fax: 817-531-4231. E-mail: financialaid@txwes.edu.
Website: http://www.txwes.edu/.

UNDERGRADUATE EXPENSES for 2018–2019 **Application fee:** $50. **Tuition, state resident:** full-time $6450; part-time $215 per credit hour. **Tuition, nonresident:** full-time $18,630; part-time $621 per credit hour. **Required fees:** full-time $2910; $87.13 per credit hour or $290 per term. Full-time tuition and fees vary according to course level, course load, program, and reciprocity agreements. Part-time tuition and fees vary according to course level, course load, program, and reciprocity agreements. **College room and board:** $8181; **Room only:** $4470. Room and board charges vary according to board plan and housing facility. **Payment plan:** Guaranteed tuition.
FRESHMAN FINANCIAL AID (Fall 2017, est.) 1,083 applied for aid; of those 85% were deemed to have need. 99% of freshmen with need received aid; of those 34% had need fully met. **Average percent of need met:** 87% (excluding resources awarded to replace EFC). **Average financial aid package:** $14,927 (excluding resources awarded to replace EFC). 9% of all full-time freshmen had no need and received non-need-based gift aid.
UNDERGRADUATE FINANCIAL AID (Fall 2017, est.) 5,396 applied for aid; of those 87% were deemed to have need. 99% of undergraduates with need received aid; of those 30% had need fully met. **Average percent of need met:** 84% (excluding resources awarded to replace EFC). **Average financial aid package:** $13,486 (excluding resources awarded to replace EFC). 6% of all full-time undergraduates had no need and received non-need-based gift aid.
GIFT AID (NEED-BASED) Total amount: $40,500,594 (43% federal, 24% state, 30% institutional, 3% external sources). **Receiving aid:** Freshmen: 70% (866); all full-time undergraduates: 62% (4,333). **Average award:** Freshmen: $9446; Undergraduates: $7381. **Scholarships, grants, and awards:** Federal Pell, FSEOG, state, private, college/university gift aid from institutional funds, United Negro College Fund, Federal Nursing.
GIFT AID (NON-NEED-BASED) Total amount: $9,520,491 (100% institutional). **Receiving aid:** Freshmen: 26% (318). Undergraduates: 20% (1,361). **Average award:** Freshmen: $3978. Undergraduates: $4526. **Scholarships, grants, and awards by category:** Academic interests/achievement: biological sciences, business, communication, computer science, education, English, foreign languages, general academic interests/achievements, health fields, home economics, humanities, library science, mathematics, physical sciences, premedicine, social sciences. Creative arts/performance: applied art and design, art/fine arts, cinema/film/broadcasting, dance, journalism/publications, music, theater/drama. Special characteristics: international students. **Tuition waivers:** Full or partial for senior citizens. **ROTC:** Army cooperative, Naval cooperative, Air Force cooperative.
LOANS Student loans: $33,288,452 (100% need-based). 72% of past graduating class borrowed through all loan programs. **Average indebtedness per student:** $23,983. **Average need-based loan:** Freshmen: $5223. Undergraduates: $6825. **Parent loans:** $1,285,809 (100% need-based). **Programs:** Federal Direct (Subsidized and Unsubsidized Stafford, PLUS), Perkins, Federal Nursing, state, college/university, alternative loans.
WORK-STUDY Federal work-study: Total amount: $1,141,219; jobs available. **State or other work-study/employment:** Total amount: $1,001,141 (100% non-need-based). Part-time jobs available.
ATHLETIC AWARDS Total amount: $524,845 (100% need-based).
APPLYING FOR FINANCIAL AID Required financial aid form: FAFSA. **Financial aid deadline:** 3/15. **Notification date:** Continuous beginning 3/15. Students must reply by 8/31.
CONTACT Mr. Governor Jackson, Executive Director of Financial Aid, Texas Woman's University, PO Box 425408, Denton, TX 76204-5408, 940-898-3051 or toll-free 866-809-6130. Fax: 940-898-3068. E-mail: gjackson@twu.edu.
Website: http://www.twu.edu/.

TEXAS WOMAN'S UNIVERSITY
Denton, TX

Tuition & fees (TX res): $9360	Average undergraduate aid package: $13,486

ABOUT THE INSTITUTION State-supported, coed, primarily women. **Awards:** certificates, bachelor's, master's, and doctoral degrees. 42 undergraduate majors. **Total enrollment:** 15,472. Undergraduates: 10,309. Freshmen: 1,272. Both federal and institutional methodology are used as a basis for awarding need-based institutional aid.

THEOLOGICAL UNIVERSITY OF THE CARIBBEAN
Saint Just, PR

Tuition & fees: $5442	Average undergraduate aid package: $2356

ABOUT THE INSTITUTION Independent Pentecostal, coed. **Awards:** certificates, diplomas, associate, bachelor's, and master's degrees. 4 undergraduate majors. **Total enrollment:** 371. Undergraduates: 279. Freshmen: 49. Federal methodology is used as a basis for awarding need-based institutional aid.

UNDERGRADUATE EXPENSES for 2018–2019 *Application fee:* $45. *Comprehensive fee:* $7842 includes full-time tuition ($4442), mandatory fees ($1000), and room and board ($2400). *College room only:* $1200. Full-time tuition and fees vary according to course load. Room and board charges vary according to board plan. *Part-time tuition:* $19.73 per credit hour. *Part-time fees:* $148 per credit hour; $3552 per term. Part-time tuition and fees vary according to course load.
FRESHMAN FINANCIAL AID (Fall 2016) 27 applied for aid; of those 100% were deemed to have need. 100% of freshmen with need received aid. *Average financial aid package:* $2356 (excluding resources awarded to replace EFC).
UNDERGRADUATE FINANCIAL AID (Fall 2016) 269 applied for aid; of those 100% were deemed to have need. 100% of undergraduates with need received aid. *Average financial aid package:* $2356 (excluding resources awarded to replace EFC).
GIFT AID (NEED-BASED) *Total amount:* $1,033,393 (100% federal). *Receiving aid:* Freshmen: 77% (27); all full-time undergraduates: 100% (269). *Average award:* Freshmen: $2356; Undergraduates: $2356. *Scholarships, grants, and awards:* Federal Pell.
GIFT AID (NON-NEED-BASED) *Tuition waivers:* Full or partial for employees or children of employees.
LOANS *Student loans:* $312,077 (100% need-based). 37% of past graduating class borrowed through all loan programs. *Average indebtedness per student:* $8906. *Average need-based loan:* Freshmen: $2195. Undergraduates: $2195. *Programs:* Federal Direct (Subsidized and Unsubsidized Stafford).
APPLYING FOR FINANCIAL AID *Required financial aid form:* FAFSA. *Financial aid deadline:* 6/30 (priority: 1/1). *Notification date:* 10/1.
CONTACT Mrs. Claudia M. Rodriguez, Financial Aid Officer, Theological University of the Caribbean, PO Box 901, Saint Just, PR 00978-0901, 787-761-0640 Ext. 224. *Fax:* 787-748-9220. *E-mail:* asistenciaeconomica@utcpr.edu. *Website:* http://www.utcpr.edu/.

THIEL COLLEGE
Greenville, PA

ABOUT THE INSTITUTION Independent Evangelical Lutheran Church in America, coed. 43 undergraduate majors.
GIFT AID (NEED-BASED) *Scholarships, grants, and awards:* Federal Pell, FSEOG, state, private, college/university gift aid from institutional funds.
GIFT AID (NON-NEED-BASED) *Scholarships, grants, and awards by category:* Academic interests/achievement: biological sciences, business, communication, computer science, education, English, general academic interests/achievements, mathematics, physical sciences, religion/biblical studies. Creative arts/performance: music, theater/drama. Special achievements/activities: leadership. Special characteristics: children and siblings of alumni, children of faculty/staff, international students, local/state students, relatives of clergy, religious affiliation, siblings of current students, veterans.
LOANS *Programs:* Federal Direct (Subsidized and Unsubsidized Stafford, PLUS), Perkins.
WORK-STUDY *Federal work-study:* 76 jobs averaging $1395. *State or other work-study/employment:* Total amount: $570,538 (96% need-based, 4% non-need-based). 375 part-time jobs averaging $1456.
APPLYING FOR FINANCIAL AID *Required financial aid forms:* FAFSA, state aid form.
CONTACT Ms. Cynthia H. Farrell, Director of Financial Aid, Thiel College, 75 College Avenue, Greenville, PA 16125-2181, 724-589-2178 or toll-free 800-248-4435. *Fax:* 724-589-2790. *E-mail:* cfarrell@thiel.edu. *Website:* http://www.thiel.edu/.

THOMAS AQUINAS COLLEGE
Santa Paula, CA

Tuition & fees: $24,500	Average undergraduate aid package: $20,095

ABOUT THE INSTITUTION Independent Roman Catholic, coed. *Awards:* bachelor's degrees. 1 undergraduate major. *Total enrollment:* 370. Undergraduates: 370. Freshmen: 90. Both federal and institutional methodology are used as a basis for awarding need-based institutional aid.
UNDERGRADUATE EXPENSES for 2017–2018 *Comprehensive fee:* $32,450 includes full-time tuition ($24,500) and room and board ($7950).
FRESHMAN FINANCIAL AID (Fall 2017, est.) 58 applied for aid; of those 98% were deemed to have need. 100% of freshmen with need received aid; of those 100% had need fully met. *Average percent of need met:* 100% (excluding resources awarded to replace EFC). *Average financial aid package:* $19,352 (excluding resources awarded to replace EFC).
UNDERGRADUATE FINANCIAL AID (Fall 2017, est.) 262 applied for aid; of those 98% were deemed to have need. 100% of undergraduates with need received aid; of those 100% had need fully met. *Average percent of need met:* 100% (excluding resources awarded to replace EFC). *Average financial aid package:* $20,095 (excluding resources awarded to replace EFC).
GIFT AID (NEED-BASED) *Total amount:* $3,002,252 (13% federal, 11% state, 75% institutional, 1% external sources). *Receiving aid:* Freshmen: 53% (48); all full-time undergraduates: 60% (221). *Average award:* Freshmen: $14,359; Undergraduates: $13,585. *Scholarships, grants, and awards:* Federal Pell, state, private, college/university gift aid from institutional funds, Canadian federal and provincial grants and scholarships.
GIFT AID (NON-NEED-BASED) *Total amount:* $11,050 (100% external sources).
LOANS *Student loans:* $1,282,592 (82% need-based, 18% non-need-based). 86% of past graduating class borrowed through all loan programs. *Average indebtedness per student:* $19,269. *Average need-based loan:* Freshmen: $2975. Undergraduates: $4650. *Parent loans:* $262,918 (100% non-need-based). *Programs:* Federal Direct (Subsidized and Unsubsidized Stafford, PLUS), college/university, Canadian student loans.
WORK-STUDY *State or other work-study/employment:* Total amount: $1,131,757 (100% need-based). 236 part-time jobs averaging $4796.
APPLYING FOR FINANCIAL AID *Required financial aid forms:* FAFSA, institution's own form, state aid form, federal income tax form(s), W-2 forms, institution's own Non-Custodial Parent Statement. *Financial aid deadline:* 3/2. *Notification date:* Continuous beginning 2/1. Students must reply by 5/1 or within 2 weeks of notification.
CONTACT Mr. Gregory Becher, Director of Financial Aid, Thomas Aquinas College, 10000 Ojai Road, Santa Paula, CA 93060-9980, 805-525-4419 Ext. 5936 or toll-free 800-634-9797. *Fax:* 805-525-9342. *E-mail:* gbecher@thomasaquinas.edu. *Website:* http://www.thomasaquinas.edu/.

THOMAS COLLEGE
Waterville, ME

Tuition & fees: N/R	Average undergraduate aid package: $20,266

ABOUT THE INSTITUTION Independent, coed. 23 undergraduate majors. Federal methodology is used as a basis for awarding need-based institutional aid.
FRESHMAN FINANCIAL AID (Fall 2017, est.) 215 applied for aid; of those 92% were deemed to have need. 100% of freshmen with need received aid; of those 12% had need fully met. *Average percent of need met:* 85% (excluding resources awarded to replace EFC). *Average financial aid package:* $21,043 (excluding resources awarded to replace EFC). 11% of all full-time freshmen had no need and received non-need-based gift aid.
UNDERGRADUATE FINANCIAL AID (Fall 2017, est.) 718 applied for aid; of those 93% were deemed to have need. 100% of undergraduates with need received aid; of those 12% had need fully met. *Average percent of need met:* 85% (excluding resources awarded to replace EFC). *Average financial aid package:* $20,266 (excluding resources awarded to replace EFC). 12% of all full-time undergraduates had no need and received non-need-based gift aid.
GIFT AID (NEED-BASED) *Total amount:* $10,311,370 (18% federal, 3% state, 79% institutional). *Receiving aid:* Freshmen: 89% (197); all full-time undergraduates: 86% (662). *Average award:* Freshmen: $16,772; Undergraduates: $15,172. *Scholarships, grants, and awards:* Federal Pell, FSEOG, state, private, college/university gift aid from institutional funds.
GIFT AID (NON-NEED-BASED) *Total amount:* $1,230,785 (65% institutional, 35% external sources). *Receiving aid:* Freshmen: 33% (74). Undergraduates: 18% (143). *Average award:* Freshmen: $11,665. Undergraduates: $10,216. *Scholarships, grants, and awards by category:* Academic interests/achievement: 572

awards ($5,413,428 total): general academic interests/achievements. *Special characteristics:* children and siblings of alumni, children of current students, children of faculty/staff, international students, local/state students, out-of-state students, veterans, veterans' children.

LOANS *Student loans:* $7,497,284 (36% need-based, 64% non-need-based). 96% of past graduating class borrowed through all loan programs. *Average indebtedness per student:* $31,142. *Average need-based loan:* Freshmen: $3744. Undergraduates: $4406. *Parent loans:* $1,156,272 (100% non-need-based). *Programs:* Federal Direct (Subsidized and Unsubsidized Stafford, PLUS), Perkins.

WORK-STUDY *Federal work-study:* Total amount: $198,931; 84 jobs averaging $2368.

APPLYING FOR FINANCIAL AID *Required financial aid form:* FAFSA. *Financial aid deadline (priority):* 2/15. *Notification date:* Continuous beginning 1/15. Students must reply within 2 weeks of notification.

CONTACT Jeannine Bosse, Director of Student Financial Services, Thomas College, 180 West River Road, Waterville, ME 04901-5097, 800-339-7001. *Fax:* 207-859-1115. *E-mail:* sfsdir@thomas.edu. *Website:* http://www.thomas.edu/.

THOMAS EDISON STATE UNIVERSITY
Trenton, NJ

Tuition & fees (NJ res): $7300	Average undergraduate aid package: N/A

ABOUT THE INSTITUTION State-supported, coed. *Awards:* certificates, associate, bachelor's, master's, and doctoral degrees (offers only distance learning degree programs). 27 undergraduate majors. *Total enrollment:* 16,233. Undergraduates: 15,238. Federal methodology is used as a basis for awarding need-based institutional aid.

UNDERGRADUATE EXPENSES for 2017–2018 *Application fee:* $75. *Tuition, state resident:* full-time $7300; part-time $396 per credit hour. *Tuition, nonresident:* full-time $9820; part-time $499 per credit hour.

GIFT AID (NEED-BASED) *Total amount:* $4,448,691 (93% federal, 3% state, 4% external sources). *Scholarships, grants, and awards:* Federal Pell, state.

GIFT AID (NON-NEED-BASED) *Scholarships, grants, and awards by category: Academic interests/achievement:* general academic interests/achievements. *Tuition waivers:* Full or partial for employees or children of employees.

LOANS *Student loans:* $17,575,946 (100% need-based). *Programs:* Federal Direct (Subsidized and Unsubsidized Stafford, PLUS), state, private loans.

APPLYING FOR FINANCIAL AID *Required financial aid form:* FAFSA. *Financial aid deadline:* Continuous. *Notification date:* Continuous. Students must reply within 4 weeks of notification.

CONTACT Mr. James Owens, Director of Financial Aid, Thomas Edison State University, 111 West State Street, Trenton, NJ 08608, 888-442-8372. *E-mail:* finaid@tesu.edu. *Website:* http://www.tesu.edu/.

THOMAS JEFFERSON UNIVERSITY
Philadelphia, PA

Tuition & fees: N/R	Average undergraduate aid package: $29,481

ABOUT THE INSTITUTION Independent, coed. *Awards:* certificates, associate, bachelor's, master's, and doctoral degrees. 7 undergraduate majors. *Total enrollment:* 3,326. Undergraduates: 1,131. Institutional methodology is used as a basis for awarding need-based institutional aid.

FRESHMAN FINANCIAL AID (Fall 2017, est.) 459 applied for aid; of those 89% were deemed to have need. 100% of freshmen with need received aid; of those 18% had need fully met. *Average percent of need met:* 83% (excluding resources awarded to replace EFC). *Average financial aid package:* $36,481 (excluding resources awarded to replace EFC). 14% of all full-time freshmen had no need and received non-need-based gift aid.

UNDERGRADUATE FINANCIAL AID (Fall 2017, est.) 2,108 applied for aid; of those 90% were deemed to have need. 100% of undergraduates with need received aid; of those 15% had need fully met. *Average percent of need met:* 72%

(excluding resources awarded to replace EFC). *Average financial aid package:* $29,481 (excluding resources awarded to replace EFC). 14% of all full-time undergraduates had no need and received non-need-based gift aid.

GIFT AID (NEED-BASED) *Total amount:* $42,486,914 (10% federal, 5% state, 84% institutional, 1% external sources). *Receiving aid:* Freshmen: 85% (408); all full-time undergraduates: 79% (1,856). *Average award:* Freshmen: $30,647; Undergraduates: $24,155. *Scholarships, grants, and awards:* Federal Pell, FSEOG, state, private, college/university gift aid from institutional funds.

GIFT AID (NON-NEED-BASED) *Total amount:* $5,473,578 (2% federal, 96% institutional, 2% external sources). *Receiving aid:* Freshmen: 10% (50). Undergraduates: 8% (188). *Average award:* Freshmen: $14,955. Undergraduates: $12,646. *Scholarships, grants, and awards by category: Academic interests/achievement:* general academic interests/achievements. *Special characteristics:* members of minority groups, veterans. *ROTC:* Air Force cooperative.

LOANS *Student loans:* $17,960,598 (75% need-based, 25% non-need-based). 79% of past graduating class borrowed through all loan programs. *Average indebtedness per student:* $40,100. *Average need-based loan:* Freshmen: $3804. Undergraduates: $4370. *Parent loans:* $8,066,405 (46% need-based, 54% non-need-based). *Programs:* Federal Direct (Subsidized and Unsubsidized Stafford, PLUS), Perkins, private loans.

WORK-STUDY *Federal work-study:* Total amount: $1,928,114; jobs available. *State or other work-study/employment:* Total amount: $547,027 (82% need-based, 18% non-need-based). Part-time jobs available.

ATHLETIC AWARDS Total amount: $3,193,811 (53% need-based, 47% non-need-based).

APPLYING FOR FINANCIAL AID *Required financial aid forms:* FAFSA, state aid form. *Financial aid deadline:* 4/15 (priority: 12/15). *Notification date:* Continuous beginning 12/15. Students must reply by 5/1.

CONTACT Office of Financial Aid, Thomas Jefferson University, 4201 Henry Avenue, Philadelphia, PA 19144, 215-951-2800 or toll-free 877-533-3247. *E-mail:* financial.aid@jefferson.edu. *Website:* http://www.jefferson.edu/university.html.

THOMAS MORE COLLEGE
Crestview Hills, KY

Tuition & fees: $30,270	Average undergraduate aid package: $20,806

ABOUT THE INSTITUTION Independent Roman Catholic, coed. *Awards:* certificates, associate, bachelor's, and master's degrees. 48 undergraduate majors. *Total enrollment:* 1,959. Undergraduates: 1,821. Freshmen: 414. Federal methodology is used as a basis for awarding need-based institutional aid.

UNDERGRADUATE EXPENSES for 2017–2018 *Application fee:* $25. *One-time required fee:* $125. *Comprehensive fee:* $37,862 includes full-time tuition ($28,850), mandatory fees ($1420), and room and board ($7592). *College room only:* $4200. Room and board charges vary according to board plan and housing facility. *Part-time tuition:* $635 per credit hour. *Part-time fees:* $71 per credit hour.

FRESHMAN FINANCIAL AID (Fall 2017, est.) 342 applied for aid; of those 90% were deemed to have need. 99% of freshmen with need received aid; of those 26% had need fully met. *Average percent of need met:* 73% (excluding resources awarded to replace EFC). *Average financial aid package:* $23,123 (excluding resources awarded to replace EFC). 11% of all full-time freshmen had no need and received non-need-based gift aid.

UNDERGRADUATE FINANCIAL AID (Fall 2017, est.) 1,175 applied for aid; of those 91% were deemed to have need. 95% of undergraduates with need received aid; of those 24% had need fully met. *Average percent of need met:* 68% (excluding resources awarded to replace EFC). *Average financial aid package:* $20,806 (excluding resources awarded to replace EFC). 16% of all full-time undergraduates had no need and received non-need-based gift aid.

GIFT AID (NEED-BASED) *Total amount:* $16,475,174 (13% federal, 13% state, 73% institutional, 1% external sources). *Receiving aid:* Freshmen: 88% (307); all full-time undergraduates: 72% (978). *Average award:* Freshmen: $18,634; Undergraduates: $16,765. *Scholarships, grants, and awards:* Federal Pell, FSEOG, state, private, college/university gift aid from institutional funds, Federal Nursing.

GIFT AID (NON-NEED-BASED) *Total amount:* $4,529,058 (4% state, 95% institutional, 1% external sources). *Receiving aid:* Freshmen: 15% (53). Undergrad-

uates: 11% (151). *Average award:* Freshmen: $15,410. Undergraduates: $14,643. *Scholarships, grants, and awards by category:* *Academic interests/achievement:* 989 awards ($10,982,955 total): biological sciences, business, communication, computer science, education, English, general academic interests/achievements, mathematics, physical sciences, premedicine, religion/biblical studies, social sciences. *Creative arts/performance:* 163 awards ($387,231 total): art/fine arts, dance, music, theater/drama. *Special achievements/activities:* 72 awards ($165,020 total): cheerleading/drum major, community service, leadership, memberships, religious involvement. *Special characteristics:* 718 awards ($4,369,593 total): adult students, children and siblings of alumni, children of current students, children of faculty/staff, children of union members/company employees, international students, members of minority groups, out-of-state students, religious affiliation, siblings of current students, veterans, veterans' children. *Tuition waivers:* Full or partial for employees or children of employees, senior citizens. *ROTC:* Army cooperative, Air Force cooperative.

LOANS *Student loans:* $7,260,698 (67% need-based, 33% non-need-based). 69% of past graduating class borrowed through all loan programs. *Average indebtedness per student:* $32,908. *Average need-based loan:* Freshmen: $2974. Undergraduates: $3672. *Parent loans:* $2,089,688 (52% need-based, 48% non-need-based). *Programs:* Federal Direct (Subsidized and Unsubsidized Stafford, PLUS), Perkins, Federal Nursing, college/university.

WORK-STUDY *Federal work-study:* Total amount: $136,144; 134 jobs averaging $1016. *State or other work-study/employment:* 241 part-time jobs averaging $1150.

APPLYING FOR FINANCIAL AID *Required financial aid form:* FAFSA. *Financial aid deadline (priority):* 3/15. *Notification date:* Continuous beginning 3/1. Students must reply by 5/1.

CONTACT Mr. Mark Messingschlager, Director of Financial Aid, Thomas More College, 333 Thomas More Parkway, Crestview Hills, KY 41017-3495, 859-344-3506 or toll-free 800-825-4557. *Fax:* 859-344-4050. *E-mail:* messinm@thomasmore.edu. *Website:* http://www.thomasmore.edu/.

THOMAS MORE COLLEGE OF LIBERAL ARTS
Merrimack, NH

Tuition & fees: $21,600	Average undergraduate aid package: $18,718

ABOUT THE INSTITUTION Independent Roman Catholic Church, coed. *Awards:* bachelor's degrees. 1 undergraduate major. *Total enrollment:* 90. Undergraduates: 90. Freshmen: 13. Federal methodology is used as a basis for awarding need-based institutional aid.

UNDERGRADUATE EXPENSES for 2018–2019 *Comprehensive fee:* $31,300 includes full-time tuition ($21,600) and room and board ($9700). Full-time tuition and fees vary according to course load, program, and reciprocity agreements. Room and board charges vary according to board plan. *Part-time tuition:* $900 per credit hour. Part-time tuition and fees vary according to course load, program, and reciprocity agreements.

FRESHMAN FINANCIAL AID (Fall 2016) 24 applied for aid; of those 96% were deemed to have need. 100% of freshmen with need received aid; of those 9% had need fully met. *Average percent of need met:* 73% (excluding resources awarded to replace EFC). *Average financial aid package:* $18,012 (excluding resources awarded to replace EFC). 75% of all full-time freshmen had no need and received non-need-based gift aid.

UNDERGRADUATE FINANCIAL AID (Fall 2016) 81 applied for aid; of those 99% were deemed to have need. 100% of undergraduates with need received aid; of those 21% had need fully met. *Average percent of need met:* 75% (excluding resources awarded to replace EFC). *Average financial aid package:* $18,718 (excluding resources awarded to replace EFC). 36% of all full-time undergraduates had no need and received non-need-based gift aid.

GIFT AID (NEED-BASED) *Total amount:* $1,210,497 (17% federal, 1% state, 82% institutional). *Receiving aid:* Freshmen: 96% (23); all full-time undergraduates: 52% (48). *Average award:* Freshmen: $15,789; Undergraduates: $16,730. *Scholarships, grants, and awards:* Federal Pell, FSEOG, state, private, college/university gift aid from institutional funds.

GIFT AID (NON-NEED-BASED) *Total amount:* $283,685 (100% institutional). *Receiving aid:* Freshmen: 67% (16). Undergraduates: 42% (39). *Average award:*

Freshmen: $3772. Undergraduates: $6643. *Scholarships, grants, and awards by category:* *Special characteristics:* 9 awards ($9000 total): siblings of current students. *Tuition waivers:* Full or partial for employees or children of employees.

LOANS *Student loans:* $441,119 (63% need-based, 37% non-need-based). 29% of past graduating class borrowed through all loan programs. *Average indebtedness per student:* $26,828. *Average need-based loan:* Freshmen: $2534. Undergraduates: $4490. *Parent loans:* $113,485 (100% need-based). *Programs:* Federal Direct (Subsidized and Unsubsidized Stafford, PLUS).

WORK-STUDY *State or other work-study/employment:* Total amount: $62,808 (87% need-based, 13% non-need-based). Part-time jobs available.

APPLYING FOR FINANCIAL AID *Required financial aid form:* FAFSA. *Financial aid deadline:* Continuous. *Notification date:* Continuous beginning 2/15. Students must reply within 4 weeks of notification.

CONTACT Clinton A. Hanson Jr., Coordinator of Financial Aid, Thomas More College of Liberal Arts, 6 Manchester Street, Merrimack, NH 03054-4818, 603-880-8308 Ext. 23 or toll-free 800-880-8308. *Fax:* 603-880-9280. *E-mail:* chanson@thomasmorecollege.edu. *Website:* http://www.thomasmorecollege.edu/.

THOMAS UNIVERSITY
Thomasville, GA

Tuition & fees: $16,940	Average undergraduate aid package: N/A

ABOUT THE INSTITUTION Independent, coed. *Awards:* certificates, associate, bachelor's, and master's degrees. 23 undergraduate majors. *Total enrollment:* 1,596. Undergraduates: 1,114. Freshmen: 79. Federal methodology is used as a basis for awarding need-based institutional aid.

UNDERGRADUATE EXPENSES for 2018–2019 *Application fee:* $25. *Comprehensive fee:* $23,980 includes full-time tuition ($15,940), mandatory fees ($1000), and room and board ($7040). *College room only:* $6000. Room and board charges vary according to housing facility. *Part-time tuition:* $630 per credit hour. *Part-time fees:* $550 per year.

FRESHMAN FINANCIAL AID (Fall 2016) 47 applied for aid; of those 85% were deemed to have need. 100% of freshmen with need received aid. 79% of all full-time freshmen had no need and received non-need-based gift aid.

UNDERGRADUATE FINANCIAL AID (Fall 2016) 101 applied for aid.

GIFT AID (NEED-BASED) *Total amount:* $2,255,398 (62% federal, 17% state, 21% institutional). *Receiving aid:* Freshmen: 52% (35). *Scholarships, grants, and awards:* Federal Pell, FSEOG, state, private, college/university gift aid from institutional funds.

GIFT AID (NON-NEED-BASED) *Receiving aid:* Freshmen: 52% (35). *Average award:* Freshmen: $3834. *Scholarships, grants, and awards by category:* *Academic interests/achievement:* biological sciences, business, education, English, general academic interests/achievements, humanities, mathematics, physical sciences, social sciences. *Creative arts/performance:* art/fine arts, debating, music, theater/drama. *Special characteristics:* children and siblings of alumni, children of faculty/staff, ethnic background, out-of-state students, veterans.

LOANS *Student loans:* $6,751,331 (100% need-based). *Parent loans:* $466,832 (100% need-based). *Programs:* Federal Direct (Subsidized and Unsubsidized Stafford, PLUS), state, alternative loans.

WORK-STUDY *Federal work-study:* 41 jobs averaging $1584.

ATHLETIC AWARDS Total amount: $2,298,356 (100% need-based).

APPLYING FOR FINANCIAL AID *Required financial aid forms:* FAFSA, state aid form. *Financial aid deadline:* Continuous. *Notification date:* Continuous beginning 1/1.

CONTACT Mr. Clifton L. Mitchell Jr., Director of Financial Aid, Thomas University, 1501 Millpond Road, Thomasville, GA 31792-7499, 229-226-1621 Ext. 1002 or toll-free 800-538-9784. *Fax:* 229-584-2400. *E-mail:* cmitchell@thomasu.edu. *Website:* http://www.thomasu.edu/.

TIFFIN UNIVERSITY
Tiffin, OH

Tuition & fees: $25,000	Average undergraduate aid package: $18,067

ABOUT THE INSTITUTION Independent, coed. *Awards:* certificates, associate, bachelor's, and master's degrees. 47 undergraduate majors. *Total enrollment:* 3,149. Undergraduates: 2,243. Freshmen: 452. Federal methodology is used as a basis for awarding need-based institutional aid.

UNDERGRADUATE EXPENSES for 2018–2019 *Application fee:* $20. *Comprehensive fee:* $36,200 includes full-time tuition ($24,600), mandatory fees ($400), and room and board ($11,200). *College room only:* $6000. Full-time tuition and fees vary according to course load, degree level, location, program, and reciprocity agreements. Room and board charges vary according to board plan and housing facility. *Part-time tuition:* $820 per credit hour. Part-time tuition and fees vary according to course load, degree level, location, program, and reciprocity agreements.

FRESHMAN FINANCIAL AID (Fall 2017, est.) 424 applied for aid; of those 92% were deemed to have need. 100% of freshmen with need received aid; of those 16% had need fully met. *Average percent of need met:* 65% (excluding resources awarded to replace EFC). *Average financial aid package:* $19,092 (excluding resources awarded to replace EFC).

UNDERGRADUATE FINANCIAL AID (Fall 2017, est.) 1,398 applied for aid; of those 92% were deemed to have need. 100% of undergraduates with need received aid; of those 17% had need fully met. *Average percent of need met:* 67% (excluding resources awarded to replace EFC). *Average financial aid package:* $18,067 (excluding resources awarded to replace EFC).

GIFT AID (NEED-BASED) *Total amount:* $19,174,206 (21% federal, 8% state, 70% institutional, 1% external sources). *Receiving aid:* Freshmen: 87% (388); all full-time undergraduates: 71% (1,254). *Average award:* Freshmen: $15,933; Undergraduates: $14,483. *Scholarships, grants, and awards:* Federal Pell, FSEOG, state, private, college/university gift aid from institutional funds, United Negro College Fund.

GIFT AID (NON-NEED-BASED) *Receiving aid:* Freshmen: 9% (40). Undergraduates: 8% (137). *Scholarships, grants, and awards by category:* Academic interests/achievement: general academic interests/achievements. Creative arts/performance: music, performing arts, theater/drama. Special achievements/activities: cheerleading/drum major. Special characteristics: children of faculty/staff. *Tuition waivers:* Full or partial for employees or children of employees, senior citizens. *ROTC:* Army cooperative, Air Force cooperative.

LOANS *Student loans:* $13,298,472 (100% need-based). 82% of past graduating class borrowed through all loan programs. *Average indebtedness per student:* $36,819. *Average need-based loan:* Freshmen: $3097. Undergraduates: $3960. *Parent loans:* $3,648,365 (100% need-based). *Programs:* Federal Direct (Subsidized and Unsubsidized Stafford, PLUS), Perkins, college/university, private loans.

WORK-STUDY *Federal work-study:* Total amount: $309,693; jobs available.

ATHLETIC AWARDS Total amount: $3,695,296 (100% need-based).

APPLYING FOR FINANCIAL AID *Required financial aid form:* FAFSA. *Financial aid deadline:* Continuous. *Notification date:* Continuous beginning 11/1. Students must reply within 2 weeks of notification.

CONTACT Ms. Cindy Little, Director of Financial Aid Operations, Tiffin University, 155 Miami Street, Tiffin, OH 44883, 419-448-3415 or toll-free 800-968-6446. *Fax:* 419-443-5006. *E-mail:* clittle@tiffin.edu. *Website:* http://www.tiffin.edu/.

TOCCOA FALLS COLLEGE
Toccoa Falls, GA

Tuition & fees: $22,744	Average undergraduate aid package: $16,791

ABOUT THE INSTITUTION Independent interdenominational, coed. *Awards:* certificates, associate, and bachelor's degrees. 31 undergraduate majors. *Total enrollment:* 1,411. Undergraduates: 1,411. Freshmen: 217. Federal methodology is used as a basis for awarding need-based institutional aid.

UNDERGRADUATE EXPENSES for 2018–2019 *Application fee:* $30. *Comprehensive fee:* $31,074 includes full-time tuition ($21,974), mandatory fees ($770), and room and board ($8330). Full-time tuition and fees vary according to location. Room and board charges vary according to board plan. *Part-time tuition:* $916 per credit hour. *Part-time fees:* $770 per year. Part-time tuition and fees vary according to location.

FRESHMAN FINANCIAL AID (Fall 2016) 191 applied for aid; of those 89% were deemed to have need. 100% of freshmen with need received aid; of those 14% had need fully met. *Average percent of need met:* 63% (excluding resources awarded to replace EFC). *Average financial aid package:* $17,190 (excluding resources awarded to replace EFC). 10% of all full-time freshmen had no need and received non-need-based gift aid.

UNDERGRADUATE FINANCIAL AID (Fall 2016) 688 applied for aid; of those 92% were deemed to have need. 100% of undergraduates with need received aid; of those 13% had need fully met. *Average percent of need met:* 66% (excluding resources awarded to replace EFC). *Average financial aid package:* $16,791 (excluding resources awarded to replace EFC). 8% of all full-time undergraduates had no need and received non-need-based gift aid.

GIFT AID (NEED-BASED) *Total amount:* $8,578,225 (21% federal, 12% state, 64% institutional, 3% external sources). *Receiving aid:* Freshmen: 86% (170); all full-time undergraduates: 88% (628). *Average award:* Freshmen: $14,577; Undergraduates: $13,571. *Scholarships, grants, and awards:* Federal Pell, FSEOG, state, private, college/university gift aid from institutional funds.

GIFT AID (NON-NEED-BASED) *Total amount:* $1,061,288 (23% state, 73% institutional, 4% external sources). *Receiving aid:* Freshmen: 10% (20). Undergraduates: 8% (59). *Average award:* Freshmen: $8736. Undergraduates: $10,284. *Scholarships, grants, and awards by category:* Academic interests/achievement: business, communication, education, general academic interests/achievements, religion/biblical studies. Creative arts/performance: music. Special achievements/activities: leadership. Special characteristics: children of faculty/staff, ethnic background, general special characteristics, international students, married students, relatives of clergy, religious affiliation, siblings of current students. *Tuition waivers:* Full or partial for employees or children of employees.

LOANS *Student loans:* $3,864,637 (81% need-based, 19% non-need-based). 79% of past graduating class borrowed through all loan programs. *Average indebtedness per student:* $26,653. *Average need-based loan:* Freshmen: $3242. Undergraduates: $3670. *Parent loans:* $1,163,044 (64% need-based, 36% non-need-based). *Programs:* Federal Direct (Subsidized and Unsubsidized Stafford, PLUS), state.

WORK-STUDY *Federal work-study:* jobs available. *State or other work-study/employment:* Part-time jobs available.

APPLYING FOR FINANCIAL AID *Required financial aid forms:* FAFSA, institution's own form. *Financial aid deadline (priority):* 5/1. *Notification date:* Continuous beginning 3/15. Students must reply within 2 weeks of notification.

CONTACT Wanda V. Pickens, Director of Student Financial Services, Toccoa Falls College, 107 Kincaid Drive, Box 900, Toccoa Falls, GA 30598, 706-886-7299 Ext. 5435 or toll-free 888-785-5624. *Fax:* 706-282-6041. *E-mail:* wpickens@tfc.edu. *Website:* http://www.tfc.edu/.

TORAH TEMIMAH TALMUDICAL SEMINARY
Brooklyn, NY

CONTACT Financial Aid Office, Torah Temimah Talmudical Seminary, 507 Ocean Parkway, Brooklyn, NY 11218-5913, 718-853-8500.

TOUGALOO COLLEGE
Tougaloo, MS

CONTACT Director of Financial Aid, Tougaloo College, 500 West County Line Road, Tougaloo, MS 39174, 601-977-6134 or toll-free 888-42GALOO. *Fax:* 601-977-6164. *Website:* http://www.tougaloo.edu/.

TOURO COLLEGE
New York, NY

ABOUT THE INSTITUTION Independent, coed. 26 undergraduate majors.

GIFT AID (NEED-BASED) *Scholarships, grants, and awards:* Federal Pell, FSEOG, state, private, college/university gift aid from institutional funds.

GIFT AID (NON-NEED-BASED) *Scholarships, grants, and awards by category:* Academic interests/achievement: general academic interests/achievements. *Special characteristics:* children of faculty/staff.

LOANS *Programs:* Federal Direct (Subsidized and Unsubsidized Stafford, PLUS), Perkins, alternative loans.

WORK-STUDY Federal work-study jobs available. *State or other work-study/employment:* Total amount: $17,930 (100% non-need-based). Part-time jobs available.

APPLYING FOR FINANCIAL AID *Required financial aid forms:* FAFSA, institution's own form.

CONTACT Karyn Wright-Moore, Office of Financial Aid, Touro College, 27 West 23rd Street, New York, NY 10010, 212-463-0400 Ext. 5108. *E-mail:* karyn.wright-moore4@touro.edu.
Website: http://www.touro.edu/.

TOURO COLLEGE LOS ANGELES
West Hollywood, CA

CONTACT Financial Aid Office, Touro College Los Angeles, 1317 North Crescent Heights Boulevard, West Hollywood, CA 90046, 323-822-9700.
Website: http://www.touro.edu/losangeles/.

TOURO UNIVERSITY WORLDWIDE
Los Alamitos, CA

CONTACT Financial Aid Office, Touro University Worldwide, 10601 Calle Lee, Suite 179, Los Alamitos, CA 90720, 818-575-6800.
Website: http://www.tuw.edu/.

TOWSON UNIVERSITY
Towson, MD

Tuition & fees (MD res): $9694	Average undergraduate aid package: $10,468

ABOUT THE INSTITUTION State-supported, coed. *Awards:* certificates, bachelor's, master's, and doctoral degrees. 63 undergraduate majors. *Total enrollment:* 22,705. Undergraduates: 19,596. Freshmen: 2,741. Federal methodology is used as a basis for awarding need-based institutional aid.

UNDERGRADUATE EXPENSES for 2017–2018 *Application fee:* $45. *Tuition, state resident:* full-time $6692; part-time $288 per credit hour. *Tuition, nonresident:* full-time $19,138; part-time $806 per credit hour. *Required fees:* full-time $3002; $130 per credit hour. Full-time tuition and fees vary according to course load and location. Part-time tuition and fees vary according to course load and location. *College room and board:* $12,544; *Room only:* $6984. Room and board charges vary according to board plan and housing facility.

FRESHMAN FINANCIAL AID (Fall 2017, est.) 2,399 applied for aid; of those 72% were deemed to have need. 94% of freshmen with need received aid; of those 12% had need fully met. *Average percent of need met:* 56% (excluding resources awarded to replace EFC). *Average financial aid package:* $10,462 (excluding resources awarded to replace EFC). 8% of all full-time freshmen had no need and received non-need-based gift aid.

UNDERGRADUATE FINANCIAL AID (Fall 2017, est.) 12,624 applied for aid; of those 78% were deemed to have need. 95% of undergraduates with need received aid; of those 10% had need fully met. *Average percent of need met:* 57% (excluding resources awarded to replace EFC). *Average financial aid package:* $10,468 (excluding resources awarded to replace EFC). 6% of all full-time undergraduates had no need and received non-need-based gift aid.

GIFT AID (NEED-BASED) *Total amount:* $61,432,064 (44% federal, 22% state, 33% institutional, 1% external sources). *Receiving aid:* Freshmen: 35% (948); all full-time undergraduates: 35% (6,042). *Average award:* Freshmen: $9830; Undergrad-

uates: $9180. *Scholarships, grants, and awards:* Federal Pell, FSEOG, state, private, college/university gift aid from institutional funds.

GIFT AID (NON-NEED-BASED) *Total amount:* $13,719,077 (2% federal, 9% state, 72% institutional, 17% external sources). *Receiving aid:* Freshmen: 24% (670). Undergraduates: 15% (2,475). *Average award:* Freshmen: $4356. Undergraduates: $5099. *Scholarships, grants, and awards by category:* Academic interests/achievement: 1,943 awards ($8,521,386 total): biological sciences, business, communication, computer science, education, English, foreign languages, general academic interests/achievements, home economics, mathematics, physical sciences. *Creative arts/performance:* 145 awards ($489,404 total): art/fine arts, cinema/film/broadcasting, dance, debating, music, performing arts, theater/drama. *Special achievements/activities:* 131 awards ($177,062 total): community service, memberships. *Special characteristics:* 492 awards ($1,704,636 total): adult students, children and siblings of alumni, children of faculty/staff, ethnic background, first-generation college students, handicapped students, international students, members of minority groups, previous college experience, veterans. *Tuition waivers:* Full or partial for employees or children of employees, senior citizens. *ROTC:* Army cooperative, Air Force cooperative.

LOANS *Student loans:* $77,540,268 (49% need-based, 51% non-need-based). 60% of past graduating class borrowed through all loan programs. *Average indebtedness per student:* $26,460. *Average need-based loan:* Freshmen: $3206. Undergraduates: $4055. *Parent loans:* $37,614,843 (1% need-based, 99% non-need-based). *Programs:* Federal Direct (Subsidized and Unsubsidized Stafford, PLUS).

WORK-STUDY *Federal work-study:* Total amount: $1,266,288; 708 jobs averaging $1763.

ATHLETIC AWARDS Total amount: $6,490,354 (2% need-based, 98% non-need-based).

APPLYING FOR FINANCIAL AID *Required financial aid forms:* FAFSA, state aid form. *Financial aid deadline (priority):* 1/17. *Notification date:* Continuous beginning 3/15. Students must reply by 5/1 or within 2 weeks of notification.

CONTACT Mr. David Horne, Director of Financial Aid, Towson University, 8000 York Road, Towson, MD 21252-0001, 410-704-4236. *E-mail:* finaid@towson.edu.
Website: http://www.towson.edu/.

TRANSYLVANIA UNIVERSITY
Lexington, KY

Tuition & fees: $38,750	Average undergraduate aid package: $28,380

ABOUT THE INSTITUTION Independent Christian Church (Disciples of Christ), coed. *Awards:* bachelor's degrees. 35 undergraduate majors. *Total enrollment:* 963. Undergraduates: 963. Freshmen: 281. Federal methodology is used as a basis for awarding need-based institutional aid.

UNDERGRADUATE EXPENSES for 2018–2019 *Comprehensive fee:* $49,210 includes full-time tuition ($37,170), mandatory fees ($1580), and room and board ($10,460). *College room only:* $5920. Room and board charges vary according to board plan and housing facility. *Part-time tuition:* $4130 per course. Part-time tuition and fees vary according to course load.

FRESHMAN FINANCIAL AID (Fall 2017, est.) 266 applied for aid; of those 83% were deemed to have need. 100% of freshmen with need received aid; of those 26% had need fully met. *Average percent of need met:* 80% (excluding resources awarded to replace EFC). *Average financial aid package:* $29,177 (excluding resources awarded to replace EFC). 22% of all full-time freshmen had no need and received non-need-based gift aid.

UNDERGRADUATE FINANCIAL AID (Fall 2017, est.) 761 applied for aid; of those 86% were deemed to have need. 100% of undergraduates with need received aid; of those 23% had need fully met. *Average percent of need met:* 78% (excluding resources awarded to replace EFC). *Average financial aid package:* $28,380 (excluding resources awarded to replace EFC). 30% of all full-time undergraduates had no need and received non-need-based gift aid.

GIFT AID (NEED-BASED) *Total amount:* $15,634,519 (8% federal, 14% state, 76% institutional, 2% external sources). *Receiving aid:* Freshmen: 78% (220); all full-time undergraduates: 69% (658). *Average award:* Freshmen: $25,956; Undergraduates: $24,474. *Scholarships, grants, and awards:* Federal Pell, FSEOG, state, private, college/university gift aid from institutional funds.

GIFT AID (NON-NEED-BASED) *Total amount:* $6,606,064 (9% state, 87% institutional, 4% external sources). *Receiving aid:* Freshmen: 14% (40). Undergrad-

uates: 11% (108). *Average award:* Freshmen: $17,309. Undergraduates: $17,591. *Scholarships, grants, and awards by category:* Academic interests/achievement: $13,175,952 total: general academic interests/achievements. *Creative arts/performance:* $238,875 total: art/fine arts, music, theater/drama. *Special achievements/activities:* $3,566,557 total: general special achievements/activities. *Special characteristics:* $1,353,380 total: children of faculty/staff, members of minority groups, out-of-state students, relatives of clergy, religious affiliation. *Tuition waivers:* Full or partial for employees or children of employees. *ROTC:* Army cooperative, Air Force cooperative.

LOANS *Student loans:* $5,252,192 (67% need-based, 33% non-need-based). 65% of past graduating class borrowed through all loan programs. *Average indebtedness per student:* $30,595. *Average need-based loan:* Freshmen: $3350. Undergraduates: $4240. *Parent loans:* $2,256,254 (42% need-based, 58% non-need-based). *Programs:* Federal Direct (Subsidized and Unsubsidized Stafford, PLUS).

WORK-STUDY *Federal work-study:* Total amount: $376,025; 313 jobs averaging $1682. *State or other work-study/employment:* Total amount: $182,700 (32% need-based, 68% non-need-based). 30 part-time jobs averaging $6363.

APPLYING FOR FINANCIAL AID *Required financial aid form:* FAFSA. *Financial aid deadline (priority):* 10/31. *Notification date:* Continuous beginning 12/20. Students must reply within 2 weeks of notification.

CONTACT Ms. Jennifer Priest, Director of Financial Aid, Transylvania University, 300 North Broadway, Lexington, KY 40508-1797, 859-233-8239 or toll-free 800-872-6798. *Fax:* 859-281-3650. *E-mail:* jpriest@transy.edu. *Website:* http://www.transy.edu/.

TREVECCA NAZARENE UNIVERSITY
Nashville, TN

Tuition & fees: $25,598	Average undergraduate aid package: N/A

ABOUT THE INSTITUTION Independent Nazarene, coed. *Awards:* certificates, associate, bachelor's, master's, and doctoral degrees. 70 undergraduate majors. *Total enrollment:* 3,620. Undergraduates: 2,219. Freshmen: 421. Institutional methodology is used as a basis for awarding need-based institutional aid.

UNDERGRADUATE EXPENSES for 2018–2019 *Application fee:* $25. *Comprehensive fee:* $33,998 includes full-time tuition ($24,698), mandatory fees ($900), and room and board ($8400). *College room only:* $4200. Full-time tuition and fees vary according to course load and program. Room and board charges vary according to board plan. *Part-time tuition:* $955 per credit hour. Part-time tuition and fees vary according to course load and program. *Payment plan:* Tuition prepayment.

GIFT AID (NEED-BASED) *Total amount:* $4,517,601 (78% federal, 22% state). *Scholarships, grants, and awards:* Federal Pell, FSEOG, state, private, college/university gift aid from institutional funds.

GIFT AID (NON-NEED-BASED) *Total amount:* $15,471,452 (11% state, 81% institutional, 8% external sources). *Scholarships, grants, and awards by category:* Academic interests/achievement: biological sciences, business, communication, education, English, general academic interests/achievements, physical sciences, religion/biblical studies, social sciences. *Creative arts/performance:* cinema/film/broadcasting, music, theater/drama. *Special achievements/activities:* general special achievements/activities, leadership. *Special characteristics:* children of faculty/staff, general special characteristics, relatives of clergy, religious affiliation, siblings of current students. *Tuition waivers:* Full or partial for employees or children of employees, senior citizens. *ROTC:* Army cooperative.

LOANS *Student loans:* $10,053,146 (43% need-based, 57% non-need-based). 68% of past graduating class borrowed through all loan programs. *Average indebtedness per student:* $29,487. *Parent loans:* $1,483,219 (100% non-need-based). *Programs:* Federal Direct (Subsidized and Unsubsidized Stafford, PLUS), Perkins.

WORK-STUDY *Federal work-study:* jobs available. *State or other work-study/employment:* Total amount: $946,323 (100% non-need-based). Part-time jobs available.

ATHLETIC AWARDS Total amount: $2,065,133 (100% non-need-based).

APPLYING FOR FINANCIAL AID *Financial aid deadline (priority):* 1/1. *Notification date:* Continuous beginning 12/1.

CONTACT Eddie White, Director of Financial Aid, Trevecca Nazarene University, 333 Murfreesboro Road, Nashville, TN 37210, 615-248-1242 or toll-free 888-210-4TNU. *Fax:* 615-248-7728. *E-mail:* ewhite@trevecca.edu. *Website:* http://www.trevecca.edu/.

TRIDENT UNIVERSITY INTERNATIONAL
Cypress, CA

CONTACT Taisha Azlin, Director of Financial Aid, Trident University International, 5665 Plaza Drive, Third Floor, Cypress, CA 90630, 800-375-9878 Ext. 1061. *Fax:* 714-484-7621. *E-mail:* financialaid@tuiu.edu. *Website:* http://www.trident.edu/.

TRINE UNIVERSITY
Angola, IN

Tuition & fees: $31,540	Average undergraduate aid package: $27,853

ABOUT THE INSTITUTION Independent, coed. *Awards:* associate, bachelor's, master's, and doctoral degrees. 61 undergraduate majors. *Total enrollment:* 4,302. Undergraduates: 4,104. Freshmen: 602. Federal methodology is used as a basis for awarding need-based institutional aid.

UNDERGRADUATE EXPENSES for 2017–2018 *Comprehensive fee:* $42,110 includes full-time tuition ($31,080), mandatory fees ($460), and room and board ($10,570). Full-time tuition and fees vary according to degree level, location, and program. Room and board charges vary according to board plan and housing facility. *Part-time tuition:* $970 per credit hour. Part-time tuition and fees vary according to degree level, location, and program.

FRESHMAN FINANCIAL AID (Fall 2017, est.) 578 applied for aid; of those 88% were deemed to have need. 100% of freshmen with need received aid; of those 17% had need fully met. *Average percent of need met:* 81% (excluding resources awarded to replace EFC). *Average financial aid package:* $28,583 (excluding resources awarded to replace EFC). 16% of all full-time freshmen had no need and received non-need-based gift aid.

UNDERGRADUATE FINANCIAL AID (Fall 2017, est.) 1,761 applied for aid; of those 90% were deemed to have need. 100% of undergraduates with need received aid; of those 21% had need fully met. *Average percent of need met:* 81% (excluding resources awarded to replace EFC). *Average financial aid package:* $27,853 (excluding resources awarded to replace EFC). 13% of all full-time undergraduates had no need and received non-need-based gift aid.

GIFT AID (NEED-BASED) *Total amount:* $11,392,520 (23% federal, 27% state, 50% institutional). *Receiving aid:* Freshmen: 84% (506); all full-time undergraduates: 86% (1,573). *Average award:* Freshmen: $23,331; Undergraduates: $21,962. *Scholarships, grants, and awards:* Federal Pell, FSEOG, state, private, college/university gift aid from institutional funds.

GIFT AID (NON-NEED-BASED) *Total amount:* $28,519,222 (91% institutional, 9% external sources). *Receiving aid:* Freshmen: 10% (61). Undergraduates: 12% (219). *Average award:* Freshmen: $15,455. Undergraduates: $14,882. *Scholarships, grants, and awards by category:* Academic interests/achievement: 123 awards ($285,900 total): education, general academic interests/achievements, home economics, premedicine. *Creative arts/performance:* 153 awards ($173,437 total): dance, music, theater/drama. *Special achievements/activities:* 25 awards ($28,333 total): cheerleading/drum major. *Special characteristics:* 304 awards ($845,535 total): children and siblings of alumni, children of educators, children of faculty/staff, members of minority groups, siblings of current students, twins. *Tuition waivers:* Full or partial for employees or children of employees, senior citizens. *ROTC:* Air Force cooperative.

LOANS *Student loans:* $12,921,015 (38% need-based, 62% non-need-based). 82% of past graduating class borrowed through all loan programs. *Average indebtedness per student:* $38,161. *Average need-based loan:* Freshmen: $4170. Undergraduates: $5053. *Parent loans:* $5,245,838 (100% non-need-based). *Programs:* Federal Direct (Subsidized and Unsubsidized Stafford, PLUS), alternative loans.

WORK-STUDY *Federal work-study:* Total amount: $225,000; jobs available.

APPLYING FOR FINANCIAL AID *Required financial aid form:* FAFSA. *Financial aid deadline (priority):* 3/1. *Notification date:* Continuous beginning 3/10. Students must reply by 5/1.

CONTACT Kim Bennett, Assistant Vice President of Enrollment Management, Trine University, 1 University Avenue, Angola, IN 46703-1764, 260-665-4438 or toll-free 800-347-4878. *Fax:* 260-665-4511. *E-mail:* bennettk@trine.edu. *Website:* http://www.trine.edu/.

TRINITY BAPTIST COLLEGE
Jacksonville, FL

CONTACT Mr. Mark Elkins, Financial Aid Administrator, Trinity Baptist College, 800 Hammond Boulevard, Jacksonville, FL 32221, 904-596-2445 or toll-free 800-786-2206. *Fax:* 904-596-2531. *E-mail:* financialaid@tbc.edu. *Website:* http://www.tbc.edu/.

TRINITY BIBLE COLLEGE AND GRADUATE SCHOOL
Ellendale, ND

CONTACT Mary Anne Whitman, Director of Financial Aid, Trinity Bible College and Graduate School, 50 South 6th Avenue, Ellendale, ND 58436-7150, 701-349-5403 or toll-free 800-523-1603. *Fax:* 701-349-5786. *E-mail:* mwhitman@ trinitybiblecollege.edu. *Website:* http://www.trinitybiblecollege.edu/.

TRINITY CHRISTIAN COLLEGE
Palos Heights, IL

Tuition & fees: $29,950	Average undergraduate aid package: $20,865

ABOUT THE INSTITUTION Independent Christian Reformed, coed. *Awards:* bachelor's and master's degrees. 56 undergraduate majors. *Total enrollment:* 1,192. Undergraduates: 1,107. Freshmen: 192. Federal methodology is used as a basis for awarding need-based institutional aid.

UNDERGRADUATE EXPENSES for 2018–2019 *Application fee:* $30. *One-time required fee:* $225. *Comprehensive fee:* $39,740 includes full-time tuition ($29,700), mandatory fees ($250), and room and board ($9790). Full-time tuition and fees vary according to course load and degree level. Room and board charges vary according to board plan and housing facility. *Part-time tuition:* $942 per credit hour. Part-time tuition and fees vary according to course load and degree level.

FRESHMAN FINANCIAL AID (Fall 2017, est.) 173 applied for aid; of those 87% were deemed to have need. 100% of freshmen with need received aid; of those 23% had need fully met. *Average percent of need met:* 78% (excluding resources awarded to replace EFC). *Average financial aid package:* $23,576 (excluding resources awarded to replace EFC). 11% of all full-time freshmen had no need and received non-need-based gift aid.

UNDERGRADUATE FINANCIAL AID (Fall 2017, est.) 770 applied for aid; of those 91% were deemed to have need. 100% of undergraduates with need received aid; of those 16% had need fully met. *Average percent of need met:* 73% (excluding resources awarded to replace EFC). *Average financial aid package:* $20,865 (excluding resources awarded to replace EFC). 11% of all full-time undergraduates had no need and received non-need-based gift aid.

GIFT AID (NEED-BASED) *Total amount:* $10,576,677 (17% federal, 11% state, 70% institutional, 2% external sources). *Receiving aid:* Freshmen: 79% (150); all full-time undergraduates: 79% (688). *Average award:* Freshmen: $20,735; Undergraduates: $16,760. *Scholarships, grants, and awards:* Federal Pell, FSEOG, state, private, college/university gift aid from institutional funds, Federal Nursing.

GIFT AID (NON-NEED-BASED) *Total amount:* $1,677,411 (3% federal, 96% institutional, 1% external sources). *Receiving aid:* Freshmen: 10% (20). Undergraduates: 9% (77). *Average award:* Freshmen: $12,569. Undergraduates: $10,560. *Scholarships, grants, and awards by category: Academic interests/ achievement:* biological sciences, business, communication, computer science, education, engineering/technologies, English, general academic interests/achievements, humanities, international studies, mathematics, physical sciences, premedicine, religion/ biblical studies, social sciences. *Creative arts/performance:* applied art and design, art/ fine arts, general creative arts/performance, journalism/publications, music, performing arts, theater/drama. *Special achievements/activities:* community service, general special achievements/activities, leadership, religious involvement. *Special characteristics:* adult students, children and siblings of alumni, children of faculty/staff, ethnic background, first-generation college students, local/state students, members of minority groups, out-of-state students, religious affiliation, veterans. *Tuition waivers:* Full or partial for employees or children of employees.

LOANS *Student loans:* $6,913,322 (44% need-based, 56% non-need-based). 78% of past graduating class borrowed through all loan programs. *Average indebtedness per student:* $29,978. *Average need-based loan:* Freshmen: $3594. Undergraduates: $4589. *Parent loans:* $1,230,128 (100% non-need-based). *Programs:* Federal Direct (Subsidized and Unsubsidized Stafford, PLUS), Perkins, Federal Nursing.

WORK-STUDY *Federal work-study:* Total amount: $123,475; jobs available. *State or other work-study/employment:* Total amount: $590,089 (100% non-need-based). Part-time jobs available.

ATHLETIC AWARDS Total amount: $1,934,160 (77% need-based, 23% non-need-based).

APPLYING FOR FINANCIAL AID *Required financial aid form:* FAFSA. *Financial aid deadline (priority):* 12/1. *Notification date:* Continuous beginning 12/15. Students must reply by 5/1 or within 2 weeks of notification.

CONTACT Mr. Ryan P. Zantingh, Director of Financial Aid, Trinity Christian College, 6601 West College Drive, Palos Heights, IL 60463-0929, 708-239-4872 or toll-free 866-TRIN-4-ME. *Fax:* 708-239-4814. *E-mail:* ryan.zantingh@trnty.edu. *Website:* http://www.trnty.edu/.

TRINITY COLLEGE
Hartford, CT

Tuition & fees: N/R	Average undergraduate aid package: $50,520

ABOUT THE INSTITUTION Independent, coed. 48 undergraduate majors. Both federal and institutional methodology are used as a basis for awarding need-based institutional aid.

FRESHMAN FINANCIAL AID (Fall 2017, est.) 347 applied for aid; of those 84% were deemed to have need. 100% of freshmen with need received aid; of those 100% had need fully met. *Average percent of need met:* 100% (excluding resources awarded to replace EFC). *Average financial aid package:* $50,836 (excluding resources awarded to replace EFC). 4% of all full-time freshmen had no need and received non-need-based gift aid.

UNDERGRADUATE FINANCIAL AID (Fall 2017, est.) 1,288 applied for aid; of those 81% were deemed to have need. 100% of undergraduates with need received aid; of those 98% had need fully met. *Average percent of need met:* 100% (excluding resources awarded to replace EFC). *Average financial aid package:* $50,520 (excluding resources awarded to replace EFC). 6% of all full-time undergraduates had no need and received non-need-based gift aid.

GIFT AID (NEED-BASED) *Total amount:* $48,426,171 (4% federal, 94% institutional, 2% external sources). *Receiving aid:* Freshmen: 50% (285); all full-time undergraduates: 48% (1,026). *Average award:* Freshmen: $47,478; Undergraduates: $47,156. *Scholarships, grants, and awards:* Federal Pell, FSEOG, state, private, college/university gift aid from institutional funds.

GIFT AID (NON-NEED-BASED) *Total amount:* $4,118,026 (93% institutional, 7% external sources). *Receiving aid:* Freshmen: 2% (12). Undergraduates: 2% (39). *Average award:* Freshmen: $25,841. Undergraduates: $28,738. *Scholarships, grants, and awards by category: Academic interests/achievement:* general academic interests/achievements. *Special achievements/activities:* leadership.

LOANS *Student loans:* $8,327,138 (37% need-based, 63% non-need-based). 45% of past graduating class borrowed through all loan programs. *Average indebtedness per student:* $25,958. *Average need-based loan:* Freshmen: $3179. Undergraduates: $4266. *Parent loans:* $4,322,536 (100% non-need-based). *Programs:* Federal Direct (Subsidized and Unsubsidized Stafford, PLUS), Perkins, state, college/university.

WORK-STUDY *Federal work-study:* Total amount: $761,869; jobs available. *State or other work-study/employment:* Part-time jobs available.

APPLYING FOR FINANCIAL AID *Required financial aid forms:* FAFSA, CSS Financial Aid PROFILE, noncustodial (divorced/separated) parent's statement, federal income tax returns. *Financial aid deadline:* 3/1 (priority: 1/15). *Notification date:* 4/1. Students must reply by 5/1.

CONTACT Carolyn LeGeyt, Interim Director of Financial Aid, Trinity College, 300 Summit Street, Hartford, CT 06106-3100, 860-297-2046. *Fax:* 860-987-6296. *E-mail:* financial-aid@trincoll.edu. *Website:* http://www.trincoll.edu/.

TRINITY COLLEGE OF FLORIDA
Trinity, FL

Tuition & fees: $16,340	Average undergraduate aid package: $11,276

ABOUT THE INSTITUTION Independent nondenominational, coed. *Awards:* certificates, associate, and bachelor's degrees. 13 undergraduate majors. *Total enrollment:* 189. Undergraduates: 189. Freshmen: 38. Both federal and institutional methodology are used as a basis for awarding need-based institutional aid.

UNDERGRADUATE EXPENSES for 2018–2019 *Application fee:* $35. *Comprehensive fee:* $23,315 includes full-time tuition ($15,300), mandatory fees ($1040), and room and board ($6975). Full-time tuition and fees vary according to course load and program. *Part-time tuition:* $510 per credit hour. *Part-time fees:* $520 per term. Part-time tuition and fees vary according to course load and program.

FRESHMAN FINANCIAL AID (Fall 2017, est.) 33 applied for aid; of those 97% were deemed to have need. 100% of freshmen with need received aid; of those 9% had need fully met. *Average percent of need met:* 61% (excluding resources awarded to replace EFC). *Average financial aid package:* $11,294 (excluding resources awarded to replace EFC). 6% of all full-time freshmen had no need and received non-need-based gift aid.

UNDERGRADUATE FINANCIAL AID (Fall 2017, est.) 140 applied for aid; of those 93% were deemed to have need. 100% of undergraduates with need received aid; of those 11% had need fully met. *Average percent of need met:* 60% (excluding resources awarded to replace EFC). *Average financial aid package:* $11,276 (excluding resources awarded to replace EFC). 10% of all full-time undergraduates had no need and received non-need-based gift aid.

GIFT AID (NEED-BASED) *Total amount:* $1,076,405 (57% federal, 8% state, 34% institutional, 1% external sources). *Receiving aid:* Freshmen: 94% (32); all full-time undergraduates: 82% (125). *Average award:* Freshmen: $8313; Undergraduates: $8024. *Scholarships, grants, and awards:* Federal Pell, FSEOG, state, college/university gift aid from institutional funds.

GIFT AID (NON-NEED-BASED) *Total amount:* $75,805 (11% state, 88% institutional, 1% external sources). *Receiving aid:* Undergraduates: 1% (2). *Average award:* Freshmen: $4200. Undergraduates: $3987. *Scholarships, grants, and awards by category:* Academic interests/achievement: 19 awards ($48,423 total): general academic interests/achievements, religion/biblical studies. *Special achievements/activities:* 7 awards ($18,440 total): community service, leadership, religious involvement. *Special characteristics:* 2 awards ($3674 total): children of faculty/staff, relatives of clergy, spouses of current students. *Tuition waivers:* Full or partial for employees or children of employees, senior citizens.

LOANS *Student loans:* $996,966 (86% need-based, 14% non-need-based). 82% of past graduating class borrowed through all loan programs. *Average indebtedness per student:* $31,757. *Average need-based loan:* Freshmen: $3390. Undergraduates: $3878. *Parent loans:* $179,057 (59% need-based, 41% non-need-based). *Programs:* Federal Direct (Subsidized and Unsubsidized Stafford, PLUS), private loans.

WORK-STUDY *Federal work-study:* Total amount: $35,012; 14 jobs averaging $2501. *State or other work-study/employment:* Total amount: $4860 (100% need-based). 1 part-time job averaging $4860.

APPLYING FOR FINANCIAL AID *Required financial aid forms:* FAFSA, institution's own form. *Financial aid deadline:* Continuous. *Notification date:* Continuous beginning 1/1. Students must reply within 6 weeks of notification.

CONTACT Sue Wayne, Director of Financial Aid, Trinity College of Florida, 2430 Welbilt Boulevard, Trinity, FL 34655, 727-569-1413 or toll-free 800-388-0869. *Fax:* 573-376-0781. *E-mail:* swayne@trinitycollege.edu. *Website:* http://www.trinitycollege.edu/.

TRINITY COLLEGE OF NURSING AND HEALTH SCIENCES
Rock Island, IL

CONTACT Mrs. Christine Carol Christopherson, Financial Aid Specialist, Trinity College of Nursing and Health Sciences, 2122 25th Avenue, Rock Island, IL 61201, 309-779-7740. *Fax:* 309-779-7748. *E-mail:* c.christopherson@trinitycollegeqc.edu. *Website:* http://www.trinitycollegeqc.edu/.

TRINITY INTERNATIONAL UNIVERSITY
Deerfield, IL

CONTACT Pat Coles, Interim Director of Financial Aid, Trinity International University, 2065 Half Day Road, Deerfield, IL 60015-1284, 847-317-8060 or toll-free 800-822-3225. *Fax:* 847-317-7081. *E-mail:* finaid@tiu.edu. *Website:* http://www.tiu.edu/.

TRINITY UNIVERSITY
San Antonio, TX

Tuition & fees: $42,976	Average undergraduate aid package: $38,968

ABOUT THE INSTITUTION Independent Presbyterian Church, coed. *Awards:* bachelor's and master's degrees. 60 undergraduate majors. *Total enrollment:* 2,604. Undergraduates: 2,424. Freshmen: 642. Both federal and institutional methodology are used as a basis for awarding need-based institutional aid.

UNDERGRADUATE EXPENSES for 2018–2019 *Comprehensive fee:* $56,440 includes full-time tuition ($42,360), mandatory fees ($616), and room and board ($13,464). *College room only:* $8690. Full-time tuition and fees vary according to course load. Room and board charges vary according to board plan. *Part-time tuition:* $1765 per credit hour. *Part-time fees:* $12.50 per credit hour. Part-time tuition and fees vary according to course load.

FRESHMAN FINANCIAL AID (Fall 2016) 492 applied for aid; of those 62% were deemed to have need. 100% of freshmen with need received aid; of those 68% had need fully met. *Average percent of need met:* 98% (excluding resources awarded to replace EFC). *Average financial aid package:* $40,226 (excluding resources awarded to replace EFC). 51% of all full-time freshmen had no need and received non-need-based gift aid.

UNDERGRADUATE FINANCIAL AID (Fall 2016) 1,395 applied for aid; of those 78% were deemed to have need. 100% of undergraduates with need received aid; of those 45% had need fully met. *Average percent of need met:* 93% (excluding resources awarded to replace EFC). *Average financial aid package:* $38,968 (excluding resources awarded to replace EFC). 49% of all full-time undergraduates had no need and received non-need-based gift aid.

GIFT AID (NEED-BASED) *Total amount:* $33,882,421 (7% federal, 5% state, 86% institutional, 2% external sources). *Receiving aid:* Freshmen: 47% (302); all full-time undergraduates: 46% (1,080). *Average award:* Freshmen: $32,078; Undergraduates: $31,374. *Scholarships, grants, and awards:* Federal Pell, FSEOG, state, private, college/university gift aid from institutional funds.

GIFT AID (NON-NEED-BASED) *Total amount:* $26,864,100 (97% institutional, 3% external sources). *Receiving aid:* Freshmen: 17% (111). Undergraduates: 9% (215). *Average award:* Freshmen: $21,659. Undergraduates: $20,549. *Scholarships, grants, and awards by category:* Academic interests/achievement: general academic interests/achievements. *Creative arts/performance:* art/fine arts, debating, music, theater/drama. *Special characteristics:* children and siblings of alumni, children of educators, international students, veterans, veterans' children. *Tuition waivers:* Full or partial for employees or children of employees. *ROTC:* Army cooperative, Air Force cooperative.

LOANS *Student loans:* $8,771,592 (56% need-based, 44% non-need-based). 44% of past graduating class borrowed through all loan programs. *Average indebtedness per student:* $40,800. *Average need-based loan:* Freshmen: $4143. Undergraduates: $4828. *Parent loans:* $2,214,672 (17% need-based, 83% non-need-based). *Programs:* Federal Direct (Subsidized and Unsubsidized Stafford, PLUS), Perkins, state, college/university.

WORK-STUDY *Federal work-study:* jobs available. *State or other work-study/employment:* Part-time jobs available.

APPLYING FOR FINANCIAL AID *Required financial aid forms:* FAFSA, CSS Financial Aid PROFILE. *Financial aid deadline (priority):* 2/15. *Notification date:* 3/15. Students must reply by 5/1.

CONTACT Office of Student Financial Services, Trinity University, One Trinity Place, San Antonio, TX 78212-7200, 210-999-8898 or toll-free 800-TRINITY. *Fax:* 210-999-8316. *E-mail:* studentfinancialservices@trinity.edu. *Website:* http://www.trinity.edu/.

TRINITY WASHINGTON UNIVERSITY
Washington, DC

CONTACT Catherine H. Geier, Director of Student Financial Services, Trinity Washington University, 125 Michigan Avenue, NE, Washington, DC 20017-1094, 202-884-9530 or toll-free 800-IWANTTC. *Fax:* 202-884-9524. *E-mail:* financialaid@trinitydc.edu.
Website: http://www.trinitydc.edu/.

TRI-STATE BIBLE COLLEGE
South Point, OH

CONTACT Mrs. Roberta Mercer, Financial Aid Director, Tri-State Bible College, 506 Margaret Street, PO Box 445, South Point, OH 45680, 740-377-2520 Ext. 23. *Fax:* 740-377-0001. *E-mail:* tsbc@zoominternet.net.
Website: http://www.tsbc.edu/.

TROY UNIVERSITY
Troy, AL

Tuition & fees (AL res): $12,155	Average undergraduate aid package: $4356

ABOUT THE INSTITUTION State-supported, coed. *Awards:* certificates, associate, bachelor's, master's, and doctoral degrees. 44 undergraduate majors. *Total enrollment:* 17,521. Undergraduates: 14,000. Freshmen: 2,160. Federal methodology is used as a basis for awarding need-based institutional aid.
UNDERGRADUATE EXPENSES for 2017–2018 *Application fee:* $30. *Tuition, state resident:* full-time $10,112; part-time $316 per credit hour. *Tuition, nonresident:* full-time $20,224; part-time $632 per credit hour. *Required fees:* full-time $2043; $39 per credit hour or $50 per term. Full-time tuition and fees vary according to location and program. Part-time tuition and fees vary according to location and program. *College room and board:* $7946; *Room only:* $4458. Room and board charges vary according to board plan and housing facility.
FRESHMAN FINANCIAL AID (Fall 2017, est.) 1,539 applied for aid; of those 100% were deemed to have need. 100% of freshmen with need received aid. *Average financial aid package:* $3648 (excluding resources awarded to replace EFC). 20% of all full-time freshmen had no need and received non-need-based gift aid.
UNDERGRADUATE FINANCIAL AID (Fall 2017, est.) 6,534 applied for aid; of those 99% were deemed to have need. 100% of undergraduates with need received aid. *Average financial aid package:* $4356 (excluding resources awarded to replace EFC). 22% of all full-time undergraduates had no need and received non-need-based gift aid.
GIFT AID (NEED-BASED) *Total amount:* $35,211,173 (100% federal). *Receiving aid:* Freshmen: 45% (861); all full-time undergraduates: 42% (4,013). *Average award:* Freshmen: $4738; Undergraduates: $4757. *Scholarships, grants, and awards:* Federal Pell, FSEOG, state, private, college/university gift aid from institutional funds.
GIFT AID (NON-NEED-BASED) *Total amount:* $66,268,784 (65% institutional, 35% external sources). *Receiving aid:* Freshmen: 50% (950). Undergraduates: 33% (3,121). *Average award:* Freshmen: $5918. Undergraduates: $7439. *Scholarships, grants, and awards by category:* Academic interests/achievement: general academic interests/achievements. Creative arts/performance: applied art and design, music, theater/drama. Special achievements/activities: leadership. Special characteristics: general special characteristics. *Tuition waivers:* Full or partial for employees or children of employees. *ROTC:* Army, Air Force.
LOANS *Student loans:* $141,392,226 (100% need-based). *Average need-based loan:* Freshmen: $3328. Undergraduates: $4245. *Parent loans:* $11,073,545 (100% need-based). *Programs:* Federal Direct (Subsidized and Unsubsidized Stafford, PLUS), Perkins.
WORK-STUDY *Federal work-study:* Total amount: $863,372; jobs available.
ATHLETIC AWARDS Total amount: $6,033,082 (100% non-need-based).
APPLYING FOR FINANCIAL AID *Required financial aid forms:* FAFSA, institution's own form. *Financial aid deadline (priority):* 3/1. *Notification date:* Continuous beginning 6/1. Students must reply within 2 weeks of notification.

CONTACT Ms. Angela Johnson, Associate Vice Chancellor of Financial Aid, Troy University, 131 Adams Administration Building, Troy, AL 36082, 334-670-3186 or toll-free 800-551-9716. *Fax:* 334-670-3702. *E-mail:* ajohnson@troy.edu.
Website: http://www.troy.edu/.

TRUETT MCCONNELL UNIVERSITY
Cleveland, GA

Tuition & fees: $19,480	Average undergraduate aid package: $15,836

ABOUT THE INSTITUTION Independent Baptist, coed. *Awards:* bachelor's and master's degrees. 19 undergraduate majors. *Total enrollment:* 2,187. Undergraduates: 2,152. Freshmen: 222. Federal methodology is used as a basis for awarding need-based institutional aid.
UNDERGRADUATE EXPENSES for 2017–2018 *Comprehensive fee:* $26,880 includes full-time tuition ($18,570), mandatory fees ($910), and room and board ($7400). Full-time tuition and fees vary according to course load, degree level, location, and program. Room and board charges vary according to housing facility. *Part-time tuition:* $774 per credit hour. *Part-time fees:* $455 per term. Part-time tuition and fees vary according to course load, degree level, location, and program.
FRESHMAN FINANCIAL AID (Fall 2017, est.) 194 applied for aid; of those 86% were deemed to have need. 100% of freshmen with need received aid; of those 16% had need fully met. *Average percent of need met:* 70% (excluding resources awarded to replace EFC). *Average financial aid package:* $16,788 (excluding resources awarded to replace EFC). 18% of all full-time freshmen had no need and received non-need-based gift aid.
UNDERGRADUATE FINANCIAL AID (Fall 2017, est.) 661 applied for aid; of those 88% were deemed to have need. 99% of undergraduates with need received aid; of those 19% had need fully met. *Average percent of need met:* 70% (excluding resources awarded to replace EFC). *Average financial aid package:* $15,836 (excluding resources awarded to replace EFC). 15% of all full-time undergraduates had no need and received non-need-based gift aid.
GIFT AID (NEED-BASED) *Total amount:* $6,143,989 (23% federal, 23% state, 50% institutional, 4% external sources). *Receiving aid:* Freshmen: 79% (166); all full-time undergraduates: 81% (577). *Average award:* Freshmen: $13,677; Undergraduates: $12,437. *Scholarships, grants, and awards:* Federal Pell, FSEOG, state, private, college/university gift aid from institutional funds, Georgia Baptist Convention scholarships.
GIFT AID (NON-NEED-BASED) *Total amount:* $1,480,556 (37% state, 59% institutional, 4% external sources). *Receiving aid:* Freshmen: 11% (24). Undergraduates: 12% (84). *Average award:* Freshmen: $6085. Undergraduates: $6850. *Scholarships, grants, and awards by category:* Academic interests/achievement: $1,818,004 total: biological sciences, business, education, general academic interests/achievements, home economics, religion/biblical studies. Creative arts/performance: $188,499 total: music. Special achievements/activities: $2,040,117 total: community service, general special achievements/activities, leadership, religious involvement. Special characteristics: $1,076,400 total: children of current students, children of faculty/staff, general special characteristics, international students, local/state students, married students, out-of-state students, parents of current students, relatives of clergy, religious affiliation, siblings of current students, spouses of current students. *Tuition waivers:* Full or partial for employees or children of employees.
LOANS *Student loans:* $3,965,638 (78% need-based, 22% non-need-based). 73% of past graduating class borrowed through all loan programs. *Average indebtedness per student:* $29,757. *Average need-based loan:* Freshmen: $4631. Undergraduates: $4826. *Parent loans:* $741,272 (42% need-based, 58% non-need-based). *Programs:* Federal Direct (Subsidized and Unsubsidized Stafford, PLUS), state, private loans.
WORK-STUDY *Federal work-study:* Total amount: $38,841; 24 jobs averaging $1834.
ATHLETIC AWARDS Total amount: $1,507,322 (64% need-based, 36% non-need-based).
APPLYING FOR FINANCIAL AID *Required financial aid forms:* FAFSA, institution's own form. *Financial aid deadline:* Continuous. *Notification date:* Continuous beginning 1/3. Students must reply within 4 weeks of notification.

CONTACT Mrs. Trista Blankenship, Financial Aid Assistant, Truett McConnell University, 100 Alumni Drive, Cleveland, GA 30528, 706-865-2134 Ext. 4203 or toll-free 800-226-8621. *Fax:* 706-243-4642. *E-mail:* tblankenship@truett.edu. *Website:* http://www.truett.edu/.

CONTACT Robin White, Interim Director of Financial Aid, Truman State University, 103 McClain Hall, Kirksville, MO 63501-4221, 660-785-4130 or toll-free 800-892-7792. *Fax:* 660-785-7389. *E-mail:* rpillen@truman.edu. *Website:* http://www.truman.edu/.

TRUMAN STATE UNIVERSITY
Kirksville, MO

Tuition & fees (MO res): $7656	Average undergraduate aid package: $12,518

ABOUT THE INSTITUTION State-supported, coed. *Awards:* bachelor's and master's degrees. 36 undergraduate majors. *Total enrollment:* 6,272. Undergraduates: 5,898. Freshmen: 1,328. Federal methodology is used as a basis for awarding need-based institutional aid.

UNDERGRADUATE EXPENSES for 2017–2018 One-time required fee: $350. *Tuition, state resident:* full-time $7352; part-time $306 per credit hour. *Tuition, nonresident:* full-time $14,136; part-time $589 per credit hour. *Required fees:* full-time $304; $304 per year. Full-time tuition and fees vary according to course load, degree level, and program. Part-time tuition and fees vary according to course load, degree level, and program. *College room and board:* $8630; *Room only:* $5730. Room and board charges vary according to board plan and housing facility.

FRESHMAN FINANCIAL AID (Fall 2016) 1,057 applied for aid; of those 65% were deemed to have need. 100% of freshmen with need received aid; of those 41% had need fully met. *Average percent of need met:* 88% (excluding resources awarded to replace EFC). *Average financial aid package:* $13,306 (excluding resources awarded to replace EFC). 44% of all full-time freshmen had no need and received non-need-based gift aid.

UNDERGRADUATE FINANCIAL AID (Fall 2016) 3,666 applied for aid; of those 71% were deemed to have need. 100% of undergraduates with need received aid; of those 36% had need fully met. *Average percent of need met:* 84% (excluding resources awarded to replace EFC). *Average financial aid package:* $12,518 (excluding resources awarded to replace EFC). 38% of all full-time undergraduates had no need and received non-need-based gift aid.

GIFT AID (NEED-BASED) Total amount: $18,871,640 (27% federal, 17% state, 52% institutional, 4% external sources). *Receiving aid:* Freshmen: 54% (684); all full-time undergraduates: 48% (2,437). *Average award:* Freshmen: $8717; Undergraduates: $7824. *Scholarships, grants, and awards:* Federal Pell, FSEOG, state, private, college/university gift aid from institutional funds, TEACH Grants.

GIFT AID (NON-NEED-BASED) Total amount: $16,264,886 (1% federal, 12% state, 81% institutional, 6% external sources). *Receiving aid:* Freshmen: 53% (672). Undergraduates: 40% (2,075). *Average award:* Freshmen: $5759. Undergraduates: $5992. *Scholarships, grants, and awards by category: Academic interests/achievement:* 8,779 awards ($22,721,863 total): agriculture, biological sciences, business, communication, computer science, education, English, foreign languages, general academic interests/achievements, health fields, humanities, mathematics, military science, physical sciences, premedicine, social sciences. *Creative arts/performance:* 172 awards ($190,735 total): art/fine arts, debating, music, theater/drama. *Special achievements/activities:* 412 awards ($2,082,643 total): leadership. *Special characteristics:* 626 awards ($1,634,423 total): children and siblings of alumni, children of faculty/staff, ethnic background, first-generation college students, international students, out-of-state students, previous college experience. *Tuition waivers:* Full or partial for children of alumni, employees or children of employees, senior citizens. *ROTC:* Army.

LOANS Student loans: $24,942,836 (48% need-based, 52% non-need-based). 57% of past graduating class borrowed through all loan programs. *Average indebtedness per student:* $24,938. *Average need-based loan:* Freshmen: $3578. Undergraduates: $4431. *Parent loans:* $1,494,826 (13% need-based, 87% non-need-based). *Programs:* Federal Direct (Subsidized and Unsubsidized Stafford, PLUS), Perkins, Federal Nursing, college/university.

WORK-STUDY Federal work-study: 449 jobs averaging $1491. *State or other work-study/employment:* Total amount: $1,621,728 (3% need-based, 97% non-need-based). 1,399 part-time jobs averaging $1129.

ATHLETIC AWARDS Total amount: $1,456,379 (32% need-based, 68% non-need-based).

APPLYING FOR FINANCIAL AID Required financial aid form: FAFSA. *Financial aid deadline (priority):* 2/1. *Notification date:* Continuous beginning 1/1.

TUFTS UNIVERSITY
Medford, MA

Tuition & fees: $54,318	Average undergraduate aid package: $45,107

ABOUT THE INSTITUTION Independent, coed. *Awards:* certificates, bachelor's, master's, and doctoral degrees. 100 undergraduate majors. *Total enrollment:* 11,449. Undergraduates: 5,541. Freshmen: 1,410. Both federal and institutional methodology are used as a basis for awarding need-based institutional aid.

UNDERGRADUATE EXPENSES for 2017–2018 Application fee: $75. *Comprehensive fee:* $68,372 includes full-time tuition ($53,152), mandatory fees ($1166), and room and board ($14,054). *College room only:* $7658. Room and board charges vary according to board plan. *Payment plan:* Tuition prepayment.

FRESHMAN FINANCIAL AID (Fall 2017, est.) 713 applied for aid; of those 78% were deemed to have need. 97% of freshmen with need received aid; of those 100% had need fully met. *Average percent of need met:* 100% (excluding resources awarded to replace EFC). *Average financial aid package:* $46,384 (excluding resources awarded to replace EFC). 1% of all full-time freshmen had no need and received non-need-based gift aid.

UNDERGRADUATE FINANCIAL AID (Fall 2017, est.) 2,361 applied for aid; of those 88% were deemed to have need. 99% of undergraduates with need received aid; of those 98% had need fully met. *Average percent of need met:* 98% (excluding resources awarded to replace EFC). *Average financial aid package:* $45,107 (excluding resources awarded to replace EFC). 3% of all full-time undergraduates had no need and received non-need-based gift aid.

GIFT AID (NEED-BASED) Total amount: $89,361,337 (4% federal, 1% state, 92% institutional, 3% external sources). *Receiving aid:* Freshmen: 37% (514); all full-time undergraduates: 35% (1,944). *Average award:* Freshmen: $44,967; Undergraduates: $42,763. *Scholarships, grants, and awards:* Federal Pell, FSEOG, state, private, college/university gift aid from institutional funds.

GIFT AID (NON-NEED-BASED) Total amount: $2,102,226 (4% federal, 31% institutional, 65% external sources). *Receiving aid:* Freshmen: 1% (16). Undergraduates: 3% (164). *Average award:* Freshmen: $500. Undergraduates: $4000. *Scholarships, grants, and awards by category: Academic interests/achievement:* 93 awards ($46,500 total): general academic interests/achievements. *Creative arts/performance:* 46 awards ($437,000 total): art/fine arts. *Special achievements/activities:* 139 awards ($483,500 total). *Tuition waivers:* Full or partial for employees or children of employees. *ROTC:* Army cooperative, Naval cooperative, Air Force cooperative.

LOANS Student loans: $11,660,198 (50% need-based, 50% non-need-based). 34% of past graduating class borrowed through all loan programs. *Average indebtedness per student:* $27,367. *Average need-based loan:* Freshmen: $2128. Undergraduates: $3112. *Parent loans:* $6,253,366 (100% non-need-based). *Programs:* Federal Direct (Subsidized and Unsubsidized Stafford, PLUS), college/university.

WORK-STUDY Federal work-study: Total amount: $2,897,613; 1,463 jobs averaging $1924. *State or other work-study/employment:* Total amount: $316,166 (100% need-based). 166 part-time jobs averaging $1914.

APPLYING FOR FINANCIAL AID Required financial aid forms: FAFSA, CSS Financial Aid PROFILE, noncustodial (divorced/separated) parent's statement, federal income tax form(s). *Financial aid deadline:* 2/1. *Notification date:* 4/5. Students must reply by 5/1.

CONTACT Patricia C. Reilly, Director of Financial Aid, Tufts University, Dowling Hall, Medford, MA 02155, 617-627-2000. *Fax:* 617-627-3987. *E-mail:* patricia.reilly@tufts.edu. *Website:* http://www.tufts.edu/.

TULANE UNIVERSITY
New Orleans, LA

Tuition & fees: $52,960	Average undergraduate aid package: $47,540

ABOUT THE INSTITUTION Independent, coed. **Awards:** certificates, bachelor's, master's, and doctoral degrees. 86 undergraduate majors. **Total enrollment:** 11,248. Undergraduates: 6,571. Freshmen: 1,905. Both federal and institutional methodology are used as a basis for awarding need-based institutional aid.

UNDERGRADUATE EXPENSES for 2017–2018 Comprehensive fee: $67,496 includes full-time tuition ($48,920), mandatory fees ($4040), and room and board ($14,536). **College room only:** $8342. Room and board charges vary according to board plan, housing facility, and student level. **Payment plan:** Tuition prepayment.

FRESHMAN FINANCIAL AID (Fall 2017, est.) 1,119 applied for aid; of those 61% were deemed to have need. 100% of freshmen with need received aid; of those 67% had need fully met. **Average percent of need met:** 97% (excluding resources awarded to replace EFC). **Average financial aid package:** $45,405 (excluding resources awarded to replace EFC). 40% of all full-time freshmen had no need and received non-need-based gift aid.

UNDERGRADUATE FINANCIAL AID (Fall 2017, est.) 2,894 applied for aid; of those 73% were deemed to have need. 100% of undergraduates with need received aid; of those 69% had need fully met. **Average percent of need met:** 96% (excluding resources awarded to replace EFC). **Average financial aid package:** $47,540 (excluding resources awarded to replace EFC). 39% of all full-time undergraduates had no need and received non-need-based gift aid.

GIFT AID (NEED-BASED) Total amount: $69,134,938 (5% federal, 2% state, 93% institutional). **Receiving aid:** Freshmen: 35% (666); all full-time undergraduates: 31% (2,049). **Average award:** Freshmen: $32,464; Undergraduates: $34,996. **Scholarships, grants, and awards:** Federal Pell, FSEOG, state, private, college/university gift aid from institutional funds.

GIFT AID (NON-NEED-BASED) Total amount: $76,026,507 (5% state, 94% institutional, 1% external sources). **Receiving aid:** Freshmen: 13% (250). Undergraduates: 9% (591). **Average award:** Freshmen: $23,999. Undergraduates: $26,091. **Scholarships, grants, and awards by category:** Creative arts/performance: 108 awards ($212,400 total): music. **Special achievements/activities:** 26 awards ($504,600 total): community service. **Special characteristics:** 267 awards ($12,524,453 total): children of faculty/staff, international students, local/state students. **Tuition waivers:** Full or partial for employees or children of employees. **ROTC:** Army, Naval, Air Force.

LOANS Student loans: $28,249,786 (52% need-based, 48% non-need-based). 37% of past graduating class borrowed through all loan programs. **Average indebtedness per student:** $33,717. **Average need-based loan:** Freshmen: $6776. Undergraduates: $7766. **Parent loans:** $8,295,298 (6% need-based, 94% non-need-based). **Programs:** Federal Direct (Subsidized and Unsubsidized Stafford, PLUS).

WORK-STUDY Federal work-study: Total amount: $3,847,679; 1,020 jobs averaging $3772. **State or other work-study/employment:** Total amount: $1,376,164 (21% need-based, 79% non-need-based). 130 part-time jobs averaging $8598.

ATHLETIC AWARDS Total amount: $12,728,971 (26% need-based, 74% non-need-based).

APPLYING FOR FINANCIAL AID Required financial aid forms: FAFSA, CSS Financial Aid PROFILE, noncustodial (divorced/separated) parent's statement, business/farm supplement. **Financial aid deadline (priority):** 2/15. **Notification date:** Continuous beginning 3/15. Students must reply by 5/1.

CONTACT Mr. Michael T. Goodman, Director of Financial Aid, Tulane University, 6823 St. Charles Avenue, New Orleans, LA 70118-5669, 504-865-5723 or toll-free 800-873-9283. Fax: 504-862-8750. E-mail: finaid@tulane.edu. Website: http://www.tulane.edu/.

TUSCULUM COLLEGE
Greeneville, TN

ABOUT THE INSTITUTION Independent Presbyterian, coed. **Awards:** associate, bachelor's, and master's degrees. 22 undergraduate majors. **Total enrollment:** 1,767. Undergraduates: 1,488. Freshmen: 337.

GIFT AID (NEED-BASED) Scholarships, grants, and awards: Federal Pell, FSEOG, state, private, college/university gift aid from institutional funds.

GIFT AID (NON-NEED-BASED) Scholarships, grants, and awards by category: Academic interests/achievement: general academic interests/achievements. Creative arts/performance: general creative arts/performance, music. Special achievements/activities: cheerleading/drum major, community service, leadership. Special characteristics: adult students, children of faculty/staff, local/state students.

LOANS Programs: Federal Direct (Subsidized and Unsubsidized Stafford, PLUS), Perkins.

WORK-STUDY Federal work-study: 293 jobs averaging $963. **State or other work-study/employment:** Part-time jobs available.

APPLYING FOR FINANCIAL AID Required financial aid form: FAFSA.

CONTACT Karen Sartain, Director of Financial Aid, Tusculum College, PO Box 5049, 60 Shiloh Road, Greeneville, TN 37743-9997, 423-636-7377 or toll-free 800-729-0256. Fax: 615-250-4968. E-mail: ksartain@tusculum.edu. Website: http://www.tusculum.edu/.

TUSKEGEE UNIVERSITY
Tuskegee, AL

Tuition & fees: N/R	Average undergraduate aid package: $20,500

ABOUT THE INSTITUTION Independent, coed. 43 undergraduate majors. Federal methodology is used as a basis for awarding need-based institutional aid.

FRESHMAN FINANCIAL AID (Fall 2017, est.) 655 applied for aid; of those 88% were deemed to have need. 100% of freshmen with need received aid; of those 50% had need fully met. **Average percent of need met:** 85% (excluding resources awarded to replace EFC). **Average financial aid package:** $20,500 (excluding resources awarded to replace EFC). 39% of all full-time freshmen had no need and received non-need-based gift aid.

UNDERGRADUATE FINANCIAL AID (Fall 2017, est.) 2,618 applied for aid; of those 85% were deemed to have need. 95% of undergraduates with need received aid; of those 50% had need fully met. **Average percent of need met:** 85% (excluding resources awarded to replace EFC). **Average financial aid package:** $20,500 (excluding resources awarded to replace EFC). 26% of all full-time undergraduates had no need and received non-need-based gift aid.

GIFT AID (NEED-BASED) Total amount: $12,852,409 (97% federal, 1% state, 2% institutional). **Receiving aid:** Freshmen: 56% (416); all full-time undergraduates: 57% (1,610). **Average award:** Freshmen: $950; Undergraduates: $950. **Scholarships, grants, and awards:** Federal Pell, FSEOG, state, private, college/university gift aid from institutional funds, United Negro College Fund.

GIFT AID (NON-NEED-BASED) Total amount: $4,634,960 (54% institutional, 46% external sources). **Receiving aid:** Freshmen: 40% (301). Undergraduates: 32% (905). **Average award:** Freshmen: $6500. Undergraduates: $6500. **Scholarships, grants, and awards by category:** Academic interests/achievement: 1,469 awards ($1,115,650 total): agriculture, architecture, business, computer science, engineering/technologies, general academic interests/achievements. Creative arts/performance: 150 awards ($190,000 total): music. Special characteristics: 28 awards ($425,660 total): children of faculty/staff, local/state students.

LOANS Student loans: $6,467,150 (23% need-based, 77% non-need-based). 92% of past graduating class borrowed through all loan programs. **Average indebtedness per student:** $26,500. **Average need-based loan:** Freshmen: $5500. Undergraduates: $6000. **Parent loans:** $1,225,600 (100% non-need-based). **Programs:** Federal Direct (Subsidized and Unsubsidized Stafford, PLUS).

WORK-STUDY Federal work-study: Total amount: $1,013,699; 590 jobs averaging $2610. **State or other work-study/employment:** Total amount: $711,525 (100% non-need-based). 225 part-time jobs averaging $2000.

ATHLETIC AWARDS Total amount: $2,012,200 (100% non-need-based).

APPLYING FOR FINANCIAL AID Required financial aid forms: FAFSA, institution's own form. **Financial aid deadline (priority):** 2/1. **Notification date:** Continuous beginning 2/1. Students must reply within 2 weeks of notification.

CONTACT Mr. A. D. James Jr., Executive Director of Student Financial Services, Tuskegee University, Carnegie Hall, 2nd Floor, Tuskegee, AL 36088, 334-727-8088 or toll-free 800-622-6531. Fax: 334-724-4078. E-mail: ajames@tuskegee.edu. Website: http://www.tuskegee.edu/.

UNILATINA INTERNATIONAL COLLEGE
Miramar, FL

CONTACT Financial Aid Office, Unilatina International College, 3130 Commerce Parkway, Miramar, FL 33025.
Website: http://www.unilatina.edu/.

UNION COLLEGE
Barbourville, KY

Tuition & fees: $26,080	Average undergraduate aid package: $23,031

ABOUT THE INSTITUTION Independent United Methodist, coed. *Awards:* certificates, bachelor's, and master's degrees. 40 undergraduate majors. *Total enrollment:* 1,202. Undergraduates: 975. Freshmen: 264. Federal methodology is used as a basis for awarding need-based institutional aid.
UNDERGRADUATE EXPENSES for 2017–2018 *Application fee:* $10. *Comprehensive fee:* $33,480 includes full-time tuition ($24,590), mandatory fees ($1490), and room and board ($7400). *College room only:* $3300. Full-time tuition and fees vary according to location and program. Room and board charges vary according to housing facility. *Part-time tuition:* $345 per credit hour. Part-time tuition and fees vary according to location and program.
FRESHMAN FINANCIAL AID (Fall 2016) 242 applied for aid; of those 96% were deemed to have need. 90% of freshmen with need received aid; of those 12% had need fully met. *Average percent of need met:* 60% (excluding resources awarded to replace EFC). *Average financial aid package:* $20,956 (excluding resources awarded to replace EFC). 18% of all full-time freshmen had no need and received non-need-based gift aid.
UNDERGRADUATE FINANCIAL AID (Fall 2016) 744 applied for aid; of those 95% were deemed to have need. 91% of undergraduates with need received aid; of those 13% had need fully met. *Average percent of need met:* 65% (excluding resources awarded to replace EFC). *Average financial aid package:* $23,031 (excluding resources awarded to replace EFC). 9% of all full-time undergraduates had no need and received non-need-based gift aid.
GIFT AID (NEED-BASED) *Total amount:* $12,324,099 (17% federal, 16% state, 65% institutional, 2% external sources). *Receiving aid:* Freshmen: 70% (201); all full-time undergraduates: 80% (631). *Average award:* Freshmen: $18,603; Undergraduates: $19,313. *Scholarships, grants, and awards:* Federal Pell, FSEOG, state, private, college/university gift aid from institutional funds.
GIFT AID (NON-NEED-BASED) *Total amount:* $1,714,807 (6% state, 90% institutional, 4% external sources). *Receiving aid:* Freshmen: 6% (17). Undergraduates: 6% (51). *Average award:* Freshmen: $17,186. Undergraduates: $16,840. *Scholarships, grants, and awards by category: Academic interests/achievement:* 502 awards ($4,987,638 total): general academic interests/achievements. *Creative arts/performance:* 60 awards ($110,826 total): music, theater/drama. *Special achievements/activities:* 168 awards ($489,100 total): cheerleading/drum major, community service, general special achievements/activities, hobbies/interests, leadership, memberships, religious involvement. *Special characteristics:* 100 awards ($252,300 total): adult students, children and siblings of alumni, children of current students, children of faculty/staff, members of minority groups, religious affiliation, siblings of current students, veterans, veterans' children. *Tuition waivers:* Full or partial for employees or children of employees.
LOANS *Student loans:* $4,548,576 (87% need-based, 13% non-need-based). 84% of past graduating class borrowed through all loan programs. *Average indebtedness per student:* $32,691. *Average need-based loan:* Freshmen: $3270. Undergraduates: $4235. *Parent loans:* $2,124,066 (59% need-based, 41% non-need-based). *Programs:* Federal Direct (Subsidized and Unsubsidized Stafford, PLUS), Perkins, college/university.
WORK-STUDY *Federal work-study:* 111 jobs averaging $1500. *State or other work-study/employment:* 28 part-time jobs averaging $1500.
ATHLETIC AWARDS Total amount: $3,856,280 (100% need-based).
APPLYING FOR FINANCIAL AID *Required financial aid form:* FAFSA. *Financial aid deadline:* Continuous. *Notification date:* Continuous beginning 2/25. Students must reply within 2 weeks of notification.

CONTACT Mrs. Andra Butler, Director of Financial Aid, Union College, 310 College Street, Barbourville, KY 40906-1499, 606-546-1224 or toll-free 800-489-8646. *Fax:* 606-546-1229. *E-mail:* abutler@unionky.edu.
Website: http://www.unionky.edu/.

UNION COLLEGE
Lincoln, NE

Tuition & fees: $23,780	Average undergraduate aid package: $17,707

ABOUT THE INSTITUTION Independent Seventh-day Adventist, coed. *Awards:* associate, bachelor's, and master's degrees. 54 undergraduate majors. *Total enrollment:* 868. Undergraduates: 781. Freshmen: 157. Federal methodology is used as a basis for awarding need-based institutional aid.
UNDERGRADUATE EXPENSES for 2018–2019 *Comprehensive fee:* $30,850 includes full-time tuition ($22,680), mandatory fees ($1100), and room and board ($7070). *College room only:* $4020. Full-time tuition and fees vary according to course load, degree level, and program. Room and board charges vary according to board plan and housing facility. *Part-time tuition:* $945 per credit hour. *Part-time fees:* $550 per term. Part-time tuition and fees vary according to program.
FRESHMAN FINANCIAL AID (Fall 2016) 134 applied for aid; of those 88% were deemed to have need. 100% of freshmen with need received aid; of those 25% had need fully met. *Average percent of need met:* 75% (excluding resources awarded to replace EFC). *Average financial aid package:* $19,425 (excluding resources awarded to replace EFC). 24% of all full-time freshmen had no need and received non-need-based gift aid.
UNDERGRADUATE FINANCIAL AID (Fall 2016) 552 applied for aid; of those 90% were deemed to have need. 100% of undergraduates with need received aid; of those 15% had need fully met. *Average percent of need met:* 65% (excluding resources awarded to replace EFC). *Average financial aid package:* $17,707 (excluding resources awarded to replace EFC). 28% of all full-time undergraduates had no need and received non-need-based gift aid.
GIFT AID (NEED-BASED) *Total amount:* $6,625,318 (22% federal, 1% state, 59% institutional, 18% external sources). *Receiving aid:* Freshmen: 76% (118); all full-time undergraduates: 71% (499). *Average award:* Freshmen: $16,224; Undergraduates: $13,017. *Scholarships, grants, and awards:* Federal Pell, FSEOG, state, private, college/university gift aid from institutional funds, United Negro College Fund.
GIFT AID (NON-NEED-BASED) *Total amount:* $2,394,214 (75% institutional, 25% external sources). *Receiving aid:* Freshmen: 18% (28). Undergraduates: 8% (59). *Average award:* Freshmen: $11,647. Undergraduates: $8063. *Scholarships, grants, and awards by category: Academic interests/achievement:* general academic interests/achievements. *Creative arts/performance:* music. *Special achievements/activities:* community service, leadership, religious involvement. *Tuition waivers:* Full or partial for employees or children of employees.
LOANS *Student loans:* $4,174,527 (82% need-based, 18% non-need-based). 65% of past graduating class borrowed through all loan programs. *Average indebtedness per student:* $35,893. *Average need-based loan:* Freshmen: $3970. Undergraduates: $5000. *Parent loans:* $857,871 (62% need-based, 38% non-need-based). *Programs:* Federal Direct (Subsidized and Unsubsidized Stafford, PLUS), Perkins, Federal Nursing, college/university.
WORK-STUDY *Federal work-study:* jobs available.
APPLYING FOR FINANCIAL AID *Required financial aid forms:* FAFSA, institution's own form. *Financial aid deadline:* Continuous. *Notification date:* Continuous beginning 2/1.
CONTACT Mrs. Taryn A. Rouse, Director of Student Financial Services, Union College, 3800 South 48th Street, Lincoln, NE 68506-4300, 402-486-2600 Ext. 2505 or toll-free 800-228-4600. *Fax:* 402-486-2952. *E-mail:* sfs@ucollege.edu.
Website: http://www.ucollege.edu/.

UNION COLLEGE
Schenectady, NY

Tuition & fees: $53,490	Average undergraduate aid package: $44,649

ABOUT THE INSTITUTION Independent, coed. *Awards:* bachelor's degrees. 40 undergraduate majors. *Total enrollment:* 2,267. Undergraduates: 2,272. Freshmen: 570. Both federal and institutional methodology are used as a basis for awarding need-based institutional aid.

UNDERGRADUATE EXPENSES for 2017–2018 *Comprehensive fee:* $66,609 includes full-time tuition ($53,019), mandatory fees ($471), and room and board ($13,119). *College room only:* $7194.

FRESHMAN FINANCIAL AID (Fall 2017, est.) 354 applied for aid; of those 80% were deemed to have need. 100% of freshmen with need received aid; of those 100% had need fully met. *Average percent of need met:* 100% (excluding resources awarded to replace EFC). *Average financial aid package:* $43,345 (excluding resources awarded to replace EFC). 29% of all full-time freshmen had no need and received non-need-based gift aid.

UNDERGRADUATE FINANCIAL AID (Fall 2017, est.) 1,176 applied for aid; of those 90% were deemed to have need. 100% of undergraduates with need received aid; of those 100% had need fully met. *Average percent of need met:* 100% (excluding resources awarded to replace EFC). *Average financial aid package:* $44,649 (excluding resources awarded to replace EFC). 29% of all full-time undergraduates had no need and received non-need-based gift aid.

GIFT AID (NEED-BASED) *Total amount:* $40,535,623 (5% federal, 2% state, 92% institutional, 1% external sources). *Receiving aid:* Freshmen: 48% (275); all full-time undergraduates: 49% (1,053). *Average award:* Freshmen: $37,841; Undergraduates: $37,748. *Scholarships, grants, and awards:* Federal Pell, FSEOG, state, private, college/university gift aid from institutional funds.

GIFT AID (NON-NEED-BASED) *Total amount:* $9,115,762 (6% federal, 1% state, 90% institutional, 3% external sources). *Receiving aid:* Freshmen: 4% (23). Undergraduates: 4% (93). *Average award:* Freshmen: $14,464. Undergraduates: $11,741. *Scholarships, grants, and awards by category:* Academic interests/achievement: general academic interests/achievements. Special characteristics: children of faculty/staff. *Tuition waivers:* Full or partial for employees or children of employees, senior citizens. *ROTC:* Army cooperative, Naval cooperative, Air Force cooperative.

LOANS *Student loans:* $11,017,355 (47% need-based, 53% non-need-based). 56% of past graduating class borrowed through all loan programs. *Average indebtedness per student:* $34,221. *Average need-based loan:* Freshmen: $3953. Undergraduates: $5067. *Parent loans:* $3,134,728 (100% non-need-based). *Programs:* Federal Direct (Subsidized and Unsubsidized Stafford, PLUS), Perkins, college/university.

WORK-STUDY *Federal work-study:* Total amount: $770,472; jobs available. *State or other work-study/employment:* Total amount: $405,000 (100% need-based). Part-time jobs available.

APPLYING FOR FINANCIAL AID *Required financial aid forms:* FAFSA, CSS Financial Aid PROFILE, state aid form, noncustodial (divorced/separated) parent's statement. *Financial aid deadline:* 1/15. *Notification date:* 3/25. Students must reply by 5/1.

CONTACT Ms. Linda Parker, Director of Financial Aid, Union College, Grant Hall, 807 Union Street, Schenectady, NY 12308-2311, 518-388-6123 or toll-free 888-843-6688. *Fax:* 518-388-8052. *E-mail:* finaid@union.edu.
Website: http://www.union.edu/.

UNION INSTITUTE & UNIVERSITY
Cincinnati, OH

CONTACT Ms. Lisa Perdomo, Director of Financial Aid, Union Institute & University, 440 East McMillan Street, Cincinnati, OH 45206-1925, 513-861-6400 Ext. 1261 or toll-free 800-486-3116. *Fax:* 513-487-1078.
Website: http://www.myunion.edu/.

UNION UNIVERSITY
Jackson, TN

Tuition & fees: $32,890	Average undergraduate aid package: $26,805

ABOUT THE INSTITUTION Independent Southern Baptist, coed. *Awards:* certificates, associate, bachelor's, master's, and doctoral degrees. 66 undergraduate majors. *Total enrollment:* 2,189. Undergraduates: 1,581. Freshmen: 344. Federal methodology is used as a basis for awarding need-based institutional aid.

UNDERGRADUATE EXPENSES for 2018–2019 *Application fee:* $35. *Comprehensive fee:* $43,090 includes full-time tuition ($31,550), mandatory fees ($1340), and room and board ($10,200). *College room only:* $7900. Full-time tuition and fees vary according to class time, course load, degree level, location, and program. Room and board charges vary according to board plan and housing facility. *Part-time tuition:* $1015 per credit hour. *Part-time fees:* $45 per credit hour. Part-time tuition and fees vary according to class time, course load, degree level, location, and program.

FRESHMAN FINANCIAL AID (Fall 2017, est.) 303 applied for aid; of those 84% were deemed to have need. 100% of freshmen with need received aid; of those 26% had need fully met. *Average percent of need met:* 81% (excluding resources awarded to replace EFC). *Average financial aid package:* $30,695 (excluding resources awarded to replace EFC). 18% of all full-time freshmen had no need and received non-need-based gift aid.

UNDERGRADUATE FINANCIAL AID (Fall 2017, est.) 1,292 applied for aid; of those 88% were deemed to have need. 100% of undergraduates with need received aid; of those 18% had need fully met. *Average percent of need met:* 70% (excluding resources awarded to replace EFC). *Average financial aid package:* $26,805 (excluding resources awarded to replace EFC). 21% of all full-time undergraduates had no need and received non-need-based gift aid.

GIFT AID (NEED-BASED) *Total amount:* $6,843,615 (39% federal, 20% state, 41% institutional). *Receiving aid:* Freshmen: 72% (227); all full-time undergraduates: 56% (817). *Average award:* Freshmen: $5380; Undergraduates: $6434. *Scholarships, grants, and awards:* Federal Pell, FSEOG, state, private, college/university gift aid from institutional funds, Federal Nursing.

GIFT AID (NON-NEED-BASED) *Total amount:* $21,882,794 (2% federal, 13% state, 83% institutional, 2% external sources). *Receiving aid:* Freshmen: 81% (256). Undergraduates: 65% (957). *Average award:* Freshmen: $14,168. Undergraduates: $14,733. *Scholarships, grants, and awards by category:* Academic interests/achievement: $13,761,491 total: biological sciences, business, communication, computer science, education, engineering/technologies, English, foreign languages, general academic interests/achievements, health fields, humanities, international studies, mathematics, military science, physical sciences, premedicine, religion/biblical studies, social sciences. Creative arts/performance: $329,565 total: art/fine arts, cinema/film/broadcasting, debating, journalism/publications, music, theater/drama. Special achievements/activities: $1,412,785 total: cheerleading/drum major, community service, general special achievements/activities, leadership, memberships, religious involvement. Special characteristics: $2,237,946 total: children and siblings of alumni, children of current students, children of educators, children of faculty/staff, ethnic background, first-generation college students, general special characteristics, handicapped students, international students, members of minority groups, relatives of clergy, religious affiliation, siblings of current students, spouses of current students, twins, veterans, veterans' children. *Tuition waivers:* Full or partial for children of alumni, employees or children of employees. *ROTC:* Army cooperative.

LOANS *Student loans:* $21,935,319 (14% need-based, 86% non-need-based). 58% of past graduating class borrowed through all loan programs. *Average indebtedness per student:* $39,022. *Average need-based loan:* Freshmen: $3352. Undergraduates: $4264. *Parent loans:* $3,342,786 (100% non-need-based). *Programs:* Federal Direct (Subsidized and Unsubsidized Stafford, PLUS), state, alternative loans.

WORK-STUDY *Federal work-study:* Total amount: $1,581,194; jobs available. *State or other work-study/employment:* Total amount: $1,200,200 (100% need-based). Part-time jobs available.

ATHLETIC AWARDS Total amount: $2,739,948 (100% non-need-based).

APPLYING FOR FINANCIAL AID *Required financial aid forms:* FAFSA, institution's own form. *Financial aid deadline (priority):* 12/1. *Notification date:* Continuous beginning 12/1. Students must reply by 5/1.

CONTACT Mr. John Windham, Director of Student Financial Planning, Union University, 1050 Union University Drive, Jackson, TN 38305-3697, 731-661-5015 or toll-free 800-33-UNION. *Fax:* 731-661-5570. *E-mail:* jwindham@uu.edu.
Website: http://www.uu.edu/.

UNITED STATES SPORTS ACADEMY
Daphne, AL

Tuition & fees: $15,972	Average undergraduate aid package: $6025

ABOUT THE INSTITUTION Independent, coed. *Awards:* bachelor's, master's, and doctoral degrees. 4 undergraduate majors. *Total enrollment:* 291. Undergraduates: 124. Federal methodology is used as a basis for awarding need-based institutional aid.

UNDERGRADUATE EXPENSES for 2018–2019 *Tuition:* full-time $14,652; part-time $407 per credit hour.

UNDERGRADUATE FINANCIAL AID (Fall 2016) 44 applied for aid; of those 100% were deemed to have need. 100% of undergraduates with need received aid; of those 95% had need fully met. *Average percent of need met:* 95% (excluding resources awarded to replace EFC). *Average financial aid package:* $6025 (excluding resources awarded to replace EFC).

GIFT AID (NEED-BASED) *Total amount:* $244,076 (91% federal, 3% state, 6% external sources). *Receiving aid:* All full-time undergraduates: 72% (44). *Average award:* Undergraduates: $1877. *Scholarships, grants, and awards:* Federal Pell, FSEOG, state.

GIFT AID (NON-NEED-BASED) *Tuition waivers:* Full or partial for employees or children of employees.

LOANS *Student loans:* $539,239 (100% need-based). *Average need-based loan:* Undergraduates: $3596. *Parent loans:* $2750 (100% need-based). *Programs:* Federal Direct (Subsidized and Unsubsidized Stafford, PLUS).

APPLYING FOR FINANCIAL AID *Required financial aid form:* FAFSA. *Financial aid deadline:* Continuous. *Notification date:* Continuous.

CONTACT Office of Financial Aid, United States Sports Academy, One Academy Drive, Daphne, AL 36526, 800-223-2668. *E-mail:* financialaid@ussa.edu. *Website:* http://www.ussa.edu/.

UNITED STATES UNIVERSITY
San Diego, CA

CONTACT Financial Aid Office, United States University, 7675 Mission Valley Road, San Diego, CA 92108, 619-477-6310 or toll-free 888-422-3381. *Website:* http://www.usuniversity.edu/.

UNITED TALMUDICAL SEMINARY
Brooklyn, NY

CONTACT Financial Aid Office, United Talmudical Seminary, 82 Lee Avenue, Brooklyn, NY 11211-7900, 718-963-9770 Ext. 309.

UNITY COLLEGE
Unity, ME

Tuition & fees: $28,350	Average undergraduate aid package: $20,848

ABOUT THE INSTITUTION Independent, coed. *Awards:* certificates, bachelor's, and master's degrees. 17 undergraduate majors. *Total enrollment:* 733. Undergraduates: 704. Freshmen: 175. Federal methodology is used as a basis for awarding need-based institutional aid.

UNDERGRADUATE EXPENSES for 2017–2018 *Comprehensive fee:* $38,750 includes full-time tuition ($27,150), mandatory fees ($1200), and room and board ($10,400). Room and board charges vary according to board plan and housing facility. *Part-time tuition:* $980 per credit.

FRESHMAN FINANCIAL AID (Fall 2017, est.) 167 applied for aid; of those 93% were deemed to have need. 100% of freshmen with need received aid; of those 13% had need fully met. *Average percent of need met:* 71% (excluding resources awarded to replace EFC). *Average financial aid package:* $21,099 (excluding resources awarded to replace EFC). 10% of all full-time freshmen had no need and received non-need-based gift aid.

UNDERGRADUATE FINANCIAL AID (Fall 2017, est.) 641 applied for aid; of those 91% were deemed to have need. 100% of undergraduates with need received aid; of those 11% had need fully met. *Average percent of need met:* 72% (excluding resources awarded to replace EFC). *Average financial aid package:* $20,848 (excluding resources awarded to replace EFC). 15% of all full-time undergraduates had no need and received non-need-based gift aid.

GIFT AID (NEED-BASED) *Total amount:* $8,024,243 (17% federal, 1% state, 79% institutional, 3% external sources). *Receiving aid:* Freshmen: 89% (156); all full-time undergraduates: 84% (584). *Average award:* Freshmen: $14,862; Undergraduates: $13,718. *Scholarships, grants, and awards:* Federal Pell, FSEOG, state, private, college/university gift aid from institutional funds.

GIFT AID (NON-NEED-BASED) *Total amount:* $1,262,937 (96% institutional, 4% external sources). *Receiving aid:* Freshmen: 7% (13). Undergraduates: 5% (37). *Average award:* Freshmen: $10,555. Undergraduates: $9602. *Scholarships, grants, and awards by category:* Academic interests/achievement: general academic interests/achievements. Special achievements/activities: 4 awards ($7500 total): community service, general special achievements/activities. Special characteristics: 27 awards ($79,550 total): children of educators, general special characteristics, local/state students, members of minority groups. *Tuition waivers:* Full or partial for employees or children of employees.

LOANS *Student loans:* $6,626,185 (75% need-based, 25% non-need-based). *Average need-based loan:* Freshmen: $6209. Undergraduates: $7120. *Parent loans:* $2,127,225 (56% need-based, 44% non-need-based). *Programs:* Federal Direct (Subsidized and Unsubsidized Stafford, PLUS).

WORK-STUDY *Federal work-study:* Total amount: $613,063; 429 jobs averaging $1429. *State or other work-study/employment:* Total amount: $28,950 (100% non-need-based). 16 part-time jobs averaging $1597.

APPLYING FOR FINANCIAL AID *Required financial aid form:* FAFSA. *Financial aid deadline:* Continuous. *Notification date:* Continuous beginning 11/26.

CONTACT Mr. Rand E. Newell, Director of Financial Aid, Unity College, 90 Quaker Hill Road, Unity, ME 04988, 207-509-7201. *Fax:* 207-512-1168. *E-mail:* rnewell@unity.edu. *Website:* http://www.unity.edu/.

UNIVERSIDAD ADVENTISTA DE LAS ANTILLAS
Mayagüez, PR

CONTACT Mrs. Awilda Matos, Director of Financial Aid, Universidad Adventista de las Antillas, Box 118, Mayaguez, PR 00681-0118, 787-834-9595 Ext. 2263. *Fax:* 787-834-9597. *E-mail:* amatos@uaa.edu. *Website:* http://www.uaa.edu/.

UNIVERSIDAD CENTRAL DEL CARIBE
Bayamón, PR

CONTACT Financial Aid Office, Universidad Central del Caribe, PO Box 60-327, Bayamón, PR 00960-6032, 787-798-3001. *Website:* http://www.uccaribe.edu/.

UNIVERSIDAD DEL ESTE
Carolina, PR

CONTACT Mrs. Eigna De Jess Molinari, Director of Financial Aid, Universidad del Este, Apartado 2010, Carolina, PR 00928, 787-257-7373 Ext. 3301. *E-mail:* eidejesus@suagm.edu. *Website:* http://www.suagm.edu/une/.

UNIVERSIDAD DEL TURABO
Gurabo, PR

CONTACT Ms. Carmen J. Rivera Lopez, Directora de la Oficina de Asistencia Economica, Universidad del Turabo, Apartado 3030, Gurabo, PR 00778-3030, 787-743-7979 Ext. 4352. *Fax:* 787-746-6777.
Website: http://www.suagm.edu/ut/.

UNIVERSIDAD METROPOLITANA
San Juan, PR

CONTACT Economic Assistant Director, Universidad Metropolitana, Call Box 21150, Rio Piedras, PR 00928-1150, 787-766-1717 Ext. 6586 or toll-free 800-747-8362 (out-of-state).
Website: http://www.suagm.edu/umet/.

UNIVERSIDAD PENTECOSTAL MIZPA
San Juan, PR

CONTACT Mrs. Myriam Juarbe, Director of Financial Aid, Universidad Pentecostal Mizpa, PO Box 20966, San Juan, PR 00928, 787-720-4476. *Fax:* 787-720-2012. *E-mail:* asistenciaeconomica@colmizpa.edu.
Website: http://www.mizpa.edu/.

UNIVERSITY AT ALBANY, STATE UNIVERSITY OF NEW YORK
Albany, NY

Tuition & fees (NY res): $9490	Average undergraduate aid package: $11,415

ABOUT THE INSTITUTION State-supported, coed. *Awards:* certificates, bachelor's, master's, and doctoral degrees. 64 undergraduate majors. **Total enrollment:** 17,743. Undergraduates: 13,508. Freshmen: 2,815. Federal methodology is used as a basis for awarding need-based institutional aid.

UNDERGRADUATE EXPENSES for 2018–2019 Application fee: $50. *Tuition, state resident:* full-time $6670; part-time $278 per credit hour. *Tuition, nonresident:* full-time $21,550; part-time $898 per credit hour. *Required fees:* full-time $2820; $75.51 per credit hour. Part-time tuition and fees vary according to course load. *College room and board:* $13,864; *Room only:* $8364. Room and board charges vary according to board plan and housing facility.

FRESHMAN FINANCIAL AID (Fall 2017, est.) 2,519 applied for aid; of those 80% were deemed to have need. 95% of freshmen with need received aid; of those 7% had need fully met. *Average percent of need met:* 58% (excluding resources awarded to replace EFC). *Average financial aid package:* $11,672 (excluding resources awarded to replace EFC). 7% of all full-time freshmen had no need and received non-need-based gift aid.

UNDERGRADUATE FINANCIAL AID (Fall 2017, est.) 10,350 applied for aid; of those 83% were deemed to have need. 97% of undergraduates with need received aid; of those 7% had need fully met. *Average percent of need met:* 60% (excluding resources awarded to replace EFC). *Average financial aid package:* $11,415 (excluding resources awarded to replace EFC). 6% of all full-time undergraduates had no need and received non-need-based gift aid.

GIFT AID (NEED-BASED) Total amount: $61,373,942 (44% federal, 39% state, 15% institutional, 2% external sources). *Receiving aid:* Freshmen: 61% (1,705); all full-time undergraduates: 57% (7,287). *Average award:* Freshmen: $9274; Undergraduates: $8387. *Scholarships, grants, and awards:* Federal Pell, FSEOG, state, private, college/university gift aid from institutional funds, Excelsior Scholarship (for qualified NY state students).

GIFT AID (NON-NEED-BASED) Total amount: $4,958,900 (7% federal, 23% state, 64% institutional, 6% external sources). *Receiving aid:* Freshmen: 2% (48). Undergraduates: 2% (204). *Average award:* Freshmen: $4028. Undergraduates:

$3839. *Scholarships, grants, and awards by category: Academic interests/ achievement:* general academic interests/achievements. *ROTC:* Army, Air Force cooperative.

LOANS Student loans: $63,138,159 (46% need-based, 54% non-need-based). 65% of past graduating class borrowed through all loan programs. *Average indebtedness per student:* $27,329. *Average need-based loan:* Freshmen: $3811. Undergraduates: $4570. *Parent loans:* $21,017,179 (100% non-need-based). *Programs:* Federal Direct (Subsidized and Unsubsidized Stafford, PLUS), Perkins.

WORK-STUDY Federal work-study: Total amount: $875,000; 610 jobs averaging $1434. *State or other work-study/employment:* Total amount: $1,867,746 (76% need-based, 24% non-need-based). 234 part-time jobs averaging $7502.

ATHLETIC AWARDS Total amount: $6,754,578 (4% need-based, 96% non-need-based).

APPLYING FOR FINANCIAL AID Required financial aid forms: FAFSA, Tuition Assistance Program (TAP) for NY State residents. *Financial aid deadline (priority):* 12/1. *Notification date:* Continuous beginning 3/2.

CONTACT Stephen Kudzin, Director of Financial Aid, University at Albany, State University of New York, Student Financial Center, Campus Center G-26, 1400 Washington Avenue, Albany, NY 12222-0001, 518-442-3202. *Fax:* 518-442-5295. *E-mail:* sfc@albany.edu.
Website: http://www.albany.edu/.

UNIVERSITY AT BUFFALO, THE STATE UNIVERSITY OF NEW YORK
Buffalo, NY

Tuition & fees (NY res): $9828	Average undergraduate aid package: $10,466

ABOUT THE INSTITUTION State-supported, coed. *Awards:* certificates, bachelor's, master's, and doctoral degrees. 76 undergraduate majors. **Total enrollment:** 30,648. Undergraduates: 21,020. Freshmen: 4,179. Federal methodology is used as a basis for awarding need-based institutional aid.

UNDERGRADUATE EXPENSES for 2017–2018 Application fee: $50. *Tuition, state resident:* full-time $6670; part-time $278 per credit hour. *Tuition, nonresident:* full-time $24,180; part-time $1008 per credit hour. *Required fees:* full-time $3158; $136.18 per credit hour. Part-time tuition and fees vary according to course load. *College room and board:* $13,782; *Room only:* $8032. Room and board charges vary according to board plan and housing facility.

FRESHMAN FINANCIAL AID (Fall 2016) 3,299 applied for aid; of those 73% were deemed to have need. 91% of freshmen with need received aid; of those 6% had need fully met. *Average percent of need met:* 49% (excluding resources awarded to replace EFC). *Average financial aid package:* $10,937 (excluding resources awarded to replace EFC). 9% of all full-time freshmen had no need and received non-need-based gift aid.

UNDERGRADUATE FINANCIAL AID (Fall 2016) 13,326 applied for aid; of those 76% were deemed to have need. 96% of undergraduates with need received aid; of those 99% had need fully met. *Average percent of need met:* 50% (excluding resources awarded to replace EFC). *Average financial aid package:* $10,466 (excluding resources awarded to replace EFC). 4% of all full-time undergraduates had no need and received non-need-based gift aid.

GIFT AID (NEED-BASED) Total amount: $76,076,465 (42% federal, 32% state, 22% institutional, 4% external sources). *Receiving aid:* Freshmen: 40% (1,650); all full-time undergraduates: 40% (7,422). *Average award:* Freshmen: $8182; Undergraduates: $7389. *Scholarships, grants, and awards:* Federal Pell, FSEOG, state, private, college/university gift aid from institutional funds, Federal Nursing.

GIFT AID (NON-NEED-BASED) Total amount: $5,921,518 (23% state, 66% institutional, 11% external sources). *Receiving aid:* Freshmen: 21% (858). Undergraduates: 13% (2,374). *Average award:* Freshmen: $4026. Undergraduates: $4253. *Tuition waivers:* Full or partial for minority students. *ROTC:* Army cooperative.

LOANS Student loans: $64,101,284 (82% need-based, 18% non-need-based). 57% of past graduating class borrowed through all loan programs. *Average indebtedness per student:* $25,598. *Average need-based loan:* Freshmen: $3922. Undergraduates: $4519. *Parent loans:* $15,611,202 (63% need-based, 37% non-need-based). *Programs:* Federal Direct (Subsidized and Unsubsidized Stafford, PLUS), Perkins, Federal Nursing, college/university.

WORK-STUDY *Federal work-study:* 848 jobs averaging $1139. *State or other work-study/employment:* Total amount: $6,195,631 (100% need-based). Part-time jobs available.
ATHLETIC AWARDS Total amount: $9,194,925 (86% need-based, 14% non-need-based).
APPLYING FOR FINANCIAL AID *Required financial aid form:* FAFSA. *Financial aid deadline (priority):* 3/1. *Notification date:* Continuous beginning 2/1. Students must reply by 5/1.
CONTACT John Gottardy, Director of Financial Aid, University at Buffalo, the State University of New York, 232 Capen Hall, Buffalo, NY 14260, 716-645-8232 or toll-free 888-UB-ADMIT. *Fax:* 716-645-6566. *E-mail:* johngott@buffalo.edu. *Website:* http://www.buffalo.edu/.

UNIVERSITY OF ADVANCING TECHNOLOGY
Tempe, AZ

CONTACT Financial Aid Office, University of Advancing Technology, 2625 West Baseline Road, Tempe, AZ 85283-1042, 602-383-8228 or toll-free 800-658-5744. *Fax:* 602-383-8222. *E-mail:* fa@uat.edu. *Website:* http://www.uat.edu/.

THE UNIVERSITY OF AKRON
Akron, OH

Tuition & fees (OH res): $10,270	Average undergraduate aid package: $7811

ABOUT THE INSTITUTION State-supported, coed. *Awards:* certificates, associate, bachelor's, master's, and doctoral degrees. 153 undergraduate majors. *Total enrollment:* 20,169. Undergraduates: 16,871. Freshmen: 3,440. Federal methodology is used as a basis for awarding need-based institutional aid.
UNDERGRADUATE EXPENSES for 2018–2019 *Application fee:* $45. *Tuition, state resident:* full-time $8618; part-time $359 per credit hour. *Tuition, nonresident:* full-time $17,149; part-time $715 per credit hour. *Required fees:* full-time $1652. Full-time tuition and fees vary according to course load, degree level, location, and program. Part-time tuition and fees vary according to course load, degree level, location, and program. *College room and board:* $12,296; *Room only:* $8026. Room and board charges vary according to board plan and housing facility.
FRESHMAN FINANCIAL AID (Fall 2017, est.) 2,878 applied for aid; of those 80% were deemed to have need. 100% of freshmen with need received aid; of those 14% had need fully met. *Average percent of need met:* 56% (excluding resources awarded to replace EFC). *Average financial aid package:* $9343 (excluding resources awarded to replace EFC). 16% of all full-time freshmen had no need and received non-need-based gift aid.
UNDERGRADUATE FINANCIAL AID (Fall 2017, est.) 11,799 applied for aid; of those 79% were deemed to have need. 100% of undergraduates with need received aid; of those 11% had need fully met. *Average percent of need met:* 52% (excluding resources awarded to replace EFC). *Average financial aid package:* $7811 (excluding resources awarded to replace EFC). 13% of all full-time undergraduates had no need and received non-need-based gift aid.
GIFT AID (NEED-BASED) *Total amount:* $30,766,023 (84% federal, 16% state). *Receiving aid:* Freshmen: 43% (1,290); all full-time undergraduates: 38% (5,038). *Average award:* Freshmen: $5240; Undergraduates: $5276. *Scholarships, grants, and awards:* Federal Pell, FSEOG.
GIFT AID (NON-NEED-BASED) *Total amount:* $42,643,140 (1% federal, 4% state, 79% institutional, 16% external sources). *Receiving aid:* Freshmen: 68% (2,037). Undergraduates: 52% (6,963). *Average award:* Freshmen: $6453. Undergraduates: $5150. *Scholarships, grants, and awards by category:* Academic interests/achievement: 3,889 awards ($14,988,468 total): biological sciences, business, communication, computer science, education, engineering/technologies, English, foreign languages, general academic interests/achievements, health fields, home economics, humanities, international studies, mathematics, military science, physical sciences, premedicine, social sciences. *Creative arts/performance:* 101 awards ($152,009 total): applied art and design, art/fine arts, creative writing, dance, debating, general creative arts/performance, journalism/publications, music, performing arts, theater/

drama. *Special achievements/activities:* 109 awards ($279,327 total): community service, general special achievements/activities, leadership, memberships. *Special characteristics:* 3,471 awards ($9,254,539 total): adult students, general special characteristics, handicapped students, international students, local/state students, members of minority groups, out-of-state students. *Tuition waivers:* Full or partial for employees or children of employees, senior citizens. *ROTC:* Army, Air Force cooperative.
LOANS *Student loans:* $61,637,356 (51% need-based, 49% non-need-based). 68% of past graduating class borrowed through all loan programs. *Average indebtedness per student:* $32,033. *Average need-based loan:* Freshmen: $3241. Undergraduates: $3927. *Parent loans:* $21,281,548 (100% non-need-based). *Programs:* Federal Direct (Subsidized and Unsubsidized Stafford, PLUS), Perkins, Federal Nursing, college/university.
WORK-STUDY *Federal work-study:* Total amount: $998,713; 302 jobs averaging $3307. *State or other work-study/employment:* Total amount: $13,609,346 (100% non-need-based). Part-time jobs available.
ATHLETIC AWARDS Total amount: $91,665 (100% non-need-based).
APPLYING FOR FINANCIAL AID *Required financial aid forms:* FAFSA, institution's own form. *Financial aid deadline (priority):* 3/1. *Notification date:* Continuous beginning 3/15. Students must reply within 2 weeks of notification.
CONTACT Mrs. Jennifer E. Harpham, Director of Student Financial Aid, The University of Akron, 302 Buchtel Mall, Akron, OH 44325-6211, 330-972-5860 or toll-free 800-655-4884. *Fax:* 330-972-7139. *E-mail:* jharpham@uakron.edu. *Website:* http://www.uakron.edu/.

THE UNIVERSITY OF ALABAMA
Tuscaloosa, AL

Tuition & fees (AL res): $10,780	Average undergraduate aid package: $14,459

ABOUT THE INSTITUTION State-supported, coed. *Awards:* certificates, bachelor's, master's, and doctoral degrees. 67 undergraduate majors. *Total enrollment:* 38,563. Undergraduates: 33,305. Freshmen: 7,407. Federal methodology is used as a basis for awarding need-based institutional aid.
UNDERGRADUATE EXPENSES for 2017–2018 *Application fee:* $40. *Tuition, state resident:* full-time $10,780. *Tuition, nonresident:* full-time $28,100. Full-time tuition and fees vary according to course load. Part-time tuition and fees vary according to course load. *College room and board:* $9974; *Room only:* $6300. Room and board charges vary according to board plan, housing facility, and location.
FRESHMAN FINANCIAL AID (Fall 2016) 5,077 applied for aid; of those 74% were deemed to have need. 96% of freshmen with need received aid; of those 29% had need fully met. *Average percent of need met:* 58% (excluding resources awarded to replace EFC). *Average financial aid package:* $16,254 (excluding resources awarded to replace EFC). 27% of all full-time freshmen had no need and received non-need-based gift aid.
UNDERGRADUATE FINANCIAL AID (Fall 2016) 15,985 applied for aid; of those 79% were deemed to have need. 97% of undergraduates with need received aid; of those 21% had need fully met. *Average percent of need met:* 54% (excluding resources awarded to replace EFC). *Average financial aid package:* $14,459 (excluding resources awarded to replace EFC). 26% of all full-time undergraduates had no need and received non-need-based gift aid.
GIFT AID (NEED-BASED) *Total amount:* $103,996,060 (30% federal, 3% state, 65% institutional, 2% external sources). *Receiving aid:* Freshmen: 38% (2,862); all full-time undergraduates: 32% (9,238). *Average award:* Freshmen: $15,053; Undergraduates: $12,730. *Scholarships, grants, and awards:* Federal Pell, FSEOG, state, private, college/university gift aid from institutional funds, Federal Nursing.
GIFT AID (NON-NEED-BASED) *Total amount:* $155,934,188 (6% federal, 4% state, 87% institutional, 3% external sources). *Receiving aid:* Freshmen: 31% (2,325). Undergraduates: 22% (6,472). *Average award:* Freshmen: $16,777. Undergraduates: $15,945. *Scholarships, grants, and awards by category:* Academic interests/achievement: agriculture, area/ethnic studies, biological sciences, business, communication, computer science, education, engineering/technologies, English, foreign languages, general academic interests/achievements, home economics, library science, mathematics, military science, physical sciences, premedicine, social sciences. *Creative arts/performance:* art/fine arts, cinema/film/broadcasting, creative writing, dance, debating, journalism/publications, music, theater/drama. *Special achievements/activities:* cheerleading/drum major, community service, general special achievements/activ-

ities, hobbies/interests, junior miss. *Special characteristics:* children of union members/ company employees, general special characteristics, international students, out-of-state students, spouses of deceased or disabled public servants. *Tuition waivers:* Full or partial for employees or children of employees. *ROTC:* Army, Air Force.

LOANS *Student loans:* $138,994,329 (64% need-based, 36% non-need-based). 46% of past graduating class borrowed through all loan programs. *Average indebtedness per student:* $34,305. *Average need-based loan:* Freshmen: $3514. Undergraduates: $4303. *Parent loans:* $84,155,595 (53% need-based, 47% non-need-based). *Programs:* Federal Direct (Subsidized and Unsubsidized Stafford, PLUS), Perkins, Federal Nursing, college/university.

WORK-STUDY *Federal work-study:* 681 jobs averaging $2702.

ATHLETIC AWARDS Total amount: $13,462,822 (3% need-based, 97% non-need-based).

APPLYING FOR FINANCIAL AID *Required financial aid forms:* FAFSA, scholarship application form. *Financial aid deadline (priority):* 3/1. *Notification date:* Continuous beginning 4/1. Students must reply within 3 weeks of notification.

CONTACT Helen Allen, Director of Student Financial Aid, The University of Alabama, Box 870162, Tuscaloosa, AL 35487-0162, 205-348-7949 or toll-free 800-933-BAMA. *Fax:* 205-348-2989. *E-mail:* helen.allen@ua.edu. *Website:* http://www.ua.edu/.

THE UNIVERSITY OF ALABAMA AT BIRMINGHAM

Birmingham, AL

Tuition & fees (AL res): $10,635	Average undergraduate aid package: $10,787

ABOUT THE INSTITUTION State-supported, coed. *Awards:* certificates, bachelor's, master's, and doctoral degrees. 46 undergraduate majors. *Total enrollment:* 20,902. Undergraduates: 13,134. Freshmen: 2,299. Federal methodology is used as a basis for awarding need-based institutional aid.

UNDERGRADUATE EXPENSES for 2017–2018 *Application fee:* $30. *Tuition, state resident:* full-time $10,410; part-time $347 per semester hour. *Tuition, nonresident:* full-time $23,790; part-time $793 per semester hour. *Required fees:* full-time $225. Full-time tuition and fees vary according to course load, degree level, program, and reciprocity agreements. Part-time tuition and fees vary according to course load, degree level, program, and reciprocity agreements. *College room and board:* $11,682; *Room only:* $6200. Room and board charges vary according to board plan and housing facility.

FRESHMAN FINANCIAL AID (Fall 2017, est.) 1,904 applied for aid; of those 76% were deemed to have need. 99% of freshmen with need received aid; of those 17% had need fully met. *Average percent of need met:* 56% (excluding resources awarded to replace EFC). *Average financial aid package:* $10,049 (excluding resources awarded to replace EFC). 27% of all full-time freshmen had no need and received non-need-based gift aid.

UNDERGRADUATE FINANCIAL AID (Fall 2017, est.) 7,091 applied for aid; of those 83% were deemed to have need. 98% of undergraduates with need received aid; of those 11% had need fully met. *Average percent of need met:* 50% (excluding resources awarded to replace EFC). *Average financial aid package:* $10,787 (excluding resources awarded to replace EFC). 21% of all full-time undergraduates had no need and received non-need-based gift aid.

GIFT AID (NEED-BASED) *Total amount:* $24,155,958 (98% federal, 1% institutional, 1% external sources). *Receiving aid:* Freshmen: 38% (844); all full-time undergraduates: 40% (3,852). *Average award:* Freshmen: $5262; Undergraduates: $5250. *Scholarships, grants, and awards:* Federal Pell, FSEOG, state, private, college/university gift aid from institutional funds, United Negro College Fund.

GIFT AID (NON-NEED-BASED) *Total amount:* $31,939,447 (1% state, 93% institutional, 6% external sources). *Receiving aid:* Freshmen: 47% (1,052). Undergraduates: 27% (2,629). *Average award:* Freshmen: $7399. Undergraduates: $7651. *Scholarships, grants, and awards by category:* Academic interests/ achievement: business, communication, computer science, engineering/technologies, general academic interests/achievements, health fields, mathematics. *Creative arts/performance:* art/fine arts, music, performing arts, theater/drama. *Special achievements/activities:* cheerleading/drum major, junior miss, leadership, memberships, religious involvement. *Special characteristics:* adult students, children and siblings of alumni,

---

children of current students, children of educators, children of faculty/staff, children of public servants, children of union members/company employees, children of workers in trades, children with a deceased or disabled parent, ethnic background, first-generation college students, general special characteristics, handicapped students, international students, married students, members of minority groups, out-of-state students, parents of current students, previous college experience, public servants, relatives of clergy, siblings of current students, spouses of current students, spouses of deceased or disabled public servants, twins, veterans, veterans' children. *Tuition waivers:* Full or partial for employees or children of employees. *ROTC:* Army, Air Force cooperative.

LOANS *Student loans:* $47,565,078 (47% need-based, 53% non-need-based). 61% of past graduating class borrowed through all loan programs. *Average indebtedness per student:* $34,872. *Average need-based loan:* Freshmen: $3856. Undergraduates: $4370. *Parent loans:* $10,887,947 (100% non-need-based). *Programs:* Federal Direct (Subsidized and Unsubsidized Stafford, PLUS), Perkins, state, college/university.

WORK-STUDY *Federal work-study:* Total amount: $637,215; jobs available.

ATHLETIC AWARDS Total amount: $8,142,154 (100% non-need-based).

APPLYING FOR FINANCIAL AID *Required financial aid form:* FAFSA. *Financial aid deadline (priority):* 3/1. *Notification date:* Continuous beginning 3/15. Students must reply within 4 weeks of notification.

CONTACT Ms. Helen M. McIntyre, Office of Student Financial Aid, The University of Alabama at Birmingham, LHL 120, 1720 2nd Avenue South, Birmingham, AL 35294-0013, 205-934-8132 or toll-free 800-421-8743. *E-mail:* finaid@uab.edu. *Website:* http://www.uab.edu/.

THE UNIVERSITY OF ALABAMA IN HUNTSVILLE

Huntsville, AL

Tuition & fees (AL res): $10,280	Average undergraduate aid package: $11,385

ABOUT THE INSTITUTION State-supported, coed. *Awards:* certificates, bachelor's, master's, and doctoral degrees. 35 undergraduate majors. *Total enrollment:* 8,468. Undergraduates: 6,507. Freshmen: 1,213. Both federal and institutional methodology are used as a basis for awarding need-based institutional aid.

UNDERGRADUATE EXPENSES for 2017–2018 *Application fee:* $30. *Tuition, state resident:* full-time $9356; part-time $411 per credit hour. *Tuition, nonresident:* full-time $20,556; part-time $908 per credit hour. *Required fees:* full-time $924. Full-time tuition and fees vary according to course load and program. Part-time tuition and fees vary according to course load and program. *College room and board:* $9748; *Room only:* $6608. Room and board charges vary according to board plan and housing facility.

FRESHMAN FINANCIAL AID (Fall 2017, est.) 1,340 applied for aid; of those 60% were deemed to have need. 99% of freshmen with need received aid; of those 30% had need fully met. *Average percent of need met:* 73% (excluding resources awarded to replace EFC). *Average financial aid package:* $14,044 (excluding resources awarded to replace EFC). 31% of all full-time freshmen had no need and received non-need-based gift aid.

UNDERGRADUATE FINANCIAL AID (Fall 2017, est.) 5,882 applied for aid; of those 53% were deemed to have need. 98% of undergraduates with need received aid; of those 19% had need fully met. *Average percent of need met:* 63% (excluding resources awarded to replace EFC). *Average financial aid package:* $11,385 (excluding resources awarded to replace EFC). 26% of all full-time undergraduates had no need and received non-need-based gift aid.

GIFT AID (NEED-BASED) *Total amount:* $20,853,356 (41% federal, 57% institutional, 2% external sources). *Receiving aid:* Freshmen: 56% (749); all full-time undergraduates: 44% (2,579). *Average award:* Freshmen: $10,257; Undergraduates: $8102. *Scholarships, grants, and awards:* Federal Pell, FSEOG, state, private, college/university gift aid from institutional funds, Federal Nursing.

GIFT AID (NON-NEED-BASED) *Total amount:* $17,430,443 (97% institutional, 3% external sources). *Receiving aid:* Freshmen: 14% (186). Undergraduates: 6% (378). *Average award:* Freshmen: $10,675. Undergraduates: $9638. *Scholarships, grants, and awards by category:* Academic interests/achievement: biological sciences, business, communication, computer science, education, engineering/technologies, English, foreign languages, general academic interests/achievements, health fields, humanities, mathematics, physical sciences, social sciences. *Creative arts/*

---

performance: art/fine arts, music. *Special achievements/activities:* cheerleading/drum major, community service, general special achievements/activities, junior miss, leadership. *Special characteristics:* general special characteristics, local/state students, members of minority groups. *Tuition waivers:* Full or partial for employees or children of employees. *ROTC:* Army cooperative.

LOANS *Student loans:* $27,996,631 (75% need-based, 25% non-need-based). 56% of past graduating class borrowed through all loan programs. *Average indebtedness per student:* $29,396. *Average need-based loan:* Freshmen: $5531. Undergraduates: $7164. *Parent loans:* $4,551,938 (44% need-based, 56% non-need-based). *Programs:* Federal Direct (Subsidized and Unsubsidized Stafford, PLUS).

WORK-STUDY *Federal work-study:* Total amount: $357,276; 82 jobs averaging $4357.

ATHLETIC AWARDS Total amount: $3,013,764 (24% need-based, 76% non-need-based).

APPLYING FOR FINANCIAL AID *Required financial aid form:* FAFSA. *Financial aid deadline:* 7/31 (priority: 4/1). *Notification date:* Continuous beginning 4/1. Students must reply within 2 weeks of notification.

CONTACT Mr. Patrick James, Director of Financial Aid, The University of Alabama in Huntsville, 301 Sparkman Drive, CTC Room 212, Huntsville, AL 35899, 256-824-6650 or toll-free 800-UAH-CALL. *Fax:* 256-824-6212. *E-mail:* finaid@uah.edu. *Website:* http://www.uah.edu/.

UNIVERSITY OF ALASKA ANCHORAGE
Anchorage, AK

Tuition & fees (AK res): $6186	Average undergraduate aid package: $9779

ABOUT THE INSTITUTION State-supported, coed. 107 undergraduate majors. Federal methodology is used as a basis for awarding need-based institutional aid.

UNDERGRADUATE EXPENSES for 2017–2018 *Tuition, state resident:* full-time $6186. *Tuition, nonresident:* full-time $18,990. Full-time tuition and fees vary according to course level and location. Part-time tuition and fees vary according to course level and location. *College room and board:* $11,962. Room and board charges vary according to board plan and housing facility.

FRESHMAN FINANCIAL AID (Fall 2017, est.) 1,166 applied for aid; of those 69% were deemed to have need. 97% of freshmen with need received aid; of those 20% had need fully met. *Average percent of need met:* 69% (excluding resources awarded to replace EFC). *Average financial aid package:* $9685 (excluding resources awarded to replace EFC). 9% of all full-time freshmen had no need and received non-need-based gift aid.

UNDERGRADUATE FINANCIAL AID (Fall 2017, est.) 4,853 applied for aid; of those 74% were deemed to have need. 96% of undergraduates with need received aid; of those 14% had need fully met. *Average percent of need met:* 62% (excluding resources awarded to replace EFC). *Average financial aid package:* $9779 (excluding resources awarded to replace EFC). 9% of all full-time undergraduates had no need and received non-need-based gift aid.

GIFT AID (NEED-BASED) *Total amount:* $28,595,909 (50% federal, 22% state, 15% institutional, 13% external sources). *Receiving aid:* Freshmen: 52% (697); all full-time undergraduates: 46% (2,938). *Average award:* Freshmen: $3423; Undergraduates: $3262. *Scholarships, grants, and awards:* Federal Pell, FSEOG, state, private, college/university gift aid from institutional funds.

GIFT AID (NON-NEED-BASED) *Total amount:* $6,869,635 (44% state, 27% institutional, 29% external sources). *Average award:* Freshmen: $2500. Undergraduates: $2246. *Scholarships, grants, and awards by category: Academic interests/achievement:* biological sciences, business, communication, computer science, education, engineering/technologies, English, general academic interests/achievements, health fields, humanities, mathematics, social sciences. *Creative arts/performance:* art/fine arts, dance, debating, music, performing arts. *Special achievements/activities:* general special achievements/activities, leadership. *Special characteristics:* children and siblings of alumni, children of current students, children of educators, children of faculty/staff.

LOANS *Student loans:* $47,972,608 (75% need-based, 25% non-need-based). 51% of past graduating class borrowed through all loan programs. *Average indebtedness per student:* $27,188. *Average need-based loan:* Freshmen: $3211. Undergraduates: $4088. *Parent loans:* $4,782,658 (61% need-based, 39% non-need-based).

Programs: Federal Direct (Subsidized and Unsubsidized Stafford, PLUS), state, private loans.

WORK-STUDY *Federal work-study:* Total amount: $387,917; jobs available.

ATHLETIC AWARDS Total amount: $1,803,751 (22% need-based, 78% non-need-based).

APPLYING FOR FINANCIAL AID *Required financial aid form:* FAFSA. *Financial aid deadline (priority):* 4/1. *Notification date:* Continuous beginning 2/1. Students must reply within 4 weeks of notification.

CONTACT Sonya F. Stein, Director of Student Financial Assistance, University of Alaska Anchorage, PO Box 141608, Anchorage, AK 99514-1608, 907-786-1517. *Fax:* 907-786-6122. *E-mail:* sfstein@alaska.edu. *Website:* http://www.uaa.alaska.edu/.

UNIVERSITY OF ALASKA FAIRBANKS
Fairbanks, AK

Tuition & fees (AK res): $8800	Average undergraduate aid package: $8233

ABOUT THE INSTITUTION State-supported, coed. *Awards:* certificates, associate, bachelor's, master's, and doctoral degrees. 77 undergraduate majors. *Total enrollment:* 7,744. Undergraduates: 6,718. Freshmen: 804. Federal methodology is used as a basis for awarding need-based institutional aid.

UNDERGRADUATE EXPENSES for 2018–2019 *Application fee:* $50. *Tuition, state resident:* full-time $7020; part-time $212 per credit hour. *Tuition, nonresident:* full-time $23,190; part-time $751 per credit hour. *Required fees:* full-time $1780. Full-time tuition and fees vary according to course level, course load, location, program, and reciprocity agreements. Part-time tuition and fees vary according to course level, course load, location, program, and reciprocity agreements. *College room and board:* $8930; *Room only:* $4200. Room and board charges vary according to board plan, housing facility, and location.

FRESHMAN FINANCIAL AID (Fall 2016) 607 applied for aid; of those 59% were deemed to have need. 96% of freshmen with need received aid; of those 22% had need fully met. *Average percent of need met:* 61% (excluding resources awarded to replace EFC). *Average financial aid package:* $8457 (excluding resources awarded to replace EFC). 17% of all full-time freshmen had no need and received non-need-based gift aid.

UNDERGRADUATE FINANCIAL AID (Fall 2016) 2,554 applied for aid; of those 65% were deemed to have need. 96% of undergraduates with need received aid; of those 16% had need fully met. *Average percent of need met:* 54% (excluding resources awarded to replace EFC). *Average financial aid package:* $8233 (excluding resources awarded to replace EFC). 14% of all full-time undergraduates had no need and received non-need-based gift aid.

GIFT AID (NEED-BASED) *Total amount:* $12,416,142 (44% federal, 21% state, 20% institutional, 15% external sources). *Receiving aid:* Freshmen: 47% (315); all full-time undergraduates: 46% (1,416). *Average award:* Freshmen: $7711; Undergraduates: $7056. *Scholarships, grants, and awards:* Federal Pell, FSEOG, state, private, college/university gift aid from institutional funds.

GIFT AID (NON-NEED-BASED) *Total amount:* $5,707,696 (44% state, 29% institutional, 27% external sources). *Receiving aid:* Freshmen: 8% (54). Undergraduates: 6% (172). *Average award:* Freshmen: $3679. Undergraduates: $3653. *Scholarships, grants, and awards by category: Academic interests/achievement:* biological sciences, business, computer science, education, engineering/technologies, general academic interests/achievements, mathematics, military science, physical sciences. *Special achievements/activities:* community service, general special achievements/activities, leadership. *Special characteristics:* local/state students. *Tuition waivers:* Full or partial for employees or children of employees, senior citizens. *ROTC:* Army.

LOANS *Student loans:* $13,162,901 (79% need-based, 21% non-need-based). 38% of past graduating class borrowed through all loan programs. *Average indebtedness per student:* $22,155. *Average need-based loan:* Freshmen: $2928. Undergraduates: $3809. *Parent loans:* $677,317 (51% need-based, 49% non-need-based). *Programs:* Federal Direct (Subsidized and Unsubsidized Stafford, PLUS), state.

WORK-STUDY *Federal work-study:* 33 jobs averaging $4765.

ATHLETIC AWARDS Total amount: $1,023,467 (33% need-based, 67% non-need-based).

APPLYING FOR FINANCIAL AID *Required financial aid forms:* FAFSA, institution's own form. *Financial aid deadline:* 7/1 (priority: 2/15). *Notification date:* Continuous beginning 3/1. Students must reply within 2 weeks of notification.

CONTACT Deanna Dieringer, Director of Financial Aid, University of Alaska Fairbanks, PO Box 756360, Fairbanks, AK 99775-6360, 907-474-7256 or toll-free 800-478-1823. *Fax:* 907-474-7065. *E-mail:* uaf-financialaid@alaska.edu. *Website:* http://www.uaf.edu/.

UNIVERSITY OF ALASKA SOUTHEAST
Juneau, AK

ABOUT THE INSTITUTION State-supported, coed. 27 undergraduate majors.
GIFT AID (NEED-BASED) *Scholarships, grants, and awards:* Federal Pell, FSEOG, state, private, college/university gift aid from institutional funds.
GIFT AID (NON-NEED-BASED) *Scholarships, grants, and awards by category:* Academic interests/achievement: general academic interests/achievements. Creative arts/performance: general creative arts/performance. Special achievements/activities: leadership. Special characteristics: local/state students.
LOANS *Programs:* Federal Direct (Subsidized and Unsubsidized Stafford, PLUS), state.
APPLYING FOR FINANCIAL AID *Required financial aid form:* FAFSA.

CONTACT Ms. Corinne Soltis, Director of Financial Aid, University of Alaska Southeast, 11120 Glacier Highway, Juneau, AK 99801-8680, 907-796-6255 or toll-free 877-465-4827. *Fax:* 907-796-6250. *E-mail:* casoltis@uas.alaska.edu. *Website:* http://www.uas.alaska.edu/.

UNIVERSITY OF ANTELOPE VALLEY
Lancaster, CA

CONTACT Financial Aid Office, University of Antelope Valley, 44055 North Sierra Highway, Lancaster, CA 93534, 661-726-1911. *Website:* http://www.uav.edu/.

THE UNIVERSITY OF ARIZONA
Tucson, AZ

Tuition & fees (AZ res): $12,200	Average undergraduate aid package: $13,288

ABOUT THE INSTITUTION State-supported, coed. *Awards:* certificates, bachelor's, master's, and doctoral degrees. 120 undergraduate majors. *Total enrollment:* 44,831. Undergraduates: 35,123. Freshmen: 7,362. Both federal and institutional methodology are used as a basis for awarding need-based institutional aid.
UNDERGRADUATE EXPENSES for 2017–2018 *Application fee:* $50. *Tuition, state resident:* full-time $12,200. *Tuition, nonresident:* full-time $35,700. Full-time tuition and fees vary according to class time, course level, course load, degree level, location, program, reciprocity agreements, and student level. Part-time tuition and fees vary according to class time, course level, course load, degree level, location, program, reciprocity agreements, and student level. *College room and board:* $12,550. Room and board charges vary according to board plan and housing facility. *Payment plan:* Guaranteed tuition.
FRESHMAN FINANCIAL AID (Fall 2016) 4,411 applied for aid; of those 73% were deemed to have need. 99% of freshmen with need received aid; of those 18% had need fully met. *Average percent of need met:* 68% (excluding resources awarded to replace EFC). *Average financial aid package:* $16,047 (excluding resources awarded to replace EFC). 30% of all full-time freshmen had no need and received non-need-based gift aid.
UNDERGRADUATE FINANCIAL AID (Fall 2016) 18,155 applied for aid; of those 82% were deemed to have need. 97% of undergraduates with need received aid; of those 11% had need fully met. *Average percent of need met:* 58% (excluding resources awarded to replace EFC). *Average financial aid package:* $13,288 (excluding resources awarded to replace EFC). 22% of all full-time undergraduates had no need and received non-need-based gift aid.

GIFT AID (NEED-BASED) *Total amount:* $153,923,652 (33% federal, 3% state, 52% institutional, 12% external sources). *Receiving aid:* Freshmen: 53% (3,162); all full-time undergraduates: 46% (13,474). *Average award:* Freshmen: $13,402; Undergraduates: $10,555. *Scholarships, grants, and awards:* Federal Pell, FSEOG, state, private, college/university gift aid from institutional funds.
GIFT AID (NON-NEED-BASED) *Total amount:* $77,347,455 (4% federal, 69% institutional, 27% external sources). *Receiving aid:* Freshmen: 9% (518). Undergraduates: 4% (1,278). *Average award:* Freshmen: $8171. Undergraduates: $7974. *Scholarships, grants, and awards by category:* Academic interests/achievement: general academic interests/achievements. *Creative arts/performance:* 668 awards ($1,510,016 total): art/fine arts, dance, music, performing arts, theater/drama. *Special achievements/activities:* 338 awards ($118,300 total): leadership. *Special characteristics:* 161 awards ($476,438 total): international students. *Tuition waivers:* Full or partial for employees or children of employees. *ROTC:* Army, Naval, Air Force.
LOANS *Student loans:* $115,981,419 (82% need-based, 18% non-need-based). 54% of past graduating class borrowed through all loan programs. *Average indebtedness per student:* $23,956. *Average need-based loan:* Freshmen: $2983. Undergraduates: $5160. *Parent loans:* $81,657,293 (79% need-based, 21% non-need-based). *Programs:* Federal Direct (Subsidized and Unsubsidized Stafford, PLUS), Perkins, Federal Nursing, college/university.
WORK-STUDY *Federal work-study:* 1,117 jobs averaging $2581. *State or other work-study/employment:* Total amount: $21,235,923 (65% need-based, 35% non-need-based). 7,384 part-time jobs averaging $2892.
ATHLETIC AWARDS Total amount: $9,818,595 (39% need-based, 61% non-need-based).
APPLYING FOR FINANCIAL AID *Required financial aid form:* FAFSA. *Financial aid deadline:* Continuous. *Notification date:* Continuous beginning 2/1.

CONTACT Financial Aid Office, The University of Arizona, Tucson, AZ 85721, 520-621-2211. *Website:* http://www.arizona.edu/.

UNIVERSITY OF ARKANSAS
Fayetteville, AR

Tuition & fees (AR res): $9062	Average undergraduate aid package: $9830

ABOUT THE INSTITUTION State-supported, coed. *Awards:* certificates, bachelor's, master's, and doctoral degrees. 83 undergraduate majors. *Total enrollment:* 27,558. Undergraduates: 23,044. Freshmen: 5,065. Federal methodology is used as a basis for awarding need-based institutional aid.
UNDERGRADUATE EXPENSES for 2017–2018 *Application fee:* $40. *Tuition, state resident:* full-time $7384; part-time $246.12 per credit hour. *Tuition, nonresident:* full-time $22,630; part-time $754.31 per credit hour. *Required fees:* full-time $1678; $55.95 per credit hour. Full-time tuition and fees vary according to course load, location, and program. Part-time tuition and fees vary according to course load, location, and program. *College room and board:* $10,704; *Room only:* $6884. Room and board charges vary according to board plan and housing facility.
FRESHMAN FINANCIAL AID (Fall 2017, est.) 4,110 applied for aid; of those 57% were deemed to have need. 94% of freshmen with need received aid; of those 13% had need fully met. *Average percent of need met:* 56% (excluding resources awarded to replace EFC). *Average financial aid package:* $9398 (excluding resources awarded to replace EFC). 18% of all full-time freshmen had no need and received non-need-based gift aid.
UNDERGRADUATE FINANCIAL AID (Fall 2017, est.) 13,111 applied for aid; of those 67% were deemed to have need. 95% of undergraduates with need received aid; of those 13% had need fully met. *Average percent of need met:* 57% (excluding resources awarded to replace EFC). *Average financial aid package:* $9830 (excluding resources awarded to replace EFC). 15% of all full-time undergraduates had no need and received non-need-based gift aid.
GIFT AID (NEED-BASED) *Total amount:* $49,359,520 (41% federal, 25% state, 27% institutional, 7% external sources). *Receiving aid:* Freshmen: 36% (1,827); all full-time undergraduates: 32% (6,561). *Average award:* Freshmen: $7281; Undergraduates: $7650. *Scholarships, grants, and awards:* Federal Pell, FSEOG, state, private, college/university gift aid from institutional funds.

GIFT AID (NON-NEED-BASED) *Total amount:* $37,523,587 (1% federal, 43% state, 49% institutional, 7% external sources). *Receiving aid:* Freshmen: 5% (242). Undergraduates: 4% (741). *Average award:* Freshmen: $4192. Undergraduates: $5273. *Scholarships, grants, and awards by category: Academic interests/achievement:* agriculture, architecture, area/ethnic studies, biological sciences, business, communication, computer science, education, engineering/technologies, English, foreign languages, general academic interests/achievements, health fields, home economics, humanities, international studies, mathematics, military science, physical sciences, premedicine, social sciences. *Creative arts/performance:* art/fine arts, journalism/publications, music, theater/drama. *Special achievements/activities:* cheerleading/drum major, community service, general special achievements/activities, leadership. *Special characteristics:* adult students, children and siblings of alumni, children of faculty/staff, children of union members/company employees, children of workers in trades, children with a deceased or disabled parent, ethnic background, first-generation college students, handicapped students, international students, local/state students, married students, members of minority groups, out-of-state students, previous college experience, veterans, veterans' children. *Tuition waivers:* Full or partial for employees or children of employees, senior citizens. *ROTC:* Army, Air Force.

LOANS *Student loans:* $74,659,556 (68% need-based, 32% non-need-based). 47% of past graduating class borrowed through all loan programs. *Average indebtedness per student:* $26,242. *Average need-based loan:* Freshmen: $4932. Undergraduates: $5249. *Parent loans:* $27,425,489 (38% need-based, 62% non-need-based). *Programs:* Federal Direct (Subsidized and Unsubsidized Stafford, PLUS), Perkins, state, college/university, alternative loans.

WORK-STUDY *Federal work-study:* Total amount: $2,648,640; 1,004 jobs averaging $2638.

ATHLETIC AWARDS Total amount: $7,869,864 (36% need-based, 64% non-need-based).

APPLYING FOR FINANCIAL AID *Required financial aid form:* FAFSA. *Financial aid deadline (priority):* 3/15. *Notification date:* Continuous beginning 4/1. Students must reply within 4 weeks of notification.

CONTACT Phillip Blevins, Director of Financial Aid and Academic Scholarships, University of Arkansas, 114 Silas H. Hunt Hall, Fayetteville, AR 72701-1201, 479-575-3806 or toll-free 800-377-8632. *Fax:* 479-575-7790. *E-mail:* pblevin@uark.edu. *Website:* http://www.uark.edu/.

UNIVERSITY OF ARKANSAS AT LITTLE ROCK
Little Rock, AR

Tuition & fees (AR res): $9430	Average undergraduate aid package: $13,138

ABOUT THE INSTITUTION State-supported, coed. 57 undergraduate majors. Both federal and institutional methodology are used as a basis for awarding need-based institutional aid.

UNDERGRADUATE EXPENSES for 2017–2018 *Tuition, state resident:* full-time $9430; part-time $216.50 per credit hour. *Tuition, nonresident:* full-time $21,430; part-time $625 per credit hour. *Required fees:* $147.40 per term. Full-time tuition and fees vary according to course load, degree level, and program. Part-time tuition and fees vary according to course load, degree level, and program. *College room and board:* $5900. Room and board charges vary according to board plan and housing facility.

FRESHMAN FINANCIAL AID (Fall 2016) 759 applied for aid; of those 62% were deemed to have need. 100% of freshmen with need received aid. *Average financial aid package:* $13,731 (excluding resources awarded to replace EFC).

UNDERGRADUATE FINANCIAL AID (Fall 2016) 3,875 applied for aid; of those 65% were deemed to have need. 100% of undergraduates with need received aid. *Average financial aid package:* $13,138 (excluding resources awarded to replace EFC).

GIFT AID (NEED-BASED) *Total amount:* $14,387,862 (100% federal). *Receiving aid:* Freshmen: 58% (469); all full-time undergraduates: 54% (2,496). *Average award:* Freshmen: $4736; Undergraduates: $4482. *Scholarships, grants, and awards:* Federal Pell, FSEOG, state, private, college/university gift aid from institutional funds.

GIFT AID (NON-NEED-BASED) *Total amount:* $21,777,905 (2% federal, 31% state, 54% institutional, 13% external sources). *Receiving aid:* Freshmen: 49% (401).

Undergraduates: 34% (1,572). *Scholarships, grants, and awards by category: Academic interests/achievement:* biological sciences, business, communication, computer science, education, engineering/technologies, English, foreign languages, general academic interests/achievements, health fields, humanities, international studies, mathematics, physical sciences, social sciences. *Creative arts/performance:* art/fine arts, music, theater/drama. *Special achievements/activities:* community service, leadership, memberships. *Special characteristics:* local/state students, members of minority groups, previous college experience. *Tuition waivers:* Full or partial for employees or children of employees, senior citizens.

LOANS *Student loans:* $33,642,626 (100% non-need-based). *Programs:* Federal Direct (Subsidized and Unsubsidized Stafford, PLUS).

WORK-STUDY *Federal work-study:* jobs available.

ATHLETIC AWARDS Total amount: $2,379,773 (100% non-need-based).

APPLYING FOR FINANCIAL AID *Required financial aid form:* FAFSA. *Financial aid deadline (priority):* 3/1. *Notification date:* 4/15.

CONTACT Financial Aid Office, University of Arkansas at Little Rock, 2801 South University Avenue, Little Rock, AR 72204-1099, 501-569-3035 or toll-free 800-482-8892. *E-mail:* financialaid@ualr.edu. *Website:* http://www.ualr.edu/.

UNIVERSITY OF ARKANSAS AT MONTICELLO
Monticello, AR

CONTACT Susan Brewer, Director of Financial Aid, University of Arkansas at Monticello, PO Box 3470, Monticello, AR 71656, 870-460-1050 or toll-free 800-844-1826. *Fax:* 870-460-1450. *E-mail:* brewers@uamont.edu. *Website:* http://www.uamont.edu/.

UNIVERSITY OF ARKANSAS AT PINE BLUFF
Pine Bluff, AR

CONTACT Mrs. Carolyn Iverson, Director of Financial Aid, University of Arkansas at Pine Bluff, 1200 North University Drive, PO Box 4985, Pine Bluff, AR 71601, 870-575-8303 or toll-free 800-264-6585. *Fax:* 870-575-4622. *E-mail:* iverson_c@uapb.edu. *Website:* http://www.uapb.edu/.

UNIVERSITY OF ARKANSAS FOR MEDICAL SCIENCES
Little Rock, AR

CONTACT Ms. Gloria Kemp, Director of Student Financial Aid, University of Arkansas for Medical Sciences, 4301 West Markham Street, MS 601, Little Rock, AR 72205, 501-686-6936. *Fax:* 501-686-8798. *E-mail:* pvcarter@uams.edu. *Website:* http://www.uams.edu/.

UNIVERSITY OF ARKANSAS–FORT SMITH
Fort Smith, AR

CONTACT Tammy Malone, Interim Financial Aid Director, University of Arkansas–Fort Smith, 5210 Grand Avenue, Fort Smith, AR 72913, 479-788-7099 or toll-free 888-512-5466. *Fax:* 479-788-7095. *E-mail:* tmalone@uafortsmith.edu. *Website:* http://uafs.edu/.

UNIVERSITY OF BALTIMORE
Baltimore, MD

CONTACT Financial Aid Office, University of Baltimore, 1420 North Charles Street, CH 123, Baltimore, MD 21201-5779, 410-837-4763. *Fax:* 410-837-5493. *E-mail:* financial-aid@ubalt.edu.
Website: http://www.ubalt.edu/.

UNIVERSITY OF BRIDGEPORT
Bridgeport, CT

Tuition & fees: $32,250	Average undergraduate aid package: $28,677

ABOUT THE INSTITUTION Independent, coed. *Awards:* certificates, associate, bachelor's, master's, and doctoral degrees. 40 undergraduate majors. *Total enrollment:* 5,434. Undergraduates: 3,129. Freshmen: 550. Federal methodology is used as a basis for awarding need-based institutional aid.

UNDERGRADUATE EXPENSES for 2017–2018 *Application fee:* $25. *Comprehensive fee:* $45,840 includes full-time tuition ($30,150), mandatory fees ($2100), and room and board ($13,590). Full-time tuition and fees vary according to course load and program. Room and board charges vary according to board plan and housing facility. *Part-time tuition:* $1005 per credit hour. *Part-time fees:* $215 per term. Part-time tuition and fees vary according to course load and program.

FRESHMAN FINANCIAL AID (Fall 2016) 494 applied for aid; of those 98% were deemed to have need. 100% of freshmen with need received aid; of those 6% had need fully met. *Average percent of need met:* 63% (excluding resources awarded to replace EFC). *Average financial aid package:* $30,815 (excluding resources awarded to replace EFC). 20% of all full-time freshmen had no need and received non-need-based gift aid.

UNDERGRADUATE FINANCIAL AID (Fall 2016) 2,185 applied for aid; of those 86% were deemed to have need. 100% of undergraduates with need received aid; of those 12% had need fully met. *Average percent of need met:* 60% (excluding resources awarded to replace EFC). *Average financial aid package:* $28,677 (excluding resources awarded to replace EFC). 13% of all full-time undergraduates had no need and received non-need-based gift aid.

GIFT AID (NEED-BASED) *Total amount:* $42,999,640 (15% federal, 2% state, 82% institutional, 1% external sources). *Receiving aid:* Freshmen: 77% (423); all full-time undergraduates: 72% (1,656). *Average award:* Freshmen: $17,429; Undergraduates: $14,193. *Scholarships, grants, and awards:* Federal Pell, FSEOG, state, private, college/university gift aid from institutional funds.

GIFT AID (NON-NEED-BASED) *Total amount:* $3,064,000 (100% institutional). *Receiving aid:* Freshmen: 88% (483). Undergraduates: 82% (1,886). *Average award:* Freshmen: $17,775. Undergraduates: $14,220. *Scholarships, grants, and awards by category:* Academic interests/achievement: biological sciences, business, communication, computer science, engineering/technologies, general academic interests/achievements, mathematics, social sciences. *Creative arts/performance:* applied art and design, music. *Special characteristics:* children of faculty/staff, international students, local/state students, previous college experience, veterans. *Tuition waivers:* Full or partial for employees or children of employees, senior citizens.

LOANS *Student loans:* $93,025,906 (17% need-based, 83% non-need-based). 68% of past graduating class borrowed through all loan programs. *Average indebtedness per student:* $21,200. *Average need-based loan:* Freshmen: $5500. Undergraduates: $7000. *Parent loans:* $5,742,769 (95% need-based, 5% non-need-based). *Programs:* Federal Direct (Subsidized and Unsubsidized Stafford, PLUS), Perkins.

WORK-STUDY *Federal work-study:* jobs available. *State or other work-study/employment:* Part-time jobs available.

ATHLETIC AWARDS Total amount: $1,713,912 (80% need-based, 20% non-need-based).

APPLYING FOR FINANCIAL AID *Required financial aid form:* FAFSA. *Financial aid deadline (priority):* 3/1. *Notification date:* Continuous beginning 3/1. Students must reply by 5/15 or within 4 weeks of notification.

CONTACT Ms. Christine E. Falzerano, Director of Student Financial Services, University of Bridgeport, 126 Park Avenue, Bridgeport, CT 06604, 203-576-4568 or toll-free 800-EXCEL-UB. *Fax:* 203-576-4570. *E-mail:* finaid@bridgeport.edu. *Website:* http://www.bridgeport.edu/.

UNIVERSITY OF CALIFORNIA, BERKELEY
Berkeley, CA

Tuition & fees (CA res): $14,170	Average undergraduate aid package: $24,048

ABOUT THE INSTITUTION State-supported, coed. 90 undergraduate majors. Both federal and institutional methodology are used as a basis for awarding need-based institutional aid.

UNDERGRADUATE EXPENSES for 2017–2018 *Tuition, state resident:* full-time $11,502. *Tuition, nonresident:* full-time $39,516. *Required fees:* full-time $2668. *College room and board:* $15,716. Room and board charges vary according to board plan and housing facility.

FRESHMAN FINANCIAL AID (Fall 2017, est.) 4,490 applied for aid; of those 64% were deemed to have need. 93% of freshmen with need received aid; of those 23% had need fully met. *Average percent of need met:* 78% (excluding resources awarded to replace EFC). *Average financial aid package:* $24,668 (excluding resources awarded to replace EFC). 5% of all full-time freshmen had no need and received non-need-based gift aid.

UNDERGRADUATE FINANCIAL AID (Fall 2017, est.) 17,359 applied for aid; of those 81% were deemed to have need. 96% of undergraduates with need received aid; of those 25% had need fully met. *Average percent of need met:* 81% (excluding resources awarded to replace EFC). *Average financial aid package:* $24,048 (excluding resources awarded to replace EFC). 5% of all full-time undergraduates had no need and received non-need-based gift aid.

GIFT AID (NEED-BASED) *Total amount:* $285,619,850 (15% federal, 30% state, 52% institutional, 3% external sources). *Receiving aid:* Freshmen: 41% (2,575); all full-time undergraduates: 44% (13,056). *Average award:* Freshmen: $21,384; Undergraduates: $20,900. *Scholarships, grants, and awards:* Federal Pell, FSEOG, state, private, college/university gift aid from institutional funds.

GIFT AID (NON-NEED-BASED) *Total amount:* $28,592,341 (6% federal, 3% state, 51% institutional, 40% external sources). *Receiving aid:* Freshmen: 2% (123). Undergraduates: 1% (348). *Average award:* Freshmen: $5868. Undergraduates: $8628. *Scholarships, grants, and awards by category:* Academic interests/achievement: general academic interests/achievements.

LOANS *Student loans:* $42,929,040 (70% need-based, 30% non-need-based). 35% of past graduating class borrowed through all loan programs. *Average indebtedness per student:* $18,197. *Average need-based loan:* Freshmen: $7864. Undergraduates: $6866. *Parent loans:* $27,451,903 (32% need-based, 68% non-need-based). *Programs:* Federal Direct (Subsidized and Unsubsidized Stafford, PLUS), Perkins.

WORK-STUDY *Federal work-study:* Total amount: $6,767,989; jobs available. *State or other work-study/employment:* Total amount: $4,421,786 (100% need-based). Part-time jobs available.

ATHLETIC AWARDS Total amount: $14,415,796 (24% need-based, 76% non-need-based).

APPLYING FOR FINANCIAL AID *Required financial aid forms:* FAFSA, noncustodial (divorced/separated) parent's statement, Cal Grant forms, GPA verification form (CA residents only). *Financial aid deadline:* 3/2. *Notification date:* 3/31. Students must reply by 5/1.

CONTACT Financial Aid and Scholarships Office, University of California, Berkeley, 201 Sproul Hall #1960, Berkeley, CA 94720-1960, 510-642-0649. *Fax:* 510-643-5526. *Website:* http://www.berkeley.edu/.

UNIVERSITY OF CALIFORNIA, DAVIS
Davis, CA

Tuition & fees (CA res): $14,463	Average undergraduate aid package: $21,951

ABOUT THE INSTITUTION State-supported, coed. *Awards:* certificates, bachelor's, master's, and doctoral degrees. 83 undergraduate majors. *Total enrollment:* 37,278. Undergraduates: 30,145. Freshmen: 5,852. Both federal and institutional methodology are used as a basis for awarding need-based institutional aid.

UNDERGRADUATE EXPENSES for 2018–2019 *Application fee:* $70. *Tuition, state resident:* full-time $11,502. *Tuition, nonresident:* full-time

$40,497. *Required fees:* full-time $2961. *College room and board:* $15,765. Room and board charges vary according to board plan.

FRESHMAN FINANCIAL AID (Fall 2017, est.) 4,154 applied for aid; of those 78% were deemed to have need. 99% of freshmen with need received aid; of those 25% had need fully met. *Average percent of need met:* 84% (excluding resources awarded to replace EFC). *Average financial aid package:* $25,819 (excluding resources awarded to replace EFC). 5% of all full-time freshmen had no need and received non-need-based gift aid.

UNDERGRADUATE FINANCIAL AID (Fall 2017, est.) 20,459 applied for aid; of those 87% were deemed to have need. 99% of undergraduates with need received aid; of those 22% had need fully met. *Average percent of need met:* 81% (excluding resources awarded to replace EFC). *Average financial aid package:* $21,951 (excluding resources awarded to replace EFC). 4% of all full-time undergraduates had no need and received non-need-based gift aid.

GIFT AID (NEED-BASED) *Total amount:* $324,808,713 (19% federal, 36% state, 43% institutional, 2% external sources). *Receiving aid:* Freshmen: 54% (3,122); all full-time undergraduates: 58% (17,090). *Average award:* Freshmen: $21,987; Undergraduates: $18,761. *Scholarships, grants, and awards:* Federal Pell, FSEOG, state, private, college/university gift aid from institutional funds, The UC Davis Aggie Grant Plan (for middle-income California students).

GIFT AID (NON-NEED-BASED) *Total amount:* $18,964,605 (17% federal, 6% state, 40% institutional, 37% external sources). *Receiving aid:* Freshmen: 2% (90). Undergraduates: 1% (366). *Average award:* Freshmen: $6040. Undergraduates: $6623. *Scholarships, grants, and awards by category: Academic interests/ achievement:* agriculture, area/ethnic studies, biological sciences, business, communication, computer science, engineering/technologies, English, foreign languages, general academic interests/achievements, health fields, home economics, humanities, international studies, mathematics, premedicine, religion/biblical studies, social sciences. *ROTC:* Army, Naval cooperative, Air Force cooperative.

LOANS *Student loans:* $61,625,292 (82% need-based, 18% non-need-based). 49% of past graduating class borrowed through all loan programs. *Average indebtedness per student:* $19,124. *Average need-based loan:* Freshmen: $6838. Undergraduates: $6165. *Parent loans:* $35,248,760 (22% need-based, 78% non-need-based). *Programs:* Federal Direct (Subsidized and Unsubsidized Stafford, PLUS), Perkins, state, college/university.

WORK-STUDY *Federal work-study:* Total amount: $2,070,819; jobs available. *State or other work-study/employment:* Total amount: $308,693 (100% need-based). Part-time jobs available.

ATHLETIC AWARDS Total amount: $7,811,739 (33% need-based, 67% non-need-based).

APPLYING FOR FINANCIAL AID *Required financial aid forms:* FAFSA, state aid form. *Financial aid deadline (priority):* 3/2. *Notification date:* Continuous beginning 3/10.

CONTACT Deborah G. Agee, Director of Financial Aid and Scholarships, University of California, Davis, One Shields Avenue, 2116 Dutton Hall, Davis, CA 95616, 530-752-2396. *Fax:* 530-752-7339. *E-mail:* dgagee@ucdavis.edu.

Website: http://www.ucdavis.edu/.

UNIVERSITY OF CALIFORNIA, IRVINE
Irvine, CA

Tuition & fees (CA res): $15,516	Average undergraduate aid package: $23,438

ABOUT THE INSTITUTION State-supported, coed. *Awards:* certificates, bachelor's, master's, and doctoral degrees. 83 undergraduate majors. *Total enrollment:* 35,242. Undergraduates: 29,307. Freshmen: 6,545. Federal methodology is used as a basis for awarding need-based institutional aid.

UNDERGRADUATE EXPENSES for 2017–2018 *Application fee:* $70. *Tuition, state resident:* full-time $11,502. *Tuition, nonresident:* full-time $39,516. *Required fees:* full-time $4014. *College room and board:* $14,829. Room and board charges vary according to board plan and housing facility.

FRESHMAN FINANCIAL AID (Fall 2017, est.) 4,963 applied for aid; of those 81% were deemed to have need. 98% of freshmen with need received aid; of those 25% had need fully met. *Average percent of need met:* 84% (excluding resources awarded to replace EFC). *Average financial aid package:* $23,886 (excluding resources awarded to replace EFC). 3% of all full-time freshmen had no need and received non-need-based gift aid.

UNDERGRADUATE FINANCIAL AID (Fall 2017, est.) 20,662 applied for aid; of those 90% were deemed to have need. 98% of undergraduates with need received aid; of those 19% had need fully met. *Average percent of need met:* 81% (excluding resources awarded to replace EFC). *Average financial aid package:* $23,438 (excluding resources awarded to replace EFC). 2% of all full-time undergraduates had no need and received non-need-based gift aid.

GIFT AID (NEED-BASED) *Total amount:* $350,214,558 (18% federal, 43% state, 38% institutional, 1% external sources). *Receiving aid:* Freshmen: 59% (3,850); all full-time undergraduates: 61% (17,705). *Average award:* Freshmen: $19,767; Undergraduates: $19,731. *Scholarships, grants, and awards:* Federal Pell, FSEOG, state, private, college/university gift aid from institutional funds.

GIFT AID (NON-NEED-BASED) *Total amount:* $8,537,256 (8% federal, 10% state, 61% institutional, 21% external sources). *Receiving aid:* Freshmen: 1% (89). Undergraduates: 1% (270). *Average award:* Freshmen: $6272. Undergraduates: $7783. *Scholarships, grants, and awards by category: Academic interests/ achievement:* area/ethnic studies, biological sciences, business, communication, computer science, education, engineering/technologies, English, foreign languages, general academic interests/achievements, health fields, humanities, international studies, mathematics, physical sciences, premedicine, social sciences. *Creative arts/performance:* art/fine arts, cinema/film/broadcasting, creative writing, dance, general creative arts/performance, music, performing arts, theater/drama. *Special achievements/activities:* community service, general special achievements/activities, leadership. *Special characteristics:* international students, out-of-state students. *Tuition waivers:* Full or partial for employees or children of employees. *ROTC:* Army, Air Force cooperative.

LOANS *Student loans:* $64,886,453 (85% need-based, 15% non-need-based). 55% of past graduating class borrowed through all loan programs. *Average indebtedness per student:* $19,745. *Average need-based loan:* Freshmen: $6482. Undergraduates: $6956. *Parent loans:* $38,309,543 (31% need-based, 69% non-need-based). *Programs:* Federal Direct (Subsidized and Unsubsidized Stafford, PLUS), Perkins, college/university, private loans.

WORK-STUDY *Federal work-study:* Total amount: $5,358,619; jobs available. *State or other work-study/employment:* Total amount: $3,932,720 (100% need-based). Part-time jobs available.

ATHLETIC AWARDS Total amount: $3,725,334 (37% need-based, 63% non-need-based).

APPLYING FOR FINANCIAL AID *Required financial aid forms:* FAFSA, state aid form. *Financial aid deadline:* 6/26 (priority: 3/2). *Notification date:* Continuous beginning 4/1. Students must reply within 2 weeks of notification.

CONTACT Ms. Lindsay Crowell, Senior Associate Director, University of California, Irvine, 102 Aldrich Hall, Irvine, CA 92697-2825, 949-824-4898. *Fax:* 949-824-2820. *E-mail:* finaid@uci.edu.

Website: http://www.uci.edu/.

UNIVERSITY OF CALIFORNIA, LOS ANGELES
Los Angeles, CA

Tuition & fees (CA res): $13,584	Average undergraduate aid package: $23,980

ABOUT THE INSTITUTION State-supported, coed. *Awards:* bachelor's, master's, and doctoral degrees. 94 undergraduate majors. *Total enrollment:* 45,428. Undergraduates: 31,002. Freshmen: 6,038. Both federal and institutional methodology are used as a basis for awarding need-based institutional aid.

UNDERGRADUATE EXPENSES for 2017–2018 *Application fee:* $70. *One-time required fee:* $165. *Tuition, state resident:* full-time $11,502. *Tuition, nonresident:* full-time $39,516. *Required fees:* full-time $2082. *College room and board:* $15,143. Room and board charges vary according to board plan and housing facility.

FRESHMAN FINANCIAL AID (Fall 2017, est.) 3,693 applied for aid; of those 86% were deemed to have need. 100% of freshmen with need received aid; of those 28% had need fully met. *Average percent of need met:* 83% (excluding resources awarded to replace EFC). *Average financial aid package:* $24,405 (excluding resources awarded to replace EFC). 3% of all full-time freshmen had no need and received non-need-based gift aid.

UNDERGRADUATE FINANCIAL AID (Fall 2017, est.) 17,808 applied for aid; of those 92% were deemed to have need. 100% of undergraduates with need received aid; of those 26% had need fully met. *Average percent of need met:* 83%

(excluding resources awarded to replace EFC). *Average financial aid package:* $23,980 (excluding resources awarded to replace EFC). 3% of all full-time undergraduates had no need and received non-need-based gift aid.

GIFT AID (NEED-BASED) *Total amount:* $324,135,708 (16% federal, 38% state, 44% institutional, 2% external sources). *Receiving aid:* Freshmen: 51% (3,056); all full-time undergraduates: 52% (15,739). *Average award:* Freshmen: $20,953; Undergraduates: $20,489. *Scholarships, grants, and awards:* Federal Pell, FSEOG, state, private, college/university gift aid from institutional funds, United Negro College Fund, Federal Nursing.

GIFT AID (NON-NEED-BASED) *Total amount:* $10,526,598 (14% federal, 8% state, 60% institutional, 18% external sources). *Receiving aid:* Freshmen: 2% (100). Undergraduates: 1% (330). *Average award:* Freshmen: $4856. Undergraduates: $5633. *Scholarships, grants, and awards by category:* Academic interests/achievement: general academic interests/achievements. Creative arts/performance: general creative arts/performance. Special achievements/activities: general special achievements/activities. Special characteristics: general special characteristics. ROTC: Army, Naval, Air Force.

LOANS *Student loans:* $70,041,434 (80% need-based, 20% non-need-based). 43% of past graduating class borrowed through all loan programs. *Average indebtedness per student:* $22,013. *Average need-based loan:* Freshmen: $7334. Undergraduates: $7488. *Parent loans:* $40,287,646 (28% need-based, 72% non-need-based). *Programs:* Federal Direct (Subsidized and Unsubsidized Stafford, PLUS), Perkins, Federal Nursing, state, college/university.

WORK-STUDY *Federal work-study:* Total amount: $5,300,000; jobs available. *State or other work-study/employment:* Total amount: $116,282 (100% need-based). Part-time jobs available.

ATHLETIC AWARDS Total amount: $12,854,726 (27% need-based, 73% non-need-based).

APPLYING FOR FINANCIAL AID *Required financial aid form:* FAFSA. *Financial aid deadline (priority):* 3/2. *Notification date:* Continuous beginning 3/15.

CONTACT Ms. Carolyn Turpin, Budget Officer, University of California, Los Angeles, A-129 Murphy Hall, Los Angeles, CA 90095-1435, 310-206-0407. *E-mail:* finaid@saonet.ucla.edu. *Website:* http://www.ucla.edu/.

UNIVERSITY OF CALIFORNIA, MERCED
Merced, CA

Tuition & fees (CA res): $13,598	Average undergraduate aid package: $25,198

ABOUT THE INSTITUTION State-supported, coed. 24 undergraduate majors. Both federal and institutional methodology are used as a basis for awarding need-based institutional aid.

UNDERGRADUATE EXPENSES for 2017–2018 *Tuition, state resident:* full-time $11,502; part-time $2875 per term. *Tuition, nonresident:* full-time $39,516; part-time $9879 per term. *Required fees:* full-time $2096; $2096 per year. Full-time tuition and fees vary according to course load. Part-time tuition and fees vary according to course load. *College room and board:* $16,790. Room and board charges vary according to board plan.

FRESHMAN FINANCIAL AID (Fall 2017, est.) 2,221 applied for aid; of those 95% were deemed to have need. 100% of freshmen with need received aid; of those 26% had need fully met. *Average percent of need met:* 87% (excluding resources awarded to replace EFC). *Average financial aid package:* $29,416 (excluding resources awarded to replace EFC). 1% of all full-time freshmen had no need and received non-need-based gift aid.

UNDERGRADUATE FINANCIAL AID (Fall 2017, est.) 6,901 applied for aid; of those 95% were deemed to have need. 99% of undergraduates with need received aid; of those 23% had need fully met. *Average percent of need met:* 83% (excluding resources awarded to replace EFC). *Average financial aid package:* $25,198 (excluding resources awarded to replace EFC). 1% of all full-time undergraduates had no need and received non-need-based gift aid.

GIFT AID (NEED-BASED) *Total amount:* $140,065,403 (18% federal, 44% state, 37% institutional, 1% external sources). *Receiving aid:* Freshmen: 91% (2,086); all full-time undergraduates: 88% (6,439). *Average award:* Freshmen: $25,176;

Undergraduates: $21,698. *Scholarships, grants, and awards:* Federal Pell, FSEOG, state, private, college/university gift aid from institutional funds.

GIFT AID (NON-NEED-BASED) *Total amount:* $1,377,514 (6% federal, 14% state, 70% institutional, 10% external sources). *Receiving aid:* Freshmen: 1% (17). Undergraduates: 1% (54). *Average award:* Freshmen: $14,841. Undergraduates: $10,363. *Scholarships, grants, and awards by category:* Academic interests/achievement: general academic interests/achievements. *Tuition waivers:* Full or partial for employees or children of employees.

LOANS *Student loans:* $19,633,040 (86% need-based, 14% non-need-based). 70% of past graduating class borrowed through all loan programs. *Average indebtedness per student:* $19,551. *Average need-based loan:* Freshmen: $4649. Undergraduates: $5093. *Parent loans:* $7,241,958 (16% need-based, 84% non-need-based). *Programs:* Federal Direct (Subsidized and Unsubsidized Stafford, PLUS), alternative loans.

WORK-STUDY *Federal work-study:* Total amount: $6,421,398; jobs available.

ATHLETIC AWARDS Total amount: $46,125 (85% need-based, 15% non-need-based).

APPLYING FOR FINANCIAL AID *Required financial aid form:* FAFSA. *Financial aid deadline (priority):* 3/2. *Notification date:* Continuous beginning 3/2.

CONTACT Dr. Ron Radney, Director of Financial Aid and Scholarships, University of California, Merced, Kolligian Library, Room 127, 5200 North Lake Road, Merced, CA 95343, 209-228-2257. *Fax:* 209-228-7861. *E-mail:* finaid@ucmerced.edu. *Website:* http://www.ucmerced.edu/.

UNIVERSITY OF CALIFORNIA, RIVERSIDE
Riverside, CA

Tuition & fees (CA res): $15,642	Average undergraduate aid package: $23,578

ABOUT THE INSTITUTION State-supported, coed. *Awards:* bachelor's, master's, and doctoral degrees. 56 undergraduate majors. *Total enrollment:* 23,278. Undergraduates: 20,069. Freshmen: 4,598. Federal methodology is used as a basis for awarding need-based institutional aid.

UNDERGRADUATE EXPENSES for 2017–2018 *Application fee:* $70. *Tuition, state resident:* full-time $11,502; part-time $5751 per year. *Tuition, nonresident:* full-time $39,516; part-time $19,758 per year. *Required fees:* full-time $4140. Full-time tuition and fees vary according to course load. Part-time tuition and fees vary according to course load. *College room and board:* $17,000. Room and board charges vary according to board plan and housing facility.

FRESHMAN FINANCIAL AID (Fall 2017, est.) 4,094 applied for aid; of those 88% were deemed to have need. 100% of freshmen with need received aid; of those 22% had need fully met. *Average percent of need met:* 91% (excluding resources awarded to replace EFC). *Average financial aid package:* $26,448 (excluding resources awarded to replace EFC). 5% of all full-time freshmen had no need and received non-need-based gift aid.

UNDERGRADUATE FINANCIAL AID (Fall 2017, est.) 16,943 applied for aid; of those 92% were deemed to have need. 100% of undergraduates with need received aid; of those 25% had need fully met. *Average percent of need met:* 89% (excluding resources awarded to replace EFC). *Average financial aid package:* $23,578 (excluding resources awarded to replace EFC). 4% of all full-time undergraduates had no need and received non-need-based gift aid.

GIFT AID (NEED-BASED) *Total amount:* $277,577,329 (20% federal, 48% state, 31% institutional, 1% external sources). *Receiving aid:* Freshmen: 77% (3,513); all full-time undergraduates: 77% (15,193). *Average award:* Freshmen: $20,892; Undergraduates: $18,125. *Scholarships, grants, and awards:* Federal Pell, FSEOG, state, private, college/university gift aid from institutional funds.

GIFT AID (NON-NEED-BASED) *Total amount:* $9,021,154 (5% federal, 11% state, 81% institutional, 3% external sources). *Receiving aid:* Freshmen: 2% (70). Undergraduates: 1% (268). *Average award:* Freshmen: $9123. Undergraduates: $8154. *Scholarships, grants, and awards by category:* Academic interests/achievement: agriculture, area/ethnic studies, biological sciences, business, education, engineering/technologies, English, general academic interests/achievements, humanities, mathematics, physical sciences, premedicine, social sciences. Creative arts/performance: art/fine arts, creative writing, dance, music, theater/drama. Special characteristics: out-of-state students, religious affiliation, veterans, veterans' children. **ROTC:** Army cooperative, Air Force cooperative.

LOANS Student loans: $67,151,234 (82% need-based, 18% non-need-based). 66% of past graduating class borrowed through all loan programs. *Average indebtedness per student:* $21,104. *Average need-based loan:* Freshmen: $4863. Undergraduates: $5547. *Parent loans:* $70,911,102 (39% need-based, 61% non-need-based). *Programs:* Federal Direct (Subsidized and Unsubsidized Stafford, PLUS), Perkins, college/university.

WORK-STUDY Federal work-study: Total amount: $4,817,209; 2,972 jobs averaging $1621.

ATHLETIC AWARDS Total amount: $3,890,628 (31% need-based, 69% non-need-based).

APPLYING FOR FINANCIAL AID Required financial aid forms: FAFSA, state aid form. *Financial aid deadline (priority):* 3/2. *Notification date:* Continuous beginning 3/1. Students must reply by 5/1 or within 3 weeks of notification.

CONTACT Mr. Jose A. Aguilar, Director of Financial Aid, University of California, Riverside, 2106 Student Services Building, Riverside, CA 92521-0209, 951-827-7249. *Fax:* 951-827-5619. *E-mail:* finaid@ucr.edu.
Website: http://www.ucr.edu/.

UNIVERSITY OF CALIFORNIA, SAN DIEGO
La Jolla, CA

Tuition & fees (CA res): $14,050	Average undergraduate aid package: $24,288

ABOUT THE INSTITUTION State-supported, coed. *Awards:* bachelor's, master's, and doctoral degrees. 94 undergraduate majors. *Total enrollment:* 35,772. Undergraduates: 28,492. Freshmen: 5,694. Both federal and institutional methodology are used as a basis for awarding need-based institutional aid.

UNDERGRADUATE EXPENSES for 2017–2018 *Application fee:* $70. *One-time required fee:* $174. *Tuition, state resident:* full-time $12,630. *Tuition, nonresident:* full-time $40,644. *Required fees:* full-time $1420. *College room and board:* $13,307. Room and board charges vary according to board plan and housing facility.

FRESHMAN FINANCIAL AID (Fall 2017, est.) 4,271 applied for aid; of those 81% were deemed to have need. 94% of freshmen with need received aid; of those 36% had need fully met. *Average percent of need met:* 88% (excluding resources awarded to replace EFC). *Average financial aid package:* $24,736 (excluding resources awarded to replace EFC). 1% of all full-time freshmen had no need and received non-need-based gift aid.

UNDERGRADUATE FINANCIAL AID (Fall 2017, est.) 17,846 applied for aid; of those 89% were deemed to have need. 97% of undergraduates with need received aid; of those 42% had need fully met. *Average percent of need met:* 88% (excluding resources awarded to replace EFC). *Average financial aid package:* $24,288 (excluding resources awarded to replace EFC). 2% of all full-time undergraduates had no need and received non-need-based gift aid.

GIFT AID (NEED-BASED) Total amount: $301,047,779 (19% federal, 37% state, 43% institutional, 1% external sources). *Receiving aid:* Freshmen: 55% (3,141); all full-time undergraduates: 54% (14,920). *Average award:* Freshmen: $20,567; Undergraduates: $19,929. *Scholarships, grants, and awards:* Federal Pell, FSEOG, state, private, college/university gift aid from institutional funds, TEACH Grants.

GIFT AID (NON-NEED-BASED) Total amount: $12,564,048 (21% federal, 7% state, 57% institutional, 15% external sources). *Receiving aid:* Freshmen: 2% (87). Undergraduates: 1% (231). *Average award:* Freshmen: $10,784. Undergraduates: $11,855. *Scholarships, grants, and awards by category:* Academic interests/achievement: biological sciences, business, communication, computer science, engineering/technologies, general academic interests/achievements, mathematics, physical sciences, premedicine, social sciences. Creative arts/performance: applied art and design, cinema/film/broadcasting, dance, journalism/publications, music, performing arts, theater/drama. Special achievements/activities: community service, leadership. Special characteristics: ethnic background, first-generation college students, handicapped students, members of minority groups, veterans' children. **ROTC:** Army cooperative, Naval cooperative, Air Force cooperative.

LOANS Student loans: $63,088,589 (81% need-based, 19% non-need-based). 48% of past graduating class borrowed through all loan programs. *Average indebtedness*

per student: $21,430. *Average need-based loan:* Freshmen: $5567. Undergraduates: $5907. *Parent loans:* $20,883,161 (29% need-based, 71% non-need-based). *Programs:* Federal Direct (Subsidized and Unsubsidized Stafford, PLUS), Perkins, college/university, alternative loans.

WORK-STUDY Federal work-study: Total amount: $18,661,524; jobs available. *State or other work-study/employment:* Total amount: $234,591 (100% need-based). Part-time jobs available.

ATHLETIC AWARDS Total amount: $498,347 (48% need-based, 52% non-need-based).

APPLYING FOR FINANCIAL AID Required financial aid forms: FAFSA, state aid form. *Financial aid deadline (priority):* 3/2. *Notification date:* Continuous beginning 3/15.

CONTACT Ms. Vonda Garcia, Director of Financial Aid and Scholarships, University of California, San Diego, 9500 Gilman Drive, Mail Code 0013, La Jolla, CA 92093-0013, 858-534-4480. *Fax:* 858-534-5459. *E-mail:* vonda@ucsd.edu.
Website: http://www.ucsd.edu/.

UNIVERSITY OF CALIFORNIA, SANTA BARBARA
Santa Barbara, CA

Tuition & fees (CA res): $14,472	Average undergraduate aid package: $23,771

ABOUT THE INSTITUTION State-supported, coed. *Awards:* certificates, bachelor's, master's, and doctoral degrees. 74 undergraduate majors. *Total enrollment:* 25,057. Undergraduates: 22,186. Freshmen: 4,538. Both federal and institutional methodology are used as a basis for awarding need-based institutional aid.

UNDERGRADUATE EXPENSES for 2018–2019 *Application fee:* $70. *Tuition, state resident:* full-time $11,502. *Tuition, nonresident:* full-time $39,516. *Required fees:* full-time $2970. *College room and board:* $15,673. Room and board charges vary according to board plan and housing facility.

FRESHMAN FINANCIAL AID (Fall 2017, est.) 3,399 applied for aid; of those 73% were deemed to have need. 97% of freshmen with need received aid; of those 25% had need fully met. *Average percent of need met:* 82% (excluding resources awarded to replace EFC). *Average financial aid package:* $25,612 (excluding resources awarded to replace EFC). 2% of all full-time freshmen had no need and received non-need-based gift aid.

UNDERGRADUATE FINANCIAL AID (Fall 2017, est.) 15,113 applied for aid; of those 86% were deemed to have need. 98% of undergraduates with need received aid; of those 20% had need fully met. *Average percent of need met:* 81% (excluding resources awarded to replace EFC). *Average financial aid package:* $23,771 (excluding resources awarded to replace EFC). 2% of all full-time undergraduates had no need and received non-need-based gift aid.

GIFT AID (NEED-BASED) Total amount: $247,112,328 (17% federal, 42% state, 40% institutional, 1% external sources). *Receiving aid:* Freshmen: 52% (2,345); all full-time undergraduates: 57% (12,311). *Average award:* Freshmen: $21,041; Undergraduates: $20,029. *Scholarships, grants, and awards:* Federal Pell, FSEOG, state, private, college/university gift aid from institutional funds, endowed and restricted scholarships and grants.

GIFT AID (NON-NEED-BASED) Total amount: $5,388,794 (7% federal, 9% state, 72% institutional, 12% external sources). *Receiving aid:* Freshmen: 1% (50). Undergraduates: 1% (191). *Average award:* Freshmen: $8792. Undergraduates: $8181. *Scholarships, grants, and awards by category:* Academic interests/achievement: general academic interests/achievements. **ROTC:** Army, Air Force cooperative.

LOANS Student loans: $51,141,793 (80% need-based, 20% non-need-based). 51% of past graduating class borrowed through all loan programs. *Average indebtedness per student:* $20,665. *Average need-based loan:* Freshmen: $6935. Undergraduates: $6510. *Parent loans:* $25,896,982 (25% need-based, 75% non-need-based). *Programs:* Federal Direct (Subsidized and Unsubsidized Stafford, PLUS), Perkins.

WORK-STUDY Federal work-study: Total amount: $6,847,756; jobs available. *State or other work-study/employment:* Total amount: $293,479 (100% need-based). Part-time jobs available.

ATHLETIC AWARDS Total amount: $4,835,576 (26% need-based, 74% non-need-based).

APPLYING FOR FINANCIAL AID *Required financial aid form:* FAFSA. *Financial aid deadline:* 5/31 (priority: 3/2). *Notification date:* Continuous beginning 3/15. Students must reply within 2 weeks of notification.

CONTACT Mike Miller, Office of Financial Aid, University of California, Santa Barbara, 2103 SAASB, Santa Barbara, CA 93106-3180, 805-893-2432. *Fax:* 805-893-8793.
Website: http://www.ucsb.edu/.

UNIVERSITY OF CALIFORNIA, SANTA CRUZ
Santa Cruz, CA

Tuition & fees (CA res): $14,028	Average undergraduate aid package: $25,754

ABOUT THE INSTITUTION State-supported, coed. *Awards:* certificates, bachelor's, master's, and doctoral degrees. 53 undergraduate majors. *Total enrollment:* 19,457. Undergraduates: 17,577. Freshmen: 4,047. Both federal and institutional methodology are used as a basis for awarding need-based institutional aid.

UNDERGRADUATE EXPENSES for 2017–2018 *Application fee:* $70. *Tuition, state resident:* full-time $11,502. *Tuition, nonresident:* full-time $39,516. *Required fees:* full-time $2526. Part-time tuition and fees vary according to course load. *College room and board:* $16,055. Room and board charges vary according to board plan and housing facility.

FRESHMAN FINANCIAL AID (Fall 2017, est.) 3,108 applied for aid; of those 76% were deemed to have need. 96% of freshmen with need received aid; of those 23% had need fully met. *Average percent of need met:* 83% (excluding resources awarded to replace EFC). *Average financial aid package:* $25,549 (excluding resources awarded to replace EFC). 11% of all full-time freshmen had no need and received non-need-based gift aid.

UNDERGRADUATE FINANCIAL AID (Fall 2017, est.) 12,285 applied for aid; of those 86% were deemed to have need. 96% of undergraduates with need received aid; of those 27% had need fully met. *Average percent of need met:* 84% (excluding resources awarded to replace EFC). *Average financial aid package:* $25,754 (excluding resources awarded to replace EFC). 8% of all full-time undergraduates had no need and received non-need-based gift aid.

GIFT AID (NEED-BASED) *Total amount:* $214,860,006 (15% federal, 36% state, 48% institutional, 1% external sources). *Receiving aid:* Freshmen: 54% (2,176); all full-time undergraduates: 59% (9,871). *Average award:* Freshmen: $20,794; Undergraduates: $21,030. *Scholarships, grants, and awards:* Federal Pell, FSEOG, state, private, college/university gift aid from institutional funds.

GIFT AID (NON-NEED-BASED) *Total amount:* $9,201,480 (4% federal, 5% state, 86% institutional, 5% external sources). *Receiving aid:* Freshmen: 1% (41). Undergraduates: 1% (149). *Average award:* Freshmen: $5456. Undergraduates: $5392. *Scholarships, grants, and awards by category:* Academic interests/achievement: 316 awards ($854,865 total): agriculture, area/ethnic studies, computer science, general academic interests/achievements, humanities, mathematics, physical sciences, social sciences. *Creative arts/performance:* 119 awards ($103,236 total): art/fine arts, cinema/film/broadcasting, creative writing, music, performing arts, theater/drama. *Special achievements/activities:* 66 awards ($71,701 total): community service, hobbies/interests, leadership, memberships. *Special characteristics:* 1,178 awards ($5,357,888 total): first-generation college students, international students, out-of-state students, veterans. *ROTC:* Army cooperative, Naval cooperative, Air Force cooperative.

LOANS *Student loans:* $50,806,807 (80% need-based, 20% non-need-based). 64% of past graduating class borrowed through all loan programs. *Average indebtedness per student:* $22,804. *Average need-based loan:* Freshmen: $6660. Undergraduates: $6726. *Parent loans:* $24,620,536 (22% need-based, 78% non-need-based). *Programs:* Federal Direct (Subsidized and Unsubsidized Stafford, PLUS), Perkins, college/university.

WORK-STUDY *Federal work-study:* Total amount: $9,040,046; 1,163 jobs averaging $2549. *State or other work-study/employment:* Total amount: $786,850 (100% need-based). Part-time jobs available.

APPLYING FOR FINANCIAL AID *Required financial aid forms:* FAFSA, state aid form, California Dream Act Application. *Financial aid deadline:* 3/2. *Notification date:* Continuous beginning 3/15. Students must reply by 5/1 or within 4 weeks of notification.

CONTACT John Patrick Register, Director of Financial Aid, University of California, Santa Cruz, 201 Hahn Student Services Building, Santa Cruz, CA 95064, 831-459-4404. *Fax:* 831-459-3628. *E-mail:* jpregis@ucsc.edu.
Website: http://www.ucsc.edu/.

UNIVERSITY OF CENTRAL ARKANSAS
Conway, AR

Tuition & fees (AR res): $8524	Average undergraduate aid package: N/A

ABOUT THE INSTITUTION State-supported, coed. *Awards:* certificates, bachelor's, master's, and doctoral degrees. 61 undergraduate majors. *Total enrollment:* 11,350. Undergraduates: 9,542. Freshmen: 1,937. Federal methodology is used as a basis for awarding need-based institutional aid.

UNDERGRADUATE EXPENSES for 2017–2018 *Application fee:* $25. *Tuition, state resident:* full-time $6523; part-time $217.43 per credit hour. *Tuition, nonresident:* full-time $13,046; part-time $434.86 per credit hour. *Required fees:* full-time $2001. Full-time tuition and fees vary according to course load. Part-time tuition and fees vary according to course load. *College room and board:* $6518. Room and board charges vary according to board plan and housing facility.

GIFT AID (NEED-BASED) *Scholarships, grants, and awards:* Federal Pell, FSEOG, state, private, college/university gift aid from institutional funds, Federal Nursing.

GIFT AID (NON-NEED-BASED) *Scholarships, grants, and awards by category:* Academic interests/achievement: general academic interests/achievements. *Tuition waivers:* Full or partial for employees or children of employees, senior citizens. *ROTC:* Army.

LOANS *Programs:* Perkins, Federal Nursing, state, alternative loans.

WORK-STUDY Federal work-study jobs available. *State or other work-study/employment:* Part-time jobs available.

APPLYING FOR FINANCIAL AID *Required financial aid form:* FAFSA. *Financial aid deadline:* 7/1 (priority: 4/15). *Notification date:* Continuous.

CONTACT Cheryl Lyons, Director of Student Aid, University of Central Arkansas, 201 Donaghey Avenue, Conway, AR 72035, 501-450-3140 or toll-free 800-243-8245. *Fax:* 501-450-5168. *E-mail:* clyons@uca.edu.
Website: http://www.uca.edu/.

UNIVERSITY OF CENTRAL FLORIDA
Orlando, FL

Tuition & fees (FL res): $6368	Average undergraduate aid package: $8655

ABOUT THE INSTITUTION State-supported, coed. *Awards:* certificates, associate, bachelor's, master's, and doctoral degrees. 83 undergraduate majors. *Total enrollment:* 66,183. Undergraduates: 56,972. Freshmen: 6,860. Federal methodology is used as a basis for awarding need-based institutional aid.

UNDERGRADUATE EXPENSES for 2017–2018 *Application fee:* $30. *Tuition, state resident:* full-time $6368; part-time $212.28 per credit hour. *Tuition, nonresident:* full-time $22,467; part-time $748.89 per credit hour. Full-time tuition and fees vary according to course load. Part-time tuition and fees vary according to course load. *College room and board:* $10,011; *Room only:* $5400. Room and board charges vary according to board plan and housing facility. *Payment plan:* Tuition prepayment.

FRESHMAN FINANCIAL AID (Fall 2016) 5,452 applied for aid; of those 67% were deemed to have need. 95% of freshmen with need received aid; of those 9% had need fully met. *Average percent of need met:* 55% (excluding resources awarded to replace EFC). *Average financial aid package:* $8544 (excluding resources awarded to replace EFC). 9% of all full-time freshmen had no need and received non-need-based gift aid.

UNDERGRADUATE FINANCIAL AID (Fall 2016) 30,552 applied for aid; of those 78% were deemed to have need. 95% of undergraduates with need received aid; of those 7% had need fully met. *Average percent of need met:* 55% (excluding resources awarded to replace EFC). *Average financial aid package:* $8655

(excluding resources awarded to replace EFC). 4% of all full-time undergraduates had no need and received non-need-based gift aid.

GIFT AID (NEED-BASED) *Total amount:* $119,484,887 (73% federal, 9% state, 18% institutional). *Receiving aid:* Freshmen: 36% (2,208); all full-time undergraduates: 43% (16,516). *Average award:* Freshmen: $6002; Undergraduates: $5796. *Scholarships, grants, and awards:* Federal Pell, FSEOG, state, private, college/university gift aid from institutional funds.

GIFT AID (NON-NEED-BASED) *Total amount:* $58,569,929 (1% federal, 59% state, 27% institutional, 13% external sources). *Receiving aid:* Freshmen: 38% (2,317). Undergraduates: 25% (9,497). *Average award:* Freshmen: $4041. Undergraduates: $4041. *Scholarships, grants, and awards by category: Academic interests/achievement:* general academic interests/achievements. *Creative arts/performance:* cinema/film/broadcasting, music, theater/drama. *Special achievements/activities:* general special achievements/activities, leadership. *Special characteristics:* first-generation college students. *Tuition waivers:* Full or partial for employees or children of employees, senior citizens. *ROTC:* Army, Air Force.

LOANS *Student loans:* $176,250,525 (50% need-based, 50% non-need-based). 50% of past graduating class borrowed through all loan programs. *Average indebtedness per student:* $21,818. *Average need-based loan:* Freshmen: $3592. Undergraduates: $4645. *Parent loans:* $13,532,963 (100% non-need-based). *Programs:* Federal Direct (Subsidized and Unsubsidized Stafford, PLUS), Perkins.

WORK-STUDY *Federal work-study:* 997 jobs averaging $3335. *State or other work-study/employment:* Part-time jobs available.

ATHLETIC AWARDS Total amount: $4,928,754 (100% non-need-based).

APPLYING FOR FINANCIAL AID *Required financial aid form:* FAFSA. *Financial aid deadline:* 6/30 (priority: 12/1). *Notification date:* Continuous beginning 3/15. Students must reply within 3 weeks of notification.

CONTACT Ms. Alicia Keaton, Director of Student Financial Assistance, University of Central Florida, 4000 Central Florida Boulevard, Orlando, FL 32816-0113, 407-823-2827. *Fax:* 407-823-5241. *E-mail:* alicia.keaton@ucf.edu.

Website: http://www.ucf.edu/.

UNIVERSITY OF CENTRAL MISSOURI
Warrensburg, MO

Tuition & fees (MO res): $7520	Average undergraduate aid package: $8622

ABOUT THE INSTITUTION State-supported, coed. *Awards:* certificates, bachelor's, and master's degrees. 63 undergraduate majors. *Total enrollment:* 12,333. Undergraduates: 9,801. Freshmen: 1,691. Federal methodology is used as a basis for awarding need-based institutional aid.

UNDERGRADUATE EXPENSES for 2017–2018 *Application fee:* $30. *Tuition, state resident:* full-time $6630; part-time $221 per credit hour. *Tuition, nonresident:* full-time $13,260; part-time $442 per credit hour. *Required fees:* full-time $890; $29.65 per credit hour. Full-time tuition and fees vary according to course load and location. Part-time tuition and fees vary according to location. *College room and board:* $8536; *Room only:* $5394. Room and board charges vary according to board plan, housing facility, and student level.

FRESHMAN FINANCIAL AID (Fall 2016) 1,444 applied for aid; of those 71% were deemed to have need. 100% of freshmen with need received aid; of those 14% had need fully met. *Average percent of need met:* 64% (excluding resources awarded to replace EFC). *Average financial aid package:* $8853 (excluding resources awarded to replace EFC). 26% of all full-time freshmen had no need and received non-need-based gift aid.

UNDERGRADUATE FINANCIAL AID (Fall 2016) 4,949 applied for aid; of those 75% were deemed to have need. 100% of undergraduates with need received aid; of those 10% had need fully met. *Average percent of need met:* 62% (excluding resources awarded to replace EFC). *Average financial aid package:* $8622 (excluding resources awarded to replace EFC). 28% of all full-time undergraduates had no need and received non-need-based gift aid.

GIFT AID (NEED-BASED) *Total amount:* $25,509,797 (54% federal, 20% state, 26% external sources). *Receiving aid:* Freshmen: 39% (615); all full-time undergraduates: 36% (2,218). *Average award:* Freshmen: $615; Undergraduates: $2833. *Scholarships, grants, and awards:* Federal Pell, FSEOG, state, private, college/university gift aid from institutional funds.

GIFT AID (NON-NEED-BASED) *Total amount:* $8,308,644 (4% federal, 5% state, 91% institutional). *Receiving aid:* Freshmen: 64% (1,008). Undergraduates:

57% (3,516). *Average award:* Freshmen: $3580. Undergraduates: $3474. *Tuition waivers:* Full or partial for employees or children of employees. *ROTC:* Army, Air Force cooperative.

LOANS *Student loans:* $40,408,428 (41% need-based, 59% non-need-based). 74% of past graduating class borrowed through all loan programs. *Average indebtedness per student:* $27,481. *Parent loans:* $6,274,291 (100% non-need-based). *Programs:* Federal Direct (Subsidized and Unsubsidized Stafford, PLUS), Perkins, state, private loans.

WORK-STUDY *Federal work-study:* 87 jobs averaging $1522. *State or other work-study/employment:* Total amount: $3,262,633 (100% non-need-based). 1,690 part-time jobs averaging $1931.

ATHLETIC AWARDS Total amount: $2,517,269 (100% non-need-based).

APPLYING FOR FINANCIAL AID *Required financial aid forms:* FAFSA, institution's own form. *Financial aid deadline (priority):* 4/1. *Notification date:* Continuous beginning 3/20.

CONTACT Mr. Tony Lubbers, Director of Student Financial Assistance, University of Central Missouri, Ward Edwards Building 1100, Warrensburg, MO 64093, 660-543-8266 or toll-free 800-729-8266. *Fax:* 660-543-8080. *E-mail:* lubbers@ucmo.edu. *Website:* http://www.ucmo.edu/.

UNIVERSITY OF CENTRAL OKLAHOMA
Edmond, OK

Tuition & fees (OK res): $7099	Average undergraduate aid package: $9809

ABOUT THE INSTITUTION State-supported, coed. *Awards:* certificates, associate, bachelor's, and master's degrees. 102 undergraduate majors. *Total enrollment:* 15,973. Undergraduates: 14,337. Freshmen: 2,250. Federal methodology is used as a basis for awarding need-based institutional aid.

UNDERGRADUATE EXPENSES for 2017–2018 *Application fee:* $50. *Tuition, state resident:* full-time $6160; part-time $206.35 per credit hour. *Tuition, nonresident:* full-time $16,508; part-time $581.55 per credit hour. *Required fees:* full-time $939; $31.30 per credit hour. Full-time tuition and fees vary according to course level, course load, degree level, location, and program. Part-time tuition and fees vary according to course level, course load, degree level, location, and program. *College room and board:* $8050; *Room only:* $3900. Room and board charges vary according to board plan and housing facility. *Payment plan:* Guaranteed tuition.

FRESHMAN FINANCIAL AID (Fall 2016) 1,776 applied for aid; of those 78% were deemed to have need. 96% of freshmen with need received aid; of those 16% had need fully met. *Average percent of need met:* 62% (excluding resources awarded to replace EFC). *Average financial aid package:* $10,459 (excluding resources awarded to replace EFC). 10% of all full-time freshmen had no need and received non-need-based gift aid.

UNDERGRADUATE FINANCIAL AID (Fall 2016) 7,448 applied for aid; of those 85% were deemed to have need. 96% of undergraduates with need received aid; of those 10% had need fully met. *Average percent of need met:* 52% (excluding resources awarded to replace EFC). *Average financial aid package:* $9809 (excluding resources awarded to replace EFC). 4% of all full-time undergraduates had no need and received non-need-based gift aid.

GIFT AID (NEED-BASED) *Total amount:* $31,819,052 (65% federal, 35% state). *Receiving aid:* Freshmen: 43% (927); all full-time undergraduates: 41% (4,327). *Average award:* Freshmen: $7176; Undergraduates: $6245. *Scholarships, grants, and awards:* Federal Pell, FSEOG, state, private, college/university gift aid from institutional funds.

GIFT AID (NON-NEED-BASED) *Total amount:* $10,879,365 (22% federal, 4% state, 13% institutional, 61% external sources). *Receiving aid:* Freshmen: 21% (467). Undergraduates: 15% (1,538). *Average award:* Freshmen: $1421. Undergraduates: $1541. *Scholarships, grants, and awards by category: Academic interests/achievement:* biological sciences, business, communication, computer science, education, English, foreign languages, general academic interests/achievements, health fields, home economics, humanities, mathematics, military science, physical sciences, social sciences. *Creative arts/performance:* applied art and design, art/fine arts, journalism/publications, music, theater/drama. *Special achievements/activities:* general special achievements/activities, junior miss, leadership. *Special characteristics:* children of faculty/staff, ethnic background, international students, members of minority groups.

Tuition waivers: Full or partial for employees or children of employees. **ROTC:** Army.

LOANS Student loans: $52,015,738 (39% need-based, 61% non-need-based). 51% of past graduating class borrowed through all loan programs. *Average indebtedness per student:* $26,939. **Average need-based loan:** Freshmen: $3136. Undergraduates: $3959. **Parent loans:** $3,190,523 (100% non-need-based). **Programs:** Federal Direct (Subsidized and Unsubsidized Stafford, PLUS), Perkins.

WORK-STUDY Federal work-study: 3,125 jobs averaging $4739. **State or other work-study/employment:** Total amount: $4,733,235 (100% non-need-based). Part-time jobs available.

ATHLETIC AWARDS Total amount: $2,317,299 (100% non-need-based).

APPLYING FOR FINANCIAL AID Required financial aid forms: FAFSA, institution's own form. **Financial aid deadline:** Continuous. **Notification date:** Continuous beginning 5/1. Students must reply within 4 weeks of notification.

CONTACT Ms. Kerry Housley, Assistant Director of Technical Services, University of Central Oklahoma, 100 North University Drive, Edmond, OK 73034-5209, 405-974-5325. *Fax:* 405-340-7658. *E-mail:* khousley@uco.edu. *Website:* http://www.uco.edu/.

UNIVERSITY OF CHARLESTON
Charleston, WV

CONTACT Ms. Nina Morton, Director of Financial Aid, University of Charleston, 2300 MacCorkle Avenue SE, Charleston, WV 25304-1099, 304-357-4947 or toll-free 800-995-GOUC. *E-mail:* ninamorton@ucwv.edu. *Website:* http://www.ucwv.edu/.

UNIVERSITY OF CHICAGO
Chicago, IL

Tuition & fees: $54,825	Average undergraduate aid package: $52,643

ABOUT THE INSTITUTION Independent, coed. **Awards:** bachelor's, master's, and doctoral degrees. 44 undergraduate majors. **Total enrollment:** 13,736. Undergraduates: 6,264. Freshmen: 1,736. Both federal and institutional methodology are used as a basis for awarding need-based institutional aid.

UNDERGRADUATE EXPENSES for 2017–2018 Application fee: $75. **One-time required fee:** $1209. **Comprehensive fee:** $70,551 includes full-time tuition ($53,292), mandatory fees ($1533), and room and board ($15,726). Full-time tuition and fees vary according to course load. Room and board charges vary according to board plan and housing facility. Part-time tuition and fees vary according to course load.

FRESHMAN FINANCIAL AID (Fall 2017, est.) 1,047 applied for aid; of those 70% were deemed to have need. 100% of freshmen with need received aid; of those 100% had need fully met. **Average percent of need met:** 100% (excluding resources awarded to replace EFC). **Average financial aid package:** $54,438 (excluding resources awarded to replace EFC).

UNDERGRADUATE FINANCIAL AID (Fall 2017, est.) 3,289 applied for aid; of those 81% were deemed to have need. 100% of undergraduates with need received aid; of those 100% had need fully met. **Average percent of need met:** 100% (excluding resources awarded to replace EFC). **Average financial aid package:** $52,643 (excluding resources awarded to replace EFC).

GIFT AID (NEED-BASED) Total amount: $127,810,937 (4% federal, 1% state, 95% institutional). **Receiving aid:** Freshmen: 42% (724); all full-time undergraduates: 42% (2,625). **Average award:** Freshmen: $48,113; Undergraduates: $46,460. **Scholarships, grants, and awards:** Federal Pell, FSEOG, state, private, college/university gift aid from institutional funds.

GIFT AID (NON-NEED-BASED) Scholarships, grants, and awards by category: *Academic interests/achievement:* general academic interests/achievements. *Special achievements/activities:* community service, leadership. **Tuition waivers:** Full or partial for employees or children of employees. **ROTC:** Army cooperative, Air Force cooperative.

LOANS Student loans: $1,194,309 (100% need-based). 29% of past graduating class borrowed through all loan programs. *Average indebtedness per student:*

$23,401. **Average need-based loan:** Undergraduates: $3777. **Programs:** Federal Direct (Subsidized and Unsubsidized Stafford, PLUS), Perkins.

WORK-STUDY Federal work-study: Total amount: $5,295,462; jobs available. **State or other work-study/employment:** Part-time jobs available.

APPLYING FOR FINANCIAL AID Required financial aid forms: FAFSA, institution's own form, CSS Financial Aid PROFILE, federal income tax form(s). **Financial aid deadline (priority):** 2/15. **Notification date:** 3/15. Students must reply by 5/1.

CONTACT Office of College Aid, University of Chicago, 1101 East 58th Street, Chicago, IL 60637, 773-702-8666. *Fax:* 773-834-4300. *E-mail:* college-aid@uchicago.edu. *Website:* http://www.uchicago.edu/.

UNIVERSITY OF CINCINNATI
Cincinnati, OH

Tuition & fees (OH res): $11,000	Average undergraduate aid package: $8514

ABOUT THE INSTITUTION State-supported, coed. **Awards:** certificates, associate, bachelor's, master's, and doctoral degrees. 142 undergraduate majors. **Total enrollment:** 37,204. Undergraduates: 26,608. Freshmen: 5,400. Federal methodology is used as a basis for awarding need-based institutional aid.

UNDERGRADUATE EXPENSES for 2018–2019 Application fee: $50. **Tuition, state resident:** full-time $9322; part-time $389 per credit hour. **Tuition, nonresident:** full-time $24,656; part-time $1098 per credit hour. **Required fees:** full-time $1678; $70 per credit hour. Full-time tuition and fees vary according to course load, location, program, and reciprocity agreements. Part-time tuition and fees vary according to course load, location, program, and reciprocity agreements. **College room and board:** $11,118; **Room only:** $6624. Room and board charges vary according to board plan and housing facility.

FRESHMAN FINANCIAL AID (Fall 2016) 4,175 applied for aid; of those 71% were deemed to have need. 93% of freshmen with need received aid; of those 7% had need fully met. **Average percent of need met:** 44% (excluding resources awarded to replace EFC). **Average financial aid package:** $8688 (excluding resources awarded to replace EFC). 18% of all full-time freshmen had no need and received non-need-based gift aid.

UNDERGRADUATE FINANCIAL AID (Fall 2016) 14,728 applied for aid; of those 79% were deemed to have need. 95% of undergraduates with need received aid; of those 5% had need fully met. **Average percent of need met:** 39% (excluding resources awarded to replace EFC). **Average financial aid package:** $8514 (excluding resources awarded to replace EFC). 19% of all full-time undergraduates had no need and received non-need-based gift aid.

GIFT AID (NEED-BASED) Total amount: $52,781,703 (45% federal, 8% state, 37% institutional, 10% external sources). **Receiving aid:** Freshmen: 41% (2,059); all full-time undergraduates: 36% (7,805). **Average award:** Freshmen: $6413; Undergraduates: $6116. **Scholarships, grants, and awards:** Federal Pell, FSEOG, state, private, college/university gift aid from institutional funds, United Negro College Fund, Federal Nursing, TEACH Grants.

GIFT AID (NON-NEED-BASED) Total amount: $30,764,342 (15% state, 65% institutional, 20% external sources). **Receiving aid:** Freshmen: 31% (1,519). Undergraduates: 22% (4,847). **Average award:** Freshmen: $5172. Undergraduates: $4549. **Tuition waivers:** Full or partial for employees or children of employees. **ROTC:** Army, Air Force.

LOANS Student loans: $100,347,565 (77% need-based, 23% non-need-based). 63% of past graduating class borrowed through all loan programs. *Average indebtedness per student:* $25,877. **Average need-based loan:** Freshmen: $3800. Undergraduates: $4472. **Parent loans:** $55,690,553 (52% need-based, 48% non-need-based). **Programs:** Federal Direct (Subsidized and Unsubsidized Stafford, PLUS), Perkins, Federal Nursing, state, college/university.

WORK-STUDY Federal work-study: jobs available.

ATHLETIC AWARDS Total amount: $6,755,020 (39% need-based, 61% non-need-based).

APPLYING FOR FINANCIAL AID Required financial aid form: FAFSA. **Financial aid deadline:** Continuous. **Notification date:** Continuous beginning 2/15. Students must reply within 2 weeks of notification.

CONTACT Mr. Randy Ulses, Director of Scholarships and Enrollment, University of Cincinnati, PO Box 210125, Cincinnati, OH 45221-0125, 513-556-1000. *Fax:* 513-556-9171. *E-mail:* financeaid@uc.edu. *Website:* http://www.uc.edu/.

UNIVERSITY OF COLORADO BOULDER
Boulder, CO

Tuition & fees (CO res): $12,086	Average undergraduate aid package: $16,699

ABOUT THE INSTITUTION State-supported, coed. *Awards:* certificates, bachelor's, master's, and doctoral degrees. 75 undergraduate majors. *Total enrollment:* 35,230. Undergraduates: 29,091. Freshmen: 6,570. Federal methodology is used as a basis for awarding need-based institutional aid.

UNDERGRADUATE EXPENSES for 2017–2018 *Application fee:* $50. *One-time required fee:* $182. *Tuition, state resident:* full-time $10,248. *Tuition, nonresident:* full-time $34,382. *Required fees:* full-time $1838. Full-time tuition and fees vary according to program. Part-time tuition and fees vary according to course load and program. *College room and board:* $13,998. Room and board charges vary according to board plan, housing facility, and location. *Payment plan:* Guaranteed tuition.

FRESHMAN FINANCIAL AID (Fall 2017, est.) 4,431 applied for aid; of those 59% were deemed to have need. 98% of freshmen with need received aid; of those 46% had need fully met. *Average percent of need met:* 82% (excluding resources awarded to replace EFC). *Average financial aid package:* $15,834 (excluding resources awarded to replace EFC). 34% of all full-time freshmen had no need and received non-need-based gift aid.

UNDERGRADUATE FINANCIAL AID (Fall 2017, est.) 13,509 applied for aid; of those 72% were deemed to have need. 97% of undergraduates with need received aid; of those 40% had need fully met. *Average percent of need met:* 80% (excluding resources awarded to replace EFC). *Average financial aid package:* $16,699 (excluding resources awarded to replace EFC). 27% of all full-time undergraduates had no need and received non-need-based gift aid.

GIFT AID (NEED-BASED) Total amount: $84,089,782 (27% federal, 10% state, 58% institutional, 5% external sources). *Receiving aid:* Freshmen: 30% (1,953); all full-time undergraduates: 27% (7,310). *Average award:* Freshmen: $11,013; Undergraduates: $11,091. *Scholarships, grants, and awards:* Federal Pell, FSEOG, state, private, college/university gift aid from institutional funds.

GIFT AID (NON-NEED-BASED) Total amount: $39,383,705 (1% state, 69% institutional, 30% external sources). *Receiving aid:* Freshmen: 2% (132). Undergraduates: 1% (353). *Average award:* Freshmen: $8704. *Scholarships, grants, and awards by category:* Academic interests/achievement: architecture, area/ethnic studies, biological sciences, business, communication, computer science, education, engineering/technologies, English, foreign languages, general academic interests/achievements, home economics, humanities, international studies, mathematics, military science, physical sciences, premedicine, religion/biblical studies, social sciences. Creative arts/performance: art/fine arts, cinema/film/broadcasting, creative writing, dance, general creative arts/performance, journalism/publications, music, performing arts, theater/drama. Special achievements/activities: community service, general special achievements/activities, leadership. Special characteristics: first-generation college students, general special characteristics, local/state students, veterans. *Tuition waivers:* Full or partial for employees or children of employees, senior citizens. *ROTC:* Army, Naval, Air Force.

LOANS Student loans: $94,899,144 (59% need-based, 41% non-need-based). 42% of past graduating class borrowed through all loan programs. *Average indebtedness per student:* $27,680. *Average need-based loan:* Freshmen: $5509. Undergraduates: $6578. *Parent loans:* $106,199,621 (34% need-based, 66% non-need-based). *Programs:* Federal Direct (Subsidized and Unsubsidized Stafford, PLUS), Perkins, college/university, private loans.

WORK-STUDY Federal work-study: Total amount: $879,781; 882 jobs averaging $1729. *State or other work-study/employment:* Total amount: $1,910,556 (97% need-based, 3% non-need-based). 869 part-time jobs averaging $2653.

ATHLETIC AWARDS Total amount: $9,663,330 (23% need-based, 77% non-need-based).

APPLYING FOR FINANCIAL AID *Required financial aid forms:* FAFSA, federal income tax form(s). *Financial aid deadline (priority):* 2/15. *Notifi-*

cation date: Continuous beginning 3/15. Students must reply within 3 weeks of notification.

CONTACT Gwen E. Pomper, Director of Financial Aid, University of Colorado Boulder, 556 UCB, Boulder, CO 80309-0556, 303-492-5091. *Fax:* 303-492-0838. *E-mail:* finaid@colorado.edu. *Website:* http://www.colorado.edu/.

UNIVERSITY OF COLORADO COLORADO SPRINGS
Colorado Springs, CO

Tuition & fees (CO res): $10,201	Average undergraduate aid package: $8629

ABOUT THE INSTITUTION State-supported, coed. *Awards:* certificates, bachelor's, master's, and doctoral degrees. 34 undergraduate majors. *Total enrollment:* 12,932. Undergraduates: 10,808. Freshmen: 2,045. Federal methodology is used as a basis for awarding need-based institutional aid.

UNDERGRADUATE EXPENSES for 2017–2018 *Application fee:* $50. *One-time required fee:* $140. *Tuition, state resident:* full-time $8610; part-time $287 per credit hour. *Tuition, nonresident:* full-time $22,590; part-time $753 per credit hour. *Required fees:* full-time $1591. Full-time tuition and fees vary according to course load, degree level, location, program, reciprocity agreements, and student level. Part-time tuition and fees vary according to course load, degree level, location, program, reciprocity agreements, and student level. *College room and board:* $10,100. Room and board charges vary according to board plan, housing facility, and student level.

FRESHMAN FINANCIAL AID (Fall 2016) 1,848 applied for aid; of those 70% were deemed to have need. 93% of freshmen with need received aid; of those 4% had need fully met. *Average percent of need met:* 41% (excluding resources awarded to replace EFC). *Average financial aid package:* $7880 (excluding resources awarded to replace EFC). 14% of all full-time freshmen had no need and received non-need-based gift aid.

UNDERGRADUATE FINANCIAL AID (Fall 2016) 4,783 applied for aid; of those 78% were deemed to have need. 93% of undergraduates with need received aid; of those 4% had need fully met. *Average percent of need met:* 43% (excluding resources awarded to replace EFC). *Average financial aid package:* $8629 (excluding resources awarded to replace EFC). 9% of all full-time undergraduates had no need and received non-need-based gift aid.

GIFT AID (NEED-BASED) Total amount: $30,953,437 (43% federal, 16% state, 31% institutional, 10% external sources). *Receiving aid:* Freshmen: 33% (654); all full-time undergraduates: 39% (2,323). *Average award:* Freshmen: $6529; Undergraduates: $7237. *Scholarships, grants, and awards:* Federal Pell, FSEOG, state, private, college/university gift aid from institutional funds.

GIFT AID (NON-NEED-BASED) Receiving aid: Freshmen: 35% (689). Undergraduates: 13% (746). *Average award:* Freshmen: $2844. Undergraduates: $2823. *Scholarships, grants, and awards by category:* Academic interests/achievement: general academic interests/achievements. *Tuition waivers:* Full or partial for employees or children of employees. *ROTC:* Army.

LOANS Student loans: $38,154,637 (100% need-based). 56% of past graduating class borrowed through all loan programs. *Average indebtedness per student:* $25,042. *Average need-based loan:* Freshmen: $3243. Undergraduates: $4363. *Parent loans:* $17,019,435 (100% need-based). *Programs:* Federal Direct (Subsidized and Unsubsidized Stafford, PLUS).

WORK-STUDY Federal work-study: 189 jobs averaging $2848. *State or other work-study/employment:* Total amount: $1,013,001 (100% need-based). 246 part-time jobs averaging $3703.

ATHLETIC AWARDS Total amount: $1,442,769 (100% non-need-based).

APPLYING FOR FINANCIAL AID *Required financial aid form:* FAFSA. *Financial aid deadline (priority):* 3/1. *Notification date:* Continuous beginning 12/15.

CONTACT Jevita Rogers, Executive Director of Financial Aid, University of Colorado Colorado Springs, 1420 Austin Bluffs Parkway, Colorado Springs, CO 80918, 719-255-3460 or toll-free 800-990-8227 Ext. 3383. *Fax:* 719-255-3650. *E-mail:* jrogers3@uccs.edu. *Website:* http://www.uccs.edu/.

UNIVERSITY OF COLORADO DENVER
Denver, CO

Tuition & fees (CO res): $11,258	Average undergraduate aid package: $9482

ABOUT THE INSTITUTION State-supported, coed. **Awards:** certificates, bachelor's, master's, and doctoral degrees. 38 undergraduate majors. **Total enrollment:** 24,839. Undergraduates: 15,586. Freshmen: 1,513. Federal methodology is used as a basis for awarding need-based institutional aid.

UNDERGRADUATE EXPENSES for 2017–2018 Application fee: $50. **Tuition, state resident:** full-time $9720; part-time $324 per credit hour. **Tuition, nonresident:** full-time $29,910; part-time $997 per credit hour. **Required fees:** full-time $1538; $918 per year. Full-time tuition and fees vary according to course level, course load, degree level, location, program, reciprocity agreements, and student level. Part-time tuition and fees vary according to course level, course load, degree level, location, program, reciprocity agreements, and student level. **College room and board:** $12,190; **Room only:** $8290. Room and board charges vary according to board plan.

FRESHMAN FINANCIAL AID (Fall 2016) 1,177 applied for aid; of those 77% were deemed to have need. 90% of freshmen with need received aid; of those 2% had need fully met. **Average percent of need met:** 47% (excluding resources awarded to replace EFC). **Average financial aid package:** $8889 (excluding resources awarded to replace EFC). 9% of all full-time freshmen had no need and received non-need-based gift aid.

UNDERGRADUATE FINANCIAL AID (Fall 2016) 6,088 applied for aid; of those 85% were deemed to have need. 94% of undergraduates with need received aid; of those 1% had need fully met. **Average percent of need met:** 49% (excluding resources awarded to replace EFC). **Average financial aid package:** $9482 (excluding resources awarded to replace EFC). 6% of all full-time undergraduates had no need and received non-need-based gift aid.

GIFT AID (NEED-BASED) Total amount: $32,673,844 (48% federal, 23% state, 23% institutional, 6% external sources). **Receiving aid:** Freshmen: 49% (667); all full-time undergraduates: 45% (3,822). **Average award:** Freshmen: $7742; Undergraduates: $7466. **Scholarships, grants, and awards:** Federal Pell, FSEOG, state, private, college/university gift aid from institutional funds, College Access Challenge Grants, TEACH Grants, Armed Services Scholarships.

GIFT AID (NON-NEED-BASED) Total amount: $2,720,341 (4% state, 66% institutional, 30% external sources). **Receiving aid:** Freshmen: 5% (63). Undergraduates: 2% (193). **Average award:** Freshmen: $2407. Undergraduates: $2614. **Scholarships, grants, and awards by category:** Academic interests/achievement: 1,310 awards ($2,153,934 total): biological sciences, business, communication, education, engineering/technologies, English, general academic interests/achievements, home economics, humanities, international studies, mathematics, physical sciences, premedicine, social sciences. Creative arts/performance: 76 awards ($72,383 total): applied art and design, art/fine arts, cinema/film/broadcasting, general creative arts/performance, music, performing arts, theater/drama. Special achievements/activities: 10 awards ($5003 total): general special achievements/activities. Special characteristics: 495 awards ($1,196,564 total): children of faculty/staff, ethnic background, first-generation college students, general special characteristics, handicapped students, international students, members of minority groups, out-of-state students, veterans. **Tuition waivers:** Full or partial for employees or children of employees. **ROTC:** Army cooperative, Air Force cooperative.

LOANS Student loans: $38,169,264 (78% need-based, 22% non-need-based). 52% of past graduating class borrowed through all loan programs. **Average indebtedness per student:** $20,941. **Average need-based loan:** Freshmen: $2680. Undergraduates: $3815. **Parent loans:** $13,134,348 (17% need-based, 83% non-need-based). **Programs:** Federal Direct (Subsidized and Unsubsidized Stafford, PLUS), Perkins, Federal Nursing.

WORK-STUDY Federal work-study: 332 jobs averaging $3396. **State or other work-study/employment:** Total amount: $1,176,680 (97% need-based, 3% non-need-based). 321 part-time jobs averaging $3666.

APPLYING FOR FINANCIAL AID Required financial aid form: FAFSA. **Financial aid deadline:** Continuous. **Notification date:** Continuous beginning 5/1.

CONTACT Justin Jaramillo, Interim Director of Financial Aid, University of Colorado Denver, PO Box 173364, Denver, CO 80217-3364, 303-315-1850. Fax: 303-315-1835. E-mail: financialaid@ucdenver.edu.
Website: http://www.ucdenver.edu/.

UNIVERSITY OF CONNECTICUT
Storrs, CT

CONTACT Mona L. Lucas, Director of Financial Aid, University of Connecticut, 233 Glenbrook Road, Unit 4116, Storrs, CT 06269-4116, 860-486-2819. Fax: 860-486-6629. E-mail: financialaid@uconn.edu.
Website: http://www.uconn.edu/.

UNIVERSITY OF DALLAS
Irving, TX

Tuition & fees: $38,716	Average undergraduate aid package: $32,804

ABOUT THE INSTITUTION Independent Roman Catholic, coed. **Awards:** certificates, bachelor's, master's, and doctoral degrees. 33 undergraduate majors. **Total enrollment:** 2,520. Undergraduates: 1,450. Freshmen: 419. Federal methodology is used as a basis for awarding need-based institutional aid.

UNDERGRADUATE EXPENSES for 2017–2018 Application fee: $50. **Comprehensive fee:** $50,676 includes full-time tuition ($36,000), mandatory fees ($2716), and room and board ($11,960). **College room only:** $6580. Full-time tuition and fees vary according to course load. Room and board charges vary according to board plan and housing facility. **Part-time tuition:** $1485 per credit hour. **Part-time fees:** $2716 per year. Part-time tuition and fees vary according to course load.

FRESHMAN FINANCIAL AID (Fall 2017, est.) 349 applied for aid; of those 91% were deemed to have need. 100% of freshmen with need received aid; of those 28% had need fully met. **Average percent of need met:** 85% (excluding resources awarded to replace EFC). **Average financial aid package:** $34,091 (excluding resources awarded to replace EFC). 24% of all full-time freshmen had no need and received non-need-based gift aid.

UNDERGRADUATE FINANCIAL AID (Fall 2017, est.) 998 applied for aid; of those 91% were deemed to have need. 100% of undergraduates with need received aid; of those 20% had need fully met. **Average percent of need met:** 79% (excluding resources awarded to replace EFC). **Average financial aid package:** $32,804 (excluding resources awarded to replace EFC). 34% of all full-time undergraduates had no need and received non-need-based gift aid.

GIFT AID (NEED-BASED) Total amount: $25,590,473 (6% federal, 5% state, 88% institutional, 1% external sources). **Receiving aid:** Freshmen: 75% (316); all full-time undergraduates: 63% (894). **Average award:** Freshmen: $30,746; Undergraduates: $28,420. **Scholarships, grants, and awards:** Federal Pell, FSEOG, state, private, college/university gift aid from institutional funds.

GIFT AID (NON-NEED-BASED) Total amount: $10,031,057 (99% institutional, 1% external sources). **Receiving aid:** Freshmen: 45% (189). Undergraduates: 42% (601). **Average award:** Freshmen: $23,470. Undergraduates: $20,613. **Scholarships, grants, and awards by category:** Academic interests/achievement: 1,615 awards ($14,535,000 total): area/ethnic studies, biological sciences, business, computer science, education, English, foreign languages, general academic interests/achievements, home economics, mathematics, military science, physical sciences, premedicine. Creative arts/performance: 69 awards ($147,315 total): art/fine arts, music, theater/drama. Special characteristics: 34 awards ($460,700 total): children of faculty/staff, religious affiliation. **Tuition waivers:** Full or partial for employees or children of employees. **ROTC:** Army cooperative, Air Force cooperative.

LOANS Student loans: $6,823,536 (88% need-based, 12% non-need-based). 57% of past graduating class borrowed through all loan programs. **Average indebtedness per student:** $35,161. **Average need-based loan:** Freshmen: $4001. Undergraduates: $5403. **Parent loans:** $1,740,018 (93% need-based, 7% non-need-based). **Programs:** Federal Direct (Subsidized and Unsubsidized Stafford, PLUS), Perkins, state.

WORK-STUDY Federal work-study: Total amount: $392,054; 253 jobs averaging $1550. **State or other work-study/employment:** Total amount: $9300 (100% need-based). 6 part-time jobs averaging $1550.

APPLYING FOR FINANCIAL AID Required financial aid form: FAFSA. **Financial aid deadline (priority):** 1/15. **Notification date:** Continuous beginning 12/1. Students must reply by 5/1 or within 2 weeks of notification.

CONTACT Mrs. Iaryn Anderson, Director of Financial Aid, University of Dallas, 1845 East Northgate Drive, Irving, TX 75062, 972-721-5266 or toll-free 800-628-6999. *Fax:* 972-721-5017. *E-mail:* ugadmis@udallas.edu.
Website: http://www.udallas.edu/.

UNIVERSITY OF DAYTON
Dayton, OH

Tuition & fees: N/R	Average undergraduate aid package: $31,029

ABOUT THE INSTITUTION Independent Roman Catholic, coed. **Awards:** certificates, bachelor's, master's, and doctoral degrees. 82 undergraduate majors. **Total enrollment:** 10,882. Undergraduates: 8,499. Freshmen: 2,226. Federal methodology is used as a basis for awarding need-based institutional aid.

UNDERGRADUATE EXPENSES for 2018–2019 Payment plan: Guaranteed tuition.

FRESHMAN FINANCIAL AID (Fall 2017, est.) 2,078 applied for aid; of those 73% were deemed to have need. 100% of freshmen with need received aid; of those 100% had need fully met. **Average percent of need met:** 82% (excluding resources awarded to replace EFC). **Average financial aid package:** $30,372 (excluding resources awarded to replace EFC). 31% of all full-time freshmen had no need and received non-need-based gift aid.

UNDERGRADUATE FINANCIAL AID (Fall 2017, est.) 6,359 applied for aid; of those 75% were deemed to have need. 96% of undergraduates with need received aid; of those 100% had need fully met. **Average percent of need met:** 83% (excluding resources awarded to replace EFC). **Average financial aid package:** $31,029 (excluding resources awarded to replace EFC). 40% of all full-time undergraduates had no need and received non-need-based gift aid.

GIFT AID (NEED-BASED) Total amount: $121,095,339 (4% federal, 1% state, 94% institutional, 1% external sources). **Receiving aid:** Freshmen: 68% (1,517); all full-time undergraduates: 58% (4,573). **Average award:** Freshmen: $28,208; Undergraduates: $27,594. **Scholarships, grants, and awards:** Federal Pell, FSEOG, state, private, college/university gift aid from institutional funds.

GIFT AID (NON-NEED-BASED) Total amount: $51,700,632 (1% federal, 98% institutional, 1% external sources). **Receiving aid:** Freshmen: 6% (132). Undergraduates: 5% (421). **Average award:** Freshmen: $17,549. Undergraduates: $18,131. **Scholarships, grants, and awards by category:** Academic interests/achievement: biological sciences, business, communication, computer science, education, engineering/technologies, English, foreign languages, general academic interests/achievements, health fields, humanities, international studies, mathematics, military science, physical sciences, premedicine, religion/biblical studies, social sciences. Creative arts/performance: art/fine arts, music. Special achievements/activities: community service, leadership. Special characteristics: children and siblings of alumni, children of faculty/staff, local/state students, members of minority groups, out-of-state students, religious affiliation. **Tuition waivers:** Full or partial for employees or children of employees. **ROTC:** Army, Air Force cooperative.

LOANS Student loans: $54,548,246 (76% need-based, 24% non-need-based). 55% of past graduating class borrowed through all loan programs. *Average indebtedness per student:* $35,689. **Average need-based loan:** Freshmen: $3412. Undergraduates: $3325. **Parent loans:** $15,055,354 (52% need-based, 48% non-need-based). **Programs:** Federal Direct (Subsidized and Unsubsidized Stafford, PLUS), Perkins.

WORK-STUDY Federal work-study: Total amount: $1,000,000; jobs available. **State or other work-study/employment:** Total amount: $7,000,000 (29% need-based, 71% non-need-based). Part-time jobs available.

ATHLETIC AWARDS Total amount: $5,176,779 (45% need-based, 55% non-need-based).

APPLYING FOR FINANCIAL AID Required financial aid form: FAFSA. **Financial aid deadline:** 5/1 (priority: 2/1). **Notification date:** Continuous beginning 2/17. Students must reply within 2 weeks of notification.

CONTACT Catherine Mix, Director of Financial Aid, University of Dayton, 300 College Park, Dayton, OH 45469-1668, 937-229-4358 or toll-free 800-837-7433. *Fax:* 937-229-4338. *E-mail:* cmix01@udayton.edu.
Website: http://www.udayton.edu/.

UNIVERSITY OF DELAWARE
Newark, DE

Tuition & fees (DE res): $13,160	Average undergraduate aid package: $13,017

ABOUT THE INSTITUTION State-related, coed. **Awards:** associate, bachelor's, master's, and doctoral degrees. 126 undergraduate majors. **Total enrollment:** 21,463. Undergraduates: 18,374. Freshmen: 3,952. Federal methodology is used as a basis for awarding need-based institutional aid.

UNDERGRADUATE EXPENSES for 2017–2018 Application fee: $75. **Tuition, state resident:** full-time $11,870; part-time $495 per credit hour. **Tuition, nonresident:** full-time $31,860; part-time $1328 per credit hour. **Required fees:** full-time $1290. **College room and board:** $12,332; **Room only:** $7462. Room and board charges vary according to board plan and housing facility.

FRESHMAN FINANCIAL AID (Fall 2016) 3,233 applied for aid; of those 65% were deemed to have need. 98% of freshmen with need received aid; of those 11% had need fully met. **Average percent of need met:** 56% (excluding resources awarded to replace EFC). **Average financial aid package:** $13,284 (excluding resources awarded to replace EFC). 24% of all full-time freshmen had no need and received non-need-based gift aid.

UNDERGRADUATE FINANCIAL AID (Fall 2016) 11,568 applied for aid; of those 71% were deemed to have need. 98% of undergraduates with need received aid; of those 10% had need fully met. **Average percent of need met:** 55% (excluding resources awarded to replace EFC). **Average financial aid package:** $13,017 (excluding resources awarded to replace EFC). 20% of all full-time undergraduates had no need and received non-need-based gift aid.

GIFT AID (NEED-BASED) Total amount: $65,518,418 (16% federal, 12% state, 67% institutional, 5% external sources). **Receiving aid:** Freshmen: 49% (1,942); all full-time undergraduates: 40% (6,846). **Average award:** Freshmen: $9842; Undergraduates: $9506. **Scholarships, grants, and awards:** Federal Pell, FSEOG, state, private, college/university gift aid from institutional funds.

GIFT AID (NON-NEED-BASED) Total amount: $32,175,790 (2% state, 86% institutional, 12% external sources). **Receiving aid:** Freshmen: 4% (172). Undergraduates: 3% (525). **Average award:** Freshmen: $7018. Undergraduates: $7523. **Scholarships, grants, and awards by category:** Academic interests/achievement: agriculture, biological sciences, business, communication, computer science, education, engineering/technologies, English, foreign languages, general academic interests/achievements, health fields, humanities, international studies, mathematics, military science, physical sciences, premedicine, religion/biblical studies, social sciences. Creative arts/performance: applied art and design, art/fine arts, music, theater/drama. Special achievements/activities: cheerleading/drum major, community service, general special achievements/activities, leadership. Special characteristics: children and siblings of alumni, children of faculty/staff, children of public servants, ethnic background, first-generation college students, general special characteristics, local/state students, members of minority groups. **Tuition waivers:** Full or partial for employees or children of employees, senior citizens. **ROTC:** Army, Air Force.

LOANS Student loans: $97,344,022 (57% need-based, 43% non-need-based). 62% of past graduating class borrowed through all loan programs. *Average indebtedness per student:* $34,144. **Average need-based loan:** Freshmen: $3645. Undergraduates: $4483. **Parent loans:** $34,534,808 (37% need-based, 63% non-need-based). **Programs:** Federal Direct (Subsidized and Unsubsidized Stafford, PLUS), Perkins, Federal Nursing.

WORK-STUDY Federal work-study: jobs available. **State or other work-study/employment:** Total amount: $151,143 (88% need-based, 12% non-need-based). Part-time jobs available.

ATHLETIC AWARDS Total amount: $11,265,423 (23% need-based, 77% non-need-based).

APPLYING FOR FINANCIAL AID Required financial aid form: FAFSA. **Financial aid deadline:** 3/15 (priority: 1/15). **Notification date:** Continuous beginning 3/15. Students must reply by 5/1 or within 3 weeks of notification.

CONTACT Mr. James Holloway, Manager of Student Financial Services Compliance, University of Delaware, 140 Student Services Building, Newark, DE 19716, 302-831-0520. *Fax:* 302-831-4334. *E-mail:* holloway@udel.edu.
Website: http://www.udel.edu/.

UNIVERSITY OF DENVER
Denver, CO

Tuition & fees: $50,556	Average undergraduate aid package: $40,587

ABOUT THE INSTITUTION Independent, coed. *Awards:* certificates, bachelor's, master's, and doctoral degrees. 78 undergraduate majors. *Total enrollment:* 11,434. Undergraduates: 5,765. Freshmen: 1,504. Institutional methodology is used as a basis for awarding need-based institutional aid.

UNDERGRADUATE EXPENSES for 2018–2019 *Application fee:* $65. *Comprehensive fee:* $63,561 includes full-time tuition ($49,392), mandatory fees ($1164), and room and board ($13,005). *College room only:* $8100. Full-time tuition and fees vary according to course load and program. Room and board charges vary according to board plan and housing facility. *Part-time tuition:* $1372 per credit hour. Part-time tuition and fees vary according to course load and program.

FRESHMAN FINANCIAL AID (Fall 2017, est.) 983 applied for aid; of those 70% were deemed to have need. 99% of freshmen with need received aid; of those 31% had need fully met. *Average percent of need met:* 88% (excluding resources awarded to replace EFC). *Average financial aid package:* $41,860 (excluding resources awarded to replace EFC). 38% of all full-time freshmen had no need and received non-need-based gift aid.

UNDERGRADUATE FINANCIAL AID (Fall 2017, est.) 3,010 applied for aid; of those 78% were deemed to have need. 99% of undergraduates with need received aid; of those 34% had need fully met. *Average percent of need met:* 86% (excluding resources awarded to replace EFC). *Average financial aid package:* $40,587 (excluding resources awarded to replace EFC). 40% of all full-time undergraduates had no need and received non-need-based gift aid.

GIFT AID (NEED-BASED) *Total amount:* $76,783,520 (7% federal, 2% state, 87% institutional, 4% external sources). *Receiving aid:* Freshmen: 46% (677); all full-time undergraduates: 42% (2,290). *Average award:* Freshmen: $34,932; Undergraduates: $34,077. *Scholarships, grants, and awards:* Federal Pell, FSEOG, state, private, college/university gift aid from institutional funds.

GIFT AID (NON-NEED-BASED) *Total amount:* $44,069,227 (94% institutional, 6% external sources). *Receiving aid:* Freshmen: 11% (158). Undergraduates: 10% (550). *Average award:* Freshmen: $20,744. Undergraduates: $18,280. *Scholarships, grants, and awards by category:* Academic interests/achievement: biological sciences, business, communication, computer science, engineering/technologies, English, general academic interests/achievements, humanities, international studies, mathematics, physical sciences, social sciences. *Creative arts/performance:* art/fine arts, debating, music, theater/drama. *Special achievements/activities:* community service, leadership. *Tuition waivers:* Full or partial for employees or children of employees, senior citizens. *ROTC:* Army cooperative, Air Force cooperative.

LOANS *Student loans:* $18,420,913 (55% need-based, 45% non-need-based). 42% of past graduating class borrowed through all loan programs. *Average indebtedness per student:* $31,526. *Average need-based loan:* Freshmen: $3390. Undergraduates: $4291. *Parent loans:* $10,747,960 (20% need-based, 80% non-need-based). *Programs:* Federal Direct (Subsidized and Unsubsidized Stafford, PLUS), Perkins, college/university.

WORK-STUDY *Federal work-study:* Total amount: $1,301,352; 471 jobs averaging $2825. *State or other work-study/employment:* Total amount: $498,232 (84% need-based, 16% non-need-based). 195 part-time jobs averaging $3128.

ATHLETIC AWARDS Total amount: $10,658,347 (18% need-based, 82% non-need-based).

APPLYING FOR FINANCIAL AID *Required financial aid forms:* FAFSA, institution's own form, CSS Financial Aid PROFILE, noncustodial (divorced/separated) parent's statement. *Financial aid deadline (priority):* 2/15. *Notification date:* 3/1. Students must reply by 5/1.

CONTACT Mr. John Gudvangen, Director of Financial Aid, University of Denver, University Hall, 2197 South University Boulevard, Denver, CO 80208, 303-871-4020 or toll-free 800-525-9495. *Fax:* 303-871-2341. *E-mail:* finaid@du.edu. *Website:* http://www.du.edu/.

UNIVERSITY OF DETROIT MERCY
Detroit, MI

Tuition & fees: $41,158	Average undergraduate aid package: $34,929

ABOUT THE INSTITUTION Independent Roman Catholic (Jesuit), coed. *Awards:* certificates, diplomas, bachelor's, master's, and doctoral degrees. 50 undergraduate majors. *Total enrollment:* 4,875. Undergraduates: 2,646. Freshmen: 532. Federal methodology is used as a basis for awarding need-based institutional aid.

UNDERGRADUATE EXPENSES for 2017–2018 *Comprehensive fee:* $50,610 includes full-time tuition ($41,158) and room and board ($9452). Full-time tuition and fees vary according to program. Room and board charges vary according to board plan and housing facility. *Part-time tuition:* $1049 per credit hour. Part-time tuition and fees vary according to location and program.

FRESHMAN FINANCIAL AID (Fall 2017, est.) 473 applied for aid; of those 78% were deemed to have need. 100% of freshmen with need received aid; of those 8% had need fully met. *Average percent of need met:* 80% (excluding resources awarded to replace EFC). *Average financial aid package:* $37,388 (excluding resources awarded to replace EFC). 29% of all full-time freshmen had no need and received non-need-based gift aid.

UNDERGRADUATE FINANCIAL AID (Fall 2017, est.) 1,905 applied for aid; of those 85% were deemed to have need. 100% of undergraduates with need received aid; of those 5% had need fully met. *Average percent of need met:* 73% (excluding resources awarded to replace EFC). *Average financial aid package:* $34,929 (excluding resources awarded to replace EFC). 26% of all full-time undergraduates had no need and received non-need-based gift aid.

GIFT AID (NEED-BASED) *Total amount:* $45,135,469 (11% federal, 6% state, 80% institutional, 3% external sources). *Receiving aid:* Freshmen: 68% (366); all full-time undergraduates: 68% (1,588). *Average award:* Freshmen: $32,183; Undergraduates: $27,922. *Scholarships, grants, and awards:* Federal Pell, FSEOG, state, private, college/university gift aid from institutional funds.

GIFT AID (NON-NEED-BASED) *Total amount:* $13,449,309 (99% institutional, 1% external sources). *Receiving aid:* Freshmen: 3% (18). Undergraduates: 1% (30). *Average award:* Freshmen: $23,247. Undergraduates: $21,556. *Scholarships, grants, and awards by category:* Academic interests/achievement: general academic interests/achievements. *Creative arts/performance:* theater/drama. *Special achievements/activities:* religious involvement. *Special characteristics:* children and siblings of alumni, children of faculty/staff. *Tuition waivers:* Full or partial for children of alumni, employees or children of employees, senior citizens.

LOANS *Student loans:* $15,086,124 (90% need-based, 10% non-need-based). 73% of past graduating class borrowed through all loan programs. *Average indebtedness per student:* $36,968. *Average need-based loan:* Freshmen: $2695. Undergraduates: $5073. *Parent loans:* $6,350,794 (82% need-based, 18% non-need-based). *Programs:* Federal Direct (Subsidized and Unsubsidized Stafford, PLUS), Perkins, Federal Nursing, alternative loans.

WORK-STUDY *Federal work-study:* Total amount: $1,188,880; jobs available.

ATHLETIC AWARDS Total amount: $5,673,307 (39% need-based, 61% non-need-based).

APPLYING FOR FINANCIAL AID *Required financial aid form:* FAFSA. *Financial aid deadline (priority):* 4/1. *Notification date:* Continuous beginning 3/1.

CONTACT Jenny McAlonan, Director of Financial Aid and Scholarships, University of Detroit Mercy, 4001 West McNichols Road, Detroit, MI 48221-3038, 313-993-3350 or toll-free 800-635-5020. *Fax:* 313-993-3347. *E-mail:* mcalonjl@udmercy.edu. *Website:* http://www.udmercy.edu/.

UNIVERSITY OF DUBUQUE
Dubuque, IA

Tuition & fees: $29,710	Average undergraduate aid package: $25,561

ABOUT THE INSTITUTION Independent Presbyterian, coed. *Awards:* associate, bachelor's, master's, and doctoral degrees. 42 undergraduate majors. *Total enrollment:* 2,340. Undergraduates: 1,965. Freshmen: 518. Federal methodology is used as a basis for awarding need-based institutional aid.

UNDERGRADUATE EXPENSES for 2017–2018 *Application fee:* $25. *One-time required fee:* $100. *Comprehensive fee:* $39,160 includes full-time tuition ($28,360), mandatory fees ($1350), and room and board ($9450). Room and board charges vary according to board plan and housing facility. *Part-time tuition:* $850 per credit hour.
FRESHMAN FINANCIAL AID (Fall 2017, est.) 565 applied for aid; of those 93% were deemed to have need. 99% of freshmen with need received aid; of those 14% had need fully met. *Average percent of need met:* 74% (excluding resources awarded to replace EFC). *Average financial aid package:* $27,325 (excluding resources awarded to replace EFC). 14% of all full-time freshmen had no need and received non-need-based gift aid.
UNDERGRADUATE FINANCIAL AID (Fall 2017, est.) 1,583 applied for aid; of those 94% were deemed to have need. 99% of undergraduates with need received aid; of those 15% had need fully met. *Average percent of need met:* 61% (excluding resources awarded to replace EFC). *Average financial aid package:* $25,561 (excluding resources awarded to replace EFC). 11% of all full-time undergraduates had no need and received non-need-based gift aid.
GIFT AID (NEED-BASED) *Total amount:* $29,431,240 (15% federal, 8% state, 59% institutional, 18% external sources). *Receiving aid:* Freshmen: 82% (513); all full-time undergraduates: 86% (1,470). *Average award:* Freshmen: $21,846; Undergraduates: $19,452. *Scholarships, grants, and awards:* Federal Pell, FSEOG, state, private, college/university gift aid from institutional funds.
GIFT AID (NON-NEED-BASED) *Total amount:* $6,348,474 (1% state, 45% institutional, 54% external sources). *Receiving aid:* Freshmen: 10% (64). Undergraduates: 11% (183). *Average award:* Freshmen: $13,158. Undergraduates: $11,896. *Scholarships, grants, and awards by category:* Academic interests/achievement: 728 awards ($6,698,044 total): general academic interests/achievements. *Creative arts/performance:* dance, music, performing arts, theater/drama. *Special characteristics:* 396 awards ($363,125 total): children and siblings of alumni, children of educators, children of faculty/staff, out-of-state students, relatives of clergy, religious affiliation, siblings of current students, spouses of current students. *Tuition waivers:* Full or partial for employees or children of employees. *ROTC:* Army.
LOANS *Student loans:* $15,527,388 (79% need-based, 21% non-need-based). 72% of past graduating class borrowed through all loan programs. *Average indebtedness per student:* $30,353. *Average need-based loan:* Freshmen: $5942. Undergraduates: $6673. *Parent loans:* $2,325,480 (53% need-based, 47% non-need-based). *Programs:* Federal Direct (Subsidized and Unsubsidized Stafford, PLUS), Perkins, college/university.
WORK-STUDY *Federal work-study:* Total amount: $1,092,602; 193 jobs averaging $2000. *State or other work-study/employment:* Total amount: $489,420 (53% need-based, 47% non-need-based). 180 part-time jobs averaging $2000.
APPLYING FOR FINANCIAL AID *Required financial aid form:* FAFSA. *Financial aid deadline (priority):* 4/1. *Notification date:* Continuous beginning 3/1. Students must reply within 3 weeks of notification.
CONTACT Teresa Brahm, Director of Student Financial Planning, University of Dubuque, 2000 University Avenue, Dubuque, IA 52001-5050, 563-589-3170 or toll-free 800-722-5583. *Fax:* 563-589-3690. *E-mail:* tbrahm@dbq.edu.
Website: http://www.dbq.edu/.

awarded to replace EFC). *Average financial aid package:* $31,459 (excluding resources awarded to replace EFC). 38% of all full-time freshmen had no need and received non-need-based gift aid.
UNDERGRADUATE FINANCIAL AID (Fall 2017, est.) 1,460 applied for aid; of those 89% were deemed to have need. 100% of undergraduates with need received aid; of those 49% had need fully met. *Average percent of need met:* 87% (excluding resources awarded to replace EFC). *Average financial aid package:* $31,270 (excluding resources awarded to replace EFC). 27% of all full-time undergraduates had no need and received non-need-based gift aid.
GIFT AID (NEED-BASED) *Total amount:* $28,955,195 (9% federal, 10% state, 76% institutional, 5% external sources). *Receiving aid:* Freshmen: 67% (298); all full-time undergraduates: 62% (1,224). *Average award:* Freshmen: $25,202; Undergraduates: $23,566. *Scholarships, grants, and awards:* Federal Pell, FSEOG, state, private, college/university gift aid from institutional funds.
GIFT AID (NON-NEED-BASED) *Total amount:* $13,329,170 (93% institutional, 7% external sources). *Receiving aid:* Freshmen: 14% (62). Undergraduates: 10% (189). *Average award:* Freshmen: $18,287. Undergraduates: $20,251. *Scholarships, grants, and awards by category:* Academic interests/achievement: 2,018 awards ($26,113,185 total): biological sciences, business, communication, computer science, education, engineering/technologies, English, foreign languages, general academic interests/achievements, humanities, international studies, mathematics, physical sciences, premedicine, religion/biblical studies, social sciences. *Creative arts/performance:* 311 awards ($3,401,595 total): art/fine arts, music, performing arts, theater/drama. *Special achievements/activities:* 211 awards ($638,863 total): general special achievements/activities, junior miss, leadership, memberships. *Special characteristics:* 399 awards ($2,924,804 total): children and siblings of alumni, children of educators, children of faculty/staff, international students, local/state students, members of minority groups, religious affiliation, siblings of current students, veterans, veterans' children. *Tuition waivers:* Full or partial for minority students, children of alumni, employees or children of employees, adult students, senior citizens. *ROTC:* Army cooperative.
LOANS *Student loans:* $9,972,825 (72% need-based, 28% non-need-based). 56% of past graduating class borrowed through all loan programs. *Average indebtedness per student:* $30,533. *Average need-based loan:* Freshmen: $3417. Undergraduates: $4795. *Parent loans:* $2,654,687 (70% need-based, 30% non-need-based). *Programs:* Federal Direct (Subsidized and Unsubsidized Stafford, PLUS), Federal Nursing.
WORK-STUDY *Federal work-study:* Total amount: $523,774; 385 jobs averaging $1656. *State or other work-study/employment:* Total amount: $112,619 (2% need-based, 98% non-need-based). 98 part-time jobs averaging $1745.
ATHLETIC AWARDS Total amount: $4,955,043 (33% need-based, 67% non-need-based).
APPLYING FOR FINANCIAL AID *Required financial aid form:* FAFSA. *Financial aid deadline (priority):* 4/1. *Notification date:* Continuous beginning 12/15. Students must reply by 5/1 or within 6 weeks of notification.
CONTACT Ms. Cathleen Wright, Director of Financial Aid, University of Evansville, 1800 Lincoln Avenue, Evansville, IN 47722, 812-488-2364 or toll-free 800-423-8633 Ext. 2468. *Fax:* 812-488-2028. *E-mail:* financialaid@evansville.edu.
Website: http://www.evansville.edu/.

UNIVERSITY OF EVANSVILLE
Evansville, IN

Tuition & fees: $36,416	Average undergraduate aid package: $31,270

ABOUT THE INSTITUTION Independent United Methodist Church, coed. *Awards:* associate, bachelor's, master's, and doctoral degrees. 79 undergraduate majors. *Total enrollment:* 2,516. Undergraduates: 2,342. Freshmen: 442. Both federal and institutional methodology are used as a basis for awarding need-based institutional aid.
UNDERGRADUATE EXPENSES for 2018–2019 *Comprehensive fee:* $48,876 includes full-time tuition ($35,300), mandatory fees ($1116), and room and board ($12,460). *College room only:* $6540. Full-time tuition and fees vary according to location. Room and board charges vary according to board plan, housing facility, and location. *Part-time tuition:* $990 per credit hour. Part-time tuition and fees vary according to course load.
FRESHMAN FINANCIAL AID (Fall 2017, est.) 376 applied for aid; of those 83% were deemed to have need. 100% of freshmen with need received aid; of those 46% had need fully met. *Average percent of need met:* 88% (excluding resources

THE UNIVERSITY OF FINDLAY
Findlay, OH

Tuition & fees: $33,320	Average undergraduate aid package: $29,186

ABOUT THE INSTITUTION Independent Church of God, coed. *Awards:* certificates, associate, bachelor's, master's, and doctoral degrees. 68 undergraduate majors. *Total enrollment:* 4,888. Undergraduates: 3,562. Freshmen: 595. Both federal and institutional methodology are used as a basis for awarding need-based institutional aid.
UNDERGRADUATE EXPENSES for 2017–2018 *Comprehensive fee:* $43,040 includes full-time tuition ($32,330), mandatory fees ($990), and room and board ($9720). *College room only:* $4850. Full-time tuition and fees vary according to program. Room and board charges vary according to board plan and housing facility. *Part-time tuition:* $715 per semester hour. *Part-time fees:* $430 per term. Part-time tuition and fees vary according to course load and program.
FRESHMAN FINANCIAL AID (Fall 2016) 521 applied for aid; of those 87% were deemed to have need. 100% of freshmen with need received aid; of those 27% had need fully met. *Average percent of need met:* 79% (excluding resources awarded

to replace EFC). *Average financial aid package:* $28,326 (excluding resources awarded to replace EFC). 95% of all full-time freshmen had no need and received non-need-based gift aid.

UNDERGRADUATE FINANCIAL AID (Fall 2016) 2,212 applied for aid; of those 86% were deemed to have need. 100% of undergraduates with need received aid; of those 27% had need fully met. *Average percent of need met:* 79% (excluding resources awarded to replace EFC). *Average financial aid package:* $29,186 (excluding resources awarded to replace EFC). 72% of all full-time undergraduates had no need and received non-need-based gift aid.

GIFT AID (NEED-BASED) *Total amount:* $66,883,072 (8% federal, 2% state, 88% institutional, 2% external sources). *Receiving aid:* Freshmen: 83% (452); all full-time undergraduates: 69% (1,909). *Average award:* Freshmen: $27,361; Undergraduates: $25,592. *Scholarships, grants, and awards:* Federal Pell, FSEOG, state, private, college/university gift aid from institutional funds.

GIFT AID (NON-NEED-BASED) *Total amount:* $5,653,335 (1% state, 82% institutional, 17% external sources). *Receiving aid:* Freshmen: 83% (452). Undergraduates: 69% (1,909). *Average award:* Freshmen: $21,948. Undergraduates: $21,595. *Scholarships, grants, and awards by category:* Academic interests/achievement: general academic interests/achievements. Creative arts/performance: music, theater/drama. Special characteristics: children of faculty/staff. *Tuition waivers:* Full or partial for employees or children of employees, senior citizens. *ROTC:* Army cooperative, Air Force cooperative.

LOANS *Student loans:* $32,555,140 (41% need-based, 59% non-need-based). 81% of past graduating class borrowed through all loan programs. *Average indebtedness per student:* $37,424. *Average need-based loan:* Freshmen: $3220. Undergraduates: $4146. *Parent loans:* $10,249,456 (12% need-based, 88% non-need-based). *Programs:* Federal Direct (Subsidized and Unsubsidized Stafford, PLUS), Perkins, private loans.

WORK-STUDY *Federal work-study:* jobs available. *State or other work-study/employment:* Total amount: $1,354,268 (100% need-based). Part-time jobs available.

ATHLETIC AWARDS Total amount: $6,584,483 (21% need-based, 79% non-need-based).

APPLYING FOR FINANCIAL AID *Required financial aid form:* FAFSA. *Financial aid deadline:* 9/1 (priority: 8/1). *Notification date:* Continuous beginning 3/1. Students must reply within 2 weeks of notification.

CONTACT Mr. Joseph F. Spencer, Director of Financial Aid, The University of Findlay, 1000 North Main Street, Findlay, OH 45840-3695, 419-434-5678 or toll-free 800-548-0932. *Fax:* 419-434-4344. *E-mail:* spencer@findlay.edu.
Website: http://www.findlay.edu/.

UNIVERSITY OF FLORIDA
Gainesville, FL

Tuition & fees (FL res): $6381	Average undergraduate aid package: $12,982

ABOUT THE INSTITUTION State-supported, coed. *Awards:* certificates, associate, bachelor's, master's, and doctoral degrees. 99 undergraduate majors. *Total enrollment:* 52,668. Undergraduates: 35,246. Freshmen: 6,423. Federal methodology is used as a basis for awarding need-based institutional aid.

UNDERGRADUATE EXPENSES for 2017–2018 *Application fee:* $30. *Tuition, state resident:* full-time $4477; part-time $149.24 per credit hour. *Tuition, nonresident:* full-time $25,694; part-time $856.45 per credit hour. *Required fees:* full-time $1904. Full-time tuition and fees vary according to course level, course load, location, program, and reciprocity agreements. Part-time tuition and fees vary according to course level, course load, location, program, and reciprocity agreements. *College room and board:* $9910. *Room only:* $5440. Room and board charges vary according to board plan and housing facility.

FRESHMAN FINANCIAL AID (Fall 2016) 5,641 applied for aid; of those 59% were deemed to have need. 98% of freshmen with need received aid; of those 28% had need fully met. *Average percent of need met:* 99% (excluding resources awarded to replace EFC). *Average financial aid package:* $13,685 (excluding resources awarded to replace EFC). 7% of all full-time freshmen had no need and received non-need-based gift aid.

UNDERGRADUATE FINANCIAL AID (Fall 2016) 21,465 applied for aid; of those 75% were deemed to have need. 97% of undergraduates with need received aid; of those 23% had need fully met. *Average percent of need met:* 97% (excluding

resources awarded to replace EFC). *Average financial aid package:* $12,982 (excluding resources awarded to replace EFC). 6% of all full-time undergraduates had no need and received non-need-based gift aid.

GIFT AID (NEED-BASED) *Total amount:* $77,049,372 (57% federal, 9% state, 34% institutional). *Receiving aid:* Freshmen: 30% (1,898); all full-time undergraduates: 31% (10,113). *Average award:* Freshmen: $8328; Undergraduates: $7612. *Scholarships, grants, and awards:* Federal Pell, FSEOG, state, private, college/university gift aid from institutional funds, United Negro College Fund.

GIFT AID (NON-NEED-BASED) *Total amount:* $104,229,932 (2% federal, 67% state, 21% institutional, 10% external sources). *Receiving aid:* Freshmen: 44% (2,845). Undergraduates: 34% (10,988). *Average award:* Freshmen: $2946. Undergraduates: $2717. *Scholarships, grants, and awards by category:* Academic interests/achievement: agriculture, architecture, business, communication, computer science, education, engineering/technologies, general academic interests/achievements, home economics, military science. Creative arts/performance: art/fine arts, dance, general creative arts/performance, journalism/publications, music, performing arts, theater/drama. Special achievements/activities: community service, general special achievements/activities, leadership. Special characteristics: children of faculty/staff, members of minority groups, out-of-state students. *Tuition waivers:* Full or partial for employees or children of employees, senior citizens. *ROTC:* Army, Naval, Air Force.

LOANS *Student loans:* $64,520,549 (49% need-based, 51% non-need-based). 38% of past graduating class borrowed through all loan programs. *Average indebtedness per student:* $22,192. *Average need-based loan:* Freshmen: $3480. Undergraduates: $4472. *Parent loans:* $20,908,610 (100% non-need-based). *Programs:* Federal Direct (Subsidized and Unsubsidized Stafford, PLUS), Perkins, college/university.

WORK-STUDY *Federal work-study:* 1,048 jobs averaging $1970. *State or other work-study/employment:* Total amount: $13,430,600 (1% need-based, 99% non-need-based). 5,059 part-time jobs averaging $1856.

ATHLETIC AWARDS Total amount: $11,487,460 (100% non-need-based).

APPLYING FOR FINANCIAL AID *Required financial aid form:* FAFSA. *Financial aid deadline (priority):* 3/15. *Notification date:* Continuous beginning 4/4.

CONTACT Mr. Richard D. Wilder, Director of Student Financial Affairs, University of Florida, S-107 Criser Hall, Gainesville, FL 32611-4025, 352-294-3220. *Fax:* 352-392-2861. *E-mail:* rwilder@ufl.edu.
Website: http://www.ufl.edu/.

UNIVERSITY OF FORT LAUDERDALE
Lauderhill, FL

CONTACT Financial Aid Office, University of Fort Lauderdale, 4093 NW 16th Street, Lauderhill, FL 33313, 954-486-7728.
Website: http://uftl.edu/.

UNIVERSITY OF GEORGIA
Athens, GA

Tuition & fees (GA res): $11,818	Average undergraduate aid package: $12,182

ABOUT THE INSTITUTION State-supported, coed. *Awards:* certificates, bachelor's, master's, and doctoral degrees. 121 undergraduate majors. *Total enrollment:* 37,606. Undergraduates: 28,848. Freshmen: 5,826. Federal methodology is used as a basis for awarding need-based institutional aid.

UNDERGRADUATE EXPENSES for 2017–2018 *Application fee:* $60. *Tuition, state resident:* full-time $9552. *Tuition, nonresident:* full-time $28,126. *Required fees:* full-time $2266. Full-time tuition and fees vary according to course load, location, and program. Part-time tuition and fees vary according to course load, location, and program. *College room and board:* $10,060; *Room only:* $6104. Room and board charges vary according to board plan and housing facility.

FRESHMAN FINANCIAL AID (Fall 2017, est.) 5,001 applied for aid; of those 53% were deemed to have need. 99% of freshmen with need received aid; of those 28% had need fully met. *Average percent of need met:* 77% (excluding resources

awarded to replace EFC). *Average financial aid package:* $13,999 (excluding resources awarded to replace EFC). 4% of all full-time freshmen had no need and received non-need-based gift aid.

UNDERGRADUATE FINANCIAL AID (Fall 2017, est.) 19,275 applied for aid; of those 62% were deemed to have need. 98% of undergraduates with need received aid; of those 23% had need fully met. *Average percent of need met:* 72% (excluding resources awarded to replace EFC). *Average financial aid package:* $12,182 (excluding resources awarded to replace EFC). 4% of all full-time undergraduates had no need and received non-need-based gift aid.

GIFT AID (NEED-BASED) *Total amount:* $102,028,975 (28% federal, 63% state, 6% institutional, 3% external sources). *Receiving aid:* Freshmen: 44% (2,589); all full-time undergraduates: 41% (11,064). *Average award:* Freshmen: $10,769; Undergraduates: $9317. *Scholarships, grants, and awards:* Federal Pell, FSEOG, state, private, college/university gift aid from institutional funds.

GIFT AID (NON-NEED-BASED) *Total amount:* $101,283,531 (93% state, 4% institutional, 3% external sources). *Receiving aid:* Freshmen: 11% (630). Undergraduates: 8% (2,050). *Average award:* Freshmen: $3636. Undergraduates: $2640. *Scholarships, grants, and awards by category:* Academic interests/achievement: 26,962 awards ($175,405,138 total): agriculture, business, education, general academic interests/achievements. *Creative arts/performance:* 123 awards ($100,780 total): music. *Special characteristics:* 255 awards ($355,999 total): local/state students. *Tuition waivers:* Full or partial for senior citizens. *ROTC:* Army, Air Force.

LOANS *Student loans:* $73,121,002 (60% need-based, 40% non-need-based). 44% of past graduating class borrowed through all loan programs. *Average indebtedness per student:* $23,403. *Average need-based loan:* Freshmen: $3299. Undergraduates: $4191. *Parent loans:* $36,761,989 (28% need-based, 72% non-need-based). *Programs:* Federal Direct (Subsidized and Unsubsidized Stafford, PLUS), state, college/university.

WORK-STUDY *Federal work-study:* Total amount: $1,033,313; 388 jobs averaging $2414.

ATHLETIC AWARDS Total amount: $10,087,286 (29% need-based, 71% non-need-based).

APPLYING FOR FINANCIAL AID *Required financial aid form:* FAFSA. *Financial aid deadline (priority):* 12/15. *Notification date:* Continuous beginning 12/1. Students must reply within 2 weeks of notification.

CONTACT Ms. Bonnie C. Joerschke, Director of Financial Aid, University of Georgia, 220 Holmes/Hunter Academic Building, Athens, GA 30602-6114, 706-542-6147. *Fax:* 706-542-8217. *E-mail:* osfa@uga.edu.
Website: http://www.uga.edu/.

UNIVERSITY OF GUAM
Mangilao, GU

CONTACT Office of Financial Aid, University of Guam, UOG Station, Mangilao, GU 96923, 671-735-2288. *Fax:* 671-734-2907.
Website: http://www.uog.edu/.

UNIVERSITY OF HARTFORD
West Hartford, CT

Tuition & fees: $40,694	Average undergraduate aid package: $27,599

ABOUT THE INSTITUTION Independent, coed. *Awards:* certificates, diplomas, associate, bachelor's, master's, and doctoral degrees. 80 undergraduate majors. *Total enrollment:* 6,561. Undergraduates: 5,069. Freshmen: 1,334. Federal methodology is used as a basis for awarding need-based institutional aid.

UNDERGRADUATE EXPENSES for 2018–2019 *Application fee:* $35. *Comprehensive fee:* $53,170 includes full-time tuition ($37,802), mandatory fees ($2892), and room and board ($12,476). *College room only:* $8008. Full-time tuition and fees vary according to program. Room and board charges vary according to board plan and housing facility. Part-time tuition and fees vary according to course load and program. *Payment plan:* Tuition prepayment.

FRESHMAN FINANCIAL AID (Fall 2017, est.) 1,174 applied for aid; of those 89% were deemed to have need. 100% of freshmen with need received aid; of those

14% had need fully met. *Average percent of need met:* 67% (excluding resources awarded to replace EFC). *Average financial aid package:* $27,225 (excluding resources awarded to replace EFC). 16% of all full-time freshmen had no need and received non-need-based gift aid.

UNDERGRADUATE FINANCIAL AID (Fall 2017, est.) 3,590 applied for aid; of those 91% were deemed to have need. 100% of undergraduates with need received aid; of those 13% had need fully met. *Average percent of need met:* 68% (excluding resources awarded to replace EFC). *Average financial aid package:* $27,599 (excluding resources awarded to replace EFC). 19% of all full-time undergraduates had no need and received non-need-based gift aid.

GIFT AID (NEED-BASED) *Total amount:* $70,281,985 (10% federal, 1% state, 88% institutional, 1% external sources). *Receiving aid:* Freshmen: 80% (1,033); all full-time undergraduates: 72% (3,227). *Average award:* Freshmen: $23,015; Undergraduates: $22,152. *Scholarships, grants, and awards:* Federal Pell, FSEOG, state, private, college/university gift aid from institutional funds.

GIFT AID (NON-NEED-BASED) *Total amount:* $17,320,825 (99% institutional, 1% external sources). *Receiving aid:* Freshmen: 9% (117). Undergraduates: 7% (295). *Average award:* Freshmen: $17,578. Undergraduates: $16,666. *Scholarships, grants, and awards by category:* Academic interests/achievement: architecture, area/ethnic studies, biological sciences, business, communication, computer science, education, engineering/technologies, English, foreign languages, general academic interests/achievements, home economics, humanities, international studies, mathematics, premedicine, religion/biblical studies, social sciences. *Creative arts/performance:* applied art and design, art/fine arts, cinema/film/broadcasting, creative writing, dance, debating, general creative arts/performance, journalism/publications, music, performing arts, theater/drama. *Special achievements/activities:* community service, leadership. *Special characteristics:* adult students, children of current students, children of faculty/staff, children of union members/company employees, children with a deceased or disabled parent, ethnic background, first-generation college students, handicapped students, international students, local/state students, members of minority groups, parents of current students, previous college experience, religious affiliation, siblings of current students, spouses of current students, twins, veterans, veterans' children. *Tuition waivers:* Full or partial for employees or children of employees, senior citizens. *ROTC:* Army cooperative, Air Force cooperative.

LOANS *Student loans:* $38,222,746 (72% need-based, 28% non-need-based). *Average need-based loan:* Freshmen: $3362. Undergraduates: $4621. *Parent loans:* $17,536,660 (63% need-based, 37% non-need-based). *Programs:* Federal Direct (Subsidized and Unsubsidized Stafford, PLUS), Perkins.

WORK-STUDY *Federal work-study:* Total amount: $988,747; 516 jobs averaging $1916. *State or other work-study/employment:* Total amount: $1,491,703 (74% need-based, 26% non-need-based). Part-time jobs available.

ATHLETIC AWARDS Total amount: $5,641,720 (32% need-based, 68% non-need-based).

APPLYING FOR FINANCIAL AID *Required financial aid form:* FAFSA. *Financial aid deadline (priority):* 2/15. *Notification date:* Continuous beginning 3/1. Students must reply by 5/1 or within 2 weeks of notification.

CONTACT Victoria Hampton, Office of Financial Aid, University of Hartford, 200 Bloomfield Avenue, West Hartford, CT 06117-1599, 860-768-4296 or toll-free 800-947-4303. *Fax:* 860-768-4961. *E-mail:* finaid@hartford.edu.
Website: http://www.hartford.edu/.

UNIVERSITY OF HAWAII AT HILO
Hilo, HI

CONTACT Financial Aid Office, University of Hawaii at Hilo, 200 West Kawili Street, Hilo, HI 96720-4091, 808-932-7449 or toll-free 800-897-4456. *Fax:* 808-932-7459. *E-mail:* uhhfao@hawaii.edu.
Website: http://hilo.hawaii.edu/.

UNIVERSITY OF HAWAII AT MANOA
Honolulu, HI

Tuition & fees (HI res): $11,970	Average undergraduate aid package: $14,944

ABOUT THE INSTITUTION State-supported, coed. *Awards:* certificates, bachelor's, master's, and doctoral degrees. 90 undergraduate majors. *Total*

enrollment: 17,612. Undergraduates: 12,881. Freshmen: 1,959. Federal methodology is used as a basis for awarding need-based institutional aid.

UNDERGRADUATE EXPENSES for 2018–2019 *Application fee:* $70. *Tuition, state resident:* full-time $11,088; part-time $462 per credit hour. *Tuition, nonresident:* full-time $33,120; part-time $1380 per credit hour. *Required fees:* full-time $882; $462 per term. Full-time tuition and fees vary according to class time, course level, course load, degree level, program, reciprocity agreements, and student level. Part-time tuition and fees vary according to class time, course level, course load, degree level, program, reciprocity agreements, and student level. *College room and board:* $13,689; *Room only:* $9663. Room and board charges vary according to board plan and housing facility.

FRESHMAN FINANCIAL AID (Fall 2017, est.) 1,534 applied for aid; of those 64% were deemed to have need. 99% of freshmen with need received aid; of those 36% had need fully met. *Average percent of need met:* 75% (excluding resources awarded to replace EFC). *Average financial aid package:* $15,477 (excluding resources awarded to replace EFC). 28% of all full-time freshmen had no need and received non-need-based gift aid.

UNDERGRADUATE FINANCIAL AID (Fall 2017, est.) 8,894 applied for aid; of those 69% were deemed to have need. 98% of undergraduates with need received aid; of those 30% had need fully met. *Average percent of need met:* 71% (excluding resources awarded to replace EFC). *Average financial aid package:* $14,944 (excluding resources awarded to replace EFC). 23% of all full-time undergraduates had no need and received non-need-based gift aid.

GIFT AID (NEED-BASED) *Total amount:* $43,966,207 (39% federal, 4% state, 51% institutional, 6% external sources). *Receiving aid:* Freshmen: 58% (961); all full-time undergraduates: 53% (5,800). *Average award:* Freshmen: $10,392; Undergraduates: $10,011. *Scholarships, grants, and awards:* Federal Pell, FSEOG, state, private, college/university gift aid from institutional funds.

GIFT AID (NON-NEED-BASED) *Total amount:* $18,026,140 (62% institutional, 38% external sources). *Receiving aid:* Freshmen: 16% (262). Undergraduates: 12% (1,335). *Average award:* Freshmen: $12,121. Undergraduates: $13,434. *Scholarships, grants, and awards by category:* Academic interests/achievement: general academic interests/achievements. *Creative arts/performance:* general creative arts/performance. *Special achievements/activities:* general special achievements/activities. *Special characteristics:* general special characteristics. *Tuition waivers:* Full or partial for minority students, employees or children of employees, adult students, senior citizens. *ROTC:* Army, Air Force.

LOANS *Student loans:* $37,552,442 (53% need-based, 47% non-need-based). 45% of past graduating class borrowed through all loan programs. *Average indebtedness per student:* $24,233. *Average need-based loan:* Freshmen: $4487. Undergraduates: $4877. *Parent loans:* $28,142,814 (100% non-need-based). *Programs:* Federal Direct (Subsidized and Unsubsidized Stafford, PLUS), state.

WORK-STUDY *Federal work-study:* Total amount: $1,230,670; 432 jobs averaging $2849. *State or other work-study/employment:* Part-time jobs available.

ATHLETIC AWARDS Total amount: $7,997,107 (1% need-based, 99% non-need-based).

APPLYING FOR FINANCIAL AID *Required financial aid form:* FAFSA. *Financial aid deadline (priority):* 2/1. *Notification date:* Continuous beginning 3/1. Students must reply by 5/1 or within 4 weeks of notification.

CONTACT Jodie Kuba, Director of Financial Aid Services, University of Hawaii at Manoa, 2600 Campus Road, Suite 112, Honolulu, HI 96822, 808-956-7251 or toll-free 800-823-9771. *Fax:* 808-956-3985. *E-mail:* finaid@hawaii.edu. *Website:* http://manoa.hawaii.edu/.

UNIVERSITY OF HAWAII–WEST OAHU
Kapolei, HI

CONTACT Lester Ishimoto, Office of Financial Aid, University of Hawaii–West Oahu, 91-1001 Farrington Highway, Kapolei, HI 96707, 808-689-2689 or toll-free 866-299-8656. *Fax:* 808-689-2691. *E-mail:* uhwo-finaid-l@lists.hawaii.edu. *Website:* http://www.uhwo.hawaii.edu/.

UNIVERSITY OF HOLY CROSS
New Orleans, LA

ABOUT THE INSTITUTION Independent Roman Catholic, coed. 17 undergraduate majors.

GIFT AID (NEED-BASED) *Scholarships, grants, and awards:* Federal Pell, FSEOG, state, private, college/university gift aid from institutional funds, United Negro College Fund.

GIFT AID (NON-NEED-BASED) *Scholarships, grants, and awards by category:* Academic interests/achievement: biological sciences, business, education, English, general academic interests/achievements, health fields, home economics, humanities, premedicine, religion/biblical studies, social sciences. *Special characteristics:* children of faculty/staff, general special characteristics, relatives of clergy, religious affiliation.

LOANS *Programs:* Federal Direct (Subsidized and Unsubsidized Stafford, PLUS), state.

APPLYING FOR FINANCIAL AID *Required financial aid form:* FAFSA.

CONTACT Ms. Hayden Wagar, Director of Financial Aid, University of Holy Cross, 4123 Woodland Drive, New Orleans, LA 70131-7399, 504-398-2133 or toll-free 800-259-7744. *Fax:* 504-394-1237. *E-mail:* hwagar@uhcno.edu. *Website:* http://www.uhcno.edu/.

UNIVERSITY OF HOUSTON
Houston, TX

Tuition & fees (TX res): $11,887	Average undergraduate aid package: $12,374

ABOUT THE INSTITUTION State-supported, coed. *Awards:* bachelor's, master's, and doctoral degrees. 87 undergraduate majors. *Total enrollment:* 45,364. Undergraduates: 37,215. Freshmen: 4,959. Federal methodology is used as a basis for awarding need-based institutional aid.

UNDERGRADUATE EXPENSES for 2017–2018 *Application fee:* $75. *Tuition, state resident:* full-time $10,905; part-time $364 per credit hour. *Tuition, nonresident:* full-time $26,355; part-time $879 per credit hour. *Required fees:* full-time $982. Full-time tuition and fees vary according to course level, course load, degree level, program, and student level. Part-time tuition and fees vary according to course level, course load, degree level, program, and student level. *College room and board:* $9984. Room and board charges vary according to board plan and housing facility. *Payment plan:* Guaranteed tuition.

FRESHMAN FINANCIAL AID (Fall 2017, est.) 3,944 applied for aid; of those 81% were deemed to have need. 96% of freshmen with need received aid; of those 17% had need fully met. *Average percent of need met:* 63% (excluding resources awarded to replace EFC). *Average financial aid package:* $12,712 (excluding resources awarded to replace EFC). 8% of all full-time freshmen had no need and received non-need-based gift aid.

UNDERGRADUATE FINANCIAL AID (Fall 2017, est.) 19,203 applied for aid; of those 88% were deemed to have need. 94% of undergraduates with need received aid; of those 15% had need fully met. *Average percent of need met:* 60% (excluding resources awarded to replace EFC). *Average financial aid package:* $12,374 (excluding resources awarded to replace EFC). 3% of all full-time undergraduates had no need and received non-need-based gift aid.

GIFT AID (NEED-BASED) *Total amount:* $138,582,315 (49% federal, 17% state, 28% institutional, 6% external sources). *Receiving aid:* Freshmen: 59% (2,822); all full-time undergraduates: 52% (13,797). *Average award:* Freshmen: $9811; Undergraduates: $8306. *Scholarships, grants, and awards:* Federal Pell, FSEOG, state, private, college/university gift aid from institutional funds.

GIFT AID (NON-NEED-BASED) *Total amount:* $6,282,181 (1% state, 76% institutional, 23% external sources). *Receiving aid:* Freshmen: 3% (155). Undergraduates: 2% (532). *Average award:* Freshmen: $5191. Undergraduates: $4697. *Scholarships, grants, and awards by category:* Academic interests/achievement: architecture, area/ethnic studies, biological sciences, business, communication, computer science, education, engineering/technologies, English, foreign languages, general academic interests/achievements, health fields, humanities, international studies, library science, mathematics, physical sciences, premedicine, social sciences. *Creative arts/performance:* art/fine arts, creative writing, dance, journalism/publications, music, performing arts, theater/drama. *Special achievements/activities:* cheerleading/drum major, community service, general special achievements/activities, hobbies/interests, leadership. *Special characteristics:* children and siblings of alumni, first-generation college students, handicapped students, international students, local/state students, out-of-state students, previous college experience. *ROTC:* Army, Naval cooperative, Air Force.

LOANS *Student loans:* $117,330,716 (83% need-based, 17% non-need-based). 50% of past graduating class borrowed through all loan programs. *Average indebtedness per student:* $23,746. *Average need-based loan:* Freshmen: $5477. Undergraduates: $7226. *Parent loans:* $12,531,287 (45% need-based, 55% non-need-based). *Programs:* Federal Direct (Subsidized and Unsubsidized Stafford, PLUS), Perkins, state.

WORK-STUDY *Federal work-study:* Total amount: $3,267,128; 781 jobs averaging $4173. *State or other work-study/employment:* Total amount: $174,936 (100% need-based). 45 part-time jobs averaging $3887.

ATHLETIC AWARDS Total amount: $6,612,966 (73% need-based, 27% non-need-based).

APPLYING FOR FINANCIAL AID *Required financial aid form:* FAFSA. *Financial aid deadline (priority):* 3/15. *Notification date:* Continuous beginning 3/1. Students must reply by 8/1.

CONTACT Office of Scholarships and Financial Aid, University of Houston, 4800 Calhoun Road, Houston, TX 77204, 713-743-1010. *Fax:* 713-743-9098. *Website:* http://www.uh.edu/.

UNIVERSITY OF HOUSTON–CLEAR LAKE
Houston, TX

Tuition & fees (TX res): $6873	Average undergraduate aid package: $8767

ABOUT THE INSTITUTION State-supported, coed. *Awards:* certificates, bachelor's, master's, and doctoral degrees. 36 undergraduate majors. *Total enrollment:* 8,542. Undergraduates: 5,798. Freshmen: 218. Federal methodology is used as a basis for awarding need-based institutional aid.

UNDERGRADUATE EXPENSES for 2017–2018 *Application fee:* $45. *Tuition, state resident:* full-time $6240; part-time $215 per credit hour. *Tuition, nonresident:* full-time $18,630; part-time $738 per credit hour. *Required fees:* full-time $633; $602 per term. Full-time tuition and fees vary according to course load, degree level, and program. Part-time tuition and fees vary according to course load, degree level, and program. *Room only:* $4852. Room and board charges vary according to housing facility.

FRESHMAN FINANCIAL AID (Fall 2016) 165 applied for aid; of those 85% were deemed to have need. 91% of freshmen with need received aid; of those 12% had need fully met. *Average percent of need met:* 64% (excluding resources awarded to replace EFC). *Average financial aid package:* $11,771 (excluding resources awarded to replace EFC). 15% of all full-time freshmen had no need and received non-need-based gift aid.

UNDERGRADUATE FINANCIAL AID (Fall 2016) 1,916 applied for aid; of those 94% were deemed to have need. 94% of undergraduates with need received aid; of those 4% had need fully met. *Average percent of need met:* 45% (excluding resources awarded to replace EFC). *Average financial aid package:* $8767 (excluding resources awarded to replace EFC). 6% of all full-time undergraduates had no need and received non-need-based gift aid.

GIFT AID (NEED-BASED) *Total amount:* $13,840,450 (64% federal, 13% state, 21% institutional, 2% external sources). *Receiving aid:* Freshmen: 48% (94); all full-time undergraduates: 31% (1,286). *Average award:* Freshmen: $12,039; Undergraduates: $6891. *Scholarships, grants, and awards:* Federal Pell, FSEOG, state, private, college/university gift aid from institutional funds.

GIFT AID (NON-NEED-BASED) *Total amount:* $2,401,435 (6% federal, 77% institutional, 17% external sources). *Receiving aid:* Freshmen: 24% (47). Undergraduates: 15% (634). *Average award:* Freshmen: $5360. Undergraduates: $2149. *Scholarships, grants, and awards by category: Academic interests/achievement:* biological sciences, business, computer science, education, humanities, mathematics, social sciences. *Creative arts/performance:* art/fine arts. *Special achievements/activities:* community service, general special achievements/activities, leadership. *Special characteristics:* local/state students, veterans, veterans' children. *Tuition waivers:* Full or partial for senior citizens.

LOANS *Student loans:* $16,456,730 (45% need-based, 55% non-need-based). 18% of past graduating class borrowed through all loan programs. *Average need-based*

loan: Freshmen: $3245. Undergraduates: $4452. *Parent loans:* $191,176 (100% non-need-based). *Programs:* Federal Direct (Subsidized and Unsubsidized Stafford, PLUS), Perkins, state, college/university.

WORK-STUDY *Federal work-study:* jobs available. *State or other work-study/employment:* Total amount: $55,726 (100% need-based). Part-time jobs available.

APPLYING FOR FINANCIAL AID *Required financial aid form:* FAFSA. *Financial aid deadline (priority):* 3/15. *Notification date:* Continuous beginning 4/1. Students must reply within 2 weeks of notification.

CONTACT Dr. Billy Satterfield, Executive Director of Student Financial Aid, University of Houston–Clear Lake, 2700 Bay Area Boulevard, Houston, TX 77058-1098, 281-283-2480. *Fax:* 281-283-2502. *E-mail:* satterfield@uhcl.edu. *Website:* http://www.uhcl.edu/.

UNIVERSITY OF HOUSTON–DOWNTOWN
Houston, TX

Tuition & fees (TX res): $7832	Average undergraduate aid package: $9634

ABOUT THE INSTITUTION State-supported, coed. *Awards:* certificates, bachelor's, and master's degrees. 36 undergraduate majors. *Total enrollment:* 13,919. Undergraduates: 12,407. Freshmen: 967. Federal methodology is used as a basis for awarding need-based institutional aid.

UNDERGRADUATE EXPENSES for 2018–2019 *Application fee:* $50. *Tuition, state resident:* full-time $6660; part-time $222 per credit hour. *Tuition, nonresident:* full-time $19,110; part-time $637 per credit hour. *Required fees:* full-time $1172. Full-time tuition and fees vary according to course load and program. Part-time tuition and fees vary according to course load and program.

FRESHMAN FINANCIAL AID (Fall 2017, est.) 785 applied for aid; of those 90% were deemed to have need. 95% of freshmen with need received aid; of those 2% had need fully met. *Average percent of need met:* 54% (excluding resources awarded to replace EFC). *Average financial aid package:* $8871 (excluding resources awarded to replace EFC). 1% of all full-time freshmen had no need and received non-need-based gift aid.

UNDERGRADUATE FINANCIAL AID (Fall 2017, est.) 5,116 applied for aid; of those 92% were deemed to have need. 95% of undergraduates with need received aid; of those 40% had need fully met. *Average percent of need met:* 58% (excluding resources awarded to replace EFC). *Average financial aid package:* $9634 (excluding resources awarded to replace EFC). 5% of all full-time undergraduates had no need and received non-need-based gift aid.

GIFT AID (NEED-BASED) *Total amount:* $35,920,113 (81% federal, 11% state, 8% institutional). *Receiving aid:* Freshmen: 67% (572); all full-time undergraduates: 56% (3,532). *Average award:* Freshmen: $5372; Undergraduates: $4453. *Scholarships, grants, and awards:* Federal Pell, FSEOG, state, private, college/university gift aid from institutional funds.

GIFT AID (NON-NEED-BASED) *Total amount:* $5,172,709 (12% state, 80% institutional, 8% external sources). *Receiving aid:* Undergraduates: 1. *Average award:* Freshmen: $3035. Undergraduates: $2300. *Scholarships, grants, and awards by category: Academic interests/achievement:* business, general academic interests/achievements. *Special achievements/activities:* community service, general special achievements/activities, leadership. *Special characteristics:* general special characteristics. *Tuition waivers:* Full or partial for senior citizens. *ROTC:* Army cooperative, Air Force cooperative.

LOANS *Student loans:* $37,521,540 (99% need-based, 1% non-need-based). 53% of past graduating class borrowed through all loan programs. *Average indebtedness per student:* $25,747. *Average need-based loan:* Freshmen: $1063. Undergraduates: $8160. *Parent loans:* $133,453 (100% need-based). *Programs:* Federal Direct (Subsidized and Unsubsidized Stafford, PLUS), state.

WORK-STUDY *Federal work-study:* Total amount: $761,915; jobs available. *State or other work-study/employment:* Total amount: $102,546 (100% need-based). Part-time jobs available.

APPLYING FOR FINANCIAL AID *Required financial aid form:* FAFSA. *Financial aid deadline (priority):* 4/1. *Notification date:* Continuous beginning 4/15. Students must reply within 4 weeks of notification.

CONTACT Office of Scholarships and Financial Aid, University of Houston–Downtown, One Main Street S330, Houston, TX 77002, 713-221-8041. *Fax:* 713-223-7483. *E-mail:* uhdfinaid@uhd.edu. *Website:* http://www.uhd.edu/.

UNIVERSITY OF HOUSTON–VICTORIA
Victoria, TX

Tuition & fees (TX res): $7627	Average undergraduate aid package: $9972

ABOUT THE INSTITUTION State-supported, coed. 16 undergraduate majors. Federal methodology is used as a basis for awarding need-based institutional aid.
UNDERGRADUATE EXPENSES for 2017–2018 Tuition, state resident: full-time $5929; part-time $197.62 per credit hour. *Tuition, nonresident:* full-time $18,379; part-time $612.62 per credit hour. *Required fees:* full-time $1698; $84.50 per credit hour. Full-time tuition and fees vary according to course level and course load. Part-time tuition and fees vary according to course level and course load. *College room and board:* $7698; *Room only:* $4250. Room and board charges vary according to board plan and housing facility. *Payment plan:* Guaranteed tuition.
UNDERGRADUATE FINANCIAL AID (Fall 2016) 1,324 applied for aid; of those 90% were deemed to have need. 98% of undergraduates with need received aid; of those 16% had need fully met. *Average percent of need met:* 70% (excluding resources awarded to replace EFC). *Average financial aid package:* $9972 (excluding resources awarded to replace EFC). 4% of all full-time undergraduates had no need and received non-need-based gift aid.
GIFT AID (NEED-BASED) Total amount: $9,106,272 (66% federal, 18% state, 16% institutional). *Receiving aid:* Entering class: 77% (230); all full-time undergraduates: 70% (1,111). *Average award:* Freshmen: $8188; Undergraduates: $5963. *Scholarships, grants, and awards:* Federal Pell, FSEOG, state, private, college/university gift aid from institutional funds.
GIFT AID (NON-NEED-BASED) Total amount: $1,117,242 (4% federal, 76% institutional, 20% external sources). *Receiving aid:* Freshmen: 67% (202). Undergraduates: 30% (482). *Average award:* Freshmen: $1381. Undergraduates: $1489. *Scholarships, grants, and awards by category:* Academic interests/achievement: biological sciences, business, communication, computer science, education, general academic interests/achievements, humanities, mathematics, social sciences. *Special achievements/activities:* community service, leadership, memberships. *Tuition waivers:* Full or partial for senior citizens.
LOANS Student loans: $11,862,032 (44% need-based, 56% non-need-based). *Parent loans:* $293,208 (100% non-need-based). *Programs:* Federal Direct (Subsidized and Unsubsidized Stafford, PLUS), state.
WORK-STUDY Federal work-study: jobs available. *State or other work-study/employment:* Total amount: $25,188 (100% need-based). Part-time jobs available.
ATHLETIC AWARDS Total amount: $261,500 (100% non-need-based).
APPLYING FOR FINANCIAL AID Required financial aid forms: FAFSA, institution's own form. *Financial aid deadline (priority):* 3/15. *Notification date:* Continuous beginning 3/30. Students must reply within 3 weeks of notification.
CONTACT Carolyn Mallory, Director of Financial Aid, University of Houston–Victoria, 3007 North Ben Wilson, Victoria, TX 77901-5731, 361-570-4131 or toll-free 877-970-4848 Ext. 110. *Fax:* 361-580-5555. *E-mail:* malloryc@uhv.edu. *Website:* http://www.uhv.edu/.

UNIVERSITY OF IDAHO
Moscow, ID

Tuition & fees (ID res): $7488	Average undergraduate aid package: $13,785

ABOUT THE INSTITUTION State-supported, coed. *Awards:* certificates, bachelor's, master's, and doctoral degrees. 98 undergraduate majors. *Total enrollment:* 12,072. Undergraduates: 9,885. Freshmen: 1,538. Federal methodology is used as a basis for awarding need-based institutional aid.

UNDERGRADUATE EXPENSES for 2017–2018 Application fee: $60. *Tuition, state resident:* full-time $5346; part-time $312 per credit hour. *Tuition, nonresident:* full-time $21,670; part-time $1129 per credit hour. *Required fees:* full-time $2142; $62 per credit hour. Full-time tuition and fees vary according to course load, program, and reciprocity agreements. Part-time tuition and fees vary according to program and reciprocity agreements. *College room and board:* $8670. Room and board charges vary according to board plan and housing facility.
FRESHMAN FINANCIAL AID (Fall 2016) 1,535 applied for aid; of those 74% were deemed to have need. 99% of freshmen with need received aid; of those 34% had need fully met. *Average percent of need met:* 80% (excluding resources awarded to replace EFC). *Average financial aid package:* $13,930 (excluding resources awarded to replace EFC). 28% of all full-time freshmen had no need and received non-need-based gift aid.
UNDERGRADUATE FINANCIAL AID (Fall 2016) 6,228 applied for aid; of those 81% were deemed to have need. 97% of undergraduates with need received aid; of those 32% had need fully met. *Average percent of need met:* 78% (excluding resources awarded to replace EFC). *Average financial aid package:* $13,785 (excluding resources awarded to replace EFC). 21% of all full-time undergraduates had no need and received non-need-based gift aid.
GIFT AID (NEED-BASED) Total amount: $19,384,317 (71% federal, 18% state, 11% institutional). *Receiving aid:* Freshmen: 40% (699); all full-time undergraduates: 44% (3,463). *Average award:* Freshmen: $4537; Undergraduates: $4596. *Scholarships, grants, and awards:* Federal Pell, FSEOG, state, private, college/university gift aid from institutional funds.
GIFT AID (NON-NEED-BASED) Total amount: $13,623,604 (1% state, 81% institutional, 18% external sources). *Receiving aid:* Freshmen: 55% (963). Undergraduates: 40% (3,175). *Average award:* Freshmen: $5608. Undergraduates: $5239. *Scholarships, grants, and awards by category:* Academic interests/achievement: agriculture, architecture, biological sciences, business, communication, computer science, education, engineering/technologies, English, foreign languages, general academic interests/achievements, health fields, home economics, humanities, international studies, library science, mathematics, military science, physical sciences, premedicine, social sciences. *Creative arts/performance:* applied art and design, art/fine arts, creative writing, dance, general creative arts/performance, journalism/publications, music, performing arts, theater/drama. *Special achievements/activities:* cheerleading/drum major, general special achievements/activities, junior miss, leadership, rodeo. *Special characteristics:* adult students, children and siblings of alumni, children of faculty/staff, ethnic background, first-generation college students, general special characteristics, handicapped students, international students, local/state students, members of minority groups, out-of-state students, veterans, veterans' children. *Tuition waivers:* Full or partial for employees or children of employees. *ROTC:* Army, Naval, Air Force cooperative.
LOANS Student loans: $33,784,159 (50% need-based, 50% non-need-based). 59% of past graduating class borrowed through all loan programs. *Average indebtedness per student:* $25,145. *Average need-based loan:* Freshmen: $5432. Undergraduates: $6671. *Parent loans:* $9,538,684 (100% non-need-based). *Programs:* Federal Direct (Subsidized and Unsubsidized Stafford, PLUS), Perkins.
WORK-STUDY Federal work-study: 464 jobs averaging $1335. *State or other work-study/employment:* Total amount: $217,024 (100% need-based). 146 part-time jobs averaging $1486.
ATHLETIC AWARDS Total amount: $6,166,595 (100% non-need-based).
APPLYING FOR FINANCIAL AID Required financial aid form: FAFSA. *Financial aid deadline (priority):* 12/1. *Notification date:* Continuous beginning 12/21. Students must reply within 4 weeks of notification.
CONTACT Mr. Dan D. Davenport, Director of Student Financial Aid Services, University of Idaho, 875 Perimeter Drive, MS-4291, Moscow, ID 83844-4291, 208-885-6312 or toll-free 888-884-3246. *Fax:* 208-885-5592. *E-mail:* dand@uidaho.edu. *Website:* http://www.uidaho.edu/.

UNIVERSITY OF ILLINOIS AT CHICAGO
Chicago, IL

Tuition & fees (IL res): $13,614	Average undergraduate aid package: $14,729

ABOUT THE INSTITUTION State-supported, coed. *Awards:* certificates, bachelor's, master's, and doctoral degrees. 86 undergraduate majors. *Total*

enrollment: 30,538. Undergraduates: 19,447. Freshmen: 4,050. Federal methodology is used as a basis for awarding need-based institutional aid.

UNDERGRADUATE EXPENSES for 2018–2019 *Application fee:* $50. *Tuition, state resident:* full-time $10,584; part-time $394.16 per credit hour. *Tuition, nonresident:* full-time $23,440; part-time $803.14 per credit hour. *Required fees:* full-time $3030. Full-time tuition and fees vary according to degree level and program. Part-time tuition and fees vary according to course load, degree level, and program. *College room and board:* $10,960; *Room only:* $7930. Room and board charges vary according to board plan and housing facility. *Payment plan:* Guaranteed tuition.

FRESHMAN FINANCIAL AID (Fall 2016) 3,000 applied for aid; of those 89% were deemed to have need. 95% of freshmen with need received aid; of those 9% had need fully met. *Average percent of need met:* 61% (excluding resources awarded to replace EFC). *Average financial aid package:* $14,792 (excluding resources awarded to replace EFC). 3% of all full-time freshmen had no need and received non-need-based gift aid.

UNDERGRADUATE FINANCIAL AID (Fall 2016) 13,775 applied for aid; of those 91% were deemed to have need. 97% of undergraduates with need received aid; of those 9% had need fully met. *Average percent of need met:* 61% (excluding resources awarded to replace EFC). *Average financial aid package:* $14,729 (excluding resources awarded to replace EFC). 4% of all full-time undergraduates had no need and received non-need-based gift aid.

GIFT AID (NEED-BASED) *Total amount:* $124,994,097 (34% federal, 28% state, 36% institutional, 2% external sources). *Receiving aid:* Freshmen: 68% (2,204); all full-time undergraduates: 62% (10,178). *Average award:* Freshmen: $13,795; Undergraduates: $12,993. *Scholarships, grants, and awards:* Federal Pell, FSEOG, state, private, college/university gift aid from institutional funds.

GIFT AID (NON-NEED-BASED) *Total amount:* $2,804,947 (17% state, 65% institutional, 18% external sources). *Receiving aid:* Freshmen: 2% (81). Undergraduates: 2% (307). *Average award:* Freshmen: $6086. Undergraduates: $5663. *Scholarships, grants, and awards by category:* Academic interests/achievement: 1,251 awards ($7,506,010 total): architecture, business, general academic interests/achievements. Creative arts/performance: 184 awards ($664,824 total): applied art and design, art/fine arts, creative writing, music, performing arts, theater/drama. *Tuition waivers:* Full or partial for employees or children of employees, senior citizens. *ROTC:* Army, Naval cooperative, Air Force cooperative.

LOANS *Student loans:* $62,313,075 (89% need-based, 11% non-need-based). 63% of past graduating class borrowed through all loan programs. *Average indebtedness per student:* $23,076. *Average need-based loan:* Freshmen: $3326. Undergraduates: $4349. *Parent loans:* $18,617,812 (87% need-based, 13% non-need-based). *Programs:* Federal Direct (Subsidized and Unsubsidized Stafford, PLUS), Perkins, Federal Nursing, college/university, private loans.

WORK-STUDY *Federal work-study:* 856 jobs averaging $3000. *State or other work-study/employment:* Total amount: $8,419,375 (76% need-based, 24% non-need-based). 3,162 part-time jobs averaging $2500.

ATHLETIC AWARDS Total amount: $4,469,930 (40% need-based, 60% non-need-based).

APPLYING FOR FINANCIAL AID *Required financial aid form:* FAFSA. *Financial aid deadline (priority):* 2/15. *Notification date:* Continuous beginning 3/15. Students must reply by 5/1.

CONTACT Deidre Rush, Associate Director of Financial Aid, University of Illinois at Chicago, 1200 West Harrison, M/C 334, Suite 1800, Chicago, IL 60607-7128, 312-996-5563. *Fax:* 312-996-3385. *E-mail:* deidreb@uic.edu. *Website:* http://www.uic.edu/.

UNIVERSITY OF ILLINOIS AT SPRINGFIELD
Springfield, IL

Tuition & fees (IL res): $12,445	Average undergraduate aid package: $13,348

ABOUT THE INSTITUTION State-supported, coed. *Awards:* certificates, bachelor's, master's, and doctoral degrees. 31 undergraduate majors. *Total enrollment:* 4,956. Undergraduates: 2,932. Freshmen: 278. Federal methodology is used as a basis for awarding need-based institutional aid.

UNDERGRADUATE EXPENSES for 2017–2018 *Application fee:* $50. *Tuition, state resident:* full-time $9405; part-time $313.50 per credit hour.

Tuition, nonresident: full-time $18,930; part-time $631 per credit hour. *Required fees:* full-time $3040; $18.40 per credit hour or $1110 per term. Full-time tuition and fees vary according to course load. Part-time tuition and fees vary according to course load. *College room and board:* $11,660; *Room only:* $7460. Room and board charges vary according to board plan and housing facility. *Payment plan:* Guaranteed tuition.

FRESHMAN FINANCIAL AID (Fall 2016) 276 applied for aid; of those 74% were deemed to have need. 100% of freshmen with need received aid; of those 25% had need fully met. *Average percent of need met:* 80% (excluding resources awarded to replace EFC). *Average financial aid package:* $16,424 (excluding resources awarded to replace EFC). 23% of all full-time freshmen had no need and received non-need-based gift aid.

UNDERGRADUATE FINANCIAL AID (Fall 2016) 1,559 applied for aid; of those 82% were deemed to have need. 99% of undergraduates with need received aid; of those 13% had need fully met. *Average percent of need met:* 69% (excluding resources awarded to replace EFC). *Average financial aid package:* $13,348 (excluding resources awarded to replace EFC). 15% of all full-time undergraduates had no need and received non-need-based gift aid.

GIFT AID (NEED-BASED) *Total amount:* $11,888,764 (37% federal, 28% state, 32% institutional, 3% external sources). *Receiving aid:* Freshmen: 67% (198); all full-time undergraduates: 59% (1,131). *Average award:* Freshmen: $14,131; Undergraduates: $10,770. *Scholarships, grants, and awards:* Federal Pell, FSEOG, state, private, college/university gift aid from institutional funds.

GIFT AID (NON-NEED-BASED) *Total amount:* $2,463,793 (3% federal, 16% state, 72% institutional, 9% external sources). *Receiving aid:* Freshmen: 21% (62). Undergraduates: 11% (201). *Average award:* Freshmen: $8690. Undergraduates: $8323. *Tuition waivers:* Full or partial for employees or children of employees, senior citizens.

LOANS *Student loans:* $11,366,350 (88% need-based, 12% non-need-based). 70% of past graduating class borrowed through all loan programs. *Average indebtedness per student:* $25,313. *Average need-based loan:* Freshmen: $3227. Undergraduates: $4159. *Parent loans:* $1,650,493 (78% need-based, 22% non-need-based). *Programs:* Federal Direct (Subsidized and Unsubsidized Stafford, PLUS), Perkins, college/university.

WORK-STUDY *Federal work-study:* jobs available. *State or other work-study/employment:* Total amount: $479,921 (73% need-based, 27% non-need-based). Part-time jobs available.

ATHLETIC AWARDS Total amount: $1,329,178 (51% need-based, 49% non-need-based).

APPLYING FOR FINANCIAL AID *Required financial aid form:* FAFSA. *Financial aid deadline:* 11/15 (priority: 3/1). *Notification date:* Continuous beginning 1/1. Students must reply within 3 weeks of notification.

CONTACT Ms. Carolyn Schloemann, Acting Director of Financial Assistance, University of Illinois at Springfield, One University Plaza, MS UHB 1015, Springfield, IL 62703-5407, 217-206-6724 or toll-free 888-977-4847. *Fax:* 217-206-7376. *E-mail:* finaid@uis.edu. *Website:* http://www.uis.edu/.

UNIVERSITY OF ILLINOIS AT URBANA–CHAMPAIGN
Champaign, IL

Tuition & fees (IL res): $15,868	Average undergraduate aid package: $16,728

ABOUT THE INSTITUTION State-supported, coed. 219 undergraduate majors. Federal methodology is used as a basis for awarding need-based institutional aid.

UNDERGRADUATE EXPENSES for 2017–2018 *Tuition, state resident:* full-time $12,036. *Tuition, nonresident:* full-time $28,156. *Required fees:* full-time $3832. Full-time tuition and fees vary according to program and student level. *College room and board:* $11,308. Room and board charges vary according to board plan, housing facility, and location. *Payment plan:* Guaranteed tuition.

FRESHMAN FINANCIAL AID (Fall 2016) 5,654 applied for aid; of those 68% were deemed to have need. 93% of freshmen with need received aid; of those 12% had need fully met. *Average percent of need met:* 68% (excluding resources awarded to replace EFC). *Average financial aid package:* $17,394 (excluding resources awarded to replace EFC). 10% of all full-time freshmen had no need and received non-need-based gift aid.

UNDERGRADUATE FINANCIAL AID (Fall 2016) 18,963 applied for aid; of those 78% were deemed to have need. 95% of undergraduates with need received aid; of those 10% had need fully met. *Average percent of need met:* 64% (excluding resources awarded to replace EFC). *Average financial aid package:* $16,728 (excluding resources awarded to replace EFC). 12% of all full-time undergraduates had no need and received non-need-based gift aid.

GIFT AID (NEED-BASED) *Total amount:* $159,729,160 (22% federal, 20% state, 54% institutional, 4% external sources). *Receiving aid:* Freshmen: 41% (3,143); all full-time undergraduates: 38% (12,181). *Average award:* Freshmen: $14,957; Undergraduates: $14,580. *Scholarships, grants, and awards:* Federal Pell, FSEOG, state, private, college/university gift aid from institutional funds, United Negro College Fund.

GIFT AID (NON-NEED-BASED) *Total amount:* $19,714,076 (3% federal, 2% state, 80% institutional, 15% external sources). *Receiving aid:* Freshmen: 9% (662). Undergraduates: 5% (1,534). *Average award:* Freshmen: $5670. Undergraduates: $5392. *Scholarships, grants, and awards by category: Academic interests/achievement:* agriculture, architecture, area/ethnic studies, biological sciences, business, communication, computer science, education, engineering/technologies, English, foreign languages, general academic interests/achievements, health fields, home economics, humanities, international studies, library science, mathematics, military science, physical sciences, premedicine, religion/biblical studies, social sciences, *Creative arts/performance:* applied art and design, art/fine arts, dance, general creative arts/performance, journalism/publications, music, performing arts, theater/drama. *Special achievements/activities:* general special achievements/activities, leadership. *Special characteristics:* children of faculty/staff, first-generation college students, general special characteristics, international students, local/state students, members of minority groups, veterans. *Tuition waivers:* Full or partial for employees or children of employees, senior citizens.

LOANS *Student loans:* $96,088,648 (82% need-based, 18% non-need-based). 45% of past graduating class borrowed through all loan programs. *Average indebtedness per student:* $25,550. *Average need-based loan:* Freshmen: $4404. Undergraduates: $4657. *Parent loans:* $75,037,615 (76% need-based, 24% non-need-based). *Programs:* Federal Direct (Subsidized and Unsubsidized Stafford, PLUS), Perkins, college/university.

WORK-STUDY *Federal work-study:* jobs available. *State or other work-study/employment:* Total amount: $20,675,470 (53% need-based, 47% non-need-based). Part-time jobs available.

ATHLETIC AWARDS Total amount: $10,780,026 (31% need-based, 69% non-need-based).

APPLYING FOR FINANCIAL AID *Required financial aid form:* FAFSA. *Financial aid deadline (priority):* 3/15. *Notification date:* Continuous beginning 2/15. Students must reply by 5/1 or within 3 weeks of notification.

CONTACT Daniel Mann, Director of Student Financial Aid, University of Illinois at Urbana–Champaign, Student Services Arcade Building, 620 East John Street, Champaign, IL 61820-5711, 217-333-0100. *Website:* http://www.illinois.edu/.

UNIVERSITY OF INDIANAPOLIS
Indianapolis, IN

Tuition & fees: $28,390	Average undergraduate aid package: $19,908

ABOUT THE INSTITUTION Independent United Methodist Church, coed. *Awards:* associate, bachelor's, master's, and doctoral degrees. 62 undergraduate majors. *Total enrollment:* 5,711. Undergraduates: 4,346. Freshmen: 994. Federal methodology is used as a basis for awarding need-based institutional aid.

UNDERGRADUATE EXPENSES for 2017–2018 *Application fee:* $25. *Comprehensive fee:* $38,378 includes full-time tuition ($27,860), mandatory fees ($530), and room and board ($9988). *College room only:* $5126. Full-time tuition and fees vary according to class time. Room and board charges vary according to board plan and housing facility. *Part-time tuition:* $1152 per credit hour. *Part-time fees:* $50 per term. Part-time tuition and fees vary according to class time and course load.

FRESHMAN FINANCIAL AID (Fall 2016) 935 applied for aid; of those 89% were deemed to have need. 100% of freshmen with need received aid; of those 12% had need fully met. *Average percent of need met:* 70% (excluding resources awarded to replace EFC). *Average financial aid package:* $21,998 (excluding resources awarded to replace EFC). 12% of all full-time freshmen had no need and received non-need-based gift aid.

UNDERGRADUATE FINANCIAL AID (Fall 2016) 3,352 applied for aid; of those 88% were deemed to have need. 99% of undergraduates with need received aid; of those 11% had need fully met. *Average percent of need met:* 65% (excluding resources awarded to replace EFC). *Average financial aid package:* $19,908 (excluding resources awarded to replace EFC). 14% of all full-time undergraduates had no need and received non-need-based gift aid.

GIFT AID (NEED-BASED) *Total amount:* $19,089,559 (33% federal, 40% state, 27% institutional). *Receiving aid:* Freshmen: 56% (560); all full-time undergraduates: 47% (1,917). *Average award:* Freshmen: $11,217; Undergraduates: $9538. *Scholarships, grants, and awards:* Federal Pell, FSEOG, state, private, college/university gift aid from institutional funds.

GIFT AID (NON-NEED-BASED) *Total amount:* $32,065,553 (99% institutional, 1% external sources). *Receiving aid:* Freshmen: 75% (747). Undergraduates: 59% (2,415). *Average award:* Freshmen: $13,769. Undergraduates: $11,712. *Scholarships, grants, and awards by category: Academic interests/achievement:* business, communication, general academic interests/achievements, health fields, physical sciences, religion/biblical studies. *Creative arts/performance:* art/fine arts, debating, music, theater/drama. *Special achievements/activities:* community service, religious involvement. *Special characteristics:* children of faculty/staff, international students, out-of-state students, relatives of clergy, religious affiliation, veterans. *Tuition waivers:* Full or partial for employees or children of employees, senior citizens. *ROTC:* Army cooperative.

LOANS *Student loans:* $41,493,733 (100% need-based). 80% of past graduating class borrowed through all loan programs. *Average indebtedness per student:* $36,320. *Average need-based loan:* Freshmen: $3322. Undergraduates: $4403. *Parent loans:* $10,035,063 (100% non-need-based). *Programs:* Federal Direct (Subsidized and Unsubsidized Stafford, PLUS), Perkins.

WORK-STUDY *Federal work-study:* 374 jobs averaging $866. *State or other work-study/employment:* Total amount: $1,353,006 (100% need-based). 182 part-time jobs averaging $7434.

ATHLETIC AWARDS Total amount: $6,792,555 (100% non-need-based).

APPLYING FOR FINANCIAL AID *Required financial aid forms:* FAFSA, institution's own form. *Financial aid deadline (priority):* 4/15. *Notification date:* Continuous beginning 2/1.

CONTACT Ms. Linda B. Handy, Associate Vice President of Financial Aid, University of Indianapolis, 1400 East Hanna Avenue, Indianapolis, IN 46227-3697, 317-788-3217 or toll-free 800-232-8634 Ext. 3216. *Fax:* 317-788-6136. *E-mail:* handy@uindy.edu. *Website:* http://www.uindy.edu/.

THE UNIVERSITY OF IOWA
Iowa City, IA

Tuition & fees (IA res): $7486	Average undergraduate aid package: $16,084

ABOUT THE INSTITUTION State-supported, coed. 138 undergraduate majors. Federal methodology is used as a basis for awarding need-based institutional aid.

UNDERGRADUATE EXPENSES for 2017–2018 *Tuition, state resident:* full-time $7486; part-time $312 per credit hour. *Tuition, nonresident:* full-time $29,130; part-time $1214 per credit hour. *Required fees:* $307 per term. Full-time tuition and fees vary according to course level, course load, degree level, program, and student level. Part-time tuition and fees vary according to course level, course load, degree level, program, and student level. *College room and board:* $10,450. Room and board charges vary according to board plan and housing facility.

FRESHMAN FINANCIAL AID (Fall 2016) 4,045 applied for aid; of those 67% were deemed to have need. 100% of freshmen with need received aid; of those 34% had need fully met. *Average percent of need met:* 65% (excluding resources awarded to replace EFC). *Average financial aid package:* $15,835 (excluding resources awarded to replace EFC). 20% of all full-time freshmen had no need and received non-need-based gift aid.

UNDERGRADUATE FINANCIAL AID (Fall 2016) 13,553 applied for aid; of those 72% were deemed to have need. 100% of undergraduates with need received aid; of those 30% had need fully met. *Average percent of need met:* 67% (excluding resources awarded to replace EFC). *Average financial aid package:* $16,084 (excluding resources awarded to replace EFC). 11% of all full-time undergraduates had no need and received non-need-based gift aid.

GIFT AID (NEED-BASED) *Total amount:* $79,174,565 (26% federal, 2% state, 68% institutional, 4% external sources). *Receiving aid:* Freshmen: 37% (1,930); all full-time undergraduates: 35% (7,144). *Average award:* Freshmen: $6800; Undergraduates: $7208. *Scholarships, grants, and awards:* Federal Pell, FSEOG, state, private, college/university gift aid from institutional funds.
GIFT AID (NON-NEED-BASED) *Total amount:* $40,033,572 (1% state, 88% institutional, 11% external sources). *Receiving aid:* Freshmen: 39% (2,019). Undergraduates: 26% (5,408). *Average award:* Freshmen: $5277. Undergraduates: $5055. *Scholarships, grants, and awards by category:* Academic interests/achievement: business, engineering/technologies, general academic interests/achievements, military science. *Creative arts/performance:* applied art and design, art/fine arts, cinema/film/broadcasting, creative writing, dance, debating, general creative arts/performance, journalism/publications, music, performing arts, theater/drama. *Special achievements/activities:* cheerleading/drum major, general special achievements/activities, leadership. *Special characteristics:* children and siblings of alumni, ethnic background, first-generation college students, handicapped students, local/state students, out-of-state students, veterans, veterans' children.
LOANS *Student loans:* $94,672,299 (68% need-based, 32% non-need-based). 49% of past graduating class borrowed through all loan programs. *Average indebtedness per student:* $28,405. *Average need-based loan:* Freshmen: $4097. Undergraduates: $4727. *Parent loans:* $32,060,053 (34% need-based, 66% non-need-based). *Programs:* Federal Direct (Subsidized and Unsubsidized Stafford, PLUS), Perkins, Federal Nursing, college/university.
WORK-STUDY *Federal work-study:* 1,169 jobs averaging $2661. *State or other work-study/employment:* Part-time jobs available.
ATHLETIC AWARDS Total amount: $12,141,094 (100% non-need-based).
APPLYING FOR FINANCIAL AID *Required financial aid form:* FAFSA. *Financial aid deadline (priority):* 11/15. *Notification date:* Continuous beginning 1/15. Students must reply by 5/1 or within 2 weeks of notification.
CONTACT Kathy Bialk, Director of Student Financial Aid, The University of Iowa, 208 Calvin Hall, Iowa City, IA 52242, 319-335-3127 or toll-free 800-553-4692. *E-mail:* kathy-bialk@uiowa.edu.
Website: http://www.uiowa.edu/.

UNIVERSITY OF JAMESTOWN
Jamestown, ND

Tuition & fees: $21,976	Average undergraduate aid package: $15,700

ABOUT THE INSTITUTION Independent Presbyterian, coed. *Awards:* bachelor's, master's, and doctoral degrees. 45 undergraduate majors. *Total enrollment:* 1,136. Undergraduates: 915. Freshmen: 235. Federal methodology is used as a basis for awarding need-based institutional aid.
UNDERGRADUATE EXPENSES for 2018–2019 *Comprehensive fee:* $29,546 includes full-time tuition ($21,196), mandatory fees ($780), and room and board ($7570). *College room only:* $3570. Full-time tuition and fees vary according to course load, degree level, and program. Room and board charges vary according to housing facility. *Part-time tuition:* $435 per credit hour. Part-time tuition and fees vary according to course load, degree level, and program.
FRESHMAN FINANCIAL AID (Fall 2016) 207 applied for aid; of those 74% were deemed to have need. 100% of freshmen with need received aid; of those 32% had need fully met. *Average percent of need met:* 76% (excluding resources awarded to replace EFC). *Average financial aid package:* $14,942 (excluding resources awarded to replace EFC). 40% of all full-time freshmen had no need and received non-need-based gift aid.
UNDERGRADUATE FINANCIAL AID (Fall 2016) 705 applied for aid; of those 82% were deemed to have need. 100% of undergraduates with need received aid; of those 26% had need fully met. *Average percent of need met:* 75% (excluding resources awarded to replace EFC). *Average financial aid package:* $15,700 (excluding resources awarded to replace EFC). 35% of all full-time undergraduates had no need and received non-need-based gift aid.
GIFT AID (NEED-BASED) *Total amount:* $5,855,905 (22% federal, 7% state, 69% institutional, 2% external sources). *Receiving aid:* Freshmen: 58% (153); all full-time undergraduates: 62% (576). *Average award:* Freshmen: $12,752; Undergraduates: $12,546. *Scholarships, grants, and awards:* Federal Pell, FSEOG, state, private, college/university gift aid from institutional funds.

GIFT AID (NON-NEED-BASED) *Total amount:* $3,517,940 (5% state, 89% institutional, 6% external sources). *Receiving aid:* Freshmen: 17% (45). Undergraduates: 13% (117). *Average award:* Freshmen: $9071. Undergraduates: $8618. *Scholarships, grants, and awards by category:* Academic interests/achievement: 713 awards ($5,105,082 total): general academic interests/achievements, physical sciences. *Creative arts/performance:* 68 awards ($176,955 total): art/fine arts, music, theater/drama. *Special achievements/activities:* 58 awards ($93,392 total): cheerleading/drum major, community service, leadership. *Special characteristics:* 267 awards ($729,659 total): children and siblings of alumni, children of faculty/staff, religious affiliation, siblings of current students, spouses of current students. *Tuition waivers:* Full or partial for employees or children of employees.
LOANS *Student loans:* $5,754,081 (52% need-based, 48% non-need-based). 73% of past graduating class borrowed through all loan programs. *Average indebtedness per student:* $27,238. *Average need-based loan:* Freshmen: $3069. Undergraduates: $3926. *Parent loans:* $648,592 (46% need-based, 54% non-need-based). *Programs:* Federal Direct (Subsidized and Unsubsidized Stafford, PLUS), Perkins, alternative loans.
WORK-STUDY *Federal work-study:* 259 jobs averaging $669. *State or other work-study/employment:* Total amount: $38,868 (100% non-need-based). 81 part-time jobs averaging $472.
ATHLETIC AWARDS Total amount: $2,182,241 (51% need-based, 49% non-need-based).
APPLYING FOR FINANCIAL AID *Required financial aid form:* FAFSA. *Financial aid deadline:* Continuous. *Notification date:* Continuous beginning 10/15.
CONTACT Judy Hager, Director of Financial Aid, University of Jamestown, 6085 College Lane, Jamestown, ND 58405, 701-252-3467 Ext. 5548 or toll-free 800-336-2554. *Fax:* 701-253-4318. *E-mail:* jhager@uj.edu.
Website: http://www.uj.edu/.

THE UNIVERSITY OF KANSAS
Lawrence, KS

Tuition & fees (KS res): $10,824	Average undergraduate aid package: $15,412

ABOUT THE INSTITUTION State-supported, coed. *Awards:* certificates, bachelor's, master's, and doctoral degrees (University of Kansas is a single institution with academic programs and facilities at two primary locations: Lawrence and Kansas City). 115 undergraduate majors. *Total enrollment:* 27,625. Undergraduates: 19,338. Freshmen: 4,153. Federal methodology is used as a basis for awarding need-based institutional aid.
UNDERGRADUATE EXPENSES for 2017–2018 *Application fee:* $40. *Tuition, state resident:* full-time $9818; part-time $327.25 per credit hour. *Tuition, nonresident:* full-time $25,586; part-time $852.85 per credit hour. *Required fees:* full-time $1006; $79.29 per credit hour. Full-time tuition and fees vary according to reciprocity agreements. Part-time tuition and fees vary according to reciprocity agreements. *College room and board:* $10,060; *Room only:* $5910. Room and board charges vary according to board plan and housing facility.
FRESHMAN FINANCIAL AID (Fall 2016) 3,258 applied for aid; of those 67% were deemed to have need. 98% of freshmen with need received aid; of those 45% had need fully met. *Average percent of need met:* 79% (excluding resources awarded to replace EFC). *Average financial aid package:* $16,455 (excluding resources awarded to replace EFC). 27% of all full-time freshmen had no need and received non-need-based gift aid.
UNDERGRADUATE FINANCIAL AID (Fall 2016) 11,064 applied for aid; of those 73% were deemed to have need. 97% of undergraduates with need received aid; of those 39% had need fully met. *Average percent of need met:* 76% (excluding resources awarded to replace EFC). *Average financial aid package:* $15,412 (excluding resources awarded to replace EFC). 20% of all full-time undergraduates had no need and received non-need-based gift aid.
GIFT AID (NEED-BASED) *Total amount:* $47,718,289 (39% federal, 5% state, 50% institutional, 6% external sources). *Receiving aid:* Freshmen: 45% (1,863); all full-time undergraduates: 37% (6,259). *Average award:* Freshmen: $8743; Undergraduates: $7340. *Scholarships, grants, and awards:* Federal Pell, FSEOG, state, private, college/university gift aid from institutional funds, Bureau of Indian Affairs Grants.
GIFT AID (NON-NEED-BASED) *Total amount:* $25,051,215 (1% federal, 92% institutional, 7% external sources). *Receiving aid:* Freshmen: 6% (267). Undergrad-

uates: 3% (590). *Average award:* Freshmen: $6643. Undergraduates: $5896. *Scholarships, grants, and awards by category: Academic interests/achievement:* architecture, area/ethnic studies, biological sciences, business, communication, computer science, education, engineering/technologies, English, foreign languages, general academic interests/achievements, home economics, humanities, international studies, mathematics, military science, physical sciences, premedicine, religion/biblical studies, social sciences. *Creative arts/performance:* applied art and design, art/fine arts, cinema/film/broadcasting, creative writing, dance, debating, general creative arts/performance, journalism/publications, music, performing arts, theater/drama. *Special achievements/activities:* community service, general special achievements/activities, leadership. *Special characteristics:* adult students, children and siblings of alumni, children of faculty/staff, ethnic background, first-generation college students, general special characteristics, international students, local/state students, married students, members of minority groups, out-of-state students, previous college experience, veterans. *Tuition waivers:* Full or partial for employees or children of employees. *ROTC:* Army, Naval, Air Force.

LOANS *Student loans:* $73,320,011 (69% need-based, 31% non-need-based). 50% of past graduating class borrowed through all loan programs. *Average indebtedness per student:* $28,462. *Average need-based loan:* Freshmen: $3587. Undergraduates: $4494. *Parent loans:* $50,624,495 (37% need-based, 63% non-need-based). *Programs:* Federal Direct (Subsidized and Unsubsidized Stafford, PLUS), Perkins, Federal Nursing, college/university, Health Professions Student Loans (HPSL), Federal Loan for Disadvantaged Students, private loans.

WORK-STUDY *Federal work-study:* 693 jobs averaging $2097. *State or other work-study/employment:* Total amount: $205,500 (61% need-based, 39% non-need-based). 58 part-time jobs averaging $4425.

ATHLETIC AWARDS Total amount: $9,753,535 (29% need-based, 71% non-need-based).

APPLYING FOR FINANCIAL AID *Required financial aid form:* FAFSA. *Financial aid deadline (priority):* 3/1. *Notification date:* Continuous beginning 4/1. Students must reply within 4 weeks of notification.

CONTACT Ms. Angela Karlin, Director of Financial Aid and Scholarships, The University of Kansas, KU Visitor Center, 1502 Iowa Street, Lawrence, KS 66045-7576, 785-864-4700 or toll-free 888-686-7323 (in-state). *Fax:* 785-864-5469. *E-mail:* financialaid@ku.edu.

Website: http://www.ku.edu/.

UNIVERSITY OF KENTUCKY
Lexington, KY

Tuition & fees (KY res): $13,134	Average undergraduate aid package: $12,392

ABOUT THE INSTITUTION State-supported, coed. *Awards:* certificates, bachelor's, master's, and doctoral degrees. 100 undergraduate majors. *Total enrollment:* 29,465. Undergraduates: 22,425. Freshmen: 4,855. Federal methodology is used as a basis for awarding need-based institutional aid.

UNDERGRADUATE EXPENSES for 2017–2018 *Application fee:* $50. *Tuition, state resident:* full-time $11,772; part-time $477 per credit hour. *Tuition, nonresident:* full-time $27,856; part-time $1145 per credit hour. *Required fees:* full-time $1362; $42.50 per credit hour. Full-time tuition and fees vary according to location, program, reciprocity agreements, and student level. Part-time tuition and fees vary according to course load, program, reciprocity agreements, and student level. *College room and board:* $12,184. Room and board charges vary according to board plan and housing facility.

FRESHMAN FINANCIAL AID (Fall 2016) 4,012 applied for aid; of those 73% were deemed to have need. 100% of freshmen with need received aid; of those 19% had need fully met. *Average percent of need met:* 53% (excluding resources awarded to replace EFC). *Average financial aid package:* $12,112 (excluding resources awarded to replace EFC).

UNDERGRADUATE FINANCIAL AID (Fall 2016) 13,213 applied for aid; of those 79% were deemed to have need. 100% of undergraduates with need received aid; of those 18% had need fully met. *Average percent of need met:* 54% (excluding resources awarded to replace EFC). *Average financial aid package:* $12,392 (excluding resources awarded to replace EFC). 29% of all full-time undergraduates had no need and received non-need-based gift aid.

GIFT AID (NEED-BASED) *Total amount:* $159,052,437 (15% federal, 18% state, 62% institutional, 5% external sources). *Receiving aid:* Freshmen: 26% (1,241);

all full-time undergraduates: 27% (4,940). *Average award:* Freshmen: $5557; Undergraduates: $5664. *Scholarships, grants, and awards:* Federal Pell, FSEOG, state, private, college/university gift aid from institutional funds.

GIFT AID (NON-NEED-BASED) *Receiving aid:* Freshmen: 38% (1,817). Undergraduates: 43% (7,998). *Average award:* Freshmen: $9694. Undergraduates: $9475. *Scholarships, grants, and awards by category: Academic interests/achievement:* agriculture, architecture, area/ethnic studies, biological sciences, business, communication, computer science, education, engineering/technologies, English, foreign languages, general academic interests/achievements, health fields, home economics, international studies, mathematics, military science, physical sciences. *Creative arts/performance:* applied art and design, art/fine arts, cinema/film/broadcasting, creative writing, dance, debating, general creative arts/performance, journalism/publications, music, performing arts, theater/drama. *Special achievements/activities:* cheerleading/drum major, general special achievements/activities, leadership. *Special characteristics:* adult students, children and siblings of alumni, children of educators, children of faculty/staff, children of public servants, children of union members/company employees, children of workers in trades, children with a deceased or disabled parent, ethnic background, first-generation college students, general special characteristics, handicapped students, international students, members of minority groups, out-of-state students, public servants, spouses of deceased or disabled public servants, veterans, veterans' children. *Tuition waivers:* Full or partial for employees or children of employees. *ROTC:* Army, Air Force.

LOANS *Student loans:* $93,287,308 (100% need-based). 54% of past graduating class borrowed through all loan programs. *Average indebtedness per student:* $31,374. *Average need-based loan:* Freshmen: $4488. Undergraduates: $4502. *Parent loans:* $37,249,349 (100% need-based). *Programs:* Federal Direct (Subsidized and Unsubsidized Stafford, PLUS), Perkins, college/university, private loans.

WORK-STUDY *Federal work-study:* jobs available. *State or other work-study/employment:* Part-time jobs available.

ATHLETIC AWARDS Total amount: $11,437,663 (100% need-based).

APPLYING FOR FINANCIAL AID *Required financial aid form:* FAFSA. *Financial aid deadline (priority):* 2/15. *Notification date:* Continuous beginning 3/15. Students must reply within 3 weeks of notification.

CONTACT Mrs. Nimmi Wiggins, Student Services Director, University of Kentucky, 128 Funkhouser Building, Lexington, KY 40506-0054, 859-257-2000 or toll-free 866-900-GO-UK. *E-mail:* admission@uky.edu.

Website: http://www.uky.edu/.

UNIVERSITY OF LA VERNE
La Verne, CA

Tuition & fees: $41,450	Average undergraduate aid package: $32,166

ABOUT THE INSTITUTION Independent, coed. *Awards:* certificates, bachelor's, master's, and doctoral degrees (also offers continuing education program with significant enrollment not reflected in profile). 54 undergraduate majors. *Total enrollment:* 4,803. Undergraduates: 2,753. Freshmen: 606. Federal methodology is used as a basis for awarding need-based institutional aid.

UNDERGRADUATE EXPENSES for 2017–2018 *Application fee:* $50. *Comprehensive fee:* $54,590 includes full-time tuition ($39,916), mandatory fees ($1534), and room and board ($13,140). *College room only:* $7030. Full-time tuition and fees vary according to location. Room and board charges vary according to board plan and housing facility. *Part-time tuition:* $1180 per credit hour. Part-time tuition and fees vary according to location.

FRESHMAN FINANCIAL AID (Fall 2017, est.) 554 applied for aid; of those 94% were deemed to have need. 100% of freshmen with need received aid; of those 5% had need fully met. *Average percent of need met:* 65% (excluding resources awarded to replace EFC). *Average financial aid package:* $34,198 (excluding resources awarded to replace EFC). 12% of all full-time freshmen had no need and received non-need-based gift aid.

UNDERGRADUATE FINANCIAL AID (Fall 2017, est.) 2,357 applied for aid; of those 95% were deemed to have need. 100% of undergraduates with need received aid; of those 6% had need fully met. *Average percent of need met:* 68% (excluding resources awarded to replace EFC). *Average financial aid package:* $32,166 (excluding resources awarded to replace EFC). 14% of all full-time undergraduates had no need and received non-need-based gift aid.

GIFT AID (NEED-BASED) *Total amount:* $62,804,664 (11% federal, 17% state, 72% institutional). *Receiving aid:* Freshmen: 86% (519); all full-time undergraduates: 83% (2,219). *Average award:* Freshmen: $19,877; Undergraduates: $18,335. *Scholarships, grants, and awards:* Federal Pell, FSEOG, state, private.
GIFT AID (NON-NEED-BASED) *Total amount:* $4,351,195 (100% institutional). *Receiving aid:* Freshmen: 86% (517). Undergraduates: 83% (2,213). *Average award:* Freshmen: $11,020. Undergraduates: $8,687. *Scholarships, grants, and awards by category:* Academic interests/achievement: general academic interests/achievements. Creative arts/performance: art/fine arts, cinema/film/broadcasting, journalism/publications, music, performing arts, theater/drama. Special achievements/activities: community service, leadership. *Tuition waivers:* Full or partial for employees or children of employees. *ROTC:* Army cooperative.
LOANS *Student loans:* $12,921,502 (98% need-based, 2% non-need-based). 77% of past graduating class borrowed through all loan programs. *Average indebtedness per student:* $33,384. *Average need-based loan:* Freshmen: $3485. Undergraduates: $4646. *Parent loans:* $11,173,313 (96% need-based, 4% non-need-based). *Programs:* Federal Direct (Subsidized and Unsubsidized Stafford, PLUS), Perkins, college/university.
WORK-STUDY *Federal work-study:* Total amount: $880,524; jobs available. *State or other work-study/employment:* Total amount: $73,000 (45% need-based, 55% non-need-based). Part-time jobs available.
APPLYING FOR FINANCIAL AID *Required financial aid forms:* FAFSA, state aid form. *Financial aid deadline (priority):* 3/2. *Notification date:* Continuous beginning 3/1. Students must reply by 5/1 or within 2 weeks of notification.
CONTACT Office of Financial Aid, University of La Verne, 1950 3rd Street, La Verne, CA 91750-4443, 800-649-0160 or toll-free 800-876-4858. *Fax:* 909-448-1629. *E-mail:* finaid@laverne.edu.
Website: http://www.laverne.edu/.

UNIVERSITY OF LOUISIANA AT LAFAYETTE
Lafayette, LA

Tuition & fees: N/R	Average undergraduate aid package: $9503

ABOUT THE INSTITUTION State-supported, coed. 61 undergraduate majors. Federal methodology is used as a basis for awarding need-based institutional aid.
FRESHMAN FINANCIAL AID (Fall 2016) 2,879 applied for aid; of those 71% were deemed to have need. 100% of freshmen with need received aid; of those 13% had need fully met. *Average percent of need met:* 71% (excluding resources awarded to replace EFC). *Average financial aid package:* $10,178 (excluding resources awarded to replace EFC). 17% of all full-time freshmen had no need and received non-need-based gift aid.
UNDERGRADUATE FINANCIAL AID (Fall 2016) 10,781 applied for aid; of those 74% were deemed to have need. 99% of undergraduates with need received aid; of those 11% had need fully met. *Average percent of need met:* 65% (excluding resources awarded to replace EFC). *Average financial aid package:* $9503 (excluding resources awarded to replace EFC). 12% of all full-time undergraduates had no need and received non-need-based gift aid.
GIFT AID (NEED-BASED) *Total amount:* $25,264,531 (91% federal, 9% state). *Receiving aid:* Freshmen: 56% (1,690); all full-time undergraduates: 53% (6,856). *Average award:* Freshmen: $5617; Undergraduates: $5226. *Scholarships, grants, and awards:* Federal Pell, FSEOG, state, college/university gift aid from institutional funds.
GIFT AID (NON-NEED-BASED) *Total amount:* $45,360,186 (57% state, 38% institutional, 5% external sources). *Receiving aid:* Freshmen: 57% (1,733). Undergraduates: 39% (4,958). *Average award:* Freshmen: $1454. Undergraduates: $1781. *Scholarships, grants, and awards by category:* Academic interests/achievement: general academic interests/achievements. Creative arts/performance: general creative arts/performance. Special achievements/activities: general special achievements/activities.
LOANS *Student loans:* $50,817,659 (41% need-based, 59% non-need-based). *Average need-based loan:* Freshmen: $2261. Undergraduates: $2921. *Parent loans:* $6,568,486 (100% need-based). *Programs:* Federal Direct (Subsidized and Unsubsidized Stafford, PLUS), Perkins, Federal Nursing.

WORK-STUDY Federal work-study jobs available. *State or other work-study/employment:* Part-time jobs available.
ATHLETIC AWARDS Total amount: $5,499,493 (100% need-based).
APPLYING FOR FINANCIAL AID *Required financial aid form:* FAFSA. *Financial aid deadline (priority):* 5/1. *Notification date:* Continuous beginning 4/1. Students must reply within 2 weeks of notification.
CONTACT Cindy S. Perez, Director of Financial Aid, University of Louisiana at Lafayette, PO Box 41206, Lafayette, LA 70504-1206, 337-482-6497 or toll-free 800-752-6553. *Fax:* 337-482-6502. *E-mail:* cperez@louisiana.edu.
Website: http://www.louisiana.edu/.

UNIVERSITY OF LOUISIANA AT MONROE
Monroe, LA

Tuition & fees (LA res): $8470	Average undergraduate aid package: $7821

ABOUT THE INSTITUTION State-supported, coed. *Awards:* certificates, associate, bachelor's, master's, and doctoral degrees. 44 undergraduate majors. *Total enrollment:* 9,181. Undergraduates: 7,948. Freshmen: 1,364. Federal methodology is used as a basis for awarding need-based institutional aid.
UNDERGRADUATE EXPENSES for 2017–2018 *Application fee:* $20. *Tuition, state resident:* full-time $5788; part-time $364.11 per credit hour. *Tuition, nonresident:* full-time $17,888; part-time $364.11 per credit hour. *Required fees:* full-time $2682; $320.42 per credit hour. Full-time tuition and fees vary according to course load, degree level, and program. Part-time tuition and fees vary according to course load, degree level, and program. *College room and board:* $7454; *Room only:* $4282. Room and board charges vary according to board plan and housing facility.
FRESHMAN FINANCIAL AID (Fall 2017, est.) 1,218 applied for aid; of those 79% were deemed to have need. 99% of freshmen with need received aid; of those 20% had need fully met. *Average percent of need met:* 64% (excluding resources awarded to replace EFC). *Average financial aid package:* $8402 (excluding resources awarded to replace EFC). 27% of all full-time freshmen had no need and received non-need-based gift aid.
UNDERGRADUATE FINANCIAL AID (Fall 2017, est.) 4,317 applied for aid; of those 79% were deemed to have need. 98% of undergraduates with need received aid; of those 18% had need fully met. *Average percent of need met:* 56% (excluding resources awarded to replace EFC). *Average financial aid package:* $7821 (excluding resources awarded to replace EFC). 29% of all full-time undergraduates had no need and received non-need-based gift aid.
GIFT AID (NEED-BASED) *Total amount:* $7,592,176 (91% federal, 9% state). *Receiving aid:* Freshmen: 49% (655); all full-time undergraduates: 45% (2,299). *Average award:* Freshmen: $2677; Undergraduates: $2658. *Scholarships, grants, and awards:* Federal Pell, FSEOG, state, private, college/university gift aid from institutional funds, Leveraging Educational Assistance Program (LEAP).
GIFT AID (NON-NEED-BASED) *Total amount:* $15,442,097 (53% state, 35% institutional, 12% external sources). *Receiving aid:* Freshmen: 52% (697). Undergraduates: 40% (2,068). *Average award:* Freshmen: $6007. Undergraduates: $3854. *Scholarships, grants, and awards by category:* Academic interests/achievement: agriculture, biological sciences, business, communication, computer science, education, English, foreign languages, general academic interests/achievements, health fields, home economics, library science, mathematics, military science, physical sciences, social sciences. Creative arts/performance: art/fine arts, creative writing, debating, journalism/publications, music, performing arts, theater/drama. Special achievements/activities: cheerleading/drum major, community service, leadership. Special characteristics: children of faculty/staff, children with a deceased or disabled parent, international students, out-of-state students. *Tuition waivers:* Full or partial for employees or children of employees, senior citizens. *ROTC:* Army cooperative.
LOANS *Student loans:* $11,861,439 (42% need-based, 58% non-need-based). *Average need-based loan:* Freshmen: $1611. Undergraduates: $1987. *Programs:* Federal Direct (Subsidized and Unsubsidized Stafford, PLUS), Perkins, college/university, Federal Health Professions Student Loans.
WORK-STUDY *Federal work-study:* Total amount: $461,001; 404 jobs averaging $1159. *State or other work-study/employment:* Part-time jobs available.
ATHLETIC AWARDS Total amount: $2,440,757 (100% non-need-based).

APPLYING FOR FINANCIAL AID *Required financial aid forms:* FAFSA, institution's own form. *Financial aid deadline (priority):* 4/1. *Notification date:* Continuous beginning 6/15. Students must reply within 2 weeks of notification. **CONTACT** Ms. Frankie Everett, Director of Financial Aid Services, University of Louisiana at Monroe, 700 University Avenue, Monroe, LA 71209, 318-342-5329 or toll-free 800-372-5127. *Fax:* 318-342-1047. *E-mail:* everett@ulm.edu. *Website:* http://www.ulm.edu/.

UNIVERSITY OF LOUISVILLE
Louisville, KY

Tuition & fees (KY res): $11,264	Average undergraduate aid package: $12,382

ABOUT THE INSTITUTION State-supported, coed. *Awards:* certificates, associate, bachelor's, master's, and doctoral degrees. 55 undergraduate majors. *Total enrollment:* 21,403. Undergraduates: 15,547. Freshmen: 2,796. Both federal and institutional methodology are used as a basis for awarding need-based institutional aid.
UNDERGRADUATE EXPENSES for 2017–2018 *Application fee:* $50. *Tuition, state resident:* full-time $11,068; part-time $462 per credit hour. *Tuition, nonresident:* full-time $26,090; part-time $1088 per credit hour. *Required fees:* full-time $196. Full-time tuition and fees vary according to reciprocity agreements. Part-time tuition and fees vary according to course load and reciprocity agreements. *College room and board:* $8700; *Room only:* $5970. Room and board charges vary according to board plan and housing facility.
FRESHMAN FINANCIAL AID (Fall 2017, est.) 2,384 applied for aid; of those 77% were deemed to have need. 99% of freshmen with need received aid; of those 22% had need fully met. *Average percent of need met:* 62% (excluding resources awarded to replace EFC). *Average financial aid package:* $13,208 (excluding resources awarded to replace EFC). 15% of all full-time freshmen had no need and received non-need-based gift aid.
UNDERGRADUATE FINANCIAL AID (Fall 2017, est.) 9,001 applied for aid; of those 82% were deemed to have need. 98% of undergraduates with need received aid; of those 19% had need fully met. *Average percent of need met:* 60% (excluding resources awarded to replace EFC). *Average financial aid package:* $12,382 (excluding resources awarded to replace EFC). 19% of all full-time undergraduates had no need and received non-need-based gift aid.
GIFT AID (NEED-BASED) *Total amount:* $66,319,748 (31% federal, 20% state, 37% institutional, 12% external sources). *Receiving aid:* Freshmen: 68% (1,785); all full-time undergraduates: 57% (6,872). *Average award:* Freshmen: $10,365; Undergraduates: $9548. *Scholarships, grants, and awards:* Federal Pell, FSEOG, state, private, college/university gift aid from institutional funds, Federal Nursing.
GIFT AID (NON-NEED-BASED) *Total amount:* $32,124,140 (22% state, 61% institutional, 17% external sources). *Receiving aid:* Freshmen: 11% (297). Undergraduates: 8% (912). *Average award:* Freshmen: $7981. Undergraduates: $6750. *Tuition waivers:* Full or partial for employees or children of employees, senior citizens. *ROTC:* Army, Air Force.
LOANS *Student loans:* $46,562,337 (72% need-based, 28% non-need-based). 55% of past graduating class borrowed through all loan programs. *Average indebtedness per student:* $23,556. *Average need-based loan:* Freshmen: $3571. Undergraduates: $4206. *Parent loans:* $10,487,374 (41% need-based, 59% non-need-based). *Programs:* Federal Direct (Subsidized and Unsubsidized Stafford, PLUS), Perkins, Federal Nursing.
WORK-STUDY *Federal work-study:* Total amount: $1,217,023; 355 jobs averaging $3682.
ATHLETIC AWARDS Total amount: $11,560,693 (28% need-based, 72% non-need-based).
APPLYING FOR FINANCIAL AID *Required financial aid form:* FAFSA. *Financial aid deadline (priority):* 2/15. *Notification date:* Continuous beginning 4/1. Students must reply by 5/1.
CONTACT Ms. Sandra J. Neel, Director of Financial Aid, University of Louisville, 2301 South Third Street, Louisville, KY 40292-0001, 502-852-5511 or toll-free 800-334-8635. *Fax:* 502-852-0182. *E-mail:* finaid@louisville.edu. *Website:* http://www.louisville.edu/.

UNIVERSITY OF MAINE
Orono, ME

Tuition & fees (ME res): $10,902	Average undergraduate aid package: $13,589

ABOUT THE INSTITUTION State-supported, coed. *Awards:* certificates, bachelor's, master's, and doctoral degrees. 82 undergraduate majors. *Total enrollment:* 11,240. Undergraduates: 9,279. Freshmen: 2,299. Federal methodology is used as a basis for awarding need-based institutional aid.
UNDERGRADUATE EXPENSES for 2017–2018 *Application fee:* $40. *Tuition, state resident:* full-time $8580; part-time $286 per credit hour. *Tuition, nonresident:* full-time $27,960; part-time $932 per credit hour. *Required fees:* full-time $2322. Full-time tuition and fees vary according to course load. Part-time tuition and fees vary according to course load. *College room and board:* $10,136; *Room only:* $5272. Room and board charges vary according to board plan and housing facility.
FRESHMAN FINANCIAL AID (Fall 2017, est.) 2,068 applied for aid; of those 78% were deemed to have need. 100% of freshmen with need received aid; of those 20% had need fully met. *Average percent of need met:* 69% (excluding resources awarded to replace EFC). *Average financial aid package:* $14,897 (excluding resources awarded to replace EFC). 29% of all full-time freshmen had no need and received non-need-based gift aid.
UNDERGRADUATE FINANCIAL AID (Fall 2017, est.) 6,857 applied for aid; of those 82% were deemed to have need. 99% of undergraduates with need received aid; of those 17% had need fully met. *Average percent of need met:* 67% (excluding resources awarded to replace EFC). *Average financial aid package:* $13,589 (excluding resources awarded to replace EFC). 21% of all full-time undergraduates had no need and received non-need-based gift aid.
GIFT AID (NEED-BASED) *Total amount:* $46,367,670 (33% federal, 5% state, 57% institutional, 5% external sources). *Receiving aid:* Freshmen: 71% (1,601); all full-time undergraduates: 62% (5,085). *Average award:* Freshmen: $10,258; Undergraduates: $8803. *Scholarships, grants, and awards:* Federal Pell, FSEOG, state, private, college/university gift aid from institutional funds.
GIFT AID (NON-NEED-BASED) *Total amount:* $13,910,298 (1% federal, 90% institutional, 9% external sources). *Receiving aid:* Freshmen: 8% (190). Undergraduates: 5% (445). *Average award:* Freshmen: $7213. Undergraduates: $6280. *Scholarships, grants, and awards by category: Academic interests/achievement:* agriculture, biological sciences, business, communication, computer science, education, engineering/technologies, English, general academic interests/achievements, home economics, international studies, mathematics, military science, physical sciences, premedicine, social sciences. *Creative arts/performance:* art/fine arts, creative writing, dance, general creative arts/performance, journalism/publications, music, theater/drama. *Special achievements/activities:* community service, general special achievements/activities, leadership, memberships. *Special characteristics:* adult students, children and siblings of alumni, children of faculty/staff, children of union members/company employees, children of workers in trades, ethnic background, first-generation college students, general special characteristics, handicapped students, international students, local/state students, members of minority groups, out-of-state students, previous college experience, religious affiliation, spouses of current students, veterans, veterans' children. *Tuition waivers:* Full or partial for employees or children of employees, senior citizens. *ROTC:* Army, Naval.
LOANS *Student loans:* $58,884,535 (66% need-based, 34% non-need-based). 76% of past graduating class borrowed through all loan programs. *Average indebtedness per student:* $34,741. *Average need-based loan:* Freshmen: $3752. Undergraduates: $4510. *Parent loans:* $11,483,723 (48% need-based, 52% non-need-based). *Programs:* Federal Direct (Subsidized and Unsubsidized Stafford, PLUS), Perkins, state, college/university, private loans.
WORK-STUDY *Federal work-study:* Total amount: $3,727,232; 727 jobs averaging $2383.
ATHLETIC AWARDS Total amount: $6,036,703 (31% need-based, 69% non-need-based).
APPLYING FOR FINANCIAL AID *Required financial aid form:* FAFSA. *Financial aid deadline (priority):* 3/1. *Notification date:* Continuous beginning 1/1. Students must reply by 5/1.
CONTACT Ms. Sarah Doheny, Director of Student Financial Aid, University of Maine, 5781 Wingate Hall, Orono, ME 04469-5781, 207-581-1324 or toll-free 877-486-2364. *Fax:* 207-581-3261. *E-mail:* sarah.doheny@maine.edu. *Website:* http://www.umaine.edu/.

UNIVERSITY OF MAINE AT AUGUSTA
Augusta, ME

ABOUT THE INSTITUTION State-supported, coed. 28 undergraduate majors.

GIFT AID (NEED-BASED) *Scholarships, grants, and awards:* Federal Pell, FSEOG, state, private, college/university gift aid from institutional funds.

GIFT AID (NON-NEED-BASED) *Scholarships, grants, and awards by category: Academic interests/achievement:* biological sciences, business, general academic interests/achievements, mathematics. *Creative arts/performance:* music. *Special achievements/activities:* general special achievements/activities, leadership. *Special characteristics:* children of faculty/staff, ethnic background, international students, local/state students, veterans' children.

LOANS *Programs:* Federal Direct (Subsidized and Unsubsidized Stafford, PLUS), Perkins, Federal Nursing.

WORK-STUDY *Federal work-study:* jobs available. *State or other work-study/employment:* Total amount: $41,000 (100% non-need-based). Part-time jobs available.

APPLYING FOR FINANCIAL AID *Required financial aid form:* FAFSA.

CONTACT Financial Aid Office, University of Maine at Augusta, 46 University Drive, Augusta, ME 04330-9410, 207-621-3185 or toll-free 877-862-1234 Ext. 3185 (in-state), 877-862-1234 (out-of-state). *Fax:* 207-621-3116. *E-mail:* umafa@maine.edu. *Website:* http://www.uma.edu/.

UNIVERSITY OF MAINE AT FARMINGTON
Farmington, ME

CONTACT Mr. Ronald P. Milliken, Director of Financial Aid, University of Maine at Farmington, 224 Main Street, Farmington, ME 04938-1990, 207-778-7105. *Fax:* 207-778-8178. *E-mail:* milliken@maine.edu. *Website:* http://www.umf.maine.edu/.

UNIVERSITY OF MAINE AT FORT KENT
Fort Kent, ME

Tuition & fees (ME res): $8115	Average undergraduate aid package: $11,258

ABOUT THE INSTITUTION State-supported, coed. *Awards:* associate and bachelor's degrees. 19 undergraduate majors. *Total enrollment:* 1,760. Undergraduates: 1,760. Freshmen: 135. Both federal and institutional methodology are used as a basis for awarding need-based institutional aid.

UNDERGRADUATE EXPENSES for 2018–2019 *Application fee:* $40. *Tuition, state resident:* full-time $6990; part-time $233 per credit hour. *Tuition, nonresident:* full-time $11,190; part-time $373 per credit hour. *Required fees:* full-time $1125; $75 per credit hour. *College room and board:* $7910; *Room only:* $4250. Room and board charges vary according to board plan and housing facility.

FRESHMAN FINANCIAL AID (Fall 2016) 116 applied for aid; of those 80% were deemed to have need. 100% of freshmen with need received aid; of those 46% had need fully met. *Average percent of need met:* 74% (excluding resources awarded to replace EFC). *Average financial aid package:* $10,644 (excluding resources awarded to replace EFC). 5% of all full-time freshmen had no need and received non-need-based gift aid.

UNDERGRADUATE FINANCIAL AID (Fall 2016) 478 applied for aid; of those 81% were deemed to have need. 100% of undergraduates with need received aid; of those 50% had need fully met. *Average percent of need met:* 79% (excluding resources awarded to replace EFC). *Average financial aid package:* $11,258 (excluding resources awarded to replace EFC). 5% of all full-time undergraduates had no need and received non-need-based gift aid.

GIFT AID (NEED-BASED) *Total amount:* $3,230,229 (52% federal, 13% state, 27% institutional, 8% external sources). *Receiving aid:* Freshmen: 67% (87); all full-time undergraduates: 58% (334). *Average award:* Freshmen: $6647; Undergrad-

uates: $6324. *Scholarships, grants, and awards:* Federal Pell, FSEOG, state, private, college/university gift aid from institutional funds, Federal Nursing.

GIFT AID (NON-NEED-BASED) *Total amount:* $96,291 (3% state, 97% institutional). *Receiving aid:* Freshmen: 2% (2). Undergraduates: 1% (6). *Average award:* Freshmen: $2964. Undergraduates: $2813. *Scholarships, grants, and awards by category: Academic interests/achievement:* biological sciences, business, communication, computer science, education, English, foreign languages, general academic interests/achievements, health fields, humanities, mathematics, social sciences. *Creative arts/performance:* general creative arts/performance, performing arts. *Special achievements/activities:* general special achievements/activities. *Special characteristics:* adult students, children of faculty/staff, ethnic background, general special characteristics, international students, members of minority groups. *Tuition waivers:* Full or partial for employees or children of employees, senior citizens.

LOANS *Student loans:* $4,248,818 (73% need-based, 27% non-need-based). 76% of past graduating class borrowed through all loan programs. *Average indebtedness per student:* $24,096. *Average need-based loan:* Freshmen: $5252. Undergraduates: $6502. *Parent loans:* $161,280 (40% need-based, 60% non-need-based). *Programs:* Federal Direct (Subsidized and Unsubsidized Stafford, PLUS), Perkins, Federal Nursing, state, college/university.

WORK-STUDY *Federal work-study:* 98 jobs averaging $1143. *State or other work-study/employment:* Part-time jobs available.

APPLYING FOR FINANCIAL AID *Required financial aid forms:* FAFSA, institution's own form, CSS Financial Aid PROFILE, state aid form. *Financial aid deadline (priority):* 3/1. *Notification date:* Continuous beginning 3/1.

CONTACT Lisa Michaud, Interim Director of Financial Aid, University of Maine at Fort Kent, 23 University Drive, Fort Kent, ME 04743-1292, 207-834-7607 or toll-free 888-TRY-UMFK. *Fax:* 207-834-7841. *E-mail:* lisa.michaud@maine.edu. *Website:* http://www.umfk.maine.edu/.

UNIVERSITY OF MAINE AT MACHIAS
Machias, ME

Tuition & fees (ME res): $7726	Average undergraduate aid package: $14,175

ABOUT THE INSTITUTION State-supported, coed. *Awards:* certificates, associate, and bachelor's degrees. 37 undergraduate majors. *Total enrollment:* 701. Undergraduates: 701. Freshmen: 99. Federal methodology is used as a basis for awarding need-based institutional aid.

UNDERGRADUATE EXPENSES for 2017–2018 *Application fee:* $40. *Tuition, state resident:* full-time $6840; part-time $228 per semester hour. *Tuition, nonresident:* full-time $18,480; part-time $616 per semester hour. *Required fees:* full-time $886. Full-time tuition and fees vary according to course load and reciprocity agreements. Part-time tuition and fees vary according to course load and reciprocity agreements. *College room and board:* $8490; *Room only:* $4330. Room and board charges vary according to housing facility.

FRESHMAN FINANCIAL AID (Fall 2016) 106 applied for aid; of those 92% were deemed to have need. 100% of freshmen with need received aid; of those 65% had need fully met. *Average percent of need met:* 80% (excluding resources awarded to replace EFC). *Average financial aid package:* $14,303 (excluding resources awarded to replace EFC).

UNDERGRADUATE FINANCIAL AID (Fall 2016) 394 applied for aid; of those 90% were deemed to have need. 100% of undergraduates with need received aid; of those 61% had need fully met. *Average percent of need met:* 83% (excluding resources awarded to replace EFC). *Average financial aid package:* $14,175 (excluding resources awarded to replace EFC). 1% of all full-time undergraduates had no need and received non-need-based gift aid.

GIFT AID (NEED-BASED) *Total amount:* $3,616,546 (45% federal, 12% state, 32% institutional, 11% external sources). *Receiving aid:* Freshmen: 82% (97); all full-time undergraduates: 81% (354). *Average award:* Freshmen: $9433; Undergraduates: $8858. *Scholarships, grants, and awards:* Federal Pell, FSEOG, state, private, college/university gift aid from institutional funds.

GIFT AID (NON-NEED-BASED) *Total amount:* $19,628 (100% institutional). *Receiving aid:* Freshmen: 1% (1). Undergraduates: 2% (9). *Average award:* Undergraduates: $750. *Scholarships, grants, and awards by category: Academic interests/achievement:* general academic interests/achievements. *Tuition waivers:* Full or partial for employees or children of employees, senior citizens.

LOANS *Student loans:* $2,164,652 (79% need-based, 21% non-need-based). 69% of past graduating class borrowed through all loan programs. *Average indebtedness per student:* $25,702. *Average need-based loan:* Freshmen: $5704. Undergraduates: $6053. *Parent loans:* $196,737 (36% need-based, 64% non-need-based). *Programs:* Federal Direct (Subsidized and Unsubsidized Stafford, PLUS), Perkins, state.

WORK-STUDY *Federal work-study:* jobs available. *State or other work-study/employment:* Part-time jobs available.

APPLYING FOR FINANCIAL AID *Required financial aid form:* FAFSA. *Financial aid deadline (priority):* 3/1. *Notification date:* Continuous beginning 2/1.

CONTACT Ms. Stephanie Larrabee, Director of Financial Aid, University of Maine at Machias, 9 O'Brien Avenue, Machias, ME 04654, 207-255-1203 or toll-free 888-GOTOUMM (in-state), 888-468-6866 (out-of-state). *Fax:* 207-255-4864. *Website:* http://www.machias.edu/.

UNIVERSITY OF MAINE AT PRESQUE ISLE
Presque Isle, ME

Tuition & fees (ME res): $8034	Average undergraduate aid package: $11,451

ABOUT THE INSTITUTION State-supported, coed. *Awards:* certificates, associate, and bachelor's degrees. 27 undergraduate majors. *Total enrollment:* 1,408. Undergraduates: 1,408. Freshmen: 171. Federal methodology is used as a basis for awarding need-based institutional aid.

UNDERGRADUATE EXPENSES for 2018–2019 *Tuition, state resident:* full-time $6990. *Tuition, nonresident:* full-time $11,190. *Required fees:* full-time $1044. Full-time tuition and fees vary according to course load. Part-time tuition and fees vary according to course load. *College room and board:* $8406; *Room only:* $4850. Room and board charges vary according to board plan.

FRESHMAN FINANCIAL AID (Fall 2017, est.) 148 applied for aid; of those 91% were deemed to have need. 100% of freshmen with need received aid; of those 50% had need fully met. *Average percent of need met:* 82% (excluding resources awarded to replace EFC). *Average financial aid package:* $12,155 (excluding resources awarded to replace EFC). 6% of all full-time freshmen had no need and received non-need-based gift aid.

UNDERGRADUATE FINANCIAL AID (Fall 2017, est.) 559 applied for aid; of those 90% were deemed to have need. 100% of undergraduates with need received aid; of those 59% had need fully met. *Average percent of need met:* 82% (excluding resources awarded to replace EFC). *Average financial aid package:* $11,451 (excluding resources awarded to replace EFC). 3% of all full-time undergraduates had no need and received non-need-based gift aid.

GIFT AID (NEED-BASED) *Total amount:* $3,701,072 (61% federal, 12% state, 20% institutional, 7% external sources). *Receiving aid:* Freshmen: 84% (133); all full-time undergraduates: 72% (492). *Average award:* Freshmen: $6994; Undergraduates: $6592. *Scholarships, grants, and awards:* Federal Pell, FSEOG, state, private, college/university gift aid from institutional funds.

GIFT AID (NON-NEED-BASED) *Receiving aid:* Freshmen: 3% (4). Undergraduates: 2% (14). *Average award:* Freshmen: $3711. Undergraduates: $3047. *Scholarships, grants, and awards by category:* Academic interests/achievement: general academic interests/achievements. *Special achievements/activities:* community service. *Special characteristics:* children of faculty/staff, ethnic background, international students, local/state students, out-of-state students, veterans' children. *Tuition waivers:* Full or partial for employees or children of employees, senior citizens.

LOANS *Student loans:* $2,867,096 (71% need-based, 29% non-need-based). *Average indebtedness per student:* $23,574. *Average need-based loan:* Freshmen: $5164. Undergraduates: $5063. *Parent loans:* $85,902 (31% need-based, 69% non-need-based). *Programs:* Federal Direct (Subsidized and Unsubsidized Stafford, PLUS), Perkins, state, college/university.

WORK-STUDY *Federal work-study:* Total amount: $643,409; jobs available.

APPLYING FOR FINANCIAL AID *Required financial aid form:* FAFSA. *Financial aid deadline (priority):* 4/1. *Notification date:* Continuous beginning 1/10. Students must reply within 2 weeks of notification.

CONTACT Christopher A.R. Bell, Director of Student Financial Services, University of Maine at Presque Isle, 181 Main Street, Presque Isle, ME 04769-2888, 207-768-9511. *Fax:* 207-768-9509. *E-mail:* chris@maine.edu. *Website:* http://www.umpi.edu/.

UNIVERSITY OF MANAGEMENT AND TECHNOLOGY
Arlington, VA

CONTACT Financial Aid Administrator, University of Management and Technology, 1901 North Fort Myer Drive, Suite 700, Arlington, VA 22209, 703-516-0035 or toll-free 800-924-4883. *Fax:* 703-516-0985. *E-mail:* info@umtweb.edu. *Website:* http://www.umtweb.edu/.

UNIVERSITY OF MARY
Bismarck, ND

CONTACT Janell Thomas, Financial Assistance Director, University of Mary, 7500 University Drive, Bismarck, ND 58504-9652, 701-355-8244 or toll-free 800-288-6279. *Fax:* 701-255-7687. *E-mail:* jdthomas@umary.edu. *Website:* http://www.umary.edu/.

UNIVERSITY OF MARY HARDIN-BAYLOR
Belton, TX

Tuition & fees: $26,890	Average undergraduate aid package: $17,854

ABOUT THE INSTITUTION Independent Southern Baptist, coed. *Awards:* certificates, bachelor's, master's, and doctoral degrees. 59 undergraduate majors. *Total enrollment:* 3,914. Undergraduates: 3,333. Freshmen: 754. Federal methodology is used as a basis for awarding need-based institutional aid.

UNDERGRADUATE EXPENSES for 2018–2019 *Application fee:* $35. *Comprehensive fee:* $35,336 includes full-time tuition ($24,640), mandatory fees ($2250), and room and board ($8446). Full-time tuition and fees vary according to course load and degree level. Room and board charges vary according to board plan and housing facility. *Part-time tuition:* $880 per credit hour. Part-time tuition and fees vary according to course load and degree level.

FRESHMAN FINANCIAL AID (Fall 2017, est.) 653 applied for aid; of those 89% were deemed to have need. 100% of freshmen with need received aid; of those 10% had need fully met. *Average percent of need met:* 62% (excluding resources awarded to replace EFC). *Average financial aid package:* $18,700 (excluding resources awarded to replace EFC). 11% of all full-time freshmen had no need and received non-need-based gift aid.

UNDERGRADUATE FINANCIAL AID (Fall 2017, est.) 2,682 applied for aid; of those 90% were deemed to have need. 100% of undergraduates with need received aid; of those 7% had need fully met. *Average percent of need met:* 57% (excluding resources awarded to replace EFC). *Average financial aid package:* $17,854 (excluding resources awarded to replace EFC). 12% of all full-time undergraduates had no need and received non-need-based gift aid.

GIFT AID (NEED-BASED) *Total amount:* $34,247,312 (19% federal, 13% state, 66% institutional, 2% external sources). *Receiving aid:* Freshmen: 77% (578); all full-time undergraduates: 78% (2,378). *Average award:* Freshmen: $15,493; Undergraduates: $13,995. *Scholarships, grants, and awards:* Federal Pell, FSEOG, state, private, college/university gift aid from institutional funds.

GIFT AID (NON-NEED-BASED) *Total amount:* $3,698,119 (1% federal, 95% institutional, 4% external sources). *Receiving aid:* Freshmen: 6% (42). Undergraduates: 4% (115). *Average award:* Freshmen: $8044. Undergraduates: $7698. *Scholarships, grants, and awards by category:* Academic interests/achievement: agriculture, biological sciences, business, communication, computer science, education, English, foreign languages, general academic interests/achievements, health fields, home economics, humanities, international studies, mathematics, military science, physical sciences, premedicine, religion/biblical studies, social sciences. *Creative arts/performance:* art/fine arts, music. *Special achievements/activities:* cheerleading/drum major, community service, leadership, religious involvement. *Special characteristics:* children and siblings of alumni, children of faculty/staff, ethnic background, handicapped students, international students, local/state students, members of minority groups, out-of-state students, relatives of clergy, religious affiliation. *Tuition waivers:* Full or partial for employees or children of employees. *ROTC:* Army, Air Force cooperative.

LOANS *Student loans:* $21,041,111 (83% need-based, 17% non-need-based). 76% of past graduating class borrowed through all loan programs. *Average indebtedness per student:* $43,344. *Average need-based loan:* Freshmen: $3349. Undergraduates: $4385. *Parent loans:* $11,228,921 (50% need-based, 50% non-need-based). *Programs:* Federal Direct (Subsidized and Unsubsidized Stafford, PLUS), Perkins, state, private loans.

WORK-STUDY *Federal work-study:* Total amount: $810,739; jobs available. *State or other work-study/employment:* Total amount: $435,852 (26% need-based, 74% non-need-based). Part-time jobs available.

APPLYING FOR FINANCIAL AID *Required financial aid form:* FAFSA. *Financial aid deadline (priority):* 1/1. *Notification date:* Continuous beginning 11/1. Students must reply within 2 weeks of notification.

CONTACT Mr. David Orsag, Associate Director of Financial Aid, University of Mary Hardin-Baylor, 900 College Street, Box 8080, Belton, TX 76513, 254-295-4517 or toll-free 800-727-8642. *Fax:* 254-295-5009. *E-mail:* dorsag@umhb.edu. *Website:* http://www.umhb.edu/.

UNIVERSITY OF MARYLAND, BALTIMORE COUNTY
Baltimore, MD

Tuition & fees (MD res): $11,518	Average undergraduate aid package: $11,033

ABOUT THE INSTITUTION State-supported, coed. *Awards:* certificates, bachelor's, master's, and doctoral degrees. 53 undergraduate majors. *Total enrollment:* 13,662. Undergraduates: 11,234. Freshmen: 1,772. Federal methodology is used as a basis for awarding need-based institutional aid.

UNDERGRADUATE EXPENSES for 2017–2018 *Application fee:* $50. *One-time required fee:* $125. *Tuition, state resident:* full-time $8368; part-time $347 per credit hour. *Tuition, nonresident:* full-time $22,504; part-time $934 per credit hour. *Required fees:* full-time $3150; $136 per credit hour. Full-time tuition and fees vary according to location and program. Part-time tuition and fees vary according to location and program. *College room and board:* $11,486; *Room only:* $6966. Room and board charges vary according to board plan and housing facility.

FRESHMAN FINANCIAL AID (Fall 2017, est.) 1,405 applied for aid; of those 70% were deemed to have need. 96% of freshmen with need received aid; of those 19% had need fully met. *Average percent of need met:* 59% (excluding resources awarded to replace EFC). *Average financial aid package:* $11,914 (excluding resources awarded to replace EFC). 34% of all full-time freshmen had no need and received non-need-based gift aid.

UNDERGRADUATE FINANCIAL AID (Fall 2017, est.) 6,424 applied for aid; of those 82% were deemed to have need. 94% of undergraduates with need received aid; of those 11% had need fully met. *Average percent of need met:* 55% (excluding resources awarded to replace EFC). *Average financial aid package:* $11,033 (excluding resources awarded to replace EFC). 17% of all full-time undergraduates had no need and received non-need-based gift aid.

GIFT AID (NEED-BASED) *Total amount:* $38,422,034 (42% federal, 20% state, 35% institutional, 3% external sources). *Receiving aid:* Freshmen: 48% (852); all full-time undergraduates: 42% (3,963). *Average award:* Freshmen: $10,488; Undergraduates: $9312. *Scholarships, grants, and awards:* Federal Pell, FSEOG, state, private, college/university gift aid from institutional funds.

GIFT AID (NON-NEED-BASED) *Total amount:* $13,490,747 (12% federal, 2% state, 65% institutional, 21% external sources). *Receiving aid:* Freshmen: 19% (339). Undergraduates: 6% (612). *Average award:* Freshmen: $5905. Undergraduates: $8128. *Scholarships, grants, and awards by category:* Academic interests/achievement: 3,301 awards ($19,106,419 total): biological sciences, computer science, education, engineering/technologies, English, foreign languages, general academic interests/achievements, humanities, mathematics, physical sciences, social sciences. *Creative arts/performance:* 31 awards ($42,275 total): art/fine arts, cinema/film/broad-

casting, creative writing, dance, music, performing arts, theater/drama. *Tuition waivers:* Full or partial for employees or children of employees, senior citizens. *ROTC:* Army cooperative, Naval, Air Force cooperative.

LOANS *Student loans:* $34,379,764 (42% need-based, 58% non-need-based). 45% of past graduating class borrowed through all loan programs. *Average indebtedness per student:* $27,221. *Average need-based loan:* Freshmen: $3319. Undergraduates: $4310. *Parent loans:* $12,237,659 (76% need-based, 24% non-need-based). *Programs:* Federal Direct (Subsidized and Unsubsidized Stafford, PLUS), Perkins.

WORK-STUDY *Federal work-study:* Total amount: $254,182; 163 jobs averaging $1559. *State or other work-study/employment:* Total amount: $1,228,488 (55% need-based, 45% non-need-based). 118 part-time jobs averaging $10,410.

ATHLETIC AWARDS Total amount: $2,576,342 (37% need-based, 63% non-need-based).

APPLYING FOR FINANCIAL AID *Required financial aid form:* FAFSA. *Financial aid deadline (priority):* 2/14. *Notification date:* Continuous beginning 3/15.

CONTACT Jane Hickey, Director of Financial Aid, University of Maryland, Baltimore County, 1000 Hilltop Circle, Baltimore, MD 21250, 410-455-2387 or toll-free 800-UMBC-4U2 (in-state), 800-862-2402 (out-of-state). *Fax:* 410-455-3322. *Website:* http://www.umbc.edu/.

UNIVERSITY OF MARYLAND, COLLEGE PARK
College Park, MD

Tuition & fees (MD res): $10,399	Average undergraduate aid package: $12,410

ABOUT THE INSTITUTION State-supported, coed. *Awards:* certificates, bachelor's, master's, and doctoral degrees. 89 undergraduate majors. *Total enrollment:* 40,521. Undergraduates: 29,868. Freshmen: 4,141. Federal methodology is used as a basis for awarding need-based institutional aid.

UNDERGRADUATE EXPENSES for 2017–2018 *Application fee:* $65. *Tuition, state resident:* full-time $8481; part-time $353 per credit hour. *Tuition, nonresident:* full-time $31,688; part-time $1321 per credit hour. *Required fees:* full-time $1918; $446.50 per term. Full-time tuition and fees vary according to location, program, and student level. Part-time tuition and fees vary according to course load, location, program, and student level. *College room and board:* $12,082; *Room only:* $7190. Room and board charges vary according to board plan and housing facility.

FRESHMAN FINANCIAL AID (Fall 2016) 3,470 applied for aid; of those 52% were deemed to have need. 100% of freshmen with need received aid; of those 19% had need fully met. *Average percent of need met:* 64% (excluding resources awarded to replace EFC). *Average financial aid package:* $11,813 (excluding resources awarded to replace EFC). 19% of all full-time freshmen had no need and received non-need-based gift aid.

UNDERGRADUATE FINANCIAL AID (Fall 2016) 15,508 applied for aid; of those 70% were deemed to have need. 100% of undergraduates with need received aid; of those 16% had need fully met. *Average percent of need met:* 66% (excluding resources awarded to replace EFC). *Average financial aid package:* $12,410 (excluding resources awarded to replace EFC). 14% of all full-time undergraduates had no need and received non-need-based gift aid.

GIFT AID (NEED-BASED) *Total amount:* $78,540,103 (31% federal, 20% state, 44% institutional, 5% external sources). *Receiving aid:* Freshmen: 30% (1,364); all full-time undergraduates: 31% (8,234). *Average award:* Freshmen: $10,122; Undergraduates: $9978. *Scholarships, grants, and awards:* Federal Pell, FSEOG, state, private, college/university gift aid from institutional funds.

GIFT AID (NON-NEED-BASED) *Total amount:* $33,794,662 (4% state, 78% institutional, 18% external sources). *Receiving aid:* Freshmen: 4% (171). Undergraduates: 2% (575). *Average award:* Freshmen: $5982. Undergraduates: $6919. *Scholarships, grants, and awards by category:* Academic interests/achievement: agriculture, architecture, biological sciences, business, communication, computer science, education, engineering/technologies, English, foreign languages, general academic interests/achievements, health fields, humanities, international studies, library science, mathematics, military science, physical sciences, premedicine, social sciences. *Creative arts/performance:* applied art and design, art/fine arts, dance, music, performing arts, theater/drama. *Special achievements/activities:* cheerleading/drum major. *Special characteristics:* adult students, out-of-state students. *Tuition waivers:* Full or partial for employees or children of employees. *ROTC:* Army, Naval cooperative, Air Force.

LOANS *Student loans:* $136,611,939 (50% need-based, 50% non-need-based). 42% of past graduating class borrowed through all loan programs. *Average indebtedness per student:* $28,122. *Average need-based loan:* Freshmen: $3481. Undergraduates: $4775. *Parent loans:* $30,625,232 (32% need-based, 68% non-need-based). *Programs:* Federal Direct (Subsidized and Unsubsidized Stafford, PLUS), Perkins, private loans.

WORK-STUDY *Federal work-study:* jobs available.

ATHLETIC AWARDS Total amount: $14,735,986 (31% need-based, 69% non-need-based).

APPLYING FOR FINANCIAL AID *Required financial aid form:* FAFSA. *Financial aid deadline (priority):* 2/15. *Notification date:* Continuous beginning 4/1. Students must reply by 5/1.

CONTACT Monique Boyd, Director of Financial Aid, University of Maryland, College Park, 0102 Lee Building, College Park, MD 20742, 301-314-9000 or toll-free 800-422-5867. *Fax:* 301-314-9265. *E-mail:* umfinaid@umd.edu.
Website: http://www.maryland.edu/.

UNIVERSITY OF MARYLAND EASTERN SHORE
Princess Anne, MD

ABOUT THE INSTITUTION State-supported, coed. *Awards:* certificates, bachelor's, master's, and doctoral degrees. 51 undergraduate majors. *Total enrollment:* 3,492. Undergraduates: 2,862. Freshmen: 565.

GIFT AID (NEED-BASED) *Scholarships, grants, and awards:* Federal Pell, FSEOG, state, private, college/university gift aid from institutional funds, United Negro College Fund.

GIFT AID (NON-NEED-BASED) *Scholarships, grants, and awards by category:* Academic interests/achievement: agriculture, biological sciences, business, computer science, education, engineering/technologies, English, general academic interests/achievements, health fields, home economics, humanities, mathematics, physical sciences, social sciences. *Creative arts/performance:* applied art and design, art/fine arts. *Special achievements/activities:* general special achievements/activities, memberships. *Special characteristics:* children of faculty/staff, children of public servants, children of union members/company employees, general special characteristics, local/state students, public servants, veterans, veterans' children.

LOANS *Programs:* Federal Direct (Subsidized and Unsubsidized Stafford, PLUS), Perkins.

APPLYING FOR FINANCIAL AID *Required financial aid form:* FAFSA.

CONTACT Mr. Al J. Dorsett, Director of Financial Aid, University of Maryland Eastern Shore, 1 Backbone Road, SDC, Suite 1100, Princess Anne, MD 21853-1299, 410-651-6172. *Fax:* 410-651-7670. *E-mail:* ajdorsett@umes.edu.
Website: http://www.umes.edu/.

UNIVERSITY OF MARYLAND UNIVERSITY COLLEGE
Adelphi, MD

Tuition & fees (MD res): $7296	Average undergraduate aid package: $6959

ABOUT THE INSTITUTION State-supported, coed. *Awards:* certificates, associate, bachelor's, master's, and doctoral degrees (offers primarily part-time evening and weekend degree programs at more than 30 off-campus locations in Maryland and the Washington, DC area, and more than 180 military communities in Europe and Asia with military enrollment not reflected in this profile; associate of arts program available to military students only). 28 undergraduate majors. *Total enrollment:* 59,379. Undergraduates: 45,604. Freshmen: 676. Federal methodology is used as a basis for awarding need-based institutional aid.

UNDERGRADUATE EXPENSES for 2018–2019 *Application fee:* $50. *Tuition, state resident:* full-time $6936; part-time $289 per credit hour. *Tuition, nonresident:* full-time $11,976; part-time $499 per credit hour. *Required fees:* full-time $360.

FRESHMAN FINANCIAL AID (Fall 2016) 210 applied for aid; of those 93% were deemed to have need. 76% of freshmen with need received aid. *Average percent of need met:* 21% (excluding resources awarded to replace EFC). *Average financial aid package:* $5144 (excluding resources awarded to replace EFC).

UNDERGRADUATE FINANCIAL AID (Fall 2016) 5,932 applied for aid; of those 95% were deemed to have need. 89% of undergraduates with need received aid; of those 1% had need fully met. *Average percent of need met:* 27% (excluding resources awarded to replace EFC). *Average financial aid package:* $6959 (excluding resources awarded to replace EFC).

GIFT AID (NEED-BASED) *Total amount:* $44,513,551 (86% federal, 6% state, 8% institutional). *Receiving aid:* Freshmen: 41% (116); all full-time undergraduates: 39% (3,743). *Average award:* Freshmen: $3668; Undergraduates: $4776. *Scholarships, grants, and awards:* Federal Pell, FSEOG, state, private, college/university gift aid from institutional funds.

GIFT AID (NON-NEED-BASED) *Total amount:* $7,224,497 (2% state, 91% institutional, 7% external sources). *Receiving aid:* Freshmen: 8% (22). Undergraduates: 13% (1,219). *Scholarships, grants, and awards by category:* Academic interests/achievement: general academic interests/achievements. *Special achievements/activities:* general special achievements/activities. *Tuition waivers:* Full or partial for employees or children of employees, senior citizens.

LOANS *Student loans:* $92,547,577 (41% need-based, 59% non-need-based). *Average need-based loan:* Freshmen: $2961. Undergraduates: $4244. *Parent loans:* $320,653 (100% non-need-based). *Programs:* Federal Direct (Subsidized and Unsubsidized Stafford, PLUS), Perkins.

WORK-STUDY Federal work-study jobs available. *State or other work-study/ employment:* Part-time jobs available.

APPLYING FOR FINANCIAL AID *Required financial aid form:* FAFSA. *Financial aid deadline (priority):* 6/1. *Notification date:* Continuous beginning 5/1. Students must reply within 2 weeks of notification.

CONTACT Cheryl Storie, Associate Vice President of Financial Aid, University of Maryland University College, 3501 University Boulevard East, Adelphi, MD 20783, 301-985-7847 or toll-free 800-888-8682. *Fax:* 301-985-7462. *E-mail:* finaid@umuc.edu.
Website: http://www.umuc.edu/.

UNIVERSITY OF MARY WASHINGTON
Fredericksburg, VA

Tuition & fees (VA res): $11,630	Average undergraduate aid package: $9485

ABOUT THE INSTITUTION State-supported, coed. *Awards:* certificates, bachelor's, and master's degrees. 28 undergraduate majors. *Total enrollment:* 4,808. Undergraduates: 4,398. Freshmen: 950. Federal methodology is used as a basis for awarding need-based institutional aid.

UNDERGRADUATE EXPENSES for 2018–2019 *Application fee:* $50. *Tuition, state resident:* full-time $5772. *Tuition, nonresident:* full-time $20,362. *Required fees:* full-time $5858. Full-time tuition and fees vary according to course load, degree level, and location. Part-time tuition and fees vary according to course load, degree level, and location. *College room and board:* $11,118; *Room only:* $7326. Room and board charges vary according to board plan and housing facility.

FRESHMAN FINANCIAL AID (Fall 2016) 759 applied for aid; of those 61% were deemed to have need. 99% of freshmen with need received aid; of those 11% had need fully met. *Average percent of need met:* 44% (excluding resources awarded to replace EFC). *Average financial aid package:* $9573 (excluding resources awarded to replace EFC). 37% of all full-time freshmen had no need and received non-need-based gift aid.

UNDERGRADUATE FINANCIAL AID (Fall 2016) 2,517 applied for aid; of those 69% were deemed to have need. 97% of undergraduates with need received aid; of those 11% had need fully met. *Average percent of need met:* 45% (excluding resources awarded to replace EFC). *Average financial aid package:* $9485 (excluding resources awarded to replace EFC). 25% of all full-time undergraduates had no need and received non-need-based gift aid.

GIFT AID (NEED-BASED) *Total amount:* $8,243,451 (42% federal, 39% state, 19% institutional). *Receiving aid:* Freshmen: 34% (314); all full-time undergraduates: 29% (1,119). *Average award:* Freshmen: $3603; Undergraduates: $3555. *Scholarships, grants, and awards:* Federal Pell, FSEOG, state, private, college/university gift aid from institutional funds.

GIFT AID (NON-NEED-BASED) *Total amount:* $6,700,500 (85% institutional, 15% external sources). *Receiving aid:* Freshmen: 36% (341). Undergraduates: 22% (849). *Average award:* Freshmen: $3004. Undergraduates: $3054. *Scholarships, grants, and awards by category: Academic interests/achievement:* architecture, biological sciences, business, computer science, education, English, foreign languages, general academic interests/achievements, humanities, international studies, library science, mathematics, physical sciences, religion/biblical studies, social sciences. *Creative arts/performance:* art/fine arts, dance, journalism/publications, music, theater/drama. *Special achievements/activities:* leadership. *Special characteristics:* adult students, children and siblings of alumni, children of faculty/staff, local/state students, religious affiliation. *Tuition waivers:* Full or partial for senior citizens. *ROTC:* Army cooperative.

LOANS *Student loans:* $12,615,068 (47% need-based, 53% non-need-based). 54% of past graduating class borrowed through all loan programs. *Average indebtedness per student:* $29,964. *Average need-based loan:* Freshmen: $3299. Undergraduates: $4177. *Parent loans:* $4,726,438 (100% non-need-based). *Programs:* Federal Direct (Subsidized and Unsubsidized Stafford, PLUS), Perkins.

WORK-STUDY *Federal work-study:* 91 jobs averaging $1156. *State or other work-study/employment:* Total amount: $1,812,780 (100% non-need-based). 813 part-time jobs averaging $1757.

APPLYING FOR FINANCIAL AID *Required financial aid form:* FAFSA. *Financial aid deadline:* 6/1 (priority: 2/1). *Notification date:* Continuous beginning 12/1. Students must reply by 5/1 or within 2 weeks of notification.

CONTACT Ms. Heidi Hunter-Goldsworthy, Director of Financial Aid, University of Mary Washington, 1301 College Avenue, Fredericksburg, VA 22401-5358, 540-654-2468 or toll-free 800-468-5614. *Fax:* 540-654-1858. *E-mail:* hhunterg@umw.edu. *Website:* http://www.umw.edu/.

UNIVERSITY OF MASSACHUSETTS AMHERST
Amherst, MA

Tuition & fees (MA res): $15,411	Average undergraduate aid package: $17,687

ABOUT THE INSTITUTION State-supported, coed. *Awards:* certificates, associate, bachelor's, master's, and doctoral degrees. 88 undergraduate majors. *Total enrollment:* 30,340. Undergraduates: 22,630. Freshmen: 4,761. Federal methodology is used as a basis for awarding need-based institutional aid.

UNDERGRADUATE EXPENSES for 2017–2018 *Application fee:* $80. *One-time required fee:* $185. *Tuition, state resident:* full-time $15,030; part-time $5264 per term. *Tuition, nonresident:* full-time $33,096; part-time $11,685 per term. *Required fees:* full-time $381; $191 per term. Full-time tuition and fees vary according to class time, location, program, reciprocity agreements, and student level. Part-time tuition and fees vary according to class time, course load, location, program, reciprocity agreements, and student level. *College room and board:* $12,258; *Room only:* $6862. Room and board charges vary according to board plan and housing facility.

FRESHMAN FINANCIAL AID (Fall 2016) 3,989 applied for aid; of those 65% were deemed to have need. 99% of freshmen with need received aid; of those 14% had need fully met. *Average percent of need met:* 83% (excluding resources awarded to replace EFC). *Average financial aid package:* $17,495 (excluding resources awarded to replace EFC). 28% of all full-time freshmen had no need and received non-need-based gift aid.

UNDERGRADUATE FINANCIAL AID (Fall 2016) 16,906 applied for aid; of those 71% were deemed to have need. 99% of undergraduates with need received aid; of those 14% had need fully met. *Average percent of need met:* 86% (excluding resources awarded to replace EFC). *Average financial aid package:* $17,687 (excluding resources awarded to replace EFC). 23% of all full-time undergraduates had no need and received non-need-based gift aid.

GIFT AID (NEED-BASED) *Total amount:* $109,234,650 (23% federal, 7% state, 67% institutional, 3% external sources). *Receiving aid:* Freshmen: 51% (2,386); all full-time undergraduates: 49% (10,493). *Average award:* Freshmen: $10,965; Undergraduates: $10,708. *Scholarships, grants, and awards:* Federal Pell, FSEOG, state, private, college/university gift aid from institutional funds.

GIFT AID (NON-NEED-BASED) *Total amount:* $29,415,596 (1% federal, 2% state, 87% institutional, 10% external sources). *Receiving aid:* Freshmen: 5% (234). Undergraduates: 4% (869). *Average award:* Freshmen: $4848. Undergraduates:

$4707. *Scholarships, grants, and awards by category: Academic interests/achievement:* agriculture, architecture, biological sciences, business, communication, computer science, education, engineering/technologies, English, health fields, humanities, mathematics, military science, physical sciences, premedicine, social sciences. *Creative arts/performance:* art/fine arts, dance, journalism/publications, music, theater/drama. *Special achievements/activities:* cheerleading/drum major, general special achievements/activities, leadership. *Special characteristics:* children and siblings of alumni, children of faculty/staff, handicapped students, veterans. *Tuition waivers:* Full or partial for employees or children of employees, senior citizens. *ROTC:* Army, Air Force.

LOANS *Student loans:* $150,090,445 (60% need-based, 40% non-need-based). 68% of past graduating class borrowed through all loan programs. *Average indebtedness per student:* $31,860. *Average need-based loan:* Freshmen: $3957. Undergraduates: $4856. *Parent loans:* $33,582,916 (32% need-based, 68% non-need-based). *Programs:* Federal Direct (Subsidized and Unsubsidized Stafford, PLUS), Perkins, Federal Nursing.

WORK-STUDY *Federal work-study:* 2,100 jobs averaging $1454.

ATHLETIC AWARDS *Total amount:* $10,792,804 (32% need-based, 68% non-need-based).

APPLYING FOR FINANCIAL AID *Required financial aid form:* FAFSA. *Financial aid deadline (priority):* 3/1. *Notification date:* Continuous beginning 12/15. Students must reply by 5/1.

CONTACT Lauren Lamica, Office of Financial Aid Services, University of Massachusetts Amherst, 255 Whitmore Administration Building, 181 Presidents Drive, Amherst, MA 01003, 413-545-0801. *Fax:* 413-545-1700. *Website:* http://www.umass.edu/.

UNIVERSITY OF MASSACHUSETTS BOSTON
Boston, MA

Tuition & fees (MA res): $13,828	Average undergraduate aid package: $15,935

ABOUT THE INSTITUTION State-supported, coed. *Awards:* certificates, bachelor's, master's, and doctoral degrees. 46 undergraduate majors. *Total enrollment:* 16,415. Undergraduates: 12,660. Freshmen: 1,881. Federal methodology is used as a basis for awarding need-based institutional aid.

UNDERGRADUATE EXPENSES for 2017–2018 *Application fee:* $60. *Tuition, state resident:* full-time $13,503; part-time $562.25 per credit hour. *Tuition, nonresident:* full-time $32,660; part-time $1360.85 per credit hour. *Required fees:* full-time $325; $13.54 per credit hour. Full-time tuition and fees vary according to program. Part-time tuition and fees vary according to program.

FRESHMAN FINANCIAL AID (Fall 2016) 1,282 applied for aid; of those 83% were deemed to have need. 97% of freshmen with need received aid; of those 38% had need fully met. *Average percent of need met:* 88% (excluding resources awarded to replace EFC). *Average financial aid package:* $15,304 (excluding resources awarded to replace EFC). 9% of all full-time freshmen had no need and received non-need-based gift aid.

UNDERGRADUATE FINANCIAL AID (Fall 2016) 6,820 applied for aid; of those 88% were deemed to have need. 97% of undergraduates with need received aid; of those 41% had need fully met. *Average percent of need met:* 88% (excluding resources awarded to replace EFC). *Average financial aid package:* $15,935 (excluding resources awarded to replace EFC). 6% of all full-time undergraduates had no need and received non-need-based gift aid.

GIFT AID (NEED-BASED) *Total amount:* $58,708,313 (37% federal, 10% state, 51% institutional, 2% external sources). *Receiving aid:* Freshmen: 63% (975); all full-time undergraduates: 59% (5,430). *Average award:* Freshmen: $11,159; Undergraduates: $9773. *Scholarships, grants, and awards:* Federal Pell, FSEOG, state, private, college/university gift aid from institutional funds, TEACH Grants.

GIFT AID (NON-NEED-BASED) *Total amount:* $5,304,018 (1% state, 95% institutional, 4% external sources). *Receiving aid:* Freshmen: 5% (71). Undergraduates: 2% (187). *Average award:* Freshmen: $8732. Undergraduates: $7959. *Scholarships, grants, and awards by category: Academic interests/achievement:* general academic interests/achievements. *Special achievements/activities:* general special achievements/activities, leadership. *Special characteristics:* adult students, children of faculty/staff, children of union members/company employees, first-gener-

ation college students, local/state students, out-of-state students, veterans, veterans' children. **ROTC:** Army cooperative, Naval cooperative, Air Force cooperative.
LOANS Student loans: $64,134,993 (76% need-based, 24% non-need-based). 59% of past graduating class borrowed through all loan programs. *Average indebtedness per student:* $27,109. **Average need-based loan:** Freshmen: $3076. Undergraduates: $4198. **Parent loans:** $3,579,504 (35% need-based, 65% non-need-based). **Programs:** Federal Direct (Subsidized and Unsubsidized Stafford, PLUS), Perkins.
WORK-STUDY Federal work-study: jobs available.
APPLYING FOR FINANCIAL AID Required financial aid form: FAFSA. **Financial aid deadline (priority):** 3/1. **Notification date:** Continuous beginning 12/15.
CONTACT Katherine N. Lynch, Director of Financial Aid Services, University of Massachusetts Boston, 100 Morrissey Boulevard, Boston, MA 02125-3393, 617-287-6300. *Fax:* 617-287-6323. *E-mail:* katherine.lynch@umb.edu.
Website: http://www.umb.edu/.

LOANS Student loans: $41,200,000 (68% need-based, 32% non-need-based). 79% of past graduating class borrowed through all loan programs. *Average indebtedness per student:* $31,992. **Average need-based loan:** Freshmen: $6841. Undergraduates: $8707. **Parent loans:** $11,500,000 (43% need-based, 57% non-need-based). **Programs:** Federal Direct (Subsidized and Unsubsidized Stafford, PLUS), Federal Nursing, state.
WORK-STUDY Federal work-study: Total amount: $1,400,000; 1,128 jobs averaging $1272. **State or other work-study/employment:** Part-time jobs available.
APPLYING FOR FINANCIAL AID Required financial aid form: FAFSA. **Financial aid deadline:** 6/30 (priority: 3/1). **Notification date:** Continuous beginning 2/1. Students must reply within 3 weeks of notification.
CONTACT Ms. Korinne Peterson, Director of Financial Aid, University of Massachusetts Dartmouth, 285 Old Westport Road, North Dartmouth, MA 02747-2300, 508-999-8643. *Fax:* 508-999-8935. *E-mail:* financialaid@umassd.edu.
Website: http://www.umassd.edu/.

UNIVERSITY OF MASSACHUSETTS DARTMOUTH
North Dartmouth, MA

Tuition & fees (MA res): $13,571	Average undergraduate aid package: $17,361

ABOUT THE INSTITUTION State-supported, coed. **Awards:** certificates, bachelor's, master's, and doctoral degrees. 47 undergraduate majors. **Total enrollment:** 8,406. Undergraduates: 6,763. Freshmen: 1,333. Federal methodology is used as a basis for awarding need-based institutional aid.
UNDERGRADUATE EXPENSES for 2017–2018 Application fee: $60. **One-time required fee:** $100. **Tuition, state resident:** full-time $13,166; part-time $548.58 per credit. **Tuition, nonresident:** full-time $27,880; part-time $1161.67 per credit. **Required fees:** full-time $405; $25.88 per credit. Full-time tuition and fees vary according to class time, program, and reciprocity agreements. Part-time tuition and fees vary according to class time, course load, program, and reciprocity agreements. **College room and board:** $12,936; **Room only:** $4475. Room and board charges vary according to board plan and housing facility.
FRESHMAN FINANCIAL AID (Fall 2017, est.) 1,236 applied for aid; of those 83% were deemed to have need. 100% of freshmen with need received aid; of those 33% had need fully met. **Average percent of need met:** 81% (excluding resources awarded to replace EFC). **Average financial aid package:** $17,203 (excluding resources awarded to replace EFC). 14% of all full-time freshmen had no need and received non-need-based gift aid.
UNDERGRADUATE FINANCIAL AID (Fall 2017, est.) 4,884 applied for aid; of those 86% were deemed to have need. 100% of undergraduates with need received aid; of those 35% had need fully met. **Average percent of need met:** 83% (excluding resources awarded to replace EFC). **Average financial aid package:** $17,361 (excluding resources awarded to replace EFC). 10% of all full-time undergraduates had no need and received non-need-based gift aid.
GIFT AID (NEED-BASED) Total amount: $36,950,000 (32% federal, 11% state, 54% institutional, 3% external sources). **Receiving aid:** Freshmen: 72% (948); all full-time undergraduates: 65% (3,735). **Average award:** Freshmen: $10,113; Undergraduates: $10,333. **Scholarships, grants, and awards:** Federal Pell, FSEOG, state, private, college/university gift aid from institutional funds.
GIFT AID (NON-NEED-BASED) Total amount: $3,810,000 (2% state, 92% institutional, 6% external sources). **Receiving aid:** Freshmen: 4% (52). Undergraduates: 3% (155). **Average award:** Freshmen: $4387. Undergraduates: $4476. **Scholarships, grants, and awards by category:** Academic interests/achievement: biological sciences, business, computer science, education, engineering/technologies, foreign languages, general academic interests/achievements, home economics, humanities, mathematics, physical sciences, social sciences. *Creative arts/performance:* applied art and design, art/fine arts. *Special achievements/activities:* community service. *Special characteristics:* adult students, children of faculty/staff, children of union members/company employees, children with a deceased or disabled parent, ethnic background, first-generation college students, local/state students, members of minority groups, previous college experience, public servants, veterans. **Tuition waivers:** Full or partial for employees or children of employees, senior citizens. **ROTC:** Army cooperative.

UNIVERSITY OF MASSACHUSETTS LOWELL
Lowell, MA

Tuition & fees (MA res): $14,800	Average undergraduate aid package: $15,884

ABOUT THE INSTITUTION State-supported, coed. **Awards:** certificates, associate, bachelor's, master's, and doctoral degrees. 46 undergraduate majors. **Total enrollment:** 18,316. Undergraduates: 14,013. Freshmen: 2,004. Federal methodology is used as a basis for awarding need-based institutional aid.
UNDERGRADUATE EXPENSES for 2017–2018 Application fee: $60. **Tuition, state resident:** full-time $14,350; part-time $598 per credit hour. **Tuition, nonresident:** full-time $31,415; part-time $1309 per credit hour. **Required fees:** full-time $450; $19 per credit hour. Part-time tuition and fees vary according to course load. **College room and board:** $12,496; **Room only:** $8254. Room and board charges vary according to board plan and housing facility.
FRESHMAN FINANCIAL AID (Fall 2016) 1,541 applied for aid; of those 71% were deemed to have need. 99% of freshmen with need received aid; of those 43% had need fully met. **Average percent of need met:** 89% (excluding resources awarded to replace EFC). **Average financial aid package:** $16,799 (excluding resources awarded to replace EFC). 21% of all full-time freshmen had no need and received non-need-based gift aid.
UNDERGRADUATE FINANCIAL AID (Fall 2016) 8,053 applied for aid; of those 76% were deemed to have need. 98% of undergraduates with need received aid; of those 44% had need fully met. **Average percent of need met:** 89% (excluding resources awarded to replace EFC). **Average financial aid package:** $15,884 (excluding resources awarded to replace EFC). 16% of all full-time undergraduates had no need and received non-need-based gift aid.
GIFT AID (NEED-BASED) Total amount: $47,495,241 (31% federal, 9% state, 57% institutional, 3% external sources). **Receiving aid:** Freshmen: 59% (987); all full-time undergraduates: 52% (5,183). **Average award:** Freshmen: $10,789; Undergraduates: $9151. **Scholarships, grants, and awards:** Federal Pell, FSEOG, state, private, college/university gift aid from institutional funds.
GIFT AID (NON-NEED-BASED) Total amount: $8,150,262 (91% institutional, 9% external sources). **Receiving aid:** Freshmen: 3% (56). Undergraduates: 3% (266). **Average award:** Freshmen: $6840. Undergraduates: $6877. **Scholarships, grants, and awards by category:** Academic interests/achievement: biological sciences, business, computer science, education, engineering/technologies, English, general academic interests/achievements, health fields, humanities, mathematics. *Creative arts/performance:* art/fine arts, music. *Special achievements/activities:* community service, general special achievements/activities. *Special characteristics:* children and siblings of alumni, children of faculty/staff, children of public servants, children of union members/company employees, general special characteristics, out-of-state students, veterans. **Tuition waivers:** Full or partial for employees or children of employees, senior citizens. **ROTC:** Army, Air Force.
LOANS Student loans: $72,857,615 (66% need-based, 34% non-need-based). 78% of past graduating class borrowed through all loan programs. *Average indebtedness per student:* $32,744. **Average need-based loan:** Freshmen: $3352. Undergraduates: $4350. **Parent loans:** $13,727,483 (30% need-based, 70% non-need-based). **Programs:** Federal Direct (Subsidized and Unsubsidized Stafford, PLUS), Perkins.

WORK-STUDY *Federal work-study:* jobs available. *State or other work-study/employment:* Total amount: $2,113,816 (95% need-based, 5% non-need-based). Part-time jobs available.
ATHLETIC AWARDS Total amount: $5,595,571 (29% need-based, 71% non-need-based).
APPLYING FOR FINANCIAL AID *Required financial aid form:* FAFSA. *Financial aid deadline (priority):* 3/1. *Notification date:* Continuous beginning 1/10.
CONTACT Joyce McLaughlin, Director of Financial Aid, University of Massachusetts Lowell, University Crossing, 220 Pawtucket Street, Suite 280, Lowell, MA 01854, 978-934-4220. *Fax:* 978-934-3009. *E-mail:* joyce_mclaughlin@uml.edu.
Website: http://www.uml.edu/.

UNIVERSITY OF MEMPHIS
Memphis, TN

Tuition & fees (TN res): $9701	Average undergraduate aid package: $10,102

ABOUT THE INSTITUTION State-supported, coed. *Awards:* certificates, bachelor's, master's, and doctoral degrees. 67 undergraduate majors. *Total enrollment:* 21,521. Undergraduates: 17,394. Freshmen: 2,669. Federal methodology is used as a basis for awarding need-based institutional aid.
UNDERGRADUATE EXPENSES for 2017–2018 *Application fee:* $25. *Tuition, state resident:* full-time $8064; part-time $320 per credit hour. *Tuition, nonresident:* full-time $21,413; part-time $808 per credit hour. *Required fees:* full-time $1637; $114 per credit hour. Full-time tuition and fees vary according to course load, degree level, program, and reciprocity agreements. Part-time tuition and fees vary according to course load, degree level, and program. *College room and board:* $9366; *Room only:* $5460. Room and board charges vary according to board plan, housing facility, and location.
FRESHMAN FINANCIAL AID (Fall 2017, est.) 2,460 applied for aid; of those 83% were deemed to have need. 99% of freshmen with need received aid; of those 6% had need fully met. *Average percent of need met:* 78% (excluding resources awarded to replace EFC). *Average financial aid package:* $13,037 (excluding resources awarded to replace EFC). 11% of all full-time freshmen had no need and received non-need-based gift aid.
UNDERGRADUATE FINANCIAL AID (Fall 2017, est.) 11,407 applied for aid; of those 83% were deemed to have need. 98% of undergraduates with need received aid; of those 5% had need fully met. *Average percent of need met:* 74% (excluding resources awarded to replace EFC). *Average financial aid package:* $10,102 (excluding resources awarded to replace EFC). 8% of all full-time undergraduates had no need and received non-need-based gift aid.
GIFT AID (NEED-BASED) *Total amount:* $47,699,659 (76% federal, 22% state, 2% institutional). *Receiving aid:* Freshmen: 77% (2,020); all full-time undergraduates: 65% (8,057). *Average award:* Freshmen: $7037; Undergraduates: $6667. *Scholarships, grants, and awards:* Federal Pell, FSEOG, state, private, college/university gift aid from institutional funds.
GIFT AID (NON-NEED-BASED) *Total amount:* $33,229,247 (55% state, 39% institutional, 6% external sources). *Receiving aid:* Freshmen: 62% (1,617). Undergraduates: 28% (3,406). *Average award:* Freshmen: $4589. Undergraduates: $4799. *Scholarships, grants, and awards by category:* Academic interests/achievement: architecture, biological sciences, business, communication, computer science, education, engineering/technologies, English, general academic interests/achievements, health fields, home economics, humanities, international studies, mathematics, military science, physical sciences, premedicine, social sciences. *Creative arts/performance:* applied art and design, art/fine arts, cinema/film/broadcasting, creative writing, dance, journalism/publications, music, theater/drama. *Special achievements/activities:* cheerleading/drum major, community service, general special achievements/activities, leadership. *Special characteristics:* adult students, children of educators, children of faculty/staff, children of public servants, first-generation college students, handicapped students, international students, local/state students, members of minority groups, public servants, veterans. *Tuition waivers:* Full or partial for employees or children of employees, senior citizens. *ROTC:* Army, Naval, Air Force.
LOANS *Student loans:* $71,830,229 (47% need-based, 53% non-need-based). 67% of past graduating class borrowed through all loan programs. *Average indebtedness per student:* $27,002. *Average need-based loan:* Freshmen: $3060. Undergraduates: $3964. *Parent loans:* $10,950,326 (100% non-need-based). *Programs:* Federal Direct (Subsidized and Unsubsidized Stafford, PLUS).

WORK-STUDY *Federal work-study:* Total amount: $324,918; 179 jobs averaging $2574. *State or other work-study/employment:* Total amount: $3,154,508 (100% non-need-based). Part-time jobs available.
ATHLETIC AWARDS Total amount: $8,073,734 (100% non-need-based).
APPLYING FOR FINANCIAL AID *Required financial aid form:* FAFSA. *Financial aid deadline (priority):* 3/1. *Notification date:* Continuous beginning 12/1. Students must reply by 8/1.
CONTACT Karen Smith, Director of Financial Aid, University of Memphis, Wilder Tower 103, Memphis, TN 38152, 901-678-3687 or toll-free 800-669-2678. *Fax:* 901-678-3590. *E-mail:* kasmith@memphis.edu.
Website: http://www.memphis.edu/.

UNIVERSITY OF MIAMI
Coral Gables, FL

Tuition & fees: $48,484	Average undergraduate aid package: $45,111

ABOUT THE INSTITUTION Independent, coed. *Awards:* certificates, bachelor's, master's, and doctoral degrees. 113 undergraduate majors. *Total enrollment:* 17,003. Undergraduates: 10,832. Freshmen: 2,211. Both federal and institutional methodology are used as a basis for awarding need-based institutional aid.
UNDERGRADUATE EXPENSES for 2017–2018 *Application fee:* $70. *Comprehensive fee:* $62,150 includes full-time tuition ($47,040), mandatory fees ($1444), and room and board ($13,666). *College room only:* $7880. Full-time tuition and fees vary according to course load. Room and board charges vary according to board plan and housing facility. *Part-time tuition:* $1960 per credit hour. Part-time tuition and fees vary according to course load and program.
FRESHMAN FINANCIAL AID (Fall 2016) 1,279 applied for aid; of those 71% were deemed to have need. 99% of freshmen with need received aid; of those 74% had need fully met. *Average percent of need met:* 96% (excluding resources awarded to replace EFC). *Average financial aid package:* $46,432 (excluding resources awarded to replace EFC). 30% of all full-time freshmen had no need and received non-need-based gift aid.
UNDERGRADUATE FINANCIAL AID (Fall 2016) 5,292 applied for aid; of those 80% were deemed to have need. 99% of undergraduates with need received aid; of those 83% had need fully met. *Average percent of need met:* 86% (excluding resources awarded to replace EFC). *Average financial aid package:* $45,111 (excluding resources awarded to replace EFC). 29% of all full-time undergraduates had no need and received non-need-based gift aid.
GIFT AID (NEED-BASED) *Total amount:* $102,588,058 (9% federal, 6% state, 81% institutional, 4% external sources). *Receiving aid:* Freshmen: 35% (709); all full-time undergraduates: 34% (3,410). *Average award:* Freshmen: $32,486; Undergraduates: $29,853. *Scholarships, grants, and awards:* Federal Pell, FSEOG, state, private, college/university gift aid from institutional funds.
GIFT AID (NON-NEED-BASED) *Total amount:* $75,959,360 (13% state, 79% institutional, 8% external sources). *Receiving aid:* Freshmen: 23% (466). Undergraduates: 18% (1,829). *Average award:* Freshmen: $19,482. Undergraduates: $18,825. *Scholarships, grants, and awards by category:* Academic interests/achievement: 5,400 awards ($116,207,501 total): architecture, biological sciences, business, communication, computer science, education, engineering/technologies, English, foreign languages, general academic interests/achievements, home economics, humanities, international studies, library science, mathematics, physical sciences, pre-medicine, religion/biblical studies, social sciences. *Creative arts/performance:* 321 awards ($7,690,118 total): music, performing arts, theater/drama. *Special achievements/activities:* 145 awards ($1,945,545 total): leadership, religious involvement. *Special characteristics:* 934 awards ($30,099,547 total): children of faculty/staff, first-generation college students, international students, veterans, veterans' children. *Tuition waivers:* Full or partial for employees or children of employees. *ROTC:* Army, Air Force.
LOANS *Student loans:* $15,830,731 (69% need-based, 31% non-need-based). 35% of past graduating class borrowed through all loan programs. *Average indebtedness per student:* $25,000. *Average need-based loan:* Freshmen: $1600. Undergraduates: $2325. *Parent loans:* $15,336,009 (19% need-based, 81% non-need-based). *Programs:* Federal Direct (Subsidized and Unsubsidized Stafford, PLUS), Perkins, Federal Nursing, college/university, private loans.

WORK-STUDY *Federal work-study:* 2,539 jobs averaging $3086. *State or other work-study/employment:* Total amount: $683,301 (3% need-based, 97% non-need-based). 209 part-time jobs averaging $3269.
ATHLETIC AWARDS Total amount: $19,309,252 (8% need-based, 92% non-need-based).
APPLYING FOR FINANCIAL AID *Required financial aid forms:* FAFSA, CSS Financial Aid PROFILE, state aid form, noncustodial (divorced/separated) parent's statement, business/farm supplement, parent and student federal income tax form(s), W-2 forms. *Financial aid deadline:* 4/15 (priority: 1/1). *Notification date:* Continuous beginning 1/20. Students must reply by 5/1.
CONTACT Mr. Raymond Nault-Hix, Executive Director for Financial Assistance Services, University of Miami, 1306 Stanford Drive, University Center, Suite 2275, Coral Gables, FL 33146, 305-284-5212. *Fax:* 305-284-8641. *E-mail:* rnaulthix@ miami.edu.
Website: http://www.miami.edu/.

UNIVERSITY OF MICHIGAN
Ann Arbor, MI

Tuition & fees (MI res): $14,826	Average undergraduate aid package: $26,477

ABOUT THE INSTITUTION State-supported, coed. *Awards:* certificates, bachelor's, master's, and doctoral degrees. 127 undergraduate majors. *Total enrollment:* 44,718. Undergraduates: 28,983. Freshmen: 6,689. Both federal and institutional methodology are used as a basis for awarding need-based institutional aid.
UNDERGRADUATE EXPENSES for 2017–2018 *Application fee:* $75. *Tuition, state resident:* full-time $14,498; part-time $573 per credit hour. *Tuition, nonresident:* full-time $47,148; part-time $1934 per credit hour. *Required fees:* full-time $328; $164 per term. Full-time tuition and fees vary according to course load, degree level, program, and student level. Part-time tuition and fees vary according to course load, degree level, program, and student level. *College room and board:* $11,198. Room and board charges vary according to board plan and housing facility.
FRESHMAN FINANCIAL AID (Fall 2016) 4,541 applied for aid; of those 60% were deemed to have need. 95% of freshmen with need received aid; of those 75% had need fully met. *Average percent of need met:* 92% (excluding resources awarded to replace EFC). *Average financial aid package:* $27,050 (excluding resources awarded to replace EFC). 14% of all full-time freshmen had no need and received non-need-based gift aid.
UNDERGRADUATE FINANCIAL AID (Fall 2016) 14,512 applied for aid; of those 74% were deemed to have need. 97% of undergraduates with need received aid; of those 80% had need fully met. *Average percent of need met:* 93% (excluding resources awarded to replace EFC). *Average financial aid package:* $26,477 (excluding resources awarded to replace EFC). 13% of all full-time undergraduates had no need and received non-need-based gift aid.
GIFT AID (NEED-BASED) *Total amount:* $171,291,670 (13% federal, 87% institutional). *Receiving aid:* Freshmen: 32% (2,145); all full-time undergraduates: 31% (8,533). *Average award:* Freshmen: $19,099; Undergraduates: $19,648. *Scholarships, grants, and awards:* Federal Pell, FSEOG, state, private, college/university gift aid from institutional funds, TEACH Grants; Iraq and Afghanistan Service Grants, Michigan Competitive Scholarships.
GIFT AID (NON-NEED-BASED) *Total amount:* $86,364,382 (9% federal, 2% state, 70% institutional, 19% external sources). *Receiving aid:* Freshmen: 30% (1,971). Undergraduates: 25% (6,836). *Average award:* Freshmen: $4732. Undergraduates: $5568. *Scholarships, grants, and awards by category: Academic interests/achievement:* architecture, area/ethnic studies, biological sciences, business, communication, computer science, education, engineering/technologies, English, foreign languages, general academic interests/achievements, health fields, humanities, international studies, library science, mathematics, military science, physical sciences, premedicine, social sciences. *Creative arts/performance:* art/fine arts, cinema/film/ broadcasting, creative writing, dance, journalism/publications, music, performing arts, theater/drama. *Special achievements/activities:* community service, general special achievements/activities, leadership. *Special characteristics:* children of faculty/staff, children of workers in trades, handicapped students, international students, local/state students, members of minority groups, out-of-state students. *ROTC:* Army, Naval, Air Force.
LOANS *Student loans:* $71,899,503 (50% need-based, 50% non-need-based). 41% of past graduating class borrowed through all loan programs. *Average indebtedness*

per student: $25,712. *Average need-based loan:* Freshmen: $4295. Undergraduates: $5314. *Parent loans:* $27,542,137 (100% non-need-based). *Programs:* Federal Direct (Subsidized and Unsubsidized Stafford, PLUS), Perkins, Federal Nursing, college/university, Health Professions Student Loans (HPSL).
WORK-STUDY *Federal work-study:* 5,120 jobs averaging $2745.
ATHLETIC AWARDS Total amount: $22,134,910 (100% non-need-based).
APPLYING FOR FINANCIAL AID *Required financial aid forms:* FAFSA, CSS Financial Aid PROFILE. *Financial aid deadline:* 4/30. *Notification date:* Continuous beginning 3/15.
CONTACT Office of Financial Aid, University of Michigan, 2500 Student Activities Building, 515 East Jefferson Street, Ann Arbor, MI 48109-1316, 734-763-6600. *Fax:* 734-647-3081. *E-mail:* financial.aid@umich.edu.
Website: http://www.umich.edu/.

UNIVERSITY OF MICHIGAN–DEARBORN
Dearborn, MI

Tuition & fees (MI res): $12,472	Average undergraduate aid package: $10,215

ABOUT THE INSTITUTION State-supported, coed. *Awards:* certificates, bachelor's, master's, and doctoral degrees. 70 undergraduate majors. *Total enrollment:* 9,339. Undergraduates: 7,141. Freshmen: 1,106. Federal methodology is used as a basis for awarding need-based institutional aid.
UNDERGRADUATE EXPENSES for 2017–2018 *Tuition, state resident:* full-time $11,718; part-time $463 per credit hour. *Tuition, nonresident:* full-time $23,952; part-time $953 per credit hour. *Required fees:* full-time $754; $377 per term. Full-time tuition and fees vary according to course level, course load, degree level, program, and student level. Part-time tuition and fees vary according to course level, course load, degree level, program, and student level.
FRESHMAN FINANCIAL AID (Fall 2016) 909 applied for aid; of those 78% were deemed to have need. 99% of freshmen with need received aid; of those 10% had need fully met. *Average percent of need met:* 64% (excluding resources awarded to replace EFC). *Average financial aid package:* $10,866 (excluding resources awarded to replace EFC). 17% of all full-time freshmen had no need and received non-need-based gift aid.
UNDERGRADUATE FINANCIAL AID (Fall 2016) 3,825 applied for aid; of those 88% were deemed to have need. 98% of undergraduates with need received aid; of those 8% had need fully met. *Average percent of need met:* 56% (excluding resources awarded to replace EFC). *Average financial aid package:* $10,215 (excluding resources awarded to replace EFC). 14% of all full-time undergraduates had no need and received non-need-based gift aid.
GIFT AID (NEED-BASED) *Total amount:* $23,276,876 (56% federal, 3% state, 40% institutional, 1% external sources). *Receiving aid:* Freshmen: 54% (560); all full-time undergraduates: 51% (2,543). *Average award:* Freshmen: $6419; Undergraduates: $6028. *Scholarships, grants, and awards:* Federal Pell, FSEOG, state, private, college/university gift aid from institutional funds.
GIFT AID (NON-NEED-BASED) *Total amount:* $4,454,432 (96% institutional, 4% external sources). *Receiving aid:* Freshmen: 39% (411). Undergraduates: 32% (1,579). *Average award:* Freshmen: $5124. Undergraduates: $5760. *Scholarships, grants, and awards by category: Academic interests/achievement:* 2,181 awards ($8,809,655 total): biological sciences, business, communication, computer science, education, engineering/technologies, foreign languages, general academic interests/ achievements, international studies, mathematics, physical sciences, social sciences. *Creative arts/performance:* 17 awards ($17,675 total): art/fine arts, cinema/film/broadcasting, creative writing, debating, general creative arts/performance, journalism/publications. *Special achievements/activities:* 186 awards ($538,698 total): community service, general special achievements/activities, leadership, memberships. *Special characteristics:* 268 awards ($2,104,604 total): adult students, children and siblings of alumni, children of faculty/staff, ethnic background, general special characteristics, handicapped students, international students, members of minority groups, out-of-state students, previous college experience, public servants. *Tuition waivers:* Full or partial for employees or children of employees, senior citizens. *ROTC:* Army cooperative.
LOANS *Student loans:* $26,377,050 (91% need-based, 9% non-need-based). 57% of past graduating class borrowed through all loan programs. *Average indebtedness*

per student: $25,759. *Average need-based loan:* Freshmen: $3315. Undergraduates: $4383. *Parent loans:* $3,802,411 (41% need-based, 59% non-need-based). *Programs:* Federal Direct (Subsidized and Unsubsidized Stafford, PLUS), alternative loans.

WORK-STUDY *Federal work-study:* 221 jobs averaging $1193. *State or other work-study/employment:* 732 part-time jobs averaging $3974.

ATHLETIC AWARDS Total amount: $373,646 (65% need-based, 35% non-need-based).

APPLYING FOR FINANCIAL AID *Required financial aid form:* FAFSA. *Financial aid deadline (priority):* 1/1. *Notification date:* Continuous beginning 12/10. Students must reply by 5/1 or within 4 weeks of notification.

CONTACT Ms. Katherine M. Allen, Director of Financial Aid and Scholarships, University of Michigan–Dearborn, 4901 Evergreen Road, 1183 University Center, Dearborn, MI 48128-2406, 313-593-5300. *Fax:* 313-593-5313. *E-mail:* umd-ask-ofa@umich.edu.

Website: http://www.umdearborn.edu/.

UNIVERSITY OF MICHIGAN–FLINT
Flint, MI

Tuition & fees (MI res): $11,334	Average undergraduate aid package: $12,813

ABOUT THE INSTITUTION State-supported, coed. *Awards:* certificates, bachelor's, master's, and doctoral degrees. 79 undergraduate majors. *Total enrollment:* 7,836. Undergraduates: 6,434. Freshmen: 688. Federal methodology is used as a basis for awarding need-based institutional aid.

UNDERGRADUATE EXPENSES for 2017–2018 *Application fee:* $30. *Tuition, state resident:* full-time $10,902; part-time $430.75 per credit hour. *Tuition, nonresident:* full-time $21,222; part-time $857.75 per credit hour. *Required fees:* full-time $432; $167 per term. Full-time tuition and fees vary according to course level, course load, degree level, program, and student level. Part-time tuition and fees vary according to course level, course load, degree level, program, and student level. *College room and board:* $8437; *Room only:* $5437. Room and board charges vary according to housing facility.

FRESHMAN FINANCIAL AID (Fall 2016) 554 applied for aid; of those 82% were deemed to have need. 97% of freshmen with need received aid; of those 2% had need fully met. *Average percent of need met:* 68% (excluding resources awarded to replace EFC). *Average financial aid package:* $11,613 (excluding resources awarded to replace EFC). 11% of all full-time freshmen had no need and received non-need-based gift aid.

UNDERGRADUATE FINANCIAL AID (Fall 2016) 3,132 applied for aid; of those 89% were deemed to have need. 97% of undergraduates with need received aid; of those 3% had need fully met. *Average percent of need met:* 68% (excluding resources awarded to replace EFC). *Average financial aid package:* $12,813 (excluding resources awarded to replace EFC). 3% of all full-time undergraduates had no need and received non-need-based gift aid.

GIFT AID (NEED-BASED) *Total amount:* $16,241,023 (64% federal, 2% state, 34% institutional). *Receiving aid:* Freshmen: 52% (314); all full-time undergraduates: 55% (2,097). *Average award:* Freshmen: $7293; Undergraduates: $6312. *Scholarships, grants, and awards:* Federal Pell, FSEOG, state, private, college/university gift aid from institutional funds.

GIFT AID (NON-NEED-BASED) *Total amount:* $4,441,973 (4% state, 83% institutional, 13% external sources). *Receiving aid:* Freshmen: 42% (256). Undergraduates: 21% (791). *Average award:* Freshmen: $4243. Undergraduates: $4168. *Scholarships, grants, and awards by category:* Academic interests/achievement: biological sciences, business, communication, computer science, education, engineering/technologies, English, foreign languages, general academic interests/achievements, humanities, international studies, mathematics, physical sciences, pre-medicine, social sciences. *Creative arts/performance:* art/fine arts, music, performing arts, theater/drama. *Special achievements/activities:* community service, general special achievements/activities, hobbies/interests, leadership. *Special characteristics:* adult students, children and siblings of alumni, children of faculty/staff, children of union members/company employees, first-generation college students, general special characteristics, handicapped students, international students, local/state students, members of minority groups, veterans, veterans' children. *Tuition waivers:* Full or partial for senior citizens. *ROTC:* Army cooperative, Naval cooperative, Air Force cooperative.

LOANS *Student loans:* $29,309,363 (92% need-based, 8% non-need-based). 58% of past graduating class borrowed through all loan programs. *Average indebtedness*

per student: $33,258. *Average need-based loan:* Freshmen: $4394. Undergraduates: $4632. *Parent loans:* $2,030,657 (100% non-need-based). *Programs:* Federal Direct (Subsidized and Unsubsidized Stafford, PLUS), Perkins.

WORK-STUDY *Federal work-study:* 124 jobs averaging $2029.

APPLYING FOR FINANCIAL AID *Required financial aid forms:* FAFSA, institution's own financial aid form (for spring and summer applicants only). *Financial aid deadline (priority):* 12/1. *Notification date:* Continuous beginning 12/15.

CONTACT Lori Vedder, Office of Financial Aid, University of Michigan–Flint, Room 277 Pavilion, 303 East Kearsley Street, Flint, MI 48502-1950, 810-762-3444 or toll-free 800-942-5636. *Fax:* 810-766-6757. *E-mail:* financialaid@umflint.edu.

Website: http://www.umflint.edu/.

UNIVERSITY OF MINNESOTA, CROOKSTON
Crookston, MN

Tuition & fees (MN res): $12,202	Average undergraduate aid package: $13,339

ABOUT THE INSTITUTION State-supported, coed. *Awards:* bachelor's degrees. 43 undergraduate majors. *Total enrollment:* 2,823. Undergraduates: 2,823. Freshmen: 239. Federal methodology is used as a basis for awarding need-based institutional aid.

UNDERGRADUATE EXPENSES for 2017–2018 *Application fee:* $30. *Tuition, state resident:* full-time $10,282; part-time $395.47 per credit. *Tuition, nonresident:* full-time $10,282; part-time $395.47 per credit. *Required fees:* full-time $1920; $960 per term. *College room and board:* $7658; *Room only:* $3470. Room and board charges vary according to board plan and housing facility.

FRESHMAN FINANCIAL AID (Fall 2017, est.) 170 applied for aid; of those 82% were deemed to have need. 100% of freshmen with need received aid; of those 31% had need fully met. *Average percent of need met:* 85% (excluding resources awarded to replace EFC). *Average financial aid package:* $14,771 (excluding resources awarded to replace EFC). 11% of all full-time freshmen had no need and received non-need-based gift aid.

UNDERGRADUATE FINANCIAL AID (Fall 2017, est.) 902 applied for aid; of those 85% were deemed to have need. 99% of undergraduates with need received aid; of those 28% had need fully met. *Average percent of need met:* 81% (excluding resources awarded to replace EFC). *Average financial aid package:* $13,339 (excluding resources awarded to replace EFC). 6% of all full-time undergraduates had no need and received non-need-based gift aid.

GIFT AID (NEED-BASED) *Total amount:* $7,748,789 (36% federal, 24% state, 36% institutional, 4% external sources). *Receiving aid:* Freshmen: 72% (138); all full-time undergraduates: 65% (732). *Average award:* Freshmen: $11,401; Undergraduates: $9708. *Scholarships, grants, and awards:* Federal Pell, FSEOG, state, private, college/university gift aid from institutional funds, Academic Competitiveness Grants.

GIFT AID (NON-NEED-BASED) *Total amount:* $375,105 (7% state, 68% institutional, 25% external sources). *Receiving aid:* Freshmen: 5% (10). Undergraduates: 4% (41). *Average award:* Freshmen: $2710. Undergraduates: $2466. *Scholarships, grants, and awards by category:* Academic interests/achievement: agriculture, biological sciences, general academic interests/achievements. *Creative arts/performance:* general creative arts/performance. *Special achievements/activities:* leadership. *Special characteristics:* children and siblings of alumni, children of faculty/staff, ethnic background, first-generation college students, general special characteristics, local/state students, members of minority groups. *Tuition waivers:* Full or partial for senior citizens. *ROTC:* Air Force cooperative.

LOANS *Student loans:* $8,701,321 (62% need-based, 38% non-need-based). 66% of past graduating class borrowed through all loan programs. *Average indebtedness per student:* $26,696. *Average need-based loan:* Freshmen: $3378. Undergraduates: $4000. *Parent loans:* $376,243 (23% need-based, 77% non-need-based). *Programs:* Federal Direct (Subsidized and Unsubsidized Stafford, PLUS), Perkins, state, private loans.

WORK-STUDY *Federal work-study:* Total amount: $371,692; jobs available. *State or other work-study/employment:* Total amount: $281,793 (100% need-based). Part-time jobs available.

ATHLETIC AWARDS Total amount: $1,235,269 (77% need-based, 23% non-need-based).

APPLYING FOR FINANCIAL AID *Required financial aid form:* FAFSA. *Financial aid deadline (priority):* 3/1. *Notification date:* Continuous beginning 3/1. Students must reply within 8 weeks of notification.

CONTACT Cynthia Prom, Director of Financial Aid, University of Minnesota, Crookston, 4 Hill Hall, 2900 University Avenue, Crookston, MN 56716-5001, 218-281-8576 or toll-free 800-862-6466. *Fax:* 218-281-8575. *E-mail:* cprom@crk.umn.edu. *Website:* http://www.umcrookston.edu/.

UNIVERSITY OF MINNESOTA, DULUTH
Duluth, MN

Tuition & fees (MN res): $13,344	Average undergraduate aid package: $12,652

ABOUT THE INSTITUTION State-supported, coed. *Awards:* certificates, bachelor's, master's, and doctoral degrees. 85 undergraduate majors. *Total enrollment:* 11,168. Undergraduates: 10,135. Freshmen: 2,275. Federal methodology is used as a basis for awarding need-based institutional aid.

UNDERGRADUATE EXPENSES for 2017–2018 *Application fee:* $40. *Tuition, state resident:* full-time $12,016; part-time $462 per credit. *Tuition, nonresident:* full-time $17,134; part-time $659 per credit. *Required fees:* full-time $1328. Full-time tuition and fees vary according to course load, program, and reciprocity agreements. Part-time tuition and fees vary according to course load, program, and reciprocity agreements. *College room and board:* $7608. Room and board charges vary according to board plan and housing facility.

FRESHMAN FINANCIAL AID (Fall 2016) 1,892 applied for aid; of those 67% were deemed to have need. 99% of freshmen with need received aid; of those 29% had need fully met. *Average percent of need met:* 74% (excluding resources awarded to replace EFC). *Average financial aid package:* $13,155 (excluding resources awarded to replace EFC). 17% of all full-time freshmen had no need and received non-need-based gift aid.

UNDERGRADUATE FINANCIAL AID (Fall 2016) 6,922 applied for aid; of those 71% were deemed to have need. 98% of undergraduates with need received aid; of those 27% had need fully met. *Average percent of need met:* 72% (excluding resources awarded to replace EFC). *Average financial aid package:* $12,652 (excluding resources awarded to replace EFC). 15% of all full-time undergraduates had no need and received non-need-based gift aid.

GIFT AID (NEED-BASED) *Total amount:* $35,579,885 (26% federal, 33% state, 34% institutional, 7% external sources). *Receiving aid:* Freshmen: 55% (1,167); all full-time undergraduates: 50% (4,273). *Average award:* Freshmen: $8190; Undergraduates: $8032. *Scholarships, grants, and awards:* Federal Pell, FSEOG, state, private, college/university gift aid from institutional funds.

GIFT AID (NON-NEED-BASED) *Total amount:* $2,650,456 (2% state, 74% institutional, 24% external sources). *Receiving aid:* Freshmen: 12% (261). Undergraduates: 10% (828). *Average award:* Freshmen: $1889. Undergraduates: $2316. *Scholarships, grants, and awards by category:* Academic interests/achievement: general academic interests/achievements. *Tuition waivers:* Full or partial for children of alumni, employees or children of employees. *ROTC:* Air Force.

LOANS *Student loans:* $50,459,489 (72% need-based, 28% non-need-based). 73% of past graduating class borrowed through all loan programs. *Average indebtedness per student:* $30,445. *Average need-based loan:* Freshmen: $6579. Undergraduates: $6501. *Parent loans:* $9,023,280 (62% need-based, 38% non-need-based). *Programs:* Federal Direct (Subsidized and Unsubsidized Stafford, PLUS), Perkins, state.

WORK-STUDY *Federal work-study:* 499 jobs averaging $814. *State or other work-study/employment:* Total amount: $866,373 (100% need-based). 1,340 part-time jobs averaging $647.

ATHLETIC AWARDS Total amount: $2,120,204 (82% need-based, 18% non-need-based).

APPLYING FOR FINANCIAL AID *Required financial aid form:* FAFSA. *Financial aid deadline:* Continuous. *Notification date:* Continuous beginning 2/1.

CONTACT Ms. Brenda Herzig, Director of Financial Aid, University of Minnesota, Duluth, 10 University Drive, 184 Darland Administration Building, Duluth, MN 55812-2496, 218-726-8000 or toll-free 800-232-1339. *Fax:* 218-726-8219. *Website:* http://www.d.umn.edu/.

UNIVERSITY OF MINNESOTA, MORRIS
Morris, MN

ABOUT THE INSTITUTION State-supported, coed. *Awards:* bachelor's degrees. 39 undergraduate majors. *Total enrollment:* 1,627. Undergraduates: 1,627. Freshmen: 356.

GIFT AID (NEED-BASED) *Scholarships, grants, and awards:* Federal Pell, FSEOG, state, private, college/university gift aid from institutional funds.

GIFT AID (NON-NEED-BASED) *Scholarships, grants, and awards by category:* Academic interests/achievement: general academic interests/achievements. Creative arts/performance: music. Special achievements/activities: general special achievements/activities. Special characteristics: ethnic background, international students, members of minority groups, veterans, veterans' children.

LOANS *Programs:* Federal Direct (Subsidized and Unsubsidized Stafford, PLUS), Perkins, state, non-federal education loans.

WORK-STUDY *Federal work-study:* 307 jobs averaging $1317. *State or other work-study/employment:* Total amount: $159,093 (100% need-based). 96 part-time jobs averaging $1515.

APPLYING FOR FINANCIAL AID *Required financial aid forms:* FAFSA, noncustodial (divorced/separated) parent's statement.

CONTACT Ms. Jill Beauregard, Director of Financial Aid, University of Minnesota, Morris, 600 East 4th Street, Morris, MN 56267, 320-589-6046 or toll-free 888-866-3382. *Fax:* 320-589-1673. *E-mail:* morrisfa@morris.umn.edu. *Website:* http://www.morris.umn.edu/.

UNIVERSITY OF MINNESOTA ROCHESTER
Rochester, MN

CONTACT Financial Aid Office, University of Minnesota Rochester, 111 South Broadway, Suite 300, Rochester, MN 55904, 877-280-4699. *Website:* http://www.r.umn.edu/.

UNIVERSITY OF MINNESOTA, TWIN CITIES CAMPUS
Minneapolis, MN

Tuition & fees (MN res): $14,417	Average undergraduate aid package: $13,381

ABOUT THE INSTITUTION State-supported, coed. *Awards:* certificates, diplomas, bachelor's, master's, and doctoral degrees. 118 undergraduate majors. *Total enrollment:* 51,848. Undergraduates: 35,433. Freshmen: 6,195. Federal methodology is used as a basis for awarding need-based institutional aid.

UNDERGRADUATE EXPENSES for 2017–2018 *Application fee:* $55. *Tuition, state resident:* full-time $12,800; part-time $492 per credit hour. *Tuition, nonresident:* full-time $24,986; part-time $884 per credit hour. *Required fees:* full-time $1617. Full-time tuition and fees vary according to program and reciprocity agreements. Part-time tuition and fees vary according to course load, program, and reciprocity agreements. *College room and board:* $9852; *Room only:* $5586. Room and board charges vary according to board plan, housing facility, and location.

FRESHMAN FINANCIAL AID (Fall 2017, est.) 5,066 applied for aid; of those 61% were deemed to have need. 99% of freshmen with need received aid; of those 26% had need fully met. *Average percent of need met:* 76% (excluding resources awarded to replace EFC). *Average financial aid package:* $13,686 (excluding resources awarded to replace EFC). 14% of all full-time freshmen had no need and received non-need-based gift aid.

UNDERGRADUATE FINANCIAL AID (Fall 2017, est.) 19,869 applied for aid; of those 72% were deemed to have need. 98% of undergraduates with need received aid; of those 22% had need fully met. *Average percent of need met:* 72% (excluding resources awarded to replace EFC). *Average financial aid package:* $13,381 (excluding resources awarded to replace EFC). 8% of all full-time undergraduates had no need and received non-need-based gift aid.

GIFT AID (NEED-BASED) *Total amount:* $138,440,038 (24% federal, 29% state, 41% institutional, 6% external sources). *Receiving aid:* Freshmen: 43% (2,634); all full-time undergraduates: 41% (12,080). *Average award:* Freshmen: $11,119; Undergraduates: $10,444. *Scholarships, grants, and awards:* Federal Pell, FSEOG, state, private, college/university gift aid from institutional funds, Federal Nursing, ROTC Scholarships, academic merit scholarships.

GIFT AID (NON-NEED-BASED) *Total amount:* $17,660,196 (80% institutional, 20% external sources). *Receiving aid:* Freshmen: 5% (289). Undergraduates: 3% (992). *Average award:* Freshmen: $5139. Undergraduates: $5006. *Scholarships, grants, and awards by category: Academic interests/achievement:* agriculture, architecture, area/ethnic studies, biological sciences, business, communication, computer science, education, engineering/technologies, English, foreign languages, general academic interests/achievements, health fields, home economics, humanities, international studies, library science, mathematics, military science, physical sciences, premedicine, religion/biblical studies, social sciences. *Creative arts/performance:* art/fine arts, general creative arts/performance. *Special achievements/activities:* hobbies/interests, leadership. *Special characteristics:* general special characteristics, local/state students, members of minority groups. *Tuition waivers:* Full or partial for senior citizens. *ROTC:* Army, Naval, Air Force.

LOANS *Student loans:* $119,129,467 (62% need-based, 38% non-need-based). 58% of past graduating class borrowed through all loan programs. *Average indebtedness per student:* $26,568. *Average need-based loan:* Freshmen: $3809. Undergraduates: $4734. *Parent loans:* $51,444,652 (27% need-based, 73% non-need-based). *Programs:* Federal Direct (Subsidized and Unsubsidized Stafford, PLUS), Perkins, Federal Nursing, state, college/university, Health Professions Student Loans (HPSL).

WORK-STUDY *Federal work-study:* Total amount: $4,633,900; jobs available. *State or other work-study/employment:* Total amount: $13,597,235 (100% need-based). Part-time jobs available.

ATHLETIC AWARDS Total amount: $10,911,991 (89% need-based, 11% non-need-based).

APPLYING FOR FINANCIAL AID *Required financial aid forms:* FAFSA, institution's own form. *Financial aid deadline (priority):* 3/1. *Notification date:* Continuous beginning 2/15.

CONTACT Office of Student Finance, University of Minnesota, Twin Cities Campus, 200 Fraser Hall, 106 Pleasant Street SE, Minneapolis, MN 55455, 612-624-1111 or toll-free 800-752-1000. *Fax:* 612-624-9584. *E-mail:* onestop@umn.edu. *Website:* http://www.twin-cities.umn.edu/.

UNIVERSITY OF MISSISSIPPI
Oxford, MS

Tuition & fees (MS res): $8290	Average undergraduate aid package: $10,630

ABOUT THE INSTITUTION State-supported, coed. 73 undergraduate majors. Federal methodology is used as a basis for awarding need-based institutional aid.

UNDERGRADUATE EXPENSES for 2017–2018 *Tuition, state resident:* full-time $8190; part-time $341.25 per credit hour. *Tuition, nonresident:* full-time $23,454; part-time $977.25 per credit hour. *Required fees:* full-time $100; $4.17 per credit hour. Full-time tuition and fees vary according to course load and program. Part-time tuition and fees vary according to course load and program. *College room and board:* $10,502. Room and board charges vary according to board plan and housing facility.

FRESHMAN FINANCIAL AID (Fall 2016) 2,873 applied for aid; of those 66% were deemed to have need. 97% of freshmen with need received aid; of those 19% had need fully met. *Average percent of need met:* 79% (excluding resources awarded to replace EFC). *Average financial aid package:* $13,656 (excluding resources awarded to replace EFC). 36% of all full-time freshmen had no need and received non-need-based gift aid.

UNDERGRADUATE FINANCIAL AID (Fall 2016) 11,136 applied for aid; of those 77% were deemed to have need. 97% of undergraduates with need received aid; of those 14% had need fully met. *Average percent of need met:* 75% (excluding resources awarded to replace EFC). *Average financial aid package:* $10,630 (excluding resources awarded to replace EFC). 27% of all full-time undergraduates had no need and received non-need-based gift aid.

GIFT AID (NEED-BASED) *Total amount:* $59,663,852 (36% federal, 9% state, 52% institutional, 3% external sources). *Receiving aid:* Freshmen: 44% (1,729); all full-time undergraduates: 42% (7,226). *Average award:* Freshmen: $10,013; Under-

graduates: $8954. *Scholarships, grants, and awards:* Federal Pell, FSEOG, state, private, college/university gift aid from institutional funds.

GIFT AID (NON-NEED-BASED) *Total amount:* $49,559,821 (5% state, 91% institutional, 4% external sources). *Receiving aid:* Freshmen: 8% (295). Undergraduates: 5% (871). *Average award:* Freshmen: $9026. Undergraduates: $8805. *Scholarships, grants, and awards by category: Academic interests/achievement:* $64,122,198 total: biological sciences, business, communication, computer science, education, engineering/technologies, English, foreign languages, general academic interests/achievements, health fields, home economics, humanities, international studies, mathematics, military science, physical sciences, premedicine, social sciences. *Creative arts/performance:* $1,464,236 total: art/fine arts, cinema/film/broadcasting, creative writing, debating, journalism/publications, music, performing arts, theater/drama. *Special achievements/activities:* $12,640,590 total: cheerleading/drum major, community service, general special achievements/activities, junior miss, leadership, memberships. *Special characteristics:* $20,430,656 total: adult students, children and siblings of alumni, children of faculty/staff, first-generation college students, general special characteristics, handicapped students, international students, local/state students, members of minority groups, out-of-state students, previous college experience, spouses of current students, veterans, veterans' children. *Tuition waivers:* Full or partial for children of alumni, employees or children of employees, senior citizens.

LOANS *Student loans:* $74,691,688 (65% need-based, 35% non-need-based). 50% of past graduating class borrowed through all loan programs. *Average indebtedness per student:* $30,731. *Average need-based loan:* Freshmen: $3462. Undergraduates: $4522. *Parent loans:* $32,606,063 (44% need-based, 56% non-need-based). *Programs:* Federal Direct (Subsidized and Unsubsidized Stafford, PLUS), Perkins, college/university, private loans, Health Professions Student Loans (HPSL).

WORK-STUDY *Federal work-study:* 376 jobs averaging $1381.

ATHLETIC AWARDS Total amount: $9,727,772 (43% need-based, 57% non-need-based).

APPLYING FOR FINANCIAL AID *Required financial aid form:* FAFSA. *Financial aid deadline (priority):* 3/1. *Notification date:* Continuous beginning 4/1. Students must reply within 4 weeks of notification.

CONTACT Ms. Laura Diven-Brown, Director of Financial Aid, University of Mississippi, 257 Martindale Center, University, MS 38677, 662-915-5788 or toll-free 800-653-6477 (in-state). *Fax:* 662-915-1164. *E-mail:* ldivenbr@olemiss.edu. *Website:* http://www.olemiss.edu/.

UNIVERSITY OF MISSISSIPPI MEDICAL CENTER
Jackson, MS

CONTACT Minetta Veazey, Administrative Secretary, University of Mississippi Medical Center, 2500 North State Street, Jackson, MS 39216, 601-984-1117. *Fax:* 601-984-6984. *E-mail:* mveazey@registrar.umsmed.edu. *Website:* http://www.umc.edu/.

UNIVERSITY OF MISSOURI
Columbia, MO

Tuition & fees (MO res): $9787	Average undergraduate aid package: $12,070

ABOUT THE INSTITUTION State-supported, coed. *Awards:* certificates, bachelor's, master's, and doctoral degrees. 115 undergraduate majors. *Total enrollment:* 30,870. Undergraduates: 23,817. Freshmen: 4,134. Federal methodology is used as a basis for awarding need-based institutional aid.

UNDERGRADUATE EXPENSES for 2017–2018 *Application fee:* $65. *Tuition, state resident:* full-time $8460; part-time $282 per credit hour. *Tuition, nonresident:* full-time $25,179; part-time $839.30 per credit hour. *Required fees:* full-time $1327. Full-time tuition and fees vary according to course load, program, and reciprocity agreements. Part-time tuition and fees vary according to course load, program, and reciprocity agreements. *College room and board:* $10,676; *Room only:* $7641. Room and board charges vary according to board plan and housing facility.

FRESHMAN FINANCIAL AID (Fall 2017, est.) 3,400 applied for aid; of those 68% were deemed to have need. 96% of freshmen with need received aid; of those 17%

had need fully met. *Average percent of need met:* 61% (excluding resources awarded to replace EFC). *Average financial aid package:* $12,455 (excluding resources awarded to replace EFC). 23% of all full-time freshmen had no need and received non-need-based gift aid.

UNDERGRADUATE FINANCIAL AID (Fall 2017, est.) 14,461 applied for aid; of those 74% were deemed to have need. 97% of undergraduates with need received aid; of those 14% had need fully met. *Average percent of need met:* 60% (excluding resources awarded to replace EFC). *Average financial aid package:* $12,070 (excluding resources awarded to replace EFC). 18% of all full-time undergraduates had no need and received non-need-based gift aid.

GIFT AID (NEED-BASED) *Total amount:* $77,292,421 (27% federal, 12% state, 54% institutional, 7% external sources). *Receiving aid:* Freshmen: 48% (1,983); all full-time undergraduates: 39% (8,641). *Average award:* Freshmen: $11,175; Undergraduates: $10,146. *Scholarships, grants, and awards:* Federal Pell, FSEOG, state, private, college/university gift aid from institutional funds, Federal Nursing.

GIFT AID (NON-NEED-BASED) *Total amount:* $30,784,357 (1% federal, 11% state, 71% institutional, 17% external sources). *Receiving aid:* Freshmen: 5% (209). Undergraduates: 3% (577). *Average award:* Freshmen: $6773. Undergraduates: $6338. *Scholarships, grants, and awards by category: Academic interests/achievement:* agriculture, area/ethnic studies, biological sciences, business, communication, computer science, education, engineering/technologies, English, foreign languages, general academic interests/achievements, health fields, home economics, humanities, international studies, library science, mathematics, physical sciences, premedicine, religion/biblical studies, social sciences. *Creative arts/performance:* art/fine arts, cinema/film/broadcasting, creative writing, journalism/publications, music, theater/drama. *Special achievements/activities:* cheerleading/drum major, general special achievements/activities, memberships. *Special characteristics:* adult students, children and siblings of alumni, children of faculty/staff, ethnic background, first-generation college students, international students, local/state students, members of minority groups, out-of-state students, veterans, veterans' children. *Tuition waivers:* Full or partial for employees or children of employees, senior citizens. *ROTC:* Army, Naval, Air Force.

LOANS *Student loans:* $83,268,800 (67% need-based, 33% non-need-based). 52% of past graduating class borrowed through all loan programs. *Average indebtedness per student:* $27,364. *Average need-based loan:* Freshmen: $3936. Undergraduates: $5091. *Parent loans:* $46,107,436 (48% need-based, 52% non-need-based). *Programs:* Federal Direct (Subsidized and Unsubsidized Stafford, PLUS), Perkins, Federal Nursing, state, college/university, alternative loans.

WORK-STUDY *Federal work-study:* Total amount: $1,170,617; jobs available.

ATHLETIC AWARDS Total amount: $9,798,713 (34% need-based, 66% non-need-based).

APPLYING FOR FINANCIAL AID *Required financial aid form:* FAFSA. *Financial aid deadline (priority):* 2/1. *Notification date:* Continuous beginning 12/15. Students must reply within 4 weeks of notification.

CONTACT Nicholas Prewett, Director of Student Financial Aid, University of Missouri, 11 Jesse Hall, Columbia, MO 65211, 573-882-7506 or toll-free 800-225-6075 (in-state). *Fax:* 573-884-5335. *E-mail:* finaidinfo@missouri.edu. *Website:* http://www.missouri.edu/.

UNIVERSITY OF MISSOURI–KANSAS CITY
Kansas City, MO

ABOUT THE INSTITUTION State-supported, coed. *Awards:* certificates, bachelor's, master's, and doctoral degrees. 52 undergraduate majors. *Total enrollment:* 16,944. Undergraduates: 11,708. Freshmen: 1,212.

GIFT AID (NEED-BASED) *Scholarships, grants, and awards:* Federal Pell, FSEOG, state, private, college/university gift aid from institutional funds, United Negro College Fund, Federal Nursing.

GIFT AID (NON-NEED-BASED) *Scholarships, grants, and awards by category: Academic interests/achievement:* general academic interests/achievements. *Creative arts/performance:* art/fine arts, debating, general creative arts/performance, music, performing arts. *Special achievements/activities:* general special achievements/activities, leadership. *Special characteristics:* children and siblings of alumni, ethnic background, local/state students, members of minority groups, out-of-state students.

LOANS *Programs:* Federal Direct (Subsidized and Unsubsidized Stafford, PLUS), Perkins, Federal Nursing, state, college/university.

WORK-STUDY *Federal work-study:* 632 jobs averaging $4144.

APPLYING FOR FINANCIAL AID *Required financial aid form:* FAFSA.

CONTACT Scott Young, Director of Financial Aid and Scholarships, University of Missouri–Kansas City, 5100 Rockhill Road, Kansas City, MO 64110-2499, 816-235-1154 or toll-free 800-775-8652. *Fax:* 816-235-5511. *E-mail:* youngsc@umkc.edu. *Website:* http://www.umkc.edu/.

UNIVERSITY OF MISSOURI–ST. LOUIS
St. Louis, MO

Tuition & fees (MO res): $10,275	Average undergraduate aid package: $11,989

ABOUT THE INSTITUTION State-supported, coed. *Awards:* certificates, bachelor's, master's, and doctoral degrees. 40 undergraduate majors. *Total enrollment:* 16,740. Undergraduates: 13,842. Freshmen: 482. Federal methodology is used as a basis for awarding need-based institutional aid.

UNDERGRADUATE EXPENSES for 2017–2018 *Application fee:* $35. *Tuition, state resident:* full-time $10,275; part-time $342.50 per credit hour. *Tuition, nonresident:* full-time $27,327; part-time $910.90 per credit hour. Full-time tuition and fees vary according to course level, course load, location, program, and reciprocity agreements. Part-time tuition and fees vary according to course level, course load, location, program, and reciprocity agreements. *College room and board:* $9363; *Room only:* $5340. Room and board charges vary according to board plan and housing facility.

FRESHMAN FINANCIAL AID (Fall 2017, est.) 416 applied for aid; of those 85% were deemed to have need. 99% of freshmen with need received aid; of those 29% had need fully met. *Average percent of need met:* 77% (excluding resources awarded to replace EFC). *Average financial aid package:* $14,284 (excluding resources awarded to replace EFC). 13% of all full-time freshmen had no need and received non-need-based gift aid.

UNDERGRADUATE FINANCIAL AID (Fall 2017, est.) 4,245 applied for aid; of those 87% were deemed to have need. 99% of undergraduates with need received aid; of those 20% had need fully met. *Average percent of need met:* 66% (excluding resources awarded to replace EFC). *Average financial aid package:* $11,989 (excluding resources awarded to replace EFC). 10% of all full-time undergraduates had no need and received non-need-based gift aid.

GIFT AID (NEED-BASED) *Total amount:* $28,554,296 (48% federal, 11% state, 36% institutional, 5% external sources). *Receiving aid:* Freshmen: 64% (301); all full-time undergraduates: 57% (2,998). *Average award:* Freshmen: $11,276; Undergraduates: $8292. *Scholarships, grants, and awards:* Federal Pell, FSEOG, state, private, college/university gift aid from institutional funds, United Negro College Fund, Federal Nursing, TEACH Grants.

GIFT AID (NON-NEED-BASED) *Total amount:* $6,290,648 (3% federal, 4% state, 63% institutional, 30% external sources). *Receiving aid:* Freshmen: 19% (89). Undergraduates: 10% (511). *Average award:* Freshmen: $6951. Undergraduates: $5614. *Scholarships, grants, and awards by category: Academic interests/achievement:* biological sciences, business, communication, computer science, education, engineering/technologies, English, foreign languages, general academic interests/achievements, home economics, humanities, international studies, mathematics, physical sciences, premedicine, social sciences. *Creative arts/performance:* art/fine arts, dance, music, theater/drama. *Special achievements/activities:* cheerleading/drum major, memberships. *Special characteristics:* adult students, children and siblings of alumni, children of faculty/staff, children with a deceased or disabled parent, ethnic background, first-generation college students, general special characteristics, international students, local/state students, members of minority groups, out-of-state students, previous college experience, spouses of deceased or disabled public servants, veterans, veterans' children. *Tuition waivers:* Full or partial for employees or children of employees, senior citizens. *ROTC:* Army, Air Force cooperative.

LOANS *Student loans:* $42,122,732 (80% need-based, 20% non-need-based). 62% of past graduating class borrowed through all loan programs. *Average indebtedness per student:* $25,873. *Average need-based loan:* Freshmen: $3182. Undergraduates: $4450. *Parent loans:* $2,125,949 (32% need-based, 68% non-need-based). *Programs:* Federal Direct (Subsidized and Unsubsidized Stafford, PLUS), Perkins, Federal Nursing, state.

WORK-STUDY *Federal work-study:* 83 jobs averaging $4307.

ATHLETIC AWARDS Total amount: $2,315,209 (88% need-based, 12% non-need-based).

APPLYING FOR FINANCIAL AID *Required financial aid form:* FAFSA. *Financial aid deadline (priority):* 2/1. *Notification date:* Continuous beginning 12/1. Students must reply within 2 weeks of notification.

CONTACT Ms. Svetlana Vejkovich, Associate Director, University of Missouri–St. Louis, One University Boulevard, 327 Millennium Student Center, St. Louis, MO 63121-4400, 314-516-5526 or toll-free 888-GO2-UMSL (in-state), 888-GO2-USML (out-of-state). *Fax:* 314-516-5408. *E-mail:* financialaid@umsl.edu. *Website:* http://www.umsl.edu/.

UNIVERSITY OF MOBILE
Mobile, AL

ABOUT THE INSTITUTION Independent Southern Baptist, coed. *Awards:* associate, bachelor's, and master's degrees. 37 undergraduate majors. *Total enrollment:* 1,604. Undergraduates: 1,443. Freshmen: 228.

GIFT AID (NEED-BASED) *Scholarships, grants, and awards:* Federal Pell, FSEOG, state, private, college/university gift aid from institutional funds, Federal Nursing.

GIFT AID (NON-NEED-BASED) *Scholarships, grants, and awards by category:* Creative arts/performance: art/fine arts, music, performing arts. *Special achievements/activities:* religious involvement. *Special characteristics:* children of faculty/staff, relatives of clergy.

LOANS *Programs:* Federal Direct (Subsidized and Unsubsidized Stafford, PLUS), Perkins, college/university.

WORK-STUDY *Federal work-study:* 55 jobs averaging $1575.

APPLYING FOR FINANCIAL AID *Required financial aid forms:* FAFSA, institution's own form, state aid form.

CONTACT Mrs. Marie Thomas Batson, Associate Vice President for Enrollment, University of Mobile, 5735 College Parkway, Mobile, AL 36613, 251-442-2370 or toll-free 800-946-7267. *E-mail:* mbatson@umobile.edu. *Website:* http://www.umobile.edu/.

UNIVERSITY OF MONTANA
Missoula, MT

Tuition & fees (MT res): $7244	Average undergraduate aid package: $11,594

ABOUT THE INSTITUTION State-supported, coed. *Awards:* certificates, associate, bachelor's, master's, and doctoral degrees. 90 undergraduate majors. *Total enrollment:* 11,865. Undergraduates: 9,323. Freshmen: 1,681. Federal methodology is used as a basis for awarding need-based institutional aid.

UNDERGRADUATE EXPENSES for 2018–2019 *Application fee:* $36. *Tuition, state resident:* full-time $5347; part-time $223 per credit hour. *Tuition, nonresident:* full-time $23,062; part-time $961 per credit hour. *Required fees:* full-time $1897; $115 per credit hour. Full-time tuition and fees vary according to degree level, location, program, reciprocity agreements, and student level. Part-time tuition and fees vary according to course load, degree level, location, and student level. *College room and board:* $9544. Room and board charges vary according to board plan and housing facility.

FRESHMAN FINANCIAL AID (Fall 2017, est.) 1,350 applied for aid; of those 74% were deemed to have need. 100% of freshmen with need received aid; of those 12% had need fully met. *Average percent of need met:* 67% (excluding resources awarded to replace EFC). *Average financial aid package:* $12,033 (excluding resources awarded to replace EFC). 22% of all full-time freshmen had no need and received non-need-based gift aid.

UNDERGRADUATE FINANCIAL AID (Fall 2017, est.) 5,478 applied for aid; of those 81% were deemed to have need. 99% of undergraduates with need received aid; of those 9% had need fully met. *Average percent of need met:* 62% (excluding resources awarded to replace EFC). *Average financial aid package:* $11,594 (excluding resources awarded to replace EFC). 18% of all full-time undergraduates had no need and received non-need-based gift aid.

GIFT AID (NEED-BASED) *Total amount:* $26,151,548 (63% federal, 32% institutional, 5% external sources). *Receiving aid:* Freshmen: 42% (649); all full-time undergraduates: 40% (2,936). *Average award:* Freshmen: $5319; Undergraduates: $5094. *Scholarships, grants, and awards:* Federal Pell, FSEOG, state, private, college/university gift aid from institutional funds.

GIFT AID (NON-NEED-BASED) *Total amount:* $5,769,167 (88% institutional, 12% external sources). *Receiving aid:* Freshmen: 38% (584). Undergraduates: 27% (1,967). *Average award:* Freshmen: $5134. Undergraduates: $4509. *Scholarships, grants, and awards by category:* Academic interests/achievement: biological sciences, business, computer science, education, English, foreign languages, general academic interests/achievements, health fields, humanities, international studies, mathematics, military science, physical sciences, premedicine, social sciences. *Creative arts/performance:* creative writing, dance, journalism/publications, music, performing arts, theater/drama. *Special achievements/activities:* cheerleading/drum major, leadership, rodeo. *Special characteristics:* children and siblings of alumni, children with a deceased or disabled parent, general special characteristics, international students, local/state students, out-of-state students, veterans. *Tuition waivers:* Full or partial for minority students, employees or children of employees, senior citizens. *ROTC:* Army.

LOANS *Student loans:* $54,096,425 (86% need-based, 14% non-need-based). 60% of past graduating class borrowed through all loan programs. *Average indebtedness per student:* $30,000. *Average need-based loan:* Freshmen: $3998. Undergraduates: $4698. *Parent loans:* $48,629,375 (67% need-based, 33% non-need-based). *Programs:* Federal Direct (Subsidized and Unsubsidized Stafford, PLUS), Perkins.

WORK-STUDY *Federal work-study:* Total amount: $6,773,240; 2,286 jobs averaging $2952. *State or other work-study/employment:* Total amount: $1,029,829 (63% need-based, 37% non-need-based). 10 part-time jobs averaging $2810.

ATHLETIC AWARDS Total amount: $1,987,450 (35% need-based, 65% non-need-based).

APPLYING FOR FINANCIAL AID *Required financial aid forms:* FAFSA, UM Supplemental Information Sheet. *Financial aid deadline (priority):* 12/31. *Notification date:* Continuous beginning 3/16. Students must reply within 4 weeks of notification.

CONTACT Mr. Kent McGowan, Director of Financial Aid, University of Montana, Lommasson Center 218, Missoula, MT 59812, 406-243-5373 or toll-free 800-462-8636. *Fax:* 406-243-4930. *E-mail:* faid@mso.umt.edu. *Website:* http://www.umt.edu/.

THE UNIVERSITY OF MONTANA WESTERN
Dillon, MT

Tuition & fees (MT res): $5502	Average undergraduate aid package: $3756

ABOUT THE INSTITUTION State-supported, coed. *Awards:* certificates, associate, and bachelor's degrees. 27 undergraduate majors. *Total enrollment:* 1,505. Undergraduates: 1,505. Freshmen: 336. Institutional methodology is used as a basis for awarding need-based institutional aid.

UNDERGRADUATE EXPENSES for 2017–2018 *Application fee:* $30. *Tuition, state resident:* full-time $4308; part-time $183 per credit hour. *Tuition, nonresident:* full-time $15,450; part-time $643.75 per course. *Required fees:* full-time $1194. Full-time tuition and fees vary according to course load, location, program, reciprocity agreements, and student level. Part-time tuition and fees vary according to course load, location, program, reciprocity agreements, and student level. *College room and board:* $7744; *Room only:* $2944. Room and board charges vary according to housing facility.

FRESHMAN FINANCIAL AID (Fall 2017, est.) 252 applied for aid; of those 87% were deemed to have need. 88% of freshmen with need received aid. *Average percent of need met:* 14% (excluding resources awarded to replace EFC). *Average financial aid package:* $3603 (excluding resources awarded to replace EFC). 1% of all full-time freshmen had no need and received non-need-based gift aid.

UNDERGRADUATE FINANCIAL AID (Fall 2017, est.) 1,064 applied for aid; of those 88% were deemed to have need. 88% of undergraduates with need received aid. *Average percent of need met:* 16% (excluding resources awarded to replace EFC). *Average financial aid package:* $3756 (excluding resources awarded to replace EFC). 1% of all full-time undergraduates had no need and received non-need-based gift aid.

GIFT AID (NEED-BASED) *Total amount:* $11,032,009 (52% federal, 3% state, 38% institutional, 7% external sources). *Receiving aid:* Freshmen: 54% (145); all full-time undergraduates: 48% (589). *Average award:* Freshmen: $2222; Undergraduates: $3382. *Scholarships, grants, and awards:* Federal Pell, FSEOG, state, private, college/university gift aid from institutional funds, Western Undergraduate Exchange (WUE) Scholarships.

GIFT AID (NON-NEED-BASED) *Total amount:* $4,293,180 (6% state, 78% institutional, 16% external sources). *Receiving aid:* Freshmen: 19% (52). Undergraduates: 19% (235). *Average award:* Freshmen: $1300. Undergraduates: $990. *Scholarships, grants, and awards by category:* Academic interests/achievement: biological sciences, business, education, English, general academic interests/achievements, humanities, mathematics, physical sciences, premedicine, social sciences. *Creative arts/performance:* art/fine arts. *Special achievements/activities:* general special achievements/activities, rodeo. *Special characteristics:* children of faculty/staff, first-generation college students, international students, members of minority groups, out-of-state students, veterans. *Tuition waivers:* Full or partial for minority students, employees or children of employees, senior citizens.

LOANS *Student loans:* $12,086,034 (80% need-based, 20% non-need-based). *Average need-based loan:* Freshmen: $3594. Undergraduates: $4058. *Parent loans:* $2,056,536 (72% need-based, 28% non-need-based). *Programs:* Federal Direct (Subsidized and Unsubsidized Stafford, PLUS), Perkins, college/university.

WORK-STUDY *Federal work-study:* Total amount: $557,253; jobs available. *State or other work-study/employment:* Total amount: $99,000 (72% need-based, 28% non-need-based). Part-time jobs available.

ATHLETIC AWARDS Total amount: $7,941,312 (39% need-based, 61% non-need-based).

APPLYING FOR FINANCIAL AID *Required financial aid forms:* FAFSA, Student Data Form. *Financial aid deadline (priority):* 3/1. *Notification date:* Continuous beginning 3/1. Students must reply by 7/1.

CONTACT Louise Driver, Director of Financial Aid, The University of Montana Western, 710 South Atlantic Street, Dillon, MT 59725, 406-683-7511 or toll-free 877-683-7331. *Fax:* 406-683-7510. *E-mail:* louise.driver@umwestern.edu. *Website:* http://www.umwestern.edu/.

UNIVERSITY OF MONTEVALLO
Montevallo, AL

Tuition & fees (AL res): $12,400	Average undergraduate aid package: $12,058

ABOUT THE INSTITUTION State-supported, coed. *Awards:* certificates, bachelor's, and master's degrees. 26 undergraduate majors. *Total enrollment:* 2,717. Undergraduates: 2,346. Freshmen: 487. Federal methodology is used as a basis for awarding need-based institutional aid.

UNDERGRADUATE EXPENSES for 2017–2018 *Application fee:* $30. *Tuition, state resident:* full-time $11,730; part-time $391 per credit hour. *Tuition, nonresident:* full-time $24,360; part-time $812 per credit hour. *Required fees:* full-time $670. *College room and board:* $7512; *Room only:* $4762. Room and board charges vary according to housing facility.

FRESHMAN FINANCIAL AID (Fall 2017, est.) 397 applied for aid; of those 83% were deemed to have need. 100% of freshmen with need received aid; of those 21% had need fully met. *Average percent of need met:* 62% (excluding resources awarded to replace EFC). *Average financial aid package:* $13,266 (excluding resources awarded to replace EFC). 27% of all full-time freshmen had no need and received non-need-based gift aid.

UNDERGRADUATE FINANCIAL AID (Fall 2017, est.) 1,630 applied for aid; of those 87% were deemed to have need. 99% of undergraduates with need received aid; of those 18% had need fully met. *Average percent of need met:* 57% (excluding resources awarded to replace EFC). *Average financial aid package:* $12,058 (excluding resources awarded to replace EFC). 23% of all full-time undergraduates had no need and received non-need-based gift aid.

GIFT AID (NEED-BASED) *Total amount:* $12,622,051 (37% federal, 8% state, 50% institutional, 5% external sources). *Receiving aid:* Freshmen: 66% (317); all full-time undergraduates: 61% (1,280). *Average award:* Freshmen: $10,903; Undergraduates: $9413. *Scholarships, grants, and awards:* Federal Pell, FSEOG, state, private, college/university gift aid from institutional funds.

GIFT AID (NON-NEED-BASED) *Total amount:* $4,476,680 (10% state, 86% institutional, 4% external sources). *Receiving aid:* Freshmen: 10% (50). Undergraduates: 7% (142). *Average award:* Freshmen: $14,172. Undergraduates: $11,534. *Scholarships, grants, and awards by category:* Academic interests/achievement: 1,195 awards ($7,693,607 total): biological sciences, business, communication, education, English, foreign languages, general academic interests/achievements,

health fields, humanities, mathematics, physical sciences, social sciences. *Creative arts/performance:* 109 awards ($259,245 total): art/fine arts, cinema/film/broadcasting, creative writing, journalism/publications, music, theater/drama. *Special achievements/activities:* 388 awards ($1,602,106 total): cheerleading/drum major, hobbies/interests, junior miss, leadership. *Special characteristics:* 285 awards ($3,364,867 total): children of faculty/staff, international students, out-of-state students. *Tuition waivers:* Full or partial for employees or children of employees. *ROTC:* Army cooperative, Air Force cooperative.

LOANS *Student loans:* $10,514,376 (44% need-based, 56% non-need-based). 66% of past graduating class borrowed through all loan programs. *Average indebtedness per student:* $33,755. *Average need-based loan:* Freshmen: $3200, Undergraduates: $3993. *Parent loans:* $2,869,133 (87% need-based, 13% non-need-based). *Programs:* Federal Direct (Subsidized and Unsubsidized Stafford, PLUS).

WORK-STUDY *Federal work-study:* Total amount: $204,203; 111 jobs averaging $1828.

ATHLETIC AWARDS Total amount: $2,329,272 (45% need-based, 55% non-need-based).

APPLYING FOR FINANCIAL AID *Required financial aid form:* FAFSA. *Financial aid deadline (priority):* 3/1. *Notification date:* Continuous beginning 12/1.

CONTACT Mr. Bob Walker, Director of Student Aid, University of Montevallo, Station 6050, Montevallo, AL 35115, 205-665-6048 or toll-free 800-292-4349. *Fax:* 205-665-6047. *E-mail:* rwalker7@montevallo.edu. *Website:* http://www.montevallo.edu/.

UNIVERSITY OF MOUNT OLIVE
Mount Olive, NC

ABOUT THE INSTITUTION Independent Free Will Baptist, coed. 24 undergraduate majors.

GIFT AID (NEED-BASED) *Scholarships, grants, and awards:* Federal Pell, FSEOG, state, private, college/university gift aid from institutional funds.

GIFT AID (NON-NEED-BASED) *Scholarships, grants, and awards by category:* Academic interests/achievement: general academic interests/achievements. Creative arts/performance: art/fine arts, general creative arts/performance. *Special achievements/activities:* general special achievements/activities, leadership. *Special characteristics:* children of faculty/staff, local/state students, religious affiliation, veterans, veterans' children.

LOANS *Programs:* Federal Direct (Subsidized and Unsubsidized Stafford, PLUS), Perkins, state.

APPLYING FOR FINANCIAL AID *Required financial aid forms:* FAFSA, institution's own form, state aid form.

CONTACT Mrs. Katrina K. Lee, Director of Financial Aid, University of Mount Olive, 634 Henderson Street, Mount Olive, NC 28365, 919-658-2502 or toll-free 800-653-0854. *Fax:* 919-658-9816. *E-mail:* klee@umo.edu. *Website:* http://www.umo.edu/.

UNIVERSITY OF MOUNT UNION
Alliance, OH

ABOUT THE INSTITUTION Independent United Methodist, coed. *Awards:* bachelor's, master's, and doctoral degrees. 64 undergraduate majors. *Total enrollment:* 2,257. Undergraduates: 2,095. Freshmen: 540.

GIFT AID (NEED-BASED) *Scholarships, grants, and awards:* Federal Pell, FSEOG, state, private, college/university gift aid from institutional funds.

GIFT AID (NON-NEED-BASED) *Scholarships, grants, and awards by category:* Academic interests/achievement: general academic interests/achievements. Creative arts/performance: art/fine arts, journalism/publications, music, performing arts, theater/drama. *Special characteristics:* children and siblings of alumni, children of faculty/staff, ethnic background, international students, members of minority groups, relatives of clergy, religious affiliation, veterans.

LOANS *Programs:* Federal Direct (Subsidized and Unsubsidized Stafford, PLUS), Perkins, state, private loans.

APPLYING FOR FINANCIAL AID *Required financial aid form:* FAFSA.

CONTACT Mrs. Emily J. Mattison, Director of Student Financial Services, University of Mount Union, 1972 Clark Avenue, Alliance, OH 44601-3993, 330-823-2674 or toll-free 800-334-6682. *Fax:* 330-829-2814. *E-mail:* mattisej@mountunion.edu. *Website:* http://www.mountunion.edu/.

CONTACT Mary Sommers, Financial Aid Office, University of Nebraska at Kearney, Memorial Student Affairs Building, 2510 11th Avenue, Kearney, NE 68849-0001, 308-865-8520 or toll-free 800-532-7639. *Fax:* 308-865-8096. *E-mail:* finaid1@unk.edu. *Website:* http://www.unk.edu/.

UNIVERSITY OF NEBRASKA AT KEARNEY
Kearney, NE

Tuition & fees (NE res): $7326	Average undergraduate aid package: $10,769

ABOUT THE INSTITUTION State-supported, coed. *Awards:* certificates, bachelor's, and master's degrees. 38 undergraduate majors. *Total enrollment:* 6,644. Undergraduates: 4,843. Freshmen: 904. Federal methodology is used as a basis for awarding need-based institutional aid.

UNDERGRADUATE EXPENSES for 2017–2018 *Application fee:* $45. *Tuition, state resident:* full-time $5753; part-time $191.75 per credit hour. *Tuition, nonresident:* full-time $12,533; part-time $417.75 per credit hour. *Required fees:* full-time $1573. Full-time tuition and fees vary according to course level, course load, degree level, location, and program. Part-time tuition and fees vary according to course level, course load, degree level, location, and program. *College room and board:* $9688; *Room only:* $4962. Room and board charges vary according to board plan and housing facility.

FRESHMAN FINANCIAL AID (Fall 2016) 856 applied for aid; of those 82% were deemed to have need. 99% of freshmen with need received aid; of those 30% had need fully met. *Average percent of need met:* 74% (excluding resources awarded to replace EFC). *Average financial aid package:* $12,008 (excluding resources awarded to replace EFC). 14% of all full-time freshmen had no need and received non-need-based gift aid.

UNDERGRADUATE FINANCIAL AID (Fall 2016) 3,287 applied for aid; of those 83% were deemed to have need. 98% of undergraduates with need received aid; of those 24% had need fully met. *Average percent of need met:* 68% (excluding resources awarded to replace EFC). *Average financial aid package:* $10,769 (excluding resources awarded to replace EFC). 17% of all full-time undergraduates had no need and received non-need-based gift aid.

GIFT AID (NEED-BASED) *Total amount:* $19,235,635 (34% federal, 6% state, 33% institutional, 27% external sources). *Receiving aid:* Freshmen: 64% (640); all full-time undergraduates: 56% (2,344). *Average award:* Freshmen: $8795; Undergraduates: $7946. *Scholarships, grants, and awards:* Federal Pell, FSEOG, state, private, college/university gift aid from institutional funds.

GIFT AID (NON-NEED-BASED) *Total amount:* $5,807,976 (1% state, 72% institutional, 27% external sources). *Receiving aid:* Freshmen: 10% (102). Undergraduates: 8% (321). *Average award:* Freshmen: $5065. Undergraduates: $4975. *Scholarships, grants, and awards by category: Academic interests/ achievement:* communication, general academic interests/achievements, military science. *Creative arts/performance:* applied art and design, art/fine arts, debating, journalism/publications, music, theater/drama. *Special achievements/activities:* cheerleading/drum major, leadership. *Special characteristics:* children and siblings of alumni, children of faculty/staff, ethnic background, first-generation college students, international students, local/state students, members of minority groups, out-of-state students, veterans, veterans' children. *Tuition waivers:* Full or partial for employees or children of employees. *ROTC:* Army.

LOANS *Student loans:* $15,062,287 (71% need-based, 29% non-need-based). 53% of past graduating class borrowed through all loan programs. *Average indebtedness per student:* $19,538. *Average need-based loan:* Freshmen: $3610. Undergraduates: $4001. *Parent loans:* $5,225,971 (31% need-based, 69% non-need-based). *Programs:* Federal Direct (Subsidized and Unsubsidized Stafford, PLUS), Perkins, college/university.

WORK-STUDY *Federal work-study:* jobs available.

ATHLETIC AWARDS Total amount: $1,844,218 (34% need-based, 66% non-need-based).

APPLYING FOR FINANCIAL AID *Required financial aid form:* FAFSA. *Financial aid deadline (priority):* 4/1. *Notification date:* Continuous beginning 3/15.

UNIVERSITY OF NEBRASKA AT OMAHA
Omaha, NE

ABOUT THE INSTITUTION State-supported, coed. 84 undergraduate majors.

GIFT AID (NEED-BASED) *Scholarships, grants, and awards:* Federal Pell, FSEOG, state, private, college/university gift aid from institutional funds.

GIFT AID (NON-NEED-BASED) *Scholarships, grants, and awards by category: Academic interests/achievement:* biological sciences, business, communication, computer science, education, engineering/technologies, English, foreign languages, general academic interests/achievements, home economics, mathematics, physical sciences, premedicine, social sciences. *Creative arts/performance:* art/fine arts, creative writing, debating, journalism/publications, music, performing arts, theater/drama. *Special achievements/activities:* general special achievements/activities, leadership, memberships. *Special characteristics:* adult students, children and siblings of alumni, children of faculty/staff, ethnic background, first-generation college students, handicapped students, international students, members of minority groups, out-of-state students, veterans' children.

LOANS *Programs:* Perkins, college/university.

APPLYING FOR FINANCIAL AID *Required financial aid form:* FAFSA.

CONTACT Marty Habrock, Office of Financial Aid, University of Nebraska at Omaha, 103 Eppley Administration Building, Omaha, NE 68182-0187, 402-554-2327 or toll-free 800-858-8648 (in-state). *Fax:* 402-554-3472. *E-mail:* finaid@unomaha.edu. *Website:* http://www.unomaha.edu/.

UNIVERSITY OF NEBRASKA–LINCOLN
Lincoln, NE

Tuition & fees (NE res): $8887	Average undergraduate aid package: $14,021

ABOUT THE INSTITUTION State-supported, coed. *Awards:* certificates, bachelor's, master's, and doctoral degrees. 118 undergraduate majors. *Total enrollment:* 26,079. Undergraduates: 20,954. Freshmen: 4,905. Both federal and institutional methodology are used as a basis for awarding need-based institutional aid.

UNDERGRADUATE EXPENSES for 2017–2018 *Application fee:* $45. *Tuition, state resident:* full-time $7125; part-time $237.50 per credit hour. *Tuition, nonresident:* full-time $22,425; part-time $747.50 per credit hour. *Required fees:* full-time $1762; $17.25 per credit hour or $375 per term. Full-time tuition and fees vary according to course load, location, program, and reciprocity agreements. Part-time tuition and fees vary according to course load, location, program, and reciprocity agreements. *College room and board:* $11,044. Room and board charges vary according to board plan and housing facility.

FRESHMAN FINANCIAL AID (Fall 2016) 3,718 applied for aid; of those 74% were deemed to have need. 98% of freshmen with need received aid; of those 20% had need fully met. *Average percent of need met:* 79% (excluding resources awarded to replace EFC). *Average financial aid package:* $14,958 (excluding resources awarded to replace EFC). 12% of all full-time freshmen had no need and received non-need-based gift aid.

UNDERGRADUATE FINANCIAL AID (Fall 2016) 11,534 applied for aid; of those 76% were deemed to have need. 97% of undergraduates with need received aid; of those 17% had need fully met. *Average percent of need met:* 74% (excluding resources awarded to replace EFC). *Average financial aid package:* $14,021 (excluding resources awarded to replace EFC). 7% of all full-time undergraduates had no need and received non-need-based gift aid.

GIFT AID (NEED-BASED) *Total amount:* $68,123,163 (28% federal, 5% state, 46% institutional, 21% external sources). *Receiving aid:* Freshmen: 47% (2,250); all full-time undergraduates: 36% (6,900). *Average award:* Freshmen: $8007; Undergraduates: $7482. *Scholarships, grants, and awards:* Federal Pell, FSEOG, state, private, college/university gift aid from institutional funds.

GIFT AID (NON-NEED-BASED) Total amount: $36,587,414 (90% institutional, 10% external sources). **Receiving aid:** Freshmen: 5% (222). Undergraduates: 3% (546). **Average award:** Freshmen: $7765. Undergraduates: $7438. **Scholarships, grants, and awards by category:** Academic interests/achievement: agriculture, architecture, biological sciences, business, computer science, education, engineering/technologies, English, foreign languages, general academic interests/achievements, health fields, home economics, humanities, international studies, mathematics, physical sciences, premedicine, social sciences. Creative arts/performance: art/fine arts, cinema/film/broadcasting, dance, journalism/publications, music, performing arts, theater/drama. Special achievements/activities: cheerleading/drum major, community service, leadership. Special characteristics: children and siblings of alumni, ethnic background, handicapped students, international students, members of minority groups, out-of-state students, veterans' children. **Tuition waivers:** Full or partial for employees or children of employees. **ROTC:** Army, Naval, Air Force.

LOANS Student loans: $54,113,528 (75% need-based, 25% non-need-based). 52% of past graduating class borrowed through all loan programs. Average indebtedness per student: $22,918. **Average need-based loan:** Freshmen: $3787. Undergraduates: $4386. **Parent loans:** $37,636,207 (55% need-based, 45% non-need-based). **Programs:** Federal Direct (Subsidized and Unsubsidized Stafford, PLUS), Perkins, college/university.

WORK-STUDY Federal work-study: 1,332 jobs averaging $2688.

ATHLETIC AWARDS Total amount: $9,857,581 (100% non-need-based).

APPLYING FOR FINANCIAL AID Required financial aid form: FAFSA. **Financial aid deadline (priority):** 4/1. **Notification date:** Continuous beginning 4/1.

CONTACT Ms. Jo Tederman, Assistant Director of Scholarships and Financial Aid, University of Nebraska–Lincoln, 12 Canfield Administration Building, Lincoln, NE 68588-0411, 402-472-2030 or toll-free 800-742-8800. Fax: 402-472-9826. Website: http://www.unl.edu/.

UNIVERSITY OF NEBRASKA MEDICAL CENTER
Omaha, NE

CONTACT Judy D. Walker, Director of Financial Aid, University of Nebraska Medical Center, 984265 Nebraska Medical Center, Omaha, NE 68198-4265, 402-559-6409 or toll-free 800-626-8431 Ext. 6468. Fax: 402-559-6796. E-mail: jdwalker@unmc.edu. Website: http://www.unmc.edu/.

UNIVERSITY OF NEVADA, LAS VEGAS
Las Vegas, NV

Tuition & fees (NV res): $7800	Average undergraduate aid package: $8852

ABOUT THE INSTITUTION State-supported, coed. **Awards:** certificates, bachelor's, master's, and doctoral degrees. 85 undergraduate majors. **Total enrollment:** 30,471. Undergraduates: 25,279. Freshmen: 3,958. Federal methodology is used as a basis for awarding need-based institutional aid.

UNDERGRADUATE EXPENSES for 2018–2019 Application fee: $60. **One-time required fee:** $120. **Tuition, state resident:** full-time $7154; part-time $224 per credit hour. **Tuition, nonresident:** full-time $21,626; part-time $470.50 per credit hour. **Required fees:** full-time $646; $14.47 per credit hour or $323 per term. Full-time tuition and fees vary according to course level, program, and reciprocity agreements. Part-time tuition and fees vary according to course level, program, and reciprocity agreements. **College room and board:** $10,780; **Room only:** $5880. Room and board charges vary according to board plan and housing facility.

FRESHMAN FINANCIAL AID (Fall 2017, est.) 3,649 applied for aid; of those 77% were deemed to have need. 99% of freshmen with need received aid; of those 21% had need fully met. **Average percent of need met:** 68% (excluding resources awarded to replace EFC). **Average financial aid package:** $8288 (excluding resources awarded to replace EFC). 16% of all full-time freshmen had no need and received non-need-based gift aid.

UNDERGRADUATE FINANCIAL AID (Fall 2017, est.) 14,430 applied for aid; of those 81% were deemed to have need. 98% of undergraduates with need received

aid; of those 16% had need fully met. **Average percent of need met:** 67% (excluding resources awarded to replace EFC). **Average financial aid package:** $8852 (excluding resources awarded to replace EFC). 8% of all full-time undergraduates had no need and received non-need-based gift aid.

GIFT AID (NEED-BASED) Total amount: $86,541,702 (49% federal, 19% state, 27% institutional, 5% external sources). **Receiving aid:** Freshmen: 49% (1,982); all full-time undergraduates: 45% (8,511). **Average award:** Freshmen: $6296; Undergraduates: $6697. **Scholarships, grants, and awards:** Federal Pell, FSEOG, state, private, college/university gift aid from institutional funds.

GIFT AID (NON-NEED-BASED) Total amount: $13,486,903 (31% federal, 25% state, 34% institutional, 10% external sources). **Receiving aid:** Freshmen: 57% (2,293). Undergraduates: 31% (5,905). **Average award:** Freshmen: $3650. Undergraduates: $4158. **Scholarships, grants, and awards by category:** Academic interests/achievement: architecture, biological sciences, business, communication, computer science, education, engineering/technologies, English, foreign languages, general academic interests/achievements, health fields, humanities, international studies, mathematics, physical sciences, premedicine, social sciences. Creative arts/performance: applied art and design, art/fine arts, cinema/film/broadcasting, creative writing, dance, debating, general creative arts/performance, journalism/publications, music, performing arts, theater/drama. Special achievements/activities: cheerleading/drum major, community service, general special achievements/activities, leadership, rodeo. Special characteristics: adult students, children and siblings of alumni, children of faculty/staff, children of public servants, children of union members/company employees, children with a deceased or disabled parent, ethnic background, first-generation college students, general special characteristics, handicapped students, international students, local/state students, members of minority groups, out-of-state students, previous college experience, veterans, veterans' children. **Tuition waivers:** Full or partial for employees or children of employees. **ROTC:** Army, Air Force.

LOANS Student loans: $93,387,829 (82% need-based, 17% non-need-based). 46% of past graduating class borrowed through all loan programs. Average indebtedness per student: $21,333. **Average need-based loan:** Freshmen: $3306. Undergraduates: $4189. **Parent loans:** $16,690,400 (63% need-based, 37% non-need-based). **Programs:** Federal Direct (Subsidized and Unsubsidized Stafford, PLUS), Perkins, Federal Nursing, state, college/university.

WORK-STUDY Federal work-study: Total amount: $850,000; jobs available. **State or other work-study/employment:** Total amount: $325,000 (100% need-based). Part-time jobs available.

ATHLETIC AWARDS Total amount: $6,758,960 (86% need-based, 14% non-need-based).

APPLYING FOR FINANCIAL AID Required financial aid form: FAFSA. **Financial aid deadline (priority):** 11/1. **Notification date:** Continuous beginning 12/1. Students must reply within 6 weeks of notification.

CONTACT Norm Bedford, Director of Financial Aid and Scholarships, University of Nevada, Las Vegas, 4505 South Maryland Parkway, Las Vegas, NV 89154-2016, 702-895-3424. Fax: 702-895-1353. Website: http://www.unlv.edu/.

UNIVERSITY OF NEVADA, RENO
Reno, NV

Tuition & fees (NV res): $7764	Average undergraduate aid package: $8800

ABOUT THE INSTITUTION State-supported, coed. **Awards:** certificates, bachelor's, master's, and doctoral degrees. 68 undergraduate majors. **Total enrollment:** 21,657. Undergraduates: 18,348. Freshmen: 3,354. Both federal and institutional methodology are used as a basis for awarding need-based institutional aid.

UNDERGRADUATE EXPENSES for 2018–2019 Application fee: $60. **Tuition, state resident:** full-time $6990; part-time $224 per credit. **Tuition, nonresident:** full-time $21,462; part-time $470 per credit. **Required fees:** full-time $774; $282 per term. Full-time tuition and fees vary according to course level, course load, degree level, and program. Part-time tuition and fees vary according to course level, course load, degree level, and program. **College room and board:** $10,868; **Room only:** $6100. Room and board charges vary according to board plan and housing facility.

FRESHMAN FINANCIAL AID (Fall 2016) 2,640 applied for aid; of those 71% were deemed to have need. 100% of freshmen with need received aid; of those 10% had need fully met. **Average percent of need met:** 61% (excluding resources awarded to replace EFC). *Average financial aid package:* $8300 (excluding resources awarded to replace EFC). 15% of all full-time freshmen had no need and received non-need-based gift aid.

UNDERGRADUATE FINANCIAL AID (Fall 2016) 10,001 applied for aid; of those 78% were deemed to have need. 100% of undergraduates with need received aid; of those 99% had need fully met. *Average percent of need met:* 60% (excluding resources awarded to replace EFC). *Average financial aid package:* $8800 (excluding resources awarded to replace EFC). 10% of all full-time undergraduates had no need and received non-need-based gift aid.

GIFT AID (NEED-BASED) *Total amount:* $43,101,475 (47% federal, 21% state, 28% institutional, 4% external sources). *Receiving aid:* Freshmen: 48% (1,682); all full-time undergraduates: 43% (6,621). *Average award:* Freshmen: $6885; Undergraduates: $6642. *Scholarships, grants, and awards:* Federal Pell, FSEOG, state, private, college/university gift aid from institutional funds.

GIFT AID (NON-NEED-BASED) *Total amount:* $15,609,072 (58% state, 25% institutional, 17% external sources). *Receiving aid:* Freshmen: 42% (1,449). Undergraduates: 28% (4,349). *Average award:* Freshmen: $2050. Undergraduates: $2650. *Scholarships, grants, and awards by category: Academic interests/achievement:* agriculture, biological sciences, business, communication, computer science, education, engineering/technologies, English, foreign languages, general academic interests/achievements, health fields, mathematics, physical sciences. *Creative arts/performance:* art/fine arts, general creative arts/performance, journalism/publications, theater/drama. *Special characteristics:* adult students, children and siblings of alumni, ethnic background, first-generation college students, married students. *Tuition waivers:* Full or partial for employees or children of employees, senior citizens. *ROTC:* Army.

LOANS *Student loans:* $48,086,827 (64% need-based, 36% non-need-based). 51% of past graduating class borrowed through all loan programs. *Average indebtedness per student:* $22,650. *Average need-based loan:* Freshmen: $3350. Undergraduates: $4220. *Parent loans:* $17,433,381 (71% need-based, 29% non-need-based). *Programs:* Federal Direct (Subsidized and Unsubsidized Stafford, PLUS), Perkins, Federal Nursing, college/university.

WORK-STUDY *Federal work-study:* jobs available. *State or other work-study/employment:* Total amount: $328,205 (26% need-based, 74% non-need-based). Part-time jobs available.

ATHLETIC AWARDS Total amount: $7,013,415 (37% need-based, 63% non-need-based).

APPLYING FOR FINANCIAL AID *Required financial aid forms:* FAFSA, institution's own form. *Financial aid deadline (priority):* 2/1. *Notification date:* Continuous beginning 3/1. Students must reply by 5/1.

CONTACT Mr. Tom Wolfe, Director of Student Financial Aid, University of Nevada, Reno, Mail Stop 076, Reno, NV 89557, 775-784-4666 or toll-free 866-263-8232. *Fax:* 775-784-1025. *E-mail:* tawolfe@unr.edu. *Website:* http://www.unr.edu/.

UNIVERSITY OF NEW ENGLAND
Biddeford, ME

Tuition & fees: $36,530	Average undergraduate aid package: N/A

ABOUT THE INSTITUTION Independent, coed. *Awards:* certificates, bachelor's, master's, and doctoral degrees. 39 undergraduate majors. *Total enrollment:* 8,291. Undergraduates: 4,423. Freshmen: 651. Federal methodology is used as a basis for awarding need-based institutional aid.

UNDERGRADUATE EXPENSES for 2017–2018 *Application fee:* $40. *Comprehensive fee:* $50,110 includes full-time tuition ($35,240), mandatory fees ($1290), and room and board ($13,580). Full-time tuition and fees vary according to course load and program. Room and board charges vary according to board plan and housing facility. *Part-time tuition:* $1240 per credit hour. *Part-time fees:* $1290 per term. Part-time tuition and fees vary according to course load and program.

GIFT AID (NEED-BASED) *Scholarships, grants, and awards:* Federal Pell, FSEOG, state, private, college/university gift aid from institutional funds.

GIFT AID (NON-NEED-BASED) *Scholarships, grants, and awards by category: Academic interests/achievement:* general academic interests/achievements. *Special achievements/activities:* leadership. *Special characteristics:* children and siblings of alumni, siblings of current students. *Tuition waivers:* Full or partial for children of alumni, employees or children of employees. *ROTC:* Army cooperative.

LOANS *Programs:* Federal Direct (Subsidized and Unsubsidized Stafford, PLUS), Perkins, Federal Nursing, state.

WORK-STUDY Federal work-study jobs available. *State or other work-study/employment:* Part-time jobs available.

APPLYING FOR FINANCIAL AID *Required financial aid form:* FAFSA. *Financial aid deadline (priority):* 5/1. *Notification date:* Continuous beginning 2/1.

CONTACT Paul Henderson, Assistant Vice President of Student Financial Services, University of New England, 11 Hills Beach Road, Biddeford, ME 04005, 207-602-2302 or toll-free 800-477-4863. *Fax:* 207-602-5968. *E-mail:* phenderson@une.edu. *Website:* http://www.une.edu/.

UNIVERSITY OF NEW HAMPSHIRE
Durham, NH

Tuition & fees (NH res): $18,499	Average undergraduate aid package: $23,953

ABOUT THE INSTITUTION State-supported, coed. *Awards:* certificates, associate, bachelor's, master's, and doctoral degrees. 93 undergraduate majors. *Total enrollment:* 15,364. Undergraduates: 12,966. Freshmen: 3,018. Federal methodology is used as a basis for awarding need-based institutional aid.

UNDERGRADUATE EXPENSES for 2018–2019 *Application fee:* $50. *Tuition, state resident:* full-time $15,140. *Tuition, nonresident:* full-time $30,520. *Required fees:* full-time $3359. Full-time tuition and fees vary according to program. Part-time tuition and fees vary according to course load and program. *College room and board:* $11,588; *Room only:* $7220. Room and board charges vary according to board plan and housing facility.

FRESHMAN FINANCIAL AID (Fall 2016) 2,489 applied for aid; of those 80% were deemed to have need. 99% of freshmen with need received aid; of those 17% had need fully met. *Average percent of need met:* 78% (excluding resources awarded to replace EFC). *Average financial aid package:* $24,020 (excluding resources awarded to replace EFC). 15% of all full-time freshmen had no need and received non-need-based gift aid.

UNDERGRADUATE FINANCIAL AID (Fall 2016) 9,820 applied for aid; of those 82% were deemed to have need. 99% of undergraduates with need received aid; of those 16% had need fully met. *Average percent of need met:* 75% (excluding resources awarded to replace EFC). *Average financial aid package:* $23,953 (excluding resources awarded to replace EFC). 16% of all full-time undergraduates had no need and received non-need-based gift aid.

GIFT AID (NEED-BASED) *Total amount:* $73,429,104 (19% federal, 73% institutional, 8% external sources). *Receiving aid:* Freshmen: 56% (1,554); all full-time undergraduates: 48% (5,820). *Average award:* Freshmen: $6851; Undergraduates: $6124. *Scholarships, grants, and awards:* Federal Pell, FSEOG, state, college/university gift aid from institutional funds, Veterans Education Benefits (GI Bill).

GIFT AID (NON-NEED-BASED) *Total amount:* $20,835,681 (100% institutional). *Receiving aid:* Freshmen: 6% (162). Undergraduates: 4% (514). *Average award:* Freshmen: $6054. Undergraduates: $6651. *Scholarships, grants, and awards by category: Academic interests/achievement:* agriculture, biological sciences, business, computer science, education, engineering/technologies, English, foreign languages, general academic interests/achievements, health fields, humanities, mathematics, military science, physical sciences. *Creative arts/performance:* art/fine arts, dance, music, performing arts, theater/drama. *Special achievements/activities:* community service, leadership. *Special characteristics:* children and siblings of alumni, children of faculty/staff, handicapped students, international students, local/state students. *Tuition waivers:* Full or partial for employees or children of employees. *ROTC:* Army, Air Force.

LOANS *Student loans:* $115,305,747 (30% need-based, 70% non-need-based). 77% of past graduating class borrowed through all loan programs. *Average indebtedness per student:* $33,013. *Average need-based loan:* Freshmen: $2637. Undergraduates: $3295. *Parent loans:* $28,375,360 (100% non-need-based). *Programs:* Federal Direct (Subsidized and Unsubsidized Stafford, PLUS), state, college/university.

WORK-STUDY *Federal work-study:* 5,723 jobs averaging $2477. *State or other work-study/employment:* Total amount: $7,680,468 (100% non-need-based). 4,114 part-time jobs averaging $1629.

ATHLETIC AWARDS Total amount: $9,190,991 (100% non-need-based).

APPLYING FOR FINANCIAL AID *Required financial aid form:* FAFSA. *Financial aid deadline (priority):* 3/1. *Notification date:* Continuous beginning 12/1.

CONTACT Mr. Joel B. Carstens, Director of Financial Aid, University of New Hampshire, 11 Garrison Avenue, Durham, NH 03824, 603-862-3600. *Fax:* 603-862-1947. *E-mail:* financial.aid@unh.edu.

Website: http://www.unh.edu/.

UNIVERSITY OF NEW HAMPSHIRE AT MANCHESTER
Manchester, NH

Tuition & fees (NH res): $14,860	Average undergraduate aid package: $13,943

ABOUT THE INSTITUTION State-supported, coed. *Awards:* associate, bachelor's, and master's degrees. 21 undergraduate majors. *Total enrollment:* 1,045. Undergraduates: 762. Freshmen: 72. Federal methodology is used as a basis for awarding need-based institutional aid.

UNDERGRADUATE EXPENSES for 2017–2018 *Application fee:* $65. *Tuition, state resident:* full-time $14,430; part-time $437 per credit hour. *Tuition, nonresident:* full-time $28,990; part-time $481 per credit hour. *Required fees:* full-time $430. Full-time tuition and fees vary according to course load and program. Part-time tuition and fees vary according to course load and program. Room and board charges vary according to housing facility.

FRESHMAN FINANCIAL AID (Fall 2016) 63 applied for aid; of those 63% were deemed to have need. 100% of freshmen with need received aid; of those 20% had need fully met. *Average percent of need met:* 73% (excluding resources awarded to replace EFC). *Average financial aid package:* $13,266 (excluding resources awarded to replace EFC). 16% of all full-time freshmen had no need and received non-need-based gift aid.

UNDERGRADUATE FINANCIAL AID (Fall 2016) 570 applied for aid; of those 82% were deemed to have need. 99% of undergraduates with need received aid; of those 10% had need fully met. *Average percent of need met:* 60% (excluding resources awarded to replace EFC). *Average financial aid package:* $13,943 (excluding resources awarded to replace EFC). 6% of all full-time undergraduates had no need and received non-need-based gift aid.

GIFT AID (NEED-BASED) *Total amount:* $1,860,461 (48% federal, 42% institutional, 10% external sources). *Receiving aid:* Freshmen: 35% (24); all full-time undergraduates: 39% (279). *Average award:* Freshmen: $2918; Undergraduates: $1970. *Scholarships, grants, and awards:* Federal Pell, FSEOG, state, private, college/university gift aid from institutional funds.

GIFT AID (NON-NEED-BASED) *Total amount:* $594,800 (100% institutional). *Receiving aid:* Freshmen: 15% (10). Undergraduates: 5% (36). *Average award:* Freshmen: $2914. Undergraduates: $2157. *Scholarships, grants, and awards by category: Academic interests/achievement:* biological sciences, business, communication, computer science, engineering/technologies, English, general academic interests/achievements, humanities. *Special characteristics:* children of faculty/staff. *Tuition waivers:* Full or partial for employees or children of employees. *ROTC:* Army cooperative, Air Force cooperative.

LOANS *Student loans:* $4,246,505 (42% need-based, 58% non-need-based). 78% of past graduating class borrowed through all loan programs. *Average indebtedness per student:* $30,423. *Average need-based loan:* Freshmen: $2959. Undergraduates: $3852. *Parent loans:* $264,348 (100% non-need-based). *Programs:* Federal Direct (Subsidized and Unsubsidized Stafford, PLUS), Perkins, state, college/university.

WORK-STUDY *Federal work-study:* 206 jobs averaging $2402.

APPLYING FOR FINANCIAL AID *Required financial aid form:* FAFSA. *Financial aid deadline (priority):* 3/1. *Notification date:* Continuous beginning 12/1.

CONTACT Sharon Eaton, Associate Director of Financial Aid, University of New Hampshire at Manchester, 400 Commercial Street, Student Services Suite, 4th Floor, Manchester, NH 03101-1113, 603-641-4114. *Fax:* 603-641-4125.

Website: http://manchester.unh.edu/.

UNIVERSITY OF NEW HAVEN
West Haven, CT

Tuition & fees: $38,170	Average undergraduate aid package: $23,082

ABOUT THE INSTITUTION Independent, coed. *Awards:* certificates, associate, bachelor's, master's, and doctoral degrees. 62 undergraduate majors. *Total enrollment:* 6,984. Undergraduates: 5,216. Freshmen: 1,449. Federal methodology is used as a basis for awarding need-based institutional aid.

UNDERGRADUATE EXPENSES for 2017–2018 *Application fee:* $50. *Comprehensive fee:* $53,780 includes full-time tuition ($36,770), mandatory fees ($1400), and room and board ($15,610). *College room only:* $9860. Full-time tuition and fees vary according to course load, location, and program. Room and board charges vary according to board plan, housing facility, and location. *Part-time tuition:* $1225 per credit hour. *Part-time fees:* $65 per term. Part-time tuition and fees vary according to class time, course load, location, and program.

FRESHMAN FINANCIAL AID (Fall 2017, est.) 1,290 applied for aid; of those 91% were deemed to have need. 100% of freshmen with need received aid; of those 14% had need fully met. *Average percent of need met:* 60% (excluding resources awarded to replace EFC). *Average financial aid package:* $23,746 (excluding resources awarded to replace EFC). 16% of all full-time freshmen had no need and received non-need-based gift aid.

UNDERGRADUATE FINANCIAL AID (Fall 2017, est.) 4,032 applied for aid; of those 92% were deemed to have need. 100% of undergraduates with need received aid; of those 15% had need fully met. *Average percent of need met:* 59% (excluding resources awarded to replace EFC). *Average financial aid package:* $23,082 (excluding resources awarded to replace EFC). 14% of all full-time undergraduates had no need and received non-need-based gift aid.

GIFT AID (NEED-BASED) *Total amount:* $69,669,617 (10% federal, 1% state, 88% institutional, 1% external sources). *Receiving aid:* Freshmen: 82% (1,177); all full-time undergraduates: 76% (3,681). *Average award:* Freshmen: $20,963; Undergraduates: $19,708. *Scholarships, grants, and awards:* Federal Pell, FSEOG, state, private, college/university gift aid from institutional funds.

GIFT AID (NON-NEED-BASED) *Total amount:* $14,459,568 (100% institutional). *Receiving aid:* Freshmen: 10% (141). Undergraduates: 9% (437). *Average award:* Freshmen: $17,063. Undergraduates: $16,299. *Tuition waivers:* Full or partial for employees or children of employees, senior citizens. *ROTC:* Army, Air Force cooperative.

LOANS *Student loans:* $45,817,719 (71% need-based, 29% non-need-based). 79% of past graduating class borrowed through all loan programs. *Average indebtedness per student:* $49,941. *Average need-based loan:* Freshmen: $3331. Undergraduates: $4267. *Parent loans:* $25,537,447 (100% non-need-based). *Programs:* Federal Direct (Subsidized and Unsubsidized Stafford, PLUS), Perkins, state.

WORK-STUDY *Federal work-study:* Total amount: $284,828; jobs available.

ATHLETIC AWARDS Total amount: $2,946,235 (57% need-based, 43% non-need-based).

APPLYING FOR FINANCIAL AID *Required financial aid form:* FAFSA. *Financial aid deadline (priority):* 1/1. *Notification date:* Continuous beginning 1/15. Students must reply by 5/1 or within 2 weeks of notification.

CONTACT Karen Flynn, Associate Vice President for Financial Aid, University of New Haven, 300 Boston Post Road, West Haven, CT 06516-1916, 203-932-7315 or toll-free 800-342-5864. *Fax:* 203-931-6050. *E-mail:* financialaid@newhaven.edu.

Website: http://www.newhaven.edu/.

UNIVERSITY OF NEW MEXICO
Albuquerque, NM

CONTACT Brian Malone, Office of Student Financial Aid, University of New Mexico, MSC 11 6315, 1 University of New Mexico, Albuquerque, NM 87131, 505-277-8900 or toll-free 800-CALL-UNM. *Fax:* 505-277-6326. *E-mail:* finaid@unm.edu.

Website: http://www.unm.edu/.

UNIVERSITY OF NEW ORLEANS
New Orleans, LA

Tuition & fees (LA res): $8694	Average undergraduate aid package: $9587

ABOUT THE INSTITUTION State-supported, coed. *Awards:* certificates, bachelor's, master's, and doctoral degrees. 34 undergraduate majors. *Total enrollment:* 7,964. Undergraduates: 6,472. Freshmen: 960. Federal methodology is used as a basis for awarding need-based institutional aid.

UNDERGRADUATE EXPENSES for 2017–2018 *Application fee:* $25. *Tuition, state resident:* full-time $6090. *Tuition, nonresident:* full-time $10,926. *Required fees:* full-time $2604. Full-time tuition and fees vary according to course load. Part-time tuition and fees vary according to course load. *College room and board:* $10,575. Room and board charges vary according to board plan and housing facility.

FRESHMAN FINANCIAL AID (Fall 2016) 792 applied for aid; of those 83% were deemed to have need. 97% of freshmen with need received aid; of those 17% had need fully met. *Average percent of need met:* 67% (excluding resources awarded to replace EFC). *Average financial aid package:* $9946 (excluding resources awarded to replace EFC). 10% of all full-time freshmen had no need and received non-need-based gift aid.

UNDERGRADUATE FINANCIAL AID (Fall 2016) 3,680 applied for aid; of those 84% were deemed to have need. 93% of undergraduates with need received aid; of those 13% had need fully met. *Average percent of need met:* 64% (excluding resources awarded to replace EFC). *Average financial aid package:* $9587 (excluding resources awarded to replace EFC). 7% of all full-time undergraduates had no need and received non-need-based gift aid.

GIFT AID (NEED-BASED) *Total amount:* $10,700,219 (90% federal, 10% state). *Receiving aid:* Freshmen: 62% (526); all full-time undergraduates: 52% (2,417). *Average award:* Freshmen: $5550; Undergraduates: $5126. *Scholarships, grants, and awards:* Federal Pell, FSEOG, state, private, college/university gift aid from institutional funds, United Negro College Fund.

GIFT AID (NON-NEED-BASED) *Total amount:* $12,163,793 (52% state, 40% institutional, 8% external sources). *Receiving aid:* Freshmen: 50% (429). Undergraduates: 34% (1,584). *Average award:* Freshmen: $2203. Undergraduates: $2605. *Tuition waivers:* Full or partial for employees or children of employees, senior citizens. *ROTC:* Army cooperative, Naval cooperative, Air Force cooperative.

LOANS *Student loans:* $17,165,808 (43% need-based, 57% non-need-based). 48% of past graduating class borrowed through all loan programs. *Average indebtedness per student:* $20,723. *Average need-based loan:* Freshmen: $3070. Undergraduates: $3813. *Parent loans:* $1,006,510 (100% non-need-based). *Programs:* Federal Direct (Subsidized and Unsubsidized Stafford, PLUS), private loans.

WORK-STUDY *Federal work-study:* jobs available. *State or other work-study/employment:* Total amount: $228,253 (100% non-need-based). Part-time jobs available.

ATHLETIC AWARDS Total amount: $1,470,804 (3% need-based, 97% non-need-based).

APPLYING FOR FINANCIAL AID *Required financial aid forms:* FAFSA, institution's own form. *Financial aid deadline:* 6/30 (priority: 5/1). *Notification date:* Continuous beginning 1/15. Students must reply by 5/1.

CONTACT Ms. Ann Lockridge, Director of Financial Aid, Scholarships, and Veterans Services, University of New Orleans, Privateer Enrollment Center, 2000 Lakeshore Drive, 105 Earl K. Long Library, 1st Floor, New Orleans, LA 70148, 504-280-6603 or toll-free 888-514-4275. *Fax:* 504-280-3973. *E-mail:* alockrid@uno.edu. *Website:* http://www.uno.edu/.

UNIVERSITY OF NORTH ALABAMA
Florence, AL

Tuition & fees (AL res): $10,370	Average undergraduate aid package: $8629

ABOUT THE INSTITUTION State-supported, coed. *Awards:* certificates, bachelor's, and master's degrees. 43 undergraduate majors. *Total enrollment:* 7,457. Undergraduates: 6,221. Freshmen: 1,128. Federal methodology is used as a basis for awarding need-based institutional aid.

UNDERGRADUATE EXPENSES for 2017–2018 *Application fee:* $35. *Tuition, state resident:* full-time $8310; part-time $277 per credit hour. *Tuition, nonresident:* full-time $16,620; part-time $554 per credit hour. *Required fees:* full-time $2060; $238 per credit hour. Full-time tuition and fees vary according to course load, program, and student level. Part-time tuition and fees vary according to course load and program. *College room and board:* $7684. Room and board charges vary according to board plan, housing facility, and student level.

FRESHMAN FINANCIAL AID (Fall 2017, est.) 980 applied for aid; of those 99% were deemed to have need. 96% of freshmen with need received aid; of those 3% had need fully met. *Average percent of need met:* 50% (excluding resources awarded to replace EFC). *Average financial aid package:* $8735 (excluding resources awarded to replace EFC). 14% of all full-time freshmen had no need and received non-need-based gift aid.

UNDERGRADUATE FINANCIAL AID (Fall 2017, est.) 3,958 applied for aid; of those 99% were deemed to have need. 97% of undergraduates with need received aid; of those 4% had need fully met. *Average percent of need met:* 50% (excluding resources awarded to replace EFC). *Average financial aid package:* $8629 (excluding resources awarded to replace EFC). 8% of all full-time undergraduates had no need and received non-need-based gift aid.

GIFT AID (NEED-BASED) *Total amount:* $10,812,594 (97% federal, 1% state, 2% institutional). *Receiving aid:* Freshmen: 45% (495); all full-time undergraduates: 43% (2,180). *Average award:* Freshmen: $3605; Undergraduates: $3677. *Scholarships, grants, and awards:* Federal Pell, FSEOG, state, private.

GIFT AID (NON-NEED-BASED) *Total amount:* $11,086,521 (98% institutional, 2% external sources). *Receiving aid:* Freshmen: 54% (597). Undergraduates: 37% (1,892). *Average award:* Freshmen: $2917. Undergraduates: $2870. *Scholarships, grants, and awards by category:* Academic interests/achievement: general academic interests/achievements, military science. Creative arts/performance: art/fine arts, dance, journalism/publications, music, theater/drama. Special achievements/activities: cheerleading/drum major, general special achievements/activities, leadership. Special characteristics: children and siblings of alumni, first-generation college students, general special characteristics, international students, out-of-state students. *Tuition waivers:* Full or partial for employees or children of employees, senior citizens. *ROTC:* Army.

LOANS *Student loans:* $20,380,436 (45% need-based, 55% non-need-based). 57% of past graduating class borrowed through all loan programs. *Average indebtedness per student:* $28,283. *Average need-based loan:* Freshmen: $3076. Undergraduates: $3852. *Parent loans:* $4,527,249 (100% non-need-based). *Programs:* Federal Direct (Subsidized and Unsubsidized Stafford, PLUS).

WORK-STUDY *Federal work-study:* Total amount: $115,409; jobs available. *State or other work-study/employment:* Total amount: $344,857 (100% non-need-based). Part-time jobs available.

ATHLETIC AWARDS Total amount: $2,273,463 (100% non-need-based).

APPLYING FOR FINANCIAL AID *Financial aid deadline (priority):* 6/1. *Notification date:* Continuous beginning 3/30.

CONTACT Ms. Shauna L. James, Director of Student Financial Services, University of North Alabama, UNA Box 5014, Florence, AL 35632-0001, 256-765-4279 or toll-free 800-TALK-UNA. *E-mail:* sljames@una.edu. *Website:* http://www.una.edu/.

UNIVERSITY OF NORTH CAROLINA AT ASHEVILLE
Asheville, NC

Tuition & fees (NC res): $7145	Average undergraduate aid package: $12,231

ABOUT THE INSTITUTION State-supported, coed. *Awards:* certificates, bachelor's, and master's degrees. 36 undergraduate majors. *Total enrollment:* 3,852. Undergraduates: 3,826. Freshmen: 648. Federal methodology is used as a basis for awarding need-based institutional aid.

UNDERGRADUATE EXPENSES for 2018–2019 *Application fee:* $75. *One-time required fee:* $150. *Tuition, state resident:* full-time $4122; part-time $139.26 per credit hour. *Tuition, nonresident:* full-time $20,845; part-time $704.22 per credit hour. *Required fees:* full-time $3023; $15.98 per credit hour. Full-time tuition and fees vary according to course load and degree level. Part-time tuition and fees vary according to course load and degree level. *College room and board:*

$9106; *Room only:* $5134. Room and board charges vary according to board plan and housing facility.

FRESHMAN FINANCIAL AID (Fall 2016) 583 applied for aid; of those 67% were deemed to have need. 98% of freshmen with need received aid; of those 26% had need fully met. *Average percent of need met:* 78% (excluding resources awarded to replace EFC). *Average financial aid package:* $12,857 (excluding resources awarded to replace EFC). 10% of all full-time freshmen had no need and received non-need-based gift aid.

UNDERGRADUATE FINANCIAL AID (Fall 2016) 2,471 applied for aid; of those 73% were deemed to have need. 98% of undergraduates with need received aid; of those 27% had need fully met. *Average percent of need met:* 75% (excluding resources awarded to replace EFC). *Average financial aid package:* $12,231 (excluding resources awarded to replace EFC). 8% of all full-time undergraduates had no need and received non-need-based gift aid.

GIFT AID (NEED-BASED) *Total amount:* $11,771,536 (45% federal, 24% state, 31% institutional). *Receiving aid:* Freshmen: 53% (354); all full-time undergraduates: 50% (1,564). *Average award:* Freshmen: $7410; Undergraduates: $7071. *Scholarships, grants, and awards:* Federal Pell, FSEOG, state, private, college/university gift aid from institutional funds.

GIFT AID (NON-NEED-BASED) *Total amount:* $716,492 (4% federal, 3% state, 92% institutional, 1% external sources). *Receiving aid:* Freshmen: 10% (67). Undergraduates: 9% (271). *Average award:* Freshmen: $2066. Undergraduates: $2248. *Scholarships, grants, and awards by category: Academic interests/ achievement:* 1,240 awards ($594,332 total): area/ethnic studies, biological sciences, business, communication, computer science, education, engineering/technologies, English, foreign languages, general academic interests/achievements, health fields, home economics, humanities, international studies, mathematics, physical sciences, religion/ biblical studies, social sciences. *Creative arts/performance:* 1 award ($800 total): art/ fine arts, dance, general creative arts/performance, music, theater/drama. *Special achievements/activities:* community service, general special achievements/activities, leadership. *Tuition waivers:* Full or partial for employees or children of employees.

LOANS *Student loans:* $12,235,293 (71% need-based, 29% non-need-based). 57% of past graduating class borrowed through all loan programs. *Average indebtedness per student:* $23,824. *Average need-based loan:* Freshmen: $4261. Undergraduates: $4625. *Parent loans:* $2,172,882 (26% need-based, 74% non-need-based). *Programs:* Federal Direct (Subsidized and Unsubsidized Stafford, PLUS), Perkins, state, college/university.

WORK-STUDY *Federal work-study:* 55 jobs averaging $2572. *State or other work-study/employment:* 1,921 part-time jobs averaging $1289.

ATHLETIC AWARDS Total amount: $2,188,981 (44% need-based, 56% non-need-based).

APPLYING FOR FINANCIAL AID *Required financial aid form:* FAFSA. *Financial aid deadline (priority):* 3/1. *Notification date:* Continuous beginning 3/1. Students must reply within 2 weeks of notification.

CONTACT Financial Aid Office, University of North Carolina at Asheville, One University Heights, 215 Brown Hall, CPO 1330, Asheville, NC 28804, 828-251-6535 or toll-free 800-531-9842. *Fax:* 828-232-2294. *E-mail:* finaid@unca.edu. *Website:* http://www.unca.edu/.

THE UNIVERSITY OF NORTH CAROLINA AT CHAPEL HILL
Chapel Hill, NC

Tuition & fees (NC res): $8986	Average undergraduate aid package: $19,626

ABOUT THE INSTITUTION State-supported, coed. *Awards:* certificates, bachelor's, master's, and doctoral degrees. 57 undergraduate majors. *Total enrollment:* 29,911. Undergraduates: 18,862. Freshmen: 4,356. Both federal and institutional methodology are used as a basis for awarding need-based institutional aid.

UNDERGRADUATE EXPENSES for 2018–2019 *Application fee:* $80. *Tuition, state resident:* full-time $7019. *Tuition, nonresident:* full-time $33,202. *Required fees:* full-time $1967. Full-time tuition and fees vary according to program. Part-time tuition and fees vary according to course load and program. *College room and board:* $11,190; *Room only:* $6610. Room and board charges vary according to board plan, housing facility, and location.

FRESHMAN FINANCIAL AID (Fall 2016) 3,186 applied for aid; of those 62% were deemed to have need. 100% of freshmen with need received aid; of those 83% had need fully met. *Average percent of need met:* 100% (excluding resources awarded to replace EFC). *Average financial aid package:* $17,732 (excluding resources awarded to replace EFC). 2% of all full-time freshmen had no need and received non-need-based gift aid.

UNDERGRADUATE FINANCIAL AID (Fall 2016) 10,433 applied for aid; of those 77% were deemed to have need. 100% of undergraduates with need received aid; of those 80% had need fully met. *Average percent of need met:* 100% (excluding resources awarded to replace EFC). *Average financial aid package:* $19,626 (excluding resources awarded to replace EFC). 4% of all full-time undergraduates had no need and received non-need-based gift aid.

GIFT AID (NEED-BASED) *Total amount:* $125,316,508 (15% federal, 10% state, 69% institutional, 6% external sources). *Receiving aid:* Freshmen: 43% (1,804); all full-time undergraduates: 40% (7,205). *Average award:* Freshmen: $15,882; Undergraduates: $17,607. *Scholarships, grants, and awards:* Federal Pell, FSEOG, state, private, college/university gift aid from institutional funds.

GIFT AID (NON-NEED-BASED) *Total amount:* $17,265,264 (3% state, 39% institutional, 58% external sources). *Receiving aid:* Freshmen: 5% (222). Undergraduates: 2% (417). *Average award:* Freshmen: $11,495. Undergraduates: $7924. *Scholarships, grants, and awards by category: Academic interests/ achievement:* business, communication, education, English, general academic interests/ achievements, health fields, mathematics. *Creative arts/performance:* applied art and design, art/fine arts, journalism/publications, music, theater/drama. *Special achievements/activities:* community service, general special achievements/activities, leadership. *Special characteristics:* children of faculty/staff, international students, out-of-state students, relatives of clergy, religious affiliation. *Tuition waivers:* Full or partial for employees or children of employees. *ROTC:* Army, Naval, Air Force.

LOANS *Student loans:* $43,179,792 (64% need-based, 36% non-need-based). 40% of past graduating class borrowed through all loan programs. *Average indebtedness per student:* $22,214. *Average need-based loan:* Freshmen: $4233. Undergraduates: $4993. *Parent loans:* $10,092,206 (8% need-based, 92% non-need-based). *Programs:* Federal Direct (Subsidized and Unsubsidized Stafford, PLUS), Perkins, state, college/university, alternative loans.

WORK-STUDY *Federal work-study:* 2,134 jobs averaging $1767.

ATHLETIC AWARDS Total amount: $15,111,864 (19% need-based, 81% non-need-based).

APPLYING FOR FINANCIAL AID *Required financial aid forms:* FAFSA, CSS Financial Aid PROFILE. *Financial aid deadline (priority):* 3/1. *Notification date:* Continuous beginning 1/31. Students must reply by 5/1.

CONTACT Ms. Rachelle Feldman, Director of Scholarships and Student Aid, The University of North Carolina at Chapel Hill, 300 Pettigrew Hall, CB # 2300, PO Box 1080, Chapel Hill, NC 27514-1080, 919-962-8396. *Fax:* 919-962-2716. *E-mail:* aidinfo@unc.edu. *Website:* http://www.unc.edu/.

THE UNIVERSITY OF NORTH CAROLINA AT CHARLOTTE
Charlotte, NC

Tuition & fees (NC res): $7023	Average undergraduate aid package: $9124

ABOUT THE INSTITUTION State-supported, coed. *Awards:* certificates, bachelor's, master's, and doctoral degrees. 67 undergraduate majors. *Total enrollment:* 29,317. Undergraduates: 23,914. Freshmen: 3,373. Federal methodology is used as a basis for awarding need-based institutional aid.

UNDERGRADUATE EXPENSES for 2017–2018 *Application fee:* $60. *Tuition, state resident:* full-time $3812. *Tuition, nonresident:* full-time $17,246. *Required fees:* full-time $3211. Full-time tuition and fees vary according to course load and program. Part-time tuition and fees vary according to course load and program. *College room and board:* $10,780; *Room only:* $6150. Room and board charges vary according to board plan and housing facility.

FRESHMAN FINANCIAL AID (Fall 2017, est.) 2,912 applied for aid; of those 72% were deemed to have need. 97% of freshmen with need received aid; of those 11% had need fully met. *Average percent of need met:* 55% (excluding resources awarded to replace EFC). *Average financial aid package:* $9103 (excluding

resources awarded to replace EFC). 2% of all full-time freshmen had no need and received non-need-based gift aid.

UNDERGRADUATE FINANCIAL AID (Fall 2017, est.) 16,417 applied for aid; of those 81% were deemed to have need. 97% of undergraduates with need received aid; of those 11% had need fully met. *Average percent of need met:* 55% (excluding resources awarded to replace EFC). *Average financial aid package:* $9124 (excluding resources awarded to replace EFC). 1% of all full-time undergraduates had no need and received non-need-based gift aid.

GIFT AID (NEED-BASED) *Total amount:* $72,906,646 (54% federal, 26% state, 15% institutional, 5% external sources). *Receiving aid:* Freshmen: 44% (1,484); all full-time undergraduates: 47% (9,987). *Average award:* Freshmen: $6968; Undergraduates: $6414. *Scholarships, grants, and awards:* Federal Pell, FSEOG, state, private, college/university gift aid from institutional funds.

GIFT AID (NON-NEED-BASED) *Total amount:* $4,085,050 (4% state, 95% institutional, 1% external sources). *Receiving aid:* Freshmen: 5% (165). Undergraduates: 4% (753). *Average award:* Freshmen: $7855. Undergraduates: $8248. *Scholarships, grants, and awards by category:* Academic interests/achievement: architecture, biological sciences, business, computer science, education, engineering/technologies, foreign languages, general academic interests/achievements, health fields, home economics, international studies, mathematics, physical sciences, religion/biblical studies, social sciences. *Creative arts/performance:* art/fine arts, dance, music, theater/drama. *Special characteristics:* adult students, children of public servants, children of union members/company employees, first-generation college students, handicapped students, international students, local/state students, members of minority groups, veterans. *Tuition waivers:* Full or partial for employees or children of employees. *ROTC:* Army, Air Force.

LOANS *Student loans:* $115,261,831 (42% need-based, 58% non-need-based). 68% of past graduating class borrowed through all loan programs. *Average indebtedness per student:* $27,453. *Average need-based loan:* Freshmen: $3407. Undergraduates: $4144. *Parent loans:* $23,282,632 (100% non-need-based). *Programs:* Federal Direct (Subsidized and Unsubsidized Stafford, PLUS), Perkins, state, college/university.

WORK-STUDY *Federal work-study:* Total amount: $1,801,317; 766 jobs averaging $2352.

ATHLETIC AWARDS Total amount: $6,435,046 (100% non-need-based).

APPLYING FOR FINANCIAL AID *Required financial aid form:* FAFSA. *Financial aid deadline (priority):* 3/1. *Notification date:* Continuous beginning 3/29. Students must reply by 9/30.

CONTACT Mr. Bruce Blackmon, Office of Financial Aid, The University of North Carolina at Charlotte, 9201 University City Boulevard, Charlotte, NC 28223-0001, 704-687-7010. *Fax:* 704-687-1461. *E-mail:* ablackm8@uncc.edu. *Website:* http://www.uncc.edu/.

aid; of those 17% had need fully met. *Average percent of need met:* 72% (excluding resources awarded to replace EFC). *Average financial aid package:* $11,508 (excluding resources awarded to replace EFC). 2% of all full-time undergraduates had no need and received non-need-based gift aid.

GIFT AID (NEED-BASED) *Total amount:* $50,919,744 (72% federal, 3% state, 25% institutional). *Receiving aid:* Freshmen: 62% (1,704); all full-time undergraduates: 56% (7,793). *Average award:* Freshmen: $7149; Undergraduates: $6224. *Scholarships, grants, and awards:* Federal Pell, FSEOG, state, private, college/university gift aid from institutional funds.

GIFT AID (NON-NEED-BASED) *Total amount:* $26,489,591 (72% state, 13% institutional, 15% external sources). *Receiving aid:* Freshmen: 58% (1,606). Undergraduates: 52% (7,210). *Average award:* Freshmen: $3757. Undergraduates: $3728. *Scholarships, grants, and awards by category:* Academic interests/achievement: biological sciences, business, communication, computer science, education, English, foreign languages, general academic interests/achievements, health fields, home economics, humanities, international studies, library science, mathematics, physical sciences, premedicine, religion/biblical studies, social sciences. *Creative arts/performance:* art/fine arts, cinema/film/broadcasting, dance, music, performing arts, theater/drama. *Special achievements/activities:* community service, general special achievements/activities, junior miss, leadership, religious involvement. *Special characteristics:* adult students, children and siblings of alumni, children of faculty/staff, general special characteristics, handicapped students, international students, local/state students, out-of-state students, religious affiliation, veterans, veterans' children. *Tuition waivers:* Full or partial for employees or children of employees, senior citizens. *ROTC:* Army cooperative, Air Force cooperative.

LOANS *Student loans:* $66,929,380 (52% need-based, 48% non-need-based). 89% of past graduating class borrowed through all loan programs. *Average indebtedness per student:* $26,841. *Average need-based loan:* Freshmen: $3369. Undergraduates: $4220. *Parent loans:* $13,438,620 (100% non-need-based). *Programs:* Federal Direct (Subsidized and Unsubsidized Stafford, PLUS), Perkins, state, college/university.

WORK-STUDY *Federal work-study:* Total amount: $1,045,778; 321 jobs averaging $2204.

ATHLETIC AWARDS Total amount: $3,127,851 (100% non-need-based).

APPLYING FOR FINANCIAL AID *Required financial aid form:* FAFSA. *Financial aid deadline (priority):* 3/1. *Notification date:* Continuous beginning 3/15. Students must reply within 3 weeks of notification.

CONTACT Mr. Bruce Cabiness, Associate Director of Financial Aid, The University of North Carolina at Greensboro, PO Box 26170, Greensboro, NC 27402-6170, 336-334-5702. *Fax:* 336-334-3010. *E-mail:* finaid@uncg.edu. *Website:* http://www.uncg.edu/.

THE UNIVERSITY OF NORTH CAROLINA AT GREENSBORO
Greensboro, NC

Tuition & fees (NC res): $7164	Average undergraduate aid package: $11,508

ABOUT THE INSTITUTION State-supported, coed. *Awards:* certificates, bachelor's, master's, and doctoral degrees. 89 undergraduate majors. *Total enrollment:* 19,922. Undergraduates: 16,439. Freshmen: 2,791. Federal methodology is used as a basis for awarding need-based institutional aid.

UNDERGRADUATE EXPENSES for 2018–2019 *Application fee:* $65. *Tuition, state resident:* full-time $4336; part-time $552.75 per credit hour. *Tuition, nonresident:* full-time $19,582; part-time $2447.63 per credit hour. *Required fees:* full-time $2828; $105.13 per credit hour. Part-time tuition and fees vary according to course load. *College room and board:* $8834; *Room only:* $5250. Room and board charges vary according to board plan and housing facility.

FRESHMAN FINANCIAL AID (Fall 2017, est.) 2,584 applied for aid; of those 99% were deemed to have need. 91% of freshmen with need received aid; of those 22% had need fully met. *Average percent of need met:* 78% (excluding resources awarded to replace EFC). *Average financial aid package:* $12,287 (excluding resources awarded to replace EFC). 2% of all full-time freshmen had no need and received non-need-based gift aid.

UNDERGRADUATE FINANCIAL AID (Fall 2017, est.) 12,019 applied for aid; of those 98% were deemed to have need. 95% of undergraduates with need received

THE UNIVERSITY OF NORTH CAROLINA AT PEMBROKE
Pembroke, NC

Tuition & fees (NC res): $5955	Average undergraduate aid package: $10,050

ABOUT THE INSTITUTION State-supported, coed. *Awards:* bachelor's and master's degrees. 43 undergraduate majors. *Total enrollment:* 6,252. Undergraduates: 5,481. Freshmen: 1,033. Federal methodology is used as a basis for awarding need-based institutional aid.

UNDERGRADUATE EXPENSES for 2018–2019 *Application fee:* $45. *Tuition, state resident:* full-time $3602; part-time $132 per credit hour. *Tuition, nonresident:* full-time $15,193; part-time $502 per credit hour. *Required fees:* full-time $2353. Full-time tuition and fees vary according to course load, location, and program. Part-time tuition and fees vary according to course load, location, and program. *College room and board:* $8782; *Room only:* $4890. Room and board charges vary according to board plan, housing facility, and location. *Payment plan:* Tuition prepayment.

FRESHMAN FINANCIAL AID (Fall 2017, est.) 998 applied for aid; of those 87% were deemed to have need. 98% of freshmen with need received aid; of those 7% had need fully met. *Average percent of need met:* 59% (excluding resources awarded to replace EFC). *Average financial aid package:* $9498 (excluding resources awarded to replace EFC). 1% of all full-time freshmen had no need and received non-need-based gift aid.

UNDERGRADUATE FINANCIAL AID (Fall 2017, est.) 4,080 applied for aid; of those 90% were deemed to have need. 98% of undergraduates with need received aid; of those 7% had need fully met. *Average percent of need met:* 62% (excluding resources awarded to replace EFC). *Average financial aid package:* $10,050 (excluding resources awarded to replace EFC). 1% of all full-time undergraduates had no need and received non-need-based gift aid.

GIFT AID (NEED-BASED) *Total amount:* $23,501,933 (66% federal, 24% state, 10% institutional). *Receiving aid:* Freshmen: 71% (736); all full-time undergraduates: 69% (3,102). *Average award:* Freshmen: $6837; Undergraduates: $6683. *Scholarships, grants, and awards:* Federal Pell, FSEOG, state, college/university gift aid from institutional funds.

GIFT AID (NON-NEED-BASED) *Total amount:* $765,385 (1% institutional, 99% external sources). *Receiving aid:* Freshmen: 20% (207). Undergraduates: 15% (674). *Average award:* Freshmen: $1533. Undergraduates: $1819. *Scholarships, grants, and awards by category: Academic interests/achievement:* 186 awards ($149,479 total): education, general academic interests/achievements. *Creative arts/performance:* art/fine arts. *Special characteristics:* children and siblings of alumni. *Tuition waivers:* Full or partial for employees or children of employees. **ROTC:** Army, Air Force.

LOANS *Student loans:* $31,200,866 (96% need-based, 4% non-need-based). 84% of past graduating class borrowed through all loan programs. *Average indebtedness per student:* $25,831. *Average need-based loan:* Freshmen: $3392. Undergraduates: $4221. *Parent loans:* $4,093,951 (67% need-based, 33% non-need-based). *Programs:* Federal Direct (Subsidized and Unsubsidized Stafford, PLUS), Perkins.

WORK-STUDY *Federal work-study:* Total amount: $164,840; 82 jobs averaging $2000.

ATHLETIC AWARDS Total amount: $1,463,932 (95% need-based, 5% non-need-based).

APPLYING FOR FINANCIAL AID *Required financial aid form:* FAFSA. *Financial aid deadline (priority):* 3/1. *Notification date:* Continuous beginning 4/15. Students must reply by 7/31.

CONTACT Mildred Weber, Associate Director of Financial Aid, The University of North Carolina at Pembroke, PO Box 1510, Pembroke, NC 28372, 910-521-6612 or toll-free 800-949-UNCP. *Fax:* 910-775-4159. *E-mail:* mildred.weber@uncp.edu. *Website:* http://www.uncp.edu/.

UNIVERSITY OF NORTH CAROLINA SCHOOL OF THE ARTS
Winston-Salem, NC

Tuition & fees: N/R	Average undergraduate aid package: $14,145

ABOUT THE INSTITUTION State-supported, coed. *Awards:* certificates, bachelor's, and master's degrees. 5 undergraduate majors. *Total enrollment:* 1,014. Undergraduates: 873. Freshmen: 173. Federal methodology is used as a basis for awarding need-based institutional aid.

UNDERGRADUATE EXPENSES for 2018–2019 *Application fee:* $95. *Tuition, state resident:* part-time $271 per credit hour. *Tuition, nonresident:* part-time $927 per credit hour. *Required fees:* full-time $2861. *College room and board:* $9021; *Room only:* $4502. Room and board charges vary according to board plan and housing facility. *Payment plan:* Guaranteed tuition.

FRESHMAN FINANCIAL AID (Fall 2017, est.) 141 applied for aid; of those 62% were deemed to have need. 100% of freshmen with need received aid; of those 11% had need fully met. *Average percent of need met:* 62% (excluding resources awarded to replace EFC). *Average financial aid package:* $13,267 (excluding resources awarded to replace EFC). 12% of all full-time freshmen had no need and received non-need-based gift aid.

UNDERGRADUATE FINANCIAL AID (Fall 2017, est.) 624 applied for aid; of those 76% were deemed to have need. 99% of undergraduates with need received aid; of those 13% had need fully met. *Average percent of need met:* 67% (excluding resources awarded to replace EFC). *Average financial aid package:* $14,145 (excluding resources awarded to replace EFC). 6% of all full-time undergraduates had no need and received non-need-based gift aid.

GIFT AID (NEED-BASED) *Total amount:* $5,186,147 (23% federal, 45% state, 29% institutional, 3% external sources). *Receiving aid:* Freshmen: 42% (72); all full-time undergraduates: 48% (406). *Average award:* Freshmen: $9188; Undergraduates: $9222. *Scholarships, grants, and awards:* Federal Pell, FSEOG, state, private, college/university gift aid from institutional funds.

GIFT AID (NON-NEED-BASED) *Total amount:* $20,510 (100% institutional). *Receiving aid:* Freshmen: 37% (63). Undergraduates: 29% (242). *Average award:* Freshmen: $2760. Undergraduates: $3313. *Scholarships, grants, and awards by category: Creative arts/performance:* applied art and design, cinema/film/broadcasting, dance, music, performing arts, theater/drama. *Tuition waivers:* Full or partial for employees or children of employees.

LOANS *Student loans:* $4,606,903 (91% need-based, 9% non-need-based). 64% of past graduating class borrowed through all loan programs. *Average indebtedness per student:* $28,551. *Average need-based loan:* Freshmen: $3389. Undergraduates: $4590. *Parent loans:* $2,114,705 (63% need-based, 37% non-need-based). *Programs:* Federal Direct (Subsidized and Unsubsidized Stafford, PLUS), Perkins.

WORK-STUDY *Federal work-study:* Total amount: $141,544; 177 jobs averaging $800.

APPLYING FOR FINANCIAL AID *Required financial aid form:* FAFSA. *Financial aid deadline (priority):* 3/1. *Notification date:* Continuous beginning 4/1. Students must reply within 2 weeks of notification.

CONTACT Jane C. Kamiab, Director of Financial Aid, University of North Carolina School of the Arts, 1533 South Main Street, Winston-Salem, NC 27127, 336-770-3297. *Fax:* 336-770-1489. *Website:* http://www.uncsa.edu/.

THE UNIVERSITY OF NORTH CAROLINA WILMINGTON
Wilmington, NC

Tuition & fees (NC res): $7048	Average undergraduate aid package: $9398

ABOUT THE INSTITUTION State-supported, coed. *Awards:* certificates, bachelor's, master's, and doctoral degrees. 49 undergraduate majors. *Total enrollment:* 16,487. Undergraduates: 14,502. Freshmen: 2,145. Federal methodology is used as a basis for awarding need-based institutional aid.

UNDERGRADUATE EXPENSES for 2017–2018 *Application fee:* $80. *Tuition, state resident:* full-time $4400; part-time $160.28 per credit hour. *Tuition, nonresident:* full-time $18,416; part-time $667.68 per credit hour. *Required fees:* full-time $2648; $76.64 per credit hour. Full-time tuition and fees vary according to course load and location. Part-time tuition and fees vary according to course load and location. *College room and board:* $9736; *Room only:* $6056. Room and board charges vary according to board plan and housing facility.

FRESHMAN FINANCIAL AID (Fall 2016) 1,792 applied for aid; of those 67% were deemed to have need. 96% of freshmen with need received aid; of those 16% had need fully met. *Average financial aid package:* $8348 (excluding resources awarded to replace EFC). 2% of all full-time freshmen had no need and received non-need-based gift aid.

UNDERGRADUATE FINANCIAL AID (Fall 2016) 8,578 applied for aid; of those 79% were deemed to have need. 96% of undergraduates with need received aid; of those 14% had need fully met. *Average financial aid package:* $9398 (excluding resources awarded to replace EFC). 1% of all full-time undergraduates had no need and received non-need-based gift aid.

GIFT AID (NEED-BASED) *Total amount:* $34,850,589 (46% federal, 21% state, 28% institutional, 5% external sources). *Receiving aid:* Freshmen: 44% (983); all full-time undergraduates: 44% (5,501). *Average award:* Freshmen: $6224; Undergraduates: $6020. *Scholarships, grants, and awards:* Federal Pell, FSEOG, state, private, college/university gift aid from institutional funds, United Negro College Fund, Federal Nursing.

GIFT AID (NON-NEED-BASED) *Total amount:* $3,863,539 (1% federal, 3% state, 74% institutional, 22% external sources). *Receiving aid:* Freshmen: 19% (425). Undergraduates: 10% (1,204). *Average award:* Freshmen: $2608. Undergraduates: $3096. *Scholarships, grants, and awards by category: Academic interests/achievement:* biological sciences, business, communication, computer science, education, engineering/technologies, English, foreign languages, general academic interests/achievements, home economics, humanities, international studies, mathematics, physical sciences, premedicine, social sciences. *Creative arts/performance:* art/fine arts, cinema/film/broadcasting, creative writing, music, theater/drama. *Special achievements/activities:* general special achievements/activities, leadership. *Special character-*

istics: local/state students, out-of-state students. **Tuition waivers:** Full or partial for employees or children of employees.

LOANS Student loans: $53,694,962 (41% need-based, 59% non-need-based). 60% of past graduating class borrowed through all loan programs. *Average indebtedness per student:* $24,605. *Average need-based loan:* Freshmen: $3318. Undergraduates: $4622. **Parent loans:** $18,194,828 (100% non-need-based). **Programs:** Federal Direct (Subsidized and Unsubsidized Stafford, PLUS), Perkins, state, college/university, private loans.

WORK-STUDY Federal work-study: jobs available.

ATHLETIC AWARDS Total amount: $2,577,695 (100% non-need-based).

APPLYING FOR FINANCIAL AID Required financial aid forms: FAFSA, institution's own form. *Financial aid deadline (priority):* 3/1. *Notification date:* Continuous beginning 3/29. Students must reply by 5/1 or within 3 weeks of notification.

CONTACT Mr. Frederick Holding, Director of the Office of Scholarships and Financial Aid, The University of North Carolina Wilmington, 601 South College Road, Wilmington, NC 28403-5951, 910-962-3177. *Fax:* 910-962-3851. *E-mail:* finaid@uncw.edu.

Website: http://www.uncw.edu/.

UNIVERSITY OF NORTH DAKOTA
Grand Forks, ND

Tuition & fees (ND res): $8447	Average undergraduate aid package: $13,661

ABOUT THE INSTITUTION State-supported, coed. **Awards:** certificates, bachelor's, master's, and doctoral degrees. 91 undergraduate majors. **Total enrollment:** 14,406. Undergraduates: 11,000. Freshmen: 1,939. Federal methodology is used as a basis for awarding need-based institutional aid.

UNDERGRADUATE EXPENSES for 2017–2018 Application fee: $35. **Tuition, state resident:** full-time $6946; part-time $289 per credit hour. **Tuition, nonresident:** full-time $18,546; part-time $773 per credit hour. **Required fees:** full-time $1501. Full-time tuition and fees vary according to degree level, program, and reciprocity agreements. Part-time tuition and fees vary according to course load, degree level, program, and reciprocity agreements. **College room and board:** $8226. Room and board charges vary according to board plan and housing facility.

FRESHMAN FINANCIAL AID (Fall 2016) 1,591 applied for aid; of those 57% were deemed to have need. 99% of freshmen with need received aid; of those 49% had need fully met. *Average percent of need met:* 64% (excluding resources awarded to replace EFC). *Average financial aid package:* $14,780 (excluding resources awarded to replace EFC). 22% of all full-time freshmen had no need and received non-need-based gift aid.

UNDERGRADUATE FINANCIAL AID (Fall 2016) 6,413 applied for aid; of those 65% were deemed to have need. 99% of undergraduates with need received aid; of those 44% had need fully met. *Average percent of need met:* 60% (excluding resources awarded to replace EFC). *Average financial aid package:* $13,661 (excluding resources awarded to replace EFC). 10% of all full-time undergraduates had no need and received non-need-based gift aid.

GIFT AID (NEED-BASED) Total amount: $17,244,239 (51% federal, 18% state, 21% institutional, 10% external sources). **Receiving aid:** Freshmen: 40% (760); all full-time undergraduates: 36% (3,118). **Average award:** Freshmen: $5284; Undergraduates: $5293. **Scholarships, grants, and awards:** Federal Pell, FSEOG, state, private, college/university gift aid from institutional funds, Federal Nursing.

GIFT AID (NON-NEED-BASED) Total amount: $4,291,630 (3% federal, 21% state, 48% institutional, 28% external sources). **Receiving aid:** Freshmen: 5% (86). Undergraduates: 3% (277). **Average award:** Freshmen: $2097. Undergraduates: $2068. **Scholarships, grants, and awards by category:** *Academic interests/achievement:* biological sciences, business, communication, computer science, education, engineering/technologies, English, foreign languages, general academic interests/achievements, home economics, humanities, international studies, mathematics, physical sciences, premedicine, social sciences. *Creative arts/performance:* art/fine arts, music, theater/drama. *Special achievements/activities:* community service, general special achievements/activities, leadership, memberships. *Special characteristics:* children of faculty/staff, ethnic background, first-generation college students, general special characteristics, handicapped students, international students, members of minority groups, veterans, veterans' children. **Tuition waivers:** Full or partial for minority students, employees or children of employees. **ROTC:** Army, Air Force.

LOANS Student loans: $56,048,536 (53% need-based, 47% non-need-based). 65% of past graduating class borrowed through all loan programs. *Average need-based loan:* Freshmen: $7473. Undergraduates: $7607. **Parent loans:** $2,949,095 (28% need-based, 72% non-need-based). **Programs:** Federal Direct (Subsidized and Unsubsidized Stafford, PLUS), Federal Nursing, alternative loans.

WORK-STUDY Federal work-study: 1,471 jobs averaging $3000.

ATHLETIC AWARDS Total amount: $4,891,735 (85% need-based, 15% non-need-based).

APPLYING FOR FINANCIAL AID Required financial aid forms: FAFSA, Scholarship Central Application. *Financial aid deadline (priority):* 2/1. *Notification date:* Continuous beginning 3/15. Students must reply within 4 weeks of notification.

CONTACT Janelle Kilgore, Interim Director of Student Financial Aid, University of North Dakota, 264 Centennial Drive, Stop 8371, Grand Forks, ND 58202, 701-777-3121 or toll-free 800-CALL-UND. *Fax:* 701-777-2040. *E-mail:* janelle.kilgore@und.edu.

Website: http://www.und.edu/.

UNIVERSITY OF NORTHERN COLORADO
Greeley, CO

Tuition & fees (CO res): $9545	Average undergraduate aid package: $13,815

ABOUT THE INSTITUTION State-supported, coed. **Awards:** bachelor's, master's, and doctoral degrees. 45 undergraduate majors. **Total enrollment:** 12,968. Undergraduates: 9,977. Freshmen: 2,047. Federal methodology is used as a basis for awarding need-based institutional aid.

UNDERGRADUATE EXPENSES for 2018–2019 Application fee: $45. **One-time required fee:** $250. **Tuition, state resident:** full-time $7374; part-time $294.75 per credit hour. **Tuition, nonresident:** full-time $18,960; part-time $755 per credit hour. **Required fees:** full-time $2171; $127.13 per credit hour. Full-time tuition and fees vary according to course load, location, program, and reciprocity agreements. Part-time tuition and fees vary according to course load, location, program, and reciprocity agreements. **College room and board:** $10,982; **Room only:** $5202. Room and board charges vary according to board plan and housing facility.

FRESHMAN FINANCIAL AID (Fall 2016) 1,914 applied for aid; of those 73% were deemed to have need. 100% of freshmen with need received aid; of those 24% had need fully met. *Average percent of need met:* 77% (excluding resources awarded to replace EFC). *Average financial aid package:* $14,042 (excluding resources awarded to replace EFC). 20% of all full-time freshmen had no need and received non-need-based gift aid.

UNDERGRADUATE FINANCIAL AID (Fall 2016) 6,847 applied for aid; of those 77% were deemed to have need. 100% of undergraduates with need received aid; of those 22% had need fully met. *Average percent of need met:* 72% (excluding resources awarded to replace EFC). *Average financial aid package:* $13,815 (excluding resources awarded to replace EFC). 16% of all full-time undergraduates had no need and received non-need-based gift aid.

GIFT AID (NEED-BASED) Total amount: $43,749,556 (32% federal, 14% state, 41% institutional, 13% external sources). **Receiving aid:** Freshmen: 57% (1,176); all full-time undergraduates: 46% (3,829). **Average award:** Freshmen: $7188; Undergraduates: $7228. **Scholarships, grants, and awards:** Federal Pell, FSEOG, state, private, college/university gift aid from institutional funds.

GIFT AID (NON-NEED-BASED) Total amount: $7,023,531 (1% federal, 72% institutional, 27% external sources). **Receiving aid:** Freshmen: 49% (1,010). Undergraduates: 38% (3,167). **Average award:** Freshmen: $3190. Undergraduates: $3141. **Scholarships, grants, and awards by category:** *Academic interests/achievement:* biological sciences, business, communication, education, English, foreign languages, general academic interests/achievements, health fields, home economics, humanities, international studies, mathematics, military science, physical sciences, premedicine, social sciences. *Creative arts/performance:* applied art and design, art/fine arts, dance, journalism/publications, music, performing arts, theater/drama. *Special achievements/activities:* community service, general special achievements/activities, leadership, memberships. *Special characteristics:* adult students, children and siblings of alumni, children of faculty/staff, children of union members/company employees, children of workers in trades, ethnic background, first-generation college students,

---

general special characteristics, handicapped students, international students, local/state students, married students, members of minority groups, out-of-state students, previous college experience, veterans. *Tuition waivers:* Full or partial for employees or children of employees. *ROTC:* Army, Air Force.

LOANS *Student loans:* $60,818,782 (78% need-based, 22% non-need-based). 67% of past graduating class borrowed through all loan programs. *Average indebtedness per student:* $24,844. *Average need-based loan:* Freshmen: $3450. Undergraduates: $4561. *Parent loans:* $78,454,733 (56% need-based, 44% non-need-based). *Programs:* Federal Direct (Subsidized and Unsubsidized Stafford, PLUS), Perkins, Federal Nursing.

WORK-STUDY *Federal work-study:* 191 jobs averaging $2436. *State or other work-study/employment:* Total amount: $4,396,375 (97% need-based, 3% non-need-based). 566 part-time jobs averaging $2331.

ATHLETIC AWARDS Total amount: $5,084,495 (44% need-based, 56% non-need-based).

APPLYING FOR FINANCIAL AID *Required financial aid form:* FAFSA. *Financial aid deadline (priority):* 3/1. *Notification date:* 3/15. Students must reply within 4 weeks of notification.

CONTACT Marty Somero, Director of Financial Aid, University of Northern Colorado, Carter Hall 1005, Greeley, CO 80639, 970-351-2502 or toll-free 888-700-4UNC. *Fax:* 970-351-3737. *E-mail:* ofa@unco.edu.
Website: http://www.unco.edu/.

UNIVERSITY OF NORTHERN IOWA
Cedar Falls, IA

Tuition & fees (IA res): $8699	Average undergraduate aid package: $8499

ABOUT THE INSTITUTION State-supported, coed. *Awards:* bachelor's, master's, and doctoral degrees. 92 undergraduate majors. *Total enrollment:* 11,907. Undergraduates: 10,005. Freshmen: 1,834. Federal methodology is used as a basis for awarding need-based institutional aid.

UNDERGRADUATE EXPENSES for 2017–2018 *Application fee:* $40. *Tuition, state resident:* full-time $7456; part-time $311 per credit hour. *Tuition, nonresident:* full-time $17,998; part-time $750 per credit hour. *Required fees:* full-time $1243. Full-time tuition and fees vary according to course load and program. Part-time tuition and fees vary according to course load and program. *College room and board:* $8781; *Room only:* $4473. Room and board charges vary according to board plan and housing facility.

FRESHMAN FINANCIAL AID (Fall 2016) 1,653 applied for aid; of those 70% were deemed to have need. 97% of freshmen with need received aid; of those 16% had need fully met. *Average percent of need met:* 65% (excluding resources awarded to replace EFC). *Average financial aid package:* $8210 (excluding resources awarded to replace EFC). 22% of all full-time freshmen had no need and received non-need-based gift aid.

UNDERGRADUATE FINANCIAL AID (Fall 2016) 6,943 applied for aid; of those 78% were deemed to have need. 95% of undergraduates with need received aid; of those 14% had need fully met. *Average percent of need met:* 64% (excluding resources awarded to replace EFC). *Average financial aid package:* $8499 (excluding resources awarded to replace EFC). 11% of all full-time undergraduates had no need and received non-need-based gift aid.

GIFT AID (NEED-BASED) *Total amount:* $27,412,491 (46% federal, 4% state, 43% institutional, 7% external sources). *Receiving aid:* Freshmen: 33% (646); all full-time undergraduates: 34% (3,122). *Average award:* Freshmen: $4964; Undergraduates: $4844. *Scholarships, grants, and awards:* Federal Pell, FSEOG, state, private, college/university gift aid from institutional funds, TEACH Grants.

GIFT AID (NON-NEED-BASED) *Total amount:* $3,583,085 (10% federal, 7% state, 65% institutional, 18% external sources). *Receiving aid:* Freshmen: 42% (828). Undergraduates: 28% (2,574). *Average award:* Freshmen: $3224. Undergraduates: $3256. *Scholarships, grants, and awards by category:* Academic interests/achievement: biological sciences, business, communication, computer science, education, general academic interests/achievements, mathematics, physical sciences, social sciences. Creative arts/performance: applied art and design, art/fine arts, debating, music, theater/drama. Special achievements/activities: leadership. Special characteristics: general special characteristics, members of minority groups, veterans. *ROTC:* Army.

LOANS *Student loans:* $44,855,975 (41% need-based, 59% non-need-based). 66% of past graduating class borrowed through all loan programs. *Average indebtedness per student:* $23,887. *Average need-based loan:* Freshmen: $3364. Undergraduates: $4296. *Parent loans:* $12,106,670 (100% non-need-based). *Programs:* Federal Direct (Subsidized and Unsubsidized Stafford, PLUS), Perkins, private loans.

WORK-STUDY *Federal work-study:* jobs available. *State or other work-study/employment:* Part-time jobs available.

ATHLETIC AWARDS Total amount: $3,782,266 (91% need-based, 9% non-need-based).

APPLYING FOR FINANCIAL AID *Required financial aid form:* FAFSA. *Financial aid deadline:* Continuous. *Notification date:* Continuous beginning 1/15.

CONTACT Heather Stalzer, Associate Director of Student Financial Aid, University of Northern Iowa, 105 Gilchrist Hall, Cedar Falls, IA 50614-0024, 319-273-2701 or toll-free 800-772-2037. *Fax:* 319-273-6950. *E-mail:* heather.stalzer@uni.edu. *Website:* http://www.uni.edu/.

UNIVERSITY OF NORTH FLORIDA
Jacksonville, FL

Tuition & fees (FL res): $6394	Average undergraduate aid package: $8820

ABOUT THE INSTITUTION State-supported, coed. *Awards:* certificates, associate, bachelor's, master's, and doctoral degrees (doctoral degree in education only). 58 undergraduate majors. *Total enrollment:* 16,309. Undergraduates: 14,255. Freshmen: 2,291. Federal methodology is used as a basis for awarding need-based institutional aid.

UNDERGRADUATE EXPENSES for 2017–2018 *Application fee:* $30. *Tuition, state resident:* full-time $4281; part-time $142.70 per credit hour. *Tuition, nonresident:* full-time $17,999; part-time $599.97 per credit hour. *Required fees:* full-time $2113; $70.43 per credit hour. Full-time tuition and fees vary according to course load. Part-time tuition and fees vary according to course load. *College room and board:* $9772; *Room only:* $5772. Room and board charges vary according to board plan and housing facility.

FRESHMAN FINANCIAL AID (Fall 2017, est.) 1,849 applied for aid; of those 58% were deemed to have need. 94% of freshmen with need received aid; of those 10% had need fully met. *Average percent of need met:* 90% (excluding resources awarded to replace EFC). *Average financial aid package:* $9495 (excluding resources awarded to replace EFC). 12% of all full-time freshmen had no need and received non-need-based gift aid.

UNDERGRADUATE FINANCIAL AID (Fall 2017, est.) 7,083 applied for aid; of those 60% were deemed to have need. 92% of undergraduates with need received aid; of those 8% had need fully met. *Average percent of need met:* 89% (excluding resources awarded to replace EFC). *Average financial aid package:* $8820 (excluding resources awarded to replace EFC). 14% of all full-time undergraduates had no need and received non-need-based gift aid.

GIFT AID (NEED-BASED) *Total amount:* $36,623,271 (56% federal, 25% state, 17% institutional, 2% external sources). *Receiving aid:* Freshmen: 31% (663); all full-time undergraduates: 27% (2,747). *Average award:* Freshmen: $6702; Undergraduates: $6444. *Scholarships, grants, and awards:* Federal Pell, FSEOG, state, private, college/university gift aid from institutional funds.

GIFT AID (NON-NEED-BASED) *Total amount:* $10,128,366 (58% state, 37% institutional, 5% external sources). *Receiving aid:* Freshmen: 27% (573). Undergraduates: 13% (1,366). *Average award:* Freshmen: $3191. Undergraduates: $3092. *Scholarships, grants, and awards by category:* Academic interests/achievement: 229 awards ($695,726 total): business, computer science, education, engineering/technologies, general academic interests/achievements, health fields, international studies. Creative arts/performance: 30 awards ($95,200 total): art/fine arts, music. Special achievements/activities: 13 awards ($25,700 total): community service, general special achievements/activities, leadership. Special characteristics: 31 awards ($46,000 total): first-generation college students, general special characteristics, international students, members of minority groups, out-of-state students. *Tuition waivers:* Full or partial for employees or children of employees, senior citizens. *ROTC:* Army, Naval cooperative.

LOANS *Student loans:* $35,610,639 (72% need-based, 28% non-need-based). 49% of past graduating class borrowed through all loan programs. *Average indebtedness per student:* $18,787. *Average need-based loan:* Freshmen: $3255. Undergrad-

uates: $4140. *Parent loans:* $2,691,513 (56% need-based, 44% non-need-based). *Programs:* Federal Direct (Subsidized and Unsubsidized Stafford, PLUS).

WORK-STUDY *Federal work-study:* Total amount: $463,885; 143 jobs averaging $3244.

ATHLETIC AWARDS Total amount: $1,809,310 (22% need-based, 78% non-need-based).

APPLYING FOR FINANCIAL AID *Required financial aid form:* FAFSA. *Financial aid deadline (priority):* 4/1. *Notification date:* Continuous beginning 3/15. Students must reply within 2 weeks of notification.

CONTACT Ms. Anissa Agne, Director of Financial Aid, University of North Florida, 1 UNF Drive, Jacksonville, FL 32224-7699, 904-620-5555. *E-mail:* anissa.agne@unf.edu. *Website:* http://www.unf.edu/.

UNIVERSITY OF NORTH GEORGIA
Dahlonega, GA

Tuition & fees (GA res): $7395	Average undergraduate aid package: $14,234

ABOUT THE INSTITUTION State-supported, coed. *Awards:* certificates, associate, bachelor's, master's, and doctoral degrees. 41 undergraduate majors. *Total enrollment:* 18,782. Undergraduates: 18,173. Freshmen: 3,964. Federal methodology is used as a basis for awarding need-based institutional aid.

UNDERGRADUATE EXPENSES for 2018–2019 *Application fee:* $30. *Tuition, state resident:* full-time $5569; part-time $182 per credit hour. *Tuition, nonresident:* full-time $19,657; part-time $642.40 per credit hour. *Required fees:* full-time $1826. Full-time tuition and fees vary according to course load, degree level, and location. Part-time tuition and fees vary according to course load, degree level, and location. *College room and board:* $10,800; *Room only:* $5520. Room and board charges vary according to board plan and housing facility.

FRESHMAN FINANCIAL AID (Fall 2017, est.) 3,190 applied for aid; of those 73% were deemed to have need. 94% of freshmen with need received aid; of those 63% had need fully met. *Average percent of need met:* 68% (excluding resources awarded to replace EFC). *Average financial aid package:* $10,077 (excluding resources awarded to replace EFC). 9% of all full-time freshmen had no need and received non-need-based gift aid.

UNDERGRADUATE FINANCIAL AID (Fall 2017, est.) 9,980 applied for aid; of those 76% were deemed to have need. 95% of undergraduates with need received aid; of those 61% had need fully met. *Average percent of need met:* 63% (excluding resources awarded to replace EFC). *Average financial aid package:* $14,234 (excluding resources awarded to replace EFC). 5% of all full-time undergraduates had no need and received non-need-based gift aid.

GIFT AID (NEED-BASED) *Total amount:* $29,639,149 (95% federal, 2% state, 2% institutional, 1% external sources). *Receiving aid:* Freshmen: 55% (1,998); all full-time undergraduates: 56% (6,952). *Average award:* Freshmen: $6059; Undergraduates: $5948. *Scholarships, grants, and awards:* Federal Pell, FSEOG, state, private, college/university gift aid from institutional funds.

GIFT AID (NON-NEED-BASED) *Total amount:* $29,830,187 (1% federal, 92% state, 2% institutional, 5% external sources). *Receiving aid:* Freshmen: 54% (1,952). Undergraduates: 57% (7,132). *Average award:* Freshmen: $1212. Undergraduates: $1349. *Scholarships, grants, and awards by category: Academic interests/achievement:* biological sciences, business, education, English, general academic interests/achievements, health fields, humanities, mathematics, military science, physical sciences, premedicine. *Creative arts/performance:* applied art and design, general creative arts/performance, music. *Special achievements/activities:* cheerleading/drum major, community service, general special achievements/activities, leadership. *Special characteristics:* general special characteristics. *Tuition waivers:* Full or partial for employees or children of employees, senior citizens. *ROTC:* Army.

LOANS *Student loans:* $44,095,140 (39% need-based, 61% non-need-based). 53% of past graduating class borrowed through all loan programs. *Average indebtedness per student:* $12,345. *Average need-based loan:* Freshmen: $3875. Undergraduates: $5230. *Parent loans:* $3,791,770 (100% need-based). *Programs:* Federal Direct (Subsidized and Unsubsidized Stafford, PLUS), Perkins, state, college/university.

WORK-STUDY *Federal work-study:* Total amount: $251,913; 178 jobs averaging $1195. *State or other work-study/employment:* Part-time jobs available.

ATHLETIC AWARDS Total amount: $823,689 (100% non-need-based).

APPLYING FOR FINANCIAL AID *Required financial aid form:* FAFSA. *Financial aid deadline (priority):* 2/20. *Notification date:* Continuous beginning 4/1. Students must reply within 2 weeks of notification.

CONTACT Jill Rayner, Director of Financial Aid, University of North Georgia, 82 College Circle, Dahlonega, GA 30597-1001, 706-864-1688 or toll-free 800-498-9581. *Fax:* 706-864-1411. *E-mail:* jill.rayner@ung.edu. *Website:* http://www.ung.edu/.

UNIVERSITY OF NORTH TEXAS
Denton, TX

Tuition & fees (TX res): $11,514	Average undergraduate aid package: $10,975

ABOUT THE INSTITUTION State-supported, coed. *Awards:* certificates, bachelor's, master's, and doctoral degrees. 87 undergraduate majors. *Total enrollment:* 38,081. Undergraduates: 31,405. Freshmen: 4,905. Federal methodology is used as a basis for awarding need-based institutional aid.

UNDERGRADUATE EXPENSES for 2018–2019 *Application fee:* $75. *Tuition, state resident:* full-time $8404. *Tuition, nonresident:* full-time $21,214. *Required fees:* full-time $3110. Full-time tuition and fees vary according to course load. Part-time tuition and fees vary according to course load. *College room and board:* $9610. Room and board charges vary according to board plan and housing facility. *Payment plan:* Guaranteed tuition.

FRESHMAN FINANCIAL AID (Fall 2017, est.) 4,067 applied for aid; of those 77% were deemed to have need. 98% of freshmen with need received aid; of those 10% had need fully met. *Average percent of need met:* 64% (excluding resources awarded to replace EFC). *Average financial aid package:* $13,131 (excluding resources awarded to replace EFC). 14% of all full-time freshmen had no need and received non-need-based gift aid.

UNDERGRADUATE FINANCIAL AID (Fall 2017, est.) 18,991 applied for aid; of those 84% were deemed to have need. 96% of undergraduates with need received aid; of those 9% had need fully met. *Average percent of need met:* 53% (excluding resources awarded to replace EFC). *Average financial aid package:* $10,975 (excluding resources awarded to replace EFC). 12% of all full-time undergraduates had no need and received non-need-based gift aid.

GIFT AID (NEED-BASED) *Total amount:* $135,477,800 (38% federal, 19% state, 28% institutional, 15% external sources). *Receiving aid:* Freshmen: 44% (2,028); all full-time undergraduates: 42% (10,739). *Average award:* Freshmen: $11,205; Undergraduates: $8311. *Scholarships, grants, and awards:* Federal Pell, FSEOG, state, private, college/university gift aid from institutional funds.

GIFT AID (NON-NEED-BASED) *Total amount:* $7,667,649 (56% institutional, 44% external sources). *Receiving aid:* Freshmen: 32% (1,499). Undergraduates: 17% (4,281). *Average award:* Freshmen: $6491. Undergraduates: $6712. *Tuition waivers:* Full or partial for employees or children of employees, senior citizens. *ROTC:* Army, Air Force.

LOANS *Student loans:* $111,467,663 (87% need-based, 13% non-need-based). 63% of past graduating class borrowed through all loan programs. *Average indebtedness per student:* $25,203. *Average need-based loan:* Freshmen: $3128. Undergraduates: $4087. *Parent loans:* $105,144,705 (74% need-based, 26% non-need-based). *Programs:* Federal Direct (Subsidized and Unsubsidized Stafford, PLUS), Perkins, state.

WORK-STUDY *Federal work-study:* Total amount: $6,796,367; jobs available. *State or other work-study/employment:* Total amount: $1,220,560 (100% need-based). Part-time jobs available.

ATHLETIC AWARDS Total amount: $4,682,788 (39% need-based, 61% non-need-based).

APPLYING FOR FINANCIAL AID *Required financial aid form:* FAFSA. *Financial aid deadline (priority):* 3/15. *Notification date:* Continuous beginning 12/15.

CONTACT Mrs. Zelma DeLeon, Executive Director of Student Financial Aid and Scholarships, University of North Texas, 1155 Union Circle #311370, Denton, TX 76203-5017, 940-565-2302 or toll-free 800-868-8211. *Fax:* 940-565-2738. *E-mail:* zelma.deleon@unt.edu. *Website:* http://www.unt.edu/.

UNIVERSITY OF NORTH TEXAS AT DALLAS
Dallas, TX

Tuition & fees (TX res): $7848	Average undergraduate aid package: $9152

ABOUT THE INSTITUTION State-supported, coed. **Awards:** bachelor's, master's, and doctoral degrees. **Total enrollment:** 3,509. Undergraduates: 2,727. Freshmen: 316. Federal methodology is used as a basis for awarding need-based institutional aid.

UNDERGRADUATE EXPENSES for 2018–2019 **Application fee:** $50. **Tuition, state resident:** full-time $7548; part-time $251.63 per credit hour. **Tuition, nonresident:** full-time $19,788; part-time $659.63 per credit hour. **Required fees:** full-time $300; $10 per credit hour. Full-time tuition and fees vary according to degree level. Part-time tuition and fees vary according to degree level. **College room and board:** $8948. Room and board charges vary according to board plan and housing facility. **Payment plan:** Guaranteed tuition.

FRESHMAN FINANCIAL AID (Fall 2016) 222 applied for aid; of those 95% were deemed to have need. 95% of freshmen with need received aid; of those 11% had need fully met. **Average percent of need met:** 54% (excluding resources awarded to replace EFC). **Average financial aid package:** $10,964 (excluding resources awarded to replace EFC). 5% of all full-time freshmen had no need and received non-need-based gift aid.

UNDERGRADUATE FINANCIAL AID (Fall 2016) 1,168 applied for aid; of those 95% were deemed to have need. 95% of undergraduates with need received aid; of those 6% had need fully met. **Average percent of need met:** 46% (excluding resources awarded to replace EFC). **Average financial aid package:** $9152 (excluding resources awarded to replace EFC). 8% of all full-time undergraduates had no need and received non-need-based gift aid.

GIFT AID (NEED-BASED) Total amount: $9,606,893 (49% federal, 21% state, 22% institutional, 8% external sources). **Receiving aid:** Freshmen: 74% (190); all full-time undergraduates: 69% (959). **Average award:** Freshmen: $8948; Undergraduates: $6263. **Scholarships, grants, and awards:** Federal Pell, FSEOG, state, college/university gift aid from institutional funds, TEACH Grants.

GIFT AID (NON-NEED-BASED) Total amount: $808,387 (31% federal, 16% state, 21% institutional, 32% external sources). **Receiving aid:** Freshmen: 35% (90). Undergraduates: 24% (334). **Average award:** Freshmen: $4784. Undergraduates: $5108. **Tuition waivers:** Full or partial for employees or children of employees, senior citizens.

LOANS Student loans: $7,782,179 (90% need-based, 10% non-need-based). 79% of past graduating class borrowed through all loan programs. **Average indebtedness per student:** $6927. **Average need-based loan:** Freshmen: $3385. Undergraduates: $4186. **Parent loans:** $757,425 (79% need-based, 21% non-need-based). **Programs:** Federal Direct (Subsidized and Unsubsidized Stafford, PLUS), state, private loans.

WORK-STUDY Federal work-study: jobs available.

APPLYING FOR FINANCIAL AID Required financial aid forms: FAFSA, state aid form. **Financial aid deadline:** Continuous. **Notification date:** Continuous beginning 12/1.

CONTACT Office of Financial Aid and Scholarships, University of North Texas at Dallas, 7300 University Hills Boulevard, Dallas, TX 75241, 972-780-3662. *E-mail:* financialaid@untdallas.edu. *Website:* http://untdallas.edu/.

UNIVERSITY OF NORTHWESTERN OHIO
Lima, OH

CONTACT Financial Aid Office, University of Northwestern Ohio, 1441 North Cable Road, Lima, OH 45805-1498, 419-227-3141. *Website:* http://www.unoh.edu/.

UNIVERSITY OF NORTHWESTERN–ST. PAUL
St. Paul, MN

CONTACT Mr. Richard L. Blatchley, Director of Financial Aid, University of Northwestern–St. Paul, 3003 Snelling Avenue North, St. Paul, MN 55113-1598, 651-631-5321 or toll-free 800-827-6827. *Fax:* 651-628-3332. *E-mail:* rlb@nwc.edu. *Website:* http://www.unwsp.edu/.

UNIVERSITY OF NOTRE DAME
Notre Dame, IN

Tuition & fees: $53,391	Average undergraduate aid package: $49,410

ABOUT THE INSTITUTION Independent Roman Catholic, coed. **Awards:** bachelor's, master's, and doctoral degrees. 64 undergraduate majors. **Total enrollment:** 12,467. Undergraduates: 8,576. Freshmen: 2,051. Both federal and institutional methodology are used as a basis for awarding need-based institutional aid.

UNDERGRADUATE EXPENSES for 2018–2019 **Application fee:** $75. **Comprehensive fee:** $68,801 includes full-time tuition ($52,884), mandatory fees ($507), and room and board ($15,410). **Part-time tuition:** $2201 per credit hour.

FRESHMAN FINANCIAL AID (Fall 2017, est.) 1,432 applied for aid; of those 71% were deemed to have need. 100% of freshmen with need received aid; of those 99% had need fully met. **Average percent of need met:** 100% (excluding resources awarded to replace EFC). **Average financial aid package:** $47,455 (excluding resources awarded to replace EFC). 2% of all full-time freshmen had no need and received non-need-based gift aid.

UNDERGRADUATE FINANCIAL AID (Fall 2017, est.) 4,937 applied for aid; of those 84% were deemed to have need. 100% of undergraduates with need received aid; of those 99% had need fully met. **Average percent of need met:** 100% (excluding resources awarded to replace EFC). **Average financial aid package:** $49,410 (excluding resources awarded to replace EFC). 5% of all full-time undergraduates had no need and received non-need-based gift aid.

GIFT AID (NEED-BASED) Total amount: $192,032,195 (4% federal, 75% institutional, 21% external sources). **Receiving aid:** Freshmen: 48% (980); all full-time undergraduates: 47% (4,014). **Average award:** Freshmen: $38,673; Undergraduates: $38,921. **Scholarships, grants, and awards:** Federal Pell, FSEOG, state, private, college/university gift aid from institutional funds.

GIFT AID (NON-NEED-BASED) Total amount: $19,296,211 (41% federal, 40% institutional, 19% external sources). **Receiving aid:** Freshmen: 8% (166). Undergraduates: 8% (656). **Average award:** Freshmen: $25,299. Undergraduates: $13,517. **Scholarships, grants, and awards by category:** Special characteristics: children of faculty/staff. **Tuition waivers:** Full or partial for employees or children of employees. **ROTC:** Army, Naval, Air Force.

LOANS Student loans: $33,030,576 (52% need-based, 48% non-need-based). 46% of past graduating class borrowed through all loan programs. **Average indebtedness per student:** $29,254. **Average need-based loan:** Freshmen: $3781. Undergraduates: $493. **Parent loans:** $12,066,805 (2% need-based, 98% non-need-based). **Programs:** Federal Direct (Subsidized and Unsubsidized Stafford, PLUS), Perkins, college/university, private loans.

WORK-STUDY Federal work-study: Total amount: $2,051,793; jobs available. **State or other work-study/employment:** Total amount: $10,991,310 (20% need-based, 80% non-need-based). 3,231 part-time jobs averaging $3402.

ATHLETIC AWARDS Total amount: $22,377,216 (18% need-based, 82% non-need-based).

APPLYING FOR FINANCIAL AID Required financial aid forms: FAFSA, CSS Financial Aid PROFILE, noncustodial (divorced/separated) parent's statement, business/farm supplement, federal income tax form(s), W-2 forms, verification worksheet. **Financial aid deadline (priority):** 2/15. **Notification date:** Continuous beginning 3/28. Students must reply by 5/1.

CONTACT Mrs. Mary Nucciarone, Director, Financial Aid, University of Notre Dame, 115 Main Building, Notre Dame, IN 46556, 574-631-6436. *Fax:* 574-631-6899. *E-mail:* finaid@nd.edu. *Website:* http://www.nd.edu/.

UNIVERSITY OF OKLAHOMA
Norman, OK

Tuition & fees (OK res): $9063	Average undergraduate aid package: $13,031

ABOUT THE INSTITUTION State-supported, coed. **Awards:** certificates, bachelor's, master's, and doctoral degrees. 102 undergraduate majors. **Total enrollment:** 28,527. Undergraduates: 22,032. Freshmen: 4,473. Federal methodology is used as a basis for awarding need-based institutional aid.

UNDERGRADUATE EXPENSES for 2017–2018 Application fee: $40. **Tuition, state resident:** full-time $4788; part-time $159.60 per credit hour. **Tuition, nonresident:** full-time $20,169; part-time $672.30 per credit hour. **Required fees:** full-time $4275; $134.05 per credit hour or $126.50 per term. Full-time tuition and fees vary according to course load, location, and program. Part-time tuition and fees vary according to course load, location, and program. **College room and board:** $10,588; **Room only:** $6192. Room and board charges vary according to board plan and housing facility. **Payment plan:** Guaranteed tuition.

FRESHMAN FINANCIAL AID (Fall 2016) 2,763 applied for aid; of those 67% were deemed to have need. 98% of freshmen with need received aid; of those 77% had need fully met. **Average percent of need met:** 77% (excluding resources awarded to replace EFC). **Average financial aid package:** $13,004 (excluding resources awarded to replace EFC). 16% of all full-time freshmen had no need and received non-need-based gift aid.

UNDERGRADUATE FINANCIAL AID (Fall 2016) 10,648 applied for aid; of those 77% were deemed to have need. 98% of undergraduates with need received aid; of those 84% had need fully met. **Average percent of need met:** 83% (excluding resources awarded to replace EFC). **Average financial aid package:** $13,031 (excluding resources awarded to replace EFC). 14% of all full-time undergraduates had no need and received non-need-based gift aid.

GIFT AID (NEED-BASED) Total amount: $52,882,705 (40% federal, 26% state, 22% institutional, 12% external sources). **Receiving aid:** Freshmen: 23% (843); all full-time undergraduates: 25% (4,603). **Average award:** Freshmen: $6946; Undergraduates: $6142. **Scholarships, grants, and awards:** Federal Pell, FSEOG, state, private, college/university gift aid from institutional funds, United Negro College Fund.

GIFT AID (NON-NEED-BASED) Total amount: $13,991,547 (32% state, 44% institutional, 24% external sources). **Receiving aid:** Freshmen: 32% (1,170). Undergraduates: 25% (4,535). **Average award:** Freshmen: $2896. Undergraduates: $2464. **Scholarships, grants, and awards by category:** Academic interests/achievement: 13,183 awards: architecture, area/ethnic studies, biological sciences, business, communication, computer science, education, engineering/technologies, English, foreign languages, general academic interests/achievements, humanities, international studies, mathematics, military science, physical sciences, social sciences. Creative arts/performance: 736 awards: art/fine arts, cinema/film/broadcasting, dance, debating, journalism/publications, music, performing arts, theater/drama. Special achievements/activities: 144 awards: leadership. Special characteristics: 1,012 awards: children and siblings of alumni, children of faculty/staff, members of minority groups, previous college experience, public servants. **Tuition waivers:** Full or partial for employees or children of employees, senior citizens. **ROTC:** Army, Naval, Air Force.

LOANS Student loans: $67,527,187 (80% need-based, 20% non-need-based). 45% of past graduating class borrowed through all loan programs. Average indebtedness per student: $29,283. **Average need-based loan:** Freshmen: $3790. Undergraduates: $4427. **Parent loans:** $23,486,253 (76% need-based, 24% non-need-based). **Programs:** Federal Direct (Subsidized and Unsubsidized Stafford, PLUS), Perkins, college/university, alternative loans.

WORK-STUDY Federal work-study: 539 jobs averaging $3225. **State or other work-study/employment:** Total amount: $887,714 (63% need-based, 37% non-need-based). 99 part-time jobs averaging $10,145.

ATHLETIC AWARDS Total amount: $12,554,734 (36% need-based, 64% non-need-based).

APPLYING FOR FINANCIAL AID Required financial aid form: FAFSA. **Financial aid deadline:** Continuous. **Notification date:** Continuous beginning 1/15. Students must reply within 6 weeks of notification.

CONTACT Office of Financial Aid, University of Oklahoma, 1000 Asp Avenue, Room 216, Norman, OK 73019-4078, 405-325-4521 or toll-free 800-234-6868. Fax: 405-325-0819. E-mail: financialaid@ou.edu. Website: http://www.ou.edu/.

UNIVERSITY OF OKLAHOMA HEALTH SCIENCES CENTER
Oklahoma City, OK

CONTACT Ms. Janice Osburn, Director, Financial Aid Office, University of Oklahoma Health Sciences Center, PO Box 26901, Oklahoma City, OK 73190, 405-271-2118. Fax: 405-271-5446. Website: http://www.ouhsc.edu/.

UNIVERSITY OF OREGON
Eugene, OR

Tuition & fees (OR res): $11,571	Average undergraduate aid package: $11,187

ABOUT THE INSTITUTION State-supported, coed. **Awards:** certificates, bachelor's, master's, and doctoral degrees. 75 undergraduate majors. **Total enrollment:** 22,887. Undergraduates: 19,340. Freshmen: 3,938. Federal methodology is used as a basis for awarding need-based institutional aid.

UNDERGRADUATE EXPENSES for 2017–2018 Application fee: $65. **One-time required fee:** $430. **Tuition, state resident:** full-time $9495; part-time $211 per credit hour. **Tuition, nonresident:** full-time $32,535; part-time $723 per credit hour. **Required fees:** full-time $2076. Full-time tuition and fees vary according to course load. Part-time tuition and fees vary according to course load. **College room and board:** $12,450. Room and board charges vary according to board plan and housing facility.

FRESHMAN FINANCIAL AID (Fall 2016) 2,940 applied for aid; of those 68% were deemed to have need. 92% of freshmen with need received aid; of those 7% had need fully met. **Average percent of need met:** 58% (excluding resources awarded to replace EFC). **Average financial aid package:** $11,038 (excluding resources awarded to replace EFC). 17% of all full-time freshmen had no need and received non-need-based gift aid.

UNDERGRADUATE FINANCIAL AID (Fall 2016) 10,804 applied for aid; of those 76% were deemed to have need. 95% of undergraduates with need received aid; of those 7% had need fully met. **Average percent of need met:** 59% (excluding resources awarded to replace EFC). **Average financial aid package:** $11,187 (excluding resources awarded to replace EFC). 14% of all full-time undergraduates had no need and received non-need-based gift aid.

GIFT AID (NEED-BASED) Total amount: $54,724,808 (42% federal, 11% state, 35% institutional, 12% external sources). **Receiving aid:** Freshmen: 37% (1,441); all full-time undergraduates: 32% (5,873). **Average award:** Freshmen: $9826; Undergraduates: $8886. **Scholarships, grants, and awards:** Federal Pell, FSEOG, state, private, college/university gift aid from institutional funds.

GIFT AID (NON-NEED-BASED) Total amount: $18,485,192 (100% institutional). **Receiving aid:** Freshmen: 3% (103). Undergraduates: 1% (220). **Average award:** Freshmen: $6173. Undergraduates: $6140. **Scholarships, grants, and awards by category:** Academic interests/achievement: 7,847 awards ($31,236,000 total): architecture, biological sciences, business, education, English, foreign languages, general academic interests/achievements, health fields, humanities, international studies, mathematics, military science, physical sciences, premedicine, social sciences. Creative arts/performance: 253 awards ($621,749 total): applied art and design, art/fine arts, creative writing, dance, debating, journalism/publications, music, performing arts, theater/drama. Special characteristics: 369 awards ($1,947,036 total): children of faculty/staff, general special characteristics, international students, local/state students, veterans, veterans' children. **Tuition waivers:** Full or partial for employees or children of employees. **ROTC:** Army, Air Force cooperative.

LOANS Student loans: $62,456,472 (62% need-based, 38% non-need-based). 44% of past graduating class borrowed through all loan programs. Average indebtedness per student: $26,164. **Average need-based loan:** Freshmen: $3872. Undergraduates: $4764. **Parent loans:** $63,083,871 (43% need-based, 57% non-need-based). **Programs:** Federal Direct (Subsidized and Unsubsidized Stafford, PLUS), Perkins, college/university.

WORK-STUDY Federal work-study: 2,364 jobs averaging $1762. **State or other work-study/employment:** Total amount: $269,000 (100% non-need-based). 78 part-time jobs averaging $3295.

ATHLETIC AWARDS Total amount: $11,079,350 (20% need-based, 80% non-need-based).

APPLYING FOR FINANCIAL AID *Required financial aid form:* FAFSA. *Financial aid deadline (priority):* 3/1. *Notification date:* Continuous beginning 4/15. Students must reply within 4 weeks of notification.

CONTACT Jim Brooks, Director of Financial Aid and Scholarships, University of Oregon, 1278 University of Oregon, 260 Oregon Hall, Eugene, OR 97403-1278, 800-760-6953 or toll-free 800-232-3825. *Fax:* 541-346-1175. *E-mail:* financialaid@uoregon.edu.
Website: http://www.uoregon.edu/.

UNIVERSITY OF PENNSYLVANIA
Philadelphia, PA

Tuition & fees: $55,584	Average undergraduate aid package: $48,971

ABOUT THE INSTITUTION Independent, coed. *Awards:* certificates, associate, bachelor's, master's, and doctoral degrees (also offers evening program with significant enrollment not reflected in profile). 96 undergraduate majors. *Total enrollment:* 21,907. Undergraduates: 10,033. Freshmen: 2,412. Both federal and institutional methodology are used as a basis for awarding need-based institutional aid.

UNDERGRADUATE EXPENSES for 2018–2019 *Application fee:* $75. *Comprehensive fee:* $71,200 includes full-time tuition ($49,220), mandatory fees ($6364), and room and board ($15,616). Room and board charges vary according to board plan and housing facility. Part-time tuition and fees vary according to course load. *Payment plan:* Tuition prepayment.

FRESHMAN FINANCIAL AID (Fall 2016) 1,304 applied for aid; of those 84% were deemed to have need. 100% of freshmen with need received aid; of those 100% had need fully met. *Average percent of need met:* 100% (excluding resources awarded to replace EFC). *Average financial aid package:* $49,401 (excluding resources awarded to replace EFC).

UNDERGRADUATE FINANCIAL AID (Fall 2016) 4,851 applied for aid; of those 92% were deemed to have need. 100% of undergraduates with need received aid; of those 100% had need fully met. *Average percent of need met:* 100% (excluding resources awarded to replace EFC). *Average financial aid package:* $48,971 (excluding resources awarded to replace EFC).

GIFT AID (NEED-BASED) *Total amount:* $203,881,763 (5% federal, 1% state, 92% institutional, 2% external sources). *Receiving aid:* Freshmen: 44% (1,074); all full-time undergraduates: 46% (4,429). *Average award:* Freshmen: $47,114; Undergraduates: $46,177. *Scholarships, grants, and awards:* Federal Pell, FSEOG, state, private, college/university gift aid from institutional funds.

GIFT AID (NON-NEED-BASED) *Total amount:* $5,375,863 (3% federal, 97% external sources). *Tuition waivers:* Full or partial for employees or children of employees. *ROTC:* Army cooperative, Naval, Air Force cooperative.

LOANS *Student loans:* $14,743,641 (8% need-based, 92% non-need-based). 27% of past graduating class borrowed through all loan programs. *Average indebtedness per student:* $23,224. *Average need-based loan:* Freshmen: $3495. Undergraduates: $3922. *Parent loans:* $10,333,194 (100% non-need-based). *Programs:* Federal Direct (Subsidized and Unsubsidized Stafford, PLUS), Perkins, Federal Nursing, college/university, supplemental third-party loans (guaranteed by institution).

WORK-STUDY *Federal work-study:* jobs available. *State or other work-study/employment:* Total amount: $3,590,253 (100% need-based). Part-time jobs available.

APPLYING FOR FINANCIAL AID *Required financial aid forms:* FAFSA, institution's own form, CSS Financial Aid PROFILE, noncustodial (divorced/separated) parent's statement, business/farm supplement, federal income tax form(s). *Financial aid deadline (priority):* 2/15. *Notification date:* 4/1. Students must reply by 5/1.

CONTACT Elaine Papas Varas, Director of Financial Aid, University of Pennsylvania, 3451 Walnut Street, 100 Franklin Building, Philadelphia, PA 19104-6270, 215-898-1988. *E-mail:* varas@upenn.edu.
Website: http://www.upenn.edu/.

UNIVERSITY OF PHOENIX–BAY AREA CAMPUS
San Jose, CA

CONTACT ACS/AFS, University of Phoenix–Bay Area Campus, 875 West Elliot Road, Tempe, AZ 85284, 480-735-3000 or toll-free 866-766-0766. *Fax:* 480-940-2060.
Website: http://www.phoenix.edu/.

UNIVERSITY OF PHOENIX–CENTRAL VALLEY CAMPUS
Fresno, CA

CONTACT ACS/AFS, University of Phoenix–Central Valley Campus, 875 West Elliot Road, Tempe, AZ 85284, 480-735-3000 or toll-free 866-766-0766. *Fax:* 480-940-2060.
Website: http://www.phoenix.edu/.

UNIVERSITY OF PHOENIX–DALLAS CAMPUS
Dallas, TX

CONTACT ACS/AFS, University of Phoenix–Dallas Campus, 875 West Elliot Road, Tempe, AZ 85284, 480-735-3000 or toll-free 866-766-0766. *Fax:* 480-940-2060.
Website: http://www.phoenix.edu/.

UNIVERSITY OF PHOENIX–HAWAII CAMPUS
Honolulu, HI

CONTACT ACS/AFS, University of Phoenix–Hawaii Campus, 875 West Elliot Road, Tempe, AZ 85284, 480-735-3000 or toll-free 866-766-0766. *Fax:* 480-940-2060.
Website: http://www.phoenix.edu/.

UNIVERSITY OF PHOENIX–HOUSTON CAMPUS
Houston, TX

CONTACT ACS/AFS, University of Phoenix–Houston Campus, 875 West Elliot Road, Tempe, AZ 85284, 480-735-3000 or toll-free 866-766-0766. *Fax:* 480-940-2060.
Website: http://www.phoenix.edu/.

UNIVERSITY OF PHOENIX–LAS VEGAS CAMPUS
Las Vegas, NV

CONTACT ACS/AFS, University of Phoenix–Las Vegas Campus, 875 West Elliot Road, Tempe, AZ 85284, 480-735-3000 or toll-free 866-766-0766. *Fax:* 480-940-2060.
Website: http://www.phoenix.edu/.

UNIVERSITY OF PHOENIX–ONLINE CAMPUS

Phoenix, AZ

CONTACT Office of Financial Aid, University of Phoenix–Online Campus, 3157 East Elwood Street, Phoenix, AZ 85034-7209, 866-766-0766. *Website:* http://www.phoenix.edu/.

UNIVERSITY OF PHOENIX–PHOENIX CAMPUS

Tempe, AZ

CONTACT Office of Financial Aid, University of Phoenix–Phoenix Campus, 1625 West Fountainhead Parkway, Tempe, AZ 85282-2371, 866-766-0766. *Website:* http://www.phoenix.edu/.

UNIVERSITY OF PHOENIX–SACRAMENTO VALLEY CAMPUS

Sacramento, CA

CONTACT ACS/AFS, University of Phoenix–Sacramento Valley Campus, 875 West Elliot Road, Tempe, AZ 85284, 480-735-3000 or toll-free 866-766-0766. *Fax:* 480-940-2060. *Website:* http://www.phoenix.edu/.

UNIVERSITY OF PHOENIX–SAN DIEGO CAMPUS

San Diego, CA

CONTACT ACS/AFS, University of Phoenix–San Diego Campus, 875 West Elliot Road, Tempe, AZ 85284, 480-735-3000 or toll-free 866-766-0766. *Fax:* 480-940-2060. *Website:* http://www.phoenix.edu/.

UNIVERSITY OF PIKEVILLE

Pikeville, KY

Tuition & fees: $20,950	Average undergraduate aid package: $20,102

ABOUT THE INSTITUTION Independent Presbyterian Church (U.S.A.), coed. *Awards:* associate, bachelor's, master's, and doctoral degrees. 21 undergraduate majors. *Total enrollment:* 2,335. Undergraduates: 1,559. Freshmen: 279. Federal methodology is used as a basis for awarding need-based institutional aid.
UNDERGRADUATE EXPENSES for 2018–2019 *Comprehensive fee:* $28,750 includes full-time tuition ($20,800), mandatory fees ($150), and room and board ($7800). Full-time tuition and fees vary according to course load. Room and board charges vary according to housing facility. *Part-time tuition:* $867 per semester hour. Part-time tuition and fees vary according to course load.
FRESHMAN FINANCIAL AID (Fall 2017, est.) 279 applied for aid; of those 100% were deemed to have need. 100% of freshmen with need received aid; of those 50% had need fully met. *Average percent of need met:* 90% (excluding resources awarded to replace EFC). *Average financial aid package:* $20,100 (excluding resources awarded to replace EFC).
UNDERGRADUATE FINANCIAL AID (Fall 2017, est.) 1,043 applied for aid; of those 99% were deemed to have need. 100% of undergraduates with need received aid; of those 59% had need fully met. *Average percent of need met:* 90% (excluding resources awarded to replace EFC). *Average financial aid package:* $20,102 (excluding resources awarded to replace EFC).

GIFT AID (NEED-BASED) *Total amount:* $15,659,143 (24% federal, 25% state, 48% institutional, 3% external sources). *Receiving aid:* Freshmen: 100% (279); all full-time undergraduates: 98% (1,032). *Average award:* Freshmen: $18,081; Undergraduates: $17,433. *Scholarships, grants, and awards:* Federal Pell, FSEOG, state, private, college/university gift aid from institutional funds.
GIFT AID (NON-NEED-BASED) *Receiving aid:* Freshmen: 57% (159). Undergraduates: 44% (463). *Tuition waivers:* Full or partial for employees or children of employees, senior citizens. *ROTC:* Army.
LOANS *Student loans:* $4,729,183 (100% need-based). 83% of past graduating class borrowed through all loan programs. *Average indebtedness per student:* $23,876. *Average need-based loan:* Freshmen: $3387. Undergraduates: $4255. *Parent loans:* $640,289 (100% need-based). *Programs:* Federal Direct (Subsidized and Unsubsidized Stafford, PLUS), Perkins, college/university.
WORK-STUDY *Federal work-study:* Total amount: $473,357; 255 jobs averaging $1852.
ATHLETIC AWARDS Total amount: $2,257,379 (100% need-based).
APPLYING FOR FINANCIAL AID *Required financial aid form:* FAFSA. *Financial aid deadline (priority):* 2/1. *Notification date:* Continuous. Students must reply by 5/1.
CONTACT Ms. Jennifer Bates, Director of Student Financial Services, University of Pikeville, 147 Sycamore Street, Pikeville, KY 41501, 606-218-5254 or toll-free 866-232-7700. *Fax:* 606-218-5255. *E-mail:* jenniferbates@upike.edu. *Website:* http://www.upike.edu/.

UNIVERSITY OF PITTSBURGH

Pittsburgh, PA

Tuition & fees (PA res): $19,080	Average undergraduate aid package: $12,192

ABOUT THE INSTITUTION State-related, coed. *Awards:* certificates, associate, bachelor's, master's, and doctoral degrees. 96 undergraduate majors. *Total enrollment:* 28,642. Undergraduates: 19,326. Freshmen: 4,019. Federal methodology is used as a basis for awarding need-based institutional aid.
UNDERGRADUATE EXPENSES for 2017–2018 *Application fee:* $45. *Tuition, state resident:* full-time $18,130; part-time $755 per credit hour. *Tuition, nonresident:* full-time $29,692; part-time $1237 per credit hour. *Required fees:* full-time $950; $279 per term. Full-time tuition and fees vary according to location and program. Part-time tuition and fees vary according to location and program. *College room and board:* $10,950; *Room only:* $6300. Room and board charges vary according to board plan, housing facility, and location.
FRESHMAN FINANCIAL AID (Fall 2016) 3,269 applied for aid; of those 65% were deemed to have need. 96% of freshmen with need received aid; of those 18% had need fully met. *Average percent of need met:* 55% (excluding resources awarded to replace EFC). *Average financial aid package:* $12,960 (excluding resources awarded to replace EFC). 9% of all full-time freshmen had no need and received non-need-based gift aid.
UNDERGRADUATE FINANCIAL AID (Fall 2016) 12,404 applied for aid; of those 77% were deemed to have need. 96% of undergraduates with need received aid; of those 13% had need fully met. *Average percent of need met:* 53% (excluding resources awarded to replace EFC). *Average financial aid package:* $12,192 (excluding resources awarded to replace EFC). 3% of all full-time undergraduates had no need and received non-need-based gift aid.
GIFT AID (NEED-BASED) *Total amount:* $60,801,753 (21% federal, 17% state, 50% institutional, 12% external sources). *Receiving aid:* Freshmen: 42% (1,664); all full-time undergraduates: 38% (6,976). *Average award:* Freshmen: $10,945; Undergraduates: $9771. *Scholarships, grants, and awards:* Federal Pell, FSEOG, state, private, college/university gift aid from institutional funds, Federal Nursing.
GIFT AID (NON-NEED-BASED) *Total amount:* $31,733,359 (81% institutional, 19% external sources). *Receiving aid:* Freshmen: 7% (277). Undergraduates: 4% (775). *Average award:* Freshmen: $12,110. Undergraduates: $11,092. *Scholarships, grants, and awards by category:* Academic interests/achievement: general academic interests/achievements. *Special characteristics:* children of faculty/staff, children of union members/company employees. *Tuition waivers:* Full or partial for employees or children of employees. *ROTC:* Army, Naval cooperative, Air Force.
LOANS *Student loans:* $110,798,762 (64% need-based, 36% non-need-based). 62% of past graduating class borrowed through all loan programs. *Average indebtedness*

per student: $38,322. **Average need-based loan:** Freshmen: $3693. Undergraduates: $4718. **Parent loans:** $37,896,693 (48% need-based, 52% non-need-based).
Programs: Federal Direct (Subsidized and Unsubsidized Stafford, PLUS), Federal Nursing, state, college/university.
WORK-STUDY *Federal work-study:* jobs available.
ATHLETIC AWARDS Total amount: $10,759,288 (37% need-based, 63% non-need-based).
APPLYING FOR FINANCIAL AID *Required financial aid forms:* FAFSA, state aid form. **Financial aid deadline (priority):** 3/1. **Notification date:** Continuous beginning 2/1.
CONTACT Mr. Marc Harding, Chief Enrollment Officer, University of Pittsburgh, 4227 Fifth Avenue, First Floor, Pittsburgh, PA 15260, 412-624-7488. *E-mail:* oafa@pitt.edu.
Website: http://www.pitt.edu/.

UNIVERSITY OF PITTSBURGH AT BRADFORD
Bradford, PA

Tuition & fees (PA res): $13,900	Average undergraduate aid package: $13,763

ABOUT THE INSTITUTION State-related, coed. **Awards:** associate and bachelor's degrees. 36 undergraduate majors. **Total enrollment:** 1,340. Undergraduates: 1,340. Freshmen: 348. Federal methodology is used as a basis for awarding need-based institutional aid.
UNDERGRADUATE EXPENSES for 2017–2018 One-time required fee: $90. **Tuition, state resident:** full-time $12,940; part-time $539 per credit hour. **Tuition, nonresident:** full-time $24,184; part-time $1007 per credit hour. **Required fees:** full-time $960; $165 per term. Full-time tuition and fees vary according to course load and program. Part-time tuition and fees vary according to course load and program. **College room and board:** $9058; **Room only:** $5490. Room and board charges vary according to board plan and housing facility.
FRESHMAN FINANCIAL AID (Fall 2016) 367 applied for aid; of those 92% were deemed to have need. 99% of freshmen with need received aid; of those 9% had need fully met. **Average percent of need met:** 59% (excluding resources awarded to replace EFC). **Average financial aid package:** $13,499 (excluding resources awarded to replace EFC). 6% of all full-time freshmen had no need and received non-need-based gift aid.
UNDERGRADUATE FINANCIAL AID (Fall 2016) 1,236 applied for aid; of those 92% were deemed to have need. 98% of undergraduates with need received aid; of those 10% had need fully met. **Average percent of need met:** 61% (excluding resources awarded to replace EFC). **Average financial aid package:** $13,763 (excluding resources awarded to replace EFC). 5% of all full-time undergraduates had no need and received non-need-based gift aid.
GIFT AID (NEED-BASED) Total amount: $10,279,197 (28% federal, 18% state, 47% institutional, 7% external sources). **Receiving aid:** Freshmen: 82% (320); all full-time undergraduates: 78% (1,054). **Average award:** Freshmen: $10,786; Undergraduates: $10,081. **Scholarships, grants, and awards:** Federal Pell, FSEOG, state, private, college/university gift aid from institutional funds, United Negro College Fund, Academic Competitiveness Grants, National SMART Grants.
GIFT AID (NON-NEED-BASED) Total amount: $1,053,584 (3% state, 86% institutional, 11% external sources). **Receiving aid:** Freshmen: 6% (22). Undergraduates: 5% (70). **Average award:** Freshmen: $6263. Undergraduates: $5890. **Scholarships, grants, and awards by category:** Academic interests/achievement: 162 awards ($152,500 total): biological sciences, business, communication, computer science, education, engineering/technologies, English, general academic interests/achievements, health fields, humanities, international studies, mathematics, physical sciences, premedicine, social sciences. Creative arts/performance: 7 awards ($2000 total): art/fine arts, cinema/film/broadcasting, creative writing, music, theater/drama. Special characteristics: 1,092 awards ($5,402,854 total): adult students, children of faculty/staff, children of union members/company employees, general special characteristics, international students, local/state students, members of minority groups, out-of-state students, veterans. **Tuition waivers:** Full or partial for employees or children of employees. **ROTC:** Army cooperative.
LOANS Student loans: $10,599,819 (78% need-based, 22% non-need-based). 85% of past graduating class borrowed through all loan programs. *Average indebtedness per student:* $36,250. **Average need-based loan:** Freshmen: $3266. Undergrad-

uates: $4373. **Parent loans:** $3,309,389 (61% need-based, 39% non-need-based).
Programs: Federal Direct (Subsidized and Unsubsidized Stafford, PLUS), Perkins.
WORK-STUDY *Federal work-study:* 165 jobs averaging $1980. **State or other work-study/employment:** 67 part-time jobs averaging $1978.
APPLYING FOR FINANCIAL AID *Required financial aid form:* FAFSA. **Financial aid deadline (priority):** 3/1. **Notification date:** Continuous beginning 4/1. Students must reply within 2 weeks of notification.
CONTACT Melissa Ibanez, Associate Vice-President of Enrollment Management/Director of Financial Aid, University of Pittsburgh at Bradford, 300 Campus Drive, Bradford, PA 16701-2812, 814-362-7550 or toll-free 800-872-1787. *Fax:* 814-362-7578. *E-mail:* ibanez@pitt.edu.
Website: http://www.upb.pitt.edu/.

UNIVERSITY OF PITTSBURGH AT GREENSBURG
Greensburg, PA

Tuition & fees (PA res): $13,870	Average undergraduate aid package: $11,618

ABOUT THE INSTITUTION State-related, coed. **Awards:** certificates and bachelor's degrees. 25 undergraduate majors. **Total enrollment:** 1,523. Undergraduates: 1,523. Freshmen: 433. Federal methodology is used as a basis for awarding need-based institutional aid.
UNDERGRADUATE EXPENSES for 2017–2018 Application fee: $45. **Tuition, state resident:** full-time $12,940; part-time $539 per credit hour. **Tuition, nonresident:** full-time $24,184; part-time $1007 per credit hour. **Required fees:** full-time $930; $174 per term. **College room and board:** $10,270; **Room only:** $6280. Room and board charges vary according to board plan and housing facility.
FRESHMAN FINANCIAL AID (Fall 2016) 442 applied for aid; of those 84% were deemed to have need. 98% of freshmen with need received aid; of those 15% had need fully met. **Average percent of need met:** 64% (excluding resources awarded to replace EFC). **Average financial aid package:** $12,438 (excluding resources awarded to replace EFC). 12% of all full-time freshmen had no need and received non-need-based gift aid.
UNDERGRADUATE FINANCIAL AID (Fall 2016) 1,246 applied for aid; of those 87% were deemed to have need. 98% of undergraduates with need received aid; of those 10% had need fully met. **Average percent of need met:** 60% (excluding resources awarded to replace EFC). **Average financial aid package:** $11,618 (excluding resources awarded to replace EFC). 5% of all full-time undergraduates had no need and received non-need-based gift aid.
GIFT AID (NEED-BASED) Total amount: $7,147,065 (35% federal, 25% state, 31% institutional, 9% external sources). **Receiving aid:** Freshmen: 74% (347); all full-time undergraduates: 64% (918). **Average award:** Freshmen: $10,013; Undergraduates: $8667. **Scholarships, grants, and awards:** Federal Pell, FSEOG, state, private, college/university gift aid from institutional funds, United Negro College Fund.
GIFT AID (NON-NEED-BASED) Total amount: $1,002,992 (4% state, 79% institutional, 17% external sources). **Receiving aid:** Freshmen: 9% (43). Undergraduates: 6% (80). **Average award:** Freshmen: $6196. Undergraduates: $5533. **Scholarships, grants, and awards by category:** Academic interests/achievement: general academic interests/achievements. Creative arts/performance: music, theater/drama. Special achievements/activities: leadership. Special characteristics: local/state students, members of minority groups. **Tuition waivers:** Full or partial for employees or children of employees, senior citizens. **ROTC:** Army, Air Force cooperative.
LOANS Student loans: $9,384,943 (70% need-based, 30% non-need-based). 82% of past graduating class borrowed through all loan programs. *Average indebtedness per student:* $36,358. **Average need-based loan:** Freshmen: $3180. Undergraduates: $4433. **Parent loans:** $1,958,667 (44% need-based, 56% non-need-based).
Programs: Federal Direct (Subsidized and Unsubsidized Stafford, PLUS), Perkins.
WORK-STUDY *Federal work-study:* jobs available.
APPLYING FOR FINANCIAL AID *Required financial aid forms:* FAFSA, state aid form. **Financial aid deadline:** Continuous. **Notification date:** Continuous beginning 3/15. Students must reply within 3 weeks of notification.
CONTACT Ms. Brandi S. Darr, Director of Financial Aid, University of Pittsburgh at Greensburg, 150 Finoli Drive, Greensburg, PA 15601-5898, 724-836-7167. *E-mail:* upgfnaid@pitt.edu.
Website: http://www.greensburg.pitt.edu/.

UNIVERSITY OF PITTSBURGH AT JOHNSTOWN
Johnstown, PA

Tuition & fees (PA res): $13,388	Average undergraduate aid package: $10,434

ABOUT THE INSTITUTION State-related, coed. *Awards:* certificates, associate, and bachelor's degrees. 52 undergraduate majors. *Total enrollment:* 2,769. Undergraduates: 2,769. Freshmen: 715. Federal methodology is used as a basis for awarding need-based institutional aid.

UNDERGRADUATE EXPENSES for 2017–2018 *Tuition, state resident:* full-time $12,452; part-time $518 per credit. *Tuition, nonresident:* full-time $23,268; part-time $969 per credit. *Required fees:* full-time $936; $127 per term. Full-time tuition and fees vary according to program. Part-time tuition and fees vary according to program. *College room and board:* $9684; *Room only:* $5470. Room and board charges vary according to board plan and housing facility.

FRESHMAN FINANCIAL AID (Fall 2016) 654 applied for aid; of those 82% were deemed to have need. 98% of freshmen with need received aid; of those 15% had need fully met. *Average percent of need met:* 56% (excluding resources awarded to replace EFC). *Average financial aid package:* $9892 (excluding resources awarded to replace EFC). 9% of all full-time freshmen had no need and received non-need-based gift aid.

UNDERGRADUATE FINANCIAL AID (Fall 2016) 2,398 applied for aid; of those 84% were deemed to have need. 98% of undergraduates with need received aid; of those 15% had need fully met. *Average percent of need met:* 59% (excluding resources awarded to replace EFC). *Average financial aid package:* $10,434 (excluding resources awarded to replace EFC). 6% of all full-time undergraduates had no need and received non-need-based gift aid.

GIFT AID (NEED-BASED) *Total amount:* $10,467,147 (32% federal, 31% state, 30% institutional, 7% external sources). *Receiving aid:* Freshmen: 66% (471); all full-time undergraduates: 61% (1,649). *Average award:* Freshmen: $7529; Undergraduates: $7762. *Scholarships, grants, and awards:* Federal Pell, FSEOG, state, private, college/university gift aid from institutional funds, United Negro College Fund.

GIFT AID (NON-NEED-BASED) *Total amount:* $1,458,787 (4% state, 78% institutional, 18% external sources). *Receiving aid:* Freshmen: 7% (50). Undergraduates: 6% (163). *Average award:* Freshmen: $3663. Undergraduates: $3513. *Scholarships, grants, and awards by category:* Academic interests/achievement: biological sciences, business, communication, computer science, education, engineering/technologies, English, general academic interests/achievements, health fields, humanities, mathematics, physical sciences, premedicine, social sciences. *Creative arts/performance:* journalism/publications, theater/drama. *Special achievements/activities:* leadership. *Special characteristics:* children of faculty/staff. *Tuition waivers:* Full or partial for employees or children of employees.

LOANS *Student loans:* $19,603,858 (66% need-based, 34% non-need-based). 81% of past graduating class borrowed through all loan programs. *Average indebtedness per student:* $37,239. *Average need-based loan:* Freshmen: $3122. Undergraduates: $4139. *Parent loans:* $4,827,388 (50% need-based, 50% non-need-based). *Programs:* Federal Direct (Subsidized and Unsubsidized Stafford, PLUS), Perkins, college/university.

WORK-STUDY *Federal work-study:* 78 jobs averaging $2400. *State or other work-study/employment:* Part-time jobs available.

ATHLETIC AWARDS Total amount: $1,139,366 (61% need-based, 39% non-need-based).

APPLYING FOR FINANCIAL AID *Required financial aid forms:* FAFSA, state aid form. *Financial aid deadline (priority):* 4/1. *Notification date:* Continuous beginning 2/15. Students must reply by 5/1 or within 2 weeks of notification.

CONTACT Ms. Joni L. Trovato, Director of Student Financial Aid, University of Pittsburgh at Johnstown, 450 Schoolhouse Road, 114 Blackington Hall, Johnstown, PA 15904-2990, 814-269-7045 or toll-free 800-765-4875. *Fax:* 814-269-7061. *Website:* http://www.upj.pitt.edu/.

UNIVERSITY OF PORTLAND
Portland, OR

Tuition & fees: N/R	Average undergraduate aid package: $31,578

ABOUT THE INSTITUTION Independent Roman Catholic, coed. 38 undergraduate majors. Federal methodology is used as a basis for awarding need-based institutional aid.

FRESHMAN FINANCIAL AID (Fall 2017, est.) 868 applied for aid; of those 76% were deemed to have need. 99% of freshmen with need received aid; of those 7% had need fully met. *Average percent of need met:* 70% (excluding resources awarded to replace EFC). *Average financial aid package:* $30,658 (excluding resources awarded to replace EFC). 32% of all full-time freshmen had no need and received non-need-based gift aid.

UNDERGRADUATE FINANCIAL AID (Fall 2017, est.) 2,696 applied for aid; of those 81% were deemed to have need. 100% of undergraduates with need received aid; of those 6% had need fully met. *Average percent of need met:* 74% (excluding resources awarded to replace EFC). *Average financial aid package:* $31,578 (excluding resources awarded to replace EFC). 38% of all full-time undergraduates had no need and received non-need-based gift aid.

GIFT AID (NEED-BASED) *Total amount:* $55,500,300 (6% federal, 1% state, 88% institutional, 5% external sources). *Receiving aid:* Freshmen: 52% (524); all full-time undergraduates: 46% (1,743). *Average award:* Freshmen: $26,161; Undergraduates: $24,216. *Scholarships, grants, and awards:* Federal Pell, FSEOG, state, private, college/university gift aid from institutional funds, Federal Nursing, TEACH Grants.

GIFT AID (NON-NEED-BASED) *Total amount:* $27,671,021 (99% institutional, 1% external sources). *Receiving aid:* Freshmen: 63% (634). Undergraduates: 54% (2,048). *Average award:* Freshmen: $18,907. Undergraduates: $17,838. *Scholarships, grants, and awards by category:* Academic interests/achievement: 2,279 awards ($41,842,068 total): biological sciences, business, communication, computer science, education, engineering/technologies, English, foreign languages, general academic interests/achievements, health fields, humanities, mathematics, military science, physical sciences, premedicine, religion/biblical studies, social sciences. *Creative arts/performance:* 88 awards ($287,398 total): music, performing arts, theater/drama. *Special achievements/activities:* 36 awards ($30,932 total): general special achievements/activities. *Special characteristics:* 38 awards ($1,631,961 total): children of faculty/staff, relatives of clergy, religious affiliation.

LOANS *Student loans:* $17,659,023 (89% need-based, 11% non-need-based). 59% of past graduating class borrowed through all loan programs. *Average indebtedness per student:* $31,815. *Average need-based loan:* Freshmen: $3694. Undergraduates: $5131. *Parent loans:* $16,932,903 (90% need-based, 10% non-need-based). *Programs:* Federal Direct (Subsidized and Unsubsidized Stafford, PLUS), Federal Nursing, college/university, private loans.

WORK-STUDY *Federal work-study:* Total amount: $43,528; jobs available. *State or other work-study/employment:* Total amount: $2,250,000 (100% non-need-based). 1,133 part-time jobs averaging $1142.

ATHLETIC AWARDS Total amount: $5,578,829 (32% need-based, 68% non-need-based).

APPLYING FOR FINANCIAL AID *Required financial aid form:* FAFSA. *Financial aid deadline:* 3/1 (priority: 1/15). *Notification date:* Continuous beginning 11/15. Students must reply by 5/1.

CONTACT Ms. Janet Turner, Director of Financial Aid, University of Portland, 5000 North Willamette Boulevard, Portland, OR 97203-5798, 503-943-7311 or toll-free 888-627-5601. *Fax:* 503-943-7508. *E-mail:* finaid@up.edu. *Website:* http://www.up.edu/.

UNIVERSITY OF PROVIDENCE
Great Falls, MT

Tuition & fees: $25,318	Average undergraduate aid package: $20,968

ABOUT THE INSTITUTION Independent Roman Catholic, coed. *Awards:* certificates, associate, bachelor's, and master's degrees. 73 undergraduate majors. *Total enrollment:* 1,063. Undergraduates: 927. Freshmen: 101. Federal methodology is used as a basis for awarding need-based institutional aid.

UNDERGRADUATE EXPENSES for 2018–2019 *Application fee:* $35. *Comprehensive fee:* $34,518 includes full-time tuition ($24,968), mandatory fees ($350), and room and board ($9200). *College room only:* $4800. Full-time tuition and fees vary according to course load. Room and board charges vary according to board plan. *Part-time tuition:* $814 per credit hour. Part-time tuition and fees vary according to course load.

FRESHMAN FINANCIAL AID (Fall 2017, est.) 86 applied for aid; of those 91% were deemed to have need. 100% of freshmen with need received aid; of those 8% had need fully met. *Average percent of need met:* 70% (excluding resources awarded to replace EFC). *Average financial aid package:* $21,363 (excluding resources awarded to replace EFC). 7% of all full-time freshmen had no need and received non-need-based gift aid.

UNDERGRADUATE FINANCIAL AID (Fall 2017, est.) 401 applied for aid; of those 89% were deemed to have need. 100% of undergraduates with need received aid; of those 2% had need fully met. *Average percent of need met:* 68% (excluding resources awarded to replace EFC). *Average financial aid package:* $20,968 (excluding resources awarded to replace EFC). 9% of all full-time undergraduates had no need and received non-need-based gift aid.

GIFT AID (NEED-BASED) *Total amount:* $3,387,335 (35% federal, 65% institutional). *Receiving aid:* Freshmen: 60% (55); all full-time undergraduates: 61% (286). *Average award:* Freshmen: $10,600; Undergraduates: $10,611. *Scholarships, grants, and awards:* Federal Pell, FSEOG, private, college/university gift aid from institutional funds.

GIFT AID (NON-NEED-BASED) *Total amount:* $2,287,707 (2% federal, 98% institutional). *Receiving aid:* Freshmen: 10% (9). Undergraduates: 8% (36). *Average award:* Freshmen: $8328. Undergraduates: $9270. *Scholarships, grants, and awards by category: Academic interests/achievement:* biological sciences, business, computer science, education, general academic interests/achievements, humanities, mathematics, physical sciences, premedicine, religion/biblical studies, social sciences. *Creative arts/performance:* dance, general creative arts/performance. *Special achievements/activities:* cheerleading/drum major, religious involvement. *Special characteristics:* children and siblings of alumni, children of current students, children of faculty/staff, ethnic background, first-generation college students, international students, local/state students, parents of current students, religious affiliation, siblings of current students, spouses of current students. *Tuition waivers:* Full or partial for employees or children of employees.

LOANS *Student loans:* $3,306,193 (78% need-based, 22% non-need-based). 70% of past graduating class borrowed through all loan programs. *Average indebtedness per student:* $31,642. *Average need-based loan:* Freshmen: $2759. Undergraduates: $3929. *Parent loans:* $457,945 (69% need-based, 31% non-need-based). *Programs:* Federal Direct (Subsidized and Unsubsidized Stafford, PLUS), Perkins.

WORK-STUDY *Federal work-study:* Total amount: $63,519; jobs available. *State or other work-study/employment:* Total amount: $147,000 (100% need-based). Part-time jobs available.

ATHLETIC AWARDS Total amount: $4,408,794 (64% need-based, 36% non-need-based).

APPLYING FOR FINANCIAL AID *Required financial aid form:* FAFSA. *Financial aid deadline (priority):* 3/1. *Notification date:* Continuous beginning 12/1.

CONTACT Kelli Engelhardt, Director of Financial Aid, University of Providence, 1301 20th Street South, Great Falls, MT 59405, 406-791-5237 or toll-free 800-856-9544. *Fax:* 406-791-5242. *E-mail:* kengelhardt01@ugf.edu. *Website:* http://www.uprovidence.edu/.

UNIVERSITY OF PUERTO RICO– AGUADILLA
Aguadilla, PR

CONTACT Director of Financial Aid, University of Puerto Rico–Aguadilla, PO Box 250-160, Aguadilla, PR 00604-0160, 787-890-2681 Ext. 273. *Website:* http://www.uprag.edu/.

UNIVERSITY OF PUERTO RICO– ARECIBO
Arecibo, PR

CONTACT Myrta F. Salcedo-Ortiz, Director of Financial Aid, University of Puerto Rico–Arecibo, PO Box 4010, Arecibo, PR 00613, 787-878-2830 Ext. 2008. *E-mail:* myrta.ortiz@upr.edu. *Website:* http://www.upra.edu/.

UNIVERSITY OF PUERTO RICO– BAYAMÓN
Bayamón, PR

Tuition & fees (PR res): $2082	Average undergraduate aid package: N/A

ABOUT THE INSTITUTION Commonwealth-supported, coed. *Awards:* associate and bachelor's degrees. 16 undergraduate majors. *Total enrollment:* 4,927. Undergraduates: 4,927. Freshmen: 1,246. Federal methodology is used as a basis for awarding need-based institutional aid.

UNDERGRADUATE EXPENSES for 2017–2018 *Application fee:* $30. *Tuition, state resident:* full-time $1938; part-time $57 per credit. *Tuition, non-resident:* full-time $3960; part-time $115.46 per credit. *Required fees:* full-time $144. Full-time tuition and fees vary according to class time, course load, and program. Part-time tuition and fees vary according to class time, course load, and program. *Payment plan:* Guaranteed tuition.

GIFT AID (NEED-BASED) *Total amount:* $18,473,679 (99% federal, 1% state). *Scholarships, grants, and awards:* Federal Pell, FSEOG, state, college/university gift aid from institutional funds.

GIFT AID (NON-NEED-BASED) *Scholarships, grants, and awards by category: Academic interests/achievement:* general academic interests/achievements. *Creative arts/performance:* 74 awards ($60,796 total): music, theater/drama. *Special achievements/activities:* 56 awards ($46,690 total): cheerleading/drum major, community service. *Special characteristics:* 322 awards ($177,038 total): children of educators, children of faculty/staff, children of union members/company employees, handicapped students, veterans, veterans' children. *Tuition waivers:* Full or partial for employees or children of employees.

LOANS *Student loans:* $867,670 (100% need-based). *Programs:* Federal Direct (Unsubsidized Stafford, PLUS), Perkins.

WORK-STUDY *Federal work-study:* 315 jobs averaging $1111. *State or other work-study/employment:* Total amount: $80,562 (100% need-based). Part-time jobs available.

ATHLETIC AWARDS Total amount: $253,235 (100% need-based).

APPLYING FOR FINANCIAL AID *Required financial aid forms:* FAFSA, state income tax form(s). *Notification date:* Continuous.

CONTACT Mr. Marcos Cesar De Jesus Rosado, Financial Aid Director, University of Puerto Rico–Bayamón, Industrial Minillas Park 170 Road 174, Bayamon, PR 00959-1919, 787-993-8953 Ext. 4031. *Fax:* 787-993-8930. *E-mail:* marcos.dejesus@upr.edu. *Website:* http://www.uprb.edu/.

UNIVERSITY OF PUERTO RICO– CAROLINA
Carolina, PR

CONTACT Financial Aid Office, University of Puerto Rico–Carolina, PO Box 4800, Carolina, PR 00984-4800, 787-257-0000. *Website:* http://www.uprc.edu/.

UNIVERSITY OF PUERTO RICO–CAYEY
Cayey, PR

CONTACT Mr. Hector Maldonado Otero, Director of Financial Aid, University of Puerto Rico–Cayey, Antonio Barcelo, Cayey, PR 00736, 787-738-2161. *Fax:* 787-263-0676.
Website: http://www.cayey.upr.edu/.

UNIVERSITY OF PUERTO RICO–HUMACAO
Humacao, PR

CONTACT Alfredo Aponte Serrano, Director of Financial Aid, University of Puerto Rico–Humacao, HUC Station, Humacao, PR 00791-4300, 787-850-9362. *E-mail:* alfredo.aponte@upr.edu.
Website: http://www.uprh.edu/.

UNIVERSITY OF PUERTO RICO–MAYAGÜEZ
Mayagüez, PR

Tuition & fees: N/R	Average undergraduate aid package: $5830

ABOUT THE INSTITUTION Commonwealth-supported, coed. 54 undergraduate majors. Federal methodology is used as a basis for awarding need-based institutional aid.
FRESHMAN FINANCIAL AID (Fall 2016) 2,119 applied for aid; of those 96% were deemed to have need. 87% of freshmen with need received aid. *Average percent of need met:* 83% (excluding resources awarded to replace EFC). *Average financial aid package:* $5552 (excluding resources awarded to replace EFC).
UNDERGRADUATE FINANCIAL AID (Fall 2016) 9,999 applied for aid; of those 99% were deemed to have need. 83% of undergraduates with need received aid. *Average percent of need met:* 83% (excluding resources awarded to replace EFC). *Average financial aid package:* $5830 (excluding resources awarded to replace EFC).
GIFT AID (NEED-BASED) Total amount: $50,226,309 (97% federal, 2% state, 1% external sources). *Receiving aid:* Freshmen: 77% (1,766); all full-time undergraduates: 67% (8,261). *Average award:* Freshmen: $5552; Undergraduates: $5830. *Scholarships, grants, and awards:* Federal Pell, FSEOG, state, private, college/university gift aid from institutional funds.
GIFT AID (NON-NEED-BASED) Total amount: $220,650 (100% external sources).
LOANS Student loans: $7,510,132 (96% need-based, 4% non-need-based). 49% of past graduating class borrowed through all loan programs. *Average indebtedness per student:* $7550. *Average need-based loan:* Freshmen: $2204. Undergraduates: $2833. *Programs:* Federal Direct (Subsidized and Unsubsidized Stafford).
WORK-STUDY Federal work-study: 1,088 jobs averaging $608. *State or other work-study/employment:* Total amount: $664,488 (100% need-based). Part-time jobs available.
ATHLETIC AWARDS Total amount: $913,810 (34% need-based, 66% non-need-based).
APPLYING FOR FINANCIAL AID Required financial aid form: FAFSA. *Financial aid deadline:* Continuous. *Notification date:* Continuous. Students must reply within 2 weeks of notification.
CONTACT Ms. Hilda M. Tamariz Vargas, Director of Financial Aid, University of Puerto Rico–Mayagüez, PO Box 9000, Mayaguez, PR 00681, 787-265-3863. *Fax:* 787-265-1920. *E-mail:* hildam.tamariz@upr.edu.
Website: http://www.uprm.edu/.

UNIVERSITY OF PUERTO RICO–MEDICAL SCIENCES CAMPUS
San Juan, PR

CONTACT Mrs. Zoraida Figueroa, Financial Aid Director, University of Puerto Rico–Medical Sciences Campus, Terreno Centro Medico-Edificio Decanato Farmacia y Estudiantes, San Juan, PR 00936-5067, 787-763-2525. *Fax:* 787-282-7117. *E-mail:* zoraida.figueroa@upr.edu.
Website: http://www.rcm.upr.edu/.

UNIVERSITY OF PUERTO RICO–PONCE
Ponce, PR

CONTACT Carmelo Vega Montes, Director of Financial Aid, University of Puerto Rico–Ponce, Box 7186, Ponce, PR 00732-7186, 787-844-8181. *Fax:* 787-840-8108.
Website: http://www.uprp.edu/.

UNIVERSITY OF PUERTO RICO–RÍO PIEDRAS
San Juan, PR

CONTACT Mr. Efraim Williams, EDP Manager, University of Puerto Rico–Río Piedras, PO Box 23300, San Juan, PR 00931-3300, 787-764-0000 Ext. 5573.
Website: http://www.uprrp.edu/.

UNIVERSITY OF PUERTO RICO–UTUADO
Utuado, PR

CONTACT Edgar Salv, Director of Financial Assistance, University of Puerto Rico–Utuado, PO Box 2500, Utuado, PR 00641, 787-894-2828 Ext. 2603. *Fax:* 787-894-3810. *E-mail:* esalva@uprutuado.edu.
Website: http://www.uprutuado.edu/.

UNIVERSITY OF PUGET SOUND
Tacoma, WA

Tuition & fees: $49,776	Average undergraduate aid package: $34,720

ABOUT THE INSTITUTION Independent, coed. *Awards:* bachelor's, master's, and doctoral degrees. 52 undergraduate majors. *Total enrollment:* 2,701. Undergraduates: 2,413. Freshmen: 593. Federal methodology is used as a basis for awarding need-based institutional aid.
UNDERGRADUATE EXPENSES for 2018–2019 Application fee: $60. *Comprehensive fee:* $62,316 includes full-time tuition ($49,510), mandatory fees ($266), and room and board ($12,540). *College room only:* $6820. Full-time tuition and fees vary according to course load. Room and board charges vary according to board plan and housing facility. Part-time tuition and fees vary according to course load.
FRESHMAN FINANCIAL AID (Fall 2017, est.) 465 applied for aid; of those 78% were deemed to have need. 100% of freshmen with need received aid; of those 16% had need fully met. *Average percent of need met:* 79% (excluding resources awarded to replace EFC). *Average financial aid package:* $35,650 (excluding resources awarded to replace EFC). 39% of all full-time freshmen had no need and received non-need-based gift aid.
UNDERGRADUATE FINANCIAL AID (Fall 2017, est.) 1,512 applied for aid; of those 83% were deemed to have need. 100% of undergraduates with need received aid; of those 18% had need fully met. *Average percent of need met:* 77%

(excluding resources awarded to replace EFC). *Average financial aid package:* $34,720 (excluding resources awarded to replace EFC). 47% of all full-time undergraduates had no need and received non-need-based gift aid.

GIFT AID (NEED-BASED) *Total amount:* $33,608,421 (7% federal, 3% state, 85% institutional, 5% external sources). *Receiving aid:* Freshmen: 61% (361); all full-time undergraduates: 52% (1,240). *Average award:* Freshmen: $29,392; Undergraduates: $27,487. *Scholarships, grants, and awards:* Federal Pell, FSEOG, state, private, college/university gift aid from institutional funds.

GIFT AID (NON-NEED-BASED) *Total amount:* $19,244,629 (95% institutional, 5% external sources). *Receiving aid:* Freshmen: 6% (34). Undergraduates: 5% (121). *Average award:* Freshmen: $17,530. Undergraduates: $16,352. *Scholarships, grants, and awards by category:* Academic interests/achievement: 1,221 awards ($16,645,499 total): biological sciences, business, communication, computer science, English, foreign languages, general academic interests/achievements, humanities, international studies, mathematics, physical sciences, premedicine, social sciences. *Creative arts/performance:* 76 awards ($596,450 total): art/fine arts, debating, music, theater/drama. *Special achievements/activities:* community service, leadership, religious involvement. *Special characteristics:* 20 awards ($546,175 total): children of faculty/staff, international students, veterans, veterans' children. *Tuition waivers:* Full or partial for employees or children of employees. *ROTC:* Army cooperative.

LOANS *Student loans:* $11,100,205 (89% need-based, 11% non-need-based). 49% of past graduating class borrowed through all loan programs. *Average indebtedness per student:* $34,791. *Average need-based loan:* Freshmen: $5584. Undergraduates: $6961. *Parent loans:* $5,520,645 (90% need-based, 10% non-need-based). *Programs:* Federal Direct (Subsidized and Unsubsidized Stafford, PLUS), Perkins.

WORK-STUDY *Federal work-study:* Total amount: $1,866,294; 505 jobs averaging $3070. *State or other work-study/employment:* Total amount: $2,559,730 (100% need-based). 894 part-time jobs averaging $2624.

APPLYING FOR FINANCIAL AID *Required financial aid form:* FAFSA. *Financial aid deadline (priority):* 1/15. *Notification date:* Continuous beginning 3/15. Students must reply by 5/1.

CONTACT Maggie A. Mittuch, Associate Vice President for Student Financial Services, University of Puget Sound, 1500 North Warner Street #1039, Tacoma, WA 98416-1039, 253-879-3214 or toll-free 800-396-7191. *Fax:* 253-879-8508. *E-mail:* mmittuch@pugetsound.edu.
Website: http://www.pugetsound.edu/.

UNIVERSITY OF REDLANDS
Redlands, CA

ABOUT THE INSTITUTION Independent, coed. 45 undergraduate majors.

GIFT AID (NEED-BASED) *Scholarships, grants, and awards:* Federal Pell, FSEOG, state, private, college/university gift aid from institutional funds.

GIFT AID (NON-NEED-BASED) *Scholarships, grants, and awards by category:* Academic interests/achievement: general academic interests/achievements. *Creative arts/performance:* art/fine arts, creative writing, debating, music. *Special achievements/activities:* general special achievements/activities. *Special characteristics:* international students.

LOANS *Programs:* Perkins, college/university.

APPLYING FOR FINANCIAL AID *Required financial aid forms:* FAFSA, state aid form.

CONTACT Alisha Aguilar, Director of Financial Aid, University of Redlands, 1200 East Colton Avenue, PO Box 3080, Redlands, CA 92373-0999, 909-748-8047 or toll-free 800-455-5064. *Fax:* 909-335-4089. *E-mail:* financialaid@redlands.edu.
Website: http://www.redlands.edu/.

UNIVERSITY OF RHODE ISLAND
Kingston, RI

Tuition & fees (RI res): $13,792	Average undergraduate aid package: $16,362

ABOUT THE INSTITUTION State-supported, coed. *Awards:* certificates, bachelor's, master's, and doctoral degrees. 86 undergraduate majors. *Total*

---

enrollment: 18,098. Undergraduates: 15,092. Freshmen: 3,172. Federal methodology is used as a basis for awarding need-based institutional aid.

UNDERGRADUATE EXPENSES for 2017–2018 *Application fee:* $65. *Tuition, state resident:* full-time $12,002; part-time $500 per credit hour. *Tuition, nonresident:* full-time $28,252; part-time $1177 per credit hour. *Required fees:* full-time $1790; $44 per credit hour or $58 per term. Full-time tuition and fees vary according to course load, location, and reciprocity agreements. Part-time tuition and fees vary according to course load, location, and reciprocity agreements. *College room and board:* $7774; *Room only:* $4500. Room and board charges vary according to board plan and housing facility.

FRESHMAN FINANCIAL AID (Fall 2017, est.) 2,480 applied for aid; of those 80% were deemed to have need. 98% of freshmen with need received aid; of those 62% had need fully met. *Average percent of need met:* 65% (excluding resources awarded to replace EFC). *Average financial aid package:* $17,526 (excluding resources awarded to replace EFC). 11% of all full-time freshmen had no need and received non-need-based gift aid.

UNDERGRADUATE FINANCIAL AID (Fall 2017, est.) 12,831 applied for aid; of those 87% were deemed to have need. 91% of undergraduates with need received aid; of those 49% had need fully met. *Average percent of need met:* 56% (excluding resources awarded to replace EFC). *Average financial aid package:* $16,362 (excluding resources awarded to replace EFC). 8% of all full-time undergraduates had no need and received non-need-based gift aid.

GIFT AID (NEED-BASED) *Total amount:* $103,465,482 (16% federal, 3% state, 78% institutional, 3% external sources). *Receiving aid:* Freshmen: 59% (1,855); all full-time undergraduates: 73% (9,656). *Average award:* Freshmen: $10,304; Undergraduates: $10,371. *Scholarships, grants, and awards:* Federal Pell, FSEOG, state, private, college/university gift aid from institutional funds.

GIFT AID (NON-NEED-BASED) *Total amount:* $7,429,833 (2% federal, 94% institutional, 4% external sources). *Receiving aid:* Freshmen: 11% (343). Undergraduates: 9% (1,165). *Average award:* Freshmen: $6921. Undergraduates: $6673. *Scholarships, grants, and awards by category:* Academic interests/achievement: 1,164 awards ($1,780,011 total): agriculture, area/ethnic studies, biological sciences, business, communication, computer science, education, engineering/technologies, English, foreign languages, general academic interests/achievements, health fields, home economics, humanities, international studies, library science, mathematics, military science, physical sciences, premedicine, religion/biblical studies, social sciences. *Creative arts/performance:* 49 awards ($106,344 total): art/fine arts, journalism/publications, music, theater/drama. *Special achievements/activities:* 5 awards ($4772 total): leadership. *Special characteristics:* 12 awards ($11,995 total): children and siblings of alumni, children of public servants, children of union members/company employees. *Tuition waivers:* Full or partial for minority students, employees or children of employees, senior citizens. *ROTC:* Army.

LOANS *Student loans:* $84,597,306 (77% need-based, 23% non-need-based). 76% of past graduating class borrowed through all loan programs. *Average indebtedness per student:* $33,335. *Average need-based loan:* Freshmen: $6793. Undergraduates: $6366. *Parent loans:* $26,467,788 (67% need-based, 33% non-need-based). *Programs:* Federal Direct (Subsidized and Unsubsidized Stafford, PLUS), Perkins, Federal Nursing, college/university.

WORK-STUDY *Federal work-study:* Total amount: $2,214,116; jobs available.

ATHLETIC AWARDS Total amount: $8,608,395 (95% need-based, 5% non-need-based).

APPLYING FOR FINANCIAL AID *Required financial aid form:* FAFSA. *Financial aid deadline (priority):* 3/1. *Notification date:* Continuous beginning 3/15. Students must reply by 5/1.

CONTACT Mr. Paul Langhammer, Senior Associate Director of Enrollment Services, University of Rhode Island, Green Hall, 35 Campus Avenue, Kingston, RI 02881, 401-874-5526.
Website: http://www.uri.edu/.

UNIVERSITY OF RICHMOND
Richmond, VA

Tuition & fees: $52,610	Average undergraduate aid package: $47,968

ABOUT THE INSTITUTION Independent, coed. *Awards:* certificates, bachelor's, master's, and doctoral degrees. 52 undergraduate majors. *Total* *enrollment:* 3,503. Undergraduates: 2,999. Freshmen: 801. Institutional methodology is used as a basis for awarding need-based institutional aid.

UNDERGRADUATE EXPENSES for 2018–2019 *Application fee:* $50. *Comprehensive fee:* $64,860 includes full-time tuition ($52,610) and room and board ($12,250). *College room only:* $5620. Full-time tuition and fees vary according to course load. Room and board charges vary according to board plan and housing facility. *Part-time tuition:* $2631 per credit hour. Part-time tuition and fees vary according to course load.

FRESHMAN FINANCIAL AID (Fall 2017, est.) 488 applied for aid; of those 68% were deemed to have need. 100% of freshmen with need received aid; of those 84% had need fully met. *Average percent of need met:* 100% (excluding resources awarded to replace EFC). *Average financial aid package:* $48,645 (excluding resources awarded to replace EFC). 11% of all full-time freshmen had no need and received non-need-based gift aid.

UNDERGRADUATE FINANCIAL AID (Fall 2017, est.) 1,643 applied for aid; of those 82% were deemed to have need. 100% of undergraduates with need received aid; of those 80% had need fully met. *Average percent of need met:* 100% (excluding resources awarded to replace EFC). *Average financial aid package:* $47,968 (excluding resources awarded to replace EFC). 18% of all full-time undergraduates had no need and received non-need-based gift aid.

GIFT AID (NEED-BASED) *Total amount:* $51,991,692 (6% federal, 2% state, 91% institutional, 1% external sources). *Receiving aid:* Freshmen: 41% (327); all full-time undergraduates: 41% (1,312). *Average award:* Freshmen: $42,218; Undergraduates: $41,831. *Scholarships, grants, and awards:* Federal Pell, FSEOG, state, private, college/university gift aid from institutional funds.

GIFT AID (NON-NEED-BASED) *Total amount:* $17,641,032 (4% federal, 5% state, 84% institutional, 7% external sources). *Receiving aid:* Freshmen: 9% (74). Undergraduates: 7% (237). *Average award:* Freshmen: $33,994. Undergraduates: $23,009. *Scholarships, grants, and awards by category:* Academic interests/achievement: 178 awards ($8,259,240 total): biological sciences, computer science, general academic interests/achievements, mathematics, physical sciences, social sciences. *Creative arts/performance:* 36 awards ($1,226,470 total): art/fine arts, dance, music, performing arts, theater/drama. *Special achievements/activities:* 96 awards ($240,000 total): community service. *Special characteristics:* 310 awards ($9,725,700 total). *Tuition waivers:* Full or partial for employees or children of employees. *ROTC:* Army.

LOANS *Student loans:* $11,764,042 (37% need-based, 63% non-need-based). 40% of past graduating class borrowed through all loan programs. *Average indebtedness per student:* $27,125. *Average need-based loan:* Freshmen: $2884. Undergraduates: $3858. *Parent loans:* $3,838,779 (2% need-based, 98% non-need-based). *Programs:* Federal Direct (Subsidized and Unsubsidized Stafford, PLUS).

WORK-STUDY *Federal work-study:* Total amount: $929,216; 638 jobs averaging $1375.

ATHLETIC AWARDS Total amount: $11,097,950 (16% need-based, 84% non-need-based).

APPLYING FOR FINANCIAL AID *Required financial aid forms:* FAFSA, CSS Financial Aid PROFILE, noncustodial (divorced/separated) parent's statement, federal income tax form(s). *Financial aid deadline:* 2/1. *Notification date:* 4/1. Students must reply within 4 weeks of notification.

CONTACT Office of Financial Aid, University of Richmond, 28 Westhampton Way, University of Richmond, VA 23173, 804-289-8438 or toll-free 800-700-1662. *Fax:* 804-484-1650. *E-mail:* finaid@richmond.edu.
Website: http://www.richmond.edu/.

UNIVERSITY OF RIO GRANDE
Rio Grande, OH

CONTACT Ms. Meghann Fraley, Assistant Director of Financial Aid, University of Rio Grande, PO Box 500, 218 North College Avenue, Rio Grande, OH 45674, 740-245-7218 or toll-free 800-282-7201. *Fax:* 740-245-7102.
Website: http://www.rio.edu/.

UNIVERSITY OF ROCHESTER
Rochester, NY

Tuition & fees: $53,825	Average undergraduate aid package: $47,340

ABOUT THE INSTITUTION Independent, coed. *Awards:* certificates, bachelor's, master's, and doctoral degrees. 67 undergraduate majors. *Total enrollment:* 7,121. Undergraduates: 5,796. Freshmen: 1,432. Institutional methodology is used as a basis for awarding need-based institutional aid.

UNDERGRADUATE EXPENSES for 2018–2019 *Application fee:* $50. *Comprehensive fee:* $69,685 includes full-time tuition ($52,867), mandatory fees ($958), and room and board ($15,860). Room and board charges vary according to board plan and housing facility. *Part-time tuition:* $1652 per credit hour. Part-time tuition and fees vary according to course load.

FRESHMAN FINANCIAL AID (Fall 2017, est.) 1,099 applied for aid; of those 79% were deemed to have need. 100% of freshmen with need received aid; of those 93% had need fully met. *Average percent of need met:* 98% (excluding resources awarded to replace EFC). *Average financial aid package:* $50,139 (excluding resources awarded to replace EFC). 30% of all full-time freshmen had no need and received non-need-based gift aid.

UNDERGRADUATE FINANCIAL AID (Fall 2017, est.) 3,803 applied for aid; of those 85% were deemed to have need. 100% of undergraduates with need received aid; of those 91% had need fully met. *Average percent of need met:* 96% (excluding resources awarded to replace EFC). *Average financial aid package:* $47,340 (excluding resources awarded to replace EFC). 30% of all full-time undergraduates had no need and received non-need-based gift aid.

GIFT AID (NEED-BASED) *Total amount:* $130,425,099 (5% federal, 2% state, 90% institutional, 3% external sources). *Receiving aid:* Freshmen: 56% (868); all full-time undergraduates: 53% (3,202). *Average award:* Freshmen: $46,015; Undergraduates: $42,106. *Scholarships, grants, and awards:* Federal Pell, FSEOG, state, college/university gift aid from institutional funds.

GIFT AID (NON-NEED-BASED) *Total amount:* $33,710,543 (1% federal, 83% institutional, 16% external sources). *Receiving aid:* Freshmen: 7% (109). Undergraduates: 6% (379). *Average award:* Freshmen: $14,344. Undergraduates: $15,124. *Scholarships, grants, and awards by category:* Academic interests/achievement: engineering/technologies, general academic interests/achievements, military science. *Creative arts/performance:* general creative arts/performance, music, performing arts. *Special achievements/activities:* general special achievements/activities, leadership. *Special characteristics:* children and siblings of alumni, children of faculty/staff, general special characteristics, international students, veterans. *Tuition waivers:* Full or partial for employees or children of employees. *ROTC:* Army cooperative, Naval, Air Force cooperative.

LOANS *Student loans:* $23,873,008 (65% need-based, 35% non-need-based). 51% of past graduating class borrowed through all loan programs. *Average indebtedness per student:* $29,013. *Average need-based loan:* Freshmen: $3351. Undergraduates: $4492. *Parent loans:* $7,438,870 (20% need-based, 80% non-need-based). *Programs:* Federal Direct (Subsidized and Unsubsidized Stafford, PLUS), Perkins, Federal Nursing.

WORK-STUDY *Federal work-study:* Total amount: $7,038,789; jobs available. *State or other work-study/employment:* Total amount: $1,835,891 (45% need-based, 55% non-need-based). Part-time jobs available.

APPLYING FOR FINANCIAL AID *Required financial aid forms:* FAFSA, CSS Financial Aid PROFILE, state aid form, noncustodial (divorced/separated) parent's statement. *Financial aid deadline (priority):* 2/15. *Notification date:* 3/1. Students must reply by 5/1.

CONTACT Samantha Veeder, Director of Financial Aid, University of Rochester, Wallis Hall, PO Box 270261, Rochester, NY 14627-0250, 585-275-3226 or toll-free 888-822-2256. *Fax:* 585-756-7664. *E-mail:* samantha.veeder@rochester.edu.
Website: http://www.rochester.edu/.

UNIVERSITY OF ST. FRANCIS
Joliet, IL

Tuition & fees: $32,320	Average undergraduate aid package: $24,259

ABOUT THE INSTITUTION Independent Roman Catholic, coed. *Awards:* certificates, bachelor's, master's, and doctoral degrees. 57 undergraduate majors. *Total enrollment:* 2,479. Undergraduates: 1,369. Freshmen: 229. Federal methodology is used as a basis for awarding need-based institutional aid.

UNDERGRADUATE EXPENSES for 2018–2019 *Tuition:* full-time $32,000; part-time $825 per credit hour. *Required fees:* full-time $320; $75 per term. Full-time tuition and fees vary according to degree level, location, and program. Part-time tuition and fees vary according to degree level and program. Room and board charges vary according to housing facility.

FRESHMAN FINANCIAL AID (Fall 2017, est.) 207 applied for aid; of those 91% were deemed to have need. 100% of freshmen with need received aid; of those 22% had need fully met. *Average percent of need met:* 85% (excluding resources awarded to replace EFC). *Average financial aid package:* $27,256 (excluding resources awarded to replace EFC). 13% of all full-time freshmen had no need and received non-need-based gift aid.

UNDERGRADUATE FINANCIAL AID (Fall 2017, est.) 1,153 applied for aid; of those 92% were deemed to have need. 100% of undergraduates with need received aid; of those 20% had need fully met. *Average percent of need met:* 80% (excluding resources awarded to replace EFC). *Average financial aid package:* $24,259 (excluding resources awarded to replace EFC). 14% of all full-time undergraduates had no need and received non-need-based gift aid.

GIFT AID (NEED-BASED) *Receiving aid:* Freshmen: 82% (188); all full-time undergraduates: 82% (1,043). *Average award:* Freshmen: $23,833; Undergraduates: $20,129. *Scholarships, grants, and awards:* Federal Pell, FSEOG, state, private, college/university gift aid from institutional funds, Federal Nursing.

GIFT AID (NON-NEED-BASED) *Receiving aid:* Freshmen: 34% (78). Undergraduates: 29% (369). *Average award:* Freshmen: $13,904. Undergraduates: $10,691. *Scholarships, grants, and awards by category: Academic interests/achievement:* 1,183 awards ($10,924,819 total): biological sciences, communication, education, general academic interests/achievements, health fields, international studies, premedicine, social sciences. *Creative arts/performance:* 40 awards ($72,230 total): applied art and design, art/fine arts, general creative arts/performance, music, performing arts. *Special achievements/activities:* 522 awards ($4,653,922 total): cheerleading/drum major, community service, general special achievements/activities, leadership, religious involvement. *Special characteristics:* 334 awards ($1,058,635 total): adult students, children and siblings of alumni, children of educators, children of faculty/staff, ethnic background, first-generation college students, general special characteristics, religious affiliation, siblings of current students, veterans, veterans' children. *Tuition waivers:* Full or partial for children of alumni, employees or children of employees. *ROTC:* Army cooperative.

LOANS *Student loans:* 81% of past graduating class borrowed through all loan programs. *Average indebtedness per student:* $32,838. *Average need-based loan:* Freshmen: $3400. Undergraduates: $4662. *Programs:* Federal Direct (Subsidized and Unsubsidized Stafford, PLUS), Perkins, alternative loans.

WORK-STUDY *Federal work-study:* 126 jobs averaging $2477. *State or other work-study/employment:* 300 part-time jobs averaging $2500.

APPLYING FOR FINANCIAL AID *Required financial aid forms:* FAFSA, institution's own form. *Financial aid deadline (priority):* 11/15. *Notification date:* Continuous beginning 10/15. Students must reply within 8 weeks of notification.

CONTACT Mr. Bruce A. Foote, Executive Director of Financial Aid Services, University of St. Francis, 500 North Wilcox Street, Joliet, IL 60435-6188, 815-740-5097 or toll-free 800-735-7500. *Fax:* 815-740-3822. *E-mail:* bfoote@stfrancis.edu. *Website:* http://www.stfrancis.edu/.

UNIVERSITY OF SAINT FRANCIS
Fort Wayne, IN

CONTACT Office of Financial Aid, University of Saint Francis, 2701 Spring Street, Fort Wayne, IN 46808, 260-399-8003 or toll-free 800-729-4732. *Fax:* 260-399-8162. *E-mail:* finaid@sf.edu. *Website:* http://www.sf.edu/.

UNIVERSITY OF SAINT JOSEPH
West Hartford, CT

Tuition & fees: $39,172	Average undergraduate aid package: $27,986

ABOUT THE INSTITUTION Independent Roman Catholic, coed, primarily women. *Awards:* certificates, bachelor's, master's, and doctoral degrees. 25 undergraduate majors. *Total enrollment:* 2,405. Undergraduates: 810. Freshmen: 134. Federal methodology is used as a basis for awarding need-based institutional aid.

UNDERGRADUATE EXPENSES for 2018–2019 *Application fee:* $50. *Comprehensive fee:* $50,600 includes full-time tuition ($37,360), mandatory fees ($1812), and room and board ($11,428). *College room only:* $6438. Full-time tuition and fees vary according to course load, degree level, location, program, and student level. Room and board charges vary according to board plan and housing facility. *Part-time tuition:* $818 per credit hour. *Part-time fees:* $58 per credit hour. Part-time tuition and fees vary according to course load, degree level, location, program, and student level.

FRESHMAN FINANCIAL AID (Fall 2017, est.) 125 applied for aid; of those 98% were deemed to have need. 100% of freshmen with need received aid; of those 19% had need fully met. *Average percent of need met:* 79% (excluding resources awarded to replace EFC). *Average financial aid package:* $29,484 (excluding resources awarded to replace EFC). 5% of all full-time freshmen had no need and received non-need-based gift aid.

UNDERGRADUATE FINANCIAL AID (Fall 2017, est.) 598 applied for aid; of those 96% were deemed to have need. 100% of undergraduates with need received aid; of those 14% had need fully met. *Average percent of need met:* 73% (excluding resources awarded to replace EFC). *Average financial aid package:* $27,986 (excluding resources awarded to replace EFC). 7% of all full-time undergraduates had no need and received non-need-based gift aid.

GIFT AID (NEED-BASED) *Total amount:* $12,958,052 (11% federal, 4% state, 74% institutional, 11% external sources). *Receiving aid:* Freshmen: 95% (122); all full-time undergraduates: 90% (554). *Average award:* Freshmen: $25,847; Undergraduates: $22,970. *Scholarships, grants, and awards:* Federal Pell, FSEOG, state, private, college/university gift aid from institutional funds.

GIFT AID (NON-NEED-BASED) *Total amount:* $1,067,474 (93% institutional, 7% external sources). *Receiving aid:* Freshmen: 15% (19). Undergraduates: 7% (44). *Average award:* Freshmen: $17,350. Undergraduates: $15,954. *Scholarships, grants, and awards by category: Academic interests/achievement:* general academic interests/achievements. *Special achievements/activities:* leadership. *Special characteristics:* local/state students, members of minority groups, siblings of current students. *Tuition waivers:* Full or partial for employees or children of employees.

LOANS *Student loans:* $6,418,336 (79% need-based, 21% non-need-based). 90% of past graduating class borrowed through all loan programs. *Average indebtedness per student:* $38,916. *Average need-based loan:* Freshmen: $3666. Undergraduates: $5814. *Parent loans:* $1,942,888 (57% need-based, 43% non-need-based). *Programs:* Federal Direct (Subsidized and Unsubsidized Stafford, PLUS), Perkins.

WORK-STUDY *Federal work-study:* Total amount: $101,887; 166 jobs averaging $1711. *State or other work-study/employment:* Total amount: $250,533 (57% need-based, 43% non-need-based). 121 part-time jobs averaging $1792.

APPLYING FOR FINANCIAL AID *Required financial aid form:* FAFSA. *Financial aid deadline (priority):* 3/1. *Notification date:* Continuous beginning 11/15. Students must reply by 5/1.

CONTACT Student Financial Services, University of Saint Joseph, 1678 Asylum Avenue, West Hartford, CT 06117, 860-231-5223 or toll-free 866-442-8752. *E-mail:* financialaid@usj.edu. *Website:* http://www.usj.edu/.

UNIVERSITY OF SAINT KATHERINE
San Marcos, CA

CONTACT Financial Aid Office, University of Saint Katherine, 1637 Capalina Road, San Marcos, CA 92069, 760-471-1316. *Website:* http://www.usk.edu/.

UNIVERSITY OF SAINT MARY
Leavenworth, KS

CONTACT Mrs. Judy Wiedower, Financial Aid Director, University of Saint Mary, 4100 South Fourth Street, Leavenworth, KS 66048, 913-758-6314 or toll-free 800-752-7043. *Fax:* 913-758-6146. *E-mail:* wiedower@hub.smcks.edu. *Website:* http://www.stmary.edu/.

UNIVERSITY OF ST. THOMAS
St. Paul, MN

Tuition & fees: $41,133	Average undergraduate aid package: $28,746

ABOUT THE INSTITUTION Independent Roman Catholic, coed. *Awards:* certificates, associate, bachelor's, master's, and doctoral degrees. 69 undergraduate majors. *Total enrollment:* 9,878. Undergraduates: 6,189. Freshmen: 1,498. Federal methodology is used as a basis for awarding need-based institutional aid.

UNDERGRADUATE EXPENSES for 2017–2018 *Comprehensive fee:* $51,187 includes full-time tuition ($40,224), mandatory fees ($909), and room and board ($10,054). *College room only:* $6304. Room and board charges vary according to board plan and housing facility. *Part-time tuition:* $1257 per credit.

FRESHMAN FINANCIAL AID (Fall 2017, est.) 1,266 applied for aid; of those 76% were deemed to have need. 100% of freshmen with need received aid; of those 26% had need fully met. *Average percent of need met:* 86% (excluding resources awarded to replace EFC). *Average financial aid package:* $29,564 (excluding resources awarded to replace EFC). 18% of all full-time freshmen had no need and received non-need-based gift aid.

UNDERGRADUATE FINANCIAL AID (Fall 2017, est.) 3,991 applied for aid; of those 81% were deemed to have need. 100% of undergraduates with need received aid; of those 21% had need fully met. *Average percent of need met:* 84% (excluding resources awarded to replace EFC). *Average financial aid package:* $28,746 (excluding resources awarded to replace EFC). 11% of all full-time undergraduates had no need and received non-need-based gift aid.

GIFT AID (NEED-BASED) *Total amount:* $70,318,988 (7% federal, 9% state, 82% institutional, 2% external sources). *Receiving aid:* Freshmen: 63% (943); all full-time undergraduates: 53% (3,170). *Average award:* Freshmen: $23,620; Undergraduates: $22,068. *Scholarships, grants, and awards:* Federal Pell, FSEOG, state, private, college/university gift aid from institutional funds.

GIFT AID (NON-NEED-BASED) *Total amount:* $17,252,457 (95% institutional, 5% external sources). *Receiving aid:* Freshmen: 14% (211). Undergraduates: 9% (509). *Average award:* Freshmen: $21,831. Undergraduates: $19,563. *Scholarships, grants, and awards by category:* Academic interests/achievement: 2,296 awards ($47,200,769 total): biological sciences, business, education, English, general academic interests/achievements, humanities, international studies, mathematics, physical sciences, religion/biblical studies, social sciences. *Creative arts/performance:* 30 awards ($120,143 total): journalism/publications, music. *Special characteristics:* 169 awards ($5,672,955 total): children of educators, children of faculty/staff, general special characteristics. *Tuition waivers:* Full or partial for employees or children of employees, senior citizens. *ROTC:* Army cooperative, Naval cooperative, Air Force.

LOANS *Student loans:* $35,037,867 (59% need-based, 41% non-need-based). 64% of past graduating class borrowed through all loan programs. *Average indebtedness per student:* $40,983. *Average need-based loan:* Freshmen: $6837. Undergraduates: $8121. *Parent loans:* $3,005,860 (48% need-based, 52% non-need-based). *Programs:* Federal Direct (Subsidized and Unsubsidized Stafford, PLUS), Perkins, state, private loans.

WORK-STUDY *Federal work-study:* Total amount: $3,141,449; 1,033 jobs averaging $3041. *State or other work-study/employment:* Total amount: $3,965,276 (57% need-based, 43% non-need-based). 903 part-time jobs averaging $3017.

APPLYING FOR FINANCIAL AID *Required financial aid form:* FAFSA. *Financial aid deadline:* Continuous. *Notification date:* Continuous beginning 1/15. Students must reply within 3 weeks of notification.

CONTACT Ms. Paula Benson, Associate Director of Student Financial Services, University of St. Thomas, 2115 Summit Avenue, MHC 152, St. Paul, MN 55105-1096, 651-962-6547 or toll-free 800-328-6819. *Fax:* 651-962-6599. *E-mail:* paula.benson@stthomas.edu. *Website:* http://www.stthomas.edu/.

UNIVERSITY OF ST. THOMAS
Houston, TX

Tuition & fees: $33,580	Average undergraduate aid package: $24,587

ABOUT THE INSTITUTION Independent Roman Catholic, coed. *Awards:* certificates, diplomas, bachelor's, master's, and doctoral degrees. 37 undergraduate majors. *Total enrollment:* 3,312. Undergraduates: 1,814. Freshmen: 277. Federal methodology is used as a basis for awarding need-based institutional aid.

UNDERGRADUATE EXPENSES for 2018–2019 *Tuition:* full-time $33,000. Full-time tuition and fees vary according to course load. Part-time tuition and fees vary according to course load. Room and board charges vary according to board plan and housing facility.

FRESHMAN FINANCIAL AID (Fall 2017, est.) 246 applied for aid; of those 91% were deemed to have need. 100% of freshmen with need received aid; of those 10% had need fully met. *Average percent of need met:* 75% (excluding resources awarded to replace EFC). *Average financial aid package:* $27,619 (excluding resources awarded to replace EFC). 21% of all full-time freshmen had no need and received non-need-based gift aid.

UNDERGRADUATE FINANCIAL AID (Fall 2017, est.) 1,030 applied for aid; of those 96% were deemed to have need. 99% of undergraduates with need received aid; of those 9% had need fully met. *Average percent of need met:* 65% (excluding resources awarded to replace EFC). *Average financial aid package:* $24,587 (excluding resources awarded to replace EFC). 23% of all full-time undergraduates had no need and received non-need-based gift aid.

GIFT AID (NEED-BASED) *Total amount:* $21,585,517 (15% federal, 10% state, 73% institutional, 2% external sources). *Receiving aid:* Freshmen: 77% (223); all full-time undergraduates: 67% (954). *Average award:* Freshmen: $25,352; Undergraduates: $21,750. *Scholarships, grants, and awards:* Federal Pell, FSEOG, state, private, college/university gift aid from institutional funds, Academic Competitiveness Grants, National SMART Grants.

GIFT AID (NON-NEED-BASED) *Total amount:* $4,273,603 (97% institutional, 3% external sources). *Receiving aid:* Freshmen: 6% (16). Undergraduates: 4% (51). *Average award:* Freshmen: $12,504. Undergraduates: $12,308. *Scholarships, grants, and awards by category:* Academic interests/achievement: biological sciences, business, communication, computer science, education, English, foreign languages, general academic interests/achievements, health fields, humanities, international studies, mathematics, physical sciences, premedicine, religion/biblical studies, social sciences. *Creative arts/performance:* applied art and design, art/fine arts, general creative arts/performance, music, performing arts, theater/drama. *Special achievements/activities:* general special achievements/activities, leadership, religious involvement. *Special characteristics:* children of faculty/staff, general special characteristics, previous college experience, religious affiliation. *Tuition waivers:* Full or partial for employees or children of employees, senior citizens. *ROTC:* Army cooperative, Air Force cooperative.

LOANS *Student loans:* $5,522,001 (86% need-based, 14% non-need-based). 50% of past graduating class borrowed through all loan programs. *Average indebtedness per student:* $29,857. *Average need-based loan:* Freshmen: $3396. Undergraduates: $4604. *Parent loans:* $1,429,733 (54% need-based, 46% non-need-based). *Programs:* Federal Direct (Subsidized and Unsubsidized Stafford, PLUS), Perkins, state, private loans.

WORK-STUDY *Federal work-study:* Total amount: $356,077; 92 jobs averaging $3870. *State or other work-study/employment:* Total amount: $10,000 (100% need-based). 3 part-time jobs averaging $3333.

ATHLETIC AWARDS Total amount: $543,265 (53% need-based, 47% non-need-based).

APPLYING FOR FINANCIAL AID *Required financial aid form:* FAFSA. *Financial aid deadline (priority):* 4/15. *Notification date:* Continuous beginning 2/15. Students must reply within 2 weeks of notification.

CONTACT Lynda McKendree, Dean of Scholarships and Financial Aid, University of St. Thomas, 3800 Montrose Boulevard, Houston, TX 77006-4696, 713-525-2170 or toll-free 800-856-8565. *Fax:* 713-525-2142. *E-mail:* finaid@stthom.edu. *Website:* http://www.stthom.edu/.

UNIVERSITY OF SAN DIEGO
San Diego, CA

Tuition & fees: $49,358	Average undergraduate aid package: $33,737

ABOUT THE INSTITUTION Independent Roman Catholic, coed. *Awards:* certificates, bachelor's, master's, and doctoral degrees. 44 undergraduate majors. *Total enrollment:* 8,905. Undergraduates: 5,774. Freshmen: 1,210. Federal methodology is used as a basis for awarding need-based institutional aid.

UNDERGRADUATE EXPENSES for 2018–2019 *Application fee:* $55. *Comprehensive fee:* $62,338 includes full-time tuition ($48,750), mandatory fees ($608), and room and board ($12,980). Room and board charges vary according to board plan and housing facility. *Part-time tuition:* $1680 per credit. *Part-time fees:* $376 per year. Part-time tuition and fees vary according to course load.

FRESHMAN FINANCIAL AID (Fall 2016) 814 applied for aid; of those 75% were deemed to have need. 98% of freshmen with need received aid; of those 17% had need fully met. *Average percent of need met:* 75% (excluding resources awarded to replace EFC). *Average financial aid package:* $33,801 (excluding resources awarded to replace EFC). 28% of all full-time freshmen had no need and received non-need-based gift aid.

UNDERGRADUATE FINANCIAL AID (Fall 2016) 3,214 applied for aid; of those 86% were deemed to have need. 98% of undergraduates with need received aid; of those 14% had need fully met. *Average percent of need met:* 71% (excluding resources awarded to replace EFC). *Average financial aid package:* $33,737 (excluding resources awarded to replace EFC). 20% of all full-time undergraduates had no need and received non-need-based gift aid.

GIFT AID (NEED-BASED) *Total amount:* $69,312,597 (13% federal, 7% state, 78% institutional, 2% external sources). *Receiving aid:* Freshmen: 52% (592); all full-time undergraduates: 48% (2,630). *Average award:* Freshmen: $27,519; Undergraduates: $26,679. *Scholarships, grants, and awards:* Federal Pell, FSEOG, state, private, college/university gift aid from institutional funds, Federal Nursing, TEACH Grants.

GIFT AID (NON-NEED-BASED) *Total amount:* $23,150,964 (19% federal, 79% institutional, 2% external sources). *Receiving aid:* Freshmen: 35% (394). Undergraduates: 26% (1,396). *Average award:* Freshmen: $14,503. Undergraduates: $15,419. *Scholarships, grants, and awards by category: Academic interests/achievement:* 1,651 awards: general academic interests/achievements. *Creative arts/performance:* 21 awards: music. *Special achievements/activities:* 755 awards: leadership, religious involvement. *Special characteristics:* 77 awards: children of faculty/staff. *Tuition waivers:* Full or partial for employees or children of employees. *ROTC:* Army cooperative, Naval, Air Force cooperative.

LOANS *Student loans:* $22,862,018 (90% need-based, 10% non-need-based). 49% of past graduating class borrowed through all loan programs. *Average indebtedness per student:* $30,854. *Average need-based loan:* Freshmen: $6151. Undergraduates: $7488. *Parent loans:* $30,805,728 (45% need-based, 55% non-need-based). *Programs:* Federal Direct (Subsidized and Unsubsidized Stafford, PLUS), Perkins, college/university, private loans.

WORK-STUDY *Federal work-study:* 508 jobs averaging $2294. *State or other work-study/employment:* Total amount: $3,333,446 (15% need-based, 85% non-need-based). Part-time jobs available.

ATHLETIC AWARDS Total amount: $7,473,900 (21% need-based, 79% non-need-based).

APPLYING FOR FINANCIAL AID *Required financial aid form:* FAFSA. *Financial aid deadline (priority):* 3/2. *Notification date:* Continuous beginning 3/1. Students must reply by 5/1 or within 3 weeks of notification.

CONTACT Judith Lewis Logue, Director of Financial Aid Services, University of San Diego, 5998 Alcala Park, San Diego, CA 92110-2492, 619-260-2700 or toll-free 800-248-4873. *E-mail:* jllogue@sandiego.edu.
Website: http://www.sandiego.edu/.

UNIVERSITY OF SAN FRANCISCO
San Francisco, CA

Tuition & fees: $48,066	Average undergraduate aid package: $35,212

ABOUT THE INSTITUTION Independent Roman Catholic (Jesuit), coed. *Awards:* certificates, bachelor's, master's, and doctoral degrees. 87 undergraduate majors. *Total enrollment:* 11,080. Undergraduates: 6,847. Freshmen: 1,532. Federal methodology is used as a basis for awarding need-based institutional aid.

UNDERGRADUATE EXPENSES for 2018–2019 *Application fee:* $65. *Comprehensive fee:* $62,896 includes full-time tuition ($47,550), mandatory fees ($516), and room and board ($14,830). *College room only:* $10,010. Full-time tuition and fees vary according to course load, degree level, location, program, and reciprocity agreements. Room and board charges vary according to board plan and housing facility. *Part-time tuition:* $1690 per credit hour. *Part-time fees:* $258 per term. Part-time tuition and fees vary according to course load, degree level, location, program, and reciprocity agreements.

FRESHMAN FINANCIAL AID (Fall 2017, est.) 1,181 applied for aid; of those 86% were deemed to have need. 100% of freshmen with need received aid; of those 7% had need fully met. *Average percent of need met:* 75% (excluding resources awarded to replace EFC). *Average financial aid package:* $40,446 (excluding resources awarded to replace EFC). 17% of all full-time freshmen had no need and received non-need-based gift aid.

UNDERGRADUATE FINANCIAL AID (Fall 2017, est.) 4,202 applied for aid; of those 90% were deemed to have need. 100% of undergraduates with need received aid; of those 5% had need fully met. *Average percent of need met:* 68% (excluding resources awarded to replace EFC). *Average financial aid package:* $35,212 (excluding resources awarded to replace EFC). 17% of all full-time undergraduates had no need and received non-need-based gift aid.

GIFT AID (NEED-BASED) *Total amount:* $105,114,539 (9% federal, 11% state, 79% institutional, 1% external sources). *Receiving aid:* Freshmen: 65% (996); all full-time undergraduates: 55% (3,627). *Average award:* Freshmen: $34,598; Undergraduates: $29,058. *Scholarships, grants, and awards:* Federal Pell, FSEOG, state, private, college/university gift aid from institutional funds, Federal Nursing.

GIFT AID (NON-NEED-BASED) *Total amount:* $16,870,334 (99% institutional, 1% external sources). *Receiving aid:* Freshmen: 4% (60). Undergraduates: 2% (154). *Average award:* Freshmen: $14,651. Undergraduates: $13,838. *Scholarships, grants, and awards by category: Academic interests/achievement:* general academic interests/achievements. *Tuition waivers:* Full or partial for employees or children of employees. *ROTC:* Army, Air Force cooperative.

LOANS *Student loans:* $38,845,243 (78% need-based, 22% non-need-based). 51% of past graduating class borrowed through all loan programs. *Average indebtedness per student:* $48,201. *Average need-based loan:* Freshmen: $3150. Undergraduates: $4449. *Parent loans:* $18,713,100 (48% need-based, 52% non-need-based). *Programs:* Federal Direct (Subsidized and Unsubsidized Stafford, PLUS), Perkins, Federal Nursing, college/university.

WORK-STUDY *Federal work-study:* Total amount: $6,180,613; jobs available. *State or other work-study/employment:* Total amount: $4,752,745 (100% need-based). Part-time jobs available.

ATHLETIC AWARDS Total amount: $6,242,276 (17% need-based, 83% non-need-based).

APPLYING FOR FINANCIAL AID *Required financial aid forms:* FAFSA, CSS Financial Aid PROFILE. *Financial aid deadline:* 2/15. *Notification date:* Continuous beginning 4/1. Students must reply within 4 weeks of notification.

CONTACT Norman Caito, Director of Financial Aid Operations and Services, University of San Francisco, 2130 Fulton Street, LM 258, San Francisco, CA 94117-1080, 415-422-2624 or toll-free 800-CALL-USF. *E-mail:* caiton@usfca.edu. *Website:* http://www.usfca.edu/.

UNIVERSITY OF SCIENCE AND ARTS OF OKLAHOMA
Chickasha, OK

Tuition & fees (OK res): $7200 | **Average undergraduate aid package: $11,420**

ABOUT THE INSTITUTION State-supported, coed. *Awards:* bachelor's degrees. 25 undergraduate majors. *Total enrollment:* 888. Undergraduates: 888. Freshmen: 223. Federal methodology is used as a basis for awarding need-based institutional aid.

UNDERGRADUATE EXPENSES for 2017–2018 *Application fee:* $40. *Tuition, state resident:* full-time $6030; part-time $201 per credit hour. *Tuition, nonresident:* full-time $16,380; part-time $546 per credit hour. *Required fees:* full-time $1170; $39 per credit hour. Room and board charges vary according to board plan and housing facility. *Payment plan:* Guaranteed tuition.

FRESHMAN FINANCIAL AID (Fall 2017, est.) 170 applied for aid; of those 87% were deemed to have need. 98% of freshmen with need received aid; of those 21% had need fully met. *Average percent of need met:* 68% (excluding resources awarded to replace EFC). *Average financial aid package:* $11,011 (excluding resources awarded to replace EFC). 12% of all full-time freshmen had no need and received non-need-based gift aid.

UNDERGRADUATE FINANCIAL AID (Fall 2017, est.) 612 applied for aid; of those 88% were deemed to have need. 98% of undergraduates with need received aid; of those 16% had need fully met. *Average percent of need met:* 68% (excluding resources awarded to replace EFC). *Average financial aid package:* $11,420 (excluding resources awarded to replace EFC). 13% of all full-time undergraduates had no need and received non-need-based gift aid.

GIFT AID (NEED-BASED) *Total amount:* $3,687,004 (51% federal, 24% state, 17% institutional, 8% external sources). *Receiving aid:* Freshmen: 71% (145); all full-time undergraduates: 64% (505). *Average award:* Freshmen: $9087; Undergraduates: $9417. *Scholarships, grants, and awards:* Federal Pell, FSEOG, state, private, college/university gift aid from institutional funds, USAO Foundation Grants.

GIFT AID (NON-NEED-BASED) *Total amount:* $534,265 (24% state, 58% institutional, 18% external sources). *Receiving aid:* Freshmen: 10% (20). Undergraduates: 7% (53). *Average award:* Freshmen: $2792. Undergraduates: $2805. *Scholarships, grants, and awards by category:* Academic interests/achievement: 535 awards ($1,431,162 total): general academic interests/achievements. *Creative arts/performance:* 13 awards ($24,000 total): art/fine arts, music, theater/drama. *Special achievements/activities:* 13 awards ($10,000 total): cheerleading/drum major. *Special characteristics:* 58 awards ($210,378 total): children of faculty/staff, international students, out-of-state students, previous college experience. *Tuition waivers:* Full or partial for employees or children of employees, senior citizens.

LOANS *Student loans:* $2,233,051 (75% need-based, 25% non-need-based). 69% of past graduating class borrowed through all loan programs. *Average indebtedness per student:* $22,351. *Average need-based loan:* Freshmen: $2678. Undergraduates: $2906. *Parent loans:* $227,922 (25% need-based, 75% non-need-based). *Programs:* Federal Direct (Subsidized and Unsubsidized Stafford, PLUS), college/university.

WORK-STUDY *Federal work-study:* Total amount: $227,947; 157 jobs averaging $1399.

ATHLETIC AWARDS Total amount: $2,138,065 (37% need-based, 63% non-need-based).

APPLYING FOR FINANCIAL AID *Financial aid deadline (priority):* 12/1. *Notification date:* Continuous beginning 11/1. Students must reply within 4 weeks of notification.

CONTACT Laura D. Coponiti, Dean of Admissions and Financial Aid, University of Science and Arts of Oklahoma, 1727 West Alabama, Chickasha, OK 73018-5322, 405-574-1350 or toll-free 800-933-8726. *Fax:* 405-574-1220. *E-mail:* lcoponiti@usao.edu. *Website:* http://www.usao.edu/.

THE UNIVERSITY OF SCRANTON
Scranton, PA

Tuition & fees: $43,310 | **Average undergraduate aid package: $27,055**

ABOUT THE INSTITUTION Independent Roman Catholic (Jesuit), coed. *Awards:* certificates, bachelor's, master's, and doctoral degrees. 66 undergraduate majors. *Total enrollment:* 4,993. Undergraduates: 3,810. Freshmen: 903. Federal methodology is used as a basis for awarding need-based institutional aid.

UNDERGRADUATE EXPENSES for 2017–2018 *Comprehensive fee:* $57,928 includes full-time tuition ($42,910), mandatory fees ($400), and room and board ($14,618). *College room only:* $8562. Room and board charges vary according to board plan and housing facility.

FRESHMAN FINANCIAL AID (Fall 2016) 885 applied for aid; of those 82% were deemed to have need. 100% of freshmen with need received aid; of those 14% had need fully met. *Average percent of need met:* 71% (excluding resources awarded to replace EFC). *Average financial aid package:* $27,728 (excluding resources awarded to replace EFC). 23% of all full-time freshmen had no need and received non-need-based gift aid.

UNDERGRADUATE FINANCIAL AID (Fall 2016) 2,933 applied for aid; of those 86% were deemed to have need. 100% of undergraduates with need received aid; of those 12% had need fully met. *Average percent of need met:* 69% (excluding resources awarded to replace EFC). *Average financial aid package:* $27,055 (excluding resources awarded to replace EFC). 23% of all full-time undergraduates had no need and received non-need-based gift aid.

GIFT AID (NEED-BASED) *Total amount:* $55,512,526 (6% federal, 4% state, 88% institutional, 2% external sources). *Receiving aid:* Freshmen: 71% (716); all full-time undergraduates: 67% (2,438). *Average award:* Freshmen: $24,665; Undergraduates: $23,408. *Scholarships, grants, and awards:* Federal Pell, FSEOG, state, private, college/university gift aid from institutional funds.

GIFT AID (NON-NEED-BASED) *Total amount:* $15,654,914 (9% federal, 90% institutional, 1% external sources). *Receiving aid:* Freshmen: 8% (78). Undergraduates: 6% (204). *Average award:* Freshmen: $15,740. Undergraduates: $14,820. *Scholarships, grants, and awards by category:* Academic interests/achievement: general academic interests/achievements, military science. *Special characteristics:* children of educators, children of faculty/staff, ethnic background, members of minority groups, religious affiliation, siblings of current students, veterans, veterans' children. *Tuition waivers:* Full or partial for employees or children of employees, senior citizens. *ROTC:* Army, Air Force cooperative.

LOANS *Student loans:* $28,903,446 (63% need-based, 37% non-need-based). 77% of past graduating class borrowed through all loan programs. *Average indebtedness per student:* $43,530. *Average need-based loan:* Freshmen: $6806. Undergraduates: $8330. *Parent loans:* $14,798,752 (42% need-based, 58% non-need-based). *Programs:* Federal Direct (Subsidized and Unsubsidized Stafford, PLUS), Perkins.

WORK-STUDY *Federal work-study:* jobs available. *State or other work-study/employment:* Total amount: $1,115,295 (46% need-based, 54% non-need-based). Part-time jobs available.

APPLYING FOR FINANCIAL AID *Required financial aid forms:* FAFSA, state aid form. *Financial aid deadline (priority):* 2/15. *Notification date:* Continuous beginning 1/15. Students must reply by 5/1.

CONTACT Office of Financial Aid, The University of Scranton, St. Thomas Hall, Scranton, PA 18510, 570-941-7701 or toll-free 888-SCRANTON. *Fax:* 570-941-4370. *E-mail:* finaid@scranton.edu. *Website:* http://www.scranton.edu/.

UNIVERSITY OF SIOUX FALLS
Sioux Falls, SD

Tuition & fees: $18,280 | **Average undergraduate aid package: $21,132**

ABOUT THE INSTITUTION Independent American Baptist Churches in the USA, coed. *Awards:* certificates, associate, bachelor's, and master's degrees. 51 undergraduate majors. *Total enrollment:* 1,453. Undergraduates: 1,215. Freshmen: 280. Federal methodology is used as a basis for awarding need-based institutional aid.

UNDERGRADUATE EXPENSES for 2018–2019 *Application fee:* $25. *Comprehensive fee:* $25,630 includes full-time tuition ($17,980), mandatory fees ($300), and room and board ($7350). **College room only:** $3850. Full-time tuition and fees vary according to course load and program. Room and board charges vary according to board plan and housing facility. **Part-time tuition:** $370 per semester hour.

FRESHMAN FINANCIAL AID (Fall 2017, est.) 267 applied for aid; of those 85% were deemed to have need. 100% of freshmen with need received aid; of those 31% had need fully met. **Average percent of need met:** 88% (excluding resources awarded to replace EFC). **Average financial aid package:** $22,378 (excluding resources awarded to replace EFC). 16% of all full-time freshmen had no need and received non-need-based gift aid.

UNDERGRADUATE FINANCIAL AID (Fall 2017, est.) 866 applied for aid; of those 88% were deemed to have need. 100% of undergraduates with need received aid; of those 26% had need fully met. **Average percent of need met:** 83% (excluding resources awarded to replace EFC). **Average financial aid package:** $21,132 (excluding resources awarded to replace EFC). 20% of all full-time undergraduates had no need and received non-need-based gift aid.

GIFT AID (NEED-BASED) Total amount: $11,884,621 (14% federal, 1% state, 82% institutional, 3% external sources). **Receiving aid:** Freshmen: 80% (222), all full-time undergraduates: 70% (728). **Average award:** Freshmen: $18,249; Undergraduates: $16,412. **Scholarships, grants, and awards:** Federal Pell, FSEOG, state, private, college/university gift aid from institutional funds.

GIFT AID (NON-NEED-BASED) Total amount: $3,618,344 (4% state, 87% institutional, 9% external sources). **Receiving aid:** Freshmen: 41% (112). Undergraduates: 31% (316). **Average award:** Freshmen: $13,675. Undergraduates: $13,117. **Scholarships, grants, and awards by category:** *Academic interests/achievement:* biological sciences, business, communication, computer science, education, engineering/technologies, English, general academic interests/achievements, humanities, mathematics, physical sciences, premedicine, religion/biblical studies, social sciences. *Creative arts/performance:* art/fine arts, music, theater/drama. *Special achievements/activities:* cheerleading/drum major, leadership. *Special characteristics:* children and siblings of alumni, children of faculty/staff, international students, local/state students, out-of-state students, religious affiliation, siblings of current students, spouses of current students. **Tuition waivers:** Full or partial for employees or children of employees. **ROTC:** Air Force cooperative.

LOANS Student loans: $6,885,343 (69% need-based, 31% non-need-based). 81% of past graduating class borrowed through all loan programs. *Average indebtedness per student:* $33,297. **Average need-based loan:** Freshmen: $3828. Undergraduates: $4700. **Parent loans:** $772,676 (61% need-based, 39% non-need-based). **Programs:** Federal Direct (Subsidized and Unsubsidized Stafford, PLUS), Perkins, alternative loans.

WORK-STUDY Federal work-study: Total amount: $174,734; jobs available.

ATHLETIC AWARDS Total amount: $3,030,830 (47% need-based, 53% non-need-based).

APPLYING FOR FINANCIAL AID Required financial aid form: FAFSA. *Financial aid deadline (priority):* 1/1. **Notification date:** Continuous beginning 11/1. Students must reply within 4 weeks of notification.

CONTACT Rachel Gunn, Financial Aid Counselor, University of Sioux Falls, 1101 West 22nd Street, Sioux Falls, SD 57105-1699, 605-331-6623 or toll-free 800-888-1047. *Fax:* 605-331-6615. *E-mail:* rachel.gunn@usiouxfalls.edu. *Website:* http://www.usiouxfalls.edu/.

UNIVERSITY OF SOUTH ALABAMA
Mobile, AL

ABOUT THE INSTITUTION State-supported, coed. **Awards:** certificates, bachelor's, master's, and doctoral degrees. 52 undergraduate majors. **Total enrollment:** 15,569. Undergraduates: 10,988. Freshmen: 1,886.

GIFT AID (NEED-BASED) Scholarships, grants, and awards: Federal Pell, FSEOG, state, private, college/university gift aid from institutional funds.

LOANS Programs: Federal Direct (Subsidized and Unsubsidized Stafford, PLUS), Perkins, college/university.

APPLYING FOR FINANCIAL AID Required financial aid form: FAFSA.

CONTACT Financial Aid Office, University of South Alabama, 390 Alumni Circle, Meisler Hall, Suite 1200, Mobile, AL 36688-0001, 800-305-6828 or toll-free 800-872-5247. *Fax:* 251-460-6517. *E-mail:* finaid@southalabama.edu. *Website:* http://www.southalabama.edu/.

UNIVERSITY OF SOUTH CAROLINA
Columbia, SC

Tuition & fees (SC res): $12,262	Average undergraduate aid package: $9482

ABOUT THE INSTITUTION State-supported, coed. **Awards:** certificates, associate, bachelor's, master's, and doctoral degrees. 76 undergraduate majors. **Total enrollment:** 34,731. Undergraduates: 26,362. Freshmen: 5,879. Federal methodology is used as a basis for awarding need-based institutional aid.

UNDERGRADUATE EXPENSES for 2017–2018 Application fee: $65. **Tuition, state resident:** full-time $11,862; part-time $494 per credit hour. **Tuition, nonresident:** full-time $31,962; part-time $1331 per credit hour. **Required fees:** full-time $400; $17 per term. Full-time tuition and fees vary according to program and reciprocity agreements. Part-time tuition and fees vary according to course load. **College room and board:** $11,200; **Room only:** $7500. Room and board charges vary according to board plan, housing facility, and location.

FRESHMAN FINANCIAL AID (Fall 2017, est.) 4,101 applied for aid; of those 65% were deemed to have need. 97% of freshmen with need received aid; of those 35% had need fully met. **Average percent of need met:** 78% (excluding resources awarded to replace EFC). **Average financial aid package:** $8327 (excluding resources awarded to replace EFC). 33% of all full-time freshmen had no need and received non-need-based gift aid.

UNDERGRADUATE FINANCIAL AID (Fall 2017, est.) 15,867 applied for aid; of those 75% were deemed to have need. 97% of undergraduates with need received aid; of those 26% had need fully met. **Average percent of need met:** 71% (excluding resources awarded to replace EFC). **Average financial aid package:** $9482 (excluding resources awarded to replace EFC). 36% of all full-time undergraduates had no need and received non-need-based gift aid.

GIFT AID (NEED-BASED) Total amount: $66,553,222 (36% federal, 42% state, 16% institutional, 6% external sources). **Receiving aid:** Freshmen: 15% (858); all full-time undergraduates: 22% (5,284). **Average award:** Freshmen: $5727; Undergraduates: $5189. **Scholarships, grants, and awards:** Federal Pell, FSEOG, state, private, college/university gift aid from institutional funds, Federal Nursing, USC Access Grants, Gamecock Guarantee.

GIFT AID (NON-NEED-BASED) Total amount: $63,459,723 (47% state, 29% institutional, 24% external sources). **Receiving aid:** Freshmen: 39% (2,304). Undergraduates: 34% (7,925). **Average award:** Freshmen: $6202. Undergraduates: $6586. **Scholarships, grants, and awards by category:** *Academic interests/achievement:* area/ethnic studies, biological sciences, business, communication, computer science, education, engineering/technologies, English, foreign languages, general academic interests/achievements, health fields, humanities, international studies, library science, mathematics, military science, physical sciences, premedicine, religion/biblical studies, social sciences. *Creative arts/performance:* art/fine arts, dance, debating, journalism/publications, music, theater/drama. *Special achievements/activities:* cheerleading/drum major, community service, general special achievements/activities, leadership, memberships, religious involvement. *Special characteristics:* adult students, children and siblings of alumni, children of faculty/staff, children of union members/company employees, children of workers in trades, children with a deceased or disabled parent, ethnic background, first-generation college students, general special characteristics, handicapped students, international students, local/state students, members of minority groups, out-of-state students, religious affiliation, spouses of deceased or disabled public servants. **Tuition waivers:** Full or partial for employees or children of employees, senior citizens. **ROTC:** Army, Naval, Air Force.

LOANS Student loans: $118,141,647 (67% need-based, 33% non-need-based). 52% of past graduating class borrowed through all loan programs. *Average indebtedness per student:* $28,972. **Average need-based loan:** Freshmen: $3444. Undergraduates: $4476. **Parent loans:** $40,928,240 (69% need-based, 31% non-need-based). **Programs:** Federal Direct (Subsidized and Unsubsidized Stafford, PLUS), Perkins, Federal Nursing.

WORK-STUDY Federal work-study: Total amount: $2,010,720; jobs available.

ATHLETIC AWARDS Total amount: $7,618,445 (33% need-based, 67% non-need-based).

APPLYING FOR FINANCIAL AID Required financial aid form: FAFSA. *Financial aid deadline (priority):* 4/1. **Notification date:** Continuous beginning 4/1.

CONTACT Joey C. Derrick, Director of Student Financial Aid and Scholarships, University of South Carolina, 1714 College Street, Columbia, SC 29208, 803-777-8134 or toll-free 800-868-5872. *Fax:* 803-777-0941. *E-mail:* jcderric@mailbox.sc.edu. *Website:* http://www.sc.edu/.

UNIVERSITY OF SOUTH CAROLINA AIKEN
Aiken, SC

Tuition & fees (SC res): $10,502	Average undergraduate aid package: $11,155

ABOUT THE INSTITUTION State-supported, coed. *Awards:* bachelor's and master's degrees. 22 undergraduate majors. *Total enrollment:* 3,506. Undergraduates: 3,354. Freshmen: 573. Federal methodology is used as a basis for awarding need-based institutional aid.

UNDERGRADUATE EXPENSES for 2017–2018 *Application fee:* $45. *Tuition, state resident:* full-time $10,164; part-time $423.50 per credit hour. *Tuition, nonresident:* full-time $20,364; part-time $848.50 per credit hour. *Required fees:* full-time $338; $12 per credit hour or $25 per term. Full-time tuition and fees vary according to reciprocity agreements. Part-time tuition and fees vary according to course load and reciprocity agreements. *College room and board:* $7592; *Room only:* $4942. Room and board charges vary according to board plan and housing facility.

FRESHMAN FINANCIAL AID (Fall 2016) 616 applied for aid; of those 72% were deemed to have need. 99% of freshmen with need received aid; of those 19% had need fully met. *Average percent of need met:* 63% (excluding resources awarded to replace EFC). *Average financial aid package:* $11,184 (excluding resources awarded to replace EFC). 5% of all full-time freshmen had no need and received non-need-based gift aid.

UNDERGRADUATE FINANCIAL AID (Fall 2016) 2,815 applied for aid; of those 71% were deemed to have need. 98% of undergraduates with need received aid; of those 16% had need fully met. *Average percent of need met:* 60% (excluding resources awarded to replace EFC). *Average financial aid package:* $11,155 (excluding resources awarded to replace EFC). 6% of all full-time undergraduates had no need and received non-need-based gift aid.

GIFT AID (NEED-BASED) *Total amount:* $11,815,210 (53% federal, 39% state, 6% institutional, 2% external sources). *Receiving aid:* Freshmen: 68% (421); all full-time undergraduates: 59% (1,668). *Average award:* Freshmen: $7334; Undergraduates: $6841. *Scholarships, grants, and awards:* Federal Pell, FSEOG, state, college/university gift aid from institutional funds.

GIFT AID (NON-NEED-BASED) *Total amount:* $4,898,080 (15% federal, 47% state, 8% institutional, 30% external sources). *Receiving aid:* Freshmen: 10% (62). Undergraduates: 7% (185). *Average award:* Freshmen: $2303. Undergraduates: $2163. *Scholarships, grants, and awards by category: Academic interests/achievement:* biological sciences, business, communication, computer science, education, engineering/technologies, English, general academic interests/achievements, humanities, mathematics, physical sciences, premedicine, social sciences. *Creative arts/performance:* art/fine arts, journalism/publications, music, theater/drama. *Special achievements/activities:* cheerleading/drum major, community service, hobbies/interests, leadership, memberships. *Special characteristics:* adult students, children and siblings of alumni, children of faculty/staff, children of public servants, ethnic background, first-generation college students, handicapped students, international students, local/state students, married students, members of minority groups, out-of-state students, previous college experience, veterans. *Tuition waivers:* Full or partial for employees or children of employees, senior citizens.

LOANS *Student loans:* $14,878,472 (74% need-based, 26% non-need-based). 73% of past graduating class borrowed through all loan programs. *Average indebtedness per student:* $27,739. *Average need-based loan:* Freshmen: $3117. Undergraduates: $3957. *Parent loans:* $2,911,704 (54% need-based, 46% non-need-based). *Programs:* Federal Direct (Subsidized and Unsubsidized Stafford, PLUS), state.

WORK-STUDY *Federal work-study:* 71 jobs averaging $1769. *State or other work-study/employment:* Total amount: $698,928 (31% need-based, 69% non-need-based). 433 part-time jobs averaging $1553.

ATHLETIC AWARDS Total amount: $777,909 (41% need-based, 59% non-need-based).

APPLYING FOR FINANCIAL AID *Required financial aid form:* FAFSA. *Financial aid deadline (priority):* 3/15. *Notification date:* Continuous beginning 4/20. Students must reply within 2 weeks of notification.

CONTACT Mrs. Tammie Minter, Director of Financial Aid, University of South Carolina Aiken, 471 University Parkway, Aiken, SC 29801, 803-641-3476 or toll-free 888-WOW-USCA. *Fax:* 803-643-6840. *E-mail:* tammiem@usca.edu. *Website:* http://www.usca.edu/.

UNIVERSITY OF SOUTH CAROLINA BEAUFORT
Bluffton, SC

CONTACT Heather Robinson, Financial Aid Administrative Assistant, University of South Carolina Beaufort, 801 Carteret Street, Beaufort, SC 29902, 843-521-3104. *Fax:* 843-521-3194. *E-mail:* uscbfina@uscb.edu. *Website:* http://www.uscb.edu/.

UNIVERSITY OF SOUTH CAROLINA UPSTATE
Spartanburg, SC

Tuition & fees: N/R	Average undergraduate aid package: $9733

ABOUT THE INSTITUTION State-supported, coed. 31 undergraduate majors. Federal methodology is used as a basis for awarding need-based institutional aid.

FRESHMAN FINANCIAL AID (Fall 2017, est.) 737 applied for aid; of those 87% were deemed to have need. 100% of freshmen with need received aid; of those 6% had need fully met. *Average percent of need met:* 52% (excluding resources awarded to replace EFC). *Average financial aid package:* $10,456 (excluding resources awarded to replace EFC). 3% of all full-time freshmen had no need and received non-need-based gift aid.

UNDERGRADUATE FINANCIAL AID (Fall 2017, est.) 3,576 applied for aid; of those 89% were deemed to have need. 98% of undergraduates with need received aid; of those 4% had need fully met. *Average percent of need met:* 46% (excluding resources awarded to replace EFC). *Average financial aid package:* $9733 (excluding resources awarded to replace EFC). 3% of all full-time undergraduates had no need and received non-need-based gift aid.

GIFT AID (NEED-BASED) *Total amount:* $13,462,507 (88% federal, 12% state). *Receiving aid:* Freshmen: 57% (452); all full-time undergraduates: 52% (2,187). *Average award:* Freshmen: $5740; Undergraduates: $5210. *Scholarships, grants, and awards:* Federal Pell, FSEOG, state, private, college/university gift aid from institutional funds.

GIFT AID (NON-NEED-BASED) *Total amount:* $10,416,000 (1% federal, 93% state, 6% institutional). *Receiving aid:* Freshmen: 73% (576). Undergraduates: 36% (1,529). *Average award:* Freshmen: $1708. Undergraduates: $1701. *Scholarships, grants, and awards by category: Academic interests/achievement:* 440 awards ($627,369 total): general academic interests/achievements. *Special characteristics:* first-generation college students.

LOANS *Student loans:* $27,864,983 (46% need-based, 54% non-need-based). 79% of past graduating class borrowed through all loan programs. *Average indebtedness per student:* $27,163. *Average need-based loan:* Freshmen: $3216. Undergraduates: $4101. *Parent loans:* $5,070,918 (100% non-need-based). *Programs:* Federal Direct (Subsidized and Unsubsidized Stafford, PLUS), Perkins, state, private loans.

WORK-STUDY *Federal work-study:* Total amount: $47,056; 52 jobs averaging $4041.

ATHLETIC AWARDS Total amount: $1,460,360 (100% non-need-based).

APPLYING FOR FINANCIAL AID *Required financial aid form:* FAFSA. *Financial aid deadline:* 7/1 (priority: 3/9). *Notification date:* Continuous beginning 5/31. Students must reply within 2 weeks of notification.

CONTACT Bonnie Carson-Durham, Director of Financial Aid, University of South Carolina Upstate, 800 University Way, Spartanburg, SC 29303, 864-503-5349 or toll-free 800-277-8727. *Fax:* 864-503-5974. *E-mail:* bcarson@uscupstate.edu. *Website:* http://www.uscupstate.edu/.

UNIVERSITY OF SOUTH DAKOTA
Vermillion, SD

Tuition & fees (SD res): $8772	Average undergraduate aid package: $8631

ABOUT THE INSTITUTION State-supported, coed. **Awards:** certificates, associate, bachelor's, master's, and doctoral degrees. 73 undergraduate majors. **Total enrollment:** 10,261. Undergraduates: 7,648. Freshmen: 1,341. Federal methodology is used as a basis for awarding need-based institutional aid.

UNDERGRADUATE EXPENSES for 2017–2018 *Application fee:* $20. *Tuition, state resident:* full-time $7191; part-time $239.70 per credit hour. *Tuition, nonresident:* full-time $10,439; part-time $347.95 per credit hour. *Required fees:* full-time $1581; $52.70 per credit hour. Full-time tuition and fees vary according to course load, location, and reciprocity agreements. Part-time tuition and fees vary according to course load, location, and reciprocity agreements. *College room and board:* $7672; *Room only:* $4114. Room and board charges vary according to housing facility.

FRESHMAN FINANCIAL AID (Fall 2016) 999 applied for aid; of those 73% were deemed to have need. 99% of freshmen with need received aid; of those 20% had need fully met. *Average percent of need met:* 59% (excluding resources awarded to replace EFC). *Average financial aid package:* $8620 (excluding resources awarded to replace EFC). 23% of all full-time freshmen had no need and received non-need-based gift aid.

UNDERGRADUATE FINANCIAL AID (Fall 2016) 3,872 applied for aid; of those 75% were deemed to have need. 99% of undergraduates with need received aid; of those 15% had need fully met. *Average percent of need met:* 57% (excluding resources awarded to replace EFC). *Average financial aid package:* $8631 (excluding resources awarded to replace EFC). 20% of all full-time undergraduates had no need and received non-need-based gift aid.

GIFT AID (NEED-BASED) Total amount: $7,836,801 (100% federal). *Receiving aid:* Freshmen: 28% (331); all full-time undergraduates: 28% (1,367). *Average award:* Freshmen: $4661; Undergraduates: $4482. *Scholarships, grants, and awards:* Federal Pell, FSEOG, state, private, college/university gift aid from institutional funds, United Negro College Fund.

GIFT AID (NON-NEED-BASED) Total amount: $9,201,193 (4% federal, 13% state, 58% institutional, 25% external sources). *Receiving aid:* Freshmen: 47% (546). Undergraduates: 33% (1,648). *Average award:* Freshmen: $2292. Undergraduates: $2202. *Scholarships, grants, and awards by category:* Academic interests/achievement: biological sciences, business, communication, computer science, education, English, foreign languages, general academic interests/achievements, humanities, mathematics, military science, premedicine, social sciences. Creative arts/performance: art/fine arts, creative writing, debating, music, theater/drama. Special achievements/activities: leadership. Special characteristics: members of minority groups. *Tuition waivers:* Full or partial for children of alumni, employees or children of employees, senior citizens. *ROTC:* Army.

LOANS Student loans: $32,462,256 (40% need-based, 60% non-need-based). 74% of past graduating class borrowed through all loan programs. *Average indebtedness per student:* $29,686. *Average need-based loan:* Freshmen: $3599. Undergraduates: $4434. *Parent loans:* $6,512,623 (100% non-need-based). *Programs:* Federal Direct (Subsidized and Unsubsidized Stafford, PLUS), Perkins, Federal Nursing.

WORK-STUDY *Federal work-study:* jobs available. *State or other work-study/employment:* Total amount: $458,699 (100% non-need-based). Part-time jobs available.

ATHLETIC AWARDS Total amount: $4,149,000 (100% non-need-based).

APPLYING FOR FINANCIAL AID *Required financial aid form:* FAFSA. *Financial aid deadline (priority):* 4/1. *Notification date:* Continuous beginning 3/1.

CONTACT Julie Pier, Director of Student Financial Aid, University of South Dakota, Belbas Center, 414 East Clark Street, Vermillion, SD 57069, 605-677-5446 or toll-free 877-269-6837. *Fax:* 605-677-5238.
Website: http://www.usd.edu/.

UNIVERSITY OF SOUTHERN CALIFORNIA
Los Angeles, CA

Tuition & fees: $54,323	Average undergraduate aid package: $49,835

ABOUT THE INSTITUTION Independent, coed. **Awards:** certificates, bachelor's, master's, and doctoral degrees. 106 undergraduate majors. **Total enrollment:** 45,687. Undergraduates: 19,170. Freshmen: 3,358. Both federal and institutional methodology are used as a basis for awarding need-based institutional aid.

UNDERGRADUATE EXPENSES for 2018–2019 *Application fee:* $85. *One-time required fee:* $350. *Comprehensive fee:* $69,208 includes full-time tuition ($53,448), mandatory fees ($875), and room and board ($14,885). *College room only:* $8985. Full-time tuition and fees vary according to program. Room and board charges vary according to board plan and housing facility. *Part-time tuition:* $1800 per credit hour. Part-time tuition and fees vary according to course load and program. *Payment plan:* Tuition prepayment.

FRESHMAN FINANCIAL AID (Fall 2016) 1,781 applied for aid; of those 62% were deemed to have need. 100% of freshmen with need received aid; of those 88% had need fully met. *Average percent of need met:* 100% (excluding resources awarded to replace EFC). *Average financial aid package:* $52,795 (excluding resources awarded to replace EFC). 21% of all full-time freshmen had no need and received non-need-based gift aid.

UNDERGRADUATE FINANCIAL AID (Fall 2016) 8,830 applied for aid; of those 75% were deemed to have need. 100% of undergraduates with need received aid; of those 84% had need fully met. *Average percent of need met:* 100% (excluding resources awarded to replace EFC). *Average financial aid package:* $49,835 (excluding resources awarded to replace EFC). 19% of all full-time undergraduates had no need and received non-need-based gift aid.

GIFT AID (NEED-BASED) Total amount: $264,014,127 (7% federal, 8% state, 81% institutional, 4% external sources). *Receiving aid:* Freshmen: 31% (957); all full-time undergraduates: 33% (5,961). *Average award:* Freshmen: $38,196; Undergraduates: $36,496. *Scholarships, grants, and awards:* Federal Pell, FSEOG, state, private, college/university gift aid from institutional funds.

GIFT AID (NON-NEED-BASED) Total amount: $81,015,143 (87% institutional, 13% external sources). *Receiving aid:* Freshmen: 24% (734). Undergraduates: 18% (3,208). *Average award:* Freshmen: $23,474. Undergraduates: $20,209. *Scholarships, grants, and awards by category:* Academic interests/achievement: general academic interests/achievements. Creative arts/performance: art/fine arts, debating, music, theater/drama. Special achievements/activities: leadership. Special characteristics: children and siblings of alumni, children of faculty/staff. *Tuition waivers:* Full or partial for employees or children of employees. *ROTC:* Army, Naval, Air Force.

LOANS Student loans: $56,180,025 (57% need-based, 43% non-need-based). 36% of past graduating class borrowed through all loan programs. *Average indebtedness per student:* $29,080. *Average need-based loan:* Freshmen: $5592. Undergraduates: $7043. *Parent loans:* $65,271,833 (100% non-need-based). *Programs:* Federal Direct (Subsidized and Unsubsidized Stafford, PLUS), Perkins, college/university.

WORK-STUDY *Federal work-study:* jobs available.

ATHLETIC AWARDS Total amount: $21,373,986 (32% need-based, 68% non-need-based).

APPLYING FOR FINANCIAL AID *Required financial aid forms:* FAFSA, CSS Financial Aid PROFILE, noncustodial (divorced/separated) parent's statement, business/farm supplement, federal income tax form(s). *Financial aid deadline (priority):* 2/17. *Notification date:* 4/1. Students must reply by 5/1.

CONTACT Thomas McWhorter, Office of Financial Aid, University of Southern California, 700 Childs Way, Los Angeles, CA 90089-0914, 213-740-5445. *Fax:* 213-821-3796. *E-mail:* faodean@usc.edu.
Website: http://www.usc.edu/.

UNIVERSITY OF SOUTHERN INDIANA
Evansville, IN

Tuition & fees (IN res): $7970	Average undergraduate aid package: $9456

ABOUT THE INSTITUTION State-supported, coed. *Awards:* certificates, associate, bachelor's, master's, and doctoral degrees. 59 undergraduate majors. *Total enrollment:* 9,014. Undergraduates: 7,706. Freshmen: 1,722. Federal methodology is used as a basis for awarding need-based institutional aid.

UNDERGRADUATE EXPENSES for 2017–2018 *Application fee:* $40. *One-time required fee:* $450. *Tuition, state resident:* full-time $7460; part-time $248.66 per credit hour. *Tuition, nonresident:* full-time $18,116; part-time $603.87 per credit hour. *Required fees:* full-time $510; $22.75 per term. Full-time tuition and fees vary according to course level, course load, program, and reciprocity agreements. Part-time tuition and fees vary according to course level, course load, program, and reciprocity agreements. *College room and board:* $8838; *Room only:* $4668. Room and board charges vary according to board plan and housing facility.

FRESHMAN FINANCIAL AID (Fall 2017, est.) 1,575 applied for aid; of those 75% were deemed to have need. 100% of freshmen with need received aid; of those 26% had need fully met. *Average percent of need met:* 82% (excluding resources awarded to replace EFC). *Average financial aid package:* $9426 (excluding resources awarded to replace EFC). 22% of all full-time freshmen had no need and received non-need-based gift aid.

UNDERGRADUATE FINANCIAL AID (Fall 2017, est.) 5,450 applied for aid; of those 77% were deemed to have need. 99% of undergraduates with need received aid; of those 30% had need fully met. *Average percent of need met:* 80% (excluding resources awarded to replace EFC). *Average financial aid package:* $9456 (excluding resources awarded to replace EFC). 17% of all full-time undergraduates had no need and received non-need-based gift aid.

GIFT AID (NEED-BASED) *Total amount:* $26,952,377 (42% federal, 35% state, 20% institutional, 3% external sources). *Receiving aid:* Freshmen: 43% (727); all full-time undergraduates: 39% (2,554). *Average award:* Freshmen: $8982; Undergraduates: $8140. *Scholarships, grants, and awards:* Federal Pell, FSEOG, state, private, college/university gift aid from institutional funds, United Negro College Fund, Federal Nursing.

GIFT AID (NON-NEED-BASED) *Total amount:* $7,533,493 (16% state, 70% institutional, 14% external sources). *Receiving aid:* Freshmen: 53% (893). Undergraduates: 54% (3,494). *Average award:* Freshmen: $4208. Undergraduates: $3931. *Scholarships, grants, and awards by category:* Academic interests/achievement: 2,532 awards ($4,942,328 total): biological sciences, business, education, engineering/technologies, general academic interests/achievements, health fields, humanities, mathematics, premedicine, social sciences. *Creative arts/performance:* 52 awards ($94,193 total): art/fine arts, creative writing, theater/drama. *Special achievements/activities:* leadership. *Special characteristics:* 637 awards ($5,142,126 total): adult students, children of faculty/staff, first-generation college students, general special characteristics, international students, members of minority groups, out-of-state students, veterans, veterans' children. *Tuition waivers:* Full or partial for employees or children of employees. *ROTC:* Army.

LOANS *Student loans:* $36,997,288 (75% need-based, 25% non-need-based). 64% of past graduating class borrowed through all loan programs. *Average indebtedness per student:* $24,568. *Average need-based loan:* Freshmen: $3021. Undergraduates: $3273. *Parent loans:* $4,179,299 (66% need-based, 34% non-need-based). *Programs:* Federal Direct (Subsidized and Unsubsidized Stafford, PLUS).

WORK-STUDY *Federal work-study:* Total amount: $152,066; 98 jobs averaging $1995.

ATHLETIC AWARDS Total amount: $1,277,056 (16% need-based, 84% non-need-based).

APPLYING FOR FINANCIAL AID *Required financial aid form:* FAFSA. *Financial aid deadline (priority):* 4/15. *Notification date:* Continuous beginning 4/1. Students must reply by 4/1.

CONTACT Mrs. Mary Harper, Financial Aid Office, University of Southern Indiana, 8600 University Boulevard, Evansville, IN 47712-3590, 812-464-1767 or toll-free 800-467-1965. *Fax:* 812-461-5305. *E-mail:* finaid@usi.edu. *Website:* http://www.usi.edu/.

UNIVERSITY OF SOUTHERN MAINE
Portland, ME

Tuition & fees (ME res): $9220	Average undergraduate aid package: $14,493

ABOUT THE INSTITUTION State-supported, coed. *Awards:* certificates, bachelor's, master's, and doctoral degrees. 47 undergraduate majors. *Total enrollment:* 7,855. Undergraduates: 6,189. Freshmen: 805. Federal methodology is used as a basis for awarding need-based institutional aid.

UNDERGRADUATE EXPENSES for 2017–2018 *Application fee:* $40. *Tuition, state resident:* full-time $7860; part-time $262 per credit hour. *Tuition, nonresident:* full-time $20,670; part-time $689 per credit hour. *Required fees:* full-time $1360; $1360 per year. Full-time tuition and fees vary according to course load, degree level, and reciprocity agreements. Part-time tuition and fees vary according to course load, degree level, and reciprocity agreements. *College room and board:* $9200; *Room only:* $5000. Room and board charges vary according to board plan and housing facility.

FRESHMAN FINANCIAL AID (Fall 2016) 832 applied for aid; of those 83% were deemed to have need. 100% of freshmen with need received aid; of those 40% had need fully met. *Average percent of need met:* 83% (excluding resources awarded to replace EFC). *Average financial aid package:* $14,808 (excluding resources awarded to replace EFC). 13% of all full-time freshmen had no need and received non-need-based gift aid.

UNDERGRADUATE FINANCIAL AID (Fall 2016) 3,328 applied for aid; of those 84% were deemed to have need. 100% of undergraduates with need received aid; of those 49% had need fully met. *Average percent of need met:* 81% (excluding resources awarded to replace EFC). *Average financial aid package:* $14,493 (excluding resources awarded to replace EFC). 7% of all full-time undergraduates had no need and received non-need-based gift aid.

GIFT AID (NEED-BASED) *Total amount:* $27,117,741 (43% federal, 9% state, 41% institutional, 7% external sources). *Receiving aid:* Freshmen: 77% (685); all full-time undergraduates: 65% (2,524). *Average award:* Freshmen: $10,474; Undergraduates: $9010. *Scholarships, grants, and awards:* Federal Pell, FSEOG, state, private, college/university gift aid from institutional funds.

GIFT AID (NON-NEED-BASED) *Total amount:* $1,916,434 (77% institutional, 23% external sources). *Receiving aid:* Freshmen: 6% (57). Undergraduates: 4% (159). *Average award:* Freshmen: $4593. Undergraduates: $4234. *Scholarships, grants, and awards by category:* Academic interests/achievement: general academic interests/achievements. *Creative arts/performance:* music, theater/drama. *Tuition waivers:* Full or partial for employees or children of employees. *ROTC:* Army cooperative, Air Force cooperative.

LOANS *Student loans:* $23,783,143 (74% need-based, 26% non-need-based). *Average need-based loan:* Freshmen: $5470. Undergraduates: $6963. *Parent loans:* $2,104,261 (30% need-based, 70% non-need-based). *Programs:* Federal Direct (Subsidized and Unsubsidized Stafford, PLUS), Perkins, Federal Nursing, college/university.

WORK-STUDY *Federal work-study:* jobs available.

APPLYING FOR FINANCIAL AID *Required financial aid form:* FAFSA. *Financial aid deadline (priority):* 2/15. *Notification date:* Continuous beginning 3/15.

CONTACT Mr. Keith P. Dubois, Director of Financial Aid, University of Southern Maine, 37 College Avenue, 107 Baily Hall, Gorham, ME 04038, 207-780-5122 or toll-free 800-800-4USM Ext. 5670. *Fax:* 207-780-5143. *E-mail:* dubois@maine.edu. *Website:* http://www.usm.maine.edu/.

UNIVERSITY OF SOUTHERN MISSISSIPPI
Hattiesburg, MS

Tuition & fees (MS res): $8108	Average undergraduate aid package: $11,603

ABOUT THE INSTITUTION State-supported, coed. *Awards:* certificates, bachelor's, master's, and doctoral degrees. 74 undergraduate majors. *Total enrollment:* 14,478. Undergraduates: 11,815. Freshmen: 1,903. Federal methodology is used as a basis for awarding need-based institutional aid.

UNDERGRADUATE EXPENSES for 2018–2019 *Application fee:* $40. *Tuition, state resident:* full-time $8108; part-time $338 per credit hour. *Tuition, nonresident:* full-time $10,108. Part-time tuition and fees vary according to course load and degree level. *College room and board:* $10,638; *Room only:* $6598. Room and board charges vary according to board plan and housing facility.
FRESHMAN FINANCIAL AID (Fall 2016) 1,320 applied for aid; of those 85% were deemed to have need. 99% of freshmen with need received aid; of those 31% had need fully met. *Average percent of need met:* 76% (excluding resources awarded to replace EFC). *Average financial aid package:* $13,096 (excluding resources awarded to replace EFC). 11% of all full-time freshmen had no need and received non-need-based gift aid.
UNDERGRADUATE FINANCIAL AID (Fall 2016) 8,547 applied for aid; of those 88% were deemed to have need. 97% of undergraduates with need received aid; of those 23% had need fully met. *Average percent of need met:* 69% (excluding resources awarded to replace EFC). *Average financial aid package:* $11,603 (excluding resources awarded to replace EFC). 7% of all full-time undergraduates had no need and received non-need-based gift aid.
GIFT AID (NEED-BASED) *Total amount:* $37,989,320 (64% federal, 10% state, 22% institutional, 4% external sources). *Receiving aid:* Freshmen: 45% (696); all full-time undergraduates: 51% (5,172). *Average award:* Freshmen: $4724; Undergraduates: $4589. *Scholarships, grants, and awards:* Federal Pell, FSEOG, state, private, college/university gift aid from institutional funds.
GIFT AID (NON-NEED-BASED) *Total amount:* $20,326,586 (13% federal, 9% state, 70% institutional, 8% external sources). *Receiving aid:* Freshmen: 52% (802). Undergraduates: 43% (4,305). *Average award:* Freshmen: $5738. Undergraduates: $5788. *Scholarships, grants, and awards by category: Academic interests/achievement:* general academic interests/achievements. *Creative arts/performance:* art/fine arts, dance, music, theater/drama. *Special achievements/activities:* cheerleading/drum major, leadership. *Special characteristics:* children and siblings of alumni, children of faculty/staff, ethnic background, local/state students, out-of-state students, veterans. *Tuition waivers:* Full or partial for children of alumni, employees or children of employees, senior citizens. *ROTC:* Army cooperative, Air Force.
LOANS *Student loans:* $56,560,168 (55% need-based, 45% non-need-based). 71% of past graduating class borrowed through all loan programs. *Average indebtedness per student:* $27,859. *Average need-based loan:* Freshmen: $4991. Undergraduates: $5029. *Parent loans:* $7,083,981 (50% need-based, 50% non-need-based). *Programs:* Federal Direct (Subsidized and Unsubsidized Stafford, PLUS).
WORK-STUDY *Federal work-study:* jobs available.
ATHLETIC AWARDS Total amount: $5,177,635 (44% need-based, 56% non-need-based).
APPLYING FOR FINANCIAL AID *Required financial aid forms:* FAFSA, institution's own form. *Financial aid deadline (priority):* 12/1. *Notification date:* Continuous beginning 12/15.
CONTACT Mr. David Williamson, Director of Financial Aid, University of Southern Mississippi, 118 College Drive #5101, Hattiesburg, MS 39406-0001, 601-266-4774. *Fax:* 601-266-5769. *E-mail:* financial.aid@usm.edu.
Website: http://www.usm.edu/.

need fully met. *Average percent of need met:* 63% (excluding resources awarded to replace EFC). *Average financial aid package:* $11,668 (excluding resources awarded to replace EFC). 13% of all full-time freshmen had no need and received non-need-based gift aid.
UNDERGRADUATE FINANCIAL AID (Fall 2016) 20,584 applied for aid; of those 84% were deemed to have need. 95% of undergraduates with need received aid; of those 10% had need fully met. *Average percent of need met:* 58% (excluding resources awarded to replace EFC). *Average financial aid package:* $11,260 (excluding resources awarded to replace EFC). 9% of all full-time undergraduates had no need and received non-need-based gift aid.
GIFT AID (NEED-BASED) *Total amount:* $110,416,477 (52% federal, 19% state, 26% institutional, 3% external sources). *Receiving aid:* Freshmen: 56% (2,635); all full-time undergraduates: 52% (14,153). *Average award:* Freshmen: $9151; Undergraduates: $7417. *Scholarships, grants, and awards:* Federal Pell, FSEOG, state, private, college/university gift aid from institutional funds, United Negro College Fund.
GIFT AID (NON-NEED-BASED) *Total amount:* $17,869,353 (50% state, 43% institutional, 7% external sources). *Receiving aid:* Freshmen: 4% (188). Undergraduates: 2% (557). *Average award:* Freshmen: $3393. Undergraduates: $2844. *Scholarships, grants, and awards by category: Academic interests/achievement:* 2,381 awards ($6,317,532 total): architecture, biological sciences, business, communication, computer science, education, engineering/technologies, English, foreign languages, general academic interests/achievements, home economics, humanities, international studies, library science, mathematics, military science, physical sciences, premedicine, religion/biblical studies, social sciences. *Creative arts/performance:* 333 awards ($389,908 total): applied art and design, art/fine arts, creative writing, dance, music, performing arts, theater/drama. *Tuition waivers:* Full or partial for employees or children of employees, senior citizens. *ROTC:* Army, Naval, Air Force.
LOANS *Student loans:* $108,777,870 (85% need-based, 15% non-need-based). 55% of past graduating class borrowed through all loan programs. *Average indebtedness per student:* $21,799. *Average need-based loan:* Freshmen: $4823. Undergraduates: $6609. *Parent loans:* $16,532,754 (44% need-based, 56% non-need-based). *Programs:* Federal Direct (Subsidized and Unsubsidized Stafford, PLUS), Perkins, college/university.
WORK-STUDY *Federal work-study:* 761 jobs averaging $3219. *State or other work-study/employment:* Total amount: $416,690 (100% need-based). 258 part-time jobs averaging $1615.
ATHLETIC AWARDS Total amount: $5,115,006 (42% need-based, 58% non-need-based).
APPLYING FOR FINANCIAL AID *Required financial aid form:* FAFSA. *Financial aid deadline (priority):* 1/1. *Notification date:* Continuous beginning 12/1.
CONTACT Ms. Billie Jo Hamilton, Director of Student Financial Aid, University of South Florida, 4202 East Fowler Avenue, SVC 1102, Tampa, FL 33620-6960, 813-974-4700. *Fax:* 813-974-5144. *E-mail:* bjhamilton@usf.edu.
Website: http://www.usf.edu/.

UNIVERSITY OF SOUTH FLORIDA
Tampa, FL

Tuition & fees (FL res): $6410	Average undergraduate aid package: $11,260

ABOUT THE INSTITUTION State-supported, coed. *Awards:* associate, bachelor's, master's, and doctoral degrees. 80 undergraduate majors. *Total enrollment:* 42,861. Undergraduates: 31,461. Freshmen: 4,049. Federal methodology is used as a basis for awarding need-based institutional aid.
UNDERGRADUATE EXPENSES for 2017–2018 *Application fee:* $30. *Tuition, state resident:* full-time $6336; part-time $211.19 per credit hour. *Tuition, nonresident:* full-time $17,250; part-time $575.01 per credit hour. *Required fees:* full-time $74; $74 per year. Full-time tuition and fees vary according to location. Part-time tuition and fees vary according to location. *College room and board:* $10,325; *Room only:* $6588. Room and board charges vary according to board plan, housing facility, and location.
FRESHMAN FINANCIAL AID (Fall 2016) 4,023 applied for aid; of those 77% were deemed to have need. 95% of freshmen with need received aid; of those 13% had

UNIVERSITY OF SOUTH FLORIDA, ST. PETERSBURG
St. Petersburg, FL

CONTACT Financial Aid Office, University of South Florida, St. Petersburg, 140 Seventh Ave S., St. Petersburg, FL 33701, 727-873-7748.
Website: http://www.usfsp.edu/.

UNIVERSITY OF SOUTH FLORIDA SARASOTA-MANATEE
Sarasota, FL

CONTACT Financial Aid Office, University of South Florida Sarasota-Manatee, 8350 N Tamiami Trail, Sarasota, FL 34243, 941-359-4200.
Website: http://www.usfsm.edu/.

THE UNIVERSITY OF TAMPA
Tampa, FL

Tuition & fees: $28,426	Average undergraduate aid package: $17,438

ABOUT THE INSTITUTION Independent, coed. *Awards:* certificates, bachelor's, and master's degrees. 62 undergraduate majors. *Total enrollment:* 8,839. Undergraduates: 7,974. Freshmen: 2,141. Federal methodology is used as a basis for awarding need-based institutional aid.

UNDERGRADUATE EXPENSES for 2017–2018 *Application fee:* $40. *One-time required fee:* $85. *Comprehensive fee:* $38,928 includes full-time tuition ($26,504), mandatory fees ($1922), and room and board ($10,502). *College room only:* $5546. Full-time tuition and fees vary according to class time, course load, and program. Room and board charges vary according to board plan and housing facility. *Part-time tuition:* $564 per credit hour. *Part-time fees:* $40 per term. Part-time tuition and fees vary according to class time, course load, and program.

FRESHMAN FINANCIAL AID (Fall 2017, est.) 1,807 applied for aid; of those 77% were deemed to have need. 100% of freshmen with need received aid; of those 10% had need fully met. *Average percent of need met:* 61% (excluding resources awarded to replace EFC). *Average financial aid package:* $17,346 (excluding resources awarded to replace EFC). 28% of all full-time freshmen had no need and received non-need-based gift aid.

UNDERGRADUATE FINANCIAL AID (Fall 2017, est.) 5,605 applied for aid; of those 82% were deemed to have need. 100% of undergraduates with need received aid; of those 8% had need fully met. *Average percent of need met:* 60% (excluding resources awarded to replace EFC). *Average financial aid package:* $17,438 (excluding resources awarded to replace EFC). 29% of all full-time undergraduates had no need and received non-need-based gift aid.

GIFT AID (NEED-BASED) *Total amount:* $57,606,527 (14% federal, 9% state, 75% institutional, 2% external sources). *Receiving aid:* Freshmen: 64% (1,360); all full-time undergraduates: 58% (4,483). *Average award:* Freshmen: $14,320; Undergraduates: $13,686. *Scholarships, grants, and awards:* Federal Pell, FSEOG, state, private, college/university gift aid from institutional funds.

GIFT AID (NON-NEED-BASED) *Total amount:* $20,636,483 (11% state, 87% institutional, 2% external sources). *Receiving aid:* Freshmen: 61% (1,309). Undergraduates: 56% (4,362). *Average award:* Freshmen: $8568. Undergraduates: $7997. *Scholarships, grants, and awards by category:* Academic interests/achievement: 6,248 awards ($51,140,128 total): biological sciences, English, general academic interests/achievements, international studies, military science, physical sciences, premedicine, social sciences. *Creative arts/performance:* 152 awards ($332,400 total): art/fine arts, creative writing, dance, journalism/publications, music, performing arts, theater/drama. *Special achievements/activities:* 249 awards ($253,500 total): general special achievements/activities, leadership, memberships. *Special characteristics:* 517 awards ($3,638,516 total): children and siblings of alumni, children of faculty/staff, first-generation college students, international students, veterans. *Tuition waivers:* Full or partial for employees or children of employees. *ROTC:* Army, Naval cooperative, Air Force cooperative.

LOANS *Student loans:* $42,223,257 (85% need-based, 15% non-need-based). 61% of past graduating class borrowed through all loan programs. *Average indebtedness per student:* $32,048. *Average need-based loan:* Freshmen: $3434. Undergraduates: $4279. *Parent loans:* $27,447,704 (88% need-based, 12% non-need-based). *Programs:* Federal Direct (Subsidized and Unsubsidized Stafford, PLUS), college/university, private loans.

WORK-STUDY *Federal work-study:* Total amount: $640,857; 404 jobs averaging $2000. *State or other work-study/employment:* Total amount: $168,549 (100% need-based). 248 part-time jobs averaging $2000.

ATHLETIC AWARDS Total amount: $2,952,123 (46% need-based, 54% non-need-based).

APPLYING FOR FINANCIAL AID *Required financial aid form:* FAFSA. *Financial aid deadline:* Continuous. *Notification date:* Continuous beginning 10/1. Students must reply by 5/1.

CONTACT Jacqueline M. LaTorella, Director of Financial Aid, The University of Tampa, 401 West Kennedy Boulevard, Box E, Tampa, FL 33606-1490, 813-253-6219 or toll-free 888-646-2738 (in-state), 888-MINARET (out-of-state). *Fax:* 813-258-7439. *E-mail:* finaid@ut.edu. *Website:* http://www.ut.edu/.

THE UNIVERSITY OF TENNESSEE
Knoxville, TN

Tuition & fees (TN res): $12,970	Average undergraduate aid package: $13,351

ABOUT THE INSTITUTION State-supported, coed. *Awards:* certificates, bachelor's, master's, and doctoral degrees. 76 undergraduate majors. *Total enrollment:* 28,321. Undergraduates: 22,317. Freshmen: 4,895. Federal methodology is used as a basis for awarding need-based institutional aid.

UNDERGRADUATE EXPENSES for 2017–2018 *Application fee:* $50. *Tuition, state resident:* full-time $11,110; part-time $371 per credit hour. *Tuition, nonresident:* full-time $29,300; part-time $1130 per credit hour. *Required fees:* full-time $1860. Full-time tuition and fees vary according to course level, location, program, reciprocity agreements, and student level. Part-time tuition and fees vary according to course level, location, program, reciprocity agreements, and student level. *College room and board:* $10,696. Room and board charges vary according to board plan and housing facility.

FRESHMAN FINANCIAL AID (Fall 2017, est.) 4,686 applied for aid; of those 64% were deemed to have need. 100% of freshmen with need received aid; of those 22% had need fully met. *Average percent of need met:* 64% (excluding resources awarded to replace EFC). *Average financial aid package:* $14,137 (excluding resources awarded to replace EFC). 18% of all full-time freshmen had no need and received non-need-based gift aid.

UNDERGRADUATE FINANCIAL AID (Fall 2017, est.) 18,421 applied for aid; of those 66% were deemed to have need. 99% of undergraduates with need received aid; of those 20% had need fully met. *Average percent of need met:* 53% (excluding resources awarded to replace EFC). *Average financial aid package:* $13,351 (excluding resources awarded to replace EFC). 14% of all full-time undergraduates had no need and received non-need-based gift aid.

GIFT AID (NEED-BASED) *Total amount:* $150,158,141 (19% federal, 38% state, 40% institutional, 3% external sources). *Receiving aid:* Freshmen: 58% (2,812); all full-time undergraduates: 51% (10,577). *Average award:* Freshmen: $12,128; Undergraduates: $10,498. *Scholarships, grants, and awards:* Federal Pell, FSEOG, state, private, college/university gift aid from institutional funds.

GIFT AID (NON-NEED-BASED) *Average award:* Freshmen: $6577. Undergraduates: $5988. *Scholarships, grants, and awards by category:* Academic interests/achievement: 2,492 awards ($6,271,994 total): agriculture, architecture, business, communication, computer science, education, engineering/technologies, general academic interests/achievements, home economics, humanities, international studies, library science, military science, social sciences. *Creative arts/performance:* 256 awards ($298,570 total): art/fine arts. *Tuition waivers:* Full or partial for employees or children of employees, senior citizens. *ROTC:* Army, Air Force.

LOANS *Student loans:* $81,830,064 (74% need-based, 26% non-need-based). 50% of past graduating class borrowed through all loan programs. *Average indebtedness per student:* $21,872. *Average need-based loan:* Freshmen: $5355. Undergraduates: $6814. *Parent loans:* $33,764,451 (100% need-based). *Programs:* Federal Direct (Subsidized and Unsubsidized Stafford, PLUS), Perkins, state, college/university.

WORK-STUDY *Federal work-study:* Total amount: $1,556,653; 539 jobs averaging $2792.

ATHLETIC AWARDS Total amount: $9,126,892 (100% need-based).

APPLYING FOR FINANCIAL AID *Required financial aid form:* FAFSA. *Financial aid deadline (priority):* 2/15. *Notification date:* Continuous beginning 3/15. Students must reply within 3 weeks of notification.

CONTACT Jeffery Gerkin, Office of Financial Aid and Scholarships, The University of Tennessee, 116 Student Services Building, Knoxville, TN 37996-0210, 865-974-1111. *Fax:* 865-974-2175. *E-mail:* finaid@utk.edu. *Website:* http://www.utk.edu/.

THE UNIVERSITY OF TENNESSEE AT CHATTANOOGA
Chattanooga, TN

Tuition & fees (TN res): $8664	Average undergraduate aid package: $10,084

ABOUT THE INSTITUTION State-supported, coed. *Awards:* certificates, bachelor's, master's, and doctoral degrees. 40 undergraduate majors. *Total enrollment:* 11,587. Undergraduates: 10,176. Freshmen: 2,147. Federal methodology is used as a basis for awarding need-based institutional aid.

UNDERGRADUATE EXPENSES for 2017–2018 *Application fee:* $30. *Tuition, state resident:* full-time $6888; part-time $287 per credit hour. *Tuition, nonresident:* full-time $23,006; part-time $984 per credit hour. *Required fees:* full-time $1776; $264 per credit hour. Full-time tuition and fees vary according to degree level. Part-time tuition and fees vary according to degree level. *College room and board:* $8676; *Room only:* $5226. Room and board charges vary according to board plan, housing facility, and location.

FRESHMAN FINANCIAL AID (Fall 2017, est.) 2,036 applied for aid; of those 67% were deemed to have need. 100% of freshmen with need received aid; of those 19% had need fully met. *Average percent of need met:* 72% (excluding resources awarded to replace EFC). *Average financial aid package:* $10,822 (excluding resources awarded to replace EFC). 14% of all full-time freshmen had no need and received non-need-based gift aid.

UNDERGRADUATE FINANCIAL AID (Fall 2017, est.) 7,928 applied for aid; of those 70% were deemed to have need. 100% of undergraduates with need received aid; of those 15% had need fully met. *Average percent of need met:* 65% (excluding resources awarded to replace EFC). *Average financial aid package:* $10,084 (excluding resources awarded to replace EFC). 11% of all full-time undergraduates had no need and received non-need-based gift aid.

GIFT AID (NEED-BASED) *Total amount:* $37,028,177 (41% federal, 44% state, 14% institutional, 1% external sources). *Receiving aid:* Freshmen: 62% (1,320); all full-time undergraduates: 54% (4,806). *Average award:* Freshmen: $8818; Undergraduates: $8116. *Scholarships, grants, and awards:* Federal Pell, FSEOG, state, private, college/university gift aid from institutional funds.

GIFT AID (NON-NEED-BASED) *Total amount:* $11,575,381 (1% federal, 63% state, 30% institutional, 6% external sources). *Receiving aid:* Freshmen: 1% (20). Undergraduates: 2% (175). *Average award:* Freshmen: $3284. Undergraduates: $3258. *Scholarships, grants, and awards by category: Academic interests/achievement:* biological sciences, business, communication, education, engineering/technologies, English, general academic interests/achievements, home economics, mathematics, military science, physical sciences. *Creative arts/performance:* art/fine arts, cinema/film/broadcasting, journalism/publications, music, performing arts, theater/drama. *Special achievements/activities:* cheerleading/drum major, community service, memberships, religious involvement. *Special characteristics:* children and siblings of alumni, children of faculty/staff, children of union members/company employees, children with a deceased or disabled parent, ethnic background, handicapped students, religious affiliation. *Tuition waivers:* Full or partial for employees or children of employees, senior citizens. *ROTC:* Army.

LOANS *Student loans:* $45,059,778 (64% need-based, 36% non-need-based). 56% of past graduating class borrowed through all loan programs. *Average indebtedness per student:* $22,293. *Average need-based loan:* Freshmen: $3128. Undergraduates: $3935. *Parent loans:* $6,580,831 (38% need-based, 62% non-need-based). *Programs:* Federal Direct (Subsidized and Unsubsidized Stafford, PLUS), Perkins, private loans.

WORK-STUDY *Federal work-study:* Total amount: $338,465; jobs available. *State or other work-study/employment:* Total amount: $176,400 (25% need-based, 75% non-need-based). Part-time jobs available.

ATHLETIC AWARDS Total amount: $4,508,364 (43% need-based, 57% non-need-based).

APPLYING FOR FINANCIAL AID *Required financial aid forms:* FAFSA, institutional scholarship application form. *Financial aid deadline:* 5/1. *Notification date:* Continuous beginning 1/20. Students must reply by 5/1 or within 4 weeks of notification.

CONTACT Jennifer Buckles, Director of Financial Aid, The University of Tennessee at Chattanooga, 615 McCallie Avenue, Chattanooga, TN 37403-2598, 423-425-4677 or toll-free 800-882-6627. *Fax:* 423-425-2292. *E-mail:* jennifer-buckles@utc.edu. *Website:* http://www.utc.edu/.

THE UNIVERSITY OF TENNESSEE AT MARTIN
Martin, TN

Tuition & fees (TN res): $9236	Average undergraduate aid package: $11,501

ABOUT THE INSTITUTION State-supported, coed. *Awards:* bachelor's and master's degrees. 85 undergraduate majors. *Total enrollment:* 6,800. Undergraduates: 6,358. Freshmen: 1,052. Federal methodology is used as a basis for awarding need-based institutional aid.

UNDERGRADUATE EXPENSES for 2017–2018 *Application fee:* $30. *Tuition, state resident:* full-time $7818; part-time $299 per credit hour. *Tuition, nonresident:* full-time $13,578; part-time $539 per credit hour. *Required fees:* full-time $1418; $59 per credit hour. Full-time tuition and fees vary according to student level. Part-time tuition and fees vary according to course level and course load. *College room and board:* $5976; *Room only:* $2730. Room and board charges vary according to board plan and housing facility.

FRESHMAN FINANCIAL AID (Fall 2017, est.) 1,024 applied for aid; of those 79% were deemed to have need. 100% of freshmen with need received aid; of those 23% had need fully met. *Average percent of need met:* 42% (excluding resources awarded to replace EFC). *Average financial aid package:* $12,512 (excluding resources awarded to replace EFC). 10% of all full-time freshmen had no need and received non-need-based gift aid.

UNDERGRADUATE FINANCIAL AID (Fall 2017, est.) 4,568 applied for aid; of those 82% were deemed to have need. 99% of undergraduates with need received aid; of those 21% had need fully met. *Average percent of need met:* 45% (excluding resources awarded to replace EFC). *Average financial aid package:* $11,501 (excluding resources awarded to replace EFC). 6% of all full-time undergraduates had no need and received non-need-based gift aid.

GIFT AID (NEED-BASED) *Total amount:* $18,435,125 (74% federal, 24% state, 2% external sources). *Receiving aid:* Freshmen: 54% (561); all full-time undergraduates: 52% (2,551). *Average award:* Freshmen: $6748; Undergraduates: $6649. *Scholarships, grants, and awards:* Federal Pell, FSEOG, state, private, college/university gift aid from institutional funds.

GIFT AID (NON-NEED-BASED) *Total amount:* $16,516,943 (53% state, 26% institutional, 21% external sources). *Receiving aid:* Freshmen: 72% (752). Undergraduates: 51% (2,509). *Average award:* Freshmen: $1805. Undergraduates: $2065. *Scholarships, grants, and awards by category: Academic interests/achievement:* 234 awards ($248,624 total): agriculture, biological sciences, business, communication, computer science, education, engineering/technologies, English, foreign languages, general academic interests/achievements, health fields, home economics, humanities, international studies, mathematics, military science, physical sciences, premedicine, social sciences. *Creative arts/performance:* 9 awards ($13,400 total): art/fine arts, cinema/film/broadcasting, creative writing, journalism/publications, music, theater/drama. *Special achievements/activities:* 24 awards ($63,326 total): cheerleading/drum major, general special achievements/activities, junior miss, leadership, rodeo. *Special characteristics:* 220 awards ($539,270 total): adult students, children and siblings of alumni, children of educators, children of faculty/staff, children of public servants, children of union members/company employees, ethnic background, general special characteristics, local/state students, members of minority groups, out-of-state students, previous college experience. *Tuition waivers:* Full or partial for employees or children of employees, senior citizens. *ROTC:* Army.

LOANS *Student loans:* $22,038,420 (49% need-based, 51% non-need-based). 65% of past graduating class borrowed through all loan programs. *Average indebtedness per student:* $27,335. *Average need-based loan:* Freshmen: $3404. Undergraduates: $4315. *Parent loans:* $2,336,246 (100% non-need-based). *Programs:* Federal Direct (Subsidized and Unsubsidized Stafford, PLUS), Perkins.

WORK-STUDY *Federal work-study:* Total amount: $771,393; 308 jobs averaging $2505.

ATHLETIC AWARDS Total amount: $3,783,818 (100% non-need-based).

APPLYING FOR FINANCIAL AID *Required financial aid form:* FAFSA. *Financial aid deadline (priority):* 2/15. *Notification date:* Continuous beginning 3/15.

CONTACT Amy J. Mistric, Assistant Director of Financial Aid, The University of Tennessee at Martin, 205 Administration Building, Martin, TN 38238-1000, 731-881-7031 or toll-free 800-829-8861. *Fax:* 731-881-7036. *E-mail:* amistric@utm.edu. *Website:* http://www.utm.edu/.

THE UNIVERSITY OF TEXAS AT ARLINGTON
Arlington, TX

ABOUT THE INSTITUTION State-supported, coed. 66 undergraduate majors.

GIFT AID (NEED-BASED) *Scholarships, grants, and awards:* Federal Pell, FSEOG, state, private, college/university gift aid from institutional funds, United Negro College Fund.

GIFT AID (NON-NEED-BASED) *Scholarships, grants, and awards by category:* *Academic interests/achievement:* architecture, biological sciences, business, communication, computer science, education, engineering/technologies, English, foreign languages, general academic interests/achievements, health fields, humanities, international studies, mathematics, military science, physical sciences, social sciences. *Creative arts/performance:* journalism/publications, music, theater/drama. *Special achievements/activities:* cheerleading/drum major, community service, general special achievements/activities, leadership. *Special characteristics:* children with a deceased or disabled parent, first-generation college students, general special characteristics, handicapped students, public servants.

LOANS *Programs:* Federal Direct (Subsidized and Unsubsidized Stafford, PLUS), Perkins, state.

APPLYING FOR FINANCIAL AID *Required financial aid form:* FAFSA.

CONTACT Karen Krause, Director of Financial Aid, The University of Texas at Arlington, UTA Box 19199, Arlington, TX 76019, 817-272-3561. *Fax:* 817-272-3555. *E-mail:* kkrause@uta.edu.
Website: http://www.uta.edu/.

THE UNIVERSITY OF TEXAS AT AUSTIN
Austin, TX

Tuition & fees (TX res): $10,398	Average undergraduate aid package: $12,313

ABOUT THE INSTITUTION State-supported, coed. *Awards:* certificates, bachelor's, master's, and doctoral degrees. 164 undergraduate majors. *Total enrollment:* 51,525. Undergraduates: 40,492. Freshmen: 8,381. Federal methodology is used as a basis for awarding need-based institutional aid.

UNDERGRADUATE EXPENSES for 2017–2018 *Application fee:* $75. *Tuition, state resident:* full-time $10,398. *Tuition, nonresident:* full-time $36,744. Full-time tuition and fees vary according to course load and program. Part-time tuition and fees vary according to course load and program. *College room and board:* $10,070. Room and board charges vary according to housing facility. *Payment plan:* Guaranteed tuition.

FRESHMAN FINANCIAL AID (Fall 2016) 6,446 applied for aid; of those 53% were deemed to have need. 99% of freshmen with need received aid; of those 21% had need fully met. *Average percent of need met:* 70% (excluding resources awarded to replace EFC). *Average financial aid package:* $11,704 (excluding resources awarded to replace EFC). 1% of all full-time freshmen had no need and received non-need-based gift aid.

UNDERGRADUATE FINANCIAL AID (Fall 2016) 22,096 applied for aid; of those 68% were deemed to have need. 100% of undergraduates with need received aid; of those 23% had need fully met. *Average percent of need met:* 71% (excluding resources awarded to replace EFC). *Average financial aid package:* $12,313 (excluding resources awarded to replace EFC). 1% of all full-time undergraduates had no need and received non-need-based gift aid.

GIFT AID (NEED-BASED) *Total amount:* $179,950,508 (23% federal, 17% state, 39% institutional, 21% external sources). *Receiving aid:* Freshmen: 31% (2,681); all full-time undergraduates: 33% (12,067). *Average award:* Freshmen: $9596; Undergraduates: $9457. *Scholarships, grants, and awards:* Federal Pell, FSEOG, state, private, college/university gift aid from institutional funds.

GIFT AID (NON-NEED-BASED) *Total amount:* $7,001,110 (7% institutional, 93% external sources). *Receiving aid:* Freshmen: 17% (1,424). Undergraduates: 10% (3,618). *Average award:* Freshmen: $2227. Undergraduates: $2444. *Scholarships, grants, and awards by category:* *Academic interests/achievement:* general academic interests/achievements. *Creative arts/performance:* art/fine arts, general creative arts/performance, music, theater/drama. *Special achievements/activities:* leadership. *Special characteristics:* local/state students. *Tuition waivers:* Full or partial for employees or children of employees, senior citizens. *ROTC:* Army, Naval, Air Force.

LOANS *Student loans:* $97,574,199 (69% need-based, 31% non-need-based). 43% of past graduating class borrowed through all loan programs. *Average indebtedness per student:* $24,883. *Average need-based loan:* Freshmen: $3466. Undergraduates: $4725. *Parent loans:* $62,051,332 (24% need-based, 76% non-need-based). *Programs:* Federal Direct (Subsidized and Unsubsidized Stafford, PLUS), Perkins, state.

WORK-STUDY *Federal work-study:* jobs available. *State or other work-study/employment:* Total amount: $307,176 (100% need-based). Part-time jobs available.

ATHLETIC AWARDS Total amount: $3,176,857 (100% non-need-based).

APPLYING FOR FINANCIAL AID *Required financial aid forms:* FAFSA, institution's own form. *Financial aid deadline (priority):* 3/15. *Notification date:* Continuous beginning 3/15. Students must reply by 5/1 or within 3 weeks of notification.

CONTACT Ms. Diane Sprague, Director of Student Financial Services, The University of Texas at Austin, PO Box 7758, Student Services Building, Suite 3.214, Austin, TX 78713-7758, 512-475-6282. *Fax:* 512-475-6296. *E-mail:* ask@finaid.utexas.edu.
Website: http://www.utexas.edu/.

THE UNIVERSITY OF TEXAS AT DALLAS
Richardson, TX

Tuition & fees (TX res): $12,528	Average undergraduate aid package: $13,220

ABOUT THE INSTITUTION State-supported, coed. *Awards:* certificates, bachelor's, master's, and doctoral degrees. 48 undergraduate majors. *Total enrollment:* 27,642. Undergraduates: 18,388. Freshmen: 3,177. Both federal and institutional methodology are used as a basis for awarding need-based institutional aid.

UNDERGRADUATE EXPENSES for 2017–2018 *Application fee:* $50. *Tuition, state resident:* full-time $12,528; part-time $417.60 per credit hour. *Tuition, nonresident:* full-time $34,644; part-time $1155 per credit hour. Full-time tuition and fees vary according to course load and degree level. Part-time tuition and fees vary according to course load and degree level. *College room and board:* $11,112. Room and board charges vary according to board plan and housing facility. *Payment plan:* Guaranteed tuition.

FRESHMAN FINANCIAL AID (Fall 2016) 2,206 applied for aid; of those 70% were deemed to have need. 98% of freshmen with need received aid; of those 25% had need fully met. *Average percent of need met:* 71% (excluding resources awarded to replace EFC). *Average financial aid package:* $14,538 (excluding resources awarded to replace EFC). 22% of all full-time freshmen had no need and received non-need-based gift aid.

UNDERGRADUATE FINANCIAL AID (Fall 2016) 8,877 applied for aid; of those 84% were deemed to have need. 97% of undergraduates with need received aid; of those 17% had need fully met. *Average percent of need met:* 65% (excluding resources awarded to replace EFC). *Average financial aid package:* $13,220 (excluding resources awarded to replace EFC). 21% of all full-time undergraduates had no need and received non-need-based gift aid.

GIFT AID (NEED-BASED) *Total amount:* $95,002,566 (24% federal, 10% state, 63% institutional, 3% external sources). *Receiving aid:* Freshmen: 43% (1,354); all full-time undergraduates: 47% (6,590). *Average award:* Freshmen: $10,751; Undergraduates: $9183. *Scholarships, grants, and awards:* Federal Pell, FSEOG, state, private, college/university gift aid from institutional funds.

GIFT AID (NON-NEED-BASED) *Total amount:* $10,968,137 (89% institutional, 11% external sources). *Receiving aid:* Freshmen: 6% (184). Undergraduates: 3% (444). *Average award:* Freshmen: $13,975. Undergraduates: $11,953. *Scholarships, grants, and awards by category:* *Academic interests/achievement:* biological sciences, business, computer science, engineering/technologies, general academic interests/achievements, mathematics, physical sciences. *Special achievements/activities:* general special achievements/activities, leadership. *Special characteristics:* adult students, children of public servants, general special characteristics, handicapped students, international students, local/state students, members of minority groups, out-of-state students, public servants, veterans, veterans' children.

Tuition waivers: Full or partial for employees or children of employees, senior citizens. *ROTC:* Army cooperative, Air Force cooperative.

LOANS Student loans: $46,992,291 (78% need-based, 22% non-need-based). 33% of past graduating class borrowed through all loan programs. *Average indebtedness per student:* $23,565. *Average need-based loan:* Freshmen: $3363. Undergraduates: $4414. *Parent loans:* $4,807,933 (32% need-based, 68% non-need-based). *Programs:* Federal Direct (Subsidized and Unsubsidized Stafford, PLUS), Perkins, state, college/university.

WORK-STUDY Federal work-study: jobs available. *State or other work-study/employment:* Total amount: $65,992 (100% need-based). Part-time jobs available.

APPLYING FOR FINANCIAL AID Required financial aid form: FAFSA. *Financial aid deadline (priority):* 3/15. *Notification date:* Continuous beginning 3/15. Students must reply within 2 weeks of notification.

CONTACT M. Beth Tolan, Director of Financial Aid, The University of Texas at Dallas, 800 West Campbell Road, SS22, Richardson, TX 75080-3021, 972-883-2941 or toll-free 800-889-2443. *Fax:* 972-883-2947. *E-mail:* bnt031000@utdallas.edu. *Website:* http://www.utdallas.edu/.

THE UNIVERSITY OF TEXAS AT EL PASO
El Paso, TX

Tuition & fees (TX res): $7651	Average undergraduate aid package: $11,820

ABOUT THE INSTITUTION State-supported, coed. *Awards:* certificates, diplomas, bachelor's, master's, and doctoral degrees. 42 undergraduate majors. *Total enrollment:* 25,078. Undergraduates: 21,341. Freshmen: 3,066. Federal methodology is used as a basis for awarding need-based institutional aid.

UNDERGRADUATE EXPENSES for 2017–2018 Tuition, state resident: full-time $5931; part-time $192.71 per credit hour. *Tuition, nonresident:* full-time $19,676; part-time $655.85 per credit hour. *Required fees:* full-time $1720; $52 per credit hour or $126.40 per term. *College room and board:* $9495; *Room only:* $4914. *Payment plan:* Guaranteed tuition.

FRESHMAN FINANCIAL AID (Fall 2017, est.) 2,549 applied for aid; of those 79% were deemed to have need. *Average percent of need met:* 57% (excluding resources awarded to replace EFC). *Average financial aid package:* $11,631 (excluding resources awarded to replace EFC). 4% of all full-time freshmen had no need and received non-need-based gift aid.

UNDERGRADUATE FINANCIAL AID (Fall 2017, est.) 12,305 applied for aid; of those 84% were deemed to have need. *Average percent of need met:* 55% (excluding resources awarded to replace EFC). *Average financial aid package:* $11,820 (excluding resources awarded to replace EFC). 5% of all full-time undergraduates had no need and received non-need-based gift aid.

GIFT AID (NEED-BASED) Total amount: $53,685,022 (69% federal, 25% state, 6% institutional). *Receiving aid:* Freshmen: 56% (1,612); all full-time undergraduates: 64% (8,500). *Average award:* Freshmen: $9469; Undergraduates: $7873. *Scholarships, grants, and awards:* Federal Pell, FSEOG, state, private, college/university gift aid from institutional funds, United Negro College Fund, Federal Nursing.

GIFT AID (NON-NEED-BASED) Total amount: $6,153,329 (6% federal, 80% institutional, 14% external sources). *Receiving aid:* Freshmen: 9% (249). Undergraduates: 12% (1,623). *Average award:* Freshmen: $4222. Undergraduates: $4229. *Scholarships, grants, and awards by category:* Academic interests/achievement: biological sciences, business, communication, computer science, education, engineering/technologies, English, general academic interests/achievements, health fields, humanities, international studies, mathematics, military science, physical sciences. *Creative arts/performance:* applied art and design, art/fine arts, journalism/publications, music, performing arts, theater/drama. *Special achievements/activities:* cheerleading/drum major, leadership. *Special characteristics:* ethnic background, international students, local/state students, members of minority groups, out-of-state students. *ROTC:* Army.

LOANS Student loans: $62,147,295 (100% need-based). 65% of past graduating class borrowed through all loan programs. *Average indebtedness per student:* $22,938. *Average need-based loan:* Freshmen: $4312. Undergraduates: $6172. *Parent loans:* $1,138,951 (100% non-need-based). *Programs:* Federal Direct (Sub-

sidized and Unsubsidized Stafford, PLUS), Perkins, Federal Nursing, state, college/university.

WORK-STUDY Federal work-study: Total amount: $1,605,933; jobs available. *State or other work-study/employment:* Total amount: $424,981 (80% need-based, 20% non-need-based). Part-time jobs available.

ATHLETIC AWARDS Total amount: $4,526,803 (100% non-need-based).

APPLYING FOR FINANCIAL AID Required financial aid forms: FAFSA, institution's own form. *Financial aid deadline (priority):* 3/15. *Notification date:* Continuous beginning 3/30. Students must reply within 2 weeks of notification.

CONTACT Mr. Ron Williams, Interim Director of Financial Aid, The University of Texas at El Paso, 500 West University Avenue, El Paso, TX 79968-0001, 915-747-5204 or toll-free 877-74MINER. *Fax:* 915-747-5631. *E-mail:* rwilliams@utep.edu. *Website:* http://www.utep.edu/.

THE UNIVERSITY OF TEXAS AT SAN ANTONIO
San Antonio, TX

Tuition & fees (TX res): $9380	Average undergraduate aid package: $10,013

ABOUT THE INSTITUTION State-supported, coed. *Awards:* certificates, bachelor's, master's, and doctoral degrees. 71 undergraduate majors. *Total enrollment:* 30,768. Undergraduates: 26,444. Freshmen: 5,029. Federal methodology is used as a basis for awarding need-based institutional aid.

UNDERGRADUATE EXPENSES for 2017–2018 Application fee: $60. *Tuition, state resident:* full-time $6635; part-time $221.15 per credit hour. *Tuition, nonresident:* full-time $20,634; part-time $687.80 per credit hour. *Required fees:* full-time $2745. Full-time tuition and fees vary according to course load and degree level. Part-time tuition and fees vary according to course load and degree level. *College room and board:* $7190; *Room only:* $4490. Room and board charges vary according to board plan and housing facility. *Payment plan:* Guaranteed tuition.

FRESHMAN FINANCIAL AID (Fall 2016) 3,699 applied for aid; of those 78% were deemed to have need. 97% of freshmen with need received aid; of those 12% had need fully met. *Average percent of need met:* 59% (excluding resources awarded to replace EFC). *Average financial aid package:* $10,722 (excluding resources awarded to replace EFC). 5% of all full-time freshmen had no need and received non-need-based gift aid.

UNDERGRADUATE FINANCIAL AID (Fall 2016) 15,734 applied for aid; of those 85% were deemed to have need. 97% of undergraduates with need received aid; of those 9% had need fully met. *Average percent of need met:* 53% (excluding resources awarded to replace EFC). *Average financial aid package:* $10,013 (excluding resources awarded to replace EFC). 4% of all full-time undergraduates had no need and received non-need-based gift aid.

GIFT AID (NEED-BASED) Total amount: $95,651,806 (48% federal, 23% state, 22% institutional, 7% external sources). *Receiving aid:* Freshmen: 52% (2,232); all full-time undergraduates: 54% (10,885). *Average award:* Freshmen: $8927; Undergraduates: $7576. *Scholarships, grants, and awards:* Federal Pell, FSEOG, state, private, college/university gift aid from institutional funds.

GIFT AID (NON-NEED-BASED) Total amount: $5,235,790 (7% federal, 1% state, 71% institutional, 21% external sources). *Receiving aid:* Freshmen: 1% (27). Undergraduates: 1% (196). *Average award:* Freshmen: $3075. Undergraduates: $3734. *Scholarships, grants, and awards by category:* Academic interests/achievement: agriculture, area/ethnic studies, biological sciences, business, communication, computer science, education, engineering/technologies, English, foreign languages, general academic interests/achievements, humanities, international studies, mathematics, physical sciences, social sciences. *Creative arts/performance:* art/fine arts, creative writing, debating, music. *Special achievements/activities:* cheerleading/drum major, general special achievements/activities. *Special characteristics:* ethnic background, first-generation college students, general special characteristics, handicapped students, local/state students, members of minority groups, out-of-state students. *Tuition waivers:* Full or partial for employees or children of employees. *ROTC:* Army, Air Force.

LOANS Student loans: $87,978,811 (52% need-based, 48% non-need-based). 63% of past graduating class borrowed through all loan programs. *Average indebtedness per student:* $26,089. *Average need-based loan:* Freshmen: $3384. Undergraduates: $4169. **Parent loans:** $14,553,179 (100% non-need-based). **Programs:** Federal Direct (Subsidized and Unsubsidized Stafford, PLUS), Perkins, state, college/university.

WORK-STUDY *Federal work-study:* 379 jobs averaging $2586. **State or other work-study/employment:** Total amount: $1,239,176 (100% need-based). 926 part-time jobs averaging $2014.

ATHLETIC AWARDS Total amount: $5,145,798 (34% need-based, 66% non-need-based).

APPLYING FOR FINANCIAL AID *Required financial aid form:* FAFSA. *Financial aid deadline (priority):* 3/15. *Notification date:* Continuous beginning 3/1. Students must reply within 4 weeks of notification.

CONTACT One Stop Enrollment Center, The University of Texas at San Antonio, One UTSA Circle, San Antonio, TX 78249, 210-458-8000 or toll-free 800-669-0919. *Fax:* 210-458-4638. *E-mail:* onestop@utsa.edu.
Website: http://www.utsa.edu/.

THE UNIVERSITY OF TEXAS AT TYLER
Tyler, TX

Tuition & fees: N/R	Average undergraduate aid package: $7758

ABOUT THE INSTITUTION State-supported, coed. 41 undergraduate majors. Federal methodology is used as a basis for awarding need-based institutional aid.

FRESHMAN FINANCIAL AID (Fall 2016) 689 applied for aid; of those 99% were deemed to have need. 92% of freshmen with need received aid; of those 4% had need fully met. *Average percent of need met:* 40% (excluding resources awarded to replace EFC). *Average financial aid package:* $7321 (excluding resources awarded to replace EFC). 1% of all full-time freshmen had no need and received non-need-based gift aid.

UNDERGRADUATE FINANCIAL AID (Fall 2016) 3,721 applied for aid; of those 97% were deemed to have need. 95% of undergraduates with need received aid; of those 3% had need fully met. *Average percent of need met:* 37% (excluding resources awarded to replace EFC). *Average financial aid package:* $7758 (excluding resources awarded to replace EFC). 1% of all full-time undergraduates had no need and received non-need-based gift aid.

GIFT AID (NEED-BASED) *Total amount:* $22,497,903 (45% federal, 15% state, 28% institutional, 12% external sources). *Receiving aid:* Freshmen: 66% (535); all full-time undergraduates: 60% (2,858). *Average award:* Freshmen: $7015; Undergraduates: $6497. *Scholarships, grants, and awards:* Federal Pell, FSEOG, state, private, college/university gift aid from institutional funds, Texas Grants, Institutional Grants (Education Affordability Program).

GIFT AID (NON-NEED-BASED) *Total amount:* $277,639 (1% state, 45% institutional, 54% external sources). *Receiving aid:* Freshmen: 2% (20). Undergraduates: 1% (69). *Average award:* Freshmen: $1000. Undergraduates: $2704. *Scholarships, grants, and awards by category:* Academic interests/achievement: communication, engineering/technologies, general academic interests/achievements, health fields. Creative arts/performance: art/fine arts, music. Special characteristics: children of faculty/staff.

LOANS *Student loans:* $21,442,131 (93% need-based, 7% non-need-based). 51% of past graduating class borrowed through all loan programs. *Average indebtedness per student:* $17,916. *Average need-based loan:* Freshmen: $2255. Undergraduates: $3510. *Parent loans:* $4,329,670 (54% need-based, 46% non-need-based). *Programs:* Federal Direct (Subsidized and Unsubsidized Stafford, PLUS).

WORK-STUDY *Federal work-study:* jobs available. *State or other work-study/employment:* Total amount: $98,989 (81% need-based, 19% non-need-based). Part-time jobs available.

APPLYING FOR FINANCIAL AID *Required financial aid forms:* FAFSA, state aid form. *Financial aid deadline (priority):* 3/15. *Notification date:* Continuous beginning 4/15. Students must reply within 2 weeks of notification.

CONTACT Candice A. Lindsey, Assistant Vice President for Enrollment Management, Marketing and Customer Relations, The University of Texas at Tyler, 3900 University Boulevard, Tyler, TX 75799, 903-566-7221 or toll-free 800-UTTYLER. *Fax:* 903-566-7183. *E-mail:* enroll@uttyler.edu.
Website: http://www.uttyler.edu/.

THE UNIVERSITY OF TEXAS HEALTH SCIENCE CENTER AT HOUSTON
Houston, TX

ABOUT THE INSTITUTION State-supported, coed. 2 undergraduate majors.

GIFT AID (NEED-BASED) *Scholarships, grants, and awards:* Federal Pell, FSEOG, state, private, college/university gift aid from institutional funds.

GIFT AID (NON-NEED-BASED) *Scholarships, grants, and awards by category:* Academic interests/achievement: home economics.

LOANS *Programs:* Federal Direct (Subsidized and Unsubsidized Stafford, PLUS), Perkins, Federal Nursing, state, college/university, alternative loans.

CONTACT Ms. Araceli Alvarez, Director of Student Financial Services, The University of Texas Health Science Center at Houston, PO Box 20036, Houston, TX 77225, 713-500-3860. *Fax:* 713-500-3863. *E-mail:* araceli.alvarez@uth.tmc.edu. *Website:* http://www.uthouston.edu/.

THE UNIVERSITY OF TEXAS HEALTH SCIENCE CENTER AT SAN ANTONIO
San Antonio, TX

CONTACT Robert T. Lawson, Financial Aid Administrator, The University of Texas Health Science Center at San Antonio, 7703 Floyd Curl Drive, MSC 7708, San Antonio, TX 78284, 210-567-0025. *Fax:* 210-567-6643.
Website: http://www.uthscsa.edu/.

THE UNIVERSITY OF TEXAS MD ANDERSON CANCER CENTER
Houston, TX

CONTACT Financial Aid Office, The University of Texas MD Anderson Cancer Center, 1515 Holcombe Boulevard, Houston, TX 77030, 713-792-2121.
Website: http://www.mdanderson.org/education-and-research/.

THE UNIVERSITY OF TEXAS MEDICAL BRANCH
Galveston, TX

CONTACT Mrs. Carol A. Cromie, University Financial Aid Officer, The University of Texas Medical Branch, 301 University Boulevard, Galveston, TX 77555-1305, 409-772-9795. *Fax:* 409-772-4466. *E-mail:* cacromie@umtb.edu.
Website: http://www.utmb.edu/.

THE UNIVERSITY OF TEXAS OF THE PERMIAN BASIN
Odessa, TX

Tuition & fees (TX res): $7124	Average undergraduate aid package: $8486

ABOUT THE INSTITUTION State-supported, coed. **Awards:** certificates, bachelor's, and master's degrees. 31 undergraduate majors. **Total enrollment:** 7,022. Undergraduates: 6,065. Freshmen: 396. Federal methodology is used as a basis for awarding need-based institutional aid.

UNDERGRADUATE EXPENSES for 2018–2019 *Application fee:* $40. *Tuition, state resident:* full-time $5662; part-time $188.73 per credit hour. *Tuition, nonresident:* full-time $6812. *Required fees:* full-time $1462; $69.56 per credit hour. Full-time tuition and fees vary according to course load, degree level, and location. Part-time tuition and fees vary according to course load, degree level, and location. **College room and board:** $10,944; **Room only:** $7200. Room and board charges vary according to board plan and housing facility. **Payment plan:** Guaranteed tuition.

FRESHMAN FINANCIAL AID (Fall 2016) 366 applied for aid; of those 79% were deemed to have need. 97% of freshmen with need received aid; of those 24% had need fully met. **Average percent of need met:** 63% (excluding resources awarded to replace EFC). **Average financial aid package:** $9562 (excluding resources awarded to replace EFC). 47% of all full-time freshmen had no need and received non-need-based gift aid.

UNDERGRADUATE FINANCIAL AID (Fall 2016) 2,117 applied for aid; of those 85% were deemed to have need. 97% of undergraduates with need received aid; of those 18% had need fully met. **Average percent of need met:** 58% (excluding resources awarded to replace EFC). **Average financial aid package:** $8486 (excluding resources awarded to replace EFC). 20% of all full-time undergraduates had no need and received non-need-based gift aid.

GIFT AID (NEED-BASED) Total amount: $9,574,294 (73% federal, 22% state, 5% institutional). **Receiving aid:** Freshmen: 58% (262); all full-time undergraduates: 60% (1,524). **Average award:** Freshmen: $9750; Undergraduates: $8142. **Scholarships, grants, and awards:** Federal Pell, FSEOG, state, private, college/university gift aid from institutional funds.

GIFT AID (NON-NEED-BASED) Total amount: $642,192 (26% federal, 1% state, 73% institutional). **Receiving aid:** Freshmen: 40% (180). Undergraduates: 28% (696). **Average award:** Freshmen: $2423. Undergraduates: $2489.

LOANS Student loans: $11,837,415 (39% need-based, 61% non-need-based). 26% of past graduating class borrowed through all loan programs. **Average indebtedness per student:** $19,578. **Average need-based loan:** Freshmen: $3004. Undergraduates: $3950. **Parent loans:** $537,044 (100% non-need-based). **Programs:** Federal Direct (Subsidized and Unsubsidized Stafford, PLUS), state.

WORK-STUDY Federal work-study: jobs available. **State or other work-study/employment:** Total amount: $336,117 (100% need-based). Part-time jobs available.

ATHLETIC AWARDS Total amount: $1,051,703 (100% non-need-based).

APPLYING FOR FINANCIAL AID Required financial aid form: FAFSA. **Financial aid deadline:** Continuous. **Notification date:** Continuous beginning 3/15.

CONTACT Gary Byers, Interim Director of Financial Aid, The University of Texas of the Permian Basin, 4901 East University Boulevard, Odessa, TX 79762, 432-552-2620 or toll-free 866-552-UTPB. **Fax:** 432-552-2621. **E-mail:** byers_g@utpb.edu. **Website:** http://www.utpb.edu/.

THE UNIVERSITY OF TEXAS RIO GRANDE VALLEY
Edinburg, TX

Tuition & fees (TX res): $9055	Average undergraduate aid package: $9987

ABOUT THE INSTITUTION State-supported, coed. **Awards:** certificates, bachelor's, master's, and doctoral degrees. 53 undergraduate majors. **Total enrollment:** 27,708. Undergraduates: 24,634. Freshmen: 4,504. Federal methodology is used as a basis for awarding need-based institutional aid.

UNDERGRADUATE EXPENSES for 2017–2018 Tuition, state resident: full-time $7588; part-time $366.80 per credit hour. **Tuition, nonresident:** full-time $17,548; part-time $781.80 per credit hour. **Required fees:** full-time $1467; $184.93 per semester hour. Full-time tuition and fees vary according to course load, degree level, program, and student level. Part-time tuition and fees vary according to course load, degree level, program, and student level. **College room and board:** $7986. Room and board charges vary according to board plan, housing facility, and location. **Payment plan:** Guaranteed tuition.

FRESHMAN FINANCIAL AID (Fall 2016) 3,182 applied for aid; of those 94% were deemed to have need. 100% of freshmen with need received aid; of those 4% had need fully met. **Average percent of need met:** 84% (excluding resources awarded to replace EFC). **Average financial aid package:** $10,357 (excluding resources awarded to replace EFC). 4% of all full-time freshmen had no need and received non-need-based gift aid.

UNDERGRADUATE FINANCIAL AID (Fall 2016) 12,806 applied for aid; of those 95% were deemed to have need. 100% of undergraduates with need received aid; of those 5% had need fully met. **Average percent of need met:** 79% (excluding

resources awarded to replace EFC). **Average financial aid package:** $9987 (excluding resources awarded to replace EFC). 2% of all full-time undergraduates had no need and received non-need-based gift aid.

GIFT AID (NEED-BASED) Total amount: $125,902,182 (53% federal, 30% state, 15% institutional, 2% external sources). **Receiving aid:** Freshmen: 81% (2,932); all full-time undergraduates: 66% (11,753). **Average award:** Freshmen: $10,487; Undergraduates: $10,455. **Scholarships, grants, and awards:** Federal Pell, FSEOG, state, private, college/university gift aid from institutional funds.

GIFT AID (NON-NEED-BASED) Total amount: $2,507,493 (7% federal, 1% state, 79% institutional, 13% external sources). **Receiving aid:** Freshmen: 16. Undergraduates: 1% (90). **Average award:** Freshmen: $3492. Undergraduates: $3174. **Scholarships, grants, and awards by category:** Academic interests/achievement: 1,993 awards ($5,292,604 total): biological sciences, business, communication, computer science, education, engineering/technologies, English, general academic interests/achievements, health fields, mathematics, military science, premedicine, social sciences. Creative arts/performance: 182 awards ($164,458 total): art/fine arts, dance, journalism/publications, music, theater/drama. Special achievements/activities: 73 awards ($34,032 total): cheerleading/drum major, community service, general special achievements/activities, leadership, memberships. Special characteristics: 118 awards ($210,319 total): general special characteristics, international students, local/state students, out-of-state students, veterans, veterans' children. **ROTC:** Army.

LOANS Student loans: $46,149,866 (87% need-based, 13% non-need-based). 59% of past graduating class borrowed through all loan programs. **Average indebtedness per student:** $14,291. **Average need-based loan:** Freshmen: $2649. Undergraduates: $4392. **Parent loans:** $628,752 (7% need-based, 93% non-need-based). **Programs:** Federal Direct (Subsidized and Unsubsidized Stafford, PLUS), Perkins, state.

WORK-STUDY Federal work-study: 785 jobs averaging $2732. **State or other work-study/employment:** Total amount: $812,794 (100% need-based). 426 part-time jobs averaging $1908.

ATHLETIC AWARDS Total amount: $1,878,348 (25% need-based, 75% non-need-based).

APPLYING FOR FINANCIAL AID Required financial aid forms: FAFSA, state aid form. **Financial aid deadline (priority):** 3/15. **Notification date:** Continuous beginning 3/15. Students must reply by 7/1 or within 2 weeks of notification.

CONTACT Mr. Elias Ozuna, Director of Student Financial Services, The University of Texas Rio Grande Valley, 1201 West University Drive, Edinburg, TX 78539, 956-665-5372 or toll-free 888-882-4026 (in-state). **Fax:** 956-665-2396. **E-mail:** elias.ozuna@utrgv.edu. **Website:** http://www.utrgv.edu/.

THE UNIVERSITY OF THE ARTS
Philadelphia, PA

Tuition & fees: $44,780	Average undergraduate aid package: $29,310

ABOUT THE INSTITUTION Independent, coed. **Awards:** certificates, diplomas, bachelor's, and master's degrees. 22 undergraduate majors. **Total enrollment:** 1,860. Undergraduates: 1,681. Freshmen: 410. Federal methodology is used as a basis for awarding need-based institutional aid.

UNDERGRADUATE EXPENSES for 2018–2019 Application fee: $60. **Comprehensive fee:** $61,102 includes full-time tuition ($44,780) and room and board ($16,322). **College room only:** $10,540. Room and board charges vary according to board plan and housing facility. **Part-time tuition:** $1866 per credit hour. Part-time tuition and fees vary according to course load.

FRESHMAN FINANCIAL AID (Fall 2017, est.) 435 applied for aid; of those 100% were deemed to have need. 100% of freshmen with need received aid; of those 23% had need fully met. **Average percent of need met:** 57% (excluding resources awarded to replace EFC). **Average financial aid package:** $28,871 (excluding resources awarded to replace EFC). 17% of all full-time freshmen had no need and received non-need-based gift aid.

UNDERGRADUATE FINANCIAL AID (Fall 2017, est.) 1,305 applied for aid; of those 100% were deemed to have need. 100% of undergraduates with need received aid; of those 11% had need fully met. **Average percent of need met:** 62% (excluding resources awarded to replace EFC). **Average financial aid package:**

$29,310 (excluding resources awarded to replace EFC). 26% of all full-time undergraduates had no need and received non-need-based gift aid.

GIFT AID (NEED-BASED) Total amount: $7,208,120 (38% federal, 14% state, 39% institutional, 9% external sources). **Receiving aid:** Freshmen: 100% (435); all full-time undergraduates: 100% (1,301). **Average award:** Freshmen: $24,982; Undergraduates: $24,377. **Scholarships, grants, and awards:** Federal Pell, FSEOG, state, private, college/university gift aid from institutional funds.

GIFT AID (NON-NEED-BASED) Total amount: $5,378,724 (97% institutional, 3% external sources). **Receiving aid:** Freshmen: 99% (432). Undergraduates: 98% (1,282). **Average award:** Freshmen: $17,725. Undergraduates: $16,427. **Scholarships, grants, and awards by category:** Academic interests/achievement: general academic interests/achievements. Creative arts/performance: applied art and design, art/fine arts, creative writing, dance, music, performing arts, theater/drama. **Tuition waivers:** Full or partial for children of alumni, employees or children of employees.

LOANS Student loans: $16,552,677 (94% need-based, 6% non-need-based). 93% of past graduating class borrowed through all loan programs. Average indebtedness per student: $37,575. **Average need-based loan:** Freshmen: $2865. Undergraduates: $4103. **Parent loans:** $11,258,568 (98% need-based, 2% non-need-based). **Programs:** Federal Direct (Subsidized and Unsubsidized Stafford, PLUS), Perkins.

WORK-STUDY Federal work-study: Total amount: $1,424,320; jobs available. **State or other work-study/employment:** Part-time jobs available.

APPLYING FOR FINANCIAL AID Required financial aid forms: FAFSA, state aid form. **Financial aid deadline (priority):** 3/1. **Notification date:** Continuous beginning 2/15. Students must reply within 2 weeks of notification.

CONTACT Dr. Michelle H. Brown-Nevers, Associate Vice President, Student Financial Services, The University of the Arts, 320 South Broad Street, Philadelphia, PA 19102-4944, 800-616-ARTS Ext. 6170 or toll-free 800-616-ARTS. E-mail: finaid@uarts.edu.

Website: http://www.uarts.edu/.

UNIVERSITY OF THE CUMBERLANDS
Williamsburg, KY

CONTACT Mr. Steve Allen, Vice President for Student Financial Planning, University of the Cumberlands, 6190 College Station Drive, Williamsburg, KY 40769-1372, 606-549-2200 or toll-free 800-343-1609. Fax: 606-539-4515. E-mail: finplan@ucumberlands.edu.

Website: http://www.ucumberlands.edu/.

UNIVERSITY OF THE DISTRICT OF COLUMBIA
Washington, DC

ABOUT THE INSTITUTION District-supported, coed. 85 undergraduate majors.

GIFT AID (NEED-BASED) Scholarships, grants, and awards: Federal Pell, FSEOG, state, private, college/university gift aid from institutional funds, United Negro College Fund, Federal Nursing.

GIFT AID (NON-NEED-BASED) Scholarships, grants, and awards by category: Academic interests/achievement: agriculture, education, health fields. Special achievements/activities: general special achievements/activities, junior miss. Special characteristics: children of faculty/staff.

LOANS Programs: Federal Direct (Subsidized and Unsubsidized Stafford, PLUS), private loans.

WORK-STUDY Federal work-study: 32 jobs averaging $1325. **State or other work-study/employment:** Part-time jobs available.

APPLYING FOR FINANCIAL AID Required financial aid form: FAFSA.

CONTACT Mrs. Nailah Williams, Director of Financial Aid, University of the District of Columbia, 4200 Connecticut Avenue NW, Washington, DC 20008-1175, 202-274-5618. Fax: 202-274-6060. E-mail: finaid@udc.edu.

Website: http://www.udc.edu/.

UNIVERSITY OF THE INCARNATE WORD
San Antonio, TX

Tuition & fees: $29,990   **Average undergraduate aid package:** $20,142

ABOUT THE INSTITUTION Independent Roman Catholic, coed. **Awards:** diplomas, associate, bachelor's, master's, and doctoral degrees. 72 undergraduate majors. **Total enrollment:** 8,603. Undergraduates: 5,994. Freshmen: 758. Federal methodology is used as a basis for awarding need-based institutional aid.

UNDERGRADUATE EXPENSES for 2017–2018 Application fee: $20. **Comprehensive fee:** $42,426 includes full-time tuition ($27,900), mandatory fees ($2090), and room and board ($12,436). Full-time tuition and fees vary according to course load, degree level, location, program, and reciprocity agreements. Room and board charges vary according to board plan and housing facility. **Part-time tuition:** $915 per credit hour. Part-time tuition and fees vary according to course load, degree level, location, program, and reciprocity agreements.

FRESHMAN FINANCIAL AID (Fall 2016) 692 applied for aid; of those 93% were deemed to have need. 100% of freshmen with need received aid; of those 12% had need fully met. **Average percent of need met:** 62% (excluding resources awarded to replace EFC). **Average financial aid package:** $28,638 (excluding resources awarded to replace EFC). 6% of all full-time freshmen had no need and received non-need-based gift aid.

UNDERGRADUATE FINANCIAL AID (Fall 2016) 3,613 applied for aid; of those 93% were deemed to have need. 100% of undergraduates with need received aid; of those 8% had need fully met. **Average percent of need met:** 59% (excluding resources awarded to replace EFC). **Average financial aid package:** $20,142 (excluding resources awarded to replace EFC).

GIFT AID (NEED-BASED) Total amount: $59,153,019 (21% federal, 12% state, 65% institutional, 2% external sources). **Receiving aid:** Freshmen: 83% (641); all full-time undergraduates: 72% (3,284). **Average award:** Freshmen: $17,514; Undergraduates: $15,340. **Scholarships, grants, and awards:** Federal Pell, FSEOG, state, private, college/university gift aid from institutional funds, Federal Nursing.

GIFT AID (NON-NEED-BASED) Total amount: $25,140 (37% federal, 63% institutional). **Receiving aid:** Freshmen: 7% (52). Undergraduates: 4% (160). **Average award:** Freshmen: $9134. **Scholarships, grants, and awards by category:** Academic interests/achievement: general academic interests/achievements. Creative arts/performance: art/fine arts, music, theater/drama. Special achievements/activities: leadership, religious involvement. Special characteristics: children and siblings of alumni, children of faculty/staff. **Tuition waivers:** Full or partial for employees or children of employees, senior citizens. **ROTC:** Army cooperative.

LOANS Student loans: $32,814,894 (87% need-based, 13% non-need-based). 68% of past graduating class borrowed through all loan programs. Average indebtedness per student: $6271. **Average need-based loan:** Freshmen: $2614. Undergraduates: $3960. **Parent loans:** $9,920,621 (61% need-based, 39% non-need-based). **Programs:** Federal Direct (Subsidized and Unsubsidized Stafford, PLUS), Perkins, Federal Nursing, state, college/university, alternative loans.

WORK-STUDY Federal work-study: jobs available. **State or other work-study/employment:** Part-time jobs available.

ATHLETIC AWARDS Total amount: $9,036,513 (19% need-based, 81% non-need-based).

APPLYING FOR FINANCIAL AID Required financial aid form: FAFSA. **Financial aid deadline (priority):** 4/1. **Notification date:** Continuous beginning 11/1. Students must reply within 2 weeks of notification.

CONTACT Ms. Amy Carcanagues, Director of Financial Assistance, University of the Incarnate Word, 4301 Broadway, San Antonio, TX 78209, 210-829-6008 or toll-free 800-749-WORD. Fax: 210-283-5053. E-mail: finaid@uiwtx.edu.

Website: http://www.uiw.edu/.

UNIVERSITY OF THE OZARKS
Clarksville, AR

CONTACT Ms. Jana D. Hart, Director of Financial Aid, University of the Ozarks, 415 North College Avenue, Clarksville, AR 72830-2880, 479-979-1221 or toll-free 800-264-8636. Fax: 479-979-1417. E-mail: jhart@ozarks.edu.

Website: http://www.ozarks.edu/.

UNIVERSITY OF THE PACIFIC
Stockton, CA

Tuition & fees: $46,346	Average undergraduate aid package: $34,876

ABOUT THE INSTITUTION Independent, coed. *Awards:* bachelor's, master's, and doctoral degrees. 54 undergraduate majors. *Total enrollment:* 6,255. Undergraduates: 3,548. Freshmen: 899. Federal methodology is used as a basis for awarding need-based institutional aid.

UNDERGRADUATE EXPENSES for 2017–2018 *Application fee:* $35. *Comprehensive fee:* $59,702 includes full-time tuition ($45,786), mandatory fees ($560), and room and board ($13,356). Room and board charges vary according to board plan and housing facility. *Part-time tuition:* $1579 per credit hour. Part-time tuition and fees vary according to course load.

FRESHMAN FINANCIAL AID (Fall 2017, est.) 776 applied for aid; of those 89% were deemed to have need. 100% of freshmen with need received aid; of those 15% had need fully met. *Average percent of need met:* 67% (excluding resources awarded to replace EFC). *Average financial aid package:* $37,952 (excluding resources awarded to replace EFC). 19% of all full-time freshmen had no need and received non-need-based gift aid.

UNDERGRADUATE FINANCIAL AID (Fall 2017, est.) 2,654 applied for aid; of those 93% were deemed to have need. 100% of undergraduates with need received aid; of those 12% had need fully met. *Average percent of need met:* 56% (excluding resources awarded to replace EFC). *Average financial aid package:* $34,876 (excluding resources awarded to replace EFC). 16% of all full-time undergraduates had no need and received non-need-based gift aid.

GIFT AID (NEED-BASED) *Total amount:* $67,745,121 (10% federal, 16% state, 74% institutional). *Receiving aid:* Freshmen: 77% (686); all full-time undergraduates: 69% (2,386). *Average award:* Freshmen: $33,112; Undergraduates: $28,134. *Scholarships, grants, and awards:* Federal Pell, FSEOG, state, private, college/university gift aid from institutional funds.

GIFT AID (NON-NEED-BASED) *Total amount:* $8,013,995 (100% institutional). *Average award:* Freshmen: $16,381. Undergraduates: $14,033. *Scholarships, grants, and awards by category:* Academic interests/achievement: general academic interests/achievements. Creative arts/performance: debating, music. Special achievements/activities: leadership, religious involvement. Special characteristics: religious affiliation. *Tuition waivers:* Full or partial for employees or children of employees. *ROTC:* Air Force cooperative.

LOANS *Student loans:* $22,046,438 (92% need-based, 8% non-need-based). 67% of past graduating class borrowed through all loan programs. *Average indebtedness per student:* $28,759. *Average need-based loan:* Freshmen: $5729. Undergraduates: $8596. *Parent loans:* $55,013,581 (88% need-based, 12% non-need-based). *Programs:* Federal Direct (Subsidized and Unsubsidized Stafford, PLUS), Perkins, alternative loans.

WORK-STUDY *Federal work-study:* Total amount: $2,101,017; jobs available.

ATHLETIC AWARDS Total amount: $8,945,093 (30% need-based, 70% non-need-based).

APPLYING FOR FINANCIAL AID *Required financial aid form:* FAFSA. *Financial aid deadline (priority):* 2/15. *Notification date:* Continuous beginning 3/1.

CONTACT Lynn Fox, Director of Financial Aid, University of the Pacific, 3601 Pacific Avenue, Stockton, CA 95211-0197, 209-946-2421.
Website: http://www.pacific.edu/.

UNIVERSITY OF THE PEOPLE
Pasadena, CA

CONTACT Financial Aid Office, University of the People, 225 South Lake Avenue, Suite 300, Pasadena, CA 91101.
Website: http://www.uopeople.edu/.

UNIVERSITY OF THE POTOMAC
Washington, DC

CONTACT Phyllis Crews, Financial Aid Counselor, University of the Potomac, 4000 Chesapeake Street NW, Washington, DC 20016, 202-686-0876 or toll-free 888-686-0876. *Fax:* 202-686-0818. *E-mail:* pcrews@potomac.edu.
Website: http://www.potomac.edu/.

UNIVERSITY OF THE SACRED HEART
San Juan, PR

CONTACT Ms. Maria Torres, Director of Financial Aid, University of the Sacred Heart, PO Box 12383, San Juan, PR 00914-0383, 787-728-1515 Ext. 3605.
Website: http://www.sagrado.edu/.

UNIVERSITY OF THE SCIENCES
Philadelphia, PA

ABOUT THE INSTITUTION Independent, coed. 18 undergraduate majors.

GIFT AID (NEED-BASED) *Scholarships, grants, and awards:* Federal Pell, FSEOG, state, private, college/university gift aid from institutional funds.

GIFT AID (NON-NEED-BASED) *Scholarships, grants, and awards by category:* Academic interests/achievement: general academic interests/achievements. Special achievements/activities: general special achievements/activities.

LOANS *Programs:* Federal Direct (Subsidized and Unsubsidized Stafford, PLUS), Perkins, college/university, Health Professions Student Loans (HPSL), Loans for Disadvantaged Students.

APPLYING FOR FINANCIAL AID *Required financial aid form:* FAFSA.

CONTACT Ms. Pamela Ramanathan, Director of Financial Aid, University of the Sciences, 600 South 43rd Street, Philadelphia, PA 19104, 215-596-8894 or toll-free 888-996-8747. *Fax:* 215-596-8554. *E-mail:* p.ramanathan@usciences.edu.
Website: http://www.usciences.edu/.

UNIVERSITY OF THE SOUTHWEST
Hobbs, NM

Tuition & fees: N/R	Average undergraduate aid package: N/A

ABOUT THE INSTITUTION Independent Christian, coed. *Awards:* bachelor's and master's degrees. 20 undergraduate majors. *Total enrollment:* 1,059. Undergraduates: 450. Freshmen: 100. Both federal and institutional methodology are used as a basis for awarding need-based institutional aid.

FRESHMAN FINANCIAL AID (Fall 2016) 96 applied for aid; of those 100% were deemed to have need.

GIFT AID (NEED-BASED) *Total amount:* $1,496,346 (85% federal, 2% state, 13% external sources). *Scholarships, grants, and awards:* Federal Pell, FSEOG, state, private, college/university gift aid from institutional funds.

GIFT AID (NON-NEED-BASED) *Scholarships, grants, and awards by category:* Academic interests/achievement: biological sciences, business, education, English, general academic interests/achievements, humanities, mathematics, physical sciences, premedicine, religion/biblical studies, social sciences. Special achievements/activities: community service, general special achievements/activities, leadership, religious involvement. Special characteristics: adult students, children of faculty/staff.

LOANS *Student loans:* $1,847,017 (100% need-based). *Parent loans:* $562,591 (100% need-based). *Programs:* Federal Direct (Subsidized and Unsubsidized Stafford, PLUS).

WORK-STUDY *Federal work-study:* 36 jobs averaging $1500. *State or other work-study/employment:* Total amount: $21,752 (100% need-based). 17 part-time jobs averaging $1500.

ATHLETIC AWARDS Total amount: $2,480,716 (100% need-based).

APPLYING FOR FINANCIAL AID *Required financial aid form:* FAFSA. *Financial aid deadline:* Continuous. *Notification date:* Continuous beginning 4/1. Students must reply within 2 weeks of notification.

CONTACT Dawny Kringel, Director of Financial Aid, University of the Southwest, 6610 North Lovington Highway, Hobbs, NM 88240-9129, 575-492-2114 or toll-free 800-530-4400. *Fax:* 575-392-6006. *E-mail:* dkringel@usw.edu. *Website:* http://www.usw.edu/.

UNIVERSITY OF THE VIRGIN ISLANDS
St. Thomas, VI

CONTACT Mavis M. Gilchrist, Director of Financial Aid, University of the Virgin Islands, RR #2, Box 10,000, Kingshill, St. Thomas, VI 00850, 340-692-4186 or toll-free 877-468-6884. *Fax:* 340-692-4145. *E-mail:* mgilchr@uvi.edu. *Website:* http://www.uvi.edu/.

UNIVERSITY OF THE WEST
Rosemead, CA

CONTACT Jamie Johnston, Financial Aid Officer, University of the West, 1409 Walnut Grove Avenue, Rosemead, CA 91770, 626-571-8811 Ext. 122. *Fax:* 626-571-1413. *E-mail:* jamiej@uwest.edu. *Website:* http://www.uwest.edu/.

THE UNIVERSITY OF TOLEDO
Toledo, OH

Tuition & fees (OH res): $9240	Average undergraduate aid package: $10,938

ABOUT THE INSTITUTION State-supported, coed. *Awards:* certificates, bachelor's, master's, and doctoral degrees. 88 undergraduate majors. *Total enrollment:* 20,579. Undergraduates: 16,194. Freshmen: 3,228. Federal methodology is used as a basis for awarding need-based institutional aid.

UNDERGRADUATE EXPENSES for 2017–2018 *Application fee:* $40. *Tuition, state resident:* full-time $8050; part-time $335.49 per credit hour. *Tuition, nonresident:* full-time $17,388; part-time $724.57 per credit hour. *Required fees:* full-time $1190; $49.60 per credit hour. Full-time tuition and fees vary according to course load, program, reciprocity agreements, and student level. Part-time tuition and fees vary according to course load, program, reciprocity agreements, and student level. *College room and board:* $11,151; *Room only:* $7471. Room and board charges vary according to board plan and housing facility.

FRESHMAN FINANCIAL AID (Fall 2017, est.) 2,926 applied for aid; of those 78% were deemed to have need. 100% of freshmen with need received aid; of those 9% had need fully met. *Average percent of need met:* 59% (excluding resources awarded to replace EFC). *Average financial aid package:* $10,896 (excluding resources awarded to replace EFC). 21% of all full-time freshmen had no need and received non-need-based gift aid.

UNDERGRADUATE FINANCIAL AID (Fall 2017, est.) 10,240 applied for aid; of those 80% were deemed to have need. 99% of undergraduates with need received aid; of those 9% had need fully met. *Average percent of need met:* 57% (excluding resources awarded to replace EFC). *Average financial aid package:* $10,938 (excluding resources awarded to replace EFC). 23% of all full-time undergraduates had no need and received non-need-based gift aid.

GIFT AID (NEED-BASED) *Total amount:* $67,966,910 (35% federal, 8% state, 53% institutional, 4% external sources). *Receiving aid:* Freshmen: 70% (2,217); all full-time undergraduates: 59% (7,618). *Average award:* Freshmen: $8827; Undergraduates: $8810. *Scholarships, grants, and awards:* Federal Pell, FSEOG, state, private, college/university gift aid from institutional funds, TEACH Grants.

GIFT AID (NON-NEED-BASED) *Total amount:* $30,974,742 (1% federal, 2% state, 61% institutional, 36% external sources). *Receiving aid:* Freshmen: 17% (545). Undergraduates: 12% (1,556). *Average award:* Freshmen: $5515. Undergraduates: $5995. *Scholarships, grants, and awards by category: Academic interests/ achievement:* biological sciences, business, communication, computer science, education, engineering/technologies, English, foreign languages, general academic interests/ achievements, health fields, humanities, international studies, library science, mathematics, military science, physical sciences, premedicine, religion/biblical studies, social

sciences. *Creative arts/performance:* art/fine arts, cinema/film/broadcasting, creative writing, general creative arts/performance, music, performing arts, theater/drama. *Special achievements/activities:* cheerleading/drum major, community service, general special achievements/activities, hobbies/interests, leadership, memberships, religious involvement. *Special characteristics:* adult students, children and siblings of alumni, children of faculty/staff, children of public servants, children of union members/ company employees, ethnic background, first-generation college students, general special characteristics, handicapped students, international students, members of minority groups, out-of-state students, previous college experience, public servants, religious affiliation, siblings of current students, veterans, veterans' children. *Tuition waivers:* Full or partial for employees or children of employees. *ROTC:* Army, Air Force cooperative.

LOANS *Student loans:* $58,002,509 (86% need-based, 14% non-need-based). 72% of past graduating class borrowed through all loan programs. *Average indebtedness per student:* $28,260. *Average need-based loan:* Freshmen: $3482. Undergraduates: $4106. *Parent loans:* $18,024,754 (86% need-based, 14% non-need-based). *Programs:* Federal Direct (Subsidized and Unsubsidized Stafford, PLUS), Perkins, state, college/university, private loans, Primary Care Loans.

WORK-STUDY *Federal work-study:* Total amount: $1,117,653; jobs available.

ATHLETIC AWARDS Total amount: $7,251,196 (38% need-based, 62% non-need-based).

APPLYING FOR FINANCIAL AID *Required financial aid form:* FAFSA. *Financial aid deadline (priority):* 3/1. *Notification date:* Continuous beginning 4/1. Students must reply within 8 weeks of notification.

CONTACT Stephen Schissler, Director of Financial Aid, The University of Toledo, 2801 West Bancroft Street, MS-314, Toledo, OH 43606, 419-530-5812 or toll-free 800-5TOLEDO. *Fax:* 419-530-5835. *E-mail:* stephen.schissler@utoledo.edu. *Website:* http://www.utoledo.edu/.

THE UNIVERSITY OF TULSA
Tulsa, OK

Tuition & fees: $41,024	Average undergraduate aid package: $31,580

ABOUT THE INSTITUTION Independent, coed. *Awards:* certificates, bachelor's, master's, and doctoral degrees. 70 undergraduate majors. *Total enrollment:* 4,433. Undergraduates: 3,343. Freshmen: 743. Federal methodology is used as a basis for awarding need-based institutional aid.

UNDERGRADUATE EXPENSES for 2018–2019 *Application fee:* $50. *One-time required fee:* $485. *Comprehensive fee:* $52,140 includes full-time tuition ($40,484), mandatory fees ($540), and room and board ($11,116). *College room only:* $6394. Full-time tuition and fees vary according to course load and program. Room and board charges vary according to board plan and housing facility. *Part-time tuition:* $1453 per credit hour. Part-time tuition and fees vary according to course load and program.

FRESHMAN FINANCIAL AID (Fall 2017, est.) 580 applied for aid; of those 78% were deemed to have need. 100% of freshmen with need received aid; of those 38% had need fully met. *Average percent of need met:* 88% (excluding resources awarded to replace EFC). *Average financial aid package:* $34,596 (excluding resources awarded to replace EFC). 32% of all full-time freshmen had no need and received non-need-based gift aid.

UNDERGRADUATE FINANCIAL AID (Fall 2017, est.) 1,752 applied for aid; of those 86% were deemed to have need. 100% of undergraduates with need received aid; of those 35% had need fully met. *Average percent of need met:* 82% (excluding resources awarded to replace EFC). *Average financial aid package:* $31,580 (excluding resources awarded to replace EFC). 39% of all full-time undergraduates had no need and received non-need-based gift aid.

GIFT AID (NEED-BASED) *Total amount:* $9,231,911 (32% federal, 14% state, 48% institutional, 6% external sources). *Receiving aid:* Freshmen: 56% (417); all full-time undergraduates: 42% (1,346). *Average award:* Freshmen: $8034; Undergraduates: $7945. *Scholarships, grants, and awards:* Federal Pell, FSEOG, state, private, college/university gift aid from institutional funds.

GIFT AID (NON-NEED-BASED) *Total amount:* $58,387,967 (2% state, 96% institutional, 2% external sources). *Receiving aid:* Freshmen: 61% (452). Undergraduates: 44% (1,420). *Average award:* Freshmen: $21,860. Undergraduates: $21,531. *Scholarships, grants, and awards by category: Academic interests/ achievement:* 1,934 awards ($40,825,414 total): biological sciences, business, communication, computer science, education, engineering/technologies, English, foreign languages, general academic interests/achievements, health fields, international studies, mathematics, physical sciences, premedicine, religion/biblical studies, social sciences. *Creative arts/performance:* 265 awards ($2,722,578 total): art/fine arts, music, performing arts, theater/drama. *Special achievements/activities:* cheerleading/drum major, community service, leadership. *Special characteristics:* children and siblings of alumni, children of faculty/staff, relatives of clergy, religious affiliation, siblings of current students. *Tuition waivers:* Full or partial for employees or children of employees. *ROTC:* Air Force cooperative.

LOANS *Student loans:* $10,090,682 (47% need-based, 53% non-need-based). 50% of past graduating class borrowed through all loan programs. *Average indebtedness per student:* $34,869. *Average need-based loan:* Freshmen: $5698. Undergraduates: $5820. *Parent loans:* $6,544,032 (100% non-need-based). *Programs:* Federal Direct (Subsidized and Unsubsidized Stafford, PLUS), Perkins.

WORK-STUDY *Federal work-study:* Total amount: $874,803; 335 jobs averaging $2481. *State or other work-study/employment:* Part-time jobs available.

ATHLETIC AWARDS Total amount: $12,952,939 (100% non-need-based).

APPLYING FOR FINANCIAL AID *Required financial aid form:* FAFSA. *Financial aid deadline (priority):* 1/15. *Notification date:* Continuous beginning 2/1. Students must reply by 5/1 or within 2 weeks of notification.

CONTACT Ms. Vicki Hendrickson, Director of Student Financial Services, The University of Tulsa, 800 South Tucker Drive, Tulsa, OK 74104, 918-631-2526 or toll-free 800-331-3050. *Fax:* 918-631-5105. *E-mail:* finaid@utulsa.edu. *Website:* http://www.utulsa.edu/.

UNIVERSITY OF UTAH
Salt Lake City, UT

Tuition & fees (UT res): $8824	Average undergraduate aid package: $21,290

ABOUT THE INSTITUTION State-supported, coed. *Awards:* certificates, bachelor's, master's, and doctoral degrees. 85 undergraduate majors. *Total enrollment:* 32,760. Undergraduates: 24,635. Freshmen: 4,119. Federal methodology is used as a basis for awarding need-based institutional aid.

UNDERGRADUATE EXPENSES for 2017–2018 *Application fee:* $55. *Tuition, state resident:* full-time $7697; part-time $216.22 per credit hour. *Tuition, nonresident:* full-time $26,940; part-time $743.38 per credit hour. *Required fees:* full-time $1127; $464.11 per term. Full-time tuition and fees vary according to course level, course load, degree level, location, program, and student level. Part-time tuition and fees vary according to course level, course load, degree level, location, program, and student level. *College room and board:* $9867; *Room only:* $5118. Room and board charges vary according to board plan, housing facility, and location.

FRESHMAN FINANCIAL AID (Fall 2017, est.) 2,880 applied for aid; of those 67% were deemed to have need. 98% of freshmen with need received aid; of those 20% had need fully met. *Average percent of need met:* 66% (excluding resources awarded to replace EFC). *Average financial aid package:* $22,575 (excluding resources awarded to replace EFC). 56% of all full-time freshmen had no need and received non-need-based gift aid.

UNDERGRADUATE FINANCIAL AID (Fall 2017, est.) 10,810 applied for aid; of those 80% were deemed to have need. 95% of undergraduates with need received aid; of those 15% had need fully met. *Average percent of need met:* 65% (excluding resources awarded to replace EFC). *Average financial aid package:* $21,290 (excluding resources awarded to replace EFC). 29% of all full-time undergraduates had no need and received non-need-based gift aid.

GIFT AID (NEED-BASED) *Total amount:* $34,292,523 (89% federal, 2% state, 5% institutional, 4% external sources). *Receiving aid:* Freshmen: 44% (1,677); all full-time undergraduates: 39% (6,999). *Average award:* Freshmen: $7754; Undergraduates: $7178. *Scholarships, grants, and awards:* Federal Pell, FSEOG, state, private, college/university gift aid from institutional funds, Federal Nursing.

GIFT AID (NON-NEED-BASED) *Total amount:* $60,917,345 (7% state, 67% institutional, 26% external sources). *Receiving aid:* Freshmen: 7% (251). Undergraduates: 3% (559). *Average award:* Freshmen: $7276. Undergraduates: $6410. *Scholarships, grants, and awards by category:* Academic interests/achievement: architecture, area/ethnic studies, biological sciences, business, communication, computer science, education, engineering/technologies, English, foreign languages, general academic interests/achievements, health fields, humanities, international studies, mathematics, military science, physical sciences, social sciences. *Creative arts/performance:*

art/fine arts, cinema/film/broadcasting, creative writing, dance, journalism/publications, music, performing arts, theater/drama. *Special achievements/activities:* cheerleading/drum major, general special achievements/activities, leadership. *Special characteristics:* children of faculty/staff, children of public servants, children with a deceased or disabled parent, ethnic background, first-generation college students, handicapped students, out-of-state students, spouses of deceased or disabled public servants, veterans' children. *Tuition waivers:* Full or partial for employees or children of employees, senior citizens. *ROTC:* Army, Naval, Air Force.

LOANS *Student loans:* $75,528,559 (91% need-based, 9% non-need-based). 39% of past graduating class borrowed through all loan programs. *Average indebtedness per student:* $21,188. *Average need-based loan:* Freshmen: $3305. Undergraduates: $4184. *Parent loans:* $5,255,661 (100% need-based). *Programs:* Federal Direct (Subsidized and Unsubsidized Stafford, PLUS), Perkins, Federal Nursing, state, college/university.

WORK-STUDY *Federal work-study:* Total amount: $1,369,886; 350 jobs averaging $3999. *State or other work-study/employment:* Part-time jobs available.

ATHLETIC AWARDS Total amount: $10,519,814 (100% non-need-based).

APPLYING FOR FINANCIAL AID *Required financial aid form:* FAFSA. *Financial aid deadline (priority):* 2/1. *Notification date:* Continuous beginning 3/1. Students must reply within 6 weeks of notification.

CONTACT Karen Henriquez, Office of Financial Aid, University of Utah, 201 South 1460 East, Room 105, Salt Lake City, UT 84112-9055, 801-581-6211 or toll-free 800-685-8856. *Fax:* 801-585-6350. *E-mail:* financialaid@sa.utah.edu. *Website:* http://www.utah.edu/.

UNIVERSITY OF VALLEY FORGE
Phoenixville, PA

ABOUT THE INSTITUTION Independent Assemblies of God, coed. *Awards:* associate, bachelor's, and master's degrees. 28 undergraduate majors. *Total enrollment:* 764. Undergraduates: 704. Freshmen: 81.

GIFT AID (NEED-BASED) *Scholarships, grants, and awards:* Federal Pell, FSEOG, state, private, college/university gift aid from institutional funds.

GIFT AID (NON-NEED-BASED) *Scholarships, grants, and awards by category:* Academic interests/achievement: general academic interests/achievements. *Creative arts/performance:* art/fine arts, music. *Special achievements/activities:* community service, general special achievements/activities, leadership, religious involvement. *Special characteristics:* children of current students, children of faculty/staff, general special characteristics, local/state students, married students, parents of current students, relatives of clergy, siblings of current students, spouses of current students.

LOANS *Programs:* Federal Direct (Subsidized and Unsubsidized Stafford, PLUS), Perkins.

WORK-STUDY *Federal work-study:* 18 jobs averaging $2671.

APPLYING FOR FINANCIAL AID *Required financial aid form:* FAFSA.

CONTACT Mrs. Linda Stein, Director of Financial Aid, University of Valley Forge, 1401 Charlestown Road, Phoenixville, PA 19460-2399, 610-917-1416 or toll-free 800-432-8322. *Fax:* 610-917-2069. *E-mail:* llstein@vfcc.edu. *Website:* http://www.valleyforge.edu/.

UNIVERSITY OF VERMONT
Burlington, VT

Tuition & fees (VT res): $17,740	Average undergraduate aid package: $25,251

ABOUT THE INSTITUTION State-supported, coed. *Awards:* certificates, bachelor's, master's, and doctoral degrees. 96 undergraduate majors. *Total enrollment:* 13,340. Undergraduates: 11,339. Freshmen: 2,642. Federal methodology is used as a basis for awarding need-based institutional aid.

UNDERGRADUATE EXPENSES for 2017–2018 *Application fee:* $55. *Tuition, state resident:* full-time $15,504; part-time $646 per credit hour. *Tuition, nonresident:* full-time $39,120; part-time $1630 per credit hour. *Required fees:* full-time $2236. Full-time tuition and fees vary according to reciprocity agreements. Part-time tuition and fees vary according to course load and reciprocity agreements.

College room and board: $12,022; **Room only:** $7900. Room and board charges vary according to board plan and housing facility.
FRESHMAN FINANCIAL AID (Fall 2016) 2,044 applied for aid; of those 74% were deemed to have need. 100% of freshmen with need received aid; of those 18% had need fully met. **Average percent of need met:** 71% (excluding resources awarded to replace EFC). **Average financial aid package:** $26,574 (excluding resources awarded to replace EFC). 33% of all full-time freshmen had no need and received non-need-based gift aid.
UNDERGRADUATE FINANCIAL AID (Fall 2016) 6,734 applied for aid; of those 80% were deemed to have need. 99% of undergraduates with need received aid; of those 16% had need fully met. **Average percent of need met:** 66% (excluding resources awarded to replace EFC). **Average financial aid package:** $25,251 (excluding resources awarded to replace EFC). 31% of all full-time undergraduates had no need and received non-need-based gift aid.
GIFT AID (NEED-BASED) Total amount: $83,610,597 (11% federal, 5% state, 80% institutional, 4% external sources). **Receiving aid:** Freshmen: 60% (1,492); all full-time undergraduates: 52% (5,185). **Average award:** Freshmen: $18,236; Undergraduates: $16,278. **Scholarships, grants, and awards:** Federal Pell, FSEOG, state, private, college/university gift aid from institutional funds, Federal Nursing.
GIFT AID (NON-NEED-BASED) Total amount: $36,811,258 (2% federal, 1% state, 88% institutional, 9% external sources). **Receiving aid:** Freshmen: 8% (209). Undergraduates: 6% (598). **Average award:** Freshmen: $14,650. Undergraduates: $12,751. **Scholarships, grants, and awards by category:** Academic interests/achievement: agriculture, area/ethnic studies, business, computer science, education, engineering/technologies, English, foreign languages, general academic interests/achievements, health fields, home economics, humanities, international studies, mathematics, military science, physical sciences, premedicine, social sciences. Creative arts/performance: debating, music, theater/drama. Special achievements/activities: community service, leadership, memberships. Special characteristics: adult students, ethnic background, first-generation college students. **Tuition waivers:** Full or partial for employees or children of employees. **ROTC:** Army.
LOANS Student loans: $48,488,654 (34% need-based, 66% non-need-based). 55% of past graduating class borrowed through all loan programs. Average indebtedness per student: $28,894. **Average need-based loan:** Freshmen: $3556. Undergraduates: $4562. **Parent loans:** $21,873,485 (100% non-need-based). **Programs:** Federal Direct (Subsidized and Unsubsidized Stafford, PLUS), Perkins, Federal Nursing, college/university.
WORK-STUDY Federal work-study: 1,412 jobs averaging $1600.
ATHLETIC AWARDS Total amount: $7,213,623 (23% need-based, 77% non-need-based).
APPLYING FOR FINANCIAL AID Required financial aid form: FAFSA. Financial aid deadline (priority): 2/1. **Notification date:** Continuous beginning 3/15. Students must reply within 4 weeks of notification.
CONTACT Office of Student Financial Services, University of Vermont, 223 Waterman Building, Burlington, VT 05405-0160, 802-656-5700. Fax: 802-656-4076. E-mail: sfs@uvm.edu.
Website: http://www.uvm.edu/.

UNIVERSITY OF VIRGINIA
Charlottesville, VA

Tuition & fees (VA res): $16,146	Average undergraduate aid package: $27,936

ABOUT THE INSTITUTION State-supported, coed. **Awards:** certificates, bachelor's, master's, and doctoral degrees. 50 undergraduate majors. **Total enrollment:** 24,360. Undergraduates: 16,655. Freshmen: 3,788. Both federal and institutional methodology are used as a basis for awarding need-based institutional aid.
UNDERGRADUATE EXPENSES for 2017–2018 Application fee: $60. **Tuition, state resident:** full-time $13,412; part-time $445 per credit hour. **Tuition, nonresident:** full-time $44,241; part-time $1440 per credit hour. **Required fees:** full-time $2734; $2720 per year. Full-time tuition and fees vary according to location, program, and student level. Part-time tuition and fees vary according to location, program, and student level. **College room and board:** $11,220; **Room only:** $6270. Room and board charges vary according to board plan and housing facility.
FRESHMAN FINANCIAL AID (Fall 2017, est.) 2,938 applied for aid; of those 50% were deemed to have need. 100% of freshmen with need received aid; of those 100% had need fully met. **Average percent of need met:** 100% (excluding resources awarded to replace EFC). **Average financial aid package:** $29,009

(excluding resources awarded to replace EFC). 2% of all full-time freshmen had no need and received non-need-based gift aid.
UNDERGRADUATE FINANCIAL AID (Fall 2017, est.) 9,414 applied for aid; of those 56% were deemed to have need. 100% of undergraduates with need received aid; of those 100% had need fully met. **Average percent of need met:** 100% (excluding resources awarded to replace EFC). **Average financial aid package:** $27,936 (excluding resources awarded to replace EFC). 4% of all full-time undergraduates had no need and received non-need-based gift aid.
GIFT AID (NEED-BASED) Total amount: $100,271,599 (12% federal, 7% state, 75% institutional, 6% external sources). **Receiving aid:** Freshmen: 34% (1,291); all full-time undergraduates: 29% (4,561). **Average award:** Freshmen: $22,594; Undergraduates: $22,284. **Scholarships, grants, and awards:** Federal Pell, FSEOG, state, private, college/university gift aid from institutional funds, Federal Nursing.
GIFT AID (NON-NEED-BASED) Total amount: $24,630,947 (12% federal, 21% institutional, 67% external sources). **Receiving aid:** Freshmen: 4% (148). Undergraduates: 2% (358). **Average award:** Freshmen: $3506. Undergraduates: $4185. **Scholarships, grants, and awards by category:** Academic interests/achievement: general academic interests/achievements. Creative arts/performance: music, theater/drama. Special achievements/activities: leadership. **Tuition waivers:** Full or partial for employees or children of employees, senior citizens. **ROTC:** Army, Naval, Air Force.
LOANS Student loans: $35,939,186 (51% need-based, 49% non-need-based). 35% of past graduating class borrowed through all loan programs. Average indebtedness per student: $24,501. **Average need-based loan:** Freshmen: $5054. Undergraduates: $5695. **Parent loans:** $12,459,597 (12% need-based, 88% non-need-based). **Programs:** Federal Direct (Subsidized and Unsubsidized Stafford, PLUS), Perkins, Federal Nursing, college/university, private loans.
WORK-STUDY Federal work-study: Total amount: $3,023,115; jobs available.
ATHLETIC AWARDS Total amount: $16,040,216 (18% need-based, 82% non-need-based).
APPLYING FOR FINANCIAL AID Required financial aid forms: FAFSA, CSS Financial Aid PROFILE. **Financial aid deadline (priority):** 3/1. **Notification date:** 4/5. Students must reply by 5/1.
CONTACT Mr. Scott Miller, Director of Financial Aid, University of Virginia, PO Box 400204, Charlottesville, VA 22904-4204, 434-982-6000. Fax: 434-924-0063. E-mail: faid@virginia.edu.
Website: http://www.virginia.edu/.

THE UNIVERSITY OF VIRGINIA'S COLLEGE AT WISE
Wise, VA

Tuition & fees (VA res): $9825	Average undergraduate aid package: $13,971

ABOUT THE INSTITUTION State-supported, coed. **Awards:** bachelor's degrees. 25 undergraduate majors. **Total enrollment:** 2,095. Undergraduates: 2,095. Freshmen: 261. Federal methodology is used as a basis for awarding need-based institutional aid.
UNDERGRADUATE EXPENSES for 2017–2018 Application fee: $25. **Tuition, state resident:** full-time $5366; part-time $229 per credit hour. **Tuition, nonresident:** full-time $21,926; part-time $927 per credit hour. **Required fees:** full-time $4459; $144 per credit hour or $35.75 per term. Part-time tuition and fees vary according to course load. **College room and board:** $10,314. Room and board charges vary according to board plan and housing facility.
FRESHMAN FINANCIAL AID (Fall 2017, est.) 264 applied for aid; of those 86% were deemed to have need. 100% of freshmen with need received aid; of those 17% had need fully met. **Average percent of need met:** 92% (excluding resources awarded to replace EFC). **Average financial aid package:** $13,128 (excluding resources awarded to replace EFC). 7% of all full-time freshmen had no need and received non-need-based gift aid.
UNDERGRADUATE FINANCIAL AID (Fall 2017, est.) 1,072 applied for aid; of those 88% were deemed to have need. 100% of undergraduates with need received aid; of those 15% had need fully met. **Average percent of need met:** 73% (excluding resources awarded to replace EFC). **Average financial aid package:** $13,971 (excluding resources awarded to replace EFC). 11% of all full-time undergraduates had no need and received non-need-based gift aid.

GIFT AID (NEED-BASED) *Total amount:* $7,462,805 (40% federal, 37% state, 16% institutional, 7% external sources). *Receiving aid:* Freshmen: 77% (207); all full-time undergraduates: 73% (854). *Average award:* Freshmen: $8039; Undergraduates: $7767. *Scholarships, grants, and awards:* Federal Pell, FSEOG, state, private, college/university gift aid from institutional funds.

GIFT AID (NON-NEED-BASED) *Total amount:* $2,550,401 (2% federal, 9% state, 89% institutional). *Receiving aid:* Freshmen: 72% (192). Undergraduates: 50% (591). *Average award:* Freshmen: $6247. Undergraduates: $6509. *Scholarships, grants, and awards by category: Academic interests/achievement:* agriculture, biological sciences, business, computer science, education, English, general academic interests/achievements, health fields, humanities, mathematics, physical sciences, premedicine, social sciences. *Creative arts/performance:* creative writing, general creative arts/performance, journalism/publications, music, performing arts, theater/drama. *Special achievements/activities:* community service, religious involvement. *Special characteristics:* children with a deceased or disabled parent, ethnic background, local/state students, veterans, veterans' children. *Tuition waivers:* Full or partial for employees or children of employees, senior citizens. *ROTC:* Army.

LOANS *Student loans:* $3,812,663 (50% need-based, 50% non-need-based). 58% of past graduating class borrowed through all loan programs. *Average indebtedness per student:* $21,389. *Average need-based loan:* Freshmen: $2712. Undergraduates: $3455. *Parent loans:* $972,593 (100% non-need-based). *Programs:* Perkins, state, college/university.

WORK-STUDY *Federal work-study:* Total amount: $239,244; jobs available.

ATHLETIC AWARDS Total amount: $1,267,667 (47% need-based, 53% non-need-based).

APPLYING FOR FINANCIAL AID *Required financial aid form:* FAFSA. *Financial aid deadline (priority):* 4/1. *Notification date:* Continuous. Students must reply within 4 weeks of notification.

CONTACT Mrs. Rebecca Huffman, Director of Financial Aid, The University of Virginia's College at Wise, 1 College Avenue, Wise, VA 24293, 276-328-0277 or toll-free 888-282-9324. *Fax:* 276-328-0251. *E-mail:* reg5a@uvawise.edu. *Website:* http://www.uvawise.edu/.

GIFT AID (NON-NEED-BASED) *Total amount:* $13,300,000 (65% institutional, 35% external sources). *Receiving aid:* Freshmen: 11% (712). Undergraduates: 6% (1,786). *Average award:* Freshmen: $3920. Undergraduates: $5000. *Scholarships, grants, and awards by category: Academic interests/achievement:* architecture, area/ethnic studies, biological sciences, business, communication, computer science, education, engineering/technologies, English, foreign languages, general academic interests/achievements, health fields, home economics, humanities, international studies, library science, mathematics, military science, physical sciences, premedicine, social sciences. *Creative arts/performance:* art/fine arts, dance, general creative arts/performance, music, performing arts, theater/drama. *Special achievements/activities:* general special achievements/activities, leadership, memberships. *Tuition waivers:* Full or partial for employees or children of employees, senior citizens. *ROTC:* Army, Naval, Air Force.

LOANS *Student loans:* $62,360,000 (70% need-based, 30% non-need-based). 35% of past graduating class borrowed through all loan programs. *Average indebtedness per student:* $19,880. *Average need-based loan:* Freshmen: $3400. Undergraduates: $4620. *Parent loans:* $37,190,000 (30% need-based, 70% non-need-based). *Programs:* Federal Direct (Subsidized and Unsubsidized Stafford, PLUS), Federal Nursing, college/university.

WORK-STUDY *Federal work-study:* Total amount: $2,037,000; 561 jobs averaging $4000. *State or other work-study/employment:* Total amount: $277,000 (100% need-based). 59 part-time jobs averaging $4618.

ATHLETIC AWARDS Total amount: $11,640,000 (22% need-based, 78% non-need-based).

APPLYING FOR FINANCIAL AID *Required financial aid forms:* FAFSA, WAFSA form (for Washington residents only). *Financial aid deadline (priority):* 1/15. *Notification date:* 4/1. Students must reply by 5/1 or within 3 weeks of notification.

CONTACT Office of Student Financial Aid, University of Washington, Box 355880, Seattle, WA 98195-5880, 206-543-6101. *Fax:* 206-685-1338. *E-mail:* osfa@u.washington.edu. *Website:* http://www.washington.edu/.

UNIVERSITY OF WASHINGTON
Seattle, WA

Tuition & fees (WA res): $10,753	Average undergraduate aid package: $17,380

ABOUT THE INSTITUTION State-supported, coed. *Awards:* certificates, bachelor's, master's, and doctoral degrees. 149 undergraduate majors. *Total enrollment:* 46,166. Undergraduates: 31,331. Freshmen: 6,793. Federal methodology is used as a basis for awarding need-based institutional aid.

UNDERGRADUATE EXPENSES for 2017–2018 *Application fee:* $70. *Tuition, state resident:* full-time $9694; part-time $323 per credit. *Tuition, nonresident:* full-time $33,732; part-time $1124 per credit. *Required fees:* full-time $1059; $27 per credit or $84 per term. Full-time tuition and fees vary according to course load and location. Part-time tuition and fees vary according to course load and location. *College room and board:* $11,691. Room and board charges vary according to board plan and housing facility. *Payment plan:* Tuition prepayment.

FRESHMAN FINANCIAL AID (Fall 2017, est.) 4,739 applied for aid; of those 63% were deemed to have need. 94% of freshmen with need received aid; of those 34% had need fully met. *Average percent of need met:* 79% (excluding resources awarded to replace EFC). *Average financial aid package:* $17,500 (excluding resources awarded to replace EFC). 9% of all full-time freshmen had no need and received non-need-based gift aid.

UNDERGRADUATE FINANCIAL AID (Fall 2017, est.) 16,288 applied for aid; of those 75% were deemed to have need. 95% of undergraduates with need received aid; of those 26% had need fully met. *Average percent of need met:* 77% (excluding resources awarded to replace EFC). *Average financial aid package:* $17,380 (excluding resources awarded to replace EFC). 8% of all full-time undergraduates had no need and received non-need-based gift aid.

GIFT AID (NEED-BASED) *Total amount:* $167,280,000 (21% federal, 27% state, 48% institutional, 4% external sources). *Receiving aid:* Freshmen: 39% (2,618); all full-time undergraduates: 36% (10,395). *Average award:* Freshmen: $15,650; Undergraduates: $15,550. *Scholarships, grants, and awards:* Federal Pell, FSEOG, state, private, college/university gift aid from institutional funds.

UNIVERSITY OF WASHINGTON, BOTHELL
Bothell, WA

Tuition & fees (WA res): $10,690	Average undergraduate aid package: $15,500

ABOUT THE INSTITUTION State-supported, coed. *Awards:* bachelor's and master's degrees. 34 undergraduate majors. *Total enrollment:* 5,990. Undergraduates: 5,365. Freshmen: 800. Federal methodology is used as a basis for awarding need-based institutional aid.

UNDERGRADUATE EXPENSES for 2017–2018 *Application fee:* $60. *Tuition, state resident:* full-time $9694; part-time $323 per credit. *Tuition, nonresident:* full-time $33,732; part-time $1124 per credit. *Required fees:* full-time $996; $33 per credit. Full-time tuition and fees vary according to course load. Part-time tuition and fees vary according to course load. *College room and board:* $10,833. Room and board charges vary according to board plan, housing facility, and location. *Payment plan:* Tuition prepayment.

FRESHMAN FINANCIAL AID (Fall 2017, est.) 642 applied for aid; of those 72% were deemed to have need. 91% of freshmen with need received aid; of those 15% had need fully met. *Average percent of need met:* 78% (excluding resources awarded to replace EFC). *Average financial aid package:* $15,350 (excluding resources awarded to replace EFC). 1% of all full-time freshmen had no need and received non-need-based gift aid.

UNDERGRADUATE FINANCIAL AID (Fall 2017, est.) 3,208 applied for aid; of those 81% were deemed to have need. 94% of undergraduates with need received aid; of those 15% had need fully met. *Average percent of need met:* 74% (excluding resources awarded to replace EFC). *Average financial aid package:* $15,500 (excluding resources awarded to replace EFC). 1% of all full-time undergraduates had no need and received non-need-based gift aid.

GIFT AID (NEED-BASED) *Total amount:* $31,925,000 (27% federal, 34% state, 36% institutional, 3% external sources). *Receiving aid:* Freshmen: 51% (392); all full-time undergraduates: 48% (2,216). *Average award:* Freshmen: $14,700; Undergrad-

uates: $14,220. **Scholarships, grants, and awards:** Federal Pell, FSEOG, state, private, college/university gift aid from institutional funds.

GIFT AID (NON-NEED-BASED) *Total amount:* $720,000 (54% institutional, 46% external sources). *Receiving aid:* Freshmen: 4% (33). Undergraduates: 3% (126). *Average award:* Freshmen: $8100. Undergraduates: $7200. **Scholarships, grants, and awards by category:** *Academic interests/achievement:* area/ethnic studies, biological sciences, business, communication, computer science, education, engineering/technologies, English, general academic interests/achievements, home economics, humanities, international studies, mathematics, physical sciences, premedicine, social sciences. *Tuition waivers:* Full or partial for employees or children of employees, senior citizens. *ROTC:* Army cooperative, Naval cooperative, Air Force cooperative.

LOANS *Student loans:* $11,870,000 (76% need-based, 24% non-need-based). 48% of past graduating class borrowed through all loan programs. *Average indebtedness per student:* $18,850. *Average need-based loan:* Freshmen: $3200. Undergraduates: $4550. *Parent loans:* $2,630,000 (20% need-based, 80% non-need-based). *Programs:* Federal Direct (Subsidized and Unsubsidized Stafford), Federal Nursing, college/university.

WORK-STUDY *Federal work-study:* Total amount: $163,000; 44 jobs averaging $3750. *State or other work-study/employment:* Total amount: $48,000 (100% need-based). 14 part-time jobs averaging $4014.

APPLYING FOR FINANCIAL AID *Required financial aid forms:* FAFSA, WAFSA form (for Washington residents only). *Financial aid deadline (priority):* 1/15. *Notification date:* 4/1. Students must reply by 5/1 or within 3 weeks of notification.

CONTACT Office of Student Financial Aid, University of Washington, Bothell, Box 358500, 18115 Campus Way NE, Bothell, WA 98011-8246, 425-352-5240. *Fax:* 425-352-3217. *E-mail:* finaid@uwb.edu.
Website: http://www.uwb.edu/.

UNIVERSITY OF WASHINGTON, TACOMA
Tacoma, WA

Tuition & fees (WA res): $10,831	Average undergraduate aid package: $15,770

ABOUT THE INSTITUTION State-supported, coed. **Awards:** certificates, bachelor's, master's, and doctoral degrees. 37 undergraduate majors. **Total enrollment:** 5,164. Undergraduates: 4,436. Freshmen: 588. Federal methodology is used as a basis for awarding need-based institutional aid.

UNDERGRADUATE EXPENSES for 2017–2018 *Application fee:* $60. *Tuition, state resident:* full-time $9694; part-time $323 per credit. *Tuition, nonresident:* full-time $33,732; part-time $1124 per credit. *Required fees:* full-time $1137; $38 per credit. Full-time tuition and fees vary according to course load. Part-time tuition and fees vary according to course load. *College room and board:* $10,230. Room and board charges vary according to housing facility and location. *Payment plan:* Tuition prepayment.

FRESHMAN FINANCIAL AID (Fall 2017, est.) 510 applied for aid; of those 84% were deemed to have need. 93% of freshmen with need received aid; of those 24% had need fully met. *Average percent of need met:* 79% (excluding resources awarded to replace EFC). *Average financial aid package:* $15,150 (excluding resources awarded to replace EFC). 8% of all full-time freshmen had no need and received non-need-based gift aid.

UNDERGRADUATE FINANCIAL AID (Fall 2017, est.) 3,208 applied for aid; of those 90% were deemed to have need. 95% of undergraduates with need received aid; of those 13% had need fully met. *Average percent of need met:* 73% (excluding resources awarded to replace EFC). *Average financial aid package:* $15,770 (excluding resources awarded to replace EFC). 4% of all full-time undergraduates had no need and received non-need-based gift aid.

GIFT AID (NEED-BASED) *Total amount:* $36,281,000 (28% federal, 33% state, 36% institutional, 3% external sources). *Receiving aid:* Freshmen: 66% (373); all full-time undergraduates: 64% (2,506). *Average award:* Freshmen: $14,350; Undergraduates: $14,120. **Scholarships, grants, and awards:** Federal Pell, FSEOG, state, private, college/university gift aid from institutional funds.

GIFT AID (NON-NEED-BASED) *Total amount:* $1,110,000 (68% institutional, 32% external sources). *Receiving aid:* Freshmen: 9% (49). Undergraduates: 3% (136). *Average award:* Freshmen: $2200. Undergraduates: $3600. **Scholarships,**

grants, and awards by category:** *Academic interests/achievement:* area/ethnic studies, biological sciences, business, communication, computer science, education, engineering/technologies, foreign languages, general academic interests/achievements, home economics, humanities, international studies, mathematics, military science, physical sciences, social sciences. *Tuition waivers:* Full or partial for employees or children of employees, senior citizens. *ROTC:* Army cooperative, Naval cooperative, Air Force cooperative.

LOANS *Student loans:* $13,990,000 (82% need-based, 18% non-need-based). 50% of past graduating class borrowed through all loan programs. *Average indebtedness per student:* $17,480. *Average need-based loan:* Freshmen: $3500. Undergraduates: $4820. *Parent loans:* $2,610,000 (35% need-based, 65% non-need-based). *Programs:* Federal Direct (Subsidized and Unsubsidized Stafford, PLUS), Federal Nursing, college/university.

WORK-STUDY *Federal work-study:* Total amount: $170,000; 44 jobs averaging $4500. *State or other work-study/employment:* Total amount: $87,000 (100% need-based). 26 part-time jobs averaging $3912.

APPLYING FOR FINANCIAL AID *Required financial aid forms:* FAFSA, WAFSA form (for Washington residents only). *Financial aid deadline (priority):* 1/15. *Notification date:* 4/1. Students must reply by 5/1 or within 3 weeks of notification.

CONTACT Office of Student Financial Aid, University of Washington, Tacoma, 1900 Commerce Street, Box 358400, Tacoma, WA 98402-3100, 253-692-4374 or toll-free 800-736-7750. *Fax:* 253-692-4788. *E-mail:* uwtfa@uw.edu.
Website: http://www.tacoma.uw.edu/.

THE UNIVERSITY OF WEST ALABAMA
Livingston, AL

Tuition & fees (AL res): $9204	Average undergraduate aid package: $10,427

ABOUT THE INSTITUTION State-supported, coed. **Awards:** certificates, associate, bachelor's, and master's degrees. 31 undergraduate majors. **Total enrollment:** 4,646. Undergraduates: 2,111. Freshmen: 461. Federal methodology is used as a basis for awarding need-based institutional aid.

UNDERGRADUATE EXPENSES for 2017–2018 *Application fee:* $40. *Tuition, state resident:* full-time $7614; part-time $324 per hour. *Tuition, nonresident:* full-time $15,228; part-time $648 per hour. *Required fees:* full-time $1590. Full-time tuition and fees vary according to course load. Part-time tuition and fees vary according to course load. *College room and board:* $7080; *Room only:* $4480. Room and board charges vary according to board plan, housing facility, and student level.

FRESHMAN FINANCIAL AID (Fall 2016) 334 applied for aid; of those 88% were deemed to have need. 99% of freshmen with need received aid; of those 2% had need fully met. *Average percent of need met:* 21% (excluding resources awarded to replace EFC). *Average financial aid package:* $11,087 (excluding resources awarded to replace EFC). 8% of all full-time freshmen had no need and received non-need-based gift aid.

UNDERGRADUATE FINANCIAL AID (Fall 2016) 1,490 applied for aid; of those 87% were deemed to have need. 100% of undergraduates with need received aid; of those 8% had need fully met. *Average percent of need met:* 21% (excluding resources awarded to replace EFC). *Average financial aid package:* $10,427 (excluding resources awarded to replace EFC). 4% of all full-time undergraduates had no need and received non-need-based gift aid.

GIFT AID (NEED-BASED) *Total amount:* $4,818,353 (99% federal, 1% state). *Receiving aid:* Freshmen: 54% (203); all full-time undergraduates: 55% (948). *Average award:* Freshmen: $4872; Undergraduates: $4812. **Scholarships, grants, and awards:** Federal Pell, FSEOG, state, private, college/university gift aid from institutional funds, United Negro College Fund.

GIFT AID (NON-NEED-BASED) *Total amount:* $3,252,024 (90% institutional, 10% external sources). *Receiving aid:* Freshmen: 47% (179). Undergraduates: 31% (542). *Average award:* Freshmen: $6260. Undergraduates: $5456. **Scholarships, grants, and awards by category:** *Academic interests/achievement:* English, general academic interests/achievements. *Creative arts/performance:* dance, music, theater/drama. *Special achievements/activities:* cheerleading/drum major, general special achievements/activities, junior miss, leadership, memberships, rodeo. *Special characteristics:* children and siblings of alumni, children of faculty/staff, first-generation college students, previous college experience. *Tuition waivers:* Full or partial for employees or children of employees. *ROTC:* Air Force cooperative.

LOANS *Student loans:* $9,370,753 (49% need-based, 51% non-need-based). 80% of past graduating class borrowed through all loan programs. *Average indebtedness per student:* $25,114. *Parent loans:* $3,996,852 (100% non-need-based). *Programs:* Federal Direct (Subsidized and Unsubsidized Stafford, PLUS), Perkins.

WORK-STUDY *Federal work-study:* 73 jobs averaging $3338. *State or other work-study/employment:* Part-time jobs available.

ATHLETIC AWARDS Total amount: $2,041,008 (100% non-need-based).

APPLYING FOR FINANCIAL AID *Required financial aid form:* FAFSA. *Financial aid deadline (priority):* 3/1. *Notification date:* Continuous beginning 4/15. Students must reply within 2 weeks of notification.

CONTACT Mr. Steve Smith, Director of Financial Aid Operations, The University of West Alabama, Station 3, Livingston, AL 35470, 205-652-3576 or toll-free 888-636-8800. *Fax:* 205-652-3847. *E-mail:* sdsmith@uwa.edu.
Website: http://www.uwa.edu/.

UNIVERSITY OF WEST FLORIDA
Pensacola, FL

Tuition & fees (FL res): $6359	Average undergraduate aid package: $10,166

ABOUT THE INSTITUTION State-supported, coed. 56 undergraduate majors. Federal methodology is used as a basis for awarding need-based institutional aid.

UNDERGRADUATE EXPENSES for 2017–2018 *Tuition, state resident:* full-time $4318; part-time $143.95 per credit hour. *Tuition, nonresident:* full-time $16,587; part-time $552.89 per credit hour. *Required fees:* full-time $2041; $68.03 per credit hour. Full-time tuition and fees vary according to location and reciprocity agreements. Part-time tuition and fees vary according to location and reciprocity agreements. *College room and board:* $9942; *Room only:* $5880. Room and board charges vary according to board plan, housing facility, and student level. *Payment plan:* Tuition prepayment.

FRESHMAN FINANCIAL AID (Fall 2016) 895 applied for aid; of those 37% were deemed to have need. 96% of freshmen with need received aid; of those 16% had need fully met. *Average percent of need met:* 66% (excluding resources awarded to replace EFC). *Average financial aid package:* $10,648 (excluding resources awarded to replace EFC). 28% of all full-time freshmen had no need and received non-need-based gift aid.

UNDERGRADUATE FINANCIAL AID (Fall 2016) 5,297 applied for aid; of those 45% were deemed to have need. 96% of undergraduates with need received aid; of those 13% had need fully met. *Average percent of need met:* 64% (excluding resources awarded to replace EFC). *Average financial aid package:* $10,166 (excluding resources awarded to replace EFC). 13% of all full-time undergraduates had no need and received non-need-based gift aid.

GIFT AID (NEED-BASED) *Total amount:* $23,780,738 (63% federal, 13% state, 23% institutional, 1% external sources). *Receiving aid:* Freshmen: 29% (313); all full-time undergraduates: 32% (2,251). *Average award:* Freshmen: $8384; Undergraduates: $7347. *Scholarships, grants, and awards:* Federal Pell, FSEOG, state, private, college/university gift aid from institutional funds.

GIFT AID (NON-NEED-BASED) *Total amount:* $4,951,205 (48% state, 38% institutional, 14% external sources). *Receiving aid:* Freshmen: 1% (14). Undergraduates: 1% (92). *Average award:* Freshmen: $979. Undergraduates: $1722. *Scholarships, grants, and awards by category:* Academic interests/achievement: biological sciences, business, communication, computer science, education, engineering/technologies, general academic interests/achievements, mathematics, military science, physical sciences, social sciences. *Creative arts/performance:* applied art and design, art/fine arts, music, theater/drama. *Special achievements/activities:* leadership. *Special characteristics:* children and siblings of alumni, children of faculty/staff, handicapped students, international students, out-of-state students, veterans. *Tuition waivers:* Full or partial for employees or children of employees, senior citizens.

LOANS *Student loans:* $29,396,677 (62% need-based, 38% non-need-based). *Average need-based loan:* Freshmen: $3243. Undergraduates: $4092. *Parent loans:* $1,770,480 (21% need-based, 79% non-need-based). *Programs:* Federal Direct (Subsidized and Unsubsidized Stafford, PLUS), Perkins.

WORK-STUDY *Federal work-study:* jobs available. *State or other work-study/employment:* Part-time jobs available.

ATHLETIC AWARDS Total amount: $1,122,121 (21% need-based, 79% non-need-based).

APPLYING FOR FINANCIAL AID *Required financial aid form:* FAFSA. *Financial aid deadline:* Continuous. *Notification date:* Continuous beginning 3/1.

CONTACT Ms. Shana Gore, Coordinator of Financial Aid, University of West Florida, 11000 University Parkway, Pensacola, FL 32514-5750, 850-474-2398 or toll-free 800-263-1074. *E-mail:* sgore1@uwf.edu.
Website: http://www.uwf.edu/.

UNIVERSITY OF WEST GEORGIA
Carrollton, GA

Tuition & fees (GA res): $7292	Average undergraduate aid package: $8828

ABOUT THE INSTITUTION State-supported, coed. *Awards:* certificates, bachelor's, master's, and doctoral degrees. 39 undergraduate majors. *Total enrollment:* 13,520. Undergraduates: 11,252. Freshmen: 2,264. Federal methodology is used as a basis for awarding need-based institutional aid.

UNDERGRADUATE EXPENSES for 2018–2019 *Application fee:* $40. *Tuition, state resident:* full-time $5330; part-time $177.67 per semester hour. *Tuition, nonresident:* full-time $18,812; part-time $627.07 per semester hour. *Required fees:* full-time $1962. Full-time tuition and fees vary according to course load, degree level, location, and program. Part-time tuition and fees vary according to course load, degree level, location, and program. *College room and board:* $10,218; *Room only:* $5450. Room and board charges vary according to board plan and housing facility.

FRESHMAN FINANCIAL AID (Fall 2017, est.) 2,172 applied for aid; of those 80% were deemed to have need. 100% of freshmen with need received aid; of those 70% had need fully met. *Average percent of need met:* 50% (excluding resources awarded to replace EFC). *Average financial aid package:* $8411 (excluding resources awarded to replace EFC). 7% of all full-time freshmen had no need and received non-need-based gift aid.

UNDERGRADUATE FINANCIAL AID (Fall 2017, est.) 8,113 applied for aid; of those 82% were deemed to have need. 99% of undergraduates with need received aid; of those 63% had need fully met. *Average percent of need met:* 53% (excluding resources awarded to replace EFC). *Average financial aid package:* $8828 (excluding resources awarded to replace EFC). 6% of all full-time undergraduates had no need and received non-need-based gift aid.

GIFT AID (NEED-BASED) *Total amount:* $26,293,619 (99% federal, 1% institutional). *Receiving aid:* Freshmen: 55% (1,198); all full-time undergraduates: 52% (4,645). *Average award:* Freshmen: $4957; Undergraduates: $5013. *Scholarships, grants, and awards:* Federal Pell, FSEOG, state, private, college/university gift aid from institutional funds, United Negro College Fund, Federal Nursing.

GIFT AID (NON-NEED-BASED) *Total amount:* $20,719,238 (90% state, 6% institutional, 4% external sources). *Receiving aid:* Freshmen: 16% (346). Undergraduates: 11% (1,014). *Average award:* Freshmen: $1871. Undergraduates: $2299. *Scholarships, grants, and awards by category:* Academic interests/achievement: biological sciences, business, communication, computer science, education, English, foreign languages, general academic interests/achievements, home economics, humanities, mathematics, physical sciences, premedicine, social sciences. *Creative arts/performance:* applied art and design, art/fine arts, debating, general creative arts/performance, journalism/publications, music, performing arts, theater/drama. *Special achievements/activities:* community service, leadership, memberships, religious involvement. *Special characteristics:* adult students, children and siblings of alumni, general special characteristics, handicapped students, international students, local/state students, members of minority groups. *Tuition waivers:* Full or partial for employees or children of employees, senior citizens. *ROTC:* Air Force cooperative.

LOANS *Student loans:* $44,361,839 (47% need-based, 53% non-need-based). 78% of past graduating class borrowed through all loan programs. *Average indebtedness per student:* $29,000. *Average need-based loan:* Freshmen: $3369. Undergraduates: $3964. *Parent loans:* $12,469,034 (100% non-need-based). *Programs:* Federal Direct (Subsidized and Unsubsidized Stafford, PLUS), Perkins, Federal Nursing, state.

WORK-STUDY *Federal work-study:* Total amount: $762,324; jobs available. *State or other work-study/employment:* Part-time jobs available.

ATHLETIC AWARDS Total amount: $1,557,226 (100% non-need-based).

APPLYING FOR FINANCIAL AID *Required financial aid form:* FAFSA. *Financial aid deadline:* 7/1 (priority: 4/1). *Notification date:* 5/1.
CONTACT Leigh Ann Hussey, Director of Financial Aid, University of West Georgia, 1601 Maple Street, Aycock Hall, Carrollton, GA 30118, 678-839-6421. *Fax:* 678-839-6422. *E-mail:* finaid@westga.edu. *Website:* http://www.westga.edu/.

CONTACT Nicole Andrews, Interim Director of Financial Aid, University of Wisconsin–Eau Claire, Old Library 1113, Eau Claire, WI 54701, 715-836-5606. *E-mail:* andrewns@uwec.edu. *Website:* http://www.uwec.edu/.

UNIVERSITY OF WISCONSIN–EAU CLAIRE

Eau Claire, WI

Tuition & fees (WI res): $8816	Average undergraduate aid package: $9479

ABOUT THE INSTITUTION State-supported, coed. *Awards:* certificates, associate, bachelor's, master's, and doctoral degrees. 52 undergraduate majors. *Total enrollment:* 10,737. Undergraduates: 10,022. Freshmen: 2,337. Federal methodology is used as a basis for awarding need-based institutional aid.

UNDERGRADUATE EXPENSES for 2017–2018 *Application fee:* $50. *Tuition, state resident:* full-time $7361; part-time $307 per credit. *Tuition, nonresident:* full-time $15,281; part-time $637 per credit. *Required fees:* full-time $1455; $61 per credit. Full-time tuition and fees vary according to program and reciprocity agreements. Part-time tuition and fees vary according to program and reciprocity agreements. *College room and board:* $7538; *Room only:* $4436. Room and board charges vary according to board plan and housing facility.

FRESHMAN FINANCIAL AID (Fall 2016) 1,961 applied for aid; of those 63% were deemed to have need. 99% of freshmen with need received aid; of those 21% had need fully met. *Average percent of need met:* 83% (excluding resources awarded to replace EFC). *Average financial aid package:* $9343 (excluding resources awarded to replace EFC). 6% of all full-time freshmen had no need and received non-need-based gift aid.

UNDERGRADUATE FINANCIAL AID (Fall 2016) 7,013 applied for aid; of those 69% were deemed to have need. 99% of undergraduates with need received aid; of those 21% had need fully met. *Average percent of need met:* 84% (excluding resources awarded to replace EFC). *Average financial aid package:* $9479 (excluding resources awarded to replace EFC). 5% of all full-time undergraduates had no need and received non-need-based gift aid.

GIFT AID (NEED-BASED) *Total amount:* $22,494,872 (44% federal, 24% state, 19% institutional, 13% external sources). *Receiving aid:* Freshmen: 43% (995); all full-time undergraduates: 41% (3,843). *Average award:* Freshmen: $6160; Undergraduates: $6043. *Scholarships, grants, and awards:* Federal Pell, FSEOG, state, private, college/university gift aid from institutional funds, Federal Nursing, Bureau of Indian Affairs Grants, Student Support Services Grants.

GIFT AID (NON-NEED-BASED) *Total amount:* $1,993,480 (9% state, 36% institutional, 55% external sources). *Receiving aid:* Freshmen: 2% (57). Undergraduates: 1% (130). *Average award:* Freshmen: $1735. Undergraduates: $2135. *Scholarships, grants, and awards by category:* Academic interests/achievement: area/ethnic studies, biological sciences, business, communication, computer science, education, English, foreign languages, general academic interests/achievements, health fields, humanities, international studies, library science, mathematics, physical sciences, premedicine, religion/biblical studies, social sciences. *Creative arts/performance:* art/fine arts, debating, journalism/publications, music, performing arts, theater/drama. *Special achievements/activities:* community service, general special achievements/activities, hobbies/interests, leadership, memberships. *Special characteristics:* adult students, ethnic background, first-generation college students, general special characteristics, international students, local/state students, members of minority groups, previous college experience. *ROTC:* Army.

LOANS *Student loans:* $41,778,213 (53% need-based, 47% non-need-based). 68% of past graduating class borrowed through all loan programs. *Average indebtedness per student:* $26,244. *Average need-based loan:* Freshmen: $4107. Undergraduates: $4405. *Parent loans:* $2,087,113 (62% need-based, 38% non-need-based). *Programs:* Federal Direct (Subsidized and Unsubsidized Stafford, PLUS), college/university, private loans.

WORK-STUDY *Federal work-study:* 4,020 jobs averaging $1142.

APPLYING FOR FINANCIAL AID *Required financial aid form:* FAFSA. *Financial aid deadline (priority):* 4/15. *Notification date:* Continuous beginning 4/15.

UNIVERSITY OF WISCONSIN–GREEN BAY

Green Bay, WI

Tuition & fees (WI res): $7878	Average undergraduate aid package: $9497

ABOUT THE INSTITUTION State-supported, coed. *Awards:* associate, bachelor's, and master's degrees. 47 undergraduate majors. *Total enrollment:* 7,030. Undergraduates: 6,758. Freshmen: 872. Federal methodology is used as a basis for awarding need-based institutional aid.

UNDERGRADUATE EXPENSES for 2017–2018 *Application fee:* $50. *One-time required fee:* $212. *Tuition, state resident:* full-time $6298; part-time $262 per credit hour. *Tuition, nonresident:* full-time $14,148; part-time $589 per credit hour. *Required fees:* full-time $1580; $66 per credit hour. Full-time tuition and fees vary according to course load and reciprocity agreements. Part-time tuition and fees vary according to reciprocity agreements. *College room and board:* $7306; *Room only:* $4380. Room and board charges vary according to board plan and housing facility.

FRESHMAN FINANCIAL AID (Fall 2017, est.) 841 applied for aid; of those 69% were deemed to have need. 100% of freshmen with need received aid; of those 37% had need fully met. *Average percent of need met:* 80% (excluding resources awarded to replace EFC). *Average financial aid package:* $9325 (excluding resources awarded to replace EFC). 5% of all full-time freshmen had no need and received non-need-based gift aid.

UNDERGRADUATE FINANCIAL AID (Fall 2017, est.) 3,443 applied for aid; of those 75% were deemed to have need. 100% of undergraduates with need received aid; of those 41% had need fully met. *Average percent of need met:* 76% (excluding resources awarded to replace EFC). *Average financial aid package:* $9497 (excluding resources awarded to replace EFC). 3% of all full-time undergraduates had no need and received non-need-based gift aid.

GIFT AID (NEED-BASED) *Total amount:* $14,705,925 (53% federal, 30% state, 4% institutional, 13% external sources). *Receiving aid:* Freshmen: 50% (460); all full-time undergraduates: 51% (2,018). *Average award:* Freshmen: $6092; Undergraduates: $5974. *Scholarships, grants, and awards:* Federal Pell, FSEOG, state, private, college/university gift aid from institutional funds.

GIFT AID (NON-NEED-BASED) *Total amount:* $699,598 (1% federal, 6% state, 29% institutional, 64% external sources). *Receiving aid:* Freshmen: 2% (19). Undergraduates: 3% (118). *Average award:* Freshmen: $1379. Undergraduates: $1581. *Scholarships, grants, and awards by category:* Academic interests/achievement: area/ethnic studies, biological sciences, business, communication, education, engineering/technologies, general academic interests/achievements, health fields, humanities, physical sciences, premedicine, social sciences. *Creative arts/performance:* art/fine arts, dance, journalism/publications, music, theater/drama. *Special achievements/activities:* community service, general special achievements/activities, leadership. *Special characteristics:* adult students, children of public servants, ethnic background, handicapped students, members of minority groups, veterans. *Tuition waivers:* Full or partial for senior citizens. *ROTC:* Army cooperative.

LOANS *Student loans:* $22,684,071 (67% need-based, 33% non-need-based). 72% of past graduating class borrowed through all loan programs. *Average indebtedness per student:* $22,664. *Average need-based loan:* Freshmen: $5000. Undergraduates: $5782. *Parent loans:* $1,457,634 (21% need-based, 79% non-need-based). *Programs:* Federal Direct (Subsidized and Unsubsidized Stafford, PLUS), Perkins.

WORK-STUDY *Federal work-study:* Total amount: $297,236; jobs available. *State or other work-study/employment:* Total amount: $74,400 (100% need-based). Part-time jobs available.

ATHLETIC AWARDS Total amount: $2,443,300 (78% need-based, 22% non-need-based).

APPLYING FOR FINANCIAL AID *Required financial aid form:* FAFSA. *Financial aid deadline (priority):* 4/1. *Notification date:* Continuous beginning 1/1. Students must reply within 3 weeks of notification.

CONTACT Mr. James Rohan, Director of Financial Aid, University of Wisconsin–Green Bay, 2420 Nicolet Drive, Green Bay, WI 54311-7001, 920-465-2073. *E-mail:* rohanj@uwgb.edu.
Website: http://www.uwgb.edu/.

CONTACT Louise Janke, Director of Financial Aid, University of Wisconsin–La Crosse, 1725 State Street, La Crosse, WI 54601-3742, 608-785-8604. *Fax:* 608-785-8843. *E-mail:* finaid@uwlax.edu.
Website: http://www.uwlax.edu/.

UNIVERSITY OF WISCONSIN–LA CROSSE
La Crosse, WI

Tuition & fees (WI res): $8922	Average undergraduate aid package: $8016

ABOUT THE INSTITUTION State-supported, coed. *Awards:* certificates, associate, bachelor's, master's, and doctoral degrees. 47 undergraduate majors. *Total enrollment:* 10,473. Undergraduates: 9,655. Freshmen: 2,106. Federal methodology is used as a basis for awarding need-based institutional aid.

UNDERGRADUATE EXPENSES for 2017–2018 Application fee: $50. *Tuition, state resident:* full-time $7585; part-time $370 per credit. *Tuition, nonresident:* full-time $16,254; part-time $725 per credit. *Required fees:* full-time $1337. Full-time tuition and fees vary according to reciprocity agreements. Part-time tuition and fees vary according to course load and reciprocity agreements. *College room and board:* $6206; *Room only:* $3750. Room and board charges vary according to board plan and housing facility.

FRESHMAN FINANCIAL AID (Fall 2016) 1,849 applied for aid; of those 60% were deemed to have need. 97% of freshmen with need received aid; of those 26% had need fully met. *Average percent of need met:* 66% (excluding resources awarded to replace EFC). *Average financial aid package:* $7857 (excluding resources awarded to replace EFC). 7% of all full-time freshmen had no need and received non-need-based gift aid.

UNDERGRADUATE FINANCIAL AID (Fall 2016) 7,341 applied for aid; of those 65% were deemed to have need. 97% of undergraduates with need received aid; of those 26% had need fully met. *Average percent of need met:* 69% (excluding resources awarded to replace EFC). *Average financial aid package:* $8016 (excluding resources awarded to replace EFC). 3% of all full-time undergraduates had no need and received non-need-based gift aid.

GIFT AID (NEED-BASED) Total amount: $15,388,537 (53% federal, 35% state, 2% institutional, 10% external sources). *Receiving aid:* Freshmen: 44% (910); all full-time undergraduates: 42% (3,820). *Average award:* Freshmen: $4752; Undergraduates: $4672. *Scholarships, grants, and awards:* Federal Pell, FSEOG, state, private, college/university gift aid from institutional funds.

GIFT AID (NON-NEED-BASED) Total amount: $5,236,528 (3% federal, 11% state, 33% institutional, 53% external sources). *Receiving aid:* Freshmen: 4% (76). Undergraduates: 3% (240). *Average award:* Freshmen: $1819. Undergraduates: $1300. *Scholarships, grants, and awards by category: Academic interests/achievement:* area/ethnic studies, biological sciences, business, communication, computer science, education, English, foreign languages, general academic interests/achievements, health fields, humanities, international studies, mathematics, military science, physical sciences, social sciences. *Creative arts/performance:* art/fine arts, music, theater/drama. *Special achievements/activities:* community service, leadership, memberships. *Special characteristics:* adult students, children and siblings of alumni, children of union members/company employees, ethnic background, first-generation college students, general special characteristics, international students, local/state students, members of minority groups, out-of-state students, veterans, veterans' children. *ROTC:* Army.

LOANS Student loans: $39,665,415 (43% need-based, 57% non-need-based). 68% of past graduating class borrowed through all loan programs. *Average indebtedness per student:* $26,768. *Average need-based loan:* Freshmen: $4988. Undergraduates: $5452. *Parent loans:* $4,887,188 (13% need-based, 87% non-need-based). *Programs:* Federal Direct (Subsidized and Unsubsidized Stafford, PLUS), Perkins.

WORK-STUDY Federal work-study: jobs available. *State or other work-study/employment:* Total amount: $3,129,723 (100% non-need-based). Part-time jobs available.

APPLYING FOR FINANCIAL AID Required financial aid form: FAFSA. *Financial aid deadline (priority):* 3/15. *Notification date:* Continuous beginning 4/1.

UNIVERSITY OF WISCONSIN–MADISON
Madison, WI

Tuition & fees (WI res): $10,533	Average undergraduate aid package: $16,308

ABOUT THE INSTITUTION State-supported, coed. *Awards:* certificates, bachelor's, master's, and doctoral degrees. 121 undergraduate majors. *Total enrollment:* 43,820. Undergraduates: 32,198. Freshmen: 6,612. Federal methodology is used as a basis for awarding need-based institutional aid.

UNDERGRADUATE EXPENSES for 2017–2018 Application fee: $60. *Tuition, state resident:* full-time $9273; part-time $386.39 per credit hour. *Tuition, nonresident:* full-time $33,523; part-time $1396.79 per credit hour. *Required fees:* full-time $1260; $99.26 per credit hour. Full-time tuition and fees vary according to program and reciprocity agreements. Part-time tuition and fees vary according to course load, program, and reciprocity agreements. *College room and board:* $10,842. Room and board charges vary according to board plan and housing facility.

FRESHMAN FINANCIAL AID (Fall 2017, est.) 4,649 applied for aid; of those 57% were deemed to have need. 94% of freshmen with need received aid; of those 45% had need fully met. *Average percent of need met:* 79% (excluding resources awarded to replace EFC). *Average financial aid package:* $16,644 (excluding resources awarded to replace EFC). 7% of all full-time freshmen had no need and received non-need-based gift aid.

UNDERGRADUATE FINANCIAL AID (Fall 2017, est.) 15,904 applied for aid; of those 69% were deemed to have need. 96% of undergraduates with need received aid; of those 42% had need fully met. *Average percent of need met:* 80% (excluding resources awarded to replace EFC). *Average financial aid package:* $16,308 (excluding resources awarded to replace EFC). 7% of all full-time undergraduates had no need and received non-need-based gift aid.

GIFT AID (NEED-BASED) Total amount: $93,160,204 (22% federal, 12% state, 60% institutional, 6% external sources). *Receiving aid:* Freshmen: 31% (2,074); all full-time undergraduates: 30% (8,563). *Average award:* Freshmen: $12,746; Undergraduates: $11,806. *Scholarships, grants, and awards:* Federal Pell, FSEOG, state, private, college/university gift aid from institutional funds.

GIFT AID (NON-NEED-BASED) Total amount: $20,407,334 (1% federal, 12% state, 67% institutional, 20% external sources). *Receiving aid:* Freshmen: 4% (256). Undergraduates: 4% (1,180). *Average award:* Freshmen: $5954. Undergraduates: $5265. *Scholarships, grants, and awards by category: Academic interests/achievement:* general academic interests/achievements. *Creative arts/performance:* general creative arts/performance. *Special achievements/activities:* general special achievements/activities. *Special characteristics:* general special characteristics. *ROTC:* Army, Naval, Air Force.

LOANS Student loans: $93,434,982 (59% need-based, 41% non-need-based). 45% of past graduating class borrowed through all loan programs. *Average indebtedness per student:* $27,979. *Average need-based loan:* Freshmen: $5618. Undergraduates: $6458. *Parent loans:* $13,853,337 (35% need-based, 65% non-need-based). *Programs:* Federal Direct (Subsidized and Unsubsidized Stafford, PLUS), Perkins, Federal Nursing.

WORK-STUDY Federal work-study: Total amount: $9,690,603; jobs available. *State or other work-study/employment:* Part-time jobs available.

ATHLETIC AWARDS Total amount: $14,695,119 (11% need-based, 89% non-need-based).

APPLYING FOR FINANCIAL AID Required financial aid form: FAFSA. *Financial aid deadline (priority):* 12/1. *Notification date:* Continuous beginning 3/1. Students must reply within 3 weeks of notification.

CONTACT Office of Student Financial Aid, University of Wisconsin–Madison, 333 East Campus Mall #9701, Madison, WI 53715-1382, 608-262-3060. *Fax:* 608-262-9068. *E-mail:* finaid@finaid.wisc.edu.
Website: http://www.wisc.edu/.

UNIVERSITY OF WISCONSIN–MILWAUKEE
Milwaukee, WI

Tuition & fees (WI res): $11,010	Average undergraduate aid package: $7858

ABOUT THE INSTITUTION State-supported, coed. *Awards:* certificates, bachelor's, master's, and doctoral degrees. 102 undergraduate majors. *Total enrollment:* 25,381. Undergraduates: 20,750. Freshmen: 3,230. Federal methodology is used as a basis for awarding need-based institutional aid.

UNDERGRADUATE EXPENSES for 2018–2019 Application fee: $50. *Tuition, state resident:* full-time $9566; part-time $398 per credit hour. *Tuition, nonresident:* full-time $20,844; part-time $868 per credit hour. *Required fees:* full-time $1444. Full-time tuition and fees vary according to course load, degree level, location, program, and reciprocity agreements. Part-time tuition and fees vary according to course load, degree level, location, program, and reciprocity agreements. *College room and board:* $10,728; *Room only:* $6602. Room and board charges vary according to board plan, housing facility, and location.

FRESHMAN FINANCIAL AID (Fall 2016) 2,561 applied for aid; of those 78% were deemed to have need. 97% of freshmen with need received aid; of those 28% had need fully met. *Average percent of need met:* 38% (excluding resources awarded to replace EFC). *Average financial aid package:* $7153 (excluding resources awarded to replace EFC). 2% of all full-time freshmen had no need and received non-need-based gift aid.

UNDERGRADUATE FINANCIAL AID (Fall 2016) 15,406 applied for aid; of those 86% were deemed to have need. 85% of undergraduates with need received aid; of those 25% had need fully met. *Average percent of need met:* 46% (excluding resources awarded to replace EFC). *Average financial aid package:* $7858 (excluding resources awarded to replace EFC). 1% of all full-time undergraduates had no need and received non-need-based gift aid.

GIFT AID (NEED-BASED) Total amount: $54,500,746 (60% federal, 34% state, 3% institutional, 3% external sources). *Receiving aid:* Freshmen: 39% (1,112); all full-time undergraduates: 45% (7,432). *Average award:* Freshmen: $6485; Undergraduates: $6117. *Scholarships, grants, and awards:* Federal Pell, FSEOG, state, private, college/university gift aid from institutional funds, Federal Nursing.

GIFT AID (NON-NEED-BASED) Total amount: $17,402,075 (63% federal, 10% state, 8% institutional, 19% external sources). *Receiving aid:* Freshmen: 16% (464). Undergraduates: 14% (2,283). *Average award:* Freshmen: $1947. Undergraduates: $2086. *Scholarships, grants, and awards by category:* Academic interests/achievement: business, education, general academic interests/achievements. Creative arts/performance: art/fine arts, general creative arts/performance, music, theater/drama. Special achievements/activities: general special achievements/activities, leadership. Special characteristics: general special characteristics, veterans, veterans' children. *Tuition waivers:* Full or partial for senior citizens. *ROTC:* Army cooperative, Naval cooperative, Air Force cooperative.

LOANS Student loans: $101,514,718 (83% need-based, 17% non-need-based). 76% of past graduating class borrowed through all loan programs. *Average indebtedness per student:* $37,131. *Average need-based loan:* Freshmen: $3664. Undergraduates: $4343. *Parent loans:* $13,062,853 (70% need-based, 30% non-need-based). *Programs:* Federal Direct (Subsidized and Unsubsidized Stafford, PLUS), Perkins, Federal Nursing, state, alternative loans.

WORK-STUDY Federal work-study: jobs available.

ATHLETIC AWARDS Total amount: $551,466 (50% need-based, 50% non-need-based).

APPLYING FOR FINANCIAL AID Required financial aid form: FAFSA. *Financial aid deadline (priority):* 3/1. *Notification date:* Continuous beginning 1/15. Students must reply within 4 weeks of notification.

CONTACT Tim Opgenorth, Director of Financial Aid, University of Wisconsin–Milwaukee, Mellencamp Hall 162, Milwaukee, WI 53201, 414-229-6300. *Fax:* 414-229-5699. *E-mail:* opgenort@uwm.edu.
Website: http://www.uwm.edu/.

UNIVERSITY OF WISCONSIN–OSHKOSH
Oshkosh, WI

ABOUT THE INSTITUTION State-supported, coed. 56 undergraduate majors.

GIFT AID (NEED-BASED) Scholarships, grants, and awards: Federal Pell, FSEOG, state, private, college/university gift aid from institutional funds, United Negro College Fund, Federal Nursing.

GIFT AID (NON-NEED-BASED) Scholarships, grants, and awards by category: Academic interests/achievement: general academic interests/achievements. Creative arts/performance: art/fine arts, general creative arts/performance. Special achievements/activities: leadership. Special characteristics: local/state students, members of minority groups.

LOANS Programs: Federal Direct (Subsidized and Unsubsidized Stafford, PLUS), Perkins, Federal Nursing, state, college/university.

WORK-STUDY Federal work-study: jobs available. *State or other work-study/employment:* Part-time jobs available.

APPLYING FOR FINANCIAL AID Required financial aid form: FAFSA.

CONTACT Ms. Stacy Drews, Financial Aid Counselor, University of Wisconsin–Oshkosh, 800 Algoma Boulevard, Oshkosh, WI 54901, 920-424-3379. *E-mail:* drewss@uwosh.edu.
Website: http://www.uwosh.edu/.

UNIVERSITY OF WISCONSIN–PARKSIDE
Kenosha, WI

Tuition & fees (WI res): $7649	Average undergraduate aid package: $9703

ABOUT THE INSTITUTION State-supported, coed. *Awards:* certificates, associate, bachelor's, and master's degrees. 49 undergraduate majors. *Total enrollment:* 4,308. Undergraduates: 4,168. Freshmen: 712. Federal methodology is used as a basis for awarding need-based institutional aid.

UNDERGRADUATE EXPENSES for 2018–2019 Application fee: $50. *One-time required fee:* $260. *Tuition, state resident:* full-time $6298; part-time $262.43 per credit hour. *Tuition, nonresident:* full-time $14,287; part-time $595.31 per credit hour. *Required fees:* full-time $1351; $45.44 per credit hour. Full-time tuition and fees vary according to course load, program, and reciprocity agreements. Part-time tuition and fees vary according to course load, program, and reciprocity agreements. *College room and board:* $7924; *Room only:* $4494. Room and board charges vary according to board plan and housing facility.

FRESHMAN FINANCIAL AID (Fall 2016) 526 applied for aid; of those 79% were deemed to have need. 95% of freshmen with need received aid; of those 15% had need fully met. *Average percent of need met:* 68% (excluding resources awarded to replace EFC). *Average financial aid package:* $9687 (excluding resources awarded to replace EFC). 3% of all full-time freshmen had no need and received non-need-based gift aid.

UNDERGRADUATE FINANCIAL AID (Fall 2016) 2,537 applied for aid; of those 82% were deemed to have need. 97% of undergraduates with need received aid; of those 14% had need fully met. *Average percent of need met:* 66% (excluding resources awarded to replace EFC). *Average financial aid package:* $9703 (excluding resources awarded to replace EFC). 3% of all full-time undergraduates had no need and received non-need-based gift aid.

GIFT AID (NEED-BASED) Total amount: $12,374,453 (61% federal, 36% state, 3% external sources). *Receiving aid:* Freshmen: 45% (287); all full-time undergraduates: 40% (1,289). *Average award:* Freshmen: $6660; Undergraduates: $6311. *Scholarships, grants, and awards:* Federal Pell, FSEOG, state, private, college/university gift aid from institutional funds.

GIFT AID (NON-NEED-BASED) Total amount: $800,264 (3% state, 44% institutional, 53% external sources). *Receiving aid:* Freshmen: 28% (180). Undergraduates: 23% (758). *Average award:* Freshmen: $2288. Undergraduates: $2149. *Scholarships, grants, and awards by category:* Academic interests/achievement: biological sciences, business, communication, computer science, education, engineering/technologies, English, foreign languages, general academic interests/achievements, home economics, humanities, mathematics, physical sciences, premedicine, social sciences. Creative arts/performance: applied art and design, art/fine arts, music, performing arts, theater/drama. *Special achievements/activities:* community service, leadership. *Special characteristics:* adult students, children of union members/company employees, children of workers in trades, ethnic background, general special characteristics, international students, local/state students, members of minority groups, out-of-state students, veterans. *Tuition waivers:* Full or partial for senior citizens. *ROTC:* Army, Air Force cooperative.

LOANS *Student loans:* $16,245,423 (45% need-based, 55% non-need-based). 75% of past graduating class borrowed through all loan programs. *Average indebtedness per student:* $28,504. *Average need-based loan:* Freshmen: $3463. Undergraduates: $4494. *Parent loans:* $1,901,899 (100% non-need-based). *Programs:* Federal Direct (Subsidized and Unsubsidized Stafford, PLUS), Perkins.

WORK-STUDY *Federal work-study:* 117 jobs averaging $1564. *State or other work-study/employment:* Part-time jobs available.

ATHLETIC AWARDS Total amount: $38,112 (100% non-need-based).

APPLYING FOR FINANCIAL AID *Required financial aid form:* FAFSA. *Financial aid deadline (priority):* 3/15. *Notification date:* Continuous beginning 3/15.

CONTACT Kristina Klemens, Director of Student Financial Aid, University of Wisconsin–Parkside, 900 Wood Road, Kenosha, WI 53141-2000, 262-595-2004. *Fax:* 262-595-2216. *E-mail:* klemens@uwp.edu.

Website: http://www.uwp.edu/.

UNIVERSITY OF WISCONSIN–PLATTEVILLE
Platteville, WI

CONTACT Elizabeth Tucker, Director of Financial Aid, University of Wisconsin–Platteville, 1 University Plaza, Platteville, WI 53818-3099, 608-342-1836 or toll-free 877-897-5288. *Fax:* 608-342-1281. *E-mail:* tucker@uwplatt.edu.

Website: http://www.uwplatt.edu/.

UNIVERSITY OF WISCONSIN–RIVER FALLS
River Falls, WI

Tuition & fees (WI res): $8013	Average undergraduate aid package: $6820

ABOUT THE INSTITUTION State-supported, coed. *Awards:* certificates, bachelor's, and master's degrees. 52 undergraduate majors. *Total enrollment:* 6,110. Undergraduates: 5,678. Freshmen: 1,325. Federal methodology is used as a basis for awarding need-based institutional aid.

UNDERGRADUATE EXPENSES for 2017–2018 *Application fee:* $44. *Tuition, state resident:* full-time $6428; part-time $267.85 per credit hour. *Tuition, nonresident:* full-time $14,001; part-time $583.39 per credit hour. *Required fees:* full-time $1585; $165.97 per credit hour. Full-time tuition and fees vary according to course load, degree level, program, and reciprocity agreements. Part-time tuition and fees vary according to course load, degree level, program, and reciprocity agreements. *College room and board:* $6576; *Room only:* $4136. Room and board charges vary according to board plan and housing facility.

FRESHMAN FINANCIAL AID (Fall 2016) 934 applied for aid; of those 73% were deemed to have need. 93% of freshmen with need received aid; of those 2% had need fully met. *Average percent of need met:* 47% (excluding resources awarded to replace EFC). *Average financial aid package:* $6216 (excluding resources awarded to replace EFC). 13% of all full-time freshmen had no need and received non-need-based gift aid.

UNDERGRADUATE FINANCIAL AID (Fall 2016) 3,984 applied for aid; of those 75% were deemed to have need. 93% of undergraduates with need received aid; of those 2% had need fully met. *Average percent of need met:* 52% (excluding resources awarded to replace EFC). *Average financial aid package:* $6820 (excluding resources awarded to replace EFC). 6% of all full-time undergraduates had no need and received non-need-based gift aid.

GIFT AID (NEED-BASED) *Total amount:* $9,017,943 (72% federal, 23% state, 2% institutional, 3% external sources). *Receiving aid:* Freshmen: 34% (341); all full-

time undergraduates: 35% (1,588). *Average award:* Freshmen: $4744; Undergraduates: $4882. *Scholarships, grants, and awards:* Federal Pell, FSEOG, state, private, college/university gift aid from institutional funds.

GIFT AID (NON-NEED-BASED) *Total amount:* $1,955,219 (4% state, 96% institutional). *Receiving aid:* Freshmen: 23% (231). Undergraduates: 18% (830). *Average award:* Freshmen: $1574. Undergraduates: $1752. *Scholarships, grants, and awards by category:* Academic interests/achievement: agriculture, area/ethnic studies, biological sciences, business, communication, computer science, education, English, foreign languages, general academic interests/achievements, health fields, humanities, international studies, mathematics, physical sciences, premedicine, social sciences. *Creative arts/performance:* art/fine arts, music, theater/drama. *Special achievements/activities:* leadership. *Special characteristics:* local/state students, members of minority groups. *ROTC:* Army.

LOANS *Student loans:* $24,601,654 (85% need-based, 15% non-need-based). 73% of past graduating class borrowed through all loan programs. *Average indebtedness per student:* $27,428. *Average need-based loan:* Freshmen: $3757. Undergraduates: $4187. *Parent loans:* $1,545,060 (100% need-based). *Programs:* Federal Direct (Subsidized and Unsubsidized Stafford, PLUS), Perkins, state, alternative loans.

WORK-STUDY *Federal work-study:* jobs available. *State or other work-study/employment:* Part-time jobs available.

APPLYING FOR FINANCIAL AID *Required financial aid form:* FAFSA. *Financial aid deadline:* Continuous. *Notification date:* Continuous beginning 4/15.

CONTACT Mr. Robert Bode, Director of Financial Aid, University of Wisconsin–River Falls, 410 South Third Street, River Falls, WI 54022-5001, 715-425-3141. *Fax:* 715-425-0708. *E-mail:* robert.bode@uwrf.edu.

Website: http://www.uwrf.edu/.

UNIVERSITY OF WISCONSIN–STEVENS POINT
Stevens Point, WI

Tuition & fees (WI res): $9734	Average undergraduate aid package: $9543

ABOUT THE INSTITUTION State-supported, coed. *Awards:* associate, bachelor's, master's, and doctoral degrees. 85 undergraduate majors. *Total enrollment:* 8,109. Undergraduates: 7,788. Federal methodology is used as a basis for awarding need-based institutional aid.

UNDERGRADUATE EXPENSES for 2018–2019 *Application fee:* $50. *Tuition, state resident:* full-time $8308; part-time $407.37 per credit. *Tuition, nonresident:* full-time $16,576; part-time $751.81 per credit. *Required fees:* full-time $1426. Full-time tuition and fees vary according to course load, location, program, reciprocity agreements, and student level. Part-time tuition and fees vary according to course load, location, program, reciprocity agreements, and student level. *College room and board:* $7290; *Room only:* $4420. Room and board charges vary according to board plan and housing facility.

FRESHMAN FINANCIAL AID (Fall 2016) 1,369 applied for aid; of those 64% were deemed to have need. 100% of freshmen with need received aid; of those 7% had need fully met. *Average percent of need met:* 67% (excluding resources awarded to replace EFC). *Average financial aid package:* $8688 (excluding resources awarded to replace EFC). 15% of all full-time freshmen had no need and received non-need-based gift aid.

UNDERGRADUATE FINANCIAL AID (Fall 2016) 6,468 applied for aid; of those 71% were deemed to have need. 100% of undergraduates with need received aid; of those 9% had need fully met. *Average percent of need met:* 73% (excluding resources awarded to replace EFC). *Average financial aid package:* $9543 (excluding resources awarded to replace EFC). 8% of all full-time undergraduates had no need and received non-need-based gift aid.

GIFT AID (NEED-BASED) *Total amount:* $20,569,210 (59% federal, 34% state, 4% institutional, 3% external sources). *Receiving aid:* Freshmen: 41% (635); all full-time undergraduates: 43% (3,440). *Average award:* Freshmen: $5875; Undergraduates: $5678. *Scholarships, grants, and awards:* Federal Pell, FSEOG, state, private, college/university gift aid from institutional funds.

GIFT AID (NON-NEED-BASED) *Total amount:* $2,038,012 (2% state, 73% institutional, 25% external sources). *Receiving aid:* Freshmen: 16% (251). Undergraduates: 10% (770). *Average award:* Freshmen: $1466. Undergraduates: $1520.

Scholarships, grants, and awards by category: Academic interests/achievement: 12 awards ($8469 total): agriculture, architecture, biological sciences, business, communication, computer science, education, engineering/technologies, English, foreign languages, general academic interests/achievements, health fields, home economics, humanities, international studies, mathematics, military science, physical sciences, premedicine, social sciences. *Creative arts/performance:* applied art and design, creative writing, dance, music, performing arts, theater/drama. *Special achievements/activities:* general special achievements/activities, leadership. *Special characteristics:* adult students, ethnic background, general special characteristics, international students, members of minority groups, out-of-state students, veterans. **Tuition waivers:** Full or partial for senior citizens. *ROTC:* Army.

LOANS Student loans: $38,316,314 (60% need-based, 40% non-need-based). 75% of past graduating class borrowed through all loan programs. *Average indebtedness per student:* $25,918. **Average need-based loan:** Freshmen: $4438. Undergraduates: $5416. **Parent loans:** $3,361,370 (12% need-based, 88% non-need-based). **Programs:** Federal Direct (Subsidized and Unsubsidized Stafford, PLUS), Perkins.

WORK-STUDY Federal work-study: jobs available. **State or other work-study/employment:** Part-time jobs available.

APPLYING FOR FINANCIAL AID Required financial aid form: FAFSA. **Financial aid deadline:** 5/1 (priority: 3/15). **Notification date:** Continuous beginning 3/1. Students must reply within 4 weeks of notification.

CONTACT Ms. Mandy Slowinski, Director of Financial Aid, University of Wisconsin–Stevens Point, 106 Student Services Center, Stevens Point, WI 54481-3897, 715-346-4771. *Fax:* 715-346-3526. *E-mail:* finaid@uwsp.edu. *Website:* http://www.uwsp.edu/.

UNIVERSITY OF WISCONSIN–STOUT
Menomonie, WI

Tuition & fees (WI res): $9456	Average undergraduate aid package: $11,237

ABOUT THE INSTITUTION State-supported, coed. **Awards:** certificates, bachelor's, master's, and doctoral degrees. 43 undergraduate majors. **Total enrollment:** 9,401. Undergraduates: 8,116. Freshmen: 1,528. Federal methodology is used as a basis for awarding need-based institutional aid.

UNDERGRADUATE EXPENSES for 2017–2018 Application fee: $50. **Tuition, state resident:** full-time $7014; part-time $234 per credit hour. **Tuition, nonresident:** full-time $14,981; part-time $499 per credit hour. **Required fees:** full-time $2442. Full-time tuition and fees vary according to degree level and reciprocity agreements. Part-time tuition and fees vary according to degree level and reciprocity agreements. **College room and board:** $6744; **Room only:** $4140. Room and board charges vary according to board plan and housing facility.

FRESHMAN FINANCIAL AID (Fall 2017, est.) 1,315 applied for aid; of those 66% were deemed to have need. 97% of freshmen with need received aid; of those 14% had need fully met. **Average percent of need met:** 81% (excluding resources awarded to replace EFC). **Average financial aid package:** $10,396 (excluding resources awarded to replace EFC). 7% of all full-time freshmen had no need and received non-need-based gift aid.

UNDERGRADUATE FINANCIAL AID (Fall 2017, est.) 5,154 applied for aid; of those 72% were deemed to have need. 98% of undergraduates with need received aid; of those 16% had need fully met. **Average percent of need met:** 85% (excluding resources awarded to replace EFC). **Average financial aid package:** $11,237 (excluding resources awarded to replace EFC). 3% of all full-time undergraduates had no need and received non-need-based gift aid.

GIFT AID (NEED-BASED) Total amount: $13,774,360 (69% federal, 27% state, 4% external sources). **Receiving aid:** Freshmen: 30% (453); all full-time undergraduates: 31% (2,058). **Average award:** Freshmen: $6047; Undergraduates: $6033. **Scholarships, grants, and awards:** Federal Pell, FSEOG, state, private, college/university gift aid from institutional funds, Bureau of Indian Affairs Grants, GEAR UP Scholarships.

GIFT AID (NON-NEED-BASED) Total amount: $3,851,037 (8% state, 44% institutional, 48% external sources). **Receiving aid:** Freshmen: 23% (348). Undergraduates: 15% (987). **Average award:** Freshmen: $1973. Undergraduates: $1865. **Scholarships, grants, and awards by category:** *Academic interests/achievement:* 286 awards ($399,918 total): business, computer science, education, engineering/technologies, general academic interests/achievements, home economics, international studies, mathematics, physical sciences. *Creative arts/performance:* 14

awards ($17,000 total): applied art and design, art/fine arts, music. *Special achievements/activities:* 42 awards ($47,900 total): community service, general special achievements/activities, leadership, memberships, religious involvement. *Special characteristics:* 51 awards ($58,200 total): adult students, first-generation college students, handicapped students, international students, local/state students, members of minority groups, out-of-state students, previous college experience, veterans, veterans' children. *ROTC:* Army, Air Force cooperative.

LOANS Student loans: $42,948,125 (40% need-based, 60% non-need-based). 73% of past graduating class borrowed through all loan programs. *Average indebtedness per student:* $30,409. **Average need-based loan:** Freshmen: $3892. Undergraduates: $4729. **Parent loans:** $2,240,236 (100% non-need-based). **Programs:** Federal Direct (Subsidized and Unsubsidized Stafford, PLUS), Perkins, state, alternative loans.

WORK-STUDY Federal work-study: Total amount: $2,950,353; 1,726 jobs averaging $1627. **State or other work-study/employment:** Part-time jobs available.

APPLYING FOR FINANCIAL AID Required financial aid form: FAFSA. **Financial aid deadline (priority):** 3/15. **Notification date:** Continuous beginning 1/27. Students must reply within 4 weeks of notification.

CONTACT Beth Boisen, Director of Financial Aid, University of Wisconsin–Stout, 712 South Broadway Street, Menomonie, WI 54751, 715-232-1363 or toll-free 800-HI-STOUT. *Fax:* 715-232-5246. *E-mail:* boisenb@uwstout.edu. *Website:* http://www.uwstout.edu/.

UNIVERSITY OF WISCONSIN–SUPERIOR
Superior, WI

Tuition & fees (WI res): $8109	Average undergraduate aid package: $11,252

ABOUT THE INSTITUTION State-supported, coed. **Awards:** certificates, associate, bachelor's, and master's degrees. 55 undergraduate majors. **Total enrollment:** 2,590. Undergraduates: 2,368. Freshmen: 345. Federal methodology is used as a basis for awarding need-based institutional aid.

UNDERGRADUATE EXPENSES for 2018–2019 Application fee: $44. **Tuition, state resident:** full-time $6535. **Tuition, nonresident:** full-time $14,108. **Required fees:** full-time $1574. Full-time tuition and fees vary according to course load and reciprocity agreements. Part-time tuition and fees vary according to course load and reciprocity agreements. **College room and board:** $6730; **Room only:** $3600. Room and board charges vary according to board plan and housing facility.

FRESHMAN FINANCIAL AID (Fall 2017, est.) 277 applied for aid; of those 75% were deemed to have need. 99% of freshmen with need received aid; of those 21% had need fully met. **Average percent of need met:** 83% (excluding resources awarded to replace EFC). **Average financial aid package:** $10,795 (excluding resources awarded to replace EFC). 6% of all full-time freshmen had no need and received non-need-based gift aid.

UNDERGRADUATE FINANCIAL AID (Fall 2017, est.) 1,416 applied for aid; of those 83% were deemed to have need. 98% of undergraduates with need received aid; of those 15% had need fully met. **Average percent of need met:** 82% (excluding resources awarded to replace EFC). **Average financial aid package:** $11,252 (excluding resources awarded to replace EFC). 3% of all full-time undergraduates had no need and received non-need-based gift aid.

GIFT AID (NEED-BASED) Total amount: $5,754,506 (66% federal, 20% state, 12% institutional, 2% external sources). **Receiving aid:** Freshmen: 39% (132); all full-time undergraduates: 42% (765). **Average award:** Freshmen: $5891; Undergraduates: $5693. **Scholarships, grants, and awards:** Federal Pell, FSEOG, state, private, college/university gift aid from institutional funds.

GIFT AID (NON-NEED-BASED) Total amount: $652,901 (8% state, 20% institutional, 72% external sources). **Receiving aid:** Freshmen: 29% (99). Undergraduates: 17% (305). **Average award:** Freshmen: $2272. Undergraduates: $1699. **Scholarships, grants, and awards by category:** *Academic interests/achievement:* biological sciences, business, communication, computer science, education, English, general academic interests/achievements, humanities, mathematics, physical sciences, social sciences. *Creative arts/performance:* general creative arts/performance. *Special characteristics:* general special characteristics, international students, members of minority groups, veterans. *ROTC:* Air Force cooperative.

LOANS Student loans: $10,669,623 (44% need-based, 56% non-need-based). 72% of past graduating class borrowed through all loan programs. *Average indebtedness per student:* $30,285. **Average need-based loan:** Freshmen: $3475. Undergraduates: $4494. **Parent loans:** $426,228 (100% non-need-based). **Programs:** Federal Direct (Subsidized and Unsubsidized Stafford, PLUS), Perkins, state, college/university.

WORK-STUDY Federal work-study: Total amount: $322,175; jobs available. **State or other work-study/employment:** Total amount: $1,228,980 (10% need-based, 90% non-need-based). Part-time jobs available.

APPLYING FOR FINANCIAL AID Required financial aid form: FAFSA. **Financial aid deadline (priority):** 12/15. **Notification date:** Continuous beginning 12/1. Students must reply by 5/1 or within 4 weeks of notification.

CONTACT Office of Financial Aid, University of Wisconsin–Superior, Belknap and Catlin, Old Main 110, PO Box 2000, Superior, WI 54880, 715-394-8200. Fax: 715-394-8027. E-mail: finaid@uwsuper.edu.
Website: http://www.uwsuper.edu/.

UNIVERSITY OF WISCONSIN– WHITEWATER
Whitewater, WI

Tuition & fees (WI res): $7662	Average undergraduate aid package: $8582

ABOUT THE INSTITUTION State-supported, coed. **Awards:** associate, bachelor's, master's, and doctoral degrees. 70 undergraduate majors. **Total enrollment:** 12,430. Undergraduates: 11,128. Freshmen: 1,972. Federal methodology is used as a basis for awarding need-based institutional aid.

UNDERGRADUATE EXPENSES for 2017–2018 Application fee: $50. **Tuition, state resident:** full-time $6519; part-time $272 per credit hour. **Tuition, nonresident:** full-time $15,092; part-time $629 per credit hour. **Required fees:** full-time $1143. Full-time tuition and fees vary according to course load, degree level, and reciprocity agreements. **College room and board:** $6492; **Room only:** $3992. Room and board charges vary according to board plan and housing facility.

FRESHMAN FINANCIAL AID (Fall 2017, est.) 1,903 applied for aid; of those 69% were deemed to have need. 95% of freshmen with need received aid; of those 38% had need fully met. **Average percent of need met:** 57% (excluding resources awarded to replace EFC). **Average financial aid package:** $7834 (excluding resources awarded to replace EFC). 6% of all full-time freshmen had no need and received non-need-based gift aid.

UNDERGRADUATE FINANCIAL AID (Fall 2017, est.) 7,790 applied for aid; of those 73% were deemed to have need. 92% of undergraduates with need received aid; of those 44% had need fully met. **Average percent of need met:** 62% (excluding resources awarded to replace EFC). **Average financial aid package:** $8582 (excluding resources awarded to replace EFC). 6% of all full-time undergraduates had no need and received non-need-based gift aid.

GIFT AID (NEED-BASED) Total amount: $21,487,000 (63% federal, 33% state, 4% external sources). **Receiving aid:** Freshmen: 36% (710); all full-time undergraduates: 34% (3,364). **Average award:** Freshmen: $6183; Undergraduates: $5874. **Scholarships, grants, and awards:** Federal Pell, FSEOG, state, private, college/university gift aid from institutional funds.

GIFT AID (NON-NEED-BASED) Total amount: $4,858,000 (3% federal, 47% institutional, 50% external sources). **Receiving aid:** Freshmen: 21% (417). Undergraduates: 12% (1,157). **Average award:** Freshmen: $1961. Undergraduates: $2154. **Scholarships, grants, and awards by category:** Academic interests/achievement: biological sciences, business, communication, computer science, education, English, foreign languages, general academic interests/achievements, humanities, mathematics, physical sciences, premedicine, social sciences. Creative arts/performance: art/fine arts, cinema/film/broadcasting, creative writing, journalism/publications, music, theater/drama. Special achievements/activities: leadership. Special characteristics: adult students, ethnic background, handicapped students, international students, local/state students, members of minority groups, out-of-state students. **Tuition waivers:** Full or partial for senior citizens. **ROTC:** Army, Air Force.

LOANS Student loans: $60,500,000 (36% need-based, 64% non-need-based). 77% of past graduating class borrowed through all loan programs. Average indebtedness per student: $24,704. **Average need-based loan:** Freshmen: $3563. Undergraduates: $4350. **Parent loans:** $8,500,000 (100% non-need-based). **Programs:** Federal Direct (Subsidized and Unsubsidized Stafford, PLUS), Perkins.

WORK-STUDY Federal work-study: Total amount: $625,000; 545 jobs averaging $1309. **State or other work-study/employment:** Total amount: $4,500,000 (100% non-need-based). 2,365 part-time jobs averaging $1903.

APPLYING FOR FINANCIAL AID Required financial aid form: FAFSA. **Financial aid deadline (priority):** 1/1. **Notification date:** Continuous beginning 2/1. Students must reply within 3 weeks of notification.

CONTACT Ms. Carol Miller, Director of Financial Aid, University of Wisconsin–Whitewater, 800 West Main Street, Whitewater, WI 53190-1790, 262-472-1130. Fax: 262-472-5655. E-mail: millerc@uww.edu.
Website: http://www.uww.edu/.

UNIVERSITY OF WYOMING
Laramie, WY

Tuition & fees (WY res): $5217	Average undergraduate aid package: $9904

ABOUT THE INSTITUTION State-supported, coed. **Awards:** certificates, bachelor's, master's, and doctoral degrees. 83 undergraduate majors. **Total enrollment:** 12,397. Undergraduates: 9,791. Freshmen: 1,696. Federal methodology is used as a basis for awarding need-based institutional aid.

UNDERGRADUATE EXPENSES for 2018–2019 Application fee: $40. **One-time required fee:** $40. **Tuition, state resident:** full-time $3870; part-time $129 per credit hour. **Tuition, nonresident:** full-time $15,480; part-time $516 per credit hour. **Required fees:** full-time $1347. Full-time tuition and fees vary according to course load, location, and reciprocity agreements. Part-time tuition and fees vary according to course load, location, and reciprocity agreements. **College room and board:** $10,320; **Room only:** $4493. Room and board charges vary according to board plan and housing facility.

FRESHMAN FINANCIAL AID (Fall 2016) 1,196 applied for aid; of those 64% were deemed to have need. 98% of freshmen with need received aid; of those 26% had need fully met. **Average percent of need met:** 66% (excluding resources awarded to replace EFC). **Average financial aid package:** $10,701 (excluding resources awarded to replace EFC). 25% of all full-time freshmen had no need and received non-need-based gift aid.

UNDERGRADUATE FINANCIAL AID (Fall 2016) 5,116 applied for aid; of those 72% were deemed to have need. 98% of undergraduates with need received aid; of those 17% had need fully met. **Average percent of need met:** 60% (excluding resources awarded to replace EFC). **Average financial aid package:** $9904 (excluding resources awarded to replace EFC). 21% of all full-time undergraduates had no need and received non-need-based gift aid.

GIFT AID (NEED-BASED) Total amount: $17,621,458 (49% federal, 37% state, 10% institutional, 4% external sources). **Receiving aid:** Freshmen: 33% (512); all full-time undergraduates: 32% (2,569). **Average award:** Freshmen: $4977; Undergraduates: $5158. **Scholarships, grants, and awards:** Federal Pell, FSEOG, state, private, college/university gift aid from institutional funds.

GIFT AID (NON-NEED-BASED) Total amount: $27,468,582 (4% federal, 35% state, 46% institutional, 15% external sources). **Receiving aid:** Freshmen: 44% (672). Undergraduates: 31% (2,524). **Average award:** Freshmen: $4082. Undergraduates: $4182. **Scholarships, grants, and awards by category:** Academic interests/achievement: agriculture, architecture, area/ethnic studies, biological sciences, business, communication, computer science, education, engineering/technologies, English, foreign languages, general academic interests/achievements, health fields, home economics, humanities, international studies, mathematics, physical sciences, religion/biblical studies, social sciences. Creative arts/performance: applied art and design, art/fine arts, cinema/film/broadcasting, creative writing, dance, debating, general creative arts/performance, journalism/publications, music, performing arts, theater/drama. Special achievements/activities: cheerleading/drum major, community service, general special achievements/activities, hobbies/interests, junior miss, leadership, memberships, rodeo. Special characteristics: adult students, children and siblings of alumni, children of public servants, ethnic background, first-generation college students, general special characteristics, handicapped students, international students, local/state students, members of minority groups, out-of-state students, previous college experience, spouses of current students, veterans, veterans' children. **Tuition waivers:** Full or partial for children of alumni, employees or children of employees, senior citizens. **ROTC:** Army, Air Force.

LOANS Student loans: $27,261,252 (36% need-based, 64% non-need-based). 47% of past graduating class borrowed through all loan programs. Average indebtedness per student: $22,524. **Average need-based loan:** Freshmen: $3306. Undergraduates: $4060. **Parent loans:** $3,140,921 (100% non-need-based). **Programs:** Federal

Direct (Subsidized and Unsubsidized Stafford, PLUS), Perkins, state, college/university, alternative loans.
WORK-STUDY *Federal work-study:* 287 jobs averaging $2045.
ATHLETIC AWARDS Total amount: $5,727,815 (73% need-based, 27% non-need-based).
APPLYING FOR FINANCIAL AID *Required financial aid form:* FAFSA. *Financial aid deadline (priority):* 3/1. *Notification date:* Continuous beginning 3/16.
CONTACT Debra Hintz, Director of Student Financial Aid, University of Wyoming, Department 3335, 1000 East University Avenue, Laramie, WY 82071, 307-766-2116 or toll-free 800-342-5996. *Fax:* 307-766-3800. *E-mail:* finaid@uwyo.edu.
Website: http://www.uwyo.edu/.

UPPER IOWA UNIVERSITY
Fayette, IA

Tuition & fees: $30,450	Average undergraduate aid package: $14,614

ABOUT THE INSTITUTION Independent, coed. *Awards:* certificates, associate, bachelor's, and master's degrees (enrollment figures include extended learning centers and online and distance education programs). 43 undergraduate majors. *Total enrollment:* 4,944. Undergraduates: 4,275. Freshmen: 221. Federal methodology is used as a basis for awarding need-based institutional aid.
UNDERGRADUATE EXPENSES for 2018–2019 *Comprehensive fee:* $38,910 includes full-time tuition ($29,700), mandatory fees ($750), and room and board ($8460). *College room only:* $3900. Full-time tuition and fees vary according to degree level, location, and program. Room and board charges vary according to board plan, housing facility, and location.
FRESHMAN FINANCIAL AID (Fall 2016) 83 applied for aid; of those 96% were deemed to have need. 100% of freshmen with need received aid. *Average percent of need met:* 39% (excluding resources awarded to replace EFC). *Average financial aid package:* $28,429 (excluding resources awarded to replace EFC).
UNDERGRADUATE FINANCIAL AID (Fall 2016) 1,838 applied for aid; of those 89% were deemed to have need. 100% of undergraduates with need received aid; of those 10% had need fully met. *Average percent of need met:* 58% (excluding resources awarded to replace EFC). *Average financial aid package:* $14,614 (excluding resources awarded to replace EFC). 1% of all full-time undergraduates had no need and received non-need-based gift aid.
GIFT AID (NEED-BASED) *Total amount:* $21,034,218 (43% federal, 15% state, 38% institutional, 4% external sources). *Receiving aid:* Freshmen: 78% (78); all full-time undergraduates: 64% (1,402). *Average award:* Freshmen: $12,217; Undergraduates: $4907. *Scholarships, grants, and awards:* Federal Pell, FSEOG, state, private, college/university gift aid from institutional funds.
GIFT AID (NON-NEED-BASED) *Total amount:* $2,026,297 (1% federal, 2% state, 94% institutional, 3% external sources). *Receiving aid:* Freshmen: 1% (1). Undergraduates: 3% (56). *Average award:* Undergraduates: $938. *Scholarships, grants, and awards by category:* Academic interests/achievement: 275 awards ($597,297 total): biological sciences, business, computer science, education, general academic interests/achievements, humanities, physical sciences, social sciences. *Special characteristics:* 24 awards ($10,687 total): children and siblings of alumni. *Tuition waivers:* Full or partial for employees or children of employees.
LOANS *Student loans:* $37,754,801 (95% need-based, 5% non-need-based). 49% of past graduating class borrowed through all loan programs. *Average indebtedness per student:* $26,488. *Average need-based loan:* Freshmen: $2611. Undergraduates: $4740. *Parent loans:* $4,056,675 (88% need-based, 12% non-need-based). *Programs:* Federal Direct (Subsidized and Unsubsidized Stafford, PLUS), Perkins, alternative loans.
WORK-STUDY *Federal work-study:* 371 jobs averaging $1877. *State or other work-study/employment:* Part-time jobs available.
ATHLETIC AWARDS Total amount: $2,651,296 (71% need-based, 29% non-need-based).
APPLYING FOR FINANCIAL AID *Required financial aid form:* FAFSA. *Financial aid deadline:* Continuous. *Notification date:* Continuous beginning 3/1. Students must reply within 1 week of notification.

CONTACT Kelli Bell, Financial Aid Director, Upper Iowa University, 605 Washington Street, Fayette, IA 52142-1857, 800-553-4150. *Fax:* 563-425-5277. *E-mail:* financialaid@uiu.edu.
Website: http://www.uiu.edu/.

URBANA UNIVERSITY–A BRANCH CAMPUS OF FRANKLIN UNIVERSITY
Urbana, OH

CONTACT Mrs. Amy M. Barnhart, Director of Financial Aid, Urbana University–A Branch Campus of Franklin University, 579 College Way, Urbana, OH 43078-2091, 937-484-1359 or toll-free 800-7-URBANA. *Fax:* 937-652-6870. *E-mail:* abarnhart@urbana.edu.
Website: http://www.urbana.edu/.

URSINUS COLLEGE
Collegeville, PA

Tuition & fees: $52,050	Average undergraduate aid package: $40,845

ABOUT THE INSTITUTION Independent, coed. *Awards:* bachelor's degrees. 32 undergraduate majors. *Total enrollment:* 1,507. Undergraduates: 1,507. Freshmen: 402. Federal methodology is used as a basis for awarding need-based institutional aid.
UNDERGRADUATE EXPENSES for 2018–2019 *Comprehensive fee:* $64,800 includes full-time tuition ($52,050) and room and board ($12,750). *Part-time tuition:* $1626 per credit hour.
FRESHMAN FINANCIAL AID (Fall 2017, est.) 361 applied for aid; of those 84% were deemed to have need. 100% of freshmen with need received aid; of those 30% had need fully met. *Average percent of need met:* 84% (excluding resources awarded to replace EFC). *Average financial aid package:* $41,196 (excluding resources awarded to replace EFC). 22% of all full-time freshmen had no need and received non-need-based gift aid.
UNDERGRADUATE FINANCIAL AID (Fall 2017, est.) 1,256 applied for aid; of those 89% were deemed to have need. 100% of undergraduates with need received aid; of those 25% had need fully met. *Average percent of need met:* 83% (excluding resources awarded to replace EFC). *Average financial aid package:* $40,845 (excluding resources awarded to replace EFC). 23% of all full-time undergraduates had no need and received non-need-based gift aid.
GIFT AID (NEED-BASED) *Total amount:* $38,040,731 (4% federal, 3% state, 93% institutional). *Receiving aid:* Freshmen: 75% (303); all full-time undergraduates: 75% (1,115). *Average award:* Freshmen: $35,326; Undergraduates: $34,433. *Scholarships, grants, and awards:* Federal Pell, FSEOG, state, private, college/university gift aid from institutional funds.
GIFT AID (NON-NEED-BASED) *Total amount:* $11,327,965 (94% institutional, 6% external sources). *Receiving aid:* Freshmen: 21% (85). Undergraduates: 16% (236). *Average award:* Freshmen: $25,457. Undergraduates: $24,065. *Scholarships, grants, and awards by category:* Academic interests/achievement: general academic interests/achievements. *Creative arts/performance:* creative writing, dance, music, performing arts, theater/drama. *Special achievements/activities:* community service, general special achievements/activities, leadership. *Special characteristics:* children and siblings of alumni, children of faculty/staff, general special characteristics, international students, siblings of current students, veterans, veterans' children. *Tuition waivers:* Full or partial for employees or children of employees.
LOANS *Student loans:* $10,897,292 (34% need-based, 66% non-need-based). 73% of past graduating class borrowed through all loan programs. *Average indebtedness per student:* $39,026. *Average need-based loan:* Freshmen: $3419. Undergraduates: $4792. *Parent loans:* $4,840,393 (100% non-need-based). *Programs:* Federal Direct (Subsidized and Unsubsidized Stafford, PLUS).
WORK-STUDY *Federal work-study:* Total amount: $1,170,500; 623 jobs averaging $1879.
APPLYING FOR FINANCIAL AID *Required financial aid forms:* FAFSA, state aid form, verification worksheet. *Financial aid deadline:* 2/1. *Notification date:* 2/1. Students must reply by 5/1 or within 2 weeks of notification.

CONTACT Ms. Suzanne Sparrow, Director of Scholarships and Financial Aid, Ursinus College, 601 East Main Street, Collegeville, PA 19426-1000, 610-409-3600. *Fax:* 610-409-3662. *E-mail:* finaid@ursinus.edu.
Website: http://www.ursinus.edu/.

URSULINE COLLEGE
Pepper Pike, OH

Tuition & fees: $32,390	Average undergraduate aid package: $24,765

ABOUT THE INSTITUTION Independent Roman Catholic, coed, primarily women. *Awards:* certificates, bachelor's, master's, and doctoral degrees (applications from men are also accepted). 37 undergraduate majors. *Total enrollment:* 1,123. Undergraduates: 621. Freshmen: 79. Federal methodology is used as a basis for awarding need-based institutional aid.

UNDERGRADUATE EXPENSES for 2018–2019 *Comprehensive fee:* $43,166 includes full-time tuition ($32,070), mandatory fees ($320), and room and board ($10,776). Full-time tuition and fees vary according to class time, course load, degree level, location, and program. Room and board charges vary according to housing facility. *Part-time tuition:* $1069 per credit hour. *Part-time fees:* $120 per term. Part-time tuition and fees vary according to class time, course load, degree level, location, and program.

FRESHMAN FINANCIAL AID (Fall 2017, est.) 74 applied for aid; of those 97% were deemed to have need. 100% of freshmen with need received aid; of those 12% had need fully met. *Average percent of need met:* 84% (excluding resources awarded to replace EFC). *Average financial aid package:* $29,874 (excluding resources awarded to replace EFC). 5% of all full-time freshmen had no need and received non-need-based gift aid.

UNDERGRADUATE FINANCIAL AID (Fall 2017, est.) 403 applied for aid; of those 94% were deemed to have need. 100% of undergraduates with need received aid; of those 10% had need fully met. *Average percent of need met:* 71% (excluding resources awarded to replace EFC). *Average financial aid package:* $24,765 (excluding resources awarded to replace EFC). 9% of all full-time undergraduates had no need and received non-need-based gift aid.

GIFT AID (NEED-BASED) *Total amount:* $6,499,461 (19% federal, 8% state, 71% institutional, 2% external sources). *Receiving aid:* Freshmen: 92% (72); all full-time undergraduates: 73% (332). *Average award:* Freshmen: $25,334; Undergraduates: $21,408. *Scholarships, grants, and awards:* Federal Pell, FSEOG, state, private, college/university gift aid from institutional funds, United Negro College Fund.

GIFT AID (NON-NEED-BASED) *Total amount:* $418,473 (96% institutional, 4% external sources). *Receiving aid:* Freshmen: 12% (9). Undergraduates: 6% (29). *Average award:* Freshmen: $10,625. Undergraduates: $9026. *Scholarships, grants, and awards by category:* Academic interests/achievement: general academic interests/achievements. Creative arts/performance: general creative arts/performance. Special achievements/activities: community service, leadership. Special characteristics: children and siblings of alumni, children of faculty/staff, first-generation college students, relatives of clergy, religious affiliation, siblings of current students, veterans. *Tuition waivers:* Full or partial for employees or children of employees. *ROTC:* Army cooperative.

LOANS *Student loans:* $5,297,802 (85% need-based, 15% non-need-based). 88% of past graduating class borrowed through all loan programs. *Average indebtedness per student:* $34,189. *Average need-based loan:* Freshmen: $4402. Undergraduates: $5942. *Parent loans:* $733,016 (48% need-based, 52% non-need-based). *Programs:* Federal Direct (Subsidized and Unsubsidized Stafford, PLUS), Perkins, state, college/university.

WORK-STUDY *Federal work-study:* Total amount: $166,930; jobs available.

ATHLETIC AWARDS Total amount: $1,589,415 (58% need-based, 42% non-need-based).

APPLYING FOR FINANCIAL AID *Required financial aid form:* FAFSA. *Financial aid deadline:* Continuous. *Notification date:* Continuous beginning 1/1. Students must reply within 3 weeks of notification.

CONTACT Ms. Mary Lynn Perri, Assistant Dean of Enrollment Management and Director of Financial Aid, Ursuline College, 2550 Lander Road, Pepper Pike, OH 44124-4398, 440-646-8330 or toll-free 888-URSULINE. *Fax:* 440-684-6114. *E-mail:* mperri@ursuline.edu.
Website: http://www.ursuline.edu/.

UTAH STATE UNIVERSITY
Logan, UT

Tuition & fees (UT res): $7174	Average undergraduate aid package: $10,263

ABOUT THE INSTITUTION State-supported, coed. *Awards:* certificates, associate, bachelor's, master's, and doctoral degrees. 115 undergraduate majors. *Total enrollment:* 27,679. Undergraduates: 24,618. Freshmen: 4,242. Federal methodology is used as a basis for awarding need-based institutional aid.

UNDERGRADUATE EXPENSES for 2017–2018 *Application fee:* $50. *Tuition, state resident:* full-time $6104. *Tuition, nonresident:* full-time $19,657. *Required fees:* full-time $1070. Full-time tuition and fees vary according to course level, course load, program, and reciprocity agreements. Part-time tuition and fees vary according to course level, course load, program, and reciprocity agreements. *College room and board:* $6060; *Room only:* $2160. Room and board charges vary according to board plan and housing facility.

FRESHMAN FINANCIAL AID (Fall 2017, est.) 2,664 applied for aid; of those 75% were deemed to have need. 100% of freshmen with need received aid; of those 18% had need fully met. *Average percent of need met:* 69% (excluding resources awarded to replace EFC). *Average financial aid package:* $9312 (excluding resources awarded to replace EFC). 19% of all full-time freshmen had no need and received non-need-based gift aid.

UNDERGRADUATE FINANCIAL AID (Fall 2017, est.) 11,221 applied for aid; of those 86% were deemed to have need. 99% of undergraduates with need received aid; of those 8% had need fully met. *Average percent of need met:* 57% (excluding resources awarded to replace EFC). *Average financial aid package:* $10,263 (excluding resources awarded to replace EFC). 11% of all full-time undergraduates had no need and received non-need-based gift aid.

GIFT AID (NEED-BASED) *Total amount:* $47,584,427 (93% federal, 6% state, 1% institutional). *Receiving aid:* Freshmen: 34% (1,319); all full-time undergraduates: 42% (7,165). *Average award:* Freshmen: $5069; Undergraduates: $5141. *Scholarships, grants, and awards:* Federal Pell, FSEOG, state, private.

GIFT AID (NON-NEED-BASED) *Total amount:* $18,596,396 (78% institutional, 22% external sources). *Receiving aid:* Freshmen: 31% (1,236). Undergraduates: 26% (4,507). *Average award:* Freshmen: $2458. Undergraduates: $3145. *Scholarships, grants, and awards by category:* Academic interests/achievement: agriculture, architecture, biological sciences, business, communication, computer science, education, engineering/technologies, English, foreign languages, general academic interests/achievements, health fields, home economics, humanities, international studies, library science, mathematics, physical sciences, premedicine, social sciences. Creative arts/performance: applied art and design, art/fine arts, general creative arts/performance, journalism/publications, music, performing arts, theater/drama. Special achievements/activities: leadership. Special characteristics: children and siblings of alumni, children of faculty/staff, international students, local/state students, members of minority groups, religious affiliation. *Tuition waivers:* Full or partial for minority students, children of alumni, employees or children of employees, adult students, senior citizens. *ROTC:* Army, Air Force.

LOANS *Student loans:* $97,988,446 (54% need-based, 46% non-need-based). 44% of past graduating class borrowed through all loan programs. *Average indebtedness per student:* $21,328. *Average need-based loan:* Freshmen: $3640. Undergraduates: $4660. *Parent loans:* $1,650,106 (100% non-need-based). *Programs:* Federal Direct (Subsidized and Unsubsidized Stafford, PLUS), Perkins, college/university.

WORK-STUDY *Federal work-study:* Total amount: $753,518; jobs available. *State or other work-study/employment:* Total amount: $667,295 (100% need-based). Part-time jobs available.

ATHLETIC AWARDS Total amount: $3,481,383 (100% non-need-based).

APPLYING FOR FINANCIAL AID *Required financial aid form:* FAFSA. *Financial aid deadline:* Continuous. *Notification date:* Continuous beginning 4/1. Students must reply within 4 weeks of notification.

CONTACT Office of Financial Aid, Utah State University, 1800 Old Main Hill, Logan, UT 84322-1800, 435-797-0173 or toll-free 800-488-8108. *Fax:* 435-797-0654. *E-mail:* finaid@usu.edu.
Website: http://www.usu.edu/.

UTAH VALLEY UNIVERSITY
Orem, UT

Tuition & fees (UT res): $5652	Average undergraduate aid package: $8129

ABOUT THE INSTITUTION State-supported, coed. **Awards:** certificates, diplomas, associate, bachelor's, and master's degrees. 83 undergraduate majors. **Total enrollment:** 37,282. Undergraduates: 36,868. Freshmen: 4,176. Federal methodology is used as a basis for awarding need-based institutional aid.

UNDERGRADUATE EXPENSES for 2017–2018 *Application fee:* $35. *Tuition, state resident:* full-time $4962; part-time $216 per credit. *Tuition, nonresident:* full-time $15,376; part-time $671 per credit. *Required fees:* full-time $690; $345 per term. Full-time tuition and fees vary according to course load and program. Part-time tuition and fees vary according to course load.

FRESHMAN FINANCIAL AID (Fall 2017, est.) 1,973 applied for aid; of those 73% were deemed to have need. 95% of freshmen with need received aid; of those 20% had need fully met. *Average percent of need met:* 70% (excluding resources awarded to replace EFC). *Average financial aid package:* $7947 (excluding resources awarded to replace EFC). 1% of all full-time freshmen had no need and received non-need-based gift aid.

UNDERGRADUATE FINANCIAL AID (Fall 2017, est.) 11,792 applied for aid; of those 86% were deemed to have need. 96% of undergraduates with need received aid; of those 10% had need fully met. *Average percent of need met:* 64% (excluding resources awarded to replace EFC). *Average financial aid package:* $8129 (excluding resources awarded to replace EFC). 1% of all full-time undergraduates had no need and received non-need-based gift aid.

GIFT AID (NEED-BASED) Total amount: $59,786,319 (91% federal, 5% state, 3% institutional, 1% external sources). *Receiving aid:* Freshmen: 29% (884); all full-time undergraduates: 45% (7,808). *Average award:* Freshmen: $5067; Undergraduates: $5187. *Scholarships, grants, and awards:* Federal Pell, FSEOG, state, private, college/university gift aid from institutional funds.

GIFT AID (NON-NEED-BASED) Total amount: $4,825,969 (1% federal, 62% state, 18% institutional, 19% external sources). *Receiving aid:* Freshmen: 20% (594). Undergraduates: 13% (2,264). *Average award:* Freshmen: $1015. Undergraduates: $1509. *Tuition waivers:* Full or partial for employees or children of employees. *ROTC:* Army, Air Force cooperative.

LOANS Student loans: $87,352,564 (78% need-based, 22% non-need-based). 47% of past graduating class borrowed through all loan programs. *Average indebtedness per student:* $20,832. *Average need-based loan:* Freshmen: $2291. Undergraduates: $2863. *Parent loans:* $441,056 (53% need-based, 47% non-need-based). *Programs:* Federal Direct (Subsidized and Unsubsidized Stafford, PLUS), Perkins.

WORK-STUDY Federal work-study: Total amount: $1,008,776; jobs available. *State or other work-study/employment:* Part-time jobs available.

ATHLETIC AWARDS Total amount: $2,653,222 (32% need-based, 68% non-need-based).

APPLYING FOR FINANCIAL AID *Required financial aid form:* FAFSA. *Financial aid deadline:* Continuous. *Notification date:* Continuous beginning 1/1.

CONTACT John Curl, Director of Financial Aid and Scholarships, Utah Valley University, 800 West University Parkway, Orem, UT 84058, 801-863-8442. *Fax:* 801-863-8448. *E-mail:* jcurl@uvu.edu. *Website:* http://www.uvu.edu/.

U.T.A. MESIVTA OF KIRYAS JOEL
Monroe, NY

CONTACT Financial Aid Office, U.T.A. Mesivta of Kiryas Joel, 48 Bakertown Road, Suite 501, Monroe, NY 10950, 845-783-9901.

UTICA COLLEGE
Utica, NY

Tuition & fees: $20,676	Average undergraduate aid package: $13,958

ABOUT THE INSTITUTION Independent, coed. **Awards:** certificates, bachelor's, master's, and doctoral degrees. 47 undergraduate majors. **Total enrollment:** 5,258. Undergraduates: 3,685. Freshmen: 548. Federal methodology is used as a basis for awarding need-based institutional aid.

UNDERGRADUATE EXPENSES for 2017–2018 *Application fee:* $40. **Comprehensive fee:** $31,510 includes full-time tuition ($20,126), mandatory fees ($550), and room and board ($10,834). Full-time tuition and fees vary according to course load, degree level, and location. Room and board charges vary according to board plan. *Part-time tuition:* $671 per credit hour. *Part-time fees:* $50 per term. Part-time tuition and fees vary according to course load, degree level, and location.

FRESHMAN FINANCIAL AID (Fall 2017, est.) 524 applied for aid; of those 90% were deemed to have need. 100% of freshmen with need received aid; of those 6% had need fully met. *Average percent of need met:* 58% (excluding resources awarded to replace EFC). *Average financial aid package:* $14,484 (excluding resources awarded to replace EFC). 10% of all full-time freshmen had no need and received non-need-based gift aid.

UNDERGRADUATE FINANCIAL AID (Fall 2017, est.) 2,655 applied for aid; of those 91% were deemed to have need. 99% of undergraduates with need received aid; of those 7% had need fully met. *Average percent of need met:* 51% (excluding resources awarded to replace EFC). *Average financial aid package:* $13,958 (excluding resources awarded to replace EFC). 9% of all full-time undergraduates had no need and received non-need-based gift aid.

GIFT AID (NEED-BASED) Total amount: $22,379,293 (29% federal, 17% state, 52% institutional, 2% external sources). *Receiving aid:* Freshmen: 82% (447); all full-time undergraduates: 72% (2,074). *Average award:* Freshmen: $5043; Undergraduates: $4805. *Scholarships, grants, and awards:* Federal Pell, FSEOG, state, private, college/university gift aid from institutional funds.

GIFT AID (NON-NEED-BASED) Total amount: $1,496,859 (2% state, 81% institutional, 17% external sources). *Receiving aid:* Freshmen: 8% (45). Undergraduates: 6% (183). *Average award:* Freshmen: $4009. Undergraduates: $4896. *Scholarships, grants, and awards by category:* Academic interests/achievement: general academic interests/achievements. *Tuition waivers:* Full or partial for employees or children of employees. *ROTC:* Army, Air Force cooperative.

LOANS Student loans: $31,138,536 (90% need-based, 10% non-need-based). 87% of past graduating class borrowed through all loan programs. *Average indebtedness per student:* $31,694. *Average need-based loan:* Freshmen: $3380. Undergraduates: $4403. *Parent loans:* $7,442,143 (87% need-based, 13% non-need-based). *Programs:* Federal Direct (Subsidized and Unsubsidized Stafford, PLUS), Perkins.

WORK-STUDY Federal work-study: Total amount: $1,211,817; jobs available. *State or other work-study/employment:* Part-time jobs available.

APPLYING FOR FINANCIAL AID *Required financial aid form:* FAFSA. *Financial aid deadline (priority):* 2/15. *Notification date:* Continuous. Students must reply by 5/1 or within 4 weeks of notification.

CONTACT Karolina Holl, Director of Financial Aid, Utica College, 1600 Burrstone Road, Utica, NY 13502-4892, 315-792-3179 or toll-free 800-782-8884. *Fax:* 315-792-3368. *E-mail:* kmholl@utica.edu. *Website:* http://www.utica.edu/.

VALDOSTA STATE UNIVERSITY
Valdosta, GA

Tuition & fees (GA res): $6410	Average undergraduate aid package: $16,647

ABOUT THE INSTITUTION State-supported, coed. **Awards:** certificates, associate, bachelor's, master's, and doctoral degrees. 52 undergraduate majors. **Total enrollment:** 11,341. Undergraduates: 8,778. Freshmen: 1,628. Both federal and institutional methodology are used as a basis for awarding need-based institutional aid.

UNDERGRADUATE EXPENSES for 2018–2019 *Application fee:* $40. *Tuition, state resident:* full-time $4264; part-time $177.67 per credit hour. *Tuition, nonresident:* full-time $15,050; part-time $627.07 per credit hour.

Required fees: full-time $2146. Full-time tuition and fees vary according to course load, location, program, and reciprocity agreements. Part-time tuition and fees vary according to course load, location, program, and reciprocity agreements. **College room and board:** $7900; **Room only:** $4060. Room and board charges vary according to board plan and housing facility.

FRESHMAN FINANCIAL AID (Fall 2016) 1,373 applied for aid; of those 82% were deemed to have need. 100% of freshmen with need received aid; of those 16% had need fully met. **Average percent of need met:** 98% (excluding resources awarded to replace EFC). **Average financial aid package:** $16,833 (excluding resources awarded to replace EFC). 2% of all full-time freshmen had no need and received non-need-based gift aid.

UNDERGRADUATE FINANCIAL AID (Fall 2016) 6,502 applied for aid; of those 82% were deemed to have need. 99% of undergraduates with need received aid; of those 13% had need fully met. **Average percent of need met:** 84% (excluding resources awarded to replace EFC). **Average financial aid package:** $16,647 (excluding resources awarded to replace EFC). 1% of all full-time undergraduates had no need and received non-need-based gift aid.

GIFT AID (NEED-BASED) Total amount: $35,614,804 (62% federal, 36% state, 1% institutional, 1% external sources). **Receiving aid:** Freshmen: 67% (987); all full-time undergraduates: 56% (4,482). **Average award:** Freshmen: $7118; Undergraduates: $6517. **Scholarships, grants, and awards:** Federal Pell, FSEOG, state, private, college/university gift aid from institutional funds, United Negro College Fund, Federal Nursing.

GIFT AID (NON-NEED-BASED) Total amount: $4,212,409 (90% state, 5% institutional, 5% external sources). **Receiving aid:** Freshmen: 4% (54). Undergraduates: 2% (201). **Average award:** Freshmen: $2332. Undergraduates: $2331. **Scholarships, grants, and awards by category:** Academic interests/achievement: biological sciences, communication, education, general academic interests/achievements, health fields, library science, mathematics, physical sciences, social sciences. Creative arts/performance: art/fine arts, general creative arts/performance, journalism/publications, music, performing arts, theater/drama. Special achievements/activities: general special achievements/activities, religious involvement. Special characteristics: general special characteristics, local/state students, members of minority groups. **Tuition waivers:** Full or partial for employees or children of employees. **ROTC:** Air Force.

LOANS Student loans: $56,168,195 (79% need-based, 21% non-need-based). 75% of past graduating class borrowed through all loan programs. Average indebtedness per student: $28,318. **Average need-based loan:** Freshmen: $3390. Undergraduates: $4056. **Parent loans:** $54,593,178 (44% need-based, 56% non-need-based). **Programs:** Federal Direct (Subsidized and Unsubsidized Stafford, PLUS), state, college/university.

WORK-STUDY Federal work-study: jobs available. **State or other work-study/employment:** Part-time jobs available.

ATHLETIC AWARDS Total amount: $1,606,409 (47% need-based, 53% non-need-based).

APPLYING FOR FINANCIAL AID Required financial aid form: FAFSA. **Financial aid deadline (priority):** 3/1. **Notification date:** Continuous beginning 5/1.

CONTACT Mr. Douglas R. Tanner, Director of Financial Aid, Valdosta State University, 1500 North Patterson Street, Valdosta, GA 31698; 229-333-5935 or toll-free 800-618-1878. Fax: 229-333-5430.

Website: http://www.valdosta.edu/.

VALENCIA COLLEGE
Orlando, FL

Tuition & fees (FL res): $2473	Average undergraduate aid package: N/A

ABOUT THE INSTITUTION State-supported, coed. **Awards:** certificates, diplomas, associate, and bachelor's degrees. 31 undergraduate majors. **Total enrollment:** 44,833. Undergraduates: 44,833. Freshmen: 8,959. Federal methodology is used as a basis for awarding need-based institutional aid.

UNDERGRADUATE EXPENSES for 2018–2019 Application fee: $35. **Tuition, state resident:** full-time $2473. **Tuition, nonresident:** full-time $9383. Full-time tuition and fees vary according to degree level. Part-time tuition and fees vary according to degree level.

GIFT AID (NEED-BASED) Total amount: $73,978,982 **Scholarships, grants, and awards:** Federal Pell, FSEOG, state, private, college/university gift aid from institutional funds.

GIFT AID (NON-NEED-BASED) Scholarships, grants, and awards by category: Creative arts/performance: art/fine arts, music, theater/drama. Special achievements/activities: community service, leadership. **Tuition waivers:** Full or partial for employees or children of employees, senior citizens. **ROTC:** Army cooperative, Naval cooperative.

LOANS Programs: Federal Direct (Subsidized and Unsubsidized Stafford, PLUS).

WORK-STUDY Federal work-study: 335 jobs averaging $1516. **State or other work-study/employment:** Part-time jobs available.

APPLYING FOR FINANCIAL AID Required financial aid forms: FAFSA, state aid form. **Financial aid deadline (priority):** 3/15. **Notification date:** Continuous beginning 5/1.

CONTACT College Answer Center Specialists, Valencia College, PO Box 3028, Orlando, FL 32802-3028, 407-299-5000.

Website: http://valenciacollege.edu/.

VALLEY CITY STATE UNIVERSITY
Valley City, ND

Tuition & fees (ND res): $7406	Average undergraduate aid package: $12,648

ABOUT THE INSTITUTION State-supported, coed. **Awards:** bachelor's and master's degrees. 40 undergraduate majors. **Total enrollment:** 1,522. Undergraduates: 1,372. Freshmen: 190. Federal methodology is used as a basis for awarding need-based institutional aid.

UNDERGRADUATE EXPENSES for 2017–2018 Application fee: $35. **Tuition, state resident:** full-time $5493; part-time $183.10 per semester hour. **Tuition, nonresident:** full-time $14,666; part-time $488.88 per semester hour. **Required fees:** full-time $1913; $79.70 per semester hour. Full-time tuition and fees vary according to course load, location, program, and reciprocity agreements. Part-time tuition and fees vary according to course load, location, program, and reciprocity agreements. **College room and board:** $6328; **Room only:** $2378. Room and board charges vary according to board plan and housing facility.

FRESHMAN FINANCIAL AID (Fall 2017, est.) 145 applied for aid; of those 62% were deemed to have need. 100% of freshmen with need received aid; of those 56% had need fully met. **Average percent of need met:** 88% (excluding resources awarded to replace EFC). **Average financial aid package:** $13,848 (excluding resources awarded to replace EFC). 40% of all full-time freshmen had no need and received non-need-based gift aid.

UNDERGRADUATE FINANCIAL AID (Fall 2017, est.) 617 applied for aid; of those 71% were deemed to have need. 99% of undergraduates with need received aid; of those 50% had need fully met. **Average percent of need met:** 82% (excluding resources awarded to replace EFC). **Average financial aid package:** $12,648 (excluding resources awarded to replace EFC). 21% of all full-time undergraduates had no need and received non-need-based gift aid.

GIFT AID (NEED-BASED) Total amount: $2,354,474 (55% federal, 20% state, 19% institutional, 6% external sources). **Receiving aid:** Freshmen: 56% (89); all full-time undergraduates: 52% (392). **Average award:** Freshmen: $7880; Undergraduates: $6379. **Scholarships, grants, and awards:** Federal Pell, FSEOG, state, private, college/university gift aid from institutional funds, TEACH Grants.

GIFT AID (NON-NEED-BASED) Total amount: $763,917 (1% federal, 20% state, 63% institutional, 16% external sources). **Receiving aid:** Freshmen: 6% (10). Undergraduates: 5% (36). **Average award:** Freshmen: $2738. Undergraduates: $2699. **Scholarships, grants, and awards by category:** Academic interests/achievement: biological sciences, business, communication, computer science, education, engineering/technologies, English, general academic interests/achievements, humanities, library science, mathematics, physical sciences, social sciences. Creative arts/performance: applied art and design, art/fine arts, journalism/publications, music, theater/drama. Special achievements/activities: general special achievements/activities. Special characteristics: children and siblings of alumni, children of faculty/staff, ethnic background, general special characteristics, international students, members of minority groups. **Tuition waivers:** Full or partial for employees or children of employees.

LOANS Student loans: $4,790,811 (54% need-based, 46% non-need-based). 79% of past graduating class borrowed through all loan programs. Average indebtedness

per student: $27,050. *Average need-based loan:* Freshmen: $4503. Undergraduates: $6008. *Parent loans:* $42,106 (10% need-based, 90% non-need-based). *Programs:* Federal Direct (Subsidized and Unsubsidized Stafford, PLUS), Perkins.
WORK-STUDY *Federal work-study:* Total amount: $75,894; 40 jobs averaging $2143. *State or other work-study/employment:* Part-time jobs available.
ATHLETIC AWARDS Total amount: $510,228 (55% need-based, 45% non-need-based).
APPLYING FOR FINANCIAL AID *Required financial aid form:* FAFSA. *Financial aid deadline (priority):* 3/15. *Notification date:* Continuous beginning 12/1. Students must reply within 4 weeks of notification.
CONTACT Ms. Marcia Lee Pritchert, Director of Student Financial Aid, Valley City State University, 101 College Street SW, Valley City, ND 58072, 701-845-7541 or toll-free 800-532-8641 Ext. 7101. *Fax:* 701-845-7545. *E-mail:* marcia.pritchert@vcsu.edu. *Website:* http://www.vcsu.edu/.

VALPARAISO UNIVERSITY
Valparaiso, IN

Tuition & fees: $40,260	Average undergraduate aid package: $30,984

ABOUT THE INSTITUTION Independent Lutheran Church, coed. *Awards:* certificates, associate, bachelor's, master's, and doctoral degrees. 88 undergraduate majors. *Total enrollment:* 4,053. Undergraduates: 3,251. Freshmen: 807. Both federal and institutional methodology are used as a basis for awarding need-based institutional aid.
UNDERGRADUATE EXPENSES for 2018–2019 *Comprehensive fee:* $52,120 includes full-time tuition ($39,000), mandatory fees ($1260), and room and board ($11,860). *College room only:* $7280. Full-time tuition and fees vary according to course load and program. Room and board charges vary according to housing facility and student level. *Part-time tuition:* $1715 per credit hour. Part-time tuition and fees vary according to course load and program. *Payment plan:* Tuition prepayment.
FRESHMAN FINANCIAL AID (Fall 2016) 821 applied for aid; of those 88% were deemed to have need. 100% of freshmen with need received aid; of those 45% had need fully met. *Average percent of need met:* 94% (excluding resources awarded to replace EFC). *Average financial aid package:* $31,812 (excluding resources awarded to replace EFC). 15% of all full-time freshmen had no need and received non-need-based gift aid.
UNDERGRADUATE FINANCIAL AID (Fall 2016) 2,707 applied for aid; of those 90% were deemed to have need. 100% of undergraduates with need received aid; of those 40% had need fully met. *Average percent of need met:* 93% (excluding resources awarded to replace EFC). *Average financial aid package:* $30,984 (excluding resources awarded to replace EFC). 19% of all full-time undergraduates had no need and received non-need-based gift aid.
GIFT AID (NEED-BASED) *Total amount:* $71,299,131 (8% federal, 4% state, 87% institutional, 1% external sources). *Receiving aid:* Freshmen: 84% (722); all full-time undergraduates: 76% (2,434). *Average award:* Freshmen: $30,370; Undergraduates: $28,710. *Scholarships, grants, and awards:* Federal Pell, FSEOG, state, private, college/university gift aid from institutional funds.
GIFT AID (NON-NEED-BASED) *Total amount:* $13,820,652 (94% institutional, 6% external sources). *Receiving aid:* Freshmen: 18% (154). Undergraduates: 14% (437). *Average award:* Freshmen: $20,002. Undergraduates: $17,064. *Scholarships, grants, and awards by category:* Academic interests/achievement: business, engineering/technologies, foreign languages, general academic interests/achievements, military science, physical sciences, religion/biblical studies. *Creative arts/performance:* art/fine arts, music, performing arts, theater/drama. *Special achievements/activities:* religious involvement. *Special characteristics:* children and siblings of alumni, children of faculty/staff, international students, relatives of clergy, religious affiliation. *Tuition waivers:* Full or partial for employees or children of employees. *ROTC:* Army cooperative, Air Force cooperative.
LOANS *Student loans:* $18,063,584 (46% need-based, 54% non-need-based). 68% of past graduating class borrowed through all loan programs. *Average indebtedness per student:* $37,978. *Average need-based loan:* Freshmen: $4600. Undergraduates: $4948. *Parent loans:* $4,250,478 (13% need-based, 87% non-need-based). *Programs:* Federal Direct (Subsidized and Unsubsidized Stafford, PLUS), Perkins, college/university, private loans.

WORK-STUDY *Federal work-study:* 556 jobs averaging $1375. *State or other work-study/employment:* Total amount: $1,941,501 (15% need-based, 85% non-need-based). 940 part-time jobs averaging $2065.
ATHLETIC AWARDS Total amount: $4,400,879 (46% need-based, 54% non-need-based).
APPLYING FOR FINANCIAL AID *Required financial aid form:* FAFSA. *Financial aid deadline (priority):* 3/1. *Notification date:* Continuous beginning 12/15.
CONTACT Ms. Karen Klimczyk, Director of Financial Aid, Valparaiso University, 1700 Chapel Drive, Valparaiso, IN 46383-6493, 219-464-5015 or toll-free 888-GO-VALPO. *Fax:* 219-464-5012. *E-mail:* karen.klimczyk@valpo.edu. *Website:* http://www.valpo.edu/.

VANDERBILT UNIVERSITY
Nashville, TN

Tuition & fees: $47,664	Average undergraduate aid package: $49,242

ABOUT THE INSTITUTION Independent, coed. *Awards:* bachelor's, master's, and doctoral degrees. 70 undergraduate majors. *Total enrollment:* 12,587. Undergraduates: 6,871. Freshmen: 1,601. Both federal and institutional methodology are used as a basis for awarding need-based institutional aid.
UNDERGRADUATE EXPENSES for 2017–2018 *Application fee:* $50. *One-time required fee:* $865. *Comprehensive fee:* $63,248 includes full-time tuition ($46,500), mandatory fees ($1164), and room and board ($15,584). *College room only:* $10,212. Room and board charges vary according to board plan. *Part-time tuition:* $1938 per credit hour. *Payment plan:* Tuition prepayment.
FRESHMAN FINANCIAL AID (Fall 2017, est.) 1,097 applied for aid; of those 80% were deemed to have need. 99% of freshmen with need received aid; of those 100% had need fully met. *Average percent of need met:* 100% (excluding resources awarded to replace EFC). *Average financial aid package:* $50,356 (excluding resources awarded to replace EFC). 8% of all full-time freshmen had no need and received non-need-based gift aid.
UNDERGRADUATE FINANCIAL AID (Fall 2017, est.) 3,878 applied for aid; of those 89% were deemed to have need. 99% of undergraduates with need received aid; of those 100% had need fully met. *Average percent of need met:* 100% (excluding resources awarded to replace EFC). *Average financial aid package:* $49,242 (excluding resources awarded to replace EFC). 10% of all full-time undergraduates had no need and received non-need-based gift aid.
GIFT AID (NEED-BASED) *Total amount:* $156,199,163 (4% federal, 1% state, 94% institutional, 1% external sources). *Receiving aid:* Freshmen: 53% (849); all full-time undergraduates: 49% (3,379). *Average award:* Freshmen: $48,559; Undergraduates: $47,294. *Scholarships, grants, and awards:* Federal Pell, FSEOG, state, private, college/university gift aid from institutional funds, United Negro College Fund.
GIFT AID (NON-NEED-BASED) *Total amount:* $22,446,268 (9% federal, 3% state, 82% institutional, 6% external sources). *Receiving aid:* Freshmen: 5% (77). Undergraduates: 3% (205). *Average award:* Freshmen: $23,629. Undergraduates: $24,444. *Scholarships, grants, and awards by category:* Academic interests/achievement: agriculture, general academic interests/achievements. *Creative arts/performance:* general creative arts/performance. *Special achievements/activities:* community service, general special achievements/activities, leadership. *Special characteristics:* general special characteristics, local/state students, members of minority groups, veterans, veterans' children. *Tuition waivers:* Full or partial for employees or children of employees. *ROTC:* Army, Naval, Air Force cooperative.
LOANS *Student loans:* $7,812,302 (17% need-based, 83% non-need-based). 21% of past graduating class borrowed through all loan programs. *Average indebtedness per student:* $23,973. *Average need-based loan:* Freshmen: $2961. Undergraduates: $3534. *Parent loans:* $5,843,665 (100% non-need-based). *Programs:* Federal Direct (Subsidized and Unsubsidized Stafford, PLUS), Federal Nursing.
WORK-STUDY *Federal work-study:* Total amount: $3,854,001; 1,570 jobs averaging $2386. *State or other work-study/employment:* Total amount: $973,064 (100% need-based). Part-time jobs available.
ATHLETIC AWARDS Total amount: $12,780,125 (28% need-based, 72% non-need-based).
APPLYING FOR FINANCIAL AID *Required financial aid forms:* FAFSA, CSS Financial Aid PROFILE. *Financial aid deadline (priority):* 2/1. *Notification date:* 4/1. Students must reply by 5/1.

CONTACT Mr. Brent Tener, Director of Financial Aid, Vanderbilt University, 2309 West End Avenue, Nashville, TN 37203, 615-322-3591 or toll-free 800-288-0432. *Fax:* 615-343-8512. *E-mail:* b.tener@vanderbilt.edu. *Website:* http://www.vanderbilt.edu/.

VANDERCOOK COLLEGE OF MUSIC
Chicago, IL

Tuition & fees: $28,434	Average undergraduate aid package: $15,524

ABOUT THE INSTITUTION Independent, coed. *Awards:* bachelor's and master's degrees. 1 undergraduate major. *Total enrollment:* 262. Undergraduates: 122. Freshmen: 15. Federal methodology is used as a basis for awarding need-based institutional aid.

UNDERGRADUATE EXPENSES for 2018–2019 *Application fee:* $35. *Comprehensive fee:* $40,508 includes full-time tuition ($26,548), mandatory fees ($1886), and room and board ($12,074). *College room only:* $6150. Full-time tuition and fees vary according to course level, course load, and program. Room and board charges vary according to board plan and housing facility. *Part-time tuition:* $1115 per semester hour. *Part-time fees:* $1115 per credit. Part-time tuition and fees vary according to course level, course load, and program.

FRESHMAN FINANCIAL AID (Fall 2016) 21 applied for aid; of those 86% were deemed to have need. 100% of freshmen with need received aid. *Average financial aid package:* $14,295 (excluding resources awarded to replace EFC). 14% of all full-time freshmen had no need and received non-need-based gift aid.

UNDERGRADUATE FINANCIAL AID (Fall 2016) 98 applied for aid; of those 86% were deemed to have need. 100% of undergraduates with need received aid. *Average financial aid package:* $15,524 (excluding resources awarded to replace EFC). 18% of all full-time undergraduates had no need and received non-need-based gift aid.

GIFT AID (NEED-BASED) *Total amount:* $318,576 (54% federal, 41% state, 5% institutional). *Receiving aid:* Freshmen: 67% (14); all full-time undergraduates: 50% (51). *Average award:* Freshmen: $9402; Undergraduates: $10,190. *Scholarships, grants, and awards:* Federal Pell, FSEOG, state, private, college/university gift aid from institutional funds.

GIFT AID (NON-NEED-BASED) *Total amount:* $764,173 (5% federal, 2% state, 90% institutional, 3% external sources). *Receiving aid:* Freshmen: 86% (18). Undergraduates: 83% (84). *Average award:* Freshmen: $5967. Undergraduates: $8927. *Scholarships, grants, and awards by category:* Academic interests/achievement: $644,750 total: education, general academic interests/achievements. Creative arts/performance: $200,250 total: music. Special characteristics: $34,200 total: ethnic background, out-of-state students, religious affiliation. *Tuition waivers:* Full or partial for employees or children of employees.

LOANS *Student loans:* $917,109 (40% need-based, 60% non-need-based). 78% of past graduating class borrowed through all loan programs. *Average indebtedness per student:* $42,886. *Average need-based loan:* Freshmen: $3340. Undergraduates: $4523. *Parent loans:* $788,656 (100% non-need-based). *Programs:* Federal Direct (Subsidized and Unsubsidized Stafford, PLUS).

WORK-STUDY *Federal work-study:* 27 jobs averaging $748. *State or other work-study/employment:* Total amount: $4698 (100% non-need-based). 7 part-time jobs averaging $611.

APPLYING FOR FINANCIAL AID *Required financial aid form:* FAFSA. *Financial aid deadline (priority):* 12/1. *Notification date:* Continuous beginning 2/1. Students must reply within 2 weeks of notification.

CONTACT Ms. Sirena Covington, Director of Financial Aid, VanderCook College of Music, 3140 South Federal Street, Chicago, IL 60616, 312-788-1146. *Fax:* 312-225-5211. *E-mail:* scovington@vandercook.edu. *Website:* http://www.vandercook.edu/.

VANGUARD UNIVERSITY OF SOUTHERN CALIFORNIA
Costa Mesa, CA

Tuition & fees: $33,700	Average undergraduate aid package: $14,614

ABOUT THE INSTITUTION Independent Assemblies of God, coed. *Awards:* certificates, associate, bachelor's, and master's degrees. 45 undergraduate majors. *Total enrollment:* 2,116. Undergraduates: 1,805. Freshmen: 433. Federal methodology is used as a basis for awarding need-based institutional aid.

UNDERGRADUATE EXPENSES for 2018–2019 *Application fee:* $45. *Tuition:* full-time $33,200; part-time $1384 per credit hour. Full-time tuition and fees vary according to class time, course level, course load, degree level, location, and program. Part-time tuition and fees vary according to class time, course level, course load, degree level, and program. Room and board charges vary according to board plan, gender, housing facility, and student level.

FRESHMAN FINANCIAL AID (Fall 2017, est.) 405 applied for aid; of those 100% were deemed to have need. 100% of freshmen with need received aid; of those 100% had need fully met. *Average financial aid package:* $16,513 (excluding resources awarded to replace EFC). 99% of all full-time freshmen had no need and received non-need-based gift aid.

UNDERGRADUATE FINANCIAL AID (Fall 2017, est.) 1,319 applied for aid; of those 99% were deemed to have need. 100% of undergraduates with need received aid; of those 100% had need fully met. *Average financial aid package:* $14,614 (excluding resources awarded to replace EFC). 92% of all full-time undergraduates had no need and received non-need-based gift aid.

GIFT AID (NEED-BASED) *Total amount:* $31,622,380 (13% federal, 25% state, 62% institutional). *Receiving aid:* Freshmen: 61% (268); all full-time undergraduates: 54% (817). *Average award:* Freshmen: $8003; Undergraduates: $7303. *Scholarships, grants, and awards:* Federal Pell, FSEOG, state, private, college/university gift aid from institutional funds.

GIFT AID (NON-NEED-BASED) *Total amount:* $1,125,756 (96% institutional, 4% external sources). *Receiving aid:* Freshmen: 26% (113). Undergraduates: 27% (413). *Average award:* Freshmen: $8749. Undergraduates: $8075. *Scholarships, grants, and awards by category:* Academic interests/achievement: general academic interests/achievements. Creative arts/performance: debating, music, theater/drama. Special characteristics: children of faculty/staff, religious affiliation. *Tuition waivers:* Full or partial for employees or children of employees. *ROTC:* Army cooperative, Air Force cooperative.

LOANS *Student loans:* $12,968,296 (100% need-based). 77% of past graduating class borrowed through all loan programs. *Average indebtedness per student:* $31,614. *Parent loans:* $4,522,268 (100% non-need-based). *Programs:* Federal Direct (Subsidized and Unsubsidized Stafford, PLUS), Perkins.

WORK-STUDY *Federal work-study:* Total amount: $601,311; jobs available.

ATHLETIC AWARDS Total amount: $1,874,580 (100% non-need-based).

APPLYING FOR FINANCIAL AID *Required financial aid form:* FAFSA. *Financial aid deadline:* 3/2. *Notification date:* Continuous beginning 3/15. Students must reply within 3 weeks of notification.

CONTACT Financial Aid Office, Vanguard University of Southern California, 55 Fair Drive, Costa Mesa, CA 92626, 714-966-5490 or toll-free 800-722-6279. *Fax:* 714-619-6655. *E-mail:* financialaid@vanguard.edu. *Website:* http://www.vanguard.edu/.

VASSAR COLLEGE
Poughkeepsie, NY

Tuition & fees: $55,210	Average undergraduate aid package: $53,642

ABOUT THE INSTITUTION Independent, coed. *Awards:* bachelor's and master's degrees. 51 undergraduate majors. *Total enrollment:* 2,353. Undergraduates: 2,352. Freshmen: 624. Institutional methodology is used as a basis for awarding need-based institutional aid.

UNDERGRADUATE EXPENSES for 2017–2018 *Application fee:* $70. *One-time required fee:* $80. *Comprehensive fee:* $68,110 includes full-time tuition ($54,410), mandatory fees ($800), and room and board ($12,900). *College room* only: $9000. Room and board charges vary according to housing facility. **Part-time tuition:** $6480 per unit.

FRESHMAN FINANCIAL AID (Fall 2017, est.) 486 applied for aid; of those 83% were deemed to have need. 100% of freshmen with need received aid; of those 100% had need fully met. **Average percent of need met:** 100% (excluding resources awarded to replace EFC). **Average financial aid package:** $52,284 (excluding resources awarded to replace EFC).

UNDERGRADUATE FINANCIAL AID (Fall 2017, est.) 1,621 applied for aid; of those 89% were deemed to have need. 100% of undergraduates with need received aid; of those 100% had need fully met. **Average percent of need met:** 100% (excluding resources awarded to replace EFC). **Average financial aid package:** $53,642 (excluding resources awarded to replace EFC).

GIFT AID (NEED-BASED) Total amount: $73,105,875 (4% federal, 1% state, 93% institutional, 2% external sources). **Receiving aid:** Freshmen: 64% (401); all full-time undergraduates: 62% (1,440). **Average award:** Freshmen: $46,709; Undergraduates: $48,194. **Scholarships, grants, and awards:** Federal Pell, FSEOG, state, private, college/university gift aid from institutional funds.

GIFT AID (NON-NEED-BASED) Total amount: $185,719 (12% federal, 3% state, 85% external sources). **Tuition waivers:** Full or partial for employees or children of employees.

LOANS Student loans: $6,368,557 (52% need-based, 48% non-need-based). 45% of past graduating class borrowed through all loan programs. **Average indebtedness per student:** $19,439. **Average need-based loan:** Freshmen: $2517. Undergraduates: $3462. **Parent loans:** $3,196,043 (100% non-need-based). **Programs:** Federal Direct (Subsidized and Unsubsidized Stafford, PLUS), Perkins.

WORK-STUDY Federal work-study: Total amount: $2,920,012; 1,119 jobs averaging $2539. **State or other work-study/employment:** Total amount: $872,770 (100% need-based). 346 part-time jobs averaging $2521.

APPLYING FOR FINANCIAL AID Required financial aid forms: FAFSA, CSS Financial Aid PROFILE, noncustodial (divorced/separated) parent's statement. **Financial aid deadline:** 2/1. **Notification date:** 3/30. Students must reply by 5/1.

CONTACT Ms. Jessica L. Bernier, Director of Student Financial Services, Vassar College, 124 Raymond Avenue, Box 8, Poughkeepsie, NY 12604, 845-437-5320 or toll-free 800-827-7270. Fax: 845-437-5325. E-mail: jebernier@vassar.edu. Website: http://www.vassar.edu/.

VAUGHN COLLEGE OF AERONAUTICS AND TECHNOLOGY
Flushing, NY

Tuition & fees: $24,877	Average undergraduate aid package: $8245

ABOUT THE INSTITUTION Independent, coed, primarily men. **Awards:** certificates, diplomas, associate, bachelor's, and master's degrees. 11 undergraduate majors. **Total enrollment:** 1,501. Undergraduates: 1,496. Freshmen: 253. Federal methodology is used as a basis for awarding need-based institutional aid.

UNDERGRADUATE EXPENSES for 2017–2018 Application fee: $40. **One-time required fee:** $160. **Comprehensive fee:** $39,062 includes full-time tuition ($23,877), mandatory fees ($1000), and room and board ($14,185). **College room only:** $10,983. Full-time tuition and fees vary according to course load, degree level, and program. Room and board charges vary according to board plan. **Part-time tuition:** $800 per credit hour. **Part-time fees:** $400 per term. Part-time tuition and fees vary according to course load, degree level, and program.

FRESHMAN FINANCIAL AID (Fall 2016) 256 applied for aid; of those 88% were deemed to have need. 100% of freshmen with need received aid; of those 15% had need fully met. **Average percent of need met:** 70% (excluding resources awarded to replace EFC). **Average financial aid package:** $8084 (excluding resources awarded to replace EFC). 7% of all full-time freshmen had no need and received non-need-based gift aid.

UNDERGRADUATE FINANCIAL AID (Fall 2016) 1,203 applied for aid; of those 83% were deemed to have need. 100% of undergraduates with need received aid; of those 16% had need fully met. **Average percent of need met:** 74% (excluding resources awarded to replace EFC). **Average financial aid package:** $8245 (excluding resources awarded to replace EFC). 6% of all full-time undergraduates had no need and received non-need-based gift aid.

GIFT AID (NEED-BASED) Total amount: $4,517,632 (50% federal, 32% state, 18% institutional). **Receiving aid:** Freshmen: 75% (196); all full-time undergraduates:

69% (885). **Average award:** Freshmen: $5424; Undergraduates: $4804. **Scholarships, grants, and awards:** Federal Pell, FSEOG, state, private, college/university gift aid from institutional funds, Academic Competitiveness Grants, National SMART Grants, TEACH Grants.

GIFT AID (NON-NEED-BASED) Total amount: $3,682,700 (51% federal, 1% state, 44% institutional, 4% external sources). **Receiving aid:** Freshmen: 27% (71). Undergraduates: 30% (387). **Average award:** Freshmen: $6146. Undergraduates: $2948. **Scholarships, grants, and awards by category:** Academic interests/achievement: computer science, education, engineering/technologies. **Special characteristics:** veterans, veterans' children. **Tuition waivers:** Full or partial for employees or children of employees. **ROTC:** Army cooperative, Air Force cooperative.

LOANS Student loans: $3,872,486 (84% need-based, 16% non-need-based). 75% of past graduating class borrowed through all loan programs. **Average indebtedness per student:** $32,014. **Average need-based loan:** Freshmen: $1709. Undergraduates: $2067. **Parent loans:** $889,333 (100% need-based). **Programs:** Federal Direct (Subsidized and Unsubsidized Stafford, PLUS), private loans.

WORK-STUDY Federal work-study: jobs available. **State or other work-study/employment:** Part-time jobs available.

APPLYING FOR FINANCIAL AID Required financial aid forms: FAFSA, state aid form. **Financial aid deadline:** Continuous. **Notification date:** Continuous beginning 4/15. Students must reply within 2 weeks of notification.

CONTACT Office of Financial Aid, Vaughn College of Aeronautics and Technology, 86-01 23rd Avenue, Flushing, NY 11369, 866-682-8446 Ext. 100 or toll-free 866-6VAUGHN. Fax: 718-779-2231. E-mail: financialaid@vaughn.edu. Website: http://www.vaughn.edu/.

VERMONT TECHNICAL COLLEGE
Randolph Center, VT

Tuition & fees (VT res): $15,510	Average undergraduate aid package: $14,736

ABOUT THE INSTITUTION State-supported, coed. **Awards:** certificates, associate, bachelor's, and master's degrees. 24 undergraduate majors. **Total enrollment:** 1,621. Undergraduates: 1,615. Freshmen: 219. Federal methodology is used as a basis for awarding need-based institutional aid.

UNDERGRADUATE EXPENSES for 2018–2019 Application fee: $47. **Tuition, state resident:** full-time $13,896; part-time $579 per credit hour. **Tuition, nonresident:** full-time $26,568; part-time $1107 per credit hour. **Required fees:** full-time $1614; $48 per credit hour. Full-time tuition and fees vary according to course load and program. Part-time tuition and fees vary according to program. **College room and board:** $10,598; **Room only:** $6312. Room and board charges vary according to board plan.

FRESHMAN FINANCIAL AID (Fall 2016) 205 applied for aid; of those 81% were deemed to have need. 100% of freshmen with need received aid; of those 8% had need fully met. **Average percent of need met:** 58% (excluding resources awarded to replace EFC). **Average financial aid package:** $12,492 (excluding resources awarded to replace EFC). 14% of all full-time freshmen had no need and received non-need-based gift aid.

UNDERGRADUATE FINANCIAL AID (Fall 2016) 902 applied for aid; of those 90% were deemed to have need. 98% of undergraduates with need received aid; of those 9% had need fully met. **Average percent of need met:** 61% (excluding resources awarded to replace EFC). **Average financial aid package:** $14,736 (excluding resources awarded to replace EFC). 6% of all full-time undergraduates had no need and received non-need-based gift aid.

GIFT AID (NEED-BASED) Total amount: $6,511,729 (36% federal, 22% state, 29% institutional, 13% external sources). **Receiving aid:** Freshmen: 72% (153); all full-time undergraduates: 60% (662). **Average award:** Freshmen: $3080; Undergraduates: $5648. **Scholarships, grants, and awards:** Federal Pell, FSEOG, state, private, college/university gift aid from institutional funds.

GIFT AID (NON-NEED-BASED) Total amount: $198,942 (83% institutional, 17% external sources). **Receiving aid:** Freshmen: 39% (83). Undergraduates: 23% (253). **Average award:** Freshmen: $4620. Undergraduates: $4740. **Scholarships, grants, and awards by category:** Academic interests/achievement: 9 awards ($58,320 total): agriculture. **Tuition waivers:** Full or partial for employees or children of employees, senior citizens. **ROTC:** Army cooperative.

LOANS Student loans: $10,903,591 (94% need-based, 6% non-need-based). 86% of past graduating class borrowed through all loan programs. **Average indebtedness**

per student: $29,988. **Average need-based loan:** Freshmen: $3340. Undergraduates: $3920. **Parent loans:** $1,489,350 (92% need-based, 8% non-need-based). **Programs:** Federal Direct (Subsidized and Unsubsidized Stafford, PLUS).

WORK-STUDY *Federal work-study:* 177 jobs averaging $1260.

APPLYING FOR FINANCIAL AID *Required financial aid forms:* FAFSA, state aid form. **Financial aid deadline (priority):** 3/1. **Notification date:** Continuous beginning 11/20.

CONTACT Catherine R. McCullough, Director of Financial Aid, Vermont Technical College, PO Box 500, Randolph Center, VT 05061-0500, 802-728-1248 or toll-free 800-442-VTCI. *Fax:* 802-728-1436.

Website: http://www.vtc.edu/.

VILLA MARIA COLLEGE
Buffalo, NY

Tuition & fees: $22,080	Average undergraduate aid package: N/A

ABOUT THE INSTITUTION Independent Roman Catholic Church, coed. **Awards:** certificates, associate, and bachelor's degrees. 20 undergraduate majors. **Total enrollment:** 596. Undergraduates: 596. Freshmen: 133. Federal methodology is used as a basis for awarding need-based institutional aid.

UNDERGRADUATE EXPENSES for 2017–2018 *Tuition:* full-time $20,830; part-time $695 per credit hour. Full-time tuition and fees vary according to degree level, program, and reciprocity agreements. Part-time tuition and fees vary according to course load, degree level, program, and reciprocity agreements.

GIFT AID (NEED-BASED) *Total amount:* $6,379,494 (29% federal, 21% state, 48% institutional, 2% external sources). **Scholarships, grants, and awards:** Federal Pell, FSEOG, state, private, college/university gift aid from institutional funds.

GIFT AID (NON-NEED-BASED) *Total amount:* $754,957 (25% federal, 52% institutional, 23% external sources). *Tuition waivers:* Full or partial for employees or children of employees.

LOANS *Student loans:* $3,730,782 (95% need-based, 5% non-need-based). 91% of past graduating class borrowed through all loan programs. *Average indebtedness per student:* $22,658. *Parent loans:* $392,242 (95% need-based, 5% non-need-based). *Programs:* Federal Direct (Subsidized and Unsubsidized Stafford, PLUS), private loans.

WORK-STUDY *Federal work-study:* jobs available. **State or other work-study/employment:** Part-time jobs available.

APPLYING FOR FINANCIAL AID *Required financial aid forms:* FAFSA, state aid form. **Financial aid deadline:** Continuous. **Notification date:** Continuous beginning 4/1. Students must reply within 2 weeks of notification.

CONTACT Aimee Murch, Director of Financial Aid, Villa Maria College, 240 Pine Ridge Road, Buffalo, NY 14225, 716-961-1828. *Fax:* 716-896-0705. *E-mail:* murcha@villa.edu.

Website: http://www.villa.edu/.

VILLANOVA UNIVERSITY
Villanova, PA

Tuition & fees: $51,284	Average undergraduate aid package: $36,683

ABOUT THE INSTITUTION Independent Roman Catholic, coed. **Awards:** certificates, bachelor's, master's, and doctoral degrees. 51 undergraduate majors. **Total enrollment:** 10,983. Undergraduates: 6,966. Freshmen: 1,725. Both federal and institutional methodology are used as a basis for awarding need-based institutional aid.

UNDERGRADUATE EXPENSES for 2017–2018 *Application fee:* $80. **Comprehensive fee:** $64,832 includes full-time tuition ($50,554), mandatory fees ($730), and room and board ($13,548). **College room only:** $7218. Full-time tuition and fees vary according to degree level, location, and student level. Room and board charges vary according to board plan and housing facility. *Part-time tuition:* $2809 per credit hour. *Part-time fees:* $20 per credit hour. Part-time tuition and fees vary according to class time, course load, degree level, location, and program.

FRESHMAN FINANCIAL AID (Fall 2017, est.) 1,204 applied for aid; of those 71% were deemed to have need. 97% of freshmen with need received aid; of those 12%

had need fully met. **Average percent of need met:** 81% (excluding resources awarded to replace EFC). **Average financial aid package:** $38,853 (excluding resources awarded to replace EFC). 6% of all full-time freshmen had no need and received non-need-based gift aid.

UNDERGRADUATE FINANCIAL AID (Fall 2017, est.) 3,919 applied for aid; of those 82% were deemed to have need. 96% of undergraduates with need received aid; of those 10% had need fully met. **Average percent of need met:** 75% (excluding resources awarded to replace EFC). **Average financial aid package:** $36,683 (excluding resources awarded to replace EFC). 8% of all full-time undergraduates had no need and received non-need-based gift aid.

GIFT AID (NEED-BASED) *Total amount:* $92,493,532 (7% federal, 1% state, 91% institutional, 1% external sources). **Receiving aid:** Freshmen: 46% (786); all full-time undergraduates: 45% (2,912). **Average award:** Freshmen: $34,470; Undergraduates: $32,405. **Scholarships, grants, and awards:** Federal Pell, FSEOG, state, private, college/university gift aid from institutional funds, endowed and restricted scholarships and grants.

GIFT AID (NON-NEED-BASED) *Total amount:* $12,823,903 (30% federal, 64% institutional, 6% external sources). **Receiving aid:** Freshmen: 5% (78). Undergraduates: 2% (157). **Average award:** Freshmen: $16,710. Undergraduates: $16,497. **Scholarships, grants, and awards by category:** Academic interests/achievement: 882 awards ($11,427,344 total): general academic interests/achievements, international studies, military science. *Special achievements/activities:* 25 awards ($21,250 total): general special achievements/activities. *Special characteristics:* 261 awards ($10,543,855 total): children of educators, children of faculty/staff, general special characteristics, religious affiliation. **Tuition waivers:** Full or partial for employees or children of employees, senior citizens. **ROTC:** Army, Naval, Air Force cooperative.

LOANS *Student loans:* $33,739,002 (84% need-based, 16% non-need-based). 60% of past graduating class borrowed through all loan programs. *Average indebtedness per student:* $34,752. **Average need-based loan:** Freshmen: $4187. Undergraduates: $5104. **Parent loans:** $14,894,814 (82% need-based, 18% non-need-based). *Programs:* Federal Direct (Subsidized and Unsubsidized Stafford, PLUS), Perkins, Federal Nursing, alternative loans.

WORK-STUDY *Federal work-study:* Total amount: $6,172,875; 2,059 jobs averaging $2842. **State or other work-study/employment:** Total amount: $136,500 (100% need-based). 46 part-time jobs averaging $2967.

ATHLETIC AWARDS Total amount: $13,314,713 (23% need-based, 77% non-need-based).

APPLYING FOR FINANCIAL AID *Required financial aid forms:* FAFSA, CSS Financial Aid PROFILE, noncustodial (divorced/separated) parent's statement, federal income tax form(s), W-2 forms. **Financial aid deadline:** 1/15. **Notification date:** 4/1. Students must reply by 5/1.

CONTACT Bonnie Lee Behm, Director of Financial Assistance, Villanova University, 800 Lancaster Avenue, Villanova, PA 19085-1699, 610-519-4010. *Fax:* 610-519-7599. *E-mail:* bonnie.behm@villanova.edu.

Website: http://www.villanova.edu/.

VIRGINIA BAPTIST COLLEGE
Fredericksburg, VA

CONTACT Financial Aid Office, Virginia Baptist College, 4111 Plank Road, Fredericksburg, VA 22407.

Website: http://www.vbc.edu/.

VIRGINIA COLLEGE IN BIRMINGHAM
Birmingham, AL

CONTACT Vice President, Campus Administration, Virginia College in Birmingham, 65 Bagby Drive, Birmingham, AL 35209, 205-802-1200. *Fax:* 205-271-8273.

Website: http://www.vc.edu/.

VIRGINIA COMMONWEALTH UNIVERSITY
Richmond, VA

Tuition & fees (VA res): $13,570	Average undergraduate aid package: $11,623

ABOUT THE INSTITUTION State-supported, coed. **Awards:** certificates, bachelor's, master's, and doctoral degrees. 58 undergraduate majors. **Total enrollment:** 31,036. Undergraduates: 24,010. Freshmen: 4,201. Federal methodology is used as a basis for awarding need-based institutional aid.

UNDERGRADUATE EXPENSES for 2017–2018 Application fee: $65. **Tuition, state resident:** full-time $11,340; part-time $391 per credit hour. **Tuition, nonresident:** full-time $30,712; part-time $1059 per credit hour. **Required fees:** full-time $2230. **College room and board:** $10,187. Room and board charges vary according to board plan and housing facility.

FRESHMAN FINANCIAL AID (Fall 2016) 3,443 applied for aid; of those 80% were deemed to have need. 97% of freshmen with need received aid; of those 8% had need fully met. **Average percent of need met:** 55% (excluding resources awarded to replace EFC). **Average financial aid package:** $12,175 (excluding resources awarded to replace EFC). 9% of all full-time freshmen had no need and received non-need-based gift aid.

UNDERGRADUATE FINANCIAL AID (Fall 2016) 14,387 applied for aid; of those 84% were deemed to have need. 97% of undergraduates with need received aid; of those 6% had need fully met. **Average percent of need met:** 53% (excluding resources awarded to replace EFC). **Average financial aid package:** $11,623 (excluding resources awarded to replace EFC). 7% of all full-time undergraduates had no need and received non-need-based gift aid.

GIFT AID (NEED-BASED) Total amount: $80,916,172 (37% federal, 34% state, 19% institutional, 10% external sources). **Receiving aid:** Freshmen: 59% (2,480); all full-time undergraduates: 50% (10,086). **Average award:** Freshmen: $9893; Undergraduates: $8758. **Scholarships, grants, and awards:** Federal Pell, FSEOG, state, private, college/university gift aid from institutional funds, United Negro College Fund.

GIFT AID (NON-NEED-BASED) Total amount: $23,517,629 (1% state, 13% institutional, 86% external sources). **Receiving aid:** Freshmen: 3% (124). Undergraduates: 2% (344). **Average award:** Freshmen: $6564. Undergraduates: $7245. **Tuition waivers:** Full or partial for employees or children of employees. **ROTC:** Army cooperative.

LOANS Student loans: $114,731,124 (78% need-based, 22% non-need-based). 62% of past graduating class borrowed through all loan programs. **Average indebtedness per student:** $31,919. **Average need-based loan:** Freshmen: $3376. Undergraduates: $4413. **Parent loans:** $25,003,893 (51% need-based, 49% non-need-based). **Programs:** Federal Direct (Subsidized and Unsubsidized Stafford, PLUS), Perkins, Federal Nursing, college/university.

WORK-STUDY Federal work-study: 759 jobs averaging $2397. **State or other work-study/employment:** Total amount: $1322 (38% need-based, 62% non-need-based). 7 part-time jobs averaging $161.

ATHLETIC AWARDS Total amount: $5,171,702 (69% need-based, 31% non-need-based).

APPLYING FOR FINANCIAL AID Required financial aid form: FAFSA. **Financial aid deadline (priority):** 3/1. **Notification date:** Continuous beginning 4/1. Students must reply within 2 weeks of notification.

CONTACT Financial Aid Office, Virginia Commonwealth University, PO Box 843026, 1015 Floyd Avenue, Richmond, VA 23284-3026, 804-828-1550 or toll-free 800-841-3638. Fax: 804-827-0060.
Website: http://www.vcu.edu/.

VIRGINIA INTERNATIONAL UNIVERSITY
Fairfax, VA

CONTACT Financial Aid Office, Virginia International University, 4401 Village Drive, Fairfax, VA 22030, 703-591-7042 or toll-free 800-514-6848.
Website: http://www.viu.edu/.

VIRGINIA MARTI COLLEGE OF ART AND DESIGN
Lakewood, OH

CONTACT Financial Aid Office, Virginia Marti College of Art and Design, 11724 Detroit Avenue, Lakewood, OH 44107, 216-221-8584.
Website: http://www.vmcad.edu/.

VIRGINIA MILITARY INSTITUTE
Lexington, VA

Tuition & fees (VA res): $18,214	Average undergraduate aid package: $24,778

ABOUT THE INSTITUTION State-supported, coed. **Awards:** bachelor's degrees. 14 undergraduate majors. **Total enrollment:** 1,722. Undergraduates: 1,722. Freshmen: 424. Federal methodology is used as a basis for awarding need-based institutional aid.

UNDERGRADUATE EXPENSES for 2017–2018 Application fee: $40. **Tuition, state resident:** full-time $8884; part-time $336 per credit hour. **Tuition, nonresident:** full-time $34,572; part-time $1155 per credit hour. **Required fees:** full-time $9330; $71 per term. **College room and board:** $9236.

FRESHMAN FINANCIAL AID (Fall 2016) 369 applied for aid; of those 76% were deemed to have need. 98% of freshmen with need received aid; of those 32% had need fully met. **Average percent of need met:** 85% (excluding resources awarded to replace EFC). **Average financial aid package:** $23,915 (excluding resources awarded to replace EFC). 3% of all full-time freshmen had no need and received non-need-based gift aid.

UNDERGRADUATE FINANCIAL AID (Fall 2016) 1,145 applied for aid; of those 79% were deemed to have need. 99% of undergraduates with need received aid; of those 39% had need fully met. **Average percent of need met:** 85% (excluding resources awarded to replace EFC). **Average financial aid package:** $24,778 (excluding resources awarded to replace EFC). 3% of all full-time undergraduates had no need and received non-need-based gift aid.

GIFT AID (NEED-BASED) Total amount: $8,375,939 (13% federal, 12% state, 71% institutional, 4% external sources). **Receiving aid:** Freshmen: 57% (248); all full-time undergraduates: 40% (685). **Average award:** Freshmen: $13,124; Undergraduates: $12,449. **Scholarships, grants, and awards:** Federal Pell, FSEOG, state, private, college/university gift aid from institutional funds.

GIFT AID (NON-NEED-BASED) Total amount: $14,509,819 (82% federal, 18% institutional). **Receiving aid:** Freshmen: 26% (115). Undergraduates: 28% (472). **Average award:** Freshmen: $7811. Undergraduates: $4284. **Scholarships, grants, and awards by category:** Academic interests/achievement: biological sciences, business, computer science, engineering/technologies, English, foreign languages, general academic interests/achievements, humanities, international studies, mathematics, military science, physical sciences, premedicine. Creative arts/performance: music. Special achievements/activities: general special achievements/activities. Special characteristics: children and siblings of alumni, general special characteristics, local/state students, out-of-state students, veterans' children. **ROTC:** Army, Naval, Air Force.

LOANS Student loans: $8,813,616 (32% need-based, 68% non-need-based). 66% of past graduating class borrowed through all loan programs. **Average indebtedness per student:** $30,367. **Average need-based loan:** Freshmen: $3762. Undergraduates: $4113. **Parent loans:** $3,043,758 (100% non-need-based). **Programs:** Federal Direct (Subsidized and Unsubsidized Stafford, PLUS), Perkins, college/university.

ATHLETIC AWARDS Total amount: $4,027,545 (100% non-need-based).

APPLYING FOR FINANCIAL AID Required financial aid forms: FAFSA, institution's own form. **Financial aid deadline:** 3/1. **Notification date:** Continuous beginning 4/1. Students must reply by 5/1.

CONTACT Capt. Brian Quisenerry, Director of Financial Aid, Virginia Military Institute, 302A Carroll Hall, Lexington, VA 24450, 540-464-7626 or toll-free 800-767-4207. Fax: 540-464-7629. E-mail: quisenberrybl@vmi.edu.
Website: http://www.vmi.edu/.

VIRGINIA POLYTECHNIC INSTITUTE AND STATE UNIVERSITY
Blacksburg, VA

Tuition & fees (VA res): $13,230	Average undergraduate aid package: $17,772

ABOUT THE INSTITUTION State-supported, coed. **Awards:** certificates, bachelor's, master's, and doctoral degrees. 80 undergraduate majors. **Total enrollment:** 34,440. Undergraduates: 27,193. Freshmen: 6,836. Federal methodology is used as a basis for awarding need-based institutional aid.

UNDERGRADUATE EXPENSES for 2017–2018 Application fee: $60. **Tuition, state resident:** full-time $11,093; part-time $462.25 per hour. **Tuition, nonresident:** full-time $28,272; part-time $1178 per hour. **Required fees:** full-time $2137; $351 per term. **College room and board:** $8690. Room and board charges vary according to board plan and housing facility.

FRESHMAN FINANCIAL AID (Fall 2016) 4,676 applied for aid; of those 55% were deemed to have need. 94% of freshmen with need received aid; of those 20% had need fully met. **Average percent of need met:** 66% (excluding resources awarded to replace EFC). **Average financial aid package:** $17,549 (excluding resources awarded to replace EFC). 10% of all full-time freshmen had no need and received non-need-based gift aid.

UNDERGRADUATE FINANCIAL AID (Fall 2016) 16,298 applied for aid; of those 67% were deemed to have need. 96% of undergraduates with need received aid; of those 17% had need fully met. **Average percent of need met:** 64% (excluding resources awarded to replace EFC). **Average financial aid package:** $17,772 (excluding resources awarded to replace EFC). 9% of all full-time undergraduates had no need and received non-need-based gift aid.

GIFT AID (NEED-BASED) Total amount: $38,490,877 (47% federal, 42% state, 11% institutional). **Receiving aid:** Freshmen: 29% (1,703); all full-time undergraduates: 31% (7,704). **Average award:** Freshmen: $7664; Undergraduates: $7097. **Scholarships, grants, and awards:** Federal Pell, FSEOG, state, private, college/university gift aid from institutional funds, United Negro College Fund.

GIFT AID (NON-NEED-BASED) Total amount: $41,074,422 (38% federal, 30% institutional, 32% external sources). **Receiving aid:** Freshmen: 23% (1,344). Undergraduates: 23% (5,763). **Average award:** Freshmen: $4027. Undergraduates: $4064. **Scholarships, grants, and awards by category:** Academic interests/achievement: general academic interests/achievements, library science. Creative arts/performance: applied art and design, art/fine arts, cinema/film/broadcasting, creative writing, journalism/publications, music, performing arts, theater/drama. Special achievements/activities: cheerleading/drum major, community service, general special achievements/activities, leadership, memberships, religious involvement. Special characteristics: children of faculty/staff, first-generation college students, local/state students, members of minority groups, out-of-state students, twins, veterans' children. **Tuition waivers:** Full or partial for senior citizens. **ROTC:** Army, Naval, Air Force.

LOANS Student loans: $99,566,680 (35% need-based, 65% non-need-based). 49% of past graduating class borrowed through all loan programs. **Average indebtedness per student:** $30,221. **Average need-based loan:** Freshmen: $3902. Undergraduates: $4528. **Parent loans:** $35,038,396 (100% non-need-based). **Programs:** Federal Direct (Subsidized and Unsubsidized Stafford, PLUS), Perkins, state, college/university.

WORK-STUDY Federal work-study: jobs available. **State or other work-study/employment:** Total amount: $13,512,378 (100% non-need-based). Part-time jobs available.

ATHLETIC AWARDS Total amount: $11,975,701 (100% non-need-based).

APPLYING FOR FINANCIAL AID Required financial aid form: FAFSA. **Financial aid deadline:** 1/15. **Notification date:** 4/1. Students must reply by 5/1 or within 4 weeks of notification.

CONTACT Ms. Beth Armstrong, Director of University Scholarships and Financial Aid, Virginia Polytechnic Institute and State University, Student Services Building, Suite 200, 800 Washington Street SW, Blacksburg, VA 24061, 540-231-5179. *Fax:* 540-231-9139. *E-mail:* finaid@vt.edu.
Website: http://www.vt.edu/.

VIRGINIA STATE UNIVERSITY
Petersburg, VA

Tuition & fees (VA res): $8726	Average undergraduate aid package: $11,600

ABOUT THE INSTITUTION State-supported, coed. **Awards:** certificates, bachelor's, master's, and doctoral degrees. 31 undergraduate majors. **Total enrollment:** 4,584. Undergraduates: 4,165. Freshmen: 1,024. Federal methodology is used as a basis for awarding need-based institutional aid.

UNDERGRADUATE EXPENSES for 2017–2018 Application fee: $25. **Tuition, state resident:** full-time $5327; part-time $380 per credit hour. **Tuition, nonresident:** full-time $15,442; part-time $842 per credit hour. **Required fees:** full-time $3399; $10 per credit hour. Full-time tuition and fees vary according to course load. Part-time tuition and fees vary according to course load. **College room and board:** $10,880; **Room only:** $6356. Room and board charges vary according to board plan and housing facility.

FRESHMAN FINANCIAL AID (Fall 2016) 943 applied for aid; of those 100% were deemed to have need. 100% of freshmen with need received aid; of those 31% had need fully met. **Average percent of need met:** 60% (excluding resources awarded to replace EFC). **Average financial aid package:** $11,000 (excluding resources awarded to replace EFC). 21% of all full-time freshmen had no need and received non-need-based gift aid.

UNDERGRADUATE FINANCIAL AID (Fall 2016) 3,828 applied for aid; of those 100% were deemed to have need. 100% of undergraduates with need received aid; of those 16% had need fully met. **Average percent of need met:** 60% (excluding resources awarded to replace EFC). **Average financial aid package:** $11,600 (excluding resources awarded to replace EFC). 10% of all full-time undergraduates had no need and received non-need-based gift aid.

GIFT AID (NEED-BASED) Total amount: $25,675,843 (54% federal, 32% state, 14% institutional). **Receiving aid:** Freshmen: 73% (753); all full-time undergraduates: 74% (3,062). **Average award:** Freshmen: $6494; Undergraduates: $6948. **Scholarships, grants, and awards:** Federal Pell, FSEOG, state, private, college/university gift aid from institutional funds, United Negro College Fund.

GIFT AID (NON-NEED-BASED) Total amount: $6,500,274 (34% state, 53% institutional, 13% external sources). **Receiving aid:** Freshmen: 31% (321). Undergraduates: 20% (841). **Average award:** Freshmen: $500. Undergraduates: $1000. **Scholarships, grants, and awards by category:** Academic interests/achievement: 125 awards: biological sciences, computer science, engineering/technologies, mathematics, physical sciences, premedicine. Creative arts/performance: 15 awards: applied art and design, art/fine arts, dance, music, performing arts. Special achievements/activities: 20 awards: cheerleading/drum major, community service, hobbies/interests, leadership, religious involvement. Special characteristics: 4,165 awards. **Tuition waivers:** Full or partial for senior citizens. **ROTC:** Army.

LOANS Student loans: $36,636,036 (93% need-based, 7% non-need-based). 92% of past graduating class borrowed through all loan programs. **Average indebtedness per student:** $28,250. **Average need-based loan:** Freshmen: $3500. Undergraduates: $5500. **Parent loans:** $12,952,366 (100% need-based). **Programs:** Federal Direct (Subsidized and Unsubsidized Stafford, PLUS), Perkins, college/university.

WORK-STUDY Federal work-study: 300 jobs averaging $2000. **State or other work-study/employment:** Total amount: $332,139 (100% need-based). 150 part-time jobs averaging $3000.

ATHLETIC AWARDS Total amount: $1,133,330 (100% need-based).

APPLYING FOR FINANCIAL AID Required financial aid forms: FAFSA, institution's own form. **Financial aid deadline (priority):** 3/31. **Notification date:** Continuous beginning 3/15. Students must reply within 2 weeks of notification.

CONTACT Mrs. Sheila Allen, Scholarship Manager, Virginia State University, PO Box 9031, Petersburg, VA 23806-2096, 800-823-7214 or toll-free 800-871-7611. *Fax:* 804-524-6818. *E-mail:* finaid@vsu.edu.
Website: http://www.vsu.edu/.

VIRGINIA UNION UNIVERSITY
Richmond, VA

ABOUT THE INSTITUTION Independent Baptist, coed. **Awards:** bachelor's, master's, and doctoral degrees. 35 undergraduate majors. **Total enrollment:** 1,922. Undergraduates: 1,509. Freshmen: 456.

GIFT AID (NEED-BASED) *Scholarships, grants, and awards:* Federal Pell, FSEOG, state, private, college/university gift aid from institutional funds.
GIFT AID (NON-NEED-BASED) *Scholarships, grants, and awards by category: Academic interests/achievement:* general academic interests/achievements. *Creative arts/performance:* music. *Special characteristics:* children of faculty/staff.
LOANS *Programs:* Federal Direct (Subsidized and Unsubsidized Stafford).
WORK-STUDY *Federal work-study:* jobs available.
APPLYING FOR FINANCIAL AID *Required financial aid forms:* FAFSA, state aid form.
CONTACT Mrs. Karen Gee, Director of Financial Aid, Virginia Union University, 1500 North Lombardy Street, Richmond, VA 23220-1170, 804-257-5854 or toll-free 800-368-3227. *E-mail:* klgee@vuu.edu.
Website: http://www.vuu.edu/.

VIRGINIA UNIVERSITY OF LYNCHBURG

Lynchburg, VA

CONTACT Mrs. Charlene P. Scruggs, Financial Aid Director, Virginia University of Lynchburg, 2058 Garfield Avenue, Lynchburg, VA 24572, 434-528-5276. *Fax:* 434-455-5958. *E-mail:* cscruggs@vul.edu.
Website: http://www.vul.edu/.

VIRGINIA WESLEYAN UNIVERSITY

Virginia Beach, VA

Tuition & fees: $36,660	Average undergraduate aid package: $24,597

ABOUT THE INSTITUTION Independent United Methodist, coed. *Awards:* certificates, bachelor's, and master's degrees. 51 undergraduate majors. *Total enrollment:* 1,470. Undergraduates: 1,436. Freshmen: 423. Federal methodology is used as a basis for awarding need-based institutional aid.
UNDERGRADUATE EXPENSES for 2018–2019 *One-time required fee:* $1520. *Comprehensive fee:* $45,916 includes full-time tuition ($36,010), mandatory fees ($650), and room and board ($9256). Full-time tuition and fees vary according to course load. Room and board charges vary according to board plan and housing facility. *Part-time tuition:* $1500 per credit hour. Part-time tuition and fees vary according to course load.
FRESHMAN FINANCIAL AID (Fall 2016) 368 applied for aid; of those 86% were deemed to have need. 100% of freshmen with need received aid; of those 12% had need fully met. *Average percent of need met:* 68% (excluding resources awarded to replace EFC). *Average financial aid package:* $26,090 (excluding resources awarded to replace EFC). 10% of all full-time freshmen had no need and received non-need-based gift aid.
UNDERGRADUATE FINANCIAL AID (Fall 2016) 1,315 applied for aid; of those 85% were deemed to have need. 100% of undergraduates with need received aid; of those 13% had need fully met. *Average percent of need met:* 65% (excluding resources awarded to replace EFC). *Average financial aid package:* $24,597 (excluding resources awarded to replace EFC). 14% of all full-time undergraduates had no need and received non-need-based gift aid.
GIFT AID (NEED-BASED) *Total amount:* $23,097,507 (11% federal, 9% state, 79% institutional, 1% external sources). *Receiving aid:* Freshmen: 86% (318); all full-time undergraduates: 84% (1,116). *Average award:* Freshmen: $22,369; Undergraduates: $20,792. *Scholarships, grants, and awards:* Federal Pell, FSEOG, state, private, college/university gift aid from institutional funds, United Negro College Fund.
GIFT AID (NON-NEED-BASED) *Total amount:* $4,340,451 (12% state, 85% institutional, 3% external sources). *Receiving aid:* Freshmen: 10% (36). Undergraduates: 14% (186). *Average award:* Freshmen: $19,709. Undergraduates: $17,682. *Scholarships, grants, and awards by category: Academic interests/achievement:* general academic interests/achievements. *Special achievements/activities:* religious involvement. *Special characteristics:* 12 awards ($324,878 total): children of faculty/staff, relatives of clergy, religious affiliation. *Tuition waivers:* Full or partial for employees or children of employees, adult students, senior citizens. *ROTC:* Army cooperative.

LOANS *Student loans:* $8,243,321 (80% need-based, 20% non-need-based). 83% of past graduating class borrowed through all loan programs. *Average indebtedness per student:* $34,212. *Average need-based loan:* Freshmen: $6779. Undergraduates: $7866. *Parent loans:* $3,713,926 (100% need-based). *Programs:* Federal Direct (Subsidized and Unsubsidized Stafford, PLUS), Perkins, alternative loans.
WORK-STUDY *Federal work-study:* 196 jobs averaging $1243.
APPLYING FOR FINANCIAL AID *Required financial aid forms:* FAFSA, state aid form. *Financial aid deadline (priority):* 3/1. *Notification date:* Continuous beginning 10/15. Students must reply by 5/1 or within 2 weeks of notification.
CONTACT Financial Aid Office, Virginia Wesleyan University, 5817 Wesleyan Drive, Virginia Beach, VA 23455, 757-455-3200 or toll-free 800-737-8684.
Website: http://www.vwu.edu/.

VISIBLE MUSIC COLLEGE

Memphis, TN

CONTACT Financial Aid Office, Visible Music College, 200 Madison Avenue, Memphis, TN 38103, 901-381-3939.
Website: http://visible.edu/.

VITERBO UNIVERSITY

La Crosse, WI

ABOUT THE INSTITUTION Independent Roman Catholic, coed. *Awards:* certificates, associate, bachelor's, master's, and doctoral degrees. 71 undergraduate majors. *Total enrollment:* 2,761. Undergraduates: 1,875. Freshmen: 320.
GIFT AID (NEED-BASED) *Scholarships, grants, and awards:* state, college/university gift aid from institutional funds.
LOANS *Programs:* alternative loans.
WORK-STUDY Federal work-study jobs available. *State or other work-study/employment:* Part-time jobs available.
CONTACT Terry Norman, Director of Financial Aid, Viterbo University, 900 Viterbo Drive, La Crosse, WI 54601-4797, 608-796-3900 or toll-free 800-VITERBO. *Fax:* 608-796-3050. *E-mail:* twnorman@viterbo.edu.
Website: http://www.viterbo.edu/.

VOORHEES COLLEGE

Denmark, SC

CONTACT Augusta L. Kitchen, Director of Financial Aid, Voorhees College, PO Box 678, Denmark, SC 29042, 803-703-7109 Ext. 7106 or toll-free 866-237-4570. *Fax:* 803-793-0831. *E-mail:* akitchen@voorhees.edu.
Website: http://www.voorhees.edu/.

WABASH COLLEGE

Crawfordsville, IN

Tuition & fees: $43,650	Average undergraduate aid package: $37,666

ABOUT THE INSTITUTION Independent, men only. *Awards:* bachelor's degrees. 25 undergraduate majors. *Total enrollment:* 864. Undergraduates: 864. Freshmen: 232. Federal methodology is used as a basis for awarding need-based institutional aid.
UNDERGRADUATE EXPENSES for 2018–2019 *Application fee:* $50. *Comprehensive fee:* $53,500 includes full-time tuition ($42,800), mandatory fees ($850), and room and board ($9850). *College room only:* $5250. Room and board charges vary according to board plan and housing facility. *Part-time tuition:* $1783 per semester hour. *Part-time fees:* $50 per term. Part-time tuition and fees vary according to course load. *Payment plan:* Tuition prepayment.
FRESHMAN FINANCIAL AID (Fall 2017, est.) 209 applied for aid; of those 90% were deemed to have need. 100% of freshmen with need received aid; of those 94%

had need fully met. *Average percent of need met:* 97% (excluding resources awarded to replace EFC). *Average financial aid package:* $40,879 (excluding resources awarded to replace EFC). 19% of all full-time freshmen had no need and received non-need-based gift aid.

UNDERGRADUATE FINANCIAL AID (Fall 2017, est.) 798 applied for aid; of those 82% were deemed to have need. 100% of undergraduates with need received aid; of those 81% had need fully met. *Average percent of need met:* 94% (excluding resources awarded to replace EFC). *Average financial aid package:* $37,666 (excluding resources awarded to replace EFC). 24% of all full-time undergraduates had no need and received non-need-based gift aid.

GIFT AID (NEED-BASED) *Total amount:* $19,785,629 (6% federal, 7% state, 85% institutional, 2% external sources). *Receiving aid:* Freshmen: 81% (188); all full-time undergraduates: 75% (649). *Average award:* Freshmen: $34,044; Undergraduates: $30,123. *Scholarships, grants, and awards:* Federal Pell, FSEOG, state, private, college/university gift aid from institutional funds, United Negro College Fund.

GIFT AID (NON-NEED-BASED) *Total amount:* $5,740,298 (93% institutional, 7% external sources). *Receiving aid:* Freshmen: 13% (31). Undergraduates: 11% (98). *Average award:* Freshmen: $28,340. Undergraduates: $22,589. *Scholarships, grants, and awards by category: Academic interests/achievement:* 814 awards ($14,894,581 total). *Creative arts/performance:* 46 awards ($136,000 total): art/fine arts, cinema/film/broadcasting, creative writing, journalism/publications, music, theater/drama. *Special achievements/activities:* 77 awards ($774,730 total): community service, leadership. *Special characteristics:* 10 awards ($414,900 total): children of faculty/staff. *Tuition waivers:* Full or partial for employees or children of employees.

LOANS *Student loans:* $6,170,035 (40% need-based, 60% non-need-based). 94% of past graduating class borrowed through all loan programs. *Average indebtedness per student:* $35,726. *Average need-based loan:* Freshmen: $3143. Undergraduates: $4348. *Parent loans:* $1,741,914 (18% need-based, 82% non-need-based). *Programs:* Federal Direct (Subsidized and Unsubsidized Stafford, PLUS).

WORK-STUDY *Federal work-study:* Total amount: $604,015; 207 jobs averaging $2912. *State or other work-study/employment:* Total amount: $843,725 (74% need-based, 26% non-need-based). 312 part-time jobs averaging $2876.

APPLYING FOR FINANCIAL AID *Required financial aid forms:* FAFSA, verification items such as federal income tax transcripts and W-2 forms. *Financial aid deadline (priority):* 1/15. *Notification date:* Continuous beginning 12/15. Students must reply by 5/1.

CONTACT Ms. Heidi Carl, Director of Financial Aid, Wabash College, PO Box 352, Crawfordsville, IN 47933-0352, 800-718-9746 or toll-free 800-345-5385. *Fax:* 765-361-6166. *E-mail:* financialaid@wabash.edu.
Website: http://www.wabash.edu/.

WAGNER COLLEGE
Staten Island, NY

ABOUT THE INSTITUTION Independent, coed. *Awards:* certificates, bachelor's, master's, and doctoral degrees. 38 undergraduate majors. *Total enrollment:* 2,289. Undergraduates: 1,812. Freshmen: 432.

GIFT AID (NEED-BASED) *Scholarships, grants, and awards:* Federal Pell, FSEOG, state, private, college/university gift aid from institutional funds.

GIFT AID (NON-NEED-BASED) *Scholarships, grants, and awards by category: Academic interests/achievement:* general academic interests/achievements. *Creative arts/performance:* music, theater/drama. *Special characteristics:* children of faculty/staff, siblings of current students.

LOANS *Programs:* Federal Direct (Subsidized and Unsubsidized Stafford, PLUS), Perkins, Federal Nursing, alternative loans.

WORK-STUDY *Federal work-study:* jobs available.

APPLYING FOR FINANCIAL AID *Required financial aid forms:* FAFSA, state aid form.

CONTACT Ms. Theresa Weimer, Director of Financial Aid, Wagner College, One Campus Road, Staten Island, NY 10301, 718-390-3122 or toll-free 800-221-1010. *Fax:* 718-390-3203. *E-mail:* tweimer@wagner.edu.
Website: http://www.wagner.edu/.

WAKE FOREST UNIVERSITY
Winston-Salem, NC

Tuition & fees: $53,322	Average undergraduate aid package: $49,309

ABOUT THE INSTITUTION Independent, coed. *Awards:* certificates, bachelor's, master's, and doctoral degrees. 38 undergraduate majors. *Total enrollment:* 8,116. Undergraduates: 5,102. Freshmen: 1,349. Institutional methodology is used as a basis for awarding need-based institutional aid.

UNDERGRADUATE EXPENSES for 2018–2019 *Application fee:* $65. *Comprehensive fee:* $69,354 includes full-time tuition ($52,348), mandatory fees ($974), and room and board ($16,032). *College room only:* $9282. *Part-time tuition:* $2170 per credit hour.

FRESHMAN FINANCIAL AID (Fall 2017, est.) 613 applied for aid; of those 67% were deemed to have need. 100% of freshmen with need received aid; of those 100% had need fully met. *Average percent of need met:* 100% (excluding resources awarded to replace EFC). *Average financial aid package:* $49,145 (excluding resources awarded to replace EFC). 4% of all full-time freshmen had no need and received non-need-based gift aid.

UNDERGRADUATE FINANCIAL AID (Fall 2017, est.) 1,910 applied for aid; of those 82% were deemed to have need. 100% of undergraduates with need received aid; of those 100% had need fully met. *Average percent of need met:* 100% (excluding resources awarded to replace EFC). *Average financial aid package:* $49,309 (excluding resources awarded to replace EFC). 9% of all full-time undergraduates had no need and received non-need-based gift aid.

GIFT AID (NEED-BASED) *Total amount:* $60,625,891 (5% federal, 3% state, 89% institutional, 3% external sources). *Receiving aid:* Freshmen: 29% (393); all full-time undergraduates: 30% (1,501). *Average award:* Freshmen: $45,652; Undergraduates: $44,338. *Scholarships, grants, and awards:* Federal Pell, FSEOG, state, private, college/university gift aid from institutional funds, United Negro College Fund.

GIFT AID (NON-NEED-BASED) *Total amount:* $9,406,949 (16% federal, 66% institutional, 18% external sources). *Receiving aid:* Freshmen: 29% (390). Undergraduates: 29% (1,475). *Average award:* Freshmen: $20,377. Undergraduates: $12,792. *Scholarships, grants, and awards by category: Academic interests/achievement:* general academic interests/achievements. *Creative arts/performance:* art/fine arts, general creative arts/performance. *Special achievements/activities:* leadership. *Special characteristics:* children and siblings of alumni, local/state students, religious affiliation. *ROTC:* Army.

LOANS *Student loans:* $19,741,992 (77% need-based, 23% non-need-based). 33% of past graduating class borrowed through all loan programs. *Average indebtedness per student:* $35,434. *Average need-based loan:* Freshmen: $9056. Undergraduates: $10,118. *Parent loans:* $6,013,352 (71% need-based, 29% non-need-based). *Programs:* Federal Direct (Subsidized and Unsubsidized Stafford, PLUS), Perkins, state, college/university.

WORK-STUDY *Federal work-study:* Total amount: $1,951,068; jobs available. *State or other work-study/employment:* Part-time jobs available.

ATHLETIC AWARDS Total amount: $14,291,116 (33% need-based, 67% non-need-based).

APPLYING FOR FINANCIAL AID *Required financial aid forms:* FAFSA, CSS Financial Aid PROFILE, state aid form, noncustodial (divorced/separated) parent's statement. *Financial aid deadline:* 1/1. *Notification date:* Continuous beginning 4/1. Students must reply by 5/1 or within 4 weeks of notification.

CONTACT Bill Wells, Director of Student Financial Aid, Wake Forest University, PO Box 7246, Winston-Salem, NC 27109-7246, 336-758-5154. *Fax:* 336-758-4924. *E-mail:* financial-aid@wfu.edu.
Website: http://www.wfu.edu/.

WALDEN UNIVERSITY
Minneapolis, MN

CONTACT Office of Financial Aid, Walden University, 100 Washington South, Suite 900, Minneapolis, MN 55401, 800-444-6795 or toll-free 866-492-5336. *Fax:* 410-843-6211. *E-mail:* finaid@waldenu.edu.
Website: http://www.waldenu.edu/.

WALDORF UNIVERSITY
Forest City, IA

ABOUT THE INSTITUTION Independent Lutheran, coed. *Awards:* certificates, associate, bachelor's, and master's degrees. 31 undergraduate majors. *Total enrollment:* 2,487. Undergraduates: 2,126. Freshmen: 131.

GIFT AID (NEED-BASED) *Scholarships, grants, and awards:* Federal Pell, FSEOG, state, private, college/university gift aid from institutional funds.

GIFT AID (NON-NEED-BASED) *Scholarships, grants, and awards by category: Academic interests/achievement:* communication, general academic interests/achievements. *Creative arts/performance:* music, theater/drama. *Special achievements/activities:* cheerleading/drum major, junior miss, leadership. *Special characteristics:* children of faculty/staff, religious affiliation.

LOANS *Programs:* Federal Direct (Subsidized and Unsubsidized Stafford, PLUS), Perkins, state, alternative loans.

APPLYING FOR FINANCIAL AID *Required financial aid forms:* FAFSA, institution's own form.

CONTACT Duane Polsdofer, Director of Financial Aid, Waldorf University, 106 South 6th Street, Forest City, IA 50436, 641-585-8120 or toll-free 800-292-1903. *Fax:* 641-585-8125. *E-mail:* polsdofed@waldorf.edu.

Website: http://www.waldorf.edu/.

WALLA WALLA UNIVERSITY
College Place, WA

Tuition & fees: $27,495	Average undergraduate aid package: $22,645

ABOUT THE INSTITUTION Independent Seventh-day Adventist, coed. *Awards:* associate, bachelor's, and master's degrees. 80 undergraduate majors. *Total enrollment:* 1,894. Undergraduates: 1,700. Freshmen: 387. Both federal and institutional methodology are used as a basis for awarding need-based institutional aid.

UNDERGRADUATE EXPENSES for 2017–2018 *Application fee:* $40. *Comprehensive fee:* $34,845 includes full-time tuition ($26,595), mandatory fees ($900), and room and board ($7350). *College room only:* $4185. *Part-time tuition:* $738 per quarter hour.

FRESHMAN FINANCIAL AID (Fall 2016) 293 applied for aid; of those 84% were deemed to have need. 100% of freshmen with need received aid; of those 30% had need fully met. *Average percent of need met:* 94% (excluding resources awarded to replace EFC). *Average financial aid package:* $23,317 (excluding resources awarded to replace EFC). 32% of all full-time freshmen had no need and received non-need-based gift aid.

UNDERGRADUATE FINANCIAL AID (Fall 2016) 1,148 applied for aid; of those 85% were deemed to have need. 100% of undergraduates with need received aid; of those 27% had need fully met. *Average percent of need met:* 92% (excluding resources awarded to replace EFC). *Average financial aid package:* $22,645 (excluding resources awarded to replace EFC). 31% of all full-time undergraduates had no need and received non-need-based gift aid.

GIFT AID (NEED-BASED) *Total amount:* $16,102,285 (18% federal, 5% state, 61% institutional, 16% external sources). *Receiving aid:* Freshmen: 49% (175); all full-time undergraduates: 51% (766). *Average award:* Freshmen: $5679; Undergraduates: $6491. *Scholarships, grants, and awards:* Federal Pell, FSEOG, state, private, college/university gift aid from institutional funds, Federal Nursing.

GIFT AID (NON-NEED-BASED) *Total amount:* $7,625,408 (2% federal, 62% institutional, 36% external sources). *Receiving aid:* Freshmen: 68% (243). Undergraduates: 58% (883). *Average award:* Freshmen: $10,907. Undergraduates: $8950. *Scholarships, grants, and awards by category: Academic interests/achievement:* biological sciences, business, communication, education, engineering/technologies, English, foreign languages, general academic interests/achievements, humanities, mathematics, religion/biblical studies. *Creative arts/performance:* general creative arts/performance, music, theater/drama. *Special achievements/activities:* leadership. *Special characteristics:* children of faculty/staff, veterans.

LOANS *Student loans:* $9,476,154 (72% need-based, 28% non-need-based). 66% of past graduating class borrowed through all loan programs. *Average indebtedness per student:* $33,577. *Average need-based loan:* Freshmen: $4021. Undergraduates: $4586. *Parent loans:* $1,444,804 (25% need-based, 75% non-need-based).

Programs: Federal Direct (Subsidized and Unsubsidized Stafford, PLUS), Perkins, Federal Nursing, college/university.

WORK-STUDY *Federal work-study:* jobs available. *State or other work-study/employment:* Total amount: $113,340 (100% need-based). Part-time jobs available.

APPLYING FOR FINANCIAL AID *Required financial aid forms:* FAFSA, institution's own form. *Financial aid deadline (priority):* 4/30. *Notification date:* Continuous beginning 2/15.

CONTACT Ms. Cassie Ragenovich, Director of Student Financial Services, Walla Walla University, 204 South College Avenue, College Place, WA 99324-1198, 509-527-2315 or toll-free 800-541-8900. *Fax:* 509-527-2556. *E-mail:* financial.aid@wallawalla.edu.

Website: http://www.wallawalla.edu/.

WALSH COLLEGE OF ACCOUNTANCY AND BUSINESS ADMINISTRATION
Troy, MI

Tuition & fees: $16,935	Average undergraduate aid package: N/A

ABOUT THE INSTITUTION Independent, coed. *Awards:* certificates, bachelor's, and master's degrees. 6 undergraduate majors. *Total enrollment:* 2,299. Undergraduates: 893. Federal methodology is used as a basis for awarding need-based institutional aid.

UNDERGRADUATE EXPENSES for 2017–2018 *Application fee:* $35. *Tuition:* full-time $16,560; part-time $8280 per year. *Required fees:* full-time $375; $375 per year. Full-time tuition and fees vary according to course level and degree level. Part-time tuition and fees vary according to course level and degree level.

GIFT AID (NEED-BASED) *Total amount:* $1,575,649 (57% federal, 17% state, 26% institutional). *Scholarships, grants, and awards:* Federal Pell, FSEOG, state, private, college/university gift aid from institutional funds.

GIFT AID (NON-NEED-BASED) *Total amount:* $115,667 (100% institutional). *Scholarships, grants, and awards by category: Academic interests/achievement:* business, computer science. *Special characteristics:* previous college experience. *Tuition waivers:* Full or partial for employees or children of employees.

LOANS *Student loans:* $3,716,197 (52% need-based, 48% non-need-based). *Parent loans:* $83,986 (100% non-need-based). *Programs:* Federal Direct (Subsidized and Unsubsidized Stafford, PLUS), private loans.

APPLYING FOR FINANCIAL AID *Financial aid deadline:* Continuous. *Notification date:* Continuous.

CONTACT Catherine Duff Berrahou, Director of Student Financial Resources, Walsh College of Accountancy and Business Administration, 3838 Livernois Road, PO Box 7006, Troy, MI 48007-7006, 248-823-1285 or toll-free 800-925-7401. *Fax:* 248-524-2520. *E-mail:* hthomas@walshcollege.edu.

Website: http://www.walshcollege.edu/.

WALSH UNIVERSITY
North Canton, OH

CONTACT Holly Van Gilder, Director of Financial Aid, Walsh University, 2020 East Maple NW, North Canton, OH 44720-3396, 330-490-7147 or toll-free 800-362-9846 (in-state), 800-362-8846 (out-of-state). *Fax:* 330-490-7372. *E-mail:* hvangilder@walsh.edu.

Website: http://www.walsh.edu/.

WARNER PACIFIC COLLEGE
Portland, OR

Tuition & fees: $24,500	Average undergraduate aid package: $21,056

ABOUT THE INSTITUTION Independent Church of God, coed. *Awards:* certificates, associate, bachelor's, and master's degrees. 32 undergraduate majors. *Total enrollment:* 409. Undergraduates: 400. Freshmen: 58. Federal methodology is used as a basis for awarding need-based institutional aid.

UNDERGRADUATE EXPENSES for 2017–2018 *Application fee:* $25. *Comprehensive fee:* $33,800 includes full-time tuition ($23,840), mandatory fees ($660), and room and board ($9300). *College room only:* $3870. Room and board charges vary according to board plan and housing facility. *Part-time tuition:* $1085 per semester hour. *Part-time fees:* $330 per term. Part-time tuition and fees vary according to course load.

FRESHMAN FINANCIAL AID (Fall 2017, est.) 60 applied for aid; of those 92% were deemed to have need. 100% of freshmen with need received aid; of those 20% had need fully met. *Average percent of need met:* 68% (excluding resources awarded to replace EFC). *Average financial aid package:* $22,286 (excluding resources awarded to replace EFC). 7% of all full-time freshmen had no need and received non-need-based gift aid.

UNDERGRADUATE FINANCIAL AID (Fall 2017, est.) 354 applied for aid; of those 94% were deemed to have need. 100% of undergraduates with need received aid; of those 18% had need fully met. *Average percent of need met:* 66% (excluding resources awarded to replace EFC). *Average financial aid package:* $21,056 (excluding resources awarded to replace EFC). 12% of all full-time undergraduates had no need and received non-need-based gift aid.

GIFT AID (NEED-BASED) *Total amount:* $3,268,898 (40% federal, 10% state, 47% institutional, 3% external sources). *Receiving aid:* Freshmen: 67% (41); all full-time undergraduates: 64% (253). *Average award:* Freshmen: $8476; Undergraduates: $7072. *Scholarships, grants, and awards:* Federal Pell, FSEOG, state, private, college/university gift aid from institutional funds.

GIFT AID (NON-NEED-BASED) *Total amount:* $404,390 (2% state, 92% institutional, 6% external sources). *Receiving aid:* Freshmen: 79% (48). Undergraduates: 76% (297). *Average award:* Freshmen: $6000. Undergraduates: $7065. *Scholarships, grants, and awards by category:* Academic interests/achievement: 306 awards ($1,380,558 total): general academic interests/achievements. Creative arts/performance: 27 awards ($62,500 total): music, theater/drama. Special achievements/activities: 73 awards ($104,000 total): leadership, memberships. Special characteristics: 11 awards ($9500 total): children and siblings of alumni, international students, local/state students, religious affiliation. *Tuition waivers:* Full or partial for children of alumni, employees or children of employees. *ROTC:* Air Force cooperative.

LOANS *Student loans:* $2,011,448 (90% need-based, 10% non-need-based). 83% of past graduating class borrowed through all loan programs. *Average indebtedness per student:* $28,471. *Average need-based loan:* Freshmen: $2786. Undergraduates: $3823. *Parent loans:* $740,206 (58% need-based, 42% non-need-based). *Programs:* Federal Direct (Subsidized and Unsubsidized Stafford, PLUS), Perkins.

WORK-STUDY *Federal work-study:* Total amount: $648,073; 270 jobs averaging $2391.

ATHLETIC AWARDS Total amount: $1,118,866 (79% need-based, 21% non-need-based).

APPLYING FOR FINANCIAL AID *Required financial aid form:* FAFSA. *Financial aid deadline (priority):* 3/1. *Notification date:* Continuous beginning 12/1. Students must reply within 2 weeks of notification.

CONTACT Cynthia D. Pollard, Executive Director of Student Financial Services and Financial Aid, Warner Pacific College, 2219 Southeast 68th Avenue, Portland, OR 97215-4099, 503-517-1018 or toll-free 800-804-1510. *Fax:* 503-517-1352. *E-mail:* cpollard@warnerpacific.edu. *Website:* http://www.warnerpacific.edu/.

WARNER UNIVERSITY
Lake Wales, FL

ABOUT THE INSTITUTION Independent Church of God, coed. 24 undergraduate majors.

GIFT AID (NEED-BASED) *Scholarships, grants, and awards:* Federal Pell, FSEOG, state, private, college/university gift aid from institutional funds.

GIFT AID (NON-NEED-BASED) *Scholarships, grants, and awards by category:* Academic interests/achievement: agriculture, biological sciences, business, communication, education, English, general academic interests/achievements, home economics, humanities, physical sciences, social sciences. Creative arts/performance: music. Special achievements/activities: cheerleading/drum major, leadership, religious involvement. Special characteristics: adult students, children and siblings of alumni, children of educators, children of faculty/staff, general special characteristics, international students, out-of-state students, previous college experience, relatives of clergy, siblings of current students, veterans, veterans' children.

LOANS *Programs:* Federal Direct (Subsidized and Unsubsidized Stafford, PLUS), Perkins, alternative loans.

APPLYING FOR FINANCIAL AID *Required financial aid forms:* FAFSA, state aid form, verification worksheet.

CONTACT Lorrie Steedley, Student Financial Services, Warner University, 13895 Highway 27, Lake Wales, FL 33859, 863-638-7202 or toll-free 800-309-9563. *Fax:* 863-638-7603. *E-mail:* financialaid@warner.edu. *Website:* http://www.warner.edu/.

WARREN WILSON COLLEGE
Swannanoa, NC

ABOUT THE INSTITUTION Independent Presbyterian Church (U.S.A.), coed. 19 undergraduate majors.

GIFT AID (NEED-BASED) *Scholarships, grants, and awards:* Federal Pell, FSEOG, state, college/university gift aid from institutional funds.

GIFT AID (NON-NEED-BASED) *Scholarships, grants, and awards by category:* Academic interests/achievement: general academic interests/achievements. Creative arts/performance: art/fine arts, creative writing. Special achievements/activities: community service, leadership. Special characteristics: children of faculty/staff, general special characteristics, local/state students, previous college experience, relatives of clergy, religious affiliation.

LOANS *Programs:* Federal Direct (Subsidized and Unsubsidized Stafford, PLUS).

WORK-STUDY *Federal work-study:* jobs available. *State or other work-study/employment:* Total amount: $413,317 (29% need-based, 71% non-need-based). Part-time jobs available.

APPLYING FOR FINANCIAL AID *Required financial aid forms:* FAFSA, state aid form.

CONTACT Financial Aid Office, Warren Wilson College, PO Box 9000, Asheville, NC 28815-9000, 828-771-2082 or toll-free 800-934-3536. *Fax:* 828-771-2030. *E-mail:* finaid@warren-wilson.edu. *Website:* http://www.warren-wilson.edu/.

WARTBURG COLLEGE
Waverly, IA

Tuition & fees: $41,280	Average undergraduate aid package: $30,082

ABOUT THE INSTITUTION Independent Lutheran, coed. *Awards:* bachelor's degrees. 58 undergraduate majors. *Total enrollment:* 1,527. Undergraduates: 1,527. Freshmen: 451. Federal methodology is used as a basis for awarding need-based institutional aid.

UNDERGRADUATE EXPENSES for 2018–2019 *Comprehensive fee:* $51,275 includes full-time tuition ($40,220), mandatory fees ($1060), and room and board ($9995). *College room only:* $5075. Room and board charges vary according to board plan and housing facility. *Part-time tuition:* $2100 per course. *Part-time fees:* $120 per year. Part-time tuition and fees vary according to course load.

FRESHMAN FINANCIAL AID (Fall 2016) 402 applied for aid; of those 83% were deemed to have need. 100% of freshmen with need received aid; of those 20% had need fully met. *Average percent of need met:* 81% (excluding resources awarded to replace EFC). *Average financial aid package:* $30,254 (excluding resources awarded to replace EFC). 23% of all full-time freshmen had no need and received non-need-based gift aid.

UNDERGRADUATE FINANCIAL AID (Fall 2016) 1,214 applied for aid; of those 86% were deemed to have need. 100% of undergraduates with need received aid; of those 20% had need fully met. *Average percent of need met:* 82% (excluding resources awarded to replace EFC). *Average financial aid package:* $30,082 (excluding resources awarded to replace EFC). 26% of all full-time undergraduates had no need and received non-need-based gift aid.

GIFT AID (NEED-BASED) *Total amount:* $26,446,468 (7% federal, 9% state, 73% institutional, 11% external sources). *Receiving aid:* Freshmen: 76% (335); all full-time undergraduates: 74% (1,043). *Average award:* Freshmen: $26,666; Undergraduates: $25,286. *Scholarships, grants, and awards:* Federal Pell, FSEOG, state, private, college/university gift aid from institutional funds.

GIFT AID (NON-NEED-BASED) *Total amount:* $12,633,126 (1% federal, 1% state, 74% institutional, 24% external sources). *Receiving aid:* Freshmen: 15% (65). Undergraduates: 15% (206). *Average award:* Freshmen: $23,534. Undergraduates: $22,209. *Scholarships, grants, and awards by category: Academic interests/achievement:* 1,414 awards ($19,560,550 total): biological sciences, business, communication, computer science, education, engineering/technologies, English, foreign languages, general academic interests/achievements, humanities, mathematics, physical sciences, premedicine, religion/biblical studies, social sciences. *Creative arts/performance:* 341 awards ($1,110,143 total): art/fine arts, cinema/film/broadcasting, journalism/publications, music, performing arts, theater/drama. *Special achievements/activities:* 30 awards ($30,000 total): junior miss, leadership. *Special characteristics:* 706 awards ($5,226,939 total): children and siblings of alumni, children of faculty/staff, international students, previous college experience, religious affiliation, siblings of current students. *Tuition waivers:* Full or partial for employees or children of employees.

LOANS *Student loans:* $11,802,369 (55% need-based, 45% non-need-based). 82% of past graduating class borrowed through all loan programs. *Average indebtedness per student:* $37,551. *Average need-based loan:* Freshmen: $4386. Undergraduates: $5502. *Parent loans:* $2,384,852 (62% need-based, 38% non-need-based). *Programs:* Federal Direct (Subsidized and Unsubsidized Stafford, PLUS), Perkins, college/university, private loans.

WORK-STUDY *Federal work-study:* 523 jobs averaging $885. *State or other work-study/employment:* Total amount: $955,572 (100% non-need-based). 462 part-time jobs averaging $1962.

APPLYING FOR FINANCIAL AID *Required financial aid form:* FAFSA. *Financial aid deadline (priority):* 3/1. *Notification date:* Continuous beginning 1/15. Students must reply within 2 weeks of notification.

CONTACT Ms. Jennifer Sassman, Director of Financial Aid, Wartburg College, 100 Wartburg Boulevard, PO Box 1003, Waverly, IA 50677-0903, 319-352-8262 or toll-free 800-772-2085. *Fax:* 319-352-8514. *E-mail:* jennifer.sassman@wartburg.edu. *Website:* http://www.wartburg.edu/.

WASHBURN UNIVERSITY
Topeka, KS

ABOUT THE INSTITUTION City-supported, coed. *Awards:* certificates, associate, bachelor's, master's, and doctoral degrees. 87 undergraduate majors. *Total enrollment:* 6,615. Undergraduates: 5,793. Freshmen: 813.

GIFT AID (NEED-BASED) *Scholarships, grants, and awards:* Federal Pell, FSEOG, state, private, college/university gift aid from institutional funds.

GIFT AID (NON-NEED-BASED) *Scholarships, grants, and awards by category: Academic interests/achievement:* biological sciences, business, communication, computer science, education, engineering/technologies, English, foreign languages, general academic interests/achievements, health fields, humanities, international studies, mathematics, physical sciences, premedicine, religion/biblical studies, social sciences. *Creative arts/performance:* art/fine arts, cinema/film/broadcasting, debating, general creative arts/performance, journalism/publications, music, performing arts, theater/drama. *Special achievements/activities:* cheerleading/drum major, community service, leadership. *Special characteristics:* adult students, children and siblings of alumni, children of faculty/staff, ethnic background, international students, local/state students.

LOANS *Programs:* Federal Direct (Subsidized and Unsubsidized Stafford, PLUS), college/university.

WORK-STUDY *Federal work-study:* jobs available. *State or other work-study/employment:* Total amount: $65,531 (100% need-based). Part-time jobs available.

APPLYING FOR FINANCIAL AID *Required financial aid form:* FAFSA.

CONTACT Dawn Boman, Associate Director of Financial Aid, Washburn University, 1700 SW College Avenue, Topeka, KS 66621, 785-670-1151 or toll-free 800-332-0291. *Fax:* 785-670-1079. *E-mail:* dawn.boman@washburn.edu. *Website:* http://www.washburn.edu/.

WASHINGTON ADVENTIST UNIVERSITY
Takoma Park, MD

CONTACT Sharon Conway, Director of Student Financial Services, Washington Adventist University, 7600 Flower Avenue, Takoma Park, MD 20912, 301-891-4005 or toll-free 800-835-4212. *Fax:* 301-891-4167. *E-mail:* sconway@wau.edu. *Website:* http://www.wau.edu/.

WASHINGTON & JEFFERSON COLLEGE
Washington, PA

Tuition & fees: $46,628	Average undergraduate aid package: $37,503

ABOUT THE INSTITUTION Independent, coed. *Awards:* certificates, bachelor's, and master's degrees. 33 undergraduate majors. *Total enrollment:* 1,412. Undergraduates: 1,405. Freshmen: 339. Both federal and institutional methodology are used as a basis for awarding need-based institutional aid.

UNDERGRADUATE EXPENSES for 2017–2018 *Application fee:* $25. *Comprehensive fee:* $58,946 includes full-time tuition ($46,048), mandatory fees ($580), and room and board ($12,318). *College room only:* $7228. Full-time tuition and fees vary according to reciprocity agreements. Room and board charges vary according to board plan and housing facility. *Part-time tuition:* $1155 per credit hour. Part-time tuition and fees vary according to course load. *Payment plan:* Tuition prepayment.

FRESHMAN FINANCIAL AID (Fall 2017, est.) 318 applied for aid; of those 87% were deemed to have need. 100% of freshmen with need received aid; of those 13% had need fully met. *Average percent of need met:* 67% (excluding resources awarded to replace EFC). *Average financial aid package:* $38,035 (excluding resources awarded to replace EFC). 18% of all full-time freshmen had no need and received non-need-based gift aid.

UNDERGRADUATE FINANCIAL AID (Fall 2017, est.) 1,178 applied for aid; of those 92% were deemed to have need. 100% of undergraduates with need received aid; of those 10% had need fully met. *Average percent of need met:* 77% (excluding resources awarded to replace EFC). *Average financial aid package:* $37,503 (excluding resources awarded to replace EFC). 20% of all full-time undergraduates had no need and received non-need-based gift aid.

GIFT AID (NEED-BASED) *Total amount:* $33,331,247 (6% federal, 5% state, 87% institutional, 2% external sources). *Receiving aid:* Freshmen: 80% (272); all full-time undergraduates: 77% (1,075). *Average award:* Freshmen: $10,960; Undergraduates: $12,202. *Scholarships, grants, and awards:* Federal Pell, FSEOG, state, private, college/university gift aid from institutional funds.

GIFT AID (NON-NEED-BASED) *Total amount:* $6,592,208 (99% institutional, 1% external sources). *Receiving aid:* Freshmen: 80% (270). Undergraduates: 70% (974). *Average award:* Freshmen: $22,234. Undergraduates: $20,989. *Scholarships, grants, and awards by category: Academic interests/achievement:* 1,206 awards ($22,283,352 total): business, general academic interests/achievements, humanities. *Special characteristics:* 94 awards ($2,007,993 total): children and siblings of alumni, children of faculty/staff, international students, local/state students, members of minority groups, veterans, veterans' children. *Tuition waivers:* Full or partial for employees or children of employees. *ROTC:* Army, Air Force cooperative.

LOANS *Student loans:* $12,201,376 (63% need-based, 37% non-need-based). 77% of past graduating class borrowed through all loan programs. *Average indebtedness per student:* $54,184. *Average need-based loan:* Freshmen: $3623. Undergraduates: $4631. *Parent loans:* $4,921,983 (83% need-based, 17% non-need-based). *Programs:* Federal Direct (Subsidized and Unsubsidized Stafford, PLUS), Perkins, college/university.

WORK-STUDY *Federal work-study:* Total amount: $1,086,842; 672 jobs averaging $1579. *State or other work-study/employment:* Total amount: $203,000 (100% non-need-based). 195 part-time jobs averaging $1476.

APPLYING FOR FINANCIAL AID *Required financial aid form:* FAFSA. *Financial aid deadline (priority):* 2/15. *Notification date:* Continuous beginning 12/15. Students must reply by 5/1.

CONTACT Ms. Charlene Bedillion, Director of Financial Aid, Washington & Jefferson College, 60 South Lincoln Street, Washington, PA 15301-4801, 724-503-1001 Ext. 6019 or toll-free 888-WANDJAY. *Fax:* 724-250-3340. *E-mail:* cbedillion@washjeff.edu. *Website:* http://www.washjeff.edu/.

WASHINGTON AND LEE UNIVERSITY
Lexington, VA

Tuition & fees: $50,170	Average undergraduate aid package: $50,827

ABOUT THE INSTITUTION Independent, coed. *Awards:* bachelor's and doctoral degrees. 36 undergraduate majors. *Total enrollment:* 2,220. Undergraduates: 1,827. Freshmen: 471. Both federal and institutional methodology are used as a basis for awarding need-based institutional aid.

UNDERGRADUATE EXPENSES for 2017–2018 *Application fee:* $60. *Comprehensive fee:* $61,900 includes full-time tuition ($49,170), mandatory fees ($1000), and room and board ($11,730). *College room only:* $5600. Full-time tuition and fees vary according to degree level. Room and board charges vary according to board plan and housing facility. *Part-time tuition:* $1756 per credit hour. Part-time tuition and fees vary according to course load and degree level.

FRESHMAN FINANCIAL AID (Fall 2017, est.) 259 applied for aid; of those 83% were deemed to have need. 100% of freshmen with need received aid; of those 100% had need fully met. *Average percent of need met:* 100% (excluding resources awarded to replace EFC). *Average financial aid package:* $51,751 (excluding resources awarded to replace EFC). 7% of all full-time freshmen had no need and received non-need-based gift aid.

UNDERGRADUATE FINANCIAL AID (Fall 2017, est.) 844 applied for aid; of those 92% were deemed to have need. 100% of undergraduates with need received aid; of those 100% had need fully met. *Average percent of need met:* 100% (excluding resources awarded to replace EFC). *Average financial aid package:* $50,827 (excluding resources awarded to replace EFC). 8% of all full-time undergraduates had no need and received non-need-based gift aid.

GIFT AID (NEED-BASED) *Total amount:* $34,248,287 (3% federal, 97% institutional). *Receiving aid:* Freshmen: 46% (214); all full-time undergraduates: 43% (778). *Average award:* Freshmen: $42,732; Undergraduates: $43,766. *Scholarships, grants, and awards:* Federal Pell, FSEOG, state, private, college/university gift aid from institutional funds.

GIFT AID (NON-NEED-BASED) *Total amount:* $9,851,826 (5% federal, 8% state, 81% institutional, 6% external sources). *Receiving aid:* Freshmen: 25% (117). Undergraduates: 18% (324). *Average award:* Freshmen: $51,874. Undergraduates: $39,088. *Scholarships, grants, and awards by category:* Academic interests/achievement: 266 awards ($7,950,681 total): general academic interests/achievements. *Tuition waivers:* Full or partial for employees or children of employees. *ROTC:* Army cooperative.

LOANS *Student loans:* $2,633,274 (29% need-based, 71% non-need-based). 28% of past graduating class borrowed through all loan programs. *Average indebtedness per student:* $22,651. *Average need-based loan:* Freshmen: $907. Undergraduates: $804. *Parent loans:* $5,717,160 (100% non-need-based). *Programs:* Federal Direct (Subsidized and Unsubsidized Stafford, PLUS), college/university.

WORK-STUDY *Federal work-study:* Total amount: $511,878; 220 jobs averaging $2000. *State or other work-study/employment:* Total amount: $745,377 (3% need-based, 97% non-need-based). 296 part-time jobs averaging $2000.

APPLYING FOR FINANCIAL AID *Required financial aid forms:* FAFSA, CSS Financial Aid PROFILE, noncustodial (divorced/separated) parent's statement, federal income tax form(s). *Financial aid deadline:* 2/15. *Notification date:* 4/1. Students must reply by 5/1.

CONTACT James D. Kaster, Director of Financial Aid, Washington and Lee University, 204 West Washington Street, Lexington, VA 24450, 540-458-8720. *Fax:* 540-458-8614. *E-mail:* financialaid@wlu.edu. *Website:* http://www.wlu.edu/.

WASHINGTON COLLEGE
Chestertown, MD

Tuition & fees: $47,006	Average undergraduate aid package: $32,393

ABOUT THE INSTITUTION Independent, coed. *Awards:* bachelor's degrees. 34 undergraduate majors. *Total enrollment:* 1,484. Undergraduates: 1,484. Freshmen: 368. Institutional methodology is used as a basis for awarding need-based institutional aid.

UNDERGRADUATE EXPENSES for 2018–2019 *Comprehensive fee:* $59,196 includes full-time tuition ($45,888), mandatory fees ($1118), and room and board ($12,190). *College room only:* $5776. Room and board charges vary according to board plan, housing facility, and location. *Part-time tuition:* $1912 per credit hour. Part-time tuition and fees vary according to course load. *Payment plans:* Guaranteed tuition, tuition prepayment.

FRESHMAN FINANCIAL AID (Fall 2017, est.) 319 applied for aid; of those 88% were deemed to have need. 100% of freshmen with need received aid; of those 18% had need fully met. *Average percent of need met:* 83% (excluding resources awarded to replace EFC). *Average financial aid package:* $35,772 (excluding resources awarded to replace EFC). 21% of all full-time freshmen had no need and received non-need-based gift aid.

UNDERGRADUATE FINANCIAL AID (Fall 2017, est.) 1,077 applied for aid; of those 89% were deemed to have need. 100% of undergraduates with need received aid; of those 17% had need fully met. *Average percent of need met:* 76% (excluding resources awarded to replace EFC). *Average financial aid package:* $32,393 (excluding resources awarded to replace EFC). 26% of all full-time undergraduates had no need and received non-need-based gift aid.

GIFT AID (NEED-BASED) *Total amount:* $27,154,083 (5% federal, 4% state, 89% institutional, 2% external sources). *Receiving aid:* Freshmen: 76% (278); all full-time undergraduates: 66% (949). *Average award:* Freshmen: $33,601; Undergraduates: $29,254. *Scholarships, grants, and awards:* Federal Pell, FSEOG, state, private, college/university gift aid from institutional funds.

GIFT AID (NON-NEED-BASED) *Total amount:* $8,889,746 (96% institutional, 4% external sources). *Receiving aid:* Freshmen: 11% (41). Undergraduates: 9% (131). *Average award:* Freshmen: $19,835. Undergraduates: $18,106. *Scholarships, grants, and awards by category:* Academic interests/achievement: general academic interests/achievements. *Creative arts/performance:* art/fine arts, creative writing, music, performing arts, theater/drama. *Special characteristics:* 29 awards ($1,223,656 total): children of faculty/staff. *Tuition waivers:* Full or partial for employees or children of employees.

LOANS *Student loans:* $8,130,121 (39% need-based, 61% non-need-based). 66% of past graduating class borrowed through all loan programs. *Average indebtedness per student:* $30,462. *Average need-based loan:* Freshmen: $3138. Undergraduates: $4293. *Parent loans:* $5,257,647 (100% non-need-based). *Programs:* Federal Direct (Subsidized and Unsubsidized Stafford, PLUS).

WORK-STUDY *Federal work-study:* Total amount: $242,836; 163 jobs averaging $1484.

APPLYING FOR FINANCIAL AID *Required financial aid form:* FAFSA. *Financial aid deadline (priority):* 3/1. *Notification date:* Continuous beginning 2/1. Students must reply by 5/1.

CONTACT Mrs. Doryann Barnhardt, Director of Student Financial Aid, Washington College, 300 Washington Avenue, Chestertown, MD 21620-1197, 410-778-7214 or toll-free 800-422-1782. *Fax:* 410-801-7160. *E-mail:* dbarnhardt2@washcoll.edu. *Website:* http://www.washcoll.edu/.

WASHINGTON STATE UNIVERSITY
Pullman, WA

Tuition & fees (WA res): $11,391	Average undergraduate aid package: $12,694

ABOUT THE INSTITUTION State-supported, coed. *Awards:* certificates, bachelor's, master's, and doctoral degrees. 148 undergraduate majors. *Total enrollment:* 20,508. Undergraduates: 17,868. Freshmen: 3,938. Federal methodology is used as a basis for awarding need-based institutional aid.

UNDERGRADUATE EXPENSES for 2017–2018 *Application fee:* $50. *Tuition, state resident:* full-time $9530; part-time $494 per credit. *Tuition, nonresident:* full-time $23,956; part-time $1226 per credit. *Required fees:* full-time $1861. Full-time tuition and fees vary according to course load, location, and reciprocity agreements. Part-time tuition and fees vary according to course load, location, and reciprocity agreements. *College room and board:* $11,356; *Room only:* $6858. Room and board charges vary according to board plan, housing facility, and location.

FRESHMAN FINANCIAL AID (Fall 2016) 3,728 applied for aid; of those 70% were deemed to have need. 97% of freshmen with need received aid; of those 17% had need fully met. *Average percent of need met:* 65% (excluding resources awarded to replace EFC). *Average financial aid package:* $12,969 (excluding resources awarded to replace EFC). 30% of all full-time freshmen had no need and received non-need-based gift aid.

UNDERGRADUATE FINANCIAL AID (Fall 2016) 15,952 applied for aid; of those 80% were deemed to have need. 96% of undergraduates with need received aid; of those 12% had need fully met. *Average percent of need met:* 63% (excluding resources awarded to replace EFC). *Average financial aid package:* $12,694 (excluding resources awarded to replace EFC). 18% of all full-time undergraduates had no need and received non-need-based gift aid.

GIFT AID (NEED-BASED) *Total amount:* $91,403,795 (37% federal, 54% state, 9% institutional). *Receiving aid:* Freshmen: 54% (2,395); all full-time undergraduates: 50% (10,842). *Average award:* Freshmen: $10,895; Undergraduates: $10,650. *Scholarships, grants, and awards:* Federal Pell, FSEOG, state, private, college/university gift aid from institutional funds, Federal Nursing.

GIFT AID (NON-NEED-BASED) *Total amount:* $21,440,484 (8% state, 56% institutional, 36% external sources). *Receiving aid:* Freshmen: 44% (1,963). Undergraduates: 29% (6,310). *Average award:* Freshmen: $4069. Undergraduates: $3922. *Scholarships, grants, and awards by category: Academic interests/achievement:* agriculture, architecture, area/ethnic studies, biological sciences, business, communication, computer science, education, engineering/technologies, English, foreign languages, general academic interests/achievements, health fields, home economics, humanities, international studies, mathematics, military science, physical sciences, premedicine, social sciences. *Creative arts/performance:* applied art and design, art/fine arts, cinema/film/broadcasting, creative writing, general creative arts/performance, journalism/publications, music, performing arts, theater/drama. *Special achievements/activities:* community service, general special achievements/activities, junior miss, leadership, memberships, religious involvement, rodeo. *Special characteristics:* children and siblings of alumni, children of faculty/staff, children of public servants, children with a deceased or disabled parent, first-generation college students, handicapped students, international students, local/state students, out-of-state students, previous college experience, public servants, religious affiliation, veterans, veterans' children. *Tuition waivers:* Full or partial for employees or children of employees, senior citizens. *ROTC:* Army, Naval cooperative, Air Force.

LOANS *Student loans:* $89,104,012 (42% need-based, 58% non-need-based). 58% of past graduating class borrowed through all loan programs. *Average indebtedness per student:* $26,807. *Average need-based loan:* Freshmen: $3481. Undergraduates: $4219. *Parent loans:* $41,994,086 (100% non-need-based). *Programs:* Federal Direct (Subsidized and Unsubsidized Stafford, PLUS), Perkins, Federal Nursing, private loans.

WORK-STUDY *Federal work-study:* jobs available. *State or other work-study/employment:* Total amount: $954,123 (100% need-based). Part-time jobs available.

ATHLETIC AWARDS Total amount: $8,189,942 (100% non-need-based).

APPLYING FOR FINANCIAL AID *Required financial aid form:* FAFSA. *Financial aid deadline:* 1/31. *Notification date:* Continuous beginning 2/1. Students must reply within 2 weeks of notification.

CONTACT Mr. Brian Dixon, Office of Financial Aid and Scholarships, Washington State University, PO Box 641068, Pullman, WA 99164-1068, 509-335-9711 or toll-free 888-468-6978. *Fax:* 509-335-1385. *E-mail:* finaid@wsu.edu. *Website:* http://www.wsu.edu/.

WASHINGTON STATE UNIVERSITY–GLOBAL CAMPUS
Pullman, WA

CONTACT Financial Aid Office, Washington State University–Global Campus, PO Box 645220, Washington State University, Pullman, WA 99164-5220 or toll-free 800-222-4978.
Website: http://www.globalcampus.wsu.edu/.

WASHINGTON UNIVERSITY IN ST. LOUIS
St. Louis, MO

Tuition & fees: $53,399	Average undergraduate aid package: $46,638

ABOUT THE INSTITUTION Independent, coed. *Awards:* certificates, bachelor's, master's, and doctoral degrees. 178 undergraduate majors. *Total enrollment:* 15,303. Undergraduates: 7,675. Freshmen: 1,778. Institutional methodology is used as a basis for awarding need-based institutional aid.

UNDERGRADUATE EXPENSES for 2018–2019 *Application fee:* $75. *Comprehensive fee:* $69,839 includes full-time tuition ($52,400), mandatory fees ($999), and room and board ($16,440). *College room only:* $11,310. Room and board charges vary according to board plan and housing facility. *Payment plan:* Tuition prepayment.

FRESHMAN FINANCIAL AID (Fall 2017, est.) 906 applied for aid; of those 80% were deemed to have need. 98% of freshmen with need received aid; of those 100% had need fully met. *Average percent of need met:* 100% (excluding resources awarded to replace EFC). *Average financial aid package:* $48,169 (excluding resources awarded to replace EFC). 10% of all full-time freshmen had no need and received non-need-based gift aid.

UNDERGRADUATE FINANCIAL AID (Fall 2017, est.) 3,204 applied for aid; of those 91% were deemed to have need. 99% of undergraduates with need received aid; of those 100% had need fully met. *Average percent of need met:* 100% (excluding resources awarded to replace EFC). *Average financial aid package:* $46,638 (excluding resources awarded to replace EFC). 8% of all full-time undergraduates had no need and received non-need-based gift aid.

GIFT AID (NEED-BASED) *Total amount:* $124,433,008 (3% federal, 1% state, 92% institutional, 4% external sources). *Receiving aid:* Freshmen: 39% (683); all full-time undergraduates: 41% (2,833). *Average award:* Freshmen: $45,567; Undergraduates: $43,745. *Scholarships, grants, and awards:* Federal Pell, FSEOG, state, private, college/university gift aid from institutional funds, United Negro College Fund.

GIFT AID (NON-NEED-BASED) *Total amount:* $2,937,260 (21% state, 29% institutional, 50% external sources). *Receiving aid:* Freshmen: 4% (68). Undergraduates: 2% (169). *Average award:* Freshmen: $11,182. Undergraduates: $5305. *Scholarships, grants, and awards by category: Academic interests/achievement:* 814 awards ($23,350,094 total): architecture, biological sciences, business, communication, computer science, education, engineering/technologies, English, foreign languages, general academic interests/achievements, home economics, humanities, international studies, mathematics, military science, physical sciences, premedicine, religion/biblical studies, social sciences. *Creative arts/performance:* 43 awards ($293,552 total): applied art and design, art/fine arts, creative writing. *Tuition waivers:* Full or partial for employees or children of employees. *ROTC:* Army, Air Force cooperative.

LOANS *Student loans:* $9,382,131 (84% need-based, 16% non-need-based). 29% of past graduating class borrowed through all loan programs. *Average indebtedness per student:* $22,592. *Average need-based loan:* Freshmen: $3298. Undergraduates: $4698. *Parent loans:* $14,856,556 (16% need-based, 84% non-need-based). *Programs:* Federal Direct (Subsidized and Unsubsidized Stafford, PLUS), Perkins, state, college/university, private loans.

WORK-STUDY *Federal work-study:* Total amount: $3,165,418; 1,374 jobs averaging $2304.

APPLYING FOR FINANCIAL AID *Required financial aid forms:* FAFSA, noncustodial (divorced/separated) parent's statement, CSS/Financial Aid PROFILE or institution's own financial aid form. *Financial aid deadline:* 2/1. *Notification date:* 4/1. Students must reply by 5/1.

CONTACT Mr. Michael Runiewicz, Director of Financial Aid, Washington University in St. Louis, Campus Box 1041, One Brookings Drive, St. Louis, MO 63130-4899, 314-935-5900 or toll-free 800-638-0700. *Fax:* 314-935-4037. *E-mail:* financial@wustl.edu. *Website:* http://www.wustl.edu/.

WATKINS COLLEGE OF ART, DESIGN, & FILM
Nashville, TN

CONTACT Lyle Jones, Financial Aid Coordinator, Watkins College of Art, Design, & Film, 2298 Rosa L. Parks Boulevard, Nashville, TN 37228, 615-383-4848 Ext. 7421. *Fax:* 615-383-4849. *E-mail:* financialaid@watkins.edu. *Website:* http://www.watkins.edu/.

WAYLAND BAPTIST UNIVERSITY
Plainview, TX

Tuition & fees: $19,430	Average undergraduate aid package: $11,880

ABOUT THE INSTITUTION Independent Baptist, coed. *Awards:* associate, bachelor's, master's, and doctoral degrees (branch locations in Anchorage, AK; Amarillo, TX; Luke Air Force Base, AZ; Glorieta, NM; Aiea, HI; Lubbock, TX; San Antonio, TX; Wichita Falls, TX). 46 undergraduate majors. *Total enrollment:* 4,827. Undergraduates: 3,543. Freshmen: 297. Federal methodology is used as a basis for awarding need-based institutional aid.

UNDERGRADUATE EXPENSES for 2017–2018 *Application fee:* $35. *Comprehensive fee:* $26,964 includes full-time tuition ($18,150), mandatory fees ($1280), and room and board ($7534). *College room only:* $3044. Full-time tuition and fees vary according to course load and location. Room and board charges vary according to board plan and housing facility. *Part-time tuition:* $605 per credit hour. Part-time tuition and fees vary according to course load and location.

FRESHMAN FINANCIAL AID (Fall 2017, est.) 271 applied for aid; of those 100% were deemed to have need. 100% of freshmen with need received aid; of those 6% had need fully met. *Average percent of need met:* 43% (excluding resources awarded to replace EFC). *Average financial aid package:* $13,003 (excluding resources awarded to replace EFC). 12% of all full-time freshmen had no need and received non-need-based gift aid.

UNDERGRADUATE FINANCIAL AID (Fall 2017, est.) 977 applied for aid; of those 100% were deemed to have need. 100% of undergraduates with need received aid; of those 6% had need fully met. *Average percent of need met:* 44% (excluding resources awarded to replace EFC). *Average financial aid package:* $11,880 (excluding resources awarded to replace EFC). 10% of all full-time undergraduates had no need and received non-need-based gift aid.

GIFT AID (NEED-BASED) *Total amount:* $10,239,872 (55% federal, 15% state, 19% institutional, 11% external sources). *Receiving aid:* Freshmen: 100% (271); all full-time undergraduates: 100% (977). *Average award:* Freshmen: $10,489; Undergraduates: $9079. *Scholarships, grants, and awards:* Federal Pell, FSEOG, state, private, college/university gift aid from institutional funds.

GIFT AID (NON-NEED-BASED) *Total amount:* $931,567 (1% federal, 4% state, 71% institutional, 24% external sources). *Receiving aid:* Freshmen: 5% (14). Undergraduates: 5% (46). *Average award:* Freshmen: $4879. Undergraduates: $5321. *Scholarships, grants, and awards by category:* Academic interests/achievement: 689 awards ($1,642,501 total): biological sciences, business, communication, education, English, foreign languages, general academic interests/achievements, home economics, mathematics, physical sciences, premedicine, religion/biblical studies, social sciences. *Creative arts/performance:* 84 awards ($259,741 total): art/fine arts, music, theater/drama. *Special achievements/activities:* 196 awards ($410,935 total): cheerleading/drum major, community service, leadership. *Special characteristics:* 238 awards ($757,747 total): children of faculty/staff, relatives of clergy, religious affiliation. *ROTC:* Army cooperative, Air Force cooperative.

LOANS *Student loans:* $13,957,026 (89% need-based, 11% non-need-based). 59% of past graduating class borrowed through all loan programs. *Average indebtedness per student:* $29,555. *Average need-based loan:* Freshmen: $3584. Undergraduates: $4154. *Parent loans:* $1,326,570 (58% need-based, 42% non-need-based).

Programs: Federal Direct (Subsidized and Unsubsidized Stafford, PLUS), Perkins, state, private loans.

WORK-STUDY *Federal work-study:* Total amount: $132,446; 123 jobs averaging $1447. *State or other work-study/employment:* Total amount: $153,219 (44% need-based, 56% non-need-based). 225 part-time jobs averaging $2171.

ATHLETIC AWARDS Total amount: $2,597,411 (59% need-based, 41% non-need-based).

APPLYING FOR FINANCIAL AID *Required financial aid forms:* FAFSA, institution's own form, state aid form. *Financial aid deadline:* Continuous. *Notification date:* Continuous beginning 1/1.

CONTACT Karen LaQuey, Director of Financial Aid, Wayland Baptist University, 1900 West 7th Street, Plainview, TX 79072-6998, 806-291-3520 or toll-free 800-588-1928. *Fax:* 806-291-1956. *E-mail:* laquey@wbu.edu. *Website:* http://www.wbu.edu/.

WAYNESBURG UNIVERSITY
Waynesburg, PA

Tuition & fees: $24,010	Average undergraduate aid package: $19,900

ABOUT THE INSTITUTION Independent Presbyterian Church (U.S.A.), coed. *Awards:* bachelor's, master's, and doctoral degrees. 52 undergraduate majors. *Total enrollment:* 1,736. Undergraduates: 1,376. Freshmen: 400. Federal methodology is used as a basis for awarding need-based institutional aid.

UNDERGRADUATE EXPENSES for 2017–2018 *Application fee:* $20. *Comprehensive fee:* $33,830 includes full-time tuition ($23,160), mandatory fees ($850), and room and board ($9820). *College room only:* $4970. Full-time tuition and fees vary according to class time. Room and board charges vary according to board plan and housing facility. *Part-time tuition:* $960 per credit hour. *Part-time fees:* $16 per credit hour. Part-time tuition and fees vary according to class time, course load, and location.

FRESHMAN FINANCIAL AID (Fall 2017, est.) 387 applied for aid; of those 92% were deemed to have need. 100% of freshmen with need received aid; of those 27% had need fully met. *Average percent of need met:* 79% (excluding resources awarded to replace EFC). *Average financial aid package:* $20,026 (excluding resources awarded to replace EFC). 11% of all full-time freshmen had no need and received non-need-based gift aid.

UNDERGRADUATE FINANCIAL AID (Fall 2017, est.) 1,242 applied for aid; of those 89% were deemed to have need. 100% of undergraduates with need received aid; of those 30% had need fully met. *Average percent of need met:* 80% (excluding resources awarded to replace EFC). *Average financial aid package:* $19,900 (excluding resources awarded to replace EFC). 15% of all full-time undergraduates had no need and received non-need-based gift aid.

GIFT AID (NEED-BASED) *Total amount:* $16,585,000 (13% federal, 13% state, 68% institutional, 6% external sources). *Receiving aid:* Freshmen: 88% (354); all full-time undergraduates: 72% (1,084). *Average award:* Freshmen: $16,000; Undergraduates: $15,250. *Scholarships, grants, and awards:* Federal Pell, FSEOG, state, private, college/university gift aid from institutional funds, United Negro College Fund.

GIFT AID (NON-NEED-BASED) *Total amount:* $3,412,892 (91% institutional, 9% external sources). *Receiving aid:* Freshmen: 9% (38). Undergraduates: 8% (122). *Average award:* Freshmen: $12,170. Undergraduates: $11,200. *Scholarships, grants, and awards by category:* Academic interests/achievement: 1,345 awards ($14,700,000 total): communication, general academic interests/achievements. *Creative arts/performance:* 15 awards ($15,000 total): art/fine arts, music, theater/drama. *Special achievements/activities:* 60 awards ($200,000 total): community service. *Special characteristics:* 50 awards ($550,000 total): children of faculty/staff, siblings of current students. *Tuition waivers:* Full or partial for employees or children of employees. *ROTC:* Army cooperative.

LOANS *Student loans:* $10,929,000 (57% need-based, 43% non-need-based). 84% of past graduating class borrowed through all loan programs. *Average indebtedness per student:* $31,000. *Average need-based loan:* Freshmen: $3900. Undergraduates: $5000. *Parent loans:* $3,233,000 (63% need-based, 37% non-need-based). *Programs:* Federal Direct (Subsidized and Unsubsidized Stafford, PLUS), Federal Nursing, college/university.

WORK-STUDY *Federal work-study:* Total amount: $149,000; 600 jobs averaging $1500.

APPLYING FOR FINANCIAL AID *Required financial aid forms:* FAFSA, state aid form. *Financial aid deadline:* Continuous. *Notification date:* Continuous beginning 12/1. Students must reply within 2 weeks of notification.

CONTACT Mr. Matthew C. Stokan, Director of Financial Aid, Waynesburg University, 51 West College Street, Waynesburg, PA 15370-1222, 724-852-3208 Ext. 227 or toll-free 800-225-7393. *Fax:* 724-852-6312. *E-mail:* mstokan@waynesburg.edu. *Website:* http://www.waynesburg.edu/.

WAYNE STATE COLLEGE
Wayne, NE

Tuition & fees (NE res): $6824	Average undergraduate aid package: $9494

ABOUT THE INSTITUTION State-supported, coed. *Awards:* certificates, bachelor's, and master's degrees. 53 undergraduate majors. *Total enrollment:* 3,292. Undergraduates: 2,757. Freshmen: 606. Federal methodology is used as a basis for awarding need-based institutional aid.

UNDERGRADUATE EXPENSES for 2017–2018 *Tuition, state resident:* full-time $5160; part-time $172 per credit hour. *Tuition, nonresident:* full-time $10,320; part-time $344 per credit hour. *Required fees:* full-time $1664; $64.25 per credit hour. Full-time tuition and fees vary according to course level, course load, and location. Part-time tuition and fees vary according to course level, course load, and location. *College room and board:* $7430; *Room only:* $3640. Room and board charges vary according to board plan and housing facility.

FRESHMAN FINANCIAL AID (Fall 2017, est.) 557 applied for aid; of those 75% were deemed to have need. 99% of freshmen with need received aid; of those 50% had need fully met. *Average percent of need met:* 60% (excluding resources awarded to replace EFC). *Average financial aid package:* $9940 (excluding resources awarded to replace EFC). 7% of all full-time freshmen had no need and received non-need-based gift aid.

UNDERGRADUATE FINANCIAL AID (Fall 2017, est.) 2,180 applied for aid; of those 78% were deemed to have need. 99% of undergraduates with need received aid; of those 44% had need fully met. *Average percent of need met:* 61% (excluding resources awarded to replace EFC). *Average financial aid package:* $9494 (excluding resources awarded to replace EFC). 4% of all full-time undergraduates had no need and received non-need-based gift aid.

GIFT AID (NEED-BASED) *Total amount:* $5,271,237 (81% federal, 15% state, 4% institutional). *Receiving aid:* Freshmen: 50% (303); all full-time undergraduates: 54% (1,307). *Average award:* Freshmen: $5868; Undergraduates: $5464. *Scholarships, grants, and awards:* Federal Pell, FSEOG, state, private, college/university gift aid from institutional funds.

GIFT AID (NON-NEED-BASED) *Total amount:* $4,058,005 (1% federal, 30% institutional, 69% external sources). *Receiving aid:* Freshmen: 51% (310). Undergraduates: 37% (892). *Average award:* Freshmen: $2149. Undergraduates: $2470. *Scholarships, grants, and awards by category:* Academic interests/achievement: biological sciences, business, communication, computer science, education, English, foreign languages, general academic interests/achievements, health fields, home economics, humanities, international studies, mathematics, physical sciences, premedicine, social sciences. *Creative arts/performance:* applied art and design, art/fine arts, creative writing, general creative arts/performance, journalism/publications, music, performing arts, theater/drama. *Special achievements/activities:* general special achievements/activities, leadership. *Special characteristics:* children of faculty/staff, ethnic background, general special characteristics, local/state students, members of minority groups, out-of-state students, veterans, veterans' children. *Tuition waivers:* Full or partial for employees or children of employees. *ROTC:* Army.

LOANS *Student loans:* $9,685,925 (44% need-based, 56% non-need-based). *Average need-based loan:* Freshmen: $3157. Undergraduates: $3893. *Parent loans:* $1,134,696 (100% non-need-based). *Programs:* Federal Direct (Subsidized and Unsubsidized Stafford, PLUS), Perkins.

WORK-STUDY *Federal work-study:* Total amount: $392,035; jobs available.

ATHLETIC AWARDS Total amount: $581,228 (100% non-need-based).

APPLYING FOR FINANCIAL AID *Required financial aid form:* FAFSA. *Financial aid deadline (priority):* 4/1. *Notification date:* Continuous beginning 2/1. Students must reply within 4 weeks of notification.

CONTACT Annette Kaus, Director of Financial Aid, Wayne State College, 1111 Main Street, Wayne, NE 68787, 402-375-7230 or toll-free 866-WSC-CATS. *Fax:* 402-375-7067. *E-mail:* ankaus1@wsc.edu. *Website:* http://www.wsc.edu/.

WAYNE STATE UNIVERSITY
Detroit, MI

Tuition & fees (MI res): $13,776	Average undergraduate aid package: $10,934

ABOUT THE INSTITUTION State-supported, coed. *Awards:* certificates, bachelor's, master's, and doctoral degrees. 83 undergraduate majors. *Total enrollment:* 27,089. Undergraduates: 17,322. Freshmen: 2,653. Federal methodology is used as a basis for awarding need-based institutional aid.

UNDERGRADUATE EXPENSES for 2017–2018 *Application fee:* $25. *One-time required fee:* $250. *Tuition, state resident:* full-time $12,264; part-time $408.81 per credit hour. *Tuition, nonresident:* full-time $28,151; part-time $938.35 per credit hour. *Required fees:* full-time $1512; $35.62 per credit hour or $221.45 per term. Full-time tuition and fees vary according to course load, program, and student level. Part-time tuition and fees vary according to course load, program, and student level. *College room and board:* $10,106; *Room only:* $6308. Room and board charges vary according to board plan and housing facility.

FRESHMAN FINANCIAL AID (Fall 2016) 2,037 applied for aid; of those 84% were deemed to have need. 99% of freshmen with need received aid; of those 9% had need fully met. *Average percent of need met:* 64% (excluding resources awarded to replace EFC). *Average financial aid package:* $12,247 (excluding resources awarded to replace EFC). 22% of all full-time freshmen had no need and received non-need-based gift aid.

UNDERGRADUATE FINANCIAL AID (Fall 2016) 9,644 applied for aid; of those 90% were deemed to have need. 98% of undergraduates with need received aid; of those 4% had need fully met. *Average percent of need met:* 49% (excluding resources awarded to replace EFC). *Average financial aid package:* $10,934 (excluding resources awarded to replace EFC). 17% of all full-time undergraduates had no need and received non-need-based gift aid.

GIFT AID (NEED-BASED) *Total amount:* $49,474,306 (67% federal, 33% institutional). *Receiving aid:* Freshmen: 51% (1,218); all full-time undergraduates: 52% (6,201). *Average award:* Freshmen: $8068; Undergraduates: $6798. *Scholarships, grants, and awards:* Federal Pell, FSEOG, state, private, college/university gift aid from institutional funds, United Negro College Fund.

GIFT AID (NON-NEED-BASED) *Total amount:* $35,032,880 (1% federal, 4% state, 92% institutional, 3% external sources). *Receiving aid:* Freshmen: 52% (1,253). Undergraduates: 46% (5,449). *Average award:* Freshmen: $6386. Undergraduates: $5383. *Scholarships, grants, and awards by category:* Academic interests/achievement: area/ethnic studies, biological sciences, business, communication, computer science, education, engineering/technologies, English, foreign languages, general academic interests/achievements, health fields, humanities, international studies, library science, mathematics, military science, physical sciences, premedicine, social sciences. *Creative arts/performance:* art/fine arts, dance, debating, general creative arts/performance, journalism/publications, music, performing arts, theater/drama. *Special achievements/activities:* leadership, memberships. *Special characteristics:* children of current students, children of faculty/staff, children with a deceased or disabled parent, ethnic background, international students, local/state students, out-of-state students, spouses of current students. *Tuition waivers:* Full or partial for employees or children of employees, senior citizens. *ROTC:* Army, Air Force cooperative.

LOANS *Student loans:* $73,866,946 (89% need-based, 11% non-need-based). 63% of past graduating class borrowed through all loan programs. *Average indebtedness per student:* $27,960. *Average need-based loan:* Freshmen: $3461. Undergraduates: $4406. *Parent loans:* $8,848,784 (100% non-need-based). *Programs:* Federal Direct (Subsidized and Unsubsidized Stafford, PLUS), Perkins, college/university.

WORK-STUDY *Federal work-study:* jobs available. *State or other work-study/employment:* Part-time jobs available.

ATHLETIC AWARDS Total amount: $3,393,973 (100% non-need-based).

APPLYING FOR FINANCIAL AID *Required financial aid forms:* FAFSA, federal income tax form(s), W-2 forms. *Financial aid deadline:* 6/30 (priority: 1/1). *Notification date:* Continuous beginning 3/31.

CONTACT Catherine Kay, Director of Financial Aid, Wayne State University, 42 West Warren Avenue, Detroit, MI 48202, 313-577-2100 or toll-free 877-WSU-INFO. *Fax:* 313-577-6648. *E-mail:* financialaid@wayne.edu. *Website:* http://www.wayne.edu/.

CONTACT Ms. Kathleen Wilson, Vice President of Student Record Services, Webber International University, PO Box 96, 1201 Scenic Highway, Babson Park, FL 33827-0096, 863-638-2930 or toll-free 800-741-1844. *Fax:* 863-638-1513. *E-mail:* wilsonka@webber.edu. *Website:* http://www.webber.edu/.

WEBBER INTERNATIONAL UNIVERSITY
Babson Park, FL

Tuition & fees: $26,116	Average undergraduate aid package: $20,525

ABOUT THE INSTITUTION Independent, coed. *Awards:* associate, bachelor's, and master's degrees. 12 undergraduate majors. *Total enrollment:* 683. Undergraduates: 626. Freshmen: 173. Federal methodology is used as a basis for awarding need-based institutional aid.

UNDERGRADUATE EXPENSES for 2018–2019 *Application fee:* $35. *Comprehensive fee:* $35,410 includes full-time tuition ($23,380), mandatory fees ($2736), and room and board ($9294). Full-time tuition and fees vary according to class time, course load, and program. Room and board charges vary according to board plan, gender, and housing facility. *Part-time tuition:* $366 per credit hour. Part-time tuition and fees vary according to class time, course load, and program.

FRESHMAN FINANCIAL AID (Fall 2017, est.) 153 applied for aid; of those 92% were deemed to have need. 100% of freshmen with need received aid; of those 9% had need fully met. *Average percent of need met:* 60% (excluding resources awarded to replace EFC). *Average financial aid package:* $20,282 (excluding resources awarded to replace EFC). 15% of all full-time freshmen had no need and received non-need-based gift aid.

UNDERGRADUATE FINANCIAL AID (Fall 2017, est.) 453 applied for aid; of those 94% were deemed to have need. 100% of undergraduates with need received aid; of those 7% had need fully met. *Average percent of need met:* 62% (excluding resources awarded to replace EFC). *Average financial aid package:* $20,525 (excluding resources awarded to replace EFC). 21% of all full-time undergraduates had no need and received non-need-based gift aid.

GIFT AID (NEED-BASED) *Total amount:* $3,766,312 (40% federal, 36% state, 22% institutional, 2% external sources). *Receiving aid:* Freshmen: 81% (140); all full-time undergraduates: 73% (426). *Average award:* Freshmen: $17,537; Undergraduates: $17,076. *Scholarships, grants, and awards:* Federal Pell, FSEOG, state, private, college/university gift aid from institutional funds.

GIFT AID (NON-NEED-BASED) *Total amount:* $2,265,176 (49% state, 50% institutional, 1% external sources). *Receiving aid:* Freshmen: 7% (12). Undergraduates: 6% (32). *Average award:* Freshmen: $5824. Undergraduates: $9199. *Scholarships, grants, and awards by category: Academic interests/achievement:* 380 awards ($1,037,443 total): business, general academic interests/achievements. *Creative arts/performance:* 3 awards ($3000 total): debating, journalism/publications. *Special achievements/activities:* 32 awards ($26,229 total): community service, general special achievements/activities, leadership, memberships. *Special characteristics:* 81 awards ($1,021,300 total): children and siblings of alumni, children of faculty/staff, general special characteristics, international students, local/state students, siblings of current students, veterans. *Tuition waivers:* Full or partial for children of alumni, employees or children of employees, adult students, senior citizens.

LOANS *Student loans:* $3,212,171 (85% need-based, 15% non-need-based). 65% of past graduating class borrowed through all loan programs. *Average indebtedness per student:* $26,682. *Average need-based loan:* Freshmen: $3339. Undergraduates: $4028. *Parent loans:* $1,688,487 (71% need-based, 29% non-need-based). *Programs:* Federal Direct (Subsidized and Unsubsidized Stafford, PLUS).

WORK-STUDY *Federal work-study:* Total amount: $51,114; 49 jobs averaging $1008. *State or other work-study/employment:* Total amount: $47,698 (19% need-based, 81% non-need-based). 44 part-time jobs averaging $1218.

ATHLETIC AWARDS Total amount: $4,340,809 (79% need-based, 21% non-need-based).

APPLYING FOR FINANCIAL AID *Required financial aid forms:* FAFSA, state aid form. *Financial aid deadline:* 8/1 (priority: 4/1). *Notification date:* Continuous beginning 12/1. Students must reply within 4 weeks of notification.

WEBB INSTITUTE
Glen Cove, NY

Tuition & fees: $50,175	Average undergraduate aid package: $52,750

ABOUT THE INSTITUTION Independent, coed. *Awards:* bachelor's degrees. 1 undergraduate major. *Total enrollment:* 98. Undergraduates: 98. Freshmen: 26. Both federal and institutional methodology are used as a basis for awarding need-based institutional aid.

UNDERGRADUATE EXPENSES for 2018–2019 *Application fee:* $60. *One-time required fee:* $3000. *Comprehensive fee:* $65,225 includes full-time tuition ($49,750), mandatory fees ($425), and room and board ($15,050). Webb provides scholarships that will fully cover the tuition expenses of U.S. citizens and permanent residents. One-time required fee is for a laptop charged in the first year only.

FRESHMAN FINANCIAL AID (Fall 2016) 7 applied for aid; of those 100% were deemed to have need. 100% of freshmen with need received aid. *Average percent of need met:* 95% (excluding resources awarded to replace EFC). *Average financial aid package:* $50,500 (excluding resources awarded to replace EFC). 75% of all full-time freshmen had no need and received non-need-based gift aid.

UNDERGRADUATE FINANCIAL AID (Fall 2016) 29 applied for aid; of those 100% were deemed to have need. 100% of undergraduates with need received aid. *Average percent of need met:* 95% (excluding resources awarded to replace EFC). *Average financial aid package:* $52,750 (excluding resources awarded to replace EFC). 67% of all full-time undergraduates had no need and received non-need-based gift aid.

GIFT AID (NEED-BASED) *Total amount:* $1,458,836 (2% federal, 95% institutional, 3% external sources). *Receiving aid:* Freshmen: 25% (7); all full-time undergraduates: 32% (29). *Average award:* Freshmen: $570; Undergraduates: $1950. *Scholarships, grants, and awards:* Federal Pell, state, private, college/university gift aid from institutional funds.

GIFT AID (NON-NEED-BASED) *Total amount:* $2,895,189 (100% institutional). *Receiving aid:* Freshmen: 25% (7). Undergraduates: 32% (29). *Average award:* Freshmen: $47,000. Undergraduates: $47,000. *Scholarships, grants, and awards by category: Academic interests/achievement:* 62 awards ($2,914,000 total): engineering/technologies, general academic interests/achievements. *Special achievements/activities:* 2 awards ($12,500 total): community service, leadership.

LOANS *Student loans:* $177,275 (100% need-based). 43% of past graduating class borrowed through all loan programs. *Average indebtedness per student:* $17,870. *Average need-based loan:* Freshmen: $3500. Undergraduates: $4710. *Parent loans:* $56,226 (100% need-based). *Programs:* Federal Direct (Subsidized and Unsubsidized Stafford, PLUS).

APPLYING FOR FINANCIAL AID *Required financial aid form:* FAFSA. *Financial aid deadline:* 5/1. *Notification date:* Continuous beginning 5/1. Students must reply by 5/15 or within 2 weeks of notification.

CONTACT Jocelyn Wilson, Director of Financial Aid, Webb Institute, 298 Crescent Beach Road, Glen Cove, NY 11542-1398, 516-403-5928 Ext. 1108. *Fax:* 516-674-9838. *E-mail:* jwilson@webb.edu. *Website:* http://www.webb.edu/.

WEBER STATE UNIVERSITY
Ogden, UT

Tuition & fees (UT res): $5712	Average undergraduate aid package: $6004

ABOUT THE INSTITUTION State-supported, coed. *Awards:* certificates, associate, bachelor's, and master's degrees. 155 undergraduate majors. *Total enrollment:* 27,949. Undergraduates: 27,111. Freshmen: 3,118. Both federal and institutional methodology are used as a basis for awarding need-based institutional aid.

UNDERGRADUATE EXPENSES for 2017–2018 *Application fee:* $30. *Tuition, state resident:* full-time $4773; part-time $2816 per year. *Tuition, non-resident:* full-time $14,321; part-time $8450 per year. *Required fees:* full-time $939; $575 per year. Full-time tuition and fees vary according to course level, course load, degree level, and program. Part-time tuition and fees vary according to course level, course load, degree level, and program. *College room and board:* $8400. Room and board charges vary according to board plan and housing facility.
FRESHMAN FINANCIAL AID (Fall 2016) 2,265 applied for aid; of those 81% were deemed to have need. 76% of freshmen with need received aid; of those 89% had need fully met. *Average financial aid package:* $5144 (excluding resources awarded to replace EFC). 23% of all full-time freshmen had no need and received non-need-based gift aid.
UNDERGRADUATE FINANCIAL AID (Fall 2016) 7,423 applied for aid; of those 87% were deemed to have need. 88% of undergraduates with need received aid; of those 75% had need fully met. *Average financial aid package:* $6004 (excluding resources awarded to replace EFC). 20% of all full-time undergraduates had no need and received non-need-based gift aid.
GIFT AID (NEED-BASED) *Total amount:* $30,957,879 (83% federal, 10% state, 7% external sources). *Receiving aid:* Freshmen: 33% (1,037); all full-time undergraduates: 41% (4,451). *Average award:* Freshmen: $4024; Undergraduates: $4232. *Scholarships, grants, and awards:* Federal Pell, FSEOG, state, private, college/university gift aid from institutional funds.
GIFT AID (NON-NEED-BASED) *Total amount:* $3,811,563 (100% institutional). *Receiving aid:* Freshmen: 7% (220). Undergraduates: 19% (2,023). *Average award:* Freshmen: $3259. Undergraduates: $3732. *Tuition waivers:* Full or partial for employees or children of employees, senior citizens. *ROTC:* Army, Naval cooperative, Air Force cooperative.
LOANS *Student loans:* $39,776,371 (45% need-based, 55% non-need-based). 44% of past graduating class borrowed through all loan programs. *Average indebtedness per student:* $22,657. *Average need-based loan:* Freshmen: $2669. Undergraduates: $3684. *Parent loans:* $34,411 (100% non-need-based). *Programs:* Federal Direct (Subsidized and Unsubsidized Stafford, PLUS), Perkins, college/university.
WORK-STUDY *Federal work-study:* jobs available. *State or other work-study/employment:* Total amount: $323,864 (100% need-based). Part-time jobs available.
ATHLETIC AWARDS Total amount: $5,916,110 (10% need-based, 90% non-need-based).
APPLYING FOR FINANCIAL AID *Required financial aid forms:* FAFSA, institution's own form. *Financial aid deadline (priority):* 3/1. *Notification date:* Continuous beginning 3/15. Students must reply within 2 weeks of notification.
CONTACT Mr. Jed Spencer, Financial Aid Director, Weber State University, Student Service Center, Suite 120, 3885 West Campus Drive, Department 1136, Ogden, UT 84408-1136, 801-626-7569 or toll-free 800-848-7700 (in-state), 800-848-7770 (out-of-state). *E-mail:* finaid@weber.edu.
Website: http://www.weber.edu/.

WEBSTER UNIVERSITY
St. Louis, MO

Tuition & fees: $27,100	Average undergraduate aid package: $23,727

ABOUT THE INSTITUTION Independent, coed. *Awards:* certificates, bachelor's, master's, and doctoral degrees. 68 undergraduate majors. *Total enrollment:* 4,090. Undergraduates: 2,544. Freshmen: 514. Federal methodology is used as a basis for awarding need-based institutional aid.
UNDERGRADUATE EXPENSES for 2017–2018 *Application fee:* $35. *One-time required fee:* $125. *Comprehensive fee:* $38,150 includes full-time tuition ($26,900), mandatory fees ($200), and room and board ($11,050). *College room only:* $6050. Full-time tuition and fees vary according to program. Room and board charges vary according to board plan and housing facility. *Part-time tuition:* $690 per credit hour.
FRESHMAN FINANCIAL AID (Fall 2017, est.) 486 applied for aid; of those 79% were deemed to have need. 100% of freshmen with need received aid; of those 21% had need fully met. *Average percent of need met:* 69% (excluding resources awarded to replace EFC). *Average financial aid package:* $27,407 (excluding resources awarded to replace EFC). 9% of all full-time freshmen had no need and received non-need-based gift aid.

UNDERGRADUATE FINANCIAL AID (Fall 2017, est.) 1,846 applied for aid; of those 81% were deemed to have need. 100% of undergraduates with need received aid; of those 19% had need fully met. *Average percent of need met:* 63% (excluding resources awarded to replace EFC). *Average financial aid package:* $23,727 (excluding resources awarded to replace EFC). 6% of all full-time undergraduates had no need and received non-need-based gift aid.
GIFT AID (NEED-BASED) *Total amount:* $26,182,288 (19% federal, 4% state, 76% institutional, 1% external sources). *Receiving aid:* Freshmen: 65% (330); all full-time undergraduates: 60% (1,320). *Average award:* Freshmen: $8045; Undergraduates: $8574. *Scholarships, grants, and awards:* Federal Pell, FSEOG, state, private, college/university gift aid from institutional funds.
GIFT AID (NON-NEED-BASED) *Total amount:* $10,840,625 (2% state, 94% institutional, 4% external sources). *Receiving aid:* Freshmen: 70% (359). Undergraduates: 58% (1,282). *Average award:* Freshmen: $15,982. Undergraduates: $13,621. *Scholarships, grants, and awards by category:* Academic interests/achievement: biological sciences, business, communication, computer science, education, English, foreign languages, general academic interests/achievements, humanities, international studies. *Creative arts/performance:* art/fine arts, creative writing, debating, music, theater/drama. *Special achievements/activities:* community service, leadership. *Special characteristics:* children of faculty/staff, ethnic background, international students, members of minority groups, out-of-state students, public servants, siblings of current students, spouses of deceased or disabled public servants, veterans, veterans' children. *Tuition waivers:* Full or partial for employees or children of employees. *ROTC:* Army cooperative, Air Force cooperative.
LOANS *Student loans:* $15,921,879 (77% need-based, 23% non-need-based). 72% of past graduating class borrowed through all loan programs. *Average indebtedness per student:* $29,867. *Average need-based loan:* Freshmen: $3673. Undergraduates: $4629. *Parent loans:* $3,370,237 (77% need-based, 23% non-need-based). *Programs:* Federal Direct (Subsidized and Unsubsidized Stafford, PLUS), Perkins, state, private loans.
WORK-STUDY *Federal work-study:* Total amount: $3,534,594; 1,291 jobs averaging $2738.
APPLYING FOR FINANCIAL AID *Required financial aid forms:* FAFSA, institution's own form. *Financial aid deadline (priority):* 2/1. *Notification date:* Continuous beginning 1/5.
CONTACT Office of Financial Aid, Webster University, 470 East Lockwood Avenue, St. Louis, MO 63119, 314-968-6992 or toll-free 800-753-6765. *Fax:* 314-968-7125. *E-mail:* financialaid@webster.edu.
Website: http://www.webster.edu/.

WELCH COLLEGE
Gallatin, TN

CONTACT Angie Edgmon, Financial Aid Coordinator, Welch College, 3606 West End Avenue, Nashville, TN 37205, 615-844-5000 Ext. 5249 or toll-free 800-763-9222. *Fax:* 615-269-6028. *E-mail:* finaid@fwbbc.edu.
Website: http://www.welch.edu/.

WELLESLEY COLLEGE
Wellesley, MA

Tuition & fees: $51,148	Average undergraduate aid package: $49,713

ABOUT THE INSTITUTION Independent, women only. *Awards:* bachelor's degrees (double bachelor's degree with Massachusetts Institute of Technology). 58 undergraduate majors. *Total enrollment:* 2,508. Undergraduates: 2,508. Freshmen: 603. Both federal and institutional methodology are used as a basis for awarding need-based institutional aid.
UNDERGRADUATE EXPENSES for 2017–2018 *Comprehensive fee:* $66,984 includes full-time tuition ($50,840), mandatory fees ($308), and room and board ($15,836). *College room only:* $8040. *Part-time tuition:* $6355 per course. *Part-time fees:* $38.50 per course. Part-time tuition and fees vary according to course load. *Payment plan:* Tuition prepayment.
FRESHMAN FINANCIAL AID (Fall 2017, est.) 427 applied for aid; of those 83% were deemed to have need. 100% of freshmen with need received aid; of those 100%

had need fully met. *Average percent of need met:* 100% (excluding resources awarded to replace EFC). *Average financial aid package:* $49,612 (excluding resources awarded to replace EFC).

UNDERGRADUATE FINANCIAL AID (Fall 2017, est.) 1,636 applied for aid; of those 86% were deemed to have need. 100% of undergraduates with need received aid; of those 100% had need fully met. *Average percent of need met:* 100% (excluding resources awarded to replace EFC). *Average financial aid package:* $49,713 (excluding resources awarded to replace EFC).

GIFT AID (NEED-BASED) *Total amount:* $66,637,876 (5% federal, 93% institutional, 2% external sources). *Receiving aid:* Freshmen: 57% (341); all full-time undergraduates: 58% (1,372). *Average award:* Freshmen: $48,433; Undergraduates: $47,375. *Scholarships, grants, and awards:* Federal Pell, FSEOG, state, private, college/university gift aid from institutional funds.

GIFT AID (NON-NEED-BASED) *Total amount:* $789,312 (100% external sources). *Tuition waivers:* Full or partial for employees or children of employees. *ROTC:* Army cooperative, Air Force cooperative.

LOANS *Student loans:* $3,816,952 (69% need-based, 31% non-need-based). 49% of past graduating class borrowed through all loan programs. *Average indebtedness per student:* $18,370. *Average need-based loan:* Freshmen: $2932. Undergraduates: $3726. *Parent loans:* $2,521,949 (100% non-need-based). *Programs:* Federal Direct (Subsidized and Unsubsidized Stafford, PLUS), Perkins, state, college/university.

WORK-STUDY *Federal work-study:* Total amount: $1,906,683; jobs available. *State or other work-study/employment:* Total amount: $655,377 (100% need-based). Part-time jobs available.

APPLYING FOR FINANCIAL AID *Required financial aid forms:* FAFSA, CSS Financial Aid PROFILE, noncustodial (divorced/separated) parent's statement, federal income tax form(s), W-2 forms. *Financial aid deadline (priority):* 2/15. *Notification date:* 4/1. Students must reply by 5/1.

CONTACT Office of Student Financial Services, Wellesley College, 106 Central Street, Wellesley, MA 02481-8203, 781-283-2360. *Fax:* 781-283-3946. *E-mail:* sfs@wellesley.edu. *Website:* http://www.wellesley.edu/.

WELLS COLLEGE
Aurora, NY

Tuition & fees: $39,600	Average undergraduate aid package: $34,750

ABOUT THE INSTITUTION Independent, coed. *Awards:* bachelor's degrees. 36 undergraduate majors. *Total enrollment:* 488. Undergraduates: 488. Freshmen: 137. Federal methodology is used as a basis for awarding need-based institutional aid.

UNDERGRADUATE EXPENSES for 2018–2019 *Comprehensive fee:* $53,330 includes full-time tuition ($38,100), mandatory fees ($1500), and room and board ($13,730). Room and board charges vary according to housing facility. *Part-time tuition:* $800 per credit hour. Part-time tuition and fees vary according to course load.

FRESHMAN FINANCIAL AID (Fall 2016) 128 applied for aid; of those 96% were deemed to have need. 100% of freshmen with need received aid; of those 19% had need fully met. *Average percent of need met:* 80% (excluding resources awarded to replace EFC). *Average financial aid package:* $32,620 (excluding resources awarded to replace EFC). 7% of all full-time freshmen had no need and received non-need-based gift aid.

UNDERGRADUATE FINANCIAL AID (Fall 2016) 491 applied for aid; of those 97% were deemed to have need. 100% of undergraduates with need received aid; of those 18% had need fully met. *Average percent of need met:* 82% (excluding resources awarded to replace EFC). *Average financial aid package:* $34,750 (excluding resources awarded to replace EFC). 6% of all full-time undergraduates had no need and received non-need-based gift aid.

GIFT AID (NEED-BASED) *Total amount:* $14,090,413 (8% federal, 6% state, 83% institutional, 3% external sources). *Receiving aid:* Freshmen: 93% (123); all full-time undergraduates: 94% (474). *Average award:* Freshmen: $28,623; Undergraduates: $29,240. *Scholarships, grants, and awards:* Federal Pell, FSEOG, state, private, college/university gift aid from institutional funds.

GIFT AID (NON-NEED-BASED) *Total amount:* $585,259 (98% institutional, 2% external sources). *Receiving aid:* Freshmen: 80% (106). Undergraduates: 80% (401). *Average award:* Freshmen: $19,444. Undergraduates: $19,731. *Scholarships, grants, and awards by category:* Academic interests/achievement: 395

awards ($7,445,400 total): general academic interests/achievements. *Special achievements/activities:* 58 awards ($580,000 total): leadership. *Special characteristics:* 20 awards ($113,000 total): children and siblings of alumni, international students. *Tuition waivers:* Full or partial for employees or children of employees, senior citizens.

LOANS *Student loans:* $3,157,750 (98% need-based, 2% non-need-based). 97% of past graduating class borrowed through all loan programs. *Average indebtedness per student:* $35,287. *Average need-based loan:* Freshmen: $2937. Undergraduates: $3783. *Parent loans:* $1,642,648 (98% need-based, 2% non-need-based). *Programs:* Federal Direct (Subsidized and Unsubsidized Stafford, PLUS), Perkins, state.

WORK-STUDY *Federal work-study:* 68 jobs averaging $1850. *State or other work-study/employment:* Total amount: $229,029 (93% need-based, 7% non-need-based). 175 part-time jobs averaging $1850.

APPLYING FOR FINANCIAL AID *Required financial aid form:* FAFSA. *Financial aid deadline (priority):* 12/1. *Notification date:* 12/15. Students must reply by 5/1.

CONTACT Ms. Laura Burns, Director of Financial Aid, Wells College, Route 90, Aurora, NY 13026, 315-364-3289 or toll-free 800-952-9355. *Fax:* 315-364-3445. *E-mail:* lburns@wells.edu. *Website:* http://www.wells.edu/.

WENTWORTH INSTITUTE OF TECHNOLOGY
Boston, MA

Tuition & fees: $34,977	Average undergraduate aid package: $20,181

ABOUT THE INSTITUTION Independent, coed. *Awards:* certificates, associate, bachelor's, and master's degrees. 20 undergraduate majors. *Total enrollment:* 4,454. Undergraduates: 4,262. Freshmen: 967. Federal methodology is used as a basis for awarding need-based institutional aid.

UNDERGRADUATE EXPENSES for 2017–2018 *Application fee:* $50. *Comprehensive fee:* $48,821 includes full-time tuition ($32,954), mandatory fees ($2023), and room and board ($13,844). Full-time tuition and fees vary according to class time, course load, and program. Room and board charges vary according to board plan and housing facility. *Part-time tuition:* $1030 per credit hour. Part-time tuition and fees vary according to class time, course load, and program.

FRESHMAN FINANCIAL AID (Fall 2017, est.) 962 applied for aid; of those 78% were deemed to have need. 100% of freshmen with need received aid; of those 10% had need fully met. *Average percent of need met:* 55% (excluding resources awarded to replace EFC). *Average financial aid package:* $19,571 (excluding resources awarded to replace EFC). 21% of all full-time freshmen had no need and received non-need-based gift aid.

UNDERGRADUATE FINANCIAL AID (Fall 2017, est.) 3,711 applied for aid; of those 75% were deemed to have need. 99% of undergraduates with need received aid; of those 7% had need fully met. *Average percent of need met:* 52% (excluding resources awarded to replace EFC). *Average financial aid package:* $20,181 (excluding resources awarded to replace EFC). 22% of all full-time undergraduates had no need and received non-need-based gift aid.

GIFT AID (NEED-BASED) *Total amount:* $35,088,364 (15% federal, 3% state, 82% institutional). *Receiving aid:* Freshmen: 69% (670); all full-time undergraduates: 63% (2,448). *Average award:* Freshmen: $13,589; Undergraduates: $14,111. *Scholarships, grants, and awards:* Federal Pell, FSEOG, state, private, college/university gift aid from institutional funds.

GIFT AID (NON-NEED-BASED) *Total amount:* $17,057,908 (100% institutional). *Receiving aid:* Freshmen: 28% (272). Undergraduates: 19% (730). *Average award:* Freshmen: $10,446. Undergraduates: $10,487. *Scholarships, grants, and awards by category:* Academic interests/achievement: general academic interests/achievements. *Tuition waivers:* Full or partial for employees or children of employees. *ROTC:* Army cooperative, Air Force cooperative.

LOANS *Student loans:* $32,015,041 (62% need-based, 38% non-need-based). 78% of past graduating class borrowed through all loan programs. *Average indebtedness per student:* $59,419. *Average need-based loan:* Freshmen: $3565. Undergraduates: $4585. *Parent loans:* $15,795,762 (30% need-based, 70% non-need-based). *Programs:* Federal Direct (Subsidized and Unsubsidized Stafford, PLUS), Perkins, state.

WORK-STUDY *Federal work-study:* Total amount: $1,490,721; jobs available. *State or other work-study/employment:* Total amount: $1,565,180 (100% need-based). Part-time jobs available.

APPLYING FOR FINANCIAL AID *Required financial aid form:* FAFSA. *Financial aid deadline:* Continuous. *Notification date:* Continuous beginning 3/15. Students must reply by 5/1 or within 2 weeks of notification.

CONTACT Anne-Marie Caruso, Director of Financial Aid, Wentworth Institute of Technology, 550 Huntington Avenue, Boston, MA 02115-5998, 617-989-4174 or toll-free 800-556-0610. *Fax:* 617-989-4201. *E-mail:* carusoa@wit.edu. *Website:* http://www.wit.edu/.

WORK-STUDY *Federal work-study:* Total amount: $26,923; jobs available. *State or other work-study/employment:* Total amount: $123,613 (19% need-based, 81% non-need-based). Part-time jobs available.

APPLYING FOR FINANCIAL AID *Required financial aid forms:* FAFSA, institution's own form. *Financial aid deadline:* 6/1 (priority: 3/15). *Notification date:* Continuous beginning 10/1. Students must reply within 2 weeks of notification.

CONTACT Daniel Miller, Acting Director of Financial Aid, Wesleyan College, 4760 Forsyth Road, Macon, GA 31210-4462, 478-757-5146 or toll-free 800-447-6610. *Fax:* 478-757-4030. *E-mail:* financialaid@wesleyancollege.edu. *Website:* http://www.wesleyancollege.edu/.

WESLEYAN COLLEGE
Macon, GA

Tuition & fees: $22,370	Average undergraduate aid package: $21,610

ABOUT THE INSTITUTION Independent United Methodist, undergraduate: women only; graduate: coed. *Awards:* bachelor's and master's degrees. 28 undergraduate majors. *Total enrollment:* 682. Undergraduates: 635. Freshmen: 104. Federal methodology is used as a basis for awarding need-based institutional aid.

UNDERGRADUATE EXPENSES for 2017–2018 *Application fee:* $30. *One-time required fee:* $250. *Comprehensive fee:* $31,940 includes full-time tuition ($21,370), mandatory fees ($1000), and room and board ($9570). Full-time tuition and fees vary according to class time, course load, and program. Room and board charges vary according to housing facility. *Part-time tuition:* $510 per semester hour. *Part-time fees:* $40 per semester hour. Part-time tuition and fees vary according to class time and course load.

FRESHMAN FINANCIAL AID (Fall 2017, est.) 71 applied for aid; of those 82% were deemed to have need. 100% of freshmen with need received aid; of those 26% had need fully met. *Average percent of need met:* 79% (excluding resources awarded to replace EFC). *Average financial aid package:* $22,740 (excluding resources awarded to replace EFC). 18% of all full-time freshmen had no need and received non-need-based gift aid.

UNDERGRADUATE FINANCIAL AID (Fall 2017, est.) 335 applied for aid; of those 91% were deemed to have need. 100% of undergraduates with need received aid; of those 19% had need fully met. *Average percent of need met:* 75% (excluding resources awarded to replace EFC). *Average financial aid package:* $21,610 (excluding resources awarded to replace EFC). 19% of all full-time undergraduates had no need and received non-need-based gift aid.

GIFT AID (NEED-BASED) *Total amount:* $5,078,598 (25% federal, 13% state, 60% institutional, 2% external sources). *Receiving aid:* Freshmen: 34% (56); all full-time undergraduates: 63% (298). *Average award:* Freshmen: $20,781; Undergraduates: $17,077. *Scholarships, grants, and awards:* Federal Pell, FSEOG, state, private, college/university gift aid from institutional funds.

GIFT AID (NON-NEED-BASED) *Total amount:* $1,563,907 (1% federal, 16% state, 80% institutional, 3% external sources). *Receiving aid:* Freshmen: 8% (13). Undergraduates: 11% (50). *Average award:* Freshmen: $13,076. Undergraduates: $11,724. *Scholarships, grants, and awards by category: Academic interests/achievement:* biological sciences, business, communication, education, engineering/technologies, English, foreign languages, general academic interests/achievements, home economics, humanities, international studies, mathematics, premedicine, religion/biblical studies, social sciences. *Creative arts/performance:* art/fine arts, music, theater/drama. *Special achievements/activities:* community service, general special achievements/activities, hobbies/interests, leadership, memberships, religious involvement. *Special characteristics:* adult students, children and siblings of alumni, children of current students, children of educators, children of faculty/staff, ethnic background, first-generation college students, general special characteristics, local/state students, parents of current students, previous college experience, relatives of clergy, religious affiliation, siblings of current students, spouses of current students, veterans. *Tuition waivers:* Full or partial for employees or children of employees. *ROTC:* Army cooperative.

LOANS *Student loans:* $2,759,670 (89% need-based, 11% non-need-based). 65% of past graduating class borrowed through all loan programs. *Average indebtedness per student:* $31,565. *Average need-based loan:* Freshmen: $3456. Undergraduates: $5777. *Parent loans:* $539,237 (68% need-based, 32% non-need-based). *Programs:* Federal Direct (Subsidized and Unsubsidized Stafford, PLUS), Perkins, state, college/university, private loans.

WESLEYAN UNIVERSITY
Middletown, CT

Tuition & fees: $52,474	Average undergraduate aid package: $51,397

ABOUT THE INSTITUTION Independent, coed. *Awards:* certificates, bachelor's, master's, and doctoral degrees. 39 undergraduate majors. *Total enrollment:* 3,213. Undergraduates: 2,976. Freshmen: 761. Institutional methodology is used as a basis for awarding need-based institutional aid.

UNDERGRADUATE EXPENSES for 2017–2018 *Application fee:* $55. *Comprehensive fee:* $66,940 includes full-time tuition ($52,174), mandatory fees ($300), and room and board ($14,466). Room and board charges vary according to board plan and student level.

FRESHMAN FINANCIAL AID (Fall 2017, est.) 345 applied for aid; of those 96% were deemed to have need. 100% of freshmen with need received aid; of those 100% had need fully met. *Average percent of need met:* 100% (excluding resources awarded to replace EFC). *Average financial aid package:* $51,412 (excluding resources awarded to replace EFC). 1% of all full-time freshmen had no need and received non-need-based gift aid.

UNDERGRADUATE FINANCIAL AID (Fall 2017, est.) 1,316 applied for aid; of those 97% were deemed to have need. 100% of undergraduates with need received aid; of those 100% had need fully met. *Average percent of need met:* 100% (excluding resources awarded to replace EFC). *Average financial aid package:* $51,397 (excluding resources awarded to replace EFC). 1% of all full-time undergraduates had no need and received non-need-based gift aid.

GIFT AID (NEED-BASED) *Total amount:* $58,876,127 (6% federal, 90% institutional, 4% external sources). *Receiving aid:* Freshmen: 41% (310); all full-time undergraduates: 41% (1,194). *Average award:* Freshmen: $47,653; Undergraduates: $47,206. *Scholarships, grants, and awards:* Federal Pell, FSEOG, state, private, college/university gift aid from institutional funds.

GIFT AID (NON-NEED-BASED) *Total amount:* $1,439,928 (62% institutional, 38% external sources). *Receiving aid:* Freshmen: 1% (9). Undergraduates: 1% (34). *Average award:* Freshmen: $52,774. Undergraduates: $43,431. *Scholarships, grants, and awards by category: Special characteristics:* 25 awards ($890,845 total): international students, veterans, veterans' children. *ROTC:* Air Force cooperative.

LOANS *Student loans:* $5,771,713 (55% need-based, 45% non-need-based). 39% of past graduating class borrowed through all loan programs. *Average indebtedness per student:* $22,930. *Average need-based loan:* Freshmen: $3186. Undergraduates: $4306. *Parent loans:* $3,812,995 (100% non-need-based). *Programs:* Federal Direct (Subsidized and Unsubsidized Stafford, PLUS), college/university.

WORK-STUDY *Federal work-study:* Total amount: $2,473,796; 994 jobs averaging $2502. *State or other work-study/employment:* Total amount: $416,721 (100% need-based). 166 part-time jobs averaging $2564.

APPLYING FOR FINANCIAL AID *Required financial aid forms:* FAFSA, CSS Financial Aid PROFILE, noncustodial (divorced/separated) parent's statement, parent and student federal income tax form(s), W-2 forms, business tax returns. *Financial aid deadline:* 2/15. *Notification date:* 4/1. Students must reply by 5/1.

CONTACT Robert Coughlin, Director of Financial Aid, Wesleyan University, 237 High Street, Middletown, CT 06459-0260, 860-685-2800. *Fax:* 860-685-2801. *E-mail:* finaid@wesleyan.edu. *Website:* http://www.wesleyan.edu/.

WESLEY COLLEGE
Dover, DE

CONTACT Mr. Michael Hall, Director of Student Financial Planning, Wesley College, 120 North State Street, Dover, DE 19901-3875, 302-736-2334 or toll-free 800-937-5398. *Fax:* 302-736-2594. *E-mail:* halljmic@wesley.edu.
Website: http://www.wesley.edu/.

WEST CHESTER UNIVERSITY OF PENNSYLVANIA
West Chester, PA

Tuition & fees (PA res): $10,111	Average undergraduate aid package: $8180

ABOUT THE INSTITUTION State-supported, coed. *Awards:* certificates, bachelor's, master's, and doctoral degrees. 51 undergraduate majors. *Total enrollment:* 17,306. Undergraduates: 14,451. Freshmen: 2,630. Federal methodology is used as a basis for awarding need-based institutional aid.

UNDERGRADUATE EXPENSES for 2017–2018 *Application fee:* $45. *Tuition, state resident:* full-time $7492; part-time $312 per credit. *Tuition, nonresident:* full-time $18,730; part-time $780 per credit. *Required fees:* full-time $2619; $109.77 per credit. Full-time tuition and fees vary according to location. Part-time tuition and fees vary according to location. *College room and board:* $9060; *Room only:* $5408. Room and board charges vary according to board plan and housing facility.

FRESHMAN FINANCIAL AID (Fall 2016) 2,185 applied for aid; of those 70% were deemed to have need. 100% of freshmen with need received aid; of those 7% had need fully met. *Average percent of need met:* 42% (excluding resources awarded to replace EFC). *Average financial aid package:* $7231 (excluding resources awarded to replace EFC). 2% of all full-time freshmen had no need and received non-need-based gift aid.

UNDERGRADUATE FINANCIAL AID (Fall 2016) 10,070 applied for aid; of those 75% were deemed to have need. 100% of undergraduates with need received aid; of those 9% had need fully met. *Average percent of need met:* 49% (excluding resources awarded to replace EFC). *Average financial aid package:* $8180 (excluding resources awarded to replace EFC). 2% of all full-time undergraduates had no need and received non-need-based gift aid.

GIFT AID (NEED-BASED) *Total amount:* $33,026,141 (48% federal, 32% state, 9% institutional, 11% external sources). *Receiving aid:* Freshmen: 33% (803); all full-time undergraduates: 35% (4,487). *Average award:* Freshmen: $5809; Undergraduates: $5651. *Scholarships, grants, and awards:* Federal Pell, FSEOG, state, private, college/university gift aid from institutional funds.

GIFT AID (NON-NEED-BASED) *Total amount:* $2,669,983 (3% state, 42% institutional, 55% external sources). *Receiving aid:* Freshmen: 16% (398). Undergraduates: 10% (1,335). *Average award:* Freshmen: $4212. Undergraduates: $4265. *Scholarships, grants, and awards by category: Academic interests/achievement:* business, general academic interests/achievements, mathematics, social sciences. *Creative arts/performance:* art/fine arts, music, theater/drama. *Special achievements/activities:* leadership. *Special characteristics:* children of faculty/staff. *Tuition waivers:* Full or partial for employees or children of employees, senior citizens. *ROTC:* Army, Air Force cooperative.

LOANS *Student loans:* $110,363,788 (76% need-based, 24% non-need-based). 73% of past graduating class borrowed through all loan programs. *Average indebtedness per student:* $34,160. *Average need-based loan:* Freshmen: $3318. Undergraduates: $4227. *Parent loans:* $23,553,244 (100% non-need-based). *Programs:* Federal Direct (Subsidized and Unsubsidized Stafford, PLUS), Federal Nursing.

WORK-STUDY *Federal work-study:* 295 jobs averaging $1644. *State or other work-study/employment:* Part-time jobs available.

ATHLETIC AWARDS Total amount: $1,391,503 (79% need-based, 21% non-need-based).

APPLYING FOR FINANCIAL AID *Required financial aid form:* FAFSA. *Financial aid deadline (priority):* 2/15. *Notification date:* Continuous beginning 3/1. Students must reply within 4 weeks of notification.

CONTACT Mr. Daniel McIlhenny, Interim Financial Aid Director, West Chester University of Pennsylvania, 25 University Avenue, Suite 030, West Chester, PA 19383, 610-436-2627 or toll-free 877-315-2165 (in-state). *Fax:* 610-436-2574. *E-mail:* finaid@wcupa.edu.
Website: http://www.wcupa.edu/.

WEST COAST UNIVERSITY
Anaheim, CA

CONTACT Financial Aid Office, West Coast University, 1477 S. Manchester Avenue, Anaheim, CA 92802, 714-782-1700.
Website: http://westcoastuniversity.edu/.

WEST COAST UNIVERSITY
North Hollywood, CA

CONTACT Financial Aid Office, West Coast University, 12215 Victory Boulevard, North Hollywood, CA 91606, 323-315-5207 or toll-free 866-508-2684.
Website: http://www.westcoastuniversity.edu/.

WEST COAST UNIVERSITY
Ontario, CA

CONTACT Financial Aid Office, West Coast University, 2855 E. Guasti Road, Ontario, CA 91761, 909-467-6100.
Website: http://westcoastuniversity.edu/.

WEST COAST UNIVERSITY
Doral, FL

CONTACT Financial Aid Office, West Coast University, 9250 NW 36th Street, Doral, FL 33178, 786-501-7070.
Website: http://westcoastuniversity.edu/.

WEST COAST UNIVERSITY
Dallas, TX

CONTACT Financial Aid Office, West Coast University, 8435 N. Stemmons Freeway, Dallas, TX 75247, 214-453-4533 or toll-free 866-508-2684.
Website: http://www.westcoastuniversity.edu/.

WESTERN CAROLINA UNIVERSITY
Cullowhee, NC

Tuition & fees (NC res): $7191	Average undergraduate aid package: $11,395

ABOUT THE INSTITUTION State-supported, coed. *Awards:* certificates, bachelor's, master's, and doctoral degrees. 70 undergraduate majors. *Total enrollment:* 10,805. Undergraduates: 9,171. Freshmen: 1,925. Federal methodology is used as a basis for awarding need-based institutional aid.

UNDERGRADUATE EXPENSES for 2017–2018 *Application fee:* $65. *Tuition, state resident:* full-time $3971. *Tuition, nonresident:* full-time $14,364. *Required fees:* full-time $3220. Full-time tuition and fees vary according to degree level. Part-time tuition and fees vary according to course load and degree level. *College room and board:* $9164; *Room only:* $4616. Room and board charges vary according to board plan and housing facility.

FRESHMAN FINANCIAL AID (Fall 2016) 1,727 applied for aid; of those 78% were deemed to have need. 98% of freshmen with need received aid; of those 12% had need fully met. *Average percent of need met:* 65% (excluding resources awarded to replace EFC). *Average financial aid package:* $11,338 (excluding resources awarded to replace EFC). 4% of all full-time freshmen had no need and received non-need-based gift aid.

UNDERGRADUATE FINANCIAL AID (Fall 2016) 6,554 applied for aid; of those 81% were deemed to have need. 99% of undergraduates with need received aid; of those 12% had need fully met. *Average percent of need met:* 65% (excluding resources awarded to replace EFC). *Average financial aid package:* $11,395 (excluding resources awarded to replace EFC). 4% of all full-time undergraduates had no need and received non-need-based gift aid.

GIFT AID (NEED-BASED) *Total amount:* $31,776,153 (47% federal, 27% state, 20% institutional, 6% external sources). *Receiving aid:* Freshmen: 67% (1,280); all full-time undergraduates: 63% (4,938). *Average award:* Freshmen: $6710; Undergraduates: $6131. *Scholarships, grants, and awards:* Federal Pell, FSEOG, state, private, college/university gift aid from institutional funds.

GIFT AID (NON-NEED-BASED) *Total amount:* $2,352,549 (3% federal, 11% state, 45% institutional, 41% external sources). *Receiving aid:* Freshmen: 3% (54). Undergraduates: 2% (143). *Average award:* Freshmen: $3546. Undergraduates: $2601. *Scholarships, grants, and awards by category: Academic interests/achievement:* biological sciences, business, communication, education, English, general academic interests/achievements, mathematics. *Creative arts/performance:* art/fine arts, music, theater/drama. *Special characteristics:* ethnic background, handicapped students, local/state students, members of minority groups.

LOANS *Student loans:* $39,471,319 (74% need-based, 26% non-need-based). 61% of past graduating class borrowed through all loan programs. *Average indebtedness per student:* $15,669. *Average need-based loan:* Freshmen: $5580. Undergraduates: $6375. *Parent loans:* $17,930,909 (28% need-based, 72% non-need-based). *Programs:* Federal Direct (Subsidized and Unsubsidized Stafford, PLUS), Perkins.

WORK-STUDY *Federal work-study:* jobs available.

ATHLETIC AWARDS Total amount: $3,048,246 (48% need-based, 52% non-need-based).

APPLYING FOR FINANCIAL AID *Required financial aid forms:* FAFSA, institution's own form. *Financial aid deadline (priority):* 3/15. *Notification date:* Continuous beginning 4/1.

CONTACT Ms. Trina F. Orr, Director of Financial Aid, Western Carolina University, 123 Killian Annex, Cullowhee, NC 28723, 828-227-7292 or toll-free 877-WCU4YOU. *Fax:* 828-227-7042. *E-mail:* torr@email.wcu.edu. *Website:* http://www.wcu.edu/.

WESTERN CONNECTICUT STATE UNIVERSITY
Danbury, CT

Tuition & fees (CT res): $10,458	Average undergraduate aid package: $8593

ABOUT THE INSTITUTION State-supported, coed. *Awards:* certificates, associate, bachelor's, master's, and doctoral degrees. 37 undergraduate majors. *Total enrollment:* 5,664. Undergraduates: 5,064. Freshmen: 827. Federal methodology is used as a basis for awarding need-based institutional aid.

UNDERGRADUATE EXPENSES for 2017–2018 *Application fee:* $50. *Tuition, state resident:* full-time $10,458; part-time $226 per credit hour. *Tuition, nonresident:* full-time $23,147; part-time $226 per credit hour. *Required fees:* $269 per credit hour or $60 per term. Full-time tuition and fees vary according to course load, program, and reciprocity agreements. *College room and board:* $12,416; *Room only:* $7108. Room and board charges vary according to board plan and housing facility.

FRESHMAN FINANCIAL AID (Fall 2016) 755 applied for aid; of those 81% were deemed to have need. 96% of freshmen with need received aid; of those 14% had need fully met. *Average percent of need met:* 46% (excluding resources awarded to replace EFC). *Average financial aid package:* $8838 (excluding resources awarded to replace EFC). 2% of all full-time freshmen had no need and received non-need-based gift aid.

UNDERGRADUATE FINANCIAL AID (Fall 2016) 3,416 applied for aid; of those 83% were deemed to have need. 97% of undergraduates with need received aid; of those 13% had need fully met. *Average percent of need met:* 42% (excluding resources awarded to replace EFC). *Average financial aid package:* $8593 (excluding resources awarded to replace EFC). 2% of all full-time undergraduates had no need and received non-need-based gift aid.

GIFT AID (NEED-BASED) *Total amount:* $14,755,581 (48% federal, 10% state, 33% institutional, 9% external sources). *Receiving aid:* Freshmen: 63% (520); all full-time undergraduates: 57% (2,327). *Average award:* Freshmen: $5762; Undergraduates: $5302. *Scholarships, grants, and awards:* Federal Pell, FSEOG, state, private, college/university gift aid from institutional funds.

GIFT AID (NON-NEED-BASED) *Total amount:* $581,040 (100% institutional). *Receiving aid:* Freshmen: 24% (198). Undergraduates: 15% (604). *Average award:* Freshmen: $10,020. Undergraduates: $9223. *Scholarships, grants, and awards by category: Academic interests/achievement:* 110 awards ($645,697 total): general academic interests/achievements. *Tuition waivers:* Full or partial for employees or children of employees, senior citizens. *ROTC:* Army cooperative, Air Force cooperative.

LOANS *Student loans:* $23,936,922 (100% need-based). 74% of past graduating class borrowed through all loan programs. *Average indebtedness per student:* $35,177. *Average need-based loan:* Freshmen: $3306. Undergraduates: $4368. *Parent loans:* $5,783,030 (100% need-based). *Programs:* Federal Direct (Subsidized and Unsubsidized Stafford, PLUS), Perkins, Federal Nursing.

WORK-STUDY *Federal work-study:* 61 jobs averaging $1810. *State or other work-study/employment:* Total amount: $98,232 (100% need-based). Part-time jobs available.

APPLYING FOR FINANCIAL AID *Required financial aid form:* FAFSA. *Financial aid deadline:* 3/15 (priority: 3/1). *Notification date:* Continuous beginning 3/20. Students must reply by 5/1 or within 2 weeks of notification.

CONTACT Melissa Stephens, Director of Student Financial Services, Western Connecticut State University, 181 White Street, Danbury, CT 06810-6860, 203-837-8582 or toll-free 877-837-WCSU. *Fax:* 203-837-8528. *E-mail:* stephensm@wcsu.edu. *Website:* http://www.wcsu.edu/.

WESTERN GOVERNORS UNIVERSITY
Salt Lake City, UT

CONTACT Robert Collins, Vice President of Financial Aid, Western Governors University, 4001 South 700 East, Suite 700, Salt Lake City, UT 84107, 877-435-7948 or toll-free 866-225-5948. *Fax:* 801-907-7727. *E-mail:* robert.collins@wgu.edu. *Website:* http://www.wgu.edu/.

WESTERN ILLINOIS UNIVERSITY
Macomb, IL

Tuition & fees (IL res): $11,267	Average undergraduate aid package: $12,356

ABOUT THE INSTITUTION State-supported, coed. *Awards:* certificates, bachelor's, master's, and doctoral degrees. 65 undergraduate majors. *Total enrollment:* 9,441. Undergraduates: 7,599. Freshmen: 1,206. Federal methodology is used as a basis for awarding need-based institutional aid.

UNDERGRADUATE EXPENSES for 2017–2018 *Application fee:* $30. *One-time required fee:* $200. *Tuition, state resident:* full-time $8541; part-time $284.70 per credit hour. *Tuition, nonresident:* full-time $8541; part-time $284.70 per credit hour. *Required fees:* full-time $2726; $90.12 per credit hour. Full-time tuition and fees vary according to course load, location, and student level. Part-time tuition and fees vary according to course load, location, and student level. *College room and board:* $9630; *Room only:* $5880. Room and board charges vary according to board plan, housing facility, and student level. *Payment plan:* Guaranteed tuition.

FRESHMAN FINANCIAL AID (Fall 2017, est.) 1,121 applied for aid; of those 89% were deemed to have need. 98% of freshmen with need received aid; of those 21% had need fully met. *Average percent of need met:* 65% (excluding resources awarded to replace EFC). *Average financial aid package:* $13,592 (excluding resources awarded to replace EFC). 6% of all full-time freshmen had no need and received non-need-based gift aid.

UNDERGRADUATE FINANCIAL AID (Fall 2017, est.) 5,747 applied for aid; of those 89% were deemed to have need. 98% of undergraduates with need received aid;

of those 26% had need fully met. *Average percent of need met:* 62% (excluding resources awarded to replace EFC). *Average financial aid package:* $12,356 (excluding resources awarded to replace EFC). 5% of all full-time undergraduates had no need and received non-need-based gift aid.

GIFT AID (NEED-BASED) *Total amount:* $41,705,434 (42% federal, 37% state, 19% institutional, 2% external sources). *Receiving aid:* Freshmen: 70% (830); all full-time undergraduates: 55% (3,651). *Average award:* Freshmen: $11,001; Undergraduates: $9653. *Scholarships, grants, and awards:* Federal Pell, FSEOG, state, private, college/university gift aid from institutional funds.

GIFT AID (NON-NEED-BASED) *Total amount:* $3,615,892 (1% federal, 26% state, 63% institutional, 10% external sources). *Receiving aid:* Freshmen: 54% (640). Undergraduates: 36% (2,394). *Average award:* Freshmen: $4484. Undergraduates: $3401. *Scholarships, grants, and awards by category:* Academic interests/achievement: 5,948 awards ($7,954,448 total): agriculture, area/ethnic studies, biological sciences, business, communication, computer science, education, engineering/technologies, English, foreign languages, general academic interests/achievements, health fields, home economics, international studies, library science, mathematics, military science, physical sciences, religion/biblical studies, social sciences. *Creative arts/performance:* 609 awards ($710,072 total): applied art and design, art/fine arts, cinema/film/broadcasting, creative writing, dance, debating, general creative arts/performance, journalism/publications, music, performing arts, theater/drama. *Special achievements/activities:* 222 awards ($157,358 total): community service, general special achievements/activities, leadership. *Special characteristics:* 1,041 awards ($2,650,589 total): children of faculty/staff, general special characteristics, international students, members of minority groups, veterans' children. *Tuition waivers:* Full or partial for employees or children of employees, senior citizens. *ROTC:* Army.

LOANS *Student loans:* $44,649,521 (43% need-based, 57% non-need-based). 84% of past graduating class borrowed through all loan programs. *Average indebtedness per student:* $29,422. *Average need-based loan:* Freshmen: $3441. Undergraduates: $4286. *Parent loans:* $7,046,445 (84% need-based, 16% non-need-based). *Programs:* Federal Direct (Subsidized and Unsubsidized Stafford, PLUS), Perkins, college/university, private loans.

WORK-STUDY *Federal work-study:* Total amount: $481,486; 175 jobs averaging $2754. *State or other work-study/employment:* Total amount: $1,179,017 (82% need-based, 18% non-need-based). Part-time jobs available.

ATHLETIC AWARDS Total amount: $3,350,573 (47% need-based, 53% non-need-based).

APPLYING FOR FINANCIAL AID *Required financial aid form:* FAFSA. *Financial aid deadline (priority):* 2/15. *Notification date:* Continuous beginning 10/15.

CONTACT Office of Financial Aid, Western Illinois University, 1 University Circle, Macomb, IL 61455-1390, 309-298-2446 or toll-free 877-742-5948. *Fax:* 309-298-2353. *E-mail:* finaid@wiu.edu.
Website: http://www.wiu.edu/.

WESTERN KENTUCKY UNIVERSITY
Bowling Green, KY

Tuition & fees (KY res): $10,202	Average undergraduate aid package: $14,550

ABOUT THE INSTITUTION State-supported, coed. *Awards:* certificates, associate, bachelor's, master's, and doctoral degrees. 98 undergraduate majors. *Total enrollment:* 20,257. Undergraduates: 17,656. Freshmen: 3,116. Federal methodology is used as a basis for awarding need-based institutional aid.

UNDERGRADUATE EXPENSES for 2017–2018 *Application fee:* $45. *Tuition, state resident:* full-time $10,202; part-time $425 per credit hour. *Tuition, nonresident:* full-time $25,512; part-time $1063 per credit hour. Full-time tuition and fees vary according to reciprocity agreements. Part-time tuition and fees vary according to reciprocity agreements. *College room and board:* $8350; *Room only:* $4600. Room and board charges vary according to board plan and housing facility.

FRESHMAN FINANCIAL AID (Fall 2016) 2,810 applied for aid; of those 78% were deemed to have need. 98% of freshmen with need received aid; of those 24% had need fully met. *Average percent of need met:* 24% (excluding resources awarded to replace EFC). *Average financial aid package:* $13,958 (excluding resources awarded to replace EFC). 13% of all full-time freshmen had no need and received non-need-based gift aid.

UNDERGRADUATE FINANCIAL AID (Fall 2016) 10,216 applied for aid; of those 79% were deemed to have need. 98% of undergraduates with need received aid; of those 23% had need fully met. *Average percent of need met:* 23% (excluding resources awarded to replace EFC). *Average financial aid package:* $14,550 (excluding resources awarded to replace EFC). 13% of all full-time undergraduates had no need and received non-need-based gift aid.

GIFT AID (NEED-BASED) *Total amount:* $29,043,834 (76% federal, 19% state, 5% institutional). *Receiving aid:* Freshmen: 42% (1,317); all full-time undergraduates: 39% (5,020). *Average award:* Freshmen: $5272; Undergraduates: $5169. *Scholarships, grants, and awards:* Federal Pell, FSEOG, state, private, college/university gift aid from institutional funds, United Negro College Fund.

GIFT AID (NON-NEED-BASED) *Total amount:* $44,564,288 (8% federal, 27% state, 60% institutional, 5% external sources). *Receiving aid:* Freshmen: 59% (1,858). Undergraduates: 43% (5,605). *Average award:* Freshmen: $6438. Undergraduates: $6561. *Scholarships, grants, and awards by category:* Academic interests/achievement: 4,715 awards ($19,543,231 total): agriculture, biological sciences, business, communication, education, engineering/technologies, English, foreign languages, general academic interests/achievements, health fields, home economics, mathematics, military science, physical sciences, premedicine, religion/biblical studies, social sciences. *Creative arts/performance:* 497 awards ($1,297,661 total): art/fine arts, cinema/film/broadcasting, dance, debating, general creative arts/performance, journalism/publications, music, theater/drama. *Special achievements/activities:* 647 awards ($1,764,271 total): general special achievements/activities, leadership, memberships. *Special characteristics:* 1,185 awards ($3,212,138 total): children of union members/company employees, ethnic background, general special characteristics, handicapped students, international students, local/state students, members of minority groups, out-of-state students, religious affiliation, veterans, veterans' children. *Tuition waivers:* Full or partial for employees or children of employees, senior citizens. *ROTC:* Army, Air Force cooperative.

LOANS *Student loans:* $57,122,166 (41% need-based, 59% non-need-based). 60% of past graduating class borrowed through all loan programs. *Average indebtedness per student:* $27,654. *Average need-based loan:* Freshmen: $3076. Undergraduates: $3864. *Parent loans:* $17,225,743 (100% non-need-based). *Programs:* Federal Direct (Subsidized and Unsubsidized Stafford, PLUS), Perkins.

WORK-STUDY *Federal work-study:* 795 jobs averaging $1754. *State or other work-study/employment:* Total amount: $4,715,559 (100% non-need-based). 1,911 part-time jobs averaging $2502.

ATHLETIC AWARDS Total amount: $5,514,117 (100% non-need-based).

APPLYING FOR FINANCIAL AID *Required financial aid form:* FAFSA. *Financial aid deadline (priority):* 2/15. *Notification date:* Continuous beginning 3/1.

CONTACT Cindy Burnette, Director of Student Financial Assistance, Western Kentucky University, Potter Hall, Room 317, Bowling Green, KY 42101-1018, 270-745-2758 or toll-free 800-495-8463. *Fax:* 270-745-6586. *E-mail:* cindy.burnette@wku.edu.
Website: http://www.wku.edu/.

WESTERN MICHIGAN UNIVERSITY
Kalamazoo, MI

Tuition & fees (MI res): $11,943	Average undergraduate aid package: $13,679

ABOUT THE INSTITUTION State-supported, coed. *Awards:* certificates, bachelor's, master's, and doctoral degrees. 151 undergraduate majors. *Total enrollment:* 22,894. Undergraduates: 17,936. Freshmen: 3,178. Federal methodology is used as a basis for awarding need-based institutional aid.

UNDERGRADUATE EXPENSES for 2017–2018 *Application fee:* $40. *One-time required fee:* $300. *Tuition, state resident:* full-time $11,020; part-time $422.86 per credit hour. *Tuition, nonresident:* full-time $13,776; part-time $528.58 per credit hour. *Required fees:* full-time $923; $258.50 per term. Full-time tuition and fees vary according to course load, location, program, reciprocity agreements, and student level. Part-time tuition and fees vary according to course load, location, program, reciprocity agreements, and student level. *College room and board:* $9848; *Room only:* $5079. Room and board charges vary according to board plan and housing facility.

FRESHMAN FINANCIAL AID (Fall 2016) 2,516 applied for aid; of those 55% were deemed to have need. 98% of freshmen with need received aid; of those 30% had need fully met. *Average percent of need met:* 77% (excluding resources awarded

to replace EFC). *Average financial aid package:* $14,180 (excluding resources awarded to replace EFC). 19% of all full-time freshmen had no need and received non-need-based gift aid.

UNDERGRADUATE FINANCIAL AID (Fall 2016) 11,273 applied for aid; of those 59% were deemed to have need. 99% of undergraduates with need received aid; of those 20% had need fully met. *Average percent of need met:* 73% (excluding resources awarded to replace EFC). *Average financial aid package:* $13,679 (excluding resources awarded to replace EFC). 9% of all full-time undergraduates had no need and received non-need-based gift aid.

GIFT AID (NEED-BASED) *Total amount:* $38,198,239 (69% federal, 5% state, 26% institutional). *Receiving aid:* Freshmen: 41% (1,171); all full-time undergraduates: 39% (5,838). *Average award:* Freshmen: $5020; Undergraduates: $5382. *Scholarships, grants, and awards:* Federal Pell, FSEOG, state, private, college/university gift aid from institutional funds.

GIFT AID (NON-NEED-BASED) *Total amount:* $25,275,123 (65% institutional, 35% external sources). *Receiving aid:* Freshmen: 31% (882). Undergraduates: 13% (1,936). *Average award:* Freshmen: $6901. Undergraduates: $6692. *Scholarships, grants, and awards by category: Academic interests/achievement:* general academic interests/achievements. *Creative arts/performance:* art/fine arts, dance, general creative arts/performance, music, theater/drama. *Special characteristics:* children and siblings of alumni, children of faculty/staff, international students, local/state students, out-of-state students, previous college experience, veterans. *Tuition waivers:* Full or partial for employees or children of employees, senior citizens. *ROTC:* Army.

LOANS *Student loans:* $112,492,064 (67% need-based, 33% non-need-based). 48% of past graduating class borrowed through all loan programs. *Average indebtedness per student:* $35,602. *Average need-based loan:* Freshmen: $3298. Undergraduates: $4002. *Parent loans:* $51,989,344 (50% need-based, 50% non-need-based). *Programs:* Federal Direct (Subsidized and Unsubsidized Stafford, PLUS), Perkins, private loans.

WORK-STUDY *Federal work-study:* jobs available. *State or other work-study/employment:* Part-time jobs available.

ATHLETIC AWARDS Total amount: $8,248,197 (100% non-need-based).

APPLYING FOR FINANCIAL AID *Required financial aid form:* FAFSA. *Financial aid deadline (priority):* 3/1. *Notification date:* Continuous beginning 12/10.

CONTACT Ms. Shashanta James, Interim Director of Financial Aid, Western Michigan University, Faunce Student Services, 1903 West Michigan Avenue, Kalamazoo, MI 49008-5337, 269-387-6000. *E-mail:* finaid-info@wmich.edu. *Website:* http://www.wmich.edu/.

WESTERN NEW ENGLAND UNIVERSITY
Springfield, MA

Tuition & fees: $35,740	Average undergraduate aid package: $26,004

ABOUT THE INSTITUTION Independent, coed. *Awards:* certificates, associate, bachelor's, master's, and doctoral degrees. 51 undergraduate majors. *Total enrollment:* 3,813. Undergraduates: 2,736. Freshmen: 770. Federal methodology is used as a basis for awarding need-based institutional aid.

UNDERGRADUATE EXPENSES for 2017–2018 *Application fee:* $40. *Comprehensive fee:* $49,182 includes full-time tuition ($33,338), mandatory fees ($2402), and room and board ($13,442). Full-time tuition and fees vary according to course load and program. Room and board charges vary according to board plan and housing facility. *Part-time tuition:* $628 per credit. Part-time tuition and fees vary according to course load and program. *Payment plan:* Tuition prepayment.

FRESHMAN FINANCIAL AID (Fall 2017, est.) 763 applied for aid; of those 86% were deemed to have need. 100% of freshmen with need received aid; of those 14% had need fully met. *Average percent of need met:* 73% (excluding resources awarded to replace EFC). *Average financial aid package:* $26,141 (excluding resources awarded to replace EFC). 14% of all full-time freshmen had no need and received non-need-based gift aid.

UNDERGRADUATE FINANCIAL AID (Fall 2017, est.) 2,514 applied for aid; of those 82% were deemed to have need. 100% of undergraduates with need received aid; of those 14% had need fully met. *Average percent of need met:* 73% (excluding resources awarded to replace EFC). *Average financial aid package:*

$26,004 (excluding resources awarded to replace EFC). 16% of all full-time undergraduates had no need and received non-need-based gift aid.

GIFT AID (NEED-BASED) *Total amount:* $38,256,175 (11% federal, 1% state, 86% institutional, 2% external sources). *Receiving aid:* Freshmen: 85% (655); all full-time undergraduates: 78% (2,046). *Average award:* Freshmen: $21,670; Undergraduates: $20,940. *Scholarships, grants, and awards:* Federal Pell, FSEOG, state, private, college/university gift aid from institutional funds.

GIFT AID (NON-NEED-BASED) *Total amount:* $9,509,848 (9% federal, 90% institutional, 1% external sources). *Receiving aid:* Freshmen: 9% (72). Undergraduates: 7% (194). *Average award:* Freshmen: $14,876. Undergraduates: $14,123. *Scholarships, grants, and awards by category: Academic interests/achievement:* business, computer science, general academic interests/achievements, home economics. *Creative arts/performance:* music. *Special achievements/activities:* leadership. *Special characteristics:* children of faculty/staff, siblings of current students. *Tuition waivers:* Full or partial for employees or children of employees. *ROTC:* Army, Air Force cooperative.

LOANS *Student loans:* $26,256,353 (51% need-based, 49% non-need-based). 81% of past graduating class borrowed through all loan programs. *Average indebtedness per student:* $36,517. *Average need-based loan:* Freshmen: $3404. Undergraduates: $4373. *Parent loans:* $7,489,907 (22% need-based, 78% non-need-based). *Programs:* Federal Direct (Subsidized and Unsubsidized Stafford, PLUS), Perkins.

WORK-STUDY *Federal work-study:* Total amount: $1,857,932; 959 jobs averaging $1935. *State or other work-study/employment:* Total amount: $300,000 (100% non-need-based). Part-time jobs available.

APPLYING FOR FINANCIAL AID *Required financial aid forms:* FAFSA, FAFSA using IRS Data Retrieval Tool. *Financial aid deadline (priority):* 4/1. *Notification date:* Continuous beginning 12/15. Students must reply by 5/1 or within 2 weeks of notification.

CONTACT Ms. Kathy M. Chambers, Director of Financial Aid, Western New England University, 1215 Wilbraham Road, Springfield, MA 01119-2684, 413-796-2080 or toll-free 800-325-1122 Ext. 1321. *Fax:* 413-796-2081. *E-mail:* finaid@wne.edu. *Website:* http://www.wne.edu/.

WESTERN NEW MEXICO UNIVERSITY
Silver City, NM

CONTACT Debra Reyes, Assistant Director, Western New Mexico University, PO Box 680, Silver City, NM 88062, 575-538-6173 or toll-free 800-872-WNMU. *Fax:* 575-538-6189. *E-mail:* reyesd@wnmu.edu. *Website:* http://www.wnmu.edu/.

WESTERN OREGON UNIVERSITY
Monmouth, OR

Tuition & fees (OR res): $9198	Average undergraduate aid package: $9865

ABOUT THE INSTITUTION State-supported, coed. *Awards:* certificates, bachelor's, and master's degrees. 35 undergraduate majors. *Total enrollment:* 5,285. Undergraduates: 4,776. Freshmen: 727. Federal methodology is used as a basis for awarding need-based institutional aid.

UNDERGRADUATE EXPENSES for 2017–2018 *Application fee:* $60. *Tuition, state resident:* full-time $7440; part-time $171 per credit hour. *Tuition, nonresident:* full-time $23,895; part-time $531 per credit hour. *Required fees:* full-time $1758. Full-time tuition and fees vary according to course load. Part-time tuition and fees vary according to course load. *College room and board:* $10,203; *Room only:* $8148. Room and board charges vary according to board plan and housing facility. *Payment plan:* Guaranteed tuition.

FRESHMAN FINANCIAL AID (Fall 2016) 605 applied for aid; of those 79% were deemed to have need. 100% of freshmen with need received aid; of those 10% had need fully met. *Average percent of need met:* 58% (excluding resources awarded to replace EFC). *Average financial aid package:* $9878 (excluding resources awarded to replace EFC). 10% of all full-time freshmen had no need and received non-need-based gift aid.

UNDERGRADUATE FINANCIAL AID (Fall 2016) 3,087 applied for aid; of those 84% were deemed to have need. 100% of undergraduates with need received aid; of those 9% had need fully met. *Average percent of need met:* 55% (excluding resources awarded to replace EFC). *Average financial aid package:* $9865 (excluding resources awarded to replace EFC). 7% of all full-time undergraduates had no need and received non-need-based gift aid.

GIFT AID (NEED-BASED) *Total amount:* $13,982,608 (60% federal, 18% state, 8% institutional, 14% external sources). *Receiving aid:* Freshmen: 67% (414); all full-time undergraduates: 66% (2,149). *Average award:* Freshmen: $7851; Undergraduates: $7374. *Scholarships, grants, and awards:* Federal Pell, FSEOG, state, private, college/university gift aid from institutional funds, United Negro College Fund, TEACH Grants.

GIFT AID (NON-NEED-BASED) *Total amount:* $1,340,547 (3% federal, 17% state, 41% institutional, 39% external sources). *Receiving aid:* Freshmen: 4% (25). Undergraduates: 2% (78). *Average award:* Freshmen: $1617. Undergraduates: $2317. *Scholarships, grants, and awards by category: Academic interests/achievement:* 1,035 awards ($1,343,071 total): biological sciences, business, communication, computer science, education, English, foreign languages, general academic interests/achievements, home economics, humanities, international studies, library science, mathematics, physical sciences, premedicine, social sciences. *Creative arts/performance:* 60 awards ($56,166 total): art/fine arts, dance, general creative arts/performance, music, performing arts, theater/drama. *Special achievements/activities:* 106 awards ($104,333 total): community service, general special achievements/activities, hobbies/interests, leadership. *Special characteristics:* 779 awards ($1,333,675 total): adult students, children of union members/company employees, ethnic background, first-generation college students, general special characteristics, handicapped students, international students, local/state students, members of minority groups, previous college experience, veterans, veterans' children. *ROTC:* Army cooperative.

LOANS *Student loans:* $21,328,019 (77% need-based, 23% non-need-based). 79% of past graduating class borrowed through all loan programs. *Average indebtedness per student:* $29,565. *Average need-based loan:* Freshmen: $3198. Undergraduates: $4030. *Parent loans:* $6,842,970 (38% need-based, 62% non-need-based). *Programs:* Federal Direct (Subsidized and Unsubsidized Stafford, PLUS), Perkins.

WORK-STUDY *Federal work-study:* 283 jobs averaging $953.

ATHLETIC AWARDS Total amount: $636,290 (56% need-based, 44% non-need-based).

APPLYING FOR FINANCIAL AID *Required financial aid form:* FAFSA. *Financial aid deadline:* Continuous. *Notification date:* Continuous beginning 3/19. Students must reply within 8 weeks of notification.

CONTACT Ms. Kella Helyer, Director of Financial Aid, Western Oregon University, 345 Monmouth Avenue North, Monmouth, OR 97361, 503-838-8679 or toll-free 877-877-1593. *Fax:* 503-838-8200. *E-mail:* finaid@wou.edu. *Website:* http://www.wou.edu/.

WESTERN STATE COLORADO UNIVERSITY
Gunnison, CO

Tuition & fees (CO res): $9802	Average undergraduate aid package: $11,207

ABOUT THE INSTITUTION State-supported, coed. *Awards:* certificates, bachelor's, and master's degrees. 70 undergraduate majors. *Total enrollment:* 2,814. Undergraduates: 2,429. Freshmen: 447. Federal methodology is used as a basis for awarding need-based institutional aid.

UNDERGRADUATE EXPENSES for 2017–2018 *Application fee:* $30. *Tuition, state resident:* full-time $6624; part-time $276 per credit hour. *Tuition, nonresident:* full-time $18,096; part-time $754 per credit hour. *Required fees:* full-time $3178. Full-time tuition and fees vary according to course load and reciprocity agreements. Part-time tuition and fees vary according to course load and reciprocity agreements. *College room and board:* $9546; *Room only:* $5030. Room and board charges vary according to board plan and housing facility.

FRESHMAN FINANCIAL AID (Fall 2017, est.) 421 applied for aid; of those 64% were deemed to have need. 100% of freshmen with need received aid; of those 3% had need fully met. *Average percent of need met:* 61% (excluding resources awarded to replace EFC). *Average financial aid package:* $11,049 (excluding resources awarded to replace EFC). 29% of all full-time freshmen had no need and received non-need-based gift aid.

UNDERGRADUATE FINANCIAL AID (Fall 2017, est.) 1,619 applied for aid; of those 64% were deemed to have need. 100% of undergraduates with need received

---

aid; of those 2% had need fully met. *Average percent of need met:* 60% (excluding resources awarded to replace EFC). *Average financial aid package:* $11,207 (excluding resources awarded to replace EFC). 26% of all full-time undergraduates had no need and received non-need-based gift aid.

GIFT AID (NEED-BASED) *Total amount:* $9,165,082 (29% federal, 11% state, 53% institutional, 7% external sources). *Receiving aid:* Freshmen: 56% (250); all full-time undergraduates: 52% (940). *Average award:* Freshmen: $9266; Undergraduates: $8821. *Scholarships, grants, and awards:* Federal Pell, FSEOG, state, private, college/university gift aid from institutional funds.

GIFT AID (NON-NEED-BASED) *Total amount:* $3,680,301 (1% state, 79% institutional, 20% external sources). *Receiving aid:* Freshmen: 56% (250). Undergraduates: 27% (482). *Average award:* Freshmen: $4480. Undergraduates: $2403. *Scholarships, grants, and awards by category: Academic interests/achievement:* general academic interests/achievements. *Creative arts/performance:* art/fine arts, music, performing arts. *Special achievements/activities:* leadership. *Special characteristics:* children and siblings of alumni. *Tuition waivers:* Full or partial for employees or children of employees, senior citizens.

LOANS *Student loans:* $11,039,772 (84% need-based, 16% non-need-based). 61% of past graduating class borrowed through all loan programs. *Average indebtedness per student:* $26,950. *Average need-based loan:* Freshmen: $3319. Undergraduates: $4142. *Parent loans:* $3,896,228 (66% need-based, 34% non-need-based). *Programs:* Federal Direct (Subsidized and Unsubsidized Stafford, PLUS), Perkins.

WORK-STUDY *Federal work-study:* Total amount: $31,519; jobs available. *State or other work-study/employment:* Total amount: $88,768 (62% need-based, 38% non-need-based). Part-time jobs available.

ATHLETIC AWARDS Total amount: $2,173,612 (72% need-based, 28% non-need-based).

APPLYING FOR FINANCIAL AID *Required financial aid form:* FAFSA. *Financial aid deadline (priority):* 4/1. *Notification date:* Continuous beginning 3/15. Students must reply within 3 weeks of notification.

CONTACT Carrie Shaw, Director of Financial Aid, Western State Colorado University, Taylor Hall, Gunnison, CO 81231, 970-943-3026 or toll-free 800-876-5309. *Fax:* 970-943-3086. *E-mail:* cshaw@western.edu. *Website:* http://www.western.edu/.

WESTERN WASHINGTON UNIVERSITY
Bellingham, WA

Tuition & fees (WA res): $7933	Average undergraduate aid package: $15,563

ABOUT THE INSTITUTION State-supported, coed. *Awards:* certificates, bachelor's, and master's degrees. 101 undergraduate majors. *Total enrollment:* 15,915. Undergraduates: 14,968. Freshmen: 3,114. Federal methodology is used as a basis for awarding need-based institutional aid.

UNDERGRADUATE EXPENSES for 2017–2018 *Application fee:* $60. *One-time required fee:* $250. *Tuition, state resident:* full-time $6879. *Tuition, nonresident:* full-time $21,391. *Required fees:* full-time $1054; $208 per credit hour. Full-time tuition and fees vary according to course load, location, and reciprocity agreements. Part-time tuition and fees vary according to course load, location, and reciprocity agreements. *College room and board:* $11,400; *Room only:* $7187. Room and board charges vary according to board plan, housing facility, and location.

FRESHMAN FINANCIAL AID (Fall 2017, est.) 2,612 applied for aid; of those 62% were deemed to have need. 99% of freshmen with need received aid; of those 16% had need fully met. *Average percent of need met:* 94% (excluding resources awarded to replace EFC). *Average financial aid package:* $16,369 (excluding resources awarded to replace EFC). 3% of all full-time freshmen had no need and received non-need-based gift aid.

UNDERGRADUATE FINANCIAL AID (Fall 2017, est.) 9,503 applied for aid; of those 72% were deemed to have need. 99% of undergraduates with need received aid; of those 15% had need fully met. *Average percent of need met:* 91% (excluding resources awarded to replace EFC). *Average financial aid package:* $15,563 (excluding resources awarded to replace EFC). 2% of all full-time undergraduates had no need and received non-need-based gift aid.

GIFT AID (NEED-BASED) *Total amount:* $42,663,892 (42% federal, 41% state, 12% institutional, 5% external sources). *Receiving aid:* Freshmen: 47% (1,440); all

---

full-time undergraduates: 39% (5,387). *Average award:* Freshmen: $8830; Undergraduates: $9138. *Scholarships, grants, and awards:* Federal Pell, FSEOG, state, private, college/university gift aid from institutional funds.

GIFT AID (NON-NEED-BASED) *Total amount:* $2,058,902 (1% federal, 5% state, 36% institutional, 58% external sources). *Receiving aid:* Freshmen: 4% (108). Undergraduates: 2% (271). *Average award:* Freshmen: $2105. Undergraduates: $1194. *Scholarships, grants, and awards by category:* Academic interests/ achievement: biological sciences, business, communication, computer science, education, engineering/technologies, English, foreign languages, general academic interests/ achievements, health fields, humanities, library science, mathematics, physical sciences, premedicine, social sciences. *Creative arts/performance:* applied art and design, art/ fine arts, cinema/film/broadcasting, creative writing, dance, general creative arts/performance, journalism/publications, music, performing arts, theater/drama. *Special achievements/activities:* community service, leadership, memberships. *Special characteristics:* children of public servants, children of union members/company employees, ethnic background, general special characteristics, international students, local/state students, members of minority groups, previous college experience, veterans. *Tuition waivers:* Full or partial for minority students, employees or children of employees, senior citizens.

LOANS *Student loans:* $56,824,109 (63% need-based, 37% non-need-based). 51% of past graduating class borrowed through all loan programs. *Average indebtedness per student:* $15,663. *Average need-based loan:* Freshmen: $3646. Undergraduates: $4486. *Parent loans:* $94,171,873 (22% need-based, 78% non-need-based). *Programs:* Federal Direct (Subsidized and Unsubsidized Stafford, PLUS), Perkins, college/university, alternative loans.

WORK-STUDY *Federal work-study:* Total amount: $965,870; 219 jobs averaging $4438. *State or other work-study/employment:* Total amount: $1,642,176 (100% need-based). 395 part-time jobs averaging $4304.

ATHLETIC AWARDS Total amount: $1,504,963 (38% need-based, 62% non-need-based).

APPLYING FOR FINANCIAL AID *Required financial aid form:* FAFSA. *Financial aid deadline (priority):* 1/31. *Notification date:* Continuous beginning 3/20. Students must reply by 5/1 or within 3 weeks of notification.

CONTACT Mrs. Christina Jensen, Associate Director of Financial Aid, Systems, Western Washington University, Old Main 260C, MS 9006, 516 High Street, Bellingham, WA 98225-9006, 360-650-4088. *E-mail:* christina.jensen@wwu.edu. *Website:* http://www.wwu.edu/.

WESTFIELD STATE UNIVERSITY
Westfield, MA

Tuition & fees (MA res): $9715	Average undergraduate aid package: $8746

ABOUT THE INSTITUTION State-supported, coed. *Awards:* certificates, bachelor's, and master's degrees. 39 undergraduate majors. *Total enrollment:* 6,237. Undergraduates: 5,552. Freshmen: 1,011. Federal methodology is used as a basis for awarding need-based institutional aid.

UNDERGRADUATE EXPENSES for 2017–2018 *Application fee:* $50. *Tuition, state resident:* full-time $970; part-time $306 per credit hour. *Tuition, nonresident:* full-time $7050; part-time $306 per credit hour. *Required fees:* full-time $8745; $75 per term. Full-time tuition and fees vary according to program and reciprocity agreements. Part-time tuition and fees vary according to course load. *College room and board:* $10,689. Room and board charges vary according to board plan and housing facility.

FRESHMAN FINANCIAL AID (Fall 2016) 1,009 applied for aid; of those 69% were deemed to have need. 97% of freshmen with need received aid; of those 9% had need fully met. *Average percent of need met:* 57% (excluding resources awarded to replace EFC). *Average financial aid package:* $8186 (excluding resources awarded to replace EFC). 2% of all full-time freshmen had no need and received non-need-based gift aid.

UNDERGRADUATE FINANCIAL AID (Fall 2016) 4,339 applied for aid; of those 72% were deemed to have need. 98% of undergraduates with need received aid; of those 11% had need fully met. *Average percent of need met:* 62% (excluding resources awarded to replace EFC). *Average financial aid package:* $8746 (excluding resources awarded to replace EFC). 2% of all full-time undergraduates had no need and received non-need-based gift aid.

GIFT AID (NEED-BASED) *Total amount:* $14,976,228 (52% federal, 27% state, 16% institutional, 5% external sources). *Receiving aid:* Freshmen: 47% (501); all full-

time undergraduates: 42% (2,143). *Average award:* Freshmen: $5865; Undergraduates: $5798. *Scholarships, grants, and awards:* Federal Pell, FSEOG, state, private, college/university gift aid from institutional funds.

GIFT AID (NON-NEED-BASED) *Total amount:* $702,473 (25% state, 43% institutional, 32% external sources). *Receiving aid:* Freshmen: 18% (196). Undergraduates: 11% (554). *Average award:* Freshmen: $4514. Undergraduates: $3408. *Tuition waivers:* Full or partial for employees or children of employees, senior citizens. *ROTC:* Army cooperative, Air Force cooperative.

LOANS *Student loans:* $32,565,877 (65% need-based, 35% non-need-based). 82% of past graduating class borrowed through all loan programs. *Average indebtedness per student:* $29,050. *Average need-based loan:* Freshmen: $3198. Undergraduates: $4133. *Parent loans:* $6,828,388 (32% need-based, 68% non-need-based). *Programs:* Federal Direct (Subsidized and Unsubsidized Stafford, PLUS), Perkins.

WORK-STUDY *Federal work-study:* 299 jobs averaging $1454. *State or other work-study/employment:* Part-time jobs available.

APPLYING FOR FINANCIAL AID *Required financial aid form:* FAFSA. *Financial aid deadline (priority):* 3/1. *Notification date:* 1/15. Students must reply within 2 weeks of notification.

CONTACT Catherine Ryan, Director of Financial Aid, Westfield State University, 333 Western Avenue, Westfield, MA 01086, 413-572-5218. *E-mail:* cryan@ westfield.ma.edu. *Website:* http://www.westfield.ma.edu/.

WEST LIBERTY UNIVERSITY
West Liberty, WV

CONTACT Christ Taskalines, Financial Aid Manager, West Liberty University, PO Box 295, West Liberty, WV 26074-0295, 304-336-8016 or toll-free 800-732-6204 (in-state), 866-WESTLIB (out-of-state). *Fax:* 304-336-8088. *E-mail:* taskalic@ westliberty.edu. *Website:* http://www.westliberty.edu/.

WESTMINSTER COLLEGE
Fulton, MO

Tuition & fees: N/R	Average undergraduate aid package: $22,895

ABOUT THE INSTITUTION Independent Presbyterian Church, coed. 33 undergraduate majors. Federal methodology is used as a basis for awarding need-based institutional aid.

FRESHMAN FINANCIAL AID (Fall 2017, est.) 157 applied for aid; of those 86% were deemed to have need. 100% of freshmen with need received aid; of those 68% had need fully met. *Average percent of need met:* 94% (excluding resources awarded to replace EFC). *Average financial aid package:* $24,896 (excluding resources awarded to replace EFC). 19% of all full-time freshmen had no need and received non-need-based gift aid.

UNDERGRADUATE FINANCIAL AID (Fall 2017, est.) 614 applied for aid; of those 84% were deemed to have need. 100% of undergraduates with need received aid; of those 68% had need fully met. *Average percent of need met:* 92% (excluding resources awarded to replace EFC). *Average financial aid package:* $22,895 (excluding resources awarded to replace EFC). 27% of all full-time undergraduates had no need and received non-need-based gift aid.

GIFT AID (NEED-BASED) *Total amount:* $13,503,578 (8% federal, 4% state, 79% institutional, 9% external sources). *Receiving aid:* Freshmen: 76% (135); all full-time undergraduates: 66% (517). *Average award:* Freshmen: $20,941; Undergraduates: $18,428. *Scholarships, grants, and awards:* Federal Pell, FSEOG, state, private, college/university gift aid from institutional funds.

GIFT AID (NON-NEED-BASED) *Total amount:* $129,436 (100% federal). *Average award:* Freshmen: $11,003. Undergraduates: $13,819. *Scholarships, grants, and awards by category:* Academic interests/achievement: general academic interests/achievements. *Creative arts/performance:* music. *Special achievements/activities:* general special achievements/activities, leadership. *Special characteristics:* children and siblings of alumni, children of faculty/staff, ethnic background, international students, local/state students, relatives of clergy, religious affiliation, siblings of current students, twins.

LOANS *Student loans:* $4,700,346 (38% need-based, 62% non-need-based). 73% of past graduating class borrowed through all loan programs. *Average indebtedness per student:* $29,691. *Average need-based loan:* Freshmen: $2955. Undergraduates: $3909. *Parent loans:* $1,515,963 (100% non-need-based). *Programs:* Federal Direct (Subsidized and Unsubsidized Stafford, PLUS), Perkins.

WORK-STUDY *Federal work-study:* Total amount: $489,476; jobs available. *State or other work-study/employment:* Total amount: $223,470 (100% non-need-based). Part-time jobs available.

APPLYING FOR FINANCIAL AID *Required financial aid form:* FAFSA. *Financial aid deadline (priority):* 11/15. *Notification date:* Continuous beginning 11/15. Students must reply within 3 weeks of notification.

CONTACT Ms. Aimee Bristow, Senior Director of Student Financial Aid, Westminster College, 501 Westminster Avenue, Fulton, MO 65251-1299, 800-475-3361. *Fax:* 573-592-5255. *E-mail:* aimee.bristow@westminster-mo.edu. *Website:* http://www.westminster-mo.edu/.

WESTMINSTER COLLEGE
New Wilmington, PA

Tuition & fees: $36,230	Average undergraduate aid package: $29,959

ABOUT THE INSTITUTION Independent Presbyterian Church (U.S.A.), coed. *Awards:* bachelor's and master's degrees. 51 undergraduate majors. *Total enrollment:* 1,254. Undergraduates: 1,192. Freshmen: 332. Federal methodology is used as a basis for awarding need-based institutional aid.

UNDERGRADUATE EXPENSES for 2017–2018 *Application fee:* $35. *Comprehensive fee:* $47,250 includes full-time tuition ($34,830), mandatory fees ($1400), and room and board ($11,020). Room and board charges vary according to board plan and housing facility. *Part-time tuition:* $1125 per credit hour.

FRESHMAN FINANCIAL AID (Fall 2016) 354 applied for aid; of those 91% were deemed to have need. 100% of freshmen with need received aid; of those 16% had need fully met. *Average percent of need met:* 80% (excluding resources awarded to replace EFC). *Average financial aid package:* $29,849 (excluding resources awarded to replace EFC). 10% of all full-time freshmen had no need and received non-need-based gift aid.

UNDERGRADUATE FINANCIAL AID (Fall 2016) 1,047 applied for aid; of those 93% were deemed to have need. 100% of undergraduates with need received aid; of those 19% had need fully met. *Average percent of need met:* 83% (excluding resources awarded to replace EFC). *Average financial aid package:* $29,959 (excluding resources awarded to replace EFC). 15% of all full-time undergraduates had no need and received non-need-based gift aid.

GIFT AID (NEED-BASED) *Total amount:* $24,881,491 (8% federal, 6% state, 82% institutional, 4% external sources). *Receiving aid:* Freshmen: 88% (322); all full-time undergraduates: 83% (955). *Average award:* Freshmen: $26,044; Undergraduates: $25,465. *Scholarships, grants, and awards:* Federal Pell, FSEOG, state, private, college/university gift aid from institutional funds.

GIFT AID (NON-NEED-BASED) *Total amount:* $2,978,275 (97% institutional, 3% external sources). *Receiving aid:* Freshmen: 87% (317). Undergraduates: 81% (938). *Average award:* Freshmen: $19,394. Undergraduates: $18,337. *Scholarships, grants, and awards by category:* Academic interests/achievement: $18,082,941 total: general academic interests/achievements, premedicine. *Creative arts/performance:* $101,760 total: cinema/film/broadcasting, general creative arts/performance, music, theater/drama. *Special characteristics:* $4,407,943 total: children and siblings of alumni, general special characteristics, religious affiliation. *Tuition waivers:* Full or partial for employees or children of employees. *ROTC:* Army cooperative.

LOANS *Student loans:* $7,627,795 (96% need-based, 4% non-need-based). 85% of past graduating class borrowed through all loan programs. *Average indebtedness per student:* $43,241. *Average need-based loan:* Freshmen: $3636. Undergraduates: $4508. *Parent loans:* $3,848,743 (98% need-based, 2% non-need-based). *Programs:* Federal Direct (Subsidized and Unsubsidized Stafford, PLUS), Perkins, alternative loans.

WORK-STUDY *Federal work-study:* 304 jobs averaging $1711. *State or other work-study/employment:* Total amount: $129,678 (70% need-based, 30% non-need-based). 77 part-time jobs averaging $1706.

APPLYING FOR FINANCIAL AID *Required financial aid forms:* FAFSA, W-2 forms. *Financial aid deadline (priority):* 5/1. *Notification date:* Continuous beginning 12/15. Students must reply by 5/1 or within 3 weeks of notification.

CONTACT Mrs. Cheryl A. Gerber, Director of Financial Aid, Westminster College, 319 South Market Street, New Wilmington, PA 16172-0001, 724-946-7102 or toll-free 800-942-8033. *Fax:* 724-946-6171. *E-mail:* gerberca@westminster.edu. *Website:* http://www.westminster.edu/.

WESTMINSTER COLLEGE
Salt Lake City, UT

Tuition & fees: $34,040	Average undergraduate aid package: $25,833

ABOUT THE INSTITUTION Independent, coed. *Awards:* certificates, bachelor's, and master's degrees. 40 undergraduate majors. *Total enrollment:* 2,570. Undergraduates: 2,030. Freshmen: 369. Federal methodology is used as a basis for awarding need-based institutional aid.

UNDERGRADUATE EXPENSES for 2018–2019 *Application fee:* $50. *One-time required fee:* $300. *Comprehensive fee:* $44,285 includes full-time tuition ($33,480), mandatory fees ($560), and room and board ($10,245). *College room only:* $5526. Full-time tuition and fees vary according to course load and program. Room and board charges vary according to board plan. *Part-time tuition:* $1395 per credit hour. *Part-time fees:* $154 per credit hour. Part-time tuition and fees vary according to course load and program.

FRESHMAN FINANCIAL AID (Fall 2017, est.) 316 applied for aid; of those 81% were deemed to have need. 100% of freshmen with need received aid; of those 27% had need fully met. *Average percent of need met:* 80% (excluding resources awarded to replace EFC). *Average financial aid package:* $27,193 (excluding resources awarded to replace EFC). 25% of all full-time freshmen had no need and received non-need-based gift aid.

UNDERGRADUATE FINANCIAL AID (Fall 2017, est.) 1,346 applied for aid; of those 86% were deemed to have need. 100% of undergraduates with need received aid; of those 23% had need fully met. *Average percent of need met:* 77% (excluding resources awarded to replace EFC). *Average financial aid package:* $25,833 (excluding resources awarded to replace EFC). 25% of all full-time undergraduates had no need and received non-need-based gift aid.

GIFT AID (NEED-BASED) *Total amount:* $24,009,431 (11% federal, 83% institutional, 6% external sources). *Receiving aid:* Freshmen: 69% (255); all full-time undergraduates: 60% (1,152). *Average award:* Freshmen: $22,807; Undergraduates: $20,809. *Scholarships, grants, and awards:* Federal Pell, FSEOG, state, private, college/university gift aid from institutional funds.

GIFT AID (NON-NEED-BASED) *Total amount:* $10,734,717 (89% institutional, 11% external sources). *Receiving aid:* Freshmen: 12% (44). Undergraduates: 8% (143). *Average award:* Freshmen: $15,795. Undergraduates: $15,120. *Tuition waivers:* Full or partial for employees or children of employees. *ROTC:* Army cooperative, Naval cooperative, Air Force cooperative.

LOANS *Student loans:* $12,890,111 (91% need-based, 9% non-need-based). 53% of past graduating class borrowed through all loan programs. *Average indebtedness per student:* $28,774. *Average need-based loan:* Freshmen: $3343. Undergraduates: $4762. *Parent loans:* $1,298,497 (91% need-based, 9% non-need-based). *Programs:* Federal Direct (Subsidized and Unsubsidized Stafford, PLUS), Perkins.

WORK-STUDY *Federal work-study:* Total amount: $1,269,714; jobs available. *State or other work-study/employment:* Total amount: $600,000 (100% non-need-based). Part-time jobs available.

ATHLETIC AWARDS Total amount: $1,271,039 (62% need-based, 38% non-need-based).

APPLYING FOR FINANCIAL AID *Required financial aid form:* FAFSA. *Financial aid deadline (priority):* 11/1. *Notification date:* Continuous beginning 2/1. Students must reply by 5/1 or within 3 weeks of notification.

CONTACT Joshua Montavon, Director of Financial Aid, Westminster College, 1840 South 1300 East, Salt Lake City, UT 84105, 801-832-2500 or toll-free 800-748-4753. *Fax:* 801-832-2501. *E-mail:* jmontavon@westminstercollege.edu. *Website:* http://www.westminstercollege.edu/.

WESTMONT COLLEGE
Santa Barbara, CA

Tuition & fees: $44,044	Average undergraduate aid package: $33,174

ABOUT THE INSTITUTION Independent nondenominational, coed. *Awards:* certificates and bachelor's degrees. 42 undergraduate majors. *Total enrollment:* 1,303. Undergraduates: 1,303. Freshmen: 353. Federal methodology is used as a basis for awarding need-based institutional aid.

UNDERGRADUATE EXPENSES for 2017–2018 *Application fee:* $50. *One-time required fee:* $300. *Comprehensive fee:* $57,930 includes full-time tuition ($42,890), mandatory fees ($1154), and room and board ($13,886). *College room only:* $8610. Room and board charges vary according to board plan and housing facility.

FRESHMAN FINANCIAL AID (Fall 2017, est.) 320 applied for aid; of those 83% were deemed to have need. 100% of freshmen with need received aid; of those 27% had need fully met. *Average percent of need met:* 85% (excluding resources awarded to replace EFC). *Average financial aid package:* $35,292 (excluding resources awarded to replace EFC). 22% of all full-time freshmen had no need and received non-need-based gift aid.

UNDERGRADUATE FINANCIAL AID (Fall 2017, est.) 1,027 applied for aid; of those 87% were deemed to have need. 100% of undergraduates with need received aid; of those 23% had need fully met. *Average percent of need met:* 80% (excluding resources awarded to replace EFC). *Average financial aid package:* $33,174 (excluding resources awarded to replace EFC). 23% of all full-time undergraduates had no need and received non-need-based gift aid.

GIFT AID (NEED-BASED) *Total amount:* $26,901,928 (4% federal, 8% state, 70% institutional, 18% external sources). *Receiving aid:* Freshmen: 75% (266); all full-time undergraduates: 69% (894). *Average award:* Freshmen: $30,092; Undergraduates: $27,067. *Scholarships, grants, and awards:* Federal Pell, FSEOG, state, private, college/university gift aid from institutional funds.

GIFT AID (NON-NEED-BASED) *Total amount:* $6,068,740 (97% institutional, 3% external sources). *Receiving aid:* Freshmen: 13% (45). Undergraduates: 9% (116). *Average award:* Freshmen: $18,779. Undergraduates: $16,606. *Scholarships, grants, and awards by category:* Academic interests/achievement: general academic interests/achievements. Creative arts/performance: art/fine arts, dance, music, theater/drama. Special achievements/activities: general special achievements/activities, leadership. Special characteristics: children of faculty/staff, ethnic background, international students. *Tuition waivers:* Full or partial for employees or children of employees. *ROTC:* Army cooperative, Air Force cooperative.

LOANS *Student loans:* $9,905,560 (69% need-based, 31% non-need-based). 70% of past graduating class borrowed through all loan programs. *Average indebtedness per student:* $33,407. *Average need-based loan:* Freshmen: $4381. Undergraduates: $6011. *Parent loans:* $3,950,548 (34% need-based, 66% non-need-based). *Programs:* Federal Direct (Subsidized and Unsubsidized Stafford, PLUS), college/university, alternative loans.

WORK-STUDY *Federal work-study:* Total amount: $810,127; 389 jobs averaging $1900.

ATHLETIC AWARDS Total amount: $1,723,237 (57% need-based, 43% non-need-based).

APPLYING FOR FINANCIAL AID *Required financial aid forms:* FAFSA, institution's own form. *Financial aid deadline (priority):* 3/1. *Notification date:* Continuous beginning 12/1. Students must reply by 5/1 or within 2 weeks of notification.

CONTACT Mr. Sean Smith, Director of Financial Aid, Westmont College, 955 La Paz Road, Santa Barbara, CA 93108, 805-565-6063 or toll-free 800-777-9011. *Fax:* 805-565-7157. *E-mail:* finaid@westmont.edu. *Website:* http://www.westmont.edu/.

WEST TEXAS A&M UNIVERSITY
Canyon, TX

Tuition & fees (TX res): $7885	Average undergraduate aid package: $8975

ABOUT THE INSTITUTION State-supported, coed. *Awards:* bachelor's, master's, and doctoral degrees. 61 undergraduate majors. *Total enrollment:* 10,060. Undergraduates: 7,394. Freshmen: 1,245. Federal methodology is used as a basis for awarding need-based institutional aid.

UNDERGRADUATE EXPENSES for 2017–2018 *Application fee:* $40. *Tuition, state resident:* full-time $5414; part-time $50 per credit hour. *Tuition, nonresident:* full-time $7047; part-time $80 per credit hour. *Required fees:* full-time $2471; $224 per credit hour. Full-time tuition and fees vary according to course load, degree level, program, and student level. Part-time tuition and fees vary according to course load, degree level, program, and student level. *College room and board:* $7196. Room and board charges vary according to board plan and housing facility. *Payment plan:* Guaranteed tuition.

FRESHMAN FINANCIAL AID (Fall 2017, est.) 1,078 applied for aid; of those 76% were deemed to have need. 97% of freshmen with need received aid; of those 11% had need fully met. *Average percent of need met:* 64% (excluding resources awarded to replace EFC). *Average financial aid package:* $9767 (excluding resources awarded to replace EFC). 14% of all full-time freshmen had no need and received non-need-based gift aid.

UNDERGRADUATE FINANCIAL AID (Fall 2017, est.) 4,354 applied for aid; of those 81% were deemed to have need. 97% of undergraduates with need received aid; of those 9% had need fully met. *Average percent of need met:* 58% (excluding resources awarded to replace EFC). *Average financial aid package:* $8975 (excluding resources awarded to replace EFC). 12% of all full-time undergraduates had no need and received non-need-based gift aid.

GIFT AID (NEED-BASED) *Total amount:* $22,126,402 (50% federal, 35% state, 9% institutional, 6% external sources). *Receiving aid:* Freshmen: 52% (644); all full-time undergraduates: 49% (2,763). *Average award:* Freshmen: $7298; Undergraduates: $6088. *Scholarships, grants, and awards:* Federal Pell, FSEOG, state, private, college/university gift aid from institutional funds.

GIFT AID (NON-NEED-BASED) *Total amount:* $2,708,444 (63% institutional, 37% external sources). *Receiving aid:* Freshmen: 36% (441). Undergraduates: 22% (1,249). *Average award:* Freshmen: $1599. Undergraduates: $2286. *Scholarships, grants, and awards by category:* Academic interests/achievement: 3,550 awards ($2,203,885 total): agriculture, business, communication, computer science, education, engineering/technologies, English, foreign languages, general academic interests/achievements, home economics, humanities, mathematics, physical sciences, premedicine, social sciences. Creative arts/performance: 389 awards ($220,542 total): art/fine arts, cinema/film/broadcasting, creative writing, dance, debating, general creative arts/performance, journalism/publications, music, theater/drama. Special achievements/activities: 684 awards ($338,187 total): cheerleading/drum major, community service, general special achievements/activities, hobbies/interests, leadership, memberships, religious involvement, rodeo. Special characteristics: 529 awards ($325,055 total): children and siblings of alumni, children of faculty/staff, children of union members/company employees, children of workers in trades, first-generation college students, general special characteristics, handicapped students, international students, local/state students, out-of-state students, public servants, religious affiliation, veterans, veterans' children. *Tuition waivers:* Full or partial for employees or children of employees.

LOANS *Student loans:* $24,999,162 (74% need-based, 26% non-need-based). 61% of past graduating class borrowed through all loan programs. *Average indebtedness per student:* $22,569. *Average need-based loan:* Freshmen: $2991. Undergraduates: $3893. *Parent loans:* $2,219,657 (22% need-based, 78% non-need-based). *Programs:* Federal Direct (Subsidized and Unsubsidized Stafford, PLUS), state.

WORK-STUDY *Federal work-study:* Total amount: $580,126; 212 jobs averaging $2749. *State or other work-study/employment:* Total amount: $35,295 (100% need-based). 13 part-time jobs averaging $2941.

ATHLETIC AWARDS Total amount: $2,094,869 (38% need-based, 62% non-need-based).

APPLYING FOR FINANCIAL AID *Required financial aid form:* FAFSA. *Financial aid deadline:* Continuous. *Notification date:* Continuous beginning 3/1. Students must reply within 2 weeks of notification.

CONTACT Marian Giesecke, Director of Financial Aid, West Texas A&M University, WTAMU Box 60939, Canyon, TX 79016-0001, 806-651-2055 or toll-free 800-99-WTAMU. *Fax:* 806-651-2924. *E-mail:* mgiesecke@mail.wtamu.edu. *Website:* http://www.wtamu.edu/.

WEST VIRGINIA STATE UNIVERSITY
Institute, WV

CONTACT Mrs. JoAnn L. Ross, Director of Student Financial Assistance, West Virginia State University, PO Box 1000, Ferrell Hall 324, Institute, WV 25112-1000, 304-204-4361 or toll-free 800-987-2112.
Website: http://www.wvstateu.edu/.

WEST VIRGINIA UNIVERSITY
Morgantown, WV

Tuition & fees (WV res): $8376	Average undergraduate aid package: $7292

ABOUT THE INSTITUTION State-supported, coed. *Awards:* bachelor's, master's, and doctoral degrees. 74 undergraduate majors. *Total enrollment:* 28,410. Undergraduates: 22,504. Freshmen: 5,225. Federal methodology is used as a basis for awarding need-based institutional aid.
UNDERGRADUATE EXPENSES for 2017–2018 *Application fee:* $45. *Tuition, state resident:* full-time $8376; part-time $349 per credit hour. *Tuition, nonresident:* full-time $23,616; part-time $984 per credit hour. Full-time tuition and fees vary according to location, program, and reciprocity agreements. Part-time tuition and fees vary according to course load, location, program, and reciprocity agreements. *College room and board:* $10,576. Room and board charges vary according to board plan, housing facility, and location.
FRESHMAN FINANCIAL AID (Fall 2016) 4,500 applied for aid; of those 63% were deemed to have need. 100% of freshmen with need received aid; of those 4% had need fully met. *Average financial aid package:* $6752 (excluding resources awarded to replace EFC). 15% of all full-time freshmen had no need and received non-need-based gift aid.
UNDERGRADUATE FINANCIAL AID (Fall 2016) 16,234 applied for aid; of those 65% were deemed to have need. 100% of undergraduates with need received aid; of those 6% had need fully met. *Average financial aid package:* $7292 (excluding resources awarded to replace EFC). 13% of all full-time undergraduates had no need and received non-need-based gift aid.
GIFT AID (NEED-BASED) *Total amount:* $40,327,157 (63% federal, 21% state, 16% institutional). *Receiving aid:* Freshmen: 44% (2,249); all full-time undergraduates: 37% (7,571). *Average award:* Freshmen: $5357; Undergraduates: $5212. *Scholarships, grants, and awards:* Federal Pell, FSEOG, state, private, college/university gift aid from institutional funds, Federal Nursing.
GIFT AID (NON-NEED-BASED) *Total amount:* $45,924,881 (47% state, 43% institutional, 10% external sources). *Receiving aid:* Freshmen: 39% (1,994). Undergraduates: 28% (5,672). *Average award:* Freshmen: $3590. Undergraduates: $3127. *Scholarships, grants, and awards by category: Academic interests/achievement:* agriculture, architecture, area/ethnic studies, biological sciences, business, communication, computer science, education, engineering/technologies, English, foreign languages, general academic interests/achievements, health fields, home economics, humanities, international studies, library science, mathematics, military science, physical sciences, premedicine, religion/biblical studies, social sciences. *Creative arts/performance:* art/fine arts, debating, music, theater/drama. *Special achievements/activities:* general special achievements/activities, leadership. *Special characteristics:* children of faculty/staff, children of union members/company employees, children of workers in trades, ethnic background, general special characteristics, international students, local/state students, members of minority groups. *Tuition waivers:* Full or partial for employees or children of employees, senior citizens. *ROTC:* Army, Air Force.
LOANS *Student loans:* $104,624,361 (35% need-based, 65% non-need-based). 60% of past graduating class borrowed through all loan programs. *Average indebtedness per student:* $29,358. *Average need-based loan:* Freshmen: $3123. Undergraduates: $4290. *Parent loans:* $6,798,659 (100% non-need-based). *Programs:* Federal Direct (Subsidized and Unsubsidized Stafford, PLUS), Perkins, Federal Nursing, college/university.
WORK-STUDY *Federal work-study:* jobs available. *State or other work-study/employment:* Total amount: $22,047,631 (100% non-need-based). Part-time jobs available.
ATHLETIC AWARDS Total amount: $9,307,570 (100% non-need-based).

APPLYING FOR FINANCIAL AID *Required financial aid forms:* FAFSA, state aid form. *Financial aid deadline:* 3/1. *Notification date:* Continuous beginning 11/1. Students must reply within 2 weeks of notification.
CONTACT Sandra Bennett, Executive Director of Financial Aid, West Virginia University, PO Box 6004, Morgantown, WV 26506-6004, 304-293-5242 or toll-free 800-344-9881. *Fax:* 304-293-4890. *E-mail:* sybennett@mail.wvu.edu.
Website: http://www.wvu.edu/.

WEST VIRGINIA UNIVERSITY INSTITUTE OF TECHNOLOGY
Beckley, WV

Tuition & fees (WV res): $6960	Average undergraduate aid package: $8238

ABOUT THE INSTITUTION State-supported, coed. *Awards:* certificates and bachelor's degrees. 33 undergraduate majors. *Total enrollment:* 1,623. Undergraduates: 1,623. Freshmen: 351. Federal methodology is used as a basis for awarding need-based institutional aid.
UNDERGRADUATE EXPENSES for 2017–2018 *Tuition, state resident:* full-time $6960; part-time $290 per credit hour. *Tuition, nonresident:* full-time $17,544; part-time $731 per credit hour. Full-time tuition and fees vary according to program. Part-time tuition and fees vary according to course load and program. *College room and board:* $11,304. Room and board charges vary according to board plan and housing facility.
FRESHMAN FINANCIAL AID (Fall 2016) 266 applied for aid; of those 72% were deemed to have need. 100% of freshmen with need received aid; of those 6% had need fully met. *Average financial aid package:* $7400 (excluding resources awarded to replace EFC). 12% of all full-time freshmen had no need and received non-need-based gift aid.
UNDERGRADUATE FINANCIAL AID (Fall 2016) 820 applied for aid; of those 75% were deemed to have need. 100% of undergraduates with need received aid; of those 7% had need fully met. *Average financial aid package:* $8238 (excluding resources awarded to replace EFC). 7% of all full-time undergraduates had no need and received non-need-based gift aid.
GIFT AID (NEED-BASED) *Total amount:* $3,233,601 (69% federal, 26% state, 5% institutional). *Receiving aid:* Freshmen: 58% (173); all full-time undergraduates: 56% (546). *Average award:* Freshmen: $5812; Undergraduates: $5793. *Scholarships, grants, and awards:* Federal Pell, FSEOG, state, private, college/university gift aid from institutional funds, Federal Nursing.
GIFT AID (NON-NEED-BASED) *Total amount:* $1,926,887 (1% federal, 47% state, 42% institutional, 10% external sources). *Receiving aid:* Freshmen: 31% (91). Undergraduates: 24% (232). *Average award:* Freshmen: $3990. Undergraduates: $3454. *Scholarships, grants, and awards by category: Academic interests/achievement:* general academic interests/achievements. *Special achievements/activities:* cheerleading/drum major, leadership. *Special characteristics:* first-generation college students. *Tuition waivers:* Full or partial for senior citizens. *ROTC:* Army.
LOANS *Student loans:* $4,056,801 (46% need-based, 54% non-need-based). 67% of past graduating class borrowed through all loan programs. *Average indebtedness per student:* $25,155. *Average need-based loan:* Freshmen: $2916. Undergraduates: $5848. *Parent loans:* $930,173 (100% non-need-based). *Programs:* Federal Direct (Subsidized and Unsubsidized Stafford, PLUS), Perkins, Federal Nursing, college/university.
WORK-STUDY *Federal work-study:* jobs available. *State or other work-study/employment:* Total amount: $275,283 (100% non-need-based). Part-time jobs available.
ATHLETIC AWARDS Total amount: $49,974 (100% non-need-based).
APPLYING FOR FINANCIAL AID *Required financial aid form:* FAFSA. *Financial aid deadline (priority):* 3/1. *Notification date:* Continuous. Students must reply within 2 weeks of notification.
CONTACT Mr. Michael A. White, Director of Financial Aid Services, West Virginia University Institute of Technology, 410 Neville Street, Beckley, WV 25801, 304-929-1440 or toll-free 888-554-8324. *E-mail:* michael.white@mail.wvu.edu.
Website: http://www.wvutech.edu/.

WEST VIRGINIA WESLEYAN COLLEGE
Buckhannon, WV

Tuition & fees: $31,640	Average undergraduate aid package: $25,260

ABOUT THE INSTITUTION Independent United Methodist Church, coed. **Awards:** certificates, bachelor's, and master's degrees. 61 undergraduate majors. **Total enrollment:** 1,449. Undergraduates: 1,320. Freshmen: 366. Federal methodology is used as a basis for awarding need-based institutional aid.

UNDERGRADUATE EXPENSES for 2018–2019 Application fee: $35. **Comprehensive fee:** $40,496 includes full-time tuition ($30,462), mandatory fees ($1178), and room and board ($8856). **College room only:** $4326. Full-time tuition and fees vary according to course load and student level. Room and board charges vary according to housing facility. Part-time tuition and fees vary according to course load.

FRESHMAN FINANCIAL AID (Fall 2017, est.) 345 applied for aid; of those 90% were deemed to have need. 100% of freshmen with need received aid; of those 26% had need fully met. **Average percent of need met:** 82% (excluding resources awarded to replace EFC). **Average financial aid package:** $29,339 (excluding resources awarded to replace EFC). 16% of all full-time freshmen had no need and received non-need-based gift aid.

UNDERGRADUATE FINANCIAL AID (Fall 2017, est.) 1,141 applied for aid; of those 90% were deemed to have need. 100% of undergraduates with need received aid; of those 24% had need fully met. **Average percent of need met:** 80% (excluding resources awarded to replace EFC). **Average financial aid package:** $25,260 (excluding resources awarded to replace EFC). 20% of all full-time undergraduates had no need and received non-need-based gift aid.

GIFT AID (NEED-BASED) Total amount: $20,945,360 (10% federal, 5% state, 85% institutional). **Receiving aid:** Freshmen: 84% (309); all full-time undergraduates: 80% (1,031). **Average award:** Freshmen: $26,762; Undergraduates: $28,139. **Scholarships, grants, and awards:** Federal Pell, FSEOG, private, college/university gift aid from institutional funds, Federal Nursing.

GIFT AID (NON-NEED-BASED) Total amount: $6,857,647 (31% state, 61% institutional, 8% external sources). **Average award:** Freshmen: $17,730. Undergraduates: $17,879. **Scholarships, grants, and awards by category:** Academic interests/achievement: general academic interests/achievements. Creative arts/performance: art/fine arts, creative writing, dance, music, performing arts, theater/drama. Special achievements/activities: community service, leadership, religious involvement. Special characteristics: children and siblings of alumni, children of faculty/staff, general special characteristics, international students, relatives of clergy, religious affiliation, veterans. **Tuition waivers:** Full or partial for employees or children of employees.

LOANS Student loans: $7,489,169 (40% need-based, 60% non-need-based). 68% of past graduating class borrowed through all loan programs. **Average indebtedness per student:** $31,996. **Average need-based loan:** Freshmen: $3291. Undergraduates: $4225. **Parent loans:** $2,108,031 (100% non-need-based). **Programs:** Federal Direct (Subsidized and Unsubsidized Stafford, PLUS), Perkins, Federal Nursing.

WORK-STUDY Federal work-study: Total amount: $304,142; jobs available. **State or other work-study/employment:** Total amount: $3,643,719 (39% need-based, 61% non-need-based). Part-time jobs available.

ATHLETIC AWARDS Total amount: $3,611,574 (95% need-based, 5% non-need-based).

APPLYING FOR FINANCIAL AID Required financial aid form: FAFSA. **Financial aid deadline (priority):** 2/1. **Notification date:** Continuous beginning 3/1. Students must reply within 3 weeks of notification.

CONTACT Susan George, Director of Financial Aid, West Virginia Wesleyan College, 59 College Avenue, Buckhannon, WV 26201, 304-473-8080 or toll-free 800-722-9933. E-mail: george_s@wvwc.edu. Website: http://www.wvwc.edu/.

WHEATON COLLEGE
Wheaton, IL

Tuition & fees: $36,420	Average undergraduate aid package: $25,883

ABOUT THE INSTITUTION Independent nondenominational, coed. **Awards:** certificates, bachelor's, master's, and doctoral degrees. 41 undergraduate majors.

Total enrollment: 2,900. Undergraduates: 2,391. Freshmen: 580. Both federal and institutional methodology are used as a basis for awarding need-based institutional aid.

UNDERGRADUATE EXPENSES for 2018–2019 Application fee: $50. **Comprehensive fee:** $46,600 includes full-time tuition ($36,420) and room and board ($10,180). **College room only:** $6000. Full-time tuition and fees vary according to program. Room and board charges vary according to board plan and housing facility. **Part-time tuition:** $1518 per credit hour. Part-time tuition and fees vary according to course load and program.

FRESHMAN FINANCIAL AID (Fall 2017, est.) 432 applied for aid; of those 80% were deemed to have need. 100% of freshmen with need received aid; of those 18% had need fully met. **Average percent of need met:** 84% (excluding resources awarded to replace EFC). **Average financial aid package:** $27,369 (excluding resources awarded to replace EFC). 22% of all full-time freshmen had no need and received non-need-based gift aid.

UNDERGRADUATE FINANCIAL AID (Fall 2017, est.) 1,468 applied for aid; of those 88% were deemed to have need. 99% of undergraduates with need received aid; of those 22% had need fully met. **Average percent of need met:** 84% (excluding resources awarded to replace EFC). **Average financial aid package:** $25,883 (excluding resources awarded to replace EFC). 23% of all full-time undergraduates had no need and received non-need-based gift aid.

GIFT AID (NEED-BASED) Total amount: $28,245,039 (9% federal, 2% state, 85% institutional, 4% external sources). **Receiving aid:** Freshmen: 59% (344); all full-time undergraduates: 55% (1,275). **Average award:** Freshmen: $23,361; Undergraduates: $21,171. **Scholarships, grants, and awards:** Federal Pell, FSEOG, state, private, college/university gift aid from institutional funds.

GIFT AID (NON-NEED-BASED) Total amount: $4,741,608 (83% institutional, 17% external sources). **Receiving aid:** Freshmen: 17% (98). Undergraduates: 15% (351). **Average award:** Freshmen: $8995. Undergraduates: $7358. **Scholarships, grants, and awards by category:** Academic interests/achievement: 1,243 awards ($4,731,464 total): area/ethnic studies, biological sciences, business, communication, education, engineering/technologies, English, foreign languages, general academic interests/achievements, home economics, humanities, international studies, mathematics, military science, physical sciences, premedicine, religion/biblical studies, social sciences. Creative arts/performance: 183 awards ($657,623 total): applied art and design, art/fine arts, cinema/film/broadcasting, creative writing, music. Special achievements/activities: 102 awards ($594,346 total): community service, general special achievements/activities, leadership, religious involvement. Special characteristics: 265 awards ($2,652,838 total): children and siblings of alumni, children of public servants, first-generation college students, general special characteristics, handicapped students, international students, local/state students, members of minority groups, out-of-state students, relatives of clergy, veterans' children. **ROTC:** Army, Air Force cooperative.

LOANS Student loans: $10,058,489 (88% need-based, 12% non-need-based). 57% of past graduating class borrowed through all loan programs. **Average indebtedness per student:** $27,543. **Average need-based loan:** Freshmen: $5019. Undergraduates: $5422. **Parent loans:** $3,110,771 (71% need-based, 29% non-need-based). **Programs:** Federal Direct (Subsidized and Unsubsidized Stafford, PLUS), Perkins.

WORK-STUDY Federal work-study: Total amount: $194,981; 143 jobs averaging $1374. **State or other work-study/employment:** Total amount: $1,650,000 (100% non-need-based). Part-time jobs available.

APPLYING FOR FINANCIAL AID Required financial aid form: FAFSA. **Financial aid deadline (priority):** 12/1. **Notification date:** Continuous beginning 1/15.

CONTACT Ms. Karen Belling, Director of Student Financial Services, Wheaton College, 501 College Avenue, Wheaton, IL 60187-5593, 630-752-5700 or toll-free 800-222-2419. E-mail: sfs@wheaton.edu. Website: http://www.wheaton.edu/.

WHEATON COLLEGE
Norton, MA

Tuition & fees: $52,626	Average undergraduate aid package: $41,564

ABOUT THE INSTITUTION Independent, coed. **Awards:** bachelor's degrees. 46 undergraduate majors. **Total enrollment:** 1,688. Undergraduates: 1,688. Freshmen: 502. Institutional methodology is used as a basis for awarding need-based institutional aid.

UNDERGRADUATE EXPENSES for 2018–2019 Application fee: $60. **One-time required fee:** $50. **Comprehensive fee:** $66,050 includes full-time tuition

($52,288), mandatory fees ($338), and room and board ($13,424). *College room only:* $7160. *Part-time tuition:* $6536 per course.

FRESHMAN FINANCIAL AID (Fall 2017, est.) 399 applied for aid; of those 85% were deemed to have need. 100% of freshmen with need received aid; of those 84% had need fully met. *Average percent of need met:* 95% (excluding resources awarded to replace EFC). *Average financial aid package:* $44,651 (excluding resources awarded to replace EFC). 30% of all full-time freshmen had no need and received non-need-based gift aid.

UNDERGRADUATE FINANCIAL AID (Fall 2017, est.) 1,268 applied for aid; of those 91% were deemed to have need. 100% of undergraduates with need received aid; of those 51% had need fully met. *Average percent of need met:* 94% (excluding resources awarded to replace EFC). *Average financial aid package:* $41,564 (excluding resources awarded to replace EFC). 29% of all full-time undergraduates had no need and received non-need-based gift aid.

GIFT AID (NEED-BASED) *Total amount:* $40,720,672 (5% federal, 1% state, 93% institutional, 1% external sources). *Receiving aid:* Freshmen: 68% (341); all full-time undergraduates: 67% (1,118). *Average award:* Freshmen: $38,565; Undergraduates: $34,058. *Scholarships, grants, and awards:* Federal Pell, FSEOG, state, private, college/university gift aid from institutional funds.

GIFT AID (NON-NEED-BASED) *Total amount:* $10,063,320 (97% institutional, 3% external sources). *Receiving aid:* Freshmen: 4% (19). Undergraduates: 2% (26). *Average award:* Freshmen: $21,402. Undergraduates: $19,953. *Scholarships, grants, and awards by category:* Academic interests/achievement: 558 awards ($11,417,950 total): general academic interests/achievements. *Tuition waivers:* Full or partial for employees or children of employees. *ROTC:* Army cooperative.

LOANS *Student loans:* $11,395,600 (68% need-based, 32% non-need-based). 65% of past graduating class borrowed through all loan programs. *Average indebtedness per student:* $35,058. *Average need-based loan:* Freshmen: $3446. Undergraduates: $4983. *Parent loans:* $3,214,715 (100% non-need-based). *Programs:* Federal Direct (Subsidized and Unsubsidized Stafford, PLUS), Perkins.

WORK-STUDY *Federal work-study:* Total amount: $1,250,425; 640 jobs averaging $1900. *State or other work-study/employment:* Total amount: $448,350 (69% need-based, 31% non-need-based). 358 part-time jobs averaging $1770.

APPLYING FOR FINANCIAL AID *Required financial aid forms:* FAFSA, CSS Financial Aid PROFILE, noncustodial (divorced/separated) parent's statement, business/farm supplement, parent and student federal income tax form(s), W-2 forms. *Financial aid deadline:* 2/1. *Notification date:* 3/15. Students must reply by 5/1.

CONTACT Ms. Susan Beard, Director of Financial Aid, Wheaton College, 26 East Main Street, Norton, MA 02766, 508-286-8232 or toll-free 800-394-6003. *Fax:* 508-286-3787. *E-mail:* sfs@wheatoncollege.edu. *Website:* http://www.wheatoncollege.edu/.

WHEELING JESUIT UNIVERSITY
Wheeling, WV

Tuition & fees: $28,110	Average undergraduate aid package: $27,281

ABOUT THE INSTITUTION Independent Roman Catholic (Jesuit), coed. *Awards:* certificates, bachelor's, master's, and doctoral degrees. 33 undergraduate majors. *Total enrollment:* 1,289. Undergraduates: 945. Freshmen: 222. Federal methodology is used as a basis for awarding need-based institutional aid.

UNDERGRADUATE EXPENSES for 2017–2018 *Application fee:* $25. *Comprehensive fee:* $37,106 includes full-time tuition ($27,000), mandatory fees ($1110), and room and board ($8996). *College room only:* $5006. Room and board charges vary according to board plan, housing facility, and student level. *Part-time tuition:* $735 per credit hour.

FRESHMAN FINANCIAL AID (Fall 2017, est.) 170 applied for aid; of those 85% were deemed to have need. 100% of freshmen with need received aid; of those 26% had need fully met. *Average percent of need met:* 88% (excluding resources awarded to replace EFC). *Average financial aid package:* $29,063 (excluding resources awarded to replace EFC). 20% of all full-time freshmen had no need and received non-need-based gift aid.

UNDERGRADUATE FINANCIAL AID (Fall 2017, est.) 589 applied for aid; of those 88% were deemed to have need. 100% of undergraduates with need received aid; of those 29% had need fully met. *Average percent of need met:* 85% (excluding resources awarded to replace EFC). *Average financial aid package:*

$27,281 (excluding resources awarded to replace EFC). 21% of all full-time undergraduates had no need and received non-need-based gift aid.

GIFT AID (NEED-BASED) *Total amount:* $3,717,130 (36% federal, 5% state, 59% institutional). *Receiving aid:* Freshmen: 54% (98); all full-time undergraduates: 52% (352). *Average award:* Freshmen: $12,685; Undergraduates: $10,589. *Scholarships, grants, and awards:* Federal Pell, FSEOG, state, private, college/university gift aid from institutional funds, Federal Nursing.

GIFT AID (NON-NEED-BASED) *Total amount:* $7,546,773 (1% federal, 5% state, 91% institutional, 3% external sources). *Receiving aid:* Freshmen: 80% (144). Undergraduates: 72% (487). *Average award:* Freshmen: $10,918. Undergraduates: $12,711. *Scholarships, grants, and awards by category:* Academic interests/achievement: 620 awards ($4,946,062 total): general academic interests/achievements, premedicine. *Creative arts/performance:* 26 awards ($65,500 total): music. *Special achievements/activities:* 44 awards ($257,469 total): community service, general special achievements/activities. *Special characteristics:* 165 awards ($781,307 total): children and siblings of alumni, children of faculty/staff, general special characteristics, religious affiliation. *Tuition waivers:* Full or partial for employees or children of employees.

LOANS *Student loans:* $4,515,074 (41% need-based, 59% non-need-based). 76% of past graduating class borrowed through all loan programs. *Average indebtedness per student:* $32,428. *Average need-based loan:* Freshmen: $4764. Undergraduates: $4645. *Parent loans:* $611,424 (100% non-need-based). *Programs:* Federal Direct (Subsidized and Unsubsidized Stafford, PLUS), alternative loans.

WORK-STUDY *Federal work-study:* Total amount: $190,355; 140 jobs averaging $2800. *State or other work-study/employment:* 25 part-time jobs averaging $2800.

ATHLETIC AWARDS Total amount: $2,873,863 (100% non-need-based).

APPLYING FOR FINANCIAL AID *Required financial aid form:* FAFSA. *Financial aid deadline:* 8/1 (priority: 11/1). *Notification date:* Continuous beginning 11/1. Students must reply within 2 weeks of notification.

CONTACT Christie Tomczyk, Director of Financial Aid, Wheeling Jesuit University, 316 Washington Avenue, Wheeling, WV 26003-6295, 304-243-2304 or toll-free 800-624-6992 Ext. 2359. *Fax:* 304-243-4397. *E-mail:* finaid@wju.edu. *Website:* http://www.wju.edu/.

WHITMAN COLLEGE
Walla Walla, WA

Tuition & fees: $51,746	Average undergraduate aid package: $41,281

ABOUT THE INSTITUTION Independent, coed. *Awards:* bachelor's degrees. 54 undergraduate majors. *Total enrollment:* 1,510. Undergraduates: 1,510. Freshmen: 389. Both federal and institutional methodology are used as a basis for awarding need-based institutional aid.

UNDERGRADUATE EXPENSES for 2018–2019 *Application fee:* $50. *Comprehensive fee:* $64,920 includes full-time tuition ($51,370), mandatory fees ($376), and room and board ($13,174). *College room only:* $5844. Part-time tuition and fees vary according to course load.

FRESHMAN FINANCIAL AID (Fall 2017, est.) 245 applied for aid; of those 76% were deemed to have need. 100% of freshmen with need received aid; of those 27% had need fully met. *Average percent of need met:* 91% (excluding resources awarded to replace EFC). *Average financial aid package:* $40,519 (excluding resources awarded to replace EFC). 36% of all full-time freshmen had no need and received non-need-based gift aid.

UNDERGRADUATE FINANCIAL AID (Fall 2017, est.) 738 applied for aid; of those 85% were deemed to have need. 100% of undergraduates with need received aid; of those 36% had need fully met. *Average percent of need met:* 93% (excluding resources awarded to replace EFC). *Average financial aid package:* $41,281 (excluding resources awarded to replace EFC). 32% of all full-time undergraduates had no need and received non-need-based gift aid.

GIFT AID (NEED-BASED) *Total amount:* $23,003,875 (4% federal, 2% state, 94% institutional). *Receiving aid:* Freshmen: 48% (184); all full-time undergraduates: 44% (623). *Average award:* Freshmen: $36,322; Undergraduates: $36,371. *Scholarships, grants, and awards:* Federal Pell, FSEOG, state, private, college/university gift aid from institutional funds.

GIFT AID (NON-NEED-BASED) *Total amount:* $6,051,315 (86% institutional, 14% external sources). *Receiving aid:* Freshmen: 20% (76). Undergraduates: 14%

(204). **Average award:** Freshmen: $11,859. Undergraduates: $11,279. **Scholarships, grants, and awards by category:** Academic interests/achievement: 373 awards ($4,361,911 total): general academic interests/achievements. Creative arts/performance: 39 awards ($461,137 total): art/fine arts, debating, music, theater/drama. Special characteristics: ethnic background, first-generation college students, international students, veterans, veterans' children.

LOANS Student loans: $4,188,303 (57% need-based, 43% non-need-based). 46% of past graduating class borrowed through all loan programs. *Average indebtedness per student:* $23,254. **Average need-based loan:** Freshmen: $3666. Undergraduates: $4485. **Parent loans:** $1,353,436 (100% non-need-based). **Programs:** Federal Direct (Subsidized and Unsubsidized Stafford, PLUS), Perkins.

WORK-STUDY Federal work-study: Total amount: $930,945; jobs available. **State or other work-study/employment:** Total amount: $179,658 (55% need-based, 45% non-need-based). Part-time jobs available.

APPLYING FOR FINANCIAL AID Required financial aid forms: FAFSA, CSS Financial Aid PROFILE, noncustodial (divorced/separated) parent's statement, federal income tax form(s), W-2 forms. **Financial aid deadline:** 2/1 (priority: 11/15). **Notification date:** 4/1. Students must reply by 5/1.

CONTACT Tyson Harlow, Assistant Director, Whitman College, 345 Boyer Avenue, Walla Walla, WA 99362-2046, 509-527-5178 or toll-free 877-462-9448. Fax: 509-527-4967.

Website: http://www.whitman.edu/.

WHITTIER COLLEGE
Whittier, CA

Tuition & fees: $46,120	Average undergraduate aid package: $37,931

ABOUT THE INSTITUTION Independent, coed. **Awards:** bachelor's, master's, and doctoral degrees. 36 undergraduate majors. **Total enrollment:** 1,904. Undergraduates: 1,681. Freshmen: 520. Federal methodology is used as a basis for awarding need-based institutional aid.

UNDERGRADUATE EXPENSES for 2017–2018 Application fee: $50. **Comprehensive fee:** $59,448 includes full-time tuition ($45,730), mandatory fees ($390), and room and board ($13,328). **College room only:** $7198. Full-time tuition and fees vary according to course load. Room and board charges vary according to board plan. **Part-time tuition:** $1905 per semester hour. Part-time tuition and fees vary according to course load.

FRESHMAN FINANCIAL AID (Fall 2017, est.) 471 applied for aid; of those 92% were deemed to have need. 100% of freshmen with need received aid; of those 18% had need fully met. **Average percent of need met:** 80% (excluding resources awarded to replace EFC). **Average financial aid package:** $39,034 (excluding resources awarded to replace EFC). 16% of all full-time freshmen had no need and received non-need-based gift aid.

UNDERGRADUATE FINANCIAL AID (Fall 2017, est.) 1,376 applied for aid; of those 93% were deemed to have need. 100% of undergraduates with need received aid; of those 16% had need fully met. **Average percent of need met:** 79% (excluding resources awarded to replace EFC). **Average financial aid package:** $37,931 (excluding resources awarded to replace EFC). 18% of all full-time undergraduates had no need and received non-need-based gift aid.

GIFT AID (NEED-BASED) Total amount: $32,351,145 (10% federal, 15% state, 75% institutional). **Receiving aid:** Freshmen: 71% (371); all full-time undergraduates: 69% (1,139). **Average award:** Freshmen: $35,855; Undergraduates: $34,151. **Scholarships, grants, and awards:** Federal Pell, FSEOG, state, private, college/university gift aid from institutional funds.

GIFT AID (NON-NEED-BASED) Total amount: $15,079,473 (99% institutional, 1% external sources). **Receiving aid:** Freshmen: 12% (61). Undergraduates: 9% (140). **Average award:** Freshmen: $22,517. Undergraduates: $22,612. **Scholarships, grants, and awards by category:** Academic interests/achievement: 1,521 awards ($33,917,331 total): general academic interests/achievements. Creative arts/performance: 78 awards ($254,000 total): art/fine arts, music, theater/drama. Special characteristics: children and siblings of alumni, children of faculty/staff, international students. **Tuition waivers:** Full or partial for employees or children of employees. **ROTC:** Army cooperative.

LOANS Student loans: $10,678,445 (61% need-based, 39% non-need-based). 75% of past graduating class borrowed through all loan programs. *Average indebtedness per student:* $32,258. **Average need-based loan:** Freshmen: $4947. Undergrad-

uates: $5687. **Parent loans:** $3,763,325 (74% need-based, 26% non-need-based). **Programs:** Federal Direct (Subsidized and Unsubsidized Stafford, PLUS), Perkins, college/university, alternative loans.

WORK-STUDY Federal work-study: Total amount: $512,024; 238 jobs averaging $2270. **State or other work-study/employment:** Total amount: $1,620,226 (75% need-based, 25% non-need-based). 580 part-time jobs averaging $1952.

APPLYING FOR FINANCIAL AID Required financial aid form: FAFSA. **Financial aid deadline:** 6/30 (priority: 3/1). **Notification date:** Continuous beginning 2/15. Students must reply within 2 weeks of notification.

CONTACT Mrs. Julie Aldama, Director of Financial Aid, Whittier College, 13406 East Philadelphia Street, Whittier, CA 90608-0634, 562-907-4285. Fax: 562-464-4560. *E-mail:* jaldama@whittier.edu.

Website: http://www.whittier.edu/.

WHITWORTH UNIVERSITY
Spokane, WA

Tuition & fees: $43,640	Average undergraduate aid package: $36,320

ABOUT THE INSTITUTION Independent Presbyterian, coed. **Awards:** certificates, bachelor's, and master's degrees. 91 undergraduate majors. **Total enrollment:** 2,627. Undergraduates: 2,251. Freshmen: 505. Federal methodology is used as a basis for awarding need-based institutional aid.

UNDERGRADUATE EXPENSES for 2018–2019 Comprehensive fee: $55,136 includes full-time tuition ($42,540), mandatory fees ($1100), and room and board ($11,496). **College room only:** $6250. Room and board charges vary according to board plan and housing facility. **Part-time tuition:** $1773 per credit hour. **Part-time fees:** $490 per term. Part-time tuition and fees vary according to course load.

FRESHMAN FINANCIAL AID (Fall 2017, est.) 459 applied for aid; of those 87% were deemed to have need. 99% of freshmen with need received aid; of those 20% had need fully met. **Average percent of need met:** 82% (excluding resources awarded to replace EFC). **Average financial aid package:** $38,628 (excluding resources awarded to replace EFC). 20% of all full-time freshmen had no need and received non-need-based gift aid.

UNDERGRADUATE FINANCIAL AID (Fall 2017, est.) 1,699 applied for aid; of those 90% were deemed to have need. 100% of undergraduates with need received aid; of those 15% had need fully met. **Average percent of need met:** 79% (excluding resources awarded to replace EFC). **Average financial aid package:** $36,320 (excluding resources awarded to replace EFC). 27% of all full-time undergraduates had no need and received non-need-based gift aid.

GIFT AID (NEED-BASED) Total amount: $41,918,398 (7% federal, 9% state, 81% institutional, 3% external sources). **Receiving aid:** Freshmen: 78% (391); all full-time undergraduates: 69% (1,498). **Average award:** Freshmen: $30,206; Undergraduates: $27,827. **Scholarships, grants, and awards:** Federal Pell, FSEOG, state, private, college/university gift aid from institutional funds.

GIFT AID (NON-NEED-BASED) Total amount: $13,788,863 (2% federal, 96% institutional, 2% external sources). **Receiving aid:** Freshmen: 10% (49). Undergraduates: 7% (142). **Average award:** Freshmen: $22,555. Undergraduates: $20,509. **Scholarships, grants, and awards by category:** Academic interests/achievement: 1,783 awards ($29,879,190 total): general academic interests/achievements, military science. Creative arts/performance: 250 awards ($1,104,568 total): art/fine arts, creative writing, debating, journalism/publications, music, theater/drama. Special achievements/activities: 27 awards ($26,500 total): religious involvement. Special characteristics: 794 awards ($2,442,969 total): children and siblings of alumni, ethnic background, international students, members of minority groups, religious affiliation, siblings of current students, veterans, veterans' children. **Tuition waivers:** Full or partial for employees or children of employees, senior citizens. **ROTC:** Army cooperative.

LOANS Student loans: $11,384,483 (81% need-based, 19% non-need-based). 69% of past graduating class borrowed through all loan programs. *Average indebtedness per student:* $26,940. **Average need-based loan:** Freshmen: $4787. Undergraduates: $5184. **Parent loans:** $4,334,960 (44% need-based, 56% non-need-based). **Programs:** Federal Direct (Subsidized and Unsubsidized Stafford, PLUS), Perkins, college/university.

WORK-STUDY *Federal work-study:* Total amount: $2,328,329; 806 jobs averaging $2810. *State or other work-study/employment:* Total amount: $281,471 (100% need-based). 92 part-time jobs averaging $3507.

APPLYING FOR FINANCIAL AID *Required financial aid form:* FAFSA. *Financial aid deadline (priority):* 12/1. *Notification date:* Continuous beginning 1/17.

CONTACT Mrs. Traci L. Spoon Stensland, Director of Financial Aid, Whitworth University, 300 West Hawthorne Road, Spokane, WA 99251-0001, 509-777-4335 or toll-free 800-533-4668. *Fax:* 509-777-4601. *E-mail:* tstensland@whitworth.edu. *Website:* http://www.whitworth.edu/.

WICHITA STATE UNIVERSITY
Wichita, KS

Tuition & fees (KS res): $8325	Average undergraduate aid package: $7927

ABOUT THE INSTITUTION State-supported, coed. *Awards:* certificates, associate, bachelor's, master's, and doctoral degrees. 70 undergraduate majors. *Total enrollment:* 15,081. Undergraduates: 12,398. Freshmen: 1,510. Federal methodology is used as a basis for awarding need-based institutional aid.

UNDERGRADUATE EXPENSES for 2017–2018 *Application fee:* $30. *Tuition, state resident:* full-time $6545; part-time $218.16 per credit hour. *Tuition, nonresident:* full-time $15,503; part-time $516.76 per credit hour. *Required fees:* full-time $1780; $7.75 per credit hour. Full-time tuition and fees vary according to course level, course load, degree level, and program. Part-time tuition and fees vary according to course level, course load, degree level, and program. *College room and board:* $6782. Room and board charges vary according to board plan and housing facility.

FRESHMAN FINANCIAL AID (Fall 2016) 1,192 applied for aid; of those 66% were deemed to have need. 98% of freshmen with need received aid; of those 25% had need fully met. *Average percent of need met:* 68% (excluding resources awarded to replace EFC). *Average financial aid package:* $7704 (excluding resources awarded to replace EFC). 24% of all full-time freshmen had no need and received non-need-based gift aid.

UNDERGRADUATE FINANCIAL AID (Fall 2016) 6,289 applied for aid; of those 77% were deemed to have need. 98% of undergraduates with need received aid; of those 17% had need fully met. *Average percent of need met:* 63% (excluding resources awarded to replace EFC). *Average financial aid package:* $7927 (excluding resources awarded to replace EFC). 16% of all full-time undergraduates had no need and received non-need-based gift aid.

GIFT AID (NEED-BASED) *Total amount:* $19,383,679 (81% federal, 7% state, 11% institutional, 1% external sources). *Receiving aid:* Freshmen: 33% (484); all full-time undergraduates: 37% (3,202). *Average award:* Freshmen: $5274; Undergraduates: $4838. *Scholarships, grants, and awards:* Federal Pell, FSEOG, state, private, college/university gift aid from institutional funds, United Negro College Fund, Bureau of Indian Affairs Grants, GEAR UP Scholarships.

GIFT AID (NON-NEED-BASED) *Total amount:* $11,960,170 (1% state, 86% institutional, 13% external sources). *Receiving aid:* Freshmen: 35% (502). Undergraduates: 24% (2,071). *Average award:* Freshmen: $1329. Undergraduates: $1235. *Scholarships, grants, and awards by category: Academic interests/ achievement:* area/ethnic studies, biological sciences, business, communication, computer science, education, engineering/technologies, English, foreign languages, general academic interests/achievements, home economics, humanities, international studies, mathematics, physical sciences, premedicine, social sciences. *Creative arts/performance:* applied art and design, art/fine arts, cinema/film/broadcasting, creative writing, dance, debating, general creative arts/performance, journalism/publications, music, performing arts, theater/drama. *Special achievements/activities:* cheerleading/drum major, community service, general special achievements/activities, hobbies/interests, leadership, memberships. *Special characteristics:* adult students, children and siblings of alumni, children of faculty/staff, ethnic background, first-generation college students, general special characteristics, handicapped students, international students, local/state students, members of minority groups, out-of-state students, previous college experience, veterans. *Tuition waivers:* Full or partial for employees or children of employees, senior citizens.

LOANS *Student loans:* $42,116,464 (47% need-based, 53% non-need-based). 58% of past graduating class borrowed through all loan programs. *Average indebtedness per student:* $25,380. *Average need-based loan:* Freshmen: $1611. Undergrad-

uates: $2134. *Parent loans:* $4,624,384 (100% non-need-based). *Programs:* Federal Direct (Subsidized and Unsubsidized Stafford, PLUS), Perkins, private loans.

WORK-STUDY *Federal work-study:* 106 jobs averaging $2623. *State or other work-study/employment:* Total amount: $78,989 (100% need-based). 87 part-time jobs averaging $908.

ATHLETIC AWARDS Total amount: $2,234,734 (100% non-need-based).

APPLYING FOR FINANCIAL AID *Required financial aid forms:* FAFSA, state aid form, university department scholarship application(s). *Financial aid deadline (priority):* 12/1. *Notification date:* Continuous beginning 8/1. Students must reply by 5/1.

CONTACT Sheelu Surender, Director of Financial Aid, Wichita State University, 1845 Fairmount Street, Wichita, KS 67260-0024, 316-978-3430 or toll-free 800-362-2594. *E-mail:* finaid@wichita.edu. *Website:* http://www.wichita.edu/.

WIDENER UNIVERSITY
Chester, PA

Tuition & fees: $44,166	Average undergraduate aid package: $33,521

ABOUT THE INSTITUTION Independent, coed. *Awards:* certificates, associate, bachelor's, master's, and doctoral degrees. 74 undergraduate majors. *Total enrollment:* 6,518. Undergraduates: 3,427. Freshmen: 787. Both federal and institutional methodology are used as a basis for awarding need-based institutional aid.

UNDERGRADUATE EXPENSES for 2017–2018 *Comprehensive fee:* $58,190 includes full-time tuition ($43,296), mandatory fees ($870), and room and board ($14,024). *College room only:* $7300. Full-time tuition and fees vary according to class time, course load, and program. Room and board charges vary according to board plan and housing facility. *Part-time tuition:* $1442 per credit hour.

FRESHMAN FINANCIAL AID (Fall 2017, est.) 722 applied for aid; of those 91% were deemed to have need. 100% of freshmen with need received aid; of those 20% had need fully met. *Average percent of need met:* 79% (excluding resources awarded to replace EFC). *Average financial aid package:* $35,505 (excluding resources awarded to replace EFC). 14% of all full-time freshmen had no need and received non-need-based gift aid.

UNDERGRADUATE FINANCIAL AID (Fall 2017, est.) 2,543 applied for aid; of those 91% were deemed to have need. 100% of undergraduates with need received aid; of those 23% had need fully met. *Average percent of need met:* 79% (excluding resources awarded to replace EFC). *Average financial aid package:* $33,521 (excluding resources awarded to replace EFC). 15% of all full-time undergraduates had no need and received non-need-based gift aid.

GIFT AID (NEED-BASED) *Total amount:* $63,180,192 (7% federal, 4% state, 88% institutional, 1% external sources). *Receiving aid:* Freshmen: 85% (651); all full-time undergraduates: 78% (2,267). *Average award:* Freshmen: $30,417; Undergraduates: $27,827. *Scholarships, grants, and awards:* Federal Pell, FSEOG, state, private, college/university gift aid from institutional funds.

GIFT AID (NON-NEED-BASED) *Total amount:* $10,578,827 (97% institutional, 3% external sources). *Receiving aid:* Freshmen: 81% (627). Undergraduates: 74% (2,159). *Average award:* Freshmen: $26,563. Undergraduates: $23,211. *Scholarships, grants, and awards by category: Academic interests/achievement:* 2,561 awards ($59,299,158 total): biological sciences, business, communication, computer science, education, engineering/technologies, English, foreign languages, general academic interests/achievements, health fields, humanities, international studies, mathematics, military science, physical sciences, premedicine, social sciences. *Creative arts/performance:* 88 awards ($215,250 total): dance, music. *Special achievements/activities:* 49 awards ($245,000 total): community service, general special achievements/activities, leadership. *Special characteristics:* 54 awards ($1,124,435 total): adult students, children of faculty/staff, ethnic background, international students. *Tuition waivers:* Full or partial for employees or children of employees, senior citizens. *ROTC:* Army, Naval cooperative, Air Force cooperative.

LOANS *Student loans:* $24,071,917 (93% need-based, 7% non-need-based). *Average need-based loan:* Freshmen: $3885. Undergraduates: $4815. *Parent loans:* $8,344,255 (95% need-based, 5% non-need-based). *Programs:* Federal Direct (Subsidized and Unsubsidized Stafford, PLUS), Perkins, college/university.

WORK-STUDY *Federal work-study:* Total amount: $3,072,743; 1,574 jobs averaging $1950. *State or other work-study/employment:* Part-time jobs available.

APPLYING FOR FINANCIAL AID *Required financial aid form:* FAFSA. *Financial aid deadline (priority):* 12/15. *Notification date:* Continuous beginning 1/30. Students must reply within 4 weeks of notification.

CONTACT Thomas K. Malloy, Executive Director of Enrollment Management, Widener University, One University Place, Chester, PA 19013-5792, 610-499-4161 or toll-free 888-WIDENER. *Fax:* 610-499-4687. *E-mail:* finaidmc@mail.widener.edu. *Website:* http://www.widener.edu/.

WILBERFORCE UNIVERSITY
Wilberforce, OH

CONTACT Director of Financial Aid, Wilberforce University, 1055 North Bickett Road, Wilberforce, OH 45384, 937-708-5727 or toll-free 800-367-8568. *Fax:* 937-376-4752.

Website: http://www.wilberforce.edu/.

WILEY COLLEGE
Marshall, TX

CONTACT Mr. Alan D. Jackson Jr., Director of Financial Aid, Wiley College, 711 Wiley Avenue, Marshall, TX 75670-5199, 903-927-3217 or toll-free 800-658-6889. *E-mail:* adjackson2@wileyc.edu. *Website:* http://www.wileyc.edu/.

WILKES UNIVERSITY
Wilkes-Barre, PA

Tuition & fees: $34,896	Average undergraduate aid package: $25,457

ABOUT THE INSTITUTION Independent, coed. *Awards:* bachelor's, master's, and doctoral degrees. 41 undergraduate majors. *Total enrollment:* 5,545. Undergraduates: 2,491. Freshmen: 607. Federal methodology is used as a basis for awarding need-based institutional aid.

UNDERGRADUATE EXPENSES for 2017–2018 *Application fee:* $40. *Comprehensive fee:* $49,166 includes full-time tuition ($33,208), mandatory fees ($1688), and room and board ($14,270). *College room only:* $8600. Room and board charges vary according to board plan and housing facility. *Part-time tuition:* $922 per credit hour. *Part-time fees:* $74 per credit hour.

FRESHMAN FINANCIAL AID (Fall 2017, est.) 523 applied for aid; of those 93% were deemed to have need. 100% of freshmen with need received aid; of those 15% had need fully met. *Average percent of need met:* 74% (excluding resources awarded to replace EFC). *Average financial aid package:* $25,631 (excluding resources awarded to replace EFC). 10% of all full-time freshmen had no need and received non-need-based gift aid.

UNDERGRADUATE FINANCIAL AID (Fall 2017, est.) 1,887 applied for aid; of those 94% were deemed to have need. 100% of undergraduates with need received aid; of those 13% had need fully met. *Average percent of need met:* 71% (excluding resources awarded to replace EFC). *Average financial aid package:* $25,457 (excluding resources awarded to replace EFC). 10% of all full-time undergraduates had no need and received non-need-based gift aid.

GIFT AID (NEED-BASED) *Total amount:* $39,831,192 (10% federal, 8% state, 80% institutional, 2% external sources). *Receiving aid:* Freshmen: 84% (488); all full-time undergraduates: 79% (1,756). *Average award:* Freshmen: $23,573; Undergraduates: $21,706. *Scholarships, grants, and awards:* Federal Pell, FSEOG, state, private, college/university gift aid from institutional funds.

GIFT AID (NON-NEED-BASED) *Total amount:* $3,309,681 (1% federal, 96% institutional, 3% external sources). *Receiving aid:* Freshmen: 48% (279). Undergraduates: 60% (1,330). *Average award:* Freshmen: $16,992. Undergraduates: $14,482. *Scholarships, grants, and awards by category:* Academic interests/achievement: general academic interests/achievements. Creative arts/performance: performing arts, theater/drama. Special achievements/activities: general special achievements/activities, leadership. Special characteristics: children of faculty/staff.

Tuition waivers: Full or partial for employees or children of employees. *ROTC:* Army cooperative, Air Force.

LOANS *Student loans:* $20,382,679 (90% need-based, 10% non-need-based). 83% of past graduating class borrowed through all loan programs. *Average indebtedness per student:* $47,907. *Average need-based loan:* Freshmen: $3440. Undergraduates: $4348. *Parent loans:* $6,556,088 (88% need-based, 12% non-need-based). *Programs:* Federal Direct (Subsidized and Unsubsidized Stafford, PLUS), Perkins, Federal Nursing, college/university, Gulf Oil Loan Fund, Rulison Evans Loan Fund.

WORK-STUDY *Federal work-study:* Total amount: $744,285; jobs available. *State or other work-study/employment:* Part-time jobs available.

APPLYING FOR FINANCIAL AID *Required financial aid form:* FAFSA. *Financial aid deadline (priority):* 3/1. *Notification date:* Continuous beginning 3/1.

CONTACT Jane Dessoye, Interim Executive Director of Financial Aid, Wilkes University, 84 West South Street, Wilkes-Barre, PA 18766, 570-408-2000 or toll-free 800-945-5378 Ext. 4400. *Fax:* 570-408-4004. *E-mail:* jane.dessoye@wilkes.edu. *Website:* http://www.wilkes.edu/.

WILLAMETTE UNIVERSITY
Salem, OR

Tuition & fees: $50,074	Average undergraduate aid package: $36,235

ABOUT THE INSTITUTION Independent United Methodist, coed. *Awards:* bachelor's, master's, and doctoral degrees. 56 undergraduate majors. *Total enrollment:* 2,819. Undergraduates: 2,112. Freshmen: 440. Federal methodology is used as a basis for awarding need-based institutional aid.

UNDERGRADUATE EXPENSES for 2018–2019 *Application fee:* $50. *Comprehensive fee:* $62,514 includes full-time tuition ($49,750), mandatory fees ($324), and room and board ($12,440). Full-time tuition and fees vary according to course load. Room and board charges vary according to board plan and housing facility. *Part-time tuition:* $6218.75 per credit. Part-time tuition and fees vary according to course load. *Payment plan:* Tuition prepayment.

FRESHMAN FINANCIAL AID (Fall 2017, est.) 393 applied for aid; of those 80% were deemed to have need. 100% of freshmen with need received aid; of those 30% had need fully met. *Average percent of need met:* 80% (excluding resources awarded to replace EFC). *Average financial aid package:* $35,088 (excluding resources awarded to replace EFC). 29% of all full-time freshmen had no need and received non-need-based gift aid.

UNDERGRADUATE FINANCIAL AID (Fall 2017, est.) 1,283 applied for aid; of those 86% were deemed to have need. 100% of undergraduates with need received aid; of those 21% had need fully met. *Average percent of need met:* 79% (excluding resources awarded to replace EFC). *Average financial aid package:* $36,235 (excluding resources awarded to replace EFC). 35% of all full-time undergraduates had no need and received non-need-based gift aid.

GIFT AID (NEED-BASED) *Total amount:* $34,515,857 (7% federal, 1% state, 89% institutional, 3% external sources). *Receiving aid:* Freshmen: 69% (305); all full-time undergraduates: 62% (1,089). *Average award:* Freshmen: $30,353; Undergraduates: $30,571. *Scholarships, grants, and awards:* Federal Pell, FSEOG, state, private, college/university gift aid from institutional funds.

GIFT AID (NON-NEED-BASED) *Total amount:* $13,359,380 (99% institutional, 1% external sources). *Receiving aid:* Freshmen: 18% (81). Undergraduates: 10% (174). *Average award:* Freshmen: $22,792. Undergraduates: $21,358. *Scholarships, grants, and awards by category:* Academic interests/achievement: general academic interests/achievements. Creative arts/performance: general creative arts/performance. Special achievements/activities: general special achievements/activities. Special characteristics: general special characteristics. *Tuition waivers:* Full or partial for employees or children of employees. *ROTC:* Army cooperative, Air Force cooperative.

LOANS *Student loans:* $10,464,141 (89% need-based, 11% non-need-based). 65% of past graduating class borrowed through all loan programs. *Average indebtedness per student:* $32,117. *Average need-based loan:* Freshmen: $3420. Undergraduates: $5054. *Parent loans:* $3,432,945 (95% need-based, 5% non-need-based). *Programs:* Federal Direct (Subsidized and Unsubsidized Stafford, PLUS), Perkins.

WORK-STUDY *Federal work-study:* Total amount: $1,013,616; jobs available. *State or other work-study/employment:* Part-time jobs available.

APPLYING FOR FINANCIAL AID *Required financial aid form:* FAFSA. *Financial aid deadline (priority):* 2/1. *Notification date:* 3/15. Students must reply by 5/1 or within 2 weeks of notification.

CONTACT Patty Hoban, Director of Financial Aid, Willamette University, 900 State Street, Salem, OR 97301-3931, 503-370-6273 or toll-free 877-542-2787. *Fax:* 503-370-6588. *E-mail:* phoban@willamette.edu. *Website:* http://www.willamette.edu/.

WILLIAM CAREY UNIVERSITY
Hattiesburg, MS

CONTACT Ms. Brenda Pittman, Associate Director of Financial Aid, William Carey University, 498 Tuscan Avenue, Hattiesburg, MS 39401-5499, 601-318-6153 or toll-free 800-962-5991. *Website:* http://www.wmcarey.edu/.

WILLIAM JESSUP UNIVERSITY
Rocklin, CA

Tuition & fees: $30,550	Average undergraduate aid package: $23,400

ABOUT THE INSTITUTION Independent nondenominational, coed. 19 undergraduate majors. Federal methodology is used as a basis for awarding need-based institutional aid.

UNDERGRADUATE EXPENSES for 2017–2018 *One-time required fee:* $75. *Comprehensive fee:* $41,625 includes full-time tuition ($29,950), mandatory fees ($600), and room and board ($11,075). Full-time tuition and fees vary according to course load. Room and board charges vary according to board plan and housing facility. *Part-time tuition:* $1260 per unit. Part-time tuition and fees vary according to course load.

FRESHMAN FINANCIAL AID (Fall 2017, est.) 153 applied for aid; of those 87% were deemed to have need. 100% of freshmen with need received aid; of those 17% had need fully met. *Average percent of need met:* 72% (excluding resources awarded to replace EFC). *Average financial aid package:* $25,313 (excluding resources awarded to replace EFC). 16% of all full-time freshmen had no need and received non-need-based gift aid.

UNDERGRADUATE FINANCIAL AID (Fall 2017, est.) 863 applied for aid; of those 92% were deemed to have need. 100% of undergraduates with need received aid; of those 12% had need fully met. *Average percent of need met:* 65% (excluding resources awarded to replace EFC). *Average financial aid package:* $23,400 (excluding resources awarded to replace EFC). 14% of all full-time undergraduates had no need and received non-need-based gift aid.

GIFT AID (NEED-BASED) *Total amount:* $14,877,459 (16% federal, 20% state, 59% institutional, 5% external sources). *Receiving aid:* Freshmen: 77% (132); all full-time undergraduates: 80% (792). *Average award:* Freshmen: $22,968; Undergraduates: $20,184. *Scholarships, grants, and awards:* Federal Pell, FSEOG, state, private, college/university gift aid from institutional funds.

GIFT AID (NON-NEED-BASED) *Total amount:* $1,866,595 (82% institutional, 18% external sources). *Receiving aid:* Freshmen: 9% (15). Undergraduates: 7% (64). *Average award:* Freshmen: $10,393. Undergraduates: $9803. *Scholarships, grants, and awards by category: Academic interests/achievement:* 674 awards ($5,056,611 total): area/ethnic studies, biological sciences, business, computer science, education, English, general academic interests/achievements, humanities, international studies, mathematics, physical sciences, religion/biblical studies, social sciences. *Creative arts/performance:* 180 awards ($778,551 total): applied art and design, art/fine arts, general creative arts/performance, music, performing arts, theater/drama. *Special achievements/activities:* 351 awards ($1,214,989 total): general special achievements/activities, leadership, religious involvement. *Special characteristics:* 467 awards ($1,653,629 total): adult students, children of faculty/staff, ethnic background, first-generation college students, general special characteristics, international students, out-of-state students, previous college experience, relatives of clergy, siblings of current students, veterans, veterans' children. *Tuition waivers:* Full or partial for employees or children of employees.

LOANS *Student loans:* $6,962,988 (52% need-based, 48% non-need-based). 74% of past graduating class borrowed through all loan programs. *Average indebtedness*

per student: $25,670. *Average need-based loan:* Freshmen: $3382. Undergraduates: $4561. *Parent loans:* $1,945,199 (60% need-based, 40% non-need-based). *Programs:* Federal Direct (Subsidized and Unsubsidized Stafford, PLUS).

WORK-STUDY *Federal work-study:* Total amount: $84,621; 84 jobs averaging $1000. *State or other work-study/employment:* Total amount: $515,000 (100% non-need-based). 125 part-time jobs averaging $1500.

ATHLETIC AWARDS Total amount: $2,187,259 (75% need-based, 25% non-need-based).

APPLYING FOR FINANCIAL AID *Required financial aid form:* FAFSA. *Financial aid deadline (priority):* 3/2. *Notification date:* Continuous beginning 3/2. Students must reply within 3 weeks of notification.

CONTACT Mr. John T. Swan, Director of Financial Aid, William Jessup University, 2121 University Avenue, Rocklin, CA 95765, 916-577-2233. *Fax:* 916-577-2230. *E-mail:* finaid@jessup.edu. *Website:* http://www.jessup.edu/.

WILLIAM JEWELL COLLEGE
Liberty, MO

Tuition & fees: $34,400	Average undergraduate aid package: $30,556

ABOUT THE INSTITUTION Independent, coed. *Awards:* certificates, bachelor's, and master's degrees (also offers evening program with significant enrollment not reflected in profile). 35 undergraduate majors. *Total enrollment:* 933. Undergraduates: 928. Freshmen: 198. Federal methodology is used as a basis for awarding need-based institutional aid.

UNDERGRADUATE EXPENSES for 2018–2019 *Comprehensive fee:* $44,330 includes full-time tuition ($33,500), mandatory fees ($900), and room and board ($9930). Full-time tuition and fees vary according to program. Room and board charges vary according to board plan and housing facility. *Part-time tuition:* $980 per credit hour.

FRESHMAN FINANCIAL AID (Fall 2017, est.) 169 applied for aid; of those 83% were deemed to have need. 100% of freshmen with need received aid; of those 60% had need fully met. *Average percent of need met:* 74% (excluding resources awarded to replace EFC). *Average financial aid package:* $31,927 (excluding resources awarded to replace EFC). 14% of all full-time freshmen had no need and received non-need-based gift aid.

UNDERGRADUATE FINANCIAL AID (Fall 2017, est.) 719 applied for aid; of those 86% were deemed to have need. 100% of undergraduates with need received aid; of those 27% had need fully met. *Average percent of need met:* 72% (excluding resources awarded to replace EFC). *Average financial aid package:* $30,556 (excluding resources awarded to replace EFC). 15% of all full-time undergraduates had no need and received non-need-based gift aid.

GIFT AID (NEED-BASED) *Total amount:* $12,383,786 (12% federal, 3% state, 82% institutional, 3% external sources). *Receiving aid:* Freshmen: 71% (141); all full-time undergraduates: 64% (582). *Average award:* Freshmen: $26,878; Undergraduates: $24,739. *Scholarships, grants, and awards:* Federal Pell, FSEOG, state, college/university gift aid from institutional funds.

GIFT AID (NON-NEED-BASED) *Total amount:* $4,563,497 (2% state, 94% institutional, 4% external sources). *Receiving aid:* Freshmen: 68% (135). Undergraduates: 59% (532). *Average award:* Freshmen: $18,954. Undergraduates: $19,039. *Scholarships, grants, and awards by category: Academic interests/achievement:* 768 awards ($11,471,250 total): general academic interests/achievements. *Creative arts/performance:* 131 awards ($401,500 total): dance, debating, journalism/publications, music, theater/drama. *Special achievements/activities:* 17 awards ($33,000 total): cheerleading/drum major, religious involvement. *Special characteristics:* 117 awards ($224,000 total): children and siblings of alumni, children of faculty/staff, siblings of current students. *Tuition waivers:* Full or partial for employees or children of employees. *ROTC:* Army cooperative.

LOANS *Student loans:* $4,122,209 (96% need-based, 4% non-need-based). 70% of past graduating class borrowed through all loan programs. *Average indebtedness per student:* $33,326. *Average need-based loan:* Freshmen: $3265. Undergraduates: $5582. *Parent loans:* $1,538,967 (89% need-based, 11% non-need-based). *Programs:* Federal Direct (Subsidized and Unsubsidized Stafford, PLUS), Perkins, Federal Nursing, alternative loans.

WORK-STUDY *Federal work-study:* Total amount: $1,027,228; 427 jobs averaging $2349. *State or other work-study/employment:* 117 part-time jobs averaging $444.

ATHLETIC AWARDS Total amount: $3,999,895 (64% need-based, 36% non-need-based).

APPLYING FOR FINANCIAL AID *Required financial aid form:* FAFSA. *Financial aid deadline (priority):* 2/1. *Notification date:* Continuous beginning 11/1. Students must reply within 2 weeks of notification.

CONTACT Mr. Daniel Holt, Director of Financial Aid and Scholarship Services, William Jewell College, 500 College Hill, Liberty, MO 64068, 816-415-5977 or toll-free 888-2JEWELL. *Fax:* 816-415-5006. *E-mail:* holtd@william.jewell.edu. *Website:* http://www.jewell.edu/.

WILLIAM PATERSON UNIVERSITY OF NEW JERSEY
Wayne, NJ

Tuition & fees (NJ res): $12,804	Average undergraduate aid package: $11,535

ABOUT THE INSTITUTION State-supported, coed. *Awards:* certificates, bachelor's, master's, and doctoral degrees. 51 undergraduate majors. *Total enrollment:* 10,252. Undergraduates: 8,832. Freshmen: 1,317. Federal methodology is used as a basis for awarding need-based institutional aid.

UNDERGRADUATE EXPENSES for 2017–2018 *Application fee:* $50. *Tuition, state resident:* full-time $12,680; part-time $406 per credit. *Tuition, nonresident:* full-time $20,718; part-time $671 per credit. *Required fees:* full-time $124; $4 per credit. Full-time tuition and fees vary according to course load. Part-time tuition and fees vary according to course load. *College room and board:* $11,218; *Room only:* $6998. Room and board charges vary according to board plan, housing facility, and location.

FRESHMAN FINANCIAL AID (Fall 2017, est.) 1,297 applied for aid; of those 84% were deemed to have need. 99% of freshmen with need received aid; of those 29% had need fully met. *Average financial aid package:* $11,881 (excluding resources awarded to replace EFC). 6% of all full-time freshmen had no need and received non-need-based gift aid.

UNDERGRADUATE FINANCIAL AID (Fall 2017, est.) 6,620 applied for aid; of those 83% were deemed to have need. 99% of undergraduates with need received aid; of those 30% had need fully met. *Average financial aid package:* $11,535 (excluding resources awarded to replace EFC). 7% of all full-time undergraduates had no need and received non-need-based gift aid.

GIFT AID (NEED-BASED) *Total amount:* $36,821,563 (57% federal, 42% state, 1% institutional). *Receiving aid:* Freshmen: 62% (811); all full-time undergraduates: 54% (3,919). *Average award:* Freshmen: $9511; Undergraduates: $8781. *Scholarships, grants, and awards:* Federal Pell, FSEOG, state, private, college/university gift aid from institutional funds.

GIFT AID (NON-NEED-BASED) *Total amount:* $8,850,691 (2% state, 94% institutional, 4% external sources). *Receiving aid:* Freshmen: 19% (249). Undergraduates: 19% (1,416). *Average award:* Freshmen: $7292. Undergraduates: $5441. *Scholarships, grants, and awards by category:* Academic interests/achievement: 2,664 awards ($7,793,685 total): general academic interests/achievements. Creative arts/performance: 106 awards ($347,822 total): art/fine arts, music. Special characteristics: 101 awards ($725,102 total): children of faculty/staff, veterans. *Tuition waivers:* Full or partial for employees or children of employees, senior citizens. *ROTC:* Air Force cooperative.

LOANS *Student loans:* $44,439,454 (45% need-based, 55% non-need-based). 74% of past graduating class borrowed through all loan programs. *Average indebtedness per student:* $33,355. *Average need-based loan:* Freshmen: $3388. Undergraduates: $4330. *Parent loans:* $8,414,682 (100% non-need-based). *Programs:* Federal Direct (Subsidized and Unsubsidized Stafford, PLUS), Federal Nursing, state.

WORK-STUDY *Federal work-study:* Total amount: $347,270; 210 jobs averaging $1800.

APPLYING FOR FINANCIAL AID *Required financial aid form:* FAFSA. *Financial aid deadline (priority):* 3/1. *Notification date:* Continuous beginning 2/15.

CONTACT Mr. Michael Corso, Director of Financial Aid, William Paterson University of New Jersey, 300 Pompton Road, Morris Hall, 1st Floor, Wayne, NJ 07470, 973-720-2202 or toll-free 877-WPU-EXCEL. *Fax:* 973-720-3133. *E-mail:* finaid@wpunj.edu. *Website:* http://www.wpunj.edu/.

WILLIAM PEACE UNIVERSITY
Raleigh, NC

ABOUT THE INSTITUTION Independent Presbyterian Church (U.S.A.), coed. *Awards:* bachelor's degrees. 21 undergraduate majors. *Total enrollment:* 930. Undergraduates: 930. Freshmen: 203.

GIFT AID (NEED-BASED) *Scholarships, grants, and awards:* Federal Pell, FSEOG, state, private, college/university gift aid from institutional funds.

GIFT AID (NON-NEED-BASED) *Scholarships, grants, and awards by category:* Academic interests/achievement: general academic interests/achievements. Creative arts/performance: art/fine arts, performing arts. Special achievements/activities: community service, leadership. Special characteristics: children of faculty/staff, siblings of current students.

LOANS *Programs:* Federal Direct (Subsidized and Unsubsidized Stafford, PLUS), state, alternative loans.

WORK-STUDY *Federal work-study:* 93 jobs averaging $2000.

APPLYING FOR FINANCIAL AID *Required financial aid form:* FAFSA.

CONTACT Miss Michelle Hemmer, Director of Financial Aid, William Peace University, 15 East Peace Street, Raleigh, NC 27604, 919-508-2284. *Fax:* 919-508-2325. *E-mail:* michelle.hemmer@peace.edu. *Website:* http://www.peace.edu/.

WILLIAM PENN UNIVERSITY
Oskaloosa, IA

CONTACT Cyndi Peiffer, Director of Financial Aid, William Penn University, 201 Trueblood Avenue, Oskaloosa, IA 52577-1799, 641-673-1060. *Fax:* 641-673-1115. *E-mail:* peifferc@wmpenn.edu. *Website:* http://www.wmpenn.edu/.

WILLIAMS BAPTIST COLLEGE
Walnut Ridge, AR

Tuition & fees: $17,320	Average undergraduate aid package: $17,498

ABOUT THE INSTITUTION Independent Southern Baptist, coed. *Awards:* associate, bachelor's, and master's degrees. 26 undergraduate majors. *Total enrollment:* 469. Undergraduates: 469. Freshmen: 113. Federal methodology is used as a basis for awarding need-based institutional aid.

UNDERGRADUATE EXPENSES for 2017–2018 *Comprehensive fee:* $24,920 includes full-time tuition ($16,200), mandatory fees ($1120), and room and board ($7600). Room and board charges vary according to board plan. *Part-time tuition:* $675 per credit hour. *Part-time fees:* $81 per term. Part-time tuition and fees vary according to course load.

FRESHMAN FINANCIAL AID (Fall 2016) 98 applied for aid; of those 73% were deemed to have need. 100% of freshmen with need received aid. *Average financial aid package:* $16,169 (excluding resources awarded to replace EFC).

UNDERGRADUATE FINANCIAL AID (Fall 2016) 370 applied for aid; of those 77% were deemed to have need. 100% of undergraduates with need received aid. *Average financial aid package:* $17,498 (excluding resources awarded to replace EFC).

GIFT AID (NEED-BASED) *Total amount:* $1,050,779 (97% federal, 3% state). *Receiving aid:* Freshmen: 52% (59); all full-time undergraduates: 50% (210). *Average award:* Freshmen: $4962; Undergraduates: $4856. *Scholarships, grants, and awards:* Federal Pell, FSEOG, state, private, college/university gift aid from institutional funds.

GIFT AID (NON-NEED-BASED) *Total amount:* $2,261,601 (31% state, 53% institutional, 16% external sources). *Receiving aid:* Freshmen: 50% (56). Undergraduates: 50% (211). *Scholarships, grants, and awards by category: Academic interests/achievement:* 194 awards ($1,098,711 total): biological sciences, business, education, general academic interests/achievements, humanities, religion/biblical studies. *Creative arts/performance:* 41 awards ($41,900 total): art/fine arts, music, theater/drama. *Special achievements/activities:* 9 awards ($5600 total): cheerleading/drum major. *Special characteristics:* 53 awards ($129,585 total): children of faculty/staff, international students, members of minority groups, relatives of clergy, religious affiliation. *Tuition waivers:* Full or partial for employees or children of employees. *ROTC:* Army cooperative.

LOANS *Student loans:* $1,884,589 (51% need-based, 49% non-need-based). 75% of past graduating class borrowed through all loan programs. *Average indebtedness per student:* $22,747. *Average need-based loan:* Freshmen: $3074. Undergraduates: $3915. *Parent loans:* $506,231 (100% non-need-based). *Programs:* Federal Direct (Subsidized and Unsubsidized Stafford, PLUS).

WORK-STUDY *Federal work-study:* 169 jobs averaging $1580. *State or other work-study/employment:* Total amount: $49,745 (100% non-need-based). 21 part-time jobs averaging $1597.

ATHLETIC AWARDS Total amount: $2,281,032 (100% non-need-based).

APPLYING FOR FINANCIAL AID *Required financial aid form:* FAFSA. *Financial aid deadline:* Continuous. *Notification date:* Continuous beginning 4/1. Students must reply within 2 weeks of notification.

CONTACT Mrs. Barbara Turner, Director of Financial Aid, Williams Baptist College, 60 West Fulbright Avenue, Walnut Ridge, AR 72476, 870-759-4112 or toll-free 800-722-4434. *Fax:* 870-759-4209. *E-mail:* bturner@wbcoll.edu.
Website: http://www.wbcoll.edu/.

WILLIAMS COLLEGE
Williamstown, MA

Tuition & fees: $53,550	Average undergraduate aid package: $54,932

ABOUT THE INSTITUTION Independent, coed. *Awards:* bachelor's and master's degrees. 41 undergraduate majors. *Total enrollment:* 2,117. Undergraduates: 2,061. Freshmen: 548. Institutional methodology is used as a basis for awarding need-based institutional aid.

UNDERGRADUATE EXPENSES for 2017–2018 *Application fee:* $65. *Comprehensive fee:* $67,700 includes full-time tuition ($53,240), mandatory fees ($310), and room and board ($14,150). *College room only:* $7170. Room and board charges vary according to board plan.

FRESHMAN FINANCIAL AID (Fall 2017, est.) 352 applied for aid; of those 82% were deemed to have need. 100% of freshmen with need received aid; of those 100% had need fully met. *Average percent of need met:* 100% (excluding resources awarded to replace EFC). *Average financial aid package:* $56,486 (excluding resources awarded to replace EFC).

UNDERGRADUATE FINANCIAL AID (Fall 2017, est.) 1,175 applied for aid; of those 87% were deemed to have need. 100% of undergraduates with need received aid; of those 100% had need fully met. *Average percent of need met:* 100% (excluding resources awarded to replace EFC). *Average financial aid package:* $54,932 (excluding resources awarded to replace EFC).

GIFT AID (NEED-BASED) *Total amount:* $53,426,853 (4% federal, 93% institutional, 3% external sources). *Receiving aid:* Freshmen: 52% (287); all full-time undergraduates: 51% (1,026). *Average award:* Freshmen: $53,866; Undergraduates: $51,773. *Scholarships, grants, and awards:* Federal Pell, FSEOG, state, private, college/university gift aid from institutional funds.

GIFT AID (NON-NEED-BASED) *Total amount:* $1,011,358 (2% federal, 98% external sources). *ROTC:* Air Force cooperative.

LOANS *Student loans:* $2,550,757 (43% need-based, 57% non-need-based). 35% of past graduating class borrowed through all loan programs. *Average indebtedness per student:* $16,230. *Average need-based loan:* Freshmen: $2838. Undergraduates: $3012. *Parent loans:* $2,700,565 (100% non-need-based). *Programs:* Federal Direct (Subsidized and Unsubsidized Stafford, PLUS), Perkins, college/university.

WORK-STUDY *Federal work-study:* Total amount: $1,111,422; jobs available. *State or other work-study/employment:* Total amount: $2,812,066 (37% need-based, 63% non-need-based). Part-time jobs available.

APPLYING FOR FINANCIAL AID *Required financial aid forms:* FAFSA, CSS Financial Aid PROFILE, noncustodial (divorced/separated) parent's statement, federal income tax form(s). *Financial aid deadline:* 1/15. *Notification date:* 4/1. Students must reply by 5/1.

CONTACT Mr. Paul J. Boyer, Director of Financial Aid, Williams College, PO Box 37, Weston Hall, 995 Main Street, Williamstown, MA 01267, 413-597-4181. *Fax:* 413-597-2999. *E-mail:* paul.j.boyer@williams.edu.
Website: http://www.williams.edu/.

WILLIAMSON COLLEGE
Franklin, TN

CONTACT Jeanie Maguire, Director of Financial Aid, Williamson College, 200 Seaboard Lane, Franklin, TN 37067, 615-771-7821. *Fax:* 615-771-7810. *E-mail:* info@williamsoncc.edu.
Website: http://www.williamsoncc.edu/.

WILLIAM WOODS UNIVERSITY
Fulton, MO

Tuition & fees: $24,185	Average undergraduate aid package: $16,149

ABOUT THE INSTITUTION Independent Christian Church (Disciples of Christ), coed. *Awards:* certificates, associate, bachelor's, master's, and doctoral degrees. 35 undergraduate majors. *Total enrollment:* 2,281. Undergraduates: 958. Freshmen: 195. Federal methodology is used as a basis for awarding need-based institutional aid.

UNDERGRADUATE EXPENSES for 2018–2019 *Comprehensive fee:* $33,885 includes full-time tuition ($23,230), mandatory fees ($955), and room and board ($9700). *College room only:* $5050. Full-time tuition and fees vary according to course load and program. Room and board charges vary according to board plan and housing facility. *Part-time tuition:* $425 per credit hour. *Part-time fees:* $50 per term. Part-time tuition and fees vary according to course load and program.

FRESHMAN FINANCIAL AID (Fall 2017, est.) 197 applied for aid; of those 100% were deemed to have need. 100% of freshmen with need received aid. *Average financial aid package:* $18,004 (excluding resources awarded to replace EFC).

UNDERGRADUATE FINANCIAL AID (Fall 2017, est.) 768 applied for aid; of those 100% were deemed to have need. 100% of undergraduates with need received aid. *Average financial aid package:* $16,149 (excluding resources awarded to replace EFC). 1% of all full-time undergraduates had no need and received non-need-based gift aid.

GIFT AID (NEED-BASED) *Total amount:* $8,169,014 (17% federal, 4% state, 77% institutional, 2% external sources). *Receiving aid:* Freshmen: 98% (197); all full-time undergraduates: 95% (750). *Average award:* Freshmen: $14,475; Undergraduates: $13,497. *Scholarships, grants, and awards:* Federal Pell, FSEOG, state, private, college/university gift aid from institutional funds.

GIFT AID (NON-NEED-BASED) *Total amount:* $198,596 (54% institutional, 46% external sources). *Receiving aid:* Freshmen: 42% (84). Undergraduates: 31% (243). *Average award:* Undergraduates: $1899. *Scholarships, grants, and awards by category: Academic interests/achievement:* general academic interests/achievements. *Creative arts/performance:* art/fine arts, theater/drama. *Special characteristics:* children and siblings of alumni, local/state students, siblings of current students. *Tuition waivers:* Full or partial for children of alumni, employees or children of employees, senior citizens. *ROTC:* Army cooperative, Naval cooperative, Air Force cooperative.

LOANS *Student loans:* $4,615,185 (62% need-based, 38% non-need-based). 70% of past graduating class borrowed through all loan programs. *Average indebtedness per student:* $32,728. *Parent loans:* $1,373,288 (100% non-need-based). *Programs:* Federal Direct (Subsidized and Unsubsidized Stafford, PLUS), Perkins, college/university.

WORK-STUDY *Federal work-study:* Total amount: $422,390; jobs available. *State or other work-study/employment:* Total amount: $119,000 (100% need-based). Part-time jobs available.

ATHLETIC AWARDS Total amount: $3,505,795 (100% need-based).

APPLYING FOR FINANCIAL AID *Required financial aid forms:* FAFSA, institution's own form. *Financial aid deadline (priority):* 3/1. *Notification date:* Continuous beginning 3/15. Students must reply within 2 weeks of notification.

CONTACT Deana Ready, Director of Student Financial Services, William Woods University, One University Avenue, Fulton, MO 65251, 573-592-4236 or toll-free 800-995-3159 Ext. 4221. *Fax:* 573-592-1180. *E-mail:* deana.ready@williamwoods.edu. *Website:* http://www.williamwoods.edu/.

WILMINGTON COLLEGE
Wilmington, OH

CONTACT Donna Barton, Coordinator of Financial Aid, Wilmington College, Pyle Center Box 1184, Wilmington, OH 45177, 937-382-6661 Ext. 466 or toll-free 800-341-9318. *Fax:* 937-383-8564. *Website:* http://www.wilmington.edu/.

WILMINGTON UNIVERSITY
New Castle, DE

CONTACT J. Lynn Iocono, Director of Financial Aid, Wilmington University, 320 DuPont Highway, New Castle, DE 19720, 302-328-9437 or toll-free 877-967-5464. *Fax:* 302-328-5902. *Website:* http://www.wilmu.edu/.

WILSON COLLEGE
Chambersburg, PA

Tuition & fees: $24,452	Average undergraduate aid package: $21,720

ABOUT THE INSTITUTION Independent Presbyterian Church (U.S.A.), coed, primarily women. *Awards:* associate, bachelor's, and master's degrees. 23 undergraduate majors. *Total enrollment:* 662. Undergraduates: 571. Freshmen: 70. Federal methodology is used as a basis for awarding need-based institutional aid.

UNDERGRADUATE EXPENSES for 2017–2018 *Comprehensive fee:* $35,816 includes full-time tuition ($23,745), mandatory fees ($707), and room and board ($11,364). *College room only:* $5390. Full-time tuition and fees vary according to location and program. Room and board charges vary according to board plan and housing facility. *Part-time tuition:* $792 per semester hour. *Part-time fees:* $40 per semester hour. Part-time tuition and fees vary according to course load, location, and program.

FRESHMAN FINANCIAL AID (Fall 2017, est.) 146 applied for aid; of those 92% were deemed to have need. 100% of freshmen with need received aid; of those 7% had need fully met. *Average percent of need met:* 73% (excluding resources awarded to replace EFC). *Average financial aid package:* $20,606 (excluding resources awarded to replace EFC). 7% of all full-time freshmen had no need and received non-need-based gift aid.

UNDERGRADUATE FINANCIAL AID (Fall 2017, est.) 542 applied for aid; of those 98% were deemed to have need. 100% of undergraduates with need received aid; of those 15% had need fully met. *Average percent of need met:* 75% (excluding resources awarded to replace EFC). *Average financial aid package:* $21,720 (excluding resources awarded to replace EFC). 5% of all full-time undergraduates had no need and received non-need-based gift aid.

GIFT AID (NEED-BASED) *Total amount:* $8,434,314 (14% federal, 11% state, 70% institutional, 5% external sources). *Receiving aid:* Freshmen: 82% (134); all full-time undergraduates: 83% (467). *Average award:* Freshmen: $10,244; Undergraduates: $11,457. *Scholarships, grants, and awards:* Federal Pell, FSEOG, state, private, college/university gift aid from institutional funds.

GIFT AID (NON-NEED-BASED) *Receiving aid:* Freshmen: 72% (118). Undergraduates: 61% (348). *Average award:* Freshmen: $10,083. Undergraduates: $8240. *Scholarships, grants, and awards by category:* Academic interests/achievement: biological sciences, business, communication, computer science, education, English, foreign languages, general academic interests/achievements, humanities, international studies, mathematics, physical sciences, premedicine, religion/biblical studies, social sciences. *Creative arts/performance:* music. *Special achievements/activities:* community service, general special achievements/activities, leadership. *Special characteristics:* adult students, children and siblings of alumni, children of current students, children of faculty/staff, international students, local/state students, relatives of clergy, religious affiliation, veterans, veterans' children. *Tuition waivers:* Full or partial for employees or children of employees. *ROTC:* Army cooperative.

LOANS *Student loans:* $5,476,346 (100% need-based). 84% of past graduating class borrowed through all loan programs. *Average indebtedness per student:* $40,623. *Average need-based loan:* Freshmen: $4608. Undergraduates: $4946. *Parent loans:* $1,901,605 (100% need-based). *Programs:* Federal Direct (Subsidized and Unsubsidized Stafford, PLUS), college/university.

WORK-STUDY *Federal work-study:* Total amount: $54,840; jobs available. *State or other work-study/employment:* Total amount: $80,937 (100% need-based). Part-time jobs available.

APPLYING FOR FINANCIAL AID *Required financial aid form:* FAFSA. *Financial aid deadline (priority):* 4/30. *Notification date:* Continuous beginning 11/15.

CONTACT Ms. Linda Brittain, Dean of Financial Aid/Senior Enrollment Associate, Wilson College, 1015 Philadelphia Avenue, Chambersburg, PA 17201-1285, 717-264-3787 or toll-free 800-421-8402. *Fax:* 717-262-2530. *E-mail:* finaid@wilson.edu. *Website:* http://www.wilson.edu/.

WINGATE UNIVERSITY
Wingate, NC

ABOUT THE INSTITUTION Independent Baptist, coed. *Awards:* certificates, bachelor's, master's, and doctoral degrees. 39 undergraduate majors. *Total enrollment:* 3,193. Undergraduates: 2,084. Freshmen: 625.

GIFT AID (NEED-BASED) *Scholarships, grants, and awards:* Federal Pell, FSEOG, state, private, college/university gift aid from institutional funds.

GIFT AID (NON-NEED-BASED) *Scholarships, grants, and awards by category:* Academic interests/achievement: general academic interests/achievements. Creative arts/performance: art/fine arts, music, theater/drama. *Special characteristics:* children and siblings of alumni, relatives of clergy.

LOANS *Programs:* Federal Direct (Subsidized and Unsubsidized Stafford, PLUS).

APPLYING FOR FINANCIAL AID *Required financial aid forms:* FAFSA, state aid form.

CONTACT Teresa G. Williams, Director of Student Financial Planning, Wingate University, Campus Box 3001, Wingate, NC 28174, 704-233-8209 or toll-free 800-755-5550. *Fax:* 704-233-9396. *E-mail:* tgwilliam@wingate.edu. *Website:* http://www.wingate.edu/.

WINONA STATE UNIVERSITY
Winona, MN

Tuition & fees (MN res): $9379	Average undergraduate aid package: $7250

ABOUT THE INSTITUTION State-supported, coed. *Awards:* certificates, associate, bachelor's, master's, and doctoral degrees. 66 undergraduate majors. *Total enrollment:* 7,953. Undergraduates: 7,437. Freshmen: 1,610. Federal methodology is used as a basis for awarding need-based institutional aid.

UNDERGRADUATE EXPENSES for 2017–2018 *Application fee:* $20. *Tuition, state resident:* full-time $7377; part-time $243.98 per credit hour. *Tuition, nonresident:* full-time $13,300; part-time $442.95 per credit hour. *Required fees:* full-time $2002; $38.99 per credit hour or $485 per term. Full-time tuition and fees vary according to location, program, and reciprocity agreements. Part-time tuition and fees vary according to course load, location, program, and reciprocity agreements. *College room and board:* $8730. Room and board charges vary according to board plan, housing facility, and location.

FRESHMAN FINANCIAL AID (Fall 2016) 1,417 applied for aid; of those 70% were deemed to have need. 98% of freshmen with need received aid; of those 11% had need fully met. *Average percent of need met:* 54% (excluding resources awarded to replace EFC). *Average financial aid package:* $6613 (excluding resources awarded to replace EFC). 20% of all full-time freshmen had no need and received non-need-based gift aid.

UNDERGRADUATE FINANCIAL AID (Fall 2016) 5,306 applied for aid; of those 73% were deemed to have need. 98% of undergraduates with need received aid; of those 12% had need fully met. *Average percent of need met:* 53% (excluding resources awarded to replace EFC). *Average financial aid package:* $7250 (excluding resources awarded to replace EFC). 13% of all full-time undergraduates had no need and received non-need-based gift aid.

GIFT AID (NEED-BASED) *Total amount:* $15,780,364 (52% federal, 28% state, 13% institutional, 7% external sources). *Receiving aid:* Freshmen: 46% (719); all full-time undergraduates: 40% (2,651). *Average award:* Freshmen: $5165; Undergraduates: $5581. *Scholarships, grants, and awards:* Federal Pell, FSEOG, state, private, college/university gift aid from institutional funds.

GIFT AID (NON-NEED-BASED) *Total amount:* $4,147,349 (9% federal, 53% institutional, 38% external sources). *Receiving aid:* Freshmen: 13% (200). Undergraduates: 7% (464). *Average award:* Freshmen: $1500. Undergraduates: $1900. *Scholarships, grants, and awards by category:* Academic interests/achievement: 1,541 awards ($2,321,127 total): general academic interests/achievements. Creative arts/performance: 101 awards ($129,850 total): art/fine arts, debating, music, theater/drama. Special characteristics: 312 awards ($1,668,989 total): children and siblings of alumni, children of faculty/staff, local/state students, members of minority groups, out-of-state students. *Tuition waivers:* Full or partial for employees or children of employees. *ROTC:* Army cooperative.

LOANS *Student loans:* $42,856,280 (57% need-based, 43% non-need-based). 76% of past graduating class borrowed through all loan programs. *Average indebtedness per student:* $33,873. *Average need-based loan:* Freshmen: $3500. Undergraduates: $4152. *Parent loans:* $4,008,886 (26% need-based, 74% non-need-based). *Programs:* Federal Direct (Subsidized and Unsubsidized Stafford, PLUS), Perkins, state, college/university.

WORK-STUDY *Federal work-study:* 284 jobs averaging $2750. *State or other work-study/employment:* Total amount: $839,133 (100% need-based). 521 part-time jobs averaging $1750.

ATHLETIC AWARDS Total amount: $1,039,217 (33% need-based, 67% non-need-based).

APPLYING FOR FINANCIAL AID *Required financial aid form:* FAFSA. *Financial aid deadline:* Continuous. *Notification date:* Continuous beginning 4/1. Students must reply within 3 weeks of notification.

CONTACT Mari Livingston, Associate Director of Financial Aid, Winona State University, PO Box 5838, Winona, MN 55987-5838, 507-457-5090 Ext. 2398 or toll-free 800-DIAL WSU.
Website: http://www.winona.edu/.

WINSTON-SALEM STATE UNIVERSITY
Winston-Salem, NC

CONTACT Raymond Solomon, Director of Financial Aid Office, Winston-Salem State University, 601 Martin Luther King Jr. Drive, PO Box 19524, Winston-Salem, NC 27110-0003, 336-750-3299 or toll-free 800-257-4052. *Fax:* 336-750-3297.
Website: http://www.wssu.edu/.

WINTHROP UNIVERSITY
Rock Hill, SC

Tuition & fees (SC res): $15,350	Average undergraduate aid package: $13,569

ABOUT THE INSTITUTION State-supported, coed. *Awards:* certificates, bachelor's, and master's degrees. 28 undergraduate majors. *Total enrollment:* 6,073. Undergraduates: 5,014. Freshmen: 1,050. Federal methodology is used as a basis for awarding need-based institutional aid.

UNDERGRADUATE EXPENSES for 2017–2018 *Application fee:* $40. *Tuition, state resident:* full-time $14,870; part-time $620 per credit hour. *Tuition, nonresident:* full-time $28,786; part-time $1200 per credit hour. *Required fees:* full-time $480. Full-time tuition and fees vary according to degree level, reciprocity agreements, and student level. Part-time tuition and fees vary according to degree level and student level. *College room and board:* $8740; *Room only:* $5290. Room and board charges vary according to board plan and housing facility.

FRESHMAN FINANCIAL AID (Fall 2017, est.) 975 applied for aid; of those 85% were deemed to have need. 100% of freshmen with need received aid; of those 14% had need fully met. *Average percent of need met:* 60% (excluding resources awarded to replace EFC). *Average financial aid package:* $14,033 (excluding resources awarded to replace EFC). 13% of all full-time freshmen had no need and received non-need-based gift aid.

UNDERGRADUATE FINANCIAL AID (Fall 2017, est.) 3,884 applied for aid; of those 87% were deemed to have need. 100% of undergraduates with need received aid; of those 13% had need fully met. *Average percent of need met:* 57% (excluding resources awarded to replace EFC). *Average financial aid package:* $13,569 (excluding resources awarded to replace EFC). 13% of all full-time undergraduates had no need and received non-need-based gift aid.

GIFT AID (NEED-BASED) *Total amount:* $30,512,341 (32% federal, 35% state, 30% institutional, 3% external sources). *Receiving aid:* Freshmen: 79% (826); all full-time undergraduates: 69% (3,112). *Average award:* Freshmen: $10,360; Undergraduates: $9187. *Scholarships, grants, and awards:* Federal Pell, FSEOG, state, private, college/university gift aid from institutional funds, TEACH Grants.

GIFT AID (NON-NEED-BASED) *Total amount:* $10,203,530 (43% state, 53% institutional, 4% external sources). *Receiving aid:* Freshmen: 9% (92). Undergraduates: 8% (355). *Average award:* Freshmen: $4948. Undergraduates: $4788. *Scholarships, grants, and awards by category:* Academic interests/achievement: general academic interests/achievements. Creative arts/performance: art/fine arts, dance, music, performing arts, theater/drama. Special characteristics: children of faculty/staff. *Tuition waivers:* Full or partial for employees or children of employees, senior citizens. *ROTC:* Army cooperative, Air Force cooperative.

LOANS *Student loans:* $29,126,478 (75% need-based, 25% non-need-based). 74% of past graduating class borrowed through all loan programs. *Average indebtedness per student:* $36,147. *Average need-based loan:* Freshmen: $3377. Undergraduates: $4348. *Parent loans:* $9,309,535 (61% need-based, 39% non-need-based). *Programs:* Federal Direct (Subsidized and Unsubsidized Stafford, PLUS), Perkins, private loans.

WORK-STUDY *Federal work-study:* Total amount: $294,028; 148 jobs averaging $1987.

ATHLETIC AWARDS Total amount: $2,398,770 (30% need-based, 70% non-need-based).

APPLYING FOR FINANCIAL AID *Required financial aid form:* FAFSA. *Financial aid deadline (priority):* 2/1. *Notification date:* Continuous beginning 3/15.

CONTACT Michelle K. Hare, Director of Financial Aid, Winthrop University, Sykes House, 638 Oakland Avenue, Rock Hill, SC 29733, 803-323-2189 or toll-free 800-763-0230. *Fax:* 803-323-2557. *E-mail:* finaid@winthrop.edu.
Website: http://www.winthrop.edu/.

WISCONSIN LUTHERAN COLLEGE
Milwaukee, WI

Tuition & fees: $29,725	Average undergraduate aid package: $22,824

ABOUT THE INSTITUTION Independent Wisconsin Evangelical Lutheran Synod, coed. *Awards:* bachelor's and master's degrees. 42 undergraduate majors. *Total enrollment:* 1,114. Undergraduates: 992. Freshmen: 232. Federal methodology is used as a basis for awarding need-based institutional aid.

UNDERGRADUATE EXPENSES for 2018–2019 *Comprehensive fee:* $39,915 includes full-time tuition ($29,410), mandatory fees ($315), and room and board ($10,190). Room and board charges vary according to board plan and housing facility. *Part-time tuition:* $765 per credit hour.

FRESHMAN FINANCIAL AID (Fall 2017, est.) 220 applied for aid; of those 88% were deemed to have need. 100% of freshmen with need received aid; of those 17% had need fully met. *Average percent of need met:* 81% (excluding resources awarded to replace EFC). *Average financial aid package:* $24,748 (excluding resources awarded to replace EFC). 16% of all full-time freshmen had no need and received non-need-based gift aid.

UNDERGRADUATE FINANCIAL AID (Fall 2017, est.) 829 applied for aid; of those 91% were deemed to have need. 100% of undergraduates with need received aid; of those 18% had need fully met. *Average percent of need met:* 80% (excluding resources awarded to replace EFC). *Average financial aid package:*

$22,824 (excluding resources awarded to replace EFC). 16% of all full-time undergraduates had no need and received non-need-based gift aid.

GIFT AID (NEED-BASED) *Total amount:* $13,583,231 (10% federal, 6% state, 81% institutional, 3% external sources). *Receiving aid:* Freshmen: 84% (194); all full-time undergraduates: 80% (740). *Average award:* Freshmen: $20,899; Undergraduates: $18,668. *Scholarships, grants, and awards:* Federal Pell, FSEOG, state, private, college/university gift aid from institutional funds.

GIFT AID (NON-NEED-BASED) *Total amount:* $2,237,232 (1% state, 91% institutional, 8% external sources). *Receiving aid:* Freshmen: 10% (23). Undergraduates: 9% (79). *Average award:* Freshmen: $14,376. Undergraduates: $11,730. *Scholarships, grants, and awards by category:* Academic interests/achievement: 879 awards ($8,975,225 total): biological sciences, business, communication, education, foreign languages, general academic interests/achievements, home economics, mathematics, physical sciences. *Creative arts/performance:* 77 awards ($96,475 total): art/fine arts, cinema/film/broadcasting, general creative arts/performance, music, theater/drama. *Special achievements/activities:* 20 awards ($39,050 total): community service, general special achievements/activities, leadership. *Special characteristics:* 764 awards ($1,451,120 total): children of faculty/staff, general special characteristics, international students, religious affiliation, veterans, veterans' children. *Tuition waivers:* Full or partial for employees or children of employees. *ROTC:* Air Force cooperative.

LOANS *Student loans:* $6,950,355 (69% need-based, 31% non-need-based). 87% of past graduating class borrowed through all loan programs. *Average indebtedness per student:* $32,549. *Average need-based loan:* Freshmen: $3185. Undergraduates: $4135. *Parent loans:* $1,636,377 (34% need-based, 66% non-need-based). *Programs:* Federal Direct (Subsidized and Unsubsidized Stafford, PLUS), state, private loans.

WORK-STUDY *Federal work-study:* Total amount: $214,387; 76 jobs averaging $2239. *State or other work-study/employment:* Total amount: $542,167 (78% need-based, 22% non-need-based). 341 part-time jobs averaging $2133.

APPLYING FOR FINANCIAL AID *Required financial aid forms:* FAFSA, institution's own form. *Financial aid deadline (priority):* 12/1. *Notification date:* Continuous beginning 12/1. Students must reply within 4 weeks of notification.

CONTACT Mrs. Linda Loeffel, Director of Financial Aid, Wisconsin Lutheran College, 8800 West Bluemound Road, Milwaukee, WI 53226-4699, 414-443-8856. *Fax:* 414-443-8514. *E-mail:* financial.aid@wlc.edu.
Website: http://www.wlc.edu/.

WITTENBERG UNIVERSITY
Springfield, OH

Tuition & fees: $39,500	Average undergraduate aid package: $32,409

ABOUT THE INSTITUTION Independent Evangelical Lutheran Church, coed. *Awards:* bachelor's and master's degrees. 45 undergraduate majors. *Total enrollment:* 1,884. Undergraduates: 1,857. Freshmen: 539. Federal methodology is used as a basis for awarding need-based institutional aid.

UNDERGRADUATE EXPENSES for 2018–2019 *Application fee:* $40. *Comprehensive fee:* $49,856 includes full-time tuition ($38,680), mandatory fees ($820), and room and board ($10,356). *College room only:* $5288. Room and board charges vary according to board plan and housing facility. *Part-time tuition:* $1289 per credit hour. Part-time tuition and fees vary according to course load.

FRESHMAN FINANCIAL AID (Fall 2017, est.) 528 applied for aid; of those 90% were deemed to have need. 100% of freshmen with need received aid; of those 27% had need fully met. *Average percent of need met:* 84% (excluding resources awarded to replace EFC). *Average financial aid package:* $34,185 (excluding resources awarded to replace EFC). 12% of all full-time freshmen had no need and received non-need-based gift aid.

UNDERGRADUATE FINANCIAL AID (Fall 2017, est.) 1,652 applied for aid; of those 88% were deemed to have need. 100% of undergraduates with need received aid; of those 27% had need fully met. *Average percent of need met:* 83% (excluding resources awarded to replace EFC). *Average financial aid package:* $32,409 (excluding resources awarded to replace EFC). 18% of all full-time undergraduates had no need and received non-need-based gift aid.

GIFT AID (NEED-BASED) *Total amount:* $37,958,944 (8% federal, 3% state, 87% institutional, 2% external sources). *Receiving aid:* Freshmen: 88% (473); all full-time undergraduates: 80% (1,427). *Average award:* Freshmen: $28,991; Undergrad-

uates: $26,551. *Scholarships, grants, and awards:* Federal Pell, FSEOG, state, private, college/university gift aid from institutional funds, United Negro College Fund.

GIFT AID (NON-NEED-BASED) *Total amount:* $6,822,406 (1% federal, 96% institutional, 3% external sources). *Average award:* Freshmen: $22,667. Undergraduates: $20,649. *Scholarships, grants, and awards by category:* Academic interests/achievement: general academic interests/achievements. *Creative arts/performance:* art/fine arts, dance, music, theater/drama. *Special achievements/activities:* community service, general special achievements/activities, leadership. *Special characteristics:* adult students, children and siblings of alumni, children of faculty/staff, ethnic background, international students, members of minority groups, relatives of clergy, religious affiliation. *Tuition waivers:* Full or partial for minority students, children of alumni, employees or children of employees, adult students, senior citizens. *ROTC:* Army cooperative, Air Force cooperative.

LOANS *Student loans:* $14,015,779 (90% need-based, 10% non-need-based). 74% of past graduating class borrowed through all loan programs. *Average indebtedness per student:* $35,242. *Average need-based loan:* Freshmen: $3417. Undergraduates: $4444. *Parent loans:* $5,657,822 (94% need-based, 6% non-need-based). *Programs:* Federal Direct (Subsidized and Unsubsidized Stafford, PLUS), Perkins, college/university.

WORK-STUDY *Federal work-study:* Total amount: $1,157,548; jobs available. *State or other work-study/employment:* Total amount: $1,181,972 (70% need-based, 30% non-need-based). Part-time jobs available.

APPLYING FOR FINANCIAL AID *Required financial aid form:* FAFSA. *Financial aid deadline (priority):* 3/1. *Notification date:* Continuous beginning 3/1. Students must reply by 5/1.

CONTACT Mr. J. Randy Green, Executive Director of Financial Aid, Wittenberg University, PO Box 720, Springfield, OH 45501-0720, 937-327-7321 or toll-free 800-677-7558 Ext. 6314. *Fax:* 937-327-6379. *E-mail:* jgreen@wittenberg.edu. *Website:* http://www.wittenberg.edu/.

WOFFORD COLLEGE
Spartanburg, SC

Tuition & fees: $43,865	Average undergraduate aid package: $36,140

ABOUT THE INSTITUTION Independent United Methodist Church, coed. *Awards:* bachelor's degrees. 26 undergraduate majors. *Total enrollment:* 1,592. Undergraduates: 1,592. Freshmen: 452. Federal methodology is used as a basis for awarding need-based institutional aid.

UNDERGRADUATE EXPENSES for 2018–2019 *Application fee:* $35. *Comprehensive fee:* $56,550 includes full-time tuition ($42,355), mandatory fees ($1510), and room and board ($12,685).

FRESHMAN FINANCIAL AID (Fall 2017, est.) 381 applied for aid; of those 74% were deemed to have need. 100% of freshmen with need received aid; of those 47% had need fully met. *Average percent of need met:* 86% (excluding resources awarded to replace EFC). *Average financial aid package:* $37,760 (excluding resources awarded to replace EFC). 26% of all full-time freshmen had no need and received non-need-based gift aid.

UNDERGRADUATE FINANCIAL AID (Fall 2017, est.) 1,203 applied for aid; of those 82% were deemed to have need. 100% of undergraduates with need received aid; of those 39% had need fully met. *Average percent of need met:* 82% (excluding resources awarded to replace EFC). *Average financial aid package:* $36,140 (excluding resources awarded to replace EFC). 28% of all full-time undergraduates had no need and received non-need-based gift aid.

GIFT AID (NEED-BASED) *Total amount:* $26,326,095 (5% federal, 17% state, 75% institutional, 3% external sources). *Receiving aid:* Freshmen: 63% (283); all full-time undergraduates: 63% (988). *Average award:* Freshmen: $32,581; Undergraduates: $32,355. *Scholarships, grants, and awards:* Federal Pell, FSEOG, state, private, college/university gift aid from institutional funds.

GIFT AID (NON-NEED-BASED) *Total amount:* $12,598,101 (16% state, 72% institutional, 12% external sources). *Receiving aid:* Freshmen: 25% (114). Undergraduates: 19% (303). *Average award:* Freshmen: $17,949. Undergraduates: $17,161. *Scholarships, grants, and awards by category:* Academic interests/achievement: general academic interests/achievements. *Creative arts/performance:* art/fine arts, music. *Special achievements/activities:* leadership. *Special characteristics:* children of faculty/staff, general special characteristics, local/state students, members of minority groups, relatives of clergy. *Tuition waivers:* Full or partial for employees or children of employees. *ROTC:* Army.

LOANS *Student loans:* $7,226,372 (60% need-based, 40% non-need-based). 50% of past graduating class borrowed through all loan programs. *Average indebtedness per student:* $32,043. *Average need-based loan:* Freshmen: $3342. Undergraduates: $4410. *Parent loans:* $2,829,788 (48% need-based, 52% non-need-based). *Programs:* Federal Direct (Subsidized and Unsubsidized Stafford, PLUS), Perkins.

WORK-STUDY *Federal work-study:* Total amount: $206,740; jobs available.

ATHLETIC AWARDS Total amount: $8,600,006 (39% need-based, 61% non-need-based).

APPLYING FOR FINANCIAL AID *Required financial aid form:* FAFSA. *Financial aid deadline (priority):* 3/1. *Notification date:* Continuous beginning 3/15. Students must reply by 5/1.

CONTACT Carolyn B. Sparks, Director of Financial Aid, Wofford College, 429 North Church Street, Spartanburg, SC 29303-3663, 864-597-4160. *Fax:* 864-597-4149. *E-mail:* finaid@wofford.edu.

Website: http://www.wofford.edu/.

WOODBURY UNIVERSITY
Burbank, CA

ABOUT THE INSTITUTION Independent, coed. *Awards:* bachelor's and master's degrees. 19 undergraduate majors. *Total enrollment:* 1,160. Undergraduates: 1,024. Freshmen: 116.

GIFT AID (NEED-BASED) *Scholarships, grants, and awards:* Federal Pell, FSEOG, state, private, college/university gift aid from institutional funds.

GIFT AID (NON-NEED-BASED) *Scholarships, grants, and awards by category: Academic interests/achievement:* architecture, business, general academic interests/achievements.

LOANS *Programs:* Federal Direct (Subsidized and Unsubsidized Stafford, PLUS), Perkins, alternative loans.

WORK-STUDY *Federal work-study:* jobs available.

APPLYING FOR FINANCIAL AID *Required financial aid forms:* FAFSA, institution's own form, CSS Financial Aid PROFILE.

CONTACT Celeastia Williams, Director of Enrollment Services, Woodbury University, 7500 Glenoaks Boulevard, Burbank, CA 91510, 818-767-0888 Ext. 273 or toll-free 800-784-WOOD. *Fax:* 818-767-4816.

Website: http://www.woodbury.edu/.

WORCESTER POLYTECHNIC INSTITUTE
Worcester, MA

Tuition & fees: $48,628	Average undergraduate aid package: $35,614

ABOUT THE INSTITUTION Independent, coed. *Awards:* certificates, bachelor's, master's, and doctoral degrees. 32 undergraduate majors. *Total enrollment:* 6,642. Undergraduates: 4,435. Freshmen: 1,124. Both federal and institutional methodology are used as a basis for awarding need-based institutional aid.

UNDERGRADUATE EXPENSES for 2017–2018 *Application fee:* $65. *One-time required fee:* $200. *Comprehensive fee:* $62,846 includes full-time tuition ($47,988), mandatory fees ($640), and room and board ($14,218). *College room only:* $8122. Room and board charges vary according to board plan and housing facility. *Part-time tuition:* $1333 per credit hour. Part-time tuition and fees vary according to course load. *Payment plan:* Tuition prepayment.

FRESHMAN FINANCIAL AID (Fall 2016) 943 applied for aid; of those 79% were deemed to have need. 100% of freshmen with need received aid; of those 58% had need fully met. *Average percent of need met:* 80% (excluding resources awarded to replace EFC). *Average financial aid package:* $34,841 (excluding resources awarded to replace EFC). 31% of all full-time freshmen had no need and received non-need-based gift aid.

UNDERGRADUATE FINANCIAL AID (Fall 2016) 3,136 applied for aid; of those 85% were deemed to have need. 99% of undergraduates with need received aid; of those 47% had need fully met. *Average percent of need met:* 81% (excluding resources awarded to replace EFC). *Average financial aid package:* $35,614 (excluding resources awarded to replace EFC). 35% of all full-time undergraduates had no need and received non-need-based gift aid.

GIFT AID (NEED-BASED) *Total amount:* $62,143,136 (5% federal, 1% state, 88% institutional, 6% external sources). *Receiving aid:* Freshmen: 66% (737); all full-time undergraduates: 62% (2,598). *Average award:* Freshmen: $22,795; Undergraduates: $22,942. *Scholarships, grants, and awards:* Federal Pell, FSEOG, state, private, college/university gift aid from institutional funds.

GIFT AID (NON-NEED-BASED) *Total amount:* $28,243,855 (82% institutional, 18% external sources). *Receiving aid:* Freshmen: 18% (203). Undergraduates: 18% (765). *Average award:* Freshmen: $12,797. Undergraduates: $15,800. *Scholarships, grants, and awards by category: Academic interests/achievement:* 4,420 awards ($50,285,084 total): general academic interests/achievements. *Special achievements/activities:* leadership. *Special characteristics:* 25 awards ($150,050 total): children of workers in trades. *Tuition waivers:* Full or partial for employees or children of employees. *ROTC:* Army, Naval cooperative, Air Force.

LOANS *Student loans:* $30,193,577 (38% need-based, 62% non-need-based). *Average need-based loan:* Freshmen: $1931. Undergraduates: $2267. *Parent loans:* $11,016,907 (100% non-need-based). *Programs:* Federal Direct (Subsidized and Unsubsidized Stafford, PLUS), Perkins, state, college/university.

WORK-STUDY *Federal work-study:* 466 jobs averaging $1503.

APPLYING FOR FINANCIAL AID *Required financial aid forms:* FAFSA, CSS Financial Aid PROFILE, noncustodial (divorced/separated) parent's statement. *Financial aid deadline:* 2/1. *Notification date:* 4/1. Students must reply by 5/1.

CONTACT Monica Blondin, Executive Director of Student Aid and Financial Literacy, Worcester Polytechnic Institute, 100 Institute Road, Worcester, MA 01609-2280, 508-831-5469. *Fax:* 508-831-5039. *E-mail:* finaid@wpi.edu.

Website: http://www.wpi.edu/.

WORCESTER STATE UNIVERSITY
Worcester, MA

Tuition & fees (MA res): $9532	Average undergraduate aid package: $14,842

ABOUT THE INSTITUTION State-supported, coed. *Awards:* certificates, bachelor's, and master's degrees. 30 undergraduate majors. *Total enrollment:* 6,434. Undergraduates: 5,495. Freshmen: 909. Federal methodology is used as a basis for awarding need-based institutional aid.

UNDERGRADUATE EXPENSES for 2017–2018 *Application fee:* $50. *Tuition, state resident:* full-time $970; part-time $40.42 per credit hour. *Tuition, nonresident:* full-time $7050; part-time $293.75 per credit hour. *Required fees:* full-time $8562; $356.75 per credit hour. Full-time tuition and fees vary according to class time, course load, degree level, and reciprocity agreements. Part-time tuition and fees vary according to class time, course load, degree level, and reciprocity agreements. *College room and board:* $12,006; *Room only:* $8256. Room and board charges vary according to board plan and housing facility.

FRESHMAN FINANCIAL AID (Fall 2016) 740 applied for aid; of those 70% were deemed to have need. 98% of freshmen with need received aid; of those 36% had need fully met. *Average percent of need met:* 77% (excluding resources awarded to replace EFC). *Average financial aid package:* $16,144 (excluding resources awarded to replace EFC). 2% of all full-time freshmen had no need and received non-need-based gift aid.

UNDERGRADUATE FINANCIAL AID (Fall 2016) 3,433 applied for aid; of those 72% were deemed to have need. 97% of undergraduates with need received aid; of those 40% had need fully met. *Average percent of need met:* 80% (excluding resources awarded to replace EFC). *Average financial aid package:* $14,842 (excluding resources awarded to replace EFC). 3% of all full-time undergraduates had no need and received non-need-based gift aid.

GIFT AID (NEED-BASED) *Total amount:* $10,545,101 (62% federal, 24% state, 14% institutional). *Receiving aid:* Freshmen: 58% (450); all full-time undergraduates: 50% (1,992). *Average award:* Freshmen: $5299; Undergraduates: $5116. *Scholarships, grants, and awards:* Federal Pell, state, private, college/university gift aid from institutional funds.

GIFT AID (NON-NEED-BASED) *Total amount:* $2,253,303 (18% state, 52% institutional, 30% external sources). *Receiving aid:* Freshmen: 29% (223). Undergraduates: 22% (879). *Average award:* Freshmen: $3711. Undergraduates: $2659.

Tuition waivers: Full or partial for employees or children of employees, senior citizens. *ROTC:* Army cooperative, Naval cooperative, Air Force cooperative.
LOANS Student loans: $22,661,862 (35% need-based, 65% non-need-based). 76% of past graduating class borrowed through all loan programs. *Average indebtedness per student:* $29,137. *Average need-based loan:* Freshmen: $2523. Undergraduates: $3082. *Parent loans:* $3,125,886 (100% non-need-based). *Programs:* Federal Direct (Subsidized and Unsubsidized Stafford, PLUS), Perkins, Federal Nursing, state, college/university.
WORK-STUDY *Federal work-study:* jobs available.
APPLYING FOR FINANCIAL AID *Required financial aid form:* FAFSA. *Financial aid deadline:* 5/1 (priority: 3/1). *Notification date:* Continuous beginning 12/15. Students must reply within 3 weeks of notification.
CONTACT Ms. Jayne McGinn, Director of Financial Aid, Worcester State University, 486 Chandler Street, Worcester, MA 01602, 508-929-8058. *Fax:* 508-929-8194. *E-mail:* jayne.mcginn@worcester.edu.
Website: http://www.worcester.edu/.

WORLD MISSION UNIVERSITY
Los Angeles, CA

CONTACT Financial Aid Office, World Mission University, 500 Shatto Place, Suite 600, Los Angeles, CA 90020, 213-385-2322.
Website: http://www.wmu.edu/.

WRIGHT STATE UNIVERSITY
Dayton, OH

Tuition & fees (OH res): $8730	Average undergraduate aid package: $10,526

ABOUT THE INSTITUTION State-supported, coed. *Awards:* certificates, bachelor's, master's, and doctoral degrees. 81 undergraduate majors. *Total enrollment:* 15,957. Undergraduates: 12,115. Freshmen: 2,281. Federal methodology is used as a basis for awarding need-based institutional aid.
UNDERGRADUATE EXPENSES for 2017–2018 *Application fee:* $30. *Tuition, state resident:* full-time $8730; part-time $394 per credit hour. *Tuition, nonresident:* full-time $17,608; part-time $803 per credit hour. Full-time tuition and fees vary according to course load, location, and reciprocity agreements. Part-time tuition and fees vary according to course load, location, and reciprocity agreements. *College room and board:* $11,376; *Room only:* $6380. Room and board charges vary according to board plan, housing facility, and location.
FRESHMAN FINANCIAL AID (Fall 2017, est.) 1,974 applied for aid; of those 77% were deemed to have need. 99% of freshmen with need received aid; of those 21% had need fully met. *Average percent of need met:* 63% (excluding resources awarded to replace EFC). *Average financial aid package:* $9870 (excluding resources awarded to replace EFC). 16% of all full-time freshmen had no need and received non-need-based gift aid.
UNDERGRADUATE FINANCIAL AID (Fall 2017, est.) 7,246 applied for aid; of those 81% were deemed to have need. 98% of undergraduates with need received aid; of those 17% had need fully met. *Average percent of need met:* 62% (excluding resources awarded to replace EFC). *Average financial aid package:* $10,526 (excluding resources awarded to replace EFC). 18% of all full-time undergraduates had no need and received non-need-based gift aid.
GIFT AID (NEED-BASED) *Total amount:* $36,637,444 (53% federal, 16% state, 27% institutional, 4% external sources). *Receiving aid:* Freshmen: 58% (1,289); all full-time undergraduates: 53% (4,950). *Average award:* Freshmen: $6532; Undergraduates: $6586. *Scholarships, grants, and awards:* Federal Pell, FSEOG, state, private, college/university gift aid from institutional funds, United Negro College Fund, Federal Nursing, Choose Ohio First scholarships.
GIFT AID (NON-NEED-BASED) *Total amount:* $11,355,368 (15% state, 77% institutional, 8% external sources). *Receiving aid:* Freshmen: 8% (176). Undergraduates: 5% (504). *Average award:* Freshmen: $4413. Undergraduates: $4185. *Scholarships, grants, and awards by category:* Academic interests/achievement: area/ethnic studies, biological sciences, business, communication, computer science, education, engineering/technologies, English, foreign languages, general academic interests/achievements, home economics, humanities, international studies, mathematics, military science, physical sciences, premedicine, religion/biblical studies, social

sciences. *Creative arts/performance:* applied art and design, art/fine arts, cinema/film/broadcasting, creative writing, dance, general creative arts/performance, music, performing arts, theater/drama. *Special achievements/activities:* cheerleading/drum major, community service, general special achievements/activities, leadership, memberships. *Special characteristics:* adult students, children and siblings of alumni, children of educators, children of faculty/staff, ethnic background, first-generation college students, handicapped students, international students, members of minority groups, out-of-state students. *Tuition waivers:* Full or partial for employees or children of employees, senior citizens. *ROTC:* Army, Air Force.
LOANS Student loans: $63,210,396 (73% need-based, 27% non-need-based). 61% of past graduating class borrowed through all loan programs. *Average indebtedness per student:* $30,677. *Average need-based loan:* Freshmen: $3198. Undergraduates: $4024. *Parent loans:* $5,557,747 (46% need-based, 54% non-need-based). *Programs:* Federal Direct (Subsidized and Unsubsidized Stafford, PLUS), Perkins, Federal Nursing, state, college/university, private loans.
WORK-STUDY *Federal work-study:* Total amount: $3,395,204; jobs available.
ATHLETIC AWARDS Total amount: $2,707,666 (37% need-based, 63% non-need-based).
APPLYING FOR FINANCIAL AID *Required financial aid form:* FAFSA. *Financial aid deadline (priority):* 12/15. *Notification date:* Continuous beginning 1/15.
CONTACT Raider Connect, Wright State University, 130 Student Union, 3640 Colonel Glenn Highway, Dayton, OH 45435, 937-775-1000 or toll-free 800-247-1770. *Fax:* 937-775-4410. *E-mail:* raiderconnect@wright.edu.
Website: http://www.wright.edu/.

WRIGHT STATE UNIVERSITY–LAKE CAMPUS
Celina, OH

Tuition & fees (OH res): $5842	Average undergraduate aid package: $7922

ABOUT THE INSTITUTION State-supported, coed. *Awards:* certificates, associate, and bachelor's degrees. 76 undergraduate majors. *Total enrollment:* 1,037. Undergraduates: 1,037. Freshmen: 242. Federal methodology is used as a basis for awarding need-based institutional aid.
UNDERGRADUATE EXPENSES for 2017–2018 *Application fee:* $30. *Tuition, state resident:* full-time $5842; part-time $265 per credit hour. *Tuition, nonresident:* full-time $14,720; part-time $674 per credit hour. Full-time tuition and fees vary according to course load, location, and reciprocity agreements. Part-time tuition and fees vary according to course load, location, and reciprocity agreements. *College room and board:* $10,584; *Room only:* $4996. Room and board charges vary according to board plan, housing facility, and location.
FRESHMAN FINANCIAL AID (Fall 2017, est.) 200 applied for aid; of those 74% were deemed to have need. 96% of freshmen with need received aid; of those 30% had need fully met. *Average percent of need met:* 72% (excluding resources awarded to replace EFC). *Average financial aid package:* $7143 (excluding resources awarded to replace EFC). 15% of all full-time freshmen had no need and received non-need-based gift aid.
UNDERGRADUATE FINANCIAL AID (Fall 2017, est.) 555 applied for aid; of those 75% were deemed to have need. 97% of undergraduates with need received aid; of those 25% had need fully met. *Average percent of need met:* 69% (excluding resources awarded to replace EFC). *Average financial aid package:* $7922 (excluding resources awarded to replace EFC). 19% of all full-time undergraduates had no need and received non-need-based gift aid.
GIFT AID (NEED-BASED) *Total amount:* $1,767,480 (69% federal, 3% state, 24% institutional, 4% external sources). *Receiving aid:* Freshmen: 52% (119); all full-time undergraduates: 49% (335). *Average award:* Freshmen: $4234; Undergraduates: $4609. *Scholarships, grants, and awards:* Federal Pell, FSEOG, state, private, college/university gift aid from institutional funds, United Negro College Fund, Federal Nursing, Choose Ohio First scholarships.
GIFT AID (NON-NEED-BASED) *Total amount:* $511,573 (5% state, 80% institutional, 15% external sources). *Receiving aid:* Freshmen: 7% (16). Undergraduates: 6% (42). *Average award:* Freshmen: $2336. Undergraduates: $2567. *Scholarships, grants, and awards by category:* Academic interests/achievement: area/ethnic studies, biological sciences, business, communication, computer science, education, engineering/technologies, English, foreign languages, general academic interests/

achievements, home economics, humanities, international studies, mathematics, military science, physical sciences, premedicine, religion/biblical studies, social sciences. *Creative arts/performance:* applied art and design, art/fine arts, cinema/film/broadcasting, creative writing, dance, general creative arts/performance, music, performing arts, theater/drama. *Special achievements/activities:* cheerleading/drum major, community service, general special achievements/activities, leadership, memberships. *Special characteristics:* adult students, children and siblings of alumni, children of educators, children of faculty/staff, ethnic background, first-generation college students, handicapped students, international students, members of minority groups, out-of-state students. *Tuition waivers:* Full or partial for employees or children of employees, senior citizens.
LOANS *Student loans:* $4,136,602 (66% need-based, 34% non-need-based). 42% of past graduating class borrowed through all loan programs. *Average indebtedness per student:* $22,549. *Average need-based loan:* Freshmen: $3181. Undergraduates: $3658. *Parent loans:* $92,868 (27% need-based, 73% non-need-based). *Programs:* Federal Direct (Subsidized and Unsubsidized Stafford, PLUS), Perkins, Federal Nursing, state, college/university, private loans.
WORK-STUDY *Federal work-study:* Total amount: $166,437; jobs available. *State or other work-study/employment:* Part-time jobs available.
APPLYING FOR FINANCIAL AID *Required financial aid form:* FAFSA. *Financial aid deadline (priority):* 12/15. *Notification date:* Continuous beginning 1/15.
CONTACT Amy Barnhart, Assistant Vice President/Director of Financial Aid, Wright State University–Lake Campus, 3640 Colonel Glenn Highway, 216 Medical Sciences Building, Dayton, OH 45435, 937-775-5405 or toll-free 800-237-1477. *E-mail:* amy.barnhart@wright.edu.
Website: http://www.wright.edu/lake/.

XAVIER UNIVERSITY
Cincinnati, OH

Tuition & fees: $37,230	Average undergraduate aid package: $24,513

ABOUT THE INSTITUTION Independent Roman Catholic, coed. 73 undergraduate majors. Federal methodology is used as a basis for awarding need-based institutional aid.
UNDERGRADUATE EXPENSES for 2017–2018 *Comprehensive fee:* $49,380 includes full-time tuition ($37,000), mandatory fees ($230), and room and board ($12,150). *College room only:* $6750. Full-time tuition and fees vary according to course load, location, and program. Room and board charges vary according to board plan and housing facility. *Part-time tuition:* $694 per credit hour. *Part-time fees:* $9 per credit hour. Part-time tuition and fees vary according to course load, location, and program.
FRESHMAN FINANCIAL AID (Fall 2016) 958 applied for aid; of those 75% were deemed to have need. 100% of freshmen with need received aid; of those 11% had need fully met. *Average percent of need met:* 67% (excluding resources awarded to replace EFC). *Average financial aid package:* $24,999 (excluding resources awarded to replace EFC). 21% of all full-time freshmen had no need and received non-need-based gift aid.
UNDERGRADUATE FINANCIAL AID (Fall 2016) 3,011 applied for aid; of those 82% were deemed to have need. 100% of undergraduates with need received aid; of those 7% had need fully met. *Average percent of need met:* 66% (excluding resources awarded to replace EFC). *Average financial aid package:* $24,513 (excluding resources awarded to replace EFC). 12% of all full-time undergraduates had no need and received non-need-based gift aid.
GIFT AID (NEED-BASED) *Total amount:* $32,704,754 (9% federal, 2% state, 88% institutional, 1% external sources). *Receiving aid:* Freshmen: 44% (487); all full-time undergraduates: 37% (1,580). *Average award:* Freshmen: $22,459; Undergraduates: $22,424. *Scholarships, grants, and awards:* Federal Pell, FSEOG, state, private, college/university gift aid from institutional funds.
GIFT AID (NON-NEED-BASED) *Total amount:* $45,894,818 (1% federal, 98% institutional, 1% external sources). *Receiving aid:* Freshmen: 19% (210). Undergraduates: 19% (814). *Average award:* Freshmen: $17,937. Undergraduates: $17,530. *Scholarships, grants, and awards by category:* Academic interests/achievement: foreign languages, general academic interests/achievements, mathematics, military science, physical sciences, social sciences. *Creative arts/performance:* art/fine arts, music, performing arts, theater/drama. *Special characteristics:* children

and siblings of alumni, international students, members of minority groups, siblings of current students. *Tuition waivers:* Full or partial for employees or children of employees, senior citizens.
LOANS *Student loans:* $25,727,173 (58% need-based, 42% non-need-based). 53% of past graduating class borrowed through all loan programs. *Average indebtedness per student:* $10,217. *Average need-based loan:* Freshmen: $3294. Undergraduates: $2082. *Parent loans:* $10,956,509 (46% need-based, 54% non-need-based). *Programs:* Federal Direct (Subsidized and Unsubsidized Stafford, PLUS), Perkins.
WORK-STUDY *Federal work-study:* jobs available. *State or other work-study/employment:* Part-time jobs available.
ATHLETIC AWARDS Total amount: $3,544,367 (10% need-based, 90% non-need-based).
APPLYING FOR FINANCIAL AID *Required financial aid form:* FAFSA. *Financial aid deadline (priority):* 2/15. *Notification date:* Continuous beginning 12/15. Students must reply by 5/1.
CONTACT Office of Financial Aid, Xavier University, 3800 Victory Parkway, Cincinnati, OH 45207-5111, 513-745-3142 or toll-free 877-XUADMIT. *Fax:* 513-745-2806.
Website: http://www.xavier.edu/.

XAVIER UNIVERSITY OF LOUISIANA
New Orleans, LA

ABOUT THE INSTITUTION Independent Roman Catholic, coed. *Awards:* bachelor's, master's, and doctoral degrees. 49 undergraduate majors. *Total enrollment:* 3,044. Undergraduates: 2,293. Freshmen: 716.
GIFT AID (NEED-BASED) *Scholarships, grants, and awards:* Federal Pell, FSEOG, state, private, college/university gift aid from institutional funds, United Negro College Fund.
GIFT AID (NON-NEED-BASED) *Scholarships, grants, and awards by category:* Academic interests/achievement: biological sciences, business, communication, computer science, education, engineering/technologies, English, foreign languages, general academic interests/achievements, health fields, humanities, mathematics, physical sciences, premedicine, religion/biblical studies, social sciences. *Creative arts/performance:* art/fine arts, music. *Special characteristics:* children of faculty/staff, spouses of current students.
LOANS *Programs:* Federal Direct (Subsidized and Unsubsidized Stafford, PLUS), Perkins.
APPLYING FOR FINANCIAL AID *Required financial aid form:* FAFSA.
CONTACT Mrs. Emily Jones, Financial Aid Director, Xavier University of Louisiana, One Drexel Drive, New Orleans, LA 70125-1098, 504-520-7517 or toll-free 877-XAVIERU. *E-mail:* ejones@xula.edu.
Website: http://www.xula.edu/.

YALE UNIVERSITY
New Haven, CT

Tuition & fees: $51,400	Average undergraduate aid package: $55,828

ABOUT THE INSTITUTION Independent, coed. *Awards:* certificates, bachelor's, master's, and doctoral degrees. 69 undergraduate majors. *Total enrollment:* 12,458. Undergraduates: 5,472. Freshmen: 1,367. Both federal and institutional methodology are used as a basis for awarding need-based institutional aid.
UNDERGRADUATE EXPENSES for 2017–2018 *Application fee:* $80. *Comprehensive fee:* $66,900 includes full-time tuition ($51,400) and room and board ($15,500). *College room only:* $8700. Room and board charges vary according to board plan.
FRESHMAN FINANCIAL AID (Fall 2017, est.) 1,006 applied for aid; of those 81% were deemed to have need. 100% of freshmen with need received aid; of those 100% had need fully met. *Average percent of need met:* 100% (excluding resources awarded to replace EFC). *Average financial aid package:* $56,320 (excluding resources awarded to replace EFC).
UNDERGRADUATE FINANCIAL AID (Fall 2017, est.) 3,129 applied for aid; of those 92% were deemed to have need. 100% of undergraduates with need received aid; of those 100% had need fully met. *Average percent of need met:* 100%

(excluding resources awarded to replace EFC). *Average financial aid package:* $55,828 (excluding resources awarded to replace EFC).

GIFT AID (NEED-BASED) *Total amount:* $148,998,481 (4% federal, 96% institutional). *Receiving aid:* Freshmen: 52% (816); all full-time undergraduates: 50% (2,869). *Average award:* Freshmen: $54,568; Undergraduates: $53,412. *Scholarships, grants, and awards:* Federal Pell, FSEOG, state, private, college/university gift aid from institutional funds, United Negro College Fund, Federal Nursing.

GIFT AID (NON-NEED-BASED) *Total amount:* $433,023 (100% external sources). *Tuition waivers:* Full or partial for employees or children of employees. *ROTC:* Army cooperative, Naval, Air Force.

LOANS *Student loans:* $2,427,457 (39% need-based, 61% non-need-based). 16% of past graduating class borrowed through all loan programs. *Average indebtedness per student:* $13,050. *Average need-based loan:* Freshmen: $2423. Undergraduates: $2929. *Programs:* Federal Direct (Subsidized and Unsubsidized Stafford, PLUS), Perkins, state, college/university.

WORK-STUDY *Federal work-study:* Total amount: $2,446,026; jobs available. *State or other work-study/employment:* Total amount: $3,542,877 (100% need-based). Part-time jobs available.

APPLYING FOR FINANCIAL AID *Required financial aid forms:* FAFSA, institution's own form, CSS Financial Aid PROFILE, noncustodial (divorced/separated) parent's statement, federal income tax form(s). *Financial aid deadline:* 3/1. *Notification date:* 4/1. Students must reply by 5/1 or within 1 week of notification.

CONTACT Mr. Caesar T. Storlazzi, University Director of Financial Aid, Yale University, PO Box 208288, New Haven, CT 06520-8288, 203-432-0371. *Fax:* 203-777-6100. *E-mail:* sfs@yale.edu. *Website:* http://www.yale.edu/.

YESHIVA AND KOLEL BAIS MEDRASH ELYON
Monsey, NY

CONTACT Financial Aid Office, Yeshiva and Kolel Bais Medrash Elyon, 73 Main Street, Monsey, NY 10952, 845-356-7064.

YESHIVA AND KOLLEL HARBOTZAS TORAH
Brooklyn, NY

CONTACT Financial Aid Office, Yeshiva and Kollel Harbotzas Torah, 1049 East 15th Street, Brooklyn, NY 11230, 718-692-0208.

YESHIVA BETH MOSHE
Scranton, PA

CONTACT Financial Aid Office, Yeshiva Beth Moshe, 930 Hickory Street, Scranton, PA 18505-2124, 717-346-1747.

YESHIVA BETH YEHUDA–YESHIVA GEDOLAH OF GREATER DETROIT
Oak Park, MI

CONTACT Rabbi P. Rushnawitz, Executive Administrator, Yeshiva Beth Yehuda–Yeshiva Gedolah of Greater Detroit, 24600 Greenfield Road, Oak Park, MI 48237-1544, 810-968-3360. *Fax:* 810-968-8613.

YESHIVA COLLEGE OF THE NATION'S CAPITAL
Silver Spring, MD

CONTACT Financial Aid Office, Yeshiva College of the Nation's Capital, 1216 Arcola Avenue, Silver Spring, MD 20902, 301-593-2534. *Website:* http://www.yeshiva.edu/.

YESHIVA DERECH CHAIM
Brooklyn, NY

CONTACT Financial Aid Office, Yeshiva Derech Chaim, 1573 39th Street, Brooklyn, NY 11218, 718-438-5426.

YESHIVA D'MONSEY RABBINICAL COLLEGE
Monsey, NY

CONTACT Financial Aid Office, Yeshiva D'Monsey Rabbinical College, 2 Roman Boulevard, Monsey, NY 10952, 914-352-5852.

YESHIVA GEDOLAH IMREI YOSEF D'SPINKA
Brooklyn, NY

CONTACT Financial Aid Office, Yeshiva Gedolah Imrei Yosef D'Spinka, 1466 56th Street, Brooklyn, NY 11219, 718-851-8721.

YESHIVA GEDOLAH RABBINICAL COLLEGE
Miami Beach, FL

CONTACT Financial Aid Office, Yeshiva Gedolah Rabbinical College, 1140 Alton Road, Miami Beach, FL 33139, 305-673-5664.

YESHIVA GEDOLAH SHAAREI SHMUEL
Lakewood, NJ

CONTACT Financial Aid Office, Yeshiva Gedolah Shaarei Shmuel, 511 Ocean Avenue, Lakewood, NJ 08701. *Website:* http://www.yeshivagedolahshaareishmuel.com/.

YESHIVA GEDOLAH ZICHRON LEYMA
Linden, NJ

CONTACT Financial Aid Office, Yeshiva Gedolah Zichron Leyma, 1000 Orchard Terrace, Linden, NJ 07036, 908-587-0502.

YESHIVA GEDOLA OHR YISRAEL
Brooklyn, NY

CONTACT Financial Aid Office, Yeshiva Gedola Ohr Yisrael, 2899 Nostrand Avenue, Brooklyn, NY 11229.
Website: http://www.ohryisroel.org/.

YESHIVA KARLIN STOLIN
Brooklyn, NY

CONTACT Mr. Daniel Ross, Financial Aid Administrator, Yeshiva Karlin Stolin, 1818 Fifty-fourth Street, Brooklyn, NY 11204, 718-232-7800 Ext. 116. *Fax:* 718-331-4833.

YESHIVA OF FAR ROCKAWAY DERECH AYSON RABBINICAL SEMINARY
Far Rockaway, NY

CONTACT Financial Aid Office, Yeshiva of Far Rockaway Derech Ayson Rabbinical Seminary, 802 Hicksville Road, Far Rockaway, NY 11691, 718-327-7600.
Website: http://www.yofr.org/.

YESHIVA OF MACHZIKAI HADAS
Brooklyn, NY

CONTACT Financial Aid Office, Yeshiva of Machzikai Hadas, 1321 43rd Street, Brooklyn, NY 11219, 718-853-2442.

YESHIVA OF NITRA RABBINICAL COLLEGE
Mount Kisco, NY

CONTACT Mr. Yosef Rosen, Financial Aid Administrator, Yeshiva of Nitra Rabbinical College, 194 Division Avenue, Mount Kisco, NY 10549, 718-384-5460. *Fax:* 718-387-9400.

YESHIVA OF THE TELSHE ALUMNI
Riverdale, NY

CONTACT Financial Aid Office, Yeshiva of the Telshe Alumni, 4904 Independence Avenue, Riverdale, NY 10471, 718-601-3523.

YESHIVA OHR ELCHONON CHABAD/ WEST COAST TALMUDICAL SEMINARY
Los Angeles, CA

CONTACT Ms. Hendy Tauber, Director of Financial Aid, Yeshiva Ohr Elchonon Chabad/West Coast Talmudical Seminary, 7215 Waring Avenue, Los Angeles, CA 90046-7660, 213-937-3763. *Fax:* 213-937-9456.
Website: http://www.yoec.edu/.

YESHIVAS BE'ER YITZCHOK
Elizabeth, NJ

CONTACT Financial Aid Office, Yeshivas Be'er Yitzchok, 1391 North Avenue, Elizabeth, NJ 07208, 908-354-6057.
Website: http://www.elizabethkollel.org/.

YESHIVA SHAAREI TORAH OF ROCKLAND
Suffern, NY

CONTACT Financial Aid Office, Yeshiva Shaarei Torah of Rockland, 91 West Carlton Road, Suffern, NY 10901, 845-352-3431.

YESHIVA SHAAR HATORAH TALMUDIC RESEARCH INSTITUTE
Kew Gardens, NY

CONTACT Mr. Yoel Yankelewitz, Executive Director, Financial Aid, Yeshiva Shaar Hatorah Talmudic Research Institute, 117-06 84th Avenue, Kew Gardens, NY 11418-1469, 718-846-1940.

YESHIVAS MAHARIT D'SATMAR
Monroe, NY

CONTACT Financial Aid Office, Yeshivas Maharit D'Satmar, 475 County Route 105, Monroe, NY 10950.
Website: http://www.yeshivasmaharit.com/.

YESHIVAS NOVOMINSK
Brooklyn, NY

CONTACT Financial Aid Office, Yeshivas Novominsk, 1569 47th Street, Brooklyn, NY 11219, 718-438-2727.

YESHIVATH VIZNITZ
Monsey, NY

CONTACT Financial Aid Office, Yeshivath Viznitz, Phyllis Terrace, PO Box 446, Monsey, NY 10952, 914-356-1010.

YESHIVATH ZICHRON MOSHE
South Fallsburg, NY

CONTACT Ms. Miryom R. Miller, Director of Financial Aid, Yeshivath Zichron Moshe, Laurel Park Road, South Fallsburg, NY 12779, 914-434-5240. *Fax:* 914-434-1009. *E-mail:* lehus@aol.com.

YESHIVAT MIKDASH MELECH
Brooklyn, NY

CONTACT Financial Aid Office, Yeshivat Mikdash Melech, 1326 Ocean Parkway, Brooklyn, NY 11230-5601, 718-339-1090.

YESHIVA TORAS CHAIM
Lakewood, NJ

CONTACT Financial Aid Office, Yeshiva Toras Chaim, 999 Ridge Avenue, Lakewood, NJ 08701, 732-942-3090.

YESHIVA UNIVERSITY
New York, NY

CONTACT Marianela Cabral, Director of Student Aid Operations, Yeshiva University, 500 West 185th Street, Room 121, New York, NY 10033, 212-960-5399. *Fax:* 212-960-0037. *E-mail:* mcabral@yu.edu. *Website:* http://www.yu.edu/.

YESHIVA ZICHRON ARYEH
Far Rockaway, NY

CONTACT Financial Aid Office, Yeshiva Zichron Aryeh, 1213 Bay 25th Street, Far Rockaway, NY 11691. *Website:* http://www.yeshivazichronaryeh.com/.

YORK COLLEGE
York, NE

CONTACT Brien Alley, Director of Financial Aid, York College, 1125 East 8th Street, York, NE 68467, 402-363-5624 or toll-free 800-950-9675. *Fax:* 402-363-5623. *E-mail:* balley@york.edu. *Website:* http://www.york.edu/.

YORK COLLEGE OF PENNSYLVANIA
York, PA

Tuition & fees: $20,100	Average undergraduate aid package: $12,845

ABOUT THE INSTITUTION Independent, coed. *Awards:* certificates, associate, bachelor's, master's, and doctoral degrees. 56 undergraduate majors. *Total enrollment:* 4,415. Undergraduates: 4,171. Freshmen: 990. Federal methodology is used as a basis for awarding need-based institutional aid.

UNDERGRADUATE EXPENSES for 2018–2019 *Comprehensive fee:* $31,300 includes full-time tuition ($18,180), mandatory fees ($1920), and room and board ($11,200). *College room only:* $6330. Full-time tuition and fees vary according to program. Room and board charges vary according to board plan and housing facility. *Part-time tuition:* $555 per credit hour.

FRESHMAN FINANCIAL AID (Fall 2017, est.) 923 applied for aid; of those 81% were deemed to have need. 100% of freshmen with need received aid; of those 15% had need fully met. *Average percent of need met:* 61% (excluding resources awarded to replace EFC). *Average financial aid package:* $13,712 (excluding resources awarded to replace EFC). 24% of all full-time freshmen had no need and received non-need-based gift aid.

UNDERGRADUATE FINANCIAL AID (Fall 2017, est.) 3,193 applied for aid; of those 83% were deemed to have need. 100% of undergraduates with need received aid; of those 15% had need fully met. *Average percent of need met:* 57% (excluding resources awarded to replace EFC). *Average financial aid package:* $12,845 (excluding resources awarded to replace EFC). 26% of all full-time undergraduates had no need and received non-need-based gift aid.

GIFT AID (NEED-BASED) *Total amount:* $23,854,132 (21% federal, 12% state, 64% institutional, 3% external sources). *Receiving aid:* Freshmen: 54% (535); all full-time undergraduates: 46% (1,758). *Average award:* Freshmen: $6010; Undergraduates: $5621. *Scholarships, grants, and awards:* Federal Pell, FSEOG, state, private, college/university gift aid from institutional funds.

GIFT AID (NON-NEED-BASED) *Total amount:* $6,105,612 (1% state, 96% institutional, 3% external sources). *Receiving aid:* Freshmen: 75% (738). Undergraduates: 61% (2,333). *Average award:* Freshmen: $7213. Undergraduates: $5800. *Scholarships, grants, and awards by category:* Academic interests/achievement: engineering/technologies, general academic interests/achievements. Creative arts/performance: music. *Special characteristics:* children and siblings of alumni, children of union members/company employees, international students, members of minority groups. *Tuition waivers:* Full or partial for employees or children of employees.

LOANS *Student loans:* $31,742,522 (81% need-based, 19% non-need-based). 79% of past graduating class borrowed through all loan programs. *Average indebtedness per student:* $41,969. *Average need-based loan:* Freshmen: $3213. Undergraduates: $4070. *Parent loans:* $7,850,149 (88% need-based, 12% non-need-based). *Programs:* Federal Direct (Subsidized and Unsubsidized Stafford, PLUS), Perkins, Federal Nursing, college/university.

WORK-STUDY *Federal work-study:* Total amount: $443,163; jobs available. *State or other work-study/employment:* Total amount: $25,881 (54% need-based, 46% non-need-based). Part-time jobs available.

APPLYING FOR FINANCIAL AID *Required financial aid form:* FAFSA. *Financial aid deadline:* Continuous. *Notification date:* Continuous beginning 3/1. Students must reply within 4 weeks of notification.

CONTACT Office of Financial Aid, York College of Pennsylvania, 441 Country Club Road, York, PA 17403, 717-849-1682 or toll-free 800-455-8018. *Fax:* 717-849-1685. *E-mail:* financialaid@ycp.edu. *Website:* http://www.ycp.edu/.

YORK COLLEGE OF THE CITY UNIVERSITY OF NEW YORK
Jamaica, NY

ABOUT THE INSTITUTION State and locally supported, coed. *Awards:* bachelor's and master's degrees. 46 undergraduate majors. *Total enrollment:* 8,360. Undergraduates: 8,258. Freshmen: 971.

GIFT AID (NEED-BASED) *Scholarships, grants, and awards:* Federal Pell, FSEOG, state, private, college/university gift aid from institutional funds, Federal Nursing.

LOANS *Programs:* Federal Direct (Subsidized and Unsubsidized Stafford, PLUS), Perkins.

WORK-STUDY *Federal work-study:* jobs available.

APPLYING FOR FINANCIAL AID *Required financial aid forms:* FAFSA, state aid form.

CONTACT Ms. Beverly Brown, Director of Student Financial Services, York College of the City University of New York, 94-20 Guy R. Brewer Boulevard, Jamaica, NY 11451-0001, 718-262-2240. *E-mail:* bbrown@york.cuny.edu. *Website:* http://www.york.cuny.edu/.

YOUNG HARRIS COLLEGE
Young Harris, GA

Tuition & fees: N/R	Average undergraduate aid package: $24,466

ABOUT THE INSTITUTION Independent United Methodist, coed. 30 undergraduate majors. Both federal and institutional methodology are used as a basis for awarding need-based institutional aid.

FRESHMAN FINANCIAL AID (Fall 2016) 308 applied for aid; of those 93% were deemed to have need. 100% of freshmen with need received aid; of those 23% had need fully met. *Average percent of need met:* 74% (excluding resources awarded to replace EFC). *Average financial aid package:* $23,810 (excluding resources awarded to replace EFC). 44% of all full-time freshmen had no need and received non-need-based gift aid.

UNDERGRADUATE FINANCIAL AID (Fall 2016) 935 applied for aid; of those 83% were deemed to have need. 100% of undergraduates with need received aid; of those 20% had need fully met. *Average percent of need met:* 75% (excluding resources awarded to replace EFC). *Average financial aid package:* $24,466

(excluding resources awarded to replace EFC). 28% of all full-time undergraduates had no need and received non-need-based gift aid.

GIFT AID (NEED-BASED) Total amount: $16,718,596 (12% federal, 11% state, 76% institutional, 1% external sources). **Receiving aid:** Freshmen: 89% (287); all full-time undergraduates: 68% (778). **Average award:** Freshmen: $21,380; Undergraduates: $21,373. **Scholarships, grants, and awards:** Federal Pell, FSEOG, state, private, college/university gift aid from institutional funds.

GIFT AID (NON-NEED-BASED) Total amount: $9,423,553 (15% state, 83% institutional, 2% external sources). **Receiving aid:** Freshmen: 20% (64). Undergraduates: 13% (151). **Average award:** Freshmen: $19,703. Undergraduates: $20,373. **Scholarships, grants, and awards by category:** Academic interests/achievement: 1,079 awards ($12,739,389 total): general academic interests/achievements. Creative arts/performance: 119 awards ($375,094 total): art/fine arts, music, performing arts, theater/drama. Special characteristics: 17 awards ($293,968 total): children of faculty/staff, religious affiliation.

LOANS Student loans: $4,742,461 (80% need-based, 20% non-need-based). 69% of past graduating class borrowed through all loan programs. Average indebtedness per student: $27,173. **Average need-based loan:** Freshmen: $3311. Undergraduates: $3784. **Parent loans:** $2,089,602 (46% need-based, 54% non-need-based). **Programs:** Federal Direct (Subsidized and Unsubsidized Stafford, PLUS), state, college/university.

WORK-STUDY Federal work-study: 109 jobs averaging $878. **State or other work-study/employment:** Total amount: $359,988 (43% need-based, 57% non-need-based). 359 part-time jobs averaging $1002.

APPLYING FOR FINANCIAL AID Required financial aid forms: FAFSA, state aid form. **Financial aid deadline (priority):** 5/1. **Notification date:** Continuous beginning 2/1. Students must reply within 2 weeks of notification.

CONTACT Michelle Bernard, Director of Financial Aid, Young Harris College, 1 College Street, Young Harris, GA 30582, 706-379-5188 or toll-free 800-241-3754 (in-state). *Fax:* 706-379-4594. *E-mail:* mmbernard@yhc.edu. *Website:* http://www.yhc.edu/.

YOUNGSTOWN STATE UNIVERSITY
Youngstown, OH

Tuition & fees (OH res): $8899	Average undergraduate aid package: $9147

ABOUT THE INSTITUTION State-supported, coed. **Awards:** certificates, diplomas, associate, bachelor's, master's, and doctoral degrees. 144 undergraduate majors. **Total enrollment:** 12,642. Undergraduates: 11,386. Freshmen: 2,215. Federal methodology is used as a basis for awarding need-based institutional aid.

UNDERGRADUATE EXPENSES for 2018–2019 Application fee: $45. **Tuition, state resident:** full-time $8899; part-time $371 per credit hour. **Tuition, nonresident:** full-time $14,899; part-time $621 per credit hour. Full-time tuition and fees vary according to course load. Part-time tuition and fees vary according to course load. Room and board charges vary according to board plan and housing facility.

FRESHMAN FINANCIAL AID (Fall 2016) 1,907 applied for aid; of those 82% were deemed to have need. 100% of freshmen with need received aid; of those 13% had need fully met. **Average percent of need met:** 37% (excluding resources awarded to replace EFC). **Average financial aid package:** $9269 (excluding resources awarded to replace EFC). 17% of all full-time freshmen had no need and received non-need-based gift aid.

UNDERGRADUATE FINANCIAL AID (Fall 2016) 7,411 applied for aid; of those 84% were deemed to have need. 99% of undergraduates with need received aid; of those 9% had need fully met. **Average percent of need met:** 33% (excluding resources awarded to replace EFC). **Average financial aid package:** $9147 (excluding resources awarded to replace EFC). 13% of all full-time undergraduates had no need and received non-need-based gift aid.

GIFT AID (NEED-BASED) Total amount: $29,044,727 (74% federal, 15% state, 1% institutional, 10% external sources). **Receiving aid:** Freshmen: 59% (1,221); all full-time undergraduates: 54% (4,695). **Average award:** Freshmen: $5306; Undergraduates: $5362. **Scholarships, grants, and awards:** Federal Pell, FSEOG, state, private, college/university gift aid from institutional funds, Advanced Education Nursing Scholarships.

GIFT AID (NON-NEED-BASED) Total amount: $14,141,505 (3% federal, 7% state, 30% institutional, 60% external sources). **Receiving aid:** Freshmen: 44% (920). Undergraduates: 33% (2,827). **Average award:** Freshmen: $4349. Undergraduates:

$3587. **Scholarships, grants, and awards by category:** Academic interests/achievement: biological sciences, business, communication, computer science, education, engineering/technologies, English, foreign languages, general academic interests/achievements, health fields, humanities, mathematics, military science, physical sciences, premedicine, religion/biblical studies, social sciences. Creative arts/performance: art/fine arts, creative writing, journalism/publications, music, performing arts, theater/drama. Special achievements/activities: cheerleading/drum major, community service, leadership, memberships, religious involvement. Special characteristics: adult students, children and siblings of alumni, children of faculty/staff, children of union members/company employees, children of workers in trades, children with a deceased or disabled parent, ethnic background, handicapped students, international students, local/state students, members of minority groups, out-of-state students, public servants, religious affiliation, spouses of deceased or disabled public servants, veterans, veterans' children. **Tuition waivers:** Full or partial for employees or children of employees, senior citizens. **ROTC:** Army, Air Force cooperative.

LOANS Student loans: $52,484,394 (43% need-based, 57% non-need-based). 73% of past graduating class borrowed through all loan programs. Average indebtedness per student: $31,759. **Average need-based loan:** Freshmen: $3041. Undergraduates: $3760. **Parent loans:** $40,953,606 (100% non-need-based). **Programs:** Federal Direct (Subsidized and Unsubsidized Stafford, PLUS), Perkins, Charles E. Schell Foundation loans, George W. Wright Student Aid loans, Rogers student loans.

WORK-STUDY Federal work-study: jobs available. **State or other work-study/employment:** Total amount: $4,048,425 (100% non-need-based). Part-time jobs available.

ATHLETIC AWARDS Total amount: $4,614,408 (100% non-need-based).

APPLYING FOR FINANCIAL AID Required financial aid form: FAFSA. **Financial aid deadline (priority):** 12/1. **Notification date:** Continuous beginning 12/15. Students must reply within 2 weeks of notification.

CONTACT Barbara Greene, Associate Director of Financial Analysis and Reporting, Youngstown State University, One University Plaza, Youngstown, OH 44555, 330-941-3504 or toll-free 877-468-6978. *Fax:* 330-941-1659. *E-mail:* bgreene@ysu.edu. *Website:* http://www.ysu.edu/.

ZAYTUNA COLLEGE
Berkeley, CA

CONTACT Financial Aid Office, Zaytuna College, 2401 Le Conte Avenue, Berkeley, CA 94709, 510-356-4760. *Website:* http://www.zaytuna.edu/.

Appendix

State Scholarship and Grant Programs

E ach state government has established one or more state-administered financial aid programs for qualified students. In many instances, these state programs are restricted to legal residents of the state. However, they often are available to out-of-state students who will be or are attending colleges or universities within the state. In addition to residential status, other qualifications frequently exist.

Gift aid and forgivable loan programs open to undergraduate students for all states and the District of Columbia are described on the following pages. They are arranged in alphabetical order, first by state name, then by program name. The annotation for each program provides information about the program, eligibility, and the contact addresses for applications or further information. Unless otherwise stated, this information refers to awards for 2015–16. Information is provided by the state-sponsoring agency in response to *Peterson's Annual Survey of Non-institutional Aid*, which was conducted between December 2015 and April 2016. Information is accurate when Peterson's receives it. However, it is always advisable to check with the sponsor to ascertain that the information remains correct.

You should write to the address given for each program to request that award details for 2017–18 be sent to you as soon as they are available. Descriptive information, brochures, and application forms for state scholarship programs are usually available from the financial aid offices of public colleges or universities within the specific state. High school guidance offices often have information and relevant forms for awards for which high school seniors may be eligible. Increasingly, state government agencies are putting state scholarship information on state government agency websites. In searching state government websites, however, you should be aware that the higher education agency in many states is separate from the state's general education office, which is often responsible only for elementary and secondary education. Also, the page at public university websites that provides information about student financial aid frequently has a list of state-sponsored scholarships and financial aid programs.

Names of scholarship programs are frequently used inconsistently or become abbreviated in popular usage. Many programs have variant names by which they are known. The program's sponsor has approved the title of the program that Peterson's uses in this guide, yet this name may differ from the program's official name or from its most commonly used name.

In addition to the grant aid and forgivable loan programs listed on the following pages, states may also offer internship or work-study programs, graduate fellowships and grants, or low-interest loans. If you are interested in learning more about these other kinds of programs, the state education office that supplies information or applications for the undergraduate scholarship programs listed here should be able to provide information about other kinds of higher education financial aid programs that are sponsored by the state.

ALABAMA

Air Force ROTC College Scholarship. Scholarship program provides three- and four-year scholarships in three different types to high school seniors. All scholarship cadets receive a nontaxable monthly allowance (stipend) during the academic year. For more details refer to web site http://www.afrotc.com/scholarships/hsschol/types.php. *Award:* Scholarship for use in freshman, sophomore, junior, or senior years; renewable. *Award amount:* $9000–$15,000. *Number of awards:* 2000–4000. *Eligibility Requirements:* Applicant must be age 17-30 and enrolled or expecting to enroll full-time at a two-year or four-year institution or university. Applicant must have 3.0 GPA or higher. Available to U.S. citizens. Applicant or parent must meet one or more of the following requirements: Air Force experience; retired from active duty; disabled or killed as a result of military service; prisoner of war; or missing in action. *Application Requirements:* Application form, interview, test scores, transcript. **Deadline:** December 1.

Contact Ty Christian, Chief Air Force ROTC Advertising Manager, Air Force Reserve Officer Training Corps, 551 East Maxwell Boulevard, Maxwell Air Force Base, AL 36112-6106. *E-mail:* ty.christian@maxwell.af.mil. *Phone:* 334-953-2278. *Fax:* 334-953-4384. *Website:* http://www.afrotc.com/.

Alabama G.I. Dependents Scholarship Program. The scholarship is for dependents of eligible disabled Alabama veterans. This scholarship will be the payer of last resort after all other grants and scholarships have been utilized for required education expenses. The scholarship pays up to the DoD Tuition Assistance Cap (currently $250 per credit hour) and up to $1,000 for the combination of required textbooks and laboratory fees per semester. Child or stepchild must initiate training before 26th birthday; age 30 deadline may apply in certain situations. No age deadline for spouses or widows. The veteran and the step child's parent must have been married prior the child's 19th birthday. *Award:* Scholarship for use in freshman, sophomore, junior, or senior years; renewable. *Eligibility Requirements:* Applicant must be enrolled or expecting to enroll full- or part-time at a two-year or four-year or technical insti-tution or university; resident of Alabama and studying in Alabama. Available to U.S. citizens. *Application Requirements:* Application form.

Contact Kayla Kyle, Department Operations Manager, Alabama Department of Veterans Affairs, PO Box 1509, Montgomery, AL 36102-1509. *Phone:* 334-242-5077. *Website:* http://www.va.alabama.gov/.

Alabama National Guard Educational Assistance Program. Renewable award aids Alabama residents who are members of the Alabama National Guard and are enrolled in a nationally recognized accredited college in Alabama. Forms must be signed by a representative of the Alabama Military Department and financial aid officer. Recipient must be in a degree-seeking program. *Award:* Scholarship for use in freshman, sophomore, junior, senior, or graduate years; not renewable. *Award amount:* $100–$2000. *Number of awards:* 400–800. *Eligibility Requirements:* Applicant must be enrolled or expecting to enroll full- or part-time at a two-year or four-year or technical institution or university; resident of Alabama and studying in Alabama. Available to U.S. citizens. Applicant must have national guard experience. *Application Requirements:* Application form, financial need analysis. **Deadline:** continuous.

Contact Cheryl Newton, Grants Coordinator. *E-mail:* cheryl.newton@ache.alabama.gov. *Phone:* 334-242-2273. *Fax:* 334-242-2269. *Website:* http://www.ache.alabama.gov/.

Alabama Student Assistance Program. Scholarship award of $300 to $5000 per academic year given to undergraduate students residing in the state of Alabama and attending a college or university in Alabama. *Award:* Grant for use in freshman, sophomore, junior, or senior years; not renewable. *Award amount:* $300–$5000. *Number of awards:* 3500–4500. *Eligibility Requirements:* Applicant must be enrolled or expecting to enroll full- or part-time at a two-year or four-year or technical institution or university; resident of Alabama and studying in Alabama. Available to U.S. citizens. *Application Requirements:* Application form, financial need analysis. **Deadline:** continuous.

Contact Cheryl Newton, Grants Coordinator. *E-mail:* cheryl.newton@ache.alabama.gov. *Phone:* 334-242-2273. *Fax:* 334-242-2269. *Website:* http://www.ache.alabama.gov/.

Alabama Student Assistance Program. Grant award of $300 to $5000 per academic year given to undergraduate students residing in the state of Alabama and attending a college or university in Alabama. *Award:* Grant for use in freshman, sophomore, junior, or senior years; not renewable. *Award amount:* $300–$5000. *Number of awards:* 3500–4500. *Eligibility Requirements:* Applicant must be enrolled or expecting to enroll full- or part-time at a two-year or four-year or technical institution or university; resident of Alabama and studying in Alabama. Available to U.S. citizens. *Application Requirements:* **Deadline:** continuous.

Contact Cheryl Newton, Grants Coordinator. *E-mail:* cheryl.newton@ache.alabama.gov. *Phone:* 334-242-2273. *Fax:* 334-242-2269. *Website:* http://www.ache.alabama.gov/.

Alabama Student Grant Program. Nonrenewable awards available to Alabama residents for undergraduate study at certain independent colleges within the state. Both full and half-time students are eligible. Deadlines: September 15, January 15, and February 15. *Award:* Grant for use in freshman, sophomore, junior, or senior years; not renewable. *Award amount:* $200–$1200. *Number of awards:* 3500–5500. *Eligibility Requirements:* Applicant must be enrolled or expecting to enroll full- or part-time at a four-year institution or university; resident of Alabama and studying in Alabama. Available to U.S. citizens. *Application Requirements:* Application form. **Deadline:** continuous.

Contact Cheryl Newton, Grants Coordinator. *E-mail:* cheryl.newton@ache.alabama.gov. *Phone:* 334-242-2273. *Fax:* 334-242-2269. *Website:* http://www.ache.alabama.gov/.

Police Officers and Firefighters Survivors Education Assistance Program-Alabama. Provides tuition, fees, books, and supplies to dependents of full-time police officers and firefighters killed or totally disabled in the line of duty. Must attend an Alabama public college as an undergraduate. Must be Alabama resident. *Award:* Scholarship for use in freshman, sophomore, junior, or senior years; renewable. *Award amount:* $1600–$12,000. *Number of awards:* 15–

30. *Eligibility Requirements:* Applicant must be enrolled or expecting to enroll full- or part-time at a two-year or technical institution or university; resident of Alabama and studying in Alabama. Available to U.S. citizens. *Application Requirements:* Application form. **Deadline:** continuous.

Contact Cheryl Newton, Grants Coordinator. *E-mail:* cheryl.newton@ ache.alabama.gov. *Phone:* 334-242-2273. *Fax:* 334-242-2269. *Website:* http://www.ache.alabama.gov/.

ALASKA

Alaska Performance Scholarship. To qualify, students must take a specific, rigorous high school curriculum; earn a minimum 2.5 GPA; and do well on college or career readiness exam. Students apply by completing the FAFSA by the annual deadline. Awards can be used at any regionally accredited college or university in Alaska, or for approved career and technical education programs in the state. Students must use scholarship within 6 years of high school graduation. Students cannot receive award for more than 8 semesters. *Award:* Scholarship for use in freshman, sophomore, junior, senior, graduate, or postgraduate years; not renewable. *Award amount:* $500–$4755. *Eligibility Requirements:* Applicant must be enrolled or expecting to enroll full- or part-time at a two-year or four-year or technical institution or university; resident of Alaska and studying in Alaska. Applicant must have 2.5 GPA or higher. Available to U.S. and non-U.S. citizens. *Application Requirements:* **Deadline:** continuous.

Contact Adam Weed, Special Programs Coordinator, Alaska Commission on Postsecondary Education, 3030 Vintage Blvd, Juneau, AK 99801. *E-mail:* customer_service@acpe.state. ak.us. *Phone:* 907-465-6685. *Website:* http://www.acpe.alaska.gov.

Alask Education Grant. The Alaska legislature created the Alask Education Grant Program (AEG) to provide need-based financial assistance to eligible Alaska students attending qualifying postsecondary educational institutions in Alaska. Students apply by completing the FAFSA annually. *Award:* Grant for use in freshman, sophomore, junior, or senior years; not renewable. *Award amount:* $500–$4000. *Eligibility Requirements:* Applicant must be

enrolled or expecting to enroll full- or part-time at a two-year or four-year institution or university; resident of Alaska and studying in Alaska. Available to U.S. and non-U.S. citizens. *Application Requirements:* **Deadline:** continuous.

Contact Adam Weed, Special Programs Coordinator, Alaska Commission on Postsecondary Education, 3030 Vintage Blvd, Juneau, AK 99801. *E-mail:* customer_service@acpe.state. ak.us. *Phone:* 907-465-6685. *Website:* http://www.acpe.alaska.gov.

ARIZONA

Leveraging Educational Assistance Partnership. Grants to financially needy students, who enroll in and attend postsecondary education or training in Arizona schools. Program was formerly known as the State Student Incentive Grant or SSIG Program. *Award:* Grant for use in freshman, sophomore, junior, senior, or graduate years; not renewable. *Award amount:* $100–$2500. *Eligibility Requirements:* Applicant must be enrolled or expecting to enroll full- or part-time at a two-year or four-year or technical institution or university; resident of Arizona and studying in Arizona. Available to U.S. citizens. *Application Requirements:* Application form, financial need analysis, transcript. **Deadline:** April 30.

Contact Mila Zaporteza, Business Manager and LEAP Financial Aid Manager, Arizona Commission for Postsecondary Education, 2020 North Central Avenue, Suite 650, Phoenix, AZ 85004-4503. *E-mail:* mila@azhighered. gov. *Phone:* 602-258-2435 Ext. 102. *Fax:* 602-258-2483. *Website:* https:// highered.az.gov/.

ARKANSAS

Arkansas Academic Challenge Scholarship Program. Awards for Arkansas residents who are graduating high school seniors, currently enrolled college students and nontraditional students to study at an approved Arkansas institution. Must have at least a 19 ACT composite score (or the equivalent). Renewable up to three additional years. *Award:* Scholarship for use in freshman, sophomore, junior, senior, or graduate years; renewable. *Award amount:* $1000–$5000. *Number of awards:* 30,000–35,000. *Eligibility Require-*

ments: Applicant must be enrolled or expecting to enroll full- or part-time at a two-year or four-year institution or university; resident of Arkansas and studying in Arkansas. Available to U.S. citizens. *Application Requirements:* Application form, financial need analysis. **Deadline:** June 1.

Contact Jonathan Coleman, Financial Aid Manager. *E-mail:* jonathan. coleman@adhe.edu. *Phone:* 501-371-2000. *Website:* http://www.adhe.edu/.

Arkansas Governor's Scholars Program. Awards for outstanding Arkansas high school seniors. Applicants who attain 32 or above on ACT, 1410 or above on SAT and have an academic 3.5 GPA, or are selected as National Merit or National Achievement finalists may receive an award equal to tuition, mandatory fees, room, and board up to $10,000 per year at any Arkansas institution. If any of the seventy-five (75) counties is not represented, the Department of Higher Education shall select a student from each non-represented county with the highest qualifications who was not initially qualified. Students from these counties will be awarded $5000 per year at any Arkansas institution. *Award:* Scholarship for use in freshman, sophomore, junior, senior, or graduate years; renewable. *Award amount:* $4000–$10,000. *Number of awards:* 75–375. *Eligibility Requirements:* Applicant must be high school student; planning to enroll or expecting to enroll full-time at a two-year or four-year institution or university; resident of Arkansas and studying in Arkansas. Applicant must have 3.5 GPA or higher. Available to U. S. citizens. *Application Requirements:* Application form, community service. **Deadline:** February 1.

Contact Jonathan Coleman, Financial Aid Manager. *E-mail:* jonathan. coleman@adhe.edu. *Phone:* 501-371-2000. *Website:* http://www.adhe.edu/.

Arkansas Single Parent Scholarship Fund. Visit our website for full eligibility and program information: http:// www.aspsf.org/scholarships/how-to-apply/ *Award:* Scholarship for use in freshman, sophomore, junior, or senior years; not renewable. *Award amount:* $1–$2000. *Number of awards:* 1–2400. *Eligibility Requirements:* Applicant must be enrolled or expecting to enroll full- or part-time at a two-year or four-year or technical institution or university and resident of Arkansas, Texas. Available to U.S. and non-U.S. citizens. *Application Requirements:* Application form, essay, financial need analysis, interview. **Deadline:** continuous.

Law Enforcement Officers' Dependents Scholarship&-Arkansas. Scholarship for dependents, under 23 years old, of Arkansas law-enforcement officers killed or permanently disabled in the line of duty. Renewable award is a waiver of tuition, fees, and room at two- or four-year Arkansas institution. Submit birth certificate, death certificate, and claims commission report of findings of fact. Proof of disability from State Claims Commission may also be submitted. *Award:* Scholarship for use in freshman, sophomore, junior, or senior ycars; renewable. *Eligibility Requirements:* Applicant must be enrolled or expecting to enroll full- or part-time at a two-year or four-year or technical institution or university; resident of Arkansas and studying in Arkansas. Available to U.S. citizens. *Application Requirements:* Application form. **Deadline:** June 1.

Contact Lisa Smith, Program Specialist, Arkansas Department of Higher Education, 423 Main Street Suite 400, Little Rock, AR 72201-3818. *E-mail:* lisa.smith@adhe.edu. *Phone:* 501-371-2000. *Website:* http://www.adhe.edu/.

Military Dependent's Scholarship Program. Renewable waiver of tuition, fees, room and board undergraduate students seeking a bachelor's degree or certificate of completion at any public college, university or technical school in Arkansas who qualify as a spouse or dependent child of an Arkansas resident who has been declared to be missing in action, killed in action, a POW, or killed on ordnance delivery, or a veteran who has been declared to be 100 percent totally and permanently disabled during, or as a result of, active military service. *Award:* Scholarship for use in freshman, sophomore, junior, or senior years; renewable. *Eligibility Requirements:* Applicant must be enrolled or expecting to enroll full-time at a two-year or four-year or technical institution or university; resident of Arkansas and studying in Arkansas. Available to U.S. citizens. Applicant or parent must meet one or more of the following requirements: general military experience; retired from active duty; disabled or killed as a result of military service;

prisoner of war; or missing in action. *Application Requirements:* Application form. **Deadline:** June 1.

Contact Lisa Smith, Director of Financial Aid, Arkansas Department of Higher Education, 423 Main Street Suite 400, Little Rock, AR 72201-3818. *E-mail:* lisa.smith@adhe.edu. *Phone:* 501-371-2000. *Website:* http://www.adhe.edu/.

CALIFORNIA

Cal Grant C. Award for California residents who are enrolled in a short-term vocational training program. Program must lead to a recognized degree or certificate. Course length must be a minimum of 4 months and no longer than 24 months. Students must be attending an approved California institution and show financial need. *Award:* Grant for use in freshman or sophomore years; renewable. *Award amount:* $576–$3168. *Number of awards:* up to 7761. *Eligibility Requirements:* Applicant must be enrolled or expecting to enroll full- or part-time at a two-year or technical institution; resident of California and studying in California. Available to U.S. citizens. *Application Requirements:* Application form, financial need analysis, GPA verification. **Deadline:** March 2.

Contact Catalina Mistler, Chief, Program Administration and Services Division, California Student Aid Commission, PO Box 419026, Rancho Cordova, CA 95741-9026. *E-mail:* studentsupport@csac.ca.gov. *Phone:* 916-464-7268. *Fax:* 916-526-8004. *Website:* http://www.csac.ca.gov/.

Child Development Teacher and Supervisor Grant Program. Award is for those students pursuing an approved course of study leading to a Child Development Permit issued by the California Commission on Teacher Credentialing. In exchange for each year funding is received, recipients agree to provide one year of service in a licensed childcare center. Child and Family Studies; Education. *Award:* Grant for use in freshman, sophomore, junior, senior, or graduate years; renewable. *Award amount:* $1000–$2000. *Number of awards:* up to 300. *Eligibility Requirements:* Applicant must be enrolled or expecting to enroll full- or part-time at a two-year or four-year institution or university; resident of Cal-

ifornia and studying in California. Applicant or parent of applicant must have employment or volunteer experience in teaching/education. Available to U.S. citizens. *Application Requirements:* Application form, financial need analysis, GPA verification, recommendations or references. **Deadline:** April 16.

Contact Catalina Mistler, Chief, Program Administration and Services Division, California Student Aid Commission, PO Box 419026, Rancho Cordova, CA 95741-9026. *E-mail:* studentsupport@csac.ca.gov. *Phone:* 916-464-7268. *Fax:* 916-526-8004. *Website:* http://www.csac.ca.gov/.

Competitive Cal Grant A. Award for California residents who are not recent high school graduates attending an approved college or university within the state. Must show financial need and meet minimum 3.00 GPA requirement. *Award:* Grant for use in freshman, sophomore, junior, or senior years; renewable. *Award amount:* $5472–$12,192. *Number of awards:* 1000–2000. *Eligibility Requirements:* Applicant must be enrolled or expecting to enroll full- or part-time at a two-year or four-year institution or university; resident of California and studying in California. Applicant must have 3.0 GPA or higher. Available to U.S. citizens. *Application Requirements:* Application form, financial need analysis, GPA verification. **Deadline:** March 2.

Contact Catalina Mistler, Chief, Program Administration and Services Division, California Student Aid Commission, PO Box 419026, Rancho Cordova, CA 95741-9026. *E-mail:* studentsupport@csac.ca.gov. *Phone:* 916-464-7268. *Fax:* 916-526-8004. *Website:* http://www.csac.ca.gov/.

Entitlement Cal Grant B. Provide grant funds for access costs for low-income students in an amount not to exceed $1648 and tuition/fee expenses of up to $12,192. Must be California residents and enroll in an undergraduate academic program of not less than one academic year at a qualifying postsecondary institution. Must show financial need and meet the minimum 2.00 GPA requirement. *Award:* Grant for use in freshman, sophomore, junior, or senior years; renewable. *Award amount:* $700–$13,665. *Number of awards:* 61,340. *Eligibility Requirements:* Applicant must be enrolled or expecting to enroll full- or part-time at a two-year or four-year or technical institution or university; resident of California and studying in California. Available to U.S. citizens. *Application Requirements:* Application form, financial need analysis. **Deadline:** March 2.

Contact Catalina Mistler, Chief, Program Administration and Services Division, California Student Aid Commission, PO Box 419026, Rancho Cordova, CA 95741-9026. *E-mail:* studentsupport@csac.ca.gov. *Phone:* 916-464-7268. *Fax:* 916-526-8004. *Website:* http://www.csac.ca.gov/.

EOPS (Extended Opportunity Programs and Services)/CARE (Cooperative Agencies Resources for Education). Renewable award available to California residents and individuals who are exempt from paying nonresident tuition. Individuals must be enrolled as a full-time student at a two-year publicly-funded California community college. EOPS students must fulfill program-specific income and educational disadvantage eligibility requirements. CARE students must be in EOPS, currently receive CalWORKs/TANF, have at least one child under fourteen years of age at time of acceptance into CARE program, be a single head of household, and age 18 or older. EOPS students may also qualify for CARE if their dependent child(ren) receive CalWORKs/TANF cash aid even if the student (i.e., parent) is not a cash aid recipient. Contact local college EOPS/CARE office for an application and more information about supportive services and grants. To locate nearest community college campus, see http://www.cccco.edu/ *Award:* Grant for use in freshman or sophomore years; renewable. *Award amount:* $100–$1000. *Number of awards:* 10,000–85,000. *Eligibility Requirements:* Applicant must be enrolled or expecting to enroll full-time at a two-year institution; single; resident of California and studying in California. Available to U.S. citizens. *Application Requirements:* Application form, financial need analysis. **Deadline:** continuous.

Law Enforcement Personnel Dependents Scholarship. Provides college grants to needy dependents of California law enforcement officers, officers and employees of the Department of Corrections and Department of Youth Authority, and firefighters killed or disabled in the line of duty. *Award:* Grant for use in freshman, sophomore, junior, or senior years; renewable. *Award amount:* $100–$13,665. *Eligibility Requirements:* Applicant must be enrolled or expecting to enroll full- or part-time at a two-year or four-year institution or university; resident of California and studying in California. Applicant or parent of applicant must have employment or volunteer experience in police/firefighting. Available to U.S. citizens. *Application Requirements:* Application form, birth certificate, death certificate of parents or spouse, police report, financial need analysis, transcript. **Deadline:** continuous.

Contact Catalina Mistler, Chief, Program Administration and Services Division, California Student Aid Commission, PO Box 419026, Rancho Cordova, CA 95741-9026. *E-mail:* studentsupport@csac.ca.gov. *Phone:* 916-464-7268. *Fax:* 916-526-8004. *Website:* http://www.csac.ca.gov/.

COLORADO

Colorado Student Grant. Grants for Colorado residents attending eligible public, private, or vocational institutions within the state. Students must complete a Free Application for Federal Student Aid (FAFSA) and demonstrate need. Application deadlines vary by institution. Renewable award for undergraduates. Contact the financial aid office at the college/institution for application and more information. *Award:* Grant for use in freshman, sophomore, junior, or senior years; not renewable. *Award amount:* $300–$5000. *Eligibility Requirements:* Applicant must be enrolled or expecting to enroll full- or part-time at a two-year or four-year or technical institution; resident of Colorado and studying in Colorado. Available to U.S. citizens. *Application Requirements:* Application form, financial need analysis. **Deadline:** continuous.

Contact Celina Duran, Financial Aid Administrator, Colorado Commission on Higher Education, 1560 Broadway, Suite 1600, Denver, CO 80202. *E-mail:* celina.duran@dhe.state.co.us. *Phone:* 303-866-2723. *Website:* http://highered.colorado.gov/cche/mission.html.

CONNECTICUT

AIFS-HACU Scholarships. Scholarships to outstanding Hispanic students to study abroad with AIFS. Available to students attending HACU member schools. Students will receive scholarships of up to 50 percent of the full program fee. Students must meet all standard AIFS eligibility requirements. Deadlines: April 15 for fall, October 1 for spring, and March 15 for summer. *Award:* Scholarship for use in freshman, sophomore, junior, or senior years; not renewable. *Award amount:* $6000–$8000. *Number of awards:* up to 1. *Eligibility Requirements:* Applicant must be Hispanic; enrolled or expecting to enroll full-time at a two-year or four-year institution or university and must have an interest in international exchange. Applicant must have 3.0 GPA or higher. Available to U.S. and non-U.S. citizens. *Application Requirements:* Application form, essay, personal photograph, recommendations or references, transcript. *Fee:* $95. **Deadline:** varies.

Contact David Mauro, Admissions Counselor, American Institute for Foreign Study, 1 High Ridge Park, Stamford, CT 06905. *E-mail:* dmauro@aifs.com. *Phone:* 800-727-2437 Ext. 5163. *Fax:* 203-399-5463. *Website:* http://www.aifsabroad.com/.

Connecticut Army National Guard 100% Tuition Waiver. Program is for any active member of the Connecticut Army National Guard in good standing. Must be a resident of Connecticut attending any Connecticut state (public) university, community-technical college or regional vocational-technical school. The total number of available awards is unlimited. *Award:* Scholarship for use in freshman, sophomore, junior, or senior years; not renewable. *Award amount:* $16,000. *Eligibility Requirements:* Applicant must be age 17-65; enrolled or expecting to enroll full- or part-time at a two-year or four-year or technical institution or university; resident of Connecticut and studying in Connecticut. Available to U.S. and non-U.S. citizens. Applicant or parent must meet one or more of the following requirements: national guard experience; retired from active duty; disabled or killed as a result of military service; prisoner of war; or missing in action. *Application Requirements:* Application form. **Deadline:** July 1.

Contact Capt. Jeremy Lingenfelser, Education Services Officer, Connecticut Army National Guard, 360 Broad Street, Hartford, CT 06105-3795. *E-mail:* education@ct.ngb.army.mil. *Phone:* 860-524-4816. *Fax:* 860-524-4904. *Website:* http://ct.ng.mil/Pages/default.aspx.

Governor's Scholarship Program—Need/Merit Scholarship. This program provides scholarships to eligible Connecticut residents attending eligible institutions of higher education in Connecticut. Eligibility is based on a minimum SAT score of 1800, or a minimum ACT score of 27 and/or top 20% ranking in the students junior year high school class. Applications must be filed through the students high school counseling office. In addition, all students must file a Free Application for Federal Student Aid (FAFSA) and, as a result, have an Expected Family Contribution (EFC) equal to or less than the annual allowable maximum EFC. Both the application and FAFSA must be processed by February 15th. *Award:* Scholarship for use in sophomore, junior, or senior years; renewable. *Award amount:* $2275–$5250. *Number of awards:* 1967. *Eligibility Requirements:* Applicant must be enrolled or expecting to enroll full- or part-time at a two-year or four-year institution or university; resident of Connecticut and studying in Connecticut. Applicant must have 3.5 GPA or higher. Available to U.S. citizens. *Application Requirements:* Application form, financial need analysis. **Deadline:** February 15.

Contact Ms. Lynne Goodwin, Student Financial Aid Consultant, Connecticut Office of Higher Education, 450 Columbus Boulevard, Suite 510, Hartford, CT 06103. *E-mail:* sfa@ctohe.org. *Phone:* 860-947-1855. *Website:* http://www.ctohe.org.

Minority Teacher Incentive Grant Program. Program provides up to $5,000 a year for two years of full-time study in a teacher preparation program for the junior or senior year at a Connecticut college or university. Applicant must be African-American, Hispanic/Latino, Asian American or Native American heritage and be nominated by the Education Dean. Program graduates who teach in Connecticut public schools may be eligible for loan reimbursement stipends up to $2,500 per year for up to four years. Education. *Award:* Grant for use in junior or senior years; renewable. *Award amount:* $2500–$5000. *Number of awards:* 87. *Eligibility Requirements:* Applicant must be American Indian/Alaska Native, Asian/Pacific Islander, Black (non-Hispanic), Hispanic; enrolled or expecting to enroll full-time at a four-year institution or university; resident of Connecticut and studying in Connecticut. Available to U.S. citizens. *Application Requirements:* Application form. **Deadline:** October 15.

Contact Ms. Lynne Goodwin, Executive Assistant, Connecticut Office of Higher Education, 450 Columbus Boulevard, Suite 510, Hartford, CT 06103. *E-mail:* mtip@ctohe.org. *Phone:* 860-947-1855. *Website:* http://www.ctohe.org.

Roberta B. Willis Scholarship Program—Need-Based Grant. This program provides need-based grants to eligible Connecticut residents attending eligible institutions of higher education in Connecticut. Students must file a Free Application for Federal Student Aid (FAFSA) by their college's deadline, if applicable. Students, as a result of filing the FAFSA, must have an Expected Family Contribution (EFC) equal to or less than the allowable annual EFC. There is no application to fill out. *Award:* Grant for use in freshman, sophomore, junior, or senior years; renewable. *Award amount:* $1–$4500. *Eligibility Requirements:* Applicant must be enrolled or expecting to enroll full- or part-time at a two-year or four-year institution or university; resident of Connecticut and studying in Connecticut. Available to U.S. citizens. *Application Requirements:* Financial need analysis. **Deadline:** continuous.

Contact Ms. Lynne Goodwin, Financial Aid Consultant, Connecticut Office of Higher Education, 450 Columbus Boulevard, Suite 510, Hartford, CT 06103. *E-mail:* sfa@ctohe.org. *Phone:* 860-947-1855. *Website:* http://www.ctohe.org.

DELAWARE

B. Bradford Barnes Memorial Scholarship. Must be a legal resident of Delaware; a high school senior who ranks in upper quarter of class and has a combined score of 1290 on the SAT; and enrolled full-time at the University of Delaware. File the Free Application for Federal Student Aid (FAFSA) prior to the application deadline. *Award:* Scholarship for use in freshman, sophomore, junior, or senior years; renewable. *Award amount:* $15,000–$20,000. *Number of awards:* 1. *Eligibility Requirements:* Applicant must be high school student; planning to enroll or expecting to enroll full-time at an institution or university; resident of Delaware and studying in Delaware. Applicant must have 3.5 GPA or higher. Available to U.S. citizens. *Application Requirements:* Application form, essay, financial need analysis. **Deadline:** March 5.

Contact Ms. Juliet Murawski, Program Administrator, Delaware Higher Education Office, 401 Federal Street, Suite 2, Dover, DE 19901. *E-mail:* dheo@doe.k12.de.us. *Phone:* 302-735-4120. *Fax:* 302-739-5894. *Website:* http://www.doe.k12.de.us.

Charles L. Hebner Memorial Scholarship. Must be a legal resident of Delaware; a U.S. citizen or eligible non-citizen; a high school senior who ranks in upper half of class and has a combined score of 1000 on the SAT; enrolled full-time at the University of Delaware or Delaware State University; and majoring in the humanities or social sciences. Preference will be given to political science majors. Must file the Free Application for Federal Student Aid (FAFSA) prior to the application deadline. *Award:* Scholarship for use in freshman, sophomore, junior, or senior years; renewable. *Award amount:* $15,000–$20,000. *Number of awards:* 2. *Eligibility Requirements:* Applicant must be high school student; planning to enroll or expecting to enroll full-time at an institution or university; resident of Delaware and studying in Delaware. Applicant must have 2.5 GPA or higher. Available to U.S. citizens. *Application Requirements:* Application form, essay, financial need analysis. **Deadline:** March 5.

Contact Ms. Juliet Murawski, Program Administrator, Delaware Higher Education Office, 401 Federal Street, Suite 2, Dover, DE 19901. *E-mail:* dheo@doe.k12.de.us. *Phone:* 302-735-4120. *Fax:* 302-739-5894. *Website:* http://www.doe.k12.de.us.

Diamond State Scholarship. Award for legal residents of Delaware who are U.S. citizens or eligible non-citizens. Must be enrolled as a full-time student in a degree program at a nonprofit, regionally accredited institution. Minimum 3.0 GPA required. High school seniors should rank in upper quarter of class and have a combined score of at least 1290 on the SAT. *Award:* Scholarship for use in freshman year; renewable. *Award amount:* $1250. *Number of awards:* 30–50. *Eligibility Requirements:* Applicant must be high school student; planning to enroll or expecting to enroll full-time at a four-year institution or university and resident of Delaware. Applicant must have 3.0 GPA or higher. Available to U.S. citizens. *Application Requirements:* Application form, essay. **Deadline:** March 5.

Contact Ms. Juliet Murawski, Program Administrator, Delaware Higher Education Office, 401 Federal Street, Suite 2, Dover, DE 19901. *E-mail:* dheo@doe.k12.de.us. *Phone:* 302-735-4120. *Fax:* 302-739-5894. *Website:* http://www.doe.k12.de.us.

Educational Benefits for Children of Deceased Veterans. Applicant must have been a resident of the state of Delaware for three or more consecutive years prior to the date of application. If the applicant's parent is a member of the armed forces, the parent must have been a resident of Delaware at the time of death or declaration of missing in action or prisoner of war status. Applicant must be a U.S. citizen or eligible non-citizen. Applicant must be between the ages of 16 and 24. Applicant must be the child of one of the following: member of the armed forces whose cause of death was service-related; member of the armed forces who is being held or was held as a prisoner of war; member of the armed forces who is officially declared missing in action; state police officer whose cause of death was service-related; or state employee of the Department of Transportation routinely employed in job-related activities upon the state highway system whose cause of death was job-related. *Award:* Grant for use in freshman, sophomore, junior, or senior years; renewable. *Award amount:* $10,000–$12,000. *Eligibility Requirements:* Applicant must be age 16-24; enrolled or expecting to enroll full-time at a two-year or four-year institution or university and resident of Delaware. Applicant or parent of applicant must have employment or volunteer experience in police/firefighting. Available to U.S. citizens. Applicant or parent must meet one or more of the following requirements: general military

experience; retired from active duty; disabled or killed as a result of military service; prisoner of war; or missing in action. *Application Requirements:* Application form. **Deadline:** June 4.

Contact Ms. Juliet Murawski, Program Administrator, Delaware Higher Education Office, 401 Federal Street, Suite 2, Dover, DE 19901. *E-mail:* dheo@doe.k12.de.us. *Phone:* 302-735-4120. *Fax:* 302-739-5894. *Website:* http://www.doe.k12.de.us.

Herman M. Holloway, Sr. Memorial Scholarship. Must be a legal resident of Delaware; a U.S. citizen or eligible non-citizen; a high school senior who is ranked in upper half of class and has a combined score of at least 1000 on the SAT; and enrolled full-time at Delaware State University. Must file the Free Application for Federal Student Aid (FAFSA) prior to the application deadline. *Award:* Scholarship for use in freshman, sophomore, junior, or senior years; renewable. *Award amount:* $15,000–$20,000. *Number of awards:* 1. *Eligibility Requirements:* Applicant must be high school student; planning to enroll or expecting to enroll full-time at an institution or university; resident of Delaware and studying in Delaware. Applicant must have 2.5 GPA or higher. Available to U.S. citizens. *Application Requirements:* Application form, essay, financial need analysis. **Deadline:** March 5.

Contact Ms. Juliet Murawski, Program Administrator, Delaware Higher Education Office, 401 Federal Street, Suite 2, Dover, DE 19901. *E-mail:* dheo@doe.k12.de.us. *Phone:* 302-735-4120. *Fax:* 302-739-5894. *Website:* http://www.doe.k12.de.us.

Scholarship Incentive Program (ScIP). Award for legal residents of Delaware who are U.S. citizens or eligible non-citizens. The application process for ScIP requires three steps: 1. Complete the Free Application for Federal Student Aid (FAFSA) by April 15, 2018, 2. Provide your academic records to the Delaware Higher Education Office by July 2, 2018 to dheo@doe.k12.de.us, 3. Log onto your student account at www.de.gov/scholarships to provide your anticipated college enrollment information for 2018-2019 by July 2, 2018. Applicants must demonstrate substantial financial need, as determined using the Free Application for Federal Student Aid (FAFSA); have

a minimum cumulative, unweighted grade point average of 2.5 on a 4.0 scale, (grades submitted on a weighted scale will be recalculated to unweighted); enroll full-time in an undergraduate degree program at a non-profit, regionally accredited institution in Delaware; or enroll full-time in an out-of-state, nonprofit, regionally accredited college in an undergraduate or graduate degree program that is not offered at the University of Delaware, Delaware State University of Delaware Technical Community College. *Award:* Grant for use in freshman, sophomore, junior, senior, or graduate years; not renewable. *Award amount:* $1000. *Number of awards:* 700–1000. *Eligibility Requirements:* Applicant must be enrolled or expecting to enroll full-time at a two-year or four-year institution or university; resident of Delaware and studying in Delaware. Applicant must have 2.5 GPA or higher. Available to U. S. citizens. *Application Requirements:* Application form, financial need analysis. **Deadline:** April 15.

Contact Ms. Juliet Murawski, Program Administrator, Delaware Higher Education Office, 401 Federal Street, Suite 2, Dover, DE 19901. *E-mail:* dheo@doe.k12.de.us. *Phone:* 302-735-4120. *Fax:* 302-739-5894. *Website:* http://www.doe.k12.de.us.

State Tuition Assistance. You must enlist in the Delaware Air or Army National Guard to be eligible for this scholarship award. Award providing tuition assistance for any member of the Air or Army National Guard attending a Delaware two-year or four-year college. Awards are renewable. Applicant's minimum GPA must be 2.0. *Award:* Scholarship for use in freshman, sophomore, junior, or senior years; renewable. *Award amount:* $1–$10,000. *Number of awards:* 1–200. *Eligibility Requirements:* Applicant must be enrolled or expecting to enroll full- or part-time at a two-year or four-year institution or university and studying in Delaware. Available to U.S. citizens. Applicant or parent must meet one or more of the following requirements: national guard experience; retired from active duty; disabled or killed as a result of military service; prisoner of war; or missing in action. *Application Requirements:* Application form. **Deadline:** continuous.

Contact Robert Csizmadia, State Tuition Assistance Manager, Delaware

Army National Guard, 1 Vavala Way, New Castle, DE 19720. *E-mail:* robert.l.csizmadianfg@mail.mil. *Phone:* 302-326-7012. *Website:* http://www.delawarenationalguard.com/.

DISTRICT OF COLUMBIA

American Indian Nurse Scholarship Program. Since 1928 The National Society of The Colonial Dames of America has provided a small number of scholarship awards to assist students of American Indian heritage who are pursuing degrees in nursing or in the field of health care and health education. Eligible students receive $1,500 per semester and the money is to be used strictly for tuition, books or fees applicable to the students approved program. The grant is sent to the school and credited to the students account. Once a student is accepted, he or she may reapply for continued funds each semester as long as the student remains in academic good standing. Health Administration; Nursing. *Award:* Scholarship for use in freshman, sophomore, junior, senior, graduate, or postgraduate years; renewable. *Award amount:* $500–$1500. *Number of awards:* 2. *Eligibility Requirements:* Applicant must be American Indian/Alaska Native and enrolled or expecting to enroll full-time at a two-year or four-year or technical institution or university. Applicant must have 2.5 GPA or higher. Available to U.S. citizens. *Application Requirements:* Application form, autobiography, driver's license, financial need analysis, personal photograph. **Deadline:** June 1.

Bureau of Indian Education Grant Program. Grants are provided to supplement financial assistance to eligible American Indian/Alaska Native students entering college seeking a Baccalaureate degree. A student must be a member of, or at least one-quarter degree Indian blood descendent of a member of an American Indian tribe who are eligible for the special programs and services provided by the United States through the Bureau of Indian Affairs to Indians because of their status as Indians. *Award:* Grant for use in freshman year; not renewable. *Eligibility Requirements:* Applicant must be American Indian/Alaska Native; high school student and planning to enroll or expecting to enroll full-time at a two-year or four-year institution or university. Available to U.S.

citizens. *Application Requirements:* Application form, recommendations or references, test scores, transcript. **Deadline:** varies.

Contact Paulina Bell, Office Automation Assistant. *Phone:* 202-208-6123. *Fax:* 202-208-3312. *Website:* http://www.bie.edu/.

Costas G. Lemonopoulos Scholarship. Scholarships to children of NALC members attending public, four-year colleges or universities supported by the state of Florida or St. Petersburg Junior College. Scholarships are renewable one time. *Award:* Scholarship for use in freshman, sophomore, junior, or senior years; renewable. *Number of awards:* 1–20. *Eligibility Requirements:* Applicant must be enrolled or expecting to enroll full-time at a two-year or four-year institution or university and studying in Florida. Applicant or parent of applicant must be member of National Association of Letter Carriers. Available to U.S. citizens. *Application Requirements:* Application form, recommendations or references, transcript. **Deadline:** June 1.

Contact Ann Porch, Membership Committee. *E-mail:* nalcinf@nalc.org. *Phone:* 202-393-4695. *Website:* http://www.nalc.org/.

Harry S. Truman Scholarship. Scholarships for U.S. citizens or U.S. nationals who are college or university students with junior-level academic standing and who wish to attend professional or graduate school to prepare for careers in government or the nonprofit and advocacy sectors. Candidates must be nominated by their institution. Public service and leadership record considered. Visit web site http://www.truman.gov for further information and application. Political Science; Public Policy and Administration. *Award:* Scholarship for use in junior year; renewable. *Award amount:* $30,000. *Number of awards:* 65. *Eligibility Requirements:* Applicant must be enrolled or expecting to enroll full-time at a four-year institution or university and must have an interest in leadership. Available to U.S. citizens. *Application Requirements:* Application form, interview, policy proposal, recommendations or references. **Deadline:** February 5.

Contact Tonji Wade, Program Officer, Harry S. Truman Scholarship Foundation, 712 Jackson Place, NW, Washington, DC 20006. *E-mail:*

office@truman.gov. *Phone:* 202-395-4831. *Fax:* 202-395-6995. *Website:* http://www.truman.gov/.

Montgomery GI Bill (Active Duty) Chapter 30. Award provides up to thirty-six months of education benefits to eligible veterans for college, business school, technical courses, vocational courses, correspondence courses, apprenticeships/job training, or flight training. Must be an eligible veteran with an Honorable Discharge and have high school diploma or GED before applying for benefits. *Award:* Scholarship for use in freshman, sophomore, junior, senior, or graduate years; renewable. *Eligibility Requirements:* Applicant must be enrolled or expecting to enroll full- or part-time at a two-year or four-year or technical institution or university. Available to U.S. citizens. Applicant or parent must meet one or more of the following requirements: general military experience; retired from active duty; disabled or killed as a result of military service; prisoner of war; or missing in action. *Application Requirements:* Application form. **Deadline:** continuous.

Contact Keith Wilson, Director, Education Service. *Phone:* 888-442-4551. *Website:* http://www.gibill.va.gov/.

Montgomery GI Bill (Selected Reserve). Educational assistance program for members of the selected reserve of the Army, Navy, Air Force, Marine Corps and Coast Guard, as well as the Army and Air National Guard. Available to all reservists and National Guard personnel who commit to a six-year obligation, and remain in the Reserve or Guard during the six years. Award is renewable. Monthly benefit is $309 for up to thirty-six months for full-time. *Award:* Scholarship for use in freshman, sophomore, junior, senior, or postgraduate years; renewable. *Eligibility Requirements:* Applicant must be enrolled or expecting to enroll full- or part-time at a two-year or four-year or technical institution or university. Available to U.S. citizens. Applicant or parent must meet one or more of the following requirements: general military experience; retired from active duty; disabled or killed as a result of military service; prisoner of war; or missing in action. *Application Requirements:* Application form. **Deadline:** continuous.

Contact Keith Wilson, Director, Education Service. *Phone:* 888-442-4551. *Website:* http://www.gibill.va.gov/.

Reserve Education Assistance Program. The program provides educational assistance to members of National Guard and reserve components. Selected Reserve and Individual Ready Reserve (IRR) who are called or ordered to active duty service in response to a war or national emergency as declared by the president or Congress are eligible. For further information see web site http://www.GIBILL.va.gov. *Award:* Scholarship for use in freshman, sophomore, junior, senior, graduate, or postgraduate years; renewable. *Eligibility Requirements:* Applicant must be enrolled or expecting to enroll full- or part-time at a two-year or four-year or technical institution or university. Available to U.S. citizens. Applicant or parent must meet one or more of the following requirements: general military experience; retired from active duty; disabled or killed as a result of military service; prisoner of war; or missing in action. *Application Requirements:* Application form. **Deadline:** continuous.

Contact Keith Wilson, Director, Education Service. *Phone:* 888-442-4551. *Website:* http://www.gibill.va.gov/.

Survivors and Dependents Educational Assistance (Chapter 35)-VA. Monthly $860 benefits for up to 45 months. Must be spouses or children under age 26 of current veterans missing in action or of deceased or totally and permanently disabled (service-related) service persons. For more information visit the following web site http://www.gibill.va.gov. *Award:* Scholarship for use in freshman, sophomore, junior, or senior years; renewable. *Eligibility Requirements:* Applicant must be enrolled or expecting to enroll full- or part-time at a two-year or four-year or technical institution or university. Available to U.S. and non-U.S. citizens. Applicant or parent must meet one or more of the following requirements: general military experience; retired from active duty; disabled or killed as a result of military service; prisoner of war; or missing in action. *Application Requirements:* Application form. **Deadline:** continuous.

Contact Keith Wilson, Director, Education Service. *Phone:* 888-442-4551. *Website:* http://www.gibill.va.gov/.

FLORIDA

Access to Better Learning and Education Grant. Grant program provides tuition assistance to Florida undergraduate students enrolled in degree programs at eligible private Florida colleges or universities. Must be a U.S. citizen or eligible non-citizen and must meet Florida residency requirements. The participating institution determines application procedures, deadlines, and student eligibility. An eligible student must complete and submit the FAFSA in order to receive program funding. For more details, visit the web site at http://www.FloridaStudentFinancialAid.org/SSFAD/home/uamain.htm. *Award:* Grant for use in freshman, sophomore, junior, or senior years; renewable. *Award amount:* up to $1500. *Eligibility Requirements:* Applicant must be enrolled or expecting to enroll full-time at a four-year institution or university; resident of Florida and studying in Florida. Available to U.S. citizens. *Application Requirements:* Application form.

First Generation Matching Grant Program. Need-based grants to Florida resident undergraduate students who are enrolled in state universities and community colleges in Florida and whose parents have not earned baccalaureate degrees. Available state funds are contingent upon matching contributions from private sources on a dollar-for-dollar basis. Institutions determine application procedures, deadlines, and student eligibility. For more details, visit the web site at http://www.FloridaStudentFinancialAid.org/SSFAD/home/uamain.htm. *Award:* Grant for use in freshman, sophomore, junior, or senior years; renewable. *Eligibility Requirements:* Applicant must be enrolled or expecting to enroll full- or part-time at a two-year or four-year institution or university; resident of Florida and studying in Florida. Available to U.S. citizens. *Application Requirements:* Application form, financial need analysis.

Florida Bright Futures Scholarship Program. Three lottery-funded scholarships reward Florida high school graduates for high academic achievement. Program is comprised of the following three awards: Florida Academic Scholars Award, Florida Medallion Scholars Award and Florida Gold Seal Vocational Scholars Award. An eligible student must complete and submit the FAFSA in order to receive program funding. For more details, visit the web site at http://www.FloridaStudentFinancialAid.org/SSFAD/home/uamain.htm. *Award:* Scholarship for use in freshman, sophomore, junior, or senior years; renewable. *Eligibility Requirements:* Applicant must be high school student; planning to enroll or expecting to enroll full- or part-time at a two-year or four-year or technical institution or university; resident of Florida and studying in Florida. Applicant must have 3.0 GPA or higher. Available to U.S. citizens. *Application Requirements:* Application form, application form may be submitted online, community service, test scores, transcript.

Florida Postsecondary Student Assistance Grant. Scholarships to degree-seeking, resident, undergraduate students who demonstrate substantial financial need and are enrolled in eligible degree-granting private colleges and universities not eligible under the Florida Private Student Assistance Grant. FSAG is a decentralized program, and each participating institution determines application procedures, deadlines and student eligibility. Number of awards varies. For more details, visit the web site at http://www.FloridaStudentFinancialAid.org/SSFAD/home/uamain.htm. *Award:* Grant for use in freshman, sophomore, junior, or senior years; renewable. *Award amount:* $200–$2610. *Eligibility Requirements:* Applicant must be enrolled or expecting to enroll full-time at a two-year or four-year institution or university; resident of Florida and studying in Florida. Available to U.S. citizens. *Application Requirements:* Financial need analysis.

Florida Private Student Assistance Grant. Grants for Florida residents who are U.S. citizens or eligible non-citizens attending eligible private, nonprofit, four-year colleges and universities in Florida. Must be a full-time student and demonstrate substantial financial need. For renewal, must have earned a minimum cumulative GPA of 2.0 at the last institution attended. For more details, visit the web site at http://www.FloridaStudentFinancialAid.org/SSFAD/home/uamain.htm. *Award:* Grant for use in freshman, sophomore, junior, or senior years; renewable. *Award amount:* $200–$2610. *Eligibility Requirements:* Applicant must be enrolled or expecting to enroll full-time at a four-year institution or university; resident of Florida and studying in Florida. Available to U.S. citizens. *Application Requirements:* Application form, financial need analysis.

Florida Public Student Assistance Grant. Grants for Florida residents, U.S. citizens or eligible non-citizens who attend state universities and public community colleges and demonstrate substantial financial need. For renewal, must have earned a minimum cumulative GPA of 2.0 at the last institution attended. For more details, visit the web site at http://www.FloridaStudentFinancialAid.org/SSFAD/home/uamain.htm. *Award:* Grant for use in freshman, sophomore, junior, or senior years; renewable. *Award amount:* $200–$2610. *Eligibility Requirements:* Applicant must be enrolled or expecting to enroll full- or part-time at a two-year or four-year institution or university; resident of Florida and studying in Florida. Available to U.S. citizens. *Application Requirements:* Application form, financial need analysis.

Florida Space Research Program. Grants for faculty researchers from Florida public and private universities and community colleges. One-time award for aerospace and technology research. Submit research proposal with budget. Aviation/Aerospace; Earth Science; Education; Electrical Engineering/Electronics; Engineering/Technology; Marine/Ocean Engineering; Materials Science, Engineering, and Metallurgy; Mathematics; Mechanical Engineering; Meteorology/Atmospheric Science; Physical Sciences. *Award:* Grant for use in junior, senior, graduate, or postgraduate years; not renewable. *Award amount:* $12,500–$25,000. *Number of awards:* 13–15. *Eligibility Requirements:* Applicant must be enrolled or expecting to enroll full- or part-time at a two-year or four-year institution or university; resident of Florida and studying in Florida. Available to U.S. citizens. *Application Requirements:* Application form. **Deadline:** May 17.

Contact Dr. Jaydeep Mukherjee, FSGC Director, NASA Florida Space Grant Consortium, PO Box 160650, 12354 Research Parkway, Room 218, Orlando, FL 32826. *E-mail:* fsgc@ucf.edu. *Phone:* 407-823-6177. *Website:* http://www.floridaspacegrant.org/.

Florida Student Assistance Grant-Career Education. Need-based grant program available to Florida residents enrolled in certificate programs of 450 or more clock hours at participating community colleges or career centers operated by district school boards. FSAG-CE is a decentralized state of Florida program, which means that each participating institution determines application procedures, deadlines, student eligibility, and award amounts. For more details, visit the web site at http://www.FloridaStudentFinancialAid.org/SSFAD/home/uamain.htm. *Award:* Grant for use in freshman, sophomore, junior, or senior years; renewable. *Award amount:* $200–$2610. *Eligibility Requirements:* Applicant must be enrolled or expecting to enroll full- or part-time at a two-year or technical institution; resident of Florida and studying in Florida. Available to U.S. citizens. *Application Requirements:* Application form may be submitted online, financial need analysis.

Florida Work Experience Program. Need-based program providing eligible Florida residents work experiences that will complement and reinforce their educational and career goals. Must maintain GPA of 2.0. Postsecondary institution will determine applicant's eligibility, number of hours to be worked per week, and the award amount. For more details, visit the web site at http://www.FloridaStudentFinancialAid.org/SSFAD/home/uamain.htm. *Award:* Grant for use in freshman, sophomore, junior, or senior years; renewable. *Eligibility Requirements:* Applicant must be enrolled or expecting to enroll full- or part-time at a two-year or four-year institution or university; resident of Florida and studying in Florida. Available to U.S. citizens. *Application Requirements:* Financial need analysis.

Jose Marti Scholarship Challenge Grant Fund. Award available to Hispanic-American students who were born in, or whose parent was born in a Hispanic country. Must be a Florida resident, be enrolled full-time in Florida at an eligible school, and have a GPA of 3.0 or above. Must be U.S. citizen or eligible non-citizen. FAFSA must be processed by May 15. For more details, visit the web site at http://www.FloridaStudentFinancialAid.org/SSFAD/home/uamain.htm. *Award:* Scholarship for use in freshman, sophomore, junior,

or senior years; renewable. *Award amount:* $2000. *Eligibility Requirements:* Applicant must be of Hispanic heritage; high school student; planning to enroll or expecting to enroll full-time at a two-year or four-year institution or university; resident of Florida and studying in Florida. Applicant must have 3.0 GPA or higher. Available to U.S. citizens. *Application Requirements:* Application form, financial need analysis. **Deadline:** April 1.

Mary McLeod Bethune Scholarship. Renewable award to Florida residents with a GPA of 3.0 or above, who will attend Bethune-Cookman University, Edward Waters College, Florida A&M University, or Florida Memorial University. Must not have previously received a baccalaureate degree. Must demonstrate financial need as specified by the institution. For more details, visit the web site at http://www.FloridaStudentFinancialAid.org/SSFAD/home/uamain.htm. *Award:* Scholarship for use in freshman, sophomore, junior, or senior years; renewable. *Award amount:* $3000. *Eligibility Requirements:* Applicant must be enrolled or expecting to enroll full-time at a four-year institution or university; resident of Florida and studying in Florida. Applicant must have 3.0 GPA or higher. Available to U.S. citizens. *Application Requirements:* Financial need analysis.

Rosewood Family Scholarship Fund. Renewable award for eligible direct descendants of African-American Rosewood families affected by the incident of January 1923. Must not have previously received a baccalaureate degree. For more details, visit the web site at http://www.FloridaStudentFinancialAid.org/SSFAD/home/uamain.htm. *Award:* Scholarship for use in freshman, sophomore, junior, or senior years; renewable. *Award amount:* up to $6100. *Number of awards:* up to 50. *Eligibility Requirements:* Applicant must be enrolled or expecting to enroll full- or part-time at a two-year or four-year or technical institution or university and studying in Florida. Available to U.S. citizens. *Application Requirements:* Application form, documentation of Rosewood ancestry, financial need analysis. **Deadline:** April 1.

Scholarships for Children & Spouses of Deceased or Disabled Veterans. Renewable scholarships for children and spouses of deceased or disabled veterans. Children must be between the ages of 16 and 22, and attend an eligible Florida postsecondary institution and enrolled at least part-time. Must ensure that the Florida Department of Veterans Affairs certifies the applicant's eligibility. Must maintain GPA of 2.0. For more details, visit the web site at http://www.FloridaStudentFinancialAid.org/SSFAD/home/uamain.htm. *Award:* Scholarship for use in freshman, sophomore, junior, or senior years; renewable. *Eligibility Requirements:* Applicant must be age 16-22; enrolled or expecting to enroll full- or part-time at a two-year or four-year or technical institution or university; resident of Florida and studying in Florida. Available to U.S. citizens. Applicant or parent must meet one or more of the following requirements: general military experience; retired from active duty; disabled or killed as a result of military service; prisoner of war; or missing in action. *Application Requirements:* Application form. **Deadline:** April 1.

William L. Boyd IV Florida Resident Access Grant. Renewable awards to Florida undergraduate residents attending an eligible private, nonprofit Florida college or university. Postsecondary institution will determine applicant's eligibility. Renewal applicant must have earned a minimum institutional GPA of 2.0. An eligible student must complete and submit the FAFSA in order to receive program funding. For more details, visit the web site at http://www.FloridaStudentFinancialAid.org/SSFAD/home/uamain.htm. *Award:* Grant for use in freshman, sophomore, junior, or senior years; renewable. *Award amount:* up to $3000. *Eligibility Requirements:* Applicant must be enrolled or expecting to enroll full-time at a four-year institution or university; resident of Florida and studying in Florida. Available to U.S. citizens. *Application Requirements:* Application form.

GEORGIA

Georgia HERO Scholarship. Provides assistance with cost of attendance to members of the Georgia National Guard and U.S. Military Reservists who were deployed overseas on active duty service, on or after February 1, 2003, to a location designated as a combat zone, and the children and spouses of such members of the Georgia National Guard and U.S. Military Reserves. Students must be attending an eligible college or university in Georgia. *Award:* Scholarship for use in freshman, sophomore, junior, or senior years; not renewable. *Award amount:* $2000. *Number of awards:* 200–350. *Eligibility Requirements:* Applicant must be enrolled or expecting to enroll full- or part-time at a two-year or four-year or technical institution or university; resident of Georgia and studying in Georgia. Available to U.S. citizens. *Application Requirements:* Application form.

Contact Ms. Pennie Strong, Vice President, Student Aid Services, Georgia Student Finance Commission, 2082 East Exchange Place, Tucker, GA 30084. *E-mail:* pennies@gsfc.org. *Phone:* 770-724-9014. *Fax:* 770-724-9249. *Website:* http://www.GAfutures.org.

Georgia Public Safety Memorial Grant. Public Safety Memorial Grant provides assistance to the dependent children of Georgia public safety officers who were permanently disabled or killed in the line of duty. Funds may be used toward the cost of attendance at eligible colleges or universities in Georgia. *Award:* Grant for use in freshman, sophomore, junior, or senior years; not renewable. *Award amount:* $2000–$18,000. *Number of awards:* 20–40. *Eligibility Requirements:* Applicant must be enrolled or expecting to enroll full-time at a two-year or four-year or technical institution or university; resident of Georgia and studying in Georgia. Applicant or parent of applicant must have employment or volunteer experience in police/firefighting. Available to U.S. citizens. *Application Requirements:* Application form. **Deadline:** continuous.

Contact Ms. Pennie Strong, Vice President, Student Aid Services, Georgia Student Finance Commission, 2082 East Exchange Place, Tucker, GA 30084. *E-mail:* pennies@gsfc.org. *Phone:* 770-724-9014. *Fax:* 770-724-9249. *Website:* http://www.GAfutures.org.

Georgia Tuition Equalization Grant (GTEG). The Georgia Tuition Equalization Grant (GTEG) provides grant assistance toward educational costs to Georgia residents enrolled at an eligible private college or university. Students must be enrolled full-time in an undergraduate program of study leading to an undergraduate *Award:* Grant for use in freshman, sophomore, junior, or senior years; renewable. *Award amount:* $317–$475. *Number of awards:* 46,000. *Eligibility Requirements:* Applicant must be enrolled or expecting to enroll full-time at a two-year or four-year institution or university; resident of Georgia and studying in Georgia. Available to U.S. citizens. *Application Requirements:* Application form.

Contact Ms. Pennie Strong, Vice President, Student Aid Services, Georgia Student Finance Commission, 2082 East Exchange Place, Tucker, GA 30084. *E-mail:* pennies@gsfc.org. *Phone:* 770-724-9014. *Fax:* 770-724-9249. *Website:* http://www.GAfutures.org.

Paper and Board Division Scholarships. Award to TAPPI student member or an undergraduate member of a TAPPI Student Chapter enrolled as a college or university undergraduate in an engineering or science program. Must be sophomore, junior, or senior and able to show a significant interest in the paper industry. Information can be found at http://www.tappi.org/s_tappi/sec.asp?CID=6101&DID=546695. Engineering/Technology; Paper and Pulp Engineering. *Award:* Scholarship for use in sophomore, junior, or senior years; not renewable. *Award amount:* $1000–$1500. *Number of awards:* 1–4. *Eligibility Requirements:* Applicant must be enrolled or expecting to enroll full-time at a four-year institution or university. Available to U.S. and non-U.S. citizens. *Application Requirements:* Application form. **Deadline:** February 15.

Contact Mr. Laurence Womack, Director of Standards and Awards, Technical Association of the Pulp & Paper Industry (TAPPI), 15 Technology Parkway South, Peachtree Corners, GA 30092. *E-mail:* standards@tappi.org. *Phone:* 770-209-7276. *Website:* http://www.tappi.org/.

Physicians for Rural Areas Assistance Program. Service repayable medical school scholarship for a maximum of $20,000 per year for four years available to Georgia residents enrolled in U.S. accredited medical school. Repay by practicing medicine for one year in rural Georgia for each year that the scholarship is received. Service payment begins upon completion of residency training. Health and Medical Sciences. *Award:* Scholarship for use in freshman, sophomore, junior, or senior years; renewable. *Award amount:* up to $20,000. *Number of awards:* 20–25. *Eligibility Requirements:* Applicant must be enrolled or expecting to enroll full-time at an institution or university and resident of Georgia. Available to U.S. citizens. *Application Requirements:* Application form, essay, financial need analysis, interview, personal photograph, proof of GA residency, test scores, transcript. **Deadline:** June 1.

Contact Ms. Pamela Smith, Administration Manager, Georgia Board for Physician Workforce (GBPW), 2 Peachtree Street, NW, 36th Floor, Atlanta, GA 30303. *E-mail:* psmith@dch.ga.gov. *Phone:* 404-232-7972. *Website:* http://www.gbpw.georgia.gov.

Zell Miller Scholarship Program. Zell Miller Scholarship is a merit-based award available to Georgia residents, similar to the HOPE Scholarship, but with more stringent academic requirements and a higher level of tuition assistance. A Zell Miller Scholarship recipient must graduate from high school with a minimum 3.7 HOPE Calculated (approved core courses) grade point average combined and earned 4 credits of academic rigor, with a minimum SAT score of 1,200 on the math and reading portions or a minimum composite ACT score of 26 in single national test administration. Students must maintain a minimum 3.3 cumulative postsecondary grade point average to remain eligible. Students are provided full-tuition assistance while pursuing an undergraduate degree and they must attend an eligible college or university in Georgia. A seven-year limit exists for students first receiving the Zell Miller Scholarship during the 2011-2012 academic year (FY12) or later. *Award:* Scholarship for use in freshman, sophomore, junior, or senior years; renewable. *Award amount:* $534–$5004. *Number of awards:* 200,000. *Eligibility Requirements:* Applicant must be enrolled or expecting to enroll full- or part-time at a two-year or four-year or technical institution or university; resident of Georgia and studying in Georgia. Applicant must have 3.5 GPA or higher. Available to U.S. citizens. *Application Requirements:* Application form.

Contact Ms. Pennie Strong, Vice President, Student Aid Services, Georgia Student Finance Commission, 2082 East Exchange Place, Tucker, GA 30084. *E-mail:* pennies@gsfc.org. *Phone:* 770-724-9014. *Fax:* 770-724-9249. *Website:* http://www.GAfutures.org.

HAWAII

Hawaii State Student Incentive Grant. Grants are given to residents of Hawaii who are enrolled in a participating Hawaiian state school. Funds are for undergraduate tuition only. Applicants must submit a financial need analysis. *Award:* Grant for use in freshman, sophomore, junior, or senior years; renewable. *Award amount:* $200–$2000. *Number of awards:* 470. *Eligibility Requirements:* Applicant must be enrolled or expecting to enroll full- or part-time at a two year or four-year or technical institution or university; resident of Hawaii and studying in Hawaii. Available to U.S. citizens. *Application Requirements:* Application form, financial need analysis. **Deadline:** continuous.

Contact Janine Oyama, Financial Aid Specialist, Hawaii State Postsecondary Education Commission, University of Hawaii, Honolulu, HI 96822. *Phone:* 808-956-6066.

IDAHO

Idaho Opportunity Scholarship. The Idaho Opportunity Scholarship is an award open to Idaho citizens who have graduated from Idaho high schools. The application is open to any high school or college students who attended an Idaho high school, are Idaho residents, and are attending or who are planning on attending an eligible Idaho college or university. Students must be earning their first undergraduate degree. The required GPA is a 3.0 and applicants must show need by completing the FAFSA by March 1 each year. The award is renewable for a total of 4 years. *Award:* Scholarship for use in freshman, sophomore, junior, or senior years; renewable. *Award amount:* $1–$3500. *Number of awards:* 700–2000. *Eligibility Requirements:* Applicant must be enrolled or expecting to enroll full-time at a two-year or four-year or technical institution or university; resident of Idaho and studying in Idaho. Applicant

must have 3.0 GPA or higher. Available to U.S. citizens. *Application Requirements:* Application form, financial need analysis. **Deadline:** March 1.

Contact Joy Miller, Scholarships Program Manager, Idaho State Board of Education, 650 W. State St., #307, Boise, ID 83720. *E-mail:* joy.miller@osbe.idaho.gov. *Phone:* 208-332 Ext. 1595. *Website:* http://www.boardofed.idaho.gov/.

ILLINOIS

Golden Apple Scholars of Illinois. Applicants must be between the ages of 16 and 21 and maintain a GPA of 2.5. Eligible applicants must be residents of Illinois studying education in Illinois. Recipients must agree to teach in an Illinois school school-of-need for 5 years. Education. *Award:* Scholarship for use in freshman, sophomore, junior, or senior years; renewable. *Award amount:* $23,000. *Number of awards:* 200. *Eligibility Requirements:* Applicant must be age 16-21; enrolled or expecting to enroll full-time at a two-year or four-year institution or university; resident of Illinois and studying in Illinois. Applicant must have 2.5 GPA or higher. Available to U.S. citizens. *Application Requirements:* Application form, essay, interview, personal photograph. **Deadline:** February 15.

Contact Ms. Patricia Kilduff, Director of Recruitment and Placement. *E-mail:* kilduff@goldenapple.org. *Phone:* 312-477-7515. *Website:* http://www.goldenapple.org/.

Grant Program for Dependents of Police, Fire, or Correctional Officers. Awards available to Illinois residents who are dependents of police, fire, and correctional officers killed or disabled in line of duty. Provides for tuition and fees at approved Illinois institutions. Number of grants and individual dollar amount awarded vary. *Award:* Grant for use in freshman, sophomore, junior, senior, graduate, or postgraduate years; renewable. *Eligibility Requirements:* Applicant must be enrolled or expecting to enroll full- or part-time at a two-year or four-year or technical institution or university; resident of Illinois and studying in Illinois. Available to U.S. citizens. *Application Requirements:* Application form. **Deadline:** October 1.

Higher Education License Plate Program-HELP. Grants for students who attend Illinois colleges for which the special collegiate license plates are available. The Illinois Secretary of State issues the license plates, and part of the proceeds are used for grants for undergraduate students attending these colleges, to pay tuition and mandatory fees. *Award:* Grant for use in freshman, sophomore, junior, or senior years; not renewable. *Eligibility Requirements:* Applicant must be enrolled or expecting to enroll full- or part-time at a two-year or four-year institution or university; resident of Illinois and studying in Illinois. Available to U.S. citizens. *Application Requirements:* Application form, financial need analysis. **Deadline:** continuous.

Illinois Monetary Award Program. Awards to Illinois residents enrolled in a minimum of 3 hours per term in a degree program at an approved Illinois institution. See web site for complete list of participating schools. Must demonstrate financial need, based on the information provided on the Free Application for Federal Student Aid. Number of grants and the individual dollar amount awarded vary. Deadline: As soon as possible after October 1 of the year before the student will enter college. *Award:* Grant for use in freshman, sophomore, junior, or senior years; renewable. *Award amount:* $2850. *Eligibility Requirements:* Applicant must be enrolled or expecting to enroll full- or part-time at a two-year or four-year or technical institution or university; resident of Illinois and studying in Illinois. Available to U.S. citizens. *Application Requirements:* Application form, financial need analysis. **Deadline:** June 30.

Illinois National Guard Grant Program. Active duty members of the Illinois National Guard, or who are within 12 months of discharge, and who have completed one full year of service are eligible. May be used for study at Illinois two- or four-year public colleges for a maximum of the equivalent of four academic years of full-time enrollment. Deadlines: October 1 of the academic year for full year, March 1 for second/third term, or June 15 for the summer term. *Award:* Grant for use in freshman, sophomore, junior, senior, or graduate years; not renewable. *Eligibility Requirements:* Applicant must be enrolled or expecting to enroll full- or part-time at a two-year or four-year

institution or university; resident of Illinois and studying in Illinois. Available to U.S. citizens. Applicant or parent must meet one or more of the following requirements: national guard experience; retired from active duty; disabled or killed as a result of military service; prisoner of war; or missing in action. *Application Requirements:* Application form. **Deadline:** October 1.

Illinois Veteran Grant Program-IVG. Awards qualified veterans and pays eligible tuition and fees for study in Illinois public universities or community colleges. Program eligibility units are based on the enrolled hours for a particular term, not the dollar amount of the benefits paid. Applications are available at college financial aid office and can be submitted any time during the academic year for which assistance is being requested. *Award:* Grant for use in freshman, sophomore, junior, senior, or graduate years; renewable. *Eligibility Requirements:* Applicant must be enrolled or expecting to enroll full- or part-time at a two-year or four-year institution or university; resident of Illinois and studying in Illinois. Available to U.S. citizens. Applicant or parent must meet one or more of the following requirements: general military experience; retired from active duty; disabled or killed as a result of military service; prisoner of war; or missing in action. *Application Requirements:* Application form. **Deadline:** continuous.

Jill S. Tietjen P.E. Scholarship. $1750 award for a woman pursuing an ABET-accredited Baccalaureate program in preparation for a career in engineering and engineering technology in the United States and Mexico. Must be a U.S. citizen and have minimum 3.0 GPA. Engineering/Technology. *Award:* Scholarship for use in sophomore, junior, or senior years; not renewable. *Award amount:* $1750. *Number of awards:* 1. *Eligibility Requirements:* Applicant must be enrolled or expecting to enroll full-time at a four-year institution or university and female. Applicant must have 3.0 GPA or higher. Available to U.S. citizens. *Application Requirements:* Application form. **Deadline:** February 15.

MIA/POW Scholarship. Any spouse, natural child, adopted child, or any step child of a veteran. Child must attend school prior to 26th birthday. No age

limit for spouse. Veteran must be MIA, POW, died as the result of service connected disability determined by the U.S. Department of Veterans' Affairs or is 100% service connected disabled permanent and total established by the U.S. Department of Veterans' Affairs. Veteran must have been an Illinois resident at time of entry into service or became an Illinois resident within 6 months after entering service. Scholarship is equivalent to four full years of college, including summer terms. Based on a point system with 120 points as the maximum. Applicant has 12 years to utilize scholarship from the date they begin using it. *Award:* Scholarship for use in freshman, sophomore, junior, senior, graduate, or postgraduate years; renewable. *Eligibility Requirements:* Applicant must be enrolled or expecting to enroll full- or part-time at a two-year or four-year institution or university and studying in Illinois. Available to U.S. and non-U.S. citizens. *Application Requirements:* Application form. **Deadline:** continuous.

Contact Mr. Dan Wellman, Administrator, Illinois Department of Veterans' Affairs, 833 South Spring Street, Springfield, IL 62794-9432. *Phone:* 217-782-7838. *Website:* https://www.illinois.gov/veterans/Pages/default.aspx.

Minority Teachers of Illinois Scholarship Program. Award for minority students intending to become school teachers; teaching commitment attached to receipt. Number of scholarships and the individual dollar amounts vary. Education. *Award:* Scholarship for use in freshman, sophomore, junior, senior, graduate, or postgraduate years; not renewable. *Eligibility Requirements:* Applicant must be American Indian/Alaska Native, Asian/Pacific Islander, Black (non-Hispanic), Hispanic; enrolled or expecting to enroll full- or part-time at a two-year or four-year institution or university; resident of Illinois and studying in Illinois. Available to U.S. citizens. *Application Requirements:* Application form. **Deadline:** March 1.

SWE Baltimore-Washington Section Scholarship. One $2000 award for a woman pursuing an ABET-accredited Baccalaureate or graduate program in preparation for a career in engineering, engineering technology, or computer science in the United States and Mexico. For use at a school in DC, MD, or VA.

U.S. citizenship and SWE membership required. Chemical Engineering; Civil Engineering; Construction Engineering/ Management; Electrical Engineering/ Electronics; Energy and Power Engineering; Engineering/Technology; Marine/Ocean Engineering; Materials Science, Engineering, and Metallurgy; Mechanical Engineering; Paper and Pulp Engineering. *Award:* Scholarship for use in sophomore, junior, senior, or graduate years; not renewable. *Award amount:* $2000. *Number of awards:* 1. *Eligibility Requirements:* Applicant must be enrolled or expecting to enroll full-time at a four-year institution or university; female and studying in District of Columbia, Maryland, Virginia. Applicant or parent of applicant must be member of Society of Women Engineers. Applicant must have 3.0 GPA or higher. Available to U.S. citizens. *Application Requirements:* Application form. **Deadline:** February 15.

SWE Central New Mexico Pioneers Scholarship. Renewable $1500 scholarship for a woman pursuing an ABET-accredited Baccalaureate program in preparation for a career in engineering, engineering technology, or computer science in the United States and Mexico. Must attend a NM university or 4-year engineering/technology school. U.S. citizenship, SWE membership, and minimum 3.0 GPA required. Renewable up to three years. Availability dependent upon renewal. Chemical Engineering; Civil Engineering; Construction Engineering/Management; Electrical Engineering/Electronics; Energy and Power Engineering; Engineering/Technology; Marine/Ocean Engineering; Materials Science, Engineering, and Metallurgy; Mechanical Engineering; Paper and Pulp Engineering. *Award:* Scholarship for use in sophomore, junior, or senior years; renewable. *Award amount:* $1500. *Number of awards:* 1. *Eligibility Requirements:* Applicant must be enrolled or expecting to enroll full-time at a four-year institution or university; female and studying in New Mexico. Applicant or parent of applicant must be member of Society of Women Engineers. Applicant must have 3.0 GPA or higher. Available to U.S. citizens. *Application Requirements:* Application form. **Deadline:** February 15.

INDIANA

Child of Disabled Veteran Grant or Purple Heart Recipient Grant. Free tuition at Indiana state-supported colleges or universities for children of disabled veterans or Purple Heart recipients. Must submit form DD214 or service record. Covers tuition and mandatory fees. *Award:* Grant for use in freshman, sophomore, junior, senior, graduate, or postgraduate years; renewable. *Eligibility Requirements:* Applicant must be enrolled or expecting to enroll full- or part-time at a two-year or four-year institution or university; resident of Indiana and studying in Indiana. Available to U.S. citizens. Applicant must have general military experience. *Application Requirements:* Application form. **Deadline:** continuous.

Contact Michael Hamm, State Service Officer. *E-mail:* mhamm@dva.in.gov. *Phone:* 317-232-3910. *Fax:* 317-232-7721. *Website:* http://www.in.gov/dva.

Department of Veterans Affairs Free Tuition for Children of POW/MIA's in Vietnam. Renewable award for residents of Indiana who are the children of veterans declared missing in action or prisoner-of-war after January 1, 1960. Provides tuition at Indiana state-supported institutions for undergraduate study. *Award:* Grant for use in freshman, sophomore, junior, senior, graduate, or postgraduate years; renewable. *Eligibility Requirements:* Applicant must be enrolled or expecting to enroll full- or part-time at a two-year or four-year institution or university; resident of Indiana and studying in Indiana. Available to U.S. citizens. Applicant must have general military experience. *Application Requirements:* Application form. **Deadline:** continuous.

Contact Michael Hamm, State Service Officer. *E-mail:* mhamm@dva.in.gov. *Phone:* 317-232-3910. *Fax:* 317-232-7721. *Website:* http://www.in.gov/dva.

Frank O'Bannon Grant Program. A need-based, tuition-restricted program for students attending Indiana public, private, or proprietary institutions seeking a first undergraduate degree. Students (and parents of dependent students) who are U.S. citizens and Indiana residents must file the FAFSA yearly by the March 10 deadline. *Award:* Grant for use in freshman, sophomore, junior, or senior years; not renewable. *Award amount:* $200–$10,992. *Number of awards:* 48,408–70,239. *Eligibility Requirements:* Applicant must be enrolled or expecting to enroll full-time at a two-year or four-year or technical institution or university; resident of Indiana and studying in Indiana. Available to U.S. citizens. *Application Requirements:* Application form, FAFSA, financial need analysis. **Deadline:** March 10.

Indiana National Guard Supplemental Grant. The award is a supplement to the Indiana Higher Education Grant program. Applicants must be members of the Indiana National Guard. All Guard paperwork must be completed prior to the start of each semester. The FAFSA must be received by March 10. Award covers certain tuition and fees at select public colleges. *Award:* Grant for use in freshman, sophomore, junior, or senior years; not renewable. *Award amount:* $20–$7110. *Number of awards:* 503–925. *Eligibility Requirements:* Applicant must be enrolled or expecting to enroll full- or part-time at a two-year or four-year institution or university; resident of Indiana and studying in Indiana. Available to U.S. citizens. Applicant or parent must meet one or more of the following requirements: national guard experience; retired from active duty; disabled or killed as a result of military service; prisoner of war; or missing in action. *Application Requirements:* Application form. **Deadline:** March 10.

Contact Kathryn Moore, Grants Counselor, Indiana Commission for Higher Education, 150 West Market Street, Suite 500, Indianapolis, IN 46204-2805. *E-mail:* kmoore@ssaci.in.gov. *Phone:* 317-232-2350. *Fax:* 317-232-2360. *Website:* http://www.in.gov/che.

National Guard Scholarship Extension Program. A scholarship extension applicant is eligible for a tuition scholarship under Indiana Code 21-13-5-4 for a period not to exceed the period of scholarship extension the applicant served on active duty as a member of the National Guard (mobilized and deployed). Must apply not later than one (1) year after the applicant ceases to be a member of the Indiana National Guard. Applicant should apply through the education officer of their last unit of assignment. *Award:* Grant for use in freshman, sophomore, junior, or senior years; renewable. *Eligibility Requirements:* Applicant must be enrolled or expecting to enroll full- or part-time at a two-year or four-year or technical institution or university; resident of Indiana and studying in Indiana. Available to U.S. citizens. Applicant must have national guard experience. *Application Requirements:* Application form. **Deadline:** continuous.

Contact Pamela Moody, National Guard Education Officer, Indiana Department of Veterans Affairs, 302 West Washington Street, Room E-120, Indianapolis, IN 46204. *E-mail:* pamela.moody@in.ngb.army.mil. *Phone:* 317-964-7017. *Website:* http://www.in.gov/dva.

National Guard Tuition Supplement Program. Applicant must be a member of the Indiana National Guard, in active drilling status, who has not been AWOL during the last 12 months, does not possess a bachelor's degree, possesses the requisite academic qualifications, meets the requirements of the state-supported college or university, and meets all National Guard requirements. *Award:* Grant for use in freshman, sophomore, junior, or senior years; renewable. *Eligibility Requirements:* Applicant must be enrolled or expecting to enroll full- or part-time at a two-year or four-year or technical institution or university; resident of Indiana and studying in Indiana. Available to U.S. citizens. Applicant must have national guard experience. *Application Requirements:* Application form. **Deadline:** continuous.

Contact Michael Hamm, State Service Officer. *E-mail:* mhamm@dva.in.gov. *Phone:* 317-232-3910. *Fax:* 317-232-7721. *Website:* http://www.in.gov/dva.

Part-Time Grant Program. Program is designed to encourage part-time undergraduates to start and complete their Associate or Baccalaureate degrees or certificates by subsidizing part-time tuition costs. It is a term-based award that is based on need. State residency requirements must be met and a FAFSA must be filed. Eligibility is determined at the institutional level subject to approval by SSACI. *Award:* Grant for use in freshman, sophomore, junior, or senior years; not renewable. *Award amount:* $20–$4000. *Number of awards:* 4680–6700. *Eligibility Requirements:* Applicant must be enrolled or expecting to enroll part-time at a two-year or four-year or technical institution or university; resident of Indiana and studying in Indiana. Available to U.S. citizens. *Application Requirements:* Application form, financial need analysis. **Deadline:** continuous.

Resident Tuition for Active Duty Military Personnel. Applicant must be a nonresident of Indiana serving on active duty and stationed in Indiana and attending any state-supported college or university. Dependents remain eligible for the duration of their enrollment, even if the active duty person is no longer in Indiana. Entitlement is to the resident tuition rate. *Award:* Grant for use in freshman, sophomore, junior, senior, graduate, or postgraduate years; renewable. *Eligibility Requirements:* Applicant must be enrolled or expecting to enroll full- or part-time at a two-year or four-year or technical institution or university and studying in Indiana. Available to U.S. citizens. Applicant or parent must meet one or more of the following requirements: Air Force or Army experience; retired from active duty; disabled or killed as a result of military service; prisoner of war; or missing in action. *Application Requirements:* Application form. **Deadline:** continuous.

Contact Michael Hamm, State Service Officer. *E-mail:* mhamm@dva.in.gov. *Phone:* 317-232-3910. *Fax:* 317-232-7721. *Website:* http://www.in.gov/dva.

Tuition and Fee Remission for Children and Spouses of National Guard Members. Award to an individual whose father, mother or spouse was a member of the Indiana National Guard and suffered a service-connected death while serving on state active duty (which includes mobilized and deployed for federal active duty). The student must be eligible to pay the resident tuition rate at the state-supported college or university and must possess the requisite academic qualifications. *Award:* Grant for use in freshman, sophomore, junior, or senior years; renewable. *Eligibility Requirements:* Applicant must be enrolled or expecting to enroll full- or part-time at a two-year or four-year or technical institution or university and studying in Indiana. Available to U.S. citizens. Applicant or parent must meet one or more of the following requirements: national guard experience; retired from active duty; disabled or killed as a result of military service; prisoner of war; or missing in action. *Application Requirements:* Application form. **Deadline:** continuous.

Contact Courtney Carr, Adjutant General, Indiana Department of Veterans Affairs, 2002 South Holt Road, Indianapolis, IN 46241. *E-mail:* c.carr@in.ngb.army.mil. *Phone:* 317-247-3559. *Website:* http://www.in.gov/dva.

IOWA

Iowa National Guard Education Assistance Program. Program provides postsecondary grant assistance to members of Iowa National Guard Units. Must study at a postsecondary institution in Iowa. *Award:* Grant for use in freshman, sophomore, junior, or senior years; not renewable. *Eligibility Requirements:* Applicant must be enrolled or expecting to enroll full- or part-time at a two-year or four-year or technical institution or university; resident of Iowa and studying in Iowa. Available to U.S. citizens. Applicant must have national guard experience. *Application Requirements:* Application form. **Deadline:** July 1.

Contact Tracy Davis, Executive Officer 1, Iowa College Student Aid Commission, 430 E Grand Avenue, FL 3, Des Moines, IA 50309-1920. *Phone:* 877-272-4456. *Website:* http://www.iowacollegeaid.gov/.

Iowa Tuition Grant Program. Program assists students who attend independent postsecondary institutions in Iowa. Iowa residents currently enrolled, or planning to enroll, for at least 3 semester hours at one of the eligible Iowa postsecondary institutions may apply. Awards currently range from $100 to $5650. Grants may not exceed the difference between independent college and university tuition fees and the average tuition fees at the three public Regent universities. *Award:* Grant for use in freshman, sophomore, junior, or senior years; not renewable. *Award amount:* $100–$5650. *Number of awards:* 16,500–19,000. *Eligibility Requirements:* Applicant must be enrolled or expecting to enroll full- or part-time at a two-year or four-year institution or university; resident of

Iowa and studying in Iowa. Available to U.S. citizens. *Application Requirements:* Financial need analysis. **Deadline:** July 1.

Contact Tristan Lynn, Executive Officer 1, Iowa College Student Aid Commission, 430 E Grand Avenue, FL 3, Des Moines, IA 50309-1920. *E-mail:* tristan.lynn@iowa.gov. *Phone:* 515-725-3409. *Website:* http://www.iowacollegeaid.gov/.

Iowa Vocational-Technical Tuition Grant Program. Program provides need-based financial assistance to Iowa residents enrolled in career education (vocational-technical), and career option programs at Iowa area community colleges. Grants range from $150 to $1200, depending on the length of the program, financial need, and available funds. *Award:* Grant for use in freshman or sophomore years; not renewable. *Award amount:* $150–$1200. *Number of awards:* 2500–3500. *Eligibility Requirements:* Applicant must be enrolled or expecting to enroll full- or part-time at a two-year or technical institution; resident of Iowa and studying in Iowa. Available to U.S. citizens. *Application Requirements:* Financial need analysis. **Deadline:** July 1.

Contact Tristan Lynn, Executive Officer 1, Iowa College Student Aid Commission, 430 E Grand Avenue, FL 3, Des Moines, IA 50309-1920. *E-mail:* tristan.lynn@iowa.gov. *Phone:* 515-725-3409. *Website:* http://www.iowacollegeaid.gov/.

KANSAS

Kansas Educational Benefits for Children of MIA, POW, and Deceased Veterans of the Vietnam War. Scholarship awarded to students who are children of veterans. Must show proof of parent's status as missing in action, prisoner-of-war, or killed in action in the Vietnam War. Kansas residence required of veteran at time of entry to service. Must attend a state-supported postsecondary school. *Award:* Scholarship for use in freshman, sophomore, junior, or senior years; not renewable. *Number of awards:* 1. *Eligibility Requirements:* Applicant must be enrolled or expecting to enroll full-time at a two-year or four-year or technical institution or university and studying in Kansas. Available to U.S. citizens. Applicant or parent must meet one or more of the following

requirements: general military experience; retired from active duty; disabled or killed as a result of military service; prisoner of war; or missing in action. *Application Requirements:* Application form, birth certificate, school acceptance letter, military discharge of veteran. **Deadline:** varies.

Contact Wayne Bollig, Program Director. *E-mail:* wbollig@kcva.org. *Phone:* 785-296-3976. *Fax:* 785-296-1462. *Website:* http://www.kcva.org/.

Kansas Ethnic Minority Scholarship. Scholarship program designed to assist financially needy, academically competitive students who are identified as members of any of the following ethnic/racial groups: African-American, American Indian or Alaskan Native, Asian or Pacific Islander, or Hispanic. Priority is given to applicants who are freshmen. Students must be Kansas residents attending postsecondary institutions in Kansas. For more details refer to web site http://www.kansasregents.org/students/student_financial_aid/scholarships_and_grants. *Award:* Scholarship for use in freshman, sophomore, junior, or senior years; renewable. *Award amount:* $50–$1850. *Number of awards:* 100–250. *Eligibility Requirements:* Applicant must be American Indian/Alaska Native, Asian/Pacific Islander, Black (non-Hispanic), Hispanic; enrolled or expecting to enroll full-time at a two-year or four-year institution or university; resident of Kansas and studying in Kansas. Applicant must have 3.0 GPA or higher. Available to U.S. citizens. *Application Requirements:* Application form, financial need analysis. **Deadline:** May 1.

Contact Diane Lindeman, Director of Student Financial Assistance, Kansas Board of Regents, 1000 SW Jackson, Suite 520, Topeka, KS 66612. *E-mail:* dlindeman@ksbor.org. *Phone:* 785-430-4255. *Fax:* 785-430-4233. *Website:* http://www.kansasregents.org/.

Kansas Teacher Service Scholarship. Scholarship to encourage talented students to enter the teaching profession and teach in Kansas in specific curriculum areas or in underserved areas of Kansas. Students must be Kansas residents attending a postsecondary institution in Kansas. For more details, refer to web site http://www.kansasregents.org. Education. *Award:* Scholarship for use in junior, senior, or graduate years; renewable. *Award amount:* $2214

$5536. *Eligibility Requirements:* Applicant must be enrolled or expecting to enroll full- or part-time at a four-year institution or university; resident of Kansas and studying in Kansas. Applicant must have 3.0 GPA or higher. Available to U.S. citizens. *Application Requirements:* Application form, essay, financial need analysis. **Deadline:** May 1.

Contact Diane Lindeman, Director of Student Financial Assistance, Kansas Board of Regents, 1000 SW Jackson, Suite 520, Topeka, KS 66612. *E-mail:* dlindeman@ksbor.org. *Phone:* 785-430-4255. *Fax:* 785-430-4233. *Website:* http://www.kansasregents.org/.

KENTUCKY

College Access Program (CAP) Grant. Award for U.S. citizens and Kentucky residents seeking their first undergraduate degree. Applicants enrolled in sectarian institutions are not eligible. Must submit Free Application for Federal Student Aid to demonstrate financial need. Funding is limited. Awards are made on a first-come, first-serve basis. *Award:* Grant for use in freshman, sophomore, junior, or senior years; not renewable. *Award amount:* $475–$1900. *Number of awards:* 45,500–47,000. *Eligibility Requirements:* Applicant must be enrolled or expecting to enroll full- or part-time at a two-year or four-year or technical institution or university; resident of Kentucky and studying in Kentucky. Available to U.S. citizens. *Application Requirements:* Application form. **Deadline:** continuous.

Contact Sheila Roe, Program Coordinator, Kentucky Higher Education Assistance Authority (KHEAA), PO Box 798, Frankfort, KY 40602-0798. *E-mail:* sroe@kheaa.com. *Phone:* 800-928-8926 Ext. 67393. *Website:* http://www.kheaa.com/.

Department of Veterans Affairs Tuition Waiver-KY KRS 164-507. Scholarship available to college students who are residents of Kentucky under the age of 26. *Award:* Scholarship for use in freshman, sophomore, junior, or senior years; not renewable. *Number of awards:* 400. *Eligibility Requirements:* Applicant must be enrolled or expecting to enroll full- or part-time at a two-year or four-year institution or university and resident of Kentucky. Available to U.S.

citizens. *Application Requirements:* Application form. **Deadline:** varies.

Contact Barbara Sipek, Tuition Waiver Coordinator. *E-mail:* barbaraa. sipek@ky.gov. *Phone:* 502-595-4447. *Website:* http://www.veterans.ky.gov/.

Early Childhood Development Scholarship. Awards scholarship with conditional service commitment for part-time students currently employed by participating ECD facility or providing training in ECD for an approved organization. For more information, visit web site http://www.kheaa.com. *Award:* Scholarship for use in freshman, sophomore, junior, or senior years; not renewable. *Award amount:* $100–$1800. *Number of awards:* 500–1100. *Eligibility Requirements:* Applicant must be enrolled or expecting to enroll part-time at a two-year or four-year institution or university; resident of Kentucky and studying in Kentucky. Available to U.S. citizens. *Application Requirements:* Application form. **Deadline:** continuous.

Contact Danny Prather, Program Coordinator, Kentucky Higher Education Assistance Authority (KHEAA), PO Box 798, Frankfort, KY 40602-0798. *E-mail:* danprather@kheaa.com. *Phone:* 800-928-8926 Ext. 67399. *Website:* http://www.kheaa.com/.

Environmental Protection Scholarship. Renewable awards for college juniors, seniors, and graduate students for in-state tuition, fees, room and board, and a book allowance at a Kentucky public university. Minimum 3.0 GPA required. Must work full-time for the Kentucky Department for Environmental Protection upon graduation (six months for each semester of scholarship support received). Interview required. Program not generally appropriate for non-residents. Biology; Chemical Engineering; Civil Engineering; Earth Science; Environmental Science; Hydrology; Mechanical Engineering; Natural Sciences. *Award:* Scholarship for use in junior, senior, or graduate years; renewable. *Award amount:* $10,000–$13,000. *Number of awards:* 1–4. *Eligibility Requirements:* Applicant must be enrolled or expecting to enroll full-time at a four-year institution or university; resident of Kentucky and studying in Kentucky. Applicant must have 3.0 GPA or higher. Available to U. S. citizens. *Application Requirements:* Application form, essay, interview. **Deadline:** February 15.

Contact James Kipp, Scholarship Program Coordinator, Kentucky Energy and Environment Cabinet, 233 Mining/Mineral Resources Building, Lexington, KY 40506-0107. *E-mail:* kipp@uky.edu. *Phone:* 859-257-1299. *Website:* http://dep.ky.gov.

Kentucky Educational Excellence Scholarship (KEES). Annual award based on yearly high school GPA and highest ACT or SAT score received by high school graduation. Awards are renewable, if required cumulative GPA is maintained at a Kentucky postsecondary school. Must be a Kentucky resident, and a graduate of a Kentucky high school. Low-income students who qualify for the free/reduced lunch program at least one year of high school may receive supplemental awards for passing scores on Advanced Placement (AP) or International Baccalaureate (IB) exams. *Award:* Scholarship for use in freshman, sophomore, junior, or senior years; renewable. *Award amount:* $125–$2500. *Number of awards:* 70,500. *Eligibility Requirements:* Applicant must be enrolled or expecting to enroll full- or part-time at a two-year or four-year or technical institution or university; resident of Kentucky and studying in British Columbia. Available to U.S. citizens. *Application Requirements:* **Deadline:** continuous.

Contact Becky Gilpatrick, Director of Student Aid Services, Kentucky Higher Education Assistance Authority (KHEAA), PO Box 798, Frankfort, KY 40602. *E-mail:* rgilpatrick@kheaa.com. *Phone:* 800-928-8926 Ext. 67394. *Website:* http://www.kheaa.com/.

Kentucky National Guard Tuition Award. Provides tuition assistance for active members of the Kentucky National Guard to attend a Kentucky college or university. Guard members may apply through their unit. *Award:* Grant for use in freshman, sophomore, junior, or senior years; renewable. *Award amount:* $100–$11,500. *Number of awards:* 1000–1500. *Eligibility Requirements:* Applicant must be enrolled or expecting to enroll full- or part-time at a two-year or four-year or technical institution or university; resident of Kentucky and studying in Kentucky. Available to U.S. citizens. Applicant must have national guard experience. *Application Requirements:* Application form. **Deadline:** continuous.

Kentucky Transportation Cabinet Civil Engineering Scholarship Program. Scholarships awarded to qualified Kentucky residents who wish to study civil engineering at University of Kentucky, Western Kentucky University, University of Louisville or Kentucky State University. Applicant should be a graduate of an accredited Kentucky high school or a Kentucky resident. Scholarship recipients are given opportunities to work for the Cabinet during summers and job opportunities upon graduation within the state of KY. Civil Engineering. *Award:* Scholarship for use in freshman, sophomore, junior, or senior years; renewable. *Award amount:* $12,400–$51,200. *Number of awards:* 15–30. *Eligibility Requirements:* Applicant must be enrolled or expecting to enroll full-time at a four-year institution or university; resident of Kentucky and studying in Kentucky. Applicant must have 2.5 GPA or higher. Available to U.S. and non-U.S. citizens. *Application Requirements:* Application form, essay, interview. **Deadline:** February 1.

Contact Cherie Mertz, Scholarship Program Coordinator, Kentucky Transportation Cabinet, 200 Mero Street, 6th Floor East, Frankfort, KY 40622. *E-mail:* Cherie.Mertz@ky.gov. *Phone:* 502-564-3730. *Website:* http://transportation.ky.gov/Education/Pages/Scholarships.aspx.

Kentucky Tuition Grant (KTG). Grants available to Kentucky residents who are full-time undergraduates at an independent college within the state. Based on financial need. Must submit FAFSA. *Award:* Grant for use in freshman, sophomore, junior, or senior years; not renewable. *Award amount:* $200–$2920. *Number of awards:* 10,000–12,500. *Eligibility Requirements:* Applicant must be enrolled or expecting to enroll full-time at a two-year or four-year institution or university; resident of Kentucky and studying in Kentucky. Available to U.S. citizens. *Application Requirements:* Application form. **Deadline:** continuous.

Contact Sheila Roe, Grant Program Coordinator, Kentucky Higher Education Assistance Authority (KHEAA), PO Box 798, Frankfort, KY 40602-0798. *E-mail:* sroe@kheaa.com. *Phone:* 800-928-8926 Ext. 67393. *Website:* http://www.kheaa.com/.

LOUISIANA

Louisiana National Guard State Tuition Exemption Program. Renewable award for college undergraduates to receive tuition exemption upon satisfactory performance in the Louisiana National Guard. Applicant must attend a state-funded institution in Louisiana, be a resident and registered voter in Louisiana, meet the academic and residency requirements of the university attended, and provide documentation of Louisiana National Guard enlistment. The exemption can be used for up to 15 semesters. Minimum 2.5 GPA required. *Award:* Scholarship for use in freshman, sophomore, junior, or senior years; renewable. *Eligibility Requirements:* Applicant must be enrolled or expecting to enroll full- or part-time at a two-year or four-year or technical institution or university; resident of Louisiana and studying in Louisiana. Applicant must have 2.5 GPA or higher. Available to U.S. citizens. Applicant or parent must meet one or more of the following requirements: national guard experience; retired from active duty; disabled or killed as a result of military service; prisoner of war; or missing in action. *Application Requirements:* Application form, test scores, transcript. **Deadline:** continuous.

Contact Jona Hughes, Education Services Officer, Louisiana National Guard, Joint Task Force LA, Building 35, Jackson Barracks, JI-PD, New Orleans, LA 70146-0330. *E-mail:* hughesj@la-arng.ngb.army.mil. *Phone:* 504-278-8531 Ext. 8304. *Fax:* 504-278-8025. *Website:* http://geauxguard.com/organization/joint-force-headquarters-jfhq-la/.

Rockefeller State Wildlife Scholarship. For college undergraduates with a minimum of 60 credit hours who are majoring in Forestry, Wildlife, or Marine Science, and for college graduate students who are majoring in Forestry, Wildlife, or Marine Science. College undergraduates must have a grade point average of at least 2.50 to apply. College graduate students must have a grade point average of at least 3.00 in order to apply. Renewable up to three years as an undergraduate and two years as a graduate student. Biology; Marine Biology; Marine/Ocean Engineering; Natural Resources; Oceanography. *Award:* Scholarship for use in freshman, sophomore, junior, senior,

graduate, or postgraduate years; renewable. *Award amount:* $2000–$3000. *Number of awards:* 20–30. *Eligibility Requirements:* Applicant must be enrolled or expecting to enroll full-time at a four-year institution or university; resident of Louisiana and studying in Louisiana. Applicant must have 2.5 GPA or higher. Available to U.S. citizens. *Application Requirements:* Application form, application form may be submitted online (http://www.osfa.la.gov for Rockefeller app), FAFSA, test scores, transcript. **Deadline:** July 1.

Contact Bonnie Lavergne, Public Information, Louisiana Office of Student Financial Assistance, PO Box 91202, Baton Rouge, LA 70821-9202. *E-mail:* custserv@osfa.la.gov. *Phone:* 800-259-5626 Ext. 7714. *Fax:* 225-612-6508. *Website:* http://www.osfa.la.gov/.

Taylor Opportunity Program for Students Honors Level. Program awards 8 semesters or 12 terms of tuition to any Louisiana State postsecondary institution plus $400 stipend per semester. Program awards 8 semesters or 12 terms of an amount equal to the weighted average public tuition to students attending a LAICU (Louisiana Association of Independent Colleges and Universities) institution plus $400 stipend per semester. Program awards 8 semesters or 12 terms of an amount equal to the weighted average public tuition to two out-of-state Institutions for Hearing Impaired Students: Gallaudet University and Rochester Institute of Technology plus $400 stipend per semester. Program awards $1744 per year to Approved Proprietary and Cosmetology schools plus a stipend of $800 per year. When you submit the FAFSA, you have automatically applied for all four levels of TOPS, for Federal Pell Grants and Go Grants and for Federal Student Loans. Please do not send separate letters of application to the TOPS office. *Award:* Scholarship for use in freshman, sophomore, junior, or senior years; renewable. *Award amount:* $836–$6736. *Number of awards:* 9661. *Eligibility Requirements:* Applicant must be enrolled or expecting to enroll full-time at a two-year or four-year or technical institution or university; resident of Louisiana and studying in Louisiana. Applicant must have 3.0 GPA or higher. Available to U.S. citizens. *Application Requirements:* Application form, application form may be submitted

online (http://www.osfa.la.gov), FAFSA, test scores, transcript. **Deadline:** July 1.

Taylor Opportunity Program for Students Opportunity Level. Program awards 8 semesters or 12 terms of tuition to any Louisiana State postsecondary institution. Program awards 8 semesters or 12 terms of an amount equal to the weighted average public tuition to students attending a LAICU (Louisiana Association of Independent Colleges and Universities) institution. Program awards 8 semesters or 12 terms of an amount equal to the weighted average public tuition to two out-of-state Institutions for Hearing Impaired Students: Gallaudet University and Rochester Institute of Technology. Program awards $1744 per year to Approved Proprietary and Cosmetology schools. When you submit the FAFSA, you have automatically applied for all four levels of TOPS, and for Federal Pell Grants and Go Grants. Please do not send separate letters of application to the TOPS office. *Award:* Scholarship for use in freshman, sophomore, junior, or senior years; renewable. *Award amount:* $436–$5936. *Number of awards:* 24,633. *Eligibility Requirements:* Applicant must be enrolled or expecting to enroll full-time at a two-year or four-year or technical institution or university; resident of Louisiana and studying in Louisiana. Applicant must have 2.5 GPA or higher. Available to U.S. citizens. *Application Requirements:* Application form, application form may be submitted online (http://www.osfa.la.gov), FAFSA, test scores, transcript. **Deadline:** July 1.

Taylor Opportunity Program for Students Performance Level. Program awards 8 semesters or 12 terms of tuition to any Louisiana State postsecondary institution plus $200 stipend per semester. Program awards 8 semesters or 12 terms of an amount equal to the weighted average public tuition to students attending a LAICU (Louisiana Association of Independent Colleges and Universities) institution plus $200 stipend per semester. Program awards 8 semesters or 12 terms of an amount equal to the weighted average public tuition to two out-of-state Institutions for Hearing Impaired Students: Gallaudet University and Rochester Institute of Technology plus $200 stipend per semester. Program awards

$1744 plus $400 per year to Approved Proprietary and Cosmetology schools. When you submit the FAFSA, you have automatically applied for all four levels of TOPS, for Federal Pell Grants and Go Grants and for Federal Student Loans. Please do not send separate letters of application to the TOPS office. *Award:* Scholarship for use in freshman, sophomore, junior, or senior years; renewable. *Award amount:* $636–$6336. *Number of awards:* 11,928. *Eligibility Requirements:* Applicant must be enrolled or expecting to enroll full-time at a two-year or four-year or technical institution or university; resident of Louisiana and studying in Louisiana. Applicant must have 3.0 GPA or higher. Available to U.S. citizens. *Application Requirements:* Application form, application form may be submitted online (http://www.osfa.la.gov), FAFSA, test scores, transcript. **Deadline:** July 1.

Taylor Opportunity Program for Students Tech Level. Program awards an amount equal to tuition for up to 4 semesters and two summers of technical training at a Louisiana postsecondary institution that offers a vocational or technical education certificate or diploma program, or a non-academic degree program; or up to $1744 to an approved Proprietary or Cosmetology school. Must have completed the TOPS Opportunity core curriculum or the TOPS Tech core curriculum, must have achieved a 2.50 grade point average over the core curriculum only, and must have achieved an ACT score of 17 or an SAT score of 810. Program awards an amount equal to the weighted average public tuition for technical programs to students attending a LAICU private institution for technical training. When you submit the FAFSA, you have automatically applied for all four levels of TOPS, for Federal Pell Grants and Go Grants and Federal Student Loans. Please do not send separate letters of application to the TOPS office. *Award:* Scholarship for use in freshman or sophomore years; renewable. *Award amount:* $436–$3985. *Number of awards:* 1671. *Eligibility Requirements:* Applicant must be enrolled or expecting to enroll full-time at a technical institution; resident of Louisiana and studying in Louisiana. Applicant must have 2.5 GPA or higher. Available to U.S. citizens. *Application Requirements:* Application form, application form may be submitted online (http://www.osfa.la.gov),

FAFSA, test scores, transcript. **Deadline:** July 1.

MAINE

American Legion Auxiliary Department of Maine Daniel E. Lambert Memorial Scholarship. Scholarships to assist young men and women in continuing their education beyond high school. Must demonstrate financial need, must be a resident of the State of Maine, U.S. citizen, and parent must be a veteran. *Award:* Scholarship for use in freshman year; not renewable. *Award amount:* $1000. *Number of awards:* up to 2. *Eligibility Requirements:* Applicant must be high school student; planning to enroll or expecting to enroll full-time at a four-year institution or university and resident of Maine. Available to U.S. citizens. Applicant or parent must meet one or more of the following requirements: general military experience; retired from active duty; disabled or killed as a result of military service; prisoner of war; or missing in action. *Application Requirements:* Application form, financial need analysis. **Deadline:** May 1.

Contact Mary Wells, Education Chairman. *E-mail:* aladeptsecme@verizon.net. *Phone:* 207-532-6007. *Website:* http://www.mainelegion.org/.

American Legion Auxiliary Department of Maine Past Presidents' Parley Nurses Scholarship. One-time award for child, grandchild, sister, or brother of veteran. Must be resident of Maine and wishing to continue education at accredited school in medical field. Must submit photo, doctor's statement, and evidence of civic activity. Minimum 3.5 GPA required. Health and Medical Sciences; Nursing. *Award:* Scholarship for use in freshman, sophomore, junior, or senior years; not renewable. *Award amount:* $300. *Number of awards:* 1. *Eligibility Requirements:* Applicant must be enrolled or expecting to enroll full-time at a two-year or four-year or technical institution or university and resident of Maine. Applicant or parent of applicant must have employment or volunteer experience in community service. Applicant must have 2.5 GPA or higher. Available to U.S. citizens. Applicant or parent must meet one or more of the following requirements: general military experience; retired from active duty; disabled or killed as a result of military

service; prisoner of war; or missing in action. *Application Requirements:* Application form, doctor's statement, personal photograph, recommendations or references, transcript. **Deadline:** March 31.

Contact Mary Wells, Education Chairman. *E-mail:* aladeptsecme@verizon.net. *Phone:* 207-532-6007. *Website:* http://www.mainelegion.org/.

EMBARK-Support for the College Journey. Scholarship for high school students who in their junior year have not made plans for college but are academically capable of success in college. Recipients are selected by their school principal or Guidance Director. Students must be entering a Maine Community College. Refer to web site http://www.mccs.me.edu/our-programs/programs-for-high-school-students/early-college/ *Award:* Scholarship for use in freshman or sophomore years; renewable. *Award amount:* $2000. *Number of awards:* 400–500. *Eligibility Requirements:* Applicant must be high school student; planning to enroll or expecting to enroll full-time at a two-year institution; resident of Maine and studying in Maine. Available to U.S. citizens. *Application Requirements:* Application form, financial need analysis. **Deadline:** April 15.

Contact Mercedes Pour, Director of College Access, Maine Community College System, 54 Lighthouse Circle, South Portland, ME 04106. *E-mail:* mpour@mccs.me.edu. *Phone:* 207-699-4897. *Website:* http://www.mccs.me.edu/.

Maine Rural Rehabilitation Fund Scholarship Program. One-time scholarship open to Maine residents enrolled in or accepted by any school, college, or university. Must be full-time and demonstrate financial need. Those opting for a Maine institution given preference. Major must lead to an agricultural career. Minimum 3.0 GPA required. Agribusiness; Agriculture; Animal/Veterinary Sciences. *Award:* Scholarship for use in freshman, sophomore, junior, senior, graduate, or postgraduate years; not renewable. *Award amount:* $800–$2000. *Number of awards:* 10–20. *Eligibility Requirements:* Applicant must be enrolled or expecting to enroll full-time at a two-year or four-year or technical institution or university and resident of Maine. Applicant must have 3.0 GPA or higher. Available to U.S. citizens. *Appli-*

cation Requirements: Application form, driver's license, financial need analysis, transcript. **Deadline:** June 15.

Contact Jane Aiudi, Director of Marketing. *E-mail:* jane.aiudi@maine.gov. *Phone:* 207-287-7628. *Fax:* 207-287-5576. *Website:* http://www.maine.gov/agriculture.

State of Maine Grant Program. Scholarship for residents of Maine, attending an eligible school in Maine, Connecticut, Massachusetts, New Hampshire, Rhode Island, or Vermont. Award based on need. Students attending out-of-state institutions must be participating in the New England Regional Tuition Break Program to be eligible. Students must apply annually. Complete free application for Federal Student Aid to apply. One-time award for undergraduate study. For further information see web site http://www.famemaine.com. *Award:* Grant for use in freshman, sophomore, junior, or senior years; not renewable. *Award amount:* $1700. *Number of awards:* 14,096. *Eligibility Requirements:* Applicant must be enrolled or expecting to enroll full- or part-time at a two-year or four-year or technical institution or university; resident of Maine and studying in Connecticut, Maine, Massachusetts, New Hampshire, Rhode Island, Vermont. Available to U.S. citizens. *Application Requirements:* Financial need analysis. **Deadline:** May 1.

Contact Jennifer Lanphear, Education Programs Officer, Finance Authority of Maine, 5 Community Drive, Augusta, ME 04332. *E-mail:* education@famemaine.com. *Phone:* 207-620-3548. *Website:* http://www.famemaine.com/.

Tuition Waiver Programs. Provides tuition waivers for children and spouses of EMS personnel, firefighters, and law enforcement officers who have been killed in the line of duty and for students who were foster children under the custody of the Department of Human Services when they graduated from high school. Waivers valid at the University of Maine System, the Maine Technical College System, and Maine Maritime Academy. Applicant must reside and study in Maine. *Award:* Grant for use in freshman, sophomore, junior, or senior years; renewable. *Number of awards:* 30. *Eligibility Requirements:* Applicant must be enrolled or expecting to enroll full- or part-time at a two-year or four-

year institution or university; resident of Maine and studying in Maine. Applicant or parent of applicant must have employment or volunteer experience in police/firefighting. Available to U.S. citizens. *Application Requirements:* Application form. **Deadline:** continuous.

Contact Jennifer Lanphear, Education Programs Officer, Finance Authority of Maine, 5 Community Drive, Augusta, ME 04332. *E-mail:* education@famemaine.com. *Phone:* 207-620-3548. *Website:* http://www.famemaine.com/.

Veterans Dependents Educational Benefits-Maine. Tuition waiver award for dependent children who have not reached their 22nd birthday or spouses of veterans permanently and totally disabled resulting from service-connected disability; died from a service-connected disability; at time of death was totally and permanently disabled due to service-connected disability, but whose death was not related to the service-connected disability; or member of the Armed Forces on active duty who has been listed for more than 90 days as missing in action, captured or forcibly detained or interned in the line of duty. Benefits apply only to the University of Maine System, Maine community colleges and Maine Maritime Academy. Must be high school graduate. Must submit with application proof of veteran's VA disability along with dependent verification paperwork such as birth, marriage, or adoption certificate and proof of enrollment in degree program. *Award:* Scholarship for use in freshman, sophomore, junior, or senior years; not renewable. *Eligibility Requirements:* Applicant must be enrolled or expecting to enroll full- or part-time at a two-year or four-year institution or university; resident of Maine and studying in Maine. Available to U.S. citizens. Applicant or parent must meet one or more of the following requirements: general military experience; retired from active duty; disabled or killed as a result of military service; prisoner of war; or missing in action. *Application Requirements:* Application form, see application.

Contact Mrs. Paula Gagnon, Office Associate II, Maine Veterans Services, State House Station 117, Augusta, ME 04333-0117. *E-mail:* mainebvs@maine.gov. *Phone:* 207-430-6035. *Fax:* 207-

626-4471. *Website:* http://www.maine.gov/dvem/bvs.

MARYLAND

Charles W. Riley Fire and Emergency Medical Services Tuition Reimbursement Program. Award intended to reimburse members of rescue organizations serving Maryland communities for tuition costs of course work towards a degree or certificate in fire service or medical technology. Must attend a two- or four-year school in Maryland. Minimum 2.0 GPA. The scholarship is worth up to $6500. Fire Sciences; Health and Medical Sciences; Trade/Technical Specialties. *Award:* Scholarship for use in freshman, sophomore, junior, or senior years; not renewable. *Award amount:* $1-$6500. *Number of awards:* 1–150. *Eligibility Requirements:* Applicant must be enrolled or expecting to enroll full- or part-time at a two-year or four-year institution or university; resident of Maryland and studying in Maryland. Applicant or parent of applicant must have employment or volunteer experience in police/firefighting. Available to U.S. citizens. *Application Requirements:* Application form. **Deadline:** June 1.

Contact Donna Thomas, Office of Student Financial Assistance, Maryland State Higher Education Commission, 6 North Liberty Street, Baltimore, MD 21202. *E-mail:* donnae.thomas@maryland.gov. *Phone:* 410-767-3109. *Website:* http://www.mhec.state.md.us/.

Delegate Scholarship Program-Maryland. Delegate scholarships help Maryland residents attending Maryland degree-granting institutions, certain career schools, or nursing diploma schools. May attend out-of-state institution if Maryland Higher Education Commission deems major to be unique and not offered at a Maryland institution. Free Application for Federal Student Aid may be required. Students interested in this program should apply by contacting their legislative district delegate. *Award:* Scholarship for use in freshman, sophomore, junior, or senior years; not renewable. *Award amount:* $200–$8650. *Number of awards:* up to 3500. *Eligibility Requirements:* Applicant must be enrolled or expecting to enroll full- or part-time at a two-year or four-year or technical institution or university; resident of Maryland and studying in Maryland. Available to U.S. citizens. *Application Requirements:* Application form, FAFSA. **Deadline:** continuous.

Contact Monica Wheatley, Office of Student Financial Assistance, Maryland State Higher Education Commission, 839 Bestgate Road, Suite 400, Annapolis, MD 21401-3013. *E-mail:* osfamail@mhec.state.md.us. *Phone:* 800-974-1024. *Fax:* 410-260-3200. *Website:* http://www.mhec.state.md.us/.

Edward T. Conroy Memorial Scholarship Program. Scholarship for dependents of deceased or 100 percent disabled U.S. Armed Forces personnel; the son, daughter, or surviving spouse of a victim of the September 11, 2001 terrorist attacks who died as a result of the attacks on the World Trade Center in New York City, the attack on the Pentagon in Virginia, or the crash of United Airlines Flight 93 in Pennsylvania; a POW/MIA of the Vietnam Conflict or his/her son or daughter; the son, daughter or surviving spouse (who has not remarried) of a state or local public safety employee or volunteer who died in the line of duty; or a state or local public safety employee or volunteer who was 100 percent disabled in the line of duty. Must be Maryland resident at time of disability. Submit applicable VA certification. Must be at least 16 years of age and attend Maryland institution. *Award:* Scholarship for use in freshman, sophomore, junior, or senior years; renewable. *Award amount:* $7200–$9000. *Number of awards:* up to 121. *Eligibility Requirements:* Applicant must be age 16-24; enrolled or expecting to enroll full- or part-time at a two-year or four-year institution or university; resident of Maryland and studying in Maryland. Applicant or parent of applicant must have employment or volunteer experience in police/firefighting. Available to U.S. citizens. Applicant or parent must meet one or more of the following requirements: general military experience; retired from active duty; disabled or killed as a result of military service; prisoner of war; or missing in action. *Application Requirements:* Application form, birth and death certificate, disability papers. **Deadline:** July 15.

Contact Linda Asplin, Office of Student Financial Assistance, Maryland State Higher Education Commission, 839 Bestgate Road, Suite 400, Annapolis, MD 21401-3013. *E-mail:* lasplin@mhec.state.md.us. *Phone:* 410-260-4563. *Fax:* 410-260-3203. *Website:* http://www.mhec.state.md.us/.

Graduate and Professional Scholarship Program-Maryland. Graduate and professional scholarships provide need-based financial assistance to students attending a Maryland school of medicine, dentistry, law, pharmacy, social work, or nursing. Funds are provided to specific Maryland colleges and universities. Students must demonstrate financial need and be Maryland residents. Contact institution financial aid office for more information. Dental Health/Services; Health and Medical Sciences; Law/Legal Services; Nursing; Social Services. *Award:* Scholarship for use in freshman, sophomore, junior, or senior years; renewable. *Award amount:* $1000–$5000. *Number of awards:* up to 584. *Eligibility Requirements:* Applicant must be enrolled or expecting to enroll full- or part-time at a four-year institution or university; resident of Maryland and studying in Maryland. Available to U.S. citizens. *Application Requirements:* Application form, contact institution financial aid office, financial need analysis. **Deadline:** March 1.

Contact Monica Wheatley, Program Manager, Maryland State Higher Education Commission, 839 Bestgate Road, Suite 400, Annapolis, MD 21401. *E-mail:* mwheatle@mhec.state.md.us. *Phone:* 410-260-4560. *Fax:* 410-260-3202. *Website:* http://www.mhec.state.md.us/.

Howard P. Rawlings Educational Excellence Awards Educational Assistance Grant. Award for Maryland residents accepted or enrolled in a full-time undergraduate degree or certificate program at a Maryland institution or hospital nursing school. Must submit financial aid form by March 1. Must earn 2.0 GPA in college to maintain award. *Award:* Grant for use in freshman, sophomore, junior, or senior years; renewable. *Award amount:* $400–$2700. *Number of awards:* 15,000–30,000. *Eligibility Requirements:* Applicant must be enrolled or expecting to enroll full-time at a two-year or four-year institution or university; resident of Maryland and studying in Maryland. Available to U.S. citizens. *Application Requirements:* Application form, financial need analysis. **Deadline:** March 1.

Howard P. Rawlings Educational Excellence Awards Guaranteed Access Grant. Award for Maryland resident enrolling full-time in an undergraduate program at a Maryland institution. Must be under 21 at time of first award and begin college within one year of completing high school in Maryland with a minimum 2.5 GPA. Must have an annual family income less than 130 percent of the federal poverty level guideline. *Award:* Grant for use in freshman, sophomore, junior, or senior years; renewable. *Award amount:* $400–$14,800. *Number of awards:* up to 1000. *Eligibility Requirements:* Applicant must be enrolled or expecting to enroll full-time at a two-year or four-year institution or university; resident of Maryland and studying in Maryland. Applicant must have 3.5 GPA or higher. Available to U.S. citizens. *Application Requirements:* Application form, financial need analysis, transcript. **Deadline:** March 1.

Contact Theresa Lowe, Office of Student Financial Assistance, Maryland State Higher Education Commission, 839 Bestgate Road, Suite 400, Annapolis, MD 21401-3013. *E-mail:* osfamail@mhec.state.md.us. *Phone:* 410-260-4555. *Fax:* 410-260-3200. *Website:* http://www.mhec.state.md.us/.

Janet L. Hoffmann Loan Assistance Repayment Program. Provides assistance for repayment of loan debt to Maryland residents working full-time in nonprofit organizations and state or local governments. Must submit Employment Verification Form and Lender Verification Form. Education; Law/Legal Services; Nursing; Social Services; Therapy/Rehabilitation. *Award:* Grant for use in freshman, sophomore, junior, or senior years; not renewable. *Award amount:* $1500–$10,000. *Number of awards:* up to 700. *Eligibility Requirements:* Applicant must be enrolled or expecting to enroll full-time at a four-year institution or university; resident of Maryland and studying in Maryland. Applicant or parent of applicant must have employment or volunteer experience in government/politics. Available to U.S. citizens. *Application Requirements:* Application form, IRS 1040 form, transcript. **Deadline:** September 30.

Contact Tamika McKelvin, Office of Student Financial Assistance, Maryland State Higher Education Commission, 839 Bestgate Road, Suite 400,

Annapolis, MD 21401. *E-mail:* tmckelvil@mhec.state.md.us. *Phone:* 410-260-4546. *Fax:* 410-260-3203. *Website:* http://www.mhcc.state.md.us/.

J.F. Tolbert Memorial Student Grant Program. Awards of $500 granted to Maryland residents attending a private career school in Maryland. The scholarship deadline continues. *Award:* Grant for use in freshman or sophomore years; not renewable. *Award amount:* $500. *Number of awards:* 522. *Eligibility Requirements:* Applicant must be enrolled or expecting to enroll full-time at a technical institution; resident of Maryland and studying in Maryland. Available to U.S. citizens. *Application Requirements:* Application form, financial need analysis. **Deadline:** continuous.

Contact Glenda Hamlet, Office of Student Financial Assistance, Maryland State Higher Education Commission, 839 Bestgate Road, Suite 400, Annapolis, MD 21401-3013. *E-mail:* osfamail@mhec.state.md.us. *Phone:* 800-974-1024. *Fax:* 410-260-3200. *Website:* http://www.mhec.state.md.us/.

Part-Time Grant Program-Maryland. Funds provided to Maryland colleges and universities. Eligible students must be enrolled on a part-time basis (6 to 11 credits) in an undergraduate degree program. Must demonstrate financial need and also be Maryland resident. Contact financial aid office at institution for more information. *Award:* Grant for use in freshman, sophomore, junior, or senior years; renewable. *Award amount:* $200–$1500. *Number of awards:* 1800–9000. *Eligibility Requirements:* Applicant must be enrolled or expecting to enroll part-time at a two-year or four-year institution or university; resident of Maryland and studying in Maryland. Available to U.S. citizens. *Application Requirements:* Application form, financial need analysis. **Deadline:** March 1.

Contact Monica Wheatley, Program Manager, Maryland State Higher Education Commission, 839 Bestgate Road, Suite 400, Annapolis, MD 21401. *E-mail:* mwheatle@mhec.state.md.us. *Phone:* 410-260-4560. *Fax:* 410-260-3202. *Website:* http://www.mhec.state.md.us/.

Senatorial Scholarships-Maryland. Renewable award for Maryland residents attending a Maryland degree-granting institution, nursing diploma school, or certain private career schools. May be used out-of-state only if Maryland Higher Education Commission deems major to be unique and not offered at Maryland institution. The scholarship value is $400 to $7000. *Award:* Scholarship for use in freshman, sophomore, junior, or senior years; renewable. *Award amount:* $400–$7000. *Number of awards:* up to 7000. *Eligibility Requirements:* Applicant must be enrolled or expecting to enroll full- or part-time at a two-year or four-year or technical institution or university; resident of Maryland and studying in Maryland. Available to U.S. citizens. *Application Requirements:* Application form, financial need analysis, test scores. **Deadline:** March 1.

Contact Monica Wheatley, Office of Student Financial Assistance, Maryland State Higher Education Commission, 839 Bestgate Road, Suite 400, Annapolis, MD 21401-3013. *E-mail:* osfamail@mhec.state.md.us. *Phone:* 800-974-1024. *Fax:* 410-260-3200. *Website:* http://www.mhec.state.md.us/.

Tuition Reduction for Non-Resident Nursing Students. Available to nonresidents of Maryland who attend a two-year or four-year public institution in Maryland. It is renewable provided student maintains academic requirements designated by institution attended. Recipient must agree to serve as a full-time nurse in a hospital or related institution for two to four years. Nursing. *Award:* Scholarship for use in freshman, sophomore, junior, or senior years; renewable. *Eligibility Requirements:* Applicant must be enrolled or expecting to enroll full- or part-time at a two-year or four-year institution and studying in Maryland. Available to U.S. citizens. *Application Requirements:* Application form. **Deadline:** varies.

Contact Robert Parker, Director. *E-mail:* rparker@mhec.state.md.us. *Phone:* 410-260-4558. *Website:* http://www.mhec.state.md.us/.

Tuition Waiver for Foster Care Recipients. Applicant must be a high school graduate or GED recipient and under the age of 21. Must either have resided in a foster care home in Maryland at the time of high school graduation or GED reception, or until 14th birthday, and been adopted after 14th birthday. Applicant, if status approved, will be exempt from paying tuition and mandatory fees at a public college in Maryland. *Award:* Grant for use in freshman, sophomore, junior, senior, or graduate years; renewable. *Eligibility Requirements:* Applicant must be enrolled or expecting to enroll full- or part-time at a two-year or four-year institution or university; resident of Maryland and studying in Maryland. Available to U.S. citizens. *Application Requirements:* Application form, financial need analysis, must inquire at financial aid office of schools. **Deadline:** March 1.

Contact Robert Parker, Director. *E-mail:* rparker@mhec.state.md.us. *Phone:* 410-260-4558. *Website:* http://www.mhec.state.md.us/.

Veterans of the Afghanistan and Iraq Conflicts Scholarship Program. Provides financial assistance to Maryland resident U.S. Armed Forces personnel who served in Afghanistan or Iraq conflicts and their children or spouses who are attending Maryland institutions. *Award:* Scholarship for use in freshman, sophomore, junior, or senior years; renewable. *Award amount:* $8850. *Number of awards:* 123. *Eligibility Requirements:* Applicant must be enrolled or expecting to enroll full- or part-time at a two-year or four-year institution or university; resident of Maryland and studying in Maryland. Available to U.S. citizens. Applicant or parent must meet one or more of the following requirements: general military experience; retired from active duty; disabled or killed as a result of military service; prisoner of war; or missing in action. *Application Requirements:* Application form, birth certificate/marriage certificate, documentation of military order, financial need analysis. **Deadline:** March 1.

Contact Linda Asplin, Program Administrator, Maryland State Higher Education Commission, 839 Bestgate Road, Suite 400, Annapolis, MD 21401-3013. *E-mail:* lasplin@mhec.state.md.us. *Phone:* 410-260-4563. *Fax:* 410-260-3203. *Website:* http://www.mhec.state.md.us/.

Workforce Shortage Student Assistance Grant Program. Scholarship of $4000 available to students who will be required to major in specific areas and will be obligated to serve in the state of Maryland after completion of degree. *Award:* Scholarship for use in freshman, sophomore, junior, or senior years;

renewable. *Award amount:* $4000. *Number of awards:* 1300. *Eligibility Requirements:* Applicant must be enrolled or expecting to enroll full- or part-time at a two-year or four-year institution or university; resident of Maryland and studying in Maryland. Available to U.S. citizens. *Application Requirements:* Application form, certain majors require additional documentation, essay, financial need analysis, recommendations or references, resume, transcript. **Deadline:** July 1.

Contact Maura Sappington, Program Manager, Maryland State Higher Education Commission, 839 Bestgate Road, Suite 400, Annapolis, MD 21401-3013. *E-mail:* msapping@mhec.state.md.us. *Phone:* 410-260-4569. *Fax:* 410-260-3203. *Website:* http://www.mhec.state.md.us/.

MASSACHUSETTS

Christian A. Herter Memorial Scholarship. Renewable award for Massachusetts residents who are in the tenth and eleventh grades, and whose socio-economic backgrounds and environment may inhibit their ability to attain educational goals. Must exhibit severe personal or family-related difficulties, medical problems, or have overcome a personal obstacle. Provides up to 50 percent of the student's calculated need, as determined by federal methodology, at the college of their choice within the continental United States. *Award:* Scholarship for use in freshman, sophomore, junior, or senior years; renewable. *Award amount:* $500–$20,000. *Number of awards:* 25–100. *Eligibility Requirements:* Applicant must be high school student; planning to enroll or expecting to enroll full-time at a two-year or four-year or technical institution or university; resident of Massachusetts and studying in Illinois, Indiana, Iowa, Kansas, Kentucky, Louisiana, Maine, Manitoba, Maryland, Massachusetts. Applicant must have 2.5 GPA or higher. Available to U.S. citizens. *Application Requirements:* Application form, community service, financial need analysis, interview. **Deadline:** February 1.

Contact Robert Brun, Director of Scholarships and Grants. *E-mail:* osfa@osfa.mass.edu. *Phone:* 617-727-9420. *Fax:* 617-727-0667. *Website:* http://www.osfa.mass.edu/.

DSS Adopted Children Tuition Waiver. Need-based tuition waiver for Massachusetts residents who are full-time undergraduate students. Must attend a Massachusetts public institution of higher education and be under 24 years of age. File the FAFSA after January 1. Contact school financial aid office for more information. *Award:* Scholarship for use in freshman, sophomore, junior, or senior years; renewable. *Eligibility Requirements:* Applicant must be enrolled or expecting to enroll full-time at a two-year or four-year institution; resident of Massachusetts and studying in District of Columbia, Massachusetts, Pennsylvania, Vermont. Available to U.S. and non-Canadian citizens. *Application Requirements:* Application form.

Contact Robert Brun, Director of Scholarships and Grants. *E-mail:* osfa@osfa.mass.edu. *Phone:* 617-727-9420. *Fax:* 617-727-0667. *Website:* http://www.osfa.mass.edu/.

Early Childhood Educators Scholarship Program. Scholarship to provide financial assistance for currently employed early childhood educators and providers who enroll in an associate or bachelor degree program in Early Childhood Education or related programs. Awards are not based on financial need. Individuals taking their first college-level ECE course are eligible for 100 percent tuition, while subsequent ECE courses are awarded at 50 percent tuition. Can be used for one class each semester. Child and Family Studies; Education. *Award:* Scholarship for use in freshman, sophomore, junior, or senior years; not renewable. *Award amount:* $150–$3600. *Eligibility Requirements:* Applicant must be enrolled or expecting to enroll full- or part-time at a two-year or four-year institution or university; resident of Massachusetts and studying in Massachusetts. Available to U.S. citizens. *Application Requirements:* Application form. **Deadline:** June 1.

Contact Ms. Jean Szymaniak, Senior Program Assistant, Massachusetts Office of Student Financial Assistance, 75 Pleasant Street, Malden, MA 02148. *E-mail:* jszymaniak@dhe.mass.edu. *Phone:* 617-391-6083. *Website:* http://www.osfa.mass.edu/.

John and Abigail Adams Scholarship. Scholarship to reward and inspire student achievement, attract more high-performing students to Massachusetts public higher education, and provide families of college-bound students with financial assistance. Must be a U.S. citizen or an eligible non-citizen. There is no application process for the scholarship. Students who are eligible will be notified in the fall of their senior year in high school. *Award:* Scholarship for use in freshman, sophomore, junior, or senior years; renewable. *Award amount:* $125–$1742. *Eligibility Requirements:* Applicant must be high school student; planning to enroll or expecting to enroll full-time at a two-year or four-year institution or university; resident of Massachusetts and studying in Massachusetts. Applicant must have 3.0 GPA or higher. Available to U.S. citizens. *Application Requirements:* **Deadline:** continuous.

Contact Clantha McCurdy, Senior Deputy Commissioner, Massachusetts Office of Student Financial Assistance, 75 Pleasant Street, 3rd Floor, Malden, MA 02148. *Phone:* 617-391-6098. *Website:* http://www.osfa.mass.edu/.

Massachusetts Assistance for Student Success Program. Provides need-based financial assistance to Massachusetts residents to attend undergraduate postsecondary institutions in Massachusetts, Pennsylvania, Vermont, and District of Columbia. High school seniors may apply. Expected Family Contribution (EFC) should be $3850. Timely filing of FAFSA required. *Award:* Grant for use in freshman, sophomore, junior, or senior years; not renewable. *Award amount:* $400–$1600. *Number of awards:* 47,000–50,000. *Eligibility Requirements:* Applicant must be enrolled or expecting to enroll full-time at a two-year or four-year or technical institution or university; resident of Massachusetts and studying in District of Columbia, Massachusetts, Pennsylvania, Vermont. Available to U.S. citizens. *Application Requirements:* Financial need analysis. **Deadline:** May 1.

Contact Robert Brun, Director of Scholarships and Grants. *E-mail:* osfa@osfa.mass.edu. *Phone:* 617-727-9420. *Fax:* 617-727-0667. *Website:* http://www.osfa.mass.edu/.

Massachusetts Cash Grant Program. A need-based grant to assist with mandatory fees and non-state supported tuition. This supplemental award is available to Massachusetts residents, who are undergraduates at public two-year, four-year colleges and universities in Massachusetts. Must file FAFSA before May 1. Contact college financial aid office for information. *Award:* Grant for use in freshman, sophomore, junior, or senior years; renewable. *Award amount:* $200–$2500. *Eligibility Requirements:* Applicant must be enrolled or expecting to enroll full- or part-time at a two-year or four-year institution or university; resident of Massachusetts and studying in Massachusetts. Available to U.S. citizens. *Application Requirements:* Financial need analysis. **Deadline:** continuous.

Contact Robert Brun, Director of Scholarships and Grants. *E-mail:* osfa@osfa.mass.edu. *Phone:* 617-727-9420. *Fax:* 617-727-0667. *Website:* http://www.osfa.mass.edu/.

Massachusetts Gilbert Matching Student Grant Program. Grants for permanent Massachusetts residents attending an independent, regionally accredited Massachusetts school or school of nursing full time. Must be U.S. citizen and permanent legal resident of Massachusetts. File the Free Application for Federal Student Aid after January 1. Contact college financial aid office for complete details and deadlines. *Award:* Grant for use in freshman, sophomore, junior, or senior years; not renewable. *Award amount:* $200–$2500. *Number of awards:* 8000–9500. *Eligibility Requirements:* Applicant must be enrolled or expecting to enroll full-time at a four-year institution or university; resident of Massachusetts and studying in Massachusetts. Available to U.S. citizens. *Application Requirements:* Financial need analysis.

Contact Robert Brun, Senior Associate Commissioner, Massachusetts Office of Student Financial Assistance, 75 Pleasant Street, 3rd Floor, Malden, MA 02148. *E-mail:* rbrub@dhe.mass.edu. *Phone:* 617-391-6099. *Website:* http://www.osfa.mass.edu/.

Massachusetts Part-Time Grant Program. Award for permanent Massachusetts residents who have enrolled part-time for at least one year in a state-approved postsecondary school. The recipient must not have a bachelor's degree. FAFSA must be filed before May 1. Contact college financial aid office for further information. *Award:* Grant for use in freshman, sophomore, junior, or senior years; not renewable. *Award amount:* $200–$1700. *Eligibility*

Requirements: Applicant must be enrolled or expecting to enroll part-time at a two-year or four-year or technical institution or university; resident of Massachusetts and studying in Massachusetts. Available to U.S. citizens. *Application Requirements:* Financial need analysis. **Deadline:** May 1.

Contact Robert Brun, Director of Scholarships and Grants. *E-mail:* osfa@osfa.mass.edu. *Phone:* 617-727-9420. *Fax:* 617-727-0667. *Website:* http://www.osfa.mass.edu/.

Massachusetts Public Service Grant Program. Scholarships for children and/or spouses of deceased members of fire, police, and corrections departments, who were killed in the line of duty. Awards Massachusetts residents attending Massachusetts institutions. Applicant should have not received a prior bachelor's degree or its equivalent. *Award:* Grant for use in freshman, sophomore, junior, or senior years; not renewable. *Award amount:* $6360–$15,411. *Eligibility Requirements:* Applicant must be enrolled or expecting to enroll full-time at a two-year or four-year institution or university; resident of Massachusetts and studying in Massachusetts. Applicant or parent of applicant must have employment or volunteer experience in police/firefighting. Available to U.S. citizens. *Application Requirements:* Application form, financial need analysis. **Deadline:** May 1.

New England Regional Student Program-Tuition Break. Tuition discount for residents of six New England states (Connecticut, Maine, Massachusetts, New Hampshire, Rhode Island, Vermont). Students pay reduced out-of-state tuition at public colleges or universities in other New England states when enrolling in certain majors not offered at public institutions in home state. Details are available at http://www.nebhe.org/tuitionbreak. *Award:* Scholarship for use in freshman, sophomore, junior, senior, or graduate years; renewable. *Eligibility Requirements:* Applicant must be enrolled or expecting to enroll full- or part-time at a two-year or four-year institution or university; resident of Connecticut, Maine, Massachusetts, New Hampshire, Rhode Island, Vermont and studying in Connecticut, Maine, Massachusetts, New Hampshire, Rhode Island, Vermont. Available to U.S. cit-

izens. *Application Requirements:* Application form. **Deadline:** continuous.

Contact Wendy Lindsay, Senior Director of Regional Student Program, New England Board of Higher Education, 45 Temple Place, Boston, MA 02111. *E-mail:* tuitionbreak@nebhe.org. *Phone:* 617-533-9511. *Website:* http://www.nebhe.org/tuitionbreak.

Paraprofessional Teacher Preparation Grant Program. Grant providing financial aid assistance to Massachusetts residents, who are currently employed as paraprofessionals in Massachusetts public schools and wish to obtain higher education and become certified as full-time teachers. Education. *Award:* Grant for use in freshman, sophomore, junior, or senior years; not renewable. *Award amount:* $250–$7500. *Eligibility Requirements:* Applicant must be enrolled or expecting to enroll full- or part-time at a two-year or four-year institution or university; resident of Massachusetts and studying in Massachusetts. Available to U.S. citizens. *Application Requirements:* Application form. **Deadline:** June 1.

Contact Ms. Jean Szymaniak, Senior Program Assistant, Massachusetts Office of Student Financial Assistance, 75 Pleasant Street Third Floor, Malden, MA 02148. *E-mail:* jszymaniak@dhe.mass.edu. *Phone:* 617-391-6083 Ext. 6083. *Website:* http://www.osfa.mass.edu/.

MICHIGAN

American Legion Auxiliary Department of Michigan Medical Career Scholarship. Award for training in Michigan as registered nurse, licensed practical nurse, physical therapist, respiratory therapist, or in any medical career. Must be child, grandchild, great-grandchild, wife, or widow of honorably discharged or deceased veteran who has served during the eligibility dates for American Legion membership. Must be Michigan resident attending a Michigan school. Health and Medical Sciences; Nursing; Therapy/Rehabilitation. *Award:* Scholarship for use in freshman year; not renewable. *Award amount:* $500. *Number of awards:* 10–20. *Eligibility Requirements:* Applicant must be enrolled or expecting to enroll full-time at a two-year or four-year or technical institution or university; resident of Michigan and studying in Michigan. Applicant must have 3.5 GPA or higher. Available to U. S. citizens. Applicant must have general military experience. *Application Requirements:* Application form, financial need analysis. **Deadline:** March 15.

American Legion Auxiliary Department of Michigan Memorial Scholarship. Scholarship for daughter, granddaughter, and great-granddaughter of any honorably discharged or deceased veteran of U.S. wars or conflicts. Must be Michigan resident for minimum of one year, female between 16 and 21 years, and attend college in Michigan. Must include copy of military discharge and copy of parent or guardian's IRS 1040 form. *Award:* Scholarship for use in freshman or sophomore years; not renewable. *Award amount:* $500. *Number of awards:* 10–20. *Eligibility Requirements:* Applicant must be age 16-21; enrolled or expecting to enroll full-time at a two-year or four-year or technical institution or university; female; resident of Michigan and studying in Michigan. Applicant must have 3.5 GPA or higher. Available to U.S. citizens. Applicant must have general military experience. *Application Requirements:* Application form, financial need analysis. **Deadline:** March 15.

American Legion Auxiliary Department of Michigan Scholarship for Non-Traditional Student. Applicant must be a dependent of a veteran. Must be one of the following: nontraditional student returning to classroom after some period of time in which their education was interrupted, student over the age of 22 attending college for the first time to pursue a degree, or student over the age of 22 attending a trade or vocational school. Applicants must be Michigan residents only and attend Michigan institution. Judging based on need, character/leadership, scholastic standing, and initiative/goal. *Award:* Scholarship for use in freshman, sophomore, junior, or senior years; renewable. *Award amount:* $500. *Number of awards:* 1. *Eligibility Requirements:* Applicant must be age 22-99; enrolled or expecting to enroll full- or part-time at a two-year or four-year or technical institution or university; resident of Michigan and studying in Michigan. Available to U.S. citizens. Applicant must have general

military experience. *Application Requirements:* Application form, financial need analysis. **Deadline:** March 15.

Children of Veterans Tuition Grant. The program is designed to provide undergraduate tuition assistance to certain children older than 16 and less than 26 years of age who have been Michigan residents for the 12 months prior to application. To be eligible, a student must be the natural or adopted child of a Michigan veteran. Stepchildren of the veteran are not eligible. The veteran must have been a legal resident of Michigan immediately before entering military service and must not have later resided outside of Michigan for more than two years; or the veteran must have established legal residency in Michigan after entering military service. *Award:* Grant for use in freshman, sophomore, junior, or senior years; renewable. *Eligibility Requirements:* Applicant must be age 16-26; enrolled or expecting to enroll full- or part-time at a four-year institution or university; resident of Michigan and studying in Michigan. Available to U.S. citizens. *Application Requirements:* Application form.

Michigan Competitive Scholarship. Renewable awards for Michigan resident to pursue undergraduate study at a Michigan institution. Awards limited to tuition. Must attain SAT score of at least 1200. Must maintain at least a 2.0 grade point average and meet the college's academic progress requirements. Must file Free Application for Federal Student Aid. *Award:* Scholarship for use in freshman, sophomore, junior, or senior years; renewable. *Eligibility Requirements:* Applicant must be enrolled or expecting to enroll full- or part-time at a two-year or four-year institution or university; resident of Michigan and studying in Michigan. Available to U.S. citizens. *Application Requirements:* Application form, financial need analysis.

Michigan Tuition Grant. Need-based program. Students must be Michigan residents and attend a Michigan private, nonprofit, degree-granting college. Must file the Free Application for Federal Student Aid and meet the college's academic progress requirements. *Award:* Grant for use in freshman, sophomore, junior, or senior years; renewable. *Eligibility Requirements:* Applicant must be

enrolled or expecting to enroll full- or part-time at a four-year institution or university; resident of Michigan and studying in Michigan. Available to U.S. citizens. *Application Requirements:* Application form, financial need analysis. **Deadline:** June 30.

Tuition Incentive Program. The Tuition Incentive Program (TIP) was established in 1987 under the Annual Higher Education Appropriations Act as an incentive program that encourages eligible students to complete high school by providing tuition assistance for the first two years of college and beyond. Students must be enrolled in courses leading to an associate degree or certificate. Certificate courses are defined as at least a one-year training program that leads to a certificate (or other recognized educational credential), which prepares students for gainful employment in a recognized occupation. Students must meet a Medicaid eligibility history requirement. Eligible students must apply prior to high school graduation (high school diploma or its recognized equivalent). The program targets students with financial need so students are encouraged to also complete the FAFSA. Funds are appropriated annually in the Higher Education Appropriations Act. This program is administered by the Student Scholarships and Grants Division. http://www.michigan.gov/mistudentaid/0,4636,7-128-60969_61016-274565—,00.html *Award:* Grant for use in freshman, sophomore, junior, or senior years; renewable. *Eligibility Requirements:* Applicant must be enrolled or expecting to enroll full- or part-time at a two-year or four-year institution or university; resident of Michigan and studying in Michigan. Available to U.S. citizens. *Application Requirements:* Application form. **Deadline:** continuous.

MINNESOTA

Minnesota GI Bill Program. The Minnesota GI Bill program provides postsecondary financial assistance to eligible Minnesota veterans and service members as well as eligible spouses and children of deceased or severely disabled eligible Minnesota veterans. Full-time undergraduate or graduate students may be eligible to receive up to $1,000 per semester or term and part-time students may be eligible to receive up to $500 per semester or term. Eligible students may receive up to $3,000 per award year and up to the lifetime maximum of $10,000. *Award:* Grant for use in freshman, sophomore, junior, senior, graduate, or postgraduate years; not renewable. *Award amount:* $50–$3000. *Eligibility Requirements:* Applicant must be enrolled or expecting to enroll full- or part-time at a two-year or four-year or technical institution or university; resident of Minnesota and studying in Minnesota. Available to U.S. citizens. *Application Requirements:* Application form. **Deadline:** continuous.

Contact Meghan Flores, State Grant Manager. *E-mail:* meghan.flores@state. mn.us. *Phone:* 651-355-0610. *Website:* http://www.ohe.state.mn.us.

Minnesota Indian Scholarship. The Minnesota Indian Scholarship Program provides postsecondary financial assistance to eligible Minnesota resident students who are of one-fourth or more American Indian ancestry and demonstrate financial need for an award. Scholarships are available to eligible American Indian undergraduate students enrolled at least time and graduate students enrolled at least half time. The award amount is based on need up to $4,000 per year for undergraduate students and up to $6,000 for graduate students. *Award:* Scholarship for use in freshman, sophomore, junior, senior, graduate, or postgraduate years; not renewable. *Eligibility Requirements:* Applicant must be of Arumanian/ Ulacedo-Romanian heritage; American Indian/Alaska Native; high school student; planning to enroll or expecting to enroll full- or part-time at a two-year or four-year or technical institution or university; resident of Minnesota and studying in Minnesota. Available to U.S. and Canadian citizens. *Application Requirements:* Application form, financial need analysis. **Deadline:** continuous.

Contact Meghan Flores, State Grant Manager. *E-mail:* meghan.flores@state. mn.us. *Phone:* 651-355-0610. *Website:* http://www.ohe.state.mn.us.

Minnesota State Grant Program. Need-based grant program available for Minnesota residents attending Minnesota colleges. Student covers 50% of cost with remainder covered by Pell Grant, parent contribution and state grant. Students apply with FAFSA and colleges administer the program on campus. *Award:* Grant for use in freshman, sophomore, junior, or senior years; not renewable. *Award amount:* $100–$11,334. *Number of awards:* 71,000–120,000. *Eligibility Requirements:* Applicant must be enrolled or expecting to enroll full- or part-time at a two-year or four-year or technical institution or university; resident of Minnesota and studying in Minnesota. Available to U.S. citizens. *Application Requirements:* Application form, financial need analysis. **Deadline:** continuous.

Minnesota State Veterans' Dependents Assistance Program. Tuition assistance to dependents of persons considered to be prisoner-of-war or missing in action after August 1, 1958. Must be Minnesota resident attending Minnesota two- or four-year school. *Award:* Scholarship for use in freshman, sophomore, junior, or senior years; renewable. *Award amount:* $249–$250. *Number of awards:* 100–200. *Eligibility Requirements:* Applicant must be enrolled or expecting to enroll full- or part-time at a two-year or four-year institution; resident of Minnesota and studying in Minnesota. Available to U.S. citizens. *Application Requirements:* Application form. **Deadline:** continuous.

Contact Meghan Flores, State Grant Manager. *E-mail:* meghan.flores@state. mn.us. *Phone:* 651-355-0610. *Website:* http://www.ohe.state.mn.us.

Postsecondary Child Care Grant Program-Minnesota. Grant available for students who are not receiving MFIP (TANF) and have children in day care. Based on financial need. Cannot exceed actual child care costs or maximum award chart (based on income). Must be Minnesota resident. For use at Minnesota two- or four-year school, including public technical colleges. Available until student has attended college for the equivalent of four full-time academic years. *Award:* Grant for use in freshman, sophomore, junior, or senior years; not renewable. *Award amount:* $100–$2800. *Number of awards:* 1–3500. *Eligibility Requirements:* Applicant must be enrolled or expecting to enroll full- or part-time at a two-year or four-year or technical institution or university; resident of Minnesota and studying in Minnesota. Available to U.S. citizens. *Application Requirements:* Application form, financial need analysis. **Deadline:** continuous.

Contact Brenda Larter, Program Administrator, Minnesota Office of Higher Education, 1450 Energy Park Drive, Suite 350, St. Paul, MN 55108-5227. *E-mail:* brenda.larter@state.mn. us. *Phone:* 651-355-0612. *Website:* http://www.ohe.state.mn.us.

Safety Officers' Survivor Grant Program. Grant for eligible survivors of Minnesota public safety officers killed in the line of duty. Safety officers who have been permanently or totally disabled in the line of duty are also eligible. Must be used at a Minnesota institution participating in State Grant Program. Write for details. Must submit proof of death or disability and Public Safety Officers Benefit Fund Certificate. Must apply for renewal each year. Five-year limit on awards. *Award:* Grant for use in freshman, sophomore, junior, senior, or graduate years; not renewable. *Award amount:* $1–$13,840. *Number of awards:* 1–10. *Eligibility Requirements:* Applicant must be enrolled or expecting to enroll full- or part-time at a two-year or four-year or technical institution or university; resident of Minnesota and studying in Minnesota. Applicant or parent of applicant must have employment or volunteer experience in police/firefighting. Available to U.S. citizens. *Application Requirements:* Application form. **Deadline:** continuous.

Contact Brenda Larter, Program Administrator. *E-mail:* brenda.larter@ state.mn.us. *Phone:* 651-355-0612. *Website:* http://www.ohe.state.mn.us.

MISSISSIPPI

Higher Education Legislative Plan (HELP). Eligible applicant must be resident of Mississippi and apply for the first time as a freshman and/or sophomore student who graduated from high school within the immediate past two years. Must demonstrate need as determined by the results of the FAFSA, documenting an average family adjusted gross income of $36,500 or less over the prior two years. Must be enrolled full-time at a Mississippi college or university, have a GPA of 2.5, have completed a specific high school core curriculum, and have scored 20 on the ACT. *Award:* Grant for use in freshman, sophomore, junior, or senior years; renewable. *Award amount:* $340–$7344.

Number of awards: 2912. *Eligibility Requirements:* Applicant must be enrolled or expecting to enroll full-time at a two-year or four-year institution or university; resident of Mississippi and studying in Mississippi. Applicant must have 3.0 GPA or higher. Available to U. S. citizens. *Application Requirements:* Application form, financial need analysis. **Deadline:** March 31.

Law Enforcement Officers/Firemen Scholarship. Financial assistance to dependent children and spouses of any Mississippi law enforcement officer, full-time fire fighter or volunteer fire fighter who has suffered fatal injuries or wounds or become permanently and totally disabled as a result of injuries or wounds which occurred in the performance of the official and appointed duties of his or her office. This financial assistance is offered as an eight semester tuition and room scholarship at any state-supported college or university in Mississippi. *Award:* Scholarship for use in freshman, sophomore, junior, or senior years; renewable. *Award amount:* $2010–$12,854. *Number of awards:* 18–30. *Eligibility Requirements:* Applicant must be enrolled or expecting to enroll full-time at a two-year or four-year institution or university; resident of Mississippi and studying in Mississippi. Applicant or parent of applicant must have employment or volunteer experience in police/firefighting. Applicant must have 2.5 GPA or higher. Available to U.S. citizens. *Application Requirements:* Application form. **Deadline:** continuous.

Mississippi Eminent Scholars Grant. Award for an entering freshmen or as a renewal for sophomore, junior or senior, who are residents of Mississippi. Applicants must achieve a GPA of 3.5 and must have scored 29 on the ACT. Must enroll full-time at an eligible Mississippi college or university. *Award:* Grant for use in freshman, sophomore, junior, or senior years; not renewable. *Award amount:* $1157–$2500. *Number of awards:* 2726. *Eligibility Requirements:* Applicant must be enrolled or expecting to enroll full-time at a two-year or four-year institution or university; resident of Mississippi and studying in Mississippi. Applicant must have 3.5 GPA or higher. Available to U.S. citizens. *Application Requirements:* Application form. **Deadline:** September 15.

Mississippi Resident Tuition Assistance Grant. Must be a resident of Mississippi enrolled full-time at an eligible Mississippi college or university. Must maintain a minimum 2.5 GPA each semester. MTAG awards may be up to $500 per academic year for freshman and sophomores and $1000 per academic year for juniors and seniors. *Award:* Grant for use in freshman, sophomore, junior, or senior years; not renewable. *Award amount:* $17–$1000. *Eligibility Requirements:* Applicant must be enrolled or expecting to enroll full-time at a two-year or four-year institution or university; resident of Mississippi and studying in Mississippi. Applicant must have 2.5 GPA or higher. Available to U.S. citizens. *Application Requirements:* Application form. **Deadline:** September 15.

MISSOURI

Access Missouri Financial Assistance Program. Need-based program that provides awards to students who are enrolled full-time and have an expected family contribution (EFC) of $12,000 or less based on their Free Application for Federal Student Aid (FAFSA). Awards vary depending on EFC and the type of postsecondary school. *Award:* Grant for use in freshman, sophomore, junior, or senior years; not renewable. *Eligibility Requirements:* Applicant must be enrolled or expecting to enroll full-time at a two-year or technical institution or university; resident of Missouri and studying in Missouri. Applicant must have 2.5 GPA or higher. Available to U. S. citizens. *Application Requirements:* FAFSA on file by April 1.

Lillie Lois Ford Scholarship Fund. Two awards of $1000 each are given each year to one boy and one girl. Applicant must have attended a full session of Missouri Boys/Girls State or Missouri Cadet Patrol Academy. Must be a Missouri resident below age 21, attending an accredited college/university as a full-time student. Must be an unmarried descendant of a veteran having served at least 90 days on active duty in the Army, Air Force, Navy, Marine Corps, or Coast Guard of the United States. *Award:* Scholarship for use in freshman year; not renewable. *Award amount:* $1000. *Number of awards:* 2. *Eligibility Requirements:* Applicant must be high school student; planning to enroll or expecting to enroll

full-time at a two-year or four-year institution or university; single and resident of Missouri. Available to U.S. citizens. Applicant or parent must meet one or more of the following requirements: general military experience; retired from active duty; disabled or killed as a result of military service; prisoner of war; or missing in action. *Application Requirements:* Application form, copy of the veteran's discharge certificate, financial need analysis, test scores. **Deadline:** April 20.

Contact John Doane, Chairman, Education and Scholarship Committee, American Legion Department of Missouri, PO Box 179, Jefferson City, MO 65102-0179. *Phone:* 417-924-8186. *Website:* http://www.missourilegion.org/

Marguerite Ross Barnett Memorial Scholarship. Scholarship was established for students who are employed while attending school part-time. Must be enrolled at least half-time but less than full-time at a participating Missouri postsecondary school, be employed and compensated for at least 20 hours per week, be 18 years of age, be a Missouri resident and a U.S. citizen or a permanent resident. *Award:* Scholarship for use in freshman, sophomore, junior, or senior years; renewable. *Eligibility Requirements:* Applicant must be enrolled or expecting to enroll part-time at a two-year or four-year or technical institution or university; resident of Missouri and studying in Missouri. Applicant must have 2.5 GPA or higher. Available to U.S. citizens. *Application Requirements:* FAFSA on file by August 1. **Deadline:** August 1.

Missouri Higher Education Academic Scholarship (Bright Flight). Program encourages top-ranked high school seniors to attend approved Missouri postsecondary schools. Must be a Missouri resident and a U.S. citizen or permanent resident. Must have a composite score on the ACT or SAT in the top 5 percent of all Missouri students taking those tests. Students with scores in the top 3 percent are eligible for an annual award of up to $3000 (up to $1500 each semester). Students with scores in the top 4% and 5% are eligible for an annual award of up to $1000 (up to $500 each semester). Award amounts, and the availability of the award for students in the 4% and 5%, are subject to change based on the amount of funding allocated for the program in the legislative session. *Award:* Scholarship for use in freshman, sophomore, junior, or senior years; renewable. *Award amount:* $1000–$3000. *Eligibility Requirements:* Applicant must be enrolled or expecting to enroll full-time at a two-year or four-year or technical institution or university; resident of Missouri and studying in Missouri. Applicant must have 2.5 GPA or higher. Available to U.S. citizens. *Application Requirements:* Test scores.

MONTANA

Montana University System Honor Scholarship. Scholarship will be awarded annually to high school seniors graduating from accredited Montana high schools. The MUS Honor Scholarship is a four year renewable scholarship that waives tuition at one of the Montana University System campuses or one of the three community colleges (Flathead Valley in Kalispell, Miles in Miles City or Dawson in Glendive). The scholarship must be used within 9 months after high school graduation. Applicant must have a minimum GPA of 3.4. *Award:* Scholarship for use in freshman, sophomore, junior, or senior years; renewable. *Award amount:* $16,000–$24,000. *Number of awards:* 200. *Eligibility Requirements:* Applicant must be high school student; planning to enroll or expecting to enroll full-time at a two-year or four-year institution or university; resident of Montana and studying in Montana. Applicant must have 3.5 GPA or higher. Available to U.S. citizens. *Application Requirements:* Application form. **Deadline:** March 15.

Contact Sheila Newlun, Grants and Scholarship Coordinator. *E-mail:* snewlun@montana.edu. *Phone:* 406-449-9168. *Fax:* 406-444-1869. *Website:* http://www.mus.edu.

NEBRASKA

Nebraska Opportunity Grant. Available to undergraduates attending a participating postsecondary institution in Nebraska. Must demonstrate financial need. Nebraska residency required. Awards determined by each participating institution. Student must complete the Free Application for Federal Student Aid (FAFSA) to apply. Contact financial aid office at institution for additional information. *Award:* Grant for use in freshman, sophomore, junior, or senior years; not renewable. *Award amount:* $100–$4139. *Eligibility Requirements:* Applicant must be enrolled or expecting to enroll full- or part-time at a two-year or four-year or technical institution or university; resident of Nebraska and studying in Nebraska. Available to U.S. citizens. *Application Requirements:* Application form, financial need analysis. **Deadline:** continuous.

Contact Mr. J. Ritchie Morrow, Financial Aid Officer, Nebraska's Coordinating Commission for Postsecondary Education, 140 North 8th Street, Suite 300, PO Box 95005, Lincoln, NE 68509-5005. *E-mail:* Ritchie.Morrow@nebraska.gov. *Phone:* 402-471-2847. *Website:* https://ccpe.nebraska.gov/.

NEVADA

CouponChief.com Scholarship Program. We at CouponChief.com want to support young leaders that understand frugality and saving money, and how the skills and knowledge of using coupons can contribute to that end. We will award 1 scholarship winner with $1000 to put towards education every year. *Award:* Scholarship for use in freshman, sophomore, junior, senior, graduate, or postgraduate years; not renewable. *Award amount:* $1000. *Number of awards:* 1. *Eligibility Requirements:* Applicant must be enrolled or expecting to enroll full- or part-time at a two-year or four-year or technical institution or university. Available to U.S. citizens. *Application Requirements:* **Deadline:** July 31.

Governor Guinn Millennium Scholarship. Scholarship for Nevada residents. Student must graduate from a public or private high school within Nevada with a minimum GPA of 3.25. Must complete core curriculum. Maximum award is $10,000. Student must acknowledge award and use it within 6 years of high school graduation. *Award:* Scholarship for use in freshman, sophomore, junior, or senior years; renewable. *Award amount:* up to $10,000. *Number of awards:* 1. *Eligibility Requirements:* Applicant must be enrolled or expecting to enroll full-time at a two-year or four-year institution or university; resident of Nevada and studying in Nevada. Available to U.S. citizens. *Application Requirements:*

Application form may be submitted online (http://nevadatreasurer.gov), high schools determine eligibility; student must accept award. **Deadline:** varies.

Contact Linda English, Executive Director. *E-mail:* info@nevadatreasurer.gov. *Phone:* 702-486-3889. *Fax:* 702-486-3246. *Website:* http://www.nevadatreasurer.gov/.

NEW HAMPSHIRE

Scholarships for Orphans of Veterans. Scholarship to provide financial assistance (room, board, books and supplies) to children of parents who served in World War II, Korean Conflict, Vietnam (Southeast Asian Conflict) or the Gulf Wars, or any other operation for which the armed forces expeditionary medal or theater of operations service medal was awarded to the veteran. Must be between the ages of 16 and 25 to qualify and be residents of New Hampshire studying at public New Hampshire colleges and universities. *Award:* Scholarship for use in freshman, sophomore, junior, senior, graduate, or postgraduate years; renewable. *Award amount:* $1000–$2500. *Number of awards:* 1. *Eligibility Requirements:* Applicant must be age 16-25; enrolled or expecting to enroll full-time at a two-year or four-year institution or university; resident of New Hampshire and studying in New Hampshire. Available to U.S. citizens. Applicant or parent must meet one or more of the following requirements: general military experience; retired from active duty; disabled or killed as a result of military service; prisoner of war; or missing in action. *Application Requirements:* Application form. **Deadline:** September 1.

Contact Mrs. Pat Moquin, Program Assistant II, N.H. Department of Education, Division of Higher Education - Higher Education Commission, 101 Pleasant Street, Concord, NH 03301. *E-mail:* patricia.moquin@doe.nh.gov. *Phone:* 603-271-0289. *Website:* http://www.education.nh.gov/highered.

NEW JERSEY

Law Enforcement Officer Memorial Scholarship. Scholarships for full-time undergraduate study at approved New Jersey institutions for the dependent children of New Jersey law enforcement officers killed in the line of duty. Value of scholarship will be established annually. Deadline varies. *Award:* Scholarship for use in freshman, sophomore, or junior years; not renewable. *Eligibility Requirements:* Applicant must be enrolled or expecting to enroll full-time at a two-year or four-year institution or university; resident of New Jersey and studying in New Jersey. Applicant or parent of applicant must have employment or volunteer experience in police/firefighting. Available to U.S. citizens. *Application Requirements:* Application form.

Contact Jean Hathoway, Assistant Director of Special Grants and Scholarships, New Jersey Higher Education Student Assistance Authority, PO Box 540, Trenton, NJ 08625. *Phone:* 609-588-3266. *Website:* http://www.hesaa. org/.

New Jersey Student Tuition Assistance Reward Scholarship II. Earn an associate degree from the home New Jersey county college as an NJ STARS recipient and graduate with a cumulative GPA of 3.25 or higher. Family income (taxable and untaxed income) must be less than $250,000 as derived from the FAFSA. NJ STARS II students may receive up to $1,250 per semester, paid completely by the State, after all other sources of federal and State grants and scholarships are applied to tuition charges. *Award:* Scholarship for use in junior or senior years; renewable. *Eligibility Requirements:* Applicant must be enrolled or expecting to enroll full-time at a four-year institution or university; resident of New Jersey and studying in New Jersey. Applicant must have 3.0 GPA or higher. Available to U.S. citizens. *Application Requirements:* Application form. **Deadline:** continuous.

Contact Jossette Greene, Program Officer. *E-mail:* jgreene@hesaa.org. *Phone:* 609-584-4480. *Website:* http:// www.hesaa.org/.

New Jersey War Orphans Tuition Assistance. $500 scholarship to children of those service personnel who died while in the military or due to service-connected disabilities, or who are officially listed as missing in action by the U.S. Department of Defense. Must be a resident of New Jersey for at least one year immediately preceding the filing of the application and be between the ages of 16 and 21 at the time of application. *Award:* Scholarship for use in freshman, sophomore, junior, or senior years; renewable. *Award*

amount: $500. *Eligibility Requirements:* Applicant must be age 16-21; enrolled or expecting to enroll full-time at a four-year institution or university and resident of New Jersey. Available to U.S. citizens. Applicant or parent must meet one or more of the following requirements: general military experience; retired from active duty; disabled or killed as a result of military service; prisoner of war; or missing in action. *Application Requirements:* Application form, transcript. **Deadline:** varies.

Contact Patricia Richter, Grants Manager, New Jersey Department of Military and Veterans Affairs, PO Box 340, Trenton, NJ 08625-0340. *E-mail:* patricia.richter@njdmava.state.nj.us. *Phone:* 609-530-6854. *Fax:* 609-530-6970. *Website:* http://www.state.nj.us/ military.

New Jersey World Trade Center Scholarship. Scholarship was established by the legislature to aid the dependent children and surviving spouses of New Jersey residents who were killed in the terrorist attacks, or who are missing and officially presumed dead as a direct result of the attacks; applies to instate and out-of-state institutions for students seeking undergraduate degrees. *Award:* Scholarship for use in freshman, sophomore, junior, or senior years; not renewable. *Award amount:* $1–$6500. *Eligibility Requirements:* Applicant must be enrolled or expecting to enroll full-time at a two-year or four-year institution or university and resident of New Jersey. Available to U.S. citizens. *Application Requirements:* Application form.

Contact Jean Hathaway, Assistant Director of Special Grants and Scholarships, New Jersey Higher Education Student Assistance Authority, PO Box 540, Trenton, NJ 08625. *E-mail:* jhathaway@hesaa.org. *Phone:* 609-588-3266. *Website:* http://www.hesaa.org/.

NJ Student Tuition Assistance Reward Scholarship. Students must enroll in a full time course of study at their home county colleges. The award covers tuition charges for up to 18 credit hours per term. *Award:* Scholarship for use in freshman or sophomore years; renewable. *Award amount:* $500–$2600. *Eligibility Requirements:* Applicant must be enrolled or expecting to enroll full-time at a two-year institution; resident of New Jersey and studying in New Jersey. Applicant must have 3.0 GPA or higher. Available to U.S. cit-

izens. *Application Requirements:* Application form.

Contact Ms. Jossette Greene, Program Officer, New Jersey Higher Education Student Assistance Authority, PO Box 540, Trenton, NJ 08625. *E-mail:* jgreene@hessa.org. *Phone:* 609-584-4480. *Website:* http://www.hesaa. org/.

Part-Time Tuition Aid Grant for County Colleges. Provides financial aid to eligible part-time undergraduate students enrolled for 9 to 11 credits at New Jersey community colleges. *Award:* Grant for use in freshman or sophomore years; not renewable. *Award amount:* $500–$1900. *Eligibility Requirements:* Applicant must be enrolled or expecting to enroll part-time at a two-year institution; resident of New Jersey and studying in New Jersey. Available to U. S. citizens. *Application Requirements:* Application form, financial need analysis.

Contact Jean Hathoway, AS of Grants and Scholarships, New Jersey Higher Education Student Assistance Authority, PO Box 540, Trenton, NJ 08625. *E-mail:* jhathaway@hesaa.org. *Phone:* 609-584-4480. *Website:* http:// www.hesaa.org/.

POW-MIA Tuition Benefit Program. Free undergraduate college tuition provided to any child born or adopted before or during the period of time his or her parent was officially declared a prisoner of war or person missing in action after January 1, 1960. The POW-MIA must have been a New Jersey resident at the time he or she entered the service. Child of veteran must attend either a public or private institution in New Jersey. A copy of DD 1300 must be furnished with the application. Minimum 2.5 GPA required. *Award:* Scholarship for use in freshman, sophomore, junior, or senior years; renewable. *Eligibility Requirements:* Applicant must be enrolled or expecting to enroll full-time at a two-year or four-year or technical institution or university; resident of New Jersey and studying in New Jersey. Applicant must have 2.5 GPA or higher. Available to U. S. citizens. Applicant or parent must meet one or more of the following requirements: general military experience; retired from active duty; disabled or killed as a result of military service; prisoner of war; or missing in action. *Application Requirements:* Application form, copy of DD 1300, transcript. **Deadline:** varies.

Contact Patricia Richter, Grants Manager, New Jersey Department of Military and Veterans Affairs, PO Box 340, Trenton, NJ 08625-0340. *E-mail:* patricia.richter@njdmava.state.nj.us. *Phone:* 609-530-6854. *Fax:* 609-530-6970. *Website:* http://www.state.nj.us/military.

Survivor Tuition Benefits Program. The scholarship provides tuition fees for spouses and dependents of law enforcement officers, fire, or emergency services personnel killed in the line of duty. Eligible recipients may attend any independent institution in the state; however, the annual value of the grant cannot exceed the highest tuition charged at a New Jersey public institution. *Award:* Scholarship for use in freshman, sophomore, junior, or senior years; renewable. *Eligibility Requirements:* Applicant must be enrolled or expecting to enroll full- or part-time at a two-year or four-year institution or university; resident of New Jersey and studying in New Jersey. Applicant or parent of applicant must have employment or volunteer experience in police/firefighting. Available to U.S. citizens. *Application Requirements:* Application form.

Contact Jean Hathaway, Assistant Director of Special Grants and Scholarships, New Jersey Higher Education Student Assistance Authority, PO Box 540, Trenton, NJ 08625. *E-mail:* jhathaway@hesaa.org. *Phone:* 609-588-3266. *Website:* http://www.hesaa.org/.

Tuition Aid Grant. The program provides grants to eligible undergraduate students attending participating in-state institutions. *Award:* Grant for use in freshman, sophomore, junior, or senior years; not renewable. *Award amount:* $1012–$12,190. *Eligibility Requirements:* Applicant must be enrolled or expecting to enroll full-time at a two-year or four-year institution or university; resident of New Jersey and studying in New Jersey. Available to U.S. citizens. *Application Requirements:* Application form, financial need analysis.

Contact Kathyrn Safran, Director of Grants and Scholarships, New Jersey Higher Education Student Assistance Authority, PO Box 540, Trenton, NJ 08625. *E-mail:* ksafran@hesaa.org.

Phone: 609-584-4480. *Website:* http://www.hesaa.org/.

Veterans Tuition Credit Program-New Jersey. Award for New Jersey resident veterans who served in the armed forces between December 31, 1960, and May 7, 1975. Must have been a New Jersey resident at time of induction or discharge or for two years immediately prior to application. *Award:* Scholarship for use in freshman, sophomore, junior, or senior years; renewable. *Award amount:* $200–$400. *Eligibility Requirements:* Applicant must be enrolled or expecting to enroll full- or part-time at a two-year or four-year or technical institution or university and resident of New Jersey. Available to U.S. citizens. Applicant or parent must meet one or more of the following requirements: general military experience; retired from active duty; disabled or killed as a result of military service; prisoner of war; or missing in action. *Application Requirements:* Application form. **Deadline:** varies.

Contact Patricia Richter, Grants Manager, New Jersey Department of Military and Veterans Affairs, PO Box 340, Trenton, NJ 08625-0340. *E-mail:* patricia.richter@njdmava.state.nj.us. *Phone:* 609-530-6854. *Fax:* 609-530-6970. *Website:* http://www.state.nj.us/military.

NEW MEXICO

Children of Deceased Veterans Scholarship-New Mexico. Award for New Mexico residents who are children of veterans killed as a result of service, prisoner of war, or veterans missing in action. Must be between ages 16 and 26. For use at New Mexico schools for undergraduate study. Must submit parent's death certificate and DD form 214. *Award:* Scholarship for use in freshman, sophomore, junior, or senior years; not renewable. *Award amount:* $300. *Number of awards:* 49–50. *Eligibility Requirements:* Applicant must be age 16-26; enrolled or expecting to enroll full- or part-time at a two-year or four-year or technical institution or university; resident of New Mexico and studying in New Mexico. Available to U.S. citizens. *Application Requirements:* Application form.

Contact Mr. Dale Movius, Director, State Benefits, New Mexico Department of Veterans' Services, 407 Galisteo St,

Room 134, Santa Fe, NM 87501. *E-mail:* dalej.movius@state.nm.us. *Phone:* 505-827-6300. *Website:* http://www.nmdvs.org.

College Affordability Grant. Grant available to New Mexico students with financial need who do not qualify for other state grants and scholarships to attend and complete educational programs at a New Mexico public college or university. Student must have unmet need after all other financial aid has been awarded. Student may not be receiving any other state grants or scholarships. Renewable upon satisfactory academic progress. *Award:* Grant for use in freshman, sophomore, junior, or senior years; renewable. *Award amount:* up to $1000. *Number of awards:* 1. *Eligibility Requirements:* Applicant must be enrolled or expecting to enroll full- or part-time at a two-year or four-year institution or university; resident of New Mexico and studying in New Mexico. Available to U.S. citizens. *Application Requirements:* Application form, FAFSA, financial need analysis. **Deadline:** continuous.

Contact Tashina Acker, Director of Financial Aid, New Mexico Commission on Higher Education, 1068 Cerrillos Road, Santa Fe, NM 87505-1650. *E-mail:* tashina.banks-moore@state.nm.us. *Phone:* 505-476-6549. *Fax:* 505-476-6511. *Website:* http://www.hed.state.nm.us/.

Legislative Endowment Scholarships. Renewable scholarships to provide aid for undergraduate students with substantial financial need who are attending public postsecondary institutions in New Mexico. Four-year schools may award up to $2500 per academic year, two-year schools may award up to $1000 per academic year. Deadlines varies. *Award:* Scholarship for use in freshman, sophomore, junior, or senior years; renewable. *Award amount:* $1000–$2500. *Number of awards:* 1. *Eligibility Requirements:* Applicant must be enrolled or expecting to enroll full- or part-time at a two-year or four-year institution or university; resident of New Mexico and studying in New Mexico. Available to U.S. citizens. *Application Requirements:* Application form, FAFSA, financial need analysis. **Deadline:** varies.

Contact Tashina Moore, Director of Financial Aid, New Mexico Commission on Higher Education, 1068 Cerrillos Road, Santa Fe, NM 87505-1650. *E-mail:* tashina.banks-moore@state.nm. us. *Phone:* 505-475-6549. *Fax:* 505-476-6511. *Website:* http://www.hed. state.nm.us/.

Legislative Lottery Scholarship. Renewable Scholarship for New Mexico high school graduates or GED recipients who plan to attend an eligible New Mexico public college or university. Must be enrolled full-time and maintain 2.5 GPA. *Award:* Scholarship for use in freshman year; renewable. *Number of awards:* 1. *Eligibility Requirements:* Applicant must be high school student; planning to enroll or expecting to enroll full-time at a four-year institution or university; resident of New Mexico and studying in New Mexico. Applicant must have 3.5 GPA or higher. Available to U.S. citizens. *Application Requirements:* Application form, FAFSA. **Deadline:** varies.

Contact Tashina Moore, Director of Financial Aid, New Mexico Commission on Higher Education, 1068 Cerrillos Road, Santa Fe, NM 87505. *E-mail:* tashina.banks-moore@state.nm. us. *Phone:* 505-476-6549. *Fax:* 505-476-6511. *Website:* http://www.hed. state.nm.us/.

New Mexico Competitive Scholarship. Scholarships for non-residents or non-citizens of the United States to encourage out-of-state students who have demonstrated high academic achievement in high school to enroll in public four-year universities in New Mexico. Renewable for up to four years. For details visit http://fin.hed.state.nm. us. *Award:* Scholarship for use in freshman year; renewable. *Eligibility Requirements:* Applicant must be high school student; planning to enroll or expecting to enroll full-time at a four-year institution or university and studying in New Mexico. Available to Canadian and non-U.S. citizens. *Application Requirements:* Application form, essay, recommendations or references, test scores. **Deadline:** varies.

Contact Tashina Moore, Director of Financial Aid, New Mexico Commission on Higher Education, 1068 Cerrillos Road, Santa Fe, NM 87505. *E-mail:* tashina.banks-moore@state.nm. us. *Phone:* 505-476-6549. *Fax:* 505-476-6511. *Website:* http://www.hed. state.nm.us/.

New Mexico Scholars' Program. Renewable award program created to encourage New Mexico high school students to attend public postsecondary institutions or the following private colleges in New Mexico: College of Santa Fe, St. John's College, College of the Southwest. For details visit http://fin. hed.state.nm.us. *Award:* Scholarship for use in freshman year; renewable. *Number of awards:* 1. *Eligibility Requirements:* Applicant must be high school student; planning to enroll or expecting to enroll full-time at a two-year or four-year institution; resident of New Mexico and studying in New Mexico. Available to U.S. citizens. *Application Requirements:* Application form, FAFSA, financial need analysis, test scores. **Deadline:** varies.

Contact Tashina Moore, Director of Financial Aid, New Mexico Commission on Higher Education, 1068 Cerrillos Road, Santa Fe, NM 87505-1650. *E-mail:* tashina.banks-moore@state.nm. us. *Phone:* 505-476-6549. *Fax:* 505-476-6511. *Website:* http://www.hed. state.nm.us/.

New Mexico Student Incentive Grant. Grant created to provide aid for undergraduate students with substantial financial need who are attending public colleges or universities or the following eligible colleges in New Mexico: College of Santa Fe, St. John's College, College of the Southwest, Institute of American Indian Art, Crownpoint Institute of Technology, Dine College and Southwestern Indian Polytechnic Institute. Part-time students are eligible for pro-rated awards. *Award:* Grant for use in freshman, sophomore, junior, or senior years; not renewable. *Award amount:* $200–$2500. *Number of awards:* 1. *Eligibility Requirements:* Applicant must be enrolled or expecting to enroll full- or part-time at a two-year or four-year or technical institution or university; resident of New Mexico and studying in New Mexico. Available to U.S. citizens. *Application Requirements:* Application form, FAFSA, financial need analysis. **Deadline:** varies.

Contact Tashina Moore, Director of Financial Aid, New Mexico Commission on Higher Education, 1068 Cerrillos Road, Santa Fe, NM 87505-1650. *E-mail:* tashina.banks-moore@state.nm. us. *Phone:* 505-476-6549. *Fax:* 505-476-6511. *Website:* http://www.hed. state.nm.us/.

New Mexico Vietnam Veteran Scholarship. Award for Vietnam veterans who have been New Mexico residents for a minimum of ten years and are attending state-funded postsecondary schools. Must have been awarded the Vietnam Campaign medal. Must submit DD 214 and discharge papers. *Award:* Scholarship for use in freshman, sophomore, junior, or senior years; renewable. *Award amount:* $3500–$4000. *Number of awards:* 100. *Eligibility Requirements:* Applicant must be enrolled or expecting to enroll full- or part-time at a two-year or four-year or technical institution or university; resident of New Mexico and studying in New Mexico. Available to U.S. citizens. *Application Requirements:* Application form.

Contact Mr. Dale Movius, Director, State Benefits, New Mexico Department of Veterans' Services, 407 Galisteo St, Room 134, Santa Fe, NM 87501. *E-mail:* Dalej.movius@state.nm.us. *Phone:* 505-827-6300. *Website:* http://www.nmdvs.org.

New Mexico Wartime Veterans Scholarship. Award for Wartime Veterans who have been a New Mexico resident for a minimum of ten years and are attending state-funded postsecondary schools. Must have been awarded a campaign medal such as the Southwest Asia Service Medal, Global War on Terrorism Expeditionary Medal, Iraq Campaign Medal, Afghanistan Campaign Medal or any other medal issued for service in the Armed Forces of the United States in support of any U.S. Military Campaign or armed conflict as defined by congress or presidential order or service after August 1, 1990. *Award:* Scholarship for use in freshman, sophomore, junior, senior, or graduate years; renewable. *Award amount:* $3500–$4000. *Number of awards:* 100. *Eligibility Requirements:* Applicant must be enrolled or expecting to enroll full- or part-time at a two-year or four-year or technical institution or university; resident of New Mexico and studying in New Mexico. Available to U.S. citizens. Applicant must have general military experience. *Application Requirements:* Application form.

Contact Mr. Dale Movius, Director, State Benefits, New Mexico Department of Veterans' Services, 407 Galiesteo St, Room 134, Santa Fe, NM 87501. *E-mail:* dalej.movius@state.nm.us.

Phone: 505-827-6374. *Website:* http://www.nmdvs.org.

Vietnam Veterans' Scholarship Program. Renewable scholarship program created to provide aid for Vietnam veterans who are undergraduate and graduate students attending public postsecondary institutions or select private colleges in New Mexico. Private colleges include: College of Santa Fe, St. John's College and College of the Southwest. *Award:* Scholarship for use in freshman, sophomore, junior, or senior years; renewable. *Number of awards:* 1. *Eligibility Requirements:* Applicant must be enrolled or expecting to enroll full-time at a two-year or four-year institution; resident of New Mexico and studying in New Mexico. Available to U.S. citizens. Applicant or parent must meet one or more of the following requirements: general military experience; retired from active duty; disabled or killed as a result of military service; prisoner of war; or missing in action. *Application Requirements:* Application form, certification by the NM Veteran's commission. **Deadline:** varies.

Contact Tashina Moore, Director of Financial Aid, New Mexico Commission on Higher Education, 1068 Cerrillos Road, Santa Fe, NM 87505-1650. *E-mail:* tashina.banks-moore@state.nm.us. *Phone:* 505-476-6549. *Fax:* 505-476-6511. *Website:* http://www.hed.state.nm.us/.

NEW YORK

Alexander and Maude Hadden Scholarship. Youth Foundation offers exceptional students with financial need an award of $2500 to $4000 per year which is renewable for four years at the foundation's discretion. Minimum GPA of 3.5 required, community service and extra curricular activities expected. Must write Foundation for information and application request form. *Award:* Scholarship for use in freshman, sophomore, junior, or senior years; renewable. *Award amount:* $2500–$4000. *Number of awards:* 96–108. *Eligibility Requirements:* Applicant must be enrolled or expecting to enroll full-time at a four-year institution or university and resident of Yukon. Applicant or parent of applicant must have employment or volunteer experience in community service. Applicant must have 3.5 GPA or higher.

Available to U.S. citizens. *Application Requirements:* Application form, community service, essay, financial need analysis, personal photograph. **Deadline:** February 28.

Contact Ms. Johanna Lee, Executive Administrator. *E-mail:* YouthFdn@aol.com. *Phone:* 212-840-6291. *Fax:* 212-840-6747. *Website:* http://fdnweb.org/youthfdn.

DAAD University Summer Course Grant. Scholarships are awarded to full-time degree students of Canadian or U.S. colleges, sophomore/2nd year and higher, for the pursuit of summer courses at universities in Germany. It is open to applicants of any major but there is a prerequisite of at least two years of college-level German (B1) or the equivalent German language fluency. Courses are three to four weeks in duration, take place at many locations in Germany (universities), are taught in German, and topics include German language, literature, current affairs, political science, history, culture, arts, film and media, economics, linguistics, law, translation and interpretation, and test prep for German language proficiency examinations. Accommodations are arranged by the host institution. Foreign Language. *Award:* Grant for use in sophomore, junior, or senior years; not renewable. *Eligibility Requirements:* Applicant must be enrolled or expecting to enroll full-time at a four-year institution or university and must have an interest in German language/culture. Available to U.S. and non-U.S. citizens. *Application Requirements:* Application form, essay.

Gardiner Foundation Scholarship. For a young person, losing a family member can be a devastating experience. However, losing multiple family members all at once is almost unthinkable. That's what happened to Dexter Gardiner, who on July 9, 2006 lost six family members in a tragic car accident on the Bronx River Parkway. Yet despite the loss, Dexter chose to use the tragedy as a way to help others who have experienced similar situations in losing beloved family members unexpectedly. Needless to say, for those left behind, especially children whose college education may suddenly be in doubt due to financial concerns, the world can suddenly seem very uncertain. *Award:* Scholarship for use in sophomore or senior years; renewable.

Award amount: $1500. *Number of awards:* 4–5. *Eligibility Requirements:* Applicant must be enrolled or expecting to enroll full-time at an institution or university. Available to U.S. citizens. *Application Requirements:* Application form, essay. **Deadline:** July 15.

New York Aid for Part-Time Study (APTS). Renewable scholarship provides tuition assistance to part-time undergraduate students who are New York residents, meet income eligibility requirements and are attending New York accredited institutions. Deadline varies. Must be U.S. citizen. *Award:* Grant for use in freshman, sophomore, junior, or senior years; renewable. *Award amount:* up to $2000. *Eligibility Requirements:* Applicant must be enrolled or expecting to enroll part-time at a two-year or four-year institution or university; resident of New York and studying in New York. Available to U.S. citizens. *Application Requirements:* Application form, financial need analysis. **Deadline:** varies.

New York Memorial Scholarships for Families of Deceased Police Officers, Fire Fighters, and Peace Officers. Renewable scholarship for children, spouses and financial dependents of deceased fire fighters, volunteer firefighters, police officers, peace officers and emergency medical service workers who died in the line of duty. Provides up to the cost of SUNY educational expenses. *Award:* Scholarship for use in freshman, sophomore, junior, or senior years; renewable. *Eligibility Requirements:* Applicant must be enrolled or expecting to enroll full-time at a four-year institution or university; resident of New York and studying in New York. Available to U.S. citizens. *Application Requirements:* Application form, financial need analysis, transcript. **Deadline:** May 1.

New York State Aid to Native Americans. Award for enrolled members of a New York State tribe and their children who are attending or planning to attend a New York State college and who are New York State residents. Deadlines: July 15 for the fall semester, December 31 for the spring semester, and May 20 for summer session. *Award:* Scholarship for use in freshman, sophomore, junior, or senior years; renewable. *Award amount:* $85–$2000. *Eligibility Requirements:* Applicant must be

American Indian/Alaska Native; enrolled or expecting to enroll full- or part-time at a two-year or four-year or technical institution or university; resident of New York and studying in New York. Available to U.S. citizens. *Application Requirements:* Application form, financial need analysis, recommendations or references, transcript. **Deadline:** varies.

New York State Tuition Assistance Program. Award for New York state residents attending a New York postsecondary institution. Must be full-time student in approved program with tuition over $200 per year. Must show financial need and not be in default in any other state program. Renewable award of $500 to $5000 dependent on family income and tuition charged. *Award:* Grant for use in freshman, sophomore, junior, or senior years; renewable. *Award amount:* $500–$5000. *Number of awards:* 350,000–360,000. *Eligibility Requirements:* Applicant must be enrolled or expecting to enroll full-time at a two-year or four-year institution or university; resident of New York and studying in New York. Available to U.S. citizens. *Application Requirements:* Application form, financial need analysis. **Deadline:** May 1.

New York Vietnam/Persian Gulf/Afghanistan Veterans Tuition Awards. Scholarship for veterans who served in Vietnam, the Persian Gulf, or Afghanistan. Must be a New York resident attending a New York institution. Must establish eligibility by September 1. *Award:* Scholarship for use in freshman, sophomore, junior, or senior years; renewable. *Eligibility Requirements:* Applicant must be enrolled or expecting to enroll full- or part-time at a two-year or four-year or technical institution or university; resident of New York and studying in New York. Available to U.S. citizens. Applicant or parent must meet one or more of the following requirements: general military experience; retired from active duty; disabled or killed as a result of military service; prisoner of war; or missing in action. *Application Requirements:* Application form, financial need analysis. **Deadline:** May 1.

Regents Award for Child of Veteran. Award for students whose parent, as a result of service in U.S. Armed Forces during war or national emergency, died;

suffered a 40 percent or more disability; or is classified as missing in action or a prisoner of war. Veteran must be current New York State resident or have been so at time of death. Student must be a New York resident, attending, or planning to attend, college in New York State. Must establish eligibility before applying for payment. *Award:* Scholarship for use in freshman, sophomore, junior, or senior years; not renewable. *Award amount:* up to $450. *Eligibility Requirements:* Applicant must be enrolled or expecting to enroll full-time at a two-year or four-year institution or university; resident of New York and studying in New York. Available to U.S. citizens. Applicant or parent must meet one or more of the following requirements: general military experience; retired from active duty; disabled or killed as a result of military service; prisoner of war; or missing in action. *Application Requirements:* Application form, proof of eligibility. **Deadline:** May 1.

Contact Rita McGivern, Student Information, New York State Higher Education Services Corporation, 99 Washington Avenue, Room 1320, Albany, NY 12255. *E-mail:* rmcgivern@hesc.com. *Website:* http://www.hesc.ny.gov.

Scholarship for Academic Excellence. Renewable award for New York residents. Scholarship winners must attend a college or university in New York. 2000 scholarships are for $1500 and 6000 are for $500. The selection criteria used are based on Regents test scores or rank in class or local exam. Must be U.S. citizen or permanent resident. *Award:* Scholarship for use in freshman year; renewable. *Award amount:* $500–$1500. *Number of awards:* up to 8000. *Eligibility Requirements:* Applicant must be high school student; planning to enroll or expecting to enroll full-time at a two-year or four-year institution or university; resident of New York and studying in New York. Available to U.S. citizens. *Application Requirements:* Application form. **Deadline:** December 19.

Contact Lewis Hall, Supervisor. *E-mail:* scholar@mail.nysed.gov. *Phone:* 518-486-1319. *Fax:* 518-486-5346. *Website:* http://www.highered.nysed.gov/.

Scholarships for Academic Excellence. Renewable awards of up to $1500 for academically outstanding

New York State high school graduates planning to attend an approved postsecondary institution in New York State. For full-time study only. Contact high school guidance counselor to apply. *Award:* Scholarship for use in freshman, sophomore, junior, or senior years; renewable. *Award amount:* $500–$1500. *Number of awards:* up to 8000. *Eligibility Requirements:* Applicant must be high school student; planning to enroll or expecting to enroll full-time at a four-year institution or university; resident of New York and studying in New York. Available to U.S. citizens. *Application Requirements:* Application form. **Deadline:** varies.

Contact Rita McGivern, Student Information, New York State Higher Education Services Corporation, 99 Washington Avenue, Room 1320, Albany, NY 12255. *E-mail:* scholarship@hesc.com. *Website:* http://www.hesc.ny.gov.

World Trade Center Memorial Scholarship. Renewable awards of up to the cost of educational expenses at a State University of New York four-year college. Available to the children, spouses and financial dependents of victims who died or were severely disabled as a result of the September 11, 2001 terrorist attacks on the U.S. and the rescue and recovery efforts. *Award:* Scholarship for use in freshman, sophomore, junior, or senior years; renewable. *Eligibility Requirements:* Applicant must be enrolled or expecting to enroll full-time at a four-year institution or university and studying in New York. Available to U.S. and non-U.S. citizens. *Application Requirements:* Application form, financial need analysis, recommendations or references, transcript. **Deadline:** May 1.

NORTH CAROLINA

North Carolina Community College Grant Program. Grants are available to North Carolina residents who demonstrate financial need and are enrolled at NC community colleges. The applicant must be a NC resident for tuition purposes; enroll for at least six credit hours per semester in a curriculum program; meet the Satisfactory Academic Progress requirements of the institution. Eligibility is determined based on the same criteria as the Federal Pell Grant; students not eligible for the Federal Pell Grant may be considered for the grant based on the expected family contribution (EFC). Student who have earned a Bachelor's (four-year) degree already are ineligible. Applicants must complete the Free Application for Federal Student Aid (FAFSA). Consideration is automatic once the FAFSA is filed. Please contact the financial aid office at the local community college for more specific information regarding institutional processes. *Award:* Grant for use in freshman or sophomore years; not renewable. *Eligibility Requirements:* Applicant must be enrolled or expecting to enroll full- or part-time at a two-year or technical institution; resident of North Carolina and studying in North Carolina. Available to U.S. citizens. *Application Requirements:* Financial need analysis. **Deadline:** continuous.

Contact Edna Williams, Manager, Award & Loan Origination Services, North Carolina State Education Assistance Authority, PO Box 13663, Research Triangle Park, NC 27709-3663. *E-mail:* ewilliams@ncseaa.edu. *Phone:* 919-549-8614. *Fax:* 919-248-4687. *Website:* http://www.ncseaa.edu/.

North Carolina National Guard Tuition Assistance Program. Scholarship for members of the North Carolina Air and Army National Guard who will remain in the service for two years following the period for which assistance is provided. Must reapply for each academic period. For use at approved North Carolina institutions. *Award:* Grant for use in freshman, sophomore, junior, senior, or graduate years; not renewable. *Award amount:* $100–$3440. *Eligibility Requirements:* Applicant must be enrolled or expecting to enroll full- or part-time at a two-year or four-year or technical institution or university; resident of North Carolina and studying in North Carolina. Available to U.S. citizens. Applicant or parent must meet one or more of the following requirements: national guard experience; retired from active duty; disabled or killed as a result of military service; prisoner of war; or missing in action. *Application Requirements:* Application form. **Deadline:** continuous.

Contact Ms. Stacy Steinmetz, NCTAP Manager, North Carolina National Guard, 1636 Gold Star Drive, Raleigh, NC 27607. *E-mail:* stacy.m.steinmetz.nfg@mail.mil. *Phone:* 919-664-6272. *Website:* http://nc.ng.mil/Pages/default.aspx.

North Carolina Sheriffs' Association Undergraduate Criminal Justice Scholarships. One-time award for full-time North Carolina resident undergraduate students majoring in criminal justice at a University of North Carolina school. Priority given to child of any North Carolina law enforcement officer. Letter of recommendation from county sheriff required. Criminal Justice/Criminology; Law Enforcement/Police Administration. *Award:* Scholarship for use in freshman, sophomore, junior, or senior years; not renewable. *Award amount:* $1000–$2000. *Number of awards:* 10. *Eligibility Requirements:* Applicant must be enrolled or expecting to enroll full-time at a four-year institution or university; resident of North Carolina and studying in North Carolina. Applicant or parent of applicant must have employment or volunteer experience in police/firefighting. Available to U.S. citizens. *Application Requirements:* Application form, financial need analysis.

Contact Michele Goldston, Assistant, Scholarship and Grant Division, North Carolina State Education Assistance Authority, PO Box 13663, Research Triangle Park, NC 27709. *E-mail:* mgoldston@ncseaa.edu. *Phone:* 919-549-8614. *Website:* http://www.ncseaa.edu/.

North Carolina Veterans Scholarships Class I-A. Scholarships for children of certain deceased, disabled or POW/MIA veterans. Award value is $4500 per nine-month academic year in private colleges and junior colleges. No limit on number awarded each year. *Award:* Scholarship for use in freshman, sophomore, junior, or senior years; renewable. *Award amount:* $4500. *Eligibility Requirements:* Applicant must be enrolled or expecting to enroll full-time at a two-year or four-year or technical institution or university; resident of North Carolina and studying in North Carolina. Available to U.S. citizens. Applicant or parent must meet one or more of the following requirements: general military experience; retired from active duty; disabled or killed as a result of military service; prisoner of war; or missing in action. *Application Requirements:* Application form, financial need analysis, interview, transcript. **Deadline:** continuous.

Contact Charles Smith, Assistant Secretary. *E-mail:* charlie.smith@ncmail.net. *Phone:* 919-733-3851. *Fax:* 919-733-2834. *Website:* http://www.milvets.nc.gov/.

North Carolina Veterans Scholarships Class I-B. Awards for children of veterans rated by USDVA as 100 percent disabled due to wartime service as defined in the law, and currently or at time of death drawing compensation for such disability. Parent must have been a North Carolina resident at time of entry into service. Duration of the scholarship is four academic years (8 semesters) if used within 8 years. No limit on number awarded each year. *Award:* Scholarship for use in freshman, sophomore, junior, or senior years; renewable. *Award amount:* $1500. *Eligibility Requirements:* Applicant must be enrolled or expecting to enroll full- or part-time at a two-year or four-year or technical institution or university; resident of North Carolina and studying in North Carolina. Available to U.S. citizens. Applicant or parent must meet one or more of the following requirements: general military experience; retired from active duty; disabled or killed as a result of military service; prisoner of war; or missing in action. *Application Requirements:* Application form, financial need analysis, interview, transcript. **Deadline:** continuous.

Contact Charles Smith, Assistant Secretary. *E-mail:* charlie.smith@ncmail.net. *Phone:* 919-733-3851. *Fax:* 919-733-2834. *Website:* http://www.milvets.nc.gov/.

North Carolina Veterans Scholarships Class II. Awards for children of veterans rated by USDVA as much as 20 percent but less than 100 percent disabled due to wartime service as defined in the law, or awarded Purple Heart Medal for wounds received. Parent must have been a North Carolina resident at time of entry into service. Duration of the scholarship is four academic years (8 semesters) if used within 8 years. Free tuition and exemption from certain mandatory fees as set forth in the law in Public, Community and Technical Colleges. *Award:* Scholarship for use in freshman, sophomore, junior, or senior years; renewable. *Award amount:* $4500. *Number of awards:* up to 100. *Eligibility Requirements:* Applicant must be enrolled or expecting to enroll full- or part-time at a two-year or four-year or technical institution or university; resident of North Carolina and studying in North Carolina. Available to U.S. citizens. Applicant or parent must meet one or more of the following requirements: general military experience; retired from active duty; disabled or killed as a result of military service; prisoner of war; or missing in action. *Application Requirements:* Application form, financial need analysis, interview, transcript. **Deadline:** March 1.

Contact Charles Smith, Assistant Secretary. *E-mail:* charlie.smith@ncmail.net. *Phone:* 919-733-3851. *Fax:* 919-733-2834. *Website:* http://www.milvets.nc.gov/.

North Carolina Veterans Scholarships Class III. Awards for children of a deceased war veteran, who was honorably discharged and who does not qualify under any other provision within this synopsis or veteran who served in a combat zone or waters adjacent to a combat zone and received a campaign badge or medal and who does not qualify under any other provision within this synopsis. Duration of the scholarship is four academic years (8 semesters) if used within 8 years. *Award:* Scholarship for use in freshman, sophomore, junior, or senior years; renewable. *Award amount:* $4500. *Number of awards:* up to 100. *Eligibility Requirements:* Applicant must be enrolled or expecting to enroll full- or part-time at a two-year or four-year or technical institution or university; resident of North Carolina and studying in North Carolina. Available to U.S. citizens. Applicant or parent must meet one or more of the following requirements: general military experience; retired from active duty; disabled or killed as a result of military service; prisoner of war; or missing in action. *Application Requirements:* Application form, financial need analysis, interview, transcript. **Deadline:** March 1.

Contact Charles Smith, Assistant Secretary. *E-mail:* charlie.smith@ncmail.net. *Phone:* 919-733-3851. *Fax:* 919-733-2834. *Website:* http://www.milvets.nc.gov/.

North Carolina Veterans Scholarships Class IV. Awards for children of veterans, who were prisoner of war or missing in action. Duration of the scholarship is four academic years (8 semesters) if used within 8 years. No limit on number awarded each year. Award value is $4500 per nine-month academic year in private colleges and

junior colleges. *Award:* Scholarship for use in freshman, sophomore, junior, or senior years; renewable. *Award amount:* $4500. *Eligibility Requirements:* Applicant must be enrolled or expecting to enroll full- or part-time at a two-year or four-year or technical institution or university; resident of North Carolina and studying in North Carolina. Available to U.S. citizens. Applicant or parent must meet one or more of the following requirements: general military experience; retired from active duty; disabled or killed as a result of military service; prisoner of war; or missing in action. *Application Requirements:* Application form, financial need analysis, interview, transcript. **Deadline:** continuous.

Contact Charles Smith, Assistant Secretary. *E-mail:* charlie.smith@ncmail.net. *Phone:* 919-733-3851. *Fax:* 919-733-2834. *Website:* http://www.milvets.nc.gov/.

Training Support for Youth with Disabilities. Public service program that helps persons with disabilities obtain competitive employment. To qualify: student must have a mental, physical or learning disability that is an impediment to employment. A Rehabilitation Counselor along with the eligible student individually develops a rehabilitation program to achieve an employment outcome which requires post secondary training. Financial assistance is based on NC Division of Vocational Rehabilitation demonstrated financial need and type of program in which the student enrolls. *Award:* Grant for use in freshman, sophomore, junior, senior, or graduate years; renewable. *Eligibility Requirements:* Applicant must be hearing impaired, learning disabled, physically disabled, or visually impaired; enrolled or expecting to enroll full- or part-time at a two-year or four-year or technical institution or university and resident of North Carolina. Applicant must be hearing impaired, learning disabled, physically disabled, or visually impaired. Available to U.S. citizens. *Application Requirements:* Application form, financial need analysis, interview. **Deadline:** continuous.

Contact Stephanie Hanes, Program Specialist for Transition, North Carolina Division of Vocational Rehabilitation Services, 2801 Mail Service Center, Raleigh, NC 27699-2801. *E-mail:* stephanie.hanes@dhhs.nc.gov. *Phone:*

919-855-3576. *Website:* http://www.dhhs.state.nc.us/.

University of North Carolina Need-Based Grant. Applicants must be enrolled in at least 6 credit hours at one of sixteen UNC system universities. Eligibility based on need; award varies, consideration for grant automatic when FAFSA is filed. Late applications may be denied due to insufficient funds. *Award:* Grant for use in freshman, sophomore, junior, or senior years; renewable. *Eligibility Requirements:* Applicant must be enrolled or expecting to enroll full- or part-time at an institution or university; resident of North Carolina and studying in North Carolina. Available to U.S. citizens. *Application Requirements:* Application form, financial need analysis.

Contact Edna Williams, Manager, Award and Loan Origination Services, North Carolina State Education Assistance Authority, PO Box 13663, Research Triangle Park, NC 27709. *E-mail:* ewilliams@ncseaa.edu. *Phone:* 919-549-8614. *Website:* http://www.ncseaa.edu/.

NORTH DAKOTA

North Dakota Academic Scholarship. This scholarship rewards ND resident high school students for taking rigorous coursework, and meeting minimum grade and testing requirements in high school. To qualify for payment, students must be enrolled full time, meet the minimum cumulative GPA requirement of 2.75 and be maintaining degree progress. Awards are $750/sem or $500/qtr up to a total of $6,000 lifetime. Students have up to 6 years following high school to utilize the scholarship. *Award:* Scholarship for use in freshman, sophomore, junior, senior, or graduate years; renewable. *Award amount:* $500–$2250. *Number of awards:* 1–3000. *Eligibility Requirements:* Applicant must be high school student; planning to enroll or expecting to enroll full-time at a two-year or four-year institution or university; resident of North Dakota and studying in North Dakota. Applicant must have 3.0 GPA or higher. Available to U.S. citizens. *Application Requirements:* Application form.

Contact Brenda Zastoupil, Director of Financial Aid, North Dakota University System, 600 E Blvd Ave, Dept. 21, Bismarck, ND 58505-0602. *E-mail:* brenda.zastoupil@ndus.edu. *Phone:*

701-328-2906. *Fax:* 701-328-2979. *Website:* http://www.ndus.edu/.

North Dakota Career and Technical Education Scholarship. This scholarship rewards ND resident high school students for taking rigorous coursework, and meeting minimum grade and testing requirements in high school. To qualify for payment, students must be enrolled full time, meet the minimum cumulative GPA requirements of 2.75 and be maintaining degree progress. Awards are $750/sem. or $500/qtr. up to a total of $6,000 lifetime. Students have up to 6 years following high school to utilize the scholarship. *Award:* Scholarship for use in freshman, sophomore, junior, senior, or graduate years; renewable. *Award amount:* $500–$2250. *Number of awards:* 1–3000. *Eligibility Requirements:* Applicant must be high school student; planning to enroll or expecting to enroll full-time at a two-year or four-year institution or university; resident of North Dakota and studying in North Dakota. Applicant must have 3.0 GPA or higher. Available to U.S. citizens. *Application Requirements:* Application form.

Contact Brenda Zastoupil, Director of Financial Aid, North Dakota University System, 600 E Blvd Ave, Dept. 21, Bismarck, ND 58505-0602. *E-mail:* brenda.zastoupil@ndus.edu. *Phone:* 701-328-2906. *Fax:* 701-328-2979. *Website:* http://www.ndus.edu/.

North Dakota Indian Scholarship Program. The North Dakota Indian Scholarship program was established to provide scholarship awards to Native American Students attending qualifying colleges or universities within North Dakota. Students must be ND residents as defined by the college, enrolled full time, and maintain a GPA of at least 2.0. Awards are available to both undergraduate and graduate students. Students who maintain a 3.50 cumulative GPA qualify for the scholarship based on merit. Students who have a GPA lower than 3.50 must show unmet need. The priority application date is July 15. Not all eligible applicants are awarded due to limited appropriations. *Award:* Scholarship for use in freshman, sophomore, junior, senior, or graduate years; not renewable. *Award amount:* $1–$2000. *Number of awards:* 1–270. *Eligibility Requirements:* Applicant must be American Indian/Alaska Native; enrolled or expecting to enroll full-time

at a two-year or four-year or technical institution or university; resident of North Dakota and studying in North Dakota. Available to U.S. citizens. *Application Requirements:* Application form, financial need analysis. **Deadline:** July 15.

Contact Brenda Zastoupil, Director of Financial Aid, North Dakota University System, 600 E Blvd Ave, Dept. 21, Bismarck, ND 58505-0602. *E-mail:* brenda.zastoupil@ndus.edu. *Phone:* 701-328-2906. *Fax:* 701-328-2979. *Website:* http://www.ndus.edu/.

North Dakota Scholars Program. The purpose of the ND Scholars Scholarship is to retain within ND, the brightest and best students who are pursuing post-secondary education. The scholarship amount equates to the tuition charged at the Scholar's eligible institution, not to exceed the highest regular resident undergraduate tuition rate in the NDUS system. This program provides merit-based, full-tuition scholarships to ND high school graduates who attend a qualifying college within ND. High school juniors who score in the top 95th percentile of all ND ACT test-takers prior to July 1 of the year preceding their freshman year of college will be considered as a candidate for this award. Not all eligible students will qualify due to limited appropriations. This scholarship is renewable for up to three years. Recipients must be enrolled at qualifying institutions in ND at full-time status (12 cr. minimum per semester) and must maintain a cumulative GPA of 3.50. *Award:* Scholarship for use in freshman, sophomore, junior, or senior years; renewable. *Award amount:* $3462–$11,666. *Number of awards:* 1–140. *Eligibility Requirements:* Applicant must be high school student; planning to enroll or expecting to enroll full-time at a two-year or four-year institution or university; resident of North Dakota and studying in North Dakota. Available to U.S. citizens. *Application Requirements:* **Deadline:** June 30.

Contact Brenda Zastoupil, Director of Financial Aid, North Dakota University System, 600 E Blvd Ave, Dept. 21, Bismarck, ND 58505-0602. *E-mail:* brenda.zastoupil@ndus.edu. *Phone:* 701-328-2906. *Fax:* 701-328-2979. *Website:* http://www.ndus.edu/.

North Dakota State Student Incentive Grant Program. The North Dakota State Grant is the premier need-based

state grant in North Dakota. Maximum award of $975 per semester or $650 per quarter. The North Dakota State Grant supports ND residents attending an eligible college or university within North Dakota in a program of study that is at least one year in length. The FAFSA is required annually. Awards are available for up to 8 full-time equivalent semesters or 12 full-time equivalent quarters of undergraduate study. Students must meet the SAP guidelines of their institution and meet all title IV eligibility criteria, including having verification complete, if required. *Award:* Grant for use in freshman, sophomore, junior, or senior years; not renewable. *Award amount:* $1–$2925. *Number of awards:* 1–7000. *Eligibility Requirements:* Applicant must be enrolled or expecting to enroll full- or part-time at a two-year or four-year institution or university; resident of North Dakota and studying in North Dakota. Available to U.S. citizens. *Application Requirements:* **Deadline:** continuous.

Contact Brenda Zastoupil, Director of Financial Aid, North Dakota University System, 600 E Blvd Ave, Dept. 21, Bismarck, ND 58505-0602. *E-mail:* brenda.zastoupil@ndus.edu. *Phone:* 701-328-2906. *Fax:* 701-328-2979. *Website:* http://www.ndus.edu/.

OHIO

Choose Ohio First Scholarship. Choose Ohio First awards competitive scholarship funding to Ohio's colleges and universities to support undergraduate and qualifying graduate students in innovative STEMM academic programs. Designated Choose Ohio First programs are integrated with regional economies, meeting statewide educational needs, facilitating the completion of baccalaureate degrees in cost effective manners, and recruiting underrepresented STEMM student groups including women and students of color. *Award:* Scholarship for use in freshman, sophomore, junior, or senior years; renewable. *Award amount:* $1500–$7368. *Number of awards:* 2643. *Eligibility Requirements:* Applicant must be enrolled or expecting to enroll full- or part-time at a two-year or four-year institution or university; resident of Ohio and studying in Ohio. Available to U.S. and non-U.S. citizens. *Application Requirements:* **Deadline:** continuous.

Contact Ms. Mandie Maxwell, Assistant Director, Ohio Department of Higher Education, Ohio Department of Higher Education, 25 South Front Street, Columbus, OH 43215. *E-mail:* amaxwell@highered.ohio.gov. *Phone:* 614-644-9602. *Website:* http://www.ohiohighered.org.

Ohio College Opportunity Grant. OCOG provides grant money to Ohio residents who demonstrate the highest levels of financial need (as determined by the results of the FAFSA) who are enrolled at Ohio public colleges or universities; Ohio private, non-profit colleges or universities; Ohio private, for-profit institutions; or eligible Pennsylvania institutions. *Award:* Grant for use in freshman, sophomore, junior, or senior years; not renewable. *Award amount:* $1056–$2832. *Eligibility Requirements:* Applicant must be enrolled or expecting to enroll full- or part-time at a two-year or four-year institution or university; resident of Ohio and studying in Ohio, Pennsylvania. *Application Requirements:* **Deadline:** October 1.

Contact Tamika Braswell, Director, Ohio Department of Higher Education, 25 South Front Street, Columbus, OH 43215. *E-mail:* ocog_admin@highered.ohio.gov. *Phone:* 614-728-8862. *Website:* http://www.ohiohighered.org.

Ohio Environmental Science & Engineering Scholarships. Merit-based, non-renewable, tuition-only scholarships awarded to undergraduate students admitted to Ohio state or private colleges and universities. Must be able to demonstrate knowledge of, and commitment to, careers in environmental sciences or environmental engineering. Environmental Science. *Award:* Scholarship for use in senior year; not renewable. *Award amount:* $1250–$2500. *Number of awards:* 18. *Eligibility Requirements:* Applicant must be enrolled or expecting to enroll full- or part-time at a two-year or four-year institution or university and studying in Ohio. Applicant must have 3.0 GPA or higher. Available to U.S. citizens. *Application Requirements:* Application form, application form may be submitted online(https://mc04.manuscriptcentral.com/oas), community service, essay, recommendations or references, resume, self-addressed stamped envelope with application, transcript. **Deadline:** April 15.

Contact Dr. Stephen McConoughey, Chief Executive Officer, Ohio Academy of Science/Ohio Environmental Education Fund, 1500 West Third Avenue, Suite 228, Columbus, OH 43212-2817. *E-mail:* smcconoughey@ohiosci.org. *Phone:* 614-488-2228. *Fax:* 614-488-7629. *Website:* http://www.ohiosci.org/.

Ohio National Guard Scholarship Program. Scholarships are for undergraduate studies at an approved Ohio post-secondary institution. Applicants must enlist for six or three years of Selective Service Reserve Duty in the Ohio National Guard. Scholarship pays 100% instructional and general fees for public institutions and an average of cost of public universities is available for private schools. May reapply up to four years of studies (12 quarters or 8 semesters) for six year enlistment and two years of studies (6 quarters or 4 semesters) for three year enlistment. Deadlines: July 1 (fall), November 1 (winter quarter/spring semester), February 1 (spring quarter), April 1 (summer). *Award:* Scholarship for use in freshman, sophomore, junior, or senior years; not renewable. *Award amount:* up to $4006. *Number of awards:* up to 3500. *Eligibility Requirements:* Applicant must be enrolled or expecting to enroll full- or part-time at a two-year or four-year or technical institution or university; resident of Ohio and studying in Ohio. Available to U.S. citizens. Applicant must have national guard experience. *Application Requirements:* Application form. **Deadline:** varies.

Contact Mrs. Toni Davis, Grants Administrator, Ohio National Guard, 2825 West Dublin Granville Road, ONGSP, Columbus, OH 43235-2789. *E-mail:* toni.davis7@us.army.mil. *Phone:* 614-336-7143. *Fax:* 614-336-7318. *Website:* http://www.ong.ohio.gov/.

Ohio Safety Officers College Memorial Fund. Renewable award covering up to full tuition is available to children and surviving spouses of peace officers, other safety officers and fire fighters killed in the line of duty in any state. Children must be under 26 years of age. Dollar value of each award varies. Must be an Ohio resident and enroll full-time or part-time at an Ohio college or university. Any spouse/child of a member of the armed services of the U.S., who has been killed in the line duty during Operation Enduring Freedom, Operation Iraqi Freedom or a combat zone designated by the President of the United States. Dollar value of each award varies. *Award:* Scholarship for use in freshman, sophomore, junior, or senior years; renewable. *Award amount:* $8115. *Eligibility Requirements:* Applicant must be enrolled or expecting to enroll full- or part-time at a two-year or four-year institution or university; resident of Ohio and studying in Ohio. Available to U.S. citizens. *Application Requirements:* **Deadline:** continuous.

Contact Ramah Church, Program Manager, Ohio Department of Higher Education, 25 South Front Street, Columbus, OH 43215. *E-mail:* osom_admin@highered.ohio.gov. *Phone:* 614-752-9528. *Website:* http://www.ohiohighered.org.

Ohio War Orphans Scholarship. Aids Ohio residents attending an eligible college in Ohio. Must be between the ages of 16 and 25, the child of a disabled or deceased veteran, and enrolled full-time. Must maintain a minimum GPA of 2.0. Renewable up to five years. Amount of award varies. Must include Form DD214. *Award:* Scholarship for use in freshman, sophomore, junior, or senior years; renewable. *Eligibility Requirements:* Applicant must be age 16-25; enrolled or expecting to enroll full-time at a two-year or four-year institution or university; resident of Ohio and studying in Ohio. Available to U.S. citizens. Applicant must have general military experience. *Application Requirements:* Application form. **Deadline:** May 15.

Contact Ramah Church, Program Manager, Ohio Department of Higher Education, 25 South Front Street, Columbus, OH 43215. *E-mail:* rchurch@highered.ohio.gov. *Phone:* 614-752-9528. *Website:* http://www.ohiohighered.org.

OKLAHOMA

Academic Scholars Program. Awards for students of high academic ability to attend institutions in Oklahoma. Renewable up to four years. ACT or SAT scores must fall between 99.5 and 100th percentiles, or applicant must be designated as a National Merit scholar or finalist. Oklahoma public institutions can also select institutional nominees. *Award:* Scholarship for use in freshman, sophomore, junior, senior, or graduate years; renewable. *Award amount:* $1800–$5500. *Eligibility Requirements:* Applicant must be high school student; planning to enroll or expecting to enroll full-time at a two-year or four-year institution or university and studying in Oklahoma. Available to U.S. citizens. *Application Requirements:* Application form.

Future Teacher Scholarship-Oklahoma. Open to outstanding Oklahoma high school graduates who agree to teach in shortage areas. Must rank in top 15 percent of graduating class or score above 85th percentile on ACT or similar test, or be accepted in an educational program. Students nominated by institution. Reapply to renew. Must attend college/university in Oklahoma. Education. *Award:* Scholarship for use in freshman, sophomore, junior, senior, or graduate years; not renewable. *Award amount:* $500–$1500. *Eligibility Requirements:* Applicant must be enrolled or expecting to enroll full- or part-time at a two-year or four-year institution or university; resident of Oklahoma and studying in Oklahoma. Available to U.S. citizens. *Application Requirements:* Application form, essay.

Oklahoma Tuition Aid Grant. Award for Oklahoma residents enrolled at an Oklahoma institution at least part time each semester in a degree program. May be enrolled in two- or four-year or approved vocational-technical institution. Award for students attending public institutions or private colleges. Application is made through FAFSA. *Award:* Grant for use in freshman, sophomore, junior, or senior years; not renewable. *Award amount:* $1000–$1300. *Eligibility Requirements:* Applicant must be enrolled or expecting to enroll full- or part-time at a two-year or four-year or technical institution or university; resident of Oklahoma and studying in Oklahoma. Available to U.S. citizens. *Application Requirements:* Application form, financial need analysis.

Contact Mrs. Linette McMurtrey, Scholarship Programs Coordinator, Oklahoma State Regents for Higher Education, 655 Research Parkway, Suite 200, Oklahoma City, OK 73104. *E-mail:* lmcmurtrey@osrhe.edu. *Phone:* 405-225-9131. *Website:* http://www.okhighered.org/.

Regional University Baccalaureate Scholarship. Renewable award for Oklahoma residents attending one of 11 participating Oklahoma public universities. Must have an ACT composite score of at least 30 or be a National Merit semifinalist or commended student. In addition to the award amount, each recipient will receive a resident tuition waiver from the institution. Must maintain a 3.25 GPA. Deadlines vary depending upon the institution attended. *Award:* Scholarship for use in freshman, sophomore, junior, or senior years; renewable. *Award amount:* $3000. *Eligibility Requirements:* Applicant must be enrolled or expecting to enroll full-time at an institution or university; resident of Oklahoma and studying in Oklahoma. Available to U.S. citizens. *Application Requirements:* Application form.

OREGON

American Legion Auxiliary Department of Oregon Department Grants. One-time award for educational use in the state of Oregon. Must be a resident of Oregon who is the child or widow of a veteran or the wife of a disabled veteran. *Award:* Scholarship for use in freshman year; not renewable. *Award amount:* $1000. *Number of awards:* 2. *Eligibility Requirements:* Applicant must be enrolled or expecting to enroll full- or part-time at a two-year or four-year or technical institution or university and resident of Oregon. Available to U.S. citizens. *Application Requirements:* Application form, essay, financial need analysis, interview. **Deadline:** February 10.

Contact Virginia Biddle, Secretary/Treasurer, American Legion Auxiliary Department of Oregon, PO Box 1730, Wilsonville, OR 97070. *E-mail:* alaor@pcez.com. *Phone:* 503-682-3162. *Website:* http://www.alaoregon.org/.

American Legion Auxiliary Department of Oregon Nurses Scholarship. One-time award for Oregon residents who are in their senior year of high school, who are the children of veterans who served during eligibility dates for American Legion membership. Must enroll in a nursing program. Contact local units for application. Nursing. *Award:* Scholarship for use in freshman year; not renewable. *Award amount:* $1500. *Number of awards:* 1. *Eligibility*

Requirements: Applicant must be high school student; planning to enroll or expecting to enroll full- or part-time at a four-year institution or university and resident of Oregon. Available to U.S. citizens. *Application Requirements:* Application form, essay, financial need analysis, interview. **Deadline:** March 20.

Contact Virginia Biddle, Secretary/Treasurer, American Legion Auxiliary Department of Oregon, PO Box 1730, Wilsonville, OR 97070. *E-mail:* alaor@pcez.com. *Phone:* 503-682-3162. *Website:* http://www.alaoregon.org/.

Better A Life Scholarship. Scholarship award available to single parents age 17-25. High schools seniors must have at least 3.0 GPA and college students must have at least a 2.5 GPA or GED equivalent. For use at Oregon public and non-profit colleges and universities. Applicants may not already possess a Bachelor's degree. May reapply for one additional year of funding. Financial need may or may not be considered. *Award:* Scholarship for use in freshman, sophomore, junior, or senior years; not renewable. *Eligibility Requirements:* Applicant must be age 17-25; enrolled or expecting to enroll full- or part-time at a two-year or four-year institution or university; single and studying in Oregon. Applicant must have 2.5 GPA or higher. Available to U.S. citizens. *Application Requirements:* Application form, financial need analysis. **Deadline:** March 1.

Contact Melissa Adams, Scholarship Processing Coordinator. *E-mail:* melissa.adams@state.or.us. *Phone:* 541-687-7409. *Website:* https://oregonstudentaid.gov/.

Glenn Jackson Scholars Scholarships. Renewable award for Oregon graduating high school seniors who are dependents of employees or retirees of Oregon Department of Transportation or Parks and Recreation Department. Employees must have worked in their department at least three years as of the scholarship deadline. Must enroll in a public or non-profit college. Scholarship is automatically renewable if renewal criteria met. Financial need may or may not be considered. *Award:* Scholarship for use in freshman, sophomore, junior, or senior years; renewable. *Eligibility Requirements:* Applicant must be high school student; planning to enroll or expecting to enroll full- or part-time at a two-year or four-year institution or university and resident of Oregon. Applicant or parent of applicant must be affiliated with Oregon Department of Transportation Parks and Recreation. Available to U.S. citizens. *Application Requirements:* Application form, financial need analysis. **Deadline:** March 1.

Contact Melissa Adams, Scholarship Processing Coordinator. *E-mail:* melissa.adams@state.or.us. *Phone:* 541-687-7409. *Website:* https://oregonstudentaid.gov/.

Laurence R. Foster Memorial Scholarship. One-time award to students enrolled or planning to enroll in a public health degree program. First preference given to those working in the public health field and those pursuing a graduate degree in public health. Second preference given to undergraduates entering junior or senior year health programs may apply if seeking a public health career, and not private practice. Applicants from diverse environments preferred. Based on financial need. Public Health. *Award:* Scholarship for use in junior, senior, or graduate years; not renewable. *Eligibility Requirements:* Applicant must be enrolled or expecting to enroll full- or part-time at a four-year institution or university. Available to U. S. citizens. *Application Requirements:* Application form, essay, financial need analysis. **Deadline:** March 1.

Contact Melissa Adams, Scholarship Processing Coordinator. *E-mail:* melissa.adams@state.or.us. *Phone:* 541-687-7409. *Website:* https://oregonstudentaid.gov/.

Oregon Scholarship Fund Community College Student Award. Scholarship open to students enrolled or planning to enroll at least half time in Oregon community college programs. Recipients may reapply for one additional year. Based on financial need. *Award:* Scholarship for use in freshman or sophomore years; renewable. *Eligibility Requirements:* Applicant must be enrolled or expecting to enroll full- or part-time at a two-year institution and studying in Oregon. Available to U.S. citizens. *Application Requirements:* Application form, financial need analysis. **Deadline:** March 1.

Contact Melissa Adams, Scholarship Processing Coordinator. *E-mail:* melissa.adams@state.or.us. *Phone:* 541-

687-7409. *Website:* https://oregonstudentaid.gov/.

Oregon Scholarship Fund Transfer Student Award. Award open to students who are currently enrolled in their second year at a community college and are planning to transfer to a four-year college in Oregon. Must enroll at least half-time. Based on financial need. *Award:* Scholarship for use in junior or senior years; renewable. *Eligibility Requirements:* Applicant must be enrolled or expecting to enroll full- or part-time at a four-year institution or university and studying in Oregon. Available to U.S. citizens. *Application Requirements:* Application form, financial need analysis. **Deadline:** March 1.

Contact Melissa Adams, Scholarship Processing Coordinator. *E-mail:* melissa.adams@state.or.us. *Phone:* 541-687-7409. *Website:* https://oregonstudentaid.gov/.

Oregon Trucking Association Safety Management Council Scholarship. One-time award available to a child of an Oregon Trucking Association member, or child of an employee of OTA member. Applicants must be graduating high school seniors planning to attend a public or nonprofit college or university. Oregon residency is not required. *Award:* Scholarship for use in freshman year; not renewable. *Eligibility Requirements:* Applicant must be high school student and planning to enroll or expecting to enroll full-time at a four-year institution. Applicant or parent of applicant must be affiliated with Oregon Trucking Association. Available to U.S. citizens. *Application Requirements:* Application form. **Deadline:** March 1.

Contact Melissa Adams, Scholarship Processing Coordinator. *E-mail:* melissa.adams@state.or.us. *Phone:* 541-687-7409. *Website:* https://oregonstudentaid.gov/.

Peter Connacher Memorial Scholarship. Renewable award for American prisoners-of-war and their descendants. Written proof of prisoner-of-war status and discharge papers from the U.S. Armed Forces must accompany application. Statement of relationship between applicant and former prisoner-of-war is required. Oregon residency preferred but not required. Financial need may or may not be considered. *Award:* Scholarship for use in freshman,

sophomore, junior, senior, or graduate years; renewable. *Eligibility Requirements:* Applicant must be enrolled or expecting to enroll full-time at a two-year or four-year institution. Available to U.S. citizens. *Application Requirements:* Application form, financial need analysis. **Deadline:** March 1.

Contact Melissa Adams, Scholarship Processing Coordinator. *E-mail:* melissa.adams@state.or.us. *Phone:* 541-687-7409. *Website:* https://oregonstudentaid.gov/.

PENNSYLVANIA

Blind or Deaf Beneficiary Grant Program. This state-funded program provides financial aid to blind or deaf students attending a postsecondary institution. This program awards funds on a first-come, first-served basis. *Award:* Grant for use in freshman, sophomore, junior, or senior years; not renewable. *Award amount:* $500. *Eligibility Requirements:* Applicant must be hearing impaired or visually impaired; enrolled or expecting to enroll full- or part-time at a two-year or four-year or technical institution or university and resident of Pennsylvania. Applicant must be hearing impaired or visually impaired. *Application Requirements:* Application form. **Deadline:** March 31.

Contact Keith New, Director of Public Relations. *E-mail:* knew@pheaa.org. *Phone:* 717-720-2509. *Website:* http://www.pheaa.org/.

Pennsylvania State Grant Program. Award for Pennsylvania residents attending an approved postsecondary institution as undergraduates in a program of at least two years duration. Renewable for up to eight semesters if applicants show continued need and academic progress. Must submit FAFSA. Number of awards granted varies annually. Scholarship value is $200 to $4340. Deadlines: May 1 and August 1. *Award:* Grant for use in freshman, sophomore, junior, or senior years; renewable. *Award amount:* $200–$4340. *Eligibility Requirements:* Applicant must be enrolled or expecting to enroll full- or part-time at a two-year or four-year or technical institution or university and resident of Pennsylvania. Available to U.S. citizens. *Application Requirements:* Application form, financial need analysis.

Contact Keith New, Director of Public Relations, Pennsylvania Higher

Education Assistance Agency, 1200 North Seventh Street, Harrisburg, PA 17102-1444. *Phone:* 717-720-2509. *Website:* http://www.pheaa.org/.

Postsecondary Education Gratuity Program. The program offers waiver of tuition and fees for children of Pennsylvania police officers, firefighters, rescue or ambulance squad members, corrections facility employees, or National Guard members who died in line of duty after January 1, 1976. *Award:* Grant for use in freshman, sophomore, junior, or senior years; renewable. *Eligibility Requirements:* Applicant must be enrolled or expecting to enroll full-time at a two-year or four-year institution or university; resident of Pennsylvania and studying in Pennsylvania. Available to U.S. citizens. Applicant or parent must meet one or more of the following requirements: national guard experience; retired from active duty; disabled or killed as a result of military service; prisoner of war; or missing in action. *Application Requirements:* Application form. **Deadline:** July 1.

Contact Keith New, Director of Public Relations. *E-mail:* knew@pheaa.org. *Phone:* 717-720-2509. *Website:* http://www.pheaa.org/.

Ready to Succeed Scholarship Program. RTSS provides scholarships to high academic achievers that, in combination with the Pennsylvania State Grant Program, offer a total award up to $2,000 for full-time and $1,000 for part-time students. The minimum award is $500. Awards can be used to cover tuition, books, fees, supplies, and living expenses. Students must be nominated by their post-secondary institution for participation in the program. Funding is limited for the program and awards are made on a first-come, first-served basis. The program, which is funded by the Pennsylvania General Assembly, provides awards to high-achieving students whose annual family income does not exceed $110,000. *Award:* Scholarship for use in sophomore, junior, or senior years; not renewable. *Award amount:* $500–$2000. *Eligibility Requirements:* Applicant must be enrolled or expecting to enroll full- or part-time at a two-year or four-year or technical institution or university; resident of Pennsylvania and studying in Pennsylvania. Applicant must have 3.5 GPA or higher. *Application Requirements:* Application form, financial need analysis.

Contact Keith New, Director of Public Relations. *E-mail:* knew@pheaa.org. *Phone:* 717-720-2509. *Website:* http://www.pheaa.org/.

SOUTH CAROLINA

Palmetto Fellows Scholarship Program. Renewable award for qualified high school seniors in South Carolina to attend a four-year South Carolina institution. The scholarship must be applied directly towards the cost of attendance, less any other gift aid received. *Award:* Scholarship for use in freshman year; renewable. *Award amount:* $6700–$7500. *Number of awards:* 4846. *Eligibility Requirements:* Applicant must be high school student; planning to enroll or expecting to enroll full-time at a four-year institution or university; resident of South Carolina and studying in South Carolina. Applicant must have 3.5 GPA or higher. Available to U.S. citizens. *Application Requirements:* Application form, test scores, transcript. **Deadline:** December 15.

Contact Dr. Karen Woodfaulk, Director of Student Services, South Carolina Commission on Higher Education, 1333 Main Street, Suite 200, Columbia, SC 29201. *E-mail:* kwoodfaulk@che.sc.gov. *Phone:* 803-737-2244. *Fax:* 803-737-3610. *Website:* http://www.che.sc.gov/.

South Carolina HOPE Scholarship. A merit-based scholarship for eligible first-time entering freshman attending a four-year South Carolina institution. Minimum GPA of 3.0 required. Must be a resident of South Carolina. *Award:* Scholarship for use in freshman year; not renewable. *Award amount:* $2800. *Number of awards:* 2605. *Eligibility Requirements:* Applicant must be high school student; planning to enroll or expecting to enroll full-time at a four-year institution or university; resident of South Carolina and studying in South Carolina. Applicant must have 3.0 GPA or higher. Available to U.S. citizens. *Application Requirements:* Transcript. **Deadline:** continuous.

Contact Gerrick Hampton, Scholarship Coordinator, South Carolina Commission on Higher Education, 1333 Main Street, Suite 200, Columbia, SC 29201. *E-mail:* ghampton@che.sc.gov. *Phone:* 803-737-4544. *Fax:* 803-737-3610. *Website:* http://www.che.sc.gov/.

South Carolina Need-Based Grants Program. Award based on FAFSA. A student may receive up to $2500 annually for full-time and up to $1250 annually for part-time study. The grant must be applied directly towards the cost of college attendance for a maximum of eight full-time equivalent terms. *Award:* Grant for use in freshman, sophomore, junior, senior, or graduate years; renewable. *Award amount:* $1250–$2500. *Number of awards:* 1–26,730. *Eligibility Requirements:* Applicant must be enrolled or expecting to enroll full- or part-time at a two-year or four-year or technical institution or university; resident of South Carolina and studying in South Carolina. Available to U.S. citizens. *Application Requirements:* Application form, financial need analysis. **Deadline:** continuous.

Contact Dr. Karen Woodfaulk, Director of Student Service, South Carolina Commission on Higher Education, 1333 Main Street, Suite 200, Columbia, SC 29201. *E-mail:* kwoodfaulk@che.sc.gov. *Phone:* 803-737-2244. *Fax:* 803-737-2297. *Website:* http://www.che.sc.gov/.

South Carolina Tuition Grants Program. Need-based grant set aside for students attending eligible independent colleges in South Carolina. Student must be a South Carolina resident. Must apply annually by submitting the Free Application for Federal Student Aid (FAFSA). Freshmen must graduate in top 75% of high school class OR score 900 on SAT/19 on ACT OR graduate with at least 2.0 on SC Uniform Grading Scale. Upperclassmen must pass a minimum of 24 credit hours annually. *Award:* Grant for use in freshman, sophomore, junior, or senior years; renewable. *Award amount:* $100–$3200. *Eligibility Requirements:* Applicant must be enrolled or expecting to enroll full-time at a two-year or four-year institution or university; resident of South Carolina and studying in South Carolina. Available to U.S. citizens. *Application Requirements:* Financial need analysis. **Deadline:** June 30.

Contact Zachary Christian, Financial Aid Counselor, South Carolina Tuition Grants Commission, 115 Atrium Way, Suite 102, Columbia, SC 29223. *E-mail:* zachary@sctuitiongrants.org. *Phone:* 803-896-1120. *Website:* http://www.sctuitiongrants.org/.

Tuition Assistance for Certain War Veterans' Children. Free tuition for South Carolina residents whose parent is a resident, wartime veteran, and meets one of these criteria; awarded Purple Heart or Congressional Medal of Honor; permanently and totally disabled by VA or killed as a result of military service; prisoner of war; or missing in action. Must be age 18?26 and enrolled or expecting to enroll full or part-time at a state supported two-year or four-year technical institution or university in South Carolina. Complete information and qualifications for this award are on web site http://www.govoepp.state.sc. us. *Award:* Scholarship for use in freshman, sophomore, junior, or senior years; not renewable. *Eligibility Requirements:* Applicant must be age 18-26; enrolled or expecting to enroll full- or part-time at a two-year or four-year or technical institution or university; resident of South Carolina and studying in South Carolina. Available to U.S. citizens. Applicant or parent must meet one or more of the following requirements: general military experience; retired from active duty; disabled or killed as a result of military service; prisoner of war; or missing in action. *Application Requirements:* Application form. **Deadline:** continuous.

Contact Adm. Dorian Sease-Phillips, Free Tuition Coordinator, South Carolina Division of Veterans Affairs, 6437 Garners Ferry Rd, Columbia, SC 29209. *E-mail:* dorian.sease-phillips@va.gov. *Phone:* 803-647-2434. *Fax:* 803-647 Ext. 2312. *Website:* http://www. govoepp.state.sc.us/vetaff.htm.

SOUTH DAKOTA

South Dakota Opportunity Scholarship. Renewable scholarship may be worth up to $6200 over four years to students who take a rigorous college-prep curriculum while in high school and stay in the state for their postsecondary education. *Award:* Scholarship for use in freshman, sophomore, junior, or senior years; renewable. *Award amount:* $1300–$2300. *Number of awards:* 1000–4100. *Eligibility Requirements:* Applicant must be high school student; planning to enroll or expecting to enroll full-time at a two-year or four-year or technical institution or university; resident of South Dakota and studying in South Dakota. Applicant must have 3.0 GPA or higher. Available

to U.S. citizens. *Application Requirements:* Application form. **Deadline:** September 1.

Contact Kerri Richards, Student Services Coordinator, South Dakota Board of Regents, 306 East Capitol, Suite 200, Pierre, SD 57501. *E-mail:* info@sdbor. edu. *Phone:* 605-773-3455. *Website:* http://www.sdbor.edu/.

TENNESSEE

Dependent Children Scholarship Program. Scholarship for Tennessee residents who are dependent children of a Tennessee law enforcement officer, fireman, or an emergency medical service technician who have been killed or totally and permanently disabled while performing duties within the scope of such employment. The scholarship is awarded to full-time undergraduate students for a maximum of four academic years or the period required for the completion of the program of study. *Award:* Scholarship for use in freshman, sophomore, junior, or senior years; renewable. *Eligibility Requirements:* Applicant must be enrolled or expecting to enroll full-time at a two-year or four-year institution or university; resident of Tennessee and studying in Tennessee. Available to U.S. citizens. *Application Requirements:* Application form. **Deadline:** July 15.

Contact Ms. Kathy Stripling, Grant and Scholarship Analyst, Tennessee Student Assistance Corporation, Parkway Towers, 404 James Robertson Parkway, Suite 1510, Nashville, TN 37243-0820. *E-mail:* kathy.stripling@ tn.gov. *Phone:* 615-253-7480. *Website:* http://www.tn.gov/collegepays.

Helping Heroes Grant. Provides assistance to Tennessee veterans who have been awarded the Iraq Campaign Medal, Afghanistan Campaign Medal, or Global War on Terrorism Expeditionary Medal (on or after 9/11/01) and who meet eligibility requirements for the program. Award is $1,000 per semester for 12 or more semester hours or $500 for 6-11 semester hours. For more information, visit http://www.TN.gov/collegepays. *Award:* Grant for use in freshman, sophomore, junior, or senior years; renewable. *Award amount:* $1000–$2000. *Eligibility Requirements:* Applicant must be enrolled or expecting to enroll full- or part-time at a two-year or four-year institution or university; resident of Tennessee and

studying in Tennessee. Available to U.S. citizens. Applicant must have general military experience. *Application Requirements:* Application form. **Deadline:** September 1.

Contact Mr. Robert Biggers, Assistant Executive Director of Grant & Scholarship Programs, Tennessee Student Assistance Corporation, Parkway Towers, 404 James Robertson Parkway, Suite 1510, Nashville, TN 37243. *E-mail:* robert.biggers@tn.gov. *Phone:* 615-253-7453. *Website:* http:// www.tn.gov/collegepays.

HOPE Aspire Award. $750 supplement per semester for four-year institutions, $250 per semester for two-year instititutions. Must meet Tennessee HOPE Scholarship requirements and Adjusted Gross Income (AGI) attributable to the parents or to the independent student must be $36,000 or less. *Award:* Scholarship for use in freshman, sophomore, junior, or senior years; renewable. *Award amount:* $500–$1500. *Eligibility Requirements:* Applicant must be enrolled or expecting to enroll full- or part-time at a two-year or four-year institution or university; resident of Tennessee and studying in Tennessee. Applicant must have 3.0 GPA or higher. Available to U.S. citizens.

Contact Mr. Robert Biggers, Assistant Executive Director of Grant & Scholarships Programs, Tennessee Student Assistance Corporation, Parkway Towers, 404 James Robertson Parkway, Suite 1510, Nashville, TN 37243-0820. *E-mail:* robert.biggers@tn. gov. *Phone:* 615-253-7453. *Website:* http://www.tn.gov/collegepays.

Ned McWherter Scholars Program. Award for Tennessee high school seniors with high academic ability. Must have minimum high school GPA of 3.5 and a score of 29 on the ACT or SAT equivalent. Must attend a college or university in Tennessee. Must be a Tennessee resident and U.S. citizen or permanent resident. For more information, visit web site http://tn.gov/collegepays. *Award:* Scholarship for use in freshman, sophomore, junior, or senior years; renewable. *Award amount:* $6000. *Eligibility Requirements:* Applicant must be enrolled or expecting to enroll full-time at a two-year or four-year or technical institution or university; resident of Tennessee and studying in Tennessee. Applicant must have 3.5 GPA or higher. Available to U.

S. citizens. *Application Requirements:* Application form. **Deadline:** February 15.

Contact Ms. Kathy Stripling, Grants and Scholarship Analyst, Tennessee Student Assistance Corporation, 404 James Robertson Parkway, Suite 1510, Parkway Towers, Nashville, TN 37243-0820. *E-mail:* kathy.stripling@tn.gov. *Phone:* 615-253-7480. *Website:* http://www.tn.gov/collegepays.

Reduction in Force Tuition Assistance Benefit. Tuition assistance of up to $11,600 ($5,800 per year) at the schools, institutions, and entities governed by the Tennessee Board of Regents and the University of Tennessee Board of Trustees, as well as state certified apprenticeship programs. Tuition assistance benefits are available for a two-year period beginning when an employee is separated due to a reduction in force. GED classes are also available through the Tennessee Department of Labor and Workforce Development's Career Centers, and testing fees will be covered under the tuition assistance benefit. This program is NOT offered to the general public, but only as one of the benefits provided to State employees who are impacted by the Reduction in Force. *Award:* Scholarship for use in freshman, sophomore, junior, or senior years; not renewable. *Eligibility Requirements:* Applicant must be enrolled or expecting to enroll full- or part-time at a two-year or four-year or technical institution or university; resident of Tennessee and studying in Tennessee. Available to U.S. citizens. *Application Requirements:* Application form.

Contact Mr. Tim Phelps, Associate Executive Director, Grants and Scholarships, Tennessee Student Assistance Corporation, 404 James Robertson Parkway, Nashville, TN 37243. *E-mail:* tim.phelps@tn.gov. *Phone:* 615-253-7441. *Fax:* 615-741-6101. *Website:* http://www.tn.gov/collegepays.

TELS -HOPE with General Assembly Merit Scholarship (GAMS). Students who qualify for the HOPE Scholarship can receive GAMS by earning a minimum 3.75 GPA and a 29 or above on the ACT (or SAT equivalent). The supplemental award is $500 per semester. Must be a Tennessee resident. For more information, visit www.tn.gov/collegepays. *Award:* Scholarship for use in freshman, sophomore, junior, or

senior years; renewable. *Eligibility Requirements:* Applicant must be enrolled or expecting to enroll full- or part-time at a two-year or four-year institution or university; resident of Tennessee and studying in Tennessee. Applicant must have 3.5 GPA or higher. Available to U.S. citizens.

Contact Mr. Robert Biggers, Assistant Executive Director of Grant & Scholarship Programs, Tennessee Student Assistance Corporation, Parkway Towers, 404 James Robertson Parkway, Suite 1510, Nashville, TN 37243-0820. *E-mail:* robert.biggers@tn.gov. *Phone:* 615-253-7453. *Website:* http://www.tn.gov/collegepays.

Tennessee Dual Enrollment Grant. Grant for study at an eligible Tennessee postsecondary institution awarded to juniors and seniors in a Tennessee high school who have been admitted to undergraduate study while still pursuing a high school diploma. For more information, visit web site http://www.tn.gov/collegepays. *Award:* Grant for use in freshman year; renewable. *Eligibility Requirements:* Applicant must be high school student; planning to enroll or expecting to enroll part-time at a two-year or four-year or technical institution or university; resident of Tennessee and studying in Tennessee. Available to U.S. citizens. *Application Requirements:* Application form. **Deadline:** continuous.

Contact Mr. Robert Biggers, Assistant Executive Director of Grant & Scholarship Programs, Tennessee Student Assistance Corporation, Parkway Towers, 404 James Robertson Parkway, Suite 1510, Nashville, TN 37243-0820. *E-mail:* robert.biggers@tn.gov. *Phone:* 615-253-7453. *Website:* http://www.tn.gov/collegepays.

Tennessee HOPE Access Grant. Non-renewable award of $2,750 for students at four-year colleges or $1,750 for students at two-year colleges. Entering freshmen must have a minimum GPA of 2.75, ACT score of 18-20 (or SAT equivalent), and adjusted gross income attributable to the student must be $36,000 or less. Recipients will become eligible for Tennessee HOPE Scholarship by meeting HOPE Scholarship renewal criteria. TN residents may graduate from high schools located in states other than Tennessee in certain exceptions. *Award:* Grant for use in freshman, sophomore, junior, or senior

years; not renewable. *Award amount:* $1750–$2750. *Eligibility Requirements:* Applicant must be enrolled or expecting to enroll full- or part-time at a two-year or four-year institution or university; resident of Tennessee and studying in Tennessee. Applicant must have 3.0 GPA or higher. Available to U.S. citizens. *Application Requirements:* Application form, financial need analysis. **Deadline:** September 1.

Contact Mr. Robert Biggers, Assistant Executive Director of Grant & Scholarship Programs, Tennessee Student Assistance Corporation, Parkway Towers, 404 James Robertson Parkway, Suite 1510, Nashville, TN 37243-0820. *E-mail:* robert.biggers@tn.gov. *Phone:* 615-253-7453. *Website:* http://www.tn.gov/collegepays.

Tennessee HOPE Foster Child Tuition Grant. Renewable tuition award available for recipients of the HOPE Scholarship or HOPE Access Grant. Student must have been in Tennessee state custody as a foster child for at least one year after reaching age 14. Award amount varies and shall not exceed the tuition and mandatory fees at an eligible Tennessee public postsecondary institution. For additional information, visit web site http://www.tn.gov/collegepays. *Award:* Scholarship for use in freshman, sophomore, junior, or senior years; renewable. *Eligibility Requirements:* Applicant must be enrolled or expecting to enroll full- or part-time at a two-year or four-year institution or university; resident of Tennessee and studying in Tennessee. Applicant must have 3.0 GPA or higher. Available to U.S. citizens. *Application Requirements:* Application form.

Contact Mr. Robert Biggers, Assistant Executive Director of Grant & Scholarship Programs, Tennessee Student Assistance Corporation, Parkway Towers, 404 James Robertson Parkway, Suite 1510, Nashville, TN 37243-0820. *E-mail:* robert.biggers@tn.gov. *Phone:* 615-253-7453. *Website:* http://www.tn.gov/collegepays.

Tennessee HOPE Scholarship. Students must achieve a minimum 3.0 GPA or 21 or above on the ACT to qualify for the scholarship. Award amount is $1,750 for per semester at four-year institutions and $1,500 per semester at two-year institutions for entering freshmen who first received HOPE in fall 2015 and thereafter. Award amount is $2,000 per semester at four-year institutions and $1,000 per semester at two-year institutions for students who first received HOPE between fall 2009 and summer 2015. Must be a Tennessee resident attending an eligible postsecondary institution in Tennessee. For more information, visit http://www.TN.gov/CollegePays. *Award:* Scholarship for use in freshman, sophomore, junior, or senior years; renewable. *Award amount:* $2000–$4500. *Eligibility Requirements:* Applicant must be enrolled or expecting to enroll full-time at a two-year or four-year institution or university; resident of Tennessee and studying in Tennessee. Applicant must have 3.0 GPA or higher. Available to U. S. citizens. *Application Requirements:* **Deadline:** September 1.

Contact Mr. Robert Biggers, Assistant Executive Director of Grant & Scholarship Programs, Tennessee Student Assistance Corporation, Parkway Towers, 404 James Robertson Parkway, Suite 1510, Nashville, TN 37243-0820. *E-mail:* robert.biggers@tn. gov. *Phone:* 615-253-7453. *Website:* http://www.tn.gov/collegepays.

Tennessee HOPE Scholarship for Nontraditional Students. Nontraditional students must be age 25 or older and be an entering freshman in an eligible post-secondary institution or have not been enrolled for at least two (2) years after last attending any post-secondary institution and is now enrolled at an eligible post-secondary institution. Student's and spouse's adjusted gross income must be $36,000 or less on IRS tax form. Students at four-year institutions and two-year institutions with on-campus housing: up to $1750 per full-time semester as a freshmen and sophomore; then up to $2,250 per full-time enrollment semester as a junior and senior. Students at two-year Institutions: up to $1,500 per full-time enrollment semester as a freshman and sophomore. *Award:* Scholarship for use in freshman, sophomore, junior, or senior years; renewable. *Eligibility Requirements:* Applicant must be enrolled or expecting to enroll full-time at a two-year or four-year institution or university; resident of Tennessee and studying in Tennessee. Applicant must have 2.5 GPA or higher. Available to U.S. citizens. *Application Requirements:* Application form. **Deadline:** continuous.

Contact Mr. Tim Phelps, Associate Executive Director, Grants and Scholar-ships, Tennessee Student Assistance Corporation, 404 James Robertson Parkway, Nashville, TN 37243. *E-mail:* tim.phelps@tn.gov. *Phone:* 615-253-7441. *Fax:* 615-741-6101. *Website:* http://www.tn.gov/collegepays.

Tennessee Reconnect Grant. Applicants must be enrolled in a federal Title IV eligible curriculum of courses leading to a certificate or associate degree. Must not have previously earned an Associate degree or Baccalaureate degree and enroll in and attend at least six (6) hours at an eligible institution. Must maintain a minimum 2.0 cumulative GPA at the end of the academic year as determined by the institution and participate in a college success program, as determined by the Tennessee Higher Education Commission. *Award:* Scholarship for use in freshman, sophomore, junior, or senior years; renewable. *Eligibility Requirements:* Applicant must be enrolled or expecting to enroll at an institution or university; resident of Tennessee and studying in Tennessee. Available to U.S. citizens. *Application Requirements:* Application form. **Deadline:** continuous.

Contact Mr. Tim Phelps, Associate Executive Director, Grants and Scholarships, Tennessee Student Assistance Corporation, 404 James Robertson Parkway, Nashville, TN 37243. *E-mail:* tim.phelps@tn.gov. *Phone:* 615-253-7441. *Fax:* 615-741-6101. *Website:* http://www.tn.gov/collegepays.

Tennessee Student Assistance Award. Award to assist financially-needy Tennessee residents attending an approved college or university within the state. Applicants must have a valid Expected Family Contribution (EFC) of $2100 or less. Students are encourage to complete the FAFSA as soon as possible after October 1 for priority consideration. To apply, go to http://www.fafsa.gov. For more information, go to www.tn.gov/collegepays *Award:* Grant for use in freshman, sophomore, junior, or senior years; renewable. *Award amount:* $1000–$4000. *Eligibility Requirements:* Applicant must be enrolled or expecting to enroll full- or part-time at a two-year or four-year or technical institution or university; resident of Tennessee and studying in Tennessee. Available to U.S. citizens. *Application Requirements:* Financial need analysis.

Contact Mrs. Leah Louallen, Director of Grants and Scholarship Programs, Tennessee Student Assistance Corporation, Parkway Towers, 404 James Robertson Parkway, Suite 1510, Nashville, TN 37243-0820. *E-mail:* leah.louallen@tn.gov. *Phone:* 615-253-7478. *Website:* http://www.tn.gov/collegepays.

TEXAS

Conditional Grant Program. Renewable award to students who are considered economically disadvantaged based on federal guidelines. The maximum amount awarded per semester is $3,000 not to exceed $6000 per academic year. Students already enrolled in an undergraduate program should have minimum GPA 2.5 and students newly enrolling should have minimum GPA 3. 0. Civil Engineering; Computer Science/Data Processing; Occupational Safety and Health. *Award:* Grant for use in freshman, sophomore, junior, or senior years; renewable. *Award amount:* $3000–$6000. *Number of awards:* 10–20. *Eligibility Requirements:* Applicant must be enrolled or expecting to enroll full-time at a four-year institution or university; resident of Texas and studying in Texas. Available to U.S. citizens. *Application Requirements:* Application form, essay, financial need analysis, interview. **Deadline:** March 1.

Contact Sheila Brooks, Program Coordinator, Texas Department of Transportation, 125 East 11th Street, Austin, TX 78701-2483. *E-mail:* hrd_recruitment@txdot.gov. *Phone:* 512-416-4979. *Website:* http://www.txdot.gov/.

Texas Educational Opportunity Grant (TEOG). Provides grant aid to students with financial need attending public two-year colleges. For initial award, student must be enrolled at least half-time and awarded in the first 30 hours (or its equivalent) of an associate's degree or certificate program (excluding credits for dual enrollment or by examination). For renewal award, student must also maintain a minimum overall GPA of 2.50 and successfully complete a minimum of 75% of classes attempted during the school year. *Award:* Grant for use in freshman, sophomore, junior, or senior years; renewable. *Award amount:* $1–$8000. *Eligibility Requirements:* Applicant must be enrolled or expecting to enroll full- or part-time at a two-year institution; resident of Texas and studying in Texas. Available to U.S. citizens. *Application Requirements:* Financial need analysis.

Top 10% Scholarship Program. Funding for Initial Awards is not available for the 2018-19 academic year and only renewal award students are eligible for this program. Renewal students must demonstrate financial need and complete the FAFSA by the state priority deadline of March 15. Renewal students must maintain a minimum overall GPA of 3.25, successfully complete at least 30 SCH each year, and successfully complete at least 75% of the hours attempted each year. *Award:* Scholarship for use in junior or senior years; renewable. *Award amount:* up to $2000. *Eligibility Requirements:* Applicant must be enrolled or expecting to enroll full-time at a two-year or four-year institution or university; resident of Texas and studying in Texas. Applicant must have 3.0 GPA or higher. Available to U.S. citizens. *Application Requirements:* Financial need analysis.

Toward EXcellence, Access, and Success (TEXAS) Grant. Renewable aid for students enrolled at least three-quarter time in a public four-year college or university in Texas within sixteen months of graduation from high school. Must demonstrate financial need and have completed the Foundation, Recommended, or DAP Curriculum in high school. For renewal awards, must also maintain a minimum GPA of 2.5 and complete a minimum of 24 SCH's each year. Amount of award is determined by the financial aid office of each school. Priority FAFSA completion deadline is March 15. Contact the college/university financial aid office for additional eligibility information. *Award:* Grant for use in freshman, sophomore, junior, or senior years; renewable. *Award amount:* $1–$8000. *Eligibility Requirements:* Applicant must be enrolled or expecting to enroll full- or part-time at a four-year institution or university; resident of Texas and studying in Texas. Available to U.S. citizens. *Application Requirements:* Financial need analysis. **Deadline:** March 15.

Tuition Equalization Grant (TEG) Program. Renewable award for Texas residents enrolled at least three-quarter time at an independent college or private university in Texas in a degree program that does not lead to ordination or licensure to preach. Awards are based on financial need. Renewal awards also require the student to maintain a minimum overall college GPA of at least 2.5, complete at least 24 SCH's each year (18 SCH's for students in graduate programs), and complete a minimum of 75% of classes attempted each year. Priority deadline to complete the FAFSA is March 15. Must not be receiving athletic scholarship concurrently. Contact college/university financial aid office for application information. *Award:* Grant for use in freshman, sophomore, junior, senior, or graduate years; renewable. *Award amount:* $1–$5046. *Eligibility Requirements:* Applicant must be enrolled or expecting to enroll full- or part-time at a four-year institution or university and studying in Texas. Available to U.S. citizens. *Application Requirements:* Financial need analysis.

The Urban Scholarships Fund. Eligibility - United States citizen or eligible non-citizen (permanent resident card I-551 front and back copy) Texas resident, graduate of high school from 29 urban cities: Abilene, Amarillo, Arlington, Austin, Beaumont, Brownsville, Carrollton, Corpus Christi, Dallas, Denton, El Paso, Fort Worth, Frisco, Garland, Grand Prairie, Houston, Irving, Killeen, Laredo, Lubbock, McAllen, McKinney, Mesquite, Midland, Pasadena, Plano, San Antonio, Waco and Wichita Falls *Award:* Scholarship for use in freshman, sophomore, junior, or senior years; not renewable. *Award amount:* $700–$1000. *Number of awards:* 450–500. *Eligibility Requirements:* Applicant must be age 16-65; enrolled or expecting to enroll full-time at a two-year or four-year or technical institution or university and resident of Texas. Available to U.S. citizens. *Application Requirements:* Financial need analysis. **Deadline:** July 10.

Contact Ms. Janice Jackson, Office Programs Administrator, Texas Association of Developing Colleges, 1140 Empire Central Drive 550, Dallas, TX 75247. *E-mail:* janice.jackson@txadc.org. *Phone:* 214-630-2511. *Website:* http://www.txadc.org.

UTAH

Higher Education Success Stipend Program. Award available to students with substantial financial need for use at any of the participating Utah institutions. The student must be a Utah resident. Contact the financial aid office of the participating institution for requirements and deadlines. *Award:* Grant for use in freshman, sophomore, junior, or senior years; not renewable. *Award amount:* $300–$4000. *Number of awards:* 1000–5000. *Eligibility Requirements:* Applicant must be enrolled or expecting to enroll full- or part-time at a two-year or four-year or technical institution or university; resident of Utah and studying in Utah. Available to U.S. citizens. *Application Requirements:* Financial need analysis. **Deadline:** continuous.

VERMONT

Vermont Incentive Grants. Grants for Vermont residents based on financial need. Must meet needs test. Must be college undergraduate enrolled full-time at an approved post secondary institution. Only available to Vermont residents. *Award:* Grant for use in freshman, sophomore, junior, or senior years; not renewable. *Award amount:* $850–$12,050. *Eligibility Requirements:* Applicant must be enrolled or expecting to enroll full-time at a two-year or four-year or technical institution or university and resident of Vermont. Available to U. S. citizens. *Application Requirements:* Application form, financial need analysis. **Deadline:** continuous.

Vermont Part-Time Student Grants. For undergraduates carrying less than twelve credits per semester who have not received a bachelor's degree. Must be Vermont resident. Based on financial need. Complete Vermont Financial Aid Packet to apply. May be used at any approved post-secondary institution. *Award:* Grant for use in freshman, sophomore, junior, or senior years; not renewable. *Award amount:* $425–$9040. *Eligibility Requirements:* Applicant must be enrolled or expecting to enroll part-time at a two-year or four-year or technical institution or university and resident of Vermont. Available to U.S. citizens. *Application Requirements:* Application form, financial need analysis. **Deadline:** continuous.

VIRGINIA

Mary Marshall Practical Nursing Scholarship (LPN). Awards for students who are accepted or enrolled as a full-time or part-time student in a practical school of nursing in the state of Virginia. Must be a Virginia resident for at least one year and have submitted a completed application form and a recommendation from the Director regarding scholastic attainment and financial need prior to June 30. Students pursuing a nursing degree not available in Virginia, are not eligible for the scholarship. Scholarship amount varies. Nursing. *Award:* Scholarship for use in freshman, sophomore, junior, or senior years; not renewable. *Award amount:* $600–$1200. *Number of awards:* 26–88. *Eligibility Requirements:* Applicant must be enrolled or expecting to enroll full- or part-time at a two-year or four-year or technical institution or university; resident of Virginia and studying in Virginia. Applicant must have 2.5 GPA or higher. Available to U.S. citizens. *Application Requirements:* Application form, driver's license, essay, financial need analysis, recommendations or references, transcript. **Deadline:** June 30.

Contact Miss. Sarahbeth Jones, Communications Specialist, Virginia Department of Health, Office of Minority Health and Health Equity, PO Box 2448, 109 Governor Street, Suite 1016-E, Richmond, VA 23218-2448. *E-mail:* IncentivePrograms@vdh.virginia.gov. *Phone:* 804-864-7422. *Fax:* 804-864-7440. *Website:* http://www.vdh.virginia.gov/.

Mary Marshall Registered Nursing Scholarships. Scholarship for Virginia residents who have been accepted or is enrollment as a full-time or part-time student in a school of nursing in the state of Virginia. Must demonstrate financial need, verified by the Financial Aid Office/authorized person at the applicant's nursing school. Must also be a resident of Virginia for at least one year and have a minimum 3.0 GPA in required courses. Must have submitted a completed application form and an official grade transcript to The Office of Minority Health and Public Health Policy prior to June 30. If no college courses attempted an official high school transcript or equivalent must be submitted. Nursing. *Award:* Scholarship for use in freshman, sophomore, junior, or senior years; not renewable. *Award amount:* $600–$2000. *Number of awards:* 28–95. *Eligibility Requirements:* Applicant must be enrolled or

expecting to enroll full- or part-time at a two-year or four-year institution or university; resident of Virginia and studying in Virginia. Applicant must have 2.5 GPA or higher. Available to U.S. citizens. *Application Requirements:* Application form, driver's license, essay, financial need analysis, recommendations or references, transcript. **Deadline:** June 30.

Contact Miss. Sarahbeth Jones, Communications Specialist, Virginia Department of Health, Office of Minority Health and Health Equity, PO Box 2448, 109 Governor Street, Suite 1016-E, Richmond, VA 23218-2448. *E-mail:* IncentivePrograms@vdh.virginia.gov. *Phone:* 804-864-7422. *Fax:* 804-864-7440. *Website:* http://www.vdh.virginia.gov/.

State Department Federal Credit Union Annual Scholarship Program. Scholarships available to members who are currently enrolled in a degree program and have completed 12 credit hours of coursework at an accredited college or university. Must have own account in good standing with SDFCU, have a minimum 2.5 GPA, submit official cumulative transcripts, and describe need for financial assistance to continue their education. Scholarship only open to members of State Department Federal Credit Union. *Award:* Scholarship for use in sophomore, junior, senior, or graduate years; not renewable. *Award amount:* $2500. *Eligibility Requirements:* Applicant must be enrolled or expecting to enroll full-time at a four-year institution or university. Applicant must have 2.5 GPA or higher. Available to U.S. and non-U.S. citizens. *Application Requirements:* Application form, financial need analysis. **Deadline:** April 29.

Virginia Commonwealth Award. Need-based award for undergraduate or graduate study at a Virginia public two- or four-year college, or university. Undergraduates must be Virginia residents. The application and awards process are administered by the financial aid office at the Virginia public institution where the student is enrolled. Dollar value of each award varies. Contact college financial aid office for application and deadlines. *Award:* Grant for use in freshman, sophomore, junior, or senior years; not renewable. *Eligibility Requirements:* Applicant must be enrolled or expecting to enroll full- or

part-time at a two-year or four-year institution or university; resident of Virginia and studying in Virginia. Available to U.S. citizens. *Application Requirements:* Financial need analysis.

Virginia Guaranteed Assistance Program. Awards to undergraduate students proportional to their need, up to full tuition, fees and book allowance. Must be a graduate of a Virginia high school. High school GPA of 2.5 required. Must be enrolled full-time in a public Virginia two- or four-year institution and demonstrate financial need. Must maintain minimum college GPA of 2.0 for renewal awards. *Award:* Grant for use in freshman, sophomore, junior, or senior years; not renewable. *Eligibility Requirements:* Applicant must be enrolled or expecting to enroll full-time at a two-year or four-year institution or university; resident of Virginia and studying in Virginia. Available to U.S. citizens. *Application Requirements:* Financial need analysis.

Virginia Military Survivors and Dependents Education Program. Scholarships for post-secondary students between ages 16 and 29 to attend Virginia state-supported institutions. Must be child or surviving spouse of veteran who has either been permanently or totally disabled due to war or other armed conflict; died as a result of war or other armed conflict; or been listed as a POW or MIA. Parent must also meet Virginia residency requirements. *Award:* Scholarship for use in freshman, sophomore, junior, senior, or graduate years; renewable. *Eligibility Requirements:* Applicant must be age 16-29; enrolled or expecting to enroll full-time at a two-year or four-year or technical institution or university; resident of Virginia and studying in Virginia. Available to U.S. citizens. Applicant or parent must meet one or more of the following requirements: general military experience; retired from active duty; disabled or killed as a result of military service; prisoner of war; or missing in action. *Application Requirements:* Application form, DD214 of service member, birth certificate of applicant, marriage certificate, acceptance letter from institution. **Deadline:** varies.

Contact Mrs. Doris Sullivan, Coordinator, Virginia Department of Veterans Services, 1351 Hershberger Road, Suite 220, Roanoke, VA 24012. *Phone:* 540-

561-6625. *Fax:* 540-857-7573. *Website:* http://www.dvs.virginia.gov/.

Virginia Tuition Assistance Grant Program (Private Institutions). Awards for undergraduate students. Also available to graduate and first professional degree students pursuing a health-related degree program. Not to be used for religious study. Must be U.S. citizen or eligible non-citizen, Virginia domiciled, and enrolled full-time at an approved private, nonprofit college within Virginia. Information and application available from participating Virginia colleges financial aid office. Visit http://www.schev.edu and click on Financial Aid. *Award:* Grant for use in freshman, sophomore, junior, senior, or graduate years; renewable. *Award amount:* $800–$3200. *Eligibility Requirements:* Applicant must be enrolled or expecting to enroll full-time at a four-year institution or university; resident of Virginia and studying in Virginia. Available to U.S. citizens. *Application Requirements:* Application form. **Deadline:** July 31.

WEST VIRGINIA

West Virginia Higher Education Grant Program. Award available for West Virginia resident for one year immediately preceding the date of application, high school graduate or the equivalent, demonstrate financial need, and enroll as a full-time undergraduate at an approved university or college located in West Virginia or Pennsylvania. *Award:* Grant for use in freshman, sophomore, junior, or senior years; not renewable. *Award amount:* $300–$2700. *Number of awards:* 18,000–21,000. *Eligibility Requirements:* Applicant must be enrolled or expecting to enroll full-time at a two-year or four-year institution or university; resident of West Virginia and studying in Pennsylvania, West Virginia. Available to U.S. citizens. *Application Requirements:* Financial need analysis. **Deadline:** April 15.

Contact Judy Smith, Senior Project Coordinator, West Virginia Higher Education Policy Commission-Student Services, 1018 Kanawha Boulevard East, Suite 700, Charleston, WV 25301-2827. *E-mail:* judy.kee@wvhepc.edu. *Phone:* 304-558-4618. *Website:* http://www.wvhepc.edu.

WISCONSIN

Handicapped Student Grant-Wisconsin. One-time award available to residents of Wisconsin who have severe or profound hearing or visual impairment. Must be enrolled at least half-time at a nonprofit institution. If the handicap prevents the student from attending a Wisconsin school, the award may be used out-of-state in a specialized college. Refer to web site for further details http://www.heab.state.wi.us. *Award:* Grant for use in freshman, sophomore, junior, or senior years; not renewable. *Award amount:* $250–$1800. *Eligibility Requirements:* Applicant must be hearing impaired or visually impaired; enrolled or expecting to enroll full- or part-time at a four-year institution or university and resident of Wisconsin. Applicant must be hearing impaired or visually impaired. Available to U.S. citizens. *Application Requirements:* Application form, financial need analysis. **Deadline:** continuous.

Contact Sandy Thomas, Program Coordinator, Wisconsin Higher Educational Aid Board, PO Box 7885, Madison, WI 53707-7885. *E-mail:* sandy.thomas@wi.gov. *Phone:* 608-266-0888. *Fax:* 608-267-2808. *Website:* http://www.heab.wi.gov/.

Minority Undergraduate Retention Grant-Wisconsin. The grant provides financial assistance to African-American, Native-American, Hispanic, and former citizens of Laos, Vietnam, and Cambodia, for study in Wisconsin. Must be Wisconsin resident, enrolled at least half-time in Wisconsin Technical College System schools, non-profit independent colleges and universities, and tribal colleges. Refer to web site for further details http://www.heab.state.wi.us. *Award:* Grant for use in sophomore, junior, or senior years; not renewable. *Award amount:* $250–$2500. *Eligibility Requirements:* Applicant must be American Indian/Alaska Native, Asian/Pacific Islander, Black (non-Hispanic), Hispanic; enrolled or expecting to enroll full- or part-time at a two-year or four-year or technical institution or university; resident of Wisconsin and studying in Wisconsin. Available to U.S. and non-U.S. citizens. *Application Requirements:* Application form, financial need analysis. **Deadline:** continuous.

Contact Mary Lou Kuzdas, Program Coordinator, Wisconsin Higher Educational Aid Board, PO Box 7885, Madison, WI 53707-7885. *E-mail:* mary.kuzdas@wi.gov. *Phone:* 608-267-2212. *Fax:* 608-267-2808. *Website:* http://www.heab.wi.gov/.

Talent Incentive Program Grant. Grant assists residents of Wisconsin who are attending a nonprofit institution in Wisconsin, and who have substantial financial need. Must meet income criteria, be considered economically and educationally disadvantaged, and be enrolled at least half-time. Refer to web site for further details http://www.heab.state.wi.us. *Award:* Grant for use in freshman, sophomore, junior, or senior years; renewable. *Award amount:* $250–$1800. *Eligibility Requirements:* Applicant must be enrolled or expecting to enroll full- or part-time at a two-year or four-year or technical institution or university; resident of Wisconsin and studying in Wisconsin. Available to U.S. citizens. *Application Requirements:* Application form, financial need analysis, nomination by financial aid office. **Deadline:** continuous.

Contact Colette Brown, Program Coordinator, Wisconsin Higher Educational Aid Board, PO Box 7885, Madison, WI 53707-7885. *E-mail:* colette.brown@wi.gov. *Phone:* 608-266-1665. *Fax:* 608-267-2808. *Website:* http://www.heab.wi.gov/.

Veterans Education (VetEd) Reimbursement Grant. The grant is for eligible Wisconsin veterans enrolled at approved schools who have not yet earned a BS/BA. Reimburses up to 120 credits or eight semesters at the UW Madison rate for the same number of credits taken in one semester or term. The number of credits or semesters is based on length of time serving on active duty in the armed forces (active duty for training does not apply). Application is due no later than 60 days after the course start date. The student must earn a 2.0 or better for the semester. An eligible veteran will have entered active duty as a Wisconsin resident or lived in state for twelve consecutive months since entering active duty. *Award:* Grant for use in freshman, sophomore, junior, or senior years; renewable. *Award amount:* $1340–$4000. *Eligibility Requirements:* Applicant must be hearing impaired, learning disabled, physically disabled, or visually impaired, age 18-73; enrolled or expecting to enroll full- or part-time at a two-year or four-year or technical institution or university; resident of Wisconsin and studying in Minnesota, Wisconsin. Applicant must be hearing impaired, learning disabled, physically disabled, or visually impaired. Applicant must have 3.5 GPA or higher. Available to U.S. citizens. Applicant must have general military experience. *Application Requirements:* Application form. **Deadline:** July 15.

Contact Miss. Leslie Busby-Amegashie, Agency Liaison and Regional Coordinator, Wisconsin Department of Veterans Affairs (WDVA), 201 West Washington Street, PO Box 7843, Madison, WI 53707-7843. *E-mail:* leslie.busby-amegashie@dva.wisconsin.gov. *Phone:* 800-947-8387 Ext. 63575. *Fax:* 608-267-0403 Ext. 3575. *Website:* http://www.dva.state.wi.us/.

Wisconsin Academic Excellence Scholarship. Renewable award for high school seniors with the highest GPA in graduating class. Must be a Wisconsin resident attending a nonprofit Wisconsin institution full-time. Scholarship value is $2250 toward tuition each year for up to four years. Must maintain 3.0 GPA for renewal. Refer to your high school counselor for more details. *Award:* Scholarship for use in freshman year; renewable. *Award amount:* up to $2250. *Eligibility Requirements:* Applicant must be high school student; planning to enroll or expecting to enroll full-time at a two-year or four-year or technical institution or university; resident of Wisconsin and studying in Wisconsin. Applicant must have 3.0 GPA or higher. Available to U.S. citizens. *Application Requirements:* Application form, test scores, transcript. **Deadline:** continuous.

Contact Nancy Wilkison, Program Coordinator, Wisconsin Higher Educational Aid Board, PO Box 7885, Madison, WI 53707-7885. *E-mail:* nancy.wilkison@wi.gov. *Phone:* 608-267-2213. *Fax:* 608-267-2808. *Website:* http://www.heab.wi.gov/.

Wisconsin Higher Education Grants (WHEG). Grants for residents of Wisconsin enrolled at least half-time in degree or certificate programs at a University of Wisconsin Institution, Wisconsin Technical College or an approved Tribal College. Must show financial need. Refer to web site for

further details http://www.heab.wi.gov. *Award:* Grant for use in freshman, sophomore, junior, or senior years; not renewable. *Award amount:* $250–$3000. *Eligibility Requirements:* Applicant must be enrolled or expecting to enroll full- or part-time at a two-year or four-year or technical institution or university; resident of Wisconsin and studying in Wisconsin. Available to U.S. citizens. *Application Requirements:* Application form, financial need analysis. **Deadline:** continuous.

Contact Sandra Thomas, Program Coordinator, Wisconsin Higher Educational Aid Board, PO Box 7885, Madison, WI 53707-7885. *E-mail:* sandy.thomas@heab.state.wi.us. *Phone:* 608-266-0888. *Fax:* 608-267-2808. *Website:* http://www.heab.wi.gov/.

Wisconsin Native American/Indian Student Assistance Grant. Grants for Wisconsin residents who are at least one-quarter American Indian. Must be attending a college or university within the state. Refer to web site for further details, http://www.heab.state.wi.us. *Award:* Grant for use in freshman, sophomore, junior, or senior years; not renewable. *Award amount:* $250–$1100. *Eligibility Requirements:* Applicant must be American Indian/Alaska Native; enrolled or expecting to enroll full- or part-time at a two-year or four-year or technical institution or university; resident of Wisconsin and studying in Wisconsin. Available to U.S. citizens. *Application Requirements:* Application form, financial need analysis. **Deadline:** continuous.

Contact Sandra Thomas, Program Coordinator, Wisconsin Higher Educational Aid Board, PO Box 7885, Madison, WI 53707-7885. *E-mail:* sandy.thomas@wi.gov. *Phone:* 608-266-0888. *Fax:* 608-267-2808. *Website:* http://www.heab.wi.gov/.

WYOMING

Douvas Memorial Scholarship. Available to Wyoming residents who are first-generation Americans. Must be between 18 and 22 years old. Must be used at any Wyoming public institution of higher education for study in freshman year. *Award:* Scholarship for use in freshman year; not renewable. *Award amount:* $500. *Number of awards:* 1. *Eligibility Requirements:* Applicant must be age 18-22; enrolled or expecting to enroll full- or part-time

at a two-year or four-year institution or university; resident of Wyoming and studying in Wyoming. Available to U.S. citizens. *Application Requirements:* Application form. **Deadline:** April 30.

Contact Bruce Hayes, Education Consultant, Wyoming Department of Education, 2300 Capitol Avenue, Hathaway Building, 2nd Floor, Cheyenne, WY 82002. *E-mail:* bruce.hayes@wyo.gov. *Phone:* 307-777-6198. *Website:* http://edu.wyoming.gov/.

Hathaway Scholarship. Scholarship for Wyoming students to pursue postsecondary education within the state. Award ranges from $840 to $1680 per semester. Deadline varies. *Award:* Scholarship for use in freshman, sophomore, junior, senior, or graduate years; renewable. *Award amount:* $840–$1680. *Eligibility Requirements:* Applicant must be enrolled or expecting to enroll full- or part-time at a two-year or four-year institution or university; resident of Wyoming and studying in Wyoming. Applicant must have 2.5 GPA or higher. Available to U.S. citizens. *Application Requirements:* Application form. **Deadline:** continuous.

Contact Mr. Bradley Barker III, Hathaway Scholarship Consultant, Wyoming Department of Education, 2300 Capitol Avenue, Hathaway Building, Cheyenne, WY 82002. *E-mail:* hathawayscholarship@wyo.gov. *Phone:* 307-777-6226. *Website:* http://edu.wyoming.gov/.

Superior Student in Education Scholarship-Wyoming. Scholarship available each year to sixteen Wyoming high school graduates who plan to teach in Wyoming. The award covers costs of undergraduate tuition at the University of Wyoming or any Wyoming community college. Education. *Award:* Scholarship for use in freshman, sophomore, junior, or senior years; renewable. *Award amount:* $1000. *Number of awards:* 16–16. *Eligibility Requirements:* Applicant must be enrolled or expecting to enroll full-time at a two-year or four-year institution or university; resident of Wyoming and studying in Wyoming. Applicant must have 3.0 GPA or higher. Available to U. S. citizens. *Application Requirements:* Application form, recommendations or references, test scores, transcript. **Deadline:** October 31.

Contact Tammy Mack, Assistant Director, Scholarships, University of

Wyoming, Department 3335, 1000 East University Avenue, Laramie, WY 82071. *E-mail:* FinAid@uwyo.edu. *Phone:* 307-766-2412. *Fax:* 307-766-3800. *Website:* http://www.uwyo.edu/scholarships.

Vietnam Veterans Award-Wyoming. Scholarship available to Wyoming residents who served in the armed forces between August 5, 1964 and May 7, 1975, and received a Vietnam service medal. *Award:* Scholarship for use in freshman, sophomore, junior, or senior years; renewable. *Eligibility Requirements:* Applicant must be enrolled or expecting to enroll full- or part-time at a two-year or four-year institution or university and resident of Wyoming. Available to U.S. citizens. Applicant or parent must meet one or more of the following requirements: general military experience; retired from active duty; disabled or killed as a result of military service; prisoner of war; or missing in action. *Application Requirements:* Application form. **Deadline:** continuous.

Contact Tammy Mack, Assistant Director, Scholarships, University of Wyoming, Department 3335, 1000 East University Avenue, Laramie, WY 82071. *E-mail:* FinAid@uwyo.edu. *Phone:* 307-766-2412. *Fax:* 307-766-3800. *Website:* http://www.uwyo.edu/scholarships.

Indexes

Non-Need Scholarships for Undergraduates

Academic Interests/Achievements

Agriculture

Abilene Christian University, TX
Angelo State University, TX
Arkansas Tech University, AR
Auburn University, AL
Austin Peay State University, TN
Berry College, GA
California Polytechnic State University, San Luis Obispo, CA
California State Polytechnic University, Pomona, CA
California State University, Chico, CA
California State University, Fresno, CA
California State University, Stanislaus, CA
Cameron University, OK
Clemson University, SC
Dordt College, IA
Eastern Michigan University, MI
Ferris State University, MI
Florida Agricultural and Mechanical University, FL
Florida Southern College, FL
Fort Hays State University, KS
Huntington University, IN
Iowa State University of Science and Technology, IA
Lincoln University, MO
Louisiana State University and Agricultural & Mechanical College, LA
Louisiana Tech University, LA
Lubbock Christian University, TX
Michigan State University, MI
Middle Tennessee State University, TN
Mississippi State University, MS
Montana State University, MT
Morehead State University, KY
Murray State University, KY
New Mexico State University, NM
North Carolina Agricultural and Technical State University, NC
North Carolina State University, NC
Northern State University, SD
Northwest Missouri State University, MO
The Ohio State University, OH
Oklahoma State University, OK
Post University, CT
Purdue University, IN
Saint Louis University, MO
Sam Houston State University, TX
South Dakota State University, SD
Southeast Missouri State University, MO
Southern Arkansas University–Magnolia, AR
Southern Illinois University Carbondale, IL
State University of New York College of Environmental Science and Forestry, NY
Stephen F. Austin State University, TX
Tennessee Technological University, TN
Texas A&M University, TX
Texas A&M University–Commerce, TX
Texas Christian University, TX
Texas State University, TX

Texas Tech University, TX
Truman State University, MO
Tuskegee University, AL
The University of Alabama, AL
University of Arkansas, AR
University of California, Davis, CA
University of California, Riverside, CA
University of California, Santa Cruz, CA
University of Delaware, DE
University of Florida, FL
University of Georgia, GA
University of Idaho, ID
University of Illinois at Urbana–Champaign, IL
University of Kentucky, KY
University of Louisiana at Monroe, LA
University of Maine, ME
University of Mary Hardin-Baylor, TX
University of Maryland, College Park, MD
University of Massachusetts Amherst, MA
University of Minnesota, Crookston, MN
University of Minnesota, Twin Cities Campus, MN
University of Missouri, MO
University of Nebraska–Lincoln, NE
University of Nevada, Reno, NV
University of New Hampshire, NH
University of Rhode Island, RI
The University of Tennessee, TN
The University of Tennessee at Martin, TN
The University of Texas at San Antonio, TX
University of Vermont, VT
The University of Virginia's College at Wise, VA
University of Wisconsin–River Falls, WI
University of Wisconsin–Stevens Point, WI
University of Wyoming, WY
Utah State University, UT
Vanderbilt University, TN
Vermont Technical College, VT
Washington State University, WA
Western Illinois University, IL
Western Kentucky University, KY
West Texas A&M University, TX
West Virginia University, WV

Architecture

Auburn University, AL
Ball State University, IN
Boise State University, ID
Boston Architectural College, MA
California Baptist University, CA
California Polytechnic State University, San Luis Obispo, CA
California State Polytechnic University, Pomona, CA
Calvin College, MI
City College of the City University of New York, NY
Clemson University, SC
Cooper Union for the Advancement of Science and Art, NY
Drury University, MO
Eastern Michigan University, MI
Fairmont State University, WV

Ferris State University, MI
Florida Agricultural and Mechanical University, FL
Florida International University, FL
Georgia Institute of Technology, GA
Hampton University, VA
Idaho State University, ID
Illinois Institute of Technology, IL
Iowa State University of Science and Technology, IA
James Madison University, VA
Kean University, NJ
Kent State University, OH
Louisiana State University and Agricultural & Mechanical College, LA
Louisiana Tech University, LA
Marywood University, PA
Miami University, OH
Mississippi State University, MS
Missouri Western State University, MO
Montana State University, MT
New Jersey Institute of Technology, NJ
North Carolina State University, NC
The Ohio State University, OH
Oklahoma State University, OK
Portland State University, OR
Samford University, AL
San Jose State University, CA
Savannah College of Art and Design, GA
Southern California Institute of Architecture, CA
Southern Illinois University Carbondale, IL
State University of New York College of Environmental Science and Forestry, NY
Texas A&M University, TX
Texas Tech University, TX
Tuskegee University, AL
University of Arkansas, AR
University of Colorado Boulder, CO
University of Florida, FL
University of Hartford, CT
University of Houston, TX
University of Idaho, ID
University of Illinois at Chicago, IL
University of Illinois at Urbana–Champaign, IL
The University of Kansas, KS
University of Kentucky, KY
University of Maryland, College Park, MD
University of Mary Washington, VA
University of Massachusetts Amherst, MA
University of Memphis, TN
University of Miami, FL
University of Michigan, MI
University of Minnesota, Twin Cities Campus, MN
University of Nebraska–Lincoln, NE
University of Nevada, Las Vegas, NV
The University of North Carolina at Charlotte, NC
University of Oklahoma, OK
University of Oregon, OR
University of South Florida, FL
The University of Tennessee, TN
University of Utah, UT

University of Washington, WA
University of Wisconsin–Stevens Point, WI
University of Wyoming, WY
Utah State University, UT
Washington State University, WA
Washington University in St. Louis, MO
West Virginia University, WV

Area/Ethnic Studies
Alaska Pacific University, AK
Augustana College, IL
Binghamton University, State University of New York, NY
Birmingham-Southern College, AL
Boise State University, ID
California State Polytechnic University, Pomona, CA
California State University, Chico, CA
California State University, Fresno, CA
California State University, Fullerton, CA
California State University, Stanislaus, CA
Calvin College, MI
City College of the City University of New York, NY
The College of New Rochelle, NY
College of Staten Island of the City University of New York, NY
Eastern Washington University, WA
Edgewood College, WI
Florida Agricultural and Mechanical University, FL
Fort Hays State University, KS
Fort Lewis College, CO
Furman University, SC
Indiana State University, IN
Indiana University of Pennsylvania, PA
Iowa State University of Science and Technology, IA
Kean University, NJ
Kent State University, OH
Loyola Marymount University, CA
Middle Tennessee State University, TN
Mississippi State University, MS
Montana State University, MT
Moravian College, PA
New Jersey Institute of Technology, NJ
New Mexico State University, NM
Northern Illinois University, IL
The Ohio State University, OH
Ohio University, OH
Ohio University–Chillicothe, OH
Ohio University–Eastern, OH
Ohio University–Lancaster, OH
Ohio University–Southern Campus, OH
Ohio University–Zanesville, OH
Oklahoma State University, OK
Old Dominion University, VA
Ouachita Baptist University, AR
Portland State University, OR
Saint Louis University, MO
San Diego State University, CA
Sonoma State University, CA
South Dakota State University, SD
Southern Illinois University Carbondale, IL
State University of New York at New Paltz, NY
State University of New York at Oswego, NY
State University of New York at Plattsburgh, NY
State University of New York College at Geneseo, NY
Stetson University, FL
Stockton University, NJ
Stony Brook University, State University of New York, NY

The University of Alabama, AL
University of Arkansas, AR
University of California, Davis, CA
University of California, Irvine, CA
University of California, Riverside, CA
University of California, Santa Cruz, CA
University of Colorado Boulder, CO
University of Dallas, TX
University of Hartford, CT
University of Houston, TX
University of Illinois at Urbana–Champaign, IL
The University of Kansas, KS
University of Kentucky, KY
University of Michigan, MI
University of Minnesota, Twin Cities Campus, MN
University of Missouri, MO
University of North Carolina at Asheville, NC
University of Oklahoma, OK
University of Rhode Island, RI
University of South Carolina, SC
The University of Texas at San Antonio, TX
University of Utah, UT
University of Vermont, VT
University of Washington, WA
University of Washington, Bothell, WA
University of Washington, Tacoma, WA
University of Wisconsin–Eau Claire, WI
University of Wisconsin–Green Bay, WI
University of Wisconsin–La Crosse, WI
University of Wisconsin–River Falls, WI
University of Wyoming, WY
Washington State University, WA
Wayne State University, MI
Western Illinois University, IL
West Virginia University, WV
Wheaton College, IL
Wichita State University, KS
William Jessup University, CA
Wright State University, OH
Wright State University–Lake Campus, OH

Biological Sciences
Abilene Christian University, TX
Alaska Pacific University, AK
Albany State University, GA
Albertus Magnus College, CT
Alfred University, NY
Angelo State University, TX
Arkansas Tech University, AR
Auburn University, AL
Augsburg University, MN
Augustana College, IL
Augustana University, SD
Austin College, TX
Austin Peay State University, TN
Averett University, VA
Ball State University, IN
Barton College, NC
Belhaven University, MS
Bellarmine University, KY
Belmont University, TN
Bemidji State University, MN
Bethel College, KS
Binghamton University, State University of New York, NY
Biola University, CA
Birmingham-Southern College, AL
Black Hills State University, SD
Bloomsburg University of Pennsylvania, PA
Blue Mountain College, MS
Bluffton University, OH
Boise State University, ID
Bowie State University, MD

Bowling Green State University, OH
Brenau University, GA
Bryan College, TN
Buena Vista University, IA
Buffalo State College, State University of New York, NY
Butler University, IN
California Lutheran University, CA
California Polytechnic State University, San Luis Obispo, CA
California State Polytechnic University, Pomona, CA
California State University, Bakersfield, CA
California State University, Chico, CA
California State University, Fresno, CA
California State University, Fullerton, CA
California State University, San Bernardino, CA
California State University, Stanislaus, CA
Calvin College, MI
Cameron University, OK
Campbellsville University, KY
Carlow University, PA
Carroll University, WI
Carson-Newman University, TN
Case Western Reserve University, OH
Cedar Crest College, PA
Centenary College of Louisiana, LA
Central College, IA
Central Methodist University, MO
Central Michigan University, MI
Chaminade University of Honolulu, HI
Chapman University, CA
Christopher Newport University, VA
The Citadel, The Military College of South Carolina, SC
City College of the City University of New York, NY
Clarion University of Pennsylvania, PA
Clarkson University, NY
Clemson University, SC
Cleveland State University, OH
Coastal Carolina University, SC
Coker College, SC
The College at Brockport, State University of New York, NY
College of Charleston, SC
College of Coastal Georgia, GA
The College of Idaho, ID
The College of New Rochelle, NY
College of Saint Mary, NE
College of Staten Island of the City University of New York, NY
The Colorado College, CO
Colorado Mesa University, CO
Columbia College, MO
Columbus State University, GA
Concordia University Chicago, IL
Concordia University, Nebraska, NE
Concordia University Texas, TX
Dakota State University, SD
Dallas Baptist University, TX
Davidson College, NC
Defiance College, OH
Denison University, OH
DeSales University, PA
Dordt College, IA
Drury University, MO
East Carolina University, NC
Eastern Illinois University, IL
Eastern Mennonite University, VA
Eastern Michigan University, MI
Eastern Washington University, WA
East Texas Baptist University, TX
Elizabethtown College, PA
Elmhurst College, IL

Elon University, NC
Emporia State University, KS
Evangel University, MO
Fairmont State University, WV
Ferris State University, MI
Florida Agricultural and Mechanical
   University, FL
Florida Gulf Coast University, FL
Florida International University, FL
Florida Southern College, FL
Fordham University, NY
Fort Hays State University, KS
Fort Lewis College, CO
Framingham State University, MA
Francis Marion University, SC
Frostburg State University, MD
Furman University, SC
Gannon University, PA
Gardner-Webb University, NC
George Fox University, OR
Georgia Institute of Technology, GA
Georgian Court University, NJ
Georgia Southern University, GA
Glenville State College, WV
Governors State University, IL
Grambling State University, LA
Greenville University, IL
Grove City College, PA
Hamline University, MN
Hampden-Sydney College, VA
Hampton University, VA
Hardin-Simmons University, TX
Harrisburg University of Science and
   Technology, PA
Henderson State University, AR
High Point University, NC
Hillsdale College, MI
Hood College, MD
Howard Payne University, TX
Huntingdon College, AL
Idaho State University, ID
Illinois Institute of Technology, IL
Indiana State University, IN
Indiana University of Pennsylvania, PA
Indiana Wesleyan University, IN
Iowa State University of Science and
   Technology, IA
Jacksonville State University, AL
James Madison University, VA
Jefferson College of Health Sciences, VA
John Carroll University, OH
Johnson C. Smith University, NC
Juniata College, PA
Kansas Wesleyan University, KS
Kean University, NJ
Kennesaw State University, GA
Kent State University, OH
Kenyon College, OH
King's College, PA
Kutztown University of Pennsylvania, PA
La Sierra University, CA
Lebanon Valley College, PA
Lee University, TN
Lewis-Clark State College, ID
Liberty University, VA
Lindenwood University, MO
Lindsey Wilson College, KY
Linfield College, OR
Lipscomb University, TN
Lock Haven University of Pennsylvania, PA
Longwood University, VA
Loras College, IA
Louisiana State University and Agricultural
   & Mechanical College, LA
Louisiana Tech University, LA

Loyola Marymount University, CA
Lycoming College, PA
Lynn University, FL
Malone University, OH
Manhattan College, NY
Mansfield University of Pennsylvania, PA
Marquette University, WI
Marymount Manhattan College, NY
Marymount University, VA
Maryville University of Saint Louis, MO
Marywood University, PA
Massachusetts College of Liberal Arts, MA
McKendree University, IL
McMurry University, TX
Mercer University, GA
Meredith College, NC
Metropolitan State University of Denver, CO
Michigan State University, MI
Middle Georgia State University, GA
Middle Tennessee State University, TN
Midwestern State University, TX
Millersville University of Pennsylvania, PA
Millikin University, IL
Mills College, CA
Minnesota State University Moorhead, MN
Minot State University, ND
Mississippi State University, MS
Missouri University of Science and
   Technology, MO
Missouri Valley College, MO
Missouri Western State University, MO
Molloy College, NY
Monmouth University, NJ
Montana State University, MT
Montana State University Billings, MT
Montana Tech of The University of
   Montana, MT
Montclair State University, NJ
Moravian College, PA
Morehead State University, KY
Morehouse College, GA
Murray State University, KY
Muskingum University, OH
Nazareth College of Rochester, NY
Newberry College, SC
New England College, NH
New Jersey Institute of Technology, NJ
New Mexico Highlands University, NM
New Mexico State University, NM
North Carolina State University, NC
North Central College, IL
Northeastern Illinois University, IL
Northeastern State University, OK
Northern Illinois University, IL
Northern Kentucky University, KY
Northern Michigan University, MI
Northern State University, SD
Northwestern College, IA
Northwest Missouri State University, MO
Northwest Nazarene University, ID
Oglethorpe University, GA
Ohio Northern University, OH
The Ohio State University, OH
Ohio University, OH
Ohio University–Chillicothe, OH
Ohio University–Eastern, OH
Ohio University–Lancaster, OH
Ohio University–Southern Campus, OH
Ohio University–Zanesville, OH
Oklahoma Baptist University, OK
Oklahoma State University, OK
Old Dominion University, VA
Oral Roberts University, OK
Ouachita Baptist University, AR
Pacific University, OR

Piedmont College, GA
Pittsburg State University, KS
Plymouth State University, NH
Point Loma Nazarene University, CA
Point Park University, PA
Post University, CT
Randolph College, VA
Regis University, CO
Rochester Institute of Technology, NY
Rockford University, IL
Rockhurst University, MO
Sacred Heart University, CT
Saginaw Valley State University, MI
St. Ambrose University, IA
Saint Augustine's University, NC
St. Edward's University, TX
St. John Fisher College, NY
St. John's University, NY
Saint Joseph's University, PA
Saint Louis University, MO
Saint Vincent College, PA
Samford University, AL
Sam Houston State University, TX
San Diego State University, CA
San Jose State University, CA
Schreiner University, TX
Shenandoah University, VA
Shepherd University, WV
Shippensburg University of Pennsylvania,
   PA
Siena College, NY
Skidmore College, NY
Slippery Rock University of Pennsylvania,
   PA
Sonoma State University, CA
South Dakota State University, SD
Southeastern Oklahoma State University,
   OK
Southeast Missouri State University, MO
Southern Adventist University, TN
Southern Arkansas University–Magnolia,
   AR
Southern Illinois University Carbondale, IL
Southern Oregon University, OR
Southwestern College, KS
Southwestern Oklahoma State University,
   OK
State University of New York at Fredonia,
   NY
State University of New York at New Paltz,
   NY
State University of New York at Oswego,
   NY
State University of New York at Plattsburgh,
   NY
State University of New York College at
   Geneseo, NY
State University of New York College at
   Potsdam, NY
State University of New York College of
   Environmental Science and Forestry, NY
Stephen F. Austin State University, TX
Stetson University, FL
Stockton University, NJ
Stony Brook University, State University of
   New York, NY
Tennessee Technological University, TN
Texas A&M University, TX
Texas A&M University–Commerce, TX
Texas A&M University–Texarkana, TX
Texas Christian University, TX
Texas Lutheran University, TX
Texas State University, TX
Texas Tech University, TX
Texas Wesleyan University, TX

Texas Woman's University, TX
Thomas More College, KY
Thomas University, GA
Towson University, MD
Trevecca Nazarene University, TN
Trinity Christian College, IL
Truett McConnell University, GA
Truman State University, MO
Union University, TN
The University of Akron, OH
The University of Alabama, AL
The University of Alabama in Huntsville, AL
University of Alaska Anchorage, AK
University of Alaska Fairbanks, AK
University of Arkansas, AR
University of Arkansas at Little Rock, AR
University of Bridgeport, CT
University of California, Davis, CA
University of California, Irvine, CA
University of California, Riverside, CA
University of California, San Diego, CA
University of Central Oklahoma, OK
University of Colorado Boulder, CO
University of Colorado Denver, CO
University of Dallas, TX
University of Dayton, OH
University of Delaware, DE
University of Denver, CO
University of Evansville, IN
University of Hartford, CT
University of Houston, TX
University of Houston–Clear Lake, TX
University of Houston–Victoria, TX
University of Idaho, ID
University of Illinois at Urbana–Champaign, IL
The University of Kansas, KS
University of Kentucky, KY
University of Louisiana at Monroe, LA
University of Maine, ME
University of Maine at Fort Kent, ME
University of Mary Hardin-Baylor, TX
University of Maryland, Baltimore County, MD
University of Maryland, College Park, MD
University of Mary Washington, VA
University of Massachusetts Amherst, MA
University of Massachusetts Dartmouth, MA
University of Massachusetts Lowell, MA
University of Memphis, TN
University of Miami, FL
University of Michigan, MI
University of Michigan–Dearborn, MI
University of Michigan–Flint, MI
University of Minnesota, Crookston, MN
University of Minnesota, Twin Cities Campus, MN
University of Mississippi, MS
University of Missouri, MO
University of Missouri–St. Louis, MO
University of Montana, MT
The University of Montana Western, MT
University of Montevallo, AL
University of Nebraska–Lincoln, NE
University of Nevada, Las Vegas, NV
University of Nevada, Reno, NV
University of New Hampshire, NH
University of New Hampshire at Manchester, NH
University of North Carolina at Asheville, NC
The University of North Carolina at Charlotte, NC
The University of North Carolina at Greensboro, NC

The University of North Carolina Wilmington, NC
University of North Dakota, ND
University of Northern Colorado, CO
University of Northern Iowa, IA
University of North Georgia, GA
University of Oklahoma, OK
University of Oregon, OR
University of Pittsburgh at Bradford, PA
University of Pittsburgh at Johnstown, PA
University of Portland, OR
University of Providence, MT
University of Puget Sound, WA
University of Rhode Island, RI
University of Richmond, VA
University of St. Francis, IL
University of St. Thomas, MN
University of St. Thomas, TX
University of Sioux Falls, SD
University of South Carolina, SC
University of South Carolina Aiken, SC
University of South Dakota, SD
University of Southern Indiana, IN
University of South Florida, FL
The University of Tampa, FL
The University of Tennessee at Chattanooga, TN
The University of Tennessee at Martin, TN
The University of Texas at Dallas, TX
The University of Texas at El Paso, TX
The University of Texas at San Antonio, TX
The University of Texas Rio Grande Valley, TX
University of the Southwest, NM
The University of Toledo, OH
The University of Tulsa, OK
University of Utah, UT
The University of Virginia's College at Wise, VA
University of Washington, WA
University of Washington, Bothell, WA
University of Washington, Tacoma, WA
University of West Florida, FL
University of West Georgia, GA
University of Wisconsin–Eau Claire, WI
University of Wisconsin–Green Bay, WI
University of Wisconsin–La Crosse, WI
University of Wisconsin–Parkside, WI
University of Wisconsin–River Falls, WI
University of Wisconsin–Stevens Point, WI
University of Wisconsin–Superior, WI
University of Wisconsin–Whitewater, WI
University of Wyoming, WY
Upper Iowa University, IA
Utah State University, UT
Valdosta State University, GA
Valley City State University, ND
Virginia Military Institute, VA
Virginia State University, VA
Walla Walla University, WA
Wartburg College, IA
Washington State University, WA
Washington University in St. Louis, MO
Wayland Baptist University, TX
Wayne State College, NE
Wayne State University, MI
Webster University, MO
Wesleyan College, GA
Western Carolina University, NC
Western Illinois University, IL
Western Kentucky University, KY
Western Oregon University, OR
Western Washington University, WA
West Virginia University, WV
Wheaton College, IL
Wichita State University, KS

Widener University, PA
William Jessup University, CA
Williams Baptist College, AR
Wilson College, PA
Wisconsin Lutheran College, WI
Wright State University, OH
Wright State University–Lake Campus, OH
Youngstown State University, OH

Business
Abilene Christian University, TX
Adelphi University, NY
Alaska Pacific University, AK
Albertus Magnus College, CT
Alfred University, NY
Alliant International University–San Diego, CA
American Jewish University, CA
Anderson University, SC
Angelo State University, TX
Arkansas Tech University, AR
Auburn University, AL
Auburn University at Montgomery, AL
Augsburg University, MN
Augustana College, IL
Augustana University, SD
Aurora University, IL
Austin College, TX
Austin Peay State University, TN
Ave Maria University, FL
Averett University, VA
Babson College, MA
Ball State University, IN
Barton College, NC
Baylor University, TX
Belhaven University, MS
Bellarmine University, KY
Belmont Abbey College, NC
Belmont University, TN
Bemidji State University, MN
Berry College, GA
Bethel College, KS
Binghamton University, State University of New York, NY
Birmingham-Southern College, AL
Black Hills State University, SD
Bloomsburg University of Pennsylvania, PA
Blue Mountain College, MS
Boise State University, ID
Bowie State University, MD
Bowling Green State University, OH
Brenau University, GA
Bryan College, TN
Bucknell University, PA
Buena Vista University, IA
Buffalo State College, State University of New York, NY
Butler University, IN
California Lutheran University, CA
California Polytechnic State University, San Luis Obispo, CA
California State Polytechnic University, Pomona, CA
California State University, Bakersfield, CA
California State University, Chico, CA
California State University, Fresno, CA
California State University, Fullerton, CA
California State University Maritime Academy, CA
California State University, Monterey Bay, CA
California State University, Northridge, CA
California State University, San Bernardino, CA
California State University, Stanislaus, CA
Calvin College, MI

Cameron University, OK
Campbellsville University, KY
Carlow University, PA
Carroll University, WI
Carson-Newman University, TN
Case Western Reserve University, OH
Catawba College, NC
Cedar Crest College, PA
Centenary College of Louisiana, LA
Central College, IA
Central Methodist University, MO
Central Michigan University, MI
Central State University, OH
Champlain College, VT
Christopher Newport University, VA
The Citadel, The Military College of South
    Carolina, SC
Clarion University of Pennsylvania, PA
Clarkson University, NY
Clemson University, SC
Cleveland State University, OH
Coastal Carolina University, SC
The College at Brockport, State University
    of New York, NY
College of Charleston, SC
College of Coastal Georgia, GA
The College of Idaho, ID
The College of New Rochelle, NY
College of Staten Island of the City
    University of New York, NY
Colorado Mesa University, CO
Colorado School of Mines, CO
Columbia College, MO
Columbia College Chicago, IL
Columbus State University, GA
Concordia University Chicago, IL
Concordia University, Nebraska, NE
Concordia University Texas, TX
Concord University, WV
Corban University, OR
Cornerstone University, MI
Creighton University, NE
Dakota State University, SD
Dallas Baptist University, TX
Davidson College, NC
Defiance College, OH
DeSales University, PA
Dordt College, IA
Drury University, MO
East Carolina University, NC
Eastern Illinois University, IL
Eastern Mennonite University, VA
Eastern Michigan University, MI
Eastern Washington University, WA
East Texas Baptist University, TX
Elizabethtown College, PA
Elmhurst College, IL
Elon University, NC
Emmanuel College, GA
Emory University, GA
Emporia State University, KS
Endicott College, MA
Evangel University, MO
Fairmont State University, WV
Felician University, NJ
Ferris State University, MI
Flagler College, FL
Florida Agricultural and Mechanical
    University, FL
Florida Atlantic University, FL
Florida Gulf Coast University, FL
Florida Institute of Technology, FL
Florida International University, FL
Florida Southern College, FL
Fordham University, NY

Fort Hays State University, KS
Fort Lewis College, CO
Francis Marion University, SC
Frostburg State University, MD
Furman University, SC
Gannon University, PA
Gardner-Webb University, NC
George Fox University, OR
Georgia College & State University, GA
Georgian Court University, NJ
Georgia Southern University, GA
Glenville State College, WV
Gonzaga University, WA
Goshen College, IN
Governors State University, IL
Grambling State University, LA
Grand Valley State University, MI
Grove City College, PA
Hamline University, MN
Hampden-Sydney College, VA
Hampton University, VA
Hardin-Simmons University, TX
Harrisburg University of Science and
    Technology, PA
Hawai`i Pacific University, HI
High Point University, NC
Hillsdale College, MI
Hood College, MD
Howard Payne University, TX
Hult International Business School, MA
Huntington University, IN
Idaho State University, ID
Illinois Institute of Technology, IL
Indiana State University, IN
Indiana University of Pennsylvania, PA
Indiana Wesleyan University, IN
Iowa State University of Science and
    Technology, IA
Iowa Wesleyan University, IA
Jacksonville State University, AL
James Madison University, VA
John Carroll University, OH
Johnson University, TN
Juniata College, PA
Kansas Wesleyan University, KS
Kean University, NJ
Kennesaw State University, GA
Kent State University, OH
Kent State University at Geauga, OH
Kent State University at Stark, OH
King's College, PA
Kutztown University of Pennsylvania, PA
Kuyper College, MI
La Sierra University, CA
Lee University, TN
Lehigh University, PA
Lewis-Clark State College, ID
Liberty University, VA
Lindenwood University, MO
Lindsey Wilson College, KY
Linfield College, OR
Lipscomb University, TN
Lock Haven University of Pennsylvania, PA
Longwood University, VA
Loras College, IA
Louisiana College, LA
Louisiana State University and Agricultural
    & Mechanical College, LA
Louisiana Tech University, LA
Loyola Marymount University, CA
Lubbock Christian University, TX
Lycoming College, PA
Lynn University, FL
Lyon College, AR
Malone University, OH

Manhattan College, NY
Marquette University, WI
Marymount University, VA
Maryville University of Saint Louis, MO
Marywood University, PA
Massachusetts College of Liberal Arts, MA
McKendree University, IL
McMurry University, TX
Mercer University, GA
Mercy College, NY
Meredith College, NC
Metropolitan State University of Denver, CO
Michigan State University, MI
Michigan Technological University, MI
Middle Georgia State University, GA
Middle Tennessee State University, TN
Midwestern State University, TX
Millersville University of Pennsylvania, PA
Millikin University, IL
Millsaps College, MS
Milwaukee School of Engineering, WI
Minnesota State University Moorhead, MN
Minot State University, ND
Mississippi State University, MS
Missouri University of Science and
    Technology, MO
Missouri Valley College, MO
Missouri Western State University, MO
Molloy College, NY
Monmouth University, NJ
Montana State University, MT
Montana State University Billings, MT
Montana Tech of The University of
    Montana, MT
Montclair State University, NJ
Moravian College, PA
Morehead State University, KY
Morehouse College, GA
Mount Mary University, WI
Murray State University, KY
Nazareth College of Rochester, NY
Newberry College, SC
New England College, NH
New Jersey Institute of Technology, NJ
New Mexico Highlands University, NM
New Mexico State University, NM
North Carolina Agricultural and Technical
    State University, NC
North Carolina State University, NC
North Central College, IL
Northeastern Illinois University, IL
Northeastern State University, OK
Northern Illinois University, IL
Northern Kentucky University, KY
Northern Michigan University, MI
Northern State University, SD
Northwestern College, IA
Northwest Missouri State University, MO
Northwest Nazarene University, ID
Northwood University, Michigan Campus,
    MI
Oglethorpe University, GA
Ohio Northern University, OH
The Ohio State University, OH
Ohio University, OH
Ohio University–Chillicothe, OH
Ohio University–Eastern, OH
Ohio University–Lancaster, OH
Ohio University–Southern Campus, OH
Ohio University–Zanesville, OH
Ohio Valley University, WV
Ohio Wesleyan University, OH
Oklahoma Baptist University, OK
Oklahoma City University, OK
Oklahoma State University, OK

Old Dominion University, VA
Olivet College, MI
Oral Roberts University, OK
Ouachita Baptist University, AR
Pacific University, OR
Peirce College, PA
Piedmont College, GA
Pittsburg State University, KS
Point Loma Nazarene University, CA
Point Park University, PA
Portland State University, OR
Post University, CT
Providence College, RI
Rochester Institute of Technology, NY
Rockford University, IL
Rockhurst University, MO
Rogers State University, OK
Sacred Heart University, CT
The Sage Colleges, NY
Saginaw Valley State University, MI
St. Andrews University, NC
St. Bonaventure University, NY
St. Catherine University, MN
St. Edward's University, TX
St. John Fisher College, NY
St. John's University, NY
Saint Leo University, FL
Saint Louis University, MO
Saint Martin's University, WA
St. Thomas Aquinas College, NY
Saint Vincent College, PA
Samford University, AL
Sam Houston State University, TX
San Diego State University, CA
San Jose State University, CA
Santa Clara University, CA
Schreiner University, TX
Shenandoah University, VA
Shepherd University, WV
Shippensburg University of Pennsylvania, PA
Siena College, NY
Slippery Rock University of Pennsylvania, PA
Sonoma State University, CA
South Dakota State University, SD
Southeastern Louisiana University, LA
Southeastern Oklahoma State University, OK
Southeast Missouri State University, MO
Southern Adventist University, TN
Southern Arkansas University–Magnolia, AR
Southern Illinois University Carbondale, IL
Southern New Hampshire University, NH
Southern Oregon University, OR
Southwestern College, KS
Southwestern Oklahoma State University, OK
Southwestern University, TX
State University of New York at Fredonia, NY
State University of New York at New Paltz, NY
State University of New York at Oswego, NY
State University of New York at Plattsburgh, NY
State University of New York College at Geneseo, NY
State University of New York College at Potsdam, NY
Stephen F. Austin State University, TX
Stetson University, FL
Stockton University, NJ

Stony Brook University, State University of New York, NY
Suffolk University, MA
Susquehanna University, PA
Tennessee Technological University, TN
Texas A&M International University, TX
Texas A&M University, TX
Texas A&M University–Commerce, TX
Texas A&M University–Texarkana, TX
Texas Christian University, TX
Texas Lutheran University, TX
Texas State University, TX
Texas Tech University, TX
Texas Wesleyan University, TX
Texas Woman's University, TX
Thomas More College, KY
Thomas University, GA
Toccoa Falls College, GA
Towson University, MD
Trevecca Nazarene University, TN
Trinity Christian College, IL
Truett McConnell University, GA
Truman State University, MO
Tuskegee University, AL
Union University, TN
The University of Akron, OH
The University of Alabama, AL
The University of Alabama at Birmingham, AL
The University of Alabama in Huntsville, AL
University of Alaska Anchorage, AK
University of Alaska Fairbanks, AK
University of Arkansas, AR
University of Arkansas at Little Rock, AR
University of Bridgeport, CT
University of California, Davis, CA
University of California, Irvine, CA
University of California, Riverside, CA
University of California, San Diego, CA
University of Central Oklahoma, OK
University of Colorado Boulder, CO
University of Colorado Denver, CO
University of Dallas, TX
University of Dayton, OH
University of Delaware, DE
University of Denver, CO
University of Evansville, IN
University of Florida, FL
University of Georgia, GA
University of Hartford, CT
University of Houston, TX
University of Houston–Clear Lake, TX
University of Houston–Downtown, TX
University of Houston–Victoria, TX
University of Idaho, ID
University of Illinois at Chicago, IL
University of Illinois at Urbana–Champaign, IL
University of Indianapolis, IN
The University of Iowa, IA
The University of Kansas, KS
University of Kentucky, KY
University of Louisiana at Monroe, LA
University of Maine, ME
University of Maine at Fort Kent, ME
University of Mary Hardin-Baylor, TX
University of Maryland, College Park, MD
University of Mary Washington, VA
University of Massachusetts Amherst, MA
University of Massachusetts Dartmouth, MA
University of Massachusetts Lowell, MA
University of Memphis, TN
University of Miami, FL
University of Michigan, MI
University of Michigan–Dearborn, MI

University of Michigan–Flint, MI
University of Minnesota, Twin Cities Campus, MN
University of Mississippi, MS
University of Missouri, MO
University of Missouri–St. Louis, MO
University of Montana, MT
The University of Montana Western, MT
University of Montevallo, AL
University of Nebraska–Lincoln, NE
University of Nevada, Las Vegas, NV
University of Nevada, Reno, NV
University of New Hampshire, NH
University of New Hampshire at Manchester, NH
University of North Carolina at Asheville, NC
The University of North Carolina at Chapel Hill, NC
The University of North Carolina at Charlotte, NC
The University of North Carolina at Greensboro, NC
The University of North Carolina Wilmington, NC
University of North Dakota, ND
University of Northern Colorado, CO
University of Northern Iowa, IA
University of North Florida, FL
University of North Georgia, GA
University of Oklahoma, OK
University of Oregon, OR
University of Pittsburgh at Bradford, PA
University of Pittsburgh at Johnstown, PA
University of Portland, OR
University of Providence, MT
University of Puget Sound, WA
University of Rhode Island, RI
University of St. Thomas, MN
University of St. Thomas, TX
University of Sioux Falls, SD
University of South Carolina, SC
University of South Carolina Aiken, SC
University of South Dakota, SD
University of Southern Indiana, IN
University of South Florida, FL
The University of Tennessee, TN
The University of Tennessee at Chattanooga, TN
The University of Tennessee at Martin, TN
The University of Texas at Dallas, TX
The University of Texas at El Paso, TX
The University of Texas at San Antonio, TX
The University of Texas Rio Grande Valley, TX
University of the Southwest, NM
The University of Toledo, OH
The University of Tulsa, OK
University of Utah, UT
University of Vermont, VT
The University of Virginia's College at Wise, VA
University of Washington, WA
University of Washington, Bothell, WA
University of Washington, Tacoma, WA
University of West Florida, FL
University of West Georgia, GA
University of Wisconsin–Eau Claire, WI
University of Wisconsin–Green Bay, WI
University of Wisconsin–La Crosse, WI
University of Wisconsin–Milwaukee, WI
University of Wisconsin–Parkside, WI
University of Wisconsin–River Falls, WI
University of Wisconsin–Stevens Point, WI
University of Wisconsin–Stout, WI
University of Wisconsin–Superior, WI

University of Wisconsin–Whitewater, WI
University of Wyoming, WY
Upper Iowa University, IA
Utah State University, UT
Valley City State University, ND
Valparaiso University, IN
Virginia Military Institute, VA
Walla Walla University, WA
Walsh College of Accountancy and Business Administration, MI
Wartburg College, IA
Washington & Jefferson College, PA
Washington State University, WA
Washington University in St. Louis, MO
Wayland Baptist University, TX
Wayne State College, NE
Wayne State University, MI
Webber International University, FL
Webster University, MO
Wesleyan College, GA
West Chester University of Pennsylvania, PA
Western Carolina University, NC
Western Illinois University, IL
Western Kentucky University, KY
Western New England University, MA
Western Oregon University, OR
Western Washington University, WA
West Texas A&M University, TX
West Virginia University, WV
Wheaton College, IL
Wichita State University, KS
Widener University, PA
William Jessup University, CA
Williams Baptist College, AR
Wilson College, PA
Wisconsin Lutheran College, WI
Wright State University, OH
Wright State University–Lake Campus, OH
Youngstown State University, OH

Communication

Abilene Christian University, TX
Adelphi University, NY
Alaska Pacific University, AK
Albertus Magnus College, CT
Albion College, MI
Alfred University, NY
Angelo State University, TX
Arkansas Tech University, AR
Auburn University, AL
Augsburg University, MN
Augustana College, IL
Augustana University, SD
Austin College, TX
Austin Peay State University, TN
Ball State University, IN
Barton College, NC
Baylor University, TX
Belhaven University, MS
Bemidji State University, MN
Berry College, GA
Bethel College, KS
Biola University, CA
Birmingham-Southern College, AL
Black Hills State University, SD
Bloomsburg University of Pennsylvania, PA
Boise State University, ID
Bowie State University, MD
Bowling Green State University, OH
Brenau University, GA
Bryan College, TN
Buffalo State College, State University of New York, NY
Butler University, IN
California Lutheran University, CA

California Polytechnic State University, San Luis Obispo, CA
California State Polytechnic University, Pomona, CA
California State University, Bakersfield, CA
California State University, Chico, CA
California State University, Fresno, CA
California State University, Fullerton, CA
California State University, Northridge, CA
California State University, Stanislaus, CA
Calvin College, MI
Cameron University, OK
Campbellsville University, KY
Carlow University, PA
Carroll University, WI
Case Western Reserve University, OH
Cedar Crest College, PA
Centenary College of Louisiana, LA
Central Methodist University, MO
Central Michigan University, MI
Champlain College, VT
Christopher Newport University, VA
City College of the City University of New York, NY
Clarion University of Pennsylvania, PA
Clarkson University, NY
Clemson University, SC
Cleveland State University, OH
Coastal Carolina University, SC
The College at Brockport, State University of New York, NY
College of Charleston, SC
The College of New Rochelle, NY
College of Staten Island of the City University of New York, NY
Colorado Mesa University, CO
Columbia College, MO
Columbia College Chicago, IL
Columbus State University, GA
Concordia University Chicago, IL
Concordia University, Nebraska, NE
Concordia University Texas, TX
Concord University, WV
Corban University, OR
Cornerstone University, MI
Dakota State University, SD
Dallas Baptist University, TX
Defiance College, OH
DeSales University, PA
Dordt College, IA
Drury University, MO
East Carolina University, NC
East Central University, OK
Eastern Illinois University, IL
Eastern Michigan University, MI
Eastern Washington University, WA
East Texas Baptist University, TX
Elizabethtown College, PA
Elmhurst College, IL
Elon University, NC
Emmanuel College, GA
Emory & Henry College, VA
Emporia State University, KS
Evangel University, MO
Ferris State University, MI
Flagler College, FL
Florida Agricultural and Mechanical University, FL
Florida International University, FL
Florida Southern College, FL
Fordham University, NY
Fort Hays State University, KS
Fort Lewis College, CO
Francis Marion University, SC
Franklin Pierce University, NH

Frostburg State University, MD
Furman University, SC
Gardner-Webb University, NC
George Fox University, OR
Georgian Court University, NJ
Georgia Southern University, GA
Goshen College, IN
Governors State University, IL
Grambling State University, LA
Grand Valley State University, MI
Grove City College, PA
Hamline University, MN
Hampton University, VA
Harding University, AR
Hardin-Simmons University, TX
High Point University, NC
Hillsdale College, MI
Hofstra University, NY
Hood College, MD
Howard Payne University, TX
Huntington University, IN
Idaho State University, ID
Illinois Institute of Technology, IL
Indiana State University, IN
Indiana University of Pennsylvania, PA
Indiana Wesleyan University, IN
Iowa State University of Science and Technology, IA
Ithaca College, NY
Jacksonville State University, AL
John Carroll University, OH
Johnson University, TN
Juniata College, PA
Kansas Wesleyan University, KS
Kean University, NJ
Kennesaw State University, GA
Kent State University, OH
Kent State University at Stark, OH
King's College, PA
Kutztown University of Pennsylvania, PA
Kuyper College, MI
Lee University, TN
Lehigh University, PA
Lewis-Clark State College, ID
Liberty University, VA
Lindenwood University, MO
Linfield College, OR
Lipscomb University, TN
Lock Haven University of Pennsylvania, PA
Loras College, IA
Louisiana College, LA
Loyola Marymount University, CA
Lubbock Christian University, TX
Lycoming College, PA
Lynn University, FL
Malone University, OH
Mansfield University of Pennsylvania, PA
Marquette University, WI
Marywood University, PA
Massachusetts College of Liberal Arts, MA
Metropolitan State University of Denver, CO
Michigan State University, MI
Middle Georgia State University, GA
Middle Tennessee State University, TN
Midwestern State University, TX
Millersville University of Pennsylvania, PA
Millikin University, IL
Milwaukee School of Engineering, WI
Minnesota State University Moorhead, MN
Minot State University, ND
Mississippi State University, MS
Missouri University of Science and Technology, MO
Missouri Valley College, MO
Missouri Western State University, MO

Molloy College, NY
Monmouth University, NJ
Montana State University, MT
Montana State University Billings, MT
Montana Tech of The University of
   Montana, MT
Montclair State University, NJ
Moravian College, PA
Morehead State University, KY
Mount Mary University, WI
Murray State University, KY
Nazareth College of Rochester, NY
Newberry College, SC
New England College, NH
New Jersey Institute of Technology, NJ
New Mexico Highlands University, NM
New Mexico State University, NM
North Central College, IL
Northeastern Illinois University, IL
Northeastern State University, OK
Northern Illinois University, IL
Northern Kentucky University, KY
Northern Michigan University, MI
Northern State University, SD
Northwestern College, IA
Northwest Missouri State University, MO
Northwest Nazarene University, ID
Oglethorpe University, GA
Ohio Northern University, OH
The Ohio State University, OH
Ohio University, OH
Ohio University–Chillicothe, OH
Ohio University–Eastern, OH
Ohio University–Lancaster, OH
Ohio University–Southern Campus, OH
Ohio University–Zanesville, OH
Oklahoma City University, OK
Oklahoma State University, OK
Old Dominion University, VA
Olivet College, MI
Oral Roberts University, OK
Ouachita Baptist University, AR
Pacific University, OR
Piedmont College, GA
Pittsburg State University, KS
Point Loma Nazarene University, CA
Point Park University, PA
Post University, CT
Rochester Institute of Technology, NY
Rockhurst University, MO
St. Ambrose University, IA
St. Edward's University, TX
St. John's University, NY
Saint Louis University, MO
St. Thomas Aquinas College, NY
Samford University, AL
Sam Houston State University, TX
San Diego State University, CA
Schreiner University, TX
Shenandoah University, VA
Shepherd University, WV
Shippensburg University of Pennsylvania,
   PA
Siena College, NY
Slippery Rock University of Pennsylvania,
   PA
Sonoma State University, CA
South Dakota State University, SD
Southeastern Louisiana University, LA
Southeastern Oklahoma State University,
   OK
Southeastern University, FL
Southeast Missouri State University, MO
Southern Adventist University, TN
Southern Illinois University Carbondale, IL
Southwestern College, KS

Southwestern Oklahoma State University,
   OK
State University of New York at Fredonia,
   NY
State University of New York at New Paltz,
   NY
State University of New York at Oswego,
   NY
State University of New York at Plattsburgh,
   NY
State University of New York College at
   Geneseo, NY
State University of New York College at
   Potsdam, NY
Stephen F. Austin State University, TX
Stetson University, FL
Stockton University, NJ
Tennessee Technological University, TN
Texas A&M International University, TX
Texas A&M University–Commerce, TX
Texas A&M University–Texarkana, TX
Texas Christian University, TX
Texas Lutheran University, TX
Texas State University, TX
Texas Tech University, TX
Texas Wesleyan University, TX
Texas Woman's University, TX
Thomas More College, KY
Toccoa Falls College, GA
Towson University, MD
Trevecca Nazarene University, TN
Trinity Christian College, IL
Truman State University, MO
Union University, TN
The University of Akron, OH
The University of Alabama, AL
The University of Alabama at Birmingham,
   AL
The University of Alabama in Huntsville,
   AL
University of Alaska Anchorage, AK
University of Arkansas, AR
University of Arkansas at Little Rock, AR
University of Bridgeport, CT
University of California, Davis, CA
University of California, Irvine, CA
University of California, San Diego, CA
University of Central Oklahoma, OK
University of Colorado Boulder, CO
University of Colorado Denver, CO
University of Dayton, OH
University of Delaware, DE
University of Denver, CO
University of Evansville, IN
University of Florida, FL
University of Hartford, CT
University of Houston, TX
University of Houston–Victoria, TX
University of Idaho, ID
University of Illinois at Urbana–Champaign,
   IL
University of Indianapolis, IN
The University of Kansas, KS
University of Kentucky, KY
University of Louisiana at Monroe, LA
University of Maine, ME
University of Maine at Fort Kent, ME
University of Mary Hardin-Baylor, TX
University of Maryland, College Park, MD
University of Massachusetts Amherst, MA
University of Memphis, TN
University of Miami, FL
University of Michigan, MI
University of Michigan–Dearborn, MI
University of Michigan–Flint, MI

University of Minnesota, Twin Cities
   Campus, MN
University of Mississippi, MS
University of Missouri, MO
University of Missouri–St. Louis, MO
University of Montevallo, AL
University of Nebraska at Kearney, NE
University of Nevada, Las Vegas, NV
University of Nevada, Reno, NV
University of New Hampshire at
   Manchester, NH
University of North Carolina at Asheville,
   NC
The University of North Carolina at Chapel
   Hill, NC
The University of North Carolina at
   Greensboro, NC
The University of North Carolina
   Wilmington, NC
University of North Dakota, ND
University of Northern Colorado, CO
University of Northern Iowa, IA
University of Oklahoma, OK
University of Pittsburgh at Bradford, PA
University of Pittsburgh at Johnstown, PA
University of Portland, OR
University of Puget Sound, WA
University of Rhode Island, RI
University of St. Francis, IL
University of St. Thomas, TX
University of Sioux Falls, SD
University of South Carolina, SC
University of South Carolina Aiken, SC
University of South Dakota, SD
University of South Florida, FL
The University of Tennessee, TN
The University of Tennessee at Chattanooga,
   TN
The University of Tennessee at Martin, TN
The University of Texas at El Paso, TX
The University of Texas at San Antonio, TX
The University of Texas at Tyler, TX
The University of Texas Rio Grande Valley,
   TX
The University of Toledo, OH
The University of Tulsa, OK
University of Utah, UT
University of Washington, WA
University of Washington, Bothell, WA
University of Washington, Tacoma, WA
University of West Florida, FL
University of West Georgia, GA
University of Wisconsin–Eau Claire, WI
University of Wisconsin–Green Bay, WI
University of Wisconsin–La Crosse, WI
University of Wisconsin–Parkside, WI
University of Wisconsin–River Falls, WI
University of Wisconsin–Stevens Point, WI
University of Wisconsin–Superior, WI
University of Wisconsin–Whitewater, WI
University of Wyoming, WY
Utah State University, UT
Valdosta State University, GA
Valley City State University, ND
Walla Walla University, WA
Wartburg College, IA
Washington State University, WA
Washington University in St. Louis, MO
Wayland Baptist University, TX
Waynesburg University, PA
Wayne State College, NE
Wayne State University, MI
Webster University, MO
Wesleyan College, GA
Western Carolina University, NC
Western Illinois University, IL

Western Kentucky University, KY
Western Oregon University, OR
Western Washington University, WA
West Texas A&M University, TX
West Virginia University, WV
Wheaton College, IL
Wichita State University, KS
Widener University, PA
Wilson College, PA
Wisconsin Lutheran College, WI
Wright State University, OH
Wright State University–Lake Campus, OH
Youngstown State University, OH

Computer Science

Adelphi University, NY
Albany State University, GA
Albertus Magnus College, CT
Angelo State University, TX
Arkansas Tech University, AR
Auburn University, AL
Augsburg University, MN
Augustana College, IL
Augustana University, SD
Austin College, TX
Austin Peay State University, TN
Baylor University, TX
Bemidji State University, MN
Binghamton University, State University of New York, NY
Birmingham-Southern College, AL
Black Hills State University, SD
Bloomsburg University of Pennsylvania, PA
Boise State University, ID
Bowie State University, MD
Bowling Green State University, OH
Bryan College, TN
Buena Vista University, IA
Buffalo State College, State University of New York, NY
Butler University, IN
California Lutheran University, CA
California Polytechnic State University, San Luis Obispo, CA
California State Polytechnic University, Pomona, CA
California State University, Chico, CA
California State University, Fullerton, CA
California State University, Northridge, CA
California State University, San Bernardino, CA
California State University, Stanislaus, CA
Calvin College, MI
Cameron University, OK
Campbellsville University, KY
Carlow University, PA
Carroll University, WI
Case Western Reserve University, OH
Central College, IA
Central Methodist University, MO
Central Michigan University, MI
Central State University, OH
Champlain College, VT
Christian Brothers University, TN
Christopher Newport University, VA
City College of the City University of New York, NY
Clarion University of Pennsylvania, PA
Clarkson University, NY
Clemson University, SC
Cleveland State University, OH
Coastal Carolina University, SC
The College at Brockport, State University of New York, NY
College of Charleston, SC

College of Saint Benedict, MN
College of Staten Island of the City University of New York, NY
Colorado Mesa University, CO
Colorado School of Mines, CO
Columbia College, MO
Columbus State University, GA
Concordia University Chicago, IL
Concordia University, Nebraska, NE
Concordia University Texas, TX
Dakota State University, SD
Dallas Baptist University, TX
DeSales University, PA
DigiPen Institute of Technology, WA
Dordt College, IA
Drury University, MO
East Carolina University, NC
Eastern Illinois University, IL
Eastern Michigan University, MI
Eastern Washington University, WA
Elizabethtown College, PA
Elmhurst College, IL
Elon University, NC
Emporia State University, KS
Evangel University, MO
Fairmont State University, WV
Ferris State University, MI
Florida Agricultural and Mechanical University, FL
Florida International University, FL
Fort Hays State University, KS
Francis Marion University, SC
Frostburg State University, MD
Furman University, SC
Gardner-Webb University, NC
George Fox University, OR
Georgia Institute of Technology, GA
Georgian Court University, NJ
Georgia Southern University, GA
Graceland University, IA
Grambling State University, LA
Grand Valley State University, MI
Hampton University, VA
Harding University, AR
Hardin-Simmons University, TX
Harrisburg University of Science and Technology, PA
Hood College, MD
Huntingdon College, AL
Idaho State University, ID
Illinois Institute of Technology, IL
Indiana State University, IN
Indiana Tech, IN
Indiana University of Pennsylvania, PA
Indiana Wesleyan University, IN
Iowa State University of Science and Technology, IA
Jacksonville State University, AL
James Madison University, VA
John Carroll University, OH
Johnson C. Smith University, NC
Juniata College, PA
Kansas Wesleyan University, KS
Kean University, NJ
Kennesaw State University, GA
Kent State University, OH
Kenyon College, OH
King's College, PA
Kutztown University of Pennsylvania, PA
Liberty University, VA
Lindenwood University, MO
Linfield College, OR
Lock Haven University of Pennsylvania, PA
Longwood University, VA
Loras College, IA

Louisiana State University and Agricultural & Mechanical College, LA
Louisiana Tech University, LA
Loyola Marymount University, CA
Lubbock Christian University, TX
Lycoming College, PA
Manhattan College, NY
Marymount University, VA
Marywood University, PA
Massachusetts College of Liberal Arts, MA
McMurry University, TX
Meredith College, NC
Metropolitan State University of Denver, CO
Michigan State University, MI
Middle Tennessee State University, TN
Midwestern State University, TX
Millersville University of Pennsylvania, PA
Mills College, CA
Milwaukee School of Engineering, WI
Minnesota State University Moorhead, MN
Minot State University, ND
Mississippi State University, MS
Missouri University of Science and Technology, MO
Missouri Valley College, MO
Missouri Western State University, MO
Monmouth University, NJ
Montana State University, MT
Montana State University Billings, MT
Montana Tech of The University of Montana, MT
Montreat College, NC
Moravian College, PA
Morehouse College, GA
Murray State University, KY
Muskingum University, OH
New England College, NH
New Jersey Institute of Technology, NJ
New Mexico Highlands University, NM
New Mexico State University, NM
North Carolina State University, NC
North Central College, IL
Northeastern Illinois University, IL
Northeastern State University, OK
Northern Illinois University, IL
Northern Kentucky University, KY
Northern Michigan University, MI
Northern State University, SD
Northwestern College, IA
Northwest Missouri State University, MO
Northwest Nazarene University, ID
Ohio Northern University, OH
The Ohio State University, OH
Ohio University, OH
Ohio University–Chillicothe, OH
Ohio University–Eastern, OH
Ohio University–Lancaster, OH
Ohio University–Southern Campus, OH
Ohio University–Zanesville, OH
Ohio Valley University, WV
Oklahoma Baptist University, OK
Oklahoma State University, OK
Old Dominion University, VA
Ouachita Baptist University, AR
Peirce College, PA
Pittsburg State University, KS
Plymouth State University, NH
Point Loma Nazarene University, CA
Point Park University, PA
Portland State University, OR
Post University, CT
Purdue University, IN
Rochester Institute of Technology, NY
Rockford University, IL
Rockhurst University, MO

Rollins College, FL
Sacred Heart University, CT
Saginaw Valley State University, MI
St. Edward's University, TX
St. John's University, NY
Saint Joseph's University, PA
Saint Louis University, MO
St. Thomas Aquinas College, NY
Samford University, AL
Sam Houston State University, TX
San Diego State University, CA
Shenandoah University, VA
Shepherd University, WV
Shippensburg University of Pennsylvania, PA
Siena College, NY
Skidmore College, NY
Slippery Rock University of Pennsylvania, PA
Sonoma State University, CA
South Dakota State University, SD
Southeastern Louisiana University, LA
Southeastern Oklahoma State University, OK
Southeast Missouri State University, MO
Southern Adventist University, TN
Southern Arkansas University–Magnolia, AR
Southern Illinois University Carbondale, IL
Southern New Hampshire University, NH
Southwestern College, KS
Southwestern Oklahoma State University, OK
State University of New York at Fredonia, NY
State University of New York at Oswego, NY
State University of New York at Plattsburgh, NY
State University of New York College at Potsdam, NY
Stephen F. Austin State University, TX
Stetson University, FL
Stockton University, NJ
Stony Brook University, State University of New York, NY
Tennessee Technological University, TN
Texas A&M University, TX
Texas A&M University–Commerce, TX
Texas A&M University–Texarkana, TX
Texas Lutheran University, TX
Texas State University, TX
Texas Tech University, TX
Texas Woman's University, TX
Thomas More College, KY
Towson University, MD
Trinity Christian College, IL
Truman State University, MO
Tuskegee University, AL
Union University, TN
The University of Akron, OH
The University of Alabama, AL
The University of Alabama at Birmingham, AL
The University of Alabama in Huntsville, AL
University of Alaska Anchorage, AK
University of Alaska Fairbanks, AK
University of Arkansas, AR
University of Arkansas at Little Rock, AR
University of Bridgeport, CT
University of California, Davis, CA
University of California, Irvine, CA
University of California, San Diego, CA
University of California, Santa Cruz, CA
University of Central Oklahoma, OK

University of Colorado Boulder, CO
University of Dallas, TX
University of Dayton, OH
University of Delaware, DE
University of Denver, CO
University of Evansville, IN
University of Florida, FL
University of Hartford, CT
University of Houston, TX
University of Houston–Clear Lake, TX
University of Houston–Victoria, TX
University of Idaho, ID
University of Illinois at Urbana–Champaign, IL
The University of Kansas, KS
University of Kentucky, KY
University of Louisiana at Monroe, LA
University of Maine, ME
University of Maine at Fort Kent, ME
University of Mary Hardin-Baylor, TX
University of Maryland, Baltimore County, MD
University of Maryland, College Park, MD
University of Mary Washington, VA
University of Massachusetts Amherst, MA
University of Massachusetts Dartmouth, MA
University of Massachusetts Lowell, MA
University of Memphis, TN
University of Miami, FL
University of Michigan, MI
University of Michigan–Dearborn, MI
University of Michigan–Flint, MI
University of Minnesota, Twin Cities Campus, MN
University of Mississippi, MS
University of Missouri, MO
University of Missouri–St. Louis, MO
University of Montana, MT
University of Nebraska–Lincoln, NE
University of Nevada, Las Vegas, NV
University of Nevada, Reno, NV
University of New Hampshire, NH
University of New Hampshire at Manchester, NH
University of North Carolina at Asheville, NC
The University of North Carolina at Charlotte, NC
The University of North Carolina at Greensboro, NC
The University of North Carolina Wilmington, NC
University of North Dakota, ND
University of Northern Iowa, IA
University of North Florida, FL
University of Oklahoma, OK
University of Pittsburgh at Bradford, PA
University of Pittsburgh at Johnstown, PA
University of Portland, OR
University of Providence, MT
University of Puget Sound, WA
University of Rhode Island, RI
University of Richmond, VA
University of St. Thomas, TX
University of Sioux Falls, SD
University of South Carolina, SC
University of South Carolina Aiken, SC
University of South Dakota, SD
University of South Florida, FL
The University of Tennessee, TN
The University of Tennessee at Martin, TN
The University of Texas at Dallas, TX
The University of Texas at El Paso, TX
The University of Texas at San Antonio, TX
The University of Texas Rio Grande Valley, TX

The University of Toledo, OH
The University of Tulsa, OK
University of Utah, UT
University of Vermont, VT
The University of Virginia's College at Wise, VA
University of Washington, WA
University of Washington, Bothell, WA
University of Washington, Tacoma, WA
University of West Florida, FL
University of West Georgia, GA
University of Wisconsin–Eau Claire, WI
University of Wisconsin–La Crosse, WI
University of Wisconsin–Parkside, WI
University of Wisconsin–River Falls, WI
University of Wisconsin–Stevens Point, WI
University of Wisconsin–Stout, WI
University of Wisconsin–Superior, WI
University of Wisconsin–Whitewater, WI
University of Wyoming, WY
Upper Iowa University, IA
Utah State University, UT
Valley City State University, ND
Vaughn College of Aeronautics and Technology, NY
Virginia Military Institute, VA
Virginia State University, VA
Walsh College of Accountancy and Business Administration, MI
Wartburg College, IA
Washington State University, WA
Washington University in St. Louis, MO
Wayne State College, NE
Wayne State University, MI
Webster University, MO
Western Illinois University, IL
Western New England University, MA
Western Oregon University, OR
Western Washington University, WA
West Texas A&M University, TX
West Virginia University, WV
Wichita State University, KS
Widener University, PA
William Jessup University, CA
Wilson College, PA
Wright State University, OH
Wright State University–Lake Campus, OH
Youngstown State University, OH

Education
Abilene Christian University, TX
Alaska Pacific University, AK
Albany State University, GA
Albertus Magnus College, CT
Alfred University, NY
Alliant International University–San Diego, CA
Alverno College, WI
Anderson University, SC
Angelo State University, TX
Appalachian Bible College, WV
Arkansas Tech University, AR
Auburn University, AL
Auburn University at Montgomery, AL
Augsburg University, MN
Augustana College, IL
Augustana University, SD
Aurora University, IL
Austin College, TX
Austin Peay State University, TN
Averett University, VA
Ball State University, IN
The Baptist College of Florida, FL
Barton College, NC
Baylor University, TX
Belhaven University, MS

Bellarmine University, KY
Belmont Abbey College, NC
Bemidji State University, MN
Berklee College of Music, MA
Berry College, GA
Binghamton University, State University of New York, NY
Birmingham-Southern College, AL
Black Hills State University, SD
Bloomsburg University of Pennsylvania, PA
Blue Mountain College, MS
Boise State University, ID
Bowling Green State University, OH
Brenau University, GA
Bryan College, TN
Buena Vista University, IA
Buffalo State College, State University of New York, NY
Butler University, IN
California Lutheran University, CA
California Polytechnic State University, San Luis Obispo, CA
California State Polytechnic University, Pomona, CA
California State University, Bakersfield, CA
California State University, Chico, CA
California State University, Fresno, CA
California State University, Fullerton, CA
California State University, Northridge, CA
California State University, San Bernardino, CA
California State University, Stanislaus, CA
Calvin College, MI
Cameron University, OK
Campbellsville University, KY
Carlow University, PA
Carroll University, WI
Carson-Newman University, TN
Catawba College, NC
Cedar Crest College, PA
Centenary College of Louisiana, LA
Central College, IA
Central Methodist University, MO
Central Michigan University, MI
Central State University, OH
Champlain College, VT
Charlotte Christian College and Theological Seminary, NC
Christopher Newport University, VA
City College of the City University of New York, NY
Clarion University of Pennsylvania, PA
Clemson University, SC
Cleveland State University, OH
Coastal Carolina University, SC
The College at Brockport, State University of New York, NY
College of Charleston, SC
College of Coastal Georgia, GA
The College of Idaho, ID
The College of New Rochelle, NY
College of Saint Mary, NE
College of Staten Island of the City University of New York, NY
Colorado Mesa University, CO
Columbia College, MO
Columbia College Chicago, IL
Columbus State University, GA
Concordia University Chicago, IL
Concordia University, Nebraska, NE
Concordia University Texas, TX
Concord University, WV
Corban University, OR
Cornerstone University, MI
Creighton University, NE

Daemen College, NY
Dakota State University, SD
Dallas Baptist University, TX
Davidson College, NC
Defiance College, OH
DeSales University, PA
Dominican College, NY
Dordt College, IA
Drury University, MO
Duquesne University, PA
East Carolina University, NC
Eastern Illinois University, IL
Eastern Mennonite University, VA
Eastern Michigan University, MI
Eastern Washington University, WA
East Texas Baptist University, TX
Elizabethtown College, PA
Elmhurst College, IL
Elon University, NC
Emmanuel College, GA
Emporia State University, KS
Endicott College, MA
Evangel University, MO
Fairmont State University, WV
Felician University, NJ
Ferris State University, MI
Flagler College, FL
Florida Agricultural and Mechanical University, FL
Florida Gulf Coast University, FL
Florida International University, FL
Florida Southern College, FL
Fort Hays State University, KS
Fort Lewis College, CO
Framingham State University, MA
Francis Marion University, SC
Frostburg State University, MD
Furman University, SC
Gannon University, PA
Gardner-Webb University, NC
George Fox University, OR
Georgia College & State University, GA
Georgian Court University, NJ
Georgia Southern University, GA
Glenville State College, WV
Goshen College, IN
Governors State University, IL
Grambling State University, LA
Grand Valley State University, MI
Grove City College, PA
Hamline University, MN
Hampden-Sydney College, VA
Hampton University, VA
Hardin-Simmons University, TX
Hawai`i Pacific University, HI
Henderson State University, AR
High Point University, NC
Hillsdale College, MI
Hood College, MD
Howard Payne University, TX
Idaho State University, ID
Indiana State University, IN
Indiana Tech, IN
Indiana University of Pennsylvania, PA
Indiana Wesleyan University, IN
Iowa State University of Science and Technology, IA
Iowa Wesleyan University, IA
Jacksonville State University, AL
James Madison University, VA
John Carroll University, OH
Johnson University, TN
Johnson University Florida, FL
Juniata College, PA
Kansas Wesleyan University, KS

Kean University, NJ
Kennesaw State University, GA
Kent State University, OH
Kent State University at Geauga, OH
Kent State University at Stark, OH
Keuka College, NY
King's College, PA
Kutztown University of Pennsylvania, PA
LaGrange College, GA
La Sierra University, CA
Lee University, TN
Lewis-Clark State College, ID
Liberty University, VA
Lindenwood University, MO
Lindsey Wilson College, KY
Linfield College, OR
Lipscomb University, TN
Lock Haven University of Pennsylvania, PA
Longwood University, VA
Loras College, IA
Louisiana State University and Agricultural & Mechanical College, LA
Louisiana Tech University, LA
Loyola Marymount University, CA
Lubbock Christian University, TX
Lycoming College, PA
Malone University, OH
Mansfield University of Pennsylvania, PA
Marquette University, WI
Maryville University of Saint Louis, MO
Marywood University, PA
Massachusetts College of Liberal Arts, MA
McMurry University, TX
Mercer University, GA
Meredith College, NC
Methodist University, NC
Metropolitan State University of Denver, CO
Miami University, OH
Michigan State University, MI
Middle Georgia State University, GA
Middle Tennessee State University, TN
Midwestern State University, TX
Millersville University of Pennsylvania, PA
Millikin University, IL
Minnesota State University Moorhead, MN
Minot State University, ND
Mississippi State University, MS
Missouri University of Science and Technology, MO
Missouri Valley College, MO
Missouri Western State University, MO
Molloy College, NY
Monmouth University, NJ
Montana State University, MT
Montana State University Billings, MT
Montclair State University, NJ
Moravian College, PA
Morehead State University, KY
Mount Mary University, WI
Murray State University, KY
Nazareth College of Rochester, NY
Newberry College, SC
New England College, NH
New Jersey Institute of Technology, NJ
New Mexico Highlands University, NM
New Mexico State University, NM
North Carolina State University, NC
North Central College, IL
Northeastern Illinois University, IL
Northeastern State University, OK
Northern Illinois University, IL
Northern Kentucky University, KY
Northern Michigan University, MI
Northern State University, SD
Northwestern College, IA

Northwest Missouri State University, MO
Northwest Nazarene University, ID
Ohio Northern University, OH
The Ohio State University, OH
Ohio University, OH
Ohio University–Chillicothe, OH
Ohio University–Eastern, OH
Ohio University–Lancaster, OH
Ohio University–Southern Campus, OH
Ohio University–Zanesville, OH
Ohio Valley University, WV
Ohio Wesleyan University, OH
Oklahoma Baptist University, OK
Oklahoma City University, OK
Oklahoma State University, OK
Old Dominion University, VA
Olivet College, MI
Oral Roberts University, OK
Ouachita Baptist University, AR
Ozark Christian College, MO
Pacific University, OR
Piedmont College, GA
Pittsburg State University, KS
Point Loma Nazarene University, CA
Point Park University, PA
Portland State University, OR
Post University, CT
Purdue University, IN
Randolph College, VA
Rockford University, IL
Rockhurst University, MO
Sacred Heart University, CT
The Sage Colleges, NY
Saginaw Valley State University, MI
St. Bonaventure University, NY
St. Catherine University, MN
St. Edward's University, TX
Saint Louis University, MO
Saint Martin's University, WA
St. Mary's College of Maryland, MD
St. Thomas Aquinas College, NY
Samford University, AL
Sam Houston State University, TX
San Diego State University, CA
San Jose State University, CA
Schreiner University, TX
Shenandoah University, VA
Shepherd University, WV
Shippensburg University of Pennsylvania, PA
Siena College, NY
Slippery Rock University of Pennsylvania, PA
Sonoma State University, CA
South Dakota State University, SD
Southeastern Louisiana University, LA
Southeastern Oklahoma State University, OK
Southeastern University, FL
Southeast Missouri State University, MO
Southern Adventist University, TN
Southern Arkansas University–Magnolia, AR
Southern Illinois University Carbondale, IL
Southern New Hampshire University, NH
Southern Oregon University, OR
Southwestern College, KS
Southwestern Oklahoma State University, OK
State University of New York at Fredonia, NY
State University of New York at New Paltz, NY
State University of New York at Oswego, NY

State University of New York at Plattsburgh, NY
State University of New York College at Cortland, NY
State University of New York College at Geneseo, NY
State University of New York College at Potsdam, NY
Stephen F. Austin State University, TX
Stetson University, FL
Stockton University, NJ
Susquehanna University, PA
Tennessee Technological University, TN
Texas A&M International University, TX
Texas A&M University, TX
Texas A&M University–Commerce, TX
Texas A&M University–Texarkana, TX
Texas Christian University, TX
Texas Lutheran University, TX
Texas State University, TX
Texas Tech University, TX
Texas Wesleyan University, TX
Texas Woman's University, TX
Thomas More College, KY
Thomas University, GA
Toccoa Falls College, GA
Towson University, MD
Trevecca Nazarene University, TN
Trine University, IN
Trinity Christian College, IL
Truett McConnell University, GA
Truman State University, MO
Union University, TN
The University of Akron, OH
The University of Alabama, AL
The University of Alabama in Huntsville, AL
University of Alaska Anchorage, AK
University of Alaska Fairbanks, AK
University of Arkansas, AR
University of Arkansas at Little Rock, AR
University of California, Irvine, CA
University of California, Riverside, CA
University of Central Oklahoma, OK
University of Colorado Boulder, CO
University of Colorado Denver, CO
University of Dallas, TX
University of Dayton, OH
University of Delaware, DE
University of Evansville, IN
University of Florida, FL
University of Georgia, GA
University of Hartford, CT
University of Houston, TX
University of Houston–Clear Lake, TX
University of Houston–Victoria, TX
University of Idaho, ID
University of Illinois at Urbana–Champaign, IL
The University of Kansas, KS
University of Kentucky, KY
University of Louisiana at Monroe, LA
University of Maine, ME
University of Maine at Fort Kent, ME
University of Mary Hardin-Baylor, TX
University of Maryland, Baltimore County, MD
University of Maryland, College Park, MD
University of Mary Washington, VA
University of Massachusetts Amherst, MA
University of Massachusetts Dartmouth, MA
University of Massachusetts Lowell, MA
University of Memphis, TN
University of Miami, FL
University of Michigan, MI
University of Michigan–Dearborn, MI

University of Michigan–Flint, MI
University of Minnesota, Twin Cities Campus, MN
University of Mississippi, MS
University of Missouri, MO
University of Missouri–St. Louis, MO
University of Montana, MT
The University of Montana Western, MT
University of Montevallo, AL
University of Nebraska–Lincoln, NE
University of Nevada, Las Vegas, NV
University of Nevada, Reno, NV
University of New Hampshire, NH
University of North Carolina at Asheville, NC
The University of North Carolina at Chapel Hill, NC
The University of North Carolina at Charlotte, NC
The University of North Carolina at Greensboro, NC
The University of North Carolina at Pembroke, NC
The University of North Carolina Wilmington, NC
University of North Dakota, ND
University of Northern Colorado, CO
University of Northern Iowa, IA
University of North Florida, FL
University of North Georgia, GA
University of Oklahoma, OK
University of Oregon, OR
University of Pittsburgh at Bradford, PA
University of Pittsburgh at Johnstown, PA
University of Portland, OR
University of Providence, MT
University of Rhode Island, RI
University of St. Francis, IL
University of St. Thomas, MN
University of St. Thomas, TX
University of Sioux Falls, SD
University of South Carolina, SC
University of South Carolina Aiken, SC
University of South Dakota, SD
University of Southern Indiana, IN
University of South Florida, FL
The University of Tennessee, TN
The University of Tennessee at Chattanooga, TN
The University of Tennessee at Martin, TN
The University of Texas at El Paso, TX
The University of Texas at San Antonio, TX
The University of Texas Rio Grande Valley, TX
University of the Southwest, NM
The University of Toledo, OH
The University of Tulsa, OK
University of Utah, UT
University of Vermont, VT
The University of Virginia's College at Wise, VA
University of Washington, WA
University of Washington, Bothell, WA
University of Washington, Tacoma, WA
University of West Florida, FL
University of West Georgia, GA
University of Wisconsin–Eau Claire, WI
University of Wisconsin–Green Bay, WI
University of Wisconsin–La Crosse, WI
University of Wisconsin–Milwaukee, WI
University of Wisconsin–Parkside, WI
University of Wisconsin–River Falls, WI
University of Wisconsin–Stevens Point, WI
University of Wisconsin–Stout, WI
University of Wisconsin–Superior, WI
University of Wisconsin–Whitewater, WI

University of Wyoming, WY
Upper Iowa University, IA
Utah State University, UT
Valdosta State University, GA
Valley City State University, ND
VanderCook College of Music, IL
Vaughn College of Aeronautics and
  Technology, NY
Walla Walla University, WA
Wartburg College, IA
Washington State University, WA
Washington University in St. Louis, MO
Wayland Baptist University, TX
Wayne State College, NE
Wayne State University, MI
Webster University, MO
Wesleyan College, GA
Western Carolina University, NC
Western Illinois University, IL
Western Kentucky University, KY
Western Oregon University, OR
Western Washington University, WA
West Texas A&M University, TX
West Virginia University, WV
Wheaton College, IL
Wichita State University, KS
Widener University, PA
William Jessup University, CA
Williams Baptist College, AR
Wilson College, PA
Wisconsin Lutheran College, WI
Wright State University, OH
Wright State University–Lake Campus, OH
Youngstown State University, OH

Engineering/Technologies

Abilene Christian University, TX
Alfred University, NY
Arkansas Tech University, AR
Auburn University, AL
Austin College, TX
Averett University, VA
Ball State University, IN
Baylor University, TX
Bemidji State University, MN
Berklee College of Music, MA
Binghamton University, State University of
  New York, NY
Birmingham-Southern College, AL
Bluefield State College, WV
Boise State University, ID
Boston University, MA
Bowie State University, MD
Bowling Green State University, OH
Bucknell University, PA
Buffalo State College, State University of
  New York, NY
Butler University, IN
California Baptist University, CA
California Polytechnic State University, San
  Luis Obispo, CA
California State Polytechnic University,
  Pomona, CA
California State University, Chico, CA
California State University, Fresno, CA
California State University, Fullerton, CA
California State University Maritime
  Academy, CA
California State University, Northridge, CA
Calvin College, MI
Cameron University, OK
Carroll University, WI
Case Western Reserve University, OH
Centenary College of Louisiana, LA
Central College, IA

Central Michigan University, MI
Central State University, OH
Christian Brothers University, TN
Christopher Newport University, VA
The Citadel, The Military College of South
  Carolina, SC
City College of the City University of New
  York, NY
Clarkson University, NY
Clemson University, SC
Cleveland State University, OH
College of Charleston, SC
College of Saint Benedict, MN
College of Staten Island of the City
  University of New York, NY
Colorado Mesa University, CO
Colorado School of Mines, CO
Cooper Union for the Advancement of
  Science and Art, NY
DigiPen Institute of Technology, WA
Dordt College, IA
East Carolina University, NC
Eastern Illinois University, IL
Eastern Mennonite University, VA
Eastern Michigan University, MI
Eastern University, PA
Eastern Washington University, WA
Elizabethtown College, PA
Elon University, NC
Emporia State University, KS
Evangel University, MO
Fairmont State University, WV
Ferris State University, MI
Florida Agricultural and Mechanical
  University, FL
Florida Atlantic University, FL
Florida Gulf Coast University, FL
Florida International University, FL
Fort Hays State University, KS
Framingham State University, MA
Francis Marion University, SC
Frostburg State University, MD
Furman University, SC
Gannon University, PA
George Fox University, OR
Georgia Institute of Technology, GA
Georgia Southern University, GA
Gonzaga University, WA
Graceland University, IA
Grambling State University, LA
Grand Valley State University, MI
Greenville University, IL
Grove City College, PA
Hampton University, VA
Harding University, AR
Hillsdale College, MI
Hofstra University, NY
Idaho State University, ID
Illinois Institute of Technology, IL
Indiana State University, IN
Indiana Tech, IN
Indiana University of Pennsylvania, PA
Iowa State University of Science and
  Technology, IA
James Madison University, VA
Johnson C. Smith University, NC
Kean University, NJ
Kennesaw State University, GA
Kent State University, OH
King's College, PA
Lehigh University, PA
Lewis-Clark State College, ID
Liberty University, VA
Lindenwood University, MO
Lipscomb University, TN

Loras College, IA
Louisiana State University and Agricultural
  & Mechanical College, LA
Louisiana Tech University, LA
Loyola Marymount University, CA
Lycoming College, PA
Manhattan College, NY
Marquette University, WI
Mercer University, GA
Metropolitan State University of Denver, CO
Miami University, OH
Michigan State University, MI
Middle Georgia State University, GA
Middle Tennessee State University, TN
Midwestern State University, TX
Milligan College, TN
Milwaukee School of Engineering, WI
Minnesota State University Moorhead, MN
Mississippi State University, MS
Missouri University of Science and
  Technology, MO
Missouri Western State University, MO
Montana State University, MT
Montana State University Billings, MT
Montana Tech of The University of
  Montana, MT
Moravian College, PA
Morehead State University, KY
Morehouse College, GA
Murray State University, KY
Muskingum University, OH
New Jersey Institute of Technology, NJ
New Mexico Highlands University, NM
New Mexico State University, NM
North Carolina Agricultural and Technical
  State University, NC
North Carolina State University, NC
Northern Illinois University, IL
Northern Kentucky University, KY
Northern Michigan University, MI
Northwest Nazarene University, ID
Ohio Northern University, OH
The Ohio State University, OH
Ohio University, OH
Ohio University–Chillicothe, OH
Ohio University–Eastern, OH
Ohio University–Lancaster, OH
Ohio University–Southern Campus, OH
Ohio University–Zanesville, OH
Oklahoma Christian University, OK
Oklahoma State University, OK
Old Dominion University, VA
Oral Roberts University, OK
Ouachita Baptist University, AR
Pittsburg State University, KS
Plymouth State University, NH
Point Loma Nazarene University, CA
Point Park University, PA
Portland State University, OR
Purdue University, IN
Rice University, TX
Rochester Institute of Technology, NY
Rockhurst University, MO
Rollins College, FL
Saginaw Valley State University, MI
St. Ambrose University, IA
Saint Louis University, MO
Saint Martin's University, WA
St. Thomas Aquinas College, NY
Sam Houston State University, TX
San Diego State University, CA
San Jose State University, CA
Santa Clara University, CA
Seattle Pacific University, WA
Shepherd University, WV

Slippery Rock University of Pennsylvania, PA
Sonoma State University, CA
South Dakota State University, SD
Southeastern Oklahoma State University, OK
Southeast Missouri State University, MO
Southern Illinois University Carbondale, IL
Southwestern Oklahoma State University, OK
State University of New York at New Paltz, NY
State University of New York at Plattsburgh, NY
State University of New York College at Potsdam, NY
State University of New York College of Environmental Science and Forestry, NY
Stony Brook University, State University of New York, NY
Suffolk University, MA
Tennessee Technological University, TN
Texas A&M International University, TX
Texas A&M University, TX
Texas A&M University–Commerce, TX
Texas A&M University–Texarkana, TX
Texas Christian University, TX
Texas State University, TX
Texas Tech University, TX
Trinity Christian College, IL
Tuskegee University, AL
Union University, TN
The University of Akron, OH
The University of Alabama, AL
The University of Alabama at Birmingham, AL
The University of Alabama in Huntsville, AL
University of Alaska Anchorage, AK
University of Alaska Fairbanks, AK
University of Arkansas, AR
University of Arkansas at Little Rock, AR
University of Bridgeport, CT
University of California, Davis, CA
University of California, Irvine, CA
University of California, Riverside, CA
University of California, San Diego, CA
University of Colorado Boulder, CO
University of Colorado Denver, CO
University of Dayton, OH
University of Delaware, DE
University of Denver, CO
University of Evansville, IN
University of Florida, FL
University of Hartford, CT
University of Houston, TX
University of Idaho, ID
University of Illinois at Urbana–Champaign, IL
The University of Iowa, IA
The University of Kansas, KS
University of Kentucky, KY
University of Maine, ME
University of Maryland, Baltimore County, MD
University of Maryland, College Park, MD
University of Massachusetts Amherst, MA
University of Massachusetts Dartmouth, MA
University of Massachusetts Lowell, MA
University of Memphis, TN
University of Miami, FL
University of Michigan, MI
University of Michigan–Dearborn, MI
University of Michigan–Flint, MI
University of Minnesota, Twin Cities Campus, MN

University of Mississippi, MS
University of Missouri, MO
University of Missouri–St. Louis, MO
University of Nebraska–Lincoln, NE
University of Nevada, Las Vegas, NV
University of Nevada, Reno, NV
University of New Hampshire, NH
University of New Hampshire at Manchester, NH
University of North Carolina at Asheville, NC
The University of North Carolina at Charlotte, NC
The University of North Carolina Wilmington, NC
University of North Dakota, ND
University of North Florida, FL
University of Oklahoma, OK
University of Pittsburgh at Bradford, PA
University of Pittsburgh at Johnstown, PA
University of Portland, OR
University of Rhode Island, RI
University of Rochester, NY
University of Sioux Falls, SD
University of South Carolina, SC
University of South Carolina Aiken, SC
University of Southern Indiana, IN
University of South Florida, FL
The University of Tennessee, TN
The University of Tennessee at Chattanooga, TN
The University of Tennessee at Martin, TN
The University of Texas at Dallas, TX
The University of Texas at El Paso, TX
The University of Texas at San Antonio, TX
The University of Texas at Tyler, TX
The University of Texas Rio Grande Valley, TX
The University of Toledo, OH
The University of Tulsa, OK
University of Utah, UT
University of Vermont, VT
University of Washington, WA
University of Washington, Bothell, WA
University of Washington, Tacoma, WA
University of West Florida, FL
University of Wisconsin–Green Bay, WI
University of Wisconsin–Parkside, WI
University of Wisconsin–Stevens Point, WI
University of Wisconsin–Stout, WI
University of Wyoming, WY
Utah State University, UT
Valley City State University, ND
Valparaiso University, IN
Vaughn College of Aeronautics and Technology, NY
Virginia Military Institute, VA
Virginia State University, VA
Walla Walla University, WA
Wartburg College, IA
Washington State University, WA
Washington University in St. Louis, MO
Wayne State University, MI
Webb Institute, NY
Wesleyan College, GA
Western Illinois University, IL
Western Kentucky University, KY
Western Washington University, WA
West Texas A&M University, TX
West Virginia University, WV
Wheaton College, IL
Wichita State University, KS
Widener University, PA
Wright State University, OH
Wright State University–Lake Campus, OH
York College of Pennsylvania, PA

Youngstown State University, OH

English
Abilene Christian University, TX
Alaska Pacific University, AK
Albertus Magnus College, CT
Alfred University, NY
Alliant International University–San Diego, CA
Angelo State University, TX
Arkansas Tech University, AR
Auburn University, AL
Augsburg University, MN
Augustana College, IL
Augustana University, SD
Austin College, TX
Austin Peay State University, TN
Averett University, VA
Ball State University, IN
Barton College, NC
Baylor University, TX
Belhaven University, MS
Bemidji State University, MN
Berry College, GA
Binghamton University, State University of New York, NY
Birmingham-Southern College, AL
Black Hills State University, SD
Bloomsburg University of Pennsylvania, PA
Blue Mountain College, MS
Boise State University, ID
Bowling Green State University, OH
Brenau University, GA
Bryan College, TN
Butler University, IN
California Lutheran University, CA
California Polytechnic State University, San Luis Obispo, CA
California State Polytechnic University, Pomona, CA
California State University, Chico, CA
California State University, Fresno, CA
California State University, Fullerton, CA
California State University, Northridge, CA
California State University, Stanislaus, CA
Calvin College, MI
Cameron University, OK
Campbellsville University, KY
Carlow University, PA
Case Western Reserve University, OH
Cedar Crest College, PA
Centenary College of Louisiana, LA
Central Methodist University, MO
Central Michigan University, MI
Christopher Newport University, VA
City College of the City University of New York, NY
Clarion University of Pennsylvania, PA
Clemson University, SC
Cleveland State University, OH
Coastal Carolina University, SC
The College at Brockport, State University of New York, NY
College of Charleston, SC
The College of Idaho, ID
The College of New Rochelle, NY
College of Staten Island of the City University of New York, NY
Colorado Mesa University, CO
Columbia College, MO
Columbia College Chicago, IL
Columbus State University, GA
Concordia University Chicago, IL
Concordia University, Nebraska, NE
Concordia University Texas, TX
Concord University, WV

Cornerstone University, MI
Dakota State University, SD
Dallas Baptist University, TX
Defiance College, OH
Denison University, OH
DeSales University, PA
Dordt College, IA
Drury University, MO
East Carolina University, NC
Eastern Illinois University, IL
Eastern Mennonite University, VA
Eastern Michigan University, MI
Eastern Washington University, WA
East Texas Baptist University, TX
Elizabethtown College, PA
Elmhurst College, IL
Emmanuel College, GA
Emporia State University, KS
Evangel University, MO
Fairmont State University, WV
Felician University, NJ
Flagler College, FL
Florida Agricultural and Mechanical
    University, FL
Florida International University, FL
Fort Hays State University, KS
Fort Lewis College, CO
Framingham State University, MA
Francis Marion University, SC
Frostburg State University, MD
Furman University, SC
Gannon University, PA
Gardner-Webb University, NC
George Fox University, OR
Georgian Court University, NJ
Georgia Southern University, GA
Glenville State College, WV
Governors State University, IL
Graceland University, IA
Grambling State University, LA
Grand Valley State University, MI
Grove City College, PA
Hamline University, MN
Harding University, AR
Hardin-Simmons University, TX
High Point University, NC
Hillsdale College, MI
Hood College, MD
Howard Payne University, TX
Idaho State University, ID
Indiana State University, IN
Indiana University of Pennsylvania, PA
Indiana Wesleyan University, IN
Iowa State University of Science and
    Technology, IA
Iowa Wesleyan University, IA
Jacksonville State University, AL
James Madison University, VA
John Carroll University, OH
Kansas Wesleyan University, KS
Kean University, NJ
Kennesaw State University, GA
Kent State University, OH
Kenyon College, OH
King's College, PA
Kutztown University of Pennsylvania, PA
La Sierra University, CA
Lebanon Valley College, PA
Lewis-Clark State College, ID
Liberty University, VA
Lindenwood University, MO
Lindsey Wilson College, KY
Linfield College, OR
Lipscomb University, TN
Lock Haven University of Pennsylvania, PA

Longwood University, VA
Loras College, IA
Louisiana College, LA
Louisiana State University and Agricultural
    & Mechanical College, LA
Louisiana Tech University, LA
Loyola Marymount University, CA
Lubbock Christian University, TX
Lycoming College, PA
Marquette University, WI
Maryville University of Saint Louis, MO
Marywood University, PA
Massachusetts College of Liberal Arts, MA
McMurry University, TX
Mercer University, GA
Meredith College, NC
Methodist University, NC
Metropolitan State University of Denver, CO
Michigan State University, MI
Middle Tennessee State University, TN
Midwestern State University, TX
Millersville University of Pennsylvania, PA
Millikin University, IL
Minnesota State University Moorhead, MN
Minot State University, ND
Mississippi State University, MS
Missouri University of Science and
    Technology, MO
Missouri Valley College, MO
Missouri Western State University, MO
Molloy College, NY
Monmouth University, NJ
Montana State University, MT
Montana State University Billings, MT
Montclair State University, NJ
Moravian College, PA
Mount Mary University, WI
Murray State University, KY
Nazareth College of Rochester, NY
New Mexico Highlands University, NM
New Mexico State University, NM
North Central College, IL
Northeast Catholic College, NH
Northeastern Illinois University, IL
Northeastern State University, OK
Northern Illinois University, IL
Northern Kentucky University, KY
Northern Michigan University, MI
Northern State University, SD
Northwestern College, IA
Northwest Missouri State University, MO
Northwest Nazarene University, ID
Oglethorpe University, GA
Ohio Northern University, OH
The Ohio State University, OH
Ohio University, OH
Ohio University-Chillicothe, OH
Ohio University-Eastern, OH
Ohio University-Lancaster, OH
Ohio University-Southern Campus, OH
Ohio University-Zanesville, OH
Ohio Valley University, WV
Oklahoma Baptist University, OK
Oklahoma State University, OK
Old Dominion University, VA
Olivet College, MI
Ouachita Baptist University, AR
Pacific University, OR
Piedmont College, GA
Pittsburg State University, KS
Point Loma Nazarene University, CA
Point Park University, PA
Randolph College, VA
Rockford University, IL
Rockhurst University, MO

Sacred Heart University, CT
The Sage Colleges, NY
St. Catherine University, MN
St. Edward's University, TX
St. John Fisher College, NY
St. John's University, NY
Saint Louis University, MO
Saint Mary's College of California, CA
St. Thomas Aquinas College, NY
Samford University, AL
Sam Houston State University, TX
San Diego State University, CA
Schreiner University, TX
Shenandoah University, VA
Shepherd University, WV
Shippensburg University of Pennsylvania,
    PA
Siena College, NY
Slippery Rock University of Pennsylvania,
    PA
Sonoma State University, CA
South Dakota State University, SD
Southeastern Louisiana University, LA
Southeastern Oklahoma State University,
    OK
Southeast Missouri State University, MO
Southern Adventist University, TN
Southern Arkansas University–Magnolia,
    AR
Southern Illinois University Carbondale, IL
Southern Oregon University, OR
Southwestern College, KS
Southwestern Oklahoma State University,
    OK
State University of New York at Fredonia,
    NY
State University of New York at New Paltz,
    NY
State University of New York at Oswego,
    NY
State University of New York at Plattsburgh,
    NY
State University of New York College at
    Geneseo, NY
State University of New York College at
    Potsdam, NY
Stetson University, FL
Stony Brook University, State University of
    New York, NY
Tennessee Technological University, TN
Texas A&M International University, TX
Texas A&M University–Commerce, TX
Texas A&M University–Texarkana, TX
Texas Christian University, TX
Texas State University, TX
Texas Tech University, TX
Texas Wesleyan University, TX
Texas Woman's University, TX
Thomas More College, KY
Thomas University, GA
Towson University, MD
Trevecca Nazarene University, TN
Trinity Christian College, IL
Truman State University, MO
Union University, TN
The University of Akron, OH
The University of Alabama, AL
The University of Alabama in Huntsville,
    AL
University of Alaska Anchorage, AK
University of Arkansas, AR
University of Arkansas at Little Rock, AR
University of California, Davis, CA
University of California, Irvine, CA
University of California, Riverside, CA

University of Central Oklahoma, OK
University of Colorado Boulder, CO
University of Colorado Denver, CO
University of Dallas, TX
University of Dayton, OH
University of Delaware, DE
University of Denver, CO
University of Evansville, IN
University of Hartford, CT
University of Houston, TX
University of Idaho, ID
University of Illinois at Urbana–Champaign, IL
The University of Kansas, KS
University of Kentucky, KY
University of Louisiana at Monroe, LA
University of Maine, ME
University of Maine at Fort Kent, ME
University of Mary Hardin-Baylor, TX
University of Maryland, Baltimore County, MD
University of Maryland, College Park, MD
University of Mary Washington, VA
University of Massachusetts Amherst, MA
University of Massachusetts Lowell, MA
University of Memphis, TN
University of Miami, FL
University of Michigan, MI
University of Michigan–Flint, MI
University of Minnesota, Twin Cities Campus, MN
University of Mississippi, MS
University of Missouri, MO
University of Missouri–St. Louis, MO
University of Montana, MT
The University of Montana Western, MT
University of Montevallo, AL
University of Nebraska–Lincoln, NE
University of Nevada, Las Vegas, NV
University of Nevada, Reno, NV
University of New Hampshire, NH
University of New Hampshire at Manchester, NH
University of North Carolina at Asheville, NC
The University of North Carolina at Chapel Hill, NC
The University of North Carolina at Greensboro, NC
The University of North Carolina Wilmington, NC
University of North Dakota, ND
University of Northern Colorado, CO
University of North Georgia, GA
University of Oklahoma, OK
University of Oregon, OR
University of Pittsburgh at Bradford, PA
University of Pittsburgh at Johnstown, PA
University of Portland, OR
University of Puget Sound, WA
University of Rhode Island, RI
University of St. Thomas, MN
University of St. Thomas, TX
University of Sioux Falls, SD
University of South Carolina, SC
University of South Carolina Aiken, SC
University of South Dakota, SD
University of South Florida, FL
The University of Tampa, FL
The University of Tennessee at Chattanooga, TN
The University of Tennessee at Martin, TN
The University of Texas at El Paso, TX
The University of Texas at San Antonio, TX
The University of Texas Rio Grande Valley, TX

University of the Southwest, NM
The University of Toledo, OH
The University of Tulsa, OK
University of Utah, UT
University of Vermont, VT
The University of Virginia's College at Wise, VA
University of Washington, WA
University of Washington, Bothell, WA
The University of West Alabama, AL
University of West Georgia, GA
University of Wisconsin–Eau Claire, WI
University of Wisconsin–La Crosse, WI
University of Wisconsin–Parkside, WI
University of Wisconsin–River Falls, WI
University of Wisconsin–Stevens Point, WI
University of Wisconsin–Superior, WI
University of Wisconsin–Whitewater, WI
University of Wyoming, WY
Utah State University, UT
Valley City State University, ND
Virginia Military Institute, VA
Walla Walla University, WA
Wartburg College, IA
Washington State University, WA
Washington University in St. Louis, MO
Wayland Baptist University, TX
Wayne State College, NE
Wayne State University, MI
Webster University, MO
Wesleyan College, GA
Western Carolina University, NC
Western Illinois University, IL
Western Kentucky University, KY
Western Oregon University, OR
Western Washington University, WA
West Texas A&M University, TX
West Virginia University, WV
Wheaton College, IL
Wichita State University, KS
Widener University, PA
William Jessup University, CA
Wilson College, PA
Wright State University, OH
Wright State University–Lake Campus, OH
Youngstown State University, OH

Foreign Languages
Abilene Christian University, TX
Adelphi University, NY
Albertus Magnus College, CT
Alfred University, NY
Angelo State University, TX
Arkansas Tech University, AR
Auburn University, AL
Augsburg University, MN
Augustana College, IL
Augustana University, SD
Austin College, TX
Austin Peay State University, TN
Averett University, VA
Ball State University, IN
Baylor University, TX
Belhaven University, MS
Bemidji State University, MN
Binghamton University, State University of New York, NY
Birmingham-Southern College, AL
Black Hills State University, SD
Bloomsburg University of Pennsylvania, PA
Boise State University, ID
Bowling Green State University, OH
Bryan College, TN
Buffalo State College, State University of New York, NY
Butler University, IN

California Lutheran University, CA
California Polytechnic State University, San Luis Obispo, CA
California State Polytechnic University, Pomona, CA
California State University, Bakersfield, CA
California State University, Chico, CA
California State University, Fresno, CA
California State University, Fullerton, CA
California State University, San Bernardino, CA
California State University, Stanislaus, CA
Calvin College, MI
Cameron University, OK
Case Western Reserve University, OH
Centenary College of Louisiana, LA
Central College, IA
Central Methodist University, MO
Central Michigan University, MI
Centre College, KY
Charlotte Christian College and Theological Seminary, NC
Christopher Newport University, VA
City College of the City University of New York, NY
Clarion University of Pennsylvania, PA
Clemson University, SC
Coastal Carolina University, SC
The College at Brockport, State University of New York, NY
College of Charleston, SC
The College of Idaho, ID
College of Staten Island of the City University of New York, NY
Colorado Mesa University, CO
Concordia University Chicago, IL
Concordia University Texas, TX
Corban University, OR
Davidson College, NC
Denison University, OH
DeSales University, PA
Dordt College, IA
Drury University, MO
East Carolina University, NC
Eastern Illinois University, IL
Eastern Mennonite University, VA
Eastern Michigan University, MI
Eastern Washington University, WA
Edgewood College, WI
Elizabethtown College, PA
Elmhurst College, IL
Emporia State University, KS
Evangel University, MO
Flagler College, FL
Florida Agricultural and Mechanical University, FL
Florida International University, FL
Fordham University, NY
Fort Hays State University, KS
Francis Marion University, SC
Frostburg State University, MD
Furman University, SC
Gannon University, PA
Gardner-Webb University, NC
George Fox University, OR
Georgian Court University, NJ
Georgia Southern University, GA
Grambling State University, LA
Grand Valley State University, MI
Grove City College, PA
Hamline University, MN
Hardin-Simmons University, TX
High Point University, NC
Hillsdale College, MI
Hood College, MD
Idaho State University, ID

Indiana State University, IN
Indiana University of Pennsylvania, PA
Indiana Wesleyan University, IN
Iowa State University of Science and
    Technology, IA
John Carroll University, OH
Juniata College, PA
Kansas Wesleyan University, KS
Kean University, NJ
Kennesaw State University, GA
Kent State University, OH
Kent State University at Stark, OH
Kenyon College, OH
King's College, PA
Kutztown University of Pennsylvania, PA
La Sierra University, CA
Lindenwood University, MO
Linfield College, OR
Lock Haven University of Pennsylvania, PA
Louisiana State University and Agricultural
    & Mechanical College, LA
Louisiana Tech University, LA
Loyola Marymount University, CA
Lubbock Christian University, TX
Lycoming College, PA
Manhattan College, NY
Marquette University, WI
Marywood University, PA
McMurry University, TX
Mercer University, GA
Meredith College, NC
Metropolitan State University of Denver, CO
Michigan State University, MI
Middle Tennessee State University, TN
Midwestern State University, TX
Millersville University of Pennsylvania, PA
Millikin University, IL
Minot State University, ND
Mississippi State University, MS
Missouri Western State University, MO
Monmouth College, IL
Monmouth University, NJ
Montana State University, MT
Montana State University Billings, MT
Montclair State University, NJ
Moravian College, PA
Nazareth College of Rochester, NY
Newberry College, SC
New Mexico Highlands University, NM
New Mexico State University, NM
North Central College, IL
Northeastern Illinois University, IL
Northeastern State University, OK
Northern Illinois University, IL
Northern Kentucky University, KY
Northern Michigan University, MI
Northern State University, SD
Northwestern College, IA
Northwest Missouri State University, MO
Oglethorpe University, GA
Ohio Northern University, OH
The Ohio State University, OH
Ohio University, OH
Ohio University–Chillicothe, OH
Ohio University–Eastern, OH
Ohio University–Lancaster, OH
Ohio University–Southern Campus, OH
Ohio University–Zanesville, OH
Oklahoma Baptist University, OK
Oklahoma State University, OK
Old Dominion University, VA
Olivet College, MI
Ouachita Baptist University, AR
Pacific University, OR
Piedmont College, GA

Pittsburg State University, KS
Point Loma Nazarene University, CA
Portland State University, OR
Rockford University, IL
Rockhurst University, MO
St. Ambrose University, IA
St. Catherine University, MN
St. Edward's University, TX
St. John Fisher College, NY
St. John's University, NY
Saint Louis University, MO
St. Thomas Aquinas College, NY
Samford University, AL
Sam Houston State University, TX
San Diego State University, CA
Shenandoah University, VA
Shippensburg University of Pennsylvania,
    PA
Siena College, NY
Slippery Rock University of Pennsylvania,
    PA
Sonoma State University, CA
South Dakota State University, SD
Southeastern Louisiana University, LA
Southeast Missouri State University, MO
Southern Adventist University, TN
Southern Arkansas University–Magnolia,
    AR
Southern Illinois University Carbondale, IL
Southern Oregon University, OR
Southwestern College, KS
Southwestern Oklahoma State University,
    OK
State University of New York at Fredonia,
    NY
State University of New York at New Paltz,
    NY
State University of New York at Oswego,
    NY
State University of New York College at
    Geneseo, NY
State University of New York College at
    Potsdam, NY
Stetson University, FL
Stony Brook University, State University of
    New York, NY
Suffolk University, MA
Tennessee Technological University, TN
Texas A&M International University, TX
Texas A&M University–Commerce, TX
Texas Christian University, TX
Texas State University, TX
Texas Tech University, TX
Texas Wesleyan University, TX
Texas Woman's University, TX
Towson University, MD
Truman State University, MO
Union University, TN
The University of Akron, OH
The University of Alabama, AL
The University of Alabama in Huntsville,
    AL
University of Arkansas, AR
University of Arkansas at Little Rock, AR
University of California, Davis, CA
University of California, Irvine, CA
University of Central Oklahoma, OK
University of Colorado Boulder, CO
University of Dallas, TX
University of Dayton, OH
University of Delaware, DE
University of Evansville, IN
University of Hartford, CT
University of Houston, TX
University of Idaho, ID

University of Illinois at Urbana–Champaign,
    IL
The University of Kansas, KS
University of Kentucky, KY
University of Louisiana at Monroe, LA
University of Maine at Fort Kent, ME
University of Mary Hardin-Baylor, TX
University of Maryland, Baltimore County,
    MD
University of Maryland, College Park, MD
University of Mary Washington, VA
University of Massachusetts Dartmouth, MA
University of Miami, FL
University of Michigan, MI
University of Michigan–Dearborn, MI
University of Michigan–Flint, MI
University of Minnesota, Twin Cities
    Campus, MN
University of Mississippi, MS
University of Missouri, MO
University of Missouri–St. Louis, MO
University of Montana, MT
University of Montevallo, AL
University of Nebraska–Lincoln, NE
University of Nevada, Las Vegas, NV
University of Nevada, Reno, NV
University of New Hampshire, NH
University of North Carolina at Asheville,
    NC
The University of North Carolina at
    Charlotte, NC
The University of North Carolina at
    Greensboro, NC
The University of North Carolina
    Wilmington, NC
University of North Dakota, ND
University of Northern Colorado, CO
University of Oklahoma, OK
University of Oregon, OR
University of Portland, OR
University of Puget Sound, WA
University of Rhode Island, RI
University of St. Thomas, TX
University of South Carolina, SC
University of South Dakota, SD
University of South Florida, FL
The University of Tennessee at Martin, TN
The University of Texas at San Antonio, TX
The University of Toledo, OH
The University of Tulsa, OK
University of Utah, UT
University of Vermont, VT
University of Washington, WA
University of Washington, Tacoma, WA
University of West Georgia, GA
University of Wisconsin–Eau Claire, WI
University of Wisconsin–La Crosse, WI
University of Wisconsin–Parkside, WI
University of Wisconsin–River Falls, WI
University of Wisconsin–Stevens Point, WI
University of Wisconsin–Whitewater, WI
University of Wyoming, WY
Utah State University, UT
Valparaiso University, IN
Virginia Military Institute, VA
Walla Walla University, WA
Wartburg College, IA
Washington State University, WA
Washington University in St. Louis, MO
Wayland Baptist University, TX
Wayne State College, NE
Wayne State University, MI
Webster University, MO
Wesleyan College, GA
Western Illinois University, IL

Western Kentucky University, KY
Western Oregon University, OR
Western Washington University, WA
West Texas A&M University, TX
West Virginia University, WV
Wheaton College, IL
Wichita State University, KS
Widener University, PA
Wilson College, PA
Wisconsin Lutheran College, WI
Wright State University, OH
Wright State University–Lake Campus, OH
Xavier University, OH
Youngstown State University, OH

Health Fields

Alaska Pacific University, AK
Albany State University, GA
Arkansas Tech University, AR
Auburn University, AL
Augsburg University, MN
Augustana University, SD
Austin Peay State University, TN
Averett University, VA
Ball State University, IN
Baylor University, TX
Belmont University, TN
Bemidji State University, MN
Birmingham-Southern College, AL
Black Hills State University, SD
Bloomsburg University of Pennsylvania, PA
Boise State University, ID
Bowling Green State University, OH
Buffalo State College, State University of
New York, NY
California Polytechnic State University, San
Luis Obispo, CA
California State University, Bakersfield, CA
California State University, Chico, CA
California State University, Fresno, CA
California State University, Fullerton, CA
California State University, San Bernardino,
CA
California State University, Stanislaus, CA
Calvin College, MI
Campbellsville University, KY
Carroll University, WI
Case Western Reserve University, OH
Central College, IA
Central Methodist University, MO
Central Michigan University, MI
Clarion University of Pennsylvania, PA
Clemson University, SC
College of Charleston, SC
The College of New Rochelle, NY
Colorado Mesa University, CO
Columbus State University, GA
Concordia University, Nebraska, NE
DeSales University, PA
Drury University, MO
East Carolina University, NC
Eastern Illinois University, IL
Eastern Michigan University, MI
Elizabethtown College, PA
Emmanuel College, GA
Emporia State University, KS
Endicott College, MA
Fairmont State University, WV
Felician University, NJ
Ferris State University, MI
Florida Agricultural and Mechanical
University, FL
Florida Gulf Coast University, FL
Florida Institute of Technology, FL
Florida International University, FL
Florida Southern College, FL

Fort Hays State University, KS
Furman University, SC
Gardner-Webb University, NC
George Fox University, OR
Georgia Southern University, GA
Governors State University, IL
Grambling State University, LA
Grand Valley State University, MI
Hampton University, VA
Harding University, AR
Hardin-Simmons University, TX
Indiana State University, IN
Indiana University of Pennsylvania, PA
Indiana Wesleyan University, IN
Iowa State University of Science and
Technology, IA
Iowa Wesleyan University, IA
Jacksonville State University, AL
James Madison University, VA
John Carroll University, OH
Kennesaw State University, GA
Kent State University, OH
Lewis-Clark State College, ID
Lindenwood University, MO
Lock Haven University of Pennsylvania, PA
Louisiana College, LA
Louisiana State University and Agricultural
& Mechanical College, LA
Louisiana Tech University, LA
Loyola Marymount University, CA
Lycoming College, PA
Malone University, OH
Mansfield University of Pennsylvania, PA
Maryville University of Saint Louis, MO
Marywood University, PA
Massachusetts College of Liberal Arts, MA
Michigan State University, MI
Middle Georgia State University, GA
Middle Tennessee State University, TN
Midwestern State University, TX
Minot State University, ND
Mississippi State University, MS
Missouri Valley College, MO
Montana State University, MT
Montana State University Billings, MT
Morehead State University, KY
Murray State University, KY
New Mexico Highlands University, NM
New Mexico State University, NM
Northeastern State University, OK
Northern Illinois University, IL
Northern Kentucky University, KY
Northern Michigan University, MI
Northwest Missouri State University, MO
Ohio Northern University, OH
The Ohio State University, OH
Ohio University, OH
Ohio University–Chillicothe, OH
Ohio University–Eastern, OH
Ohio University–Lancaster, OH
Ohio University–Southern Campus, OH
Ohio University–Zanesville, OH
Oklahoma Baptist University, OK
Old Dominion University, VA
Oral Roberts University, OK
Ouachita Baptist University, AR
Pacific University, OR
Peirce College, PA
Piedmont College, GA
Pittsburg State University, KS
Point Park University, PA
Purdue University, IN
Sacred Heart University, CT
Saginaw Valley State University, MI
St. Ambrose University, IA
St. Catherine University, MN

Saint Francis Medical Center College of
Nursing, IL
St. John's University, NY
Samford University, AL
Sam Houston State University, TX
San Diego State University, CA
Shepherd University, WV
Sonoma State University, CA
South Dakota State University, SD
Southeast Missouri State University, MO
Southern Arkansas University–Magnolia,
AR
Southern Illinois University Carbondale, IL
Southern Oregon University, OR
State University of New York at Plattsburgh,
NY
Stephen F. Austin State University, TX
Stockton University, NJ
Stony Brook University, State University of
New York, NY
Tennessee Technological University, TN
Texas A&M International University, TX
Texas A&M University, TX
Texas A&M University–Commerce, TX
Texas Christian University, TX
Texas State University, TX
Texas Wesleyan University, TX
Texas Woman's University, TX
Truman State University, MO
Union University, TN
The University of Akron, OH
The University of Alabama at Birmingham,
AL
The University of Alabama in Huntsville,
AL
University of Alaska Anchorage, AK
University of Arkansas, AR
University of Arkansas at Little Rock, AR
University of California, Davis, CA
University of California, Irvine, CA
University of Central Oklahoma, OK
University of Dayton, OH
University of Delaware, DE
University of Houston, TX
University of Idaho, ID
University of Illinois at Urbana–Champaign,
IL
University of Indianapolis, IN
University of Kentucky, KY
University of Louisiana at Monroe, LA
University of Maine at Fort Kent, ME
University of Mary Hardin-Baylor, TX
University of Maryland, College Park, MD
University of Massachusetts Amherst, MA
University of Massachusetts Lowell, MA
University of Memphis, TN
University of Michigan, MI
University of Minnesota, Twin Cities
Campus, MN
University of Mississippi, MS
University of Missouri, MO
University of Montana, MT
University of Montevallo, AL
University of Nebraska–Lincoln, NE
University of Nevada, Las Vegas, NV
University of Nevada, Reno, NV
University of New Hampshire, NH
University of North Carolina at Asheville,
NC
The University of North Carolina at Chapel
Hill, NC
The University of North Carolina at
Charlotte, NC
The University of North Carolina at
Greensboro, NC
University of Northern Colorado, CO

University of North Florida, FL
University of North Georgia, GA
University of Oregon, OR
University of Pittsburgh at Bradford, PA
University of Pittsburgh at Johnstown, PA
University of Portland, OR
University of Rhode Island, RI
University of St. Francis, IL
University of St. Thomas, TX
University of South Carolina, SC
University of Southern Indiana, IN
The University of Tennessee at Martin, TN
The University of Texas at El Paso, TX
The University of Texas at Tyler, TX
The University of Texas Rio Grande Valley, TX
The University of Toledo, OH
The University of Tulsa, OK
University of Utah, UT
University of Vermont, VT
The University of Virginia's College at Wise, VA
University of Washington, WA
University of Wisconsin–Eau Claire, WI
University of Wisconsin–Green Bay, WI
University of Wisconsin–La Crosse, WI
University of Wisconsin–River Falls, WI
University of Wisconsin–Stevens Point, WI
University of Wyoming, WY
Utah State University, UT
Valdosta State University, GA
Washington State University, WA
Wayne State College, NE
Wayne State University, MI
Western Illinois University, IL
Western Kentucky University, KY
Western Washington University, WA
West Virginia University, WV
Widener University, PA
Youngstown State University, OH

Home Economics

Alaska Pacific University, AK
Allen College, IA
Alliant International University–San Diego, CA
Arkansas Tech University, AR
Auburn University, AL
Augustana University, SD
Austin College, TX
Averett University, VA
Baylor University, TX
Bethel College, KS
Binghamton University, State University of New York, NY
Birmingham-Southern College, AL
Boise State University, ID
Bowling Green State University, OH
Brenau University, GA
Buffalo State College, State University of New York, NY
Butler University, IN
Caldwell University, NJ
California Baptist University, CA
California Polytechnic State University, San Luis Obispo, CA
California State University, Fresno, CA
California State University, Fullerton, CA
Calvin College, MI
Cameron University, OK
Carson-Newman University, TN
Case Western Reserve University, OH
Catawba College, NC
Cedar Crest College, PA
Central Michigan University, MI

Chaminade University of Honolulu, HI
Cleveland State University, OH
The College at Brockport, State University of New York, NY
College of Coastal Georgia, GA
College of Staten Island of the City University of New York, NY
Concordia University Texas, TX
Corban University, OR
Cornerstone University, MI
Cox College, MO
Daemen College, NY
Dakota State University, SD
DeSales University, PA
Dominican University, IL
East Carolina University, NC
Eastern Illinois University, IL
Eastern Michigan University, MI
Eastern Washington University, WA
East Texas Baptist University, TX
Evangel University, MO
Fort Hays State University, KS
Framingham State University, MA
Francis Marion University, SC
George Fox University, OR
Georgian Court University, NJ
Georgia Southern University, GA
Grambling State University, LA
Hampden-Sydney College, VA
Idaho State University, ID
Indiana University of Pennsylvania, PA
Iowa State University of Science and Technology, IA
Jacksonville State University, AL
Juniata College, PA
Kansas Wesleyan University, KS
Kean University, NJ
Kent State University, OH
Kent State University at Geauga, OH
Kent State University at Stark, OH
Lewis-Clark State College, ID
Lipscomb University, TN
Long Island University–LIU Brooklyn, NY
Long Island University–LIU Post, NY
Loras College, IA
Louisiana College, LA
Louisiana Tech University, LA
Loyola Marymount University, CA
Marquette University, WI
Marymount University, VA
Maryville University of Saint Louis, MO
Marywood University, PA
Medical University of South Carolina, SC
Metropolitan State University of Denver, CO
Michigan State University, MI
Middle Tennessee State University, TN
Millersville University of Pennsylvania, PA
Millikin University, IL
Milwaukee School of Engineering, WI
Minnesota State University Moorhead, MN
Minot State University, ND
Mississippi State University, MS
Missouri Western State University, MO
Monmouth University, NJ
Montana State University, MT
Montana Tech of The University of Montana, MT
Montclair State University, NJ
Moravian College, PA
Murray State University, KY
Nazareth College of Rochester, NY
Nebraska Methodist College, NE
New Mexico State University, NM
Northeastern State University, OK
Northern Kentucky University, KY

Northern Michigan University, MI
Northwest Missouri State University, MO
Northwest Nazarene University, ID
The Ohio State University, OH
Ohio University, OH
Ohio University–Chillicothe, OH
Ohio University–Eastern, OH
Ohio University–Lancaster, OH
Ohio University–Southern Campus, OH
Ohio University–Zanesville, OH
Oklahoma City University, OK
Oklahoma State University, OK
Oregon Health & Science University, OR
Ouachita Baptist University, AR
Piedmont College, GA
Pittsburg State University, KS
Point Loma Nazarene University, CA
Rochester Institute of Technology, NY
Rockhurst University, MO
The Sage Colleges, NY
St. Catherine University, MN
St. Edward's University, TX
Saint Louis University, MO
Saint Vincent College, PA
Samford University, AL
Sam Houston State University, TX
San Diego State University, CA
San Jose State University, CA
Shenandoah University, VA
Shepherd University, WV
Siena College, NY
Slippery Rock University of Pennsylvania, PA
South Dakota State University, SD
Southeast Missouri State University, MO
Southern Adventist University, TN
Southern Illinois University Carbondale, IL
Southwestern College, KS
State University of New York at Plattsburgh, NY
Stephen F. Austin State University, TX
Stockton University, NJ
Tennessee Technological University, TN
Texas A&M University–Texarkana, TX
Texas State University, TX
Texas Tech University, TX
Texas Woman's University, TX
Towson University, MD
Trine University, IN
Truett McConnell University, GA
The University of Akron, OH
The University of Alabama, AL
University of Arkansas, AR
University of California, Davis, CA
University of Central Oklahoma, OK
University of Colorado Boulder, CO
University of Colorado Denver, CO
University of Dallas, TX
University of Florida, FL
University of Hartford, CT
University of Idaho, ID
University of Illinois at Urbana–Champaign, IL
The University of Kansas, KS
University of Kentucky, KY
University of Louisiana at Monroe, LA
University of Maine, ME
University of Mary Hardin-Baylor, TX
University of Massachusetts Dartmouth, MA
University of Memphis, TN
University of Miami, FL
University of Minnesota, Twin Cities Campus, MN
University of Mississippi, MS
University of Missouri, MO

University of Missouri–St. Louis, MO
University of Nebraska–Lincoln, NE
University of North Carolina at Asheville, NC
The University of North Carolina at Charlotte, NC
The University of North Carolina at Greensboro, NC
The University of North Carolina Wilmington, NC
University of North Dakota, ND
University of Northern Colorado, CO
University of Rhode Island, RI
University of South Florida, FL
The University of Tennessee, TN
The University of Tennessee at Chattanooga, TN
The University of Tennessee at Martin, TN
University of Vermont, VT
University of Washington, WA
University of Washington, Bothell, WA
University of Washington, Tacoma, WA
University of West Georgia, GA
University of Wisconsin–Parkside, WI
University of Wisconsin–Stevens Point, WI
University of Wisconsin–Stout, WI
University of Wyoming, WY
Utah State University, UT
Washington State University, WA
Washington University in St. Louis, MO
Wayland Baptist University, TX
Wayne State College, NE
Wesleyan College, GA
Western Illinois University, IL
Western Kentucky University, KY
Western New England University, MA
Western Oregon University, OR
West Texas A&M University, TX
West Virginia University, WV
Wheaton College, IL
Wichita State University, KS
Wisconsin Lutheran College, WI
Wright State University, OH
Wright State University–Lake Campus, OH

Humanities

Alaska Pacific University, AK
Albertus Magnus College, CT
Alfred University, NY
Alliant International University–San Diego, CA
Angelo State University, TX
Arkansas Tech University, AR
Auburn University, AL
Augustana College, IL
Augustana University, SD
Austin College, TX
Austin Peay State University, TN
Averett University, VA
Ball State University, IN
Barton College, NC
Baylor University, TX
Belhaven University, MS
Belmont Abbey College, NC
Bemidji State University, MN
Berry College, GA
Binghamton University, State University of New York, NY
Birmingham-Southern College, AL
Black Hills State University, SD
Bloomsburg University of Pennsylvania, PA
Blue Mountain College, MS
Boise State University, ID
Bowling Green State University, OH
Brenau University, GA
Bryan College, TN

Buena Vista University, IA
Butler University, IN
California Lutheran University, CA
California Polytechnic State University, San Luis Obispo, CA
California State Polytechnic University, Pomona, CA
California State University, Bakersfield, CA
California State University, Chico, CA
California State University, Fresno, CA
California State University, Fullerton, CA
California State University, Stanislaus, CA
Calvin College, MI
Campbellsville University, KY
Carlow University, PA
Carroll University, WI
Case Western Reserve University, OH
Centenary College of Louisiana, LA
Central College, IA
Central Methodist University, MO
Central Michigan University, MI
Christopher Newport University, VA
The Citadel, The Military College of South Carolina, SC
City College of the City University of New York, NY
Clarion University of Pennsylvania, PA
Clarkson University, NY
Clemson University, SC
Cleveland State University, OH
Coastal Carolina University, SC
The College at Brockport, State University of New York, NY
College of Charleston, SC
The College of Idaho, ID
The College of New Rochelle, NY
College of Staten Island of the City University of New York, NY
Colorado Mesa University, CO
Columbia College, MO
Columbia College Chicago, IL
Columbus State University, GA
Concordia University, Nebraska, NE
Cornerstone University, MI
Dallas Baptist University, TX
Defiance College, OH
DeSales University, PA
Dominican University of California, CA
Dordt College, IA
Drury University, MO
East Carolina University, NC
Eastern Illinois University, IL
Eastern Mennonite University, VA
Eastern Michigan University, MI
Eastern Washington University, WA
East Texas Baptist University, TX
Elizabethtown College, PA
Elmhurst College, IL
Emory University, GA
Emporia State University, KS
Evangel University, MO
Fairmont State University, WV
Flagler College, FL
Florida Agricultural and Mechanical University, FL
Florida Gulf Coast University, FL
Florida International University, FL
Fort Hays State University, KS
Fort Lewis College, CO
Francis Marion University, SC
Frostburg State University, MD
Furman University, SC
Gannon University, PA
Gardner-Webb University, NC
George Fox University, OR
Georgian Court University, NJ

Georgia Southern University, GA
Governors State University, IL
Grambling State University, LA
Grand Valley State University, MI
Grove City College, PA
Hamline University, MN
Hardin-Simmons University, TX
High Point University, NC
Hiram College, OH
Hood College, MD
Idaho State University, ID
Illinois Institute of Technology, IL
Indiana State University, IN
Indiana University of Pennsylvania, PA
Iowa State University of Science and Technology, IA
Jacksonville State University, AL
James Madison University, VA
Juniata College, PA
Kansas Wesleyan University, KS
Kean University, NJ
Kennesaw State University, GA
Kent State University, OH
Kent State University at Geauga, OH
Kenyon College, OH
King's College, PA
Kutztown University of Pennsylvania, PA
Lewis-Clark State College, ID
Lindenwood University, MO
Linfield College, OR
Longwood University, VA
Louisiana College, LA
Louisiana State University and Agricultural & Mechanical College, LA
Loyola Marymount University, CA
Lubbock Christian University, TX
Lycoming College, PA
Marymount University, VA
Massachusetts College of Liberal Arts, MA
Messiah College, PA
Metropolitan State University of Denver, CO
Middle Tennessee State University, TN
Midwestern State University, TX
Millersville University of Pennsylvania, PA
Millikin University, IL
Minot State University, ND
Mississippi State University, MS
Missouri University of Science and Technology, MO
Missouri Valley College, MO
Missouri Western State University, MO
Molloy College, NY
Monmouth University, NJ
Montana State University, MT
Montana State University Billings, MT
Montana Tech of The University of Montana, MT
Montclair State University, NJ
Moravian College, PA
Mount Mary University, WI
Murray State University, KY
Nazareth College of Rochester, NY
Newberry College, SC
New England College, NH
New Jersey Institute of Technology, NJ
New Mexico Highlands University, NM
New Mexico State University, NM
North Carolina State University, NC
North Central College, IL
Northeast Catholic College, NH
Northeastern State University, OK
Northern Illinois University, IL
Northern Michigan University, MI
Northern State University, SD
Northwestern College, IA
Northwest Missouri State University, MO

Oglethorpe University, GA
Ohio Northern University, OH
The Ohio State University, OH
Ohio University, OH
Ohio University–Chillicothe, OH
Ohio University–Eastern, OH
Ohio University–Lancaster, OH
Ohio University–Southern Campus, OH
Ohio University–Zanesville, OH
Oklahoma Baptist University, OK
Oklahoma State University, OK
Old Dominion University, VA
Ouachita Baptist University, AR
Pacific University, OR
Piedmont College, GA
Point Park University, PA
Portland State University, OR
Post University, CT
Purdue University, IN
Rensselaer Polytechnic Institute, NY
Rochester Institute of Technology, NY
Rockhurst University, MO
Sacred Heart University, CT
St. Catherine University, MN
St. Edward's University, TX
St. John Fisher College, NY
St. John's University, NY
Saint Louis University, MO
Saint Mary's College of California, CA
St. Thomas Aquinas College, NY
Samford University, AL
Sam Houston State University, TX
San Diego State University, CA
San Jose State University, CA
Shenandoah University, VA
Shepherd University, WV
Shippensburg University of Pennsylvania,
PA
Siena College, NY
Sonoma State University, CA
South Dakota State University, SD
Southeastern Louisiana University, LA
Southeast Missouri State University, MO
Southern Adventist University, TN
Southern Illinois University Carbondale, IL
Southwestern College, KS
Southwestern University, TX
State University of New York at Fredonia,
NY
State University of New York at Oswego,
NY
State University of New York at Plattsburgh,
NY
State University of New York College at
Geneseo, NY
State University of New York College at
Potsdam, NY
Stetson University, FL
Stockton University, NJ
Tennessee Technological University, TN
Texas A&M University–Commerce, TX
Texas Christian University, TX
Texas State University, TX
Texas Tech University, TX
Texas Wesleyan University, TX
Texas Woman's University, TX
Thomas University, GA
Trinity Christian College, IL
Truman State University, MO
Union University, TN
The University of Akron, OH
The University of Alabama in Huntsville,
AL
University of Alaska Anchorage, AK
University of Arkansas, AR

University of Arkansas at Little Rock, AR
University of California, Davis, CA
University of California, Irvine, CA
University of California, Riverside, CA
University of California, Santa Cruz, CA
University of Central Oklahoma, OK
University of Colorado Boulder, CO
University of Colorado Denver, CO
University of Dayton, OH
University of Delaware, DE
University of Denver, CO
University of Evansville, IN
University of Hartford, CT
University of Houston, TX
University of Houston–Clear Lake, TX
University of Houston–Victoria, TX
University of Idaho, ID
University of Illinois at Urbana–Champaign,
IL
The University of Kansas, KS
University of Maine at Fort Kent, ME
University of Mary Hardin-Baylor, TX
University of Maryland, Baltimore County,
MD
University of Maryland, College Park, MD
University of Mary Washington, VA
University of Massachusetts Amherst, MA
University of Massachusetts Dartmouth, MA
University of Massachusetts Lowell, MA
University of Memphis, TN
University of Miami, FL
University of Michigan, MI
University of Michigan–Flint, MI
University of Minnesota, Twin Cities
Campus, MN
University of Mississippi, MS
University of Missouri, MO
University of Missouri–St. Louis, MO
University of Montana, MT
The University of Montana Western, MT
University of Montevallo, AL
University of Nebraska–Lincoln, NE
University of Nevada, Las Vegas, NV
University of New Hampshire, NH
University of New Hampshire at
Manchester, NH
University of North Carolina at Asheville,
NC
The University of North Carolina at
Greensboro, NC
The University of North Carolina
Wilmington, NC
University of North Dakota, ND
University of Northern Colorado, CO
University of North Georgia, GA
University of Oklahoma, OK
University of Oregon, OR
University of Pittsburgh at Bradford, PA
University of Pittsburgh at Johnstown, PA
University of Portland, OR
University of Providence, MT
University of Puget Sound, WA
University of Rhode Island, RI
University of St. Thomas, MN
University of St. Thomas, TX
University of Sioux Falls, SD
University of South Carolina, SC
University of South Carolina Aiken, SC
University of South Dakota, SD
University of Southern Indiana, IN
University of South Florida, FL
The University of Tennessee, TN
The University of Tennessee at Martin, TN
The University of Texas at El Paso, TX
The University of Texas at San Antonio, TX

University of the Southwest, NM
The University of Toledo, OH
University of Utah, UT
University of Vermont, VT
The University of Virginia's College at Wise,
VA
University of Washington, WA
University of Washington, Bothell, WA
University of Washington, Tacoma, WA
University of West Georgia, GA
University of Wisconsin–Eau Claire, WI
University of Wisconsin Green Bay, WI
University of Wisconsin–La Crosse, WI
University of Wisconsin–Parkside, WI
University of Wisconsin–River Falls, WI
University of Wisconsin–Stevens Point, WI
University of Wisconsin–Superior, WI
University of Wisconsin–Whitewater, WI
University of Wyoming, WY
Upper Iowa University, IA
Utah State University, UT
Valley City State University, ND
Virginia Military Institute, VA
Walla Walla University, WA
Wartburg College, IA
Washington & Jefferson College, PA
Washington State University, WA
Washington University in St. Louis, MO
Wayne State College, NE
Wayne State University, MI
Webster University, MO
Wesleyan College, GA
Western Oregon University, OR
Western Washington University, WA
West Texas A&M University, TX
West Virginia University, WV
Wheaton College, IL
Wichita State University, KS
Widener University, PA
William Jessup University, CA
Williams Baptist College, AR
Wilson College, PA
Wright State University, OH
Wright State University–Lake Campus, OH
Youngstown State University, OH

International Studies

Albertus Magnus College, CT
Alfred University, NY
Alliant International University–San Diego,
CA
Angelo State University, TX
Arkansas Tech University, AR
Augsburg University, MN
Augustana University, SD
Austin College, TX
Austin Peay State University, TN
Ball State University, IN
Baylor University, TX
Belhaven University, MS
Bemidji State University, MN
Binghamton University, State University of
New York, NY
Birmingham-Southern College, AL
Bloomsburg University of Pennsylvania, PA
Boise State University, ID
Bowling Green State University, OH
Buena Vista University, IA
Butler University, IN
California Lutheran University, CA
California Polytechnic State University, San
Luis Obispo, CA
California State Polytechnic University,
Pomona, CA
California State University, Chico, CA

California State University, Fullerton, CA
California State University, San Bernardino, CA
California State University, Stanislaus, CA
Calvin College, MI
Carroll University, WI
Case Western Reserve University, OH
Central College, IA
Central Michigan University, MI
City College of the City University of New York, NY
Clarion University of Pennsylvania, PA
Clemson University, SC
Coastal Carolina University, SC
The College at Brockport, State University of New York, NY
College of Staten Island of the City University of New York, NY
Columbus State University, GA
Concordia University Texas, TX
Davidson College, NC
Defiance College, OH
Drury University, MO
East Carolina University, NC
Eastern Illinois University, IL
Eastern Washington University, WA
Elizabethtown College, PA
Elmhurst College, IL
Evangel University, MO
Fairmont State University, WV
Fort Hays State University, KS
Frostburg State University, MD
Furman University, SC
Gannon University, PA
George Fox University, OR
Georgetown College, KY
Georgia Institute of Technology, GA
Georgian Court University, NJ
Georgia Southern University, GA
Glenville State College, WV
Grand Valley State University, MI
Grove City College, PA
Hampden-Sydney College, VA
Henderson State University, AR
High Point University, NC
Idaho State University, ID
Indiana University of Pennsylvania, PA
Indiana Wesleyan University, IN
Iowa State University of Science and Technology, IA
James Madison University, VA
Juniata College, PA
Kean University, NJ
Kennesaw State University, GA
Kent State University, OH
King's College, PA
Kutztown University of Pennsylvania, PA
Lehigh University, PA
Lindenwood University, MO
Linfield College, OR
Lock Haven University of Pennsylvania, PA
Long Island University–LIU Brooklyn, NY
Long Island University–LIU Post, NY
Longwood University, VA
Louisiana Tech University, LA
Loyola Marymount University, CA
Lycoming College, PA
Lynn University, FL
Maryville University of Saint Louis, MO
Mercer University, GA
Michigan State University, MI
Middle Tennessee State University, TN
Midwestern State University, TX
Millikin University, IL
Minnesota State University Moorhead, MN
Mississippi State University, MS

Missouri University of Science and Technology, MO
Molloy College, NY
Montclair State University, NJ
Moravian College, PA
Morehead State University, KY
Murray State University, KY
Nazareth College of Rochester, NY
New England College, NH
New Jersey Institute of Technology, NJ
North Central College, IL
Northern Illinois University, IL
Northern Kentucky University, KY
Northern Michigan University, MI
Northern State University, SD
Oglethorpe University, GA
Ohio Northern University, OH
The Ohio State University, OH
Ohio University, OH
Ohio University–Eastern, OH
Ohio University–Lancaster, OH
Ohio University–Southern Campus, OH
Ohio University–Zanesville, OH
Oklahoma State University, OK
Old Dominion University, VA
Ouachita Baptist University, AR
Ozark Christian College, MO
Point Loma Nazarene University, CA
Point Park University, PA
Portland State University, OR
Post University, CT
Rochester Institute of Technology, NY
Rockhurst University, MO
St. Ambrose University, IA
St. Edward's University, TX
Saint Louis University, MO
Saint Martin's University, WA
Saint Mary's College of California, CA
Samford University, AL
San Diego State University, CA
San Jose State University, CA
Shenandoah University, VA
Siena College, NY
South Dakota State University, SD
Southeast Missouri State University, MO
Southern Illinois University Carbondale, IL
Southwestern University, TX
State University of New York at Fredonia, NY
State University of New York at New Paltz, NY
State University of New York at Oswego, NY
State University of New York at Plattsburgh, NY
State University of New York College at Cortland, NY
State University of New York College at Geneseo, NY
Stony Brook University, State University of New York, NY
Tennessee Technological University, TN
Texas A&M International University, TX
Texas A&M University–Commerce, TX
Texas A&M University–Texarkana, TX
Texas Christian University, TX
Texas State University, TX
Texas Tech University, TX
Texas Wesleyan University, TX
Trinity Christian College, IL
Union University, TN
The University of Akron, OH
University of Arkansas, AR
University of Arkansas at Little Rock, AR
University of California, Davis, CA
University of California, Irvine, CA

University of Colorado Boulder, CO
University of Colorado Denver, CO
University of Dayton, OH
University of Delaware, DE
University of Denver, CO
University of Evansville, IN
University of Hartford, CT
University of Houston, TX
University of Idaho, ID
University of Illinois at Urbana–Champaign, IL
The University of Kansas, KS
University of Kentucky, KY
University of Maine, ME
University of Mary Hardin-Baylor, TX
University of Maryland, College Park, MD
University of Mary Washington, VA
University of Memphis, TN
University of Miami, FL
University of Michigan, MI
University of Michigan–Dearborn, MI
University of Michigan–Flint, MI
University of Minnesota, Twin Cities Campus, MN
University of Mississippi, MS
University of Missouri, MO
University of Missouri–St. Louis, MO
University of Montana, MT
University of Nebraska–Lincoln, NE
University of Nevada, Las Vegas, NV
University of North Carolina at Asheville, NC
The University of North Carolina at Charlotte, NC
The University of North Carolina at Greensboro, NC
The University of North Carolina Wilmington, NC
University of North Dakota, ND
University of Northern Colorado, CO
University of North Florida, FL
University of Oklahoma, OK
University of Oregon, OR
University of Pittsburgh at Bradford, PA
University of Puget Sound, WA
University of Rhode Island, RI
University of St. Francis, IL
University of St. Thomas, MN
University of St. Thomas, TX
University of South Carolina, SC
University of South Florida, FL
The University of Tampa, FL
The University of Tennessee, TN
The University of Tennessee at Martin, TN
The University of Texas at El Paso, TX
The University of Texas at San Antonio, TX
The University of Toledo, OH
The University of Tulsa, OK
University of Utah, UT
University of Vermont, VT
University of Washington, WA
University of Washington, Bothell, WA
University of Washington, Tacoma, WA
University of Wisconsin–Eau Claire, WI
University of Wisconsin–La Crosse, WI
University of Wisconsin–River Falls, WI
University of Wisconsin–Stevens Point, WI
University of Wisconsin–Stout, WI
University of Wyoming, WY
Utah State University, UT
Villanova University, PA
Virginia Military Institute, VA
Washington State University, WA
Washington University in St. Louis, MO
Wayne State College, NE
Wayne State University, MI

Webster University, MO
Wesleyan College, GA
Western Illinois University, IL
Western Oregon University, OR
West Virginia University, WV
Wheaton College, IL
Wichita State University, KS
Widener University, PA
William Jessup University, CA
Wilson College, PA
Wright State University, OH
Wright State University–Lake Campus, OH

Library Science

Alverno College, WI
Bluefield College, VA
California Polytechnic State University, San Luis Obispo, CA
Clarion University of Pennsylvania, PA
East Carolina University, NC
Iowa State University of Science and Technology, IA
Kent State University, OH
Kutztown University of Pennsylvania, PA
Lindenwood University, MO
Lock Haven University of Pennsylvania, PA
Mississippi State University, MS
Moravian College, PA
Northeastern State University, OK
Northern Illinois University, IL
Old Dominion University, VA
Sam Houston State University, TX
Southern Arkansas University–Magnolia, AR
Texas Woman's University, TX
The University of Alabama, AL
University of Houston, TX
University of Idaho, ID
University of Illinois at Urbana–Champaign, IL
University of Louisiana at Monroe, LA
University of Maryland, College Park, MD
University of Mary Washington, VA
University of Miami, FL
University of Michigan, MI
University of Minnesota, Twin Cities Campus, MN
University of Missouri, MO
The University of North Carolina at Greensboro, NC
University of Rhode Island, RI
University of South Carolina, SC
University of South Florida, FL
The University of Tennessee, TN
The University of Toledo, OH
University of Washington, WA
University of Wisconsin–Eau Claire, WI
Utah State University, UT
Valdosta State University, GA
Valley City State University, ND
Virginia Polytechnic Institute and State University, VA
Wayne State University, MI
Western Illinois University, IL
Western Oregon University, OR
Western Washington University, WA
West Virginia University, WV

Mathematics

Abilene Christian University, TX
Adelphi University, NY
Alaska Pacific University, AK
Albany State University, GA
Albertus Magnus College, CT
Alfred University, NY
Angelo State University, TX

Arkansas Tech University, AR
Auburn University, AL
Augsburg University, MN
Augustana College, IL
Augustana University, SD
Austin College, TX
Austin Peay State University, TN
Averett University, VA
Ball State University, IN
Barton College, NC
Baylor University, TX
Belhaven University, MS
Bemidji State University, MN
Bethel College, KS
Binghamton University, State University of New York, NY
Birmingham-Southern College, AL
Black Hills State University, SD
Bloomsburg University of Pennsylvania, PA
Blue Mountain College, MS
Bluffton University, OH
Boise State University, ID
Bowie State University, MD
Bowling Green State University, OH
Bryan College, TN
Bucknell University, PA
Buena Vista University, IA
Buffalo State College, State University of New York, NY
Butler University, IN
California Lutheran University, CA
California Polytechnic State University, San Luis Obispo, CA
California State Polytechnic University, Pomona, CA
California State University, Bakersfield, CA
California State University, Chico, CA
California State University, Fresno, CA
California State University, Fullerton, CA
California State University, Northridge, CA
California State University, San Bernardino, CA
California State University, San Marcos, CA
California State University, Stanislaus, CA
Calvin College, MI
Cameron University, OK
Campbellsville University, KY
Carlow University, PA
Carroll University, WI
Carson-Newman University, TN
Case Western Reserve University, OH
Cedar Crest College, PA
Centenary College of Louisiana, LA
Central College, IA
Central Methodist University, MO
Central Michigan University, MI
Christian Brothers University, TN
Christopher Newport University, VA
City College of the City University of New York, NY
Clarion University of Pennsylvania, PA
Clarkson University, NY
Clemson University, SC
Cleveland State University, OH
Coastal Carolina University, SC
The College at Brockport, State University of New York, NY
College of Charleston, SC
College of Coastal Georgia, GA
The College of Idaho, ID
The College of New Rochelle, NY
College of Saint Benedict, MN
College of Saint Mary, NE
College of Staten Island of the City University of New York, NY

The Colorado College, CO
Colorado Mesa University, CO
Colorado School of Mines, CO
Columbia College, MO
Columbia College Chicago, IL
Columbus State University, GA
Concordia University Chicago, IL
Concordia University, Nebraska, NE
Concordia University Texas, TX
Concord University, WV
Cornerstone University, MI
Dakota State University, SD
Dallas Baptist University, TX
Davidson College, NC
Defiance College, OH
Denison University, OH
DeSales University, PA
DigiPen Institute of Technology, WA
Dordt College, IA
Drury University, MO
Duke University, NC
East Carolina University, NC
Eastern Illinois University, IL
Eastern Mennonite University, VA
Eastern Michigan University, MI
Eastern Washington University, WA
East Texas Baptist University, TX
Elizabethtown College, PA
Elmhurst College, IL
Elon University, NC
Emporia State University, KS
Evangel University, MO
Fairmont State University, WV
Ferris State University, MI
Florida Agricultural and Mechanical University, FL
Florida Gulf Coast University, FL
Florida International University, FL
Fort Hays State University, KS
Fort Lewis College, CO
Framingham State University, MA
Francis Marion University, SC
Frostburg State University, MD
Furman University, SC
Gannon University, PA
Gardner-Webb University, NC
George Fox University, OR
Georgian Court University, NJ
Georgia Southern University, GA
Glenville State College, WV
Governors State University, IL
Grambling State University, LA
Grand Valley State University, MI
Greenville University, IL
Grove City College, PA
Hamline University, MN
Hardin-Simmons University, TX
Henderson State University, AR
High Point University, NC
Hillsdale College, MI
Hood College, MD
Howard Payne University, TX
Huntingdon College, AL
Idaho State University, ID
Illinois Institute of Technology, IL
Indiana State University, IN
Indiana University of Pennsylvania, PA
Indiana Wesleyan University, IN
Iowa State University of Science and Technology, IA
Jacksonville State University, AL
James Madison University, VA
John Carroll University, OH
Johnson C. Smith University, NC
Juniata College, PA

Kansas Wesleyan University, KS
Kean University, NJ
Kennesaw State University, GA
Kent State University, OH
Kenyon College, OH
King's College, PA
Knox College, IL
Kutztown University of Pennsylvania, PA
Lebanon Valley College, PA
Lewis-Clark State College, ID
Liberty University, VA
Lindenwood University, MO
Lindsey Wilson College, KY
Linfield College, OR
Lipscomb University, TN
Lock Haven University of Pennsylvania, PA
Longwood University, VA
Loras College, IA
Louisiana College, LA
Louisiana State University and Agricultural
    & Mechanical College, LA
Louisiana Tech University, LA
Loyola Marymount University, CA
Lycoming College, PA
Malone University, OH
Manhattan College, NY
Mansfield University of Pennsylvania, PA
Marquette University, WI
Marymount University, VA
Maryville University of Saint Louis, MO
Marywood University, PA
Massachusetts College of Liberal Arts, MA
McMurry University, TX
Meredith College, NC
Metropolitan State University of Denver, CO
Michigan State University, MI
Middle Tennessee State University, TN
Midwestern State University, TX
Millersville University of Pennsylvania, PA
Millikin University, IL
Mills College, CA
Milwaukee School of Engineering, WI
Minnesota State University Moorhead, MN
Minot State University, ND
Mississippi State University, MS
Missouri University of Science and
    Technology, MO
Missouri Valley College, MO
Missouri Western State University, MO
Molloy College, NY
Monmouth University, NJ
Montana State University, MT
Montana State University Billings, MT
Montana Tech of The University of
    Montana, MT
Montclair State University, NJ
Moravian College, PA
Morehouse College, GA
Mount Mary University, WI
Murray State University, KY
Muskingum University, OH
Nazareth College of Rochester, NY
Newberry College, SC
New Jersey Institute of Technology, NJ
New Mexico Highlands University, NM
New Mexico State University, NM
North Carolina State University, NC
North Central College, IL
Northeastern Illinois University, IL
Northeastern State University, OK
Northern Illinois University, IL
Northern Kentucky University, KY
Northern Michigan University, MI
Northern State University, SD
Northwestern College, IA
Northwest Missouri State University, MO

Northwest Nazarene University, ID
Oglethorpe University, GA
Ohio Northern University, OH
The Ohio State University, OH
Ohio University, OH
Ohio University–Chillicothe, OH
Ohio University–Eastern, OH
Ohio University–Lancaster, OH
Ohio University–Southern Campus, OH
Ohio University–Zanesville, OH
Ohio Valley University, WV
Oklahoma Baptist University, OK
Oklahoma State University, OK
Old Dominion University, VA
Ouachita Baptist University, AR
Pacific University, OR
Piedmont College, GA
Pittsburg State University, KS
Plymouth State University, NH
Point Loma Nazarene University, CA
Point Park University, PA
Purdue University, IN
Randolph College, VA
Regis University, CO
Rensselaer Polytechnic Institute, NY
Rochester Institute of Technology, NY
Rockford University, IL
Rockhurst University, MO
Rollins College, FL
Sacred Heart University, CT
Saginaw Valley State University, MI
St. Catherine University, MN
St. Edward's University, TX
St. John Fisher College, NY
St. John's University, NY
Saint Joseph's University, PA
Saint Louis University, MO
Saint Mary's College of California, CA
St. Thomas Aquinas College, NY
Saint Vincent College, PA
Samford University, AL
Sam Houston State University, TX
San Diego State University, CA
San Jose State University, CA
Schreiner University, TX
Shenandoah University, VA
Shepherd University, WV
Shippensburg University of Pennsylvania,
    PA
Siena College, NY
Skidmore College, NY
Slippery Rock University of Pennsylvania,
    PA
Sonoma State University, CA
South Dakota State University, SD
Southeastern Louisiana University, LA
Southeastern Oklahoma State University,
    OK
Southeast Missouri State University, MO
Southern Adventist University, TN
Southern Arkansas University–Magnolia,
    AR
Southern Illinois University Carbondale, IL
Southern Oregon University, OR
Southwestern College, KS
Southwestern Oklahoma State University,
    OK
Southwestern University, TX
State University of New York at Fredonia,
    NY
State University of New York at New Paltz,
    NY
State University of New York at Oswego,
    NY
State University of New York at Plattsburgh,
    NY

State University of New York College at
    Cortland, NY
State University of New York College at
    Geneseo, NY
State University of New York College at
    Potsdam, NY
Stephen F. Austin State University, TX
Stetson University, FL
Stockton University, NJ
Stony Brook University, State University of
    New York, NY
Suffolk University, MA
Tennessee Technological University, TN
Texas A&M International University, TX
Texas A&M University, TX
Texas A&M University–Commerce, TX
Texas A&M University–Texarkana, TX
Texas Christian University, TX
Texas Lutheran University, TX
Texas State University, TX
Texas Tech University, TX
Texas Wesleyan University, TX
Texas Woman's University, TX
Thomas More College, KY
Thomas University, GA
Towson University, MD
Trinity Christian College, IL
Truman State University, MO
Union University, TN
The University of Akron, OH
The University of Alabama, AL
The University of Alabama at Birmingham,
    AL
The University of Alabama in Huntsville,
    AL
University of Alaska Anchorage, AK
University of Alaska Fairbanks, AK
University of Arkansas, AR
University of Arkansas at Little Rock, AR
University of Bridgeport, CT
University of California, Davis, CA
University of California, Irvine, CA
University of California, Riverside, CA
University of California, San Diego, CA
University of California, Santa Cruz, CA
University of Central Oklahoma, OK
University of Colorado Boulder, CO
University of Colorado Denver, CO
University of Dallas, TX
University of Dayton, OH
University of Delaware, DE
University of Denver, CO
University of Evansville, IN
University of Hartford, CT
University of Houston, TX
University of Houston–Clear Lake, TX
University of Houston–Victoria, TX
University of Idaho, ID
University of Illinois at Urbana–Champaign,
    IL
The University of Kansas, KS
University of Kentucky, KY
University of Louisiana at Monroe, LA
University of Maine, ME
University of Maine at Fort Kent, ME
University of Mary Hardin-Baylor, TX
University of Maryland, Baltimore County,
    MD
University of Maryland, College Park, MD
University of Mary Washington, VA
University of Massachusetts Amherst, MA
University of Massachusetts Dartmouth, MA
University of Massachusetts Lowell, MA
University of Memphis, TN
University of Miami, FL
University of Michigan, MI

University of Michigan–Dearborn, MI
University of Michigan–Flint, MI
University of Minnesota, Twin Cities Campus, MN
University of Mississippi, MS
University of Missouri, MO
University of Missouri–St. Louis, MO
University of Montana, MT
The University of Montana Western, MT
University of Montevallo, AL
University of Nebraska–Lincoln, NE
University of Nevada, Las Vegas, NV
University of Nevada, Reno, NV
University of New Hampshire, NH
University of North Carolina at Asheville, NC
The University of North Carolina at Chapel Hill, NC
The University of North Carolina at Charlotte, NC
The University of North Carolina at Greensboro, NC
The University of North Carolina Wilmington, NC
University of North Dakota, ND
University of Northern Colorado, CO
University of Northern Iowa, IA
University of North Georgia, GA
University of Oklahoma, OK
University of Oregon, OR
University of Pittsburgh at Bradford, PA
University of Pittsburgh at Johnstown, PA
University of Portland, OR
University of Providence, MT
University of Puget Sound, WA
University of Rhode Island, RI
University of Richmond, VA
University of St. Thomas, MN
University of St. Thomas, TX
University of Sioux Falls, SD
University of South Carolina, SC
University of South Carolina Aiken, SC
University of South Dakota, SD
University of Southern Indiana, IN
University of South Florida, FL
The University of Tennessee at Chattanooga, TN
The University of Tennessee at Martin, TN
The University of Texas at Dallas, TX
The University of Texas at El Paso, TX
The University of Texas at San Antonio, TX
The University of Texas Rio Grande Valley, TX
University of the Southwest, NM
The University of Toledo, OH
The University of Tulsa, OK
University of Utah, UT
University of Vermont, VT
The University of Virginia's College at Wise, VA
University of Washington, WA
University of Washington, Bothell, WA
University of Washington, Tacoma, WA
University of West Florida, FL
University of West Georgia, GA
University of Wisconsin–Eau Claire, WI
University of Wisconsin–La Crosse, WI
University of Wisconsin–Parkside, WI
University of Wisconsin–River Falls, WI
University of Wisconsin–Stevens Point, WI
University of Wisconsin–Stout, WI
University of Wisconsin–Superior, WI
University of Wisconsin–Whitewater, WI
University of Wyoming, WY
Utah State University, UT

Valdosta State University, GA
Valley City State University, ND
Virginia Military Institute, VA
Virginia State University, VA
Walla Walla University, WA
Wartburg College, IA
Washington State University, WA
Washington University in St. Louis, MO
Wayland Baptist University, TX
Wayne State College, NE
Wayne State University, MI
Wesleyan College, GA
West Chester University of Pennsylvania, PA
Western Carolina University, NC
Western Illinois University, IL
Western Kentucky University, KY
Western Oregon University, OR
Western Washington University, WA
West Texas A&M University, TX
West Virginia University, WV
Wheaton College, IL
Wichita State University, KS
Widener University, PA
William Jessup University, CA
Wilson College, PA
Wisconsin Lutheran College, WI
Wright State University, OH
Wright State University–Lake Campus, OH
Xavier University, OH
Youngstown State University, OH

Military Science
Angelo State University, TX
Arkansas Tech University, AR
Auburn University at Montgomery, AL
Austin Peay State University, TN
Ball State University, IN
Baylor University, TX
Black Hills State University, SD
Boise State University, ID
Boston College, MA
Boston University, MA
Bowie State University, MD
Bowling Green State University, OH
California Polytechnic State University, San Luis Obispo, CA
California State University, Fullerton, CA
Cameron University, OK
Carson-Newman University, TN
Central Michigan University, MI
Christopher Newport University, VA
The Citadel, The Military College of South Carolina, SC
Claremont McKenna College, CA
Clarion University of Pennsylvania, PA
Clarkson University, NY
Clemson University, SC
The College at Brockport, State University of New York, NY
College of Saint Benedict, MN
Colorado School of Mines, CO
Columbus State University, GA
Creighton University, NE
Dickinson College, PA
East Carolina University, NC
Eastern Washington University, WA
Elon University, NC
Florida Agricultural and Mechanical University, FL
Florida Institute of Technology, FL
Fort Hays State University, KS
Furman University, SC
Georgia Southern University, GA
Gonzaga University, WA
Grambling State University, LA

Idaho State University, ID
Indiana University of Pennsylvania, PA
Iowa State University of Science and Technology, IA
Jacksonville State University, AL
James Madison University, VA
John Carroll University, OH
Kent State University, OH
Lehigh University, PA
Lincoln University, MO
Lindenwood University, MO
Longwood University, VA
Louisiana Tech University, LA
Manhattan College, NY
Mercer University, GA
Methodist University, NC
Michigan State University, MI
Middle Tennessee State University, TN
Mississippi State University, MS
Missouri University of Science and Technology, MO
Missouri Valley College, MO
Missouri Western State University, MO
Montana State University, MT
Moravian College, PA
Morehead State University, KY
Morehouse College, GA
Murray State University, KY
New Mexico State University, NM
North Carolina State University, NC
Northern Illinois University, IL
Northern Michigan University, MI
Northwest Nazarene University, ID
The Ohio State University, OH
Ohio University, OH
Ohio University–Chillicothe, OH
Ohio University–Eastern, OH
Ohio University–Lancaster, OH
Ohio University–Southern Campus, OH
Ohio University–Zanesville, OH
Oklahoma State University, OK
Old Dominion University, VA
Olivet Nazarene University, IL
Pittsburg State University, KS
Providence College, RI
Purdue University, IN
Rensselaer Polytechnic Institute, NY
Rochester Institute of Technology, NY
Rogers State University, OK
Saint Augustine's University, NC
St. Edward's University, TX
St. John's University, NY
Saint Leo University, FL
Saint Louis University, MO
St. Mary's University, TX
Sam Houston State University, TX
San Diego State University, CA
Santa Clara University, CA
Siena College, NY
Slippery Rock University of Pennsylvania, PA
South Dakota State University, SD
Southeast Missouri State University, MO
Southern Illinois University Carbondale, IL
Stephen F. Austin State University, TX
Stetson University, FL
Tennessee Technological University, TN
Texas Christian University, TX
Texas State University, TX
Texas Tech University, TX
Texas Wesleyan University, TX
Truman State University, MO
Union University, TN
The University of Akron, OH
The University of Alabama, AL

University of Alaska Fairbanks, AK
University of Arkansas, AR
University of Central Oklahoma, OK
University of Colorado Boulder, CO
University of Dallas, TX
University of Dayton, OH
University of Delaware, DE
University of Florida, FL
University of Houston, TX
University of Idaho, ID
University of Illinois at Urbana–Champaign, IL
The University of Iowa, IA
The University of Kansas, KS
University of Kentucky, KY
University of Louisiana at Monroe, LA
University of Maine, ME
University of Mary Hardin-Baylor, TX
University of Maryland, College Park, MD
University of Massachusetts Amherst, MA
University of Memphis, TN
University of Michigan, MI
University of Minnesota, Twin Cities Campus, MN
University of Mississippi, MS
University of Montana, MT
University of Nebraska at Kearney, NE
University of New Hampshire, NH
University of North Alabama, AL
University of Northern Colorado, CO
University of North Georgia, GA
University of Oklahoma, OK
University of Oregon, OR
University of Portland, OR
University of Rhode Island, RI
University of Rochester, NY
The University of Scranton, PA
University of South Carolina, SC
University of South Dakota, SD
University of South Florida, FL
The University of Tampa, FL
The University of Tennessee, TN
The University of Tennessee at Chattanooga, TN
The University of Tennessee at Martin, TN
The University of Texas at El Paso, TX
The University of Texas Rio Grande Valley, TX
The University of Toledo, OH
University of Utah, UT
University of Vermont, VT
University of Washington, WA
University of Washington, Tacoma, WA
University of West Florida, FL
University of Wisconsin–La Crosse, WI
University of Wisconsin–Stevens Point, WI
Valparaiso University, IN
Villanova University, PA
Virginia Military Institute, VA
Washington State University, WA
Washington University in St. Louis, MO
Wayne State University, MI
Western Illinois University, IL
Western Kentucky University, KY
West Virginia University, WV
Wheaton College, IL
Whitworth University, WA
Widener University, PA
Wright State University, OH
Wright State University–Lake Campus, OH
Xavier University, OH
Youngstown State University, OH

Physical Sciences
Abilene Christian University, TX
Adelphi University, NY

Alaska Pacific University, AK
Albertus Magnus College, CT
Alfred University, NY
Angelo State University, TX
Arkansas Tech University, AR
Auburn University, AL
Augsburg University, MN
Augustana College, IL
Augustana University, SD
Austin College, TX
Austin Peay State University, TN
Averett University, VA
Ball State University, IN
Barton College, NC
Baylor University, TX
Bellarmine University, KY
Bemidji State University, MN
Binghamton University, State University of New York, NY
Birmingham-Southern College, AL
Black Hills State University, SD
Bloomsburg University of Pennsylvania, PA
Blue Mountain College, MS
Bluffton University, OH
Boise State University, ID
Bowling Green State University, OH
Bryan College, TN
Bucknell University, PA
Buffalo State College, State University of New York, NY
Butler University, IN
California Lutheran University, CA
California Polytechnic State University, San Luis Obispo, CA
California State Polytechnic University, Pomona, CA
California State University, Bakersfield, CA
California State University, Chico, CA
California State University, Fresno, CA
California State University, Fullerton, CA
California State University, San Bernardino, CA
California State University, Stanislaus, CA
Calvin College, MI
Cameron University, OK
Campbellsville University, KY
Carroll University, WI
Case Western Reserve University, OH
Catawba College, NC
Cedar Crest College, PA
Centenary College of Louisiana, LA
Central College, IA
Central Methodist University, MO
Central Michigan University, MI
Central State University, OH
Chapman University, CA
Christopher Newport University, VA
Clarion University of Pennsylvania, PA
Clarkson University, NY
Clemson University, SC
Cleveland State University, OH
Coastal Carolina University, SC
The College at Brockport, State University of New York, NY
College of Charleston, SC
The College of Idaho, ID
The College of New Rochelle, NY
College of Saint Benedict, MN
College of Staten Island of the City University of New York, NY
The Colorado College, CO
Colorado Mesa University, CO
Colorado School of Mines, CO
Columbia College, MO
Columbus State University, GA
Concordia University, Nebraska, NE

Concordia University Texas, TX
Concord University, WV
Cornerstone University, MI
Dakota State University, SD
Dallas Baptist University, TX
Davidson College, NC
Defiance College, OH
Denison University, OH
DeSales University, PA
Dordt College, IA
Drury University, MO
East Carolina University, NC
Eastern Illinois University, IL
Eastern Mennonite University, VA
Eastern Michigan University, MI
Eastern Washington University, WA
East Texas Baptist University, TX
Elizabethtown College, PA
Elmhurst College, IL
Elon University, NC
Emory University, GA
Emporia State University, KS
Evangel University, MO
Fairmont State University, WV
Flagler College, FL
Florida Agricultural and Mechanical University, FL
Florida Atlantic University, FL
Florida Gulf Coast University, FL
Florida International University, FL
Florida Southern College, FL
Fort Hays State University, KS
Fort Lewis College, CO
Framingham State University, MA
Francis Marion University, SC
Frostburg State University, MD
Furman University, SC
Gardner-Webb University, NC
George Fox University, OR
Georgia College & State University, GA
Georgia Institute of Technology, GA
Georgian Court University, NJ
Governors State University, IL
Graceland University, IA
Grambling State University, LA
Grand Valley State University, MI
Greenville University, IL
Grove City College, PA
Hamline University, MN
Hampton University, VA
Hardin-Simmons University, TX
Harrisburg University of Science and Technology, PA
High Point University, NC
Hillsdale College, MI
Hiram College, OH
Howard Payne University, TX
Idaho State University, ID
Indiana State University, IN
Indiana University of Pennsylvania, PA
Indiana Wesleyan University, IN
Iowa State University of Science and Technology, IA
Jacksonville State University, AL
James Madison University, VA
John Carroll University, OH
Juniata College, PA
Kansas Wesleyan University, KS
Kean University, NJ
Kennesaw State University, GA
Kent State University, OH
King's College, PA
Kutztown University of Pennsylvania, PA
Lebanon Valley College, PA
Lewis-Clark State College, ID
Lindenwood University, MO

Linfield College, OR
Lock Haven University of Pennsylvania, PA
Loras College, IA
Louisiana State University and Agricultural
& Mechanical College, LA
Louisiana Tech University, LA
Loyola Marymount University, CA
Lubbock Christian University, TX
Lycoming College, PA
Mansfield University of Pennsylvania, PA
Marquette University, WI
Massachusetts College of Liberal Arts, MA
McMurry University, TX
Meredith College, NC
Metropolitan State University of Denver, CO
Michigan State University, MI
Middle Tennessee State University, TN
Midwestern State University, TX
Millersville University of Pennsylvania, PA
Millikin University, IL
Mills College, CA
Minnesota State University Moorhead, MN
Mississippi State University, MS
Missouri University of Science and
Technology, MO
Missouri Valley College, MO
Missouri Western State University, MO
Monmouth University, NJ
Montana State University, MT
Montana State University Billings, MT
Montana Tech of The University of
Montana, MT
Montclair State University, NJ
Moravian College, PA
Morehead State University, KY
Murray State University, KY
Muskingum University, OH
Nazareth College of Rochester, NY
Newberry College, SC
New Jersey Institute of Technology, NJ
New Mexico Highlands University, NM
New Mexico State University, NM
North Carolina State University, NC
North Central College, IL
Northeastern Illinois University, IL
Northeastern State University, OK
Northern Illinois University, IL
Northern Kentucky University, KY
Northern Michigan University, MI
Northern State University, SD
Northwestern College, IA
Northwest Missouri State University, MO
Northwest Nazarene University, ID
Oberlin College, OH
Ohio Northern University, OH
The Ohio State University, OH
Ohio University, OH
Ohio University–Chillicothe, OH
Ohio University–Eastern, OH
Ohio University–Lancaster, OH
Ohio University–Southern Campus, OH
Ohio University–Zanesville, OH
Oklahoma Baptist University, OK
Oklahoma State University, OK
Old Dominion University, VA
Ouachita Baptist University, AR
Pacific University, OR
Piedmont College, GA
Pittsburg State University, KS
Point Loma Nazarene University, CA
Point Park University, PA
Portland State University, OR
Purdue University, IN
Randolph College, VA
Regis University, CO

Rhodes College, TN
Rochester Institute of Technology, NY
Rockford University, IL
Rockhurst University, MO
Rollins College, FL
Sacred Heart University, CT
Saginaw Valley State University, MI
St. Catherine University, MN
St. Edward's University, TX
St. John Fisher College, NY
St. John's University, NY
Saint Joseph's University, PA
Saint Louis University, MO
Saint Mary's College of California, CA
Saint Vincent College, PA
Samford University, AL
Sam Houston State University, TX
San Diego State University, CA
San Jose State University, CA
Schreiner University, TX
Shenandoah University, VA
Shepherd University, WV
Shippensburg University of Pennsylvania,
PA
Siena College, NY
Skidmore College, NY
Slippery Rock University of Pennsylvania,
PA
Sonoma State University, CA
South Dakota State University, SD
Southeastern Oklahoma State University,
OK
Southeast Missouri State University, MO
Southern Adventist University, TN
Southern Arkansas University–Magnolia,
AR
Southern Illinois University Carbondale, IL
Southern Oregon University, OR
Southwestern College, KS
Southwestern Oklahoma State University,
OK
State University of New York at Fredonia,
NY
State University of New York at New Paltz,
NY
State University of New York at Oswego,
NY
State University of New York at Plattsburgh,
NY
State University of New York College at
Cortland, NY
State University of New York College at
Geneseo, NY
State University of New York College at
Potsdam, NY
State University of New York College of
Environmental Science and Forestry, NY
Stephen F. Austin State University, TX
Stetson University, FL
Stockton University, NJ
Stony Brook University, State University of
New York, NY
Tennessee Technological University, TN
Texas A&M International University, TX
Texas A&M University, TX
Texas A&M University–Commerce, TX
Texas Christian University, TX
Texas State University, TX
Texas Tech University, TX
Texas Wesleyan University, TX
Texas Woman's University, TX
Thomas More College, KY
Thomas University, GA
Towson University, MD
Trevecca Nazarene University, TN

Trinity Christian College, IL
Truman State University, MO
Union University, TN
The University of Akron, OH
The University of Alabama, AL
The University of Alabama in Huntsville,
AL
University of Alaska Fairbanks, AK
University of Arkansas, AR
University of Arkansas at Little Rock, AR
University of California, Irvine, CA
University of California, Riverside, CA
University of California, San Diego, CA
University of California, Santa Cruz, CA
University of Central Oklahoma, OK
University of Colorado Boulder, CO
University of Colorado Denver, CO
University of Dallas, TX
University of Dayton, OH
University of Delaware, DE
University of Denver, CO
University of Evansville, IN
University of Houston, TX
University of Idaho, ID
University of Illinois at Urbana–Champaign,
IL
University of Indianapolis, IN
University of Jamestown, ND
The University of Kansas, KS
University of Kentucky, KY
University of Louisiana at Monroe, LA
University of Maine, ME
University of Mary Hardin-Baylor, TX
University of Maryland, Baltimore County,
MD
University of Maryland, College Park, MD
University of Mary Washington, VA
University of Massachusetts Amherst, MA
University of Massachusetts Dartmouth, MA
University of Memphis, TN
University of Miami, FL
University of Michigan, MI
University of Michigan–Dearborn, MI
University of Michigan–Flint, MI
University of Minnesota, Twin Cities
Campus, MN
University of Mississippi, MS
University of Missouri, MO
University of Missouri–St. Louis, MO
University of Montana, MT
The University of Montana Western, MT
University of Montevallo, AL
University of Nebraska–Lincoln, NE
University of Nevada, Las Vegas, NV
University of Nevada, Reno, NV
University of New Hampshire, NH
University of North Carolina at Asheville,
NC
The University of North Carolina at
Charlotte, NC
The University of North Carolina at
Greensboro, NC
The University of North Carolina
Wilmington, NC
University of North Dakota, ND
University of Northern Colorado, CO
University of Northern Iowa, IA
University of North Georgia, GA
University of Oklahoma, OK
University of Oregon, OR
University of Pittsburgh at Bradford, PA
University of Pittsburgh at Johnstown, PA
University of Portland, OR
University of Providence, MT
University of Puget Sound, WA

University of Rhode Island, RI
University of Richmond, VA
University of St. Thomas, MN
University of St. Thomas, TX
University of Sioux Falls, SD
University of South Carolina, SC
University of South Carolina Aiken, SC
University of South Florida, FL
The University of Tampa, FL
The University of Tennessee at Chattanooga, TN
The University of Tennessee at Martin, TN
The University of Texas at Dallas, TX
The University of Texas at El Paso, TX
The University of Texas at San Antonio, TX
University of the Southwest, NM
The University of Toledo, OH
The University of Tulsa, OK
University of Utah, UT
University of Vermont, VT
The University of Virginia's College at Wise, VA
University of Washington, WA
University of Washington, Bothell, WA
University of Washington, Tacoma, WA
University of West Florida, FL
University of West Georgia, GA
University of Wisconsin–Eau Claire, WI
University of Wisconsin–Green Bay, WI
University of Wisconsin–La Crosse, WI
University of Wisconsin–Parkside, WI
University of Wisconsin–River Falls, WI
University of Wisconsin–Stevens Point, WI
University of Wisconsin–Stout, WI
University of Wisconsin–Superior, WI
University of Wisconsin–Whitewater, WI
University of Wyoming, WY
Upper Iowa University, IA
Utah State University, UT
Valdosta State University, GA
Valley City State University, ND
Valparaiso University, IN
Virginia Military Institute, VA
Virginia State University, VA
Wartburg College, IA
Washington State University, WA
Washington University in St. Louis, MO
Wayland Baptist University, TX
Wayne State College, NE
Wayne State University, MI
Western Illinois University, IL
Western Kentucky University, KY
Western Oregon University, OR
Western Washington University, WA
West Texas A&M University, TX
West Virginia University, WV
Wheaton College, IL
Wichita State University, KS
Widener University, PA
William Jessup University, CA
Wilson College, PA
Wisconsin Lutheran College, WI
Wright State University, OH
Wright State University–Lake Campus, OH
Xavier University, OH
Youngstown State University, OH

Premedicine

Albertus Magnus College, CT
Alfred University, NY
American Jewish University, CA
Angelo State University, TX
Arkansas Tech University, AR
Auburn University, AL
Augustana University, SD
Austin College, TX

Averett University, VA
Baylor University, TX
Belhaven University, MS
Bemidji State University, MN
Bethel College, KS
Binghamton University, State University of New York, NY
Birmingham-Southern College, AL
Blue Mountain College, MS
Bluffton University, OH
Boise State University, ID
Bryan College, TN
Butler University, IN
California State University, Bakersfield, CA
California State University, Stanislaus, CA
Calvin College, MI
Campbellsville University, KY
Carroll University, WI
Case Western Reserve University, OH
Catawba College, NC
Centenary College of Louisiana, LA
Central College, IA
Central Methodist University, MO
Central Michigan University, MI
Chaminade University of Honolulu, HI
Christopher Newport University, VA
City College of the City University of New York, NY
Clarion University of Pennsylvania, PA
Clemson University, SC
Cleveland State University, OH
The College at Brockport, State University of New York, NY
College of Charleston, SC
College of Coastal Georgia, GA
The College of Idaho, ID
The College of New Rochelle, NY
College of Staten Island of the City University of New York, NY
Concordia University, Nebraska, NE
Concord University, WV
Dallas Baptist University, TX
Davidson College, NC
Defiance College, OH
DeSales University, PA
Dordt College, IA
Drury University, MO
Eastern Illinois University, IL
Eastern Mennonite University, VA
Eastern Washington University, WA
Elizabethtown College, PA
Elmhurst College, IL
Elon University, NC
Emory & Henry College, VA
Emporia State University, KS
Evangel University, MO
Florida Agricultural and Mechanical University, FL
Florida Institute of Technology, FL
Fort Hays State University, KS
Francis Marion University, SC
Frostburg State University, MD
Furman University, SC
Gannon University, PA
Gardner-Webb University, NC
Georgian Court University, NJ
Grambling State University, LA
Grand Valley State University, MI
Hamline University, MN
Hampden-Sydney College, VA
Hardin-Simmons University, TX
High Point University, NC
Hillsdale College, MI
Hobart and William Smith Colleges, NY
Howard Payne University, TX
Idaho State University, ID

Illinois Institute of Technology, IL
Indiana State University, IN
Indiana University of Pennsylvania, PA
Indiana Wesleyan University, IN
Iowa State University of Science and Technology, IA
James Madison University, VA
John Carroll University, OH
Juniata College, PA
Kansas Wesleyan University, KS
Kean University, NJ
Kennesaw State University, GA
Kent State University, OH
King's College, PA
Liberty University, VA
Lindenwood University, MO
Lindsey Wilson College, KY
Lipscomb University, TN
Lock Haven University of Pennsylvania, PA
Loras College, IA
Lycoming College, PA
Malone University, OH
Marywood University, PA
McMurry University, TX
Middle Tennessee State University, TN
Midwestern State University, TX
Millikin University, IL
Mills College, CA
Minnesota State University Moorhead, MN
Mississippi State University, MS
Missouri University of Science and Technology, MO
Missouri Valley College, MO
Missouri Western State University, MO
Montana State University Billings, MT
Moravian College, PA
Murray State University, KY
Muskingum University, OH
Nazareth College of Rochester, NY
New Jersey Institute of Technology, NJ
North Central College, IL
Northeastern State University, OK
Northern Kentucky University, KY
Northern Michigan University, MI
Northwestern College, IA
Northwest Nazarene University, ID
Ohio Northern University, OH
The Ohio State University, OH
Ohio University, OH
Ohio University–Chillicothe, OH
Ohio University–Eastern, OH
Ohio University–Lancaster, OH
Ohio University–Southern Campus, OH
Ohio University–Zanesville, OH
Oklahoma Baptist University, OK
Oklahoma State University, OK
Ouachita Baptist University, AR
Pacific University, OR
Piedmont College, GA
Plymouth State University, NH
Point Park University, PA
Providence College, RI
Randolph College, VA
Rochester Institute of Technology, NY
Rockford University, IL
Rockhurst University, MO
Rogers State University, OK
Sacred Heart University, CT
St. Catherine University, MN
St. Edward's University, TX
St. John's University, NY
Saint Joseph's University, PA
Saint Louis University, MO
Saint Martin's University, WA
Samford University, AL
Schreiner University, TX

Shepherd University, WV
Siena College, NY
Sonoma State University, CA
South Dakota State University, SD
Southeastern Louisiana University, LA
Southeast Missouri State University, MO
Southern Adventist University, TN
Southern Illinois University Carbondale, IL
Southwestern College, KS
Southwestern University, TX
State University of New York at Oswego, NY
State University of New York at Plattsburgh, NY
State University of New York College at Geneseo, NY
State University of New York College of Environmental Science and Forestry, NY
Stephen F. Austin State University, TX
Stetson University, FL
Sweet Briar College, VA
Tennessee Technological University, TN
Texas A&M International University, TX
Texas A&M University, TX
Texas A&M University Commerce, TX
Texas Christian University, TX
Texas Tech University, TX
Texas Wesleyan University, TX
Texas Woman's University, TX
Thomas More College, KY
Trine University, IN
Trinity Christian College, IL
Truman State University, MO
Union University, TN
The University of Akron, OH
The University of Alabama, AL
University of Arkansas, AR
University of California, Davis, CA
University of California, Irvine, CA
University of California, Riverside, CA
University of California, San Diego, CA
University of Colorado Boulder, CO
University of Colorado Denver, CO
University of Dallas, TX
University of Dayton, OH
University of Delaware, DE
University of Evansville, IN
University of Hartford, CT
University of Houston, TX
University of Idaho, ID
University of Illinois at Urbana–Champaign, IL
The University of Kansas, KS
University of Maine, ME
University of Mary Hardin-Baylor, TX
University of Maryland, College Park, MD
University of Massachusetts Amherst, MA
University of Memphis, TN
University of Miami, FL
University of Michigan, MI
University of Michigan–Flint, MI
University of Minnesota, Twin Cities Campus, MN
University of Mississippi, MS
University of Missouri, MO
University of Missouri–St. Louis, MO
University of Montana, MT
The University of Montana Western, MT
University of Nebraska–Lincoln, NE
University of Nevada, Las Vegas, NV
The University of North Carolina at Greensboro, NC
The University of North Carolina Wilmington, NC
University of North Dakota, ND

University of Northern Colorado, CO
University of North Georgia, GA
University of Oregon, OR
University of Pittsburgh at Bradford, PA
University of Pittsburgh at Johnstown, PA
University of Portland, OR
University of Providence, MT
University of Puget Sound, WA
University of Rhode Island, RI
University of St. Francis, IL
University of St. Thomas, TX
University of Sioux Falls, SD
University of South Carolina, SC
University of South Carolina Aiken, SC
University of South Dakota, SD
University of Southern Indiana, IN
University of South Florida, FL
The University of Tampa, FL
The University of Tennessee at Martin, TN
The University of Texas Rio Grande Valley, TX
University of the Southwest, NM
The University of Toledo, OH
The University of Tulsa, OK
University of Vermont, VT
The University of Virginia's College at Wise, VA
University of Washington, WA
University of Washington, Bothell, WA
University of West Georgia, GA
University of Wisconsin–Eau Claire, WI
University of Wisconsin–Green Bay, WI
University of Wisconsin–Parkside, WI
University of Wisconsin–River Falls, WI
University of Wisconsin–Stevens Point, WI
University of Wisconsin–Whitewater, WI
Utah State University, UT
Virginia Military Institute, VA
Virginia State University, VA
Wartburg College, IA
Washington State University, WA
Washington University in St. Louis, MO
Wayland Baptist University, TX
Wayne State College, NE
Wayne State University, MI
Wesleyan College, GA
Western Kentucky University, KY
Western Oregon University, OR
Western Washington University, WA
Westminster College, PA
West Texas A&M University, TX
West Virginia University, WV
Wheaton College, IL
Wheeling Jesuit University, WV
Wichita State University, KS
Widener University, PA
Wilson College, PA
Wright State University, OH
Wright State University–Lake Campus, OH
Youngstown State University, OH

Religion/Biblical Studies

Abilene Christian University, TX
Alaska Bible College, AK
Alaska Pacific University, AK
Albertus Magnus College, CT
Anderson University, SC
Appalachian Bible College, WV
Augsburg University, MN
Augustana College, IL
Augustana University, SD
Austin College, TX
Austin Graduate School of Theology, TX
Averett University, VA
The Baptist College of Florida, FL

Barton College, NC
Baylor University, TX
Belhaven University, MS
Belmont University, TN
Berry College, GA
Birmingham-Southern College, AL
Bloomsburg University of Pennsylvania, PA
Blue Mountain College, MS
Boise State University, ID
Boston Baptist College, MA
Bryan College, TN
Butler University, IN
California Baptist University, CA
California Lutheran University, CA
California State University, Bakersfield, CA
California State University, Fullerton, CA
Calvin College, MI
Campbellsville University, KY
Carolina Christian College, NC
Carson-Newman University, TN
Case Western Reserve University, OH
Centenary College of Louisiana, LA
Central College, IA
Central Methodist University, MO
Central Michigan University, MI
Charlotte Christian College and Theological Seminary, NC
The Citadel, The Military College of South Carolina, SC
The College of Idaho, ID
The College of New Rochelle, NY
Columbia College, MO
Concordia University Chicago, IL
Concordia University, Nebraska, NE
Concordia University, St. Paul, MN
Concordia University Texas, TX
Concordia University Wisconsin, WI
Corban University, OR
Cornerstone University, MI
Criswell College, TX
Crossroads Bible College, IN
Dallas Baptist University, TX
Davis College, NY
Defiance College, OH
DeSales University, PA
Dordt College, IA
Eastern Mennonite University, VA
Eastern Michigan University, MI
East Texas Baptist University, TX
Elizabethtown College, PA
Elmhurst College, IL
Elon University, NC
Emmanuel College, GA
Evangel University, MO
Faulkner University, AL
Felician University, NJ
Flagler College, FL
Florida Gulf Coast University, FL
Florida Southern College, FL
Furman University, SC
Gannon University, PA
Gardner-Webb University, NC
George Fox University, OR
Georgian Court University, NJ
Grove City College, PA
Hamline University, MN
Harding University, AR
Hardin-Simmons University, TX
High Point University, NC
Hiram College, OH
Hood College, MD
Howard Payne University, TX
Indiana University of Pennsylvania, PA
Indiana Wesleyan University, IN
James Madison University, VA

John Carroll University, OH
Johnson University, TN
Johnson University Florida, FL
Kansas Wesleyan University, KS
Kent State University, OH
King's College, PA
La Sierra University, CA
Lebanon Valley College, PA
Lee University, TN
Liberty University, VA
Lindenwood University, MO
Lindsey Wilson College, KY
Linfield College, OR
Lipscomb University, TN
Loras College, IA
Louisiana College, LA
Loyola Marymount University, CA
Lubbock Christian University, TX
Lycoming College, PA
Malone University, OH
Marywood University, PA
McKendree University, IL
McMurry University, TX
Mercer University, GA
Meredith College, NC
MidAmerica Nazarene University, KS
Mississippi State University, MS
Missouri Baptist University, MO
Missouri Western State University, MO
Montclair State University, NJ
Moravian College, PA
Nazareth College of Rochester, NY
Nebraska Christian College of Hope
    International University, NE
Newberry College, SC
North Central College, IL
Northeast Catholic College, NH
Northwest Christian University, OR
Northwestern College, IA
Northwest Nazarene University, ID
Ohio Northern University, OH
Ohio Valley University, WV
Oklahoma Baptist University, OK
Oklahoma Christian University, OK
Oklahoma City University, OK
Oral Roberts University, OK
Ouachita Baptist University, AR
Ozark Christian College, MO
Piedmont College, GA
Point Loma Nazarene University, CA
Randolph-Macon College, VA
Rockhurst University, MO
St. Ambrose University, IA
St. Edward's University, TX
Saint Louis University, MO
Saint Mary's College of California, CA
St. Thomas Aquinas College, NY
Samford University, AL
San Diego State University, CA
San Jose State University, CA
Schreiner University, TX
Shenandoah University, VA
Siena College, NY
Southeastern University, FL
Southeast Missouri State University, MO
Southern Adventist University, TN
Southwestern College, KS
Stetson University, FL
Texas Christian University, TX
Texas Wesleyan University, TX
Thomas More College, KY
Toccoa Falls College, GA
Trevecca Nazarene University, TN
Trinity Christian College, IL
Trinity College of Florida, FL
Truett McConnell University, GA

Union University, TN
University of California, Davis, CA
University of Colorado Boulder, CO
University of Dayton, OH
University of Delaware, DE
University of Evansville, IN
University of Hartford, CT
University of Illinois at Urbana–Champaign,
    IL
University of Indianapolis, IN
The University of Kansas, KS
University of Mary Hardin-Baylor, TX
University of Mary Washington, VA
University of Miami, FL
University of Minnesota, Twin Cities
    Campus, MN
University of Missouri, MO
University of North Carolina at Asheville,
    NC
The University of North Carolina at
    Charlotte, NC
The University of North Carolina at
    Greensboro, NC
University of Portland, OR
University of Providence, MT
University of Rhode Island, RI
University of St. Thomas, MN
University of St. Thomas, TX
University of Sioux Falls, SD
University of South Carolina, SC
University of South Florida, FL
University of the Southwest, NM
The University of Toledo, OH
The University of Tulsa, OK
University of Wisconsin–Eau Claire, WI
University of Wyoming, WY
Valparaiso University, IN
Walla Walla University, WA
Wartburg College, IA
Washington University in St. Louis, MO
Wayland Baptist University, TX
Wesleyan College, GA
Western Illinois University, IL
Western Kentucky University, KY
West Virginia University, WV
Wheaton College, IL
William Jessup University, CA
Williams Baptist College, AR
Wilson College, PA
Wright State University, OH
Wright State University–Lake Campus, OH
Youngstown State University, OH

Social Sciences

Abilene Christian University, TX
Alaska Pacific University, AK
Albany State University, GA
Albertus Magnus College, CT
Alfred University, NY
Alliant International University–San Diego,
    CA
Angelo State University, TX
Arkansas Tech University, AR
Auburn University, AL
Augsburg University, MN
Augustana College, IL
Augustana University, SD
Austin College, TX
Austin Peay State University, TN
Ball State University, IN
Barton College, NC
Baylor University, TX
Belhaven University, MS
Belmont University, TN
Bemidji State University, MN
Bethel College, KS

Binghamton University, State University of
    New York, NY
Birmingham-Southern College, AL
Black Hills State University, SD
Bloomsburg University of Pennsylvania, PA
Blue Mountain College, MS
Boise State University, ID
Bowling Green State University, OH
Bryan College, TN
Buffalo State College, State University of
    New York, NY
Butler University, IN
California Lutheran University, CA
California Polytechnic State University, San
    Luis Obispo, CA
California State Polytechnic University,
    Pomona, CA
California State University, Bakersfield, CA
California State University, Chico, CA
California State University, Fresno, CA
California State University, Fullerton, CA
California State University, Northridge, CA
California State University, San Bernardino,
    CA
California State University, Stanislaus, CA
Calvin College, MI
Cameron University, OK
Campbellsville University, KY
Carlos Albizu University, PR
Carlow University, PA
Carroll University, WI
Case Western Reserve University, OH
Centenary College of Louisiana, LA
Central College, IA
Central Methodist University, MO
Central Michigan University, MI
Champlain College, VT
Christopher Newport University, VA
City College of the City University of New
    York, NY
Clarion University of Pennsylvania, PA
Clarkson University, NY
Clemson University, SC
Cleveland State University, OH
Coastal Carolina University, SC
The College at Brockport, State University
    of New York, NY
College of Charleston, SC
College of Coastal Georgia, GA
The College of Idaho, ID
The College of New Rochelle, NY
College of Staten Island of the City
    University of New York, NY
Colorado Mesa University, CO
Columbia College, MO
Concordia University, Nebraska, NE
Concordia University Texas, TX
Concord University, WV
Corban University, OR
Cornerstone University, MI
Dallas Baptist University, TX
Davidson College, NC
Defiance College, OH
DeSales University, PA
Dordt College, IA
Drury University, MO
East Carolina University, NC
Eastern Illinois University, IL
Eastern Mennonite University, VA
Eastern Michigan University, MI
Eastern Washington University, WA
East Texas Baptist University, TX
Elizabethtown College, PA
Elmhurst College, IL
Elon University, NC
Emporia State University, KS

Evangel University, MO
Fairmont State University, WV
Flagler College, FL
Florida Agricultural and Mechanical University, FL
Florida Atlantic University, FL
Florida Gulf Coast University, FL
Florida International University, FL
Florida Southern College, FL
Fort Hays State University, KS
Fort Lewis College, CO
Francis Marion University, SC
Frostburg State University, MD
Furman University, SC
Gannon University, PA
Gardner-Webb University, NC
George Fox University, OR
Georgia College & State University, GA
Georgian Court University, NJ
Georgia Southern University, GA
Glenville State College, WV
Governors State University, IL
Grambling State University, LA
Grand Valley State University, MI
Grove City College, PA
Hamline University, MN
Hardin-Simmons University, TX
Hillsdale College, MI
Hiram College, OH
Hood College, MD
Howard Payne University, TX
Idaho State University, ID
Illinois Institute of Technology, IL
Indiana State University, IN
Indiana University of Pennsylvania, PA
Indiana Wesleyan University, IN
Iowa State University of Science and Technology, IA
Iowa Wesleyan University, IA
Jacksonville State University, AL
James Madison University, VA
John Carroll University, OH
Juniata College, PA
Kansas Wesleyan University, KS
Kean University, NJ
Kennesaw State University, GA
Kent State University, OH
Kent State University at Stark, OH
Kenyon College, OH
King's College, PA
Lebanon Valley College, PA
Lewis-Clark State College, ID
Lindenwood University, MO
Linfield College, OR
Lock Haven University of Pennsylvania, PA
Longwood University, VA
Louisiana College, LA
Louisiana Tech University, LA
Loyola Marymount University, CA
Lubbock Christian University, TX
Lycoming College, PA
Malone University, OH
Marymount University, VA
Maryville University of Saint Louis, MO
Marywood University, PA
Massachusetts College of Liberal Arts, MA
McMurry University, TX
Metropolitan State University of Denver, CO
Michigan State University, MI
Middle Georgia State University, GA
Middle Tennessee State University, TN
Midwestern State University, TX
Millersville University of Pennsylvania, PA
Minnesota State University Moorhead, MN
Minot State University, ND

Mississippi State University, MS
Missouri University of Science and Technology, MO
Missouri Valley College, MO
Missouri Western State University, MO
Molloy College, NY
Monmouth University, NJ
Montana State University, MT
Montana State University Billings, MT
Montclair State University, NJ
Moravian College, PA
Morehead State University, KY
Mount Mary University, WI
Murray State University, KY
Nazareth College of Rochester, NY
Newberry College, SC
New England College, NH
New Mexico Highlands University, NM
New Mexico State University, NM
North Carolina State University, NC
North Central College, IL
Northeastern Illinois University, IL
Northeastern State University, OK
Northern Illinois University, IL
Northern Kentucky University, KY
Northern Michigan University, MI
Northern State University, SD
Northwestern College, IA
Northwest Missouri State University, MO
Northwest Nazarene University, ID
Oglethorpe University, GA
Ohio Northern University, OH
The Ohio State University, OH
Ohio University, OH
Ohio University–Chillicothe, OH
Ohio University–Eastern, OH
Ohio University–Lancaster, OH
Ohio University–Southern Campus, OH
Ohio University–Zanesville, OH
Oklahoma Baptist University, OK
Oklahoma State University, OK
Old Dominion University, VA
Ouachita Baptist University, AR
Pacific University, OR
Piedmont College, GA
Pittsburg State University, KS
Point Loma Nazarene University, CA
Point Park University, PA
Portland State University, OR
Post University, CT
Randolph College, VA
Rochester Institute of Technology, NY
Rockford University, IL
Rockhurst University, MO
St. Catherine University, MN
St. Edward's University, TX
St. John Fisher College, NY
St. John's University, NY
Saint Louis University, MO
St. Thomas Aquinas College, NY
Samford University, AL
Sam Houston State University, TX
San Diego State University, CA
San Jose State University, CA
Schreiner University, TX
Shenandoah University, VA
Shepherd University, WV
Shippensburg University of Pennsylvania, PA
Siena College, NY
Slippery Rock University of Pennsylvania, PA
Sonoma State University, CA
South Dakota State University, SD
Southeastern Louisiana University, LA

Southeastern Oklahoma State University, OK
Southeast Missouri State University, MO
Southern Adventist University, TN
Southern Arkansas University–Magnolia, AR
Southern Illinois University Carbondale, IL
Southern New Hampshire University, NH
Southern Oregon University, OR
Southwestern College, KS
Southwestern Oklahoma State University, OK
Southwestern University, TX
State University of New York at Fredonia, NY
State University of New York at Oswego, NY
State University of New York at Plattsburgh, NY
State University of New York College at Geneseo, NY
State University of New York College at Potsdam, NY
Stetson University, FL
Stockton University, NJ
Stony Brook University, State University of New York, NY
Tennessee Technological University, TN
Texas A&M International University, TX
Texas A&M University–Commerce, TX
Texas A&M University–Texarkana, TX
Texas Christian University, TX
Texas State University, TX
Texas Tech University, TX
Texas Wesleyan University, TX
Texas Woman's University, TX
Thomas More College, KY
Thomas University, GA
Trevecca Nazarene University, TN
Trinity Christian College, IL
Truman State University, MO
Union University, TN
The University of Akron, OH
The University of Alabama, AL
The University of Alabama in Huntsville, AL
University of Alaska Anchorage, AK
University of Arkansas, AR
University of Arkansas at Little Rock, AR
University of Bridgeport, CT
University of California, Davis, CA
University of California, Irvine, CA
University of California, Riverside, CA
University of California, San Diego, CA
University of California, Santa Cruz, CA
University of Central Oklahoma, OK
University of Colorado Boulder, CO
University of Colorado Denver, CO
University of Dayton, OH
University of Delaware, DE
University of Denver, CO
University of Evansville, IN
University of Hartford, CT
University of Houston, TX
University of Houston–Clear Lake, TX
University of Houston–Victoria, TX
University of Idaho, ID
University of Illinois at Urbana–Champaign, IL
The University of Kansas, KS
University of Louisiana at Monroe, LA
University of Maine, ME
University of Maine at Fort Kent, ME
University of Mary Hardin-Baylor, TX

University of Maryland, Baltimore County, MD
University of Maryland, College Park, MD
University of Mary Washington, VA
University of Massachusetts Amherst, MA
University of Massachusetts Dartmouth, MA
University of Memphis, TN
University of Miami, FL
University of Michigan, MI
University of Michigan–Dearborn, MI
University of Michigan–Flint, MI
University of Minnesota, Twin Cities Campus, MN
University of Mississippi, MS
University of Missouri, MO
University of Missouri–St. Louis, MO
University of Montana, MT
The University of Montana Western, MT
University of Montevallo, AL
University of Nebraska–Lincoln, NE
University of Nevada, Las Vegas, NV
University of North Carolina at Asheville, NC
The University of North Carolina at Charlotte, NC
The University of North Carolina at Greensboro, NC
The University of North Carolina Wilmington, NC
University of North Dakota, ND
University of Northern Colorado, CO
University of Northern Iowa, IA
University of Oklahoma, OK
University of Oregon, OR
University of Pittsburgh at Bradford, PA
University of Pittsburgh at Johnstown, PA
University of Portland, OR
University of Providence, MT
University of Puget Sound, WA
University of Rhode Island, RI
University of Richmond, VA
University of St. Francis, IL
University of St. Thomas, MN
University of St. Thomas, TX
University of Sioux Falls, SD
University of South Carolina, SC
University of South Carolina Aiken, SC
University of South Dakota, SD
University of Southern Indiana, IN
University of South Florida, FL
The University of Tampa, FL
The University of Tennessee, TN
The University of Tennessee at Martin, TN
The University of Texas at San Antonio, TX
The University of Texas Rio Grande Valley, TX
University of the Southwest, NM
The University of Toledo, OH
The University of Tulsa, OK
University of Utah, UT
University of Vermont, VT
The University of Virginia's College at Wise, VA
University of Washington, WA
University of Washington, Bothell, WA
University of Washington, Tacoma, WA
University of West Florida, FL
University of West Georgia, GA
University of Wisconsin–Eau Claire, WI
University of Wisconsin–Green Bay, WI
University of Wisconsin–La Crosse, WI
University of Wisconsin–Parkside, WI
University of Wisconsin–River Falls, WI
University of Wisconsin–Stevens Point, WI
University of Wisconsin–Superior, WI
University of Wisconsin–Whitewater, WI

University of Wyoming, WY
Upper Iowa University, IA
Utah State University, UT
Valdosta State University, GA
Valley City State University, ND
Wartburg College, IA
Washington State University, WA
Washington University in St. Louis, MO
Wayland Baptist University, TX
Wayne State College, NE
Wayne State University, MI
Wesleyan College, GA
West Chester University of Pennsylvania, PA
Western Illinois University, IL
Western Kentucky University, KY
Western Oregon University, OR
Western Washington University, WA
West Texas A&M University, TX
West Virginia University, WV
Wheaton College, IL
Wichita State University, KS
Widener University, PA
William Jessup University, CA
Wilson College, PA
Wright State University, OH
Wright State University–Lake Campus, OH
Xavier University, OH
Youngstown State University, OH

Creative Arts/Performance

Applied Art and Design
Anderson University, SC
Auburn University, AL
Belhaven University, MS
Belmont University, TN
Bemidji State University, MN
Bethel College, KS
Bowie State University, MD
Brenau University, GA
Buffalo State College, State University of New York, NY
Butler University, IN
California Baptist University, CA
California Polytechnic State University, San Luis Obispo, CA
California State University, Chico, CA
Calvin College, MI
Central Michigan University, MI
Chatham University, PA
City College of the City University of New York, NY
Claflin University, SC
Clemson University, SC
Cleveland Institute of Art, OH
College of Staten Island of the City University of New York, NY
Columbia College Chicago, IL
Concordia University, Nebraska, NE
Converse College, SC
Defiance College, OH
Dominican University, IL
East Carolina University, NC
Eastern Illinois University, IL
Eastern Michigan University, MI
Emmanuel College, GA
Ferris State University, MI
FIDM/Fashion Institute of Design & Merchandising, Los Angeles Campus, CA
Flagler College, FL
Florida Agricultural and Mechanical University, FL
Fort Hays State University, KS
Georgian Court University, NJ

Graceland University, IA
Grand Valley State University, MI
Greenville University, IL
Hamline University, MN
Hardin-Simmons University, TX
Hofstra University, NY
Huntington University, IN
Illinois Institute of Technology, IL
Indiana State University, IN
Indiana University of Pennsylvania, PA
Iowa State University of Science and Technology, IA
Kansas Wesleyan University, KS
Kean University, NJ
Keene State College, NH
Kent State University, OH
Kutztown University of Pennsylvania, PA
Lafayette College, PA
Laguna College of Art & Design, CA
La Sierra University, CA
Lindenwood University, MO
Lindsey Wilson College, KY
Louisiana State University and Agricultural & Mechanical College, LA
Louisiana Tech University, LA
Loyola Marymount University, CA
Lycoming College, PA
Marymount California University, CA
Maryville University of Saint Louis, MO
Massachusetts College of Liberal Arts, MA
Meredith College, NC
Mississippi State University, MS
Missouri Valley College, MO
Morehead State University, KY
Mount Mary University, WI
Muskingum University, OH
Nazareth College of Rochester, NY
New England College, NH
New Jersey Institute of Technology, NJ
New Mexico State University, NM
Northeastern State University, OK
Northern Illinois University, IL
Northern Michigan University, MI
Northwest College of Art & Design, WA
Ohio Northern University, OH
Ohio University, OH
Ohio University–Chillicothe, OH
Ohio University–Eastern, OH
Ohio University–Lancaster, OH
Ohio University–Southern Campus, OH
Ohio University–Zanesville, OH
Ohio Wesleyan University, OH
Oklahoma Baptist University, OK
Oklahoma Christian University, OK
Oklahoma City University, OK
Old Dominion University, VA
Oral Roberts University, OK
Piedmont College, GA
Ringling College of Art and Design, FL
Robert Morris University Illinois, IL
Rochester Institute of Technology, NY
Sacred Heart University, CT
Saint Mary-of-the-Woods College, IN
San Diego State University, CA
San Jose State University, CA
Savannah College of Art and Design, GA
Schreiner University, TX
Seton Hill University, PA
Shepherd University, WV
Slippery Rock University of Pennsylvania, PA
Sonoma State University, CA
Southern Illinois University Carbondale, IL
Southwestern Oklahoma State University, OK

State University of New York at Fredonia, NY
State University of New York College at Geneseo, NY
Stetson University, FL
Stockton University, NJ
Texas A&M University–Commerce, TX
Texas Christian University, TX
Texas State University, TX
Texas Tech University, TX
Texas Woman's University, TX
Trinity Christian College, IL
Troy University, AL
The University of Akron, OH
University of Bridgeport, CT
University of California, San Diego, CA
University of Central Oklahoma, OK
University of Colorado Denver, CO
University of Delaware, DE
University of Hartford, CT
University of Idaho, ID
University of Illinois at Chicago, IL
University of Illinois at Urbana–Champaign, IL
The University of Iowa, IA
The University of Kansas, KS
University of Kentucky, KY
University of Maryland, College Park, MD
University of Massachusetts Dartmouth, MA
University of Memphis, TN
University of Nebraska at Kearney, NE
University of Nevada, Las Vegas, NV
The University of North Carolina at Chapel Hill, NC
University of North Carolina School of the Arts, NC
University of Northern Colorado, CO
University of Northern Iowa, IA
University of North Georgia, GA
University of Oregon, OR
University of St. Francis, IL
University of St. Thomas, TX
University of South Florida, FL
The University of Texas at El Paso, TX
The University of the Arts, PA
University of West Florida, FL
University of West Georgia, GA
University of Wisconsin–Parkside, WI
University of Wisconsin–Stevens Point, WI
University of Wisconsin–Stout, WI
University of Wyoming, WY
Utah State University, UT
Valley City State University, ND
Virginia Polytechnic Institute and State University, VA
Virginia State University, VA
Washington State University, WA
Washington University in St. Louis, MO
Wayne State College, NE
Western Illinois University, IL
Western Washington University, WA
Wheaton College, IL
Wichita State University, KS
William Jessup University, CA
Wright State University, OH
Wright State University–Lake Campus, OH

Art/Fine Arts

Abilene Christian University, TX
Adelphi University, NY
Alaska Pacific University, AK
Albertus Magnus College, CT
Albion College, MI
Albright College, PA
Alfred University, NY

Allegheny College, PA
Alma College, MI
Alverno College, WI
Anderson University, SC
Arizona State University at the Tempe campus, AZ
Arkansas Tech University, AR
Auburn University, AL
Augsburg University, MN
Augustana College, IL
Augustana University, SD
Aurora University, IL
Austin College, TX
Austin Peay State University, TN
Averett University, VA
Baker University, KS
Barton College, NC
Baylor University, TX
Belhaven University, MS
Bellarmine University, KY
Belmont University, TN
Bemidji State University, MN
Berry College, GA
Bethany Lutheran College, MN
Bethel College, IN
Bethel College, KS
Bethel University, MN
Binghamton University, State University of New York, NY
Birmingham-Southern College, AL
Black Hills State University, SD
Bluefield College, VA
Blue Mountain College, MS
Bluffton University, OH
Boise State University, ID
Boston University, MA
Bowie State University, MD
Bowling Green State University, OH
Bradley University, IL
Brenau University, GA
Brigham Young University, UT
Bucknell University, PA
Buena Vista University, IA
Butler University, IN
Caldwell University, NJ
California Baptist University, CA
California Lutheran University, CA
California Polytechnic State University, San Luis Obispo, CA
California State University, Bakersfield, CA
California State University, Chico, CA
California State University, Fresno, CA
California State University, Fullerton, CA
California State University, San Bernardino, CA
California State University, San Marcos, CA
California State University, Stanislaus, CA
Calumet College of Saint Joseph, IN
Calvin College, MI
Cameron University, OK
Campbellsville University, KY
Campbell University, NC
Canisius College, NY
Cardinal Stritch University, WI
Carroll College, MT
Carroll University, WI
Carson-Newman University, TN
Case Western Reserve University, OH
Cedar Crest College, PA
Centenary College of Louisiana, LA
Central College, IA
Central Michigan University, MI
Central Washington University, WA
Chapman University, CA
Chatham University, PA

Christopher Newport University, VA
City College of the City University of New York, NY
Claflin University, SC
Clarion University of Pennsylvania, PA
Clarke University, IA
Clemson University, SC
Cleveland Institute of Art, OH
Cleveland State University, OH
Coastal Carolina University, SC
Coe College, IA
Coker College, SC
The College at Brockport, State University of New York, NY
College of Charleston, SC
College of Coastal Georgia, GA
The College of Idaho, ID
The College of New Jersey, NJ
The College of New Rochelle, NY
College of Saint Benedict, MN
The College of Saint Rose, NY
College of Staten Island of the City University of New York, NY
Colorado Mesa University, CO
Colorado State University, CO
Columbia College, MO
Columbia College Chicago, IL
Columbus College of Art & Design, OH
Columbus State University, GA
Concordia College, MN
Concordia University, Nebraska, NE
Concord University, WV
Cooper Union for the Advancement of Science and Art, NY
Cornell College, IA
Creighton University, NE
Culver-Stockton College, MO
Daemen College, NY
Dallas Baptist University, TX
Davidson College, NC
DePaul University, IL
DigiPen Institute of Technology, WA
Doane University, NE
Dominican University, IL
Drake University, IA
Drew University, NJ
Drury University, MO
East Carolina University, NC
Eastern Illinois University, IL
Eastern Mennonite University, VA
Eastern Michigan University, MI
Eastern Oregon University, OR
Eastern Washington University, WA
Eckerd College, FL
Edgewood College, WI
Elizabethtown College, PA
Elmhurst College, IL
Elon University, NC
Emmanuel College, GA
Emory & Henry College, VA
Emory University, GA
Emporia State University, KS
Endicott College, MA
Eureka College, IL
Evangel University, MO
Fairmont State University, WV
Ferris State University, MI
Flagler College, FL
Florida Agricultural and Mechanical University, FL
Florida Gulf Coast University, FL
Florida International University, FL
Florida Southern College, FL
Fort Hays State University, KS
Fort Lewis College, CO

Francis Marion University, SC
Franklin College, IN
Frostburg State University, MD
Furman University, SC
Gardner-Webb University, NC
George Fox University, OR
Georgetown College, KY
Georgia College & State University, GA
Georgian Court University, NJ
Georgia Southern University, GA
Georgia Southwestern State University, GA
Glenville State College, WV
Gordon College, MA
Goucher College, MD
Graceland University, IA
Grand Valley State University, MI
Greenville University, IL
Gustavus Adolphus College, MN
Hamline University, MN
Harding University, AR
Hardin-Simmons University, TX
Hartwick College, NY
Henderson State University, AR
Hendrix College, AR
High Point University, NC
Hillsdale College, MI
Hobart and William Smith Colleges, NY
Hofstra University, NY
Hood College, MD
Hope College, MI
Houston Baptist University, TX
Howard Payne University, TX
Huntington University, IN
Idaho State University, ID
Illinois College, IL
Illinois Wesleyan University, IL
Indiana State University, IN
Indiana University of Pennsylvania, PA
Indiana Wesleyan University, IN
Iowa State University of Science and
    Technology, IA
Iowa Wesleyan University, IA
Jacksonville State University, AL
Jacksonville University, FL
James Madison University, VA
John Brown University, AR
Johnson University, TN
Judson University, IL
Juniata College, PA
Kalamazoo College, MI
Kansas City Art Institute, MO
Kansas Wesleyan University, KS
Kean University, NJ
Keene State College, NH
Kennesaw State University, GA
Kent State University, OH
Kentucky State University, KY
Kenyon College, OH
King University, TN
Knox College, IL
Kutztown University of Pennsylvania, PA
Lafayette College, PA
LaGrange College, GA
Laguna College of Art & Design, CA
La Sierra University, CA
Lewis-Clark State College, ID
Lewis University, IL
Lincoln University, MO
Lincoln University, PA
Lindenwood University, MO
Lipscomb University, TN
Lock Haven University of Pennsylvania, PA
Long Island University–LIU Brooklyn, NY
Long Island University–LIU Post, NY
Longwood University, VA
Louisiana College, LA

Louisiana State University and Agricultural
    & Mechanical College, LA
Louisiana Tech University, LA
Loyola Marymount University, CA
Loyola University Chicago, IL
Loyola University New Orleans, LA
Lubbock Christian University, TX
Lycoming College, PA
Lynchburg College, VA
Lyon College, AR
Manhattanville College, NY
Mansfield University of Pennsylvania, PA
Marietta College, OH
Marlboro College, VT
Marshall University, WV
Marymount Manhattan College, NY
Maryville College, TN
Maryville University of Saint Louis, MO
Marywood University, PA
Massachusetts College of Liberal Arts, MA
McMurry University, TX
Mercer University, GA
Meredith College, NC
Messiah College, PA
Miami University, OH
Michigan State University, MI
Michigan Technological University, MI
MidAmerica Nazarene University, KS
Middle Tennessee State University, TN
Midwestern State University, TX
Millersville University of Pennsylvania, PA
Milligan College, TN
Millikin University, IL
Millsaps College, MS
Minnesota State University Mankato, MN
Minnesota State University Moorhead, MN
Minot State University, ND
Mississippi State University, MS
Missouri Southern State University, MO
Missouri Valley College, MO
Missouri Western State University, MO
Molloy College, NY
Monmouth College, IL
Montana State University, MT
Montana State University Billings, MT
Montclair State University, NJ
Moravian College, PA
Morehead State University, KY
Morehouse College, GA
Morningside College, IA
Mount Marty College, SD
Mount Mary University, WI
Mount Mercy University, IA
Mount St. Joseph University, OH
Mount St. Mary's University, MD
Mount Vernon Nazarene University, OH
Muhlenberg College, PA
Murray State University, KY
Muskingum University, OH
Nazareth College of Rochester, NY
New England College, NH
New Jersey Institute of Technology, NJ
Newman University, KS
New Mexico Highlands University, NM
New Mexico State University, NM
North Central College, IL
Northeastern Illinois University, IL
Northeastern State University, OK
Northern Arizona University, AZ
Northern Illinois University, IL
Northern Kentucky University, KY
Northern State University, SD
Northwest College of Art & Design, WA
Northwestern College, IA
Northwest Missouri State University, MO
Oakland City University, IN

Oglethorpe University, GA
Ohio Northern University, OH
Ohio University, OH
Ohio University–Chillicothe, OH
Ohio University–Eastern, OH
Ohio University–Lancaster, OH
Ohio University–Southern Campus, OH
Ohio University–Zanesville, OH
Ohio Wesleyan University, OH
Oklahoma Baptist University, OK
Oklahoma City University, OK
Oklahoma State University, OK
Old Dominion University, VA
Olivet College, MI
Olivet Nazarene University, IL
Oral Roberts University, OK
Ouachita Baptist University, AR
Pacific Lutheran University, WA
Pacific University, OR
Park University, MO
Piedmont College, GA
Point Loma Nazarene University, CA
Portland State University, OR
Rhode Island College, RI
Rhodes College, TN
Rice University, TX
Ringling College of Art and Design, FL
Roanoke College, VA
Roberts Wesleyan College, NY
Rochester Institute of Technology, NY
Rockford University, IL
Rogers State University, OK
Rollins College, FL
Rosemont College, PA
Sacred Heart University, CT
The Sage Colleges, NY
Saginaw Valley State University, MI
St. Ambrose University, IA
St. Catherine University, MN
St. Edward's University, TX
Saint John's University, MN
St. John's University, NY
Saint Louis University, MO
Saint Mary-of-the-Woods College, IN
Saint Mary's University of Minnesota, MN
Saint Michael's College, VT
St. Norbert College, WI
St. Olaf College, MN
Salve Regina University, RI
Samford University, AL
Sam Houston State University, TX
San Diego State University, CA
San Francisco Art Institute, CA
Savannah College of Art and Design, GA
School of the Art Institute of Chicago, IL
School of Visual Arts, NY
Schreiner University, TX
Seattle Pacific University, WA
Seattle University, WA
Seton Hill University, PA
Shepherd University, WV
Shippensburg University of Pennsylvania,
    PA
Simpson College, IA
Slippery Rock University of Pennsylvania,
    PA
Sonoma State University, CA
South Dakota State University, SD
Southeastern Louisiana University, LA
Southeastern Oklahoma State University,
    OK
Southeastern University, FL
Southern Adventist University, TN
Southern Arkansas University–Magnolia,
    AR
Southern Illinois University Carbondale, IL

Southern Oregon University, OR
Southern Utah University, UT
Southwest Baptist University, MO
Southwestern Oklahoma State University, OK
Southwestern University, TX
State University of New York at Fredonia, NY
State University of New York at New Paltz, NY
State University of New York at Plattsburgh, NY
State University of New York College at Cortland, NY
State University of New York College at Geneseo, NY
State University of New York College at Potsdam, NY
Sterling College, KS
Stetson University, FL
Stevenson University, MD
Stockton University, NJ
Syracuse University, NY
Temple University, PA
Tennessee Technological University, TN
Texas A&M International University, TX
Texas A&M University–Commerce, TX
Texas A&M University–Corpus Christi, TX
Texas Christian University, TX
Texas State University, TX
Texas Tech University, TX
Texas Wesleyan University, TX
Texas Woman's University, TX
Thomas More College, KY
Thomas University, GA
Towson University, MD
Transylvania University, KY
Trinity Christian College, IL
Trinity University, TX
Truman State University, MO
Tufts University, MA
Union University, TN
The University of Akron, OH
The University of Alabama, AL
The University of Alabama at Birmingham, AL
The University of Alabama in Huntsville, AL
University of Alaska Anchorage, AK
The University of Arizona, AZ
University of Arkansas, AR
University of Arkansas at Little Rock, AR
University of California, Irvine, CA
University of California, Riverside, CA
University of California, Santa Cruz, CA
University of Central Oklahoma, OK
University of Colorado Boulder, CO
University of Colorado Denver, CO
University of Dallas, TX
University of Dayton, OH
University of Delaware, DE
University of Denver, CO
University of Evansville, IN
University of Florida, FL
University of Hartford, CT
University of Houston, TX
University of Houston–Clear Lake, TX
University of Idaho, ID
University of Illinois at Chicago, IL
University of Illinois at Urbana–Champaign, IL
University of Indianapolis, IN
The University of Iowa, IA
University of Jamestown, ND
The University of Kansas, KS

University of Kentucky, KY
University of La Verne, CA
University of Louisiana at Monroe, LA
University of Maine, ME
University of Mary Hardin-Baylor, TX
University of Maryland, Baltimore County, MD
University of Maryland, College Park, MD
University of Mary Washington, VA
University of Massachusetts Amherst, MA
University of Massachusetts Dartmouth, MA
University of Massachusetts Lowell, MA
University of Memphis, TN
University of Michigan, MI
University of Michigan–Dearborn, MI
University of Michigan–Flint, MI
University of Minnesota, Twin Cities Campus, MN
University of Mississippi, MS
University of Missouri, MO
University of Missouri–St. Louis, MO
The University of Montana Western, MT
University of Montevallo, AL
University of Nebraska at Kearney, NE
University of Nebraska–Lincoln, NE
University of Nevada, Las Vegas, NV
University of Nevada, Reno, NV
University of New Hampshire, NH
University of North Alabama, AL
University of North Carolina at Asheville, NC
The University of North Carolina at Chapel Hill, NC
The University of North Carolina at Charlotte, NC
The University of North Carolina at Greensboro, NC
The University of North Carolina at Pembroke, NC
The University of North Carolina Wilmington, NC
University of North Dakota, ND
University of Northern Colorado, CO
University of Northern Iowa, IA
University of North Florida, FL
University of Oklahoma, OK
University of Oregon, OR
University of Pittsburgh at Bradford, PA
University of Puget Sound, WA
University of Rhode Island, RI
University of Richmond, VA
University of St. Francis, IL
University of St. Thomas, TX
University of Science and Arts of Oklahoma, OK
University of Sioux Falls, SD
University of South Carolina, SC
University of South Carolina Aiken, SC
University of South Dakota, SD
University of Southern California, CA
University of Southern Indiana, IN
University of Southern Mississippi, MS
University of South Florida, FL
The University of Tampa, FL
The University of Tennessee, TN
The University of Tennessee at Chattanooga, TN
The University of Tennessee at Martin, TN
The University of Texas at Austin, TX
The University of Texas at El Paso, TX
The University of Texas at San Antonio, TX
The University of Texas at Tyler, TX
The University of Texas Rio Grande Valley, TX
The University of the Arts, PA

University of the Incarnate Word, TX
The University of Toledo, OH
The University of Tulsa, OK
University of Utah, UT
University of Washington, WA
University of West Florida, FL
University of West Georgia, GA
University of Wisconsin–Eau Claire, WI
University of Wisconsin–Green Bay, WI
University of Wisconsin–La Crosse, WI
University of Wisconsin–Milwaukee, WI
University of Wisconsin–Parkside, WI
University of Wisconsin–River Falls, WI
University of Wisconsin–Stout, WI
University of Wisconsin–Whitewater, WI
University of Wyoming, WY
Utah State University, UT
Valdosta State University, GA
Valencia College, FL
Valley City State University, ND
Valparaiso University, IN
Virginia Polytechnic Institute and State University, VA
Virginia State University, VA
Wabash College, IN
Wake Forest University, NC
Wartburg College, IA
Washington College, MD
Washington State University, WA
Washington University in St. Louis, MO
Wayland Baptist University, TX
Waynesburg University, PA
Wayne State College, NE
Wayne State University, MI
Webster University, MO
Wesleyan College, GA
West Chester University of Pennsylvania, PA
Western Carolina University, NC
Western Illinois University, IL
Western Kentucky University, KY
Western Michigan University, MI
Western Oregon University, OR
Western State Colorado University, CO
Western Washington University, WA
Westmont College, CA
West Texas A&M University, TX
West Virginia University, WV
West Virginia Wesleyan College, WV
Wheaton College, IL
Whitman College, WA
Whittier College, CA
Whitworth University, WA
Wichita State University, KS
William Jessup University, CA
William Paterson University of New Jersey, NJ
Williams Baptist College, AR
William Woods University, MO
Winona State University, MN
Winthrop University, SC
Wisconsin Lutheran College, WI
Wittenberg University, OH
Wofford College, SC
Wright State University, OH
Wright State University–Lake Campus, OH
Xavier University, OH
Young Harris College, GA
Youngstown State University, OH

Cinema/Film/Broadcasting
Adelphi University, NY
Arkansas Tech University, AR
Auburn University, AL
Baker University, KS
Ball State University, IN

Baylor University, TX
Belhaven University, MS
Belmont University, TN
Bemidji State University, MN
Binghamton University, State University of
  New York, NY
Biola University, CA
Bowling Green State University, OH
Butler University, IN
California Baptist University, CA
California Polytechnic State University, San
  Luis Obispo, CA
California State University, Chico, CA
California State University, Fullerton, CA
Calvin College, MI
Cameron University, OK
Central Michigan University, MI
Chapman University, CA
City College of the City University of New
  York, NY
The College at Brockport, State University
  of New York, NY
College of Staten Island of the City
  University of New York, NY
Columbia College Chicago, IL
DeSales University, PA
Eastern Illinois University, IL
Eastern Michigan University, MI
Eastern Washington University, WA
Emory University, GA
Flagler College, FL
Florida Agricultural and Mechanical
  University, FL
Florida State University, FL
Fort Hays State University, KS
George Fox University, OR
Georgia Southern University, GA
Grand Valley State University, MI
Harding University, AR
Henderson State University, AR
Hofstra University, NY
Huntington University, IN
Ithaca College, NY
James Madison University, VA
Kansas Wesleyan University, KS
Kean University, NJ
Keene State College, NH
Kent State University, OH
Lafayette College, PA
Liberty University, VA
Lindenwood University, MO
Long Island University–LIU Brooklyn, NY
Long Island University–LIU Post, NY
Loyola Marymount University, CA
Massachusetts College of Liberal Arts, MA
Milligan College, TN
Minnesota State University Moorhead, MN
Minot State University, ND
Mississippi State University, MS
Missouri Valley College, MO
Missouri Western State University, MO
Montana State University, MT
Montclair State University, NJ
Muhlenberg College, PA
New Mexico State University, NM
North Central College, IL
Northwest Missouri State University, MO
Ohio University, OH
Ohio University–Chillicothe, OH
Ohio University–Eastern, OH
Ohio University–Lancaster, OH
Ohio University–Southern Campus, OH
Ohio University–Zanesville, OH
Old Dominion University, VA
Oral Roberts University, OK
Piedmont College, GA

Point Park University, PA
Rhode Island College, RI
Ringling College of Art and Design, FL
Rochester Institute of Technology, NY
Sacred Heart University, CT
St. John's University, NY
Saint Mary's College of California, CA
Samford University, AL
Sam Houston State University, TX
San Diego State University, CA
San Jose State University, CA
Savannah College of Art and Design, GA
Sonoma State University, CA
Southeastern University, FL
Southern Illinois University Carbondale, IL
Southwestern College, KS
Sterling College, KS
Stony Brook University, State University of
  New York, NY
Texas Christian University, TX
Texas Woman's University, TX
Towson University, MD
Trevecca Nazarene University, TN
Union University, TN
The University of Alabama, AL
University of California, Irvine, CA
University of California, San Diego, CA
University of California, Santa Cruz, CA
University of Central Florida, FL
University of Colorado Boulder, CO
University of Colorado Denver, CO
University of Hartford, CT
The University of Iowa, IA
The University of Kansas, KS
University of Kentucky, KY
University of La Verne, CA
University of Maryland, Baltimore County,
  MD
University of Memphis, TN
University of Michigan, MI
University of Michigan–Dearborn, MI
University of Mississippi, MS
University of Missouri, MO
University of Montevallo, AL
University of Nebraska–Lincoln, NE
University of Nevada, Las Vegas, NV
The University of North Carolina at
  Greensboro, NC
University of North Carolina School of the
  Arts, NC
The University of North Carolina
  Wilmington, NC
University of Oklahoma, OK
University of Pittsburgh at Bradford, PA
The University of Tennessee at Chattanooga,
  TN
The University of Tennessee at Martin, TN
The University of Toledo, OH
University of Utah, UT
University of Wisconsin–Whitewater, WI
University of Wyoming, WY
Virginia Polytechnic Institute and State
  University, VA
Wabash College, IN
Wartburg College, IA
Washington State University, WA
Western Illinois University, IL
Western Kentucky University, KY
Western Washington University, WA
Westminster College, PA
West Texas A&M University, TX
Wheaton College, IL
Wichita State University, KS
Wisconsin Lutheran College, WI
Wright State University, OH
Wright State University–Lake Campus, OH

Creative Writing
Arkansas Tech University, AR
Auburn University, AL
Augustana College, IL
Augustana University, SD
Austin Peay State University, TN
Belhaven University, MS
Belmont University, TN
Bemidji State University, MN
Binghamton University, State University of
  New York, NY
Bowling Green State University, OH
Brenau University, GA
Bucknell University, PA
California Lutheran University, CA
California Polytechnic State University, San
  Luis Obispo, CA
California State University, Chico, CA
Calumet College of Saint Joseph, IN
Calvin College, MI
Cameron University, OK
Campbell University, NC
Carroll College, MT
Case Western Reserve University, OH
Cedar Crest College, PA
Central College, IA
Central Michigan University, MI
Chapman University, CA
City College of the City University of New
  York, NY
Cleveland State University, OH
Coe College, IA
Coker College, SC
The College at Brockport, State University
  of New York, NY
The College of New Rochelle, NY
College of Staten Island of the City
  University of New York, NY
Colorado Mesa University, CO
Colorado State University, CO
Columbia College, MO
Columbia College Chicago, IL
Davidson College, NC
Drury University, MO
Eastern Illinois University, IL
Eastern Michigan University, MI
Eastern Washington University, WA
Eckerd College, FL
Edgewood College, WI
Emmanuel College, GA
Emporia State University, KS
Fairmont State University, WV
Flagler College, FL
Florida Agricultural and Mechanical
  University, FL
Fort Hays State University, KS
Frostburg State University, MD
Furman University, SC
Georgia Southern University, GA
Graceland University, IA
Grove City College, PA
Hamline University, MN
Hardin-Simmons University, TX
Hobart and William Smith Colleges, NY
Hollins University, VA
Hope College, MI
Huntington University, IN
Kent State University, OH
Kenyon College, OH
Knox College, IL
Lafayette College, PA
Lebanon Valley College, PA
Lewis-Clark State College, ID
Long Island University–LIU Brooklyn, NY
Long Island University–LIU Post, NY
Louisiana Tech University, LA

Loyola Marymount University, CA
Lycoming College, PA
Malone University, OH
Manhattanville College, NY
Meredith College, NC
Michigan State University, MI
Middle Tennessee State University, TN
Midwestern State University, TX
Millikin University, IL
Minnesota State University Moorhead, MN
Mississippi State University, MS
Missouri Western State University, MO
Molloy College, NY
Morningside College, IA
Mount Mercy University, IA
New England College, NH
New Mexico State University, NM
Northeastern Illinois University, IL
Northern Illinois University, IL
Ohio Northern University, OH
The Ohio State University, OH
Ohio University, OH
Ohio University–Chillicothe, OH
Ohio University–Eastern, OH
Ohio University–Lancaster, OH
Ohio University–Southern Campus, OH
Ohio University–Zanesville, OH
Oklahoma State University, OK
Old Dominion University, VA
Plymouth State University, NH
Rockhurst University, MO
Sacred Heart University, CT
St. John's University, NY
Saint Mary-of-the-Woods College, IN
St. Thomas Aquinas College, NY
San Diego State University, CA
Savannah College of Art and Design, GA
Siena College, NY
Sonoma State University, CA
Southern Illinois University Carbondale, IL
Southern Oregon University, OR
Southwestern College, KS
State University of New York College at Geneseo, NY
Sterling College, KS
Stockton University, NJ
Susquehanna University, PA
Texas Christian University, TX
Texas Wesleyan University, TX
The University of Akron, OH
The University of Alabama, AL
University of California, Irvine, CA
University of California, Riverside, CA
University of California, Santa Cruz, CA
University of Colorado Boulder, CO
University of Hartford, CT
University of Houston, TX
University of Idaho, ID
University of Illinois at Chicago, IL
The University of Iowa, IA
The University of Kansas, KS
University of Kentucky, KY
University of Louisiana at Monroe, LA
University of Maine, ME
University of Maryland, Baltimore County, MD
University of Memphis, TN
University of Michigan, MI
University of Michigan–Dearborn, MI
University of Mississippi, MS
University of Missouri, MO
University of Montana, MT
University of Montevallo, AL
University of Nevada, Las Vegas, NV

The University of North Carolina Wilmington, NC
University of Oregon, OR
University of Pittsburgh at Bradford, PA
University of South Dakota, SD
University of Southern Indiana, IN
University of South Florida, FL
The University of Tampa, FL
The University of Tennessee at Martin, TN
The University of Texas at San Antonio, TX
The University of the Arts, PA
The University of Toledo, OH
University of Utah, UT
The University of Virginia's College at Wise, VA
University of Wisconsin–Stevens Point, WI
University of Wisconsin–Whitewater, WI
University of Wyoming, WY
Ursinus College, PA
Virginia Polytechnic Institute and State University, VA
Wabash College, IN
Washington College, MD
Washington State University, WA
Washington University in St. Louis, MO
Wayne State College, NE
Webster University, MO
Western Illinois University, IL
Western Washington University, WA
West Texas A&M University, TX
West Virginia Wesleyan College, WV
Wheaton College, IL
Whitworth University, WA
Wichita State University, KS
Wright State University, OH
Wright State University–Lake Campus, OH
Youngstown State University, OH

Dance

Adelphi University, NY
Allegheny College, PA
Alma College, MI
Arizona State University at the Tempe campus, AZ
Augustana University, SD
Baker University, KS
Ball State University, IN
Belhaven University, MS
Belmont University, TN
Benedictine College, KS
Berklee College of Music, MA
Binghamton University, State University of New York, NY
Birmingham-Southern College, AL
Boise State University, ID
Bowling Green State University, OH
Brenau University, GA
Bucknell University, PA
Butler University, IN
California Polytechnic State University, San Luis Obispo, CA
California State University, Chico, CA
California State University, Fullerton, CA
Case Western Reserve University, OH
Cedar Crest College, PA
Centenary College of Louisiana, LA
Central Michigan University, MI
Chapman University, CA
Cleveland State University, OH
Coker College, SC
The College at Brockport, State University of New York, NY
The College of Wooster, OH
Colorado Mesa University, CO
Colorado State University, CO

Columbia College Chicago, IL
Columbus State University, GA
Concordia University, Nebraska, NE
Cornell College, IA
Creighton University, NE
Culver-Stockton College, MO
DeSales University, PA
Dominican University of California, CA
Drexel University, PA
Duquesne University, PA
East Carolina University, NC
Eastern Michigan University, MI
Emmanuel College, GA
Florida Agricultural and Mechanical University, FL
Florida International University, FL
Florida State University, FL
Fordham University, NY
Fort Hays State University, KS
Georgian Court University, NJ
Goucher College, MD
Graceland University, IA
Grambling State University, LA
Grand Valley State University, MI
Gustavus Adolphus College, MN
Hawai`i Pacific University, HI
Henderson State University, AR
Hendrix College, AR
Hobart and William Smith Colleges, NY
Hofstra University, NY
Hollins University, VA
Hope College, MI
Huntingdon College, AL
Idaho State University, ID
Indiana University of Pennsylvania, PA
Ithaca College, NY
James Madison University, VA
The Juilliard School, NY
Kansas Wesleyan University, KS
Kean University, NJ
Keene State College, NH
Kennesaw State University, GA
Kent State University, OH
Knox College, IL
Kutztown University of Pennsylvania, PA
Lafayette College, PA
Lindenwood University, MO
Long Island University–LIU Brooklyn, NY
Long Island University–LIU Post, NY
Loyola Marymount University, CA
Manhattanville College, NY
Marymount Manhattan College, NY
McKendree University, IL
Messiah College, PA
Methodist University, NC
Middle Tennessee State University, TN
Milligan College, TN
Millikin University, IL
Mississippi State University, MS
Missouri Valley College, MO
Missouri Western State University, MO
Montana State University, MT
Montclair State University, NJ
Morningside College, IA
Muhlenberg College, PA
Murray State University, KY
Nazareth College of Rochester, NY
New Mexico State University, NM
Nicholls State University, LA
Northeastern Illinois University, IL
Northeastern State University, OK
Northern Illinois University, IL
Northwestern College, IA
Northwest Missouri State University, MO
Ohio Northern University, OH

The Ohio State University, OH
Ohio University, OH
Ohio University–Chillicothe, OH
Ohio University–Eastern, OH
Ohio University–Lancaster, OH
Ohio University–Southern Campus, OH
Ohio University–Zanesville, OH
Ohio Wesleyan University, OH
Oklahoma City University, OK
Old Dominion University, VA
Pacific Lutheran University, WA
Palm Beach Atlantic University, FL
Plymouth State University, NH
Point Park University, PA
Rhode Island College, RI
Robert Morris University Illinois, IL
Rockford University, IL
Rogers State University, OK
Sacred Heart University, CT
St. Ambrose University, IA
St. John's University, NY
Saint Mary-of-the-Woods College, IN
Saint Mary's College of California, CA
St. Olaf College, MN
Sam Houston State University, TX
San Diego State University, CA
San Jose State University, CA
Santa Clara University, CA
Savannah College of Art and Design, GA
Seton Hill University, PA
Shenandoah University, VA
Slippery Rock University of Pennsylvania, PA
Sonoma State University, CA
Southeastern Oklahoma State University, OK
Southeast Missouri State University, MO
Southern Arkansas University–Magnolia, AR
Southern Illinois University Carbondale, IL
Southwestern College, KS
State University of New York at Fredonia, NY
State University of New York College at Geneseo, NY
State University of New York College at Potsdam, NY
Stockton University, NJ
Temple University, PA
Texas A&M International University, TX
Texas Christian University, TX
Texas State University, TX
Texas Tech University, TX
Texas Wesleyan University, TX
Texas Woman's University, TX
Thomas More College, KY
Towson University, MD
Trine University, IN
The University of Akron, OH
The University of Alabama, AL
The University of Arizona, AZ
University of California, Irvine, CA
University of California, Riverside, CA
University of California, San Diego, CA
University of Colorado Boulder, CO
University of Dubuque, IA
University of Florida, FL
University of Hartford, CT
University of Houston, TX
University of Idaho, ID
University of Illinois at Urbana–Champaign, IL
The University of Iowa, IA
The University of Kansas, KS
University of Kentucky, KY

University of Maine, ME
University of Maryland, Baltimore County, MD
University of Maryland, College Park, MD
University of Mary Washington, VA
University of Massachusetts Amherst, MA
University of Memphis, TN
University of Michigan, MI
University of Missouri–St. Louis, MO
University of Montana, MT
University of Nebraska–Lincoln, NE
University of Nevada, Las Vegas, NV
University of New Hampshire, NH
University of North Alabama, AL
University of North Carolina at Asheville, NC
The University of North Carolina at Charlotte, NC
The University of North Carolina at Greensboro, NC
University of North Carolina School of the Arts, NC
University of Northern Colorado, CO
University of Oklahoma, OK
University of Oregon, OR
University of Providence, MT
University of Richmond, VA
University of South Carolina, SC
University of Southern Mississippi, MS
University of South Florida, FL
The University of Tampa, FL
The University of Texas Rio Grande Valley, TX
The University of the Arts, PA
University of Utah, UT
University of Washington, WA
The University of West Alabama, AL
University of Wisconsin–Green Bay, WI
University of Wisconsin–Stevens Point, WI
University of Wyoming, WY
Ursinus College, PA
Virginia State University, VA
Wayne State University, MI
Western Illinois University, IL
Western Kentucky University, KY
Western Michigan University, MI
Western Oregon University, OR
Western Washington University, WA
Westmont College, CA
West Texas A&M University, TX
West Virginia Wesleyan College, WV
Wichita State University, KS
Widener University, PA
William Jewell College, MO
Winthrop University, SC
Wittenberg University, OH
Wright State University, OH
Wright State University–Lake Campus, OH

Debating

Abilene Christian University, TX
Austin Peay State University, TN
Baker University, KS
Ball State University, IN
Baylor University, TX
Berry College, GA
Bethany Lutheran College, MN
Bethel College, KS
Bethel University, MN
Boise State University, ID
Bowling Green State University, OH
California Baptist University, CA
California Polytechnic State University, San Luis Obispo, CA
California State University, Chico, CA
Cameron University, OK

Carroll College, MT
Carson-Newman University, TN
Cedarville University, OH
Clarion University of Pennsylvania, PA
The College of Idaho, ID
College of Saint Mary, NE
Concordia College, MN
Concordia University Irvine, CA
Concordia University, Nebraska, NE
Corban University, OR
Culver-Stockton College, MO
Doane University, NE
Dordt College, IA
Drury University, MO
Eastern Illinois University, IL
Eastern Michigan University, MI
Emory University, GA
Emporia State University, KS
Evangel University, MO
Fairmont State University, WV
Ferris State University, MI
George Fox University, OR
Gonzaga University, WA
Gustavus Adolphus College, MN
Harding University, AR
Hawai'i Pacific University, HI
Henderson State University, AR
Hillsdale College, MI
Idaho State University, ID
Kansas Wesleyan University, KS
Lewis & Clark College, OR
Lewis-Clark State College, ID
Liberty University, VA
Lindenwood University, MO
Linfield College, OR
Louisiana Tech University, LA
Loyola Marymount University, CA
Loyola University Chicago, IL
Malone University, OH
McKendree University, IL
Mercer University, GA
Methodist University, NC
Michigan State University, MI
Middle Tennessee State University, TN
Mississippi State University, MS
Monmouth College, IL
Muskingum University, OH
North Central College, IL
Northeastern State University, OK
Northern Illinois University, IL
Northwest Missouri State University, MO
Northwest Nazarene University, ID
Northwest University, WA
Ohio University, OH
Ohio University–Chillicothe, OH
Ohio University–Eastern, OH
Ohio University–Lancaster, OH
Ohio University–Southern Campus, OH
Ohio University–Zanesville, OH
Oklahoma City University, OK
Pacific Lutheran University, WA
Pacific University, OR
Piedmont College, GA
Point Loma Nazarene University, CA
Regis University, CO
St. John's University, NY
Saint Joseph's University, PA
Saint Mary's College of California, CA
Samford University, AL
San Diego State University, CA
Santa Clara University, CA
Savannah College of Art and Design, GA
Simpson College, IA
South Dakota State University, SD
Southeastern Oklahoma State University, OK

Southern Illinois University Carbondale, IL
Southwest Baptist University, MO
Sterling College, KS
Tennessee Technological University, TN
Texas Wesleyan University, TX
Thomas University, GA
Towson University, MD
Trinity University, TX
Truman State University, MO
Union University, TN
The University of Akron, OH
The University of Alabama, AL
University of Alaska Anchorage, AK
University of Denver, CO
University of Hartford, CT
University of Indianapolis, IN
The University of Iowa, IA
The University of Kansas, KS
University of Kentucky, KY
University of Louisiana at Monroe, LA
University of Michigan–Dearborn, MI
University of Mississippi, MS
University of Nebraska at Kearney, NE
University of Nevada, Las Vegas, NV
University of Northern Iowa, IA
University of Oklahoma, OK
University of Oregon, OR
University of Puget Sound, WA
University of South Carolina, SC
University of South Dakota, SD
University of Southern California, CA
The University of Texas at San Antonio, TX
University of the Pacific, CA
University of Vermont, VT
University of West Georgia, GA
University of Wisconsin–Eau Claire, WI
University of Wyoming, WY
Vanguard University of Southern California, CA
Wayne State University, MI
Webber International University, FL
Webster University, MO
Western Illinois University, IL
Western Kentucky University, KY
West Texas A&M University, TX
West Virginia University, WV
Whitman College, WA
Whitworth University, WA
Wichita State University, KS
William Jewell College, MO
Winona State University, MN

Journalism/Publications

Abilene Christian University, TX
Alaska Pacific University, AK
Albright College, PA
Arkansas Tech University, AR
Auburn University, AL
Augustana University, SD
Austin Peay State University, TN
Averett University, VA
Baker University, KS
Ball State University, IN
Baylor University, TX
Belhaven University, MS
Belmont University, TN
Bemidji State University, MN
Benedictine College, KS
Berry College, GA
Bethany Lutheran College, MN
Binghamton University, State University of New York, NY
Biola University, CA
Boise State University, ID
Bowling Green State University, OH

Brenau University, GA
Bryan College, TN
Butler University, IN
California Baptist University, CA
California Lutheran University, CA
California Polytechnic State University, San Luis Obispo, CA
California State University, Chico, CA
California State University, Fresno, CA
California State University, Fullerton, CA
California State University, Northridge, CA
California State University, San Bernardino, CA
Calvin College, MI
Cameron University, OK
Campbellsville University, KY
Campbell University, NC
Carroll University, WI
Carson-Newman University, TN
Central Michigan University, MI
The Citadel, The Military College of South Carolina, SC
Cleveland State University, OH
The College at Brockport, State University of New York, NY
The College of New Rochelle, NY
College of Staten Island of the City University of New York, NY
Colorado Mesa University, CO
Columbia College Chicago, IL
Concord University, WV
Corban University, OR
Dordt College, IA
Eastern Illinois University, IL
Eastern Washington University, WA
Elon University, NC
Emmanuel College, GA
Fairmont State University, WV
Faulkner University, AL
Ferris State University, MI
Florida Agricultural and Mechanical University, FL
Florida International University, FL
Fort Hays State University, KS
Fort Lewis College, CO
Francis Marion University, SC
Franklin College, IN
Frostburg State University, MD
Georgia College & State University, GA
Glenville State College, WV
Grand Valley State University, MI
Hamline University, MN
Harding University, AR
Hardin-Simmons University, TX
Hawai`i Pacific University, HI
Henderson State University, AR
Hillsdale College, MI
Hofstra University, NY
Huntington University, IN
Idaho State University, ID
Indiana University of Pennsylvania, PA
Iowa State University of Science and Technology, IA
Ithaca College, NY
Jacksonville State University, AL
James Madison University, VA
John Brown University, AR
Kansas Wesleyan University, KS
Kent State University, OH
Kent State University at Stark, OH
Lehigh University, PA
Liberty University, VA
Lincoln University, MO
Lindenwood University, MO
Lipscomb University, TN

Lock Haven University of Pennsylvania, PA
Long Island University–LIU Brooklyn, NY
Long Island University–LIU Post, NY
Louisiana College, LA
Louisiana State University and Agricultural & Mechanical College, LA
Louisiana Tech University, LA
Loyola Marymount University, CA
Loyola University Chicago, IL
Lubbock Christian University, TX
Malone University, OH
Mansfield University of Pennsylvania, PA
Massachusetts College of Liberal Arts, MA
Michigan State University, MI
Middle Georgia State University, GA
Middle Tennessee State University, TN
Midwestern State University, TX
Mississippi State University, MS
Missouri Southern State University, MO
Missouri Valley College, MO
Missouri Western State University, MO
Morehead State University, KY
Murray State University, KY
Muskingum University, OH
New Jersey Institute of Technology, NJ
Newman University, KS
New Mexico State University, NM
North Central College, IL
Northeastern Illinois University, IL
Northeastern State University, OK
Northern Illinois University, IL
Northern Michigan University, MI
Northwest Missouri State University, MO
Oglethorpe University, GA
Ohio Northern University, OH
The Ohio State University, OH
Ohio University, OH
Ohio University–Chillicothe, OH
Ohio University–Eastern, OH
Ohio University–Lancaster, OH
Ohio University–Southern Campus, OH
Ohio University–Zanesville, OH
Ohio Valley University, WV
Oklahoma Christian University, OK
Oklahoma State University, OK
Old Dominion University, VA
Olivet College, MI
Oral Roberts University, OK
Ouachita Baptist University, AR
Pacific University, OR
Piedmont College, GA
Rhode Island College, RI
Robert Morris University Illinois, IL
St. Ambrose University, IA
St. Bonaventure University, NY
St. Edward's University, TX
St. John's University, NY
Saint Mary-of-the-Woods College, IN
Samford University, AL
Sam Houston State University, TX
San Diego State University, CA
San Jose State University, CA
Savannah College of Art and Design, GA
Schreiner University, TX
Siena College, NY
Sonoma State University, CA
South Dakota State University, SD
Southeastern University, FL
Southern Adventist University, TN
Southern Illinois University Carbondale, IL
Southern Oregon University, OR
Southwestern College, KS
State University of New York at Plattsburgh, NY

State University of New York College at Geneseo, NY
Stephen F. Austin State University, TX
Sterling College, KS
Stockton University, NJ
Stony Brook University, State University of New York, NY
Suffolk University, MA
Texas A&M University, TX
Texas A&M University–Commerce, TX
Texas Christian University, TX
Texas Lutheran University, TX
Texas State University, TX
Texas Tech University, TX
Texas Wesleyan University, TX
Texas Woman's University, TX
Trinity Christian College, IL
Union University, TN
The University of Akron, OH
The University of Alabama, AL
University of Arkansas, AR
University of California, San Diego, CA
University of Central Oklahoma, OK
University of Colorado Boulder, CO
University of Florida, FL
University of Hartford, CT
University of Houston, TX
University of Idaho, ID
University of Illinois at Urbana–Champaign, IL
The University of Iowa, IA
The University of Kansas, KS
University of Kentucky, KY
University of La Verne, CA
University of Louisiana at Monroe, LA
University of Maine, ME
University of Mary Washington, VA
University of Massachusetts Amherst, MA
University of Memphis, TN
University of Michigan, MI
University of Michigan–Dearborn, MI
University of Mississippi, MS
University of Missouri, MO
University of Montana, MT
University of Montevallo, AL
University of Nebraska at Kearney, NE
University of Nebraska–Lincoln, NE
University of Nevada, Las Vegas, NV
University of Nevada, Reno, NV
University of North Alabama, AL
The University of North Carolina at Chapel Hill, NC
University of Northern Colorado, CO
University of Oklahoma, OK
University of Oregon, OR
University of Pittsburgh at Johnstown, PA
University of Rhode Island, RI
University of St. Thomas, MN
University of South Carolina, SC
University of South Carolina Aiken, SC
The University of Tampa, FL
The University of Tennessee at Chattanooga, TN
The University of Tennessee at Martin, TN
The University of Texas at El Paso, TX
The University of Texas Rio Grande Valley, TX
University of Utah, UT
The University of Virginia's College at Wise, VA
University of West Georgia, GA
University of Wisconsin–Eau Claire, WI
University of Wisconsin–Green Bay, WI
University of Wisconsin–Whitewater, WI
University of Wyoming, WY
Utah State University, UT

Valdosta State University, GA
Valley City State University, ND
Virginia Polytechnic Institute and State University, VA
Wabash College, IN
Wartburg College, IA
Washington State University, WA
Wayne State College, NE
Wayne State University, MI
Webber International University, FL
Western Illinois University, IL
Western Kentucky University, KY
Western Washington University, WA
West Texas A&M University, TX
Whitworth University, WA
Wichita State University, KS
William Jewell College, MO
Youngstown State University, OH

Music

Abilene Christian University, TX
Adelphi University, NY
Agnes Scott College, GA
Alabama State University, AL
Alaska Bible College, AK
Alaska Pacific University, AK
Albany State University, GA
Albion College, MI
Albright College, PA
Alcorn State University, MS
Allegheny College, PA
Allegheny Wesleyan College, OH
Alma College, MI
Alverno College, WI
Anderson University, SC
Andrews University, MI
Appalachian Bible College, WV
Arizona Christian University, AZ
Arizona State University at the Tempe campus, AZ
Arkansas Tech University, AR
Assumption College, MA
Auburn University, AL
Augsburg University, MN
Augustana College, IL
Augustana University, SD
Aurora University, IL
Austin College, TX
Austin Peay State University, TN
Ave Maria University, FL
Averett University, VA
Baker University, KS
Baldwin Wallace University, OH
Ball State University, IN
The Baptist College of Florida, FL
Barton College, NC
Baylor University, TX
Belhaven University, MS
Bellarmine University, KY
Belmont University, TN
Beloit College, WI
Bemidji State University, MN
Benedictine College, KS
Benedictine University, IL
Berklee College of Music, MA
Berry College, GA
Bethany Lutheran College, MN
Bethel College, IN
Bethel College, KS
Bethel University, MN
Binghamton University, State University of New York, NY
Biola University, CA
Birmingham-Southern College, AL
Black Hills State University, SD
Bluefield College, VA

Blue Mountain College, MS
Bluffton University, OH
Boise State University, ID
Boston University, MA
Bowie State University, MD
Bowling Green State University, OH
Bradley University, IL
Brenau University, GA
Bridgewater College, VA
Brigham Young University, UT
Bryan College, TN
Bucknell University, PA
Buena Vista University, IA
Buffalo State College, State University of New York, NY
Butler University, IN
Cairn University, PA
Caldwell University, NJ
California Baptist University, CA
California Lutheran University, CA
California Polytechnic State University, San Luis Obispo, CA
California State University, Bakersfield, CA
California State University, Chico, CA
California State University, Fresno, CA
California State University, Fullerton, CA
California State University, Northridge, CA
California State University, San Bernardino, CA
California State University, Stanislaus, CA
Calvin College, MI
Cameron University, OK
Campbellsville University, KY
Campbell University, NC
Canisius College, NY
Capital University, OH
Cardinal Stritch University, WI
Carleton College, MN
Carroll College, MT
Carroll University, WI
Carson-Newman University, TN
Case Western Reserve University, OH
Catawba College, NC
The Catholic University of America, DC
Cedarville University, OH
Centenary College of Louisiana, LA
Central College, IA
Central Methodist University, MO
Central Michigan University, MI
Central State University, OH
Central Washington University, WA
Centre College, KY
Chapman University, CA
Chatham University, PA
Chowan University, NC
Christopher Newport University, VA
The Citadel, The Military College of South Carolina, SC
City College of the City University of New York, NY
Claflin University, SC
Clarion University of Pennsylvania, PA
Clarke University, IA
Clear Creek Baptist Bible College, KY
Cleveland Institute of Music, OH
Cleveland State University, OH
Coastal Carolina University, SC
Coe College, IA
Coker College, SC
The College at Brockport, State University of New York, NY
College of Charleston, SC
The College of Idaho, ID
The College of New Jersey, NJ
The College of New Rochelle, NY
College of Saint Benedict, MN

The College of Saint Rose, NY
The College of St. Scholastica, MN
College of Staten Island of the City
    University of New York, NY
College of the Holy Cross, MA
The College of William and Mary, VA
The College of Wooster, OH
Colorado Mesa University, CO
Colorado State University, CO
Columbia College, MO
Columbia College Chicago, IL
Columbus State University, GA
Concordia College, MN
Concordia University Chicago, IL
Concordia University Irvine, CA
Concordia University, Nebraska, NE
Concordia University, St. Paul, MN
Concordia University Texas, TX
Concordia University Wisconsin, WI
Concord University, WV
Converse College, SC
Corban University, OR
Cornell College, IA
Cornerstone University, MI
Covenant College, GA
Creighton University, NE
Culver-Stockton College, MO
Dakota State University, SD
Dallas Baptist University, TX
Davidson College, NC
Defiance College, OH
Delaware State University, DE
Delaware Valley University, PA
DePaul University, IL
Doane University, NE
Dominican University of California, CA
Dordt College, IA
Drake University, IA
Drew University, NJ
Drexel University, PA
Drury University, MO
Duquesne University, PA
East Carolina University, NC
East Central University, OK
Eastern Illinois University, IL
Eastern Kentucky University, KY
Eastern Mennonite University, VA
Eastern Michigan University, MI
Eastern University, PA
Eastern Washington University, WA
East Texas Baptist University, TX
Eckerd College, FL
Edgewood College, WI
Elizabethtown College, PA
Elmhurst College, IL
Elon University, NC
Emmanuel College, GA
Emory & Henry College, VA
Emory University, GA
Emporia State University, KS
Endicott College, MA
Eureka College, IL
Evangel University, MO
Fairmont State University, WV
Faulkner University, AL
Ferris State University, MI
Florida Agricultural and Mechanical
    University, FL
Florida Atlantic University, FL
Florida Gulf Coast University, FL
Florida Institute of Technology, FL
Florida International University, FL
Florida Southern College, FL
Florida State University, FL
Fordham University, NY

Fort Hays State University, KS
Fort Lewis College, CO
Francis Marion University, SC
Franklin & Marshall College, PA
Franklin College, IN
Frostburg State University, MD
Furman University, SC
Gannon University, PA
Gardner-Webb University, NC
Geneva College, PA
George Fox University, OR
Georgetown College, KY
Georgia College & State University, GA
Georgia Southern University, GA
Georgia Southwestern State University, GA
Gettysburg College, PA
Glenville State College, WV
Gonzaga University, WA
Gordon College, MA
Goshen College, IN
Goucher College, MD
Graceland University, IA
Grambling State University, LA
Grand Valley State University, MI
Greenville University, IL
Grove City College, PA
Gustavus Adolphus College, MN
Hamline University, MN
Hampton University, VA
Harding University, AR
Hardin-Simmons University, TX
Harris-Stowe State University, MO
Hartwick College, NY
Hawai`i Pacific University, HI
Heidelberg University, OH
Henderson State University, AR
Hendrix College, AR
High Point University, NC
Hillsdale College, MI
Hiram College, OH
Hobart and William Smith Colleges, NY
Hofstra University, NY
Hollins University, VA
Hood College, MD
Hope College, MI
Hope International University, CA
Houston Baptist University, TX
Howard Payne University, TX
Huntingdon College, AL
Huntington University, IN
Idaho State University, ID
Illinois College, IL
Illinois Wesleyan University, IL
Indiana State University, IN
Indiana University of Pennsylvania, PA
Indiana Wesleyan University, IN
Iona College, NY
Iowa State University of Science and
    Technology, IA
Iowa Wesleyan University, IA
Ithaca College, NY
Jackson State University, MS
Jacksonville State University, AL
Jacksonville University, FL
James Madison University, VA
John Brown University, AR
Johnson C. Smith University, NC
Johnson University, TN
Johnson University Florida, FL
Judson University, IL
The Juilliard School, NY
Juniata College, PA
Kalamazoo College, MI
Kansas Wesleyan University, KS
Kean University, NJ

Keene State College, NH
Kennesaw State University, GA
Kent State University, OH
Kent State University at Stark, OH
Kentucky State University, KY
Kenyon College, OH
King University, TN
Knox College, IL
Kutztown University of Pennsylvania, PA
Kuyper College, MI
Lafayette College, PA
LaGrange College, GA
Lancaster Bible College, PA
La Sierra University, CA
Lawrence University, WI
Lebanon Valley College, PA
Lee University, TN
Lehigh University, PA
Le Moyne College, NY
Lenoir-Rhyne University, NC
Lewis & Clark College, OR
Lewis-Clark State College, ID
Lewis University, IL
Liberty University, VA
Lincoln Memorial University, TN
Lincoln University, MO
Lincoln University, PA
Lindenwood University, MO
Lindsey Wilson College, KY
Linfield College, OR
Lipscomb University, TN
Lock Haven University of Pennsylvania, PA
Long Island University–LIU Brooklyn, NY
Long Island University–LIU Post, NY
Longwood University, VA
Loras College, IA
Louisiana College, LA
Louisiana State University and Agricultural
    & Mechanical College, LA
Louisiana Tech University, LA
Loyola Marymount University, CA
Loyola University Chicago, IL
Lubbock Christian University, TX
Luther College, IA
Lycoming College, PA
Lynchburg College, VA
Lynn University, FL
Lyon College, AR
Malone University, OH
Manchester University, IN
Manhattan College, NY
Manhattanville College, NY
Mansfield University of Pennsylvania, PA
Marietta College, OH
Marist College, NY
Martin Luther College, MN
Maryville College, TN
Maryville University of Saint Louis, MO
Marywood University, PA
Massachusetts College of Liberal Arts, MA
McKendree University, IL
McMurry University, TX
Mercer University, GA
Meredith College, NC
Messiah College, PA
Methodist University, NC
Metropolitan State University of Denver, CO
Miami University, OH
Michigan State University, MI
MidAmerica Nazarene University, KS
Middle Tennessee State University, TN
Midwestern State University, TX
Millersville University of Pennsylvania, PA
Milligan College, TN
Millikin University, IL

Millsaps College, MS
Mills College, CA
Minnesota State University Moorhead, MN
Minot State University, ND
Mississippi State University, MS
Missouri Baptist University, MO
Missouri Southern State University, MO
Missouri University of Science and
   Technology, MO
Missouri Valley College, MO
Missouri Western State University, MO
Molloy College, NY
Monmouth College, IL
Montana State University, MT
Montana State University Billings, MT
Montclair State University, NJ
Montreat College, NC
Moravian College, PA
Morehead State University, KY
Morehouse College, GA
Morningside College, IA
Mount Aloysius College, PA
Mount Marty College, SD
Mount Mary University, WI
Mount Mercy University, IA
Mount St. Joseph University, OH
Mount Saint Mary's University, CA
Mount Vernon Nazarene University, OH
Muhlenberg College, PA
Murray State University, KY
Muskingum University, OH
Nazareth College of Rochester, NY
Newberry College, SC
New England Conservatory of Music, MA
Newman University, KS
New Mexico Highlands University, NM
New Mexico State University, NM
Nicholls State University, LA
North Carolina Agricultural and Technical
   State University, NC
North Central College, IL
Northeastern Illinois University, IL
Northeastern State University, OK
Northern Arizona University, AZ
Northern Illinois University, IL
Northern Kentucky University, KY
Northern Michigan University, MI
Northern State University, SD
Northwest Christian University, OR
Northwestern College, IA
Northwestern University, IL
Northwest Missouri State University, MO
Northwest Nazarene University, ID
Northwest University, WA
Oakland City University, IN
Oberlin College, OH
Occidental College, CA
Oglethorpe University, GA
Ohio Northern University, OH
The Ohio State University, OH
Ohio University, OH
Ohio University–Chillicothe, OH
Ohio University–Eastern, OH
Ohio University–Lancaster, OH
Ohio University–Southern Campus, OH
Ohio University–Zanesville, OH
Ohio Valley University, WV
Ohio Wesleyan University, OH
Oklahoma Baptist University, OK
Oklahoma Christian University, OK
Oklahoma City University, OK
Oklahoma State University, OK
Old Dominion University, VA
Olivet College, MI
Olivet Nazarene University, IL
Oral Roberts University, OK

Ouachita Baptist University, AR
Ozark Christian College, MO
Pacific Lutheran University, WA
Pacific University, OR
Palm Beach Atlantic University, FL
Park University, MO
Peabody Conservatory of The Johns Hopkins
   University, MD
Pfeiffer University, NC
Philander Smith College, AR
Piedmont College, GA
Pittsburg State University, KS
Plymouth State University, NH
Point Loma Nazarene University, CA
Portland State University, OR
Presbyterian College, SC
Purdue University, IN
Regis University, CO
Rhode Island College, RI
Rhodes College, TN
Rice University, TX
Roanoke College, VA
Robert Morris University Illinois, IL
Roberts Wesleyan College, NY
Rockford University, IL
Rockhurst University, MO
Rocky Mountain College, MT
Rogers State University, OK
Rollins College, FL
Rowan University, NJ
Sacred Heart University, CT
Saginaw Valley State University, MI
St. Ambrose University, IA
Saint Augustine's University, NC
St. Bonaventure University, NY
St. Catherine University, MN
Saint John's University, MN
St. John's University, NY
Saint Louis University, MO
Saint Martin's University, WA
Saint Mary's College, IN
Saint Mary's College of California, CA
St. Mary's University, TX
Saint Mary's University of Minnesota, MN
St. Norbert College, WI
St. Olaf College, MN
Salem College, NC
Samford University, AL
Sam Houston State University, TX
San Diego State University, CA
San Francisco Conservatory of Music, CA
San Jose State University, CA
Santa Clara University, CA
Savannah College of Art and Design, GA
Schreiner University, TX
Seattle University, WA
Seton Hill University, PA
Shenandoah University, VA
Shepherd University, WV
Shippensburg University of Pennsylvania,
   PA
Siena College, NY
Simpson College, IA
Skidmore College, NY
Slippery Rock University of Pennsylvania,
   PA
Sonoma State University, CA
South Dakota State University, SD
Southeastern Louisiana University, LA
Southeastern Oklahoma State University,
   OK
Southeastern University, FL
Southeast Missouri State University, MO
Southern Adventist University, TN
Southern Arkansas University–Magnolia,
   AR

Southern Illinois University Carbondale, IL
Southern New Hampshire University, NH
Southern Oregon University, OR
Southern Utah University, UT
Southwest Baptist University, MO
Southwestern Christian College, TX
Southwestern College, KS
Southwestern Oklahoma State University,
   OK
Southwestern University, TX
State University of New York at Fredonia,
   NY
State University of New York at New Paltz,
   NY
State University of New York at Plattsburgh,
   NY
State University of New York College at
   Cortland, NY
State University of New York College at
   Geneseo, NY
State University of New York College at
   Potsdam, NY
Stephen F. Austin State University, TX
Sterling College, KS
Stetson University, FL
Stockton University, NJ
Stony Brook University, State University of
   New York, NY
Susquehanna University, PA
Sweet Briar College, VA
Syracuse University, NY
Tarleton State University, TX
Taylor University, IN
Temple University, PA
Tennessee Technological University, TN
Tennessee Wesleyan University, TN
Texas A&M International University, TX
Texas A&M University–Commerce, TX
Texas Christian University, TX
Texas Lutheran University, TX
Texas State University, TX
Texas Tech University, TX
Texas Wesleyan University, TX
Texas Woman's University, TX
Thomas More College, KY
Thomas University, GA
Tiffin University, OH
Toccoa Falls College, GA
Towson University, MD
Transylvania University, KY
Trevecca Nazarene University, TN
Trine University, IN
Trinity Christian College, IL
Trinity University, TX
Troy University, AL
Truett McConnell University, GA
Truman State University, MO
Tulane University, LA
Tuskegee University, AL
Union College, KY
Union College, NE
Union University, TN
The University of Akron, OH
The University of Alabama, AL
The University of Alabama at Birmingham,
   AL
The University of Alabama in Huntsville,
   AL
University of Alaska Anchorage, AK
The University of Arizona, AZ
University of Arkansas, AR
University of Arkansas at Little Rock, AR
University of Bridgeport, CT
University of California, Irvine, CA
University of California, Riverside, CA
University of California, San Diego, CA

University of California, Santa Cruz, CA
University of Central Florida, FL
University of Central Oklahoma, OK
University of Colorado Boulder, CO
University of Colorado Denver, CO
University of Dallas, TX
University of Dayton, OH
University of Delaware, DE
University of Denver, CO
University of Dubuque, IA
University of Evansville, IN
The University of Findlay, OH
University of Florida, FL
University of Georgia, GA
University of Hartford, CT
University of Houston, TX
University of Idaho, ID
University of Illinois at Chicago, IL
University of Illinois at Urbana–Champaign, IL
University of Indianapolis, IN
The University of Iowa, IA
University of Jamestown, ND
The University of Kansas, KS
University of Kentucky, KY
University of La Verne, CA
University of Louisiana at Monroe, LA
University of Maine, ME
University of Mary Hardin-Baylor, TX
University of Maryland, Baltimore County, MD
University of Maryland, College Park, MD
University of Mary Washington, VA
University of Massachusetts Amherst, MA
University of Massachusetts Lowell, MA
University of Memphis, TN
University of Miami, FL
University of Michigan, MI
University of Michigan–Flint, MI
University of Mississippi, MS
University of Missouri, MO
University of Missouri–St. Louis, MO
University of Montana, MT
University of Montevallo, AL
University of Nebraska at Kearney, NE
University of Nebraska–Lincoln, NE
University of Nevada, Las Vegas, NV
University of New Hampshire, NH
University of North Alabama, AL
University of North Carolina at Asheville, NC
The University of North Carolina at Chapel Hill, NC
The University of North Carolina at Charlotte, NC
The University of North Carolina at Greensboro, NC
University of North Carolina School of the Arts, NC
The University of North Carolina Wilmington, NC
University of North Dakota, ND
University of Northern Colorado, CO
University of Northern Iowa, IA
University of North Florida, FL
University of North Georgia, GA
University of Oklahoma, OK
University of Oregon, OR
University of Pittsburgh at Bradford, PA
University of Pittsburgh at Greensburg, PA
University of Portland, OR
University of Puerto Rico–Bayamón, PR
University of Puget Sound, WA
University of Rhode Island, RI
University of Richmond, VA

University of Rochester, NY
University of St. Francis, IL
University of St. Thomas, MN
University of St. Thomas, TX
University of San Diego, CA
University of Science and Arts of Oklahoma, OK
University of Sioux Falls, SD
University of South Carolina, SC
University of South Carolina Aiken, SC
University of South Dakota, SD
University of Southern California, CA
University of Southern Maine, ME
University of Southern Mississippi, MS
University of South Florida, FL
The University of Tampa, FL
The University of Tennessee at Chattanooga, TN
The University of Tennessee at Martin, TN
The University of Texas at Austin, TX
The University of Texas at El Paso, TX
The University of Texas at San Antonio, TX
The University of Texas at Tyler, TX
The University of Texas Rio Grande Valley, TX
The University of the Arts, PA
University of the Incarnate Word, TX
University of the Pacific, CA
The University of Toledo, OH
The University of Tulsa, OK
University of Utah, UT
University of Vermont, VT
University of Virginia, VA
The University of Virginia's College at Wise, VA
University of Washington, WA
The University of West Alabama, AL
University of West Florida, FL
University of West Georgia, GA
University of Wisconsin–Eau Claire, WI
University of Wisconsin–Green Bay, WI
University of Wisconsin–La Crosse, WI
University of Wisconsin–Milwaukee, WI
University of Wisconsin–Parkside, WI
University of Wisconsin–River Falls, WI
University of Wisconsin–Stevens Point, WI
University of Wisconsin–Stout, WI
University of Wisconsin–Whitewater, WI
University of Wyoming, WY
Ursinus College, PA
Utah State University, UT
Valdosta State University, GA
Valencia College, FL
Valley City State University, ND
Valparaiso University, IN
VanderCook College of Music, IL
Vanguard University of Southern California, CA
Virginia Military Institute, VA
Virginia Polytechnic Institute and State University, VA
Virginia State University, VA
Wabash College, IN
Walla Walla University, WA
Warner Pacific College, OR
Wartburg College, IA
Washington College, MD
Washington State University, WA
Wayland Baptist University, TX
Waynesburg University, PA
Wayne State College, NE
Wayne State University, MI
Webster University, MO
Wesleyan College, GA
West Chester University of Pennsylvania, PA

Western Carolina University, NC
Western Illinois University, IL
Western Kentucky University, KY
Western Michigan University, MI
Western New England University, MA
Western Oregon University, OR
Western State Colorado University, CO
Western Washington University, WA
Westminster College, MO
Westminster College, PA
Westmont College, CA
West Texas A&M University, TX
West Virginia University, WV
West Virginia Wesleyan College, WV
Wheaton College, IL
Wheeling Jesuit University, WV
Whitman College, WA
Whittier College, CA
Whitworth University, WA
Wichita State University, KS
Widener University, PA
William Jessup University, CA
William Jewell College, MO
William Paterson University of New Jersey, NJ
Williams Baptist College, AR
Wilson College, PA
Winona State University, MN
Winthrop University, SC
Wisconsin Lutheran College, WI
Wittenberg University, OH
Wofford College, SC
Wright State University, OH
Wright State University–Lake Campus, OH
Xavier University, OH
York College of Pennsylvania, PA
Young Harris College, GA
Youngstown State University, OH

Performing Arts
Adelphi University, NY
Albertus Magnus College, CT
Albion College, MI
Allegheny College, PA
Alma College, MI
Anderson University, SC
Auburn University, AL
Augsburg University, MN
Augustana University, SD
Austin Peay State University, TN
Ball State University, IN
Belhaven University, MS
Belmont University, TN
Bemidji State University, MN
Berklee College of Music, MA
Binghamton University, State University of New York, NY
Birmingham-Southern College, AL
Bluefield College, VA
Bluffton University, OH
Boise State University, ID
Bowling Green State University, OH
Brenau University, GA
Bryan College, TN
Bucknell University, PA
Buffalo State College, State University of New York, NY
Butler University, IN
California Lutheran University, CA
California Polytechnic State University, San Luis Obispo, CA
California State University, Chico, CA
California State University, Fullerton, CA
Calvin College, MI
Cameron University, OK

Capital University, OH
Carroll College, MT
Carroll University, WI
Case Western Reserve University, OH
Cedar Crest College, PA
Centenary College of Louisiana, LA
Central Michigan University, MI
Chapman University, CA
Christian Brothers University, TN
Christopher Newport University, VA
City College of the City University of New York, NY
Clemson University, SC
Cleveland State University, OH
Coastal Carolina University, SC
Coe College, IA
College of Charleston, SC
The College of Idaho, ID
College of Staten Island of the City University of New York, NY
Colorado Mesa University, CO
Colorado State University, CO
Columbia College Chicago, IL
Columbus State University, GA
Corban University, OR
Cornell College, IA
Creighton University, NE
Davidson College, NC
DeSales University, PA
Doane University, NE
Drew University, NJ
Drexel University, PA
East Carolina University, NC
East Central University, OK
Eastern Illinois University, IL
Eastern Michigan University, MI
Edgewood College, WI
Elizabethtown College, PA
Elon University, NC
Emmanuel College, GA
Emory & Henry College, VA
Endicott College, MA
Eureka College, IL
Flagler College, FL
Florida Agricultural and Mechanical University, FL
Florida Atlantic University, FL
Florida International University, FL
Fort Hays State University, KS
Fort Lewis College, CO
Francis Marion University, SC
Franklin College, IN
Franklin Pierce University, NH
Frostburg State University, MD
Gannon University, PA
Georgetown College, KY
Gonzaga University, WA
Goucher College, MD
Grambling State University, LA
Greenville University, IL
Hardin-Simmons University, TX
Hawai`i Pacific University, HI
Heidelberg University, OH
Henderson State University, AR
Hobart and William Smith Colleges, NY
Hofstra University, NY
Huntingdon College, AL
Huntington University, IN
Idaho State University, ID
Indiana State University, IN
Indiana University of Pennsylvania, PA
Ithaca College, NY
The Juilliard School, NY
Juniata College, PA
Kalamazoo College, MI
Kansas Wesleyan University, KS

Kean University, NJ
Kennesaw State University, GA
Kent State University, OH
Kent State University at Stark, OH
Kentucky State University, KY
King University, TN
Lafayette College, PA
Lawrence University, WI
Lees-McRae College, NC
Lehigh University, PA
Liberty University, VA
Lincoln University, MO
Lindenwood University, MO
Lock Haven University of Pennsylvania, PA
Long Island University–LIU Brooklyn, NY
Long Island University–LIU Post, NY
Louisiana College, LA
Louisiana State University and Agricultural & Mechanical College, LA
Louisiana Tech University, LA
Loyola Marymount University, CA
Lubbock Christian University, TX
Manhattanville College, NY
Marietta College, OH
Marymount Manhattan College, NY
Massachusetts College of Liberal Arts, MA
Metropolitan State University of Denver, CO
Michigan State University, MI
Michigan Technological University, MI
Middle Tennessee State University, TN
Minot State University, ND
Mississippi State University, MS
Missouri Valley College, MO
Missouri Western State University, MO
Molloy College, NY
Montclair State University, NJ
Mount Aloysius College, PA
Mount Marty College, SD
Muhlenberg College, PA
Nazareth College of Rochester, NY
New Jersey Institute of Technology, NJ
New Mexico Highlands University, NM
New Mexico State University, NM
Northeastern Illinois University, IL
Northeastern State University, OK
Northern Illinois University, IL
Northwestern College, IA
Oglethorpe University, GA
Ohio Northern University, OH
The Ohio State University, OH
Ohio University, OH
Ohio University–Chillicothe, OH
Ohio University–Eastern, OH
Ohio University–Lancaster, OH
Ohio University–Southern Campus, OH
Ohio University–Zanesville, OH
Ohio Valley University, WV
Ohio Wesleyan University, OH
Oklahoma Baptist University, OK
Oklahoma City University, OK
Old Dominion University, VA
Olivet Nazarene University, IL
Ouachita Baptist University, AR
Piedmont College, GA
Point Park University, PA
Robert Morris University Illinois, IL
Rockford University, IL
Rockhurst University, MO
Sacred Heart University, CT
The Sage Colleges, NY
St. Andrews University, NC
Saint Augustine's University, NC
St. Bonaventure University, NY
Saint Louis University, MO
Saint Mary-of-the-Woods College, IN
Saint Mary's College of California, CA

Saint Michael's College, VT
Samford University, AL
Sam Houston State University, TX
San Diego State University, CA
Savannah College of Art and Design, GA
Seattle Pacific University, WA
Seton Hill University, PA
Shenandoah University, VA
Shepherd University, WV
Siena College, NY
Simpson College, IA
Slippery Rock University of Pennsylvania, PA
Sonoma State University, CA
South Dakota State University, SD
Southeastern Oklahoma State University, OK
Southeastern University, FL
Southeast Missouri State University, MO
Southern Illinois University Carbondale, IL
Southwestern College, KS
State University of New York at Fredonia, NY
State University of New York College at Geneseo, NY
State University of New York College at Potsdam, NY
Sterling College, KS
Stockton University, NJ
Temple University, PA
Texas A&M International University, TX
Texas A&M University, TX
Texas A&M University–Commerce, TX
Texas Christian University, TX
Texas Lutheran University, TX
Texas Tech University, TX
Texas Wesleyan University, TX
Tiffin University, OH
Towson University, MD
Trinity Christian College, IL
The University of Akron, OH
The University of Alabama at Birmingham, AL
University of Alaska Anchorage, AK
The University of Arizona, AZ
University of California, Irvine, CA
University of California, San Diego, CA
University of California, Santa Cruz, CA
University of Colorado Boulder, CO
University of Colorado Denver, CO
University of Dubuque, IA
University of Evansville, IN
University of Florida, FL
University of Hartford, CT
University of Houston, TX
University of Idaho, ID
University of Illinois at Chicago, IL
University of Illinois at Urbana–Champaign, IL
The University of Iowa, IA
The University of Kansas, KS
University of Kentucky, KY
University of La Verne, CA
University of Louisiana at Monroe, LA
University of Maine at Fort Kent, ME
University of Maryland, Baltimore County, MD
University of Maryland, College Park, MD
University of Miami, FL
University of Michigan, MI
University of Michigan–Flint, MI
University of Mississippi, MS
University of Montana, MT
University of Nebraska–Lincoln, NE
University of Nevada, Las Vegas, NV
University of New Hampshire, NH

The University of North Carolina at
Greensboro, NC
University of North Carolina School of the
Arts, NC
University of Northern Colorado, CO
University of Oklahoma, OK
University of Oregon, OR
University of Portland, OR
University of Richmond, VA
University of Rochester, NY
University of St. Francis, IL
University of St. Thomas, TX
University of South Florida, FL
The University of Tampa, FL
The University of Tennessee at Chattanooga,
TN
The University of Texas at El Paso, TX
The University of the Arts, PA
The University of Toledo, OH
The University of Tulsa, OK
University of Utah, UT
The University of Virginia's College at Wise,
VA
University of Washington, WA
University of West Georgia, GA
University of Wisconsin–Eau Claire, WI
University of Wisconsin–Parkside, WI
University of Wisconsin–Stevens Point, WI
University of Wyoming, WY
Ursinus College, PA
Utah State University, UT
Valdosta State University, GA
Valparaiso University, IN
Virginia Polytechnic Institute and State
University, VA
Virginia State University, VA
Wartburg College, IA
Washington College, MD
Washington State University, WA
Wayne State College, NE
Wayne State University, MI
Western Illinois University, IL
Western Oregon University, OR
Western State Colorado University, CO
Western Washington University, WA
West Virginia Wesleyan College, WV
Wichita State University, KS
Wilkes University, PA
William Jessup University, CA
Winthrop University, SC
Wright State University, OH
Wright State University–Lake Campus, OH
Xavier University, OH
Young Harris College, GA
Youngstown State University, OH

Theater/Drama
Abilene Christian University, TX
Adelphi University, NY
Alabama State University, AL
Alaska Pacific University, AK
Albertus Magnus College, CT
Albion College, MI
Albright College, PA
Allegheny College, PA
Alma College, MI
Anderson University, SC
Arizona State University at the Tempe
campus, AZ
Arkansas Tech University, AR
Auburn University, AL
Augsburg University, MN
Augustana College, IL
Augustana University, SD
Aurora University, IL

Austin College, TX
Austin Peay State University, TN
Averett University, VA
Baker University, KS
Ball State University, IN
Barton College, NC
Baylor University, TX
Belhaven University, MS
Belmont Abbey College, NC
Belmont University, TN
Benedictine College, KS
Berklee College of Music, MA
Berry College, GA
Bethany Lutheran College, MN
Bethel College, IN
Bethel College, KS
Bethel University, MN
Binghamton University, State University of
New York, NY
Biola University, CA
Birmingham-Southern College, AL
Black Hills State University, SD
Bluefield College, VA
Blue Mountain College, MS
Boise State University, ID
Boston University, MA
Bowling Green State University, OH
Bradley University, IL
Brenau University, GA
Brigham Young University, UT
Bryan College, TN
Bucknell University, PA
Buena Vista University, IA
Buffalo State College, State University of
New York, NY
Butler University, IN
California Baptist University, CA
California Lutheran University, CA
California Polytechnic State University, San
Luis Obispo, CA
California State University, Bakersfield, CA
California State University, Chico, CA
California State University, Fresno, CA
California State University, Fullerton, CA
California State University, San Bernardino,
CA
Calumet College of Saint Joseph, IN
Calvin College, MI
Cameron University, OK
Campbellsville University, KY
Campbell University, NC
Cardinal Stritch University, WI
Carroll College, MT
Carroll University, WI
Case Western Reserve University, OH
Catawba College, NC
The Catholic University of America, DC
Cedar Crest College, PA
Centenary College of Louisiana, LA
Central College, IA
Central Methodist University, MO
Central Michigan University, MI
Central Washington University, WA
Centre College, KY
Chapman University, CA
Christopher Newport University, VA
Clarion University of Pennsylvania, PA
Clarke University, IA
Clemson University, SC
Cleveland State University, OH
Coastal Carolina University, SC
Coe College, IA
Coker College, SC
The College at Brockport, State University
of New York, NY

College of Charleston, SC
The College of Idaho, ID
College of Saint Benedict, MN
College of Staten Island of the City
University of New York, NY
The College of William and Mary, VA
The College of Wooster, OH
Colorado Mesa University, CO
Colorado State University, CO
Columbia College Chicago, IL
Columbus State University, GA
Concordia College, MN
Concordia University Irvine, CA
Concordia University, Nebraska, NE
Concordia University, St. Paul, MN
Concord University, WV
Converse College, SC
Corban University, OR
Cornell College, IA
Creighton University, NE
Culver-Stockton College, MO
Davidson College, NC
DePaul University, IL
DeSales University, PA
Doane University, NE
Dordt College, IA
Drake University, IA
Drew University, NJ
Drexel University, PA
Drury University, MO
East Central University, OK
Eastern Illinois University, IL
Eastern Michigan University, MI
Eastern Washington University, WA
East Texas Baptist University, TX
Eckerd College, FL
Edgewood College, WI
Elizabethtown College, PA
Elmhurst College, IL
Elon University, NC
Emmanuel College, GA
Emory & Henry College, VA
Emory University, GA
Emporia State University, KS
Eureka College, IL
Evangel University, MO
Fairmont State University, WV
Faulkner University, AL
Ferris State University, MI
Flagler College, FL
Florida Agricultural and Mechanical
University, FL
Florida International University, FL
Florida Southern College, FL
Florida State University, FL
Fort Hays State University, KS
Fort Lewis College, CO
Francis Marion University, SC
Franklin College, IN
Franklin Pierce University, NH
Frostburg State University, MD
Furman University, SC
Gannon University, PA
Gardner-Webb University, NC
George Fox University, OR
Georgetown College, KY
Georgia Southern University, GA
Georgia Southwestern State University, GA
Gordon College, MA
Goshen College, IN
Goucher College, MD
Graceland University, IA
Grambling State University, LA
Grand Valley State University, MI
Gustavus Adolphus College, MN

Hamline University, MN
Hardin-Simmons University, TX
Harris-Stowe State University, MO
Heidelberg University, OH
Henderson State University, AR
Hendrix College, AR
High Point University, NC
Hillsdale College, MI
Hofstra University, NY
Hollins University, VA
Hope College, MI
Howard Payne University, TX
Huntington University, IN
Idaho State University, ID
Illinois College, IL
Illinois Wesleyan University, IL
Indiana State University, IN
Indiana University of Pennsylvania, PA
Indiana Wesleyan University, IN
Iowa State University of Science and
    Technology, IA
Ithaca College, NY
Jacksonville State University, AL
Jacksonville University, FL
James Madison University, VA
John Brown University, AR
Judson University, IL
The Juilliard School, NY
Juniata College, PA
Kansas Wesleyan University, KS
Kean University, NJ
Keene State College, NH
Kennesaw State University, GA
Kent State University, OH
Kent State University at Stark, OH
King University, TN
Knox College, IL
Lafayette College, PA
LaGrange College, GA
La Sierra University, CA
Lawrence University, WI
Lees-McRae College, NC
Lee University, TN
Lehigh University, PA
Lewis-Clark State College, ID
Lewis University, IL
Lincoln University, MO
Lindenwood University, MO
Linfield College, OR
Lipscomb University, TN
Long Island University–LIU Brooklyn, NY
Long Island University–LIU Post, NY
Longwood University, VA
Louisiana College, LA
Louisiana State University and Agricultural
    & Mechanical College, LA
Louisiana Tech University, LA
Loyola Marymount University, CA
Loyola University Chicago, IL
Lubbock Christian University, TX
Lycoming College, PA
Lynchburg College, VA
Lyon College, AR
Malone University, OH
Manhattanville College, NY
Marietta College, OH
Marist College, NY
Marquette University, WI
Marymount Manhattan College, NY
Maryville College, TN
Massachusetts College of Liberal Arts, MA
McMurry University, TX
Mercer University, GA
Meredith College, NC
Messiah College, PA
Metropolitan State University of Denver, CO

Miami University, OH
Michigan State University, MI
Michigan Technological University, MI
Middle Tennessee State University, TN
Midwestern State University, TX
Milligan College, TN
Millikin University, IL
Millsaps College, MS
Minnesota State University Moorhead, MN
Minot State University, ND
Mississippi State University, MS
Missouri Baptist University, MO
Missouri Southern State University, MO
Missouri University of Science and
    Technology, MO
Missouri Valley College, MO
Missouri Western State University, MO
Molloy College, NY
Monmouth College, IL
Montana State University, MT
Montana State University Billings, MT
Montclair State University, NJ
Morehead State University, KY
Morningside College, IA
Mount Marty College, SD
Mount Mercy University, IA
Muhlenberg College, PA
Murray State University, KY
Muskingum University, OH
Nazareth College of Rochester, NY
Newberry College, SC
New England College, NH
New Jersey Institute of Technology, NJ
Newman University, KS
New Mexico State University, NM
Niagara University, NY
North Central College, IL
Northeastern Illinois University, IL
Northeastern State University, OK
Northern Arizona University, AZ
Northern Illinois University, IL
Northern Kentucky University, KY
Northern Michigan University, MI
Northern State University, SD
Northwestern College, IA
Northwest Missouri State University, MO
Northwest Nazarene University, ID
Oglethorpe University, GA
Ohio Northern University, OH
The Ohio State University, OH
Ohio University, OH
Ohio University–Chillicothe, OH
Ohio University–Eastern, OH
Ohio University–Lancaster, OH
Ohio University–Southern Campus, OH
Ohio University–Zanesville, OH
Ohio Valley University, WV
Ohio Wesleyan University, OH
Oklahoma Baptist University, OK
Oklahoma Christian University, OK
Oklahoma City University, OK
Oklahoma State University, OK
Old Dominion University, VA
Olivet Nazarene University, IL
Ouachita Baptist University, AR
Ozark Christian College, MO
Pacific Lutheran University, WA
Pacific University, OR
Palm Beach Atlantic University, FL
Park University, MO
Piedmont College, GA
Plymouth State University, NH
Point Loma Nazarene University, CA
Point Park University, PA
Portland State University, OR
Providence College, RI

Rhode Island College, RI
Rhodes College, TN
Rider University, NJ
Robert Morris University Illinois, IL
Rockford University, IL
Rockhurst University, MO
Rogers State University, OK
Rollins College, FL
Sacred Heart University, CT
The Sage Colleges, NY
Saginaw Valley State University, MI
St. Ambrose University, IA
St. Andrews University, NC
St. Edward's University, TX
Saint John's University, MN
Saint Joseph's University, PA
Saint Louis University, MO
Saint Martin's University, WA
Saint Mary's College of California, CA
Saint Mary's University of Minnesota, MN
Saint Michael's College, VT
St. Norbert College, WI
St. Olaf College, MN
Samford University, AL
Sam Houston State University, TX
San Diego State University, CA
San Jose State University, CA
Santa Clara University, CA
Savannah College of Art and Design, GA
Schreiner University, TX
Seattle University, WA
Seton Hill University, PA
Shenandoah University, VA
Shepherd University, WV
Shippensburg University of Pennsylvania,
    PA
Siena College, NY
Simpson College, IA
Slippery Rock University of Pennsylvania,
    PA
Sonoma State University, CA
South Dakota State University, SD
Southeastern Louisiana University, LA
Southeastern Oklahoma State University,
    OK
Southeast Missouri State University, MO
Southern Adventist University, TN
Southern Arkansas University–Magnolia,
    AR
Southern Illinois University Carbondale, IL
Southern Oregon University, OR
Southern Utah University, UT
Southwest Baptist University, MO
Southwestern College, KS
Southwestern Oklahoma State University,
    OK
Southwestern University, TX
State University of New York at Fredonia,
    NY
State University of New York at New Paltz,
    NY
State University of New York at Plattsburgh,
    NY
State University of New York College at
    Geneseo, NY
State University of New York College at
    Potsdam, NY
Stephen F. Austin State University, TX
Sterling College, KS
Stetson University, FL
Stockton University, NJ
Susquehanna University, PA
Syracuse University, NY
Tarleton State University, TX
Taylor University, IN
Temple University, PA

Texas A&M University, TX
Texas A&M University–Commerce, TX
Texas Christian University, TX
Texas Lutheran University, TX
Texas State University, TX
Texas Tech University, TX
Texas Wesleyan University, TX
Texas Woman's University, TX
Thomas More College, KY
Thomas University, GA
Tiffin University, OH
Towson University, MD
Transylvania University, KY
Trevecca Nazarene University, TN
Trine University, IN
Trinity Christian College, IL
Trinity University, TX
Troy University, AL
Truman State University, MO
Union College, KY
Union University, TN
The University of Akron, OH
The University of Alabama, AL
The University of Alabama at Birmingham, AL
The University of Arizona, AZ
University of Arkansas, AR
University of Arkansas at Little Rock, AR
University of California, Irvine, CA
University of California, Riverside, CA
University of California, San Diego, CA
University of California, Santa Cruz, CA
University of Central Florida, FL
University of Central Oklahoma, OK
University of Colorado Boulder, CO
University of Colorado Denver, CO
University of Dallas, TX
University of Delaware, DE
University of Denver, CO
University of Detroit Mercy, MI
University of Dubuque, IA
University of Evansville, IN
The University of Findlay, OH
University of Florida, FL
University of Hartford, CT
University of Houston, TX
University of Idaho, ID
University of Illinois at Chicago, IL
University of Illinois at Urbana–Champaign, IL
University of Indianapolis, IN
The University of Iowa, IA
University of Jamestown, ND
The University of Kansas, KS
University of Kentucky, KY
University of La Verne, CA
University of Louisiana at Monroe, LA
University of Maine, ME
University of Maryland, Baltimore County, MD
University of Maryland, College Park, MD
University of Mary Washington, VA
University of Massachusetts Amherst, MA
University of Memphis, TN
University of Miami, FL
University of Michigan, MI
University of Michigan–Flint, MI
University of Mississippi, MS
University of Missouri, MO
University of Missouri–St. Louis, MO
University of Montana, MT
University of Montevallo, AL
University of Nebraska at Kearney, NE
University of Nebraska–Lincoln, NE
University of Nevada, Las Vegas, NV

University of Nevada, Reno, NV
University of New Hampshire, NH
University of North Alabama, AL
University of North Carolina at Asheville, NC
The University of North Carolina at Chapel Hill, NC
The University of North Carolina at Charlotte, NC
The University of North Carolina at Greensboro, NC
University of North Carolina School of the Arts, NC
The University of North Carolina Wilmington, NC
University of North Dakota, ND
University of Northern Colorado, CO
University of Northern Iowa, IA
University of Oklahoma, OK
University of Oregon, OR
University of Pittsburgh at Bradford, PA
University of Pittsburgh at Greensburg, PA
University of Pittsburgh at Johnstown, PA
University of Portland, OR
University of Puerto Rico–Bayamón, PR
University of Puget Sound, WA
University of Rhode Island, RI
University of Richmond, VA
University of St. Thomas, TX
University of Science and Arts of Oklahoma, OK
University of Sioux Falls, SD
University of South Carolina, SC
University of South Carolina Aiken, SC
University of South Dakota, SD
University of Southern California, CA
University of Southern Indiana, IN
University of Southern Maine, ME
University of Southern Mississippi, MS
University of South Florida, FL
The University of Tampa, FL
The University of Tennessee at Chattanooga, TN
The University of Tennessee at Martin, TN
The University of Texas at Austin, TX
The University of Texas at El Paso, TX
The University of Texas Rio Grande Valley, TX
The University of the Arts, PA
University of the Incarnate Word, TX
The University of Toledo, OH
The University of Tulsa, OK
University of Utah, UT
University of Vermont, VT
University of Virginia, VA
The University of Virginia's College at Wise, VA
University of Washington, WA
The University of West Alabama, AL
University of West Florida, FL
University of West Georgia, GA
University of Wisconsin–Eau Claire, WI
University of Wisconsin–Green Bay, WI
University of Wisconsin–La Crosse, WI
University of Wisconsin–Milwaukee, WI
University of Wisconsin–Parkside, WI
University of Wisconsin–River Falls, WI
University of Wisconsin–Stevens Point, WI
University of Wisconsin–Whitewater, WI
University of Wyoming, WY
Ursinus College, PA
Utah State University, UT
Valdosta State University, GA
Valencia College, FL
Valley City State University, ND

Valparaiso University, IN
Vanguard University of Southern California, CA
Virginia Polytechnic Institute and State University, VA
Wabash College, IN
Walla Walla University, WA
Warner Pacific College, OR
Wartburg College, IA
Washington College, MD
Washington State University, WA
Wayland Baptist University, TX
Waynesburg University, PA
Wayne State College, NE
Wayne State University, MI
Webster University, MO
Wesleyan College, GA
West Chester University of Pennsylvania, PA
Western Carolina University, NC
Western Illinois University, IL
Western Kentucky University, KY
Western Michigan University, MI
Western Oregon University, OR
Western Washington University, WA
Westminster College, PA
Westmont College, CA
West Texas A&M University, TX
West Virginia University, WV
West Virginia Wesleyan College, WV
Whitman College, WA
Whittier College, CA
Whitworth University, WA
Wichita State University, KS
Wilkes University, PA
William Jessup University, CA
William Jewell College, MO
Williams Baptist College, AR
William Woods University, MO
Winona State University, MN
Winthrop University, SC
Wisconsin Lutheran College, WI
Wittenberg University, OH
Wright State University, OH
Wright State University–Lake Campus, OH
Xavier University, OH
Young Harris College, GA
Youngstown State University, OH

Special Achievements/Activities

Cheerleading/Drum Major
Abilene Christian University, TX
Anderson University, SC
Arkansas Tech University, AR
Auburn University, AL
Augustana University, SD
Baker University, KS
Belhaven University, MS
Bellarmine University, KY
Belmont Abbey College, NC
Belmont University, TN
Benedictine College, KS
Bethel College, KS
Bluefield College, VA
Bluefield State College, WV
Blue Mountain College, MS
Boise State University, ID
Brenau University, GA
California Baptist University, CA
Cameron University, OK
Campbellsville University, KY
Campbell University, NC
Carroll College, MT
Catawba College, NC

Central Methodist University, MO
Claflin University, SC
Cleveland State University, OH
Coastal Carolina University, SC
Coker College, SC
Columbus State University, GA
Concordia University, Nebraska, NE
Culver-Stockton College, MO
Drexel University, PA
Drury University, MO
East Central University, OK
Eastern Kentucky University, KY
East Texas Baptist University, TX
Emmanuel College, GA
Emory & Henry College, VA
Evangel University, MO
Fairmont State University, WV
Faulkner University, AL
Florida Agricultural and Mechanical University, FL
Florida Institute of Technology, FL
Fort Hays State University, KS
Francis Marion University, SC
Gardner-Webb University, NC
Georgia Institute of Technology, GA
Georgia Southern University, GA
Graceland University, IA
Grambling State University, LA
Greenville University, IL
Harding University, AR
Hawai`i Pacific University, HI
Henderson State University, AR
Hofstra University, NY
Hope International University, CA
Houston Baptist University, TX
Huntingdon College, AL
Huntington University, IN
Idaho State University, ID
Indiana Wesleyan University, IN
James Madison University, VA
Kansas Wesleyan University, KS
Kentucky State University, KY
Lee University, TN
Lenoir-Rhyne University, NC
Lewis University, IL
Liberty University, VA
Lincoln Memorial University, TN
Lincoln University, MO
Lindenwood University, MO
Lindsey Wilson College, KY
Lipscomb University, TN
Long Island University–LIU Brooklyn, NY
Long Island University–LIU Post, NY
Louisiana College, LA
Louisiana Tech University, LA
Lyon College, AR
Malone University, OH
Maryville University of Saint Louis, MO
McKendree University, IL
Methodist University, NC
MidAmerica Nazarene University, KS
Middle Tennessee State University, TN
Midwestern State University, TX
Milligan College, TN
Mississippi State University, MS
Missouri Baptist University, MO
Missouri Southern State University, MO
Missouri Valley College, MO
Missouri Western State University, MO
Montana State University Billings, MT
Morehead State University, KY
Morehouse College, GA
Morningside College, IA
Newberry College, SC
New Mexico State University, NM
Nicholls State University, LA

North Carolina State University, NC
Northeastern State University, OK
Northern Illinois University, IL
Northern Kentucky University, KY
Northern Michigan University, MI
Northwest Missouri State University, MO
Northwood University, Michigan Campus, MI
The Ohio State University, OH
Oklahoma Baptist University, OK
Oklahoma Christian University, OK
Oklahoma State University, OK
Old Dominion University, VA
Olivet Nazarene University, IL
Oral Roberts University, OK
Ouachita Baptist University, AR
Robert Morris University Illinois, IL
Rocky Mountain College, MT
Rogers State University, OK
St. Ambrose University, IA
St. Edward's University, TX
St. John's University, NY
Saint Louis University, MO
St. Mary's University, TX
Samford University, AL
San Diego State University, CA
Seton Hill University, PA
Southeastern Louisiana University, LA
Southeastern Oklahoma State University, OK
Southeastern University, FL
Southeast Missouri State University, MO
Southern Arkansas University–Magnolia, AR
Southern Illinois University Carbondale, IL
Southwestern College, KS
Southwestern Oklahoma State University, OK
Stephen F. Austin State University, TX
Sterling College, KS
Stetson University, FL
Temple University, PA
Tennessee Technological University, TN
Tennessee Wesleyan University, TN
Texas A&M University–Commerce, TX
Texas Wesleyan University, TX
Thomas More College, KY
Tiffin University, OH
Trine University, IN
Union College, KY
Union University, TN
The University of Alabama, AL
The University of Alabama at Birmingham, AL
The University of Alabama in Huntsville, AL
University of Arkansas, AR
University of Delaware, DE
University of Houston, TX
University of Idaho, ID
The University of Iowa, IA
University of Jamestown, ND
University of Kentucky, KY
University of Louisiana at Monroe, LA
University of Mary Hardin-Baylor, TX
University of Maryland, College Park, MD
University of Massachusetts Amherst, MA
University of Memphis, TN
University of Mississippi, MS
University of Missouri, MO
University of Missouri–St. Louis, MO
University of Montana, MT
University of Montevallo, AL
University of Nebraska at Kearney, NE
University of Nebraska–Lincoln, NE
University of Nevada, Las Vegas, NV

University of North Alabama, AL
University of North Georgia, GA
University of Providence, MT
University of Puerto Rico–Bayamón, PR
University of St. Francis, IL
University of Science and Arts of Oklahoma, OK
University of Sioux Falls, SD
University of South Carolina, SC
University of South Carolina Aiken, SC
University of Southern Mississippi, MS
The University of Tennessee at Chattanooga, TN
The University of Tennessee at Martin, TN
The University of Texas at El Paso, TX
The University of Texas at San Antonio, TX
The University of Texas Rio Grande Valley, TX
The University of Toledo, OH
The University of Tulsa, OK
University of Utah, UT
The University of West Alabama, AL
University of Wyoming, WY
Virginia Polytechnic Institute and State University, VA
Virginia State University, VA
Wayland Baptist University, TX
West Texas A&M University, TX
West Virginia University Institute of Technology, WV
Wichita State University, KS
William Jewell College, MO
Williams Baptist College, AR
Wright State University, OH
Wright State University–Lake Campus, OH
Youngstown State University, OH

Community Service

Adelphi University, NY
Agnes Scott College, GA
Alaska Pacific University, AK
Albertus Magnus College, CT
Allen College, IA
Alliant International University–San Diego, CA
Alverno College, WI
Appalachian Bible College, WV
Arizona Christian University, AZ
Augsburg University, MN
Augustana University, SD
Austin College, TX
Ball State University, IN
Baylor University, TX
Bellarmine University, KY
Belmont University, TN
Beloit College, WI
Benedictine University, IL
Bentley University, MA
Berry College, GA
Bethel College, KS
Bethel University, MN
Binghamton University, State University of New York, NY
Biola University, CA
Boise State University, ID
Bradley University, IL
Brenau University, GA
Bryan College, TN
Caldwell University, NJ
California Lutheran University, CA
California Polytechnic State University, San Luis Obispo, CA
California State University, Bakersfield, CA
California State University, Chico, CA
California State University, Fresno, CA

California State University, San Bernardino, CA
California State University, Stanislaus, CA
Calvin College, MI
Centenary College of Louisiana, LA
Central College, IA
Centre College, KY
Chaminade University of Honolulu, HI
Christopher Newport University, VA
The Citadel, The Military College of South Carolina, SC
City College of the City University of New York, NY
Clarion University of Pennsylvania, PA
Clarke University, IA
Clemson University, SC
The College at Brockport, State University of New York, NY
College of Coastal Georgia, GA
The College of New Rochelle, NY
The College of Saint Rose, NY
College of Staten Island of the City University of New York, NY
The College of Wooster, OH
Columbia College, MO
Columbus State University, GA
Concord University, WV
Dallas Baptist University, TX
Davidson College, NC
Defiance College, OH
DePaul University, IL
DePauw University, IN
Dominican University of California, CA
Dordt College, IA
Drew University, NJ
Edgewood College, WI
Elon University, NC
Emory & Henry College, VA
Endicott College, MA
Eureka College, IL
Flagler College, FL
Florida Agricultural and Mechanical University, FL
Florida Gulf Coast University, FL
Florida Southern College, FL
Francis Marion University, SC
Franklin College, IN
Frostburg State University, MD
Furman University, SC
Gannon University, PA
Georgian Court University, NJ
Georgia Southern University, GA
Gonzaga University, WA
Goshen College, IN
Grove City College, PA
Hamline University, MN
Hawai`i Pacific University, HI
Hendrix College, AR
Hillsdale College, MI
Hobart and William Smith Colleges, NY
Hollins University, VA
Howard Payne University, TX
Huntingdon College, AL
Illinois Institute of Technology, IL
Indiana University of Pennsylvania, PA
Indiana Wesleyan University, IN
Iona College, NY
Iowa State University of Science and Technology, IA
John Carroll University, OH
Johnson University, TN
Juniata College, PA
Kean University, NJ
Kennesaw State University, GA
Kent State University, OH

Kent State University at Stark, OH
Keuka College, NY
King's College, PA
Knox College, IL
Kutztown University of Pennsylvania, PA
La Salle University, PA
Lawrence University, WI
Lewis & Clark College, OR
Lewis-Clark State College, ID
Lewis University, IL
Lindenwood University, MO
Linfield College, OR
Lipscomb University, TN
Lock Haven University of Pennsylvania, PA
Longwood University, VA
Loyola Marymount University, CA
Loyola University Chicago, IL
Lycoming College, PA
Manhattan College, NY
Manhattanville College, NY
Marymount University, VA
Maryville College, TN
Maryville University of Saint Louis, MO
Marywood University, PA
McKendree University, IL
Mercer University, GA
Meredith College, NC
Michigan State University, MI
Millersville University of Pennsylvania, PA
Milligan College, TN
Millikin University, IL
Millsaps College, MS
Minnesota State University Moorhead, MN
Misericordia University, PA
Missouri Valley College, MO
Missouri Western State University, MO
Molloy College, NY
Montana Tech of The University of Montana, MT
Montclair State University, NJ
Moravian College, PA
Morehead State University, KY
Morehouse College, GA
Mount Carmel College of Nursing, OH
Mount Marty College, SD
Mount St. Joseph University, OH
Mount Saint Mary's University, CA
Murray State University, KY
Muskingum University, OH
Neumont College of Computer Science, UT
New England College, NH
New Jersey Institute of Technology, NJ
Newman University, KS
Niagara University, NY
Nichols College, MA
North Central College, IL
Northeastern State University, OK
Northern Illinois University, IL
Northern Kentucky University, KY
Northwest Christian University, OR
Oglethorpe University, GA
Ohio Northern University, OH
Ohio Valley University, WV
Oklahoma State University, OK
Old Dominion University, VA
Olivet College, MI
Oral Roberts University, OK
Pacific University, OR
Philander Smith College, AR
Piedmont College, GA
Point Park University, PA
Portland State University, OR
Principia College, IL
Providence College, RI
Randolph College, VA

Ringling College of Art and Design, FL
Robert Morris University Illinois, IL
Rochester Institute of Technology, NY
Rockford University, IL
Rockhurst University, MO
Sacred Heart University, CT
The Sage Colleges, NY
Saginaw Valley State University, MI
St. Andrews University, NC
St. Catherine University, MN
St. Edward's University, TX
St. John Fisher College, NY
St. John's University, NY
St. Joseph's College, Long Island Campus, NY
St. Joseph's College, New York, NY
Saint Joseph's University, PA
St. Lawrence University, NY
St. Louis College of Pharmacy, MO
Saint Louis University, MO
Saint Martin's University, WA
Saint Mary-of-the-Woods College, IN
St. Olaf College, MN
St. Thomas Aquinas College, NY
Samford University, AL
San Jose State University, CA
Schreiner University, TX
Shippensburg University of Pennsylvania, PA
Siena College, NY
Simmons College, MA
Simpson College, IA
Slippery Rock University of Pennsylvania, PA
Sonoma State University, CA
South Dakota State University, SD
Southern Adventist University, TN
Southern Illinois University Carbondale, IL
Southern New Hampshire University, NH
Southern Oregon University, OR
Southern Vermont College, VT
Southwestern College, KS
Spring Hill College, AL
State University of New York at Plattsburgh, NY
State University of New York College at Cortland, NY
State University of New York College at Geneseo, NY
State University of New York College at Potsdam, NY
State University of New York College of Environmental Science and Forestry, NY
Stetson University, FL
Stockton University, NJ
Stony Brook University, State University of New York, NY
Suffolk University, MA
Texas A&M University, TX
Texas A&M University–Texarkana, TX
Texas Christian University, TX
Texas Tech University, TX
Texas Wesleyan University, TX
Thomas More College, KY
Towson University, MD
Trinity Christian College, IL
Trinity College of Florida, FL
Truett McConnell University, GA
Tulane University, LA
Union College, KY
Union College, NE
Union University, TN
Unity College, ME
The University of Akron, OH
The University of Alabama, AL

The University of Alabama in Huntsville, AL
University of Alaska Fairbanks, AK
University of Arkansas, AR
University of Arkansas at Little Rock, AR
University of California, Irvine, CA
University of California, San Diego, CA
University of California, Santa Cruz, CA
University of Chicago, IL
University of Colorado Boulder, CO
University of Dayton, OH
University of Delaware, DE
University of Denver, CO
University of Florida, FL
University of Hartford, CT
University of Houston, TX
University of Houston–Clear Lake, TX
University of Houston–Downtown, TX
University of Houston–Victoria, TX
University of Indianapolis, IN
University of Jamestown, ND
The University of Kansas, KS
University of La Verne, CA
University of Louisiana at Monroe, LA
University of Maine, ME
University of Maine at Presque Isle, ME
University of Mary Hardin-Baylor, TX
University of Massachusetts Dartmouth, MA
University of Massachusetts Lowell, MA
University of Memphis, TN
University of Michigan, MI
University of Michigan–Dearborn, MI
University of Michigan–Flint, MI
University of Mississippi, MS
University of Nebraska–Lincoln, NE
University of Nevada, Las Vegas, NV
University of New Hampshire, NH
University of North Carolina at Asheville, NC
The University of North Carolina at Chapel Hill, NC
The University of North Carolina at Greensboro, NC
University of North Dakota, ND
University of Northern Colorado, CO
University of North Florida, FL
University of North Georgia, GA
University of Puerto Rico–Bayamón, PR
University of Puget Sound, WA
University of Richmond, VA
University of St. Francis, IL
University of South Carolina, SC
University of South Carolina Aiken, SC
The University of Tennessee at Chattanooga, TN
The University of Texas Rio Grande Valley, TX
University of the Southwest, NM
The University of Toledo, OH
The University of Tulsa, OK
University of Vermont, VT
The University of Virginia's College at Wise, VA
University of West Georgia, GA
University of Wisconsin–Eau Claire, WI
University of Wisconsin–Green Bay, WI
University of Wisconsin–La Crosse, WI
University of Wisconsin–Parkside, WI
University of Wisconsin–Stout, WI
University of Wyoming, WY
Ursinus College, PA
Ursuline College, OH
Valencia College, FL
Vanderbilt University, TN
Virginia Polytechnic Institute and State University, VA

Virginia State University, VA
Wabash College, IN
Washington State University, WA
Wayland Baptist University, TX
Waynesburg University, PA
Webber International University, FL
Webb Institute, NY
Webster University, MO
Wesleyan College, GA
Western Illinois University, IL
Western Oregon University, OR
Western Washington University, WA
West Texas A&M University, TX
West Virginia Wesleyan College, WV
Wheaton College, IL
Wheeling Jesuit University, WV
Wichita State University, KS
Widener University, PA
Wilson College, PA
Wisconsin Lutheran College, WI
Wittenberg University, OH
Wright State University, OH
Wright State University–Lake Campus, OH
Youngstown State University, OH

Hobbies/Interests

California State Polytechnic University, Pomona, CA
California State University, Chico, CA
California State University, San Bernardino, CA
Capital University, OH
Centenary College of Louisiana, LA
The College at Brockport, State University of New York, NY
The College of New Rochelle, NY
College of Staten Island of the City University of New York, NY
Colorado Mesa University, CO
Emmanuel College, GA
Florida Institute of Technology, FL
Francis Marion University, SC
Hawai`i Pacific University, HI
Hollins University, VA
Illinois Institute of Technology, IL
Indiana University of Pennsylvania, PA
Indiana Wesleyan University, IN
Michigan State University, MI
Middle Tennessee State University, TN
Millsaps College, MS
Missouri Valley College, MO
Montana Tech of The University of Montana, MT
New Jersey Institute of Technology, NJ
New Mexico State University, NM
The Ohio State University, OH
Sacred Heart University, CT
St. John's University, NY
Saint Martin's University, WA
San Diego State University, CA
Siena College, NY
South Dakota State University, SD
Southern New Hampshire University, NH
Southern Oregon University, OR
State University of New York College at Cortland, NY
Stephen F. Austin State University, TX
Texas Tech University, TX
Union College, KY
The University of Alabama, AL
University of California, Santa Cruz, CA
University of Houston, TX
University of Michigan–Flint, MI
University of Minnesota, Twin Cities Campus, MN
University of Montevallo, AL

University of South Carolina Aiken, SC
The University of Toledo, OH
University of Wisconsin–Eau Claire, WI
University of Wyoming, WY
Virginia State University, VA
Wesleyan College, GA
Western Oregon University, OR
West Texas A&M University, TX
Wichita State University, KS

Junior Miss

Arkansas Tech University, AR
Augsburg University, MN
Belhaven University, MS
Birmingham-Southern College, AL
Bluefield State College, WV
Campbellsville University, KY
Carroll University, WI
Cedar Crest College, PA
Concordia University Texas, TX
Georgetown College, KY
Georgia Southern University, GA
Goshen College, IN
Grambling State University, LA
Gustavus Adolphus College, MN
Kansas Wesleyan University, KS
Lewis-Clark State College, ID
Lindenwood University, MO
Lindsey Wilson College, KY
Louisiana Tech University, LA
Mississippi State University, MS
Missouri Valley College, MO
Morehead State University, KY
Muskingum University, OH
New Mexico State University, NM
Northeastern State University, OK
Ohio Northern University, OH
Oklahoma City University, OK
Roberts Wesleyan College, NY
Rogers State University, OK
South Dakota State University, SD
Stetson University, FL
Tennessee Wesleyan University, TN
Texas A&M University–Commerce, TX
Texas Lutheran University, TX
The University of Alabama, AL
The University of Alabama at Birmingham, AL
The University of Alabama in Huntsville, AL
University of Central Oklahoma, OK
University of Evansville, IN
University of Idaho, ID
University of Mississippi, MS
University of Montevallo, AL
The University of North Carolina at Greensboro, NC
The University of Tennessee at Martin, TN
The University of West Alabama, AL
University of Wyoming, WY
Wartburg College, IA
Washington State University, WA

Leadership

Abilene Christian University, TX
Adelphi University, NY
Agnes Scott College, GA
Alabama State University, AL
Alaska Pacific University, AK
Albertus Magnus College, CT
Alcorn State University, MS
Allen College, IA
Alliant International University–San Diego, CA
American Jewish University, CA
American University, DC
Anderson University, SC

Andrews University, MI
Appalachian Bible College, WV
Aquinas College, MI
Arizona Christian University, AZ
Arizona State University at the Downtown
　　Phoenix campus, AZ
Arizona State University at the Polytechnic
　　campus, AZ
Arizona State University at the Tempe
　　campus, AZ
Arizona State University at the West campus,
　　AZ
Auburn University, AL
Auburn University at Montgomery, AL
Augsburg University, MN
Augustana College, IL
Augustana University, SD
Aurora University, IL
Austin College, TX
Austin Peay State University, TN
Ave Maria University, FL
Averett University, VA
Babson College, MA
Baker University, KS
Ball State University, IN
Barton College, NC
Baylor University, TX
Becker College, MA
Belhaven University, MS
Bellarmine University, KY
Belmont University, TN
Beloit College, WI
Bemidji State University, MN
Benedictine College, KS
Benedictine University, IL
Bentley University, MA
Berry College, GA
Bethel University, MN
Binghamton University, State University of
　　New York, NY
Biola University, CA
Birmingham-Southern College, AL
Bluefield State College, WV
Blue Mountain College, MS
Bluffton University, OH
Boise State University, ID
Bowdoin College, ME
Bowling Green State University, OH
Bradley University, IL
Brenau University, GA
Brigham Young University, UT
Bryan College, TN
Bryn Mawr College, PA
Bucknell University, PA
Buena Vista University, IA
Caldwell University, NJ
California Lutheran University, CA
California Polytechnic State University, San
　　Luis Obispo, CA
California State Polytechnic University,
　　Pomona, CA
California State University, Bakersfield, CA
California State University, Chico, CA
California State University, Fresno, CA
California State University, Fullerton, CA
California State University, Monterey Bay,
　　CA
California State University, Northridge, CA
California State University, San Marcos, CA
California State University, Stanislaus, CA
Calumet College of Saint Joseph, IN
Calvin College, MI
Cameron University, OK
Campbellsville University, KY
Capital University, OH

Carlow University, PA
Carroll College, MT
Carroll University, WI
Carson-Newman University, TN
Case Western Reserve University, OH
Catawba College, NC
Cedarville University, OH
Central Methodist University, MO
Central Michigan University, MI
Central Washington University, WA
Champlain College, VT
Chatham University, PA
Chowan University, NC
Christian Brothers University, TN
Christopher Newport University, VA
The Citadel, The Military College of South
　　Carolina, SC
City College of the City University of New
　　York, NY
Claremont McKenna College, CA
Clarion University of Pennsylvania, PA
Clarke University, IA
Clarkson University, NY
Clemson University, SC
Cleveland Institute of Art, OH
Coker College, SC
The College at Brockport, State University
　　of New York, NY
College of Coastal Georgia, GA
The College of Idaho, ID
The College of New Rochelle, NY
College of Saint Mary, NE
College of Staten Island of the City
　　University of New York, NY
Colorado Mesa University, CO
Columbia College, MO
Columbia International University, SC
Columbus State University, GA
Concord University, WV
Corban University, OR
Covenant College, GA
Culver-Stockton College, MO
Daemen College, NY
Dallas Baptist University, TX
Davidson College, NC
Davis College, NY
Defiance College, OH
DePaul University, IL
DeSales University, PA
DigiPen Institute of Technology, WA
Dominican University of California, CA
Dordt College, IA
Drury University, MO
Duke University, NC
Eastern Illinois University, IL
Eastern Michigan University, MI
Eastern Oregon University, OR
Eastern University, PA
East Texas Baptist University, TX
Elmira College, NY
Elon University, NC
Embry-Riddle Aeronautical University–
　　Daytona, FL
Emmanuel College, GA
Emory University, GA
Emporia State University, KS
Endicott College, MA
Eugene Lang College of Liberal Arts, NY
Eureka College, IL
Evangel University, MO
Fairmont State University, WV
Faulkner University, AL
Flagler College, FL
Florida Agricultural and Mechanical
　　University, FL

Florida Gulf Coast University, FL
Florida Institute of Technology, FL
Florida Southern College, FL
Fort Hays State University, KS
Fort Lewis College, CO
Francis Marion University, SC
Franklin College, IN
Franklin Pierce University, NH
Frostburg State University, MD
Furman University, SC
Gannon University, PA
Geneva College, PA
George Fox University, OR
Georgia Institute of Technology, GA
Georgian Court University, NJ
Georgia Southern University, GA
Georgia Southwestern State University, GA
Gonzaga University, WA
Gordon College, MA
Goucher College, MD
Graceland University, IA
Grambling State University, LA
Greenville University, IL
Grove City College, PA
Hamline University, MN
Hampden-Sydney College, VA
Hampton University, VA
Harding University, AR
Hawai'i Pacific University, HI
Henderson State University, AR
Hendrix College, AR
High Point University, NC
Hilbert College, NY
Hillsdale College, MI
Hobart and William Smith Colleges, NY
Hofstra University, NY
Hollins University, VA
Hood College, MD
Hope International University, CA
Howard Payne University, TX
Huntington University, IN
Husson University, ME
Illinois Institute of Technology, IL
Indiana University of Pennsylvania, PA
Iowa State University of Science and
　　Technology, IA
Ithaca College, NY
Jackson State University, MS
Jacksonville State University, AL
Jacksonville University, FL
James Madison University, VA
John Carroll University, OH
John Paul the Great Catholic University, CA
Johnson University, TN
Judson University, IL
Juniata College, PA
Kalamazoo College, MI
Kean University, NJ
Keene State College, NH
Kennesaw State University, GA
Kent State University, OH
Keuka College, NY
The King's College, NY
King's College, PA
Kutztown University of Pennsylvania, PA
Kuyper College, MI
LaGrange College, GA
Lancaster Bible College, PA
La Sierra University, CA
Lawrence University, WI
Lee University, TN
Le Moyne College, NY
Lenoir-Rhyne University, NC
Lewis & Clark College, OR
Lewis-Clark State College, ID

Lewis University, IL
Liberty University, VA
Life University, GA
LIM College, NY
Lindenwood University, MO
Lindsey Wilson College, KY
Linfield College, OR
Lipscomb University, TN
Lock Haven University of Pennsylvania, PA
Longwood University, VA
Loras College, IA
Louisiana College, LA
Loyola Marymount University, CA
Loyola University Chicago, IL
Loyola University New Orleans, LA
Lubbock Christian University, TX
Lycoming College, PA
Lynn University, FL
Malone University, OH
Manhattan College, NY
Mansfield University of Pennsylvania, PA
Marlboro College, VT
Marymount Manhattan College, NY
Marymount University, VA
Maryville College, TN
Maryville University of Saint Louis, MO
Marywood University, PA
Massachusetts College of Liberal Arts, MA
Massachusetts Maritime Academy, MA
McDaniel College, MD
McKendree University, IL
Mercer University, GA
Meredith College, NC
Merrimack College, MA
Messiah College, PA
Methodist University, NC
Metropolitan State University of Denver, CO
Miami University, OH
Michigan State University, MI
MidAmerica Nazarene University, KS
Middle Tennessee State University, TN
Midwestern State University, TX
Millikin University, IL
Millsaps College, MS
Mills College, CA
Minnesota State University Mankato, MN
Misericordia University, PA
Mississippi State University, MS
Missouri Southern State University, MO
Missouri State University, MO
Missouri Valley College, MO
Missouri Western State University, MO
Mitchell College, CT
Molloy College, NY
Monmouth University, NJ
Montana State University, MT
Montana Tech of The University of Montana, MT
Montclair State University, NJ
Montreat College, NC
Moravian College, PA
Morehead State University, KY
Morehouse College, GA
Morrisville State College, NY
Mount Aloysius College, PA
Mount Marty College, SD
Mount Mary University, WI
Mount St. Joseph University, OH
Mount Saint Mary College, NY
Mount Saint Mary's University, CA
Muskingum University, OH
Nazareth College of Rochester, NY
Nebraska Methodist College, NE
New England College, NH
New Jersey Institute of Technology, NJ
Newman University, KS

New Mexico State University, NM
Nicholls State University, LA
Nichols College, MA
North Carolina State University, NC
Northeastern Illinois University, IL
Northeastern State University, OK
Northern Arizona University, AZ
Northern Illinois University, IL
Northern Kentucky University, KY
Northern Michigan University, MI
Northern State University, SD
Northwest Christian University, OR
Northwest Missouri State University, MO
Northwest Nazarene University, ID
Northwest University, WA
Occidental College, CA
Oglethorpe University, GA
Ohio Northern University, OH
The Ohio State University, OH
Ohio Valley University, WV
Ohio Wesleyan University, OH
Oklahoma Baptist University, OK
Oklahoma City University, OK
Oklahoma State University, OK
Old Dominion University, VA
Olivet College, MI
Oral Roberts University, OK
Oregon State University, OR
Pacific Lutheran University, WA
Palm Beach Atlantic University, FL
Parsons School of Design, NY
Peirce College, PA
Pfeiffer University, NC
Piedmont College, GA
Portland State University, OR
Principia College, IL
Purdue University, IN
Randolph College, VA
Regent University, VA
Regis University, CO
Rice University, TX
Robert Morris University Illinois, IL
Rochester Institute of Technology, NY
Rockford University, IL
Rockhurst University, MO
Rogers State University, OK
Sacred Heart University, CT
The Sage Colleges, NY
Saginaw Valley State University, MI
St. Ambrose University, IA
St. Andrews University, NC
St. Catherine University, MN
St. Edward's University, TX
St. John's University, NY
St. Joseph's College, Long Island Campus, NY
St. Joseph's College, New York, NY
St. Lawrence University, NY
Saint Leo University, FL
St. Louis College of Pharmacy, MO
Saint Louis University, MO
Saint Martin's University, WA
Saint Mary's College of California, CA
Saint Mary's University of Minnesota, MN
St. Olaf College, MN
Saint Peter's University, NJ
St. Thomas Aquinas College, NY
St. Thomas University, FL
Salem College, NC
Samford University, AL
Sam Houston State University, TX
San Diego State University, CA
San Jose State University, CA
Schreiner University, TX
Seattle University, WA
Shepherd University, WV

Shippensburg University of Pennsylvania, PA
Siena College, NY
Simpson College, IA
Slippery Rock University of Pennsylvania, PA
Soka University of America, CA
Sonoma State University, CA
South Dakota State University, SD
Southeastern Louisiana University, LA
Southeastern Oklahoma State University, OK
Southeastern University, FL
Southeast Missouri State University, MO
Southern Adventist University, TN
Southern Arkansas University–Magnolia, AR
Southern Illinois University Carbondale, IL
Southern New Hampshire University, NH
Southern Oregon University, OR
Southern Utah University, UT
Southern Vermont College, VT
Southwestern College, KS
Southwestern Oklahoma State University, OK
Southwestern University, TX
State University of New York at Fredonia, NY
State University of New York at Plattsburgh, NY
State University of New York College at Cortland, NY
State University of New York College at Geneseo, NY
State University of New York College at Potsdam, NY
State University of New York College of Agriculture and Technology at Cobleskill, NY
State University of New York College of Environmental Science and Forestry, NY
State University of New York Maritime College, NY
Stephen F. Austin State University, TX
Stetson University, FL
Stockton University, NJ
Stony Brook University, State University of New York, NY
Suffolk University, MA
Susquehanna University, PA
Taylor University, IN
Texas A&M University, TX
Texas A&M University–Commerce, TX
Texas A&M University–Texarkana, TX
Texas Christian University, TX
Texas Lutheran University, TX
Texas State University, TX
Texas Tech University, TX
Texas Wesleyan University, TX
Thomas More College, KY
Toccoa Falls College, GA
Trevecca Nazarene University, TN
Trinity Christian College, IL
Trinity College, CT
Trinity College of Florida, FL
Troy University, AL
Truett McConnell University, GA
Truman State University, MO
Union College, KY
Union College, NE
Union University, TN
The University of Akron, OH
The University of Alabama at Birmingham, AL
The University of Alabama in Huntsville, AL

University of Alaska Anchorage, AK
University of Alaska Fairbanks, AK
The University of Arizona, AZ
University of Arkansas, AR
University of Arkansas at Little Rock, AR
University of California, Irvine, CA
University of California, San Diego, CA
University of California, Santa Cruz, CA
University of Central Florida, FL
University of Central Oklahoma, OK
University of Chicago, IL
University of Colorado Boulder, CO
University of Dayton, OH
University of Delaware, DE
University of Denver, CO
University of Evansville, IN
University of Florida, FL
University of Hartford, CT
University of Houston, TX
University of Houston–Clear Lake, TX
University of Houston–Downtown, TX
University of Houston–Victoria, TX
University of Idaho, ID
University of Illinois at Urbana–Champaign, IL
The University of Iowa, IA
University of Jamestown, ND
The University of Kansas, KS
University of Kentucky, KY
University of La Verne, CA
University of Louisiana at Monroe, LA
University of Maine, ME
University of Mary Hardin-Baylor, TX
University of Mary Washington, VA
University of Massachusetts Amherst, MA
University of Massachusetts Boston, MA
University of Memphis, TN
University of Miami, FL
University of Michigan, MI
University of Michigan–Dearborn, MI
University of Michigan–Flint, MI
University of Minnesota, Crookston, MN
University of Minnesota, Twin Cities Campus, MN
University of Mississippi, MS
University of Montana, MT
University of Montevallo, AL
University of Nebraska at Kearney, NE
University of Nebraska–Lincoln, NE
University of Nevada, Las Vegas, NV
University of New England, ME
University of New Hampshire, NH
University of North Alabama, AL
University of North Carolina at Asheville, NC
The University of North Carolina at Chapel Hill, NC
The University of North Carolina at Greensboro, NC
The University of North Carolina Wilmington, NC
University of North Dakota, ND
University of Northern Colorado, CO
University of Northern Iowa, IA
University of North Florida, FL
University of North Georgia, GA
University of Oklahoma, OK
University of Pittsburgh at Greensburg, PA
University of Pittsburgh at Johnstown, PA
University of Puget Sound, WA
University of Rhode Island, RI
University of Rochester, NY
University of St. Francis, IL
University of Saint Joseph, CT
University of St. Thomas, TX

University of San Diego, CA
University of Sioux Falls, SD
University of South Carolina, SC
University of South Carolina Aiken, SC
University of South Dakota, SD
University of Southern California, CA
University of Southern Indiana, IN
University of Southern Mississippi, MS
The University of Tampa, FL
The University of Tennessee at Martin, TN
The University of Texas at Austin, TX
The University of Texas at Dallas, TX
The University of Texas at El Paso, TX
The University of Texas Rio Grande Valley, TX
University of the Incarnate Word, TX
University of the Pacific, CA
University of the Southwest, NM
The University of Toledo, OH
The University of Tulsa, OK
University of Utah, UT
University of Vermont, VT
University of Virginia, VA
University of Washington, WA
The University of West Alabama, AL
University of West Florida, FL
University of West Georgia, GA
University of Wisconsin–Eau Claire, WI
University of Wisconsin–Green Bay, WI
University of Wisconsin–La Crosse, WI
University of Wisconsin–Milwaukee, WI
University of Wisconsin–Parkside, WI
University of Wisconsin–River Falls, WI
University of Wisconsin–Stevens Point, WI
University of Wisconsin–Stout, WI
University of Wisconsin–Whitewater, WI
University of Wyoming, WY
Ursinus College, PA
Ursuline College, OH
Utah State University, UT
Valencia College, FL
Vanderbilt University, TN
Virginia Polytechnic Institute and State University, VA
Virginia State University, VA
Wabash College, IN
Wake Forest University, NC
Walla Walla University, WA
Warner Pacific College, OR
Wartburg College, IA
Washington State University, WA
Wayland Baptist University, TX
Wayne State College, NE
Wayne State University, MI
Webber International University, FL
Webb Institute, NY
Webster University, MO
Wells College, NY
Wesleyan College, GA
West Chester University of Pennsylvania, PA
Western Illinois University, IL
Western Kentucky University, KY
Western New England University, MA
Western Oregon University, OR
Western State Colorado University, CO
Western Washington University, WA
Westminster College, MO
Westmont College, CA
West Texas A&M University, TX
West Virginia University, WV
West Virginia University Institute of Technology, WV
West Virginia Wesleyan College, WV
Wheaton College, IL
Wichita State University, KS

Widener University, PA
Wilkes University, PA
William Jessup University, CA
Wilson College, PA
Wisconsin Lutheran College, WI
Wittenberg University, OH
Wofford College, SC
Worcester Polytechnic Institute, MA
Wright State University, OH
Wright State University–Lake Campus, OH
Youngstown State University, OH

Memberships
Adelphi University, NY
Albright College, PA
Alverno College, WI
American University, DC
Anderson University, SC
Auburn University, AL
Austin Peay State University, TN
Ave Maria University, FL
Averett University, VA
Benedictine University, IL
Birmingham-Southern College, AL
Blue Mountain College, MS
Boston University, MA
Caldwell University, NJ
California State University, Chico, CA
California State University, San Bernardino, CA
California State University, Stanislaus, CA
Carroll University, WI
Carson-Newman University, TN
Chaminade University of Honolulu, HI
Charlotte Christian College and Theological Seminary, NC
Christian Brothers University, TN
The College of New Rochelle, NY
College of Staten Island of the City University of New York, NY
Corban University, OR
Dallas Baptist University, TX
Eastern Michigan University, MI
Emmanuel College, GA
Emporia State University, KS
Ferris State University, MI
Flagler College, FL
Florida Institute of Technology, FL
Francis Marion University, SC
Franklin College, IN
Geneva College, PA
Georgian Court University, NJ
Georgia Southern University, GA
Gonzaga University, WA
Greenville University, IL
Grove City College, PA
Hamline University, MN
Hawai`i Pacific University, HI
Hiram College, OH
Huntington University, IN
Illinois Institute of Technology, IL
Kansas Wesleyan University, KS
Kean University, NJ
Kennesaw State University, GA
Lewis-Clark State College, ID
Lewis University, IL
LIM College, NY
Lock Haven University of Pennsylvania, PA
Longwood University, VA
Loyola Marymount University, CA
Loyola University Chicago, IL
Marymount University, VA
Massachusetts College of Liberal Arts, MA
Michigan State University, MI
Middle Tennessee State University, TN

Mississippi State University, MS
Missouri Baptist University, MO
Missouri Western State University, MO
Molloy College, NY
Montana Tech of The University of
Montana, MT
Morrisville State College, NY
Murray State University, KY
Nebraska Methodist College, NE
Newman University, KS
New Mexico State University, NM
Northern Illinois University, IL
Northern Michigan University, MI
Northwest Missouri State University, MO
Oglethorpe University, GA
The Ohio State University, OH
Oklahoma State University, OK
Old Dominion University, VA
Olivet College, MI
Oral Roberts University, OK
Pacific University, OR
Peirce College, PA
Point Park University, PA
Portland State University, OR
Regent University, VA
Sacred Heart University, CT
St. Catherine University, MN
Saint Louis University, MO
Saint Mary-of-the-Woods College, IN
Saint Mary's College of California, CA
San Diego State University, CA
Schreiner University, TX
Siena College, NY
Sonoma State University, CA
South Dakota State University, SD
Southeastern Louisiana University, LA
Southeast Missouri State University, MO
Southern New Hampshire University, NH
Southern Oregon University, OR
Southwestern College, KS
State University of New York College at
Geneseo, NY
State University of New York College of
Environmental Science and Forestry, NY
Tennessee Wesleyan University, TN
Texas A&M University, TX
Texas A&M University–Commerce, TX
Texas A&M University–Texarkana, TX
Texas Christian University, TX
Texas Tech University, TX
Texas Wesleyan University, TX
Thomas More College, KY
Towson University, MD
Union College, KY
Union University, TN
The University of Akron, OH
The University of Alabama at Birmingham,
AL
University of Arkansas at Little Rock, AR
University of California, Santa Cruz, CA
University of Evansville, IN
University of Houston–Victoria, TX
University of Maine, ME
University of Michigan–Dearborn, MI
University of Mississippi, MS
University of Missouri, MO
University of Missouri–St. Louis, MO
University of North Dakota, ND
University of Northern Colorado, CO
University of South Carolina, SC
University of South Carolina Aiken, SC
The University of Tampa, FL
The University of Tennessee at Chattanooga,
TN
The University of Texas Rio Grande Valley,
TX

The University of Toledo, OH
University of Vermont, VT
University of Washington, WA
The University of West Alabama, AL
University of West Georgia, GA
University of Wisconsin–Eau Claire, WI
University of Wisconsin–La Crosse, WI
University of Wisconsin–Stout, WI
University of Wyoming, WY
Virginia Polytechnic Institute and State
University, VA
Warner Pacific College, OR
Washington State University, WA
Wayne State University, MI
Webber International University, FL
Wesleyan College, GA
Western Kentucky University, KY
Western Washington University, WA
West Texas A&M University, TX
Wichita State University, KS
Wright State University, OH
Wright State University–Lake Campus, OH
Youngstown State University, OH

Religious Involvement
Alaska Bible College, AK
Alaska Pacific University, AK
Albright College, PA
Alma College, MI
Amridge University, AL
Andrews University, MI
Appalachian Bible College, WV
Augsburg University, MN
Augustana College, IL
Augustana University, SD
Austin College, TX
Austin Graduate School of Theology, TX
Ave Maria University, FL
Averett University, VA
Baker University, KS
Barton College, NC
Baylor University, TX
Bellarmine University, KY
Belmont Abbey College, NC
Belmont University, TN
Berry College, GA
Bethel University, MN
Birmingham-Southern College, AL
Blue Mountain College, MS
Brigham Young University, UT
Bryan College, TN
Caldwell University, NJ
California Lutheran University, CA
Calvin College, MI
Campbellsville University, KY
Campbell University, NC
Canisius College, NY
Capital University, OH
Carlow University, PA
Carroll College, MT
Carroll University, WI
Cedar Crest College, PA
Centenary College of Louisiana, LA
Central College, IA
Central Methodist University, MO
Chaminade University of Honolulu, HI
Charlotte Christian College and Theological
Seminary, NC
The Citadel, The Military College of South
Carolina, SC
Clarke University, IA
The College at Brockport, State University
of New York, NY
The College of New Rochelle, NY
The College of Wooster, OH
Columbia College, MO

Columbia International University, SC
Concordia University Texas, TX
Criswell College, TX
Crossroads Bible College, IN
Dallas Baptist University, TX
Davidson College, NC
Defiance College, OH
Drury University, MO
Earlham College, IN
Eastern Mennonite University, VA
Eastern Michigan University, MI
East Texas Baptist University, TX
Edgewood College, WI
Elizabethtown College, PA
Elon University, NC
Emmanuel College, GA
Emory & Henry College, VA
Endicott College, MA
Eureka College, IL
Evangel University, MO
Faulkner University, AL
Flagler College, FL
Franciscan University of Steubenville, OH
Franklin College, IN
Furman University, SC
Gardner-Webb University, NC
Geneva College, PA
George Fox University, OR
Georgetown College, KY
Georgian Court University, NJ
Georgia Southern University, GA
Graceland University, IA
Greenville University, IL
Grove City College, PA
Harding University, AR
Hawai`i Pacific University, HI
Hendrix College, AR
High Point University, NC
Houston Baptist University, TX
Howard Payne University, TX
Huntington University, IN
Indiana Wesleyan University, IN
Johnson University, TN
Kansas Wesleyan University, KS
King's College, PA
Kutztown University of Pennsylvania, PA
Lancaster Bible College, PA
Lee University, TN
Lewis University, IL
Lindsey Wilson College, KY
Lipscomb University, TN
Loras College, IA
Loyola Marymount University, CA
Malone University, OH
Marymount University, VA
Maryville University of Saint Louis, MO
McMurry University, TX
Millsaps College, MS
Missouri Baptist University, MO
Missouri Western State University, MO
Molloy College, NY
Monmouth College, IL
Moravian College, PA
Morehouse College, GA
Mount Marty College, SD
Mount St. Mary's University, MD
Mount Vernon Nazarene University, OH
Neumont College of Computer Science, UT
Newberry College, SC
New Jersey Institute of Technology, NJ
Newman University, KS
North Central College, IL
Northwest Christian University, OR
Northwest Nazarene University, ID
Northwest University, WA
Oakland City University, IN

Oglethorpe University, GA
Ohio Valley University, WV
Oklahoma Baptist University, OK
Oklahoma City University, OK
Oral Roberts University, OK
Ozark Christian College, MO
Pacific University, OR
Pfeiffer University, NC
Philander Smith College, AR
Piedmont College, GA
Piedmont International University, NC
Principia College, IL
Randolph-Macon College, VA
Regent University, VA
Roberts Wesleyan College, NY
Sacred Heart University, CT
St. John's University, NY
Saint Leo University, FL
Saint Louis University, MO
Saint Martin's University, WA
Saint Mary-of-the-Woods College, IN
St. Olaf College, MN
Samford University, AL
Schreiner University, TX
Shenandoah University, VA
Siena College, NY
Simpson College, IA
Southeastern University, FL
Southern Adventist University, TN
Southwest Baptist University, MO
Southwestern College, KS
Sterling College, KS
Stetson University, FL
Texas Christian University, TX
Texas Lutheran University, TX
Texas Wesleyan University, TX
Thomas More College, KY
Trinity Christian College, IL
Trinity College of Florida, FL
Truett McConnell University, GA
Union College, KY
Union College, NE
Union University, TN
The University of Alabama at Birmingham, AL
University of Detroit Mercy, MI
University of Indianapolis, IN
University of Mary Hardin-Baylor, TX
University of Miami, FL
The University of North Carolina at Greensboro, NC
University of Providence, MT
University of Puget Sound, WA
University of St. Francis, IL
University of St. Thomas, TX
University of San Diego, CA
University of South Carolina, SC
The University of Tennessee at Chattanooga, TN
University of the Incarnate Word, TX
University of the Pacific, CA
University of the Southwest, NM
The University of Toledo, OH
The University of Virginia's College at Wise, VA
University of West Georgia, GA
University of Wisconsin–Stout, WI
Valdosta State University, GA
Valparaiso University, IN
Virginia Polytechnic Institute and State University, VA
Virginia State University, VA
Virginia Wesleyan University, VA
Washington State University, WA
Wesleyan College, GA

West Texas A&M University, TX
West Virginia Wesleyan College, WV
Wheaton College, IL
Whitworth University, WA
William Jessup University, CA
William Jewell College, MO
Youngstown State University, OH

Rodeo

Boise State University, ID
California Polytechnic State University, San Luis Obispo, CA
East Texas Baptist University, TX
Fort Hays State University, KS
Lewis-Clark State College, ID
Michigan State University, MI
Missouri Valley College, MO
Murray State University, KY
New Mexico State University, NM
Oklahoma State University, OK
Sam Houston State University, TX
South Dakota State University, SD
Southeastern Oklahoma State University, OK
Southern Arkansas University–Magnolia, AR
Southwestern Oklahoma State University, OK
Stephen F. Austin State University, TX
Texas A&M University, TX
Texas A&M University–Commerce, TX
Texas A&M University–Kingsville, TX
Texas Tech University, TX
University of Idaho, ID
University of Montana, MT
The University of Montana Western, MT
University of Nevada, Las Vegas, NV
The University of Tennessee at Martin, TN
The University of West Alabama, AL
University of Wyoming, WY
Washington State University, WA
West Texas A&M University, TX

Special Characteristics

Adult Students

Adelphi University, NY
Agnes Scott College, GA
Alaska Pacific University, AK
Allegheny College, PA
Augustana University, SD
Averett University, VA
Ball State University, IN
Barton College, NC
Bay Path University, MA
Bellarmine University, KY
Berry College, GA
Binghamton University, State University of New York, NY
Birmingham-Southern College, AL
Bluefield College, VA
Blue Mountain College, MS
Caldwell University, NJ
California Baptist University, CA
California Lutheran University, CA
California State University, Chico, CA
Calvin College, MI
Campbellsville University, KY
Carroll University, WI
Christopher Newport University, VA
Claflin University, SC
Coe College, IA
Coker College, SC
The College at Brockport, State University of New York, NY

College of Staten Island of the City University of New York, NY
Colorado Mesa University, CO
Columbia College, MO
Concordia University Texas, TX
Dominican University of California, CA
East Carolina University, NC
Eastern Washington University, WA
East Texas Baptist University, TX
Elon University, NC
Emmanuel College, GA
Evangel University, MO
The Evergreen State College, WA
Fairmont State University, WV
Faulkner University, AL
Ferris State University, MI
Florida Gulf Coast University, FL
Fordham University, NY
Fort Hays State University, KS
Fort Lewis College, CO
Francis Marion University, SC
Franklin Pierce University, NH
Frostburg State University, MD
Gannon University, PA
Georgia College & State University, GA
Georgian Court University, NJ
Georgia Southern University, GA
Grand Valley State University, MI
Hampton University, VA
Hollins University, VA
Indiana University of Pennsylvania, PA
Iowa State University of Science and Technology, IA
Kean University, NJ
Kent State University, OH
Kent State University at Stark, OH
Kentucky State University, KY
La Sierra University, CA
Lewis-Clark State College, ID
Lincoln University, MO
Lipscomb University, TN
Lock Haven University of Pennsylvania, PA
Loyola Marymount University, CA
Loyola University Chicago, IL
Maryville University of Saint Louis, MO
McMurry University, TX
Mercer University, GA
Meredith College, NC
Messiah College, PA
Metropolitan State University of Denver, CO
Middle Tennessee State University, TN
Millsaps College, MS
Minnesota State University Moorhead, MN
Mississippi State University, MS
Missouri Baptist University, MO
Missouri Western State University, MO
Monmouth University, NJ
Montana State University Billings, MT
Moravian College, PA
Morehead State University, KY
Mount St. Joseph University, OH
Murray State University, KY
New Jersey Institute of Technology, NJ
New Mexico State University, NM
North Central College, IL
Northeastern Illinois University, IL
Northern Illinois University, IL
Northern Kentucky University, KY
Northern State University, SD
The Ohio State University, OH
Ohio Valley University, WV
Oklahoma Baptist University, OK
Oklahoma State University, OK
Palm Beach Atlantic University, FL
Piedmont College, GA

Portland State University, OR
Randolph College, VA
Regis University, CO
Robert Morris University Illinois, IL
Rogers State University, OK
Sacred Heart University, CT
The Sage Colleges, NY
Saginaw Valley State University, MI
St. Ambrose University, IA
St. Catherine University, MN
St. Edward's University, TX
Saint Mary-of-the-Woods College, IN
San Diego State University, CA
San Jose State University, CA
Siena College, NY
Simpson College, IA
Sonoma State University, CA
South Dakota State University, SD
Southeastern Louisiana University, LA
Southern Arkansas University–Magnolia, AR
Southern Oregon University, OR
Southwestern College, KS
State University of New York College at Cortland, NY
State University of New York College at Geneseo, NY
State University of New York College at Potsdam, NY
Stephen F. Austin State University, TX
Stockton University, NJ
Texas A&M University–Commerce, TX
Texas Christian University, TX
Texas Wesleyan University, TX
Thomas More College, KY
Towson University, MD
Trinity Christian College, IL
Union College, KY
The University of Akron, OH
The University of Alabama at Birmingham, AL
University of Arkansas, AR
University of Hartford, CT
University of Idaho, ID
The University of Kansas, KS
University of Kentucky, KY
University of Maine, ME
University of Maine at Fort Kent, ME
University of Maryland, College Park, MD
University of Mary Washington, VA
University of Massachusetts Boston, MA
University of Massachusetts Dartmouth, MA
University of Memphis, TN
University of Michigan–Dearborn, MI
University of Michigan–Flint, MI
University of Mississippi, MS
University of Missouri, MO
University of Missouri–St. Louis, MO
University of Nevada, Las Vegas, NV
University of Nevada, Reno, NV
The University of North Carolina at Charlotte, NC
The University of North Carolina at Greensboro, NC
University of Northern Colorado, CO
University of Pittsburgh at Bradford, PA
University of St. Francis, IL
University of South Carolina, SC
University of South Carolina Aiken, SC
University of Southern Indiana, IN
The University of Tennessee at Martin, TN
The University of Texas at Dallas, TX
University of the Southwest, NM
The University of Toledo, OH
University of Vermont, VT
University of West Georgia, GA

University of Wisconsin–Eau Claire, WI
University of Wisconsin–Green Bay, WI
University of Wisconsin–La Crosse, WI
University of Wisconsin–Parkside, WI
University of Wisconsin–Stevens Point, WI
University of Wisconsin–Stout, WI
University of Wisconsin–Whitewater, WI
University of Wyoming, WY
Wesleyan College, GA
Western Oregon University, OR
Wichita State University, KS
Widener University, PA
William Jessup University, CA
Wilson College, PA
Wittenberg University, OH
Wright State University, OH
Wright State University–Lake Campus, OH
Youngstown State University, OH

Children and Siblings of Alumni

Adelphi University, NY
Alaska Pacific University, AK
Albany State University, GA
Albion College, MI
Albright College, PA
Alliant International University–San Diego, CA
Alma College, MI
Alverno College, WI
Appalachian Bible College, WV
Aquinas College, MI
Auburn University, AL
Augsburg University, MN
Augustana College, IL
Augustana University, SD
Aurora University, IL
Averett University, VA
Baker University, KS
Baldwin Wallace University, OH
Barton College, NC
Belhaven University, MS
Bellarmine University, KY
Belmont University, TN
Bemidji State University, MN
Benedictine University, IL
Bethel College, KS
Bethel University, MN
Binghamton University, State University of New York, NY
Birmingham-Southern College, AL
Blue Mountain College, MS
Bluffton University, OH
Boston Baptist College, MA
Boston University, MA
Bowling Green State University, OH
Bradley University, IL
Brenau University, GA
Bryan College, TN
Caldwell University, NJ
California Lutheran University, CA
California Polytechnic State University, San Luis Obispo, CA
California State Polytechnic University, Pomona, CA
California State University, Monterey Bay, CA
Calumet College of Saint Joseph, IN
Calvin College, MI
Canisius College, NY
Capital University, OH
Cardinal Stritch University, WI
Carlow University, PA
Carroll University, WI
Carson-Newman University, TN
The Catholic University of America, DC
Cedar Crest College, PA

Centenary College of Louisiana, LA
Central College, IA
Central Methodist University, MO
Central Michigan University, MI
Central Washington University, WA
Centre College, KY
Chapman University, CA
Chatham University, PA
Christian Brothers University, TN
The Citadel, The Military College of South Carolina, SC
City College of the City University of New York, NY
Clarke University, IA
Clarkson University, NY
Coe College, IA
Coker College, SC
Coleman University, CA
The College at Brockport, State University of New York, NY
The College of Idaho, ID
The College of New Rochelle, NY
College of Saint Benedict, MN
The College of Saint Rose, NY
The College of St. Scholastica, MN
College of Staten Island of the City University of New York, NY
Columbia College, MO
Columbia International University, SC
Concordia University Chicago, IL
Concordia University, Nebraska, NE
Concordia University Texas, TX
Converse College, SC
Corban University, OR
Cornell College, IA
Culver-Stockton College, MO
Curry College, MA
Daemen College, NY
Davis College, NY
Defiance College, OH
DePauw University, IN
Dickinson College, PA
Doane University, NE
Dominican University, IL
Dominican University of California, CA
Dordt College, IA
Drake University, IA
Drexel University, PA
Drury University, MO
Duke University, NC
Duquesne University, PA
East Carolina University, NC
Eastern Kentucky University, KY
Eastern Mennonite University, VA
Eastern Michigan University, MI
Eastern University, PA
Eastern Washington University, WA
East Texas Baptist University, TX
Edgewood College, WI
Elmhurst College, IL
Elmira College, NY
Emory & Henry College, VA
Emporia State University, KS
Endicott College, MA
Eureka College, IL
Evangel University, MO
Fairfield University, CT
Fairmont State University, WV
Faulkner University, AL
Ferris State University, MI
Florida Institute of Technology, FL
Florida Southern College, FL
Fordham University, NY
Fort Hays State University, KS
Fort Lewis College, CO
Francis Marion University, SC

Franklin College, IN
Franklin Pierce University, NH
George Fox University, OR
Georgetown College, KY
Georgian Court University, NJ
Georgia Southern University, GA
Georgia Southwestern State University, GA
Gonzaga University, WA
Gordon College, MA
Graceland University, IA
Grambling State University, LA
Grand Valley State University, MI
Greenville University, IL
Gustavus Adolphus College, MN
Gwynedd Mercy University, PA
Hamline University, MN
Hanover College, IN
Hardin-Simmons University, TX
Hartwick College, NY
Heidelberg University, OH
Henderson State University, AR
Hilbert College, NY
Hillsdale College, MI
Hiram College, OH
Hobart and William Smith Colleges, NY
Hofstra University, NY
Hollins University, VA
Hood College, MD
Hope College, MI
Howard Payne University, TX
Huntingdon College, AL
Huntington University, IN
Husson University, ME
Illinois College, IL
Illinois Institute of Technology, IL
Indiana State University, IN
Indiana Wesleyan University, IN
Iona College, NY
Iowa State University of Science and
    Technology, IA
Iowa Wesleyan University, IA
Ithaca College, NY
Jackson State University, MS
Jacksonville State University, AL
James Madison University, VA
Johnson University Florida, FL
Juniata College, PA
Kalamazoo College, MI
Kansas Wesleyan University, KS
Keene State College, NH
Kennesaw State University, GA
Kent State University, OH
Kent State University at Stark, OH
Keuka College, NY
The King's College, NY
King's College, PA
Kuyper College, MI
Lancaster Bible College, PA
Lasell College, MA
Lawrence University, WI
Lebanon Valley College, PA
Lees-McRae College, NC
Le Moyne College, NY
Lenoir-Rhyne University, NC
Lewis-Clark State College, ID
Lewis University, IL
Life University, GA
Lincoln Memorial University, TN
Lincoln University, PA
Lindenwood University, MO
Lindsey Wilson College, KY
Linfield College, OR
Long Island University–LIU Brooklyn, NY
Long Island University–LIU Post, NY
Longwood University, VA

Louisiana Tech University, LA
Loyola Marymount University, CA
Loyola University New Orleans, LA
Lubbock Christian University, TX
Luther College, IA
Lynn University, FL
Lyon College, AR
Malone University, OH
Manchester University, IN
Mansfield University of Pennsylvania, PA
Marietta College, OH
Marshall University, WV
Marymount University, VA
Maryville College, TN
Maryville University of Saint Louis, MO
McKendree University, IL
Methodist University, NC
Michigan State University, MI
Michigan Technological University, MI
Middle Tennessee State University, TN
Midwestern State University, TX
Millikin University, IL
Minot State University, ND
Misericordia University, PA
Mississippi State University, MS
Missouri Baptist University, MO
Missouri State University, MO
Missouri University of Science and
    Technology, MO
Missouri Valley College, MO
Missouri Western State University, MO
Monmouth University, NJ
Montana State University, MT
Montana State University Billings, MT
Montana Tech of The University of
    Montana, MT
Montclair State University, NJ
Montreat College, NC
Moravian College, PA
Morehead State University, KY
Morehouse College, GA
Morningside College, IA
Mount Mary University, WI
Mount Mercy University, IA
Mount St. Joseph University, OH
Mount Saint Mary's University, CA
Muskingum University, OH
Nazareth College of Rochester, NY
Newberry College, SC
New England College, NH
Newman University, KS
New Mexico State University, NM
Nichols College, MA
North Carolina State University, NC
Northeastern State University, OK
Northern Arizona University, AZ
Northern Illinois University, IL
Northern Kentucky University, KY
Northern Michigan University, MI
Northwestern College, IA
Northwest Missouri State University, MO
Northwest Nazarene University, ID
Northwood University, Michigan Campus,
    MI
Oakland City University, IN
Ohio Northern University, OH
The Ohio State University, OH
Ohio University, OH
Ohio University–Chillicothe, OH
Ohio University–Eastern, OH
Ohio University–Lancaster, OH
Ohio University–Southern Campus, OH
Ohio University–Zanesville, OH
Ohio Wesleyan University, OH
Oklahoma Baptist University, OK

Oklahoma State University, OK
Olivet College, MI
Oral Roberts University, OK
Oregon State University, OR
Ouachita Baptist University, AR
Pacific Lutheran University, WA
Pacific University, OR
Palm Beach Atlantic University, FL
Peirce College, PA
Penn State Abington, PA
Penn State Altoona, PA
Penn State Beaver, PA
Penn State Berks, PA
Penn State Brandywine, PA
Penn State Erie, The Behrend College, PA
Penn State Harrisburg, PA
Penn State Hazleton, PA
Penn State New Kensington, PA
Penn State Shenango, PA
Penn State York, PA
Pfeiffer University, NC
Piedmont International University, NC
Pine Manor College, MA
Pittsburg State University, KS
Post University, CT
Principia College, IL
Randolph-Macon College, VA
Regent University, VA
Rensselaer Polytechnic Institute, NY
Rhode Island College, RI
Roberts Wesleyan College, NY
Rockford University, IL
Sacred Heart University, CT
The Sage Colleges, NY
St. Ambrose University, IA
Saint Anselm College, NH
St. Catherine University, MN
St. John Fisher College, NY
St. Joseph's College, Long Island Campus,
    NY
St. Joseph's College, New York, NY
Saint Joseph's University, PA
St. Lawrence University, NY
Saint Martin's University, WA
Saint Mary-of-the-Woods College, IN
Saint Mary's College of California, CA
Saint Mary's University of Minnesota, MN
Salve Regina University, RI
Samford University, AL
San Diego State University, CA
San Francisco Art Institute, CA
Santa Clara University, CA
Seattle Pacific University, WA
Seattle University, WA
Seton Hill University, PA
Shippensburg University of Pennsylvania,
    PA
Siena College, NY
Simmons College, MA
Simpson College, IA
Slippery Rock University of Pennsylvania,
    PA
Sonoma State University, CA
Southeastern Louisiana University, LA
Southeastern Oklahoma State University,
    OK
Southern Adventist University, TN
Southern Arkansas University–Magnolia,
    AR
Southern Illinois University Carbondale, IL
Southern New Hampshire University, NH
Southern Utah University, UT
Southwestern Oklahoma State University,
    OK
Springfield College, MA

State University of New York at Fredonia, NY

State University of New York College at Potsdam, NY

State University of New York College of Agriculture and Technology at Cobleskill, NY

State University of New York College of Environmental Science and Forestry, NY

Stephen F. Austin State University, TX

Sterling College, KS

Stetson University, FL

Suffolk University, MA

Susquehanna University, PA

Taylor University, IN

Tennessee Technological University, TN

Tennessee Wesleyan University, TN

Texas A&M University–Commerce, TX

Texas Lutheran University, TX

Texas Wesleyan University, TX

Thomas College, ME

Thomas More College, KY

Thomas University, GA

Towson University, MD

Trine University, IN

Trinity Christian College, IL

Trinity University, TX

Truman State University, MO

Union College, KY

Union University, TN

The University of Alabama at Birmingham, AL

University of Alaska Anchorage, AK

University of Arkansas, AR

University of Dayton, OH

University of Delaware, DE

University of Detroit Mercy, MI

University of Dubuque, IA

University of Evansville, IN

University of Houston, TX

University of Idaho, ID

The University of Iowa, IA

University of Jamestown, ND

The University of Kansas, KS

University of Kentucky, KY

University of Maine, ME

University of Mary Hardin-Baylor, TX

University of Mary Washington, VA

University of Massachusetts Amherst, MA

University of Massachusetts Lowell, MA

University of Michigan–Dearborn, MI

University of Michigan–Flint, MI

University of Minnesota, Crookston, MN

University of Mississippi, MS

University of Missouri, MO

University of Missouri–St. Louis, MO

University of Montana, MT

University of Nebraska at Kearney, NE

University of Nebraska–Lincoln, NE

University of Nevada, Las Vegas, NV

University of Nevada, Reno, NV

University of New England, ME

University of New Hampshire, NH

University of North Alabama, AL

The University of North Carolina at Greensboro, NC

The University of North Carolina at Pembroke, NC

University of Northern Colorado, CO

University of Oklahoma, OK

University of Providence, MT

University of Rhode Island, RI

University of Rochester, NY

University of St. Francis, IL

University of Sioux Falls, SD

University of South Carolina, SC

University of South Carolina Aiken, SC

University of Southern California, CA

University of Southern Mississippi, MS

The University of Tampa, FL

The University of Tennessee at Chattanooga, TN

The University of Tennessee at Martin, TN

University of the Incarnate Word, TX

The University of Toledo, OH

The University of Tulsa, OK

The University of West Alabama, AL

University of West Florida, FL

University of West Georgia, GA

University of Wisconsin–La Crosse, WI

University of Wyoming, WY

Upper Iowa University, IA

Ursinus College, PA

Ursuline College, OH

Utah State University, UT

Valley City State University, ND

Valparaiso University, IN

Virginia Military Institute, VA

Wake Forest University, NC

Warner Pacific College, OR

Wartburg College, IA

Washington & Jefferson College, PA

Washington State University, WA

Webber International University, FL

Wells College, NY

Wesleyan College, GA

Western Michigan University, MI

Western State Colorado University, CO

Westminster College, MO

Westminster College, PA

West Texas A&M University, TX

West Virginia Wesleyan College, WV

Wheaton College, IL

Wheeling Jesuit University, WV

Whittier College, CA

Whitworth University, WA

Wichita State University, KS

William Jewell College, MO

William Woods University, MO

Wilson College, PA

Winona State University, MN

Wittenberg University, OH

Wright State University, OH

Wright State University–Lake Campus, OH

Xavier University, OH

York College of Pennsylvania, PA

Youngstown State University, OH

Children of Current Students

Augustana University, SD

Aurora University, IL

Bethel College, KS

Blue Mountain College, MS

Bryan College, TN

Caldwell University, NJ

California State Polytechnic University, Pomona, CA

Cardinal Stritch University, WI

Carroll University, WI

Central College, IA

Columbia College, MO

Curry College, MA

Elmhurst College, IL

Emmanuel College, GA

Franklin College, IN

Franklin Pierce University, NH

Indiana Tech, IN

Johnson University, TN

Kansas Wesleyan University, KS

Lancaster Bible College, PA

Long Island University–LIU Brooklyn, NY

Long Island University–LIU Post, NY

Misericordia University, PA

Missouri Baptist University, MO

Mount Aloysius College, PA

Mount Marty College, SD

Newman University, KS

New Mexico State University, NM

Northwest University, WA

Palm Beach Atlantic University, FL

Robert Morris University Illinois, IL

Rockford University, IL

Sacred Heart University, CT

St. Catherine University, MN

Saint Mary-of-the-Woods College, IN

Springfield College, MA

Texas Wesleyan University, TX

Thomas College, ME

Thomas More College, KY

Truett McConnell University, GA

Union College, KY

Union University, TN

The University of Alabama at Birmingham, AL

University of Alaska Anchorage, AK

University of Hartford, CT

University of Providence, MT

Wayne State University, MI

Wesleyan College, GA

Wilson College, PA

Children of Educators

Agnes Scott College, GA

Alfred University, NY

Allegheny College, PA

Amridge University, AL

Appalachian Bible College, WV

Austin Peay State University, TN

Bard College, NY

Bridgewater College, VA

Bryan College, TN

Caldwell University, NJ

Campbellsville University, KY

Canisius College, NY

Carlow University, PA

Centenary College of Louisiana, LA

Chowan University, NC

Coe College, IA

The College of Idaho, ID

The College of Wooster, OH

Columbia College, MO

Columbus College of Art & Design, OH

Concordia University, Nebraska, NE

Davis College, NY

Emmanuel College, GA

Emory & Henry College, VA

Endicott College, MA

Evangel University, MO

Flagler College, FL

Franklin Pierce University, NH

Goshen College, IN

Hardin-Simmons University, TX

Hillsdale College, MI

Jacksonville University, FL

John Carroll University, OH

Johnson University, TN

Kansas Wesleyan University, KS

King's College, PA

Lipscomb University, TN

Lycoming College, PA

Lynn University, FL

Mary Baldwin University, VA

McDaniel College, MD

MidAmerica Nazarene University, KS

Mississippi State University, MS

Moravian College, PA

New England College, NH

Northwest University, WA

Occidental College, CA
Palm Beach Atlantic University, FL
Pfeiffer University, NC
Rockford University, IL
St. Ambrose University, IA
Saint Anselm College, NH
St. Catherine University, MN
Saint Mary's College of California, CA
Salem College, NC
Seattle University, WA
Simpson College, IA
Sonoma State University, CA
Southeastern University, FL
Southern Illinois University Carbondale, IL
Southern New Hampshire University, NH
Tarleton State University, TX
Tennessee Technological University, TN
Texas Christian University, TX
Texas Lutheran University, TX
Texas Wesleyan University, TX
Trine University, IN
Trinity University, TX
Union University, TN
Unity College, ME
The University of Alabama at Birmingham, AL
University of Alaska Anchorage, AK
University of Dubuque, IA
University of Evansville, IN
University of Kentucky, KY
University of Memphis, TN
University of Puerto Rico–Bayamón, PR
University of St. Francis, IL
University of St. Thomas, MN
The University of Scranton, PA
The University of Tennessee at Martin, TN
Villanova University, PA
Wesleyan College, GA
Wright State University, OH
Wright State University–Lake Campus, OH

Children of Faculty/Staff
Abilene Christian University, TX
Adelphi University, NY
Agnes Scott College, GA
Alaska Bible College, AK
Alaska Pacific University, AK
Alcorn State University, MS
Alfred University, NY
Allegheny College, PA
Allen College, IA
Alliant International University–San Diego, CA
Alverno College, WI
Amridge University, AL
Anderson University, SC
Andrews University, MI
Appalachian Bible College, WV
Aquinas College, MI
Arizona State University at the Downtown Phoenix campus, AZ
Arizona State University at the Polytechnic campus, AZ
Arizona State University at the Tempe campus, AZ
Arizona State University at the West campus, AZ
Arkansas Tech University, AR
Auburn University, AL
Augustana College, IL
Augustana University, SD
Aurora University, IL
Austin College, TX
Austin Peay State University, TN
Ave Maria University, FL

Baker University, KS
Ball State University, IN
Bard College, NY
Barton College, NC
Baylor University, TX
Bay Path University, MA
Becker College, MA
Belhaven University, MS
Bellarmine University, KY
Belmont Abbey College, NC
Belmont University, TN
Bemidji State University, MN
Benedictine College, KS
Benedictine University, IL
Berry College, GA
Bethany Lutheran College, MN
Bethel College, IN
Bethel College, KS
Bethel University, MN
Binghamton University, State University of New York, NY
Biola University, CA
Birmingham-Southern College, AL
Bloomsburg University of Pennsylvania, PA
Bluefield College, VA
Blue Mountain College, MS
Bluffton University, OH
Boston Baptist College, MA
Boston University, MA
Bowdoin College, ME
Bowling Green State University, OH
Bradley University, IL
Brenau University, GA
Bridgewater College, VA
Bryan College, TN
Buena Vista University, IA
Cairn University, PA
Caldwell University, NJ
California Baptist University, CA
California Lutheran University, CA
California State University, Bakersfield, CA
California State University, Chico, CA
California State University, Stanislaus, CA
Calumet College of Saint Joseph, IN
Calvin College, MI
Cameron University, OK
Campbellsville University, KY
Campbell University, NC
Canisius College, NY
Capital University, OH
Cardinal Stritch University, WI
Carlos Albizu University, Miami Campus, FL
Carlow University, PA
Carnegie Mellon University, PA
Carroll College, MT
Carroll University, WI
Case Western Reserve University, OH
Catawba College, NC
The Catholic University of America, DC
Cedarville University, OH
Centenary College of Louisiana, LA
Central College, IA
Central Methodist University, MO
Central Michigan University, MI
Central State University, OH
Central Washington University, WA
Centre College, KY
Chaminade University of Honolulu, HI
Chatham University, PA
Chowan University, NC
Claflin University, SC
Clarion University of Pennsylvania, PA
Clarke University, IA
Clarkson University, NY

Clemson University, SC
Cleveland Institute of Music, OH
Cleveland State University, OH
Coastal Carolina University, SC
Coe College, IA
Coker College, SC
The College at Brockport, State University of New York, NY
The College of Idaho, ID
The College of New Rochelle, NY
College of Saint Mary, NE
The College of Saint Rose, NY
The College of St. Scholastica, MN
College of the Holy Cross, MA
The College of Wooster, OH
The Colorado College, CO
Colorado State University, CO
Columbia College, MO
Columbia College Chicago, IL
Columbia International University, SC
Columbus College of Art & Design, OH
Concordia University Chicago, IL
Concordia University Irvine, CA
Concordia University, Nebraska, NE
Concordia University, St. Paul, MN
Concordia University Texas, TX
Concord University, WV
Converse College, SC
Corban University, OR
Cornell College, IA
Cornerstone University, MI
Covenant College, GA
Crossroads Bible College, IN
Culver-Stockton College, MO
Curry College, MA
Daemen College, NY
Dallas Baptist University, TX
Davis College, NY
Defiance College, OH
Denison University, OH
DePaul University, IL
Dickinson College, PA
Doane University, NE
Dominican College, NY
Dominican University, IL
Dominican University of California, CA
Dordt College, IA
Drury University, MO
Duquesne University, PA
East Carolina University, NC
East Central University, OK
Eastern Kentucky University, KY
Eastern Mennonite University, VA
Eastern University, PA
East Texas Baptist University, TX
Eckerd College, FL
Edgewood College, WI
Elizabethtown College, PA
Elmira College, NY
Elms College, MA
Elon University, NC
Emmanuel College, GA
Emmanuel College, MA
Emory & Henry College, VA
Emory University, GA
Emporia State University, KS
Eureka College, IL
Evangel University, MO
Fairfield University, CT
Fairmont State University, WV
Faulkner University, AL
Felician University, NJ
Flagler College, FL
Florida Institute of Technology, FL
Florida Southern College, FL

Fordham University, NY
Fort Hays State University, KS
Fort Lewis College, CO
Framingham State University, MA
Franciscan University of Steubenville, OH
Francis Marion University, SC
Franklin College, IN
Franklin Pierce University, NH
Furman University, SC
Gardner-Webb University, NC
Geneva College, PA
George Fox University, OR
Georgetown College, KY
Georgetown University, DC
Georgia College & State University, GA
Georgian Court University, NJ
Glenville State College, WV
Gonzaga University, WA
Gordon College, MA
Goshen College, IN
Governors State University, IL
Graceland University, IA
Grambling State University, LA
Grand Valley State University, MI
Greenville University, IL
Gwynedd Mercy University, PA
Hampden-Sydney College, VA
Hampton University, VA
Hanover College, IN
Harding University, AR
Hardin-Simmons University, TX
Hartwick College, NY
Heidelberg University, OH
Henderson State University, AR
Hendrix College, AR
High Point University, NC
Hillsdale College, MI
Hofstra University, NY
Hollins University, VA
Hood College, MD
Hope International University, CA
Houston Baptist University, TX
Howard Payne University, TX
Huntingdon College, AL
Huntington University, IN
Husson University, ME
Idaho State University, ID
Illinois College, IL
Illinois Institute of Technology, IL
Illinois Wesleyan University, IL
Indiana State University, IN
Indiana Tech, IN
Indiana University of Pennsylvania, PA
Indiana Wesleyan University, IN
Iowa Wesleyan University, IA
Ithaca College, NY
Jackson State University, MS
Jacksonville University, FL
James Madison University, VA
John Carroll University, OH
Johnson C. Smith University, NC
Johnson University, TN
Johnson University Florida, FL
Juniata College, PA
Kansas Wesleyan University, KS
Kent State University, OH
Kent State University at Geauga, OH
Kent State University at Stark, OH
Kentucky State University, KY
Keuka College, NY
King's College, PA
King University, TN
Knox College, IL
Kutztown University of Pennsylvania, PA
Kuyper College, MI
LaGrange College, GA

Lancaster Bible College, PA
La Salle University, PA
Lasell College, MA
La Sierra University, CA
Lebanon Valley College, PA
Lees-McRae College, NC
Lee University, TN
Lehigh University, PA
Lenoir-Rhyne University, NC
Lewis & Clark College, OR
Lewis-Clark State College, ID
Lewis University, IL
Liberty University, VA
LIM College, NY
Lincoln Memorial University, TN
Lincoln University, MO
Lincoln University, PA
Lindenwood University, MO
Lindsey Wilson College, KY
Linfield College, OR
Lipscomb University, TN
Long Island University–LIU Brooklyn, NY
Long Island University–LIU Post, NY
Louisiana College, LA
Louisiana Tech University, LA
Loyola Marymount University, CA
Loyola University New Orleans, LA
Lubbock Christian University, TX
Lycoming College, PA
Lynn University, FL
Lyon College, AR
Manchester University, IN
Manhattan College, NY
Manhattanville College, NY
Marquette University, WI
Marshall University, WV
Mary Baldwin University, VA
Marymount University, VA
Maryville College, TN
Massachusetts College of Art and Design, MA
McKendree University, IL
McMurry University, TX
Mercer University, GA
Mercy College, NY
Meredith College, NC
Merrimack College, MA
Messiah College, PA
Methodist University, NC
Miami University, OH
Michigan State University, MI
Michigan Technological University, MI
MidAmerica Nazarene University, KS
Midwestern State University, TX
Milligan College, TN
Millikin University, IL
Millsaps College, MS
Milwaukee School of Engineering, WI
Minnesota State University Moorhead, MN
Minot State University, ND
Misericordia University, PA
Mississippi State University, MS
Missouri Baptist University, MO
Missouri University of Science and Technology, MO
Missouri Valley College, MO
Monmouth University, NJ
Montana State University Billings, MT
Montana Tech of The University of Montana, MT
Montreat College, NC
Moravian College, PA
Morehouse College, GA
Morningside College, IA
Morrisville State College, NY
Mount Carmel College of Nursing, OH

Mount Marty College, SD
Mount Mary University, WI
Mount St. Joseph University, OH
Mount Saint Mary College, NY
Mount St. Mary's University, MD
Mount Vernon Nazarene University, OH
Murray State University, KY
Nazareth College of Rochester, NY
Nebraska Christian College of Hope International, NE
Nebraska Methodist College, NE
Neumont College of Computer Science, UT
Newberry College, SC
New England College, NH
New Jersey Institute of Technology, NJ
Newman University, KS
New Mexico State University, NM
New York Institute of Technology, NY
Niagara University, NY
Nicholls State University, LA
Nichols College, MA
North Carolina State University, NC
North Central College, IL
Northeastern Illinois University, IL
Northeastern State University, OK
Northern Illinois University, IL
Northern Kentucky University, KY
Northern Michigan University, MI
Northwest Christian University, OR
Northwestern College, IA
Northwest Missouri State University, MO
Northwest Nazarene University, ID
Northwest University, WA
Northwood University, Michigan Campus, MI
Nova Southeastern University, FL
Oakland City University, IN
Occidental College, CA
Oglethorpe University, GA
Ohio Northern University, OH
The Ohio State University, OH
Ohio University, OH
Ohio University–Chillicothe, OH
Ohio University–Eastern, OH
Ohio University–Lancaster, OH
Ohio University–Southern Campus, OH
Ohio University–Zanesville, OH
Ohio Valley University, WV
Oklahoma Baptist University, OK
Oklahoma Christian University, OK
Oklahoma City University, OK
Oklahoma State University, OK
Old Dominion University, VA
Olivet College, MI
Olivet Nazarene University, IL
Oral Roberts University, OK
Ouachita Baptist University, AR
Our Lady of the Lake University, TX
Ozark Christian College, MO
Pacific Lutheran University, WA
Pacific University, OR
Palm Beach Atlantic University, FL
Park University, MO
Peirce College, PA
Pfeiffer University, NC
Philander Smith College, AR
Piedmont College, GA
Piedmont International University, NC
Pine Manor College, MA
Plymouth State University, NH
Point Park University, PA
Post University, CT
Presbyterian College, SC
Principia College, IL
Purdue University, IN
Quinnipiac University, CT

Ramapo College of New Jersey, NJ
Randolph College, VA
Randolph-Macon College, VA
Regent University, VA
Regis University, CO
Rensselaer Polytechnic Institute, NY
Rhodes College, TN
Robert Morris University, PA
Robert Morris University Illinois, IL
Roberts Wesleyan College, NY
Rochester Institute of Technology, NY
Rockford University, IL
Rockhurst University, MO
Rocky Mountain College, MT
Sacred Heart University, CT
St. Ambrose University, IA
Saint Anselm College, NH
Saint Augustine's University, NC
St. Bonaventure University, NY
St. Catherine University, MN
St. Edward's University, TX
St. John Fisher College, NY
St. John's College, NM
St. John's University, NY
St. Joseph's College, Long Island Campus, NY
St. Joseph's College, New York, NY
Saint Joseph's University, PA
St. Louis College of Pharmacy, MO
Saint Louis University, MO
Saint Martin's University, WA
Saint Mary-of-the-Woods College, IN
Saint Mary's College of California, CA
St. Mary's College of Maryland, MD
St. Mary's University, TX
Saint Mary's University of Minnesota, MN
St. Norbert College, WI
Saint Peter's University, NJ
Saint Vincent College, PA
Salem College, NC
Samford University, AL
San Diego State University, CA
San Jose State University, CA
Santa Clara University, CA
Schreiner University, TX
Seattle Pacific University, WA
Seattle University, WA
Seton Hill University, PA
Shawnee State University, OH
Shenandoah University, VA
Siena College, NY
Simpson College, IA
Skidmore College, NY
Slippery Rock University of Pennsylvania, PA
Sonoma State University, CA
South Dakota State University, SD
Southeastern Louisiana University, LA
Southeastern University, FL
Southeast Missouri State University, MO
Southern Arkansas University–Magnolia, AR
Southern Illinois University Carbondale, IL
Southern Vermont College, VT
Southwestern Christian College, TX
Southwestern College, KS
Southwestern Oklahoma State University, OK
Southwestern University, TX
Springfield College, MA
Spring Hill College, AL
State University of New York at New Paltz, NY
State University of New York College at Potsdam, NY

Stephen F. Austin State University, TX
Sterling College, KS
Stetson University, FL
Stockton University, NJ
Stonehill College, MA
Suffolk University, MA
Susquehanna University, PA
Tarleton State University, TX
Taylor University, IN
Temple University, PA
Tennessee Technological University, TN
Tennessee Wesleyan University, TN
Texas A&M University, TX
Texas Christian University, TX
Texas Lutheran University, TX
Texas Tech University, TX
Texas Wesleyan University, TX
Thomas College, ME
Thomas More College, KY
Thomas University, GA
Tiffin University, OH
Toccoa Falls College, GA
Towson University, MD
Transylvania University, KY
Trevecca Nazarene University, TN
Trine University, IN
Trinity Christian College, IL
Trinity College of Florida, FL
Truett McConnell University, GA
Truman State University, MO
Tulane University, LA
Tuskegee University, AL
Union College, KY
Union College, NY
Union University, TN
The University of Alabama at Birmingham, AL
University of Alaska Anchorage, AK
University of Arkansas, AR
University of Bridgeport, CT
University of Central Oklahoma, OK
University of Colorado Denver, CO
University of Dallas, TX
University of Dayton, OH
University of Delaware, DE
University of Detroit Mercy, MI
University of Dubuque, IA
University of Evansville, IN
The University of Findlay, OH
University of Florida, FL
University of Hartford, CT
University of Idaho, ID
University of Illinois at Urbana–Champaign, IL
University of Indianapolis, IN
University of Jamestown, ND
The University of Kansas, KS
University of Kentucky, KY
University of Louisiana at Monroe, LA
University of Maine, ME
University of Maine at Fort Kent, ME
University of Maine at Presque Isle, ME
University of Mary Hardin-Baylor, TX
University of Mary Washington, VA
University of Massachusetts Amherst, MA
University of Massachusetts Boston, MA
University of Massachusetts Dartmouth, MA
University of Massachusetts Lowell, MA
University of Memphis, TN
University of Miami, FL
University of Michigan, MI
University of Michigan–Dearborn, MI
University of Michigan–Flint, MI
University of Minnesota, Crookston, MN
University of Mississippi, MS

University of Missouri, MO
University of Missouri–St. Louis, MO
The University of Montana Western, MT
University of Montevallo, AL
University of Nebraska at Kearney, NE
University of Nevada, Las Vegas, NV
University of New Hampshire, NH
University of New Hampshire at Manchester, NH
The University of North Carolina at Chapel Hill, NC
The University of North Carolina at Greensboro, NC
University of North Dakota, ND
University of Northern Colorado, CO
University of Notre Dame, IN
University of Oklahoma, OK
University of Oregon, OR
University of Pittsburgh, PA
University of Pittsburgh at Bradford, PA
University of Pittsburgh at Johnstown, PA
University of Portland, OR
University of Providence, MT
University of Puerto Rico–Bayamón, PR
University of Puget Sound, WA
University of Rochester, NY
University of St. Francis, IL
University of St. Thomas, MN
University of St. Thomas, TX
University of San Diego, CA
University of Science and Arts of Oklahoma, OK
The University of Scranton, PA
University of Sioux Falls, SD
University of South Carolina, SC
University of South Carolina Aiken, SC
University of Southern California, CA
University of Southern Indiana, IN
University of Southern Mississippi, MS
The University of Tampa, FL
The University of Tennessee at Chattanooga, TN
The University of Tennessee at Martin, TN
The University of Texas at Tyler, TX
University of the Incarnate Word, TX
University of the Southwest, NM
The University of Toledo, OH
The University of Tulsa, OK
University of Utah, UT
The University of West Alabama, AL
University of West Florida, FL
Ursinus College, PA
Ursuline College, OH
Utah State University, UT
Valley City State University, ND
Valparaiso University, IN
Vanguard University of Southern California, CA
Villanova University, PA
Virginia Polytechnic Institute and State University, VA
Virginia Wesleyan University, VA
Wabash College, IN
Walla Walla University, WA
Wartburg College, IA
Washington & Jefferson College, PA
Washington College, MD
Washington State University, WA
Wayland Baptist University, TX
Waynesburg University, PA
Wayne State College, NE
Wayne State University, MI
Webber International University, FL
Webster University, MO
Wesleyan College, GA

West Chester University of Pennsylvania, PA
Western Illinois University, IL
Western Michigan University, MI
Western New England University, MA
Westminster College, MO
Westmont College, CA
West Texas A&M University, TX
West Virginia University, WV
West Virginia Wesleyan College, WV
Wheeling Jesuit University, WV
Whittier College, CA
Wichita State University, KS
Widener University, PA
Wilkes University, PA
William Jessup University, CA
William Jewell College, MO
William Paterson University of New Jersey, NJ
Williams Baptist College, AR
Wilson College, PA
Winona State University, MN
Winthrop University, SC
Wisconsin Lutheran College, WI
Wittenberg University, OH
Wofford College, SC
Wright State University, OH
Wright State University–Lake Campus, OH
Young Harris College, GA
Youngstown State University, OH

Children of Public Servants
California State University, San Bernardino, CA
Central Washington University, WA
Chowan University, NC
Christian Brothers University, TN
Framingham State University, MA
Georgia Southern University, GA
Grambling State University, LA
Illinois Institute of Technology, IL
Louisiana Tech University, LA
Mercer University, GA
Mississippi State University, MS
Missouri Western State University, MO
Monmouth University, NJ
New Mexico State University, NM
Northern Kentucky University, KY
The Ohio State University, OH
Peirce College, PA
Regent University, VA
Robert Morris University Illinois, IL
Siena College, NY
Sonoma State University, CA
Southern Illinois University Carbondale, IL
Tennessee Technological University, TN
Texas Wesleyan University, TX
The University of Alabama at Birmingham, AL
University of Delaware, DE
University of Kentucky, KY
University of Massachusetts Lowell, MA
University of Memphis, TN
University of Nevada, Las Vegas, NV
The University of North Carolina at Charlotte, NC
University of Rhode Island, RI
University of South Carolina Aiken, SC
The University of Tennessee at Martin, TN
The University of Texas at Dallas, TX
The University of Toledo, OH
University of Utah, UT
University of Wisconsin–Green Bay, WI
University of Wyoming, WY
Washington State University, WA
Western Washington University, WA
Wheaton College, IL

Children of Union Members/Company Employees
Auburn University, AL
Averett University, VA
California State University, Bakersfield, CA
Calvin College, MI
Carroll College, MT
Chowan University, NC
Clarion University of Pennsylvania, PA
The College of New Rochelle, NY
The College of Saint Rose, NY
Columbia College, MO
Eastern Washington University, WA
Emporia State University, KS
Framingham State University, MA
Francis Marion University, SC
Frostburg State University, MD
Grand Valley State University, MI
Hofstra University, NY
Husson University, ME
Kennesaw State University, GA
Kent State University, OH
Kentucky State University, KY
Kutztown University of Pennsylvania, PA
Lindenwood University, MO
Massachusetts College of Art and Design, MA
Michigan State University, MI
Midwestern State University, TX
Millersville University of Pennsylvania, PA
Millikin University, IL
Missouri University of Science and Technology, MO
Missouri Western State University, MO
Montana State University Billings, MT
Moravian College, PA
New Jersey Institute of Technology, NJ
New Mexico State University, NM
Northeastern Illinois University, IL
Northern Michigan University, MI
The Ohio State University, OH
Sacred Heart University, CT
Sam Houston State University, TX
Siena College, NY
Slippery Rock University of Pennsylvania, PA
Sonoma State University, CA
Stephen F. Austin State University, TX
Stockton University, NJ
Stonehill College, MA
Texas Christian University, TX
Texas Wesleyan University, TX
Thomas More College, KY
The University of Alabama, AL
The University of Alabama at Birmingham, AL
University of Arkansas, AR
University of Hartford, CT
University of Kentucky, KY
University of Maine, ME
University of Massachusetts Boston, MA
University of Massachusetts Dartmouth, MA
University of Massachusetts Lowell, MA
University of Michigan–Flint, MI
University of Nevada, Las Vegas, NV
The University of North Carolina at Charlotte, NC
University of Northern Colorado, CO
University of Pittsburgh, PA
University of Pittsburgh at Bradford, PA
University of Puerto Rico–Bayamón, PR
University of Rhode Island, RI
University of South Carolina, SC
The University of Tennessee at Chattanooga, TN
The University of Tennessee at Martin, TN
The University of Toledo, OH

University of Wisconsin–La Crosse, WI
University of Wisconsin–Parkside, WI
Western Kentucky University, KY
Western Oregon University, OR
Western Washington University, WA
West Texas A&M University, TX
West Virginia University, WV
York College of Pennsylvania, PA
Youngstown State University, OH

Children of Workers in Trades
Calvin College, MI
The College of New Rochelle, NY
Grand Valley State University, MI
Huntingdon College, AL
Kennesaw State University, GA
Midwestern State University, TX
Missouri Western State University, MO
New Mexico State University, NM
The Ohio State University, OH
San Diego State University, CA
Siena College, NY
Sonoma State University, CA
South Dakota State University, SD
Texas Christian University, TX
The University of Alabama at Birmingham, AL
University of Arkansas, AR
University of Kentucky, KY
University of Maine, ME
University of Michigan, MI
University of Northern Colorado, CO
University of South Carolina, SC
University of Wisconsin–Parkside, WI
West Texas A&M University, TX
West Virginia University, WV
Worcester Polytechnic Institute, MA
Youngstown State University, OH

Children with a Deceased or Disabled Parent
Appalachian Bible College, WV
The Baptist College of Florida, FL
Bay Path University, MA
California State University, San Bernardino, CA
Calvin College, MI
The Citadel, The Military College of South Carolina, SC
Clarion University of Pennsylvania, PA
The College of New Jersey, NJ
Elmhurst College, IL
Fairfield University, CT
Fordham University, NY
Georgia Institute of Technology, GA
Harding University, AR
Idaho State University, ID
Kentucky State University, KY
La Salle University, PA
Lees-McRae College, NC
Lipscomb University, TN
Louisiana State University and Agricultural & Mechanical College, LA
Midwestern State University, TX
Millikin University, IL
New Mexico State University, NM
Northeastern State University, OK
Northern Illinois University, IL
Northern Kentucky University, KY
San Jose State University, CA
Santa Clara University, CA
Siena College, NY
Southern Illinois University Carbondale, IL
Texas Wesleyan University, TX
The University of Alabama at Birmingham, AL
University of Arkansas, AR
University of Hartford, CT

University of Kentucky, KY
University of Louisiana at Monroe, LA
University of Massachusetts Dartmouth, MA
University of Missouri–St. Louis, MO
University of Montana, MT
University of Nevada, Las Vegas, NV
University of South Carolina, SC
The University of Tennessee at Chattanooga, TN
University of Utah, UT
The University of Virginia's College at Wise, VA
Washington State University, WA
Wayne State University, MI
Youngstown State University, OH

Ethnic Background

Abilene Christian University, TX
Alaska Pacific University, AK
Albright College, PA
Alverno College, WI
American University, DC
Auburn University, AL
Augustana College, IL
Augustana University, SD
Austin Peay State University, TN
Baker University, KS
Ball State University, IN
Bellarmine University, KY
Berry College, GA
Bethel College, KS
Binghamton University, State University of New York, NY
Biola University, CA
Birmingham-Southern College, AL
Boise State University, ID
Buena Vista University, IA
California State University, Bakersfield, CA
California State University, Chico, CA
California University of Pennsylvania, PA
Calvin College, MI
Capital University, OH
Cedarville University, OH
Centenary College of Louisiana, LA
Central Michigan University, MI
Centre College, KY
Chaminade University of Honolulu, HI
Christian Brothers University, TN
Claflin University, SC
Clemson University, SC
Coe College, IA
The College at Brockport, State University of New York, NY
The College of Saint Rose, NY
College of Staten Island of the City University of New York, NY
Columbia College, MO
Columbia International University, SC
Cornerstone University, MI
Delaware Valley University, PA
DeSales University, PA
Drury University, MO
Duke University, NC
Duquesne University, PA
East Carolina University, NC
Eastern Mennonite University, VA
Eastern Michigan University, MI
Eastern Washington University, WA
Elmhurst College, IL
Elon University, NC
The Evergreen State College, WA
Fairfield University, CT
Fairmont State University, WV
Ferris State University, MI
Flagler College, FL

Florida Agricultural and Mechanical University, FL
Florida Gulf Coast University, FL
Fort Lewis College, CO
Franklin College, IN
Furman University, SC
Gannon University, PA
George Fox University, OR
Georgian Court University, NJ
Goshen College, IN
Grambling State University, LA
Grove City College, PA
Gustavus Adolphus College, MN
Hardin-Simmons University, TX
Hawai`i Pacific University, HI
Hood College, MD
Hope College, MI
Huntington University, IN
Husson University, ME
Idaho State University, ID
Indiana University of Pennsylvania, PA
Iowa State University of Science and Technology, IA
Johnson C. Smith University, NC
Johnson University, TN
Juniata College, PA
Kennesaw State University, GA
Kent State University, OH
Kentucky State University, KY
LaGrange College, GA
Lenoir-Rhyne University, NC
Lesley University, MA
Lewis-Clark State College, ID
Lock Haven University of Pennsylvania, PA
Loyola Marymount University, CA
Lyon College, AR
Macalester College, MN
Maryville University of Saint Louis, MO
Massachusetts Maritime Academy, MA
McMurry University, TX
Medical University of South Carolina, SC
Meredith College, NC
Middle Tennessee State University, TN
Millsaps College, MS
Minot State University, ND
Molloy College, NY
Montana State University Billings, MT
Morehead State University, KY
Muskingum University, OH
Nazareth College of Rochester, NY
New England College, NH
New Jersey Institute of Technology, NJ
New Mexico State University, NM
Northern Illinois University, IL
Northern State University, SD
Northwestern College, IA
Oakland City University, IN
Ohio Northern University, OH
The Ohio State University, OH
Ohio Valley University, WV
Oklahoma State University, OK
Ouachita Baptist University, AR
Pacific University, OR
Piedmont International University, NC
Portland State University, OR
Randolph-Macon College, VA
Rensselaer Polytechnic Institute, NY
Sacred Heart University, CT
The Sage Colleges, NY
St. Catherine University, MN
St. John Fisher College, NY
Saint Martin's University, WA
Saint Mary-of-the-Woods College, IN
Saint Mary's University of Minnesota, MN
Samford University, AL

Sam Houston State University, TX
San Jose State University, CA
Shepherd University, WV
Siena College, NY
Simpson College, IA
Slippery Rock University of Pennsylvania, PA
Sonoma State University, CA
South Dakota State University, SD
Southern Adventist University, TN
Southwestern University, TX
State University of New York at Fredonia, NY
State University of New York at New Paltz, NY
State University of New York College at Geneseo, NY
State University of New York College at Potsdam, NY
Stetson University, FL
Stockton University, NJ
Stony Brook University, State University of New York, NY
Taylor University, IN
Tennessee Technological University, TN
Texas Christian University, TX
Texas Wesleyan University, TX
Thomas University, GA
Toccoa Falls College, GA
Towson University, MD
Trinity Christian College, IL
Truman State University, MO
Union University, TN
The University of Alabama at Birmingham, AL
University of Arkansas, AR
University of California, San Diego, CA
University of Central Oklahoma, OK
University of Colorado Denver, CO
University of Delaware, DE
University of Hartford, CT
University of Idaho, ID
The University of Iowa, IA
The University of Kansas, KS
University of Kentucky, KY
University of Maine, ME
University of Maine at Fort Kent, ME
University of Maine at Presque Isle, ME
University of Mary Hardin-Baylor, TX
University of Massachusetts Dartmouth, MA
University of Michigan–Dearborn, MI
University of Minnesota, Crookston, MN
University of Missouri, MO
University of Missouri–St. Louis, MO
University of Nebraska at Kearney, NE
University of Nebraska–Lincoln, NE
University of Nevada, Las Vegas, NV
University of Nevada, Reno, NV
University of North Dakota, ND
University of Northern Colorado, CO
University of Providence, MT
University of St. Francis, IL
The University of Scranton, PA
University of South Carolina, SC
University of South Carolina Aiken, SC
University of Southern Mississippi, MS
The University of Tennessee at Chattanooga, TN
The University of Tennessee at Martin, TN
The University of Texas at El Paso, TX
The University of Texas at San Antonio, TX
The University of Toledo, OH
University of Utah, UT
University of Vermont, VT

The University of Virginia's College at Wise, VA
University of Wisconsin–Eau Claire, WI
University of Wisconsin–Green Bay, WI
University of Wisconsin–La Crosse, WI
University of Wisconsin–Parkside, WI
University of Wisconsin–Stevens Point, WI
University of Wisconsin–Whitewater, WI
University of Wyoming, WY
Valley City State University, ND
VanderCook College of Music, IL
Wayne State College, NE
Wayne State University, MI
Webster University, MO
Wesleyan College, GA
Western Carolina University, NC
Western Kentucky University, KY
Western Oregon University, OR
Western Washington University, WA
Westminster College, MO
Westmont College, CA
West Virginia University, WV
Whitman College, WA
Whitworth University, WA
Wichita State University, KS
Widener University, PA
William Jessup University, CA
Wittenberg University, OH
Wright State University, OH
Wright State University–Lake Campus, OH
Youngstown State University, OH

First-Generation College Students
Abilene Christian University, TX
Augustana College, IL
Austin College, TX
Averett University, VA
Berry College, GA
Binghamton University, State University of New York, NY
Birmingham-Southern College, AL
Bluefield College, VA
Boise State University, ID
Bowie State University, MD
Brenau University, GA
California State Polytechnic University, Pomona, CA
California State University, Bakersfield, CA
California State University, Chico, CA
California State University, San Bernardino, CA
California State University, Stanislaus, CA
Calvin College, MI
Centenary College of Louisiana, LA
Centre College, KY
Champlain College, VT
Chowan University, NC
Christopher Newport University, VA
Claflin University, SC
Clarion University of Pennsylvania, PA
The College at Brockport, State University of New York, NY
College of Coastal Georgia, GA
The College of Idaho, ID
Colorado Mesa University, CO
Colorado State University, CO
Columbia College, MO
Concordia University Irvine, CA
Culver-Stockton College, MO
Eastern Washington University, WA
Elon University, NC
Emmanuel College, GA
Emporia State University, KS
The Evergreen State College, WA
Fairfield University, CT
Fairmont State University, WV

Flagler College, FL
Florida Agricultural and Mechanical University, FL
Florida International University, FL
Fort Lewis College, CO
Franklin College, IN
Georgian Court University, NJ
Georgia Southern University, GA
Glenville State College, WV
Graceland University, IA
Grove City College, PA
Gustavus Adolphus College, MN
Hamline University, MN
High Point University, NC
Hillsdale College, MI
Hood College, MD
Idaho State University, ID
Indiana University of Pennsylvania, PA
Iowa State University of Science and Technology, IA
Juniata College, PA
Kean University, NJ
Kent State University, OH
Kent State University at Stark, OH
Keuka College, NY
Kutztown University of Pennsylvania, PA
LaGrange College, GA
Lewis & Clark College, OR
Lewis-Clark State College, ID
Loras College, IA
Loyola Marymount University, CA
Lyon College, AR
Maryville University of Saint Louis, MO
McMurry University, TX
Meredith College, NC
Metropolitan State University of Denver, CO
Michigan State University, MI
Middle Tennessee State University, TN
Midwestern State University, TX
Millsaps College, MS
Minnesota State University Moorhead, MN
Mississippi State University, MS
Missouri Baptist University, MO
Missouri Western State University, MO
Monmouth University, NJ
Montana State University Billings, MT
Montana Tech of The University of Montana, MT
Montreat College, NC
Moravian College, PA
New Jersey Institute of Technology, NJ
Northern Illinois University, IL
Northwestern College, IA
Ohio University, OH
Ohio University–Chillicothe, OH
Ohio University–Eastern, OH
Ohio University–Lancaster, OH
Ohio University–Southern Campus, OH
Ohio University–Zanesville, OH
Oklahoma State University, OK
Ouachita Baptist University, AR
Pacific University, OR
The Sage Colleges, NY
St. John Fisher College, NY
Saint Louis University, MO
Saint Mary-of-the-Woods College, IN
Saint Vincent College, PA
Sam Houston State University, TX
San Diego State University, CA
San Francisco Art Institute, CA
San Jose State University, CA
Simpson College, IA
Sonoma State University, CA
South Dakota State University, SD
Southeastern Louisiana University, LA
Southeast Missouri State University, MO

Southern Illinois University Carbondale, IL
State University of New York at New Paltz, NY
State University of New York College at Geneseo, NY
Stephen F. Austin State University, TX
Stetson University, FL
Stockton University, NJ
Tennessee Technological University, TN
Texas A&M University, TX
Texas A&M University–Commerce, TX
Texas A&M University–Corpus Christi, TX
Texas Tech University, TX
Texas Wesleyan University, TX
Towson University, MD
Trinity Christian College, IL
Truman State University, MO
Union University, TN
The University of Alabama at Birmingham, AL
University of Arkansas, AR
University of California, San Diego, CA
University of California, Santa Cruz, CA
University of Central Florida, FL
University of Colorado Boulder, CO
University of Colorado Denver, CO
University of Delaware, DE
University of Hartford, CT
University of Houston, TX
University of Idaho, ID
University of Illinois at Urbana–Champaign, IL
The University of Iowa, IA
The University of Kansas, KS
University of Kentucky, KY
University of Maine, ME
University of Massachusetts Boston, MA
University of Massachusetts Dartmouth, MA
University of Memphis, TN
University of Miami, FL
University of Michigan–Flint, MI
University of Minnesota, Crookston, MN
University of Mississippi, MS
University of Missouri, MO
University of Missouri–St. Louis, MO
The University of Montana Western, MT
University of Nebraska at Kearney, NE
University of Nevada, Las Vegas, NV
University of Nevada, Reno, NV
University of North Alabama, AL
The University of North Carolina at Charlotte, NC
University of North Dakota, ND
University of Northern Colorado, CO
University of North Florida, FL
University of Providence, MT
University of St. Francis, IL
University of South Carolina, SC
University of South Carolina Aiken, SC
University of South Carolina Upstate, SC
University of Southern Indiana, IN
The University of Tampa, FL
The University of Texas at San Antonio, TX
The University of Toledo, OH
University of Utah, UT
University of Vermont, VT
The University of West Alabama, AL
University of Wisconsin–Eau Claire, WI
University of Wisconsin–La Crosse, WI
University of Wisconsin–Stout, WI
University of Wyoming, WY
Ursuline College, OH
Virginia Polytechnic Institute and State University, VA
Washington State University, WA
Wesleyan College, GA

Western Oregon University, OR
West Texas A&M University, TX
West Virginia University Institute of
Technology, WV
Wheaton College, IL
Whitman College, WA
Wichita State University, KS
William Jessup University, CA
Wright State University, OH
Wright State University–Lake Campus, OH

Handicapped Students

Bemidji State University, MN
Binghamton University, State University of
New York, NY
Boise State University, ID
Bryan College, TN
California State University, Chico, CA
California State University, Fresno, CA
California State University, San Bernardino,
CA
Calvin College, MI
Central College, IA
Chowan University, NC
Clear Creek Baptist Bible College, KY
The College of St. Scholastica, MN
College of Staten Island of the City
University of New York, NY
Dordt College, IA
East Carolina University, NC
Eastern Washington University, WA
Emporia State University, KS
Fairmont State University, WV
Florida Gulf Coast University, FL
Fordham University, NY
Fort Lewis College, CO
Francis Marion University, SC
Franklin College, IN
Gardner-Webb University, NC
Georgia Southern University, GA
Grand Valley State University, MI
Grove City College, PA
Hardin-Simmons University, TX
Hofstra University, NY
Idaho State University, ID
James Madison University, VA
Kennesaw State University, GA
Kent State University, OH
Kutztown University of Pennsylvania, PA
Kuyper College, MI
Lock Haven University of Pennsylvania, PA
Long Island University–LIU Brooklyn, NY
Long Island University–LIU Post, NY
Louisiana Tech University, LA
Loyola Marymount University, CA
Malone University, OH
Michigan State University, MI
Middle Tennessee State University, TN
Midwestern State University, TX
Mississippi State University, MS
Morehead State University, KY
New Jersey Institute of Technology, NJ
New Mexico State University, NM
Northern Illinois University, IL
Northern Kentucky University, KY
Northern State University, SD
Northwestern College, IA
The Ohio State University, OH
Oklahoma State University, OK
Ouachita Baptist University, AR
Portland State University, OR
Sacred Heart University, CT
San Diego State University, CA
Santa Clara University, CA
Shepherd University, WV

Shippensburg University of Pennsylvania,
PA
Sonoma State University, CA
South Dakota State University, SD
Southern Illinois University Carbondale, IL
Southern New Hampshire University, NH
Southwest Baptist University, MO
State University of New York College at
Geneseo, NY
State University of New York College at
Potsdam, NY
Texas Christian University, TX
Texas Tech University, TX
Texas Wesleyan University, TX
Towson University, MD
Union University, TN
The University of Akron, OH
The University of Alabama at Birmingham,
AL
University of Arkansas, AR
University of California, San Diego, CA
University of Colorado Denver, CO
University of Hartford, CT
University of Houston, TX
University of Idaho, ID
The University of Iowa, IA
University of Kentucky, KY
University of Maine, ME
University of Mary Hardin-Baylor, TX
University of Massachusetts Amherst, MA
University of Memphis, TN
University of Michigan, MI
University of Michigan–Dearborn, MI
University of Michigan–Flint, MI
University of Mississippi, MS
University of Nebraska–Lincoln, NE
University of Nevada, Las Vegas, NV
University of New Hampshire, NH
The University of North Carolina at
Charlotte, NC
The University of North Carolina at
Greensboro, NC
University of North Dakota, ND
University of Northern Colorado, CO
University of Puerto Rico–Bayamón, PR
University of South Carolina, SC
University of South Carolina Aiken, SC
The University of Tennessee at Chattanooga,
TN
The University of Texas at Dallas, TX
The University of Texas at San Antonio, TX
The University of Toledo, OH
University of Utah, UT
University of West Florida, FL
University of West Georgia, GA
University of Wisconsin–Green Bay, WI
University of Wisconsin–Stout, WI
University of Wisconsin–Whitewater, WI
University of Wyoming, WY
Washington State University, WA
Western Carolina University, NC
Western Kentucky University, KY
Western Oregon University, OR
West Texas A&M University, TX
Wheaton College, IL
Wichita State University, KS
Wright State University, OH
Wright State University–Lake Campus, OH
Youngstown State University, OH

International Students

Agnes Scott College, GA
Alaska Pacific University, AK
Albion College, MI
Allegheny College, PA

Alliant International University–San Diego,
CA
Alverno College, WI
Anderson University, SC
Andrews University, MI
Appalachian Bible College, WV
Arizona State University at the Downtown
Phoenix campus, AZ
Arizona State University at the Polytechnic
campus, AZ
Arizona State University at the Tempe
campus, AZ
Arizona State University at the West campus,
AZ
Arkansas Tech University, AR
Auburn University at Montgomery, AL
Augsburg University, MN
Augustana College, IL
Augustana University, SD
Austin College, TX
Averett University, VA
Baker University, KS
Ball State University, IN
Barton College, NC
Bay Path University, MA
Belhaven University, MS
Bellarmine University, KY
Bemidji State University, MN
Benedictine University, IL
Bentley University, MA
Berry College, GA
Bethel College, IN
Bethel College, KS
Binghamton University, State University of
New York, NY
Biola University, CA
Birmingham-Southern College, AL
Bloomsburg University of Pennsylvania, PA
Bluffton University, OH
Boise State University, ID
Bowling Green State University, OH
Brenau University, GA
Bridgewater College, VA
Bryan College, TN
Bryant University, RI
Buena Vista University, IA
Buffalo State College, State University of
New York, NY
California Baptist University, CA
California Lutheran University, CA
California State University, Chico, CA
California University of Pennsylvania, PA
Calvin College, MI
Cameron University, OK
Campbellsville University, KY
Canisius College, NY
Capital University, OH
Cardinal Stritch University, WI
Carlow University, PA
Carroll College, MT
Carroll University, WI
Centenary College of Louisiana, LA
Central College, IA
Central Methodist University, MO
Central Michigan University, MI
Champlain College, VT
Chapman University, CA
Chowan University, NC
Christian Brothers University, TN
Claflin University, SC
Clarkson University, NY
Clear Creek Baptist Bible College, KY
Coastal Carolina University, SC
Coe College, IA
Coker College, SC

The College at Brockport, State University
    of New York, NY
College of Coastal Georgia, GA
The College of Idaho, ID
College of Saint Benedict, MN
College of Saint Mary, NE
The College of St. Scholastica, MN
College of Staten Island of the City
    University of New York, NY
The College of Wooster, OH
Colorado State University, CO
Columbia College, MO
Columbia International University, SC
Concordia College, MN
Concordia University Chicago, IL
Concordia University, Nebraska, NE
Concordia University Texas, TX
Corban University, OR
Cornerstone University, MI
Covenant College, GA
Culver-Stockton College, MO
Daemen College, NY
Davis College, NY
Defiance College, OH
DeSales University, PA
Dominican University of California, CA
Dordt College, IA
Drake University, IA
Drury University, MO
Duke University, NC
Duquesne University, PA
East Central University, OK
Eastern Mennonite University, VA
Eastern Michigan University, MI
Eastern University, PA
East Texas Baptist University, TX
Eckerd College, FL
Elizabethtown College, PA
Elmira College, NY
Elon University, NC
Emmanuel College, GA
Emporia State University, KS
Endicott College, MA
Fairmont State University, WV
Ferris State University, MI
Flagler College, FL
Florida Gulf Coast University, FL
Florida Institute of Technology, FL
Fort Hays State University, KS
Fort Lewis College, CO
Franciscan University of Steubenville, OH
Francis Marion University, SC
Franklin Pierce University, NH
Frostburg State University, MD
Furman University, SC
Gannon University, PA
George Fox University, OR
Gonzaga University, WA
Gordon College, MA
Goshen College, IN
Graceland University, IA
Grambling State University, LA
Grand Valley State University, MI
Greenville University, IL
Gustavus Adolphus College, MN
Hamline University, MN
Hampden-Sydney College, VA
Hampton University, VA
Hanover College, IN
Harding University, AR
Hartwick College, NY
Harvey Mudd College, CA
Hawai`i Pacific University, HI
Henderson State University, AR
Hendrix College, AR
Hillsdale College, MI

Hollins University, VA
Hood College, MD
Huntington University, IN
Husson University, ME
Idaho State University, ID
Illinois College, IL
Illinois Institute of Technology, IL
Illinois Wesleyan University, IL
Indiana University of Pennsylvania, PA
Iowa State University of Science and
    Technology, IA
Iowa Wesleyan University, IA
Jacksonville University, FL
James Madison University, VA
Johnson C. Smith University, NC
Johnson University, TN
Juniata College, PA
Kansas Wesleyan University, KS
Kennesaw State University, GA
Kent State University, OH
Keuka College, NY
The King's College, NY
King's College, PA
Kuyper College, MI
Lancaster Bible College, PA
Lawrence University, WI
Lebanon Valley College, PA
Liberty University, VA
Life University, GA
Lincoln University, MO
Linfield College, OR
Lipscomb University, TN
Lock Haven University of Pennsylvania, PA
Long Island University–LIU Brooklyn, NY
Long Island University–LIU Post, NY
Louisiana Tech University, LA
Loyola Marymount University, CA
Malone University, OH
Manchester University, IN
Marymount Manhattan College, NY
Maryville University of Saint Louis, MO
McKendree University, IL
McMurry University, TX
Mercer University, GA
Meredith College, NC
Merrimack College, MA
Methodist University, NC
Michigan State University, MI
Middle Tennessee State University, TN
Midwestern State University, TX
Millersville University of Pennsylvania, PA
Millikin University, IL
Minot State University, ND
Missouri Western State University, MO
Monmouth College, IL
Monmouth University, NJ
Montclair State University, NJ
Montreat College, NC
Moravian College, PA
Morehead State University, KY
Morningside College, IA
Mount Marty College, SD
Mount Mary University, WI
Mount Mercy University, IA
Mount Vernon Nazarene University, OH
Muskingum University, OH
Nebraska Christian College of Hope
    International University, NE
Neumont College of Computer Science, UT
Newberry College, SC
New England College, NH
New Jersey Institute of Technology, NJ
Newman University, KS
New Mexico State University, NM
North Central College, IL
Northern Illinois University, IL

Northern Michigan University, MI
Northern State University, SD
Northwest Christian University, OR
Northwestern College, IA
Northwestern University, IL
Northwest Nazarene University, ID
Northwest University, WA
Oakland City University, IN
Ohio Northern University, OH
Ohio Valley University, WV
Ohio Wesleyan University, OH
Oklahoma Baptist University, OK
Oklahoma Christian University, OK
Oklahoma State University, OK
Old Dominion University, VA
Olivet College, MI
Oral Roberts University, OK
Ouachita Baptist University, AR
Ozark Christian College, MO
Pacific Lutheran University, WA
Pacific University, OR
Peirce College, PA
Piedmont College, GA
Piedmont International University, NC
Plymouth State University, NH
Point Park University, PA
Portland State University, OR
Quinnipiac University, CT
Ramapo College of New Jersey, NJ
Randolph College, VA
Roberts Wesleyan College, NY
Rockford University, IL
Sacred Heart University, CT
St. Ambrose University, IA
St. Catherine University, MN
Saint Louis University, MO
Saint Martin's University, WA
Saint Mary-of-the-Woods College, IN
Saint Mary's University of Minnesota, MN
St. Norbert College, WI
San Jose State University, CA
Schreiner University, TX
Seattle Pacific University, WA
Seton Hill University, PA
Simpson College, IA
Sonoma State University, CA
South Dakota State University, SD
Southeastern University, FL
Southeast Missouri State University, MO
Southern Adventist University, TN
Southern Illinois University Carbondale, IL
Southern New Hampshire University, NH
Southern Oregon University, OR
Southwest Baptist University, MO
Southwestern College, KS
State University of New York at Fredonia,
    NY
State University of New York at Plattsburgh,
    NY
State University of New York College at
    Geneseo, NY
State University of New York College of
    Environmental Science and Forestry, NY
Stetson University, FL
Stockton University, NJ
Taylor University, IN
Texas A&M University, TX
Texas A&M University–Corpus Christi, TX
Texas Christian University, TX
Texas State University, TX
Texas Wesleyan University, TX
Texas Woman's University, TX
Thomas College, ME
Thomas More College, KY
Toccoa Falls College, GA
Towson University, MD

Trinity University, TX
Truett McConnell University, GA
Truman State University, MO
Tulane University, LA
Union University, TN
The University of Akron, OH
The University of Alabama, AL
The University of Alabama at Birmingham, AL
The University of Arizona, AZ
University of Arkansas, AR
University of Bridgeport, CT
University of California, Irvine, CA
University of California, Santa Cruz, CA
University of Central Oklahoma, OK
University of Colorado Denver, CO
University of Evansville, IN
University of Hartford, CT
University of Houston, TX
University of Idaho, ID
University of Illinois at Urbana–Champaign, IL
University of Indianapolis, IN
The University of Kansas, KS
University of Kentucky, KY
University of Louisiana at Monroe, LA
University of Maine, ME
University of Maine at Fort Kent, ME
University of Maine at Presque Isle, ME
University of Mary Hardin-Baylor, TX
University of Memphis, TN
University of Miami, FL
University of Michigan, MI
University of Michigan–Dearborn, MI
University of Michigan–Flint, MI
University of Mississippi, MS
University of Missouri, MO
University of Missouri–St. Louis, MO
University of Montana, MT
The University of Montana Western, MT
University of Montevallo, AL
University of Nebraska at Kearney, NE
University of Nebraska–Lincoln, NE
University of Nevada, Las Vegas, NV
University of New Hampshire, NH
University of North Alabama, AL
The University of North Carolina at Chapel Hill, NC
The University of North Carolina at Charlotte, NC
The University of North Carolina at Greensboro, NC
University of North Dakota, ND
University of Northern Colorado, CO
University of North Florida, FL
University of Oregon, OR
University of Pittsburgh at Bradford, PA
University of Providence, MT
University of Puget Sound, WA
University of Rochester, NY
University of Science and Arts of Oklahoma, OK
University of Sioux Falls, SD
University of South Carolina, SC
University of South Carolina Aiken, SC
University of Southern Indiana, IN
The University of Tampa, FL
The University of Texas at Dallas, TX
The University of Texas at El Paso, TX
The University of Texas Rio Grande Valley, TX
The University of Toledo, OH
University of West Florida, FL
University of West Georgia, GA
University of Wisconsin–Eau Claire, WI

University of Wisconsin–La Crosse, WI
University of Wisconsin–Parkside, WI
University of Wisconsin–Stevens Point, WI
University of Wisconsin–Stout, WI
University of Wisconsin–Superior, WI
University of Wisconsin–Whitewater, WI
University of Wyoming, WY
Ursinus College, PA
Utah State University, UT
Valley City State University, ND
Valparaiso University, IN
Warner Pacific College, OR
Wartburg College, IA
Washington & Jefferson College, PA
Washington State University, WA
Wayne State University, MI
Webber International University, FL
Webster University, MO
Wells College, NY
Wesleyan University, CT
Western Illinois University, IL
Western Kentucky University, KY
Western Michigan University, MI
Western Oregon University, OR
Western Washington University, WA
Westminster College, MO
Westmont College, CA
West Texas A&M University, TX
West Virginia University, WV
West Virginia Wesleyan College, WV
Wheaton College, IL
Whitman College, WA
Whittier College, CA
Whitworth University, WA
Wichita State University, KS
Widener University, PA
William Jessup University, CA
Williams Baptist College, AR
Wilson College, PA
Wisconsin Lutheran College, WI
Wittenberg University, OH
Wright State University, OH
Wright State University–Lake Campus, OH
Xavier University, OH
York College of Pennsylvania, PA
Youngstown State University, OH

Local/State Students
Abilene Christian University, TX
Agnes Scott College, GA
Alaska Pacific University, AK
Albany State University, GA
Albertus Magnus College, CT
Albright College, PA
Allen College, IA
Alliant International University–San Diego, CA
Appalachian Bible College, WV
Arizona State University at the Downtown Phoenix campus, AZ
Arizona State University at the Polytechnic campus, AZ
Arizona State University at the Tempe campus, AZ
Arizona State University at the West campus, AZ
Auburn University, AL
Augustana University, SD
Aurora University, IL
Austin College, TX
Averett University, VA
Ball State University, IN
Barton College, NC
Belhaven University, MS
Bellarmine University, KY

Belmont University, TN
Benedictine University, IL
Berry College, GA
Bethel College, KS
Binghamton University, State University of New York, NY
Birmingham-Southern College, AL
Bluefield College, VA
Boise State University, ID
Boston University, MA
Bridgewater State University, MA
Brigham Young University, UT
Bryan College, TN
Caldwell University, NJ
California Polytechnic State University, San Luis Obispo, CA
California State University, Bakersfield, CA
California State University, Chico, CA
California State University, Fresno, CA
California State University, Monterey Bay, CA
California State University, San Marcos, CA
California State University, Stanislaus, CA
Calvin College, MI
Campbell University, NC
Centenary College of Louisiana, LA
Central College, IA
Central Michigan University, MI
Central Washington University, WA
Chowan University, NC
Christopher Newport University, VA
The Citadel, The Military College of South Carolina, SC
City College of the City University of New York, NY
Claflin University, SC
Clarion University of Pennsylvania, PA
Clarkson University, NY
Clemson University, SC
Coastal Carolina University, SC
Coker College, SC
College of Coastal Georgia, GA
The College of Idaho, ID
The College of St. Scholastica, MN
College of Staten Island of the City University of New York, NY
Colorado Mesa University, CO
Colorado Mountain College, CO
Columbia College, MO
Columbia International University, SC
Columbus College of Art & Design, OH
Concordia University, Nebraska, NE
Culver-Stockton College, MO
DePaul University, IL
Dordt College, IA
Duke University, NC
Eastern Oregon University, OR
Eastern Washington University, WA
Eckerd College, FL
Elizabethtown College, PA
Elmira College, NY
Emmanuel College, GA
Emory University, GA
Endicott College, MA
Eugene Lang College of Liberal Arts, NY
The Evergreen State College, WA
Fairmont State University, WV
Faulkner University, AL
Ferris State University, MI
Flagler College, FL
Florida Agricultural and Mechanical University, FL
Florida Gulf Coast University, FL
Florida Southern College, FL
Florida State University, FL

Fort Lewis College, CO
Franciscan University of Steubenville, OH
Francis Marion University, SC
Franklin College, IN
Franklin Pierce University, NH
Frostburg State University, MD
Furman University, SC
Gardner-Webb University, NC
Georgetown College, KY
Georgia College & State University, GA
Georgia Institute of Technology, GA
Georgian Court University, NJ
Georgia Southwestern State University, GA
Graceland University, IA
Grambling State University, LA
Grand Valley State University, MI
Greenville University, IL
Hamline University, MN
Hawai`i Pacific University, HI
Hofstra University, NY
Hollins University, VA
Hood College, MD
Howard Payne University, TX
Huntingdon College, AL
Huntington University, IN
Idaho State University, ID
Illinois Institute of Technology, IL
Indiana Tech, IN
Indiana University of Pennsylvania, PA
Iowa State University of Science and
    Technology, IA
Jacksonville State University, AL
James Madison University, VA
Jefferson College of Health Sciences, VA
John Carroll University, OH
Juniata College, PA
Kansas Wesleyan University, KS
Kean University, NJ
Kennesaw State University, GA
Kent State University, OH
Kentucky State University, KY
Kutztown University of Pennsylvania, PA
Lees-McRae College, NC
Lee University, TN
Lenoir-Rhyne University, NC
Liberty University, VA
Life University, GA
LIM College, NY
Lincoln Memorial University, TN
Lipscomb University, TN
Lock Haven University of Pennsylvania, PA
Longwood University, VA
Loras College, IA
Loyola Marymount University, CA
Lycoming College, PA
Lyon College, AR
Malone University, OH
Mansfield University of Pennsylvania, PA
Marist College, NY
Marshall University, WV
Marymount Manhattan College, NY
Marymount University, VA
McDaniel College, MD
McMurry University, TX
Medical University of South Carolina, SC
Messiah College, PA
Methodist University, NC
Metropolitan State University of Denver, CO
Miami University, OH
Michigan State University, MI
Middle Georgia State University, GA
Middle Tennessee State University, TN
Millsaps College, MS
Minot State University, ND
Mississippi State University, MS
Missouri State University, MO

Missouri Western State University, MO
Monmouth University, NJ
Montana State University, MT
Montana State University Billings, MT
Montana Tech of The University of
    Montana, MT
Montreat College, NC
Morehead State University, KY
Morehouse College, GA
Morrisville State College, NY
Murray State University, KY
Muskingum University, OH
Neumont College of Computer Science, UT
Newberry College, SC
New England College, NH
New Jersey Institute of Technology, NJ
New Mexico State University, NM
Nicholls State University, LA
North Carolina State University, NC
Northeastern State University, OK
Northern Arizona University, AZ
Northern Kentucky University, KY
Northern Michigan University, MI
Northern State University, SD
Ohio Valley University, WV
Ohio Wesleyan University, OH
Oklahoma Baptist University, OK
Oklahoma State University, OK
Old Dominion University, VA
Oregon State University, OR
Ouachita Baptist University, AR
Post University, CT
Randolph College, VA
Regis University, CO
Rice University, TX
Robert Morris University Illinois, IL
Sacred Heart University, CT
Saginaw Valley State University, MI
Saint Augustine's University, NC
St. Bonaventure University, NY
St. Catherine University, MN
St. Edward's University, TX
St. John Fisher College, NY
St. John's University, NY
Saint Martin's University, WA
Saint Mary's University of Minnesota, MN
San Diego State University, CA
San Jose State University, CA
Schreiner University, TX
Shenandoah University, VA
Shepherd University, WV
Shippensburg University of Pennsylvania,
    PA
Siena College, NY
Slippery Rock University of Pennsylvania,
    PA
Smith College, MA
Sonoma State University, CA
Southern Adventist University, TN
Southern Illinois University Carbondale, IL
Southern New Hampshire University, NH
Southern Utah University, UT
Southwest Baptist University, MO
Southwestern Christian College, TX
Southwestern College, KS
Southwestern Oklahoma State University,
    OK
State University of New York at Fredonia,
    NY
State University of New York at New Paltz,
    NY
State University of New York College at
    Cortland, NY
State University of New York College at
    Geneseo, NY

State University of New York College at
    Potsdam, NY
State University of New York College of
    Agriculture and Technology at
    Cobleskill, NY
State University of New York College of
    Environmental Science and Forestry, NY
State University of New York Polytechnic
    Institute, NY
Stephen F. Austin State University, TX
Stetson University, FL
Stockton University, NJ
Swarthmore College, PA
Tennessee Technological University, TN
Texas A&M University, TX
Texas Christian University, TX
Texas Lutheran University, TX
Texas Wesleyan University, TX
Thomas College, ME
Trinity Christian College, IL
Truett McConnell University, GA
Tulane University, LA
Tuskegee University, AL
Unity College, ME
The University of Akron, OH
The University of Alabama in Huntsville,
    AL
University of Alaska Fairbanks, AK
University of Arkansas, AR
University of Arkansas at Little Rock, AR
University of Bridgeport, CT
University of Colorado Boulder, CO
University of Dayton, OH
University of Delaware, DE
University of Evansville, IN
University of Georgia, GA
University of Hartford, CT
University of Houston, TX
University of Houston–Clear Lake, TX
University of Idaho, ID
University of Illinois at Urbana–Champaign,
    IL
The University of Iowa, IA
The University of Kansas, KS
University of Maine, ME
University of Maine at Presque Isle, ME
University of Mary Hardin-Baylor, TX
University of Mary Washington, VA
University of Massachusetts Boston, MA
University of Massachusetts Dartmouth, MA
University of Memphis, TN
University of Michigan, MI
University of Michigan–Flint, MI
University of Minnesota, Crookston, MN
University of Minnesota, Twin Cities
    Campus, MN
University of Mississippi, MS
University of Missouri, MO
University of Missouri–St. Louis, MO
University of Montana, MT
University of Nebraska at Kearney, NE
University of Nevada, Las Vegas, NV
University of New Hampshire, NH
The University of North Carolina at
    Charlotte, NC
The University of North Carolina at
    Greensboro, NC
The University of North Carolina
    Wilmington, NC
University of Northern Colorado, CO
University of Oregon, OR
University of Pittsburgh at Bradford, PA
University of Pittsburgh at Greensburg, PA
University of Providence, MT
University of Saint Joseph, CT
University of Sioux Falls, SD

University of South Carolina, SC
University of South Carolina Aiken, SC
University of Southern Mississippi, MS
The University of Tennessee at Martin, TN
The University of Texas at Austin, TX
The University of Texas at Dallas, TX
The University of Texas at El Paso, TX
The University of Texas at San Antonio, TX
The University of Texas Rio Grande Valley, TX
The University of Virginia's College at Wise, VA
University of West Georgia, GA
University of Wisconsin–Eau Claire, WI
University of Wisconsin–La Crosse, WI
University of Wisconsin–Parkside, WI
University of Wisconsin–River Falls, WI
University of Wisconsin–Stout, WI
University of Wisconsin–Whitewater, WI
University of Wyoming, WY
Utah State University, UT
Valdosta State University, GA
Vanderbilt University, TN
Virginia Military Institute, VA
Virginia Polytechnic Institute and State University, VA
Wake Forest University, NC
Warner Pacific College, OR
Washington & Jefferson College, PA
Washington State University, WA
Wayne State College, NE
Wayne State University, MI
Webber International University, FL
Wesleyan College, GA
Western Carolina University, NC
Western Kentucky University, KY
Western Michigan University, MI
Western Oregon University, OR
Western Washington University, WA
Westminster College, MO
West Texas A&M University, TX
West Virginia University, WV
Wheaton College, IL
Wichita State University, KS
William Woods University, MO
Wilson College, PA
Winona State University, MN
Wofford College, SC
Youngstown State University, OH

Married Students

Alaska Bible College, AK
Appalachian Bible College, WV
Auburn University, AL
Binghamton University, State University of New York, NY
Blue Mountain College, MS
California State University, Chico, CA
The College at Brockport, State University of New York, NY
The College of Idaho, ID
Crossroads Bible College, IN
Davis College, NY
Eastern Washington University, WA
Emmanuel College, GA
Franklin Pierce University, NH
Georgian Court University, NJ
Georgia Southern University, GA
Indiana Tech, IN
Indiana University of Pennsylvania, PA
Johnson University, TN
Lock Haven University of Pennsylvania, PA
Montana Tech of The University of Montana, MT
Murray State University, KY

Newman University, KS
New Mexico State University, NM
Northwest University, WA
Ouachita Baptist University, AR
Sonoma State University, CA
Texas Wesleyan University, TX
Toccoa Falls College, GA
Truett McConnell University, GA
The University of Alabama at Birmingham, AL
University of Arkansas, AR
The University of Kansas, KS
University of Nevada, Reno, NV
University of Northern Colorado, CO
University of South Carolina Aiken, SC

Members of Minorities

Abilene Christian University, TX
Alabama State University, AL
Alaska Pacific University, AK
Alice Lloyd College, KY
Allen College, IA
Alma College, MI
American University, DC
Anderson University, SC
Assumption College, MA
Augsburg University, MN
Augustana College, IL
Augustana University, SD
Austin Peay State University, TN
Baker University, KS
Baldwin Wallace University, OH
Ball State University, IN
Bellarmine University, KY
Belmont University, TN
Bemidji State University, MN
Bentley University, MA
Berry College, GA
Bethel College, IN
Binghamton University, State University of New York, NY
Biola University, CA
Bluffton University, OH
Boise State University, ID
Boston University, MA
Bowling Green State University, OH
Brenau University, GA
Bridgewater College, VA
Bridgewater State University, MA
Brigham Young University, UT
Bryan College, TN
Bryant University, RI
Buffalo State College, State University of New York, NY
California State Polytechnic University, Pomona, CA
California State University, Chico, CA
California University of Pennsylvania, PA
Calvin College, MI
Cameron University, OK
Capital University, OH
Carson-Newman University, TN
Centenary College of Louisiana, LA
Central College, IA
Central Connecticut State University, CT
Central Washington University, WA
Champlain College, VT
Christian Brothers University, TN
Christopher Newport University, VA
Clarion University of Pennsylvania, PA
Clarkson University, NY
Clemson University, SC
Coe College, IA
The College at Brockport, State University of New York, NY

The College of Idaho, ID
The College of New Jersey, NJ
The College of Saint Rose, NY
College of Staten Island of the City University of New York, NY
The College of Wooster, OH
Colorado State University, CO
Columbia College, MO
Columbia International University, SC
Concordia University, Nebraska, NE
Cornerstone University, MI
Covenant College, GA
Creighton University, NE
Delaware Valley University, PA
Dominican University of California, CA
Dordt College, IA
Drury University, MO
Duquesne University, PA
East Central University, OK
Eastern Kentucky University, KY
Eastern Michigan University, MI
Eastern Oregon University, OR
Elizabethtown College, PA
Elmhurst College, IL
Elon University, NC
Emporia State University, KS
Eugene Lang College of Liberal Arts, NY
Fairfield University, CT
Fairmont State University, WV
Ferris State University, MI
Flagler College, FL
Florida Gulf Coast University, FL
Francis Marion University, SC
Franklin College, IN
Gannon University, PA
Gardner-Webb University, NC
George Fox University, OR
Georgetown College, KY
Georgia Institute of Technology, GA
Georgian Court University, NJ
Georgia Southern University, GA
Gonzaga University, WA
Goshen College, IN
Graceland University, IA
Grambling State University, LA
Grove City College, PA
Gustavus Adolphus College, MN
Hamline University, MN
Hampton University, VA
Hanover College, IN
Hilbert College, NY
Hiram College, OH
Hofstra University, NY
Husson University, ME
Idaho State University, ID
Indiana State University, IN
Iowa State University of Science and Technology, IA
Ithaca College, NY
James Madison University, VA
Johnson University, TN
Judson University, IL
Kennesaw State University, GA
Kent State University, OH
Kent State University at Stark, OH
Keuka College, NY
Lehigh University, PA
Le Moyne College, NY
Lenoir-Rhyne University, NC
Lewis-Clark State College, ID
Life University, GA
Lincoln Memorial University, TN
Linfield College, OR
Lipscomb University, TN
Lock Haven University of Pennsylvania, PA

Louisiana Tech University, LA
Loyola Marymount University, CA
Luther College, IA
Lyon College, AR
Malone University, OH
Manchester University, IN
Mansfield University of Pennsylvania, PA
Marietta College, OH
Marshall University, WV
Maryville College, TN
Maryville University of Saint Louis, MO
McMurry University, TX
Medical University of South Carolina, SC
Meredith College, NC
Miami University, OH
MidAmerica Nazarene University, KS
Middle Tennessee State University, TN
Midwestern State University, TX
Minnesota State University Mankato, MN
Minnesota State University Moorhead, MN
Minot State University, ND
Misericordia University, PA
Missouri State University, MO
Missouri University of Science and
Technology, MO
Molloy College, NY
Monmouth University, NJ
Montana State University, MT
Montana State University Billings, MT
Morehead State University, KY
Morrisville State College, NY
Mount Carmel College of Nursing, OH
Mount Vernon Nazarene University, OH
Murray State University, KY
Muskingum University, OH
New Jersey Institute of Technology, NJ
New Mexico State University, NM
Nicholls State University, LA
Northeastern State University, OK
Northern Arizona University, AZ
Northern Illinois University, IL
Northern Kentucky University, KY
Northern Michigan University, MI
Northern State University, SD
Northwest Missouri State University, MO
Oakland City University, IN
The Ohio State University, OH
Ohio Wesleyan University, OH
Oklahoma Baptist University, OK
Oregon State University, OR
Ouachita Baptist University, AR
Piedmont International University, NC
Portland State University, OR
Rensselaer Polytechnic Institute, NY
Rhodes College, TN
Rice University, TX
Rider University, NJ
Sacred Heart University, CT
The Sage Colleges, NY
Saginaw Valley State University, MI
St. Ambrose University, IA
St. Bonaventure University, NY
St. John Fisher College, NY
Saint Joseph's University, PA
Saint Louis University, MO
Saint Martin's University, WA
Saint Mary's University of Minnesota, MN
Saint Michael's College, VT
Samford University, AL
Sam Houston State University, TX
San Jose State University, CA
Seattle University, WA
Shepherd University, WV
Simpson College, IA
Slippery Rock University of Pennsylvania,
PA

Sonoma State University, CA
South Dakota State University, SD
Southeast Missouri State University, MO
Southern Adventist University, TN
Southern Illinois University Carbondale, IL
Southern Oregon University, OR
Southern Utah University, UT
Southwestern College, KS
Southwestern University, TX
State University of New York at Fredonia,
NY
State University of New York at New Paltz,
NY
State University of New York College at
Cortland, NY
State University of New York College at
Geneseo, NY
State University of New York College at
Potsdam, NY
State University of New York College of
Agriculture and Technology at
Cobleskill, NY
State University of New York College of
Environmental Science and Forestry, NY
State University of New York Polytechnic
Institute, NY
Stetson University, FL
Stockton University, NJ
Tennessee Technological University, TN
Texas Christian University, TX
Texas Wesleyan University, TX
Thomas Jefferson University, PA
Thomas More College, KY
Towson University, MD
Transylvania University, KY
Trine University, IN
Trinity Christian College, IL
Union College, KY
Union University, TN
Unity College, ME
The University of Akron, OH
The University of Alabama at Birmingham,
AL
The University of Alabama in Huntsville,
AL
University of Arkansas, AR
University of Arkansas at Little Rock, AR
University of California, San Diego, CA
University of Central Oklahoma, OK
University of Colorado Denver, CO
University of Dayton, OH
University of Delaware, DE
University of Evansville, IN
University of Florida, FL
University of Hartford, CT
University of Idaho, ID
University of Illinois at Urbana–Champaign,
IL
The University of Kansas, KS
University of Kentucky, KY
University of Maine, ME
University of Maine at Fort Kent, ME
University of Mary Hardin-Baylor, TX
University of Massachusetts Dartmouth, MA
University of Memphis, TN
University of Michigan, MI
University of Michigan–Dearborn, MI
University of Michigan–Flint, MI
University of Minnesota, Crookston, MN
University of Minnesota, Twin Cities
Campus, MN
University of Mississippi, MS
University of Missouri, MO
University of Missouri–St. Louis, MO
The University of Montana Western, MT
University of Nebraska at Kearney, NE

University of Nebraska–Lincoln, NE
University of Nevada, Las Vegas, NV
The University of North Carolina at
Charlotte, NC
University of North Dakota, ND
University of Northern Colorado, CO
University of Northern Iowa, IA
University of North Florida, FL
University of Oklahoma, OK
University of Pittsburgh at Bradford, PA
University of Pittsburgh at Greensburg, PA
University of Saint Joseph, CT
The University of Scranton, PA
University of South Carolina, SC
University of South Carolina Aiken, SC
University of South Dakota, SD
University of Southern Indiana, IN
The University of Tennessee at Martin, TN
The University of Texas at Dallas, TX
The University of Texas at El Paso, TX
The University of Texas at San Antonio, TX
The University of Toledo, OH
University of West Georgia, GA
University of Wisconsin–Eau Claire, WI
University of Wisconsin–Green Bay, WI
University of Wisconsin–La Crosse, WI
University of Wisconsin–Parkside, WI
University of Wisconsin–River Falls, WI
University of Wisconsin–Stevens Point, WI
University of Wisconsin–Stout, WI
University of Wisconsin–Superior, WI
University of Wisconsin–Whitewater, WI
University of Wyoming, WY
Utah State University, UT
Valdosta State University, GA
Valley City State University, ND
Vanderbilt University, TN
Virginia Polytechnic Institute and State
University, VA
Washington & Jefferson College, PA
Wayne State College, NE
Webster University, MO
Western Carolina University, NC
Western Illinois University, IL
Western Kentucky University, KY
Western Oregon University, OR
Western Washington University, WA
West Virginia University, WV
Wheaton College, IL
Whitworth University, WA
Wichita State University, KS
Williams Baptist College, AR
Winona State University, MN
Wittenberg University, OH
Wofford College, SC
Wright State University, OH
Wright State University–Lake Campus, OH
Xavier University, OH
York College of Pennsylvania, PA
Youngstown State University, OH

Out-of-State Students
Abilene Christian University, TX
Alaska Pacific University, AK
Albion College, MI
Allen College, IA
Alma College, MI
Alverno College, WI
Anderson University, SC
Arizona State University at the Downtown
Phoenix campus, AZ
Arizona State University at the Polytechnic
campus, AZ
Arizona State University at the Tempe
campus, AZ

Arizona State University at the West campus, AZ
Arkansas Tech University, AR
Auburn University, AL
Augustana College, IL
Aurora University, IL
Austin College, TX
Averett University, VA
Baker University, KS
Ball State University, IN
Bellarmine University, KY
Bemidji State University, MN
Benedictine University, IL
Berry College, GA
Bethel University, MN
Binghamton University, State University of New York, NY
Bluefield College, VA
Bluffton University, OH
Boise State University, ID
Bradley University, IL
Brenau University, GA
Bridgewater College, VA
Buena Vista University, IA
California State University, Chico, CA
Calvin College, MI
Cameron University, OK
Campbell University, NC
Canisius College, NY
Capital University, OH
Centenary College of Louisiana, LA
Central College, IA
Central Michigan University, MI
Central Washington University, WA
Chowan University, NC
Christian Brothers University, TN
The Citadel, The Military College of South Carolina, SC
Cleveland State University, OH
Coastal Carolina University, SC
Coker College, SC
The College of Idaho, ID
The College of New Rochelle, NY
College of Saint Benedict, MN
The College of Saint Rose, NY
College of Staten Island of the City University of New York, NY
Colorado Mesa University, CO
Concordia University Wisconsin, WI
Davidson College, NC
Davis College, NY
Delaware State University, DE
Dordt College, IA
East Central University, OK
Eastern Michigan University, MI
East Texas Baptist University, TX
Elmira College, NY
Emory & Henry College, VA
Evangel University, MO
The Evergreen State College, WA
Fairmont State University, WV
Faulkner University, AL
Flagler College, FL
Florida Gulf Coast University, FL
Florida Southern College, FL
Fort Lewis College, CO
Francis Marion University, SC
Franklin College, IN
Frostburg State University, MD
Gardner-Webb University, NC
George Fox University, OR
Georgetown College, KY
Georgia College & State University, GA
Georgia Institute of Technology, GA
Georgian Court University, NJ

Glenville State College, WV
Graceland University, IA
Grambling State University, LA
Grand Valley State University, MI
Greenville University, IL
Gustavus Adolphus College, MN
Hamline University, MN
Hampden-Sydney College, VA
Hanover College, IN
Hardin-Simmons University, TX
Hawai`i Pacific University, HI
Heidelberg University, OH
Henderson State University, AR
Hollins University, VA
Hood College, MD
Husson University, ME
Idaho State University, ID
Iowa State University of Science and Technology, IA
Iowa Wesleyan University, IA
James Madison University, VA
Johnson C. Smith University, NC
Kent State University, OH
Kent State University at Geauga, OH
Kent State University at Stark, OH
King University, TN
Lewis-Clark State College, ID
Lincoln University, MO
Lipscomb University, TN
Loras College, IA
Louisiana State University and Agricultural & Mechanical College, LA
Louisiana Tech University, LA
Loyola Marymount University, CA
Lynn University, FL
Manchester University, IN
Marymount Manhattan College, NY
Marymount University, VA
Maryville University of Saint Louis, MO
McMurry University, TX
Meredith College, NC
Miami University, OH
Michigan State University, MI
Minnesota State University Moorhead, MN
Minot State University, ND
Misericordia University, PA
Mississippi State University, MS
Missouri University of Science and Technology, MO
Missouri Western State University, MO
Monmouth University, NJ
Montana State University Billings, MT
Montana Tech of The University of Montana, MT
Moravian College, PA
Morehead State University, KY
Morrisville State College, NY
Mount Mercy University, IA
Murray State University, KY
Nazareth College of Rochester, NY
New College of Florida, FL
New Jersey Institute of Technology, NJ
New Mexico State University, NM
Nicholls State University, LA
Northeastern State University, OK
Northern Michigan University, MI
Northwest Missouri State University, MO
Ohio Northern University, OH
The Ohio State University, OH
Oklahoma Baptist University, OK
Oklahoma State University, OK
Ouachita Baptist University, AR
Pacific Lutheran University, WA
Piedmont College, GA
Portland State University, OR

Ramapo College of New Jersey, NJ
Randolph-Macon College, VA
Robert Morris University Illinois, IL
Roberts Wesleyan College, NY
Rockford University, IL
Rogers State University, OK
Sacred Heart University, CT
St. Ambrose University, IA
St. Bonaventure University, NY
St. Catherine University, MN
St. Edward's University, TX
Saint John's University, MN
Saint Martin's University, WA
Saint Mary-of-the-Woods College, IN
Saint Michael's College, VT
Saint Vincent College, PA
Shawnee State University, OH
Shepherd University, WV
Siena College, NY
Simpson College, IA
Slippery Rock University of Pennsylvania, PA
Sonoma State University, CA
Southeastern Louisiana University, LA
Southeastern Oklahoma State University, OK
Southeast Missouri State University, MO
Southern Adventist University, TN
Southern Arkansas University–Magnolia, AR
Southern Oregon University, OR
Southwestern Oklahoma State University, OK
State University of New York at Fredonia, NY
State University of New York at Plattsburgh, NY
State University of New York College of Environmental Science and Forestry, NY
Stetson University, FL
Tennessee Technological University, TN
Tennessee Wesleyan University, TN
Texas A&M University–Commerce, TX
Texas Tech University, TX
Texas Wesleyan University, TX
Thomas College, ME
Thomas More College, KY
Thomas University, GA
Transylvania University, KY
Trinity Christian College, IL
Truett McConnell University, GA
Truman State University, MO
The University of Akron, OH
The University of Alabama, AL
The University of Alabama at Birmingham, AL
University of Arkansas, AR
University of California, Irvine, CA
University of California, Riverside, CA
University of California, Santa Cruz, CA
University of Colorado Denver, CO
University of Dayton, OH
University of Dubuque, IA
University of Florida, FL
University of Houston, TX
University of Idaho, ID
University of Indianapolis, IN
The University of Iowa, IA
The University of Kansas, KS
University of Kentucky, KY
University of Louisiana at Monroe, LA
University of Maine, ME
University of Maine at Presque Isle, ME
University of Mary Hardin-Baylor, TX
University of Maryland, College Park, MD

University of Massachusetts Boston, MA
University of Massachusetts Lowell, MA
University of Michigan, MI
University of Michigan–Dearborn, MI
University of Mississippi, MS
University of Missouri, MO
University of Missouri–St. Louis, MO
University of Montana, MT
The University of Montana Western, MT
University of Montevallo, AL
University of Nebraska at Kearney, NE
University of Nebraska–Lincoln, NE
University of Nevada, Las Vegas, NV
University of North Alabama, AL
The University of North Carolina at Chapel Hill, NC
The University of North Carolina at Greensboro, NC
The University of North Carolina Wilmington, NC
University of Northern Colorado, CO
University of North Florida, FL
University of Pittsburgh at Bradford, PA
University of Science and Arts of Oklahoma, OK
University of Sioux Falls, SD
University of South Carolina, SC
University of South Carolina Aiken, SC
University of Southern Indiana, IN
University of Southern Mississippi, MS
The University of Tennessee at Martin, TN
The University of Texas at Dallas, TX
The University of Texas at El Paso, TX
The University of Texas at San Antonio, TX
The University of Texas Rio Grande Valley, TX
The University of Toledo, OH
University of Utah, UT
University of West Florida, FL
University of Wisconsin–La Crosse, WI
University of Wisconsin–Parkside, WI
University of Wisconsin–Stevens Point, WI
University of Wisconsin–Stout, WI
University of Wisconsin–Whitewater, WI
University of Wyoming, WY
VanderCook College of Music, IL
Virginia Military Institute, VA
Virginia Polytechnic Institute and State University, VA
Washington State University, WA
Wayne State College, NE
Wayne State University, MI
Webster University, MO
Western Kentucky University, KY
Western Michigan University, MI
West Texas A&M University, TX
Wheaton College, IL
Wichita State University, KS
William Jessup University, CA
Winona State University, MN
Wright State University, OH
Wright State University–Lake Campus, OH
Youngstown State University, OH

Parents of Current Students
Arkansas Tech University, AR
Aurora University, IL
Blue Mountain College, MS
Caldwell University, NJ
The College of New Rochelle, NY
Columbia College, MO
Emmanuel College, GA
Franklin Pierce University, NH
Johnson University, TN
Manchester University, IN
Maryville University of Saint Louis, MO

Millikin University, IL
Missouri Baptist University, MO
Mount Aloysius College, PA
Mount Marty College, SD
New England College, NH
Northwest University, WA
Rockford University, IL
St. Joseph's College, Long Island Campus, NY
St. Joseph's College, New York, NY
Saint Mary-of-the-Woods College, IN
State University of New York at Fredonia, NY
Texas Wesleyan University, TX
Truett McConnell University, GA
The University of Alabama at Birmingham, AL
University of Hartford, CT
University of Providence, MT
Wesleyan College, GA

Previous College Experience
Abilene Christian University, TX
Alaska Pacific University, AK
Anderson University, SC
Appalachian Bible College, WV
Arkansas Tech University, AR
Austin College, TX
Bellarmine University, KY
Bemidji State University, MN
Bethel College, KS
Birmingham-Southern College, AL
Boise State University, ID
Bridgewater College, VA
Caldwell University, NJ
Calumet College of Saint Joseph, IN
Central College, IA
Clarion University of Pennsylvania, PA
Coker College, SC
The College at Brockport, State University of New York, NY
The College of New Rochelle, NY
The College of St. Scholastica, MN
College of Staten Island of the City University of New York, NY
Columbia College, MO
Eastern Michigan University, MI
Eastern University, PA
East Texas Baptist University, TX
Elmira College, NY
Fairmont State University, WV
Ferris State University, MI
Florida Institute of Technology, FL
Gardner-Webb University, NC
Georgian Court University, NJ
Hamline University, MN
Hawai`i Pacific University, HI
Hendrix College, AR
Hollins University, VA
Hood College, MD
Illinois College, IL
Illinois Institute of Technology, IL
Indiana State University, IN
Kansas Wesleyan University, KS
Kean University, NJ
Kent State University, OH
Lewis-Clark State College, ID
Lewis University, IL
Linfield College, OR
Lock Haven University of Pennsylvania, PA
Loyola Marymount University, CA
Manhattanville College, NY
McDaniel College, MD
McMurry University, TX
Meredith College, NC
Millikin University, IL

Misericordia University, PA
Mississippi State University, MS
Missouri Western State University, MO
Monmouth University, NJ
Morehead State University, KY
Mount Mercy University, IA
Muskingum University, OH
New Mexico State University, NM
New York Institute of Technology, NY
Nicholls State University, LA
Northwest Missouri State University, MO
The Ohio State University, OH
Oklahoma State University, OK
Old Dominion University, VA
Ouachita Baptist University, AR
Palm Beach Atlantic University, FL
Point Park University, PA
St. Ambrose University, IA
St. John's University, NY
Saint Louis University, MO
Saint Vincent College, PA
San Diego State University, CA
Shepherd University, WV
Siena College, NY
Slippery Rock University of Pennsylvania, PA
Sonoma State University, CA
Southeast Missouri State University, MO
Southern New Hampshire University, NH
Southern Oregon University, OR
State University of New York at Fredonia, NY
State University of New York College at Potsdam, NY
State University of New York Polytechnic Institute, NY
Stephen F. Austin State University, TX
Stockton University, NJ
Texas A&M University–Commerce, TX
Texas Christian University, TX
Texas Wesleyan University, TX
Towson University, MD
Truman State University, MO
The University of Alabama at Birmingham, AL
University of Arkansas, AR
University of Arkansas at Little Rock, AR
University of Bridgeport, CT
University of Hartford, CT
University of Houston, TX
The University of Kansas, KS
University of Maine, ME
University of Massachusetts Dartmouth, MA
University of Michigan–Dearborn, MI
University of Mississippi, MS
University of Missouri–St. Louis, MO
University of Nevada, Las Vegas, NV
University of Northern Colorado, CO
University of Oklahoma, OK
University of St. Thomas, TX
University of Science and Arts of Oklahoma, OK
University of South Carolina Aiken, SC
The University of Tennessee at Martin, TN
The University of Toledo, OH
The University of West Alabama, AL
University of Wisconsin–Eau Claire, WI
University of Wisconsin–Stout, WI
University of Wyoming, WY
Walsh College of Accountancy and Business Administration, MI
Wartburg College, IA
Washington State University, WA
Wesleyan College, GA
Western Michigan University, MI
Western Oregon University, OR

Western Washington University, WA
Wichita State University, KS
William Jessup University, CA

Public Servants
Alliant International University–San Diego, CA
Arkansas Tech University, AR
Caldwell University, NJ
Central Washington University, WA
Chowan University, NC
College of Staten Island of the City University of New York, NY
Francis Marion University, SC
Georgia College & State University, GA
Grambling State University, LA
Grand Valley State University, MI
Hardin-Simmons University, TX
Hofstra University, NY
Kent State University at Stark, OH
Kentucky State University, KY
La Sierra University, CA
Lindenwood University, MO
Missouri Baptist University, MO
Missouri Western State University, MO
New Mexico State University, NM
Nicholls State University, LA
Peirce College, PA
Regent University, VA
Regis University, CO
St. John's University, NY
St. Joseph's College, Long Island Campus, NY
St. Joseph's College, New York, NY
Southern Illinois University Carbondale, IL
Sterling College, KS
Tennessee Technological University, TN
Texas Wesleyan University, TX
The University of Alabama at Birmingham, AL
University of Kentucky, KY
University of Massachusetts Dartmouth, MA
University of Memphis, TN
University of Michigan–Dearborn, MI
University of Oklahoma, OK
The University of Texas at Dallas, TX
The University of Toledo, OH
Washington State University, WA
Webster University, MO
West Texas A&M University, TX
Youngstown State University, OH

Relatives of Clergy
Abilene Christian University, TX
Albion College, MI
American University, DC
Appalachian Bible College, WV
Augsburg University, MN
Austin College, TX
Averett University, VA
Baker University, KS
Barton College, NC
Benedictine University, IL
Bethel College, KS
Bethel University, MN
Biola University, CA
Birmingham-Southern College, AL
Blue Mountain College, MS
Boston University, MA
Bryan College, TN
Cairn University, PA
Caldwell University, NJ
California Baptist University, CA
California Lutheran University, CA
Campbellsville University, KY
Capital University, OH

Carson-Newman University, TN
Centenary College of Louisiana, LA
Central Methodist University, MO
Chapman University, CA
Chowan University, NC
Claflin University, SC
Clarke University, IA
Corban University, OR
Cornerstone University, MI
Dallas Baptist University, TX
Davidson College, NC
Davis College, NY
Dominican College, NY
Drury University, MO
Duquesne University, PA
Eastern University, PA
Elon University, NC
Emmanuel College, GA
Eureka College, IL
Evangel University, MO
Faulkner University, AL
Florida Southern College, FL
Franciscan University of Steubenville, OH
Franklin College, IN
Furman University, SC
Gardner-Webb University, NC
George Fox University, OR
Georgetown College, KY
Gordon College, MA
Hamline University, MN
Harding University, AR
Hardin-Simmons University, TX
Hawai`i Pacific University, HI
Heidelberg University, OH
Hendrix College, AR
High Point University, NC
Hiram College, OH
Hobart and William Smith Colleges, NY
Houston Baptist University, TX
Howard Payne University, TX
Huntington University, IN
Indiana Wesleyan University, IN
Johnson University, TN
Johnson University Florida, FL
King's College, PA
Kuyper College, MI
LaGrange College, GA
Lancaster Bible College, PA
La Salle University, PA
La Sierra University, CA
Lenoir-Rhyne University, NC
Lindsey Wilson College, KY
Lipscomb University, TN
Lycoming College, PA
Malone University, OH
McMurry University, TX
Mercer University, GA
Merrimack College, MA
Methodist University, NC
MidAmerica Nazarene University, KS
Millikin University, IL
Misericordia University, PA
Missouri Baptist University, MO
Montreat College, NC
Moravian College, PA
Mount Vernon Nazarene University, OH
Muhlenberg College, PA
Muskingum University, OH
Nebraska Christian College of Hope International University, NE
Newberry College, SC
New Jersey Institute of Technology, NJ
Niagara University, NY
North Central College, IL
Northwest Christian University, OR

Northwest Nazarene University, ID
Northwest University, WA
Ohio Northern University, OH
Ohio Valley University, WV
Ohio Wesleyan University, OH
Oklahoma Baptist University, OK
Oklahoma City University, OK
Olivet Nazarene University, IL
Oral Roberts University, OK
Ouachita Baptist University, AR
Ozark Christian College, MO
Pacific Lutheran University, WA
Pacific University, OR
Piedmont International University, NC
Presbyterian College, SC
Randolph College, VA
Randolph-Macon College, VA
Rhodes College, TN
Roberts Wesleyan College, NY
Saint Anselm College, NH
St. Bonaventure University, NY
St. John's University, NY
Saint Mary's College of California, CA
Saint Peter's University, NJ
Salem College, NC
Samford University, AL
Schreiner University, TX
Seattle Pacific University, WA
Siena College, NY
Simpson College, IA
Southwest Baptist University, MO
Southwestern University, TX
Stonehill College, MA
Susquehanna University, PA
Tennessee Wesleyan University, TN
Texas Christian University, TX
Texas Lutheran University, TX
Texas Wesleyan University, TX
Toccoa Falls College, GA
Transylvania University, KY
Trevecca Nazarene University, TN
Trinity College of Florida, FL
Truett McConnell University, GA
Union University, TN
The University of Alabama at Birmingham, AL
University of Dubuque, IA
University of Indianapolis, IN
University of Mary Hardin-Baylor, TX
The University of North Carolina at Chapel Hill, NC
University of Portland, OR
The University of Tulsa, OK
Ursuline College, OH
Valparaiso University, IN
Virginia Wesleyan University, VA
Wayland Baptist University, TX
Wesleyan College, GA
Westminster College, MO
West Virginia Wesleyan College, WV
Wheaton College, IL
William Jessup University, CA
Williams Baptist College, AR
Wilson College, PA
Wittenberg University, OH
Wofford College, SC

Religious Affiliation
Abilene Christian University, TX
Agnes Scott College, GA
Alaska Pacific University, AK
Albertus Magnus College, CT
Alverno College, WI
Anderson University, SC
Appalachian Bible College, WV

Augustana College, IL
Augustana University, SD
Aurora University, IL
Austin College, TX
Ave Maria University, FL
Averett University, VA
Baker University, KS
Baldwin Wallace University, OH
The Baptist College of Florida, FL
Barton College, NC
Belhaven University, MS
Bellarmine University, KY
Bethel College, KS
Binghamton University, State University of New York, NY
Birmingham-Southern College, AL
Bluefield College, VA
Blue Mountain College, MS
Bluffton University, OH
Boston University, MA
Bridgewater College, VA
Brigham Young University, UT
Buena Vista University, IA
Caldwell University, NJ
California Baptist University, CA
California Lutheran University, CA
Calumet College of Saint Joseph, IN
Calvin College, MI
Campbellsville University, KY
Canisius College, NY
Capital University, OH
Cardinal Stritch University, WI
Carlow University, PA
Carroll College, MT
The Catholic University of America, DC
Cedarville University, OH
Centenary College of Louisiana, LA
Central College, IA
Central Methodist University, MO
Chaminade University of Honolulu, HI
Charlotte Christian College and Theological Seminary, NC
Chowan University, NC
Christopher Newport University, VA
Claflin University, SC
Coe College, IA
The College at Brockport, State University of New York, NY
The College of St. Scholastica, MN
Columbia College, MO
Conception Seminary College, MO
Concordia University Chicago, IL
Concordia University Irvine, CA
Concordia University, Nebraska, NE
Concordia University, St. Paul, MN
Concordia University Texas, TX
Covenant College, GA
Culver-Stockton College, MO
Dallas Baptist University, TX
Davidson College, NC
Defiance College, OH
Doane University, NE
Dordt College, IA
Drury University, MO
Duquesne University, PA
Eastern Mennonite University, VA
Eastern Michigan University, MI
East Texas Baptist University, TX
Eckerd College, FL
Elizabethtown College, PA
Elmhurst College, IL
Elms College, MA
Emmanuel College, GA
Emory & Henry College, VA
Emory University, GA
Emporia State University, KS

Endicott College, MA
Eureka College, IL
Evangel University, MO
Faulkner University, AL
Florida Southern College, FL
Franciscan University of Steubenville, OH
Franklin College, IN
Furman University, SC
Gannon University, PA
Geneva College, PA
George Fox University, OR
Georgetown College, KY
Georgian Court University, NJ
Georgia Southern University, GA
Graceland University, IA
Greenville University, IL
Hamline University, MN
Hanover College, IN
Hardin-Simmons University, TX
Hawai`i Pacific University, HI
Heidelberg University, OH
Hiram College, OH
Hood College, MD
Hope College, MI
Houston Baptist University, TX
Howard Payne University, TX
Huntington University, IN
Indiana Wesleyan University, IN
Iona College, NY
Johnson University, TN
Johnson University Florida, FL
Kansas Wesleyan University, KS
Kennesaw State University, GA
Keuka College, NY
LaGrange College, GA
La Sierra University, CA
Lees-McRae College, NC
Lenoir-Rhyne University, NC
Lewis University, IL
Liberty University, VA
Lindsey Wilson College, KY
Lipscomb University, TN
Loras College, IA
Loyola Marymount University, CA
Loyola University Chicago, IL
Luther College, IA
Lyon College, AR
Malone University, OH
Manchester University, IN
Mansfield University of Pennsylvania, PA
Marymount University, VA
Maryville College, TN
McKendree University, IL
McMurry University, TX
Meredith College, NC
Merrimack College, MA
Messiah College, PA
Methodist University, NC
MidAmerica Nazarene University, KS
Millsaps College, MS
Missouri Baptist University, MO
Missouri Western State University, MO
Molloy College, NY
Montreat College, NC
Moravian College, PA
Mount Aloysius College, PA
Mount Marty College, SD
Mount Vernon Nazarene University, OH
Muskingum University, OH
Nebraska Methodist College, NE
Newberry College, SC
New Jersey Institute of Technology, NJ
Northeastern State University, OK
Northwest Christian University, OR
Northwestern College, IA
Northwest Nazarene University, ID

Northwest University, WA
Oakland City University, IN
Ohio Northern University, OH
Ohio Valley University, WV
Ohio Wesleyan University, OH
Oklahoma Baptist University, OK
Oklahoma City University, OK
Olivet College, MI
Olivet Nazarene University, IL
Ouachita Baptist University, AR
Our Lady of the Lake University, TX
Ozark Christian College, MO
Pacific Lutheran University, WA
Park University, MO
Randolph College, VA
Regent University, VA
Rhodes College, TN
Roberts Wesleyan College, NY
Sacred Heart University, CT
St. Ambrose University, IA
St. Bonaventure University, NY
St. Catherine University, MN
St. Edward's University, TX
St. John's University, NY
Saint Louis University, MO
Saint Peter's University, NJ
Saint Vincent College, PA
Samford University, AL
Schreiner University, TX
Seattle Pacific University, WA
Seattle University, WA
Siena College, NY
Simpson College, IA
Southeastern University, FL
Southern Adventist University, TN
Southwest Baptist University, MO
Southwestern College, KS
Southwestern University, TX
State University of New York College at Geneseo, NY
Taylor University, IN
Tennessee Wesleyan University, TN
Texas Christian University, TX
Texas Lutheran University, TX
Texas Wesleyan University, TX
Thomas More College, KY
Toccoa Falls College, GA
Transylvania University, KY
Trevecca Nazarene University, TN
Trinity Christian College, IL
Truett McConnell University, GA
Union College, KY
Union University, TN
University of California, Riverside, CA
University of Dallas, TX
University of Dayton, OH
University of Dubuque, IA
University of Evansville, IN
University of Hartford, CT
University of Indianapolis, IN
University of Jamestown, ND
University of Maine, ME
University of Mary Hardin-Baylor, TX
University of Mary Washington, VA
The University of North Carolina at Chapel Hill, NC
The University of North Carolina at Greensboro, NC
University of Portland, OR
University of Providence, MT
University of St. Francis, IL
University of St. Thomas, TX
The University of Scranton, PA
University of Sioux Falls, SD
University of South Carolina, SC

The University of Tennessee at Chattanooga, TN
University of the Pacific, CA
The University of Toledo, OH
The University of Tulsa, OK
Ursuline College, OH
Utah State University, UT
Valparaiso University, IN
VanderCook College of Music, IL
Vanguard University of Southern California, CA
Villanova University, PA
Virginia Wesleyan University, VA
Wake Forest University, NC
Warner Pacific College, OR
Wartburg College, IA
Washington State University, WA
Wayland Baptist University, TX
Wesleyan College, GA
Western Kentucky University, KY
Westminster College, MO
Westminster College, PA
West Texas A&M University, TX
West Virginia Wesleyan College, WV
Wheeling Jesuit University, WV
Whitworth University, WA
Williams Baptist College, AR
Wilson College, PA
Wisconsin Lutheran College, WI
Wittenberg University, OH
Young Harris College, GA
Youngstown State University, OH

Siblings of Current Students
Albertus Magnus College, CT
Albright College, PA
Alliant International University–San Diego, CA
Alma College, MI
Appalachian Bible College, WV
Augsburg University, MN
Augustana College, IL
Augustana University, SD
Aurora University, IL
Ave Maria University, FL
Baldwin Wallace University, OH
Barton College, NC
Bay Path University, MA
Becker College, MA
Belhaven University, MS
Belmont University, TN
Beloit College, WI
Benedictine University, IL
Bethel College, KS
Blue Mountain College, MS
Bryant University, RI
Buena Vista University, IA
Caldwell University, NJ
California Baptist University, CA
Campbell University, NC
Capital University, OH
Cardinal Stritch University, WI
Carlow University, PA
Carroll College, MT
Carroll University, WI
Carson-Newman University, TN
Catawba College, NC
The Catholic University of America, DC
Cedar Crest College, PA
Centenary College of Louisiana, LA
Central College, IA
Central Methodist University, MO
Chaminade University of Honolulu, HI
Chatham University, PA
Christendom College, VA

Clarke University, IA
Coe College, IA
The College of Idaho, ID
The College of New Rochelle, NY
The College of Saint Rose, NY
The College of St. Scholastica, MN
Columbia College, MO
Concordia University Texas, TX
Corban University, OR
Crossroads Bible College, IN
Culver-Stockton College, MO
Curry College, MA
Davis College, NY
Delaware Valley University, PA
DeSales University, PA
Doane University, NE
Dominican University, IL
Drexel University, PA
Drury University, MO
Eastern University, PA
Elizabethtown College, PA
Elmhurst College, IL
Elmira College, NY
Elms College, MA
Emmanuel College, GA
Emmanuel College, MA
Emory & Henry College, VA
Eureka College, IL
Faulkner University, AL
Felician University, NJ
Florida Institute of Technology, FL
Florida Southern College, FL
Franciscan University of Steubenville, OH
Franklin College, IN
Franklin Pierce University, NH
Georgian Court University, NJ
Gonzaga University, WA
Greenville University, IL
Gustavus Adolphus College, MN
Gwynedd Mercy University, PA
Hanover College, IN
Harding University, AR
Hardin-Simmons University, TX
Hartwick College, NY
Hilbert College, NY
Hood College, MD
Hope College, MI
Howard Payne University, TX
Illinois College, IL
Indiana Tech, IN
Indiana Wesleyan University, IN
Iona College, NY
Iowa Wesleyan University, IA
Ithaca College, NY
James Madison University, VA
Johnson C. Smith University, NC
Johnson University, TN
Juniata College, PA
Kansas Wesleyan University, KS
Keuka College, NY
King's College, PA
Kuyper College, MI
Lancaster Bible College, PA
Lasell College, MA
La Sierra University, CA
Lawrence University, WI
Lees-McRae College, NC
Lee University, TN
Lenoir-Rhyne University, NC
LIM College, NY
Linfield College, OR
Long Island University–LIU Brooklyn, NY
Long Island University–LIU Post, NY
Lubbock Christian University, TX
Lynn University, FL

Manchester University, IN
McDaniel College, MD
Mercer University, GA
Merrimack College, MA
Methodist University, NC
Millikin University, IL
Misericordia University, PA
Missouri Baptist University, MO
Mitchell College, CT
Molloy College, NY
Moravian College, PA
Mount Aloysius College, PA
Mount Marty College, SD
Mount Mary University, WI
Mount Mercy University, IA
Mount St. Mary's University, MD
Muskingum University, OH
Nazareth College of Rochester, NY
Newberry College, SC
New England College, NH
New Jersey Institute of Technology, NJ
Newman University, KS
Nichols College, MA
Northwest Christian University, OR
Northwestern College, IA
Northwest University, WA
Northwood University, Michigan Campus, MI
Oglethorpe University, GA
Ohio Northern University, OH
Olivet College, MI
Oral Roberts University, OK
Park University, MO
Peirce College, PA
Piedmont College, GA
Point Park University, PA
Providence College, RI
Quinnipiac University, CT
Randolph-Macon College, VA
Regent University, VA
Rockford University, IL
Rockhurst University, MO
Sacred Heart University, CT
Saint Anselm College, NH
St. Bonaventure University, NY
St. Catherine University, MN
St. Joseph's College, Long Island Campus, NY
St. Joseph's College, New York, NY
Saint Joseph's University, PA
St. Lawrence University, NY
Saint Leo University, FL
Saint Louis University, MO
Saint Martin's University, WA
Saint Mary-of-the-Woods College, IN
Saint Mary's College, IN
Saint Michael's College, VT
St. Thomas Aquinas College, NY
Samford University, AL
Schreiner University, TX
Seton Hill University, PA
Simpson College, IA
Southern New Hampshire University, NH
Southwest Baptist University, MO
Springfield College, MA
Spring Hill College, AL
Sterling College, KS
Stonehill College, MA
Suffolk University, MA
Tennessee Wesleyan University, TN
Texas Wesleyan University, TX
Thomas More College, KY
Thomas More College of Liberal Arts, NH
Toccoa Falls College, GA
Trevecca Nazarene University, TN

Trine University, IN
Truett McConnell University, GA
Union College, KY
Union University, TN
The University of Alabama at Birmingham, AL
University of Dubuque, IA
University of Evansville, IN
University of Hartford, CT
University of Jamestown, ND
University of New England, ME
University of Providence, MT
University of St. Francis, IL
University of Saint Joseph, CT
The University of Scranton, PA
University of Sioux Falls, SD
The University of Toledo, OH
The University of Tulsa, OK
Ursinus College, PA
Ursuline College, OH
Wartburg College, IA
Waynesburg University, PA
Webber International University, FL
Webster University, MO
Wesleyan College, GA
Western New England University, MA
Westminster College, MO
Whitworth University, WA
William Jessup University, CA
William Jewell College, MO
William Woods University, MO
Xavier University, OH

Spouses of Current Students

Alaska Bible College, AK
Alliant International University–San Diego, CA
Andrews University, MI
Appalachian Bible College, WV
Augustana University, SD
Aurora University, IL
The Baptist College of Florida, FL
Bethel College, KS
Blue Mountain College, MS
Boise State University, ID
Bryan College, TN
Caldwell University, NJ
Cardinal Stritch University, WI
Carroll College, MT
Carroll University, WI
Central Methodist University, MO
Clarion University of Pennsylvania, PA
The College of New Rochelle, NY
The College of St. Scholastica, MN
Columbia College, MO
Columbia International University, SC
Crossroads Bible College, IN
Curry College, MA
Davis College, NY
Elmhurst College, IL
Emmanuel College, GA
Emmanuel College, MA
Franklin College, IN
Franklin Pierce University, NH
Huntingdon College, AL
Indiana Tech, IN
Johnson University, TN
Johnson University Florida, FL
Kansas Wesleyan University, KS
Lee University, TN
Lubbock Christian University, TX
Manchester University, IN
Missouri Baptist University, MO
Mount Aloysius College, PA
Mount Marty College, SD
Newman University, KS

New Mexico State University, NM
Northwest University, WA
Ozark Christian College, MO
Piedmont International University, NC
Post University, CT
Regent University, VA
St. Catherine University, MN
St. Joseph's College, Long Island Campus, NY
St. Joseph's College, New York, NY
Saint Louis University, MO
Saint Mary-of-the-Woods College, IN
St. Thomas Aquinas College, NY
Samford University, AL
Texas Wesleyan University, TX
Trinity College of Florida, FL
Truett McConnell University, GA
Union University, TN
The University of Alabama at Birmingham, AL
University of Dubuque, IA
University of Hartford, CT
University of Jamestown, ND
University of Maine, ME
University of Mississippi, MS
University of Providence, MT
University of Sioux Falls, SD
University of Wyoming, WY
Wayne State University, MI
Wesleyan College, GA

Spouses of Deceased or Disabled Public Servants

The College of New Rochelle, NY
Eastern Washington University, WA
Francis Marion University, SC
Grand Valley State University, MI
Louisiana Tech University, LA
Michigan State University, MI
Mississippi State University, MS
New Mexico State University, NM
Northeastern State University, OK
Northern Kentucky University, KY
Southern Illinois University Carbondale, IL
Texas State University, TX
Texas Wesleyan University, TX
The University of Alabama, AL
The University of Alabama at Birmingham, AL
University of Kentucky, KY
University of Missouri–St. Louis, MO
University of South Carolina, SC
University of Utah, UT
Webster University, MO
Youngstown State University, OH

Twins

Blue Mountain College, MS
Caldwell University, NJ
Calvin College, MI
The Catholic University of America, DC
Central College, IA
The College of New Rochelle, NY
The College of Saint Rose, NY
Drexel University, PA
Elmira College, NY
Emmanuel College, GA
Long Island University–LIU Brooklyn, NY
Long Island University–LIU Post, NY
Mount Aloysius College, PA
Ohio Wesleyan University, OH
Ouachita Baptist University, AR
Randolph College, VA
Sacred Heart University, CT
St. Joseph's College, Long Island Campus, NY
St. Joseph's College, New York, NY
St. Thomas Aquinas College, NY

Simpson College, IA
Southern New Hampshire University, NH
Sterling College, KS
Texas Wesleyan University, TX
Trine University, IN
Union University, TN
The University of Alabama at Birmingham, AL
University of Hartford, CT
Virginia Polytechnic Institute and State University, VA
Westminster College, MO

Veterans

Adelphi University, NY
Agnes Scott College, GA
Alaska Pacific University, AK
Alliant International University–San Diego, CA
Amridge University, AL
Anderson University, SC
Arkansas Tech University, AR
Augustana University, SD
Aurora University, IL
Austin College, TX
Austin Peay State University, TN
Babson College, MA
Ball State University, IN
Barton College, NC
Baylor University, TX
Belhaven University, MS
Belmont University, TN
Beloit College, WI
Benedictine University, IL
Berry College, GA
Bethel University, MN
Binghamton University, State University of New York, NY
Birmingham-Southern College, AL
Bluefield College, VA
Boise State University, ID
Boston University, MA
Brown University, RI
Bryant University, RI
Buffalo State College, State University of New York, NY
Butler University, IN
Caldwell University, NJ
California Baptist University, CA
California Lutheran University, CA
California State University, Bakersfield, CA
California State University, San Bernardino, CA
California University of Pennsylvania, PA
Calvin College, MI
Cameron University, OK
Campbellsville University, KY
Campbell University, NC
Canisius College, NY
Cardinal Stritch University, WI
Carroll College, MT
The Catholic University of America, DC
Cedarville University, OH
Centenary College of Louisiana, LA
Central College, IA
Central State University, OH
Central Washington University, WA
Chowan University, NC
Christian Brothers University, TN
The Citadel, The Military College of South Carolina, SC
Claflin University, SC
Claremont McKenna College, CA
Clarion University of Pennsylvania, PA
Clarkson University, NY
Clemson University, SC

Coe College, IA
Coker College, SC
Colgate University, NY
The College at Brockport, State University
of New York, NY
The College of New Rochelle, NY
College of Staten Island of the City
University of New York, NY
Colorado State University, CO
Columbia College, MO
Columbia International University, SC
Concordia University, Nebraska, NE
Concordia University, St. Paul, MN
Concordia University Texas, TX
Concord University, WV
Corban University, OR
Culver-Stockton College, MO
Daemen College, NY
Dakota State University, SD
Dallas Baptist University, TX
Defiance College, OH
Delaware Valley University, PA
Denison University, OH
DePaul University, IL
Dickinson College, PA
Dominican University of California, CA
Drury University, MO
Duquesne University, PA
East Central University, OK
Eastern University, PA
Eastern Washington University, WA
East Texas Baptist University, TX
Elmhurst College, IL
Elmira College, NY
Elon University, NC
Emmanuel College, MA
Emory University, GA
Emporia State University, KS
The Evergreen State College, WA
Fairfield University, CT
Fairmont State University, WV
Ferris State University, MI
Florida International University, FL
Fort Hays State University, KS
Framingham State University, MA
Francis Marion University, SC
Franklin College, IN
Frostburg State University, MD
Furman University, SC
Gannon University, PA
Georgetown College, KY
Georgia Institute of Technology, GA
Georgian Court University, NJ
Georgia Southern University, GA
Glenville State College, WV
Gordon College, MA
Governors State University, IL
Grambling State University, LA
Grand Valley State University, MI
Gwynedd Mercy University, PA
Hamline University, MN
Hampden-Sydney College, VA
Hampton University, VA
Hardin-Simmons University, TX
Hartwick College, NY
High Point University, NC
Hillsdale College, MI
Hofstra University, NY
Hollins University, VA
Hood College, MD
Hope International University, CA
Huntingdon College, AL
Illinois Institute of Technology, IL
Indiana State University, IN
Indiana Tech, IN

Indiana Wesleyan University, IN
Iona College, NY
Iowa State University of Science and
Technology, IA
John Carroll University, OH
Kansas Wesleyan University, KS
Kean University, NJ
Kennesaw State University, GA
Kent State University, OH
Kent State University at Stark, OH
Kentucky State University, KY
Keuka College, NY
King's College, PA
King University, TN
Knox College, IL
La Salle University, PA
Lasell College, MA
Lawrence University, WI
Lebanon Valley College, PA
Lees-McRae College, NC
Lewis University, IL
Liberty University, VA
Lindenwood University, MO
Linfield College, OR
Long Island University–LIU Brooklyn, NY
Long Island University–LIU Post, NY
Louisiana State University and Agricultural
& Mechanical College, LA
Louisiana Tech University, LA
Loyola Marymount University, CA
Lynn University, FL
Malone University, OH
Manhattanville College, NY
Marymount Manhattan College, NY
Marymount University, VA
Maryville College, TN
Massachusetts College of Art and Design,
MA
McDaniel College, MD
McKendree University, IL
McMurry University, TX
Merrimack College, MA
Metropolitan State University of Denver, CO
Michigan State University, MI
Michigan Technological University, MI
MidAmerica Nazarene University, KS
Midwestern State University, TX
Millikin University, IL
Minot State University, ND
Missouri Baptist University, MO
Missouri Southern State University, MO
Missouri Western State University, MO
Molloy College, NY
Monmouth College, IL
Monmouth University, NJ
Montana State University Billings, MT
Montana Tech of The University of
Montana, MT
Montreat College, NC
Moravian College, PA
Morehead State University, KY
Mount Mary University, WI
Mount Mercy University, IA
Murray State University, KY
Nazareth College of Rochester, NY
Neumont College of Computer Science, UT
New England College, NH
New Jersey Institute of Technology, NJ
New Mexico State University, NM
New York Institute of Technology, NY
Nicholls State University, LA
Northern Illinois University, IL
Northern Kentucky University, KY
Northwestern College, IA
Nova Southeastern University, FL

Occidental College, CA
Ohio Northern University, OH
Oklahoma Baptist University, OK
Olivet Nazarene University, IL
Pacific University, OR
Palm Beach Atlantic University, FL
Park University, MO
Peirce College, PA
Piedmont College, GA
Piedmont International University, NC
Portland State University, OR
Post University, CT
Randolph-Macon College, VA
Regent University, VA
Robert Morris University, PA
Robert Morris University Illinois, IL
Rochester Institute of Technology, NY
Rocky Mountain College, MT
Rogers State University, OK
Sacred Heart University, CT
The Sage Colleges, NY
Saginaw Valley State University, MI
St. Ambrose University, IA
St. Edward's University, TX
St. John's College, NM
St. John's University, NY
Saint Joseph's University, PA
Saint Louis University, MO
Saint Martin's University, WA
Saint Mary's College, IN
Saint Mary's College of California, CA
St. Mary's University, TX
Saint Michael's College, VT
St. Thomas Aquinas College, NY
Samford University, AL
Sam Houston State University, TX
San Diego State University, CA
San Jose State University, CA
Savannah College of Art and Design, GA
Schreiner University, TX
Seattle Pacific University, WA
Shawnee State University, OH
Simpson College, IA
Sonoma State University, CA
South Dakota State University, SD
Southeastern Louisiana University, LA
Southeast Missouri State University, MO
Southern Adventist University, TN
Southern Illinois University Carbondale, IL
Southern New Hampshire University, NH
Southern Oregon University, OR
Southwestern College, KS
Southwestern University, TX
State University of New York College at
Geneseo, NY
Stephen F. Austin State University, TX
Stetson University, FL
Stonehill College, MA
Suffolk University, MA
Susquehanna University, PA
Tarleton State University, TX
Texas A&M University, TX
Texas A&M University–Commerce, TX
Texas A&M University–Texarkana, TX
Texas Christian University, TX
Texas Lutheran University, TX
Texas State University, TX
Texas Tech University, TX
Texas Wesleyan University, TX
Thomas College, ME
Thomas Jefferson University, PA
Thomas More College, KY
Thomas University, GA
Towson University, MD
Trinity Christian College, IL

Trinity University, TX
Union College, KY
Union University, TN
The University of Alabama at Birmingham, AL
University of Arkansas, AR
University of Bridgeport, CT
University of California, Riverside, CA
University of California, Santa Cruz, CA
University of Colorado Boulder, CO
University of Colorado Denver, CO
University of Evansville, IN
University of Hartford, CT
University of Houston–Clear Lake, TX
University of Idaho, ID
University of Illinois at Urbana–Champaign, IL
University of Indianapolis, IN
The University of Iowa, IA
The University of Kansas, KS
University of Kentucky, KY
University of Maine, ME
University of Massachusetts Amherst, MA
University of Massachusetts Boston, MA
University of Massachusetts Dartmouth, MA
University of Massachusetts Lowell, MA
University of Memphis, TN
University of Miami, FL
University of Michigan–Flint, MI
University of Mississippi, MS
University of Missouri, MO
University of Missouri–St. Louis, MO
University of Montana, MT
The University of Montana Western, MT
University of Nebraska at Kearney, NE
University of Nevada, Las Vegas, NV
The University of North Carolina at Charlotte, NC
The University of North Carolina at Greensboro, NC
University of North Dakota, ND
University of Northern Colorado, CO
University of Northern Iowa, IA
University of Oregon, OR
University of Pittsburgh at Bradford, PA
University of Puerto Rico–Bayamón, PR
University of Puget Sound, WA
University of Rochester, NY
University of St. Francis, IL
The University of Scranton, PA
University of South Carolina Aiken, SC
University of Southern Indiana, IN
University of Southern Mississippi, MS
The University of Tampa, FL
The University of Texas at Dallas, TX
The University of Texas Rio Grande Valley, TX
The University of Toledo, OH
The University of Virginia's College at Wise, VA
University of West Florida, FL
University of Wisconsin–Green Bay, WI
University of Wisconsin–La Crosse, WI
University of Wisconsin–Milwaukee, WI
University of Wisconsin–Parkside, WI
University of Wisconsin–Stevens Point, WI
University of Wisconsin–Stout, WI
University of Wisconsin–Superior, WI
University of Wyoming, WY
Ursinus College, PA
Ursuline College, OH
Vanderbilt University, TN
Vaughn College of Aeronautics and Technology, NY
Walla Walla University, WA
Washington & Jefferson College, PA

Washington State University, WA
Wayne State College, NE
Webber International University, FL
Webster University, MO
Wesleyan College, GA
Wesleyan University, CT
Western Kentucky University, KY
Western Michigan University, MI
Western Oregon University, OR
Western Washington University, WA
West Texas A&M University, TX
West Virginia Wesleyan College, WV
Whitman College, WA
Whitworth University, WA
Wichita State University, KS
William Jessup University, CA
William Paterson University of New Jersey, NJ
Wilson College, PA
Wisconsin Lutheran College, WI
Youngstown State University, OH

Veterans' Children

Agnes Scott College, GA
Alliant International University–San Diego, CA
Anderson University, SC
Arkansas Tech University, AR
Aurora University, IL
Ball State University, IN
Baylor University, TX
Belhaven University, MS
Belmont University, TN
Benedictine University, IL
Berry College, GA
Bethel University, MN
Binghamton University, State University of New York, NY
Birmingham-Southern College, AL
Bluefield College, VA
Boise State University, ID
Boston University, MA
Brown University, RI
Buffalo State College, State University of New York, NY
Butler University, IN
Caldwell University, NJ
California Baptist University, CA
California Lutheran University, CA
California State University, San Bernardino, CA
Calvin College, MI
Cameron University, OK
The Catholic University of America, DC
Centenary College of Louisiana, LA
Central College, IA
Central State University, OH
Central Washington University, WA
Chowan University, NC
Christian Brothers University, TN
The Citadel, The Military College of South Carolina, SC
Claflin University, SC
Claremont McKenna College, CA
Clarion University of Pennsylvania, PA
Coastal Carolina University, SC
Coe College, IA
Colgate University, NY
The College of Idaho, ID
The College of New Rochelle, NY
College of Staten Island of the City University of New York, NY
Columbia College, MO
Columbia International University, SC
Concordia University, Nebraska, NE
Concordia University, St. Paul, MN

Concordia University Texas, TX
Concord University, WV
Corban University, OR
Culver-Stockton College, MO
Dallas Baptist University, TX
Defiance College, OH
DePaul University, IL
DeSales University, PA
Dickinson College, PA
Dominican University of California, CA
Duquesne University, PA
East Central University, OK
Eastern University, PA
Eastern Washington University, WA
Elmhurst College, IL
Emory University, GA
Emporia State University, KS
The Evergreen State College, WA
Fairfield University, CT
Fairmont State University, WV
Florida International University, FL
Fort Hays State University, KS
Fort Lewis College, CO
Francis Marion University, SC
Franklin College, IN
Frostburg State University, MD
Georgetown College, KY
Georgia Institute of Technology, GA
Georgia Southern University, GA
Glenville State College, WV
Gordon College, MA
Grambling State University, LA
Grand Valley State University, MI
Gwynedd Mercy University, PA
Hampden-Sydney College, VA
Hampton University, VA
Hardin-Simmons University, TX
Hobart and William Smith Colleges, NY
Hofstra University, NY
Hood College, MD
Huntingdon College, AL
Illinois Institute of Technology, IL
Indiana Tech, IN
Iona College, NY
Iowa State University of Science and Technology, IA
John Carroll University, OH
Kansas Wesleyan University, KS
Kennesaw State University, GA
Kent State University, OH
Keuka College, NY
King University, TN
Lasell College, MA
Lawrence University, WI
Lees-McRae College, NC
Lewis University, IL
Lindenwood University, MO
Long Island University–LIU Brooklyn, NY
Long Island University–LIU Post, NY
Louisiana Tech University, LA
Loyola Marymount University, CA
Loyola University New Orleans, LA
Marymount Manhattan College, NY
Marymount University, VA
McKendree University, IL
McMurry University, TX
Michigan Technological University, MI
Midwestern State University, TX
Minot State University, ND
Missouri Baptist University, MO
Monmouth University, NJ
Montreat College, NC
Moravian College, PA
Morehead State University, KY
Muhlenberg College, PA
Murray State University, KY

New England College, NH
New Jersey Institute of Technology, NJ
New Mexico State University, NM
Northern Illinois University, IL
Northern Kentucky University, KY
Occidental College, CA
Old Dominion University, VA
Peirce College, PA
Piedmont College, GA
Post University, CT
Randolph-Macon College, VA
Regent University, VA
Sacred Heart University, CT
Saginaw Valley State University, MI
St. Edward's University, TX
St. John's University, NY
Saint Joseph's University, PA
St. Lawrence University, NY
Saint Martin's University, WA
Saint Mary's College of California, CA
St. Mary's University, TX
Saint Michael's College, VT
Samford University, AL
San Diego State University, CA
Savannah College of Art and Design, GA
Seattle Pacific University, WA
Siena College, NY
Simpson College, IA
South Dakota State University, SD
Southeastern Louisiana University, LA
Southern Illinois University Carbondale, IL
Southern Oregon University, OR
Southwestern University, TX
Stephen F. Austin State University, TX
Sterling College, KS
Stetson University, FL
Stonehill College, MA
Tarleton State University, TX
Texas A&M University, TX

Texas A&M University–Commerce, TX
Texas A&M University–Texarkana, TX
Texas Christian University, TX
Texas Lutheran University, TX
Texas State University, TX
Texas Tech University, TX
Texas Wesleyan University, TX
Thomas College, ME
Thomas More College, KY
Trinity University, TX
Union College, KY
Union University, TN
The University of Alabama at Birmingham, AL
University of Arkansas, AR
University of California, Riverside, CA
University of California, San Diego, CA
University of Evansville, IN
University of Hartford, CT
University of Houston–Clear Lake, TX
University of Idaho, ID
The University of Iowa, IA
University of Kentucky, KY
University of Maine, ME
University of Maine at Presque Isle, ME
University of Massachusetts Boston, MA
University of Miami, FL
University of Michigan–Flint, MI
University of Mississippi, MS
University of Missouri, MO
University of Missouri–St. Louis, MO
University of Nebraska at Kearney, NE
University of Nebraska–Lincoln, NE
University of Nevada, Las Vegas, NV
The University of North Carolina at Greensboro, NC
University of North Dakota, ND
University of Oregon, OR
University of Puerto Rico–Bayamón, PR

University of Puget Sound, WA
University of St. Francis, IL
The University of Scranton, PA
University of Southern Indiana, IN
The University of Texas at Dallas, TX
The University of Texas Rio Grande Valley, TX
The University of Toledo, OH
University of Utah, UT
The University of Virginia's College at Wise, VA
University of Wisconsin–La Crosse, WI
University of Wisconsin–Milwaukee, WI
University of Wisconsin–Stout, WI
University of Wyoming, WY
Ursinus College, PA
Vanderbilt University, TN
Vaughn College of Aeronautics and Technology, NY
Virginia Military Institute, VA
Virginia Polytechnic Institute and State University, VA
Washington & Jefferson College, PA
Washington State University, WA
Wayne State College, NE
Webster University, MO
Wesleyan University, CT
Western Illinois University, IL
Western Kentucky University, KY
Western Oregon University, OR
West Texas A&M University, TX
Wheaton College, IL
Whitman College, WA
Whitworth University, WA
William Jessup University, CA
Wilson College, PA
Wisconsin Lutheran College, WI
Youngstown State University, OH

Athletic Grants for Undergraduates

Archery

Blue Mountain College, MS	M,W
Campbellsville University, KY	M,W
Emmanuel College, GA	M,W
University of Pikeville, KY	M,W

Baseball

Abilene Christian University, TX	M
Academy of Art University, CA	M
Adams State University, CO	M
Adelphi University, NY	M
Alabama State University, AL	M
Alcorn State University, MS	M
Alice Lloyd College, KY	M
Anderson University, SC	M
Angelo State University, TX	M
Appalachian State University, NC	M
Aquinas College, MI	M
Arizona Christian University, AZ	M
Arizona State University at the Downtown Phoenix campus, AZ	M
Arizona State University at the Polytechnic campus, AZ	M
Arizona State University at the Tempe campus, AZ	M
Arizona State University at the West campus, AZ	M
Arkansas Tech University, AR	M
Auburn University, AL	M
Auburn University at Montgomery, AL	M
Augustana University, SD	M
Austin Peay State University, TN	M
Azusa Pacific University, CA	M
Baker University, KS	M
Ball State University, IN	M
Barry University, FL	M
Barton College, NC	M
Baylor University, TX	M
Bellarmine University, KY	M
Belmont University, TN	M
Bemidji State University, MN	M
Benedictine College, KS	M
Bethel College, IN	M
Bethune-Cookman University, FL	M
Binghamton University, State University of New York, NY	M
Biola University, CA	M
Bloomsburg University of Pennsylvania, PA	M
Bluefield College, VA	M
Blue Mountain College, MS	M
Boston College, MA	M
Bowling Green State University, OH	M
Bradley University, IL	M
Brigham Young University, UT	M
Bryan College, TN	M
Bryant University, RI	M
Butler University, IN	M
Caldwell University, NJ	M
California Baptist University, CA	M
California Polytechnic State University, San Luis Obispo, CA	M
California State Polytechnic University, Pomona, CA	M
California State University, Dominguez Hills, CA	M
California State University, Fullerton, CA	M
California State University, Long Beach, CA	M
California State University, Monterey Bay, CA	M
California State University, Northridge, CA	M
California State University, Sacramento, CA	M
California State University, San Bernardino, CA	M
California State University, Stanislaus, CA	M
Calumet College of Saint Joseph, IN	M
Cameron University, OK	M
Campbellsville University, KY	M
Canisius College, NY	M
Carson-Newman University, TN	M
Catawba College, NC	M
Cedarville University, OH	M
Central Connecticut State University, CT	M
Central Methodist University, MO	M
Central Michigan University, MI	M
Chestnut Hill College, PA	M
Chowan University, NC	M
Christian Brothers University, TN	M
The Citadel, The Military College of South Carolina, SC	M
Clarion University of Pennsylvania, PA	M
Clarke University, IA	M
Clemson University, SC	M
Coastal Carolina University, SC	M
Coker College, SC	M
College of Charleston, SC	M
The College of Idaho, ID	M
The College of Saint Rose, NY	M
College of the Ozarks, MO	M
The College of William and Mary, VA	M
Colorado Mesa University, CO	M
Columbia College, MO	M
Columbus State University, GA	M
Concordia University Irvine, CA	M
Concordia University, Nebraska, NE	M
Concordia University, St. Paul, MN	M
Concord University, WV	M
Corban University, OR	M
Cornerstone University, MI	M
Creighton University, NE	M
Culver-Stockton College, MO	M
Dakota State University, SD	M
Dallas Baptist University, TX	M
Davidson College, NC	M
Delaware State University, DE	M
Doane University, NE	M
Dominican College, NY	M
Drury University, MO	M
East Carolina University, NC	M
East Central University, OK	M
Eastern Michigan University, MI	M
East Stroudsburg University of Pennsylvania, PA	M
Eckerd College, FL	M
Elon University, NC	M
Embry-Riddle Aeronautical University–Daytona, FL	M
Emmanuel College, GA	M
Emporia State University, KS	M
Evangel University, MO	M
Fairfield University, CT	M
Fairleigh Dickinson University, Metropolitan Campus, NJ	M
Felician University, NJ	M
Flagler College, FL	M
Florida Agricultural and Mechanical University, FL	M
Florida Atlantic University, FL	M
Florida Gulf Coast University, FL	M
Florida Institute of Technology, FL	M
Florida International University, FL	M
Florida National University, FL	M
Florida Southern College, FL	M
Florida State University, FL	M
Fordham University, NY	M
Francis Marion University, SC	M
Franklin Pierce University, NH	M
Furman University, SC	M
Gannon University, PA	M
George Mason University, VA	M
Georgetown College, KY	M
Georgetown University, DC	M
The George Washington University, DC	M
Georgia College & State University, GA	M
Georgia Institute of Technology, GA	M
Georgia Southern University, GA	M
Georgia Southwestern State University, GA	M
Georgia State University, GA	M
Gonzaga University, WA	M
Goshen College, IN	M
Graceland University, IA	M
Grambling State University, LA	M
Grand Valley State University, MI	M
Harding University, AR	M
Harris-Stowe State University, MO	M
Hawai`i Pacific University, HI	M
High Point University, NC	M
Hillsdale College, MI	M
Hofstra University, NY	M
Houston Baptist University, TX	M
Indiana State University, IN	M
Indiana Tech, IN	M
Indiana University Bloomington, IN	M

College	
Indiana University of Pennsylvania, PA	M
Indiana University South Bend, IN	M
Indiana University Southeast, IN	M
Indiana Wesleyan University, IN	M
Inter American University of Puerto Rico, Bayamón Campus, PR	M
Iona College, NY	M
Jackson State University, MS	M
Jacksonville University, FL	M
James Madison University, VA	M
Judson University, IL	M
Kansas State University, KS	M
Kansas Wesleyan University, KS	M
Kennesaw State University, GA	M
Kent State University, OH	M
Kentucky State University, KY	M
King University, TN	M
Kutztown University of Pennsylvania, PA	M
Lamar University, TX	M
La Salle University, PA	M
Lawrence Technological University, MI	M
Lee University, TN	M
Lehigh University, PA	M
Le Moyne College, NY	M
Lenoir-Rhyne University, NC	M
Lewis University, IL	M
Liberty University, VA	M
Lincoln Memorial University, TN	M
Lincoln University, PA	M
Lindenwood University, MO	M
Lindsey Wilson College, KY	M
Lipscomb University, TN	M
Lock Haven University of Pennsylvania, PA	M
Long Island University–LIU Brooklyn, NY	M
Long Island University–LIU Post, NY	M
Longwood University, VA	M
Louisiana State University and Agricultural & Mechanical College, LA	M
Loyola Marymount University, CA	M
Lubbock Christian University, TX	M
Lynn University, FL	M
Lyon College, AR	M
Malone University, OH	M
Manhattan College, NY	M
Mansfield University of Pennsylvania, PA	M
Marist College, NY	M
Marshall University, WV	M
Marymount California University, CA	M
Maryville University of Saint Louis, MO	M
McKendree University, IL	M
Mercer University, GA	M
Mercy College, NY	M
Merrimack College, MA	M
Metropolitan State University of Denver, CO	M
Miami University, OH	M
Michigan State University, MI	M
MidAmerica Nazarene University, KS	M
Middle Georgia State University, GA	M
Middle Tennessee State University, TN	M
Millersville University of Pennsylvania, PA	M
Milligan College, TN	M
Minot State University, ND	M
Mississippi State University, MS	M
Missouri Baptist University, MO	M
Missouri State University, MO	M
Missouri University of Science and Technology, MO	M
Missouri Valley College, MO	M
Missouri Western State University, MO	M
Molloy College, NY	M
Morehead State University, KY	M
Morehouse College, GA	M
Morningside College, IA	M
Mount Marty College, SD	M
Mount Mercy University, IA	M
Mount St. Mary's University, MD	M
Mount Vernon Nazarene University, OH	M
Murray State University, KY	M
Newberry College, SC	M
New Jersey Institute of Technology, NJ	M
Newman University, KS	M
New Mexico Highlands University, NM	M
New Mexico State University, NM	M
New York Institute of Technology, NY	M
Niagara University, NY	M
North Carolina State University, NC	M
Northeastern State University, OK	M
Northern Illinois University, IL	M
Northern Kentucky University, KY	M
Northern State University, SD	M
Northwestern College, IA	M
Northwest Nazarene University, ID	M
Nova Southeastern University, FL	M
Oakland City University, IN	M
The Ohio State University, OH	M
Ohio University, OH	M
Oklahoma Baptist University, OK	M
Oklahoma Christian University, OK	M
Oklahoma City University, OK	M
Oklahoma State University, OK	M
Old Dominion University, VA	M
Olivet Nazarene University, IL	M
Oral Roberts University, OK	M
Oregon State University, OR	M
Ouachita Baptist University, AR	M
Our Lady of the Lake University, TX	M
Palm Beach Atlantic University, FL	M
Penn State University Park, PA	M
Pepperdine University, CA	M
Pfeiffer University, NC	M
Pittsburg State University, KS	M
Point Loma Nazarene University, CA	M
Point Park University, PA	M
Post University, CT	M
Prairie View A&M University, TX	M
Presbyterian College, SC	M
Purdue University, IN	M
Queens College of the City University of New York, NY	M
Quinnipiac University, CT	M
Radford University, VA	M
Regis University, CO	M
Rice University, TX	M
Rider University, NJ	M
Robert Morris University Illinois, IL	M
Rockhurst University, MO	M
Rogers State University, OK	M
Rollins College, FL	M
Rutgers University–New Brunswick, NJ	M
Sacred Heart University, CT	M
Saginaw Valley State University, MI	M
St. Ambrose University, IA	M
St. Andrews University, NC	M
Saint Augustine's University, NC	M
St. Bonaventure University, NY	M
St. John's University, NY	M
Saint Joseph's University, PA	M
Saint Leo University, FL	M
Saint Louis University, MO	M
Saint Martin's University, WA	M
Saint Mary's College of California, CA	M
St. Mary's University, TX	M
Saint Peter's University, NJ	M
St. Thomas Aquinas College, NY	M
St. Thomas University, FL	M
Samford University, AL	M
Sam Houston State University, TX	M
San Diego State University, CA	M
San Francisco State University, CA	M
Santa Clara University, CA	M
Seton Hill University, PA	M
Shawnee State University, OH	M
Shepherd University, WV	M
Shippensburg University of Pennsylvania, PA	M
Siena College, NY	M
Slippery Rock University of Pennsylvania, PA	M
Sonoma State University, CA	M
Southeastern Louisiana University, LA	M
Southeastern Oklahoma State University, OK	M
Southeastern University, FL	M
Southeast Missouri State University, MO	M
Southern Arkansas University–Magnolia, AR	M
Southern Illinois University Carbondale, IL	M
Southwest Baptist University, MO	M
Southwestern College, KS	M
Spring Hill College, AL	M
Stanford University, CA	M
Stephen F. Austin State University, TX	M
Stetson University, FL	M
Stonehill College, MA	M
Stony Brook University, State University of New York, NY	M
Tarleton State University, TX	M
Taylor University, IN	M
Tennessee Technological University, TN	M
Tennessee Wesleyan University, TN	M
Texas A&M International University, TX	M
Texas A&M University, TX	M

Texas A&M University–Corpus Christi, TX	M	University of Minnesota, Duluth, MN	M	University of Washington, WA	M
Texas A&M University–Texarkana, TX	M,W	University of Minnesota, Twin Cities Campus, MN	M	The University of West Alabama, AL	M
Texas Christian University, TX	M	University of Missouri, MO	M	University of West Georgia, GA	M
Texas State University, TX	M	University of Missouri–St. Louis, MO	M	University of Wisconsin–Milwaukee, WI	M
Texas Tech University, TX	M	University of Montevallo, AL	M	University of Wisconsin–Parkside, WI	M
Thomas University, GA	M	University of Nebraska at Kearney, NE	M	Upper Iowa University, IA	M
Tiffin University, OH	M	University of Nebraska–Lincoln, NE	M	Utah Valley University, UT	M
Towson University, MD	M	University of Nevada, Las Vegas, NV	M	Valdosta State University, GA	M
Trevecca Nazarene University, TN	M	University of Nevada, Reno, NV	M	Valley City State University, ND	M
Trinity Christian College, IL	M	University of New Haven, CT	M	Valparaiso University, IN	M
Troy University, AL	M	University of New Orleans, LA	M	Vanderbilt University, TN	M
Truett McConnell University, GA	M	University of North Alabama, AL	M	Vanguard University of Southern California, CA	M
Truman State University, MO	M	University of North Carolina at Asheville, NC	M	Villanova University, PA	M
Tulane University, LA	M	The University of North Carolina at Chapel Hill, NC	M	Virginia Commonwealth University, VA	M
Union University, TN	M	The University of North Carolina at Charlotte, NC	M	Virginia Military Institute, VA	M
University at Albany, State University of New York, NY	M	The University of North Carolina at Greensboro, NC	M	Wake Forest University, NC	M
The University of Alabama, AL	M	The University of North Carolina at Pembroke, NC	M	Washington State University, WA	M
The University of Alabama at Birmingham, AL	M	The University of North Carolina Wilmington, NC	M	Wayland Baptist University, TX	M
University of Arkansas, AR	M	University of Northern Colorado, CO	M	Wayne State College, NE	M
University of Bridgeport, CT	M	University of North Florida, FL	M	Wayne State University, MI	M
University of California, Davis, CA	M	University of North Georgia, GA	M	Webber International University, FL	M
University of California, Irvine, CA	M	University of Notre Dame, IN	M	West Chester University of Pennsylvania, PA	M
University of California, Los Angeles, CA	M	University of Oklahoma, OK	M	Western Illinois University, IL	M
University of California, Riverside, CA	M	University of Oregon, OR	M	Western Kentucky University, KY	M
University of California, Santa Barbara, CA	M	University of Pikeville, KY	M	Western Michigan University, MI	M
University of Central Arkansas, AR	M	University of Pittsburgh, PA	M	Western Oregon University, OR	M
University of Central Florida, FL	M	University of Rhode Island, RI	M	Westmont College, CA	M
University of Central Missouri, MO	M	University of Richmond, VA	M	West Texas A&M University, TX	M
University of Central Oklahoma, OK	M	University of St. Francis, IL	M	West Virginia University, WV	M
University of Cincinnati, OH	M	University of San Diego, CA	M	West Virginia University Institute of Technology, WV	M
University of Colorado Colorado Springs, CO	M	University of San Francisco, CA	M	West Virginia Wesleyan College, WV	M
University of Dayton, OH	M	University of Science and Arts of Oklahoma, OK	M	Wichita State University, KS	M
University of Evansville, IN	M	University of Sioux Falls, SD	M	William Jewell College, MO	M
The University of Findlay, OH	M	University of South Carolina, SC	M	William Woods University, MO	M
University of Florida, FL	M	University of South Carolina Aiken, SC	M	Winona State University, MN	M
University of Georgia, GA	M	University of Southern California, CA	M	Winthrop University, SC	M
University of Hartford, CT	M	University of Southern Indiana, IN	M	Wofford College, SC	M
University of Hawaii at Manoa, HI	M	University of Southern Mississippi, MS	M	Wright State University, OH	M
University of Houston, TX	M	The University of Tampa, FL	M	Youngstown State University, OH	M
University of Illinois at Chicago, IL	M	The University of Tennessee, TN	M		
University of Illinois at Springfield, IL	M	The University of Tennessee at Martin, TN	M	**Basketball**	
University of Jamestown, ND	M	The University of Texas at Austin, TX	M	Abilene Christian University, TX	M,W
The University of Kansas, KS	M	The University of Texas at San Antonio, TX	M	Academy of Art University, CA	M,W
University of Kentucky, KY	M	The University of Texas of the Permian Basin, TX	M	Adams State University, CO	M,W
University of Louisiana at Monroe, LA	M	University of the Incarnate Word, TX	M	Adelphi University, NY	M,W
University of Louisville, KY	M	University of the Pacific, CA	M	Alabama State University, AL	M,W
University of Maine, ME	M	The University of Toledo, OH	M	Alcorn State University, MS	M,W
University of Maryland, Baltimore County, MD	M	University of Utah, UT	M	Alice Lloyd College, KY	M,W
University of Maryland, College Park, MD	M	University of Virginia, VA	M	American University, DC	M,W
University of Massachusetts Amherst, MA	M	The University of Virginia's College at Wise, VA	M	Anderson University, SC	M,W
University of Massachusetts Lowell, MA	M			Angelo State University, TX	M,W
University of Memphis, TN	M			Appalachian State University, NC	M,W
University of Miami, FL	M			Aquinas College, MI	M,W
University of Michigan, MI	M			Arizona Christian University, AZ	M,W
University of Minnesota, Crookston, MN	M			Arizona State University at the Downtown Phoenix campus, AZ	M,W
				Arizona State University at the Polytechnic campus, AZ	M,W
				Arizona State University at the Tempe campus, AZ	M,W
				Arizona State University at the West campus, AZ	M,W
				Arkansas Tech University, AR	M,W
				Assumption College, MA	M,W
				Auburn University, AL	M,W

College	
Auburn University at Montgomery, AL	M,W
Augustana University, SD	M,W
Austin Peay State University, TN	M,W
Azusa Pacific University, CA	M,W
Baker University, KS	M,W
Ball State University, IN	M,W
Barry University, FL	M,W
Barton College, NC	M,W
Baylor University, TX	M,W
Bellarmine University, KY	M,W
Belmont University, TN	M,W
Bemidji State University, MN	M,W
Benedictine College, KS	M,W
Bentley University, MA	M,W
Bethel College, IN	M,W
Bethel College, KS	M,W
Bethune-Cookman University, FL	M,W
Binghamton University, State University of New York, NY	M,W
Biola University, CA	M,W
Black Hills State University, SD	M,W
Bloomsburg University of Pennsylvania, PA	M,W
Bluefield College, VA	M,W
Blue Mountain College, MS	M,W
Boise State University, ID	M,W
Boston College, MA	M,W
Boston University, MA	M,W
Bowie State University, MD	M,W
Bowling Green State University, OH	M,W
Bradley University, IL	M,W
Brenau University, GA	W
Brigham Young University, UT	M,W
Bryan College, TN	M,W
Bryant University, RI	M,W
Bucknell University, PA	M,W
Butler University, IN	M,W
Caldwell University, NJ	M,W
California Baptist University, CA	M,W
California Polytechnic State University, San Luis Obispo, CA	M,W
California State Polytechnic University, Pomona, CA	M,W
California State University, Dominguez Hills, CA	M,W
California State University, Fullerton, CA	M,W
California State University, Long Beach, CA	M,W
California State University Maritime Academy, CA	M,W
California State University, Monterey Bay, CA	M,W
California State University, Northridge, CA	M,W
California State University, Sacramento, CA	M,W
California State University, San Bernardino, CA	M,W
California State University, Stanislaus, CA	M,W
Calumet College of Saint Joseph, IN	M,W
Cameron University, OK	M,W
Campbellsville University, KY	M,W
Canisius College, NY	M,W
Cardinal Stritch University, WI	M,W
Carlow University, PA	M,W
Carroll College, MT	M,W
Carson-Newman University, TN	M,W
Catawba College, NC	M,W
Cedarville University, OH	M,W

College	
Central Connecticut State University, CT	M,W
Central Methodist University, MO	M,W
Central Michigan University, MI	M,W
Central State University, OH	M,W
Chaminade University of Honolulu, HI	M,W
Chestnut Hill College, PA	M,W
Chowan University, NC	M,W
Christian Brothers University, TN	M,W
The Citadel, The Military College of South Carolina, SC	M
Clarion University of Pennsylvania, PA	M,W
Clarke University, IA	M,W
Clayton State University, GA	M,W
Clemson University, SC	M,W
Cleveland State University, OH	M,W
Coastal Carolina University, SC	M,W
Coker College, SC	M,W
Colgate University, NY	M,W
College of Charleston, SC	M,W
College of Coastal Georgia, GA	M,W
The College of Idaho, ID	M,W
College of Saint Mary, NE	W
The College of Saint Rose, NY	M,W
College of the Holy Cross, MA	M,W
College of the Ozarks, MO	M,W
The College of William and Mary, VA	M,W
Colorado Mesa University, CO	M,W
Colorado State University, CO	M,W
Columbia College, MO	M,W
Columbus State University, GA	M,W
Concordia University Irvine, CA	M,W
Concordia University, Nebraska, NE	M,W
Concordia University, St. Paul, MN	M,W
Concord University, WV	M,W
Converse College, SC	W
Corban University, OR	M,W
Cornerstone University, MI	M,W
Creighton University, NE	M,W
Culver-Stockton College, MO	M,W
Daemen College, NY	M,W
Dakota State University, SD	M,W
Dallas Baptist University, TX	M
Davidson College, NC	M,W
Delaware State University, DE	M,W
DePaul University, IL	M,W
Doane University, NE	M,W
Dominican College, NY	M,W
Dominican University of California, CA	M,W
Drake University, IA	M,W
Drexel University, PA	M,W
Drury University, MO	M,W
Duquesne University, PA	M,W
East Carolina University, NC	M,W
East Central University, OK	M,W
Eastern Michigan University, MI	M,W
Eastern Oregon University, OR	M,W
Eastern Washington University, WA	M,W
East Stroudsburg University of Pennsylvania, PA	M,W
Eckerd College, FL	M,W
Elon University, NC	M,W
Embry-Riddle Aeronautical University–Daytona, FL	M,W
Emmanuel College, GA	M,W
Emporia State University, KS	M,W
Evangel University, MO	M,W
The Evergreen State College, WA	M,W
Fairfield University, CT	M,W

College	
Fairleigh Dickinson University, Metropolitan Campus, NJ	M,W
Felician University, NJ	M,W
Ferris State University, MI	M,W
Flagler College, FL	M,W
Florida Agricultural and Mechanical University, FL	M,W
Florida Atlantic University, FL	M,W
Florida Gulf Coast University, FL	M,W
Florida Institute of Technology, FL	M,W
Florida International University, FL	M,W
Florida National University, FL	M
Florida Southern College, FL	M,W
Florida State University, FL	M,W
Fordham University, NY	M,W
Fort Lewis College, CO	M,W
Francis Marion University, SC	M,W
Franklin Pierce University, NH	M,W
Furman University, SC	M,W
Gannon University, PA	M,W
George Mason University, VA	M,W
Georgetown College, KY	M,W
Georgetown University, DC	M,W
The George Washington University, DC	M,W
Georgia College & State University, GA	M,W
Georgia Institute of Technology, GA	M,W
Georgian Court University, NJ	M,W
Georgia Southern University, GA	M,W
Georgia Southwestern State University, GA	M,W
Georgia State University, GA	M,W
Gonzaga University, WA	M,W
Goshen College, IN	M,W
Governors State University, IL	M,W
Graceland University, IA	M,W
Grambling State University, LA	M,W
Grand Valley State University, MI	M,W
Hampton University, VA	M,W
Harding University, AR	M,W
Harris-Stowe State University, MO	M,W
Hawai`i Pacific University, HI	M,W
High Point University, NC	M,W
Hillsdale College, MI	M,W
Hofstra University, NY	M,W
Holy Family University, PA	M,W
Hope International University, CA	M,W
Houston Baptist University, TX	M,W
Humboldt State University, CA	M,W
Idaho State University, ID	M,W
Indiana State University, IN	M,W
Indiana Tech, IN	M,W
Indiana University Bloomington, IN	M,W
Indiana University Northwest, IN	M,W
Indiana University of Pennsylvania, PA	M,W
Indiana University–Purdue University Indianapolis, IN	M,W
Indiana University South Bend, IN	M,W
Indiana University Southeast, IN	M,W
Indiana Wesleyan University, IN	M,W
Inter American University of Puerto Rico, Bayamón Campus, PR	M,W
Iona College, NY	M,W
Iowa State University of Science and Technology, IA	M,W
Jackson State University, MS	M,W
Jacksonville University, FL	M,W

James Madison University, VA	M,W
John Brown University, AR	M,W
Johnson C. Smith University, NC	M,W
Judson University, IL	M,W
Kansas State University, KS	M,W
Kansas Wesleyan University, KS	M,W
Kennesaw State University, GA	M,W
Kent State University, OH	M,W
Kentucky State University, KY	M,W
King University, TN	M,W
Kutztown University of Pennsylvania, PA	M,W
Lamar University, TX	M,W
La Salle University, PA	M,W
Lawrence Technological University, MI	M,W
Lee University, TN	M,W
Lehigh University, PA	M,W
Le Moyne College, NY	M,W
Lenoir-Rhyne University, NC	M,W
Lewis University, IL	M,W
Liberty University, VA	M,W
Life University, GA	M,W
Lincoln Memorial University, TN	M,W
Lincoln University, MO	M,W
Lincoln University, PA	M,W
Lindenwood University, MO	M,W
Lindsey Wilson College, KY	M,W
Lipscomb University, TN	M,W
Lock Haven University of Pennsylvania, PA	M,W
Long Island University–LIU Brooklyn, NY	M,W
Long Island University–LIU Post, NY	M,W
Longwood University, VA	M,W
Louisiana State University and Agricultural & Mechanical College, LA	M,W
Loyola Marymount University, CA	M,W
Loyola University Chicago, IL	M,W
Loyola University New Orleans, LA	M,W
Lubbock Christian University, TX	M,W
Lynn University, FL	M,W
Lyon College, AR	M,W
Malone University, OH	M,W
Manhattan College, NY	M,W
Mansfield University of Pennsylvania, PA	M,W
Marist College, NY	M,W
Marquette University, WI	M,W
Marshall University, WV	M,W
Maryville University of Saint Louis, MO	M,W
McKendree University, IL	M,W
Mercer University, GA	M,W
Mercy College, NY	M,W
Merrimack College, MA	M,W
Metropolitan State University of Denver, CO	M,W
Miami University, OH	M,W
Michigan State University, MI	M,W
Michigan Technological University, MI	M,W
MidAmerica Nazarene University, KS	M,W
Middle Georgia State University, GA	M,W
Middle Tennessee State University, TN	M,W
Millersville University of Pennsylvania, PA	M,W
Milligan College, TN	M,W

Minnesota State University Moorhead, MN	M,W
Minot State University, ND	M,W
Mississippi State University, MS	M,W
Missouri Baptist University, MO	M,W
Missouri State University, MO	M,W
Missouri University of Science and Technology, MO	M,W
Missouri Valley College, MO	M,W
Missouri Western State University, MO	M,W
Molloy College, NY	M,W
Montana Tech of The University of Montana, MT	M,W
Morehead State University, KY	M,W
Morehouse College, GA	M
Morningside College, IA	M,W
Mount Marty College, SD	M,W
Mount Mercy University, IA	M,W
Mount St. Mary's University, MD	M,W
Mount Vernon Nazarene University, OH	M,W
Murray State University, KY	M,W
Newberry College, SC	M,W
New Jersey Institute of Technology, NJ	M,W
Newman University, KS	M,W
New Mexico Highlands University, NM	M,W
New Mexico State University, NM	M,W
New York Institute of Technology, NY	M,W
Niagara University, NY	M,W
North Carolina State University, NC	M,W
Northeastern State University, OK	M,W
Northern Arizona University, AZ	M,W
Northern Illinois University, IL	M,W
Northern Kentucky University, KY	M,W
Northern State University, SD	M,W
Northwest Christian University, OR	M,W
Northwestern College, IA	M,W
Northwest Missouri State University, MO	M,W
Northwest Nazarene University, ID	M,W
Northwest University, WA	M,W
Nova Southeastern University, FL	M,W
Oakland City University, IN	M,W
The Ohio State University, OH	M,W
Ohio University, OH	M,W
Oklahoma Baptist University, OK	M,W
Oklahoma Christian University, OK	M,W
Oklahoma City University, OK	M,W
Oklahoma State University, OK	M,W
Old Dominion University, VA	M,W
Olivet Nazarene University, IL	M,W
Oral Roberts University, OK	M,W
Oregon State University, OR	M,W
Ouachita Baptist University, AR	M,W
Our Lady of the Lake University, TX	M,W
Palm Beach Atlantic University, FL	M,W
Penn State University Park, PA	M,W
Pepperdine University, CA	M,W
Pfeiffer University, NC	M,W
Pittsburg State University, KS	M,W
Point Loma Nazarene University, CA	M,W
Point Park University, PA	M,W
Post University, CT	M,W
Prairie View A&M University, TX	M,W
Presbyterian College, SC	M,W
Providence College, RI	M,W

Purdue University, IN	M,W
Queens College of the City University of New York, NY	M,W
Quinnipiac University, CT	M,W
Radford University, VA	M,W
Regis University, CO	M,W
Rice University, TX	M,W
Rider University, NJ	M,W
Robert Morris University, PA	M,W
Robert Morris University Illinois, IL	M,W
Roberts Wesleyan College, NY	M,W
Rockhurst University, MO	M,W
Rocky Mountain College, MT	M,W
Rogers State University, OK	M,W
Rollins College, FL	M,W
Rutgers University–New Brunswick, NJ	M,W
Sacred Heart University, CT	M,W
Saginaw Valley State University, MI	M,W
St. Ambrose University, IA	M,W
St. Andrews University, NC	M,W
Saint Augustine's University, NC	M,W
St. Bonaventure University, NY	M,W
St. John's University, NY	M,W
Saint Joseph's University, PA	M,W
Saint Leo University, FL	M,W
St. Louis College of Pharmacy, MO	M,W
Saint Louis University, MO	M,W
Saint Martin's University, WA	M,W
Saint Mary-of-the-Woods College, IN	W
Saint Mary's College of California, CA	M,W
St. Mary's University, TX	M,W
Saint Michael's College, VT	M,W
Saint Peter's University, NJ	M,W
St. Thomas Aquinas College, NY	M,W
St. Thomas University, FL	M,W
Samford University, AL	M,W
Sam Houston State University, TX	M,W
San Diego State University, CA	M,W
San Francisco State University, CA	M,W
Santa Clara University, CA	M,W
Seattle Pacific University, WA	M,W
Seattle University, WA	M,W
Seton Hill University, PA	M,W
Shawnee State University, OH	M,W
Shepherd University, WV	M,W
Shippensburg University of Pennsylvania, PA	M,W
Siena College, NY	M,W
Slippery Rock University of Pennsylvania, PA	M,W
Sonoma State University, CA	M,W
Southeastern Louisiana University, LA	M,W
Southeastern Oklahoma State University, OK	M,W
Southeastern University, FL	M,W
Southeast Missouri State University, MO	M,W
Southern Arkansas University–Magnolia, AR	M,W
Southern Illinois University Carbondale, IL	M,W
Southern Methodist University, TX	M,W
Southern Utah University, UT	M,W
Southwest Baptist University, MO	M,W
Southwestern College, KS	M,W

Spring Hill College, AL	M,W	University of Idaho, ID	M,W	University of Richmond, VA	M,W
Stanford University, CA	M,W	University of Illinois at Chicago, IL	M,W	University of St. Francis, IL	M,W
Stephen F. Austin State University, TX	M,W	University of Illinois at Springfield, IL	M,W	University of St. Thomas, TX	M,W
Stetson University, FL	M,W	University of Jamestown, ND	M,W	University of San Diego, CA	M,W
Stonehill College, MA	M,W	The University of Kansas, KS	M,W	University of San Francisco, CA	M,W
Stony Brook University, State University of New York, NY	M,W	University of Kentucky, KY	M,W	University of Science and Arts of Oklahoma, OK	M,W
Syracuse University, NY	M,W	University of Louisiana at Monroe, LA	M,W	University of Sioux Falls, SD	M,W
Tarleton State University, TX	M,W	University of Louisville, KY	M,W	University of South Carolina, SC	M,W
Taylor University, IN	M,W	University of Maine, ME	M,W	University of South Carolina Aiken, SC	M,W
Temple University, PA	M,W	University of Maryland, Baltimore County, MD	M,W	University of South Dakota, SD	M,W
Tennessee Technological University, TN	M,W	University of Maryland, College Park, MD	M,W	University of Southern California, CA	M,W
Tennessee Wesleyan University, TN	M,W	University of Massachusetts Amherst, MA	M,W	University of Southern Indiana, IN	M,W
Texas A&M International University, TX	M,W	University of Massachusetts Lowell, MA	M,W	University of Southern Mississippi, MS	M,W
Texas A&M University, TX	M,W	University of Memphis, TN	M,W	The University of Tampa, FL	M,W
Texas A&M University–Commerce, TX	M,W	University of Miami, FL	M,W	The University of Tennessee, TN	M,W
Texas A&M University–Corpus Christi, TX	M,W	University of Michigan, MI	M,W	The University of Tennessee at Chattanooga, TN	M,W
Texas Christian University, TX	M,W	University of Michigan–Dearborn, MI	M,W	The University of Tennessee at Martin, TN	M,W
Texas State University, TX	M,W	University of Minnesota, Crookston, MN	M,W	The University of Texas at Austin, TX	M,W
Texas Tech University, TX	M,W	University of Minnesota, Duluth, MN	M,W	The University of Texas at El Paso, TX	M,W
Texas Woman's University, TX	W	University of Minnesota, Twin Cities Campus, MN	M,W	The University of Texas at San Antonio, TX	M,W
Tiffin University, OH	M,W	University of Missouri, MO	M,W	The University of Texas of the Permian Basin, TX	M,W
Towson University, MD	M,W	University of Missouri–St. Louis, MO	M,W	University of the Incarnate Word, TX	M,W
Trevecca Nazarene University, TN	M,W	University of Montana, MT	M,W	University of the Pacific, CA	M,W
Trinity Christian College, IL	M,W	University of Montevallo, AL	M,W	The University of Toledo, OH	M,W
Troy University, AL	M,W	University of Nebraska at Kearney, NE	M,W	The University of Tulsa, OK	M,W
Truett McConnell University, GA	M,W	University of Nebraska–Lincoln, NE	M,W	University of Utah, UT	M,W
Truman State University, MO	M,W	University of Nevada, Las Vegas, NV	M,W	University of Vermont, VT	M,W
Tulane University, LA	M,W	University of Nevada, Reno, NV	M,W	University of Virginia, VA	M,W
Union University, TN	M,W	University of New Hampshire, NH	M,W	The University of Virginia's College at Wise, VA	M,W
University at Albany, State University of New York, NY	M,W	University of New Haven, CT	M,W	University of Washington, WA	M,W
University at Buffalo, the State University of New York, NY	M,W	University of New Orleans, LA	M,W	The University of West Alabama, AL	M,W
The University of Akron, OH	M,W	University of North Alabama, AL	M,W	University of West Georgia, GA	M,W
The University of Alabama, AL	M,W	University of North Carolina at Asheville, NC	M,W	University of Wisconsin–Madison, WI	M,W
The University of Alabama at Birmingham, AL	M,W	The University of North Carolina at Chapel Hill, NC	M,W	University of Wisconsin–Milwaukee, WI	M,W
University of Alaska Fairbanks, AK	M,W	The University of North Carolina at Charlotte, NC	M,W	University of Wisconsin–Parkside, WI	M,W
University of Arkansas, AR	M,W	The University of North Carolina at Greensboro, NC	M,W	University of Wyoming, WY	M,W
University of Bridgeport, CT	M,W	The University of North Carolina at Pembroke, NC	M,W	Upper Iowa University, IA	M,W
University of California, Davis, CA	M,W	The University of North Carolina Wilmington, NC	M,W	Ursuline College, OH	W
University of California, Irvine, CA	M,W	University of North Dakota, ND	M,W	Utah State University, UT	M,W
University of California, Los Angeles, CA	M,W	University of Northern Colorado, CO	M,W	Utah Valley University, UT	M,W
University of California, Riverside, CA	M,W	University of Northern Iowa, IA	M,W	Valdosta State University, GA	M,W
University of California, Santa Barbara, CA	M,W	University of North Florida, FL	M,W	Valley City State University, ND	M,W
University of Central Arkansas, AR	M,W	University of North Georgia, GA	M,W	Valparaiso University, IN	M,W
University of Central Florida, FL	M,W	University of North Texas, TX	M,W	Vanderbilt University, TN	M,W
University of Central Missouri, MO	M,W	University of Notre Dame, IN	M,W	Vanguard University of Southern California, CA	M,W
University of Central Oklahoma, OK	M,W	University of Oklahoma, OK	M,W	Villanova University, PA	M,W
University of Cincinnati, OH	M,W	University of Oregon, OR	M,W	Virginia Commonwealth University, VA	M,W
University of Colorado Boulder, CO	M,W	University of Pikeville, KY	M,W	Virginia Military Institute, VA	M
University of Colorado Colorado Springs, CO	M,W	University of Pittsburgh, PA	M,W	Wake Forest University, NC	M,W
University of Dayton, OH	M,W	University of Providence, MT	M,W	Warner Pacific College, OR	M,W
University of Denver, CO	M,W	University of Rhode Island, RI	M	Washington State University, WA	M,W
University of Evansville, IN	M,W			Wayland Baptist University, TX	M,W
The University of Findlay, OH	M,W			Wayne State College, NE	M,W
University of Florida, FL	M,W			Wayne State University, MI	M,W
University of Georgia, GA	M,W			Webber International University, FL	M,W
University of Hartford, CT	M,W				
University of Hawaii at Manoa, HI	M,W				
University of Houston, TX	M,W				

Weber State University, UT	M,W
West Chester University of Pennsylvania, PA	M,W
Western Illinois University, IL	M,W
Western Kentucky University, KY	M,W
Western Michigan University, MI	M,W
Western Oregon University, OR	M,W
Western State Colorado University, CO	M,W
Western Washington University, WA	M,W
Westminster College, UT	M,W
Westmont College, CA	M,W
West Texas A&M University, TX	M,W
West Virginia University, WV	M,W
West Virginia University Institute of Technology, WV	M,W
West Virginia Wesleyan College, WV	M,W
Wichita State University, KS	M,W
William Jewell College, MO	M,W
William Woods University, MO	M,W
Winona State University, MN	M,W
Winthrop University, SC	M,W
Wofford College, SC	M,W
Wright State University, OH	M,W
Youngstown State University, OH	M,W

Bowling

Adelphi University, NY	W
Alabama State University, AL	W
Aquinas College, MI	M,W
Baker University, KS	W
Bethune-Cookman University, FL	W
Blue Mountain College, MS	M,W
Caldwell University, NJ	W
Calumet College of Saint Joseph, IN	M,W
Campbellsville University, KY	M,W
Chestnut Hill College, PA	W
Chowan University, NC	W
Clarke University, IA	M,W
College of Saint Mary, NE	W
Cornerstone University, MI	M,W
Culver-Stockton College, MO	M,W
Daemen College, NY	W
Delaware State University, DE	W
Duquesne University, PA	W
Emmanuel College, GA	M,W
Fairleigh Dickinson University, Metropolitan Campus, NJ	W
Felician University, NJ	W
Florida Agricultural and Mechanical University, FL	W
Grambling State University, LA	W
Hampton University, VA	W
Indiana Tech, IN	M,W
Jackson State University, MS	W
Johnson C. Smith University, NC	W
Judson University, IL	M,W
Kansas Wesleyan University, KS	M,W
Kutztown University of Pennsylvania, PA	W
Lawrence Technological University, MI	M,W
Lewis University, IL	W
Lincoln Memorial University, TN	M,W
Lincoln University, MO	W
Lindenwood University, MO	M,W
Lindsey Wilson College, KY	M,W
Long Island University–LIU Brooklyn, NY	W
Long Island University–LIU Post, NY	W

Maryville University of Saint Louis, MO	W
McKendree University, IL	W
Missouri Baptist University, MO	M,W
Molloy College, NY	W
Mount Mercy University, IA	M,W
Mount St. Mary's University, MD	W
Newman University, KS	M,W
Post University, CT	W
Prairie View A&M University, TX	W
Robert Morris University Illinois, IL	M,W
Roberts Wesleyan College, NY	W
Sacred Heart University, CT	W
St. Ambrose University, IA	M,W
Saint Augustine's University, NC	W
Sam Houston State University, TX	W
Savannah College of Art and Design, GA	M,W
Stephen F. Austin State University, TX	W
Tennessee Wesleyan University, TN	M,W
The University of Alabama at Birmingham, AL	W
University of Central Missouri, MO	M,W
University of Nebraska–Lincoln, NE	W
University of Pikeville, KY	M,W
University of St. Francis, IL	M,W
Ursuline College, OH	W
Valparaiso University, IN	W
Vanderbilt University, TN	W
Webber International University, FL	M,W
West Texas A&M University, TX	M,W
Wichita State University, KS	M,W

Cheerleading

Adelphi University, NY	W
Alabama State University, AL	M,W
Anderson University, SC	W
Aquinas College, MI	M,W
Arizona Christian University, AZ	W
Arkansas Tech University, AR	M,W
Auburn University at Montgomery, AL	M,W
Austin Peay State University, TN	M,W
Baker University, KS	M,W
Baylor University, TX	M,W
Bellarmine University, KY	M,W
Benedictine College, KS	W
Bethel College, IN	M,W
Biola University, CA	W
Bluefield College, VA	M,W
Blue Mountain College, MS	M,W
Brenau University, GA	W
Brigham Young University, UT	M,W
California Baptist University, CA	W
Cameron University, OK	M,W
Campbellsville University, KY	M,W
Carroll College, MT	M,W
Central Methodist University, MO	M,W
Central State University, OH	M,W
Clayton State University, GA	M,W
Concordia University, Nebraska, NE	M,W
Cornerstone University, MI	W
Culver-Stockton College, MO	M,W
Delaware State University, DE	M,W
Doane University, NE	W
Drake University, IA	M,W
Drury University, MO	M,W

Eastern Oregon University, OR	W
East Texas Baptist University, TX	W
Emporia State University, KS	M,W
Gannon University, PA	W
Georgetown College, KY	W
Georgia Institute of Technology, GA	M,W
Graceland University, IA	M,W
Harris-Stowe State University, MO	M,W
Hofstra University, NY	M,W
Indiana Tech, IN	M,W
Indiana Wesleyan University, IN	M,W
John Brown University, AR	W
Judson University, IL	M,W
Kansas Wesleyan University, KS	M,W
Kentucky State University, KY	W
King University, TN	M,W
Lenoir-Rhyne University, NC	M,W
Lewis University, IL	W
Liberty University, VA	M,W
Lincoln Memorial University, TN	M,W
Lincoln University, PA	W
Lindenwood University, MO	M,W
Lindsey Wilson College, KY	M,W
Lipscomb University, TN	W
Loyola University New Orleans, LA	M,W
Maryville University of Saint Louis, MO	M,W
McKendree University, IL	M,W
MidAmerica Nazarene University, KS	M,W
Middle Tennessee State University, TN	M,W
Milligan College, TN	W
Mississippi State University, MS	M,W
Missouri Baptist University, MO	M,W
Missouri Valley College, MO	M,W
Morehead State University, KY	M,W
Mount Mercy University, IA	M,W
Newberry College, SC	M,W
North Carolina State University, NC	M,W
Northern Kentucky University, KY	M,W
Northwestern College, IA	M,W
Northwest Missouri State University, MO	M,W
Oakland City University, IN	W
The Ohio State University, OH	M,W
Oklahoma City University, OK	M,W
Oklahoma State University, OK	M,W
Old Dominion University, VA	M,W
Olivet Nazarene University, IL	M,W
Pfeiffer University, NC	M,W
Pittsburg State University, KS	M,W
Point Park University, PA	W
Prairie View A&M University, TX	M,W
Presbyterian College, SC	M,W
Robert Morris University Illinois, IL	M,W
Rocky Mountain College, MT	M,W
Rogers State University, OK	M,W
St. Ambrose University, IA	M,W
Saint Augustine's University, NC	W
St. Thomas University, FL	M,W
Sam Houston State University, TX	M,W
Southeast Missouri State University, MO	M,W
Southern Arkansas University–Magnolia, AR	M,W
Southern Methodist University, TX	M,W
Southwestern College, KS	M,W
Stephen F. Austin State University, TX	M,W

Tarleton State University, TX	M,W	Nova Southeastern University, FL	W	Barton College, NC	M,W
Tennessee Technological University, TN	M,W	Oklahoma City University, OK	M,W	Baylor University, TX	M,W
Tennessee Wesleyan University, TN	M,W	Old Dominion University, VA	W	Bellarmine University, KY	M,W
Texas A&M University–Commerce, TX	M,W	Robert Morris University, PA	W	Belmont University, TN	M,W
Union University, TN	W	Rutgers University–New Brunswick, NJ	W	Bemidji State University, MN	W
The University of Alabama, AL	M,W	Sacred Heart University, CT	W	Benedictine College, KS	M,W
University of Central Arkansas, AR	M,W	Saint Joseph's University, PA	M,W	Bethel College, IN	M,W
University of Central Florida, FL	M,W	Saint Mary's College of California, CA	W	Bethel College, KS	M,W
University of Florida, FL	M,W	Seattle Pacific University, WA	W	Bethune-Cookman University, FL	M,W
University of Hawaii at Manoa, HI	M,W	Southern Methodist University, TX	W	Binghamton University, State University of New York, NY	M,W
University of Illinois at Springfield, IL	M,W	Stanford University, CA	M,W	Biola University, CA	M,W
University of Jamestown, ND	M,W	Stetson University, FL	M,W	Black Hills State University, SD	M,W
University of Louisville, KY	M,W	Syracuse University, NY	M,W	Bloomsburg University of Pennsylvania, PA	M,W
University of Memphis, TN	M,W	Temple University, PA	M,W	Bluefield College, VA	M,W
University of Michigan, MI	M,W	The University of Alabama, AL	W	Blue Mountain College, MS	M,W
University of Nevada, Las Vegas, NV	M,W	University of California, Los Angeles, CA	W	Boise State University, ID	M,W
University of North Alabama, AL	M,W	University of Central Florida, FL	W	Boston College, MA	M,W
The University of North Carolina at Charlotte, NC	M,W	The University of Kansas, KS	W	Boston University, MA	M,W
University of Oklahoma, OK	M,W	University of Massachusetts Amherst, MA	W	Bowie State University, MD	M,W
University of Pikeville, KY	M,W	University of Miami, FL	W	Bowling Green State University, OH	M,W
University of Providence, MT	M,W	University of Michigan, MI	W	Bradley University, IL	M,W
University of St. Francis, IL	M,W	The University of North Carolina at Chapel Hill, NC	W	Brenau University, GA	W
University of Science and Arts of Oklahoma, OK	M,W	University of Notre Dame, IN	W	Brigham Young University, UT	M,W
University of Sioux Falls, SD	M,W	University of Oklahoma, OK	W	Bryan College, TN	M,W
The University of Tennessee at Martin, TN	W	University of Rhode Island, RI	M	Bryant University, RI	M,W
The University of Texas of the Permian Basin, TX	M,W	University of San Diego, CA	W	Bucknell University, PA	W
University of the Incarnate Word, TX	W	University of Southern California, CA	W	Butler University, IN	M,W
University of Utah, UT	M,W	The University of Tampa, FL	W	Caldwell University, NJ	M,W
University of Washington, WA	M,W	The University of Tennessee, TN	W	California Baptist University, CA	M,W
University of West Georgia, GA	W	The University of Texas at Austin, TX	W	California Polytechnic State University, San Luis Obispo, CA	M,W
Wayland Baptist University, TX	M,W	The University of Tulsa, OK	W	California State Polytechnic University, Pomona, CA	M,W
Weber State University, UT	M,W	University of Virginia, VA	W	California State University, Fullerton, CA	M,W
Wichita State University, KS	M,W	University of Washington, WA	M,W	California State University, Long Beach, CA	M,W
William Jewell College, MO	M,W	Washington State University, WA	W	California State University, Monterey Bay, CA	M,W
William Woods University, MO	W	Western Washington University, WA	W	California State University, Northridge, CA	M,W
Wright State University, OH	M,W	West Virginia University, WV	W	California State University, Sacramento, CA	M,W
				California State University, Stanislaus, CA	M,W
Crew		**Cross-country running**		Calumet College of Saint Joseph, IN	M,W
Barry University, FL	W	Abilene Christian University, TX	M,W	Cameron University, OK	M
Boston College, MA	W	Academy of Art University, CA	M,W	Campbellsville University, KY	M,W
Boston University, MA	M,W	Adams State University, CO	M,W	Canisius College, NY	M,W
California State University, Sacramento, CA	M,W	Adelphi University, NY	M,W	Cardinal Stritch University, WI	M,W
Clemson University, SC	W	Alabama State University, AL	M,W	Carlow University, PA	M,W
College of the Holy Cross, MA	W	Alcorn State University, MS	M,W	Carroll College, MT	M,W
Creighton University, NE	W	American University, DC	M,W	Carson-Newman University, TN	M,W
Drexel University, PA	M,W	Anderson University, SC	M,W	Catawba College, NC	M,W
Duquesne University, PA	W	Angelo State University, TX	M,W	Cedarville University, OH	M,W
Eastern Michigan University, MI	W	Appalachian State University, NC	M,W	Central Connecticut State University, CT	M,W
Fairfield University, CT	M,W	Aquinas College, MI	M,W	Central Methodist University, MO	M,W
Florida Institute of Technology, FL	M,W	Arizona Christian University, AZ	M,W	Central Michigan University, MI	M,W
George Mason University, VA	W	Arizona State University at the Downtown Phoenix campus, AZ	M,W	Central State University, OH	M,W
Georgetown University, DC	M,W	Arizona State University at the Polytechnic campus, AZ	M,W	Chaminade University of Honolulu, HI	M,W
The George Washington University, DC	M,W	Arizona State University at the Tempe campus, AZ	M,W	Chestnut Hill College, PA	M,W
Indiana University Bloomington, IN	W	Arizona State University at the West campus, AZ	M,W	Chowan University, NC	M,W
Jacksonville University, FL	M,W	Arkansas Tech University, AR	W	Christian Brothers University, TN	M,W
Kansas State University, KS	W	Auburn University, AL	M,W	The Citadel, The Military College of South Carolina, SC	M,W
La Salle University, PA	M,W	Auburn University at Montgomery, AL	M,W	Clarion University of Pennsylvania, PA	W
Lehigh University, PA	W	Augustana University, SD	M,W		
Loyola Marymount University, CA	W	Austin Peay State University, TN	M,W		
Marist College, NY	W	Azusa Pacific University, CA	M,W		
Merrimack College, MA	W	Baker University, KS	M,W		
Michigan State University, MI	W	Ball State University, IN	W	Clarke University, IA	M,W

Clayton State University, GA	M,W	Georgetown College, KY	M,W	Lindsey Wilson College, KY	M,W
Clemson University, SC	M,W	Georgetown University, DC	M,W	Lipscomb University, TN	M,W
Cleveland State University, OH	W	The George Washington		Lock Haven University of	
Coastal Carolina University, SC	M,W	University, DC	M,W	Pennsylvania, PA	M,W
Coker College, SC	M,W	Georgia College & State		Long Island University–LIU	
College of Charleston, SC	M,W	University, GA	M,W	Brooklyn, NY	W
The College of Idaho, ID	M,W	Georgia Institute of Technology,		Long Island University–LIU	
College of Saint Mary, NE	W	GA	M,W	Post, NY	M,W
The College of Saint Rose, NY	M,W	Georgian Court University, NJ	M,W	Longwood University, VA	M,W
College of the Holy Cross, MA	W	Georgia Southern University, GA	W	Louisiana State University and	
The College of William and Mary,		Georgia Southwestern State		Agricultural & Mechanical	
VA	M,W	University, GA	W	College, LA	M,W
Colorado Mesa University, CO	M,W	Georgia State University, GA	W	Loyola Marymount University, CA	M,W
Colorado State University, CO	M,W	Gonzaga University, WA	M,W	Loyola University Chicago, IL	M,W
Columbia College, MO	M,W	Goshen College, IN	M,W	Loyola University New Orleans, LA	M,W
Columbus State University, GA	M,W	Governors State University, IL	M,W	Lubbock Christian University, TX	M,W
Concordia University Irvine, CA	M,W	Graceland University, IA	M,W	Lynn University, FL	M,W
Concordia University, Nebraska, NE	M,W	Grand Valley State University, MI	M,W	Lyon College, AR	M,W
Concordia University, St. Paul, MN	M,W	Hampton University, VA	M,W	Malone University, OH	M,W
Concord University, WV	M,W	Harding University, AR	M,W	Manhattan College, NY	M,W
Converse College, SC	W	Hawai`i Pacific University, HI	M,W	Mansfield University of	
Corban University, OR	M,W	High Point University, NC	M,W	Pennsylvania, PA	M,W
Cornerstone University, MI	M,W	Hillsdale College, MI	M,W	Marist College, NY	M,W
Creighton University, NE	M,W	Hofstra University, NY	M,W	Marquette University, WI	M,W
Culver-Stockton College, MO	M,W	Holy Family University, PA	M,W	Marshall University, WV	M,W
Daemen College, NY	M,W	Hope International University, CA	M,W	Maryville University of Saint	
Dakota State University, SD	M,W	Houston Baptist University, TX	M,W	Louis, MO	M,W
Dallas Baptist University, TX	W	Humboldt State University, CA	M,W	McKendree University, IL	M,W
Davidson College, NC	M,W	Idaho State University, ID	M,W	Mercer University, GA	M,W
Delaware State University, DE	M,W	Indiana State University, IN	M,W	Merrimack College, MA	M,W
DePaul University, IL	M,W	Indiana Tech, IN	M,W	Miami University, OH	M,W
Doane University, NE	M,W	Indiana University Bloomington, IN	M,W	Michigan State University, MI	M,W
Dominican College, NY	M,W	Indiana University Northwest, IN	M,W	Michigan Technological	
Dominican University of		Indiana University of		University, MI	M,W
California, CA	M,W	Pennsylvania, PA	M,W	MidAmerica Nazarene University, KS	M,W
Drake University, IA	M,W	Indiana University–Purdue		Middle Georgia State University,	
Drury University, MO	M,W	University Indianapolis, IN	M,W	GA	W
Duquesne University, PA	M,W	Indiana University South Bend, IN	M,W	Middle Tennessee State	
East Carolina University, NC	M,W	Indiana Wesleyan University, IN	M,W	University, TN	M,W
East Central University, OK	M,W	Inter American University of		Millersville University of	
Eastern Michigan University, MI	M,W	Puerto Rico, Bayamón Campus,		Pennsylvania, PA	W
Eastern Oregon University, OR	M,W	PR	M,W	Milligan College, TN	M,W
Eastern Washington University, WA	M,W	Iona College, NY	M,W	Minnesota State University	
East Stroudsburg University of		Iowa State University of Science		Moorhead, MN	M,W
Pennsylvania, PA	M,W	and Technology, IA	M,W	Minot State University, ND	M,W
Elon University, NC	M,W	Jackson State University, MS	M,W	Mississippi State University, MS	W
Embry-Riddle Aeronautical		Jacksonville University, FL	W	Missouri Baptist University, MO	M,W
University–Daytona, FL	M,W	James Madison University, VA	W	Missouri State University, MO	W
Emmanuel College, GA	M,W	John Brown University, AR	M,W	Missouri University of Science	
Emporia State University, KS	M,W	Johnson C. Smith University, NC	M,W	and Technology, MO	M,W
Evangel University, MO	M,W	Judson University, IL	M,W	Missouri Valley College, MO	M,W
Fairfield University, CT	M,W	Kansas State University, KS	M,W	Missouri Western State	
Fairleigh Dickinson University,		Kansas Wesleyan University, KS	M,W	University, MO	M,W
Metropolitan Campus, NJ	M,W	Kennesaw State University, GA	M,W	Molloy College, NY	M,W
Felician University, NJ	M,W	Kent State University, OH	M,W	Morehead State University, KY	M,W
Ferris State University, MI	M,W	Kentucky State University, KY	M,W	Morehouse College, GA	M
Flagler College, FL	M,W	King University, TN	M,W	Morningside College, IA	M,W
Florida Agricultural and		Kutztown University of		Mount Marty College, SD	M,W
Mechanical University, FL	M,W	Pennsylvania, PA	M,W	Mount Mercy University, IA	M,W
Florida Gulf Coast University, FL	M,W	Lamar University, TX	M,W	Mount St. Mary's	
Florida Institute of Technology,		La Salle University, PA	M,W	University, MD	M,W
FL	M,W	Lawrence Technological		Mount Vernon Nazarene	
Florida International		University, MI	M,W	University, OH	M,W
University, FL	M,W	Lee University, TN	M,W	Murray State University, KY	W
Florida Southern College, FL	M,W	Lehigh University, PA	M,W	Newberry College, SC	M,W
Florida State University, FL	M,W	Le Moyne College, NY	M,W	New Jersey Institute of	
Fordham University, NY	M,W	Lenoir-Rhyne University, NC	M,W	Technology, NJ	M,W
Fort Lewis College, CO	M,W	Lewis University, IL	M,W	Newman University, KS	M,W
Francis Marion University, SC	M,W	Liberty University, VA	M,W	New Mexico Highlands University,	
Franklin Pierce University, NH	M,W	Life University, GA	W	NM	M,W
Furman University, SC	M,W	Lincoln Memorial University, TN	M,W	New Mexico State University, NM	M,W
Gannon University, PA	M,W	Lincoln University, MO	W	New York Institute of	
George Mason University, VA	M,W	Lindenwood University, MO	M,W	Technology, NY	M,W

Niagara University, NY	M,W	Sam Houston State University, TX	M,W	University of Arkansas, AR	M,W
North Carolina State University, NC	M,W	San Diego State University, CA	W	University of Bridgeport, CT	M,W
Northern Arizona University, AZ	M,W	San Francisco State University, CA	M,W	University of California, Davis, CA	M,W
Northern Kentucky University, KY	M,W	Santa Clara University, CA	M,W	University of California, Irvine, CA	M,W
Northern State University, SD	M,W	Savannah College of Art and Design, GA	M,W	University of California, Los Angeles, CA	M,W
Northwest Christian University, OR	M,W	Seattle Pacific University, WA	M,W	University of California, Riverside, CA	M,W
Northwestern College, IA	M,W	Seattle University, WA	M,W	University of California, Santa Barbara, CA	M,W
Northwest Nazarene University, ID	M,W	Seton Hill University, PA	M,W	University of Central Arkansas, AR	M,W
Northwest University, WA	M,W	Shawnee State University, OH	M,W	University of Central Florida, FL	W
Nova Southeastern University, FL	M,W	Shippensburg University of Pennsylvania, PA	M,W	University of Central Missouri, MO	M,W
Oakland City University, IN	M,W	Siena College, NY	M,W	University of Central Oklahoma, OK	W
The Ohio State University, OH	M,W	Slippery Rock University of Pennsylvania, PA	M,W	University of Cincinnati, OH	M,W
Ohio University, OH	M,W	Soka University of America, CA	M,W	University of Colorado Boulder, CO	M,W
Oklahoma Baptist University, OK	M,W	Southeastern Louisiana University, LA	M,W	University of Colorado Colorado Springs, CO	M,W
Oklahoma Christian University, OK	M,W	Southeastern Oklahoma State University, OK	W	University of Dayton, OH	M,W
Oklahoma State University, OK	M,W	Southeastern University, FL	M,W	University of Evansville, IN	M,W
Olivet Nazarene University, IL	M,W	Southeast Missouri State University, MO	M,W	The University of Findlay, OH	M,W
Oral Roberts University, OK	M,W	Southern Arkansas University–Magnolia, AR	M,W	University of Florida, FL	M,W
Oregon State University, OR	W	Southern Illinois University Carbondale, IL	M,W	University of Georgia, GA	M,W
Ouachita Baptist University, AR	W	Southern Methodist University, TX	W	University of Hartford, CT	M,W
Our Lady of the Lake University, TX	M,W	Southern Utah University, UT	M,W	University of Hawaii at Manoa, HI	W
Palm Beach Atlantic University, FL	M,W	Southwest Baptist University, MO	M,W	University of Houston, TX	M,W
Penn State University Park, PA	M,W	Southwestern College, KS	M,W	University of Idaho, ID	M,W
Pepperdine University, CA	M,W	Spring Hill College, AL	M,W	University of Illinois at Chicago, IL	M,W
Pfeiffer University, NC	M,W	Stanford University, CA	M,W	University of Illinois at Springfield, IL	M,W
Pittsburg State University, KS	M,W	Stephen F. Austin State University, TX	M,W	University of Jamestown, ND	M,W
Point Loma Nazarene University, CA	W	Stetson University, FL	M,W	The University of Kansas, KS	M,W
Point Park University, PA	M,W	Stonehill College, MA	M,W	University of Kentucky, KY	M,W
Post University, CT	M,W	Stony Brook University, State University of New York, NY	M,W	University of Louisiana at Monroe, LA	M,W
Prairie View A&M University, TX	M,W	Syracuse University, NY	M,W	University of Louisville, KY	M,W
Presbyterian College, SC	M,W	Tarleton State University, TX	M,W	University of Maine, ME	M,W
Providence College, RI	M,W	Taylor University, IN	M,W	University of Maryland, Baltimore County, MD	M,W
Purdue University, IN	M,W	Temple University, PA	M,W	University of Maryland, College Park, MD	W
Queens College of the City University of New York, NY	M,W	Tennessee Technological University, TN	M,W	University of Massachusetts Amherst, MA	M,W
Quinnipiac University, CT	M,W	Tennessee Wesleyan University, TN	M,W	University of Massachusetts Lowell, MA	M,W
Radford University, VA	M,W	Texas A&M International University, TX	M,W	University of Memphis, TN	M,W
Regis University, CO	M,W	Texas A&M University–Commerce, TX	M,W	University of Miami, FL	M,W
Rice University, TX	M,W	Texas A&M University–Corpus Christi, TX	M,W	University of Michigan, MI	M,W
Rider University, NJ	M,W	Texas Christian University, TX	M,W	University of Michigan–Dearborn, MI	M,W
Robert Morris University, PA	W	Texas State University, TX	M,W	University of Minnesota, Duluth, MN	M,W
Robert Morris University Illinois, IL	M,W	Texas Tech University, TX	M,W	University of Minnesota, Twin Cities Campus, MN	M,W
Roberts Wesleyan College, NY	M,W	Tiffin University, OH	M,W	University of Missouri, MO	M,W
Rockhurst University, MO	W	Towson University, MD	W	University of Montana, MT	M,W
Rocky Mountain College, MT	M,W	Trevecca Nazarene University, TN	M,W	University of Nebraska at Kearney, NE	M,W
Rogers State University, OK	M,W	Trinity Christian College, IL	M,W	University of Nebraska–Lincoln, NE	M,W
Rutgers University–New Brunswick, NJ	M,W	Troy University, AL	M,W	University of Nevada, Las Vegas, NV	W
Sacred Heart University, CT	M,W	Truett McConnell University, GA	M,W	University of Nevada, Reno, NV	W
Saginaw Valley State University, MI	M,W	Truman State University, MO	M,W	University of New Hampshire, NH	M,W
St. Ambrose University, IA	M,W	Tulane University, LA	M,W	University of New Haven, CT	M,W
St. Andrews University, NC	M,W	Union University, TN	M,W	University of New Orleans, LA	M,W
Saint Augustine's University, NC	M,W	University at Albany, State University of New York, NY	M,W	University of North Alabama, AL	M,W
St. Bonaventure University, NY	M,W	University at Buffalo, the State University of New York, NY	M,W	University of North Carolina at Asheville, NC	M,W
St. John's University, NY	W	The University of Akron, OH	M,W		
Saint Joseph's University, PA	M,W	The University of Alabama, AL	M,W		
Saint Leo University, FL	M,W	The University of Alabama at Birmingham, AL	W		
St. Louis College of Pharmacy, MO	M,W	University of Alaska Fairbanks, AK	M,W		
Saint Louis University, MO	M,W				
Saint Martin's University, WA	M,W				
Saint Mary-of-the-Woods College, IN	W				
Saint Mary's College of California, CA	M,W				
Saint Peter's University, NJ	M,W				
St. Thomas Aquinas College, NY	M,W				
St. Thomas University, FL	M,W				
Samford University, AL					

The University of North Carolina at Chapel Hill, NC	M,W
The University of North Carolina at Charlotte, NC	M,W
The University of North Carolina at Greensboro, NC	M,W
The University of North Carolina at Pembroke, NC	M,W
The University of North Carolina Wilmington, NC	M,W
University of North Dakota, ND	M,W
University of Northern Colorado, CO	M,W
University of Northern Iowa, IA	M,W
University of North Florida, FL	M,W
University of North Georgia, GA	W
University of North Texas, TX	M,W
University of Notre Dame, IN	M,W
University of Oklahoma, OK	M,W
University of Oregon, OR	M,W
University of Pikeville, KY	M,W
University of Pittsburgh, PA	M,W
University of Rhode Island, RI	M,W
University of Richmond, VA	W
University of St. Francis, IL	M,W
University of St. Thomas, TX	M,W
University of San Diego, CA	M,W
University of San Francisco, CA	M,W
University of Sioux Falls, SD	M,W
University of South Carolina, SC	W
University of South Carolina Aiken, SC	W
University of South Dakota, SD	M,W
University of Southern California, CA	W
University of Southern Indiana, IN	M,W
University of Southern Mississippi, MS	W
The University of Tampa, FL	M,W
The University of Tennessee at Chattanooga, TN	M,W
The University of Tennessee at Martin, TN	M,W
The University of Texas at Austin, TX	M,W
The University of Texas at El Paso, TX	M,W
The University of Texas at San Antonio, TX	M,W
The University of Texas of the Permian Basin, TX	M,W
University of the Incarnate Word, TX	M,W
University of the Pacific, CA	W
The University of Toledo, OH	M,W
The University of Tulsa, OK	M,W
University of Utah, UT	W
University of Vermont, VT	M,W
University of Virginia, VA	M,W
The University of Virginia's College at Wise, VA	M,W
University of Washington, WA	M,W
The University of West Alabama, AL	M,W
University of West Georgia, GA	M,W
University of Wisconsin–Madison, WI	M,W
University of Wisconsin–Milwaukee, WI	M,W
University of Wisconsin–Parkside, WI	M,W
University of Wyoming, WY	M,W
Upper Iowa University, IA	W
Ursuline College, OH	W

Utah State University, UT	M,W
Utah Valley University, UT	M,W
Valdosta State University, GA	M,W
Valley City State University, ND	M,W
Valparaiso University, IN	M,W
Vanderbilt University, TN	M,W
Vanguard University of Southern California, CA	M,W
Villanova University, PA	M,W
Virginia Commonwealth University, VA	M,W
Virginia Military Institute, VA	M,W
Wake Forest University, NC	M,W
Warner Pacific College, OR	M,W
Washington State University, WA	M,W
Wayland Baptist University, TX	M,W
Wayne State College, NE	M,W
Wayne State University, MI	M,W
Webber International University, FL	M,W
Weber State University, UT	M,W
Western Illinois University, IL	M,W
Western Kentucky University, KY	M,W
Western Michigan University, MI	W
Western Oregon University, OR	M,W
Western State Colorado University, CO	M,W
Western Washington University, WA	M,W
Westminster College, UT	M,W
Westmont College, CA	M,W
West Texas A&M University, TX	M,W
West Virginia University, WV	W
West Virginia University Institute of Technology, WV	M,W
West Virginia Wesleyan College, WV	M,W
Wichita State University, KS	M,W
William Jewell College, MO	M,W
William Woods University, MO	M,W
Winona State University, MN	M,W
Winthrop University, SC	M,W
Wofford College, SC	M,W
Wright State University, OH	M,W
Youngstown State University, OH	M,W

Equestrian sports

Auburn University, AL	W
Baylor University, TX	W
Converse College, SC	W
Delaware State University, DE	W
Long Island University–LIU Post, NY	W
Maryville College, TN	M,W
Oklahoma State University, OK	W
Sacred Heart University, CT	W
St. Andrews University, NC	M,W
Saint Mary-of-the-Woods College, IN	W
Savannah College of Art and Design, GA	M,W
Seton Hill University, PA	W
Southern Methodist University, TX	W
Texas A&M University, TX	W
Texas Christian University, TX	W
University of Georgia, GA	W
University of Minnesota, Crookston, MN	W
University of Providence, MT	M,W
University of South Carolina, SC	W
The University of Tennessee at Martin, TN	W
West Texas A&M University, TX	W

Fencing

Cleveland State University, OH	M,W
Fairleigh Dickinson University, Metropolitan Campus, NJ	W
New Jersey Institute of Technology, NJ	M,W
The Ohio State University, OH	M,W
Penn State University Park, PA	M,W
Queens College of the City University of New York, NY	W
Sacred Heart University, CT	M
St. John's University, NY	M,W
Stanford University, CA	M,W
Temple University, PA	W
The University of North Carolina at Chapel Hill, NC	M,W
University of Notre Dame, IN	M,W
Wayne State University, MI	M,W

Field hockey

Adelphi University, NY	W
American University, DC	W
Appalachian State University, NC	W
Ball State University, IN	W
Bellarmine University, KY	W
Bloomsburg University of Pennsylvania, PA	W
Boston College, MA	W
Boston University, MA	W
Bryant University, RI	W
Bucknell University, PA	W
Central Michigan University, MI	W
Colgate University, NY	W
College of the Holy Cross, MA	W
The College of William and Mary, VA	W
Davidson College, NC	W
Drexel University, PA	W
East Stroudsburg University of Pennsylvania, PA	W
Fairfield University, CT	W
Franklin Pierce University, NH	W
Georgetown University, DC	W
Hofstra University, NY	W
Indiana University of Pennsylvania, PA	W
James Madison University, VA	W
Kent State University, OH	W
Kutztown University of Pennsylvania, PA	W
La Salle University, PA	W
Lehigh University, PA	W
Liberty University, VA	W
Lindenwood University, MO	W
Lock Haven University of Pennsylvania, PA	W
Long Island University–LIU Brooklyn, NY	W
Long Island University–LIU Post, NY	W
Longwood University, VA	W
Mansfield University of Pennsylvania, PA	W
Mercy College, NY	W
Merrimack College, MA	W
Miami University, OH	W
Michigan State University, MI	W
Millersville University of Pennsylvania, PA	W
Missouri State University, MO	W
Molloy College, NY	W
Newberry College, SC	W
The Ohio State University, OH	W

Institution	
Ohio University, OH	W
Old Dominion University, VA	W
Penn State University Park, PA	W
Providence College, RI	W
Quinnipiac University, CT	W
Rider University, NJ	W
Rutgers University–New Brunswick, NJ	W
Sacred Heart University, CT	W
Saint Joseph's University, PA	W
Saint Louis University, MO	W
Seton Hill University, PA	W
Shippensburg University of Pennsylvania, PA	W
Slippery Rock University of Pennsylvania, PA	W
Stanford University, CA	W
Stonehill College, MA	W
Syracuse University, NY	W
Temple University, PA	W
Towson University, MD	W
University at Albany, State University of New York, NY	W
University of California, Davis, CA	W
University of Louisville, KY	W
University of Maine, ME	W
University of Maryland, College Park, MD	W
University of Massachusetts Amherst, MA	W
University of Massachusetts Lowell, MA	W
University of Michigan, MI	W
University of New Hampshire, NH	W
University of New Haven, CT	W
The University of North Carolina at Chapel Hill, NC	W
University of Richmond, VA	W
University of the Pacific, CA	W
University of Vermont, VT	W
University of Virginia, VA	W
Villanova University, PA	W
Virginia Commonwealth University, VA	W
Wake Forest University, NC	W
West Chester University of Pennsylvania, PA	W

Football

Institution	
Abilene Christian University, TX	M
Adams State University, CO	M
Alabama State University, AL	M
Alcorn State University, MS	M
Angelo State University, TX	M
Appalachian State University, NC	M
Arizona Christian University, AZ	M
Arizona State University at the Downtown Phoenix campus, AZ	M
Arizona State University at the Polytechnic campus, AZ	M
Arizona State University at the Tempe campus, AZ	M
Arizona State University at the West campus, AZ	M
Arkansas Tech University, AR	M
Auburn University, AL	M
Augustana University, SD	M
Austin Peay State University, TN	M
Azusa Pacific University, CA	M
Baker University, KS	M
Ball State University, IN	M
Baylor University, TX	M
Bemidji State University, MN	M
Benedictine College, KS	M
Bethel College, KS	M
Bethune-Cookman University, FL	M
Black Hills State University, SD	M
Bloomsburg University of Pennsylvania, PA	M
Bluefield College, VA	M
Boise State University, ID	M
Boston College, MA	M
Bowie State University, MD	M
Bowling Green State University, OH	M
Brigham Young University, UT	M
Bryant University, RI	M
Bucknell University, PA	M
California Polytechnic State University, San Luis Obispo, CA	M
California State University, Northridge, CA	M
California State University, Sacramento, CA	M
Campbellsville University, KY	M
Carroll College, MT	M
Carson-Newman University, TN	M
Catawba College, NC	M
Central Methodist University, MO	M
Central Michigan University, MI	M
Chestnut Hill College, PA	M
Chowan University, NC	M
The Citadel, The Military College of South Carolina, SC	M
Clarion University of Pennsylvania, PA	M
Clarke University, IA	M
Clemson University, SC	M
Coastal Carolina University, SC	M
Colgate University, NY	M
College of the Holy Cross, MA	M
The College of William and Mary, VA	M
Colorado Mesa University, CO	M
Colorado State University, CO	M
Concordia University, Nebraska, NE	M
Concordia University, St. Paul, MN	M
Concord University, WV	M
Culver-Stockton College, MO	M
Dakota State University, SD	M
Davidson College, NC	M
Delaware State University, DE	M
Doane University, NE	M
Duquesne University, PA	M
East Carolina University, NC	M
East Central University, OK	M
Eastern Michigan University, MI	M
Eastern Oregon University, OR	M
Eastern Washington University, WA	M
East Stroudsburg University of Pennsylvania, PA	M
Elon University, NC	M
Emporia State University, KS	M
Evangel University, MO	M
Ferris State University, MI	M
Florida Agricultural and Mechanical University, FL	M
Florida Atlantic University, FL	M
Florida Institute of Technology, FL	M
Florida International University, FL	M
Florida State University, FL	M
Fordham University, NY	M
Fort Lewis College, CO	M
Furman University, SC	M
Gannon University, PA	M
Georgetown College, KY	M
Georgia Institute of Technology, GA	M
Georgia Southern University, GA	M
Georgia State University, GA	M
Graceland University, IA	M
Grambling State University, LA	M
Grand Valley State University, MI	M
Hampton University, VA	M
Harding University, AR	M
Hillsdale College, MI	M
Houston Baptist University, TX	M
Humboldt State University, CA	M
Idaho State University, ID	M
Indiana State University, IN	M
Indiana University Bloomington, IN	M
Indiana University of Pennsylvania, PA	M
Iowa State University of Science and Technology, IA	M
Jackson State University, MS	M
James Madison University, VA	M
Johnson C. Smith University, NC	M
Kansas State University, KS	M
Kansas Wesleyan University, KS	M
Kennesaw State University, GA	M
Kent State University, OH	M
Kentucky State University, KY	M
Kutztown University of Pennsylvania, PA	M
Lamar University, TX	M
Lawrence Technological University, MI	M
Lehigh University, PA	M
Lenoir-Rhyne University, NC	M
Liberty University, VA	M
Lincoln University, MO	M
Lincoln University, PA	M
Lindenwood University, MO	M
Lindsey Wilson College, KY	M,W
Lock Haven University of Pennsylvania, PA	M
Long Island University–LIU Post, NY	M
Louisiana State University and Agricultural & Mechanical College, LA	M
Lyon College, AR	M
Malone University, OH	M
Marshall University, WV	M
McKendree University, IL	M
Mercer University, GA	M
Merrimack College, MA	M
Miami University, OH	M
Michigan State University, MI	M
Michigan Technological University, MI	M
MidAmerica Nazarene University, KS	M
Middle Tennessee State University, TN	M
Millersville University of Pennsylvania, PA	M
Minnesota State University Moorhead, MN	M
Minot State University, ND	M
Mississippi State University, MS	M
Missouri Baptist University, MO	M
Missouri State University, MO	M
Missouri University of Science and Technology, MO	M
Missouri Valley College, MO	M
Missouri Western State University, MO	M

Montana Tech of The University of Montana, MT	M	Syracuse University, NY	M	University of North Alabama, AL	M
Morehouse College, GA	M	Tarleton State University, TX	M	The University of North Carolina at Chapel Hill, NC	M
Morningside College, IA	M	Taylor University, IN	M	The University of North Carolina at Charlotte, NC	M
Murray State University, KY	M	Temple University, PA	M	The University of North Carolina at Pembroke, NC	M
Newberry College, SC	M	Tennessee Technological University, TN	M	University of North Dakota, ND	M
New Mexico Highlands University, NM	M	Texas A&M University, TX	M	University of Northern Colorado, CO	M
New Mexico State University, NM	M	Texas A&M University–Commerce, TX	M	University of Northern Iowa, IA	M
North Carolina State University, NC	M	Texas Christian University, TX	M	University of North Texas, TX	M
Northeastern State University, OK	M	Texas State University, TX	M	University of Notre Dame, IN	M
Northern Arizona University, AZ	M	Texas Tech University, TX	M	University of Oklahoma, OK	M
Northern Illinois University, IL	M	Tiffin University, OH	M	University of Oregon, OR	M
Northern State University, SD	M	Towson University, MD	M	University of Pikeville, KY	M
Northwestern College, IA	M	Troy University, AL	M	University of Pittsburgh, PA	M
Northwest Missouri State University, MO	M	Truman State University, MO	M	University of Rhode Island, RI	M
The Ohio State University, OH	M	Tulane University, LA	M	University of Richmond, VA	M
Ohio University, OH	M	University at Albany, State University of New York, NY	M	University of St. Francis, IL	M
Oklahoma Baptist University, OK	M	University at Buffalo, the State University of New York, NY	M	University of Sioux Falls, SD	M
Oklahoma State University, OK	M	The University of Akron, OH	M	University of South Carolina, SC	M
Old Dominion University, VA	M	The University of Alabama, AL	M	University of South Dakota, SD	M
Olivet Nazarene University, IL	M	The University of Alabama at Birmingham, AL	M	University of Southern California, CA	M
Oregon State University, OR	M	University of Arkansas, AR	M	University of Southern Mississippi, MS	M
Ouachita Baptist University, AR	M	University of California, Davis, CA	M	The University of Tennessee, TN	M
Penn State University Park, PA	M	University of California, Los Angeles, CA	M	The University of Tennessee at Chattanooga, TN	M
Pittsburg State University, KS	M	University of Central Arkansas, AR	M	The University of Tennessee at Martin, TN	M
Prairie View A&M University, TX	M	University of Central Florida, FL	M		
Purdue University, IN	M	University of Central Missouri, MO	M	The University of Texas at Austin, TX	M
Rice University, TX	M	University of Central Oklahoma, OK	M	The University of Texas at El Paso, TX	M
Robert Morris University, PA	M	University of Cincinnati, OH	M	The University of Texas at San Antonio, TX	M
Robert Morris University Illinois, IL	M	University of Colorado Boulder, CO	M		
Rocky Mountain College, MT	M	The University of Findlay, OH	M	The University of Texas of the Permian Basin, TX	M
Rutgers University–New Brunswick, NJ	M	University of Florida, FL	M	University of the Incarnate Word, TX	M
Sacred Heart University, CT	M	University of Georgia, GA	M	The University of Toledo, OH	M
Saginaw Valley State University, MI	M	University of Hawaii at Manoa, HI	M	The University of Tulsa, OK	M
St. Ambrose University, IA	M	University of Houston, TX	M	University of Utah, UT	M
Saint Augustine's University, NC	M	University of Idaho, ID	M	University of Virginia, VA	M
		University of Jamestown, ND	M	The University of Virginia's College at Wise, VA	M
Samford University, AL	M	The University of Kansas, KS	M	University of Washington, WA	M
Sam Houston State University, TX	M	University of Kentucky, KY	M	The University of West Alabama, AL	M
San Diego State University, CA	M	University of Louisiana at Monroe, LA	M	University of West Georgia, GA	M
Seton Hill University, PA	M	University of Louisville, KY	M		
Shepherd University, WV	M	University of Maine, ME	M	University of Wisconsin–Madison, WI	M
Shippensburg University of Pennsylvania, PA	M	University of Maryland, College Park, MD	M	University of Wyoming, WY	M
Slippery Rock University of Pennsylvania, PA	M	University of Massachusetts Amherst, MA	M	Upper Iowa University, IA	M
				Utah State University, UT	M
Southeastern Louisiana University, LA	M	University of Memphis, TN	M	Valdosta State University, GA	M
Southeastern Oklahoma State University, OK	M	University of Miami, FL	M	Valley City State University, ND	M
		University of Michigan, MI	M	Vanderbilt University, TN	M
Southeastern University, FL	M	University of Minnesota, Crookston, MN	M	Villanova University, PA	M
Southeast Missouri State University, MO	M	University of Minnesota, Duluth, MN	M	Virginia Military Institute, VA	M
Southern Arkansas University–Magnolia, AR	M	University of Minnesota, Twin Cities Campus, MN	M	Virginia Polytechnic Institute and State University, VA	M
Southern Illinois University Carbondale, IL	M	University of Missouri, MO	M	Wake Forest University, NC	M
Southern Methodist University, TX	M	University of Montana, MT	M	Washington State University, WA	M
Southern Utah University, UT	M	University of Nebraska at Kearney, NE	M	Wayland Baptist University, TX	M
Southwest Baptist University, MO	M			Wayne State College, NE	M
Southwestern College, KS	M	University of Nebraska–Lincoln, NE	M	Wayne State University, MI	M
Stanford University, CA	M			Webber International University, FL	M
Stephen F. Austin State University, TX	M	University of Nevada, Las Vegas, NV	M		
Stonehill College, MA	M	University of Nevada, Reno, NV	M	Weber State University, UT	M
Stony Brook University, State University of New York, NY	M	University of New Hampshire, NH	M	West Chester University of Pennsylvania, PA	M
		University of New Haven, CT	M		

Western Illinois University, IL	M
Western Kentucky University, KY	M
Western Michigan University, MI	M
Western Oregon University, OR	M
Western State Colorado University, CO	M
West Texas A&M University, TX	M
West Virginia University, WV	M
West Virginia Wesleyan College, WV	M
William Jewell College, MO	M
Winona State University, MN	M
Wofford College, SC	M
Youngstown State University, OH	M

Golf

Abilene Christian University, TX	M
Academy of Art University, CA	M,W
Adams State University, CO	M,W
Adelphi University, NY	M,W
Alabama State University, AL	M,W
Alcorn State University, MS	M,W
Anderson University, SC	M,W
Angelo State University, TX	W
Appalachian State University, NC	M,W
Aquinas College, MI	M,W
Arizona Christian University, AZ	M,W
Arizona State University at the Downtown Phoenix campus, AZ	M,W
Arizona State University at the Polytechnic campus, AZ	M,W
Arizona State University at the Tempe campus, AZ	M,W
Arizona State University at the West campus, AZ	M,W
Arkansas Tech University, AR	M,W
Auburn University, AL	M,W
Augustana University, SD	M,W
Austin Peay State University, TN	M,W
Baker University, KS	M,W
Ball State University, IN	M,W
Barry University, FL	M,W
Barton College, NC	M,W
Baylor University, TX	M,W
Bellarmine University, KY	M,W
Belmont University, TN	M,W
Bemidji State University, MN	M,W
Bethel College, IN	M,W
Bethel College, KS	M,W
Bethune-Cookman University, FL	M,W
Binghamton University, State University of New York, NY	M
Biola University, CA	M,W
Bluefield College, VA	M
Blue Mountain College, MS	M,W
Boise State University, ID	M,W
Boston College, MA	M,W
Boston University, MA	W
Bowling Green State University, OH	M,W
Bradley University, IL	M,W
Brenau University, GA	W
Brigham Young University, UT	M,W
Bryan College, TN	M,W
Bryant University, RI	M
Butler University, IN	M,W
California Baptist University, CA	M,W
California Polytechnic State University, San Luis Obispo, CA	M,W
California State University, Dominguez Hills, CA	M
California State University, Fullerton, CA	M,W
California State University, Long Beach, CA	M,W
California State University Maritime Academy, CA	M
California State University, Monterey Bay, CA	M,W
California State University, Northridge, CA	M
California State University, Sacramento, CA	M
California State University, San Bernardino, CA	M
California State University, Stanislaus, CA	M
Calumet College of Saint Joseph, IN	M,W
Cameron University, OK	M,W
Campbellsville University, KY	M,W
Canisius College, NY	M
Cardinal Stritch University, WI	M,W
Carroll College, MT	M,W
Carson-Newman University, TN	M
Catawba College, NC	M,W
Cedarville University, OH	M
Central Connecticut State University, CT	M,W
Central Michigan University, MI	W
Central State University, OH	M,W
Chaminade University of Honolulu, HI	M
Chestnut Hill College, PA	M
Chowan University, NC	M,W
Christian Brothers University, TN	M,W
The Citadel, The Military College of South Carolina, SC	W
Clarion University of Pennsylvania, PA	M,W
Clarke University, IA	M,W
Clayton State University, GA	M
Clemson University, SC	M
Cleveland State University, OH	M
Coastal Carolina University, SC	M,W
Coker College, SC	M,W
College of Charleston, SC	M,W
College of Coastal Georgia, GA	M,W
The College of Idaho, ID	M,W
College of Saint Mary, NE	W
The College of Saint Rose, NY	M,W
The College of William and Mary, VA	M,W
Colorado Mesa University, CO	M,W
Colorado State University, CO	M,W
Columbia College, MO	M,W
Columbus State University, GA	M,W
Concordia University, Nebraska, NE	M,W
Concordia University, St. Paul, MN	M,W
Concord University, WV	M,W
Converse College, SC	W
Corban University, OR	M,W
Cornerstone University, MI	M,W
Creighton University, NE	M,W
Culver-Stockton College, MO	M,W
Daemen College, NY	M
Dallas Baptist University, TX	W
Davidson College, NC	M
DePaul University, IL	M
Doane University, NE	M,W
Dominican College, NY	M
Dominican University of California, CA	M,W
Drake University, IA	M
Drexel University, PA	M
Drury University, MO	M,W
East Carolina University, NC	M,W
Eastern Michigan University, MI	M,W
Eastern Washington University, WA	W
Eckerd College, FL	M,W
Elon University, NC	M,W
Embry-Riddle Aeronautical University–Daytona, FL	M,W
Emmanuel College, GA	M,W
Evangel University, MO	M,W
Fairfield University, CT	M,W
Fairleigh Dickinson University, Metropolitan Campus, NJ	M,W
Felician University, NJ	M
Ferris State University, MI	M,W
Flagler College, FL	M,W
Florida Agricultural and Mechanical University, FL	M,W
Florida Atlantic University, FL	M,W
Florida Gulf Coast University, FL	M,W
Florida Institute of Technology, FL	M,W
Florida International University, FL	W
Florida Southern College, FL	M,W
Florida State University, FL	M,W
Fordham University, NY	M
Fort Lewis College, CO	M,W
Francis Marion University, SC	M
Franklin Pierce University, NH	M,W
Furman University, SC	W
Gannon University, PA	M,W
George Mason University, VA	M
Georgetown College, KY	M,W
Georgetown University, DC	M,W
The George Washington University, DC	M
Georgia College & State University, GA	M
Georgia Institute of Technology, GA	M
Georgia Southern University, GA	M,W
Georgia Southwestern State University, GA	M
Georgia State University, GA	M,W
Gonzaga University, WA	M,W
Goshen College, IN	M
Governors State University, IL	M,W
Graceland University, IA	M,W
Grand Valley State University, MI	M,W
Hampton University, VA	M,W
Harding University, AR	M,W
Hawai`i Pacific University, HI	M,W
High Point University, NC	M,W
Hillsdale College, MI	M
Hofstra University, NY	W
Hope International University, CA	M,W
Houston Baptist University, TX	M,W
Idaho State University, ID	W
Indiana State University, IN	W
Indiana Tech, IN	M,W
Indiana University Bloomington, IN	M,W
Indiana University Northwest, IN	M,W
Indiana University of Pennsylvania, PA	M
Indiana University–Purdue University Indianapolis, IN	M,W
Indiana University South Bend, IN	M,W
Indiana Wesleyan University, IN	M,W
Iona College, NY	M
Iowa State University of Science and Technology, IA	M,W
Jackson State University, MS	M,W
Jacksonville University, FL	M,W
James Madison University, VA	M,W
Johnson C. Smith University, NC	M

Judson University, IL	M,W	Mount Vernon Nazarene		Saint Peter's University, NJ	M
Kansas State University, KS	M,W	University, OH	M,W	St. Thomas University, FL	M
Kansas Wesleyan University, KS	M,W	Murray State University, KY	M,W	Samford University, AL	M,W
Kennesaw State University, GA	M,W	Newberry College, SC	M,W	Sam Houston State University, TX	M,W
Kent State University, OH	M,W	Newman University, KS	M,W	San Diego State University, CA	M,W
Kentucky State University, KY	M	New Mexico State University, NM	M,W	Santa Clara University, CA	M,W
King University, TN	M,W	Niagara University, NY	M,W	Savannah College of Art and	
Kutztown University of		North Carolina State University,		Design, GA	M,W
Pennsylvania, PA	W	NC	M,W	Seattle University, WA	M,W
Lamar University, TX	M,W	Northeastern State University, OK	M,W	Seton Hill University, PA	W
La Salle University, PA	M,W	Northern Arizona University, AZ	W	Shawnee State University, OH	M,W
Lawrence Technological		Northern Illinois University, IL	M,W	Shepherd University, WV	M
University, MI	M,W	Northern Kentucky University, KY	M,W	Siena College, NY	M,W
Lee University, TN	M,W	Northwest Christian University, OR	M,W	Southeastern Louisiana	
Lehigh University, PA	M,W	Northwestern College, IA	M,W	University, LA	M
Le Moyne College, NY	M,W	Northwest Nazarene University, ID	M,W	Southeastern Oklahoma State	
Lenoir-Rhyne University, NC	M,W	Nova Southeastern University, FL	M,W	University, OK	M
Lewis University, IL	M,W	Oakland City University, IN	M,W	Southeastern University, FL	M,W
Liberty University, VA	M	The Ohio State University, OH	M,W	Southern Illinois University	
Lincoln Memorial University, TN	M,W	Ohio University, OH	M,W	Carbondale, IL	M,W
Lincoln University, MO	M,W	Oklahoma Baptist University, OK	M,W	Southern Methodist University, TX	M,W
Lindenwood University, MO	M,W	Oklahoma Christian University, OK	M,W	Southern Utah University, UT	M,W
Lindsey Wilson College, KY	M,W	Oklahoma City University, OK	M,W	Southwest Baptist University, MO	M,W
Lipscomb University, TN	M,W	Oklahoma State University, OK	M,W	Southwestern College, KS	M,W
Long Island University–LIU		Old Dominion University, VA	M,W	Spring Hill College, AL	M,W
Brooklyn, NY	M,W	Olivet Nazarene University, IL	M	Stanford University, CA	M,W
Longwood University, VA	M,W	Oral Roberts University, OK	M,W	Stephen F. Austin State	
Louisiana State University and		Oregon State University, OR	M,W	University, TX	M,W
Agricultural & Mechanical		Our Lady of the Lake University,		Stetson University, FL	M,W
College, LA	M,W	TX	M	Stonehill College, MA	W
Loyola Marymount University, CA	M	Palm Beach Atlantic University, FL	M,W	Tarleton State University, TX	W
Loyola University Chicago, IL	M,W	Penn State University Park, PA	M,W	Taylor University, IN	M,W
Loyola University New Orleans, LA	M,W	Pepperdine University, CA	M,W	Temple University, PA	M
Lubbock Christian University, TX	M,W	Pfeiffer University, NC	M,W	Tennessee Technological	
Lynn University, FL	M,W	Pittsburg State University, KS	M	University, TN	M,W
Lyon College, AR	M,W	Point Loma Nazarene University, CA	W	Tennessee Wesleyan University, TN	M,W
Malone University, OH	M,W	Point Park University, PA	M,W	Texas A&M International	
Manhattan College, NY	M	Post University, CT	M,W	University, TX	M,W
Marquette University, WI	M	Prairie View A&M University, TX	M,W	Texas A&M University, TX	M,W
Marshall University, WV	M,W	Presbyterian College, SC	M,W	Texas A&M University–	
Marymount California University,		Purdue University, IN	M,W	Commerce, TX	M,W
CA	M,W	Quinnipiac University, CT	W	Texas A&M University–	
Maryville University of Saint		Radford University, VA	M,W	Corpus Christi, TX	W
Louis, MO	M,W	Regis University, CO	M,W	Texas Christian University, TX	M,W
McKendree University, IL	M,W	Rice University, TX	M	Texas State University, TX	M,W
Mercer University, GA	M,W	Rider University, NJ	M	Texas Tech University, TX	M,W
Merrimack College, MA	W	Robert Morris University, PA	M	Thomas University, GA	M
Metropolitan State University of		Robert Morris University		Tiffin University, OH	M,W
Denver, CO	W	Illinois, IL	M,W	Towson University, MD	M,W
Miami University, OH	M	Roberts Wesleyan College, NY	M	Trevecca Nazarene University, TN	M,W
Michigan State University, MI	M,W	Rockhurst University, MO	M,W	Trinity Christian College, IL	M
Middle Tennessee State		Rocky Mountain College, MT	M,W	Troy University, AL	M,W
University, TN	M	Rogers State University, OK	M,W	Truett McConnell University, GA	M,W
Millersville University of		Rollins College, FL	M,W	Truman State University, MO	W
Pennsylvania, PA	M,W	Rutgers University–New		Tulane University, LA	W
Milligan College, TN	M,W	Brunswick, NJ	M,W	Union University, TN	M,W
Minnesota State University		Sacred Heart University, CT	M,W	University at Albany, State	
Moorhead, MN	W	Saginaw Valley State University,		University of New York, NY	W
Mississippi State University, MS	M,W	MI	M	The University of Akron, OH	M,W
Missouri Baptist University, MO	M,W	St. Ambrose University, IA	M,W	The University of Alabama, AL	M,W
Missouri State University, MO	M,W	St. Andrews University, NC	M,W	The University of Alabama at	
Missouri Valley College, MO	M,W	Saint Augustine's		Birmingham, AL	M,W
Missouri Western State		University, NC	M	University of Arkansas, AR	M,W
University, MO	M,W	St. Bonaventure University, NY	M	University of California, Davis,	
Montana Tech of The University		St. John's University, NY	M,W	CA	M,W
of Montana, MT	M,W	Saint Joseph's University, PA	M	University of California,	
Morehead State University, KY	M,W	Saint Leo University, FL	M,W	Irvine, CA	M,W
Morningside College, IA	M,W	Saint Martin's University, WA	M,W	University of California, Los	
Mount Marty College, SD	M,W	Saint Mary-of-the-Woods College,		Angeles, CA	M,W
Mount Mercy University, IA	M,W	IN	W	University of California,	
Mount St. Mary's		Saint Mary's College of		Riverside, CA	M
University, MD	M,W	California, CA	M	University of California, Santa	
		St. Mary's University, TX	M,W	Barbara, CA	M

University of Central Arkansas, AR	M,W	University of Rhode Island, RI	M	West Texas A&M University, TX	M,W
University of Central Florida, FL	M,W	University of Richmond, VA	M,W	West Virginia University, WV	M
University of Central Missouri, MO	M,W	University of St. Francis, IL	M,W	West Virginia University	
University of Central Oklahoma, OK	M,W	University of St. Thomas, TX	M,W	Institute of Technology, WV	M
University of Cincinnati, OH	M,W	University of San Diego, CA	M	West Virginia Wesleyan College, WV	M,W
University of Colorado Boulder, CO	M,W	University of San Francisco, CA	M,W	Wichita State University, KS	M,W
University of Colorado Colorado		University of Sioux Falls, SD	M,W	William Jewell College, MO	M,W
Springs, CO	M,W	University of South Carolina, SC	M,W	William Woods University, MO	M,W
University of Dayton, OH	M	University of South Carolina		Winona State University, MN	M,W
University of Denver, CO	M,W	Aiken, SC	M	Winthrop University, SC	M,W
University of Evansville, IN	M,W	University of South Dakota, SD	W	Wofford College, SC	M,W
The University of Findlay, OH	M,W	University of Southern		Wright State University, OH	M
University of Florida, FL	M,W	California, CA	M,W	Youngstown State University, OH	M,W
University of Georgia, GA	M,W	University of Southern Indiana, IN	M,W		
University of Hartford, CT	M,W	University of Southern		**Gymnastics**	
University of Hawaii at Manoa, HI	M,W	Mississippi, MS	M,W	Arizona State University at the	
University of Houston, TX	M,W	The University of Tampa, FL	M,W	Downtown Phoenix campus, AZ	W
University of Idaho, ID	M,W	The University of Tennessee, TN	M,W	Arizona State University at the	
University of Illinois at		The University of Tennessee at		Polytechnic campus, AZ	W
Springfield, IL	M,W	Chattanooga, TN	M,W	Arizona State University at the	
University of Jamestown, ND	M,W	The University of Tennessee at		Tempe campus, AZ	W
The University of Kansas, KS	M,W	Martin, TN	M	Arizona State University at the	
University of Kentucky, KY	M,W	The University of Texas at		West campus, AZ	W
University of Louisiana at		Austin, TX	M,W	Auburn University, AL	W
Monroe, LA	M,W	The University of Texas at El		Azusa Pacific University, CA	W
University of Louisville, KY	M,W	Paso, TX	M	Ball State University, IN	W
University of Maryland, College		The University of Texas at San		Boise State University, ID	W
Park, MD	M,W	Antonio, TX	M,W	Bowling Green State University, OH	W
University of Memphis, TN	M,W	The University of Texas of the		Brigham Young University, UT	W
University of Miami, FL	W	Permian Basin, TX	M,W	California State University,	
University of Michigan, MI	M,W	University of the Incarnate		Sacramento, CA	W
University of Minnesota,		Word, TX	M,W	Central Michigan University, MI	W
Crookston, MN	M,W	University of the Pacific, CA	M	The College of William and Mary,	
University of Minnesota, Twin		The University of Toledo, OH	M,W	VA	M,W
Cities Campus, MN	M,W	The University of Tulsa, OK	W	Eastern Michigan University, MI	W
University of Missouri, MO	M,W	University of Utah, UT	M	Gannon University, PA	W
University of Missouri–St.		University of Virginia, VA	M,W	Georgetown College, KY	W
Louis, MO	M,W	University of Washington, WA	M,W	The George Washington	
University of Montana, MT	W	The University of West Alabama, AL	M,W	University, DC	W
University of Montevallo, AL	M,W	University of West Georgia, GA	M,W	Hawai`i Pacific University, HI	W
University of Nebraska at		University of Wisconsin–		Iowa State University of Science	
Kearney, NE	M,W	Madison, WI	M,W	and Technology, IA	W
University of Nebraska–		University of Wisconsin–		Kent State University, OH	W
Lincoln, NE	M,W	Parkside, WI	M	Lindenwood University, MO	W
University of Nevada, Las Vegas,		University of Wyoming, WY	M,W	Louisiana State University and	
NV	M	Upper Iowa University, IA	M,W	Agricultural & Mechanical College,	
University of Nevada, Reno, NV	M,W	Ursuline College, OH	W	LA	W
University of New Orleans, LA	M	Utah State University, UT	M	Michigan State University, MI	W
University of North Alabama, AL	M	Utah Valley University, UT	M,W	Mount St. Mary's	
University of North Carolina at		Valdosta State University, GA	M	University, MD	M,W
Asheville, NC	W	Valley City State University, ND	M,W	North Carolina State University,	
The University of North Carolina		Valparaiso University, IN	M,W	NC	W
at Chapel Hill, NC	M,W	Vanderbilt University, TN	M,W	Northern Illinois University, IL	W
The University of North Carolina		Virginia Commonwealth		The Ohio State University, OH	M,W
at Charlotte, NC	M,W	University, VA	M	Oregon State University, OR	W
The University of North Carolina		Virginia Military Institute, VA	M	Penn State University Park, PA	M,W
at Greensboro, NC	M,W	Virginia Polytechnic Institute		Quinnipiac University, CT	W
The University of North Carolina		and State University, VA	M	Rutgers University–New	
at Pembroke, NC	W	Wake Forest University, NC	M,W	Brunswick, NJ	W
The University of North Carolina		Warner Pacific College, OR	M,W	Seattle Pacific University, WA	W
Wilmington, NC	M,W	Washington State University, WA	M,W	Southeast Missouri State	
University of North Dakota, ND	M,W	Wayland Baptist University, TX	M,W	University, MO	W
University of Northern Colorado,		Wayne State University, MI	M,W	Southern Utah University, UT	W
CO	M,W	Webber International University,		Stanford University, CA	M,W
University of Northern Iowa, IA	M,W	FL	M,W	Temple University, PA	W
University of North Florida, FL	M	Weber State University, UT	M,W	Texas Woman's University, TX	W
University of North Georgia, GA	M,W	West Chester University of		Towson University, MD	W
University of North Texas, TX	M,W	Pennsylvania, PA	M,W	The University of Alabama, AL	W
University of Notre Dame, IN	M,W	Western Illinois University, IL	M	University of Arkansas, AR	W
University of Oklahoma, OK	M,W	Western Kentucky University, KY	M,W	University of Bridgeport, CT	W
University of Oregon, OR	M,W	Western Michigan University, MI	W	University of California, Davis,	
University of Pikeville, KY	M,W	Western Washington University, WA	M,W	CA	W
University of Providence, MT	M,W	Westminster College, UT	M,W	University of California, Los	
				Angeles, CA	W

University of California, Santa
  Barbara, CA — M,W
University of Denver, CO — W
University of Florida, FL — W
University of Georgia, GA — W
University of Illinois at
  Chicago, IL — M,W
University of Kentucky, KY — W
University of Maryland, College
  Park, MD — W
University of Michigan, MI — M,W
University of Minnesota, Twin
  Cities Campus, MN — M,W
University of Missouri, MO — W
University of Nebraska–
  Lincoln, NE — M,W
University of New Hampshire, NH — W
The University of North Carolina
  at Chapel Hill, NC — W
University of Oklahoma, OK — M,W
University of Pittsburgh, PA — W
University of Utah, UT — W
University of Washington, WA — W
Utah State University, UT — W
West Chester University of
  Pennsylvania, PA — W
Western Michigan University, MI — W
West Virginia University, WV — W

Ice hockey
Arizona State University at the
  Downtown Phoenix campus, AZ — M
Arizona State University at the
  Polytechnic campus, AZ — M
Arizona State University at the
  Tempe campus, AZ — M
Arizona State University at the
  West campus, AZ — M
Bemidji State University, MN — M,W
Bentley University, MA — M
Boston College, MA — M,W
Boston University, MA — M,W
Bowling Green State University, OH — M
Canisius College, NY — M
Clarkson University, NY — M,W
Colgate University, NY — M,W
College of the Holy Cross, MA — M
The Colorado College, CO — M
Ferris State University, MI — M
Indiana Tech, IN — M
Life University, GA — M
Lindenwood University, MO — M,W
Merrimack College, MA — M,W
Miami University, OH — M
Michigan State University, MI — M
Michigan Technological
  University, MI — M
Niagara University, NY — M
The Ohio State University, OH — M,W
Penn State University Park, PA — M,W
Providence College, RI — M,W
Quinnipiac University, CT — M,W
Rensselaer Polytechnic
  Institute, NY — M,W
Robert Morris University, PA — M
Sacred Heart University, CT — M,W
St. Lawrence University, NY — W
Syracuse University, NY — W
University of Alaska Fairbanks, AK — M
University of Denver, CO — M
University of Maine, ME — M,W
University of Massachusetts
  Amherst, MA — M

University of Massachusetts
  Lowell, MA — M
University of Michigan, MI — M
University of Minnesota, Duluth,
  MN — M,W
University of Minnesota, Twin
  Cities Campus, MN — M,W
University of New Hampshire, NH — M,W
University of North Dakota, ND — M
University of Notre Dame, IN — M
University of Vermont, VT — M,W
University of Wisconsin–
  Madison, WI — M,W
Western Michigan University, MI — M

Lacrosse
Adams State University, CO — M,W
Adelphi University, NY — M,W
American University, DC — W
Aquinas College, MI — M,W
Arizona State University at the
  Downtown Phoenix campus, AZ — W
Arizona State University at the
  Polytechnic campus, AZ — W
Arizona State University at the
  Tempe campus, AZ — W
Arizona State University at the
  West campus, AZ — W
Barton College, NC — W
Bellarmine University, KY — M
Bethel College, IN — W
Binghamton University, State
  University of New York, NY — M,W
Bloomsburg University of
  Pennsylvania, PA — W
Boston College, MA — W
Boston University, MA — M,W
Bryant University, RI — M,W
Bucknell University, PA — M,W
Butler University, IN — W
Caldwell University, NJ — W
Canisius College, NY — M,W
Catawba College, NC — M,W
Central Connecticut State
  University, CT — W
Central Michigan University, MI — W
Chestnut Hill College, PA — M,W
Chowan University, NC — M,W
Clarke University, IA — M,W
Coastal Carolina University, SC — W
Coker College, SC — M,W
Colgate University, NY — M,W
The College of Saint Rose, NY — M
College of the Holy Cross, MA — M,W
The College of William and Mary,
  VA — W
Colorado Mesa University, CO — M,W
Concordia University Irvine, CA — M,W
Concordia University, St. Paul, MN — W
Converse College, SC — W
Davidson College, NC — W
Dominican College, NY — M,W
Dominican University of
  California, CA — M
Drexel University, PA — M,W
Duquesne University, PA — W
East Carolina University, NC — W
East Stroudsburg University of
  Pennsylvania, PA — W
Elon University, NC — W
Embry-Riddle Aeronautical
  University–Daytona, FL — M,W
Emmanuel College, GA — M,W

Fairfield University, CT — M,W
Florida Institute of Technology,
  FL — M,W
Florida Southern College, FL — M,W
Fort Lewis College, CO — W
Franklin Pierce University, NH — M,W
Gannon University, PA — W
George Mason University, VA — W
Georgetown College, KY — W
Georgetown University, DC — M,W
Georgian Court University, NJ — M,W
Hampton University, VA — M
High Point University, NC — M,W
Hofstra University, NY — M,W
Holy Family University, PA — W
Indiana Tech, IN — M,W
Indiana University of
  Pennsylvania, PA — W
Iona College, NY — W
Jacksonville University, FL — M,W
James Madison University, VA — W
Kennesaw State University, GA — W
Kutztown University of
  Pennsylvania, PA — W
La Salle University, PA — W
Lawrence Technological
  University, MI — M,W
Lee University, TN — W
Lehigh University, PA — M,W
Le Moyne College, NY — M,W
Lenoir-Rhyne University, NC — M,W
Lewis University, IL — W
Liberty University, VA — W
Lincoln Memorial University, TN — M,W
Lindenwood University, MO — M,W
Lock Haven University of
  Pennsylvania, PA — W
Long Island University–LIU
  Brooklyn, NY — W
Long Island University–LIU
  Post, NY — M,W
Longwood University, VA — W
Lynn University, FL — M
Manhattan College, NY — M,W
Marist College, NY — M,W
Marquette University, WI — M,W
Marymount California University,
  CA — M,W
Maryville University of Saint
  Louis, MO — M,W
McKendree University, IL — W
Mercer University, GA — M,W
Mercy College, NY — M,W
Merrimack College, MA — M,W
Millersville University of
  Pennsylvania, PA — W
Missouri Baptist University, MO — M,W
Missouri Valley College, MO — W
Molloy College, NY — M,W
Mount St. Mary's
  University, MD — M,W
Newberry College, SC — M,W
New York Institute of
  Technology, NY — M,W
Niagara University, NY — W
The Ohio State University, OH — M,W
Oklahoma Baptist University, OK — W
Old Dominion University, VA — W
Palm Beach Atlantic University, FL — M,W
Penn State University Park, PA — M,W
Pfeiffer University, NC — M,W
Post University, CT — M,W
Presbyterian College, SC — W

Providence College, RI	M
Queens College of the City University of New York, NY	W
Quinnipiac University, CT	M,W
Radford University, VA	W
Regis University, CO	W
Robert Morris University, PA	M
Robert Morris University Illinois, IL	M,W
Roberts Wesleyan College, NY	M,W
Rockhurst University, MO	M,W
Rutgers University–New Brunswick, NJ	M,W
Sacred Heart University, CT	M,W
St. Ambrose University, IA	M
St. Andrews University, NC	M,W
St. Bonaventure University, NY	M,W
St. John's University, NY	M
Saint Joseph's University, PA	M,W
Saint Leo University, FL	M,W
San Diego State University, CA	W
Savannah College of Art and Design, GA	M,W
Seton Hill University, PA	M,W
Shepherd University, WV	W
Shippensburg University of Pennsylvania, PA	W
Siena College, NY	M,W
Slippery Rock University of Pennsylvania, PA	W
Stanford University, CA	W
Stetson University, FL	W
Stonehill College, MA	W
Stony Brook University, State University of New York, NY	M,W
Syracuse University, NY	M,W
Temple University, PA	W
Tennessee Wesleyan University, TN	M,W
Tiffin University, OH	W
Towson University, MD	M,W
Truett McConnell University, GA	W
University at Albany, State University of New York, NY	M,W
University of Bridgeport, CT	W
University of California, Davis, CA	W
University of Cincinnati, OH	W
University of Colorado Boulder, CO	W
University of Colorado Colorado Springs, CO	W
University of Denver, CO	M,W
The University of Findlay, OH	W
University of Florida, FL	W
University of Hartford, CT	M
University of Louisville, KY	W
University of Maryland, Baltimore County, MD	M,W
University of Maryland, College Park, MD	M,W
University of Massachusetts Amherst, MA	M,W
University of Massachusetts Lowell, MA	M,W
University of Michigan, MI	M,W
University of Michigan–Dearborn, MI	M
University of Minnesota, Duluth, MN	M,W
University of New Hampshire, NH	W
University of New Haven, CT	W
The University of North Carolina at Chapel Hill, NC	M,W
University of Notre Dame, IN	M,W
University of Oregon, OR	W

University of Richmond, VA	M,W
University of Southern California, CA	W
The University of Tampa, FL	M,W
University of Vermont, VT	M,W
University of Virginia, VA	M,W
The University of Virginia's College at Wise, VA	W
Ursuline College, OH	W
Vanderbilt University, TN	W
Villanova University, PA	M,W
Virginia Commonwealth University, VA	W
Virginia Military Institute, VA	M
Virginia Polytechnic Institute and State University, VA	W
West Chester University of Pennsylvania, PA	W
Westminster College, UT	M,W
West Virginia Wesleyan College, WV	W
Wofford College, SC	W

Riflery

The Citadel, The Military College of South Carolina, SC	M,W
Concordia University, Nebraska, NE	M,W
Emmanuel College, GA	M,W
Georgia Southern University, GA	W
Lindenwood University, MO	M,W
Morehead State University, KY	M,W
Murray State University, KY	M,W
North Carolina State University, NC	M,W
The Ohio State University, OH	M,W
Texas Christian University, TX	W
The University of Akron, OH	W
The University of Alabama at Birmingham, AL	W
University of Alaska Fairbanks, AK	M,W
University of Kentucky, KY	M,W
University of Memphis, TN	M,W
University of Nebraska–Lincoln, NE	W
University of Nevada, Reno, NV	M,W
University of North Georgia, GA	M,W
The University of Tennessee at Martin, TN	M,W
Virginia Military Institute, VA	M,W
West Virginia University, WV	M,W
Wofford College, SC	M,W

Rowing

Boston University, MA	M,W
Embry-Riddle Aeronautical University–Daytona, FL	M,W
Fordham University, NY	W
Gonzaga University, WA	W
Indiana University Bloomington, IN	W
Michigan State University, MI	W
The Ohio State University, OH	W
Robert Morris University, PA	W
San Diego State University, CA	W
Stanford University, CA	M,W
University of Central Oklahoma, OK	W
University of Louisville, KY	W
University of Oklahoma, OK	W
University of Washington, WA	M,W

Rugby

Bethel College, IN	M
Life University, GA	M,W
Lindenwood University, MO	M,W
Molloy College, NY	W
Mount St. Mary's University, MD	W
Quinnipiac University, CT	W

Sacred Heart University, CT	W
The University of North Carolina at Pembroke, NC	M
West Chester University of Pennsylvania, PA	W

Sailing

Hampton University, VA	M,W

Sand volleyball

Arizona State University at the Downtown Phoenix campus, AZ	W
Arizona State University at the Polytechnic campus, AZ	W
Arizona State University at the Tempe campus, AZ	W
Arizona State University at the West campus, AZ	W
Austin Peay State University, TN	W
California State University, Long Beach, CA	W
Coastal Carolina University, SC	W
College of Charleston, SC	W
Colorado Mesa University, CO	W
Florida State University, FL	W
Georgia State University, GA	W
Lincoln Memorial University, TN	W
Mercer University, GA	W
Saint Mary's College of California, CA	W
St. Thomas University, FL	W
Texas Christian University, TX	W
University of Louisiana at Monroe, LA	W
University of Nebraska–Lincoln, NE	W
University of Oregon, OR	W
The University of Tennessee at Martin, TN	W
Webber International University, FL	M,W

Skiing (cross-country)

Bluefield College, VA	M,W
Michigan Technological University, MI	M,W
University of Alaska Fairbanks, AK	M,W
University of Colorado Boulder, CO	M,W
University of Denver, CO	M,W
University of New Hampshire, NH	M,W
University of Utah, UT	M,W
University of Vermont, VT	M,W

Skiing (downhill)

The College of Idaho, ID	M,W
Rocky Mountain College, MT	M,W
University of Colorado Boulder, CO	M,W
University of Denver, CO	M,W
University of New Hampshire, NH	M,W
University of Utah, UT	M,W
University of Vermont, VT	M,W
Westminster College, UT	M,W

Soccer

Abilene Christian University, TX	W
Academy of Art University, CA	M,W
Adams State University, CO	M,W
Adelphi University, NY	M,W
Alabama State University, AL	W
Alcorn State University, MS	W
American University, DC	M,W
Anderson University, SC	M,W
Angelo State University, TX	W
Appalachian State University, NC	M,W
Aquinas College, MI	M,W

Arizona Christian University, AZ	M,W	Carroll College, MT	M,W	Fairleigh Dickinson University,	
Arizona State University at the		Carson-Newman University, TN	M,W	Metropolitan Campus, NJ	M,W
Downtown Phoenix campus, AZ	W	Catawba College, NC	M,W	Felician University, NJ	M,W
Arizona State University at the		Cedarville University, OH	M,W	Ferris State University, MI	W
Polytechnic campus, AZ	W	Central Connecticut State		Flagler College, FL	M,W
Arizona State University at the		University, CT	M,W	Florida Gulf Coast University, FL	M,W
Tempe campus, AZ	W	Central Methodist University, MO	M,W	Florida Institute of Technology,	
Arizona State University at the		Central Michigan University, MI	W	FL	M,W
West campus, AZ	W	Chaminade University of		Florida International	
Auburn University, AL	W	Honolulu, HI	M,W	University, FL	M,W
Auburn University at Montgomery,		Chestnut Hill College, PA	M,W	Florida National University, FL	M,W
AL	M,W	Chowan University, NC	M,W	Florida Southern College, FL	M,W
Augustana University, SD	W	Christian Brothers University, TN	M,W	Florida State University, FL	W
Austin Peay State University, TN	W	The Citadel, The Military		Fordham University, NY	M,W
Azusa Pacific University, CA	M,W	College of South Carolina, SC	W	Fort Lewis College, CO	M,W
Baker University, KS	M,W	Clarion University of		Francis Marion University, SC	M,W
Ball State University, IN	W	Pennsylvania, PA	W	Franklin Pierce University, NH	M,W
Barry University, FL	M,W	Clarke University, IA	M,W	Furman University, SC	M,W
Barton College, NC	M,W	Clayton State University, GA	M,W	Gannon University, PA	M,W
Baylor University, TX	W	Clemson University, SC	M,W	George Mason University, VA	M,W
Bellarmine University, KY	M,W	Cleveland State University, OH	M	Georgetown College, KY	M,W
Belmont University, TN	M,W	Coastal Carolina University, SC	M,W	Georgetown University, DC	M,W
Bemidji State University, MN	W	Coker College, SC	M,W	The George Washington	
Benedictine College, KS	M,W	Colgate University, NY	M,W	University, DC	M,W
Bethel College, IN	M,W	College of Charleston, SC	M,W	Georgia College & State	
Bethel College, KS	M,W	The College of Idaho, ID	M,W	University, GA	W
Binghamton University, State		College of Saint Mary, NE	W	Georgian Court University, NJ	M,W
University of New York, NY	M,W	The College of Saint Rose, NY	M,W	Georgia Southern University, GA	M,W
Biola University, CA	M,W	College of the Holy Cross, MA	M,W	Georgia Southwestern State	
Bloomsburg University of		The College of William and Mary,		University, GA	M,W
Pennsylvania, PA	M,W	VA	M,W	Georgia State University, GA	M,W
Bluefield College, VA	M,W	The Colorado College, CO	W	Gonzaga University, WA	M,W
Boise State University, ID	W	Colorado Mesa University, CO	M,W	Goshen College, IN	M,W
Boston College, MA	M,W	Colorado State University, CO	W	Graceland University, IA	M,W
Boston University, MA	M,W	Columbia College, MO	M,W	Grand Valley State University, MI	W
Bowling Green State University, OH	M,W	Columbus State University, GA	W	Harding University, AR	M,W
Bradley University, IL	M	Concordia University Irvine, CA	M,W	Harris-Stowe State University, MO	M,W
Brenau University, GA	W	Concordia University, Nebraska, NE	M,W	Hawai`i Pacific University, HI	M,W
Brigham Young University, UT	W	Concordia University, St. Paul, MN	W	High Point University, NC	M,W
Bryan College, TN	M,W	Concord University, WV	M,W	Hofstra University, NY	M,W
Bryant University, RI	M,W	Converse College, SC	W	Holy Family University, PA	M,W
Bucknell University, PA	M	Corban University, OR	M,W	Hope International University, CA	M,W
Butler University, IN	M,W	Cornerstone University, MI	M,W	Houston Baptist University, TX	M,W
Caldwell University, NJ	M,W	Creighton University, NE	M,W	Humboldt State University, CA	M,W
California Baptist University, CA	M,W	Culver-Stockton College, MO	M,W	Idaho State University, ID	W
California Polytechnic State		Daemen College, NY	M,W	Indiana State University, IN	W
University, San Luis Obispo, CA	M,W	Dallas Baptist University, TX	W	Indiana Tech, IN	M,W
California State Polytechnic		Davidson College, NC	M,W	Indiana University Bloomington, IN	M,W
University, Pomona, CA	M,W	Delaware State University, DE	W	Indiana University of	
California State University,		DePaul University, IL	M,W	Pennsylvania, PA	W
Dominguez Hills, CA	M,W	Doane University, NE	M,W	Indiana University–Purdue	
California State University,		Dominican College, NY	M,W	University Indianapolis, IN	M,W
Fullerton, CA	M,W	Dominican University of		Indiana Wesleyan University, IN	M,W
California State University,		California, CA	M,W	Iona College, NY	M,W
Long Beach, CA	W	Drake University, IA	M,W	Iowa State University of Science	
California State University		Drexel University, PA	M,W	and Technology, IA	W
Maritime Academy, CA	M	Drury University, MO	M,W	Jackson State University, MS	W
California State University,		Duquesne University, PA	M,W	Jacksonville University, FL	M,W
Monterey Bay, CA	M,W	East Carolina University, NC	W	James Madison University, VA	M,W
California State University,		East Central University, OK	W	John Brown University, AR	M,W
Northridge, CA	M	Eastern Michigan University, MI	W	Judson University, IL	M,W
California State University,		Eastern Oregon University, OR	M,W	Kansas Wesleyan University, KS	M,W
Sacramento, CA	M,W	Eastern Washington University, WA	W	Kennesaw State University, GA	W
California State University, San		East Stroudsburg University of		Kent State University, OH	W
Bernardino, CA	M,W	Pennsylvania, PA	M,W	King University, TN	M,W
California State University,		Eckerd College, FL	M,W	Kutztown University of	
Stanislaus, CA	M,W	Elon University, NC	M,W	Pennsylvania, PA	W
Calumet College of Saint Joseph,		Embry-Riddle Aeronautical		Lamar University, TX	W
IN	M,W	University–Daytona, FL	M,W	La Salle University, PA	M,W
Campbellsville University, KY	M,W	Emmanuel College, GA	M,W	Lawrence Technological	
Canisius College, NY	M,W	Emporia State University, KS	W	University, MI	M,W
Cardinal Stritch University, WI	M,W	The Evergreen State College, WA	M,W	Lee University, TN	M,W
Carlow University, PA	W	Fairfield University, CT	M,W	Lehigh University, PA	M,W

Le Moyne College, NY	M,W	Newberry College, SC	M,W	Saint Louis University, MO	M,W
Lenoir-Rhyne University, NC	M,W	New Jersey Institute of		Saint Martin's University, WA	W
Lewis University, IL	M,W	Technology, NJ	M,W	Saint Mary-of-the-Woods College,	
Liberty University, VA	M,W	Newman University, KS	M,W	IN	W
Life University, GA	M,W	New Mexico Highlands University,		Saint Mary's College of	
Lincoln Memorial University, TN	M,W	NM	W	California, CA	M,W
Lincoln University, PA	W	New Mexico State University, NM	W	St. Mary's University, TX	M,W
Lindenwood University, MO	M,W	New York Institute of		Saint Peter's University, NJ	M,W
Lindsey Wilson College, KY	M,W	Technology, NY	M,W	St. Thomas Aquinas College, NY	M,W
Lipscomb University, TN	M,W	Niagara University, NY	M,W	St. Thomas University, FL	M,W
Lock Haven University of		North Carolina State University, NC	M,W	Samford University, AL	W
Pennsylvania, PA	M,W	Northeastern State University, OK	M,W	Sam Houston State University, TX	W
Long Island University–LIU		Northern Arizona University, AZ	W	San Diego State University, CA	M,W
Brooklyn, NY	M,W	Northern Illinois University, IL	M,W	San Francisco State University, CA	M,W
Long Island University–LIU		Northern Kentucky University, KY	M,W	Santa Clara University, CA	M,W
Post, NY	M,W	Northern State University, SD	W	Savannah College of Art and	
Longwood University, VA	M,W	Northwest Christian University, OR	M,W	Design, GA	M,W
Louisiana State University and		Northwestern College, IA	M,W	Seattle Pacific University, WA	M,W
Agricultural & Mechanical		Northwest Nazarene University, ID	W	Seattle University, WA	M,W
College, LA	W	Northwest University, WA	M,W	Seton Hill University, PA	M,W
Loyola Marymount University, CA	M,W	Nova Southeastern University, FL	M,W	Shawnee State University, OH	M,W
Loyola University Chicago, IL	M,W	Oakland City University, IN	M,W	Shepherd University, WV	M,W
Lubbock Christian University, TX	M,W	The Ohio State University, OH	M,W	Shippensburg University of	
Lynn University, FL	M,W	Ohio University, OH	W	Pennsylvania, PA	M,W
Lyon College, AR	M,W	Oklahoma Baptist University, OK	M,W	Siena College, NY	M,W
Malone University, OH	M,W	Oklahoma Christian University, OK	M,W	Slippery Rock University of	
Manhattan College, NY	M,W	Oklahoma City University, OK	M,W	Pennsylvania, PA	M,W
Mansfield University of		Oklahoma State University, OK	W	Soka University of America, CA	M,W
Pennsylvania, PA	W	Old Dominion University, VA	M,W	Sonoma State University, CA	M,W
Marist College, NY	M,W	Olivet Nazarene University, IL	M,W	Southeastern Louisiana	
Marquette University, WI	M,W	Oral Roberts University, OK	M,W	University, LA	W
Marshall University, WV	M,W	Oregon State University, OR	M,W	Southeastern University, FL	M,W
Marymount California University,		Ouachita Baptist University, AR	M,W	Southeast Missouri State	
CA	M,W	Our Lady of the Lake University,		University, MO	W
Maryville University of Saint		TX	M,W	Southern Methodist University, TX	M,W
Louis, MO	M,W	Palm Beach Atlantic University, FL	M,W	Southern Utah University, UT	W
McKendree University, IL	M,W	Penn State University Park, PA	M,W	Southwest Baptist University, MO	M,W
Mercer University, GA	M,W	Pepperdine University, CA	W	Southwestern College, KS	M,W
Mercy College, NY	M,W	Pfeiffer University, NC	M,W	Spring Hill College, AL	M,W
Merrimack College, MA	M,W	Point Loma Nazarene University, CA	M,W	Stanford University, CA	M,W
Metropolitan State University of		Point Park University, PA	M,W	Stephen F. Austin State	
Denver, CO	M,W	Post University, CT	M,W	University, TX	W
Miami University, OH	W	Prairie View A&M University, TX	M,W	Stetson University, FL	M,W
Michigan State University, MI	M,W	Presbyterian College, SC	M,W	Stonehill College, MA	M,W
Michigan Technological		Providence College, RI	M,W	Stony Brook University, State	
University, MI	W	Purdue University, IN	W	University of New York, NY	M,W
MidAmerica Nazarene University, KS	M,W	Queens College of the City		Syracuse University, NY	M,W
Middle Georgia State University, GA	W	University of New York, NY	M,W	Taylor University, IN	M,W
Middle Tennessee State		Quinnipiac University, CT	M,W	Temple University, PA	M,W
University, TN	W	Radford University, VA	M,W	Tennessee Technological	
Millersville University of		Regis University, CO	M,W	University, TN	W
Pennsylvania, PA	M,W	Rice University, TX	W	Tennessee Wesleyan University, TN	M,W
Milligan College, TN	M,W	Rider University, NJ	M,W	Texas A&M International	
Minnesota State University		Robert Morris University, PA	M,W	University, TX	M,W
Moorhead, MN	W	Robert Morris University		Texas A&M University, TX	W
Mississippi State University, MS	W	Illinois, IL	M,W	Texas A&M University–	
Missouri Baptist University, MO	M,W	Roberts Wesleyan College, NY	M,W	Commerce, TX	W
Missouri State University, MO	M,W	Rockhurst University, MO	M,W	Texas A&M University–	
Missouri University of Science		Rocky Mountain College, MT	M,W	Corpus Christi, TX	W
and Technology, MO	M,W	Rogers State University, OK	M,W	Texas A&M University–	
Missouri Valley College, MO	M,W	Rollins College, FL	M,W	Texarkana, TX	M,W
Missouri Western State		Rutgers University–New		Texas Christian University, TX	W
University, MO	W	Brunswick, NJ	M,W	Texas State University, TX	W
Molloy College, NY	M,W	Sacred Heart University, CT	M,W	Texas Tech University, TX	W
Morehead State University, KY	W	Saginaw Valley State University,		Texas Woman's University, TX	W
Morningside College, IA	M,W	MI	M,W	Thomas University, GA	M,W
Mount Marty College, SD	M,W	St. Ambrose University, IA	M,W	Tiffin University, OH	M,W
Mount Mercy University, IA	M,W	St. Andrews University, NC	M,W	Towson University, MD	M,W
Mount St. Mary's		St. Bonaventure University, NY	M,W	Trevecca Nazarene University, TN	M,W
University, MD	M,W	St. John's University, NY	M,W	Trinity Christian College, IL	M,W
Mount Vernon Nazarene		Saint Joseph's University, PA	M,W	Troy University, AL	W
University, OH	M,W	Saint Leo University, FL	M,W	Truett McConnell University, GA	M,W
Murray State University, KY	W	St. Louis College of Pharmacy, MO	M,W	Truman State University, MO	M,W

Tulane University, LA	W
Union University, TN	M,W
University at Albany, State University of New York, NY	M,W
University at Buffalo, the State University of New York, NY	W
The University of Akron, OH	M,W
The University of Alabama, AL	W
The University of Alabama at Birmingham, AL	M,W
University of Arkansas, AR	W
University of Bridgeport, CT	M,W
University of California, Davis, CA	M,W
University of California, Irvine, CA	M,W
University of California, Los Angeles, CA	M,W
University of California, Riverside, CA	M,W
University of California, Santa Barbara, CA	M,W
University of Central Arkansas, AR	M,W
University of Central Florida, FL	M,W
University of Central Missouri, MO	W
University of Central Oklahoma, OK	W
University of Cincinnati, OH	M,W
University of Colorado Boulder, CO	W
University of Colorado Colorado Springs, CO	M,W
University of Dayton, OH	M,W
University of Denver, CO	M,W
University of Evansville, IN	M,W
The University of Findlay, OH	M,W
University of Florida, FL	W
University of Georgia, GA	W
University of Hartford, CT	M,W
University of Hawaii at Manoa, HI	W
University of Houston, TX	W
University of Idaho, ID	W
University of Illinois at Chicago, IL	M
University of Illinois at Springfield, IL	M,W
University of Jamestown, ND	M,W
The University of Kansas, KS	W
University of Kentucky, KY	M,W
University of Louisiana at Monroe, LA	W
University of Louisville, KY	M,W
University of Maine, ME	W
University of Maryland, Baltimore County, MD	M,W
University of Maryland, College Park, MD	M,W
University of Massachusetts Amherst, MA	M,W
University of Massachusetts Lowell, MA	M,W
University of Memphis, TN	M,W
University of Miami, FL	W
University of Michigan, MI	M,W
University of Michigan–Dearborn, MI	M
University of Minnesota, Crookston, MN	W
University of Minnesota, Duluth, MN	W
University of Minnesota, Twin Cities Campus, MN	W
University of Missouri, MO	W
University of Missouri–St. Louis, MO	M,W
University of Montana, MT	W

University of Montevallo, AL	M,W
University of Nebraska at Kearney, NE	W
University of Nebraska–Lincoln, NE	W
University of Nevada, Las Vegas, NV	M,W
University of Nevada, Reno, NV	W
University of New Hampshire, NH	M,W
University of New Haven, CT	M,W
University of North Alabama, AL	W
University of North Carolina at Asheville, NC	M,W
The University of North Carolina at Chapel Hill, NC	M,W
The University of North Carolina at Charlotte, NC	M,W
The University of North Carolina at Greensboro, NC	M,W
The University of North Carolina at Pembroke, NC	M,W
The University of North Carolina Wilmington, NC	M,W
University of North Dakota, ND	W
University of Northern Colorado, CO	W
University of Northern Iowa, IA	W
University of North Florida, FL	M,W
University of North Georgia, GA	M,W
University of North Texas, TX	W
University of Notre Dame, IN	M,W
University of Oklahoma, OK	W
University of Oregon, OR	W
University of Pikeville, KY	M,W
University of Pittsburgh, PA	M,W
University of Providence, MT	M,W
University of Rhode Island, RI	M,W
University of Richmond, VA	W
University of St. Francis, IL	M,W
University of St. Thomas, TX	M,W
University of San Diego, CA	M,W
University of San Francisco, CA	M,W
University of Science and Arts of Oklahoma, OK	M,W
University of Sioux Falls, SD	W
University of South Carolina, SC	M,W
University of South Carolina Aiken, SC	M,W
University of South Dakota, SD	W
University of Southern California, CA	W
University of Southern Indiana, IN	M,W
University of Southern Mississippi, MS	W
The University of Tampa, FL	M,W
The University of Tennessee, TN	W
The University of Tennessee at Chattanooga, TN	W
The University of Tennessee at Martin, TN	
The University of Texas at Austin, TX	W
The University of Texas at San Antonio, TX	W
The University of Texas of the Permian Basin, TX	M,W
University of the Incarnate Word, TX	M,W
University of the Pacific, CA	W
The University of Toledo, OH	W
The University of Tulsa, OK	M,W
University of Utah, UT	W
University of Vermont, VT	M,W

University of Virginia, VA	M,W
University of Washington, WA	M,W
The University of West Alabama, AL	M,W
University of West Georgia, GA	W
University of Wisconsin–Madison, WI	M,W
University of Wisconsin–Milwaukee, WI	M,W
University of Wisconsin–Parkside, WI	M,W
University of Wyoming, WY	W
Upper Iowa University, IA	M,W
Ursuline College, OH	W
Utah State University, UT	W
Utah Valley University, UT	W
Valdosta State University, GA	W
Valparaiso University, IN	M,W
Vanderbilt University, TN	W
Vanguard University of Southern California, CA	M,W
Villanova University, PA	M,W
Virginia Commonwealth University, VA	M,W
Virginia Military Institute, VA	M
Virginia Polytechnic Institute and State University, VA	M,W
Wake Forest University, NC	M,W
Warner Pacific College, OR	M,W
Washington State University, WA	W
Wayland Baptist University, TX	M,W
Wayne State College, NE	W
Webber International University, FL	M,W
Weber State University, UT	W
West Chester University of Pennsylvania, PA	M,W
Western Illinois University, IL	M,W
Western Michigan University, MI	M,W
Western Oregon University, OR	W
Western State Colorado University, CO	W
Western Washington University, WA	M,W
Westminster College, UT	M,W
Westmont College, CA	M,W
West Texas A&M University, TX	M,W
West Virginia University, WV	M,W
West Virginia University Institute of Technology, WV	M,W
West Virginia Wesleyan College, WV	M,W
William Jewell College, MO	M,W
William Woods University, MO	M,W
Winona State University, MN	W
Winthrop University, SC	M,W
Wofford College, SC	M,W
Wright State University, OH	M,W
Youngstown State University, OH	W

Softball

Abilene Christian University, TX	W
Academy of Art University, CA	W
Adelphi University, NY	W
Alabama State University, AL	W
Alcorn State University, MS	W
Anderson University, SC	W
Angelo State University, TX	W
Appalachian State University, NC	W
Aquinas College, MI	W
Arizona Christian University, AZ	W
Arizona State University at the Downtown Phoenix campus, AZ	W
Arizona State University at the Polytechnic campus, AZ	W

Arizona State University at the Tempe campus, AZ	W	Central Michigan University, MI	W
Arizona State University at the West campus, AZ	W	Chaminade University of Honolulu, HI	W
Arkansas Tech University, AR	W	Chestnut Hill College, PA	W
Auburn University, AL	W	Chowan University, NC	W
Auburn University at Montgomery, AL	W	Christian Brothers University, TN	W
Augustana University, SD	W	Clarion University of Pennsylvania, PA	W
Austin Peay State University, TN	W	Clarke University, IA	W
Azusa Pacific University, CA	W	Clemson University, SC	W
Baker University, KS	W	Cleveland State University, OH	W
Ball State University, IN	W	Coastal Carolina University, SC	W
Barry University, FL	W	Coker College, SC	W
Barton College, NC	W	Colgate University, NY	W
Baylor University, TX	W	College of Charleston, SC	W
Bellarmine University, KY	W	College of Coastal Georgia, GA	W
Belmont University, TN	W	The College of Idaho, ID	W
Bemidji State University, MN	W	College of Saint Mary, NE	W
Benedictine College, KS	W	The College of Saint Rose, NY	W
Bethel College, IN	W	College of the Holy Cross, MA	W
Bethune-Cookman University, FL	W	Colorado Mesa University, CO	W
Binghamton University, State University of New York, NY	W	Colorado State University, CO	W
		Columbia College, MO	W
Biola University, CA	W	Columbus State University, GA	W
Bloomsburg University of Pennsylvania, PA	W	Concordia University Irvine, CA	W
		Concordia University, Nebraska, NE	W
Bluefield College, VA	W	Concordia University, St. Paul, MN	W
Blue Mountain College, MS	W	Concord University, WV	W
Boise State University, ID	W	Corban University, OR	W
Boston College, MA	W	Cornerstone University, MI	W
Boston University, MA	W	Creighton University, NE	W
Bowie State University, MD	W	Culver-Stockton College, MO	W
Bowling Green State University, OH	W	Dakota State University, SD	W
Bradley University, IL	W	Delaware State University, DE	W
Brenau University, GA	W	DePaul University, IL	W
Brigham Young University, UT	W	Doane University, NE	W
Bryan College, TN	W	Dominican College, NY	W
Bryant University, RI	W	Dominican University of California, CA	W
Bucknell University, PA	W	Drake University, IA	W
Butler University, IN	W	Drexel University, PA	W
Caldwell University, NJ	W	Drury University, MO	W
California Baptist University, CA	W	East Carolina University, NC	W
California Polytechnic State University, San Luis Obispo, CA	W	East Central University, OK	W
		Eastern Michigan University, MI	W
California State University, Dominguez Hills, CA	W	Eastern Oregon University, OR	W
		East Stroudsburg University of Pennsylvania, PA	W
California State University, Fullerton, CA	W	Eckerd College, FL	W
California State University, Long Beach, CA	W	Elon University, NC	W
		Embry-Riddle Aeronautical University–Daytona, FL	W
California State University, Monterey Bay, CA	W	Emmanuel College, GA	W
California State University, Northridge, CA	W	Emporia State University, KS	W
		Evangel University, MO	W
California State University, Sacramento, CA	W	Fairfield University, CT	W
California State University, San Bernardino, CA	W	Fairleigh Dickinson University, Metropolitan Campus, NJ	W
		Felician University, NJ	W
California State University, Stanislaus, CA	W	Ferris State University, MI	W
Calumet College of Saint Joseph, IN	W	Flagler College, FL	W
Cameron University, OK	W	Florida Agricultural and Mechanical University, FL	W
Campbellsville University, KY	W	Florida Atlantic University, FL	W
Canisius College, NY	W	Florida Gulf Coast University, FL	W
Cardinal Stritch University, WI	W	Florida Institute of Technology, FL	W
Carlow University, PA	W	Florida International University, FL	W
Carroll College, MT	W		
Carson-Newman University, TN	W	Florida Southern College, FL	W
Catawba College, NC	W	Florida State University, FL	W
Cedarville University, OH	W	Fordham University, NY	W
Central Connecticut State University, CT	W	Fort Lewis College, CO	W
Central Methodist University, MO	W	Francis Marion University, SC	W

Franklin Pierce University, NH	W
Furman University, SC	W
Gannon University, PA	W
George Mason University, VA	W
Georgetown College, KY	W
Georgetown University, DC	W
Georgia College & State University, GA	W
Georgia Institute of Technology, GA	W
Georgian Court University, NJ	W
Georgia Southern University, GA	W
Georgia Southwestern State University, GA	W
Georgia State University, GA	W
Goshen College, IN	W
Graceland University, IA	W
Grambling State University, LA	W
Grand Valley State University, MI	W
Hampton University, VA	W
Harding University, AR	W
Harris-Stowe State University, MO	W
Hawai`i Pacific University, HI	W
Hillsdale College, MI	W
Hofstra University, NY	W
Holy Family University, PA	W
Hope International University, CA	W
Houston Baptist University, TX	W
Humboldt State University, CA	W
Idaho State University, ID	W
Indiana State University, IN	W
Indiana Tech, IN	W
Indiana University Bloomington, IN	W
Indiana University of Pennsylvania, PA	W
Indiana University–Purdue University Indianapolis, IN	W
Indiana University South Bend, IN	W
Indiana University Southeast, IN	W
Indiana Wesleyan University, IN	W
Inter American University of Puerto Rico, Bayamón Campus, PR	M,W
Iona College, NY	W
Iowa State University of Science and Technology, IA	W
Jackson State University, MS	W
Jacksonville University, FL	W
James Madison University, VA	W
Johnson C. Smith University, NC	W
Judson University, IL	W
Kansas Wesleyan University, KS	W
Kennesaw State University, GA	W
Kent State University, OH	W
Kentucky State University, KY	W
King University, TN	W
Kutztown University of Pennsylvania, PA	W
La Salle University, PA	W
Lawrence Technological University, MI	W
Lee University, TN	W
Lehigh University, PA	W
Le Moyne College, NY	W
Lenoir-Rhyne University, NC	W
Lewis University, IL	W
Liberty University, VA	W
Lincoln Memorial University, TN	W
Lincoln University, MO	W
Lincoln University, PA	W
Lindenwood University, MO	W
Lindsey Wilson College, KY	W
Lipscomb University, TN	W

Lock Haven University of Pennsylvania, PA	W	Northwest University, WA	W	Southeastern Oklahoma State University, OK	W
Long Island University–LIU Brooklyn, NY	W	Nova Southeastern University, FL	W	Southeastern University, FL	W
		Oakland City University, IN	W	Southeast Missouri State	
Long Island University–LIU Post, NY	W	The Ohio State University, OH	W	University, MO	W
		Ohio University, OH	W	Southern Arkansas	
Longwood University, VA	W	Oklahoma Baptist University, OK	W	University–Magnolia, AR	W
Louisiana State University and Agricultural & Mechanical College, LA	W	Oklahoma Christian University, OK	W	Southern Illinois University Carbondale, IL	W
		Oklahoma City University, OK	W		
		Oklahoma State University, OK	W	Southern Utah University, UT	W
Loyola Marymount University, CA	W	Olivet Nazarene University, IL	W	Southwest Baptist University, MO	W
Loyola University Chicago, IL	W	Oregon State University, OR	W	Southwestern College, KS	W
Lubbock Christian University, TX	W	Ouachita Baptist University, AR	W	Spring Hill College, AL	W
Lynn University, FL	W	Our Lady of the Lake University, TX	W	Stanford University, CA	W
Lyon College, AR	W	Palm Beach Atlantic University, FL	W	Stephen F. Austin State	
Malone University, OH	W	Penn State Hazleton, PA	W	University, TX	W
Manhattan College, NY	W	Penn State University Park, PA	W	Stetson University, FL	W
Mansfield University of Pennsylvania, PA	W	Pfeiffer University, NC	W	Stonehill College, MA	W
		Pittsburg State University, KS	W	Stony Brook University, State	
Marist College, NY	W	Point Park University, PA	W	University of New York, NY	W
Marshall University, WV	W	Post University, CT	W	Syracuse University, NY	W
Maryville University of Saint Louis, MO	W	Prairie View A&M University, TX	W	Tarleton State University, TX	W
		Presbyterian College, SC	W	Taylor University, IN	W
McKendree University, IL	W	Providence College, RI	W	Tennessee Technological	
Mercer University, GA	W	Purdue University, IN	W	University, TN	W
Mercy College, NY	W	Queens College of the City University of New York, NY	W	Tennessee Wesleyan University, TN	W
Merrimack College, MA	W			Texas A&M International	
Metropolitan State University of Denver, CO	W	Quinnipiac University, CT	W	University, TX	W
		Radford University, VA	W	Texas A&M University, TX	W
Miami University, OH	W	Regis University, CO	W	Texas A&M University– Corpus Christi, TX	W
Michigan State University, MI	W	Rider University, NJ	W		
MidAmerica Nazarene University, KS	W	Robert Morris University, PA	W	Texas A&M University– Texarkana, TX	M,W
Middle Georgia State University, GA	W	Robert Morris University Illinois, IL	W		
Middle Tennessee State University, TN	W	Rockhurst University, MO	W	Texas State University, TX	W
		Rogers State University, OK	W	Texas Tech University, TX	W
Millersville University of Pennsylvania, PA	W	Rollins College, FL	W	Texas Woman's University, TX	W
		Rutgers University–New Brunswick, NJ	W	Thomas University, GA	W
Milligan College, TN	W			Tiffin University, OH	W
Minnesota State University Moorhead, MN	W	Sacred Heart University, CT	W	Towson University, MD	W
		Saginaw Valley State University, MI	W	Trevecca Nazarene University, TN	W
Minot State University, ND	W	St. Ambrose University, IA	W	Trinity Christian College, IL	W
Mississippi State University, MS	W	St. Andrews University, NC	W	Troy University, AL	W
Missouri Baptist University, MO	W	Saint Augustine's University, NC	W	Truett McConnell University, GA	W
Missouri State University, MO	W	St. Bonaventure University, NY	W	Truman State University, MO	W
Missouri University of Science and Technology, MO	W	St. John's University, NY	W	Union University, TN	W
		Saint Joseph's University, PA	W	University at Albany, State University of New York, NY	W
Missouri Valley College, MO	W	Saint Leo University, FL	W		
Missouri Western State University, MO	W	St. Louis College of Pharmacy, MO	W	University at Buffalo, the State University of New York, NY	W
		Saint Louis University, MO	W	The University of Akron, OH	W
Molloy College, NY	W	Saint Martin's University, WA	W	The University of Alabama, AL	W
Morehead State University, KY	W	Saint Mary-of-the-Woods College, IN	W	The University of Alabama at Birmingham, AL	W
Morningside College, IA	W	Saint Mary's College of California, CA	W		
Mount Marty College, SD	W			University of Arkansas, AR	W
Mount Mercy University, IA	W	Saint Peter's University, NJ	W	University of Bridgeport, CT	W
Mount St. Mary's University, MD	W	St. Thomas Aquinas College, NY	W	University of California, Davis, CA	W
		St. Thomas University, FL	W	University of California, Los Angeles, CA	W
Mount Vernon Nazarene University, OH	W	Samford University, AL	W		
		Sam Houston State University, TX	W	University of California, Riverside, CA	W
Murray State University, KY	W	San Diego State University, CA	W		
Newberry College, SC	W	San Francisco State University, CA	W	University of California, Santa Barbara, CA	W
Newman University, KS	W	Santa Clara University, CA	W		
New Mexico Highlands University, NM	W	Seattle University, WA	W	University of Central Arkansas, AR	W
New Mexico State University, NM	W	Seton Hill University, PA	W	University of Central Florida, FL	W
New York Institute of Technology, NY	W	Shawnee State University, OH	W	University of Central Missouri, MO	W
Niagara University, NY	W	Shepherd University, WV	W	University of Central Oklahoma, OK	W
North Carolina State University, NC	W	Shippensburg University of Pennsylvania, PA	W	University of Colorado Colorado Springs, CO	W
Northeastern State University, OK	W	Siena College, NY	W		
Northern Illinois University, IL	W	Slippery Rock University of Pennsylvania, PA	W	University of Dayton, OH	W
Northern Kentucky University, KY	W			University of Evansville, IN	W
Northern State University, SD	W	Sonoma State University, CA	W	The University of Findlay, OH	W
Northwest Christian University, OR	W	Southeastern Louisiana University, LA	W	University of Florida, FL	W
Northwestern College, IA	W			University of Georgia, GA	W
Northwest Nazarene University, ID	W				

University of Hartford, CT	W	University of South Carolina		**Swimming and diving**	
University of Hawaii at Manoa, HI	W	Aiken, SC	W	Adams State University, CO	M,W
University of Houston, TX	W	University of South Dakota, SD	W	Adelphi University, NY	M,W
University of Illinois at		University of Southern Indiana, IN	W	Arizona Christian University, AZ	W
Chicago, IL	W	University of Southern		Arizona State University at the	
University of Illinois at		Mississippi, MS	W	Downtown Phoenix campus, AZ	M,W
Springfield, IL	W	The University of Tampa, FL	W	Arizona State University at the	
University of Jamestown, ND	W	The University of Tennessee, TN	W	Polytechnic campus, AZ	M,W
The University of Kansas, KS	W	The University of Tennessee at		Arizona State University at the	
University of Kentucky, KY	W	Chattanooga, TN	W	Tempe campus, AZ	M,W
University of Louisiana at		The University of Tennessee at		Arizona State University at the	
Monroe, LA	W	Martin, TN	W	West campus, AZ	M,W
University of Louisville, KY	W	The University of Texas at		Auburn University, AL	M,W
University of Maine, ME	W	Austin, TX	W	Augustana University, SD	W
University of Maryland,		The University of Texas at San		Azusa Pacific University, CA	W
Baltimore County, MD	W	Antonio, TX	W	Ball State University, IN	M,W
University of Maryland, College		The University of Texas of the		Barton College, NC	M,W
Park, MD	W	Permian Basin, TX	W	Bellarmine University, KY	M,W
University of Massachusetts		University of the Incarnate		Binghamton University, State	
Amherst, MA	W	Word, TX	W	University of New York, NY	M,W
University of Massachusetts		University of the Pacific, CA	W	Biola University, CA	M,W
Lowell, MA	W	The University of Toledo, OH	W	Bloomsburg University of	
University of Memphis, TN	W	The University of Tulsa, OK	W	Pennsylvania, PA	M,W
University of Michigan, MI	W	University of Utah, UT	W	Boise State University, ID	W
University of Michigan–		University of Virginia, VA	W	Boston College, MA	M,W
Dearborn, MI	W	The University of Virginia'		Boston University, MA	M,W
University of Minnesota,		s College at Wise, VA	W	Bowling Green State University, OH	W
Crookston, MN	W	University of Washington, WA	W	Brenau University, GA	W
University of Minnesota, Duluth,		The University of West Alabama, AL	W	Brigham Young University, UT	M,W
MN	W	University of West Georgia, GA	W	Bryant University, RI	M,W
University of Minnesota, Twin		University of Wisconsin–		Bucknell University, PA	M
Cities Campus, MN	W	Madison, WI	W	California Baptist University, CA	M,W
University of Missouri, MO	W	University of Wisconsin–		California Polytechnic State	
University of Missouri–St.		Parkside, WI	W	University, San Luis Obispo, CA	M,W
Louis, MO	W	Upper Iowa University, IA	W	California State University,	
University of Montana, MT	W	Ursuline College, OH	W	Northridge, CA	M,W
University of Nebraska at		Utah State University, UT	W	Campbellsville University, KY	M,W
Kearney, NE	W	Utah Valley University, UT	W	Canisius College, NY	M,W
University of Nebraska–		Valdosta State University, GA	W	Carson-Newman University, TN	M,W
Lincoln, NE	W	Valley City State University, ND	W	Catawba College, NC	M,W
University of Nevada, Las Vegas,		Valparaiso University, IN	W	Central Connecticut State	
NV	W	Vanguard University of Southern		University, CT	W
University of Nevada, Reno, NV	W	California, CA	W	Chowan University, NC	W
University of New Haven, CT	W	Villanova University, PA	W	Clarion University of	
University of North Alabama, AL	W	Wayne State College, NE	W	Pennsylvania, PA	M,W
The University of North Carolina		Wayne State University, MI	W	Cleveland State University, OH	M,W
at Chapel Hill, NC	W	Webber International University, FL	W	Colgate University, NY	W
The University of North Carolina		Weber State University, UT	W	The College of Idaho, ID	M,W
at Charlotte, NC	W	West Chester University of		College of Saint Mary, NE	W
The University of North Carolina		Pennsylvania, PA	W	The College of Saint Rose, NY	M,W
at Greensboro, NC	W	Western Illinois University, IL	W	College of the Holy Cross, MA	W
The University of North Carolina		Western Kentucky University, KY	W	Colorado Mesa University, CO	M,W
at Pembroke, NC	W	Western Michigan University, MI	W	Colorado State University, CO	W
The University of North Carolina		Western Oregon University, OR	W	Concordia University Irvine, CA	M,W
Wilmington, NC	W	Western Washington University, WA	W	Converse College, SC	W
University of North Dakota, ND	W	West Texas A&M University, TX	W	Davidson College, NC	M,W
University of Northern Colorado, CO	W	West Virginia University		Drexel University, PA	M,W
University of Northern Iowa, IA	W	Institute of Technology, WV	W	Drury University, MO	M,W
University of North Florida, FL	W	West Virginia Wesleyan College, WV	W	Duquesne University, PA	W
University of North Georgia, GA	W	Wichita State University, KS	W	East Carolina University, NC	M,W
University of North Texas, TX	W	William Jewell College, MO	W	Eastern Michigan University, MI	M,W
University of Notre Dame, IN	W	William Woods University, MO	W	East Stroudsburg University of	
University of Oklahoma, OK	W	Winona State University, MN	W	Pennsylvania, PA	W
University of Oregon, OR	W	Winthrop University, SC	W	Emmanuel College, GA	M,W
University of Pikeville, KY	W	Wright State University, OH	W	Fairfield University, CT	M,W
University of Pittsburgh, PA	W	Youngstown State University, OH	W	Florida Agricultural and	
University of Rhode Island, RI	W			Mechanical University, FL	M,W
University of St. Francis, IL	W	**Squash**		Florida Gulf Coast University, FL	W
University of San Diego, CA	W	Drexel University, PA	M,W	Florida Institute of Technology,	
University of Science and Arts		Fordham University, NY	M	FL	M,W
of Oklahoma, OK	W	Stanford University, CA	W	Florida International	
University of Sioux Falls, SD	W	University of Providence, MT	W	University, FL	W
University of South Carolina, SC	W	University of Rochester, NY	M	Florida Southern College, FL	M,W
		University of Virginia, VA	M,W		

Florida State University, FL	M,W	Niagara University, NY	M,W	University of Houston, TX	W
Fordham University, NY	M,W	North Carolina State University,		University of Idaho, ID	W
Gannon University, PA	M,W	NC	M,W	University of Illinois at	
George Mason University, VA	M,W	Northern Arizona University, AZ	W	Chicago, IL	M,W
Georgetown University, DC	W	Northern Illinois University, IL	M,W	The University of Kansas, KS	W
The George Washington		Northern State University, SD	W	University of Kentucky, KY	M,W
University, DC	M,W	Nova Southeastern University, FL	M,W	University of Louisville, KY	M,W
Georgia Institute of Technology,		The Ohio State University, OH	M,W	University of Maine, ME	W
GA	M,W	Ohio University, OH	W	University of Maryland,	
Georgia Southern University, GA	W	Oklahoma Baptist University, OK	M,W	Baltimore County, MD	M,W
Grand Valley State University, MI	M,W	Oklahoma Christian University, OK	M,W	University of Massachusetts	
Hillsdale College, MI	W	Old Dominion University, VA	M,W	Amherst, MA	M,W
Indiana State University, IN	W	Oregon State University, OR	W	University of Miami, FL	M,W
Indiana University Bloomington, IN	M,W	Ouachita Baptist University, AR	M,W	University of Michigan, MI	M,W
Indiana University of		Penn State University Park, PA	M,W	University of Minnesota, Twin	
Pennsylvania, PA	M,W	Pepperdine University, CA	W	Cities Campus, MN	M,W
Indiana University–Purdue		Pfeiffer University, NC	M,W	University of Missouri, MO	M,W
University Indianapolis, IN	M,W	Purdue University, IN	M,W	University of Missouri–St.	
Inter American University of		Queens College of the City		Louis, MO	M,W
Puerto Rico, Bayamón Campus,		University of New York, NY	M,W	University of Nebraska at	
PR	M,W	Rice University, TX	W	Kearney, NE	W
Iona College, NY	M,W	Rider University, NJ	M,W	University of Nebraska–	
Iowa State University of Science		Roberts Wesleyan College, NY	M,W	Lincoln, NE	W
and Technology, IA	M,W	Rutgers University–New		University of Nevada, Las Vegas,	
James Madison University, VA	W	Brunswick, NJ	W	NV	M,W
King University, TN	M,W	Sacred Heart University, CT	W	University of Nevada, Reno, NV	W
Kutztown University of		Saginaw Valley State University,		University of New Hampshire, NH	W
Pennsylvania, PA	W	MI	M,W	University of North Carolina at	
La Salle University, PA	M,W	St. Ambrose University, IA	M,W	Asheville, NC	W
Lehigh University, PA	M,W	St. Bonaventure University, NY	M,W	The University of North Carolina	
Le Moyne College, NY	M,W	Saint Leo University, FL	M,W	at Chapel Hill, NC	M,W
Lenoir-Rhyne University, NC	M,W	Saint Louis University, MO	M,W	The University of North Carolina	
Lewis University, IL	M,W	Saint Peter's University, NJ	M,W	Wilmington, NC	M,W
Liberty University, VA	W	San Diego State University, CA	W	University of Northern Colorado,	
Life University, GA	W	Savannah College of Art and		CO	W
Lindenwood University, MO	M,W	Design, GA	M,W	University of Northern Iowa, IA	W
Lindsey Wilson College, KY	M,W	Seattle University, WA	M,W	University of North Florida, FL	W
Lock Haven University of		Shippensburg University of		University of North Texas, TX	W
Pennsylvania, PA	W	Pennsylvania, PA	M,W	University of Notre Dame, IN	M,W
Long Island University–LIU		Siena College, NY	W	University of Pittsburgh, PA	M,W
Brooklyn, NY	W	Soka University of America, CA	M,W	University of Rhode Island, RI	W
Long Island University–LIU		Southern Illinois University		University of Richmond, VA	W
Post, NY	W	Carbondale, IL	M,W	University of San Diego, CA	W
Louisiana State University and		Southern Methodist University, TX	M,W	University of Sioux Falls, SD	W
Agricultural & Mechanical		Stanford University, CA	M,W	University of South Carolina, SC	M,W
College, LA	M,W	Stony Brook University, State		University of South Dakota, SD	M,W
Loyola Marymount University, CA	W	University of New York, NY	W	University of Southern	
Loyola University New Orleans, LA	M,W	Texas A&M University, TX	M,W	California, CA	M,W
Lynn University, FL	W	Texas Christian University, TX	M,W	The University of Tampa, FL	M,W
Malone University, OH	M,W	Tiffin University, OH	M,W	The University of Tennessee, TN	M,W
Manhattan College, NY	M,W	Towson University, MD	M,W	The University of Texas at	
Marist College, NY	M,W	Truman State University, MO	W	Austin, TX	M,W
Marshall University, WV	W	Tulane University, LA	W	The University of Texas of the	
Maryville University of Saint		University at Buffalo, the State		Permian Basin, TX	M,W
Louis, MO	M,W	University of New York, NY	W	University of the Incarnate	
McKendree University, IL	M,W	The University of Akron, OH	W	Word, TX	M,W
Merrimack College, MA	W	The University of Alabama, AL	M,W	University of the Pacific, CA	M,W
Miami University, OH	M,W	University of Alaska Fairbanks, AK	W	The University of Toledo, OH	W
Michigan State University, MI	M,W	University of Arkansas, AR	W	University of Utah, UT	M,W
Millersville University of		University of Bridgeport, CT	M,W	University of Vermont, VT	W
Pennsylvania, PA	W	University of California, Davis,		University of Virginia, VA	M,W
Milligan College, TN	M,W	CA	W	University of Wisconsin–	
Minnesota State University		University of California, Los		Madison, WI	M,W
Moorhead, MN	W	Angeles, CA	W	University of Wisconsin–	
Missouri State University, MO	M,W	University of California, Santa		Milwaukee, WI	M,W
Missouri University of Science		Barbara, CA	M,W	University of Wyoming, WY	M,W
and Technology, MO	M	University of Cincinnati, OH	M,W	Ursuline College, OH	W
Morningside College, IA	M,W	University of Denver, CO	M,W	Valparaiso University, IN	M,W
Mount St. Mary's		University of Evansville, IN	M,W	Vanderbilt University, TN	W
University, MD	M,W	The University of Findlay, OH	M,W	Villanova University, PA	W
New Jersey Institute of		University of Florida, FL	M,W	Virginia Military Institute, VA	M
Technology, NJ	M,W	University of Georgia, GA	M,W	Virginia Polytechnic Institute	
New Mexico State University, NM	W	University of Hawaii at Manoa, HI	M,W	and State University, VA	M,W

Washington State University, WA	W	Caldwell University, NJ	W	Emporia State University, KS	M,W
Wayne State University, MI	M,W	California Polytechnic State		Evangel University, MO	M,W
West Chester University of		University, San Luis Obispo, CA	M,W	Fairfield University, CT	M,W
Pennsylvania, PA	M,W	California State University,		Fairleigh Dickinson University,	
Western Illinois University, IL	M,W	Fullerton, CA	W	Metropolitan Campus, NJ	M,W
Western State Colorado		California State University,		Ferris State University, MI	M,W
University, CO	W	Long Beach, CA	W	Flagler College, FL	M,W
West Virginia University, WV	M,W	California State University,		Florida Agricultural and	
West Virginia University		Northridge, CA	W	Mechanical University, FL	M,W
Institute of Technology, WV	M,W	California State University,		Florida Gulf Coast University, FL	M,W
West Virginia Wesleyan College, WV	M,W	Sacramento, CA	M,W	Florida Institute of Technology,	
William Jewell College, MO	M,W	California State University,		FL	M,W
Wright State University, OH	M,W	Stanislaus, CA	W	Florida International	
Youngstown State University, OH	W	Calumet College of Saint Joseph,		University, FL	W
		IN	M,W	Florida Southern College, FL	M,W
Table tennis		Cameron University, OK	M,W	Florida State University, FL	M,W
Inter American University of		Campbellsville University, KY	M,W	Fordham University, NY	M,W
Puerto Rico, Bayamón Campus,		Cardinal Stritch University, WI	M,W	Francis Marion University, SC	M,W
PR	M,W	Carlow University, PA	W	Franklin Pierce University, NH	M,W
Lindenwood University, MO	M,W	Carson-Newman University, TN	M,W	Furman University, SC	M,W
		Catawba College, NC	M,W	George Mason University, VA	M,W
Tennis		Cedarville University, OH	M,W	Georgetown College, KY	M,W
Abilene Christian University, TX	M,W	Central State University, OH	M,W	Georgetown University, DC	W
Academy of Art University, CA	W	Chaminade University of		The George Washington	
Adelphi University, NY	M,W	Honolulu, HI	W	University, DC	M,W
Alabama State University, AL	M,W	Chestnut Hill College, PA	M,W	Georgia College & State	
Alcorn State University, MS	M,W	Chowan University, NC	M,W	University, GA	M,W
Anderson University, SC	M,W	Christian Brothers University, TN	M,W	Georgia Institute of Technology,	
Appalachian State University, NC	M,W	The Citadel, The Military		GA	M,W
Aquinas College, MI	M,W	College of South Carolina, SC	M	Georgia Southern University, GA	M,W
Arizona Christian University, AZ	M,W	Clarion University of		Georgia Southwestern State	
Arizona State University at the		Pennsylvania, PA	W	University, GA	M,W
Downtown Phoenix campus, AZ	M,W	Clayton State University, GA	M,W	Georgia State University, GA	M,W
Arizona State University at the		Clemson University, SC	M,W	Gonzaga University, WA	M,W
Polytechnic campus, AZ	M,W	Cleveland State University, OH	W	Goshen College, IN	M,W
Arizona State University at the		Coastal Carolina University, SC	M,W	Grambling State University, LA	W
Tempe campus, AZ	M,W	Coker College, SC	M,W	Grand Valley State University, MI	M,W
Arizona State University at the		College of Charleston, SC	M,W	Hampton University, VA	M,W
West campus, AZ	M,W	College of Coastal Georgia, GA	M,W	Harding University, AR	M,W
Arkansas Tech University, AR	W	The College of Idaho, ID	W	Hawai`i Pacific University, HI	M,W
Auburn University, AL	M,W	College of Saint Mary, NE	W	Hillsdale College, MI	M,W
Auburn University at Montgomery,		The College of Saint Rose, NY	W	Hofstra University, NY	M,W
AL	M,W	The College of William and Mary,		Holy Family University, PA	W
Augustana University, SD	M,W	VA	M,W	Hope International University, CA	M,W
Austin Peay State University, TN	M,W	Colorado Mesa University, CO	M,W	Idaho State University, ID	M,W
Azusa Pacific University, CA	M,W	Colorado State University, CO	W	Indiana Tech, IN	M,W
Baker University, KS	M,W	Columbus State University, GA	M,W	Indiana University Bloomington, IN	M,W
Ball State University, IN	M,W	Concordia University Irvine, CA	M,W	Indiana University of	
Barry University, FL	M,W	Concordia University, Nebraska, NE	M,W	Pennsylvania, PA	W
Barton College, NC	M,W	Concord University, WV	M,W	Indiana University–Purdue	
Baylor University, TX	M,W	Converse College, SC	W	University Indianapolis, IN	M,W
Bellarmine University, KY	M,W	Creighton University, NE	M,W	Indiana University South Bend, IN	M,W
Belmont University, TN	M,W	Daemen College, NY	M,W	Indiana University Southeast, IN	M,W
Bemidji State University, MN	W	Dallas Baptist University, TX	W	Indiana Wesleyan University, IN	M,W
Bethel College, IN	M,W	Davidson College, NC	M,W	Iowa State University of Science	
Bethel College, KS	M,W	Delaware State University, DE	W	and Technology, IA	W
Bethune-Cookman University, FL	M,W	DePaul University, IL	M,W	Jackson State University, MS	M,W
Binghamton University, State		Dominican University of		James Madison University, VA	M,W
University of New York, NY	M,W	California, CA	W	John Brown University, AR	M,W
Biola University, CA	M,W	Drake University, IA	M,W	Johnson C. Smith University, NC	M,W
Bloomsburg University of		Drexel University, PA	M,W	Judson University, IL	M,W
Pennsylvania, PA	M,W	Drury University, MO	M,W	Kansas State University, KS	W
Bluefield College, VA	M,W	Duquesne University, PA	M,W	Kansas Wesleyan University, KS	M,W
Blue Mountain College, MS	M,W	East Carolina University, NC	M,W	Kennesaw State University, GA	M,W
Boise State University, ID	M,W	Eastern Michigan University, MI	M,W	King University, TN	M,W
Boston College, MA	M,W	Eastern Washington University, WA	M,W	Kutztown University of	
Boston University, MA	W	East Stroudsburg University of		Pennsylvania, PA	M,W
Bowie State University, MD	W	Pennsylvania, PA	W	Lamar University, TX	M,W
Bowling Green State University, OH	W	Eckerd College, FL	M,W	La Salle University, PA	M,W
Bradley University, IL	W	Elon University, NC	M,W	Lawrence Technological	
Brenau University, GA	W	Embry-Riddle Aeronautical		University, MI	M,W
Brigham Young University, UT	M,W	University–Daytona, FL	M,W	Lee University, TN	M,W
Bryant University, RI	M,W	Emmanuel College, GA	M,W	Lehigh University, PA	M,W
Butler University, IN	M,W				

Le Moyne College, NY	M,W	Northwest Missouri State		Southern Utah University, UT	M,W
Lenoir-Rhyne University, NC	M,W	University, MO	M,W	Southwest Baptist University, MO	M,W
Lewis University, IL	M,W	Nova Southeastern University, FL	W	Southwestern College, KS	M,W
Liberty University, VA	M,W	Oakland City University, IN	M,W	Spring Hill College, AL	M,W
Lincoln Memorial University, TN	M,W	The Ohio State University, OH	M,W	Stanford University, CA	M,W
Lindenwood University, MO	M,W	Oklahoma Baptist University, OK	M,W	Stephen F. Austin State	
Lindsey Wilson College, KY	M,W	Oklahoma State University, OK	M,W	University, TX	W
Lipscomb University, TN	M,W	Old Dominion University, VA	M,W	Stetson University, FL	M,W
Long Island University–LIU		Olivet Nazarene University, IL	M,W	Stonehill College, MA	M,W
Brooklyn, NY	W	Oral Roberts University, OK	M,W	Stony Brook University, State	
Long Island University–LIU		Ouachita Baptist University, AR	M,W	University of New York, NY	W
Post, NY	W	Our Lady of the Lake University,		Syracuse University, NY	W
Longwood University, VA	M,W	TX	M,W	Tarleton State University, TX	W
Louisiana State University and		Palm Beach Atlantic University, FL	M,W	Taylor University, IN	M,W
Agricultural & Mechanical		Penn State University Park, PA	M,W	Temple University, PA	M,W
College, LA	M,W	Pepperdine University, CA	M,W	Tennessee Technological	
Loyola Marymount University, CA	M,W	Pfeiffer University, NC	M,W	University, TN	M
Loyola University New Orleans, LA	M,W	Point Loma Nazarene University, CA	M,W	Tennessee Wesleyan University, TN	M,W
Lynn University, FL	M,W	Post University, CT	M,W	Texas A&M University, TX	M,W
Manhattan College, NY	W	Prairie View A&M University, TX	M,W	Texas A&M University–	
Marist College, NY	M,W	Presbyterian College, SC	M,W	Corpus Christi, TX	M,W
Marquette University, WI	M,W	Purdue University, IN	M,W	Texas A&M University–	
Marshall University, WV	W	Queens College of the City		Texarkana, TX	M,W
Maryville University of Saint		University of New York, NY	M,W	Texas Christian University, TX	M,W
Louis, MO	M,W	Quinnipiac University, CT	M,W	Texas State University, TX	W
McKendree University, IL	M,W	Radford University, VA	M,W	Texas Tech University, TX	M,W
Mercer University, GA	M,W	Rice University, TX	M,W	Thomas University, GA	W
Merrimack College, MA	M,W	Rider University, NJ	M,W	Tiffin University, OH	M,W
Metropolitan State University of		Roberts Wesleyan College, NY	M,W	Towson University, MD	W
Denver, CO	M,W	Rockhurst University, MO	M,W	Troy University, AL	M,W
Miami University, OH	W	Rollins College, FL	M,W	Truman State University, MO	M,W
Michigan State University, MI	M,W	Rutgers University–New		Tulane University, LA	M,W
Michigan Technological		Brunswick, NJ	M,W	University at Albany, State	
University, MI	M,W	Sacred Heart University, CT	M,W	University of New York, NY	W
Middle Georgia State University,		Saginaw Valley State University,		University at Buffalo, the State	
GA	M,W	MI	W	University of New York, NY	M,W
Middle Tennessee State		St. Ambrose University, IA	M,W	The University of Akron, OH	W
University, TN	M,W	St. Bonaventure University, NY	M,W	The University of Alabama, AL	M,W
Millersville University of		St. John's University, NY	M,W	The University of Alabama at	
Pennsylvania, PA	M,W	Saint Joseph's University, PA	M,W	Birmingham, AL	M,W
Milligan College, TN	M,W	Saint Leo University, FL	M,W	University of Arkansas, AR	M,W
Minnesota State University		St. Louis College of Pharmacy, MO	M,W	University of California, Davis,	
Moorhead, MN	W	Saint Louis University, MO	M,W	CA	M,W
Mississippi State University, MS	M,W	Saint Mary's College of		University of California,	
Missouri Baptist University, MO	M,W	California, CA	M,W	Irvine, CA	M,W
Missouri Valley College, MO	M,W	St. Mary's University, TX	M,W	University of California, Los	
Missouri Western State		Saint Peter's University, NJ	M,W	Angeles, CA	M,W
University, MO	W	St. Thomas University, FL	M,W	University of California, Santa	
Molloy College, NY	W	Samford University, AL	M,W	Barbara, CA	M,W
Morehead State University, KY	M,W	Sam Houston State University, TX	W	University of Central Arkansas, AR	W
Morehouse College, GA	M	San Diego State University, CA	M,W	University of Central Florida, FL	M,W
Morningside College, IA	M,W	Santa Clara University, CA	M,W	University of Central Oklahoma, OK	W
Mount Marty College, SD	W	Savannah College of Art and		University of Cincinnati, OH	W
Mount St. Mary's		Design, GA	M,W	University of Colorado Boulder, CO	W
University, MD	M,W	Seton Hill University, PA	W	University of Dayton, OH	M,W
Mount Vernon Nazarene		Shawnee State University, OH	W	University of Denver, CO	M,W
University, OH	M,W	Shepherd University, WV	M,W	The University of Findlay, OH	M,W
Murray State University, KY	W	Shippensburg University of		University of Florida, FL	M,W
Newberry College, SC	M,W	Pennsylvania, PA	W	University of Georgia, GA	M,W
New Jersey Institute of		Siena College, NY	M,W	University of Hawaii at Manoa, HI	M,W
Technology, NJ	M,W	Slippery Rock University of		University of Houston, TX	W
Newman University, KS	M,W	Pennsylvania, PA	W	University of Idaho, ID	M,W
New Mexico State University, NM	M,W	Sonoma State University, CA	M,W	University of Illinois at	
New York Institute of		Southeastern Louisiana		Chicago, IL	M,W
Technology, NY	M,W	University, LA	W	University of Illinois at	
Niagara University, NY	M,W	Southeastern Oklahoma State		Springfield, IL	M,W
North Carolina State University,		University, OK	M,W	The University of Kansas, KS	W
NC	M,W	Southeastern University, FL	M,W	University of Kentucky, KY	M,W
Northeastern State University, OK	W	Southeast Missouri State		University of Louisiana at	
Northern Arizona University, AZ	M,W	University, MO	W	Monroe, LA	W
Northern Illinois University, IL	M,W	Southern Arkansas		University of Louisville, KY	M,W
Northern Kentucky University, KY	M,W	University Magnolia, AR	W	University of Maryland, College	
Northwestern College, IA	M,W	Southern Methodist University, TX	M,W	Park, MD	W

University of Massachusetts Amherst, MA		
University of Memphis, TN	M,W	
University of Miami, FL	M,W	
University of Michigan, MI	M,W	
University of Minnesota, Crookston, MN	W	
University of Minnesota, Duluth, MN	W	
University of Minnesota, Twin Cities Campus, MN	M,W	
University of Missouri, MO	W	
University of Missouri–St. Louis, MO	M,W	
University of Montana, MT	M,W	
University of Montevallo, AL	W	
University of Nebraska at Kearney, NE	M,W	
University of Nebraska–Lincoln, NE	M,W	
University of Nevada, Las Vegas, NV	M,W	
University of Nevada, Reno, NV	M,W	
University of New Haven, CT	W	
University of New Orleans, LA	M,W	
University of North Alabama, AL	M,W	
University of North Carolina at Asheville, NC	M,W	
The University of North Carolina at Chapel Hill, NC	M,W	
The University of North Carolina at Charlotte, NC	M,W	
The University of North Carolina at Greensboro, NC	M,W	
The University of North Carolina Wilmington, NC	M,W	
University of North Dakota, ND	M,W	
University of Northern Colorado, CO	M,W	
University of Northern Iowa, IA	W	
University of North Florida, FL	M,W	
University of North Georgia, GA	M,W	
University of Notre Dame, IN	M,W	
University of Oklahoma, OK	M,W	
University of Oregon, OR	M,W	
University of Pikeville, KY	M,W	
University of Pittsburgh, PA	W	
University of Rhode Island, RI	W	
University of Richmond, VA	M,W	
University of St. Francis, IL	M,W	
University of San Diego, CA	M,W	
University of San Francisco, CA	M,W	
University of Sioux Falls, SD	W	
University of South Carolina, SC	M,W	
University of South Carolina Aiken, SC	M,W	
University of South Dakota, SD	W	
University of Southern California, CA	M,W	
University of Southern Indiana, IN	M,W	
University of Southern Mississippi, MS	M,W	
The University of Tampa, FL	W	
The University of Tennessee, TN	M,W	
The University of Tennessee at Chattanooga, TN	M,W	
The University of Tennessee at Martin, TN	W	
The University of Texas at Austin, TX	M,W	
The University of Texas at El Paso, TX	W	

The University of Texas at San Antonio, TX	M,W
The University of Texas of the Permian Basin, TX	M,W
University of the Incarnate Word, TX	M,W
University of the Pacific, CA	M,W
The University of Toledo, OH	M,W
The University of Tulsa, OK	M,W
University of Utah, UT	M,W
University of Virginia, VA	M,W
The University of Virginia's College at Wise, VA	M,W
University of Washington, WA	M,W
The University of West Alabama, AL	M,W
University of West Georgia, GA	W
University of Wisconsin–Madison, WI	M,W
University of Wisconsin–Milwaukee, WI	W
University of Wyoming, WY	W
Upper Iowa University, IA	W
Ursuline College, OH	W
Utah State University, UT	M,W
Valdosta State University, GA	M,W
Valparaiso University, IN	M,W
Vanderbilt University, TN	M,W
Virginia Commonwealth University, VA	M,W
Virginia Military Institute, VA	M
Virginia Polytechnic Institute and State University, VA	M,W
Wake Forest University, NC	M,W
Washington State University, WA	W
Wayne State University, MI	M,W
Webber International University, FL	M,W
Weber State University, UT	M,W
West Chester University of Pennsylvania, PA	M,W
Western Illinois University, IL	W
Western Kentucky University, KY	W
Western Michigan University, MI	M,W
Westmont College, CA	M,W
West Virginia University, WV	W
West Virginia Wesleyan College, WV	M,W
Wichita State University, KS	M,W
William Jewell College, MO	M,W
William Woods University, MO	M,W
Winona State University, MN	W
Winthrop University, SC	M,W
Wofford College, SC	M,W
Wright State University, OH	M,W
Youngstown State University, OH	M,W

Track and Field

Abilene Christian University, TX	M,W
Academy of Art University, CA	M,W
Adams State University, CO	M,W
Adelphi University, NY	M,W
Alabama State University, AL	M,W
Alcorn State University, MS	M,W
American University, DC	M,W
Anderson University, SC	M,W
Angelo State University, TX	M,W
Appalachian State University, NC	M,W
Aquinas College, MI	M,W
Arizona Christian University, AZ	M,W
Arizona State University at the Downtown Phoenix campus, AZ	M,W
Arizona State University at the Polytechnic campus, AZ	M,W
Arizona State University at the Tempe campus, AZ	M,W

Arizona State University at the West campus, AZ	M,W
Auburn University, AL	M,W
Augustana University, SD	M,W
Austin Peay State University, TN	W
Azusa Pacific University, CA	M,W
Baker University, KS	M,W
Ball State University, IN	W
Barton College, NC	M,W
Baylor University, TX	M,W
Bellarmine University, KY	M,W
Belmont University, TN	M,W
Bemidji State University, MN	W
Benedictine College, KS	M,W
Bethel College, IN	M,W
Bethel College, KS	M,W
Bethune-Cookman University, FL	M,W
Binghamton University, State University of New York, NY	M,W
Biola University, CA	M,W
Black Hills State University, SD	M,W
Bloomsburg University of Pennsylvania, PA	M,W
Boise State University, ID	M,W
Boston College, MA	M,W
Boston University, MA	M,W
Bowie State University, MD	M,W
Bowling Green State University, OH	W
Bradley University, IL	M,W
Brenau University, GA	W
Brigham Young University, UT	M,W
Bryan College, TN	M,W
Bryant University, RI	M,W
Bucknell University, PA	W
Butler University, IN	M,W
Caldwell University, NJ	M,W
California Baptist University, CA	M,W
California Polytechnic State University, San Luis Obispo, CA	M,W
California State Polytechnic University, Pomona, CA	M,W
California State University, Dominguez Hills, CA	W
California State University, Fullerton, CA	M,W
California State University, Long Beach, CA	M,W
California State University, Northridge, CA	M,W
California State University, Sacramento, CA	M,W
California State University, Stanislaus, CA	M,W
Calumet College of Saint Joseph, IN	M,W
Campbellsville University, KY	M,W
Cardinal Stritch University, WI	M,W
Carroll College, MT	M,W
Carson-Newman University, TN	M,W
Cedarville University, OH	M,W
Central Connecticut State University, CT	M,W
Central Methodist University, MO	M,W
Central Michigan University, MI	M,W
Central State University, OH	M,W
Chestnut Hill College, PA	M,W
Christian Brothers University, TN	M,W
The Citadel, The Military College of South Carolina, SC	M,W
Clarion University of Pennsylvania, PA	W
Clarke University, IA	M,W
Clayton State University, GA	M,W

Clemson University, SC	M,W	High Point University, NC	M,W	Michigan State University, MI	M,W
Cleveland State University, OH	W	Hillsdale College, MI	M,W	Michigan Technological	
Coastal Carolina University, SC	M,W	Holy Family University, PA	M,W	University, MI	M,W
Coker College, SC	M,W	Hope International University, CA	M,W	MidAmerica Nazarene University, KS	M,W
The College of Idaho, ID	M,W	Houston Baptist University, TX	M,W	Middle Tennessee State	
The College of Saint Rose, NY	M,W	Humboldt State University, CA	M,W	University, TN	M,W
College of the Holy Cross, MA	W	Idaho State University, ID	M,W	Millersville University of	
The College of William and Mary,		Indiana State University, IN	M,W	Pennsylvania, PA	W
VA	M,W	Indiana Tech, IN	M,W	Milligan College, TN	M,W
Colorado Mesa University, CO	M,W	Indiana University Bloomington, IN	M,W	Minnesota State University	
Colorado State University, CO	M,W	Indiana University of		Moorhead, MN	M,W
Columbus State University, GA	M,W	Pennsylvania, PA	M,W	Minot State University, ND	M,W
Concordia University Irvine, CA	M,W	Indiana University–Purdue		Mississippi State University, MS	M,W
Concordia University, Nebraska, NE	M,W	University Indianapolis, IN	M,W	Missouri Baptist University, MO	M,W
Concordia University, St. Paul, MN	M,W	Indiana Wesleyan University, IN	M,W	Missouri State University, MO	W
Concord University, WV	M,W	Inter American University of		Missouri University of Science	
Converse College, SC	W	Puerto Rico, Bayamón Campus,		and Technology, MO	M,W
Corban University, OR	M,W	PR	M,W	Missouri Valley College, MO	M,W
Cornerstone University, MI	M,W	Iona College, NY	M,W	Missouri Western State	
Culver-Stockton College, MO	M,W	Iowa State University of Science		University, MO	M,W
Daemen College, NY	M,W	and Technology, IA	M,W	Molloy College, NY	M,W
Dakota State University, SD	M,W	Jackson State University, MS	M,W	Morehead State University, KY	M,W
Dallas Baptist University, TX	W	Jacksonville University, FL	W	Morehouse College, GA	M
Davidson College, NC	M,W	James Madison University, VA	W	Morningside College, IA	M,W
Delaware State University, DE	M,W	Johnson C. Smith University, NC	M,W	Mount Marty College, SD	M,W
DePaul University, IL	M,W	Judson University, IL	M,W	Mount Mercy University, IA	M,W
Doane University, NE	M,W	Kansas State University, KS	M,W	Mount St. Mary's	
Dominican College, NY	M,W	Kansas Wesleyan University, KS	M,W	University, MD	M,W
Drake University, IA	M,W	Kennesaw State University, GA	M,W	Mount Vernon Nazarene	
Drury University, MO	M,W	Kent State University, OH	M,W	University, OH	M,W
Duquesne University, PA	M,W	Kentucky State University, KY	M,W	Murray State University, KY	W
East Carolina University, NC	M,W	King University, TN	M,W	Newberry College, SC	M,W
Eastern Michigan University, MI	M,W	Kutztown University of		New Mexico State University, NM	W
Eastern Oregon University, OR	M,W	Pennsylvania, PA	M,W	Niagara University, NY	W
Eastern Washington University, WA	M,W	Lamar University, TX	M,W	North Carolina State University,	
East Stroudsburg University of		La Salle University, PA	M,W	NC	M,W
Pennsylvania, PA	M,W	Lee University, TN	M,W	Northern Arizona University, AZ	M,W
Elon University, NC	W	Lehigh University, PA	M,W	Northern Kentucky University, KY	M,W
Embry-Riddle Aeronautical		Le Moyne College, NY	M,W	Northern State University, SD	M,W
University–Daytona, FL	M,W	Lenoir-Rhyne University, NC	M,W	Northwest Christian University, OR	M,W
Emmanuel College, GA	M,W	Lewis University, IL	M,W	Northwestern College, IA	M,W
Emporia State University, KS	M,W	Liberty University, VA	M,W	Northwest Missouri State	
Evangel University, MO	M,W	Life University, GA	W	University, MO	M,W
Fairleigh Dickinson University,		Lincoln University, MO	M,W	Northwest Nazarene University, ID	M,W
Metropolitan Campus, NJ	M,W	Lincoln University, PA	M,W	Northwest University, WA	M,W
Ferris State University, MI	M,W	Lindenwood University, MO	M,W	Nova Southeastern University, FL	M,W
Flagler College, FL	M,W	Lindsey Wilson College, KY	M,W	The Ohio State University, OH	M,W
Florida Agricultural and		Lipscomb University, TN	M,W	Ohio University, OH	W
Mechanical University, FL	M,W	Lock Haven University of		Oklahoma Baptist University, OK	M,W
Florida Institute of Technology,		Pennsylvania, PA	M,W	Oklahoma Christian University, OK	M,W
FL	M,W	Long Island University–LIU		Oklahoma City University, OK	M,W
Florida International		Brooklyn, NY	M,W	Oklahoma State University, OK	M,W
University, FL	M,W	Louisiana State University and		Olivet Nazarene University, IL	M,W
Florida State University, FL	M,W	Agricultural & Mechanical		Oral Roberts University, OK	M,W
Fordham University, NY	M,W	College, LA	M,W	Oregon State University, OR	W
Fort Lewis College, CO	W	Loyola University Chicago, IL	M,W	Our Lady of the Lake University,	
Franklin Pierce University, NH	M,W	Loyola University New Orleans, LA	M,W	TX	M,W
Furman University, SC	M,W	Lynn University, FL	W	Palm Beach Atlantic University, FL	M,W
George Mason University, VA	M,W	Malone University, OH	M,W	Penn State University Park, PA	M,W
Georgetown College, KY	M,W	Manhattan College, NY	M,W	Pepperdine University, CA	M,W
Georgetown University, DC	M,W	Mansfield University of		Pittsburg State University, KS	M,W
Georgia Institute of Technology,		Pennsylvania, PA	M,W	Point Loma Nazarene University, CA	W
GA	M,W	Marist College, NY	M,W	Point Park University, PA	M,W
Georgian Court University, NJ	M,W	Marquette University, WI	M,W	Post University, CT	M,W
Georgia Southern University, GA	W	Marshall University, WV	M,W	Prairie View A&M University, TX	M,W
Georgia State University, GA	W	Marymount California University,		Providence College, RI	M,W
Gonzaga University, WA	W	CA	M	Purdue University, IN	M,W
Goshen College, IN	M,W	Maryville University of Saint		Queens College of the City	
Graceland University, IA	M,W	Louis, MO	M,W	University of New York, NY	M,W
Grambling State University, LA	M,W	McKendree University, IL	M,W	Quinnipiac University, CT	W
Grand Valley State University, MI	M,W	Mercer University, GA	W	Radford University, VA	W
Hampton University, VA	M,W	Merrimack College, MA	M,W	Rice University, TX	M,W
Harding University, AR	M,W	Miami University, OH	M,W	Rider University, NJ	M,W

Robert Morris University, PA	W	Trevecca Nazarene University, TN	M,W	University of New Orleans, LA	M,W
Robert Morris University Illinois, IL	M,W	Trinity Christian College, IL	M,W	University of North Alabama, AL	W
Roberts Wesleyan College, NY	M,W	Troy University, AL	M,W	University of North Carolina at Asheville, NC	M,W
Rocky Mountain College, MT	M,W	Truman State University, MO	M,W	The University of North Carolina at Chapel Hill, NC	M,W
Rogers State University, OK	M,W	Tulane University, LA	W		
Rutgers University–New Brunswick, NJ	M,W	University at Albany, State University of New York, NY	M,W	The University of North Carolina at Charlotte, NC	M,W
Sacred Heart University, CT	M,W	University at Buffalo, the State University of New York, NY	M,W	The University of North Carolina at Greensboro, NC	M,W
Saginaw Valley State University, MI	M,W	The University of Akron, OH	M,W	The University of North Carolina at Pembroke, NC	M,W
St. Ambrose University, IA	M,W	The University of Alabama, AL	M,W		
Saint Augustine's University, NC	M,W	The University of Alabama at Birmingham, AL	W	The University of North Carolina Wilmington, NC	M,W
St. John's University, NY	W	University of Arkansas, AR	M,W	University of North Dakota, ND	M,W
Saint Joseph's University, PA	M,W	University of California, Davis, CA	M,W	University of Northern Colorado, CO	M,W
Saint Leo University, FL	M,W	University of California, Irvine, CA	M,W	University of Northern Iowa, IA	M,W
St. Louis College of Pharmacy, MO	M,W	University of California, Los Angeles, CA	M,W	University of North Florida, FL	M,W
Saint Louis University, MO	M,W			University of North Texas, TX	M,W
Saint Martin's University, WA	M,W	University of California, Santa Barbara, CA	M,W	University of Notre Dame, IN	M,W
Saint Mary's College of California, CA	M,W	University of Central Arkansas, AR	M,W	University of Oklahoma, OK	M,W
Saint Peter's University, NJ	M,W	University of Central Florida, FL	W	University of Oregon, OR	M,W
St. Thomas University, FL	M,W	University of Central Missouri, MO	M,W	University of Pikeville, KY	M,W
Samford University, AL	M,W	University of Central Oklahoma, OK	W	University of Pittsburgh, PA	M,W
Sam Houston State University, TX	M,W	University of Cincinnati, OH	M,W	University of Providence, MT	M,W
San Diego State University, CA	W	University of Colorado Boulder, CO	M,W	University of Rhode Island, RI	M,W
San Francisco State University, CA	W	University of Colorado Colorado Springs, CO	M,W	University of Richmond, VA	W
Santa Clara University, CA	M,W			University of St. Francis, IL	M,W
Seattle Pacific University, WA	M,W	University of Dayton, OH	W	University of San Diego, CA	W
Seattle University, WA	M,W	University of Evansville, IN	M,W	University of San Francisco, CA	W
Seton Hill University, PA	M,W	The University of Findlay, OH	M,W	University of Sioux Falls, SD	M,W
Shawnee State University, OH	M,W	University of Florida, FL	M,W	University of South Carolina, SC	M,W
Shippensburg University of Pennsylvania, PA	M,W	University of Georgia, GA	M,W	University of South Dakota, SD	M,W
		University of Hawaii at Manoa, HI	W	University of Southern California, CA	M,W
Slippery Rock University of Pennsylvania, PA	M,W	University of Houston, TX	M,W	University of Southern Indiana, IN	M,W
Soka University of America, CA	M,W	University of Idaho, ID	M,W	University of Southern Mississippi, MS	M,W
Southeastern Louisiana University, LA	M,W	University of Illinois at Chicago, IL	M,W	The University of Tampa, FL	M,W
Southeast Missouri State University, MO	M,W	University of Illinois at Springfield, IL	M,W	The University of Tennessee, TN	M,W
Southern Arkansas University–Magnolia, AR	M,W	University of Jamestown, ND	M,W	The University of Tennessee at Chattanooga, TN	M,W
		The University of Kansas, KS	M,W	The University of Texas at Austin, TX	M,W
Southern Illinois University Carbondale, IL	M,W	University of Kentucky, KY	M,W	The University of Texas at El Paso, TX	M,W
Southern Utah University, UT	M,W	University of Louisiana at Monroe, LA	M,W	The University of Texas at San Antonio, TX	M,W
Southwest Baptist University, MO	M,W	University of Louisville, KY	M,W		
Southwestern College, KS	M,W	University of Maine, ME	M,W	University of the Incarnate Word, TX	M,W
Spring Hill College, AL	M,W	University of Maryland, Baltimore County, MD	M,W	The University of Toledo, OH	W
Stanford University, CA	M,W	University of Maryland, College Park, MD	W	The University of Tulsa, OK	M,W
Stephen F. Austin State University, TX	M,W			University of Utah, UT	W
Stonehill College, MA	M,W	University of Massachusetts Amherst, MA	M,W	University of Vermont, VT	M,W
Stony Brook University, State University of New York, NY	M,W	University of Massachusetts Lowell, MA	M,W	University of Virginia, VA	M,W
Syracuse University, NY	M,W	University of Memphis, TN	M,W	University of Washington, WA	M,W
Tarleton State University, TX	M,W	University of Miami, FL	M,W	The University of West Alabama, AL	M,W
Taylor University, IN	M,W	University of Michigan, MI	M,W	University of West Georgia, GA	W
Temple University, PA	W	University of Minnesota, Twin Cities Campus, MN	M,W	University of Wisconsin–Madison, WI	M,W
Tennessee Technological University, TN	W	University of Missouri, MO	M,W	University of Wisconsin–Milwaukee, WI	M,W
Tennessee Wesleyan University, TN	M,W	University of Montana, MT	M,W	University of Wisconsin–Parkside, WI	M,W
Texas A&M University, TX	M,W	University of Nebraska at Kearney, NE	M,W	University of Wyoming, WY	M,W
Texas A&M University–Commerce, TX	M,W	University of Nebraska–Lincoln, NE	M,W	Upper Iowa University, IA	W
Texas A&M University–Corpus Christi, TX	M,W	University of Nevada, Las Vegas, NV	W	Ursuline College, OH	W
Texas Christian University, TX	M,W			Utah State University, UT	M,W
Texas State University, TX	M,W	University of Nevada, Reno, NV	W	Utah Valley University, UT	M,W
Texas Tech University, TX	M,W	University of New Hampshire, NH	M,W	Valley City State University, ND	M,W
Tiffin University, OH	M,W	University of New Haven, CT	M,W	Valparaiso University, IN	M,W
Towson University, MD	W			Vanderbilt University, TN	W

Vanguard University of Southern California, CA	M,W
Villanova University, PA	M,W
Virginia Commonwealth University, VA	M,W
Virginia Military Institute, VA	M,W
Virginia Polytechnic Institute and State University, VA	M,W
Wake Forest University, NC	M,W
Warner Pacific College, OR	M,W
Washington State University, WA	M,W
Wayland Baptist University, TX	M,W
Wayne State College, NE	M,W
Wayne State University, MI	W
Webber International University, FL	M,W
Weber State University, UT	M,W
West Chester University of Pennsylvania, PA	M,W
Western Illinois University, IL	M,W
Western Kentucky University, KY	M,W
Western Michigan University, MI	W
Western Oregon University, OR	W
Western State Colorado University, CO	M,W
Western Washington University, WA	M,W
Westminster College, UT	M,W
Westmont College, CA	M,W
West Texas A&M University, TX	M,W
West Virginia University, WV	W
West Virginia Wesleyan College, WV	M,W
Wichita State University, KS	M,W
William Jewell College, MO	M,W
William Woods University, MO	M,W
Winona State University, MN	W
Winthrop University, SC	M,W
Wofford College, SC	M,W
Wright State University, OH	W
Youngstown State University, OH	M,W

Triathlon

Arizona State University at the Downtown Phoenix campus, AZ	W
Arizona State University at the Polytechnic campus, AZ	W
Arizona State University at the Tempe campus, AZ	W
Arizona State University at the West campus, AZ	W
Daemen College, NY	W
Drury University, MO	M,W
University of South Dakota, SD	W
The University of West Alabama, AL	W
Webber International University, FL	M,W

Volleyball

Abilene Christian University, TX	W
Academy of Art University, CA	W
Adams State University, CO	W
Adelphi University, NY	W
Alabama State University, AL	W
Alcorn State University, MS	W
American University, DC	W
Anderson University, SC	W
Angelo State University, TX	W
Appalachian State University, NC	W
Aquinas College, MI	W
Arizona Christian University, AZ	W
Arizona State University at the Downtown Phoenix campus, AZ	W
Arizona State University at the Polytechnic campus, AZ	W

Arizona State University at the Tempe campus, AZ	W
Arizona State University at the West campus, AZ	W
Arkansas Tech University, AR	W
Auburn University, AL	W
Auburn University at Montgomery, AL	W
Augustana University, SD	W
Austin Peay State University, TN	W
Azusa Pacific University, CA	W
Baker University, KS	W
Ball State University, IN	M,W
Barry University, FL	W
Barton College, NC	M,W
Baylor University, TX	W
Bellarmine University, KY	W
Belmont University, TN	W
Bemidji State University, MN	W
Benedictine College, KS	W
Bethel College, IN	W
Bethel College, KS	W
Bethune-Cookman University, FL	W
Binghamton University, State University of New York, NY	W
Biola University, CA	W
Black Hills State University, SD	W
Bluefield College, VA	M,W
Boise State University, ID	W
Boston College, MA	W
Bowie State University, MD	W
Bowling Green State University, OH	W
Bradley University, IL	W
Brenau University, GA	W
Brigham Young University, UT	M,W
Bryan College, TN	M,W
Bryant University, RI	W
Bucknell University, PA	W
Butler University, IN	W
Caldwell University, NJ	W
California Baptist University, CA	M,W
California Polytechnic State University, San Luis Obispo, CA	W
California State Polytechnic University, Pomona, CA	W
California State University, Dominguez Hills, CA	W
California State University, Fullerton, CA	W
California State University, Long Beach, CA	M,W
California State University Maritime Academy, CA	W
California State University, Monterey Bay, CA	W
California State University, Northridge, CA	M,W
California State University, Sacramento, CA	W
California State University, San Bernardino, CA	W
California State University, Stanislaus, CA	W
Calumet College of Saint Joseph, IN	M,W
Cameron University, OK	W
Campbellsville University, KY	M,W
Canisius College, NY	W
Cardinal Stritch University, WI	M,W
Carlow University, PA	W
Carroll College, MT	W
Carson-Newman University, TN	W
Catawba College, NC	W

Cedarville University, OH	W
Central Connecticut State University, CT	W
Central Methodist University, MO	W
Central Michigan University, MI	W
Central State University, OH	W
Chaminade University of Honolulu, HI	W
Chestnut Hill College, PA	W
Chowan University, NC	W
Christian Brothers University, TN	W
The Citadel, The Military College of South Carolina, SC	W
Clarke University, IA	M,W
Clemson University, SC	W
Cleveland State University, OH	W
Coastal Carolina University, SC	W
Coker College, SC	M,W
Colgate University, NY	W
College of Charleston, SC	W
College of Coastal Georgia, GA	W
The College of Idaho, ID	W
College of Saint Mary, NE	W
The College of Saint Rose, NY	W
College of the Holy Cross, MA	W
College of the Ozarks, MO	W
The College of William and Mary, VA	W
Colorado Mesa University, CO	W
Colorado State University, CO	W
Columbia College, MO	W
Columbus State University, GA	W
Concordia University Irvine, CA	M,W
Concordia University, Nebraska, NE	W
Concordia University, St. Paul, MN	W
Concord University, WV	W
Converse College, SC	W
Corban University, OR	W
Cornerstone University, MI	W
Creighton University, NE	W
Culver-Stockton College, MO	M,W
Daemen College, NY	M,W
Dakota State University, SD	W
Dallas Baptist University, TX	W
Davidson College, NC	W
Delaware State University, DE	W
DePaul University, IL	W
Doane University, NE	W
Dominican College, NY	W
Dominican University of California, CA	W
Drake University, IA	W
Drury University, MO	W
Duquesne University, PA	W
East Carolina University, NC	W
East Central University, OK	W
Eastern Michigan University, MI	W
Eastern Oregon University, OR	W
Eastern Washington University, WA	W
East Stroudsburg University of Pennsylvania, PA	W
Eckerd College, FL	W
Elon University, NC	M,W
Embry-Riddle Aeronautical University–Daytona, FL	W
Emmanuel College, GA	M,W
Emporia State University, KS	W
Evangel University, MO	W
The Evergreen State College, WA	W
Fairfield University, CT	W
Fairleigh Dickinson University, Metropolitan Campus, NJ	W
Felician University, NJ	W

Ferris State University, MI	W	Kansas Wesleyan University, KS	W	Missouri Western State
Flagler College, FL	W	Kennesaw State University, GA	W	University, MO	W
Florida Agricultural and		Kent State University, OH	W	Molloy College, NY	W
Mechanical University, FL	W	Kentucky State University, KY	W	Montana Tech of The University	
Florida Atlantic University, FL	W	King University, TN	M,W	of Montana, MT	W
Florida Gulf Coast University, FL	W	Kutztown University of		Morehead State University, KY	W
Florida Institute of Technology,		Pennsylvania, PA	W	Morningside College, IA	W
FL	W	Lamar University, TX	W	Mount Marty College, SD	W
Florida International		La Salle University, PA	W	Mount Mercy University, IA	M,W
University, FL	W	Lawrence Technological		Mount Vernon Nazarene	
Florida National University, FL	W	University, MI	M,W	University, OH	W
Florida Southern College, FL	W	Lee University, TN	W	Murray State University, KY	W
Florida State University, FL	W	Lehigh University, PA	W	Newberry College, SC	W
Fordham University, NY	W	Le Moyne College, NY	W	New Jersey Institute of	
Fort Lewis College, CO	W	Lenoir-Rhyne University, NC	W	Technology, NJ	M,W
Francis Marion University, SC	W	Lewis University, IL	M,W	Newman University, KS	W
Franklin Pierce University, NH	W	Liberty University, VA	W	New Mexico Highlands University,	
Furman University, SC	W	Life University, GA	W	NM	W
Gannon University, PA	W	Lincoln Memorial University, TN	W	New Mexico State University, NM	W
George Mason University, VA	M,W	Lincoln University, PA	W	New York Institute of	
Georgetown College, KY	W	Lindenwood University, MO	M,W	Technology, NY	W
Georgetown University, DC	W	Lindsey Wilson College, KY	W	Niagara University, NY	W
The George Washington		Lipscomb University, TN	W	North Carolina State University,	
University, DC	W	Lock Haven University of		NC	W
Georgia College & State		Pennsylvania, PA	W	Northern Arizona University, AZ	W
University, GA	W	Long Island University–LIU		Northern Illinois University, IL	W
Georgia Institute of Technology,		Brooklyn, NY	W	Northern Kentucky University, KY	W
GA	W	Long Island University–LIU		Northern State University, SD	W
Georgian Court University, NJ	W	Post, NY	W	Northwest Christian University, OR	W
Georgia Southern University, GA	W	Louisiana State University and		Northwestern College, IA	W
Georgia State University, GA	W	Agricultural & Mechanical College,		Northwest Missouri State	
Gonzaga University, WA	W	LA	W	University, MO	W
Goshen College, IN	M,W	Loyola Marymount University, CA	W	Northwest Nazarene University, ID	W
Governors State University, IL	M,W	Loyola University Chicago, IL	M,W	Northwest University, WA	W
Graceland University, IA	M,W	Loyola University New Orleans, LA	W	Nova Southeastern University, FL	W
Grambling State University, LA	W	Lubbock Christian University, TX	W	Oakland City University, IN	W
Grand Valley State University, MI	W	Lynn University, FL	W	The Ohio State University, OH	M,W
Hampton University, VA	W	Lyon College, AR	W	Ohio University, OH	W
Harding University, AR	W	Malone University, OH	W	Oklahoma Baptist University, OK	W
Harris-Stowe State University, MO	W	Manhattan College, NY	W	Oklahoma City University, OK	W
Hawai`i Pacific University, HI	W	Marist College, NY	W	Olivet Nazarene University, IL	W
High Point University, NC	W	Marquette University, WI	W	Oral Roberts University, OK	W
Hillsdale College, MI	W	Marshall University, WV	W	Oregon State University, OR	W
Hofstra University, NY	W	Maryville University of Saint		Ouachita Baptist University, AR	W
Holy Family University, PA	W	Louis, MO	W	Our Lady of the Lake University,	
Hope International University, CA	M,W	McKendree University, IL	M,W	TX	W
Houston Baptist University, TX	W	Mercer University, GA	W	Palm Beach Atlantic University, FL	W
Humboldt State University, CA	W	Mercy College, NY	W	Penn State University Park, PA	M,W
Idaho State University, ID	W	Merrimack College, MA	W	Pepperdine University, CA	M,W
Indiana State University, IN	W	Metropolitan State University of		Pfeiffer University, NC	W
Indiana Tech, IN	W	Denver, CO	W	Pittsburg State University, KS	W
Indiana University Bloomington, IN	W	Miami University, OH	W	Point Loma Nazarene University, CA	W
Indiana University Northwest, IN	W	Michigan State University, MI	W	Point Park University, PA	W
Indiana University of		Michigan Technological		Post University, CT	W
Pennsylvania, PA	W	University, MI	W	Prairie View A&M University, TX	W
Indiana University–Purdue		MidAmerica Nazarene University, KS	W	Presbyterian College, SC	W
University Indianapolis, IN	W	Middle Georgia State University,		Providence College, RI	W
Indiana University South Bend, IN	W	GA	W	Purdue University, IN	W
Indiana University Southeast, IN	W	Middle Tennessee State		Queens College of the City	
Indiana Wesleyan University, IN	W	University, TN	W	University of New York, NY	W
Inter American University of		Millersville University of		Quinnipiac University, CT	W
Puerto Rico, Bayamón Campus,		Pennsylvania, PA	W	Radford University, VA	W
PR	M,W	Milligan College, TN	M,W	Regis University, CO	W
Iona College, NY	W	Minnesota State University		Rice University, TX	W
Iowa State University of Science		Moorhead, MN	W	Rider University, NJ	W
and Technology, IA	W	Minot State University, ND	W	Robert Morris University, PA	W
Jackson State University, MS	W	Mississippi State University, MS	W	Robert Morris University	
Jacksonville University, FL	W	Missouri Baptist University, MO	M,W	Illinois, IL	M,W
James Madison University, VA	W	Missouri State University, MO	W	Roberts Wesleyan College, NY	W
John Brown University, AR	W	Missouri University of Science		Rockhurst University, MO	W
Johnson C. Smith University, NC	W	and Technology, MO	W	Rocky Mountain College, MT	W
Judson University, IL	M,W	Missouri Valley College, MO	M,W	Rollins College, FL	W
Kansas State University, KS	W				

Rutgers University–New Brunswick, NJ	W	Texas Christian University, TX	W	University of Minnesota, Crookston, MN	W
Sacred Heart University, CT	M,W	Texas State University, TX	W	University of Minnesota, Duluth, MN	W
Saginaw Valley State University, MI	W	Texas Tech University, TX	W	University of Minnesota, Twin Cities Campus, MN	W
		Texas Woman's University, TX	W		
St. Ambrose University, IA	M,W	Tiffin University, OH	W	University of Missouri, MO	W
Saint Augustine's University, NC	W	Towson University, MD	W	University of Missouri–St. Louis, MO	W
St. John's University, NY	W	Trevecca Nazarene University, TN	W	University of Montana, MT	W
Saint Leo University, FL	W	Trinity Christian College, IL	W	University of Montevallo, AL	W
St. Louis College of Pharmacy, MO	W	Troy University, AL	W	University of Nebraska at Kearney, NE	W
Saint Louis University, MO	W	Truett McConnell University, GA	W		
Saint Martin's University, WA	W	Truman State University, MO	W	University of Nebraska–Lincoln, NE	W
		Tulane University, LA	W		
Saint Mary's College of California, CA	W	Union University, TN	W	University of Nevada, Las Vegas, NV	W
St. Mary's University, TX	W	University at Albany, State University of New York, NY	W	University of Nevada, Reno, NV	W
Saint Peter's University, NJ	W	University at Buffalo, the State University of New York, NY	W	University of New Hampshire, NH	W
St. Thomas Aquinas College, NY	W			University of New Haven, CT	W
St. Thomas University, FL	W	The University of Akron, OH	W	University of New Orleans, LA	W
Samford University, AL	W	The University of Alabama, AL	W	University of North Alabama, AL	W
Sam Houston State University, TX	W	The University of Alabama at Birmingham, AL	W	University of North Carolina at Asheville, NC	W
San Diego State University, CA	W	University of Alaska Fairbanks, AK	W		
San Francisco State University, CA	W	University of Arkansas, AR	W	The University of North Carolina at Chapel Hill, NC	W
Santa Clara University, CA	W	University of Bridgeport, CT	W		
Seattle Pacific University, WA	W	University of California, Davis, CA	W	The University of North Carolina at Charlotte, NC	W
Seattle University, WA	W	University of California, Irvine, CA	M,W	The University of North Carolina at Greensboro, NC	W
Seton Hill University, PA	W				
Shawnee State University, OH	W	University of California, Los Angeles, CA	M,W	The University of North Carolina at Pembroke, NC	W
Shepherd University, WV	W	University of California, Riverside, CA	W	The University of North Carolina Wilmington, NC	W
Shippensburg University of Pennsylvania, PA	W	University of California, Santa Barbara, CA	M,W		
Siena College, NY	W	University of Central Arkansas, AR	W	University of North Dakota, ND	W
Slippery Rock University of Pennsylvania, PA	W	University of Central Florida, FL	W	University of Northern Colorado, CO	W
Sonoma State University, CA	W	University of Central Missouri, MO	W	University of Northern Iowa, IA	W
Southeastern Louisiana University, LA	W	University of Central Oklahoma, OK	W	University of North Florida, FL	W
		University of Cincinnati, OH	W	University of North Texas, TX	W
Southeastern Oklahoma State University, OK	W	University of Colorado Boulder, CO	W	University of Notre Dame, IN	W
Southeastern University, FL	W	University of Colorado Colorado Springs, CO	W	University of Oklahoma, OK	W
Southeast Missouri State University, MO	W	University of Dayton, OH	W	University of Oregon, OR	W
		University of Denver, CO	W	University of Pikeville, KY	W
Southern Arkansas University–Magnolia, AR	W	University of Evansville, IN	W	University of Pittsburgh, PA	W
		The University of Findlay, OH	W	University of Providence, MT	W
Southern Illinois University Carbondale, IL	W	University of Florida, FL	W	University of Rhode Island, RI	W
Southern Methodist University, TX	W	University of Georgia, GA	W	University of St. Francis, IL	W
Southern Utah University, UT	W	University of Hartford, CT	W	University of St. Thomas, TX	W
Southwest Baptist University, MO	W	University of Hawaii at Manoa, HI	M,W	University of San Diego, CA	W
Southwestern College, KS	W	University of Houston, TX	W	University of San Francisco, CA	W
Spring Hill College, AL	W	University of Idaho, ID	W	University of Sioux Falls, SD	W
Stanford University, CA	M,W	University of Illinois at Chicago, IL	W	University of South Carolina, SC	W
Stephen F. Austin State University, TX	W	University of Illinois at Springfield, IL	W	University of South Carolina Aiken, SC	W
Stetson University, FL	W	University of Jamestown, ND	W	University of South Dakota, SD	W
Stonehill College, MA	W	The University of Kansas, KS	W	University of Southern California, CA	M,W
Stony Brook University, State University of New York, NY	W	University of Kentucky, KY	W	University of Southern Indiana, IN	W
		University of Louisiana at Monroe, LA	W	University of Southern Mississippi, MS	W
Syracuse University, NY	W	University of Louisville, KY	W	The University of Tampa, FL	W
Tarleton State University, TX	W			The University of Tennessee, TN	W
Taylor University, IN	W	University of Maryland, Baltimore County, MD	W		
Temple University, PA	W	University of Maryland, College Park, MD	W	The University of Tennessee at Chattanooga, TN	W
Tennessee Technological University, TN	W			The University of Tennessee at Martin, TN	W
Tennessee Wesleyan University, TN	W	University of Massachusetts Lowell, MA	W		
Texas A&M International University, TX	W	University of Memphis, TN	W	The University of Texas at Austin, TX	W
Texas A&M University, TX	W	University of Miami, FL	W	The University of Texas at El Paso, TX	W
Texas A&M University–Commerce, TX	W	University of Michigan, MI	W	The University of Texas at San Antonio, TX	W
Texas A&M University–Corpus Christi, TX	W	University of Michigan–Dearborn, MI	W		

The University of Texas of the Permian Basin, TX — W
University of the Incarnate Word, TX — W
University of the Pacific, CA — M,W
The University of Toledo, OH — W
The University of Tulsa, OK — W
University of Utah, UT — W
University of Virginia, VA — W
The University of Virginia's College at Wise, VA — W
University of Washington, WA — W
The University of West Alabama, AL — W
University of West Georgia, GA — W
University of Wisconsin–Madison, WI — W
University of Wisconsin–Milwaukee, WI — W
University of Wisconsin–Parkside, WI — W
University of Wyoming, WY — W
Upper Iowa University, IA — W
Ursuline College, OH — W
Utah State University, UT — W
Utah Valley University, UT — W
Valdosta State University, GA — W
Valley City State University, ND — W
Valparaiso University, IN — W
Vanguard University of Southern California, CA — W
Villanova University, PA — W
Virginia Commonwealth University, VA — W
Wake Forest University, NC — W
Warner Pacific College, OR — W
Washington State University, WA — W
Wayland Baptist University, TX — W
Wayne State College, NE — W
Wayne State University, MI — W
Webber International University, FL — M,W
Weber State University, UT — W
West Chester University of Pennsylvania, PA — W
Western Illinois University, IL — W
Western Kentucky University, KY — W
Western Michigan University, MI — W
Western Oregon University, OR — W
Western State Colorado University, CO — W
Western Washington University, WA — W
Westminster College, UT — W
Westmont College, CA — W
West Texas A&M University, TX — W
West Virginia University, WV — W
West Virginia University Institute of Technology, WV — W
West Virginia Wesleyan College, WV — W
Wichita State University, KS — W
William Jewell College, MO — W
William Woods University, MO — W
Winona State University, MN — W
Winthrop University, SC — W
Wofford College, SC — W
Wright State University, OH — W
Youngstown State University, OH — W

Water polo

Arizona State University at the Downtown Phoenix campus, AZ — W
Arizona State University at the Polytechnic campus, AZ — W
Arizona State University at the Tempe campus, AZ — W
Arizona State University at the West campus, AZ — W
California Baptist University, CA — M,W
California State University, Long Beach, CA — M,W
California State University, Monterey Bay, CA — W
Concordia University Irvine, CA — M,W
Fordham University, NY — M
Gannon University, PA — M,W
The George Washington University, DC — M
Indiana University Bloomington, IN — W
Iona College, NY — W
La Salle University, PA — M,W
Lindenwood University, MO — M,W
Loyola Marymount University, CA — M,W
Marist College, NY — W
McKendree University, IL — M,W
Pepperdine University, CA — M
San Diego State University, CA — W
Santa Clara University, CA — M,W
Siena College, NY — W
Stanford University, CA — M,W
University of California, Davis, CA — M,W
University of California, Irvine, CA — M,W
University of California, Los Angeles, CA — M,W
University of California, Santa Barbara, CA — M,W
University of Hawaii at Manoa, HI — W
University of Michigan, MI — W
University of Southern California, CA — M,W
University of the Pacific, CA — M,W

Weight lifting

Inter American University of Puerto Rico, Bayamón Campus, PR — M
Lindenwood University, MO — M,W

Wrestling

Adams State University, CO — M
American University, DC — M
Appalachian State University, NC — M
Arizona State University at the Downtown Phoenix campus, AZ — M
Arizona State University at the Polytechnic campus, AZ — M
Arizona State University at the Tempe campus, AZ — M
Arizona State University at the West campus, AZ — M
Augustana University, SD — M
Baker University, KS — M
Bellarmine University, KY — M
Benedictine College, KS — M
Binghamton University, State University of New York, NY — M
Bloomsburg University of Pennsylvania, PA — M
Bluefield College, VA — M
Bucknell University, PA — M
California Baptist University, CA — M
California Polytechnic State University, San Luis Obispo, CA — M
Calumet College of Saint Joseph, IN — M
Campbellsville University, KY — M,W
Central Michigan University, MI — M
The Citadel, The Military College of South Carolina, SC — M

Clarion University of Pennsylvania, PA — M
Cleveland State University, OH — M
Coker College, SC — M
Colorado Mesa University, CO — M
Concordia University, Nebraska, NE — M
Davidson College, NC — M
Drexel University, PA — M
Drury University, MO — M
Eastern Michigan University, MI — M
East Stroudsburg University of Pennsylvania, PA — M
Emmanuel College, GA — M,W
Gannon University, PA — M
George Mason University, VA — M
Graceland University, IA — M
Hofstra University, NY — M
Indiana Tech, IN — M
Indiana University Bloomington, IN — M
Iowa State University of Science and Technology, IA — M
Kansas Wesleyan University, KS — M
Kent State University, OH — M
King University, TN — M,W
Kutztown University of Pennsylvania, PA — M
Lehigh University, PA — M
Life University, GA — M,W
Lindenwood University, MO — M,W
Lindsey Wilson College, KY — M
Lock Haven University of Pennsylvania, PA — M
Long Island University–LIU Post, NY — M
Lyon College, AR — M,W
Maryville University of Saint Louis, MO — M
McKendree University, IL — M,W
Michigan State University, MI — M
Millersville University of Pennsylvania, PA — M
Minnesota State University Moorhead, MN — M
Missouri Baptist University, MO — M,W
Missouri Valley College, MO — M,W
Morningside College, IA — M
Newberry College, SC — M
Newman University, KS — M
North Carolina State University, NC — M
Northern Illinois University, IL — M
Northern State University, SD — M
Northwestern College, IA — M
The Ohio State University, OH — M
Ohio University, OH — M
Oklahoma City University, OK — M,W
Oklahoma State University, OK — M
Old Dominion University, VA — M
Oregon State University, OR — M
Ouachita Baptist University, AR — M
Penn State University Park, PA — M
Purdue University, IN — M
Rider University, NJ — M
Rutgers University–New Brunswick, NJ — M
Sacred Heart University, CT — M
San Francisco State University, CA — M
Seton Hill University, PA — M
Shippensburg University of Pennsylvania, PA — M
Southeastern University, FL — M
Southwestern College, KS — W
Stanford University, CA — M

Tiffin University, OH	M
Truett McConnell University, GA	M
Truman State University, MO	M
University at Buffalo, the State University of New York, NY	M
University of Central Missouri, MO	M
University of Central Oklahoma, OK	M
The University of Findlay, OH	M
University of Jamestown, ND	M,W
University of Maryland, College Park, MD	M
University of Michigan, MI	M
University of Minnesota, Twin Cities Campus, MN	M
University of Missouri, MO	M

University of Nebraska at Kearney, NE	M
University of Nebraska–Lincoln, NE	M
The University of North Carolina at Chapel Hill, NC	M
The University of North Carolina at Pembroke, NC	M
University of Northern Colorado, CO	M
University of Northern Iowa, IA	M
University of Oklahoma, OK	M
University of Pittsburgh, PA	M
University of Providence, MT	M
The University of Tennessee at Chattanooga, TN	M

University of Virginia, VA	M
University of Wisconsin–Madison, WI	M
University of Wisconsin–Parkside, WI	M
University of Wyoming, WY	M
Upper Iowa University, IA	M
Utah Valley University, UT	M
Virginia Military Institute, VA	M
Wayland Baptist University, TX	M,W
Western State Colorado University, CO	M
West Virginia University, WV	M
West Virginia University Institute of Technology, WV	M

Co-Op Programs

Adams State University, CO
Alabama State University, AL
Alcorn State University, MS
Alfred University, NY
Allen College, IA
Alma College, MI
American University, DC
Anderson University, SC
Andrews University, MI
Aquinas College, MI
Arizona State University at the Downtown Phoenix campus, AZ
Arizona State University at the Polytechnic campus, AZ
Arizona State University at the Tempe campus, AZ
Arizona State University at the West campus, AZ
Athens State University, AL
Auburn University, AL
Auburn University at Montgomery, AL
Augsburg University, MN
Austin Peay State University, TN
Averett University, VA
Azusa Pacific University, CA
Ball State University, IN
Bates College, ME
Bay Path University, MA
Becker College, MA
Bellarmine University, KY
Belmont University, TN
Benedictine College, KS
Bethany Lutheran College, MN
Bethel College, KS
Bethune-Cookman University, FL
Biola University, CA
Birmingham-Southern College, AL
Black Hills State University, SD
Bloomsburg University of Pennsylvania, PA
Bluefield College, VA
Boise State University, ID
Boston University, MA
Bowie State University, MD
Bowling Green State University, OH
Bradley University, IL
Buffalo State College, State University of New York, NY
Butler University, IN
California Christian College, CA
California Institute of Technology, CA
California Lutheran University, CA
California Polytechnic State University, San Luis Obispo, CA
California State Polytechnic University, Pomona, CA
California State University, Dominguez Hills, CA
California State University, Fullerton, CA
California State University, Monterey Bay, CA
California State University, Sacramento, CA
California State University, San Bernardino, CA
California State University, Stanislaus, CA
California University of Pennsylvania, PA
Calumet College of Saint Joseph, IN
Campbellsville University, KY
Canisius College, NY
Capital University, OH
Cardinal Stritch University, WI

Carlos Albizu University, PR
Carlow University, PA
Carnegie Mellon University, PA
Carroll College, MT
Case Western Reserve University, OH
The Catholic University of America, DC
Cedarville University, OH
Central Connecticut State University, CT
Central Methodist University, MO
Central State University, OH
Centre College, KY
Champlain College, VT
Charlotte Christian College and Theological Seminary, NC
Chatham University, PA
Chestnut Hill College, PA
Chowan University, NC
Christendom College, VA
Christian Brothers University, TN
The Citadel, The Military College of South Carolina, SC
Clarion University of Pennsylvania, PA
Clarke University, IA
Clarkson University, NY
Clayton State University, GA
Clemson University, SC
Cleveland State University, OH
Coastal Carolina University, SC
The College at Brockport, State University of New York, NY
College of Charleston, SC
The College of Idaho, ID
The College of New Rochelle, NY
College of Staten Island of the City University of New York, NY
College of the Atlantic, ME
Colorado State University, CO
Columbia College, MO
Columbia College Chicago, IL
Columbus State University, GA
Conception Seminary College, MO
Concord University, WV
Converse College, SC
Corban University, OR
Cornell University, NY
Dakota State University, SD
Delaware State University, DE
Delaware Valley University, PA
DePauw University, IN
DeSales University, PA
DigiPen Institute of Technology, WA
Doane University, NE
Dominican College, NY
Drake University, IA
Drexel University, PA
Drury University, MO
Earlham College, IN
East Carolina University, NC
Eastern Michigan University, MI
Eastern Oregon University, OR
Eastern Washington University, WA
Edgewood College, WI
Elmhurst College, IL
Elms College, MA
Embry-Riddle Aeronautical University–Daytona, FL
Emory & Henry College, VA
Emory University, GA
Emporia State University, KS
Endicott College, MA

Eugene Lang College of Liberal Arts, NY
Fairleigh Dickinson University, Florham Campus, NJ
Fairleigh Dickinson University, Metropolitan Campus, NJ
Farmingdale State College, NY
Felician University, NJ
Ferris State University, MI
FIDM/Fashion Institute of Design & Merchandising, Los Angeles Campus, CA
Flagler College, FL
Florida Agricultural and Mechanical University, FL
Florida Atlantic University, FL
Florida Gulf Coast University, FL
Florida Institute of Technology, FL
Florida International University, FL
Florida National University, FL
Florida State University, FL
Framingham State University, MA
Franklin College, IN
Frostburg State University, MD
Gannon University, PA
Geneva College, PA
George Mason University, VA
Georgetown College, KY
The George Washington University, DC
Georgia Institute of Technology, GA
Georgia Southern University, GA
Georgia State University, GA
Gordon College, MA
Graceland University, IA
Grambling State University, LA
Grand Valley State University, MI
Greenville University, IL
Guilford College, NC
Gustavus Adolphus College, MN
Gwynedd Mercy University, PA
Hampden-Sydney College, VA
Hampton University, VA
Harding University, AR
Harris-Stowe State University, MO
Hawai`i Pacific University, HI
Hendrix College, AR
High Point University, NC
Hilbert College, NY
Hiram College, OH
Hofstra University, NY
Hollins University, VA
Holy Family University, PA
Humboldt State University, CA
Husson University, ME
Idaho State University, ID
Indiana State University, IN
Indiana Tech, IN
Indiana University Bloomington, IN
Indiana University East, IN
Indiana University Northwest, IN
Indiana University of Pennsylvania, PA
Indiana University–Purdue University Indianapolis, IN
Inter American University of Puerto Rico, Bayamón Campus, PR
Iowa State University of Science and Technology, IA
Jackson State University, MS
Jacksonville University, FL
Jefferson College of Health Sciences, VA
John Brown University, AR

John Jay College of Criminal Justice of the City University of New York, NY
Johnson C. Smith University, NC
Johnson University, TN
Kansas State University, KS
Kean University, NJ
Keene State College, NH
Kennesaw State University, GA
Kent State University, OH
Kentucky State University, KY
Lamar University, TX
La Salle University, PA
Lasell College, MA
Lawrence Technological University, MI
Lee University, TN
Lehigh University, PA
Lehman College of the City University of New York, NY
LeTourneau University, TX
Liberty University, VA
Life University, GA
LIM College, NY
Lincoln Memorial University, TN
Lincoln University, MO
Lindsey Wilson College, KY
Lock Haven University of Pennsylvania, PA
Logan University, MO
Long Island University–LIU Brooklyn, NY
Long Island University–LIU Post, NY
Loras College, IA
Louisiana State University and Agricultural & Mechanical College, LA
Loyola University Chicago, IL
Loyola University New Orleans, LA
Lubbock Christian University, TX
Lycoming College, PA
Lynn University, FL
Manhattan College, NY
Marist College, NY
Marquette University, WI
Marshall University, WV
Marymount California University, CA
Maryville University of Saint Louis, MO
Massachusetts College of Liberal Arts, MA
Massachusetts Institute of Technology, MA
Massachusetts Maritime Academy, MA
McKendree University, IL
MCPHS University, MA
Medgar Evers College of the City University of New York, NY
Mercer University, GA
Mercy College, NY
Meredith College, NC
Merrimack College, MA
Messiah College, PA
Metropolitan College of New York, NY
Metropolitan State University of Denver, CO
Miami University, OH
Michigan State University, MI
Michigan Technological University, MI
MidAmerica Nazarene University, KS
Middle Georgia State University, GA
Millersville University of Pennsylvania, PA
Milligan College, TN
Mills College, CA
Minot State University, ND
Misericordia University, PA
Mississippi State University, MS
Missouri State University, MO
Missouri University of Science and Technology, MO
Missouri Valley College, MO
Montana Tech of The University of Montana, MT
Montclair State University, NJ
Moravian College, PA

Morehead State University, KY
Morehouse College, GA
Mount Marty College, SD
Mount St. Joseph University, OH
Mount Saint Mary College, NY
Mount Saint Mary's University, CA
Murray State University, KY
Nazareth College of Rochester, NY
Nebraska Methodist College, NE
Neumann University, PA
New Jersey City University, NJ
New Jersey Institute of Technology, NJ
Newman University, KS
New Mexico Highlands University, NM
New Mexico Institute of Mining and Technology, NM
New Mexico State University, NM
New York Institute of Technology, NY
Niagara University, NY
Nichols College, MA
North Carolina State University, NC
Northeastern State University, OK
Northeastern University, MA
Northern Arizona University, AZ
Northern Illinois University, IL
Northern Kentucky University, KY
Northern Michigan University, MI
Northern State University, SD
Northwest Christian University, OR
Northwestern College, IA
Northwestern University, IL
Northwest Nazarene University, ID
Northwest University, WA
Oglethorpe University, GA
Ohio Northern University, OH
The Ohio State University, OH
Ohio University, OH
Oklahoma Baptist University, OK
Oklahoma Christian University, OK
Oklahoma City University, OK
Old Dominion University, VA
Olivet Nazarene University, IL
Oregon State University, OR
Ouachita Baptist University, AR
Our Lady of the Lake University, TX
Pacific Lutheran University, WA
Parsons School of Design, NY
Peirce College, PA
Penn State University Park, PA
Pennsylvania College of Technology, PA
Pfeiffer University, NC
Piedmont College, GA
Pitzer College, CA
Point Park University, PA
Portland State University, OR
Post University, CT
Prairie View A&M University, TX
Purdue University, IN
Queens College of the City University of New York, NY
Ramapo College of New Jersey, NJ
Reed College, OR
Regis University, CO
Rensselaer Polytechnic Institute, NY
Rhodes College, TN
Rider University, NJ
Robert Morris University, PA
Rochester Institute of Technology, NY
Rockhurst University, MO
Rogers State University, OK
Roger Williams University, RI
Rose-Hulman Institute of Technology, IN
Rowan University, NJ
Rutgers University–Camden, NJ
Rutgers University–Newark, NJ
Rutgers University–New Brunswick, NJ

Sacred Heart University, CT
The Sage Colleges, NY
Saginaw Valley State University, MI
St. Ambrose University, IA
Saint Augustine's University, NC
Saint Joseph's University, PA
Saint Louis University, MO
Saint Martin's University, WA
St. Mary's College of Maryland, MD
St. Mary's University, TX
Saint Mary's University of Minnesota, MN
Saint Michael's College, VT
Saint Peter's University, NJ
Saint Vincent College, PA
Salisbury University, MD
Samuel Merritt University, CA
San Francisco Conservatory of Music, CA
San Francisco State University, CA
Santa Clara University, CA
Savannah College of Art and Design, GA
Schreiner University, TX
Scripps College, CA
Shepherd University, WV
Shippensburg University of Pennsylvania, PA
Siena College, NY
Simpson College, IA
Soka University of America, CA
Sonoma State University, CA
Southeastern University, FL
Southern Illinois University Carbondale, IL
Southern Methodist University, TX
Southern Utah University, UT
Southern Vermont College, VT
Southwest Baptist University, MO
Spelman College, GA
State University of New York at New Paltz, NY
State University of New York at Oswego, NY
State University of New York at Plattsburgh, NY
State University of New York College of Environmental Science and Forestry, NY
State University of New York College of Technology at Canton, NY
State University of New York Polytechnic Institute, NY
Stephen F. Austin State University, TX
Stevens Institute of Technology, NJ
Stevenson University, MD
Stony Brook University, State University of New York, NY
Suffolk University, MA
Syracuse University, NY
Tarleton State University, TX
Taylor University, IN
Temple University, PA
Tennessee Technological University, TN
Texas A&M University, TX
Texas A&M University–Commerce, TX
Texas A&M University–Corpus Christi, TX
Texas Tech University, TX
Texas Woman's University, TX
Thomas Aquinas College, CA
Thomas Jefferson University, PA
Thomas University, GA
Towson University, MD
Trine University, IN
Trinity Christian College, IL
Trinity College of Florida, FL
Truman State University, MO
Tufts University, MA
Tulane University, LA
Union College, NE
Union University, TN

Unity College, ME
University at Buffalo, the State University of New York, NY
The University of Akron, OH
The University of Alabama, AL
The University of Alabama at Birmingham, AL
University of Alaska Fairbanks, AK
The University of Arizona, AZ
University of Arkansas, AR
University of Bridgeport, CT
University of California, San Diego, CA
University of California, Santa Barbara, CA
University of California, Santa Cruz, CA
University of Central Arkansas, AR
University of Central Florida, FL
University of Cincinnati, OH
University of Colorado Boulder, CO
University of Colorado Colorado Springs, CO
University of Colorado Denver, CO
University of Dayton, OH
University of Denver, CO
University of Evansville, IN
The University of Findlay, OH
University of Florida, FL
University of Georgia, GA
University of Hartford, CT
University of Hawaii at Manoa, HI
University of Houston, TX
University of Idaho, ID
University of Illinois at Chicago, IL
University of Illinois at Springfield, IL
University of Jamestown, ND
The University of Kansas, KS
University of Kentucky, KY
University of Louisiana at Monroe, LA
University of Louisville, KY
University of Maine at Fort Kent, ME
University of Maine at Machias, ME
University of Maine at Presque Isle, ME
University of Maryland, Baltimore County, MD
University of Maryland, College Park, MD
University of Maryland University College, MD
University of Massachusetts Amherst, MA
University of Massachusetts Boston, MA
University of Massachusetts Dartmouth, MA
University of Massachusetts Lowell, MA
University of Memphis, TN
University of Miami, FL
University of Michigan, MI
University of Michigan–Dearborn, MI
University of Michigan–Flint, MI
University of Minnesota, Crookston, MN
University of Minnesota, Twin Cities Campus, MN
University of Missouri, MO
University of Missouri–St. Louis, MO

University of Montana, MT
University of Nebraska–Lincoln, NE
University of Nevada, Las Vegas, NV
University of New England, ME
University of New Haven, CT
University of New Orleans, LA
University of North Alabama, AL
University of North Carolina at Asheville, NC
The University of North Carolina at Charlotte, NC
The University of North Carolina at Pembroke, NC
The University of North Carolina Wilmington, NC
University of North Dakota, ND
University of Northern Colorado, CO
University of Northern Iowa, IA
University of North Florida, FL
University of North Georgia, GA
University of North Texas, TX
University of North Texas at Dallas, TX
University of Oklahoma, OK
University of Oregon, OR
University of Pennsylvania, PA
University of Pittsburgh, PA
University of Pittsburgh at Bradford, PA
University of Puget Sound, WA
University of Rhode Island, RI
University of Rochester, NY
University of St. Thomas, MN
University of San Francisco, CA
University of South Carolina, SC
University of South Carolina Aiken, SC
University of Southern California, CA
University of Southern Indiana, IN
University of Southern Maine, ME
University of Southern Mississippi, MS
The University of Tampa, FL
The University of Tennessee, TN
The University of Tennessee at Chattanooga, TN
The University of Tennessee at Martin, TN
The University of Texas at Austin, TX
The University of Texas at Dallas, TX
The University of Texas at San Antonio, TX
The University of Texas of the Permian Basin, TX
The University of Texas Rio Grande Valley, TX
University of the Incarnate Word, TX
University of the Pacific, CA
The University of Toledo, OH
University of Utah, UT
University of Vermont, VT
University of Virginia, VA
The University of Virginia's College at Wise, VA
University of Washington, WA
University of Washington, Bothell, WA

The University of West Alabama, AL
University of West Georgia, GA
University of Wisconsin–Eau Claire, WI
University of Wisconsin–Madison, WI
University of Wisconsin–Milwaukee, WI
University of Wisconsin–Parkside, WI
University of Wisconsin–Stevens Point, WI
University of Wisconsin–Stout, WI
University of Wisconsin–Superior, WI
University of Wisconsin–Whitewater, WI
University of Wyoming, WY
Upper Iowa University, IA
Ursinus College, PA
Utah State University, UT
Utah Valley University, UT
Utica College, NY
Valdosta State University, GA
Valencia College, FL
Valley City State University, ND
Valparaiso University, IN
Vanderbilt University, TN
Vassar College, NY
Vermont Technical College, VT
Villa Maria College, NY
Villanova University, PA
Virginia Commonwealth University, VA
Virginia Polytechnic Institute and State University, VA
Warner Pacific College, OR
Washington State University, WA
Washington University in St. Louis, MO
Wayne State College, NE
Wayne State University, MI
Webber International University, FL
Weber State University, UT
Webster University, MO
Wellesley College, MA
Wentworth Institute of Technology, MA
Western Connecticut State University, CT
Western Kentucky University, KY
Western Michigan University, MI
Western Washington University, WA
Westminster College, UT
West Texas A&M University, TX
West Virginia University Institute of Technology, WV
Wheaton College, MA
Whitman College, WA
Wichita State University, KS
Widener University, PA
Wilkes University, PA
William Jewell College, MO
Winthrop University, SC
Wittenberg University, OH
Worcester Polytechnic Institute, MA
Wright State University, OH
Wright State University–Lake Campus, OH
York College of Pennsylvania, PA
Youngstown State University, OH

ROTC Programs

Air Force

Adelphi University, NY*
Agnes Scott College, GA*
Alabama State University, AL
Alaska Pacific University, AK*
Alverno College, WI*
American University, DC*
Amherst College, MA*
Anderson University, SC*
Angelo State University, TX
Arizona Christian University, AZ*
Arizona State University at the Downtown
     Phoenix campus, AZ*
Arizona State University at the Polytechnic
     campus, AZ*
Arizona State University at the Tempe
     campus, AZ
Arizona State University at the West campus,
     AZ*
Assumption College, MA*
Auburn University, AL
Auburn University at Montgomery, AL*
Augsburg University, MN*
Augustana University, SD*
Austin Peay State University, TN*
Azusa Pacific University, CA*
Baker University, KS*
Baldwin Wallace University, OH*
Barnard College, NY*
Barry University, FL*
Baylor University, TX
Bay Path University, MA*
Becker College, MA*
Belhaven University, MS*
Bellarmine University, KY*
Belmont University, TN*
Bentley University, MA*
Bethel College, IN*
Bethel University, MN*
Bethune-Cookman University, FL*
Binghamton University, State University of
     New York, NY*
Biola University, CA*
Birmingham-Southern College, AL*
Bloomsburg University of Pennsylvania, PA*
Boston College, MA*
Boston University, MA
Bowling Green State University, OH
Brandeis University, MA*
Bridgewater State University, MA*
Brigham Young University, UT
Bryn Mawr College, PA*
Butler University, IN*
Cairn University, PA*
California Baptist University, CA*
California Institute of Technology, CA*
California Lutheran University, CA*
California State University, Dominguez Hills,
     CA*
California State University, Long Beach, CA*
California State University Maritime
     Academy, CA*
California State University, Monterey Bay,
     CA*
California State University, Northridge, CA*
California State University, Sacramento, CA
California State University, San Bernardino,
     CA
California State University, San Marcos, CA*

Capital University, OH*
Carlow University, PA*
Carnegie Mellon University, PA*
Carroll University, WI*
Case Western Reserve University, OH*
Catawba College, NC*
The Catholic University of America, DC*
Cazenovia College, NY*
Cedarville University, OH*
Central Connecticut State University, CT*
Central Methodist University, MO*
Central Michigan University, MI*
Centre College, KY*
Chaminade University of Honolulu, HI*
Chapman University, CA*
Chatham University, PA*
Christian Brothers University, TN*
The Citadel, The Military College of South
     Carolina, SC
Claremont McKenna College, CA*
Clarkson University, NY
Clark University, MA*
Clayton State University, GA*
Clemson University, SC
Cleveland State University, OH*
Coe College, IA*
The College at Brockport, State University of
     New York, NY*
College of Charleston, SC*
The College of New Jersey, NJ*
College of Saint Mary, NE*
The College of Saint Rose, NY*
The College of St. Scholastica, MN*
College of the Holy Cross, MA*
Colorado State University, CO
Columbia College, MO*
Columbia University, NY*
Concordia University, Nebraska, NE*
Concordia University, St. Paul, MN*
Corban University, OR*
Cornell University, NY
Creighton University, NE*
Dakota State University, SD*
Dallas Baptist University, TX*
Davidson College, NC*
Delaware State University, DE
DePauw University, IN*
Doane University, NE*
Drake University, IA*
Drexel University, PA*
Duquesne University, PA*
East Carolina University, NC
Eastern Michigan University, MI*
Eastern University, PA*
East Stroudsburg University of Pennsylvania,
     PA*
Eckerd College, FL*
Edgewood College, WI*
Elmhurst College, IL*
Elms College, MA*
Elon University, NC*
Embry-Riddle Aeronautical University–
     Daytona, FL
Emory University, GA*
Fairfield University, CT*
Fairleigh Dickinson University, Florham
     Campus, NJ*
Fairleigh Dickinson University, Metropolitan
     Campus, NJ*

Farmingdale State College, NY
Felician University, NJ*
Florida Agricultural and Mechanical
     University, FL*
Florida Atlantic University, FL*
Florida International University, FL
Florida Southern College, FL*
Florida State University, FL
Fordham University, NY*
Franklin Pierce University, NH*
George Mason University, VA*
Georgetown College, KY*
Georgetown University, DC*
The George Washington University, DC*
Georgia Institute of Technology, GA
Georgia State University, GA*
Governors State University, IL*
Grambling State University, LA*
Guilford College, NC*
Hamilton College, NY*
Hamline University, MN*
Harvard University, MA
Harvey Mudd College, CA*
Haverford College, PA*
Hawai`i Pacific University, HI*
Heidelberg University, OH*
High Point University, NC*
Hiram College, OH*
Hobart and William Smith Colleges, NY*
Houston Baptist University, TX*
Huntingdon College, AL*
Indiana State University, IN
Indiana University Bloomington, IN
Indiana University–Purdue University
     Indianapolis, IN*
Indiana University South Bend, IN*
Indiana University Southeast, IN*
Iona College, NY*
Iowa State University of Science and
     Technology, IA
Ithaca College, NY*
Jackson State University, MS
James Madison University, VA*
John Brown University, AR*
Kansas State University, KS
Kean University, NJ*
Keene State College, NH*
Kennesaw State University, GA*
Kent State University, OH
Kent State University at Stark, OH*
Kentucky State University, KY*
King's College, PA*
Lamar University, TX*
La Roche College, PA*
La Salle University, PA*
Lawrence Technological University, MI*
Le Moyne College, NY*
Lewis University, IL*
Liberty University, VA*
Lindenwood University, MO*
Linfield College, OR*
Lipscomb University, TN*
Louisiana State University and Agricultural &
     Mechanical College, LA
Loyola Marymount University, CA
Loyola University Chicago, IL*
Loyola University New Orleans, LA*
Lubbock Christian University, TX*
Lynn University, FL*

* program is offered at another college's campus

Macalester College, MN*
Manhattan College, NY
Marquette University, WI
Mary Baldwin University, VA*
Marymount University, VA*
Marywood University, PA*
Massachusetts Institute of Technology, MA
McKendree University, IL*
Mercy College, NY*
Meredith College, NC*
Merrimack College, MA*
Metropolitan State University of Denver, CO*
Miami University, OH
Michigan State University, MI
Michigan Technological University, MI
MidAmerica Nazarene University, KS*
Middle Tennessee State University, TN*
Millsaps College, MS*
Milwaukee School of Engineering, WI*
Minnesota State University Moorhead, MN*
Misericordia University, PA*
Mississippi State University, MS
Missouri University of Science and Technology, MO
Morehouse College, GA*
Mount Carmel College of Nursing, OH*
Mount Holyoke College, MA*
Mount St. Joseph University, OH*
Nazareth College of Rochester, NY*
Nebraska Methodist College, NE*
Neumann University, PA*
New Jersey Institute of Technology, NJ
New Mexico State University, NM
New York Institute of Technology, NY*
North Carolina State University, NC
North Central College, IL*
Northeastern University, MA*
Northern Arizona University, AZ
Northern Illinois University, IL*
Northern Kentucky University, KY*
Northwestern University, IL*
Northwest University, WA*
Occidental College, CA*
Oglethorpe University, GA*
Ohio Northern University, OH*
The Ohio State University, OH
Ohio University, OH
Ohio Wesleyan University, OH*
Oklahoma Baptist University, OK*
Oklahoma Christian University, OK*
Oklahoma City University, OK*
Oklahoma State University, OK
Oral Roberts University, OK*
Oregon State University, OR
Penn State Abington, PA*
Penn State Altoona, PA*
Penn State Brandywine, PA*
Penn State Hazleton, PA*
Penn State New Kensington, PA*
Penn State University Park, PA
Penn State Wilkes-Barre, PA*
Penn State Worthington Scranton, PA*
Pepperdine University, CA*
Pitzer College, CA*
Point Loma Nazarene University, CA*
Point Park University, PA*
Pomona College, CA*
Portland State University, OR*
Prairie View A&M University, TX*
Princeton University, NJ*
Purdue University, IN
Quinnipiac University, CT*
Ramapo College of New Jersey, NJ*
Regis University, CO*

Rensselaer Polytechnic Institute, NY
Rhodes College, TN*
Rice University, TX*
Robert Morris University, PA*
Roberts Wesleyan College, NY*
Rochester Institute of Technology, NY
Rose-Hulman Institute of Technology, IN
Rutgers University–Camden, NJ*
Rutgers University–Newark, NJ
Rutgers University–New Brunswick, NJ
Sacred Heart University, CT*
The Sage Colleges, NY*
Saint Augustine's University, NC*
St. Catherine University, MN*
St. John Fisher College, NY*
Saint Joseph's University, PA
St. Lawrence University, NY*
Saint Leo University, FL
St. Louis College of Pharmacy, MO*
Saint Louis University, MO
Saint Martin's University, WA*
Saint Mary-of-the-Woods College, IN*
St. Mary's University, TX*
Saint Michael's College, VT*
St. Thomas Aquinas College, NY*
St. Thomas University, FL*
Saint Vincent College, PA*
Salisbury University, MD*
Samford University, AL
San Diego State University, CA
San Francisco State University, CA*
Santa Clara University, CA*
Sarah Lawrence College, NY*
Scripps College, CA*
Seattle Pacific University, WA*
Seattle University, WA*
Shepherd University, WV*
Siena College, NY*
Skidmore College, NY*
Smith College, MA*
Sonoma State University, CA*
Southeast Missouri State University, MO
Southern Illinois University Carbondale, IL
Southern Methodist University, TX*
Southwestern University, TX*
Spelman College, GA*
Spring Hill College, AL*
Stanford University, CA*
State University of New York at Oswego, NY*
State University of New York College at Cortland, NY*
State University of New York College at Geneseo, NY*
State University of New York College at Potsdam, NY*
State University of New York College of Environmental Science and Forestry, NY*
State University of New York College of Technology at Canton, NY*
State University of New York Polytechnic Institute, NY*
Stevens Institute of Technology, NJ*
Stevenson University, MD*
Stony Brook University, State University of New York, NY*
Syracuse University, NY
Tarleton State University, TX*
Temple University, PA*
Tennessee Technological University, TN*
Texas A&M University, TX
Texas A&M University–Commerce, TX*
Texas Christian University, TX
Texas Lutheran University, TX*
Texas State University, TX

Texas Tech University, TX
Texas Woman's University, TX*
Thomas Jefferson University, PA*
Tiffin University, OH*
Towson University, MD*
Transylvania University, KY*
Trine University, IN*
Trinity University, TX*
Troy University, AL
Tufts University, MA*
Tulane University, LA
Union College, NY*
University at Albany, State University of New York, NY*
The University of Akron, OH*
The University of Alabama, AL
The University of Alabama at Birmingham, AL*
The University of Arizona, AZ
University of Arkansas, AR
University of California, Davis, CA*
University of California, Irvine, CA*
University of California, Los Angeles, CA
University of California, Riverside, CA*
University of California, San Diego, CA*
University of California, Santa Barbara, CA*
University of California, Santa Cruz, CA*
University of Central Florida, FL
University of Central Missouri, MO*
University of Chicago, IL*
University of Cincinnati, OH
University of Colorado Boulder, CO
University of Colorado Denver, CO*
University of Dallas, TX*
University of Dayton, OH*
University of Denver, CO*
The University of Findlay, OH*
University of Florida, FL
University of Georgia, GA
University of Hartford, CT*
University of Hawaii at Manoa, HI
University of Houston, TX
University of Houston–Downtown, TX*
University of Idaho, ID*
University of Illinois at Chicago, IL*
The University of Kansas, KS
University of Kentucky, KY
University of Louisville, KY
University of Mary Hardin-Baylor, TX*
University of Maryland, Baltimore County, MD*
University of Maryland, College Park, MD
University of Massachusetts Amherst, MA
University of Massachusetts Boston, MA*
University of Massachusetts Lowell, MA
University of Memphis, TN
University of Miami, FL
University of Michigan, MI
University of Michigan–Flint, MI*
University of Minnesota, Crookston, MN*
University of Minnesota, Duluth, MN
University of Minnesota, Twin Cities Campus, MN
University of Missouri, MO
University of Missouri–St. Louis, MO*
University of Montevallo, AL*
University of Nebraska–Lincoln, NE
University of Nevada, Las Vegas, NV
University of New Hampshire, NH
University of New Haven, CT*
University of New Orleans, LA*
The University of North Carolina at Chapel Hill, NC
The University of North Carolina at Charlotte, NC

---

* program is offered at another college's campus

The University of North Carolina at Greensboro, NC*
The University of North Carolina at Pembroke, NC
University of North Dakota, ND
University of Northern Colorado, CO
University of North Texas, TX
University of Notre Dame, IN
University of Oklahoma, OK
University of Oregon, OR*
University of Pennsylvania, PA*
University of Pittsburgh, PA
University of Pittsburgh at Greensburg, PA*
University of Rochester, NY*
University of St. Thomas, MN
University of St. Thomas, TX*
University of San Diego, CA*
University of San Francisco, CA*
The University of Scranton, PA*
University of Sioux Falls, SD*
University of South Carolina, SC
University of Southern California, CA
University of Southern Maine, ME*
University of Southern Mississippi, MS
The University of Tampa, FL*
The University of Tennessee, TN
The University of Texas at Austin, TX
The University of Texas at Dallas, TX*
The University of Texas at San Antonio, TX
University of the Pacific, CA*
The University of Toledo, OH*
The University of Tulsa, OK*
University of Utah, UT
University of Virginia, VA
University of Washington, WA
University of Washington, Bothell, WA*
University of Washington, Tacoma, WA*
The University of West Alabama, AL*
University of West Georgia, GA*
University of Wisconsin–Madison, WI
University of Wisconsin–Milwaukee, WI*
University of Wisconsin–Parkside, WI*
University of Wisconsin–Stout, WI*
University of Wisconsin–Superior, WI*
University of Wisconsin–Whitewater, WI
University of Wyoming, WY
Utah State University, UT
Utah Valley University, UT*
Utica College, NY*
Valdosta State University, GA
Valparaiso University, IN*
Vanderbilt University, TN*
Vanguard University of Southern California, CA*
Vaughn College of Aeronautics and Technology, NY*
Villanova University, PA*
Virginia Military Institute, VA
Virginia Polytechnic Institute and State University, VA
Warner Pacific College, OR*
Washington & Jefferson College, PA*
Washington State University, WA
Washington University in St. Louis, MO*
Wayland Baptist University, TX*
Wayne State University, MI*
Weber State University, UT*
Webster University, MO*
Wellesley College, MA*
Wentworth Institute of Technology, MA*
Wesleyan University, CT*
West Chester University of Pennsylvania, PA*
Western Connecticut State University, CT*
Western Kentucky University, KY*

Western New England University, MA*
Westfield State University, MA*
Westminster College, UT*
Westmont College, CA*
West Virginia University, WV
Wheaton College, IL*
Widener University, PA*
Wilkes University, PA
Willamette University, OR*
William Paterson University of New Jersey, NJ*
Williams College, MA*
William Woods University, MO*
Winthrop University, SC*
Wisconsin Lutheran College, WI*
Wittenberg University, OH*
Worcester Polytechnic Institute, MA
Worcester State University, MA*
Wright State University, OH
Youngstown State University, OH*

Army

Academy of Art University, CA*
Adelphi University, NY*
Agnes Scott College, GA*
Alabama State University, AL*
Alcorn State University, MS
Alfred University, NY*
Allegheny College, PA*
Allen College, IA*
Alma College, MI*
Alverno College, WI*
American University, DC*
Amherst College, MA*
Anderson University, SC*
Appalachian State University, NC
Arizona State University at the Downtown Phoenix campus, AZ*
Arizona State University at the Polytechnic campus, AZ*
Arizona State University at the Tempe campus, AZ
Arizona State University at the West campus, AZ*
Arkansas Tech University, AR*
Assumption College, MA*
Auburn University, AL
Auburn University at Montgomery, AL
Augsburg University, MN*
Augustana University, SD*
Aurora University, IL*
Austin Peay State University, TN
Azusa Pacific University, CA
Babson College, MA*
Baker University, KS*
Baldwin Wallace University, OH*
Ball State University, IN
Barnard College, NY*
Barry University, FL*
Baruch College of the City University of New York, NY*
Baylor University, TX
Bay Path University, MA*
Becker College, MA*
Belhaven University, MS*
Bellarmine University, KY*
Belmont University, TN*
Benedictine College, KS*
Benedictine University, IL*
Bentley University, MA*
Bethany Lutheran College, MN*
Bethel College, IN*
Bethel University, MN*
Bethune-Cookman University, FL*

Binghamton University, State University of New York, NY*
Biola University, CA*
Birmingham-Southern College, AL*
Black Hills State University, SD
Bloomsburg University of Pennsylvania, PA
Boise State University, ID
Boston College, MA*
Boston University, MA
Bowie State University, MD
Bowling Green State University, OH
Bradley University, IL
Brandeis University, MA*
Bridgewater State University, MA*
Brigham Young University, UT
Bryant University, RI*
Bucknell University, PA
Buena Vista University, IA
Buffalo State College, State University of New York, NY*
Butler University, IN*
Caldwell University, NJ*
California Baptist University, CA
California Institute of Technology, CA*
California Lutheran University, CA*
California Polytechnic State University, San Luis Obispo, CA
California State Polytechnic University, Pomona, CA
California State University, Dominguez Hills, CA
California State University, Fullerton, CA
California State University, Long Beach, CA
California State University, Northridge, CA*
California State University, Sacramento, CA*
California State University, San Bernardino, CA
California State University, San Marcos, CA
California University of Pennsylvania, PA
Calvin College, MI*
Cameron University, OK
Campbellsville University, KY*
Canisius College, NY
Capital University, OH
Carlow University, PA*
Carnegie Mellon University, PA*
Carroll College, MT
Carroll University, WI*
Carson-Newman University, TN
Case Western Reserve University, OH
Catawba College, NC*
The Catholic University of America, DC*
Cazenovia College, NY*
Cedarville University, OH*
Central Connecticut State University, CT*
Central Methodist University, MO*
Central Michigan University, MI
Central State University, OH
Centre College, KY*
Chaminade University of Honolulu, HI*
Champlain College, VT*
Chapman University, CA*
Chatham University, PA*
Christian Brothers University, TN*
Christopher Newport University, VA
The Citadel, The Military College of South Carolina, SC
City College of the City University of New York, NY
Claremont McKenna College, CA
Clarion University of Pennsylvania, PA
Clarke University, IA*
Clarkson University, NY
Clark University, MA*
Clayton State University, GA*

---

* program is offered at another college's campus

Clemson University, SC
Cleveland State University, OH*
Coastal Carolina University, SC
Coe College, IA
Colby College, ME*
Colgate University, NY*
The College at Brockport, State University of New York, NY
The College of Idaho, ID*
The College of New Jersey, NJ*
College of Saint Benedict, MN*
College of Saint Mary, NE*
The College of Saint Rose, NY*
College of the Holy Cross, MA*
College of the Ozarks, MO
The College of William and Mary, VA
The Colorado College, CO*
Colorado State University, CO
Columbia College, MO*
Columbia University, NY*
Columbus State University, GA
Concordia University, Nebraska, NE*
Concordia University, St. Paul, MN*
Converse College, SC*
Corban University, OR*
Cornell University, NY
Cornerstone University, MI*
Covenant College, GA*
Creighton University, NE
Curry College, MA*
Daemen College, NY*
Dakota State University, SD*
Dallas Baptist University, TX*
Dartmouth College, NH*
Davidson College, NC
Delaware State University, DE
Denison University, OH*
DePaul University, IL
DePauw University, IN*
DeSales University, PA*
Dickinson College, PA
Doane University, NE*
Drake University, IA*
Drew University, NJ*
Drexel University, PA
Drury University, MO*
Duquesne University, PA
East Carolina University, NC
Eastern Michigan University, MI
Eastern Oregon University, OR
Eastern University, PA*
Eastern Washington University, WA
East Stroudsburg University of Pennsylvania, PA
Eckerd College, FL*
Edgewood College, WI*
Elmhurst College, IL*
Elms College, MA*
Elon University, NC
Embry-Riddle Aeronautical University–Daytona, FL
Emmanuel College, MA*
Emory University, GA*
Endicott College, MA*
Evangel University, MO*
Fairfield University, CT*
Fairleigh Dickinson University, Florham Campus, NJ*
Fairleigh Dickinson University, Metropolitan Campus, NJ*
Farmingdale State College, NY*
Felician University, NJ*
Ferris State University, MI*
Fisher College, MA*
Fitchburg State University, MA

Florida Agricultural and Mechanical University, FL
Florida Atlantic University, FL
Florida Institute of Technology, FL
Florida International University, FL
Florida Southern College, FL
Florida State University, FL
Fordham University, NY
Francis Marion University, SC
Franklin College, IN*
Franklin Pierce University, NH*
Furman University, SC
Gannon University, PA
Geneva College, PA*
George Mason University, VA
Georgetown College, KY*
Georgetown University, DC
The George Washington University, DC*
Georgia College & State University, GA*
Georgia Institute of Technology, GA
Georgia Southern University, GA
Georgia State University, GA
Gettysburg College, PA*
Gonzaga University, WA
Gordon College, MA*
Grambling State University, LA
Guilford College, NC*
Gustavus Adolphus College, MN*
Hamilton College, NY*
Hamline University, MN*
Hampden-Sydney College, VA*
Hampton University, VA
Harding University, AR*
Harris-Stowe State University, MO*
Harvard University, MA
Harvey Mudd College, CA*
Hawai`i Pacific University, HI*
Heidelberg University, OH*
Hendrix College, AR*
High Point University, NC*
Hilbert College, NY*
Hiram College, OH*
Hobart and William Smith Colleges, NY*
Hofstra University, NY
Holy Family University, PA*
Hood College, MD
Hope College, MI*
Hope International University, CA*
Houston Baptist University, TX*
Huntingdon College, AL*
Husson University, ME
Idaho State University, ID
Illinois Wesleyan University, IL*
Indiana State University, IN
Indiana Tech, IN*
Indiana University Bloomington, IN
Indiana University Kokomo, IN
Indiana University Northwest, IN
Indiana University of Pennsylvania, PA
Indiana University–Purdue University Indianapolis, IN
Indiana University South Bend, IN*
Indiana University Southeast, IN*
Indiana Wesleyan University, IN
Inter American University of Puerto Rico, Bayamón Campus, PR*
Iona College, NY*
Iowa State University of Science and Technology, IA
Ithaca College, NY*
Jackson State University, MS
Jacksonville University, FL
James Madison University, VA
John Brown University, AR*
John Carroll University, OH

Judson University, IL*
Kalamazoo College, MI*
Kansas State University, KS
Kean University, NJ*
Keene State College, NH*
Kennesaw State University, GA*
Kent State University, OH
Kent State University at Stark, OH*
Kentucky State University, KY*
The King's College, NY*
King's College, PA
Kutztown University of Pennsylvania, PA*
Lafayette College, PA*
La Roche College, PA*
La Salle University, PA*
Lehigh University, PA
Lehman College of the City University of New York, NY*
Le Moyne College, NY*
Lewis University, IL*
Liberty University, VA
Lincoln Memorial University, TN*
Lincoln University, MO
Lincoln University, PA*
Lindenwood University, MO*
Lipscomb University, TN*
Lock Haven University of Pennsylvania, PA
Long Island University–LIU Brooklyn, NY*
Long Island University–LIU Post, NY*
Longwood University, VA
Loras College, IA*
Louisiana State University and Agricultural & Mechanical College, LA
Loyola Marymount University, CA*
Loyola University Chicago, IL
Loyola University New Orleans, LA*
Lubbock Christian University, TX*
Lycoming College, PA*
Macalester College, MN*
Manhattan College, NY*
Mansfield University of Pennsylvania, PA*
Marist College, NY
Marquette University, WI
Marshall University, WV
Mary Baldwin University, VA*
Marymount University, VA*
Maryville University of Saint Louis, MO*
Marywood University, PA*
Massachusetts Institute of Technology, MA
Massachusetts Maritime Academy, MA*
McDaniel College, MD
McKendree University, IL*
Mercer University, GA
Mercy College, NY*
Meredith College, NC*
Metropolitan State University of Denver, CO
Miami University, OH*
Michigan State University, MI
Michigan Technological University, MI
MidAmerica Nazarene University, KS*
Middlebury College, VT*
Middle Tennessee State University, TN
Millersville University of Pennsylvania, PA
Millsaps College, MS*
Mills College, CA*
Milwaukee School of Engineering, WI*
Minnesota State University Moorhead, MN*
Misericordia University, PA*
Mississippi State University, MS
Missouri Baptist University, MO*
Missouri State University, MO
Missouri University of Science and Technology, MO
Missouri Valley College, MO*
Missouri Western State University, MO

---

* program is offered at another college's campus

Molloy College, NY*
Monmouth College, IL*
Moravian College, PA*
Morehead State University, KY
Morehouse College, GA
Morningside College, IA*
Mount Carmel College of Nursing, OH*
Mount Holyoke College, MA*
Mount Marty College, SD*
Mount St. Joseph University, OH*
Mount Saint Mary College, NY*
Mount St. Mary's University, MD*
Muhlenberg College, PA*
Murray State University, KY
Nazareth College of Rochester, NY*
Neumann University, PA*
Newberry College, SC
New Jersey City University, NJ*
New Jersey Institute of Technology, NJ*
New Mexico State University, NM
New York Institute of Technology, NY*
Niagara University, NY
North Carolina State University, NC
North Central College, IL*
Northeastern State University, OK
Northeastern University, MA
Northern Arizona University, AZ
Northern Illinois University, IL
Northern Kentucky University, KY*
Northern Michigan University, MI
Northwestern University, IL*
Northwest Nazarene University, ID
Northwest University, WA*
Occidental College, CA*
Oglethorpe University, GA*
Ohio Northern University, OH*
The Ohio State University, OH
Ohio University, OH
Ohio Wesleyan University, OH*
Oklahoma Christian University, OK*
Oklahoma City University, OK*
Oklahoma State University, OK
Old Dominion University, VA
Olivet Nazarene University, IL
Oregon State University, OR
Ouachita Baptist University, AR
Our Lady of the Lake University, TX*
Pacific Lutheran University, WA
Palm Beach Atlantic University, FL*
Penn State Abington, PA*
Penn State Altoona, PA*
Penn State Berks, PA*
Penn State Brandywine, PA*
Penn State Erie, The Behrend College, PA*
Penn State Harrisburg, PA*
Penn State Lehigh Valley, PA*
Penn State University Park, PA
Penn State Wilkes-Barre, PA*
Penn State Worthington Scranton, PA*
Pennsylvania College of Technology, PA
Pepperdine University, CA*
Pfeiffer University, NC*
Pittsburg State University, KS
Pitzer College, CA*
Point Loma Nazarene University, CA*
Point Park University, PA*
Pomona College, CA*
Portland State University, OR*
Prairie View A&M University, TX
Pratt Institute, NY*
Presbyterian College, SC
Princeton University, NJ
Providence College, RI
Purdue University, IN

Queens College of the City University of
   New York, NY*
Quinnipiac University, CT*
Radford University, VA
Ramapo College of New Jersey, NJ*
Randolph-Macon College, VA*
Regent University, VA*
Regis University, CO*
Rensselaer Polytechnic Institute, NY
Rhode Island College, RI*
Rhodes College, TN*
Rice University, TX*
Rider University, NJ*
Robert Morris University, PA
Robert Morris University Illinois, IL*
Roberts Wesleyan College, NY*
Rochester Institute of Technology, NY
Rockhurst University, MO*
Rocky Mountain College, MT*
Roger Williams University, RI
Rose-Hulman Institute of Technology, IN
Rowan University, NJ*
Rutgers University–Camden, NJ*
Rutgers University–Newark, NJ
Rutgers University–New Brunswick, NJ
The Sage Colleges, NY*
Saint Anselm College, NH*
Saint Augustine's University, NC
St. Bonaventure University, NY
St. Catherine University, MN*
St. John Fisher College, NY*
Saint John's University, MN
St. John's University, NY
St. Joseph's College, Long Island Campus,
   NY*
Saint Joseph's University, PA*
St. Lawrence University, NY*
Saint Leo University, FL
St. Louis College of Pharmacy, MO*
Saint Louis University, MO*
Saint Martin's University, WA*
Saint Mary-of-the-Woods College, IN*
Saint Mary's College of California, CA*
St. Mary's University, TX
Saint Mary's University of Minnesota, MN*
Saint Michael's College, VT*
St. Norbert College, WI
Saint Peter's University, NJ*
Saint Vincent College, PA*
Salisbury University, MD
Salve Regina University, RI*
Samford University, AL*
Sam Houston State University, TX
San Diego State University, CA
San Francisco State University, CA*
Santa Clara University, CA
Scripps College, CA*
Seattle Pacific University, WA*
Seattle University, WA
Seton Hill University, PA*
Shippensburg University of Pennsylvania, PA
Siena College, NY
Simmons College, MA*
Skidmore College, NY*
Slippery Rock University of Pennsylvania,
   PA
Smith College, MA*
Sonoma State University, CA*
Southeastern Louisiana University, LA
Southeastern University, FL*
Southern Illinois University Carbondale, IL
Southern Methodist University, TX
Southern Utah University, UT
Southwest Baptist University, MO*
Spelman College, GA*

Spring Hill College, AL*
Stanford University, CA*
State University of New York at Oswego,
   NY*
State University of New York College at
   Cortland, NY*
State University of New York College at
   Geneseo, NY*
State University of New York College at
   Potsdam, NY*
State University of New York College of
   Environmental Science and Forestry, NY*
State University of New York College of
   Technology at Canton, NY*
State University of New York Maritime
   College, NY*
State University of New York Polytechnic
   Institute, NY*
Stephen F. Austin State University, TX
Stetson University, FL*
Stevens Institute of Technology, NJ*
Stevenson University, MD*
Stockton University, NJ*
Stonehill College, MA
Stony Brook University, State University of
   New York, NY
Suffolk University, MA*
Susquehanna University, PA*
Syracuse University, NY
Tarleton State University, TX
Temple University, PA
Tennessee Technological University, TN
Texas A&M International University, TX
Texas A&M University, TX
Texas A&M University–Corpus Christi, TX
Texas A&M University–Kingsville, TX
Texas Christian University, TX
Texas Lutheran University, TX*
Texas State University, TX
Texas Tech University, TX
Texas Woman's University, TX*
Tiffin University, OH*
Towson University, MD*
Transylvania University, KY*
Trevecca Nazarene University, TN*
Trinity University, TX*
Troy University, AL
Truman State University, MO
Tufts University, MA*
Tulane University, LA
Union College, NY*
Union University, TN*
University at Albany, State University of New
   York, NY
University at Buffalo, the State University of
   New York, NY*
The University of Akron, OH
The University of Alabama, AL
The University of Alabama at Birmingham,
   AL
University of Alaska Fairbanks, AK
The University of Arizona, AZ
University of Arkansas, AR
University of California, Davis, CA
University of California, Irvine, CA
University of California, Los Angeles, CA
University of California, Riverside, CA*
University of California, San Diego, CA*
University of California, Santa Barbara, CA
University of California, Santa Cruz, CA*
University of Central Arkansas, AR
University of Central Florida, FL
University of Central Missouri, MO
University of Central Oklahoma, OK
University of Chicago, IL*

---

* program is offered at another college's campus

University of Cincinnati, OH
University of Colorado Boulder, CO
University of Colorado Colorado Springs, CO
University of Colorado Denver, CO*
University of Dallas, TX*
University of Dayton, OH
University of Denver, CO*
University of Dubuque, IA
University of Evansville, IN*
The University of Findlay, OH*
University of Florida, FL
University of Georgia, GA
University of Hartford, CT*
University of Hawaii at Manoa, HI
University of Houston, TX
University of Houston–Downtown, TX*
University of Idaho, ID
University of Illinois at Chicago, IL
The University of Kansas, KS
University of Kentucky, KY
University of La Verne, CA*
University of Louisiana at Monroe, LA*
University of Louisville, KY
University of Maine, ME
University of Mary Hardin-Baylor, TX
University of Maryland, Baltimore County, MD*
University of Maryland, College Park, MD
University of Mary Washington, VA*
University of Massachusetts Amherst, MA
University of Massachusetts Boston, MA*
University of Massachusetts Dartmouth, MA*
University of Massachusetts Lowell, MA
University of Memphis, TN
University of Miami, FL
University of Michigan, MI
University of Michigan–Dearborn, MI*
University of Michigan–Flint, MI*
University of Minnesota, Twin Cities Campus, MN
University of Missouri, MO
University of Missouri–St. Louis, MO
University of Montana, MT
University of Montevallo, AL*
University of Nebraska at Kearney, NE
University of Nebraska–Lincoln, NE
University of Nevada, Las Vegas, NV
University of Nevada, Reno, NV
University of New England, ME*
University of New Hampshire, NH
University of New Haven, CT
University of New Orleans, LA*
University of North Alabama, AL
The University of North Carolina at Chapel Hill, NC
The University of North Carolina at Charlotte, NC
The University of North Carolina at Greensboro, NC*
The University of North Carolina at Pembroke, NC
University of North Dakota, ND
University of Northern Colorado, CO
University of Northern Iowa, IA
University of North Florida, FL
University of North Georgia, GA
University of North Texas, TX
University of Notre Dame, IN
University of Oklahoma, OK
University of Oregon, OR
University of Pennsylvania, PA*
University of Pikeville, KY
University of Pittsburgh, PA
University of Pittsburgh at Bradford, PA*

University of Pittsburgh at Greensburg, PA
University of Puget Sound, WA*
University of Rhode Island, RI
University of Richmond, VA
University of Rochester, NY*
University of St. Francis, IL*
University of St. Thomas, MN*
University of St. Thomas, TX*
University of San Diego, CA*
University of San Francisco, CA
The University of Scranton, PA
University of South Carolina, SC
University of South Dakota, SD
University of Southern California, CA
University of Southern Indiana, IN
University of Southern Maine, ME*
University of Southern Mississippi, MS*
The University of Tampa, FL
The University of Tennessee, TN
The University of Tennessee at Chattanooga, TN
The University of Tennessee at Martin, TN
The University of Texas at Austin, TX
The University of Texas at Dallas, TX*
The University of Texas at El Paso, TX
The University of Texas at San Antonio, TX
The University of Texas Rio Grande Valley, TX
University of the Incarnate Word, TX*
The University of Toledo, OH
University of Utah, UT
University of Vermont, VT
University of Virginia, VA
The University of Virginia's College at Wise, VA
University of Washington, WA
University of Washington, Bothell, WA*
University of Washington, Tacoma, WA*
University of Wisconsin–Eau Claire, WI
University of Wisconsin–La Crosse, WI
University of Wisconsin–Madison, WI
University of Wisconsin–Milwaukee, WI*
University of Wisconsin–Parkside, WI
University of Wisconsin–River Falls, WI
University of Wisconsin–Stevens Point, WI
University of Wisconsin–Stout, WI
University of Wisconsin–Whitewater, WI
University of Wyoming, WY
Ursuline College, OH*
Utah State University, UT
Utah Valley University, UT
Utica College, NY
Valencia College, FL*
Valparaiso University, IN*
Vanderbilt University, TN
Vanguard University of Southern California, CA*
Vaughn College of Aeronautics and Technology, NY*
Vermont Technical College, VT*
Villanova University, PA
Virginia Commonwealth University, VA*
Virginia Military Institute, VA
Virginia Polytechnic Institute and State University, VA
Virginia Wesleyan University, VA*
Wake Forest University, NC
Washington & Jefferson College, PA
Washington and Lee University, VA*
Washington State University, WA
Washington University in St. Louis, MO
Wayland Baptist University, TX*
Waynesburg University, PA*
Wayne State College, NE
Wayne State University, MI

Weber State University, UT
Webster University, MO*
Wellesley College, MA*
Wentworth Institute of Technology, MA*
West Chester University of Pennsylvania, PA
Western Connecticut State University, CT*
Western Illinois University, IL
Western Kentucky University, KY
Western Michigan University, MI
Western New England University, MA
Western Oregon University, OR*
Westfield State University, MA*
Westminster College, PA*
Westminster College, UT*
Westmont College, CA*
West Virginia University, WV
West Virginia University Institute of Technology, WV
Wheaton College, IL
Wheaton College, MA*
Whittier College, CA*
Whitworth University, WA*
Widener University, PA
Wilkes University, PA*
Willamette University, OR*
William Jewell College, MO*
William Woods University, MO*
Winona State University, MN*
Winthrop University, SC*
Wittenberg University, OH*
Wofford College, SC
Worcester Polytechnic Institute, MA
Worcester State University, MA*
Wright State University, OH
Youngstown State University, OH

Naval
Arizona State University at the Downtown Phoenix campus, AZ*
Arizona State University at the Polytechnic campus, AZ*
Arizona State University at the Tempe campus, AZ
Arizona State University at the West campus, AZ*
Auburn University, AL
Augsburg University, MN*
Barnard College, NY*
Becker College, MA*
Belmont University, TN*
Boston College, MA*
Boston University, MA
California State University Maritime Academy, CA*
California State University, San Marcos, CA*
Carlow University, PA*
Carnegie Mellon University, PA
The Catholic University of America, DC*
Chatham University, PA*
Christian Brothers University, TN*
The Citadel, The Military College of South Carolina, SC
Clayton State University, GA*
The College at Brockport, State University of New York, NY*
College of the Holy Cross, MA
Columbia College, MO*
Columbia University, NY
Cornell University, NY
Drexel University, PA*
Duquesne University, PA*
Eastern Michigan University, MI*
Edgewood College, WI*
Embry-Riddle Aeronautical University–Daytona, FL

---

* program is offered at another college's campus

Emory University, GA*
Farmingdale State College, NY*
Florida Agricultural and Mechanical
    University, FL
Florida State University, FL*
Fordham University, NY*
Georgetown University, DC*
The George Washington University, DC
Georgia Institute of Technology, GA
Georgia State University, GA*
Hampton University, VA
Harvard University, MA
Houston Baptist University, TX*
Husson University, ME*
Indiana University South Bend, IN*
Iowa State University of Science and
    Technology, IA
Jacksonville University, FL
Louisiana State University and Agricultural &
    Mechanical College, LA*
Loyola University Chicago, IL*
Loyola University New Orleans, LA*
Macalester College, MN*
Marquette University, WI
Mary Baldwin University, VA*
Massachusetts Institute of Technology, MA
Miami University, OH
Milwaukee School of Engineering, WI*
Molloy College, NY*
Morehouse College, GA
Mount Carmel College of Nursing, OH*
New Jersey City University, NJ*
North Carolina State University, NC
Northeastern University, MA*
Northwestern University, IL
Oglethorpe University, GA*
The Ohio State University, OH
Old Dominion University, VA
Oregon State University, OR
Penn State University Park, PA
Point Loma Nazarene University, CA*
Prairie View A&M University, TX
Princeton University, NJ*
Purdue University, IN

Regent University, VA*
Regis University, CO*
Rensselaer Polytechnic Institute, NY
Rhodes College, TN*
Rice University, TX
Robert Morris University, PA*
Rochester Institute of Technology, NY*
Rutgers University–Newark, NJ
Rutgers University–New Brunswick, NJ
St. John Fisher College, NY*
Saint Joseph's University, PA*
St. Louis College of Pharmacy, MO*
Saint Mary-of-the-Woods College, IN*
San Diego State University, CA
Seattle Pacific University, WA*
Seattle University, WA*
Spelman College, GA*
Stanford University, CA*
State University of New York Maritime
    College, NY
Stony Brook University, State University of
    New York, NY*
Temple University, PA*
Texas A&M University, TX
Texas Woman's University, TX*
Tufts University, MA*
Tulane University, LA
Union College, NY*
The University of Arizona, AZ
University of California, Davis, CA*
University of California, Los Angeles, CA
University of California, San Diego, CA*
University of California, Santa Cruz, CA*
University of Colorado Boulder, CO
University of Florida, FL
University of Houston, TX*
University of Idaho, ID
University of Illinois at Chicago, IL*
The University of Kansas, KS
University of Maine, ME
University of Maryland, Baltimore County,
    MD
University of Maryland, College Park, MD*
University of Massachusetts Boston, MA*

University of Memphis, TN
University of Michigan, MI
University of Michigan–Flint, MI*
University of Minnesota, Twin Cities
    Campus, MN
University of Missouri, MO
University of Nebraska–Lincoln, NE
University of New Orleans, LA*
The University of North Carolina at Chapel
    Hill, NC
University of North Florida, FL*
University of Notre Dame, IN
University of Oklahoma, OK
University of Pennsylvania, PA
University of Pittsburgh, PA*
University of Rochester, NY
University of St. Thomas, MN*
University of San Diego, CA
University of South Carolina, SC
University of Southern California, CA
The University of Tampa, FL*
The University of Texas at Austin, TX
University of Utah, UT
University of Virginia, VA
University of Washington, WA
University of Washington, Bothell, WA*
University of Washington, Tacoma, WA*
University of Wisconsin–Madison, WI
University of Wisconsin–Milwaukee, WI*
Valencia College, FL*
Vanderbilt University, TN
Villanova University, PA
Virginia Military Institute, VA
Virginia Polytechnic Institute and State
    University, VA
Washington State University, WA*
Weber State University, UT*
Westminster College, UT*
Widener University, PA*
William Woods University, MO*
Worcester Polytechnic Institute, MA*
Worcester State University, MA*

---

* program is offered at another college's campus

Tuition Waivers

Adult Students

Albright College, PA
Barton College, NC
Bluefield State College, WV
Caldwell University, NJ
Campbellsville University, KY
Carlow University, PA
Cedarville University, OH
Coe College, IA
Creighton University, NE
DeSales University, PA
Elmira College, NY
Faulkner University, AL
Hilbert College, NY
Indiana Tech, IN
Judson University, IL
Lynchburg College, VA
Marist College, NY
Messiah College, PA
New England College, NH
Randolph College, VA
Roanoke College, VA
St. Andrews University, NC
St. John's University, NY
Southeastern Oklahoma State University,
  OK
Sweet Briar College, VA
University of Evansville, IN
University of Hawaii at Manoa, HI
Utah State University, UT
Virginia Wesleyan University, VA
Webber International University, FL
Wittenberg University, OH

Children of Alumni

Alliant International University–San Diego,
  CA
Appalachian Bible College, WV
Aurora University, IL
Baldwin Wallace University, OH
Bethel College, KS
Black Hills State University, SD
Caldwell University, NJ
Calumet College of Saint Joseph, IN
Carlow University, PA
The Catholic University of America, DC
Central Methodist University, MO
Central Michigan University, MI
Christendom College, VA
Columbia College, MO
Concordia University Chicago, IL
Corban University, OR
Curry College, MA
Drake University, IA
Drury University, MO
Eastern University, PA
Florida Southern College, FL
Georgian Court University, NJ
Grambling State University, LA
Henderson State University, AR
Hilbert College, NY
Hillsdale College, MI
Huntington University, IN
Indiana Tech, IN
Iona College, NY
Ithaca College, NY
Jackson State University, MS
Kansas Wesleyan University, KS
Lasell College, MA
Lewis University, IL

Lincoln University, PA
Louisiana Tech University, LA
Manhattanville College, NY
Marshall University, WV
McKendree University, IL
Michigan Technological University, MI
Minot State University, ND
Mississippi State University, MS
Missouri Baptist University, MO
Missouri State University, MO
Missouri Valley College, MO
Morehead State University, KY
Morningside College, IA
Morrisville State College, NY
Muskingum University, OH
Nazareth College of Rochester, NY
New England College, NH
Northern Kentucky University, KY
Northern Michigan University, MI
Northern State University, SD
Northwest College of Art & Design, WA
Ohio Northern University, OH
Oklahoma State University, OK
Pacific Lutheran University, WA
Palm Beach Atlantic University, FL
Peirce College, PA
Pine Manor College, MA
Saint Augustine's University, NC
Saint Martin's University, WA
Simpson College, IA
South Dakota State University, SD
Southeastern Oklahoma State University,
  OK
Southern Arkansas University–Magnolia,
  AR
Southern Illinois University Carbondale, IL
Southern Utah University, UT
Southwestern Oklahoma State University,
  OK
Suffolk University, MA
Texas Lutheran University, TX
Truman State University, MO
Union University, TN
University of Detroit Mercy, MI
University of Evansville, IN
University of Minnesota, Duluth, MN
University of Mississippi, MS
University of New England, ME
University of St. Francis, IL
University of South Dakota, SD
University of Southern Mississippi, MS
The University of the Arts, PA
University of Wyoming, WY
Utah State University, UT
Warner Pacific College, OR
Webber International University, FL
William Woods University, MO
Wittenberg University, OH

Minority Students

Appalachian Bible College, WV
Bethel College, KS
Drury University, MO
Fort Lewis College, CO
Hilbert College, NY
Huntington University, IN
Indiana Tech, IN
Lock Haven University of Pennsylvania, PA
Minot State University, ND
Montana State University, MT

Montana Tech of The University of
  Montana, MT
Morehead State University, KY
Morrisville State College, NY
Nazareth College of Rochester, NY
Ohio Northern University, OH
Shepherd University, WV
Slippery Rock University of Pennsylvania,
  PA
Southeastern Oklahoma State University,
  OK
University at Buffalo, the State University of
  New York, NY
University of Evansville, IN
University of Hawaii at Manoa, HI
University of Montana, MT
The University of Montana Western, MT
University of North Dakota, ND
University of Rhode Island, RI
Utah State University, UT
Western Washington University, WA
Wittenberg University, OH

Senior Citizens

Adams State University, CO
Adelphi University, NY
Albertus Magnus College, CT
Albright College, PA
Andrews University, MI
Appalachian Bible College, WV
Arkansas Tech University, AR
Athens State University, AL
Auburn University at Montgomery, AL
Austin Peay State University, TN
Averett University, VA
Baker University, KS
Ball State University, IN
Baruch College of the City University of
  New York, NY
Belmont University, TN
Benedictine College, KS
Berry College, GA
Bethany Lutheran College, MN
Bethel College, KS
Black Hills State University, SD
Bloomsburg University of Pennsylvania, PA
Bluefield College, VA
Bluefield State College, WV
Boise State University, ID
Bowie State University, MD
Bowling Green State University, OH
Bradley University, IL
Bridgewater State University, MA
Caldwell University, NJ
California State University, Bakersfield, CA
California State University, Chico, CA
California State University, Dominguez
  Hills, CA
California State University, Fullerton, CA
California State University, Long Beach, CA
California State University, Northridge, CA
California State University, San Bernardino,
  CA
California State University, San Marcos, CA
Calumet College of Saint Joseph, IN
Cameron University, OK
Campbellsville University, KY
Capital University, OH
Carroll College, MT
Carson-Newman University, TN

Cedarville University, OH
Central Connecticut State University, CT
Central Michigan University, MI
Central State University, OH
Central Washington University, WA
Chestnut Hill College, PA
Christopher Newport University, VA
The Citadel, The Military College of South Carolina, SC
Clarion University of Pennsylvania, PA
Clayton State University, GA
Clemson University, SC
Cleveland State University, OH
Coastal Carolina University, SC
Coe College, IA
College of Charleston, SC
College of Coastal Georgia, GA
The College of New Jersey, NJ
College of Saint Mary, NE
The College of St. Scholastica, MN
College of Staten Island of the City University of New York, NY
The College of William and Mary, VA
Columbia College, MO
Columbus State University, GA
Concordia University Chicago, IL
Corban University, OR
Creighton University, NE
Culver-Stockton College, MO
Daemen College, NY
Dakota State University, SD
Delaware State University, DE
DeSales University, PA
Dickinson College, PA
Dixie State University, UT
Doane University, NE
Dominican College, NY
Drake University, IA
Duquesne University, PA
Eastern Illinois University, IL
Eastern Kentucky University, KY
Eastern Oregon University, OR
East Stroudsburg University of Pennsylvania, PA
Elmhurst College, IL
Elms College, MA
Emmanuel College, GA
Emporia State University, KS
Eureka College, IL
The Evergreen State College, WA
Fairleigh Dickinson University, Florham Campus, NJ
Fairleigh Dickinson University, Metropolitan Campus, NJ
Fitchburg State University, MA
Florida Agricultural and Mechanical University, FL
Florida Atlantic University, FL
Florida Institute of Technology, FL
Florida State University, FL
Fort Lewis College, CO
Framingham State University, MA
Francis Marion University, SC
Franklin College, IN
Franklin Pierce University, NH
Frostburg State University, MD
George Fox University, OR
George Mason University, VA
Georgia College & State University, GA
Georgia Institute of Technology, GA
Georgian Court University, NJ
Georgia Southern University, GA
Georgia Southwestern State University, GA
Georgia State University, GA
Gonzaga University, WA
Governors State University, IL

Graceland University, IA
Grambling State University, LA
Greenville University, IL
Hanover College, IN
Harding University, AR
Henderson State University, AR
Hilbert College, NY
Holy Family University, PA
Hood College, MD
Houston Baptist University, TX
Husson University, ME
Idaho State University, ID
Indiana State University, IN
Indiana Tech, IN
Indiana University of Pennsylvania, PA
John Carroll University, OH
Judson University, IL
Juniata College, PA
Kansas Wesleyan University, KS
Kean University, NJ
Keene State College, NH
Kennesaw State University, GA
Kent State University, OH
Kent State University at Geauga, OH
Kent State University at Stark, OH
Kentucky State University, KY
King's College, PA
King University, TN
Kutztown University of Pennsylvania, PA
LaGrange College, GA
Lamar University, TX
La Roche College, PA
Lebanon Valley College, PA
Lee University, TN
Lenoir-Rhyne University, NC
Lincoln University, MO
Lindenwood University, MO
Lindsey Wilson College, KY
Linfield College, OR
Lock Haven University of Pennsylvania, PA
Longwood University, VA
Louisiana College, LA
Louisiana Tech University, LA
Loyola University Chicago, IL
Loyola University New Orleans, LA
Lynchburg College, VA
Malone University, OH
Mansfield University of Pennsylvania, PA
Marquette University, WI
Marshall University, WV
Marymount California University, CA
Marymount Manhattan College, NY
Marymount University, VA
Maryville University of Saint Louis, MO
Marywood University, PA
Massachusetts College of Liberal Arts, MA
Mercy College, NY
Merrimack College, MA
Messiah College, PA
Methodist University, NC
Metropolitan State University of Denver, CO
Michigan Technological University, MI
MidAmerica Nazarene University, KS
Middle Georgia State University, GA
Millersville University of Pennsylvania, PA
Minnesota State University Mankato, MN
Minnesota State University Moorhead, MN
Minot State University, ND
Mississippi State University, MS
Missouri Baptist University, MO
Missouri State University, MO
Missouri Western State University, MO
Molloy College, NY
Monmouth University, NJ
Montana State University, MT
Montana State University Billings, MT

Montana Tech of The University of Montana, MT
Montclair State University, NJ
Morehead State University, KY
Morningside College, IA
Morrisville State College, NY
Mount Mary University, WI
Mount St. Joseph University, OH
Mount Vernon Nazarene University, OH
Murray State University, KY
New England College, NH
New Jersey City University, NJ
New Mexico Highlands University, NM
New Mexico Institute of Mining and Technology, NM
New Mexico State University, NM
New York Institute of Technology, NY
Nicholls State University, LA
North Central College, IL
Northeastern Illinois University, IL
Northern Illinois University, IL
Northern Kentucky University, KY
Northern Michigan University, MI
Northern State University, SD
Northwest Missouri State University, MO
Northwest Nazarene University, ID
The Ohio State University, OH
Ohio University, OH
Ohio University–Eastern, OH
Ohio University–Zanesville, OH
Oklahoma Baptist University, OK
Oklahoma State University, OK
Old Dominion University, VA
Penn State Abington, PA
Penn State Altoona, PA
Penn State Beaver, PA
Penn State Berks, PA
Penn State Brandywine, PA
Penn State Erie, The Behrend College, PA
Penn State Greater Allegheny, PA
Penn State Harrisburg, PA
Penn State Hazleton, PA
Penn State Lehigh Valley, PA
Penn State New Kensington, PA
Penn State Schuylkill, PA
Penn State Shenango, PA
Penn State University Park, PA
Penn State Wilkes-Barre, PA
Penn State Worthington Scranton, PA
Penn State York, PA
Point Loma Nazarene University, CA
Portland State University, OR
Post University, CT
Prairie View A&M University, TX
Presbyterian College, SC
Purdue University, IN
Queens College of the City University of New York, NY
Radford University, VA
Ramapo College of New Jersey, NJ
Roanoke College, VA
Roberts Wesleyan College, NY
Rockhurst University, MO
Rogers State University, OK
St. Andrews University, NC
St. Bonaventure University, NY
St. Catherine University, MN
St. John's University, NY
St. Mary's College of Maryland, MD
Saint Michael's College, VT
St. Olaf College, MN
Salisbury University, MD
San Francisco State University, CA
Seattle Pacific University, WA
Shawnee State University, OH
Shepherd University, WV

Shippensburg University of Pennsylvania, PA
Simpson College, IA
Skidmore College, NY
Slippery Rock University of Pennsylvania, PA
South Dakota State University, SD
Southeastern Oklahoma State University, OK
Southeast Missouri State University, MO
Southern Adventist University, TN
Southern Arkansas University–Magnolia, AR
Southern Illinois University Carbondale, IL
Southern New Hampshire University, NH
Southern Oregon University, OR
Southern Utah University, UT
Southern Vermont College, VT
Southwestern College, KS
Southwestern Oklahoma State University, OK
State University of New York College of Agriculture and Technology at Cobleskill, NY
Stephen F. Austin State University, TX
Sterling College, KS
Stockton University, NJ
Suffolk University, MA
Sweet Briar College, VA
Taylor University, IN
Tennessee Technological University, TN
Texas A&M International University, TX
Texas A&M University–Commerce, TX
Texas A&M University–Corpus Christi, TX
Texas A&M University–Kingsville, TX
Texas A&M University–Texarkana, TX
Texas Tech University, TX
Texas Woman's University, TX
Thomas More College, KY
Tiffin University, OH
Towson University, MD
Trevecca Nazarene University, TN
Trine University, IN
Trinity College of Florida, FL
Truman State University, MO
Union College, NY
The University of Akron, OH
University of Alaska Fairbanks, AK
University of Arkansas, AR
University of Arkansas at Little Rock, AR
University of Bridgeport, CT
University of Central Arkansas, AR
University of Central Florida, FL
University of Colorado Boulder, CO
University of Delaware, DE
University of Denver, CO
University of Detroit Mercy, MI
University of Evansville, IN
The University of Findlay, OH
University of Florida, FL

University of Georgia, GA
University of Hartford, CT
University of Hawaii at Manoa, HI
University of Houston–Clear Lake, TX
University of Houston–Downtown, TX
University of Houston–Victoria, TX
University of Illinois at Chicago, IL
University of Illinois at Springfield, IL
University of Illinois at Urbana–Champaign, IL
University of Indianapolis, IN
University of Louisiana at Monroe, LA
University of Louisville, KY
University of Maine, ME
University of Maine at Fort Kent, ME
University of Maine at Machias, ME
University of Maine at Presque Isle, ME
University of Maryland, Baltimore County, MD
University of Maryland University College, MD
University of Mary Washington, VA
University of Massachusetts Amherst, MA
University of Massachusetts Dartmouth, MA
University of Massachusetts Lowell, MA
University of Memphis, TN
University of Michigan–Dearborn, MI
University of Michigan–Flint, MI
University of Minnesota, Crookston, MN
University of Minnesota, Twin Cities Campus, MN
University of Mississippi, MS
University of Missouri, MO
University of Missouri–St. Louis, MO
University of Montana, MT
The University of Montana Western, MT
University of Nevada, Reno, NV
University of New Haven, CT
University of New Orleans, LA
University of North Alabama, AL
The University of North Carolina at Greensboro, NC
University of North Florida, FL
University of North Georgia, GA
University of North Texas, TX
University of North Texas at Dallas, TX
University of Oklahoma, OK
University of Pikeville, KY
University of Pittsburgh at Greensburg, PA
University of Rhode Island, RI
University of St. Thomas, MN
University of St. Thomas, TX
University of Science and Arts of Oklahoma, OK
The University of Scranton, PA
University of South Carolina, SC
University of South Carolina Aiken, SC
University of South Dakota, SD
University of Southern Mississippi, MS
University of South Florida, FL

The University of Tennessee, TN
The University of Tennessee at Chattanooga, TN
The University of Tennessee at Martin, TN
The University of Texas at Austin, TX
The University of Texas at Dallas, TX
University of the Incarnate Word, TX
University of Utah, UT
University of Virginia, VA
The University of Virginia's College at Wise, VA
University of Washington, WA
University of Washington, Bothell, WA
University of Washington, Tacoma, WA
University of West Florida, FL
University of West Georgia, GA
University of Wisconsin–Green Bay, WI
University of Wisconsin–Milwaukee, WI
University of Wisconsin–Parkside, WI
University of Wisconsin–Stevens Point, WI
University of Wisconsin–Whitewater, WI
University of Wyoming, WY
Utah State University, UT
Valencia College, FL
Vermont Technical College, VT
Villanova University, PA
Virginia Polytechnic Institute and State University, VA
Virginia State University, VA
Virginia Wesleyan University, VA
Washington State University, WA
Wayne State University, MI
Webber International University, FL
Weber State University, UT
Wells College, NY
West Chester University of Pennsylvania, PA
Western Connecticut State University, CT
Western Illinois University, IL
Western Kentucky University, KY
Western Michigan University, MI
Western State Colorado University, CO
Western Washington University, WA
Westfield State University, MA
West Virginia University, WV
West Virginia University Institute of Technology, WV
Whitworth University, WA
Wichita State University, KS
Widener University, PA
William Paterson University of New Jersey, NJ
William Woods University, MO
Winthrop University, SC
Wittenberg University, OH
Worcester State University, MA
Wright State University, OH
Wright State University–Lake Campus, OH
Xavier University, OH
Youngstown State University, OH

Tuition Payment Alternatives

College	Code
Abilene Christian University, TX	I,P
Academy of Art University, CA	I
Adams State University, CO	D,G,I
Adelphi University, NY	D,I,P
Agnes Scott College, GA	I
Alabama State University, AL	D
Alaska Bible College, AK	I
Alaska Pacific University, AK	D,I
Albany State University, GA	I
Albertus Magnus College, CT	I
Albion College, MI	D,I
Albright College, PA	I
Alcorn State University, MS	I
Alfred University, NY	I
Alice Lloyd College, KY	I
Allegheny College, PA	I
Allen College, IA	D
Alliant International University–San Diego, CA	D
Alma College, MI	D,I
Alverno College, WI	D,I
Amcrican University, DC	I,P
Amherst College, MA	I
Amridge University, AL	G,I,P
Anderson University, SC	I
Andrews University, MI	I
Angelo State University, TX	G,I
Appalachian Bible College, WV	D,I
Appalachian State University, NC	G,I
Aquinas College, MI	D,I
Arizona Christian University, AZ	I
Arizona State University at the Tempe campus, AZ	I
Arkansas Tech University, AR	D,I
Athens State University, AL	I
Auburn University, AL	I
Auburn University at Montgomery, AL	I
Augsburg University, MN	I
Augustana College, IL	I,P
Augustana University, SD	I
Aurora University, IL	D,I
Austin College, TX	I
Austin Graduate School of Theology, TX	I
Austin Peay State University, TN	I
Averett University, VA	I
Azusa Pacific University, CA	I
Babson College, MA	I
Baker University, KS	I
Baldwin Wallace University, OH	D,I
Ball State University, IN	I
Baptist University of the Americas, TX	I
Barclay College, KS	I
Bard College, NY	I,P
Barnard College, NY	D,I,P
Barry University, FL	D,I
Barton College, NC	I
Baruch College of the City University of New York, NY	D,I
Bates College, ME	I,P
Baylor University, TX	I
Bay Path University, MA	I
Becker College, MA	I
Belhaven University, MS	I
Bellarmine University, KY	I
Belmont University, TN	D,I
Beloit College, WI	I
Benedictine College, KS	I
Benedictine University, IL	I
Bennington College, VT	I
Bentley University, MA	I
Berry College, GA	I
Bethany Lutheran College, MN	I
Bethel College, IN	I
Bethel College, KS	D,I
Bethel University, MN	I,P
Bethune-Cookman University, FL	I
Binghamton University, State University of New York, NY	I
Biola University, CA	I
Black Hills State University, SD	D,I
Blessing-Rieman College of Nursing & Health Sciences, IL	I
Bloomsburg University of Pennsylvania, PA	I
Bluefield College, VA	I
Bluefield State College, WV	I
Blue Mountain College, MS	D,I
Bluffton University, OH	I
Bob Jones University, SC	I
Boise State University, ID	I
Boston Architectural College, MA	I
Boston Baptist College, MA	I
Boston College, MA	I
Boston University, MA	I,P
Bowdoin College, ME	D,I
Bowie State University, MD	D,I
Bowling Green State University, OH	I
Bradley University, IL	D,I
Brandeis University, MA	I
Brenau University, GA	D,I
Bridgewater College, VA	I
Bridgewater State University, MA	I
Brown University, RI	I
Bryan College, TN	I
Bryant University, RI	I
Bryn Mawr College, PA	I
Bucknell University, PA	I,P
Buena Vista University, IA	I
Buffalo State College, State University of New York, NY	I
Butler University, IN	I
Cairn University, PA	I
Caldwell University, NJ	I
California Baptist University, CA	I
California Christian College, CA	I
California College of the Arts, CA	I
California Institute of Technology, CA	D,I
California Lutheran University, CA	I
California Polytechnic State University, San Luis Obispo, CA	I
California State Polytechnic University, Pomona, CA	D,I
California State University, Bakersfield, CA	I
California State University, Chico, CA	D,I
California State University, Dominguez Hills, CA	I
California State University, Fullerton, CA	D,I
California State University, Long Beach, CA	I
California State University Maritime Academy, CA	I
California State University, Northridge, CA	I
California State University, Sacramento, CA	I
California State University, San Bernardino, CA	I
California State University, Stanislaus, CA	I
California University of Pennsylvania, PA	I
Calumet College of Saint Joseph, IN	D,G
Calvin College, MI	I
Cameron University, OK	I
Campbellsville University, KY	I
Campbell University, NC	I
Canisius College, NY	D,I
Capital University, OH	I
Cardinal Stritch University, WI	I
Carleton College, MN	I
Carlos Albizu University, Miami Campus, FL	I
Carlow University, PA	I
Carnegic Mellon University, PA	I
Carolina Christian College, NC	I
Carroll College, MT	I
Carroll University, WI	D,I
Carson-Newman University, TN	D,I
Case Western Reserve University, OH	I
Catawba College, NC	I
The Catholic University of America, DC	I
Cazenovia College, NY	I
Cedar Crest College, PA	D,I
Cedarville University, OH	I
Centenary College of Louisiana, LA	I
Central Connecticut State University, CT	I
Central Methodist University, MO	I
Central Michigan University, MI	I
Central State University, OH	I
Central Washington University, WA	I
Centre College, KY	I
Chaminade University of Honolulu, HI	I
Champlain College, VT	I,P
Chapman University, CA	D,I,P
Charlotte Christian College and Theological Seminary, NC	G,I
Charter Oak State College, CT	I
Chatham University, PA	I
Chestnut Hill College, PA	D,I
Chowan University, NC	I
Christendom College, VA	I
Christian Brothers University, TN	I
Christopher Newport University, VA	I
The Citadel, The Military College of South Carolina, SC	I
Claflin University, SC	D,I
Claremont McKenna College, CA	I
Clarion University of Pennsylvania, PA	D,I
Clarke University, IA	D,I
Clarkson University, NY	I
Clark University, MA	I,P
Clemson University, SC	I
Cleveland Institute of Art, OH	I
Cleveland State University, OH	I
Coastal Carolina University, SC	I
Coe College, IA	I
Coker College, SC	I

D = deferred payment system; *G* = guaranteed tuition rate; *I* = installment payments; *P* = prepayment locks in tuition rate

College	Code
Colby College, ME	I
Colgate University, NY	D,I,P
The College at Brockport, State University of New York, NY	D,I
College of Charleston, SC	I
College of Coastal Georgia, GA	I
The College of Idaho, ID	I
The College of New Jersey, NJ	I
The College of New Rochelle, NY	I
College of Saint Benedict, MN	I
College of Saint Mary, NE	D,I
The College of Saint Rose, NY	I
The College of St. Scholastica, MN	I
College of Staten Island of the City University of New York, NY	I
College of the Atlantic, ME	I
College of the Holy Cross, MA	I
College of the Ozarks, MO	I
The College of William and Mary, VA	I
The College of Wooster, OH	I
The Colorado College, CO	I
Colorado Mesa University, CO	I
Colorado School of Mines, CO	I
Columbia College, MO	D,G,I
Columbia College Chicago, IL	I
Columbia International University, SC	I
Columbia University, NY	I,P
Columbus College of Art & Design, OH	D,I
Conception Seminary College, MO	I
Concordia College, MN	I
Concordia University Chicago, IL	I
Concordia University Irvine, CA	I
Concordia University, Nebraska, NE	I
Concordia University, St. Paul, MN	I
Concord University, WV	I
Connecticut College, CT	I
Converse College, SC	I
Cooper Union for the Advancement of Science and Art, NY	I
Corban University, OR	I
Cornell College, IA	I
Cornell University, NY	I
Cornerstone University, MI	I
Cox College, MO	I
Creighton University, NE	I
Criswell College, TX	I
The Culinary Institute of America, NY	I
Culver-Stockton College, MO	I
Curry College, MA	I
Daemen College, NY	D,I
Dakota State University, SD	I
Dallas Baptist University, TX	D,I
Dartmouth College, NH	I,P
Davidson College, NC	I
Davis College, NY	I
Dean College, MA	I
Defiance College, OH	I
Delaware State University, DE	D,I
Delaware Valley University, PA	I
Denison University, OH	D,I
DePaul University, IL	D,I
DePauw University, IN	I
DeSales University, PA	D,I
Dickinson College, PA	I
DigiPen Institute of Technology, WA	I
Dixie State University, UT	I
Doane University, NE	I
Dominican College, NY	D,I
Dominican University, IL	D
Dominican University of California, CA	I
Drake University, IA	G,I
Drew University, NJ	D,I,P
Drexel University, PA	I
Drury University, MO	D,I
Duke University, NC	I,P
Duquesne University, PA	D,I
Earlham College, IN	D,I
East Carolina University, NC	D,G,I
East Central University, OK	G
Eastern Illinois University, IL	G,I
Eastern Kentucky University, KY	I
Eastern Mennonite University, VA	I
Eastern Michigan University, MI	I
Eastern Oregon University, OR	D,I
Eastern University, PA	I
East Stroudsburg University of Pennsylvania, PA	I
East Texas Baptist University, TX	I
Eckerd College, FL	I
Edgewood College, WI	I
Elizabethtown College, PA	I
Elmhurst College, IL	I
Elmira College, NY	I,P
Elms College, MA	I
Elon University, NC	I
Embry-Riddle Aeronautical University–Daytona, FL	I
Emmanuel College, GA	I
Emmanuel College, MA	I
Emory & Henry College, VA	G,I
Emory University, GA	I
Emporia State University, KS	D,I
Endicott College, MA	I,P
Eugene Lang College of Liberal Arts, NY	I
Eureka College, IL	I
Evangel University, MO	I
The Evergreen State College, WA	I
Excelsior College, NY	I
Fairfield University, CT	I
Fairleigh Dickinson University, Florham Campus, NJ	D,I
Fairleigh Dickinson University, Metropolitan Campus, NJ	D,I
Fairmont State University, WV	I
Farmingdale State College, NY	I
Faulkner University, AL	D,I
Felician University, NJ	I
Ferris State University, MI	I
FIDM/Fashion Institute of Design & Merchandising, Los Angeles Campus, CA	I
Fisher College, MA	I
Fitchburg State University, MA	I
Flagler College, FL	I
Florida Agricultural and Mechanical University, FL	P
Florida Atlantic University, FL	D,I
Florida Institute of Technology, FL	I
Florida International University, FL	I
Florida National University, FL	G,I,P
Florida Southern College, FL	I
Florida State University, FL	I,P
Fordham University, NY	I
Fort Hays State University, KS	D,I
Fort Lewis College, CO	I
Framingham State University, MA	I,P
Franciscan University of Steubenville, OH	I
Francis Marion University, SC	I
Franklin & Marshall College, PA	D,I
Franklin College, IN	I
Franklin Pierce University, NH	I
Franklin W. Olin College of Engineering, MA	I
Frostburg State University, MD	D,I
Furman University, SC	I
Gardner-Webb University, NC	I
Geneva College, PA	I
George Fox University, OR	I
George Mason University, VA	D,I
Georgetown College, KY	I
Georgetown University, DC	I
The George Washington University, DC	G,I
Georgia College & State University, GA	I
Georgia Institute of Technology, GA	D
Georgian Court University, NJ	I
Georgia Southern University, GA	I
Gettysburg College, PA	I
Goldfarb School of Nursing at Barnes-Jewish College, MO	I
Gonzaga University, WA	D,I
Gordon College, MA	I
Goshen College, IN	I
Goucher College, MD	I,P
Governors State University, IL	G,I
Graceland University, IA	I
Grambling State University, LA	D,I
Grand Valley State University, MI	D,I
Greenville University, IL	I
Grinnell College, IA	I
Guilford College, NC	G,I
Gustavus Adolphus College, MN	I,P
Gwynedd Mercy University, PA	I
Hamilton College, NY	I
Hamline University, MN	I
Hampden-Sydney College, VA	I
Hampton University, VA	D,I
Hanover College, IN	I
Harding University, AR	I,P
Hardin-Simmons University, TX	G,I
Harrisburg University of Science and Technology, PA	D,I
Harris-Stowe State University, MO	I
Hartwick College, NY	I
Harvard University, MA	I,P
Harvey Mudd College, CA	I
Haverford College, PA	I
Hawai`i Pacific University, HI	I
Heidelberg University, OH	I
Henderson State University, AR	I
Hendrix College, AR	I
High Point University, NC	I
Hilbert College, NY	I
Hillsdale College, MI	I
Hiram College, OH	G,I
Hobart and William Smith Colleges, NY	I,P
Hofstra University, NY	G,I
Hollins University, VA	I,P
Holy Family University, PA	D,I
Hood College, MD	I
Hope College, MI	I
Hope International University, CA	I
Houston Baptist University, TX	I
Howard Payne University, TX	I
Humboldt State University, CA	I
Hunter College of the City University of New York, NY	I
Huntingdon College, AL	I
Huntington University, IN	I
Husson University, ME	I,P
Idaho State University, ID	G,I
Illinois College, IL	I
Illinois Wesleyan University, IL	I
Indiana State University, IN	D,I
Indiana Tech, IN	G,I
Indiana University Bloomington, IN	D,I
Indiana University East, IN	D,I
Indiana University Kokomo, IN	D,I
Indiana University Northwest, IN	D,I

D = deferred payment system; *G* = guaranteed tuition rate; *I* = installment payments; *P* = prepayment locks in tuition rate

Indiana University of Pennsylvania, PA	D,I	Lindsey Wilson College, KY	I	Middle Tennessee State University, TN	I
Indiana University–Purdue University Indianapolis, IN	D	Linfield College, OR	I	Mid-South Christian College, TN	G,I
Indiana University South Bend, IN	D,I	Lipscomb University, TN	I	Millersville University of Pennsylvania, PA	I
Indiana University Southeast, IN	D,I	Lock Haven University of Pennsylvania, PA	I	Milligan College, TN	I
Indiana Wesleyan University, IN	D,I	Long Island University–LIU Brooklyn, NY	I	Millikin University, IL	I
Inter American University of Puerto Rico, Bayamón Campus, PR	D	Long Island University–LIU Post, NY	I	Mills College, CA	I
Iona College, NY	I	Longwood University, VA	I	Milwaukee School of Engineering, WI	I
Iowa State University of Science and Technology, IA	D,I	Loras College, IA	I	Minnesota State University Mankato, MN	I
Iowa Wesleyan University, IA	D,I	Louisiana College, LA	I	Minnesota State University Moorhead, MN	I
Ithaca College, NY	I	Louisiana State University and Agricultural & Mechanical College, LA	D	Minot State University, ND	I
Jackson State University, MS	I	Louisiana Tech University, LA	D,I	Misericordia University, PA	D,I
Jacksonville State University, AL	I	Loyola Marymount University, CA	I	Mississippi State University, MS	I,P
Jacksonville University, FL	D	Loyola University Chicago, IL	D,I	Missouri Baptist University, MO	I
John Brown University, AR	I	Loyola University Maryland, MD	I	Missouri State University, MO	D
John Carroll University, OH	I	Loyola University New Orleans, LA	I	Missouri University of Science and Technology, MO	I
John Paul the Great Catholic University, CA	G	Lubbock Christian University, TX	I	Missouri Valley College, MO	I,P
Johnson C. Smith University, NC	I	Luther College, IA	I	Missouri Western State University, MO	I
Johnson University, TN	I	Lycoming College, PA	I	Molloy College, NY	D,I
Johnson University Florida, FL	I	Lynchburg College, VA	I,P	Monmouth College, IL	I
Judson University, IL	D	Lynn University, FL	D,I	Monmouth University, NJ	I
The Juilliard School, NY	I	Lyon College, AR	I	Montana State University, MT	D,I
Juniata College, PA	I	Macalester College, MN	I	Montana State University Billings, MT	I
Kalamazoo College, MI	I	Malone University, OH	I	Montana Tech of The University of Montana, MT	I
Kansas City Art Institute, MO	I	Manchester University, IN	I	Montclair State University, NJ	I
Kansas State University, KS	D,I	Manhattan College, NY	D,I	Moravian College, PA	I
Kansas Wesleyan University, KS	I	Manhattanville College, NY	I	Morehead State University, KY	D,I
Kean University, NJ	I	Mansfield University of Pennsylvania, PA	D,I	Morehouse College, GA	I
Keene State College, NH	I	Marietta College, OH	I	Morgan State University, MD	D,I
Kennesaw State University, GA	D,I	Marist College, NY	I	Morningside College, IA	I
Kent State University, OH	I	Marlboro College, VT	I	Morrisville State College, NY	D,I
Kent State University at Geauga, OH	I	Marquette University, WI	I	Mount Carmel College of Nursing, OH	I
Kent State University at Stark, OH	I	Marshall University, WV	I	Mount Holyoke College, MA	I
Kentucky State University, KY	I	Martin Luther College, MN	I	Mount Marty College, SD	I
Kenyon College, OH	I	Mary Baldwin University, VA	I	Mount Mary University, WI	I
Keuka College, NY	I	Marymount California University, CA	I	Mount Mercy University, IA	I
The King's College, NY	D,I	Marymount Manhattan College, NY	I	Mount St. Joseph University, OH	D,I
King's College, PA	I	Marymount University, VA	I	Mount Saint Mary College, NY	I
King University, TN	I	Maryville College, TN	I	Mount Saint Mary's University, CA	I
Knox College, IL	I	Maryville University of Saint Louis, MO	D,I	Mount St. Mary's University, MD	I
Kutztown University of Pennsylvania, PA	D,I	Marywood University, PA	D,I	Mount Vernon Nazarene University, OH	I
Kuyper College, MI	D,I	Massachusetts College of Liberal Arts, MA	I	Muhlenberg College, PA	I
Lafayette College, PA	I	Massachusetts Institute of Technology, MA	I	Murray State University, KY	I
LaGrange College, GA	I	Massachusetts Maritime Academy, MA	I	Muskingum University, OH	I
Laguna College of Art & Design, CA	I	McDaniel College, MD	I	Nazareth College of Rochester, NY	D,I
Lakeview College of Nursing, IL	I	McKendree University, IL	D,I	Nebraska Christian College of Hope International University, NE	D,I
Lamar University, TX	G,I	McMurry University, TX	I	Nebraska Methodist College, NE	I
La Roche College, PA	I	MCPHS University, MA	I	Neumann University, PA	D,I
La Salle University, PA	D,I	Medgar Evers College of the City University of New York, NY	D,I	Neumont College of Computer Science, UT	I
Lasell College, MA	I	Mercer University, GA	I	Newberry College, SC	I
La Sierra University, CA	I	Mercy College, NY	D,I	New College of Florida, FL	I
Lawrence Technological University, MI	I	Merrimack College, MA	I	New England College, NH	I
Lawrence University, WI	I	Messiah College, PA	I	New Jersey City University, NJ	D,I
Lebanon Valley College, PA	I	Methodist University, NC	I	New Jersey Institute of Technology, NJ	D,I
Lees-McRae College, NC	G,I	Metropolitan College of New York, NY	D,G,I	Newman University, KS	I
Lee University, TN	D	Metropolitan State University of Denver, CO	D,I	New Mexico Highlands University, NM	I
Lehigh University, PA	I,P	Miami University, OH	G,I	New Mexico State University, NM	I
Le Moyne College, NY	D,I	Michigan State University, MI	D	The New School College of Performing Arts, NY	I
Lesley University, MA	I	Michigan Technological University, MI	D,I	The New School for Public Engagement, NY	I
LeTourneau University, TX	I	MidAmerica Nazarene University, KS	I	New York Institute of Technology, NY	I
Lewis & Clark College, OR	I	Middlebury College, VT	P	Niagara University, NY	D,I
Lewis University, IL	I	Middle Georgia State University, GA	I		
Liberty University, VA	I				
Life University, GA	I				
LIM College, NY	I				
Lincoln Memorial University, TN	I				
Lincoln University, MO	D,I				
Lincoln University, PA	D,G,I				
Lindenwood University, MO	D,I				

D = deferred payment system; *G* = guaranteed tuition rate; *I* = installment payments; *P* = prepayment locks in tuition rate

Nicholls State University, LA	D,I	Piedmont International University,		Saint Joseph's University, PA	I
Nichols College, MA	I	NC	I	St. Lawrence University, NY	I,P
North Carolina State University, NC	G,I	Pine Manor College, MA	I	Saint Leo University, FL	D,I
North Central College, IL	I	Pittsburg State University, KS	I	Saint Louis University, MO	D,I
Northeastern Illinois University, IL	D,G,I	Pitzer College, CA	D,I	Saint Martin's University, WA	I
Northeastern State University, OK	G,I	Point Loma Nazarene University, CA	I	Saint Mary-of-the-Woods College, IN	G,I
Northeastern University, MA	I	Point Park University, PA	D,I	Saint Mary's College, IN	I
Northern Arizona University, AZ	D,G,I	Pomona College, CA	I	Saint Mary's College of	
Northern Illinois University, IL	I	Portland State University, OR	I	California, CA	I
Northern Kentucky University, KY	I	Post University, CT	I,P	St. Mary's College of	
Northern Michigan University, MI	D,I	Prairie View A&M University, TX	G,I	Maryland, MD	I
Northern State University, SD	I	Presbyterian College, SC	I	St. Mary's University, TX	I
Northland College, WI	I	Princeton University, NJ	D,I	Saint Mary's University of	
Northwest Christian University, OR	I	Principia College, IL	I	Minnesota, MN	I
Northwest College of Art & Design,		Providence College, RI	I	Saint Michael's College, VT	I
WA	I	Purdue University, IN	I	St. Norbert College, WI	D,I
Northwestern College, IA	I,P	Queens College of the City		St. Olaf College, MN	I
Northwestern University, IL	I	University of New York, NY	I	St. Thomas Aquinas College, NY	I
Northwest Missouri State		Quinnipiac University, CT	I	St. Thomas University, FL	D,I
University, MO	D,I	Radford University, VA	I	Saint Vincent College, PA	I
Northwest Nazarene University, ID	I	Ramapo College of New Jersey, NJ	I	Salem College, NC	I
Northwest University, WA	I	Randolph College, VA	I	Salisbury University, MD	I
Northwood University, Michigan		Randolph-Macon College, VA	I	Salve Regina University, RI	I
Campus, MI	I	Reed College, OR	I	Samford University, AL	I
Nova Southeastern University, FL	D,I	Regent University, VA	I	Sam Houston State University, TX	G,I
Oakland City University, IN	D	Regis University, CO	D,I	San Diego State University, CA	I
Oberlin College, OH	I	Rensselaer Polytechnic Institute, NY	I	San Francisco Art Institute, CA	I
Occidental College, CA	I,P	Resurrection University, IL	I	San Francisco Conservatory of	
Oglethorpe University, GA	I,P	Rhode Island College, RI	I	Music, CA	I
Ohio Northern University, OH	I	Rhodes College, TN	I	San Francisco State University, CA	I
The Ohio State University, OH	G,I	Rice University, TX	I	San Jose State University, CA	D,I
Ohio University, OH	G,I	Ringling College of Art and		Santa Clara University, CA	I
Ohio University–Eastern, OH	I	Design, FL	I	Sarah Lawrence College, NY	I
Ohio University–Zanesville, OH	I	Roanoke College, VA	I	Savannah College of Art and	
Ohio Valley University, WV	I	Robert Morris University, PA	D,I	Design, GA	I
Ohio Wesleyan University, OH	I	Robert Morris University Illinois,		School of the Art Institute of	
Oklahoma Baptist University, OK	I	IL	I	Chicago, IL	I
Oklahoma Christian University, OK	I	Roberts Wesleyan College, NY	I	Schreiner University, TX	I
Oklahoma City University, OK	D,I	Rochester Institute of Technology,		Scripps College, CA	I,P
Oklahoma State University, OK	G,I	NY	D,I,P	Seattle Pacific University, WA	D,I
Old Dominion University, VA	D,I	Rockford University, IL	I	Seattle University, WA	D,I
Olivet Nazarene University, IL	I	Rockhurst University, MO	D,I	Seton Hill University, PA	I
Oral Roberts University, OK	I	Rocky Mountain College, MT	I	Sewanee: The University of the	
Oregon Health & Science		Rogers State University, OK	I	South, TN	I
University, OR	G,I	Roger Williams University, RI	D,G	Shawnee State University, OH	G,I
Ouachita Baptist University, AR	D,I	Rollins College, FL	I	Shenandoah University, VA	I
Our Lady of the Lake University, TX	D,I	Rose-Hulman Institute of		Shepherd University, WV	I
Pacific Lutheran University, WA	I	Technology, IN	I,P	Shippensburg University of	
Palm Beach Atlantic University, FL	I	Rosemont College, PA	I	Pennsylvania, PA	I
Parsons School of Design, NY	I	Rowan University, NJ	D,I	Siena College, NY	I
Peirce College, PA	D,I	Rutgers University–Camden, NJ	I	Simmons College, MA	I
Penn State Abington, PA	D,I	Rutgers University–Newark, NJ	I	Simpson College, IA	I
Penn State Altoona, PA	D,I	Rutgers University–New		Skidmore College, NY	I,P
Penn State Beaver, PA	D,I	Brunswick, NJ	I	Slippery Rock University of	
Penn State Berks, PA	D,I	Sacred Heart University, CT	I	Pennsylvania, PA	I
Penn State Brandywine, PA	D,I	The Sage Colleges, NY	I	Smith College, MA	I,P
Penn State Erie, The Behrend		Saginaw Valley State University, MI	I	Soka University of America, CA	D,I
College, PA	D,I	St. Ambrose University, IA	D,I	Sonoma State University, CA	I
Penn State Greater Allegheny, PA	D,I	St. Andrews University, NC	I	South Dakota State University, SD	D,I
Penn State Harrisburg, PA	D,I	Saint Anselm College, NH	I	Southeastern Louisiana University,	
Penn State Hazleton, PA	D,I	Saint Augustine's		LA	G,I
Penn State Lehigh Valley, PA	D,I	University, NC	D	Southeastern Oklahoma State	
Penn State New Kensington, PA	D,I	St. Catherine University, MN	I	University, OK	G,I
Penn State Schuylkill, PA	D,I	St. Edward's University, TX	I	Southeastern University, FL	I
Penn State Shenango, PA	D,I	Saint Francis Medical Center		Southeast Missouri State	
Penn State University Park, PA	D,I	College of Nursing, IL	I	University, MO	D,I
Penn State Wilkes-Barre, PA	D,I	St. John Fisher College, NY	D,I	Southern Adventist University, TN	I
Penn State Worthington Scranton, PA	D,I	St. John's College, MD	I,P	Southern Arkansas University–	
Penn State York, PA	D,I	St. John's College, NM	I	Magnolia, AR	I
Pennsylvania College of		Saint John's University, MN	I	Southern Illinois University	
Technology, PA	D	St. John's University, NY	I	Carbondale, IL	G,I
Pepperdine University, CA	I	St. Joseph's College, Long		Southern Methodist University, TX	I,P
Pfeiffer University, NC	I	Island Campus, NY	I	Southern New Hampshire University,	
Philander Smith College, AR	D,I	St. Joseph's College, New		NH	D,I
Piedmont College, GA	I	York, NY	I	Southern Oregon University, OR	D,I

D = deferred payment system; *G* = guaranteed tuition rate; *I* = installment payments; *P* = prepayment locks in tuition rate

Southern Utah University, UT	I	Theological University of the		University of Houston–	
Southern Vermont College, VT	I	Caribbean, PR	D	Victoria, TX	D,G,I
Southwest Baptist University, MO	I	Thomas Aquinas College, CA	I	University of Idaho, ID	I
Southwestern College, KS	I	Thomas Edison State University, NJ	I	University of Illinois at Chicago,	
Southwestern Oklahoma State		Thomas More College, KY	I	IL	G,I
University, OK	D,I	Thomas More College of Liberal		University of Illinois at	
Southwestern University, TX	I	Arts, NH	I	Springfield, IL	G,I
Spelman College, GA	D,I	Thomas University, GA	I	University of Illinois at	
Spring Hill College, AL	I	Tiffin University, OH	D,I	Urbana–Champaign, IL	G,I
Stanford University, CA	I	Toccoa Falls College, GA	I	University of Indianapolis, IN	D,I
State University of New York at		Towson University, MD	I	The University of Iowa, IA	I
Fredonia, NY	I	Transylvania University, KY	I	University of Jamestown, ND	I
State University of New York at		Trevecca Nazarene University, TN	I,P	The University of Kansas, KS	I
New Paltz, NY	I	Trine University, IN	I	University of Kentucky, KY	I
State University of New York at		Trinity Christian College, IL	I	University of La Verne, CA	D,I
Oswego, NY	I	Trinity College of Florida, FL	I	University of Louisiana at Monroe,	
State University of New York at		Trinity University, TX	I	LA	I
Plattsburgh, NY	D,I	Troy University, AL	I	University of Louisville, KY	I
State University of New York		Truett McConnell University, GA	I	University of Maine, ME	I
College at Cortland, NY	I	Truman State University, MO	I	University of Maine at Fort Kent, ME	I
State University of New York		Tufts University, MA	I,P	University of Maine at Machias, ME	I
College at Geneseo, NY	D,I	Tulane University, LA	I,P	University of Maine at Presque	
State University of New York		Union College, KY	I	Isle, ME	I
College at Potsdam, NY	I	Union College, NE	I	University of Mary Hardin-Baylor, TX	I
State University of New York College		Union College, NY	I	University of Maryland, Baltimore	
of Agriculture and Technology		Union University, TN	D,I	County, MD	I
at Cobleskill, NY	D,I	United States Sports Academy, AL	I	University of Maryland, College	
State University of New York College		Unity College, ME	I	Park, MD	D,I
of Environmental Science and		University at Buffalo, the State		University of Maryland University	
Forestry, NY	I	University of New York, NY	I	College, MD	I
State University of New York		The University of Akron, OH	I	University of Mary Washington, VA	I
College of Technology at Canton, NY	D,I	The University of Alabama, AL	D,I	University of Massachusetts	
State University of New York		The University of Alabama at		Amherst, MA	I
Maritime College, NY	I	Birmingham, AL	I	University of Massachusetts	
State University of New York		The University of Alabama in		Dartmouth, MA	I
Polytechnic Institute, NY	I	Huntsville, AL	I	University of Massachusetts	
Stephen F. Austin State		University of Alaska Fairbanks, AK	D,I	Lowell, MA	I
University, TX	G,I	The University of Arizona, AZ	G,I	University of Memphis, TN	I
Sterling College, KS	I	University of Arkansas, AR	I	University of Miami, FL	I
Stetson University, FL	I	University of Bridgeport, CT	D,I	University of Michigan, MI	I
Stevens Institute of Technology, NJ	I	University of California,		University of Michigan–	
Stevenson University, MD	I	Berkeley, CA	I	Dearborn, MI	I
Stockton University, NJ	D,I	University of California, Irvine, CA	I	University of Michigan–	
Stonehill College, MA	I,P	University of California, Merced, CA	D	Flint, MI	I
Stony Brook University, State		University of California,		University of Minnesota,	
University of New York, NY	I	Riverside, CA	D	Crookston, MN	I
Suffolk University, MA	D,I	University of California, Santa		University of Minnesota, Duluth, MN	I
Susquehanna University, PA	I,P	Barbara, CA	I	University of Minnesota, Twin	
Swarthmore College, PA	I	University of California, Santa		Cities Campus, MN	I
Sweet Briar College, VA	I	Cruz, CA	I	University of Missouri, MO	I
Syracuse University, NY	I,P	University of Central Arkansas, AR	I	University of Missouri–St.	
Tarleton State University, TX	G,I	University of Central Florida, FL	D,P	Louis, MO	I
Taylor University, IN	I	University of Central Missouri, MO	D,I	University of Montana, MT	I
Temple University, PA	I	University of Central Oklahoma, OK	D,G	The University of Montana Western,	
Tennessee Technological		University of Chicago, IL	I	MT	D,I
University, TN	D	University of Cincinnati, OH	I	University of Montevallo, AL	I
Tennessee Wesleyan University, TN	I	University of Colorado Boulder, CO	G,I	University of Nebraska at Kearney,	
Texas A&M International		University of Colorado Colorado		NE	I
University, TX	G,I	Springs, CO	I	University of Nebraska–	
Texas A&M University, TX	G,I	University of Colorado Denver, CO	D,I	Lincoln, NE	I
Texas A&M University–		University of Dallas, TX	I	University of Nevada, Las Vegas, NV	D,I
Commerce, TX	I	University of Dayton, OH	G,I	University of Nevada, Reno, NV	I
Texas A&M University–Corpus		University of Delaware, DE	I	University of New England, ME	I
Christi, TX	G,I	University of Denver, CO	D,I	University of New Hampshire, NH	I
Texas A&M University–		University of Detroit Mercy, MI	D,I	University of New Hampshire at	
Kingsville, TX	G,I	University of Dubuque, IA	I	Manchester, NH	I
Texas A&M University–		University of Evansville, IN	I	University of New Haven, CT	I
Texarkana, TX	G,I	The University of Findlay, OH	I	University of New Orleans, LA	D,I
Texas Christian University, TX	I	University of Hartford, CT	I,P	University of North Alabama, AL	I
Texas Lutheran University, TX	I	University of Hawaii at Manoa, HI	I	University of North Carolina at	
Texas State University, TX	G,I,P	University of Houston, TX	D,G,I	Asheville, NC	D,I
Texas Tech University, TX	I	University of Houston–Clear		The University of North Carolina	
Texas Wesleyan University, TX	D,I	Lake, TX	D,I	at Chapel Hill, NC	I
Texas Woman's University, TX	G,I	University of Houston–		The University of North Carolina	
		Downtown, TX	I	at Charlotte, NC	I

D = deferred payment system; *G* = guaranteed tuition rate; *I* = installment payments; *P* = prepayment locks in tuition rate

The University of North Carolina at Greensboro, NC	I	The University of Texas of the Permian Basin, TX	G,I	Washington & Jefferson College, PA	I,P
The University of North Carolina at Pembroke, NC	I,P	The University of Texas Rio Grande Valley, TX	G,I	Washington College, MD	G,I,P
University of North Carolina School of the Arts, NC	G,I	The University of the Arts, PA	I	Washington University in St. Louis, MO	I,P
The University of North Carolina Wilmington, NC	I	University of the Incarnate Word, TX	I	Wayland Baptist University, TX	I
University of North Dakota, ND	D	University of the Pacific, CA	D	Waynesburg University, PA	I
University of Northern Colorado, CO	I	The University of Toledo, OH	I	Wayne State College, NE	I
University of Northern Iowa, IA	I	The University of Tulsa, OK	I	Wayne State University, MI	I
University of North Florida, FL	I	University of Utah, UT	D,I	Webber International University, FL	I
University of North Georgia, GA	I	University of Vermont, VT	I	Weber State University, UT	I
University of North Texas, TX	G,I	University of Virginia, VA	I	Webster University, MO	D
University of North Texas at Dallas, TX	G	The University of Virginia's College at Wise, VA	D,I	Wellesley College, MA	I,P
University of Notre Dame, IN	I	University of Washington, WA	P	Wells College, NY	I
University of Oklahoma, OK	G,I	University of Washington, Bothell, WA	I,P	Wentworth Institute of Technology, MA	I
University of Oregon, OR	I	University of Washington, Tacoma, WA	I,P	Wesleyan College, GA	I
University of Pennsylvania, PA	I,P	The University of West Alabama, AL	I	Wesleyan University, CT	I
University of Pikeville, KY	I	University of West Florida, FL	D,P	West Chester University of Pennsylvania, PA	I
University of Pittsburgh, PA	D,I	University of West Georgia, GA	I	Western Connecticut State University, CT	I
University of Pittsburgh at Bradford, PA	I	University of Wisconsin–Eau Claire, WI	I	Western Illinois University, IL	G,I
University of Pittsburgh at Greensburg, PA	I	University of Wisconsin–Green Bay, WI	I	Western Kentucky University, KY	I
University of Pittsburgh at Johnstown, PA	I	University of Wisconsin–La Crosse, WI	I	Western Michigan University, MI	I
University of Providence, MT	D	University of Wisconsin–Madison, WI	I	Western New England University, MA	I,P
University of Puerto Rico–Bayamón, PR	D,G	University of Wisconsin–Milwaukee, WI	I	Western Oregon University, OR	G
University of Puget Sound, WA	D,I	University of Wisconsin–Parkside, WI	I	Western State Colorado University, CO	D,I
University of Rhode Island, RI	I	University of Wisconsin–Stevens Point, WI	D,I	Western Washington University, WA	I
University of Richmond, VA	I	University of Wisconsin–Superior, WI	I	Westfield State University, MA	I
University of Rochester, NY	I	University of Wisconsin–Whitewater, WI	D,I	Westminster College, PA	I
University of St. Francis, IL	D,I	University of Wyoming, WY	I	Westminster College, UT	D,I
University of Saint Joseph, CT	I	Upper Iowa University, IA	I	Westmont College, CA	I
University of St. Thomas, MN	D,I	Ursinus College, PA	I	West Texas A&M University, TX	G,I
University of St. Thomas, TX	D,I	Ursuline College, OH	I	West Virginia University, WV	I
University of San Diego, CA	I	Utah State University, UT	D	West Virginia University Institute of Technology, WV	I
University of San Francisco, CA	I	Utah Valley University, UT	D	West Virginia Wesleyan College, WV	I
University of Science and Arts of Oklahoma, OK	G,I	Valdosta State University, GA	I	Wheaton College, IL	D,I
The University of Scranton, PA	I	Valencia College, FL	I	Wheaton College, MA	I
University of Sioux Falls, SD	I	Valley City State University, ND	I	Whittier College, CA	I
University of South Carolina, SC	D	Valparaiso University, IN	I,P	Whitworth University, WA	I
University of South Carolina Aiken, SC	D	Vanderbilt University, TN	I,P	Wichita State University, KS	I
University of South Dakota, SD	D	VanderCook College of Music, IL	I	Widener University, PA	I
University of Southern California, CA	I,P	Vanguard University of Southern California, CA	I	Wilkes University, PA	D,I
University of Southern Indiana, IN	I	Vassar College, NY	I	Willamette University, OR	I,P
University of Southern Maine, ME	I	Vaughn College of Aeronautics and Technology, NY	I	William Jessup University, CA	D
University of Southern Mississippi, MS	I	Vermont Technical College, VT	I	William Jewell College, MO	I
University of South Florida, FL	D	Villa Maria College, NY	I	William Paterson University of New Jersey, NJ	I
The University of Tampa, FL	I	Villanova University, PA	I	Williams Baptist College, AR	I
The University of Tennessee, TN	I	Virginia Commonwealth University, VA	I	Williams College, MA	I
The University of Tennessee at Chattanooga, TN	I	Virginia Military Institute, VA	I	William Woods University, MO	I
The University of Tennessee at Martin, TN	D,I	Virginia Polytechnic Institute and State University, VA	I	Wilson College, PA	I
The University of Texas at Austin, TX	G,I	Virginia State University, VA	I	Winona State University, MN	I
The University of Texas at Dallas, TX	G,I	Virginia Wesleyan University, VA	I	Winthrop University, SC	I
The University of Texas at El Paso, TX	G,I	Wabash College, IN	I,P	Wisconsin Lutheran College, WI	I
The University of Texas at San Antonio, TX	D,G,I	Walsh College of Accountancy and Business Administration, MI	D	Wittenberg University, OH	I
		Warner Pacific College, OR	D,I	Wofford College, SC	I
		Wartburg College, IA	I	Worcester Polytechnic Institute, MA	D,I,P
				Worcester State University, MA	I
				Wright State University, OH	I
				Wright State University–Lake Campus, OH	I
				Xavier University, OH	D,I
				Yale University, CT	I
				York College of Pennsylvania, PA	I
				Youngstown State University, OH	D,I

D = deferred payment system; *G* = guaranteed tuition rate; *I* = installment payments; *P* = prepayment locks in tuition rate

NOTES

NOTES

NOTES